ISBN 978-0-266-05657-7
PIBN 10953122

1 MONTH OF
FREE
READING

at

www.ForgottenBooks.com

By purchasing this book you are eligible for one month membership to ForgottenBooks.com, giving you unlimited access to our entire collection of over 700,000 titles via our web site and mobile apps.

To claim your free month visit:

www.forgottenbooks.com/free953122

English
Français
Deutsche
Italiano
Español
Português

www.forgottenbooks.com

Mythology Photography **Fiction**
Fishing Christianity **Art** Cooking
Essays Buddhism Freemasonry
Medicine **Biology** Music **Ancient**
Egypt Evolution Carpentry Physics
Dance Geology **Mathematics** Fitness
Shakespeare **Folklore** Yoga Marketing
Confidence Immortality Biographies
Poetry **Psychology** Witchcraft
Electronics Chemistry History **Law**
Accounting **Philosophy** Anthropology
Alchemy Drama Quantum Mechanics
Atheism Sexual Health **Ancient History**
Entrepreneurship Languages Sport
Paleontology Needlework Islam
Metaphysics Investment Archaeology
Parenting Statistics Criminology
Motivational

National Reporter System.—State Series.

THE

SOUTHEASTERN REPORTER,

VOLUME 13,

CONTAINING ALL THE DECISIONS OF THE

SUPREME COURTS OF APPEALS OF VIRGINIA AND WEST VIRGINIA, AND SUPREME COURTS OF NORTH CAROLINA, SOUTH CAROLINA, GEORGIA.

PERMANENT EDITION.

APRIL 28, 1891—JANUARY 5, 1892.

WITH TABLES OF SOUTHEASTERN CASES PUBLISHED IN VOLS. 86 AND 87, GEORGIA REPORTS; 107 AND 108, NORTH CAROLINA REPORTS; 32 AND 33, SOUTH CAROLINA REPORTS; 87, VIRGINIA REPORTS; 34, WEST VIRGINIA REPORTS.

A TABLE OF STATUTES CITED AND CONSTRUED IS
GIVEN IN THE INDEX.

ST. PAUL:
WEST PUBLISHING CO.
1892.

JUDGES

OF THE

COURTS REPORTED DURING THE PERIOD COVERED BY THIS VOLUME.

VIRGINIA—Supreme Court of Appeals.

LUNSFORD L. LEWIS, PRESIDENT.

JUDGES.

BENJAMIN W. LACY.   THOMAS T. FAUNTLEROY.
ROBERT A. RICHARDSON. DRURY A. HINTON.

WEST VIRGINIA—Supreme Court of Appeals.

DANIEL B. LUCAS, PRESIDENT.

JUDGES.

HENRY BRANNON.   JOHN W. ENGLISH.
HOMER A. HOLT.

NORTH CAROLINA—Supreme Court.

AUGUSTUS S. MERRIMON, CHIEF JUSTICE.

ASSOCIATE JUSTICES.

ALPHONSO C. AVERY.   JAMES E. SHEPHERD.
JOSEPH J. DAVIS.   WALTER CLARK.

SOUTH CAROLINA—Supreme Court.

HENRY McIVER, CHIEF JUSTICE.

ASSOCIATE JUSTICES.

SAMUEL McGOWAN.   Y. J. POPE.[1]

GEORGIA—Supreme Court.

LOGAN E. BLECKLEY, CHIEF JUSTICE.

ASSOCIATE JUSTICES.

THOMAS J. SIMMONS.   SAMUEL LUMPKIN.

[1] Elected December, 1891.

COURT RULES.

SUPREME COURT OF NORTH CAROLINA.

Rule 53 was amended at September Term, 1891, as follows:

After the word "petitioner," in line 14, [line 19 as printed in 12 S. E. Rep. p. x,] insert, "who shall be one of the Justices who concurred in the opinion of the Court."

For the rules of the supreme court, see 12 S. E. Rep. v-xi.

13 s. e.   (iv)

CASES REPORTED.

See End of Index for Tables of Southeastern Cases in State Reports.

TOWN OF DURHAM v. RICHMOND & D. R. Co.

(Supreme Court of North Carolina. April 14, 1891.)

COSTS ON APPEAL—PRINTING RECORD AND BRIEF.

1. Sup. Ct. Rule N. C. 31, limits the costs for printing the record to 20 pages, unless otherwise specially ordered by the court. *Held,* that where the "case on appeal," as settled by the judge, exceeds 20 printed pages, the supreme court will permit the costs of the excess to be taxed in favor of the unsuccessful party, as such "case" is required to be printed as part of the record by rule 29, but no costs will be taxed for printing other parts of the record, not embraced in the "case on appeal," and presenting no question to be reviewed.

2. In settling the case on appeal, only so much of the evidence or other matters occurring on the trial as may be necessary to present and illustrate the matters excepted to should be inserted, and not the entire evidence embraced in the stenographer's minutes.

3. Where the successful party on appeal could have condensed his brief to 10 pages, for which number of pages he is permitted to tax costs by Sup. Ct. Rule N. C. 37, no costs will be allowed him for the excess.

For former report, see 12 S. E. Rep. 1040.

Batchelor & Devereux, for appellant. *T. H. Busbee,* for appellee.

CLARK, J. This is a motion by the appellant to retax the bill of costs in this court by allowing "the actual cost of printing the record and brief." Rule 29 requires the "case on appeal" to be printed, and such other parts of the record as may be necessary to present the exceptions made, the designation of such other parts to be made by counsel of the appellant. If, however, more than 20 pages are printed the costs for the excess can only be allowed by order of the court,[1] for which purpose this motion is now made. An inspection of the transcript shows 74 pages printed. Of these, 68 pages are in the "case on appeal" settled by the judge. As this the appellant was required by the rules to have printed, and could not omit any part thereof, it is but just that he should be allowed for said 68 pages, deducting the 20 pages already taxed, to-wit, 48 pages additional at 60 cents per page. The other 6 pages were not embraced in the "case on appeal," presented no exceptions to be reviewed, and were un-

necessarily printed. This case differs from Roberts *v.* Lewald, 12 S. E. Rep. 1028, (at this term,) in which the case on appeal was only 2 pages, and, the winning party having been allowed the costs of printing 20 pages, further allowance was denied.

In this connection it is proper to note that the case seems to have been made up from the stenographer's notes, and, instead of making a brief of such evidence as was material, the entire transcript of the evidence seems to have been put into the case. This may save labor to the judge, but is an unnecessary expense to parties, and is not a "case settled," within the meaning of the statute. As the use of stenographers will become more common in our courts, the attention of the trial judges should be especially called to this, which is likely, if not adverted to, to become an evil and an oppression. It is not intended that the transcript of the "case on appeal" should become a dumping-ground for the entire evidence and *minutiæ* of the trial below. The parties, if they agree on a case, or the judge, if he settles it, should eliminate the points excepted to, and only send up in connection with them so much of the evidence or other matters occurring on the trial as may be necessary to present and illustrate the matters excepted to. The judge does not do his duty in "settling the case" unless he keeps this in view. Parties ought not to be taxed and oppressed, either with the copying by the clerk below, or by the printing in this court of a vast mass of testimony, utterly irrelevant, so far as concerns the exceptions to be reviewed. This is said, not in criticism of the careful and accurate judge who tried this particular cause, but because this is a "case" somewhat more lengthy, perhaps, than was necessary, which was evidently due to reliance on the stenographer's notes, and to prevent by a timely caution what is already a growing evil from becoming a serious and fruitful source of unnecessary and oppressive costs.

As to the brief of appellant, he has already had taxed for his benefit 10 pages, as allowed by rule 37. We do not think that more was necessary, and that with a proper regard to condensation and expense, the forcible argument of the appellant could have been put within that compass. If he chose to elaborate it beyond

[1] Sup. Ct. rule 31.

that limit, it was at his own "cost and charges." To the extent herein indicated, motion allowed.

BAKER v. GARRIS.

(Supreme Court of North Carolina. April 7, 1891.)

COMPLAINT ON NOTE OF MARRIED WOMAN — DEMURRER—WAIVER—ADMINISTRATORS.

1. A complaint on a note alleging that the maker was a married woman, and died seised of certain property, but failing to allege that she was competent by statute to make the note, or to show that her separate estate was chargeable therefor, does not state a cause of action. MERRIMON, C. J., dissenting.

2. Where defendant's demurrer is overruled, the fact that he answers over, and goes to trial on the merits, does not waive the insufficiency of the complaint.

3. Defendant may take advantage of the defect in the appellate court by a motion to dismiss the case. MERRIMON, C. J., dissenting.

4. An executor may plead the coverture of his testatrix in actions to charge her separate estate with debt.

5. Oral testimony is inadmissible to show the grounds on which a preceding judge overruled a written demurrer.

Appeal from superior court, Wayne county; BOYKIN, Judge.

The complaint alleges: "(1) That on January 1, 1886. Julia J. V. Garris, wife of the defendant, for a valuable consideration, executed and delivered her promissory note, under seal, to the plaintiff, wherein she promised to pay the plaintiff on January 1, 1888, the sum of four hundred dollars, with interest at eight per cent. per annum from said January 1, 1886, and that no part of said indebtedness has been paid. (2) That in 1887 said Julia J. V. Garris died possessed of real and personal estate, leaving a will, in which her husband, the defendant, was appointed executor of the same, who qualified as such executor in August, 1887, and entered on his duties as such executor, taking said property into his possession, and omits and refuses to pay said debt. Wherefore plaintiff demands judgment against defendant for $400, with interest at eight per cent. from January 1, 1886, and for costs." The defendant demurred, assigning as ground of demurrer: "(2) That, the said Julia J. V. Garris being a married woman at the time of the execution and delivery of said sealed note, the same was void, and not binding on her or her personal representative." The court overruled the demurrer, and granted the defendant leave to answer the complaint. He excepted, and took an appeal to this court, but did not prosecute the same. Afterwards he answered alleging: "(3) That at the time of the execution of the said alleged note the defendant's testatrix was a married woman; that the consideration of the said alleged note was not for her benefit, nor for the benefit of her separate estate; that the payment of said alleged note was not charged, either expressly or by implication, on her separate estate; nor was it executed with the written consent of her husband; that said alleged note was not given for her necessary personal expenses, nor for the support of her family, nor to enable her to pay her debts

existing before her marriage." The plaintiff replied to the answer: "(1) That in the complaint in this action it was alleged that the testatrix of the defendant was a married woman at the time of the execution of said note, and the defendant demurred to said complaint upon the ground that it did not state facts sufficient to constitute a cause of action, in that it appeared from said complaint that the testatrix of the defendant was a married woman at the time of signing said note; that said demurrer was heard, and a judgment was rendered in this cause overruling said demurrer, and the plaintiff avers that said judgment was rendered upon the sole ground that the defense of coverture was not available to the defendant, and the plaintiff pleads said judgment as an estoppel." The court gave judgment as follows: "This cause coming on to be heard, and the defendant having admitted in open court the execution of the note declared on in the complaint, and that no part of the same has been paid, it is therefore considered and adjudged that the plaintiff T. M. Baker recover of the defendant Jonathan Garris, executor of J. J. Garris, the sum of five hundred and thirty-eight dollars and eighty-four cents, with interest at eight per cent. per annum on four hundred dollars until paid, and for costs." The defendant appealed. On the trial "the plaintiff offered to prove by parol that the judgment of his honor at October term, 1888, overruling the demurrer, was 'rendered upon the sole ground that the defense of coverture was not available to the defendant.' The defendant objected to this evidence, but it was admitted by the court, and the defendant excepted. It was then admitted by the defendant, subject to said exception, that said judgment was rendered on the sole ground alleged by the plaintiff." The defendant moved in this court to dismiss the action upon the ground that the complaint does not state facts sufficient to constitute a cause of action.

Aycock & Daniels, for appellant. *Faircloth & Allen,* for appellee.

SHEPHERD, J., *(after stating the facts as above.)* The defendant moves in this court to dismiss the action, for that the complaint does not state facts sufficient to constitute a cause of action. It appears on the face of the complaint that the defendant's testatrix, a married woman, executed her simple promissory note to the plaintiff in the sum of $400, and that she died "possessed of real and personal estate, leaving a will in which the defendant was appointed executor." There is an entire absence of any allegation showing that the contract was such as she was by statute competent to make, nor is there the slightest intimation of any circumstances showing that the indebtedness was charged or is chargeable upon her separate estate. Indeed, there is no pretense whatever of such a charge, and the prayer is for a judgment *in personam.* It is very clear that under the numerous decisions of this court, from Pippen v. Wesson, 74 N. C. 437, down to Flaum v. Wallace, 103 N. C. 296, 9 S. E. Rep. 567, and subsequent cases, that the complaint is fatally defective in that it does not set forth a cause of action. It is argued, however, that in certain exceptional instances (as in the case of a free trader) a married woman may make a legal contract, and therefore the court ought to assume that the contract sued upon is one of that peculiar character. This position is so utterly subversive of every principle of legal presumption that it would seem unnecessary to cite any authority in its refutation. As, however, it appears to be seriously pressed, it may not be improper to make some observations upon the subject. Very soon after the adoption of the present constitution and the passage of what is known as the "Married Woman's Act," (chapter 42 of the Code,) it became the duty of this court to determine the character of the statutory separate estate of a *feme covert*, and the manner in which it could be charged with her executory contracts. In a few of the states, where similar statutes had been passed, it was held that their effect was to remove the common-law disability of coverture, and to enable the wife to contract in all cases as if she were a *feme sole*, except where expressly prohibited. In a majority of the states the opposite view was taken, and this view, after much deliberation, was adopted by our court in Pippen v. Wesson, supra. This case settled the fundamental principles of the law of married women in North Carolina in reference to the constitutional and statutory provisions above mentioned, and its authority, so far from being questioned, has been uniformly recognized and approved by the repeated decisions of the court. The doctrine of the case is well stated by RUFFIN, J., in his carefully considered opinion in Dougherty v. Sprinkle, 88 N. C. 300, in which that learned justice discusses the manner in which the engagements of married women may be enforced. He says: "Nor was there any change wrought in this particular by the alterations made in our court system under the constitution of 1868, or by the adoption of the statute known as the 'Married Woman's Act.' It was in reference to these very alterations and the effect of the statute that the court declared in Pippen v. Wesson, and Huntley v. Whitner, 77 N. C. 392, that no deviation from the common law had been produced thereby, as respects either the power of a *feme covert* to contract, the nature of her contract, or the remedy to enforce it, that, as a contract merely, her promise is still as void as it ever was, with no power in any court to proceed to judgment against her *in personam*; that it was only through the equitable powers of the court that satisfaction of her engagements could be enforced as against her separate estate. The nature of the pleadings is substantially the same as under the former system of our courts, and it is essential, in order to establish a right to a special judgment against her separate estate, that the complaint should show not only that she has such estate, but that her promises are such as by the statute she is rendered competent to make. It was for want of just such allegations, and because the

complaint demanded a personal judgment against the *feme* defendant in Pippen v. Wesson, that the demurrer was sustained, and the action was dismissed." In Pippen v. Wesson the plaintiff sued upon a promissory note signed by the husband and wife, and the coverture appeared upon the face of the complaint. There was, as in our case, no allegation showing that the contract was of such a character as to fall within the exceptions of the statute; nor did there appear any circumstances by which the separate estate was chargeable. The *feme* defendant demurred on the ground that the complaint did not state facts sufficient to constitute a cause of action; and the court, after stating that the complaint should have contained the essential allegations above mentioned, proceeds as follows: "In the case of obligors *pleni juris* this would be immaterial; but where one of them has only a limited capacity to contract, the contract must be shown to be within her capacity. One who contracts by virtue of a power, statutory or otherwise, and who, except by such power, is incapable of contracting, must pursue the power, or her contract will be void." The demurrer was sustained, and thus we have a case directly in point, against the contention of the plaintiff. After this express decision upon the very question before us, it is quite difficult to understand how this court is at liberty to go to the extraordinary length of presuming the existence of the very circumstances which it has, in the most unequivocal terms, declared essential to be alleged. The cases cited from New York, even if they could be recognized as controlling authorities in this state, do not support the position of the plaintiff. In those cases the coverture did not appear upon the face of the complaint, and therefore it was not demurrable. Where the question, however, did arise, the court of appeals of that state (before the act of 1884, removing the disability of coverture, except as to contracts between husband and wife) ruled precisely as this court did in Pippen v. Wesson. In Broome v. Taylor, 76 N. Y. 564, the court said: "If this complaint had not shown that the defendant Helen was a married woman, it would have been good against her; and in that case, in order to avail herself of the defense of coverture, it would have been necessary for her to set it up in her answer. But the complaint shows that the bond is the obligation of a married woman, and there is no allegation showing that it was given for any purpose that would make it binding upon her. As to her, the bond is *prima facie* a nullity, and hence the complaint does not show a cause of action against her." In view of these authorities, it cannot, we think, for a moment be questioned that the complaint in this case does not state a cause of action. The proposition is so very plain that nothing but the earnest contention to the contrary would seem to justify this somewhat extended discussion in its support.

It is further insisted on the authority of Vick v. Pope, 81 N. C. 23; Newhart v. Peters, 80 N. C. 166; Nicholson v. Cox, 83

N. C. 48; and Johnston v. Cochrane, 84 N. C. 446,—that coverture must be pleaded. This is undoubtedly true, for where the disability does not appear upon the face of the complaint the plea must of course be by way of answer, as otherwise the fact of coverture can never be known. In the present case the disability appears from the complaint, and the plea of coverture, even had it been necessary, has from the beginning been insisted upon by way of demurrer. We suppose that it will hardly be contended that a demurrer in such a case is not a pleading within the principle of the above-mentioned cases. Code, §§ 238, 239; Estee, Pl. & Pr. § 3068; Oliphant v. Whitney, 34 Cal. 25; Furniss v. Ellis, 2 Brock. 14. Now, if no cause of action be stated, it is well settled that this objection and the objection to the jurisdiction may be made either by written demurrer or demurrer ore tenus. "As to the two exceptions specified there can be," says MERRIMON, J., "no waiver, and in these respects objections may be made at any time. In such cases there is an absence of anything to which the jurisdiction of the court can attach. Love v. Commissioners, 64 N. C. 706; Tucker v. Baker, 86 N. C. 1." Johnson v. Finch, 93 N. C. 205. In the face of this very plain declaration of the court it is insisted that the defendant can waive the objection, and that he cannot make it at any time. The manner in which this strange result is reached is said to be by way of estoppel growing out of a ruling at some previous term, in which the court overruled a demurrer, and gave the defendant leave to answer over. The demurrer was written, and the ground assigned was that, as the defendant's testatrix was a married woman at the time of the execution of the note, the same was void, and that the plaintiff could not recover. The defendant did not appeal, but answered, setting up the coverture. It is said that this interlocutory judgment amounts to an adjudication, and therefore the motion cannot now be insisted upon. In support of this position we are referred to such cases as Jones v. Thorne, 80 N. C. 72; Sanderson v. Daily, 83 N. C. 67; Mabry v. Henry, Id. 298; Roulhac v. Brown, 87 N. C. 1; Pasour v. Lineberger, 90 N. C. 159; and Wingo v. Hooper, 98 N. C. 482, 4 S. E. Rep. 463. In these cases certain interlocutory orders,—such as the appointment of receivers, motions to vacate attachments, orders of arrest, and the like,—were held to be res adjudicata, unless affidavits were presented showing additional facts subsequently transpiring. Provisional adjudications of this character are mere incidents to an action, the ultimate rights of the parties being tried upon issues of law or fact raised by the pleadings. Such orders are entirely independent of the general rules of pleading, and it is plain that the cases cited have no application to the question under consideration. The case of Wilson v. Lineberger, 82 N. C. 412, however, seems to be more in point, but upon an examination of the opinion we cannot regard it as authority in the present case. There the parties demurred, and it is said, "for want of equity," and after a trial before the jury and a report upon a

reference for an account—four terms having elapsed—the defendant moved that the action be dismissed for the same cause. This the court declined, and the defendant appealed. There were several reasons why the order of the court should not have been disturbed, one of which is that, while the power of the judge to thus summarily dispose of actions is well recognized, and its exercise in very clear cases commended, the practice generally is discouraged, (Wilson v. Sykes, 84 N. C. 215,) and this court will not entertain an appeal from a refusal to dismiss. McBryde v. Patterson, 78 N. C. 412. This reason was in itself sufficient to have disposed of the appeal, and is, indeed, mentioned by the court. But, apart from this, in view of the repeated decisions of this court, that a motion to dismiss upon the grounds mentioned cannot be waived, and may be taken at any time, we cannot give the effect contended for to such a merely interlocutory ruling as in this case. Again, we have held that it is the duty of this court to inspect the whole record, and pronounce such judgment as in law should be rendered. Thornton v. Brady, 100 N. C. 38, 5 S. E. Rep. 910. Now, if a complaint does not state a cause of action, this rule must be applied, and this could not be done if the expressions used in Wilson's Case are to be followed in all instances. It is very evident that the rule there stated had reference to the practice in the superior court alone, and was not intended to apply to motions made in this court, where the power is universally recognized and acted upon, and this without reference to the ruling below.

It is said that the court should not dismiss the action upon motion, but that the defect should be taken advantage of by demurrer. If we are not to reject the overwhelming weight of authority to the effect that this complaint does not state facts sufficient to constitute a cause of action, and that the objection cannot be waived, and may be made either by written demurrer or demurrer ore tenus, (Tucker v. Baker, 86 N. C. 1; Pescud v. Hawkins, 71 N. C. 299,) then it must follow that the suggestion is unfounded. Such a demurrer, written or ore tenus, is as strong a plea of coverture as can well be imagined; and it matters not at what stage of the action it is made, nor what other pleas may have been filed. It is very true that, if no demurrer had been interposed, and the case had been tried upon its merits, the evidence sustaining issues embodying the essential circumstances, the court below, (Code, § 273,) and even this court, upon motion, might have allowed an amendment conforming the pleadings to the facts proved, and refused to dismiss. But nothing of the kind appears here. In fact, the case has never been tried upon its merits, but upon the alleged legal insufficiency of the complaint, and there is therefore nothing to show the actual existence of the circumstances necessary to charge the estate. While this disposes of the appeal, we will add that we are clearly of the opinion that oral testimony is not admissible to show the grounds upon which the preceding judge placed his ruling. The demurrer was in writing, and we cannot look beyond it and the judgment. The principle which admits such testimony in aid of a record pleaded as an estoppel, where such record fails to disclose the precise point on which the case was decided, (as in Yates v. Yates, 81 N. C. 397,) has no application to rulings upon written demurrers. We will also remark that we do not concur in the proposition of the intelligent counsel that an executor cannot plead the coverture of his testatrix. This would be practically charging her estate with debts for which she was not liable in her life-time. The case of Newhart v. Peters, 80 N. C. 167, simply decides that this plea cannot be interposed by one who has no interest in the subject-matter of the suit, and who cannot be affected by its result. The action must be dismissed.

MERRIMON, C. J., (*dissenting*.) I think this court ought not to dismiss this action upon the ground that the complaint fails to state facts sufficient to constitute a cause of action. The complaint did state a cause of action, and the court might and would have given judgment for the plaintiff if the defendant had not pleaded, or in case he failed to plead the coverture of his testatrix at the time she executed the note sued upon. It is settled that the plaintiff may have judgment against a married woman upon a note or alleged indebtedness of any kind executed or incurred while she was such married woman, unless she pleads her coverture. That is a defense she may or may not avail herself of, and she must plead it. Vick v. Pope, 81 N. C. 22; Neville v. Pope, 95 N. C. 346; Newhart v. Peters, 80 N. C. 166; Nicholson v. Cox, 83 N. C. 48; Johnston v. Cochrane, 84 N. C. 446. Hence, if a married woman should simply plead in a proper case that she did not execute the note sued upon, or that she had paid the same, or that it was barred by the statute of limitations, and the plea should be determined against her, the plaintiff would clearly be entitled to judgment, as she did not plead her coverture; and if on the trial of such pleas either party should assign error as to some ruling of the court, and, after final judgment adverse to him or her, he or she should appeal to this court, the latter could not, *ex mero motu*, or upon the motion of the *feme* defendant, dismiss the action upon the ground that the complaint failed to state facts sufficient to constitute a cause of action, because it did sufficiently state a cause of action, in the absence of the defense of coverture properly pleaded. In this case, for the reasons stated above, the court below could not have dismissed the action for the cause last above mentioned, if the defendant had not availed himself of the defense of the coverture of his testatrix by demurrer or answer, and for the like reason, upon appeal in such case, this court could not upon motion dismiss the action. A mere motion to dismiss the action in such case is not sufficient because, in the absence of the coverture pleaded, the complaint would be sufficient to entitle the plaintiff to judgment. In this case the defendant pleaded by his answer the coverture of his testatrix. On the trial he assigned error as to certain rulings of the

court below, and, after final judgment adverse to him, he appealed to this court. This court should consider and dispose of the assignments of error. It cannot properly grant the motion to dismiss the action upon the ground that the complaint fails to state facts sufficient to constitute a cause of action, because, simply upon its face, it does state a cause of action. Such motion will be allowed only when no cause of action is stated, and when the court has not jurisdiction. Code, § 242. The case of Pippen v. Wesson, 74 N. C. 437, does not sustain the action of this court in this case. In that case the defendant demurred, and the court sustained the demurrer, and gave judgment for the defendant. It did not grant a motion to dismiss the action, nor did this court. On appeal, the latter court simply affirmed the judgment of the court below.

TUCKER v. TUCKER.[1]

(*Supreme Court of North Carolina.* March 24, 1891.)

TAXATION—REDEMPTION—NEXT IN TITLE—RIGHT TO INHERIT.

1. Under the statute (Acts N. C. 1885, c. 177, § 59, re-enacted in Acts 1887, c. 187, § 121) providing that when the person "seised as tenant by curtesy or dower, as tenant for life or in right of his wife," of land which is sold for taxes, shall fail to redeem the same within a year, the land shall be forfeited to the person "next in title in remainder or reversion" who may redeem within a year from such forfeiture, the homestead allotted to a widow "during widowhood" in lieu of dower may be redeemed by the person next in title when the widow allows it to be sold for non-payment of taxes.

2. The rights given by Code N. C. § 1281, rules 9, 10, permitting illegitimate children born of negroes who lived together as man and wife prior to 1868 to inherit from their mother and from one another, are not abridged by rule 13, same section, permitting such children to inherit from both parents, but not collaterally, and brothers, therefore, born of parents who lived together as man and wife prior to 1868, may inherit from each other.

Distinguishing Tucker v. Bellamy, 98 N. C. 31, 4 S. E. Rep. 34, and Jones v. Hoggard, 19 S. E. Rep. 906, 907.

AVERY, J., dissenting.

Civil action for recovery of real estate, tried before GRAVES, J., at April term, 1890, of New Hanover superior court. The case was submitted upon facts agreed, from which it appeared that William Tucker died in 1880, seised of the land in controversy, leaving the plaintiff, his only brother, leaving no children, and the defendant, his widow. By proper proceedings the premises were allotted to said widow as her homestead in lieu of dower. In 1886 she listed the land for taxes, but, failing to pay the same, the land was regularly sold, after due advertisement, January 7, 1887, and was bought by one Maria Fuller, who was the adopted daughter of the defendant. The defendant failed to redeem the land, and on January 5, 1889, the plaintiff, claiming to be the person next in title to said land, paid the tax, penalty, and cost to the clerk of New Hanover superior court, the same having been previously tendered by him to Maria Fuller, who de-

[1] Rehearing granted on question as to whether there was a valid sale of the land, and on that point only.

clined to accept it. It is further admitted that the defendant is in possession, and that the plaintiff is a colored man, formerly a slave, as was also the husband of the defendant. Their mother and father lived together as man and wife prior to 1868, and died before the abolition of slavery. Upon these facts the court rendered judgment in favor of defendant, and plaintiff appealed.

T. W. Strange, for appellee.

CLARK, J., (after stating the facts as above.) The statute (Acts 1885, c. 177, § 59) provides that when the person "seised as tenant by curtesy or dower, as tenant for life or in right of his wife," of land which is sold for taxes thereon, "shall not within one year after such sale redeem the same according to law, such person shall forfeit to the person or persons next in title to such lands in remainder or reversion" his estate in said land, and that such person next in title may redeem it within one year after forfeiture. This section is re-enacted verbatim in Acts 1887, c. 137, § 121. The allotment of the premises to the defendant as her homestead by virtue of Const. art. 10, § 5, was an extension and prolongation of the seisin and homestead right of her husband "during her widowhood." For that period she held it, was "tenant" or "holder" of it, protected against sale of it for his debts, and with the right to enjoy the "rents and profits." Indeed, in this respect she enjoys the homestead more fully than her deceased husband could have done, for the rents and profits cannot be subjected to payment of his debts, as would be the case if he were living. (Bank v. Green, 78 N. C. 247.) but "inure to her benefit." Such right of occupancy of the premises, with the absolute right to the rents and profits during widowhood, while technically not in all respects a tenancy for life, (Jones v. Britton, 102 N. C. 166, 9 S. E. Rep. 554,) is at least such within the purview and meaning of the statute. (2 Bl. Comm. 131.) It cannot be that the premises are exempt from taxation during her occupancy, since the constitution expressly provides that the homestead is subject to sale for taxes. Article 10, § 2. Nor can it be thought that the fee is subject to sale for non-payment of taxes by the widow. Ex parte Macay, 84 N. C. 63. Indeed, the statute above cited (section 42) provides that the sheriff's deed shall convey only the estate which the delinquent had in the land. It is not a reasonable construction of the statute that the remainder man should be held to payment of the taxes for the indefinite period of the life of the widow, who meantime enjoys the rents and profits, under penalty of losing his ultimate right to the fee. The reasonable and just construction is that the widow who possesses the premises, and enjoys the rents and profits thereof "during widowhood," comes within the class of "tenants for life," designated by the statute, and when she permitted her interest to be sold for non-payment of taxes, and failed to redeem, instead of the premises going out of the family, the law permitted the remainder-man, the "next in title," to redeem it, as he

elected to do, within the prescribed time. The defendant, therefore, comes within the words of the statute, and was subject to forfeiture of her estate by permitting the land to be sold for taxes, and failing to redeem it. It is, however, contended that the plaintiff was not "the next in title;" citing Tucker v. Bellamy, 98 N. C. 31, 4 S. E. Rep. 34, and Jones v. Hoggard, 12 S. E. Rep. 906, 907, (at this term.) The Code, § 1281, rule 13, legitimating the children born prior to 1868 of colored parents who lived together as man and wife, confers the right of inheriting upon the children only as to their parents' estates, and not collaterally. Prior to that act such children had only the rights of other illegitimates, and by section 1281, rules 9 and 10, could only inherit from their mother when there was no legitimate child, and from one another. The act of 1879, rule 13, did not abridge the rights given by rules 9 and 10, but extended them by conferring upon parties designated therein the right of succeeding to the father, and also to the mother, in all cases. It follows, therefore, that the husband of the defendant and the plaintiff were in the eye of the law, as to each other, vested with the rights of illegitimates, and upon the death of William Tucker the estate descended to the plaintiff, subject to the dower and homestead rights of the widow.

This case differs from the two cases above cited. In Tucker v. Bellamy the court held that the Acts of 1879, rule 13, supra, did not authorize the children legitimated by it "to inherit from collateral kindred, such as uncles and aunts." It may be noted that this did not conflict with rule 10, for, though that rule allows illegitimate children to be legitimate as between themselves and their representatives, this contemplates that such representatives shall be themselves legitimate representatives of the illegitimate child. In Tucker v. Bellamy the plaintiffs were the illegitimate representatives (being born in slavery) of the illegitimate brother, who died in slavery when incapable of inheriting, and therefore the estate could not pass to the plaintiffs unless authorized by rule 13, which, the court held, conferred no rights to inherit upon collaterals. Rule 13 made them legitimate, it is true, as to their father's estate, but they did not claim the estate of their father, but of their aunt. In the present case, by virtue of emancipation and the constitution, the plaintiff has the same civil rights as any other illegitimate, and under rule 10 can succeed to the estate of his illegitimate brother. Rule 13 has no application to this case. Jones v. Hoggard (at this term) is also materially different. In that case the decedent left a legitimate brother, who was the defendant, and several illegitimate brothers and sisters, the plaintiffs, who were only legitimated by rule 13. The court held that this last rule only conferred the right of inheriting from the parents, and not from the brother. The decedent and the defendant in that case being legitimate brothers, rule 10 did not apply to plaintiffs as here. In the present case the plaintiff and his brother were of necessity either legitimates or illegitimates; if legitimates, then the plaintiff was, of course, next in title; if illegitimates, there being no legitimate brother or sister, the plaintiff was equally next in title. Reversed.

AVERY, J., dissents.

SIMPSON et al. v. PEGRAM et al.

(Supreme Court of North Carolina. April 1, 1891.)

SALE—CONSIGNMENT—EVIDENCE.

Where a person writes, "please send me the following" goods promptly, on his letter-head paper, the printed part of which reads "general merchandise broker," "consignments solicited," and, after receiving the goods, assigns them, the letter, together with the printed letter-head, is competent evidence to go to the jury on the question whether the goods were sold or consigned to the person ordering them.

Appeal from superior court, Forsyth county; BYNUM, Judge.

The plaintiffs brought this action to recover the value of a considerable quantity of flour from the defendant Pegram and his co-defendants, who are his assignees. Pegram ordered from the plaintiffs the flour in question by letter, of which the following is a copy: "Office of T. H. Pegram, Jr., general merchandise broker. Consignments solicited. And dealer in wagons, grain, hay, mill feed, &c. Winston, N. C., Nov. 14, 1887. Messrs. Simpson, Bass & Co., Richmond, Va.—Gents: Please send me the following: 100 bags ℔98 Bob White 50 bbls.; 100 bags ℔49 Bob White 25 bbls.; 200 bags ℔24 Bob White 25 bbls.; 400 bags ℔12 Bob White 25 bbls. Ship as soon as possible, as I need the goods right now. Want fresh goods. Yours, truly, T. H. PEGRAM, Jr." The plaintiffs contend the flour was consigned to defendant Pegram, and not sold to him. The defendants admit the flour in controversy was received by the defendant Pegram, and the most of it was in his possession at the time of his assignment to Buxton and Grogan, passed into the hands of the assignees, and the proceeds of said flour is now in their hands; but the defendants contend the flour was bought by the defendant Pegram, and not consigned. The following issue was submitted to the jury: "Was the flour in controversy in this action consigned to the defendant Pegram by plaintiffs?" The plaintiffs offered in evidence and read to the jury the letter above set forth, and rested their case. His honor instructed the jury that upon the evidence offered by the plaintiffs they should render a verdict for the defendants, and answered the issue "No." Plaintiffs excepted. There was a verdict for the defendants, and thereupon the court gave judgment in favor of the plaintiffs against the defendant Pegram for the value of the flour, and that the defendants' assignees go without day. The plaintiffs, having excepted, appealed to this court.

Jones & Kerner and Glenn & Manly, for plaintiffs. J. S. Grogan, for defendants.

MERRIMON, C. J., (after stating the facts as above.) In the course of the business of trade "letter-heads," "bill-heads," and like advertising mediums, when identified and connected with the party using and giving them out for his own purposes and advantage, have point and significance, and the more when they appear directly in connection with, and give, or reasonably may give, cast and meaning to business correspondence and transactions in their nature uncertain and indeterminate and requiring explanation as to their meaning and purpose. They may, and oftentimes ought to, be taken as indicative and explanatory of the correspondence or transactions left uncertain and imperfect without them, and have more or less weight, according to their nature, connections, application, bearing, and the circumstances. Oftentimes the very purpose of the use of them is to give the public, and as well individuals, notice of the advertiser's business, its nature, where it is carried on, and to invite correspondence, business, and trade transactions. When a person thus holds himself out, declares the nature of his business and purpose to another person with whom he deals, in the absence of explanation in some way appearing to the contrary, the reasonable inference is that his contract—the transaction pertinent to his business—was of the nature contemplated by that business thus made known; and that he thus made known his business may, in a proper case, be shown by any competent evidence. Thus, if such person should, under a "letter-head" declaring the nature and place of his business, write and send a letter to a person engaged in a business at a distance from him, with whom he wished and proposed to have a business transaction pertinent to his business, without particularly specifying its nature and terms, and a transaction accordingly took place, the inference would be that it was such as his business contemplated, and the letter, including the "letter-head," would be competent evidence of the fact in a proper case. The true office of such evidence would be "to interpret the otherwise indeterminate intention of the parties, and to ascertain the nature and extent of their contracts, arising not from express stipulation, but from mere implications and presumptions and acts of a doubtful and equivocal character, and to fix and explain the meaning of words and expressions of doubtful or various senses. On this principle the usage or habit of trade or conduct of individual, which is known to the person who deals with him, may be given in evidence to prove what was the contract between them." 2 Greenl. Ev. § 251. In the notes to Wigglesworth v. Dallison, 1 Smith, Lead Cas. 594, it is said: "The usage of an individual in his own business as to the manner of performing it, and the like, if known to the party dealing with him, is competent to show that the contract was on those terms." Norris v. Fowler, 87 N. C. 9. In the case before us the defendant Pegram wrote to the plaintiff immediately under a printed "letter-head," stating the character of his business,—that of a "general merchandise broker," and soliciting "consignments" for the purpose of his business. The letter was in no wise inconsistent with such business purpose. It was in material respects indefinite in its terms. It did not contain a proposition to purchase goods, or to pay for the same presently or in the future; it simply asked that the goods specified be sent to him promptly. By his letter he represented to the plaintiffs that he was such broker; that he desired consignments of goods for the purpose of his business. He asked that certain goods pertinent for his business be sent to him at once. Taking his representations as to his business, his requests, the whole together constituted evidence to go to the jury tending to prove that he wished and intended that the goods be consigned to him to be sold, not as his own, but as the plaintiffs', in the course of his business; and that the plaintiffs so understood, intended, and agreed, and sent him the goods accordingly. Pegram's business as "general merchandise broker" did not by its nature imply that he purchased or took title to the goods he sold; on the contrary, it might be that he sold such merchandise for one person to another for compensation, and to that end, and to facilitate his business, he "solicited" consignments of goods. He sent his letter-head in connection with and as part of his letter to the plaintiffs, and the whole constituted evidence of his contract with them, and tended to prove that the flour in controversy belonged to them. The court should have so instructed the jury, leaving them to determine its weight. There is error. The plaintiffs are entitled to a new trial, and we so adjudge. To that end let this opinion be certified to the superior court. It is so ordered.

STATE v. PEEPLES.

(Supreme Court of North Carolina. April 1, 1891.)

BASTARDY—AFFIDAVIT—WARRANT.

1. It is not necessary that it should appear affirmatively in the woman's affidavit in a bastardy proceeding that she is single.

2. It is immaterial that the warrant issued upon the affidavit fails to conclude, "against the statute in such case made and provided."

Bastardy proceeding, tried before BYNUM, J., at February term, 1891, of Forsyth superior court upon appeal from a justice's court. The state introduced the affidavit of the woman, upon which the warrant had been issued, and rested its case. The defendant introduced no evidence, and asked the court to instruct the jury that the affidavit was insufficient, and not a *prima facie* case. The court refused, and instructed the jury to return a verdict against the defendant, and entered judgment thereon. Defendant appealed, and assigned as exceptions: (1) That it does not appear that the affidavit of the woman was voluntary; (2) that it did not appear by the affidavit that the mother was a single woman; (3) that the warrant did not conclude, "against the statute in such case made and provided."

J. S. Grogan, for appellant. *The Attorney General* and *R. B. Glenn*, for the State.

CLARK, J., *(after stating the facts as above.)* 1. An inspection of the affidavit shows that it was sworn out by the woman before a justice of the peace. It appears to be voluntary, and there is nothing to indicate the contrary.

2. It is not necessary that it should appear affirmatively that the woman is a single woman. If she is a married woman, that is a matter of defense, and only then to the extent of raising a presumption that the child is legitimate. State v. Pettaway, 3 Hawks, 623. There is no presumption of law that she is married rather than single; indeed, "it is to be assumed that she is a single woman until it is made to appear that she is married." State v. Allison, Phil. (N. C.) 346; State v. Higgins, 72 N. C. 226. In a very recent case, State v. McDuffie, 107 N. C. 885, 12 S. E. Rep. 83, which was an indictment for fornication and adultery, it is held that the single state, being the first in order of time, is presumed to continue till a change to the married state is shown.

3. The proceeding is in the main civil in its nature, (State v. Carson, 2 Dev. & B. 368; State v. Pate, Busb. 244; State v. Higgins, supra;) and the conclusion, "against the form of the statute," etc., is unnecessary. But, were it a criminal action, such conclusion was mere form and immaterial, as has been repeatedly held. State v. Sykes, 104 N. C. 694, 10 S. E. Rep. 191; State v. Kirkman, 104 N. C. 911, 10 S. E. Rep. 312; State v Harris, 106 N. C. 682, 11 S. E. Rep. 377; State v. Peters, 107 N. C. 876, 12 S. E. Rep. 74. No error.

BROWN et al. v. WALKER et al.

(Supreme Court of North Carolina. April 1, 1891.)

ACTION ON ADMINISTRATOR'S BOND—PARTIES—RES ADJUDICATA—ASSETS—CONCLUSIVENESS—EVIDENCE—PARTIES.

1. Under Code N. C. § 186, providing that persons severally liable upon the same obligation or instrument, including the parties to bills of exchange and promissory notes, may all or any of them be included in the same action, at the option of the plaintiff, the administrator and other sureties on his bond are not necessary parties to a suit by the distributees against one of the sureties to enforce a judgment recovered against the administrator and all of his sureties.

2. Where the administrator of a surety on an administrator's bond is sued together with the other sureties and the principal, and fails to appear, though served with process, the judgment for plaintiffs is conclusive against him, and he cannot, in a suit to enforce that judgment, set up defenses which he might have pleaded in the original action.

3. The fact that evidence is improperly admitted to show the date of administration is immaterial when the fact as established by the evidence is admitted by the answer.

4. Under the law as it existed prior to July, 1869, (Code N. C. §§ 1476, 1477,) a judgment against an administrator by default fixes him with assets with which to satisfy it, and he cannot set up in defense to a suit on such judgment that he had no assets when it was rendered.

Appeal from superior court, Mecklenburg county; PHILIPS, Judge.

Action to recover the amount of a judgment rendered in the case of Ann E. Brown and others v. T. B. McKee and others. William Walker died in 1858, and in that year T. B. McKee qualified as his administrator, and gave bond, with R. R. Rea, J. B. Walker, and J. L. Walker, as sureties. In 1882, Ann E. Brown and others, as distributees of William Walker, sued T. B. McKee and his sureties on the administration bond for their distributive shares. J. B. Walker, one of the sureties, had died in 1862, and at July term, 1862, of the county court W. H. Walker qualified as his administrator, and as such was made a party defendant to the suit of Brown v. McKee, and served with process. He failed to appear or plead. In Brown et al. v. McKee et al. there was a reference ordered to ascertain how much was due by McKee, administrator, to the plaintiffs in this, and in that suit the distributees. The referee reported $1,200 to be the amount. His report was confirmed, and it was adjudged that plaintiffs recover that amount and costs of the defendants. This action is brought against W. H. Walker, administrator of J. B. Walker, and H. K. De Armond and wife (the latter being devisee of J. B. Walker) to enforce payment of that judgment, first, to recover an amount due by W. H. Walker, administrator, and, if not sufficient to pay plaintiffs' demand, to subject the land to Mrs. De Armond to the payment of the balance.

C. Dowd & Son, for plaintiffs. G. F. Bason, Burwell & Walker, and Jones & Tillett, for defendants.

SHEPHERD, J., (after stating the facts as above.) The first exception is addressed to the refusal of the court to make T. B. McKee, administrator of William Walker, and the other sureties to his administration bond, parties to this action. This exception cannot be sustained. Flack v. Dawson, 69 N. C. 42; Syme v. Bunting, 86 N. C. 175; Code, § 186. The second exception is also without merit. The defendant W. H. Walker was sued as the administrator of J. B. Walker, who was a surety on the administration bond of T. B. McKee. He was duly served with process, but failed to appear, and, as the matters of defense which he now offers to establish could have been asserted by him in that action, he is concluded by the judgment, and cannot now litigate them. The third exception to the admission of "parol" testimony to show the date of the administration of the said W. H. Walker. It does not appear that such testimony was introduced, the case simply stating that "evidence" was admitted upon that point. Conceding, however, that such testimony was inadmissible, and that the question could only have been determined by the record of the appointment, and that it should have been tried upon inspection by the court, we are unable to see how the appellant was in any way prejudiced. The only purpose and effect of the evidence was to prove that the said defendant administered prior to the 1st of July, 1869, and this is clearly admitted by his answer, in which he states that his intestate died in 1862, and that he, as administrator, set tled the estate in August, 1864. The exception must therefore be overruled. The remaining exception involves an inquiry into the nature of the judgment rendered against the said Walker in the former action as administrator. His intestate was one of the sureties on the administration bond of T. B. McKee, and these plaintiffs brought an action on said bond against the principal and sureties. The said Walker, as administrator of J. B. Walker, was made a party defendant, but failed to appear, or make any defense whatever. Upon a reference it was found that McKee was considerably indebted as administrator to the plaintiffs, and the report was confirmed, and judgment rendered against all of the defendants. It is insisted by the defendant Walker that this judgment did not have the effect of fixing him with assets, and that he is now at liberty to show that he has properly administered the estate, and that the lands of his intestate should be subjected to the payment of the claims of the plaintiffs. While the judgment is somewhat informal, it expressly includes all of the defendants, and the most favorable view in which it can be considered as to Walker is that it is a judgment against him as administrator. As the administration was prior to the 1st day of July, 1869, this case is governed by the laws existing at that time, (Code, §§ 1476, 1477;) and we think it well settled that under the former practice "a judgment against an executor or administrator, whether by default or upon demurrer, or upon any plea pleaded by an executor or administrator except plene administravit, or admitting assets to such a sum, and riens ultra, is conclusive upon him that he has assets to satisfy such judgment." Ired. Ex'rs, 673; Eaton, Forms, note 225. In Ruggles v. Sherman, 14 Johns. 446, it was held that "if an executor or administrator confesses a judgment, or suffers judgment by default, he is estopped from denying assets to the extent of the judgment as far as regards the plaintiff therein." To the same effect are Trull v. Edwards, 6 Mod. 308; Rock v. Leighton, 1 Salk. 310; Skelton v. Hawling, 1 Wils. 268; Wheatley v. Lane, 1 Saund. 216; and numerous other cases. This doctrine is considered as firmly established by modern writers, (2 Woerner, Adm'n, 792,) and is recognized to have been the former law in this state in McDowell v. Asbury, 66 N. C. 444. In that case it is said that, "where a personal representative is sued, he must protect himself by proper pleading," and, the administrator having withdrawn his plea of "fully administered," it was held that a judgment against him for "the debt of his intestate" fixed him with assets. So in Hooks v. Moses, 8 Ired. 88, where a judgment was confessed by an administrator before a justice of the peace for the amount of the debt, and nothing was said about assets, it was held in an action upon this judgment that the plea of plene administravit was immaterial, as the former judgment was conclusive against the defendant upon that question. The case of Armistead v. Harramond, 4 Hawks, 339, is not in conflict with the above authorities, as it was there simply held that a judgment against an administrator for the debt of his intestate, while evidence of the debt and of assets, did not, as to the latter, bind his sureties, who were not parties to the action. It is also contended that the complaint in the former action should have alleged that the defendant Walker was possessed of assets, and our attention was called to the declaration in Platt v. Robins, 1 Johns. 276, which contains such an averment. The case is not in point, as it was an action of debt upon a former judgment, suggesting a *devastavit*, which was one of the methods of enforcing a judgment after a return of *nulla bona* upon an execution *de bonis testatoris*. Under the former system an action against an administrator for the recovery of a debt due by his intestate in itself implied a charge that the administrator had such assets; and, as we have seen, it was necessary for him to protect himself against liability by proper pleas. Indeed, it was a common practice to declare simply upon the debt of the intestate, and, if there was a judgment by default, or no plea as to the assets, the judgment was regarded as fixing them in the hands of the administrator. The manner of enforcing such judgments is elaborately considered in McDowell v. Asbury, supra, and need not be repeated here. Suffice it to say that, if the sheriff returned *nulla bona* to the *fieri facias de bonis testatoris*, the plaintiff must generally have proceeded by *scire facias* in order to have obtained an execution *de bonis propriis* and in such proceeding, while the defendant could make any defense arising subsequently to the judgment fixing him with assets, (as, for instance, their loss or destruction under excusable circumstances,) he would be precluded from setting up any matter which could have been pleaded before the rendition of such judgment. The same principle applies in this proceeding, but the only matter which the said defendant relied upon could have been pleaded before the judgment, and is therefore inadmissible. The objection that the former action should have been commenced in the name of the state would have been good if taken in apt time, (Carmichael v. Moore, 88 N. C. 29,) but cannot avail the defendant under the circumstances of this case. Our conclusion is that as Walker, administrator, is fixed with assets, and as it is not shown that he and his sureties are insolvent, (Latham v. Bell, 69 N. C. 135, and Lilly v. Wooley, 94 N. C. 412,) the land should not be sold, and the judgment against the said Walker should be affirmed.

STATE v. EWING et al.

(*Supreme Court of North Carolina.* April 7, 1891.)

LANDLORD AND TENANT — UNLAWFUL SEIZURE OF CROPS—APPEAL—SPECIAL VERDICT.

1. Code N. C. § 1754, provides that crops on land leased for agricultural purposes shall be deemed in possession of the lessor until all rents are paid. Section 1755 gives the lessee a civil remedy, if the lessor obtains actual possession otherwise than as mentioned in the preceding section. Section 1759 makes it a misdemeanor for the lessor to unlawfully and knowingly seize the crop when there is nothing due him. Section 1762 extends these provisions to leases of turpentine trees. *Held*, that a lessor, who, after receiving all rent due, forbade the lessee to gather part of his crop, and leased the trees to others,

before the first lease terminated, and allowed them to take the balance of the crop, was guilty of a misdemeanor under section 1759.

2. Where the jury renders a special verdict on the facts, and the court enters a verdict "not guilty" thereon, the state may appeal.

Appeal from superior court, Montgomery county; BYNUM, Judge.

Indictment under Code N. C. § 1759, for unlawfully seizing a tenant's crop of turpentine.

The Attorney General, for the State. *Pemberton & Jerome, Batchelor & Devereux*, and *J. C. Black*, for appellees.

MERRIMON, C. J. The statute (Code, § 1754) prescribes that "when lands shall be rented or leased by agreement, written or oral, for agricultural purposes, or shall be cultivated by a cropper, unless otherwise agreed between the parties to the lease or agreement, any and all crops raised on said lands shall be deemed and held to be vested in possession of the lessor or his assigns at all times until the rents for said lands shall be paid, and until all the stipulations contained in the lease or agreement shall be performed," etc., and it further gives the landlord and his assigns a civil remedy prescribed in case the lessee, cropper, or the assigns of either of them "shall remove the crop, or any part thereof, from the lands without the consent of the lessor or his assigns," etc. The same statute (Code, § 1755) gives the lessee or cropper, or the assigns of either, a like civil remedy against the lessor or his assigns in case he or they "shall get the actual possession of the crop, or any part thereof, otherwise than by the mode prescribed in the preceding section," etc., and refuse upon notice "to make a fair division of said crop, or to pay over to such lessee or cropper, or the assigns of either, such part thereof as he may be entitled to under the lease or agreement," etc. These and other statutory provisions extend to leases of turpentine trees. Id. § 1762. The purpose of the same statute, (Id. § 1759,) which makes it a misdemeanor on the part of the lessee or cropper, or the assigns of either, to remove the crop or any part thereof without the consent of the lessor or his assigns, etc., and likewise on the part of the landlord to "unlawfully, willfully, knowingly, and without process of law, and unjustly, seize the crop of his tenant when there is nothing due him," etc., is to render the statutory provisions and regulations above referred to more effective, and this penal provision must be interpreted in that light and with that view. It embraces both the landlord and the tenant, and intends the more effectually to secure their respective rights as prescribed.

It appears that the prosecutor had leased turpentine trees from the defendants, and made the crop, but had not gathered the whole thereof; that his term of lease was not over, but he was out of the actual possession of the trees and the land on which they were situate; that he had paid the defendants all the rents due them, and owed them nothing for advancements or expenses; that he sent his servants back to gather and remove the remaining ungathered part of the crop; that they went to do so, and the defendants forbade them to gather the crop so remaining, and accordingly they did not; that the defendants, before the prosecutor's lease was over, leased the same trees to tenants for the next ensuing year, and these tenants were allowed to take the balance of the prosecutor's crop, and use it for their own purposes. The defendants had possession of the land, the turpentine trees, and the boxes in them, containing the prosecutor's ungathered crop of turpentine. Such being the facts, clearly the prosecutor might have maintained his civil action as allowed by the statute above mentioned against the defendants to recover the ungathered part of his crop. The defendants had no shadow of right to detain it, or prevent the owner or his servants from gathering and removing it. We are also of opinion that the defendants, in the just sense and contemplation of the statute, (Code, § 1759) "unlawfully, willfully, knowingly, and without process of law, and unjustly," seized the crop of their tenant, the prosecutor, when there was nothing due them, and thereby committed a misdemeanor. They violated the spirit and certain purpose of the statute first above referred to, and did that which the penal provision just cited intends to prevent. They had possession of the turpentine trees, the boxes in them containing the ungathered crop of the prosecutor that he had the right to gather, and when they refused to allow his servants to gather the same, they thereby manifested their purpose to and did in contemplation of the statute "seize," take possession and control of, such ungathered crop. The word "seize" is used in the sense of taking unlawful actual possession of the crop by force actually used or plainly implied. To constitute the offense it is not necessary that the landlord shall take possession of the crop *manu forti*, or manual possession of it at all. It will be complete in this respect if he takes possession and control thereof in such way as prevents and excludes the tenant from gathering and removing his crop in a peaceable and orderly manner. This the statute intends he shall have the right to do. The defendants asserted their purpose to have and take the exclusive possession when they forbade the prosecutor to remove his crop, and the latter, on that account, desisted from doing so. That such was their purpose was made the more manifest by the fact that they let the turpentine trees to other tenants, and allowed them to take the prosecutor's remaining crop. We are therefore of opinion that upon the special verdict the court should have decided that the defendants were guilty.

It was contended on the argument that an appeal did not lie in this case in favor of the state, because, as suggested, there was a verdict of not guilty. This contention is founded in misapprehension. It very obviously appears from the record that the jury intended to, and certainly did, render a special verdict embodying all the material facts of the case. This they did, and no more, and this it was their province to do. This verdict remains and appears as part of the record, and the judgment of the court is founded upon it. The jury could not go further and render two verdicts, one special and the other general, so that both might prevail at the same time. To do so would involve practical absurdity. The court did not set the special verdict aside. It in effect simply decided that upon this verdict the defendants were not guilty, and gave judgment in their favor. The entry of the verdict "not guilty" was not the finding of the jury. It was the order of the court upon the special verdict, and was not necessary. Perhaps it might (ought to) have been omitted, as it served no useful purpose. State v. Moore, 7 Ired. 228. On the argument it was brought to our attention that some confusion and inconsistency prevailed in the numerous decisions of this court in respect to special verdicts in criminal cases. We have examined the cases cited and others, and upon mature consideration we think it better that upon the special verdict in a case the court should simply declare its opinion that the defendant is guilty or not guilty, and enter judgment accordingly. Indeed, the simple entry of judgment in favor of or against the defendant would be sufficient. This is substantially the practice as pointed out in State v. Moore, supra. It is plain and convenient, will prevent further conflict of decision, and should be observed. There is error. Let this opinion be certified to the superior court according to law. It is so ordered.

GILLIS v. WILMINGTON, O. & E. C. R. Co.[1]

(*Supreme Court of North Carolina.* April 7, 1891.)

SECONDARY EVIDENCE—LOST LETTERS—DEGREE OF PROOF.

1. In an action for breach of a contract of hiring contained in letters written by defendant's agent to plaintiff, testimony by plaintiff that he usually kept his letters in his trunk, and had searched there for those in question without finding them, is sufficient to render admissible secondary evidence of their contents, though plaintiff further testified that sometimes the letters were changed into his wife's trunk, which was not shown to have been searched, and though on his cross-examination he refused to positively testify that the letters had been lost or destroyed.

2. Where the writing and contents of alleged lost letters are denied, the proof must be clear that such letters once existed, and that their contents were such as to sustain the material allegations of the complaint; and it is error to refuse an instruction requested by defendant that, to find for plaintiff, the jury must be satisfied by more than a preponderance of testimony that defendant's agent did write to plaintiff offering to employ him, as alleged by plaintiff, that the offer was accepted by plaintiff, and that the letters were lost or destroyed. SHEPHERD, J., dissenting.

This was a civil action for damages for breach of contract, tried before MacRae, J., and a jury, at November term, 1890, of Cumberland superior court. The single issue submitted, with the response thereto, was as follows: "Is the defendant indebted to the plaintiff as alleged; if so, in what sum? Answer. The defendant is indebted $275." Rule for new trial for errors alleged as to admission of testimony and upon the following exceptions to the

[1] For concurring opinion, see 13 S. E. Rep. 1019.

charge: The defendant excepts to his honor's charge: "(1) For that his honor assumed in said charge that there was sufficient evidence of the search of the plaintiff for the alleged letters containing the alleged contract, and their loss, to justify the admission of secondary evidence of contents, although the plaintiff said he himself had destroyed them, or might have destroyed them, and afterwards said, 'They may have been destroyed; I don't know.' (2) For that his honor charged that 'if the [secondary] testimony satisfied the jury that Mr. Lamb was the chief engineer of the defendant, and wrote to plaintiff, and offered him $60 per month and board for one year for his work, and that plaintiff accepted this offer and went to work, the jury would be warranted in finding that there was a contract in writing as required by the statute;' thus assuming that because he was chief engineer he was 'authorized thereto,' and did not advert to the fact, sworn to by Lamb, that he had no authority to make such a contract as is required by statute, which was the only evidence as to his authority. (3) For that his honor charged the jury that 'if the testimony satisfied them that Mr. Lamb was chief engineer of the defendant, and wrote to plaintiff, and offered him $60 per month and board for one year for his work, and that plaintiff accepted this offer, and went to work, the jury would be warranted in finding that there was a contract in writing as required by the statute,' and did not charge the jury, as requested, that they must be clearly satisfied by more than a preponderance of testimony that said Lamb did write to the plaintiff making said offer, and that said offer was accepted by plaintiff, and said correspondence was lost or destroyed, before they could find a verdict for plaintiff. (4) For that his honor charged the jury that 'the defendant had no right to discharge plaintiff except for good cause, and no cause has been proven,' when there was evidence that plaintiff was discharged on complaint of the local engineer under whom he worked."

A. M. Waddell, for appellant. *Sutton & Cook,* for appellee.

AVERY, J., *(after stating the facts as above.)* It is within the sound discretion of the court to determine what is sufficient evidence of the loss or destruction of an original paper to make testimony as to its contents competent, and this court will assume, where nothing appears to the contrary, that the court below acted, in admitting secondary evidence to show the words or substance of the instrument, upon plenary proof that a sufficiently diligent, but fruitless, search was made, and that there was no testimony tending to show that it was fraudulently destroyed or withheld by the party proposing to prove its contents. Bonds v. Smith, 106 N. C. 564, 11 S. E. Rep. 322; 1 Whart. Ev. § 141; 1 Greenl. Ev. § 558; 1 Tayl. Ev. § 22. Mr. Greenleaf says: "The question whether the loss of the instrument is sufficiently proved to admit secondary evidence of its contents is to be determined by the court,

and not by the jury." Taylor says: "In like manner, if the question be whether a document has been duly executed or stamped, or whether it comes from the right custody; whether sufficient search has been made for it to admit secondary evidence of its contents, etc.,—in all these and the like cases the preliminary question of admissibility must, in the first instance, be exclusively decided by the judge, however complicated the circumstances may be, and though it may be necessary to weigh the conflicting testimony of numerous witnesses in order to arrive at a just conclusion." In Mauney v. Crowell, 84 N. C. 315, it was held that a general finding by the judge, without setting out the testimony, that no sufficient search had been made, would have been conclusive; thus recognizing the discretionary power of the court. But where the facts upon which the *nisi prius* judge acted are found, it is competent for this court to review his ruling, and determine whether the testimony was sufficient in law to justify his conclusion. The degree of diligence that must be shown depends largely upon the nature and circumstances of the case, and especially upon the character of the paper, as a useless document may be presumed to have been lost or destroyed on proof of much less search and for a much shorter time than an important one. Best, Ev. § 482; 1 Whart. Ev. § 140. As a rule, it is expected that deeds and records that are evidence of title will be more carefully kept than letters or papers which may or may not become material as testimony tending to establish one's rights. In Gathercole v. Miall, 15 Mees. & W. 335, ALDERSON, B., says: "The question whether there has been a loss, and whether there has been sufficient search, must depend very much on the nature of the instrument searched for. If we were speaking of an envelope in which a letter had been received, and a person said, 'I have searched for it among my papers; I cannot find it,' surely that would be sufficient. So with respect to an old newspaper, which had been at a public coffee-room; if the party who kept the public coffee-room had searched for it, where he would naturally find it, that seems to me to be amply sufficient. If he had said, 'I know it was taken away by A. B,' then you ought to go to A. B." But he concluded: "It would be very unreasonable to require you to go to every member of the club." Where a reasonable person might be satisfied, from the testimony offered, that an effort had been made in good faith to find and produce a letter, the decision of the trial judge to admit proof of its contents is not reviewable in the appellate court. Best, Ev. p. 451. The object in offering the proof is to establish a reasonable presumption of the loss of the instrument, and this is a preliminary inquiry addressed to the discretion of the judge." 1 Greenl. Ev. § 558.

The first exception is stated in the record as follows: "The plaintiff resumed, and testified: 'Richard Lamb said he was chief engineer of defendant, and he was acting as such, and I got this letter from him. I got other letters from him before

I went there. I have lost them. I have made search for them; have looked over my trunk. I had changed about so much, till I could not find them. I reckon I lost them.' Plaintiff was cross-examined upon this point, and testified: 'I kept them in my trunk, and sometimes in my wife's trunk. We would change them about, and sometimes when we got too many letters we would destroy them; these letters may have been destroyed. I don't know.' The defendant objected to plaintiff testifying as to the contents of the letters. The court, being of opinion that the witness had laid the foundation for the offer of secondary evidence by his testimony of the loss or destruction of the papers, permitted the plaintiff to testify as to their contents, and defendant excepted." We do not think, when it appears that the plaintiff usually kept his letters in his own trunk, and searched for them there without finding them, that the judge was in error in allowing him to testify as to the contents, merely because he said that sometimes the letters were changed into his wife's trunk, and it did not appear that it had also been examined, nor because the witness said on his examination in chief, "I reckon I lost them;" and on his cross-examination. "These letters may have been destroyed; I don't know." We think that his honor was warranted in drawing the inference that the letter had been lost or destroyed, and, in either event, its contents could be proven by parol. It is not essential that the testimony should have excluded the possibility that the letter was still in existence, as it was not necessary, in the case already cited, that every member of a club who had the privilege of reading or carrying off a newspaper should be offered to negative the possibility that he had it in his possession. In the case of Mauney v. Crowell, supra, it was declared error to exclude a copy of an original contract to sell land which had been shown to have been lost because it did not appear that the registry of the county in which the law required it to be registered had been examined.

In passing upon the evidence as to the preliminary question, the judge is not required to find that there is clear and satisfactory proof that a paper has been lost or destroyed before admitting testimony to show its contents. In Fisher v. Carroll, 6 Ired. Eq. 488, Judge PEARSON, speaking of a case where the execution and contents of an alleged lost note were denied, said: "In such a case, although equity would not refuse to consider the mere affidavit as sufficient to account for not producing the original note, the strictest and clearest proof of the execution and contents would be required." See, also, Mobley v. Watts, 98 N. C. 284, 3 S. E. Rep. 677, and Clifton v. Fort, 98 N. C. 178, 3 S. E. Rep. 726. It is settled by a line of authorities that, although the loss of a deed or paper relied on to prove a contract may have been sufficiently shown to justify the judge in admitting secondary evidence, such testimony must amount to clear and convincing proof that the deed or paper embodying the contract once existed, and that its contents were such as to sustain

the material allegations of the complaint or answer in support of which they are offered. Loftin v. Loftin, 96 N. C. 94, 1 S. E. Rep. 837; Fisher v. Carroll, supra. We think, therefore, that there was error in refusing to give the third instruction prayed for, for which a new trial must be granted.

While it is unnecessary to pass upon the question raised by the second exception, it may be well to add that it would not follow from the fact that Lamb was chief engineer that it was within the scope of his authority to make contracts with subordinate managers employed in grading the road-bed, and the laborers under them, in reference to wages. Wood, Ry. Law, p. 446, and note 2. There was no testimony offered as to the nature or extent of his authority, or tending to show a ratification of his agreement with the plaintiff by the corporation. Error.

SHEPHERD, J., (concurring.) I concur in the disposition made of this appeal, but I do not agree to the suggestion that what constitutes a diligent and reasonable search for an alleged lost paper writing is in any case within the sole discretion of the trial judge, and that his ruling is conclusive upon that question. If such be the law, it would be exceedingly difficult to account for the numerous decisions of appellate courts in the text-books and in our own Reports upon this important subject. The authorities cited do not, in my opinion, sustain such a principle, but, on the contrary, establish the very opposite view. When the testimony relating to the particulars of the search is conflicting, it is the duty of the court, upon the request of the objecting party, to find the facts, and, if no such request is made, that aspect of the testimony which is most favorable to the other party will be taken by this court in passing upon the ruling of the trial judge. Holden v. Purifoy, 12 S. E. Rep. 848, (decided at this term.) The findings as to the facts are conclusive, but the legal inferences are reviewable. Neither do I agree that a diligent search was made in the present case, and that oral testimony should have been admitted. Mr. Greenleaf (volume 1, § 558) says that the evidence must show that a *bona fide* and diligent search has been unsuccessfully made (for the lost instrument) in the place where it is most likely to be found, if the nature of the case admits of such proof. The party must "exhaust, in a reasonable degree, all the sources of information and means of discovery which the nature of the case would naturally suggest, and which were accessible to him." Id.; Dumas v. Powell, 3 Dev. 103; Murphy v. McNiel, 2 Dev. & B. 244; Harper v. Hancock, 6 Ired. 124; Threadgill v. White, 11 Ired. 591; McCracken v. McCrary, 5 Jones, (N. C.) 399. The foregoing cases, and many others to be found in our Reports, exemplify in a high degree the very strict application by this court of the general principle above stated. So far from the witness in this case having exhausted all of his sources of information, his examination reveals the two depositories of these very letters, and yet he has examined but one of them. He says: "I kept them in my trunk, and sometimes in my wife's trunk,"—that is to say, either in one trunk or the other; and it is but fair to assume, in the absence of an examination, that the letters were in his wife's trunk at the time of the trial. It does seem very clear to me that there has been no such diligent search as is required by the law, and that, if oral testimony can be substituted for contractual writings under such circumstances, the rule as to the primariness of documentary evidence will be practically abrogated. If, as in Davidson v. Norment, 5 Ired. 555, a party was required to go to another state, and get his deed, it would seem but reasonable that this witness should have taken a few steps, presumably in his own house, and looked into his wife's trunk for the letters in question. The case cited from 3 Dev., supra, also illustrates the great particularity of the court in applying this most salutary rule of practice. When contracts have been reduced to writing, there is an implied agreement between the parties, which the law recognizes and enforces, that such contracts shall only be proved by the selected medium of proof, and the "slippery memory of witnesses" should never be substituted, except upon the most imperative demands of necessity and justice.

As to the intensity of proof, I have never understood that, in the case of a writing evidencing a purely simple contract, where the writing is lost or destroyed, and there is no evidence of fraudulent suppression or spoliation, a party is compelled, in a court of law, to establish its contents by the same degree of proof, as is required in equity where lost bonds and other deeds are sought to be set up or corrected, as in the cases cited. The degree of proof mentioned is only applied in cases of equitable cognizance. See discussion in Harding v. Long, 103 N. C. 7, 9 S. E. Rep. 445.

CLARK, J. I concur with my Brother SHEPHERD.

STATE v. FESPERMAN.

(Supreme Court of North Carolina. April 7, 1891.)

ASSAULT—JURISDICTION OF SUPERIOR COURT.

1. Code N. C. § 892, restricting the jurisdiction of the superior courts for assault, where no deadly weapon is used, and no serious damage done, to cases where justices of the peace neglect for six months to take official cognizance of the offense, does not oust the jurisdiction of the court where the indictment charges an assault with a deadly weapon, although the evidence shows only a simple assault, committed within six months of the finding of the indictment.

2. Const. N. C. art. 4, § 27, restricts the jurisdiction of magistrates to cases where the punishment cannot exceed $50 fine or 30 days' imprisonment. Code, § 987, prescribes that an assault with a deadly weapon may be punished by fine and imprisonment, in the discretion of the court. *Held,* that section 892, as amended by chapter 152, Acts 1891, giving magistrates jurisdiction of all assaults in which no serious damage is done, where the punishment shall not exceed $50 fine or 30 days' imprisonment, does not confer jurisdiction in cases where, although no serious damage is inflicted, the use of a deadly weapon is charged.

Appeal from superior court, Stanley county; BYNUM, Judge.

Indictment for assault with a deadly weapon. Code N. C. § 892, provides that justices of the peace shall have exclusive original jurisdiction of all assaults, assaults and batteries, and affrays where no deadly weapon is used, and no serious damage done; provided, that nothing in this section shall prevent the superior courts from assuming jurisdiction if some justice of the peace, within six months after the commission of the offense, shall not have proceeded to take official cognizance of the same.

The Attorney General, for the State.

CLARK, J. The indictment charges an assault "with a certain deadly weapon, to-wit, a shovel, of the weight of 5 pounds." The special verdict finds that in fact the assault was made by the defendant with his fist and within six months before the true bill was found. It has been repeatedly held that when the indictment in the superior court charges an assault with a deadly weapon the court retains jurisdiction, although in the proof simple assault only shall be shown. State v. Ray, 89 N. C. 587; State v. Reaves, 85 N. C. 553; State v. Cunningham, 94 N. C. 824; State v. Earnest, 98 N. C. 740, 4 S. E. Rep. 495. The cases in which the jurisdiction of the superior court is ousted by showing that the assault was within six months (now twelve months) before indictment found, are limited to those in which the charge in itself is of a simple assault. State v. Porter, 101 N. C. 713, 7 S. E. Rep. 902, and cases there cited. The court below was therefore plainly in error in holding, as the law stood at the time of the trial, (1890,) that the superior court did not have jurisdiction. It is insisted, however, that by virtue of chapter 152, Acts 1891, a magistrate has now jurisdiction of an assault with a deadly weapon if no serious damage was done. There is in the act no exception as to pending actions, and the present case differs in that respect from State v. Watts, 85 N. C. 517. But if it is conceded that the act applies to pending cases, we are of opinion that it does not confer jurisdiction of assaults with a deadly weapon upon magistrates in any case. The constitution restricts the jurisdiction of magistrates in criminal matters to cases "where the punishment cannot exceed a fine of $50 or imprisonment for thirty days." Const. N. C. art. 4, § 27. It is not competent, therefore, for the legislature to confer jurisdiction upon magistrates of any offenses of which the punishment affixed by law may exceed that limit. The Code, § 987, which was not amended, still prescribes that assaults with a deadly weapon may be punished by fine and imprisonment, in the discretion of the court. It is true that the Code, § 892, as amended by chapter 152, Acts 1891, purports to give magistrates exclusive original jurisdiction of all assaults "in which no serious damage is done, and of all criminal matters arising in their counties, where the punishment prescribed by law shall not exceed a fine of fifty dollars, or imprisonment for thirty days." We might surmise that the intention was to confer jurisdiction upon magistrates in cases where, though a deadly weapon was used, no serious damage was inflicted. But the punishment for assaults with a deadly weapon in all cases, whether serious damage is or is not inflicted, being left unchanged,—"fine and imprisonment, in the discretion of the court,"—whatever may or may not have been the legislative intent in amending the Code, § 892, the amendatory act could not confer upon the justice's court jurisdiction of an offense the punishment affixed to which may exceed the constitutional limit of such court. The constitution makes the punishment which the court has authority to impose the test of a magistrate's jurisdiction. It was competent for the legislature to reduce the punishment of this offense within the jurisdiction of a justice, and the justice would *ipso facto* acquire jurisdiction without further provision; but an act in terms prescribing that a justice of the peace shall have have jurisdiction of an offense without reducing the punishment within the constitutional limitation upon that officer is of no effect. This has been often decided. State v. Perry, 71 N. C. 522; State v. Cherry, 72 N. C. 123; State v. Heidelburg, 70 N. C. 496; State v. Vermington, 71 N. C. 264. The judgment is reversed, and the case remanded, that the court below may pass sentence upon the special verdict in accordance with this opinion.

GRAVES v. HINES *et al.*

(Supreme Court of North Carolina. April 7, 1891.)

HOMESTEAD—RIGHTS OF CHILDREN—DOWER LANDS.

> Const. N. C. art. 10, § 2, provides that "every homestead, * * * not exceeding in value one thousand dollars, to be selected" by the owner, or, in lieu thereof, any town lot, with the buildings thereon of like value, owned and occupied by him, shall be exempt from debt; and section 3 provides that the homestead, after the death of the owner, shall be so exempt during the minority of any of his children. *Held*, that when a man dies without having had a homestead allotted, and dower is assigned to the widow, the minor children are not entitled to homestead in lands covered by the dower. Following Watts v. Leggett, 66 N. C. 197.

Appeal from superior court, Surry county; GILMER, Judge.

This was a proceeding by the administrator of A. Hines against his minor children for leave to sell the real estate of the testator, subject to the widow's dower, which had been assigned. No homestead had been laid off in the testator's life-time, and his children now claim a homestead in lands not covered by the widow's dower. At the trial this claim was denied, and defendants appeal. Const. N. C. art. 10, § 2, provides that "every homestead, and the dwellings and buildings used therewith, not exceeding in value one thousand dollars, to be selected by the owner thereof, or, in lieu thereof, at the option of the owner, any lot in a city, town, or village, with the dwelling and buildings used therewith, owned and occupied by any resident of this state, and not exceeding the value of one thousand dollars, shall be exempt from sale under execution or other final process obtained on any debt." Section 3 provides that "the homestead, after the death of the owner thereof, shall be

exempt from the payment of any debt during the minority of his children, or any one of them."

R. L. Haymore, for plaintiff. *S. F. Graves* and *Batchelor & Devereux*, for defendants.

PER CURIAM. The very point in this case was passed upon in Watts v. Leggett, 66 N. C. 197, and decided adversely to the claims of the defendants. The view there taken by the court has been long regarded as the settled law of this state, and has been frequently approved in subsequent decisions, notably in McAfee v. Bettis, 72 N. C. 28, and Gregory v. Ellis, 86 N. C. 579. In the latter case the opinion in Watts v. Leggett is quoted at some length by ASHE, J., and entirely approved by the court as to the particular point now in question. We have been much impressed with the able argument of the counsel for the defendants, but are of the opinion that it is better to adhere to the previous rulings of the court, and that there is nothing which imperatively demands their reversal. Affirmed.

BOYKIN *et al.* v. EPSTEIN *et al.*

(Supreme Court of Georgia. March 16, 1891.)

INJUNCTION—PLEADING—VERIFICATION.

> The refusal by a judge of the superior court to hear and determine a petition for injunction and the appointment of a receiver, before the same has been verified as required by law, was not error.

(Syllabus by the Court.)

Error from superior court, Chatham county; FALLIGANT, Judge.

J. R. Saussy, for plaintiffs in error. *Denmark, Adams & Adams*, for defendants in error.

LUMPKIN, J. The plaintiffs in error presented to the judge of the superior court of Chatham county their petition praying for the appointment of a receiver of the firm of Epstein & Wannbacher, and also for an injunction against them and a large number of their creditors. This petition was not sworn to, nor in any manner verified, when presented to the judge, who, without observing the same, granted a restraining order and rule *nisi*, and appointed a time for the hearing of the petition. At the hearing petitioners announced themselves ready to prove the allegations of the petition by affidavits, witnesses, books, and records of the court, and especially by the books of Epstein & Wannbacher, then in court. No affidavit or proof of any kind was attached to the petition itself for the purpose of verifying it; but nevertheless plaintiffs insisted that the hearing should proceed, and that they had a right to submit their proof in support of their petition while the hearing was in progress, contending that this would be such a verification thereof as the law contemplated. The judge declined to hear any part of the proof thus offered, or to permit petitioners to verify the petition in this way, set aside the temporary restraining order previously granted, and discharged the rule to show cause, upon the ground that the petition was not verified in the manner prescribed by law. The act of 1887 (Acts 1886–87, p. 65) provides "that no petition needs to be verified unless it seeks an extraordinary equitable relief or remedy, in which case it must be." This act, therefore, imperatively requires that a petition for injunction and receiver must be verified, and the judge, certainly, may demand that this be done before taking action or allowing a hearing to be had thereon. If, as contended by the learned counsel for the plaintiffs in error, proof of the allegations at and during the hearing would be sufficient verification, there would have been no need at all for passing the statute cited, because, as no injunction could be properly granted, or receiver appointed, unless facts authorizing such relief are proved to the judge, it follows that, unless the statute means to provide for a verification of the petition in some way previous to action thereon by the judge, it is useless, and serves no practical purpose. It may be said in reply to this that the judge could not appoint a receiver or grant a restraining order or other like relief before the petition has been verified, but that he could grant a rule to show cause before this was done. The statute makes no such distinction. Its evident purpose was that nothing putting in motion the extraordinary powers of the court should be done by the judge until the application for the exercise of such powers has been vouched for by some kind of proof or verification. A rule *nisi* on such a petition is as much a part of the "equitable relief or remedy" sought as a restraining order, or one appointing a receiver; and the law means that no part of this relief can be had upon an unverified petition. We do not mean to hold that the verification required by law can be made only by an affidavit attached to the petition, or that the judge may not, at the hearing, allow the verification to be made. It may be that other forms of proof could be attached to the petition or accompany and be exhibited with it, which would authorize the judge, if he saw proper, to proceed; and he may in his discretion, at the hearing, allow the petition to be verified; but he cannot, in the face of the statute, be compelled to allow the hearing to take place without any verification. In the present case the plaintiffs squarely insisted, as a matter of right, upon having their petition heard on its merits without verification of any kind preceding the hearing, and this, we think, they could not demand when the judge only required a compliance with the law. It follows, therefore, that he committed no error in refusing, under the circumstances, to proceed further with the investigation. Judgment affirmed.

MATTHEWS v. STATE.

(*Supreme Court of Georgia.* March 16, 1891.)

BURGLARY—EVIDENCE—CONFESSION.

On an indictment for burglary it was shown that a dwelling had been broken open and some bacon and meal stolen. The articles were found in defendant's possession and at first she

denied taking them, but afterwards, being told that she had better confess it if she took them, she confessed in the presence of three men that one P. helped her to burst in the door, and they got the meat and meal, and carried them off and divided them. *Held*, that a verdict of guilty was warranted.

Error from superior court, Madison county; LUMPKIN, Judge.

The official report is as follows: "Georgia Matthews was indicted for burglary. The evidence for the state tended to show the following: On August 19, 1888, the dwelling-house of one Eberhart was broken open, and some meal and bacon stolen from it. The property was found in the possession of defendant. She was asked how she came by it. She at first denied taking it, and afterwards, in the presence of three men, freely and voluntarily stated that Albert Pass helped her to burst in the door of the house, and they got the meat and meal and carried it off in the woods and divided it. No threats or force or violence were offered to make her admit it, but one of the men present told her if she did take the things it would be best for her to own it, and, if she did not, not to do it. No testimony was introduced by the defendant. She stated that when the men came up and asked her where she got that meat and meal, and if she did not break into the house, that she told them, 'No,' and then one of them said, 'If you don't own it, you had better own it;' that she said she did not break in, Albert Pass broke in; that Albert did break in, and got the meat and meal and gave her part of it. She was found guilty, and moved for a new trial on the ground that the verdict was contrary to law, evidence," etc. The motion was overruled, and she excepted.

David W. Meadow, for plaintiff in error. *W. M. Howard*, Sol. Gen., by *Z. D. Harrison*, for the State.

SIMMONS, J. There was ample evidence in this case to authorize the jury to find the defendant guilty. Judgment affirmed.

MATTHEWS v. STATE.

(*Supreme Court of Georgia.* March 16, 1891.)

BURGLARY—EVIDENCE—NEW TRIAL.

1. The burglary being fully established, and the whole contest being as to the identity of the burglar, the positive testimony of one witness that she recognized the accused as the person, and the less confident testimony of another that she also recognized him, both of them being on the premises when the offense was committed, and the moon giving considerable light, warranted a verdict of guilty.

2. The newly-discovered evidence is not such as to justify the grant of a new trial upon legal principles.

(*Syllabus by the Court.*)

Error from superior court, Madison county; LUMPKIN, Judge.

David W. Meadow, for plaintiff in error. *W. M. Howard*, Sol. Gen., by *J. H. Lumpkin*, for the State.

BLECKLEY, C. J. 1. All the facts requisite to constitute the offense of burglary were established beyond the possibility of question, and the whole contest was as to the identity of the burglar. We cannot escape a feeling of apprehension that some mistake may have been made as to whether Matthews was really the person who committed the crime; but there was moonlight, and Mrs. Phillips testified positively to his identity. Her evidence was strengthened somewhat by that of a negro woman, who was present, and who, as well as Mrs. Phillips, recognized Matthews at the time. A strange fact is that this woman seems not to have told Phillips who the person was until next day; and a still stranger fact is that, so far as appears, Mrs. Phillips did not tell him at all. Neither she nor Phillips mentions, in the testimony as it comes to us, anything of her having told him; and, after having full opportunity at night to converse with his wife, he resumed the search for tracks next morning, as he says, "to see if I could make any discovery as to who it was." If his wife knew who it was, it is strange that he remained ignorant so long. But the jury heard the witness; and, deciding according to legal rules, we cannot say that the evidence before them was not sufficient to warrant the verdict. There seems to have been no thorough sifting of the state's witnesses, but the jury were satisfied with the evidence without it; and we cannot order a new trial merely because the witnesses were not sifted on cross-examination. This was the fault of the prisoner or his counsel. Mrs. Phillips may or may not have been mistaken. The jury have found that she was not. The trial judge was satisfied with the finding; and, the evidence being sufficient, this court will acquiesce.

2. The newly-discovered evidence is not such as to justify the grant of a new trial upon legal principles. Judgment affirmed.

JOHNSTON v. PATTERSON.

(*Supreme Court of Georgia.* Feb. 23, 1891.)

DISTRESS WARRANT — ARRESTING LEVY — PAROL EVIDENCE—SET-OFF.

1. Where the entry of a levy upon a distress warrant included among other things "one crop cotton growing," allowing such levy to be read to the jury on the trial of an issue made by a counter-affidavit to the distress warrant was no ground for a new trial.

2. A written contract, silent or ambiguous as to certain matters, may, as to them, be explained by parol evidence, not conflicting with anything plainly expressed in such contract.

3. A plea of set-off alleging against the plaintiff in a distress warrant items of indebtedness entirely independent of and disconnected with the rent contract is not allowable.

4. The defendant in a distress warrant, after arresting the proceeding of a levy thereof as the statute prescribes, may, on the trial of the issue thus formed, prove, by way of recoupment against the plaintiff's demand, damages resulting from a breach by the plaintiff of his own stipulations in the rent contract, and in order to do this it is not necessary to amend his counter-affidavit to set out the grounds of such recoupment.

(*Syllabus by the Court.*)

Error from superior court, Bibb county; MILLER, Judge.

Steed & Wimberly, Claud & Hubert Estes, M. G. Bayne, and *J. A. Thomas,* for plaintiff in error. *R. W. Patterson* and *R. Hodges,* for defendant in error.

LUMPKIN, J. It appears from the record that Patterson and Johnston made a written contract, dated August 3, 1888, containing numerous mutual promises and stipulations, and among them the following: That Patterson rented to Johnston 160 acres of land, consisting of 30 acres in the "Grace Field," 120 acres in the "Big Field," and 10 acres surrounding the house. Johnston agreed to pay Patterson $480 rent for the above-described premises on the 15th of October. Patterson also rented to Johnston four mules, to be used on said plantation, for which Johnston agreed to pay as rent the sum of $80. Johnston was also to receive 5 per cent. on the collections which he might make of rents arising from lands of Patterson which Johnston rented out for Patterson; and Patterson also agreed to pay Johnston $60 on the 15th of October, provided Johnston should well and truly attend to any business which Patterson might direct on said plantation. It appears also that Johnston had been in possession of the rented premises prior to the date of the above contract, and that the contract between the parties was reduced to writing and executed the day the contract bears date. There are 27 grounds in the motion for new trial, but they may be condensed into those set out in the head-notes.

1. As appears by the entry of the officer, the distress warrant was levied on certain cotton-seed, corn, peas, potatoes, and "one crop cotton growing." The fact that the entry contained the words quoted was certainly no reason for rejecting the entire levy. Indeed, if the growing crop of cotton had been all the property levied on, we do not see, on the trial of an issue formed by a counter-affidavit to a distress warrant, how allowing this entry to be read to the jury could be of any consequence. It simply went in along with the pleadings in the case, and, though immaterial and perhaps irrelevant, on this sort of a trial, was harmless. Section 3642 of the Code might afford good ground to dismiss a levy made on a growing crop, but the reading or not reading of such a levy to the jury in this case could in no way injuriously affect the defendant's rights upon the issues pending.

2. It was seriously disputed in this case whether the land cultivated by Phillips, and for the rent of which he paid Patterson, was a part of the land for which Johnston was to pay $480 rent, and whether or not the amount paid by Phillips to Patterson should be a credit on the rent Johnston owed Patterson. The court by its rulings and charges refused to allow Johnston to go into these questions with his evidence, on the idea that he was estopped from so doing by the written contract, and would not be permitted to vary its terms by parol evidence. We think this was error. The contract was silent as to whether or not the land worked by Phillips was a part of that Johnston rented from Patterson for himself, and as Johnston was, by the contract, made the agent of Patterson to rent out his lands, it is uncertain, from the contract itself, whether, if he rented to Phillips a part of the land he had himself contracted to pay

rent for, this would reduce *pro tanto* the amount of rent due by him. Where a writing is such that something more than what is expressed therein is to be implied therefrom, parol evidence of anything not inconsistent with that unexpressed something is admissible. McMahan v. Tyson, 23 Ga. 43. It is too well settled to require further argument or authority that omissions, ambiguities, and uncertainties in written contracts may be explained by parol evidence, which does not conflict with anything the instrument plainly expresses, and parol evidence is admissible to apply all written contracts to their subject-matter.

3. The defendant undertook to set off against the plaintiff's claim for rent certain demands which were entirely independent of the rent contract. This he could not do, and the court rightly rejected all the evidence offered for this purpose. It was held in the case of McMahan v. Tyson, above cited, that while failure of consideration might be set up as a defense to a note given for rent, and sought to be collected by distress warrant, a plea of set-off would not be allowed because it admits the sum it is pleaded against is due. This ruling to the extent above stated is approved in Rountree v. Rutherford, 65 Ga. 446.

4. The defendant also sought to recoup against plaintiff's demand for rent damages resulting to him from various alleged breaches by the plaintiff of stipulations and promises by the latter contained in the rent contract itself, and immediately connected therewith, such as the plaintiff's agreements to furnish him mules; to pay commissions on rents received from land Johnston might rent out for him; to pay Johnston for his services on the plantation, etc. These defenses he ought to have been permitted to make, and for the purpose of so doing it was not necessary to amend his counter-affidavit. Guthman v. Castleberry, 48 Ga. 172, and 49 Ga. 272. When the defendant met the levy of the distress warrant by filing the affidavit required by law, and the issue thus formed was returned to court, it was his right to prove his defense. Holland v. Brown, 15 Ga. 113; Drake v. Dawson, 66 Ga. 174. The following cases are referred to as showing when recoupment is a proper defense: Mell v. Moony, 30 Ga. 413; Lufburrow v. Henderson, Id. 482; Finney v. Cadwallader, 55 Ga. 75; Latimer v. Lane, 45 Ga. 474. Judgment reversed.

WOLFE v. BAXTER et al.

(*Supreme Court of Georgia.* Feb. 28, 1891.)

TITLE TO MAINTAIN EJECTMENT.

Where one died in possession of land under a *bona fide* claim of right thereto, this was *prima facie* evidence of title in him, and his heirs or devisees may recover on proof of such possession, unless a better adverse title is shown by the defendant.

(*Syllabus by the Court.*)

Error from superior court, Bibb county; MILLER, Judge.

Alexander & Turnbull, Steed & Wimberly, and *F. A. Arnold,* for plaintiff in error. *Felton & Baxter,* for defendants in error.

LUMPKIN, J. In this case the court below granted a nonsuit, and by the bill of exceptions three questions are presented for review. The first, viz., whether or not a plaintiff in ejectment, suing for a one-fifth interest in land, and proving a right to recover a one-sixth interest therein, can recover the latter interest, needs no argument. It is well settled that a plaintiff may always recover a less amount or interest than that sued for, but never more. In the second place, we deem it unnecessary to discuss whether or not the familiar rule that in ejectment, where both parties claim under a common grantor, neither need trace title beyond that source, is applicable to the facts of this case, because the case is really controlled by the principle announced in the above headnote, and to that we will now devote our attention. The plaintiff's evidence made the following case: The land in dispute, at some time prior to the year 1853, was in possession of one Bryon Scott. Afterwards, in 1853 or 1854, it went into the possession of Robert Freeman, and so remained until his death, which occurred about the year 1855. Robert Freeman died testate, and in his will directed that his entire estate, except what was sold to pay his debts, be kept together and managed for the support and maintenance of his family, and the education of his children, during the life or widowhood of his wife, Harriet B.; and, if she should marry again, that all his estate be divided equally between his wife and children. It further provided that the wife, if she married, should take her share absolutely, and that the shares of his children should go to them during their natural lives, with remainder, at their deaths, to their children, respectively. His wife and one Andrew Comer were appointed executrix and executor of the will, but the former alone qualified. Mrs. Freeman, in 1863 or 1864, married one Fulton, and died in 1884 or 1885. She remained in possession of the land as executrix until her marriage with Fulton, and also after this marriage for a considerable length of time. The testator, Robert Freeman, left five children,—two sons and three daughters. One of his sons, James S., married the plaintiff, whose maiden name was Powell. James S. Freeman died about three years after his marriage with the plaintiff, leaving her as his widow, and one child, James E. Freeman, who lived about a year, and died, leaving his mother, the plaintiff, his sole heir at law. The evidence in the case tends to show that no division of the testator's estate, as contemplated by his will, was ever made, and this suit was brought by the plaintiff to recover a fifth interest in the lot of land in dispute, which appears to have been a part of the tract of land occupied by Robert Freeman at the time of his death. Section 3366 of the Code declares that a plaintiff in ejectment may recover upon his prior possession alone against one who subsequently acquires possession by mere entry, and without any lawful right. In Johnson v. Lancaster, 5 Ga. 39, the same rule is asserted, and also in Jones v. Scoggins, 11 Ga. 119. On page 121, Judge NISBET says: "If the plaintiff, as in this case, relies upon possession acquired bona fide, and nothing else, and the defendant is in possession as a trespasser, the defendant cannot rely upon that tortious possession, nor can he protect himself by showing a title in a third person." It was held in Jones v. Easley, 53 Ga. 454, that a plaintiff in ejectment may recover on prior possession alone against one who subsequently acquires possession without any lawful right, and this is true though the plaintiff may himself show to the jury no title. See, also, Scott v. Singer, 54 Ga 689. Again, in Jones v Nunn, 12 Ga. 472, Judge NISBET says: "As against one who can show no better title than naked possession, a plaintiff who has had prior possession may recover upon that possession." See, also, Eaton v. Freeman, 63 Ga. 535. This court ruled in Hadley v. Bean, 53 Ga. 688, that possession under a deed will cast the burden on the defendant to show he is not a trespasser, and that he has not acquired possession by mere entry without any lawful right whatever. The above case is cited approvingly in Parker v. Railroad Co., 81 Ga. 392, 8 S. E. Rep. 871. The rule stated seems, therefore, to have been fully settled both by the statute and repeated adjudications, but this court in the case of Bagley v. Kennedy has gone further, and decided definitely that evidence of such possession will change the onus, and put the defendant on proof of his title. This whole subject, in the case just cited, was thoroughly reviewed and discussed by Chief Justice BLECKLEY. The decision was rendered July 12, 1890, and may be found in 11 S. E. Rep. 1091. The head-note is as follows: "Possession of land under claim of ownership is prima facie evidence of title in the occupant. Hence, where a man died in the year 1829, in possession of the premises now in dispute, persons claiming under his heirs or devisees, and bringing suit in 1887, may recover on proof of his possession, or of title derived from him through his heirs or devisees, as the case may be, unless a better adverse title, by possession or otherwise, appears." In the opinion he quotes the case of Brown v. Colson, 41 Ga. 42, where the plaintiff's ancestor died in possession, and the premises were assigned to the widow as dower. She went into possession and died, and these facts were held sufficient, prima facie, to put the defendant upon proof of title. He also cites Buckner v. Chambliss, 30 Ga. 652, where it was held that an administrator may recover upon the possession alone of his intestate, and Boynton v. Brown, 67 Ga. 396, holding that heirs may recover upon the possession of their ancestor. That opinion also cites a large number of other authorities, to which reference is hereby made. In the case now before us, Robert Freeman died possessed of the land in controversy, having held and used it as his own. This, we have shown, was prima facie evidence of title in him. Under the facts proved in this case the widow could not, either as executrix up to the time of her second marriage, or as tenant in common with his children after her marriage, hold adversely to them, or those

claiming under them. It seems that the lands of the testator were never divided in kind. The plaintiff, therefore, as sole heir of one of the testator's devisees in remainder, upon proof of the foregoing facts, showed a prima facie right to recover her undivided interest in the land, and the nonsuit against her should not have been granted. Judgment reversed.

PHILLIPS v. TROWBRIDGE FURNITURE CO.

(Supreme Court of Georgia. Feb. 23, 1891.)

PARTNERSHIP—EVIDENCE—MORTGAGES—SECONDARY EVIDENCE.

1. On an issue as to whether defendant was a partner of one N., it is error to admit a statement made by N. to another person, not in defendant's presence or with her knowledge, that defendant was going into partnership with him.

2. A partner has the right to give a mortgage on personal property to secure a partnership debt, and also to agree to its cancellation, and the other partner is not injured thereby.

3. A blank form of a contract used by defendant's alleged partner, when he sold goods on installment, is not admissible in evidence to show the character of contracts that he made, where it is not shown that an executed original cannot be obtained nor a certified copy from the records of such contracts.

4. Nor is a memorandum of the names and amounts of customers, as shown by the books, admissible, where the books themselves are not tendered nor accounted for.

Error from superior court, Bibb county; MILLER, Judge.

L. D. Moore, for plaintiff in error. Lanier & Anderson, for defendant in error.

SIMMONS, J. 1. One of the main issues in this case was whether Mrs. Phillips was a partner of Neal. The plaintiff in its declaration alleged that she was. She denied it. It is complained of as error in the eighth ground of the motion for a new trial that, pending the trial, Kendall, the agent of the plaintiff, was allowed to testify, over objection of the defendant, "that Neal stated to him in Atlanta that Mrs. Phillips was going in with him, and would furnish security to the amount of a thousand dollars." We think the judge erred in admitting this testimony. It was a statement by Neal, made in the presence of Mrs. Phillips. The question in issue being whether Mrs. Phillips was a partner or not, she could not be bound by anything which Neal said. The rest of the evidence on the question of partnership not being conclusive, this testimony doubtless had considerable weight with the jury in finding that she was a partner. She was therefore prejudiced in her rights, and we think ought to have had a new trial on this ground.

2. The fourth ground of the motion complains of the construction placed upon the writing given by Neal to the plaintiff. Counsel for the plaintiff in error contends that it was a bill of sale, and a delivery of the goods thereunder in payment of the debt. We do not agree with him in this construction. In our opinion, under the facts, it was a written title to the property given by Neal to the plaintiff to secure the company for the purchase price of the furniture which had been sold to Neal, and a written assignment of the

notes and accounts. Biggers v. Bird, 55 Ga. 650. It being a written title for this purpose, Neal had a right to give it, even if there was a partnership, bearing his individual name. One partner has the right to give a mortgage or other security upon personal partnership property to secure a partnership debt; and, if Neal had the right to give it in the first instance as a partner, he also had the right to agree to its cancellation. Therefore, if Mrs. Phillips was a partner, and the title to the furniture and assignment of the choses in action were given to secure a partnership debt, she was not injured thereby, nor was she injured by the cancellation of the same. If she was not partner, but a security, and the title was taken by the plaintiff to the goods in the store and choses in action, and afterwards canceled without her consent, and she was damaged thereby, of course she would be released to the extent she was damaged by such cancellation. The title covered the furniture in the store and the choses in action, and if the creditor surrendered it, and the furniture and choses in action were afterwards lost, the security's liability to that extent would be increased. I will say in passing, however, that Mrs. Phillips in her answer makes no complaint of being injured in this manner, and, of course, could take no advantage of it on the next trial unless her answer be amended. She contends, as we have before remarked, that the writing is a bill of sale, and that its effect was to pay off and discharge the debt due by Neal to the plaintiff. This, we have shown, is not the correct interpretation of the instrument.

3. This being the proper construction to be given to the writing between the plaintiff and Neal, there was no error in refusing to give the requests to charge as complained of in the sixth and seventh grounds of the motion. These requests went upon the idea that it was a contract of sale between Neal and the plaintiff, and that the debt was paid off and discharged thereby.

4. It appears from the record that Neal used in his business a certain "form of a contract" when he sold furniture to people upon the installment plan, reserving title, etc. In the progress of the trial, Mrs. Phillips offered one of these forms in evidence, proposing to prove it was the same form as that used by Neal and filled out by him when he made such sales. This was excluded, and the ruling of the court is complained of as error in the ninth ground of the motion. There was no error in this ruling. The proper foundation was not laid for the introduction of this paper. One of the originals which had been executed should have been introduced, if obtainable. If none could be obtained from the original parties, or a certified copy of the same from the record, in case they had been recorded, then, perhaps, the paper presented might have been admissible. We can understand how, in case the jury upon the next trial should find that Mrs. Phillips was security, and not a partner, it might be material to show the number and amount of such

contracts Neal had at the time the title given to the plaintiff was canceled.

5. For the same reason the court did not err in excluding in evidence the "memorandum of the names and amounts of Neal's customers as shown by his books the day after the bill of sale was made." The original books should have been tendered or accounted for before secondary evidence could be offered and admitted. Judgment reversed.

BROWN v. STATE.

(*Supreme Court of Georgia.* Feb. 7, 1891.)

LARCENY—INDICTMENT.

An indictment for simple larceny, charging the theft of "one dark bay horse, with one white spot on the end of his nose and one small white spot in his forehead," did not describe the property alleged to have been stolen with the accuracy and fullness our statute requires, and a special demurrer thereto on this ground should have been sustained.

(*Syllabus by the Court.*)

Error from superior court, Bibb county; MILLER, Judge.

Hardeman & Nottingham and *Dessau & Bartlett*, for plaintiff in error. *W. H. Felton*, Sol. Gen., for the State.

LUMPKIN, J. Sections 4394 and 4395 of the Code read as follows: "Horse-stealing shall be denominated 'simple larceny,' and the term 'horse' shall include mule and ass, and each animal of both sexes, and without regard to the alterations which may be made by artificial means." "The offense shall, in all cases, be charged as simple larceny, but the indictment shall designate the nature, character, and sex of the animal, and give some other description by which its identity may be ascertained." By the first of these sections, the theft of any horse, mule, or ass is made "horse-stealing," without regard to the sex of the animal, or to any alterations which may be made by artificial means. The word "horse," as used in this section, is a generic term, which includes horse, as a species, mule, and ass. Horse, as a species, may again be subdivided into stallion, ridgling, gelding, and mare, and the same subdivision may be made as to mule and ass. Colloquially, the word "horse," among our people, usually means a male gelding of the horse species. So, if section 4394 was the only one with which we had to deal, it would be proper to sustain this indictment, on the idea that by it the defendant was sufficiently informed as to what kind of "horse" he was charged with stealing; that is to say, he would understand the word "horse" to mean what it usually does in every-day use and conversation. But the next section provides distinctly what indictments for this class of offenses shall contain, and declares that such indictments shall designate the nature, character, and sex of the animal, and also give some other description fixing its identity. The latter requirement of this section was complied with, in this case, by giving the color and flesh-marks of the animal; but we do not think the use of the word "horse," which has both a generic and a specific signification, distinctly recognized by our statute, was sufficient to give the defendant full and fair notice of the "nature, character, and sex" of the animal, as the law evidently contemplated should be done. Nor is the defect in this indictment cured by the use of the pronoun "his," because, under section 4, par. 3, of the Code, the masculine includes the feminine and neuter genders. But even if, in this case, this pronoun is to be understood as meaning a male, it still remains indefinite and uncertain whether it means a male horse, a male mule, or a male ass; and if a horse, whether he was a stallion, a ridgling, or a gelding. We regard it unnecessary to quote authorities to sustain the ruling herein made, because we think the question at issue is settled by the plain words of our own statute. To give a practical meaning to all the words used in both the sections of the Code referred to leads inevitably, we think, to the conclusion we have reached. The ruling of this court in the case of Taylor v. State, 44 Ga. 263, properly understood, is not in conflict with this conclusion. There the defendant was indicted for stealing a "chestnut sorrel horse," entered his plea of not guilty, without making any objection to the indictment, and was convicted. He then moved in arrest of judgment, the motion was denied, and this court sustained the court below in so doing. Now, inasmuch as the word "horse" may mean a male horse of the horse species, and the defendant was satisfied with the description in the indictment, and did not, by demurrer or otherwise, demand any further or more particular description, it was too late, after verdict, to make his objection to the indictment. This is all the judgment in that case amounts to, and we think it was right. We do not wish to be understood as following and adopting all that was said in that case by LOCHRANE, C. J., because we do not think some of his expressions are borne out by the statute, or a proper course of reasoning thereon. We simply mean to say we agree to what is actually adjudged in that case, and it does not conflict with our judgment in this. Here the defendant at the proper time, which was before pleading to the merits, demurred specially to the indictment, and thereby in effect demanded, as was his right, to be distinctly and accurately informed as to the nature, character, and sex of the animal he was charged with having stolen, and we do not think this right should have been denied him. Our Code, § 4629, recognizes the right of a defendant to take exception to an indictment for any formal defect, provided he does so before trial, that is, upon arraignment, and that is precisely what the defendant did in this case. Judgment reversed.

GEORGIA RAILROAD & BANKING CO. v.
MAYOR, ETC., OF MACON.

(*Supreme Court of Georgia.* Feb. 2, 1891.)

GRANT TO RAILROADS — FULFILLMENT OF CONDITIONS — BREACH — HARMLESS ERROR.

1. Where the state makes a grant of land to a city, to be absolute upon the payment of $10,000 by the city to the state, within a given time, the original receipt of the comptroller general for said sum of money was properly admitted as evidence of such payment.

2. Where land was granted to a railroad company, so long as the same should be used "for shops, depots, and other conveniences and fixtures necessary for said company," and the only use made of the land was the building and maintenance thereon of a track or tracks for the purpose of conveying freights to private parties, the storage of cars, and other like uses, this would not be a compliance by the company with the terms of the grant.

3. Where such a grant was made to the Milledgeville Railroad Company, of which the Macon & Augusta Railroad Company was the legal successor, and the latter company took possession of a portion of the land, and so built and used such tracks thereon, but did no more, and the Georgia Railroad & Banking Company afterwards took possession of the same, and it appearing that the title was in the city of Macon, except so far as it might be affected by the terms of such grant, then the city was entitled to recover the land from the Georgia Railroad as a mere wrong-doer, unless it showed some right to hold under the Macon & Augusta Company, or, if it did show such right, then the city was entitled to recover for want of compliance with the terms of the grant, and, in either event, no demand was necessary as a condition precedent to the city's bringing its action for the land.

4. Where the facts were as stated in last head-note, and a verdict in favor of the city was inevitable, a charge by the court on the law of prescription was immaterial and harmless.

(*Syllabus by the Court.*)

Error from superior court, Bibb county; MILLER, Judge.

Hardeman, Davis & Turner, for plaintiff in error. *C. L. Bartlett, R. W. Patterson,* and *Hill & Harris,* for defendant in error.

LUMPKIN, J. This case is, in many respects, similar to that of Mayor, etc., of Macon v. East Tennessee, V. & G. Ry. Co., reported in 82 Ga., beginning on page 501, and in 9 S. E. Rep. 1127. Most of the questions determined in that case are conclusive upon the main questions at issue in this. The right of the old Milledgeville Railroad Company to 10 acres of land, constituting a part of what was known as the "Macon Reserve," depended upon identically the same acts of the legislature, and the same action by the city council of Macon, as did the right of the Macon & Brunswick Railroad Company to 10 other acres of land in such reserve. In that case the East Tennessee Company claimed to be the successor of the Macon & Brunswick Company. In this case the Georgia Railroad Company claims to be the successor of the Macon & Augusta Company, which succeeded the Milledgeville Company.

1. There was no error in the admission of the comptroller general's receipt. The act of the legislature required the payment to be made to the state of Georgia. Its treasurer was the proper person to receive the money, and payments to the treasurer are legally evidenced by the receipt of the comptroller general. In point of fact the receipt now in question was actually signed by both the treasurer and the comptroller general. A certified transcript from the treasurer's books, showing that this sum of money had been paid into the treasury, would have been admissible, in case no better evidence was

attainable, to prove this payment; but the original receipt itself, conceded to be genuine, seems to us to have been evidence of the highest character of the fact of payment. See Wooten v. Nall, 18 Ga. 609.

2. In the argument of the case here, counsel for the Georgia Railroad only insisted on its right to hold so much of the land as is covered by the tracks thereon, and abandoned all claim to the remainder of said land. The question as to its right to hold any of the land has been settled by this court in the case cited. In his carefully prepared opinion, delivered in that case, BLECKLEY, C. J., stated, in effect, that it could not be supposed the authorities of Macon intended its grant as a donation or gratuity to the railroad company, but, beyond all doubt, the city expected to receive local benefits from the compliance by the company with the terms of the grant, and it is clear that something more was contemplated than the building of railroad tracks across the land. A full examination of that case will show that the identical question now being considered was there adjudicated, and further comment upon it is therefore unnecessary.

3. It seems to have been conceded in this case, or, at any rate, no serious question was raised thereon, that the Macon & Augusta Railroad Company had succeeded to all the rights and franchises of the Milledgeville Railroad Company; but it is by no means clear how the Georgia Railroad Company became the owner, if it ever did, of the property and franchises of the Macon & Augusta Company. It appears from the evidence that the Georgia Company, under some sort of a contract, took possession of the Macon & Augusta Railroad, and operated it; but the record is entirely silent as to the nature of that contract, as to whether it was in writing or in parol, and as to what legal rights, if any, it conferred upon the Georgia Railroad Company. This being true, and the city of Macon having shown a clear legal title to the property in dispute, except in so far as that title might be modified or affected by the grant to the old Milledgeville Company, clearly the city had a right to recover the property in dispute from the Georgia Company, as a mere trespasser, unless that company showed, in some legal way, it had succeeded to the rights of its predecessors under such grant. But, even if this had been shown by the Georgia Company, it would have been of no avail, because it would then have been in no better position than its predecessors, and neither of them, as has been shown, could have held this land against the city, under the facts disclosed by the record. If any of these railroads had any right to the lands mentioned, it was by reason of accepting the grant on the terms fixed by the city council of Macon, and, as was held in the case cited, this must have been with the limitation that the estate acquired was to exist only so long as the property was used for the purposes specified, and such a limitation is different from an ordinary condition subsequent, inasmuch as it marks the limit or boundary beyond which the estate conveyed could not continue to exist. Numerous authorities are there cited in support of this proposition. Under our law, no demand is necessary, as a condition precedent to the bringing of an action, except in such cases as the law distinctly declares such demand shall be made. As far as we have been able to ascertain, this case does not come within any such exceptions, and therefore no demand was necessary before bringing the action. The city's right of entry was complete, and therefore the action itself was all the demand the law required. Edmondson v. Leach, 56 Ga. 461. There are numerous assignments of error in the bill of exceptions, but all of them which we deem material have been fully covered by the rulings in the case cited and those herein made. After a careful examination of the record, we find that no errors were committed by the presiding judge. The case was fairly submitted to the jury, every right of the defendant was carefully guarded, and, in view of the facts disclosed by the record, we are satisfied that substantial justice has been done, more especially as the defendant has been relieved from the payment of all rents during the entire time it controlled and held possession of the property in dispute. We therefore affirm the judgment of the court below.

FREEMAN et al. v. STURGIS NAT. BANK.

(Supreme Court of Georgia. Feb. 7, 1891.)

REPLEVIN—WHEN LIES.

When, on trial of a claim case, there was no evidence at all showing that the property levied on either belonged to, or was in possession of, the defendant in fi. fa., the court rightly ordered the levy to be dismissed.

(Syllabus by Lumpkin, J.)

Error from superior court, Bibb county; MILLER, Judge.

M. R. Freeman, for plaintiffs in error. Steed & Wimberly, for defendant in error.

Judgment affirmed.

WATSON v. COMMONWEALTH.

(Supreme Court of Appeals of Virginia. April 2, 1891.)

RECORD ON CHANGE OF VENUE—HOMICIDE—OBJECTIONS TO GRAND JURY—EVIDENCE—INSTRUCTIONS.

1. Code Va. § 4016, providing that, where one indicted in the county court for a felony elects to be tried in the circuit court, the clerk shall transmit to the clerk of the latter court "a transcript of the record of the proceedings in said county court in relation to the prosecution, and copies of the indictment and recognizances and other papers connected with the case," does not require the record to show affirmatively that a venire facias was issued in summoning the grand jury.

2. Objection that no venire facias was issued must be made before plea to the merits.

3. On indictment for murder, where defendant testifies that he killed deceased because he had spoken insultingly of his wife, he may be asked on cross-examination whether the woman was lawfully married to him.

4. On indictment for murder it appeared that during a quarrel between defendant and deceased the latter spoke insultingly of defendant's wife, and called defendant a thief, murderer, and fugitive from justice; that defendant procured a gun, and followed deceased, who had fled, declaring that he would kill him; that deceased

secreted himself in a house, and defendant waited for him outside with the gun all night; that on another occasion he sought deceased out, declaring an intention to kill him; that about four weeks after the quarrel, while deceased was in the house of his former wife, quarreling with her, defendant went there and killed him. Under deceased was found an old, unused, and unloaded pistol, which could not have been used; and defendant testified that when he shot deceased the latter was advancing on him with the pistol, but he was contradicted by other witnesses. *Held*, that the court properly refused to set aside a verdict of murder in the first degree.

5. An instruction that if defendant was acting in the heat of passion, engendered by the slanderous words spoken of his wife, and if sufficient time had not elapsed for his passion to cool and subside, the killing was murder in the second degree; but that it was murder in the first degree, if sufficient time had elapsed for his passion to subside, and if he afterwards went after deceased with a deadly weapon for the purpose of killing him on account of the slanderous words, and did kill him willfully and with malice and premeditation,—is proper.

6. Where an instruction, asked by defendant, that if deceased had threatened to kill him, and the threats were made known to him, and if, before the fatal shot was fired, deceased did some overt act from which defendant could reasonably infer that he intended to execute the threats, the killing would be excusable homicide, is modified by the insertion of the clause, "and that defendant killed deceased to prevent him from killing him, or doing him great bodily harm," defendant cannot complain, since the modification could not injure him.

7. An instruction, asked by defendant, that if he went to the house where the killing occurred to stop a quarrel between deceased and deceased's wife, and to demand an apology for the slanderous words previously spoken by deceased, and if, when he attempted to do so, deceased attacked him with a deadly weapon, the killing of deceased is not murder, is properly modified by requiring that defendant shall have gone to the house for the purpose of "peaceably" stopping the quarrel, and demanding an apology.

FAUNTLEROY and HINTON, JJ., dissenting.

Davis & McIlwaine, for plaintiff in error. *R. Taylor Scott,* Atty. Gen., for the Commonwealth.

LACY, J. This is a writ of error to a judgment of the circuit court, Greensville county, rendered at the special term of that court held on the 8th day of January, 1890; and is to a second conviction of the plaintiff in error of murder in the first degree for a homicide committed on the 26th day of December, 1886. The first conviction was brought here on writ of error, and decided March 7, 1889, when the judgment was reversed for misdirection by the circuit court in its instructions to the jury, which is reported at page 867 of 85 Va., and page 418 of 9, S. E. Rep. Upon the second trial, which was had in the said circuit court, the plaintiff in error was again convicted of murder in the first degree, and the case was brought to this court, as before, by writ of error.

The errors assigned are, so far as exceptions appear upon the record: (1) That the accused, being sworn as a witness in his own behalf, and having testified that the deceased had abused his wife by speaking slanderous words concerning her, was asked whether the woman in question was actually lawfully married to him. (2) That the circuit court misdirected the jury

to the prejudice of the accused as to the law of the case. (3) That the circuit court overruled his motion to set aside the verdict and grant him a new trial, because the verdict was contrary to the law and the evidence as set forth in full under his second bill of exceptions; and the error assigned at the hearing here that the record does not affirmatively show that any *venire facias* was ever issued in the case for the summoning of the grand jury. The record sets forth the caption of the indictment and the indictment in full in the county court, where the indictment was found, and sets forth that in the said court, on a day named, certain named persons, at the court-house of the said county, in the said court, were sworn a special grand jury of inquest in and for the body of the county of Greensville, and, having received their charge, were sent out of court, and after some time returned into court and presented an indictment for felony, a true bill; and then follows the indictment in full. Being arraigned thereunder, the accused elected to be tried in the circuit court, as his right was, and in the said last-mentioned court he pleaded not guilty, and was convicted as stated; and there was no objection of any sort taken to the manner of summoning the grand jury, until after verdict and judgment upon appearance here to prosecute his writ of error on other grounds.

In the first place, there does not appear to be any irregularity in the mode of summoning the grand jury. Nothing upon that subject appears upon the transcript of the record as sent up to the circuit court upon the prisoner's election to be tried there. Section 4016 of the Code of Virginia provides that in such case the trial shall be in the county court, "except that a person to be tried for any felony for which he may be punished with death may, upon his arraignment in the county court, demand to be tried in the circuit court having jurisdiction over the county for which said county court is held. Upon such demand the accused shall be remanded for trial in the said circuit court, and all the material witnesses desired for the prosecution or defense shall be recognized for their attendance at such trial. When a person is remanded as aforesaid by a county court, the clerk thereof shall certify and transmit to the clerk of the court in which such person is to be tried a transcript of the record of the proceedings in said county court in relation to the prosecution, and copies of the indictment and recognizances and other papers connected with the case. Such transcript and copies shall be used with the same effect as the originals." The transcript is to begin with the indictment and recognizances, and other papers connected with the case are to follow as stated. These papers are all sent up, and all appear to be in due and regular form. No *venire facias* for the summoning of the grand jury appears on this transcript, nor does the accused make any objection on that ground, but proceeds with the trial. Are we to presume here that because no *venire facias* was sent to the circuit court with the transcript required by law, therefore no *venire facias* ever issued? It is the prosecution in this case that is to be brought up with the transcript, and that begins with the indictment, which must have been found in due course of law; and the person accused has the right to have the law complied with in the matter of summoning and in the organization of the grand jury and the impaneling of that body; and the courts afford some remedy for every violation of a person's rights. While a defendant may not go into the question of the evidence before a grand jury, nor the question of the swearing of the witnesses there, as there is then only an *ex parte* hearing of testimony, and there may be no witnesses, the grand jurors finding upon their own knowledge, not a question of guilt or innocence, but that an offense is charged to have been committed, but if there be an incompetent grand juror, to whom exception is to be taken, or when as to the whole body, as for instance that the grand jury consisted of too many members, or too few, or that it was otherwise incompetent, or an irregularity in the summoning or impaneling of the grand jury or the selecting of the jurors, or in any case where the authority of the body under the law of the land is wanting, and there is an illegal constitution or organization, an opportunity is afforded the accused who is thus unlawfully charged to effectively except to such error, because he cannot be tried for a felony until he has been legally indicted. This objection being as to matter before the trial begins and preliminary thereto, it must be drawn to the attention of the court by plea before pleading to the merits. This must be done then in some way. There are some defects that may be reached by motion to quash, but it is sometimes by challenge, and, when that method is not used or not recognized, plea in abatement is the usual and proper method. If a grand juror is incompetent to serve as such personally,—that is, when he lacks some requirement of the law, or when he has some quality which, under the law, excludes him,—and when the number is illegal, or when there is any irregularity in the summoning or impaneling of the jury which would vitiate the whole finding if not waived, then the defendant may protect himself against this infraction of the law and abridgement of his rights by plea in abatement. And objections of this sort are considered as waived by a plea to the merits; therefore they cannot be taken advantage of at the trial, and, *a fortiori*, it is too late after verdict to raise an objection of this sort. If defects appear of record which show that the grand jury was an illegal body, either having been summoned without authority or going to the extent of showing that the grand jury was not a legal body lawfully attached to the court, it would be a different question, and considered and treated differently upon a motion in arrest of judgment. But where the record is merely silent, then the presumption of law is that all will be presumed to have been rightly done; and in such case, as in this case, the whole matter is put to rest by our law. Section 3985 of the Code provides, as to the findings of grand jurors,

that "no irregularity in the time or manner of selecting the jurors or in the writ of *venire facias* or in the manner of executing the same shall vitiate any presentment, indictment, or finding of a grand jury." In this case, on this question, nothing appears upon the record to suggest any irregularity of any sort in this respect, and, as no exception has been taken or urged in the two hotly contested trials below, it is a just and reasonable presumption of law that none exists; and no doubt it is perfectly true that no such error exists in the court from which the case was originally transferred, and there is no law requiring such paper to appear in the circuit court. 1 Bish. Crim. Proc. § 872, p. 516; Durr v. State, 53 Miss. 425; State v. Carver, 49 Me. 588; McCullough v. Com., 67 Pa. St. 30, 31, 33; Mershon v. State, 51 Ind. 14; U. S. v. Hammond, 2 Woods, 197; State v. Dixon, 3 Iowa, 416; State v. Hinkle. 6 Iowa, 380; Com. v. Smith, 9 Mass. 107; People v. Roberts, 6 Cal. 214; Shropshire v. State, 12 Ark. 190; Harding v. State, 22 Ark. 210; Montgomery v. State, 3 Kan. 263; Doyle v. State, 17 Ohio, 222, McQuillen v. State, 8 Smedes & M. 587; Rawls v. State, Id. 599; Newman v. State, 14 Wis. 426.

As to the first exception,—that the question was allowed to be asked by the court of the prisoner whether the woman called his wife, and in whose behalf he claimed to have committed the homicide, was really his wife, and when and by whom they were married, if they were legitimately married,—there is no error perceived in this action. The accused had committed a homicide, and upon the witness stand had admitted it, and claimed to have done so because of insulting words spoken of and concerning his said wife. He claimed that she was his wife, and, if so, then she was legitimately so, and the place where and by whom she was married to him were inquiries in pursuance of his own assertion, and it could by no possibility injure him, except that it might turn out by cross-examination to be false, and to this, like all other witnesses, he must submit. The cross-examination was proper, and altogether admissible, and is a valuable test of truth.

The third exception is as to the refusal of the court to set aside the verdict and grant the accused a new trial on the ground that the said verdict is contrary to the law and the evidence. The evidence in this case is certified, and from it it appears that while at a party at a man's house named Lemon Carey, about four weeks before Christmas, 1886, the deceased took something from the table of his former wife, from whom he had separated, and refused to pay for it; that the accused rebuked him for this, and the deceased became angry, and accused him of doing the same thing about something else. The dispute growing warmer, a fight ensued, in which the deceased was badly used, face cut and bloody, and the throat cut. Other parties were present and interfered, and the fight was stopped. The deceased, in the heat of this quarrel, abused the wife of the accused, was very offensive as to her, and said as to the prisoner that he had stolen mules in North Carolina, and was a fugitive from justice, and had run away with another man's wife after killing the husband. The deceased then made his escape, and left the prisoner in a great rage, who went straight home and got his gun and pursued the deceased, loudly proclaiming that he would kill him unless he took back what he had said about his wife, saying nothing of the things he had said about himself. The deceased escaped into a house, and the door was held against the accused by others, but the accused, gun in hand, stood guard around the house all night, and the sun rose upon him next morning still bent upon murder; but, it being Sunday morning, the railroad section master ordered him to go off with his gun, which he did, still proclaiming his purpose to kill on sight. At another time, gun in hand, he waylaid the deceased standing in a chimney corner of a house in which the deceased was secreted, but the deceased did not come out of the house, and the prisoner, being discovered, went off. Some four weeks after the first fight, on the 26th day of December, 1886, the deceased went to the house (after night) of his wife or his former wife, which was on the same farm with the prisoner, where the prisoner was a sort of head man, and began a dispute with his former wife. The prisoner, hearing where he was and what he was doing, got his gun, and hastened to the spot, and was standing under cover of the darkness in the chimney corner close by the deceased as he stood talking with his former wife. The prisoner being thus discovered, rushed around the corner of the house, crying out "You G——d d——d son of a bitch, crack your lips, and I will blow your brains out!" shot at once, shooting the deceased through the head, and killing him instantly. An old broken, unused, and unloaded pistol was found under the leg of the deceased as he lay upon the ground, and the accused said the deceased offered to shoot him with this pistol, and he shot in self-defense only; and the doctor testified that this pistol could not have been drawn after the deceased was shot, but it does not follow that he did not attempt to draw it after the attack was made on him, or that it did not fall out of his pocket as he fell. However this may be, the accused was the attacking party, and he made this attack after numerous and often-repeated threats to kill the deceased. He has himself testified in the case; and he is studious to exclude the conclusion that he ever saw Joe Robinson after the fight without attacking him. After speaking of the quarrel, he says: "I then went home and took my gun and went down to the shanty to look for Joe Robinson. I knocked at the door and asked for Joe Robinson. Ridley said, 'Yes, he is in here,' but would not open the door. I do not remember whether I tried to break open the window or not. I told Joe Robinson I intended to shoot him if he did not take back what he had said about my wife. Being unable to get in the house, I went home, and the next morning, about sunrise, I went back there, looking for Joe Robinson. From that

time I did not see Joe Robinson until the time of the killing. I was at Wiseman's, but did not see Joe Robinson, and did not know that he was there." (This is the place where he is said to have been lying in wait, gun in hand, and where one of the witnesses told Joe Robinson· "There is Randall Watson looking for you with that same gun.") The intimation is that if he had seen him he would have killed him before he did. He constantly kept to the front the abuse spoken of his wife, but it will be remembered that Joe Robinson had intimated a dangerous knowledge of the prisoner's past life, proclaiming him a fugitive from justice, a mule thief, and a murderer at large. Whether this intimation had any effect in keeping alive for four weeks this unfailing determination to kill we do not know. The accused said that when he fired the fatal shot Joe Robinson was advancing upon him with a pistol pointed, threatening to kill him, but this is contradicted by the other witnesses, who say that Randall Watson rushed from his place behind the chimney, gun in hand, declaring his purpose to shoot at once, shouting at close quarters, and with fatal effect. The jury—the proper triers of the weight of the testimony—have found that the killing was willful and deliberate, and with malice aforethought, and was murder in the first degree, and this verdict is abundantly sustained by the evidence in the record; and we are of opinion that the circuit court did not err in overruling the motion for a new trial, and properly refused to set aside the verdict, and that there is no error in this action of the trial court.

It only remains to inquire whether there was error to the prejudice of the plaintiff in error as to the instructions given by the judge of the court to the jury as to the law of the case. The second exception is as to the refusal of the court to give the instructions asked for by the accused, numbered 1, 2, and 3, and giving in lieu thereof those numbered 9, 10, and 11. The first instruction was as follows, as asked: "The court instructs the jury that if they believe from the evidence that the prisoner at the time that he fired the fatal shot was acting in the heat of passion engendered by the slanderous words spoken by the deceased about the wife of the prisoner, which were in themselves calculated to provoke a high degree of violence, then the killing would be murder in the second degree, unless they further believe from the evidence that a sufficient time had elapsed since the slanderous words were spoken for the passions engendered thereby to have cooled and subsided, and that the prisoner then shot Joe Robinson from a willful, deliberate, and premeditated purpose to kill him." Instead of this the court gave the following: "The court instructs the jury that if they believe from the evidence that the prisoner at the time he fired the fatal shot was acting in the heat of passion engendered by slanderous and abusive words spoken by the deceased about the wife of the prisoner, which were in themselves calculated to provoke a high degree of violence; that a sufficient time had not elapsed since the words were spoken for the passions engendered thereby to cool and subside,—then the killing is murder in the second degree. But if the jury believe from the evidence that a sufficient time had elapsed since the slanderous and abusive words were spoken for the passions engendered thereby to cool and subside, and that afterwards Randall Watson went to the place of the fatal encounter, armed with a deadly weapon, for the purpose of killing Joe Robinson on account of the slanderous and abusive words so spoken of his wife, and did kill him on that account, willfully, and with malice and premeditation, then Randall Watson is guilty of murder in the first degree." There is no error in this instruction. It is correct in all respects, and clearly expounds the law upon the subject in hand. The first instruction asked and refused was substantially the same, and was in fact given when the ninth was given.

The second instruction asked by the accused was as follows: "The court instructs the jury that if they believe from the evidence that before the time of the fatal encounter Joe Robinson had threatened to beat or kill Randall Watson, that such threats had been communicated to Randall Watson, and if they further believe from the evidence that at the time of the encounter and before the fatal shot was fired Joe Robinson did some overt act from which Randall Watson could reasonably infer that Joe Robinson was about to execute the said threats by killing him or doing him some serious bodily harm, then the killing of Joe Robinson by Randall Watson would be excusable homicide, and not murder." In lieu of the words, "then the killing of Joe Robinson by Randall Watson would be excusable homicide, and not murder," the following, "and that Randall Watson killed Joe Robinson to prevent him from killing him or doing him serious bodily harm, then the jury must find the prisoner not guilty," were given. These words were not injurious to the prisoner, but more favorable than those asked by him, and his exception to them is groundless.

The third instruction asked by the prisoner was as follows: "If the jury believe from the evidence that Randall Watson went to the place of the fatal encounter for the purpose of stopping the disturbance there, and to demand an apology for the grievous and abusive words he had spoken of the wife of Randall Watson, and that he did demand of Joe Robinson an apology, but that the said Robinson, in response to a demand for an apology, gave none, but advanced upon the prisoner with a pistol, then the shooting by Randall Watson was excusable homicide, and not murder." In lieu of this the court gave the following: "The court instructs the jury that if they believe that Randall Watson went to the place of the fatal encounter for the purpose of peaceably stopping the disturbance there, and for the purpose of peaceably demanding an apology of Joe Robinson for the grievous and abusive words spoken of his wife, and that he did not go there for the purpose of killing Joe Robinson, or of having a difficulty with him in the event he should refuse to give

the required apology, and that Randall Watson did go there and peaceably endeavor to stop the disturbance, and did peaceably demand an apology of Joe Robinson, and that Joe Robinson refused to give the apology, but advanced upon Randall Watson with a pistol, and that Randall Watson killed Joe Robinson under the belief that it was necessary to save his life, or himself from some bodily injury, then the jury must find him not guilty." The plaintiff in error earnestly contends that the giving of this instruction was greatly to his prejudice, and was erroneous in that the word "peaceably" was inserted therein four times. But this instruction correctly expounds the law upon the subject. The theory of the instruction asked by the accused was that the purpose of stopping the disturbance was an act of peace, and not of battery, and only in that sense could it be given properly to the jury. The accused could not rightfully ask the court to instruct the jury that he had a right to go there to stop the disturbance by making a greater disturbance, to stop a quarrel by the act of killing the participants, to seize upon the situation into which he had surprised his enemy, whose life he had been so long and so openly seeking, to consummate his cherished purpose of murder, to cover his murderous purpose by a show of protecting the peace,—to do this was murder. But if he went on a mission of peace, to peaceably stop a disturbance, and to peaceably demand an apology for his cause of quarrel with the deceased, then, if he thus stood and acted bona fide in the attitude and played the role of peace-maker, and so peaceably acting was assaulted with a deadly weapon, drawn and aimed at his life, and killed his assailant in self-defense, then the jury, finding this to be true, should have found him not guilty. This was the claim he set up, with the addition that his purpose was to kill on sight unless the apology was promptly forth-coming, which apology he said he expected to get. The instruction, as amended, was well adapted to meet the line of evidence set up by the accused in his own defense, and was properly given by the court, and we perceive no error in that action of the court.

There were other instructions given by the court at the motion of the accused and of the commonwealth, no objection to which have been urged in this court, and which appear to be plainly right. This disposes of all the exceptions upon the record and all the assignments of error here, and upon the whole case we perceive no error in the action of the circuit court, and the judgment of that court in the case will be affirmed here.

FAUNTLEROY and HINTON, JJ., dissenting.

MOTLEY et al. v. FRANK et al.

(Supreme Court of Appeals of Virginia. Feb. 5, 1891.)

ASSIGNMENT FOR BENEFIT OF CREDITORS — PREFERENCES—INJUNCTION—FRAUD—EVIDENCE.

1. Where a creditor files a bill attacking the validity of an assignment for the benefit of cred-

itors on the ground that a preferred claim to the debtor's mother is fictitious, and that the mother was in fact a secret partner, and obtains an injunction against the payment of that claim, but fails for more than a year to adduce any evidence to substantiate the charges of the bill, which are specifically denied by the answer setting out how the debt was contracted, the injunction is properly dissolved upon the motion of the preferred creditor.

2. The failure of the court to pass upon exceptions taken to the deposition of one of defendants is immaterial, where the deposition is not considered in determining the case, but the injunction is dissolved upon the bill and answer, there being no evidence to support the bill.

3. Where the business is carried on by one visible partner, who is known to the creditor to be advertised as the sole proprietor of the firm, such partner has power to assign the firm assets to pay his individual debts in preference over partnership creditors.

Berkley & Harrison, Green & Miller, and *Rutherford & Page,* for appellants. *Peatrus & Harris* and *Guy & Gilliam,* for appellees.

FAUNTLEROY, J. This is an appeal from a decree of the circuit court of the town of Danville, Va., pronounced on the 22d of January, 1889, in an injunction suit depending in said court, in which A. H. Motley, A. H. Motley, Jr., and James A. Thomas, merchants doing business under the firm name and style of A. H. Motley & Co., are complainants, and the Frank Tobacco Company and others are defendants. The record discloses the following case: In November, 1887, L. B. Frank, who did business under the style of the Frank Tobacco Company in Danville, Va., assigned by deed all his property and assets, as well those in his business of the Frank Tobacco Company as his private property, including even his exemptions, to L. D. Wildman, in trust to secure his creditors in six classes. In the second class is a debt due to Mrs. F. Frank, the mother of the grantor, a debt due to Penn & Rison, a debt due Montoul & Co., of Charleston, S. C., and a debt due to A. H. Motley & Co., though not all of the debt due to them. This deed was recorded on the 2d day of November, 1887, and on the 8th of November, 1887, appellants filed their bill in the corporation court of Danville, which was subsequently removed to the circuit court of Danville, assailing the validity of the deed for fraud, and the *bona fides* of the debt secured to Mrs. F. Frank therein, and praying for an injunction, which they obtained on the 8th of November, 1887, restraining the execution of the said deed of trust, and, among other things, restraining and enjoining the payment of the debt of $3,090, secured to Mrs. F. Frank, until the further order of the court. On the appellant's application, also, the trustee named in the deed was removed, and a receiver was appointed in his stead, to whom the trustee turned over all the trust property. The bill charges that the Frank Tobacco Company was composed of one S. Liebman, L. B. Frank, and several others, (not named,) male and female, of the immediate relations, connections, and friends of said L. B. Frank; that S. Liebman was a secret

partner of L. B. Frank; that Mrs. Fanny Frank was also a secret partner, and that Meyer Frank was a secret partner; and that the debts secured in the deed to Mrs. F. Frank and Meyer Frank were fictitious debts, and "only pretenses to throw the assets of the Frank Tobacco Company into the hands of the relatives of L. B. Frank." Upon these allegations of the bill S. Liebman was enjoined from making any disposition of his property, real and personal, and the receiver was directed to take charge of all his property, in addition to all the property embraced in the deed of trust. At the ensuing term (January, 1888,) of the hustings court, the answers of Mrs. Fanny Frank and of L. B. Frank and Meyer Frank were filed, denying and explicitly putting to issue all the material charges made in the bill, and the case was then removed to the circuit court, the term of which began January 15, 1888. At that term the complainants were in total default of all testimony to sustain the harsh allegations of their bill, although over two months had elapsed since they obtained the injunction, and Mrs. F. Frank moved, upon her answer, to have the injunction dissolved; whereupon the complainants moved for a continuance, and filed an affidavit that they intended to take the testimony of witnesses beyond the limits of the state which was essential to their cause, and thereby they obtained a continuance. At the January term, 1889, after the injunction had been standing for 13 months and 14 days, Mrs. F. Frank again moved to dissolve the injunction, when, the complainants not having taken evidence to sustain the charge of the bill impeaching the good faith of her claim, or that she was a partner in the Frank Tobacco Company, and offering no excuse for their default, and answering the inquiry of the court whether they knew of, or expected to produce, any proof to sustain their bill against Mrs. F. Frank's claim, that they did not, the court dissolved the injunction as to her, and ordered that the amount of her claim be paid to her. From this order this appeal is taken; and the sole question for decision by this court is whether the circuit court was right in rendering the decree complained of.

The bill was filed and the injunction obtained upon a charge of fraud, November 8, 1887. It was promptly answered by all the defendants, and by Mrs. Frank, denying each and all the allegations of fraud, and substantiating her claim, and calling for proof. She not only denies the charges of the bill so far as they affected her debt and her rights, but she showed specifically when and how the debt secured to her in the deed of trust had been made, thus enabling the complainants to assail and refute her statements if they could; and she denied that she was ever a partner in the Frank Tobacco Company, or that she contributed anything to its capital as a partner, or that there was any other partner in the firm than L. B. Frank; and she showed that her money had been loaned to him for his said business, and was used by him in it. The injunction restraining her rights and charging fraud had been held against her for 14 months awaiting proof, and, when none was offered, the injunction was dissolved. A refusal or delay to dissolve the injunction as to her would have worked a protracted and harsh injustice to her, and would have indulged the complainants in systematic negligence and inexcusable wrong. See Moore v. Steelman, 80 Va. 331. Where the answer denies all the grounds of equity set up in the bill, and those grounds are unsustained by proof, the injunction must necessarily be dissolved. Hogan v. Duke, 20 Grat. 244. It is assigned as error that the court refused to pass upon exceptions taken by complainants to certain depositions filed by the defendants. The court did not consider the depositions, but dissolved the injunction because no testimony had been produced to sustain the charges in the bill that Mrs. Frank was either a member of the Frank Tobacco Company, or that her debt secured by the deed of trust was fictitious. In the total absence of all proof to sustain the bill she was entitled to a dissolution of the injunction on the record and the case of the complainants, without considering at all the depositions of the defendants; and the court stated that such had been its action. In their third alleged error the complainants say that they did not know that the case was considered upon the deposition of the witness Meyer Frank, after they had stated in their first assignment of error that it had been considered on that deposition. All the evidence taken by the appellants was upon the one single point of the alleged secret partnership between L. B. Frank and S. Liebman. They failed in this. The agreement between L. B. Frank and S. Liebman in the record shows upon what terms Liebman worked for the Frank Tobacco Company, and the complainant A. H. Motley himself admits that he knew that L. B. Frank was advertised as the sole proprietor of the firm; and if they had proved even that Liebman was a dormant partner, still the evidence shows that Mrs. Frank knew nothing of that fact or alleged secret relation of the parties, and that she dealt with L. B. Frank alone, as the ostensible sole proprietor of the concern; and the law is settled that the ostensible partner has full power to assign the firm assets to pay his individual debts in preference over the firm creditors. Cammack v. Johnson, 2 N. J. Eq. 163, and notes; 1 Colly. Partn. (6th Ed.) 188, 189. "If the firm was open, the credit was given to the firm and the goods in possession, and the partnership creditor should be first paid out of them; but, if the partner be unknown, the credit is given to the visible partner only; and in such case the discovery of a latent partner cannot give any preference to a partnership creditor." Cammack v. Johnson, supra. See, also, the case of Lord v. Baldwin, 6 Pick. 348. The answer of Mrs. Frank gives a reasonable and unsuspicious account of her debt due to her from L. B. Frank, her son,— that she loaned to L. B. Frank $3,000 in Georgia state bonds, which were bringing her interest, upon the understanding that he should pay to her the interest so soon as

he used the money, and then return to her the amount in money. This was reasonable and natural for a mother. The appellants have failed to prove the case made in their bill against the appellee Mrs. F. Frank, and our judgment is that the decree appealed from is right, and it must be affirmed.

TIMBERLAKE'S ADM'R *et al.* v. JENNINGS *et al.*

(*Supreme Court of Appeals of Virginia.* March 26, 1891.)

BEST AND SECONDARY EVIDENCE — ADMINISTRATOR'S BOND—LOSS OF RECORD.

The entry in a "fiduciary book," in which Code Va. 1849, c. 132, § 1, and Code 1860, c. 132, § 1, required the clerk of the court to keep a record of personal representatives and their sureties, is, in the absence of the bond and other records, which were lost during the war, sufficient to show the fact of the suretyship of the persons named therein. HINTON and RICHARDSON, JJ., dissenting.

W. W. Gordon, for appellants. *J. F. Hubbard, Conway Sands,* and *George P. Hard,* for appellees.

FAUNTLEROY, J. This is an appeal by the personal representative of Thomas N. Timberlake, deceased, and the personal representative of B. B. Jones, deceased, from a decree of the circuit court of New Kent county, rendered October 27, 1888, in a suit pending in the said court in the name of the heirs and distributees of Isaac S. Jennings, deceased, complainants originally, against A. I. E. Jennings, administrator of I. S. Jennings, deceased, and Thomas N. Timberlake and H. D. Vaiden; all of which parties defendant being dead, the suit is proceeding against their personal representatives. The suit was instituted to enforce a settlement of the estate accounts of said A. I. E. Jennings as administrator of the estate of I. S. Jennings, deceased, and to compel payment of the balance charged to be due from the said administrator of I. S. Jennings and said T. N. Timberlake and H. D. Vaiden, who are alleged to have been the sureties of the said A. I. E. Jennings upon his official bond as such administrator aforesaid. The said Timberlake and Vaiden in their life-time and their personal representatives since and now do not deny positively that the said Timberlake and Vaiden were ever sureties on the administration bond of the said A. I. E. Jennings, administrator of I. S. Jennings, deceased, but only to the best of their belief they were not, and A. I. E. Jennings, administrator, in his answer also says that he does "not think" that they were his sureties on his administration bond. The sole issue now before this court is whether the said T. N. Timberlake and H. D. Vaiden were sureties of said A. I. E. Jennings, as administrator of Isaac S. Jennings, deceased, on his official bond as such. The bond itself, executed by A. I. E. Jennings as administrator of Isaac S. Jennings, deceased, is not produced, nor is it or any copy of it to be found in the records of the county court of New Kent county, where said A. I. E. Jennings qualified as administrator of I S. Jennings, deceased. The only thing offered and relied on by the complainants

I. S. Jennings' distributees as record evidence of the execution of the said administrator's bond by the said T. N. Timberlake and H. D. Vaiden as sureties thereon is an entry in a book produced and claimed by the complainants to be the fiduciary book which was kept by the clerk of the county court of New Kent county as the record of the executorial and administration bonds. Is that book the genuine "fiduciary book," and is the entry in it, relied on by the complainants, conclusive evidence of the execution of said bond by A. I. E. Jennings, and T. N. Timberlake and H. D. Vaiden as his sureties, in the absence of the bond itself? The court below has said in the decree of October 27, 1888, complained of, that it is, and this appeal is, ou this issue, from that decree.

It is not disputed—but is a fact in the record—that A. I. E. Jennings did qualify as the administrator of I. S. Jennings, deceased, in the county court of New Kent county, on the 8th of December, 1859, and did then give bond as such, with some one or more as his sureties; and the only question here in issue is, who were these sureties? The Code of 1849, c. 132, § 1, and the Code of 1860, c. 132, § 1, require the clerks of the courts to keep a record in a book of all the personal representatives, their sureties, etc. The act of 1869-70, c. 293, changed this. No minute book of 1859 is produced, and no bond; but it is proved that the most important of the records of New Kent county court's clerk's office were taken to Richmond in 1862 for safety and were deposited in the state-house, and were doubtless burned there in 1865. The sole evidence adduced as record evidence is this book, called a "Fiduciary Book," which is said to have been taken to some northern state, and restored after the war. This book contains an entry of A. I. E. Jennings as administrator of Isaac S. Jennings, deceased, and of Thomas N. Timberlake and H. D. Vaiden as his sureties, in a bond in the penalty of $4,000 of 8th of December, 1859. Thomas Barham, as commissioner in chancery, says that of his own knowledge Timberlake and Vaiden were sureties upon the official bond of A. I. E. Jennings, administrator of Isaac S. Jennings, deceased, but the court sustained an exception to his *ipse dixit* as evidence. Madison I. Martin testifies that there was an entry made in this "fiduciary book" in 1866, of Andrew J. Martin, as administrator of Mary T. Timberlake, when it should have been Madison I. Martin, etc. John G. Green testifies to the burning of the state-house in Richmond, and O. M. Chandler to the removal of the records of the county court of New Kent, in 1862, to Richmond. The testimony is that this entry of A. I. Jennings as administrator of I. S. Jennings, deceased, and T. N. Timberlake and Henry D. Vaiden as his sureties, was in what was in 1859 kept as the fiduciary book in the clerk's office of the county court of New Kent county, in accordance with the requirements of the law, and was in the handwriting of John D. Christian, who was then the clerk in that office of that court. This case is one of the many occasioned by the destruction or derangement of court records and record evidence in the counties of Virginia by the casualties of war, and the extraordinary circumstances compel a departure from the strict and beaten track of record evidence. There is an entry in a book identified and fully proved to have been the one kept in the clerk's office of the county court of New Kent county, in the handwriting of the then clerk, John D. Christian, as the "list of fiduciaries," as required by the Codes of 1849 and 1860, which fully proves that A. I. E. Jennings did duly qualify as administrator of I. S. Jennings, deceased, and T. N. Timberlake and Henry D. Vaiden as his sureties as such administrator, December 8, 1859. Our judgment is that the decree complained of is without error in holding the estates of T. N. Timberlake, deceased, and Henry D. Vaiden, deceased, liable as sureties aforesaid, and the said decree must be affirmed.

LACY, J., absent. HINTON and RICHARDSON, JJ., dissent. LEWIS, J., concurs.

BARTON'S EX'R v. BRENT *et al.*
(Supreme Court of Appeals of Virginia. Jan. 29, 1891.)[1]

FRAUDULENT CONVEYANCES—ESTOPPEL.

1. In the absence of a statute prohibiting preferences by an insolvent debtor, a deed by an insolvent to his wife, in consideration of the release of *bona fide* debts due from him to third persons, is valid.

2. In 1875 defendant conveyed property to a bank to secure his notes to a third person, but the deed was not properly acknowledged. In 1878 he gave a deed of trust to secure to the bank any debt for which he should be liable jointly with M. as one of the sureties on the bond of the cashier who had defaulted. M. sought to enforce the deed of 1878 for contribution, claiming that it was paramount to the defectively acknowledged deed of 1875. *Held* that, since the bank had knowledge of the deed of 1875, and could not set up the deed of 1878 against it, M. could not do so, since he could only claim through the bank.

Appeal from circuit court, Frederick county.

Barton & Boyd and *J. J. Williams,* for appellants. *Harrison & Byrd,* for appellee.

LEWIS, P. This was a creditor's suit in the circuit court of Frederick county, brought by the executor of D. W. Burton, deceased, (the appellant here,) to subject the property of the defendant E. S. Brent to the satisfaction of the liens thereon. The bill charges, among other things, that a certain deed, dated March 6, 1886, whereby Brent assigned to his wife all his interest in the property devised to her by her father, was without consideration deemed valuable in law, and is therefore void; and the prayer is that the deed be set aside on that ground. The facts in relation to the matter are these: By his will, the late George W. Baker, the father of Mrs. Brent, devised to her a certain house and lot in Winchester, with provision that, in the event of her dying without issue, the property should pass to the children of his first wife. The property

---

[1] Rehearing refused March 11, 1891

was afterwards sold under a decree in a friendly suit in chancery, and the proceeds of sale were ordered to be invested in other property, to be held subject to the same limitation as that prescribed in the will. The money was accordingly invested in two notes of Brent, aggregating about $3,000, which were held by the Shenandoah Valley National Bank, and which were supposed to have been secured on certain real estate in Frederick county by a deed of trust from Brent to Tilman Shumate, trustee, dated November 1, 1875. The deed, however, was admitted to record upon Brent's acknowledgment, taken by Shumate as a notary public, and this acknowledgment being invalid because of Shumate's incompetency to take it, he being the trustee in the deed, it is conceded that the recordation of the deed is void. Bowden v. Parrish, 86 Va. 67, 9 S. E. Rep. 616. The testator died, and his will was admitted to probate in the year 1865. Mr. and Mrs. Brent have no children, and have never had issue, so that, under the law as it was at the testator's death, the defendant Brent took an estate in the house and lot above mentioned for the joint lives of himself and wife. Breeding v. Davis, 77 Va. 639. It does not appear that Mrs. Brent had any other property. The deed first above mentioned recites that Brent is indebted to Baker & Co. in the sum of $264, with interest from January 24, 1878, and to C. M. Gibbons in the sum of $106, with interest from March 5, 1886, and that the assignment to Mrs. Brent was made in consideration of the release of these debts. The circuit court held that this was a valuable consideration for the assignment, and upheld the assignment by the decree complained of. We are of opinon that in this particular the decree is right. There is no question that the debts were bona fide and subsisting obligations, and, looking to the substance, rather than the form, of the transaction, it is the same, in effect, as if the assignment had been taken by the above-mentioned creditors directly to themselves, and the interest had been afterwards assigned by them to Mrs. Brent. The assignor was at the time admittedly insolvent; and, had the transaction assumed the form just suggested, it would have presented the common case of an insolvent debtor making preferences as between his creditors, which this court has repeatedly held is neither illegal nor immoral when not prohibited by statute. Paul v. Baugh, 85 Va. 955, 9 S. E. Rep. 329, and cases cited. There is no proof of fraud in the transaction, nor is fraud positively charged in the bill. The only allegation in this connection is that the assignment was without a valuable consideration. Nor does the evidence show that the consideration was inadequate. If the notes in which the investment above mentioned was made were worth their par value, the commissioner's report shows that the defendant's life-interest therein would be worth $2,182.23. But the evidence does not show what their real value is, and there is evidence tending to prove that the defendant's interest does not exceed in value four or five hundred dollars. It is mani-

fest that, without first ascertaining the value of the notes, no correct estimate of the value of the husband's interest therein could be made from the life-tables, according to the rule laid down in Strayer v. Long, 86 Va. 557, 10 S. E. Rep. 574. If in fact the consideration for the assignment was so grossly inadequate as to amount to proof of fraud, it was incumbent on the appellant to show it, and, in the absence of such proof, the transaction must stand. The case is not within the principle of Blow v. Maynard, 2 Leigh, 29, and that class of cases relating to post-nuptial settlements; nor is it within the principle decided in Yates v. Law, 86 Va. 117, 9 S. E. Rep. 508, for here, as we have seen, the consideration is shown to have moved from third persons, who virtually became the purchasers of the husband's interest, and who then assigned it, or caused it to be assigned, to the wife. The case, therefore, is not that of a purchase by the wife, but rather that of a gift to the wife by creditors of the husband, the validity of whose debts is not questioned.

The next question is between the appellees Brent and wife and the appellee John M. Miller. It appears that Brent and Miller were sureties for one H. M. Brent, who was cashier of the Shenandoah Valley National Bank, of Winchester, and who, as such cashier, defaulted for a considerable sum. On the 23d of January, 1878, the appellee Brent conveyed certain property to W. L. Clark and E. H. Boyd, in trust to secure certain debts, and, among them, "whatever debt, no matter what the form or the evidence of it may be, for which E. S. Brent is bound, growing out of his liability, jointly with John M. Miller, as surety for H. M. Brent as cashier," etc. Some time after the defalcation occurred, Brent and Miller, the sureties, had what they called "a final settlement of all accounts between them relating to their debts due in the said bank by reason of their suretyship" aforesaid, and according to that settlement it appears that they were jointly liable to the bank, as such sureties, for $10,000. Of this sum it was agreed between them that Miller would assume $8,200 and Brent $1,800, which was accordingly done, Miller executing his note for $8,200, and Brent executing his note for $1,800, with Miller as indorser. Miller's note seems to have been paid; but there is still a balance due on Brent's note of $847.03, for which amount Miller claims to be entitled to a lien by virtue of the deed of trust of January 23, 1878, and which lien, he insists, is paramount to the trust-deed of November 1, 1875. The circuit sustained this contention, and in this, we think, there was error. The joint liability secured by the deed of January 23, 1878, was not to Miller, but to the bank; and the only way, therefore, by which Miller could, under any circumstances, become entitled to the security would be by virtue of the equitable doctrine of subrogation, upon his paying the money due by Brent, for whom he is indorser. But in point of fact he has not paid any part of it, and hence the doctrine of subrogation has no application to the case; and even if he had paid the money, his claim would be subordinate to the trust-deed of November 1, 1875, because he could only claim through the bank, and the bank confessedly had actual notice of that deed before the deed of January 23, 1878, was executed. Hopewell v. Bank, 10 Leigh, 206, 227. The same consideration would apply if the suit, so far as Miller's claim to the benefit of a prior lien is concerned, were treated as in the nature of a proceeding *quia timet*. In either case he could claim only through the bank, and, if the bank is affected with notice of the invalidly recorded deed,—*i. e.*, the deed of November 1, 1875,—he (Miller) could stand upon no better footing. In such a case the surety can enforce for his own exoneration only such security as the creditor has against the principal. Stephenson v. Taverners, 9 Grat. 398; 3 Pom. Eq. Jur. § 1417, note 2. Besides, the evidence is positive that Miller himself had notice of that deed before the execution of the last one. William B. Baker, president of the bank, in his examination as a witness before the commissioner, was asked this question: "Prior to the 23d day of January, 1878, was John M. Miller informed and cognizant of the deed of trust dated the 1st day of November, 1875, to Tilman Shumate, trustee?" To which he answered: "He was." The decree, in the particular last mentioned, must therefore be reversed, and in all other respects affirmed.

McVEIGH'S EX'R v. HOWARD.

(Supreme Court of Appeals of Virginia. April 2, 1891.)

INTEREST—AGREEMENT TO PAY IN PRÆSENTI.

A bond reciting, "in consideration of professional services rendered to me by H., I owe, and hereby promise to pay to him, $10,000," is a promise of payment *in præsenti*, and bears interest from date.

S. F. Beach, for plaintiff in error. *G. A. Mushbach,* for defendant in error.

RICHARDSON, J. This is a writ of error to a judgment of the circuit court of the city of Alexandria, rendered on the 23d day of September, 1890, in an action of debt, wherein John Howard was plaintiff and S. Ferguson Beach, executor of William N. McVeigh, deceased, was defendant. The action was founded on the following bond: "$10,000. Richmond, Va., Jan'y 9th, 1878. In consideration of professional services rendered to me by John Howard, Esq., I owe, and hereby promise to pay to him, ten thousand dollars. Witness my hand and seal, this day and year above written. W. N. McVEIGH. [Seal.]" On the bond was the following indorsement: "The within obligation, to the extent of nine thousand dollars, ($9,000,) is secured by a first judgment lien on ample real estate in Alexandria, this day assigned by me to Mr. Howard. W. N. McVEIGH. Richmond, Jan'y 9th, 1878." The bond was also indorsed with several credits, aggregating about $7,000. To the plaintiff's declaration the defendant pleaded as follows: "For a plea to the plaintiff's action the defendant says that his testator, William N. McVeigh, during his life-time, paid

to the plaintiff the full amount of money in the writing obligatory specified, according to the tenor and effect thereof. And this he is ready to verify. Wherefore," etc. For a further plea to the said action, the defendant says that his said testator, during his life-time, made the payments following upon the said writing obligatory, viz.:

1882.		
Feb'y 24.	Cash per Com'r C. W. Wattles	$1,343 17
Mar. 4.	" " "	698 50
1885.		
Feb'y 26.	Proceeds John T. Cox bond....	616 28
" "	Cash judgment v. Alf'd Chapman	60 00
June 24.	Cash per C. W. Wattles, com'r	4,167 68
	Total	$8,814 85

—And this he is ready to verify. Wherefore," etc. "S. FERGUSON BEACH, Executor." To which pleas the plaintiff replied generally, and issue was joined thereon; and thereupon came a jury, etc. On the trial of the cause the bond and the indorsements thereon constituted all the evidence, no other testimony having been offered on either side. The defendant's counsel moved the court to give to the jury three several instructions, as follows: "(1) On an obligation to pay money at a future day, interest runs only from the day of payment, and not from its date, unless interest from date is expressly reserved. (2) The obligation sued on in this case is an obligation to pay money at a future day, when payment should be demanded, and interest upon it runs only from the time of demand actually made. (3) In the absence of any demand, specially made and proved, the interest on said obligation runs from the date of the commencement of the suit." But the court refused each of these instructions, and the defendant excepted. Then, on the motion of the plaintiff, the court instructed the jury that the bond sued on bore interest from its date, and to this ruling the defendant also excepted. The jury found a verdict for the plaintiff, as follows: "We, the jury, find the issue joined for the plaintiff, and that the defendant is indebted to the plaintiff in the sum of $7,652.63, the debt in the declaration mentioned, with legal interest thereon from the 25th day of June, 1885." Motions were made in arrest of judgment, to set aside the verdict and grant a new trial, but the court overruled these motions, and entered judgment according to the finding of the jury; and to this action of the court the defendant also excepted, and in his bill of exceptions set forth the facts and all the evidence, as above stated, which was signed and sealed by the court, and made a part of the record; and the defendant applied for and obtained a writ of error and *supersedeas* to said judgment and rulings.

All the evidence adduced on both sides at the trial was the bond sued on and the indorsements thereon. The defense attempted to be set up by the defendant (the plaintiff in error here) is presented in the three instructions asked for by him, and refused by the court. The first instruction asserts the undeniably correct proposition as an abstract question of law that on an obligation to pay money at a future day interest runs only from the day of payment, and not from its date, unless interest from date is expressly reserved; but it has no application to the bond sued on in the present case, as will at once appear from the language of the bond, viewed in the light of repeated decisions of this court. The second and third instructions asked for by the defendant may be considered together. They were clearly founded on a misapprehension of the legal effect of the bond sued on, and were rightly refused. They are as follows: "(2) The obligation sued on in this case is an obligation to pay money at a future day, when payment should be demanded, and interest upon it runs only from the time of demand actually made;" and (3) in the absence of any demand, specially made and proved, the interest on said obligation runs from the date of the commencement of the suit." In utter disregard of the grammatical sense and plain import of the words employed in the bond it is assumed in the second and third instructions asked for by the defendant (1) that the bond sued on is one which obliges the obligor to pay money at a future day, when payment must be demanded, and, if the demand of payment be not then made, the interest runs only from the time of suit brought; (2) that, inasmuch as there was no proof of a demand of payment made prior to the bringing of the suit, interest cannot be recovered except from the time the suit was commenced. Is the bond, in tenor and effect, such an instrument as it is thus assumed to be? We think not. Let the bond be its own interpreter. It is dated January 9, 1878, and the pivotal language is: "In consideration of professional services rendered to me by John Howard, Esq., I owe, and hereby promise to pay to him," etc. The antecedent words, "in consideration of professional services rendered to me," etc., cannot by possibility be tortured into any meaning other than that the professional services referred to had been performed prior to the date of the bond. This being so, then the language, "I owe, and hereby promise to pay," etc., is purely consequential upon that preceding it, refers only to the services theretofore rendered by the obligee to the obligor, and is but the simple acknowledgment by the latter of his indebtedness, and his promise to pay for such services the sum stipulated in the bond. What possible interpretation can be given to the expression "I owe" other than that the obligor then, at the time of executing the bond, owed the debt specified therein; and so as to the language, "and hereby promise to pay to him," which can only mean that the obligor, in recognition of the obligation resting upon him, promised to pay then, at the very moment of executing the bond, the debt evidenced thereby. And the language of the instrument, taken altogether, is but a simple acknowledgment of and promise to pay a pre-existing debt,—a debt then due for services already rendered. The bond in suit stipulates for no day in the future as the day of payment. On the contrary, it is an express acknowledgment, under seal, of a precedent debt of a sum certain, and is an equally express and solemn promise of payment *in præsenti*. This obligation of present payment conferred the right of action on the bond immediately upon its execution and delivery, and interest was a legal incident of the obligation from its date. It is admitted by the learned counsel for the plaintiff in error that in the familiar case of an obligation payable "on demand" "it is payable presently, and bears interest from date, which admission is based on the express language of this court in Omohundro v. Omohundro, 21 Grat. 631, where it is said that the words "on demand" have a plain, distinct, clearly defined, legal, and popular signification, well known to the courts and to the people, and by which the parties perfectly understood that the debt is payable presently, that it is due immediately, and bears interest from date. But it is sought to distinguish such an obligation containing the words "on demand" from the one in suit, where those words are not employed: and it is argued that it was evidently in the mind of the parties not to create, in form or in effect, the ordinary "on demand" obligation; and that it is not to be supposed that they intended to do what they clearly knew how to do, what they had it perfectly in their power to do, and yet deliberately omitted to do. This argument has no solid foundation in either reason or principle. The question is not what the parties may or may not have intended, but what is the legal effect of what they actually did. If, as is admitted, an obligation to pay "on demand" legally signifies a debt presently due and payable, is it not absurdly illogical to say that an obligation which omits those words is one payable at a future day, although no day or event in the future is specified as the time of payment? If an instrument such as this, which designates no point of time in the future as the time of payment, is an obligation to pay in the future, and if interest runs only from the time of default of payment, who is to determine at what time the default occurred? And would it not have to be determined outside of the contract between the parties? And, if so, would not this be making and enforcing a contract different from that actually entered into by the parties themselves? It is the settled rule that when no day is named in a bond or note given for the payment of a precedent debt it is due and payable on the day of its date, and bears interest from date, though no interest be reserved. Such an instrument, like a bond or note payable, in Virginia, on demand, is payable presently, and bears interest from date. This doctrine is founded in good conscience and correct morals, it having been said by this court, as far back as the decision in Jones v. Williams, 2 Call, 106, that "it is natural justice that he who has the use of another's money should pay interest on it;" and in Hatcher v. Lewis, 4 Rand. (Va.) 157, interest was said to follow the principal as the shadow the substance. We are therefore clearly of opinion that the circuit court did not err in refusing the three instructions asked for by the defendant.

Having refused each of the instructions asked for by the defendant, on the motion of the plaintiff the court instructed the jury that the bond sued on bore interest from its date; and this instruction is the subject of the defendant's second bill of exceptions. From what has already been said in considering the instructions asked for by the defendant, it follows that this instruction was properly given. Its correctness, in view of the doctrine upheld by this court, cannot be questioned. See Chapman v. Shepherd, 24 Grat. 383, 384; Roberts v. Cocke, 28 Grat. 207, 217, 218; Cecil v. Hicks, 29 Grat. 4, 5; Cecil v. Deyerle, 28 Grat. 775, 783, 784; Kent v. Kent, Id. 840, 846, 847. Thus, in Roberts v. Cocke, BURKS, J., said: "It has always been lawful in Virginia for parties to contract for the payment of interest for the use or forbearance of money within the limits prescribed by statute; and, in the absence of any express agreement for the payment of interest in obligations for the payment of a certain sum of money on demand, or on a given day, interest on the principal sum from the time it becomes payable is 'a legal incident of the debt,' and the right to it is founded on the presumed intention of the parties." Citing Chapman v. Shepherd, supra, in which Judge STAPLES, speaking of the defenses which may be made to the recovery of interest on such obligations as were mentioned by BURKS, J., in Roberts v. Cocke, says: "It is true that the debtor may sometimes, under peculiar circumstances, avoid the payment of interest; but these are matters of defense, the burden of which is upon him in all cases. They are offered to show that the obligation to pay has been discharged, and not that it did not originally exist. If no valid ground of defense is shown, the judgment is as certainly rendered for the interest as for the principal. In contracts of the character just mentioned it is apparent, therefore, that interest is not given as damages, at the discretion of the court or jury, but as an incident of the debt, which the court has no discretion to refuse. Wherever there is a contract, express or implied, for the payment of legal interest, the obligation of the contract extends as well to the payment of the interest as it does to the payment of the principal sum, and neither the courts nor the juries have ever had the arbitrary power to dispense with the performance of either in whole or in part." And in Kent v. Kent, supra, MONCURE, P., said: "A bond payable on demand, or on a certain day, bears interest from the time it is payable, according to the well-settled law of this state, unless there be some contract, express or implied, between the parties, or some extraordinary or peculiar circumstances, showing that interest was not to be paid; and the burden of proving contract or circumstances devolves on the party who seeks to avoid the payment. In the absence of such proof, the obligation for the payment of interest is as much a matter of contract in the case as the obligation for the payment of the principal." In the present case there was no contract, express or implied, that interest should not be paid; and, as already

v.13s.e.no.1—3

shown, the bond in suit being for a precedent debt, and no time in the future being designated as the time of payment, and although interest was not specially reserved, yet the debt was due and payable on the day of the date of the bond, and from that time interest runs as a legal incident of the debt. It is therefore clear that the circuit court did not err in so instructing the jury.

The defendant's third exception is to the action of the circuit court overruling his motions in arrest of judgment, and to set aside the verdict, and grant a new trial. No ground whatever is shown in support of the motion in arrest of judgment. The only evidence before the jury was the bond sued on and the indorsements thereon. The verdict of the jury was for the balance due on the bond, after applying the partial payments first to the interest on said bond and then to the principal, as authorized by law. For the sum thus ascertained to be due and unpaid the jury found a verdict for the plaintiff, with interest from the 25th day of June, 1885. The finding was right, and the judgment thereon is without error; hence there could be no ground for disturbing the judgment of the circuit court, which must be affirmed.

HOLLORAN v. MEISEL et al.[1]

(*Supreme Court of Appeals of Virginia.* Jan. 29, 1891.)

EJECTMENT—PRIMA FACIE TITLE.

A grant of land by the commonwealth as waste and unappropriated gives the grantee *prima facie* title, which cannot be resisted in ejectment by a defendant who has taken possession without color of title, and relies on the fact that the land had been conveyed by an old colonial grant to a third person before the grant by the commonwealth. LACY and HINTON, JJ., dissenting.

John Howard, Edgar Allan, and *J. Sam'l Parrish,* for plaintiff in error. *W. W. & B. T. Crump,* for defendants in error.

FAUNTLEROY, J. The petition of James Holloran represents that he is aggrieved by a judgment of the circuit court of the city of Richmond, rendered on the 6th day of September, 1888, in an action of ejectment, wherein he is plaintiff, and Philip Meisel, Sr., and Philip Meisel, Jr., are defendants. The record discloses that James Holloran, the plaintiff in error, obtained from the commonwealth of Virginia a grant for a tract of land lying in the county of Henrico, near the city of Richmond, containing 3.84 acres, on the 12th day of February, 1887; that the said grant was obtained after the said James Holloran had had the said land surveyed, and he had complied fully with all the requirements of the law; that the said land was and had been on the commons, and waste and unappropriated, up to three or four years before the rendition of the said judgment, and that no one laid claim thereto; that some three or four years before said judgment was rendered the defendants in error fenced the said land in, and were in possession of the same at the time of the institution of

[1] Affirmed on rehearing, March 26, 1891.

this suit, and that the said James Holloran demanded of them possession of the said land prior to the institution of the action of ejectment; that the said land had not been on the land-books from 1813 to 1888, when it was put on by the said James Holloran; that by deed dated June 5, 1888, Thomas E. McCorkle and wife conveyed to Philip Meisel a parcel of land adjoining the said land granted to the said James Holloran, but that said last-named deed did not embrace the land granted to the said James Holloran as aforesaid, but did embrace and convey only a separate and distinct parcel of land known as "Chelsea," fully described in the said deed and the plat thereto annexed; and that the only ground upon which the defendants rested their claim to the land granted as aforesaid to James Holloran was that the said land was embraced in a grant from the colonial government of Virginia, in 1687, to Joshua Stepp (or Stapp) for 277 acres of land, without pretending, or undertaking in any way, to trace their title back to said Stapp; but, on the contrary, the record shows conclusively that the said defendants never received a conveyance for the said land from any one, and never laid any claim thereto by reason of any purchase from any one, but only inclosed it as adjoining the land which they did purchase from McCorkle some three or four years before the rendition of the judgment complained of. Upon these facts, under the instruction given by the court, the jury brought in a verdict for the defendants; and upon the said verdict the circuit court of the city of Richmond entered its judgment for the defendants and against the plaintiff, James Holloran. The plaintiff asked the court to give to the jury three instructions, which are set forth in his first bill of exceptions, and which it is not necessary to repeat here, and in regard to which we deem it sufficient to say that they do not fully and accurately state the law, and they were properly refused by the court. The defendants also asked for an instruction, which was refused; and the court gave, in lieu of those asked for by the plaintiff and that asked for by the defendants, the following instruction: "If the jury believe from the evidence that the patent dated October 21, 1687, to Joshua Stapp, for 277 acres of land, included the land in controversy, then the land was not after that waste and unappropriated, and the grant of the property in controversy to James Holloran, by the patent in evidence, was void, and they must find for the defendants. But unless the jury believe that the land in controversy was included in the patent to Stapp, they should find for the plaintiff." To which ruling of the court in giving the aforesaid instruction, and in refusing to give the instructions asked for by the plaintiff, the plaintiff excepted; and this is the ground of the first error assigned.

The instruction given by the court was erroneous. Under the facts as proved in the record, the defendant Meisel entered upon the land without title or claim, or even color of title, and as a mere intruder upon land not his own, having only "a bare and naked possession, without a

shadow of right." Holloran, the plaintiff, by his grant from the commonwealth on the 12th day of February, 1887, as shown in evidence, acquired a *prima facie* title to the land granted in fee, and was a "purchaser for valuable consideration," with both right of property and right of immediate actual possession. Clay v. White, 1 Munf. 171; Green v. Liter, 8 Cranch, 229; 1 Tuck. Comm. 274. The grant of the commonwealth confers seisin without actual entry. (1 Munf. 162,) and it is a seisin in deed, and not a mere seisin in law, which it gives. 8 Cranch, 229. Meisel's defense against the claim of Holloran by virtue of his grant from the commonwealth is that there is an outstanding title in a third person, to whom the land had been previously patented by the colonial government in 1687,—one Joshua Stapp. But the copy of the paper dated October 21, 1687, put in evidence to prove a patent for the land in controversy, granted to Joshua Stapp by Lord Howard, as colonial governor of Virginia, October 21, 1687, is without signature or seal, and shows upon its face never to have been executed, and therefore void and inoperative as a grant or instrument of conveyance. It is simply void upon its face as a grant or valid patent for the land, taking it out of the category of waste and unappropriated land; and even if the said unexecuted and incomplete paper of the 21st of October, 1687, could as a matter of law, be operative to pass the title out of the commonwealth, there was no survey or plat or map, according to the metes and bounds of said paper exhibited in evidence, to identify this 3.84 acres of land as a part of the 277 acres alleged to have been patented to Stapp 200 years ago, and which since 1813 has lain waste, without an owner, or even an occupier or claimant, and without ever appearing upon the land-books until it was squatted upon by Meisel, who claims under nobody, and traces no title from any source. Yet the court, under these circumstances, assumed that the paper of October 21, 1687, is itself a patent, though without signature or seal, and without any evidence of its ever having been executed or delivered, or of possession under it; and, by the instruction given, took the whole question from the jury as to whether a prior patent had been executed and issued for the land; and, ignoring that question, left to the jury only the question of the identity of the *locus in quo* as part of an assumed valid grant: thus positively instructing the jury that the paper of October 21, 1687, shown an outstanding title, prior and paramount to the validly executed grant of the land to the plaintiff for valuable consideration by the commonwealth, under the sign-manual of its governor and its seal of state, and setting up by the instruction given an absolute nullity, without signature or seal, as a judicially adjudicated valid prior conveyance. 1 Hen. St. at Large, p. 472, Act 87: "That all patents be drawne upp in a fitt forme relateing to the present government; and that till a seale may be procured, the governour and secretarie for the time being signeing the said pattents, they shall be accompted vallid and authentique in all courtes of justice, as any pattentsformerly granted under the colloney seale. And the like for all things that bath usually passed under the seale." Passed, April, 1652; see 2 Hen. St. at Large, p. 245, Act 19. The paper of October 21, 1687, was admissible only as a memorandum from the colonial records, tending to prove that proceedings had been taken looking to an execution and issuing of a grant, to be followed up, if possible, by evidence tending to show that the grant so contemplated and begun was actually executed, issued, and delivered; but, standing by itself, the copy was a nullity, as a grant, and proved nothing but its own abortive existence. As against the commonwealth or her grantee, Holloran, in the patent of 1887, there is no evidence in the record tending to show that a prior patent ever was actually executed, issued, or delivered. The presumption as to an actual issue of a patent stands upon grounds not existing in this case; and such an issue, and the evidence bearing upon it, are for the jury to determine, and not the court. Where there has been long possession under claim of title and long-continued payment of taxes, a patent may sometimes be presumed. In Archer v. Saddler, 2 Hen. & M. 370, there had been 60 years of peaceable and uninterrupted possession, together with payment of quitrents before and of taxes since the Revolution by the caveator and those under whom he claimed; and it was held that it was a case to be submitted to a jury to decide whether a patent should be presumed to have issued formerly, and whether the facts justified such a presumption. In the case under review there is no evidence of the possession of the *locus in quo* at an time by anybody with claim of title, nor even of possession, until Meisel squatted on it a few years ago; and the record shows that no taxes were paid or assessed by anybody for more than 75 years, until 1888, when Holloran first paid taxes on it after receiving his patent. For the error of the court in giving the instruction, and the error in overruling the motion for a new trial upon the ground that the verdict is contrary to the law and the evidence, the judgment complained of must be reversed and annulled; and the judgment of this court is that the verdict be set aside, and the case be remanded to the circuit court of the city of Richmond for a new trial, upon which, if the evidence be the same, the jury shall be instructed in accordance with this opinion. .

LACY and HINTON, JJ., dissenting.

DAVIS v. GORDON.

(Supreme Court of Appeals of Virginia. March 26, 1891.)

REAL-ESTATE AGENTS—SPECIAL AGENCY.

1. An owner of land employed real-estate agents to sell it, without fixing a definite price. These agents had previously sold other land for the owner; but in each case, before closing the contract, the offer was submitted to the owner for his approval or rejection. Not being able to sell the land, it was platted into lots, with a view of selling at auction. On consultation with the owner, he fixed the minimum price, and advised the agents to sell the property as a whole, or to first put up the lots furthest from the corner. The auction sale was abandoned. For seven months thereafter, no sale was effected, and no definite price for the lots was agreed on; but the owner on several occasions conferred with the agents about the market, asked if they had any offer to submit on the lots, and required the property to be sold as a whole, or the lots furthest from the corner first. *Held*, that the agents, being employed to effect the sale of only the one parcel of land in a specified manner, were special agents, and not general agents; that the owner was not bound by a sale of the corner lots made by them in his absence, and without his consent, at a price below the minimum fixed for the auction sale, and at a time when the demand for the lots had greatly increased on account of public improvements to be made in the vicinity; and that the purchasers from the agent could not specifically enforce the contract as against the owner.

2. The fact that the proposed auction sale was advertised in several newspapers by the real-estate agents, and that the bill for such advertising was paid by the owner, did not convert the special agency into a general agency, with authority in the agents, seven months later, to effect a private sale of the lots in a manner and at a price wholly different from what was arranged for the contemplated auction sale.

3. The fact that the real-estate agents erected a sign on the property, showing that it was for sale by them, without mentioning the owner's name, does not constitute a holding out of the agents, by the owner to the public, as having a general authority to bind him by a sale of the property.

Pollard & Sands, for appellant. *Johnson, Williams & Boulware* and *H. H. Marshall*, for appellee.

RICHARDSON, J. This is an appeal from a decree of the chancery court for the city of Richmond, pronounced on the 6th day of July, 1889, in the suit therein then pending, wherein Dr. H. Wythe Davis was plaintiff, and Col. John W. Gordon was defendant. The object of the suit was to compel specific performance of a certain contract for the sale and purchase of real estate, which contract was entered into by and between Chewning & Rose, real-estate agents, and Dr. H. Wythe Davis, on the 12th of January, 1889, whereby Chewning & Rose undertook, as agents of said John W. Gordon, to sell to said H. W. Davis 60 feet of ground at the corner of Cary and Linden streets, in the city of Richmond; and, at the time of the alleged contract, Chewning & Rose executed the following paper: "Richmond, Va., January 12th, 1889. Received of Dr. H. W. Davis five dollars, current money, on purchase of a lot at north-east corner of Cary and Linden streets, fronting sixty feet on Cary street by a depth of 100 feet to an alley, for the price of twenty-four hundred dollars, payable as follows: One-fourth cash; balance at six, twelve, and eighteen months. CHEWNING & ROSE, Agents for John W. Gordon." It was to enforce this contract that the plaintiff's bill was filed. After setting forth the contract, the plaintiff alleges that on the —— day of January, 1889, as soon as an examination of the title to said property could be conveniently made, and which was begun at once, an abstract of which is exhibited with the bill, he tendered to the said

Chewning & Rose, agents for said John W. Gordon, and afterwards to the said Gordon himself, the sum of $600 in currency, a note for $618, payable to the order of said John W. Gordon, at 6 months, a note for $636, payable to his order, at 12 months, and a note for $654, payable to his order, at 18 months, together with a deed of trust conveying said property to secure the payment of the said notes, and demanded of said Chewning & Rose, agents as aforesaid, a deed of general warranty, conveying said property to the plaintiff; that said agents refused to comply with the terms of sale, because, as they alleged, the said John W. Gordon had instructed them not to do so, and the said Gordon also declined said tender, and refused to comply with said contract, alleging as an excuse that said Chewning & Rose were not authorized to make said sale; that the plaintiff has fully complied with the terms of said contract on his part, so far as it was proper for him to do without a delivery to him of the deed demanded as aforesaid; and that the plaintiff is now, as he has always been since the making of said contract, ready and anxious to comply with its terms. And the bill charges that the said Chewning & Rose were the agents of said John W. Gordon, and authorized to make said contract of sale. And the prayer of the bill is that John W. Gordon be made a party defendant thereto, and required to answer the same, but waiving answer under oath, and that said John W. Gordon be required to specifically perform said contract, and for general relief, etc.

The defendant, John W. Gordon, answered, saying that the contract for the sale of the lot which was entered into by said Davis with Chewning & Rose, as agents, was entered into without any authority from him to said Chewning & Rose, as his agents, to make such contract or such sale, and denies that he is in any way bound by the same. He says it is true, as alleged in the bill, that said Davis offered to comply with the provisions of said contract, but that respondent declined to allow him to do so, because he repudiated said contract, and considered that he was in no way bound by the same, etc. Depositions were taken on both sides, and the cause, having been regularly matured, came on and was heard on the 6th day of July, 1889, when the said chancery court entered the following decree: "This day this cause came on to be again heard upon the bill of the plaintiff, the answer of the defendant, this day ordered to be filed by leave of the court, and the general replication thereto, and upon the depositions taken in the cause, and was argued by counsel. On consideration whereof, the court, for reasons appearing in a written opinion filed herein, doth adjudge, order, and decree that the said bill be, and the same is hereby, dismissed, but without prejudice to any legal rights or remedies the plaintiff may have; and doth further decree that the said plaintiff shall pay to the said defendant his costs in this suit." From this decree the plaintiff obtained an appeal to this court.

The sole question to be determined is, were Chewning & Rose authorized, as the agents of John W. Gordon, to make the contract in question? The answer to this question depends upon the nature and extent of the authority conferred by John W. Gordon upon Chewning & Rose, it not being denied by the former that the latter were his agents in a limited and restricted sense. Agencies are commonly divided into two sorts: (1) A general agency; (2) special agency. A general agency properly exists where there is a delegation of authority to do all acts connected with a particular trade, business, or employment. On the other hand, a special agency exists when the authority delegated is to do a single act. Thus a person who is authorized by his principal to execute all deeds, sign all contracts, or purchase all goods required in a particular trade, business, or employment, is a general agent in that trade, business, or employment. But a person who is authorized by his principal to execute a particular deed, or to sign a particular contract, or to purchase a particular parcel of merchandise, is a special agent. Story, Ag. § 17. The same author, in section 18, says: "A person is sometimes (although, perhaps, not with entire accuracy) called a general agent, who is not appointed with powers so general as those above mentioned, but who has a general authority in regard to a particular object or thing; as, for example, to buy and sell a particular parcel of goods, or to negotiate a particular note or bill,—his agency not being limited in the buying or selling such goods, or negotiating such note or bill, to any particular mode of doing it." So an agent, who is appointed to do a particular thing in a prescribed mode, is often called a special agent, as contradistinguished from a general agent; and in section 19 it is said: "On the other hand, (although this is not the ordinary commercial sense,) a person is sometimes said to be a special agent, whose authority, although it extends to acts generally in a particular business or employment, is yet qualified and restrained by limitations, conditions, and restrictions of a special nature. In such a case the agent is deemed, as to the person dealing with him in ignorance of such special limitations, conditions, and restrictions, to be a general agent; although, as between himself and his principal, he may be deemed a special agent. In short, the true distinction (as generally recognized) between a general and a special agent (or, as he is sometimes called, a particular agent) is this: A general agency does not import an unqualified authority, but that which is derived from a multitude of instances, or in the general course of an employment or business; whereas, a special agency is confined to an individual transaction."

The author, in this concise statement of the law, covers all the ground essential to the proper consideration of every practical distinction that may be taken between a general and a special agency. It is of the utmost importance to carefully discriminate between general agents and special agents, as to the rights and responsibilities, the duties and the obligations, both of principals and agents, as the principles applicable to the one frequently have no application whatever to the other. To perform this task successfully, and with due regard for the rights of all persons interested, it is important to keep constantly in mind what has been already stated, the distinction commonly taken between the case of a general agent and that of a special agent, the former being appointed to act in his principal's affairs generally, and the latter to act concerning some particular object. In the former case, the principal will be bound by the acts of his agent within the scope of the general authority conferred on him, although he violates by those acts his private instructions and directions, which are given to him by the principal, limiting, qualifying, suspending, or prohibiting the exercise of such authority under particular circumstances. But, on the contrary, in the case of a special agency, if the agent exceeds the special and limited authority conferred on him, the principal is not bound by his acts, but they become mere nullities, so far as he is concerned; unless, indeed, he has held him out as possessing a more enlarged authority. Story, Ag. § 126, and authorities there referred to; and, among them, 2 Kent, Com. § 41, (4th Ed.) pp. 620, 621; 3 Chit. Commer. Law, 196; Smith, Merc. Law, (2d Ed.) 58-62; Fenn v. Harrison, 3 Term. R. 757; Howard v. Braithwaite, 1 Ves. & B. 209-210; Whitehead v. Tuckett, 15 East, 408. "The ground of this distinction," says Story, "is the public policy of preventing frauds upon innocent persons, and the encouragement of confidence in dealings with agents. If a person is held out to third persons, or to the public at large, by the principal, as having a general authority to act for and to bind him in a particular business or employment, it would be the height of injustice, and lead to the grossest frauds, to allow him to set up his own secret and private instructions to the agent limiting that authority, and thus to defeat his acts and transactions under the agency, when the party dealing with him had, and could have, no notice of such instructions. In such cases good faith requires that the principal should be bound by the acts of the agent within the scope of his general authority; for he has held him out to the public as competent to do the acts, and to bind him thereby. The maxim of natural justice here applies with its full force, that he who, without intentional fraud, has enabled any person to do an act which must be injurious to himself, or to another innocent party, shall himself suffer the injury rather than the innocent party who has placed confidence in him. The maxim is founded in the soundest ethics, and is enforced to a large extent by courts of equity. Of course the maxim fails in its application when the party dealing with the agent has a full knowledge of the private instructions of the agent, or that he is exceeding his authority." Story, Ag. § 127. The same author, after stating the exemplification of the rule in the civil law as to the distinction between a general and a special agency, says: "The illustrations in our law of

the same distinction between general agents and limited or special agents may be familiarly seen in the common case of factors, known to be such. They possess a general authority to sell; and if, in selling, they violate their private instructions, the principal is, nevertheless, bound. And it makes no difference, in a case of this kind, whether the factor (if known to be such) has been ordinarily employed by the principal to sell, or whether it is the first and only instance of his being so employed by the principal to sell; being a known factor, he is held out by the principal as possessing, in effect, all the ordinary general authority of a factor in relation to the particular sale. But if a common person, not being a factor, should be authorized to make a like sale, and he should violate his private instructions, and deviate from his authority in the sale, the principal would not be bound. In such a case no general authority is presumed, and he who deals with such an agent deals with him at his own peril; for, in such a case, the principal has not held the agent out as a general agent." However apt the above illustration may be in the case of factors known to be such, the doctrine applicable to that class of agents can have but a limited influence in illustrating the case of agents who, as in the present case, are real-estate brokers, as a factor differs from a broker in certain important particulars. Real-estate brokers negotiate the sale or purchase of real estate. Their powers are ordinarily limited to negotiating a contract, and do not extend to the execution of a contract of purchase or sale, and in this respect they differ from merchandise brokers. The broker may be employed orally or by writing; and he may be authorized to make a contract for the sale or lease of real estate, which will be sufficient, under the statute of frauds, by an instrument not under seal, and even by parol; but he may not attach a seal to the instrument made under such an authority. An authority "to close the bargain" is not an authority to sign the name of the principal to a contract of sale. 3 Wait, Act. & Def. 286, 287, and authorities cited. The same author, discussing the case of factors and commission merchants, at page 289, says: "A factor is an agent employed to sell goods consigned or delivered to him by or for his principal for a commission usually called a 'factorage' or 'commission.' Hence he is often called a 'commission merchant' or 'consignee;' the goods received by him for sale are called a 'consignment.' There seems to be no substantial difference in law between a 'factor' and a 'commission merchant.' The words are ordinarily used interchangeably. A factor, as we have seen, differs materially from a broker. He is intrusted with the possession, management, and disposal of the consigned property. He may sell in his own name, and may receive and enforce payment." And in Story on Agency, after defining the terms "broker" and "factor" in substantially the same language as that employed in 3 Wait, § 28 et seq., it is said: "Properly speaking, a broker is a mere negotiator between the other parties, and he never acts in his own name, but in the names of those who employ him. Where he is employed to buy or sell goods, he is not intrusted with the custody or possession of them, and is not authorized to buy or to sell them in his own name. He is strictly, therefore, a middle-man, or intermediate negotiator between the parties; and, for some purposes, (as for the purpose of signing a contract within the statute of frauds,) he is treated as the agent of both parties. Hence, when he is employed to buy and sell goods, he is accustomed to give to the buyer a note of the sale, commonly called a 'sale note,' and to the seller a like note, commonly called a 'bought note,' in his own name, as agent of each, and thereby they are respectively bound, if he has not exceeded his authority. Hence, also, it is that if a broker sells the goods of his principal in his own name, (without some special authority to do so,) inasmuch as he exceeds his proper authority, the principal will have the same rights and remedies against the purchaser as if his name had been disclosed by the broker." "It has been already suggested," says the author, "that a broker is, for some purposes, treated as the agent of both parties. But primarily he is deemed merely the agent of the party by whom he is originally employed; and he becomes the agent of the other party only when the bargain or contract is definitely settled as to its terms between the principals; for, as a middle-man, he is not intrusted to fix the terms, but merely to interpret (as it is sometimes phrased) between the principals." The character of a broker is also sometimes combined in the same person with that of a factor. In such cases we should carefully distinguish between his acts in the one character and in the other, as the same rules do not always apply precisely to each. * * * A factor differs from a broker in some important particulars. A factor may buy and sell in his own name, as well as in the name of his principal. A broker, as we have seen, is always bound to buy and sell in the name of his principal. A factor is intrusted with the possession, control, and disposal of the goods to be bought or sold, and has a special property in them and a lien on them. A broker, on the contrary, usually has no such possession, management, control, or disposal of the goods, and consequently has no such special property or lien."

Guided by these principles, we must turn to the evidence in the cause in order to determine whether Chewning & Rose, as agents of John W. Gordon, had authority to make the contract of sale in question, and to bind Gordon thereby. They insist that they were his general agents, and that they had full authority from him to make the sale and to bind him thereby. He, on the other hand, contends that they were merely special agents, with limited authority, and that he never delegated to them any authority to make the contract of sale sought to be enforced in this suit nor to make any sale except subject to his approval. In the court below, the learned chancellor (FITZHUGH) dismissed the plaintiff's bill, on the ground that there was an irreconcilable conflict in the testimony as to the extent of the authority delegated by Gordon to Chewning & Rose as agents; and that there was such conflict, he stated, that it would be a waste of time to show in detail, as it was apparent on the face of the depositions. In the light of the evidence in the cause, the conclusion arrived at by the chancellor is, in our opinion, undoubtedly the correct one. The following facts may be stated as either undisputed or established by such an overwhelming weight of evidence as to render any contention to the contrary absurd: The property in controversy is part of a lot of land commencing at the north-west corner of Cary and Linden streets, extending west 120 feet, fronting on said Cary street, and extending back 100 feet to an alley. The appellee, John W. Gordon, purchased the property on or about the 1st of March, 1887, at an auction sale conducted by Chewning & Rose, real-estate agents, and was thus bought for speculation; and, having been so bought, the purchaser, Gordon, said to Chewning & Rose, "It is for sale again;" and expressed a desire that they would sell it, but no definite price was then fixed upon the property. Chewning & Rose had before this sold other properties for Gordon, and they had, in each case, before closing the contract, submitted the offer to him for his approval or rejection. Gordon had received several proposals to purchase the corner lot, and for as much as 40 feet on the corner, but always declined to sell the corner first, and was repeatedly and urgently advised by Chewning & Rose not to sell the corner first. They frequently said to Gordon they could sell the corner lot for a good price at any time, and more than once mentioned offers by parties who, for the sake of securing the corner lot, would also buy the next one or two lots to it. And they (Chewning & Rose) represented that the purchaser might put up a grog-shop there and ruin the prospects of the remaining property, and that they must make the corner lot sell the others. Not very long after the purchase of this property by Gordon, the opposite or south-eastern corner of Cary and Linden streets was mentioned in the city newspapers as a desirable site for the erection of the proposed Clay Ward Market-House, and a discussion of the subject in the papers about that time had the effect of bringing this property into favorable notice, and the subsequent action of the city council (presently to be more particularly referred to) greatly stimulated the demand therefor. The proposed erection of the Clay Ward Market met with considerable opposition, and for some months the discussion of the subject seemed to cease, and the result was a lull in the demand for property in the immediate neighborhood of the proposed site for the new market-house. During this period, in the summer of 1888, at the instance and by the persuasion of Chewning & Rose, Gordon was induced to let them try this property at public auction; consequently the property was advertised to be sold in lots of 20 feet each, fronting on Cary street. A few days prior to the day appointed for the auction sale, Gordon had a conference with Chewning & Rose in order that they might be informed as to the minimum prices at which the lots would be allowed to go at auction; and on this, as on other occasions, they advised Gordon either to sell the property as a whole, or to first put up the lots furthest from the corner. Accordingly, a rough sketch or diagram was made, dividing the property into six lots of 20 feet each, and several scales of prices were suggested and made,—some of them by Mr. Rose, of the firm of Chewning & Rose, and some by Gordon,—in which the prices varied from $55 per foot for the corner lot to $30 for the lot most remote from the corner; the object being to arrive at a price in the aggregate for all the lots, the lowest scale which Gordon agreed to accept making the aggregate price for all the lots about $4,500; the lowest price per foot being $30, which was for the lot furthest from the corner, which was to be first put up. Very few people attended the proposed auction, and Mr. Rose, who was the auctioneer of the firm of Chewning & Rose, declined to offer the property at auction, saying he would not put up the property; that he knew the crowd, and that every would-be buyer wanted the corner lot, which they were determined not to sell first. From the day of the proposed auction sale until the 12th day of January, 1889, the date of the alleged contract of sale by Chewning & Rose, agents for Gordon, a period of some seven months, the latter agreed with the former upon no price for the lots in question; but during that period he several times conferred with them about the real-estate market, and asked if they had any offer to submit for these lots. Thus the matter stood until the 7th day of March, 1889, on which day John W. Gordon left Richmond for North Carolina; and on the same day, but after Gordon left the city, there was a meeting of the common council of the city of Richmond, at which a resolution was unanimously adopted fixing the location of the Clay Ward Market at a point very near the property in question. While in North Carolina Gordon received telegrams making him offers for this property, which induced him to believe that his property had suddenly become greatly in demand. He was at a point remote from any railroad, but, by putting himself to some trouble, he secured certain Richmond papers, and, on searching them, found the action of the common council, above referred to. He thereupon by wire declined the offers made him for his property, and at once returned to Richmond, where he arrived on Sunday, the 18th of March, and after his arrival was informed that in his absence Chewning & Rose had entered into a contract of sale with Dr. H. W. Davis, by which they undertook to sell 60 feet of the Cary-Street property, commencing at the corner, at $40 per front-foot. This action was taken by Chewning & Rose in the absence of and without conferring with Col. Gordon, and, of course, without his consent. The next morning, (Monday, the 14th,) as soon as he could reach their office, he informed them that he would not ratify the sale; that they had made it without authority from him; and requested them to notify the purchaser at once

that he would not approve it. Subsequently, on the same day, Chewning & Rose, or one of them, anxious for an adjustment of the matter without further difficulty, requested Col. Gordon to permit them to propose to the purchaser that, if he would take the remaining 60 feet at $35, he (Gordon) would then ratify the sale as to the whole property, and Col. Gordon agreed that he would do that. Having on the next day (March 15th) ascertained that the board of aldermen had, on the previous evening of March 14th, approved the action of the common council, he went immediately to Chewning & Rose, and said to them that, if they had made the offer authorized by him on the day before to withdraw it, and they did so; and Gordon himself went to see the alleged purchaser, Davis, and, failing to see him, left a note at his residence, informing him that he would not ratify the sale made to him by Chewning & Rose. Mr. Chewning had informed Col. Gordon that he (Chewning) had, on Monday, the 14th, notified Dr. Davis of his (Gordon's) refusal to ratify the contract; but Dr. Davis testifies that Chewning had given him no such notification, but had only offered to sell him the residue of the property at $35 per foot, and that he (Davis) had no notice of such refusal until he received Col. Gordon's note on Tuesday.

The facts above stated are either undisputed or are not seriously controverted. There are, however, other facts and circumstances, some of which are relied upon by the appellant to show that Chewning & Rose were the general agents of Col. Gordon, and fully authorized to make the sale in question and bind him thereby; and other facts and circumstances relied on by the appellee, Gordon, to show that Chewning & Rose were his special agents as to the Cary-Street property, and none other, and had no authority to make the sale in question, nor any sale, except subject to his approval or rejection. Touching the question thus presented, three witnesses—A. J. Chewning and Edward S. Rose, who constitute the firm of Chewning & Rose, and A. J. Gray, formerly a clerk with Chewning & Rose—depose on behalf of the appellant. There is no consistency in the testimony of any two of these witnesses, nor is the testimony of either one of them consistent with the appellant's theory of the case. Chewning says that he was authorized by Col. Gordon to sell 30 feet or upwards at $40 a foot. This was on his examination in chief. On cross-examination, he says he had authority to sell 30 feet or upwards at $40, and the whole at $35 a foot. The witness Gray, on his re-examination by the plaintiff, says that the instructions of Col. Gordon to the firm were to sell at least 40 or 60 feet at $40 a foot; and that they did not have authority to sell 30 feet, for instance, as the lots were laid off in 20-foot lots, and that they did not have authority to sell less than 2 or 3 lots of 20 feet each; while the witness Rose, on his cross-examination, says that they had authority to sell the corner lot at $30, meaning, as he says, by the corner lot, 20 feet; thus showing a very wide discrepancy between the members of the firm of Chewning & Rose, and between each of them and their former clerk, who was in their office for a considerable length of time while they had this property for sale, and was cognizant of what transpired there in respect to the dealings in regard to this property. We therefore see, as respects the authority of Chewning & Rose to sell, Mr. Chewning asserting authority to sell 30 feet, but admitting that he had none to sell less than 30 feet; Mr. Gray claiming that they had authority to sell at least 40 feet, but not less than that, while Mr. Rose claims that they had authority to sell as little as 20 feet. Again, Mr. Chewning says that he never advised Col. Gordon not to sell the corner lot first, but, on the contrary, advised him to do so. Mr. Rose says he does not recollect, but he very probably did so advise him; and Mr. Gray says positively, and without hesitation, that he had frequently heard Mr. Chewning, certainly, and he thinks Mr. Rose, also, advise Col. Gordon not to sell the corner lot first; thus again exhibiting their inconsistencies of statements. Mr. Chewning again says that Col. Gordon never mentioned any special terms upon which the property was to be sold, but said, "upon the usual terms;" and Mr. Rose says that no price or terms were ever fixed by Col. Gordon, except when the auction sale was proposed, and that they were then fixed with reference alone to the proposed auction sale. What the "usual terms" are the record does not inform us, nor did the plaintiff (the appellant) in any way attempt to show what the "usual terms" are. Surely there can be no reasonable pretense for claiming authority to sell privately half of these lots, including the corner, at a price and upon terms admitted to have been arranged with reference to the proposed auction sale alone, and especially as Col. Gordon had determined, at the urgent solicitation of Chewning & Rose, to sell the property as a whole, or to sell first the lots furthest from the corner, and when they had given such excellent reasons for so doing, and when the sale in question was made six months after the time fixed for the auction sale, and with reference to which alone the only price ever agreed upon was fixed by Col. Gordon. If no price was ever fixed at any other time, or for any other purpose, as admitted by Mr. Rose, why was not the arrangement as to the proposed auction sale caried out in other respects? Why did not Chewning & Rose sell the property as a whole, or sell first the lot most remote from the corner? Can there be any question as to the fact that Col. Gordon never authorized the sale in the manner, on the terms, or at the price set forth in the contract sought to be enforced in this suit? We think not. It follows, therefore, that the sale made by Chewning & Rose to Dr. Davis was without authority from Col. Gordon, and he is not bound thereby.

Chewning & Rose claim that they were the exclusive agents for the sale of these lots, and yet it is established by indubitable proof, and they admit, that the same property was in the hands of E. A. Catlin and other real-estate agents, to whom Col. Gordon had delegated precisely the same authority as that conferred upon Chewning & Rose, and that was to watch the real-estate market, hunt up and negotiate with proposed purchasers, and to submit any offers made to him for his approval or rejection. And Mr. Chewning says if any other agent had brought Col. Gordon a satisfactory offer he supposes he would have accepted it. The forgetfulness or inaccuracy of Mr. Chewning is well illustrated in his denial, on cross-examination, that he had ever before sold any property for Col. Gordon, when, in his own deposition, Col. Gordon proves that he had made several sales for him before, and actually produced and filed the account of such sales furnished him by Chewning & Rose. And again, the same fact is illustrated by Chewning's statement (before referred to) to Col. Gordon that he had notified Dr. Davis of his (Gordon's) refusal to ratify the sale in question, when Dr. Davis testifies that Chewning gave him no such information, and that the first notice he had of the fact was when he received Col. Gordon's note, a day later. Mr. Catlin testifies as to the time and place of an interview between Chewning & Rose, Col. Gordon, and himself, and states in detail what was said. Col. Gordon at first did not, it is true, remember the interview; but when it was called to his attention he did remember it, though, with commendable candor, he states that he does not remember what occurred at it. Chewning & Rose tried to disprove the interview by showing that Mr. Catlin came to their office, where the interview took place, on business other than anything connected with Col. Gordon's affairs. But Mr. Catlin, in the outset, had said that he went to the office about another matter; but he testifies that while there Col. Gordon came in, and that Chewning & Rose then, in his presence, tried to induce Col. Gordon to withdraw this property from his hands, which he could not do. And Mr. Catlin is sustained by Col. Gordon, who, though not recollecting the particulars of the interview above referred to, does testify that soon after the discussion commenced in the newspapers as to the site for the Clay Ward Market he received, through Mr. Catlin, an offer of $35 per foot for the whole property, and that he promptly refused the offer; that Catlin then asked him to name his price, which Gordon declined to do, saying he did not care to name any price just then, but that he (Catlin) might submit any bona fide offer above $40 per foot for the whole property; that he subsequently communicated the particulars of this interview to Chewning & Rose, and told them that he had declined what he considered, or what might be considered, an offer of $35 per foot for the whole property, and that they said he had done right. And Col. Gordon testifies that this offer by Catlin was not referred to Chewning & Rose for determination as to whether it should be accepted or not, as intimated in the deposition of Mr. Gray; that he had positively declined the offer before saying anything to them, and only mentioned the offer to them that they might know that the property was being inquired for.

In addition to the depositions of Mr. Catlin and of Col. Gordon himself, on behalf of the latter, the depositions of Robert Lecky, Jr., and G. B. Picot, clerks in Col. Gordon's office, were also taken. Mr. Lecky testifies that he had heard Mr. Gray (who testified on behalf of the plaintiff) tell Col. Gordon that he had frequently heard Chewning & Rose advise him not to sell the corner lot first, and not to sell the property except as a whole. Mr. Picot testifies that he heard Mr. Gray tell Col. Gordon that he had frequently heard him tell Chewning & Rose that he would not sell this property except as a whole, or unless they sold the lots furthest from the corner first. Now, Mr. Gray was a witness introduced on behalf of the plaintiff, and on his cross-examination, the proper foundation having been laid, he was asked if he had not made the statements testified to by Lecky and Picot, and he denied having made them. It is obvious, taking the testimony of Gray, as it should be taken, in connection with that of Lecky and Picot, who distinctly, clearly, and directly state what Gray said in their presence and hearing, that the weight of evidence is very greatly in favor of the appellee as to the manner in which Col. Gordon required this property to be disposed of. In other words, the evidence clearly establishes that the property was to be sold as a whole, or the lots furthest from the corner to be sold first.

Moreover the plaintiff (appellant here) invoked the aid of established custom, and to that end took the depositions of several real-estate agents, but from them he derived no comfort. On the contrary, they, with possibly one exception, testify directly and positively that, under similar circumstances, they would by no means have felt authorized to close a sale without conferring with the owner or principal. And, further, in order to uphold his claim that Chewning & Rose were the general agents of Col. Gordon, were by him clothed with ample authority, and held out to the public as such, the appellant places much reliance on the fact that the proposed auction sale was advertised in one or more of the newspapers of the city of Richmond, and that the bill for advertising was presented by Chewning & Rose to Col. Gordon, and was paid by him. Certainly he paid the bill, for at their instance he had authorized Chewning & Rose to try the property at public auction, and, although no sale was thereby effected, he was responsible for the expense thus incurred, especially as there was no special contract to the contrary.

But the question presents itself, if Chewning & Rose were the general agents of Col. Gordon, and, as such, were clothed with full power and authority to make the sale and bind him thereby, without submitting their action to him, then why did they not arrange for the proposed auction sale without consulting him? Why was it necessary to submit their proposition for a sale at auction to him, to urge his acceptance of same, and to arrange beforehand, under his personal superintendence and direction, the terms and minimum price at which he would permit the prop-

erty to be sold at such auction? The day set for the proposed auction was more than seven months prior to the contract of sale here in question. How, then, can it be claimed, with the least degree of consistency, that an authority that was insufficient to authorize Chewning & Rose to arrange for and sell the property at auction, was yet ample, seven months later, to authorize a private sale in a manner and at a price wholly different from what was arranged for the contemplated auction, and that was not only never authorized by Col. Gordon, but was forbidden by him? Col. Gordon's name was not even mentioned in the advertisement; and, as before stated, it had reference only to the proposed auction sale, and had, and could have, no reference or application to anything else whatever.

The appellant also relies upon the fact that Chewning & Rose erected on the property in question their "board," on which was printed, in large letters, something like this, "For Sale," or "This Property for Sale. Apply to Chewning & Rose, Agents," etc; but not mentioning the name of Gordon, the owner. If acts such as these—the mere devices of real-estate agents, intended to attract notice and entice bidders—constitute holding out one to third persons, or to the public at large, by the principal, as having a general authority to bind him in a case like the present, then, indeed, is the condition of the property holder a most deplorable one, for he is, at the mere will and pleasure of any one of the army of land agents, liable at any time to have his estate administered upon, and to be sold out of house and home. If real-estate agents may, by their own interested acts, thus hold themselves out to third persons, and to the public, then, if a man employ such an agent to sell at auction a particular piece of property, or even a lot of old rubbish, the agency may, though never so special and limited, be continued and enlarged by acts of the agent alone, such as are relied on in the present case, who can, at pleasure, dispose of any man's estate on terms and at a price to suit himself. The law is as above laid down, and it tolerates no such monstrous doctrine. The true principle is, as already stated, that if a person is held out to third persons, or to the public at large, by the principal, as having a general authority to act for and to bind him in a particular business or employment, it would be grossly unjust, and tend to sanction the most unmitigated frauds, to allow such principal to set up his own secret instructions to the agent, limiting that authority, and thus to defeat his acts and transactions under the agency, when the party dealing with him had, and could have, no notice of such instructions. But while sound public policy thus encourages freedom and confidence in the dealings with agents, yet the law jealously guards against unauthorized acts, and promptly rejects, as odious, the idea that an agent may at his will act either without or in excess of the authority conferred on him, and bind his principal thereby. Hence the rule is directly the reverse of that just laid down, when, as in the present case, a special or particular agent is employed in one single transaction; for, in such case, it is the duty of the party dealing with the agent to ascertain the extent of his authority; and if he does not, he must abide the consequences. Such is the condition of the appellant in this case. He blindly confided in and contracted with agents who acted without authority from their principal. Then, looking at the case in the light of all the evidence, it is clear that Chewning & Rose were but special agents, with limited authority as to one particular piece of property; that they not only failed to communicate with Col. Gordon by telegram, when they could readily have done so, as others did, but neglected and refused to obey his positive instructions to them, and of their own will, without authority from him, undertook to sell a portion of the property, including the corner lot. How, then, was it possible for the learned chancellor below to arrive at any other conclusion than that announced in his decree? It only remains to add that the theory advanced by the appellant must necessarily fall to the ground for want of that evidence essential to show that Chewning & Rose had authority to make the contract sought to be enforced in this suit. The contract attempted to be set up was made by the appellant with Chewning & Rose, and was signed by the latter as agents for the appellee, by whom it was not authorized, and it is therefore without validity, and is incapable of enforcement. The specific execution of a contract for the sale of real estate rests in the sound legal discretion of the court. The plaintiff must establish the contract, and prove it as stated in the bill, and the contract must be certain, fair, and just in all its parts. Haskin v. Insurance Co., 78 Va. 707. In the present case all these essentials are wanting, and therefore the appellant has no case. The legal proposition asserted by the counsel for the appellant, that the owner of lands may, by parol, authorize another to make a contract for the sale thereof, as was held in Yerby v. Grigsby, 9 Leigh, 387, seems to be established law; but it is of no force in the present case, as here there was no authority, either by parol or otherwise, to make the contract. For the reasons stated, we are clearly of opinion that the decree appealed from is without error, and that the same must be affirmed.

BROWN OIL CO. v. CALDWELL et al.

(Supreme Court of Appeals of West Virginia. March 14, 1891.)

RIPARIAN RIGHTS—BOUNDARIES ON RIVERS.

1. Rights of riparian owners of land on the Ohio river extend to low-water mark.

2. A conveyance of land calls "thence N., 8 degrees W., 26 9-10 poles to a stake at Ohio river marked 'I;' thence down said river S., 62 degrees W., 81 6-10 poles, to a stake on point at mouth of French creek." The line along the river is low-water mark.

3. This is not changed by the facts that before the conveyance actual survey was made fixing the point at I just over the river bank, and running thence a straight line to point at the mouth of French creek, leaving a space between it and low-water mark, and that a diagram representing such surveying and straight line was made, and the further fact that the deed conveying three parcels of land contains the clause: "These said calls are controlled by diagram made by R. A. G., county surveyor."

(Syllabus by the Court.)

Appeal and supersedeas from circuit court, Pleasants county.
J. G. McCluer and Jackson & Yeaton, for appellants. T. I. Stealey and L. N. Tavenner, for appellee.

BRANNON, J. On a bill presented by the Brown Oil Company against R. G. Caldwell and others to the judge of the circuit court of Pleasants county, an injunction was awarded restraining the defendants from constructing derricks, boring any well, or entering or trespassing upon certain premises of the plaintiff described in the bill; and, the judge having overruled a motion to dissolve the injunction, the defendants appealed to this court. On 26th October, 1887, George Hendricks and wife conveyed to Elizabeth Jones three tracts of land. Nos. 1, 2, and 3; and on 27th March, 1890, Elizabeth Jones and her husband leased said land to Joseph S. Brown, for oil development, and he transferred his lease to the Brown Oil Company. On 14th July, 1890, George Hendricks leased to R. G. Caldwell and others, for the purpose of boring for oil, a parcel of land of about one acre, and, these lessees having entered to bore a well for oil, the Brown Oil Company obtained said injunction. Both sides claim under George Hendricks. The Brown Oil Company claims that the deed from Hendricks and wife, conveying lot No. 2, goes to low-water mark on the Ohio river, leaving no opening for the subsequent lease made to Caldwell and others; while Caldwell and his co-lessees claim that the prior deed from Hendricks to Jones is next to the river bounded by a line running practically with its bank, not including its shore and beach, leaving between this line and low-water mark an area of about one acre leased to them. Thus the only question we are to decide is whether the lot No. 2, conveyed by Hendricks and wife to Elizabeth Jones, extends to the low-water mark of the Ohio river; for, if it does, there is no room for the land he subsequently leased to Caldwell and others, he having no title to it to confer on Caldwell and others. The deed from Hendricks to Jones describes lot No. 2 as follows: "Tract No. 2. Beginning at a stake on upper bank of said French creek in edge of railroad right of way, marked 'G' on diagram; thence with said right of way N., 74 degrees E., 31 poles, to a stake at H; thence N., 8 degrees W., 26 9-10 poles, to a stake at Ohio river marked 'I;' thence down said river S., 62 degrees W., 81 6-10 poles, to a stake on point at mouth of said French creek; thence S., 28 degrees E., 1 pole, to a stake; thence up the creek, with its meanders, N., 80 degrees E., 20 poles; N., 65 degrees E., 21 7-10 poles; N., 88 degrees E., 12 3-10 poles, to the beginning,—containing six and one-half acres by survey."

Hendricks' right extended to low-water

mark of the Ohio river, as riparian owners of lands bounded by that river go to low-water mark, subject to the easement of the public in that portion between high and low water marks. Barre v. Fleming, 29 W. Va. 314, 1 S. E. Rep. 731. I think it plain, under the law, that the boundary of tract 2, as given above, carries that tract to the limit of Hendricks'; that is, low-water mark. We see that after leaving the Ohio River Railroad right of way the call is for N., 8 W., 26.9, to a stake at Ohio river. Where does this line stop? As the grantor's line was the low-water mark, in law is it not reasonable to say that he intended to sell to the outer line when he locates a corner at the river? Does he intend still to retain a narrow strip, which he could not reach except by going over the land which he sold? Of what value would it be to him? Is it reasonable that the purchaser intended to leave this strip, which would cut off all access to the river for the most of the time? Ang. Water-Courses, § 23, says: "The cases, on the whole, may be said to demonstrate the existence of the rule that a grantee bounded on a river (and it is immaterial by what mode of expression) goes *ad medium filum aquæ*, unless there be decided language showing a manifest intent to stop at the water's edge; and there seems a distinct and strong tendency in the cases to turn every doubt upon expressions which fix the boundary next the river in favor of a contact with the water." My examination satisfies me thoroughly that this statement of Angell is a fair and unquestionable presentation of the law. Surely, under this law, a line calling for a stake "at Ohio river" would carry us to the water of the river. In the case of the Ohio it is to low water; in case of streams not navigable, it would be to the middle of the stream. In Rix v. Johnson, 5 N. H. 520, a call for a stake at the river made the river the boundary, and from "stake at the river" the line was said to be "on the river," and it was said to be a strong argument to show that the river was the boundary. Note to section 29, Ang. Water-Courses. Where a line ran to a stake standing on the east bank, etc., thence down the river, it extended to the thread of the river. A line calling easterly on a creek, and down said creek to a butternut tree, was held to place the corner in the center of the stream opposite the butternut. 1 Wait, Act. & Def. 711. The cases are numerous to show that this line from the railroad goes clear to the river. Thus we are at the low-water mark, and we cannot leave it; and then the next call is: "Thence down said river S., 62 degrees W., 81 6-10 poles, to a stake on point at mouth of said French creek." Who can doubt that this expressly keeps us to the low-water mark in tracing the line? A line running on or with or along a stream goes to its middle; and, even where the call is the bank of a river, it is to its middle. Ang. Water-Courses, § 24. And this river line calls for a terminus at a stake "on point at mouth of said French creek." The mouth of French creek is the Ohio; that is, it is actual, physical contact of creek with river; a confluence of

their waters; their intermingling and union. This is the meaning of the expression "at the mouth of said French creek." The call for a stake, all surveyors know, is not a natural or fixed, immovable point, but we must yield distance to the natural call for the river, and be conducted to it by course or some other element to give it location. Here the stake is "on point at mouth of said French creek." Well, that is the point of land made by the junction of the creek and river. If we want to go to high-water mark, we would go out the point only so far as to reach that mark; while, if we want to go to low-water mark, we proceed on out this point until we get to low-water mark. In either case, we would be on the point; and, as Hendricks' right went to low-water mark, and we are not to assume that he intended the unusual thing of retaining a narrow, inaccessible strip, or that the purchaser intended to leave this strip to exclude him from valuable river privileges, what more plausible than to say that this corner also is at low water, and that thus the river line follows the low-water mark? Authorities in support of these views could be cited almost without limit. Hayes v. Bowman, 1 Rand. (Va.) 417; Mead v. Haynes, 3 Rand. (Va.) 33; Camden v. Creel, 4 W. Va 365. Thus, tested by the calls of the deed, it is safe to say that the river line of Hendrick's grant to Jones is the low-water mark.

While I do not deem it necessary to advert to all the points of argument made for the defense, yet it is just to their claim that I should refer to a fact on which they rely,—on which it may be said their defense solely rests. (The deed from Hendricks to Jones, after describing each of the tracts, says: "These said calls are controlled by diagram made by R. A. Gallaher, county surveyor of the county aforesaid;" and it is proven that before the deed was made Hendricks, Mrs. Jones' husband, acting for her, and Gallaher, the surveyor, made an actual survey of this lot 2, running the line from the railroad right of way towards the river, but not to the river; and that he stopped at 26.9 poles, point I, which is some distance over the edge of the river bank, and some distance from the water, and ran the next line from said point I down to the point at mouth of French creek, and that said line is straight, and that he made a plat giving the course and distance according to the running on the ground, and this line left a strip between it and the water of the river. Counsel for appellees concede that but for the reference in the deed to this diagram the deed would go to the water, but contend that the declaration of the deed that its calls shall be controlled by the diagram shows a contrary intent, and that the lines as shown on the plat as they were actually surveyed on the ground, and as they are short and distance can be accurately fixed, must govern. There is some force in this contention, but it is not sufficient to control the case. We have seen that the calls of the deed go to low water, and all presumptions favor the theory that the intent is to go to the water, and it must be clear that it was not the intention. Angell on Water-Courses, § 9, states the law thus: "The only mode by which a right of property in a water-course, above tide-water, can be withheld from a person who receives a grant of the land, is by a reservation directly expressed or clearly implied." And in section 17: "It matters not what may be the intention of the grantor of land described as being bounded by a water-course, or by words as comprehensive or in law equivalent; the grantee will hold to the thread of the river, even if such was not the grantor's intention." "It would require an express exception in the grant, or some clear and unequivocal declaration or certain and immemorial usage, to limit the title of the owner in such cases to the edge of the river." 3 Kent, Comm. 428. In Watson v. Peters, 26 Mich. 508, it was decided that a grant of a city lot bounded on a navigable stream, with the water as a boundary, in the absence of an express reservation, conveys to the grantee to the center of the stream; and the fact that the grantor, before conveying, platted the land into lots and blocks, with distinct lines and distances marking the boundaries of each lot, and with the water boundary of the river lots indicated by a line representing the shore-line, and conveyed by such plat, will not limit the grant to such shore-line, or operate to reserve to him proprietary rights in front of the lots conveyed. Judge Cooley said in the opinion: "The owner of city lots bounded on navigable streams, like the owner of any other land thus bounded, may limit his conveyance within specific limits, if he choose; but, where he conveys with the water as a boundary, it will never be presumed that he reserves to himself proprietary rights in front of the land conveyed, which he may grant to others for private occupation, or so occupy himself as to cut off his grantee from the privileges and conveniences which appertain to the shore of navigable water. Such privileges and conveniences constitute a part, and in many cases the principal part, of the value of the grant. * * * The rule is too valuable and important to be varied by so immaterial a circumstance as that the boundary on the water is described by a line, instead of by making use of words which to the common understanding would convey the same meaning; and what we have said of navigable waters is equally applicable to all water-courses. If on the face of the plat, by reference to which the defendant bought, there was anything which distinctly indicated an intent on the part of the proprietors to make this case exceptional, and to reserve to themselves any rights in front of the water lots marked on it, after they should have been sold, the case would have been different." Ang. Water-Courses, § 23, note 2. "There seems to be no conflict whatever in the authorities that, where a certain distance is called for from a given point on a navigable stream to another point on the stream, to be ascertained by such measurement, the measurement must be made by the meanders, not in a straight line." Tyler, Bound. 224. (Where an exception or reservation which would cut off the grantee from the

water is claimed to exist in a deed, the Maine court, in Winslow v. Patten, 34 Me. 25, has said that the doctrine pertinent to the matter is that words of doubtful import are to be construed most favorably to the grantee. See Tyler, Bound. 225. If the intention was in the case of this deed from Hendricks to Jones to reserve the land claimed by the defendants, how easy it would have been to except it plainly. It is difficult to say just what was meant by the language of the deed that the calls were to be controlled by the diagram. Was it intended to keep it from going to low-water mark, which everybody knew to be Hendricks' line? Why, then, did the deed call for a stake at the river, and run thence "down said river," which certainly would follow the river at low-water mark? Shall we allow this doubtful language to overthrow calls in the deed which in law would carry us to low-water mark, and exclude this one acre, and cut off Mrs. Jones' land from the advantages of the stream? I think not. What does this language mean with reference to lots 1 and 2? I observe that in describing lot 1 the call is from railroad land N., 8 degrees W., 28.4, to river at A; then down the river 6 poles, to I. I take it that the river line of lot 1 goes to low-water mark. It stops at this same letter "I," known, in lot 2. How long would the diagram last? It lost, where could this description be found? Shall we reject the certain calls of the deed for those of the plat, under this clause, uncertain and perishable? It is not presumed that a party granting land intends to retain a mere narrow strip between the land sold and his line, and this is much more so when it would cut off the grantee from valuable water privileges. Western M. & M. Co. v. Peytona C. C. Co., 8 W. Va. 406. There is evidence tending to show, perhaps a decided preponderance, that when the survey was made the husband of Mrs. Jones directed the surveyor not to include this piece claimed by defendants, saying he did not desire to pay for land which he could not cultivate, and that he directed where the line down the river should be run, and that the vendor acceded to it, saying he could utilize this small piece in tying up boats and rafts. Hendricks says he did not intend to sell it. Mrs. Jones and her husband say they did intend to include it in their rights, but that the agreement was that it was worth nothing for cultivation, and, the consideration of the purchase being $100 per acre, she did not wish to pay for it, and the survey was made, not to limit the land from the river, but to ascertain just how much land fit for cultivation there was, so as to count its cost. This version derives considerable support from the fact that the calls in the deed are for the river, while the lines actually run do not go to it. But there stands the deed, the repository of the agreement of the parties, conferring certain legal rights, not to be overthrown by the doubtful meaning arising from the clause of the deed that the calls were to be controlled by the plat, and I do not think we can allow any verbal agreement such as that referred to to control the effect of the deed. Order of circuit court overruling motion to dissolve is affirmed, and the injunction is perpetuated.

LUCAS, P., and ENGLISH and HOLT, JJ., concur.

SPRAGINS *et al.* v. WEST VIRGINIA, C. & P. RY. CO.

(Supreme Court of Appeals of West Virginia. March 19, 1891.)

ISSUANCE OF PROCESS.

Process to commence a civil action returnable to the first Monday in a month as a rule-day may be dated, issued, and executed on the return-day.

(Syllabus by the Court.)

Error to circuit court, Tucker county.

A. B. Parsons, for plaintiffs in error.
C. W. Dailey, for defendant in error.

LUCAS, P. This was an action at law, in which, on motion of the defendant, the circuit court quashed the summons. The following bill of exceptions was reserved: "Be it remembered that upon the calling of this case at the former term of this court, the defendant, by its attorney, appeared only for the purpose of moving to quash the summons in this cause, and moved to quash the same in these words, to-wit: 'Summons. The state of West Virginia, to the sheriff of Tucker county, greeting: You are hereby commanded to summon The West Virginia Central and Pittsburg Railroad Company to appear at the clerk's office of the circuit court of Tucker county, at rules to be held for the said court on the first Monday of August, 1889, to answer Samuel D. Buck and Stith B. Spragins, partners in trade under the firm name and style of Spragins, Buck & Co., of a plea of trespass on the case in *assumpsit;* damages, $1,000.00; and have then there this writ. Witness: JOHN J. ADAMS, clerk of our said court, at the court-house of Tucker county, the 5th day of August, 1889, and in the 27th year of the state.' '(Sheriff's return.) Executed the within summons on the W. Va. C. & P. R. R. Co. by delivering F. K. Ford, a depot agent of said company in the actual employment of said company, in the county of Tucker, at the town of Parsons, a station of said company, on the 5th day of August, 1889, the president nor any of the directors, officials of said company, or visitors being found, a copy hereof.' On the ground that it was issued on the 5th day of August, 1889, and returnable the same day, the first Monday of August, 1889, which was the 5th day of said month to which motion the plaintiffs, by their attorney, objected of which motion the court took time to consider, and at this term of the court, upon argument, it appearing to the court that the summons was returnable on the day of its date and issue, and to the same rules, the court sustained the motion of the defendant, and quashed the summons and dismissed the case; to which action and ruling of the court the plaintiffs excepted and tendered this, their bill of exceptions, and prayed that the same be signed, and enrolled, which is accordingly done. JOSEPH T. HOKE. [Seal.]" It will be perceived that

the only question to be decided in this case is whether the original process or summons to commence an action can be issued on the first rule-day of the month, and served, or executed and returned, upon the same day. The provisions in regard to rule-days and the proceedings at rules are to be found in chapter 125 of the Code, and it is provided that rules shall be held on the first Monday in every month, and continued for three days, except where such holding or continuance would interfere with a term of court. It is further provided that "the rules may be to declare, plead, reply, rejoin, or for other proceedings. They shall be given from month to month." Chapter 124, after providing for the forms of writs, provides in the second section that "process from any court, whether original, mesne, or final, may be directed to the sheriff of any county. * * * Any process may be executed on or before the return-day thereof." "Any process shall be returnable within 90 days after its date to the court on the first day of its term, or in the clerk's office to the first Monday in a month or some rule-day, except as follows: A summons for a witness shall be returnable on whatever day his attendance is desired, and an order of attachment may be returnable to the next term of the court, although more than 90 days from the date of the order, and process awarded in court may be returnable as the court shall direct." Section 5 of the same chapter provides: "The process to commence a suit shall be a writ commanding the officer to whom it is directed to summon a defendant to answer the bill or action. It shall be issued on the order of the plaintiff, or his attorney or agent, and shall not, after it is issued, be altered, nor any blank therein filled up, except by the clerk." These are the principal provisions of the Code which bear upon this subject. It will be seen that those sentences quoted from the second section of chapter 124 apply to all process in a civil action, whether original, mesne, or final, —that is to say, those provisions apply equally to the summons which is the original process to commence a suit; or to an attachment, which is frequently a mesne process; or to an execution, which is generally the final process after judgment has been obtained. It is contended for the plaintiff in error that the provision which says that "any process shall be returnable within 90 days after its date," taken in connection with section 12 of chapter 13 of the Code, which is as follows: "The time within which an act is to be done shall be computed by excluding the first day and including the last,"—does necessarily exclude the day of the issuance of the writ from those days upon which it may be executed. It will be perceived, however, that if this reasoning be correct as to the summons or original process it must necessarily be so also as to the mesne and final process, so that an attachment issued on one day could not be served immediately, but only after the intervention of a day, and an execution could not be levied on the day when issued, but would have to be levied on the following day at the earliest. Such could not possibly have been the intention of the legislature, and the reasoning upon which such a conclusion is based must necessarily be fallacious. The error in this reasoning is in overlooking that provision which declares that any process may be executed on the return-day thereof; so that a writ returnable to Monday as the first rule-day may be served upon that day, no matter when issued. Neither can the defendant suffer the slightest inconvenience from this construction, since the object of the summons is to give him notice of the suit; and it is material to him when the notice is served, but utterly immaterial and unimportant when it may have issued; that is to say, if the writ can be served on Monday, it is utterly immaterial whether it bear date on that day or on the preceding Saturday, since the defendant knows nothing of it until served. When it is provided that an act may be done within a given period after a certain date, the general construction is that it may be done the moment that date arrives. For example, if it be said that an infant may elect to set aside a decree by petition within 6 months, or 180 days, after he attains his majority, it follows he may move against the decree upon the very day that his majority is attained. Or if it be provided that the widow shall have one year after probate of the will of her husband within which to renounce the will, such election and renunciation may be made the very moment the will is probated. It follows, therefore, that under the provisions of the Code any process in a civil action, whether original, mesne, or final, may be executed upon the day of its date, and immediately after it is issued. Upon inquiry I find that the practice in the various circuits of the state has differed somewhat on this question, but no doubt in a majority of the circuits the practice which we now affirm and approve has prevailed. It is more important that it should be settled, owing to these differences of opinion which have existed in the various circuits. For these reasons we think there was error on the part of the circuit court in quashing the return, and its judgment must be reversed, the motion overruled, and the case remanded.

ENGLISH, BRANNON, and HOLT, JJ., concur.

RINGOLD et al. v. SUITER et al.

(Supreme Court of Appeals of West Virginia. March 24, 1891.)

GARNISHMENT — FINDING — PARTNERSHIP OF MARRIED WOMAN — LIEN OF ATTACHMENT — LIABILITY OF FRAUDULENT GRANTEE.

1. The remedy by garnishment is a creature of the statute, and limited by it.

2. A finding by a jury as to indebtedness of a garnishee to the attachment debtor and effects in his hands, rendered upon a suggestion of the insufficiency of the garnishee's answer, must be sufficiently definite and certain to warrant judgment against the garnishee. The finding here is too vague.

3. Evidence certified cannot be read to find facts essential to judgment, which should have been, but were not, found by verdict.

4. A partnership between a married woman, living with her husband, and another person is

void. She cannot be sued at law on a contract of such partnership; but the other member of the firm may be rendered liable therefor, and judgment given against him alone.

5. An attachment served on a garnishee indebted to or having effects of the debtor binds debts existing or effects in the garnishee's hands at the date of service of the attachment, as also debts arising or effects coming to the hands of the garnishee until the answer of such garnishee, but not later than such answer.

6. There may be a money recovery against a fraudulent grantee of property who has sold such property to a bona fide purchaser and realized money therefrom in favor of the defrauded creditor.

(Syllabus by the Court.)

Error to circuit court, Cabell county.

Campbell & Holt, for plaintiffs in error. Simms & Enslow, for defendants in error.

BRANNON, J. In an action at law by F. R. Ringold & Co. against J. K. Suiter in the circuit court of Cabell county an attachment issued and was served on Miller & Ingalls, as garnishees, on 13th November, 1889, and on 9th December, 1889, said garnishees answered that they were not indebted to Suiter, but that on 4th of November, 1889, said firm had bought certain goods and accounts of Suiter for $5,000, for which they were to pay by giving negotiable notes, and that they had given such notes. The plaintiffs suggested that the garnishees had not fully answered, and the court made an order directing that the question of the indebtedness of said garnishees be submitted to a jury, as provided by statute, to ascertain and determine what effects, if any, said garnishees had in their hands at the date of the service of the attachment, and that the jury should determine, try, and return their verdict on the following issues: "(1) Did the garnishees, Mrs. Gertrude Ingalls and W. C. Miller, doing business as partners, owe anything to or have any effects of the said J. K. Suiter in their possession at the date of the service of the attachment herein on them? (2) Was the sale of the goods of J. K. Suiter to Ingalls and Miller upon good conditions, and valid? (3) Did the said Ingalls and Miller, or either of them, at the time they purchased the stock of goods of J. K. Suiter, have any knowledge the defendant J. K. Suiter was in debt, and that the stock of goods was not paid for? (4) Was there any intent on the part of Ingalls and Miller or W. C. Miller to hinder, delay, or defraud the creditors of J. K. Suiter at the time the sale was made? (5) Did Ingalls & Miller, or either of them, have knowledge that Suiter was selling his stock of goods to them to prevent his creditors levying on it for their debts?" On March 28, 1890, the plaintiffs propounded to the jury a sixth or additional interrogatory, as follows: "Was W. C. Miller at any time indebted to J. K. Suiter between the date of service of attachment in this case, viz., November 13, 1889, and the date of his answer, this March 28, 1890? If so, in what sum?" The jury not agreeing, afterwards another trial was had, and, after the jury had fully heard the evidence and argument of counsel, the plaintiffs, against objection, propounded to the jury the sixth interrogatory given above. The jury returned the following verdict: "Answer to first interrogatory, Yes; answer to second interrogatory, No; answer to third interrogatory, Yes; answer to fourth interrogatory, Yes; answer to fifth interrogatory, Yes; answer to the additional or sixth interrogatory, Yes. $1,585.00." The defense moved the court to set aside the findings, because contrary to law and evidence, and, this motion having been overruled, the defense moved the court to arrest judgment because the findings and answers of the jury were too vague and uncertain to base judgment on; but the court overruled this motion, and rendered judgment against W. C. Miller, requiring him to pay $269.75 and costs to the sheriff holding the attachment. Miller sued out a writ of error.

I have struggled to sustain the judgment in this case, rendered after two trials, but I am unable to do so. A judgment against a garnishee must have something on which to rest, either an answer of the garnishee, sufficient to warrant it, or a verdict of a jury of legal certainty, finding facts to warrant judgment. Garnishment is purely a creature of statute, and we can only follow the procedure pointed out by the statute, and it is not within the rules of construction governing common-law actions. It cannot be resorted to except where the statute expressly authorizes it; and when the statutory limits have been reached without accomplishing the purposes for which it was invoked, we cannot extend its operations into new fields, or contrive new means of applying it to the exigencies of the particular case. Wade, Attachm. § 333; Drake, Attachm. § 451a. Our statute (section 14, c. 106, Code 1887) provides that when a garnishee under an attachment appears he shall be examined under oath; and that, if it appear from his examination that at or after service of the attachment he was indebted to the defendant, or had in his possession or control effects of the defendant, the court may order him to pay the money due from him, and deliver the effects in his hands. Section 16 provides that, if the plaintiff suggest that the garnishee has not made a full disclosure, the court shall impanel a jury to inquire as to such debts or effects, and as to any liability on the garnishee established by the verdict the court shall proceed as if it had been confessed by the garnishee. Where a garnishee does not appear the court may hear evidence under section 15 to establish his liability; but where, as in this case, the garnishee answers, and the answer does not warrant judgment, the only resource given by the statute is an inquiry by a jury, and its verdict, either alone or in connection with the answer, constitutes the only basis for judgment against the garnishee. Now, omitting the sixth interrogatory, the remaining interrogatories and their answers will not warrant a judgment for money, for they give no amount. Now, bring to the aid of those five interrogatories the answer of the garnishees. Then we have the facts that the garnishees purchased of Suiter, the debtor, a stock of goods at $5,000, and had them

in possession, and that this sale was fraudulent as to creditors. Did this justify a judgment for money? If there be a fraudulent conveyance of property for a fixed consideration it is certain that the property itself can be subjected, because the conveyance is void as to the creditor. The creditor treats it as void, and against him the purchaser acquires no title. But can the creditor waive relief as against the property, and take a judgment against the purchaser for the purchase money which he agreed to pay? It would seem at first view that there would be strong reason to say that he could do so; but when we reflect that there is not the slightest privity between the creditor and the fraudulent purchaser, and that the only theory on which the creditor has right in the matter is that property liable in his debtor's hands to his debt has been diverted from its payment by a sale to all intents void under the law as to him, just as if it had never been made, it is difficult to see how he can claim the purchase money under the sale, thus ratifying it. It is true, the supreme court of Ohio, in Bradford v. Beyer, 17 Ohio St. 388, has held that in such case the creditor might go against the goods, or compel the fraudulent vendee to account for the purchase price of the goods. No authority is cited for the proposition. I find no other cases to support it. If this were so, we could justify the money judgment in this case; but we do not think the position tenable. If the fraudulent purchaser has sold the property to an innocent purchaser, so that it cannot be reached, the injured creditor may have a money recovery to the value of the property against the purchaser, because the purchaser has thus realized from the sale of property wrongfully diverted from the payment of the seller's debts, and he cannot complain if he be made responsible. This court, in Hinton v. Ellis, 27 W. Va. 422, held a fraudulent grantee liable by decree for money for the amount realized by him from a sale to an innocent purchaser of the land which he acquired in fraud of a creditor. The soundness of the principle on which that case rests is apparent. A fraudulent grantee ought not to be protected in the possession of the proceeds of the property received by him on a sale of it. The property in his hands is in trust for the creditor, and when he converts it into money, the fund is impressed with the same trust; and equity would be balked, and the statute defeated, if it could not be followed; otherwise the fraudulent grantee has but to sell the property to an innocent purchaser, so that the creditor cannot follow the property, and pocket the money himself, and the fraud is triumphant. The case of Hinton v. Ellis is well sustained by authority. Williamson v. Goodwyn, 9 Grat. 503; Ferguson v. Hillman, 55 Wis. 190, 12 N. W. Rep. 389; Murtha v. Curley, 90 N. Y. 372; Heath v. Page, 63 Pa. St. 108; Hopkirk v. Randolph, 2 Brock. 132; Backhouse v. Jett, 1 Brock. 500; Wait, Fraud. Conv. §§ 177, 178; 2 Bigelow, Frauds, 419, and note 5; Bump, Fraud. Conv. 608, note 2. In Fullerton v. Viall, 42 How. Pr. 294, and Feary v. Cummings, 41 Mich. 376, 1 N. W. Rep. 946, it was held that the money recovery against the fraudulent grantee is not limited to what he received, but he is accountable for its value.

In this case the facts certified in the bill of exceptions on the motion to set aside the verdict show that after the purchase of the goods the garnishees, Ingalls and Miller, had sold part of them for $3,834. Clearly, if we could read the bill of exceptions to prove this fact in aid of the verdict, we would sustain the judgment; but we cannot so read it. We could read it on passing on the motion to set aside the verdict as contrary to evidence, but not to supplement a verdict, nor to help an indefinite and vague verdict, for that would be for the court to perform the jury's function by taking the evidence and incorporating in the verdict facts which the jury itself should have found. The evidence was addressed to the jury for its finding, not to the court for its finding. During the trial the court had nothing to do with the evidence, so far as finding any fact from it was concerned. As well might a court certify from the evidence the amount of the damages which in its opinion the evidence proved, and thus aid a verdict finding for the plaintiff in assumpsit, but silent as to the damages; or as well might a court certify that the evidence showed that a plaintiff in ejectment had an estate in fee, and thus help a verdict failing to find that fact. Thus, without the aid of the sixth interrogatory, the judgment cannot be sustained. Let us bring it into consideration. The evidence developed that the firm of Miller & Ingalls, the garnishees, was made up of a married woman, Mrs. Ingalls, living with her husband, and Miller; and, as such a partnership was void as to the woman, and no judgment could be rendered against her, but the man could be rendered liable alone for firm debts and liabilities because there was in law no partnership, (Carey v. Burruss, 20 W. Va. 571,) and the former interrogatories had viewed Ingalls and Miller as the purchasers of the goods, and directed inquiry to them, it was desirable to have an interrogatory directed to the ascertainment of the liability of Miller alone. And, moreover, notes given by Ingalls and Miller for the goods had been transferred to Daniels, and Miller had taken up those notes, and given his individual note in their place to Daniels, and Daniels had had it discounted by a bank, Suiter depositing $1,585 with the bank to pay the note of Miller if Miller should not pay it; and, Miller not having paid it, the bank applied Suiter's money to pay it, and thus Miller became on that score indebted to Suiter, January 19, 1890; and this sixth interrogatory was designed to catch this indebtedness arising, at any rate, from money paid by Suiter to the use of Miller. It will be seen that this sixth interrogatory asks the jury whether Miller was indebted to Suiter at any time between 13th November, 1889, the date of service of the attachment, and the 28th of March, 1890; and that the answer of the garnishees was made on 9th December, 1889, thus allowing the jury to ascertain indebtedness of Miller to Suiter not only at the date of the service of the attach-

ment or the date of the garnishee's answer, but later, until March 28th. What is the period covered by the lien of an attachment as to debts or effects in the hands of a garnishee? Section 9, c. 106, declares that the lien begins with the service of the attachment, and of course binds debts or effects then in the garnishee's hands; but how long does it continue to attach to and bind new debts arising or effects coming to the garnishee? It certainly continues to attach to new or other debts or effects after that period, for section 14 says that if it appear on examination of the garnishee "that at or after the service of the attachment he was indebted to the defendant against whom the claim is, or had in his possession or control any goods, chattels, money, securities, or other effects belonging to the said defendant, the court may order him to pay," etc. From this I think the attaching power of the attachment continues up to, but not after, the answer of the garnishee. Just here we must bear in mind the principle above stated, that the garnishment remedy is of statutory origin, and can go so far only as the words of the statute will allow. In Railroad Co. v. Gallahue, 12 Grat. 655, it is said under the Virginia statute, similar to our own as to this point, that "it seems that the statute in relation to attachments at law refers to debts due from the garnishee to the defendant at the time of the service of the process upon the garnishee." The opinion by Judge ALLEN will show how undecided his mind was on the point, and is unsatisfactory as to this.

We think under our statute that the attachment covers debts or effects down to the answer of garnishee. This interrogatory asked the jury to inquire as to indebtedness of the garnishee after the answer. This it could not do, as the attachment did not reach beyond the answer. There is another reason against this interrogatory. It is only when the garnishee has not fully disclosed that a jury acts to inquire into "such debts and effects,"—that is, such as he should have in his answer disclosed; and, as to any debts or effects found by a jury chargeable to the garnishee, section 16 says that the court shall proceed in the same manner as if "they had been confessed by the garnishee." This shows that the verdict only takes the place of the garnishee's answer. The garnishee could not on December 9th answer as to a debt arising against him January 19th, after; and, as the jury inquiry is only to find the true facts as of the date of the answer, as its office is only to find what a true and full answer from the garnishee would have shown, as it simply stands in the shoes of a true answer, it cannot find an indebtedness not existing at the date of the answer. For reasons given above, we cannot call on the evidence certified to aid the verdict in response to question 6 to show that the jury must have found the indebtedness as existing before the answer; and, even if we could read it, we should find from the purchase of the goods and the sale of a large amount of them prior to the answer, ground of a liability prior to the answer; and from the use of Suiter's money in paying Miller's note an indebtedness arising after the answer; so that we could not say the jury found on one ground and not on the other; but in truth, from the fact that the jury found the indebtedness to be $1,585, we would be compelled to say that it based its verdict on the indebtedness accruing after the answer, as that is the exact sum deposited by Suiter to pay Miller's note. True, we might be asked to treat the whole transaction as a fraud from beginning to end, including the new note and deposit for it; but we cannot so read the evidence at all. It might also be questioned whether the oath of the jury would apply to this sixth interrogatory, but, as this question will likely not arise again, we do not decide it. For these reasons we must reverse the order made April 10, 1890, requiring W. C. Miller to pay to the sheriff $269.75, with interest, and costs; and, rendering such judgment as the circuit court ought to have rendered on the motion in arrest of judgment upon the verdict of the jury, it is here considered that judgment upon the verdict of the jury be arrested, the verdict set aside, and a *venire de novo* be awarded, and the case is remanded for further proceedings.

ENGLISH and HOLT, JJ., concur. LUCAS, P., absent.

HULL'S ADM'R v. HULL'S HEIRS.

DUDLEY et al. v. SAME.

(Supreme Court of Appeals of West Virginia March 21, 1891.)

JUDICIAL SALE — RIGHTS OF PURCHASER—SALE OF LAND TO PAY DECEDENT'S DEBTS — DECREE—LIMITATIONS—COVENANT OF WARRANTY.

1. A purchaser of land under a void decree, whose money has been applied upon liens on the land valid against the owner of the land, will be entitled to charge such money upon such land by substitution to the right of the creditor, upon disaffirmance of the sale.

2. Such purchaser may maintain a bill to enforce such right, and as incident to his relief make his bill a creditors' bill.

3. A decree which simply confirms a commissioner's report of debts, and directs a sale of lands therefor in default of payment, though that report specifies the debts and priorities, is erroneous, because the decree does not itself adjudicate and declare what debts are to be paid, and fix their order and priority as to the lands to be sold therefor.

4. A record of a suit by an administrator and widow of a decedent, brought in Virginia against his heirs, to sell lands there to pay debts and satisfy the widow's dower, wherein debts are decreed against the decedent's estate and subjecting its assets, is not evidence, in a suit in this state against such heirs to subject lands of such decedent to pay such debts, to establish such debts or their amounts.

5. A decree in such suit will not save such debts from the statute of limitations for the purposes of a suit prosecuted in this state against lands here.

6. Where a bond is given for purchase money for land, and secured by a lien in the deed of conveyance, the mere giving of a new bond or note, in place of the original, does not release the lien, but the lien is good for the new bond or note.

7. The statute of limitation does not apply to a lien for purchase money reserved in a conveyance of land.

8. A deed conveys the "entire interest" of the grantor in land, and contains a covenant of general warranty. This warranty is limited and restricted to the interest conveyed, and does not warrant the land.

9. A covenant of warranty applies to the estate conveyed, and cannot enlarge that estate.

(Syllabus by the Court.)

Appeal from circuit court, Pocahontas county.

R. S. Turk, for appellant. R. S. Parrish, for appellees.

BRANNON, J. This case, if we may call it the same case, is now the second time before this court. The report of the former decision of this court will be found in 26 W. Va. 1, where will be found a full statement of the facts up to the date of the former appeal. A chancery suit had been brought in the circuit court of Pocahontas county by Sheffy, administrator under a Virginia appointment of F. H. Hull, deceased, and Elizabeth Hull, his widow, to sell lands of said decedent lying in Pocahontas county to pay debts of his estate, some of them alleged to exist as purchase-money liens on said land, and to satisfy the dower claim of said widow out of the proceeds of sale in lieu of dower in kind, and a decree of sale was rendered, and said lands sold, and their sales confirmed; and then one of the heirs, after becoming of age, filed a petition showing cause against the decrees, and asking their reversal, and the restoration of his share in the lands sold under the decree; and, such relief having been denied him, he appealed to this court, which rendered a decision holding that the plaintiffs in the suit could not maintain such a bill to sell said lands, and that the infant heirs of Hull were not parties before the court, and therefore the decrees and sales were void, and remanding the cause to the circuit court, "with instructions to put all parties *in statu quo*, by requiring all persons who have received any of the purchase money of said lands to refund the same, with interest, and by refunding to the purchasers any money which they may have paid on their purchases, with interest from the time when it was paid, and allowing them compensation for all permanent improvements put upon the land bought, and by requiring them to pay for the rents and profits of said lands from June 9, 1869, and by doing all other things necessary and proper to put all persons *in statu quo*, and, if necessary, to modify or change the above suggestions as to the mode of so doing in any way which, under the actual circumstances of the case, may be found necessary; and the court shall otherwise proceed with this cause according to the principles laid down in this opinion, and further according to principles governing courts of equity." When the cause went back to the circuit court, E. P. Hull, F. H. Hull, and Lillie E. Huff, heirs of F. H. Hull, moved the court to put them in possession of the lands of their father which had been sold under the void decree, but the court refused to do this. We think this should have been promptly done. This court had held that there was really no suit, and that the decree of sale was void; and having directed, as the chief, I may say the sole, object of remanding the cause, that

v.13S.E.no.1—4

the parties should be put *in statu quo*, manifestly a restoration of possession to these heirs of the lands improperly sold from them under the void decree was a step to said heirs—the most important step—in the line of action indicated by this court to put the parties *in statu quo*. The decree was the only right by which the purchasers had obtained, or could ask to retain, possession, and, that having fallen, what right had they to retain possession? If it be said that the money of these purchasers had gone to pay liens against the land, and the purchasers would be entitled to substitution, and ought to be allowed to retain possession in order that they might from the rents and profits reimburse themselves, these answers present themselves: (1) No decree had yet been made declaring them entitled to substitution; (2) the suit having been held to be one not properly brought to sell the lands or convene the liens, it could not, in its then state, be made the vehicle of enforcing the right of substitution, as it had no *locus standi in curia*, save only to restore the parties to the *status quo*, the only function which, by fair construction of the former opinion of this court, this court designed said cause thereafter to perform; and (3) at that time the suit of Dudley and others v. Hull and others, below more particularly referred to, had not been brought. Should said heirs hereafter ask such possession, it should be given them.

The court made a reference, at the same time this motion for a writ of possession was made, (1) to ascertain all lands of Hull; (2) all liens thereon; (3) all debts due from his estate; (4) to settle the accounts of his administrator; (5) to ascertain the persons to whom purchase money from such land sales was paid, and on what account, calculating interest from date of payment; (6) to make an account of rents and profits of each tract sold under the decree from date of confirmation of sale; (7) an account of permanent improvements, showing by whom made. Now, some of these heads of reference were pertinent to the purpose for which the cause was remanded to the circuit court, and necessary to the execution of the mandate of this court; but so far as the reference directed the lands of which Hull died seised to be ascertained, and the liens and all the estate debts thereon and the settlement of the personal estate, with the view of converting the suit into a creditors' bill, the court was making the suit perform an office which it could not be made to perform consistently with the decision of this court; and had the suit gone on alone, and been treated as a creditors' bill, the action of so treating it would have been erroneous. All that it could do was to restore possession, and compel restitution from those who had received money under a void and reversed decree, and repay those who had paid for land under it. But this action of the court, in making a reference so comprehensive, becomes immaterial, by reason of the fact that afterwards Dudley and other persons, who had purchased lands under the said void decree, filed, in the circuit court of

Pocahontas county, a bill against the heirs and administrator of Felix H. Hull, deceased, and others, alleging that Hull died in Highland county, Va., leaving a widow and three children, his heirs, owning various lands, and was largely indebted at his death, and his estate, real and personal, in Virginia had been exhausted in paying his debts, leaving some unpaid; that among those unpaid were several vendors' liens on the lands in Pocahontas, to-wit, one reserved to A. G. Matthews on certain tracts, and assigned to James H. Renick, and one to Mary Ann Matthews on certain land, and one in favor of Joseph McClung on certain lands; and alleging that Hugh Sheffy, administrator of Felix H. Hull, and Elizabeth M. Hull, his widow, had brought a suit in that court against the heirs of Felix H. Hull and others, asking to have said lands sold, and dower of said widow provided for out of their proceeds, and to have the balance of such proceeds applied to discharge such liens on said lands; and that a decree of sale had been made in said suit, and that said plaintiffs and certain defendants had purchased certain tracts, respectively, at certain prices, under such decree; and that the purchase money under such sales had been collected and applied under decree in the cause to the debts of Hull, to his widow, to attorneys and court officers for services in the cause; and that then Felix H. Hull filed a petition to set aside the decrees in the cause; that the circuit court had refused to set aside such sales; that the case was appealed to the supreme court of appeals, which had held all the proceedings in the cause void, and reversed the said decree, and remanded the cause to the circuit court for the purpose of placing the parties *in statu quo;* and alleging, further, that since the payment of their purchase money for lands sold under said void decree many of the creditors had become insolvent; and praying that the accounts of the West Virginia administrator of said Felix H. Hull, deceased, be settled, and his creditors convened, and that those who had purchased lands under such void decree, and whose money had been applied on debts and liens of said decedent, be subrogated to the rights of the creditors whose debts the money of such purchasers had gone to pay. The said two causes, that of Dudley and others v. Hull and others, and that of Hull's Adm'r et al. v. Hull's Heirs and others, (the Sheffy suit,) were heard together, and a reference was made to a commissioner to ascertain all the lands of which Felix H. Hull died seised lying in Pocahontas, and all liens thereon; all debts due from his estate; to settle the administrator's accounts; to ascertain all purchase money paid by the several purchasers of land sold under decree in the case of Hull's Adm'r v. Hull's Heirs; the amounts paid by each, and the date of payment, and to whom paid, and on what account, calculating interest from dates of payment; and to make an account of rents and profits of each tract which had been sold, and an account of all permanent improvements on each tract, showing by whom made. Upon a report the court rendered a decree in the two causes, heard together in June, 1888, by which it confirmed the report, and decreed that, unless the debts by it reported be paid, the lands should be sold; and from this decree Samuel Gibson, administrator of Felix H. Hull, has appealed to this court.

It is urged by appellant that these plaintiffs in the new bill, Dudley and others, cannot maintain a creditors' bill, because they are not creditors of Hull. Technically they are not creditors, but only entitled to substitution under those who are creditors; but, if so entitled, they get the rights of those who are creditors, and those creditors could maintain a creditors' bill, and, if the debts which their money paid were liens, they must or could convene the lienors, and, if not liens, they must convene the creditors generally, for they could only get a *pro rata* share in case of deficiency of assets. Though I do not see that the court decreed the debts against Hull's estate, or directed the money arising from the sale to be paid thereon, yet if, in fact, they were paid thereon, we must treat Dudley and others, plaintiffs in the new bill, as entitled to substitution to the debts which were paid by the moneys which they paid as purchasers under the void decree; for the case of Haymond v. Camden, 22 W. Va. 180, holds that "a purchaser of land sold under a void decree is entitled, upon the disaffirmance of the sale, to be substituted to the rights of the creditor, and charge the land with the amount of the debts paid by him." See Hudgin v. Hudgin, 6 Grat. 320.

The position of appellant's counsel, that in Haymond v. Camden substitution was allowed only because Camden and Andrews asked that the debt might be ascertained, is untenable. The court gave that as a reason why, though the proceeding was void for want of jurisdiction as to them, substitution could be made in that proceeding; holding that they thereby waived objection to jurisdiction, save in those respects they excepted to it and submitted to the jurisdiction. The court, however, held the general proposition in a separate point that a purchaser under a void decree was entitled to be substituted to the debts his money pays. Principles of justice demand this, and courts of equity have raised up this principle, a being of their creation, called "substitution," unknown to common-law forums, to accomplish the ends of justice; and I know of no more signal instance to exemplify the disposition, as well as the power, of equity to adopt means to accomplish right, than this of substitution, accorded purchasers under void proceedings, whose money has gone to satisfy liens good against the debtor.

Another point made against the decree is that the most important parties, the heirs of Hull, whose lands were to be sold, were not before the court, because the affidavit on which rested the order of publication against them as non-residents was made before a notary in Virginia, and the certificate is simply signed by him, and is without notarial seal, and also wants a certificate of a clerk or other officer of a court of record of Virginia under official seal, verifying the genuineness of the signature of the notary, and his authority to administer oaths, as required by Code, c. 130, § 31. This objection is well taken. A party must be served with process, and thus brought before the court, unless he be one against whom publication may be made, and the fact justifying such order must be made to appear as the law points out. The law requires an affidavit to establish that fact as a prerequisite or foundation for the order, and that affidavit, if made out of the state, must be certified as required by statute, to be admissible to show the fact of non-residence. Though the decree states that the non-residents had been "regularly proceeded against by order of publication, as the law provides," yet the affidavit and order, being a part of the record, show this defect. Though this be error, yet I do not think it avails the appellant, the administrator. Still it should be corrected in after-proceedings, as it might affect titles acquired under a decree hereafter. The decree does not declare on its face what particular debts shall be paid or fix their order, but simply decrees that, "unless the defendants, the administrator and heirs of the late F. H. Hull, deceased, or some one for them, shall within sixty days from the rising of this court pay to the special receiver in these causes the several debts reported by Commissioner Warwick against the estate of F. H. Hull, deceased, the lands should be sold." Such a decree is erroneous under the case of Bank v. Wilson, 25 W. Va. 242. As Judge Woods very properly said in the opinion in that case, "Upon its face it [the decree] neither ascertains the amount or priority of any debt, or the person to whom the same is to be paid;" and as he said in that case I say in this, that while the decree does refer to the report for the debts to be paid, that leaves every creditor to determine for himself, at his peril, the amount decreed him. I add that this report is complicated. A given debt is a specific lien on certain lands, and a general charge on others; another debt is a specific lien on certain lands and a general charge on others; and other debts general charges. The special commissioner and parties are to construe this report for themselves, at their peril, and fix the amounts of liens, their order, and what lands they bind; whereas, the decree should make these matters legally certain.

What debts were to be paid under this decree? The decree should have plainly declared what original debts of Hull yet remained unpaid, and what particular purchasers were entitled to substitution, and in what sums, and out of what lands, after charging them with rents and profits, less permanent improvements and taxes paid. The heirs would know then how much was chargeable upon their estate, and in whose favor, if they desired to discharge it, and, in case a sale should be made, every original creditor would know how much was coming to him, and every purchaser would know how much he was entitled to for reimbursement or substitution, and thus they could bid at the sale with their eyes full upon their adjudicated rights.

As to the debts reported against Hull's estate: It is scarcely necessary to say that the parties, claiming substitution on account of moneys paid by them under their purchases of land having been applied on debts of Hull's estate, must show debts valid and binding said estate. The appellant's counsel contends that there was no evidence to establish the debts reported as debts binding Hull's estate. And here it is certain that the pleadings, depositions, or decrees in the case of Sheffy, Adm'r, v. Hull's Heirs, in Pocahontas circuit court, cannot be read as evidence against the heirs or Administrator of Hull to establish debts, for reasons already stated. It is also clear that the record of the case of Sheffy, Adm'r, etc., v. Hull's Heirs, brought in Highland county, Va., cannot be read to establish such debts. It was the same character of suit as that brought in Pocahontas by Sheffy, administrator, and Mrs. Hull, against Hull's heirs, which this court held to be a void proceeding; but, in addition, that the Highland county suit was brought in another state to sell land and operate on personal assets there, and could by no means affect lands here; and the West Virginia administrator was not a party to it; and, if the infant heirs were parties, it could not establish debts not personally decreed against them so as to bind lands here. The decree was only that, unless the estate debts be paid, the lands be sold.

The debt in favor of James H. Renick is sustained by the agreement of sale between Andrew Matthews and Felix H. Hull, dated 13th October, 1863, in connection with Uriah Hevener's deposition.

As to the bond of $757.87 in favor of Ann M. Matthews: The evidence is not clear to show that it is a remnant of purchase money for land sold by Sampson Matthews to Hull and Warwick. The bond is of different date from the sale and deed, but is claimed to be a balance on settlement. As the deed from Mary Ann and Ann M. Matthews to Hull and Warwick, which must have been accepted by the grantees and put on record, recognizes money as yet unpaid on the land, and the bond is signed by Hull and Warwick, the same parties alleged to have purchased the land, and as John W. Warwick's deposition virtually recognizes it as a purchase-money bond, I think we should say that it is established. Though given after said deed, being for purchase money, it is entitled to the lien retained in the deed, as a release of the lien would not be presumed from the mere execution of a new bond. Hess v. Dille, 23 W. Va. 90; Coles v. Withers, 33 Grat. 186; 2 Jones, Mortg. § 927; Hopkins v. Detwiler, 25 W Va. 749.

As to debts of estate of Joseph McClung: I think the deed from McClung and wife to Hull, dated 26th September, 1855, found on record, and Hull's bond of $2,500, of same date, to McClung, justify the report in considering that debt established; but there is no evidence to sustain the item of $932.55, reported in favor of McClung's estate, except the Highland county record,

which is incompetent, and it is barred by the statute of limitations. I think the claim of Hull's administrator for abatement from McClung's debt for loss of the 500 acres was properly overruled. The deed of McClung and wife conveyed "their entire interest in the lands formerly owned by Jacob W. Matthews" in certain specified lands, "together with all their interest in the lands formerly belonging to said Matthews lying on Clover creek." Where a deed conveys the grantor's right, title, and interest, though it contains in general terms a covenant of general warranty, the covenant is regarded as a restricted one, limited to the estate conveyed, and not one defending generally the land described. The covenant of warranty is intended to defend only what is conveyed, and cannot enlarge the estate conveyed. Wait, Act. & Def. 391; 3 Washb. Real Prop. 665; Rawle, Cov. 420; Sweet v. Brown, 12 Metc. (Mass.) 175; Allen v. Holton, 20 Pick. 458; Ballard v. Child, 46 Me. 152; McNear v. McComber, 18 Iowa, 12; Kimball v. Semple, 25 Cal. 452; Blanchard v. Brooks, 12 Pick. 47; White v. Brocaw, 14 Ohio St. 339; Adams v. Ross, 30 N. J. Law, 510; Lamb v. Wakefield, 1 Sawy. 251; Hope v. Stone, 10 Minn. 141, (Gil. 114.) Here the grantors conveyed only their interest. The land was in dispute, and Porter seems to have had superior title to it; and, besides, the evidence tends to show that the deed does not cover the 500 acres claimed as lost land.

The debts of Renick, Matthews, and McClung, above mentioned, are purchase-money liens, and are not barred by the statute of limitations. Heiskell v. Powell, 23 W. Va. 718; Wayt v. Carwithen, 21 W. Va. 522. A lien for purchase money reserved in a deed is treated as a mortgage or deed of trust, and the statute of limitations does not apply. Coles v. Withers, 33 Grat. 186, 194; Smith v. Railroad Co., Id. 620; Lewis v. Hawkins, 23 Wall. 119. It is clear that the statute does not run against mortgages and deeds of trust. Criss v. Criss, 28 W. Va. 396; Camden v. Alkire, 24 W. Va. 675; Pitzer v. Burns, 7 W. Va. 63; Bowie v. School, 75 Va. 300.

The debt reported at $5,335.05, in favor of Benjamin F. Jackson, is not only not proven, except by evidence in the Highland cause, but is for an open account, the last item being in October, 1861, and is barred, and was improperly allowed. So, also, the Samuel V. Gatewood debt of $1,226.68 is not proven, except by the Highland record, and is barred by limitation. The suit in Highland county could not operate to protect debts against the statute of limitation as to assets in West Virginia. There was no personal decree against the heirs; simply a decree ascertaining certain debts as existing against Hull's estate for the purposes of that cause,—that is, against the Virginia lands of the estate,—and was only a decree adjudicating such debts as existing by confirming a report finding them. And besides, it was a suit brought by the Virginia administrator and the widow to sell lands for debts, which they could not do, as there there was no such statute as in this state allowing an administrator to main-

tain such a suit, and the widow could not
do so; and as decided in Hull v. Hull, 26
W. Va. 1, such a suit was inefficacious to
accomplish the purpose of keeping alive
these debts. The suit in Pocahontas by
said Sheffy, administrator, and the widow
of Hull, being void, could not keep alive
those debts; nor would the bringing of
the suit of Dudley and others, within one
year after the reversal by this court in the
case of Hull v. Hull, operate to save the
debts from limitation, under section 19,
c. 104, Code, as it was a void proceeding.
It does not, in fact, appear that the Dudley suit was brought within one year after
the 25th April, 1885, the date of such reversal, as the summons in it is not in the
record. I think the land owned by Hull
jointly with others should have been
divided before sale. I do not think that
the parties claiming substitution had
right to set off one-third of rents and profits as for land to which the widow of Hull
was entitled, and be charged with only
two-thirds of rents and profits. A widow
has no estate by reason of her dower
right till it is actually assigned. Tom-
linson v. Nickell, 24 W. Va. 160, 27 W.
Va. 709. I find no decree assigning her
dower, or declaring the money value of it,
or directing its payment. It was probably in the power of the court to appoint
a special receiver to receive and disburse
the moneys under the sale, but I do not
see why special commissioners could not
do so, after giving bond. The decree complained of is reversed, and the cause remanded, to be further proceeded in according to the principles herein indicated,
and further according to principles governing courts of equity.

LUCAS, P., and ENGLISH, J., concur.
HOLT, J., absent.

FEAMSTER et al. v. FEAMSTER.

(Supreme Court of Appeals of West Virginia.
March 7, 1891.)

JUDGMENT—ASSIGNMENT—LIEN—TRUSTS.

1. Where a judgment is assigned to a party for
the benefit of infant children, and the same judgment was assigned to another party for the benefit of said children, and in a chancery suit pending both of said assignees file petitions respectively, claiming to be entitled to the control of
said judgment, the successful party in said contest must be regarded as having accepted said
assignment, and subsequently as holding said
judgment as trustee for said infant children.

2. Said judgment being a lien upon the lands
of a party, and prior judgment liens existing
against the same land, which is the only estate of
the judgment debtor, said land, under the circumstances, must be regarded as the trust subject, and cannot be purchased by the trustee for
his individual benefit at a judicial sale, under
the circumstances of the case.

3. If said land is purchased by said trustee
at a price which fails to satisfy the judgment of
his *cestuis que trustent*, and is resold by said
trustee at a profit, said *cestuis que trustent* may
have said profits applied towards the payment of
their judgment so held by said trustee.

(Syllabus by the Court.)

Appeal from circuit court, Greenbrier
county.

J. M. McWhorter and Okey Johnson, for
appellants. John A. Preston, for appellee.

ENGLISH, J. Patsy Feamster, the moth-
er of Joseph A. Feamster, was the owner of a judgment
against Joseph A. Feamster amounting
to $5,249.72 as of April 20, 1885; and on
the 5th day of March, 1885, she made two
assignments of said judgment for the benefit of the children of her son Joseph A.
Feamster by his wife, Mary J. Feamster,
who are the plaintiffs in this suit, and Willie
L. Feamster, their brother, who has since
departed this life without issue. One of
said assignments was made to Joseph A.
Feamster, and the other to S. W. N. Feamster; both of said assignments being made
for the use and benefit of said children of
Joseph A. Feamster. In a chancery suit,
brought in the year 1886 by Mary J. Feamster against Joseph A. Feamster and others, the lien creditors of said Joseph A.
Feamster were convened under the provisions of the statute, and were classified
and reported by a commissioner, to whom
the cause was referred with a view of obtaining a decree for the sale of said land,
and said judgment was classed No. 6.
Said Joseph A. Feamster and S. W. N.
Feamster filed their respective assignments, each claiming control of said judgment and the proceeds thereof. These
claims were referred to a commissioner,
who took evidence and reported thereon,
and at the hearing the court decided the
controversy in favor of S. W. N. Feamster; holding that he held the valid assignment for said judgment. The land of
said Joseph A. Feamster was directed to
be sold, and the liens prior to said judgment, which was held by S. W. N. Feamster in trust for the plaintiffs, who were
children of said Joseph A. Feamster,
amounted to about $2,000. After said
land had been advertised by the commissioners appointed to make sale thereof,
one S. W. Anderson came to see one of the
commissioners about the sale thereof, and
proposed purchasing part of it, and said
he wanted about 100 acres thereof. At
said sale said S. W. N. Feamster became
the purchaser at the price of $2,300 of said
tract of land containing 320 acres, said
Anderson being present at the sale, but refusing to bid; and said sale was reported
to the court by the commissioners appointed to make the same, and, being unex-
cepted to, was confirmed. The children
of said Joseph A. Feamster, Annie C.
Feamster, Maud E. Feamster, and Pattie
Alderson Feamster—the last two of whom
are infants, and sue by their next friend—
filed their bill on the first Monday in
March, 1890, in the circuit court of Greenbrier county, against said S. W. N. Feamster, in which they set forth the above
facts, and further allege that before said
sale was confirmed by a decree of said
court to the defendant he sold a part of
the land to said Anderson for something
over $3,000; that the tract of land was
very valuable, and should have brought
a much larger price; that it had been sold
by the same commissioners at a former time
for $7,000, which sale for some cause had
been set aside; that the defendant, having
undertaken to act as trustee for plaintiffs,
should have encouraged bidders, so as to
have made the land bring as large a sum

as possible for the benefit of his *cestuis que trustent;* and that, having assumed the trust, the law made it his duty to promote the interests of plaintiffs, who were infant children of his brother, but that, instead of doing this, the land was sold at about half price, the trustee was the purchaser, and one was present wanting 160 acres of the land, but from an understanding with the defendant declined to bid, and soon after the sale was made he paid the defendant over $30 per acre for 105⅝ acres of the land; that the bidders were forestalled, and the defendant purchased the whole tract at half of its value or less, and then sold one-third of it for a sum sufficient to reimburse himself and make a profit of $1,000 or upwards, and still retains over 200 acres of the land; that in settling up their accounts of receipts and disbursements, the commissioners who made the sale had a balance of $31.75 to return to said trustee after paying costs of suit, expenses of sale, and the liens prior to the one in favor of Patsy Feamster, now for the use of plaintiffs, which sum the defendant admits the plaintiffs are entitled to on their judgment, and they charge the conduct of their said trustee constitutes a fraud upon their rights; that they are entitled to the benefit of any profit realized by him; and they call upon him to disclose the true amount for which he sold said 105⅝ acres to S. W. Anderson, and pray that he may be required to account to and pay over to plaintiffs, as they become of age, their respective shares of what he made over and above what he paid for said land, and that the 200 acres or upwards remaining in his hands may be decreed to be sold for the benefit of plaintiffs, or that he may be required to account to them for the value thereof, and the rents and profits of the same during the time he has had it in possession. On the 2d of May, 1890, the plaintiffs filed an amended bill, in which they allege that since filing their original bill they have learned that the arrangement for the sale of the land to S. W. Anderson after the defendant purchased it was made by Joseph A. Feamster, the brother of the defendant, who in that matter was acting as the agent and with the knowledge and consent of the defendant; that the defendant resided near the land sold, as did Joseph A. Feamster, and knew all about its great value, and the liens attaching to said land which were prior to the lien held in trust by the defendant for plaintiffs, which amounted to near $2,000, and then came plaintiffs' lien, amounting to over $5,000, which defendant controlled, and which he could and did use to his own advantage. They further allege that in the same class with plaintiff's judgment, viz., class 6, was reported a judgment in favor of W. P. Rucker against Joseph A. Feamster for the sum of $149.55, with interest from April 20, 1885; that one Edgar P. Rucker prepared an upset bid and offered to give good security thereon at the sum of $3,000, and was going to file it in the cause, and ask the sale to defendant to be set aside, when the defendant, through some of his friends, agreed that if the upset bid should not be put in, and if the sale

should be confirmed to him at the price he had purchased it at, viz., $2,800, he would pay the judgment of said W. P. Rucker, who was the father of said Edgar P. Rucker, and he did accordingly pay said judgment, and thereupon the sale was confirmed; and they aver and charge that this single transaction is of itself sufficient to sustain to the fullest extent the charge that the whole proceedings in the purchase of the land by their trustee, when their debt of $5,000 was the next to be paid, and gave their said trustee the entire control of the situation by virtue of his relation thereto, was a fraud upon their rights, and that he purchased the same with a view to his own advantage; and they aver and charge that the defendant knew before said sale was confirmed to him, and even when the purchase was made, about what he could sell to said Anderson for; and they pray as in their original bill and for general relief.

The defendant, S. W. N. Feamster, answered the original bill, admitting the judgment assigned to him by Patsy Feamster, its amount and priority, and that it was assigned to him for the use of plaintiffs, and that she assigned the same to Joseph A. Feamster for the same use, and that they respectively filed petitions in said cause claiming said assignment, and that on the hearing of the cause the court decided the assignment to him (S. W. N. Feamster) was the valid assignment, and he was "decreed to be the trustee for said children of whatever might be realized from said judgment;" but he denied that he accepted the trust. He also denied that said property was trust property, and alleged that it was sold at a judicial sale, brought about by another party, which he took no part in procuring, and over which he could not have had control. He also denied that before said sale was confirmed he sold a part of said land to S. W. Anderson at any price, but admitted that after said sale he did sell part of said land to said Anderson. As to the allegation that said commissioners made a sale some time previous of said land for $7,000, which for some cause was set aside, he claimed that was a negotiation for an exchange of said land for some property in the town of Alderson, and the price named was the estimated value of said Alderson property, but that no such offer was made in money, and said trade was never consummated. He also denied that he in any manner retarded or prevented any one from bidding on said property; but, on the contrary, alleged that after the sale and before confirmation thereof said commissioners sought to get some one to put in an upset bid, and he was approached by a certain man, and requested to make a contract with him for part of the tract, and he replied that he could not and would not treat with him until after the court had acted upon the sale, and then and there encouraged said party to put in an upset bid if he desired the property; and he put in issue by said answer all of the material allegations of plaintiffs' original bill. He also filed an answer to the plaintiffs' amended bill, in which he admitted that he paid the debt of $149.55

reported in favor of W. P. Rucker, but under the following circumstances, viz.: Capt. R. F. Dennis, his attorney in the Joseph A. Feamster case, wrote him that he told said Rucker that if the sale was confirmed to respondent of said tract of land said Rucker's debt should be paid; that he at first refused to pay it, but, seeing that said Dennis was in an embarrassing position in reference to the statement he had made to said Rucker, agreed to pay the same only on account of said Dennis' statement to said Rucker; that he did not authorize said Dennis to make such arrangement, and did not know he had done so until the reception of said letter, which was not received until after the sale had been confirmed, and the court had adjourned; that he never agreed with said Rucker that he would pay his debt if he would not put in an upset bid, or upon any condition, prior to the confirmation of the sale; and that he paid the same only as above stated; and he put in issue all of the material allegations of said amended bill. These answers were each replied to generally. Quite a number of depositions were taken, and on the 28th day of June, 1890, the court decreed that said S. W. N. Feamster did not occupy such relation to the plaintiffs in his trusteeship as would prevent his bidding on the land of Joseph A. Feamster, and that he could not be held to account for the excess for which he sold to S. W. Anderson above what he paid for the land, and that the plaintiffs were not entitled to the recovery of the remaining unsold land, or to a sale thereof for their benefit, and that all they were entitled to recover was the sum of $31.75, returned to said trustee by the commissioners who made the sale, with interest from the 1st day of April, 1889, to be paid to them as they respectively arrived at the age of 21 years; and from this decree the plaintiffs appealed to this court.

The defendant, in his answer to the original bill, admits that he and Joseph A. Feamster, respectively, filed petitions in the case of Mary J. Feamster v. Joseph A. Feamster, claiming the assignment of said judgment from Patsy Feamster, which contest was decided in his favor, and he was decreed upon his own petition to be a trustee for the plaintiffs of whatever might be realized from said judgment, but he denies that he accepted the trust. What more he could have done in the way of a formal acceptance of the trust it is difficult to perceive. He petitioned the court for it, and in a contest with Joseph A. Feamster it was decreed in his favor, and he does not appear in any manner to have subsequently disclaimed it; and while said decree remained in his favor he remained the trustee, and was the only person entitled to control said judgment, and in this case he must be regarded as their trustee with reference to said judgment; and, being such trustee, the question presented for our determination is whether, under the circumstances of this case, he could consistently become the purchaser of said tract of land. His interest as a purchaser was diametrically opposed to the interests of his cestuis que trustent. His interest was to purchase

the property at the least price he could, while their desire and interest were to make the property bring more than $5,000 more than it did, so that their judgment would be paid. By purchasing the land at less than its value, and selling it again at a profit, the money which would and should have gone towards the satisfaction of their judgment goes into the pocket of their trustee; not for their benefit, but for his own. S. W. N. Feamster was fully aware of the desire on the part of S. W. Anderson to become the owner of a portion of said tract of land, and the conduct of said Anderson with reference to the purchase of a portion thereof clearly indicates his anxiety to buy the same. The defendant, in his deposition, says that said Anderson came to him before the confirmation of said sale, and said he wanted a part of the land, but that he told him he could not talk to him about it until the sale was acted upon by the court; but that, if confirmed, he would probably let him have part of it at what it was worth. Why could he not talk to Anderson in regard to the matter? unless he was afraid of defeating the confirmation of the sale to himself, and depriving himself of the profit he had made by said purchase. Said Anderson was present when the land was put up for sale, and was unwilling to bid over $2,300 for the entire tract of 320 acres, but in a few days after he paid S. W. N. Feamster $3,000 for 105¾ acres,—less than one-third of it. In other words, he preferred to pay $700 more for the 105¾ acres—part of said tract—than he was willing to pay for the whole 320 acres, assigning as a reason that he did not want the remaining 200 acres, although he states it was worth $5 an acre. As a general thing, in business transactions the actions of men are controlled by their interests, and the fact that said Anderson declined to bid on said entire property under the circumstances, coupled with the additional fact that W. P. Rucker in his deposition states that he heard after said sale, and before its confirmation, that S. W. N. Feamster had sold a part of said land to said Anderson for a good deal more than the whole tract cost him, clearly indicates collusion and an understanding between said S. W. N. Feamster and said Anderson. It was the plain duty of said S. W. N. Feamster, acting as trustee for the infant children of his brother, to make said land bring every dollar it would for the benefit of his cestuis que trustent, but when approached by Mr. Anderson in regard to the purchase of part of it he says he told him "he could not talk about it until the sale was acted upon by the court, but that, if confirmed, he would probably let him have a part of it at its worth;" and when he comes to sell it we find how widely different his views were in regard to its worth from what they were when he was bidding on it at public sale. Again, the evident desire of said S. W. N. Feamster to have said sale confirmed by his conduct in reference to the upset bid of E. P. Rucker, assignee of the claim of William P. Rucker. Henry Gilmer, who was acting as attorney for Commissioner McWhorter, states in his deposition that Dr. W. P. Rucker, who held a judgment against Joseph A. Feamster, and whose judgment was not paid by the sale made, told him that his son, E. P. Rucker, intended to put in an upset bid, and to please hold the matter open, and write to S. W. N. Feamster, and tell him of the fact; that E. P. Rucker did bring him a bond to make the land bring $3,000 if a new sale was ordered, and gave it to him; that he then wrote to said Feamster, and told him of the upset bid, and also wrote him, at the request of Dr. Rucker, that if he, Feamster, would pay or secure Rucker's judgment, the bond would not be used; that Col. J. W. Davis was to go on the bond also, and told him he would do so. In the course of a few days said Feamster came to town, and the same day Dr. Rucker came to witness and told him his debt was all right, and that he, Gilmer, need not get Davis to sign the bond, but could go on, and have the order entered confirming the sale. And William P. Rucker, in his deposition, states that E. P. Rucker, at his instance, filed an upset bid, or prepared one, which was not offered because the attorney for S. W. N. Feamster assured him in court that if the upset bond was not filed, and the sale was confirmed, S. W. N. Feamster would pay his debt; that said attorney wrote a letter to Feamster, which he sent him by Samuel F. Tyree or E. P. Rucker, and he received a reply, saying he would settle it in a short time, which he did. So that it appears from this evidence that said Feamster, so far from desiring that an upset bid should be put in, was not only willing to, but did, pay E. P. Rucker. assignee of W. P. Rucker, $149.55, to prevent a reopening of the biddings.

It is contended by counsel for the appellee that the land sold was not "trust property," but was the land of Joseph A. Feamster. Suppose, by way of illustration, that the land was reasonably worth $2,000, and that the infant children of Joseph A. Feamster, instead of owning a judgment lien upon the land as they do, held a deed of trust upon it for $1,900, in one sense it would still be Joseph A. Feamster's land, although said trust-deed, if enforced, would consume almost its entire value; and, if the claim secured by said tract was in the hands of S. W. N. Feamster for the benefit of said infants, it would hardly be contended that the land itself was not the trust subject; and so with this judgment lien, the record shows that the land constituted all the estate of said Joseph A. Feamster, and in the absence of the land the judgment was worthless to said infants, as its value to them grew out of and solely depended upon the interest which said judgment lien created for them in said land, and which the law conferred upon them the right to assert by subjecting said land to its payment. This lien and this right was their property, and it was in the hands of their trustee, whose duty it was to zealously guard and protect their interest. If prior liens existed against the land which would consume in satisfaction one-half of the land at a fair sale, then they or their representative must and could only look

to the residue for satisfaction. Neither an execution issued under said judgment nor a certified copy of the judgment itself could be regarded as available trust property, unless it could be used as a lien upon something out of which money could be realized. In this instance it was the land which gave the judgment value, and when that was sacrificed to prior liens the trust subject was sacrificed; and, under the circumstances of this case, equity would regard the land as the trust subject. In Story's Equity Jurisprudence, § 321, the author says: "A trustee is never permitted to partake of the bounty of the party for whom he acts except under circumstances which would make the same valid if it were a case of guardianship. A trustee cannot purchase of his *cestui que trust* unless under like circumstances. * * * But it is difficult to make out such a case where the exception is taken, especially when there is any inadequacy of price, or any inequality in the bargain. And, therefore, if a trustee, though strictly honest, should buy for himself an estate of his *cestui que trust*, and then should sell it for more, according to the rules of a court of equity, from general policy, and not from any peculiar imputation of fraud, he would be held still to remain a trustee to all intents and purposes, and not to be permitted to sell it for himself." See Fox v. Mackreth, 2 Brown, Ch. 400; Prevost v. Grats, 1 Pet. 367; Hawley v. Cramer, 4 Cow. 717. And in section 322, vol. 1, Story, Eq. Jur., the author further says: "But we are not to understand from this last language that to entitle the *cestui que trust* to relief it is indispensable to show that the trustee has made some advantage where there has been a purchase by himself; and that, unless some advantage has been made, the sale to the trustee is good. That would not be putting the doctrine upon its true ground, which is that the prohibition arises from the subsisting relation of trusteeship. The ingredient of advantage made by him would only go to establish that the transaction might be open to the strong imputation of being tainted by imposition or selfish cunning. But the principle applies, however innocent the purchase may be, in a given case. It is poisonous in its consequences. The *cestui que trust* is not bound to prove, nor is the court bound to decide, that the trustee has made a bargain advantageous to himself. The fact may be so, and yet the party not have it in his power distinctly and clearly to show it. There may be fraud, and yet the party not be able to show it. It is to guard against this uncertainty and hazard of abuse, and to remove the trustee from temptation, that the rule does and will permit the *cestui que trust* to come at his own option, and, without showing essential injury, to insist upon having the experiment of another sale; so that in fact in all cases where a purchase has been made by a trustee on his own account of the estate of his *cestui que trust*, although sold at public auction, it is in the option of the *cestui que trust* to set aside the sale, whether *bona fide* made or not." See Davoue v. Fanning, 2 Johns. Ch. 252; Campbell v. Walker, 5 Ves.

678; Morse v. Royal, 12 Ves. 355. If this, then, be the law with reference to parties that are *sui juris*, with how much more strength should it apply where the parties represented by the trustee, as in this case, are infants. In Adams' Equity, 160, the author says: "Lastly, a trustee must not avail himself of his fiduciary character for any object of personal benefit. His fundamental duty is to do his utmost for the *cestui que trust*, and every advantage which he appropriates to himself must be acquired by a dereliction of that duty;" and on page 162, note, it is said: "It seems a trustee may not purchase the trust property for his own benefit when it is sold under a judicial decree which he was not instrumental in procuring, unless by the order of sale he was specially allowed so to purchase;" referring to Chapin v. Weed, 1 Clarke, 464; Beeson v. Beeson, 9 Pa. St. 279, etc. In Minor's Institutes, (volume 2, p. 212, § 10,) the author says: "As a general principle it is well settled that trustees, agents, auctioneers, and all persons acting in a confidential character, are disqualified from purchasing the subject committed to them. The functions of buyer and seller are incompatible, and cannot be exercised by the same person without great danger of fraud. Such transactions are constructively fraudulent, and are therefore voidable at the instance of the beneficiary, although, if he chooses to recognise them, they are binding upon the trustee," etc.; citing 1 Rob. Pr. (1st Ed.) 85; 1 Lom. Dig. 319; Carter v. Harris, 4 Rand. (Va.) 204; Seger v. Edwards, 11 Leigh, 213; Buckles v. Lafferty, 2 Rob. (Va.) 300; Howery v. Helms, 20 Grat. 1; Marsh v. Whitmore, 21 Wall 183. Again he says on page 213: "It is admitted that a trustee can legally purchase the trust subject of a *cestui que trust* who is *sui juris*, and has discharged him from the relation of trustee, although even then the transaction will be scrutinised with guarded jealousy. So in like manner he may purchase when he has from the beginning disclaimed the trust and never acted in it; and finally a trustee may buy the trust subject by leave of the court of equity." In the case under consideration, however, we find that the trustee brought himself within none of these exceptions, and, although he claims that he never accepted the trust, he asserted his claim to the subject by way of petition and was successful, and was never heard to disclaim the trust until he filed his answer in this case. In the case of Miller v. Holcombe, 9 Grat. 665, section 5 of syllabus, the court held that "a trustee making a compromise with a third person in relation to a trust subject, though he may purchase the subject for himself, is bound to account as trustee for all the profits made on the transaction;" and LEE, J., delivering the opinion of the court in that case, said, on page 679: "The principle on which the prohibition to one standing in a fiduciary character to deal with the trust subject with reference to his own individual interests rests, is that not only would it be contrary to the design under which he has obtained control of the subject, but he would be placed in such a situation as that his interests

might, in reference to the conduct of the trust, by possibility come into conflict with those of the *cestui que trust*." 2 Spence, Eq. Jur. 299; 2 Fonbl. Eq. 189. This is precisely what happened to the defendant in this case in becoming a purchaser of the property on which the judgment he held as trustee was a lien,—his interests as purchaser came in conflict with the interests of his *cestuis que trustent*. He wished to purchase the property as cheaply as he could, and their interests required that it should bring enough to satisfy their judgment. In order that he might realize a profit of $700, and still retain 200 acres of the land, he preferred to have the sale confirmed at his bid, and he was willing to pay E. P. Rucker $149.55 to bring about that result, although this course sacrificed the entire judgment he held for the plaintiffs as trustee, with the exception of $31.-75. It is the province of a court of equity to guard against these conflicting interests in which self and the weakness and greed of human nature assert themselves on the one hand, and sacred trusts and high moral obligations upon the other. It is to prevent this struggle between duty and self-interest that the law has provided that a trustee shall not be subjected to these temptations or placed in an attitude in which, in order to secure his own gain, he must place obstacles in the way to prevent those whom he should impartially represent from obtaining what they are justly entitled to. Accordingly, in the case of Newcomb v. Brooks, 16 W. Va. 32, this court has settled the law on this subject as follows, section 1, syllabus: "A person who occupies any fiduciary relation to another is bound not to exercise for his own benefit and to the prejudice of the party to whom he stands in such relation any of the powers or rights, or any knowledge or advantage of any description, which he derives from such confidential relations." Also, section 6: "A fiduciary cannot make a valid purchase of the trust property, though it be made at a judicial sale, under a decree made in an adverse proceeding. Any such purchase may be avoided at his option by any party to whom he owes such fiduciary relations." In section 8 of said syllabus it was held that "if a fiduciary purchases trust property, and then resells it to a purchaser for valuable consideration with notice of the character of his title, the person to whom the fiduciary occupied the fiduciary relation may, at his option, avoid the sale, though the property has passed into the hands of a subpurchaser with notice;" and again, in section 9, it was held as follows: "But if the subpurchaser had no notice of the vendor's title the sale cannot be set aside, but the party can have redress against the fiduciary personally to the extent of the profits he made by the resale." See, also, Lane v. Black, 21 W. Va. 617. The facts proven in this case clearly indicate that the defendant, instead of seeking to promote the interests of his *cestuis que trustent*, disregarded his plain duties as trustee, and sacrificed their interest for his individual gain, and for these reasons we are of opinion that the plaintiffs were entitled to the relief prayed for. The decree complained of must be reversed, and the cause remanded to the circuit court of Greenbrier county for further proceedings to be had therein, and the appellee must pay the costs of this appeal.

LUCAS, P., and BRANNON, J., concur. HOLT, J., absent.

KANAWHA VALLEY BANK v. WILSON et al.

(Supreme Court of Appeals of West Virginia. March 11, 1891.)

TIME OF TAKING APPEAL—ARRESTING STATUTE OF LIMITATION.

1. Under the third section of chapter 135 of the Code an appeal from a final decree entered by the circuit court must be prosecuted within two years after the same has been rendered, and the currency of this statute of limitation is arrested by the filing of the petition.

2. One of the essential qualifications necessary to a bill in chancery is that it should, either in the caption or in the body of the bill, name some person or persons as parties defendant, and describe them as having some interest in the subject-matter of the suit, and pray for some relief against them; and these requisites are as essential to a bill of review as to an original bill, and without them a paper purporting to be a bill of review should be dismissed on demurrer, or stricken from the files on motion.

3. The filing of any such abortive bill of review could not have the effect of arresting the statute of limitations, so as to extend the period within which an appeal might have been taken from the final decree, the review and reversal of which were attempted by such abortive bill.

(Syllabus by the Court.)

Appeal and *supersedeas* from circuit court. Kanawha county.

Watts & Ashby and Okey Johnson, for appellants. J. F. Brown, Price & Flournoy, and H. D. Shrewsbury, for appellee.

LUCAS, P. This case comes before this court upon a motion to dismiss the appeal as improvidently awarded. In connection with this motion, the case was brought on and heard on the merits of the appeal. If, however, we should be of opinion that the appeal to the final decree complained of was not taken in the period prescribed by law, it would not only be unnecessary, but improper, to discuss the case upon its merits, since, being without jurisdiction, such a discussion would be gratuitous, and could lead to no profitable results. The final decree complained of by the appellants was entered on the 11th day of July, 1888, by the circuit court of Kanawha county in a chancery suit in which the Kanawha Valley Bank was plaintiff and the present appellants, A. H. Wilson, and Mary E. Wilson, his wife, were, along with others, defendants. The third section of chapter 135 of the Code provides as follows: "No petition shall be presented for an appeal from or writ of error or *supersedeas* to any judgment, decree, or order, whether the state be a party thereto or not, nor to any judgment of a circuit court or municipal court rendered in an appeal from the judgment of a justice, which shall have been rendered or made more than five years before such petition is presented, if the judgment, decree, or order mentioned in the petition has been given, rendered, or made before this chapter, as amended, takes effect, but as to any judgment, decree or order given, rendered, or made after this chapter as amended takes effect, no such petition shall be presented after two years from the date of such judgment, decree, or order." It will be perceived, therefore, that with reference to final decrees rendered since the date of the above enactment any appeal therefrom must be prosecuted within two years after the same has been entered, and that the currency of the limitation of time is arrested by the filing of the petition. In the present case, as we have seen, the final decree complained of was entered on the 11th of July, 1888, and the appeal was allowed by a judge of this court in vacation on the 27th of September, 1890, at or about which time it is fair to presume the petition was presented. The statutory period, therefore, having expired before the presentation of the petition, the appeal must be dismissed as improvidently awarded. But it is contended that a bill of review was filed by leave of court in the circuit court on the 3d day of May, 1889, and that the same was only dismissed on demurrer by a final decree rendered June 28, 1890. It is supposed that the filing and pendency of this "bill of review," as it is called, had some efficacy to suspend the statute of limitation which we have been considering. The first requisite of every bill in chancery, whether original or by way of supplement or review, is that there shall be parties thereto made such by proper description and name. The form of such a bill as laid down in skeleton in our Code is as follows: "The bill of complaint of A. B. (state the names of all the plaintiffs) against C. D. (state the names of all the defendants, if known, and, if not, designate them as the unknown parties or unknown heirs, etc., as the case may be) filed in the circuit court of —— county. The plaintiff complains and says that (here state all the facts constituting a claim to relief.) The said plaintiff therefore prays that (here state the particular relief desired.) He also asks such other and general relief as the court may see fit to grant." It will thus be perceived that the briefest and most modernized form of a bill requires parties defendant to be set out in the body of the bill as those having an interest in the subject-matter, and against whom relief is prayed. A bill of review is no exception to this general rule. "Such a bill," says Judge CABELL in Laidley v. Merrifield, 7 Leigh, 346, "is a proceeding to correct a final decree in the same court for error apparent on the face of the decree, or on account of new evidence discovered since the final decree. The decree being final, the bill of review is not regarded as a part of the cause in which the decree was rendered." "Such a bill," says Mr. Barton, "cannot be filed by persons who cannot be benefited by the reversal or modification of the former decree; but the general rule is that all the parties to the original bill shall be made parties to the bill of review." Bart. Ch. Pr. § 64, p. 205. To the same effect, see Daniell, Ch. Pr. p. 1579. In the bill which we are now considering, purporting to be a bill of review, there are no parties defendant named in the caption, nor anywhere named or described in the body of the bill. It follows, therefore, in accordance with the principles laid down in McCoy v. Allen, 16 W. Va. 724, that whatever statements might be contained in the bill, or however meritorious a cause it might present, no possible relief could be obtained against any one whatever. The defendants, never having been summoned or served with any process, appeared for no other purpose than to demur to the bill, which was equivalent to a motion to have it stricken from the file. See Daniell, Ch. Pr. p. 1578. The demurrer was sustained by the circuit court, and for the reasons stated we think there was no error in such judgment by the circuit court. It is hardly necessary to say that the erroneous filing of such abortive instrument, improperly called a "bill of review," could not in any manner suspend the currency of the statute of limitations, which carried the final decree of July 11, 1888, beyond the reach of appeal at the time when the appellants filed their petition. For these reasons we find no error in the decree of the circuit court of June 28, 1890, and the same must be affirmed, and this appeal, so far as allowed to the decree of July 11, 1888, must be dismissed as improvidently awarded.

ENGLISH, BRANNON, and HOLT, JJ., concur.

CROTTY et al. v. EAGLE'S ADM'R.

(Supreme Court of Appeals of West Virginia. March 19, 1891.)

ACCOUNTING BY ADMINISTRATOR—INFANT HEIRS—POWERS OF ATTORNEYS — COMPROMISING SUIT—DUTIES OF ADMINISTRATOR.

1. Where infants sue in equity by a prochein ami to compel an administrator to settle his accounts as such administrator of an estate in which they are interested as distributees, and such prochein ami employs an attorney to represent their interests, such attorney cannot bind said infants by an agreement signed by himself or by another attorney authorized by him to waive proof of the vouchers and accounts presented by said administrator in the settlement of his administration accounts, or to allow commissions to such administrator which are not allowed by statute.

2. Where an attorney has been employed to prosecute a suit, in the absence of direction from his client he cannot delegate his authority as such to another attorney.

3. An attorney at law cannot by an agreement in pais commute the debt by his client, or compromise his suit, without express authority so to do.

4. It is the duty of an administrator to protect the estate of his decedent by interposing every legal defense, and he cannot by an agreement in pais, where infants are concerned and are made parties, either obtain commissions as administrator, to which he is not entitled by statute, or provide for the allowance of claims against said estate without proof of their correctness and validity.

(Syllabus by the Court.)

Appeal and supersedeas from circuit court, Kanawha county.

T. B. Swann, for appellant. J. M. McWhorter, for appellees.

ENGLISH, J. This suit was brought by C. P. Crotty and others against Thomas B. Swann, administrator of the estate of Stewart Eagle, deceased, in the circuit court of Kanawha county, for the purpose of obtaining a settlement of the account of said administrator, and a disbursement of the assets in his hands among the distributees entitled thereto. The plaintiffs in their bill allege that in the year 1857 the said Stewart Eagle recovered a judgment in the county court of Kanawha county, Va., against the James River & Kanawha Company for the sum of $5,400, and that before any money was realized upon said judgment the said Stewart Eagle died, and on the 9th day of April, 1866, said Thomas B. Swann qualified as the administrator of his estate; that the said Thomas B. Swann had, as attorney, obtained said judgment, and was to have one-half of the recovery, and was to pay the expenses or costs attending said suit outside of the costs following the suit, and said Stewart Eagle was to get half that might be recovered; that shortly after his qualification as such administrator said Swann recovered or received as attorney several large sums of money on said judgment,—about October 11, 1867, $183.14, January 11, 1868, $1,823.71, January 28, 1868, $1,823.70, and February 18, 1868, $1,794.06, aggregating $5,624.61; that one-half of said recovery should have gone into the hands of said Thomas B. Swann as assets of the estate of Stewart Eagle, deceased, to be administered in payment of his debts, and the residue of said half should have been disbursed among the heirs or distributees of said Stewart Eagle; that said Stewart Eagle died intestate and unmarried, and among his legal heirs were two infant children, Ada Eagle and Edward Eagle, who sue by their next friend, C. P. Crotty. The plaintiffs further allege that it has been many years since the administrator received said funds; that very little has been paid the plaintiffs; and that no settlement of the administration account has ever been made; and they pray that said administrator may be required to settle his accounts, showing what money he has received for said estate, what disposition he has made of the same, and what he still has on hand, and that he be required to disburse the same, with its accrued interest, to the distributees, etc. On the 17th day of July, 1886, this cause was ordered to be heard together with the case of Stewart Eagle's Adm'r v. Aaron Stockton's Adm'r et als., and both causes were referred to a commissioner to ascertain and report (1) what amount of money T. B. Swann had collected as administrator of Stewart Eagle, deceased, what disposition he had made of the same, and what amount, if any, was still in his hands as administrator, and to whom it was due; (2) should said commissioner find that the funds due were payable to the distributees of Stewart Eagle, he should report a distributee account showing what had been paid to each, and what is due to or from each distributee of said estate, and any other matter deemed pertinent, or required by any party to the cause. The report in pursuance of said decree appears to have been made by J. W. Kennedy, special commissioner; and the clerk certifies that a writing attached to said report is in the words and figures following, to-wit: "To Commissioner J. W. Kennedy, Esq.: Henry A. Eagle and others v. Stockton and others, in chancery, Kanawha circuit court; and Eagle's Heirs v. Eagle's Adm'r and others, in chancery, Kanawha circuit court. It is agreed that the fifteen per cent. fees to J. S. Swann provided for in the papers filed in this cause are subject to credits shown by vouchers filed for fees paid other attorneys in the controversy with C. M. Deem in Greenbrier circuit court. And it is further agreed that the administrator's commissions to adm'r of Stewart Eagle, as claimed, shall be allowed him; and the 15 per cent. fees are also to be charged with John S. Swann's personal expenses to Greenbrier; and it is admitted that the vouchers and accounts filed before Commissioner Kennedy by the adm'r of Stewart Eagle are correct, and proof thereof is waived;" which agreement was signed: "Eagle's Heirs and Distributees, by J. McWhorter, Att'y, per L. E. McWhorter, Att'y. T. B. Swann, as Adm'r of S. Eagle; and J. S. & T. B. Swann, John S. Swann, and T. B. Swann. Dated Charleston, W. Va., Oct. 10, 1888." On the 17th day of January, 1889, said special commissioner, Kennedy, filed his report in the case of Stewart Eagle's Distributees v. Stewart Eagle's Administrator, in which he says:

"Thomas B. Swann, administrator of Stewart Eagle, deceased, appeared and filed his vouchers from No. 1 to No. 86, before me; and the parties also filed before me an agreement that said vouchers and accounts are correct, and that proof thereof shall be waived, (see vouchers and accounts and agreement.) Said agreement also provides that the 15 per cent. fee to J. S. Swann provided for in the papers in this cause is subject to credits shown by vouchers filed for fees paid to other attorneys in the suit with C. M. Deem in Greenbrier circuit court; and, further, that said Swann, adm'r, shall be entitled to his administration commissions, and that the 15 per cent. fees shall also be charged with J. S. Swann's personal expenses to Greenbrier, and that no other evidence than the above was placed before him. Said commissioner then finds, in pursuance of the first requirement of said decree:

First. That the amount of money collected by T. B. Swann as administrator of Stewart Eagle, deceased, as shown by said vouchers and accounts filed before him, was the sum of................ $9,618 19

Second. The said sum of $9,618.19 was disposed of as follows: The said Swann paid out by way of costs incurred in a suit between said heirs and C. M. Deem in the Greenbrier circuit court the sum of............................... $308 96
Also 15 per cent. to J. S. Swann, att'y in said Deem Case........ 846 07
Also the administration commission on the said sum of $3,618.12 amounts to..................... 180 96

     Total paid out................ 785 99

Leaving to be divided among the heirs and distributees the net amount of.... $1,389 13

One-fourth of which goes to each distributee as follows:
To Wm. Eagle.............................. $ 458 03
     Henry Eagle.......................... 458 03
     B. F. Eagle.......................... 458 03
     C. P. Crotty.......................... 458 04

"(2) As to the second requirement, I report the following amounts paid to the several distributees, respectively, and the amounts due to and from them, respectively:

The amount due Wm. Eagle as above... $ 458 03
Amounts paid him as shown by vouchers.................... $127 25
Amount paid C. P. Crotty, guardian for his children............ 315 42

     Total paid..................... 442 67

Leaving due..................... $ 15 36
Add interest from 1872........... 15 00

     Total due Wm. Eagle's share....... $ 30 36

Amount due Henry Eagle as above...... $ 458 03
Amount paid him.............. $ 50 00
Amount paid C. P. Crotty, his assignee................... 16 66

     Total paid................... $ 66 66

Leaving due.................. $ 391 37
Add interest 1872............... 376 24

     Total due Henry Eagle's share..... $ 767 61

Amount due B. F. Eagle.............. $ 458 03
Amount paid..................... 980 00

Overpaid..................... $ 521 97

Amount due C. P. Crotty as above....... $ 458 04
Amount paid..................... 402 42

Leaving due.................. $ 55 62
Add interest 1872............... 53 00

     Total due C. P. Crotty's share..... $ 108 62

"The above amount due Henry Eagle's share—namely, $767.61—goes to C. P. Crotty and B. F. Eagle, as assignees, in the following proportions: To C. P. Crotty, $367.48; to B. F. Eagle, $400.13.
"Included in the payments above from T. B. Swann to B. F. Eagle is an amount of $675.08, agreed by said Eagle to be paid to said Swann for a tract of land (see voucher contract) which said Eagle agreed to purchase from said Swann. Respectfully submitted, J. W. KENNEDY, Special Commissioner."

Numerous exceptions were indorsed on said commissioner's report by T. B. Swann in his own right and as administrator of S. Eagle, deceased, and by J. S. and T. B. Swann, all of which are based upon the allegation that it does not carry out the agreement of the 10th of October, 1888, filed in the cause with said report between said administrator and the parties by their counsel and in person, and also because said account was not made out by J. W. Kennedy, but by William Lohmeyer, who did not have before him the agreement upon which the report ought to have been made. On the 25th day of June, 1889, said Thomas B. Swann filed his answer to the plaintiff's bill, in which he asks that his answer in the case of H. A. Eagle et al. v. H. Stockton et al., together with his accounts therewith filed, be read as a part of his answer, alleging that the agreement of J. S. and T. B. Swann for fees with Eagle in his suit with the James River & Kanawha Company is fully set out in and with said answer, but he does not file a copy of said answer as an exhibit. He further alleges that neither J. S. nor T. B. Swann ever agreed to pay one dollar of costs for S. Eagle in any of his suits, and that in their engagements for fees with S. Eagle they were entitled to and owned one-half of the judgment for $5,400 recovered by S. Eagle v. James River & Kanawha Company, and that subsequent litigation to make it availing was subject to the burden of mutual costs equally to be borne by the shares of each in the judgment for $5,400; that as administrator his disbursements exceeded his receipts by over $1,500, not counting interest; besides, the estate of A. Stockton was indebted to him $1,000, with interest since 1868, as is fully set out in an order and assignment from J. M. Laidley to T. B. Swann, all of which appears in the file of Deem v. Stockton in United States court, but he does not exhibit said order or assignment with his answer. He then details the facts in regard to the litigation with C. M. Deem in the circuit court of Greenbrier county and in this court, and its compromise; also as to the litigation with the James River & Kanawha Company, and the litigation necessary to enforce the collection of the judgment after it was obtained; and also states that he paid S. A. Miller $250 for his services in the case. He also alleges that he furnished to Commissioner Kennedy, on the 3d of March, 1888, a true account of his administration of said estate, in writing, which said commissioner returned with his report, a copy of which is exhibited with said answer. He then recites the terms of said agreement, and alleges that it was agreed in writing, signed by him and counsel for complainants, and returned with said report, admitting that said account was in all things correct, and should be so reported and allowed, and yet Commissioner Kennedy forgot to give this important paper to the stranger William Lohmeyer, whom he got to make up this account, who in its absence failed to credit him with items covered by said agreement in writing, aggregating, without interest, largely over $1,500; and he prays that a decree may be made in his favor against said heirs, to whom he paid more money than they were entitled to receive. This answer was excepted to by the plaintiffs because the exhibits referred to were not filed with the answer, no depositions were taken in the case, affidavits were filed by T. B. Swann, J. W. Kennedy, J. M. McWhorter, and L. E. McWhorter in reference to their understanding of said agreement, its meaning and intention, and as to L. E. McWhorter's authority to act in executing the same; and on the 10th day of July, 1889, a decree was rendered in said cause, confirming said report of Commissioner J. W. Kennedy, overruling all of the exceptions thereto, and directing disbursements to be made by said Thomas B. Swann as administrator, in accordance

with the findings of said report, and from this decree this appeal was obtained.

The appellant appears to rely greatly upon the agreement of October, 1888, signed "Eagle's Heirs and Distributees, by J. McWhorter, Att'y, per L. E. McWhorter, Att'y," on the one part, and T. B. Swann, as administrator of S. Eagle and in his individual capacity, and also by J. S. and T. B. Swann; and his first exception to the commissioner's report is because it does not carry out this agreement, and again he excepts to the report because the same was not made out and prepared by J. W. Kennedy, to whom the cause was referred, but by William Lohmeyer, who did not have before him this agreement upon which the report ought to have been made. The report, however on its face appears to have been made out and signed by J. W. Kennedy, special commissioner, and he states in said report that Thomas B. Swann, administrator of S. Eagle, deceased, appeared and filed his vouchers from No. 1 to No. 86 before him, and that the parties also filed before him an agreement that said vouchers were correct, and that proof thereof should be waived; and that said agreement also provided that the 15 per cent. fee to J. S. Swann, provided for in the papers, was subject to credits shown by vouchers filed for fees paid to other attorneys in the suit with C. M. Deem in Greenbrier circuit court; and further that said Swann, administrator, should be entitled to his administration commissions, and that the 15 per cent. fees should also be charged with J. S. Swann's personal expenses to Greenbrier. Was this agreement such a paper as, in the absence of all other evidence, would authorize said commissioner to settle said administration account as he did? Among the plaintiffs in this case were two infant children, Ada Eagle and Edward Eagle, who sued by their next friend, C. P. Crotty, and who were interested in the distribution of this estate; and it is the peculiar province of a court of equity to protect their interests, and we could not say that, if they had signed this agreement in person, it would have been binding upon them. Is it any more obligatory against, as it was, by their attorney by another attorney? In Ewell's Leading Cases on Infancy, in the notes to the case of Mills v. Dennis, 235, it is said: "No decree can be taken against a minor on his own admissions or those of his guardian ad litem, (except, perhaps, on admissions evidently for the benefit of the infant;) but as against him every allegation of the bill or petition must be duly proved." Mills v. Dennis, 3 Johns. Ch. 367. And in Bingham on Infancy, page 10, note 2, it is said: "Infants may avoid the sale of their lands or any contract or agreement to surrender or release their rights for which they are entitled to an equivalent, because it is a presumption of law that infants have not sufficient discretion to put a just value on their own rights." Baker v. Lovett, 6 Mass. 78. And in 5 Port. (Ala.) 393, in the case of Isaacs v. Boyd, the court, in speaking of the duties of a prochein ami, says: "The duties of a prochein ami and his power are comprised within a very narrow compass.

He may prosecute a right for an infant, but he can do nothing which can operate to its injury. He can, it is true, dismiss a suit because he is himself liable for costs, though even this may be well questioned when injury to the minor would be the result. A *prochein ami* is one admitted by the court to prosecute for the infant, because otherwise he might be prejudiced by the refusal or neglect of his guardian. 10 Petersd. Abr. 579, note. He is in fact but a species of attorney, who is permitted to act for the infant so far as to conduct his suit, but he has certainly not a more extensive authority than an attorney at law, who cannot enter into a bond, or compromise the right of his client. Holker v. Parker, 7 Cranch, 436." In the case of Smith v. Lamberts, 7 Grat. 142, DANIEL, J., delivering the opinion of the court, says: "In some of our sister states the relation of client and attorney has been held to confer upon the latter the authority even to compromise, compound, or commute demands of the former confided to him for collection. The general doctrine, however, so far as I have had it in my power to collect it from a review of the decisions, is that the attorney has no right to commute the debt of his client, to release the 'person of his debtor when in prison by virtue of a *ca. sa.*, or to enter a *retraxit* in a suit to execute a release, or to do any other act which destroys the cause of action without receiving payment." Webster defines "commutation" as follows: A substitution of a less thing for a greater, especially a substitution of one form of payment for another, or one payment for many, or a specific sum of money for conditional payments or allowances, etc. Now in the case under consideration, although there was a suit pending in the circuit court of Kanawha county in which the heirs at law of S. Eagle, deceased, were plaintiffs and Thomas B. Swann, as administrator of said Eagle's estate, was defendant, said agreement does not appear to have been made a matter of record, but appears from the affidavit of T. B. Swann to have been executed *in pais*, and not by the attorney employed in the cause, but by his son, L. E. McWhorter, who signed the agreement, "Eagle's Heirs and Distributees, by J. McWhorter, Att'y, per L. E. McWhorter, Att'y." "An act *in pais* is literally an act in the country, but the phrase is technically used to express any act which is not a matter of record, or done in a court of record." 2 Bl. Comm. 294. An agreement of this character could not have been made by the attorney who was employed and had control of the case, much less could it have been made by delegated authority from the attorney employed. Story on Agency, (section 13,) says: "For a like reason one who has a bare power or authority from another to do an act must execute it himself, and cannot delegate his authority to another; for this being a trust or confidence reposed in him personally, it cannot be assigned to a stranger, whose ability and integrity might not be known to the principal, or who, if known, might not be selected for such a purpose. * * * The same rule

applies to a broker; for he cannot delegate his authority to another to sign a contract in behalf of his principal without the assent of the latter. The reason is plain, for in each of these cases there is an exclusive personal trust and confidence reposed in the particular party, and hence is derived the maxim of the common law: *Delegata potestas non potest delegari*." In this case, a portion of the plaintiffs, being infants, could give no consent, and could only sue and employ counsel by their next friend; and, as we have seen, a *prochein ami* can do nothing that will operate to the injury of those he represents. The effect of this agreement violates this principle by allowing commissions to the administrator, which the plain provisions of the statute would prevent him from obtaining. It is admitted that the vouchers and accounts filed before Commissioner Kennedy by the administrator of Stewart Eagle were correct, and waived proof thereof, and fixed the fees of J. S. Swann at 15 per cent., subject to credits for fees paid other attorneys in the controversy with C. M. Deem in Greenbrier, and also subject to the personal expenses of said J. S. Swann in going to Greenbrier. These matters should have been established by proof, and neither the *prochein ami* nor the attorney employed by him had the right or authority to waive such proof; neither could the attorney for the adults waive such proofs unless expressly authorized so to do by them. The action of the attorney who signed this agreement was equivalent to an actual arbitration of the matters in litigation, and dispensed with proof which would have otherwise been required by the commissioner, and in this the attorney exceeded his powers, even if the attorney retained in the case could have delegated to him authority to execute such a paper. In the case of McGinnis v. Curry, 13 W. Va. 48, GREEN, J., in delivering the opinion of the court, says: "While I have found no case deciding that an attorney has a general authority to submit his client's controversies to arbitration, there are cases in which it has been decided that he does not possess such authority. See Jenkins v. Gillespie, 10 Smedes & M. 31; Scarborough v. Reynolds, 12 Ala. 252. It is true that these were cases in which there was no *lis pendens*. But it seems to me that, as it is held that an attorney by reason of his being employed to institute a suit or defend a threatened one has no authority to submit, by an agreement *in pais*, signed by the attorney, the case to arbitration, that it must follow that he has no such authority, though the suit is pending. An authority to act *in pais* could only be inferred if it exist from his employment before the institution of the suit as an' attorney; and such employment, we have seen, confers no such authority. This conclusion is not at all inconsistent with the numerous cases deciding that an attorney has authority in a pending suit by an order of court to submit the cause to arbitration." In the case in judgment the agreement which the administrator relies upon did not submit the matters in controversy to arbitration, but went further, and disposed of the matters of difference. The agreement, on the other hand, was signed by the administrator, whose plain duty under the law was to protect the estate of his intestate, and interpose every legal defense in his power to prevent encroachments upon it; and, such being the case, a court of equity would not uphold and enforce an agreement made by him which passes upon and determines the correctness and validity of the receipts and vouchers taken by him in the discharge of his duty as such administrator, and which are presented to the commissioner for the purpose of showing he has fully administered the estate, and is entitled to be discharged from liability as such. My conclusion, then, is that the said agreement is invalid, and the report of said commissioner, having been made in the absence of parol proof, and having been based to a considerable extent upon the admissions and waivers contained in said agreement, the decree confirming said report and adjudicating the cause in accordance with the findings of said commissioner must be reversed. But as the adult plaintiffs have assigned no errors, and are not complaining of said decree, and they appear to have assented to a portion of the vouchers presented to said commissioner by said administrator, and they not having excepted to said report, the cause is remanded to the circuit court of Kanawha county for further proceedings to be had therein, with directions to allow such portions of the vouchers, receipts, and accounts presented by said administrator as have been assented to by the adult distributees of said estate, except so far as they affect the interests of the infant parties, and to allow said administrator commissions on the portion of said estate represented by said adult parties only, and it is ordered that Thomas B. Swann do pay the costs of this appeal.

LUCAS, P., and BRANNON and HOLT, JJ., concur.

BRIGHT et al. v. KNIGHT et al.

(Supreme Court of Appeals of West Virginia. March 11, 1891.)

TRUST ON LAND—PAROL EVIDENCE—QUIETING TITLE.

1. Parol evidence may be received to establish a trust, but the trusts to be thus proven are confined to the cases of resulting trusts, which arise from an implication of law, as, for example, where the money is paid by one, the property purchased, and the title taken in another; in such case and similar cases the legal title is in one, and the equitable title in another, and to prevent fraud the fact of payment may be shown by parol evidence, and equity will decree the purchaser a trustee for the person who paid the purchase money.

2. Where the statute of frauds does not apply, and a trust of land is allowed to be established by parol evidence, to establish such trust the facts must be alleged, and the evidence to support them must be full, clear, and satisfactory.

3. A court of equity will not settle the title and boundaries of land when the plaintiff has no equity against the party who is holding the land.

(Syllabus by the Court.)

Appeal and supersedeas from circuit court, Greenbrier county.

J. M. McWhorter and J. W. Davis, for appellants. J. W. Harris, for appellees.

ENGLISH, J. The original bill in this cause was filed by Jennie Bright, Helen E. Bright, and others against James Knight, and Jesse Bright, in his own right, and as administrator of Margaret Bright, deceased, in the circuit court of Greenbrier county. Jesse Bright was alleged to be the husband of Margaret Bright, who died on the 5th of March, 1880, and said Jesse Bright was appointed her administrator. It was further alleged in said bill that said Margaret Bright was at the time of her death the owner and in possession of 10 acres of land near the town of Lewisburg, in said county, on which were valuable and lasting improvements; that said land was purchased by said Margaret Bright at a sale made under a deed of trust given by Matthew V. Peers to George H. Peers; that said purchase was made on credit, and said Margaret Bright executed her bonds for the purchase money, with Jesse Bright, F. H. Ludington, and James Knight as her sureties, and she failed to pay said bonds at maturity, and she and her sureties were sued thereon, and a decree was rendered for the sale of said land in 1875. It is further alleged that said land was sold in 1881, and said Knight bought it for the children and heirs at law of the said Margaret Bright, deceased; that prior to said sale said Knight had been boarding with the plaintiff Jennie Bright, and so continued until some time in April, 1882, with the agreement that the price of his board should go as a payment on the advance he had made for the children of said Margaret Bright, deceased, in payment of said Peers' decree; that the original amount due from said Margaret Bright to G. H. Peers, in 1876, was $383.94, as shown by the delivery bond taken on the execution issued on said decree, and that at the same term of court at which said decree was rendered against said Margaret Bright and her sureties a judgment was rendered in said circuit court in favor of said Margaret Bright against F. H. and James C. Ludington for the sum of $416.50, as of the 29th of June, 1876; that said James Knight was sheriff of said county during the entire year 1876, and that by an agreement between said Margaret Bright and James Knight he was to take and collect the execution to be issued in favor of said Margaret Bright against said Ludingtons, and apply enough of the proceeds thereof to discharge the said G. H. Peers decree; that said execution was issued and went into the hands of said Knight as such sheriff, and that from the time he received it until the return-day thereof the said James C. Ludington had ample personal property out of which said execution, and every part thereof, could have been made, which property was well known to said James Knight, and said execution could have been made by him if he had tried to make the same, but that, either through negligence or favoritism to the defendants therein, he failed to make the money on said execution, but that equity would hold that done which ought to have been done, and, applying this principle, the debt was paid, and the heirs of said Margaret Bright were entitled to a deed for said land; and, to show that said Knight so understood the matter, the plaintiffs allege that the children and heirs of Margaret Bright have had the exclusive disposition and use of said property from the date of her death until the time of filing said bill; and to further show that said James Knight did not set up any claim to said property, as the owner thereof, the house thereon was consumed by fire after his supposed claim, and the children and heirs at law of Margaret Bright rebuilt the same in good faith, believing that no incumbrance was on the land, which rebuilding cost seven or eight hundred dollars, which was done within the knowledge, consent, and approval of said Knight, and without any claim set up by him at the time of the rebuilding that he was the real owner of the land, and that the said Knight delayed his purpose to claim the title to said property until the July term, 1887, of the circuit court of said county, at which time he obtained a writ of possession to place him in possession of said property, said writ to issue after the 1st day of November, 1887; and they pray that said Knight be compelled to settle with them, and make them a deed for said land; and they also ask a reference to a commissioner in order that it may be shown that he has been fully paid for the advance he made to purchase said land, and that said Knight might be enjoined and restrained from taking possession of said land under said writ of possession until said account should be taken, and the further order of the court. The said James Knight answered said bill, in which he says that he, F. H. Ludington, and Jesse Bright were sureties of Margaret Bright in a bond given for purchase money of the house and lot in the bill mentioned, and that on the 30th day of October, 1875, said circuit court, in the suit of George H. Peers against said Margaret Bright and others, rendered a personal decree against said sureties for the amount due on said bond, and decreed the sale of said house and lot to satisfy said balance of purchase money, and provided in said decree that, if any of said sureties should satisfy said decree for purchase money, the sale of said house and lot should be made for his benefit; that the said Jesse Bright and F. H. Ludington were insolvent, and that he was compelled to pay the balance of the purchase money due from said Margaret Bright, and that this fact, and the amount of said payment, having been made to appear in said cause to said court, a decree was rendered therein at the November term, 1876, directing said house and lot to be sold for his benefit; that sale was made of said house and lot on the 14th day of April, 1883, and the property was purchased by him, the purchase money settled, the sale confirmed by said court on the 2d day of May, 1883, and a deed was afterwards made to him. He denies that he purchased said land for any one else than himself, or that it was bought for the children and heirs at law of Margaret

Bright, deceased, and he denies all the allegations in the bill inconsistent with the foregoing statement. Said Knight also denies that he ever boarded with said Jennie Bright, or made any agreement with her, or any one on her behalf, that any board or other things should go as a credit in payment of the Peers decree, or the amount paid by him for said Margaret Bright; that said Jesse Bright and his children, the other parties to said suit, continued to occupy said property after respondent's said purchase, and that he and several of his children are still in the occupation thereof, but that none of them ever claimed to occupy any other position than as his tenants; that when he obtained said writ of possession, in July, 1887, said Jesse Bright agreed to surrender possession on the 1st of November, 1887, and to take good care of the property until that time, if said Knight would allow him to remain until said period, which was agreed upon, and the counsel of said Bright had an addition made to said order to the effect that said order should not issue until the 1st of November, 1887, but that, instead of surrendering said property as he agreed, the said Bright caused this suit to be instituted to get further use of said property. He also denies that he could ever have made anything on the said execution in favor of Margaret Bright against F. H. and J. C. Ludington, and says that he never agreed to take and collect said execution as alleged; that he never received one cent thereon; and that said execution was afterwards fully paid to said Jesse Bright, as administrator of Margaret Bright, by G. S. Bierly, upon a portion of whose lands said judgment on which it was based was a lien; and he alleges that said house was destroyed by fire and rebuilt long before the sale to him on the 14th of April, 1883; and he denies having conceded to the plaintiffs, or said Jesse Bright, any right in said property, but alleges that they remained in said property by his permission, which he from the time of said sale claimed as his own; and he denies all of the allegations of plaintiffs' bill inconsistent with his answer. This answer was filed, and was replied to generally, and the plaintiffs filed an amended bill, in which they allege that the two acres of land on which said house is situated was dropped from the land-books for Greenbrier county in 1851, and have not been entered thereon since, unless it was included and embraced in the Peers lot, and if it was intended to be included in said lot there is no title passed for the two acres, for no title has ever been vested in the grantor; that by entering on said two-acre lot after it had become forfeited to the state for non-entry, building their house thereon, and paying the taxes thereon for more than 10 years, they have, under the laws of the state of West Virginia, acquired title against all claimants whatever; that the house was built by plaintiffs in their own right, and not as heirs of Margaret Bright, as is shown by the mechanic's lien recorded against them and others, a copy of which they exhibit, and they also exhibit the survey and plat, which they claim shows the facts alleged in their amended bill, and which is taken from the old surveyor's books. The defendant James Knight, for answer to said amended bill, denied that any portion of the land in the bill mentioned was ever dropped from the landbooks as alleged, or otherwise became forfeited. He also denied the allegation that he has no title to the two acres upon which the house mentioned in the bill is situated, but says he has a good title thereto. He also denied that the plaintiffs, or any of them, have ever had any adversary possession of any part of the land in the bill mentioned, but, on the contrary, said that the plaintiffs' original bill shows that they claim under him and Margaret Bright, which is the fact. He denies that Exhibits 1 and 2, filed with said amended bill, are evidence of anything, or are copies from the surveyor's book, and he excepts to said exhibits as evidence in the cause. Numerous depositions were taken in the cause by both plaintiffs and defendants, and on the 16th day of November, 1882, the cause was heard, and the bill dismissed, and the plaintiffs appealed.

The plaintiffs rely upon the allegation in their bill that under the decree of sale made in 1875, which was executed in 1881, the defendant James Knight bought in the 10 acres of land in the bill mentioned for the children and heirs at law of Margaret Bright, deceased; that said Knight had, prior to the said sale, been boarding with Jennie Bright, and continued to board with her until some time in the month of April, 1882, with the agreement that the price of his board should go as a payment on the advance he had made for the children of Margaret Bright, deceased, in the payment of the Peers decree. This alleged agreement is entirely unsupported by the evidence in the cause. Jesse Bright, in one of his depositions, states, in answer to a question, that "it was certainly the understanding between me and Mr. Knight that he was to bid in the property for Jennie Bright," but not, as the bill alleges, "for the children and heirs at law of Margaret Bright, deceased;" and no witness in the cause proves the alleged agreement that the price of said Knight's board should go as a payment on the advance he had made for the children of Margaret Bright, deceased, in the payment of the Peers decree. It is alleged in the bill that said sale took place in 1881, and this fact is proven by the deposition of Jesse Bright; and Thomas Pare in his deposition says James Knight boarded with the plaintiff Jennie Bright from April, 1881, to February or March, 1882; and Jesse Bright states in his deposition that he boarded there about 12 months; so that, according to the plaintiffs' allegations and proofs, a considerable, if not the greater, portion of said account for board accrued subsequent to said sale. The plaintiffs, however, allege that an execution dated the 29th day of June, 1876, in favor of Margaret Bright, and against F. H. and J. C. Ludington, for $398.15, with interest from the 15th of June, 1876, and costs, $18.35, was placed in the hands of said James Knight, as sheriff, which he, as sheriff, was to collect, and apply

the proceeds thereof to the discharge of said Peers judgment, and that said Knight, through negligence or favoritism to the defendants, failed to make the money on said execution. It, however, appears from the evidence in the cause that J. M. McWhorter, as attorney for Jesse Bright, administrator of Margaret Bright, subjected certain lands which said F. H. Ludington had conveyed to his son-in-law, Bierly, to the payment of said judgment, and paid the proceeds to said Jesse Bright as such administrator. The theory upon which the plaintiffs seek to obtain relief in this cause is that the defendant Knight had in his hands, or should have had, money of theirs sufficient to pay for said property; and that, in pursuance of an agreement with them, he purchased said property for the children and heirs at law of the said Margaret Bright, deceased; and, having so purchased the same, it created a resulting trust in their favor; and they pray that said Knight may be compelled to make a settlement with the plaintiffs, and make to them a deed for the land; and, in order to show that he has been fully paid for the advances he made to purchase said land, they pray that the cause may be referred to a commissioner to take an account between the parties.

In the case of Shaffer v. Fetty, 30 W. Va. 248, 4 S. E. Rep. 278, (section 4 of syllabus,) this court held that "a resulting trust, arising from the payment by a stranger of the whole or a part of the purchase money of land conveyed to another, is a claim to the whole or a definite portion of the land, corresponding to the portion of the purchase money paid by such stranger, and not a lien upon the land for the sum of money paid by such stranger as a part of the purchase money." And in section 5 that, "in such a suit, the bill may be demurred to if it fails to state what portion of the entire purchase money of the land was paid by the plaintiff, who is seeking to set up such resulting trust." GREEN, J., in delivering the opinion of the court in that case, says, on page 258, 30 W. Va., and on page 283, 4 S. E. Rep.: "The whole doctrine of resulting trusts arising from the payment or part payment of the purchase money has been abrogated in some few of the states by statute, but not in this state. But it is admitted that this doctrine of resulting trust, arising from the payment of the whole or part of the purchase money by a person other than the grantor, should be acted on with great caution, and the circumstances from which a trust is to be raised must be clearly proven, (Faringer v. Ramsay, 4 Md. Ch. 33:) and the payment or advance of the purchase money must be made before or at the time of the purchase, and a subsequent payment will not, by relation, attach a 'trust to the original purchaser, (see Nixon's Appeal, 63 Pa. St. 279;) for the trust arises from the fact that the money of the real, and not the nominal, purchaser formed at the time the consideration of the purchase, and thus became converted into land in view of a court of equity. See Botsford v. Burr, 2 Johns Ch. 405, 414; Steere v. Steere, 5 Johns. Ch.

1, 19, 20." So in the case of Miller v. Blose's Ex'r, 30 Grat. 745, (section 2 of syllabus,) the court held that, "where the trust does not arise on the face of the deed, but is raised upon the payment of the purchase money, which creates a trust, which is to override the deed, the proof must be very clear, and mere parol evidence ought to be received with great caution." Also, in section 3 of syllabus, the court held that "a resulting trust must arise at the time of the execution of the conveyance, payment, or advance of the purchase money, before or at the time of the purchase, is indispensable. A subsequent payment will not, by relation, attach a trust to the original purchase; for the trust arises out of the circumstance that the moneys of the real, and not the nominal, purchaser formed at the time the consideration of the purchase, and became converted into land."

If we apply the principles enunciated in the cases above quoted to the facts alleged or proven in this case, we cannot hold that a resulting trust has been created either in favor of the heirs at law of Margaret Bright, or in favor of the plaintiff Jennie Bright. It appears from the allegations of the bill, and from the proof, that the defendant Knight boarded with Jennie Bright for a year ending in April, 1882; but no witness in the cause states what portion of said board money remained unpaid at the time of said sale, and no witness proves any agreement on the part of said Knight to apply the same as a credit upon the amount paid by him for said Margaret Bright; and said James Knight in his answer "denies that he ever boarded with Jennie Bright, or ever made any agreement with her, or any one on her behalf, that any board or other things should go as a credit in payment on the Peers decree, or the amount paid by him for said Margaret Bright, so that by the pleadings in the cause the burden of proving the existence of such an agreement, or the advance of money or other thing in lieu thereof at the time of the sale, devolved upon the plaintiffs. It is true that in case of Nease v. Capehart, 8 W. Va. 95, this court held that, "when a debtor has conveyed land to a trustee to secure a debt, and afterwards another person and the debtor agree that the former shall purchase the land, and hold it as a security for the purchase money he pays, and accordingly the debtor acquiesces, and the other purchases the land, that purchase constitutes a trust, which a court of equity will enforce;" but the case under consideration is very different from that. In this Margaret Bright became the purchaser of the land in controversy at a trust sale on a credit, and the defendant James Knight, together with said Jesse Bright and F. H. Ludington, became her sureties. Said Margaret Bright failed to pay the purchase money, and a decree was obtained subjecting said land to sale for the unpaid purchase money, and the decree which directed said sale also provided that said sureties, or either of them, were entitled upon the payment of said purchase money to be subrogated to the rights of George H. Peers, the plaintiff, and directed the commissioner therein appointed to sell said land at his or their request, and for his or their benefit. This gave the said Jesse Bright an ample opportunity to raise the money, if he had the ability, and pay off the Peers debt, and have the property sold for his benefit, or for Jennie Bright, or for the heirs at law of Margaret Bright. This decree was rendered in 1875, and the sale did not take place until some time in 1881, giving him ample time to raise the money, if he had the ability. There is no allegation in the plaintiff's bill that said land brought less than its value, or that the plaintiffs, or any one interested as an heir at law of Margaret Bright, were prevented from being present, and bidding on the property, by the representations of the defendant Knight, or that they, or any of them, are ready and willing to repay him the amount he paid for said land; but they rest their case, and rely merely on the allegation that at said sale, made in 1881, said land was bought in for the children and heirs at law of said Margaret Bright, deceased, by said Knight, with the agreement that the price of his board should go as a payment on the advance he had made for the children of Margaret Bright, deceased, in the payment of the Peers decree; and both the allegation aforesaid and the evidence show that said advance or payment had been made before the boarding was furnished. In the case of Jackman v. Ringland, 4 Watts & S. 149, (a state in which the seventh section of the statute of frauds had been omitted as in our state,) I think the law is correctly propounded. Justice ROGERS, in delivering the opinion of the court, said: "That parol evidence may be received to establish a trust has been repeatedly ruled, but the question is, what is a trust which comes within the principle? It is confined, as I take it, to those cases of resulting trusts which arise from an implication of law, as, for example, where the money is paid by one, the property purchased, and the title taken in the name of another. In such and similar cases, the legal title is in one, the equitable title in another, and, to prevent fraud, the fact of payment may be established by parol evidence; equity will decree the purchaser a trustee for the use of the person who paid the purchase money. But where there is nothing more in the transaction than is implied from the violation of a parol agreement, equity will not decree the purchaser a trustee. See Robertson v. Robertson, 9 Watts, (Pa.) 32; Haines v. O'Conner, 10 Watts, 313; Kisler v. Kisler, 2 Watts, 323; Fox v. Heffner, 1 Watts & S. 372. In the case of Dyer v. Dyer, reported in 1 White & T. Lead. Cas. Eq. pt. 1, p. 354, notes, it was held "that a grant cannot be affected with an oral trust for a third person merely on the ground of contract, nor unless the evidence goes far enough to establish fraud." This, however, is still an open question in this state, and, as we regard it, unnecessary to be decided in this case. There seems to be little conflict among the authorities upon this proposition, that where the statute of frauds does not apply, and a trust of land is allowed to be established by parol evidence, to establish such trust the facts must be alleged and the evidence to support them must be full, clear, and satisfactory. See Snavely v. Pickle, 29 Grat. 31; Phelps v. Seely, 22 Grat. 573. In the case of Bier v. Smith, 25 W. Va. 837, this court held that the allegations and the proof must correspond, and a decree based on a different case from that stated therein will be reversed, (see McFarland v. Dilly, 5 W. Va. 135; Baugher v. Eichelberger, 11 W. Va. 217; Floyd v. Jones, 19 W. Va. 359;) and the plaintiffs in this case having alleged that the defendant Knight bought said property in for the children and heirs at law of Margaret Bright, deceased, who are alleged in the bill to be Jennie Bright, Helen E. Bright, John B. Bright, Frank Bright, Abe Bright, Jesse Bright, Julia, wife of W. N. Curry, Maggie, wife of W. P. Stalnaker, Katie, wife of T. H. Pare, and Thomas Bright, and Samuel C. Bright; and the only proof in regard to the matter being found in the deposition of Jesse Bright, who when asked the question, "Tell whether or no there was any agreement between Mr. Knight and yourself as to the purchase of this property at that sale, whereby Mr. Knight was to bid off the property and hold it in trust for Jennie Bright, subject to his lien for whatever he might advance on the whole purchase," answered, "it was certainly the understanding between me and Mr. Knight that he was to bid in the property for Jennie Bright,"—it could hardly be contended that this proof corresponded with the plaintiffs' allegation that the property was purchased by said Knight under an agreement so to do for the above-named heirs at law of Margaret Bright, and certainly said bill could not be sustained on such proof. The plaintiffs file an amended bill, in which they claim that since their original bill was filed they have ascertained that the two acres of land on which their house is located was dropped from the land-books in 1851, and has never been entered thereon since, unless it was included in the Peers lot, and, if it was intended to be included in said lot, that no title passed for said two-acre lot, for no title had ever been vested in the grantor, and they, by entering on said lot, improving and paying taxes on the same, acquired title thereto against all claimants whatever. This claim is diametrically opposed to the one they assert in their original bill, in that they claim under Peers and Margaret Bright, and in the amended bill against them. The evidence, however, shows that on the 13th day of May, 1858, Ophelia Cary conveyed to M. V. Peers the 10 acres of land upon which he then lived, and, so far as appears, continued to live until purchased by Margaret Bright; and, if there was a forfeiture of any superior title, it would inure to the benefit of Peers and those claiming under him. They raise a question as to the boundary, but as they all claim under Peers, and he appears to have had possession under a deed calling for 10 acres since his purchase in 1858, a court of equity will not settle the title and boundaries of land, when the plaintiff has no equity against the party who is holding the land. See

Cresap v. Kemble, 26 W. Va. 603. See, also, Hill v. Proctor, 10 W. Va. 59, where this court held that "the existence of a controverted boundary does not constitute a sufficient ground for the interposition of courts of equity to ascertain and fix that boundary. It is necessary, to maintain such a bill, that some peculiar equity should be superinduced. There must be some equitable ground attaching itself to the controversy." For these reasons I am of opinion that there is no error in the decree complained of, and the same is affirmed, with costs and damages against the appellants.

LUCAS, P., and BRANNON and HOLT, JJ., concur.

BUMGARDNER et al. v. LEAVITT et al.

(Supreme Court of Appeals of West Virginia. March 31, 1891.)

SPECIFIC PERFORMANCE — CONTRACT TO DELIVER SHARES OF STOCK—REMEDY AT LAW.

1. As a general rule equity will not enforce specific performance of contracts for the delivery of shares of stock; but when a purchaser has bargained for or taken an option upon such shares because they have to him a unique and special value, the loss of which could not be adequately compensated by damages at law, the chancellor, in the exercise of a sound discretion, may decree specific execution.

2. Where such relief would be granted to the purchaser, were he to apply, the seller, who has given to the purchaser such preference or option, is entitled to like relief by reason of the operation of the principle of mutuality of right and remedy.

3. Where the remedy at law would be incomplete and inadequate because the court of law could not give a conditional or modified judgment, and would be unable to preserve the benefit of the agreement to all the parties interested, equity has jurisdiction to enforce the agreement.

(Syllabus by the Court.)

Appeal and supersedeas from circuit court, Wood county.

Loomis & Tavener, for appellants. Barna Powell and Okey Johnson, for appellees.

LUCAS, P. This suit originated by the filing of a bill in chancery by H. E. Bumgardner, a married woman, and H. F. Bumgardner, her husband, against C. P. Leavitt and others, in the circuit court of Wood county. The female plaintiff alleges that the defendant Leavitt induced her to invest $1,000 in the steam-boat General Dawes, the proposed cost of which was $7,500. It was understood that the boat was to be put in a joint-stock company, in which the plaintiff H. E. Bumgardner was to have shares in proportion to the money she had advanced, as aforesaid. The plaintiff exhibits with her bill an agreement as follows: "This article of agreement, made and entered into this the 14th day of July, 1884, between C. P. Leavitt, county of Wood, and state of West Virginia, and H. E. Bumgardner of Hockingport, Athens Co., Ohio, witnesseth, that the said C. P. Leavitt, in case of misunderstanding, or not being able to agree, or in case of death of Herman Bumgardner, agent, said Leavitt agrees to take the said stock of Mrs. Bumgardner at not exceeding cost, or, if boat depreciates in value, at fair cash valuation. The said Mrs. H. E. Bumgardner agrees to give said C. P. Leavitt the refusal over any other purchaser. The said stock referred to above is stock in the steamer General Dawes. [Signed] C. P. Leavitt." And there is further exhibited the following notice: "To Chas. P. Leavitt—Sir: I propose to sell you my stock in the Farmer's Trans. Co. in accordance with your contract of July 14, 1884, at cost, or, if the boat has depreciated in value, at its fair cash valuation. Your early attention is called to this matter, the contingency having arisen under which you bound yourself to take said stock. [Signed] H. E. Bumgardner, by H. F. Bumgardner, Ag't. March 31, 1887." The bill supplements the above-written agreement, signed by C. P. Leavitt, by stating that it was a part of the consideration that the husband, H. F. Bumgardner, was to have regular employment on said steam-boat, of which said C. P. Leavitt was to be master. It is further alleged that all of the interests, including the stock owned by Leavitt, (which was a large majority of it,) as well as that owned by H. E. Bumgardner, was capitalized into a corporation known as the Farmer's Transportation Company, or conveyed to said company. The steamer was valued at $7,600 at that time, and 760 shares of capital stock of the par value of $10 per share were issued, of which 100 shares were given to said H. E. Bumgardner, and 1½ shares to her husband, in order that he might be represented in the company. It is further alleged that C. P. Leavitt took charge as master, and pursuant to the agreement gave H. F. Bumgardner employment, but that they soon disagreed, and said H. F. Bumgardner was discharged. Plaintiffs proceed to aver that since such disagreement they have at all times been ready to give said Leavitt the preference of purchasing said stock, and have urged him to buy said stock according to his agreement, but he has steadily and persistently refused to do so, until the 31st day of March, 1887, when the above notice was written and served. They charge that there has been no depreciation in the value of the boat, but that it has been increased in size and capacity at a large expense, and its value enhanced in consequence. It is futher alleged that one E. W. Petty, who is made a defendant, had attached the 101½ shares of stock in the circuit court of Wood county in an action at law against H. F. Bumgardner. It is further alleged that the plaintiffs were largely indebted to J W Arnold and L. H. Arnold, both of whom were made defendants, and that the female plaintiff executed a lien upon the said 100 shares of stock to secure said indebtedness. By an agreement and compromise between the plaintiffs and said E. W. Petty his debt is reduced to $422, which it is agreed shall be paid him out of the proceeds arising from the sale of said 101½ shares of stock; and by like agreement with J. W. and L. H. Arnold, they are to receive the residue of the proceeds of said sale as a compromise, and in

full settlement of the indebtedness due them from the plaintiffs. Plaintiff H. E. Bumgardner, it is alleged, has always been ready, and has offered, and now offers, to specifically perform the said agreement on her part, by assigning and transferring said 101½ shares of the stock free and unincumbered, as of the 31st day of March, 1887. The prayer of the bill is that the court will declare the plaintiff to be entitled to a specific performance and execution of the said agreement, with interest on the said amount from March 31, 1887; second, that the court will decree that the amount ascertained to be due said H. E. Bumgardner from said C. P. Leavitt may be paid over to said E. W. Petty and said J. W. and L. H. Arnold, as above set out; and, thirdly, for all proper accounts and general relief. The bill was demurred to by Leavitt, but the demurrer was overruled, whereupon C. P. Leavitt filed his answer, in which he admits the agreement as set out in the bill, so far as it goes, but he denies it was ever understood or contemplated that the said H. F. Bumgardner should have the right, at any time he might thereafter see fit, to require respondent to buy the stock of said H. E. Bumgardner, and to require respondent to pay therefor the original cost, but in truth it was intended to give respondent refusal and right to buy said stock at any time, provided he paid therefor as much as any other bidder, and provided, furthermore, that respondent so desired. He alleges that the boat is not worth more than $2,500, and one-third of what she cost at the time said stock was issued; and that the present value of said 101½ shares in the bill mentioned is not worth more than $333.33½ at the outside. He denies that the stock has ever been tendered him, or that either of the plaintiffs have ever proffered the same at anything like a fair cash valuation. He admits that on or about the ———— day of July, 1887, he offered them $850 for the stock, although he knew that they had immediately before that offered it to another party at $800. He alleges that it had been assigned by H. E. Bumgardner to Mrs. J. W. Arnold, to secure payment of a debt, and the certificate was then held by one L. N. Tavener, as attorney for said Arnold, who had notified the secretary of the corporation, and requested a transfer on the books. Respondent sets out also that the certificate was incumbered by a lien of said E. W. Petty, and he pleads that the plaintiffs had not title to said stock, and so could not carry out the agreement. Respondent further alleges that his said offer of $850 was made in good faith, and he was ever ready from the time he offered in 1887 to buy said stock to take the same, but his offer was not accepted, nor was there ever tendered to respondent the said stock at any time, nor could it be, since they had parted with the title. He denies that he ought in equity to be compelled to pay for the stock, which cannot be delivered, and is incumbered to the full amount of its value. J. W. Arnold and L. H. Arnold filed their joint and separate answer, in which they admit all that is said in the bill about the mortgage or pledge of the stock to them, and admit that they have agreed that out of the proceeds arising from the sale E. W. Petty should be first paid, and that they would accept the residue of the proceeds in full satisfaction of their lien, and that they have accordingly authorized L. N. Tavener, Esq., their attorney to execute their release, in order that said H. E. Bumgardner may execute to said defendant C. P. Leavitt an unincumbered transfer of said 100 shares of stock in fulfillment of said H. E. Bumgardner's contract on her part, as set out in Exhibit No. 1 of the bill. E. W Petty likewise answers, and admits all the averments of the bill as to his lien upon the stock by attachment, and also the agreement with reference to his payment out of the proceeds of sale.

A vast amount of testimony was taken, very little of which had anything to do with the case, the bulk of it seeming to be predicated upon some extraneous controversies as to the earnings of the boat, and Leavitt's settlement with the corporation and stockholders. On the 10th of December, 1888, the case came on to be finally heard, and the court decreed that H. E. Bumgardner was entitled to specific execution of the contract; that demand was made by her on the 31st day of March, 1887; and that the 101¼ shares of stock were then worth $866.60; and the said C. P. Leavitt is decreed to pay that amount, with interest from 31st day of March, 1887, aggregating the sum of $954.76, which he is to pay, with interest thereon from the date of decree. The money is to be distributed to the Arnolds and Petty in accordance with their respective liens, and agreements with reference to the same. The decree then proceeds to direct "that L. N. Tavener, who is authorized in a writing filed in the papers in this cause to release the lien of said J. W. Arnold and L. H. Arnold upon 100 shares of the stock aforesaid, to execute said release of said lien, and, in case said L. N. Tavener shall fail or refuse to execute said release within ten days from this date, then Barna Powell, who is hereby appointed a special commissioner for the purpose, is authorized and directed to execute a release of the lien of said J. W. Arnold and L. H. Arnold, as aforesaid, upon the 100 shares of stock held in the name of H. E. Bumgardner and filed with the papers in this cause, which certificate of 100 shares, as well as the certificate of 101¼ shares now also in the file in this cause, are to be delivered to said C. P. Leavitt upon payment by him, or some one for him, to the defendants Petty and Arnolds and plaintiffs, the sum hereinbefore decreed by him to be paid." Leave was given to the plaintiffs to sue out execution. From this decree the defendant Leavitt has appealed to this court.

The first and pivotal question to be decided in this case is whether the court of chancery had jurisdiction to decree specific performance. If not, the bill should have been dismissed on demurrer. In the first place, regarding the defendant Leavitt, as having for a consideration obtained the refusal of, or, as we may call it, the option on, this stock, could he have maintained a bill for specific performance against Mrs. H. E. Bumgardner in case she had refused to let him have the stock, and had insisted on selling it to some one else? This is an important question, because, if such relief could be granted to the purchaser were he to apply, the seller, who has given the purchaser such preference or option, is entitled to like relief by reason of the operation of the principle of mutuality of right and remedy. The general doctrine upon this subject is thus stated by Mr. Pomeroy: "It is not then sufficient in general that a valid and binding agreement exists, and that an action at law for damages will lie in favor of either party for a breach by the other; the peculiarly distinctive feature of the equitable doctrine is that the remedial right to a specific performance must be mutual." See Moore v. Fitz Randolph, 6 Leigh, 175. This is a general rule, namely, that the right to a specific execution of a contract, so far as the question of mutuality is concerned, depends upon whether the agreement itself is obligatory on both parties, so that upon the application of either against the other the court would grant a specific performance. Duvall v. Myers, 2 Md. Ch. 401. Says Mr. Pomeroy: "It is a familiar doctrine that if the right to the specific performance of a contract exists at all, it must be mutual. The remedy must be alike attainable by both parties to the agreement." Pom. Spec. Perf. § 165. In the present case it appears that the defendant Leavitt, being the owner of about three-fourths of the stock in a steamboat, entered into an agreement with a married woman with reference to $1,000 of the same stock. It is true that the contract was signed by him alone. The circumstance that it was signed by him alone is not material, since it is admitted by both parties that she entered into the contract, and was to be bound by it. Wat. Spec. Perf. §§ 268, 270. Neither is the fact that she was a married woman material in this state, since, by our married woman's act, which went into operation in 1869, (see Code, c. 66,) a married woman may not only take and hold personal property, such as stocks, but, being such a stockholder, she may vote the same in any organised company; consequently she had the right of disposition and the power to sell or contract to sell. It is also true that, according to her statement, personal services entered into a part of the consideration of the contract, and it is a rule almost universal that a contract for personal services cannot be enforced against the party promising such services, and hence for the want of the requisite mutuality specific execution will not be enforced against the opposite party, unless the services have been actually performed, and the contract to that extent been executed, as was the case here. Pom. Spec. Perf. § 310.

These obstacles being disposed of, we may inquire, had Mrs. Bumgardner persisted in selling this stock to a third party, contrary to her agreement, could Leavitt have asked the court of chancery to interfere by injunction, and to compel her to transfer the stock to him upon payment of the price stipulated in the agreement? The question of specific performance of contracts for the delivery of stock is frequently treated by the text-writers in an empirical and unsatisfactory manner, as if there were something peculiar in this character of personal property, which rendered it impossible to classify it under any general rule. Mr. Fry, for example, does not hesitate to say positively that a contract for the sale of stock will not be specifically enforced, although he afterwards admits that railway shares form an exception. Fry, Spec. Perf. §§ 24, 27. Mr. Pomeroy's treatment of the subject is equally unsatisfactory. See Pom. Spec. Perf. §§ 17-19. The true principle would seem to be that, as a general rule, courts of equity will not enforce specific performance of contracts for the delivery of shares of stock, but when a purchaser has bargained for such shares, or taken an option upon them, because they have for him a unique and special value, the loss of which could not be adequately compensated by damages at law, the chancellor, in the exercise of a sound discretion, may decree specific execution. This principle we find laid down and insisted upon in the more recent work of Mr. Waterman, (1881.) "The same principles," he says, "govern in contracts for the sale of stock as in the sale of other property,—that is, if a breach can be fully compensated in damages, equity will not interfere; while it will do so when, notwithstanding the payment of the money value of the stock, the plaintiff will still lose a substantial benefit, and thereby remain uncompensated. If a contract to convey stock is clear and definite, and the uncertain value of the stock renders it difficult to do justice by an award of damages, specific performance will be decreed." Wat. Spec. Perf. § 19. Among the many other cases cited in support of this proposition is the leading case of Doloret v. Rothschild, decided by Sir John Leach, vice-chancellor, in 1824, 1 Sim. & S. 590, in which it is said that a bill will lie for the specific performance of a contract for the purchase of government stock, where it prays for the delivery of certificates which give the legal title to the stock. There are many other cases, however, both in England and America, which sustain the correct principle as laid down above, but which it is unnecessary to cite. In the present case the purchaser of the refusal of or option upon the stock in the steam-boat was dealing for an article which he could not go upon the market and buy, and which no one could deliver to him but the holder, with whom he bargained. The shares of stock evidently had for him a peculiar value, which could not be compensated by mere damages, such as would be recovered at law. Their possession would enable him to control the company, and to retain his position as master of the vessel. For the same reason, therefore, that a contract for railway shares will frequently be specifically performed, viz., whenever such shares are being purchased for the purposes of organization and control, I think a court of equity would have interfered in this case in favor of C. P. Leavitt, had he

filed a bill praying for its intervention. It follows, therefore, upon the ground of mutuality of remedy and reciprocity of obligation, that such a bill could be maintained by Mrs. Bumgardner. There is another ground quite as apparent as that stated above, and that is that the legal title to this stock had passed into the hands of a third party, who is properly made a co-defendant. In the case cited above of Doloret v. Rothschild, 1 Sim. & S. 590, the vice-chancellor remarks: "I consider also that the plaintiff, not being the original holder of the scrip, but merely the bearer, may not be able to maintain any action at law upon the contract, and that, if he has any title, it must be in equity." So in the present case the plaintiffs are in a situation in which a court of equity sees its way clearly to administer complete and adequate remedial justice to all parties interested, whereas, if they were remitted to a court of law, if relief could be afforded at all, it could only be done by resorting to several actions, perhaps no less than three. Upon the general principle, therefore, of avoiding circuity of action, and affording relief where the remedy at law is inadequate, it was proper for the court of equity to exercise its jurisdiction. Whenever the remedy at law would be incomplete and inadequate because the court of law cannot give a conditional or modified judgment, and would be unable to preserve the benefit of the agreement to all the parties interested, equity has jurisdiction to enforce the agreement. In the case of Summers v. Bean, the general principle is thus declared by Judge Moncure, (13 Grat. 412:) "Generally an adequate remedy may be had at law for the breach of a contract concerning any other personality than slaves, and therefore, as a general rule, a court of equity will not enforce the execution of such a contract. But sometimes an adequate remedy at law cannot be had for the breach of such a contract, and then its specific execution will be enforced in equity." As it was said in May v. Le Claire, 11 Wall. 218, in order to oust the equity jurisdiction, the remedy at law must be "as effectual and complete as the chancellor can make it." The same principle is recognized by all the text-writers. See Fry, Spec. Perf. § 18; Pom. Spec. Perf. § 29. Mr. Waterman says tersely: "If, however, the remedy at law would be wholly inadequate or impracticable, specific performance will be decreed." Wat. Spec. Perf. § 17. For these reasons, therefore, we think there was no error in overruling the demurrer to the plaintiffs' bill. Upon the merits, although there was, as we have said, a great deal of unnecessary testimony taken, the plaintiffs' case might have rested, and no doubt did rest, upon the testimony of the defendant C. P. Leavitt himself. Out of the 168 questions propounded to him, of which some were frivolous, and nearly all impertinent, he is asked on the 103d question whether he did not offer Mrs. Bumgardner $850 for her stock, in order to get rid of Bumgardner, to which he replies: "Yes; I wanted to get rid of him. Here is one of the clerks right here who asked him what he would take for it at different times." 104th question: "Did you not make a proposition to buy the stock on account of your obligation under that contract? Answer. Oh, yes; several times. I guess the clerk here knows that I made offers at different times through Mr. Ritchie, and Mr. Baringer can testify to the same thing." The defendant further testifies that these offers were made in March, 1887, or a little after that time, and that the negotiations would have been concluded, except for some trivial and inconsequential dispute about matters foreign to the subject-matter. To take the defendant, therefore, at his own word, and fix the value of the stock at a price only differing by a few dollars from what he himself offered, with interest from the time of his offer, was a judgment of the circuit court of which he has no right to complain, and we think, therefore, that the decree complained of should be in all respects affirmed.

BROWN *et al.* v. BUTLER *et al.*

(Supreme Court of Appeals of Virginia. April 9, 1891.)

LIMITATIONS—EXCEPTIONS—BONA FIDE PURCHASER —LIEN OF JUDGMENT.

1. Code Va. § 3573, prohibits the enforcement of a judgment lien upon which the right to issue execution or bring *scire facias* or action is barred by sections 3577 and 3578. Section 3577 provides that execution may issue within a year, and a *scire facias* or action may be brought within 10 years after judgment, and, where execution issues within the year, other executions may be issued, or a *scire facias* or action may be brought within 10 years from the return-day of an execution on which there is no return, or within 20 years from the return-day of an execution on which there is such return. Judgment in a justice court was obtained February 23, 1866, duly docketed, but upon which no execution was issued, and a judgment of the circuit court of November 2, 1866, also was duly docketed, on which no execution was issued. Suit was brought to enforce the liens of the judgments April 30, 1887. *Held,* that the right was barred by limitation.

2. Code Va. § 2933, provides that where a right accrues against a person who had before resided in the state, and who departs therefrom, or by any other indirect means obstructs the prosecution of such right, the time such obstruction continues shall not be computed as part of the time within which the right should have been prosecuted. A judgment debtor at the date of the judgment resided in the state, and was a carpenter by trade, and for several years after judgment he went from place to place in different states, working at his trade, leaving his family all the time in the place where the judgment was obtained. His wife testified that only three months before her deposition he wrote "he was coming home," and that his family were expecting him home, had he not died. *Held,* that there was no such obstruction as contemplated by the statute, as the judgment debtor had not left the state with the purpose of changing his residence.

3. Where lands are bought under a parol agreement, and the price is paid, and visible possession taken before notice of the rendition of a judgment, the subsequent docketing of a judgment against the vendor before the deed to the land is recorded creates no lien.

Appeal from hustings court of city of Manchester.

L. O. Wendenburg, for appellants. *J. M. Gregory* and *Courtney & Patterson,* for appellees.

LEWIS, P. This was a creditors' suit in the hustings court of Manchester to subject certain lots of land situate within the present limits of that city to the satisfaction of three judgments, recovered many years ago, against Joseph Butler, now deceased. The lots in question were sold, but not conveyed, by Butler prior to the rendition of the judgments, and the question is whether, in the hands of his alienees or those claiming under them, they are subject to the lien of the judgments. At the hearing the court below dismissed the bill, whereupon the plaintiffs appealed. The judgments in question are as follows, viz.: (1) A judgment in favor of A. A. Jenks for $23.70 and costs, obtained before a justice of the peace of Chesterfield county on the 23d of February, 1866, which was duly docketed, but upon which no execution has ever issued; (2) a judgment in favor of Jenks for $500, with interest and costs, obtained in the circuit court of Chesterfield county on the 2d day of November, 1866, which also was duly docketed, but upon which no execution has ever issued; and (3) a judgment in favor of William B. Jones & Co. for $240.90, with interest and costs, obtained at the March term, 1867, of the same court. A few days thereafter an execution of *fi. fa.* was issued on this judgment, returnable to the ensuing May rules, which was returned, "No effects." The judgment was docketed on the 20th of March, 1867. As to the first two judgments, we are of opinion that the defense of the statute of limitations is well founded. No execution has ever been issued on either of them, and the present suit was not commenced until April 30, 1887. The provision of the statute (Code, § 3573) is express that no suit shall be brought to enforce the lien of a judgment, upon which the right to issue an execution or bring a *scire facias* or an action is barred by sections 3577 and 3578; and by section 3577 it is provided that "on a judgment execution may be issued within a year, and a *scire facias* or an action may be brought within ten years after the date of the judgment; and, where execution issues within the year, other executions may be issued, or a *scire facias* or an action may be brought, within ten years from the return-day of an execution on which there is no return by an officer, or within twenty years from the return-day of an execution on which there is such return," with certain exceptions not material to the present case. The appellants, however, contend that the limitation of the statute is repelled by the judgment debtor's departure without the state, and absence therefrom, and they rely upon the case of Ficklin's Ex'r v. Carrington, 31 Grat. 219. On the other hand, the appellees contend that that decision has no application to the present case—*First,* because the exception contained in the statute, which was construed in that case, applies only to the person who obstructs the prosecution of any such right as is mentioned in the statute; and, *secondly,* because there was no such departure from the state by the judgment debtor in the present case as is contemplated by the statute. The statute provides that where any such right as is mentioned therein "shall accrue against a person who had before resided in this state, if such person shall, by departing without the same, or by absconding or concealing himself, or by any other indirect ways or means, obstruct the prosecution of such right, the time that such obstruction may have continued shall not be computed as any part of the time within which the said right might or ought to have been prosecuted. But this section shall not avail against any other person than him so obstructing, notwithstanding another might have been jointly sued with him. If there had been no such obstruction." Code, § 2983.

With respect to the first branch of the appellees' contention, above stated, we are of opinion that, so long as a judgment is in existence as against the judgment debtor, the lien thereof continues, and may be enforced in equity, although the real estate sought to be subjected is in the hands of a purchaser who has in no way obstructed the prosecution of the plaintiff's right, provided, of course, the lien is in other respects enforceable against such real estate. In the present case, however, we agree with the appellees that there has been no such obstruction as is contemplated by the statute, and consequently that the case is not within the exception contained in the statute above quoted. When the judgments were obtained, the judgment debtor was confessedly a resident of this state, having a family and a home in the city of Manchester. It appears that he was, by trade, a carpenter and bridge builder, and that several years after the rendition of the judgments he left Manchester, "going first to one place and then another," working at his trade. His daughter, Mrs. Burton, who was examined as a witness in the cause, testifies that he traveled about a good deal. "I received letters from him," she says, "from Tennessee, Cincinnati, St. Louis, Norfolk, and other places." His wife and family, however, continued to reside in Manchester, to which place he occasionally returned. And the preponderance of the evidence is to the effect that he regarded that city as his home until his death, which occurred after the institution of the present suit. Mrs. Burton testifies that only three months before her deposition was taken he wrote "he was coming home,"—i. e., to Manchester,—and she added: "We were expecting him home Christmas, had he not died." He died in Baltimore, where for a number of years he spent the most of his time. That he and his wife lived unhappily together is not disputed, nor is it disputed that he left Manchester much indebted; but the evidence does not shew that he ever intended to totally abandon his family, or to become a resident of another state. "Departing without the state," within the meaning of the statute, is a removal from the state, with the intention of changing one's residence. It is different from absconding or concealing one's self, and the burden of proving such removal in the present case was on the plaintiffs. Pitson v. Bushong, 29 Grat. 229; Lindsay v. Murphy, 76 Va. 428. The case of Ficklin's Ex'r v.

Carrington is not in conflict with these views; for there it was admitted that the defendant, after the cause of action accrued, left the state, and became a resident of another state. The court, however, in deciding the case, laid down the broad doctrine that such a removal operates, *proprio vigore*, an obstruction, within the meaning of the statute, to the prosecution of the plaintiff's right during the period of the debtor's absence. It is somewhat remarkable that no allusion was made in the opinion to Wilson v. Koonts, 7 Cranch, 202. In that case a substantially similar statute of this state was the subject of construction, and it was there held by the supreme court, speaking by Chief Justice MARSHALL, that it was essential, in order to bring the case within the exception contained in the statute, that the plaintiff should have been actually obstructed by the removal of the defendant. And in 1 Rob. Pr. (old) p. 109, the author expresses the same view, saying that the mere circumstance of the defendant's removal is not sufficient where there is no evidence to show that the plaintiff intended to bring his action sooner than he did, or that he was in fact delayed by the defendant's removal. The same view is also expressed by the learned author of the Institutes, in construing the statute as it now is, and as it was when Ficklin's Ex'r v. Carrington was decided. "It must appear," he says, "that the complainant was actually defeated or obstructed in bringing his action; not merely that he might have been so;" citing Wilson v. Koonts, supra; 4 Minor, Inst. 514. Without stopping, however, to inquire whether these decisions are irreconcilable, and, if so, which is the correct one, it is enough, for the purposes of the present case, to say that upon the facts already adverted to we are of opinion that the appellants are not shown to have been obstructed in the prosecution of their rights, either actually or constructively. The bar of the statute was, therefore, complete when the suit was commenced. As to the order made by the circuit court of Chesterfield county on the 15th of November, 1887, after the commencement of the suit, purporting to revive the second judgment, above mentioned, on a *scire facias* sued out against Butler, the judgment debtor, it is clear that that order cannot affect the rights of the purchasers whose property is sought to be subjected in this suit. Not only were they not parties to the proceeding, but the judgment had been "annihilated" by time and the operation of the statute before the *scire facias* was sued out; and the principle has not only been affirmed by this court, but it is now settled by statute that the lien of a judgment ceases with the life of the judgment. Hutcheson v. Grubbs, 80 Va. 251; Code, § 3573; Ayre's Adm'r v. Burke, 82 Va. 338. The principal defense set up against the third judgment (which is not barred by the statute) is that the lots in question were purchased under parol contracts; that the purchasers at once took actual, visible, and notorious possession; and that the purchase money was fully paid before notice of the judgment, actual or constructive.

In other words, the contention is that the case is within the principle decided in Floyd v. Harding, 28 Grat. 401; and we are of opinion that this position is well taken. The most of the lots in question were sold at public auction, through Grubbs & Williams, auctioneers, on the 29th of December, 1865. The deeds, however, were not delivered until after the docketing of the judgments. There was no other contemporaneous writing evidencing the sales than the auctioneer's memorandum, which was as follows, to-wit:

"Dec. 29th. Auction sale of real estate of Jos. Butler. Terms, one-third cash; bal. at 6 and 12 mos., with int. added. Lots on Manchester and Falling Creek turnpike:

Lot 30 ft. front at $2.10—Ed. Chenault....$ 63 00
"   30 "   "   " 1.90—Wm. Heider..... 57 00
"   90 "   "   " 1.60—J. C. Laughton... 144 00
"   30 "   "   " 1.75—Stephen Ryan.... 52 50
"   60 "   " with frame house—W. T.
                    Brooks................. 306 00
"   30 "   " at $1.90—Chas. Severance.. 57 00"

This writing, although a sufficient "memorandum" to satisfy the statute of frauds, is not such a contract in writing as, by the registry acts, is required to be recorded. And as to the lot on what is now Decatur street, sold privately to S. A. Moles on the 1st day of October, 1866, we are of opinion that that transaction also is within the protection of the principle decided in Floyd v. Harding. The transaction was treated by the commissioner as a parol contract, and we think he was warranted in so treating it. Upon the other points made by the defendants, namely, that the purchasers took immediate and notorious possession of the lots purchased by them, respectively, and that the purchase money was fully paid before notice of the judgment, a great deal of testimony was taken before the commissioner, which is copied into the record. We do not deem it necessary to review it. It is enough to say we have examined it carefully, and are satisfied with the conclusion reached by the learned judge of the hustings court. The decree dismissing the bill is therefore affirmed.

CUSTIS v. COMMONWEALTH.

Supreme Court of Appeals of Virginia. April 2, 1891.

CRIMINAL LAW—HOMICIDE—TRIAL—JURY—EVIDENCE—VARIANCE.

1. Where, on indictment for murder, defendant's motion in arrest of judgment is overruled, and on the following day of the term the court, of its own motion, sets the verdict aside, and remands defendant for another trial, he is not entitled to his discharge, on the ground that his motion in arrest of judgment was sustained.

2. Setting aside a verdict and granting a new trial in a criminal case does not expunge the plea of not guilty previously entered, and it is too late for defendant, on the new trial, while the plea is standing, to plead in abatement that the record does not show that a *venire facias* was issued to summon the grand jury by which the indictment was found.

3. Act Va. Feb. 24, 1890, (Acts 1889-90, p. 79,) requiring the judge of each county and corporation court, at least 10 days before the commencement of every term, to set each criminal case for trial on a certain day, does not apply to the circuit courts.

4. The appearance of 16 of the 20 persons ordered to be summoned from the list furnished by the judge to serve as jurors is sufficient, under Code Va. § 4019, providing that in cases of felony, "where a sufficient number of jurors to constitute a panel of sixteen persons free from exception cannot be had from those summoned," additional persons may be summoned from the by-standers; and it is not error for the court to refuse to cause the appearance of the four persons originally summoned.

5. Of persons summoned on a *venire* in a felony case, six, who were found free from exception, were allowed to separate during an adjournment to a future day of the term, being cautioned not to converse about the case, and were subsequently sworn as jurors without being again examined on their *voir dire. Held,* no error.

6. Pending a murder trial defendant was taken apparently with a fit, and was removed from the court room, the trial being suspended, and examined by physicians, who testified that, in their opinion, he was sane, and merely shamming, though under great mental excitement. After walking in the court-yard he was brought back into court. *Held,* that the trial was properly resumed.

7. On indictment for murder, a physician testified that he had examined deceased, and thought death resulted from wounds which he found on his head. A witness testified that defendant confessed to him that, with others, he went to deceased's store, and struck him on the head, and killed him, and that a companion threw a mattress on him and ignited it. He also testified that defendant stated that, after the mattress was fired, he heard deceased groan, but it appeared that defendant was at the time one-third of a mile away, with the wind blowing towards deceased. *Held,* that the jury were justified in finding that death was caused by the wounds on the head.

8. Proof that deceased died from wounds on the left side of his head is not a material variance from an allegation that the wounds were on the right side.

Error to circuit court, Norfolk county.

Murdaugh & Marshall, for plaintiff in error. *R. Taylor Scott,* Atty. Gen., for the Commonwealth.

LEWIS, P. The prisoner was indicted in the county court of Norfolk county for the murder of Terrence L. Waller, and upon his arraignment demanded to be tried in the circuit court of that county. He was thereupon remanded for trial in the circuit court, pursuant to the provisions of section 4016 of the Code. At the ensuing term of that court he pleaded not guilty; and, having been put upon his trial, was found guilty by the jury of murder in the first degree. He thereupon moved for a new trial, which motion was overruled. Whereupon he moved in arrest of judgment, which motion also was overruled. But on a subsequent day of the term the court, of its own motion, set aside the verdict, and remanded the prisoner for trial at a special term, to be held on the 24th of April then next ensuing. On the last-mentioned day the prisoner was 'again led to the bar. Whereupon he moved that he be discharged, on the ground that his motion in arrest of judgment at the previous term had been sustained, but the motion was overruled; to which ruling he excepted, and this ruling is the subject of the first assignment of error here. The question thus raised is a simple one of fact, to be determined by the record, and that shows, as above stated, that the motion in arrest of judgment was overruled. Nothing more upon that point, therefore, need be said.

The prisoner next moved the court to quash the indictment, on the ground that it did not affirmatively appear from the record that a *venire facias* had been issued to summon the grand jury by which the indictment had been found, and the overruling of this motion is the subject of the second assignment of error. In support of this assignment, Hall's Case, 80 Va. 555, and a number of subsequent decisions of this court have been cited to the effect that a *venire* is an indispensable process, both at common law and under the statute, to authorize the sheriff or other officer to summon a jury in a felony case, and therefore that the record must affirmatively show that a *venire* was issued; and these decisions, it is contended, apply as well to the summoning of the grand jury as the petit jury. But this is a mistaken view. It has never been held, either in England or in Virginia, that the award of process to summon a grand jury must affirmatively appear by the record, and there is no principle for so holding. At common law the process for summoning a grand jury was a precept, either in the name of the king, or of two or more justices of the peace, directed to the sheriff. This was anterior to and independent of any action of the court, the object being to have a grand jury in attendance at the commencement of the term. The court, however, had power to have a grand jury summoned during the term, as occasion might require. Burton's Case, 4 Leigh, 645. By statute, in Virginia, until a comparatively recent period, the sheriff was required, *ex officio*, to summon a grand jury to attend to the first day of every term prescribed by law, as a substitute for the precept above mentioned. And now the statute (Code, § 3976) provides that a *venire facias* to summon a regular grand jury shall be issued by the clerk prior to the commencement of each term at which such grand jury is required. It by no means follows, however, because a *venire* is now the proper process to summon as well a grand jury as a petit jury, that the same strictness is required in each case. On the contrary, it is well settled that exceptions to the mode of summoning a grand jury, or to the disqualifications of particular grand jurors, must be made at a preliminary stage of the case,—that is, before a plea to the merits; otherwise they will be considered as waived, unless, indeed, the proceeding be void *ab initio*. "After the general issue, or any plea in bar," says Bishop, "it is too late to plead in abatement, except on leave to withdraw the former, because the plea in bar admits whatever is ground only of abatement." 1 Bish. Crim. Proc. (3d Ed.) § 756. This subject was very fully considered in U. S. v. Gale, 109 U. S. 65, 3 Sup. Ct. Rep. 1, in which case objection was made for the first time after verdict, on the ground of the alleged wrongful exclusion of four persons from the grand jury, and it was held that the objection came too late. The rule

was recognized that where the whole proceeding of forming the panel is void, as where the jury is not a jury of the court or term in which the indictment is found, or has been selected by persons having no authority whatever to select them, objection may be taken at any time. But where the objection, it was said, was founded upon an irregularity in summoning the panel, or upon the disqualification of particular jurors, it must be taken before pleading in bar. It would be trifling with justice, it was added, and would render criminal proceedings a farce, if the rule were otherwise. In State v. Carver, 49 Me. 588, the defendant, after a general plea of guilty, moved in arrest of judgment, on the ground that the grand jury had not been legally drawn, and had no power to act in the premises. But the motion was overruled, although it appeared from the return on the *venire facias* that one of the grand jurors had no authority to act as such. It was held, however, that neither the *venire* nor the return thereon constituted any part of the record, and, moreover, that, by pleading generally to the indictment, all matters in abatement were waived. The same doctrine was recently held by this court in Early's Case, 86 Va. 921, 11 S. E. Rep. 795. In that case, which was an indictment for arson, the prisoner, upon his arraignment, pleaded not guilty, and at a subsequent term asked leave to withdraw the plea, and to plead in abatement, on the ground that the grand jury had not been legally summoned, and because one of the grand jurors was disqualified. But the trial court overruled the motion, and this ruling was affirmed. In the course of its opinion, this court said: "By pleading the general issue alone, a defendant has always been understood to waive the right to interpose afterwards a plea in abatement. The settled doctrine, however, is that the judge may permit a pleading to be withdrawn, and another one to be substituted, whenever by so doing he does not violate any positive rule of law or of established practice. But such a discretion will rarely, if ever, be exercised in aid of an attempt to rely upon a merely dilatory or formal defense."

In the present case the prisoner, upon his arraignment in the circuit court, pleaded not guilty, upon which plea alone the trial was had. When the verdict was afterwards set aside and a new trial awarded, the case was in the same situation in which it was when the first trial began; that is to say, all the proceedings subsequent to the joinder of issue on the plea having been set aside, the commonwealth and the prisoner were at issue on the plea of not guilty. To say that the effect of granting a new trial is to "expunge," as has been claimed in this case, the plea previously entered, and to leave the case just as if there had been no plea entered at all, is to assert a proposition not founded in reason, and one that has never been recognized in any jurisdiction where the rules and practice of the common law prevail. If the plea of the general issue in such a case is "expunged," so also is the indictment, for the latter is no more a part of the pleadings than the former;

and will it be contended that the effect of granting a new trial is to necessitate a new indictment against the accused? Blackstone says that after the prisoner in a felony case has been arraigned, and has pleaded not guilty, "they then proceed, as soon as conveniently may be, to the trial," (Bl. Comm. bk. 4, p. 341,) which is tantamount to saying that not until after the pleadings have been made up does the trial begin. And a new trial necessarily begins where the previous one did, unless, by leave of the court, the plea of the general issue is withdrawn, and another plea substituted, or unless the accused pleads, as he may do, a special plea in bar. Hence, when the prisoner in the present case undertook, on the second trial, to contest the validity of the indictment on the ground already mentioned, he sought to assert a dilatory defense, which by the plea of not guilty had been waived, and which plea he did not ask leave to withdraw. The objection, therefore, came too late, as the circuit court held.

The subject of the next assignment of error is the refusal of the court to grant a continuance. The motion for continuance was based on the ground that the case had not been set for trial 10 days before the commencement of the term, as required by the act approved February 24, 1890, which makes it the duty of the judge of each county and corporation court, at least 10 days before the commencement of every term, to set each criminal case then pending for trial on a certain day, etc. Acts 1889-90, p. 79. But this act applies to county and corporation courts only. It was not intended, as both its terms and title indicate, to apply to circuit courts, and, even if it embraced circuit courts, the result would be the same, inasmuch as the order granting a new trial, which was entered on the 31st of March, virtually set the case for trial on the 24th of the ensuing month.

The next question arises upon the prisoner's bill of exceptions, which states that, of the 20 persons ordered to be summoned from the list furnished by the judge to serve as jurors, only 16 attended, whereupon the prisoner moved the court to compel the attendance of the remaining 4, so as to complete a panel of 20 persons; which motion the court overruled.

The statute provides that "in any case of felony, where a sufficient number of jurors to constitute a panel of sixteen persons free from exception cannot be had from those summoned and in attendance, the court may direct another *venire facias*, and cause to be summoned from the bystanders, or from a list to be furnished by the court, so many persons as may be deemed necessary to complete the said panel." Code, § 4019. And this provision of the statute was conformed into the present case. It also appears that, of the 16 persons who attended in pursuance of the original *venire*, only 6 were found free from exception. These were adjourned over until a future day of the term, and were allowed to separate, but only after being cautioned by the court not to converse, or to allow any one to converse with them, about the case. It also ap-

pears that they were subsequently sworn upon the jury with being again examined on their *voir dire*. The prisoner complains of this action of the court, but we perceive no just ground for complaint. It was not necessary to keep the six *venire* men together until the jury was completed, nor is there any suggestion in the record that they, or either of them, disobeyed the admonition of the court as to conversing, or allowing conversation to be had with them, concerning the case. And it was not the duty of the court, under these circumstances, *ex mero motu*, to again examine them on their *voir dire*. The statute does not require it, and there is no rule of practice or of the common law that required it.

The next question arises upon the prisoner's eighth bill of exceptions, which states that in the progress of the trial the prisoner was taken apparently with a fit, and fell or jumped from his seat to the floor, where he laid until carried to a private room. The court thereupon suspended the trial, and summoned two physicians, who after making an examination of the prisoner, testified that, in their opinion, he was sane and "shamming," although evidently laboring under great mental excitement. After the examination by the doctors, the prisoner, escorted by two deputy-sheriffs, walked out of the court-room into the court-house yard, and soon afterwards returned to the prisoner's box, where he remained during the further progress of the trial. Under these circumstances, the question is whether the circuit court, upon the return of the prisoner, rightly resumed and proceeded with the trial, and we are of opinion that it did. At all events, if it did not, the error is not apparent from the record, which, in the disposition of the case in the appellate court, amounts to the same thing. Harman v. City of Lynchburg, 33 Grat. 37; Early's Case, supra.

The next question relates to the action of the court in overruling the motion for a new trial. It is contended that the motion ought to have been sustained, on the ground of a variance between the allegations of the indictment and the proof. The indictment charges that the prisoner killed the deceased by means of blows inflicted on the head. At the trial one of the principal witnesses for the commonwealth, Dr. George Christian, testified that he was present at the coroner's inquest, and found a slight flesh-wound on the forehead of the deceased, and 'a wound on the left eye; that the eye was much bruised, and the frontal bone was crushed, which seemed to have been done with a blunt instrument; that, in his opinion, the last two wounds produced concussion of the brain, from which the deceased died; that the body of the deceased had been badly burned, which, by possibility, caused his death, but he did not think it probable; that in his opinion the burning was done to cover up the crime. Another witness for the commonwealth testified that the prisoner, after his arrest, confessed that he had killed the deceased by knocking him on the head with a stick of wood. To this witness the prisoner stated that about an hour before day-light, on the morning of the homicide, he went to the store of the deceased, in Norfolk county, and awakened him, telling him he wanted quinine for a sick lady; that when the deceased opened the door he struck and knocked him down, as before stated; that he was accompanied to the store by Robert Custis, John Hardy, and George Prior, their object being to kill the deceased for the purpose of stealing his money; that when he (the prisoner) knocked the deceased down Robert Custis struck him with a hatchet; that afterwards Hardy threw a mattress, saturated with kerosene oil, on his prostrate body, and then ignited it. He also stated, in his confession, that at the examination before the magistrates, that after the mattress had been set on fire he heard the deceased groan. But he admitted that that was after he had left the store, and while he was at a certain walnut tree, which, by actual measurement, is distant from the store about one-third of a mile. And it was proved, moreover, that the wind was blowing at the time in the direction of the store from the tree. In this state of the evidence the court instructed the jury as follows: "That unless the jury believe, beyond a reasonable doubt, that the death of the deceased ensued from a blow or blows received at the hands of the prisoner and not by burning, they must acquit the prisoner."

The case having been thus submitted to the jury, they found the prisoner guilty of murder in the first degree; and, as we think, correctly. The indictment, it is true, charges that the blows were inflicted on the right side of the head of the deceased, whereas the proof is they were on the left side; but this is not such a discrepancy between the *allegata* and the *probata* as amounts, in legal contemplation, to a variance. At common law, while an indictment for murder must show with certainty in what part of the body the deceased was wounded, the same strictness is not required as to the evidence necessary to support it. If, for instance, say the authorities, the wound be stated to be on the left side and proved to be on the right, or alleged to be on one part of the body and proved to be on the other, the variance is immaterial. 2 Hale. P. C. 186. In such case the substance of the issue is proved, and that is sufficient. 1 Greenl. Ev. § 65. So in Lazier's Case, 10 Grat. 708, it was held to be no more necessary to prove that the wound was in the same part of the body in which it is alleged to have been than it is to prove the length and depth of the wound as alleged in the indictment. See, also, 2 Bish. Crim. Proc. (3d Ed.) § 525. The judgment of the circuit court, approving the verdict, must therefore be affirmed.

PERRIN v. COMMONWEALTH.

(*Supreme Court of Appeals of Virginia.* March 26, 1891.)

LARCENY—EVIDENCE—JURISDICTION.

1. On trial for the larceny of a pocket-book containing $100 in money and a check for $10.79, the evidence showed that the pocket-book had been lost in a public road. The next day, defendant, a colored man, unable to either read or write, in passing along the road, saw some papers along the wayside, and picked up two of them, one of which was the check in question, which was made payable to a third person, and did not have the owner's name thereon. On the same day defendant showed the check to a neighbor, who was unable to tell him what it was. Some weeks after this defendant accidentally disclosed his possession of the check, and reluctantly parted with it in payment of a bill, stating that the check had been given him in payment for work done. *Held,* that the evidence was not sufficient to show that defendant ever had possession of the pocket-book or its contents, except the check; and that, as there was nothing to show that he knew the owner at the time of the finding, and as the owner's name did not appear on the check, a conviction would be set aside as without evidence in its support.

2. Even if the use which defendant made of the check, which was only of the value of $10.79, constituted a conversion with intent to steal, the offense is only that of petit larceny; and, as such conversion occurred in a county different from the one in which the pocket-book was lost, the county court of the latter county has no jurisdiction of the matter.

RICHARDSON, J., dissenting.

Error to circuit court, Gloucester county.

Wm. B. Taliaferro, for plaintiff in error. *R. Taylor Scott,* Atty. Gen., for the Commonwealth.

FAUNTLEROY, J. The plaintiff in error, Peter Perrin, was, on the 3d day of November, 1890, indicted in the county court of Gloucester county as follows: "That Peter Perrin, on the 20th day of October, 1890, in the said county, a certain leather pocket-book, containing one hundred dollars in United States currency of the value of one hundred dollars, one check for the payment of ten dollars and seventy-nine cents, signed by S. Toutelott & Co., and payable to R. A. Roane & Brother, of the value of ten dollars and seventy-nine cents, the said pocket-book, United States currency, and check, at the time of committing the felony, being the property of R. C. Tinsley, the proprietor thereof, feloniously did steal, take, and carry away," etc. Upon the charge formulated in the foregoing indictment the prisoner was tried, convicted, and sentenced in the county court of Gloucester county on the 14th day of January, 1891, to be confined for a term of two years in the penitentiary, to which said judgment he obtained a writ of error from the circuit court of Gloucester county, which by its judgment rendered on the 5th day of February, 1891, affirmed the said judgment of the county court aforesaid.

The evidence in the record, even that alone which was adduced by the prosecution, and excluding the conflicting testimony for the defense, is plainly insufficient to warrant the verdict of the jury and the judgment of the court. The commonwealth's chief witness, R. C. Tinsley, proves that on a Saturday evening, early in August, 1890, he lost the pocket-book and contents described in the indictment, and alleged to have been stolen out of his hippocket, on the public county road, on his way from his store to his home, 10 miles distant, both being in Gloucester county. Peter Perrin, the prisoner, a colored man, with a family, resident in Gloucester county in the neighborhood of R. C. Tinsley, who could neither read nor write, in passing along the public road on a Sunday morning early in August, (the day of the month not stated, but presumably the next day after the Saturday evening when Mr. Tinsley says he lost the pocket-book on the public road going from his store to his home,) left his house to go down to a neighbor, Moses Gayle, and saw some papers scattered by the wayside, two of which he picked up, and upon arriving at Gayle's house he told Gayle of the circumstances, and, showing one of the papers to him, asked him what it was. Gayle told him that he could not read or write, and he did not know what it was. Perrin then put the paper in his money purse, and kept it there for several weeks until he went down for his wagon or buggy to Mr. Forrest's shop in Mathews county. These facts are not contradicted, nor are they in conflict with any of the testimony for the commonwealth. R. H. Forrest, a witness for the commonwealth, testified: "I keep a work-shop in Mathews county. Some time last August Peter Perrin brought a buggy to my shop, which I repaired for him. A week or two afterwards he came after it. My bill amounted to $5. He took out $2 and offered me, and said that was all the money he had. I saw a paper in his purse, and asked him if that was not a check. He said he was sorry I had seen it; that he had not intended for me to see it. I asked him, 'Why?' He said because he did not want to break it; that if he broke it he would spend it. He objected to my having the check. I told him as he had the check and could pay me, he could not get the buggy without paying me what he owed on it. After some time he consented for me to have it. He told me that he had been working for R. A. Roane & Brother in the highlands, and that, not having the money to settle with him, they had given him the check in payment. He handed me the check, and I saw it was for $10.79. Mr. Tinsley's name was not on the check, and [I] did not know that Mr. Tinsley had any connection with it. I told him to indorse it, and I would pay him the difference between it and my bill. He said he could not write. We went over to the blacksmith's shop of Mr. Atherton, my blacksmith, to indorse it. Mr. Atherton did write his, Peter Perrin's, name on the back of the check. I paid him the difference in cash, $5.79." There is no evidence in the record that the prisoner, Peter Perrin, had ever seen or had in his possession the pocket-book, (which Mr. Tinsley says he lost on the public road, and which may have been found by any one, and some one who could read, and who took the money out of it, and threw away the papers which it contained,) or that he had possession of any of the contents of the lost pocket-book other than this check for $10.-79, not payable to Mr. Tinsley, and which did not have Mr. Tinsley's name upon its face or upon its back.

The evidence of the commonwealth not only fails to prove the felony charged in the indictment against the prisoner, but it proves the prosecution out of the jurisdiction of the county court of Gloucester county, because, even if the hesitating and unwilling yielding of Peter Perrin to the persuasion and demand of the witness Forrest to convert and pass to him the check as the only condition upon which he would let him have his buggy, weeks after he had found it, can be held to be a conversion *animo furandi*, it was not only not coincident with the finding, but it was in the county of Mathews, and, being only for the value of $10.79, it would prove only the offense of petit larceny at most. The mere possession of goods which have been actually lost does not furnish any conclusive or even *prima facie* proof of guilt,—of itself it does not raise the suspicion of guilt. "To constitute larceny in the finder of goods actually lost, it is not enough that the party has general means by the use of proper diligence of discovering the true owner. He must know the owner at the time of the finding, or the goods must have some mark about them, understood by him, or presumably known by him, by which the owner can be ascertained, and he must appropriate them at the time of finding, with intent to take entire dominion over them." Hunt v. Com., 13 Grat. 757; Tanner's Case, 14 Grat. 635; 2 Bish. Crim. Law, § 882. The verdict of the jury is contrary to the law and the evidence, and it must be set aside; and the judgment of the circuit court affirming the erroneous judgment of the county court of Gloucester county is erroneous, and both of the said judgments must be reversed and annulled.

RICHARDSON, J., dissents.

WYTHEVILLE INS. & BKG. CO. v. STULTZ.

(*Supreme Court of Appeals of Virginia.* April 9, 1891.)

FIRE INSURANCE—ACTION ON POLICY—SERVICE OF PROCESS—EVIDENCE—INSTRUCTIONS.

1. The fact that an insurance company also does a banking business does not, in an action on a policy, necessitate the service of process on it in the mode prescribed for service of process on banks; and where the action is brought in the county in which the property was situated, and there is no agent of the company resident in that county, the process may be served by publication, as provided by Code Va. § 3225, for service against corporations generally with the exception of banks.

2. In an action on a policy of fire insurance covering a lot of tobacco, a question propounded by defendant to a witness as to what commission he was to receive if he sold plaintiff's tobacco is properly excluded as irrelevant.

3. An instruction that the insured was bound to disclose every material fact which at the time of the issuance of the policy would have influenced the company in issuing or refusing it, or which would have induced the demand of a higher rate, is properly refused, as the insured must have knowledge of the existence of the fact or of its materiality before the policy can be avoided for his failure to disclose it.

4. Where the policy contains many questions as to facts deemed by the company material to the risk, the insured is bound to disclose only such matters as may be inquired about by the company; and therefore an instruction that the policy is vitiated by the failure of the insured to disclose the fact that the tobacco was damaged and unsalable when he obtained the policy is

properly refused, where no such inquiry was made by the company.

5. Neither is the insured bound to disclose the particulars of his title unless the same is inquired about, or unless it is made imperative on him by some condition of the policy; and, in the absence of such inquiry or condition, it is proper to refuse an instruction that the policy is vitiated if, at the time of its issuance, the insured owed on the tobacco an amount equal to its value.

6. Where the insured, on his application for the policy, correctly represented the building in which the tobacco was stored as a tobacco factory, an instruction that such representation amounts to a warranty by the insured as to the character of the building is properly refused as misleading.

7. In an action on the policy, defendant's evidence showed that plaintiff misrepresented the character and value of the tobacco, that the tobacco was in fact unsalable, that it was destroyed within nine days after the issuance of the policy, and that plaintiff had offered no explanation, except that he thought that the fire was the work of an incendiary. Plaintiff's evidence showed that he had made no misrepresentations, and that the tobacco was valuable and salable. *Held* that, on writ of error after a verdict in plaintiff's favor, the supreme court of appeals must reject such of defendant's evidence as is in conflict with that of plaintiff, and that the verdict could not be set aside as contrary to the evidence.

RICHARDSON, J., dissenting.

D. S. Peirce, for plaintiff in error. *Peatross & Harris*, for defendant in error.

LACY, J. This is a writ of error to a judgment of the circuit court of Henry county rendered at the July special term, 1889. The action is trespass on the case in *assumpsit* against the Wytheville Insurance & Banking Company by the defendant in error, L. B. Stults, on a policy of insurance. At the trial the defendant moved the court to quash the process, because there had been no personal service on the company in any way whatever, and that the order of publication, which was the substituted process resorted to, was insufficient, because the defendant company was a bank; which motion was overruled, and the defendant excepted. At the trial the evidence was taken and certified, and instructions given and refused, and the defendant excepted to the rulings of the court against him, and a verdict was rendered against the defendant company; whereupon the defendant moved the court to set aside the verdict, and grant it a new trial, which motion the court overruled, and the defendant excepted; whereupon the court rendered judgment in accordance with the verdict, and the defendant brought this case to this court by writ of error.

The first question we will consider is as to the motion of the defendant to quash the process in this case because the defendant is a bank. The statute provides that the service of process against a bank shall be upon the president, as provided by section 3225 of the Code of Virginia. This section provides that service of process against a bank may be on its president, cashier, treasurer, or any one of its directors; and also it is there provided that, if the process be against some other corporation chartered by this state, or by some other state, or in any case, if there be not in the county or corporation

wherein the case is commenced any other person on whom there can be service as aforesaid, or any agent of the corporation against which the case is, (unless it be a case against a bank,) or on any person declared by the laws of this state to be an agent of such corporation, and if there be no such agent in the county or corporation wherein the case is commenced, on affidavit of that fact, and that there is no other person in such county or corporation on which there can be service as aforesaid, publication of a copy of the process or notice once a week, for four weeks, shall be a sufficient service of such process or notice. The defendant was called a banking as well as an insurance company, but with its business as a bank the plaintiff has in this suit no concern. The said defendant company was and is doing business as an insurance company, and the suit is upon a contract of insurance, made by the said company in the county where this suit was commenced; and section 3214 of the Code provides that any action of law, if it be to recover a loss under a policy of insurance either upon property or life, may be commenced in the county or corporation wherein the property insured was situated, or the person whose life was insured resided, at the date of the policy. It appeared by affidavit that no agent of the company resided in this county upon whom process could be served, and, it being against an insurance company, it was properly commenced in the county where the property insured was situated; and being so commenced there, and there being no agent of the said company residing there on whom process could be served, an order of publication was proper in the case. That the defendant company at other times did business as a bank is immaterial. In this transaction it was dealing as an insurance company, and the action was upon a loss under a policy of insurance; and it was with its character as an insurance company that the plaintiff was dealing, and the motion to quash the process in the case was properly overruled, as the same was lawful, regular, and altogether proper.

The second assignment of error, and which is the subject of the second bill of exceptions, is as to the refusal of the court to compel the witness Semple to disclose, at the instance of the defendant, what commission was paid him for selling, or what commission he was to receive if he sold, the plaintiff's tobacco. The witness objected to disclosing what commission he was to receive for selling, as that was his private business, and he did not wish to tell it. It does not appear in what respect that question was germane or in any wise related to the issue to be tried. The witness was engaged in selling his own tobacco, and took along some for the plaintiff, and did not sell it. The commission to be paid him was irrelevant to the issue, and no foundation was laid for its introduction into the trial of this case, and there was no error in excluding it.

The third assignment, and the subject of the third exception, is as to the action of the circuit court in excluding the answer of the witness Terry, which disclosed a statement of third parties, made to him. This was hearsay merely, and the fact to be proved, if necessary, could have been properly proved only by the persons having the knowledge themselves, and a report of what they had said in the absence of the plaintiff did not rise to the dignity of legal evidence, and was properly excluded.

The fourth assignment of error, and the subject of the fourth exception, is as to the action of the court in refusing certain instructions asked by defendant, and giving certain others. The first instruction asked for by the defendant, and refused by the court, and which is involved herein, is as follows: "Instruction No. 3. The court instructs the jury that any fact which, if known, would have influenced the company to fix a higher rate of premium, or would have influenced the said company in issuing or refusing to issue the policy in question, is material to the risk; and it was the duty of the plaintiff to disclose every such fact when he made his application for the said policy, and the failure so to do on the part of the plaintiff vitiates his policy." The next is instruction No. 4: "The court further instructs the jury that if they believe from the evidence that at the time the plaintiff obtained the policy sued on he knew the tobacco insured was damaged, and not salable on the markets, and failed to disclose the same to the company, and if they shall further believe that the knowledge of said fact would have caused the company to refuse to issue the said policy, then the failure to disclose the same, whether fraudulent or not, vitiates the policy, and they must find for the defendant." The next is instruction No. 5: "The court instructs the jury that if they believe from the evidence that at the time the plaintiff obtained the policy sued on he owed on the tobacco insured an amount equal to the value of the same, and failed to disclose the same to the defendant company, and if they shall further believe that the knowledge of that fact would have caused the said company to refuse to issue the said policy, then the failure to disclose the same vitiates the policy, and they must find for the defendant." The next is as follows: "Instruction No. 6. The court instructs the jury that the provision in the policy that the house in which the tobacco insured was situated was occupied as a tobacco factory is a warranty, and the plaintiff is bound thereby; and if they shall believe from the evidence that the said building was at that time, and at the time of the fire, not so occupied, and that a knowledge of that fact would have caused the company to have refused to issue the policy, then they must find for the defendant." Instruction No. 7 is as follows: "The court further instructs the jury that if they believe from the evidence that at the time the plaintiff obtained the policy sued on he represented to the company that he did not owe for the tobacco insured, when in fact he owed for the same to an amount equal to the value of the tobacco,

and if they shall further believe that the knowledge of this fact would have caused the defendant company to refuse to issue the said policy, then such misrepresentation vitiates the policy, and they must find for the defendant." Instruction No. 8, as asked for by the defendant, is as follows: "The court further instructs the jury that, under the provisions of the policy, the misrepresentations of the plaintiff to the agents of the company at the time of the obtaining of the policy, as to the value of the tobacco insured, amounts to a warranty; and if they believe from the evidence that at that time he represented the tobacco to be worth greatly more than it was in fact worth, and materially overvalued the same, such representation vitiates the policy, and they must find for the defendant."

In lieu of these instructions as asked for by the defendant, the court gave others, as follows: In lieu of the foregoing instruction No. 3, the court gave the following, marked "Instruction A:" "That, in order that misrepresentations made in procuring insurance shall have the effect to make the policy void, (unless such misrepresentations be warranties,) such misrepresentations must be material to the risk, and must have influenced the issuing of the policy; and whether they be material to the risk or influenced the issuing of the policy or not are questions for the jury to determine from the evidence." In lieu of the fourth instruction asked by the defendant, the court gave the following, marked "Instruction B:" "That in order for the defendant company in this suit to be entitled to a verdict in its favor, on the ground that the policy was void because of misrepresentations by the plaintiff in procuring the insurance, the defendant company must prove to the satisfaction of the jury that the plaintiff made such misrepresentations, and that they were as to matters material to the risk." In lieu of the fifth instruction asked for by the defendant, the court gave the following, marked "Instruction C:" "That if one applying for insurance state fairly to the company, or its agent, the facts required by the contract of insurance to be stated, or if such facts be known to the company or its agent, and the facts be not truly stated by the company, or its agent writing the policy, the company will not be released from liability by such failure to state truly the facts in the policy." In lieu of the sixth instruction, as asked for by the defendant, the court gave the following, marked "Instruction D:" "A mere misrepresentation of the value of the property insured does not vitiate the policy, unless the overvaluation be gross and clear, such as must be known to be such by the insured, and not known to the insurer, and therefore false and fraudulent." In lieu of the seventh instruction, as asked for by the defendant, the court gave the following, marked "Instruction E:" "That, as a rule, the insured is only required to disclose what he is interrogated as to, unless the terms of the policy require such disclosure; but, whether interrogated or not, if the jury believe from the evidence that he withheld or omitted to state any fact material to the risk which, in honesty and good faith, he ought to have communicated, with the design and for the purpose of obtaining the issuance of the policy, or for the purpose or with the design of obtaining the same at a lower premium than the one charged, then the policy is thereby vitiated, and the jury must find for the defendant."

It is insisted that it was the duty of the insured to disclose every fact which, if known to the company at the time of the issuance of the policy, would have induced the demand for a higher rate, or would have influenced the company in issuing or refusing the said policy, and that the circuit court should have so instructed the jury, as asked in the said third instruction; but this cannot be true unless such material fact was known to the assured; otherwise the assured was incapable of disclosing them, and, if known to him, he must also have known that the supposed fact was material to the risk. The third instruction was incorrect, and, if it had been given, would have tended to mislead rather than instruct the jury.

As to the duty of the insured to make every disclosure which is material to the risk, whether questioned concerning the same or not. It is generally true that the insured is bound only to disclose such matters as may be inquired about, and not the particulars of his title, unless the same is inquired about, or unless it is made imperative upon him by some condition of the policy. The rights of the insurer are sufficiently guarded by having it in his power to exact, by inquiry, a description of the interest of the insured, and by the recovery being limited, in case of loss, to the value of the interest proved at the trial. As was said by Judge Moncure in Insurance Co. v. Sheets, 26 Grat. 872, quoting from Morrison v. Insurance Co., 18 Mo. 262: "The man who asks insurance on his property is not aware of the necessity of disclosures which long experience in insurance offices has shown to the underwriter to be necessary, and to hold his policy void, for not making disclosures of the importance of which he is not aware, would be gross injustice." And again: "What is material must be determined upon the circumstances of each case. What is material in one case may not be in another, and so a wide field for litigation will be opened. The ends of justice will be best subserved by holding the assured only responsible for fraud. Insurance companies may protect themselves by inquiries in relation to these things, and after filling their policies with so much detail, and so much *minutiae* of information in regard to other matters, as to create the impression that they are satisfied, to hold that they are not bound by their contract, unless information of another kind is communicated by the assured, which is not sought for, would be enabling them to commit the rankest injustice." And Judge Moncure adds: "These views are very strong and I am decidedly of opinion that they are correct. Nothing more need be added to them." In Clark v. Insurance

Co., 8 How. 235, it is said the relation of the parties is entirely changed, if the insurer asks no information, and the insured makes no representations. But when representations are not asked nor given, and with only this general knowledge the insurer chooses to assume the risk, he must be presumed, in point of law, to do so at his peril. In this case the policy was issued on a mere request to insure, and without any statement as to these things now contended for.

As to the sixth instruction, that the statement that the house was a tobacco factory was a warranty, this instruction was calculated only to mislead the jury by suggesting that there was some dispute upon this point, and that there was some evidence to the contrary; whereas, the evidence everywhere shows that the building was a tobacco factory, and nothing else, and there is no testimony to the contrary whatever; and moreover, the fact that the agent effecting the insurance was fully informed and entirely familiar with the building in question is proved, and not denied; and, being so known to the insurer, the said instruction was irrelevant; and when the insurer knows the situation of the building before insurance he is estopped from setting up a misstatement in reference thereto in the application. Wood, Ins. p. 299, and authorities cited. But, as we have said, there was no evidence tending to show any misrepresentations as to this, and the fact plainly appeared, and was uncontradicted, and the instruction was inapplicable to any phase of this case, and was irrelevant, and properly rejected. And we may add that an oral application for insurance, although referred to in the policy, does not thereby become a warranty. The verbal statements made by the assured are merely representations, which, if not fraudulent and material to the risk, do not avoid the policy. Nothing can be incorporated into or be said to be a part of a written contract, except it is in writing, and the danger of permitting such a doctrine to gain a foot-hold is readily perceived. It would be of very dangerous consequences to add a conversation that passed at the time as part of the written agreement. In all cases where verbal representations are made material to the risk, they may be shown for the purpose of establishing fraud on the part of the assured. But even though such statements are false, if they are honestly made, the policy is not avoided. They must be both false and fraudulent to have that effect. Wood, Ins. p. 300, and authorities cited, page 207, § 90: page 889, § 424; Insurance Co. v. Weill, 28 Grat. 389; Insurance Co. v. Wilkinson, 13 Wall. 222; Insurance Co. v. West, 76 Va. 582; National Bank v. Insurance Co., 95 U. S. 673.

Instruction No. 7 was properly refused for reasons already stated. No inquiry was made of him about what he owed, and such an inquiry would have been unusual and novel, if it had been made. There was an inquiry as to incumbrance in the policy, but there was no incumbrance thereon, and no instruction is asked concerning it. There was no error in the action of the court in giving or refusing the said instructions given or refused, and the assignment of error concerning the same must be overruled.

The next assignment of error, which is the subject of the fifth exception, is as to the action of the court in overruling the motion of the defendant to set aside the verdict in the case found by the jury, and rendering judgment thereon in accordance with its terms. In consideration of this motion we will remark that the evidence herein is certified, and under our law, upon writ of error here, we must consider the same as upon a demurrer to the evidence.

The defense made to the action is that the plaintiff misrepresented the character and value of the tobacco insured; that the insured tobacco was not salable, was unsound and sour, and growing daily worse; that the same was not stored in a tobacco factory, as represented, but in an outhouse in the country, closed for more than a year, and that the facts were not known to the agent of the company who issued the policy, but reliance was placed on the statements of the insured, and they were untrue; that the fire occurred nine days after the insurance was effected; and that the plaintiff offers no explanation, except that he thought it was the act of an incendiary; that the plaintiff left home the night of the fire, and was three miles distant, and was apprised of the fire at about 9 o'clock, and he did not go to the scene of the fire; that his tobacco had been rejected as sour by dealers in various cities; and there is in the certificate of evidence in the record certain evidence which the defendant offered to that effect. On the other hand, the plaintiff offers evidence adduced at the trial to the effect that the agent of the company was aware of the location of the factory, and all about it; that the tobacco was worth from $6,000 to $7,000; that he fully disclosed to the agent of the company the character of his tobacco, and the several grades, and the prices put on each; that he was not asked whether there was any money due on the tobacco, and that there was not any incumbrance on the said tobacco; that the insurance was placed by the agent in several companies, and that he, the insured, did not know what companies would be given the risk; that his tobacco was good, and not unsound; and that on the night of the fire he was at his brother-in-law's house, where his wife was staying; that he was sick in bed, on an inclement night, with tonsilitis; and that he did not go in the night to the scene of the fire (1) because he was sick with a disease which would have been aggravated by exposure, and (2) because he understood that the building was hopelessly burning, and he could do no good by going there in the night only to see it burn. The witness A. D. Stultz says the estimate of the value of the tobacco burned was largely less than the actual value of the tobacco; that the house where it was stored was a tobacco factory when the insurance was effected, and at the date of the fire; that the tobacco was sound and

v.13s.E.no.2—6

good, and not sour or unsound; and that he had examined it, and knew it well. Another witness, J. W. Burch, says he had examined three grades of this tobacco, and found them sound; that they were good and sound, and no sourness about them; that one grade was especially good. Upon this state of the evidence the jury, the proper triers of the facts, based their verdict upon the evidence of the plaintiff, apparently; and in considering the same here, upon writ of error, we must reject the evidence of the defendant which is in conflict with the plaintiff's evidence. This rule being applied, the verdict, in the light of the plaintiff's evidence, and of such evidence of the defendant as can be considered, appears to be right, and there is no error in the action of the circuit court in overruling the motion for a new trial, and in refusing to set aside the verdict as contrary to the law and the evidence. Upon the whole case, as disclosed by the record, we perceive no error in the judgment of the circuit court herein, and the same must be affirmed.

RICHARDSON, J., dissents.

NEW ENGLAND MORTGAGE SECURITY CO.
v. McLAUGHLIN.

(*Supreme Court of Georgia.* March 16, 1891.)

CONFLICT OF LAWS—INTEREST.

Where a note, executed in this state, is made payable in the state of New York, and is secured by a mortgage which stipulates "that the contract embodied in this mortgage, and the note secured hereby, shall in all respects be construed according to the laws of Georgia," and the note on its face bears interest at the rate of 8 per cent. per annum, the same being legal in Georgia, the entire amount of such interest is collectible in this state, notwithstanding the maximum legal rate of interest in the state of New York may be less than 8 per cent.

(*Syllabus by the Court.*)

Error from superior court, Marion county; SMITH, Judge.

W. E. Simmons, for plaintiffs in error. Thornton & Cameron and B. F. McLaughlin, for defendant in error.

LUMPKIN, J. McLaughlin gave his note to the New England Mortgage Security Company, promising therein to pay interest from its date at the rate of 8 per cent. per annum, and secured the same by a mortgage on land in Georgia, containing the stipulation quoted in the above headnote. The note was made payable in the city of New York. Plaintiffs foreclosed said mortgage in the superior court of Marion county. The defense was that, the note being made payable in New York, it must be enforced according to the laws of that state; and, as the maximum legal rate of interest in said state is 6 per cent., the note is, for this reason, on its face usurious. Plaintiffs recovered the full amount appearing to be due on the face of the note, and a motion was made for a new trial by the defendant, which was granted by the court below. We presume the new trial was granted on the ground that the note was usurious, because the motion contains no other ground upon which it could have been granted. The only question presented by the record for our determination is whether or not this note was affected with usury for the reason stated. The question whether or not a note, made payable in a different state than that in which it is executed, and bearing a given rate of interest legal in the state where made, is usurious when the contract rate of interest expressed therein is higher than the legal rate prescribed in the state where payable, has been often and fully discussed by many courts and text-writers. But for the fact that so much contrariety of opinion has been expressed upon the question, the writer would deem it a plain one, especially where the contract itself, as in the present case, provides that it shall be in all respects construed by the laws of the state in which it is made. Deferring, however, to the large number of respectable authorities entertaining a different view, some discussion of the question will be now attempted. In the first place, it would seem that the parties themselves are the best judges of what they wish to accomplish by their contract, and if such contract contains no provision *per se* illegal, vicious, or contrary to public policy, it ought to be enforced. It has often been held that parties will not be allowed to make contracts to be performed in another jurisdiction for the purpose of evading the usury laws of their own domicile, but this doctrine can have no application where the maker of a note contracts consistently with the laws of his own state. Many authors and judges have laid down the rule that, in cases of this kind, effect should be give to the actual intention of the parties as to what rate of interest should prevail, and under what law. And some go to the extent of holding that this intention may be gathered from facts and circumstances attending the transaction, and outside of the note itself. If in Georgia, where 8 per cent. interest is legal, a resident of this state desires to make himself liable for that rate upon a note to be paid in another state, and deliberately undertakes so to do, it is difficult to conceive any good reason of morals or policy why this should not be allowed. If in such a note no rate of interest were specified, the rate prevailing in the state where the contract was to be performed would be that collected; and this conclusion, it seems, is arrived at in many decisions mainly on the idea that, where the contract is silent as to the rate of interest, it is presumed that the parties intended that the legal rate of the place where the paper is payable should apply. In his work on Contracts, (section 1372,) Mr. Bishop states as a general rule that "a contract valid where made is valid everywhere, and one invalid where made is everywhere invalid." Again, in section 1388, he says: "If the agreed interest is lawful in the state where the bargain is entered into, the courts of this state will enforce the contract, though the payment is by its terms to transpire in another state, where it is unlawful;" cit-

ing Thornton v. Dean, 19 S. C. 583; Pancoast v Insurance Co., 79 Ind. 172; Richardson v. Brown, 9 Baxt. 242; Lindsay v. Hill, 66 Me. 212; Sheldon v. Haxtun, 91 N. Y. 124. In 1 Daniel, Neg. Inst. § 922, the case of Depau v. Humphreys, 8 Mart. (N. S.) 1, is mentioned, holding that a note made in Louisiana, bearing 10 per cent. interest, which was legal in that state, would not be usurious, but valid, though payable in New York, where all contracts to pay more than 7 per cent. were at that time usurious; and the author remarks that "the like view has been recognized and adopted in numerous cases, and may be regarded as a recognized principle of English and American jurisprudence;" citing many authorities. The same doctrine is set out in 2 Kent, Com. p. *460. as follows: "If, however, the rate of interest be specified in the contract, and it be according to the law of the place where the contract was made, though that rate be higher than is lawful by the law of the place where payment was to be made, the specified rate of interest at the place of the contract has been allowed by the courts of justice in that place, for that is part of the substance of the contract." Mr. Randolph, in his work on Commercial Paper, (volume 1, § 43,) says: "In determining whether a bill or note is usurious, the courts have leaned noticeably to decisions sustaining the instrument, if valid by the law of any place, whether of contract or of payment, and this somewhat in disregard of any general rule. If a different rate of interest is fixed by law in the place of contract and of payment, the parties may elect either rate to govern their contract. Thus they may choose the rate of the place of payment, that being the higher; or the rate of the place of contract, if that is the higher." The doctrine above quoted seems to proceed on the idea that the intention of the parties should govern. To the same effect, see 2 Pars. Cont. 583, 583.

All the authorities above cited refer to notes or other contracts which have not in them a distinct stipulation that the contract shall be construed according to the laws of the place where made. A recent Texas case, that of Dugan v. Lewis, 14 S. W. Rep. 1024, decides the precise question presented by the case at bar. In that case a note bearing a rate of interest which would have been usurious in New York, where it was made payable, was executed in Texas, and secured by a deed of trust which contained a stipulation identical with that in the mortgage made by McLaughlin, except that the word "other" is there introduced between the words "all" and "respects." In a carefully considered and well-prepared opinion, HENRY, J., sets forth the views of the supreme court of Texas, reaching the conclusion that the contract in question was governed by the usury laws of Texas. A large number of authorities are referred to and discussed, which need not be noticed in detail, because that opinion speaks for itself, and is a clear and able exposition of the law on this subject. We will observe, however, that the learned justice remarked, in substance. that it was not entirely clear the stipulation referred to had reference to the rate of interest, except in a general way. He further says that this expression "should be taken as a circumstance to be considered in ascertaining and giving effect to the intention of the parties." We are prepared to go further on this line, and have little doubt that the parties to this contract distinctly meant by this very stipulation that the contract as to interest and every other essential feature and particular should be not only construed, but enforced, according to the laws of the state where it was made. In the case before us we are quite sure that the parties to the note and mortgage under consideration meant and intended that they should be in all respects understood and carried out as Georgia contracts, and enforced under Georgia laws; and after all, is it not plain and simple justice to give this effect and meaning to these words? To do otherwise, it seems to us, would defeat the expressed wishes and intention of these parties. To construe this note and mortgage as we have done works injustice to no one, but puts the parties where they manifestly intended to put themselves. The defendant, having made a note and mortgage in the state of Georgia, and bound himself to pay interest at the rate of 8 per cent, and agreed that this contract should be construed in all respects according to the laws of Georgia, should stand to his promises. The contract being under our laws perfectly legal, he cannot and ought not to expect the courts of this state to release him from his solemn and deliberate undertakings. Judgment reversed.

HOPKINS v. CENTRAL RAILROAD & BANKING CO.

CENTRAL RAILROAD & BANKING CO. v. HOPKINS.

(*Supreme Court of Georgia.* Feb. 23, 1891.)

Error from superior court, Houston county; MILLER, Judge.

L. F. Garrard and *C. C. Duncan,* for plaintiff in error. *R. F. Lyon,* for defendant in error.

BLECKLEY, C. J. These cases are controlled by the act of November 11, 1889, which prescribes the manner of taking cases to the supreme court. and declares this manner the exclusive one after January 15, 1890. Writs of error dismissed.

GODBEE v. McCATHERN.

(*Supreme Court of Georgia.* March 16, 1891.)

Error from superior court, Burke county; RONEY, Judge.

Lovett & Davis, for plaintiff in error. *B. H. Perry* and *Phil. P. Johnston,* for defendant in error.

BLECKLEY, C. J. This case is controlled by Owensby v. Thompson, 69 Ga. 778, the certificate of the judge to the bill of exceptions being, according to that case, fatally defective. Writ of error dismissed.

COOK et al. v. BUCHANAN.

(*Supreme Court of Georgia.* March 4, 1891.)

FORECLOSURE OF CHATTEL MORTGAGE—AFFIDAVIT OF ILLEGALITY—VERIFICATION BY AGENT—RATIFICATION.

1. Code Ga. § 2207, provides that any act authorized or required to be done under the Code, by any person in the prosecution of his legal remedies, may be done by his agents; and for this purpose he is authorized to make an affidavit and execute any bond required, though his agency be created by parol. Plaintiff foreclosed a chattel mortgage in justice's court, and levied on the mortgaged property. A., as defendants' special agent appointed by parol, filed an affidavit of illegality. *Held,* that the verbal appointment of the agent sufficiently authorized his filing the affidavit in behalf of his principal.

2. Appealing the case, giving an appeal-bond, and offering to subscribe the affidavit in the superior court, is a ratification by the principal of his agent's acts, authorizing the lower court to hear and determine the illegality on its merits.

Error from superior court, Marion county; SMITH, Judge.

Morgan & McMichael, for plaintiffs in error. *Butt & Lumpkin,* for defendant in error.

SIMMONS, J. Buchanan foreclosed in a justice's court a chattel mortgage against Rebecca Everingham and John W. Cook. Execution was issued thereon, and levied on the mortgaged property. An affidavit of illegality was filed by McMichael as special agent of the defendants. A trial was held in the justice's court, and judgment in favor of Buchanan was rendered against the defendants, and they entered an appeal to the superior court. When the case was called in the superior court, Buchanan demurred to the affidavit of illegality on the ground that it was filed by a special agent of the defendants, the authority for so doing not accompanying and not being filed with the affidavit. The court sustained the demurrer, and dismissed the illegality, and the defendants excepted. The sole question to be decided is whether an agent can file an affidavit of illegality in behalf of his principal without a written power of attorney authorizing him to do so. Section 2207 of the Code is as follows: "Any act authorized or required to be done under this Code by any person in the prosecution of his legal remedies may be done by his agents; and for this purpose he is authorized to make an affidavit and execute any bond required, though his agency be created by parol. In all such cases, if the principal repudiate the act of the agent, the agent shall be personally bound, together with his sureties." We think that under this section of the Code an agent can make an affidavit of illegality, and that it is not necessary, in order for him to do so, that the agency should be created in writing, as contended by counsel for the defendant in error. This section expressly declares that the agency may be created by parol. The word "parol," as applied to cases of illegality, does not, in our opinion, mean a writing, but means a verbal creation of the agency. Under this section, whenever the principal is authorized or required to do an act in the prosecution of his legal remedies, he may appoint an agent verbally to do the act for him, if the agent can conscientiously depose to the same facts to which the principal could. In the case of Hadden v. Larned, 83 Ga. 636, 10 S. E. Rep. 278, this court held that under this section an agent could not interpose a claim affidavit *in forma pauperis*, because that affidavit is a personal privilege to the claimant, and the agent could not depose as to the *bona fides*, belief, and poverty of the claimant. He could not swear positively that the claim was made in good faith, or that the agent was from his poverty unable to give good bond and security. Nor can an agent created by parol under this section enter an appeal, because section 3615 expressly requires that, if an agent enters an appeal, he must be authorized in writing, and the writing filed in the court in which the case is pending. In the case of an illegality there is no reason why the agent cannot depose to the same facts as the principal could. He can have the same knowledge as to the illegality of the execution as the principal has, and can depose as positively to the grounds of illegality generally as the principal could. We think, therefore, that under this section any person, in the prosecution of his legal remedies, may appoint verbally an agent to act for him therein, unless it is apparent that the agent cannot make the affidavit required by law, as in the case of Hadden v. Larned, supra, or as in the case of an appeal, where the Code provides that the appointment shall be in writing. If the sheriff or other levying officer is satisfied that the agent has the necessary authority to make the affidavit, he may receive it, and return the paper to the court. If, however, the agent has no such authority, this section of the Code allows the principal to repudiate the action of the agent, and in that event the agent and his securities become liable; and this is the difference between this section and section 3670, which says an affidavit of illegality may be filed by an attorney in fact or an executor, administrator, or other trustee. Under the latter section a person undoubtedly would have the right to appoint an attorney in fact to file an affidavit for him. If he does appoint an attorney in fact, it must necessarily be in writing, and must be executed with the same formality as the law prescribes for the execution of the act for which the agency is created, as required by section 2182 of the Code. Where an agent is appointed in this manner, the principal cannot repudiate his acts, as he can do under the other section. The facts in this case show that, while this agent was appointed by parol, the principals ratified his action by appealing the case from the justice's court to the superior court, and giving the appeal-bond required by law, and by appearing in the superior court, and offering to subscribe their names to the affidavit. If there could be any doubt as to the legality of the agency, this ratification on the part of the principal was sufficient to authorize the court to hear and determine the illegality. Judgment reversed.

WILKINS v. McGEHEE.

(*Supreme Court of Georgia. March 4, 1891.*)

POWER—REVOCATION BY DEATH—ESTOPPEL IN PAIS.

1. A mortgage given as collateral security to a note containing a power of sale does not convey such an interest in the estate as to render the power irrevocable by the death of the mortgagor, under Code Ga. § 2183, providing that the death of a person creating a power of agency revokes it, unless the power is coupled with an interest in the agent himself.

2. Code Ga. § 2066, provides that "one who silently stands by and permits another to purchase his property without disclosing his title is guilty of such fraud as estops him from subsequently setting up such title against the purchaser." A. executed a mortgage to B. to secure her on a note, and thereafter died. At maturity of the note, plaintiffs, as the deceased mortgagor's executors, tried to borrow money to pay the note, and failed, whereupon B. paid the note, advertised the property under the power of the sale in the mortgage, and sold it. Two of plaintiffs were present at the sale, and made no objections. The purchaser, as the agent of the mortgagee, drew the notice of sale, and was a brother of deceased mortgagor in possession of the facts of title. *Held,* that the plaintiffs were not estopped from contesting the validity of the sale.

Error from superior court, Muscogee county; SMITH, Judge.

L. F. Garrard, for plaintiff in error. Peabody, Brannon & Hatcher, for defendant in error.

SIMMONS, J. There are two questions made for our decision by the record in this case: (1) The first is whether the power of sale given by Mrs. Wilkins to Mrs. Mustian survived after the death of Mrs. Wilkins, the maker. (2) If the power did not survive, or was revoked by her death, whether the plaintiffs in the court below are estopped from setting up their claim to the land.

1. The first question depends upon the nature of the conveyance to Mrs. Mustian, whether it gave her such an interest in the land as to render the power of sale irrevocable by the death of Mrs. Wilkins. As a general rule all powers are revoked by the death of the person creating the power. The exception to this general rule is where the power is coupled with an interest. If the power is coupled with an interest, then the death of the maker does not revoke it. But to render it irrevocable, the interest must be in the property itself, and not merely in the proceeds resulting from the execution of the power. Code, § 2183; Hunt v. Rousmanier, 8 Wheat. 175; Lockett v. Hill, 1 Woods, 552; Coney v. Sanders, 28 Ga. 511; Lathrop v. Brown, 65 Ga. 315. MARSHALL, C. J., says in the case first cited: "We hold it to be clear that the interest which can protect a power after the death of a person who creates it must be an interest in the thing itself. In other words, the power must be ingrafted on an estate in the thing." In this case, in order for the power to have survived, Mrs. Mustian must have had some title or estate in the land. Did she have such a title, estate, or interest as to render the power irrevocable? We think not. In our opinion, the conveyance to her by Mrs. Wilkins was nothing more than a mortgage to secure

her against loss in the event she had to pay the note on which she was security for Mrs. Wilkins. It was not the intention of either of the parties that the title to the land should pass from Mrs. Wilkins to Mrs. Mustian. The money was not borrowed by Mrs. Wilkins from Mrs. Mustian, but from another party. The conveyance was not made at the time the note was given, but subsequently thereto, for the purpose of indemnifying Mrs. Mustian in case Mrs. Wilkins failed to pay the note, and she had it to pay. There is no warranty of title in the conveyance, and it is denominated a mortgage therein. So we think the real intent and understanding of the parties were that it was a mortgage. Being a mortgage, under our Code it did not convey the title, but was only a security for the debt. Code, § 1954. As this instrument passed no title to Mrs. Mustian, she did not get any estate in the land, but only an interest in the proceeds of the sale thereof. She had an interest in the power, but none in the thing. Such an interest does not render the power irrevocable by the death of the maker, and therefore the death of Mrs. Wilkins revoked the power of sale contained in the mortgage. Lathrop v. Brown, 65 Ga. 312; Miller v. McDonald, 72 Ga. 20; Lockett v. Hill, *supra*; Hunt v. Rousmanier, *supra*; Johnson v. Johnson, 27 S C. 309, 3 S. E. Rep. 606. It was contended, however, by counsel for defendant in error that this court in the case of Calloway v. Bank, 54 Ga. 441, held that a mortgagee did have such an interest in the mortgaged property as to make the power of sale therein irrevocable. It is true that Judge McCay, in his reasoning in that case, did say that the mortgagee had an interest in the mortgaged property. While the decision in the case was right, we think from the authorities above cited that the reasoning to sustain it was not well founded. In that case, Maxwell, the mortgagor, was not dead, nor was there any effort on his part to revoke the power of sale given in the mortgage. The attack on the power of sale seems to have been made by unsecured creditors of Maxwell. Under the facts of that case the power of sale could very well be held irrevocable, because they show that the contract between Maxwell and the mortgagees was that on default, of payment of the sum of money secured by the mortgage the mortgagees were not to be delayed by the necessity of foreclosing in the courts, but either of them might sell all or any part of the lands to pay said indebtedness after advertising, etc. Maxwell was not dead at the time of the sale; and the power, being part of a contract for consideration, might for that reason be held irrevocable in the lifetime of the mortgagor. In Lathrop v. Brown, JACKSON, C. J., commenting upon that case, said: "And though Judge Mc-Cay, in 54 Ga., does express the opinion that the mortgagee has such an interest in the thing mortgaged as to make the power irrevocable, yet he could not have meant, and did not mean, that it survived the death of the mortgagor, so as to defeat costs of administration, year's sup-port, widow's dower, and trust debts." 65 Ga. 317.

2. Having determined that the power of sale given to Mrs. Mustian in the mortgage was revoked by the death of Mrs. Wilkins, it follows that the sale of the land under that power, made after the death of Mrs. Wilkins, was void, and conferred no title on the purchasers. It only remains for us to decide whether the plaintiffs were estopped by their conduct at the sale. The facts of the case show, in substance, that Mrs. Wilkins died before the note upon which Mrs. Mustian was security fell due; that when it became due, Davis, the son and agent of Mrs. Mustian, went to the plaintiffs, to see if they could raise the money to pay the note. They endeavored to do so, but failed. The note was then paid by Mrs. Mustian. Davis, as her agent, then had the land advertised for sale under the power given in the mortgage. On the day of sale he became the purchaser, and Mrs. Mustian executed to him a deed to the land. Two of the plaintiffs were present at the sale, but did not do or say anything in regard to the matter. They made no representations as to the title to the property, or the right of Mrs. Mustian to sell it. Davis knew as much about the title as they did. He, being the agent of Mrs. Mustian, and having had the property advertised, must have had the mortgage, with the power of sale, in his possession. Besides, Mrs. Wilkins, as the record shows, was his sister. He thus had as much knowledge of the true state of the title as the plaintiffs had. Indeed, he had better means of acquiring such knowledge than they had. Under this state of facts, we do not think that the plaintiffs are estopped. He was not influenced to make the purchase by any act of theirs, either of omission or of commission. They did not practice any art or deceit. There was no false suggestion, no suppression of truth, by them. They were not guilty of any fraud; but, on the contrary, it was admitted in the argument here that all parties acted in perfect good faith, under the belief that the power of sale was still valid when the sale took place. It was an honest and mutual mistake of law. The purchaser was as much bound to know the law as the plaintiffs. All of them being equally ignorant, it is now claimed in behalf of the purchaser that the plaintiffs became estopped by not informing him truly of the law. We know of no law requiring one who is present at a sale like this to act as the legal adviser of an adverse party, or else become forever estopped from contesting the validity of the sale. The law of equitable estoppel, as respects the title to real property, is clearly stated thus by the supreme court of the United States: "For the application of the doctrine of equitable estoppel there must generally be some intended deception in the conduct or declarations of the party to be estopped, or such gross negligence on his part as amounts to constructive fraud, by which another has been misled to his injury. Where the estoppel relates to the title of real property, it is essential to the appli-

cution of the doctrine that the party claiming to have been influenced by the conduct or declarations of another was himself not only destitute of knowledge of the true state of the title, but also of any convenient and available means of acquiring such knowledge. Where the condition of the title is known to both parties, or both have the same means of ascertaining the truth, there is no estoppel." Brant v. Coal, etc., Co., 93 U. S. 326. The same principles appear in the following authorities: Davis v. Davis, 26 Cal. 23, and cases cited; Chellis v. Coble, 37 Kan. 558, 15 Pac. Rep. 505; 2 Herm. Estop. §§ 957, 958, et seq. And see Canal Co. v. Hathaway, 8 Wend. 480, 24 Amer. Dec. 51, and notes; Crest v. Jack, 27 Amer. Dec. 353; Johnson v. Insurance Co., (Ky.) 2 S. W. Rep. 151; Martien v. Norris, 91 Mo. 465, 3 S. W. Rep. 849. Section 2966 of the Code is in these words: "A fraud may be committed by acts as well as words; and one who silently stands by and permits another to purchase his property without disclosing his title is guilty of such a fraud as estops him from subsequently setting up such title against the purchaser." In Brown v. Tucker, 47 Ga. 485, this court held that the section quoted only operates in favor of a bona fide purchaser without notice. Granting that the executors stand, in this respect, on the same footing as an owner, still the purchaser in this case does not fill the description, because he was fully acquainted with the facts involving the title, and there was consequently nothing more of which he could be notified. So far we have treated the executors, who are the plaintiffs in this case, as if they were the real owners of the land in dispute, and concluded that they are not estopped. If any doubt attended this conclusion, it would be overcome by considering the wide difference between estopping one who acts as an individual and one who acts in a representative capacity. Where an administrator makes an unauthorized sale of property belonging to the estate, he will not be estopped from recovering it back. Worthy v. Johnson, 10 Ga. 358; Gouldsmith v. Coleman, 57 Ga. 425. The estoppel works against the individual, so that he cannot shun personal liability by pleading his want of authority, but in many cases does not work against the estate. Thus, in Sellars v. Cheney, 70 Ga. 790, it is held: "That an administratrix stood by and saw property of the intestate sold under a void fi. fa. will not estop the administrator de bonis non, who succeeded her, from attacking the validity of the sale." In Magee v. Gregg, 11 Smedes & M. 70, it was held that an administrator, who was present at the sale of a slave belonging to his intestate, made by another person, and offered no objection to the sale, could recover the slave from the purchaser; that he might be estopped of his individual rights, but not deprived of his fiduciary right, by such implied assent. See also, Lewis v. Lusk, 35 Miss. 696, where it is said that an estate cannot be prejudiced or estopped by the mere silence of the administrator, or by his omission to assert title, or to do an act in relation to its interest. In the present case the plain-

tiffs declared on three counts,—one as executors, another as trustees under the will, and another as next friend of the minor beneficiaries; and we are asked to hold that they are estopped in all three characters. In addition to the above authorities we may, in answer, refer to the case of Groover v. King, 46 Ga. 101, in which WARNER, C. J., says: "Although the minor heirs of the intestate may have had a guardian, and that guardian may have receipted to the administrator for their share of the proceeds of the sale of the land without any knowledge of the illegality of the sale, as the evidence in the record shows, they were not estopped from asserting their claim to the land when they obtained a knowledge of such illegal sale, and it was error in the court to charge the jury that they were estopped. Estoppels are not generally favored by the courts, and it would be a very harsh rule to establish that the minor heirs in this case were estopped when their guardian had no knowledge of the illegality of the sale of the land. But in electing to set aside the sale they must account for what they have received from the sale of the land. They cannot have the land and retain the proceeds of the sale thereof." So here, in making this ruling, we do not intend to hold that the purchaser has no remedy. He can still set up his mortgage by way of cross-bill to the action of ejectment, and have it foreclosed, and the land sold, and be paid the amount of the mortgage with interest thereon.

Judgment reversed.

GILL v. STATE.

(Supreme Court of Georgia. March 4, 1891.)

SALES OF LIQUOR TO MINORS—PERMIT FROM PARENT.

Written authority from the parent or guardian for selling or furnishing intoxicating liquors to a minor must be special for each occasion. A general permit or license for the minor to drink beer and whisky in a specified barroom, without limitation as to time or quantity, is void.

(Syllabus by the Court.)

Error from superior court, Muscogee county; SMITH, Judge.

Martin & Worrill, for plaintiff in error. *A. A. Carson*, Sol. Gen., for the State.

BLECKLEY, C. J. The indictment was under section 4540a of the Code, which reads as follows: "No person or persons, by himself or another, shall sell, or cause to be sold, or furnished, or permit any other person or persons, in his, her, or their employ, to sell or furnish any minor or minors spirituous or intoxicating or malt liquors of any kind, without first obtaining written authority from the parent or guardian of such minor or minors, and such person or persons so offending shall, on conviction, be punished as prescribed in section 4310 of the Code." This statute is a police regulation, and has regard not alone to the will and wishes of parents and guardians over the conduct of children, but chiefly to the wholesome re-

straint and discipline of minors as imma-
ture members of society. It relies upon
parental discretion, and intends that that
discretion shall be exercised by the parent
or guardian, and not delegated to the
child. It has no thought of empowering
the parent to make the child the judge of
its own needs for intoxicating liquors,
without limitation as to time or quantity.
On the contrary, the foundation principle
of the law is that the minor's discretion is
not to be trusted. Hence it requires a decision of the parent or guardian, evidenced
by writing. A parental decision not founded on the circumstances of any particular
occasion, but applicable alike to all occasions, and measuring the supply of liquors
to be furnished by nothing but the desires
and appetites of the child, is simply an
effort to repeal the law *pro tanto.* To
give it effect would be in direct conflict
with the principle announced by this
court, during the prevalence of slavery, in
the case of Reinhart v. State, 29 Ga. 522, in
which it was held that the master's discretion to determine the quantity of spirituous liquors necessary for the health of a
slave could not be delegated. Consistently with the policy of the law, there can be
no general authority by the parent conferred upon any one to furnish liquors at
his own pleasure or the pleasure of the
child. The parent must hold control of
the supply, both as to time and quantity,
and the written authority must be special,
as contradistinguished from general. It
must be applicable to one occasion only,
and must be repeated separately for each
subsequent occasion. Once acted on, it is
exhausted, and is no more authority for
subsequent supplies than if it had never
existed. Parental license to run indefinitely would, if granted by a sufficient number
of rash and inconsiderate fathers, enable
one or more drinking saloons in large
cities to flourish on the patronage of minors alone. We think such a license shows
on its face an attempted evasion of the
law. It treats the parent alone as interested in the conduct of the child, and ig-
nores the wider and more important policy
of the statute, which is to rear good citizens and conserve the public order and
general welfare of the state. If we are
correct in what has been said, the instrument relied upon as a defense in this case
was void upon its face. It was no authority for selling or furnishing even in a
single instance, for it had no limitation as
to time or quantity, and was obviously
intended as a general license rather than
as a particular authority. It was an unlimited permit to drink whisky and beer in
the bar-room of which the defendant was
one of the proprietors. We have not overlooked the case of Mascowitz v. State, 49
Ark. 170, 4 S. W. Rep. 656, but, notwithstanding our high respect for the court
which decided it, we cannot accept it as
a precedent. It refers to no authority,
and to our minds its reasoning confounds
the just distinction between police and
civil liability. There was no error in excluding the evidence, nor in refusing to
grant a new trial on other grounds. Judgment affirmed.

DIXON v. STATE.

(Supreme Court of Georgia. March 4, 1891.)

IMPEACHMENT OF WITNESS — SALES OF LIQUOR TO
MINORS.

1. Unless the witness has deceived and entrapped the party introducing him, such party
cannot impeach his credit by evidence of his previous declarations at variance with his sworn
testimony. This rule applies to the state in
criminal prosecutions.

2. Written orders from a parent to a liquor
dealer, requesting him to supply beer and whisky
to a minor whenever he wants them, are void.
They contravene the police policy of section 4540a
of the Code.

(Syllabus by the Court.)

Error from superior court, Muscogee
county; SMITH, Judge.

Martin & Worrill, for plaintiff in error.
A. A. Carson, Sol. Gen., for the state.

BLECKLEY, C. J. 1. No doubt the court
erred in admitting the evidence of several
witnesses to the previous sayings of
Walsh, thereby contradicting a portion of
his testimony given in as a witness for the
state. He testified he never told them so
and so; they testified he did. The only
relevancy of their evidence was to impeach him. It proved nothing in and of
itself pertinent to the case. It was not
competent for the state to discredit its
own witness by showing that he had
made statements out of court which he
denied while testifying for the state in
court. This is the rule applicable to parties generally, and there is no good reason
why it should not affect the state in criminal prosecutions. It was applied in Mc-
Daniel v. State, 53 Ga. 253, without any
suggestion of a distinction between civil
and criminal cases. The Code, § 3869, announcing the general rule, but dispensing
with it where the party has been entrapped by the witness, is broad enough
to cover all cases alike. Here the solicit-
or general did not profess to have been
entrapped or misled.

2. But this error did no harm. The
state's case did not rest on the evidence of
Walsh in any degree, but was established
by other witnesses, who proved the minority of Willie Walsh, and that he was seen
drinking whisky and beer in the defendant's bar-room in the year 1889. The defendant replied in his statement to the
jury that he never let Willie Walsh have
whisky or beer until the written orders
were given by his father. These orders,
one bearing date December 3, 1887, the
other September 11, 1888, were void on
their face, being in their terms too general
and indefinite, as we have just ruled in
the case of Gill v. State, ante, 86. They
contravene the police policy of section
'4540a of the Code. One of them is addressed to Dixon & Herring, the other to
D. W. Dixon, each of them saying:
"Please let my son Willie have whisky
and beer whenever he wants it." This
was no judgment by the father of the
needs and wants of his son, but was an
effort to delegate to the son the power of
judging for himself both as to time and
quantity. The policeman appointed by
law cannot abdicate nor delegate his

functions to the person over whom they are to be exercised. The verdict of the jury was correct, and so was the refusal of the court to grant a new trial. Judgment affirmed.

SEATS v. GEORGIA, M. & G. R. Co.

(Supreme Court of Georgia. March 16, 1891.)

DEATH BY WRONGFUL ACT — CONTRIBUTORY NEGLIGENCE.

Under the plain provisions of our statutes, a widow cannot recover damages from a railroad company for the killing of her husband when it appears that, by ordinary care, he could have avoided the killing, and that his death was caused by his own negligence. Code, §§ 2972, 3034.

(Syllabus by Lumpkin, J.)

Error from superior court, Harris county; SMITH, Judge.

Thornton & Cameron, for plaintiff in error. *Goetchius & Chappell,* for defendant in error.

PER CURIAM. Judgment affirmed.

HARRISON et al. v. PERRY.

(Supreme Court of Georgia. March 16, 1891.)

COMPETENCY OF WITNESS—INTEREST.

1. The main issue in an action of ejectment, brought by the heirs of the grantee named in a certain deed, being whether or not this deed was delivered to such grantee, she being dead when the case was tried, the defendant, who, though not by name a party to the deed, was at the time it was signed the owner of a perfect equity in the land covered thereby, and participated in negotiations relating to its being signed by one who held the legal title, and to the disposition made of it after it was signed, was not, under the evidence act of 1866, a competent witness to prove, in his own favor, facts tending to show its non-delivery.

2. The maker of such deed, not being a party to the case, was, under said act, a competent witness to testify against his own interest as to facts connected with the delivery or non-delivery of the deed.

(Syllabus by the Court.)

Error from superior court, Harris county; SMITH, Judge.

C. J. Thornton, for plaintiffs in error. *L. L. Stanford* and *Martin & Worrill,* for defendant in error.

LUMPKIN, J. It appears from the evidence in this case that one J. J. W. Biggers at one time owned the land in dispute. He bargained said land to J. B. Perry, taking Perry's promissory note in payment for the same, and delivering to Perry his bond for titles. Afterwards Perry paid the full amount of the purchase money. The plaintiffs, who were the heirs at law of Mary L. Harrison, a daughter of J. B. Perry, relied upon a deed signed by Biggers, which purported to convey the land to said Mary L. Harrison. The main dispute in the case was whether or not this deed had ever been delivered. For the plaintiffs it was contended the proof showed that after Perry had paid for the land he surrendered the bond for titles to Biggers, and procured Biggers to make the deed called for by said

bond directly to his daughter, the said Mary L., or that after said deed was so made and delivered Perry acquiesced in and ratified what had been done. On the other hand, the contention of the defendant was that, after he had paid the purchase money to Biggers, Perry's wife, who was old and very ill, and who desired that the land should be conveyed to her daughter, the said Mary L., requested Biggers so to do, and that he accordingly made out and signed the deed to gratify the old lady, but did not deliver it to the daughter; that, on the contrary, he delivered it to the defendant Perry, stating, at the time, that he had made the deed to Mary to gratify old Mrs. Perry; that it was wrong to so make it, but for him (the defendant) to take it and keep it, and not deliver it to Mary, and at the proper time he (Biggers) would make the defendant Perry a title to the land in conformity to the bond; that with this understanding he (Perry) took the deed from Biggers, and surrendered to the latter his bond for titles; that said deed never was delivered, but was, without the knowledge or consent of the defendant Perry, abstracted from his house and put upon record.

1. On the trial the defendant, Perry, was offered as a witness to prove the facts above recited, in his own defense; and the first question presented for our determination is whether or not, under the evidence act of 1866, which was in force at the time of said trial, he was a competent witness for such purpose. We think he should have been excluded, both under the letter and spirit of that act. In the first place he was a party to the case, and had a direct personal and pecuniary interest in the result of it. The contest was between him and the heirs at law of his deceased daughter, Mary L. Harrison, and the effect of his testimony, if admitted, was to break down and destroy the validity of the paper which purported on its face to be a deed from Biggers conveying the land in dispute to her, under whom these plaintiffs claimed title. Moreover, we think that, under the undisputed facts disclosed by this record, Perry should be treated as a party to the deed itself. It is true he was not a party thereto in name, but the facts show he had bought the land from Biggers, had paid the full purchase money therefor, and had surrendered to Biggers his bond for titles. While, therefore, Biggers held the legal title, the actual ownership of the property was in Perry, and if no dispute had arisen as to the validity or delivery of the deed Perry would stand in the same attitude as if he had taken a deed from Biggers, and then himself made a deed of gift to his daughter. The deed from Biggers was signed by him, and duly attested according to law. On its face it purports to have been signed, sealed, and delivered, and such, therefore, is the legal presumption. It was incumbent on Perry to overcome his presumption, and this he sought to do by his own testimony, which we do not think should be allowed. If plaintiffs' theory is true, his position in the case is, for all practical purposes, pre-

cisely the same as if he, having the legal title, had made out and signed a deed conveying the land to his daughter, and was claiming that such deed had never been delivered to her. Treating him, therefore, not only as an interested party to the case, but also as substantially a party to the contract itself which was in issue and on trial, he could not break down plaintiffs' theory by his own testimony, and is excluded from testifying, under the first exception to the evidence act of 1866, which reads as follows: "Where one of the original parties to the contract or cause of action in issue or on trial is dead, or is shown to the court to be insane, or where an executor or administrator is a party in any suit on a contract of his testator or intestate, the other party shall not be admitted to testify in his own favor." Code, § 3854, par. 1. And this is true whether the word "party," last used in the exception quoted, means party to the case, or party to the contract; because, as we have endeavored to show, Perry was really a party to both.

2. The defendant also offered Biggers as a witness to prove the alleged facts above recited as to the non-delivery of the deed. In our opinion, Biggers was a competent witness for this purpose. He was not a party to the case, and had no immediate interest in the result thereof. It was his ultimate interest that the deed in question should be sustained, because it contained a warranty of the title from himself to Mrs. Harrison. If her heirs prevailed in this suit his warranty would be thus established, and he would be freed from further liability thereon. If they failed to recover, he might become liable to her heirs in an action for a breach of this warranty. It appears from the record that in no event could he be further liable to Perry. Perry had voluntarily surrendered to Biggers his bond for titles; had accepted from Biggers the deed in dispute; and, no matter whether the same was delivered or not delivered to Mrs. Harrison, the conduct of Perry had estopped him from asserting any further demand against Biggers concerning this land. When, therefore, Biggers was offered to prove circumstances which, if true, would tend to defeat a recovery by the heirs at law of Mrs. Harrison, he was testifying against his own interest; because, if they failed to recover the land, he was at least putting himself in a position where they might make him liable upon the warranty in the deed. In the exception to the evidence act of 1866, above quoted, no witness is prohibited from testifying against his own interest. The law simply says that witnesses coming within such exception shall not be allowed to testify in their own favor. It may be said that, if an action at law was brought by the heirs of Mrs. Harrison against Biggers upon the warranty in said deed, he would not be permitted as a witness to testify to the identical facts which he was offered to prove in the case now pending; and no doubt this is true, but for the manifest reason that in such an action Biggers

would then have a direct interest in the result of that case, and he would be forbidden by the law from testifying to facts which would aid in his defense thereto, because, under those circumstances, such testimony would be in his own favor. In the present case this reason does not apply, and we think, for the reasons already given, he was a competent witness to prove the acts recited. It will be observed that our rulings in this case, as to both the witnesses Perry and Biggers, are based upon the language of the statute in connection with the facts, without reference to previous adjudications of this court upon questions arising under this act. It seems so clear that our rulings in this case can be safely made in the manner stated, that we deem it unnecessary to review and endeavor to harmonize the various decisions already made upon this act, the more especially as a new act has been passed upon the subject, which we trust will relieve the courts from many of the embarrassments and difficulties experienced under the act of 1866. Judgment reversed.

McLENDON v. HOLLIS.

(Supreme Court of Georgia. March 4, 1891.)

Error from superior court, Talbot county; SMITH, Judge.

Willis & Matthews, for plaintiff in error. *Henry Persons* and *M. Bethune,* for defendant in error.

SIMMONS, J. This case was not brought here in compliance with the act approved November 11, 1889; and as that act provides that no case shall be brought here by bill of exceptions, except in the manner prescribed therein, we are without jurisdiction to hear and determine the case made in this bill of exceptions. Writ of error dismissed.

WEEMS v. JONES.

SAME v. AMERICAN MORTG. Co. OF SCOTLAND, Limited.

(Supreme Court of Georgia. March 4, 1891.)

USURY—COMMISSION TO AGENT.

Where the lender of money neither takes, nor contracts to take, anything beyond lawful interest, the loan is not rendered usurious because the borrower contracts with one engaged in the business of procuring loans to pay him out of the loan for his services, and does so pay him, the lender having no interest in such business or its proceeds.

Error from superior court, Chattahoochee county; SMITH, Judge.

E. J. Wynn and *C. J. Thornton,* for plaintiff in error. *W. E. Simmons,* for defendant in error.

SIMMONS, J. The material facts in both of these cases are the same, and both are ruled by the case of Merck v. Freehold Co., 79 Ga. 213, 7 S. E. Rep. 265. Judgment affirmed.

STATE v. STUBBS.

(Supreme Court of North Carolina. April 14, 1891.)

ADULTERY—ADMISSIBILITY OF EVIDENCE — SUFFICIENCY OF INDICTMENT.

1. On an indictment for adultery, evidence of a declaration of the *feme* defendant, made after the offense charged, but not as part of the *res gestæ*, that her brother had driven her from home, and her father had paid the male defendant to take her on his farm as a work-hand, was inadmissible.

2. Where the male defendant testified that he had heard the *feme* defendant's father order her to leave his house, it was not material error to exclude his testimony that he had seen letters from her father and brother, declaring that she could not stay there.

3. Evidence that the defendants had been seen driving together since the prosecution began was admissible when received with other evidence tending to show their adulterous association.

4. An indictment charging that defendants "unlawfully did associate, bed, and cohabit together, and then and there did commit fornication and adultery, contrary to the form of the statute," etc., and that they "were not united together in marriage," implies that they did "lewdly and lasciviously associate," as forbidden by Code N. C. § 1041, and sufficiently charges the offense.

Appeal from superior court, Catawba county; ARMFIELD, Judge.

The defendant (appellant) and a *feme* defendant, who did not appeal, were indicted for the offense of fornication and adultery, and pleaded not guilty. There was a trial and verdict of guilty, and judgment thereon, from which the male defendant appealed to this court. Code N. C. § 1041, provides that "if any man and woman, not being married to each other, shall lewdly and lasciviously associate and cohabit together, they shall be guilty of a misdemeanor."

The Attorney General, for the State.

MERRIMON, C. J. The *feme* defendant, on the cross-examination of a witness for the state, asked the latter whether on some occasion while she was in possession of property of the male defendant, and before the indictment, she had not told the witness that her brother had driven her from home, and that her father had paid the male defendant, who had married her cousin, to take her on his farm as a work-hand. The question had reference to declarations of the *feme* defendant, made after the offense charged in the indictment. The evidence, if material, was properly rejected. What a party says exculpatory of himself after the offense was committed, and not part of the *res gestæ*, is not evidence for him; otherwise he might make evidence for himself. State v. McNair, 93 N. C. 628, and cases there cited; State v. Ward, 103 N. C. 419, 8 S. E. Rep. 814; State v. Moore, 104 N. C. 744, 10 S. E. Rep. 183. The appellant testified in his own behalf, and was asked if he had not heard the *feme* defendant's father order her to leave his house, and if he had not seen letters from her father and brother, declaring she could not stay at her father's house. Upon objection the court excluded reference to the letters. The evidence seems to have been

of slight importance, and the mere mention of letters was simply cumulative, if evidence at all. The exclusion of such mention was in any view of it too slight to constitute ground for a new trial. Whitehurst v. Hyman, 90 N. C. 487; McGowan v. Railroad Co., 95 N. C. 417; Livingston v. Dunlap, 99 N. C. 268, 6 S. E. Rep. 200. The state produced evidence tending to show that the defendants had been seen driving together since the prosecution began, and this was received, in connection with other evidence, going to show their lascivious association within two years next before this action began. As to this evidence the court instructed the jury " that they could only find the defendants guilty upon proof of this association—bedding and cohabiting with each other—within two years next before the finding of the bill of indictment, but that the evidence offered of acts before that time, and also acts after the finding of the bill of indictment, should be considered by them as explaining the relation of the parties within the two years preceding the finding of the bill." This is assigned as error. The objection is unfounded. The evidence objected to was received in connection with other pertinent evidence, and as tending in some degree to prove the adulterous character of the association of the parties. State v. Guest, 100 N. C. 410, 6 S. E. Rep. 253; State v. Wheeler, 104 N. C. 893, 10 S. E. Rep. 491.

The motion in arrest of judgment cannot be allowed. The indictment sufficiently charges the substance of the offense. It does not charge in the terms of the statute, as regularly it should do, that the defendants did "lewdly and lasciviously associate, "etc.; but it does charge that they "unlawfully did associate, bed, and cohabit together, and then and there did commit fornication and adultery, contrary to the form of the statute," etc., and it also charged that they were "not united together in marriage." All this must imply that they did "lewdly and lasciviously associate." State v. Lashley, 84 N. C. 754. It is always safer and better to charge the statutory offense in the words of the statute when this can be conveniently done, but when the offense is charged substantially in all respects the indictment must be upheld as sufficient. There is no error, and the judgment must be affirmed.

ASHBY v. PAGE.

(Supreme Court of North Carolina. April 14, 1891.)

APPEAL—REVERSAL—PROCEEDINGS BELOW — CUSTODY OF CHILD.

1. On application by a mother for the apprenticeship of her minor child, the superior court affirmed the action of the clerk in apprenticing the child to defendant, against the mother's wishes. *Held,* that a reversal of this decision by the supreme court on appeal, which did not render a final judgment in the matter, but simply remanded the cause for a new trial to the court below, did not warrant the mother in instituting *habeas corpus* proceedings to regain the custody of the child from defendant, as the order of the superior court apprenticing the child to him still remained in force.

2. The reversal by the supreme court of the judgment of the superior court, on the ground that the facts found did not warrant the judgment that the mother was not entitled to the custody of her child, does not preclude the superior court, on a new trial, from hearing additional testimony, nor from finding the facts in accordance therewith.

3. A finding by the court, on such additional evidence, that the mother is a woman of bad character, and not a fit person to have the custody of the child, whose father is dead, brings the case within Acts N. C. 1889, c. 169, § 2, subd. 4, and authorizes the apprenticeship of the child to a stranger.

Appeal from McCorkle, J., at fall term, 1890, of Stokes superior court. This case was brought here by a former appeal, and is reported in 106 N. C. 328, 11 S. E. Rep. 283, when this court found error in the ruling below. On 21st of May, 1890, soon after said opinion had been filed, and before the next succeeding term of Stokes superior court, the plaintiff sued out a petition of *habeas corpus*, which defendant answered 26th May, but by successive continuances the matter went over to the fall term, at which time the court heard additional affidavits from the defendant, the plaintiff excepting. Counter-affidavits were then offered by the plaintiff. The court found as facts that the plaintiff had three bastard children (one of them the child in controversy) before her present marriage; that she is a woman of bad character for virtue and morality, and that she is not a fit person to have the custody of the child; that the defendant is a man of good moral character, and a suitable person to have the custody of it; and remanded it to him by virtue of the apprenticeship heretofore made by the clerk of the superior court. The plaintiff appealed, and assigned as error: (1) That the court erred in hearing additional evidence as the matter was *res judicata;* (2) that by virtue of the decision of the supreme court the plaintiff was entitled to judgment directing the child to be delivered to her; (3) that the child did not come under any of the provisions of chapter 169, Acts 1889, and plaintiff was entitled to its custody; (4) that by virtue of said act, and in the *status* of the cause, the court had no jurisdiction to pass upon the right and propriety of allowing the defendant to hold the custody of the child. The cause was submitted in this court on printed briefs, without oral argument, by counsel, under rule 10.

A. M. Stack, for appellant.   W. W. King, for appellee.

Clark, J., (*after stating the facts as above.*) The decision of this court on the former hearing (106 N. C. 328, 11 S. E. Rep. 283) was that there was error because the facts as found by the court below did not bring the case within any of the five classes which the clerk was authorized to apprentice by chapter 169, Acts 1889. There was no final judgment here, and the cause stood on the docket of the court below for a new trial at the first term held after the certificate was sent down from this court. Acts 1887, c. 192, § 3. The attempted *habeas corpus* proceeding was irregular, as the defendant had possession of the child under the order of the court, (Code, §§ 1645, 1646,) and, though this court had held there was error, no judgment had been given for plaintiff on the merits, and the matter stood for proper action at the next term. The *habeas corpus* proceeding seems to have been in the nature of a petition in the cause; it could serve no purpose, and may be treated as mere surplusage.

The plaintiff contends, however, that the opinion of this court was a finality, and that it was error in the court below to hear additional testimony. To this we do not assent. This court decided that the facts found did not warrant the judgment that the plaintiff was not entitled to the custody of the child. It was competent for the court below to hear any additional testimony, and it was its duty to find the facts before entering its judgment. In Jones v. Swepson, the court had, on the former appeal, (79 N. C. 510,) held that there was error, and the court on the second appeal (94 N. C. 700) say, (Smith, C. J.,) in passing upon the same point now before us: "We think it clear that a new trial awarded for some vitiating illegal ruling, which may be reasonably supposed to have influenced the verdict, reopens the controversy for the admission of any evidence that is itself competent, and ought to have been received if offered at the first trial. This is equally true when the judge assumes the function of passing upon the evidence and determining the facts upon which the judgment is founded." The decision of this court that there was error had the effect to set aside the former decision, and the cause stood for trial on the merits *de novo*. The present case and the one just cited differ, therefore, somewhat from Jones v. Thorne, 80 N. C. 72; Sanderson v. Daily, 83 N. C. 67; Mabry v. Henry, Id. 298; Roulhac v. Brown, 87 N. C. 1; Pasour v. Lineberger, 90 N. C. 159; Wingo v. Hooper, 98 N. C. 482, 4 S. E. Rep. 463; and the like. In those cases certain interlocutory orders as to refusing injunctions appointing receivers, vacating attachments, and the like, were held to be *res judicata*, unless affidavits were presented showing additional facts subsequently transpiring, or, at least, facts making an entirely different ground for the relief already refused. Here the court on appeal has adjudged that the facts found did not warrant the judgment, and on the new trial the appellee has made out a stronger case.

The present finding of the court below, upon the additional evidence offered, is that the plaintiff is a woman of bad character, and not a fit person to have the custody of the child, who is without a father. This brings the case within the fourth subdivision of section 2, c. 169, Acts 1889, and the clerk was authorized to apprentice the child to the defendant. This being an appeal to the superior court from the clerk, it was competent for the judge, instead of sending the case back to the clerk, to proceed to hear and determine the matters in controversy himself. Acts 1887, c. 276. No error.

FULPS v. MOCK.

(Supreme Court of North Carolina. April 14, 1891.)

PLEADING AND PROOF—VARIANCE.

A complaint alleged defendant's indebtedness for services rendered from March 1, 1881, to November 15, 1889, in the sum of $15 per month. The answer denied the allegations, pleaded the statute of limitations, and set up a counter-claim for board. Plaintiff's reply alleged that defendant agreed in consideration of the services named to board plaintiff, and leave him all his property at his decease, but that on November 15, 1889, defendant dismissed him from service. On the trial plaintiff testified that he hired to defendant in 1881, and was to be paid whatever was right, and worked a year; that in 1883 he made a contract with defendant to stay with him as long as defendant lived, he to make plaintiff heir to all his property; and that plaintiff lived with him for five years, when defendant discharged him. Plaintiff testified his services were worth from $20 to $25 per month. *Held*, that the allegations of the complaint were broad enough to cover evidence given of the special contract set up in the replication.

Appeal from MERRIMON, J., at spring term, 1891. of Alexander superior court. The complaint alleged "that defendant is justly indebted to the plaintiff in the sum of eighteen hundred dollars for services performed by the plaintiff for the defendant as miller in defendant's mill, and for attending defendant's fishery, and for services on defendant's farm, from the first day of March, 1881, to the 15th day of November, 1889, at $25 per month, "and a demand and refusal to pay. The answer denied the allegations of the complaint, pleaded the statute of limitations, and a counter-claim for board and lodging for the time specified in the complaint. The plaintiff filed a replication to the defendant's pleas of the statute of limitations and counter-claim, setting out that defendant agreed, in consideration of services named, and which plaintiff has rendered, the defendant would board him, and would convey him all the property which he (defendant) might own at his death; that on November 15, 1889, the defendant dismissed the plaintiff from his service, declined to allow him to proceed further under the contract, and denied its existence; and thereupon the plaintiff brought this action for the value of the services actually rendered by the plaintiff. By consent the following issue was submitted. "Is the defendant indebted to the plaintiff? If so, in what sum?" The plaintiff was offered as a witness in his own behalf, and, after objection by defendant, which was overruled by the court, testified as follows: "I hired to defendant in 1881. Worked one year under this contract. He was to pay me whatever was right. No agreed price. Sawed for him. I made a contract with defendant in 1883. He sent for me to go over to the mill to see him. He wanted me to stay with him as long as he lived, and he would make me an heir to everything he had, and I agreed to do it. Went to his house, and stayed there with him five years. Attended to his mill, attended to his ferry and fishery, and did other things. I quit in 1889, in November. Defendant made me quit. He cursed me, and drew his stick on me, and told me, 'Damn you, you have

to get away, and I'll get somebody that will attend to my business.' He boarded me. This was a part of the agreement. My services were worth $20 to $25 per month." This evidence was objected to by defendant "under the pleadings as they stood, unamended. The plaintiff did not ask leave to amend, nor was any amendment of the pleadings made then or at any time." The court, upon the authority of Stokes v. Taylor, 104 N. C. 394, 10 S. E. Rep. 566, overruled the objection, and defendant excepted. The plaintiff, without objection by defendant, abandoned any claim for services rendered under the contract for 1881, and sought only to recover for services rendered under the contract of 1883. There was other evidence tending to show how long plaintiff served defendant, and the value of his services. The defendant offered evidence tending to show an agreement in 1881 that plaintiff was to receive as compensation a part of the mill tolls; that he left, and when he returned in 1883, and went to work, nothing was said about terms, and plaintiff left voluntarily in 1889. The court charged the jury (1) that if the contract was as alleged by the plaintiff in his replication, then, unless the plaintiff was ready and willing to perform his part of the contract, and was prevented from doing so by defendant, they would answer the issue "No." (2) If such contract existed, and plaintiff was ready and willing to perform his part, but was prevented by defendant, plaintiff is entitled to recover the value of his services, less such sums as had been paid him, and the value of such tolls or proceeds of such as he may have retained; and that he was not barred by the statute of limitations as to any part of his claim if defendant committed a breach of the contract in November, 1889, as testified by plaintiff. (3) That if there was no contract as to length of service or rate of pay plaintiff could recover only the value of his services for three years immediately preceding the action, subject to any payments made him; and as to the statute of limitations he read to the jury what was said in Miller v. Lash, 85 N. C. on page 54, 3d paragraph. (4) If the contract between the parties was as testified to by defendant, the plaintiff was not entitled to recover anything. Defendant excepted to the instructions 1 and 2. There was a verdict for the plaintiff. Defendant moved for a new trial, on the ground "that throughout this trial the special contract set up in the replication had been treated by the court as a cause of action in itself, and sufficiently and lawfully pleaded to enable the plaintiff to have the benefit of it as a ground for recovery; that evidence had been admitted for the purpose of establishing it as such; and that his honor's charge had instructed the jury to find for plaintiff if he had proved that special contract, and defendant's breach of it; which part of his charge he respectfully assigned as error." The case on appeal further states: "His honor's charge, in the particular complained of, speaks for itself, but he did not treat the special contract set up in plaintiff's replication as a cause of action in itself, and sufficiently and lawfully pleaded to enable the plaintiff to have the benefit of it as a ground for a recovery. The evidence was not admitted for the purpose of establishing it as such. His honor was of opinion that under the ruling of the supreme court in Stokes v. Taylor it was incumbent upon him to admit the evidence objected to upon the issue submitted to the jury (there being no objection to the form or to the substance of the issue) for the purpose of proving that plaintiff rendered services for which he was entitled to be paid; and that the variance between the allegations of the complaint and the proof offered ought not to be regarded as material; and that the defendant was sufficiently informed by the complaint of the plaintiff's demand against him, and was not in any way taken by surprise. Verdict and judgment for plaintiff. Appeal by defendant.

Jones & Kerner and *W. M. Robbins*, for appellant. *R. B. Burke*, for appellee.

CLARK, J., (*after stating the facts as above.*) The defendant seems to have misconceived the scope of the action. The court below did not "allow plaintiff to abandon his cause of action set out in the complaint, and to recover on a special contract set out in the replication." The plaintiff, by his complaint, was seeking to recover the value of his services from 1881 to 1889. On the trial he abandoned any claim for services from 1881 to 1883. To this defendant did not and could not object. To prove his right to recover the value of his services from 1883 to 1889, without being subject to counter-claim for board, and to bar the application of the statute of limitations, the plaintiff introduced evidence which was also admissible to prove the allegations of his complaint. The evidence was pertinent and appropriate. It was not necessary to plead these matters of evidence in the complaint, and that the plaintiff pleaded them in his replication constituted no change or abandonment of his cause of action, which remained, as before, for the recovery of the value of his services. The plaintiff did not seek on the trial to recover the compensation alleged to have been stipulated for in the express contract. The express contract was put in evidence merely to show why the plaintiff, by defendant's abandonment of it, could recover on a *quantum meruit*, and why the statute of limitations did not run. The cause of action was so broadly stated, indeed, as to have authorized a recovery by proof either on a *quantum meruit* or express contract. Lewis v. Railroad Co., 95 N. C. 179. If the allegation was defective, the proper mode of correction (when the substantial facts which constitute the cause of action are stated in the complaint, or can be inferred therefrom by reasonable intendment) is not by demurrer, nor by excluding evidence on the trial, but by a motion before the trial to make the averments more definite by amendment. Stokes v. Taylor, 104 N. C. 394, 10 S. E. Rep. 566; Pom. Rem. § 549; Code, § 261; Moore v. Edmiston, 70 N. C. 510. No error.

MALLARD et al. v. PATTERSON.

(*Supreme Court of North Carolina.* April 14, 1891.)

FILING PLEADINGS—EXTENSION OF TIME—CLAIMS AGAINST DECEDENTS.

1. In an action against an administrator, defendant made default in answering the verified complaint, and after time was granted him to file his pleading an unverified answer appeared among the papers. After the lapse of five years defendant was allowed to file a verified answer, setting up meritorious pleas, exclusive of a plea of the running of the statute of limitations. *Held*, that leave to file the verified answer, with the limitation, was discretionary with the court below, and is not reviewable on appeal.

2. Code N. C. provides that, where an action is brought on a claim which was not presented within 12 months from the first publication of a notice to creditors, the administrator shall not be chargeable for assets he may have distributed before such action was commenced. An administrator published a notice to all persons having claims against the estate to exhibit them within 12 months thereafter. After the expiration of the year he paid part of the assets to the next of kin on account of their distributive shares. Plaintiff sued on a claim that had not been presented within 12 months from the first publication of the notice. *Held*, that defendant is not chargeable with the amount of money he paid to the distributees.

Appeal from superior court, Iredell county, BYNUM, Judge.

It appears that Ann Patterson died intestate in the county of Iredell before the 4th day of October, 1875, and on that day the defendant was appointed and qualified as administrator of her estate, and gave notice to all persons having claims against the estate to exhibit the same to him within twelve months, etc., as required by the statute. Code, § 1421. The defendant brought an action against certain parties, which was not determined until after the lapse of several years, and then adversely to him. In the mean time he had failed to wind up and administer the estate in his hands according to law. Within twelve months next after he gave notice to creditors to present their claims he paid to certain of the next of kin of the intestate considerable sums of money, on account of their respective distributive shares, and took their receipts for the same. On the 3d of February, 1883, the plaintiffs brought this special proceeding, in behalf of themselves and all other creditors of the said intestate, to compel the defendant to an account of his administration, and to pay the creditors what might be payable to them respectively. The defendant was duly served with a summons on the 19th of February, 1883. On the 3d of March, 1883, the plaintiffs filed their complaint, alleging a cause of action, and the indebtedness of the intestate to them, respectively, for divers sums of money. Thereupon the clerk advertised for all creditors of the intestate to appear before him on or before the time designated, and file evidence of their claims, etc. Afterwards, on the 9th of April, 1883, the defendant moved to dismiss the proceeding because the advertisement was not regular and was insufficient. The motion was denied, and fresh advertisement made. The defendant did not then answer the complaint, but the court gave time to answer until the 21st of May, 1883. Afterwards a further advertisement was made for creditors to present their claims on or before the 7th of September, 1889. Notice was also served upon the defendant to appear before the clerk on the same day, to exhibit on oath a list of all claims against his intestate's estate, etc. Afterwards, on the 1st of October, 1889, upon affidavit filed, the defendant moved to be allowed to file his verified answer to the complaint. The complaint was verified when filed. An answer, unverified, was found among the papers, but when it was filed did not appear. After contention of the parties, the clerk allowed the defendant to file an answer, in which he might "set up only meritorious pleas, to-wit, allowed him to set up only pleas of payment, counter-claims, or set-offs which he might have," but he was not allowed to plead the statute of limitations. The defendant excepted. Afterwards the clerk examined claims presented by creditors of the intestate, heard evidence, etc., filed his report of account stated, etc. To this report the defendant filed divers exceptions, which were not sustained. The clerk gave judgment for the plaintiffs, and the defendant appealed to the judge of the court in term-time. The court, in term-time, overruled all the defendant's exceptions, found the facts to be as found by the clerk, and affirmed his rulings, and gave judgment upon the report for the plaintiffs, and, the defendant having excepted, appealed to this court.

Armfield & Turner, for appellant. *W. M. Robbins*, for appellees.

MERRIMON, C. J., (*after stating the facts as above.*) This proceeding has been greatly delayed and neglected by the parties, particularly so by the defendant, and possibly to his prejudice in respects not remediable here. We can only deal with errors assigned, or such as appear upon the face of the record proper. The plaintiffs, in the orderly course of procedure, filed their verified complaint, alleging sufficiently a cause of action. The defendant was allowed time to file his answer. This he did not do promptly. An answer appears among the papers,—when this was placed among them does not appear,—and it was not verified. It was therefore no sufficient pleading, and could not be treated as such, certainly in the face of objection. Alford v. McCormac, 90 N. C. 151. After the lapse of five years or more, the defendant asked to be allowed to verify this answer, or to file a new one properly verified. Clearly, he was not entitled to do so as of right. It was discretionary with the court to allow or disallow his application, or grant the same, with limitations. The court allowed him to answer, alleging "meritorious" defenses, but not to avail himself of the statute of limitations. This the court might do, and its exercise of discretion in such respect is not reviewable in this court.

The first four exceptions to the account stated by the clerk relate to his refusal to allow the defendant credit for certain sums of money paid by him to certain of the next of kin of his intestate within 12 months next after his first publication of notice to creditors of his intestate to present their claims to him, etc. Regularly, the administrator should pay all debts due creditors before he distributes the estate, or any part of it, to the next of kin of his intestate. He fails to do so at his peril, unless the claim was not presented to him until after the lapse of 12 months next after the first publication of notice given by him to creditors to present their claims, as required by the statute, (Code, § 1421.) In the latter case, in an action upon such claim, he will not be chargeable with such sums of money as he may have paid in satisfaction of distributive shares. The statute (Id. § 1428) so expressly provides. In this case not a single claim sued upon or the subject of this proceeding was, so far as appears, presented to the defendant within 12 months from the first publication of the general notice to creditors to present their claims to the defendant, and the sums of money paid by him to distributees were all paid years before this proceeding began. The statute just cited provides that in such case "the executor, administrator, or collector shall not be chargeable for any assets that he may have paid in satisfaction of any debts, legacies, or distributive shares before such action was commenced." The purpose is to relieve administrators, executors, and collectors from liability for assets they may pay or distribute to a person or persons entitled to have the same, as to claims not presented within 12 months after the first publication of general notice to creditors, and as well to facilitate and encourage the prompt settlement of the estates of deceased persons. It may be that if an administrator should, with knowledge of existing debts against his intestate's estate, collusively so pay or distribute assets to creditors or distributees, he would not be relieved from liability as to debts not so presented, but, so far as we can see, no fraud or collusion is imputed to the defendant in this case. We are therefore of opinion that the defendant ought not to have been charged with the several sums of money he paid to the distributees. We have examined the other exceptions, and think that they are without merit. It will serve no useful purpose to advert to them further. There is error. The account must be corrected, in accordance with this opinion, and the judgment accordingly modified, and as so modified affirmed. To that end let this opinion be certified to the superior court. It is so ordered.

MUSE et al. v. LONDON ASSUR. CORP.

(*Supreme Court of North Carolina. April 14, 1891.*)

INSURANCE—CONDITIONS—TIME OF SUING.

A condition in a policy, that no suit against the insurer shall be sustained unless commenced "within 12 months" next after the loss, is not in contravention of Code N. C. § 3076, which forbids the insurer to limit the term within which suit shall be brought "to a period less than one year."

Appeal from superior court, Moore county: GRAVES, Judge.

Action by John C. Muse and A. H. Muse against the London Assurance Corporation on an insurance policy. The property insured was destroyed by fire August 31, 1885, and on October 11, 1887, plaintiffs commenced suit to recover for the loss. The policy stipulated that "no suit or action against this corporation for the recovery of any claim by virtue of this policy shall be sustainable in any court of law or chancery unless such suit or action be commenced within twelve months next after the loss shall occur; and, should any suit or action be commenced after the expiration of the aforesaid twelve months, the lapse of time shall be taken and deemed conclusive evidence against the validity of such claim, any statute of limitation to the contrary notwithstanding." Code N. C. § 3076, provides that "no person licensed to do insurance business under this chapter shall limit the term within which any suit shall be brought against such person to a period less than one year from the time when the loss insured against shall occur." Defendant moved for judgment upon the face of the pleadings, which was denied, and defendant appeals.

John W. Hinsdale, for appellant. *J. C. Black* and *Haywood & Haywood*, for appellees.

AVERY, J. It seems to be established that a provision in a policy that the insured may bring suit within 12 months after the loss, and not later, being in the nature of a condition precedent, is not in contravention of the policy or statutes of limitation, and will be upheld by the courts. May, Ins. § 478; O'Laughlin v. Insurance Co., 11 Fed. Rep. 280; Fullam v Insurance Co., 7 Gray, 61; Wilson v. Insurance Co., 27 Vt. 99; Riddlesbarger v. Insurance Co., 7 Wall. 386; Gray v. Insurance Co., 1 Blackf. 280. The weight of authority sustains the position also that "the rights of the parties in such cases are fixed by the contract," and that the contract must be construed as requiring that the action which is prosecuted to judgment (not a suit begun previously) must be brought within 12 months after the loss occurs, unless the conduct of the insurer has been such as to amount to a waiver of the benefit of the condition. Riddlesbarger's Case, supra; Arthur v. Insurance Co., 78 N. Y. 462; McFarland v. Insurance Co., 6 W. Va. 437; and 2 Phil. Ins. § 1983. The condition that the suit shall be instituted, if at all, within a year after the loss has been sustained as reasonable and valid in part, at least, because the tendency of speedy investigations, while the evidence is fresh, is to prevent fraudulent practices. 4 Wait, Act. & Def. 86. But such stipulations operating as forfeitures are construed strictly, and comparatively slight evidences of waiver have been held sufficient to prevent their enforcement. Ripley v. Insurance Co., 29 Barb. 552; Ames v. Insurance Co., 14 N. Y. 253. There was nothing, however, in the conduct of the company or its agents that was calculated to mislead the plaintiff as to its purposes, and induce him to postpone instituting the action, nor was there evidence of evading service, or of any act showing a purpose on the part of the company to prevent or delay the bringing of the suit after the plaintiff determined to take more active steps. We think, therefore, that there was not, under the most liberal view of the law on that subject, sufficient evidence to go to the jury as tending to show a waiver. Insurance Co. v Hall, 12 Mich. 211; Ripley's and Arthur's Cases, supra. So far our views coincide fully with these expressed by the learned judge who presided in the court below. But we do not concur in the construction given by him to section 3076 of the Code, and in the consequent conclusions that the stipulation in the policy was void because it was in conflict with that statute. If, instead of prohibiting licensed insurance companies from stipulating that actions should begin within a shorter period that one year, the legislature had, by appending an additional subsection under section 156 of the Code, prescribed one year as the limit for bringing the action for a loss sustained by the assured, there would have been good ground for the contention that the right of action would still subsist for a year after "nonsuit, reversal, or arrest of judgment," under the provisions of section 166 of the Code. But his honor's ruling rests entirely upon the idea that the stipulation that no action should be sustainable unless it should be "commenced within twelve months next after the loss shall occur" was in effect a limitation of the time within which suit might be brought "to a period less than one year," and was void, because in contravention of an express provision of the law Twelve months, in the absence of a legislative definition of the word "month," must be interpreted, according to the ordinary popular understanding, as meaning twelve calendar (not lunar) months. 2 Rap. Law Dict.; Gross v. Fowler, 21 Cal. 396; Bouv. Law Dict.; Society v. Thompson, 32 Cal. 347; Mitchell v Woodson, 37 Miss. 567; Sprague v. Norway, 31 Cal. 174; Kimball v. Lamson, 2 Vt. 142; Williamson v. Farrow, 1 Bailey, 611; Brewer v. Harris, 5 Grat. 285; Com. v. Chambre, 4 Dall. 133. The courts of this country have very generally adopted a different rule of construction from that which obtained in England before the Revolution, because the popular sense of the word "month" was in America a calendar, not a lunar, month. Kimball v. Lamson, supra. On the other hand, the word "year" is interpreted to mean 12 calendar months. See definitions of the word, 2 Abb. Law Dict.; 2 Rap. Law Dict.; 2 Bouv. Law Dict. We understand his honor, however, to hold that "within one year" is necessarily "less than one year," and therefore the stipulation is in conflict with the statute. While his construction of the language of the policy is more than plausible, we do not concur in it. The law was enacted to prohibit persons or corporations engaged in the business of insuring lives or property from inserting in policies issued a provision that an action for a loss could not be maintained unless it should be instituted before the expiration of six or ten months, or of any period less than one year or twelve months. The stipulation in this case did not fix the limit at less than one year, but precisely at twelve months, which was equivalent to a year. An agreement that the time for bringing the action should be limited to two years, or to any intermediate period down to and including one year, would have been valid. The inhibition of the statute extended only to stipulating for a time of limitation less than a year. We think that upon the face of the pleadings and upon the facts admitted it was apparent that the plaintiff could not maintain this action, and the defendant was entitled to judgment for costs. There is error.

McKESSON v SMART et al.

(*Supreme Court of North Carolina.* April 14, 1891.)

LOST DOCUMENTS—SECONDARY EVIDENCE.

The testimony of a magistrate that he had failed to enter a certain case upon his docket; that he had made diligent search for the other records in the case, but could not find them, and that they were lost or destroyed, is sufficient foundation for the admission of parol evidence of their contents.

This was an action tried before BYNUM, J., and a jury, on' an appeal from a justice's court, at spring term, 1890, of Mitchell superior court. The plaintiff alleged upon an account of $63. The defendants denied the indebtedness, and also pleaded as an estoppel that the same cause of action had been sued upon in another and different action before a justice of the peace, based upon the same cause of action, and determined in favor of the defendants, and that from such judgment the plaintiff did not appeal. In support of this plea the defendants introduced J. M. Riddle, who testified that "he was an acting justice of the peace in 1889, and that during his term of office the plaintiff's intestate brought an action against these defendants before him, and that he tried and determined the same." Defendants then asked witness where were the records of the trial referred to. To this witness replied "that he had his docket, but the case had never been put upon it; the other records of the trial were lost or destroyed; that he had made diligent search for them, but could not find them." Defendants then proposed to prove by witness the contents of the lost records. To this plaintiff's counsel objected. The objection was sustained by the court, and the defendants excepted. The court charged the jury at this point that there was no evidence of a former trial of this action, and that they would not consider this question or plea. Judgment for plaintiff. Appeal by defendants.

W. B. Councill, for appellants.

AVERY, J., (*after stating the facts as above.*) The witness, a justice of the peace, had failed to enter the case upon his docket, and testified that he had made "diligent search" for the other papers, and could not find them, and that they were lost or destroyed. He was the custodian of these *quasi* records, the contents of which were important to show a former trial and judgment, which would operate as an estoppel against the plaintiff in this action. The inevitable inference is that, being an officer, intrusted by the state of North Carolina with judicial power, and the custody of the process and papers pertaining to his position, he had sufficient knowledge of the language used in every-day life to know that he could not make diligent search for these particular documents among the papers of another person, or in any place except where he usually kept his own official papers, or actually knew that they had been deposited. Making diligent search could not imply less than a careful hunting for them there. It might have meant more,—that, in addition, he had examined some other locality, where he had, contrary to his usual custom, left them. When the clerk of a court testifies that he has made diligent search for a record belonging to the court the testimony *ex vi termini* implies an examination in the place where he usually deposits such a paper. The judge is not expected to inquire or require counsel to ask how long a time the officer consumed in the search, in what corner of the room he usually kept the paper, how many packages he opened, whether he had adopted a good system of classification and arrangement of documents, and on *ad infinitum*, in order to satisfy himself from this detailed statement that the search was in truth diligent, because every corner of an apartment, or every pigeon-hole in a desk, was ransacked. The preliminary inquiry addressed to the court is whether the evidence raises a reasonable presumption that the instrument has been lost. Best, Ev. 451; Gillis v. Railroad Co., ante, 11, (decided at this term.) In order to raise this presumption, it would not have been sufficient to have asked some person who did not appear to be charged by the law with the custody of the papers whether he had made diligent search, and to have received the answer that he had. But if the custodian had even stated how he searched the usual depository, and failed to find the papers, and had also said that A. B. had some time before the search taken them to his house, and had not, so far as he knew, returned them, it would have become necessary to call and examine A. B. Tayl. Ev. § 22. The witness testified that the papers had been in existence and in his care; that he still had his docket, upon which he had failed to enter the case. If his honor had admitted the evidence, it still remained for the jury to pass upon its sufficiency to show the contents. The finding by the judge upon the preliminary question no more establishes the sufficiency of the evidence to show the actual existence and contents of the document than does the preliminary finding upon which the declaration of an alleged conspirator is admitted establish the conspiracy. In Yount v. Miller, 91 N. C. 332, the plaintiff proved "by M. O. Sherrill, former clerk of the court of the pleas and quarter sessions, that the original papers in the case of Elizabeth Yount, widow of John Yount, against the heirs of John Yount, had been searched for by him, and had been lost." This was all of the preliminary proof offered in that case. The officer did not testify that he had searched diligently, as in our case, nor did he intimate where he searched. He was formerly the custodian, as clerk of the court of pleas and quarter sessions, and then, as clerk of the superior court, had them in charge. After objection, the court admitted secondary evidence in that case, upon the idea, of course, that sufficient proof of the loss had been offered. It would seem useless to add any other case from our own Reports. We think that it was error to refuse to admit the testimony, and allow the jury, with proper instruction, to consider it as bearing upon the issues. The defendant is entitled to a new trial.

WILLIAMS et al. v. BENET.

(*Supreme Court of South Carolina.* April 28, 1891.)

CORPORATIONS—SUBSCRIPTIONS TO STOCK.

Where a person's name is on the subscription list of a corporation with his consent, he is *prima facie* bound to pay for his stock, and his liability is not discharged by a private agreement with a third person that the latter should pay for it.

Appeal from common pleas circuit court, Abbeville county; ALDRICH, Judge.

Parker & McGowan and *Sam'l C. Cason,* for appellant. *Westmoreland & Haynsworth,* for respondents.

WALLACE, J. This is an action at law, brought to recover an unpaid balance of a subscription to the capital stock of the Georgia Construction & Investment Company. The defendant denies that he subscribed to the stock, or paid any installment thereon, and sets up a special defense, to-wit: "(1) That the defendant was the attorney and counsellor of Susong & Co. prior to the organization of the Georgia Construction and Investment Company, who were the contractors, and had the control of the Atlantic, Western & Knoxville Railway Co., and as such attorney rendered valuable services. (2) That a majority of the members of the last-mentioned company became members of the Georgia Construction and Investment Company, and held a controlling interest therein, and upon its organization the said Susong & Company, in payment of his services as attorney, was to deliver to the defendant fifty shares of the par value of one hundred dollars each of the Georgia Construction and Investment Company. (3) That it was not intended, and there was no agreement on the part of the defendant, that he should pay and put off the said sum of five thousand dollars; and the amount paid in, to-wit, fifteen hundred dollars, was paid by the said Susong & Co., in part performance of their contract with the defendant, and not by the defendant. (4) That defendant had nothing whatever to do with subscribing to the stock of said company, and he did not attend its meetings as a stockholder, but as attorney; and he denies that he is liable for any balance on the stock, but avers that the whole of the fifty shares has been paid for, so far as this defendant is concerned, by services rendered as aforesaid." The issues came on to be heard before a jury, and the plaintiff put in evidence tending to show that defendant had acted as a stockholder,—claiming to hold 50 shares; had been appointed and acted as a director of the company from the date of his appointment up to the appointment of the receivers, who are plaintiffs here; or further tending to show that defendant recognized his liability as 'a subscriber. Plaintiff put in evidence the two following letters, written in answer to a demand by the company of payment of installments for shares held by him: "Dear Mr. Sibley: Repeated and prolonged absence from home must excuse any seeming negligence in the matter of the installments you call for. Another thing: There was a little misunderstanding about the payment of it between Mr. Susong and myself, which is all cleared up now. All my dues will be paid up by the middle of this month, which Mr. Susong said would be soon enough. [Signed] Yours, truly, W. C. BENET." "Dear Mr. Sibley: Your letter came during my absence from home, and it was forwarded to me, with others, to Sumter, the very day I left Sumter; and then I did not receive it for nearly two weeks. I will try at once to arrange about my installments. I must see Mr. Susong first, and will do so at my earliest leisure. [Signed] Yours, truly, W. C. BENET." After plaintiff closed his case defendant offered to prove the allegations of his special defense copied above. Plaintiff objected, and moved to strike out the special defense as not stating facts sufficient to constitute a defense. The presiding judge—Judge ALDRICH—granted the motion in so far as it related to the defenses numbered 1 and 2, and this ruling is the first ground of appeal.

There is no question but that a contract such as is set out in the special defense was made between defendant and Susong & Co., but there is nothing in the record tending to show that the Georgia Construction & Investment Company was a party to it, or assented to it, or knew of it. Its existence, therefore, could not alter the relation between the latter company and its stockholders, or affect the rights that arose from that relation. If defendant's name was upon the stock list with his consent, *prima facie* he was bound to pay for the shares; and that liability was not discharged by a private agreement between himself and Susong & Co. that the latter would pay for them. The presiding judge, therefore, did not commit error in ruling that proof of the contract set up in the special defense was irrelevant to the issue, or by granting the motion to strike out paragraphs 1 and 2.

The remaining grounds of appeal all relate to the charge of Judge ALDRICH to the jury. The second and third grounds were not argued at the hearing. They merely state the principle that, if defendant authorized Susong & Co. to subscribe for stock for him, or if Susong & Co. made such subscription with his consent, in either case Susong & Co. would be his agents, and he would be bound. With respect to the remaining grounds of appeal it may be said that there certainly was a subscription to the stock of the company in the name of defendant, and the issue was whether he had originally authorized or subsequently approved and adopted it; and the facts of the charge excepted to confine the jury to the time of that issue. In this there was no error. The judgment of this court is that the judgment of the circuit court be affirmed.

McIVER, J., concurs.

CORBIN v. PLANTERS' NAT. BANK OF RICHMOND.

(Supreme Court of Appeals of Virginia. April 16, 1891.)

NEGOTIABLE INSTRUMENTS—NOTICE OF PROTEST—JOINT DEFENDANTS.

1. The maker and indorsers of a promissory note, executed in another state, under the laws of which it is negotiable, are not jointly liable to a holder who discounts it in Virginia, and such holder cannot, therefore, sue the maker and indorsers jointly.

2. The certificate of protest of a note payable in New York, by a notary there, is no evidence of dishonor, in a suit on it in Virginia, since there is no statute in Virginia making such protest evidence.

3. Where it appears that the note was due on the 14th of the month in New York, and that on the 17th the holder received notice of its dishonor in Richmond, Va., which on the same day he forwarded to the indorser, there is no proof of due notice of dishonor, as it does not appear when the notice was mailed in New York.

Error to corporation court of Danville.

This was an action of *assumpsit* in the corporation court of Danville, wherein the Planters' National Bank of Richmond was plaintiff, and T. J. Corbin was defendant. The case, as disclosed by the record, is as follows: On the 13th of July, 1887, one S. F. Cobbs, in the city of New York, executed his promissory note for $3,000, payable 90 days after its date, to his own order, at his office, 48 Broad street, in that city. It is admitted that by the laws of New York this note was negotiable. It does not appear, however, that by those laws it was protestable. After being indorsed by Cobbs, Corbin, and one T. S. Flournoy, Jr., it was discounted for the latter by the Planters' Bank, two days after its date, and the proceeds put to his credit in the bank. The note was not paid at maturity, and was protested by a New York notary, as appears from his certificate of protest filed with the record. On the 25th of February, 1888, the bank instituted a joint action of debt in the said corporation court against the maker and indorsers of the note, in which action process was duly served on all the defendants. The defendants Corbin and Flournoy, at the April term of the court, 1888, demurred to the declaration and also pleaded *nil debit;* whereupon the court overruled the demurrer, and continued the cause to the following July term. In the mean time—

to-wit, on the 26th of May—the defendant Flournoy confessed a judgment in the clerk's office, in the same action, for the debt claimed in the declaration and costs; and at the following July term there was a judgment by default against Cobbs, and a discontinuance as to Corbin. Afterwards the present action was instituted against Corbin alone. The declaration contains the various common counts, and also a count upon the above-mentioned note, and alleges the insolvency of Cobbs and Flournoy. The defendant pleaded *non assumpsit,* and a special plea of "former adjudication," setting up, in a rather informal manner, the defense that the cause of action asserted in the declaration was merged in the judgments above mentioned. And at the April term, 1889, neither party requiring a jury, the court, after hearing the evidence, entered up judgment for the plaintiff for $3,001.41, with interest thereon from the 14th of October, 1887, and costs, which is the judgment complained of.

Berryman Green and *Christian & Christian,* for plaintiff in error. *Berkeley & Harrison,* for defendant in error.

LEWIS, P., *(after stating the facts as above.)* The case involves several important questions of law, but their solution is free from difficulty.

1. The defendant, in support of his special plea, relies upon the decision of this court in Beasley v. Sims, 81 Va. 644. But that case is not in point. The rule, moreover, announced in that case has been changed by the new Code. That was an action against two joint obligors, in which process was served on one of the defendants only, and there was a judgment against that one, and a discontinuance as to the other; and, in a subsequent action against both, it was held that the cause of action was merged in the judgment recovered in the first suit. Afterwards, however, the present Code of Virginia was adopted, section 3396 of which—after providing that where, in any action against two or more defendants, the process is served on part of them, the plaintiff may proceed to judgment as to any so served, and either discontinue it as to the others, or from time to time, as the process is served as to such others, proceed to judgment as to them, until judgments be obtained against all—goes on further to enact that "such discontinuance of the action as to any defendant shall not operate as a bar to any subsequent action which may be brought against him for the same cause." It is obvious that the discontinuance here provided for is a discontinuance as against any one or more defendants upon whom process has not been served. In the present case, however, process in the first action was served on all the defendants, so that the case is not within the statute. And it may be conceded that the principle recognized in Beasley v. Sims would govern this case, if the first action could have been rightly maintained in this state against all the defendants. But clearly it could not, for their liability was not joint but several, and the note sued on was not

"payable at a particular bank, or at a particular office thereof for discount and deposit, or the place of business of a savings institution or savings bank, or at the place of business of a licensed banker or broker." Code, § 2853.

2. This being so, the next question is whether upon the evidence, which is set out in the bill of exceptions, the bank was entitled to recover in the present action; and we are of opinion that it was not. In the first place, there was no proof of the dishonor of the note. By the law-merchant, which is a part of the common law, protest of a dishonored foreign bill of exchange is ordinarily indispensable, and the notary's certificate of protest proves itself; that is, it is *prima facie* evidence of presentment and non-acceptance or non-payment. But the rule does not extend to promissory notes and inland bills. As to these, the protest is not regarded as an official act, and accordingly, in the absence of statute, is not receivable as evidence of demand. 2 Daniel, Neg. Inst. § 928; Young v. Bryan, 6 Wheat. 146; Bank v. Hyde, Id. 572; Nicholls v. Webb, 8 Wheat. 326; Dunn v. Adams, 1 Ala. 527; Story, Prom. Notes, § 297. And where a state statute makes the certificate of protest, when executed by a notary of that state, evidence of dishonor in such cases, it does not authorize the notary to act beyond its territorial limits, or accord the same effect to his act when beyond them. 2 Daniel, Neg. Inst. § 959; 96 Amer. Dec. 608, note, to Tate v. Sullivan. Parsons states the common-law rule as follows: "In the case of foreign bills protested in a country other than that in which the suit is brought," he says, "full faith and credit are given to the instrument of protest; and the original or a duly-certified copy are admissible in evidence of the acts therein stated, so far as those acts are within the scope of a notary's official duty. In the case of inland bills, and even foreign bills which are protested in the country where suit is brought, the protest is not admissible in evidence, unless the notary has deceased since the protest was made." 1 Pars. Notes & B. p. 635. The whole subject, however, as he goes on to say, is very generally regulated in this country by statute, and so it is in Virginia. The question, therefore, as to the effect of the certificate of the New York notary, which was the only evidence offered in the present case as to the dishonor of the note sued on, must be determined in accordance with the statute law of this state; for it is conceded that as to this matter the *lex fori* governs.

It is contended by the defendant (the plaintiff in error here) that the court below erred in treating the note sued on as negotiable. But we do not concur in this view. It is a general rule that every contract, as to its validity, nature, interpretation, and effect, is governed by the law of the place where it is made, unless it is to be performed in another place. Accordingly, it was decided by this court in Bank v. Ruckman, 16 Grat. 126, that whether a note is negotiable or not is a question which relates to its nature and effect, and is therefore to be governed by

the *lex loci contractus*, although the remedy is governed by the place where the suit is instituted. Hence the note sued on in the present case, having been executed and made payable in New York, where, it is conceded, it was negotiable, it was properly so treated by the court below. But, as already stated, the only evidence of its dishonor was the certificate of the New York notary, and that, according to the statute of this state, was not evidence for the purpose for which it was offered. The note was payable, not in this state, but in New York, and is therefore not within our statute permitting the protest of promissory notes and inland bills, which applies only to such notes as are payable in this state, at a particular bank, or at a particular office thereof, for discount and deposit, etc., and as to which the protest is made *prima facie* evidence of what is stated therein. Code, §§ 2849, 2850; McVeigh v. Bank, 26 Grat. 785, 829. The legislature has not seen fit to make the notarial certificate of protest of a promissory note, or of an inland bill, payable outside of the state, admissible in evidence in our courts as an official act, and we have not the power, even if we were so disposed, to give to it an effect which is not sanctioned either by the common law or by the statute. Besides, there is no proof that the note sued on was a protestable security by the laws of New York, and, in the absence of any such proof, the presumption is that it was not. Dunn v. Adams, 1 Ala. 527.

3. There is no proof, moreover, of due notice to the defendant of the dishonor of the note. Although there has been a diversity and fluctuation of opinion among judges as to what is reasonable time within which notice must be given by the holder to his indorser, it is now well settled that, ordinarily, where the parties reside at different places, notices should be forwarded the day after dishonor if practicable at least. "Where the notice is sent by post," says Greenleaf, "it need not be sent on the day of dishonor, but it should go by the next practicable post after that day, having due reference to all the circumstances of the case." 2 Greenl. Ev. § 187; 1 Pars. Notes & B. p. 511; 2 Daniel, Neg. Inst. §§ 1039, 1043. And the general rule is that each successive party who receives notice of dishonor is entitled to a full day to transmit it to any antecedent party who is chargeable over to him upon payment of the bill or note. 2 Daniel, Neg. Inst. § 1044. In the case at bar the only evidence on the point of notice is that of Quarles, cashier of the bank, who testifies that notices of protest were received by him from New York on Monday, October 17, 1887, and that on the same day he mailed a copy to the defendant at Danville. The note matured on Friday, the 14th of October, and there is no evidence whatever either as to the time when the notices were mailed in New York, or as to the usual course of the mail between New York and this city. For aught the record shows, the notices may have been mailed on Sunday, the 16th, or on Monday, the 17th, and, if not mailed before that time, it was too late to avail. The rule is well

expressed by Parsons, who says that "the burden of proving due notice is upon the plaintiff, whose duty it is to give it in a way capable of proof. It should also be proved distinctly. Thus, if the witness says the notice was sent in two or three days, and two are enough, but three not, and there is nothing to define this testimony, it will not be sufficient evidence to find a verdict for the plaintiff." 1 Pars. Notes & B. p. 516. And in Friend v. Wilkinson, 9 Grat. 33, it was decided that not only is the burden of proving notice on the plaintiff, but that, where notice is required, it is a condition precedent to a recovery, and that he must show a strict compliance with the rule. Hence it was held incumbent on the plaintiff in that case to show the time at which the notice was placed in the post-office to be mailed, and, there being no proof that the defendant duly received notice, the judgment of the lower court in favor of the plaintiff was reversed. The application of these elementary principles to the present case shows very clearly, we think, that the judgment here complained of is erroneous, and that the same must be reversed, and a judgment entered for the defendant.

EDICHAL BULLION CO. *et al.* v. COLUMBIA GOLD MINING CO. *et al.*

(*Supreme Court of Appeals of Virginia.* April 9, 1891.)

SPECIFIC PERFORMANCE — INSUFFICIENCY OF CONTRACT.

In an action to compel specific performance, the complaint alleged that A. procured a lease from plaintiffs, giving him the option of purchasing certain mining lands within a given period, and that he was the agent of defendants, and operating machinery on said lands for them beyond the time in which the option expired, and that defendants thereby became bound as purchasers. The complaint referred to certain letters that passed thereafter between the officers of the respective companies, and an unsigned memorandum that it alleged showed defendants had agreed to take the property on the terms of A.'s contract, and only were negotiating as to the times of making payments. *Held*, that the bill and correspondence referred to disclosed a failure on the part of the parties to agree upon a time of payment, which is essential to a contract for the sale or purchase of real estate.

Appeal from circuit court, Fluvanna county.

W. B. *Pettit* and W. W. *Henry*, for appellants. T. S. *Martin* and A. A. *Gray*, for appellees.

FAUNTLEROY, J. The petition of the Edichal Bullion Company, a corporation, and of J B. Baker, J. W. Woodside, and M. R. Kirkpatrick, as individuals, represents that they, and each of them, are aggrieved and injured by the decree rendered by the circuit court of Fluvanna county on the 12th day of April, 1889, in the chancery cause pending therein, in which the Columbia Gold Mining Company, a corporation, is complainant, and the said petitioners and one H. H. Eames are defendants. The original bill was filed against the said Edichal Bullion Company, as a non-resident and foreign corporation, for the purpose of enforcing specific perform-

ance of an alleged contract for the purchase by it, from the said Columbia Gold Mining Company, of real estate lying in the counties of Goochland and Fluvanna, Va., known as the "Tellurium Gold Mining Property;" and, simultaneously with the institution of the suit, on the 9th day of July, 1886, an attachment was sued out and levied upon the interest which it was alleged the said Edichal Bullion Company owned in about 1,100 acres of land, lying mostly in the said county of Fluvanna, known as the "Bowles Mining Property," and upon some personal property. To the original bill, and two successive amended bills filed by the complainants, the defendant company demurred and answered. The circuit court overruled the demurrer, and by the decree complained of held that there was a contract for the sale, by the Columbia Gold Mining Company to the defendant the Edichal Bullion Company, of the tellurium gold mining property, as set forth in the bill, to have been made on the 7th day of November, 1885, and decreed specific performance of the same by the defendant company; and also decreed against the individual members of the said defendant company as securities for the defendant company. The case made by the original and amended bills was demurred to, as wanting in all the essential requisites of a suit for specific performance, because it does not show that any distinct and definite contract of sale and purchase was made; nor when, where, how, and by whom it was made, and that the person making it had authority to bind the defendant company; nor whether the alleged contract was by parol or in writing: nor whether there was any express contract made by the defendant company, or by any authorized agent for it, either by parol or in writing. It is merely stated, argumentatively, that inasmuch as H. H. Eames had, on the 7th day of February, 1885, procured a contract of lease from the complainant company, giving him the option of buying the tellurium gold mining property, upon certain terms, within a limited time, and was, as they allege, the agent of the defendant company, operating its machinery on the premises which he had leased, with the option to buy on or before the 7th day of November, 1886; and inasmuch as his said experimental operations were continued beyond the day upon which, by the express terms of his contract, his said option was to cease,—therefore the said Edichal Bullion Company had become bound to buy, and had bought, the property upon the terms stipulated in the written contract between the complainant company and the lessee, H. H. Eames, made more than six months before the defendant Edichal Bullion Company had any existence in fact or in law; that the bills do not show that Eames himself, within the time limited, availed of his option to buy the property, by notice to that effect, or by offering to pay the purchase money; nor that the complainant company was, on the next day after the expiration of the option contract with Eames, under any obligation to sell to him, much less that it was under any obligation to sell the property to the defendant Edichal Bullion Company.

In the case of Iron Co. v. Gardiner, 79 Va. 305, Judge LACY, speaking for this court, said: "Can there be a contract without mutual obligation? Can there be an agreement between two parties which binds one of them absolutely and the other only at his pleasure? Upon this ground no specific performance could properly have been decreed, since the want of mutuality in the contract should be considered a valid objection to the exercise of that jurisdiction." After charging, arguendo, that the defendant company had, on the 7th of November, 1885, become the purchaser of the property in question, on the terms named in said contract, (with Eames,)—to-wit, $15,000, of which $7,500 was to be paid in cash, and the residue in three months with interest,—the bill refers to certain letters that afterwards passed between some of the officers of the respective companies, and to an unsigned memorandum, which are not exhibited with or made part of the bill, nor claimed as constituting the contract sought to be enforced, but as rendering plain that the defendant Edichal Bullion Company had agreed to take the property on the terms named in the contract with Eames, and only were negotiating for the times of making payments. The times of making payments are an important and essential element of a contract for the sale or purchase of real estate.—so essential that a failure to agree and distinctly to state as to them is a failure to agree upon any contract at all. The bill, and the correspondence referred to in it, show a failure to agree upon these important particulars of the alleged contract. And this reference further shows that no contract had been made on the 7th of November, as argued in the bill there had been; for it shows that on the 7th of November, 1885, the complainant company agreed with their lessee, Eames, to extend his option, which, under their written contract with him, would expire on that day, until the 12th of November; and that from the 18th of that month to the 31st of December, 1885, the officers of the respective corporations were in treaty about the sale and terms of purchase of the property, and were never at one about them. See Iron Co. v. U. S., 118 U. S. 40, 42, 6 Sup. Ct. Rep. 928: "Until the terms of an agreement have received the assent of both parties, the negotiation is open, and imposes no obligation on either." "If it be doubtful whether an agreement has been concluded, or is a mere negotiation, chancery will not decree a specific performance. The principle is a sound one, and especially applicable in a case like this, where the party attempting to enforce this contract has done nothing upon it." Carr v. Duval, 14 Pet. 88. The case of Carr v. Duval, supra, was one in which the contract was sought to be, like the case at bar, deduced from correspondence, which was conducted, on the side of the parties against whom a specific performance was sought, by one who, in the language of the court, "was acting not for himself only, but for his sisters and brothers, without any express

authority from them." The same learned judge, in delivering the opinion of the court in the case of Colson v. Thompson, 2 Wheat., 336, 341, said: "The contract which is sought to be specifically executed ought not only to be proved, but the terms of it should be so precise as that neither party could reasonably misunderstand them. If the contract be vague or uncertain, or the evidence to establish it be insufficient, a court of equity will not exercise its extraordinary jurisdiction to enforce it, but will leave the party to his legal remedy." In the case of Williams v. Morris, 95 U. S. 444, 456, CLIFFORD, J., said: "The proof as to the terms of the contract must be clear, definite, and conclusive, and must show a contract leaving no *jus deliberandi* or *locus penitentiæ;*" and (on page 457) must clearly and satisfactorily show "the existence of the contract as laid in the pleadings," and "the particular agreement charged in the bill or answer." Relief in suits for specific performance is not granted by courts of equity *ex debito justitiæ*, but under the sound discretion of the court. Railroad Co. v. Lewis, 76 Va. 885; Iron Co. v. Gardiner, 79 Va. 309. In granting such relief, the very first thing that is required is that the complainant shall set forth and prove a contract certain and definite in its terms. Litterall v. Jackson, 80 Va. 612. The bill for specific performance of a contract made with an agent must, on its face, distinctly state the contract that was made, and show when, where, how, and by whom it was made, and that the person making it had authority to bind the company. Haden v. Association, Id. 683. In order that a contract can exist, there must be a *consensus* between the parties. Their minds must agree at the same moment to the terms constituting the contract. "The parties must agree to the same thing at the same time." 4 Minor, Inst. 16. "The assent must be to the precise terms offered." 3 Minor, Inst. 126. "Where there is a misunderstanding as regards the terms of a contract, neither party is liable in law or equity." Bank v. Hall, 101 U. S. 50. "Contracts for sale of real estate must be in writing, signed by the party to be charged, or his agent." Code 1873, p. 985.

The case stated in the complainants' bills falls far short of measuring up to these requisites of the law in this state, as settled by the decisions of this court; and the circuit court erred in overruling the demurrer to the bills; and, as said by Judge RICHARDSON in delivering the opinion of this court in the case of Litterall v. Jackson, supra: "In no view does the alleged contract, whether looked at by itself or in the light of surrounding circumstances, as disclosed by the testimony, come up to the standard which is necessary to its capability of specific execution." Citing *Pigg v. Corder, 12 Leigh, 69; Graham v. Call, 5 Munf. 396; Wright v. Pucket, 22 Grat. 374. The demurrer to the bills should, upon these authorities, have been sustained; but, upon the answers and the proofs, the complainants' case is without facts, justice, law, or equity to support it.

The record shows that H. H. Eames

claimed to have invented a process or machinery for reducing ores, and extracting their precious metals, which was very valuable. On the 7th day of February, 1885, long before the Edichal Bullion Company was formed, or even the act of the legislature of the state of New Jersey, authorizing it to be formed, was enacted, the complainant, the Columbia Gold Mining Company, gave to the said H. H. Eames a lease and option of purchase upon their "Tellurium" property, in Fluvanna county, for six months, with a view to its development and the testing of his invention. That option to Eames expired on the 7th of August, 1885, and it was verbally extended to Eames to the 7th of November, 1885. There is not the slightest evidence in the record of any assignment of the said option, in writing, to the defendant Edichal Bullion Company, or of any determination, expressed in writing, by or on behalf of the said defendant company, on or before the 7th of November, 1885, to take the said property in accordance with the terms of Eames' said option, which terms were $15,000,—one-half cash, and the residue at three months, with interest. On the contrary, the record of the proceedings of the Columbia Gold Mining Company, at a "stockholders' meeting November 7, 1885, shows that Mr. H. H. Eames was present, and asked for and obtained 'an extension of the time on the contract with him,' which would expire to-day, until next Thursday, the 12th inst.;" and on the 13th day of November, 1885, Mr. Baker, the president of the Edichal Bullion Company, was in consultation with the officers of the Columbia Gold Mining Company, at which consultation a memorandum of the proposal of terms for the sale of the tellurium gold mining property of the Columbia Gold Mining Company to the Edichal Bullion Company was reduced to writing by Mr. Shepherd, one of the Columbia Gold Mining Company, but which was not signed by any one, to-wit, the purchase of the property by the defendant company at $15,000, one-half to be paid in three months, one-quarter to be paid in four months, and the remainder in five months, with interest from the 7th of November, 1885. This memorandum Mr. Baker, the president of the Edichal Bullion Company, took with him to Philadelphia, telling the Columbia Gold Mining Company, at the said meeting on the 13th inst., that he had no authority to contract or commit his company without a consultation with and by instructions from them; that when he left Philadelphia, on the 9th inst., to go to the mines in Fluvanna county, at the request of Mr. Eames, he had no idea of visiting Richmond, or of negotiating for the purchase of the Tellurium property; that he had arrived at the mines on the 10th inst., and had come to Richmond to see the Columbia Gold Mining Company in the interest of, and at the request of, Mr. Eames, to try to obtain an extension of his option contract, to enable him further to experiment and test the value of his machinery and mining operations: for which they, the Edichal Bullion Company, had been induced, by Eames' glowing accounts of actual and ex-

pected products, to advance to him large sums of money. This memorandum, unsigned, and not binding upon any one, Mr. Baker, upon his return to Philadelphia, laid before his company; and on the 18th of November, 1885, wrote the following letter:

"The Columbia Gold-Mining Company, Richmond, Va.—Gents: We will agree to the terms of your mem. for the sale of the tellurium property, except to the time of the payments of notes, which we propose as follows:

1st note, Nov. 7th, $8,750, 4 months.
2d   "   "   8,750, 5   "
3d   "   "   8,750, 6   "
4th   "   "   8,750, 7   "

—All these notes to bear interest at 6 per cent. per annum, we to have the privilege of taking up the notes before maturity. Trusting this will be satisfactory, yours, truly,   EDICHAL BULLION COMPANY.
        "J. W. WOODSIDE, Secretary."

To this letter, containing the only proposal in writing ever made by the Edichal Bullion Company to purchase the tellurium property of the complainant, a positive and unqualified refusal was made in a letter dated November 19, 1885, and signed "C. E. Belvin, President," addressed to Mr. J. W. Woodside, secretary, 135 Arch street, Philadelphia: "Dear Sir: 18th inst. received this P. M.," etc. "In reply, I beg to say that I at once called a meeting of our company, and I am authorized to say that they will have to decline to make any alteration in the terms as stated in the memo. handed your president, Mr. J. B. Baker, and accepted by him, at Ford's Hotel, in this city, on last Friday morning, 13th inst.," etc. To this Mr. Baker, president, replied in a letter dated Philadelphia, November 23, 1885, addressed to C. E. Belvin, president, Richmond, Va.: "On my return to Philadelphia, on the 15th inst., I laid the memo. referred to before my colleagues, stating that I said to the gentlemen I met that when I left Philadelphia I did not expect to stop in Richmond, or see any of the persons interested in the sale of tellurium mines; that I did not have any conversation with my colleagues in Philadelphia with reference to the payments for the property; and that it would be necessary to have the approval of Mr. Woodside and Mr. Kirkpatrick before any agreement could be ratified," etc. "Our board, after fully considering the terms in the memo., decided to ask your company to divide the first payment ($7,500) into two equal parts, making one to become due February 7th, '86, and the other, at six months, for Nov. 7th, '86, interest to be added in each from Nov. 7th, '85· Our company deems it injudicious to contemplate the payment of so large an amount of money in February," etc. "It hopes that the Columbia Gold Mining Company will reconsider its decision."

To this letter the Columbia Gold Mining Company, through its president, C. E. Belvin, replied as follows:

"Richmond, Va., Nov. 25th, 1885. Mr. J. B. Baker, President Edichal Bullion Company, 135 Arch St., Phila., Pa.—Dear Sir: Your letter 23d received this day; and we have considered your proposition, and our board have agreed to accept your terms of payment, which we understand to be as follows:

$3,750 and int. at 8 mos. from Nov. 7th, 1885.
$3,750   "   4   "   "
$3,750   "   5   "   "
$3,750   "   6   "   "

"If we are correct in this, please advise me promptly, and I will have the papers prepared at once."

It is seen at once that this letter of acceptance makes a material variation in the terms proposed in the letter from Baker; and Belvin, the president, speaking for his board, shows that they were uncertain as to the terms of payment offered; and, in its state of uncertainty, asked to be advised promptly whether it was correct, etc. No reply was made to this until the letter of 12th of December, 1885, written by Baker, president, addressed to C. E. Belvin, president, Richmond, Va., in which it is stated that the Edichal board of directors had and would defer action upon the proposal contained in the letter of Belvin of the 25th of November, 1885, until it could hear better accounts of the experimental working of the mine by Eames. The said terms proposed in the letter of the 25th of November, 1885, have never been accepted by the Edichal Company; and the subsequent correspondence between the two companies shows conclusively that no agreement was ever concluded between them. "Where there is a misunderstanding as regards the terms of a contract, neither party is liable in law or equity." Bank v. Hall, 101 U. S. 49. "A proposal to accept, or an acceptance on terms varying from those offered, is a rejection of the offer." Id. 50. "A subsequent acceptance upon the terms offered does not make a contract." 3 Amer. & Eng. Enc. Law, p. 853, tit. "Contract." If the offer be upon payments at certain times, and the party selling requires shorter times, the party making the proposal is not bound. Story, Cont. § 85, referring to Bruce v. Pearson, 3 Johns. 534, and cases cited.

It appears from the record that Eames, who claimed to have invented valuable machinery, and who had a lease and option of purchase from the Columbia Gold Mining Company of their tellurium property, adjoining the Bowles property, owned by the Edichal Bullion Company, had deceived the last-named company in reference to what he was doing with his machine at the mines; and that it was because of his false but glowing statements as to results obtained, that the Edichal Company ever thought of binding itself for the purchase money. But, while negotiations were pending, the Edichal Company discovered that they had been deceived by Eames, and they refused to have anything to do with the purchase; and, after the failure of his scheme with the Edichal Company, Eames became a swift witness for the Columbia Gold Mining Company in their endeavor to force the tellurium property upon the Edichal Company. The uniting of Eames as a defendant in a suit asking for a specific performance against the Edichal Company

(of which it is denied in the answer, and not proved in the evidence, that he was a member or an agent to purchase) was obviously for the advantage of his sworn answer, which was called for on oath from him, while it was waived from the defendant company. He admits, upon cross-examination, that one of the attorneys for the Columbia Gold Mining Company prepared his answer, in which he is made to say, under oath, that the Edichal Bullion Company did adopt his contract with the plaintiff company for the sale and purchase of the tellurium gold mine; and that, after the 7th of November, 1885, he was in full possession thereof, for and by the authority of said Edichal Bullion Company, and the mines were worked and operated for it, and with capital furnished by it; yet, when he is asked, "When did the Edichal Company adopt your contract?" he replied: "I do not know that they ever did." And when he is asked, "When did the Edichal Company give you authority to take possession?" he replied, "that, as a company, they never gave me such authority, but, individually, they did." And when he is asked, "Who did, and when, and what took place?" he replied: "Mr. Baker; at the time we were speaking of getting an extension of time on the option; he thought we might be able to manage the purchase if the extension was granted." There is no proof in the record of any written contract by any of the defendants for the purchase of the property; and, as to the alleged parol contract by the substitution or adoption of Eames' expired option, the answers to the original and first amended bills emphatically put in issue and deny the contract alleged; and, in the language of this court, by Lewis, P., in the case of Railroad Co. v. Lewis, 76 Va. 833, 837, "the evidence is too vague, uncertain, and contradictory upon which to found a decree in chancery for the specific performance of a contract."

In the second amended bill, Baker, Woodside, and Kirkpatrick are made defendants, and the charge against them is that they individually, through Eames, purchased the tellurium property, and turned it over to the Edichal Bullion Company; and the prayer of the bill is that "if, therefore, your honor shall be of the opinion that, for any reason, the defendant corporation is not bound by the alleged purchase of the tellurium gold mining property, then complainant is desirous of holding the said corporators personally bound by it, authorized and sanctioned as it was by each one of them individually. They are responsible if the Edichal Company is not." So far from alleging positively and clearly a precise and definite contract of purchase, showing when, where, how, and by whom, and whether in writing or by parol, the bill, as a dernier resort, doubtingly, hesitatingly, and beseechingly expresses the alternative desire of the complainants that if, by the pleadings and their proofs, they have made and sustained no case for specific performance against the defendant company, then to hold the individual corporators liable; and the decree of the court below is against both the defendant company, and the individual persons as securities,—thus establishing a liability not put in issue by the pleadings nor sustained by the proofs. The decree must be upon the case made by the pleadings, although the evidence may show a right to a further decree. Knibb v. Dixon, 1 Rand. (Va.) 249; Mundy v. Vawter, 3 Grat. 518. Neither of these individual defendants in this third bill was served with process to answer it, and neither, by plea, demurrer, or answer, or in any way, entered an appearance. The fact that they appeared before a notary in Philadelphia to give their depositions, did not authorize the court to give a personal decree against them. Smith v. Chilton, 77 Va. 535. Any individual liability of Baker, Woodside, and Kirkpatrick for the purchase price of the property, as securities for the defendant company, could not obtain under and by virtue of a contract which did not bind the company itself; and the memorandum of the 13th of November, 1885, made by Shepherd, a member of the complainant company, and unsigned by any one, and made merely tentatively, as a basis for further negotiations, will not supply the imperative requirement of the statute for a writing signed by the party to be bound or by his agent. Code 1887, § 2840. The complainant company have no equity in their case; the decree appealed from is wholly erroneous, and it is reversed and annulled; and the order of this court will be to abate the attachment, and to dismiss the bills, with costs. Decree reversed.

TERRY v. COMMONWEALTH.

(*Supreme Court of Appeals of Virginia.* April 16, 1891.)

FORGERY—WHAT CONSTITUTES.

One T. was indicted for forgery of the following instrument: "Office of H. M. Smith & Co. T.—Dear Sir: Yours of the 9th inst. to hand. * * * You owe us $7.38, and you —— the note for $412. It was canceled, * * * but it was marked 'Paid,' and canceled; so it cannot be of any use to any one. Yours, truly, SMITH & McGUIRE, Receivers." The indictment alleged that T. was at the time indebted to H. M. Smith & Co. *Held* not a forgery under Code Va. 1887, § 3737, defining as forgery the forging "any writing * * * to the prejudice of another's right."

Error to circuit court, Campbell county. *J. W. Riely* and *Henry Edmunds,* for plaintiff in error. *R. Taylor Scott,* Atty. Gen., for the Commonwealth.

FAUNTLEROY, J. The petition of Joseph O. Terry represents that he was indicted, tried, and convicted in the county court of Campbell county, at the November, 1890, term thereof, upon a charge of forgery, and was sentenced by the said court, at its said term, to confinement in the penitentiary of Virginia for the term of two years; that he presented his petition, with a copy of the record of the said prosecution against him, to the judge of the circuit court of Campbell county, asking for a writ of error and *supersedeas* to the said judgment, which said petition was, by the said judge of the circuit court of Campbell county, denied, and a writ of

error refused on the 27th day of December, 1890. The case is here upon a writ of error awarded by one of the judges of this court to the judgment aforesaid of the county court of Campbell county, and to the said judgment of the judge of the circuit court of Campbell county. The indictment is founded on section 3737 of the Code of Virginia, 1887: "If any person forge any writing * * * to the prejudice of another's right, or utter, or attempt to employ as true, such forged writing, knowing it to be forged, he shall be confined in the penitentiary not less than two nor more than ten years." This statute predicates the offense of forgery only of such writings as are, or may be, to the prejudice of another's right, or by which another may be defrauded. It must sufficiently appear, from the description given of the writing alleged to have been forged, that it is writing to the prejudice of another's right. If it be not such, it is not within the statute, and the forgery of it cannot be punished as felony. Powell v. Com., 11 Grat. 822; citing Chit. Crim. Law, 1021; 2 Russ. Crimes, 318.

The indictment in the case at bar contains two counts,—one for forging; and the other for uttering, knowing it to be forged, a certain writing of the tenor following: "Office of H. M. Smith & Co., Manufacturers of Agricultural Machinery, Richmond, Va., Feb. 18, 1886. J. O. Terry, Esq.—DEAR SIR: Yours of the 9th inst. to hand. We inclose a statement of your account. It agrees with yours very nearly, as you will see. You owe us $7.38, and you —— the note for $412. It was canceled and sent you by mail last ——. If you did not receive it it is probably in the dead-letter office at Washington; but it was mailed, marked 'paid,' and canceled; so it cannot be of any use to any one. Yours, truly, SMITH & McGUIRE, Receivers." The indictment avers that the accused, being at that time indebted to H. M. Smith & Co., forged the writing described. The paper, as set out in the indictment, shows on its face, with no averment of extrinsic circumstances to connect Smith & McGuire, receivers, with H. M. Smith & Co., that it was incapable of affecting or prejudicing the rights of H. M. Smith & Co. as defensive evidence in a suit or demand by them on any indebtedness of the accused to them; and it does not fix, nor could it operate, any pecuniary liability upon any one. It does not refer to H. M. Smith & Co., and it could not, as before said, prejudice their rights as defensive evidence. Nor could it prejudice any right of Smith & McGuire, receivers, unless the accused was indebted to them; but the indebtedness of the accused is alleged in the indictment, not to be to them, but to H. M. Smith & Co.; and if, in fact, the accused was indebted to Smith & McGuire, receivers, it should have been so alleged in the indictment. There is no such averment, and, without it, the writing is, on its face, ineffectual to prejudice their rights.

In the case of Glass v. Com., 33 Grat. 832, the court said: "To authorize a valid conviction of an offense it must be sufficiently charged in the indictment or information. Every material ingredient of the offense must be so charged, otherwise there can be no legal conviction in the case; for, admitting the charge to be literally true, it does not follow that the accused was guilty of any offense. The judgment in that case was arrested because the offense was not sufficiently alleged in the indictment. Forgery is the fraudulent making of a false writing, which, if genuine, would be apparently of legal efficacy. Bish. Crim. Law, (3d Ed.) §§ 495, 499. The instrument must appear on its face to be, or be in fact, one which, if true, would be valid, or legally capable of effecting a fraud. Writings invalid on their face are not subjects of forgery. If incomplete or uncertain on their face, so that their legal efficacy is dependent on extrinsic circumstances, then such extrinsic matters must be averred in the indictment. 2 Bish. Crim. Law, (3d Ed.) §§ 503, 505, 506, 511, 512. The writing alleged in the indictment to have been forged is signed, "Smith & McGuire, Receivers." What Smith, of all Smiths? And what McGuire? Receivers of whom? By what authority? Can Smith & McGuire, as a partnership or firm, be made receivers? The paper bearing their signature, which is alleged to be forged, is meaningless, void, and of no legal efficacy, even if it were genuine. It is not only wanting in the legal requisites of validity, were it genuine, but its meaning and terms are unintelligible from the words and characters used, and it is so incomplete and unmeaning that it cannot be the foundation of any legal liability. Fomby v. State, 6 South. Rep. 271. The indictment does not charge an offense; and the trial court erred in overruling the motion to arrest the judgment, and in not discharging the prisoner from this prosecution. The order will be entered here to reverse and annul the judgment complained of, and to discharge the prisoner. Judgment reversed.

AMERICUS, P. & L. R. R. v. LUCKIE.

(*Supreme Court of Georgia.* March 16, 1891.)

CONTRIBUTORY NEGLIGENCE — COMPARATIVE NEGLIGENCE—INSTRUCTIONS.

Upon the trial of a suit against a railroad company for personal injuries to the plaintiff, it was error to charge as follows: "If, by the exercise of ordinary care and diligence, the plaintiff could have avoided the consequences to herself of the defendant's negligence, she cannot recover; but if both parties were at fault, and the alleged injury was the result of the fault of both, then, notwithstanding the plaintiff's negligence, she would be entitled to recover, but the amount of the recovery would be abated in proportion to the amount of the default on her part." The error consisted in stating, in immediate connection with each other, and without proper explanation, two distinct rules of law, and thus qualifying the former by the latter, which is not the purpose of the statute.

(*Syllabus by the Court.*)

Error from superior court, Dooly county; FORT, Judge.

B. P. Hollis, for plaintiff in error. *C. C. Duncan* and *Hardeman & Davis*, for defendant in error.

LUMPKIN, J. Section 2972 of the Code, relating to actions for personal injuries, declares, in substance, that if the plaintiff, by ordinary care, could have avoided the consequences to himself caused by the defendant's negligence, he cannot recover. This section sets forth one of the defenses which railroad companies are permitted to make to such actions. It further provides: "But in other cases the defendant is not relieved, although the plaintiff may in some way have contributed to the injury sustained." The "other cases" referred to are manifestly those in which the plaintiff could not by ordinary care have avoided the consequences of defendant's negligence. In cases of that kind, both parties being at fault, the damages are apportioned. This also is undoubtedly the meaning of the latter sentence of section 3034 of the Code, which reads as follows: "If the complainant and the agents of the company are both at fault, the former may recover, but the damages shall be diminished by the jury in proportion to the amount of fault attributable to him." This sentence relates to the same kind of "other cases" which are referred to in section 2972; that is, cases in which it appears that the plaintiff could not, by exercising ordinary care, have avoided the injury to himself caused by defendant's negligence. It seems to be the clear meaning of our law that the plaintiff can never recover in an action for personal injuries, no matter what the negligence of the defendant may be, short of actual wantonness, when the proof shows he could, by ordinary care, after the negligence of defendant began or was existing, have avoided the consequences to himself of that negligence. The law also clearly contemplates cases in which, while the plaintiff is to some extent negligent, he nevertheless could not, by using ordinary care, have avoided an injury resulting from defendant's negligence. Of course there can be no recovery when the defendant is entirely free from negligence, and uses all proper care to prevent injury. The law of contributory negligence is applicable only where both parties are at fault, and when, also, the plaintiff could not, by ordinary care, have avoided the injury which defendant's negligence produced. The charge given by the judge below, in effect, makes the defendant liable if the jury should find both parties negligent, notwithstanding they might have believed that if the plaintiff had exercised ordinary care she would not have been hurt. He correctly charged the law set forth in section 2972, but improperly qualified it by charging the law contained in the latter half of section 3034, without making the proper explanation as to the class of cases to which this latter charge is applicable. If he had said: "But if both parties were at fault, and the alleged injury was the result of the fault of both, *and you find from the evidence that the plaintiff could not by ordinary care have avoided the alleged injury to herself, occasioned by defendant's negligence,* then, notwithstanding she may have been to some extent negligent, she would be entitled to recover, but the amount of damages should be apportioned," etc.,—the charge would have been correct, because it would have fully met all the requirements of the sections referred to. The court's attention was called to the propriety of qualifying his instructions to the jury by using such words as we have above italicised, and a request to this effect was made and refused. This request was not in writing, and the court was not therefore bound to give it as a request; but as so doing would have relieved the charge given of the error therein, and without such addition the charge does not fully and accurately present the law, we are constrained to grant a new trial. Judgment reversed.

WATSON v. GOOLSBY.

(Supreme Court of Georgia. March 16, 1891.)

PARTIES—ESTATE—INJUNCTION—RECEIVER.

1. Land was devised to a married woman for the life of her husband, with a charge thereon for the support and maintenance of her husband during his life; after his death, his minor children to take the fee. *Held,* that such a minor had not, during the lives of his parents, such an interest in the land as rendered him a necessary party to an action resulting in a verdict and judgment by consent that the claim be a special lien on the crops, to be enforced in three annual installments.

2. The action being against the wife, and having been commenced in a county court which has no equitable jurisdiction, and it being doubtful whether on appeal the superior court had authority to allow an amendment seeking equitable relief, and to enter up the judgment rendered, and it being further doubtful whether execution would not lie against the life-estate, an injunction and the appointment of a receiver for the enforcement of the judgment was properly denied.

Error from superior court, Jasper county: JENKINS, Judge.

The following is the official report: The judge put his refusal of injunction and receiver (which is the judgment excepted to) upon the ground that John K. Goolsby, Jr., the minor child of John K. Goolsby and Julia E. Goolsby, has such an interest in the income of the land conveyed by the deed below set forth as made him a necessary party to an action which resulted in a verdict and judgment taken by consent of the parties, in which it was ordered that the judgment be a special lien on the crops growing and to be grown on the land conveyed by the deed, and be enforced as against such crops in three yearly installments, the *gravamen* of the present complaint being the failure of the defendants to comply with this judgment; and that the same is void as to the minor, for the reason that the only service upon him was by acknowledgment through the attorney of his guardian *ad litem.* The deed is as follows: "Georgia, Jasper county. This indenture, made and agreed on this March 30, 1877, between Cardin Goolsby, of said state and county, of the one part, and Julia E. Goolsby, of the same county, of the second part, and the children of the said Cardin, except the said John K., of the third part, witnesseth that, subject to the conditions, and limitations, to be herein mentioned and contained, for the purpose of securing a home and a support for the said John K. and his family, and in consideration of the natural love and affection the said Cardin Goolsby has for his son John K. and his wife, the said Julia E., and also in consideration of

the love and affection he has for his other children, and also in consideration of the sum of five dollars to him in hand paid, he, the said Cardin Goolsby, has granted, given, and conveyed, and by these presents doth give, grant, and convey, unto the said Julia E., for and during the life of the said John K., or so long as he shall live, with remainder over in fee to such child or children as the said John K. may beget by his present or any future wife, the following lands. * * * But if, at the death of the said John K., he, the said John K., shall not have begotten children by his present or any future wife, in remainder over in fee to the children of the said Cardin. That is to say, the true intent and meaning of this writing is, and shall be so construed, the said Julia E. shall take an estate in the premises herein treated of, for and during the life of John K. Goolsby; an estate in remainder in fee shall revest immediately in the children of the said Cardin Goolsby, subject to be divested from the said Cardin's children upon the said John K. begetting children by his present or any future wife, in which event the children of the said John K. shall take an estate in remainder in fee: provided, always, and to this end all estate for years, life, or in remainder are subordinate and dependent, the said John K., so long as he lives, shall be supported from the rents and profits issuing out of said land; that is to say, his support and maintenance during life shall be a charge upon said estate, but not to the extent of diminishing the *corpus,* and he takes no other interest in this deed, nor shall the rents or profits issuing out of said lands be liable to any debt or contract of his. * * *" The action was originally against Julia E. Goolsby. By amendment, John K. Goolsby and John K. Goolsby, Jr., were made parties defendant. On this amendment it was ordered that John K. Goolsby be appointed guardian *ad litem* for John K. Goolsby, Jr., and be served with a copy of the amendment. Following this order is an acknowledgment of service and waiver of process "for all the defendants," signed by "F. Jordan, Atty. for J. K. Goolsby, and J. K. Goolsby, guardian *ad litem* for John K. Goolsby, minor."

Hall & Hammond, for plaintiff in error.
F. Jordan, for defendant in error.

SIMMONS, J. The trial judge placed his refusal of an injunction and the appointment of a receiver in this case upon the ground that the minor son was interested in the land and the fund; that he had not been properly served in the common-law suit; and therefore the judgment or decree sought to be enforced in this equitable petition did not bind him. We think the trial judge was wrong in holding that the infant had an interest which the judgment or decree would bind had he been properly served. Mrs. Goolsby, the mother, is the only person having a direct interest in the land. She has a life estate therein during the life of her husband, John K. Goolsby, with a charge thereon for the support and maintenance of her husband during his life. After his death, the minor, John K., Jr., and such other children as may be living at his death, take the fee.

But, while the reasoning of the judge was erroneous, his judgment refusing the injunction may be right, according to the facts disclosed in this record. There are two reasons which might have authorized him to refuse the injunction if they had been considered. The first is, did the superior court, on an appeal from the county court, have the right and power to allow the amendments making John K. Goolsby and his son parties to the action in the superior court? and did it also have power and authority to allow the amendment seeking equitable relief? Did it have the power and authority to enter up the judgment or decree which it rendered in this case? In other words, can an appeal be taken from a county court which has no equitable jurisdiction to the superior court, and the entire nature of the case be changed by an equitable amendment? The second question is, cannot this land be sold under the judgment against Mrs. Goolsby, the life-tenant, subject, of course, to the charge thereon for the support of John K. Goolsby during his life? If the superior court had no jurisdiction to allow the amendment and to enter up the decree, or if the land can be levied on and sold under the judgment against the life-tenant, the appointment of a receiver would be improper. These matters being at least doubtful, the judge was not bound to make such appointment. We therefore affirm the judgment.

STUBBS v. STATE.

(*Supreme Court of Georgia.* March 16, 1891.)

RECORD ON APPEAL—PRACTICE.

This case is controlled by the act of November 11, 1889, prescribing the method of bringing cases to the supreme court. Moreover, the brief of evidence is a mere report of the trial by questions and answers, and is not such a brief as the law contemplates.

(*Syllabus by Bleckley, C. J.*)

Error from superior court, Terrell county; GUERRY, Judge.

Hoyl & Parks, for plaintiff in error. J. M. Griggs, Sol. Gen., for the State.

Writ of error dismissed.

LAING v. MAYOR, ETC., OF CITY OF AMERICUS.

(*Supreme Court of Georgia.* March 4, 1891.)

CITIES—OBSTRUCTION OF STREET—LICENSE—DIRECTING VERDICT.

1. Without express statutory authority, a municipal government cannot grant to any person the right to erect and maintain in a public street a structure, such as a permanent fish-box, for his private and exclusive use.

2. The charter of Americus invests the city council with full power to clear the streets of all obstructions, and this power may be exercised summarily, and without granting a preliminary hearing, after notice to remove, and refusal.

3. A license from the city to carry on the business of a fish-dealer, etc., gives no vested right to keep a box in the street, and use it in the business.

4. Where the whole case turns upon a question of law, which is decisive of its merits, the court may direct a verdict for the defendant.

Even if this be irregular, it is no cause for a new trial, where a recovery would be impossible.

(*Syllabus by the Court.*)

Error from superior court, Sumter county; FORT, Judge.

Simmons & Kimbrough, L. J. Blalock, and Hoyl & Parks, for plaintiffs in error. B. P. Hollis, E. A. Hawkins, and Harrison & Peeples, for defendant in error.

BLECKLEY, C. J. The plaintiff located his fish-box, a structure nine feet long, three feet wide, and two and one-half feet high, in one of the public streets of Americus, intending it to be permanent, and believing that he had the consent of the city council so to do. Certain members of the street committee of the council gave their consent expressly, co-operated with him in selecting the site, and gave direction as to how and where the contrivance for drainage of the box should be placed. Considerable expense was incurred by the plaintiff in procuring the box, putting it in position, and supplying it with the needful apparatus for drainage. He was a licensed fish-dealer and restaurant keeper, and renewed his license while using the box in connection with his business. The renewed license had a considerable length of time to run when the city, in January, 1888, after the box had stood in the street for about 15 months, removed it without his consent, and in spite of his objection. This was not done, however, until after he had been notified to remove it, and had positively refused to do so. Having no place on any premises under his control on which such a box could be located, he could make no further use of it in his business, and the result was that his business as a fish-dealer was broken up. He brought his action against the city for damages, and, after hearing all the evidence offered by both parties, the court directed the jury to return a verdict for the defendant.

1. It is not pretended that the municipal government of Americus had any express statutory authority to farm out the public streets to fish-dealers or to any one else. Without such authority, they could not grant to any citizen the right to maintain a permanent structure for private use in any of the streets. 2 Dill. Mun. Corp. § 660. Any license, therefore, which the city granted, or could grant, to the plaintiff to occupy the street with his fish-box was necessarily temporary and revocable. Even if both parties had intended it to be permanent, such intention would be of no effect. So far from there being cause for complaint that the structure was allowed to stand only 15 months, it was matter of indulgence to the plaintiff, and something to which he had no legal right, that it was allowed to be placed there at all. His real grievance is that he made a mistake in supposing that he was securing a right which the city authorities had no power to confer upon him. In dealing with public agents, every person must take notice of the extent of their powers at his peril; and only by gross neglect to inform himself could any one having the requisite capacity to deal in fish fall into the error of supposing that he could ac-

quire for his own exclusive use the right to occupy permanently 67 cubic feet of space in a public street. It matters not that a permanent structure for private enjoyment in a street or highway is confined to a part little used, or not used at all; it becomes a nuisance, as an encroachment upon the public right. Elliott, Roads & S. 477 et seq.; Wilbur v. Tobey, 16 Pick. 177; Emerson v. Babcock, 66 Iowa, 257, 23 N. W. Rep. 656; State v. Berdetta, 73 Ind. 185. It was no reason for not removing the obstruction that the plaintiff had incurred expense in erecting and maintaining it. Winter v. City of Montgomery, 83 Ala. 589, 3 South. Rep. 235. The suggestion that the city would be estopped, as in City of Atlanta v. Gas-Light Co., 71 Ga. 107, is without relevancy, for in that case the gas company had a charter from the legislature; the city had power to give consent, and consequently could be estopped from denying that it had given it; and where the power to consent exists, and has been exercised, the city may be estopped to revoke needlessly and to the injury of the other party. Town of Spencer v. Andrew, (Iowa,) 47 N. W. Rep. 1007.

2. The charter of the city of Americus. § 20, declares that the said mayor and council of Americus shall have full power and authority to remove, or cause to be removed, any building, posts, steps, fence, or other obstruction or nuisance, in the public streets, lanes, alleys, sidewalks, or public squares of the city. Acts 1873, p. 114. This power was ample, and was duly exercised in the present instance. The plaintiff was notified, according to the city ordinance, to remove the box, and refused to do it. On the facts in evidence, looking to his testimony alone, there was good cause for removing it, and his complaint that he was denied a hearing by the city council is of no significance. To abate nuisances elsewhere than in the public streets, a preliminary hearing would generally be necessary; but to clear the streets of palpable obstructions, no such hearing is required. The plaintiff has now had a full hearing in the superior court, and has failed to show any legal reason why his box should remain in the street. It was not the want of a hearing, but the lack of any legal right, that exposed him to loss.

3. The plaintiff's license as a fish-dealer or a restaurant keeper did not confer any right upon him to use the street permanently and exclusively as an annex to his premises and an adjunct to his business. We have referred to the transcript of the record of file here in the case of City of Atlanta v. Dooly, 74 Ga. 702, and find that the bill-board involved in that case was located upon private property extending along the margin of the street, and not upon the street itself or sidewalk. It was that circumstance that made the ruling in that case correct. The license granted to Dooly as a bill-poster was not claimed to comprehend the right of maintaining bill-boards in the public streets, but only to cover the privilege of exercising the business on adjacent lands. The city officials seized and removed a board thus located. No act of merely clearing obstructions

out of a street was under consideration in that case.

4. After all the evidence was in, the plaintiff's right to recover turned exclusively upon a question of law. That question was against him. It was not possible for the jury to render any verdict in his favor which could be upheld. This being so, no good reason occurs to us why the court could not direct a verdict for the defendant. But, even if such direction was irregular, it was harmless, and it would be idle to require a new trial. Hobby v. Alford, 73 Ga. 791; Cothran v. City of Rome, 77 Ga. 582. Construing the evidence most favorably for the plaintiff, and treating all conflict in it as settled adversely to the defendant, the verdict was correct. Judgment affirmed.

POWELL et ux. v. ACHEY.

(Supreme Court of Georgia. March 16, 1891.)

REVIEW—CONFLICTING EVIDENCE — APPOINTMENT OF RECEIVER.

Where the evidence was conflicting, and no abuse of discretion by the judge below in granting an injunction and appointing a receiver appears, this court will not disturb his judgment.

(Syllabus by Lumpkin, J.)

Error from superior court, Schley county; FORT, Judge.

J. R. Williams and Hinton & Cutts, for plaintiffs in error. C. R. McCrary and P. L. Mynatt, for defendant in error.

Judgment affirmed.

GREER v. HOLDRIDGE.

(Supreme Court of Georgia. March 16, 1891.)

BILL OF EXCEPTIONS—SERVICE—LACHES.

Where plaintiff in error fails to serve his bill of exceptions on the opposing party within the time limited by the statute after the signing thereof by the judge, a subsequent certificate of the judge, to the effect that such failure of service arose through his delay, cannot be considered to relieve the party in default.

Error from superior court, Dooly county; FORT, Judge.

M. T. Hodges and Martin & Smith, for plaintiff in error. W. L. Grice, for defendant in error.

SIMMONS, J. The bill of exceptions in this case was certified by the trial judge on the 14th of April, 1890; it was served upon the opposite party on April 28, 1890, and filed in the clerk's office May 3, 1890. When the case was called here, a motion to dismiss it was made upon the ground that the bill of exceptions was not served upon opposite counsel within 10 days after the certificate was signed by the judge, or filed with the clerk within 15 days thereafter, as the law requires. In reply to this, counsel for the plaintiff in error read an additional certificate of the judge who tried the case, dated April 30, 1890, wherein he certifies that it was his fault in not returning the bill of exceptions to counsel for the plaintiff in error within the proper time after he had signed it; that, through the neglect of his office boy, the bill of exceptions was not mailed; and it was not the fault of counsel for the plaintiff in error that service was not perfected in time. We have held up this case to the present time in order to consider whether we could receive and act on this certificate or not. After a careful consideration of the matter, we have come to the conclusion that the statute does not authorize the trial judge to sign but one certificate, and that certificate is the one provided for by law. After he has once signed and certified a bill of exceptions, his power and jurisdiction over the case ceases, and we know of no law which would permit us to receive and act on a second certificate, although that certificate relieves counsel for the plaintiff in error from any charge of laches or negligence in failing to have the bill of exceptions served and filed in time. We therefore dismiss this writ of error.

CHATTANOOGA, R. & C. R. CO. v. JACKSON.

(Supreme Court of Georgia. Feb. 23, 1891.)

PLEADING—AMENDMENT—CONTINUANCE—FOREIGN LAWS — EVIDENCE — PRIOR JUDGMENT — SUIT PENDING.

1. There is no error in permitting the amendment of a petition by the substitution of a word so as to give the defendant its proper corporate name, as this is simply correcting a misnomer, and not an introduction of a new party.

2. Service having been acknowledged in defendant's proper name, such amendment was no ground for continuance.

3. Notwithstanding Code Ga. § 3824, provides that the public laws of the several states, as published by authority, shall be judicially recognized without proof, there is no error in receiving the testimony of skilled attorneys to aid in coming to a correct conclusion as to the laws, and especially as to the practice of the courts of their state.

4. Plaintiff obtained judgment against defendant in a Tennessee justice court. Defendant, after appealing to the circuit court, dismissed his appeal, and the court confirmed the justice's judgment. Plaintiff then dismissed his case. In Tennessee an appeal from a justice court vacates the judgment. The amount of the judgment was paid by defendant to the circuit court clerk. But it does not appear that the clerk was the proper party to receive it, or that it was ever paid to plaintiff. *Held,* in an action in Georgia, that a plea in abatement of prior judgment which had been satisfied was properly overruled.

5. The omission of the order dismissing the case to revoke in terms the order dismissing the appeal was a mere irregularity, which does not render the order open to collateral attack.

6. Though it does not appear by the record that notice of the dismissal of the case was served on defendant, it will be presumed that no such notice was necessary, or, if necessary, that it was in fact given.

7. Pendency of a prior suit in one state cannot be pleaded in abatement of a suit between the same parties, for the same cause, in a court of another state.

Error from superior court, Walker county; MADDOX, Judge.

W. W. Brooks and W. T. Turnbull, for plaintiff in error. Payne & Walker, for defendant in error.

SIMMONS, J. Jackson brought his action against the Chattanooga, Rome & Carrollton Railroad Company, for damages sustained by him by reason of personal injuries inflicted upon him by the negligence of the company. This action was brought to the February term, 1889,

of Walker superior court. At that term the defendant filed a plea in abatement. The first was, in substance, that the plaintiff should not have and maintain this action, because on the 18th of January, 1889, he began his action against the defendant in a justice's court in the state of Tennessee for $200, for injuries to a minor son, and that on February 20, 1889, a judgment was rendered against the defendant in said action, and on the 25th of February, 1889, the defendant paid off and discharged the judgment, and that said suit in Tennessee was for the same cause of action set up in this suit. Defendant afterwards amended this plea by alleging that said suit in Tennessee was still pending. When the case came on for trial at the February term, 1890, in Walker superior court, the plaintiff proposed to amend his declaration by striking out the word "Carrollton" in the name of the company, and inserting in lieu thereof the word "Columbus" so that the defendant's name would read, the "Chattanooga, Rome & Columbus Railroad Company." To this the defendant objected, on the ground that the proposed amendment introduced a new party. The objection was overruled, and the defendant excepted. The defendant objected to going to trial, on the ground that it had just been made a party, and that it was then the appearance term. The objection was overruled, and the defendant excepted. The case then went to trial, without the intervention of a jury, on the plea in abatement. Upon the trial of the issue made on these pleas, the plaintiff offered the interrogatories of Lewis Shepard and John A. Moon, practicing attorneys in the courts of Tennessee, for the purpose of showing what the rules of practice were in Tennessee, and also to show the effect of the orders, judgments, and decrees of the circuit courts of that state, and the law of that state on the subject of pleading in justices' courts, and the dismissal of appeals therefrom; to all of which evidence the defendant objected, on the ground that the statutes of Tennessee and the decisions of its supreme court are the highest and best evidence of its laws. This objection was overruled, and the court, after hearing the evidence on the pleas, found against the defendant, and the defendant excepted. The case was then tried upon its merits before a jury, and a verdict was rendered against the defendant. The defendant thereupon made a motion for a new trial, on the several grounds contained therein, which was overruled by the court, and it excepted. Error is assigned in the bill of exceptions on each of the above rulings.

1. There was no error in allowing the plaintiff to amend his declaration by substituting the word "Columbus" for the word "Carrollton," so as to give the defendant its proper corporate name. It was not adding a new party, but simply correcting a misnomer. This, under our Code, § 3483, the plaintiff had the right to do *instanter.* Johnson v. Railroad Co., 74 Ga. 397.

2. There was no error in requiring the defendant to go to trial after this amendment was allowed. Counsel did not state

to the court that they were less prepared for trial on account of this amendment, nor give any other reason why the trial should not proceed, except that a new party had been added,,and that it was the appearance. term as to it. Besides, it appears from the record that service was acknowledged on the writ by counsel, on behalf of the "Chattanooga & Columbus Railway Company;" and in the pleas filed in abatement the case was stated as "Jackson v. Chattanooga, Rome & Columbus Railroad Company;" showing that counsel for the defendant recognized that the true defendant had been sued and served.

3. The next exception relates to the admission, over objection, of the testimony of Shepard and Moon. It will be remembered that this testimony was offered, not only to prove the law of Tennessee on the subject of appeals and their dismissal, but also to prove the practice in the circuit courts in regard to such matters. Our Code, § 3824, declares: "The public laws of the United States, and of the several states thereof, as published by authority, shall be judicially recognized without proof." While, therefore, the trial judge might have resorted to the statutes and the decisions of the supreme court of Tennessee, we cannot say that it was error to receive the testimony of skilled attorneys, who practiced in the courts of that state, to aid him in arriving at a proper conclusion as to what was the law of the state, and especially as to the practice of the courts thereof in regard to appeals and their dismissal. The testimony was not for the jury, but for the information of the judge, and he was not bound by the opinions of these attorneys; but it was his duty at last to decide the law himself, aided by these opinions and by such other sources of information as were accessible to him. Knowing, as we do, the great difficulty under which courts labor in arriving at the true law of a case, and especially the difficulty encountered here as well as in the court below in this case, we cannot condemn a trial judge for resorting to any sources of information which will aid him in coming to a correct conclusion as to the law. The record shows that the judge in this case did not confine himself to the opinions of the attorneys, but that the statutes of Tennessee and the decisions of its supreme court were read to him. Moreover, in some states that have no statute like our own above quoted, (Code, § 3824,) evidence of this kind is the proper mode of proving the law of another state; and the supreme court of the United States has so held. Hanley v. Donoghue, 116 U. S. 1, 6 Sup. Ct. Rep. 242; Chicago & A. R. Co. v. Wiggins Ferry Co., 119 U. S. 615, 7 Sup. Ct. Rep. 398.

4. The next exception complains that the court erred in finding for the plaintiff on the pleas in abatement. It will be remembered that the first plea in abatement was filed at the February term, 1889, and alleged that the plaintiff had already recovered a judgment upon the same cause of action in the state of Tennessee, and that the judgment had been paid off and discharged. The evidence on the trial of

this plea, a year after the filing of the plea, showed that, instead of the judgment having been paid off and discharged, the defendant, on the 20th of February, five days before the plea was filed, had appealed from the justice's court to the circuit court, and on the 9th of March thereafter, in vacation, dismissed the appeal; and on the 6th of May thereafter moved in the circuit court to enter the dismissal of record, and took an order in open court, as follows: "It appearing to the court that the defendant is entitled to make said dismissal a matter of record in this court, it is therefore considered by the court that said appeal be and the same is dismissed, and the judgment of the justice's court is affirmed." This order appears to have been entered on the records of the circuit court. The evidence further showed that on the same day, and after the defendant had dismissed its appeal, the plaintiff dismissed his case against the defendant, by order of the same court; and that on June 30th thereafter the amount recovered by the plaintiff against the defendant was paid into the clerk's office of the circuit court, but the record fails to disclose that the plaintiff ever received the money; nor was there any evidence going to show that the clerk was the proper party to receive it. The dismissal of the appeal in vacation was unauthorized by the laws of Tennessee, and has no effect. Such we have ascertained is the rule in that state. In Tennessee, an appeal from a justice's court to the circuit court does not merely suspend the judgment, as it does in this state, but vacates it. Furber v. Carter, 2 Sneed, 3. When, therefore, the appeal was entered, the judgment of the justice's court was vacated; and under this law, and the above state of facts, the court did not err in finding against the plea.

But it is argued by counsel for the plaintiff in error that when the company dismissed its appeal on the 9th of March, in vacation, and took an order in open court on the 6th of May, thereafter, making the dismissal the judgment of the circuit court, and affirming the judgment of the justice of the peace, the judgment of the justice's court became final, and that the court below in the present case erred in not so holding. Counsel for the defendant in error replies to this by showing the subsequent order, wherein he dismissed in the circuit court the case he had brought in the justice's court, and which the railroad company had carried up by appeal. But counsel for the railroad company contend that this order was void, and should not have been construed to have any effect, because when the company dismissed its appeal and the judge of the circuit court, by his order, affirmed the judgment of the justice's court, there was no case in the circuit court to dismiss. It will be seen, therefore, that the present case, upon this point, turned on the question whether the order of the Tennessee circuit court dismissing the case was void, or was simply an irregularity, and erroneous. If it was void, Jackson, the plaintiff, when this case came up in the court below, had already a final judgment of the courts of Tennessee against the defendant, upon the same cause of action; but, if the order dismissing the case was simply irregular, each of the parties was bound by it until revoked or reversed on appeal or writ of error. After much reflection, we have come to the conclusion that the order dismissing the case from the circuit court was not void, but was merely irregular and erroneous. "By the common law a judgment might be altered, revised, revoked, or amended at any time during the term at which it was rendered." 12 Amer. & Eng. Enc. Law, 120. "A court may vacate its judgment at any time during the term at which it was rendered, even though the steps for taking an appeal have been perfected." Id. 126. See, also, 1 Amer. & Eng. Enc. Law, 627, and authorities cited, note 15; 1 Black, Judgm. § 305; 1 Freem. Judgm. § 69. There was no question made but that the court which rendered the judgment had jurisdiction of the subject-matter and the parties. Having this jurisdiction, it had the right at any time during that term to annul, revoke, change, or amend any judgment which it had previously rendered. While the latter judgment dismissing the case does not allude to the former judgment dismissing the appeal, and affirming the judgment of the justice's court, yet to give it effect it must necessarily be construed to revoke or annul the first judgment, and to reinstate the case. The court having acquired full jurisdiction of the case, it retained it until the case was finally disposed of. The exercise of the jurisdiction may have been suspended upon the dismissal of the appeal, but the jurisdiction itself was not suspended. "When, therefore, a court which still retains jurisdiction, but has suspended the exercise of it, assumes again to exercise its jurisdiction, its action is within its power, and cannot be collaterally impeached." 2 Black, Judgm. § 912; Audubon v. Excelsior Co., 27 N. Y. 216; Loeb v. Willis, 3 N. E. Rep. 177, 100 N. Y. 231; Blum v. Wettermark, 58 Tex. 125. While it would have been the better practice to revoke in terms the first order dismissing the appeal, we think the granting of the second order dismissing the case was a revocation of the first by indirection. 1 Black, Judgm. § 304. For instance, when a trial is had, a verdict rendered, and a judgment entered thereon, and a motion for a new trial is made and granted, the granting of the motion sets aside the judgment by indirection. It was also contended that the order was void, because there was no notice given the railroad company of the application for or the granting of the second order. In reply to this, it is said in 2 Black, Judgm. § 912, that "where, in the case of a foreign judgment, it does not appear by the record that any notice was given to the party affected by the action of the court in thus resuming its jurisdiction, it will be presumed that, according to the practice of the court, no such notice was necessary, or that, if necessary, it was in fact given."

5. The last remaining ground to be considered, as made in the bill of exceptions, is that the court erred in finding against the plea of pendency of the former suit in the Tennessee court. There was no error in this finding by the court. It is well settled that "the pendency of a prior suit in one state cannot be pleaded in abatement of a suit between the same parties, for the same cause, in a court of another state." Benn. Lis Pendens, § 347. See, also, Whart. Confl. Laws, § 784 et seq; Story, Confl. Laws, 833, note; 8 Amer. & Eng. Enc. Law, 554; Smith v. Lathrop, 44 Pa. St. 326; West v. McConnell, 25 Amer. Dec. 191, and note.

6. The only ground of a motion for a new trial insisted upon here was the third ground thereof, which is that the verdict is contrary to evidence, etc. It is claimed in support of this ground of the motion that the evidence shows that the plaintiff in the court below was negligent, and could have avoided the injury to himself by the exercise of ordinary care. We presume that the court submitted this question fairly to the jury, and the jury having found against the railroad company on that issue, and there being sufficient evidence to authorize their finding, and the trial judge being satisfied therewith, he did not abuse his discretion in refusing a new trial on this ground. Judgment affirmed.

RODMAN v. ARCHBELL.

(Supreme Court of North Carolina. April 24, 1891.)

APPEAL—DELAY IN DOCKETING—PRACTICE.

1. Where an appeal is not docketed within the time fixed by law, on account of delay in settling the case, and appellant does not apply for *certiorari* at the first term next after the trial, the appeal will be dismissed. Following Joyner v. Hines, (N. C.) 12 S. E. Rep. 901.

2. The contention that appellant's failure to docket the appeal in time was by consent of the appellee cannot be sustained, where the agreement is not in writing, and is denied by appellee's counsel.

3. Under rule 30 of the supreme court of North Carolina, an appeal will be dismissed, if the record is not printed.

On motion of appellee to dismiss appeal. *John H. Small* and *T. F. Davidson,* for appellant. *E. S. Simmons, F. H. Whitaker,* and *F. H. Busbee,* for appellee.

PER CURIAM. This case was tried at December term, 1889, of Beaufort superior court. It was not docketed here till February term, 1891. The appellant contends that the delay in settling case in time for spring term, 1890, was by no fault of his. If this were so, it was his duty to have docketed the case here at that term, and apply for a *certiorari.* Pittman v. Kimberly, 92 N. C. 562; Joyner v. Hines, 12 S. E. Rep. 901, (at this term.)

He further insists that by consent of the appellee the case was not docketed at fall term, 1890. If it be conceded that this would be regular, the agreement was not in writing, and is denied by the affidavit of appellee's counsel. The court, therefore, cannot consider it. Rule 38. The appeal must be dismissed, because not filed in time. Rule 5; Whitehead v. Blandford, 12 S. E. Rep. 908, (at this term.) The appellee is also entitled to have the appeal dismissed because the record is not printed. Rule 30. Appeal dismissed.

STATE v. JAMES.

(Supreme Court of North Carolina. April 14, 1891.)

APPEAL—DISMISSAL—FAILURE TO DOCKET APPEAL.

Where an appeal is not docketed in the supreme court at the term succeeding the trial of the case in the court below, and no excuse is shown for the delay, the appeal will be dismissed.

On motion to dismiss appeal.
The Attorney General, for the State.

PER CURIAM. This case was tried at spring term, 1890, of Alexander superior court. The appeal was not docketed here at fall term, 1890. There was no application for *certiorari* at that term, (Pittman v. Kimberly, 92 N. C. 562,) and no excuse is shown for the delay. Under the repeated decisions of this court we must direct the entry to be made, appeal dismissed.

PARDUE v. GIVENS.

(Supreme Court of North Carolina. April 14, 1891.)

PARTITION—OWELTY—VENDITIONI EXPONAS.

A decree of partition having charged the dividend of superior value with a sum of money to make equality, payment must be enforced by the writ of *venditioni exponas* granted on motion or petition in the partition proceedings, and not by independent action. Following Herman v. Watts, 12 S. E. Rep. 487

Motion by plaintiff in supreme court, where the cause was pending, for a writ of *venditioni exponas* to issue for the purpose of selling the more valuable shares in a partition proceeding, which were charged with the payment of certain sums for owelty of partition.
Covington & Adams, for petitioner.
Battle & Mordecai, opposed.

PER CURIAM. This case is governed by the decision in Herman v. Watts, 107 N. C. 646, 12 S. E. Rep. 487, and therefore let it be entered. Motion denied.

LONG et al. v. OXFORD et al.

(Supreme Court of North Carolina. April 21, 1891.)

EXECUTORS AND ADMINISTRATORS — RES ADJUDICATA—STATUTE OF LIMITATIONS—COSTS.

1. In a proceeding to sell land to make assets, a judgment previously obtained against the executor is conclusive against the heirs and devisees unless fraud and collusion is alleged and shown, and the heir or devisee cannot plead the statute of limitation or other defense which might have been set up in the original action.

2. In such proceedings the realty is liable for costs as well as the balance of the judgment, unless the court which rendered the judgment taxed the costs against the executor or administrator personally or against the plaintiff.

(Syllabus by the Court.)

Appeal from superior court, Alexander county; MERRIMON, Judge.
This was a special proceeding in the nature of a creditors' bill for the settlement of an estate, and to subject devised lands to the payment of debts. On the hearing before the clerk the plaintiffs demurred to the answers filed, on the ground that they did not allege facts sufficient to constitute

a valid defense. The clerk, sustaining the demurrer, gave judgment against the defendants, which judgment was confirmed by the judge in term, and the defendants appealed to the supreme court.
R. Z. Linney and *R. B. Burke*, for appellants. *A. C. McIntosh*, for appellees.

CLARK, J., *(after stating the facts as above.)* The plaintiffs seek to subject the lands of Samuel H. Reid to the payment of a judgment heretofore obtained against the executor. The defendants, who are the executor himself and his wife, (who is the sole devisee of Reid,) attempt in their answers to set up the statute of limitations and other matters of defense which might have been pleaded in the original action. The plaintiffs demurred on the ground that the answers did not set up any defense to the action which could avail the defendants or either of them. The court properly sustained the demurrer. "The heir (or devisee) is bound by the judgment against the administrator, (or executor,) unless he can show that it was obtained by collusion and fraud; and he is barred by it from setting up any statutory limitation or other matter which might have been pleaded by the administrator (or executor) as a bar to the action against him." Proctor v. Proctor, 105 N. C. 222, 10 S. E. Rep. 1036; Speer v. James, 94 N. C. 417; Smith v. Brown, 101 N. C. 347, 7 S. E. Rep. 890. The answer of the devisee in the present case does not aver fraud or collusion. It is admitted that the personal assets are insufficient to pay the judgment.

The defendants, however, insist that the land cannot be subjected to payment of the costs, and is exempted therefrom by virtue of the former decision of this court. It was competent for the court below in the former action to have taxed the executor personally with the costs of that action in the cases mentioned in the Code, § 1429. When the appeal from the judgment in that action was before us (104 N. C. 408, 10 S. E. Rep. 525) the question presented was as to the right of the plaintiffs to recover costs. The judgment below gave the plaintiffs costs, but did not tax the executor with them individually, and the judgment here merely affirmed the judgment below. The land is subject to pay the costs as well as the balance of the judgment. No error.

BEAM et al. v. BRIDGES et al.

(Supreme Court of North Carolina. April 21, 1891.)

WIFE'S SEPARATE ESTATE— INVESTMENT BY HUSBAND—RESULTING TRUST.

While, under the former system, the wife's money became the property of the husband *jure mariti*, the latter may agree, as between him and the wife, to treat it as the wife's property; and where there is evidence to show an agreement to that effect, and that the husband invested it in land for her benefit, and took the title in his name, there is a resulting trust.

(Syllabus by the Court.)

Appeal from superior court, Rutherford county; G. H. BROWN, Jr., Judge.
Special proceeding for partition. The only issue submitted to the jury was as

follows: "Was the first 150-acre tract described in the complaint, and conveyed by Anderson Bridges to John Beam, February 18, 1846, purchased by John Beam with the money of his wife, Elizabeth, and at her request and for her?" There was testimony tending to show that Mrs. Beam was possessed of certain money; that her husband voluntarily agreed to treat it as hers, and to waive his marital rights in respect to it, by investing the same for her in the lands above mentioned. Neither John Beam nor his wife had any children. The plaintiffs requested the court to charge that, under the testimony, the issue should be answered in the negative, and that the court should so charge. The court refused to give the instruction. There was a verdict against the plaintiffs, and they appealed.

Justice & Justice, for appellants. *Montgomery & Forney*, for appellees.

SHEPHERD, J., (*after stating the facts as above*.) The only question presented for review is whether there was sufficient evidence to sustain an affirmative finding of the second issue. We think it very clear from the testimony of James and William Bridges that John Beam purchased the land in question with his wife's money, at her request; that the purchase was intended for her benefit, and that such was the understanding and agreement of the parties. It may also be inferred that she intended that the title should be made to her. Indeed, the agreement was that the husband should purchase the land "for her," and the necessary implication is that the title was to be taken in her name. It is a well-settled principle that where, on the purchase of property, the conveyance of the legal estate is taken in the name of one person, but the purchase money is paid by another at the same time or previously, and as a part of one transaction, a trust results in favor of him who supplies the purchase money. Adams, Eq. 33; Malone, Real Prop. 509. The principle has frequently been applied where land is purchased with funds arising from the separate estate of the wife, (Cunningham v. Bell, 83 N. C. 328; Lyon v. Akin, 78 N. C. 258,) or with funds which by agreement of the husband are to be treated as such separate estate, (Hackett v. Shuford, 86 N. C. 144, and the cases cited.) It is urged, however, that in our case the money with which the land was purchased was not the separate estate of the wife, and that the agreement of the husband to treat it as such being purely voluntary, and therefore of no effect, there was nothing to prevent the operation of the principle *by which the money of the wife became the property of the husband, *jure mariti.* The argument derives some support from the intimation of the learned justice who delivered the opinion in Hackett's Case, supra, but it will appear from an examination of the Maryland cases (alone cited by him) that the rights of creditors were involved, and that, so far from any pecuniary consideration being necessary as between the parties, the contrary view was declared by the supreme court of that state. The case, upon appeal, does not

v.13 s.e.no.4—8

very clearly show how the wife acquired or held the money in question, but, granting that it was subject to the marital rights of the husband, we think that, as between him and the wife, his agreement to treat it as her separate property would be recognized in equity in cases like this: especially where there were no children to be provided for, and the claim of the wife was more meritorious than that of the collateral heirs, whom the husband was under no moral obligation to maintain. Garner v. Garner, Busb. Eq. 1. It is said by high authority that, although the presumption is that the money of the wife during the marriage becomes the husband's, such presumption is not conclusive, and the husband "may so treat it as to charge himself and his heirs, as trustees of the wife, with the duty of applying it to her separate use." Taggard v. Talcott, 2 Edw. Ch. 628; Resor v. Resor, 9 Ind. 349; Temple v. Williams, 4 Ired. Eq. 39; Woodruff v. Bowles, 104 N. C. 197, 10 S. E. Rep. 482. It is well settled that a husband may, after marriage, make gifts or presents to his wife which will be supported in equity against himself and his representatives, (Lucas v. Lucas, 1 Atk. 270; Ath. Mar. Sett. 331; Garner v. Garner, supra; Smith v. Smith, Winst. Eq. 581:) and it seems to be also well established that a trust may be raised in favor of the wife by proof that her husband paid the purchase money for her benefit, and with his own funds, (Raybold v. Raybold, 20 Pa. St. 308; Pinney v. Fellows, 15 Vt. 525; Farley v. Blood, 10 Fost. (N. H.) 354; Dyer v. Dyer, 1 White & T. Lead. Cas. 341.) In consideration of the foregoing authorities, we see no reason why the agreement of the husband in this case may not be sustained as against the parties to this action; and, this being so, it must follow that there was a resulting trust. Affirmed.

SMITH v. SMITH.

(*Supreme Court of North Carolina.* April 1, 1891.)

INSANITY—NEXT FRIENDS—LIABILITY FOR COSTS.

1. In an action to set aside a power of attorney on account of the maker's want of mental capacity, next friends, appointed by the clerk to conduct the action, may, on a verdict finding the maker sane, be taxed with costs, if they officiously and unnecessarily caused themselves to be appointed, but there must first be a special finding of such fact by the court. Modifying 12 S. E. Rep. 1045.

2. On appeal, the cause may be remanded for such finding.

Upon motion in supreme court to correct judgment. The facts are reported in same case, 12 S. E. Rep. 1045.

CLARK, J. The exceptions to the charge were taken in time when set out in appellant's statement of case on appeal, (Lowe v. Elliott, 107 N. C. 718, 12 S. E. Rep. 388,) though it is better practice and fairer, both to appellee and appellant, to make such exceptions on a motion for a new trial, since, if a slip has been made, the judge may perhaps correct it, and save parties the costs and delay of an appeal, (McKinnon v. Morrison, 104 N. C. 354, 10 S.

E. Rep. 513.) We find no error in the charge in the particulars excepted to. There are many precedents to support it. It is true that ordinarily, if insanity is found to exist, it is presumed to continue till the opposite is shown. State v. Vann, 82 N. C. 631. But here, the main contention in the action being as to the mental capacity of Larkin Smith, the preliminary action of the clerk in appointing next friends to conduct the proceeding is not such a finding as to change the burden of proof and prejudge the very question at issue. While there is no specific exception to the judgment, any error therein which is apparent upon the face of the record the court will take notice of and correct. Thornton v. Brady, 100 N. C. 38, 5 S. E. Rep. 910. The next friends are not parties to the action. Mason v. McCormick, 75 N. C. 263; George v. High, 85 N. C. 113; Tate v. Mott, 96 N. C. 19, 2 S. E. Rep. 176. They are appointed by the court to act for and represent the real party in interest. The verdict and judgment having settled that Larkin Smith was *compos mentis*, the order appointing next friends was properly set aside. He then could have continued the action as to so much of it as asked to set aside the prior power of attorney to defendant or have discontinued it. He elected to do the latter. The costs of the proceedings instituted in his behalf and by order of the court should *prima facie* be taxed against him. It is to be presumed that the order of the court appointing next friends was made regularly, after due inquiry and in the interest of Larkin Smith. He is the party plaintiff in fact and in law, and appeared by next friends, who merely represented him, under the authority and appointment of the court. Code, § 180. It is contended, however, that, though not strictly parties to the action, the next friends in the case at bar, in resisting the motion to discharge them, were in fact, as virtually found by the verdict of the jury, resisting the will of Larkin Smith, a person of full age and competent to appear for himself; that such next friends officiously and unnecessarily caused themselves to be appointed; and that they, and not Larkin Smith, should pay the costs incurred by their false clamor. There is some force in this suggestion. While "next friends" may not be embraced in the strict letter of the Code, § 535, they come within the purview of that section. It was held error to tax trustees of an express trust who are parties to the action with the costs, unless the court had adjudged that they were guilty of "mismanagement or bad faith in such action." Smith v. King, 107 N. C. 273, 12 S. E. Rep. 57. *A fortiori* it is error to tax "next friends" who are not parties, without at least a similar finding. This is not alleged here in the answer nor found by the court. Indeed, the presumption, by virtue of their appointment by the court, is that they acted in good faith, and they cannot be liable to costs, unless there is an express finding against them of the facts requisite to tax them with costs. An analogous rule obtains in criminal actions, as to which it is held that an order taxing a prosecutor with the costs is erroneous,

unless the court finds the facts which would authorize such order, and that the absence of such finding from the judgment would be an error apparent on the face of the record, which the court would correct without assignment of error. State v. Roberts, 106 N. C. 662, 10 S. E. Rep. 900. It is further held in the same case that it is notwithstanding still open to the solicitor, when the case goes back for correction of the judgment, to move in the court below that the court pass upon the facts, since the court has not found the facts either way, so as to make its judgment a finality, but has simply omitted to find them. We find no error, except in the judgment as to costs, which should not have been awarded against the next friends, without a distinct finding by the court "of mismanagement or bad faith" by them in the institution or conduct of the action. To the end that such fact may be passed upon by the court below, and the costs awarded in accordance therewith, the case is remanded. The judgment in all other respects is affirmed. Remanded.

CAMPBELL v. SHIPMAN.

(Supreme Court of Appeals of Virginia. April 16, 1891.)

BILL IN EQUITY—PARTIES—ASSIGNMENT OF PLAINTIFF'S INTEREST.

Where a creditor files a bill to set aside a voluntary conveyance by his debtor, and pending the suit the debt is paid by the indorser of the notes representing it, and the notes delivered to him, such indorser cannot prosecute the suit in the name of the original plaintiff. RICHARDSON, J., dissenting.

Edmund Burke and *A. W. Armstrong,* for appellant. *W. Willoughby,* for appellee.

LACY, J. This is an appeal from a decree of the circuit court of Alexandria city, rendered on the 4th day of February, 1890. The bill was filed by the appellant, Peter Campbell, in the circuit court of Fairfax county, against the appellee, John J. Shipman, in March, 1877, and against Priscilla J. Shipman, the wife of the said John J. Shipman, and one Joseph A. Rice, alleging that said appellant was the creditor of the said John J. Shipman to the amount of certain notes of the said John J. Shipman, set forth in the bill indorsed by one William Fletcher, which had been by the said complainant discounted in due course of his business as a banker and broker; and as such creditor seeking to set aside as fraudulent a deed executed by the said John J. Shipman to the said Rice, without consideration deemed valuable in law, by which certain real estate was conveyed to the said grantee; and to set aside, also, a deed forthwith made by the grantee, Rice, to the wife of his grantor, the said Priscilla J. Shipman. The defendant John J. Shipman answered, and admitted the debts, but claiming debts thereon, admitted the voluntary character of the deeds in question, but denied any fraudulent intent in their execution, and alleged a sufficiency of other property to pay all of his debts. A decree was rendered subsequently, the record does not disclose when, referring the cause to a commissioner to take an account of the debts of John J. Shipman existing at the date of the voluntary deed aforesaid, and an account of liens, if any, on the real estate in question. Here the matter rested, and nothing was done until November 7, 1884, when a decree was entered whereby, by the consent of parties, the cause was removed to the circuit court of Alexandria city. Nothing more appears to have been done in the cause until March 28, 1888, when a decree was again entered by consent of parties, submitting the cause to the judge of the circuit court for decision and decree therein in vacation. And it was further ordered that the said cause be referred to John S. Fowler as a special commissioner, to take proofs and make report thereon to the court with all convenient speed. This special commissioner was sufficiently expeditious to make a report in the cause on the 1st of August, 1889; the defendant Shipman in the mean time having made a motion to dismiss, on March 2, 1889, for want of prosecution. The commissioner reported a large amount of testimony, in the form of depositions taken before him and others; and reports that it is very difficult, in the midst of so much conflicting evidence, and in the absence of reliable data, to report the condition of the accounts between Campbell and Shipman, but that there was a controversy pending between Shipman and Fletcher, the indorser of these notes, who had been partners in business, and that these notes had been withdrawn from the papers in this suit, and filed by Fletcher in the papers of the Shipman & Fletcher suit, when a settlement of the partnership accounts of Shipman & Fletcher was proceeding, upon the claim by Fletcher that, as indorser of these notes, he had paid them to Campbell; and that they thus became a charge against Shipman as the maker, and first liable therefor, in favor of Fletcher. And Campbell also proves that he had kept enough money belonging to Fletcher on deposit with him to pay these notes, and had then given up the notes to Fletcher. Fletcher testified that he had paid these notes to Campbell, and Campbell testified that he had collected them out of Fletcher's money. By a decree entered in the cause in September, 1889, this report was recommitted to the same commissioner, who again reported, January 10, 1890; wherein, among other things, he reports that Fletcher, the indorser, has paid the notes in question, and has them in his possession; and that if Fletcher is allowed to prosecute this suit in the name of Campbell, who has no interest in it, charging Shipman with the notes which he owes to Fletcher, in the personal transactions between Campbell and Shipman, then, in view of the conflicting oral and somewhat uncertain documentary evidence, he finds Shipman indebted to Campbell, by virtue of these notes, $2,401.21, with interest from January 10, 1877. To all this the circuit court responded on the 4th day of February, 1890, by rendering a decree dismissing the bill of the plaintiff, with costs. From this decree in this case is here by appeal.

The appellee appears here, and moves to dismiss the appeal upon the ground that the appellant, Peter Campbell, has no interest in the suit, and cannot prosecute the appeal for the benefit of another. It is a concession in the case that the appellant in this court, the plaintiff in the circuit court, has no interest whatever in any recovery which might be had in this case. The notes sued on were executed by Shipman, and indorsed by Fletcher, and purchased by Campbell; Shipman and Fletcher being at that time partners in business, contractors, on the public and other works of the District of Columbia. The matters of business between Shipman and Fletcher had resulted in litigation, and had at one time been submitted to arbitration, and there had been an award which gave to Fletcher $1,291.96, in full of all demands up to February 7, 1877; and Fletcher appeared at one time in this suit, and filed this award against Shipman; but Shipman instituted suit in the circuit court of Alexandria city to set aside this award for misconduct of the arbitrators and for other causes, in which he finally succeeded, and which may be found reported in 82 Va. 601. The suit between Shipman and Fletcher, after the award had been finally set aside, was proceeded with in the said court, where it still is. In this suit, which is for the settlement of the partnership accounts and dealings of the said Shipman & Fletcher, the said Fletcher has filed the notes sued on in this suit by Campbell, and there he has claimed them as a credit against Shipman, because he has paid them; whereas, Shipman, as maker, was primarily liable for their payment. What the result of this suit is or will be we do not know, but, upon the ground that Campbell has no interest in this suit, and that he is sole plaintiff and sole appellant, the appellee, Shipman, moves the court to dismiss this appeal. The said Fletcher is not a party to this suit, either as plaintiff or defendant; but counsel appear here, as they did in the circuit court, and claim to represent Campbell for the benefit of Fletcher, who is the party alleged to be the real party in interest. It is a general rule in equity that every party interested in any suit must be made a party to the suit, either as plaintiff or defendant, and the real party in interest must be the complainant; and it is immaterial that the interest of the defendants are in conflict with each other, or that some of their claims are identical with those of the plaintiff. Equity deals with the real parties in interest. Castleman v. Berry, 86 Va. 606. 10 S. E. Rep. 884; Kellam v. Sayre, 30 W. Va. 198, 3 S. E. Rep. 589; Field v. Maghee, 5 Paige, 540; Mason v. Railroad Co., 52 Me. 82; Mills v. Hoag, 7 Paige, 18; 2 Daniel, Ch. Pr. 1517, note; Johnson v. Thomas, 11 Beav. 501; Solomon v. Solomon, 13 Sim. 516. In Mills v. Hoag, supra, it was said by Chancellor WALWORTH: "But even if purchasers of this kind [purchasers of the plaintiff's interest] were both legal and meritorious, the right of appeal is gone, and cannot be restored by amendment, as the appeal is not in the name of the proper parties. In this court the proceedings must be carried on in the name of the real parties, so far at least as the rights of the complainant are concerned, although there has been a change of interest subsequent to the commencement of the suit. But the rights of the adverse party cannot be prejudiced by any sale of the subject-matter of the suit, merely voluntary, *pendente lite.* When the complainant sells his whole right in the suit, or it becomes wholly vested in another by operation of law, whether before or after a decree, if there is to be any further litigation in the case, it cannot be carried on in the name of the original complainant by the person who has acquired the right. And, if the complainant's interest is determined by voluntary assignment, the assignee must make himself a party to the suit by an original bill, in the nature of a supplemental bill, before he can be permitted to proceed. Mitf. Pl. 65. The complainant, therefore, was not the proper party to appeal after he had sold all his interest to others, and this court will not permit the appeal to be carried on in his name for their benefit." In Johnson v. Thomas, supra, Lord LANGDALE, master of the rolls, said: "The suit is clearly defective. How is it possible to proceed with it in its present form, when the subject has been transferred to a person who is not a party? The defendant in truth is called on to combat a shadow, and not the real opponent. It is not possible to make any decree with the knowledge of this fact." In Solomon v. Solomon, supra, Vice-Chancellor SHADWELL said: "Here I find the fact that all the adult plaintiffs have parted *pro tanto* with the whole of their interest to a mortgagee, and my opinion is that, unless their mortgagee is made a party, the suit cannot proceed." It is clear that Campbell has no interest in the notes sued on, and that, not being a creditor of Shipman, he has no interest to serve in setting aside the voluntary deed made by Shipman to Rice, and that he was not aggrieved by a decree dismissing a bill in which he had no interest, and that his appeal here cannot be sustained; but it is equally clear, and for the same reasons, that the circuit court did not err in dismissing the bill in the cause. Campbell had no just claim of any sort against Shipman on the notes sued on, which have been paid in full, and surrendered by him to a person not a party to this suit, and who would not, therefore, be affected by any decree rendered in the cause. Campbell is without any legal demand against any defendant in the cause, and he is the sole plaintiff. It was therefore right to dismiss his bill, and there was no error in the said decree of the circuit court to that end, and the same will be affirmed.

RICHARDSON, J., dissenting　HINTON, J., not sitting.

ROME HOTEL CO. v. WARLICK et al.

(*Supreme Court of Georgia.* March 30, 1891.)

MECHANIC'S LIEN — FAILURE TO COMPLETE CONTRACT.

1. Plaintiffs contracted to furnish an apparatus at a fixed price sufficient to heat part of defendant's hotel. It was verbally agreed that the hotel halls should be kept closed, and not be in-

cluded in this contract. Plaintiffs agreed to do extra work, and furnish materials, for which no price was agreed upon. Plaintiffs sued for a lien covering the whole amount. A portion of the claim had been paid, and plaintiff quit before completing the extra work for fear he would not get his pay. There was a dispute as to the price of the extra work. The court charged: "If the plaintiffs quit the extra work for fear they would not get their pay, they had the right to do so, and a failure to complete the extra work for that reason would not defeat their lien." *Held,* that under Code Ga. § 1990, which requires that there shall be "a compliance with his contract by the person claiming a lien," the plaintiffs, having failed to do the work, are not entitled to a lien for so much of the extra work as they have done, but as to such work are entitled to a general judgment upon a *quantum meruit.*

2. Where a part of the amount is not fixed in price, and there is a contention as to the value of the services, the fact that the jury found less than was claimed for extra work does not deprive plaintiffs of their lien on the ground that they had not completed their contract.

3. It is not error to charge: "If it was the contract that the hotel company was to close up the halls by storm-doors, and if the hotel company failed to close up the halls, and if there was a failure to produce the proper degree of heat by reason of such neglect to put in storm doors, then the plaintiffs would not be responsible for the failure," though the main contract was a written one, and the contract as to the doors was in parol, where the testimony as to the closing of the halls was first brought out by defendant on cross-examination of plaintiffs' witness, and an issue was made thereon without objection.

Error from superior court, Floyd county; MADDOX, Judge.

The official report is as follows: "Warlick, Wingate & Mell sued the Rome Hotel Company for a balance on account of $2,691.63, a balance claimed to be due them for work and labor done and materials furnished on and in building the hotel of defendant, and in doing plumbing, gas-fitting, and other work thereon, and also to declare and set up a lien on the hotel building and grounds for such balance. The defendant pleaded "Not indebted;" also, that the account was unjust, and the work negligently and unskillfully done, and with inferior and defective material, damaging it in the sum of $3,000; that a steam-heating system,—one of the principal items in the account,—was so negligently done that it failed to heat the hotel arcade, parlors, and dining-room, so that coal had to be used during the winter; and the steam-heating was of no value, and its defects had damaged the hotel $1,000, etc. The principal matters in dispute between the parties was as to the steam-heating system, which, together with certain other work, was originally contracted for, and extra work done by plaintiffs for defendant. The evidence for plaintiffs tended to show the following: On March 22, 1888, the plaintiffs made a written proposition to defendant to furnish a Florida boiler, with necessary pipes, radiators, etc., to complete the system of steam-heating in the hotel, guarantying to heat the arcade, parlors, and dining-room, in the coldest weather, to 70 degrees Fahrenheit, for the sum of $1,454. The writing also contained propositions for certain other work, not necessary to be here mentioned, except that the plaintiffs proposed to furnish hot and cold water for wash-basins and bath-tubs. It was expressly understood between the parties before the contract, as stated in the writing, was closed, that the hotel halls were not to be included in the heating system, but were to be closed up with storm-doors, or curtains, or in some similar way. It was expressly understood that plaintiffs were to do nothing towards heating the halls. This was an oral understanding. These halls opened upon the arcade. The plaintiffs, in accordance with the contract, put in a Florida boiler, with the necessary pipes, radiators, etc., to complete the system of steam-heating. If properly managed, the boiler, radiators, etc., as put in by them, were more than sufficient to produce the degree of heat stipulated for in the hotel arcade, parlors, and dining-room, but were not sufficient to heat the halls, or to produce the degree of heat contracted for the halls being left open. Defendant did not properly manage the boiler, and did not use the proper kind of coal or coke, so that the heat obtained was not at all times such as it should have obtained, and so that grates in the boiler were negligently burned out. The boiler, when properly supplied with coal or coke of the right quality, and left in proper condition in the morning, would not require further attention more than once during the day, or probably not until night. It was simple, and easily operated, and did not require a person of more than ordinary intelligence to attend to it. It was economical, valuable, and furnished a first-class system of heating. Anthracite coal or good gas coke was the proper fuel to use in the boiler. A pamphlet setting forth the claims made by the manufacturers of the Florida boiler was exhibited by plaintiffs to defendant. It was represented to defendant to be one of the most economical heating apparatuses known to science. As a portion of the heating apparatus plaintiffs were to furnish radiators. Radiators were furnished, and, in order to do their work properly, they ought not to leak; but it is not absolutely necessary to their heating power that they should not leak; they can heat and still leak, and frequently do so. They are constructed with automatic valves, but require to be set, of course, regulated by hand, and then work automatically, but, of course, require some attention. They were not properly attended to by defendant, so as to obtain from them the amount of heat which could have been obtained by proper attention. If they leaked, the leaks were not important; and one leak, insisted upon as quite serious by defendant, the attention of plaintiffs had not been called to up to the trial. If a sufficient quantity of hot water was not obtained by defendant it was because defendant neglected to put in hot-water boilers of sufficient capacity. The putting in of such boilers was not a part of the contract with plaintiffs. The charges for the extra work were fair and reasonable, and that work was properly done. No definite sum for this work had been agreed upon, but it was agreed that it should be done for a reasonable

price. Defendant several times complained about the inefficiency of the heating apparatus, and plaintiffs did not complain that the halls were not closed, and never demanded that the halls should be closed up. That was left with defendant. When the Florida boiler was properly run in the hotel it made plenty of heat, and burned out no grate-bars. The work which plaintiffs did was concluded within 90 days of the time their claim of lien was filed and recorded, and their suit was brought within 12 months from the time their claim became due. The work was done and material furnished by them as plumbers, steam and gas fitters. Plaintiffs did not get to finish everything connected with the extra work which was to have been done, on account of the fact that they had done about all they could get any money for. There was some work that might have been put in if the money had held out. A tank up on top of the house, and a little steam table, (which are not charged in the accounts sued on,) might have been put in if the money had held out. Plaintiffs quit work because the money gave out. That was not on the regular work, but on the extra work, where they were paid by the day. The tank has been put in by defendant since, and was not necessary to complete the job properly, if defendant would run its elevator right. Plaintiffs quit because they were afraid about their money. They had finished up about what they had to do there, and stopped because they were apprehensive about money matters. When the radiators were full of cold air, before hot air was to be forced into them, it was proper that the radiator should be to some extent open to permit the cold air to escape, and when the valves were open, when first heated up, a little water would come out of them, but they are not continually leaking, and water running down through the floors. If they do leak and run down through the dining-room it never was reported. A witness for plaintiffs, who was overseeing the job for them, was in the hotel, and looked over everything time and again when one Jewell was in charge, and there was no leak there then. If hot water, after the completion of the building, ran up into the pipes for a month all right, and afterwards did not, and after that two additional heaters were put in the kitchen and one in the barber-shop, and after that the water went back through the pipes, one of plaintiffs' witnesses testified that he would say that was a good job; but he did not know whether the water system of the barber-shop was connected with the house or not. If the boilers for the storage of hot water were just the same now as they were before, and when first completed did not supply hot water but do now, there was something wrong about it; but the entire job of plumbing should not be condemned on that account, as there might be a stop in it, or a leak, or some such thing, etc. When one King was in charge of the hotel for defendant (and King, from the evidence, seems to have been generally in charge of it as the agent or representative of the defendant) any little imperfec tion about the work, which he called plaintiffs' attention to, was corrected. He never called attention to the leak in the dining-room. Storm-doors for the hall were not contemplated in the plan of the house, but it is possible to put them in. If a system of heating the hotel applied to the whole hotel it would apply to the halls as well as the arcade, parlors, and dining-room; and one of plaintiffs' witnesses testified that he never saw a system of heating a hotel that applied to heating up nothing but the arcade, parlor, and dining-room, that he knew of. The valves of the radiators furnished by plaintiffs are automatic; but such valves will not remain so, even if they are properly set, though it is claimed that they will. They have to be watched,—noticed occasionally. When the metal has been expanded by heat it will not come exactly back to its place when it contracts, and by a small fraction, therefore, these valves will be inclined to open, and should be turned sufficiently to adjust them as desired.

The defendant put in evidence, from the descriptive catalogue of the Florida steamboiler exhibited to it by plaintiffs, the recommendations of the radiator. Among these recommendations were that it would carry steam continuously from 12 to 18 hours without attention, in the coldest weather; that it was self-feeding; that it was more economical of fuel than other radiators; and that one man could easily give it all the attention required in a quarter of an hour at evening and the same time in the morning. Defendant also put in evidence, from the same pamphlet, the printed instructions as to the management of the heater. The only one of these instructions which contained a direction or suggestion as to what kind of coal should be used was the following, in very large letters: "Use stove coal." Among the instructions was that, when steam was required at the radiators, the valves should be open to their full capacity, and, when not required, tightly closed; that a valve half open would cause the radiator to fill with water. The oral evidence for defendant tended to show the following: The heating apparatus put in by plaintiffs was not sufficient to keep the arcade, dining-room, and parlors up to the degree of heat contracted for, but coal-fires had to be used in addition, especially in the dining-room, and at considerable expense. The dining-room is cut off from the arcade by sliding doors. It was not intended when the hotel was built that the halls should be closed up. There is no provision made for it in its construction, and it was never agreed with plaintiff that the halls should be closed. For a month or so after the system of heating was put in by plaintiffs, hot water could be obtained, but since that time, and until changes were made by defendant, it could not be, except in the most insufficient quantities. The trouble with the steam-heating system put in by plaintiffs was not that proper fuel was not used, or proper attention given, but that the heater was entirely too small to do the work agreed. The steam-pipes leaked from the registers in the dining-room until the water dripped through the ceiling to the floor below. The bills for extra work were too large. In order to perfect the system of heating, and of furnishing hot water, defendant has had to incur large expense. A plumber who is engaged to do a job, the object of which is to furnish hot water, should know beforehand, and should state before a job was turned over, whether or not the hot-water boilers were of sufficient capacity. The system for obtaining hot water was changed by defendant after it was found that hot water in sufficient quantities was not to be obtained under the system as at first used in connection with plaintiffs' contract, but no greater heating surface was used, nor hot-water boilers of greater capacity, and when the change was made a sufficient supply of hot water was obtained. The charges for extra work are unreasonable to the extent of $250; and the heating apparatus, as furnished by plaintiffs, taking into consideration the annoyance and extra expense caused by it, is worth $1,000 less than that contracted for.

The jury found for plaintiffs $2,591.63, and also set up the lien claimed. Defendant made a motion in arrest of judgment upon the ground that that part of the verdict which found for plaintiffs only the sum of $2,591.63 was a finding for the defendant, on its plea that plaintiffs failed to comply with their contract, and had damaged defendant $100; and that that part of the verdict which set up a lien on the property was inconsistent with the other part mentioned, and was null and void, and no legal or valid judgment could be entered on it. Defendant also moved for a new trial on the following grounds: (1, 2, 3) Verdict contrary to evidence, etc., and to certain specified portions of the charge. (4) Error in charging: "If it was the contract that the hotel company was to close up the halls by storm-doors, and if the hotel company failed to close up the halls, and if there was a failure to produce the proper degree of heat by reason of such neglect to put in storm-doors, then the plaintiffs would not be responsible for the failure if it was caused by the failure to close up the halls." (5) Error in charging: "If the plaintiffs quit the extra work for fear that they would not get their pay, they had the right to do so, and a failure to complete the extra work for that reason would not defeat their lien." The motions were overruled, and defendant excepted.

Dabney & Fouché, for plaintiffs in error.
J. Branham, for defendant in error.

SIMMONS, J. 1. The facts in this case will be found in the official report. Under these facts the trial judge did not err in overruling the motion in arrest of judgment set out in the bill of exceptions. A part of the lien claimed on the hotel by the defendants in error was for extra work, for which no price had been agreed upon by the parties. The plaintiffs in the court below claimed a lien for $2,591.63. This included the work and material specified in the written contract, and extra work and material for which there was no written contract and no agreed price. The jury found a verdict for $2,591.63,—$100 less than the amount claimed by the plaintiffs in the court below. The defendant in the court below moved in arrest of judgment for this reason, claiming that, the jury having found less than the plaintiffs claimed, the verdict showed that the plaintiffs had not fully complied with their contract, and therefore were not entitled to a lien. This might be true, perhaps, if the whole amount had been fixed in the written contract, but, as only a part of it was fixed therein, and as the remainder was for extra work as to which there was no agreed price, and as the parties differed in their testimony in regard to what the price should be, the fact that the jury found less than was claimed for the extra work did not deprive the plaintiffs of their lien. There was, therefore, no error in refusing to arrest the judgment on this ground.

2. The fourth ground of the motion for a new trial complains that the court erred in charging the jury as follows: "If it was the contract that the hotel company was to close up the halls by storm-doors, and if the hotel company failed to close up the halls, and if there was a failure to produce the proper degree of heat by reason of such neglect to put in storm-doors, then the plaintiffs would not be responsible for the failure if it was caused by the failure to close up the halls." This charge is alleged to be error (1) because parol testimony will not be received to vary a written contract; and (2) because, if there was such a contract as to closing the halls with storm-doors, it was merged in the written contract. The general rule is that parol testimony will not be received to vary the terms of a written contract, and that all the agreements and negotiations are merged in the written contract; but, under the facts disclosed in this record, we do not think the court erred in giving this instruction to the jury. The record discloses that the plaintiffs in the court below did not introduce or bring into the case anything as to the closing of the halls, but that it was first brought out by counsel for the defendant on his cross-examination of Bartow Warlick, one of the witnesses for the plaintiffs; and no objection was made to the testimony, and no motion to exclude it, so far as appears from the record. And from the examination of this witness and others it seems to have been made an issue in the case as to whether the contract was that the halls should be closed with storm-doors. The issue having been made by the testimony, and no objection being made to it, and no motion to exclude it, it was the right and the duty of the court to instruct the jury upon it.

3. The fifth ground complains that the court charged the jury as follows: "If the plaintiffs quit the extra work for fear that they would not get their pay, they had the right to do so, and a failure to complete the extra work for that reason would not defeat their lien." Under the evidence disclosed by the record we think the court erred in giving this charge. We do not think the law allows a contractor, mechanic, and material-man to violate a contract and claim a lien for work done because of an apprehension or fear that he will not receive his pay. So far as disclosed by the evidence, the defendant in the court below had not at the time the plaintiffs quit the work failed or refused to pay them therefor. If the contract had been that the defendant was to pay them by the day or the week or the month, and the defendant had failed to make the payment when due, then, perhaps, the plaintiffs would be justified in stopping work, and would be authorized to claim a lien for the work already done; but upon a mere apprehension or fear that they would not be paid at the time for payment, we do not think they could quit work and claim a lien. Before a lien upon real estate can be established by the Code, § 1990, requires that there shall be "a compliance with his contract by the person claiming the lien." The plaintiffs having failed to complete their contract as to the extra work, simply on account of the fear that they would receive no compensation therefor, they are not entitled to a lien for so much of the extra work as they have done, but as to such work are merely entitled to a general judgment upon a *quantum meruit;* and this only because the defendant received the benefit of the work. So far, therefore, as the verdict sets up a special lien for this extra work, it is erroneous, and to that extent the lien should be discharged. To ascertain this amount we have made a calculation, based upon the figures set out in the record, and we find that to the extent of $553.41 the verdict sets up a lien on account of extra work and material. As we have seen, the verdict is for $2,591.63, this being a balance reached after deducting payments to the amount of $2,356.98, credited by the plaintiffs on their account before this suit was brought. The aggregate account, therefore, so far as the jury found it to be correct, amounted to $4,948.-61. Of this the part which came within the written contract (to-wit, heating system, $1,452; closets and plumbing, $1,-508.50 and $322; and gas-pipe, at 10 cents per foot, $609.40) amounted to $3,891.90; leaving the amount of $1,056.71, which must have been allowed for work and material outside of the written contract. As above stated, before the account was sued, payments to the amount of $2,356.98 were made thereon, and these payments should be prorated between that part of the account which came within the written contract and that part which the jury recognized as correct for extra work and material. Thus apportioning the payments, it will be seen that of the aggregate balance for which the jury set up a lien, to-wit, $2,-591.63, the sum of $553.41 must be the proportion of the balance found to be due for extra work and material; and, as already said, the verdict was to this extent improper. We therefore reverse the judgment in this case, unless the defendants in error will write off and discharge their special lien for the $553.41. If they will do this within 30 days after the judgment of this court is made the judgment of the superior court the case will stand affirmed.

4. As to the 1st, 2d, and 3d grounds of the motion, which are the usual ones that the verdict is contrary to law, evidence,

etc., we will say that the evidence appears to be conflicting upon the points made in the pleadings; and, the trial judge being satisfied with the finding of the jury upon these issues, we will not interfere with his discretion in overruling the motion on these grounds. Judgment reversed, with direction.

IRVIN et al. v. GREGORY et al.

(Supreme Court of Georgia. Feb. 7, 1891.)

ADOPTION OF SCHOOL LAW—TAXATION—INJUNCTION — ELECTIONS — NON-RESIDENT PUPILS—CHARGE FOR TUITION—CONSTITUTIONAL LAW.

1. A majority of the complainants having voted in favor of the approval of the local school law now in question, and all of them having acquiesced in the result of the election until after a school was established and put into operation, the judge was warranted in denying an interlocutory injunction to restrain the collection of a tax authorized by the local law and levied thereunder for supporting the public school system provided for by said law. Any infirmity in the law or in the election was as good cause for enjoining the establishment of the schools before the expense was incurred as it would be now for arresting the collection of revenue with which to defray the expense.

2. The general rule is that provisions in a statute for advertising a proposed election are mandatory unless the time and place of such election are fixed by the legislature, yet where the advertisement prescribed was publication once a week for four weeks, and the last publication was inadvertently omitted, but the other three were duly made, the omission may be treated as a mere irregularity if more than two-thirds of the qualified voters actually voted, and if the result has been acquiesced in until after action has been taken on the faith thereof by which substantial rights have arisen.

3. In a local statute authorizing the establishment of public schools in a town a provision that the local board may admit pupils not residents of the town on such terms as the board may prescribe is not to be construed as allowing the board to prescribe terms which would cast upon the town or its inhabitants any part of the expense of educating non-resident pupils. Such pupils cannot be received at a less rate per scholar than the inhabitants of the town pay by taxation for their children, nor can they be received at all to the exclusion of resident children who would otherwise attend.

4. In so far as municipal public schools perform the functions of common schools, they must be free to all the children of the municipality just as the common schools in general are free to all children of the state. This results from the scheme of the constitution in regard to public schools. It follows that the action of an incidental fee to be paid by each and every pupil as a condition of admission into the public schools of a town, though constitutional, as applied to non-resident pupils, would be unconstitutional if applied to resident pupils also.

5. The main purpose of a statute passed by the general assembly, and approved by two-thirds of the qualified voters of a given town, being to establish and maintain a system of public schools in and for said town, an unconstitutional requirement therein, which exacts an incidental fee annually of all pupils, thereby including resident as well as non-resident pupils, will not necessarily vitiate the whole statute. If, as matter of fact, the means otherwise provided for establishing and maintaining the schools are sufficient for the purpose, the law can have effect, notwithstanding the failure of the legislative and the popular intent touching the universality of the requirement for the payment of incidental fees.

6. Administrative acts on the part of the local board of education, even if erroneous or wrong-ful, and amenable to proper remedial proceedings, furnish no cause for enjoining the collection of a school tax legally assessed.

(Syllabus by the Court.)

Error from superior court, Stewart county; FORT, Judge.

Steed & Wimberly, J. L. Wimberly, and Harrison & Peeples, for plaintiffs in error. R. F. Watts and Little & Wimbish, for defendants in error.

BLECKLEY, C. J. 1. The election was held on the 19th day of July, 1890. This bill was filed on the 20th of October, 1890. In the mean time the local board of education provided for by the act had gone to work, established and opened a school, and the school had been in actual operation for about six weeks before any steps were taken by the complainants to have the election declared illegal. More than half of them had voted in the election in favor of the school law, and all of them acquiesced in the result until after a school had been organized and put to work. This involved expense, and the complainants stood by and permitted the expense to be incurred, when full diligence on their part in making an application for injunction would have raised the question which they now seek to make in time to have put the question on its own merits, uncomplicated with the consequences of delay in making it. Under these circumstances the judge was warranted in denying a preliminary or interlocutory injunction on the application of these complainants, who sue, not in behalf of the citizens of the town generally, but for their own separate benefit and protection. If they have any good cause for enjoining the collection of the tax that cause would have been equally good for enjoining the establishment and opening of the school at the expense of the town,—an expense which they must have known was incurred with the expectation that a tax would be imposed to defray it. In the view of a court of equity it would not be altogether conscientious for citizens of a town to acquiesce in the establishment of a public school system for the benefit of the town until that benefit had been secured, and then object to contribute their pro rata of taxation necessary to defray its expenses for the first year. Especially is this true of most of the complainants; for they not only acquiesced, but took an active part by their votes in causing a public school system to be adopted. That the objection now urged against the tax might as well have been urged against the creation of the municipal obligation rendering the tax necessary, see Hudson v. Marietta, 64 Ga. 286; County of Dougherty v. Boyt, 71 Ga. 484; Gavin v. City of Atlanta, (Ga.) 12 S. E. Rep. 262; Crampton v. Zabriskie, 101 U. S. 601, 609; Howell v. City of Peoria, 90 Ill. 104; 1 Dill. Mun. Corp. (4th Ed.) § 197 et seq.; Cooley, Tax'n, 764. Of the thirteen complainants one is a woman, and had no vote in the election, and another is a man who voted against the measure; but these two have linked their fortunes in this bill with the other complainants, seven of whom voted in favor of the approval of the local law authorizing the establishment of the school.

2. Perhaps what we have already said would be enough to dispose of the case in so far as the element of interlocutory injunction is concerned; but as we have held it up for a considerable time for the purpose of dealing with it in a broader and more comprehensive way, we shall express our opinion upon several of the points in controversy argued at the bar, and on which a decision was invoked. Did the want of a strict compliance with the terms of the statute in advertising the election render the election void? The constitutional provision under which the act was passed reads as follows: "Authority may be granted to counties upon the recommendation of two grand juries, and to municipal corporations on the recommendation of the corporate authority, to establish and maintain public schools in their respective limits by local taxation: but no such local laws shall take effect until the same shall have been submitted to a vote of the qualified voters in each county or municipal corporation, and approved by a two-thirds vote of persons qualified to vote at such election; and the general assembly may prescribe who shall vote on such question." Code, § 5207. The provision in the act of 1889, (pages 1305, 1306,) under which the election was held, reads thus: "This act shall be submitted to an election for approval or disapproval by the qualified voters of the town of Lumpkin; said election to take place on such day as the mayor and council may determine, notice of which election shall be given by the mayor of said town by publication in any newspaper published in the town of Lumpkin once a week for four weeks previous to the day of election. Those favoring public schools shall have printed or written on their ballots, 'For public schools,' and those opposing shall have printed or written on their ballots, 'Against public schools.' That said election shall be held in the same manner as elections for mayor and council of the town of Lumpkin are held, and all those qualified to vote at an election of mayor and council of said town shall be permitted to vote at the election herein provided for. The managers of said election shall certify the number of votes cast 'for public schools' and 'against public schools' to the mayor and council of said town of Lumpkin, and if two-thirds of the qualified voters of said town shall vote 'for public schools' the mayor of said town shall so declare in writing, and publish his said declaration once in any newspaper published in said town, and upon said publication this act shall take effect and be of force, and the public schools therein provided for shall be put in operation as soon as deemed practicable by said board of education of the town of Lumpkin." The election was advertised in the proper newspaper for a period of four weeks before the day of election, but there was an omission, which seems to have been altogether casual and undesigned, to insert it in the issue of the last week of the four; that is, it was published once a week for three weeks, but in the fourth week it failed to appear. There was thus a literal departure from the requirement of the statute; for, though notice was given four weeks, it was not given by publication once a week for four weeks previous to the day of the election. When the time and place of an election are fixed by law, the requirement of notice is directory; but when they are not so fixed, and the duty of fixing them is committed to a municipal body, what the statute prescribes as to the giving of notice is mandatory. This is a general rule. Paine, Elect. § 885; 1 Dill. Mun. Corp. § 197; Cooley, Const. Lim. 759; 6 Amer. & Eng. Enc. Law, 297 et seq. The town of Lumpkin is not a large one, and there is every probability that the election, although not advertised with strict regularity, was known to every inhabitant interested in the question except one, whose affidavit is in the record. More than two-thirds of the qualified voters actually voted; and such was their unanimity in favor of the measure that only one vote was cast against it. The rule of our Code (section 4, par. 6) is that a substantial compliance with statutory requirements, especially on the part of public officers, will suffice. Where it affirmatively appears, as it does here, that the results of notice have been realized as to the great body of the voters, we feel warranted in concluding that the publication in this instance for four weeks, though there was an omission of one insertion, was a substantial compliance with the terms of the act. The purpose of the notice was to make generally known the time and place of election. This was as fully accomplished in the present case as it was in Wheat v. Smith, 50 Ark. 266, 7 S. W. Rep. 161. The law involved in that case required two modes of advertising the election, one of which was wholly omitted; nevertheless the election was upheld. In State v. Echols, (Kan.) 20 Pac. Rep. 528, the vote was not full, and one of the modes of advertising having been omitted, the election was held invalid. In each of these cases we think the substance of the matter was regarded, and rightly so. If in the present case all those who failed to vote had appeared and voted there could not by any possibility have been any change in the result of the election, even had the absentees all voted one way. Their votes would have counted for nothing on the final result. To suffer this election to be overthrown upon so slight a ground as the casual omission of one insertion of the notice in the newspaper would be to sacrifice substance to mere form. We might be obliged to do this if the election had been attacked before anything substantial had been done upon the faith of it. In Mize v. Speight, 82 Ga. 397, 9 S. E. Rep. 1080, there was an omission to advertise in strict conformity with the statute relating to the stock law, and, the question not being made until after the law had been treated by the citizens in consequence of the election as operative, this court held that the omission was a mere irregularity. In Bowen v. Mayor, etc., 79 Ga. 709, 4 S. E. Rep. 159, the application for injunction was promptly made before the election had been acted

on to the injury of any one, and the ruling here was that the injunction ought to be granted. There is no doubt that mere irregularities in executing laws touching taxation, public money, and public indebtedness ought to count for much where they are complained of promptly and properly; but where they are acquiesced in until injury would be done by recognizing them as fatal they should have no force or influence upon the substantial rights of parties litigant. They are then within the spirit of our general law touching elections, which declares that "no election shall be defeated for non-compliance with the requirements of the law, if held at the proper time and place by persons qualified to hold them, if it is not shown that by that non-compliance the result is different from what it would have been had there been proper compliance." Code, § 1334.

3. As to the constitutionality of the local act there can be no doubt, so far as its main features are concerned. Were it unconstitutional in its provisions relating to admitting pupils who are not resident of the town, those provisions would fail, but this would not interfere with the general scheme of the law. We, however, think that under a proper construction and administration of the act it is not unconstitutional in this respect. The act certainly does not contemplate that non-residents are to be educated at the expense of the tax-payers of the town. The power given to the board of education to fix the terms is not a power to be exercised so as to work that result. No terms can be fixed which will make the expense to non-residents less per scholar than the expense per scholar to the tax-payers of the town for supporting the school. In other words, non-residents are at least to pay for their own tuition, and the people of the town are not to be burdened as tax-payers with any part of the same. The board can put terms upon non-residents which will make their tuition a source of revenue to the school, but cannot allow terms which will make it an expense upon the inhabitants of the town. If the power has not been thus construed heretofore it must be so construed hereafter, as this is the only construction which the local act, in the light of general principles, will bear. The board must exclude all non-residents who fail to contribute as much per scholar for the non-resident children as the tax-payers of Lumpkin contribute per scholar to educate the children of the town. Furthermore, the board would have no power to admit non-residents at all to the exclusion of any resident applicant for tuition. It would only be to unoccupied seats in the school that non-residents could be admitted, and they could remain only so long as their seats were not called for by or on behalf of resident pupils. The sufficiency of the title of the act to cover all its provisions is disputed, but there is no ground for this contention. Hope v. Gainesville, 72 Ga. 246.

4. One provision in the sixth section of the act is clearly unconstitutional, if taken in the full breadth of its letter, and applied to the children of the town as well as to non-resident pupils. It reads as follows:

"The said board of education shall require each child, upon entering said schools, to pay to said board an incidental fee of not less than five dollars nor more than ten dollars per scholastic year, and that no child shall attend said schools or enjoy the benefit thereof in any manner until the required fee is paid: provided, that said board may require said incidental fee paid in quarterly installments." A public school system from which resident pupils can be excluded because they are unable or unwilling to pay for admission is not the system contemplated by the constitution. As will appear from the extract quoted under the second head of this opinion, authority may be granted to establish and maintain public schools by local taxation. There is no hint in the constitution that these schools are to be open to persons who pay, and closed against those who do not pay. So to treat them would put them out of harmony with the common school system of the state provided for in a preceding paragraph of the constitution, (Code, § 5204,) as to which the constitution expressly declares: "The schools shall be free to all children of the state, but separate schools shall be provided for the white and colored races." There can be no doubt that municipal public schools, in so far as they perform the functions of common schools, are to be free to the children of the municipality, just as the ordinary common schools are free to the children of the state; and that the public schools contemplated by the local statute for the town of Lumpkin were intended to perform the functions of common schools, is shown by the fact that the local board of education is authorized by the statute to receive and disburse the pro rata share of the state school fund for Stewart county for each child attending the school established by the board. It follows that, were it necessary to save the constitutionality of the local act as a whole, it would be incumbent upon the courts to construe the requirement that each child, upon entering the schools, is to pay an incidental fee, and that no child shall attend said schools or enjoy the benefit thereof until the fee is paid, as applying to non-resident children only. So construed, the requirement can have effect, whereas, by taking the language in its broad and most comprehensive sense, it would militate with the constitution.

5. It is suggested, however, that the legislature having plainly declared that "the said board of education shall require each child, upon entering said schools, to pay to said board an incidental fee of not less than five dollars nor more than ten dollars per scholastic year, and that no child shall attend said schools or enjoy the benefit thereof in any manner until the required fee is paid," and the people of the town having voted upon and approved the act with these words in it, the whole act is vitiated because the provision, in its comprehensive and obvious sense, is unconstitutional. It is altogether probable that both the legislature and the people intended the provision to be taken and understood literally; but it is a well-established principle that, unless the main pur-

pose of a statute is affected by the unconstitutionality of a particular provision, the whole act is not thereby defeated. We think this rule applies as well to statutes submitted to the people for their approval as to any other acts of the legislature. In Robinson v. Bidwell, 22 Cal. 392, it was said: "But if the vote of the people could be considered as the act of legislation the result would be the same. We must in that case apply the same considerations to determine the validity of a law passed by a direct vote of the people that are applicable to determine the validity of a law passed by the legislature." We think this sound doctrine, notwithstanding it may be supposed to be in conflict with the view of the supreme court of Ohio as manifested in State v. Commissioners, 5 Ohio St. 497. It seems to us that when the people are called in, whether by the constitution or by a statute, to assist in the act of legislation, the resulting statutory provisions must be tested by the same rules as apply to the enactments of the ordinary legislative power. Whatever can be treated as non-essential in a statute passed by the concurrent votes of the senate and the house of representatives, and approved by the governor, can be so treated when enacted into a valid law by the additional concurrence of the people to be affected thereby. The question, then, is whether, granting that the legislative purpose must fail as to exacting an annual incidental fee from all children of the town of Lumpkin attending the schools, the whole system of public schools for the town of Lumpkin must be defeated. There can be no doubt that the main purpose of the statute was to have and maintain the schools. If, therefore, they can be had and maintained without the aid of this fee, the main purpose can be made effectual; otherwise it cannot. The statute denominates the fee in question as incidental, and evidently does not look to it in other than an incidental way as a fund for the support of the schools. On the contrary, it authorises municipal taxation for that purpose annually, not to exceed one-half of one per cent. on all the property in the town subject to taxation. In addition to this, it devotes the *pro rata* share of the state school fund for the county to the general object of establishing and maintaining the schools. Whether these sources of revenue will be sufficient to uphold and execute the main purpose of the act is a question of fact, rather than of law; but we see nothing on the face of the act itself to negative their sufficiency, or to indicate that the provision relating to the incidental fee was so essential, either in the legislative or the popular mind, as to warrant the conclusion that the school system provided for by the act would not have been adopted in its main features if the legislature or the people had foreseen that the fee could not be constitutionally exacted from resident children. This being so, the unconstitutionality of the comprehensive language used by the act touching the incidental fee does not vitiate the whole act, but is to be rejected, or rather restricted in its operation, as we have above indicated. Warren v. Mayor, etc.,

2 Gray, 84; Railroad Co. v. State, 29 Ala. 573; Robinson v. Bidwell, 22 Cal. 379; Cooley, Const. Lim. 209 et seq.; Suth. St. Const. § 169 et seq.

6. Mere administrative acts on the part of the local board of education are complained of, but it is enough to say of these that they furnish no cause for enjoining the collection of the school tax. If, as public functionaries, the board fail to execute their duties conformably to law, the remedy is not to cut off their supply of money by enjoining lawful taxation or the collection of taxes legally assessed, but some other appropriate proceeding. There was no error in denying the injunction.

Judgment affirmed.

BURNS et al. v LEWIS.

(*Supreme Court of Georgia.* Feb. 7, 1891.)

DIVORCE — PROPERTY OF HUSBAND — JUDGMENT — RIGHTS OF WIFE IN HOMESTEAD — ATTACHMENT OF HOMESTEAD—SALE FOR TAXES — ISSUING FI. FA.

1. Where in a suit for divorce the verdict of the second jury finds in favor of a total divorce, and expressly disallows anything for alimony to the wife, the husband's property embraced in the schedule filed with the divorce proceedings remains his property just as though the jury had disposed of it by awarding it to him; and this is true whether any judgment or decree has been entered upon the verdict or not.

2. By the constitution of 1868, in suits for divorce the function of regulating the rights and disabilities of the parties devolved on the jury rendering the final verdict, subject only to a power of revision by the court. A final verdict in favor of a total divorce was sufficient to dissolve the marriage, though it was silent as to rights and disabilities, and though no judgment declaring the marriage dissolved was actually entered up; the verdict, so far as appears, not having been set aside or interfered with by the court.

3. On the dissolution of a marriage by total divorce the wife ceases to be a member of the husband's family as effectually as if she were dead. She is therefore no longer a beneficiary of a homestead set apart in his property. Her right to use or enjoy the property as a homestead terminates with the expiration of the coverture.

4. Where a creditor seeks to charge homestead property as such the proceedings must conform substantially to remedies enforceable against trust-estates. A trust-estate is not subject to attachment on the ground that the trustee is a non-resident of the state; nor is an alleged homestead subject to attachment as such on the ground that the owner is a non-resident. In this case there was no debt other than one contracted by a former beneficiary after the homestead had determined. The judgment founded on an attachment for such a debt was void on the face of the proceedings, and a sale under it passed no title.

5. One in possession of real estate under color of title and claim of right is subject to be assessed for the taxes accruing thereon pending such possession, and if such person allows the premises to be assessed and sold for taxes as the property of a former occupant, who has neither title nor possession, such sale being made under a general *fi. fa. in personam* not specifying any particular property to be seized, he cannot strengthen his title by purchasing at such sale, or from the purchaser at that sale. Any purchase so made by one subject to assessment will be treated as merely paying the taxes or redeeming the property.

(*a*) Sundry observations on the proper mode of issuing tax *fi. fas.* where the owner of realty assessed is unknown or doubtful.

(*Syllabus by the Court.*)

Error from superior court, Fulton county; MARSHALL J. CLARKE, Judge.

Geo. F. Fry and F. A. Arnold, for plaintiffs in error. Hillyer & Bro. and Broyles & Sons, for defendant in error.

BLECKLEY, C. J. A great many grounds are embraced in the motion for a new trial. Severally and collectively they raise the general question whether the court erred in overruling the motion. There are controlling elements of the case which will enable us to decide this general question without discussing separately the grounds of the motion in detail. The conclusion at which we have arrived is that, though errors were committed on the trial, none of them were of such a character as to warrant the court below, or this court, in setting aside the verdict.

1. For the sake of clearness we shall first consider the right of Lewis to recover in his complaint for land in the nature of ejectment against Mrs. Lewis, irrespective of the claim of Mrs. Burns. The premises in controversy consisted of a parcel of land fronting 108½ feet on Emma street, and running back (same width) 185½ feet to D'Alvigny street, the same being lot No. 25 in the subdivision of the Loyd property, in the city of Atlanta, and containing a half acre, more or less. The action was brought in September, 1874. Did Lewis, the plaintiff, have title and the right of possession at that time as against Mrs. Lewis, the defendant in the action? The lot was conveyed to Lewis in 1868, while these parties were husband and wife. On the 10th of April, 1869, she applied for it to be set aside as a homestead, reciting that the family of Lewis consisted of himself, herself, and one child. The application also recited the deed by which Lewis acquired title, and stated that she applied for exemption of the property as a homestead because he failed and refused to do so. After regular proceedings by survey, plat, etc., the homestead was approved by the ordinary on the 26th of April, 1869. This was done pending a suit for divorce which had been brought by Mrs. Lewis against Lewis upon the same day on which her application for homestead was filed. The first verdict in the divorce suit was rendered at the April term, 1871. The date of the second verdict does not appear in the transcript of the record, but from divers facts it is manifest that the second verdict was rendered prior to the commencement of the action of complaint by Lewis against Mrs. Lewis for the recovery of the premises. Neither of the verdicts makes mention of any child or children, and, as there is no such reference elsewhere in the record other than in the application for homestead, the presumption is that the child if any, had died before the parents were divorced. Should the fact be otherwise, the rights of the child under the homestead proceedings will not be affected by the result of this litigation. Its life or death may therefore be treated, and was treated below, as immaterial to a right disposition of the present controversy. This city lot was, by schedule, embraced in the pleadings in the divorce suit, and thus was before the court for disposi-

tion by the second jury. Code 1868, §§ 1719, 1721, corresponding to Code 1882, §§ 1720, 1722. The verdict of that jury granted a total divorce to both parties, and expressly declared that no alimony was to be set apart for the support of the wife. Otherwise the verdict was silent as to property, but the fair implication is that the intent of the jury was that this lot, which was the only property specified in the schedule, was to be and remain the property of the husband. The verdict is to be understood as denying the wife any enjoyment of it after the marriage was dissolved, and as leaving the ownership in the husband. Barclay v. Waring, 58 Ga. 86. So far as appears, no judgment or decree of the court was rendered in the divorce suit, either declaring the marriage dissolved or making any disposition of the scheduled property. Doubtless the law contemplates that some judgment should be rendered. Indeed, the Code is express, where the verdict disposes of property, that the court shall enter such judgment or decree, or take such other steps usual in chancery, as will effectually execute the verdict. Code 1868, § 1728; Code 1882, § 1724. But where the verdict denies alimony and in effect leaves the property unchanged in ownership, no judgment or decree is essential to carry the verdict into effect, so far as property rights are concerned. In the case above cited none such was rendered, and this court ruled that the divorce worked no change in the title.

2. After the rendition of two verdicts in favor of the divorce, was it indispensable that a judgment declaring the divorce granted should have been entered up in order for the marriage to be legally dissolved and Mrs. Lewis eliminated from the family of her husband? This might have been necessary had the proceeding been governed by the constitution of 1865, as was that in Clark v. Cassidy, 62 Ga. 408, 64 Ga. 662. Under that constitution it devolved upon the court to regulate the rights and disabilities of the parties. Irwin's Code, § 4964. But by the constitution of 1865 this function was lodged with the jury rendering the final verdict, subject only to a power of revision by the court. Code 1873, § 5116. It was under this latter constitution that the divorce suit of Mrs. Lewis against her husband was begun and terminated. The final verdict, being in favor of a total divorce, admits of no construction but that the jury intended the marriage should be dissolved, and we think the revising power of the court contemplated by the constitution of 1868 would not extend to this element of the verdict, but only to any special findings, had the verdict embraced any, touching the rights and disabilities of the parties. The verdict being silent as to the rights and disabilities of the parties, there was nothing over which the revising power of the court could be exercised. The only judgment which could have been rendered was one declaring a total divorce. This being so, we think the omission to enter up such a judgment was not matter of substance, and that the legal effect of the final verdict was to dissolve the marriage ipso facto. It may be added that Mrs. Lewis does not contro-

vert the completeness or finality of the divorce. In her answer to the bill filed by Lewis in connection with his original suit against her for the land she, by implication, admits that a decree was rendered in the divorce case, for she mentions a decree by name. As we find none, however, in the record, we dispose of the question independently of her answer.

3. The dissolution of the marriage severed Mrs. Lewis from the family, and she was no longer a beneficiary of the homestead. By the constitution of 1868 her husband, as the head of a family, had the right to a homestead, of which the sole beneficiaries were the members of his family. Code 1873, § 5135. By statute she, as his wife, was empowered to have the homestead set apart if he failed or refused to do so. This right she exercised, but the fact that the property was set apart on her application would give her no better or more durable interest in the use of it than she would have had if it had been set apart on his application. The death of a wife when there are no surviving minor children, or the majority of children where there is no surviving wife or widow, terminates the homestead. Heard v. Downer, 47 Ga. 629; Benedict v. Webb, 57 Ga. 348. A total divorce severs the wife from the family as effectually as death itself. She ceases to be a beneficiary of the homestead provision, and her relation to it from thenceforth is the same as if she had never been a member of the family. The provision which the law contemplates for a divorced wife is alimony, or such an interest in the property of the husband as the jury rendering the final verdict shall award to her. In this instance the jury thought proper to declare in express terms that no alimony was to be set apart for her support. We have already seen that the effect of this was to leave the title to the property now in question in Lewis. If her interest in it as a homestead was destroyed by the dissolution of the marriage, and the verdict conferred upon her no new interest, she was left altogether without right to use or occupy the premises; and consequently, when Lewis brought his action against her in 1874, both the title and the right of possession were in him. As between him and her, therefore, his recovery in the court below was correct.

4. The next inquiry is as to the title set up by Mrs. Burns, and the right of a recovery by Lewis as against her. Her title has two branches: First, she claims as purchaser at a sheriff's sale, which she procured to be made under an attachment issued at her instance against Lewis in 1882. The attachment was issued in May. Judgment upon it was rendered in the justice's court in July, and the property was sold by the sheriff in September, 1882. The ground alleged in the affidavit for attachment was that Lewis resided out of the state; and the petition filed in the justice's court by Mrs. Burns in support of her attachment alleged that Lewis was indebted to her in the sum of $100, besides interest, on an account for money furnished, materials provided, and labor done on his house and lot in the city of Atlanta, (describing these premises;) that the same

had been exempted and set apart as a homestead, and that the money and materials furnished and labor done were all furnished and done for repairs on said homestead, at the instance of the beneficiaries of the homestead, and were all necessary for the protection and preservation of the property. The account bore date in January, 1879, and consisted of various items aggregating $100, the items being lumber for improving and repairing house, railings for fences, digging post-holes, posts, well-bucket, pulley for well-bucket, windlass for well, well-house, and brick wall in well, brick and labor for walks, one grate and setting same, nails, and two doors. This proceeding by attachment is susceptible of only one construction, which is that it was an attempt to charge Lewis by attachment with expenses incurred by Mrs. Lewis in making repairs to the house and premises as homestead property long after the homestead terminated. The pleading shows on its face that, treated as a claim against Lewis, it was void, because the facts stated in the petition and bill of particulars would raise no debt against him personally. Treating the claim as one against the homestead property, the attachment was void, for homestead property is to be made liable for debts chargeable upon it in the same manner as ordinary trust-estates are made liable, (Willingham v. Maynard, 59 Ga. 330; Wilder v. Frederick, 67 Ga. 669;) and a trust-estate is not subject to attachment on account of the non-residence of the trustee, (Smith v. Riley, 32 Ga. 356.) The judgment founded upon this attachment was consequently void on its face, the proceedings from which it resulted showing that there was no cause of action otherwise than as a claim against the property in its homestead character, and such a claim being under the law a subject-matter for which the remedy of attachment is not available. The justice's court had no jurisdiction by attachment of the alleged cause of action, and the judgment was one which it had no legal power to render. The sale made by the sheriff was therefore void, and Mrs. Burns acquired no title as against Lewis by her purchase at that sale.

5. The other branch of Mrs. Burns' title springs out of a sale for taxes. Speaking of the sheriff's sale made in September, 1882, she states in her answer that "the sale was in every sense legal, open, and fair. Under it defendant went into possession, and has remained in it ever since." In September, 1883, an execution was issued in favor of the city of Atlanta against Catherine Lewis for six dollars, "the amount of her city tax for the year 1883." This execution mentioned no specific property, but directed generally the seizure of the goods and chattels, lands and tenements of Catherine Lewis. It was levied upon the premises now in controversy as her property. A sale took place in pursuance of this levy in November, 1883, at which the city was the purchaser, and a deed was made to the city accordingly; the purchase price recited being $15.13, which was the amount of the tax *fi. fa.,* together with the costs thereon, and the

expenses of the sale. After retaining the title thus acquired for more than one year, the city, in January, 1885, offered the property for sale at public outcry, and Mrs. Burns became the purchaser at the price of $24.10. A deed to her was executed by the mayor of the city. This is her tax-title. It appeared in evidence that according to the returns of the city assessors, the premises were assessed for the tax of 1883 as the property of Mrs. Catherine Lewis, and had been so assessed each year consecutively for 10 preceding years. It further appeared that the tax assessed on these premises for the year 1883 was six dollars, and that Mrs. Lewis was not assessed upon any other property, so that, if she was answerable to the city for any tax whatever, it was only on this particular property. It did not appear, however, that she was in possession of these premises at any time after the sheriff's sale in September, 1882. On the contrary, it appeared from the answer of Mrs. Burns that she, Mrs. Burns, was in possession when the taxes of 1883 accrued. Her answer further states that "this defendant paid the state, county, and city taxes for 1882 on the property. These taxes were then assessed against the property in the name of Catherine Lewis. In 1883 this defendant resided out of the city of Atlanta, and had omitted to have the property transferred on the city taxbooks from the name of Mrs. Lewis to her own name." Mrs. Lewis, being neither the owner nor in possession of the premises in 1883, was not chargeable with the taxes of that year; nor does it appear that she returned the property for taxation, either as agent or otherwise, so as to render herself chargeable by reason of returning it. Indeed, the taxing system as to real estate, under the charter of Atlanta, does not contemplate private returns, but only assessment by the official assessors, and the returns made by them, as the basis of taxation. Acts 1874, pp. 124, 144. The official assessors are at liberty to return property as belonging to unknown owners, but not to ascribe ownership to any and every person indifferently. Doubtless they can treat as owner any person in possession when they are unable to fix ownership on any one else, for possession is a mark of ownership; but where there is no actual possession at the time the premises are examined and assessed, they should not return any owner as known if in fact he is unknown. If they do so, and if an execution issues for the taxes against a person who has neither possession nor any interest in the property, what authority is there for selling or seizing one parcel of property more than another unless the execution points it out? Can an execution in personam sell anything as to which the defendant neither has title nor any right to represent the person who has it? We should say not. In Stokes v. State, 46 Ga. 412, the execution described the property as "the Bryan Plantation," and the court said: "If it is true that the property is bound for the taxes, it makes very little difference who the owner of that property is, or how a tax execution describes it, so it

is done with sufficient definiteness to enable the levying officer to ascertain the property." In Williams v. Roe, 51 Ga. 453, the defendant in the tax fi. fa. was in possession, and the property had been returned by him in the character in which the fi. fa. charged him, namely, as agent of the estate of a deceased owner. In Hight v. Fleming, 74 Ga. 592, it appeared that the defendant in the tax fi. fa. was the agent of the owner of the property taxed, and that the tax for which the fi. fa. issued was assessed upon the property from the sale of which the fund in court for distribution arose. The facts stated in the report would warrant the inference that the agent was in possession of the property when the tax accrued. In State v. Hancock, 79 Ga. 799, 5 S. E. Rep. 248, the defendant in the tax fi. fa. was in possession with his family, to whom the property belonged, and he had returned it in his own name as owner. In Bank v. Danforth, 80 Ga. 55, 7 S. E. Rep. 546, the defendant in the tax fi. fa. was in possession of the property, probably at first as agent for her son, the owner. The circumstances indicated that it had been returned by her or her agent for taxation for some years before she became interested in it in her own right. There were executions for three years' taxes, and the only doubtful matter was as to the taxes of the first year. The evidence warranted the conclusion that she had returned it, though informally, for taxation in each of the three years, and had a right so to do. None of these cases afford any warrant for selling property for taxes under a general fi. fa. against a person who is not the owner or occupant, nor the agent of either, and who has not returned it for taxation. On the other hand, the case of Clewis v. Hartman, 71 Ga. 810, has a strong tendency to show that such a sale will pass no title. In that case the tax fi. fa. was issued against one person as agent for another. As such agent, the defendant had returned by number two lots of land for taxation. The fi. fa., which was a general fi. fa. in personam, was levied upon a third lot not embraced in the return. It did not appear that either the agent or his principal was in possession of the lot levied upon during the year for which the tax was assessed, nor did either of them return the lot for taxation. In that case, as in this, the fi. fa. did not show on its face that it was issued for taxes due on the land which was sold. A sale was made under the levy, and a deed was executed accordingly. It was held that the purchaser acquired no title. For general authorities on this question, most of which are affected by statutory provisions, see Cooley, Tax'n. 396; 1 Blackw. Tax-Titles, §§ 256–277. In this state, the universal rule, unless some statute can be shown to vary it in particular instances, is that taxes are to be charged upon the owners of the property. Owners, therefore, have an interest in being properly designated in executions which issue for the collection of taxes upon their property, or, if they cannot be designated with reasonable certainty, that the property shall be pointed out in the executions as authority for selling it irrespective of ownership, or as the property of some particular person. In all cases of doubt the execution should specify the particular realty on which the tax has accrued, and direct the officer to seize it or so much of it as is necessary to pay its own taxes. This is especially true where the system of assessment, as in Atlanta, is by official assessors, and not by returns made to a tax receiver. Under such a system the executions issued for taxes on realty should be of a mixed nature,—that is, each execution should be a process partly *in rem* and partly *in personam*. Of course, where the owner is wholly unknown, and is unrepresented by an occupant or an agent, the execution would, from the necessity of the case, have to issue against the property only. The divorce suit was matter of public record in the superior court of Fulton county. So, too, was the result of the homestead proceedings. The two, read together, furnished notice that Mrs. Lewis ceased to have any interest in these premises when the divorce was granted. After that time the city assessors had no warrant for treating Mrs. Lewis as owner, save that she was in possession. So long as she remained in possession, they were justified, perhaps, in so treating her; but Mrs. Burns, not Mrs. Lewis, was in possession in 1883, under her purchase at the sheriff's sale made in September, 1882. What reason, then, was there for assessing the premises for the tax of 1883, as the property of Mrs. Lewis? And what propriety was there in levying upon the property and selling it as hers under a general *fi. fa.* against her? At a sale so made the city, a party to the wrong assessment, became the purchaser. Did it acquire any title whatever? We are strongly inclined to the opinion that it did not. But if it did, was not the subsequent purchase by Mrs. Burns from the city, although made after the year for redemption had expired, a redemption in substance and effect? She was in possession under claim and color of title when the tax of 1883 accrued. She was the sister of Mrs. Lewis, knew that Mrs. Lewis was neither the owner nor in possession, knew that the divorce had been granted, and she was chargeable with notice that the action in favor of Lewis for the recovery of possession was pending. She could not have been ignorant that the duty of paying the tax rested either upon herself or upon Lewis, and that the assessment to Mrs. Lewis was erroneous. As between her and Lewis, was it not her moral duty to pay the taxes for the year 1883? She obtained her color of title pending his action for possession, and by an unwarranted use of legal process in his absence from the state. She thus entered into possession, and has been in possession ever since. On her theory of ownership, the taxes for 1883 were chargeable to her. If they were chargeable to her morally, she could not better her title by a direct purchase at the tax-sale. Douglas v. Dangerfield, 10 Ohio, 152; Lacey v. Davis, 4 Mich. 140; Blackwood v. Van Vleit, 30 Mich. 118; McMinn v. Whelan, 27 Cal. 300; Barrett v. Amorein, 36 Cal. 322; Christy v. Fisher, 58 Cal. 256;

Bassett v. Welch, 22 Wis. 175; Lybrand v. Haney, 31 Wis. 230; Gaskins v. Blake, 27 Miss. 675; Jacks v. Dyer, 31 Ark. 335; Black, Tax-Titles, § 146; 1 Black w. Tax-Titles, § 581; Cooley, Tax'n, p. 500 et seq.; 2 Desty, Tax'n, p. 934 et seq. See note to Blake v. Howe, 15 Amer. Dec. 685 et seq. Nor could she strengthen her title by taking at second hand from the purchaser at that sale, the amount paid by her being inconsiderable as compared with the value of the property. Her purchase would count only as a redemption. Dubois v. Campau, 24 Mich. 360; Coppinger v. Rice, 33 Cal. 408; Whitney v. Gunderson, 31 Wis. 359; Keith v. Keith, 26 Kan. 26; Cowdry v. Cuthbert, 71 Iowa, 733, 29 N. W. Rep. 798; Wambole v. Foote, 2 Dak. 1, 2 N. W. Rep. 239. But let it be granted that Mrs. Burns might have acquired title had the property been assessed to Lewis, the owner, and sold as his, yet it would not follow that she could acquire a better title than the person had to whom it was assessed, and as whose property it was sold. Her relation to the property and to Lewis, as owner, might not cut her off from purchasing his title had it in fact been sold, but Lewis was not the defendant in execution, nor was the execution against his property, not against the goods and chattels, lands and tenements, of Mrs. Lewis. Under the special facts of the case, Mrs. Burns could not acquire the title of Lewis, because it was not sold; and, as Mrs. Lewis had no title, Mrs. Burns took nothing by her purchase from the city. She and the city were alike affected by the want of title or possession in Mrs. Lewis when the taxes of 1883 accrued. For the reasons which we have assigned the case had a right result as to Mrs. Burns, and we have already seen that there was a right of recovery against Mrs. Lewis. This being so, none of the assignments of error in the bill of exceptions can be sustained as cause for a new trial. The court was correct in denying the motion. Judgment affirmed.

PAYTON *v.* PAYTON.

(Supreme Court of Georgia. March 16, 1891.)

WIFE'S SEPARATE ESTATE—SEPARATION FROM HUSBAND.

1. A husband who paid for land with his own money, and took a conveyance in 1881, describing himself in the deed as trustee for his wife, acquired the property for her, and it became her separate estate, both legally and equitably. The trust was executed as soon as created. Sutton v. Aiken, 62 Ga. 733.

2. Interference between husband and wife, after their separation, to control by interlocutory injunction the possession of the family dwelling, though it be her property, would generally be unwise. In the present case the discretion of the judge was not abused.

(Syllabus by the Court.)

Error from superior court, Dougherty county; BOWER, Judge.

W. T. Jones, for plaintiff in error. J. W. Walters, for defendant in error.

BLECKLEY, C. J. 1. We have no doubt that Mrs. Payton, the plaintiff, has the exclusive title, legal and equitable, to the premises involved in the dispute between her and her husband. He paid for the property, but took a deed which described him as her trustee. This deed was executed in June, 1881, and is governed in all respects by the rule announced in Sutton v. Aiken, 62 Ga. 733.

2. Nevertheless, inasmuch as Mrs. Payton had separated from her husband, leaving him in possession of the property, which possession he still holds, we think he is not a trespasser in such sense as to make it obligatory upon the judge of the superior court, by a mere interlocutory injunction, to expel him from the possession, or to constrain him to admit into joint occupation with him a new tenant under Mrs. Payton. Judicial interference in a family quarrel of this nature should not be too summary. Very likely delay may have a salutary effect. The parties, left to themselves, may become reconciled, and may compose their differences. The granting of an injunction is discretionary in every case. Code, § 3220. Not unfrequently the wisest exercise of this discretion is by non-intervention. This may be so in the present case. An interlocutory injunction is no finality; it settles nothing. Only some final judgment can put an end to the controversy between these parties. When this is reached there will be no longer any discretion as to admitting the plaintiff or her tenants into possession, and turning the defendant out. It will be noticed that this is no application for the appointment of a receiver. Judgment affirmed.

MADDEN v. BLAIN.

(*Supreme Court of Georgia.* March 16, 1891.)

CONTRACTS BY MARRIED WOMEN—FREE TRADERS.

The power of a married woman to contract as a free trader, under section 1760 of the Code, is restricted by the general provision of section 1783 as to all married women, which disables them to bind their separate estate by any contract of suretyship. Hence an accommodation acceptance by a *feme covert* is not rendered obligatory by her being a free trader at the time the bill was drawn and accepted.

(*Syllabus by the Court.*)

Error from superior court, Glynn county; ATKINSON, Judge.

Courtland Symms, for plaintiff in error. *Goodyear & Kay*, for defendant in error.

BLECKLEY, C. J. An accommodation acceptor is a surety for the drawer. Such was the character of the acceptance in this case. Code, § 1783, declares that, "while the wife may contract, she cannot bind her separate estate by any contract of suretyship, nor by any assumption of the debts of her husband." We think this section applies to all married women, and that it qualifies the general language of section 1760, which says: "The wife, by consent of her husband, evidenced by notice in a public gazette for one month, may become a public or free trader; in which event she is liable as a *feme sole* for all her contracts, and may enforce the same in her own name." The phrase "all her contracts" is qualified by section 1783, and this construction reconciles the two sec-

tions, and renders them consistent. A public or free trader, according to the scheme of the Code prior to the act of 1866, was bound by all contracts connected with her trade or business, and was upon substantially the same footing as a minor who, by permission of his parent or guardian or by permission of law, practices any profession or trade or engages in any business as an adult. Code, § 2733. We can discover no good reason why married women who are free traders should have any wider discretion as to becoming sureties for other persons, or as to assuming the debts of their husbands, than married women generally. Both sections of the Code can have effect together, and construing them as we do harmonizes them with the general spirit of our law touching the rights and powers of married women. All of them are, since the act of 1866, substantially free traders. The control of their husbands over their contracting privileges is merely nominal, if not quite done away with. With or without a separate estate, they can make contracts at pleasure, except as restrained by section 1783. Hays v. Jordan, (Ga.) 11 S. E. Rep. 833. This restraint seems wise and salutary. It ought to, and we think does, apply alike to all. The court committed no error.

Judgment affirmed.

GREENWOOD v. BOYD & BAXTER FURNITURE FACTORY.

(*Supreme Court of Georgia.* Feb. 2, 1891.)

CERTIORARI — PROCEDURE — FINAL JUDGMENT—POWER OF ATTORNEY—GARNISHMENT.

1. To review the judgment of a justice's court for an amount exceeding $50, where no facts were in dispute, the writ of *certiorari* is a proper remedy.

2. Upon the hearing of a *certiorari* in the superior court, in which no issues of fact were involved, and the determination of the case depended entirely upon legal questions, it was the duty of that court to render a final judgment.

3. A power of attorney authorizing one to collect a fire insurance policy, payable to the assured, accompanied by oral instructions to apply the proceeds, when collected, to a debt due by the assured to the attorney in fact, does not operate as a transfer of such policy to the latter, or prevent the money due on such policy, and still in the company's hands, from being reached by a garnishment sued out in favor of another creditor of the assured.

(*Syllabus by the Court.*)

Error from superior court, Bibb county; MILLER, Judge.

A. Proudfit and *Dessau & Bartlett*, for plaintiff in error. *Ross & Anderson*, for defendant in error.

LUMPKIN, J. 1. Repeated adjudications of this court have settled the law as to when the judgments of justices' courts may be reviewed by *certiorari*. In all cases, where only questions of law are to be determined by the superior court, the remedy may be by that writ. Where facts are in dispute there should be an appeal, either to a jury in the justice's court, or to the superior court. In the case at bar there was a contest in the justice's court between the plaintiff in attachment and the claimant, as to which was entitled to the proceeds of a fire insurance policy issued to the defendant in attachment. After all the testimony had been introduced, the plaintiffs admitted as true all that claimant's witnesses had sworn, and made no issue at all on the facts. Their position taken in the justice's court, as the record shows, was that, conceding all the claimant proved, they were entitled to their money. The justice adjudged otherwise, and, the amount of plaintiffs' demand being over $50, they sued out a writ of *certiorari* to the superior court. The judge below rightly refused to dismiss the same. There was no office for a jury to perform in this case, there being no controversy whatever as to the facts. In determining whether or not a *certiorari* will lie in cases which are to go up from justices' courts, the test question should be, is there any disputed question of fact to be settled by a jury? If so, then there should be an appeal; but as WARNER, C. J., said in Wynn v. Knight, 53 Ga. 570: "If the only question involved is a question of law, which must necessarily control the case, then the proper remedy is by *certiorari.*" In the case now under consideration, the only question was: Taking all the facts, just as they appear, and without any controversy concerning them, are the plaintiffs, as a matter of law, entitled to have their claim paid out of this fund? Hence there was no issue for a jury to try, "which the right of appeal presupposes." Small v. Sparks, 69 Ga. 745. The ruling of the court below is fully sustained by the case of Cruse v. Express Co., 72 Ga. 184, where it was held that when "no facts were contested before the justice, and the exception is that, conceding all the facts, the judgment was erroneous, a *certiorari* may be taken directly from such judgment." See, also, Railroad v. Dyar, 70 Ga. 723, and Bostick v. Palmer, 79 Ga. 680, 4 S. E. Rep. 319. A number of other decisions, bearing more or less directly on this question, have been rendered by this court. The rule, we think, to be deduced from them all, is that *certiorari* will lie to review pure questions of law, that is, in all cases where there is no dispute as to the facts or the inferences of fact to be drawn from the testimony; but when there are such disputes, of either kind, there must be an appeal.

2. The only controversy in this case being upon questions of law, and there being but one possible legal end of such controversy, the court did right in making a final judgment.

3. The policy of insurance could not be transferred by mere delivery, or by a written power simply to collect, with oral directions as to the application of its proceeds. Turk v. Cook, 63 Ga. 681. Judgment affirmed.

WILSON v. HERRINGTON, Tax Collector.

(*Supreme Court of Georgia.* March 16, 1891.)

TAX EXECUTION—PAYMENT—FAILURE TO ENTER—LEVY ON CLAIM CASE—DISMISSAL.

1. Unless a tax execution paid off by one not a party to it is entered on the execution docket of the superior court, as required by section 891a of the Code, within 30 days after the transfer, it

v.13s.E.no.4—9

has no longer any force, except as against the defendant only. As to all third persons it is extinguished.

2. But without payment in full no legal transfer can be made, and such payment includes costs as well as taxes.

3. When, in a claim case, the levy has been improperly dismissed, the court may correct the error at the same term by reinstating the case on motion. A motion general in its language is sufficient, the error being apparent on the face of the record.

4. The omission of the tax collector to attach an unsigned receipt to the execution, as required by the act of 1885, does not render the execution void, but only irregular.

(*Syllabus by the Court.*)

Error from superior court, Pulaski county; ROBERTS, Judge.

A. C. Pate and Martin & Smith, for plaintiff in error. Jordan & Smith, for defendant in error.

BLECKLEY, C. J. 1. If the tax execution had been wholly paid off by Lewis, though this was done pending the claim, his failure to enter the execution on the execution docket of the superior court within 30 days after the transfer made to him by the sheriff would have justified the court in dismissing the levy, for the statute keeps such executions alive, as to third persons, only on condition that they are so entered. Code, § 891a. Though defendants against whom they are issued will still be affected by such executions, where there has been a failure to enter them, claimants of property levied upon are entitled to treat them as extinguished or discharged. Hoyt v. Byron, 66 Ga. 351; Murray v. Bridges, 69 Ga. 644; Bank v. Danforth, 80 Ga. 56, 7 S. E. Rep. 546; Fuller v. Dowdell, (Ga.) 11 S. E. Rep. 773; Clarke v. Douglass, (Ga.) 12 S. E. Rep. 209. It will be observed that so much of the section of the Code above cited as is taken from the act of 1879 relates alone to tax executions issued prior to February 20, 1875. The execution now in question was issued in 1889 for state and county taxes of 1888, and consequently is governed by the general terms of the prior statute, and not by the special provisions of the act of 1879.

2. But the execution was not fully paid off. There remained due upon it one dollar for costs, and to collect this unpaid balance the tax collector was entitled to proceed with the levy. He was so proceeding, and consequently the court erred in dismissing the levy because the fi. fa. had been transferred to Lewis by the sheriff, and not recorded within 30 days thereafter. The sheriff had no authority to make the transfer, inasmuch as the execution was not paid in full. Lewis is no party to the claim case, nor is he a party in this court. The tax collector is proceeding to subject the property levied upon, and he has a right to do this so long as anything remains unpaid on the execution.

3. The court having erred in dismissing the levy, the right way to correct the error was to reinstate the case on motion, and set aside the erroneous judgment. This was done at the same term of the court, and there was no error in so doing. The motion made, though very general in its language, was sufficient, the error com-

mitted in dismissing the levy being apparent on the face of the record.

4. The provision in the act of 1885, (Acts 1884-85, p. 67,) requiring tax collectors to attach an unsigned receipt to each execution issued for taxes, is directory, and the omission of that duty does not render the execution invalid. A claimant of property levied upon by virtue of an execution for taxes is not entitled to have the levy dismissed because no receipt is attached. Judgment affirmed.

BAKER *et al.* v. McDANIEL *et al.*

(Supreme Court of Georgia. March 16, 1891.)

INJUNCTION—CERTIORARI—FAILURE TO FILE BOND
—DISMISSAL.

1. Where a petition for injunction and the evidence offered to sustain it failed entirely to make a case entitling the plaintiff to the relief sought, (as fully appears from the record in this case,) the judge rightly refused to grant the same.

2. Where a petition for *certiorari* had been sanctioned by the judge and filed with the clerk of the superior court, but no bond as required by law was filed therewith, and consequently no writ of *certiorari* was issued, it was too late, after the expiration of the time allowed by law for obtaining the writ of *certiorari*, to file such bond; and under such circumstances no error was committed in dismissing the case in the absence of plaintiff's attorney, to whom the judge had granted leave of absence for the balance of the term. This was the only legal disposition that could have been made of the case, even if the attorney had been present.

(Syllabus by the Court.)

Error from superior court, Montgomery county; ROBERTS, Judge.

De Lacy & Bishop, for plaintiffs in error. *Clark & Norman,* for defendants in error.

LUMPKIN, J. The petition of Baker & Lawrence for injunction and other relief, and the evidence submitted in support thereof, made, substantially, the following case: The plaintiffs had leased certain land for the purpose of cutting timber and running a saw-mill thereon. One McDaniel swore out a warrant against them for forcible entry and detainer, and the case made by this warrant was tried before a justice of the peace and a jury, who improperly found for the plaintiff therein. Baker & Lawrence presented their petition for *certiorari* to the judge, which was sanctioned by him, and filed in the clerk's office of the superior court within the time prescribed by law. No bond was filed with the petition, but the plaintiffs in *certiorari* had made the bond required by law, and filed the same with the justice, who promised to send it to the clerk, but in fact it never reached the clerk's office. The clerk refused to issue the writ of *certiorari*, because of the absence of the bond. At the next term of the superior court, counsel for Baker & Lawrence obtained leave to withdraw the *certiorari* papers, "to examine and perfect them," stating to the court that a bond had been given, and that, if the court would grant time, would perfect the record. After this was done the court granted the counsel leave of absence for the balance of the term; and after he had left the court, and without further notice

to him, the court passed an order dismissing the *certiorari* case; reciting therein, among other reasons for such dismissal, the fact that no bond had been filed with the petition, as required by law. Soon after the term the justice before whom the forcible entry and detainer case was tried issued a writ of possession at the instance of McDaniel's attorneys, and the sheriff, acting thereunder, was about to turn Baker & Lawrence out of possession of the property. The petition prayed that this proceeding by the sheriff be enjoined; that the verdict and judgment in the forcible entry and detainer case be set aside; that the clerk of the superior court be required to issue the writ of *certiorari*; and that the *certiorari* case be reinstated and heard upon its merits. Upon the case thus made the judge refused the injunction and other relief prayed for. We are of the opinion that the judge did right. The verdict and judgment in the forcible entry and detainer case, however improper, unjust, and unsupported by testimony, were valid and binding upon the parties until set aside in the manner prescribed by law. The plaintiff had a plain remedy for the errors complained of, by obtaining the writ of *certiorari*. He took certain steps in this direction, but failed in one essential particular to comply with the law, viz., to file in the clerk's office, with the petition for *certiorari*, the bond required by the statute. Section 4054 of the Code declares that the bond must be so filed, and this, of course, must be done within the time prescribed by law, or the clerk cannot legally issue the writ of *certiorari*. It is doubtless true that at the next term of the superior court, after the forcible entry and detainer trial was had, the judge did grant counsel for Baker & Lawrence permission to take the papers in that case from the clerk's office for the purpose, as alleged, "of examining and perfecting them;" the evident purpose being to obtain and file thereafter the *certiorari* bond which counsel alleged had already been executed. The judge also granted said counsel leave of absence, and after so doing, without further notice to him, dismissed the *certiorari* case. The judge must either have overlooked the fact that he had granted this leave of absence, or considered that, even if the counsel was present, the case must in any event be dismissed, because the time in which the bond could be legally filed had long since expired, and to allow the bond to be filed, then or thereafter, would also cause an unlawful delay of six more months in disposing of the case. It is immaterial whether the judge forgot the fact that he had granted the leave of absence, or dismissed the case for the reason stated. No other legal disposition of the *certiorari* was possible, under the facts disclosed, and, even if counsel had been present, the dismissal of the case was inevitable. What then remains? A valid judgment is now of force against Baker & Lawrence in the forcible entry and detainer case, and they have not availed themselves of the proper and legal method of setting the same aside; nor did they state in their petition for injunction, etc., any good and sufficient legal reason why they failed so to do. These things being true, this judgment cannot be attacked and set aside collaterally, and therefore the judge below committed no error in refusing to grant the remedies sought by the petition. Judgment affirmed.

WASHINGTON v. STATE.

(*Supreme Court of Georgia.* March 16, 1891.)

ARSON—INSTRUCTIONS—ARGUMENTS OF COUNSEL.

1. When on the trial of a defendant for setting fire to and attempting to burn a guard-house the vital issue was whether he attempted simply to burn a hole in the door solely for the purpose of effecting his escape, or set fire to the house maliciously and with intent to burn it, and the court, in its charge, after alluding to various alleged circumstances connected with the occurrence, and stating in detail a number of alleged acts of the defendant, instructed the jury they should look to the circumstances in proof and to the conduct of the defendant in determining what his intention was, it would have been a better practice for the court, in the same connection, to also instruct the jury they might look to defendant's statement, giving it such weight as they deemed proper, and decide whether or not the statement successfully rebutted any inferences of guilty intention, provided there were such, which might be drawn from the testimony.

2. On such a trial, and involving such an issue, it was error to charge as follows: "A man has the same right to burn a hole in the house to get into it as to burn a hole into it to get out of it. He has exactly the same right to burn a hole into a dwelling-house for the purpose of getting inside of it that he would have to burn a hole into the guard-house to get out of it."

3. On the trial of an indictment for arson it was error to allow the solicitor general, over objection of defendant's counsel, to state in his concluding argument that frequent burnings had occurred throughout the country, and to urge the jury, in consequence thereof, to strictly enforce the law in the case then on trial.

(*Syllabus by the Court.*)

Error from superior court, Dougherty county; BOWER, Judge.

Jesse Walters, for plaintiff in error. W. N. Spence, Sol. Gen., for the State.

LUMPKIN, J. 1. The defendant below was tried for the crime of arson, it being alleged that he maliciously set fire to and attempted to burn a guard-house in the city of Albany. This court, in the case of Jenkins v. State, 53 Ga. 33, having settled the law that burning a hole in the door, or attempting to burn one through the floor, of a guard-house in an incorporated town, merely for the purpose of effecting his escape, and without intending "to consume or to generally injure the building," neither of such results occurring, did not make one guilty of arson, the court below, on the trial of the case at bar, recognized this rule, and accordingly the main issue submitted to the jury was whether this defendant attempted simply to burn a hole in the door of the guard-house in the purpose of escaping therefrom, or set fire to the house maliciously and with intent to burn it. In its charge to the jury the court hypothetically alluded to various circumstances connected with the occurrence which the state contended had been proved, and stated in detail a number of alleged acts on the part of the defendant,

and then in substance instructed the jury that they should look to the circumstances in proof, and to the conduct of the defendant, in determining what his intention was. It is true the judge also charged the jury concerning the defendant's statement, and informed them they could attach to it whatever weight they saw proper, and believe it in preference to the sworn testimony of the witnesses; but he did not do this in immediate connection with the instructions above referred to. Taking these instructions by themselves, their meaning would be that in arriving at the intention of the defendant, the jury should look only to the facts and circumstances brought out by the testimony; and it may be that they reached their conclusion without taking into consideration what the judge had told them concerning the defendant's statement. A trained, legal mind would doubtless understand from the entire charge that the judge meant to instruct the jury they might refer to the prisoner's statement, and, if they believed it to be true, might find that it successfully rebutted inferences of guilty intention, if there were any, deducible from the testimony; but the jurors, being unprofessional men, and not habitually accustomed to dealing with legal questions, may not have so understood the charge. We do not mean to say that the court below committed absolute error in failing to call the attention of the jury to the prisoner's statement, and the effect which might be given to it, in the same connection with the other charges referred to, or to hold that if in the case now under consideration the guilt of the defendant plainly and unmistakably appeared, a new trial should be ordered on account of such failure; but we think that in a grave case like this, involving the penalty of death or that of life imprisonment, the safer practice would be as indicated in the first head-note.

2. The charge in the second head-note was manifestly erroneous. It was irrelevant, and calculated to prejudice the defendant's case before the jury. When the judge stated that a man had the same right to burn a hole in a dwelling-house in order to get inside of it that he would have to burn one in a guard-house to get out of it, it is very likely that the jury concluded he had no right at all to do the former, and consequently no right to do the latter; and that, having no such right, burning the hole in the guard-house would necessarily be arson. In any view of it we are unable to see how such a charge could aid the jury in arriving at a proper conclusion upon the serious issue they were to determine in this case.

3. It appears that during the concluding argument of the solicitor general he alluded to the frequency of burnings throughout the country, and urged upon the jury the importance of strictly enforcing the law in this case. Upon objection being made to these remarks, the judge stated he presumed the object of the solicitor general was not to insist on convicting the defendant because numerous burnings had taken place, but that he merely intended to urge the jury to look carefully into '

case, and see whether the defendant was guilty or not; whereupon the solicitor general said this was his reason for making the remarks alluded to, and the court ruled that the argument was not out of order. It is the well-settled policy of this court that counsel in the argument of cases should confine their remarks to the law and the evidence, and that in no instance should they be permitted to comment upon extraneous facts prejudicial to the interests or rights of a party, over his objection, unless such facts be of a kind of which judicial cognizance may be taken without proof. The wisdom of this rule is well established by numerous and respectable authorities. In Weeks, Attys. § 112, it is said: "Counsel must confine themselves to the facts in evidence. This is a rule frequently violated. It is the duty of a court to check any departure from the evidence, and to stop counsel when he introduces irrelevant matters or facts not supported by the evidence. If an objection be made to this course of argument it is error for the court to permit it, and a new trial may be granted for such error; but where counsel for the state made comments outside of the evidence, and no objection was made, it was held not error." In Ferguson v. State, 49 Ind. 33, it was held: "On the trial of an indictment for murder it is error for counsel for the state, in argument to the jury, to comment on the frequent occurrence of murders in the community, and the formation of vigilance committees and mobs, and to state that the same are caused by laxity in the administration of the law, and that they should make an example of the defendant, and for the court, upon objection by the defendant to such language, to remark to the jury that such matters are proper to be commented upon." Special attention is called to the case of Bennett v. State, 12 S. E. Rep. 806, decided at the last term of this court, in which Mr. Justice Simmons delivered an able and carefully prepared opinion reviewing a decision made by the writer while on the circuit bench. The precise question made in that case was concerning the court's allowing the solicitor general to comment upon the fact that the defendant had failed to prove his good character, which the court below permitted because defendant's counsel in his argument had repeatedly reiterated that he did have a good character, and alluded to numerous facts in this connection which were not in evidence. This court held that even this improper conduct of defendant's counsel did not justify the court in allowing the solicitor general to commit a like impropriety. Many authorities are cited in the case last mentioned upon the particular subject of the defendant's character in criminal cases, and the right of counsel, in the absence of proof, to comment thereon; but the court goes further, and comments fully upon the general duty of the judge to confine counsel in their arguments to the law and evidence, especially when attempts to do otherwise are objected to by the other side. An extended extract is made from an opinion by Judge Nisbet in Mitchum v. State, 11 Ga. 615, citing Berry v. State,

10 Ga. 522, which is full, appropriate, and pointed with reference to the question now under consideration. In the case of Tucker v. Henniker, 41 N. H. 317, cited by Justice Simmons, this opinion of Judge Nisbet is cited with approbation; indeed, the New Hampshire justice adopted almost bodily Judge Nisbet's opinion. Again, in the case of Towner v. Thompson, 82 Ga. 740, 9 S. E. Rep. 672, which was a civil case, Chief Justice Bleckley said: "During the concluding argument counsel for Thompson stated a fact not in evidence, to-wit, that Towner was born in Illinois. This statement was improper, and the request made by opposing counsel to charge directly to that effect should have been granted; but the charge given, to-wit, that the jury should try the case by the evidence, and not by what counsel said in their speeches, was sufficient. No court, however, should tolerate counsel in stating any fact in argument as to which there is no evidence, unless it be some fact which can be noticed judicially without proof. Certainly that Mr. Towner was born in Illinois is not one of this class of facts. There should have been no allusion made to it in argument." A careful review of all the authorities above cited and referred to will lead to the conclusion that the rule above laid down should be carefully and strictly enforced by the courts. In the case now under consideration the fact that frequent arsons had occurred in the community, if such was the fact, could have no possible bearing upon the question whether or not the defendant maliciously set fire to the guard-house in Albany. The only effect that the making of such a statement by the solicitor general could have would be to improperly prejudice the minds of the jury against the defendant. Certainly the fact he undertook to state was not one of such public notoriety or matter of history as that the court or the jury could take judicial cognizance thereof. It was the duty of the court, when the objection was made by the defendant's counsel, to promptly and unequivocally declare that such an argument was improper, and require the solicitor general to desist therefrom. Instead of so doing, the court undertook to inform the jury what it presumed the solicitor general meant thereby, and this we do not think was the proper course to pursue. We repeat here that this court will hereafter strictly adhere to and enforce the rule upon this subject which has been stated above. Judgment reversed.

BRIMBERRY v. MANSFIELD.

(Supreme Court of Georgia. March 16, 1891.)

LANDLORD'S LIEN—SURETY FOR TENANT.

A landlord having, as surety with his tenant and another person, signed a note for supplies purchased by the tenant, but not having purchased or ordered them himself, cannot have a lien therefor on the tenant's crop, though he is obliged to pay the note at its maturity.

Error from superior court, Mitchell county; BOWER, Judge.

Spence & Twitty, for plaintiff in error. *I. A. Bush,* for defendant in error.

SIMMONS, J. Under the facts of this case as they appear from the record, we think the court erred in sustaining the *certiorari* and in awarding the money to Mansfield. We think the facts clearly show that Mansfield did not himself furnish the supplies to his tenant, but that he was merely a surety on the note which he and his tenant Faircloth gave for the supplies. Mansfield was not alone bound for the goods sold by the merchant to his tenant, but the facts show that the tenant and Faircloth were equally bound with him. In the case of Scott v. Pound, 61 Ga. 579, it was held that, "in order for a landlord to have a lien upon his tenant's crop for supplies, etc., the landlord must furnish the articles, and not merely become the tenant's surety for the price to some other person by whom they were sold to the tenant." Mansfield being only a surety for his tenant, under the law he would have no lien as landlord for supplies which his tenant purchased from a merchant, and for which he stood the tenant's security; nor would the fact that he paid the note after it became due entitle him to such lien. Of course, had he ordered the supplies from the merchant upon his own credit, and in that manner furnished them to his tenant, under the law he would have been entitled to a lien. But as the tenant himself purchased the supplies, and the landlord merely stood his security for the payment therefor, he is not entitled to a lien. Judgment reversed.

MAYOR, ETC., OF WAYCROSS v. BOARD OF EDUCATION.

(Supreme Court of Georgia. March 16, 1891.)

COLLECTION OF SCHOOL TAX—COMPENSATION.

Where a school tax was levied by town authorities, the law providing that the money so raised should be used only for establishing and maintaining public schools in said town, and making it the duty of the treasurer of the town to recover all said money from the mayor and council, and where by authority of law said mayor and council had appointed a collector of all taxes imposed by them, and provided that he should receive a certain per cent. thereof as compensation for his services, such collector had the right to retain from the school fund his commissions for collecting the same.

(Syllabus by the Court.)

Error from superior court, Ware county; ATKINSON, Judge.

J. L. Sweat, for plaintiffs in error. S. W. Hitch, for defendant in error.

LUMPKIN, J. An act was passed October 22, 1887, to establish a system of public schools for the town of Waycross. It was amended December 26, 1888. Under the law as amended, the mayor and council of said town were authorized and required to levy an *ad valorem* tax of one-fourth of 1 per cent., and the sum so raised was to be used only for the purpose of establishing and maintaining public schools in and for said town. The last recited act also provided that it should be the duty of the treasurer of said town to recover from the mayor and council all the money received by them by taxation for school purposes, and pay the same out only upon the order of the board of education. The charter of the town of Waycross authorized the town authorities to appoint a tax collector for the town, prescribe his duties, and regulate his salary or pay. In pursuance of this authority, the mayor and council appointed a tax collector, and provided that he should receive as compensation for his services 10 per cent. of all the taxes collected by him. It appears that this collector collected the sum of $1,735.30, and paid over the same to the school authorities, less his commissions of $173.53. The board of education, alleging that said collector had no legal right to retain this sum out of the school fund, demanded the same from the mayor and council, who refused to pay or cause the same to be paid to said board. Whereupon the board of education sought by *mandamus* to compel the town authorities to have this money paid to them for school purposes. The judge below granted a *mandamus* absolute, and this decision is the error complained of. The sole question made is, were the mayor and council authorized by law to apply any portion of the sum collected for school purposes to the payment of the expense of its collection? As a general proposition, it would seem just and equitable that any fund collected by taxation for a specific purpose should bear the legitimate and necessary expense of such collection, and it would follow inevitably that this school fund should be reduced by the amount of such expense, unless the law on the subject provides otherwise. We are of the opinion that this law should not be so strictly construed as to prevent this fund from being so reduced. A statute of Pennsylvania provided, in substance, that whenever school taxes assessed on unseated lands should not be paid by the owner or owners thereof, the proper county commissioners should enforce the collection thereof, and when collected the money should be paid to the district treasurer for school purposes, by orders drawn on the county treasurer. A question arose under this act as to whether or not the county treasurer should be allowed his commissions for collecting school taxes on unseated lands; and in the case of Cameron Co. v. School-Dist., 117 Pa. St. 149, 11 Atl. Rep. 534, it was held that, inasmuch as the treasurer, by the act of 1834, was entitled to receive for his services a certain per cent. on all moneys received and paid out by him, he could retain his commissions for collecting the school tax, and that the county was liable to the school-district for but the amount of school tax, less the commissions paid. The Pennsylvania act does not, it is true, expressly declare that all of the school tax on unseated lands should be paid over for school purposes, but the requirement to pay over the money is the same, in effect, as a requirement to pay over all the money. The case of People v. Wiltshire, 92 Ill. 260, is exactly in point. By a statute of Illinois it was provided that the county tax collector should pay over to the township treasurer, for school purposes, the full amount of certain school taxes, and it was held that this meant he should pay over the full amount less his commissions. Mr. Justice SCHOLFIELD remarked that the language used was imperative, and, taken by itself, would undoubtedly require all this fund to be paid over without deduction; but, inasmuch as it was provided by another statute that county collectors should be allowed a commission on all money collected by them, the two statutes should be construed *in pari materia*, and that, taken together, they should be held to mean that the school fund, like all other funds collected, should be subject to this commission. It was further held by the Illinois court that "legitimate commissions for collecting school taxes may not improperly be called 'money raised for school purposes;'" and this seems to us by no means a strained construction of the law. In the case before us the money raised by taxation for school purposes in the town of Waycross was to be used only in establishing and maintaining public schools, for the law so provided. But another law of equal force authorized the mayor and council of Waycross to pay its collector in whatever way they saw proper; and they having, under the authority of this law, fixed his compensation at 10 per cent. upon all sums collected for taxes, this provision was of equal weight and force with the law providing for the establishment of schools. Construing the two together, as did the supreme court of Illinois, they mean that the school authorities of Waycross shall have the use of the school fund, less the legitimate expense of collecting it, and that this very expense is incurred for establishing and maintaining these schools. While the question here decided may not be entirely free from doubt, our conclusion is certainly supported by two eminently respectable decisions, as shown, and doubtless others upon the same line could be found; and, on general principles, it is certainly fair that the school fund should bear the expense of its own gathering, just as all other funds raised by taxation are made to do. In the distribution of money by courts, and especially by courts of equity, the same fair rule universally prevails; and no good reason occurs to us why this principle should not control the case before us. Judgment reversed.

HOOKS v. HAYES.

(*Supreme Court of Georgia.* March 16, 1891.)

MORTGAGES—ASSIGNMENT—FORECLOSURE—PARTIES—EVIDENCE—NEW TRIAL—AMENDMENT OF PLEADING.

1. The evidence having been conflicting, and the court having been satisfied with the verdict, there is no error in refusing a new trial on the grounds that the verdict was contrary to the law and evidence.

2. It is too late on a motion for a new trial to, for the first time, complain of the allowance of amendments to a petition for foreclosure, the one adding a prayer for counsel fees, the other making the administrator of plaintiff's assignor a party plaintiff suing for the use of plaintiff.

3. The administrator having been made a party plaintiff, there was no error in allowing the admission in evidence of the original mortgage, though there was no written transfer thereof to plaintiff.

4. A witness not a party or interested in the issue can testify to a contract made in his hearing whereby defendant's mortgagee, since deceased, sold the mortgage to plaintiff.

5. As plaintiff did not claim to have purchased the note and mortgage before they came due, the admission of his testimony, after the making of the mortgagee's administrator a party plaintiff, that he was a *bona fide* holder of the note and mortgage before commencement of the suit, could not prejudice defendant.

Error from superior court, Worth county; BOWER, Judge.

Jesse W. Waters, for plaintiff in error. *D. H. Pope,* for defendant in error.

SIMMONS, J. Iverson L. Ford commenced his suit to foreclose a mortgage against J. T. Hooks, in October, 1883. The note and mortgage were payable to the order of E. F. Haily, and Ford alleged that he purchased the same from Haily before the latter's death. At a subsequent term of the court two amendments were allowed to the petition for foreclosure, one adding a prayer for a judgment of 10 per cent. counsel fees, and the other making the administrator of Haily a party plaintiff, suing for the use of I. L. Ford. No objections were made to these amendments at the time they were allowed by the court. Two years after these amendments were made, the case was tried, and the plea relied on by the defendant was payment. The jury returned a verdict in favor of the plaintiff, and the defendant made a motion for a new trial upon the several grounds contained therein, which was overruled by the court.

1. The first and second grounds of the motion were the usual ones, that the verdict is contrary to law and the evidence. The evidence was conflicting as to whether the note and mortgage had been paid by the defendant, and, the jury finding that they had not been paid, and the court being satisfied with their verdict, there was no error in refusing a new trial upon these grounds.

2. The third and eighth grounds complain of the allowance of the two amendments to the petition for foreclosure, the amendment asking for counsel fees, and the amendment making Hayes a party plaintiff, suing for the use of Ford. These two grounds of the motion cannot be considered, because the record shows that these amendments were allowed at the April term, 1888, and no objection thereto was at that time made, or exception *pendente lite* filed. It was therefore too late to complain of their allowance by the court in the motion for a new trial two years thereafter.

3. The fourth ground of the motion complains that the court erred in allowing the mortgage from Hooks to Haily to be introduced in evidence, on the ground that there was no written transfer of said mortgage from Haily to Ford. After the amendment, making Hayes, the administrator of Haily, a party, was allowed, this was not a good ground of objection. The suit, after this amendment, proceeded in the name of Hayes, as such administrator, and the mortgage was therefore admissible in evidence.

4. The fifth ground complains that the court erred in allowing plaintiff's witness, Bob Ford, to testify that Haily told him that he (Haily) had sold the mortgage to I. L. Ford. Objection was made to this testimony, on the ground that it was hearsay. We can see no objection to the admission of this testimony. Bob Ford was not a party plaintiff, appears to have been a disinterested witness, and was testifying to a contract he heard made between Haily and I. L. Ford. That contract was treated by both parties and the court as an issue on the trial, and we are at a loss to understand why Bob Ford could not testify thereto.

5. The sixth ground alleges error in allowing the plaintiff I. L. Ford to testify that he was a bona fide holder of the note and mortgage before the institution of the suit to foreclose the same. After the amendment making Hayes a party plaintiff his testimony was immaterial, and did no damage to the defendant. It was of no concern to him whether I. L. Ford was the owner of the mortgage, or whether it was a part of the assets of the estate of Haily, and belonged to Hayes as administrator. His defense was not prejudiced whether the one owned it or the other, as Ford did not claim to have purchased the note and mortgage before they fell due.

6. For the reason given in our comments on the fourth ground there was no error in refusing a new trial upon the seventh ground of the motion, which complains that the court erred in allowing the plaintiff Ford to testify that he told Hooks how he held the note and mortgage, etc., the objection being that the transfer of the mortgage should be in writing.

Judgment affirmed.

MONROE v. STIGER.

(*Supreme Court of Georgia.* March 16, 1891.)

Error from superior court, Ware county; ATKINSON, Judge.

J. L. Sweat and *L. A. Wilson,* for plaintiff in error. *S. W. Hitch,* for defendant in error.

BLECKLEY, C. J. This case is controlled by the act of November 11, 1889, prescribing the method of bringing cases to the supreme court. Writ of error dismissed.

KENNEDY v. CROMWELL.

(*Supreme Court of North Carolina.* April 21, 189?.)

STATUTE OF LIMITATIONS—ACTION ON GUARDIAN'S BOND—MARRIAGE OF FEME PLAINTIFF.

1. Where the cause of action against an executor, administrator, or guardian is for a breach of the bond it is barred, as to the sureties, after three years from the breach complained of. Code, § 155, (6.)

2. Where the cause of action is to recover the balance admitted to be due by the final account it is barred, as to sureties on the bond, after six years from auditing and filing such final account. Code, § 154, (2.)

3. When such final account is filed, and there is a demand and refusal, the action is barred, as to both the principal and sureties on said bond, in three years.

4. When such final account is filed, and there is no demand and refusal, *quære,* whether the action as to the executor, administrator, or guardian himself is barred in six years or ten years.

5. When there is no final account filed, *semble,* that the statute begins to run from the arrival of the ward of age, but whether, in such case, three years or ten years bars, *quære.*

6. When no final account has been filed, but there is a demand and refusal, the statute bars in three years thereafter, as to the principal as well as the sureties.

7. When the statute begins to run, the subsequent marriage of the *feme* plaintiff will not stop it.

MERRIMON, C. J., dissenting.

(*Syllabus by the Court.*)

Appeal from superior court, Edgecombe county; SPIER WHITAKER, Judge.

G. M. T. Fountain and *H. L. Staton,* for appellant. *John L. Bridgers,* for appellee.

CLARK, J. The Code, § 154, (2,) bars an action against an executor, administrator or guardian on his official bond within six years after filing his audited final account; while by the Code, § 155, (6,) an action against the sureties on such bond is barred within three years after breach complained of. As the action on the official bond necessarily embraces the sureties, it would seem that the distinction is that, where the final account is filed admitting a balance to be due, but no breach is alleged, such balance, as to the sureties, is conclusively presumed to be paid over after the lapse of six years if the statute of limitations is pleaded; whereas, if a breach is alleged before or after filing final account, as a *devastavit,* a failure to file final account, a demand and refusal to pay balance due by final account, or any other breach of the bond, the sureties are discharged by a delay to sue for more than three years after the breach which is complained of as the cause of action. Norman v. Walker, 101 N. C. 24, 7 S. E. Rep. 468. When the executor, administrator, or guardian files his final account, and there is a demand and refusal, the action as to him is barred in three years. Wyrick v. Wyrick, 106 N. C. 84, 10 S. E. Rep. 916. When he files such final account, and there is no demand and refusal, whether the action is barred as to him in six years under the Code, § 154, (2,) (Vaughan v. Hines, 87 N. C. 445,) or in ten years by virtue of the Code, § 158, (Wyrick v. Wyrick, supra,) we are not called on to decide in the present case. Here, though one annual account was filed, no other was subsequently filed, nor any final account. Under such circumstances, whether or not there is an unclosed express trust against which no statute runs was left an open question by PEARSON, J., in Hamlin v. Mebane, 1 Jones, Eq. 18; but SMITH, C. J., intimates strongly, in Hodges v. Council, 86 N. C. 186, that even in such case the cause of action accrued upon the ward becoming of age, and that it would be at least barred by the lapse of ten years, (Code, § 168,) and possibly in three years; citing Ang. Lim. §§ 174, 178. In Wyrick v. Wyrick, supra, the court, (SHEPHERD, J.,) say that "it was the evident purpose of the Code to prescribe a period of limitations to all actions whatsoever, and thus make it a complete statute of repose." Whether the limitation is three years or ten years it runs from the ward's majority, when no final account has been filed, and there has been no demand and refusal. In the present case there was a demand and refusal. This put an end to the trust of itself, if it was not before terminated by the ward's becoming of age, and capable of suing. The relation of the parties became adversary by the demand and refusal, and it is clear that the action would be barred by a delay to sue within three years thereafter. Robertson v. Dunn, 87 N. C. 191; Woody v. Brooks, 102 N. C. 334, 9 S. E. Rep. 294; County Board of Education v. State Board of Education, 107 N. C. 366, 12 S. E. Rep. 452. In the present case, the facts, as found by the referee and the findings approved by the court, are that the guardian qualified in 1861, made his returns in 1862, has made none since, and filed no final account. The ward, the plaintiff, married in 1872, and became of age August, 1873, before which time her husband had died. She married again in 1879. In September and October, 1877, the plaintiff wrote her former guardian, saying, in substance, that she hoped something was due her, and asking him to send it. To these letters the guardian replied that he had expended for her more than was due her. This was a demand and refusal,—a denial of any liability or trust in respect to the plaintiff. This action was begun 24th September, 1888. This was more than 15 years after the plaintiff became of age, being then discovert, and more than 10 years after the demand and refusal. The statute, having begun to run, could not be stopped by the subsequent marriage of the plaintiff. In any aspect of the case the claim of the plaintiff was barred by the statute of limitations, and the court below should have dismissed the action. Error.

MERRIMON, C. J., (*dissenting*.) I am of opinion that the plaintiff's cause of action is not barred by any statute of limitation. The intestate of the defendant was her guardian, a trustee of an express trust, which has never been closed, as required by the statute pertinent (Code, §§ 1617–1619) or otherwise; nor did the intestate at any time deny or disavow the trust. In such case no statute of limitation applies. In Grant v. Hughes. 94 N. C. 231, the court say: "The action is not brought upon the official bond as administrator of the testator of the defendant. It is brought to compel an account and settlement of the estate of the intestate of the plaintiff in his hands in his life-time. He was a trustee of an express trust, and the statute of limitations did not apply." This case was afterwards cited in Woody v. Brooks, 102 N. C. 334, 9 S. E. Rep. 294, with approval, and the late Chief Justice SMITH said, among other things: "Until a final account is filed and audited there can be no bar; nor is there any as to a balance admitted to be due by such final account, unless the executor or administrator can show that he has disposed of it in some way authorized by law, or unless there has been a demand and refusal to pay such

admitted balance, in which case the action is barred in three years after such demand and refusal." In this case the intestate never accounted by filing any final account. There was no admitted balance, nor did he ever come to an account or settlement in any way with the plaintiff. This express trust remains to this day unclosed. Other decisions to the like effect might be cited. Furthermore, in my judgment, there was no sufficient evidence—none that should be treated as evidence—of a demand on the part of the plaintiff upon the intestate, her guardian, that he come to an account and settlement with her, and a refusal on his part to do so. The intestate of the defendant was the plaintiff's guardian, and her uncle—he had never accounted as such—had neglected to state and file accounts as the statute required. Twice she wrote him, saying, in substance, that she hoped there was something due her as his ward. He simply said hastily in reply that she had already received more than was due her. What she thus said could not fairly—especially in view of the relations of the parties—be treated as a demand for a settlement, nor what the intestate said,—a refusal to account. The parties had not reached the point of demand on one side and refusal on the other. The plaintiff did not say or mean to say, "You owe me, and I demand a settlement;" nor did the guardian say, or intend to say, "I do not owe you. I will not account with you. Seek your legal remedy,"—or the substance of that. The language was not fairly that of demand and refusal. In such cases the demand and refusal should be clear and unmistakable. Here the plaintiff was the niece of her guardian. She simply made a timid inquiry and request of the latter. He did not say, "I am ready to account with you," as he ought to have done, and was bound to do; no doubt, because he did not understand that a demand of settlement was made upon him. The guardian was derelict,—never accounted. The plaintiff was truthful and confiding, and hence loses any sum due her. I do not think the law so intends.

TAYLOR v. SIKES.

(*Supreme Court of North Carolina.* May 5, 1891.)

WIFE'S SEPARATE ESTATE—CONTROL BY HUSBAND.

1. At common law a husband may, as between himself and his wife, treat the wife's choses in action as his property, and constitute himself, in respect to them, a trustee for her benefit.

2. If he can do this, he may also unite with her in their disposition, and, where this has been actually done, the proceeds cannot be recovered back by either of them.

(*Syllabus by the Court.*)

Appeal from superior court, Granville county; JAMES C. MACRAE, Judge.

Edwards & Batchelor, for appellant. *R. H. Battle* and *M. V. Lanier,* for appellee.

SHEPHERD, J. Conceding that this case is governed by the laws of Maryland, and assuming, as we must do, in the absence of proof to the contrary, that the common law prevails in that state, we are nevertheless unable to see how the plaintiff can recover. The finding of the judge is a little obscure as to whether the *feme* plaintiff had any interest in the money on deposit in the bank. His honor might very well have found upon her declarations made in the presence of the husband, together with the other circumstances in evidence, that she did not own any part of the said fund; and we are inclined to think that the case upon appeal is susceptible of the construction that such was his conclusion as a matter of fact. Putting this aside, however, and granting the husband's right to the money *jure mariti*, it is well settled that, instead of exercising his right to the fund, he could have treated it as the wife's, and constituted himself a trustee in respect to it for her benefit. See Bean v. Bridgers, ante, 112, (decided at this term,) and the cases there cited. If he could have done this, he could surely have united with her in its disposition; and this he substantially did by permitting her to relinquish her apparent right to it. The agreement has been executed, and we can see nothing in the case which entitles either of the plaintiffs to recover back the money which they have voluntarily paid to the defendant. The exceptions as to the admissibility of testimony were not pressed in this court, and we need not consider them. The judgment is affirmed.

RANDALL v. RICHMOND & D. R. Co.

(*Supreme Court of North Carolina.* April 28, 1891.)

COMMON CARRIERS—PREPAYMENT OF FREIGHT—EVIDENCE.

1. Under Code N. C. § 1963, providing that common carriers may require prepayment of freight in all cases, a railroad company may lawfully refuse to receive freight offered by a connecting railway company without prepayment, though it does not demand prepayment of others, if the connecting railroad has notice that prepayment is required.

2. In an action for damages for refusal to receive from a connecting line without prepayment freight billed to a certain flag station, defendant may show that it had a fixed regulation requiring prepayment on all freight consigned to that station, and that both plaintiff and the connecting line knew of that fact.

Appeal from superior court, Madison county; BROWN, Judge.

Action by J. W. Randall against the Richmond & Danville Railroad Company for refusal to receive freight.

F. H. Busbee, for appellee.

CLARK, J. A common carrier can demand prepayment of freight from any one and to any station. Code, § 1963; Allen v. Railroad Co., 100 N. C. 397, 5 S. E. Rep. 105. That the defendant made a general regulation that it would require prepayment on all freight to a flag station (at which there was no agent) was not only reasonable, but was a matter entirely within the defendant's powers. A common carrier may require prepayment from any shipper, at its choice, though it may not require it from others. Allen v. Railroad Co., supra. It should appear, however, that the plaintiff or his forwarding agent, the first company, had notice that prepayment was required. This the

defendant was not improperly allowed to do by showing, as it did, that all freight to this station was required to be prepaid, and, further, by the plaintiff himself that he knew of such regulation. It was also in evidence that notice was given to the East Tennessee, Virginia & Georgia Railroad, who were the agents of plaintiff for forwarding the freight beyond its own line. A witness introduced for defendant testified that the defendant did not accept the freight from the East Tennessee, Virginia & Georgia Railroad till February 28th, and that it was shipped the next day. The two companies were not shown to be under the same management, but were simply connecting roads. The defendant was not required to receive freight from the East Tennessee, Virginia & Georgia Railroad for shipment without prepayment of freight, any more than from any one else. It is in evidence, and not contradicted, that the defendant notified such company that it required prepayment, and, when it was satisfied in that regard, that it immediately received and promptly shipped the freight. If the East Tennessee, Virginia & Georgia Railroad received prepayment of freight for shipment over both lines, and negligently failed to prepay the defendant, as required by its regulations, and the plaintiff has suffered damage by the consequent detention, he must look to the company who received his money, and with whom he contracted for the shipment. Mount Pleasant Manuf'g Co. v. Cape Fear, etc., R. Co., 106 N. C. 207, 10 S. E. Rep. 1046. The court properly instructed the jury that there was no evidence that the defendant received the freight until February 28th, and to find the issues in favor of the defendant. No error.

MEREDITH v. RICHMOND & D. R. Co.

(*Supreme Court of North Carolina.* April 28, 1891.)

RAILROAD COMPANIES—PERSONAL INJURIES—BOY ON TRACK—CONTRIBUTORY NEGLIGENCE.

1. In an action against a railroad company for personal injuries, plaintiff, a bright boy of 13, showed that what had previously been a highway had been filled for a considerable distance by defendant's tracks; that while walking thereon he passed a train going in the opposite direction, and, seeing another coming along the track on which he was walking, he stepped off, and was struck and injured by the backing of the first train, which he did not see. *Held,* contributory negligence, and plaintiff was properly nonsuited.

2. Actual or implied license by a railroad company to use as a foot-way its tracks, laid on what was previously a highway, does not relieve a pedestrian of the duty of exercising care.

3. Where a boy 13 years old, and "apparently capable of appreciating the peril of his situation," is walking on the track in front of a locomotive, and there is an opportunity for him to avert the danger by stepping off, the engineer is justified in assuming that he will step off.

Appeal from superior court, Madison county; PHILIPS, Judge.

Action by W. J. Meredith against the Richmond & Danville Railroad Company for damages for personal injuries. The defendant company, in constructing its road from Hot Springs to Paint Rock, had used what had previously been the public high way, and just below Hot Springs had put in two side tracks in addition to the main line, extending some distance down the road. The plaintiff, W. J. Meredith, who sues by his next friend, Nichols Meredith, his father, was shown by all of the witnesses to be a bright boy, about 13 years old. In going from the house of his father to Hot Springs he was compelled to pass along the defendant's road, where the three tracks were laid down, and at a short distance on either side of said tracks there were lines of wire fence. When on the way from his father's house to Hot Springs he passed a train apparently heading towards Paint Rock, and not long after, seeing another train coming from Hot Springs in his front on the track on which he was walking, he stepped over to the side track on which the train first seen by him was running, but failed to see it approaching him from his rear till it ran against and injured him. He might have stepped off the track and avoided the injury, had he seen the train coming up behind him. He was struck by the engine, and his arm was crushed, and afterwards amputated. When the plaintiff rested his case the judge instructed the jury that he could not recover. The plaintiff submitted to judgment of nonsuit, and appealed.

F. H. Busbee, for appellee.

AVERY, J., (*after stating the facts as above.*) Where the engineer in charge of a moving engine sees a human being walking along the track in front of it, if such person is unknown to him, and is apparently old enough to understand the necessity for care and watchfulness, under such circumstances, the engineer may act upon the assumption that he w'll step off the track in time to avoid injury. McAdoo v. Railroad Co., 105 N. C. 140, 11 S. E. Rep. 316; Parker v. Railroad Co., 86 N. C. 221. The witnesses concur in the statement that the boy who was injured was an intelligent youth, about 13 years old. In the absence of knowledge or information to the contrary, the engineer was justified in supposing that he would look to his own safety even when trains were moving on three parallel tracks, if there was manifestly an opportunity to escape by walking across the rail to the neighboring side track. Daily v. Railroad Co., 106 N. C. 301, 11 S. E. Rep. 320. The fact that there was then no other possible route for persons walking from Paint Rock to Hot Springs, would not relieve a man or boy of his age. endowed with reason and the instinct of self-preservation, from the duty of watchfulness, when he must know and should be always mindful that carelessness will expose him to danger. Actual or implied license from the railroad company to use the track as a foot-way would not relieve him from the consequences of failing to exercise ordinary care. The license to use does not carry with it the right to obstruct the road and impede the passage of trains. McAdoo v. Railroad Co., supra. Where the engineer knows the person on the track, and has knowledge or information that he is of unsound mind, or so deaf that he cannot hear an approaching train, or where the engineer sees, or can,

by ordinary care and watchfulness, discover, that a human being is apparently lying asleep, or helplessly drunk, or an animal or wagon is entangled on the track in his front, even at a public crossing, he cannot relieve the company of liability for injury caused by running over the person or animal, except by showing that he promptly used every available means, short of imperiling the lives of passengers on his own train, to avert the danger. Deans v. Railroad Co., 107 N. C. 686, 12 S. E. Rep. 77; Bullock v. Railroad Co., 105 N. C. 189, 10 S. E. Rep. 988; Carlton v. Railroad Co., 104 N. C. 365, 10 S. E. Rep. 516. The same rule applies where the injury has been done to a child apparently too small to understand the danger, and where the engineer, had he kept a proper lookout, might have averted it without peril to passengers. The boy injured was described by witnesses as bright and "smart." but, if he was apparently capable of appreciating the peril of his situation, it is sufficient to relieve the servants of the company from the imputation of carelessness in assuming that he would step aside before the engine reached him. Considerations of public policy, such as the reasonable demand for the speedy transportation of mails, and a proper regard for the safety of passengers, forbid that trains should be stopped for trivial causes, or that the lives of those on board should be put in jeopardy even to avert manifest danger to others. We concur with the judge below in the opinion that the plaintiff was not entitled to recover because, by the undisputed facts, considered in any phase presented by them, the plaintiff was negligent in failing to see the train approaching him from behind, while the servant of the defendant was not in fault in acting on the belief that plaintiff would move out of the way of the engine before it should reach him. There is no error. The judgment is affirmed.

TAYLOR v. SHARP.

(*Supreme Court of North Carolina.* April 21, 1891.)

CONFLICT OF LAWS — CONTRACT BY MARRIED WOMAN.

1. Where a married woman enters into a contract in a state by the laws of which she may contract as if unmarried, and suit is brought in a state in which she is subjected to the common-law disability of coverture, and it appears that she was at the commencement of the suit and has since been a resident of the latter state, it will be presumed that at the time of the contract she was domiciled in the state in which it was made, and the contract will be enforced against her.

2. Under Laws N. Y. 1884, c. 381, providing that a married woman may contract as if she were a *feme sole* except where the contract is made with her husband, she is bound by the indorsement of a note executed by her husband to her order, and by her indorsed for his accommodation. Bank v. Sniffen, 7 N. Y. Supp. 520.

Appeal from superior court, Rockingham county; BYNUM, Judge.

This was a suit on two notes executed in the state of New York by Thomas Sharp to his wife, Gertrude, and by her indorsed to the plaintiff. She answered that she indorsed the notes for the accommodation and at the solicitation of her husband, and under a kind of matrimonial coercion, and without any consideration whatever to her thereunto moving, and without any benefit to her separate estate thereby arising, and this to the full knowledge of the plaintiff. It was also averred that, when the action was commenced, she was and still is a resident and citizen of the state of North Carolina. The plaintiff replied that the notes were indorsed by her to give credit to her husband, "and she had the legal right to do so under the laws of the state of New York, and she thereby rendered herself and her separate estate as liable as though she was a *feme sole*." At the trial the plaintiff introduced Laws N. Y. 1884, c. 381, providing that a married woman may contract as if she were a *feme sole*, except where the contract is made with her husband. No other evidence was offered. Under the direction of the court, the jury returned a verdict for the plaintiff. There was a judgment on the verdict, and Gertrude Sharp appealed.

Mebane & Scott, for appellant. *Haywood & Haywood,* for appellee.

SHEPHERD, J. The single question presented in this appeal is whether the judgment rendered by his honor was authorized by the facts appearing in the record. It is a general principle that all matters bearing upon the execution, the interpretation, and the validity of a contract are to be determined by the law of the place where the contract is made, and, if valid there, it is valid everywhere. Watson v. Orr, 3 Dev. 163; Davis v. Coleman, 7 Ired. 424; Anderson v. Doak, 10 Ired. 295; Scudder v. Bank, 91 U. S. 406. An exception, however, is maintained by some of the continental jurists as to the capacity of a contracting party, and they generally hold that the incapacity of the domicile attaches to and follows the person wherever he may go. This is not, says Mr. Justice Story, (Confl. Laws, 103, 104,) the doctrine of the common law; and GRAY, C. J., in Milliken v. Pratt, 125 Mass. 374, after an elaborate examination of the question, concludes that the general current of English and American authorities is in favor of holding that a contract, which by the law of the place is recognized as lawfully made, by a capable person, is valid everywhere, although the person would not, under the law of the domicile, be deemed capable of making it. This principle has been doubted in the case of a married woman, where her contract, made in another state, is sought to be enforced in the state of her domicile, where, by the laws of such state, she is under a complete common-law disability to make any contract whatever. The question, however, does not arise in the present case, as there is nothing to show that the *feme* defendant was domiciled in this state at the time of the execution of the contract sued upon. In the absence of anything to the contrary, the law presumes that she was, at the date of the contract, a resident of the state where it was made. The contract was executed in New York, and under the laws of that state (Acts

1884) a married woman may contract as if she were *feme sole*, except where the contract is made with her husband. This contract was not made with her husband, within the meaning of the act above mentioned, (Bank v. Sniffen, 7 N. Y. Supp. 520,) and was therefore valid where made. It is well settled that our courts will entertain personal actions between citizens of other states where jurisdiction has been obtained by service of process within our limits, (Code, § 192,) and we are unable to see how the defendant, by a mere change of residence, can rid herself of liability upon the contract in question. 2 Pars. Cont. 576. We have very carefully examined the authorities cited by the defendant's counsel, but they fail to convince us that in sustaining the judgment we are contravening any well-settled public policy in this state in reference to the laws of married women. Many phases of the general subject (not free from difficulty) were presented by the counsel, but we have purposely abstained from their discussion, as they are not directly presented by the record. We simply decide that we are of the opinion that this particular judgment should be affirmed.

HOUSER v. McGINNIS *et al.*

(Supreme Court of North Carolina.　April 21, 1891.)

ASSUMPSIT—MONEY PAID TO DEFENDANT'S USE.

Plaintiff was the clerk of an agent for an express company. He received a money package, and delivered it to the consignee, but neglected to take a receipt. The latter having denied receiving the package, the agent was required by the express company to make good the loss. Plaintiff paid the money to the agent, who sent it to the consignor, and the latter credited it on his account against the consignee. *Held,* in a suit to which the agent, the consignor, and the consignee were made parties, that the consignee was liable to the plaintiff for the money paid by him.

This was a civil action heard upon demurrer of the defendant P. C. Beam, at the spring term, 1891, of the superior court of Gaston county, before MERRIMON, Judge. The complaint was as follows: "That heretofore, to-wit, on the 25th day of November, 1887, the defendant W. J. McGinnis was the agent at Cherryville of the Southern Express Company, a corporation doing business as a common carrier between the towns of Shelby, in Cleveland county, N. C., and the town of Cherryville, in Gaston county, N. C., and plaintiff was on said day acting as clerk or agent of said defendant in the transaction of the business of said express company at Cherryville; he, the said defendant McGinnis, being on said day absent from Cherryville, engaged in other business. (2) That on said 25th November, 1887, plaintiff, in the course of his business as such clerk or agent, and while defendant McGinnis was still absent, received a package containing five hundred dollars in currency from said express company, the same having been transmitted by the defendant B. K. Humphreys from the said town of Shelby, through said express company, to the defendant P. C. Beam, at Cherryville. (3) That immediately upon the receipt of the package, and without entering the same on the book of the said express company, kept at Cherryville, known as the 'Delivery Book,' plaintiff carried and delivered said package of $500 to the defendant P. C. Beam, without taking the receipt of said Beam therefor, intending afterwards to make the proper entry on said book and take the same to Beam, and obtain his receipt thereon for said package, as was frequently done at said office; but plaintiff wholly forgot to make said entry or to take such receipt. (4) That afterwards, to-wit, on the 22d day of March, 1888, nearly four months after such receipt and delivery of said package, the defendant McGinnis demanded the payment of the said sum of $500 by the plaintiff, alleging that the said sum had been demanded of him, the said McGinnis, by said express company, upon the ground that said Beam denied its delivery to him by plaintiff, or that he had ever received the same from any source; that the books of the route agent or messenger of said express company showed a receipt for said package, signed by plaintiff; and that the said express delivery book showed no entry of said package, nor any receipt of said Beam therefor, and that said Beam denied the delivery of said package to him by plaintiff or any one else for him. (5) That plaintiff, upon investigation, found the allegations of McGinnis with regard to the book of the express messenger and the delivery book to be true, and further that Beam denied the receipt of said package, and having, on account of the great lapse of time since the receipt and delivery of said package to said Beam, forgotten the circumstances, thereon, in his surprise and confusion, supposed he must either have lost or mislaid said package; and by mistake and inadvertence, being misled by the appearance of said books and the denial of Beam, he then and there acknowledged his liability therefor, and agreed to pay to said McGinnis the said sum of $500 for said Humphreys, or to be delivered by said McGinnis to the express company for said Humphreys. (6) That thereupon plaintiff paid to McGinnis $245, all the money he could raise at the time, which sum was by McGinnis immediately paid to the express company for Humphreys, and the balance of the $500, to-wit, $255, was at the same time paid by McGinnis out of his own pocket to said express company to be by it delivered to Humphreys. (7) That the said sum of $500 so contributed and paid to said express company as aforesaid was by it carried and delivered to said Humphreys at Shelby, N. C., who allowed credit therefor to said Beam in the settlement of certain dealings between them, as plaintiff is informed and believes. (8) That afterwards plaintiff, having discovered with certainty that he did deliver said package of $500 to said Beam, as alleged in the first paragraph hereof, before the institution of this suit made demand upon the defendants McGinnis and Beam for the repayment of said sum of $245, which was refused. (9) That neither of said defendants, nor any one for them, have paid to plaintiff the said sum of money, nor any part thereof,

but the whole thereof remains due and unpaid. (10) That by reason of the receipt of said package of $500 on said 25th day of November, and the credit afterwards given him by said Humphreys, said defendant Beam has had the benefit of said sum of money twice, and his detention thereof is unjust and unlawful and wrongful towards the plaintiff. (11) That defendant McGinnis ought properly to have been a party plaintiff to this action, but he refused to make himself a party plaintiff at the institution of this suit, and was therefore made a party defendant. Wherefore plaintiff demands judgment against the defendants W. J. McGinnis and P. C. Beam for the said sum of $245, with interest from the 22d day of March, 1888, until paid, together with the costs of this action, and for such other and further relief as to the court may seem just."

Defendant McGinnis answered, admitting all of the material allegations of the complaint. Humphreys neither answered nor demurred. Defendant Beam demurred as follows: "(1) That the complaint does not state that the money paid by Houser to McGinnis was ever paid to the defendant Beam, or that he derived any benefit therefrom. (2) That the complaint states a cause of action against Beam in Humphreys on account of the money sent by him to P. C. Beam, which still subsists. That said cause of action has not been extinguished by the payment of the money by Houser, nor does the complaint state any facts which amount to an assignment of said cause of action to Houser. (3) That the complaint does not allege that the expressions therein made by Beam were ever made to Houser, or made with intent to influence Houser, or to affect him in any way; nor made with intent to deceive him or any one else. (4) That there are no facts or circumstances alleged in the complaint which constitute an express contract between Houser and Beam, or from which any contract could be implied, or other liability could arise on the part of Beam to Houser. Whereupon defendant demands judgment that this action be dismissed; that he go without day, and recover his costs of the plaintiff, to be taxed by the clerk." Demurrer sustained. Plaintiff appealed.

George F. Bason and *Jones & Tillett*, for appellant.

AVERY, J., (*after stating the facts as above.*) By demurring the defendant Beam admits that the plaintiff paid over to him the sum of $500 in money, consigned by express, and failed to take his receipt, and that subsequently, under a mistake as to the fact of having previously made said payment, the plaintiff, through the defendant McGinnis, paid to the defendant Humphreys $500, which Humphreys allowed as a credit on a debt due him from Beam, in order to satisfy and pay a second time the claim of Beam as assignee. The money has thus been twice paid to the consignee with no new consideration, and yet he resists the plaintiff's demand for restitution on the ground that the action could be maintained by Humphreys only, in whom the right to bring it still subsists, the company failing to show any privity between the plaintiff and Humphreys. Where money is paid and received in discharge of a debt then believed by the payer to be due, but in fact previously paid in full by or for the debtor, the creditor is not allowed to keep double the sum due him against the demand of the debtor preferred in an action in the nature of *assumpsit* for the recovery of the second payment made by mistake. Pool v. Allen, 7 Ired. 120; Mitchell v. Walker, 8 Ired. 243; Newell v. March, Id. 441; Hare, Cont. p. 104. The defendant seems to admit this principle, but insists that Humphreys paid the debt the last time, and he alone can maintain the action for the restitution of the amount wrongfully paid by him. The plaintiff has brought all of the parties who actually have claimed, or who, according to the contention of either party, can rightfully claim, an interest in the controversy. McGinnis admits the truth of plaintiff's allegations by answer and Beam by demurrer, while Humphreys confesses by failing to answer. When the money was placed by McGinnis in the hands of Humphreys, as agent, to pay the claim of the defendant Beam a second time, Humphreys retained the money, but allowed Beam credit on a debt due him from the latter. This was equivalent to paying the debt in money a second time, and the arrangement was made for plaintiff, and in consideration of funds furnished by or for him. It was in effect a second payment by Houser. *Quod facit per alium, facit per se.* If the facts stated in the complaint be true, we see no reason why the plaintiff might not have maintained his action against Beam alone, treating both McGinnis and Humphreys as his agents. Houser paid $245 in money—all that he could raise—to McGinnis to be handed over to Humphreys, who was to effect the settlement with the defendant, and induced McGinnis to pay for his benefit $255, the residue of the $500. The law implies a promise by Beam to repay it to Houser. Mason v. Waite, 17 Mass. 563. Where an agent by mistake of fact pays money for his principal, the latter may recover it back from the party who has received it. Story, Ag. § 435; Whart. Ag. § 413; Sheffer v. Montgomery, 65 Pa. St. 329; Bank v. King, 98 Amer. Dec. 215, and notes 221. It is a general rule that where the money of the principal has been wrongfully paid by his agent to a stranger, either the principal or the agent may maintain an action for its recovery. 1 Lawson, Rights, Rem. & Pr. § 121. But the principal cannot recover where the agent loans to one of his own creditors, who has no notice that it is the principal's money. Id. McGinnis, being intrusted by Houser as agent with a part of the money, and having advanced the residue for the plaintiff, might substitute Humphreys, who would be, in contemplation of law, says Mr. Wharton, "but the extension of the principal himself, introducing no new party into the contract." Whart. Ag. §§ 33, 34. As Houser might have made Humphreys directly his agent, or might in terms have authorized McGinnis to constitute him a

subagent to settle with Beam, he had the right to ratify the substitution of Humphreys by McGinnis, and thus establish a privity between Humphreys and himself; and of this Beam could not complain. But if this were not so, all of the parties being before the court, and the mistake being admitted, it would be unconscionable to allow the defendant to retain double the amount due him.

As it may possibly be insisted that, though the privity between the plaintiff and Humphreys be admitted, still the complaint does not state facts sufficient to constitute a cause of action, it is proper that we should consider this case in another aspect. We think that if the plaintiff, under the circumstances, actually knew he had paid the debt, and could not at the time prove the payment, or if his mistake of fact was negligently made, and he might by the exercise of ordinary care have avoided falling into it, still, as between him and the defendant, who admits that the money was paid to him in full a second time, not as a gratuity, but nominally in discharge of the same debt, the plaintiff is entitled to restitution when it can be made without loss or sacrifice on the part of the latter. His negligence in failing to find out the facts before paying the money does not prevent his recovery from one who does not deny the allegation that he received and retained double the sum justly due to him. Hare, Cont. p. 233; Union Nat. Bank v. Sixth Nat. Bank, 43 N. Y. 455; Lyle v. Shinnebarger, 17 Mo. App. 66; North v. Bloss, 30 N. Y. 374; Bank v. Morse, 88 Amer. Dec. 284, and notes, p. 290. It would have been otherwise if the plaintiff, by his negligence in failing to give timely notice of his demand, had prevented the defendant from recovering the sum claimed of a third party, or generally where the defendant had sustained damage which the plaintiff, by ordinary care, might have prevented. Bank v. McGillvray, 64 Amer. Dec. 92; U. S. v. Bank, 6 Fed. Rep. 854. Where the parties cannot be placed *in statu quo* the loss must fall upon the person who caused it by his negligence, though he may have made the payment under a mistake as to the facts, but without exercising due diligence in ascertaining them. Boas v. Updegrove, 47 Amer. Dec. 425. If a second payment had been made with a full knowledge of the facts, but not by compulsion of or mistake as to the law, the courts would not allow Beam, who acknowledges that he has been twice paid, to go out of a court of conscience, when all of the parties are before the court, without accounting for what is justly due to the plaintiff, when he has advanced out of his own funds a part and owes McGinnis the balance of the amount used by Humphreys in making the second payment. No wrong is imputed to any other party, and in any view of the facts the courts could not lend their sanction to fraud by allowing one who, by falsely denying a first payment, secures a second, to retain it simply because the debtor may have been guilty of even gross negligence. A payment is not necessarily voluntary, nor is it to be treated as a gift, because the debtor did not act under compulsion in paying it a second time. Pool v. Allen, supra. We conclude, therefore, that there was error in sustaining the demurrer, and the judgment of the court below is reversed.

BARRINGER v. BURNS.

(Supreme Court of North Carolina. April 21, 1891.)

REPLEVIN—BAILMENT—INSTRUCTIONS.

1. A mare was delivered to a horse trainer, who agreed to keep and train her, and, when requested by the owner, to exhibit her speed in the presence of witnesses. She was then to be sold, and the trainer paid out of the proceeds. Though several times requested to display her speed as agreed, the trainer refused to do so. *Held,* that the owner could recover possession of the mare without tendering the trainer's charge.

2. The trainer having used the mare on other occasions than for training, and for purposes of business and pleasure, the owner could determine the bailment for that reason, and recover possession without tendering the charges.

3. Though an instruction embraces only the aspects of the case favorable to. one party, it is not erroneous if the entire charge fairly presents the case to the jury.

4. Where plaintiff and defendant are the principal witnesses, and the former testifies distinctly to one contract and its breach by defendant, who testifies as distinctly to another and a different contract, it is not error to charge that, if the jury find that plaintiff has stated the contract correctly, they will find for him, but, if defendant stated it correctly, then the verdict should be for him.

Appeal from superior court, Mecklenburg county; MERRIMON, Judge.

This action is brought to recover possession of the mare specified in the complaint. The pleadings raised issues of fact. On the trial the court, among other instructions, gave the following to the jury at the request of the plaintiff: "(3) That if the jury believe from the testimony that the contract was that the defendant, Burns, was, upon request of plaintiff, to exhibit the speed which the mare had attained under his training, and, upon request by plaintiff to that effect, the defendant failed or refused so to do, that would operate as a breach of the contract, and would entitle the plaintiff to a verdict for the mare. (4) That if the jury believe from the testimony that the contract was that the defendant, Burns, was only to use the mare for training purposes, and that Burns used her, or allowed her to be used, for any other purpose, it would constitute a breach of contract on the part of defendant, and would entitle the plaintiff to a verdict for the mare, unless the use made of the mare was such as riding to town, which was necessary for the mare as exercise, and in this event it would not amount to a breach of the contract." The court further instructed the jury as follows: "(1) If Barringer states the contract correctly, the jury should answer the first issue, 'Yes.' (2) If the contract was that the defendant was to turn the mare over to the plaintiff to be sold, and to receive the compensation out of the proceeds, the answer will be, 'Yes.' (3) There is no evidence as to the damage the plaintiff sustained by reason of the defendant's wrong-

ful detention. (4) If the contract was as stated by Burns, the answer to the first issue should be, 'No,' and to the second issue, 'None.' (5) If the defendant was to be paid by the month, as testified to by Barringer, *i. e.,* $8 for training and $20 for keep, and it was not a part of the contract that defendant was to surrender possession of the mare and take his pay out of the proceeds, the answer to the third issue should be the amount accrued up to the date demand was made. (6) The plaintiff says he saw the mare here 30 times. It does not appear that he made any protest. If this was a provision of the contract, did he not waive it? (7) If the defendant has not himself paid for the shoeing of the mare, and no charge has been made against him for it, he cannot claim any lien for charges for that." The testimony on both sides, bearing upon these points, was called to the attention of the jury. The jury responded to the first issue, "Yes;" to second, "None;" to third, "None;" and to fourth, "Nothing." The defendant moved for a new trial. Motion denied. Judgment for the plaintiff, from which defendant appealed. In statement of case on appeal, the defendant assigns the following errors and exceptions: "(2) That the court gave the jury the instruction No. 3 of the plaintiff's prayers set out above. (3) That the court gave the jury the instruction No. 4 of the plaintiff's prayers set out above. (4) That the court charged the jury that, if Barringer stated the contract correctly, the jury should answer the first issue, 'Yes.' (5) That the court charged the jury that if the defendant had not paid for the shoeing of the mare, and the bill for shoeing was not charged to him, he could not claim a lien for that."

Jones & Tillett, for appellant. *McCall & Bailey* and *G. F. Bason,* for appellee.

MERRIMON, C. J., *(after stating the facts as above.)* The parties produced evidence on the trial pertinent to and bearing upon every aspect of the case to which the court directed the attention of the jury. Particularly there was evidence of the plaintiff tending to prove the breaches of the contract alleged by him, to which the third and fourth special instructions complained of as erroneous had reference. The plaintiff alleged that he placed his mare with the defendant, a horse trainer, to be trained for trotting races; that she was to be left in defendant's possession to be trained; that said defendant was to feed her as trained horses should be fed, have her comfortably stabled and well groomed, and then thoroughly trained; and that at the direction of the plaintiff the mare was to be trotted around the race-track for a nominal prize, in the presence of two or three disinterested witnesses, who were to time her with stop watches, in order that it might be discovered what speed she had attained as a racer, and she was then to be delivered to the plaintiff, and he was to sell her, and out of the proceeds of sale to pay the defendant, etc.; that the defendant, "although several times requested to display the speed of said mare as aforesaid, invariably refused so to do, in consequence whereof the plaintiff demanded her surrender from the defendant," etc.; and he further alleged that, in violation of the contract alleged, the defendant had "used and permitted another to drive said mare on other occasions than for training, and for purposes of business or mere pleasure, in which several matters the plaintiff avers the defendant broke his contract," etc. By the terms of the contract thus alleged it was material and important that the defendant, who so had the mare in training, should, upon the demand of the plaintiff, exhibit trials of her speed in the presence of witnesses. He refused, upon repeated demands of the plaintiff, to make such trials, as he was bound to do. If he did, he violated a material provision of the contract as alleged, and the plaintiff became at once entitled to have possession of his mare; and as there was evidence tending to prove the contract and a breach thereof, as alleged, the plaintiff was entitled to have the third special instruction which he demanded and the court gave. The plaintiff alleged that the defendant, by the terms of the contract, had possession of the mare only for the purposes of training her. If he went beyond that, and used her, as alleged, for other purposes, he committed a breach of the contract, and the plaintiff might demand and have possession of her. There was some evidence tending to prove such allegation, and therefore the plaintiff was entitled to have the fourth special instruction as to which error is assigned. There is nothing alleged by the plaintiff that creates a lien upon the mare in favor of the defendant, or that gives rise to a counter-claim in his favor. The instructions just referred to were asked for by the plaintiff as bearing upon certain aspects of the case favorable to him, and deemed important. They did not embrace or apply to every aspect of the case, particularly those favorable to the defendant, but other instructions given did, and all the instructions given must be taken together, certainly in so far as they have reference to and bearing upon each other. If a party asks for and special instructions are given that present certain aspects of the case distinctively and in a way misleading to the jury, unless qualified, and no qualification is given in some appropriate connection, this would be ground for a new trial. But this is not such a case. The record shows that the court distinctly gave instructions in aspects of the case favorable to the defendant, calling the attention of the jury to the evidence pertinent and bearing upon them. The instructions so given, taken in connection with others given, and the whole taken together, were not in themselves misleading, nor does it appear that they had such effect Indeed, the instructions were clear, fair, and easily understood. There were allegations and evidence that warranted them, and they were properly given.

It is further objected that the court erroneously told the jury that if the plaintiff, in his testimony on the trial, had stated the contract correctly, they should respond to the first issue in the affirmative. We do not think this instruction

was erroneous in any view of it. If the testimony of the plaintiff was true, obviously he was entitled to have possession of his mare, because it went directly to prove the contract as alleged by him and the alleged breaches thereof. We have seen above that, if the contract as alleged was the true one, and the defendant violated the same, he had no right to detain the mare. But it is insisted that it was error to thus make the case turn upon the evidence of the plaintiff himself. It appears that the plaintiff distinctively alleged and testified to one contract and breaches thereof by the defendant, and the latter, quite as distinctively, alleged and testified in his own behalf to another and different contract, favorable to himself. The plaintiff and defendant were the principal witnesses, and testified to the main facts. The other evidence tended more or less to corroborate them. Seeing this, the court told the jury that, if the plaintiff stated the contract correctly, they should answer the first issue in his favor. But almost in the same connection, and substantially in the same words, and with equal clearness, it told them that, if the defendant stated the contract correctly, they should answer the issue favorably to him. These instructions, taken together, as they must be for the present purpose, were true, plain, impartial, easily comprehended and understood. We cannot see that the defendant suffered any prejudice by either of them. They did not prevent the jury from taking any other view of the evidence in part or as a whole. The court had called their attention to and pointed out its bearings upon the various aspects of the case. It appears that it "arrayed the testimony on both sides." As to the fifth assignment of error, there was evidence bearing upon and that fully warranted the seventh instruction complained of, as well as some evidence to the contrary. The instruction left it fairly to the jury to weigh and pass upon the whole evidence pertinent. So far as appears, the instructions were pertinent, clear, fair, and very impartial. We are not at liberty to grant a new trial upon the ground that the jury possibly ought to have rendered a different verdict. The court below alone could set the verdict aside because they found it against the weight of evidence, if they did. We do not mean at all to say that they did or did not. Judgment affirmed.

SPRAGUE v. BOND et al.

(Supreme Court of North Carolina. April 21, 1894.)

SPECIFIC PERFORMANCE — PAROL TRUST — LIMITATIONS.

1. For a nominal consideration plaintiff conveyed to defendant certain lands, in which they were jointly interested. Defendant agreed orally to hold the lands in trust, and that on a sale certain advances made by the parties, respectively, were to be repaid out of the proceeds, and the balance equally divided between them. *Held* that, though no trust in the land could be established by parol, plaintiff could, after a sale by the defendant, enforce the agreement for a division of the proceeds.

2. The statute of limitations does not run until the lands are sold by the defendant.

Appeal from superior court, Caldwell county; HOKE, Judge.

In 1871 and 1872, and thereafter, the plaintiff was engaged in entering lands in Caldwell and Burke counties, N. C., when Henry F. Bond; father of the defendant Louisa N. Bond, said his daughter had some $10,000 in bonds, the money on which would soon be available, and as her agent Henry F. Bond agreed to advance the money necessary to take out certain grants. Plaintiff was to contribute part of the expenses of surveys and certain services in selling said lands, which were to be repaid him; that plaintiff did make outlays and expenditures to the amount of $500 and more, and Henry Bond, as agent of his daughter, the defendant, advanced enough money to perfect and take out grants for 18,000 acres of land, which were taken out in plaintiff's name. Afterwards Henry F. Bond said his daughter would feel safer if the plaintiff would convey the lands to her, and by such conveyance the sale and transfer of the lands would be facilitated, and he requested plaintiff to convey said lands to his daughter, Louisa N. Bond. On such request the plaintiff did, in the latter part of 1875, or January, 1876, convey all of the lands to Louisa N. Bond under a contract and agreement in parol that said Louisa N. Bond should hold the land in trust to sell same, and out of the proceeds pay plaintiff for his services and expenses and pay defendant I ouisa N. Bond the moneys advanced by her agent in procuring the grants, and divide the residue equally between plaintiff and Louisa N. Bond. The land having been sold by the defendant, the plaintiff commenced this suit to enforce a division of the proceeds in accordance with the parol agreement. At the conclusion of the plaintiff's evidence the court intimated that he could not establish the trust claimed by parol evidence in the absence of any allegation of fraud or mistake In defense to this intimation the plaintiff suffered a nonsuit, and appealed.

B. F. Long, M. Silver, W. S. Pearson, and *Avery & Ervin*, for appellant. *S. J. Ervin*, for appellees.

SHEPHERD, J. We entirely concur with the ruling of his honor that the plaintiff could not have established any trust in the lands conveyed to the defendant. This is conceded by the plaintiff's counsel, and it is therefore needless to enter into the consideration of that question. We are of the opinion, however, that upon the pleadings and evidence the plaintiff is entitled to an account of the proceeds of the sale of the land in order to ascertain the amount due him as the consideration of the conveyance, and that he may recover the same. The enforcement of the alleged agreement, after the sale of the land, does not in any respect impinge upon the terms of the conveyance, but relates entirely to the payment of the consideration. It is true that the plaintiff could not have compelled the defendant to execute her agreement to sell the land, as there was no enforceable trust, and the agreement was within the statute of frauds; but this part of the agreement has been voluntarily performed, and the other part, not being within the statute, may now be enforced. The principle is illustrated by the following cases: In Hess v. Fox, 10 Wend. 436, the plaintiff conveyed his equity of redemption to his mortgagee in consideration of the actual cancellation and discharge of the mortgage indebtedness and a promise to sell the land and pay the surplus, if any, to the plaintiff. The land was sold, and, there being a surplus, the plaintiff recovered it in an action of *assumpsit*. SAVAGE, C. J., after stating that the agreement to sell could not have been enforced, said that "no question can arise as to the validity of the agreement to sell; that was performed, and the remaining part was to pay over money supported by the consideration of land conveyed to the promisor." In Massey v. Holland, 3 Ired. 197, the plaintiff, being indebted to the defendant, conveyed certain lands to him upon the understanding that he should sell the same, satisfy his claim, and pay the surplus to the plaintiff. The land was sold and the plaintiff recovered the surplus in an action of *assumpsit*. The defendant objected to the introduction of parol testimony to prove the agreement, but it was held that it was not within the statute, the court remarking that "the plaintiff has not brought his action upon the agreement. He treats the agreement as having been executed, and claims the money which in consequence of that agreement became due to him." See, also, Browne, St. Frauds, § 117. Still more directly in point is the case of Michael v. Foil, 100 N. C. 178, 6 S. E. Rep. 264. There "the contract for the sale of the land was in writing. The land itself was sold; but the agreement that if the mineral interest in the land should be sold during the life-time of the plaintiff he should have one-half of it was not put in writing." The court said: "If the contract of sale was made subject to this agreement as an inducement to the contract the agreement, though in parol, may be enforced. The agreement did not pass, or purport to pass, any interest in the land, and does not fall within the statute of frauds." In addition to the authorities cited in the opinion in the foregoing case we will add the case of Miller v. Kendig, 55 Iowa, 174, 7 N. W. Rep. 500, in which it was held that "a parol agreement by the grantee of land that in case he sells the land for more than the price paid, one-half of the excess shall be paid to the grantor, does not create an interest in real estate within the statute of frauds." The court, after stating that the agreement to sell could not be enforced, proceeds as follows: "The agreement entered into between the parties pertained merely to the purchase price. It was to be at least $1,650, and in a certain contingency more than that. The plaintiff shows that the contingency has happened." It was held that he was entitled to recover. In Trowbridge v. Weatherbee, 11 Allen, 361, it is said that "a parol promise to pay to another a portion of the profits made by a promisor on the purchase and sale of real estate is

not within the statute of frauds, and
may be proved by parol." See, also, Ma-
hagan v. Mead, 63 N. H. 130; Sherrill v.
Hagan, 92 N. C. 345.

We have examined with great care the
cases cited by the defendant's counsel,
but in our opinion they do not shake the
authority of Michael v. Foil, supra, sustained as it is by the general current of
judicial decision. The principle there laid
down is applicable to the present case.
The plaintiff here had the legal title to the
land, and conveyed it upon an apparently
nominal consideration to the defendant.
He testifies that the inducement to the
making of such conveyance was the agreement that the defendant should sell the
land, and when sold he was to be paid for
his services and expenditures, and after
deducting the amount advanced by the
defendant he was to have one-half of the
proceeds of the sale. We think that if the
plaintiff can establish such an agreement
he will be entitled to recover. As the land
was not sold until 1890, the plaintiff's
cause of action did not accrue until then,
and is therefore not barred by the statute
of limitations. This defense was not seriously urged before us. For the reasons
given, we think there should be a new
trial.

GODDIN v. BLAND et al.

(*Supreme Court of Appeals of Virginia.* April
30, 1891.)

EQUITY—JURISDICTION—ACCOUNT.

Where one is employed at a certain
amount per cord to purchase wood to be delivered by the vendors to the purchasing agent's
employers, and the single question in dispute
between such employe and his employers is the
quantity of wood purchased and delivered, there
is no ground for equity jurisdiction, though the
account is a long one, and the delivery of a large
number of lots is disputed.

Appeal from circuit court, King William
county.

J. F. Hubbard, for appellant. Pollard
& Sands, for appellees.

LACY, J. This is an appeal from two decrees of the circuit court of King William
county, rendered, respectively, on the 4th
day of October, 1887, and on the 1st day
of July, 1889. The case is as follows. In
1884, Bland & Bro., residents of King and
Queen county, in Virginia, employed Syl-
vanus Goddin, a resident of the county of
New Kent, in the same state, to purchase
for them poplar cord-wood in the counties
of New Kent, Charles City, James City,
and York, situated in what is known as
the "Peninsula," in this state, lying between the James river and the York river,
and its affluent, the Pamunkey river, at
an agreed price, to be delivered by the vendors thereof to the said Bland & Bro., at
the river and creek landings in that section, on board of vessels and barges to
be there provided by Bland & Bro. to receive the same, Goddin to receive 25 cents
per cord for his compensation for buying
the said wood; the said Bland & Bro., the
appellees, to advance to those persons so
selling them wood, $1.50 to pay for cut-
ting and delivering this wood at the landing, to be paid for in full by the said ap-

v.13s.e.no.5—10

pellees as it should be put on board of the
vessel or barge. A large quantity of wood
was purchased by Goddin for the said appellees,—enough, by his claim, to bring his
compensation up to $1,597.10, at 25 cents
per cord. The appellees not making payment of this claim of Goddin at request,
in June, 1885, the said Goddin brought, in
New Kent county, his action of *assumpsit*
against the said Bland & Bro., to which
action the said defendants pleaded in abatement to the jurisdiction of the court, upon
which issue was joined and a jury sworn
to try the said issue, and the evidence was
partly heard, and the arguments of counsel were partly had, when the defendants
withdrew this plea, and pleaded *non assumpsit*, and issue was joined upon this
plea, and the cause continued. Subsequently, and before final judgment in this
suit at law in New Kent, in the year 1886,
the defendants in that suit brought-their
bill in chancery in the adjoining county of
King William, wherein the foregoing contract for the purchase of cord-wood was
set forth, and the delivery of 2,672¾ cords
of wood is set forth, by which it is admitted that Goddin is entitled to receive
$668.10 as compensation for his services,
whereas he is claiming against the said
Bland & Bro. the larger sum of $1,529.34
on account of his services in buying cord-
wood at 25 cents per cord, and that this
large difference is caused by the act of
Goddin in charging for large quantities
of wood never really delivered; and that
said Goddin should not be allowed to proceed with his said suit at law now pending and undetermined in New Kent county.
(1) because long and intricate accounts
are involved; (2) because he has been paid
$200 for his services, of which he has ren-
dered no account; (3) because it is still
undetermined what amount of wood the
said plaintiffs, Bland & Bro., will have
to account for; and (4) because the case
involves the trial of at least 25 cases of
dispute, and that irreparable mischief will
be done if the common-law action is allowed to proceed, (no discovery is sought,
but answer under oath is waived,) and
that said Goddin be enjoined from prosecuting his suit, etc. The injunction was
awarded, an account ordered and taken,
and a decree made substantially in accordance with the views set forth in the
plaintiff's bill, and Goddin appealed to
this court.

The first ground of error assigned here
is that the bill should have been dismissed
because a court of equity was without
jurisdiction in the premises, the remedy at
law being adequate and ample; that the
ground for relief sought by the bill against
the action pending at law does not come
within any of the recognized heads of
equity jurisdiction, there being neither accident, mistake, forfeiture, mutual or very
complicated accounts, fraud, discovery,
nor trusts. It is true, an account is
prayed for, and it is conceded that the
jurisdiction of equity in matters of account
is among the most comprehensive of those
which it has assumed. Yet it is not
every case of account of which a court of
equity has jurisdiction. As has been said:
Although I run up an account at a store,

my merchant cannot, as a matter of course, sue me before that tribunal; to entitle him to proceed there he must show some ground of interference, such as fraud, the necessity of discovery, complications in accounts, or such like (2 Tuck. Comm. Laws Va. p. 409; Lord Courteney v. Godschall, 9 Ves. 473,) or upon the ground that courts of law cannot give a remedy, or cannot give so complete a remedy, as equit, (Smith v. Marks, 2 Rand., Va., 452.)

In this case the dispute was as to the quantity of wood delivered to the plaintiffs, actually or constructively, pursuant to their contract. The plaintiffs stated it as set forth in their bill; the defendant, Goddin, claimed pay for over six thousand cords of wood purchased pursuant to the contract above referred to. While these figures may be admitted to be large, the question is at least one of fact, to be proved by legal evidence, and involved a single issue. No discovery was sought, and no account was involved which was in any degree complicated, and there were no mutual accounts in dispute, as the plaintiffs had kept and the defendant did not dispute the account of their payments on the account. The simple and single question in dispute was as to the quantity of cord-wood purchased and delivered, actually or constructively, pursuant to the contract. There was no such relation of principal and agent as justified the interference of a court of equity. The account between Goddin and his principal was not in dispute. The mere relation of principal and agent was not sufficient, there being no trust or fiduciary element in the relation here. The relation was and is rather that of employer and employe. And the action of the employe for his hire is properly cognizable in a court of law, and there the plaintiffs could, under the plea of *non assumpsit*, avail of every defense which they have really interposed in their present suit in equity. And, the bill of the plaintiffs should have been dismissed, and the parties left to liquidate their dispute in the pending action at law in the circuit court of New Kent. We have been cited by the learned counsel for the appellants to 3 Pom. Eq. Jur. § 1421; Coffman v. Sangston, 21 Grat. 269; Marvin v. Brooks, 94 N. Y. 76. See, also, Barb. Ch. Pr. 12, 13 Terrell v Dick, 1 Call, 546; Alderson v. Biggars, 4 Hen. & M. 471; Barrett v. Floyd, 3 Call, 531; Campbell v. Rust, 85 Va. 665, 8 S. E. Rep. 664, opinion of RICHARDSON, J., and cases cited; Penn v. Ingles, 82 Va. 65; Tillar v. Cook, 77 Va. 481. The case presents no ground whatever for equitable jurisdiction, and should have been dismissed at the hearing, and the decree of the circuit court of King William, granting the relief prayed for, and perpetually enjoining the defendant, Goddin, from proceeding with his action at law in the circuit court of New Kent, is erroneous, and will be reversed and annulled, and the bill dismissed. But as the case in New Kent, at law, must be tried upon the legal evidence there to be adduced, we will express no opinion upon the merits upon the evidence adduced in this case. And such decree will be rendered here as the said circuit court of King William should have rendered, and the bill of the plaintiffs dismissed, with costs.

THOMAS *et al.* v. SELLMAN *et al.*

(*Supreme Court of Appeals of Virginia.* April 23, 1891.)

EQUITY—PLEADING—MULTIFARIOUSNESS—WIFE AS WITNESS.

1. A bill which alleges that one of the defendants, a judgment debtor, has made various fraudulent transfers to the other defendants, and which seeks to have them set aside, and asks for an injunction and receiver, is not multifarious, having for its single object the subjection of the property of the judgment debtor to the lien of plaintiff's judgment and execution.

2. Where a wife and her husband are both parties to an action, but she alone is interested in the result, she is competent as a witness.

Edward Nichols and *W. W. & B. T. Cramp*, for appellants. *John H. Alexander*, for appellees.

LACY, J. This is an appeal from a decree of the circuit court of Loudoun county, rendered at the October term, 1889. The bill was filed by the appellants, judgment creditors of the appellees, Sellman & Mott, at the March rules, 1889, having for its object to enforce the said judgments against the property of the defendants, by setting aside as fraudulent a sale made by the said Sellman of a half interest in a certain valuable stallion, called "Ramoz," to Virginia L. Mott, as of February 13, 1889, and ascertain and establish the interest of the said Sellman in certain real and personal property described in the bill, and to subject the same to the payment of the said judgments. The bill sets forth the judgments; the failure in business of the debtors, Sellman, Douglas, and A. R. Mott; the sale of their property to satisfy the said debts; that, by reason of preferences and a failure of assets, no creditors would receive anything except near relatives; and that after the sale of the property of the debtor, as was supposed, subsequently one Charles R. Paxton died, and it was disclosed by his papers that the said Sellman was the half owner of a certain thoroughbred stallion, worth $2,000 or $2,500, which he had heretofore pretended to keep as agent only; that this fact of ownership transpiring, the said Sellman forthwith sold the said one-half of the said horse for $720 to his wife's mother, the said Virginia L. Mott; that, in the first place, this sale was a fraud and a pretense, and nothing was actually paid by the said fraudulent grantee, and, in the next place, the consideration was so grossly inadequate as to amount to a fraud. The bill further charges that, prior to the failure of the said firm of Douglas & Sellman, said Sellman and one Henry J. Fadeley were in partnership in farming and dairying, and, as such, owned about 250 acres of land in Loudoun county, Va., with much valuable stock, farming implements, etc., thereon. Said Sellman's share was conveyed to trustees, John H. Alexander and said H. J. Fadeley, who afterwards sold the same as a whole, and said Fadeley was announced the purchaser thereof. Since said sale said Sellman, they are informed, has continued his interest in and oversight of the said property, alleged to have been sold to said Fadeley by said trustees, and they are constrained to believe, from many events brought to their knowledge, that said Sellman has had, and now has, an interest in all said property purchased in the name of said Fadeley from said trustees, and all additions to and increase of the stock, etc., on said land, and such interests and rights of said Sellman in any property standing in the name of said Fadeley is subject to the said judgments and execution liens; and prayed that the defendants be required to answer, (answer under oath being waived;) asked for an injunction to restrain the said Sellman from collecting any debts due him, and that a receiver be appointed to take charge of the said stallion Ramos, and to collect all choses in action of the said Sellman, or in which he may be interested; that Virginia L. Mott be restrained from selling or disposing of the one-half of the horse, and that an account might be taken of all the estate, real and personal, belonging to the defendant, and any choses in action due them, and an account of all liens, and a decree for a sale of the estate, real and personal. Sellman answered, admitting the debts and his failure in business, and alleging his surrender of all of his property to his creditors, and denying that he had any property on which either judgment or execution could be any lien; that he never had any interest in the horse until it was acquired in 1888; that he did not make any pretended or fraudulent sale of the said interest in the said horse; that he sold the said interest to pay for the board of himself, his wife, and his child, which he justly owed to his mother-in-law, who kept a boarding-house; and that he had nothing now but the fruits of his daily labor, of which he should not be deprived by injunction order restraining him from collecting, and restraining his employer from paying to him. Virginia L. Mott answered that the debt was honest, and set forth in detail its history, character, and amount, and shows that the amount paid for one-half of a horse was not insignificant nor inadequate at $720. The injunction was, however, awarded, and, on the motion of Sellman to dissolve the same, it was continued in force temporarily as to all debts or amounts due Sellman over $50 in the aggregate. Depositions were taken to show the ownership of the one-half of the horse, and also to show that Sellman was still interested in the dairy farm; and depositions were taken for the defendants, among them Virginia L. Mott, to which the plaintiffs excepted, because of her husband's interest in the result of the suit. On the 25th day of October, 1889, a decree was rendered, by which it was held that the sale to Mrs. Mott of the one-half interest in the horse was valid, and not fraudulent, and that it was not shown that H. C. Sellman has any interest in the Fadeley land and personal property thereon. The court dismissed the bill as to Virginia L. Mott, H. J. Fadeley, and A. R. Mott, with costs, and referred it to a commissioner to take an account of what collections have been made since August 11, 1888, and to whom; an account of the earnings of the horse Ramos prior to the conveyance to V. L. Mott, and what is due thereon; and to settle an account between H. C. Sellman and C. R. Paxton's executrix, etc.; which report was made and returned, showing a balance due to Sellman of $113.89 of collections, and uncollected debts amounting to $210; which the court confirmed, and decreed the net balance due Sellman to be paid to his creditors, the complainants. From this decree the said complainants appealed to this court.

The appellees insist here, first, that the bill in the circuit court should have been dismissed on the demurrer and answer, because the same is clearly multifarious, and for that reason this appeal should be dismissed. But, according to the decisions of this court, this claim as to the bill is not sustained, and the bill is not multifarious. Its object was to subject the property of the defendant Sellman to the lien of the plaintiffs' judgment and execution. This was the one common object which ran through the whole bill. See Sadler v. Whitehurst, 83 Va. 46, 1 S. E. Rep. 410; Insurance Co. v. Devore, 83 Va. 267, 2 S. E. Rep. 433, and authorities cited; also Nulton v. Isaacs, 30 Grat. 726; Almond v. Wilson, 75 Va. 613, opinion of STAPLES, J.

As to the assignment of error by the appellants, that the circuit court erred in not setting aside the sale to Mrs. Mott, and in not subjecting the interest of Sellman in the dairy farm, it is clear, from an examination of the evidence herein, that no such supposed interest of Sellman was developed by the testimony; and, as to the sale to Mrs. Mott of the one-half of the horse, the consideration was distinctly proved, if Mrs. Mott was a competent witness, and this she clearly was in her own behalf, as interest no longer debars a witness, and her husband, though a party to the suit, had no interest therein, and the wife was not disqualified as a witness by reason of his being a party to the suit. Farley v. Tillar, 81 Va. 279; Hayes v. Association, 76 Va. 228. But it is insisted that, although Virginia L. Mott was a purchaser for valuable consideration, without notice of any lien, yet the executions issued against Sellman were liens on the interest in the horse, prior to and paramount to any right which Sellman could sell or Virginia L. Mott could purchase. But there was no lien under these executions which had never been levied thereon before the return-day thereof. Section 3587 of the Code of Virginia provides that "the lien of a writ of fieri facias under this section, on what is capable of being levied on, but is not levied on under the writ on or before the return-day thereof, shall cease on that day." The sale to Mrs. Mott of the horse appears to have been upon a valuable consideration of unincumbered property, and the other creditors have no valid ground of objection as against Mrs. Mott, who has paid for the property purchased at a price certainly not grossly inadequate, in any view of the question. As far as Sellman is concerned, all of the property belonging to him which was developed by the proceedings herein was paid to the creditors, and the court could not properly have gone further. There appears to be no error in the decree of the circuit court of Loudoun, appealed from here, and the same will be affirmed.

COLEMAN v. SANDS, Registrar.

(Supreme Court of Appeals of Virginia. April 30, 1891.)

ELECTIONS—REGISTRATION—MANDAMUS—OFFICE AND OFFICER—RESIGNATION.

1. Under Code Va. § 83, providing that if any person shall offer to be registered, and shall be rejected by the registrar, he may take an appeal to the court of his county or corporation, or to the judge thereof in vacation, and that on application of such appellant the registrar shall transmit to the court or judge a written statement of the ground relied on by appellant, and the reasons of the registrar for his action, the answer of the registrar that appellant did not offer to qualify as to his right to vote, and that he is not entitled to register, is no defense to an application for *mandamus* to compel him to transmit such statement to the county judge.

2. A registrar of voters cannot legally resign by merely sending his resignation to the clerk of the electoral board, and receiving from him an acknowledgment of its receipt, without an express or implied acceptance thereof by the board.

LACY and RICHARDSON, JJ., dissenting.

Edmund Waddill, Jr., and *Wm. H. Beveridge,* for plaintiff. *Sands, Pollard & Sands* and *Meredith & Cocke,* for defendant.

LEWIS, P. This is a petition for a *mandamus,* filed in the original jurisdiction of the court by George Coleman against William H. Sands, alleged registrar of Shoemaker's election district, in Henrico county. The petition alleges that the petitioner is a legally-qualified voter in the said election district, and that the defendant, Sands, is the registrar for the same district; that on the 2d day of April, 1891, the petitioner presented himself to the defendant, as registrar, and requested to be registered as a voter in said district; that he then stated to the defendant that he was a duly-qualified voter, and entitled to be registered as such in said district, and offered to make a full statement under oath of all the facts required by law to prove that he was entitled to be registered; that the defendant refused to register petitioner, whereupon he, desiring an appeal, applied to the defendant to transmit a written statement to the judge of the county court of Henrico county of the ground relied on by the petitioner, and the reasons of the defendant for his action; that petitioner thereupon appealed to the county judge, and presented his petition, setting forth all the facts, and offered to prove every allegation made by him that was necessary to be proved to show his right to be registered; that the defendant appeared by counsel, and, instead of filing the said written statement, he entered a demurrer to the petition, and declined to file said statement, or to give any reason for his failure to do so. The petition then goes on to further aver that the judge refused to consider the appeal, on the ground that he had not before him the written statement aforesaid, as required by section 83 of the Code, and because he

had no power to compel such statement to be furnished. And the prayer of the petition is that a *mandamus* be awarded by this court to compel the defendant to transmit to the judge of the county court the written statement aforesaid, pursuant to the statute in such case made and provided. To this petition the defendant demurred, and also answered. In his answer he sets up two grounds of defense, viz.: (1) That on the 2d of April, 1891, he was not the registrar for the said election district; and (2) that the petitioner did not on the said 2d day of April, or at any time thereafter, offer to qualify as to his right to vote; and, moreover, that he is not entitled to be registered in the said county. The averment of the answer as to the first point is as follows: "Your respondent states that some time in the month of March, 1891, he qualified as registrar of Shoemaker's precinct in Henrico county, under an appointment of the electoral board of said county, and that, after holding the office for a short time, he, on the morning of the 2d of April, 1891, resigned the same, and herewith files the acknowledgment of the receipt of said resignation by the clerk of the electoral board." To this answer the petitioner demurred. He also filed a general replication, and upon the issue thus joined evidence has been taken. Inasmuch, however, as the questions in controversy may be properly determined on the demurrer, we will consider the case upon the demurrer alone, and in doing so we will consider the points relied on in the answer in the inverse order in which they have just been stated.

The second point, namely, that the defendant did not offer to qualify as to his right to vote, and that he is not entitled to be registered, is clearly not a sufficient answer to the case made by the petition. The question on this branch of the case is not whether the petitioner offered to swear that he was a qualified voter, or whether he is or is not entitled to be registered, but whether the requisitions of the statute in such a case have been complied with. Section 83 of the Code provides that "if any person shall offer to be registered, and shall be rejected by the registrar, he may take an appeal to the court of his county or corporation, or to the judge thereof in vacation;" and by the same section it is made the duty of the registrar, on the application of any person so desiring an appeal, to "transmit to the court having jurisdiction over the said election district, or to the judge thereof, a written statement of the ground relied on by the appellant, and the reasons of the registrar for his action." There is no averment in the answer that an opportunity was given the petitioner to take the oath required by section 75 of the Code of every person before being registered; and, if such opportunity had been given and the petitioner declined to take the oath, that would be no just ground for the refusal of the defendant, if, as the petitioner alleges, he was the duly-qualified registrar for Shoemaker's election district at the time, to transmit the reasons for his action, as required by section 83, above alluded to. When such a statement as is required by that section is transmitted, it is for the court or judge, as the case may be, to determine whether or not the appellant is entitled to be registered. But no such question, we repeat, is presented for our consideration. The object of this proceeding is to compel the defendant to transmit a statement to the county judge, giving the reasons for his action in refusing to register the petitioner, to enable the judge to decide whether that action was right or not. Without the required statement, that question cannot be determined, and the proper tribunal to determine it is the county court in term-time, or the judge thereof in vacation.

Then the next, and only other real, question is, was the defendant in office when the application to him was made by the petitioner? or, in other words, had his resignation at that time become complete? In his answer he states that he resigned on the 2d day of April, 1891. But he does not stop there. He goes on to aver how, as he supposes, his resignation was effected; and the averment is that on that day he tendered his resignation, the receipt of which was acknowledged in writing by the clerk of the electoral board. It is not stated, however, that the resignation has ever been acted on by the board, either by formally accepting it, or by appointing a successor. He relies simply on the tender of the resignation and the acknowledgment of its receipt. The question therefore is, did that amount to a deposition of his office as registrar? After a careful consideration of the case we are of opinion that it did not. At the present day, in this country, when, as is commonly said, the man oftener seeks the office than the office the man, especially if it be an office of honor and emolument, to question the proposition that a person in office may resign at pleasure seems, at first blush, perhaps, a little strange, if not absurd. But, be that as it may, in the absence of any controlling statute on the subject, and we are aware of none, such is not the law of this case. The resignation of a public local office is by no means in all cases a matter of right. Such an office is ordinarily held, not at the will of either party, but at the will of both. And a registrar is not only a public officer, but one upon whom, in the administration of the government, most important and essential duties are imposed. He is required, moreover, to take the same oath of office as is prescribed for officers of the state generally. Code, § 76. At common law to refuse to serve in a municipal office connected with local administration, when elected or appointed thereto, was a punishable offense, of which numerous illustrations are to be found in the books. Thus in Rex v. Burder, 4 Term R. 778, the defendant was indicted for that, having been appointed to the office of overseer of the poor, he unlawfully refused to execute the office, and the indictment was sustained. So in Rex v. Lone, 2 Strange, 920, which was an indictment for not taking the office of constable, it was moved, after verdict, in arrest of judgment, that the

offense charged was not indictable; but the motion was overruled, and the conviction held good. The same principle was recognised in Rex v. Bower, 1 Barn. & C. 585. That was an application for a mandamus to compel the defendant to take upon himself the office of common councilman in the borough of Lancaster, and the defense was that by a by-law persons refusing to fill the office were subject to a certain fine, which the defendant had paid. But the return was held insufficient, as it did not state that the fine was to be in lieu of service. The court said: "It is an offense at common law to refuse to serve an office when duly elected. The by-law in this case does not say that the party paying the fine shall be exempt from serving the office, or that the fine is to be in lieu of service. As that is not declared in the by-law, we cannot say that the payment shall have any such operation." A peremptory mandamus was accordingly awarded. Whether, in view of the statute, now carried into section 69 of the Code, which empowers the electoral board, and makes it its duty, to declare vacant and to fill the office of any registrar who fails to qualify within 30 days after his appointment, an indictment would be sustainable in Virginia for a refusal to take the office of registrar, it is not necessary, for the purposes of the present case, to inquire, for here there has been no refusal to qualify, and the question is whether the defendant has legally resigned. In other words, the question is narrowed down by the record to this: Can a registrar resign at pleasure, without any acceptance, express or implied, of the resignation by the proper authority, to-wit, the electoral board of his city or county?

That an office is vacated by resignation no one will deny. But the question arises, what constitutes a resignation,—i. e., a completed resignation? Bouvier, in his Law Dictionary, after giving the definition of the term "resignation," adds these words: "As offices are held at the will of both parties, if the resignation of an officer be not accepted he remains in office;" and for this he cites the case of Hoke v. Henderson, 4 Dev. 1. In that case the opinion, which is a very able one, was delivered by Chief Justice RUFFIN, who, among other things, said: "An officer may certainly resign, but without acceptance his resignation is nothing, and he remains in office. It is not true that an office is held at the will of either party. It is held at the will of both. Generally resignations are accepted, and that has been so much a matter of course with respect to lucrative offices as to have grown into a common notion that to resign is a matter of right. But it is otherwise. The public has a right to the services of all the citizens, and may demand them in all civil departments as well as in the military. Hence there are in our statute-book several acts to compel men to serve in offices. Every man is obliged, upon a general principle, after entering upon office, to discharge the duties of it while he continues in office; and he cannot lay it down until the public, or those to whom the authority is confided, are satisfied that the office is in a proper state to be left, and the officer is discharged. The obligation is therefore strictly mutual, and neither party can forcibly violate it." Judge Dillon, speaking of the resignation of municipal officers, lays down the same doctrine. He says: "An office must be resigned either expressly or by implication. If the charter prescribes the mode in which the resignation is to be made, that mode should, of course, be complied with. Acceptance by the corporation is, at common law, necessary to a consummation of the resignation, and until acceptance by proper authority the tender or offer to resign is revocable." 1 Dill. Mun. Corp. § 163. We find this subject very fully and luminously discussed by Mr. Justice BRADLEY in delivering the opinion of the court in Edwards v U. S., 103 U. S. 471. That was an application for a *mandamus* against Edwards, as a township supervisor in the state of Michigan, to have a judgment previously recovered by the relator against the township audited and paid. The defendant answered that he had resigned his office in a written communication addressed to the township board, a copy of which he exhibited with his answer. It did not appear, however, that the resignation had been acted on, and it was therefore held not complete. In the course of the opinion it was said: "As civil officers are appointed for the purpose of exercising the functions and carrying on the operations of government, and maintaining public order, a political organization would seem to be imperfect which should allow the depositaries of its power to throw off their responsibilities at their own pleasure. This certainly was not the doctrine of the common law   In England a person elected to a municipal office was obliged to accept it and perform its duties, and be subjected himself to a penalty by refusal. An office was regarded as a burden which the appointee was bound, in the interest of the community and of good government, to bear; and from this it followed of course that, after an office was conferred and assumed, it could not be laid down without the consent of the appointing power. This was required in order that the public interests might suffer no inconvenience for the want of public servants to execute the laws. This acceptance," it was added, "may be manifested either by a formal declaration or by the appointment of a successor"   The court then went into an examination of the Michigan statutes, including one which provides that every office shall become vacant by "resignation," and continues as follows: "But it is nowhere declared when a resignation shall become complete. This is left to be determined upon general principles; and, in view of the manifest spirit and intent of the laws above cited, it seems to us apparent that the common-law requirement, namely, that a resignation must be accepted before it can be regarded as complete, was not intended to be abrogated. To hold it to be abrogated would enable every office holder to throw off his official character at will, and leave the community unprotected. We do not think that

this was the intent of the law." Many other authorities to the same effect might be cited, but we deem a citation of them unnecessary.

On the other hand, the defendant relies upon several cases, the first of which is Amy v. Watertown, 130 U. S. 301, 9 Sup. Ct. Rep. 530. But that case, as the court said in its opinion, is clearly distinguishable from the Edwards Case and other cases of that class. That was an action against the city of Watertown, and the principal question was whether process in the action had been duly served   The charter of the city required service in such cases to be had on the mayor, and also provided that "the resignation of the mayor shall be in writing, directed to the common council or city clerk, and filed with the clerk, and shall take effect at the time of filing the same." The mayor resigned, before the commencement of the action, by complying with this provision, and it was held that his resignation became complete upon being filed, and, consequently, that there had been no valid service of process. It would be an idle waste of time to say more to show that that case is no authority for the position taken by the defendant in the present case. The next case is U. S. v. Wright, 1 McLean, 509, which was a *nisi prius* decision of Mr. Justice McLEAN, and in which the resignation of a United States revenue officer was a subject of consideration. In the opinion it was said: "There can be no doubt that a civil officer has a right to resign his office at pleasure, and it is not in the power of the executive to compel him to remain in office." This is certainly a very broad statement of the doctrine, and, if correct as a universal proposition, would be decisive of the present case. But of that case we need only say (1) that it was virtually overruled by the supreme court in the Edwards Case; and (2) that the doctrine there announced has no application to officers who are chosen to carry on local government. Such was the comment upon the case by the supreme court of New Jersey in State v. Ferguson, 31 N. J. Law, 107, which remark was quoted with approval in the Edwards Case. And the same comment may be made with equal propriety upon Bunting v. Willis, 27 Grat. 144, which was decided before the Edwards Case, and in which MONCURE, P., referring to the resignation by the plaintiff in error of the office of United States deputy collector of customs, observed in language very similar to that of Mr. Justice McLEAN in the Wright Case that "he had a right to resign his federal office, and that such right does not depend upon the consent or acceptance of the government." It is observable, moreover, that, notwithstanding this broad language, the decision of the case, if we correctly understand it, proceeded on the ground that not until acceptance did the resignation become complete. That was the case of the election of a person, holding a federal office at the time, to the office of sheriff for the term commencing on the 1st of July then next ensuing. He tendered his resignation of the former office on the 19th of June, to take effect on the 30th. On the 1st day of

July he performed an official act as deputy-collector, by completing the clearance of a vessel, and on the next day he was relieved, and the office turned over to another, which was the first manifestation of an acceptance of the resignation; and this court held that not until then did he cease to hold the office. Although the resignation was tendered to take effect on the 30th of June, said the court, "it was not accepted until after that time." It was consequently held that by continuing in the federal office after the 1st of July the office of sheriff was vacated. It is obvious, to say the least, that the case is not an authority against the views we have expressed. In Pace v. People, 50 Ill. 432, also relied upon, which was the case of the resignation of a school superintendent, there was in fact an acceptance of the resignation, and therefore, as the court held, the same became complete upon its being tendered. In People v. Porter, 6 Cal. 26, it was decided by a divided court, and chiefly on the authority of the case in 1 McLean, that the resignation of an office is effectual without acceptance; and following those cases is State v. Fitts, 49 Ala. 402. To the same effect, also, is State v. Hauss, 43 Ind. 105. We have examined these cases, and are unable to yield our assent to them. They do not, in our opinion, state correctly the true principle of the common law, and are, moreover, in conflict with the great weight of authority, as we think we have already shown. Our conclusion, therefore, is that there has not been such a completed resignation on the part of the defendant as to amount to a deposition of his office as registrar, and that a *mandamus* must be awarded, as prayed for in the petition.

LACY, J., (*dissenting.*) This is upon an application by George Coleman, the petitioner, for the peremptory writ of *mandamus* to compel W. H. Sands, the respondent, to transmit to the county court of Henrico a written statement of the grounds relied on by the said petitioner to register as a voter, alleging that the respondent is a registrar of voters in the registration district in question, and that said certificate is required by law. The respondent answers that he is not now, and was not at the time application was made to him for said certificate, a registrar of voters in said district; that he had held such office, but had resigned the same unreservedly before the application was made to him for the certificate in question, and that petitioner was informed of the fact that he had resigned the said office, and was no longer authorized by law to discharge the functions of said office; that he was appointed by the electoral board of the county, as prescribed by law, and had delivered his resignation in writing to the said appointing power, through its clerk. It is set forth therein also that whereas, by law, it is provided that each registrar shall annually on the second Tuesday in May, at his voting place, proceed to register the names of all qualified voters within his election district, not previously registered, who shall apply to be registered, commencing at sunrise

and ending at sunset, (section 78, Code Va.;) and although he had notified all persons manifesting an interest in the subject that on that day all would be added to the list who were entitled to be,—that yet, as the law authorized a registrar to register applicants entitled to vote at any time previous to regular elections, numerous persons applied to him at his house at night in such manner, and with such insistence, that he had been unwilling to hold the said office, and had unconditionally resigned it. To this answer the petitioner demurred, and upon consideration of the issue thus raised I am of opinion that the answer is sufficient in law, and is indeed a complete answer to the petition, and that the same should be dismissed, and the writ of *mandamus* denied, because the respondent is not a registrar, but is out of office, and cannot lawfully perform any duty appertaining to it. In Virginia an unconditional resignation of an office is a termination of an office *proprio vigore.* I find all the books agreed upon this proposition, and I have not found anything to the contrary. Mr. Minor, in his Institutes, (volume 2, p. 26,) says: "The grounds on which offices may be determined. The circumstances which may lead to offices being determined may be enumerated as follows: (1) Resignation, expiration of term, and removal from office by competent authority." And again he says on the following page, (29:) "Mode of effecting the removal from office of one on the grounds above named. Resignation, expiration of term, and removal by competent authority, of course, terminate the office *proprio vigore.* But in the other cases of delinquency the office is not determined, *ipso facto,* by the occurrence of the cause. There must be a judgment of a motion," etc. This must be so, under our constitution and laws, which everywhere recognise and provide for vacancies in office created by resignation or otherwise; and Mr. Minor is clearly right in this view, because, if an incumbent has resigned beyond recall, he cannot again rehabilitate himself with the office; and when the resignation is accepted, which it may be either expressly or by implication, the resignation is effective, if peremptory, from its date.

This language of Mr. Minor has been adopted by this court more than once, and is by the decisions of this court the settled law upon this subject in this state. In the case in this court known as the "Bland & Giles Co. Judge Case," reported in 33 Grat. 443, it was said: "An office is terminated *proprio vigore* by resignation, expiration of term, and removal by competent authority. But in other cases the office is not determined, *ipso facto,* by the occurrence of the cause. There must be a judgment of a motion," etc.; citing 2 Minor, Inst. 322, and authorities there cited, one of which is 7 Tuck. (Amer. Ed.) p. 11, where the same doctrine is found. Judge TUCKER says: "It remains to remark that offices may be terminated by resignation, or the acceptance of an incompatible office, even though it be inferior, (Milward v. Thatcher, 2 Term R. 81; King v. Godwin, 1 Doug. 398,) or be remote," etc. Adding:

"Offices may be forfeited by misconduct or neglect, etc.; but this can only be by the judgment of a court, I apprehend, in Virginia. * * * I am not aware of any decision as to the necessity of a judgment of a motion when an office has been for feited by removal, or an incompatible office." It will be observed that the learned commentator seems to regard the case, as Mr. Minor, as obviously a matter of course. Again, in the case of Johnson v. Mann, reported in 77 Va. 265, Judge RICHARDSON, speaking of a case of expiration of term, says in delivering the unanimous opinion of this court, all the judges concurring as the court is at present constituted: "Again, in the Bland & Giles Co. Judge Case, 33 Grat. 450, Judge CHRISTIAN, in delivering the opinion of this court, in speaking of the tenure of office of a county judge, says: 'An office is terminated *proprio vigore* by resignation, expiration of term, and removal by competent authority.'" And again, in the same case, in construing a section of the Pennsylvania constitution which is as follows: "They [certain officers, including the one then in question] shall hold their offices for three years if they shall so long behave themselves well, and until their successor shall be duly qualified,"—it is said: "The obvious meaning of this provision is that such officers cannot hold for less than three years, if they so long behave well, and choose not to resign, although, on the happening of certain contingencies, they may hold for a longer period." The language relied on by the petitioner in the law, that this officer shall hold for a stated term, and until his successor is qualified, refers, I think, to a definition of "term" and "tenure." Where there had been no vacancy created in the office except by expiration of term, the end and object is enabling only.

This language has been under review here in several cases. In the case of Johnson v. Mann, supra, and in the case of Kilpatrick v. Smith, 77 Va. 358, Judge RICHARDSON says: "The twenty-fifth section of article six of the constitution is in its nature enabling. It empowers judges and all other officers elected and appointed to continue to discharge the duties of their offices after their terms of service have expired, until their successors have been qualified; no longer. * * * The clause in question in our constitution does not extend the term, but simply enables the incumbent to hold over until his successor, whether elected or appointed, is chosen in the way prescribed by law." And I think this language cannot be correctly used to do more than to enable an officer to discharge the duties, when his term has ended by expiration of the time for which he was chosen. It is not intended to compel a citizen to hold an office against his will, and after he has chosen to resign. It was intended to enable the incumbent to hold for that time, (to use the language of the unanimous opinion of this court, cited above,) unless he chose sooner to resign. There are other decisions of this court to the same effect on both propositions, but it is not necessary to further cite them.

I do not concur in the argument that the authority granted by sections 67, 69, and 84 of the Code of Virginia is intended to and does compel an officer to hold for the full term, and afterwards, whether he wishes to or not. They mean, as this court has said, that he may do so unless "he choose sooner to resign;" and he may resign during the term, if he chooses to do so, and thus create a vacancy. But the argument is that the supreme court of the United States has held in certain cases, erroneously cited as Badger v. U. S., (Badger v. Bolles,) 93 U. S. 599; Solomaka v. U. S., (Salamanca Tp. v. Wilson, 3 Sup. Ct. Rep. 344,) that an officer cannot resign when he chooses, and thus throw off his responsibilities to the public, etc., and especially that Justice BRADLEY has said so in Edwards v. U. S., 103 U. S. 471. Without pausing to myself explain or construe these cases, I will leave that where it is so well done by that learned justice himself in the later case of Amy v. Watertown, 130 U. S. 315, 319, 9 Sup. Ct. Rep. 580, merely remarking that in the case of Edwards v. U. S., supra, the justice says: "In this country, where offices of emolument and honor are commonly more eagerly sought after than shunned, a contrary doctrine (that is, contrary to the common law) with regard to such offices, and in some states with regard to offices in general, may have obtained, but we must presume that the common-law rule prevails, unless the contrary is shown;" and he goes on to show that in that state (Michigan) the common-law rule has been adopted by statute, and cites a law of that state where, if an officer declines to accept an office, and does not qualify within 10 days, he is fined $10. Of course, when acceptance of an office is made compulsory by the penal laws, and resignation is restricted by law, the question is distinguishable from this. But I have said that I would cite this learned justice in Amy v. Watertown, decided in 1889. In that case, speaking of an officer who had resigned, he said: "There was no mayor in office at the time. The last mayor had resigned, and his resignation had taken effect. Service on him was of no more avail than service on an entire stranger. The case is different from those in which we have held that a resignation of an officer did not take effect until it was accepted or until another was appointed. In these cases either the common law prevailed, or the local law provided for the case, and prevented a vacancy. Such were the cases of Badger v. U. S., 93 U. S. 599, and Edwards v. U. S., 103 U. S. 471, and Salamanca Tp. v. Wilson, 109 U. S. 627, 3 Sup. Ct. Rep. 344. "In the present case," further says the learned justice, "it is true the consolidated charter of the city of Watertown provides that 'all elective officers except aldermen shall, unless otherwise provided, hold their respective offices for one year, and until their successors are elected and qualified.' But that provision has respect to ordinary cases. It cannot apply in case of death, and does not apply in case of resignation." And it goes on to show that this resignation was to take effect by the state law from the time it was filed. And it appears that this case, like the others, proceeds upon a consideration of the law of the state where the case arose in accordance with the act of congress of June 1, 1872, (Rev. St. U. S. § 914,) since the passage of which act the practice and pleadings and forms and modes of proceeding must conform to the state law and the practice of the state courts.

In this case, therefore, if the supreme court of the United States were considering this question, the said court, in view of the foregoing decisions of this court, would, I think, decide this question as I have urged that it should be decided, and I do not find anything in that court to the contrary. We have been referred to numerous other authorities by the learned counsel for the respondent; among the cases in this court, of Bunting v. Willis, 27 Grat. 155, where MONCURE, P., speaking for this court, said, as to an officer who had resigned a federal office in Virginia: "That he had a right to resign his federal office, and that such right does not depend upon the consent or acceptance of the government or its agents, seems to be well settled. That after such a resignation becomes complete it cannot be withdrawn by the officer, even with the consent of the government, seems also to be settled, though he may receive a new appointment, which may perhaps be given to him in the form of a withdrawal by consent of his resignation of his former office." Further citations are not necessary, I think. It is clear to me that Mr. Sands, the registrar, is out of office, and is no longer capable or able to do the act required of him, and that the writ should be denied.

RICHARDSON, J., concurs.

BRUCE v. JOHN L. ROPER LUMBER CO.

(Supreme Court of Appeals of Virginia. Jan. 29, 1891.)

CUTTING TIMBER — INJUNCTION — WRITTEN CONTRACT — PAROL EVIDENCE — RIGHTS OF STRANGER.

1. Where defendant obtained a license from a land company to cut timber from its land, knowing at the time the superior rights of plaintiff lumber company, and such license is revoked, defendant will be enjoined from further cutting and removing lumber.

2. Plaintiff, being a stranger to the contract between defendant and the land company, may by parol evidence show the true meaning and scope thereof.

E. E. Holland and *S. D. Davies,* for appellant. *White & Garnett* and *Geo. McIntosh,* for appellee.

HINTON, J. This is a controversy between the appellant and appellee as to the right of the former to cut timber in that part of the Dismal swamp which, from its proximity to Suffolk, is known as the "Suffolk Side" of the swamp. The appeal is taken from a decree of the circuit court of Nansemond county, which perpetuates the injunction previously awarded, and allows the defendant, Bruce, "to remove from the lands in the bill and proceedings mentioned all the timber which he had cut thereon prior to the 14th day of August, 1886, that being the date on which he received notice from the Dismal Swamp Land Company to cease cutting on said lands. * * *" This decree, we think, after repeated and careful examinations of the record, and the able argument presented for the appellant, should be sustained; because we are satisfied that, no matter what may be the rights, if any, of the said Bruce, under his contract, to cut "down and refuse lumber," those rights were to be taken in subordination to the rights of the John L. Roper Lumber Company, and never were intended to extend to the cutting of the juniper and cypress lumber, except as a subcontractor of that company. Without going into a detailed statement of all the testimony upon these points, we think it sufficient to say all this fully appears, not only from the testimony of Loyall, Herring, and Roper, but from the testimony and acts of Bruce as well; for, after having waited some time, according to his own admission, to find out from Roper's own lips what were the rights of John L. Roper Lumber Company, and whether they had been surrendered so far as the Suffolk side of the swamp, thus impliedly admitting that, whatever those rights were, he knew that they were superior to his own, he nevertheless, without having seen Roper, went on and entered into the contract with Loyall, president of the Dismal Swamp Land Company, and commenced to cut timber, both dead and growing, under it. In answer to the thirty-third question, which is in these words: "Then you knew, both in person and by letter, from the president of the Lumber Company, that he declined to let you cut juniper and cypress timber, and you say that at your second interview Mr. Roper told you that he had a contract for all the juniper on the company's land, and that Mr. Loyall had no right to contract with me, you, or any one else. Is that so?"—he says: "Yes, sir;" thus showing in the clearest manner, as we have said before, that, although he was aware of the superior rights of the lumber company, he went on and acted in defiance of them. The court is also of opinion that, although neither Bruce nor the Dismal Swamp Land Company can be allowed, as between themselves, to introduce testimony to contradict the contract made between them, it is competent for the lumber company, a stranger to said contract, to show what was the true meaning and scope of that contract. "The rule," says Mr. Greenleaf, excluding parol proof in such cases, "is applied only [in suits] between the parties to the instrument. * * * It cannot affect third parties, who, if it were otherwise, might be prejudiced by things recited in the writings contrary to the truth, through the ignorance, carelessness, or fraud of the parties, and who, therefore, ought not to be precluded from proving the truth, however contradictory to the written statement of others." 1 Green. Ev. § 279, and cases there cited, and in Barreda v. Silsbee, 21 How. 169. And the court is further of opinion that that contract, when viewed in the light of the surrounding circumstances, amounts to a license, revocable at the will of the Dismal Swamp Land Company, and that the same was revoked on the 14th day of August, 1886, by the notice sent to them on that day. Entertaining these views as to the facts, we only deem it necessary to add that we concur in the decree entered by the lower court, and that the same must be affirmed.

SNELLING v. STATE.

(*Supreme Court of Georgia.* April 24, 1891.)

MURDER—EVIDENCE—RESISTING ARREST.

Deceased and others had come to defendant's house to arrest him for a felony committed in that county, and for which he had been indicted three years before. When they ordered the door opened, the only response was from a little girl that nobody was in there. Deceased then entered, saw defendant, and told him to get up and consider himself under arrest. He did not, however, announce that he was an officer. *Held* that, as by Code Ga. § 4724, a private person may arrest one who has committed a felony, and is escaping or attempting to escape, and defendant knew deceased's purpose, his killing deceased, by resisting and shooting him, constituted murder.

Error from superior court, Randolph county; LUMPKIN, Judge.

Jesse Walters and *Harrison & Peeples,* for plaintiff in error. *J. M. Griggs,* Sol. Gen., for the State.

CLARKE, Special Judge. At a special term of Randolph superior court held in July, 1890, Sam Snelling, the plaintiff in error, was convicted of the murder of Ed Skipper. He moved for a new trial, setting forth as the only grounds of such motion that the verdict was contrary to the evidence and contrary to the law. The motion was denied, and its denial is the error here assigned. The evidence introduced by the prosecution was substantially as follows: In 1884 a bench-warrant was issued from the superior court of Randolph county for the arrest of said Snelling for murder, he having been indicted in that court for such offense. On May 17, 1887, the sheriff placed this warrant in the hands of the deceased, for the purpose of execution. He is mentioned in the evidence as "a bailiff of the county," "officer of the justice court here," "arresting officer," and jailer of the county. Shortly after 9 o'clock in the morning of that day Skipper left Cuthbert to make the arrest, being accompanied by Joe Standley and N A. Burge. Their interest in the matter was to secure a reward which had been offered for the apprehension of Snelling. These men were all armed, Skipper and Burge each having a double-barrel shotgun, and Standley a Winchester rifle. Skipper took one route for the house where Snelling was supposed to be, and Standley and Burge another. The three met at the house. This was simply a single room, with a front and rear door, and a window in one end. The house was "pretty high" above the ground, and steps led up to the front door, which opened towards the inside. Skipper took position at the front door, Burge at the rear door, and Standley at a corner which commanded a view both of the front door

and window. Skipper three times ordered that the door be opened. The only response was from a little girl, who said there was "nobody in there." He then caught hold of the door knob, turned it, and pushed, and the door flew open. After the door opened he entered the house, and said to Snelling: "Get up, and consider yourself under arrest." When these words were spoken, Snelling fired a pistol at Skipper, the ball of which entered his stomach. Standley then ran to the door, and sprang into the house. As he did so, the pistol was fired a second time, and Snelling and Skipper then had hold of each other. The latter's gun was on the floor, with the barrel pointing to the door. Skipper cried: "Help, he has killed me!" Standley made an ineffectual effort to use his gun, when Snelling fired at him, shooting him in the shoulder. This disabled Standley so that his gun fell to the floor. It fired as it fell. Snelling then shot at Standley a second time, inflicting another wound, and then again, the last time missing his aim. Standley was still unable to discharge his gun, though "he cocked it once or twice, and snapped it." Snelling was still "snapping" his pistol at Standley. He turned to the door, and let himself down. Here Burge came up, and some dozen words were exchanged between him and Standley. About this time Skipper fell backwards out of the door. At the same time Snelling leaped through the door, and fled. Skipper neither spoke nor moved after he fell. He expired in five minutes. Upon examination it appeared that his gun had not been fired. When the shooting occurred, the only person in the house besides the three men was a negro girl about nine or ten years old. No evidence was tendered on the part of the defendant. He made a statement, which was, in substance, that on the occasion in question he was asleep in his wife's house; that the noise of some one breaking into the house awoke him; that the first thing he saw was a man in the house presenting a gun at him; that he thereupon shot at the man; that the man again presented the gun, and defendant again shot; that about this time another man entered with a gun; that neither of the men said anything to him; and that what he did was for his own protection. He mentioned further that he did not know how many shots he fired, and that he escaped after he had fired the last one. The state having introduced a witness who testified that defendant had told him that Skipper had shot him (defendant) with a double-barrel shotgun, before he fired at all, defendant made a supplemental statement, in which he said that he was shot in the difficulty, and with buckshot, and pointed out to the jury the place where he was struck. Under the evidence, the most favorable view of the case for the defendant is that he killed a private citizen who was attempting to arrest him for the commission of a felony. This view may well be taken, for the officer did not disclose his character as such, and did not exhibit or mention the warrant which he had. Supposing the facts to be thus, is there anything to relieve the defendant of the guilt of murder? We think not. A private person had a legal right to make the arrest. "If the offense is a felony, and the offender is escaping, or attempting to escape, a private person may arrest him upon reasonable and probable grounds of suspicion." Code, § 4724. This defendant's offense was a felony, for which he had been indicted three years before. Nor could he shield himself from the effect of the situation by a claim that he acted in ignorance of the purpose of the person attempting the arrest. This purpose was distinctly announced by the first and only words which were addressed to him by the deceased. This evidence cannot be overcome, and needs no support. If it needed aid, it could well receive it from the circumstances of the defendant when the killing occurred. He was in the county where the felony had been perpetrated, and there as a fugitive from justice. He must have apprehended the very thing which occurred, and might reasonably have supposed the attack on his home to have been made with that design. It is easy to believe that he did at once realize the intention of the arresting party. The response of the little girl to the demand for admission to the house is significant in this connection. The state of preparation in which he was found, and the promptness and vigor with which he availed himself of such preparation, mean much in explaining the state of his mind. If, then, Skipper, as a private citizen, had authority to apprehend the defendant, and the defendant knew that Skipper's purpose was to arrest him, it was, of course, his duty to submit. The law would not tolerate in him any form or degree of resistance, and most certainly we cannot discover the slightest excuse for the sanguinary and fatal resistance to which he did resort. The following decisions of this court were cited by counsel for defendant, to wit: O'Connor v. State, 64 Ga. 125; Phillips v. State, 66 Ga. 755; Davis v. State, 79 Ga. 767, 4 S. E. Rep. 318, and Croom v. State, 85 Ga. 718, 11 S. E. Rep. 1035. We have examined in full each one of these cases, and fail to find any adjudication at variance with this opinion. Indeed, the one last named states more strongly and clearly than the writer can the doctrines upon which we rest the present decision. Judgment affirmed.

LUMPKIN, J., being disqualified in this case, Hon MARSHALL J. CLARKE, judge of the superior courts of Atlanta circuit, was designated by the governor, and presided.

BENTLEY v. FINCH et al.

(Supreme Court of Georgia. March 16, 1891.)

DEFAULT JUDGMENT—VACATING.

Where, in an action on an unconditional contract in writing, no plea on the part of the defense is filed, and counsel's name is not marked upon the docket, a request by one of defendants to the clerk to mark the name of counsel on the docket, and the fact that such counsel was a member of the legislature in session when the case was called, are not sufficient grounds for setting aside the judgment, under the rule requiring counsel to file his pleas at the first term

of court, and to mark or have marked his name on the docket.

Error from superior court, Brooks county; ALEXANDER, Judge.

Daniel Rountree, for plaintiff in error.
W. S. Humphreys, for defendants in error.

SIMMONS, J. We think the court erred, under the facts of this case, in setting aside the judgment. There was no plea filed, the name of counsel was not marked upon the docket, nor was the attention of the court called to the fact that the absent counsel was employed in the case or expected to appear in the same. When counsel is employed in a case, especially in defense of a suit on an unconditional contract in writing, it is his duty to file his pleas at the first term of the court, and to mark, or have marked, his name upon the docket. When this is not done, it is the duty of the court to award judgment without a jury in the case. This case was doubtless called in its order, and no plea having been filed, and counsel's name not having been marked upon the docket, the court entered judgment thereon. We do not think the defendants in the court below made a sufficient showing to authorize the judge to set aside a solemn judgment made at a former term of the court. The fact that one of the defendants requested the clerk to mark the name of his counsel on the docket is not sufficient. The fact that counsel was a member of the legislature, which was then in session, is not sufficient. The fact that the defendants now say they have a meritorious defense is not sufficient. Defendants had more than six months within which to inform the court of this defense, and failed to do it in the manner prescribed by law. They, or their counsel, should have seen that such defense was filed. The least they could have done would have been to mark the name of their counsel on the docket, so as to inform the judge that there was a defense to the suit. Not having done this, and showing no sufficient reason for setting the judgment aside, the trial judge erred in granting the motion. Phillips v. Taber, 83 Ga. 565, 10 S. E. Rep. 270; McDaniel v. McLendon, 85 Ga. 614, 11 S. E. Rep. 869. Judgment reversed.

MEADOWS et al. v. TAYLOR et al.

(Supreme Court of Georgia. March 16, 1891.)

CERTIORARI TO ORDINARY—ADOPTION OF STOCK LAW.

The statute providing for elections respecting fences and stock law in and for a single militia district makes no provision for a counter-petition, or for any contest or hearing before the ordinary; and the ordinary's action upon such a petition is ministerial, and *certiorari* will not lie to correct any error or mistake in his conduct. Affirming 10 S. E. Rep. 204.

Error from superior court, Pulaski county; ROBERTS, Judge.

The official report is as follows: The exception in this case is to the ruling of the court below dismissing a *certiorari* on the ground that *certiorari* would not lie to the ministerial act of an ordinary in opening the returns of a "stock law" election for a militia district, and proclaiming the result, over the objections of the plaintiffs in *certiorari*, made before the returns were opened and result declared; and in holding that this question would not be affected by the fact that, at the time of the election and consolidation of the votes, a bill of exceptions was pending in the supreme court to a refusal of the judge of the superior court to sustain a *certiorari*, brought by the same plaintiffs to the action of the ordinary in refusing to sustain their *caveat* to the petition for the election, and in ordering the election. The case made by the bill of exceptions last referred to was heard by this court at its March term, 1889, and will be found reported in 82 Ga. 738, 10 S. E. Rep. 204. The ruling of the court below was affirmed.

Martin & Smith, for plaintiffs in error. *Jordan & Watson*, for defendants in error.

SIMMONS, J. Under the facts as they appear in this record, the court did not err in dismissing the *certiorari*. Judgment affirmed.

SAVANNAH, F. & W. R. CO. v. WATSON.

(Supreme Court of Georgia. March 16, 1891.)

AMENDMENT OF PLEADINGS.

Under Code Ga. § 3479, providing that plaintiff or defendant, in any court except the supreme court, whether at law or in equity, may, at any stage of the case, amend the pleadings in all respects, it is reversible error to refuse an amendment to defendant's plea of the general issue, by filing a plea of the statute of limitations after the cause has been submitted, and the jury have retired, and been out all night.

Error from superior court, Decatur county; BOWER, Judge.

D. A. Russell, for plaintiff in error. *Donalson & Hawes*, for defendant in error.

SIMMONS, J. The jury had been charged with this case, and had retired to their room. After they had been out all night, the defendant proposed to amend his plea of the general issue by filing a plea of the statute of limitations. Plaintiff's counsel stated that he would be surprised by the amended plea; that his client had been sent home by him before he knew of the offer to amend his plea; that, were his client present, he could testify to such facts as, in his opinion, would take the case out of the bar of the statute. The court refused to allow the plea to be filed, and this was the main ground of exception argued before us. Section 3479 of the Code provides as follows: "All parties, whether plaintiffs or defendants, in the superior or other courts, (except the supreme court,) whether at law or in equity, may, at any stage of the cause, as matter of right, amend their pleadings in all respects, whether in matter of form or of substance, provided there is enough in the pleadings to amend by." Under this section, we think the court erred in refusing to allow the amendment, even at the late stage of the case then on trial. This is a very broad provision in the law for amendments. It declares that either of the parties may, at any stage of the case, as matter of right, amend their pleadings

in all respects, etc. While the facts of this case show gross negligence on the part of the defendant in not sooner offering this amendment, yet, under this section, he had a right to make it at any time before the jury returned their verdict. Of course, had it worked a surprise upon the plaintiff, he would have had a right to continue the cause at the expense of the defendant, and the court should, before allowing the amendment, have put the defendant upon terms, as is provided for in section 3482 of the Code. While we think this is the proper construction of this section of the Code, we also think the section goes too far in allowing amendments. We think the right to amend ought, at least, to cease after the jury has been charged with the case, and have retired to their room. It frequently works a great hardship upon the courts, at great expense to the county. I have known several instances where cases have occupied the court for days, and at the last stage of the trial one of the parties would offer an amendment which would cause the case to be continued. Besides, it is an inducement to laziness and negligence on the part of counsel. Judgment reversed.

SAVANNAH & W. R. CO. et al. v. WOODRUFF.

(Supreme Court of Georgia. Nov. 10, 1890.)

RAILROAD COMPANIES — TRACKS ON STREETS—IN-
JUNCTION.

1. After railways have been connected for nearly 80 years under a special act of the legislature providing for their connection in a city with the consent of the people thereof, the people having consented by popular vote cast within the year following the passage of the act, and the connection having been made within the next year after the vote was taken, no authority can be derived from the act for holding another election giving consent to the laying of additional side tracks or turn-outs on the streets of the city by one or more of the railway companies. When the connection was completed with the side tracks, etc., then constructed, the power conferred by the act to encroach on the streets was exhausted.

2. A temporary injunction restraining the construction of a side track or turn-out for a steam railway in the streets of a city may be granted at the instance of a citizen alleging special damage to his real estate located in the vicinity of the nuisance, and, though the evidence be conflicting as to whether he will sustain special damage or not, the discretion of the judge in granting the injunction will not be controlled unless abused.

3. It is no legal bar to the injunction that the plaintiff may have acquired his title from collateral motives, and very recently before the work complained of began or was to begin.

(Syllabus by the Court.)

Error from superior court, Muscogee county; Martin, Judge.

Peabody, Brannon & Hatcher, for plaintiffs in error. *C. E. Battle* and *McNeill & Levy*, for defendant in error.

BLECKLEY, C. J. 1. Without legislative authority the city government of Columbus could not authorize the construction and use of a side track for a steam railway over and upon the public streets of the city. Kavanagh v. Railroad Co., 78

Ga. 271;[1] Daly v. Railroad Co., 80 Ga. 793, 7 S. E. Rep. 146. The needful authority is sought to be derived from the act of 1857, and from a vote of the citizens taken under that act in 1887. The title of the act is "An act to authorize the connection of the Muscogee Railroad with the Opelika Branch Railroad and the Mobile and Girard Railroad, at Columbus." Under this title the preamble and enacting clauses are as follows: "Whereas, it would promote the interest and convenience of the people of Georgia and Alabama, as well as the public generally, to connect the Muscogee Railroad with the Opelika Branch Railroad and Mobile and Girard Railroad, be it enacted, that the president and directors of said roads shall have the power of connecting their said roads by extending them through the city commons and streets of Columbus, with such side tracks, turn-outs, and sheds as may be necessary for the convenience of freights and passengers: provided, they first obtain the consent of the people of the city of Columbus, upon such terms as may be agreed on and shall be satisfactory to them." Acts 1857, p. 73. It appears from the record that the connection provided for in this act took place in 1859 under a vote of the citizens cast under the act in the previous year. Since that time the rights and franchises of the Opelika Branch Railroad have devolved upon and become vested in the Savannah & Western Railroad Company, the plaintiff in error. Looking at the title of the act of 1857 above quoted, it is manifest that the whole purpose of that act was to provide once for all for connecting the several railroads therein mentioned. In so far as side tracks, turn-outs, and sheds were embraced in and constituted a part of the scheme of connection, the act comprehended and provided for them. But that scheme was executed in 1859, and it seems plain to us that side tracks, etc., which did not become necessary for the convenience of freights or passengers until 20 or 30 years thereafter, could not have been in legislative contemplation when the act was passed. The much safer and more rational construction is that the powers conferred by the act were exhausted by their exercise and by the consequent connection of the railroads as the result of the popular vote taken in 1859. It cannot be that the work of connecting these railroads was not fully accomplished long ago. It cannot be regarded as a continuous and progressive work, not terminated in 1859, nor even within the long period since elapsed. The title of the act of 1857 is not broad enough to cover any side tracks, turn-outs, etc., which were not necessary as a part of the scheme of connection. To bring side tracks, turn-outs, etc., within the title of the act at all, they have to be treated as belonging to the scheme of connection. Without so treating them, the act as to them would be unconstitutional. The two votes taken under this act were separated by the period almost a generation. To apply the act to the later of the two, would be to regard the work of making a connection as prolonged for the term of an ordinary life-time. This court said in Kavanagh v. Railroad Co., supra: "It may be that, under this act of the legislature, a further consent of the people of Columbus might be given by them in a further vote to be taken, that such side tracks might be laid down along said street." This was a mere suggestion of a possibility, the case then in hand not requiring any adjudication of the point. The present case brings the question directly under adjudication, and we have considered it on our responsibility as a court. Thus dealing with it, we think it should be answered unhesitatingly in the negative. An affirmative answer would require us to use the act as a mere color for authorizing a vote 30 years after the passage of the act, and when a vote under it had already been taken within the next year after its passage. Our conclusion is that the city council of Columbus had no power or authority to grant permission to the Savannah & Western Railroad Company (plaintiff in error) to occupy the public streets with the side track or turn-out now in question.

2. In the absence of legal authority for placing and using this structure in the public streets, the same would be a public nuisance; and under the evidence in the record we think the judge did not abuse his discretion in granting a temporary injunction at the instance of Woodruff, the owner of real estate in the immediate vicinity. The injunction was granted upon terms, bond and security to answer for any resulting damages being required of Woodruff before the injunction would become effective. Whether he would sustain special damage or not from this threatened public nuisance is a question for trial, under our practice, by a jury. Usually such a question may be dealt with on applications for temporary injunctions, according to the sound discretion of the judge. He will not be controlled by this court where no abuse of his discretion appears. Cohen v. Bank, 81 Ga. 723, 7 S. E. Rep. 811.

3. The motive of Woodruff for purchasing the real estate which he seeks to protect, or the recency of his purchase, can have no influence on his legal rights as owner of the property. It is no answer by one who is about to erect a public nuisance that the citizen complaining of special damage would not have been injured if he had abstained from making so late a purchase, or if his motive for purchasing had been more disinterested. We do not say that these matters should have no weight upon the mind of the judge in shaping his discretionary action upon the application for injunction, but only that they present no legal bar to the exercise of his discretion favorably to the applicant. Judgment affirmed.

MACON & A. R. CO. v. MACON & D. R. CO.

(*Supreme Court of Georgia.* Oct. 27, 1890.)

RAILROADS—CONSTRUCTION—DISTANCE FROM CONSTRUCTED LINE.

The provision of Code Ga. § 1689, that, where a railroad is intended to be built between

---

[1] 2 S. E. Rep. 686.

two points where a railroad is now constructed, the general direction and location of such new railroad shall be at least 10 miles from the railroad already constructed, does not prevent the building of a railroad within less than 10 miles of a railroad in process of construction, but not completed.

Error from superior court, Twiggs county; ROBERTS, Judge.

Gustin, Guerry & Hall and *C. Anderson,* for plaintiff in error. *W. M. Wimberly, Bacon & Rutherford, J. M. Stubbs, J. D. Jones,* and *L. D. Shannon,* for defendant in error.

BLANDFORD, J. At the instance of the defendant in error, the plaintiff in error was enjoined by the judge of the superior court from making or constructing its railroad within 10 miles of the road-bed of the Macon & Dublin Railroad Company. It appears from the record in this case that the Macon & Dublin Railroad Company received its charter on the 8th day of August, 1885, under the general railroad law of this state, as embraced in section 1689 et seq. of the Code; that the Macon & Atlantic Railway Company obtained its charter likewise in April, 1890; that, at the time of the filing of the petition praying for injunction, the Macon & Dublin Railroad Company had not constructed its road-bed from Macon to Dublin by some 13 miles. So the whole question in this case turns upon the construction of section 1689t of the Code, which is as follows: "Where a railroad or branch railroad is intended to be built under this section, between two points where a railroad is now constructed, the general direction and location of such new railroad shall be at least ten miles from the railroad already constructed, but this section shall not be construed to refer to any point within ten miles of either terminus, or to prevent said roads from running as near to each other the said first ten miles from either terminus as the interest of such company building the new route may dictate." It will be perceived that this section provides that, where a railroad or branch railroad is intended to be built between two points where a railroad is now constructed, the general direction and location of the new road shall be at least 10 miles from the railroad already constructed; but that this section is not to be construed to refer to any point within 10 miles of either terminus, or to prevent the roads from running as near to each other for the first 10 miles from either terminus as the interest of the company building the new road may dictate. The terminal points of the Macon & Dublin Railroad Company are Macon, in Bibb county, and Dublin, in Laurens county. The terminal points of the Macon & Atlantic Railway Company are Sofka, in Bibb county, and Savannah and a point on the Savannah river, in Effingham county. It is contended that the words "now constructed," in this section of the act, shoud be construed to mean "now being constructed," or "in process of construction;" and this point was very ably argued by counsel for the defendant in error. We, however, are of the opinion that the words "now con-

structed" and "already constructed," which appear in this section of the act, mean one and the same thing; so we are to give these words their plain and unambiguous meaning. There can be no doubt that the legislature intended to apply this section to a new railroad chartered under this law where there was another railroad which was then constructed, and which had already been constructed at the time of the passage of this act. It seems to us that the words cannot bear a plainer meaning, whatever injustice may be done to a railroad company whose road-bed is in progress of construction by this interpretation of the statute. The words are to receive their plain and obvious import; and we think the maxim, *a verbis legis non est recedendum,* applies in this case. The judgment of the court below, therefore, in granting the injunction restraining the plaintiff in error from building its road-bed within 10 miles of the road-bed of the defendant in error, is reversed. But we do not by this opinion intimate or decide that the Macon & Atlantic Railway Company can take, use, or occupy any right of way or other property, acquired by or belonging to the Macon & Dublin Railroad Company, unless condemned by the first-named company, proper compensation being paid therefor.

Judgment reversed.

AMERICAN MORTG. CO. OF SCOTLAND, Limited, v. TENNILLE.

(*Supreme Court of Georgia.* March 28, 1891.)

FOREIGN CORPORATIONS — POWER TO HOLD LAND —AFFIDAVIT OF ILLEGALITY.

1. Under the act of February 28, 1877, providing that the state of Georgia will not consent to foreign corporations owning 5,000 or more acres of land in this state, unless they shall become incorporated under the laws of Georgia, the state alone can make the question as to the right of such corporations to hold said land.

2. A motion to dismiss an affidavit of illegality was rightly denied when at least one of the grounds thereof presented a legal defense against the further progress of the execution.

(*Syllabus by the Court.*)

Error to superior court, Quitman county; GUERRY, Judge.

Wm. E. Simmons and *W. C. Worrill,* for plaintiff in error. *W. D. Kiddoo,* for defendant in error.

LUMPKIN, J. Tennille executed and delivered to J. K. O. Sherwood a promissory note, and at the same time, in order to secure the same, made and delivered to said Sherwood a deed to certain land. Sherwood transferred the note, and conveyed the land to the American Mortgage Company of Scotland, Limited, who sued the note to judgment in the superior court of Quitman county, and an execution issued thereon was levied upon the land described in the aforesaid deed; the mortgage company having previously filed in the clerk's office a deed purporting to reconvey the land to said Tennille, for the purpose of making this levy. . To the levy of the execution Tennille filed his affidavit of illegality, containing several grounds, one of which was as follows, viz.. That "the said plaintiff was a foreign corporation, has never been incorporated by the laws of Georgia, and owned more than 5,000 acres of land in said state, (so far as to claim the same and hold deeds thereto,) in conflict with and against the laws of said state, and therefore could not hold the title to lands, or convey the same to the defendant, legally." The defendant served on the plaintiff a notice to produce at the trial a number of papers, and among them the charter of the plaintiff, and deeds from 14 persons to Sherwood, and from Sherwood to the plaintiff, covering various lands in Randolph and Quitman counties; the use intended to be made of said deeds being to prove the ground of illegality above quoted. The court held that said charter and these deeds should be produced, and, upon the plaintiff's failure to do so, ordered the levy of the execution to be dismissed. We can see no error in requiring the production of the charter, as it might contain evidence supporting one of the grounds of the illegality. The main question, therefore, upon which this court is asked to pass in this case, is whether or not the ground of illegality setting forth plaintiff's inability to hold land, in excess of 5,000 acres, is good in law, and consequently whether or not the plaintiff should have been required to produce said deeds.

1. It seems to be well settled that, in a case of this kind, the state alone is authorized to assert her policy in prohibiting foreign corporations from holding 5,000 or more acres of land in Georgia, and that individuals have no right to make the question in controversies with each other. Numerous decisions may be found to the effect that, where a corporation acquires or uses land to any extent or for any purpose not authorized by its charter, the question of its right so to do cannot be made by an individual in a legal controversy with the corporation, or with those claiming under it, but must be raised directly by a proceeding instituted for that purpose by the state wherein such corporation is exercising such powers ultra vires. Some of these decisions were made by the courts of the states in which the corporations themselves were created, and others in states outside of which the corporations involved had been chartered. None of them are directly in point as to the precise question made in the case now before us, because the disability of the corporations arose under the provisions of their own charters. They are referred to merely to show the trend of judicial opinion on this question. These cases are so numerous, and the doctrine they establish is so well recognized, we deem it unnecessary to cite them by name. The following language, used by Judge Dillon in his great work on Municipal Corporations, has some bearing on the question now being considered: "Whether a municipal corporation, with power to purchase and hold real estate for certain purposes, has acquired and is holding such property for other purposes, is a question which can only be determined in a proceeding instituted at the instance of the state. If there is capacity to purchase, the deed to the corporation divests the estate of the gran-

tor, and there is a complete sale; and whether the corporation, in purchasing, exceeds its power, is a question between it and the state, and does not concern the vendor or others." 2 Dill. Mun. Corp. (Ed. 1890,) § 574. We have been able to find some cases directly in point. In that of Barnes v. Suddard, (Ill.) 7 N. E. Rep. 477, it was held that, where a foreign corporation had power to acquire real estate so far as necessary for its business, its acquisition of realty cannot be assailed in a collateral proceeding as an act ultra vires. It appears from an examination of that case that in Illinois foreign corporations had the same rights to own and hold real estate as did domestic corporations of that state, and the case turned, not upon the charter powers of the corporation, but upon its right under the Illinois law to hold land. The Pennsylvania act approved April 26, 1855, forbade any foreign corporation to acquire and hold real estate. Notwithstanding this statute, it was held, in the case of Hickory Farm Oil Co. v. Buffalo, N. Y. & P. R. Co., 32 Fed. Rep. 22, that a deed of conveyance of land to such a corporation was not void, but passed the title, and that the corporation held the land subject to the commonwealth's right of escheat; also that the commonwealth alone could object to the legal capacity of the corporation to hold real estate. In support of this opinion, Bone v. Canal Co., (Pa.) 5 Atl. Rep. 751, and Railroad Co. v. Lewis, (Iowa,) 4 N. W. Rep. 842, are cited. Another case holding the same way is that of Carlow v. Aultman & Co., decided by the supreme court of Nebraska, and reported in 44 N. W. Rep. 873. An act of Nebraska, passed in 1887, provided that no non-resident alien foreigner, nor any corporation not incorporated by laws of that state, should acquire or own, hold or possess, any real estate in the state of Nebraska. While this law was in force, Aultman & Co., a foreign corporation, purchased land in that state at a judicial sale, and it was held that this corporation's title was valid against every one but the state, and could be divested only by proceedings brought by the state for that purpose. These foreign corporations, it seems, have been treated as aliens were in England as to purchasing and holding real estate. By the common law, while an alien might purchase, he could do so only for the benefit of the king, and the king was entitled to land purchased by him by virtue of his prerogative upon "office found;" and accordingly it was held that, upon the proceeding of "office found" was perfected, an alien had the power to hold and convey the land inter vivos. 1 Devl. Deeds, §§ 124, 125. It therefore seems clear, in view of the cases cited and the common-law foundation upon which the principle governing them is based, that the doctrine is thoroughly established in our American states that the right of foreign corporations to purchase or hold lands in excess of the authority conferred, either by their own charters or by the laws of the state in which such purchase is made, can only be questioned by the state itself in which such land may be situated. It follows, of course, that the defendant in this case had no right whatever to raise the question made in the ground of this illegality hereinbefore set forth; and, that being true, the production of the deeds called for was unnecessary and useless, because the ground of illegality, in support of which it was sought to introduce these deeds, presented no legal reason for interfering with the progress of the plaintiff's execution.

2. Another ground of the illegality alleged, in effect, that the deed purporting to be from the plaintiff to the defendant in execution, which had been filed in the clerk's office, was no sufficient deed, and would not convey title out of the plaintiff to the defendant, but would only throw a cloud upon the defendant's title, and cause the land to sell for less than its true value. If these assertions are true they amount to a good ground of illegality. It may be that such ground is not set forth with sufficient clearness, but, as there was no special demurrer or objection to it, because it was wanting in distinctness or fullness, but only a general motion, in the nature of a demurrer, to dismiss the affidavit of illegality, the point was not rightly made to the court below as to the insufficiency of this ground, and the judge, therefore, properly refused to dismiss the affidavit of illegality as a whole. If this ground failed to set forth the reasons why the deed referred to was insufficient, and failed to convey title to the defendant, this distinct objection should have been made to it. We therefore leave the case to be tried again in the court below, with such additional light shed upon the law of the case as may be gathered from this opinion.

Judgment reversed.

FREEMAN v. EXCHANGE BANK.

(*Supreme Court of Georgia.* April 20, 1891.)

BANKS — COLLECTIONS — GARNISHMENT — EXPERT TESTIMONY—JUSTICES OF THE PEACE — INSTRUCTIONS.

1. Generally the payee of a bill of exchange, by indorsing it (otherwise in blank) "For deposit to the credit of" himself, retains ownership not only of the bill, but of its proceeds, until they are so deposited. The money realized by collecting the bill is, in the hands of a disinterested bank, through whose agency the collection was made, subject to garnishment as assets belonging to such indorser.

2. Expert testimony is not admissible to aid in the interpretation of an indorsement having a definite legal import, and being expressed in terms free from ambiguity.

3. It is settled law that the presiding justice is not bound to charge the jury trying an appeal in a justice's court.

(*Syllabus by the Court.*)

Error from superior court, Bibb county; MILLER, Judge.

M. R. Freeman, by *C. L. Bartlett,* for plaintiff in error. *Bacon & Rutherford,* for defendant in error.

BLECKLEY, C. J. 1. An indorsement for collection, or the like, is not a contract of indorsement, but the creation of a power; the indorsee being a mere agent to receive or enforce payment for the indorser's use. Central R. Co. v. First Nat. Bank, 73 Ga. 383; Tied. Com. Paper, § 268; 1 Daniel,

Neg. Inst. §§ 698, 698d; 2 Rand. Com. Paper, §§ 727, 1009; 1 Morse, Banks, § 217; 2 Morse, Banks, §§ 583, 593; Bolles, Banks, §§ 220, 384e et seq.; Benj. Chalm. Bills, (2d Amer. Ed.) 182; Bank v. Armstrong, 39 Fed. Rep. 684; Bank v. Hubbell, 117 N. Y. 384, 22 N. E. Rep. 1031. A suit is not maintainable by the indorsee against the indorser. White v. Bank, 102 U. S. 658. And see Lee v. Bank, 1 Bond, 387. To sue other parties in order to enforce payment is deemed within the delegated power of the agent; and by reason of the great favor shown by the law to commercial paper the restricted indorsee is allowed in some jurisdictions to sue in his own name. Wilson v. Tolson, 79 Ga. 137;[1] Boyd v. Corbitt, 37 Mich. 52; 2 Rand. Com. Paper, § 726; Benj. Chalm. Bills, (2 Amer. Ed.) 133, 149. The maker of a restricted indorsement can follow the bill or its proceeds over any number of subsequent indorsements, the terms of his indorsement being notice of his title. Elementary works cited supra; First Nat. Bank v. Reno Co. Bank, 3 Fed. Rep. 257; Bank of the Metropolis v. First Nat. Bank, 19 Fed. Rep. 301; First Nat. Bank v. Bank of Monroe, 33 Fed. Rep. 408: In re Armstrong, Id. 405; Bank v. Hamilton, 42 Fed. Rep. 880. The last case is criticised from the stand-point of bankers, but only with reference to transmitting the proceeds of collection from the collecting bank to the intermediary through whom the bill was received. The expert opinion seems to be that transmission according to custom, by correspondence, and proper entries of debit and credit founded thereon, the entries being made after collection, will serve commercially, and therefore legally, as the equivalent of paying over the money, or forwarding it by mail or express; and, consequently, that transmission by such entries, each bank making the appropriate entry for itself, will discharge the collecting bank. See 45 Bank. Mag. 241; 4 Bank. Law J. 3. The learned United States circuit judge who decided the case which is thus criticised took a different view. The bill of exchange upon which the question in the present case arises was drawn at Kansas City, Mo., by S. A. Brown & Co. upon F. A. Ross, agent Central Railroad, Macon, Ga., payable at sight to their own order. It was indorsed by them thus: "For deposit to the credit of S. A. Brown & Co." Following this indorsement was another in these terms: "Pay Exchange Bank, or order, for collection account of National Bank of Kansas City. M. ANDMON, Cashier." The bill, after its receipt for collection under the latter indorsement, was paid to the Exchange Bank at Macon, and thereupon, while that bank had possession of the money, a garnishment, issued at the instance of Freeman as a creditor of S. A. Brown & Co., the drawers and payees of the bill, was served upon it. No facts are in evidence as to the actual ownership of the money at the time the garnishment was served except the bill itself and the indorsement thereon. The legal import of the first indorsement —that of S. A. Brown & Co.—being that

---

[1] 8 S. E. Rep. 900.

the ownership of the bill was retained by them, the terms of the second indorsement —that made by the cashier of the National Bank of Kansas City—are of no consequence. As the indorsements stand, there is no express link of connection between them, no written link naming or constituting the National Bank of Kansas City a holder of the bill for any purpose whatever. But, in virtue of being an actual holder, that bank would have the right to fill up the first indorsement so as to make it read thus: "Pay to the National Bank of Kansas City, or order, for deposit to the credit of S. A. Brown & Co." There might be other terms in which the full indorsement which that bank would be authorized to supply could be expressed; but, on the state of facts before us, that bank would have no authority to insert any terms which would vary substantially the legal import of the original indorsement, or render it other than a restrictive indorsement confining ownership of the bill and its proceeds to S. A. Brown & Co. Lee v. Bank, 1 Bond, 387. The proceeds would be impressed with this ownership until they were actually so deposited. The garnishment fastened upon them before this did or could take place, for the money was in the hands of the collecting bank, the Exchange Bank of Macon, when the garnishment was served. The agency created by the owners of the bill by means of their indorsement had not been fully executed. The Kansas City bank was still the immediate agent under them, and the Macon bank was a subagent under it. The latter held the money as a bailee for the ultimate use and benefit of the owners. It could discharge itself by transmitting to the Kansas City bank at any time before the garnishment was served, but could not do so after such service, the fund being then in gremio legis. There being in evidence no facts extrinsic to the bill itself and its indorsements to throw light upon the question of title, we are not to be understood as holding that such facts might not exert a controlling influence on the question. Indeed, there is authority for giving them such effect when duly proved. A deposit of paper in bank by a customer, he indorsing it, "For deposit," may operate to clothe the bank with title under certain circumstances. Bank v. Miller, 77 Ala. 168; 2 Morse, Banks, § 577. But the general rule is that by a restrictive indorsement the depositor retains the title. Bolles, Banks, § 230.

2. The indorsement to be construed being free from ambiguity, and having a clear and definite legal meaning, expert testimony to aid in its interpretation was not admissible. The duty of construing such an indorsement, by its own terms and without the opinion of witnesses, devolves upon the court, or upon the jury, the case being on appeal in a justice's court. Mr. Cabiniss, the cashier of the bank garnished, deposed to no fact which actually transpired in relation to this particular indorsement, but only gave his opinion, founded upon his expert knowledge, as to what had probably transpired between the Kansas City bank and the payees of

the bill, and as to the legal effect of such an indorsement. His opinion was wholly irrelevant and inadmissible. But, as no ground of objection to his evidence is stated in the petition for certiorari, we cannot say that the superior court ought to have sustained the certiorari because of this error committed by the justice's court.

3. That it is not the legal duty of the justice of the peace presiding over a jury trial in his court to instruct the jury as to the law of the case has been heretofore ruled more than once. Johnson v. Nelms, 21 Ga. 192; Adams v. Clark, 64 Ga. 648. Bendheim v. Baldwin, 73 Ga. 594. But, inasmuch as the jury, under the evidence before them, erred in finding in favor of the garnishee, the certiorari should have been sustained for that reason, and the superior court erred in not sustaining it.

Judgment reversed.

JACOBY v. KIESLING et al.

(Supreme Court of Georgia. March 16, 1891.)

APPOINTMENT OF RECEIVER.

Where a judge appointed as receiver of the assets of an insolvent firm a fit and proper person, who was the choice of a large majority, in amount and number, of the creditors, and no good reason appeared why he should have appointed another person at the instance of a single creditor, whose claim against the firm was comparatively small, such action of the judge was manifestly proper, and will not be disturbed.

(Syllabus by Lumpkin, J.)

Error from superior court, Chatham county; FALLIGANT, Judge.

Chas. N. West, for plaintiff in error. Denmark, Adams & Adams and Garrard & Meldrim, for defendant in error.

Judgment affirmed.

JONES v. COTTEN.

(Supreme Court of North Carolina. April 28, 1891.)

APPEAL IN HABEAS CORPUS PROCEEDING—CUSTODY OF CHILDREN—INSANITY AFTER JUDGMENT—REMANDING CAUSE.

Where, on appeal from a writ of habeas corpus, granted by the superior court, awarding to a mother the possession of her minor children, it appears that she has since become insane and has been committed to the insane asylum, the case will be remanded, under Code N. C. § 965, providing that a case may be remanded for further proceedings, "whenever it shall appear necessary for the purposes of justice."

Appeal from superior court, Craven county; WOMACK, Judge.

This is a proceeding in which the plaintiff applied for a writ of habeas corpus to obtain possession of three of her minor children named, alleged to be in the possession of the defendant. The writ was issued and served, and return thereof made. At the hearing of the matter the court gave judgment that the children be delivered to the plaintiff, whereupon the defendant appealed to this court, as allowed by the statute (Code, § 1662) in such cases. It appears at this term that since the appeal was taken the plaintiff has become insane, and has been committed to and is now in the appropriate insane asylum. The counsel for the defendant asks the court to make such disposition of the appeal as it may deem appropriate and proper. Code N. C. § 965, provides that the supreme court shall have power, "whenever it shall appear necessary for the purposes of justice, to allow and direct the taking of further testimony in any case which may be pending in said court, under such rules as may be prescribed, or the court may remand the case, to the intent that amendments may be made, further testimony taken, or other proceedings had in the court below."

C. R. Thomas, for appellant.

MERRIMON, C. J., (after stating the facts.) We are of opinion that the case must be remanded to the judge now riding the second judicial district, to the end that he shall have and take jurisdiction of and take such further action in the matter as the condition of the children mentioned and the circumstances of the case may warant and require. according to law. Such proceedings and matters are largely summary in their nature, and may be conducted in the sound discretion of the court in such way as, in view of the variant circumstances of the case, will promote the ends of justice, secure the rights of parties, and afford adequate protection to the children whose custody may be in question. The statute (Code, § 965) contemplates that, with a view to justice, a case may be remanded. The other statute (Code, § 1661) confers upon the court below very large powers, to "promote the interest and welfare of the children." Holley v. Holley, 96 N. C. 229, 1 S. E. Rep. 553; Knott v. Taylor, 96 N. C. 553, 2 S. E. Rep. 680. Let the case be so remanded. It is so ordered.

EULISS v. McADAMS.

(Supreme Court of North Carolina. April 28, 1891.)

DEEDS—DESCRIPTION—EVIDENCE—EXCEPTIONS—BOUNDARIES.

1. A description of land in a deed as "the Sellars Tract" is not too vague to admit of evidence aliunde of its location, for the purpose of establishing a corner.

2. Where a deed describes land as "all their land lying between Haw river and Stony creek, up to the line of" H., and refers to the title papers, evidence aliunde is admissible to identify the land.

3. It is competent to establish the lines and courses of a tract of land by showing where the surveyor actually ran when making the boundaries at the instance of the parties to the conveyance, and with a view to its execution.

4. A junior deed is not admissible as evidence to locate the corner of land conveyed by an older deed.

5. An exception to the sufficiency of evidence to identify land described in a deed cannot be raised for the first time on appeal.

This was a civil action brought to recover damage for trespass and involving title, tried at fall term, 1890, of the superior court of Alamance county, before MacRae, J. The descriptions contained in the deeds offered by the plaintiff to show title are set forth in the opinion. The defendant contended that the deeds were void for uncertainty in all of the descriptions. It was admitted that defendant

owned the land adjoining this tract; and, while the plaintiff was required to prove his title, the main contention between the parties was as to the location of their adjoining lines, as will appear by the plat attached. Plaintiff also offered a deed from D. W. Huffman and wife to defendant for 105 acres, 8th of April, 1870, and another deed from same to same for 100 acres, more or less, 21st March, 1874, and a grant to William Mebane for 400 acres, March, 1795, and a deed from John Huffman to Daniel Huffman in 1808, and much testimony as to the location of defendant's land, for the purpose of establishing as a fact that the defendant's land stopped at X on the plat and not at Y, as claimed by defendant. The defendant, during the cross-examination of one of plaintiff's witnesses, offered a grant to Benj. Rainy, 1799; and a deed from Benj. Rainy to Neill B. Rose, 1807; and a deed from William Mebane to Jos. Murray. 1799; and a deed from Wm. Mebane to Thos. Cole, 1796; and a deed from Thomas Cole to John Huffman, 1797; and a deed from John Huffman to Daniel Huffman, 1808; and the will of Daniel Huffman, devising to John Huffman the same land, and the two deeds offered by plaintiff by Huffman to McAdams,—all of these for the purpose of locating defendant's land. John J. Trollinger was examined as a witness by plaintiff for the purpose of locating defendant's S. W. corner at X, instead of at Y, and testified that at one time he had owned the land lying to the west of the defendant; that he understood that Sellars' land joined his, (witness':) that Jeffries now owns the land which witness formerly owned; that Jeffries' corner is the same as witness' corner was, though witness does not know where Jeffries claims to; that Jeffries bought from the Holts the land witness owned, no more and no less,—all that witness owned was conveyed to Holt. Defendant then proposed to offer a deed from Holt to Jeffries, in 1887, to locate this corner. Objected to by the plaintiff upon the ground that this deed was junior to plaintiff's deed, and could not be offered to locate an older tract. Objection sustained. Defendant excepted. After much evidence on both sides, the defendant offered a deed from Murray, sheriff, to E. M. Holt for the Jeffries land, 10th of January, 1872, for the purpose of locating the Jeffries corner at Y, and by this means locate defendant's corner at Y. Defendant's deed for this tract was dated 1870. Plaintiff objected, because an older deed cannot be located by a junior. Objection sustained. Defendant excepted. The jury found the issues in favor of the plaintiff, as will appear by the record. Rule for new trial for errors alleged. Rule discharged. Judgment for plaintiff. Defendant appealed to the supreme court.

F. H. Whitaker, L. M. Scott, and W. H. Carroll, for appellant. J. A. Long, for appellee.

AVERY, J., (after stating the facts as above.) The plaintiff offered two deeds, —the first from A. Murray and wife to the Falls of Neuse Manufacturing Company; and the second from W. J. Murray and wife to the same company. The defendant objected to the introduction of both, on the ground that the descriptive clauses were too vague to admit of explanation by extrinsic evidence. The descriptions were, respectively, in the following words: *First.* "A tract of land in Alamance county, state of North Carolina, adjoining the lands of John Staley, David Staley, and Joseph McAdams, known as the 'Sellars Tract,' subject to whatever rights the widow Sellars may have in it, containing one hundred and forty acres more or less." *Second.* Seven tracts or interests in seven tracts conveyed by one deed as follows: "The following tracts of land in Alamance county, state of North Carolina, their dwelling-house, and the land on which the same is situated, containing about eight acres more or less, adjoining Big Falls water-power lands, and the lands heretofore owned by Albert Murray, being the place on which we now reside. For a more specific description reference is made to our title papers. Also our undivided half of the following lands situate in said county of Alamance, to-wit: (1) The John Dixon tract, containing about one hundred and thirty acres, more or less, adjoining the lands of Austin Isley, Jesse Rippy, Jesse Grant, and others. (2) The Long tract, containing about one hundred and ten acres, more or less, situated on the east side of Haw river, adjoining the lands of W. T. Wilkins, Mrs. Kirkpatrick, and others. (3) The Sellars tract, containing about one hundred and sixteen acres, more or less, situated on the southwest side of Haw river, adjoining the lands of Joseph McAdams, John Staley, and others. (4) The Staley tract, containing twenty-seven acres, more or less, adjoining the lands of Mebane Morrow, Joseph McAdams, and others. Tracts number three and four above named are subject to the dower rights, if any, which the widow, Nancy Sellars, may have therein. (5) A tract containing about six acres, called 'Morrow Tract,' for which an exchange was made with Mebane Morrow. (6) And also their interest, being a half interest, in all their lands lying between Haw river and Stony creek up to the line of J. H. and W. E. Holt & Co., including the Big Falls water-power and mills, and all the rights, privileges, and appurtenances thereto belonging, which lands were heretofore owned by W. J. and A. Murray, as partners and tenants in common, and also all of the rights, privileges, and interests of said W. J. Murray, whether as copartners or tenants in common or in his own right, in and to the bed of Haw river and Stony creek, or either of them, and the waters thereof. For a more particular description of tracts one, two, three, four, five, and six reference is hereby made to the title papers therefor to W. J. Murray and W. J. and A. Murray." The descriptive words, "known as the 'Sellars Tract,'" (omitting as surplusage the residue of the description,) pointed with sufficient certainty to possible proof of the existence and location of a body of land which, according to general reputation, was so designated, and rendered parol proof competent to fit it to the thing. Henley v. Wilson, 81 N. C. 405; Smith v. Low, 2 Ired. 457. In the case last cited Chief Justice RUFFIN says that by the description "Mount Vernon, the late residence of General Washington," the place referred to is better known than by setting forth the metes and bounds of the tract on which his dwelling-house was located. A reference to the title papers of the grantors in the other deed from William J. Murray and wife is equivalent to incorporating the full descriptions set forth in the papers referred to into the former deed, and of course made the conveyance mentioned, together with competent evidence to locate the land aliened by them, competent. Everitt v. Thomas, 1 Ired. 252. It is unnecessary, in order to settle the question of law whether this part of the deed is void for vagueness, that we should go further, and pass upon the sufficiency of the additional designations as "their dwelling-house and the land on which the same is situated," etc., or the place on which we now reside. Carson v. Ray, 7 Jones, (N. C.) 610; Murdock v. Anderson, 4 Jones, Eq. 77. The descriptive words, "the John Dixon tract," "the Long tract," "the Sellars tract," and the "Staley tract," used in the second deed, were sufficient to point to proof *aliunde* that these distinct bodies of land were generally known by such designation. Smith v. Low, supra; Scull v. Pruden, 92 N. C. 168; Henley v. Wilson, supra. Evidence was unquestionably admissible not only to show the location of the tract "called the 'Morrow Tract,'" but to identify the boundaries by a deed of exchange from Mebane Morrow, and to consider such metes and bounds as if they were incorporated into the descriptive clause of the deed from W. J. Murray and wife. Henley v. Wilson, supra; Everitt v. Thomas, supra. The description numbered 6, is not too indefinite, because it was competent for the plaintiff under its terms to identify the land as lying between Haw river and Stony creek, and extending up to the lines of J. H. and W. E. Holt & Co., so as to include the Big Falls water-power. Horton v. Cook, 1 Jones, Eq. 270. The further designation of the land as that "owned by W. J. Murray and A. Murray, as partners and tenants in common," together with the reference to title papers, which follows and applies to all of the tracts numbered from 1 to 6, opens the door for the admission of testimony to identify the land lying between those rivers by written evidences tracing title to the two Murrays as tenants in common. It was likewise competent to show title as tenant in common or sole seisin for the beds of Haw river and Stony creek in W. J. Murray, all title and interests in these localities proven to have been in him having passed by the deed to the Falls of Neuse Company.

The judge states that the plaintiff offered the testimony of several witnesses, tending to prove his contention as to the location of the land claimed by him, and as to the alleged trespass; but this evidence is not set forth in detail in the statement. The defendant did not except in the court below to the sufficiency of the whole of the testimony to go to the jury as tending to fit any or all of the descriptions to the land claimed by the plaintiff, and to show it to be identical with that described in the complaint. We cannot, therefore, consider the exception raised here for the first time that the evidence was not in fact sufficient to locate the land. With notice of such an assignment of error we assume that the judge would have sent up much additional testimony bearing upon this question. McKinnon v. Morrison, 104 N. C. 357, 10 S. E. Rep. 513.

We find in the brief of the defendant some statements in conflict with those in the case on appeal and much *addenda* to the record, which of course we cannot consider. The case on appeal states that the defendant purposed to offer a deed from Holt to Jeffries, dated in 1887, to locate his south-west corner, and not, as contended by defendant, simply to contradict Trollinger. It is competent to establish the lines and courses of a tract of land by showing where the surveyor actually ran when making the boundaries at the instance of the parties to the conveyance, and with a view to its execution, as it is to locate a patent by showing marks, corresponding in age and course with the calls of the deed, upon a line of trees. Ingram v. Colson, 3 Dev. 520; Topping v. Sadler, 5 Jones, (N. C.) 357; Roberts v. Preston, 100 N. C. 248, 6 S. E. Rep. 574. But the junior deed from Holt to Jeffries (dated in 1887) was not competent as evidence to locate the corner of the deed previously made to the plaintiff. Sasser v. Herring, 3 Dev. 340. The objection of the plaintiff is based upon the ground of incompetency as evidence of the location of the corner of an older deed. It is too late to set up other grounds of exception in this court. There is no error in either of the rulings of the court excepted to, and the judgment must be affirmed.

DOVER et ux. v. RHEA.

(*Supreme Court of North Carolina.* April 28, 1891.)

PAROL TRUSTS—STATUTE OF FRAUDS—SUBROGATION.

1. Plaintiff's father conveyed land to defendant upon a parol trust to pay certain judgments, which were afterward discharged with the proceeds of other land, which the father had intended to convey to plaintiff, with the understanding with defendant that he should convey the land held in trust by him to plaintiff. *Held,* that a trust in the land conveyed to defendant resulted to plaintiff's father, and went to his heirs. There being no transfer of the legal title contemporaneous with the parol understanding that defendant should convey to plaintiff, no trust resulted in her favor.

2. The understanding between plaintiff's father and defendant, as an agreement to convey to plaintiff, not being in writing, was void under the statute of frauds.

3. Plaintiff is not entitled to the land by way of subrogation, since she had no interest in the land intended for her.

This was a civil action tried before PHILIPS, J., and a jury, at fall term, 1890, of the superior court of Madison county. The purpose of the action was to declare the defendant a trustee for the benefit of the plaintiff Polly as to a certain tract of land described in the complaint. The only issue submitted to the jury was as follows: "Does H. R. Rhea hold the land under a parol agreement to convey to Polly Dover?" It was in evidence that J. L. Rhea, the father of the *feme* plaintiff and defendant, conveyed the said land (it being known as the "Arrington Tract") to his son N. L. Rhea by deed absolute, upon a parol trust to sell the same, and pay certain judgments which had been obtained against the said J. L. Rhea by one Flasher, and also certain costs, etc.; that said N. L. Rhea, with the consent of his father, conveyed to the defendant by deed absolute, upon similar parol trusts, all of said tract except 12 acres, which he had sold to one Hensley, and substituting for said 12 acres 25 acres of other land, which his father had previously given him; that there was an express agreement that the defendant should hold all of said land upon the trusts above mentioned. It was also in evidence that said J. L. Rhea had divided all of his land (except that above mentioned) among his children, and conveyed to them, except a tract intended for Polly; that afterwards, being pressed upon the judgments, and being unable to sell the land conveyed in trust, and there being an offer for the tract intended for Polly, J. L. Rhea sold and conveyed the same to W. S. Rhea for $400, and that this was done upon an understanding with the defendant that he would convey the land he held in trust to said Polly whenever she called for a deed. It was also in evidence that defendant took the money, and paid off and discharged the said judgments, costs, etc. The defendant denied that he took the land in question upon any trust whatever, claiming that he purchased the same for a valuable consideration. He denies that he ever promised to convey the land to Polly. There was no evidence that Polly was ever in possession of the tract set apart and intended for her, nor was it ever conveyed to her. The Flasher judgments were against J. L. Rhea as principal, and the defendant as his surety. The defendant objected to evidence as to his declaration that he would convey the land to Polly, claiming that it was inhibited by the statute of frauds. It was admitted, and he excepted. The court, after stating the contention of the parties, etc., charged as follows: "If upon the whole evidence it is shown to the satisfaction of the jury that J. L. Rhea, in the division of his lands among his children, set apart a tract which he intended for his daughter Polly, and also set apart a tract, to be sold to pay off the judgments against him, which he conveyed to his son N. L. Rhea for that purpose, and with that understanding, and N. L. Rhea, while holding the same for that purpose, conveyed twelve acres to Hensley, and to replace the value of the twelve acres conveyed twenty-five acres spoken of in the evidence, together with the said tract, to his brother H. R. Rhea, with the consent of J. L. Rhea, and H. R. Rhea accepted the said deed from N. L. Rhea for the same purpose, and with the same understanding, then he was simply a trustee; and if before H. R. Rhea sold the land or paid the judgments, he agreed with J. L. Rhea that if J. L. Rhea would convey to W. S. Rhea the tract intended for Polly, and let him take the money and pay on the judgments, he would hold the tract (including the twenty-five acres) which N. L. Rhea had conveyed to him for Polly, and make a deed to her for the same, and J. Rhea conveyed the land to W. S. Rhea, and the purchase price was paid to H. R. Rhea, then the jury should answer the issue, 'Yes;' otherwise they will answer, 'No.' " There were several exceptions to the charge, but these are unnecessary to be stated to a proper understanding of the opinion. The jury found the issue submitted to them by the court, which appears in the record, for the plaintiff. The counsel for the defendant then moved for judgment *non obstante veredicto.* The court stated to counsel that a judgment *non obstante veredicto* was a judgment rendered in favor of the plaintiff notwithstanding the verdict for the defendant, and that this judgment was given upon motion, which can only be made by the plaintiff, and refused the motion of the defendant's counsel, to which he excepted. The counsel for the defendant moved that, notwithstanding the verdict, as it appeared that the defendant had paid several hundred dollars to discharge incumbrances upon the land in dispute he be held chargeable with such sum, and that an account be ordered to ascertain the same. Motion refused by the court, and the defendant excepted. The court denied the motion for a new trial, and gave judgment for the plaintiff. The defendant appealed, and gave notice of appeal in open court, which notice was waived, and appeal-bond fixed at $——. The following note was appended by his honor: " I sign and settle the above as the case on appeal for the supreme court, notice of time and place for settling the same being waived by the parties. I send up the entire evidence because of the defendant's motion for judgment *non obstante veredicto,* and his motion for a reference, and because of the errors assigned in his motion for a new trial. For these reasons I adopt the suggestion of the defendant's counsel to send up all the evidence, that the case and my rulings may be clearly seen and fully reviewed by the supreme court." The judgment declared that the plaintiff was the owner of the land, and that, upon the failure of the defendant to convey to her in 10 days, the decree should operate as passing the title. Defendant appealed.

W. H. Malone, for appellant.　*T. F. Davidson,* for appellees.

SHEPHERD, J., (*after stating the facts as above.*) There was evidence tending to show that J. L. Rhea, in effect, conveyed the land to the defendant upon a parol trust to sell the same, and apply the proceeds to the satisfaction and discharge of the judgments and costs mentioned in the complaint. Assuming this to be true, we are nevertheless unable to find anything

in the record which warrants the judgment of his honor declaring that the defendant held the land in trust for the *feme* plaintiff, and directing that he execute a conveyance to her. If, as contended, the purposes of the trust were effectuated by the trustor with other means furnished by him, it is plain that there was a resulting trust in his favor. 1 Perry, Trusts, § 152. This resulting trust descended to the heirs at law of the trustor, unless the *feme* plaintiff can show that he transferred it to her in his life-time. It is well settled that, while an express trust in lands may, in this state, be created by a parol declaration, made contemporaneously with the transfer of the legal title, (Pittman v. Pittman, 107 N. C. —, 12 S. E. Rep. 61,) such trust when created, together with the resultant interest of the trustor, can be conveyed only in the same manner as other equitable interests in real property. Patton v. Clendenin, 3 Murph. 68; Holmes v. Holmes, 86 N. C. 208. The question, then, to be determined is whether the resultant interest of J. L. Rhea has been acquired by his daughter, the *feme* plaintiff. The said trustor had another tract of land which he intended to give his daughter, but, instead of conveying it to her, he sold it, and with the proceeds paid off the judgments and costs above mentioned. The *feme* plaintiff had no legal or equitable interest whatever in this land, and her father was at liberty to dispose of it as he pleased. It is true that the defendant promised that, upon a sale of the same and the payment of the said indebtedness, he would convey the tract which he held to the *feme* plaintiff; but, if we consider this as a mere agreement to convey, it is void, under the statute of frauds; and, if we treat it as a declaration of trust, it must likewise fail, because it is not evidenced by any writing and was not made in connection with a conveyance of the legal title. Frey v. Ramsour, 66 N. C. 466; Pittman v. Pittman, supra. It amounted simply to a parol agreement to convey the land to the *feme* plaintiff, and this, we have seen, cannot be enforced where it is denied by the answer. Holler v. Richards, 102 N. C. 545, 9 S. E. Rep. 460; Fortesque v. Crawford, 105 N. C. 30, 10 S. E. Rep. 910. It is urged, however, that the plaintiff is entitled to relief by way of subrogation or by constructive trust; but this is founded entirely upon the idea that she had some interest in the property sold by her father, and, as such was not the case, it is clear that the position cannot be maintained. Her father relied simply upon the verbal agreement of the defendant to convey, and, as the latter denies the agreement, it must follow that there was error in holding that the plaintiff acquired the equitable title to the land in question. As the case goes back for a new trial, we think it proper to say that the other heirs at law may be made parties, and, if a resulting trust be established, the plaintiff may, upon partition, obtain substantial justice by requiring the heirs to account for the advancements made to them. New trial.

WHITEHEAD *et al.* v. WHITEHURST.

(*Supreme Court of North Carolina.* April 28, 1891.)

REVIEW ON APPEAL—MORTGAGES — PURCHASE BY MORTGAGEE—JUDICIAL SALES—REFERENCE.

1. The findings of fact by a referee, to whom a cause has been referred by consent, will not be reviewed on appeal if there is any evidence to sustain them, though the cause is equitable in its nature.

2. A purchase by a mortgagee at his own sale is not void, but voidable, and becomes binding on the mortgagee when the price is reasonable, and no exception is taken by the parties in interest.

3. Where a mortgagee purchases land at his own sale under license of the court, and afterwards there is a resale by consent of the parties, but without license of the court, for a less amount, the mortgagee is chargeable with the price bid at the first sale.

Appeal from superior court, Edgecombe county; WHITAKER, Judge.

This action is brought by creditors of the intestate of the defendant to compel him to an account of his administration, and to pay the creditors what may be payable to them respectively. The pleadings raised issues of fact and law. In the course of the action "the case" was by consent of parties referred to a referee, "to find the facts, and state the accounts, and report the result of his findings," etc. Afterwards the referee made report as directed, and the defendant filed divers exceptions thereto. Afterwards the court overruled all these exceptions, and gave judgment for the plaintiff. The defendant, having excepted, appealed to this court, assigning error as follows: "(1) That he has failed to credit the defendant with his account of five hundred and seventy dollars for rent of mill under the contract of milling, as established by the testimony of D. C. Moore and G. A. Vick. (2) That he has failed to credit the defendant with Exhibits R and S, as representing the indebtedness of B. C. Highsmith, defendant's intestate, to G. A. Vick, arising under the milling contract aforesaid, and paid by M. D. Whitehurst, the defendant, amounting to six hundred and forty-eight dollars and sixty-eight cents. (3) That he has charged the defendant with twelve hundred and eleven dollars as of 1883, proceeds from sale of land; whereas the amount proper to have been charged was eight hundred dollars, 6th day of May, 1889. The defendant excepts to the referee's conclusions of law numbered, respectively, 1, 2, 5, 6, 11." The findings of law thus referred to are the following: "(1) That, while purchase by a mortgagee at his own sale is voidable, it is not void, but when the price is reasonable, and no exception taken by the mortgagor, it becomes valid; and therefore, by virtue of the sale made by William Whitehead, under his mortgage, on February 24, 1883, he became the legal owner of the lands purchased by him, and is not chargeable with rents. (2) That the defendant is chargeable with the proceeds of the first sale of the lands." "(5) That the debt mentioned in the twenty-first finding is not a proper charge. (6) That none of the items embraced in voucher 'T,' except that of Asa Bullock, are proper charges against the estate."

"(11) That the plaintiffs are entitled to judgment that the sum of $1,261.57, remaining in the hands of the defendant administrator, and liable to the demands of the plaintiff creditors, be distributed among the several plaintiffs as follows: The plaintiff William Whitehead to recover the sum of $1,204.60; the plaintiff Piney Highsmith to recover the sum of $58.64; and the plaintiff M. G. Bryan the sum of $28.66."

Battle & Mordecai, for appellees.

MERRIMON, C. J., (*after stating the facts as above.*) In effect the court approved and sustained the findings of fact and law by the referee. The reference was by consent of parties: hence it is not the province of this court to review the findings of fact, although this action is equitable in its nature, if there is any evidence to sustain them. This is settled by many decisions. There was clearly some evidence to sustain such findings of fact; and, accepting them, as we must do, the exceptions as to them cannot be sustained. The credits claimed were, for the reasons stated by the referee, properly disallowed, and the charge complained of was a proper one. The intestate of the defendant in his lifetime owed the plaintiff Whitehead certain debts, and to secure the same executed to the latter two mortgages of the land therein specified. Under a power of sale in these mortgages the land was sold, and the mortgagee indirectly through a third party purchased the same at a "fair" sale, and they sold for their full value. This appears. This sale was made in February of 1883, and the money, the proceeds of the sale, properly applied. The mortgagor died shortly before the sale, but, so far as appears, the heir at law did not and does not at all complain of the same, nor did the defendant, until he filed his exceptions to the report; nor does it appear that he is interested in opposition to it as administrator or otherwise. This sale was not void. It was voidable at the instance of the heir, and in possible cases it may be that the administrator might in a proper way avoid it; but this does not appear to be such a case. It does not appear that the creditors of the intestate are or can be prejudiced by it, and the defendant is not—does not profess to be—interested in their behalf. Joyner v. Farmer, 78 N. C. 196; Sumner v. Sessoms, 94 N. C. 371; Gibson v. Barbour, 100 N. C. 192, 6 S. E. Rep. 766. In 1883 the defendant applied to a proper court for a license to sell certain of the lands of his intestate to make assets to pay debts. Such license was granted; the sale was made; the purchaser at the same paid the purchase money; the sale was confirmed by the court, and the defendant was directed to make title to the purchaser, which he accordingly did. Afterwards, in 1887, the counsel for the defendant and counsel for the plaintiff Whitehead agreed to set aside the sale last above mentioned, and this stipulation was handed to the clerk of the superior court in which the license to sell the land was granted; but the clerk made no such order, nor did the court in term-time or at all. What purported to be a reaale of the same land was made in 1889, after this action began, and $800 was bid for the same. The defendant insists that the referee should have charged him with this sum, and not that bid and paid for the land at the sale thereof under license from the court, as he did do. The license to sell the land, the sale thereof, and the confirmation of the sale, were not set aside. They remained and remain in full force and effect, and the defendant is properly charged with the price bid and paid for it. The second supposed sale had no judicial or authoritative sanction, and was ineffectual, certainly as to the purposes of this action. As to the exceptions 5, 6, and 11 to the findings of law, we are of opinion that they are unfounded. The findings of fact pertinent, certainly so far as we can see, warrant them. If there is error, the burden is upon the defendant to make it appear. None is pointed out, and none appears upon the face of the record. Judgment affirmed.

BROWN v. MILLER et al.
(Supreme Court of North Carolina. April 21, 1891.)

MORTGAGE ON CROPS—DESCRIPTION.

1. In January, 1889, a mortgage was given on "the entire crop of cotton to be raised by me or my tenants on all my lands during the year 1889." The mortgagor had for 15 years been in possession of a tract of land known as his. There was then pending a suit for the recovery of the land, in which judgment was entered against him 10 days after the mortgage was given. He then leased the land, and planted it in cotton. Held, that the mortgage covered the crop raised subject to the landlord's lien for rent.

2. The mortgagor gave a second mortgage to the defendants, and was directed to deliver to them a bale of cotton due his landlord for rent. The mortgagor delivered a bale to the defendants for his landlord, but they insisted on applying it on account of their mortgage. The mortgagor said he was willing if his landlord was, and the next week he delivered to the landlord another bale in payment of the rent. Held, that the defendants were liable to the first mortgagee for the conversion of the bale delivered to them.

3. Under a mortgage on a crop of cotton "for supplies," where it does not appear how, or on what account, or for what purpose, the supplies were furnished, the mortgagee acquires no preference over a prior mortgage under Code N. C. § 1799, providing for such a preference for advances for supplies.

Following Rawlings v. Hunt, 90 N. C. 270.

Appeal from superior court, Mecklenburg county; BROWN, Judge.

This action is brought to recover the value of the bale of cotton specified in the complaint, which it is alleged belonged to the plaintiff, and was converted by the defendants to their own use before the action began, etc. On the trial the plaintiff put in evidence a chattel mortgage, proved and registered on the 23d of January, 1889, executed to him by John P. Patterson, whereby the latter purported and undertook to convey to the plaintiff his "entire crop of cotton to be raised by me or my tenants on all my lands during the year 1889," etc. This mortgagor was examined as a witness for the plaintiff, and testified that "the defendants got the bale of cotton which is the subject of this controversy

from me in October, 1889." The plaintiff then asked the witness: "On whose land was that cotton raised?" Under objection the court allowed the witness to say: "On the lands I live on at home, and have been on for fifteen years. The lands were known as my lands. I paid for them as my lands. On the 2d of February, 1889, I was declared by the court (in an action) not to be the owner." One Fisher obtained judgment in his favor for the land in the action referred to, and afterwards Patterson leased the land from him in June, 1889, and agreed to pay him one bale of cotton as rent, which Fisher directed him to leave at Nesbit's gin. The bale of cotton in question was produced on the lands mentioned, and which Fisher so recovered. In March, 1889, Patterson executed to the defendants his other mortgage, which was duly registered on the 4th of the same month, to secure a debt due to them for "supplies" which they furnished to him, and the cotton in controversy was embraced by this mortgage. Patterson further testified that he delivered the bale of cotton in question to defendants as the rent he owed Fisher, and directed them to deliver it to them as such rent. Nesbit (who is one of the defendants) took the bale, and refused to so deliver it, saying that the defendants wanted it on account of their mortgage debt above mentioned. Patterson said he was willing to do this if Fisher was willing. The defendants took the bale, and Patterson the next week delivered to Fisher another bale for the rent due him. The court submitted to the jury two issues, the first of which was: "Did the defendants wrongfully convert the bale of cotton belonging to the plaintiff as alleged?" The defendants insisted that the court should instruct the jury to respond "No" to this issue, but, on the contrary, it told them that, if they believed the evidence, to respond "Yes," and the defendants excepted. There was a verdict and judgment for the plaintiff, and the defendants appealed to this court, assigning error as follows: "(1) For admission of evidence objected to as above set forth; (2) for refusal to charge that upon all the evidence the jury should answer the first issue 'No.' (3) For error in charging that if the jury believed the evidence they should answer the first issue 'Yes.'"

Jones & Tillett, for appellants. F. F. Bason, for appellee.

MERRIMON, C. J., (after stating the facts as above.) The deed of mortgage under which the plaintiff claims title to the bale of cotton in controversy sufficiently designates and identifies the land upon which it was to be produced and the cotton itself to render this deed operative and effectual for the purpose contemplated by it. The purpose of this description was not to designate land to which the mortgagor certainly had absolute or perfect title, but the land claimed by him as his at the time he executed the deed, and upon which he intended that himself or his tenants should thereafter produce the cotton crop that the mortgage was intended to embrace. The simple purpose was to identify the land claimed by him as his on which the crop of cotton was to be produced. The mere fact that a third party, after the deed was executed, recovered the land sufficiently described by it, could not affect the sufficiency of the description or the deed. The land described as "my [the mortgagor's] land" remained the same. The description—the designation of it—was not destroyed or rendered less certain. The cotton crop conveyed by the deed was sufficiently designated. It was not an indefinite part of it, but all "the entire crop of cotton to be raised by me [the mortgagor] or my tenants on all my lands during the year 1889;" that is, the "entire crop" so raised on the land described as "my [the mortgagor's] land." The deed identified the land and the cotton crop embraced by it with such definiteness as that the same could be certainly ascertained and known. Woodlief v. Harris, 95 N. C. 211; Gwathney v. Etheridge, 99 N. C. 571, 6 S. E. Rep. 411; State v. Logan, 100 N. C. 454, 6 S. E. Rep. 898. Nor could the supervenient rights of Fisher, after he recovered the lands from the mortgagor as the latter's landlord, to rent—the one bale of cotton—render the mortgage inoperative, except to the extent of the rent. As to this the statute (Code, § 1754) gave the landlord a prior lien for the rent; but the whole cotton crop belonged to the plaintiff, subject only to that lien. As between the plaintiff and the mortgagor, the mortgage remained effectual, except as to the rent. The defendants contend, however, that the mortgagor, Patterson, executed to them in March next after Fisher recovered the land from him, a mortgage to secure a debt created for "supplies," which embraced the bale of cotton in controversy, and therefore they had good title to the same. This contention is without force. The last-mentioned mortgage was in effect a mortgage second to that of the plaintiff as to the cotton crop, including the bale in question. In no aspect of this second mortgage, so far as appears, can it be treated as creating a prior lien in favor of the defendants, as allowed in certain cases, by the statute. Id. § 1799. It does not appear how or for what purpose or on what account the "supplies" were made by the defendants to the mortgagor. Rawlings v. Hunt, 90 N. C. 270, and the cases there cited. The defendants further contend that the bale of cotton in question belonged to Fisher, the landlord, as and for the rent due to h.m from Patterson. We do not think the evidence went to prove that this bale of cotton was delivered to the landlord to pay the rent so due to him. Accepting the evidence pertinent as true, it only showed that Patterson, the tenant, at first intended that it should go to pay the rent, but the defendants did not so receive it for the landlord. They insisted that they should have it on account of their mortgage debt. The tenant, their mortgage debtor, consented, and afterwards he delivered to his landlord another and different bale in discharge of the rent due to him. This certainly is the fair and just interpretation of the facts as they appear. Judgment affirmed.

GUDGER v. PENLAND.

(Supreme Court of North Carolina. April 28, 1891.)

SLANDER—PLEADING.

1. Where perjury is punishable by confinement in the penitentiary, a false charge that a person swore lies at a certain trial is actionable *per se.*

2. Where the complaint in an action for slander in making such charge does not show whether the charge was made at or after the trial, or that defendant sustained such relation to the trial as would exempt him from liability for his utterance, the complaint is not demurrable on the ground that the charge was made pending a judicial investigation.

3. In an action of slander, in that defendant accused plaintiff of false swearing at a trial, plaintiff need not set forth the language or substance of the testimony referred to by defendant, unless defendant, in uttering the slanderous words, went on to specify what plaintiff swore, or in what particulars his testimony was false.

4. Though an action could be maintained and damages recovered by proving the utterance of slanderous words set forth in more than one paragraph of the complaint, where the language used in each instance amounts to a charge of perjury in the same judicial proceeding, and at the same time, it is not necessary that a separate demand for damages be appended to each paragraph.

This was an action for slander heard on demurrer at the February term, 1890, of the superior court of Buncombe county, before PHILIPS, J. The complaint and demurrer were as follows: The plaintiff, complaining of the defendant, alleges: "(1) That he is now a good, true, and honest citizen of this state, and as such hath always conducted himself, and until the committing of the grievances hereinafter mentioned was always reputed to be a person of good fame and credit, and hath never been guilty, nor, until the committing of the said grievances, been suspected to have been guilty, of swearing falsely, or of any other crime, by means of which said premises he, (the said plaintiff,) before the committing of the said grievances, had deservedly obtained the good opinion of all of his neighbors and of all other persons to whom he is known. (2) That the said defendant, well knowing the premises, as stated in paragraph 1, but contriving and wickedly and maliciously intending to injure the plaintiff in his good fame and credit, and to bring him into public scandal, infamy, and disgrace, and to cause it to be suspected that he (the plaintiff) had been guilty of perjury and swearing falsely heretofore, to-wit, on the ——— day of January, 1890, in the county of Buncombe aforesaid, in a certain discourse which he (the said defendant) then and there had, in the presence and hearing of divers good and noted citizens of this state, concerning the plaintiff, falsely and maliciously spoke and published of and concerning the plaintiff these false, scandalous, malicious, and defamatory words following; that is to say, 'he [meaning the plaintiff,] that damned old son-of-a-bitch, Dolph Gudger, has sworn lies on him [meaning the said defendant] in the criminal court at Asheville, at the special term, 1889.' (3) That afterwards, to-wit, on the day and year aforesaid, in the county aforesaid, in a certain other discourse which he (the said defendant) then and there had, in the presence and hearing of divers other good and worthy citizens of this state, he, (the said defendant,) further contriving and intending as aforesaid, then and there, in the presence and hearing of the said last-mentioned citizens, falsely and maliciously spoke and published of and concerning the said plaintiff these other false, scandalous, malicious, and defamatory words following; that is to say, he (meaning the plaintiff A. M. Gudger) swore to a lie in the court at Asheville, and he could prove it, and he, A. M. Gudger, (meaning the plaintiff,) swore lies on him (meaning the defendant) at the court in Asheville, and he (meaning the defendant) could prove it; that the lies sworn by him (meaning the plaintiff) were in the fence case, which was an indictment tried at the November special term of the criminal court of Buncombe county, 1889. (4) That afterwards, to-wit, on the day and year aforesaid, in the county aforesaid, in a certain other discourse which he (the said defendant) then and there had, in the presence and hearing of divers other good and worthy citizens of this state, he, (the said defendant,) further contriving and intending as aforesaid, then and there, in the presence and hearing of the said last-mentioned citizens, falsely and maliciously spoke and published of and concerning the said plaintiff these other false, scandalous, malicious, and defamatory words following; that is to say, he, (meaning the plaintiff,) at the special term of the criminal court held for the county of Buncombe in November, 1889, swore to a God damn lie, and he could prove it, in a case then pending, in which the state was the plaintiff and C. L. Miller, Eugene Moss, William Plemmons, Sr., Dow Meadows, Zack Plemmons, Francis Hill, and William Plemmons, Jr., were defendants. (5) That afterwards, to-wit, on the day and year aforesaid, in the county aforesaid, in a certain other discourse which he (the said defendant) then and there had, in the presence and hearing of divers other good and worthy citizens of this state, he, (the said defendant,) further contriving and intending as aforesaid, then and there, in the presence and hearing of the said last-mentioned citizens, falsely and maliciously spoke and published of and concerning the said plaintiff these other false, scandalous, malicious, and defamatory words following; that is to say, he, (meaning the plaintiff, A. M. Gudger,) swore to a lie in the case of the State against C. L. Miller, Eugene Moss, William Plemmons, Sr., Dow Meadows, Zack Plemmons, Francis Hill, and William Plemmons, Jr., the case which was tried at the special term of the criminal court held for the county of Buncombe, 1889, in which case the plaintiff was sworn as a witness and testified in behalf of the defendants. (6) That before the speaking of the several false, scandalous, malicious, and defamatory words by the said defendant of and concerning the plaintiff, stated in the paragraphs hereinbefore mentioned, a certain action was depending in the criminal court of Buncombe county, wherein the state was plaintiff and C. L. Miller, Eugene Moss,

William Plemmons, Sr., Dow Meadows, Zack Plemmons, Francis Hill, and William Plemmons, Jr., were defendants, in which said action, before the speaking and publishing of the same words, to-wit, at the special November term, 1889, the said defendants were tried and convicted, that is to say, C. L. Miller, Eugene Moss, Dow Meadows, Zack Plemmons, and William Plemmons, Jr., for destroying the fence of the said defendant, A. M. Penland, on the trial of which said case he (the said plaintiff) was duly sworn and did take his corporal oath upon the Holy Gospels of God before the said court, the said court then and there having sufficient and competent power and authority to administer an oath to the said plaintiff in that behalf, and the said plaintiff, being so sworn, and having so taken his corporal oath, was then and there examined and did give his evidence as a witness in said case aforesaid; and the said plaintiff further saith that the said defendant, well knowing the premises, but greatly envying the reputation of the said plaintiff, and contriving and intending to injure the plaintiff in his aforesaid good name, fame, and character, and bring him into public scandal, infamy, and disgrace with all his neighbors and other good citizens to whom be was known, and to cause it to be suspected and believed by those neighbors and citizens that he (the plaintiff) had been and was guilty of perjury, and to subject him to the pains and penalties of the law, and also to vex, harass, and ruin him, the said plaintiff, on the day and year aforesaid, in a certain discourse which the said defendant then and there, in the presence and hearing of the said last-mentioned citizens, falsely and maliciously spoke and published of and concerning the said plaintiff, and of and concerning the said trial, and of and concerning the said evidence so given by the said plaintiff as aforesaid, the false, scandalous, malicious, and defamatory words following; that is to say, that he (meaning the plaintiff, A. M. Gudger) swore a lie about rails not having been put upon the fence of A. M. Penland, and that old Dolph Gudger swore a lie in testifying that there had not been a new rail on the said fence in twenty years. (7) That by means of the committing of the said grievances, and on account of the committing of the same, the said plaintiff has been and is greatly injured in his said good fame and credit, and brought into public scandal, infamy, and disgrace, and otherwise greatly injured, to the damage of the said plaintiff in the sum of ten thousand dollars. Wherefore the plaintiff prays judgment for the sum of ten thousand dollars damages, and the costs of this action." On the back of said complaint appears the following indorsement: "Filed April 10th, 1890. Demurrer. The defendant demurs to the plaintiff's complaint, and assigns for cause of demurrer that said complaint does not state facts sufficient to constitute a cause of action in that: (1) It fails to allege that the criminal court of Buncombe had jurisdiction to try the case, (State v. C. L. Miller and others,) referred to in the complaint. (2) It fails to allege that in said case re-

ferred to in said complaint the defendants were charged with any crime or
offense against the laws of this state.
(3) It fails to allege that the evidence
given by the plaintiff, the falsity of which
the defendant is alleged to have charged,
was material to the issue then on trial.
(4) It fails to allege that the language
which the complaint alleges that the defendant charged the plaintiff with having
used falsely was material to any issue arising upon an indictment for removing a
fence. (5) That it appears upon the face of
said complaint that the language which
it charges that the defendant charged
the plaintiff with having falsely uttered as
a witness on the trial of the case State
against C. L. Miller and others, mentioned
in said complaint, was not material to
any issue that could arise upon said trial.
(6) It fails to allege that the defendant
charged the plaintiff with the commission
of any crime against the laws of this
state, and it alleges no special damage.
(7) The language charged to have been
uttered by the defendant against the plaintiff is not actionable *per se*, and no special
damage is alleged. (8) That the complaint is vague, indefinite, and does not
state with sufficient clearness the language
used, nor who used it. (9) If the plaintiff
should attempt to treat the different allegations of his complaint as statements of
separate causes of action, then neither
states a cause of action, in that, in addition to the defects hereinbefore assigned,
each of said allegations fails to allege any
damage, and fails to comply with the requirements of rule 24 of the supreme court,
(104 N. C. 923, 12 S. E. Rep. vii.) Wherefore the defendant prays to be hence dismissed, with his proper costs." Demurrer
overruled. Appeal.

W. J. Peele, for appellant.   *George A.
Shuford*, for appellee.

AVERY, J., (*after stating the facts as
above.*) The charge that one has committed an infamous offense, if false, is actionable *per se*. Pegram v. Stoltz, 76 N. C.
349; McKee v. Wilson, 87 N. C. 300; Sparrow v. Maynard, 8 Jones, (N. C.) 195; Eure
v. Odom, 2 Hawks, 52. It is not material
whether the offense charged falls within the
classification of felonies or misdemeanors,
if at the time when the words are spoken a
person convicted on indictment for it
would be subject to infamous punishment.
Eure v. Odom, supra. Imprisonment in
the state-prison is infamous punishment.
McKee v. Wilson, supra; In re Hughes,
Phil. (N. C) 62. Perjury is a misdemean-
or, and is punishable by imprisonment in
the penitentiary or in the county jail, and
by fine not exceeding $1,000. Code, § 1092.
The contention of the defendant's counsel, that the slanderous language appeared
to have been used while a judicial investigation was progressing, and that under
the principle stated in Nissen v. Cramer,
104 N. C. 574, 10 S. E. Rep. 676, the defendant is absolutely exempt from liability,
finds no support in the admitted allegations of the complaint. It does not appear
affirmatively in the complaint whether
the language imputed to the defendant
in either of the paragraphs of the com-

plaint setting forth specific language,
in which the charge was couched on
different occasions, was spoken at the
time of the trial of the criminal action
or afterwards. The plaintiff was not
required to negative the idea that the
words slanderous *per se* were uttered under such circumstances that the defendant would be protected from liability on
the ground of privilege. The fact, if true,
that the words were uttered in the course
of a judicial proceeding, and were relevant
and pertinent to the matter before the
court, must be set up in the answer if the
defendant wishes to avail himself of it in
his defense, unless it be gratuitously alleged in the complaint. If it had been alleged that the language was spoken when
the defendant was being examined as a
witness on the trial of the indictment, still
it does not appear that the defendant sustained such relation to the prosecutor as
to furnish absolute or presumptive protection against liability. Nissen v. Cramer, supra; Shelfer v. Gooding, 2 Jones,
(N. C.) 175; Briggs v. Byrd, 12 Ired. 380.
There is nothing alleged in the complaint
that will support the contention of the defendant's counsel that the action cannot
be maintained.

We think that it appears with sufficient
certainty that defendant charged the
plaintiff with having sworn a lie, when he
was examined as a witness in the criminal
court of Buncombe county on the trial at
a term mentioned of an indictment (under
section 1092 of the Code) against the persons named for destroying Penland's
fence. We take judicial notice of the existence of that court and of the fact that
it had jurisdiction of the offense mentioned. State v. Ledford, 6 Ired. 5; State
v. Brown, 79 N. C. 642. It was not necessary that the plaintiff should set forth the
language or substance of the testimony
delivered by him and referred to by the defendant, as constituting the false swearing, unless the defendant, when speaking
the slanderous words, went on to specify
what the plaintiff did swear, or in what
particulars his testimony was false. Smith
v. Smith, 8 Ired. 29. A formal prayer for
relief is not now essential in any complaint, and where a plaintiff specifies, in
different paragraphs of the complaint, language used by the defendant at various
times, before the action was brought, but
amounting, in each instance, in all of its
varied forms, to a charge that the plaintiff swore falsely as a witness on the trial
of a certain suit before a court of competent jurisdiction, it is not necessary to append to each specification a separate demand for damage. Harris v. Sneeden, 104
N. C. 369, 10 S. E. Rep. 477. Though an action could be maintained and damages recovered by proving the utterance of the
slanderous words set forth in more than
one paragraph of a complaint, the language used in each instance amounting to
a charge of perjury in the same judicial
proceeding, and at the same time, it does
not follow that it is essential in this case
that a separate demand for damage
should be appended to each of such paragraphs. Harris v. Sneeden, supra. The
rule referred to in the demurrer is not sus-

ceptible of the construction that counsel seem to have given to it. For the reasons given we think that the demurrer was properly overruled. There was no error.

SPRAGINS et al. v. WHITE.

(Supreme Court of North Carolina. April 28, 1891.)

CONTRACTS — INTERPRETATION—QUESTION FOR COURT.

In an action for the price of goods sold by parol, which defendant had refused to receive, the latter swore that the goods were to be delivered in two weeks, which was denied by plaintiffs. *Held*, that it was error to charge the jury that, if they found that such agreement was made, then they must determine whether the parties understood that the plaintiffs were to insure the delivery within that time, or merely whether they were to use all due diligence in forwarding the goods by the common carrier; the interpretation of the contract was a question of law for the court. MERRIMON, C. J., dissenting.

Appeal from superior court, Bertie county; ARMFIELD, Judge.

The plaintiffs brought this action in the court of a justice of the peace to recover the price of certain goods (shoes) sold by them to the defendant. The latter denied the allegations of the complaint, and alleged that by a special agreement the plaintiffs promised to sell and deliver to him certain shoes at their place of business within a time specified, which they failed to do; that he was not bound to receive the shoes, and did not do so, etc. On the trial in the superior court the plaintiffs produced evidence tending to prove their cause of action as alleged by them. Defendant testified in his own behalf, among other things, as follows: "About the last of February, 1889, A. R. Benton, representing the plaintiffs, came to my store in Aulander, and after some conversation I agreed to buy of him a bill of shoes upon his promise to have them in Aulander in two weeks. That was the main inducement to the bargain. Without this promise I would not have taken the goods. I had a contract to fill within two weeks. Plaintiffs sent me an invoice of the goods, and shipped them, which I have. I also took down a memorandum of the order given Mr. Benton. I have that memorandum." The court, having directed the attention of the jury to the evidence and view of the case favorable to the plaintiffs, instructed them further as follows: "But the defendant contends that, at the time he purchased the plaintiffs' agent, there was an express bargain and agreement that the goods should be delivered at his house in two weeks. This plaintiffs deny. But, if you should believe that this agreement and bargain was made, then you must inquire and determine what was meant and understood by it by the parties making it. Did it mean that the plaintiffs were to insure, at all events, the delivery by the transportation company of the goods in two weeks, and that in failure of such delivery in two weeks the sale was to be void at the option of the defendant, and he might return the goods to plaintiffs? If so, plaintiffs are not entitled to recover. But if it meant that plaintiffs were to use all due

diligence in forwarding the order, in packing and shipping the goods by the common carrier, and plaintiffs did all these things, then plaintiffs are entitled to recover the bill and interest, as before stated." The defendant excepted upon the ground that "the court erred in the interpretation of the contract to the jury." There was a verdict and judgment for the plaintiffs, and the defendant appealed to this court.

F. D. Winston, for appellant. *Winston & Williams,* for appellees.

SHEPHERD, J., (*after stating the facts as above.*) "Where a contract," says Judge GASTON in Young v. Jeffreys, 4 Dev. & B. 221, "is wholly in writing, and the intention of the framers is by law to be collected from the document itself, there the entire construction of the contract—that is, the ascertainment of the intention of the parties, as well as the effect of that intention—is a pure question of law, and the whole office of the jury is to pass on the existence of the alleged written agreement. Where the contract is by parol (that is, oral) the terms of the agreement are of course a matter of fact; and if those terms be obscure or equivocal, or are susceptible of explanation from extrinsic evidence, it is for the jury to find also the meaning of the terms employed; but the effect of a parol agreement, when its terms are given and their meaning fixed, is as much a question of law as the construction of a written agreement." In speaking of oral contracts, NASH, J., remarks in Festerman v. Parker, 10 Ired. 474, that, "if there be no dispute as to the terms, and they be precise and explicit, it is for the court to declare their effect." See, also, Rhodes v. Chesson, Busb. 336; Pendleton - Jones, 82 N. C. 249. "Unless there were so, says PARKE, B., in Neilson v. Harford, 8 Mees. & W. 806, "there would be no certainty in the law, for a misconstruction by the jury cannot be set right at all effectually." We are sure that the learned judge was entirely familiar with the above principles, but we think that they were not properly applied in the present case. The terms of an oral contract must necessarily be ascertained from the testimony of the witnesses, and it is the duty of the court to instruct the jury as to the law applicable to the various phases arising upon such testimony. But where the court presents to the jury a particular view of the facts, and this embodies the terms of a contract which are in themselves precise and explicit, the court should declare their legal effect, and it would be error to leave this to be determined by the jury. In such a case the rule is the same as if the contract were in writing. After charging the jury upon the testimony of the plaintiffs, his honor presented the contention of the defendant, which was founded upon the evidence, as follows: "I agreed to buy of him [the agent of plaintiffs] a bill of shoes upon his promise to have them in Aulander in two weeks." According to the defense, this was the entire agreement as to the shipment and delivery, and it is not varied in any manner because it induced the defendant to purchase the goods. It was the contract resulting from the "express bargain and agreement" that formed the inducement, and it is this contract alone that was to be interpreted. The language used is clear and precise. It is not unusual or equivocal, nor does it involve any scientific exposition by experts, nor is it doubtful in the sense that it may be explained by evidence of usage or other extraneous circumstances. If the language, being thus free from ambiguity, leaves the meaning of the parties in doubt, it is the duty of the court, and not the jury, to determine its legal effect; and, if no definite meaning can be attached to such language, then it is the duty of the court to so hold. Silverthorn v. Fowle, 4 Jones, (N. C.) 362. His honor, after stating the terms of the contract, instructed the jury that, if such was the contract, they must further "inquire and determine what was meant and understood by it by the parties making it." Now, the charge assumes that the terms of the contract are ascertained, but at the same time leaves its interpretation to the jury. The court should have interpreted this meaning according to the terms of the assumed contract, and not according to other terms incorporated into the same by what the jury were to infer was the meaning of the parties. In this we think there was error. New trial.

MERRIMON, C. J., (dissenting.) The special contract alleged by the defendant was not in writing. If it had been so, and the writing had been admitted or proven by proper evidence, the court would have interpreted its meaning. The proper construction of contracts is matter of law, and it is the province of the court to interpret their meaning. When they are written, and cannot be explained or modified by parol, in some cases they may be, their terms are settled, and their meaning is simply a question of law to be determined by the court. When, also, a contract has not been reduced to writing, but its terms appear,—are precise, clear, and explicit,—the court must interpret their meaning and legal effect. If, however, the parties to an unwritten contract dispute about its terms, and these are not clear nor definite,—are obscure or equivocal, or their use is not certain and determinate, or it must be inferred from the conduct of the parties,—such contract—what its terms are—must be ascertained by the jury. And so, also, if the terms used are technical or unusual, and their meaning must be gathered from experts, or persons acquainted with the particular act or business to which such terms refer, and in the like cases, the jury must ascertain the meaning of such terms as used by the parties; still, when their use and what they are, are ascertained by the jury, it is the duty of the court to interpret the contract ascertained as matter of fact by the jury. The jury must ascertain as matter of fact what the contract is, and the court must determine what is its legal import and effect. In such cases the court should generally give the jury instructions as to the meaning and effect of the contract, accordingly as

they may find it to be, carefully pointing out their duty in ascertaining what the contract is. Young v. Jeffreys, 4 Dev. & B. 216; Massey v. Belisle, 2 Ired. 170; Festerman v. Parker, 10 Ired. 474; Silverthorn v. Fowle, 4 Jones, (N. C.) 362. In this case the exception is based upon a misapprehension of the instruction complained of. The court did not intend to leave it to the jury to interpret the contract in question, nor did it do so in effect. The contract alleged was not in writing; the principal evidence—that of the defendant—tending to prove it was not very explicit, unequivocal, and determinate. On the contrary, it left the real agreement to inference in material respects. The witness said: "I agreed to buy of him [the plaintiffs' agent] a bill of shoes upon his promise to have them in Aulander in two weeks;" but he did not say certainly, in terms, that the agent agreed on his part to deliver the shoes at the place mentioned within that time; that this was a substantial part of the contract; and that it was understood that the defendant would not be bound to take the shoes if they were not so delivered. This was left in doubt: to inference. He said "that this was the main inducement to the bargain: without this promise I would not have taken the goods." He does not say, in terms, that the agent so understood and agreed; that he did, was left to inference. He did not say, in terms, that the contract was special,—out of the ordinary course of trade in such cases. That was left to inference. Hence the court told the jury to inquire whether there was such special contract, and, if so, what was meant —not as matter of law, but as matter of fact—by it; by what was said and mutually understood and agreed upon by the parties. That is, the court instructed the jury to ascertain from the uncertain, undeterminate, evidence of such contract what it was as matter of fact. It submitted to them, not what was the legal meaning of the words used by the defendant or by either party, but whether the parties in fact mutually understood and agreed that the shoes should be delivered "in two weeks" at the defendant's place of business, or whether in fact it was agreed that the plaintiffs, in the ordinary course of business, sold the defendant the shoes; and this was the fact of the agreement; and the plaintiffs' agent said.—simply added,—not as part of the agreement, that he would deliver them "in two weeks," meaning no more than that he would be prompt in shipping them. The court further said, in substance, that, if the jury should find the contract to be as contended by the defendant, then, as matter of law, the plaintiffs could not recover. Thus it interpreted the contract in that view. It further said, in effect, that if the jury should find the contract to be in fact as contended by the plaintiffs, then the latter could recover. Thus it interpreted the meaning and legal effect of it in the view favorable to the plaintiffs. The evidence in this case left the terms of contract much more in doubt than did the evidence of the contract in question in

Massey v. Belisle, supra. In that case "the plaintiff stated to the defendant, as a fact, that it had been discovered that her house was two feet upon his lot. Upon this information she promised to pay him four dollars per annum while it remained there. At the expiration of the first year, when the rent was demanded, she refused to pay, alleging that the house was altogether upon her own land. After this refusal she did pay four dollars, upon his express promise to refund it if it should turn out that the house was not upon his lot. The parties then agreed upon a mode by which the boundaries of their respective lots should be determined. Unfortunately the attempt thus to determine their boundaries failed, and the plaintiff sued for the next year's rent. Now, it seems to us clear that upon what terms and upon what consideration the defendant promised to pay rent was an inquiry of fact fit for the determination of a jury." The court said that, the facts as to the terms being doubtful, it was the province of the jury to ascertain the same. They certainly were more definite than the terms in question in the present case. Perhaps the instruction given the jury might have been more precise, but it was quite intelligible, and substantially in all respects correct. The court interpreted the contract, as to its legal import and effect, accordingly as the jury might ascertain it, to be as matter of fact, and it gave them proper instructions as to their duty. The other exceptions are without merit, and it would serve no useful purpose to advert further to them.

HOWLAND et al. v. FORLAW.

(*Supreme Court of North Carolina.* May 5, 1891.)

LEASE– RENT IN KIND—LIEN—SALE TO THIRD PERSON.

Plaintiffs, the owners of a fish-scrap and oil factory, contracted to furnish W. & Co. the factory, a seine, and some boats, while W. & Co. agreed to deliver to them one-fourth of the gross product of oil and scraps, and to pay all running expenses of factory. W. & Co., instead of delivering the one-fourth of the product to plaintiffs, sold it all to defendant. *Held,* in an action to recover said one-fourth or the value thereof, that said agreement constituted a lease, rent to be paid in kind; and that as the only statutory provision giving the landlord a lien, until a division had been made and his share set apart to him in severalty, was in the case of leases for agricultural purposes, (Code N. C. § 1754,) plaintiffs' only remedy was against their lessees.

This was a civil action in the nature of trover, brought to recover the value of certain fish-scrap and oil, sold by B. L. Webb & Co., who were in charge of plaintiffs' mills, to the defendant, and tried at the fall term, 1890, of superior court of Carteret county, before ARMFIELD, J. His honor refused instructions asked, and charged the jury as follows: "That the contract between plaintiffs Howland and B. T. Webb & Co. was not a copartnership contract, but was a contract of rental of the property of plaintiffs for one-fourth of the product of the factory; that if the plaintiffs were in possession of the property in controversy, under the contract introduced in evidence, the same having

been delivered to them, and defendant purchased it and · took it away, then, whether said property (scrap and oil) was divided or not, the plaintiffs are entitled to recover, that being the effect of the contract." The · defendant requested the court, among other prayers, to give the following instruction: "(4) If said Benjamin T. Webb was the lessee of plaintiffs of the Steep Point Fish-Scrap & Oil Factory, and was in possession of said factory and fish-scrap and oil therein, under an agreement to pay, as rent therefor, a portion or percentage of the profits or the gross products of scrap and oil, and the defendant, Forlaw, purchased from said Webb, from said factory, fish-scrap and oil in bulk, or which had never been divided or set apart to plaintiffs as rent, then the plaintiffs are not entitled to recover any amount, as plaintiffs had no possession or right of property sufficient to maintain this action, nor any lien, by statute or otherwise, in the fish-scrap and oil until a division. The plaintiffs' cause of action is against Benjamin T. Webb, if any one." The defendant excepted to the instruction given, and to the refusal to charge as requested. Defendant appealed. The other material facts are stated in the opinion of the court.

C. R. Thomas, Jr., for appellant.

AVERY, J., (*after stating the facts as above.*) By the terms of the covenant entered into between the plaintiffs, Ralph Howland and L. C. Howland and B. F. Webb & Co., the plaintiffs agreed to "furnish" the firm "a purse seine and two purse-boats;" also the fish-scrap and oil works, with appurtenances, situated on Steep Point, on North river; while Webb & Co. agreed to deliver to them "one-fourth of the gross product of oil and scrap of said factory, seine oil to be barreled and scrap in bulk in scrap-house,— all to be in shipping order." B. T. Webb & Co. further covenanted to pay all of the expenses of catching fish, and that incurred in running the factory during the year, and to fill certain engagements for furnishing scrap previously made by the plaintiffs with a customer. Before it was declared by statute (Code, § 1754) that crops raised on land, leased for agricultural purposes, should be deemed vested in the landlord to secure the payment of his rents, his advancements and expenditures for making and saving crops, and the performance on the part of the tenant of the stipulations in the lease, the title to the whole of the crop was, in contemplation of law, vested in the tenant (even where the parties had agreed upon the payment as rent of a certain portion of the crop) until a division had been made, and the share of the landlord had been set apart to him in severalty. Deaver v. Rice, 4 Dev. & B. 431; Gordon v. Armstrong, 5 Ired. 409; Biggs v. Ferrell, 12 Ired. 1; Ross v. Swaringer, 9 Ired. 481. This was an agreement to pay for the rent of the manufacturing establishment, the seine and boats, a certain proportion of the oil and scrap manufactured instead of a rent in money, and constituted Webb & Co. neither partners nor servants (or croppers) of Howland, but simply renters. Biggs v. Ferrell, supra, and Ross v. Swaringer, supra. Webb & Co. were to divide the product of the mill, and set apart Howland's share. The oil-works, with all appurtenances, situated on Steep Point, were described with sufficient certainty to pass a definite interest. These provisions in the agreement are distinctive characteristics of a lease. Harrison v. Ricks, 71 N. C. 7, and Haywood v. Rogers, 73 N. C. 320. As the works, with appurtenances, were not demised for agricultural purposes, no lien in favor of the lessor attached to the scrap and oil made. The plaintiffs have only their common-law remedy. The common-law right of distress or rent was held to be inconsistent with the spirit of our statutes in North Carolina: Taylor, Landl. & Ten. § 558; Deaver v. Rice, supra. Where a plaintiff recovered in an action of ejectment, the crop growing on the land, when he was not in possession, passed with the land; but he could neither recover specific articles (whether crops or trees) that had been severed from the land during the occupancy by the trespasser in an action of replevin, nor their value in trover, of one who had bought from the latter. Brothers v. Hurdle, 10 Ired. 490; Ray v. Gardner, 82 N. C. 454; Harrison v. Hoff, 102 N. C. 128, 9 S. E. Rep. 638. The remedy in such cases was an action of trespass for mesne profits against the party evicted. The very forcible reason given by PEARSON, J., for adopting this rule, was that, in a country where there were no markets overt, public policy forbade that every one who purchased a load of wood or a bushel of corn should incur a liability to the owner of the land from which it had been severed, if it should afterwards appear that they had purchased from a tenant holding over or other trespasser. Brothers v. Hurdle, supra. The public would be subjected to the same inconvenience if every purchaser of fish-scrap or oil from the lessees of an establishment where it is made subjected himself to a liability equal to the value of the article purchased, in case of failure on the part of the lessee to pay the full amount of rent according to the stipulations of the lease. The plaintiffs abandoned the ancillary remedy, (claim and delivery,) and relied upon showing a conversion of their property by the defendant, who had bought a quantity of scrap and oil, the product of the works leased, from R. T. Webb & Co. It is manifest that they can neither maintain an action of trover against the purchaser from Webb & Co. for the value of the property, nor resort to the ancillary remedy, and thereby establish a right to seize the specific article sold by said lessees. Cooley, Torts, p. 445. Having no lien by virtue of the Code, § 1754, until the receipt of their rent in kind, plaintiffs can look only to the lessees to deliver it, or account for its value, if they sell. The lessees, until the division was made under the contract with the lessor, were, in contemplation of law, the owners of all of the scrap and oil manufactured. The effect of a sale of any part of the scrap or oil made was to subject them to liability to the lessors *pro tanto* for the value of the landlord's proportion. There was error in the refusal of the judge to charge that, under the contract, B. T. Webb & Co. were lessees, and the defendant incurred no liability by buying scrap that had not been set apart and delivered to plaintiffs or their agent as rent; and that, by a sale of any portion of the undivided products of the manufacturing establishment leased to them, B. T. Webb & Co. passed a good title to the purchaser. For the error pointed out a new trial must be awarded. It is useless to discuss the other assignments of error.

KING *et al.* v. RHEW.

(*Supreme Court of North Carolina.* April 28, 1891.)

TRUST ESTATES — ADVERSE POSSESSION — LIMITATIONS—CONTINGENT REMAINDERS.

1. Land was conveyed to W., his heirs and assigns, in trust for the sole use and enjoyment of K. during her life, and not liable for the debts of her husband; and at her death to be divided among any children she might leave surviving her. Thereafter the husband of K. executed a deed of the land, and she signed it, but her name nowhere else appeared in the deed except in the attestation clause, and the deed did not refer in any way to the trust-estate. *Held*, in an action by the children of K. after her death against a party claiming by mesne conveyances from the grantee in the deed of K. and her husband, and who had been in possession, claiming adversely for the statutory period, that, as said deed was not in fact executed by K., and her husband had no interest to convey, the trustee could have maintained an action against defendant at any time, and therefore the trustee's estate was barred.

2. As the children had but a contingent remainder, the legal title to the fee vested in the trustee, and his estate being barred that of the remainder-men was also barred.

Appeal from superior court, New Hanover county; GRAVES, Judge.

D. L. *Russell* and *Ricaud & Weill*, for appellants. *Junius Davis*, for appellee.

SHEPHERD, J. The land in question was conveyed on the 25th of April, 1863, to one "Robert Wood, Jr., and his heirs and assigns," in trust "for the sole and separate use, occupation, and enjoyment of Charlotte King during her natural life, and at her death to be equally divided between any children she may leave her surviving, born of her intermarriage with her present husband, share and share alike, and to be in no wise liable to be sold or taken for the debts of her said husband." Charlotte King died in 1889, and the plaintiffs are the only children born of her intermarriage with Isaac W. King, her said husband. The said King in 1869 conveyed the land for a valuable consideration to one Ann Eliza Orrell, and the defendant claims by mesne conveyances from her. Charlotte King executed the deed with her husband, but her name does not appear in it anywhere except in the attestation clause, nor does the deed refer in any way to the trust-estate of Wood. It is admitted that the defendant "has been in the actual and open possession of the said land since the date (16th September, 1880) of the deed to him, [by one Chadwick,] claiming adversely under said deed, and [that] such possession was adverse to the plaintiffs unless in law it was not adverse."

The first question to be considered is whether the deed executed by King and wife (the trustee being no party thereto) conveyed any interest of the wife in the said land, so that the trustee would have been prevented in equity from asserting his legal title during the nine years' occupancy of the defendant. In Bank v. Rice, 4 How. 241, it was said that, "in order to convey by grant the party possessing the right must be grantor, and use apt and proper words to convey to the grantee; and merely signing, sealing, and acknowledging an instrument in which another person is grantor, is not sufficient. The deed in question conveyed the marital interests of the husband in these lands and nothing more. In the following cases the same rule is upheld as to deeds exactly similar to the one in question, where the party signed, sealed, and acknowledged it, and was only named in the attestation clause: Lufkin v. Curtis, 13 Mass. 223; Leavitt v. Lamprey, 13 Pick. 382; Greenough v. Turner, 11 Gray, 332; Stevens v. Owen, 25 Me. 94; Cox v. Wells, 7 Blackf. 410; Hall v. Savage, 4 Mason, 273; Bruce v. Wood, 1 Metc. (Mass.) 542; Pierce v. Chase, 108 Mass. 258; Purcell v. Goshorn, 17 Ohio, 105; Chapman v. Crooks, 41 Mich. 597, 2 N. W. Rep. 924; Wildes v. Van Voorhis, 15 Gray, 148; Harper v. Gilbert, 5 Cush. 418; Hubbard v. Knous, 8 Gray, 567." See, also, 1 Bish. Mar. Wom. § 594, note; Malone, Real Prop. 528, 703. In Gray v. Mathis, 7 Jones, (N. C.) 502, several of the foregoing cases are cited, and their doctrine clearly recognised and approved. These authorities abundantly show that Mrs. King was not a party to the deed signed by her, and that it was inefficacious to pass her estate in the said land. Neither did her husband have any interest jure mariti which he could have conveyed, as the property was vested in the trustee for the "sole and separate use" of his wife. Heathman v. Hall, 3 Ired. Eq. 420; 2 Lewin, Trusts, 753–756; 2 Perry, Trusts, § 648. Even had there been no trust, he could not, under the act of 1848, (Rev. Code, c. 56,) have conveyed his interest unless the wife had joined in the conveyance, and this we have seen she failed to do. The deed then can only be regarded as that of the husband, and, as he had no interest which he could have conveyed, the trustee could have maintained an action at any time against the defendant for the possession of the property. The defendant being thus exposed to an action on the part of the trustee, (Swann v. Myers, 75 N. C. 585,) and having been in the continuous possession for over seven years under his deed from Chadwick, (which was color of title,) and it being admitted that his possession was actually adverse, it must necessarily follow that the trustee's estate is barred. It is suggested, however, though not seriously pressed, that the possession of the defendant was permissive only; but there is no evidence of this, and we have but the naked deed of the husband and the admitted adverse possession of the defendant. Indeed, there is nothing in the case to show that Ann Eliza Orrell

ever had possession of the land; nor does it appear that the defendant ever had any notice of the deed to Wood, the trustee; not does he claim under it; nor is it a part of his title. The only evidence as to the possession is the admitted fact that Rhew has had possession since 1880, claiming adversely to all persons; and, even had he actual or constructive notice of the trust, the estate which he acquired by disseisin would not be subject to it, as it is well settled that "a disseisor is not an assign of the trustee, either in the per or post, for he does not claim through or under the trustee, but holds by a wrongful title of his own, and adversely to the trust." 1 Lewin, Trusts, 250; 1 Perry, Trusts, §§ 341–346; Benzein v. Lenoir, 1 Dev. Eq. 225. This seems to be conceded by counsel. It is not insisted that the trustee would have been prevented from suing because of any equitable estoppel against Mrs. King; but we will remark that, although it had appeared that her husband had represented that the conveyance was in proper form, and she had simply remained silent while he received the purchase money, she would not have been estopped. Clayton v. Rose, 87 N. C. 110. Neither would the consideration (other lands conveyed to her) have had this effect, whatever equitable remedy, if any, Mrs. Orrell might have had as to the land conveyed by her while it remained in the hands of Mrs. King. Scott v. Battle, 85 N. C. 184; Clayton v. Rose, supra. The estate of the trustee being barred, it is well settled that the cestuis que trustent are barred also. This principle is admirably stated by SMITH, C. J., in Clayton v. Cagle, 97 N. C. 301, 1 S. E. Rep. 523: "The annexation of trusts to the legal estate cannot arrest the operation of the rule which, under the circumstances, ripens an imperfect into a perfect title, since during all this period the defendant was exposed to the action of the true owner, [that is, the trustee;] and his negligence in bringing it tolls his entry, and bars his action. The interest of the cestui que trust is, as against strangers to the deed, under the protection of the trustee, and shares the fate that befalls the legal estate by his inaction and indifference." See, also, Herndon v. Pratt, 6 Jones, Eq. 327; Wellborn v. Finley, 7 Jones, (N. C.) 233; Clayton v. Rose, and Swann v. Myers, supra.

2. It is very earnestly insisted, however, that for the purposes of the trust it was unnecessary that the trustee should have taken any greater than a life-estate, and therefore the remainder-men should not be barred. The principle has very generally been applied in cases of devise where it is held that there is more room for construction to ascertain and carry into effect the intention of the testator; and accordingly the estate of the trustee has in some cases been enlarged or restricted to conform to the purposes of the trust. The rule, however, does not seem to be recognized in this state as applicable to limitations by deed. Evans v. King, 3 Jones, Eq. 387. But conceding to the fullest extent, for the purposes of the discussion, that in such cases the estate of the trustee will be "abridged or cut down" to a life-estate where the statute of uses would generally

execute the ulterior limitations, or, as expressed by the counsel, where the legal estate is unnecessary to subserve the purposes of the trust, we are nevertheless unable to see how it can avail the plaintiffs in this action. The land was purchased from a stranger for a valuable consideration, and the plain intention of the parties was that the entire legal and beneficial interest should pass out of the grantor. Although the plaintiffs may not have been in existence at the time of the execution of the conveyance, the limitation could have been made by a deed (operating, under our statute of 1715, as a common-law conveyance) directly to the wife for life, the inheritance during the contingency being either, as the old writers say, in abeyance or *in nubibus*, (Co. Litt. 342;) or, according to Mr. Fearne, (Cont. Rem. 361,) remaining in the grantor until the ascertainment of the persons who are entitled to take. Under such a conveyance, however, the wife's estate would have been subjected to the marital rights of the husband, and the contingent limitations over could have been defeated by the destruction of the life-estate. For the purpose, therefore, of securing her in the sole and separate enjoyment of her life estate, and presumably to more effectually preserve the particular estate until the vesting of the remainders, the entire fee was conveyed to Wood and his heirs in trust for the purposes declared. Nothing remained in the grantor, and, there being a valuable consideration, there could never have been a resulting trust in his favor. Brown v. Jones, 1 Atk. 158; Perry, Trusts, 158. In whom, then, was it necessary for the fee to vest? It could not be in the wife, because she took but a life-estate; and it could not go to the children even if in existence at the execution of the deed, (and this does not appear,) for it is well settled that, if the use is contingent, the use is not *in esse* until the happening of the contingency upon which its vesting depends, and the statute will not execute it until then. Chudleigh's Case, 1 Coke, 126; Sand, Uses & T. 110; 1 Sugd. Powers, 41; 4 Kent, Comm. 241; 1 Cruise, Dig. 354. It will be observed that the limitation over is not to the children of Mrs. King provided they survive her, (in which case they would have taken a vested remainder, subject to have been divested afterwards by their death before that of their mother,) but it is to "any children she may leave surviving her." During her life there could be no one to fill the description, and it is therefore quite clear that the uses were contingent. The fee then having passed out of the grantor, the wife taking but a life-estate, and the children having but a contingent use, which could not be executed by the statute, it must follow that until the death of Mrs. King it was necessary that it should have resided in the trustee and his heirs; and this is precisely where it was placed by the express terms of the conveyance. In support of this conclusion, in reference to the facts of this particular case, we reproduce the language of RUFFIN, C. J., in Battle v. Petway, 5 Ired. 576. He says: "If the trust is not for a particular person only, but is

limited over for other persons, for whose protection the trustee's legal estate is necessary or highly useful, it is plain that the duty of the trustee to those entitled *in futuro* requires him to retain his estate; and therefore the court would not decree him to convey it." In our case it was not only useful, but, as we have seen, it was absolutely necessary, that the fee should have abided in the trustee until the happening of the contingencies mentioned. The legal fee then being in the trustee, and having been barred by his inaction, as well as that of the equitable life-tenant, there remained no estate to feed the remainders when they vested in the plaintiffs upon the death of their mother, and they are therefore not entitled to recover. If any further authority were needed to support the conclusion at which we have arrived, it will be found in Herndon's Case, supra, which is strongly in point for the defendant. There, in the words of the defendant's counsel, the purposes of the trust were simply and purely to preserve the estate for the benefit of the contingent limitation to Mary Herndon and the others during the life of Robert and Julia, and according to the contention of the counsel for plaintiff it was only necessary that the trustees should take an estate for the lives of those two, and that the statute could only run against that life-estate; but the court held that the plaintiffs were barred, and they treated the question as too clear to admit of a doubt. If there had been anything in the point now raised by the counsel for plaintiffs, it certainly would not have escaped the attention of the eminent counsel who argued the case, or of the very able lawyer and distinguished jurist who delivered the opinion. Whatever opinion may be entertained by other courts, it is yet too well settled in this state to admit of argument that, where the trustee is barred, the *cestuis que trustent* in remainder as well as those for life are barred also. Herndon v. Pratt, and Swann v. Myers, supra.

Under the view we have taken of the law as settled by this court, and its application to the present case, it is hardly necessary to review the authorities cited by the plaintiffs from other states. We will remark, however, that Ellis v. Fisher, 65 Amer. Dec. 52, related to a trust created by devise, and the same is true of the quotation from Coulter v. Robinson, 57 Amer. Dec. 168, cited by counsel. In Nicoll v. Walworth, 4 Denio, 385, the estate of the trustee was but for life, and the decision is explained by DANFORTH, J., in Bennett v. Garlock, 79 N. Y. 302. In this latter case the doctrine as contended for by the plaintiffs was recognized as to deeds, but its application was denied because, as in the present case, it was necessary for the purposes of the trust that the trustee should take the fee. The passage cited from Perry, Trusts, 858, to the effect that the statutory bar ought not to run against the *cestuis que trustent* in remainder, is not sustained in the single case (Parker v. Hall, 2 Head, 641) cited in its support. The case only decides that the *cestuis que trustent* are not barred where the trustee estops himself from suing by selling the property, and thus "uniting with the purchaser in a breach of the trust." The wrong, says the court, is to the *cestuis que trustent* and not to the trustee, and "he could not sue or represent them." It has never been insisted that the bar is effective against the *cestui que trust* except in cases where the trustee could have sued, as in this case, and failed to do so. For the reasons given we are of the opinion that his honor committed no error in holding that the plaintiffs were barred, and could not recover. Affirmed.

BANK OF OXFORD v. BOBBITT *et al.*

(Supreme Court of North Carolina. April 28, 1891.)

RIGHT TO INTEREST—ACCOUNTING—REVIEW ON APPEAL.

1. Defendants executed certain bonds to secure plaintiff, a banking corporation, for advancements to be made to a firm, not to exceed $5 000, and to "include and to secure all amounts drawn by them for any purpose whatsoever," to terminate October 31, 1886, and the obligors to be held for whatever balance thereafter appeared at 8 per cent. per annum. In an action on the bonds the referee found that plaintiff charged on the daily balances of advancements 1 per cent. per month, and compounded same from month to month, and that on October 31st there was due plaintiff $5,081.83, which was reduced by credits, leaving due $4,043.73, September 1, 1887. Judgment was entered for the latter amount without interest. *Held,* that the bonds covered any balance found due October 31st, with 8 per cent. interest therefrom, and plaintiff was entitled to interest on the amount due from September 1, 1887, at 8 per cent.

2. Where defendants excepted to the judgment, but failed to appeal, they are estopped from questioning the correctness of the balance found by the court, on an appeal by plaintiff.

MERRIMON, C. J., and CLARK, J., dissenting.

This is an appeal by the plaintiff from a judgment rendered by T. B. WOMACK, J., in a civil action tried before him at the April term, 1890, of the superior court of Granville county. The complaint alleges, in substance: (1) That on the 2d of February, 1886, the defendants William Bobbitt and R. B. Hines were copartners in the management and conduct of the Meadows warehouse in Oxford, N. C., and for the sale of leaf tobacco. (2) That said Bobbitt & Hines agreed with the plaintiff that if plaintiff would advance money, not to exceed the sum of $5,000, to enable them to carry on their said copartnership, they would secure plaintiff against loss by reason of said advances to them, and in pursuance of said agreement said Bobbitt and the defendant D. C. White executed and delivered to the plaintiff, on the said 2d day of February, 1886, their covenant in words and figures as follows, to-wit: "State of North Carolina, Granville county. Oxford, N. C., Feb. 2d, 1886. $1,000.00. For value received, we, W. A. Bobbitt and D. C. White, hereby acknowledge ourselves jointly and severally bound to the Bank of Oxford in the sum of one thousand dollars, and hereby also bind our heirs, executors, administrators, and assigns. Witness our hands and seals, this the day and

year above written. The foregoing obligation is made to secure the bank of Oxford in part for an amount not exceeding $5,000, should it agree to advance to Bobbitt & Hines, copartners in the management of the Meadows warehouse. The amount due at any time shall be evidenced by the account which the Bank of Oxford agrees to open with the said Bobbitt & Hines, and is to include and to secure all amounts drawn by them for any purpose whatsoever. All advances under this agreement may be discounted by the Bank of Oxford upon three days' notice, and the account shall stand for settlement in fifteen days thereafter, when the balance shall be considered due and payable. If not paid, interest thereafter shall be at 8 per cent. per annum. This agreement terminates on the 31st of October, 1886, and the obligors hereto shall be held bound for whatever balance may then appear to be due the said Bank of Oxford, with interest thereafter at the rate of eight (8%) per cent. per annum, not to exceed the sum of $1,000. [Signed] W. A. BOBBITT. [Seal.] D. C. WHITE. [Seal.]" (3) That afterwards, on the 12th day of February, 1886, said W. A. Bobbitt and the defendants M. E. Bobbitt and T. C. Rogers, in pursuance of said agreement with plaintiff, executed and delivered to plaintiff a like covenant, with like stipulations and conditions, for $1,500. (4) That on the 2d of February, 1886, the said R. B. Hines and the defendant L. C. Taylor, in pursuance of said agreement with the plaintiff, executed and delivered to plaintiff a like covenant with like stipulations and conditions for $2,500. (5) That on the 1st day of November, 1886, there was a balance due plaintiff from said Bobbitt & Hines, on account of their said agreement, of $5,345.08, which was secured by said covenants, which indebtedness has been reduced by sundry credits, leaving a balance due, September 1, 1887, of $4,061.77. (6) That the plaintiff is a corporation duly created, etc., and hath right to maintain this action. The plaintiff demands judgment against the defendants Bobbitt & Hines for the sum of $4,061.77, with interest at 8 per cent. from September 1, 1887, till paid, and against the other defendants, D. C. White, M. E. Bobbitt, T. C. Rogers, and L. C. Taylor, respectively, for the sums due according to their respective covenants, and for such other relief, etc. The defendants W. A. Bobbitt and the sureties on the covenants executed by him, file a separate answer, admitting allegations 1, 2, 3, 4, and 6, except that they say that the defendant D. C. White executed the bond mentioned in the second allegation as surety for W. A. Bobbitt alone, and that the defendants M. E. Bobbitt and T. C. Rogers executed the bond mentioned in the third allegation as sureties for said W. A. Bobbitt alone; and these facts were known to the plaintiff at the time of the execution of the same. They admit that plaintiff made advances to Bobbitt & Hines, as alleged in the fifth allegation, but they deny that said Bobbitt & Hines were or are indebted to the plaintiff in the amount or in any amount nearly so large as alleged. And in their answer to the complaint the de fendants say: (7) That plaintiff has charged said firm for the sums advanced as interest at a greater rate than 8 per cent., to-wit, at the rate of 1 per cent. per month, and compounded the same monthly at the same rate, contrary to the statute, and that a large part of the indebtedness claimed by plaintiff consists of said illegal interest, which is included in drafts of the firm held by plaintiff, and that plaintiff, by reason of the statute of usury, which the defendants set up against plaintiff's claim, is not entitled to receive said illegal interest or any interest on the same advanced by plaintiff to said firm. (8) Defendants further say that they admit that said firm justly owes to plaintiff a balance of principal of some amount which the bonds mentioned in the complaint were intended to secure, but much less than the plaintiff alleges, and that a just account of the dealings with plaintiff will make it so appear; that such account is necessary, and ought to be taken, so as to show the true amount of indebtedness of said firm to plaintiff; and these defendants pray that the same may be done.

The defendants Hines & Taylor file a separate answer, in which they say that defendant Taylor was surety only to the bond of R. B. Hines, and this was known to plaintiff, and, so far as is material to the question before this court, containing the same admissions and relying upon the same defenses as set out in the answer of W. A. Bobbitt and his sureties. The respective answers contain controverted matter between the defendants themselves immaterial to this controversy, and need not be stated. At September term, 1888, it was, on motion of defendants, referred to a referee to state an account "of all sums advanced by plaintiff to the firm of Bobbitt & Hines in the pleadings mentioned, so as to show the amounts so advanced and the date at which they were advanced, and also of all sums received by plaintiff from the said defendants, and the dates of the same respectively." In obedience to the order of reference, C. T. Baskerville, the referee, reported a detailed account, from which, among other things, it appeared that plaintiff, in pursuance of an agreement, made advancements from time to time to the firm of Bobbitt & Hines, and that "on the sums of money advanced by the Bank of Oxford to the firm of Bobbitt & Hines the said bank charged said firm interest on the daily balances at the rate of 1 per cent. per month, and compounded the same from month to month to the end of the account,—31st of October, 1886. There was no agreement between the bank and said firm as to rate of interest the bank should charge upon advances made, but the covenant heretofore mentioned specially provides that any balance found to be due the bank upon the cessation of dealings on the 31st of October, 1886, should bear interest at the rate of 8 per cent. The firm of Bobbitt & Hines, however, knew from statements, including interest, furnished by them to the bank from time to time between the 28th of January, 1886, and the 31st of October, 1886, during the course of these dealings, with what rate of interest the

bank was charging them." It further appears from the report that the sum of $5,031.82 was due from the firm to the plaintiff on the 31st of October, 1886. This sum, as appears, was reduced by subsequent payments, leaving a balance of $4,043.73 due on the 1st of September, 1887. To the report of the referee the defendants filed numerous exceptions, and, the action being heard upon the same, the following judgment was rendered:

"On motion of attorneys for plaintiff it is adjudged by the court that exceptions filed by said W. A. Bobbitt and D. C. White and M. E. Bobbitt be and the same are overruled. It is adjudged by the court that the exceptions from one to seven, both inclusive, filed by the defendants Hines and Taylor, be, and the same are hereby, overruled. And on motion of attorneys for defendants, and the court having found as a fact that plaintiff had received usurious interest from defendants, it is adjudged by the court that plaintiff recover from the defendants no interest on the balance due from the 31st of October, 1886, until the first day of this term. And it appearing to the court that the balance due the plaintiff (over and above all payments, including payments made since 31st October, 1886, over and above advances made since that date) is $4,043.73, which sum is secured by the several collateral bonds as stated in the pleadings. Now, on motion of plaintiff's attorneys it is adjudged by the court that plaintiff recover of the defendants W. A. Bobbitt and R. B. Hines the said sum of $4,043.73, with interest thereon from 1st day of this term (21st April, 1890) until paid, at eight per cent. It is further adjudged that plaintiff recover of defendant L. C. Taylor $2,500, with interest on that sum from said first day of this term until paid, at eight per cent., which sum when paid shall be in full of one-half of judgment against principal above said. It is further adjudged that plaintiff recover of D. C. White the sum of $1,000, with interest on that sum at eight per cent. from first day of this term until paid, which sum when paid shall be a payment pro tanto on the judgment first above rendered. It is further adjudged that plaintiff recover of M. E. Bobbitt and T. C. Rogers the sum of $1,500, with interest on that sum from first day of this court until paid, at eight per cent. interest until paid, the same which sum when paid shall be a payment pro tanto on the judgment against the principal first above rendered. It is further adjudged that plaintiff recover of defendants its costs, to be taxed by the clerk. It is further adjudged that, upon the payment by said W. A. Bobbitt and R. B. Hines, or either of them, or by either of the other parties, of the above judgment rendered against them, such payment shall be in full discharge of the said several judgments herein rendered against said Taylor and White and M. E. Bobbitt and T. C. Rogers, and any payments made on said judgment against the principals shall be a discharge of part of the judgment against ―――― parties in the proportion of the amounts thereof."

To this judgment both plaintiffs and defendants excepted, but the plaintiff only ap-

pealed, and assigned as error the following:
"The court found as a fact that the
plaintiff had received from the defendants
Bobbitt & Hines, during the year 1886, and
before the 31st day of October of that year,
usurious interest on the sums advanced
by plaintiff to said Bobbitt & Hines, in
pursuance of the parol contract between
plaintiff and said Bobbitt & Hines, and
the court thereupon adjudged that this
receiving of usurious interest by plaintiff
of said Bobbitt & Hines was a forfeiture of
all interest on this contract between plaintiff and said Bobbitt & Hines from the
31st of October, 1886, up to the time when
the judgment was rendered, and was also
a forfeiture of all interest on the bonds or
sealed obligations executed by said William
A. Bobbitt, M. E. Bobbitt, and T. C. Rogers for $1,500, and by said William A.
Bobbitt and D. C. White for $1,000, and by
said R. B. Hines and L. C. Taylor for
$2,500, to secure whatever sum might be
due to plaintiff by said Bobbitt & Hines
on the 31st day of October, 1886, on the
contract between plaintiff and said Bobbitt & Hines from said 31st of October,
1886, up to the rendition of the judgment.
The defendants excepted to this decision
and ruling of the court, and for cause of
exception show: (1) That the same was
erroneous in law. (2) That the same was
erroneous as to the said Bobbitt & Hines,
because there was no note or other evidence of debt carrying interest, on which
this alleged usurious interest was taken
and received. (3) Because the said usurious interest was paid on a parol unwritten contract, in which there was no agreement to pay interest at any rate, legal or
otherwise. (4) Because there was no
agreement between plaintiff and said Bobbitt & Hines by which the latter contracted to pay any interest to plaintiff, or to
pay interest at any stated rate, whether
legal or otherwise. (5) Because the sureties to said several collateral obligations,
to-wit, the said M. E. Bobbitt, Rogers,
White, and Taylor were not parties to the
contract between plaintiff and said Bobbitt & Hines, on which the alleged usurious interest was taken. (6) That the covenants of said sureties bound them to pay
such balance as might be due plaintiff
from said Bobbitt & Hines on the 31st
day of October, 1886, and no interest at a
rate greater than is allowed by law has
been taken, received, reserved, or charged
on the sealed obligation executed by
said sureties to plaintiff, either before or
since the said 31st day of October, 1886.
(7) That said sureties, by their said several obligations, having bound and obligated themselves to pay to plaintiff such
sum as said Bobbitt & Hines might be indebted to plaintiff on said 31st day of October, 1886, and said Bobbitt & Hines having knowingly and voluntarily paid plaintiff interest at a rate greater than is allowed by law, the said usury not being
paid on any bond, note, or other evidence
of debt, nor on any contract by which a
greater rate of interest was agreed to be
paid than is allowed by law before said
31st day of October, 1886, the said sureties
cannot avail themselves of the defense of

usury on account of usurious interest paid
before the 31st of October, 1886, but are
bound by their said obligation to pay to
plaintiff the amount due on said 31st day
of October, 1886, without reference to such
usurious interest, if any such was received
in the manner stated above."
L. C. Edwards and Batchelor & Devereux, for appellant. Graham & Winston,
for appellees.

DAVIS, J., (after stating the facts as
above.) We think the court below misapprehended the purpose of the several covenants upon which this action is brought,
and failed to interpret them correctly.
They were independent covenants, collateral to the agreement between the plaintiff bank and the defendants Bobbitt &
Hines, and were intended to secure the
former in the payment of any balance
that might be ascertained to be due to
it for advancements which it might make
from time to time to the latter in carrying on their business under an agreement
which was to terminate on the 31st of
October, 1886, (unless discontinued before
that time upon notice as stipulated,)
with interest thereafter on such balance at
the rate of 8 per cent. per annum. The
balance found to be due from the firm of
Bobbitt & Hines to the plaintiff on the 31st
day of October, 1886, as reported by the
referee, and affirmed by the court, was
$5,031.82, which, as appears from the cred-
its, was subsequently reduced to $4,043.73,
September 1, 1887; and the plaintiff insists
that the covenants were to secure this balance, with interest thereon at the rate of
8 per cent. per annum till paid, and that
they are entitled to judgment accordingly. The defendants, on the contrary, insist that the plaintiff exacted and received
usury from the firm of Bobbitt & Hines,
and thereby forfeited the interest on this
balance, and, in accordance with this contention, and upon motion of counsel for
defendants, the court adjudged "that the
plaintiff recover from the defendant no interest on the balance due from the 31st of
October, 1886, until the first of this term,
(April 21, 1890.)" In this we think his
honor erred. Whether the balance—
$4,043.73—found to be due was a correct
balance, or whether it embraced any usurious interest or other item improperly
charged, is not a question for our consideration, as that is the balance found to be
due by the referee and affirmed by the
court below, from which there was no appeal by the defendants, and the sole question presented by the plaintiff's appeal is:
Was the plaintiff entitled to interest at 8
per centum on this balance under the covenants executed by the defendants to secure the same?
It is too well settled to need citation of
authority that, except as to questions of
jurisdiction and the sufficiency of the complaint to constitute a cause of action, this
court will only consider questions presented by the appeal of the appellant, and,
even if it were agreed that exceptions tak-
en and errors alleged by the appellee
should be heard and passed upon with the
appellant's case on appeal, it could not be
done without a departure from the settled

practice of the court. If both parties appeal, the appeal of one will not bring up the appeal of the other; and this rule cannot be waived by consent. Perry v. Adams, 96 N. C. 347, 2 S. E. Rep. 659, and cases cited. In the present case the defendants' exceptions are not before us. The covenants stipulate that the obligors shall secure the Bank of Oxford in the advances made to Bobbitt & Hines, including "all amounts drawn by them for any purpose whatever." The fair and reasonable—in fact, the only legal—interpretation that can be placed upon this is that they shall secure the payment of all amounts ascertained to be legally due, and, if any usurious advances or advances upon any other illegal or improper consideration were made, not only the defendants Bobbitt & Hines, but the sureties on the collateral covenants to secure the payment of any balance that might be ascertained upon settlement to be due the plaintiff, had a right to have any illegal item or items stricken from the account which would reduce pro tanto the balance; but that balance, when ascertained, would, under the agreement, bear interest from October 31, 1886, at eight per cent. It is not pretended that the covenants contained any contract or stipulation for the payment of a greater rate of interest than is allowed by law. On the contrary, it is found that there was no such stipulation or agreement; but it is said that the bank charged Bobbitt & Hines usurious interest on advancements made to them, and thereby forfeited all interest on the balance secured by the covenant. We are not called upon in the present case to say how it would be if the balance was increased by usurious interest; but, even if it were so, and the referee and the court below erred in finding that there was a balance due of $4,043.73, the question is not presented in this appeal. If the court below failed or refused to strike any usurious or other illegal item from the account, whereby the balance due would be diminished, the defendants should have excepted and appealed; but they seem to have been satisfied with the judgment,—at all events failed to except and perfect an appeal therefrom,—and we can only consider the error assigned by the appellant.

The defendants rely upon the case of Burwell v. Burgwyn, 100 N. C. 389, 6 S. E. Rep. 409. In that case there was a usurious contract as alleged and found, and the question was presented by the appeal. In the present case we fail to see in the covenants any contract for the payment of usury; in fact, it is found there was none; they only stipulate for the payment of the balance ascertained to be due, with interest thereon at 8 per cent. till paid. The judge below had the power to review the findings of fact as well as the conclusions of law of the referee, and to overrule, change, alter, or modify them as he might think just and proper; but the findings of fact, if upon sufficient and competent evidence, are conclusive upon this court, which has no control over the facts, and can only review the questions of law presented by the appeal. The balance found to be due from Bobbitt & Hines to the plaintiff, after deducting payment made since October 31, 1886, was $4,043.73, and this sum is accepted, without appeal, as the correct balance, and by the clear, explicit, and unmistakable language of the covenants bears interest at the rate of 8 per centum per annum till paid; and without passing upon the plaintiff's exceptions seriatim, or considering in detail the points presented by the learned counsel, by whom they were forcibly and ably pressed upon our attention, we think the court below erred in construing the covenants and denying to the plaintiff interest at 8 per cent. on the balance ascertained to be due, as stipulated therein. This interest should be on $4,043.73 from September 1, 1887, the balance having been reduced by credits, subsequent to October 31, 1886, to that amount on said day, and the judgment below will be made to conform to this opinion. There is error.

CLARK, J., (dissenting.) It is found as a fact by the referee, and the finding is approved by the court, that the plaintiff exacted and received usurious interest. The Code, § 3836, provides that the "taking, receiving, or charging" a greater rate of interest than that allowed by law, when knowingly done, "shall be deemed a forfeiture of the entire interest" which "the debt carries with it, or which has been agreed to be paid thereon." Had the defendants excepted to the allowance of any interest in making up the amount found by the referee to have been due on the 31st of October, 1886, and appealed from the judgment of the court approving the report of the referee, the defendants' exceptions should be allowed, and the account reformed by striking out all interest prior to the 31st of October, 1886, it having been forfeited by the clear terms of the statute. But the defendants do not appeal, and must be taken as satisfied with the judgment. They, however, do except to the allowance of any interest subsequent to October 31, 1886. They were not estopped to do so by not insisting to the full extent of their rights that the interest prior to that date should also be stricken out. The judge held with the defendants in refusing to allow interest subsequent to the date named, and the plaintiff's exception thereto cannot be sustained.

MERRIMON, C. J., (dissenting.) The court overruled all the exceptions of the defendants to the report of the referee. It in effect approved and adopted the latter's finding of fact, particularly and affirmatively, that the plaintiff had exacted usury from Bobbitt & Hines. There was no objection to the findings of fact. Then, upon the pleadings and the report, including the findings of fact, it gave judgment for the plaintiff for the balance ascertained to be due to it from Bobbitt & Hines on the 31st day of October, 1866, less credits, but allowed no interest upon such balance, upon the ground that the plaintiff took usury from them from time to time on account of moneys advanced to them, and thereby forfeited its right to have interest on such balance agreed to be paid by the defendants. The plaintiff insists that the court erred in refusing to allow such interest. The facts were ascertained, and the court, seeing and considering the whole record, should have given such judgment thereupon as the plaintiff was entitled to have, and it was erroneous to give any other. Then, did the court give the proper judgment? I think not; that it misapprehended the purpose of the several covenants sued upon, and failed to interpret them correctly. They were not part of the contract between the plaintiff and Bobbitt & Hines, whereby the former agreed to advance money from time to time during the period specified to the latter. They were separate from and collateral to that contract, and the simple purpose of them was to render the defendants responsible to the plaintiff for any balance of such advancements that might be due to it by virtue of the contract upon its termination, not exceeding the aggregate sums of money specified in the covenants, such balance to bear interest until paid at the rate of 8 per centum per annum. The covenants so expressly declare and provide. The plaintiff did not "advance" or lend to the defendants any money during the time specified by virtue of such covenants or any stipulations contained in them, nor was it intended it should, nor did it, exact from them on such account any usury. The usury was exacted from Bobbitt & Hines, partners, on account of moneys advanced to them from time to time during the period specified under their contract as partners with the plaintiff. Nor did the latter exact usury from them as to the present cause of action, but as to the contract between it and them as partners. The liability of the defendants, the extent thereof, and particularly the measure thereof, must be determined by a just interpretation of the several covenants sued upon. They each contain this explanatory and obligatory provision: "The foregoing obligation is made to secure the Bank of Oxford in part for an amount not exceeding five thousand dollars, should it agree to advance to Bobbitt & Hines, copartners in the management of the Meadows warehouse. The amount due at any time shall be evidenced by the account which the Bank of Oxford agrees to open with the said Bobbitt & Hines, and is to include and to secure all amounts drawn by them for any purpose whatsoever. * * * This agreement terminates on the 31st of October, 1886, and the obligors hereto shall be held bound for whatever balance may then appear to be due the said Bank of Oxford, with interest thereafter at the rate of eight per cent. per annum, not to exceed the sum of one thousand dollars." Now, this plainly implies that it was contemplated by the parties that the plaintiff would from time to time, within the period designated, advance to Bobbitt & Hines, partners, money not exceeding $5,000, and, if it should do so, then the defendants respectively would each be obliged to pay the plaintiff any balance of such advancements Bobbitt & Hines might owe it at the termination of that contract with it in that respect, not exceeding the sum each of the defendants covenanted to pay, with interest at the rate stated. It was stipulated that the amount so due the plaintiff should be evidenced by the account it should open with Bobbitt & Hines, and that such account should "include and secure all amounts drawn by them for any purpose whatever." But the words "amounts drawn by them for any purpose whatever" do not imply for every possible purpose, or for any purpose legal or illegal. They imply, giving them their broadest meaning in favor of the plaintiff, amounts drawn in good faith for any legal purpose whatever. They do not imply amounts drawn for any illegal purpose within the knowledge of the plaintiff, and particularly any illegal purpose to be shared in or for the benefit of the plaintiff. It is not to be presumed or merely inferred that the parties to the covenants, whether covenantors or covenantees, contemplated or intended any such advancements of money or amounts to be drawn for illegal purposes or any illegal transactions, or that the plaintiff would knowingly make such advancements for illegal purposes. They contemplated and intended the utmost good faith on the part of the plaintiff towards the defendants, and the covenants of the latter are to be interpreted in that light. Hence the defendants did not covenant to pay to the plaintiff any usury charged against, exacted from, or paid or agreed to be paid by, Bobbitt & Hines under their contract with it, to which their covenants sued upon had reference, and to which they had relation collaterally; nor did they covenant to pay a balance of money due from them to the plaintiff, augmented by such charges, exactions, or payments of usury, or the same agreed to be paid. There is nothing in the covenants that indicates a purpose to pay a balance thus created in whole or in part. The defendants covenanted to pay the plaintiff any such balance in its favor for money advanced. It might be contended that this implied money was actually advanced,—paid directly to Bobbitt & Hines; but it must be observed that the account which the plaintiff agreed to open with them was intended to embrace "all amounts drawn by them for any purpose whatever." This fairly implies and embraces any "amount drawn" to pay the plaintiff lawful interest for the advances of money to them. The reasonable and just implication is that the defendants expected that the plaintiff would charge and require to be paid lawful interest upon such advances, and that they obliged themselves to be responsible on that account. The defendants were therefore liable, each, to the plaintiff for a sum of money not exceeding that specified in the covenant executed by them on account of any balance of such advancements made to Bobbitt & Hines, partners, which balance should be ascertained by adding interest upon advancements unpaid until the 31st day of October, 1886, at the rate of 6 per cent. per annum. The rate of 8 per cent. per annum cannot be allowed, because there was no agreement in writing for that rate. The balance ascertained to be due to the plaintiff on the day last mentioned (that was the day after which further advancements could not be made as contemplated by the covenant of defendants) bore interest until paid at the rate of 8 per cent. per annum. The covenants so expressly provided. The court, seeing the whole record, and learning from the report of the referee, approved by it, the amount of the balance due the plaintiff, should have given judgment in its favor for that balance, including interest as above indicated. It will be observed that no question as to usury paid by Bobbitt & Hines, partners, to the plaintiff properly arises in this case. The action is founded upon the covenants specified in the complaint, and, as said above, the liability of the defendants is determined by a proper interpretation of those covenants.

MARSHALL et al. v. MACON COUNTY SAV. BANK.

(*Supreme Court of North Carolina.* April 28, 1891.)

SALE—FAILURE TO ACCEPT—EVIDENCE OF INCORPORATION.

1. In an action for the price of a "ledger, index, check-books, and other stationery," it appeared that plaintiffs prepared the articles at defendant's request. They were only useful for it, and it, without cause, refused to accept and pay for them. The court charged that if defendant ordered the goods, and plaintiffs thereby prepared the same, and the order was countermanded thereafter, plaintiffs are entitled to damages, which would be the difference between the contract price and present value; and, if the goods were of no value except to defendant, the measure of damages would be the contract price. Judgment was entered for plaintiffs. *Held,* that there was evidence warranting the instructions.

2. Certified copies of letters of incorporation are *prima facie* evidence of such incorporation, under Code N. C. §§ 677–682, providing that letters of incorporation, certified by the clerk of the supreme court, shall be admissible in judicial proceedings, and be deemed *prima facie* evidence of the organization of a company purporting thereby to be established.

Appeal from superior court, Macon county; J. H. MERRIMON, Judge.

This action was brought in the court of a justice of the peace to recover from the defendant the price of a "ledger, index, check-books, and other stationery," which the plaintiffs allege they prepared at the request of the defendant, and which it afterwards, without cause, refused to accept, and refused to pay for the same; that the articles so prepared were of no value to the plaintiffs, or other person than the defendant, etc. The pleading raised issues of fact. On the trial in the superior court the defendant requested the court to instruct the jury: "(1) That the plaintiffs cannot recover of the defendant, for the reason that the goods were never delivered to the defendant. (2) The defendant is not a corporation, for the reason that the time the goods were ordered was within a few days after the defendant undertook to be incorporated, and that the notice countermanding the same was before the expiration of thirty days, the time required by law for the publication to be made, before the defendant was a corporation in law. (3) That the defendant was not a corporation in law, and therefore could not be sued, although it might be an inchoate corporation. (4)

That if a corporation, or an inchoate one, in the absence of evidence of the use of the functions conferred by law, it would not be in law a corporation. (5) That as the articles of agreement provide that none of the stockholders are responsible or liable for any debt except the subscription to the capital stock, the defendant, or any other stockholder, would not be liable for the goods sued on by the plaintiff; the evidence being that the defendant has no assets or property of any kind whatsoever in its corporate capacity, nor ever had any. (6) That if the jury believes that one Danford entered into and confederated with the plaintiffs to defraud the defendant, the plaintiffs could not recover in this action; and, as a badge of fraud, that there is no evidence that the plaintiffs ever made any inquiries as to the existence of the defendant as a corporation, nor whether the defendant had assets or property, or as to the liabilities of the alleged stockholders in said corporation, if in law the defendant was a corporation." The court refused to give the instructions as asked for, but instructed the jury, after reciting the testimony, that the copy of letters of incorporation put in evidence by the plaintiffs was *prima facie* evidence of the complete organization and incorporation of the defendant company, and that there was no evidence to rebut this *prima facie* case. That if the defendant ordered the goods from the plaintiffs, as testified by W. R. Johnson, and the plaintiffs under such order prepared the goods for the defendant according to the terms of such order, and the order was countermanded after the goods were prepared, and the defendant refused to receive and pay for the same, then the plaintiffs would be entitled to recover of the defendant the sum of damages they sustained by reason of defendant refusing to receive and pay for said goods. The measure of damages would be the difference between the contract price, which is the reasonable worth of the goods, and their present value. If the goods, in their present condition, are worthless to the plaintiffs, and are of no value to any one except the defendant, then the plaintiffs' damage would be the contract price for the goods. If the jury should find that said goods are of some value in their present condition, they should subtract their value from the contract price of the same. That it devolves upon the plaintiffs to make out their case by a preponderance of evidence. There was a verdict and judgment for the plaintiffs. Defendant appealed.

K. Elias and *T. F. Davidson,* for appellant.

MERRIMON, C. J., (*after stating the facts as above.*) The statute (Acts 1887, c. 412) authorizes the incorporation of "savings banks in the manner already provided for the formation of other corporations," etc. The general statute (Code, §§ 677–682) prescribes how corporations, with certain specified exemptions, may be formed, and it is, among other things, expressly provided that copies of the letters of incorporation, "certified by the clerk of the su-

perior court of the county where the same
are recorded, shall in all cases be admissible in evidence, and the letters aforesaid
shall in all judicial proceedings be deemed
prima facie evidence of the complete organization and incorporation of the company purporting thereby to have been established." The statute thus makes the
letters *prima facie* evidence of the incorporation of the company, and its organization; and also a certified copy of the letters, as recorded, likewise evidence in all
cases. State v. Abernathy, 94 N. C. 545.
The court, therefore, properly received in
evidence the certified copy of the letters of
incorporation, and instructed the jury
that the same was *prima facie* evidence of
the incorporation and organization of the
defendant. There was evidence that warranted the instructions given the jury,
and the defendant could not complain of
them. The defendant ordered the goods,
and they were prepared as directed, and
thus, in their nature, were useful only for
its purposes. It could not, after they
were so prepared, without any lawful excuse, be allowed to refuse to receive them;
and no such excuse was shown. The evidence went to prove that the defendant
ordered the goods; that they were manufactured as directed; that they could be
useful only to the defendant. There was
no evidence of fraud, so far as appears, as
suggested by the instructions asked for by
the defendant. Judgment affirmed.

JOHNSTON v. JOHNSTON *et al.*

(*Supreme Court of North Carolina.* April 28,
1891.)

WILLS—CONSTRUCTION — POWERS OF EXECUTOR—
DIVISION OF PROPERTY.

1. Testator at the same time executed a deed
of gift and a will disposing of all his property to
his children. By his deed he gave at the time of
its execution to each of his children in equal
amounts part of his personal property on conditions expressed therein, taking a receipt reciting
that they received the property on such conditions. The deed provided that testator's children should share equally in his property, specifying terms and conditions affecting the different
shares, and provided that his executor should
take receipts similar to that taken by him. The
will recited that in the event of testator's death
without further distribution of the remainder of
his estate it should be the basis of the final distribution, and appointed his son T. executor, who
was "fully charged with the duty and authority
of carrying out the purposes and intent expressed
in it, viz., a distribution of equal portions of
my remaining property to each of my children or
their lineal heirs, with same conditions annexed
as expressed in my deed of gift, and taken herewith, and take receipt therefor of like tenor and
manner as those bearing even date with these
presents." It further provided that property
not easily parceled out in equal portions should
be sold at public auction, and the proceeds divided among his children, but that at such sale
his executor should have the same right to purchase as the rest of his children. *Held,* that the
division and sale must be made by the executor,
it being for him in the exercise of his sound discretion to determine what property could be
easily parceled out.

2. In case of an actual division, the devisee
or legatee would take under the will, and it
would be sufficient for the executor to execute a
paper under his hand and seal specifying the
division made and the allotment, making appro-

priate reference to the will and his power thereunder, such writing to be proved and registered
as in the case of deeds.

3. In case any of the property was sold the
executor should execute a deed to the purchaser,
with reference to the will, and his power thereunder.

4. In case any of the devisees purchased, the
executor should in like manner execute a deed
to him.

5. The executor should, in case of a division
of the property or the proceeds, take receipts
from the devisees in substance and form as referred to in the will, which should be filed.

6. The executor, in dividing the property,
should set apart a share for himself equal with
the shares of the others; should execute a writing that in such division his share had been allotted to him, which should be proven and recorded; and he should also take and file his own
receipt for his share.

7. Under the provision of the will contained
in the deed of gift that in case any of testator's
children shall have issue which shall reach majority then the gift to them shall vest in such
children absolutely, "released and discharged
from all terms, limitations, and provisions herein
imposed," the receipt from a devisee or legatee
having issue of age need not specify the terms,
conditions, and limitations otherwise required,
but should recite the arrival of such issue at majority.

Appeal from superior court, Buncombe
county; BROWN, Judge.

It appears that William Johnston died
in the county of Buncombe on the 20th
day of September, 1890, leaving a last will
and testament, which was duly proven,
and the plaintiff qualified as executor
thereof. The following is so much of this
will as need be reported: "In the event of
my death without other and further distribution of the remainder of my estate, it
is my wish and desire that this paper
writing be taken as in effect and purpose
my last will and testament, and the basis
of the final distribution of my effects; and
to that end I hereby appoint my son,
Thomas D. Johnston, my executor, who
is hereby fully charged with the duty and
authority of carrying out the purposes
and intent expressed in it, viz., a distribution of equal portions of my remaining
property to each of my children or their
lineal heirs, with same conditions annexed
as expressed in my deed of gift now about
to be made, and taking herewith, and
take receipt therefor of like tenor and manner as those bearing even date with these
presents. And in regard to property not
easily parceled out and assessed in equal
portions, whether the same be lands or
stock, real or personal property, it is my
direction that the same be sold at public
auction to the highest bidder for cash, or
on time, duly advertising the time, place,
terms, etc.; and, after deducting the necessary expenses and his reasonable commission, divide the proceeds equally among
my children or their lineal heirs as herein
directed. But at said sale the said Thomas D. Johnston is not to be debarred from
becoming a purchaser on account of his
executorship, but is to be on equal footing in regard thereto with the rest of my
children; my purpose being not only to
secure equality in distribution of my effects
among my children according to the
terms and limitations and conditions expressed in my said deed of gift, but also to

hedge them in with safeguards against the contingency of litigation; it being an expressed condition of this and each bestowment that the recipient in receiving the same recognizes the validity and effect of this paper writing as my last will and testament, and thereby expressly pledges their acquiescence and assent to the provisions and conditions thereof, both now and ever hereafter. In testimony whereof I have hereunto set my hand and seal this 18th day of September, A. D. 1885. [Signed] WM. JOHNSTON. [Seal.]"

The devisees and legatees of this will each contends for a different interpretation of some of its material provisions, and insist upon different views of the powers of the executor to be exercised in the administration of the estate. The latter brings this action against the former, and asks the court to interpret the will, and particularly to advise and direct him as to his duties in the following specified respects: "(11) That the plaintiff by this action desires to obtain from the court its advice, direction, and opinion in construing said will, and as to his duty thereunder, and especially in the following particulars: *First.* Whether by the terms of said will he should divide or partition among the devisees and legatees mentioned therein the said real estate, or any part thereof, and, if so, should he assign the value of the several parts, and whether said will vests in him a discretion as to which part should be divided by metes and bounds and which part should be sold. *Second.* That if the court shall be of the opinion that any part should be divided among the said devisees and legatees, would it be the duty of the plaintiff, as executor, to make such division, and to execute deeds to the devisees for their several allotments, or would they each take as purchasers under said will simply? *Third.* That, if the court be of the opinion that the plaintiff should execute deeds as aforesaid, should the deeds so executed contain the conditions and limitations annexed to the property by the provisions of said will? *Fourth.* If the court be of the opinion that the plaintiff should execute deeds with said conditions and limitations as aforesaid, how would the plaintiff take title as one of said devisees under the will? *Fifth.* That if the said real estate, in the opinion of the court, should be sold as a whole or in part, provided in plaintiff's judgment the same cannot be divided by metes and bounds without prejudice to the parties in interest, should the plaintiff execute deed in fee-simple to the purchasers, free from all conditions and limitations contained in said will, and divide the proceeds of said sale, taking from the said legatees and devisees their receipt, with such conditions and limitations expressed therein, and of the same tenor and in like manner, as was taken from said devisees and legatees by testator in receipt dated 18th day of September, 1885, as per copy herewith annexed, marked Exhibit B? *Sixth.* If, in the opinion of the court, the said real estate or any part thereof should be sold for division under said will, and any of the said legatees and devisees should purchase at said sale, should the plaintiff, as

executor, execute to them deeds in fee-simple without the conditions and limitations expressed therein? *Seventh.* That the plaintiff is willing and ready to do and perform any and all of the opinions and directions of the court in the premises, and prays that the court will advise and direct him in each and every one of the particulars above stated, and in such other particulars as to the court may seem proper in construing said will."

Upon the facts admitted the court gave judgment, whereof the following is a copy: "Upon these facts the court is of opinion and adjudges as follows: (1) That Thomas D. Johnston is vested with the power, and it is his duty, as executor, to divide the real and personal estate devised and bequeathed in said will equally among the said devisees and legatees whenever in his judgment such estate can be easily parceled out and assessed in equal portions. But whenever in his judgment any of said real or personal estate cannot be easily parceled out and assessed in equal portions, the said executor is authorized, and it is his duty, to sell the same in the manner directed in said will. (2) That it is the duty of said executor to make such division, or cause the same to be made under his supervision, in such manner as will best conduce to perfect equality of division as nearly as possible. That any allotment of such real estate should be in writing under the hand and seal of said Thomas D. Johnston, which refers to the will under which it is made, and designates and allots to every devisee his or her part of the real estate actually divided in severalty, and states the cash value fixed upon such real estate as is in it allotted as of the time of the death of the testator, but contains no conditions, limitations, or restrictions; and this writing shall be duly proved or acknowledged and registered in said county as deeds are ordinarily proved or acknowledged and registered in said county according to law. (3) In making such division or allotment, or division and allotment, the executor shall take, signed by every devisee and legatee, six receipts of like tenor with that mentioned in findings of fact No. 4, for the amount of the value of the real and personal estate so to such devisees and legatees, respectively, allotted, as fixed by said executor in making such division or allotment, or division and allotment, as aforesaid, as by said will directed, which receipts shall contain the conditions and stipulations set forth specifically in said will. At any sale of said real or personal estate, or any part thereof, made by said executor for division as aforesaid, any of said devisees and legatees may become a purchaser, and take such property or estate so purchased as would any other person, not a devisee or legatee as aforesaid, who should purchase at said sale. (4) That the plaintiff executor pay the costs of this action, to be taxed by the clerk of this court."

F. A. Sondley, for appellants. *George A. Shuford,* for appellee.

MERRIMON, C. J., (*after stating the facts as above.*) The will before us to be interpreted is peculiar in its form and the method of the disposition of the testator's large estate. He first devised a scheme of division of his property, both real and personal, among his children, which is embodied in what he styles "my [his] deed of gift," which was executed at the same time he executed his will, and is particularly referred to in and made part of it. By this deed he gave at the time of its execution to each of his children in equal amounts considerable parts of his personal property, upon terms, conditions, and limitations expressed therein, and took from them a receipt therefor, joint and several in its form, in which they recite that they respectively received the property upon such terms, conditions, and limitations as are recited in the deed. As to further future dispositions of property to his children, to take effect in his life-time or after his death, except as to "such legacies, bequests, and devises as I [he] may make by a last will and testament under different limitations and conditions," he directs that they shall be made and received by them "upon the express provisions and conditions that the same shall be held by my [his] said children, and each of them, in their own names, respectively; and that all uses, changes, and investments of the principal of the same shall be made in their own names, respectively," etc. This deed provides and directs much in detail, that the testator's children shall severally share equally his property, and how they shall receive, have, own, and enjoy the same; and it specifies certain terms, conditions, and limitations affecting the several shares. In it the testator directs his executor to take receipts for the property so bequeathed and devised "of like tenor and manner" with that taken by himself, above mentioned. The deed above referred to is clearly made a material and substantial part of the testator's will. He refers to it in the first paragraph thereof as "my [his] deed of gift now about to be made and taking [taken] herewith," etc. Indeed, the will would be incomplete without it. In the first clause of his will he declares that "in the event of my death without other and further distribution of the remainder of my estate it is my wish and desire that this paper writing be taken as in effect and purpose my last will and testament, and the basis of the final distribution of my effects; and to that end I hereby appoint my son, Thomas D. Johnston, my executor, who is hereby fully charged with the duty and authority of carrying out the purposes and intent expressed in it, viz., a distribution of equal portions of my remaining property to each of my children or their lineal heirs, with the same conditions annexed as expressed in my deed of gift now about to be made, and taking herewith, and take receipt therefor of like tenor and manner as those bearing even date with these presents." The deed thus constituting part of the will must be so interpreted in all pertinent respects, and have due weight and force in fixing the disposition of the property and determining the powers of the executor. Siler v. Dorsett, 12 S. E. Rep. 986, decided at this term. The testator disposes of his whole property exclusively to his children.

He gives to no one of them any particular property, but plainly directs that the whole, both real and personal, shall be divided equally among them. At the time he executed the will and that part of it called the "deed of gift" he gave each of them an equal amount of personal property, and, keeping in view his purpose of just equality, he directs "a distribution of equal portions of my remaining property to each of my [his] children or their lineal heirs, with same conditions annexed as expressed in my deed of gift," etc. Indeed, the whole will manifests a deep affection for all his children alike, and a settled purpose that they shall in equal measure share his bounty.

It appears that the testator at the time of his death had large and valuable real estate, consisting of city lots, mountain land, undivided fractional mineral interests in large tracts of land, and that an actual division of all of them cannot be made among the devisees without prejudice to all or some of them. He did not devise particular tracts or parcels of land to any of his children, nor did he give any one or more of them specific legacies. He devised and bequeathed the whole of his property, both real and personal, as a whole, to be equally divided among them; and a chief purpose he had in view was equality in the division, made in such way as would most certainly promote the interests of all. Hence he made his dispositions of his property, both real and personal, very general, and the "basis of the final distribution of" the same; and hence, too, he "fully charged [his executor] with the duty and authority of carrying out the purposes and intent expressed in" his will,—that is, "a distribution of equal portion of my [his] remaining property to each of my [his] children or their lineal heirs," etc. He did not determine that his property, real and personal, other than money, could and should be actually divided among his children at all events; he intentionally left that to be determined after his death. He thought parts of it (parts of the land, stocks, and other personal property) might be actually divided, and to the advantage of his children. In such case, when it can be done, it is made the duty of the executor to make such division; otherwise he is required to sell the property, real or personal, and turn the same into a cash fund for such division. If it should turn out for any cause that such actual division cannot be made, that it would the better promote the interests of the devisees and legatees to turn the whole property into a cash fund for division, then and in that case it will be the duty of the executor to sell the whole for such purpose. It was therefore the testator said in general terms: "And in regard to property not easily parceled out and assessed in equal portions, whether the same be lands or stock or personal property, it is my direction that the same be sold at public auction," etc. It is expressly made the duty of the executor to carry "out the purposes and intent expressed in" the will,—to distribute the property, both real and personal, embraced by it. It is very obvious that the testator had great confidence in the ability, integrity, and good judgment of his son, Thomas, and his fitness to be the executor of his will. He fully charges him with the "duty and authority of carrying out the purposes and intent expressed in it, viz., a distribution of equal portions of my remaining property to each of my children," etc. He is "fully charged with the duty and authority" to effectuate such purpose. It is his duty to make the division, and he has full authority to that end; and when in good faith he has made it, it will be effectual. Thus, if the land, or parts of it, can be divided, he must make the division, and so also as to the personal property. If such actual division cannot be made, "parceled out and assessed in equal portions," then he should sell the property as directed, turn the same into a cash fund, and divide the same. It is his duty in making such division to assess the value and allot the property to the devisees and legatees. He may call to his aid the experience and observation of others if he shall see fit to do so, but the division and allotment must be his own. His judgment and action must prevail. Moreover, he is made the judge of what property cannot for any cause be "easily parceled out and assessed in equal portions." As to this, he should exercise a sound, not an arbitrary, discretion.

In case of such actual division of the property, real or personal, or any part of it, the devisee or legatee will take and have title under and by virtue of the will; and hence it will be sufficient for the executor to execute a paper writing under his hand and seal, specifying the division made, and the allotment of the same in severalty, to the particular devisee or legatee, making appropriate reference to the will, and his power as executor under the same. Such paper writing should be duly proven and registered, as in case of deeds required to be registered. Moreover, the executor should take from the devisees and legatees, in case of such division, a receipt in substance and form such as that mentioned and referred to in the will. In case the property or any part of it shall be sold, the sale should be made strictly as directed by the will, and the executor should execute to the purchaser a proper deed conveying the absolute title to the purchaser. The deed should appropriately refer to the will and the power of the executor to sell the property and make title therefor. In case the devisees, or any of them, shall purchase property at such sale, the executor should execute to him a proper deed for the property so purchased by him, just as if he were not such devisee. He should take a receipt from such devisee for his part of the fund divided, when the division shall be made. It is very apparent that the testator did not intend to put the executor at any disadvantage, but on a footing equal with the other devisees and legatees. No special provision is made for ascertaining and allotting the share of the executor. Hence, in the absence of such provision, in dividing the property, whether real or personal, he should set apart a share for himself

equal with the shares, respectively, of the other devisees or legatees, and should execute a paper writing under his hand and seal, to the effect that in such division his share had been allotted to him, and the same should be proven and registered. Thus the evidence of such division and allotment would be established and made perpetual. Furthermore, the executor should execute a "receipt"—a paper writing—in all respects like the receipts he is required to take from the other devisees and legatees, reciting in the face thereof that he had received his share or some part thereof of the estate of the testator, and such paper should be filed in the clerk's office with the other papers and records of the estate. These receipts should be carefully preserved, as they may become important in an action or actions to enforce the conditions and limitations therein specified. It is expressly provided in that part of the will specifying the terms, conditions, and limitations of the devises and bequests as follows: "And in case any or either of my said children shall have any issue which shall arrive at the age of twenty-one years, whether in the life-time or after the death or deaths of each of my said children, then the gifts and advancements herein made to such of my said children, respectively, or which may come to them on any future distribution of my estate, shall vest in such of my said children, respectively, or in their respective lineal heirs per stirpes, absolutely, and released and discharged from all the terms, limitations, and provisions herein imposed." When, therefore, it appears to the executor that one of the devisees and legatees has issue that has so arrived at the age of 21 years, the receipt required need not specify such terms, conditions, and limitations, but these may be omitted. It should, however, specify particularly that such issue had arrived at that age, thus suggesting the reason for such omission. This action is brought by the executor simply to obtain the advice and direction of the court as to his duties under the will. We are not called upon, nor would it be proper for the court below or for us, to express any opinion as to the rights of any party claiming under the will who is a party to the action. The purpose of the action is not to litigate, settle, and determine the rights of parties. The advice and direction given by the court below, so far as it extended, was substantially correct, and we approve and affirm the same. It should, however, have given the additional advice and direction indicated in this opinion, and it will amend and enlarge its entry so as to embrace the same. To that end let this opinion be certified to the superior court.

It is so ordered.

PATTERSON *et al.* v. GOOCH *et al.*

(*Supreme Court of North Carolina.* May 5, 1891.)

MARRIED WOMAN—MEMBER OF A FIRM—JUSTICE'S COURT.

1. Where suit is brought against a firm before a justice of the peace, and after appeal to the superior court it appears that the defendants are husband and wife, the action cannot be main-

tained, since the justice could have no jurisdiction of a *feme covert.*

2. Where it is not shown that goods purchased by a firm of which a *feme covert* is a member are still in the possession of the firm, or of the *feme,* when an action for the price is brought, the principle that it would be a fraud to permit her to retain the goods and set up her coverture as a defense does not apply.

Appeal from superior court, Granville county; BOYKIN, Judge.

Plaintiffs brought two actions before a justice of the peace against the defendants A. L. Gooch and E. C. Gooch, composing the firm of A. L. Gooch & Co. Defendants did not appear at the trials except by counsel, and judgments were rendered against them, from which they afterwards appealed to the superior court, and defendant E. C. Gooch gave an undertaking to stay execution on appeal. In the superior court a jury trial was waived, and both cases were tried as one by consent of parties. Plaintiffs proved their claims, and that, when the constable went to levy the executions obtained on his judgments upon the stock of goods of the defendants, they were claimed by defendant E. C. Gooch, and then introduced the following correspondence: "Baltimore, Oct. 3, 1889. Mr. A. L. Gooch, Dabney, N. C.—Dear Sir: We respectfully ask you to make a statement of your financial condition by answering the questions on the other side as a basis of credit for any present or future transaction you may have with us. PATTERSON, RENSHAW & Co. Received Oct. 11, 1889." The questions and answers on the other side were answered entirely by A. L. Gooch, there being no evidence that E. C. Gooch knew anything about them. Plaintiffs also prove that this statement had been made and delivered to plaintiffs by defendant A. L. Gooch, and that the goods, the price of which was here sued for, were sold to defendants on the faith of this statement, and rested his case. The defendants' counsel then stated that they would make no objection to judgments being entered against A. L. Gooch, but offered to show that defendant E. C. Gooch was a married woman, the wife of A. L. Gooch. Plaintiffs objected to this evidence because the plea of coverture, not having been set up in the justice's court, ought not to be allowed to be set up in the superior court; but the court admitted the plea and received the evidence and plaintiffs excepted. Defendants then proved that A. L. Gooch and E. C. Gooch were husband and wife, and were so on and since October 3, 1889. Plaintiffs insisted that, the defendants being husband and wife, and partners in trade, the husband was, as partner, the agent of the wife, and as such agent and partner had power to bind her, and that the letter to plaintiffs was such written consent to her entering into the contract as the statute law requires; that it would be a fraud upon creditors to allow her, after such representations on the part of her husband,—plainly implying that she was either a man or a *feme sole,*—to set up the defense of coverture; that the statutes and law against a *feme covert* binding herself, and against her being sued in the court of a justice of the

peace, do not apply to a case like the present, where she is engaged with her husband as a partner in trade, and when sued on a debt contracted by representations that she was a man or *feme sole.* The court ruled that the action could not be maintained against defendant E. C. Gooch on account of her coverture, and plaintiffs appeal.

T. T. Hicks, for appellants. *A. W. Graham,* for appellees.

CLARK, J. The plaintiffs contend that the statement set out in the record is in effect a written consent on the part of the husband, and, the nature of the contract being such as necessarily to imply a charge upon the wife's personal estate, that the *feme* defendant is liable, by virtue of the Code, § 1826. We need not decide how that may be, for, if we concede that it is so, the remedy cannot be sought in a court of a justice of the peace. Dougherty v. Sprinkle, 88 N. C. 300; Farthing v. Shields, 106 N. C. 289, 10 S. E. Rep. 998. The cases cited by the appellants in support of their position that it was in the discretion of the court below to allow or refuse the plea of coverture because not made at the first term—Neville v. Pope, 95 N. C. 346, and Vick v. Pope, 81 N. C. 22—only go to the extent that after judgment it is too late for the coverture to be set up, unless there has been excusable neglect, mistake, fraud, or the like. Nor will the principle laid down in Burns v. McGregor, 90 N. C. 225, that it would be a fraud to let the *feme* defendant keep the goods and set up the defense of coverture against an action for the recovery of the price of them, avail the plaintiff, for it is not shown that the *feme* defendant or the firm of which she is a member now has in possession any of the goods for the price of which this action is brought, nor is this an action of claim and delivery for the specific goods. It was competent for the judge to refuse to dismiss the appeal. Marsh v. Cohen, 68 N. C. 243; Richardson v. Railroad, 82 N. C. 343. No error.

MITCHELL *et al.* v. MITCHELL *et al.*

(*Supreme Court of North Carolina.* May 5, 1891.)

DEED—CONSTRUCTION.

A deed providing that "in consideration that he, the said J., is to live with me, the said M., and take care of me, the said M., and my wife, Sally, so long as we both live, and that I, the said M., doth give to the said J. all of the tract of land whereon I now live, at my death, containing, * * * and that I, the said M., do hereby warrant and defend the right and title of said land to J. and his heirs, forever, against the claims of all persons whatsoever," will be so construed that the words, "his heirs, forever," in the warranty, will be held to operate both to pass a remainder in fee and define the extent of the warranty.

This is a petition for partition sent up from the clerk. A trial by jury having been waived by consent, the case was heard upon facts agreed, at November term, 1890, of the superior court of Granville county, before JAMES C. MACRAE, Judge. "It is agreed that, if the presiding judge shall construe the said deed to convey a title in fee-simple to Jack E. Mitchell, the judgment shall be for the defendants that they are seised as set out in the answer. If the court shall hold that, by virtue of said deed, the grantee took only a life-estate in the land, the petitioners are tenants in common with defendants, and entitled to partition, or a sale for partition, as may be proper." Judgment for defendants. Plaintiffs appealed.

J. W. Graham, for appellants. *John W. Hays,* for appellees.

AVERY, J., *(after stating the facts as above.)* The material portion of the deed brought before us for construction by this appeal is as follows: "This indenture," etc. "witnesseth that, for and in consideration that he, the said Jack E. Mitchell, is to live with me, the said John Mitchell, and take care of me, the said John Mitchell, and my wife, Sally, so long as we both live, and that I, the said John Mitchell, doth give to the said Jack E. Mitchell all of the tract of land whereon I now live at my death, containing one hundred and sixty-nine acres, and that I, the said John Mitchell, do hereby warrant and defend the right and title of said land to Jack E. Mitchell, and his heirs, forever, against the claims of all persons whatsoever." "The courts, in order to carry out the intention of the grantor, where it could be gathered from the face of a deed, have, in a liberal spirit, construed conveyances as passing an estate of inheritance, in all cases, where the word 'heirs' was joined as a qualification to the name or designation of the bargainee, even in the clause of warranty, or where the covenant of warranty was confused with the premises or *habendum,* if by a transposition of it, or by making a parenthesis, or in any way disregarding punctuation, the word 'heirs' could be made to qualify the apt words of conveyance in the premises, or the words 'to have and to hold,' etc., in the *habendum* and *tenendum,* even though it was made thereby to do double duty as a part of the covenant of warranty also." Anderson v. Logan, 105 N. C. 266, 11 S. E. Rep. 361; Winborne v. Downing, 105 N. C. 20, 10 S. E. Rep. 888; Vickers v. Leigh, 104 N. C. 257, 10 S. E. Rep. 308. The words "his heirs, forever," used in the connection in which they occur, bring the deed within the principle stated, and will be construed as operating both to pass the remainder in fee and to define the extent of the warranty. Anderson v. Logan, supra. The judgment of the court below is affirmed.

PLEMMONS v. SOUTHERN IMP CO.

(Supreme Court of North Carolina. May 5, 1891.)

AMENDMENT OF PROCESS—WHEN APPEAL LIES.

1. The power of amendment of pleadings, process, and proceedings, given to the trial court by Code N. C. § 273, will not enable it to bring in a new party defendant without its consent, except by the issue and service of an amended summons, and where the summons commands the sheriff to summon "B., president of the Southern Improvement Co.," and it was so served, the added words are merely *descriptio personæ,* and B. alone is summoned; and an amendment striking out the words "B., president of," will not have the effect to make the improvement company a defendant.

2. No appeal lies from the denial of a motion to dismiss an action.

Appeal from superior court, Madison county; WHITAKER, Judge.

F. A. Sondley and *T. F. Davidson,* for appellant.

CLARK, J. The summons commanded the sheriff to summon "A. H. Bronson, president of the Southern Improvement Co.," and it was so served. This is legally a summons and service only upon A. H. Bronson individually. The superadded words, "president of the Southern Improvement Co.," were a mere *descriptio personæ,* as would be the words "Jr." or "Sr.," or the addition of words identifying a party by the place of his residence and the like. Code, § 273, gives the court very great powers of amendment over pleadings, process, and proceedings, "by adding or striking out the name of a party," etc. It was competent for the court below to amend the summons so as to make the Southern Improvement Company either an additional party defendant, or have substituted it as sole party defendant by at the same time striking out the name of "A. H. Bronson, president," etc.; but it could not bring the Southern Improvement Company in as a party defendant to the action without its consent (either expressed or by entering a general appearance) except by causing the amended summons to be served upon it. The service of summons, issued against "A. H. Bronson, president," etc., was not a service upon the corporation, and it cannot, in this short-hand manner, by amendment, be brought into court without service of process. Young v. Rollins, 90 N. C. 134. When additional parties plaintiff are made, or there is a substitution of parties plaintiff, no summons issues, because the plaintiff is the moving party, and comes into court voluntarily. Reynolds v. Smathers, 87 N. C. 24; Jarrett v. Gibbs, 107 N. C. 303, 12 S. E. Rep. 272. If he objects, and is a necessary party, he is made a defendant. Code, § 185. No summons was directed to issue against the corporation, and, the amendment of the summons not having the effect to make it a party without service of process, the company, by counsel appearing specially for the purposes of the motion only, moved to dismiss the proceedings as to the Southern Improvement Company. The court refused the motion, and the said company appealed. It is settled that no appeal lies from a refusal to dismiss an action. Mitchell v. Kilburn, 74 N. C. 483; Foster v. Penry, 77 N. C. 160; Crawley v. Woodfin, 78 N. C. 4. The appellant might have properly treated all subsequent proceedings as a nullity till served with process, or it may be that leave may still be granted to issue against it upon the amended summons.

Appeal dismissed.

HERNDON *et al.* v. ÆTNA INS. CO.

(Supreme Court of North Carolina. May 5, 1891.)

REMOVAL OF CAUSES — AMENDMENT OF APPLICATION—RES ADJUDICATA.

Where an application for removal to the federal court has been denied on the ground that the allegations therein as to the citizenship of the parties were insufficient, the court below might in its discretion have allowed an amendment at the proper time, but after an appeal from the order of denial, and an affirmance by the supreme court, the matter has become res adjudicata, although it was an interlocutory or incidental order, and an amendment cannot be allowed.

Appeal from superior court, Durham county; E. T. BOYKIN, Judge.

The defendant filed its petition in the action within the time allowed by law, praying that the same be removed to the circuit court of the United States in and for the western district of North Carolina, as allowed by law in appropriate cases. That petition failed to allege, and it did not appear, that one of the plaintiffs was a citizen of this state, that the others were citizens of another state, and the defendant was a citizen of a third and different state, at the time the action began, and the application was denied. Herndon v. Insurance Co., 107 N. C. 191, 12 S. E. Rep. 240. Thereupon the defendant excepted, and appealed to this court, and the latter affirmed the judgment of the court below. Thereafter, and at the last term of the superior court, the defendant moved upon affidavit "that it be allowed to amend its petition to remove this action to the United States court, which has been heretofore filed herein," etc., so as to allege such diverse citizenship at the time the action began. The court refused this motion, "not as matter of discretion, but on the ground that it is too late to amend, the defendant having heretofore filed its answer herein." From the order of the court refusing to allow the amendment the defendant appealed to this court.

J. W. Hinsdale and J. M. Manning, for appellant. Fuller & Fuller and J. W. Graham, for appellees.

MERRIMON, C. J., (after stating the facts as above.) No doubt the court below might, in its discretion, have allowed such amendment as that prayed for, if a proper motion for the purpose had been made in apt time; but it is questionable whether such motion could have been allowed after the lapse of the time within which application might be made to remove the case to the circuit court of the United States. We need not, however, decide how this might be, because the application to so remove the case was denied, the defendant appealed to this court from the order of denial, and the latter court affirmed the order. Thus the application was ended, became res adjudicata, and the court below had no authority to set the order of denial affirmed aside, or at all interfere with it, or allow such amendment as that asked for and denied upon the ground that the motion came "too late, the defendant having heretofore filed its answer." This denial does not properly rest upon the ground thus assigned, but upon the other ground above indicated. Nor does the fact that the order so appealed from and affirmed by this court was to be treated as interlocutory or incidental at all alter the case. The application was ended by a regular and orderly adjudication which was, as to it, final.

Jones v. Thorne, 80 N. C. 72; Roulhac v. Brown, 87 N. C. 1; Pasour v. Lineberger, 90 N. C. 159; Wilson v. Lineberger, 83 N. C. 412; Moore v. Grant, 92 N. C. 316; Wingo v. Hooper, 98 N. C. 482, 4 S. E. Rep. 468; Dobson v. Simonton, 100 N. C. 56, 6 S. E. Rep. 369; White v. Butcher, 97 N. C. 7, 2 S. E. Rep. 59. If it be granted that the defendant could have made a fresh application to remove the case, it did not do so; and, if it had done so, the application could not have been allowed, because it would have been made too late,—not within the time such applications might be made. Order affirmed.

STATE v. HALL.

(Supreme Court of North Carolina. May 5, 1891.)

FORGERY—EVIDENCE—SENTENCE.

1. Under indictment charging the forgery of an order upon another for goods, the essential element of the offense is that there was an intent to defraud, and evidence of the presentation of the order to the partner of the person on whom it is drawn, and the delivery of the goods by him, will not amount to a variance, but is ample evidence of such intent.

2. Under an indictment consisting of two counts, where there was no instruction refused or exception taken to the charge as to one of them, and there was a general verdict of guilty on both counts, and but one sentence imposed, the law will apply it to the verdict upon the count to which no exception was assigned.

3. Mistrials and severances being within the discretion of the trial judge, it was not error, where two defendants were jointly indicted and tried, and one only convicted, to make a mistrial as to the other, and try him alone at the next term.

4. Though the order in question is not such as to be the subject of forgery at common law, yet if the indictment is good for a misdemeanor at common law, and the sentence imposed is within the limit authorized by Code N. C. § 1097, for offenses committed with intent to defraud, the judgment will not be disturbed.

Appeal from superior court, Stanley county; BYNUM, Judge.

The defendant and one Freeman were indicted at fall term, 1889, for forgery of the following paper writing: "Mr. Miller, pleas send me 3 gals. whiskey I will send you the money DOLPH SHAVER. Dec. the 24th 1888." There were two counts in the bill of indictment,—the first charging the forgery with intent to defraud Miller, and the second with intent to defraud Shaver. At spring term, 1890, the defendants were put upon their trial. The defendant Freeman was convicted, but, the jury having failed to agree upon a verdict as to the defendant Hall, the court directed a mistrial as to him. At fall term, 1890, he was again placed on trial. It was in evidence that Miller and one Basinger were partners distilling and selling liquor; that the order set out in the bill was fraudulently signed by said Hall without the authority of Shaver; that it was presented at the place of business of Miller & Basinger to Basinger by said Freeman, who obtained the liquor on it, and delivered it subsequently to Hall. The other facts are not set out, as there was no exception taken to the evidence. The defendant asked the following instructions: (1) That there is a variance between the allegations contained in the bill of indictment and the proof, in that the bill of indictment alleges that the order alleged to be a forgery was made with an intent to defraud Manuel Miller, while the proof showed that the whisky was obtained from James Basinger. (2) That there is no proof that any whisky was obtained on the order from Miller. The court refused the instructions asked, and in lieu thereof charged the jury that, if they found the fact to be that Miller and Basinger were partners in Rowan county, and that defendant, in Stanley county, signed the order as set forth in the bill of indictment, the charge in the bill to defraud Miller would be sustained by this proof, if Basinger filled the order believing it to have been signed by Shaver. To this defendant excepted, and also to the refusal to give the special instructions asked. Verdict of guilty. Judgment. Appeal by defendant.

Batchelor & Devereux, for appellant. *The Attorney General*, for the State.

CLARK, J., (*after stating the facts as above.*) To constitute forgery, it is essential that there is an intent to defraud. It is not essential that any one be actually defrauded, or that any act be done other than the fraudulent making or altering of the writing. The forgery of the order upon Miller, and its presentation to his partner, was evidence ample of the intent to defraud. State v. Lane, 80 N. C. 407; State v. Morgan, 2 Dev. & B. 348. It was immaterial whether Miller himself, or Basinger for him, as his partner, filled the order, or, indeed, whether the order was filled at all or not. This is not an indictment for obtaining goods under false pretenses. Indeed, upon an allegation of an intent to defraud A., it is not a variance to show an attempt to defraud A. and B. 1 Whart. Crim. Law, 713, 743a. And in fact it was not necessary to allege the name of any person or corporation intended to be defrauded. Code, § 1191. Besides, there was no instruction refused or exception taken to the charge as to the second count. The alleged errors were clearly such as could not have affected the verdict on the second count. There being a general verdict of guilty on both counts, and but one sentence imposed, the law will apply it to the verdict upon the count to which no exception was assigned. State v. Toole, 106 N. C. 736, 11 S. E. Rep. 168. The defendant moves here in arrest of judgment (1) because, having been indicted jointly with Freeman, who was found guilty at the former term, it was error to make a mistrial as to the defendant, and try him alone at the next term. Mistrials (except in capital cases) and severances are matters within the discretion of the trial judge. We see, therefore, nothing to review in the course pursued here. When several defendants are indicted jointly, it is not unusual to try one or more, and issue *caplases* for others not taken, or, if taken, there may be a continuance as to some of the defendants for cause. Besides, there was no exception at the time, and it is too late to raise this exception after verdict. (2) The second ground urged in arrest of judgment is that the order is not such a one as is the subject of

forgery under the statute. That is true, but the indictment is good for misdemeanor at common law, (State v Lamb, 65 N. C. 419; State v. Leak, 80 N. C. 403; State v. Covington, 94 N. C. 913;) and, being an offense committed with intent to defraud, the sentence imposed is within the limits authorized by Code, § 1097.

There is no error.

GATLIN et al. v. HARRELL et al.

(Supreme Court of North Carolina. May 5, 1891.)

FRAUD AND DECEIT—EVIDENCE.

In an action for damages for fraud and deceit of defendants in the sale of land to plaintiff, where the proof was that the defendants pointed out to the plaintiff certain corners and line trees of the tract, and stated that it had been surveyed, and contained 115 acres, and some of the corners and line trees were not true ones, but there was nothing to show that defendants knew that they were not the true ones, or that they fraudulently intended to deceive plaintiff, or that the land had not been surveyed, or that it did not contain "115 acres, more or less" as specified in the deed, the plaintiff was properly nonsuited.

Appeal from superior court, Edgecombe county; WHITAKER, Judge.

The purpose of this action is to recover damages occasioned by the alleged fraud and deceit of the defendants perpetrated upon the *feme* plaintiff in the sale to her of the tract of land mentioned in the complaint. The pleadings raised issues of fact. The only evidence produced on the trial was as follows: "R. H. Gatlin, the plaintiff: Bought land from John H. Harrell, the defendant, about 27th of July, 1888, before the time he was to see me two or three times in regard to it, he described the land to me. I walked down the canal with him, and he pointed out to me a corner between him and his brother, George Harrell. He said the other corner was a pine stump on the road near an old steam-mill. Before that time he pointed out two trees—a pine and a maple—on the line between him and Fred Boyett. These were the lines of the land he sold me. He gave me an obligation to make title upon payment of purchase money, and he made a deed. Before deed was made he also showed me another corner on the west of this tract, or, in other words, the corner between him and Boyett. He also showed me some line trees between him and his brother, George, the corner on the road from Tarboro to Goose Nest, Boyett's land on the south of this corner, land since sold to me by Boyett on the west. He said the tract had been surveyed, and contained 115 acres. These corners and lines pointed out to me were not the true corners and lines, except the line on east side of his land between him and George Harrell. Deed from John H. Harrell and Martha E. Harrell to Penelope E. Gatlin, dated 29th August, 1888, Book 65, p. 400, introduced. Grant of 640 acres land, John Smith, dated March 1, 1780, introduced. Deed from John Smith to Blake B. Wiggins, dated 26th January, 1785, introduced. Deed from Blake B. Wiggins and wife to John Burnett, 19th February, 1782, introduced. Deed from John Burnett to

Thomas Bryan, 26th September, 1805, introduced. Deed from John Burnett to Arthur Staton, April, 1798, introduced. Deed from John Burnett to Wm. Jones, Book 8, p. 72. Edgecombe Record, introduced. Here, in answer to a question from the court, and before plaintiffs had closed their case, it was admitted that the deed from John H. Harrell and Martha E. Harrell to Penelope E. Gatlin, dated 22d August, 1888, was taken by grantees in execution of previous contract to convey land as pointed out to them by grantors. It thereupon was suggested by the court that plaintiffs could not recover in this action. The plaintiffs submitted to a nonsuit, and appealed to the supreme court."

G. M. T. Fountain, for appellants. Gilliam & Son and J. L. Bridgers, for appellees.

MERRIMON, C. J., (*after stating the facts as above.*) The gist, and largely the substance, of the plaintiffs' alleged cause of action consists in the false and fraudulent representations of the defendants to the *feme* plaintiff, in which she confided, and on which she acted, as to the lines, corner and line trees, and the quantity of the tract of land they sold and conveyed to her as alleged. The defendants, in their answer, broadly and much in detail denied the material allegations of the complaint. No question was raised before or on the trial as to whether the plaintiffs alleged or sufficiently alleged a good cause of action, as their counsel now seems to suppose. The nonsuit was not founded upon such ground, certainly so far as appears. The plaintiffs produced such evidence as they could or saw fit to do, and thereupon the court intimated the opinion that they could not recover, and they submitted to a judgment of nonsuit, as they might do. We think the suggestion of the court was well founded. The whole of the evidence accepted as true did not in any reasonable view of it prove the alleged fraud and deceit. The proof was that the defendants pointed out to the plaintiff certain corners and line trees and lines of the tract so sold, and that these, or some of them, were not the true ones; but there is nothing to prove that the defendants knew that they were not the true ones, nor that they fraudulently intended to mislead, deceive, and get advantage of the *feme* plaintiff. The proof further was that the defendants "said the tract had been surveyed, and contained one hundred and fifteen acres." There was nothing to prove that it had not been surveyed, or that it did not contain that quantity. The mere fact that the defendants pointed out corners and lines not the true ones could not of itself prove fraud and deceit, especially in the total absence of proof that the tract conveyed did not contain the quantity of land specified in the deed as "containing one hundred and fifteen acres, more or less." Indeed, there was no proof, so far as appears, as to the quantity of land the defendants contracted to sell to the *feme* plaintiff, or what quantity they conveyed, otherwise than as shown by the deed put in evidence. There was no proof to sustain the material allegations of the complaint. In the

absence of such proof it is obvious the plaintiffs could not recover, and the court hence properly intimated that they could not. There must be *probata* as well as *allegata.* Judgment affirmed.

BLACKNALL v. ROWLAND *et al.*

(*Supreme Court of North Carolina.* May 5, 1891.)

DECEIT—FRAUDULENT REPRESENTATIONS — ESTOPPEL.

In an action for fraudulent misrepresentations in the sale to plaintiff of certain shares of corporate stock, a written agreement of the parties was put in evidence, reciting that 50 per cent. of the par value had been paid in cash, and 25 per cent. by a declaration of dividend out of net profits, and setting out the alleged financial condition of the company, and providing that the trade was to be conditioned upon the representations as to the condition of the business and stock of said company, which might be verified by an examination of its affairs by an expert book-keeper of plaintiff's selection and at his expense. *Held,* that plaintiff's right to recover upon such representations, as fraudulent, is not concluded by his failure to avail himself of the right to make such examination through an expert.

Appeal from superior court, Durham county; E. T. BOYKIN, Judge.

This action is brought to recover damages occasioned by the false and fraudulent representations of the defendants to the plaintiff, whereby the latter was intentionally misled and induced to buy from the defendants certain shares of the capital stock of no value of a corporation named, and in consideration thereof to convey to the defendants his tract of land of great value, etc. Having in view the transactions referred to, the parties executed a paper writing, whereof the following is a copy: "W. H. Rowland and W. R. Cooper propose to sell, and W. O. Blacknall agrees to buy, the interest of said Rowland & Cooper in fifty shares of the capital stock of the Durham Sash, Door & Blind Manufacturing Company. As the basis of the proposition and acceptance, it is represented and understood that said stock is of the par value of fifty dollars a share; that fifty per cent. of the par value of each share has been paid thereon in cash, and twenty-five per cent. of the par value thereof has been paid by a declaration of dividend out of the net profits of the business and operations of the company, so that seventy-five per cent. of the par value of the stock of said company is now legally paid up; that the company owes for machinery $2,000, for lumber about $——, and floating debt of $600 to $700; that its assets are available and in good condition, and exceed its liabilities by $3,000; that Rowland and Cooper will be able to legally assign said stock or interest, and have the same duly transferred on the company's books, to said Blacknall. In exchange for said stock or interest said Blacknall is to convey to said Rowland and Cooper and their heirs, by good and sufficient deed in fee-simple, an unincumbered title to 28 acres of land in Durham county adjoining T. D. Lyon on the east, N. C. R. R. Co. on the south, W. O. Blacknall on the west, S. J. Hester on the north, it being just east of the 30 acres now under mortgage. This trade is conditioned upon the representations above as to condition of business and stock of said company, and other statements, being verified upon examination of its affairs by an expert book-keeper of Blacknall's selection, and at his expense, and upon the condition that his title to the land named above is good. Witness the signatures of W. H. ROWLAND and W. R. COOPER and W. O. BLACKNALL, October 4th, 1888." The defendants denied the material allegations of the complaint. On the trial the plaintiff put in evidence the paper writing above set forth, and much other evidence, oral and otherwise. The defendants also introduced several witnesses, who were examined. "After the evidence had closed, and one of the plaintiff's counsel and two of the defendants' counsel had addressed the jury, his honor stated to plaintiff's counsel that, as the plaintiff had not had the books of the corporation examined by an expert book-keeper, he would instruct the jury that the plaintiff was not entitled to recover upon the issues submitted by him to the jury. In deference to this opinion of his honor, the plaintiff submitted to a judgment of nonsuit. Judgment entered. Plaintiff appealed to supreme court."

J. S. Manning, for appellant. *John W. Graham,* for appellees.

MERRIMON, C. J., (*after stating the facts as above.*) The cause of action alleged in the complaint consists, in substance, of the alleged false and fraudulent representations of the defendants made to the plaintiff in the paper writing, a copy of which is set forth above, and otherwise, as to the condition, circumstances, and solvency of the corporation therein named, which the plaintiff reasonably believed to be true, and whereby he was fraudulently misled and induced to buy the shares of stock mentioned of the defendants in that corporation, which were really of no value, and to convey to them his tract of land mentioned, of large value; and, further, of the false and fraudulent warranty of the truth of such representations made by the defendants to the plaintiff as additional inducement to him to buy such stock of no value. There was evidence for the plaintiff on the trial tending to prove that the representations made by the defendants to him in the paper writing and otherwise were not true; that the corporation was insolvent; that it was not prosperous, but declining; that its indebtedness was greater and its resources less than represented; that the dividend mentioned was not declared out of the net earnings of the corporation, and that the defendants knew these facts; that they encouraged and induced the plaintiff to believe these representations, and to close the proposed transaction. There was evidence for the defendants tending to prove the contrary. In this state of the case, the presiding judge said "that, as the plaintiff had not had the books of the corporation examined by an expert book-keeper, he would instruct the jury that the plaintiff was not entitled to recover." In this there is error. The plaintiff was not

concluded by the fact that he did not have such examination made. He was not bound to verify the representations made. He might, as matter of caution, have done so, but he might not unreasonably believe, rely, and act upon the plain, pertinent, and material statements made by the defendants to him in the paper writing and otherwise. If the plaintiff believed them to be true, and acted upon them, and the defendants knew them to be false, and intended fraudulently thereby to induce the plaintiff to purchase their shares of stock, of no value, at the price he paid for them, he might recover, notwithstanding he did not cautiously have their representations verified. Such verification was not intended for the benefit of the defendants; much less was it intended to shield or relieve them from liability for fraud and deceit they might perpetrate upon the plaintiff. The paper writing, and particularly the last clause of it, in respect to the verification of its statements, might, taken in connection with other evidence favorable to the defendants, be evidence of their good faith, and going to prove that the plaintiff did not rely upon their representations; but, on the other hand, the same might, along with other evidence favorable to the plaintiff, be evidence of a fraudulent contrivance to deceive and mislead him. Fraud is Protean in its devices, and endless in its shifts and subterfuges. What is evidence of it or its absence oftentimes depends more or less upon the conditions of matters and things material and the attending circumstances. In one aspect of the evidence in this case, accepted as true, the material representations in the paper writing, in effect made to the plaintiff, and other like representations otherwise made to him by the defendants, were grossly false, and so within their knowledge; and it might be fairly inferred, from the nature of the matter and the evidence, that the paper writing, and particularly the last clause of it, was an artful shift to mislead and deceive the plaintiff, a man little familiar with such matters, as to the sincerity and good faith of the defendants in respect to the proposed sale of the shares of stock mentioned. In another aspect of it more favorable to the defendants, the paper writing, and especially the last clause of it, would be evidence tending to show their good faith, and that the plaintiff, in buying the shares of stock and the sale of his land, relied upon his own judgment, and information gathered from other sources than the defendants. If the defendants knew that the representations made by them in the paper writing, and otherwise, as in evidence, were false, as the evidence—much of it—tended to prove, it would be most unreasonable to infer that they intended or expected the same to be verified or scrutinized. On the other hand, in view of parts of the evidence, the reasonable and just inference would be that the last clause of the paper writing was inserted to simulate great fairness and candor on the part of the defendants, and thus the more successfully entrap, deceive, and mislead the plaintiff, a man, as the evidence tended to show, not familiar with such matters. Such view of the evidence would be strengthened by the fact that the verification suggested was to be made by an expert book-keeper at the expense of the plaintiff. Shrewd men of experience might think and expect that a man of small experience, after such flattering representations, would not have such verification made at his own cost. Hence the paper writing, including the last clause of it, was simply evidence; it did not conclude the plaintiff, as the court intimated it did. There is therefore error. The judgment of nonsuit must be set aside, and the case disposed of according to law. To that end let this opinion be certified to the superior court. It is so ordered.

FREDENHEIM et al. v. ROHR et al.[1]

(Supreme Court of Appeals of Virginia. April 30, 1891.)

COURTS OF APPEALS—JURISDICTION — INJUNCTION —APPOINTMENT OF RECEIVER.

Code Va. § 3438, provides that when a circuit or corporation court or judge thereof shall refuse to award an injunction, a copy of the proceedings in court, and the original papers presented to the judge in vacation, with his order of refusal, may be presented to a judge of the court of appeals, who may thereupon award an injunction. In an action to set aside a deed of trust an order was granted restraining the trustee from selling the goods therein conveyed. Upon the trial the order was dissolved, and the prayer for the appointment of a receiver denied. Upon the following day a judge of this court, upon the original bill, and without notice to defendants, granted the injunction and appointment of a receiver. After the entry of this order, and in the absence of counsel for defendants, a judgment of the lower court granted an order directing the sheriff to put the receiver in possession of the property. Held, that the statute confers no authority upon a judge of the court of appeals to reinstate an injunction order that has been dissolved on the merits in the lower court, and both orders are void. LACY and RICHARDSON, JJ., dissenting.

Appeal from chancery court of Richmond.

Jos. Christian and E. Y. Cannon, for appellants. Pollard & Sands, for appellees.

FAUNTLEROY, J. The petition of M. S. Fredenheim and Herman Rosenberg, trustee in a deed of trust executed by the said M. S. Fredenheim on the 27th day of April, 1889, complains of an order of the chancery court of the city of Richmond, entered on the 15th day of May, 1889, and the order of the judge of that court, entered on the 21st day of May, 1889, in a chancery suit pending in said court, in which Nathan Rohr, Carl Callman, and William H. Robertson, and others, creditors of M. S. Fredenheim, are complainants and M. S. Fredenheim and others are defendants. The bill charges that Margaret S. Fredenheim, being indebted to the complainants, with intent to hinder, delay, and defraud them and her other creditors, on the 27th of April, 1889, made a deed of conveyance of all her stock in trade to one H. Rosenberg, which deed was duly recorded in the clerk's office of the chancery court of the city of Richmond, and an official copy thereof is filed as an exhibit with the bill. The prayer of the bill, after calling for

[1] For dissenting opinion, see 13 S. E. Rep. 266.

v.13s.E.no.6—13

answers from the defendants, is that "the said H. Rosenberg, trustee as aforesaid, Margaret S. Fredenheim, and A. Fredenheim, her husband, acting as agent for the said trustee, may be enjoined and restrained from managing, controlling, or selling the stock of goods lately owned by the said M. S. Fredenheim, at her store at No. 113 East Broad street, Richmond, Va.; that a receiver may be forthwith appointed by the court to take charge of the said stock of goods and the other property conveyed by the said deed of April 27, 1889, and, after due advertisement, sell the same upon such terms as may be prescribed by the court, and to proceed to collect, without delay, the notes and other choses in action conveyed by the said deed; that the decree of the court may be entered declaring null and void the said deed of April 27, 1889, and directing the payment of the debts due your orator from the proceeds realised from the sale, etc.; and that such surplus as may remain may be administered under and by direction of the court, through a receiver to be appointed as before asked," etc. This bill, charging fraud and collusion of fraud, and praying for an injunction, and to have the deed of trust of April 27, 1889, vacated for fraud, and for the appointment of a receiver, was presented to Judge FITZHUGH in the chancery court of Richmond city on the 7th day of May, 1889, who on that day granted an injunction according to the prayer of the bill, but declared in the order that he deemed it proper that the defendants should have reasonable notice of the time and place of moving for the appointment of receiver as prayed for in the bill, and an opportunity to move to dissolve the injunction; and this accordingly took place. After this injunction had become effectual, the defendants filed their answers, denying and putting in issue all the material allegations of the bill. The case came on to be heard on the 14th day of May, 1889, upon the bill and answers, and sundry affidavits and counter-affidavits, upon due notice and motion to dissolve, before Judge WELLFORD, sitting in the chancery court in the absence of Judge FITZHUGH, who had left the city, and was fully heard upon the arguments of counsel upon the motion to dissolve the injunction and to appoint a receiver, and for no other purpose; whereupon a decree was entered dissolving the injunction which had been awarded by Judge FITZHUGH on the 7th day of May, 1889, and expressly denying the prayer of the bill for the appointment of a receiver, but requiring the trustee, H. Rosenberg, to execute a bond, with approved security, in the penalty of $10,000, for the security of the fund, and for the faithful discharge of his trust, which bond was accordingly promptly executed by the said trustee. If the complainants in the bill were dissatisfied or aggrieved by this order of the chancellor dissolving the injunction and denying the prayer of the bill for the appointment of a receiver, their plain remedy, as prescribed by section 3454, Code 1887, was by appeal or by application to the chancellor for a rehearing and reinstatement of the injunction upon notice to the defendants, and if that had been denied they could have appealed from that denial; but they neither appealed from the order of dissolution, nor did they apply for a rehearing or reinstatement, but chose to present the very same bill, without any alteration or new matter, and without notice to the defendants, to a judge of the court of appeals, who, by his order of the 15th of May, 1889, addressed to the clerk of the chancery court of the city of Richmond, awarded the injunction according to the prayer of the bill, which had been dissolved the day before by the chancellor of that court upon full hearing and argument on the merits; and, on the motion of the complainants, and without notice to the defendants, and in their absence, and in the absence of their counsel, appointed one S. L. Bloomberg, as "a receiver of the chancery court of the city of Richmond, to take into his possession all of the property mentioned in the said deed of the 27th of April, 1889, and he is directed to take an inventory as to other stock of goods at No. 113 East Broad street, and proceed to sell the same for cash, as provided by the terms of the said deed, for and during the period of sixty days from the date of said deed." After this order had been given and duly entered in the order-book of the chancery court of the city of Richmond, the complainant's counsel proceeded to the county of Fauquier, where Judge FITZHUGH, the judge of the chancery court, was sojourning with a sick family; and, without notice to the defendants or their counsel, and in the absence of their counsel, obtained from Judge FITZHUGH the following order, dated May 21, 1889: "It appearing to the judge of the chancery court of the city of Richmond, in vacation, that Sol. L. Bloomberg, who has been duly appointed and duly qualified as receiver in this cause, has made application to Herman Rosenberg, trustee in the deed of trust from M. S. Fredenheim to him, bearing date April 27, 1889, for possession of the store, and stock of goods therein, situated at 113 East Broad street, in the city of Richmond, and that said Rosenberg, trustee, has refused to give possession of the said store, and to turn over the said stock of goods therein to the said Bloomberg as such receiver, in accordance with the order herein entered, it is therefore ordered by the said judge in vacation that the sheriff of this city do forthwith proceed to put the said S. L. Bloomberg, receiver as aforesaid, in possession of the said store and stock of goods situated at 113 East Broad street, in the city of Richmond, and lately occupied by M. S. Fredenheim as a millinery establishment. EDWARD H. FITZHUGH, Judge of Said Court." From these orders of the chancery court of the city of Richmond the case is here upon appeal.

The jurisdiction of the supreme court of appeals and of the judges thereof is fixed by the constitution and statute law of Virginia. The second section of the sixth article of the constitution of the state provides that the supreme court of appeals shall have appellate jurisdiction only, except in cases of *habeas corpus, mandamus,* and prohibition; and the statute (section 3438, Code 1887,) under which the order of May 15, 1889, awarding the injunction and appointing a receiver, according to the prayer of the bill in this case, was confessedly made, is as follows: "When a circuit or corporation court, or a judge thereof, shall refuse to award an injunction, a copy of the proceedings in court and the original papers presented to the judge in vacation, with his order of refusal, may be presented to a judge of the court of appeals, who may thereupon award an injunction." This statute confers no original jurisdiction upon one of the judges of this court to award an injunction, except in the case where the application has been made first to a judge of an inferior court, either in term or in vacation, and has been refused. See the cases of Mayo v. Haines, 2 Munf. 423; Webster v. Couch, 6 Rand. (Va.) 519; Gilliam v. Allen, 1 Rand. (Va.) 415. In these cases this court has held that the court of appeals itself, sitting *in banc*, has no power to award an injunction that has been refused by a judge or court below, although a single judge of the court of appeals might, under the statute, exercise the power; but that, where an injunction has been awarded by a court below, and had been (as in the case under review) dissolved upon the merits, neither this court, nor any one judge thereof, could grant a new injunction, or reinstate the dissolved injunction, upon the case made by the bill. In the case under review we have the order of May 15, 1889, awarding an injunction and appointing a receiver, made by a judge of the court of appeals, and directed by law to be entered as the order of the same chancellor who had the day before dissolved the very same injunction, and denied the prayer of the same bill for the appointment of a receiver, upon a full hearing of the whole case presented by the bill, answers, proofs, argument, and notice of all the parties to the cause. This action of the chancery court, in dissolving the injunction and denying the prayer of the bill for the appointment of a receiver, was reviewable by appeal, under section 3454 of the Code of 1887; but on the case presented there was no power in this court, or in one of its judges, to appoint a receiver for the chancery court of the city of Richmond, and especially, as in this case, without any notice to the defendants. It is of the very essence of a motion for the appointment of a receiver, even by the court below, that notice shall be given to the defendants of the time and place of the application; and it is only in an extreme case—such that the exigency of the danger would be fatal—that a receiver can be justly appointed, even in and by the court in which the cause is pending, without reasonable notice to the defendants. See High, Rec. p. 75, § 111, and pp. 24, 25; and Kerr, Rec. pp. 147-149; and the cases of Bisson v. Curry, 35 Iowa, 72; French v. Gifford, 30 Iowa, 148; Rogers v. Dougherty, 20 Ga. 271; People v. Norton, 1 Paige, 17; Triebert v. Burgess, 11 Md. 452; Voshell v. Heaton, 26 Md. 83; Gibson v. Martin, &

Paige, 481; Sandford v. Sinclair, Id. 373; Thompson v. Dilffenderfer, 1 Md. Ch. 489, 490; Verplanck v. Insurance Co., 2 Paige, 450. In the case of Barry v. Briggs, 22 Mich. 201, CAMPBELL, C. J., says: "The effect of this order (appointing a receiver) is to divest the entire legal estate of the defendant in property over which he had the exclusive control and exclusive title. * * * The order divests the whole body of the property, and puts its management, as well as ownership, in other hands. * * * An adjudication which produces such important effects, and which actually transfers the entire estate from the defendant, is, to all intents and purposes, a decree, as far as it goes. * * * It would be a very singular thing if a court could, by anticipating the date of a decree which would be appealable, produce all the consequences of a decree, and yet deprive the party of his right to review. The statute regulating appeals has regard to the rights of parties, and not to senseless formalities." This court has been emphatic in denunciation of decrees or orders entered ex parte, and without hearing the parties affected and interested by such decrees or orders. See Underwood v. McVeigh, 23 Grat. 418. The facts of this case furnish a notable illustration of the wisdom of the well-settled policy of the law which sets its face sternly and constantly against all orders, judgments, or decrees pronounced ex parte, and without opportunity of defense; and, even had the power to make the orders appealed from obtained under the constitution and law of the state, no case is made by the pleadings and the proofs in the cause for the appointment of a receiver. A bond, with approved security in the penalty of $10,000, (the same amount required of the receiver appointed,) was required to be given, and was instantly given, by the trustee, and accepted by the court, for the preservation of the fund, and a large number of the leading merchants of the city of Richmond certified that the trustee named in the deed was, from his knowledge of the business and his character, peculiarly qualified to execute the trust for which he had been specially selected. The orders appealed from, that of May 15, 1889, awarding the injunction and appointing a receiver for the chancery court of the city of Richmond, is ultra vires and void; and the order of May 21, 1889, ordering the sheriff of Richmond city to put the receiver, S. L. Bloemberg, in possession of the store and stock of goods of the defendant at No. 118 East Broad street, is erroneous, without authority of law, and void; and the judgment of this court is to reverse and annul both of the aforesaid orders, with costs to the defendants, and to remand the case, with directions to the chancery court of the city of Richmond to restore the trustee, Rosenberg, to the possession of the store and stock of goods to which he was entitled under the deed of trust of April 27, 1889, and to the administration of the trust, and for such further proceedings as shall be necessary in the premises   Judgment reversed.

LACY and RICHARDSON, JJ., dissenting.

WHITEHEAD v. BRADLEY et al.

(Supreme Court of Appeals of Virginia. April 23, 1891.)

JUDICIAL SALES—DUTY OF PURCHASERS—INVALID PAYMENTS—ACTION TO RESELL—PARTIES—INTERLOCUTORY DECREE.

1. Where the purchase money at a judicial sale is paid to a commissioner, who has failed to give bond, as required by the decree, and also by Code Va. § 3397, such payment is invalid, and does not discharge the purchaser.

2. Code Va. § 2609, provides that the circuit court may, on the application of a guardian, order the sale of an infant's real estate, when it shall be necessary for his proper maintenance and education, and may also, from time to time, make such decrees as are proper to secure the due expenditure of the proceeds. Held, that such authority must be given before, and not after, such expenditures are made; and therefore, when a guardian, without first obtaining an order for that purpose, makes such expenditures, the court has no authority afterwards to ratify the same.

3. A decree, approving the accounts of a guardian, but failing to direct how certain moneys in bank are to be disposed of, and how costs thereafter accruing are to be provided for, is not final, but interlocutory.

4. Where the purchase money, under an order directing the sale of an infant's real estate, is paid to an unbonded commissioner, who, without previous sanction of the court, pays the same to the infant's guardian, and a petition is then filed against the purchasers to show cause why the property should not be resold, and alleging the guardian's insolvency, an objection that the remedy against the guardian and his sureties was not first exhausted comes too late when made for the first time in the appellate court.

5. Where, in such a case, the entire purchase money was paid to one of two commissioners, it was not necessary to proceed against the other, who received no part of the fund, and was therefore not liable.

6. Where payments of purchase money at a judicial sale are void, because made to an unbonded commissioner, proceedings against the purchasers to show cause why the property should not be resold are not within Code Va. § 3425, which declares that the purchaser's title at a sale made under a decree six months after the date thereof, and confirmed, shall not be affected by a subsequent reversal; since the object of such proceedings is not to set aside the sale, but to compel the purchasers to comply with their respective contracts.

Appeal from a decree of the circuit court of Henrico county, rendered on the 12th of July, 1889, in a suit in equity, wherein William Bradley was plaintiff and Ellen Briggs and others were defendants, commenced in the circuit court of Chesterfield in 1874, and afterwards removed to the first-mentioned court. The bill was filed by Bradley, as guardian of his three infant children, alleging that they were seised in fee of certain real estate situate in Manchester, the income from which was inadequate for their maintenance and education; that their interests would be promoted by a sale of the property, and an investment of the proceeds in desirable interest-bearing stocks, and praying that a sale be ordered. A guardian ad litem was appointed for the infant defendants, who answered, admitting the allegations of the bill, and submitting the interests of the infants to the protection of the court. Depositions were taken, and a sale was ordered by a decree entered on the 20th of February, 1874. The decree appointed A. C. Attkisson and Socrates Brooks commissioners of sale, and directed that before they, or either of them, should receive any money under the decree, bond should be given in a penalty of $6,000, conditioned as the law directs. It appears that there were two sales,—one in September, 1874, the other in November, 1876. At the first, at which several lots were sold, the two commissioners acted jointly. At the second, at which the residue of the property was sold, Brooks acted alone, and to him alone the whole purchase money for all the property sold at both sales was paid by the purchasers, although no bond had been executed by either of the commissioners. The sales were duly confirmed. It also appears that all the money received by Brooks, after paying certain costs, was paid over by him to the guardian, except the sum of $70.96, for which he never accounted. He afterwards died insolvent. The money thus received by the guardian was, without the previous sanction of the court, expended by him in the maintenance of his wards, which expenditures were subsequently ratified by the court, by a decree entered on the 11th day of May, 1881. Nothing further was done in the cause until the 3d of December, 1888, when the eldest of the wards, having attained his majority, filed his petition, alleging that the payments by the purchasers were void, inasmuch as they were made to Brooks, who never executed a bond as commissioner, and that the payment of the money by Brooks to the guardian was also without authority, there being no decree authorizing such payment. It was also alleged that the expenditures by the guardian were illegal, and that the subsequent decree ratifying them was without any legal effect. And the prayer of the petition was that the purchasers named therein be summoned to show cause why they should not be required to pay into court the amount of their respective purchases, or else have the property resold. Rules were accordingly issued, to which the purchasers appeared and severally answered, insisting that the payments to Brooks were valid, and, moreover, that all the matters sought to be put in controversy by the petition had been finally adjudicated and settled by the decree of May 11, 1881. The circuit court granted the prayer of the petition by the decree complained of, crediting each of the respondents, however, with his proportionate share of the moneys which had been used in the payment of costs. From this decree R. S. Whitehead, one of the purchasers, applied for an appeal, which was allowed. Code Va. § 2609, provides that the circuit or chancery courts may, on the application of a guardian, order the sale of an infant's real estate, when it shall be made to appear to the satisfaction of the court that such sale is necessary for the infant's proper maintenance and education; and may also, from time to time, make such orders and decrees as are proper to secure the due application of the proceeds.

M. M. Gilliam and *Saml. D. Davies*, for

appellant. *B. H. Nash* and *J. M. Gregory,* for appellees.

LEWIS, P.   1. It is clear, upon well-settled principles, that payment of the purchase money to Commissioner Brooks was invalid. This court has repeatedly held that an unbonded commissioner, *qua* commissioner, has no authority to collect the purchase money for property which he is directed to sell, and that payment to such a commissioner does not discharge the purchaser. In the present case not only did the decree of sale provide that no money under it should be collected by the commissioners, or either of them, without first giving bond, but the statute itself provided, as it does now, that "no special commissioner appointed by a court shall receive money under a decree or order until he gives bond before the said court or its clerk." Code 1873, c. 174, § 1; Code 1887, § 3397. It was therefore incumbent on the purchasers, before paying the money to Brooks, to have inquired whether these requirements of the decree and of the statute had been complied with, and, inasmuch as they were not complied with, payment to him was unauthorized and invalid. Hess v. Rader, 26 Grat. 746; Lloyd v. Erwin, 29 Grat. 598; Tyler v. Toms, 75 Va. 116; Woods v. Ellis, 85 Va. 471, 7 S. E. Rep. 852. There is, indeed, a recent statute which protects a purchaser who makes payment to a commissioner when there has been a certificate of the clerk, published with the advertisement of sale or renting, that such commissioner has given the required bond, whether, in point of fact, he has done so or not, and which makes the clerk and his sureties liable for a false certificate to any person injured thereby. But that statute has no bearing on the present case. Acts 1883–84, p. 213; Code, § 3399.

2. Nor was there any decree directing or authorizing the money to be paid over by Brooks to the guardian, and, although there was a decree after the money had been expended by the guardian, ratifying his expenditures, yet, so far as the *corpus* of the fund was concerned, there was no authority in the court to validate such expenditure. The jurisdiction of the circuit courts of the commonwealth to authorize the application of the principal of the proceeds of infants' real estate to their maintenance and education is altogether statutory, and, according to the statute, which, as this court has said, must be strictly construed, such authority must be given, if at all, before, and not after, the expenditure is made. Code 1873, c. 123, § 13; Code 1887, § 2609; Rinker v. Streit, 33 Grat. 663; Gayle v. Hayes, 79 Va. 542; Cumming v. Simpson, (Va.) 1 S. E. Rep. 657. In the present case, it is true, a petition was filed by the guardian at the October term, 1874, asking authority to expend a portion of the principal of the fund for the maintenance and education of his wards; but no other action appears to have been taken on the petition than merely to refer it to a commissioner for inquiry and report. At all events, there was no approval of his expenditures until after they had been made,—too late to

give validity either to the expenditure of the principal, or to the action of the commissioner in turning over the fund to the guardian.

3. It is contended, however, that the decree of May 11, 1881, was a final decree, and is not now assailable by a simple petition for rules against the purchasers to show cause why the property should not be resold. But this is a mistaken view. That decree undoubtedly settled the principles of the cause, but did not finally dispose of it. It approved the accounts of the guardian, and directed, among other things, that certain moneys be deposited in bank, but made no disposition of the fund, which could be withdrawn, after being deposited, only on the order of the court, thus leaving something further in the cause to be done by the court; and it only partially provided for the payment of costs,—that is to say, it directed how costs up to the date of the decree should be paid, leaving the matter of costs thereafter to be incurred unprovided for. The decree was, therefore, not final, but interlocutory. Rawlings v. Rawlings, 75 Va. 76; Noel's Adm'r v. Noel's Adm'r, 86 Va. 109, 9 S. E. Rep. 584.

4. Another point made by the appellant is that the remedy against the guardian and his sureties ought to have been exhausted before proceeding against the purchasers, and Lee v. Swepson, 76 Va. 173, is relied upon in support of this position. But a sufficient answer to this is that no such objection was made in the court below, and it is too late now to raise it for the first time in the appellate court. Besides, the record shows that the guardian is insolvent, and it was not necessary to proceed in the first instance against his sureties, (who are not before the court as parties to the suit,) even if, under the circumstances, they are liable at all, as to which we express no opinion.

5. Nor was it necessary to proceed against Commissioner Attkisson; for he received no part of the fund to which the present controversy relates, and is not liable in this proceeding.

6. Lastly, there was no error in proceeding against the purchasers by rule to show cause, all of whom, except the appellant, have acquiesced in the decree appealed from. The purchase money having been collected by Brooks without authority, the result is the same, so far as this appeal is concerned, as if the money had been paid to a stranger, or not at all. The case differs from Thomson v. Brooke, 76 Va. 160, for in that case the commissioner was the counsel of the parties entitled to the money, and, at their solicitation, the money was collected. Hence it was held that the purchaser, having paid the money into a hand legally entitled to receive it, i. e., to the counsel of the parties, was not responsible, the case being analogous in principle to Dixon v. McCue, 21 Grat. 373. The purchasers, then, in the present case, being in default, they were compellable to complete their respective purchases by a rule upon each to show cause why the property should not be resold. And in such a case, when a resale is ordered, the former sale is not set aside,

but the property is sold as the property of the purchaser. If it brings more than the debt, he is entitled to the surplus; if less, he is responsible for the deficiency. Tyler v Toms, 75 Va. 116; Insurance Co. v. Cottrell, 85 Va. 857, 9 S. E. Rep. 132. So that the case is not within the statute invoked by the appellant, which declares that the title of a purchaser at a sale made under a decree six months after the date of the decree, and confirmed, shall not be affected by a subsequent reversal of the decree, although there may be a restitution of the proceeds of sale to those entitled. Code, § 3425. Here the object is, not to set aside the decree of sale, or the sales made under it, but to compel the purchasers, by the process of the court, to comply with their respective contracts. We are of opinion that there is no error in the decree, and that the same must be affirmed.

* ———

* SPRAYBERRY v. CITY OF ATLANTA.

(Supreme Court of Georgia. April 20, 1891.)

INTOXICATING LIQUORS — LICENSE — REVOCATION.

1. Under the charter of the city of Atlanta, (Acts Ga. 1874, p. 122, § 27,) conferring on the mayor and council "full power and authority to regulate the retail of ardent spirits," and "at their discretion, to issue license to retail or to withhold the same," they have authority to pass an ordinance that conviction of violation of the state statute prohibiting the sale of liquor to a minor shall work an immediate revocation of the license.

2. The license, being a mere privilege to carry on the business subject to the will of the grantor, and not a contract, is not property, and such a forfeiture does not deprive the licensee of his property without due process of law.

3. Where the license itself contains the conditions of forfeiture as prescribed by the ordinance, the licensee, who has been convicted of selling liquor to a minor, is not entitled to any notice of the forfeiture of his license.

Error from superior court, Fulton county; M. J. CLARKE, Judge.

Arnold & Arnold, for plaintiff in error. J. B. Goodwin and J. A. Anderson, for defendant in error.

SIMMONS, J. The charter of the city of Atlanta provides that "the mayor and general council shall have full power and authority to pass all by-laws and ordinances for the prevention and punishment of disorderly conduct, and conduct liable to disturb the peace and tranquillity of any citizen or citizens thereof; and every other by-law, regulation, and ordinance that may seem to them proper for the security, for the peace, health, order, and good government, of said city." Acts 1874, p. 119, § 15. The charter also provides that the mayor and general council "shall have full power and authority to regulate the retail of ardent spirits within the corporate limits of said city, and, at their discretion, to issue license to retail or to withhold the same, and to fix the price to be paid for license at any sum they may think proper, not exceeding two thousand dollars." Id. p. 122, § 27. Under these provisions of the charter, the mayor and general council passed an ordinance prescribing the manner of issuing licenses for the retail of liquors, the limits or streets in which licenses might be granted, and the manner of keeping places licensed for this purpose, etc. The fourteenth section of the ordinance provided as follows: "The mayor and general council shall forfeit the license of any dealer of either spirituous or lager-beer or malt liquors, whose place becomes a nuisance by disorder, threat, or otherwise. The conviction in a state court of any person licensed to retail spirituous or malt liquors, for the violation of the state statute in relation to the sale of ardent spirits to a minor or a person already intoxicated, or the conviction of a retailer before the recorder's court for the violation of any of the provisions of this ordinance, shall work an immediate revocation of the license of such person; and for any further exercise of the privilege granted by such license he shall be punished as one retailing without license." Under this ordinance, Sprayberry, the plaintiff in error, applied for and obtained a license to retail ardent spirits in the city of Atlanta. The license contained a clause reciting that it was "subject to be revoked whenever the ordinances of the city or the laws of the state of Georgia are violated by the holder of this license." Subsequently he was convicted in the superior court of Fulton county of the offense of selling liquor to a minor. After this conviction he continued the sale of liquors, and he was summoned to appear before the recorder's court, and answer to the charge of retailing spirituous and malt liquors without license from the mayor and general council. He appeared, and in answer to the charge exhibited the license he had obtained from the mayor and general council, and claimed that he was not guilty. The recorder held that, upon his conviction in the superior court for the offense of selling liquor to a minor, his license, under the above section of the ordinance, was revoked, and that he was guilty of the offense charged; and a fine of $100 was imposed upon him, with the alternative that, upon his failure to pay the fine, he be put to labor for 30 days upon the public works. He thereupon sued out a writ of *certiorari* to the superior court, alleging as error that the judgment was contrary to law and the evidence; that the proper authorities had not revoked his license, and that no court of competent jurisdiction had adjudged the same to be forfeited; that the section of the ordinance in question was invalid and *ultra vires*, as punishing a crime by forfeiture; that he could not be punished for retailing without license until his license had been revoked in a proceeding for that purpose before some competent tribunal; that the city of Atlanta had no power to punish offenders by forfeiture of property or otherwise; that the plea of guilty and the sentence of the superior court were not final, but were subject to be set aside and annulled, and that a motion for that purpose was undisposed of; and that the city of Atlanta had no power to pass an ordinance for the punishment of persons retailing liquors without license, the statutes of the state having exhausted the subject. Upon the hearing of the case in the supe-

rior court the *certiorari* was overruled, and Sprayberry excepted.

It was insisted before us by counsel for the plaintiff in error that the mayor and general council had no power, under the charter, to pass the ordinance in question; that the effect of the ordinance was to revoke the license, which could not be done until a proceeding for that purpose had been instituted before some competent tribunal; that Sprayberry had a property right in the license, which could not be taken from him in this summary manner; and that the ordinance was invalid and *ultra vires*, as punishing a crime by forfeiture. Under the clauses of the charter above quoted, we think the mayor and general council had full power and authority to pass the ordinance complained of. They have power to pass any ordinance that may seem to them proper for the security, the peace, order, and good government of the city. They also have power to regulate the retail of ardent spirits, and, in their discretion, to issue license or withhold the same. It is now well settled that the issuing of a license to retail liquors is not a contract, but is a permission to the licensee to engage in the business, under such restrictions, conditions, and limitations as may appear judicious to the authority issuing the license. The license not being a contract, the privilege granted thereby may be revoked at any time, and the business of selling liquor prohibited, by the proper authorities. Under the charter the mayor and general council have power to grant licenses for the sale of liquors, or to prohibit the sale altogether, by refusal to issue licenses. If they have the power to prohibit the sale altogether, by refusal to issue license therefor, they certainly have the right to issue license under such restrictions, conditions, and limitations as may seem proper to them. The power to regulate also confers upon the mayor and general council the right to impose such terms and conditions upon the licensee as they may see fit and proper. They may impose a condition that he shall keep an orderly house; that he shall close his place of business at a certain hour of the night; that he shall not have a screen between the door and his counter; and we think they can also impose a condition that, upon his conviction of a violation of a state law or of a city ordinance regulating the sale of liquors, his license shall be *ipso facto* revoked. In the case of Schwuchow v. Chicago, 68 Ill. 444, it was held that "where power is conferred on a city to prohibit entirely the sale of intoxicating liquors, or to regulate and license the same, at discretion, the city may grant the privilege of selling such liquors on such terms and conditions as it may see fit to impose, and has ample power to impose, as a condition, that a license granted shall be subject to revocation on the violation of any of the ordinances regulating the traffic. In such a case, where absolute control over the whole subject of granting licenses is conferred, the city may impose any other conditions calculated to protect the community, preserve order, and suppress vice, such as the closing of the grocery on election days, holidays, or Sundays, or the closing of the same at a particular hour each evening, etc., and for a violation of any of these conditions provide for a forfeiture of the license. Such power grows out of the fact that it is discretionary to prohibit the sale or license it on such terms as the city may choose." In Wiggins v. Chicago, Id. 372, it was held that "the power to tax, license, and regulate auctioneers, etc., authorizes the city authorities to adopt any reasonable ordinance for the purpose; and the city may tax, may license, and may regulate the business, and the ordinance may properly empower the mayor to revoke the license for cause." Launder v. Chicago, 111 Ill. 291; Ottumwa v. Schaub, 52 Iowa, 515, 3 N. W. Rep. 529; Hildreth v. Crawford, (Iowa,) 21 N. W Rep. 667; In re Bickerstaff, (Cal.) 11 Pac. Rep. 393; Martin v. State, (Neb.) 36 N. W. Rep. 554; People v. Meyers, 95 N. Y. 223; Horr & B. Mun. Ord. § 266, and 7 Crim. Law Mag. 142-146.

But it is insisted by the plaintiff in error that the license to sell liquor is a property right, and that this property right cannot be taken from him without a judgment by a competent tribunal. We have already seen that a license to sell liquor is not a contract, but only a permission to enjoy the privilege on the terms named, for a specified time, unless it be sooner abrogated. The granting of the license is an exercise of police power, and does not include any contractual relations whatever. "The contracts which the constitution protects are those that relate to property rights, not governmental." Stone v. Mississippi, 101 U. S. 820. The license being a mere privilege to carry on a business subject to the will of the grantor, it is not property, in the sense which protects it under the constitution. The revocation of the license does not deprive the citizen of his liberty or his property without due process of law. "The vesting, by legislative authority, of the power to license various occupations and professions, requiring skill in their exercise, or the observance of the law of hygiene, or the like, has never been construed to be obnoxious to these objections. It has been uniformly held that laws providing by accustomed modes for the licensing of physicians, lawyers, pilots, butchers, bakers, liquor dealers, and in fact all trades, professions, and callings, interfere with no natural rights of the citizen secured by our constitution." McDonald v. State, (Ala.) 2 South. Rep. 829, and authorities there cited. In the case of Board v. Barrie, 34 N. Y. 667, the court of appeals of that state, in discussing this subject, says: "The assumption is not even plausible that the act works a deprivation of property to any one within the meaning of the constitutional restrictions upon legislative authority. It in terms, it is true, revokes licenses granted under the act of 1857, but that is no encroachment upon any right secured to the citizen as inviolable by the fundamental law. These licenses to sell liquors are not contracts between the state and the persons licensed, giving the latter vested rights, protected on general principles, and by the constitution of the United States, against subsequent

legislation; nor are they property, in any legal or constitutional sense. They have neither the qualities of a contract nor of property, but are merely temporary permits to do what otherwise would be an offense against a general law. They form a portion of the internal police system of the state; are issued in the exercise of its police powers; and are subject to the direction of the state government, which may modify, revoke, or continue them as it may deem fit. If the act of 1857 had declared that licenses under it should be irrevocable, (which it does not, but by its very terms they are revocable,) the legislatures of subsequent years would not have been bound by the declaration. The necessary powers of the legislature over all subjects of internal police, being a part of the general grant of power given by the constitution, cannot be sold, given away, or relinquished." See, also, Schwuchow v. Chicago, supra. The license to sell liquor, therefore, not being property, the mayor and general council had the right under the charter to pass the ordinance which declares that a conviction, as specified therein, shall work an immediate revocation of the license. In our opinion, this ordinance was a wise and reasonable one. The facts of this case show the necessity of it. Sprayberry violated the statute of the state by selling liquor to a minor. He was indicted, filed a plea of guilty, was sentenced by the court to pay a fine, and paid it. He was charged in the recorder's court with retailing liquors without a license on the 16th of February, and was summoned to appear for trial on the 22d. The record discloses that on the 21st of February he filed a petition in the superior court to set aside his conviction therein for the offense of selling liquor to a minor; and upon his trial in the recorder's court, on the 22d, he filed a certified copy of this petition to the superior court, and asked that the case in the recorder's court be continued until the petition in the superior court had been acted upon. If the motion to continue had been granted on this ground, he could have prolonged the litigation in the superior court until his license had expired. This shows the wisdom and the necessity of the ordinance.

But it is claimed that he ought to have been notified by the mayor and council that his license had been revoked; that unless this was done he must try the case himself, and determine for himself whether it had been revoked or not by his conviction. What was the necessity of any notice to him? His license informed him that it was subject to be revoked. The law under which the license was granted informed him that his conviction would work an immediate revocation. What more notice could he desire? What other trial could he wish than the one he had already had in the superior court? When he was convicted there, the notice was ample that it operated as a revocation of his license. Nothing that he could have said or done before the mayor and council would have changed the record of his conviction. They would have had no discretion in the matter; the law was as imperative upon them as it was upon him. Upon the subject of the immediate revocation of a license by a violation of the condition upon which it is issued, the court of appeals of New York in the case of People v. Meyers, 95 N. Y. 223, say: "Under the provision of the excise act of 1873, which provides that a conviction for a violation of any provision of said act, or of the acts thereby amended, by any person or at any place licensed as therein provided, shall forfeit the license, and authorizes the board of excise, upon being satisfied of a violation of any such provision, to cancel or revoke the license, a conviction of a bar-tender of a licensed person for an offense under the act, committed at the place licensed, operates *ipso facto* to annul the license. The act casts upon the licensee the necessity, in order to protect himself in the enjoyment of his license, of seeing to it that no violation shall be committed upon the licensed premises. * * * It is competent for the legislature to prescribe such a cause of forfeiture." In the case of People v. Tighe, 5 Hun, 25, it was held that the conviction of a licensee, under any of the provisions of the act of 1873, *ipso facto* annuls his license. Moreover, we think that, when Sprayberry applied for and accepted a license under this ordinance, he assented to the condition contained therein, and he has no right now to insist that it shall be adjudged forfeited by a judicial tribunal. He knew this to be the law when he applied for and accepted the license, and he knew that these terms, conditions, and restrictions were put upon him by his acceptance of it. He knew that, when he was indicted and convicted for a violation of the state law, it worked an immediate revocation of the license. By what right, then, can he claim that he was entitled to have any further notice, or entitled to have a trial to determine whether the license was revoked or not? In the case of Schwuchow v. Chicago, supra, it was held that, "where a party applies for and accepts a license under an ordinance imposing conditions and restrictions, and the license itself contains a condition that it may be revoked at the discretion of the mayor, he thereby assents to the terms and conditions imposed, both in the license and the ordinance under which it is issued." In the case of Wiggins v. Chicago, supra, it was held that "when a party accepts a license from the mayor of a city, under an ordinance empowering the mayor to revoke for cause, and the license recites that it may be revoked by the mayor at any time, in his discretion, he will have no ground to say that the mayor has no power, and that it can only be revoked by a judicial sentence." It was also insisted that the conviction was not final, because it was subject to be set aside, and a motion for that purpose was undisposed of. In reply, it is sufficient to say that, under the facts of this case, the judgment seems to have been treated as final until the charge was made against Sprayberry in the recorder's court. As before remarked, judgment of conviction was pronounced against him in the superior court on the 17th of January, and he paid the fine and costs, and no motion to set the judgment aside was made until the

21st of February, after the charge in the recorder's court had been preferred. After his attention was thus called to the effect of his conviction in the superior court, no doubt he wished to set aside that conviction, or to litigate about it until his license should expire. But, outside of the particular facts above mentioned, we think that the conviction in this case was final until it was properly set aside. These are the only questions in the case that we deem it necessary to discuss. Judgment affirmed.

FARKAS v. POWELL.

(Supreme Court of Georgia. March 16, 1891.)

HIRE OF HORSE — DEVIATION FROM CONTRACT—
LIABILITY OF BAILEE.

A man hired a horse to ride five miles, but he found that the person he wished to see was at a house several miles further on. After riding this extra distance, and returning within the limits of his original hiring, the horse was taken sick, and fell in the road. A day or two later it died. *Held,* in an action for damages, that the bailee was liable for any injury to which the extra ride materially contributed, even though the accident occurred without any fault whatever on his part, and after he had returned within the limits of the original hiring; and it was error to charge that, if the bailee exercised ordinary care only, he would not be liable for going such extra distance, although the horse may have been injured without his fault in so doing.

Error from superior court, Dougherty county; BOWER, Judge.

Jesse W. Walters, for plaintiff in error. *D. H. Pope,* for defendant in error.

SIMMONS, J. Powell hired from Farkas a horse to ride from Albany to the Whitehead place, in the country, a distance of five miles, and was to return by 11 o'clock at night. When he arrived at the Whitehead place, he learned that the person he wished to see was at the Bryant place, three or four miles beyond, and he rode on to that point. He remained at the Bryant place some two hours and a half, and left there for Albany about half past 9 in the evening. On his return, and after getting between the Whitehead place and Albany, the horse fell in the road. After considerable trouble, he got the horse on his feet, and led him about three miles, and, when within about a mile of Albany, the horse again fell, and he had to obtain the assistance of two colored men, living near by, to again get the horse upon his feet. He then took the horse to the lot of one of these men, and left him there; and about daylight in the morning walked on to the town, and notified Farkas' stable-man where the horse was, and of his condition. The horse died within a day or two thereafter. Farkas brought suit against Powell, alleging, in substance, that he had ridden the horse three miles beyond the place he had hired him to go, and that by negligence or cruelty the horse had been so injured that he died. The evidence for the plaintiff tended to show that, on the afternoon when the horse was hired to Powell, it was sound and in good condition, moved off briskly down the street, and showed no signs of any disease, but that when returned the next morning it was lame, and could scarcely walk, and had a halter burn around one of its feet. The evidence for the defendant tended to show that he rode the horse moderately, never going faster than a trot; that at the Bryant place he hitched it to a post; that there was no halter or rope around its foot while in his possession; and that in returning from the Bryant place he rode the horse in a walk until it suddenly fell in the road. An expert in diseases of horses testified that, in his opinion, the horse was paralyzed, and that this may have been produced by straining. There was also evidence that, a day or two before the hiring, the horse had been used in hauling dirt. Powell also testified that about a year before he had hired another horse from Farkas to go to the same place, and rode three or four miles further than he intended to go, and that when informed of it on his return Farkas said it was all right, and did not charge him for the extra time or distance.

On this state of facts the trial judge charged the jury, in substance, that if Powell exercised ordinary care in riding the horse, and attending to it while in his possession, it did not make any difference whether he rode it beyond the Whitehead place or not; that, if Powell was not at fault in riding and in his attention to the horse, he could not be held liable because he went a greater distance than he had hired the horse to go, although it may have been injured by accident or otherwise, without his fault, in going this extra distance. The jury found for the defendant, and the plaintiff made a motion for a new trial. We think this charge was error. When Powell hired the horse from Farkas to go five miles to the Whitehead place, he had no right, under his contract, to go beyond that point without the consent of Farkas; and when he did go beyond it was at least a technical conversion, or a violation of his contract and duty; and, if the horse had been injured while beyond the point to which he was hired to go, Powell undoubtedly would have been liable, whether the injury was caused by his own negligence or by the negligence of others, or even by accident, unless he was forced to go beyond that point by circumstances which he could not control. For example, if a bridge had been washed away, or the road was impassable, and in consequence he had to take a longer road in order to go to the Whitehead place, he would then be liable only for his own negligence. This principle seems to be sustained by the following authorities: Story, Bailm. § 413 et seq., and authorities there cited; Schouler, Bailm. § 139, and authorities cited.

But the nice question in this case is, would Powell, after having been guilty of a technical conversion or violation of his duty, and having returned within the limits of the original hiring, and the horse then sustained injury without other fault on his part, be liable? That would depend, in our opinion, upon whether the extra ride of six or eight miles to the Bryant place and back caused or materially contributed to the accident. If it did, we think he would be liable to the owner. The horse might have been well able to travel the five miles and return, but the six or eight miles extra may have fatigued him to such an extent as to have caused him to stumble and fall, and thus produced the injury. If, however, the extra ride did not cause or materially contribute to the injury, we do not think Powell would be liable, if guilty of no other fault. We can see no good reason to hold the hirer liable for an injury to the horse hired, which occurred, without his fault, after he had returned with it within the limits of his original contract, although he had been guilty of a technical conversion by riding it three miles beyond the point to which it was hired to go, the extra distance not causing or contributing to the injury. We have been unable to find any cause the facts of which are like the facts in this. Nearly all the cases which hold the hirer liable, when he has deviated from the terms of his contract, are cases in which he was negligent in fact, or willfully and wantonly misconducted himself, or had overdriven the horse, or destroyed or ruined the property while beyond the limit or in the course of deviation from the purpose of the hiring. The cases cited in the brief of counsel for the plaintiff in error were all of this character. See Mayor, etc., of Columbus v. Howard, 6 Ga. 213; Gorman v. Campbell, 14 Ga. 137; Collins v. Hutchins, 21 Ga. 270; Lewis v. McAfee, 32 Ga. 465; Malone v. Robinson, 77 Ga. 719. So likewise were nearly all the cases referred to in Schouler and Story, supra. The facts in those cases show that the property was injured or destroyed during the time it was being improperly used, or being used for a different purpose from that for which it was hired. The question whether this extra ride did or did not cause or materially contribute to the injury was for the jury to determine under the evidence and a proper charge by the court; and, the court by its charge having eliminated this issue from the case, we think a new trial should be granted.

Judgment reversed.

PHILLIPS v. CITY OF ATLANTA.

(Supreme Court of Georgia. March 23, 1891.)

CERTIORARI—AMENDMENT OF ANSWER—VIOLATION OF ORDINANCE—TIME

1. The judge of a police court who presided at the trial to be reviewed on *certiorari* is still competent to perfect his answer to the *certiorari* by adding thereto a copy of the ordinance on which his judgment was founded, though he has retired from judicial office, and become assistant city attorney, it not appearing that he has taken any part as counsel in the *certiorari* case.

2. Where the penalty for carrying on business without registering the same is graduated by ordinance according to the number of days the business has been carried on, the maximum fine for three days' business cannot be imposed if the accusation is by summons, which specifies one day only, and makes no charge as to more than one day.

3. The evidence being sufficient to establish a violation of the ordinance, the error of the recorder may be corrected by reducing the fine. Direction is given accordingly.

(Syllabus by the Court.)

Error from superior court, Fulton county; M. J. CLARKE, Judge.

Broyles & Sons, for plaintiff in error. *J. R. Goodwin,* for defendant in error.

BLECKLEY, C. J. Thrice this unquiet case has materialized at the sittings of this tribunal. We hope its perturbed spirit will now enter into unbroken rest. Its former appearances are registered in 78 Ga. 773, 3 S. E. Rep. 431, and in 79 Ga. 510, 4 S. E. Rep. 256.

1. That part of the law of *certiorari* embodied in section 4063 of the Code reads thus: "The answer shall not be written or dictated by either of the parties, or their attorneys, or any other person interested in the cause, and, if made after the party making the same has retired from office, it shall be verified by affidavit." The recorder's answer in this case was made before his retirement from office, but it was not full, and for that reason was excepted to by the city. Its only deficiency was that it omitted to set out the municipal ordinance on which the proceeding against Phillips in the recorder's court was founded. Before perfecting the answer, the recorder had changed his relation to the city by ceasing to be its judicial officer, and by becoming assistant city attorney. It does not appear, however, that he took any part in the management of this *certiorari,* or was ever connected with it in the capacity of counsel or attorney. His amended answer was supported by affidavit, and, had it been untrue, might have been traversed. As the ordinance was a public document, not only recorded in the city archives, but published to the world, there could be no danger that any falsehood or error in the answer as to it would pass without detection. Such an amendment as this, however it might be with others of a different character, could, we think, be made on the affidavit of the ex-recorder, notwithstanding his new relation to the city as assistant municipal attorney. If the answer could not be perfected in this way, it could not be perfected at all.

2. The original case was commenced by a written summons dated March 24, 1886, commanding Phillips to appear in the recorder's court "to answer the charge of engaging in the business of a pawnbroker, without registering the same and paying license, in the city of Atlanta, on the 23d day of March, 1886." Phillips, being tried and found guilty, was fined $300. The ordinance which he had violated declared that "any person whose duty it shall be to register their business, and who shall refuse or fail to do so, may be arrested and brought before the recorder; * * * and, on conviction, be fined in a sum not exceeding one hundred dollars and costs, or imprisonment not exceeding thirty days, or both, in the discretion of the court, for each day such business has been done, * * * without registering the same." No doubt it would have been competent to charge in one and the same proceeding that Phillips had carried on the business upon more than one day, and to convict him for as many as five days' work, if that number of days were specified in the summons. There could not be a conviction for more than

five days at full rates, because the power of the court to impose fines is limited by the city charter to $500 in each case. But the summons commanding Phillips to answer was limited to one day, and, that being so, it gave him no notice that he was threatened with punishment for more than one day's transactions. Where penalty is measured by the element of time, the length of time comprehended in the charge is material. If a more severe penalty is denounced against a criminal transaction which occupies several days than against a like transaction which occupies one day only, it is essential that the accused shall have notice that he is to be tried for the higher grade of the offense before he can be punished for that grade. In this instance the summons afforded no such warning. On the contrary, it was confined expressly to one day; and, while the particular day specified need not be proved by showing that the business was carried on upon the exact day mentioned in the summons, yet the summons was too narrow to cover a penalty for more than a single day. If the ordinance had directly declared that any person carrying on business for three days should be punishable by a fine not exceeding $300, and any person carrying on business for one day should be punishable by a fine not exceeding $100, no one would suppose that a summons embracing only one day would be sufficient to uphold a fine of $300. Now, this is precisely the substance, though not the language, of the ordinance under which M. Phillips was tried. The offense, while one and the same, is aggravated in exact proportion to the number of days through which it is continued. In this case the aggravation counted for twice as much as the original offense, and thus two-thirds of the conviction were left entirely outside of the charge. It is plain Phillips was fined either for three offenses, or for three grades of the same offense. Neither of these triplets was covered by the charge. The charge was a unit, both as to offense and grade.

3. We have carefully read the evidence. It warranted the recorder in finding that the ordinance was violated. His error was in imposing a fine of more than $100. This error may be corrected by reducing the fine to that sum. We direct that this be done. The judge of the superior court will sustain the *certiorari,* and make a final judgment disposing of the case for all time. Other questions were raised by the petition for *certiorari,* but were not argued or insisted upon by counsel. Judgment reversed, with direction.

SOUTHERN BELL TEL., ETC., CO. v JORDAN.

(Supreme Court of Georgia. March 28, 1891.)

CONTINUANCE—SURPRISE—EVIDENCE—INSTRUCTIONS.

1. The court may refuse defendant a continuance on the ground of surprise by an amendment, where a copy of the amendment was served on it in December, and the trial was not had until the following October, though the original was not filed in the clerk's office until three days before trial.

2. Where the complaint alleges injuries from a pole which struck plaintiff on the shoulder,

broke his collar-bone, and felled him to the ground, evidence of pain from injury to the muscles is admissible.

3. In the examination of an expert as to plaintiff's condition, it is proper to put hypothetical questions based on plaintiff's testimony.

4. An instruction that "the law leaves the amount of the damages to the sound discretion of the jury" is not misleading in its use of the word "discretion."

5. Nor is it misleading to refer inadvertently to the "claim for injuries made by defendant" instead of by plaintiff.

Error from city court of Atlanta; VAN EPPS, Judge.

Hoke & Burton Smith, for plaintiff in error. *R. J. Jordan*, for defendant in error.

SIMMONS, J. 1. The first ground insisted on in the motion for a new trial in this case for a reversal of the court below is that the court erred in refusing to continue the case after the plaintiff filed the amendment set out in the record. The record shows that a copy of the amendment was served on the defendant's counsel in December, 1889, but the original was not filed in office until October 27, 1890, and that the trial was had on October 30, 1890. Defendant's counsel stated in his place that "he was surprised by such amendment; that he was less prepared for trial thereby, by reason of the fact that he had made no preparation, by expert evidence or in other respects, to meet said amendment; and that such surprise was not claimed for the purpose of delay only." Counsel did not state that he had not been served with a copy of the amendment, or that he had forgotten it, or that he thought the plaintiff had abandoned it because he had not filed it in court; nor did he state what he could prove, or expected to prove, if the continuance were granted. We are inclined to think that when he received the notice of the amendment that was sufficient to put him upon some inquiry for evidence to meet it. Under the Code, the plaintiff had the right to offer the amendment at any stage of the trial, and was not compelled to offer it until the trial, and the defendant's counsel, knowing this, should have made preparation to meet it. We presume the notice was given by the plaintiff for the very purpose of preventing a surprise to the defendant and a continuance of the case by him. Moreover, the Code, § 3521, declares, in substance, that when an amendment is made, and a surprise claimed on that account, it is still in the discretion of the court whether he will grant the continuance or not; and this court will not attempt to control the discretion given by law to the trial judge, unless that discretion is abused. After a careful study of the facts in this case, we do not think the trial judge abused his discretion.

2. The second ground complains that the court erred in allowing the physician to testify that "the pain suffered by the plaintiff would perhaps be from some injury to the muscles at the time the injury was inflicted." The error assigned is that there was no allegation in the declaration under which it would be admissible, there being nothing alleged as to any injury to the muscles. There was no error in allowing

this testimony. The declaration alleges "that the pole fell with great force, striking the plaintiff on the left shoulder and the collar-bone, breaking the bones thereof, and felling him to the rock pavement." We think this allegation is sufficient to authorize proof of pain in the muscles, without alleging specifically that the muscles were lacerated and injured. We cannot see how the collar-bone could have been broken by the falling of the pole upon it, without injuring the muscles of the shoulder.

3. The third ground complains that the court allowed plaintiff's counsel, in interrogating the physician as to the condition of the plaintiff, to put hypothetical questions. There was no error in this, under the facts of the case. The proper mode of examining a physician or expert, where he is not testifying from his own knowledge, is to ask him hypothetical questions. Dr. Knott testified in this case that his attention had never been called by the plaintiff to his eye, and the questions asked him must therefore have been upon the statement made by the plaintiff in his testimony.

4. The sixth ground alleges as error that the court instructed the jury that "the law leaves the question of amount, in cases where an award is proper, to the sound discretion of the jury," and "the law declares that damages of this kind are in the discretion of enlightened jurors, whose aim is to be just, and not oppressive." There was no error in this charge, taking it in connection with the context of the charge as set out in the record. The criticism made upon it was as to the use of the word "discretion." While this word is not usual in instructions to juries upon this subject, we do not think that, when taken in connection with the remainder of the charge, the jury could have understood, as was claimed by counsel for the plaintiff in error, that they were "turned loose" to give any amount of damages they saw proper. The judge was instructing them upon the law of damages in regard to pain and suffering. He informed them that there was "no rule by which the value of a pain may be ascertained with mathematical precision. Damages of this sort are of a nature not susceptible of being calculated accurately in money;" and then added the words excepted to in this ground of the motion. This was equivalent to instructing the jury that the plaintiff could not prove in dollars and cents the value of pain and suffering; but that, in arriving at the amount of their award, they must act as fair and reasonable men, in the exercise of sound discretion and judgment, and give the plaintiff a reasonable amount for the pain he had suffered,—such an amount as would be deemed proper in the enlightened consciences of impartial jurors who were seeking to be reasonable and fair, and not oppressive, in their finding.

5. The ninth ground complains that the court erred in charging as follows: "With reference to the claim which defendant makes, that his eye suffered an injury, and his eyesight, and that this will continue in the future, I charge you that the burden is

upon the plaintiff to show to your satisfaction that an injury such as that now under consideration was either the approximate result of the defendant's wrongful act, if any, or its necessary and connected effect." The criticism on this charge is that the court used the word "defendant" in the first line thereof, instead of the word "plaintiff." We do not think that the jury could have been misled by the use of the word "defendant" for "plaintiff." The jury could very easily understand that the court meant plaintiff, taking it in connection with the other words of the sentence. It would be a reflection upon their intelligence to even suppose that they could be misled by such a slip of the tongue as this evidently was. Besides, the defendant's counsel was present and heard the charge, but did not call the attention of the court to the misuse of the word. See Wilson v. State, 66 Ga. 591.

6. It is also claimed that the verdict is excessive. The evidence shows that the defendant was grossly negligent in allowing a rotten pole to stand in a populous street, where it was subject to fall at any time and kill or injure any one traveling upon the street, and that it did fall upon the plaintiff, and break his collar-bone, and badly bruised him, by throwing him upon the hard pavement of the street; that he received a contusion of the skin upon his head, above the right eye, and a large knot above the temple; that his eye had given him trouble since the injury, had been inflamed more or less, especially when he read; and that he suffered a good deal at the time of the injury, and his shoulder and arm had given him more or less pain since then, especially in cloudy weather. Upon this state of facts we do not think the verdict is so excessive as to justify the inference of the jury's mistake or undue bias. Judgment affirmed.

LOWRY BANKING CO. v. ABBOTT et al.

(*Supreme Court of Georgia.* April 20, 1891.)

CREDITORS' BILL—LIABILITY FOR EXPENSES.

Where a petition in equity in the nature of a creditors' bill is filed, alleging the insolvency of a partnership, and praying an injunction and appointment of a receiver, creditors who on their own application are made plaintiffs after the receiver is appointed become chargeable with their proportion of counsel fees for filing the petition, as provided by Code Ga. 3149c, though the appointment of the receiver was unnecessary, because such creditors have mortgages which will absorb the entire assets.

Error from superior court, Fulton county; M. J. CLARKE, Judge.

J. L. Brown, Candler & Thomson, and Jackson & Jackson, for plaintiff in error. Abbott & Smith, for defendants in error.

SIMMONS, J. Certain creditors of Wyly & Green, through their counsel, Abbott & Smith, filed their petition in equity in the nature of a creditors' bill, under sections 3149a et seq. of the Code, alleging the insolvency of Wyly & Green, and praying for injunction, and for a receiver to take charge of their assets. The injunction was granted, and a receiver appointed,

who took charge of the assets, and administered them, and brought a fund of $30,000 into court to be distributed to the creditors. After the petition was filed and the receiver appointed, the Lowry Banking Company made itself a party complainant, alleging that it had two mortgages, given it by Wyly & Green, which were sufficient to cover the whole amount of the assets. The other creditors disputed the validity of these mortgages, but they were declared to be valid and binding upon the assets by the verdict of a jury on a trial where this issue was made. Before the fund was distributed, Abbott & Smith filed their application to the court, wherein they stated that they were the solicitors of the complainants who filed the petition against Wyly & Green, and obtained the order appointing the receiver, etc.; that the receiver had collected the sum of $30,000; and that they represented the receiver, and advised him in many matters touching his receivership. They prayed the court to tax as costs against the fund the sum of $1,500 as counsel's fees for bringing the fund into court. They alleged that they had been paid $250 on account of such service, by order of the court, and that there was still due them the sum of $1,250. They asked a rule *nisi* requiring the Lowry Banking Company and the receiver to show cause why said sum should not be allowed them. To this rule the Lowry Banking Company demurred, upon the grounds (1) "that the court had no authority, without the verdict of a jury, to take a part of the fund in the hands of the receiver, covered by the mortgages to this respondent, and apply the same to the payment of fees of counsel;" and (2) "that there was no law of Georgia authorizing fees to be paid out of a fund like this, and upon a petition like this." The Lowry Banking Company also answered the rule, setting up various reasons why the movants were not entitled to fees out of the fund. The court sustained the first ground of demurrer, and referred the matter to a jury, and upon a trial of the issue the jury returned a verdict for $150, counsel fees. Abbott & Smith moved for a new trial, and it was granted by the court, and the Lowry Banking Company excepted.

1. It was insisted by counsel for the plaintiff in error that the court erred in granting a new trial in the case, because the law does not authorize counsel fees to Abbott & Smith under the facts of the case; that the facts show that the Lowry Banking Company had mortgages which covered the entire assets of the estate; that there was really no necessity for a receiver; that the petition was filed as much to get rid of the mortgages of the Lowry Banking Company as for anything else, and that the whole contest was made by the other creditors upon the claim of the Lowry Banking Company; and it would therefore be inequitable and unjust to compel the Lowry Banking Company to pay the opposing counsel their fees, although the fund was brought into court under the petition which the latter had filed in behalf of the creditors. We would agree with counsel for the plaintiff in error

in this view of the law were it not for one fact in the record. That fact is that after the petition was filed and the receiver appointed the Lowry Banking Company, upon its own application, was made a party plaintiff. This action on the part of the Lowry Banking Company recognized the necessity for the petition, and ratified the filing of it. The third section of the act of 1880, (Code, § 3149c,) under which this proceeding was instituted, provides that "any creditor may become a party to said bill, under an order of the court, at any time before the final distribution of the assets, he becoming chargeable with his proportion of the expenses of the previous proceedings. "When, therefore, the banking company was made a party plaintiff to the petition upon its own motion, under this section of the Code, it became chargeable with its proportion of the expenses, whatever that proportion might be. If its mortgages were sufficient in amount to cover the whole assets of Wyly & Green, there was no necessity for the petition or for the appointment of a receiver, as has been held frequently by this court; and if the banking company had objected to the appointment of a receiver, and had shown to the court that its mortgages were sufficient to cover the entire assets, the receiver would not have been appointed. Instead of doing this, however, it joined in the proceeding, and thereby became chargeable with its proportion of the expenses up to the time it was made a party, and a like proportion up to the end of the litigation. In case it recovered the whole fund, it would be for the court or the jury to determine, under all the facts of the case, what amount of fees Abbott & Smith should receive out of the fund before it was paid over to the Lowry Banking Company.

2. The court did not err in granting a first new trial, as he could well conclude that the jury found contrary to the evidence. Both parties filed exceptions *pendente lite* during the trial, and assigned error on them here, but, as the case is still pending in the court below, we cannot consider them now. Code, § 4250. Judgment affirmed.

MILLS v. EAST TENNESSEE, V. & G. RY. CO.

(*Supreme Court of Georgia.* March 30, 1891.)

INJURY TO RAILROAD EMPLOYE — QUESTION FOR JURY.

Under the facts of this case, as disclosed by the record, it was error to grant a nonsuit.

(*Syllabus by the Court.*)

Error from superior court, Fulton county; M. J. CLARKE, Judge.

M. H. Blandford and *Arnold & Arnold,* for plaintiff in error. *Dorsey, Brewster & Howell,* for defendant in error.

LUMPKIN, J. George Lawshe, a flagman on a freight train of the East Tennessee, Virginia & Georgia Railway Company, whose duties were "on or about the rear end of the train," was killed in a collision in the night-time, caused by the running of the engine of a passenger train into the rear end of the freight train. His widow, who is now Lula Mills, brought suit against the railway company for the killing of her husband, on the trial of which a nonsuit was granted by the court below, and this judgment is now before this court for review. The plaintiff's evidence made substantially the following case: The accident occurred at Braswell station, some 50 feet north of which is a trestle more than a hundred feet long. The road has a heavy up-grade coming from the north to this station, and from that direction the top of a car standing on the end of the trestle could be seen 160 or more yards before reaching it. A train running up this grade at the rate of 30 miles an hour could be stopped within 50 yards. The freight train upon which Lawshe was employed as flagman was going south, and had reached Braswell after 12 o'clock on the night of the accident. The engine of that train had been derailed, and, while efforts were being made to get it back upon the track, the train of freight-cars unavoidably remained on the main line, and occupied the trestle. It was known to the employes having charge of this freight train that the south-bound passenger train was approaching, and would be due in about an hour and a half. The conductor of the freight train told Lawshe to go back and put torpedoes on the track, and then, as he had worked hard, was tired, and needed rest, to go into the cab and go to sleep; stating also that he (the conductor) would have him waked up in time to flag the approaching passenger train. On the morning succeeding the accident the remains of an exploded torpedo were found on the track about 150 yards north of the trestle. The conductor instructed one Mills, the front brakeman, to go back to the cab and wake Lawshe, and tell him to go and flag the passenger train. Mills went twice in the direction of the cab into which Lawshe had gone, and shouted the conductor's message to Lawshe, but it does not appear that Lawshe heard him, or that he awoke, if he was asleep. Lawshe certainly did not come out of the cab, and never went back to flag the passenger train. In one or two minutes after Mills had called Lawshe the second time the engine of the passenger train, running at a high rate of speed, struck the cab, and demolished it, ran through one other car, and into a third. Lawshe was thrown out of the cab and killed. His body was found on the ground below the trestle, wrapped in a blanket, in which he had doubtless been asleep. There was also evidence to show that a torpedo, when exploded, made a noise louder than a gunshot, and that it could be heard for half a mile. The following rules of the company were put in evidence: "Rule 31. An explosive cap, or torpedo, placed on the rail, is a signal to be used in addition to the regular signals. The explosion of one torpedo is a signal to stop immediately; the explosion of two torpedoes is a signal to reduce speed immediately, and look out for a danger signal." "Rule 99a. All trains will approach stations with great care, expecting to find the main track occupied between the station limits.

* * * The responsibility for accidents between limit posts (or switches) or at fuel and water stations will rest with approaching trains."

As will be seen, the evidence is quite meager as to the extent and nature of the duties of Lawshe, as flagman. About all that can be gathered from the record on this subject must be taken from the conversation had between him and the conductor, in connection with the fact that his duties, whatever they were, were to be performed "on or about the rear end of the train." Whether his duties were fixed by rules of the company, which he, as well as the conductor, was bound to obey, or were prescribed by the conductor himself, does not appear from the evidence. In the absence of distinct proof upon this subject, and in view of the fact that the conductor was the chief officer in charge of the train, and was giving orders to Lawshe, we cannot presume the existence of any rules or regulations prescribed by an officer of the company superior in authority to these men, and equally binding on both of them, but must conclude that Lawshe had to look to the conductor alone for instructions and commands regulating his duties. Just here, it seems to us, is the key to a proper determination of the question whether or not a nonsuit should have been granted. In the case of Banking Co. v. McDade, 59 Ga. 73, it was held, in effect, that where a rule was prescribed for railroad employes by a common superior, one of them could not plead, as a justification for violating such rule, the orders of the other; and, therefore, an engineer could not excuse himself for running contrary to a schedule fixed by the company's rules, on the ground that he had been ordered to do so by the conductor. In the absence of a rule or regulation prescribed by such superior officer, addressed to and binding alike on subordinates, the doctrine seems to be well settled that a conductor has the charge and control of all persons employed on his train, and that they are bound to obey his orders. In the case of Railway Co. v. Ross, 112 U. S. 390, 5 Sup. Ct. Rep. 184, Justice FIELD said: "We know from the manner in which railroads are operated that, subject to the general rules and orders of the directors of the companies, the conductor has entire control and management of the train to which he is assigned. He directs when it shall start, at what speed it shall run, at what stations it shall stop, and for what length of time, and everything essential to its successful movement; and all persons employed on it are subject to his orders. In no proper sense of the term is he a fellow-servant with the fireman, the brakeman, the porters, and the engineer. The latter are fellow-servants in the running of the train under his direction. As to them and the train he stands in the place of and represents the corporation." This doctrine has also been recognized by this court in Prather v. Railroad Co., 80 Ga. 436, 9 S. E. Rep. 530, wherein Justice SIMMONS remarked: "The conductor was in charge of the train. * * * He represented the company. It was his right and duty to give all necessary orders for the protection of the interests of the company and the safety of its servants." Other authorities could be cited, but the above are doubtless sufficient to support a proposition so well founded in common sense and experience.

It follows, then, so far as this record discloses, that Lawshe was under the orders of the conductor, and therefore was justified in obeying any reasonable command of the latter. Of course, he would not have been justified in recklessly exposing himself to danger, although commanded so to do; but do the facts of this case so conclusively show that he did this as to leave nothing for a jury to pass upon in this connection? Are not the facts disclosed such as to make it proper for a jury to decide this question? In the first place, it may be assumed that Lawshe knew of that rule of the company which required all passenger trains to approach stations with great caution, and he had a right to assume that this rule would be observed, unless some other rule, directly binding on him, provided, either in terms or by necessary implication, that he should not rely implicitly on the employes of the passenger train, but must himself do certain things to prevent accident in case they disregarded the rule as to the manner of approaching stations. He doubtless was also aware of the fact that a freight-car standing on the trestle could be seen a considerable distance, and that a train coming up that grade, even at a high rate of speed, could easily be stopped in time to avoid a collision. In the second place, if the plaintiff's inference from the testimony as to the torpedo is correct, Lawshe also knew that one of these explosives had been placed by himself on the track, which ought to have warned the approaching passenger train of danger, and caused it to stop. And in the third place, being doubtless worn out and fatigued, he had the command of his superior officer to enter the cab and go to sleep, and that officer's assurance that he should be awakened, not only in time to prevent harm to himself, but also in time to go back upon the track, and give warning to this expected train. And he may have felt the greater security because the conductor seemed satisfied with the existing situation, and to apprehend no danger. In view of all these facts, ought a court to say that his conduct was reckless, and therefore he was guilty of negligence? Our judgment is that this question had better be left for solution to a jury. As we have already intimated, if the evidence showed that it was the duty of this flagman, under any rule of the company prescribed by an officer superior both to himself and the conductor, and binding directly on the flagman himself, to go back on the track and flag this passenger train, we would hold that he had no right to obey the conductor's order to go into the cab, or any other order of the conductor which conflicted with the duty he ought to perform under such rule made by the superior officer. The argument of the learned and able counsel for the railway company proceeded upon the assumption that it was the duty of the flagman to go back and flag the passenger train, and that some rule of the company, of higher authority than any order which the conductor could give, prescribed this duty. We have carefully examined the pleadings and the evidence to ascertain whether or not this assumption is borne out thereby, but we have been unable to find in the record anything showing how the flagman's duties were defined or regulated, otherwise than by the orders of the conductor. Without expressing any opinion as to the merits of this case, we leave it to be investigated in the court below, feeling assured that, after both sides have been fully heard, and all the facts brought out, a jury can determine more accurately than ourselves or the learned trial judge whether or not the deceased was guilty of negligence in the calamity which caused his death, this being the main and vital question to be decided. Judgment reversed.

BALLARD et al. v. GAY et al.

(*Supreme Court of North Carolina.* May 5, 1891.)

APPEAL FROM JUSTICES' COURTS—DISMISSAL.

Code N. C. § 565, provides that appeals from justices of the peace shall stand for trial *de novo* on the dockets of the superior courts at the first term after the appeal is taken, and that, if defendant should make default, judgment should be rendered against him, final in some cases, and by default and inquiry in others. By an amendatory act (Laws 1889, c. 443) it is further provided that where the appellant failed to have his appeal docketed at the next term the appellee might file a transcript of the justice's record, and move to dismiss. *Held,* that where defendant failed to docket his appeal at the next term, but did so at the second term, when plaintiff, upon defendant's failure to appear, took judgment by default against him, which was subsequently set aside on the ground that his failure to appear was excusable negligence, plaintiff was still entitled to move for a dismissal for failure to docket the appeal in time.

Appeal from superior court, Durham county; MACRAE, Judge.

This was a motion to dismiss an appeal from the judgment of a justice of the peace.

J. S. Manning and *Boone & Parker,* for appellants. *Fuller & Fuller,* for appellees.

AVERY, J. The judge below heard at the October term of the court two motions. First, upon motion of the defendants, supported by numerous affidavits, he ordered that a judgment by default, entered against them at the previous June term, be vacated, on the ground that the failure to enter an appearance at last-named term was excusable neglect. So soon as the appeal was reinstated upon the docket by this judgment, and counsel had appeared for defendants, the plaintiffs moved the court to dismiss the appeal for failure of the defendants to cause it to be docketed before the term of the superior court next after the trial in the court of the justice of the peace. The plain purpose of the legislature, as manifested in the statute, (Code, § 565,) was to expedite the disposition of appeals from the courts of justices of the peace, by providing that they should stand for trial *de novo* on the dockets of the superior courts at the first term after the appeal should be taken; that if both parties should appear, judgment should be rendered against the party cast; and that, where the defendant should make default, the judgment in certain classes of cases should be final, and in other actions by default and inquiry "to be executed forthwith by a jury." This section was subsequently so amended (Laws 1889, c. 443) that where the party appealing should fail to cause his appeal to be docketed before the next term of the superior court, the opposing party should have the right to procure a transcript of the justice's record, docket it, and move to dismiss the appeal at said term. The amendment seems to have been enacted in furtherance of the same purpose to prevent unnecessary delay in disposing of these causes involving small amounts. The case was tried before the justice on the 26th of October, 1889, and his return was handed to the clerk October 26th. The next term of the superior court was held in January following. The defendants neglected to pay the clerk's fees for docketing until after that term, and consequently the appeal was not entered on the docket until the March term, 1890. Just after handing the transcript to the clerk—on the same day—the justice of the peace told the defendants that the clerk would not docket the appeal unless they should pay his fees. The clerk had the right, even under the common law, as he has under the statute, (Code, § 3758,) to demand his fees in advance. West v. Reynolds, 94 N. C. 333; Clerk v. Wagoner, 4 Ired. 131; Andrews v. Whisnant, 83 N. C. 446; Long v. Walker, 105 N. C. 97, 10 S. E. Rep. 858; Martin v. Chasteen, 75 N. C. 96. The clerk followed the suggestion of this court made in West v. Reynolds, supra, in notifying the justice of the peace that he would not enter the case upon the docket until his fees should be paid, and the latter told the defendants on the same day of the clerk's demand and purpose. Both the original provision of the Code and the amendatory statute indicate an intent on the part of the legislature to require litigants to be diligent in prosecuting appeals from justices of the peace. The purpose seems to have been to prevent parties from using their right to a new trial in an intermediate *nisi prius* court as a means of causing useless delay and subjecting the successful party meantime to the risk of losing the fruits of his victory. The plaintiffs might have docketed and dismissed the appeal at the January term, under the act of 1889. When it was entered by the clerk at the instance of the defendants at the next succeeding term, the plaintiffs, seeing that counsel had not entered an appearance, elected to ask for a judgment by default, instead of moving to dismiss. When the court subsequently declared that the failure to appear was excusable negligence, the reinstated case stood upon the docket subject to the right of the plaintiffs to move to dismiss them, just as they could have substituted that motion for the demand for judgment by default at the previous term. After the judgment had been vacated, and the parties were appearing before the court by counsel, the *status* of both in the court was the same as if the judgment by default had never been entered at all.' There was no error in the judgment dismissing the appeal, and, as that was a final disposition of the case, it was subject to review in this court. No error.

POWERS et al. v. ERWIN et al.

(Supreme Court of North Carolina. May 12, 1891.)

SALE—CONTRACT—BREACH—EVIDENCE — INSTRUCTIONS.

In an action for the price of machinery, defendants filed a counter-claim for plaintiffs' failure to deliver the machinery promptly, according to their contract. Plaintiffs replied that they were merely defendants' agents to purchase the machinery specified, and were in no wise responsible for the delay. The evidence was conflicting as to whether plaintiffs were such agents, or whether the machinery was purchased directly from them. *Held*, that it was error to instruct the jury to find that plaintiffs had not failed to comply with their contract.

Appeal from superior court, Alamance county; JAMES MACRAE, Judge.

The complaint alleges that the plaintiffs sold to the defendants certain machinery for the consideration alleged, and that there is a balance of the purchase money due them for the same, which the defendants refuse to pay, etc. The answer admits that such balance was unpaid, but it alleges a counter-claim, the cause of action being damages sustained by reason of the failure of the plaintiffs to deliver promptly to the defendants a certain important piece of machinery specified, as they agree and bound themselves to do, which piece of machinery was part of the goods the defendants purchased from the plaintiffs, the price of which, in part, they seek to recover by this action. The reply denies the alleged counter-claim, and alleges that the plaintiffs were simply the agents of the defendants, charged to purchase from the manufacturers thereof the particular piece of machinery specified; that as such agents they purchased the same for the defendants, and are in no way or manner responsible for the delay complained of in shipping and supplying it, or for its defective nature, or for the damages to the defendants occasioned by the delay complained of, etc. The court submitted to a jury these issues: "(1) Did the plaintiffs fail to comply with their contract with the defendants, as alleged in the answer? (2) What damages, if any, have defendants sustained?" The court, among other things, instructed the jury as follows: "The contention of the plaintiffs, Powers & Co., is that the 'sunder' was ordered by them from the Berlin Machine-Works at the instance of the defendants, and not on their own account, and that they, the plaintiffs, are not responsible to the defendants for any delay in the shipment of the 'sunder,' or for any defect in the 'sunder' itself. It appears by the evidence that the plaintiffs were not manufacturers of the piece of machinery called the 'sunder,' and while they were to furnish this piece of machinery they were not

to send it direct, but were to order it to be sent at once to defendants from Berlin Machine-Works. If the plaintiffs then promptly ordered the machine from the company at Berlin, Wis., and did not assent to nor participate in the delay of the Berlin Machine-Works to make prompt shipments, the plaintiffs are not responsible for the failure of the Berlin Works to send the machine forward at once. Neither are they responsible for any delay in the transportation after the same had been delivered to the railroad company. The plaintiffs, being requested to order the machine from the Berlin Works, would not be responsible to defendants for a defect, especially a hidden defect, in that piece of it which broke soon after they put it in operation. So, upon all the testimony, I shall have to instruct you that your response to the first issue should be, 'No.' To this charge the defendants except." The jury responded "No" to the first issue, and judgment was rendered for plaintiffs. Defendants appealed to supreme court, and assign for error in the charge of his honor: "(1) That he erred in charging and instructing the jury to respond to the first issue, 'No.'"

Boone & Parker, for appellants. *J. A. Long*, for appellees.

MERRIMON, C. J., *(after stating the facts as above.)* The exception must be sustained. There was evidence produced by the defendants on the trial tending directly to prove that the plaintiffs were not the agents of the defendants, but that the latter purchased the piece of machinery in question directly from them, and not from the manufacturers thereof. One of the defendants so expressly testified. The bill of charges rendered by the plaintiffs to the defendants contained an item of charge for it, and the correspondence put in evidence tended likewise to prove the same fact. There was evidence tending to prove delay in supplying the machinery in question, when by the terms of the contract it should have been shipped promptly, etc. There was evidence (correspondence) going to show that the defendants had repeatedly written the manufacturers of the machine, urging them to hasten the shipment of the same, but this correspondence did not develop—certainly not in terms—any contract of sale on the part of the manufacturers to the defendants. The mere fact that the latter urged the former to hasten the shipment of the machine could not necessarily prove that the plaintiffs were the defendants' agents to purchase the same. In any view of the evidence, the court ought not to have instructed the jury to render a verdict in the negative upon the first issue submitted to them. At least, it should have submitted the question of agency, with appropriate instructions. There is error. The defendants are entitled to a new trial, and we so adjudge. To that end let this opinion be certified to the superior court. It is so ordered.

GRANT v. RALEIGH & G. R. Co.

(*Supreme Court of North Carolina.* May 12, 1891.)

CARRIERS — INJURIES TO PASSENGERS—EVIDENCE.

1. In an action for injuries to plaintiff, a mail agent on defendant's train, received in an accident at a switch, the exclusion of a question whether there was not a subsequent accident at the same switch is harmless error where another witness testifies as to such accident.

2. It is not error to exclude a question whether, if a switch be worn, the flanges of the engine wheels might not throw it open, when the witness is not an expert, and there is no evidence that the switch was worn.

3. Evidence of the condition of defendant's track at other places and of other switches in the vicinity is inadmissible.

4. Though the accident was occasioned by the train leaving the main track at the switch, and then running into freight-cars standing on the side track leaving such freight-cars standing on the side track, is not negligence where they do not interfere with travel when the tracks are in order.

Action tried before WOMACK, J., at March term, 1890, of Halifax superior court. The plaintiff brought this action to recover damages alleged to have been occasioned by the negligence of defendant, in that, while he was in the regular discharge of his duty as mail agent in one of the cars attached to and forming part of one of defendant's regular passenger and mail trains in motion, the same was thrown violently from the track, and he sustained serious physical injuries. The defendant denied the material allegations of the complaint, and the following issues were submitted to the jury: "Was the plaintiff damaged by the negligence of defendant? (2) What damage, if any, did plaintiff sustain by the negligence of the defendant?" It was in evidence from both plaintiff and defendant that plaintiff, while in the discharge of his duties as mail agent of one of the regular passenger trains of defendant, received injuries by the train leaving the track at a switch about a half mile from Johnston-Street station in Raleigh, on Friday, February 6, 1889. That after the accident the pin which held the switch in place was missing, and has never been found. That at the place of the accident there is a decided curve, the switch being on the outside. There were three tracks,—one called a "spur track," built to hold idle cars, and unconnected with the other tracks at its end nearest the scene of the accident; one a side track, connected with the main track by the switch in question; and the main track. That at the time of the accident there were no cars on the spur track, but there were 14 cars standing on the side track, but far enough away to permit trains to pass on the main track with safety. That when the train left the main track at the switch it ran for a short distance over the crossties, and into the cars standing on the side track with great force, badly breaking the engine and several of the standing cars. That prior to the accident the road-bed and switch at the place of accident, as well as the engine and cars, were in good condition, and the employes of the defendant company whose duty it was to super-

v.13s.E.no.6—14

intend and operate them were competent and efficient.

Lewis Wrenn, who was conductor in charge of the train, was examined as a witness for the defendant. On the cross-examination, the witness was asked: "Was there not a similar accident near the same place a little before or after this accident by the train running off, run by the same engineer and conductor?" Objection by defendant. Objection sustained, and the plaintiff excepted. Subsequently Rufus Horton was examined as a witness for the defendant, and testified that he was the engineer in charge of the derailed train. On his cross-examination the plaintiff was permitted to ask this question: "Have you had another accident shortly prior to this accident?" To which he answered: "I have not for a number of years." He was then asked: "Were there any accidents shortly after this one?" To which question he answered: "I had an accident shortly afterwards, about two hundred yards above the place of this accident, at the other end of the switch. That switch was probably changed by mistake. I did not get off the track. I ran on the side track, and into cars standing on it. There was no switch broken; I was only turned on the wrong track by a mistake of some one changing the switch." Counsel for the plaintiff stated that this was the accident they desired the witness Wrenn to testify to, who was admitted to have been the conductor in charge of the train on this occasion also. On the cross-examination of T. H. Pleasants, a witness for the defendant, he was asked by the plaintiff: "If the end of the switch had worn, and the flanges of the wheels caught on it, might not the engine open the switch, coming from either direction?" Objection by the defendant, and objection sustained, for there was no evidence that this switch had worn, and the defendant excepted. J. R. Thrower, a witness for the defendant, had previously stated, in explaining a model of the switch in use: "The point of the switch would wear after a long time, but would wear thinner." Rufus Horton had testified that "the points of switches wear some." W. A. Green had testified: "I examined the switch Wednesday before the accident, and it was in good order." The plaintiff offered to prove the condition of the track at or near the "Round-House," and within the yard limit presided over by the same section-master as the road at the point of the accident. Objected to by the defendant. Objection sustained, and the plaintiff excepted. The plaintiff asked a witness, "What is the present condition of the switches in the yard limit?" Objection by the defendant. Objection sustained, and the defendant excepted.

The plaintiff asked the following special instructions: "(1) The defendant railroad is a public carrier, and is required to use the greatest care and utmost diligence and good faith in providing for the safety of its passengers, both as to life and limb. (2) The defendant is required, by the nature of its calling, to provide the safest cars, the safest engines, the safest roads, the safest switches, and the safest and best and most competent employes and servants the nature of its business permits; and if it failed to provide them, or any of them, and the plaintiff was thereby injured, he is entitled to recover to the extent of injuries. (3) If the plaintiff has shown, and the jury believe, that he was injured in the manner described by him by the accident or wreck on defendant's road, the law presumes that the injury was by the defendant's negligence, and the burden is upon the defendant to show that the wreck was not by its fault, and that it used the utmost care and diligence to prevent it. (4) The law requires that the defendant shall not only have efficient and competent servants, but should have them in sufficient numbers to provide against every reasonable contingency. (5) Switches are points and parts of a road at which accidents are liable to occur, unless closely attended to, and defendant is held to the utmost diligence, care, and watchfulness in selecting the safest patterns in the start, and in keeping them in perfect order. (6) Leaving cars on such a side track, so close to such a switch as that the train going at the usual speed of thirty or thirty-five miles an hour, and rushing out upon such side track, could not have been stopped in time to prevent a collision, is negligence. (7) If the jury believe that the accident and injury to the plaintiff occurred in consequence of a misplaced switch, then the evidence offered by the defendant is not sufficient to rebut the presumption of negligence, and the jury should find the first issue, 'Yes.'" The court gave substantially the 1st, 2d, 3d, 4th, and 5th special instructions asked by the plaintiff, and refused the 6th and 7th, and the plaintiff excepted.

The court charged the jury as follows: "In this case the burden of proof is upon the plaintiff to show by a preponderance of the evidence that he was injured by the negligence of the defendant, and, if he has not so convinced the jury, they will answer the first issue, 'No.' Unless he has shown the jury by a preponderance of the evidence that the injury was occasioned by an act which, with proper care, or by machinery which, with proper use and care, would not ordinarily produce damage, if he has so satisfied the jury, then he has made what the law terms a *prima facie* case of negligence, and the laboring oar is shifted to the defendant, and the defendant must show by preponderance of the evidence that the company has not been guilty of negligence; and the reason for this is that it is so much easier for those who do the damage to show the exculpating circumstances, if such exist, than it is for the injured to produce proof of positive negligence." To this instruction the plaintiff excepted. The court further charged the jury: "To render the defendant liable the injury must be the natural and probable consequence of the negligence,—such a consequence as, under the circumstances, might or ought to have been foreseen by the wrong-doer as likely to result from his act." To this instruction the plaintiff excepted. The court further charged the jury: "The defendant

claims to have rebutted this presumption of negligence by showing that the only way the accident could have occurred was by the pin having been taken out of the switch by some evil-disposed person other than the defendant and its agents. If the defendant has satisfied the jury that this is true, then the defendant has not been guilty of negligence, and the plaintiff cannot recover." To this charge the plaintiff excepted. The court further charged the jury: "If the defendant has not so satisfied the jury, and the jury believe that the accident may have occurred in some other manner than by the switch-pin having been so removed, then the defendant must satisfy the jury that it has not in other respects been negligent; and in that view the court charges the jury that it is not negligence in the defendant company not to have a guard or watchman at the switch." To which charge the plaintiff excepted. The court further charged: "It was not negligence to place box cars on the side track, unless they were near enough to interfere with travel on the main track." To which charge the plaintiff excepted. The court further charged: "If the jury believe that the defendant used the safest and best switches obtainable, and other safest machinery; employed competent officials in their respective capacities; caused the switch and road to be examined carefully every two or three days; that this switch was examined carefully on Wednesday preceding the accident; that a number of trains passed over the switch the same day, that the switch was operated successfully that morning, and nothing was discovered to be wrong with it; and that the engineer, in his proper place, noticed and saw that the signal showed the main track to be open, and that only human agency could enable the target to show safety when the switch was partly open, which caused the wreck,—then the defendant has not been guilty of negligence, and the plaintiff cannot recover, for the defendant must use the highest degree of care that a reasonable man could use." To which charge the plaintiff excepted. "But if the jury are not so satisfied by the defendant, they will answer the first issue, 'Yes,' and will proceed to the second issue." There was a verdict for the defendant. Rule for a new trial, and *venire de novo* by the plaintiff for error in the rejection of evidence set out in exceptions 1, 2, 3, and 4, and for refusing the special instructions asked for and set out in exceptions 5 and 6, and in those given as set out in exceptions 7, 8, 9, 10, 11, and 12. Rule discharged. Judgment upon the verdict for the defendant. Appeal by the plaintiff.

R. B. Peebles and *W. J. Peele*, for appellant. *Batchelor & Devereux* and *W. H. Day*, for appellee.

MERRIMON, C. J., *(after stating the facts as above.)* As to the first exception, if it be granted that the court should have allowed the question to be answered, it appears that another witness of the defendant upon cross-examination was afterwards allowed to testify that an accident subsequent to that alleged in the complaint had happened, and the counsel for the plaintiff said this was the same one he desired the first witness to give evidence of It was not questioned by the defendant that such second accident did occur, and hence the plaintiff had benefit of the evidence in as full measure, in every respect of the case, as if the first witness referred to had given the same. The exception is therefore without force. Nor has the second exception any merit. The witness referred to was not examined as an expert; nor does it appear that he was an expert or that he was skilled in such matters as the question had reference to. The question he was not allowed to answer was based upon a hypothetical state of facts, and was intended to elicit his opinion. The answer, if the same had been received, could have served no proper purpose, because "there was no evidence that this switch had worn." It is so stated in the case, and no such evidence appears. The evidence to which the third and fourth exceptions refer was properly excluded. The condition of the defendant's railroad track at places other than that at which the accident in question happened could not prove or disprove the condition of the track at the latter place. Such evidence would afford ground only for uncertain inference—mere conjecture—and it would certainly tend to mislead and confuse the jury. The same may be said of evidence of the "condition of the switches in the yard limit" at the time of the trial. We think the plaintiff has no just ground of exception to the instructions complained of that the court gave the jury. Indeed, it is questionable whether in some respects they were not too favorable to him. The evidence went to prove the accident whereby the plaintiff sustained injury, and that it may have been and probably was occasioned by the absence of an important bolt, the purpose and use of which were to hold the "switch" in its proper place. There was no evidence going to show what otherwise could have given rise to it. The principal inquiry was whether the defendant negligently allowed that bolt to be out of its place. It seems that only such parts of the instructions to the jury as were excepted to are set forth in the record. But it certainly appears that the court very fully, in substance, told the jury that if the plaintiff had satisfied them that his "injury was occasioned by an act which with proper care or by machinery which with proper use and care would not ordinarily produce damage," then the burden was on the defendant to prove that it was not chargeable with negligence. This was clearly sufficient, and in harmony with numerous decisions of this court. Ellis v. Railroad Co., 2 Ired. 138; Aycock v. Railroad Co., 89 N. C. 321, and cases there cited; Moore v. Parker, 91 N. C. 275; Patt. Ry. Acc. Law, 433 et seq; 3 Lawson, Rights, Rem. & Pr. § 1213; Lawrence v. Green, 70 Cal. 417, 11 Pac. Rep. 750. The court properly declined to give the jury the sixth special instruction asked for by the plaintiff. Leaving cars standing on a side track is not of itself negligence; certainly it is not when the cars are not in the way of trains passing on the main track. A train moving on the main track of a railroad cannot go upon a side track if the two tracks are respectively in order. It is not negligence to do what may be done in the regular course of business if in the nature of the matter harm does not arise therefrom, unless occasioned by some negligence. Sellars v. Railroad Co., 94 N. C. 654. The plaintiff was not entitled to the seventh instruction asked for by him, because clearly there was evidence from which the jury might find that the defendant was not chargeable with negligence. Indeed, the evidence went strongly to prove its active diligence. Other minor objections to the instructions given are groundless, and are fully met by Sellars v. Railroad Co., supra, and Doggett v. Railroad Co., 78 N. C. 305. Judgment affirmed.

WOODLIEF v. BRAGG.

(Supreme Court of North Carolina. May 12, 1891.)

CLAIMS AGAINST DECEDENT—LIMITATION—ARREST OF BAR.

1. Code N. C. § 164, provides that when a claim against decedent is filed with the personal representative within a year after the grant of letters of administration, and the same shall be admitted by him, it shall not be necessary to bring an action on such claim to prevent the bar of the statute. *Held* that, in the absence of fraud or collusion, this is sufficient to arrest the statute as to the heirs as well as to the personal representative.

2. Where a claim is filed in time, and no objection is made thereto, but the administrator files his petition to apply proceeds of the sale of real estate to its payment, this will be deemed, in the absence of evidence to the contrary, an admission of the claim by him so as to arrest the running of the statute.

Appeal from superior court, Granville county; BOYKIN, Judge.
Special proceeding commenced before the clerk.

Edwards & Batchelor, for appellant.
Graham & Graham, for appellee.

CLARK, J. The creditor presented the claims now in dispute to the administrator within one year of his qualification, and said claims were not barred by the statute of limitations at the death of the intestate. The administrator files this petition to condemn proceeds of sale of certain real estate in the clerk's office as assets to pay debts, there being an insufficiency of assets, and the defendants, the heirs at law, seek the benefit of the statute of limitations. The Code, § 164, provides that, if a claim is "filed with the personal representative within the time above specified, *i. e.*, one year after grant of letters to the personal representative, and the same shall be admitted by him, it shall not be necessary to bring an action upon such claim to prevent the bar." Code, § 1429, provides that, if action should notwithstanding be brought, the plaintiff must pay the costs, unless payment is unnecessarily delayed or neglected, or the defendant refuses to refer the matter. The first section above cited (164) provides generally that the statute, under such circumstances, ceases to run, and there is nothing which would seem to indicate a suspension of the statute as to the personal representative only, leaving the heir at law to be protected by the lapse of time. Action could only be brought against the personal representative, and the statute, (section 1429,) to discourage the bringing of such action, provides that the plaintiff shall pay the costs, except in certain instances, which do not apply to this case. When judgment is obtained against the personal representative, the heir at law cannot plead the statute of limitations, unless there is fraud and collusion. Speer v. James, 94 N. C. 417; Long v. Oxford, ante, 112, (at this term.) The reason of this is that the personal representative represents the deceased, and when a judgment is obtained against him, in the absence of fraud and collusion, it is conclusive as to the validity of the indebtedness against the heir as well as against the distributee. For the same reason, since the amendment of the Code, § 104, by chapter 80, Acts 1881, (the provision above quoted,) the heir is as much barred by the filing of the claim within the prescribed time, and its admission by the personal representative, as he would be by the latter submitting to a judgment. It will be noted that the claim in controversy in Bevers v. Park, 88 N. C. 456, was a cause of action accrued prior to Code Civil Proc., and section 164 did not apply to it at all. Hall v. Gibbs, 87 N. C. 4. Besides, a judgment had been obtained on that claim and the amendatory act, (chapter 80, Acts 1881,) now before us, could have no application. In the present case it is not expressly found that the administrator admitted the claim. We do not hold that the mere reception by an administrator of a claim, without objection, is an admission of its validity, but in Flemming v. Flemming, 85 N. C. 127, where this provision was construed, Smith, C. J., says the creditor had perhaps the right to "deem the acceptance [of the claim by the administrator] without remark as arresting the running of the statute." Here not only the claim was filed in proper time, and no objection was made, but the administrator files the petition to obtain assets to pay it. This is strong proof that he did not deny its correctness, but "admitted" it; certainly it is so, in the absence of any proof whatever to the contrary. No error.

LEACH et al. v. LINDE.

(Supreme Court of North Carolina. May 21, 1891.)

DRAWING JURY—FRAUDULENT REPRESENTATIONS.

1. When Acts 1885, c. 180, was passed, prescribing that certain terms of the superior court of the county of Wake should continue for three weeks for the trial of civil business alone, (there having previously been no longer terms than two weeks,) Code N. C. c. 89, in respect to jurors, providing in terms for the drawing of them by the county commissioners for each week of the terms of the courts lasting two weeks, was by necessary implication extended to authorize the commissioners to draw jurors for the third week of the newly-established terms.

2. If the commissioners fail to draw jurors for the third week the court may direct a jury to be drawn and summoned, as prescribed by Code N. C. § 1732, providing for drawing a jury in case the commissioners fail to do so.

3. Plaintiffs, on the representation of defendant that an ice factory was in good repair, and would make a certain quantity of ice a day at a certain cost, leased the same, and purchased of defendant bonds, the value of which depended on the truth of the representations. The representations were false. Plaintiffs made repairs without being able to bring the factory up to defendant's representations; and sued him to recover, as damages, the amount spent for repairs, and the amount paid for the bonds. Held, that plaintiffs were entitled to recover for the damage resulting from the fraud of defendant; and instructions that they could not recover the amount paid for the bonds if they could, in a reasonable time and with a reasonable outlay, have repaired the factory so as to place it in the condition required by the contract with defendant, were properly refused.

4. Instructions should be refused, unless there is evidence to which they are pertinent, and which warrants them.

Appeal from superior court, Wake county; BOYKIN, Judge.

Action by G. E. Leach and another against Charles F. Linde to recover damages of defendant for fraudulent misrepresentations by which plaintiffs were induced to lease an ice factory, and purchase certain bonds, the value of which was dependent on the value and condition of the factory. The complaint charged that defendant, to induce plaintiffs to lease the factory and purchase the bonds, represented to them that the factory was in good repair, and capable of producing 15 tons of ice per day, at a cost of not more than $2.25 per ton, whereas, in fact, the machinery was in a bad condition, and was capable of producing only 4 or 5 tons a day, and that at a cost of $6 per ton. Plaintiffs repaired the machinery at a cost of $2,400, but could not make it come up to the representations of defendant. This action is to recover, as damages, the amount of the bonds, and the amount spent in repairs. Defendant asked special instructions as follows: "(1) If the plant mentioned in the complaint could have been, in a reasonable time, with a reasonable outlay of money, so repaired and improved by the plaintiffs, after they took possession of the same, as to place it in the condition required by the contract, then the plaintiffs are not entitled to recover as damages the $4,000 paid for bonds as alleged in said complaint. (2) If the plant mentioned in the complaint could have been, within a reasonable time, and with the outlay of $2,400 mentioned in this complaint, so repaired and improved by the plaintiffs, after they took possession of the same, as to place it in the condition required by their contract of October 6, 1888, set forth in the complaint, then the plaintiffs are not entitled to recover as damages the $4,000 paid for bonds as alleged in said complaint. * * * (10) Of the damages claimed by the plaintiffs, to-wit, the sum paid for the bonds and the sum expended in repairing the plant, they are entitled to recover only such sum as was necessary to put the plant in good repair, and make it capable of producing ice as required by the contract set forth in the complaint." All of said instructions were refused.

Strong, Gray & Stamps, for appellant.

Battle & Mordecai and *Armistead Jones*, for appellees.

MERRIMON, C. J. The statute (Acts 1885, c. 180) prescribes, among other things, that certain of the terms of the superior court of the county of Wake shall continue for three weeks, "to be for the trial of civil business alone." These terms are to be devoted to the proper disposition of all kinds of civil actions and proceedings pending in the court, whether they be such as require trials by jury or not. Hence the statute just cited, taken, as it must be, in connection with the other statute, (Code, c. 39, in respect to "Jurors," especially sections 1727, 1732,) contemplates and intends that a jury shall be provided for each week of the terms of the court to which reference is thus made. The third week of such terms, as well as the two preceding weeks thereof, is devoted to the disposition of civil business,—actions that generally require jury trials. How can such trials be had without a jury? Is it not obvious that the statute creating these terms intended that each week of them should have provided for it a jury, drawn in the regular method prescribed? In extending the terms of the courts for such purpose, by plain implication the duty of the county commissioners was correspondingly enlarged so as to require them to provide regularly a jury for the third week of terms. It is true that the statute (Code, § 1727) provides generally in terms for drawing for each week of the terms of the superior courts lasting two weeks, but its chief and leading purpose is to provide juries for the regular terms of the courts, and a jury for each week of them. At the time the general statute in respect to juries was first enacted the regular terms of the superior courts did not extend beyond two weeks, and hence the county commissioners were required only to provide a jury for each week of a term of that length. Afterwards, when the terms of some of the courts were extended to three weeks, as in the case of the county of Wake, the statute in respect to juries was not in terms in pertinent respects correspondingly modified, but it was in effect. The two statutes are in important respects *in pari materia*, and must be taken and treated together. That in regard to jurors is intended in large measure to effectuate that in respect to courts. Hence, when the statute first above cited extended the terms of the court one week, it had the effect to so modify the statute in respect to juries as to require a jury to be provided for that week in the regular method. In the nature of the matter, and in view of the purpose of the law, it would be impracticable, unreasonable, and absurd to extend the terms of the court one week for general purposes, and provide no jury for that week. It appears in this case that the county commissioners for some cause failed to draw a jury for the third week of the term at which the action was tried. The court directed that a jury for the same be prescribed and allowed by the statute, (Code, § 1732,) and a jury was so drawn and summoned accordingly. A jury thus drawn was not illegal.

It was such as the law allowed, and to be so treated for all proper purposes. It is true the statute provides that a jury may be so drawn "if the commissioners for any cause fail to draw a jury for any term of the superior court, regular or special," etc. Here the commissioners provided juries for the two weeks of the term, but not for the third week. Clearly such failure came within the mischief provided against by the section of the statute just cited. The object of the statute is to provide in an orderly method unobjectionable jurors for the courts. The defendant's challenge to the array cannot, therefore, be allowed; hence, his first exception is groundless.

The issues of fact submitted to the jury were clearly raised by allegations of the complaint broadly denied in the answer. They were comprehensive, and afforded the defendant ample opportunity to introduce on the trial all evidence material for his defense, and to raise all questions of law in respect to the materiality, relevancy, and application of the same, and like opportunity as to the evidence of the plaintiffs. The verdict of the jury upon them would settle with sufficient fullness the material controverted constituent facts. The issues tendered by the defendant might have served the like purpose, but scarcely so well, because they were unnecessarily more in number, and subdivided the material inquiries to be made. This always tends more or less to confuse the jury. So the second exception is without force.

The evidence objected to and embraced by the third exception was of slight importance, not such as in its nature would prejudice the defendant. It tended in some degree to identify the contract alleged and set forth in the complaint, to show that the defendant had knowledge of its contents and meaning, and to account for the absence of the subscribing witness thereto. This exception has no substantial merit.

The defendant was not entitled to have the first, second, and tenth special instructions asked for by him given to the jury, because the plaintiffs in substance alleged, and there was evidence tending to prove, that they were induced to lease the ice manufactory mentioned, and in that connection to pay to the defendant $4,000 for certain bonds of little or no value by the false and fraudulent representations made by him to them. The plaintiffs allege that the defendant falsely and fraudulently represented to them that the ice manufactory was a good one—in good repair; that it was capable of producing a certain quantity of ice per day, at a cost of not exceeding a specified sum; that the ice plant was of great value,—$40,000. Hence they believed that the bonds, whose value depended upon the facts thus falsely represented to exist, were of substantial value, and were induced to buy them. It is alleged that the defendant knew that such representations made by him were false, and that he fraudulently induced the plaintiffs to take the lease, and pay $4,000 for the bonds they received at his instance and solicitation and for his benefit. If such allegations were true, the plaintiffs were entitled to recover damages upon the ground that they were, under the circumstances, fraudulently induced by the defendant to buy the bonds, which he represented to be of great value, whereas in fact they were of no substantial value. The damage in such respect was a direct result of the fraud alleged, and the plaintiffs were entitled to recover on account of the same.

It is stated in the case that the evidence sent up was all that bore upon the special instructions asked for by the defendant. We have examined it carefully, and are of opinion that there was no evidence that could warrant the court in giving the third, fourth, and fifth special instructions asked for. No part of the evidence, nor the whole of it together, accepted as true, in any reasonable view of it was sufficient to prove that the plaintiffs "knew that the said plant [the ice manufactory] did not come up to the representations made by this defendant;" nor that the plaintiffs would have taken the lease if they had known that the representations made by the defendant were false. The court should not give instructions, special or otherwise, in the absence of evidence to which they are pertinent, and that warrants them. It would be error to do so if they prejudiced the adverse party. The court gave the eighth and ninth special instructions asked for substantially and sufficiently in its charge to the jury, to which there was no exception. Indeed, it was very fair, and sufficiently explicit. It directed the attention of the jury particularly to the issues, their nature, and the evidence submitted to them. We are unable to discover that the defendant was prejudiced, as he complained, by any instructions the court gave or failed to give them. Judgment affirmed.

STATE v. BAKER.

(*Supreme Court of North Carolina.* May 5, 1891.)

ROAD SERVICE—WARRANT—NOTICE.

1. In proceedings before a justice of the peace, a warrant that charges that defendant was liable and duly assigned to work on a public road specified; that he was within the ages of 18 and 45 years; that he was duly summoned to work on that road at the time specified; and that he willfully and unlawfully failed and omitted to work as he was bound to do, etc.,—sufficiently discloses an offense, under Act N. C. 1885, c. 134.

2. Where, under a road law (Acts N. C. 1885, c. 134, § 3) requiring the township trustees to "divide their respective townships into suitable road-districts," and to "furnish each supervisor with a plat of his district," it appears that no new division was made, but that the trustees "adopted the districts of the old board" of supervisors, created under Code, § 2014, "making such alterations as they thought advisable, allotting certain farms to a section," and that no map or plat was furnished to the supervisors, such division into sections, and assignment of the hands liable to road service, is sufficiently definite to fix the duty and liability of the defendant for a refusal to work it.

3. It appeared from the evidence of the supervisor that he personally notified defendant to work on the road; that he told him to meet him "at Hunter's branch to work the road" on the mornings specified, but without mentioning any road; that defendant had previously received a like notice to work the same road, and had

worked as directed. *Held,* that the notice, though informal, was sufficient.

Appeal from criminal court, Mecklenburg county; MEARES, Judge.

Dowd & Harris, for appellant. *The Attorney General,* for the State.

MERRIMON, C. J. The motion here in arrest of judgment cannot be allowed. Nothing appears or fails to appear in the record that could properly prevent the entry of the judgment appealed from. The defendant was charged by a state warrant with a petty misdemeanor, before a justice of the peace, and, though the offense is not charged with great precision and particularity, the court can at once see what it is, and the defendant can learn from the warrant all that is necessary to enable him to make defense, and to defend himself in case of a subsequent prosecution. It is charged that he was liable and duly assigned to work on a public road specified, situate within a particular township and county named; that he was within the ages of 18 and 45 years; that he was duly summoned to work on that road at a time specified; and that he willfully and unlawfully failed and omitted to work as he was bound to do, etc. This was sufficient. It is not expected nor essential, in criminal proceedings before justices of the peace, that all the precision and niceties of pleading shall be observed, as required in the superior courts. It is sufficient if the substance of the offense is charged, and the court and the defendant can certainly see what it is. Moreover, when such proceedings are defective, the courts should exercise liberally the large powers conferred upon them to amend the same. A mere technicality, not affecting the substance, should not be allowed to defeat or delay the administration of criminal justice. The statute (Acts 1885, c. 134) prescribes and embodies a system in respect to "roads and highways" in the county of Mecklenburg. In many material respects it is very different from the general statute on the subject of "roads, ferries, and bridges," (Code N. C. § 2014,) and it must be so interpreted as to effectuate its purpose appearing from its terms and necessary and reasonable implication. It appeared on the trial that the board of trustees of the township had not divided the township into suitable road-districts, as required by the third section of the statute just cited, nor had they observed its requirements in other respects as they should have done, and ought to be compelled to do, with a view to better and perfect the road system prescribed; but the evidence went to prove that they "adopted the districts of the old board, making such alterations as they thought advisable, allotting certain farms to a section." This was treated as "districting the township." The court instructed the jury that the statute above cited prescribed no particular form to be observed in laying off the township road-districts, and that, if they believed the evidence above recited, the district, as described, was sufficient for the purposes of this action. The defendant excepted, contending that the provisions of the statute are mandatory in numerous particulars specified by him, and that he could not be convicted, as the statute, in these respects, had not been observed by the township board of trustees. The third section of the statute requires that the township trustees shall "divide their respective townships into suitable road-districts," and "furnish each supervisor with a plot of his district." A leading purpose of such districts is to designate with certainty the roads with which the superintendent is to be charged, the hands liable to work on public roads subject to his authority, and to fix his and their liability and amenability for any omission of duty. The evidence went to prove that the township trustees adopted the road-districts in their township as they found them when they came into office, and designated the farms, the hands on which should do road service in the particular district where the farms were situate. Now, although the township trustees had failed to discharge their duty fully and properly, as they should have done, still the public road—a section of it—was designated, and the hands liable to do road service were assigned to duty in it. There was sufficient certainty in all respects to fix the duty and liability of the defendant, and the court properly so decided. The evidence went to prove that the supervisor was appointed with instructions as to the road and hands subject to his authority. He received a list of the farms, the hands on which were assigned to the road mentioned in the warrant. He testified on the trial that he personally notified the defendant to work that road on days specified; that he told him to "meet me [himself] at Hunter's branch to work the road Wednesday and Thursday morning. [the days designated.] I don't think I mentioned any road." He further testified that the branch mentioned crossed the road mentioned in the warrant; that on a later occasion he gave the defendant like notice to work on the same road, and he went and worked as directed. The defendant insisted that this notice was not sufficient. We think it was reasonable and sufficient. The defendant was notified to meet the supervisor, on the mornings of days specified, at a branch that crossed the public road to be worked, to do road service. He knew that he was liable to do such service, and the fair implication from the notice was that he was required to do road service on the road specified in the warrant, which was the road the branch crossed, at the times mentioned to him. The notice was sufficiently definite, though informal, to inform him that he was required to meet the supervisor, and do service he knew he owed on the particular road that crossed the branch named, or certainly on one the supervisor would point out at the time appointed. What has thus been said substantially disposes of the special instructions asked for by the defendant. These were founded upon highly technical grounds, and the denial of them could not prejudice any pertinent right of the defendant. Upon the merits, the conviction was a proper one. Judgment affirmed.

BARBEE *et al.* v. BARBEE *et al.*

(Supreme Court of North Carolina. May 12, 1891.)

DEED—PAROL EVIDENCE OF CONSIDERATION—TRANSACTION WITH DECEDENT.

1. The recital in a deed of the receipt of the purchase money, not being contractual in its nature, is only *prima facie* evidence of payment, and hence, though deeds from a father to his children recite the receipt of a consideration, parol evidence is admissible to show that the conveyances were intended as advancements.

2. In partition between heirs at law evidence by some of the parties that in a division of lands by their father among them it was agreed that some of them should pay certain sums to others for owelty of partition is incompetent under Code N. C. § 590, where one of the heirs, a party to such agreement, is dead.

This is a special proceeding (before MAC-RAE, J., at Durham superior court) for the partition of real estate between the heirs at law of one Gray Barbee, and the questions presented for review relate to certain alleged advancements made by the said Barbee to the several heirs mentioned in the petition.

Guthrie, Boone & Parker, for appellants. *W. W. Fuller* and *J. W. Graham,* for appellees.

SHEPHERD, J., (*after stating the facts as above.*) Although the record is very voluminous, containing the report of the referee, a very considerable amount of testimony, and many exceptions, it seemed to be the understanding of counsel that for the purposes of this appeal but two questions were necessary to be argued by them and decided by the court.

1. The first question involves the correctness of his honor's ruling that the recitals of the payment of the considerations set forth in the deeds executed by Mr. Barbee to several of his children were, in the absence of allegations and proof of mistake, fraud, etc., so far conclusive as to preclude the introduction of parol testimony to show the true character of the transactions, and thus rebut the presumption of a sale arising from such recitals. There was abundant testimony to sustain the findings of the referee that the conveyances were intended as advancements. Indeed, it was admitted by the parties examined that they had not in fact paid the considerations mentioned, and it also appeared that Mr. Barbee had charged some of his children with the payment of certain amounts in favor of others for the purpose of equalizing the partial distribution of his property. There can really be no question that such was his intention, but it is earnestly insisted that parol testimony cannot be heard to show such intention until the conveyances are corrected in respect to the recitals above mentioned. In support of this position we are referred to the case of Wilkinson v. Wilkinson, 2 Dev. Eq. 376. There a father conveyed land to his son by a deed of bargain and sale, which recited the payment of several hundred dollars as purchase money. The court held that the proofs offered to show that the consideration had not been paid were insufficient, but it was at the same time declared that, had the testimony been satisfactory, it would not have been heard

to contradict the recital, unless it appeared "that by reason of some unfair practice, or through mistake or by surprise, the deed was made to express an intention different from that which the bargainer believed it did declare." This part of the opinion was unnecessary to the determination of the case, and is in conflict with Jones v. Spaight, 2 Murph. 89, where, for the purpose of showing that a conveyance was intended as an advancement, parol evidence was admitted, without invoking any equitable element, to prove that a recited consideration of £40 was in fact never paid, and was only mentioned, as alleged in the petition, "as a formal circumstance in the execution" of the deed. The principle stated in Wilkinson's Case is based entirely upon the idea that the recital of the payment of the consideration is a part of the contract, and, like other written contracts, cannot be contradicted or varied by parol testimony. Such seems to be the general current of the decisions in England, where it is held that the consideration cannot be recovered in a court of law in the face of a recital of this nature. This is also generally understood to be the course of judicial decision in North Carolina. Brocket v. Foscue, 1 Hawks, 64; Mendenhall v. Parish, 8 Jones, (N. C.) 105, and the cases cited. On the other hand, the overwhelming weight of American authority is in favor of treating the recital as only *prima facie* evidence of payment, as in the case of a receipt, the only effect of the consideration clause being to estop the grantor from alleging that the deed was executed without consideration in order to prevent a resulting trust. 1 Greenl. Ev. 37, and note; 2 Whart. Ev. § 1042, and note; Bigelow, Estop. 318; 3 Washb. Real Prop. 321. The English doctrine was very reluctantly assented to by Lord MANSFIELD, and it is even now claimed by some writers that the decisions of the courts of that country are not entirely harmonious in its application. Without stopping to inquire how this may be, it is very manifest from an examination of our own decisions that the principle has not always been practically followed in North Carolina. If the recital is contractual in its nature it is plain that it cannot be gotten rid of but by a correction of the deed in equity on the grounds mentioned in Wilkinson's Case, supra; and it would seem equally clear that to obtain such relief there must be allegation and proof that the clause was inserted by surprise, fraud, or mistake, etc. Nevertheless this court, in Shaw v. Williams, 100 N. C. 272, 6 S. E. Rep. 196, permitted the recovery of the consideration money in the teeth of a recital of its payment, although there was "no pretense that the plaintiff was surprised into making the deed, or was ignorant of what she was doing. It was manifest," says the court, "that she executed it with full knowledge that it passed her estate in the land, and such was her purpose. The true inquiry should have been whether it was the intent to exonerate the purchaser from his obligation to pay the consideration money by the introduction of this recital." It will be observed that the recital was pleaded as a release, and, being a part of

the deed, necessarily showed the consideration upon which it was made. It will also be noted that there was no pleading whatever impeaching the said release, (there being only the general denial to the answer implied by the law,) and yet it was held that the recital could be contradicted by parol testimony as to the intent with which it was made. It is very difficult to reconcile the decision with the principle above stated, and there are other cases where, perhaps, in view of the hardship of a rigid enforcement of the rule, a similar departure has been made. It seems to be conceded everywhere that injustice must result in some instances from a strict and logical application of the doctrine; and it is in the struggle to administer substantial justice in such cases, and at the same time adhere to the principle that such recitals are contractual, that we find the inconsistencies in this and other courts in their rulings upon the subject. In Michael v. Foil, 100 N. C. 179, 6 S. E. Rep. 264, the deed recited a consideration of $500, but the court, without any suggestion of fraud, surprise, or mistake, admitted parol evidence to vary the recital by showing that it was agreed at the time of the conveyance that the grantor should have one-half of the proceeds of the sale of the mineral interest in the land, if such a sale were made in his life-time. Athough the principle of Manning v. Jones, Busb. 368, was applied in this case, the decision can hardly be reconciled with the theory that the recital of a consideration is contractual, and the court quoted with approval a decision from the supreme court of Massachusetts, in which state the doctrine is repudiated. The non-contractual character of such recitals in executed contracts is distinctly asserted in Harper v. Harper, 92 N. C. 300, in which the following language is used: "It was contended on the argument that the parol evidence introduced by the appellees was incompetent because its effect was to explain and contradict the deed. This is a misapprehension of the purpose of the evidence. The deed was not in question at all. There was no purpose to contradict or change or modify its terms, or to change its meaning in any degree. Its office was to convey the title to the land. The evidence was introduced in respect to a matter outside of and independent of it. It was intended to show with what intent the father and bargainor made it, apart from the purpose to convey land to his son. It was put in evidence, not to prove title, but to show a particular intent on the part of the maker of it, in another respect distinct from it." Again, it was said in Melvin v. Bullard, 82 N. C. 37, that "while a gift in form raises the presumption of an intent that the donee of any considerable portion of the parent's estate shall account therefor in a settlement with the heirs and distributees after his death, while a bargain and sale does not, it is clear that if at the time of the conveyance by either mode the parent did not intend it should operate as an advancement, and this intent appears from the instrument by which the transfer is effected, or from the facts of the transaction, or is shown by other proof, the property so conveyed is not an advancement, nor its value to be accounted for afterwards." In this unsatisfactory state of the authorities we must determine whether we shall return to the principle of some of the older decisions of this court, and administer it in its original strictness and simplicity, or whether we shall continue to act upon the American doctrine, as unmistakably indicated by our later cases. If the latter view is to prevail, it would seem better to distinctly recognize it at once, and thus avoid the anomaly, as shown by some of the cases, of denying a demand upon the ground that it can only be recovered in a court of equity, and granting the relief in that court without allegation or finding as to the existence of any equitable element whatever. While the writer is doubtful of the policy of departing from the old rule, the majority of the court are of the opinion that we are committed to the American doctrine, which, in their judgment, is founded upon correct reasoning, and better adapted to the proper administration of justice. The court is therefore of the opinion that the recital in a deed of the receipt of the consideration is not contractual in its character, and is only *prima facie* evidence of the payment of the purchase money, which may be rebutted by parol testimony. In accordance with this view we must conclude that parol evidence was competent in this case to show the real intent and purpose of Mr. Barbee in executing the several conveyances to his children, and especially should this be so when it seems that they do not pretend that any actual consideration was paid by them.

2. The remaining question to be considered is whether there was error in the exclusion of the testimony of Mrs. Ladd and others. The point is thus presented by his honor in the case prepared for this court: "The plaintiffs propose to show by Mrs. C. A. Ladd, one of the defendants, that in the division of certain lands between his children by Gray Barbee an agreement was made between them and Gray Barbee by which some were to pay others certain sums for equality of partition. This was objected to by defendants upon the ground that, H. Tyler Barbee being dead, and a party to the alleged agreement, the witness is incompetent under section 590 of the Code. Other parties to this action were also offered as witnesses by the plaintiffs for a similar purpose, to whose evidence similar objection was taken by the defendants." The court held "that the witness C. A. Ladd [and the other parties to this action] is incompetent to testify as to any transaction between herself and H. Tyler Barbee, now deceased, in which his estate is sought to be charged." We are of the opinion that the testimony, in so far as it affected the lands conveyed to H. Tyler Barbee, deceased, was incompetent under section 590 of the Code, and that there was no error in its exclusion. The witnesses were parties to the action, and, if there was such an agreement as contended for between them and their father, it was clearly to their interest that the deceased brother should be included therein, so as to charge his estate. We have very carefully examined the cases cited by the plaintiffs'

counsel, but can find nothing in them which conflicts with the ruling of his honor.

STATE v BRABHAM.

(*Supreme Court of North Carolina.* May 12, 1891.)

HOMICIDE—EVIDENCE—CIRCUMSTANCES—INSTRUCTIONS.

1. On an indictment for murder, where the evidence for the state is entirely circumstantial, evidence is admissible as to the unnatural behavior of defendant shortly after the homicide took place.

2. Where it is shown that deceased was killed with an iron coupling-pin, and a witness has testified that he saw a man who looked like defendant drop the pin near the place of the homicide, and shortly after its occurrence, evidence is admissible that such a pin was seen near defendant's house the day before the homicide, which shortly disappeared therefrom.

3. Where a witness, B., at the trial identified a coat as having been worn by defendant, another witness is competent to testify that B. identified the coat at the guard-house after defendant's arrest, though B. himself was not asked whether he did so.

4. A statement by the court that defendant had offered no evidence to contradict the testimony of the state's witnesses, which is true, is relieved of any possible prejudicial effect by the further statement that it is a question for the jury whether there is any contradiction between the state's witnesses.

Appeal from criminal court, Mecklenburg county; MEARES, Judge.

McCall & Bailey, for appellant. *The Attorney General*, for the State.

SHEPHERD, J. The first exception is addressed to the admission of testimony as to the manner of the prisoner shortly after the commission of the homicide. The testimony tended to show that the homicide was committed between 11 and 12 o'clock on Saturday night, the 11th of April, 1891; that about 12 o'clock of the same night the prisoner went to the room of the witnesses Wyche and Davis; that his actions there were unnatural; that he spoke hurriedly, and in a low tone, and that his hand trembled and he seemed nervous. Such testimony alone would raise but a slight conjecture of the prisoner's guilt, but, taken in connection with the other facts in evidence, was very clearly relevant. The evidence offered by the state was entirely circumstantial in its nature, and in such cases facts which are in themselves of but trifling significance may become of serious import, in view of their relation to other circumstances attending the transaction. "Everything calculated to elucidate the transaction is admissible, since the conclusion depends upon a number of links, which alone are weak, but, taken together, are strong and able to conclude." McCann v. State, 13 Smedes & M. 471. As bearing directly upon the particular point under consideration, we cite the case of Campbell v. State, 23 Ala. 69. See. also, Whart. Crim. Law, 3520.

The second exception is to the testimony of the witness Griffith, "that the [coupling] pin was found on the sidewalk near Pemberton's house, where the prisoner boarded." There was evidence tending to show that the mortal wound was inflicted with an iron coupling-pin, which was found on the floor near the deceased. The witness stated that this coupling-pin was like the one seen by him on Saturday morning lying in the grass 28 steps from the boarding-house of the prisoner, and that on Sunday he looked for it, and it had disappeared. One R. J. Johnson testified that on the night of the 11th of April he came by Mocca's store, and saw a colored man standing against the window with his hand behind him, and that he saw him drop a piece of iron about the length of the coupling-pin introduced in evidence, and that he took it up and wrapped it in a whitish colored cloth of some kind, and put it in his pocket. This witness also stated that he did not know that the prisoner was the man he saw, but that he had the same color and height, wore a brown overcoat, and "looked in appearance like the prisoner." It was also in evidence that a handkerchief, soiled apparently with rust, was found in the pocket of the prisoner's overcoat, and that the pocket of the overcoat was "torn or ripped." For the reasons given in passing upon the first exception, we think that the testimony was admissible, and should have been submitted to the jury. State v. Christmas, 101 N. C. 749, 8 S. E. Rep 361; State v. Bruce, 106 N. C. 792, 11 S. E. Rep. 475. In this connection, we will state that the sixth exception, as to the admissibility of the testimony of Johnson, is plainly untenable, and should also be overruled.

The third exception (the only one argued in the brief of the prisoner's counsel) is that the court "allowed [the] witness Baker to testify that Benny Mocca identified the coat at the police office [or guard-house] without Benny having been first asked as to the fact, i. e., whether he did so identify it." Benny Mocca, the son of the deceased, had been examined, and testified that the overcoat produced upon the trial was the same as that worn by the prisoner at the shop of his deceased father on the night of the homicide. This overcoat was identified by other witnesses as the one taken from the valise of the prisoner, and identified by Benny at the guard-house in the presence of the witness Baker and the prisoner. Whatever may be the ruling in other states upon the subject, it is well settled in North Carolina that such testimony as Baker's is admissible for the purpose of corroborating a witness who has been impeached, or stands in such a relationship to the parties or to the action as to subject his testimony to suspicion or discredit. Jones v. Jones, 80 N. C. 247; State v. Boon, 82 N. C. 648; State v. Whitfield, 92 N. C. 831. No point, however, is made as to whether the witness Benny Mocca had been impeached, but the exception is based entirely upon the failure of the state to ask him, when on the stand, whether he had, in effect, made such a statement as to the identity of the overcoat at the guard-house. Such preliminary questions are necessary where it is proposed to discredit a witness by proof of conflicting statements concerning collateral matter indicating bias, feeling, and the like, (State v. Morton, 107 N. C. 890, 12 S. E. Rep. 112, and cases cited;) and this is because the witness should have an opportunity of explaining such statements, (State v. Wright, 75 N. C. 439;) but this reason has no application where the purpose of the testimony is to sustain the witness, and we have been unable to find any authority in support of such a principle. Testimony of this character was admitted without preliminary inquiry in State v. Dove, 10 Ired. 469, and State v. Ward, 103 N. C. 419, 8 S. E. Rep. 814; and we do not understand that any practice to the contrary has generally obtained in this state. We cannot see how the testimony is open to the grave objections urged by counsel. Benny, on the trial, identified the coat then exhibited as that worn by the prisoner. This was substantive testimony. Baker simply testified that before the trial, and at the guard-house, the same witness had, in effect, made a similar statement about the same overcoat. This was only corroborative testimony, and admitted alone for that purpose, and we must assume, in the absence of any exception in this particular, (the entire charge as to the recapitulation of the evidence not being set forth,) that as such only it was submitted to the jury. State v. Powell, 106 N. C. 637, 11 S. E. Rep. 191.

The fourth exception is "because his honor refused to give the instructions as prayed for by the prisoner, and without giving the first, instructed the jury that it was not denied by the state." The latter part of this exception seems to be founded upon a misapprehension, as the court not only stated that the propositions of law contained in the first instruction were substantially correct, but actually gave them in almost the precise language as prayed for. Upon a careful scrutiny of the charge, we are of the opinion that it substantially responded to all of the instructions requested by the prisoner. In State v. Parker, Phil. (N. C.) 475, PEARSON, C. J., said that all that the law requires is that the jury shall be clearly instructed that, unless after due consideration of all of the evidence they are "fully satisfied" or "entirely convinced" or "satisfied beyond a reasonable doubt" of the guilt of the prisoner, it is their duty to acquit, and every attempt on the part of the court to lay down a "formula" for the instruction of the jury by which to "gauge" the degrees of conviction has resulted in no good. State v. Sears, Phil. (N. C.) 146; State v. Knox, Id. 312; State v. Gee, 92 N. C. 756. His honor told the jury that every material circumstance relied upon by the state must be established beyond a reasonable doubt, and "that material circumstances were those circumstances in the case which pointed to the guilt of the prisoner, and that the material circumstances relied on, and which were established beyond a reasonable doubt by the state, must be so strong as to exclude any reasonable hypothesis of the innocence of the prisoner." This, surely, was as favorable to the prisoner as the law permits, and we have no hesitation in overruling the exception.

The fifth exception is also without merit. It was true, as stated by the court, that the prisoner had offered no evidence to contradict the testimony of the state's witnesses. This was but the statement of a fact, and was relieved of any possible prejudicial effect by its immediate connection with the remarks that "whether there was any contradiction between any of the witnesses in the case is a question to be determined by the jury; the court cannot express any opinion upon the testimony." Neither was there error in stating that, in the absence of testimony to the contrary, every witness was presumed to be of good character. It will be observed that in this connection the jury were told that, although a witness was of good character, they were not bound to believe him if his statements were unwarranted, etc.

The seventh exception "to the charge as a whole" is too general to be considered. State v. Nipper, 95 N. C. 653, and McKinnon v. Morrison, 104 N. C. 354, 10 S. E. Rep. 513.

The eighth exception: While we doubt the propriety of the remark of the court as to what some writers had said about the reliability of circumstantial testimony, we are sure that the jury could not have understood that such was the opinion of his honor in respect to this case, or that they were to be influenced by it in the slightest degree. This very clearly appears from the immediately succeeding language, in which the jury were referred to a former part of the charge as to the degree of proof requisite to a conviction.

The ninth and tenth exceptions are not sustained by the record, which very plainly fails to disclose that his honor charged "that, where a witness' character is not assailed, he is to be believed." These exceptions are also overruled. After a careful examination of the whole record, we are of the opinion that the case was fairly tried, and that there is no reason why the verdict of the jury should be disturbed.

There is no error.

STATE v. AUSTIN et al.

(Supreme Court of North Carolina. May 12, 1891.)

FORNICATION—EVIDENCE—TRIAL.

1. On indictment for fornication and adultery it is competent for a witness to testify that he met the male defendant going in the night-time towards the house of the female defendant; that defendant told him that he was going to another place, to meet a certain person; that defendant did not go there, and afterwards denied having said that he was going.

2. Evidence is admissible of the statement defendant made to his wife in regard to his whereabouts on that night, as also of the question by the wife which called forth this statement.

3. It is not competent, on the issue of defendant's character, to ask a witness how it was rumored that a "hung jury" stood on a former trial of the indictment, the witness having testified that he did not know how they stood.

4. It is not error to refuse to instruct that the jury must acquit if they do not believe the witnesses who testified that they saw defendants in the act of sexual intercourse, where there is circumstantial evidence tending to show immoral intimacy.

5. Defendants cannot complain of the reception of the verdict by clerk during the judge's absence from the court-room, where they failed to object at the time to its being so received, though they had opportunity to do so.

Appeal from criminal court, Mecklenburg county: MEARES, Judge.

Burwell & Walker, Covington & Adams, and *J. J. Vann,* for appellants. *The Attorney General,* for the State.

CLARK, J. The defendants were indicted for fornication and adultery.

Exception 1. One Helms, a witness for the state, testified that he met the male defendant one night about 200 yards from the female defendant's house, going in the direction of her house, and defendant told him he was going to Coleman Stewart's, to meet Elliott, (an Alliance lecturer;) and when this matter was tried before the Alliance the defendant denied telling him so, and denied meeting him. To this defendant objected. There was evidence by many witnesses of the defendant Austin making nocturnal visits to the female defendant's house; of being seen in the room alone with her at night; of going into her room, the light being put out; and of leaving his horse hitched out at night, and going with his shoes off to her house; of walking up a stream to conceal his tracks; of being seen embracing her, and the like. The evidence, therefore, of his being seen near her house after dark, going in that direction, and his saying he was going to meet an Alliance lecturer, which statement he denied on the Alliance trial, when it was shown that he did not meet the Alliance lecturer on that night, and also his denial of meeting the witness, was competent, as a circumstance tending to corroborate the other evidence of his visits by night to his co-defendant. "Every circumstance calculated to throw light on the alleged crime and aid the jury in coming to a correct conclusion is competent." State v. Bishop, 98 N. C. 773, 4 S. E. Rep. 357, and cases there cited; State v. Christmas, 101 N. C. 749, 8 S. E. Rep. 361.

Exception 2. The same witness stated, the defendants objecting, that at the Alliance trial (they having been on trial before the local Alliance for expulsion for this offense) the defendant Austin's wife said that she could account for her husband except that night Helms said he had met him; that her husband got on his horse that night, and rode off, saying he was going to Coleman Stewart's, and the defendant Austin had thereupon replied that he did tell his wife so, but, after riding 100 yards, he turned and rode back, unseen by any one, and went into a room, which was not his bedroom, and which he was not in the habit of occupying, and slept till nearly daylight, when he rode off to Coleman Stewart's. This evidence was competent as being a statement made by the defendant as to his whereabouts and doings, there being evidence that he did not get to Coleman Stewart's till next morning. What his wife said was competent from having been made in his presence, and from being replied to by him, and as having drawn out his statement.

Exception 3. One Winchester, witness for the defense, testified that the character of the defendants was good. On cross-examination he was asked if he would say that the character of the defendants was good at the time, notwithstanding the Alliance trial and the "hung jury" at the trial held in the superior court of Union county, and the witness answered, "Yes!" On the redirect examination the defendants' counsel asked the witness if he knew of his own knowledge how the "hung jury" stood, or how they were divided, and he answered, "No." The defendants' counsel then proposed to ask the witness how the current report or the general rumor was as to how the "hung jury" was divided. On objection by the state the question was ruled out, and the defendants excepted. The law does not countenance or permit the endless ramification and the countless collateral issues which such a course of examination would introduce. It was held incompetent, on a question as to character, to prove a general report as to any particular act done by the party whose character was being testified to. State v. Bullard, 100 N. C. 486, 6 S. E. Rep. 191. It was therefore certainly incompetent to show in what degree certain 12 men were rumored to have differed in opinion as to a certain act alleged to have been done by the defendants. It was only competent to show the general reputation for character, not the general reputation as to any particular act, still less the reputation how certain men thought as to the truth of a certain alleged particular act. As a test of the witness it is competent to ask him to name persons whom he has heard say that the character of the person in question was good or bad. State v. Perkins, 66 N. C. 126. The rule extends no further. It was therefore incompetent for the state to ask the question as to the "hung jury." The defendant did not object to it. He should have done so, or have asked the court to strike it out. It was no correction of the error to extend the error still further by incompetent and irrelevant inquiries. The court at least gave the defendant the same amount of license when it permitted him to show, if he could, if the witness knew how the jury stood. It appeared that he did not, and the court properly refused to inquire as to the reputation of how the jury had stood. The witness was one out of some 60 examined in this case. He was testifying as to the good character of the defendant, and the investigation as to how far his opinion as to the general character of the defendants should be discredited by the effect which would probably be had on the public mind by the report as to how a former jury had divided in opinion as to an act of the defendant, (for that is the only legal bearing and relevancy of the testimony,) when he had stated he did not know how they stood, is too remote from the issue, which was whether the defendants, a married man and a widow, had lewdly and lasciviously bedded and cohabited together. In no part of a trial at nisi prius is the disposition "to run rabbits" more strongly developed than in the examination of character witnesses. The courts have always repressed it. Its indulgence beyond the well-recognized legal limits can serve no good purpose. It would serve (if not repressed) to open old scandals, confuse the jury with multiplicity of issues, and prolong to a needless and expensive length the trial of causes without any compensation in the better investigation of the truth as to the real issue before the court and jury. It is better *super stare antiquas vias.*

Exception 4. The defendants asked the court to charge that the only direct evidence of criminal intimacy between the defendants which had been testified in this case was that of Bob Marsh and John Brooks, and if the jury should not believe this evidence, or should entertain a reasonable doubt as to the truth thereof, it would be their duty to acquit. These two witnesses had testified to finding the defendants in actual sexual intercourse. There was testimony by other witnesses of the male defendant stealthily visiting the chamber of the female by night, and remaining some hours; of his going to and coming from her room by night with his shoes off; of being in a room alone with her, and then extinguishing the light, and his subsequently being discovered in the act of endeavoring to escape from the room unperceived; of their riding together in a buggy, after sundown; of his kissing her; and much other evidence tending to show an immoral intimacy. The instruction asked, therefore, was in effect that, unless the jury believed the testimony as to the defendants being seen in the very act, it was their duty to acquit. The instruction was properly refused. State v. Potest, 8 Ired. 23; State v. Eliason, 91 N. C. 564. Besides, the instruction, if given, would have been a clear violation of the statute forbidding the judge to express an opinion upon the weight of the testimony. Code, § 413; Jackson v. Commissioners, 76 N. C. 282. In telling the jury the value to be given the testimony with that of these two witnesses omitted the court would necessarily have given its opinion as to the weight of their testimony, and so, by varying the prayers for instructions with the names of different witnesses, the court, by a process of elimination, might be called on to express its opinion as to the value to be given to the testimony of each and every witness.

Exception 5. As soon as the jury had retired after receiving the charge the court instructed the clerk from the bench in a clear and distinct voice to receive the verdict, and to have the defendants present. The defendants' counsel had then left the court-room, and defendants had no knowledge of and did not consent to the order. On the return of the jury the clerk received the verdict, both defendants being present. The defendants afterwards moved for a new trial and in arrest of judgment, on the ground that the verdict was received in the absence of the judge and of defendants' counsel, and in the recess of the court. The case also states that while the jury were considering their verdict the judge remarked, in the presence of one of defendants' counsel, that he had instructed the clerk to receive the verdict, and the counsel made no response; that, as the jury came into the court-house, the clerk told another of defendants' counsel that he was going in to take the verdict; that he asked if the judge was present, and the clerk replied that he was not, and had instructed him (the clerk) to receive the verdict; that the counsel then did not go into the court-room, but went to the solicitor, and told him of the conversation; that, in reply to the solicitor's inquiry if he would consent to the clerk's receiving the verdict, he replied that he would not, but before the solicitor could reach the court-room the verdict had been rendered. The defendants had the right to have the verdict rendered in the presence of the judge, and it is best that it should always be done. But it is certainly competent, except in capital cases, for it to be received by the clerk if no objection is made, and opportunity is given the defendant to object; "and such practice is very common." PEARSON, C. J., in Houston v. Potts, 65 N. C. 41. Indeed, in all cases not capital, the defendant may even waive his own right to be present, either expressly (State v. Epps, 76 N. C. 55) or by voluntarily withdrawing himself from the jurisdiction of the court, (State v. Kelly, 97 N. C. 404, 2 S. E. Rep. 185; State v. Jacobs, 107 N. C. 772, 11 S. E. Rep. 962,) though his counsel cannot waive it for him, (State v. Jenkins, 84 N. C. 812.) In the present instance the defendants were both present in the court-room when the verdict was rendered, and made no objection to the absence of the judge or of their counsel. Had they done so, doubtless the judge and counsel would have been sent for; or, if that had been refused, the defendants could have then presented the matter as ground for new trial to the court below, and, if refused, have appealed. It is true the case states that the defendants did not expressly consent to the verdict being received in the judge's absence, but they permitted it to be received in his absence without objection. They were presumably in the court-room when, on the retirement of the jury, the judge instructed the clerk to receive the verdict, and made no objection; and the judge told one of the counsel personally of such instruction, and received no indication of objection. The clerk, before receiving the verdict, told the other counsel that he was then on his way to do so, and received no objection, though an objection then from the counsel or from the defendants would have doubtless caused the judge to be sent for. It is true counsel afterwards told the solicitor he did not consent, but too late to stop the rendition of the verdict. If he wished the judge to be sent for, why did he not make that statement to the clerk? It is not suggested that the defendants were prejudiced in any way by the judge's absence. If there was any evidence indicating that they had been, we are sure their able and astute counsel would have pointed it out, and the just judge who tried the cause would have promptly set the verdict aside. The motion seems rather based upon a dislike to the tenor of the verdict itself and a desire to be relieved from it than upon any grievance sustained by the manner of its rendition The presence of counsel at the rendition of the verdict has never been held essential to its validity. State v. Jones, 91 N. C. 654. Besides, counsel had notice that the clerk was about to receive the verdict, and did not go in the court-room, nor did he object to the absence of the judge, as he might then have done had he chosen to do so. No error.

THOMAS v. HUNSUCKER.

(*Supreme Court of North Carolina.* May 19, 1891.)

EJECTMENT—DEFENSES—TITLE IN THIRD PERSONS —SHERIFF'S DEED.

1. In ejectment, since the plaintiff must recover on the strength of his own title, defendant may show that the title to the land passed from plaintiff by a sheriff's deed to a third person, without connecting himself with the title of such person.

2. A judgment rendered by a court of competent jurisdiction, and a sale under execution thereon, are not void on the ground that when the judgment was rendered and sale made defendant was insane; and cannot be collaterally attacked in ejectment by defendant, where the sheriff's deed is introduced to show that plaintiff in ejectment has no title.

Appeal from superior court, Clay county; E. T. BOYKIN, Judge.

J. W. Cooper and *T. F. Davidson,* for appellant. *Batchelor & Devereux* and *E. C. Smith,* for appellee.

SHEPHERD, J. We think there was error in refusing to give the fourth instruction, on the ground that the defendant could not show title out of the plaintiff without connecting himself with such outstanding title. This is a correct principle of law, but is applicable only where the defendant seeks to attack a title under which both himself and the plaintiff claim. Love v. Gates, 3 Dev. & B. 363; Gilliam v. Bird, 8 Ired. 280; Christenbury v. King, 85 N. C. 230; Ryan v. Martin, 91 N. C. 464. It is true that in our case both parties claim under Killian, but the defendant, under the instruction asked, does not propose to impeach Killian's title, but contends that, although the plaintiff may have derived title from him, it has been divested by sale under execution, and therefore he is not entitled to recover. In ejectment the plaintiff must recover upon the strength of his own title, and it is always competent for the defendant to show title out of him where this can be done without encountering the rule of practice commonly called estoppel. Clegg v. Fields, 7 Jones, (N. C.) 37. Even had the defendant entered as the tenant of the plaintiff, he could have shown that the title of the latter had been divested by a sale under execution, and thus have resisted a recovery. Lancashire v. Mason, 75 N. C. 455. *A fortiori,* can this be done where no such relation exists. It is urged, however, that the error is harmless, because there appears to have been no testimony identifying the land in question with that described in the sheriff's deed. The case states that the defendant offered no such testimony, but as it does not purport to set out the evidence in full, and as the ruling of his honor seems to assume the existence of such testimony, (possibly disclosed by the plaintiff's witnesses,) we do not feel warranted in saying that the error was not prejudicial to the defendant; and especially is this so when the point does not seem to have been made upon the trial below. It is further contended that the sheriff's deed is void because of the insanity of the plaintiff when the judgment was rendered, and at the time of the sale under execution. The authorities seem to be in entire accord in holding that such a judgment is voidable only. 1 Black, Judgm. § 205; Freem. Judgm. 142: Freem. Ex'ns, § 22. See, also, Wood v. Watson, 107 N. C. 52, 12 S. E. Rep. 49. It is also well settled that "whatever irregularity there may be in a judgment, if it be an act of a court of competent jurisdiction, unreversed, and in force when a sale is made by execution under it, the purchaser at such sale is safe, even though the judgment be subsequently reversed or set aside. The same principle applies to an error in the execution, the regularity of which cannot be questioned in an action against a purchaser at a sheriff's sale." See cases in Rattle, Dig. 559, and 6 Seymour, Dig. 264, and 7 Seymour, Dig. 279. It is true that, where the plaintiff in the judgment is the purchaser, the sale may be set aside on the ground of irregularity, but, unless this is done, the title passes, and cannot be attacked collaterally. Benners v. Rhinehart, 107 N. C. 705, 12 S. E. Rep. 456. For these reasons we think that there should be a new trial.

BURGWYN v. HALL et al.

(*Supreme Court of North Carolina.* May 19, 1891.)

ACTION EX DELICTO — DISCHARGE FROM ARREST UNDER INSOLVENT DEBTOR'S ACT.

Code N. C. §§ 2942-2981, entitled "Insolvent Debtors," provides that every insolvent debtor may, in a manner prescribed, assign his estate for the benefit of creditors, and be thereafter exempt from arrest or imprisonment for previously contracted debts, and prescribes (section 2952) that "every person taken or charged on any order of arrest for default of bail, or on surrender of bail in any action," and "every person taken or charged in execution of arrest for any debt or damages rendered in any action whatever," shall be entitled to the benefit of the law. *Held* that, though the statute in terms refers only to "debtors and creditors," a non-resident under arrest in an action for a tort is entitled, before judgment, to his discharge on surrendering his property in the manner prescribed. DAVIS and AVERY, JJ., dissenting.

Appeal from an order made by WHITAKER, J., in an action pending in Vance superior court. The plaintiff brought his action against the defendants, who are non-residents of this state, to recover damages for an alleged injury to his person done and procured to be done by them. In the course of the action he obtained an order for their arrest, and they were duly arrested, and, failing to give bail as allowed by law, they are held in the common jail of the county of Vance, in which county the action was brought. The defendants filed their petition, therein alleging the material facts in the superior court of said county, in which the action mentioned is pending, praying that they may be allowed the benefit of the statute (Code, c. 27) entitled "Insolvent Debtors." The plaintiff opposes the application of the defendants; denies that they are insolvent; and insists that, inasmuch as it appears that they are non-residents of this state, and the cause of action on account whereof they are arrested and held is a tort, they are not entitled to the benefits of the statute they invoke. The court gave judgment denying the application of the defendants to be discharged from custody, and they appealed to this court.

T. T. Hicks and Pittman & Shaw, for appellants. W. H. Cheek, A. C. Zollicoffer and W. R. Henry, for appellee.

MERRIMON, C. J., (*after stating the facts as above.*) The constitution (article 1, § 16) provides that "there shall be no imprisonment for debt in this state except in cases of fraud." The legislature, observing this provision, has provided by statute (Code, § 291) that in civil actions founded upon particular causes of action specified the defendant may, under an order of arrest duly obtained, be arrested and held in custody, unless he shall, as he may do in the way prescribed, give bail "by causing a written undertaking, payable to the plaintiff, to be executed by sufficient surety, to the effect that the defendant shall at all times render himself amenable to the process of the court during the pendency of the action, and to such as may be issued to enforce the judgment therein;" and he may likewise be arrested in execution upon a judgment in the cases specified, as prescribed by the statute, (Id. §§ 442, 447, 448, par. 3;) otherwise parties in civil actions cannot be arrested unless for contempt. But another statute, entitled "Insolvent Debtors," (Id. §§ 2942-2981,) provides generally that every insolvent debtor may in the way prescribed "assign"—surrender—his estate for the benefit of all his creditors, and that his person may thereafter be exempt from arrest or imprisonment on account of any judgment previously rendered, or of any debts previously contracted. It would seem that this statute is unnecessary as to honest debtors, because the constitutional provision above recited relieves such debtors from imprisonment. Such surrender of his property by an insolvent debtor for the benefit of his creditors, as to debts and judgments existing before such surrender, would relieve him from possible future annoyance and arrest on account of such debts, although property he might thereafter acquire might be liable to levy and sale to pay the same in proper cases. But the benefits of this chapter are not confined to simply insolvent debtors, so designated. Such benefits are extended to other classes of persons held in arrest in civil actions. The statute cited (Id. § 2951) prescribes that "the following persons are entitled to the benefits of this chapter: (1) Every person taken or charged on any order of arrest for default of bail, or on surrender of bail in any action; (2) every person taken or charged in execution of arrest for any debt or damages rendered in any action whatever." It is to be observed that this provision enlarges the general purpose of the statute by extending the same to the classes of persons specified: *First*, to "every person taken or charged [not yet arrested] on any order of arrest for default of bail;" *secondly*, to every person whose bail has surrendered him as allowed by the statute; *thirdly*, to "every person taken or charged [but not yet taken] in execution of arrest for any debt or damages rendered in any action whatever,"—as allowed by the statute. Id. §§ 442, 447, 448, par. 3. The terms "all of them" thus extending the purpose of the statute, are as broad and sweeping as they well can be. They do not, in any view of them, as to the purpose intended, imply limitation or discrimination. They plainly embrace "every person" taken or charged to be arrested by virtue of "any order of arrest," not specially for a tort, or for fraud, or other particular cause of action as to which a person may be arrested, but for any cause of action, no matter what may be its nature, if the person is arrested in a case wherein he may lawfully be so. They in plain, strong terms embrace any such arrest made or ordered to be made in any action whatever; that is, any action in which a person—a party—may be so arrested. There is a total absence of words or phraseology of limitation or discrimination in the section of the statute just recited, or in the statute, or elsewhere, that confines its benefits to persons so arrested or to be arrested as fraudulent debtors. Nor is there anything in the nature or purpose of the statute that reasonably, much less necessarily, implies such limitation. Its general purpose is to relieve honest insolvent debtors from arrest on account of debts and judgments against them existing at and before the time they make a surrender of their property as prescribed. The purpose of the particular section of the statute under consideration is to relieve a party to an action arrested or presently subject to arrest, or "in execution of arrest for any debt or damages rendered in any action whatever," upon a surrender of his property in the way prescribed. In such case the party arrested and so seeking relief must notify the creditors or plaintiff at whose suit he is arrested, but he may or may not notify other creditors of his application to surrender his property and be discharged from arrest, and only such creditors as may be so notified will be affected by his discharge. Id. § 2955. The principal relief sought in such case by the party arrested is to be discharged from arrest in the action brought by the creditor at whose instance he was arrested; and he is entitled to such discharge upon the honest surrender of his property in the way prescribed, whether the cause of action on account of which he was arrested was a fraudulent debt or a tort or of other nature as to which he might be arrested. The statute (Id. § 2952) so expressly provides. It in broadest terms embraces "every person taken or charged as in the preceding section [that above recited] specified."

It is insisted, however, that the several sections of the statute pertinent to that (section 2951) above recited mention and refer in terms only to debtors and creditors, and do not in like express terms mention or refer to persons arrested or to be arrested for causes of action other than a fraudulent debt, and therefore persons arrested or to be arrested for such other causes of action are not entitled to the benefits of this statute. The terms "debtor and creditor" are employed generally in varying connections throughout the statute to designate the classes of persons to be affected by it, and such terms are not modified so as to make them pertinently and expressly applicable to persons

arrested seeking benefit of the statute. It seems that the legislature, in enlarging and extending the purpose of the statute so as to embrace all persons arrested and, to be arrested in civil actions, probably by inadvertence failed to use the most appropriate terms to effectuate and harmonize the details of its purpose; but such failure, and the use of the not very precise words "debtor and creditor," in matters of detail, cannot be allowed to modify and abridge by mere implication the meaning and application of the plain, strong, and comprehensive words and phraseology employed in the section extending the benefit of the statute to all persons so arrested. As we have said, such purpose appears clearly by explicit and the most comprehensive terms; and, moreover, it appears from the nature of the matter. Why should a person guilty of fraud in contracting a debt on which an action is founded, when he shall be arrested on that account, as he may be, have the benefit of the statute under consideration, and another person arrested in an action brought to recover damages for an injury to person or character, or for injuring or for wrongfully taking, detaining, or converting property, not have the like benefit? Can any just or even plausible reason be suggested for such distinction? Clearly the legislature had no intention to exclude any person arrested in a civil action for any of the causes specified in the statute (Code, § 291) from such benefit. None appears from its terms or by reasonable inference or implication. The terms "debtor and creditor," employed generally and without precision in the statute as to persons arrested in civil actions, must be taken as meaning and applying to the plaintiff and defendant in the action in which the defendant shall be so arrested. They imply the plaintiff's claiming and suing for damages for which the defendant is liable to him. Such interpretation is allowable and reasonable with a view to effectuate the intention of the statute as to persons so arrested. When and as soon as the plaintiff obtains judgment for damages in such case he at once becomes a judgment creditor of the defendant, and then he comes within the words of the section of the statute recited above. The second clause thereof expressly embraces "every person taken or charged in execution of arrest for any debt or damages rendered in any action whatever." Thus persons "in execution of arrest" for fraudulent debts (they could not be arrested for or on account of honest debts) and for "damages rendered in any action whatever" are expressly put on the same footing. It is further said that the plaintiff in an action for injury to the person, before trial, has no debt, and may never obtain judgment; and it is asked to what end shall the defendant arrested in such action surrender his property, as contemplated by the statute, and be discharged; and how shall his property so surrendered, or the proceeds of the sale thereof by the trustee, be distributed as between the plaintiff (who has no debt or judgment) and other creditors of the defendant? It is hence insisted that the defendant is not entitled to the benefit of the statute. In such case the statute contemplates that the defendant may surrender his property and be discharged, and thus he may have benefit of the principal object to be attained. His property so surrendered will pass to a trustee, to be appointed as prescribed by the statute, (Code, §§ 2957, 2977–2981,) to be applied for the benefit of his creditors, including the plaintiff in the action, when he shall obtain judgment. The distribution of the assets of the defendant may, if need be, be stayed until the plaintiff's action shall be tried. If he shall obtain judgment he will share in the distribution of the assets; if he shall not, then the assets will be distributed to the defendant's creditors; and, if there be any surplus, the same will be returned to him. The statute so intends. The difficulty and objection suggested are no greater or otherwise substantially than they would have been if the cause of action sued upon had been a fraudulent debt contracted by the defendant. Indeed, in any case or proceeding involving a distribution of the assets of an insolvent debtor the distribution might be stayed until a disputed claim could be litigated and determined. Besides, provisions of a statute affecting its details, not altogether practicable, but not essential to its effectiveness, and the absence of like provisions, will not be allowed to defeat or abridge its purpose clearly appearing. It is the duty of the court to give it full effect if this be at all practicable, and to that end to interpret its terms and phraseology in the light of and with a view to its purpose. We think it clear that the provisions of the statute under consideration extend to and embrace every person arrested or to be arrested in a civil action on account of any cause of action specified in the statute. Id. § 291. If the contention of the plaintiff should be allowed to prevail, no person arrested before judgment in the action could have benefit of the statute, unless he should be arrested on account of a fraudulent debt. If the purpose had been to so limit its application it would have so declared. It certainly would not have employed such explicit and comprehensive terms to express its narrow and exclusive meaning.

Nor are the benefits of the statute confined to residents of this state. There is no provision in it or any other statute within our knowledge that in terms or by reasonable implication declares that a non-resident shall not be discharged from arrest in a civil action if he makes the complete surrender of his estate as prescribed. The defendants, being non-residents, are not entitled to homestead and personal property exemptions. Such exemptions are allowed only in favor of those having residence in this state. Baker v. Legget, 98 N. C. 304, 4 S. E. Rep. 37; Finley v. Saunders, 99 N. C. 462, 4 S. E. Rep. 516. Nor are they entitled to such exemptions here under any statute of the state of Georgia, they being citizens of that state. Such statute could not secure to them in this state exemptions of property against the rights of creditors here. In some respects the courts of this state, upon principles of comity, will administer the laws of another state in the distribution of the proper-

ty of deceased persons who were citizens of the latter state, but they will do so subject to the rights of citizens of this state. Medley v. Dunlap, 90 N. C. 527; Simpson v. Cureton, 97 N. C. 112, 2 S. E. Rep. 668. The defendants are entitled to be discharged from arrest when they make surrender of their property, as specified in their respective accounts of the same. To the end the same may be received and disposed of according to law the court should appoint a trustee for that purpose, as prescribed by the statute. Code, §§ 2957, 2977–2980. No harm can come from the construction we have given the statute, because it is always in the power of the plaintiff to suggest fraud, and have an issue submitted and defendant held (in default of bail) till it is found that a full disclosure has been made. There is error. The defendants are entitled to make surrender of their property and be discharged from arrest according to law. To that end let this opinion be certified to the superior court. It is so ordered.

DAVIS, J., (dissenting.) I cannot concur in the opinion that the defendants are entitled before judgment rendered to the benefit of chapter 27 of the Code. It is manifest, and I suppose will be conceded, that the relation of creditor and debtor cannot exist, if ever, till "after judgment," when, if the plaintiff shall recover damages, he will become "a judgment creditor," and the defendants will become "judgment debtors." I think chapter 27 of the Code can only apply when the relation of creditor and debtor exists by reason of a contract, express or implied, or when the relation is established by a "judgment rendered" for the recovery of unliquidated damages, or in an action *ex delicto*. I think this plainly appears from the title of the original act (Acts 1868–69, c. 162) and the context of the act. This court can only construe and declare the law. It cannot make law, and, if section 2951 of the Code is to receive the broad construction given to it without reference to the context or subject-matter of the chapter, then it must apply to any action whatever, and the person under arrest, whether debtor, tort-feasor, or criminal, is entitled to discharge, for there is nothing but the context and subject-matter that restricts the section to civil actions, and these plainly restrict it to insolvents against whom there is a "previously" rendered "judgment" or a "previously contracted debt." No one would insist that a person under arrest in a criminal action would be entitled to the benefit of the act, and yet it seems to me this would be no more in conflict with the chapter relating to crimes than with the chapter on arrest and bail. I think it is inconsistent with either. When any unadjudicated claim, whether *ex contractu* or *ex delicto*, becomes a debt by the ascertainment and judgment of court, the relation of creditor and debtor is established, and the debtor is entitled to the benefit of the act. Section 2952 provides only for the discharge upon compliance with chapter 27 of the Code; and without enumerating the provisions to be complied with, there is not one of them that is not predicated upon a previously contracted debt or a previously rendered judgment. If these defendants had been arrested at the suit of some creditor, (the plaintiff cannot be a creditor until and unless he becomes such by judgment yet to be rendered,) there can nowhere be found in the statute a provision by which they can notify the plaintiff in this action, or any one else against whom they may have committed a tort, and obtain their discharge as against the claim for damages which the person wronged may have till after judgment rendered. It is well settled that the constitutional provision prohibiting imprisonment for debt except for fraud has no application to actions for torts. Long v. McLean, 88 N. C. 3, and cases cited; Kinney v. Laughenour, 97 N. C. 326, 2 S. E. Rep. 43, and cases cited. If a person arrested upon a charge of fraud is not entitled to discharge before trial, why should one arrested for tort be so entitled? Before an order of arrest can be made the plaintiff is required to give bond, with security, for the protection of the defendant, and upon which he may have redress if it shall be found by the judgment that the plaintiff is not entitled to recover. Would the condition of this bond be canceled by the discharge of the defendant before judgment? I think not; and, if the defendant is held to bail for a tort, I think he can only be discharged before judgment by complying with section 298 of the Code, as a criminal punished by fine and costs can only be discharged after judgment for fine and costs.

Section 2951 is the only section relied on for the discharge of the defendants. That section declares what "persons shall be entitled to the benefit of this chapter." The first section of the chapter (section 2942 of the Code) provides that the insolvent may file his petition, etc., praying that his estate may be assigned for the benefit of all his creditors, and "that his person may thereafter be exempt from arrest or imprisonment on account of any judgment previously rendered, or of any debt previously contracted." Section 2950 provides that the person of the insolvent by the order of discharge "shall forever thereafter be exempted from arrest or imprisonment on account of any judgment or debt due at the time of such order, or contracted for before that time, though payable afterwards." Except the provision in section 2967, in favor of the putative father of a bastard, or person committed for fine and costs in criminal actions, I am unable, after a careful examination of the statute which we are called upon to construe, to find a section or sentence that will extend its "benefit" to any insolvent person on account of any judgment not yet rendered, or any debt not yet contracted. There is as yet no judgment rendered or debt existing against the defendants, and (give to section 2951 the broadest possible construction, and the "benefit" prescribed in sections 2942 and 2950 does not extend to them) I, think, unless we mean to extend the "benefit" of a statute which by its clear and unmistakable language limits it to judgments previously rendered or debts previously contracted to judgments for damages hereafter to be rendered, the defendants do not come within v. 13 s. e. no. 7—15

its "benefit." If the language of the statute limits the "benefit" I do not think we can extend it by construction so as to include the defendants, unless persons against whom damages are claimed and sought to be recovered for alleged torts, however grievous they may be, are to find, before judgment, and by the action of the debtor, a benefit that can nowhere be found in favor of an insolvent debtor. The defendants have been lawfully arrested, before judgment, in an action ex delicto, for a tort, and the action is still pending, which distinguishes it from Houston v. Walsh, 79 N. C. 35, which I think by the clearest implication sustains the view presented by me. Being lawfully in arrest for a tort, they cannot be discharged, except as allowed in the chapter on arrest and bail, or until it is determined by judgment whether there are damages or not, when, of course, they will be discharged if there are none, or, if there shall be judgment making them judgment debtors, when they will be entitled to the benefits of chapter 27 of the Code. In the present case the insolvent may have no assets to distribute, but, if there were, I know of no provision by which they could be distributed, except among creditors existing at the time of the ,application for discharge; but cases may arise in which our decision may be of vast interest to persons who may be greatly damaged by tort-feasors, and, having a decided conviction as to the construction to be placed upon the statute, I have felt it my duty to enter my dissent to that placed upon it by the court.

AVERY, J. I concur in the opinion of my Brother DAVIS.

STATE v. NEIS.

(*Supreme Court of North Carolina.* May 21, 1891.)

INTOXICATING LIQUORS—SALE WITHOUT LICENSE—CO-OPERATIVE CLUB.

On indictment for retailing spirituous liquors without a license it appeared that defendant, the steward of a club, was given a jug of liquor by the individual members thereof, who owned the liquor in common, and that he gave one of such members a drink from the jug, taking 10 cents in exchange. The amount received was just about the value of the liquor furnished, and with other money so received was used in replenishing the jug. *Held*, that there was a sale. Following State v. Lockyear, 95 N. C. 633.[1]

Indictment for retailing spirituous liquors without license, tried before MOORE, J., at January term, 1891, of Buncombe criminal court. The jury returned a special verdict, the nineteenth paragraph of which is as follows: "That on April 28, 1890, the defendant, at the club house of the Cosmopolitan Club, in the city of Asheville, furnished and dealt out to the said W. E. Williamson a small quantity, to-wit, a drink, of spirituous liquor, so held by the defendant as aforesaid, the said drink being a quantity less than a quart, and being taken by said defendant from a demijohn in which some other members as aforesaid had an equal quantity of liquor with said Williamson; and at the same time and place received from said

[1] See note at end of case.

Williamson the sum of ten cents, in the legal currency of the United States, which sum was about the value of the quantity of said spirituous liquor so furnished as aforesaid; and that said defendant thereupon handed the said sum of money to the said E. J. Holmes, who afterwards expended it for the purchase of other spirituous liquors for the said Williamson, and turned the same over to the custody of the defendant for the replenishment of the stock of liquor of said Williamson." The other facts sufficiently appear in the opinion. Upon the special verdict the court held that the defendant was not guilty, and ordered his discharge. Appeal by the state.

J. B. Batchelor, for the State. *F. H. Busbee,* for appellee.

CLARK, J., *(after stating the facts as above.)* The transaction presented by the special verdict, stripped of surplusage, is this: The defendant was steward of the Cosmopolitan Club of Asheville, and was indicted for selling spirituous liquor to its members. In consequence of the decision in the analogous case of State v. Lockyear, 95 N. C. 633, (the state of facts being the same,) he pleaded guilty. The club thereupon distributed a part of the liquors on hand to certain of its members, who placed them in the hands of the defendant to be held by him not for the club, as a club, but for those individual members of the club as tenants in common, the shares of each not being kept separate, but mingled in the same casks, jars, and demijohns. From time to time, as each of those members wished, he obtained drinks from the defendant for himself and friends, paying therefor, (in money, or giving tickets afterwards redeemed in money,) as near as may be, the cost price of the drinks so furnished, and with the money the defendant from time to time replenished the stock of liquors. We can see in this transaction no substantial distinction from the facts of Lockyear's Case. There the steward of the club, as a club, received the money for drinks furnished at cost, and with the money replenished the stock of liquors. Here the individuals of the club, treating themselves as unorganized, furnished through defendant to themselves, from a common stock, the drinks at cost, and with the money received therefor replenished the common stock. When in the present case an individual received drinks for himself and friends, he clearly did not receive the identical liquor which belonged to himself, but he received liquor which belonged mostly to others, and in which he had a minute undivided interest. For his money he received in exchange liquor which belonged to several others, as well as to himself, and converted it to his sole and separate use. Before the transaction the money was solely his, and the liquor belonged to several. By virtue of the transaction, and in exchange for the money, the liquor became his sole and separate property. This is surely a sale. It has every element of a sale. It cannot affect the transaction that subsequently the defendant would purchase

the same amount of liquor in value for the party paying the money, and mingle it in the common stock. This last act is that of a member of an association keeping up his quota of contribution to the common stock; the other is the purchase by a member of an association from its common agent, and the character and purport of the act are not changed by the subsequent contribution. It could make no difference that here the defendant was the agent of the individual members of the club, acting as an unorganized body, and that in Lockyear's Case the salesman was agent of individuals acting as an organized club. If an agent is appointed by several tenants in common to dispose of real or personal property, and he does dispose of any part thereof in exchange for money, it is none the less a sale because the party paying the money and receiving such part to his own use happens to be one of the tenants in common. And it would still be a sale although afterwards the money so received should be invested in the purchase of similar property held by the same tenant in common. The dealing here is simply what is known as "co-operation," which is an arrangement by which a member of an association procures supplies from the association at cost. The object and the effect of co-operation are not to abolish purchases, for the member still buys from the association, but to procure supplies at cost. This transaction is necessarily either a partition in severalty to the tenant in common or a purchase. It is clearly not a partition to each tenant in common in severalty of his undivided portion in the common stock, and it is plain that such is not the purpose and intent of the parties, for money is received in exchange, and it is to be used to obtain more liquor. Besides, the person obtaining the liquor not only does not obtain the identical liquor belonging to him, but he could very rarely, if ever, obtain his exact aliquot part, unless the stock became very low. The fact specially found that the membership of the club is "composed of gentlemen of the highest social standing" does not throw any light upon the transaction, except that it may be reasonably supposed that they have no desire to evade the law, and by this proceeding wish merely to procure a construction as to the legal nature of this transaction. No set of men have any special privileges under our constitution, and the parties interested must pay a license tax if other citizens pay it, and be prohibited altogether when others are prohibited. Nor can it make any difference that no profit was intended to be realized, but that as near as possible the drinks are to be furnished at cost. Profit is not a necessary ingredient of a sale. Indeed, many sales are made at a loss. Besides, if the defendant's contention was sound, "co-operative bar-rooms" would spring up on all sides, and the revenue act as to the sale of liquor, or the prohibition laws, where they prevail, would be a nullity. If the gentlemen composing the Cosmopolitan Club of Asheville can be exempted from the license tax by the simple device of treating themselves as unorganized tenants in common of a stock of spirituous liquors, and employing an agent to furnish drinks to any of their club and their friends, by selling at cost, the same can be done by any 500 or 5,000 patrons of a bar-room. The "dealer" would simply become an "agent," and, in lieu of profits, would receive as compensation for his services a commission on purchases or some amount out of receipts, and the money received for drinks would be invested as usual, and, as in the present case, to buy more liquor for the customer and his friends. Such an arrangement may be ingenious, but none the less a license tax is requisite to make it legal to furnish drinks in that mode. The case of State v. Lockyear has been often cited with approval in the courts of other states. State v. Social Club, (Md.) 20 Atl. Rep. 783, (November, 1890,) and other cases. These authorities, together with those cited in Lockyear's Case itself, render further citations unnecessary. Upon the facts found in the special verdict the defendant should be adjudged guilty. The case must be remanded, with directions that the judgment be so entered, and that sentence may be imposed in conformity with law. Error.

NOTE.

INTOXICATING LIQUORS—SALES BY CLUBS—WHEN UNLAWFUL. This decision is in line with the main current of recent American cases. In State v. Essex Club, 20 Atl. Rep. 769, decided by the supreme court of New Jersey, it appeared that the club was, in good faith, incorporated for "social, intellectual, and recreative purposes," and not for the purpose of evading the statutes regulating the liquor traffic. The club purchased liquors, which were kept by the butler with the other supplies. There was no wine or liquor room set apart for drinking. Liquors were procured by giving an order to a servant, who served them, and either received pay therefor at the time, or took a memorandum or check for the amount, which was incorporated in the member's account, and paid at the end of the month. None but members could thus procure liquors. No profit was intended to be made by the club. The court nevertheless held that this was a "sale," within the terms of an ordinance forbidding the sale of liquors without a license. In that case the main authority relied on by the defense was Graff v. Evans, 8 Q. B. Div. 873, in which an opposite conclusion was reached; and VAN SYCKEL, J., commenting thereon, says: "The court likens it to a purchase by a number of persons of a cask of wine to be divided between them in proportion to the sum paid by each, but it is manifestly not a parallel case. The club purchases the entire cask, and disposes of it in small quantities from time to time, to such members as may desire to be served with it. The corporation is a person, and it is the case of an individual owner of a cask of wine selling to such individuals of a selected class as may desire to have it at a stipulated price. Every quality of a sale is present in such a transaction. The liquor is not the property of the member before it is separated from the common mass, and delivered to him under his promise to pay for it, but the property of the company. * * * If he should clandestinely enter the club-house at night, and regale himself with the liquors of the club, it would prove a very shallow defense to an indictment for larceny if he set up that he was co-owner of the property. As well might a bank cashier, who was likewise a shareholder in the bank, set up a like plea to a charge of embezzlement." In State v. Easton, etc., Club, (Md.) 20 Atl. Rep. 783, the facts were practically the same, and a like conclusion was

reached. See, also, State v. Horacek, (Kan.) 21 Pac. Rep. 204, where the club sold chips to its members, each chip representing a glass of beer, which was delivered in exchange therefor. In People v. Andrews, 22 N. E. Rep. 358, the New York court of appeals (reversing the decision of the supreme court, 3 N. Y. Supp. 508) reached a similar conclusion, where the club was unincorporated, and the steward furnished drinks to a stranger, on the request of a member, who paid for them. Since this decision the supreme court has held that where the steward of an incorporated club furnished liquors to a member, and punched a ticket previously bought by him, there was a sale. People v. Bradley, 11 N. Y. Supp. 594. See, also, People v. Sinell, 12 N. Y. Supp. 40. So, in Kansas, where a club owned liquors, which by its rules were permitted to be sold only to members, a member who procured a sale to be made to a stranger was held guilty of selling in violation of the prohibitory law. State v. Nickerson, 2 Pac. Rep. 654.

A club organized under the Iowa statute, in regard to "corporations other than those for profit," is a "person," within the meaning of the statute providing a penalty for selling beer to a drunkard; and is liable for the penalty when, at a ball given by the club, a committee, composed of an officer and certain members, sells beer to those present, and the corporation receives the proceeds. Stewart v. Waterloo Turn Verein, (Iowa,) 33 N. W. Rep. 975. The Massachusetts statute of 1887, providing that "all buildings or places used by clubs for the purpose of selling, distributing, and dispensing intoxicating liquors to their members shall be deemed common nuisances," applies to a place used by an incorporated club, and where liquors bought for and owned by the individual members are dispensed to them. See, to the same effect, Com. v. Jacobs, (Mass.) 25 N. E. Rep. 463, and Com. v. Ryan, (Mass.) Id. 465.

GILCHRIST v. MIDDLETON.

(Supreme Court of North Carolina. May 12, 1891.)

PUBLIC LANDS—GRANTS FROM STATE—PRIORITY—VALIDITY—EJECTMENT.

1. In ejectment, where plaintiff claims by adverse possession under color of title, and two grants from the state are exhibited, title will be deemed to have passed by that first issued, in the absence of any direct proceeding declaring it fraudulent, as against the younger.

2. The rights of a senior grantee, without notice of a prior entry and payment, cannot be affected by subsequent legislation.

Confirming 12 S. E. Rep. 85.

On rehearing.

Burwell & Walker, for appellant. *Frank McNeill, John D. Shaw,* and *Geo. V. Strong,* for appellee.

AVERY, J. This was a petition to rehear the case argued at the February term, 1890, (107 N. C. 663, 12 S. E. Rep. 85.) The application to rehear was allowed only as to the holding of the court that the grant to McFarland, in 1847, under an entry made in 1801, was void upon its face, and as to such exceptions as were not considered by the court, by reason of the fact that the grant mentioned could be collaterally attacked on that ground. The plaintiff offered a grant to Duncan McFarland, dated January 13, 1847, issued on an entry dated July 4, 1801. The defendant offered a grant to Duncan McLaurin, dated March 31, 1842, issued by virtue of an entry made in the year 1841. It is admitted that both of these grants cover and include the land in controversy in this action. Looking only to the older grant to McLaurin as the source of title, and leaving the junior grant out of view, it is admitted by both parties that whatever interest was acquired by the original grantee passed through several mesne conveyances to one John L. Fairly, and descended upon his death to five children, three of whom were laboring under disability such that the statute did not run against them during the time when J. B. Buchanan held the possession of the land in controversy, and two of whom were under no disability during that period. The plaintiff relied solely, after showing title out of the state by the McLaurin grant, upon this possession of Buchanan under a deed for the premises from one McKay to him dated September 23, 1863. This alleged occupancy by Buchanan extended over the period from the date of his deed in 1863 till the year 1879, when the interest of John L. Fairly was sold by his administrator, and bought by one McLaurin. McLaurin conveyed it immediately to the defendant Middleton, who claims that Fairly could show a chain of title connecting him with both grants, being the deeds and evidence offered by the defendant.

The legal, and presumably the equitable, estate in the land passed by the older grant to McLaurin. His title could not, under the former practice, have been successfully attacked or impeached in a court of law by McFarland. The claimant under a junior grant, but senior entry, if he would avoid the older patent, was compelled to resort to a court of equity, and allege and prove that the prior grant was obtained by the grantee therein named with knowledge of the first entry. Plemmons v. Fore, 2 Ired. Eq. 312; Harris v. Ewing, 1 Dev. & B. 369; Stanly v. Biddle, 4 Jones, Eq. 383. Where controversies originated in such conflicting claims, it sometimes happened that the grantee under the senior grant, issued on the junior entry, brought an action of ejectment against the grantee in possession, claiming under the junior grant and senior entry; and the latter, being unable to set up his equity as a defense in a court of law, filed a bill in the court of equity, asking that the former be declared a trustee, ordered to convey the legal estate, and that, pending the investigation of his claim; for such relief, the plaintiff in the action of ejectment should be enjoined from further proceedings. In other instances the junior grantee was evicted, and subsequently filed his bill. If in such suit the plaintiff succeeded in proving that the defendant had either actual or constructive notice of the older entry when he took out his grant, and that the older entry covered the same land embraced in it, then the court would declare the defendant a trustee for the plaintiff, and compel him to convey the legal title. But the burden was upon the claimant under the junior grant then, as it is now, to establish this fraud, in a direct proceeding, in which it must be distinctly alleged. Currie v. Gibson, 4 Jones, Eq. 25; Munroe v. McCormick, 6 Ired. Eq. 85; Allen v. Gilreath, Id. 252. As there is no evidence to show that McLaurin was

ever declared a trustee, and required to convey the legal title, the grant to McFarland could, in the most favorable view, be made available only as colorable title, where continuous adverse possession was shown in those claiming under it for the statutory period. If it be conceded that the junior grant was valid upon its face, the only actual possession of which there appears to have been any evidence was that of Buchanan, the benefit of which inured to the plaintiff, if to any one, the title having been traced from Buchanan by mesne conveyances to the plaintiff, as is admitted. Buchanan occupied under the deed from McKay to him, which covered the land in dispute, and which the judge properly told the jury was colorable title.

It was not error, in any aspect of the testimony, to instruct the jury that if they should find that Buchanan held continuous adverse possession of the locus in quo for seven years, exclusive of the period when the statute of limitations was suspended, (from May 20, 1861, to January 1, 1870,) the plaintiff was entitled to recover. The older grant is in a strictly legal, as distinguished from an equitable, proceeding, paramount as evidence of title; and, if it did convey the title out of the state, it is admitted by the plaintiff that such estate as passed by it was transmitted by mesne conveyances to John L. Fairly, and on his death descended to his five children. The plaintiff claims that he is entitled to recover two undivided fifths, and concedes the defendant's right to three undivided fifths, which descended to the three children of Fairly, who were under disability, passed by the administrator's deed to McLaurin, and was conveyed by McLaurin to the defendant. Only such interest as was acquired by the junior grantee, McFarland, descended to his heirs at law, and was transmitted by the mesne conveyances offered, if all of them had been admitted to be valid, to the defendant. If McFarland's grant was available only as color of title in a court of law as against the older title, and gave him only a right of action in equity, those holding under him could acquire nothing more through a chain of conveyances and descents. Let us suppose, for the sake of the argument, that John G. Pearson became the husband of McFarland's daughter, to whom whatever title he had under that grant descended before the 1st of March, 1849, and that John G. Pearson's interest as tenant by the curtesy was regularly levied upon and sold by Buchanan, sheriff of Richmond county, and conveyed to McCall, to whom the defendant traced his title. The defendant would not thereby have shown a better title than that of plaintiff, derived through the deed from McKay to Buchanan, and the possession of the latter under it. The plaintiff had not attempted to connect himself by mesne conveyances with either of the original grants. He offered the younger grant to show title out of the state simply, and when the defendant introduced the senior grant he was not precluded from saying that he did not dispute the fact that the title passed by the last-mentioned grant, but, if it did, still the possession upon which he relied would vest the title in him as to two undivided fifths of the land. Code, § 141. But while it appears that the wife of Pearson died before April, 1852, leaving a son who died in February, 1872, the date of the marriage is not given in the statement of the case. We infer that he was married after March 1, 1849, and, if so, the sheriff's deed was void, and there would have been no error in the instruction in reference to it, if the title had actually been in his wife. Avent v. Arrington, 105 N. C. 393, 10 S. E. Rep. 991; Rev. Code, c. 56, § 1.

It is manifest that, in any aspect of the evidence, the right of the plaintiff to recover two undivided fifths of the land in dispute depended upon the question whether he had shown continuous adverse possession under color of title on the part of Buchanan, through whom he claimed. The deed from McKay to Buchanan was color of title, and the fact that the right of the heirs of Fairly, and those claiming under them, to bring an action, relying on the McFarland grant to establish title, did not accrue till Pearson died, in 1883, would not interfere with the right which the two heirs, who were sui juris, had on the 1st day of January, 1870, and for seven years thereafter, to evict Buchanan under the prima facie title shown by the defendant in this action, by means of a series of mesne conveyances connecting him with the older grant to McLaurin. Having shown that the two heirs of McFairly had a right to recover under that title, the defendant cannot avoid the consequences of their laches by saying that they could not then establish their right in equity to have the junior grant declared superior to the senior grant, because of a fraud which is neither alleged nor proven, practiced by McLaurin upon McFarland, if the plaintiff had exhibited a chain of title connecting himself with the McLaurin grant, such as the defendant has offered, instead of relying on proof of possession under color of title, the defendant would not, in that event, have been permitted, after setting up a strictly legal defense by denying the plaintiff's title, and that his own possession was tortious, to nonsuit the plaintiff, because the two heirs of Fairly could not, during Buchanan's occupancy, have instituted a suit in the nature of a bill in equity, and have tested their ability to discover and adduce such proof of fraud on the part of McLaurin as would have converted him into a trustee for McFarland. But the defendant traces his claim under both grants through Ferdinand McLeod. The testimony offered by the defendant shows that Duncan McCall, the purchaser of Pearson's interest as life-tenant under the junior grant, conveyed it to Ferdinand McLeod on the 24th of September, 1857, and that on the same day Duncan McLaurin, the grantee named in the senior grant, also conveyed all of his interest held under it to said McLeod, who subsequently, on the 16th of April, 1858, conveyed all of the title and interest acquired by the merger of the two interests to John L. Fairly. The defendant also exhibited a series of mesne conveyances showing a chain of title connecting him

with a deed from John G. Pearson to Addison Stevens, executed on the 17th of April, 1875, after he had inherited from his son Tryon Pearson whatever estate had descended to his mother under the McFarland grant. If we admit that an action might have been brought by Tryon Pearson, and after his death by his father and heir at law, John G. Pearson, between January 1, 1870, and April 17, 1875, and by Stevens between the last-named date and the 7th of January, 1878, in which the burden would have been on them to show that McLaurin practiced a fraud on McFarland in obtaining the grant, still the title was vested absolutely under the senior grant in Fairly's heirs; and in this action any person controverting the rights of claimants by virtue of Buchanan's possession must submit to the consequences of the laches of the two, who were during that period sui generis. If Buchanan occupied the land in dispute, cultivating a portion of it every year, for seven years after the 1st of January, 1870, as the testimony tended to show, under the McKay deed, which embraced it within its boundaries, then, for the purpose of showing title out of the state, the plaintiff, who claimed under Buchanan, might offer himself, or rely on when introduced by the defendant, any or all grants from the state, which included the locus in quo, for the purpose of showing title out of the state, and diminishing the statutory period requisite for the maturity of his title from 21 to 7 years. The plaintiff did not attempt to connect himself with either of the grants, nor was there any testimony tending to connect him by a chain of mesne conveyances with any source of title in common with the defendant, and thereby throw around him the trammels of any rule of evidence that would interfere with his right to avail himself of the oldest grant exhibited to prove that the state had no interest in the controversy. It being conceded that both grants covered the area upon which the trespass was shown, the defendant might elect to rely on the older and better title exhibited for the purpose mentioned, and, when he coupled with it proof of color of title and continuous possession for seven years, he was entitled to recover, even though the defendant exhibited a chain of title connecting him with both grants, unless it had appeared that no right of action accrued to the defendant, or those through whom he claimed title, under the senior grant to McLaurin, against Buchanan, during his occupancy of the premises, but did accrue afterwards. As Pearson derived all of the right or title that he had through the younger grant, if we admit that McCall got by the sheriff's deed whatever interest Pearson could claim as tenant by the curtesy, still he acquired, as against those claiming under the senior grant, at best but a bare right, which would not avail him or them as evidence of title in this action. It is not material whether the sheriff's deed was utterly void or passed only a right. As it did not, in any aspect of the evidence, tend to establish title in the defendant to the land in controversy, the defendant has no just ground of complaint, even if his honor erred (which we do not admit) in telling the jury that the deed from Buchanan, sheriff, to McCall, conveyed no title, because of irregularities in the judgment or execution, or because Pearson had but a bare right, not subject to sale under execution, or an estate by the curtesy, which the law prohibited the sheriff from selling. It is unnecessary to review the authorities cited, or pass upon the point urged by the able counsel for the plaintiff on the argument, to-wit, that John G. Pearson, as the husband of one claiming through the junior grant a mere right in equity to compel the grantee under the elder grant to convey, had no estate which is subject to sale under execution, under section 450 of the Code. It is immaterial, too, for the purpose of disposing of this appeal, whether the sheriff was prohibited from selling such estate as Pearson claimed as tenant by the curtesy because he was married after March 1, 1849, as the sale passed only such interest as he acquired through his wife, who, if living, would have had the same right of action for the fee. Where a person, after having perfected the title by possession under colorable deed, moves off the premises, he is not deemed to have abandoned his right by voluntarily leaving. The estate thus vested remains in him until it is aliened by him, or those in privity with him, lawfully sold under judicial decree or process, or another divests it by adverse possession subsequent to his departure. 1 Washb. Real Prop. p. 499; Wood. Lim. Act, § 254; Avent v. Arrington, 105 N. C. 398, 10 S. E. Rep. 991; Manfuacturing Co. v. Brooks, 106 N. C. 113, 11 S. E. Rep. 456.

If Buchanan acquired title, therefore, it passed to the plaintiff through the mesne conveyances offered, notwithstanding the fact that Buchanan left after his title was matured, and the defendant entered and took possession. It is admitted that without actual possession on the part of defendant, or of those under whom he claims, the plaintiff's title to two undivided fifths would mature, and did mature, as against the perfect chain of title offered by the defendant to connect himself with the senior grant to McLaurin, unless for some reason the running of the statute of limitation was suspended as to all of the heirs of Fairly as well as the defendant from January 1, 1870, till the action was brought, in 1882. If the possession of Buchanan would have been sufficient against McLaurin, or those claiming under him, and holding the legal and presumably the equitable title, to divest their estate, and vest it in him, it would seem absurd to hold that the statute did not run in favor of Buchanan, and for the ultimate benefit of the plaintiffs, because another grant has been exhibited which in this action could be used only as color of title, and which, at best, might furnish the basis of a claim to the equitable estate, possibly not susceptible of being established. If such were the law, the recovery of plaintiff in ejectment might be prevented by exhibiting a worse title, when a better would not subserve the purpose. The position of the defendant involves the still more startling proposition that though

he acquired the estate that passed by the older grant to McLaurin by deed from W. H. McLaurin, dated March 18, 1879, and the interest of Tryon Pearson that descended under the younger grant was conveyed to him by McCall and wife on 31st of March, 1879, he will by permitted to prevail in an action raising only the issues of title and possession, and drive the plaintiff to a nonsuit, because McFarland, and others through whom he connects himself with the junior grant, had the right in equity to demand a conveyance of the legal title from McLaurin and those claiming under the older grant to him. It is manifest that the plaintiff's right to recover two undivided fifths of the land depended solely upon the question whether Buchanan cultivated any portion of the land in controversy for seven consecutive years between January 1, 1870, and the date of the summons in this action, unless the defendant's right of action had accrued by reason of the death of John L. Fairly, and the liability of his lands to be subjected for assets by his administrator. It is familiar learning that the personal representative has no control over or connection with the land belonging to the decedent, unless and until he, under the statute, (Code, § 1436,) applies for and obtains license to sell it, in order to pay the debts and charges of administration. It was evidently the purpose of the framers of the statutes, providing for settlements by executors and administrators, that they should be required to render their final accounts within two years after qualification, if possible. Code, § 1488. For the benefit of the creditors only, and in harmony with that idea, all conveyances of real property of a decedent, by a devisee or heir at law, made within two years after the grant of letters to the personal representative, are declared "void as to creditors, executors, administrators, and collectors of such decedent;" but such conveyances, when made more than two years from the grant of letters to bona fide purchasers for value and without notice, are "valid, even as against creditors." The evident purpose was not only to allow the administrator to sell when necessary to satisfy the demands of creditors, but to restrain heirs and devisees for a reasonable time from disposing of the real property, and thereby depriving the creditors, who are represented by the executor or administrator, from making it available as assets. It will not be so construed to save the heir from the consequences of his own laches, or to deprive one who has shown more diligence of the rights acquired by him under the express provision of another statute. Id. § 141.

Thus far we have conducted this discussion upon the idea that both grants were valid upon their faces, but that, both being exhibited, the title would be deemed to have passed by that first issued, until, by a direct proceeding, the older grant should be declared fraudulent as against the younger. But it is insisted that this court erred in holding that the grant to McFarland was void upon its face. It is true that the court did not advert to the fact that the statute then in force in the year

1847 permitted one who entered land to take out his grant, provided he should pay the purchase money to the state before the "31st day of December, which should happen in the second year thereafter," but did not declare a grant void because it was issued or the survey was made after that time had elapsed. Rev. St. c. 42, § 10; Krous v. Long, 6 Ired. Eq. 259; Stanly v. Biddle, 4 Jones, Eq. 383. The result would be that while it is correct as a principle to hold that a grant, which upon its face appears to have been issued in contravention of law, is void, the particular grant to McFarland was not upon its face invalid.

Neither of the grants has come up with the record as an exhibit. Under the terms of the act of 1796, c. 455, § 13, (2 Potter's Revisal, p. 807,) a grant was not valid if taken out more than two years after the entry was made. This section was repealed by the act of 1804, c. 651. (2 Potter's Revisal, p. 1010.) At the same session of the general assembly another act was passed which is substantially the same as Code, § 2766; Acts 1804, c. 759, (2 Potter's Revisal, 1149.) So that where a grant was issued in 1847, upon an entry made in 1801, it was not upon its face void. If the purchase money was paid to the state before the 15th (now the 31st) of December of the second year after the entry was made, the grant was valid, under the statute then in force. Krous v. Long, supra. McLaurin's entry was made in 1841, and his grant was taken out in 1842. The first question suggested by the dates of the entries and grants is whether the various acts extending the time for taking out patents affect the legal *status* of the claimants under them. Though the act of 1842, c. 35, did not contain the saving clause in reference to junior entries, couched in the same terms as the other acts in relation to that subject, it was construed by the court to mean the same thing. Buchanan v. Fitzgerald, 6 Ired. Eq. 121. In the case of Bryson v. Dobson, 3 Ired. Eq. 188, (decided in 1843,) the court having previously declared that, "against another subsisting entry, one that has lapsed is revived as of the date of the statute by which it is revived." The only effect of the act of 1842, then, would be to make the rights of the parties the same as if the entry of McFarland had been made in 1842, on the day when the act was passed, thus making his entry (as well as his grant) junior in contemplation of law to that of McLaurin. But the defendant insists in his petition to rehear that this court must take notice of a resolution passed by the general assembly on the 7th of January, 1847, (Laws 1846–47, p. 381,) while the plaintiff maintains that it is a private law and the courts cannot take notice of it, unless it has been offered in evidence. Waiving all objection to its introduction and identity as authority for issuing the McFarland grant, we would encounter insuperable difficulty in declaring it a superior title to the grant issued before the passage of the resolution. The legislative recital that the purchase money was paid by McFarland in 1804 would not fix Duncan McFarland with notice. Indeed,

he could not have been affected by such notice if it had been proven in an action for possession, to which he was a party. Even if the resolution can be noticed by us, and we should go further and accept as true the statement that it is referred to in the grant as the legislative authority for issuing the grant, it will not be contended that, in the absence of a judicial declaration of fraud on McLaurin's part, the legislature had the power to divest out of McLaurin such title as had already vested in him under his grant in 1842, and transfer it to McFarland. Stanmire v. Taylor, 3 Jones, (N. C.) 207; Stanmire v. Welch, Id. 214. In Buchanan v. Fitzgerald, supra, Chief Justice RUFFIN, delivering the opinion, said, in reference to the validity of a senior grant, taken out after the purchase money had been paid by a junior grantee, who had an older entry: "Certainly without notice of it, [the payment,] the defendant might innocently and justly enter the land and lay out his money for it, after a lapse of upwards of five years from the date of the entry, and nearly three from that of the alleged payment of the money into the treasury, and therefore is entitled in consequence to hold it to his own use." In that case the defendants had brought an action of ejectment against the plaintiffs, who were heirs at law of the claimant, under the junior grant and senior entry, and had evicted them; and after being ejected the plaintiffs had filed a bill asking to have the defendant declared a trustee, but had failed, because there was "nothing in the case to affect the defendant with notice of" the payment of the purchase money. In our case about 43 years intervened between the payment of the purchase money and the issuing of the grant, instead of 5. A more marked distinction, however, arises out of the fact that while no suit had ever been brought against Duncan McLaurin to fix him with notice of the entry and payment of the purchase money, and declare him a trustee, the defendant, under a general denial in an ordinary action for title and possession, asks the court to declare that one of the grantees through whom he claims defrauded the other, through whom he claims also, and should be declared a trustee as to the land in controversy for his benefit. This relief is asked without a *scintilla* of evidence to fix McLaurin with actual or constructive notice of the entry or payment of the purchase money by McFarland, before his grant was issued, and for the purpose of transferring the legal title at this late date in an action wherein no equity is alleged on the part of the junior grantee, McFarland, and those claiming under him; and then showing that the statute of limitations did not run in favor of Buchanan, as against that title, because Pearson's life-estate had not terminated when he occupied the premises. Only such exceptions of the defendant as the court did not consider on the former hearing, because of the holding that the McFarland grant was void upon its face, are open for discussion upon the rehearing. All of these fall within the principles we have announced, and are disposed of, whether specifically mentioned or not, since we have sustained the court below in leaving only the question of possession to the jury, on the ground that, if it were admitted that the defendant could trace his title to both the grants offered, the plaintiff, in view of the other admitted facts, was entitled to recover two undivided fifths of the land, if Buchanan cultivated the land for seven years, when the statute was running as to the two heirs of Fairly, who were not under legal disability. For the reasons stated, we hold that, if it were error to tell the jury that the sheriff's deed for Pearson's interest was void, error was harmless, and no other material error was shown. The petition must be dismissed.

WATTS et al. v. WARREN et al.

FRAUDULENT CONVEYANCES—EVIDENCE—TRANSACTIONS WITH DECEDENT—ASSIGNMENTS OF ERROR.

(Supreme Court of North Carolina. May 19, 1891.)

1. Where, in an action by creditors to set aside as fraudulent an assignment of a life insurance policy to decedent's brothers, the defense was that the latter had theretofore paid a number of decedent's debts; that one of them, as co-executor with him of their father's estate, was obliged to pay large sums on account of his default; and that the sums so paid were a just and fair price for the assignment,—evidence as to such payments was material to prove the consideration for the assignment, and the bona fide character of the transaction.

2. Code N. C. § 590, provides that no one interested in an action adversely to a deceased person shall be examined as a witness in his own behalf, "concerning a personal transaction or communication between the witness and the deceased person." Held, in an action to set aside an assignment to decedent's brothers of a life insurance policy, that defendants, although incompetent under said section to prove the contract of assignment, or the consideration agreed upon therefor with decedent, could testify to their transactions with third persons in that regard, and show what money they had paid in settlement of decedent's debts, and also what sums they had been compelled to pay on account of decedent's default as co-executor of their father's estate.

3. Assignments of error in disallowing certain questions, as to what payments had been made by defendants for and on account of decedent, sufficiently suggest the materiality of the evidence proposed; and, although the evidence itself is not specifically set forth, such assignments will be considered on appeal.

Appeal from superior court, Durham county; MACRAE, Judge.

It appears that Julius B. Warren died intestate in the county of Durham, in the month of June, 1889, and the defendant W. A. Warren duly became the administrator of his estate. This action is brought by the creditors of the intestate to compel the defendant administrator to an account of his administration, and to pay the creditors what may be payable to them respectively. The other defendants are brought into the action to the end that they may be concluded in respects not necessary to be particularly mentioned here. In the life-time of this intestate, he obtained from the Provident Savings Assurance Society of New York a policy of insurance of his own life, payable to him and for his own benefit, dated the 15th of March, 1888, for the sum of $15,000. On the 29th day of March, 1889, he assigned,

transferred, and delivered this policy of insurance to his two brothers, the defendants W. A. Warren and Frank Warren, "for value received." No particular consideration is recited. At the time of the death of the intestate, he was largely indebted to divers creditors, and it is alleged that the assets of his estate are insufficient to pay his debts and the costs of administration. It is further alleged, among other things, that such assignment of the policy of insurance was made in fraud of and to defraud the creditors of the intestate, etc.; and that, at most, such assignment was intended only to secure certain debts and the payment of premiums upon the policy as the same might come due, etc. The plaintiffs allege that the policy belongs to and constitutes part of the assets of the estate, and they demand judgment that it be so declared, etc. The defendants deny the alleged fraud, and aver that such assignment was made in good faith, and for a just and fair consideration; and they further contend that, at all events, they bought the insurance policy for a just consideration, in good faith, and without knowledge or notice of any such fraudulent intent or purpose of the said intestate. The court submitted to the jury the following issues, and the jury responded to the same as indicated at the end of each: "(1) Was the assignment by J. B. Warren to W. A. Warren and F. R. Warren absolute and for full value?' Answer. No. (2) Was said assignment intended as a security for indebtedness of J. B. Warren as executor of his father's estate or otherwise? A. No. (3) Was such assignment made simply as a security for premiums paid out and to be paid thereon by W. A. Warren and F. R. Warren? A. No. (4) Was said assignment made by J. B. Warren with intent to hinder, delay, and defraud his creditors? A. Yes. (5) Did the defendants W. A. Warren and F. R. Warren have notice of such intent when the assignment was made?" There was no response to this issue. On the trial there was evidence tending to prove that the intestate and the defendant administrator were executors of their deceased father's will and that the intestate in his life-time had used very considerable sums of money—how much did not definitely appear—that belonged to legatees of the will, and that the defendant W. A. Warren had paid and had to pay the same, etc., and that such payments constituted part of the consideration paid by him for the policy of insurance. The defendant administrator was examined as a witness in his own behalf, and his counsel, among others, put to him questions as follows: "What payments have you made to other persons than J. B. Warren in consideration of that assignment? This was objected to by the plaintiffs, and, the objection being sustained, the defendants excepted. Defendants' counsel asked: What sums of money have you paid out by reason of your liability as co-executor with J. B. Warren of F. L. Warren, deceased? Objection by plaintiffs sustained, and defendants except." The defendant F. R. Warren was also examined as a witness for the defendants, and, among others, this question was put to him: "State if you have made any payment, if so, to whom, on debts of J. B. Warren. The plaintiffs objected, and, objection being sustained, the defendants except." There were numerous other exceptions, but they need not be reported. The court gave judgment upon the verdict for the plaintiffs, and the defendants thereupon appealed to this court.

John W. Graham and *Jas. S. Manning*, for appellants. *Boone & Parker*, *W. W. Fuller*, and *W. A. Guthrie*, for appellees.

MERRIMON, C. J., (*after stating the facts as above.*) Assignments of error, upon the ground that evidence tendered on the trial was improperly rejected, should distinctly specify its relevancy and materiality. The court must be able to see its nature and application with reasonable certainty; otherwise it cannot say that there is or is not error. The presumption is that the rulings of the court are correct until the contrary is made to appear in some appropriate way. Whitesides v. Twitty, 8 Ired. 431; Knight v. Killebrew, 86 N. C. 400; Summer v. Candler, 92 N. C. 634. Although the evidence which the defendants sought to elicit by the questions put to the witnesses in this case, and which the court declined to allow them to answer, is not specifically set forth in the assignments of error, still we think the questions themselves suggest with sufficient distinctness and certainty the nature, meaning, relevancy, and materiality of the evidence proposed and rejected, as will presently appear. The plaintiffs, creditors of the intestate of the defendant administrator, alleged that he assigned to the defendants the Warrens, his brothers, the policy of insurance mentioned, in fraud of and to "hinder, delay, and defraud his creditors;" and, further, that, if this was not so, then he assigned the same to them to the end they might pay the premiums that might after the assignment come due thereon, and in the end receive the money that might be paid in discharge of the policy, and apply the same to reimburse themselves for such premiums as might be paid by them: and also to the payment and discharge of certain debts and liabilities of the intestate. This the defendants broadly denied, alleging, in substance, that they bought the policy so assigned to them in good faith, paying therefor its fair value. They allege, further, that their brother, the intestate, was in his life-time the co-executor with the defendant W. A. Warren of the will of their deceased father; that the intestate, while so executor, took and used for his own purposes large sums of money that belonged to his father's estate, and were devoted by the will to the payment of legacies, etc., for all which the defendant W. A. Warren was liable, and was bound to pay the same; that they had paid other debts for their said brother; that the aggregate of the sums of money they so paid, and others they were obliged to pay, for the intestate, was intended to be and was a fair and just price for the policy of insurance so assigned to them; and that the intestate assigned the same to them in

good faith, for such consideration. It hence behooved the defendants the Warrens to prove on the trial, and to produce competent evidence for that purpose, that the intestate owed them as alleged, and what sums of money; what premiums they so paid on account of the policy of insurance; what of his debts they paid at his instance; and what sum or sums of money the defendant W. A. Warren had paid and was obliged to pay as such co-executor on account of the default of the intestate as one of the executors of his father's will. There was some evidence produced on the trial by the defendants tending to prove that such matters and things constituted the consideration for the assignment of the policy of insurance. There was likewise some evidence, in some aspects of the whole of the evidence produced, tending to prove that the assignment of the policy of insurance was made as a security for the reimbursement of the defendants the Warrens, on account of premiums they might pay as required by the policy, and to pay certain debts and discharge certain liabilities of the intestate. Therefore the evidence proposed by the defendants, and which was rejected, tending to prove what sums of money the defendant W. A. Warren had paid on account of the default of his brother, the intestate, as executor of his father's will, was relevant and material, as was also the other evidence so proposed and rejected, tending to show what debts of the intestate the defendants the Warrens had paid for him. Such evidence, if it had been received, would have tended in some measure to prove a consideration, and the amount thereof, for the assignment of the policy, and that the same was made in good faith and for a lawful purpose. Although it was not very direct, its pertinency and bearing favorable to the defendants were plainly to be seen, and, taken in connection with the whole evidence produced on the trial, (very much of it indefinite and unsatisfactory,) it might have materially changed the verdict of the jury as to one or more of the issues submitted to them. In any view of the case, the defendants were entitled to have the benefit of it.

It was insisted, however, that the evidence so rejected came within the inhibition of the statute, (Code, § 590,) and was not competent, because the witnesses were interested in the event of the action adversely to a deceased person, and the evidence it was proposed they should give was "concerning a personal transaction or communication between the witness and the deceased person,"—the intestate named. We think this contention cannot be allowed to prevail. The court properly held that the witness W. A. Warren was not a competent witness to testify as to the contract of assignment of the policy of insurance, and the consideration thereof agreed upon, because such testimony would clearly come within the inhibition of the statute just cited. But there was some evidence of the witnesses other than the defendants Warren, whose proposed testimony was rejected, going to prove that the intestate made the assignment in question, not for any fraudulent purpose, but for a valuable consideration, such as that above mentioned. The defendants the Warrens were not competent witnesses to testify as to the contract of assignment, because the deceased assignor could not testify in his own behalf. and contradict them, as to "a personal transaction or communication" between him and them. The obvious purpose of the statute is to prevent the surviving interested party in such cases from testifying as to such "personal transaction or communication," because the deceased party cannot. The witnesses were not called upon to testify "concerning a personal transaction or communication" between them and the deceased person, their brother; they were asked to testify as to transactions and communications with persons other than the deceased, and as to which such third persons could testify, if need be. The statute does not by its terms or purpose prevent the surviving party from testifying concerning transactions and communications with third persons that may affect adversely the estate of the deceased person, or the rights of persons in and to the same. The questions put to the witnesses which they were not allowed to answer obviously had reference to the pleadings, the issues, and the contentions of the parties on the trial. They were intended to elicit from the witness W. A. Warren—First, an account of what sums of money he had paid to persons other than his brother, deceased. for and on account of the latter; and, secondly, what sums of money he had paid to third persons, and for which he was liable, on account of the default of his brother as executor of his father's will. The question put to F. R. Warren was intended to elicit from him an account of any sums of money he had paid "on debts" of his brother, deceased; and such evidence was intended to apply and have force on the trial in any pertinent aspects of the case. Such payments of money for the benefit of the deceased brother were not made to the latter, but to third persons, and he may or may not have had knowledge of the same; but, however this might be, the transactions and communications concerning the same were not with him. Nor was the purpose of the evidence to prove the contract of assignment of the policy of insurance, or "concerning a personal transaction or communication between the witness and the deceased person" about the same. The purpose was to prove material facts and transactions distinctly with third persons, and to connect and apply them with other material facts and transactions by proper evidence, for pertinent purposes on the trial. The evidence was material, not to prove the contract of assignment of the policy, but to prove distinct transactions with third persons—persons other than the deceased party—that grew out of and were in a sense a consequence of such contract. In view of the pleadings, the issues submitted to the jury, the contentions of the parties, and the whole of the evidence produced on the trial, upon which the evidence rejected might have

had some material bearing favorable to the defendants, the latter evidence was relative, material, and competent, and ought to have been received by the court, unless the answers of the witnesses to the questions put to them had, contrary to expectation, been irrelevant, and not such as their nature and purpose suggested and implied. The following cited authorities are more or less in point here: Whitesides v. Green, 64 N. C. 307; Thompson v. Humphrey, 83 N. C. 416; Lockhart v. Bell, 90 N. C. 499; Peacock v. Stott, Id. 518; Waddell v. Swann, 91 N. C. 105; Sikes v. Parker, 95 N. C. 232; Loftin v. Loftin, 96 N. C. 94, 1 S. E Rep. 837; Carey v. Carey, 104 N. C. 175, 10 S. E. Rep. 156; Bunn v. Todd, 107 N. C. 266, 11 S. E. Rep. 1043. There are numerous other assignments of error, but we do not deem it useful or necessary to advert to them further than to say that most, if not all, of them cannot be sustained. There is error. The defendants are entitled to a new trial, and we so adjudge. To that end let this opinion be certified to the superior court. It is so ordered.

STEWART et al. v. REGISTER et al.

(Supreme Court of North Carolina. May 19, 1891.)

REFORMATION OF DEEDS—ESTOPPEL OF RECORD—DEPOSITION TAKEN IN FORMER ACTION—OBJECTIONS NOT TAKEN BELOW.

1. In an action to reform a deed by inserting the words "and their heirs," omitted by mistake from the proper place to pass the fee, it appeared that a special proceeding was previously brought against plaintiffs, who set this up as an equitable counter-claim, and that the question was decided in their favor, but was reversed in the supreme court. The reversal, however, was never entered below, the action and the counter-claim being withdrawn by common consent. Held, that such proceeding did not constitute an estoppel.

2. The deposition of a draughtsman, admitted to have been regularly taken, and allowed in a previous action between the same parties, and in relation to the same subject-matter, is competent, though no proceedings have been taken to make it competent in the present action.

3. On appeal, the admission of such deposition cannot be objected to on the ground of a non-identity of parties, where the record fails to show any pertinent data as to the matter, or that such objection was raised below, and there are no assignments of error in regard thereto.

Appeal from superior court, Sampson county; ARMFIELD, Judge.

This action is brought to have a deed of conveyance of land, specified in the complaint, corrected, so as to insert therein at the pertinent and appropriate place to pass the fee-simple estate in the land conveyed the words "and their heirs," which, it is alleged, were omitted from it by the inadvertence and mistake of the draughtsman thereof. It is alleged that the deed conveyed but a life-estate, whereas the grantor therein—a grandfather, sustaining the relation of loco parentis to certain of his grandchildren—intended thereby to convey to them the fee in the land conveyed. The defendants deny the material allegations of the complaint, and allege also that the plaintiffs are estopped in the action by the determination of a special proceeding specified before this action began. That proceeding came before this court by appeal, and the latter directed that the judgment appealed from be reversed. Powell v. Morisey, 98 N. C. 426, 4 S. E. Rep. 185. The judgment of this court was duly certified to the superior court. Thereupon that court, at the October term thereof of 1888, made this entry in the proceeding: "The plaintiffs are permitted to withdraw their action or special proceeding because the same was prematurely begun, and leave is given the defendants to withdraw their counterclaim." In this action the court submitted to the jury appropriate issues, and they found by their verdict that the maker of the deed in question did intend to convey the fee in the land conveyed thereby, and that the words "and their heirs" were omitted from it by the mistake and inadvertence of the draughtsman thereof; that the grantor of the deed, at the time he executed the same, had placed himself *in loco parentis* to the grantees in the deed, who were his grandchildren; and that the plaintiffs were the owners of the land. The court, on inspection of the record of the special proceeding above referred to, decided that the same did not estop the plaintiffs in this action, and the defendants excepted. The following is so much of the case settled on appeal as need be reported: "On the trial the plaintiff offered as evidence a deposition of A. A. McKoy, a copy of which is filed with this record, marked 'Exhibit A.' It was stated by the plaintiffs, and admitted by the defendants, that this deposition had been regularly taken and allowed to be read, and was read on the trial in the case set out in the defendants' answer in this action, alleging a second defense; that said McKoy had died before the commencement of this action. The defendants objected to this evidence, on the ground that said deposition had not been regularly taken in this action, and no proceeding in law or equity had been taken to make the deposition competent. The court overruled this objection, and the defendants excepted." The court gave judgment in favor of the plaintiffs, and the defendants, having excepted, as above stated, appealed to this court.

H. E. Faison and *Haywood & Haywood*, for appellants. *J. L. Stewart* and *R. H. Battle*, for appellees.

MERRIMON, C. J., (*after stating the facts as above.*) The special proceeding relied upon by the defendants does not, in any view of it, constitute an estoppel of record upon the plaintiffs in this action, for the plain reason that that proceeding was never determined upon the merits thereof by any final judgment therein. See Powell v. Morisey, 98 N. C. 426, 4 S. E. Rep. 185. This court directed the judgment therein appealed from to be reversed, but no entry of reversal ever was made. Indeed, it appears that when the decision of this court was certified to the superior court the latter court at once allowed the plaintiffs to "withdraw their action or special proceeding because the same was prematurely begun," and allowed the defendants therein "to withdraw their counter-claim." Thus the proceeding was in legal effect dismissed,—abandoned by common consent of the parties before the litigation was completed. There was no settlement of the rights of the parties, nor any judgment concluding the latter in any respect. The plaintiffs withdrew their matter of the proceeding, and the defendants did likewise, with the sanction of the court. It so appears of record. Nothing appears by the latter to estop the parties in this action or elsewhere. To create an estoppel by a former judgment it must appear that the matter, claim, or demand in litigation has been tried and determined in a former action or proceeding, and the identity in effect of the present and former cause of litigation must appear. Temple v. Williams, 91 N. C. 82. The defendants objected to the deposition read in evidence on the trial on the ground that it "had not been regularly taken in this action, and no proceeding in law or equity had been taken to make" the same competent. These objections are clearly not tenable. It was not necessary that the deposition should be taken in this action. It is sufficient if it was taken in another action or proceeding between the same parties in relation to the same subject-matter or cause of action, or involves the same material questions, and the adverse party had opportunity to cross-examine the witness. Bryan v. Malloy, 90 N. C. 508; 1 Greenl. Ev. 553; Tayl. Ev. § 434. Nor was it necessary that any proceeding should be taken in a court of law or equity to render it competent as evidence in this action. It was sufficient to take it from the files to which it properly belonged, and introduce it on the trial, properly identifying it with the former action. It could not be changed, modified, or amended. It, as it appeared on file, was sufficient or insufficient; competent or incompetent. Why, therefore, should any proceeding be taken in court to render it competent? Any proper objection might have been made to it at the time it was put in evidence. It might have been objected that it was not taken in another action between the parties, or that it was taken in respect to a different matter or cause of action. It might have been objected further that it was in no way material in the former action. The material parts of the record in the former action should have accompanied and been introduced with it, to show its pertinency or competency in this action. Indeed, it seems that such record was so introduced. It does not appear from the record that any such objections as those just suggested were made in the court below. If there were such, and the defendants intended to avail themselves of them here, they should have had the objection noted in the record; and, if the court failed to sustain the same, they should have assigned error. The exceptions made did not raise any such questions. The defendants' counsel on the argument before us insisted that several of the parties to the former action are not parties to the present one, and that several of the parties to the present one were not parties to the former one; but no such objection appears from the record to have been made in the court below. No error is assigned in such respect. Moreover, there are no pertinent *data* by which we can see who of the present action were or were not of the former action. Nor can we see by the record who of the present action are in privity with parties to the former action. The judgment, therefore, must be affirmed.

GRUBBS V. NORTH CAROLINA HOME INS. CO.

(Supreme Court of North Carolina. May 12, 1891.)

FIRE INSURANCE—STIPULATION IN POLICY—FURTHER INSURANCE — WAIVER — AUTHORITY OF AGENT—MEASURE OF DAMAGES—TRIAL—ARGUMENT OF COUNSEL.

1. One who is intrusted by an insurance company with blank applications and its policies duly signed by its officers, and is authorized to take risks without consulting the company, to issue policies by simply signing his name as agent, and to collect premiums and cancel policies, is empowered as agent to waive conditions against further insurance.

2. Stipulation in a policy against further insurance without the consent of the company indorsed on the policy is waived where the agent, in reply to the statement of the insured that he should want more insurance, says that it is all right so long as he does not insure for more than three-fourths the value of the stock. MERRIMON, C. J., dissenting.

3. Where, after the loss, the officers of the company, with knowledge of the additional insurance, still recognize the validity of the policy, and induce insured to incur expense in making proof, the condition requiring the consent of the company to be indorsed on the policy will be held to be waived. MERRIMON, C. J., dissenting.

4. There was no error in refusing to submit a special issue as to whether the fact that additional insurance was taken was made known to the company before the loss, as such inquiry was immaterial.

5. It is not error to refuse to consider written requests for instructions, unless presented to the court at or before the close of the testimony.

6. There is no error in an instruction that the measure of damages is the fair cash value of goods at the time and place of the fire.

7. The fact that a witness for defendant, who was present and aiding its counsel in the conduct of the case, was not examined to contradict the plaintiff as to what occurred when he and another came to adjust the loss, was a matter which counsel was properly allowed to use as an argument that plaintiff's testimony should be believed.

Appeal from superior court, Northampton county: T. B. WOMACK, Judge.

T. W. Mason, B. S. Gay, and *J. W. Hinsdale,* for appellant. *R. O. Burton, Jr., R. B. Peebles,* and *W. C. Bowen,* for appellee.

AVERY, J. The defendant asked the court to instruct the jury that upon consideration of all the evidence there was no waiver of the condition of the policy requiring the written consent of the defendant to be indorsed upon it, provided the plaintiff should take out additional insurance in other companies. This request was equivalent to a demurrer to the whole of the evidence, it being admitted that additional insurance was taken out in other companies after the policy sued on was issued, without first securing the written indorsement of the defendant's consent upon it in accordance with the express requirements of one of its conditions. If Dr. Ramsey, the agent with

whom the plaintiff treated, was authorized to take fire risks and issue policies, he was empowered to waive by parol a condition in a policy issued by him. Winans v. Insurance Co., 38 Wis. 342; Miner v. Insurance Co., 27 Wis. 693; Gans v. Insurance Co., 43 Wis. 108; Insurance Co. v. Spiers, 87 Ky. 285, 8 S. W. Rep. 453; Kitchen v. Insurance Co., 57 Mich. 135, 23 N. W. Rep. 616; Insurance Co. v. Earle, 33 Mich. 143; Viele v. Insurance Co., 26 Iowa, 63; Wood, Ins. § 391; Shearman v. Insurance Co., 46 N. Y. 526; Fishbeck v. Insurance Co., 54 Cal. 422. Where a general agent permits a subagent acting under his direction to receive premiums from and to fill up and deliver policies to the insured, the acts of the subagent are regarded as the acts of the general agent. Insurance Co. v. Ruckman, 127 Ill. 365, 20 N. E. Rep. 77. The powers of an agent are *prima facie* co-extensive with the apparent authority given him, and persons dealing with him may judge of their extent from the nature of the business intrusted to his care. Wood, Ins. § 500; Hornthall v. Insurance Co., 88 N. C. 71; Beal v. Insurance Co., 16 Wis. 241; Davenport v. Insurance Co., 17 Iowa, 276. Though the authorities are conflicting upon many questions that have arisen as to the powers of insurance agents generally to bind the companies for which they act, there is a growing tendency to abrogate rules laid down by some of the courts, when the insured sought the principal officers of these corporations in the larger towns, and asked the agents to forward applications for insurance, instead of waiting at their homes for agents sent to solicit their patronage and stimulated to active and persistent effort by their employers. We concur with the judge below in the opinion that, if Dr. Ramsey was intrusted by the defendant (as he testified that he was) with the blank applications and with its policies duly signed by its officers, and was authorized to take risks without consulting the company, to issue policies by simply signing his name as agent, to collect premiums, and to cancel policies, then he was empowered as agent to waive the condition that no additional insurance should be taken. In the case of Insurance Co. v. Earle, supra, an agent, when asked about the taking of additional insurance, said in substance that it would make no difference, but, without saying it in so many words, left the inference that consent in writing was not necessary, and the court held that the agent had waived a condition in the policy similar to that in plaintiff's policy, and that the insurers could not avoid liability under the contract because additional insurance was subsequently taken in another company, without asking for or securing the indorsement of its written consent on the original policy. See, also, Gans v. Insurance Co, supra. After testifying that he was permitted by the defendant to exercise all of the powers enumerated by the court in the foregoing instructions, Dr. Ramsey stated also that Grubbs did say to him that he would want further insurance, and that he (Ramsey) replied that he thought Grubbs could get it if he wished; that he did not remember any more of the conversation on that subject. The witness Gay testified that Ramsey said to Grubb, when asked about further insurance, that it was all right so that he did not insure for more than three-fourths the value of the stock. Grubbs testifies that he told Ramsey the exact amount of insurance that he proposed to place and did take in each of the other companies, which did not in the aggregate exceed three-fourths of the value of the property insured. So that the facts in our case would more naturally warrant the inference that the agent did not require his assent to be indorsed in writing on the policy than the evidence in the Michigan authority cited above, because Ramsey not only conveyed the idea that it would be all right to get additional insurance, but added the condition that the whole insurance should not in the aggregate exceed three-fourths of the value of the property insured, thereby excluding the inference that he would insist upon any other condition. But, even upon his own testimony, Ramsey was empowered to waive the indorsement; and if, after Grubbs notified him of the amount which he proposed to take and did afterwards take in each of the other companies, Ramsey by his language left Grubbs to infer that no objection would be made unless the aggregate amount of insurance in all of the companies should exceed three-fourths of the value of the insured property, and Grubbs did not exceed the limit, then, if Grubbs was induced to believe that the forfeiture would not be insisted on unless the limit in the amount of insurance should be transcended, and acted under that impression in effecting additional insurance, that condition of the policy would be considered as waived by the company. We think, therefore, that there was no error in the rulings of the judge below upon which the 6th, 14th, 15th, 16th, and 17th exceptions are founded.

It seems that some of the counsel abandoned, while other counsel insisted upon, the exceptions numbered from 1 to 8, inclusive, and so much of exception 10 as referred to the refusal of the court to give special instructions asked by defendant, and numbered 7. If after a breach of the conditions of a policy the insurers, with a knowledge of the facts constituting it, by their conduct lead the insured to believe that they still recognize the validity of the policy, and consider him as protected by it, and induce him under such impression to incur expense, they will be deemed to have waived the forfeiture, and will be estopped from setting it up as a defense. Viele v. Insurance Co., 26 Iowa, 9, and note page 68; Oshkosh Gas-Light Co. v. Germania Fire Ins. Co., 71 Wis. 454, 37 N. W. Rep. 819. Where, with a knowledge of the facts constituting the alleged waiver, the insurer, after the insured property had been destroyed by fire, requires the insured to furnish invoice of goods destroyed, proofs of loss, or plans and specifications of the building burned, or to appear for examination, such acts of its adjuster amount to a concession that the forfeiture for failure to secure the indorsement of additional risks will not be insisted upon.

Insurance Co. v. Kittle, 39 Mich. 51; Titus v. Insurance Co., 81 N. Y. 410; Cannon v. Insurance Co., 53 Wis. 585, 11 N. W. Rep. 11; Webster v. Insurance Co., 36 Wis. 67. Where, after a fire, the adjuster of a company joins the agents of other companies in the effort to adjust the loss, requires the production of books for examination, and asks for invoices from the time the insured went into business, and, the invoices not being furnished because of their destruction by fire, then asks for duplicates, which the insured endeavored by correspondence with creditors to get, and objects to settling on the ground only that he cannot agree with the insured 'as to the amount of loss, and offers to pay for his company its proportion of the loss as estimated by him, the company represented by such adjuster is estopped from insisting upon a forfeiture by reason of the breach of any conditions in the policy in reference to taking additional insurance. Fishbeck v. Insurance Co., supra; Argall v. Insurance Co., 84 N. C. 355. See, especially, opinion of COOLEY, J., in Insurance Co. v. Kittle, supra. The testimony admitted after objection, and constituting the ground of exceptions 4, 5, and 7, will therefore appear at a glance to be competent, if our view of the law in reference to waiver by conduct subsequent to the loss, and inconsistent with the idea of insisting upon a forfeiture for failure to comply with the conditions set forth in the policy, be correct. It would follow also from the principle laid down by us that there was no error in so much of his honor's charge as relates to the doctrine of waiver by the acts of the defendant's agents after the property was destroyed, and this applies to the 13th, 18th, and 19th exceptions.

The defendant excepted to the refusal of the court to submit an issue involving the question whether the fact that plaintiff had obtained additional insurance in the other four companies was made known to the defendant before the fire occurred. It does not appear that the refusal of the court to allow the jury to answer such an issue specifically deprived the defendant of the opportunity to have presented to the jury any view of the law arising out of the testimony that was material to his defense, and there was therefore no error in the ruling complained of. McAdoo v. Railroad Co., 105 N. C. 151, 11 S. E. Rep. 316; Emery v. Railroad, 102 N. C. 209, 9 S. E. Rep. 139; Lineberger v. Tidwell, 104 N. C. 510, 10 S. E. Rep. 758; Bonds v. Smith, 106 N. C. 564, 11 S. E. Rep. 322. Indeed, it is apparent that, according to our view of the law governing this case, it is not material whether Primrose and Cowper, the president and adjuster of the defendant company, or the agent, Ramsey, had notice of the additional insurance before the loss, since it is not denied that they had actual notice after the fire, and when Cowper, according to the testimony, so acted as to waive the right of the company to insist upon a forfeiture of the policy. Besides, it seems that, in order to make the issue tendered subserve the proposed purpose, it would be necessary now to amend it by interpolating the words "prior to the loss," and it is rather late to amend defective exceptions in this court.

The ninth exception is stated in the record as follows: "During the morning session of the court, and pending the argument of counsel, the court gave notice to counsel that no special instructions would be considered which were not presented at the convening of court in the afternoon session. Near the conclusion of the speech of Mr. Mason, who closed for the defendant, just at night, the defendant presented the following additional special instructions, which were not considered, for the reason that they were not presented in apt time. Upon the conclusion of the speech of Mr. Mason the court took a recess until after supper, when Mr. Burton closed for the plaintiff." "(11) That the value of the stock of goods burnt is not necessarily the original cost price, with cost of transportation added, for it is testified that the goods are more or less old, and also that a large proportion were bought on time, and that certain per cent. was added for the time price. These facts must be considered by the jury in forming their estimate of the stock. The actual value of the stock may be and should be arrived at by estimating the cash price of such goods as those destroyed at their reasonably best market, and then adding thereto the cost of transportation to Seaboard, and then deduct therefrom the amount of deterioration by reason of the age and the handling of the stock of goods. The balance will be the actual value of the goods. (12) If the plaintiff had a large lot of goods for which there was no demand or market at Seaboard, then the jury will estimate such goods at what they reasonably could have been sold for at the time at Seaboard, or at what they could in their condition have been reasonably sold at the best reasonable market, deducting the cost of transportation." It was not error to refuse to consider written requests for instruction unless presented to the court at or before the close of the testimony. Marsh v. Richardson, 106 N. C. 548, 11 S. E. Rep. 522; Taylor v. Plummer, 105 N. C. 56, 11 S. E. Rep. 266; Powell v. Railroad, 68 N. C. 395. The eleventh exception is stated in the record as follows: "There was evidence tending to support the 11th and 12th instructions asked by the defendant. The plaintiff's evidence tended to show that the costs of the goods with five per cent. added for cost of transportation, amounted to $8,218.31, made up of the amount of inventory taken of August 8, 1889, $5,852.71, and subsequent purchases shown by his ledger account, and certain stocks of goods purchased from assignees, etc., (about $475 worth,) $4,007.68, deducting the amount of sales from August 8th to the time of fire,—$1,478.01 in cash sales, and $1,582.10 in credit sales,—upon which there was an average profit of 30 per cent.; that his purchases were upon 30 days and four months, and that a discount of from 1 to 2 per cent. could have been obtained by purchasing in cash; that the value was at least $7,400. The defendant's evidence tended to show that the value of the stock of goods did not exceed $3,500 or $4,000 at the time of the fire. His honor charged the jury on the second issue that the measure of damage was the fair cash value of goods at the time and place of the fire, and recapitulated the evidence in extenso as to the respective contentions of the parties on the question of damages. The defendant excepted." The rule laid down in this court is substantially the same as that stated for the court by Justice READE in Fowler v. Insurance Co., 74 N. C. 89, and is expressed in almost identical language. In that case, as in ours, a stock of goods had been destroyed by fire, and the court held that "the measure of damages against the defendant is the market value of the goods (within the amount insured) at the time and place of the fire." His honor substituted "fair cash value" for "market value." We can see no material difference between the words used in the opinion referred to and the language of the charge. This court in that case cited May, Ins. § 424, and the authority fully sustains the rule announced. Wood (in his work on Insurance, § 445) says that one who takes out a policy on a stock of goods can recover "only such sum as the goods were actually worth at the time of the loss; not what they cost him, not necessarily what it would cost him to replace the goods, but the sum which the goods were worth when they were destroyed by the casualty insured against." The cost of the property in the market may be shown as one of the elements, but not the test of its value when destroyed; and, on the other hand, it is competent for the insurer to prove that there was a deterioration in the value of the goods after the purchase and before the loss, which, if not resulting merely from temporary depression in the market, will tend to establish the value at the time of the fire. The damage depends upon the ascertainment of the amount for which the property can be sold, and that in turn depends upon its actual value at the time and place of the fire. Wood, Ins. p. 765, § 445; Western Ins. Co. v. Transportation Co., 12 Wall. 201. In Wynne v. Insurance Co., 71 N. C. 125, the court construed the statement that the jury had found "the value of the stock on hand to be $2,600" to mean just the same as if they had found that "the damage on account of the destruction of the goods" was $2,600, thus indirectly giving sanction to the rule laid down by the judge below in this case. In Bobbitt v. Insurance Co., 66 N. C. 70, the court said: "The value of the tobacco was what it was worth then and there,—what it would have sold for then and there;" and it would seem that there is no material difference between this rule and the charge of the judge that the "measure of damage was the fair cash value at the time and place of the fire." It is not material that the court declared that the value of a staple, like tobacco, at any particular point might be determined as well in another way by ascertaining the price in the usual usual markets, and deducting stamp duty, the cost of transportation, and other usual and necessary expenses. But it was not in fact necessary to have passed upon the question of the quantum of damages in that case at all.

The fact that Mr. Johnson, who was a witness for the defendant, and who was present at the bar, and aiding the defendant's counsel in the conduct of the case, was not examined to contradict the plaintiff, Grubbs, as to what occurred when he and Cowper came to adjust the loss, was a legitimate subject of comment, and it was not error to refuse to stop counsel from using the fact as an argument to show that the testimony of Grubbs should be believed. We understand that the twelfth exception was abandoned. It was, at any rate, a waste of time to discuss it. Upon a review of all of the assignments of error we think that there is not sufficient ground for a new trial, and that the judgment below should be affirmed.

MERRIMON, C. J., (dissenting.) The policy upon which this action is founded contains this provision, which is expressly made a material part of the contract of insurance: "This company will not be liable for * * * loss if there be any prior or subsequent insurance, whether valid or invalid, without written consent of the company indorsed hereon." The plaintiffs were not inadvertent to this provision. It clearly appears that they had actual knowledge of and understood its meaning and purpose. It is clear that it was a material part of the contract. It is contended, however, by the plaintiffs that the defendant waived this provision and the condition embodied by it, and this contention is founded upon this evidence: "The witness [one of the plaintiffs] then proceeded to say that after insuring in the defendant company, he had a conversation with Dr. J. N. Ramsey, agent of the defendant company, before he took out additional insurance, telling him that he wanted additional insurance, and that Dr. Ramsey said it would be all right." This witness, in reply to further interrogatories, objected to by the defendant, said: "He told Ramsey that he wanted additional insurance in the Pelican Insurance Company and the Virginia Fire & Marine Insurance Company. The conversation was in his store. That later on he said he wanted additional insurance in the Liverpool & London & Globe Insurance Company, and in the Mt. Vernon Insurance Copmany. That he did not know who was present except his clerk, R. T. Gay. That Ramsey said it would all be right so that he did not take out policies over three-fourths value of the goods. That he had two conversations with Ramsey, and told him that he had an idea of taking additional insurance. That he said it was all right. That he told him that he wanted $2,000 in the Virginia Fire & Marine, and $1,000 in the Pelican. In the second conversation he told him that he wanted $500 in the Liverpool & London & Globe, and $500 in the Mt. Vernon. That these conversations were before the additional insurance was effected." Another witness said he 'heard the conversations between Grubbs and Ramsey. Grubbs said that he did not have insurance sufficient. That Ramsey said it was all right so that he did not get more than three-fourths value of his stock." Dr. J. N. Ramsey, mentioned, testified

"that a few days after he issued the policy to the plaintiff sued on Grubbs said to him that he would want further insurance; that he said to him that he thought that he could get it if he wished it; * * * that he did not know that Grubbs was insured in any other company until after the fire." The plaintiffs obtained additional insurance in other companies, and it was admitted that no written consent was indorsed upon the policy sued upon that the plaintiffs might take such or any additional insurance upon the property insured by the defendant. Now, it seems to me that, putting aside all question as to the authority of Ramsey as agent of the defendant to waive the condition in question, the evidence, accepted as true, did not, in any fair view of it, constitute such waiver. The plaintiffs knew of the condition that, if they took other further insurance without consent on the part of the defendant written on the policy sued upon, the latter would be void. They did not ask Ramsey, the agent, to waive the condition,—to say that further insurance might be taken without consent written on the policy; nor did they give him or the defendant notice that they had taken further insurance; nor did the defendant or its agent have such notice until after the loss. At most they only suggested their desire and purpose to obtain more. Nor did Ramsey tell them that they might take other insurance without having consent of the defendant indorsed on the policy sued upon, and that they might do so without notice to him or the defendant. The fair and just interpretation of what and all that was said by the plaintiffs and Ramsey is that the former suggested their wish and purpose to obtain further insurance, and the latter said in reply they might do so, not exceeding two-thirds of the value of the property insured, in the way and as contemplated by the policy of the defendant held by the plaintiffs. Ramsey did not say they might do otherwise. What motive or reason had he to waive the condition? And what reasonable ground was there to merely infer that he did? And what just reason had the plaintiffs to believe that the agent consented to or intended such waiver? And is it not clear that the plaintiffs carelessly and negligently failed to have the defendant's consent written on the policy, or that they felt apprehensive that the defendant would not consent? Collins v. Insurance Co., 79 N. C. 279; Sugg v. Insurance Co., 98 N. C. 143, 3 S. E. Rep. 732; Havens v. Insurance Co., 111 Ind. 90, 12 N. E. Rep. 137; Healey v. Insurance Co., 5 Nev. 268; May, Ins. §§ 369–372; Wood, Ins. § 496.

It is further contended that the defendant, after the plaintiffs sustained the loss, waived the condition in question, or is estopped to claim and have benefit of the same, in that its agents took steps to ascertain the extent of the loss, with a view to pay what it might be liable for upon the policy. But the defendant's agents did not say their purpose was to waive the condition; nor was there any fair implication that they did; nor was there any consideration for such waiver. The mere fact that such inquiry was made could not reasonably or justly be treated as such waiver or an estoppel. The defendant might, without waiving any right or defense, make such inquiry in order to learn what it ought, without regard to its legal liability, fairly to pay, if anything. It might by such inquiry ascertain whether the loss was fairly sustained, whether the insurance was too great, whether the stock of goods was as great as represented, or whether the same was overvalued, etc. Simply such inquiry ought not to conclude the defendant as to any proper defense it might have. So far as appears, there are no considerations, valuable or otherwise, that in their nature do or ought to so conclude the defendant. It does not appear that the defendant was not in some way prejudiced by the additional insurance. May, Ins. (2d Ed.) § 507. The contract of insurance is plain and unequivocal in the respect in question. The plaintiffs clearly understood its meaning and purpose. It is the duty of the court to uphold and enforce it in its integrity, as it affects the rights created by it of both parties. Reasonably and justly a waiver of any material part, provision, or condition of it, to be effectual, should appear, not by mere conjecture or inference, but by evidence that reasonably tends to prove the same; and the burden in this respect is on the plaintiffs. I do not think there was such evidence in this case.

DAVIE et al. v. DAVIS.

(*Supreme Court of North Carolina.* May 19, 1891.)

RES ADJUDICATA—DISMISSAL.

1. Where, in an action on a bond in a justice's court, it is adjudged, after hearing the evidence, that the suit be dismissed as to one of the defendants on the ground that no obligee was named in the bond at the time such defendant signed it, and plaintiff did not present on the trial any equitable claim he might have had against defendant on account of his having executed said bond, the judgment is one upon the merits, that concludes the parties to all matters that were and could have been pleaded.

2. In an action on a bond evidence is admissible as to whether the merits were inquired into upon rendering a judgment in a justice court in another action on the same bond.

Appeal from superior court, Granville county; BOYKIN, Judge.

Graham & Graham, for appellants. *Edwards & Batchelor,* for appellee.

CLARK, J. The defendant having pleaded that the matter was *res judicata,* by consent the court found the facts. It found "that there had been a trial on the issues involved in this action, and a judgment heretofore had and rendered between the parties hereto, to-wit, before a justice of the peace in this county on 9th June, 1890; that said justice rendered his said judgment solely and entirely upon the ground that it was proven to his satisfaction that there was no obligee named in the bond at the time the defendant executed the same, and that said justice did not hear or consider any equitable claim that the plaintiffs had against the defendant on account of his having executed said bond." This is conclusive; nor is the latter part of the finding contradictory. Unless the former proceeding was terminated by a nonsuit, the judgment therein is conclusive; and it is not a nonsuit, necessarily, because it was in form a judgment against the plaintiff. It is found that the plaintiff failed on the merits, and, though he may have had other merits, or an equitable ground of maintaining the action, it was his own fault he did not present it on the trial, nor appeal from the judgment. The judgment not being a nonsuit, it concludes the parties, not only as to all matters pleaded, but as to all which could or should have been. The former judgment was as follows: "This cause came on for trial after hearing the evidence. It is adjudged that this warrant be dismissed as to Jonathan Davis;" and there was further judgment that the plaintiff recover of the other defendant in that action the amount of the bond sued on, with interest and costs. The plaintiff insisted that this was, as to Jonathan Davis, merely a judgment of nonsuit, and excepted to the admission of evidence as to the proceedings had before the justice. "Evidence of what a justice meant by the judgment in the former action is improper, for the entry must speak for itself; but it is otherwise as to the fact whether the merits were inquired into upon rendering it." *Ferrall* v. *Underwood,* 2 Dev. 111. This was cited and approved in *Justice* v. *Justice,* 3 Ired. 58; *Massey* v. *Lemon,* 5 Ired. 557, and in other cases. No error.

WILLIAMS v. NEVILLE et al.

(*Supreme Court of North Carolina.* May 19, 1891.)

APPOINTMENT OF ADMINISTRATORS—NEXT OF KIN —RENUNCIATION—REMOVAL.

1. Code N. C. § 1378, provides that when any person applies for administration, and any other person has a prior right thereto, a written renunciation of such right must be filed with the clerk of the superior court. *Held,* that a verbal statement made by a person having such right, to one who desires to be appointed, that she will not administer upon an estate, does not constitute a renunciation.

2. A letter, by one having such right to administer, to the clerk of the superior court having jurisdiction, stating that she intends to renounce in favor of her nominee before the clerk of another county, does not constitute a renunciation.

3. Where a person having such right has not renounced or otherwise lost it, it is error to refuse her application to remove an administrator already appointed.

4. Where such person, within the time allowed, has renounced her right in favor of her nominee, it is error to refuse to appoint him.

5. The fact that, pending an appeal from an order refusing to appoint such nominee, the latter has not applied for appointment within the statutory period therefor, will not bar his appointment.

Appeal from an order of BOYKIN, J., overruling an order previously made by Lassiter, clerk of the superior court of Granville county, refusing to remove a creditor who had been appointed administrator, and appoint a person designated by the next of kin of the decedent. The order of the clerk appealed from was as follows: "This motion to remove Alonzo Neville, administrator of Emily Knight, coming on to be heard, and having been heard, and said Alonzo Neville having offered in evidence a letter of one Mrs. Candace Williams, dated 8th September, 1890, to R. W. Lassiter, C. S. C.; also a letter of J. S. Timberlake to him, said clerk, of said date; and the said Alonzo Neville admitting that the renunciation of said Mrs. Candace Williams was duly executed before F. P. Pierce, the subscribing witness, which paper is filed; and no charges being preferred against said administrator,—the court is of opinion that he should not be removed from his office, and that said Mrs. Candace Williams had no right or power to name the administrator of Mrs. Knight. The court finds as a fact, and it is admitted, that said Emily Knight died 8th May, 1890, in Granville Co., and that Mrs. Candace Williams is the next of kin of said deceased, and that said Alonzo Neville is the largest creditor of said estate. From this ruling said Candace Williams and her said appointee appeal," etc.

Battle & Mordecai, N. V. Lanier, and *N. B. Cannady,* for appellants. *Batchelor & Devereux,* for appellee.

AVERY, J., *(after stating the facts as above.)* It is conceded that Candace Williams, being the only sister of the decedent, who left neither husband, child, nor brother her surviving, had the right to administer within six months after her sister's death. She had also the right within that time to select and recommend such person as she might prefer, if she did not wish to administer herself: and, if her nominee was suitable in character, habits, and intellect, to demand his appointment. Little v. Berry, 94 N. C. 433; Ritchie v. McAuslin, 1 Hayw. 220; Pearce v. Castrix, 8 Jones, (N. C.) 71; Wallis v. Wallis, Winst. Eq. 78; Schouler. Ex'rs, § 113. Emily Knight died in Granville county on the 8th day of May, 1890. On the 14th of June, 1890, the clerk of the superior court of Granville county granted letters of administration to the defendant, Alonzo Neville, who was the largest creditor. Candace Williams had not filed any paper renouncing her right as next of kin to administer, but the defendant had visited her at her home in Franklin county, after the death of her sister and before the said 14th of June, and in a conversation then had with her she had declared to him "that she would not have anything to do with and would not administer upon" the estate of the decedent. Code, § 1378, provides that "when any person applies for administration, and any other person has a prior right thereto, a written renunciation of the person or persons having such prior right must be produced and filed with the clerk." It is manifest, therefore, that the language used by the plaintiff in conversation did not, in contemplation of law, amount to a renunciation. In Hill v. Alspaugh, 72 N. C. 404, the court, construing sections 6, 7, and 8 of Battle's Revisal, (Code, §§ 1378-1380,) said: "We think the true intent and meaning of the statute is that the persons primarily entitled to administration shall assert their right and comply with the law within six months after the death of the intestate, and that a party interested, wishing to quicken their diligence within that time, must do so by citation, as prescribed by statute; or if a person, not preferred, applies for administration within six months, he must produce the written renunciation of the person or persons having prior right." It was only after the lapse of six months that the clerk had the right to appoint the "most competent creditor," when plaintiff had neither renounced in writing nor applied for letters for herself or some suitable person selected by her. After the expiration of thirty days, (after June 8, 1890,) the defendant might have applied to the clerk to issue a citation to the plaintiff to show cause why she should not be decreed to have renounced. It was his own folly if, instead of pursuing the course plainly pointed out by the law, he applied for and obtained letters of administration at the expiration of only 36 days after the death of Emily Knight. It was in his power to compel her to renounce or actively assert her right within 20 days. In the absence of such citation, the law gave the plaintiff six months to deliberate and determine whether she would apply for letters of administration to be issued either to herself or her appointee. The appointment of Neville having been made contrary to law, the clerk ought first to have revoked the letters illegally issued to him, upon the motion of the person entitled to administer or to nominate, and then to have allowed a reasonable time for her or her appointee to qualify. Hughes v. Pipkin, Phil. (N. C.) 4. If the plaintiff, in answer to a citation issued in the manner indicated by the law, had claimed the right for herself or another, and the person named by her had been appointed by the court, and had failed or refused within a reasonable time to qualify, then, though the six months had not expired, the clerk would have been authorized by law to appoint another. Stoker v. Kendall, Busb. 242.

On the 8th day of September, 1890, Candace Williams wrote a letter to the clerk, (R. W. Lassiter,) stating that she claimed her right to administer within six months (four months only having then expired) from the death of her sister; that she had given that privilege to J. S. Timberlake, and wished him to revoke the letters of administration, which, as he had ascertained from reading or advertisement, had been granted to the defendant. She insisted also that, as the larger part of the property was in Franklin county, letters ought to be granted by the clerk of the superior court of that county. On the same day (September 8th) J. S. Timberlake also wrote to R. W. Lassiter, clerk, that at the request of plaintiff he had consented to administer on the estate of her sister, Mrs. Knight, and would administer within six months, as he claimed a right to do, but, as the most of her estate was in Franklin county, he expected to administer there. It was evident that J. S. Timberlake had advised her, upon such information as he had, that the clerk of the superior court of Franklin county alone had jurisdiction; whereas, in fact, the court of Granville had acquired sole jurisdiction by first moving in the matter, though its order was subject to revocation on motion of plaintiff. Code, § 1375; Clay-well v. Sudderth, 77 N. C. 287.

On the 1st day of October, 1890, the plaintiff filed before R. W. Lassiter, clerk of the superior court of Granville, the following paper, addressed to Lassiter, clerk: "I, Candace Williams, sister of Mrs. Emily Knight, and entitled to administer on her estate, hereby renounce my right to qualify as such administrator, and request that the clerk of the superior court appoint E. W. Timberlake. I further certify that I am the only sister, living, of the said Emily Knight, and that she had no brother at her death. October 1, 1890." (Signed by Candace Williams and witnessed by F. P. Pierce.) "I am well acquainted with Mrs. Candace Williams, and she is the only living sister of Mrs. Emily Knight. I further know that she has no brother living." (Signed by F. P. Pierce.) On the 27th of October, 1890, the parties, with their attorneys, appeared before said R. W. Lassiter, clerk, when he refused the motion to remove Alonzo Neville, as administrator, resting his ruling in express terms upon the ground that the letter of Candace Williams, dated September 8th, and that of J. S. Timberlake, of the same date, amounted to a total renunciation on her part, and that "Mrs. Candace Williams had no right or power to name the administrator of Mrs. Knight." This ruling was palpably erroneous. In Little v. Berry, supra, this court, conceding that no question had ever been raised as to the right of the next of kin to renounce in favor of a suitable person selected by them where a decedent had died intestate, went further, and, overruling Suttle v. Turner, 8 Jones, (N. C.) 403, declared that the same rule applied in case of the appointment of an administrator *cum testamento annexo*, whether the will was proven and the executor qualified before July 1, 1869, under the provisions of Rev. Code, c. 40, § 2, or after that date, under the Code of Civil Procedure which was then enacted. Code, § 1376; Battle's Revisal, c. 45, § 1. The appeal in that case was from an explicit ruling of the judge below that the next of kin had no right to designate the person who should be appointed in their stead.

The refusal to appoint E. W. Timberlake, who was nominated on October 1st, was error on the part of the clerk, and after the appeal to the judge of the superior court, on the 27th of October, 1890, the clerk had no further control over the matter. The previous notice, dated September 8th, to the effect that the plaintiff expected to renounce before the clerk in Franklin county, in favor of J. S. Timberlake, and ask Lassiter to revoke the letters to Neville, was not, as it was not intended to be, a renunciation of the right to administer, such as would justify the order made. The paper filed October 1st was a formal renunciation in favor of her own nominee, E. W. Timberlake, within less than five months after Mrs.

Knight's death. It was the first renunciation filed, and it was a conditional one. E. W. Timberlake was not required to go before the clerk on the 27th of October, anticipating the action of the clerk with a bond executed in the same sum named in Neville's bond. There is neither precedent nor reason for such practice. Upon his examination as an applicant, under section 1388 of the Code, the clerk might have valued the personal property at a higher figure, after acquiring such information as he could give, than he had previously done. So that the framers of the statute must have contemplated that the amount of bond should depend upon the application and examination of the principal named in it, unless the clerk preferred to examine another person. After the appeal to the superior court on October 27th, E. W. Timberlake was not required to appear before the clerk for the 12 days remaining after the expiration of the whole of the six months, pending the appeal in the higher court, and go through the vain ceremony of tendering a bond in a sum fixed by himself to a clerk who had solemnly declared, as a conclusion of law, that the plaintiff had no right to select him and demand his appointment and Neville's removal. On the 27th of October, 1890, the attorneys of the plaintiff entered the motion, which appears of record, to appoint E. W. Timberlake, in accordance with the request dated October 1, 1890, and it was this motion which was refused on that day, and from which an appeal was then and there taken, as appears from the clerk's order. The fact that Candace Williams and her husband, pending that appeal and before it was heard before BOYKIN, J., at January term, 1891, filed before the clerk a more formal renunciation in favor of E. W. Timberlake, does not affect his right, or her right for him, to insist upon the removal of Neville, and his appointment by reason of the designation on October 1st. After the controversy had been transferred to the superior court in term-time, the clerk had no jurisdiction of the matter. The paper dated "November Term" purports to be only "a ratification of the power I [she] have heretofore given him, E. W. Timberlake," to act as such; evidently referring to the paper of October 1st.

The judge finds as a fact that E. W. Timberlake has never applied for letters of administration. It was a vain and foolish thing to apply, after refusal of an application made in due time to have Neville removed. He could not be appointed till the defendant could be removed, and his removal was to be made, if at all, at the instance of the plaintiff. Garrison v. Cox, 95 N. C. 353.

It was error to refuse to remove Neville when he had been appointed contrary to law. The clerk ought to have removed him, and to have given notice to E. W. Timberlake to qualify within a reasonable time,—say 30 days from service of notice,—and such will be the proper order, when this opinion shall be certified. Wallis v. Wallis, supra. In the case of Stokes v. Kindall, supra, the facts were that a creditor gave notice, as Neville should have done in this case, to one who was the next of kin of a decedent, that he would make application at a certain term of the county court for letters of administration, and at said term the person so notified appeared before the court, and an order was entered appointing him, with the proviso that he should give bond in a sum named. This court said in that case that three months after entering the order of appointment was more than a reasonable time to allow him for filing bond, and on his failure to do so before the next February term, it was proper for the county court to then appoint the creditor. What is reasonable time, when the statute does not fix it, is a question for the court. Hughes v. Pipkin, supra. We think, for the reasons stated, that there was no error in the ruling of the court below that the clerk erred in refusing to remove the defendant, and that the plaintiff, being entitled on the 1st of October to designate a suitable person to act as administrator, and her motion being then refused, has still the right to demand the appointment of E. W. Timberlake, if he be adjudged a suitable person, or to administer herself, or designate another person.

There is no error.

TURNER v. SHUFFLER et al.

(Supreme Court of North Carolina. May 19, 1891.)

SALE OF DECEDENT'S LAND—CLAIMS AGAINST DECEDENT'S ESTATE—LIMITATIONS—PLEA OF STATUTE—PAYMENT BY ADMINISTRATOR OUT OF HIS OWN FUNDS—SUBROGATION.

1. Where, in proceedings to set aside an administrator's sale because made indirectly to the administrator, the referee finds that the sale was not in fact so made, but that it was *bona fide*, and that the purchaser, after paying a fair price, and taking a proper deed, then conveyed the property to the administrator, such finding will not be reviewed on appeal if there was any evidence to warrant it, and if the sale was approved.

2. Where an administrator, being in doubt as to what is properly assets in his hands, inadvertently pays some of the debts of his intestate out of his own funds, he does not thereby become an intermeddler, but is entitled to subrogation to the rights of those creditors whose claims he has paid.

3. Under Code N. C. § 164, providing that, if claims against a decedent's estate are filed within a year after appointment of the administrator, and allowed, it shall not be necessary to bring suit thereon to prevent a bar, claims filed within the year will not be barred by subsequent lapse of time pending the administration, and the statute of limitations cannot be pleaded against them.

4. An answer which pleads the seven-year statute of limitations as a bar to claims of creditors against decedent's estate, without alleging definitely that proceedings were not begun, as required by section 153, subsec. 2, within seven years after the appointment of the administrator, is insufficient; and, although the court might have allowed an amendment, its refusal to do so will not be reviewed.

Appeal from superior court, Burke county; HOKE, Judge.

It appears that Christopher Shuffler died intestate in the county of Burke before the 9th day of August, 1877, and that on that day the plaintiff was duly appointed and qualified as administrator of his estate; that his personal estate was of little

value; that the debts against his estate aggregated several hundred dollars; that the plaintiff applied for and obtained a license to sell certain real estate of his intestate called the "Mill Property," to make assets to pay debts; that this land was sold, and the proceeds of the sale were duly applied as assets to the payment of debts; that other debts remain unpaid; and the present is a special proceeding to obtain a license to sell another tract of land of the intestate to make additional assets to pay such unpaid debts. The defendants, heirs of the intestate, deny the material allegations of the complaint. They allege that the alleged unpaid claims are not just, and that they are barred by the statute of limitations. They further allege that the sale of the land by the plaintiff first above mentioned was void, upon the ground that the plaintiff himself in effect bought the same at his own sale. By consent of parties it was ordered by the court that all matters in controversy between them be referred to a referee named, to take testimony and report to the court the facts and the law arising thereon. The referee took evidence, took and stated an account, reported the same and his findings of fact. To the same the defendants filed divers exceptions, some of which were sustained, and others were overruled by the court. The referee, among other things, found that the claims against the estate of the intestate specified in the account were "presented to the administrator and payment demanded within twelve months from the date of his qualification as administrator, and that he told the creditors that if they would not sue on their claims he would pay all just claims as soon as he had assets in hand sufficient, and that he would not plead the statute of limitations against debts." The defendants' exceptions overruled were these: "(3) That referee's finding that Turner went strictly according to law in the sale of the mill property finds no support whatever in the evidence shown him on the trial, and is in direct conflict with a long train of judicial decisions in this and all the states that an administrator must not buy, directly or indirectly, at his own sale. (4) That the referee erred in omitting to find the plea of the three-year statute of limitations pleaded by the defendants in bar of the plaintiff administrator's right to reimbursement for debts of his intestate paid by him, as he alleged, three years before the commencement of this action, in favor of defendants; and likewise error is alleged in the refusal of the referee to permit defendants to make their former plea of the seven-year statute of limitations (Code, § 153, subsec. 2) more specific in an amended answer tendered by them, and refused by the referee at the hearing of this cause." In the case settled for this court the court says: "Third exception overruled, and report sustained, and the court finds that the sale was *bona fide*, and for fair value, to Galloway, and bought by Turner from him; and, if otherwise, cannot be impeached here. Fourth exception overruled." The defendants assigned as error the overruling of the exceptions above set forth. There was judgment for the plaintiffs, and defendants appealed.

J. T. Perkins and *W. S. Pearson,* for appellants. *S. J. Ervin,* for appellee.

MERRIMON, C. J., (*after stating the facts as above.*) The order of reference was entered by consent of the parties, and the court below, in all respects pertinent and material here, approved the findings of fact by the referee. It is not objected that there was no evidence to warrant such findings. Indeed there was some. That it is not the province of this court to review such findings of fact is well settled by many decisions. Regularly and properly the defendants could not attack collaterally, in this proceeding, the sale of the land made in the former special proceeding mentioned above to make assets to pay debts. That should be done by an action brought for the purpose. Sumner v. Sessoms, 94 N. C. 371; Garrison v. Cox, 99 N. C. 478, 6 S. E. Rep. 124; Smith v. Fort, 105 N. C. 446, 10 S. E. Rep. 914. But if this were not so the defendants' third exception could not be sustained, because the court below distinctly found the fact that the sale of the land complained of was made in good faith, and purchased by one who might buy, and who paid a fair price for it. The sale was ratified by the court, the purchaser took a proper deed therefor, and afterwards conveyed the title he thus bought to the plaintiff. This being true, the defendants' objection is clearly groundless. It seems that they were dissatisfied with the findings of fact, but, as we have said, we cannot review such findings. We can only correct errors in the application of the law to them, and in this respect no error appears in the record. It appears that the plaintiff paid several debts of his intestate with moneys other than such as constituted part of the assets of the estate in his hands, for which he was not allowed credit. It further appears in that connection that he received certain rents that he supposed to be assets, but the same were not allowed to be such, and the court sustained the exception to the allowance of the same by the referee. This and like things done by the plaintiff show that in paying debts of his intestate and charges of administration he was not officiously paying the same with his own funds simply for the purpose of creating a debt in his own favor, whereby he might annoy and prejudice the defendants, but that he did so in good faith. The debt of the estate remaining unpaid is due to the plaintiff on account of moneys advanced and used by him to pay debts of his intestate. The defendants insist that such payments were officious, and also that the same are barred by the pertinent statute of limitations, and they cite and rely in part on Bevers v. Park, 88 N. C. 456. We think such payments by the plaintiff were not officious, but were such as were made through inadvertence in part as to what constituted assets in his hands, and also such as he might have made for the convenience and benefit of the estate. In such case the administrator is entitled to be subrogated to the rights of the creditors whose

debts he so paid with his own funds. In making such payments he was not a mere intermeddler; he simply gave the estate, wherewith he was charged, the temporary benefit of his own funds in the course of administering the same. Williams v. Williams, 2 Dev. Eq. 69; Sanders v. Sanders, Id. 262. It is insisted, however, that he stands in the place of the creditors whose debts he so paid, and their debts were barred by the statute at the time he so paid them. But it does not so appear. It is found as a fact that they were not so barred at the time he paid them; and it further appears that such debts were presented to the administrator, and payment thereof demanded, within one year after the issuing of letters of administration to the plaintiff, and that he took notice of the same as contemplated by the statute, (Code, § 164,) which, among other things, provides that, "if the claim upon which such cause of action is based be filed with the personal representative within the time above specified, [within one year after the issuing of letters testamentary or of administration,] and the same shall be admitted by him, it shall not be necessary to bring action upon such claim to prevent the bar." It seems that the creditors and plaintiff, as to these claims, intended to and did substantially what the clause of the statute just recited allows to be done in such cases. This had the effect to prevent the bar of the statute. If it be said that it does not specifically appear that the claims were not barred at the time they were so presented, still it appears expressly that they were not barred at the time the plaintiff paid them; and hence it must be that they were not at the time they were so presented. They were paid after that time. It has been decided at the present term that claims not barred at the time they were filed with the administrator, as just indicated, will not be barred by subsequent lapse of time pending the administration; nor can the heir plead the statute as to them. Woodlief v. Bragg, ante, 211, (at this term.) The defendants, in their answer, say that they "plead the statutes of limitation of ten, seven, six, and three years, as prescribed in the Code, to all said claims, and aver that they are unable to plead the same more definitely to each and all of said claims." This is clearly bad and insufficient pleading. The court might, in its discretion, have allowed appropriate amendments, but it was not bound to do so; nor is the exercise of its discretion reviewable here. It declined to allow an amendment. It seems that it treated the pleading as sufficient as to the statute barring claims after the lapse of three years; but it refused, as it might do, to recognize the insufficient pleading of any other like statute. The answer is wholly insufficient, in so far as it no more than suggests its purpose to allege that the cause of action was barred by the lapse of seven years. It should, in this respect, have alleged definitely that the special proceedings were not begun "within seven years next after the qualification of the * * * administrator and his making the advertisement required by law for credit-

ors of the deceased to present their claims."
Love v. Ingram, 104 N. C. 600, 10 S. E. Rep.
77. This case is materially different from
Proctor v. Proctor, 105 N. C. 222, 10 S. E.
Rep. 1036. In that case the court did not
take notice or dispose of the imperfect
pleading at all. In this one it refused to
allow an amendment, and treated the insufficient pleading as none at all. Judgment affirmed.

ROGERS et al. v. BANK OF OXFORD.

(Supreme Court of North Carolina. May 19,
1891.)

ACCOUNTING—USURIOUS PAYMENTS—LIABILITY OF
SURETY—EXCEPTIONS TO REFEREE'S REPORT.

1. Plaintiffs sued to enjoin a foreclosure and
compel an accounting between them and defendant. The mortgage was collateral to a bond executed by plaintiffs to secure defendant for such
money as it might thereafter advance to a firm
composed of two of the obligors, in an amount not
exceeding $5,000, such advances to be discounted
after three days, with interest, and the balance
existing one year after date of the bond to become
payable at 8 per cent. interest. The account embraced dealings prior to the execution of the bond,
and also showed that defendant had charged the
firm daily on balances at the rate of 12 per cent.
interest, which it had paid monthly by checks.
Held, that the defendant is entitled to judgment
against the firm for the balance upon the whole
dealings, without regard to the usury, as plaintiffs' remedy for such illegal payments was by
action to recover the same within two years, under Code N. C. § 3836, and equity could not relieve plaintiffs, as such payments of usury were
transactions distinct from the indebtedness to defendant.

2. The surety on the bond is liable only for
the balance of the money so advanced by defendant, with interest at 8 per cent. after one year,
said balance to be ascertained by allowing defendant interest at 6 per cent. on the advances, it
not being within the meaning of the bond that
the surety should be liable for usurious interest.

3. Where plaintiffs omitted to file exceptions
to the referee's report, but, at a term when a
final amended report under a re-reference was
filed, filed a motion in writing embracing specified objections to such report, having all the effect
of exceptions thereto, and no objection is made
by defendant, the hearing and overruling of such
motion cures any irregularity as to the time of
filing same.

Appeal from superior court, Granville
county; MACRAE, Judge.

The plaintiffs executed to the defendant
a bond, whereof the following is a copy:
"$5,000. Oxford, N. C., Nov. 1, 1886. For
value received, we, John B. Booth, J. F.
Rogers, and C. M. Rogers, hereby acknowledge ourselves jointly and severally bound
to the Bank of Oxford in the sum of five
thousand dollars, and hereby also bind
our heirs, executors, administrators and
assigns. Witness our hands and seals the
day and date above written. The foregoing obligation is made to secure the
Bank of Oxford for such amounts, not exceeding five thousand dollars, as it may
advance to said John B. Booth and J. F.
Rogers, firm of Booth & Rogers, who propose to trade and deal in leaf tobacco.
The amount due at any time shall be evidenced by the account which the Bank of
Oxford agrees to open with said Booth
and Rogers, and is to include and secure
all amounts drawn by them for any pur-

pose whatsoever. All advances under this
agreement may be discontinued by the
Bank of Oxford upon three days' notice.
and the account shall stand for settlement
in fifteen days thereafter, when the balance shall be considered due and payable.
If not paid, interest thereafter shall be at
eight per cent. per annum. This agreement terminates on the 31st day of October, 1887, and the obligors hereto shall be
held bound for whatever balance may then
appear to be due the said Bank of Oxford,
with interest thereafter at the rate of
eight per cent. per annum. Witness:
JOHN B. BOOTH. [Seal.] J. F. ROGERS.
[Seal.] C. M. ROGERS. [Seal.]" The defendant had loaned to Booth & Rogers,
the firm mentioned therein, large sums of
money before the date of this bond, and
it claimed a considerable balance as due
it from them at that time on account of
former dealings. As contemplated by the
bond, the defendant advanced to the firm
large sums of money between its date and
the time the agreement therein specified
terminated. It charged the firm interest
for the money it loaned them from time to
time at the rate of 12 per centum per annum, and this was charged and paid
monthly. In addition to the bond above
set forth, the plaintiff J. F. Rogers executed to the defendant a mortgage of a valuable tract of land to secure it as to moneys
it might advance to the said firm The defendant claimed that the firm mentioned
owed it a large balance on account of such
advancements, and was proceeding to sell
the land embraced by the mortgage referred to by virtue of a power of sale therein contained to pay such balance. The
plaintiffs brought this action to prevent
such sale, and compel the defendant to an
account and settlement of the dealings
and transactions between them and it, alleging that they in fact owed it very little,
if anything, etc. The defendant admitted
some of the allegations of the complaint,
and denied many of the material ones.
The sale of the land was stayed pending
the action by injunction. The court, in
the course of the action, by order appointed a referee to find the material facts, and
to take and state an account, and make
report of the same. Accordingly, the facts
were found, the account stated, and report
thereof filed. The defendant filed exceptions thereto, which the court overruled.
At a subsequent term, on the coming in of
an amended report, the plaintiffs did not
file formal exceptions, but filed a motion
in writing, objecting to sundry items of
charge, and, among these, charges of usury exacted by the defendant, etc. The
court overruled the motion thus made,
confirmed the report, gave judgment in favor of the defendant for the balance as ascertained to be due it from the plaintiffs,
and directed a sale of the land mentioned,
etc. The plaintiffs, having excepted, appealed to this court.

Battle & Mordecai, M. V. Lanier, and *N.
B. Cannady,* for appellants. *L. C. Edwards* and *Batchelor & Devereux,* for appellee.

MERRIMON, C. J., *(after stating the facts
as above.)* The order of reference to a ref-

dree to find the material facts and state the necessary account was entered by the court without objection from either of the parties. It was therefore entered by consent. The referee filed his report, and, the defendant having filed exceptions thereto, they were overruled. There was a re-reference and an amended report. The court approved the findings of fact. These findings are not reviewable here. Wadesboro v. Atkinson, 107 N. C. 317, 12 S. E. Rep. 202, and cases there cited.

The plaintiffs did not formally file exceptions to the report of the referee, but at the term when the final amended report was filed they "moved," without objection, so far as appears, to exclude certain items of charge and other charges of interest, which the plaintiffs insisted represented certain usury exacted from them by the defendant. This motion in writing embraced several specified objections to the report, and it was, in effect, exceptions thereto, and should have been so treated. It served the purpose of exceptions as effectually as if it had been so called. It was insisted on the argument that, if it should be treated as exceptions, they were not made in apt time. They were made at the term when the completed report was filed. But, if it be granted that they should have been made when the report was at first filed, there was no objection to filing them on the part of the defendant, and the court entertained and overruled them. This had the effect to cure any irregularity as to the time of filing the same. So that such exceptions must be treated for all pertinent purposes as having been made. But, if such exceptions had not been filed, it was nevertheless competent for the plaintiffs to move and insist before the court that it should, upon the record, including the findings of fact and the report, enter a particular judgment asked for by them, and, if the court had declined to grant the same, they might have assigned error. The defendant might have done the like. This is so, because it was the duty of the court to inspect the whole record, and enter such judgment as it would properly warrant. Indeed, in such case, the appellant might take advantage of error in the judgment in this court, in the absence of any formal assignment of error, if the error appeared in the face of the record. Code, § 957; Thornton v. Brady. 100 N C. 38, 5 S. E. Rep. 910; Bush v. Hall, 95 N. C. 82; State v. Watkins, 101 N. C. 702, 8 S. E. Rep. 346; McKinnon v. Morrison, 104 N. C. 354, 10 S. E. Rep. 513.

One leading purpose of this action is to compel an account and settlement of the dealings and transactions between the plaintiffs Booth and J. F. Rogers, trading and doing business as partners under the name of Booth & Rogers, and the defendant, during the whole period beginning on the 11th day of November, 1885, and ending at the time of taking the account. Adverting, now, to this view of the case, it appears from the report of the referee that the defendant exacted from the firm considerable sums of usury. The plaintiffs insist that such sums shall be placed to their credit in stating the account. The defendant, on the contrary, objects,

and contends that this cannot be done, because, granting that the usury was exacted, it was actually paid by the firm more than two years next before this action began; and, moreover, its exaction and payment was a transaction concluded, distinct, separate, and apart from the indebtedness of the firm to the defendant on account of money advanced to them from time to time. It certainly appears that the defendant charged the firm interest daily on balances in their favor at the rate of 12 per centum per annum, and at the end of each month they paid the same by their check on their deposit with the defendant. It is clear that the firm gave their check from time to time, and the defendant received the same as payment for the interest so exacted. The mere fact that the firm paid such rate of interest reluctantly—did not want to do so— could not defeat the purpose of payment and the legal character of the transaction. The exaction was illegal, and the firm might afterwards have recovered back twice the amount of interest so paid, if it had brought its action for the purpose within two years next after such payment; but it did not do so, and it is now too late. Code, § 3836. It was insisted on the argument that the court in the exercise of its jurisdiction in equitable matters could and would grant relief to the extent of the usury exacted. This it might do, if the interest had not been actually paid as a transaction separate and distinct from the indebtedness of the firm to the defendant. There was a clear purpose of the parties to treat the matter of interest as apart and distinct from the advancement of money to the firm, however reluctantly the latter paid the usurious rate. Cobb v. Morgan, 83 N. C. 211.

A second purpose of the action is to ascertain and determine the measure of the liability of the plaintiffs to the defendant upon the bond specified in the pleadings. It was contemplated and expected by the parties that the defendant would from time to time, between the 1st day of November, 1886, and the 31st day of October, 1887, lend—"advance"—to the business firm of Booth & Rogers considerable sums of money, and the purpose of the bond in question was to secure to the defendant any balance, not exceeding $5,000, that the firm might owe it upon the termination of such loans as contemplated and provided by the bond. It did not in terms or by just implication embrace any balance or balances of money advanced to the firm before or after the period above specified; there is nothing in it that intimates such purpose. The obligation was to secure such balance of such sums of money as the defendant "may advance" to the firm, not of such sums as it had advanced, and the agreement, by its express terms, was to be at an end on a day specified. The provision of the condition of the bond, that "it is to include and secure all amounts drawn by them [the firm] for any purpose whatsoever," does not imply for all possible purposes. It must be interpreted as extending to amounts drawn for any lawful purpose pertinent to and within the meaning of the business specified of the firm. It is not to be presumed that the parties contemplated any unlawful purpose, or business transactions or practices other than such as were legitimate, if the same were within the knowledge of the defendant. Hence it was not expected that the defendant would advance to the firm from time to time large sums of money, and exact interest therefor at the rate of 12 per centum per annum. It was not within the meaning of the bond that the dealings between the defendant and the firm, as to the purpose specified, should be based upon such an unlawful rate of interest. Nor did the obligors in the bond agree to pay the balance of such advances of money ascertained by the allowance of unlawful rates of interest. In view of the nature of the matter, it may be fairly said, in the absence of any stipulated rate of interest, that they expected the defendant would charge and receive for the use of its money so advanced the lawful interest; that is, interest at the rate of 6 per centum per annum. By reasonable implication, it came within the scope of the agreement of the obligors of the bond that they would pay the balance of the money so advanced, allowing the defendant the lawful rate of interest. They certainly expecte i that the defendant would " advance"—lend —the firm money, and as certainly that the bank would demand and the firm would pay interest, and at the lawful rate Hence, in ascertaining the balance for which the obligors of the bond are liable as such, the defendant can only be allowed interest at the rate of 6 per centum per annum, and interest upon the balance ascertained at the rate of 8 per centum per annum, because the latter rate as to the balance was stipulated for in the bond. The plaintiffs Booth and J. F. Rogers are before the court as partners, composing the firm of Booth & Rogers, and also as individuals, and the defendant is entitled to judgment against them for the balance of money due it upon their whole dealings and transactions with it, embraced by the pleadings, without regard to the usury paid, and to have the mortgage specified in the pleadings foreclosed, and the land embraced by it sold to that end, if need be; but the defendant is entitled to have judgment against the plaintiff Clinton M. Rogers for the balance of moneys, not exceeding $5,000, advanced to the firm of Booth & Rogers during the period specified in the bond; that balance to be ascertained by allowing the defendant interest for the use of the money so advanced at the rate of 6 per centum per annum, and interest on such balance at the rate of 8 per centum per annum. The account and judgment must be modified in accordance with this opinion, and, as thus modified, affirmed. To that end let the opinion be certified to the superior court. It is so ordered.

<hr>

STATE v. LEWIS.

(Supreme Court of North Carolina. Dec. 22, 1890.)

For majority opinion, see 12 S. E. Rep. 457.

<hr>

SHEPHERD, J., (concurring.) I concur in the decision upon the grounds first stated in the opinion of the court. As the other questions are of much importance, and, to my mind, not free from difficulty, and as their consideration is unnecessary to the disposition of this appeal, I do not desire to be understood as agreeing to all that has been said in reference to them.

Reversed.

<hr>

OZBURN v. STATE.

(Supreme Court of Georgia. April 24, 1891.)

CRIMINAL LAW — IMPANELING JURY—JUSTIFIABLE HOMICIDE—INSTRUCTIONS — CHARACTER—ARGUMENTS OF COUNSEL.

1. When, on the trial of a felony, several of the jury have been selected, and one of them becomes sick, it is not error to excuse him, and then proceed regularly to complete the panel to the number of twelve; and this the court may do without summoning a physician to determine that the juror is sick.

2. On the trial of a murder case the court was requested in writing to give in charge to the jury the sections of the Code relating to the law of voluntary manslaughter and of justifiable homicide, and complied with the request as made, except as to justifiable homicide; and, it plainly appearing that in no view of the case the law of justifiable homicide was applicable, no error was committed.

3. When, on a trial for murder, the court failed to instruct the jury they could find the defendant guilty of voluntary manslaughter, and no error is assigned on such failure, either in the motion for a new trial or bill of exceptions, the question whether or not such failure was error is not before this court for review.

4. A witness who testifies to the good character of a defendant for peaceableness, and that he had never heard of defendant having a difficulty before, may be asked on cross-examination if he had never heard of defendant's shooting any one before, and if he had never heard of his shooting a man in another state.

5. On the trial of a murder case counsel for the state may comment before the jury upon the propriety or impropriety of their recommending imprisonment for life as a punishment.

6. A specified portion of the court's charge concerning the defendant's statement being in the main correct, an exception to the same as a whole, not alleging any particular portion thereof to be erroneous, cannot be considered. In this case there is nothing in the charge complained of requiring a new trial. In charging concerning statements made by defendants, courts should confine themselves to the language of the statute upon this subject, and not indulge in extended comments upon the effect to be given to such statements.

(Syllabus by the Court.)

Error from superior court, Fulton county; R. H. CLARK, Judge.

Hulsey & Bateman and C. T. Ladson, for plaintiff in error. C. D. Hill, Sol. Gen., and W. D. Ellis, for the State.

LUMPKIN, J. 1. After eleven jurors had been selected, but not sworn in chief, and, by direction of the court, had been kept together for a day and night, one of them became sick, and was unable to serve. The court satisfied himself of the juror's illness, which he certainly had a right to do without summoning a physician, and then discharged him, and proceeded regularly until two other jurors were selected, and the panel completed. There was no error in this conduct of the court. See Pannell v. State, 29 Ga. 681, and Hanvey v. State, 68 Ga. 612. In the latter case it appears that the juror did present a certificate of a physician that he was unable to serve; but it further appears that the judge himself, counsel consenting, heard the juror's excuse under oath, and determined therefrom that he was, on account of his sickness, unable to serve. It is immaterial how the fact of sickness is shown, if the judge is satisfied it exists. The consent of counsel was unnecessary to the validity of the court's action.

2. Defendant's counsel presented to the court a request in writing, which was as follows: "The defendant's counsel request that the court give in charge to the jury the sections of the Code defining and relating to the law of voluntary manslaughter and of justifiable homicide." It appears from an examination of the record that the court complied literally with this request, except so far as it related to justifiable homicide. He read to the jury the sections of the Code defining voluntary manslaughter, and explained to them distinctly the difference between murder and manslaughter, emphasizing the fact that the chief distinction between these two offenses was that in murder malice must exist, while in manslaughter there was an absence of malice. In no possible view of the case would a charge concerning justifiable homicide have been legal or proper. Indeed, the zealous and faithful counsel for the prisoner who argued the case before this court virtually conceded that the law of justifiable homicide had nothing to do with it. We therefore find no reason in this ground of the motion for granting a new trial.

3. The court, when instructing the jury as to the form of their verdict, did not state to them that they might find the defendant guilty of voluntary manslaughter. There was no request made to this effect; nor was any complaint made, either in the motion for a new trial or in the bill of exceptions, of the failure of the court to so instruct the jury. The question, therefore, is not made by this record, and cannot now be adjudicated, whether such failure was error or not. It was argued before us that the court ought to have distinctly told the jury that they could convict this defendant of voluntary manslaughter, but the fact that he did not do this is, as already stated, nowhere assigned as error. But suppose this had been done, would any benefit therefrom have resulted to the plaintiff in error? Taking the entire charge together, it in effect amounted to instructing the jury that if they should believe the defendant was guilty of voluntary manslaughter, they must acquit him. The judge plainly and clearly defined what was necessary to constitute murder, and told the jury, in substance, that unless they believed the defendant guilty of this offense, they must find him not guilty. In one view this charge was more favorable to the defendant than he had any right to expect or demand, because, following it, the result would have been an acquittal, even though the jury believed he was guilty of voluntary manslaughter. Be this as it may, we think it is clear from the record in this case that, if the judge had plainly instructed the jury they could convict of this offense, they would not have done so. If there had been the slightest inclination on the part of the jury to reduce this crime below the grade of murder they would most assuredly have recommended imprisonment for life, and thus have averted the penalty of death. The fact that they found the defendant guilty without making such recommendation is absolutely conclusive that in no event would they have rendered a verdict of voluntary manslaughter. This conclusion is fortified by the fact that the judge in his charge plainly and repeatedly told them that the penalty must be death unless they recommended life-time imprisonment, and used language which must have impressed upon them in the most solemn and emphatic manner the grave responsibility which rested upon them of deciding whether this man should be sent to the penitentiary or the gallows.

4. After a witness for the defendant had sworn that he knew the defendant, and had known him for a long time; that his character for peaceableness was good, and he had never heard of his having any difficulty at all,—it was not error to allow the state's counsel, on cross-examination, to ask the witness if he had never heard of defendant shooting any one before, and also, if the witness had never heard of his shooting a man in another state. A knowledge of character is derived from general reputation, and, the witness having sworn in effect that the reputation of the defendant was good as a peaceable man, and that he had never heard anything to the contrary, it was certainly allowable, on cross-examination, to sift the witness as to the accuracy of his testimony and the sincerity of the statements made by him. What the witness heard would not, of course, be evidence of the truth thereof, nor would it be proper to go into details of the occurrences referred to, but to the extent indicated the questions were proper, and the answers thereto admissible. Section 3874 of the Code, as to impeached witnesses, is as follows: "The witness may be sustained by similar proof of character; but the particular transactions, or the opinions of single individuals, cannot be inquired of on either side, except upon cross-examination, in seeking for the extent and foundation of the witness' knowledge." In Reg. v. Wood, 5 Jur. 225, the defendant put his character in issue, and a witness deposed to having known him for some years, gave him a good character, and stated that he had never heard anything against him. On cross-examination the witness was asked if he had never heard that defendant was suspected of having committed a robbery in the neighborhood some years previous. The question was allowed. PARKE, B., remarking: "The question is not whether the prisoner was guilty of that robbery, but whether he was suspected of having been implicated in it. A man's character is made up of a number of small circumstances, of which his being

suspected of misconduct is one." This case is cited approvingly in 1 Taylor on Evidence, § 352, and the author says: "But if, with the view of raising a presumption of innocence, witnesses to character are called for the defense, the counsel for the crown may then rebut this presumption by cross-examining the witnesses, either as to particular facts, or, if they deem it essential, as to the ground of their belief." Reg. v. Wood is also cited approvingly in Best on Evidence, § 261, where the doctrine is also laid down that, when a defendant in a criminal prosecution puts his character in issue, the prosecutor may encounter his evidence either by cross-examination or by contrary testimony. In Abbott's Trial Brief of Criminal Causes, § 473, we find the following: "A witness who has testified to the good character of the accused may be asked on cross-examination if he has not heard of a specific charge against the accused;" citing Ingram v. State, 67 Ala. 67, which was a murder case, wherein it was held: "The shadings, as well as the brighter hues, are to be considered in making up the estimate of character and reputation; and when a witness has testified that he knew the character of the accused for peace and quietude, and that it was good, it is not error to allow him to be asked on cross-examination if he had not been informed that the defendant had 'killed a man in the state of Georgia,' and his answer was admissible in evidence." Reg. v. Wood, supra, and De Arman v. State, 71 Ala. 351, are also cited by the author in support of this proposition. The ruling of this court in Harris v. State, 61 Ga. 359, is not in conflict with the view expressed in this case on the point under consideration. In that case the court asked the witness, who had testified to defendant's peaceable character, if he had not heard that defendant once beat his wife with a butcher's file. It was held that, while the presiding judge may ask pertinent questions, he should not exercise this right in such manner as to intimate an opinion against the prisoner, and for this reason it was decided that it was improper for the court to ask the question. Another decision of this court, seemingly at variance with our ruling on this question in the case at bar, is that rendered in Pulliam v. Cantrell, 77 Ga. 563, 3 S. E. Rep. 280. It was there held that it was proper to refuse to allow a witness who testified to the good character of another witness to be asked on cross-examination if the latter had not been found a defaulter of public funds, or if the witness testifying had never heard he had been so found; but Judge Jackson distinctly states the question was not asked to show the foundation or extent of the witness' knowledge of the character of the person of whom he was testifying, but that it was an effort to prove a conviction of embezzlement by hearsay, which was, of course, improper. Taking the ruling in connection with the fact stated, it is not at all in conflict with our decision as to the question asked the witness Camp in the present case.

5. Under our law juries trying murder cases have the right to avert the death penalty by recommending life imprisonment, and it is therefore not improper for counsel to argue before them the question whether or not they should so recommend. It may not be proper for counsel to state that they should not recommend life imprisonment because the governor of the state might pardon the defendant, and he would therefore be set free; but, if such a statement is made, and the attention of the court is not called to it, and he is not asked to make any ruling thereon, it will afford no ground for a new trial.

6. One ground of the motion for a new trial assigned as error the following charge of the court: "If, however, you choose to give the statement force, then you must consider the degree of force you will give it; and the law, in its tenderness, goes so far as to place it within the province of the jury to allow them to give it force, if they choose, to the extent of believing it in preference to the sworn testimony. But the statement should have no greater force than evidence. It is to be measured as the law measures testimony. Evidence introduced by the state against the defendant is intended to be inculpating; that is, it is meant to tend in the direction of guilt. The statement of the defendant, to have any effect, should be upon the other side. It should be exculpatory upon legal grounds." This is an extract from a lengthy charge by the court concerning the defendant's statement. So much of it as precedes the words: "But the statement should have no greater force than evidence. It is to be measured as the law measures testimony,"—is undoubtedly correct; and, as no particular portion of it is alleged to be erroneous, the exception taken is too general, in accordance with established rules, to be considered. If it means that the entire charge objected to is erroneous, this is not sound, because much of it is good law; and if complaint is intended to be made of some part thereof the same should be specified. We are therefore constrained to hold that no assignment of error is properly set forth in this ground. We gather, however, from the argument before us that the part of the charge intended to be complained of is that beginning with the words last above quoted, and extending to the end. Suppose, then, this exception had been properly taken, would it have been sufficient to require a new trial? The motion alleges that the charge is erroneous because it is dubious and misleading, because it deprived the statement of the potentiality given it by law, and because it amounts to saying the statement cannot avail defendant where not in conflict with the evidence. We do not think these objections are well taken. As to the first, it may be true that the charge was dubious, but we do not think it misled the jury as to their right to believe the statement. We have endeavored earnestly to ascertain what the court did mean by some of the expressions used. By the words: "But the statement should have no greater force than evidence. It is to be measured as the law measures testimony,"—it is obvious that the court referred to the probative value of the statement, and not

to the question of its credibility. He could not have meant to refer to the latter, because he had just told the jury they could believe the statement in preference to the evidence, and emphasized this assertion by saying the law in its tenderness allowed this much weight to be given to a prisoner's statement. In other words, we think the idea conveyed by the court's language was this: "A fact established by a statement is to have no greater value than a fact established by evidence; that is, a fact proved to the satisfaction of the jury is simply a fact for whatever it is worth, and should have no more force and effect because it is made to appear by the prisoner's statement than the same fact would have if sworn to by a credible witness." There is a manifest difference between the question: Shall the jury believe a thing asserted by the prisoner to be the truth? and the question: Assuming the thing asserted to be true, what effect has it in determining what conclusion in the case shall be reached? This is the distinction we think the court intended, and we are sustained in placing this construction upon the court's language, because he immediately proceeded, in effect, to instruct the jury that, to be available to defendant, the statement must be exculpatory in its effect. By this he undoubtedly meant to say that, no matter how true and credible a statement might be, the facts contained in it must be pertinent to the issue, and must set up a legal defense in order to be of practical benefit to the accused. Taking the entire charge together, we repeat we are satisfied that the jury were not misled as to the legal effect which they might give to the statement, and that they fully understood it to be their right and privilege, if they saw proper, to believe the statement in preference to the sworn testimony. It is quite evident that they did not believe the statement at all. If they had, they would undoubtedly have exercised the power given them by law of saving the defendant from the penalty of death by recommending imprisonment for life. The statement is improbable, inconsistent with the sworn testimony of disinterested witnesses, and made by the defendant under the strong temptation to say anything he could which might save him from death or a term in the penitentiary. Taken in the best possible view, it would make him unquestionably guilty of voluntary manslaughter, and, as we have already shown, the jury had no disposition to convict him of that offense. It is quite plain, from a careful examination of the entire record, that they believed him guilty of murder, and that they rejected his statement altogether, although they must have understood they had the right to believe it if they saw proper. In this connection we will state that it would be a much wiser and safer practice for our brethren on the circuit bench in charging concerning statements made by defendants to confine themselves to the language of the statute upon this subject, and not indulge in extended comments upon the effect to be given to such statements. This course on their part will relieve them and this court

of much embarrassment and difficulty arising from a contrary practice.

The evidence discloses that an atrocious, unprovoked, and deliberate murder was committed by the defendant. The verdict finding him guilty and imposing upon him the penalty of death, in our opinion, renders exact and substantial justice. After a thorough, careful, and anxious examination of the entire record we are fully convinced that the judgment of the court below should stand. It is well known that juries are reluctant to take away by their verdicts the lives of their fellow-creatures; and when good men, in the faithful and conscientious discharge of a painful duty, enforce and vindicate the law, as the jury in this case undoubtedly did, we do not feel authorized to discourage them, and others who may try such cases in the future, by setting aside a verdict which is manifestly right. Judgment affirmed.

JOHNSON v. BRADSTREET CO.

(Supreme Court of Georgia. March 28, 1891.)

ACTION FOR LIBEL—DEATH OF PLAINTIFF—ABATEMENT.

Under section 2967 of the Code, as amended by the act of 1889, (Acts 1889, p. 73,) an action for libel, pending at the time the act passed, does not abate upon the death of the plaintiff.

(Syllabus by the Court.)

Error from city court of Atlanta; VAN EPPS, Judge.

T. C. Mayson, J. T. Glenn, Arnold & Arnold, and *T. P. Westmoreland,* for plaintiff in error. *N. J. & T. A. Hammond* and *Candler & Thomson,* for defendant in error.

LUMPKIN, J. The question presented for our determination in this case is whether or not an action for libel, brought before the passage of the act recited in the headnote, and pending when the act was passed, is abated by the death of the plaintiff. It appears that Johnson died September 1, 1890, which was, of course, after the passage of the act. It does not appear from the particular record now before us on the present hearing of this case whether or not the suit was brought before the passage of the act referred to, but we learn from statements of counsel that such is the fact. Besides, this same case came to this court in the life-time of Johnson, the intestate of the plaintiff in error. See Johnson v. Bradstreet Co., 81 Ga. 425, 7 S. E. Rep. 867. The record there shows the case was brought before the passage of the act. It will thus be seen that the case was pending when the act passed, and that Johnson died thereafter. We have considered and determined the case with reference to these facts. The act undoubtedly applies to cases brought after its passage, and no reason appears, or was suggested to us in the argument, why it should not apply to pending suits. The language of the act is sufficiently comprehensive to include pending actions, and we hold that it does. No position to the contrary was either taken or insisted upon by counsel for the defendant in error. The only contention presented by the discussion of the case was whether or not the section as amended applied to actions for libel. It is unquestionably true that, before the section was amended, such an action would not have survived the death of the plaintiff. The amending act provides that no action "for homicide, injury to person, or injury to property shall abate by death." If the words "injury to person" are to be restricted to mere bodily or physical injuries, an action for libel would be abated by the death of the plaintiff, but if these words are held to extend to all injuries to person, then such action would not be so abated. In our opinion these words are used in a technical legal sense, and should be construed accordingly. Some light is thrown upon the question at issue by reference to the position which the amended section occupies in the Code. Title 8, pt. 2, of the Code treats of "torts, or injuries to persons or property." Chapter 2 of that article deals with "injuries to the person." This chapter is divided into three articles. The first treats of "physical injuries," the second of "injuries to reputation," and the third of "other injuries to the person." According to this classification it will be seen that injuries to reputation are included in the chapter dealing generally with injuries to the person. The article relating to physical injuries treats only of injuries to the body; that relating to reputation includes and defines libel and slander; and the remaining article of that chapter deals with still other personal injuries, such as false imprisonment, malicious arrest, and injuries to health. All of the foregoing injuries, as has been shown, are classed under the general subdivision covering injuries to the person. It is more than probable that the legislature, in making this new law a part of the Code, intended that it should harmonize with its surroundings; and in amending this section it was doubtless their deliberate purpose that the words used in the amending act should be construed and understood with reference to the existing arrangement and classification of the law of torts, in which this new law found its place. If, however, the meaning of the words "injury to person" cannot be determined by the position of the amended section in the Code, it may be arrived at by reference to the common law. At common law absolute personal rights were divided into personal security, personal liberty, and private property. The right of personal security was subdivided into protection to life, limb, body, health, and reputation. 3 Bl. Comm. 119. If the right to personal security includes reputation, then reputation is a part of the person, and an injury to the reputation is an injury to the person. Under the head of "security in person," Cooley includes the right to life, immunity from attacks and injuries, and to reputation. Cooley, Torts, (2d Ed.) 23, 24. See, also, Pol. Torts, *7. Bouvier classes among absolute injuries to the person, batteries, injuries to health, slander, libel, and malicious prosecution. 1 Bouv. Law Dict. (6th Ed.) 636. "Person" is a broad term, and legally includes, not only the physical body and members, but also every bodily sense and personal attribute, among

which is the reputation a man has acquired. Reputation is a sort of right to enjoy the good opinion of others, and is capable of growth and real existence, as an arm or leg. If it is not to be classed as a personal right, where does it belong? No provision has been made for any middle class of injuries between those to person and those to property, and the great body of wrongs arrange themselves under the one head or the other. Whether viewed from the artificial arrangement of law-writers or the stand-point of common sense, an injury to reputation is an injury to person; and oftentimes an injury of this sort causes far more pain and unhappiness, to say nothing of actual loss of money or property, than any physical injury could possibly occasion. As already suggested, it is of great importance to arrive, if possible, at the intention of the legislature as to the meaning to be given to the words "injury to person." We have endeavored to show that the legislative intent may, to some extent, be arrived at by reference to the place in the Code which the amended section occupies; and we have also endeavored to show that the common-law meaning of the words "injury to person" includes libel, slander, and the like. Having reached this point in the discussion, we may also invoke another rule for the construction of statutes, viz.: that where words have a definite and well-settled meaning at common law, it is to be presumed, unless some good reason to the contrary appears, that this same meaning attaches to them when used in a statute. In Suth. St. Const. § 253, we find the following: "Where a statute uses a word which is well known and has a definite sense at common law, or in the written law, without defining it, it will be restricted to that sense, unless it appears that it was not so intended." Again, in § 291, that author says: "In all doubtful matters, and when the statute is in general terms, it is subject to the principles of the common law. When words of definite signification therein are used in such provisions, and there is no intention manifest that they are to be taken in a different sense, they are to be deemed employed in their known and defined common-law meaning." The same rule is laid down by Endlich, who says: "Where a term used in a statute has acquired at common law a settled meaning, that is ordinarily the technical meaning which is to be given to it in construing the statute." Endl. Interp. St. § 3. And to the same effect see, also, Id. § 127. The legislature having considered this subject of sufficient importance to pass this amending act, we must presume they intended to give these words their legal meaning and effect, as there is no good reason to conclude that they intended to use them in such a restricted sense as would confine them alone to bodily or physical injuries.

After considerable labor and research, we have been unable to find many authorities outside of this state bearing directly upon the question under discussion. A Texas case seems, at first glance, to hold contrary to the doctrine we have herein asserted. In the case of Engelking v.

Von Wamel, 26 Tex. 469, it was held that an act which gave to justices' courts cognizance "over all suits for torts, trespass, and other injuries to person or property," where the amount sought to be recovered did not exceed $100, did not include actions for slander. WHEELER, C. J., remarks that, while "libel and slander, according to Blackstone and other elementary writers, are infractions of the right of personal security, and are treated by them under the general denomination of injuries affecting the rights of persons," and are, "as understood by the legal profession, injuries to the person," yet it was not to be supposed the legislature intended by the language used to give to justices of the peace jurisdiction over such actions, because it would be the exercise of a novel, difficult, and very inconvenient jurisdiction for them, such as, it was not to be conceived, the legislature had in contemplation in framing the statute. This decision, therefore, seems to be based mainly upon the idea that it was improbable the legislature of Texas intended to confer upon justices' courts jurisdiction of this kind; but it will be observed the court recognized the rule that libel and slander may, in a technical sense, be regarded as injuries to the person. The case of Ward v. Blackwood, 41 Ark. 295, holds contrary to the conclusion we have reached in this case. Construing a statute containing the words "for wrongs done to the person or property of another," they were held to relate only to bodily injuries or damages of a physical character, and not to extend to torts affecting the feelings or reputation. The case last mentioned cites Smith v. Sherman, 4 Cush. 408, Nettleton v. Dinehart, 5 Cush. 543, and Norton v. Sewall, 106 Mass. 145, and an examination of them shows that they are in point. Notwithstanding these decisions, and others on the same line which might be found, we adhere to our own conclusion, and are fortified, we think, in so doing by what has already been said concerning the place which the amended section occupies in our Code. Aside from this, the following authorities seem to sustain our judgment in the case before us: In the case of Cregin v. Railroad Co., 75 N. Y. 192, construing the meaning of the words "actions on the case for injuries to the person of the plaintiff," found in a New York statute, the court held that these words included actions for slander, libel, assault and battery, and false imprisonment, and that cases of this kind were to be treated as actions for injuries done to the person of the plaintiff. Under section 2157 of the Code of Alabama, actions for injuries to the person or reputation are abated by the death of a party. Construing this section, in the case of Garrison v. Burden, 40 Ala. 513, it was held that an action to recover damages for the seduction of the plaintiff's wife was an action for injuries to the person, and therefore, under the section cited, abated by the death of the defendant. JUDGE, J., says: "Is adultery or criminal conversation with the wife, in legal contemplation, an injury to the person of the husband? Blackstone and

Chitty both declare that it is. * * * And upon this point we are not aware there is any conflict of authority." This case, in effect, rules that injuries to the person are not confined to physical injuries. In the case of Delamater v Russell, 4 How. Pr. 234, it was held that an action for criminal conversation with the plaintiff's wife was an action for injury to the person of the plaintiff. PARKER, J., says: "Rights of persons are divided into absolute and relative. Criminal conversation is classed under actions for injuries to the latter. This classification is related by all our elementary writers." While the question here decided is certainly not free from doubt, but is one upon which plausible arguments can be made on both sides, we think, in view of the foregoing reasons and the advancing policy of our law that good causes of action should not be abated by the death of a party, the right to proceed with this case survived to the deceased plaintiff's representative, and we therefore feel constrained to reverse the judgment of the court below.

Judgment reversed.

CITY OF ATLANTA v. FIRST PRESBYTERIAN CHURCH.

(Supreme Court of Georgia. Feb. 27, 1891.)

MUNICIPAL IMPROVEMENTS— ASSESSMENTS—EXEMPTION OF CHURCH PROPERTY.

A local statute which confers upon the municipal government power and authority to assess one-third of the cost of grading, paving, macadamizing, and otherwise improving the road-way or street proper, on real estate abutting on each side of the street improved, subjects alike all real estate owned by individuals or private corporations, without respect to the purpose or use for which the property is held or to which it is devoted. Churches are not exempt; and, after paying such assessment, the religious corporation to which a church belongs cannot recover back the money so paid into the city treasury. Trustees, etc., v. City of Atlanta, 76 Ga. 181, overruled.

(Syllabus by the Court.)

Error from superior court, Fulton county; M. J. CLARKE, Judge.

J. B. Goodwin, J. T. Pendleton, and J. A. Anderson, for plaintiff in error. Hoke & Burton Smith, for defendant in error.

BLECKLEY, C. J. This was an action by the church, a body corporate and politic, against the city, brought in February, 1887, to recover the sum of $616.87, the amount paid by the plaintiff to the defendant in January, 1885, in satisfaction of a fi. fa. which the city had issued against, and caused to be levied upon, the church building and the premises on which the same was situate, said premises fronting and abutting on Marietta street. The fi. fa. was issued for the pro rata share of these premises of the cost incurred in the year 1883 by the city in paving with Belgian blocks the road-way or street proper on which the premises abutted. The payment was made under protest, and to prevent a sale of the property in pursuance of the levy. The street was paved by virtue of the act of September 3, 1881, amending the charter of the city, and the provisions of the act were fully complied with.

The church building was used only for church purposes and religious worship. At the trial the facts were agreed upon, and reduced to writing, and, by consent of parties, the only question raised was stated thus: "Is property occupied by a church, and used for church purposes only, and religious worship, liable for street improvement under the said act of 1881?" The court instructed the jury to find for the plaintiff; and after verdict the defendant moved for a new trial because of error in this instruction, and because the verdict was contrary to law and to evidence. The motion was overruled.

The act in question (Acts 1880–81, p. 358,) was construed by a majority of this court as then constituted, in Trustees, etc. v. City of Atlanta, 76 Ga. 181; and that decision was afterwards held by a full bench to be conclusive upon the parties in that case, the same case having again come up for review. The principle of *res adjudicata* made the latter ruling a necessary corollary to the former, whether the first in order was correct or incorrect. But as the present case, although it involves the same question touching the right construction of the act of 1881, is a new case, and between different parties, or with one of the parties different, the duty of construing the act *de novo* cannot be declined by the present bench, save upon the ground that the former construction is satisfactory, or, if not, that it should be acquiesced in because of some mischief or public inconvenience likely to result from adopting and promulgating a different construction after the first has stood undisturbed for a period of nearly five years. The rule of *stare decisis* is a wholesome one, but should not be used to sanctify and perpetuate error in so short a term as five years, without very weighty reasons in behalf of public policy. At the last term of this court, we recognized the rule in Scott v. Stewart, 84 Ga. 772, 11 S. E. Rep. 897, as a right rule of decision where many transactions of the public at large, based on an exposition of the law declared 10 or 11 years ago, would probably be disturbed or vitiated by expounding the law differently now. We deprecate and distrust rash innovation as much as the most conservative magistrates ought; but it has never been the doctrine of any court of last resort that the law is to be a refuge and safe asylum for all the errors that creep into it. Indeed, the mind, private or official, which closes down upon all the errors it embraces, refusing to eject them when exposed, is no longer fit for the pursuit of truth. Courts, like individuals, but with more caution and deliberation, must sometimes reconsider what has been already carefully considered, and rectify their own mistakes. If this is to be done in any case, it would seem to be a case like the present, where a change of decision would uproot no transaction founded on the prior decision, and where the effect in the particular controversy at the bar would be simply to leave the parties where they had placed themselves by doing aright what one of them now seeks to have undone. If in very truth, according to the real law of the matter, the church corporation paid to the city a debt which it justly owed, and for which it was legally liable, it could not recover back the money consistently with Christian morality, were there no other obstacle to withdrawing the cash from the city treasury. Nor does the corporation desire so to do, for it has united with the city in formulating thus the question to be decided: "Is property occupied by a church, and used for church purposes only, and religious worship, liable for street improvement under the said act of 1881?" We could not answer truly according to our judicial convictions by citing and following the case in 76 Ga., for we think that case misconstrues the act, and unduly restricts its application.

The act, after conferring power to grade, pave, macadamize, and otherwise improve the streets, invests the mayor and general council with "power and authority to assess one-third of the cost of grading, paving, macadamizing, * * * and otherwise improving the road-way or street proper, on the real estate abutting on each side of the street improved: provided, that before any street, or portion of a street, shall be so improved, the persons owning real estate which has at least one-third of the fronting on the street, or portion of a street, the improvement of which is desired, shall, in writing, request the commissioners of streets and sewers to make such improvements, and said commissioners shall have approved the same, and shall forward the same, with their approval, to the mayor and general council, with a statement of the character of the improvement proposed to be made, and an estimate of the cost of the same, and said mayor and general council shall by ordinance direct the said work to be done." Acts 1880–81, pp. 359, 360. The act proceeds to confer power to adopt by ordinance a system of equalizing assessments, and prorating the cost "on the real estate according to its frontage on the street, or portion of a street, so improved." It declares "that the amount of assessment on each piece of real estate shall be a lien on said real estate from the date of the passage of the ordinance providing for the work and making the assessment;" and it gives the mayor and general council "authority to enforce the collection of the amount of any assessment so made for work * * * upon streets * * * by executions to be issued by the clerk of council against the real estate so assessed, and against the owner thereof, at the date of the ordinance making the assessment, which execution may be levied by the marshal of said city on such real estate: and after advertisement and other proceedings, as in cases of sales for city taxes, the same may be sold at public outcry to the highest bidder, and such sale shall vest an absolute title in the purchaser: provided, that the defendant shall have a right to file an affidavit" to contest the amount due, etc. Id. p. 360. It only requires that language shall be taken in its ordinary signification, in conformity to the rule of construction laid down in section 4 of the Code, for us to be able to hold, not as a conjecture, but with absolute certainty, that the terms, "real estate abutting on each side of the street improved,",include all lands so abutting, no matter to whom they belong, nor how the buildings upon them may be occupied or used. Church property, therefore, is manifestly within the letter of the act, and as clearly within it as any other property whatsoever. The grant of power to assess it is no less express than is the grant of power to assess any other. The act neither makes nor hints at any discrimination, but uses words which embrace all real estate as appropriately and completely as they embrace any part of the same. It would be as consistent with the letter of the statute to deny that it comprehends any real estate at all as to deny that it comprehends all that abuts on the street. This is the plain truth; and yet the opinion of the court in 76 Ga. 187, 188, launches the argument by referring to the rule that no corporation can exercise any power not expressly conferred or necessarily implied; and after observing that places of religious worship, etc., are not brought directly by name within the provisions of the act, adds: "And we do not think they can be brought within it by construction or necessary implication, unless it is made to appear that the property so exempted from taxation is used for purposes of 'private or corporate profit or income.'" This seems to be the fundamental error of the opinion. It treats the city as invoking implication, whereas the city points to an express grant, and the church invokes implication to limit the words of the grant. True, church property is not brought in by its special name, nor is any other; the name applied to all alike being "real estate abutting on each side of the street improved." The property now in question, though belonging to a religious corporation, and used exclusively for worship and church purposes, is "real estate," and it abuts on Marietta street,—the street improved. The true and only problem is whether it can be taken out of the act by implication, not whether it can be brought in. The legislature, by not excepting any real estate whatever, has put it in; and no consistent and unforced construction of the act can be arrived at without setting out from this standpoint. To deny the natural import of the words of a statute, and thus exclude from them something that they evidently comprehend, and then to argue that this same thing cannot be brought in by implication, is to expel the occupant, and then keep him out because he was never in. If the words, "the real estate abutting on each side of the street improved," are not definite and free from all manner of ambiguity, no words can be. And yet, clear and definite as they are, we can be morally certain that they comprehend more than the legislature intended they should; for they cover, by their letter, public as well as private property, and subject the whole alike to assessment, lien, levy, and sale. That the public property of the United States, the state, the county, or the city was intended to be dealt with thus is so improbable that we can have no hesitation in holding that an implied exception as to all public property can and should be engrafted upon the act by construction. And just here the real question in its ultimate form emerges: Can a like exception in favor of church property—which all will agree is not public, but strictly private, property—be recognized, and the words of the statute still further narrowed by construction so as to exclude it also? No answer to this question is afforded by citing the clause of the constitution which authorizes the general assembly to exempt church property as well as public property from taxation, and citing with it the act of 1878, (Code, § 798,) by which the power was exercised throughout its whole extent, and thereby, for the time being, exhausted. This court has ruled in Hayden v. Atlanta, 70 Ga. 817,—a case which arose out of the identical statute we are now construing,—that the taxation to which that power relates is taxation for revenue, and not local assessments for the improvement of streets, which latter are in the nature of an interchange of equivalents between the public and the owners of property locally benefited by the improvement. By general and now almost unanimous concurrence throughout the jurisprudence of the American states, there is an essential difference between the two species of taxation; and many rules, whether constitutional or statutory, which govern the former are without application to the latter. See, besides the citations in Hayden v. Atlanta, supra, City of Birmingham v. Klein, 89 Ala. 461, 7 South. Rep. 386; Speer v. Athens, 85 Ga. 49, 11 S. E. Rep. 802; 2 Dill. Mun. Corp. (4th Ed.) §§ 777, 778.

Consistency requires that when the constitution has been ruled, as in Hayden v. Atlanta, not to apply to local assessments, its provisions on the subject of taxation should not be treated as authority, direct or indirect, for holding property of any kind exempt from such assessments. If it supplies no rule for levying assessments, and declares no exemption from their imposition, what control can it possibly have when a statute on the subject of assessments is under construction? To appeal to it in the discussion is either to recede from the doctrine that it is silent on assessments, or to invoke what it says on one subject to limit what the legislature has expressly said when treating of another. Surely, the mere grouping of church property with public property, first by the constitution, and then by the statute, in dealing with taxation proper, is no sufficient reason for concluding that the legislature intended that they should stand upon the same footing in the law of local assessments, where no such intention has been anywhere declared. The argument that because the legislature, under express authority granted to it by the constitution, has expressly exempted church property from taxation, therefore it has impliedly exempted it from local assessment, is manifestly fallacious. The constitution itself exempts nothing, not even public property; it only gives authority to the general assembly to make certain exemptions. Without some express promulgation of the legislative will, no private property whatever could claim exemption from general taxation. How can a system of express exemption from such taxation be a legitimate premise from which to conclude that the legislature intends a system of implied exemption as to certain private property to run through its enactments on the subject of local assessments? Having once made the distinction between the two species of taxation, and professing still to adhere to it, we ought to accept its consequences. In no other way can consistency be maintained; and nothing inconsistent is law, for the law is never in conflict with itself, nor one part with another part.

It may be said, however, that the opinion we are reviewing does not cite the constitution, and the statute under it exempting church property from taxation, as authority direct, or indirect, but only as evincing on the part of the state a friendly spirit and disposition towards religious institutions and instrumentalities. For this purpose we concede the citation would be legitimate. The constitution defines very explicitly the fiscal relation which the state is to bear to religion. It declares, on the one hand, (Code, § 5006:) "No money shall ever be taken from the public treasury, directly or indirectly, in aid of any church, sect, or denomination of religionists, or of any sectarian institution." This settles it that the state shall pay nothing to the church. It declares, on the other hand, (Id. §§ 5181, 5182, 5184:) "All taxation shall be uniform upon the same class of subjects, and ad valorem on all property subject to be taxed within the territorial limits of the authority levying the tax, and shall be levied and collected under general laws. * * * The general assembly may, by law, exempt from taxation all public property; places of religious worship or burial; all institutions of purely public charity; all buildings erected for and used as a college, incorporated academy, or other seminary of learning; the real and personal estate of any public library, and that of any other literary association, used by or connected with such library; all books and philosophical apparatus; and all paintings and statuary of any company or association kept in a public hall, and not held as merchandise, or for purposes of sale or gain: provided, the property so exempted be not used for purposes of private or corporate profit or income. * * * All laws exempting property from taxation, other than the property herein enumerated, shall be void." This settles it that the church, like other proprietors, shall pay taxes upon its whole property, unless the legislature shall think proper to exempt its places of religious worship, etc., not used for purposes of private or corporate profit or income. All property of the church not embraced in this power of exemption stands, with reference to the state, upon exactly the same footing as if it belonged to individuals, and had no connection with religious uses whatever. With respect to it, there can be no exemption from general taxation expressly granted; much less any resulting from implication only. And the scheme of the constitution evidently is

to have no implied exemptions at all; certainly none other than of public property. It may be that were the legislature to lay a tax for the benefit of the state upon all property, without having declared any exemption whatever, the statute might be construed as impliedly excepting public property; but no court, we apprehend, would feel warranted in extending the implication to church property. Thus the matter stands with reference to the species of taxation with which the constitution deals, to-wit, taxation for revenue. The policy of the state, as indicated by the constitution, is to make no discrimination in favor of property devoted to religious purposes save by express statute. While the legislature is empowered to extend favor to such property, it is expected to do so, if at all, by express provision. And such is now our whole statutory scheme with reference to churches and religion. The policy is to favor them,—favor them highly,—but to leave no favor whatever to implication. This is shown by the opinion we are reviewing. It correctly refers to a great number of topics in respect to which favors have been granted, but they have all been expressly granted. In the whole range of our state legislation since the adoption of the Code, we know of no instance in which the legislature has been understood to intend any favor or privilege in behalf of the church which it has failed to set down and specify in express terms. Taking the Code and all our statutes together, we have a comprehensive and specific enumeration of particulars, in respect to which religion and those engaged in its ministrations are preferred or favored. But surely this is no warrant for a court to add to these favors by construction or implication. On the contrary, as the legislature has expressed so much, the inference ought to be that its expressions are co-extensive with its will and intention.

Glancing now at the current of authority let us see how the stream runs. In People v. McCreery, 34 Cal. 456, the supreme court of that state say: "The meaning of taxation must be kept in view; and that is, a charge levied by the sovereign power upon the property of its subject. It is not a charge upon its own property, nor upon property over which it has no dominion. This excludes the property of the state, whether lands, revenue, or other property, and the property of the United States." Accordingly, it was held in Doyle v. Austin, 47 Cal. 358, that a statute providing for the opening of a street, and for the payment of the expenses by assessment upon the lands benefited, was not vitiated by an express exception from liability in making the assessment of lands belonging to the United States, the state of California, and the city, respectively, although it appeared by the report of the assessors that these lands would be benefited to the extent of $800,000. That property belonging to the public, and held for public uses, is exempt from taxation when not expressly subjected thereto, is held in the following cases: City of Rochester v. Town of Rush, 80 N. Y. 302; Directors of Poor v.

School Directors, 42 Pa. St. 21; City of Louisville v. Com., 1 Duv. 295. The same rule prevails as to assessments for local improvements of a public nature. Inhabitants of Worcester Co. v. Mayor, etc., of Worcester, 116 Mass. 193; County Commissioners v. Board, etc., of Maryland Hospital, 62 Md. 127; State v. City of Hartford, 3 Amer. & Eng. Corp. Cas. 610, the editor citing 49 Conn. 89, which is a miscitation. In Missouri, it would seem, an exemption is not implied in favor of all public property. St. Louis Public Schools v. St. Louis, 26 Mo. 468. And in Illinois, under the constitution of 1870, such exemptions are not implied. Adams Co. v. Quincy, (Ill.) 22 N. E. Rep. 624. In New York, certain words contained in a city charter were construed to subject property of the state to assessment for the improvement of a street. Hassan v. City of Rochester, 67 N. Y. 528. In Texas, (Harris Co. v. Boyd, 7 S. W. Rep. 713,) an exemption in the constitution protecting the property of counties, cities, and towns, held only for public purposes, from forced sale and from taxation, was ruled to extend to an assessment against a courthouse for the improvement of a street. It is manifest, however, that this decision could have been rested upon the general principle announced by the courts of Massachusetts, Maryland, and Connecticut, to the effect that public property is not included in statutes for local assessments unless specially named. Implied exceptions in favor of public property also prevail over general words in a statute founded on the exercise of the power of eminent domain. Mayor, etc., of Atlanta v. Central R., etc., Co., 53 Ga. 120; St. Louis, etc., R. Co. v. Trustees, 43 Ill. 303. We thus see that to engraft an exception upon the amended charter of Atlanta in favor of public property has the sanction of authority. But no such rule prevails, so far as we know or have been able to ascertain, in favor of private property used for religious purposes. In the following cases, churches, although not expressly named in assessment statutes, were held to be subject to assessment for local improvements, notwithstanding they were exempt by express law from general taxation: In re Mayor, etc., of New York, 11 Johns. 77; (and see Harlem P. Church v. Mayor, 5 Hun, 442;) In re Second Ave. M. E. Church, 66 N. Y. 395; People v. Mayor, etc., 2 Hun,

433; Northern Liberties v. St. John's Church, 13 Pa. St. 104; Lefevre v. Mayor, etc., 2 Mich. 586; City of Ottawa v. Trustees of Free Church, 20 Ill. 423; Broadway B. Church v. McAtee, 8 Bush, 508; Lockwood v. City of St. Louis, 24 Mo. 20. And see First P. Church v. Ft. Wayne, 36 Ind. 338; Society v. City of Providence, 6 R. I. 235. The like rule has been applied to cemeteries. Mayor, etc., v. Green Mt. Cemetery, 7 Md. 517; Buffalo City Cemetery v. Buffalo, 46 N. Y. 506; Lima v. Cemetery Ass'n, 42 Ohio St. 128. And to hospitals, asylums, and other charitable institutions. Sheehan v. Hospital, 50 Mo. 155; City of Lafayette v. Orphan Asylum, 4 La. Ann 1; Society v. Boston, 116 Mass. 181. And see City of Chicago v. Baptist Theological Union, 115 Ill. 245, 2 N. E. Rep. 254; In re St. Johns's Asylum, 69 N. Y. 353. Also, to institutions of learning, etc. In re College Street, 8 R. I. 474.

If express words are requisite to exempt private property from general taxation, there is no reason why like words are not equally necessary to exempt it from assessments. Lima v. Cemetery Ass'n, supra. Instances of such express exemption are furnished by State v. Mayor, etc., 36 N. J. Law, 478; State v. City of St. Paul, 36 Minn. 529, 32 N. W. Rep. 781. But in City of Chicago v. Baptist Theological Union, 115 Ill. 245, 2 N. E. Rep. 254, it was held that even an express exemption from assessment could not be granted under the constitution of Illinois, because violative of the principle of equality. Inasmuch as the constitution of Georgia neither expressly nor by implication lays down any principle whatever touching local assessments, being entirely silent on the subject, there would seem to be no defect of power in the legislature to spare churches from such assessments at pleasure. We rule, not that the legislature might not have granted the exemption now contended for, had it been so disposed, but that it has not done so. The question of legal discrimination in favor of church property over secular property, in the matter of bearing burdens, is one of public policy; and it is for the legislature, not the courts, to mould that policy and proclaim it. The services of religion to the state are of untold value; but it is the glory of religion in this country that it serves as a volunteer, without money and without price. Judgment reversed.

BRANTLEY v. STATE.

(Supreme Court of Georgia.　April 20, 1891.)

ASSAULT WITH INTENT TO KILL — INSTRUCTIONS—
SELF-DEFENSE—CORRECTION OF VERDICT.

1. On a trial for assault with intent to murder by shooting, where neither the evidence nor the prisoner's statement supports a theory that the defendant shot under the fears of a reasonable man that a felony or other like injury was about to be committed on him, a charge concerning such fears was properly omitted; nor was it error, in such a case, to charge that there must have been a necessity for the shooting by the defendant at the time he fired, to render the shooting justifiable.

2. It was not error to charge the jury that they should not be controlled, in making up their verdict, by any fear as to what the punishment might be, but that they were sworn to find according to the evidence.

3. The infliction of a penalty not authorized by law is no ground for a new trial.

4. When the jury return a verdict which is not in the proper form, it is not error for the court to allow them to put it in the proper form, or, at their request, to have the solicitor general do so for them; they unanimously stating that the verdict as formulated by him is their real finding.

(Syllabus by the Court.)

Error from superior court, Douglas county; R. H. CLARK, Judge.

Thos. W. Latham, for plaintiff in error.
John S. Candler, Sol. Gen., for the State.

LUMPKIN, J. Duke, the prosecutor, and Brantley, the defendant, had a quarrel in the forenoon about a dog, which resulted in nothing serious. That night, while Brantley was in a store in the town of Douglasville, having with him a shotgun with which he had been hunting in the afternoon, Duke appeared on the scene, and fired at him with a pistol, inflicting a severe wound. Brantley immediately returned the fire with his gun. By reason of the firing of the gun the light in the store was extinguished, and both parties disappeared from the store in the dark, and went down the street. A very short time thereafter Duke was shot by Brantley in an adjacent alley running out from this street. The evidence does not show clearly the circumstances under which Duke was shot in the alley. That for the state tended to show that Duke was fleeing from Brantley, had fallen over some barrels or boxes, and was shot while in this position. According to the prisoner's statement, Duke went into the alley for the purpose of waylaying him, shot at him as he came up, and he immediately returned the fire in self-defense. It seems clear from the testimony that in the shooting which occurred at the store Brantley was without fault, and Duke was to blame. If Brantley was guilty of any offense at all, it was because his shooting Duke in the alley was unlawful. He either shot a fleeing and helpless adversary without necessity, which would, of course, have been unlawful, or he shot in self-defense, which would have been justifiable. The theory of self-defense was supported by the prisoner's statement alone. The jury evidently disregarded this statement, and found the defendant guilty of shooting at another on the strength of the evidence above mentioned.

v.13s.E.no.8—17

1. From the foregoing recital it will appear that neither the evidence nor the prisoner's statement put in issue the question whether or not the defendant shot Duke while in the alley under the fear that Duke was about to shoot or otherwise assault him. If the shooting by Brantley in the alley was justifiable at all, it was upon the doctrine of actual self-defense. The prisoner does not contend in his statement that he shot because he was afraid Duke was about to attack him, but alleges that Duke actually did fire at him, and that, under the immediate and pressing danger, he shot to save his life, or to prevent the perpetration upon him of an injury amounting to a felony. The court, in his charge to the jury, gave the defendant the full benefit of the theory presented by his own statement, and, in view of the evidence and this statement, did not err in omitting to charge the law concerning reasonable fears; and it follows, of course, that it was proper for the court to charge that, in order to justify the defendant, there must have been a necessity for him to shoot at the time he actually fired.

2. While under the Code the jury have the right in all criminal cases to recommend the prisoner to the mercy of the court, and it is the duty of the court to pay proper respect to such recommendation, still the question of what the punishment may be ought never to affect the jury in deciding the naked question whether the defendant is guilty or not guilty of the charge made against him. If they respect their oaths, they must follow the evidence, giving such weight to the prisoner's statement also as they see proper, and in every case fairly and honestly determine whether or not the guilt of the accused has been established beyond a reasonable doubt. In discharging this duty they cannot be aided, and should not be influenced, by any consideration as to what punishment will be inflicted by the court. When they determine that the prisoner is guilty they may recommend mercy, and the law says the court should respect such a recommendation; but what punishment will be inflicted can in no sense aid the jury in determining the guilt or innocence of the prisoner.

3. The punishment provided by our Code for the offense of shooting at another shall be by fine, imprisonment in the common jail, or both, or by confinement in the penitentiary. The court in this case sentenced the defendant to pay a fine of $250, or, in default thereof, that he be confined in the penitentiary for 18 months. One of the grounds of the motion for a new trial assigns this sentence as error, but the sentence itself was not directly excepted to in the bill of exceptions. The question not being properly before us, we do not decide whether this penalty was illegal or not; but granting, for the sake of the argument, that it was so, it certainly affords no ground for a new trial. If the trial was in all respects regular, and the verdict right, it would never do to set it aside and order a new hearing of the whole case simply because the court inflicted a penalty which he had no authority of law to impose. If the sentence was

unlawful, the defendant should have directly excepted to it, and brought the question to this court for review; or, it may be, he could relieve himself from such unlawful sentence by writ of *habeas corpus.*

4. It is perfectly clear from the record in this case that the jury meant and intended to find the defendant guilty of the offense of shooting at another, not in his own defense. They made two or three efforts to express their finding in writing, but used language which, in the opinion of the court failed to do so with sufficient accuracy. It was certainly not error, therefore, for the court to require them to put the verdict in such form as to make its meaning entirely clear and free from objection, or to allow the solicitor general, at the request of the jury, to frame their verdict for them. Neither the judge nor the solicitor general made the verdict. The jury stated repeatedly and unmistakably what they desired to find; and after the finding was put in proper shape they ratified and approved of it, and then, upon being polled, each and every member of the jury answered that such was his verdict. Of course no court should ever intimate to a jury what their verdict should be; but when they agree upon one, and all present know exactly what they mean to find, it is mere trifling to say that the judge may not aid them in expressing their finding in legal phraseology.

Judgment affirmed.

STEWART v. JOHNSTON.

(Supreme Court of Georgia. March 30, 1891.)

RECEIVER'S BOND—LIABILITY OF SURETIES.

An order of court, passed at the instance of one of the parties to a case in which a receiver has been appointed, requiring the receiver to give a new bond in the same amount, and conditioned as his existing bond, will not operate, after the new bond has been given, to discharge the surety on the old bond from liability for future defaults of the receiver, but he will continue liable for defaults, past and future, as though no additional bond had been required or given; there being nothing in the order or in the attendant circumstances to indicate that the second bond was intended as a substitute for, rather than as supplemental to, the first.

(Syllabus by the Court.)

Error from superior court, Fulton county; MARSHALL J. CLARKE, Judge.

H. L. Culbertson and *T. P. Westmoreland,* for plaintiff in error. *Broyles & Son,* for defendant in error.

BLECKLEY, C. J. In a suit between A. and B. as partners, C. was appointed a receiver of the partnership assets. D. was the surety upon his bond. This was the first bond given by the receiver, and bore date November 20, 1884. Afterwards, upon motion of B., the court required the receiver to give a new bond, the order being in these terms: "It is further ordered that the receiver do give a new bond in the same amount and conditioned as the former one, said new bond to be filed in the clerk's office by 12 o'clock, May 8, 1886."

A bond was filed, purporting to be executed by the receiver as principal and E. as surety, and the clerk approved the same. This bond bore date May 12, 1886. Afterwards the receiver left the state, and F. was appointed receiver in his stead. An action in the nature of a bill in equity was brought by F., the second receiver, upon both of his predecessors' bonds. In defense to this action, D., the surety on the first bond, contended that the order requiring the new bond and the clerk's approval of that bond relieved him from all liability except for any waste or misconduct of his principal which occurred previously to the filing of the second bond. The court ruled that the first bond covered the whole default of the receiver, whether occurring before or after the second was given. There was no application or request by the surety to be discharged when or before the second bond was required; and, even if there had been, the general rule is that the court will not grant such a request coming from a surety upon a receiver's bond unless for special cause shown. 2 Daniell, Ch. 1766; Kerr, Rec. 251; High, Rec. § 127. The order for a new bond contained no reference to any purpose on the part of the court to discharge the surety on the first bond, or to terminate his liability, or to limit it in any way whatever. There are no words indicating that the new bond was to be substituted for the old, or that it was to stand instead thereof. The second bond was required, not at the instance of the surety on the first, but at the instance of one of the parties to the pending cause. So far as appears, it was intended as a mere strengthening of the security afforded by the first bond. It was cumulative or additional, rather than substitutional. Both upon principle and the authority of analogous cases, we think no discharge took place. 2 Amer. & Eng. Enc. Law, 466*f*; Murfree, Off. Bonds, § 221; Brandt, Sur. § 461. In the absence of affirmative evidence to that effect, there can be no presumption that the parties to the litigation or their interests would be benefited by discharging the surety on an existing bond merely because a new bond was required and given. And that the application for a new bond was made by one of the parties carries with it no implication that he or the court desired the old bond not to be fully operative after the new should be given the same as before. Having decided that by the terms of the order requiring the new bond the latter was to be cumulative security only, it is unnecessary to consider what effect forgery of the surety's name upon the new bond would have had if the terms of the order had been different. Nor is it material to notice that the order was not in fact complied with in respect to the time within which the new bond was to be filed. It would be difficult to hold that the clerk had any authority to accept it after the time for filing appointed by the order had expired, if the effect of acceptance would be to arrest the continuous operation of the prior bond. Judgment affirmed.

MOORE *et al.* v. HILL *et al.*

(Supreme Court of Georgia. March 30, 1891.)

APPEALABLE JUDGMENTS—GARNISHMENT.

A judgment allowing garnishees to file their answer after default for not answering is not final, but leaves the garnishment still pending. The same is true of a failure or refusal of the court to sustain a motion by the plaintiff to dismiss a written statement filed by the garnishees setting forth grounds of attack on the affidavit, bond, and summons of garnishment. Complaints like these being matters for exception *pendente lite* only, a writ of error based on them alone, and not assigning error upon any judgment or decision final in its nature, will not be entertained. Code, § 4250.

(Syllabus by the Court.)

Error from superior court, Fulton county; M. J. CLARKE, Judge.

Rosser & Carter, for plaintiffs in error.

Henry Jackson, for defendants in error.

BLECKLEY, C. J. "No cause shall be carried to the supreme court upon any bill of exceptions so long as the same is pending in the court below, unless the decision or judgment complained of, if it had been rendered as claimed by the plaintiff in error, would have been a final disposition of the cause. But at any stage of the cause either party may file his exceptions to any decision, sentence, or decree of the superior court, and, if the same is certified and allowed, it shall be entered of record in the cause; and should the case, at its final termination, be carried, by writ of error, to the supreme court by either party, error may be assigned upon such bills of exception, and a reversal and new trial may be allowed thereon when it is manifest that such erroneous decision of the court has or may have affected the final result of the case." Code, § 4250. The garnishment is still pending in the court below, and the main judgment excepted to is one rendered on the 20th of November, 1890, which reads thus: "On motion of the counsel of the garnishees that the within answer be now filed, and after hearing and considering the evidence submitted in connection with said motion, it is ordered that the same be allowed." Had leave to file the answer been denied instead of granted, the denial would have left the garnishment still pending. So far as appears, no adjudication final in its nature has been made in the case. Haygood v. Banking & T. Co., 60 Ga. 291. The garnishees have not been discharged, nor was it too late to traverse their answer when this writ of error was sued out, the term of the court at which the answer was filed being then unexpired. The plaintiffs resisted the filing of the answer because it came too late, but the court, on the cause shown, was of opinion that it did not come too late, and permitted it to be filed. This did not *ipso facto* terminate the garnishment proceeding, but was subject-matter for exception *pendente lite* only. The bill of exceptions contains another exception and assignment of error. It says: "The court also erred in not dismissing the grounds Nos. 1, 2, 3, and 4, shown by garnishees, why judgment should not be rendered against them, and in not holding that they presented matters of no concern to the garnishees;

and to this the plaintiffs except." The facts on which this exception is based are as follows: The garnishees had filed a written statement embracing four grounds on which they objected to judgment being entered up by the plaintiffs against them, irrespective of any question as to an answer. These grounds went to the sufficiency of the affidavit and bond on which the garnishment was sued out, and to the competency of the notary public by whom the summons of garnishment was issued. On the 15th of November, counsel for the plaintiffs moved to dismiss each and all of these grounds, "but over the objections of plaintiffs the court held up the case until November 20, 1890, and then passed an order," etc.; the order being the one copied above, allowing the answer of the garnishees to be filed. Had the court sustained the motion to dismiss, instead of passing it by without disposing of it,—that is, if the decision had been rendered as claimed by the plaintiffs,—this would not have been a final disposition of the cause, for the garnishment would have been left still pending. Obviously, therefore, the refusal of the court to pass upon or sustain the motion was matter for exception *pendente lite*, and cannot be the basis of a writ of error to this court while the cause is pending below. It appears from the bill of exceptions that the plaintiffs made a motion to enter up judgment against the garnishees for want of an answer, and that the motion was not granted; but the refusal or failure to grant this motion is not excepted to, although it could have been. The determination of the motion in the way claimed by the plaintiffs would have been a final disposition of the cause, and hence denial of the motion was ground for a writ of error. For some reason, which is not disclosed in the record, the plaintiffs have acquiesced in the only thing, affirmative or negative, which would afford them a standing in this court, and have presented for review matters proper for exception *pendente lite*. This was not the course pursued in Bearden v. Railroad Co., 82 Ga. 605, 9 S. E. Rep. 603. Writ of error dismissed.

TIM *et al.* v. FRANKLIN *et al.*

LEVI v. SAME.

(Supreme Court of Georgia. March 30, 1891.)

PROPERTY SUBJECT TO GARNISHMENT — PARTIES—
APPEAL.

1. Assets to which a debtor has no title, legal or equitable, cannot be reached by his creditors through summons of garnishment. One who, at his own expense, and in his own name, takes out a policy of insurance on the goods of another, owns the policy. Creditors who allege fraud in the transaction by way of traverse to an answer filed by the insurance company to a summons of garnishment must set forth facts constituting fraud.

2. Where a policy of insurance is outstanding in the hands of the person to whom it was issued, a garnishment which seeks an adjudication that it is, and was from the beginning, the property of another person, is not sustainable against the company, the holder of the policy being a necessary party to such an adjudication. A surety on the bond given to dissolve a garnishment is not a party to the garnishment suit save in his

character of surety, and for the purposes of that relation only.

3. Is the striking of the plaintiff's traverse to the garnishee's answer such a judgment or decision as may be brought to the supreme court for review while the garnishment is pending in the court below?

(*Syllabus by the Court.*)

Error from city court of Atlanta; VAN EPPS, Judge.

R. J. Jordan, for plaintiffs in error. *Well & Goodwin* and *C. W. Smith*, for defendants in error.

BLECKLEY, C. J. 1. As a general rule, creditors cannot reach by garnishment any assets which the debtor himself could not recover from the garnishee. Bates v. Forsyth, 69 Ga. 365. Here the policy of insurance was issued to Cohen. Franklin was no party to it. The original undertaking of the company was to pay to Cohen if a loss should occur. The presumption is that the premiums were paid by Cohen. The traverse of the company's answer suggests nothing to the contrary. It alleges that the policy covered goods belonging to Franklin, and was issued to Cohen to defraud Franklin's creditors, but does not disclose who were the parties to the fraud. It does not say that the company was one of these, or that it had notice of any fraud as between Franklin and Cohen. It does not set out any facts which would constitute fraud, and upon which the company could join issue intelligently and with a knowledge of what had to be proved or disproved. No fraudulent agreement, contract, or contrivance is set out. Nothing is alleged besides the ownership of the goods by Franklin, except the motive or object of issuing the policy to Cohen. In legal effect it would not be a fraud upon anybody but the insurance company for Cohen to take a policy at his own expense upon Franklin's goods, and it would be no fraud upon the company for him to do so, unless he represented the goods as his own in his application for the insurance.

2. But if the traverse were full and definite enough to tender an issue of fraud, Cohen, being the party to whom the insurance company is bound by its contract in the policy, would be a necessary party to any litigation seeking to establish an adverse interest in Franklin or his creditors. It is said that he became a party to the garnishment proceeding by becoming surety on the bond of Franklin dissolving the garnishment. We think otherwise. His suretyship did not connect him with the case in any relation but that of surety, or for any purpose but to render him responsible for the amount of the fund, should it be recovered as the property of Franklin in litigation carried on between Franklin and his creditors in this contest. A mere surety in such a bond has no right or power to conduct or control the litigation, but must abide passively by what is done by others, and the results thereof. That he is not a party to the case in the court below is manifest, because, if he were so, he would be a necessary party to this writ of error, and would have to be served with the bill of exceptions. He was not

so served. For us to recognize him as a party in the court below would involve, by the logic of practice in this court, that we should pronounce a judgment dismissing the writ of error for want of service upon him of the bill of exceptions.

3. We are not sure that this case has not been brought here prematurely, for the reason that the garnishment is still pending in the court below. Perhaps there is a distinction between cutting the plaintiff off in his appointed remedies for prosecuting the case and forcing upon him defensive pleadings in behalf of the garnishee. That rulings against the plaintiff in respect to obstructions put in his way by the garnishee are not final judgments, and therefore not cause for writ of error, we have just decided in Moore v. Hill, ante, 259. At present we are doubtful whether the like reason applies in its full force where the plaintiff is hindered from having a jury trial upon a traverse which he has tendered, and because of this doubt we forbear to dismiss this writ of error.

Judgment affirmed.

PHILLIPS et al. v. COLLIER.

(*Supreme Court of Georgia.* March 23, 1891.)

VACATING—DEFAULT JUDGMENT—PERSONAL SERVICE—NEGLIGENCE OF COUNSEL.

In an action on an open account, where personal service was had, a judgment by default will not be set aside because defendant's counsel neglected to appear; and the fact that such counsel is insolvent, and unable to respond in damages, is immaterial.

(*Syllabus by the Court.*)

Error from city court of Atlanta; VAN EPPS, Judge.

Mayson & Hill, for plaintiffs in error. *R. J. Jordan*, for defendant in error.

SIMMONS, J. Under the facts in this case the court did not err in refusing to set aside the judgment. There was no defect apparent on the face of the record or pleadings, nor is it alleged that there was any defect therein. We do not think the reasons assigned in the motion to set aside the judgment were sufficient to authorize the trial judge to grant the motion. While it is true that counsel for the movants had marked his name on the docket, yet when the case was called for trial neither he nor they appeared to defend the same. The suit being on an open account, and there being personal service on the defendants, the court directed the jury to find a verdict for the plaintiff. This was proper, under the decision of this court in the case of Stephens v. Gas-Light Co., 81 Ga. 150, 6 S. E. Rep. 838, where it was held that in a suit upon an open account, where there was personal service on the defendant, "he was as much concluded as if he had come into court and acknowledged the correctness of the account, and that it was unpaid." If counsel had been present, and had neglected to summon witnesses and prove his defense, the court must have taken the same action; and the defendants, under that state of facts, would have had as much right to move to set aside the judgment as they would in this case. Unfortunately for them, they employed counsel who neglected their business, and they must look to him for redress, instead of asking the court to set aside a solemn judgment because of his negligence. But it is said that counsel is insolvent, and cannot answer to the plaintiffs in error in damages for his negligent conduct. In reply to this it is sufficient to call attention to the case of Phillips v. Taber, 83 Ga. 578, 10 S. E. Rep. 270, where the same point was made, and in which this court said: "We do not think the plaintiff in error is entitled to any relief on this ground. Phillips doubtless knew the pecuniary condition of his counsel when he employed him. Whether he did or not, it would be a new doctrine to establish in Georgia that third parties are to be deprived of their rights because the defendant or the plaintiff, as the case may be, had employed an impecunious attorney." Judgment affirmed.

HOLLIDAY et al. v McLENDON.

(Supreme Court of Georgia. March 23, 1891.)

REVIEW ON APPEAL—REFUSING NEW TRIAL.

There being sufficient evidence to sustain the verdict, and the court below being satisfied therewith, this court will not interfere with its discretion in refusing a new trial.

(Syllabus by Lumpkin, J.)

Error from superior court, Fulton county; M. J. CLARKE, Judge.
R. J. Jordan, for plaintiffs in error.
Candler & Thomson, for defendant in error.

PER CURIAM. Judgment affirmed.

FALVEY et al. v. RICHMOND.

(Supreme Court of Georgia. March 30, 1891.)

SALE—ACTION FOR PRICE—TRIAL.

1. In an action for the balance due on goods, though defendant testifies that they were only worth one cent a pound, which amount he paid, a verdict for plaintiff is warranted, where defendant admits on his examination that the contract price was a cent and a half per pound

2. A charge that if a merchant in Atlanta ordered goods to be shipped to him by a railroad company from Virginia, delivery to the railroad company by the seller would be delivery to the purchaser, in contemplation of law, is correct, in the absence of a contract to deliver the goods in Atlanta.

3. The fact that the plaintiff's counsel handed the interrogatories of plaintiff to the jury when they retired, and that they kept them until the verdict was announced, is not ground for a new trial, where counsel make affidavit that they did so inadvertently, and the foreman of the jury makes affidavit that they did not examine the interrogatories, and did not know that they had them.

Error from superior court, Fulton county; M. J. CLARKE, Judge.
Simmons & Corrigan, for plaintiffs in error. Mayson & Hill, for defendant in error.

SIMMONS, J. Richmond sued Falvey & Co. in a justice's court upon an open account. The defendants pleaded the general issue and payment. The jury in the justice's court returned a verdict in favor of the plaintiff, and Falvey & Co. appealed to the superior court. The jury in that court rendered a like verdict, and Falvey

& Co. made a motion for a new trial, which was overruled by the court.
1. We think there was sufficient evidence to authorize the jury to return the verdict they did. Falvey claimed that the cabbages were worth only one cent per pound, but, in answer to a direct question, he testified that the contract was that he was to pay one and a half cents per pound; and, as he had only paid to Richmond one cent per pound, the jury, under this evidence, was authorized to find the additional amount they did find. This disposes of the 1st, 2d, 3d, and 4th grounds of the motion.
2. The motion also complains that the court erred in charging that if a merchant residing in Atlanta, and doing business there, should order goods to be shipped to him from the state of Virginia by a railroad company, and the person from whom the goods were ordered should deliver the goods to the company, such delivery would be, in contemplation of law, a delivery to the purchaser. There was no error in this charge. See Wade v. Hamilton, 30 Ga. 450; Glass Co. v. Longley, 64 Ga. 576; Dunn v. State, 82 Ga. 27, 8 S. E. Rep. 806; Phosphate Co. v. Ely, 82 Ga. 440, 9 S. E. Rep. 170; Bennett's Benj. Sales, § 693; Newmark, Sales, § 146; Tied. Sales, § 85. Of course, if the contract was that Richmond was to deliver the cabbages in Atlanta, the delivery to the carrier would not be a delivery to Falvey & Co., and so the court charged the jury.
3. The next ground of the motion complains that the plaintiff's counsel handed to the jury the interrogatories of Richmond, which were carried by them to the jury-room, and kept until they had made and published their verdict. The affidavit of the counsel, in reply to this ground of the motion, shows that while he handed the interrogatories to the jury it was inadvertently done, and that there was no attempt on his part to gain any unfair advantage thereby. The affidavit of the foreman of the jury shows that the interrogatories were not read or examined by any of the jury, and that they did not know they had the interrogatories until their return to the court-room, when the matter was first brought to their notice. Under these affidavits there was no error in the refusal of the court to grant a new trial on this ground. Schmertz v. Johnson, 72 Ga. 472; Wilkins v. Maddrey, 67 Ga. 766. Judgment affirmed.

JOHNSON et al. v. JONES et al.

(Supreme Court of Georgia. March 23, 1891.)

CONSTITUTIONAL LAW — TITLE OF ACT — DEED—VALIDITY BETWEEN PARTIES — PLEA TO JURISDICTION.

1. The act of 1885, amending section 4185 of the Code, providing for service of certain proceedings by publication, is unconstitutional, because it "contains matter different from what is expressed in the title thereof."

2. A deed without witnesses is legal and binding between the parties thereto and those claiming under them as mere volunteers.

3. Where defendants, residing in another state, were not served by publication according to law, and at the proper time filed a plea to the jurisdiction of the court upon this ground, and

it appearing that such plea was true in fact, it was error to overrule the same.

(*Syllabus by the Court.*)

Error from superior court, Fulton county; M. J. Clarke, Judge.

R. L. Rodgers, for plaintiffs in error. T. P. Westmoreland, for defendants in error.

Lumpkin, J. 1. An act was approved October 15, 1885, (Acts 1884–85, pp. 56, 57,) the title of which declared that it was an act to amend section 4185 of the Code by adding after the words "four months" therein the following words, "which order to perfect service may be granted by the judge in vacation." This is all the amending act, by its title, proposed to do to the section mentioned, viz., simply to insert the quoted words in the section at the place designated. In the body of the act it is enacted that these words shall be so added, and the act then proceeds to assert that the original section, when so amended, shall read a certain way. The difficulty about it is that the section, when so amended, does not read that way, but, on the contrary, the words, "twice a month for two months," are substituted for the words, "once a month for four months," occurring in the section. No hint is given, either in the title of the act or in the enacting part thereof, that this change or substitution will be made. Indeed, the act does not anywhere directly declare that such change shall be made; it only incorrectly says that such a change shall result from introducing certain words into the section. Therefore, as the title expresses distinctly, explicitly, and unequivocally the precise words which shall be added to the section to be amended, and the body of the act, in the indirect manner indicated, makes another and entirely distinct and important change in the section, it follows inevitably that the act "contains matter different from what is expressed in the title thereof," and this the constitution plainly forbids. Code, § 5067. An examination of the act, in connection with this section of the Code, will readily disclose the defect herein discussed.

2. The only question disclosed by the record which can be of any consequence to the plaintiffs in error is whether or not a deed having no witnesses is good between the parties thereto, and conveys title from the grantor to the grantee. This question has been virtually settled by this court in the cases of Downs v. Yonge, 17 Ga. 295, and Gardner v. Moore, 51 Ga. 268. In the first case it was held that a deed with only one witness was good between the parties; and in the second, that a mortgage of real estate. with only one witness, was likewise good. The reasoning in those cases is conclusive that a deed or mortgage of realty without witnesses would be good, as between the parties themselves, or those claiming under them as mere volunteers. On the same line, it was held in Marable v. Mayer, 78 Ga. 60,[1] that a mortgage on personalty was good, as between the original parties, without any witness at all. If the deed in the case before us, which had no witnesses, was

[1] 8 S. E. Rep. 429.

valid and binding to the extent stated, it follows, as the facts of this case show, that the plaintiffs in error have no interest whatever in the property covered thereby.

3. It appears, however, that they were never legally served. Being non-residents of the state, service was attempted by publication twice a month for two months, instead of once a month for four months, as required by section 4185 of the Code. It is obvious that service was sought to be perfected in this manner under the impression that the act mentioned in the first head-note was constitutional. This, we have shown, is not the case, and therefore the service amounted to nothing. The plaintiffs in error filed in the court below their plea to the jurisdiction for want of legal service, which plea the court overruled, and we are therefore constrained to reverse the judgment on this ground. The facts disclosed on the trial of the case cannot possibly be changed upon another hearing, and these parties could accomplish nothing, even if they were legally served. Judgment reversed.

Clay v. Ballard, Registrar.

(*Supreme Court of Appeals of Virginia. May 15, 1891.*)

Elections—Right to Copy Registration Books—Mandamus—Jurisdiction of Court of Appeals.

1. Code Va. § 3086, giving the supreme court of appeals original jurisdiction to issue writs of *mandamus* in all cases in which it may be "necessary to prevent a failure of justice," in which a *mandamus* may issue according to the principles of the common law, does not take a case of which the circuit court also has jurisdiction out of the original jurisdiction of said court on the ground that, since the circuit court has jurisdiction, the interposition of the court of appeals is not necessary to prevent a failure of justice.

2. Code Va. § 84, providing that registration books shall at all times be open to public inspection, gives also under the common law the right to take copies of them; and it is immaterial whether the legislature has provided compensation for the registrar for making copies himself, or for time consumed by others in taking copies under his observation.

3. Any qualified voter has such interest as entitles him to petition for *mandamus* to compel the registrar of voters to allow him to inspect or take copies of the registration books.

Lacy, J., dissenting.

Mandamus.

L. C. Bristow and R. C. Bickford, for petitioner. Scott & Scott and Meredith & Cocke, for respondent.

Lewis, P. The petitioner, a legally qualified voter in election district No. 1 in Newport News, Warwick county, prays a *mandamus* to compel the defendant, who is the registrar for said district, to allow petitioner to inspect and to take a copy of his registration books. The defendant demurs to the petition, and also answers. In his answer he states that he had never refused to allow an inspection of the books, but denies the right of petitioner to have or demand copies of them. The principal question we have, therefore, to determine is whether or not the petitioner has such right. On the demurrer two questions have been raised, the first of which is that this is not a proper case for the exercise of the original jurisdiction of this court. The statute, now carried into section 3086 of the Code, gives the court original jurisdiction to issue writs of *mandamus* to the circuit and other enumerated courts, "and in all other cases in which it may be *necessary to prevent a failure of justice*, in which a *mandamus* may issue according to the principles of the common law." The precise point of objection to the jurisdiction, if we correctly understand it, is that, inasmuch as the circuit court of Warwick county has jurisdiction in cases of *mandamus*, it is not shown that the interposition of this court is necessary to prevent a failure of justice. In other words, that because a subordinate, local court was open to the petitioner, he ought to have pursued his remedy in that court, and, not having done so, the case, as it is, is not within the jurisdiction of this court. This is a novel view, certainly. Although the language of the statute has long been as it now stands in the Code, we are not aware that such a suggestion has ever before emanated either from the bench or bar. The uniform practice of the court undoubtedly has been to the contrary. And apart from the practical construction which has thus been put upon the statute, we are of opinion that the position of the defendant is clearly untenable. The writ of *mandamus* issues, no matter from what court it is issued, only in those cases in which there is no other adequate legal remedy, and, therefore, to prevent a failure of justice. It is of very ancient origin, and was introduced, as Lord MANSFIELD said in Rex v. Barker, 3 Burrows, 1267, "to prevent disorder from a failure of justice and defect of police." Being, at common law, a prerogative writ, power to issue it was given to the king's bench only, where the king himself used to sit in person; and in this country the power is generally conferred upon the highest courts having original jurisdiction. Kendall v. U. S., 12 Pet. 524; 14 Amer. & Eng. Enc. Law, p. 23. Accordingly our legislature has given original jurisdiction to this court to issue the writ, and in doing so has adopted almost the identical terms used by the common-law authorities in defining the nature and office of the writ; that is to say, it has provided that the court shall have jurisdiction to issue the writ in all cases in which it may be necessary to prevent a failure of justice. This shows that the object of the legislature was not to narrow the jurisdiction, but to make it co-extensive in such cases with that of the court of king's bench in England; in other words, to give the court unrestricted original jurisdiction to issue the writ in all cases in which it may issue according to the principles of the common law. Or, stated differently, the language of the statute relied on by the defendant, and which we have italicized, was intended rather as a definition of the remedy as it exists at common law than as a restriction on the jurisdiction of the court. This is too obvious to admit of doubt. Had the intention been to make the jurisdiction contingent, or secondary, so to speak, it would surely have been expressed in clear and unmistakable terms.

Many reasons might be suggested for the action of the legislature in conferring this comprehensive original jurisdiction upon this court, but the language of the statute expresses too plainly the intention of that body to require further discussion; and it need only to be added in this connection that the exercise of the jurisdiction thus conferred is no more left to the discretion of this court than is the exercise of its jurisdiction generally. Code, § 3011 et seq. Of course, by this is meant that the court may not arbitrarily decline to take cognizance of a case properly before it. Undoubtedly cases have arisen at common law in which it has been held that where the right sought to be enforced is of a private nature, and where to grant the writ would be to decide important questions in which persons not before the court are interested, it is discretionary in the court either to grant or refuse it. And in many other cases that might be mentioned the writ is granted or withheld in the sound discretion of the court. But where the object is to enforce obedience to a public statute it has been invariably held that the writ is demandable of right. Bull. N. P. 199; Bac. Abr. tit. "Mandamus;" High, Extr. Rem. § 9. The present case is a case of that description, if the petitioner's contention be well founded; and this brings us to the main point in the case, which is whether the petitioner is entitled, as he contends, to a copy of the books in question. These books undoubtedly are of a public nature, and therefore, upon general principles, independently of any statute on the subject, any person having an interest in them would have a right to inspect them. But the legislature, out of abundant caution, and with an unmistakable object in view, has seen fit to enact expressly that they "shall at all times be open to public inspection." Code, § 84. The case turns upon the construction of this statute. In other words, what is the extent of the right of inspection thus given? Does it mean that the voter may inspect the lists only so far as to see whether or not his own name is upon them? Or does it give the right to examine and scrutinize, and, if necessary to enable him to remember and to utilize the information derived from his examination, to take notes, or, if need be, copies of the entire books? It is manifest, if the first of these propositions be, as the defendant contends, the true construction, that the right given by the statute is extremely narrow, and incapable of being used for any great advantage to the public, either in the way of the detection of fraud or otherwise. But we are of opinion that it is not the correct view. The provision of the statute was obviously intended primarily as a safeguard against fraud, and ought, therefore, to be liberally, rather than strictly, construed. At common law the right to inspect public documents is well defined and understood. The authorities on the subject are very numerous, and they uniformly hold that such a right includes the right, when necessary to the attainment of justice, to take copies. We have been referred to no case, and are aware of none, in which this has ever been denied. Hence we must presume that the legislature, in giving the right of inspection in a case like the present, intended to give it with all its common-law incidents. Greenleaf, than whom there is no more accurate text-writer in modern times, lays it down that the inspection and exemplification of the records of the king's courts is, and from a very early period has been, the common right of the subject. And as to other public documents, the custodian of them, he says, will, upon proper application, be compelled by *mandamus* to allow the applicant to inspect them, and, if desired, to take copies. 1 Greenl. Ev. §§ 471, 478. Tidd, in his Practice, gives it as a general rule, well settled, that a party has a right to inspect and take copies of all such books and records as are of a public nature wherein he has an interest. 1 Tidd, Pr. 593. And in conformity with the rule, Lord DENMAN, in Rex v. Justices, 6 Adol. & E. 84, remarked that "the court is by no means disposed to narrow its authority to enforce by *mandamus* the production of every document of a public nature in which any citizen can prove himself to be interested. For such persons, indeed, every officer appointed by law to keep records ought to deem himself for that purpose a trustee." Judge DILLON, in treating of the inspection of corporate books and records, which he says are of a public nature, states the same doctrine. "If the corporation," he says, "should refuse inspection of its books and records to any person having an interest therein, or, perhaps, for any proper purpose, to any inhabitant of the corporation, whether he had any special or private interest or not, a writ of *mandamus* would lie to command the corporation to allow such inspection and copies to be taken, under reasonable precautions to secure the safety of the originals." 2 Dill. Mun. Corp. § 684. The rule is stated in pretty much the same terms by another writer of authority, who says *mandamus* will lie in behalf of a member of a municipality entitled to an inspection of its books to permit him to make such inspection and to take copies. High, Extr. Rem. § 330. Authorities to the same effect might be multiplied almost indefinitely. We will, however, refer in this connection only to one other case, and that is Brouwer v. Cotheal, 10 Barb. 216. In that case the plaintiff, a stockholder in an incorporated insurance company, sued the defendant, an officer of the company, to recover a penalty of $250 for refusing to allow the plaintiff to take a copy of the books containing the transfers of stock and the names of the stockholders. The action was brought under a statute of New York, which required the books to be open to the examination of every stockholder, and prescribed a penalty for refusing to exhibit them for examination. When the plaintiff called to examine the books they were shown him, and he commenced copying, whereupon the defendant closed them, saying he had no right to see any but his own name. The plaintiff, under these circumstances, recovered a judgment in the action, which was af-

firmed, the supreme court saying that the right of examination included the right to take memoranda, and, if necessary to enable the stockholder to state the result of his examination, to take copies. The remarks of the court in that case seem to us sound, and they are very pertinent to the present case. This view as to the scope and extent of the right of inspection given by the statute is further enforced by other statutory provisions to which our attention was called in the argument. Thus provision is made in detail for the mode in which the registration is to be conducted, for the transfer of voters who have removed from one election precinct to another, for the striking off from the registration books the names of those who have lost the right to vote by conviction of crime, and for the purging of the books; all or most of which provisions would surely fall short of having their intended effect unless the books were put upon the footing of public records. Especially is this so with respect to those provisions relating to the purging of the books. By section 86 of the Code the right is given to any five qualified voters of any election district to post written or printed notices fifteen days before any regular day of registration, at not less than three public places in said district, of the names of all persons alleged by said votes to be improperly on the registration books of that district; and by the same section it is made the duty of the registrar on the regular day of registration to hear testimony on the subject, and, if he be satisfied that any person mentioned in said notice is not a qualified voter, to strike his name from the books. This is a most important provision, and it is obvious that a full and intelligent exercise of the right it gives is dependent upon the right not only to inspect, but to take copies of, the registration books. It was virtually conceded in the argument that the right to copies of the books could not be successfully resisted if this were a proceeding by five qualified voters having in view the exercise of the right given by the section just mentioned. But the statute no more gives the right to compel copies to be taken in the joint proceeding by five voters than in a proceeding like the present, by a single voter, nor is the right to take copies any more given for one legitimate purpose than another. That right is purely a common-law incident of the right of inspection given by the eighty-fourth section, except so far as it may be implied from other provisions of the statute. Nor does the fact that no compensation is provided for the registrar, either for making copies or for the time consumed by others in taking copies under his observation, upon which fact much stress was laid in the argument, in any way affect the case. Neither did the legislature see fit to provide compensation for keeping the books at all times open to inspection, and yet the right of the public to inspect them without charge is not disputed. The question of compensation was a matter exclusively for the legislature, and it is not for the courts to nullify a plain legal right, because certain duties are imposed upon registrars for the performance of which no compensation is provided by law. As to the right of the petitioner to a mandamus, in the present case we have no doubt. The duty, performance of which is sought to be coerced, is a public duty, and hence the interest which he as a citizen has in the enforcement of the laws is a sufficient interest to entitle him to maintain this proceeding. "Where the question," says High, "is one of public right, and the object of the mandamus is to procure the enforcement of a public duty, the people are regarded as the real party, and the relator at whose instigation the proceedings are instituted need not show that he has any legal or special interest in the result, it being sufficient to show that he is a citizen, and as such interested in the execution of the laws." High, Extr. Rem. § 431. See, also, Ferry v. Williams, 41 N. J. Law, 332. A peremptory mandamus must therefore be awarded, as prayed for in the petition.

RICHARDSON, J., absent.

LACY, J., (dissenting.) Upon the petition of the petitioner, Clay, a citizen of Warwick county, Va., the court is asked to award the peremptory writ of mandamus to compel the respondent, one of the registrars of said county, to furnish to him a copy, or to allow him, the said petitioner, to make a copy, of the registration books in his charge as a public officer of the state of Virginia. The respondent answers, and says that he is a public officer of this state. That he is the registrar of the district in question, and has duly qualified as such, and taken an oath to perform the duties of his said office according to law. That chapter 8 of the Code of Virginia sets forth in sections 71, 73–76, 78–86, plainly, what his duties are and how he shall perform them. That the law provides for a copy of the registration books in section 71, supra, and only there; and there it is provided for when the said books become so mutilated and defaced in the judgment of the electoral board of the county, under which he holds his office, as to render it proper. That as an honest, faithful, and discreet citizen and officer he has ever looked to the public good, and sought to do his duty as directed by the law of Virginia. "That within the last two or three months H. De B. Clay has made two applications to him for the purpose of inspecting, making memoranda, and copying the registration books, which were under his authority and control: that he has never refused to allow the said books to be inspected, but has ever and will ever keep and preserve the same, and have them open to the inspection of the public. But he has ever and will ever, unless compelled by authority of law, refuse to allow said registration books to be copied." He responds further that if he gave a copy to one citizen he could refuse none. That he is the lawful custodian of these books, and is required by law to them safely keep; and, as the law does not allow them to go out of his custody, his presence would be necessary whenever and wherever a copy should be made.

That he has often been requested to furnish copies by political partisans of both political parties, but that he has refused to allow copies of the registration books to be made, because it is no part of his duty to do so. That his office is a statutory office, and the duties of the same are prescribed by law; and that, when he has strictly complied with the law's prescription, he has failed in no legal duty. That the petitioner, Clay, like any other citizen of the commonwealth, has the right to inspect the registration books so far as they may concern him, but he cannot as a citizen set up any supervisory power over the said books. That the law prescribes in section 86 of chapter 8 of the Code of Virginia how these books may be purged if they are supposed to require that. That it is by law provided that it shall be lawful for any five qualified voters of any election district to give notice, and the notice to be signed by them all, when by proper proceedings, upon notice, and upon legal evidence, the questions raised can be duly considered and correctly and justly determined. That the law does not bestow upon one citizen this or any other right concerning these books except the right to inspect as one of the public, (that is, to inspect so far as they concern him;) and, not so granting, but expressly providing for the matter otherwise, the effect is to exclude the claim. But that the petitioner cannot claim the right by implication, upon the insistence that the law does not forbid. To have the right to mandamus he must not only show that the law does not forbid his claim, but he must establish a clear legal right, and be without any other adequate legal remedy. It is not the province of this writ to determine whether he or some other person has or has not such a right; his right must be clear. "To justify the issuance of the writ to enforce the performance of an act by a public officer two things must concur: The act must be one the performance of which the law especially enjoins as a duty resulting from an office, and an actual omission on the part of the respondent to perform it. It is incumbent on the relator to show not only that the respondent has failed to perform the required duty, but that the performance thereof is actually due from him at the time of the application." 14 Amer. & Eng. Enc. Law, par. 11, p. 105, and numerous authorities there cited. This is a concise and correct statement of the law upon this branch of this inquiry. Again, in the same work, at page 130, upon the same subject, it is said: "The office of the writ of mandamus, when addressed to a public officer, is to compel him to exercise such functions as the law confers upon him. When the law enjoins upon such officer the performance of a specific act or duty, obedience to the law may, in the absence of other adequate remedy, be enforced by this writ. But the writ neither creates nor confers power upon the officer to whom it is directed. It can do no more than to command the exercise of powers already existing; and in order to compel a public officer by mandamus to do an act at the instance of the relator, he must show that he has an interest in the act sought to be coerced. The writ of *mandamus* lies to compel a public officer to perform a duty concerning which he is vested with no discretionary power, and which is either imposed upon him by some express enactment or necessarily results from the office which he holds." See authorities cited, notes 1 and 2, p. 140, 14 Amer. & Eng. Enc. Law. By the law of this state (section 84, Code Va.) the registrar is required to keep and preserve the registration books, and that the said books shall at all times be open to public inspection. There is no contention that there is any duty imposed upon him by law to copy these books unless the duty is imposed by the words: "And the said registration books shall be at all times open to public inspection." But the majority of the court find in these words the right in any citizen to have a copy made of these books.

Does the right to inspect carry with it the right to have a copy? What does an inspection mean? In its most comprehensive sense, to look into, from the Latin *inspicere*, but in practice, an examination; and in this sense all public records are open for an inspection by any person having an interest in them; and the respondent does not refuse to permit an inspection of these books. But the right to a copy is not bestowed by the law, none is provided for, and no compensation allowed for making it. In the case of public judicial writings, these are open to the inspection of every one upon paying the fees of the officer charged with their custody; and if this inspection is denied, the right is enforced by rule of court where an action is pending, and by writ of *mandamus* where no action is pending. 4 Minor, Inst. p. 714; 1 Greenl. Ev. §§ 472, 477, 478. This is conceded. No person has denied that it is the duty of a public officer to allow an inspection of such public records, and by reason of our statute, which so provides, copies may be had of these, and the law prescribes the officer to make the copy, and the fees payable therefor; and, the duty being plain and prescribed by law, any citizen may have a copy upon application, and upon paying the fees prescribed by law; and a failure to perform this duty will entitle the citizen or any person to the writ of *mandamus*, against the officer. But there are public writings not judicial, such as these official registers, of the qualified voters of the district, and the right to an inspection of these is not so universal as with regard to public writings judicial in their character, and is regulated by law in this state. The writing in question is open by law to the inspection of the public, and thus far there is a public duty upon the registrar; but for obvious reasons the law does not provide for copies. These books are subject to daily changes throughout the year by section 78 of the Code. A name or names may be added or removed, as occasion requires. There is no recordation of this writing. It has no permanent official character or form. A copy would be no exemplification of the original for a single day. Necessarily, and by law actually protean in character, it changes in the midst of a shifting popula-

tion continually. It is a public writing under the sanction of the law, and its use by the law prescribed. It is not for the courts to prescribe how it shall be kept, or when copied. With the wisdom of the law we have little to do. It is not the policy of the law to require copies to be made of these books except where the originals have been destroyed. It appears to me to be wisely not provided that these books shall be copied at the instance of everybody. A copy might be obtained every week in the year, and yet no two copies be alike; one political leader or follower, having fortified himself with what he regarded as an unanswerable authority for all of his associates to demand the right to vote, might find his antagonist also armed with a supposed evidence *per contra*, and many disputes be set up at the polls, and many tribunals installed to determine questions left to the determination of a board of sworn officers. The law has wisely left such a provision out. But, however that may be, (and with that I claim not to deal,) my opinion is that a right to a copy must first be established by law, then, if the right so clearly exists, it must be appointed by law unto the respondent to make and deliver it, before it can become his duty to do so. That if there is no right established and ordained by the law, and no duty imposed upon the respondent by law to make the copy, the court cannot create the duty, and then issue the writ to compel its performance. The question is one of a legal right, and the petitioner must show the existence of such right, or the *mandamus* cannot issue. I am of opinion to deny the writ and to dismiss the petition.

FREDENHEIM et al. v. ROHR et al.

(Supreme Court of Appeals of Virginia. April 30, 1891.)

JURISDICTION OF COURT OF APPEALS—INJUNCTION APPOINTMENT OF RECEIVER—APPEAL.

1. Code Va. § 3438, provides that when a circuit or corporation court or judge thereof shall refuse to award an injunction, a copy of the proceedings in court, and the original papers presented to the judge in vacation, with his order of refusal, may be presented to a judge of the court of appeals, who may thereupon award an injunction. In an action to set aside a deed of trust, a preliminary injunction, on motion for an injunction and the appointment of a receiver, was granted, restraining the trustee from selling the goods therein conveyed until the "motion could be heard and determined." Upon the hearing the petition was denied, and the preliminary injunction was dissolved. *Held*, that under the statute a judge of the court of appeals has authority thereafter, upon the original bill, to grant such petition thus denied.

2. An appeal from the granting of such petition by a judge of the court of appeals will not lie, especially where the property is in the hands of the receiver, and no motion was made below to dissolve the injunction, and no proofs taken.

Per LACY and RICHARDSON, JJ., dissenting.

For majority opinion, see ante, 193.

LACY, J., *(dissenting.)* This is an appeal from an order of the chancery court of the city of Richmond, entered on the 15th day of May, 1889, and the order of the judge of that court, entered on the 21st day of May, 1889. The order of the 15th day of May, supra, was entered in the said chancery court by myself as one of the judges of this court in pursuance of section 3438 of the Code of Virginia, which is as follows: "When a circuit or corporation court or a judge thereof shall refuse to award an injunction, a copy of the proceedings in court, and the original papers presented to the judge in vacation, with his order of refusal, may be presented to a judge of the court of appeals, who may thereupon award the injunction." The order of 21st of May, supra, was an order entered by the judge of the chancery court, directing the sheriff to enforce the said order of the 15th of May. The said orders and the order of the chancery court of date May 14, 1889, are all the orders copied in the record presented to one of the judges for an appeal in this case; but there was one other, of date May 7th, which will be hereafter referred to, and which is made to play an important part in the opinion of the majority of the court. This order of May 7, 1889, was rendered upon the filing of the bill for an injunction and for the appointment of a receiver. The bill was filed by the appellees, creditors of the appellant M. S. Fredenheim, and all other creditors who should come in and contribute their share of the expenses, alleging that the appellant Margaret S. Fredenheim, who was conducting a millinery business in the city of Richmond as a sole trader, was indebted to the said plaintiffs in large sums of money contracted as late as March 21, 1889, to one, and to another March 1, 1889; and that, being thus so indebted by debts contracted about 30 days before, on the 27th of April, 1889, she made a deed, by which all of her stock of goods was conveyed to a trustee for the benefit of pretended debts and creditors, with intent to defraud them and her other creditors. (1) That the said Margaret S. Fredenheim was largely indebted at the time of making the said assignment. (2) That the fraudulent alienee, the trustee, was a hopelessly insolvent, broken merchant. (3) That this fraudulent alienee was the brother of the only preferred creditor of first class in any amount, one Fannie Bottigheimer. (4) That the said fraudulent alienee had actually participated in, and procured the said assignment with fraudulent intent. (5) That the deed provided by an agreement beforehand that the grantor and her husband should continue to conduct the business by the trustee for 60 days, and remain in possession for that period. (6) That after an assignment had been determined on, and its terms arranged, and preferences provided for by said deed agreed on, she made large purchases of goods, and inflated her stock to an unreasonable degree. (7) That she sold in Norfolk and other cities not named by her husband representing himself as a traveling salesman, large bills of goods for cash, at prices far below the market value and cost of said goods, when such goods are usually sold on credit, and were so bought by her on credit. (8) That in order to procure this credit for herself this fraudulent grantor had made false statements and

estimates of assets. That it was of the utmost importance to the said plaintiffs that this fraudulent grantee and trustee should be removed, and be enjoined and restrained from acting as trustee, and that a receiver be appointed to take charge of and sell the said goods under the order of the court, and praying for the appointment of the said receiver, and an injunction, etc.

Soon after the filing of this bill, his honor, Judge EDWARD H. FITZHUGH, on the 7th of May entered the order of the court as follows: "Upon reading the bill in this cause the court is of opinion that the plaintiffs should give reasonable notice to the defendants, Margaret S. Fredenheim and A. Fredenheim, her husband, and to H. Rosenberg, trustee, of the time and place of moving for the injunction and the appointment of a receiver, and the court doth so order and direct. And the court doth further order and direct that in the mean time and until the said motion can be heard and determined, [what motion was this to be determined hereafter? Obviously the motion for an injunction and the appointment of a receiver,] the above-named defendants are enjoined and restrained from removing, selling, or in any way disposing of the stock of goods in the store No. 118 East Broad street, Richmond, in the bill and proceedings mentioned," and bond required in the penalty of $500. In the opinion of the majority this order is referred to in the following language: "This bill [charging, etc., and paying, etc.] was presented to Judge FITZHUGH in the chancery court of Richmond city on the 7th day of May, 1889, who on that day granted an injunction according to the prayer of the bill, but declared in the order that he deemed it proper that the defendant should have reasonable notice of the time and place of moving for the appointment of a receiver as prayed for in the bill, and an opportunity to move to dissolve the injunction, and this accordingly took place after this injunction had become effectual." This is the language of the majority referring to the order of May 7, 1889. The order itself says: "The court is of opinion that the plaintiffs should give reasonable notice to the defendants [naming them] of the time and place of moving for the injunction prayed for in the bill, and for the appointment of a receiver, and the court doth so order and direct." But the opinion of the majority says "that the court that day granted an injunction in accordance with the prayer of the bill," and "declared that it was proper to give notice of the time and place of moving for the appointment of a receiver." I do not see in the order of May 7, 1889, above inserted in full, any justification for this construction by the opinion. It evidently does not grant an injunction in accordance with the prayer of the bill, but expressly declines to do so in words unmistakable, until notice has been given to the other side. I find, however, in the brief of the appellants the following language: "Bill was presented to Judge FITZHUGH in court on the 7th of May, 1889, and the judge of the chancery court had granted an injunction according to the prayer of the bill, but had directed that reasonable notice should be given to the defendants of the time and place of moving for the appointment of a receiver prayed for in the bill." This may be a mere coincidence, as great minds often run in the same channel, but obviously brief of counsel is not the record of the court under review. This is the fundamental error of the opinion, and prepared the way for the others which culminated in what I regard as the erroneous conclusion.

This order of May 7th was followed by the order of May 14th, when notice having been given as required by the court, the order of that day was entered as follows: "This day came the plaintiffs, Nathan Rohr and others, by counsel, and upon their motion for the appointment of a receiver, made in open court, due notice of the time and place having been given the defendants in this cause, according to the requirement of the preliminary injunction awarded herein, and on the like motion of the defendants by counsel to dissolve the said injunction, and was argued by counsel, on consideration whereof, and upon the reading of the bill and the petition heretofore filed in this cause, exhibits filed therewith, and affidavits filed in behalf of the plaintiffs in support of said motion, to-wit, S. Frautman, S. W. Gerhardt, John L. Baker, and Edgar W. Carrington, and the letter of M. S. Fredenheim, addressed to Mess. Goldsmith, Bachrach & Co., and the certificates of the clerk of the circuit court of the city of Richmond, and the clerk of the chancery court, city of Richmond, [these certificates of these clerks were certifications of unsatisfied judgments and decrees against the insolvent trustee, showing his insolvency for many thousands of dollars of long standing,] the answers of the defendants treated as affidavits, and the paper marked '1,' signed by Thos. Potts and others, to the reading of which paper and affidavit objection is made, [this paper signed by Thomas Potts and others is relied on in the opinion, and is referred to as follows: "And a large number of the leading merchants of the city of Richmond certified that the trustee named in the deed was peculiarly qualified for the trust in question,"] and the affidavit of M. S. Fredenheim and H. Rosenberg, trustee, the court doth refuse the injunction prayed for in the bill and the appointment of a receiver, and doth dissolve the preliminary injunction awarded in this cause, on the 7th day of May, 1889, [which, let us remember, by its terms was expressly limited to the time when the motion to award an injunction and for the appointment of a receiver could be heard,—"in the mean time, and until the said motion can be heard and determined;"] but the court being of opinion that upon the application of any party in interest a bond in the penalty of ten thousand dollars with approved security may be required of the trustee, H. Rosenberg, for the faithful discharge as such trustee and the performance of his duties, which bond was then tendered in open court by the said H. Rosenberg, trustee, with Thomas Potts and Fannie Bot-

tigheimer as his sureties thereon, to which security no objection was offered, but in consequence of the absence of said securities at the moment, leave is given to said Rosenberg, trustee, to execute said bond in open court to-morrow morning at ten o'clock A. M., along with his said sureties; and the court doth accordingly direct that said bond be executed at said hour accordingly." This is the full text of this order. Now, let us see what reference there is to it in the opinion of the majority. Speaking of the 7th of May order, requiring notice of the motion to award an injunction and for the appointment of a receiver, it says: "After this injunction had become effectual, [?] [which by its terms was in the mean time and until the said motion could be heard,] the case came on to be heard on the 14th day of May, 1889, upon the bill, etc., and upon due notice and motion to dissolve, and was fully heard upon the arguments of counsel, upon the motion to dissolve the injunction and appoint a receiver, and for no other purpose, whereupon a decree was entered dissolving the injunction which had been awarded by Judge FITZHUGH on the 7th of May, 1889, * * * denying the prayer of the bill for the appointment of a receiver, but requiring the trustee, H. Rosenberg, to execute a bond with approved security in the penalty of ten thousand dollars, * * * which bond was accordingly promptly executed by the said trustee."

We see that in the opinion of the majority it is said that the cause came on on the 14th day of May, on the motion to dissolve the injunction and for the appointment of a receiver, and for no other purpose, and a decree was rendered dissolving the injunction and refusing to appoint a receiver; but the order entered on that day, as appears in the printed transcript, says: "The court doth refuse the injunction prayed for in the bill, and the appointment of a receiver, and doth dissolve [not the injunction prayed for in the bill, but] the preliminary injunction awarded in this cause on the 7th of May, 1889, [that is, the injunction awarded by the court upon its own motion in the mean time, and until the motion to award the injunction prayed for in the bill could be heard upon notice.]" And again, the opinion states that the bond of the trustee referred to "was accordingly promptly executed." The decree of the court, on the other hand, as appears by the record, was not that the bond was promptly executed, but here is the very different language used by the record upon this subject: "Which bond was then tendered in open court by the said H. Rosenberg, trustee, with Thomas Potts and Fannie Bottigheimer as his sureties thereon, to which security no objection was offered, but in consequence of the absence of said securities at the moment leave is given to said Rosenberg, trustee, to execute said bond in open court to-morrow morning, along with his said securities;" so that said bond with said securities was not promptly executed, but, so far as this record discloses, such bond never was executed; the security Thomas Potts was not only absent at the moment, but remained perpetually absent, and the bond subsequently filed and copied in the record and containing his name recited as one of the obligors, was never excented by him, although he is the same Thomas Potts, no doubt, who heads the list of the "large number of business men of Richmond," referred to above, who knew H. Rosenberg for many years, etc. Does the record justify the statement in the opinion, that the case came on and was fully heard upon the arguments of counsel upon due notice and motion to dissolve the injunction and for the appointment of a receiver? On the contrary, it shows that the motion refused was one to grant an injunction and to appoint a receiver. But another inspection of the brief of counsel for the appellant will show how this misapprehension of the record came about. It is there said: "After said injunction had been awarded by Judge FITZHUGH, and had become effectual, the defendants filed their answers, * * * and the case being fully heard upon the arguments of counsel, and the decree upon its face showing that the case was brought on upon a motion to dissolve the injunction and appoint a receiver, and for no other purpose, the injunction which had been thus awarded by Judge FITZHUGH on the 7th of May, 1889, was dissolved, and the receivership asked for was denied, but the trustee, H. Rosenberg, was required to execute a bond in the penalty of $10,000, with approved security, for the faithful discharge of his duties as such trustee, which bond was accordingly executed." When this language was on the brief of counsel it was "simply executed," but when transplanted to the opinion it was, in the exuberance of the writer, "promptly executed," whereas the bond offered in court on the 14th of May with sureties to whom no objection was made was never executed at all. The only bond filed was executed by Bottigheimer, who is the preferred creditor, and chiefly interested in maintaining the alleged fraudulent deed.

The record in this case shows that a bill was filed by creditors of a defaulting debtor, who, having greatly inflated a stock of merchandise a few days before, had sold large quantities of the goods purchased recently and not paid for, not in the usual course of business, upon credit or for cash upon a profit, but below cost price, and for cash, by sending her husband out to make these secret sacrifices in distant cities, and then conveyed the unpaid-for goods, not to secure the purchase price for the same, but first to pay a large debt to the sister of the trustee, and provided that the defaulting debtor and her husband should practically continue to manage and run the business for 60 days; and the affidavits filed show that the alleged trustee was not to be found about the premises, but that the alleged fraudulent grantor and her husband were actually in charge, and when anxious inquiries were made for this trustee he could not be seen, but the husband was there, declaring that he could attend to anything, and said that his wife proposed to pay 25 cents on the dollar as a compromise. That the object of the bill was to set aside the said deed as actually fraudulent, and charged fraud upon the grantor and upon the grantee, and asked for an injunction to stop the sacrifice of the property in question, and to place the same in the bonded hands of a receiver of the court, charging and showing by judgments and decrees unsatisfied against him to the amount of thousands of dollars of long standing that the trustee was insolvent (which insolvency the trustee admitted in his answer) and irresponsible. That the hearing of this motion for an injunction and the appointment of a receiver was adjourned for a few days, to allow notice to the defendants, and in the mean time, and until this motion could be heard, an injunction was temporarily awarded until the motion to award an injunction and appoint a receiver could be heard upon notice. That upon notice being given and the motion heard the injunction was refused, but the trustee required to give a bond. That upon this refusal of the chancery court judge in open court, to award an injunction an application was made to one of the judges of this court, as is expressly authorized by section 3438, which says: "When a circuit or corporation court or a judge thereof shall refuse to award an injunction, a copy of the proceedings in court and the original papers presented to a judge in vacation, with his order of refusal, may be presented to a judge of the court of appeals, who may thereupon award the injunction," and the same was awarded accordingly. It is idle to say that such an act was *ultra vires*, as is said in the opinion of the majority. The next section of the Code directs that such order shall be certified to and become an order of the court below, and this was so ordered accordingly. Without moving to dissolve this injunction in the court below, and without a transcript of the record except the bill, the order of May 14, 1889, and the order of the judge of this court awarding the injunction, and the order of the judge of the chancery court enforcing the same, an appeal was applied for and obtained. The petition for an appeal sets forth that the judge of the chancery court, Judge WELLFORD, sitting for Judge FITZHUGH, entered an order dissolving a preliminary order entered by Judge FITZHUGH, and refusing to appoint a receiver, and also refusing to award an injunction prayed for in the bill; and yet the opinion states that this order dissolved the injunction which had been awarded according to the prayer of the bill upon full hearing and argument upon the merits. And the opinion of the majority further says: "If the complainants in the bill were dissatisfied or aggrieved by this order of the chancellor, their plain remedy, as prescribed by section 3454, Code of 1887, was by appeal." Upon turning to section 3454, Code Va., we see that it prescribes that "any person who is a party to any case in chancery wherein there is a decree or order dissolving an injunction, or to any case requiring money to be paid, or the possession or title to property to be changed, or adjudicating the principles of a cause, or in any case in which there is a final judgment, decree, or order, may present a petition," etc. Now, under this section, where could the plaintiff in this case lawfully find authority to present a petition for appeal? The decree of the court says that it refuses to award an injunction. How was the case heard and decided upon its merits? The object of the suit was to annul an alleged fraudulent deed. Was this deed annulled, or did the court refuse to annul the same? Not by any order of the decrees in this record. The bill sought to subject the property conveyed in the deed to the payment of the debts of the plaintiffs. Was this prayer granted or denied? It certainly was not granted. Did the court below do anything else than refuse to award an injunction, and refuse to appoint a receiver, and require the trustee to give a bond? This was all; and yet we are gravely told that if the plaintiffs were aggrieved by this order, deciding nothing and refusing to do anything except to require the trustee to give a bond at the suit of creditors who had brought their suit to that end, their remedy was by appeal. There is no authority for this position in the 3454th section of the Code of Virginia. This authority must be sought for somewhere else than the Code or any previous decision of this court. In a paper copied in the record signed by the appellants' counsel this supposed law is set forth as follows: "This decree of the 14th of May, 1889, was rendered upon the bill, answers, and depositions of witnesses and arguments of counsel upon a full hearing of the case upon the questions raised upon due notice. If the decree of the chancery court was erroneous, the plaintiffs' remedy was by appeal from that decree. * * * The jurisdiction of the supreme court of appeals and of the judges thereof is fixed by the constitution and statute law of the state. A judge of said court may award an appeal or writ of error upon a petition and copy of the record in a proper case. Orders dissolving an injunction or appointing a receiver by the express terms of the statute are made subjects of appeal in a proper case. See Code 1887, § 3454." If there are any such express terms in this statute they do not appear to be embodied in any of its words. No such construction had ever before been placed upon section 3454. and it was not easy to anticipate such a construction. So the plaintiffs, having been refused an injunction by the chancery court, in accordance with the prayer of the bill, as the order itself says, and not being by any law then in force entitled to an appeal under section 3438 of the Code of Virginia, applied to a judge of this court for an injunction. That section provides, as we have said, that when a circuit (which includes the chancery court of Richmond) or corporation court or judge thereof shall refuse to award an injunction, a copy of the proceedings in court and the original papers presented to the judge in vacation, with his order of refusal, may be presented to a judge of the court of appeals, who may thereupon award an injunction. Here is the authority in the law under which the judge

of this court acted, when the injunction was awarded. Yet that action is characterized as *ultra vires*. This rather high-sounding phrase, used a good deal in the brief of counsel, has no rightful place in the opinion of the majority, if everything there urged were correct. It has no application, as seems to be supposed, to a case where a court or judge has proceeded in excess of his jurisdiction, but is a phrase which refers to the exercise by corporations of powers not granted in the act of their creation. It is agreed that corporations cannot exercise their powers for purposes foreign to their creation. This is a question of no interest in this discussion, yet for the benefit of enthusiastic counsel I refer them and the learned writer of the opinion in this case to Mr. Bouvier's Dictionary (volume 3, p. 760,) "Ultra Vires;" 1 Dill. Mun. Corp. § 381; 2 Dill. Mun. Corp. §§ 749, 766; 13 Amer. Law Rev. 632; 2 Minor, Inst. 549; Ang. & A. Corp. 117. These text-writers fully explain the legitimate use of the phrase in question.

The opinion contains the following: "This statute (section 3454) confers no original jurisdiction upon one of the judges of this court to award an injunction, except in the case where the application has been made first to a judge of an inferior court, either in term-time or vacation," and cites cases. It is hard to realize that this language was seriously used with reference to this case in the light of the decrees already recited from the record, (and there are no others in it.) We have been helped to an explanation of the startling statements in the opinion several times in this discussion by turning to read the strange things to be found in the appellants' brief. On the first page of this brief we find the following: "No original jurisdiction was conferred upon any of the courts of appeal to award an injunction except in those cases in which the application has been first made to a judge of the inferior court, either in term-time or vacation, and been refused;" citing the same cases. A good deal of complaint is found in appellants' brief that the order complained of was made without notice, and Underwood v. McVeigh, 28 Grat. 418, is cited as a case in point, and all this, to the extent of whole pages of printed matter, is transferred solidly to the opinion, but an inspection of the record shows that it has not the remotest application to this case. The fullest notice was everywhere required and given, and the fullest hearing accorded. The chancery court, as we have seen, did not take the first step without notice. Nothing was done without notice, and every order entered in the case before the order granting the appeal was an order in that court. What has Underwood v. McVeigh to do with this case?

The next question raised and urged by counsel and taken up and adopted by the opinion is that a judge of this court, in awarding an injunction where it has been refused by the court below, is without authority to appoint a receiver. These are inconsistent positions taken by counsel, it being contended at one time that the court below did not refuse to award an injunction. But as the opinion adopts them, I will remark that where the question is whether a judge of this court, when awarding an injunction to go as an order in the court below, must in some cases necessarily appoint a receiver, as in this case, or destroy the rights of property involved by leaving the property without a hand to hold or protect and guard, the grant of the authority to award the injunction carries with it as a necessary incident the authority to appoint a receiver. But equally true is it that that question is not worth discussing in a dissenting opinion, as it is no longer an open question in this court, except so far as it is disturbed by this case, which is not at all, as the opinion makes this out to be a case where an injunction was granted, and dissolved upon the merits. In the case of Graeme v. Cullen, 23 Grat. 282, 285, Judge JOYNES, of this court, so acted,—awarded an injunction and appointed a receiver, as did Judge BURKS in the case of Richardson v. Willcox,[1] from the circuit court of Charles City, while I was the judge of that circuit. Beverley v. Brooke, 4 Grat. 189, 212; Penn v. Whiteheads, 12 Grat. 83. Upon the merits enough has been said already for the purposes I have in view to put myself right upon the record, and for that purpose I have quoted largely from the record.

One word as to the propriety of the order granting the appeal. The order refusing to award the injunction was rendered on the 14th of May. The order made by one of the judges of this court was made on the 15th of May. The defendants defied this order, denouncing it as ultra vires, as the opinion has done. Application was made to me to supplement it and enforce it. This I declined to do, as that was the province of the chancellor below. This the chancellor did, by decree entered on the 22d of May. On the 23d of May—the next day—one of the judges of this court—the writer of the opinion—granted an appeal, which was interpreted to reverse and nullify the order awarding the injunction, without any consultation whatever with the judge who had awarded the injunction, and this, as I have shown from the record already, without obtaining a transcript of the record, as is required by section 3457, Code Va.; one of the decrees relied on not being copied, only 11 pages being brought up, whereas it was necessary subsequently to bring up 118 pages in addition, consisting chiefly of the petitions of numerous creditors seeking to set aside the deed as fraudulent; affidavits flatly contradicting one the other; not a deposition taken in the case; no principle in the cause settled; the possession of the property unchanged, because in this case the trustee was in court and the receiver was in court as soon as he qualified, which he did do, and the possession of the property was in the hands of the court in either case; and there had been no order dissolving an injunction, and no final decree in the cause, and no motion had been made in the lower court to dissolve the decree awarding the injunction. Clearly there was no order in the case to which

by law and according to the unbroken decisions of this court up to this time an appeal would lie. See the case of Jamison v. Jamison's Adm'x, 86 Va. 54, 9 S. E. Rep. 480, and cases cited. I think the appeal was unauthorized by law, was improvidently awarded, and should have been dismissed without more, as was moved by the appellees. And for the foregoing reasons I dissent from the opinion of the majority on all points. No appeal lies in this state from an order awarding an injunction and appointing a receiver; certainly not in a case like this, when the property was in the hands of the court's officer, when there was no motion made in the lower court to dissolve this injunction, and no proofs taken, and no decision on the merits.

RICHARDSON, J., also dissents from the opinion of the court.

CLEVELAND COTTON-MILLS v. COMMISSIONERS OF CLEVELAND COUNTY.

(Supreme Court of North Carolina. May 12, 1891.)

CONTRACT BY COUNTY COMMISSIONERS—RATIFICATION BY JUSTICES OF THE PEACE.

Defendants, county commissioners, contracted in writing to pay plaintiff the actual cost of constructing a bridge upon a highway in the county. A majority of the justices of the county, not then in session, executed a writing ratifying the contract, and afterwards at a regular joint meeting of the commissioners and justices a quorum of the latter voted in ratification of said contract. Held, that under Code N. C. § 707, subsec. 10, providing that where the cost of a bridge exceeds $500 the commissioners can order its construction only with the concurrence of a majority of the justices of the peace, the approval of the contract by a majority of the justices sitting as an organized body is a sufficient compliance therewith. MERRIMON, C. J., and CLARK, J., dissenting.

Appeal from superior court, Cleveland county; G. H. BROWN, Judge.

The plaintiff contracted in writing with the defendants to construct for the latter a bridge across First-Broad river in the county of Cleveland, and the latter stipulated and promised to pay the former for the same the actual cost of the bridge. The price was not otherwise specified. A majority of the justices of the peace of that county, not in session with the defendants at the time, signed a paper writing in which they "do by our [their] signatures ratify and confirm and concur in the above contract, made on the 21st day of May, 1888, between the county commissioners of Cleveland county and Cleveland Cotton-Mills," etc. In the contract it is stipulated that "the payments [are] to be made in annual installments in amounts equal to the tax on its [the plaintiff's] property in this county each year, until full payments shall be made." Afterwards, at a regular joint meeting in June, 1890, of the commissioners and justices of the peace, a quorum of the latter being present, the plaintiffs asked in writing that the justices of the peace "ratify and concur in the contract" mentioned above. A motion in this joint meeting was made to that effect, which was adopted, 23 jus-

---

[1] Not reported.

tices of the peace voting for and 13 against it. The defendants did not vote. The plaintiff complied fully on its part with the contract, and the defendants accepted the bridge, which cost $2,730.95. A new road was established leading across this bridge, and it and the bridge have been constantly used by the public, and there is no other way of crossing the river in the northern part of the county when the water is high. The board of commissioners for 1888, after the completion and acceptance of the bridge, "made the first payment on said bridge, amounting to $185.21, an amount equal to tax on plaintiff's property in this county for that year." Between the time of this first payment and the time when, under the contract, the second payment to be made came due, a new board of county commissioners came into office, and upon demand they refused and still refuse to pay the second installment of the contract price due the plaintiff, but nevertheless they exercise control over the new road which leads to and across the said bridge, and it and the road have been constantly used by the public as a highway, and the supervisors control the road. This action is brought to recover the sum of money alleged to be due to the plaintiff upon and by virtue of the said contract. The defendants contend that the contract sued upon is void, and of no effect, because it was not made "with the concurrence of a majority of the justices of the peace" of the county, as required by the statute, (Code, § 707, subsec. 10;) and further, that it is void because it undertakes to provide in advance that a part of the regular revenues of the county coming from the plaintiff shall be devoted to a specified purpose, etc. The court gave judgment for the plaintiff for the amount due, and the defendants appealed.

Batchelor & Devereux, for appellants. *W. J. Montgomery* and *J. F. Scheuck,* for appellee.

AVERY, J., *(after stating the facts as above.)* The courts of this country have generally adopted the common-law principle that, if an act is to be done by an indefinite body, the law, resolution, or ordinance authorizing it to be done is valid if passed by a majority of those present at a legal meeting. 1 Dill. Mun. Corp. § 277, (215.) Where the law creating a municipal corporation is silent on the subject, the majority of the members-elect or officers or persons authorized to act constitute the legal body, and a majority of the members of the legally organized body can exercise the powers delegated to the municipality. 1 Dill. Mun. Corp. § 278, (216;) Heiskell v. Mayor, etc., 65 Md. 125, 4 Atl. Rep. 116; Barnert v. Paterson, 48 N. J. Law, 395, 6 Atl. Rep. 15. The same rules apply to other bodies, whether the two houses of the legislature or other organized bodies of officers or persons to whom the legislature has given authority. The powers delegated to a county can, as a general rule, be exercised only by the board of county commissioners, or in pursuance of a resolution adopted by them. Code, § 703. The commissioners, organized and

acting as a board, are the embodiment of municipal authority. In their names the county must sue and be sued. The only limitations upon their exercise of the corporate functions of the municipality is to be found in subsections 1, 10, 11, 17, and 20 of section 707 of the Code. Subsection 10 provides that, where the cost of building or repairing a bridge shall exceed $500, the commissioners can order the construction or repair only "with the concurrence of a majority of the justices of the peace," as subsection 1 imposes the restriction that taxes shall not be levied by the board except "with the concurrence of a majority of the justices of the peace sitting with them." Before the constitution of 1868 was adopted the justices of the peace in the several counties exercised the powers delegated to the counties by the legislature. The justices of the peace were the judges of the courts of pleas and quarter sessions. For convenience the various statutes specified the particular number that must sit to discharge certain judicial duties or exercise police powers of different kinds. Rev. Code, c. 31, § 1. "A majority, or twelve," were required to meet on the second and third days of the term of the county court first held after the election, to take the sheriff's bond. Rev. Code, c. 105, § 10. The justices of the peace, "a majority being present," were required, at their first court held after the 1st of January of every year, to levy a tax for county purposes. Rev. Code, c. 28, § 1. The justices being then the representatives of the county as a corporation, and recognized by the law as a body clothed with judicial authority and charged with administrative duties, it followed that powers delegated to them were to be exercised by a majority constituting a quorum according to the common-law rule, unless some statute prescribed that a smaller number would be sufficient, or more than a majority would be required to discharge a specified official duty. After the constitutional amendments had been ratified and had taken effect (on January 1, 1877) the legislature, having entire control of county government, provided (Code, § 716) that the justices should meet biennially on the first Monday in June, and, a majority being present, "should proceed to elect not more than five nor less than three county commissioners." The commissioners can call the justices of the peace together not oftener than once in three months. 1d. § 717. The justices are required, by section 719 of the Code, to fill vacancies occurring in the board of commissioners of a county. It is clear that by implication of law a majority of the majority of the whole number necessary to constitute a quorum may fill a vacancy in the board of commissioners and elect all of the commissioners in the biennial meeting ("a majority being present") by the express terms of the law in the same way. In addition to the four instances already mentioned in which the justices of the peace of the several counties are required to participate in their government, we find that it is provided in subsections 11 and 20 of section 707 that the commissioners shall be clothed with authority to meet the necessary expenses of the several counties, or to sell or lease real estate belonging to the county, only with the "assent of a majority of the justices of the peace therein." We think it is clear that the purpose of the general assembly, according to the ordinary meaning of the language employed by it, was to require the concurrence of a majority of the whole number constituting a quorum, to be expressed in the usual way by a majority of those present, where the justices should ratify or express their approval of an order for the levying of taxes for county purposes, or provide for constructing bridges, involving an expenditure of more than $500, just as a majority (under chapter 28, § 1, Rev. Code) levied the tax before 1868.

Under the system of county government established by the constitution of 1868 the several justices of the peace were made each a judicial officer with a limited jurisdiction, and those residing in each township were created a body politic for certain purposes; but there were no powers exercised by all the justices of a county as a body, and consequently no provision of law recognizing them as an organization. After the amendments had been ratified the legislature of 1876–77 provided (Code, § 717) that they might organize at their meetings, to be held not oftener than four times a year, with the register of deeds as ex officio clerk, and, in the absence of a specific requirement, empowered a majority constituting a quorum to transact business. It seems probable that the general assembly did not propose originally to recognize the justices in their organized capacity except for the purposes mentioned, and therefore, in intrusting them with the supervisory power to ratify or annul the action of the commissioners in five out of the six, it was deemed best to declare what number should be requisite for each purpose, though the number prescribed might amount to an affirmance of the common-law rule. It must be remembered that, unless a contrary intent is apparent from the words of the statute, in each case a majority of the organized body is to constitute a quorum and express their will in the usual way. We must also note the fact that the powers to levy taxes to build costly bridges and to erect houses of correction are exercised by the commissioners, subject to "the concurrence of a majority of the justices of the peace," while the authority to borrow money to meet the necessary county expenses and to sell or lease the real estate of the county is made to depend upon the "assent of a majority of the justices of the peace therein." The language used in these subsections is much more restricted than that employed in the constitution, art. 7, § 7. That section provides that "no county, city, town, or other municipal corporation shall contract any debt, pledge its faith, or loan its credit, nor shall any tax be levied or collected by any officers of the same, except for the necessary expenses thereof, unless by a vote of the majority of the qualified voters therein." The language of the constitution is very widely different from that used in any of the statutes defining

v.13s.E.no.9—18

the powers of justices of the peace, to which we have referred. The constitutional inhibition is intended to prevent the creation of any such debts as those specified, not without the assent or concurrence of a majority, (which may be expressed by an organization comprising a majority,) but unless by a vote (actually cast) of a majority of the qualified voters therein (in the county) in favor of creating it. We think that the words, "by a vote of a majority," as an entirety, cannot be interpreted as equivalent to "with the concurrence," or "with the assent, of a majority," which can be manifested just as each house of the general assembly is in the habit of giving the assent of the body to a law by a majority of a quorum. Cooley, Const. Lim. marg. p. 141. Where the word "majority" is used in the statute to define a quorum, as in the subsections cited, the concurrence of the majority is ascertained by the universal rule governing deliberative bodies. Judge Cooley says: "A simple majority of a quorum is sufficient, unless the constitution establishes some other rule; and where, by the constitution, a two-thirds or three-fourths vote is made essential to the passage of any particular class of bill, two-thirds or three-fourths of a quorum will be understood, unless the terms employed clearly indicate that this proportion of all the members or of all those elected is intended." Cooley, Const. Lim. marg. p. 141. The constitution of Michigan provided that no act of incorporation should be passed by the legislature unless with the assent of at least two-thirds of each house. The supreme court of that state held that by the phrase mentioned, two-thirds of the legislative body, comprising a majority of the members elected and qualified, was meant. Southworth v. Railroad Co., 2 Mich. 287. The custom has been, where the framers of constitutions have meant a majority of the whole number, to indicate the intent to take the provision of the organic law out of the general rule of construction by using the words "a majority (or two-thirds, as the case may be) of the members elected." Sedg. St. & Const. Law, 533. The constitution of North Carolina (article 13, § 2) provides that no part of that instrument shall be altered "unless a bill to alter the same shall have been agreed to by three-fifths of each house of the general assembly." This clause received a legislative construction from the house of representatives when an amendment was passed by the votes of 60 out of 100 present, and out of an aggregate membership of 120. House Journal, 530, 707. When a case involving the construction of a similar clause in the constitution of Missouri (Harshman v. Bates Co., 92 U. S. 569) first came before the supreme court of the United States for interpretation, upon an analysis of the language ("unless two-thirds of the qualified voters of such city or town at a regular or special election to be held therein shall assent thereto") it was held to require the affirmative vote of two-thirds of all of the registered voters, and not to mean two-thirds of those voting. In County of Cass v. Johnston,

95 U. S. 360, the court overruled that decision, but Mr. Chief Justice WAITE, delivering the opinion of the court, rested the ruling entirely upon the idea that the courts of the United States must be governed by and conform to the construction given by the supreme court of Missouri to a similar statute enacted in pursuance of the same clause in the constitution of that state. Justice BRADLEY, in an able dissenting opinion, insisted that the clause in question had received no such judicial interpretation from the court of Missouri, and that it was in fact analogous to another section of the constitution of that state, which provided that no bill should be passed "unless by the consent of a majority of all the members elected to each branch of the general assembly." In the absence of such a provision in our own constitution the majority of a quorum, under the general rule, is deemed sufficient, and without the addition of the word "elected." Article 13, § 2, was interpreted, as we have seen, to require the affirmative vote of three-fifths of the whole (being for the particular purpose a quorum) that actually voted. In Duke v. Brown, 96 N. C. 130, 1 S. E. Rep. 873, Chief Justice SMITH adverts to the conflicting rulings in construing even such strong language as that used in the constitution of Missouri, and determining whether a requirement that a municipal debt could only be incurred by a vote of a majority of the voters should be interpreted to mean a majority of the qualified voters or a majority of those voting. The ruling of the court is made to depend, in part at least, "upon the difference in the terms used" in article 7, § 7, of our constitution from those employed in statutes and clauses of constitutions that have received judicial construction in other courts. This court had previously reached the conclusion, in a case decided at the same term,—Southerland v. City of Goldsboro, 96 N. C. 49, 1 S. E. Rep. 760,—that registered voters only were qualified voters, and that no county, town, or other municipal corporation could contract any debt, pledge its faith, or loan its credit, except for necessary expenses, unless a majority of the registered vote of the municipality was actually cast in favor of creating the debt. Rigsbee v. Durham, 98 N. C. 81, 3 S. E. Rep. 749. If the language used in section 707 (10) of the Code had been "with the concurrence by their votes of a majority of the justices of the peace of the county who have been duly appointed and have qualified," it would have been analogous to that upon which the other cases turned, and would have necessitated the actual casting of an affirmative vote by a majority of all the justices in the county who have qualified. This distinction is clearly drawn in the authorities cited, and in many others that might be added, and is fully sustained by "the reason of the thing."

It may lend some additional weight to this view of the subject to add that a careful review of the statutes providing a system of county government under the constitution adopted in 1835, as collated in the Revised Code, and a comparison of them with chapter 17 of the Code, will suggest the idea to any intelligent mind that the legislature of 1876-77 (in the exercise of the power given by the constitutional amendment to provide for the government of counties) was attempting to ingraft some features of the old system upon the new by giving to the justices of the peace, a majority being present and constituting a quorum, just as under the old *régime*, the power to supervise the levying of taxes, the creation of bonded debts, the sale of real estate belonging to the county, and the creation of large indebtedness even for the necessary expense of the county. The purpose evidently was in all these cases to return to ancient landmarks, and, if the language were doubtful, this apparent intent might come to our aid in interpreting it. But, following the construction given to the same and similar phrases in our courts, we find that the legislative intent in enacting section 707 (10) is manifest from the terms of the statute. We add here, too, to the ruling in Southerland v. City of Goldsboro, Duke v. Brown, and Rigsbee v. Durham, supra, all of which are distinguishable from that at bar in that the language employed in article 7, § 7, of the constitution is clearly susceptible of no other interpretation than that it is essential to the validity of the indebtedness that an actual majority of all of the registered voters within the corporate limits should cast their vote in favor of creating it. Wherever the words used are construed to require the affirmative support of a majority of all who are qualified to act, of course their assent must be manifested, not by remaining at home, but by actual participation in the effort to carry the measure. The distinction between this case and those cases mentioned depends, therefore, solely upon the construction of the language employed. It was not the purpose of this court in Duke v. Brown, supra, to lay down a general rule subversive of the well-established principle that a majority of a body, in the absence of some words clearly showing that a majority of all persons qualified to act as members of it was intended, is always to be interpreted to mean a majority of a quorum, and that a majority of the whole number authorized to participate is in law a quorum, in the absence of a special statutory requirement to the contrary. We think that where the phrase used is "qualified voters," it should be construed just as the courts have interpreted "members-elect." We attach no importance to the paper signed by an actual majority of the whole number of justices of the peace of the county. The action contemplated by the law was that of the justices of the peace in a lawfully constituted meeting as a body, as in cases where the validity of an agreement made by the governing officials of any other corporation is drawn in question. Duke v. Markham, 105 N. C. 131, 10 S. E. Rep. 1017. It was not intended that the two bodies —the board of county commissioners and the justices of the county—should become merged, and act jointly as one assemblage. In all of the cases mentioned where the justices of the peace are clothed with the supervisory power over the acts of the commissioners it seems to be contemplated by law that the board should first exercise its judgment, just as if its action would be final, but should not give effect to such action till the justices of the peace, either at a regular meeting or at one called by the commissioners according to law, should ratify and approve the order held in abeyance to await their consideration of its merits. The law (Code, § 717) names the register of deeds as the secretary of these assemblages, but leaves the organization beyond that an open question. It would seem to be proper that as an independent supervisory body they should appoint their own chairman, and await a report from the board of commissioners as to the preliminary action upon the matters that are subject to their approval. It is not necessary, taking the view of the subject which we have expressed, that we should discuss or decide the question whether, according to the admitted facts, the justices of the peace, or the board of commissioners, or both, ratified or sanctioned the original contract by subsequent acts in such a way as to amount to a waiver of irregularities. We hold that the contract was approved by the justices of the peace sitting as an organized body in the manner required by the statute, and therefore the contract needed no further recognition to impart validity to it. The contract between the plaintiff and the board of commissioners involved no agreement to appropriate the tax collected to other purposes than those prescribed by law. Upon the principle *id certum est quod certum reddi potest*, the cost of the bridge to be paid by the county was to be ascertained by keeping and rendering a careful account of the expenditure made in constructing it, while the size of the installments was to be determined by reference to the amount of tax levied on the property of the plaintiff in the county. If the county should pay a sum of money to the plaintiff, and the identical fund should be used the same day to satisfy the claim of the tax collector, it would not amount to a misappropriation of the tax. There is no error. The judgment of the court below is affirmed.

MERRIMON, C. J., (*concurring in the judgment.*) The plain, express words of the statute, (Code, § 707, subsec. 10,) and as well its obvious purpose, exclude and forbid the interpretation that the concurrence of a majority of a simple quorum or of a majority of one of the whole number of the justices of the peace of the county shall be sufficient to make valid a contract of the board of commissioners of the county for the construction or repair of a bridge or bridges that cost exceeding $500. The words employed are, "with the concurrence of a majority of the justices of the peace." These words are significant and important. They cannot be treated as mere surplusage and meaningless, as they must be if a majority of a majority of one of the whole number is sufficient, because, if such words had not been employed, such majority would have been required and sufficient. In the absence of

such words, and in the absence of all limiting words, a majority of a quorum, or a majority of a simple majority, would be necessary when such concurrence might be required. Such is the rule in all deliberative bodies and judicial tribunals. Then what useful, effective purpose do the words cited of the statute serve? That these words imply, and were intended to imply, the concurrence of a majority of the whole number of justices of the peace of the county further appears in this: The same statute (Id. § 710) prescribes that the justices of the peace "shall assemble at the court-house of their respective counties, and, a majority being present, [at the time designated,] shall proceed to the election of not less than three nor more than five persons, to be chosen from the body of the county, who shall be styled the 'Board of Commissioners for the County,'" etc. Here, in an important respect, it is plainly contemplated that a majority of a bare majority may elect. Why were the words " a majority of the justices of the peace concurring," or like pertinent words, omitted in this connection and employed in other important connections in the same statute? It is further provided, in subsection 14, that "the action of the board in creating or altering townships shall not be operative until approved by the justices of the peace at a regular meeting." Why were these words, "a majority of the justices of the peace concurring," etc., omitted in this connection? The legislature was clearly advertent to distinctions and differences made as to the voice of the justices of the peace. It cannot reasonably be said that it incautiously and carelessly made such difference with no practical purpose in view. The same statute (Id. § 717) further prescribes that "for the proper discharge of their duties the justices of the peace shall meet annually with the board of commissioners on the first Monday in June, unless they shall be oftener convened by the board of commissioners, which is empowered to call together the justices of the peace not oftener than once in three months." It is further prescribed (section 707, subsec. 1) that at such annual meeting "the board of commissioners is authorized, with the concurrence of a majority of the justices of the peace sitting with them, to levy, in like manner with the state taxes, the necessary taxes for county purposes," etc. It is further provided in subsection 9 of the same section that, "with the concurrence of a majority of the justices of the peace," the commissioners may "erect and repair the necessary county buildings, and to raise, by taxation, the moneys therefor," etc. It is further prescribed, in subsection 11 of the same section, that the commissioners shall have power "to borrow money for the necessary expenses of the county, with the assent of a majority of the justices of the peace therein, and not otherwise, and to provide for its payment." In subsection 17 it is provided that, "with the concurrence of a majority of the justices of the peace, the commissioners may make provision for the erection in each county of a house of correction." It will be hence observed that the "concurrence of a majority of the justices of the peace" is expressly required only whenever taxes are to be levied, debts are to be contracted, and obligations incurred in and by the counties. In respect to other matters, whenever they are to co-operate with the commissioners it is only requisite that a majority of a bare majority shall concur. Thus it appears that the legislature had a settled purpose to make distinctions and differences as indicated, the object being to secure the larger voice and more reliable judgment of the county authorities in the very important matters of levying taxes and creating county obligations to pay money. It was not intended that the county commissioners and a simple majority of a bare majority of the justices of the peace should exercise such authority. Such legislation was cautious and wise, and deemed a proper restraint upon the wild and reckless spirit of the times manifested in the creation of public debts. It is very apparent that the legislature had in view and followed up the spirit and purpose of the constitution as expressed in article 7, § 7, which provides that "no county, city, town, or other municipal corporation shall contract any debt, pledge its faith, or loan its credit, nor shall any tax be levied or collected by any officers of the same, except for the necessary expenses thereof, unless by a vote of the majority of the qualified voters therein." The statutory provisions above referred to, requiring the concurrence or assent of a majority of the justices of the peace, simply in effect extended this wholesome provision of the constitution to the levying of taxes and the creation of debts for the "necessary expenses" of counties. This purpose is obvious, and hence the words of the statute, "the concurrence of a majority of the justices of the peace," should receive the same interpretation as the substantially similar words, "by a vote of the majority of the qualified voters therein," of the constitutional provision just cited. The language of the two phraseologies is in effect the same, except as to the difference in their application. In the one the language material here is "the majority of the qualified voters;" in the other it is the "majority of the justices of the peace." Can the reasonable mind see substantial difference? The clause of the constitution just recited has been interpreted by this court in numerous cases, and it is firmly settled that the "majority of the qualified voters" required by it is a majority of all the qualified voters of the county, city, town, or other municipal corporation. Southerland v. City of Goldsboro, 96 N. C. 49, 1 S. E. Rep. 760; Duke v. Brown, 96 N. C. 127, 1 S. E. Rep. 873; McDowell v. Construction Co., 96 N. C. 514, 2 S. E. Rep. 351; Wood v. Town of Oxford, 97 N. C. 227, 2 S. E. Rep. 653; Rigsbee v. Durham, 98 N. C. 81, 3 S. E. Rep. 749, and 99 N. C. 341, 6 S. E. Rep. 64; and there are other cases to the same effect. As the words of the constitution under consideration and the like words of the statute to be interpreted are substantially the same, and are used for and intended to serve and subserve the same purpose, is it not reasonable, just, and

necessary that they must and shall receive the like interpretation? It is very difficult to see how any other conclusion can be reached. Hence the words to be interpreted of the statute, "with the concurrence of a majority of the justices of the peace," imply a majority of all the justices of the peace of the county.

I nevertheless concur in the judgment of affirmance, because it was clearly within the power of the county commissioners to contract for the construction of the bridge mentioned if it should cost no more than $500; and they might contract for the same for a greater sum than that mentioned, "with the concurrence of a majority of the justices of the peace" of the county. The several statutory provisions pertinent, (Code, § 707, subsec. 10; Id. §§ 2014, 2035; Acts 1887, c. 370,) fairly interpreted, imply that the county commissioners ordinarily contract on the part of the county for the construction and repair of bridges; and, if the construction or repairs shall cost exceeding $500, they must do so subject to the concurrence of a majority of the justices of the peace. It is not essential that such contract shall be made at a joint meeting of the county commissioners and the justices of the peace; the party with whom they contract being present, it will be sufficient if such commissioners contract inchoately with such party at one time, the contract to be afterwards concurred in by the justices of the peace at a joint meeting of themselves and the commissioners. Until such concurrence the contract would not be complete and binding; it would remain in fieri, open for the concurrence or non-concurrence of the justices of the peace. It would be very cumbersome and inconvenient for the contracting parties in such case to assemble together at a time and place prescribed by law and agree upon the terms and details of the contract. It is not contemplated that they shall, but it is intended that the county commissioners and the party contracted with may make the contract, subject to the simple concurrence of the justices of the peace. This is reasonable and practicable, and the statute so contemplates. If the party contracting to construct or repair the bridge should venture to construct or repair the same before such concurrence, he would do so at the hazard of his rights that might arise under the contract. Hence the contract in question between the defendants and the plaintiff was not void at the time the justices of the peace concurred in the same (if they did;) it was until that time simply inchoate, and they might concur or refuse to concur with the defendants, and, concurring with them, render it complete and effectual. Hence, also, the argument for the defendants that the contract was absolutely void, and therefore could not be concurred in, is without force.

We are also of opinion that the justices of the peace did concur in the contract in question. After the bridge was constructed, and after it was accepted by the defendants, they paid the first installment of the price agreed to be paid for it. Regularly, under and in pursuance of the statute. (Code, § 707, subsec. 1,) a majority of the justices of the peace sitting with the defendants must have concurred in levying taxes to pay such installment paid, and thus they informally but in effect concurred in the contract for the construction of the bridge. In the absence of allegation and evidence to the contrary, it must be taken that they did. A regular formal concurrence would be better and more satisfactory, but a concurrence in such joint meeting appearing by presumption and reasonable implication is sufficient, if nothing to the contrary appears. It is not to be presumed that the justices of the peace at their regular joint meeting with the defendants on the first Monday in June, 1888, for the purpose of levying taxes for county purposes, including bridges, were ignorant of the bridge in question, and the county debt created on account of it, to pay part of which they presumedly made provision. On the contrary, the presumption is that they knew of it, and concurred in the contract under which it arose, and hence concurred in the tax-levy to pay part of it, and that afterwards the defendants, in the orderly course of their duties, paid that part; otherwise they would not have made such payment. Such presumption arose from the record of the procedure and pertinent action of the justices of the peace in the joint meeting of themselves and the defendants. It had and has permanency, and continues until in some proper way the contrary shall be made to appear. The debt could not be properly and lawfully provided for or paid without such concurrence. The presumption, further, is that such concurrence was by a majority of the justices of the peace, because the statute (Code § 707, subsec. 1) requires that such majority shall concur in the tax-levy.

CLARK, J. I concur with the chief justice that a vote of a majority of all the justices of the county is requisite, and that the vote of a majority of a quorum is not sufficient.

ATLANTA & F. R. CO. v. KIMBERLY.

(Supreme Court of Georgia. April 24, 1891.)

NUISANCE—INDEPENDENT CONTRACTOR—EVIDENCE.

1. A railroad company which has employed an independent contractor to construct its road is not liable for the damages resulting from a nuisance created by such contractor, consisting of a pond on plaintiff's land, the result of failure to drain through an embankment, and the accumulation therein of filth from the camp of the contractor's workmen; the nuisance not being one necessarily incident to the construction of the road, and the railroad company having retained no control over the manner of constructing it.

2. Where possession of the road was not yet delivered to the railroad company at the time of the injuries complained of, there is no such ratification of the contractor's acts as will render it liable therefor.

3. Plaintiff testified that the malaria of which he complained resulted from four causes, viz.: An embankment of loose earth, a dam, a horse lot, and a hog lot,—all maintained by the contractor near his house. There being no allegation in the petition as to the horse and hog lots, they were stricken from his testimony. Held, that it was error to admit the answer as changed, since

it made the injury dependent upon two causes only, while plaintiff assigned four.

Error from superior court, Clayton county; R. H. CLARKE, Judge.

J. Carroll Payne and N. J. & T. A. Hammond, for plaintiff in error. J. C. Reed and Dorsey, Brewster & Howell, for defendant in error.

SIMMONS, J. Kimberly sued the railroad company for damages, and alleged in his declaration "that while the company was constructing its road it made a deep cut, and piled the fresh earth therefrom near his dwelling-house, and dammed up a small stream, and ponded the water therefrom near the house; and that it also stationed near the house a camp of convicts, whom it was using in said construction, and permitted the filth accumulating in the sinks of this camp and otherwise therein from the convicts to flow from the camp, and be deposited a few yards from the house, by reason of which the air in and around the house became infected with noxious scents, malaria, and other substances injurious to health, whereby plaintiff and his wife both became sick, and endured great pain and suffering, and were unable to attend to their daily duties," etc. The defense of the railroad company was that it did not do the acts complained of in the declaration; that, if they were done at all, they were done by the Chattahoochee Brick Company, an independent contractor, which it had employed to build the railroad from Atlanta to Senoia. On the trial of the case the jury found a verdict for the plaintiff, and the defendant made a motion for a new trial on the various grounds set out therein, which was overruled, and it excepted.

The main question argued before us was whether under the facts of this case the railroad company was liable for the damages sustained by Kimberly. The general rule of law upon this subject is: Where an individual or corporation contracts with another individual or corporation exercising an independent employment for the latter to do a work not in itself unlawful or attended with danger to others, such work to be done according to the contractor's own methods, and not subject to the employer's control or orders except as to the results to be obtained, the employer is not liable for the wrongful or negligent acts of the contractor or of the contractor's servants. Code, § 2962; Harrison v. Kiser, 79 Ga. 588, 4 S. E. Rep. 320. And see the following text-books and cases therein cited: 1 Lawson, Rights, Rem. & Pr. § 295; 2 Thomp. Neg. 899 et seq.; Id. 909–913; 2 Wood, Ry. Law, § 284. Also, 1 Add. Torts, 302; Cooley, Torts, 644; Bish. Non-Cont. Law, § 606; Pierce, R. R. 286–291; 1 Rorer, R. R. 468–470; Whit. Smith, Neg. 171 et seq.; Wood, Nuis. 77, p. 81; Dicey, Parties, (2d Amer. Ed.) 468 et seq. See especially the following cases: Peachey v. Rowland, 22 Law J. C. P. 81, 13 C. B. 182; Cuff v. Railroad Co., 35 N. J. Law, 17; Clark v. Railroad, 39 Mo. 202; McCafferty v. Railroad Co., 61 N. Y. 178; Hughes v. Railway Co., 15 Amer. & Eng. R. Cas. 100; Hilliard v. Richardson, 3 Gray, 349; Eaton v. Railway Co., 59 Me.

520; Railway Co. v. Farver, 111 Ind. 195, 12 N. E. Rep. 296; Railway Co. v. Fitzsimmons, 18 Kan. 34; Painter v. Pittsburgh, 46 Pa. St 220.

To the general rule there are several exceptions: (1) Where the work is wrongful in itself, or, if done in the ordinary manner, would result in a nuisance, the employer will be liable for injury resulting to third persons, although the work is done by an independent contractor. This is upon the principle that if one contracts with another to commit a nuisance, he is a co-trespasser by reason of his directing or participating in the work; in other words, the rule is that, "if the act or neglect which produces the injury is purely collateral to the work contracted to be done, and entirely the result of the wrongful acts of the contractor and his workman, the proprietor is not liable; but if the injury directly results from the work which the contractor engaged and was authorised to do, he is equally liable with the contractor." 2 Thomp. Neg. 909. See, also, authorities cited supra. (2) If, according to previous knowledge and experience, the work to be done is in its nature dangerous to others, however carefully performed, the employer will be liable, and not the contractor, because, it is said, it is incumbent on him to foresee such danger, and take precautions against it; and this is the principle upon which the cases of Bower v. Peate, 1 Q. B. Div. 321; Tarry v. Ashton, Id. 314; and Pickard v. Smith, 10 C. B. (N. S.) 470,—relied on by the defendant in error, were decided. And in this exception is included the principle that where the injury is caused by defective construction which was inherent in the original plan of the employer, the latter is liable. See authorities cited supra. Also Robbins v. Chicago, 4 Wall. 657; Boswell v. Laird, 8 Cal. 469; Lancaster v. Insurance Co., 92 Mo. 460, 5 S. W. Rep. 23. For instance, if any person employs another to erect a building, and the plan of the building is defective, the walls being too thin and weak, and the building while in process of erection falls, and causes injury to a third person, the employer, and not the contractor, is liable. Or, if a contractor is employed to build a sewer, and the employer agrees to furnish the materials, and the sewer-pipe furnished by the employer is too small, and damage is sustained by reason thereof, the employer is liable. (3) The next exception is where the wrongful act is the violation of a duty imposed by express contract upon the employer; for where a person contracts to do a certain thing he cannot evade liability by employing another to do that which he has agreed to perform. For instance, where a company undertook to lay water-pipes in a city, agreeing with the city that it would "protect all persons against damages by reason of excavations made by them in laying pipes, and to be responsible for all damages which might occur by reason of the neglect of their employes in the premises," and the company let out the work to a contractor, who used a steam-drill in such a manner as to frighten a traveler's horse and injure the traveler, it was held by the supreme court of the United States that the company was liable. Water Co. v. Ware, 16 Wall. 566. (4) The next exception is where a duty is imposed by statute. The person upon whom a statutory obligation is imposed is liable for any injury that arises to others from its non-performance or in consequence of its having been negligently performed, either by himself or by a contractor employed by him. Thus, where the statute imposed upon a railroad company, as a duty to the proprietors of inclosures through which the road passed, the obligation of placing stock-guards, and preserving or supplying fences, on the right of way, and protecting the inclosure from injury, in the construction of its road, the company was held liable for the failure to perform such duty, though resulting from the negligence of a contractor. Railroad Co. v. Meador, 50 Tex. 77. And it was upon this principle that the cases of Wilson v. White, 71 Ga. 506; Gray v. Pullen, 5 Best & S. 970; Hole v. Railroad Co., 6 Hurl. & N. 488; and Railroad Co. v. McCarthy, 20 Ill. 388,—relied upon by counsel for the defendant in error, were decided. And the case of Hinde v. Navigation Co., 15 Ill. 72, also relied upon for the defendant in error, falls under the same principle. In that case the charter imposed upon the company the duty of paying for all material taken for the use of its work, and expressly gave a remedy against the company; and it was held that the company could not by delegating its work to a contractor escape liability for material taken by him for the work; especially as he was working under the immediate supervision and direction of the engineer of the company. (5) The employer may also make himself liable "by retaining the right to direct and control the time and manner of executing the work, or by interfering with the contractor and assuming control of the work, or some part of it, so that the relation of master and servant arises, or so that an injury ensues which is traceable to his interference. But merely taking steps to see that the contractor carries out his agreement, as having the work supervised by an architect or superintendent, does not make the employer liable; nor does reserving the right to dismiss incompetent workmen." 1 Lawson, Rights, Rem. & Pr. 299; Harrison v. Kiser, supra. (6) The employer may also be held liable upon the ground that he has ratified or adopted the unauthorized wrong of the independent contractor. See Harrison v. Kiser, supra; 2 Thomp. Neg. 903, 915.

Applying the foregoing principles to the facts of this case, we find that the railroad company made a contract with the Chattahoochee Brick Company, whereby the latter agreed to build the former's road from Atlanta to Senoia, according to certain specifications: and the railroad company did not retain any control over the contractor as to the method or manner of doing the work. The construction company was to furnish the labor and all the materials, including the pipes with which the sewers or culverts were to be built. All the control reserved by the road was that its superintendent was to see that the road was built according to the contract. There is no indication in the record outside of some loose and illegal declarations of third parties, the admission of which as evidence we will speak of presently, tending to show that the railroad company had any authority, power, or control over the construction, as to the manner or means of doing the work. This being true, the railroad company, under the general rule above announced, is not liable for the negligent acts done by the contractor. It was argued by the able counsel for the defendant in error that the building of a railroad necessarily results in a nuisance, unless certain precautions are taken to prevent it; that the low places by which the surrounding lands are drained and from which the water is carried off must be filled up, and, unless certain precautions are taken to provide an escape for the water, a nuisance necessarily results; and that the railroad company cannot escape liability by having the work done by an independent contractor. If the premises of counsel are true, the conclusion might also be true; but if a railroad is built properly we do not think any nuisance will result from the building. The company, under its charter, had authority of law to do this work; and when it contracted with the construction company it was of course implied that the latter would do the work in a proper and lawful manner. "A person employing another to do a lawful act is presumed, in the absence of evidence to the contrary, to have employed him to do it in a lawful and reasonable manner; and therefore, unless the parties stand in the relation of master and servant, the employer is not responsible for damages occasioned by the negligent mode in which the work is done." 1 Redf. R. R. (6th Ed.) 542. Moreover, the evidence shows that in the very place where this nuisance is said to have occurred the railroad company had provided means which, if used, would have prevented the nuisance. The superintendent directed that a waste-way should be placed there, but the contractor put in a pipe, which the defendant claims was one of the causes of the nuisance, (1) by being too small to carry off the water in proper time, and (2) because it was not put upon the bed of the stream, but several inches above the bed, thereby causing the water to pond near the plaintiff's house. Nor would the other things which it is claimed caused the nuisance, to-wit, the throwing up of the fresh dirt, the convict camp, and the hog and horse lots, render the railroad company liable. It had lawful authority for excavating the hills and filling the bottoms in order to make its road-bed; and the placing of the convict-camp and the hog and horse lots near the plaintiff's house was the act of the construction company, over which, it appears from the record, the railroad company had no power or control. So it will be seen that the work committed to the construction company was not wrongful per se, nor did it necessarily result in a nuisance; and therefore does not fall within the first exception to the general rule. Nor is there any legal evidence to show that it would fall within the second exception. It is claimed that the pond of water was caused by the sewer pipes being too small to carry it off, but there is no evidence that the railroad company directed that this particular size of pipe should be placed at that point. It is true there are some declarations of Hammond and English to the effect that the superintendent ordered it to be put there, but these declarations were illegal, and should have been excluded. If it should be shown upon the next trial that this particular size of pipe was placed at that point by direction of the company, or if the specifications in the contract required it to be placed there, and it should be further shown that this part of the plan was inherently defective, and that it caused this nuisance, and the plaintiff sustained injury thereby, the railroad company would be liable. But if the railroad company did not direct this particular size of pipe to be placed at that point, or its plans and specifications did not require it, and it was put there by the contractor according to his own judgment, and negligently placed above the bed of the stream, then the railroad company would not be liable, although it may have had notice from the plaintiff that in his opinion the pipe was too small. If the railroad company had no control over the contractor as to the manner in which he should build the sewer or put in the pipe, any notice which the plaintiff might give its officers would not make it liable. The contractor being in an independent employment, whatever he does outside of or beyond his contract is a collateral act for which the employer is not liable. He is not the servant or agent of the employer, and the employer cannot be held liable for any acts of negligence committed or omitted by him outside of his contract. Where the work he is engaged to do is lawful, the law presumes that he will do it in a lawful manner; and if he does it illegally he is liable and not the employer.

Nor do the facts of the case bring it within the third or the fourth exceptions. There was no duty imposed upon the railroad company, either by contract or by statute, to do this particular work, or to do it in a particular way. Its charter does not impose upon it the duty of building the road, and does not specify the manner in which it shall be built; nor is any liability imposed upon it for acts of the kind complained of in this case. The authorities all hold that a railroad company has the right to make a contract with other parties for the construction of its road, and it is held that a contract of this character is not such a delegation of its chartered rights as to render the company liable for unauthorized wrongs committed by the contractor or his servants while engaged in the work. "The principle that a railroad company cannot delegate to an employe its chartered rights and privileges, so as to exempt it from liability, does not extend to the use of the ordinary ways and means for the construction of the road, but to the use of such extraordinary powers only as the company itself could not exercise without having first complied with the conditions of the legislative grant of authority. Thus, after having first procured the right of way, the company can delegate to another lawful authority to enter upon the same and make its road-bed and perform other proper acts of construction; but it cannot delegate such lawful authority without having first secured the right of way by donation, purchase, or the exercise of the right of eminent domain." Cunningham v. Railroad Co., 51 Tex. 513. See Pierce, R. R. 290.

As we have already seen, the case does not come within the fifth exception, for there is no legal evidence that the railroad company had any control over the construction, as to the manner or means of doing the work. Nor does it come within the next exception, for the facts do not show any ratification of the wrongful acts of the contractor. It is not shown when the company accepted the road from the contractor. The evidence does show that the work near the plaintiff's house was done either in March, April, or May, and that about the 1st of June the plaintiff and his wife became sick. But under the contract the road was not to be turned over to the company until several months after this. The company not being in possession of the road at the time the plaintiff received the injury from the nuisance, and there being no evidence to show that it knew there was a nuisance, it cannot be said that the company ratified any act of its contractor which created a nuisance.

It only remains for us to say that we think the court should have excluded the whole answer to the interrogatory set out in the fourth ground of the motion for a new trial, and that the error was not cured by the agreement of the defendant's counsel that the whole might be read, after the court had decided that only a part of it could be read. In his answer the witness assigned four causes, which, in his opinion, produced the malaria: The embankment of loose earth, the horse lot, and the hog lot, and the dam. This answer was objected to because there was no allegation in the petition that the horse lot and hog lot produced the malaria. The court therefore ruled that these two reasons should be stricken, and the remainder of the answer read. The effect of this ruling was to make the witness testify that the loose earth and the dam alone produced the malaria, when the answer showed that in his opinion it was produced by these and the horse and hog lots. We do not think the answer of the witness ought to have been cut up in this manner. By so doing he was made to testify what he did not intend to. The plaintiff should either have amended his declaration to meet the proof, or the whole answer should have been excluded. Nor do we think the defendant waived this error by consenting, after the above ruling, that the whole should be read. The ruling of the court striking out two of the causes of malaria and leaving in two placed the defendant in a worse position than that in which it would have been if the whole

answer had remained. The court should also have excluded the declarations of English and Hammond as set out in the fifth and sixth grounds of the motion. They were not the servants or agents of the railroad company, and any declarations they may have made would not bind the company. Judgment reversed.

ADAMS v. POWELL.

(Supreme Court of Georgia. April 20, 1891.)

EJECTMENT—BOUNDARIES—CALLS IN DEED.

1. In ejectment it appeared that S. and G. divided a lot which they owned in common, and that by mesne conveyances the title to the share of S. vested in defendant. The source of plaintiff's title to G.'s portion was a deed from one A., made after the partition, but his title was not shown to be connected with G.'s. The property in dispute was a small tract claimed by each to be included in his portion of the lot. *Held* that, as plaintiff's title was not connected with S. or G., it was error to charge the jury that, if they believed that plaintiff's and defendant's titles originated in S. or G., and from them came down to plaintiff and defendant, there was a common owner under whom both claimed, and that there was no dispute as to the title being in S. or G., and those who claimed under them.

2. S. and G., owning a lot in common, divided it between them, and their portions, by mesne conveyances, became vested in plaintiff and defendant, respectively, through an intermediate grantee of both portions. The deeds of S.'s portion down to plaintiff described the tract as containing 93 acres, more or less, and the deeds from G. down to defendant described his portion as containing 100 acres, more or less. The land in dispute was a tract midway of the lot which each claimed to be included in his portion. The evidence tended to show that a boundary line had been established between S. and G., which was recognized by subsequent purchasers. *Held*, that it was error to charge that, if defendant had 100 acres without taking in the tract in dispute, and plaintiff did not have 93 acres without including it, plaintiff should recover the tract; since if S. and G. had established a boundary line, and defendant had purchased his tract with reference to it, he would be entitled to hold it, though it contained more than 100 acres.

3. In such case, if both plaintiff and defendant claimed title under the intermediate grantee, instead of under S. and G., plaintiff, having first purchased from such grantee with reference to the boundary established by S. and G., would be entitled to take up to that boundary only, whether the tract so determined contained the number of acres called for by his deed or not; but, if he purchased by an imaginary boundary, he would be entitled to 93 acres, though it might leave defendant who purchased after him, less than the number of acres called for by his deed.

Error from superior court, De Kalb county; R. H. CLARK, Judge.

Action by Thomas S. Powell, as sole heir of Julia L. Powell, deceased, against George Adams and C. H. Strong, to recover 20 acres of lot 200, in the eighteenth district of De Kalb county. In 1838 one Dobbs conveyed lot 200 to Solomon Goodwin, with the exception of 50 acres formerly conveyed to one Lunceford. On Goodwin's death, in 1864, his sons, Starling and Solomon, took possession, and divided the land; Starling taking the southern portion, and Solomon the northern portion. The source of plaintiff's title was a deed from one Austin to John M. Dorsey, made in 1865, but there was nothing to connect

Austin's title with the Goodwins. The deed described the land conveyed as the "south-west part of lot 200, * * * containing 93 acres, more or less." By mesne conveyances the title to the northern part of the lot, belonging to Solomon Goodwin, vested also in John M. Dorsey. All the deeds described the northern part as containing 100 acres, more or less. Defendant Strong, by mesne conveyances, acquired title through Dorsey. The 20 acres in dispute is midway of lot 200, and is claimed by plaintiff as included in his deeds of the southern part of the lot, and by defendant as being in the northern portion.

Candler & Thomson, for plaintiff in error. *Hall & Hammond*, for defendant in error.

SIMMONS, J. The record shows that the source of title of Powell, the plaintiff in the court below, was a deed from James M. Austin to John M. Dorsey, made on April 6th, 1865, to the south-west part of lot No. 200, in the eighteenth district of De Kalb county, containing 93 acres, more or less, and that the source of the defendant's title was a deed from Dobbs to Goodwin, and from Goodwin to Bridwell, etc. As far as appears from the record, the plaintiff's title was not connected with either Solomon or Starling Goodwin. There is no indication in the record how Austin's title originated. The court, therefore, erred in charging the jury that, if they believed that this title originated in the Goodwins, and passed from the Goodwins to the others, until it came down to Powell and Strong, there was a common owner from whom both claimed; and that there was no dispute as to the title to this lot of land being in the Goodwins, and those who claimed under the Goodwins. As we have shown, there was no evidence on which to base this charge.

2. We think the court erred also in charging the jury, under the facts of this case, that if Strong's deed specified 100 acres, more or less, of the N. ½ of this lot of land, and Powell's deed specified 93 acres in the S. ½ of the lot of land, they were then to find how many acres were in the lot, after deducting the Lunceford tract; and that if Strong had 100 acres, without taking in the 20 acres in dispute, and Powell did not have 93 acres without including the 20 acres, then Powell would be entitled to recover the 20 acres sued for. The record discloses that Solomon Goodwin, Sr., purchased the lot of land from Dobbs in 1838, and that he gave it to his two sons, Solomon and Starling. The evidence shows that these sons divided the land between them, Solomon taking the N. or N. E. ½, and Starling the S. or S. W. part of the lot, and that they resided on their respective parts for many years, recognizing the line established by them in the beginning of their possession. In all the deeds to that portion of the land which was assigned to Solomon Goodwin, it is described as the N. or N. E. "half" of lot No. 200; and in all the deeds to that part of the lot which was assigned to Starling, the land is described as the S. or S. W. "part" of lot 200, with the ex-

ception of the deed from Hagar to Julia Powell, which describes it as the S. W. "half" of said lot. This is an indication that the land was not equally divided between the two brothers, but that Solomon got the N. ½, and Starling got the balance that was left after deducting the 50 acres of Lunceford, or the S. or S. W. part of the land. This seems to be a recognition that there was a boundary line established between the two brothers, and that this boundary was recognized by subsequent purchasers. We think, therefore, that, upon the next trial of the case, the jury should be instructed to inquire whether these Goodwin brothers did establish a boundary line between them, and whether it was recognized by them, and whether subsequent purchasers and grantors recognized the same boundary line. If such a line was established and assented to by different owners for a sufficient length of time, and there were a hundred acres or more on the north side of the line thus established, and Strong purchased the land on the north side, he would be entitled to hold it, although there was more than a hundred acres on that side; for this deed calls for 100 acres, more or less. If, however, there was no such line established, or, if established, it was not assented to or recognized by the various parties claiming the two portions of the lot, then, of course, this rule will not prevail; and the rule would be that, if there was no line established and recognized, and Strong had his 100 acres, and it took 20 acres to make Powell's 93, Powell would be entitled to recover the same, provided his deed covered the 20 acres. In other words, if there was an actual physical boundary between the two portions of the lot, and Strong's purchase included the land up to that actual physical boundary, then he would be entitled to hold the land up to that boundary, although it may include more than 100 acres. If there was no such boundary line, but it was an ideal or imaginary one, the jury should find from the evidence its location; and if Powell's purchase covers the land up to that location or line, and the land in dispute is on Powell's side of that line, then he would be entitled to recover. This would be the rule in the contest between the Goodwin title and the Dorsey title. If, however, both parties claim under Dorsey as the common grantor, and Mrs. Dorsey sold the land by an actual physical boundary, Powell would be entitled to the land up to that boundary, whether it was 93 acres or not. If the land was not sold by an actual, physical boundary, but an ideal or imaginary one, then, in our opinion, Powell would be entitled to 93 acres, although it might leave Strong short of his 100 acres, because Mrs. Dorsey sold the south part of the land to Wallace, under whom Powell claims, before she sold the north part to James O. Powell, under whom Strong claims. Of course, neither of these rules would apply if either of the parties or those under whom they hold had had exclusive adverse possession of the 20 acres a sufficient length of time to give title under the statute. Judgment reversed.

JOHNSON v. STATE.

(Supreme Court of Georgia. Nov. 10, 1890.)

LARCENY—EVIDENCE—CONFESSIONS.

1. Where the charge is larceny from the house by stealing goods from a wholesale store, the corpus delicti is not established without proof that the goods disappeared by stealing, rather than by sale to retail dealers in the course of business. If the goods in question were not missed from the stock, and the stock was never ascertained to be short or deficient, the presumption is they were sold, and not stolen.

2. A doubtful or contradictory confession by a man of good moral character will not warrant a conviction where the corpus delicti is uncertain.

(Syllabus by the Court.)

Error from city court of Atlanta; VAN EPPS, Judge.

L. P. Skeen and W. T. Moyers, for plaintiff in error. F. M. O'Bryan, for the State.

BLECKLEY, C. J. 1. The charge was larceny from the house. The goods, alleged to have been stolen from the storehouse of F. E. Block, were 1 can of oysters, 1 can of milk, 1 can of lobsters, 7 boxes of sardines, 13 boxes of ham and tongue, 2 boxes of soap, 1 can of sausage, and 2 boxes of mustard sardines,—the property of said Block. The evidence established that Block had and kept such articles in his store, but it fails to establish to a reasonable certainty that any such were ever stolen therefrom, either by the accused or any one else. Block testified on the subject as follows: "I cannot say that I lost the goods mentioned in the indictment. I never missed nor searched for them, nor tried to find out if I had lost them. I run a large wholesale grocery, employ about 125 hands, and sell generally to the retail trade in Atlanta and elsewhere." Catlett testified: "I work for Block in this city and county. The first of last year we missed from Block's store a cheese; and Mr. Parks, another employe of Block's, and I, with an officer, went to search the house of our driver, whom we suspected of taking it. We didn't find it, and went to defendant's house in this city, who was not at home. His wife readily agreed to aid us, although we did not tell her what we were searching for. We did not find the cheese, but in the closet, the door of which his wife opened for us, on the top of the shelf, behind a board which was nailed to the front of the shelf so as to hold what was put on the shelf, we found a lot of canned goods, consisting of one can of condensed milk, Vienna sausage, two boxes of mustard sardines, Kennesaw oysters, etc. I believed the goods to be stolen, especially the Vienna sausage, and took them away in a gunny sack. They filled the sack about one foot high. The defendant had worked for Block in the store about one year, and had access at all times to this kind of goods. When we first went to defendant's house and told his wife we wanted to search it she excitedly threw her keys on the floor before us. We told her that, as we had to go through a woman's fixings, a woman was best to guide us. She then took the keys and unlocked the door for us. I identified

the goods found in Block's. The goods we found at Henry Johnson's consisted of 1 can of oysters, 1 can of milk, 1 can of lobsters, 7 boxes of sardines, 13 boxes of ham and tongue, 2 boxes of soap, 1 can of sausage, and 2 boxes of mustard sardines." It will be observed that Mr. Catlett does not testify that anything had been missed from the store except a cheese, and that had not been found. So far as appears, the stock of Mr. Block was intact as to all classes of goods found in Johnson's possession. If the stock had been short of these articles, the fair presumption is that Mr. Block or some of his numerous employes would either have known of it, or could have ascertained it. There is no suggestion in the evidence that the articles were short, or that there were no means of ascertaining whether they were so or not. It is not said that Mr. Block kept no books, or that he was otherwise deficient in the usual resources of merchants for determining the kind and quantity of all goods in store. It seems highly improbable that such a number of articles could be abstracted from a single stock of goods without some of them being missed. It does not appear that a single one of them was missed, either before or after they were found in Johnson's possession. Mr. Catlett testifies that he "identified the goods found in Block's." Possibly he means that he identified them as Block's goods. But this could signify no more than that they were such goods as Block had kept in stock. Block himself testified, however, that he ran a large wholesale grocery, and sold generally to the retail trade in Atlanta and elsewhere. Several of the retail dealers in Atlanta, one of whom was Mr. Karwisch, testified on behalf of the accused that he, the accused, had traded with them for a length of time, and that they had sold him similar goods to most of those found in his possession. The accused proved by two witnesses, moreover, that he was a man of excellent character, and there was no evidence to the contrary. Taking all the testimony together, we think it wholly fails to establish any corpus delicti. There is no certainty whatever that any of the goods traced to Johnson were stolen. The probability that Block had sold them to retail dealers before they reached Johnson is decidedly stronger than that they were stolen by any one from his stock.

2. As to the alleged confession, we think that cannot be relied upon to supply the want of evidence as to the corpus delicti. "A confession alone, uncorroborated by other evidence, will not justify a conviction." Code, § 3792. The wisdom of this provision of the law is well vindicated by the present case. Couch, the officer who arrested Johnson, testified that "at the station-house he confessed to Mr. Block that he stole the goods." Mr. Block, however, testified on that subject as follows: "In one conversation he twice admitted taking the goods, but immediately after stated that he bought them from Mr. Henry Karwisch. * * * I cannot say positively that he said he stole the goods, or that he merely took them. I sus-

pected somebody else had been implicated with him, and asked him who helped him take them. He twice replied that he did it himself, and afterwards added that he bought them from Karwisch." It thus appears that what was to Couch a confession of stealing the goods, was to Block a very doubtful confession, and coupled with an assertion that he bought them from Karwisch. It is not improbable that both these witnesses misunderstood the real import of. his statement. At all events there is too much uncertainty about it for it to serve as a confession to make out the *corpus delicti.* Let the state first prove that Mr. Block's goods were stolen, and then it will be in order to connect Johnson with the larceny by this so-called confession, in so far as the jury may believe it correctly understood and reported. As the case comes to us in the record, there is altogether too much uncertainty as to whether any offense was committed. The good character of the accused should count for much in such a case; and we think the trial court erred in not granting a new trial. Judgment reversed.

BLILEY v. TAYLOR.

(Supreme Court of Georgia. March 16, 1891.)

APPEAL—REVIEW — CONFLICTING EVIDENCE — OBJECTIONS NOT RAISED BELOW.

1. Where the evidence was conflicting, and no abuse of discretion by the judge below in appointing a receiver appears, this court will not disturb his judgment.

2. Where a receiver of the assets of a partnership was appointed, and the failure of the judge to appoint a member of the firm such receiver is assigned as error, and it appears that no request or prayer was made to him that such member should be so appointed, the propriety or impropriety of such failure is not before this court for adjudication.

(Syllabus by Lumpkin, J.)

Error from superior court, Fulton county; M. J. CLARKE, Judge.
For opinion on former appeal, see 12 S. E. Rep. 210.
O'Neill & Fraser, for plaintiff in error.
P. L. Mynatt, for defendant in error.
Judgment affirmed.

NEAL v. BROCKHAN.

(Supreme Court of Georgia. April 20, 1891.)

HOMESTEAD—ENTRY ON EXECUTION—INTEREST ON JUDGMENT.

1. Where a homestead is set apart to a mother and her children, on the ground that they are minors, the fact that thereafter, and before he came of age, one of the children became imbecile and dependent, will not keep the homestead alive after the mother's death, and the attainment of their majority by all the children.

2. Since an execution on a justice's judgment is directed to any constable of the county, an entry thereon by a constable is legal, though he is not an officer of the militia district in which the execution issued, and will keep the judgment alive.

3. Where a note stipulates for interest at 12 per cent. per annum, it is proper to allow interest at the same rate on the judgment thereon, since by the law of Georgia judgments bear interest at the contract rate.

Error from superior court, Fulton county; M. J. CLARKE, Judge.
T. P. Westmoreland, for plaintiff in error. *Arnold & Arnold,* for defendant in error.

SIMMONS, J. The record discloses that Mrs. Brockhan borrowed of Neal certain money, for which she gave him her six promissory notes, dated January 15, 1876, all due within less than six months, and agreed to pay interest at the rate of 1 per cent. per month. The notes were sued to judgment in a justice's court on the 8th of July, 1876. Judgment was rendered for the interest on the notes at 1 per cent. per month, and for the same rate of future interest on the judgments themselves. Mrs. Brockhan applied for a homestead, and it was granted on the 12th of July, 1879. She made the application as the head of a family, consisting of herself and her three minor children. The minor children were Annie B., Willie, and John. Willie, the youngest, attained his majority in 1889. His mother, to whom the homestead was granted, died in 1883. After the mother's death, and after all the children had arrived at their majority, Neal levied his *fi. fa.* upon the property set apart as a homestead. Annie B. filed an affidavit of illegality for herself and her infirm brother, Willie, and her brother John, and alleged that the property levied on was not subject to levy and sale, because in July, 1879, her mother had the property set apart to herself and her three minor children as a homestead, and that the homestead was still in existence, with the affiant and her brother Willie as beneficiaries; that Willie attained his majority in March, 1889, and "is now, and was long before said date, an infirm person, and wholly dependent, incapacitated in mind and body for any of the ordinary transactions of life. without power of speech and otherwise totally helpless; and he is therefore still one of the beneficiaries. His infirmity began before the death of his mother, and before he attained majority, and she is compelled to care for, support, and maintain him. Affiant makes the affidavit because her mother, one of the defendants in the judgment, died intestate, and the lands levied upon descended to John, Willie, and affiant, as her children and only heirs at law." The affiant also states that she is the legally appointed guardian of Willie, who is an imbecile. Under this state of facts the trial judge decided that the land was not subject, and Neal excepted. We think the court erred in this ruling. It will be remembered that the mother applied for and was granted a homestead for herself and her three minor children. Nothing was said in the application as to Willie's being an imbecile and dependent. The allegation was that he and the other two were minors, and it was upon this ground that the homestead was granted. When, therefore, the mother died, and the children became of age, according to the repeated rulings of this court, the homestead estate ceased, and the land became subject to the liens of creditors. We do not think the fact that one of the minors became imbecile and dependent after the homestead was set apart, but before he became of age, would change the rule, and keep the homestead estate alive. When the head of the family, to whom the homestead was set apart, died, the land descended to her children as her heirs at law; and after they became of age the homestead ceased, and, if there had been no creditors, the children would have had the right to have the property sold or divided. There being a judgment creditor in this case, his lien, which had been inactive and held off since the homestead was set apart, became active and was leviable when the homestead estate ceased.

The defendant in the court below insisted upon two other grounds of illegality, which the court overruled, and she filed a cross-bill of exceptions. The first ground taken in the cross-bill was that the judgments were dormant, because the only entry made by any officer or other person upon the *fi. fas.* within the period of seven years from June 5, 1878, was an entry made by a constable who was not an officer of the militia district wherein the *fi. fa.* was issued, and in which the defendant resided, but was an officer and constable of another district, and at the time he made this entry on the *fi. fas.* there were two duly-qualified and acting constables in the district whence the *fi. fa.* issued. and, the constable who made the entry not being an officer authorized to execute and return the *fi. fas.* there, they were dormant. There was no error in overruling this ground of illegality. We think the entry made by the officer residing and acting in a different district from the one whence the *fi. fas.* issued was a legal entry. Executions issued from a justice's court are directed to any lawful constable of the county. Therefore any lawful constable of the county would have a legal right to make an entry thereon. Moreover, if it was a *bona fide* effort on the part of the plaintiff to keep his judgment alive, by having the entry made by the constable in another district, it would prevent dormancy of the judgment, although the execution had not been directed to all the constables of the county, and although the defendant did not reside in that district and had no property therein. Long v. Wight, 82 Ga. 431, 9 S. E. Rep. 535, and cases there cited.

The next ground taken in the cross-bill of exceptions is that the notes were each given on the 15th of January, 1876, were for less than six months, and drew interest at the rate of 1 per cent. per month, and that the judgments were rendered July 8, 1876, for interest on the notes from January 15, 1876, at 1 per cent. per month, and drew interest at 1 per cent. per month from their date; and it is contended that, "in the absence of a contract to draw legal interest, the judgments only draw interest at 7 per cent. per annum, as provided by the act of 1875;" and that the claim for excess over lawful interest should therefore be disallowed. The trial judge did not err in overruling this ground. At the time these notes were given, the law allowed 12 per cent. per annum, if specified in writing. These notes specified 1 per cent. per

month, which is equivalent to 12 per cent. per annum. It was claimed, however, in the argument, that, after judgment on the notes, interest should have been computed at 7 per cent. only, instead of 12, as was done. Under our Code, and under the decisions of this court, judgments bear interest at the contract rate, and not at the rate which all contracts carry if no interest be stipulated therein. Daniel v. Gibson, 72 Ga. 367. It was claimed by counsel that, when the per cent. is split up and made payable for a short period, it must bear the same proportion to the time it runs as 12 does to 12 months; and that, as February had only 28 days, the rate of interest was more than 12 per cent. per annum. We have stated this point, and the substance of the argument upon it, not that we think there is anything in it, but to show to what fine-spun theories learned and able counsel will resort when hard pressed in their cases. It is sufficient to say that, to all practical intents and purposes, 1 per cent. per month is equivalent to 12 per cent. per annum, and that charging interest at the rate of 1 per cent. per month is not usury, although some of the months may have a less number of days than others. *De minimis non curat lex.* Judgment reversed as to the main bill of exceptions, and affirmed as to the cross-bill.

DOOLEY v. BELL.

(*Supreme Court of Georgia.* March 23, 1891.)

SALE OF MINOR'S LAND — VOID APPOINTMENT OF GUARDIAN.

1. Where land was sold by one professing to act as guardian for others, when in fact he was not, for the reason that his alleged appointment as such was absolutely void, the sale itself was likewise void, and passed no title to the purchaser thereat, although he bought in good faith, and without actual notice of any defect in the guardian's appointment or his authority to sell.

2. Such purchaser cannot recover land thus sold from one holding the legal title thereto, and the former certainly should not complain of a decree directing a sale of the property, and a return to him of the full amount he paid, with interest thereon.

(*Syllabus by the Court.*)

Error from superior court, Fulton county; M. J. CLARKE, Judge.

P. L. Mynatt & Son, for plaintiff in error. J. C. Reed, for defendant in error.

LUMPKIN, J. 1. The proposition contained in the first head note has been settled by this court in the case of Bell v. Love, 72 Ga. 125. The appointment of the guardian, and all his acts as such, were void for the reason there stated.

2. In the litigation between Dooley and Bell over the land involved in this case, a decree was finally made directing that the property be sold, and that out of the proceeds thereof the entire purchase money paid by Dooley, with interest thereon, be refunded to him. This, certainly, is all he had any right to expect. Indeed, it is doubtful, to say the least, if his equity entitled him to anything more than so much of his money, with interest, as was used in payment of demands to satisfy which a legal guardian would have been authorized, without a special order, to encroach

upon the *corpus* of the ward's estate. Some of Dooley's money was paid on claims to which the *corpus*, without such an order, was not subject. The purchaser at a guardian's sale is undoubtedly bound, at his peril, to look to the legality of the latter's appointment and his authority to sell. If he fails to exercise these precautions, no amount of good faith or fairness on his part can make his title a good one if, in fact, there was no lawful guardian, and, consequently, no authority to sell. Dooley, therefore, having obtained no title whatever by his purchase, and the record showing that a portion of the money he paid was expended in a manner which would not have been lawful even on the part of a legally appointed guardian, he is quite fortunate in receiving back all his money, with interest. This case differs from that of Milner v. Vandivere, 12 S. E. Rep. 879, (decided at the last term.) It appears from the record of that case that a sale of land made by an administratrix, who was the widow of the deceased, was at least irregular, if not void. It further appears that, at the sale made by her, the land was bid off by a person who soon thereafter quitclaimed it to her. She accounted to the estate for the purchase money by crediting the entire amount upon an allowance which had been made to her of a year's support. Afterwards she sold two separate portions of the land, at different times, to one A. G. B Vandivere, and the remaining portion to one Feemster, who subsequently sold to the said A. G. B., and the latter afterwards sold all the land to S. L. Vandivere. The Vandiveres and Feemster bought in good faith, and without notice of any defect in the title. The disputed questions of fact in the case were: (1) Whether all or only some of the minors participated in the enjoyment of the fund so applied to the year's support; and (2) whether or not the year's support itself was properly set apart. Without undertaking to settle these questions, but leaving the same to be investigated upon another trial, this court simply held that, inasmuch as the year's support was a claim of the highest dignity against the estate of the deceased, and one to which the *corpus* of that estate could be legally subjected, a *bona fide* purchaser, whose money paid for the land in the manner disclosed by the record, had an equity superior to the legal title of so many of the heirs as received and enjoyed the benefit of this money in the way of a year's support In the case at bar no question of a year's support was raised at all, and the facts show that a person assuming to act as guardian made an unauthorized use of at least a portion of the purchase money of the land which he had attempted to sell, and that, even as to the balance of said money, it was not applied to any such claim as a year's support, which is a paramount charge upon the property of a deceased person. The ruling in Milner v. Vandivere, while supported by authority, goes quite far enough in the direction of defeating a clear legal title to land by establishing a superior equity in favor of one whose right thereto is derived from

an irregular or illegal sale of a deceased person's property, and the doctrine of this case will not be extended beyond the precise principle therein stated. After a careful examination of the record in the case before us, we are satisfied that the court below committed no errors, and its judgment is therefore affirmed.

OSBORNE v. WILKES *et ux.*

(*Supreme Court of North Carolina.* May 19, 1891.)

FRAUDULENT CONVEYANCES—HUSBAND AND WIFE —CONTRACTS BY WIFE—EVIDENCE—PRACTICE—SUPPLEMENTARY PROCEEDINGS.

1. M., a creditor of W., bought at execution sale a lot belonging to the latter for $7,000. In consideration of $3,000, advanced for the benefit of W.'s wife by S., her brother, and four notes for $3,000 each, signed by W. and his wife, secured by reconveyance in trust, M., in pursuance of a previous agreement with the attorney of S., conveyed the land to W.'s wife. W. and his wife conveyed the equity of redemption to S. by deed absolute upon its face, to secure the payment of the $3,000 advanced. *Held*, that the transaction was not fraudulent in law, nor did the admitted facts raise a presumption of fraud; but it was proper for the court to leave the jury to determine, upon consideration of all the evidence, whether the purchase was made for the husband in the wife's name in order to evade the payment of his debts, and whether she participated in the fraud, or she or her agent had notice of a fraudulent purpose or combination to defraud the husband's creditors.

2. When M., S., and W. and wife subsequently joined in conveying to a purchaser, who paid a price more than sufficient to discharge the whole lien of $15,000 held by M. and S., if there was no intent to defraud in the first purchase participated in by her, the profit realized from the sale might be invested in making the first payment for a second lot, for which a conveyance was taken in the wife's name, but a reconveyance was immediately executed by her and her husband to secure the notes given by them for deferred payments.

3. Though the wife cannot bind herself by contract for the purchase money, and though she may have no separate estate, or may not bind what she has for its payment, still if the vendor will take the risk of selling to her on a credit, neither the husband nor his creditor will be allowed to question the validity of a bond for title or deed made to her in good faith.

4. Where a married woman, not being a free trader, carries on the business of manufacturing on her own property, she may employ the husband as her agent to manage the business, and the fact that she employs him raises no presumption of a purpose to defraud his creditors, but it is competent, in trying an issue of fraud, to show his manner of conducting the business.

5. While creditors may subject, in a supplementary proceeding, the debtor's choses in action, including even a claim for compensation due for service rendered under an express or implied contract, they have no lien on his skill or attainments, and cannot compel him to exact compensation for managing his wife's property, or for service rendered to any person with the understanding that it was gratuitous.

6. Where many circumstances were shown tending to prove that conveyances were made to the wife to evade the payment of a certain debt due from the husband, it was competent for him to show in rebuttal that he had voluntarily allowed the judgment in favor of that creditor to be renewed after it was barred by the statute of limitation.

7. Where such creditor testified that he was informed by the debtor in 1871 that he conducted the business in his wife's name to prevent his creditors from hampering him, the creditor ac-

knowledged that he then had notice of the fraud, and, where suit was brought and judgment rendered against the debtor alone in 1874, and under a supplementary proceeding begun soon after, though the receiver had power to bring an action in 1886 against husband and wife to have her declared a trustee, and to recover the land conveyed to her, with rents, and for specific articles of personal property alleged to have been bought with the husband's funds or on his credit, such action, both for the equitable relief and the recovery of rents and specific personal property, was barred in three years after he had notice of the fraud, according to his own testimony, as against the wife, who was a party only to the action brought by the receiver.

8. If the action had not been barred by the provisions of subsections 4 and 9 of section 155 of the Code, it would have been barred under the general section 158, and it was not error to tell the jury that the action was barred in three years or in ten years. SHEPHERD, J., dissenting.

9. Where execution was issued on another judgment, and levied on the husband's interest in a gold mine, for which he had paid $13,000, and the wife bought for $5 at the sheriff's sale, but it appeared that the judgment, as well as the debts of some other creditors, had been subsequently discharged in full, *held*, that mere inadequacy of price was not sufficient to raise a presumption of fraud; but the inadequacy of the price and the subsequent payment of the debt might be considered by the jury as suspicious circumstances tending to establish the fraud.

10. While there is a presumption that a deed from a husband, who is embarrassed with debt, conveying land to his wife, is fraudulent, yet a deed from the sheriff or any other person to her is presumed to be made in good faith, and the burden is on any one alleging the contrary to prove it.

11. Where the judge invited argument, in the presence of the jury, when the plaintiff rested, as to whether he had made a *prima facie* case, and when he directed the defendants to proceed in the development of their case, and told the jury then, and subsequently charged them, that they must not be influenced in favor of defendants by his inviting argument, nor against them by his order to proceed with the introduction of their testimony, *held* not to be error.

12. Where the jury came into court on Saturday of the first week of the term, and announced that they could not agree as to the facts, it was not error for the judge to say that there were two more weeks of the term, and he would give them plenty of time to consider, and then to direct the sheriff to provide comfortable accommodations for them.

DAVIS, J., dissenting.
(*Syllabus by the Court.*)

Civil action, brought by the receiver appointed in a supplementary proceeding under the order of the court to have the *feme* defendant declared a trustee as to some property, and to recover specifically other property, which it was alleged had been purchased with the funds of or on the credit of the male defendant, her husband, and tried at September term, 1889, of Mecklenburg superior court, before CLARK, J. In the year 1869 the Rock Island Manufacturing Company became indebted to Coates Bros. in the sum of $24,806.78, for which said company gave several notes, with the defendant John Wilkes as surety. Judgment was rendered in the superior court of Rowan county in favor of Coates Bros. against said John Wilkes at April term, 1874, of said court, and supplementary proceedings were begun on the 7th day of the following September. During the same month

Wilkes was examined, after which there was a suspension of active proceedings until he was again ordered before the clerk and examined in December, 1883. A number of other witnesses were also examined between that time and the 17th of September, 1885, when the plaintiff was appointed receiver. The plaintiff brought this action in the superior court of Mecklenburg county. In his complaint he alleges three causes of action: (1) That defendant Jane Wilkes unlawfully and fraudulently withholds the possession of the property described in the second section of the complaint, because the plaintiff is receiver, and said property is liable to the Coates Bros. judgment. The plaintiff demands judgment for possession and damages for detention. (2) That the Alexander property was purchased by Jane Wilkes with the money and credit of John Wilkes, by a scheme or plan contrived to defraud the creditors of John Wilkes. The plaintiff demands judgment for a surrender of this property, and damages for use and occupation. (3) That the Capps mine is subject to the lien of said judgment, and the title thereof is in John Wilkes individually or as partner of Jane Wilkes, and that Jane Wilkes claims said property, because her money paid therefor. Plaintiff alleges that she had no claim to it, and demands judgment for the possession and damages. The defendants positively deny all allegations of fraud, and aver that the property described in the complaint is the property of Jane Wilkes, and not in any way liable to the payment of the debts of John Wilkes. They further allege that the plaintiff's cause of action, if he has any, is barred by the statute of limitations. The first two allegations of fraud were treated as one, by agreement of the parties, and are known as the first cause of action, and that relating to the Capps mine as the second cause of action. It was in evidence that a certain lot in the city of Charlotte, known as the "Navy Yard," was sold under execution against the defendant John Wilkes, and bought by R. Y. McAden for the First National Bank of Charlotte, to which Wilkes owed a debt of about $15,000. The brothers and sisters of the *feme* defendant were residents of the state of New York, where she had a separate estate invested by trustees under her marriage settlement. They subscribed or loaned $3,000 to be used for her benefit by her brother Adolphus Swedburg. He, through Mr. J. H. Wilson, an attorney, effected an arrangement, whereby, in consideration of the payment to said bank of the $3,000 and the execution by Wilkes and his wife of several notes falling due annually for the remaining $12,000, the said Navy Yard property was conveyed to Mrs. Jane R. Wilkes, and immediately reconveyed by her and her husband by mortgage deed to secure the payment of the notes as they should fall due. The equity of redemption was conveyed by Wilkes and wife to Swedburg as a security for the $3,000. The Navy Yard property was subsequently sold at a profit, and out of the proceeds of sale the deeds to the bank and to Swedburg were discharged, leaving a balance in the hands of Mrs. Wilkes, a part of which was subsequently used in making the cash payment for a lot or tract of land in Charlotte, on which are located her dwelling-house and the Mecklenburg foundry; and a portion of the profits were used for the purchase of machinery, etc., used in said foundry. The said lot was sold to her by S. B. Alexander for $9,000. She paid out of her profits $1,000, and she and her husband gave notes for $8,000, the balance of the purchase money, taking title to herself, but immediately joining her husband in a reconveyance to secure payment of notes for purchase money. She has not paid all of the purchase money yet. The foundry has been managed by the defendant John Wilkes for her since the year 1871, and she has realized a handsome profit. He draws checks and attends to the management. She allows him a support for himself and family out of the profits of the business. The plaintiff offered circumstantial testimony tending to show that the purchase was made in the name of the wife, but really for the benefit of her husband, in order that it might be protected from the husband's creditors. The deposition of plaintiff and that of one Frank W. Hall were read in evidence, both deposing that John Wilkes told them that he conducted the business in his wife's name to save himself from annoyance by his creditors. John Wilkes, McAden, Alexander, and others testified to circumstances tending to show that the purchase and sale of the Navy Yard and the subsequent purchase from Alexander were made in good faith for the *feme* defendant. It was in evidence for the plaintiff that after the defendant John Wilkes had expended many thousands of dollars for an interest in the Capps gold mine, including the land and valuable machinery erected thereon, his interest was sold at execution sale, to satisfy an execution issued on a judgment in favor of one J. C. Burroughs, and bought by the *feme* defendant for five dollars. Burroughs also testified that after the sale the whole of his judgment was paid. John Wilkes testified that he had been permitted by his wife to pay off a number of old debts which he owed. He denied making the alleged statement to the plaintiff or the witness Hall. He testified also that more than $8,000 of his wife's separate funds held by trustees for her had been invested in the machinery, etc., at the foundry. He further testified that he had made no arrangement, either with the bank, McAden, or the sheriff, in reference to the sale or purchase of the Navy Yard property, and also to the good faith of the parties in the purchase of the Capps mine. One of many circumstances offered for plaintiff was the fact that for nine years the business of Mecklenburg foundry was advertised in the name of "John Wilkes, Proprietor."

The following issues were submitted without objection: "(1) Was there any arrangement, agreement, or understanding between the defendants John Wilkes or Jane R. Wilkes and the First National bank of Charlotte, by which the property conveyed to the bank by the sheriff under the execution sale of May 23, 1870, was thereupon conveyed to defendant Jane R. Wilkes for the purpose of preserving the property and business of John Wilkes, and hindering, delaying, or defrauding his creditors? Answer. No. (2) Was the property conveyed to Mrs. Wilkes by the bank for $15,000 paid for out of the proceeds of the sale thereof to Matthews, in whole or in part, and, if in part, how much of said proceeds were so used? A. In part; twelve thousand and interest. (3) Were the lots conveyed to the defendant Jane R. Wilkes by S. B. Alexander, trustee, and the machinery, machine tools, and appliances made for or used in the foundry and shops purchased with the money and credit of the defendant John Wilkes, and was the title to said lots procured by him to be made to his wife for the purpose of defrauding his creditors of their just debts, and especially Coates Bros.? A. No. (4) Is the plaintiff in this action entitled to possession of the property known as the 'Capps Mine,' or any interest therein, as the property of John Wilkes, defendant? A. No. (5) Is the plaintiff's first cause of action barred by the statute of limitations? A. Yes. (6) Is the plaintiff's second cause of action barred by the statute of limitations. A. No."

The plaintiff requested the court to instruct the jury: "(1) That, if the property in dispute was purchased from Alexander for the consideration of $9,000,—$1,000 in cash and the balance upon credit,—for the payment of which Wilkes and wife executed their notes and mortgage upon the same for payment of the notes as set forth in the mortgage, and only $1,000 has since been paid thereon, and there is still due of the purchase money over $8,000, then the consideration of the contract of purchase did not move from Mrs. Wilkes, she has acquired no sole and separate interest therein as to the unpaid purchase money, and the property is subject to the claims of the creditors of the husband, incumbered by the amount of the purchase money yet due. (This instruction was refused.) (2) The defendants, both, in their answer to paragraphs 6 (of answer) having admitted and averred that they invested the surplus after paying off the bank debt in the purchase of the Alexander property, now occupied by them as the Mecklenburg Iron-Works, cannot be permitted to prove the contrary, and issue 3 must be found for the plaintiff. (The court refused to give this instruction.) (3) That, even according to the evidence of Mr. Wilkes on the trial, a part of said surplus did go in part payment of the purchase money of said property. (The court gave this instruction.) (4) That according to the evidence of Mr. Wilkes he was the agent of Mrs. Wilkes, and gave the operations of the iron-works his exclusive attention and labors, and large accumulations resulted therefrom, which were applied in enlarging the buildings, increasing the machinery and plant, supporting the household to the extent of $5,000 per annum, and adding to the value of the iron-works to the amount of $35,000. Such accumulations did not become the separate property of the *feme* defendant, but inured to the benefit of

John Wilkes, and the third issue must be found for the plaintiff. (The court refused to give this instruction.) (5) That, if any of the earnings of John Wilkes went to pay for the property conveyed to Mrs. Wilkes by Alexander, they will find for the plaintiff on issue 3 [to the extent of said earnings.] (Given by the court as modified in brackets.) (6) That, if any residue or balance arising out of the sale by Mrs. Wilkes and the Swedburgs to Matthews went to pay any part of the purchase money to Alexander, they will find for the plaintiff on issue 3. (The court refused to give this instruction.) (7) That a separate estate in a married woman must be proved by the instrument making it, and that there is no evidence here of any separate estate belonging to Mrs. Wilkes, deft., sufficient to have a credit upon in the purchase of lands, and no evidence has been adduced, showing that any charge upon such estate, if it existed, could attach to the transactions set up in the answer. (The court refused to give this instruction.) (8) 'A badge of fraud is a fact or circumstance calculated to throw suspicion on a transaction and requiring explanation.' (This instruction was given.) If, therefore, there are any circumstances connected with the sale of the Navy Yard property on May 23, 1870, calculated to throw suspicion on that transaction, and which circumstances have not been satisfactorily explained by the defendants, the jury should answer the first issue 'Yes.' (The court refused to give this instruction.) (9) Fraud may be inferred from facts and circumstances tending to establish it, and less proof is required to establish fraud between husband and wife than between strangers. (This instruction was given.) (10) That stronger proof is required of parties claiming the benefit of transactions between husband and wife than from parties claiming benefits of transactions between strangers. (This instruction was given.) (11) The presumption is that the wife purchased with funds of the husband. (Refused.) Transfer of property from the husband to the wife is regarded with suspicion. (Given.) (12) Conversations of parties charged with fraud are admitted to prove the fraud. If there was any arrangement between the bank on the one hand, and either of the defendants, or any one of them, on the other, that the property should be bid in by the bank, and conveyed to Mrs. Wilkes, the answer to the first issue should be, 'Yes.' (Given.) (13) If Wilkes has devoted his industry, his knowledge of the business, his skill in its management, his name and credit to the accumulation of property to be held by his wife for the use of himself and family, to the exclusion of his creditors, the jury ought to answer issue 3 'Yes.' [But not if he was merely acting *bona fide* as agent for his wife.] (Given as modified, modification shown in brackets.) (14) To make the execution sale fraudulent, it is not necessary that the sheriff should be a party to the agreement that the property shall [should] be bid in or held for the benefit of the judgment debtor. Dobson v. Erwin, 1 Dev. & B. 569. (Given.) (15) If there was any arrangement between the bank

and either John or Jane Wilkes, to bring about the sale under execution, so as to divest John Wilkes of the title and rest it in Mrs. Wilkes, and the effect of the transaction was to hinder and delay creditors, the law will regard such transactions fraudulent, though it may not have been the intent of the parties to so hinder, delay, etc. (Given as a supplement to prayer No. 1 of defendants.)"

Defendants' prayers for instructions: "(1) [As a general rule] [amendment] in order to find that any of the transactions which are alleged to have been fraudulent were fraudulent as to the creditors of the defendant John Wilkes, the jury must first be satisfied by a preponderance of the evidence that the transactions were not only such as in their effect might delay or hinder creditors, but that they were conceived and carried on with the actual intent to hinder, delay, and defraud creditors. [Subject, however, to the proviso that if it was a combination and arrangement to do that act, etc.] (Given as amended, amendments in brackets.) (2) That the jury, in order to find that any of said transactions were fraudulent, must also find that Jane R. Wilkes participated in said interest and purpose, [or bought with notice thereof, either in person or through her husband acting for her.] (Given as amended in brackets.) (3) That, if the creditors Coates Brothers discovered the alleged fraud more than three years prior to the commencement of this action, the first cause of action is barred by the statute of limitations. (Given.) (4) That, if more than three years prior to the commencement of this action they had knowledge of facts and circumstances calculated to put a prudent man on inquiry, which, if prosecuted, would have disclosed the alleged fraud, then the law presumes a discovery of the alleged fraud at said time, and the first cause of action would be barred. (Given.) (5) That, if said discovery was made more than ten years before this action was commenced, the first cause of action is barred. (Given.) (6) Repeat the fourth prayer as to the ten-year limitation. (Given.) (7) That, if the jury should find that any of the personal property, estate, or credit of John Wilkes was invested in the property described in the first cause of action, yet if, after said investment, more than three years elapsed before the commencement of this action, plaintiff is barred. (Refused.) (8) That, if more than ten years elapsed under the facts and circumstances detailed in the seventh prayer, the plaintiff is barred. (Refused.) (9) That, if the jury believe the evidence, the plaintiff's second cause of action is barred by the statute of limitations. (Refused.) (10) That, if more than ten years elapsed after Coates Bros. obtained their judgment, and before this action was commenced, the plaintiff's first cause of action is barred by the statute of limitations. (Given.) (11) That, if more than ten years elapsed after Coates Bros. obtained their judgment, and before this action was commenced, the plaintiff's second cause of action is barred by the statute of limitations. (Refused.)"

The court, in addition to special instructions given, charged the jury as follows, in substance: It is the duty of the jury to weigh the testimony, etc., to remember if the court omits or misrecites any. The court expresses no opinion on the facts, and the jury are not to draw any conclusions against the plaintiff by reason of the stoppage of the case against the defendants nor by requiring it to go on. The jury are not to consider that argument of counsel as to the effect of verdict on the present condition of the Mecklenburg Iron-Works. The court did not stop counsel in that argument, but now cautions the jury that they are not to consider that nor the effect of their verdict upon any one, but only to find the truth of the facts submitted to them on the issues. On the first issue, the plaintiff claims that the sale of the foundry property on the 23d of May, 1870, was fraudulent, and as grounds for this contention offers evidence that sale was postponed from May 7th to May 23d; no readvertisement of property was made. John Wilkes was insolvent. The bank sold to his wife, and took mortgage back. The books of the foundry went on without change. The admission of John Wilkes to Coates and to Hall that he had put the property in his wife's name, etc., as testified by them. On the other hand, the defendants say the postponement of the sale to the 20th of May was from inadvertence, and they do not know whether readvertised or not. They admit that Wilkes was insolvent, but deny, on the testimony of McAden and Wilkes himself, that there was any arrangement by which the property was to be sold to Mrs. Wilkes, and a mortgage taken back for the purchase money; that the sale was made in good faith, and not for the purpose of defrauding creditors, and refer to the fact that afterwards the plaintiff's claim became barred by the statute of limitations and Wilkes renewed the debt by written acknowledgment. When the purchaser of the husband's property is his wife, the law looks through all disguises; and if the jury find on going to the bottom of the matter that it was an arrangement, no matter how arranged, they should answer the first issue "Yes;" otherwise "No." The burden is on the plaintiff to show such arrangement by preponderance, etc. The plaintiff claims on the second issue that the property conveyed to Mrs. Wilkes by the bank for $15,000 was paid for entirely out of the proceeds of the sale to Matthews. On the other hand, the defendants say that only $12,000 of the purchase money and interest was paid out of the proceeds of that sale. On this point it is the duty of the jury to sift and weigh the testimony, and say whether in whole or in part, and, if in part, how much of said proceeds were so used. On the third issue same charge was submitted substantially as on the first issue, except that the evidence raised a presumption of fraud in the purchase. On fourth issue: If the property known as the "Capps Mine" was bought by Mrs. Wilkes by an arrangement, contrivance, etc., and $13,000 worth of property was bought for $5, the sale would be fraudulent, the jury are to consider it in his wife, etc., but if the sale was *bona fide*, and if it

was not with consent of husband, etc., it is a good sale. The law views with suspicion the dealings of husband and wife, and the gross inadequacy of price, if bought with Wilkes' money, or by any contrivance, or if sold with intent to hinder and delay his creditors, and Mrs. Wilkes participated in such intent, or had notice of it, the sale was fraudulent, and you will answer the fourth issue "Yes;" otherwise "No."

The plaintiff excepted to the court's refusal to instruct the jury as requested by plaintiff, and to his instructing them as requested by defendant, and to the charge as given. In the trial of the cause all that part of the complaint which spoke of the Mecklenburg Iron-Works was by consent treated as the plaintiff's first cause of action, and all that part relating to the Capps mine as a second cause of action. This cause was given to the jury about 12 o'clock on Saturday of the first week of the term. About 5 o'clock P. M. of the same day they came into court, and stated to his honor that they were unable to agree. His honor inquired whether they wished instructions upon any matter of law. Stated that he would be glad to give them special instructions upon any point of law about which they were in doubt, but that if they were differing as to the facts in the case he could not help them. The jury responded that they were differing as to matters of fact, but they thought it was utterly impossible for them to agree. The court remarked that there were two weeks more of the court, and it was important to the parties that the jury should agree. He could give them plenty of time to consider the case; and upon further discussion and consideration of the case he thought they would be able to agree upon a just and proper verdict, and notified the sheriff to provide them with comfortable quarters, and keep them together in charge of an officer. They were accordingly kept at an hotel in charge of an officer till Tuesday evening following, when they rendered the verdict recorded. No exception was taken to the remark of the court till after verdict. After verdict plaintiff moved for judgment, notwithstanding the verdict, upon the grounds: (1) That the evidence as to the sale of the Capps mine property under execution to Jane R. Wilkes was sufficient to raise a presumption of fraud, and that there was no evidence in the case to rebut such presumption. (2) That the evidence showed clearly that the defendant John Wilkes had at least an interest in all the property in controversy by reason of his services and skill in operating the foundry and shops from the earnings of which all the money which had gone to pay for the said property had been derived, and that his creditors were entitled to the benefit thereof upon a proper accounting. (3) That the evidence showed that the Mecklenburg Iron-Works, as well as the old Navy Yard property, had been bought by Mrs. Wilkes largely on credit, and that, being a married woman, and not a free trader at the time of such purchase, there being no evidence that the purchase was made on the faith of her separate estate, or that her separate property was charged therewith, such purchase inured to the benefit of her husband's creditors. This motion was refused, and the plaintiff excepted. Plaintiff then moved for a new trial upon the same grounds as set out in the motion for a judgment, notwithstanding the verdict, and upon the additional grounds: (1) That the court intimated an opinion that the plaintiff had failed to make out a case when he rested. (2) Because of the court's language to the jury when the jury announced that they could not agree. (3) For failure to give the instructions asked for by the plaintiff, and for improper instructions given at request of counsel for defendants, and for error in the charge. This motion was refused, and the plaintiff excepted. There was judgment for defendants, from which plaintiff appealed.

B. C. Potts, G. F. Bason, and *W. P. Bynum,* for appellant. *Burwell & Walker* and *Jones & Tillett,* for appellees.

AVERY, J., *(after stating the facts as above.)* When the plaintiff rested upon the supposition that the testimony offered by him was sufficient to be submitted to the jury as *prima facie* evidence of his right to recover, the judge asked counsel, in presence of the jury, in effect, whether they did not think that the defendants might safely demur, and required both parties to give him the benefit of their views upon the question of law thus propounded. Wittkowsky v. Wasson, 71 N. C. 451; State v. Brown, 100 N. C. 519, 6 S. E. Rep. 568. After hearing the argument, the court directed the defendants to proceed, and told the jury then, as they were subsequently cautioned in the charge, to bear in mind the fact that the court had no right to intimate, and had not in fact intimated, an opinion in favor of the defendants by requiring argument, or against them by requiring them subsequently to develop their defense. The plaintiff had promptly objected and excepted when the inquiry was first addressed to his counsel. The statute (Code, § 413) prohibits the judge who presides at the trial from expressing an opinion, "in giving a charge to the jury, either in a civil or a criminal action," that a fact has or has not been fully proven. Neither the letter nor the spirit of the law was violated. The jury were cautioned after the argument, and warned subsequently in the instruction given them, that they must draw no inference prejudicial to either of the parties from the request for an argument on the one hand, or the order made at its conclusion on the other. There was no good ground for complaint on the part of either. State v. Chastain, 104 N. C. 904, 10 S. E. Rep. 519; McCurry v. McCurry, 82 N. C. 296. "This cause was given to the jury about 12 o'clock on Saturday of the first week of the term. About 5 o'clock P. M. of the same day they came into court, and stated to his honor that they were unable to agree. He inquired whether they wished instruction upon any matter of law, and stated that he would be glad to give them special instructions upon any point of law about which they were in doubt; but that if

they were differing as to the facts in the case he could not help them. They responded that they were differing as to matters of fact, but they thought it was utterly impossible for them to agree. The court remarked that there were two weeks more of the court, and it was important to the parties that the jury should agree. He could give them plenty of time to consider the case, and upon further discussion and consideration of the case he thought they would be able to agree upon a just and proper verdict, and notified the sheriff to provide them with comfortable quarters, and keep them together in charge of an officer. They were accordingly kept at an hotel in charge of an officer, till Tuesday evening following, when they rendered the verdict recorded. No exception was taken to the remark of the court till after the verdict." The law anticipates a verdict in every case after the jury have had a reasonable time for consideration. State v. Ephraim, 2 Dev. & B. 171. The judge had the power to discharge the jury in accordance with their request, or in the exercise of a sound discretion to detain them till the end of the term. It was not error to tell them what the law provided in reference to their detention, and direct that they should be taken to comfortable quarters for further consideration and discussion of the issues in reference to which they had not agreed. Hannon v. Grizzard, 89 N. C. 115. The jury, selected by the county commissioners on account of their high character, are supposed to have sufficient intelligence to understand the extent of the judge's power, and to have such conceptions of their own duty that they will not be driven to return a hasty and unjust verdict for fear of being kept in comfortable quarters, but separated from their families, for a few days, or for two weeks, if they could not sooner concur as to their findings. If the typical jurors chosen under our law are so wanting in intelligence and virtue that they can be swerved from the line of rectitude by such considerations, then we should so reform our system as to insure the selection of men who are guided by principle, and thus bring our practice and theory into harmony. The remark of the judge did not constitute sufficient ground for exception, if objection had been made in apt time. If the tendency of telling the jury the extent of the authority vested in the court was to induce them to agree, neither party could say in advance that it was calculated to foreshow or indicate the particular conclusion which it would be proper for them to reach. It is unreasonable to entertain this objection, made for the first time after verdict, if from the nature of the case it would have been available as a ground of exception at an earlier stage of the proceeding.

It is settled law in North Carolina that our statutes (chapter 42, Code) impose no limit upon the "wife's power to acquire property by contracting with her husband or any other person, but only operate to restrain her from or protect her in disposing of property already acquired by her." Battle v. Mayo, 102 N. C. 439, 9 S. E. Rep. 384; Stephenson v. Felton, 106 N.

C. 121, 11 S. E. Rep. 255; George v. High, 85 N. C. 99; Dula v. Young. 70 N. C. 450; Kirkman v. Bank, 77 N. C. 394. The law restricts her *jus disponendi*, not her *jus acquirendi*. Though a married woman may not be able to bind herself by a contract for the payment of the purchase money, yet, if the vendor chooses to take the risk of collecting the debt from her, neither her husband nor his creditor will be allowed to question the validity of a bond for title or deed executed to her in good faith, or to claim profits accruing from a resale of any interest in land which she may have acquired under such agreement or conveyance. No complaint was ever made by McAden or the bank, and the purchase money was ultimately paid, and the lien upon it created by the mortgage discharged. Where the wife has no separate estate, or where she does not bind such separate estate as she has, to secure the payment of the purchase money for other property bought by her on a credit, the contract nevertheless inures to her benefit, and she holds the property, when paid for, in her own right. 2 Bish. Mar. Wom. § 80; Burns v. McGregor, 90 N. C. 222; Knapp v. Smith, 27 N. Y. 277. If, therefore, after R. Y. McAden had bought at execution sale the land of her husband, known as the "Navy Yard Property," the *feme* defendant contracted through Swedburg, Wilson, or even through her husband, acting in good faith as her agent, for the purchase of the property in her own right, and Swedburg advanced $3,000 of the purchase money, taking a conveyance absolute upon its face of her equity of redemption from her husband and herself to secure its repayment, while McAden for the bank conveyed the property to her absolutely, taking at the same time a mortgage from her and her husband to secure the residue of the purchase money ($12,000) due, in four equal annual installments, these transactions vested in her the equitable title to the land, subject first to the payment of the notes for the purchase money, with interest, and then to the amount advanced by Swedburg. While her agreement to pay the purchase money could not be enforced directly, she could by joining her husband make a valid conveyance of her own land, whether by an absolute deed or a mortgage. Newhart v. Peters, 80 N. C. 168. In this way she pledged the land as security for the payment of the residue of the purchase money, though she did not bind herself personally.

Where land is conveyed to a married woman by a person other than her husband, every presumption is in favor of the validity of such a conveyance, as is the rule in reference to other deeds. 2 Bish. Mar. Wom. § 138. The burden of proving the deed of both McAden and Alexander to Mrs. Jane Wilkes to be fraudulent was upon the plaintiffs. She was not required to show affirmatively that she purchased with her own money, or upon her own credit. A different rule might have applied if the land had been conveyed by her husband, instead of by the purchaser at execution sale. While her buying on a credit from McAden does not *per se* affect

the validity of the conveyance to her, the counsel for the plaintiff had the right, which they doubtless exercised, to insist before the jury that her purchase on a credit, when her separate funds held under her marriage contract could not be invested outside of the state of New York, unless in pursuance of a judicial decree of the courts of that state, was a suspicious circumstance, which, with others, tended to show that the husband used the wife's name with her assent to buy the property for his own benefit, and prevent his creditors from again selling it to satisfy his debts. All of the circumstances enumerated in the carefully prepared brief of plaintiff's counsel are at most but badges of fraud, to be considered by the jury as tending to establish the purpose of the parties in the execution of the deed. The evidence as a whole was not even sufficient to raise the presumption in fact, much less in law, that the first conveyance (of October 14, 1870) to Mrs. Wilkes was fraudulent. State v. Mitchell, 102 N. C. 347, 9 S. E. Rep. 702; Woodruff v. Bowles, 104 N. C. 197, 10 S. E. Rep. 482; Harding v. Long, 103 N. C. 1, 9 S. E. Rep. 445; Berry v. Hall, 105 N. C. 154, 10 S. E. Rep. 903. There is no presumption arising from the testimony that she used the funds of her husband in making the purchase. The judge in his charge enumerated carefully the circumstances relied on by the plaintiff as badges of fraud, and also recapitulated the testimony offered by the defendants in explanation. There was no error in giving or refusing instruction in relation to the first issue involving the character of the deed, conveying the Navy Yard property to Mrs. Wilkes. The general principles already stated, if applied to the testimony bearing upon that issue, will dispose of all exceptions arising out of any view of it. If the *feme* defendant, through her agent, acting in good faith, had legal capacity to purchase even on a credit the Navy Yard property, it would follow that the fund realized as a profit from a subsequent sale of it would constitute a part of her separate estate, and she could use that fund, or $1,000 of it, in making a cash payment for the property on which the dwelling-house and foundry are now located, and the deed of Alexander to her would be presumptively valid, as would be the mortgage deed executed by her and her husband, by which they reconveyed the land to Alexander to secure the payment of the residue of the purchase money ($8,000.) The same reason and the same authorities that were offered to sustain the presumptive validity of the transaction with McAden applied to the later trade with Alexander. The consideration of $1,000 paid down did move from Mrs. Wilkes, as it constituted a part of her legitimate profit from the former sale, if her deed for the Navy Yard property was valid. Neither of the deeds was fraudulent as to the *feme* defendant, unless she participated in the fraud, or she or her agent had notice of a fraudulent purpose or combination to hinder, delay, or defraud the creditors of her husband before she purchased. Battle v. Mayo and Woodruff v. Bowles, supra.

Without discussing them in detail, we have disposed of the exceptions to the refusal of the court to give the instructions asked, numbered, respectively, 1, 3, 6, 7, 8, 11, 15, and those relating to instructions requested by the defendants upon the same subject, numbered 1 and 2. The objection urged in the plaintiff's brief that the verdict was against the weight of the evidence is one that is addressed entirely to the discretion of the *nisi prius* judge, when made below. His refusal to grant a new trial on that ground is not reviewable, and such motions will not be entertained when made for the first time in the appellate court. Whitehurst v. Pettipher, 105 N. C. 40, 11 S. E. Rep. 369. An appeal lies only from the refusal to set aside the verdict on the ground that there was no evidence, or not in law sufficient evidence, to support it. Inadequacy of price is not of itself in any case sufficient ground for setting aside a conveyance as fraudulent, but is a suspicious circumstance, to be considered in connection with other testimony tending to show fraud in procuring its execution. Berry v. Hall, supra; Potter v. Everitt, 7 Ired. Eq. 152; Bump. Fraud. Conv. p. 86; Kerr, Fraud & M. 189. Mrs. Wilkes had the same right to buy her husband's land with her own funds when sold at execution sale, or from a purchaser at such sale, that any other person had. If additional testimony were offered tending to show a fraudulent combination to prevent a fair competition of bidders on the part of her husband and others, in which she participated, or of which she had notice before buying, then the jury would be justified in considering the inadequacy of the price paid for the Capps mine, in connection with other badges of fraud and with the fact that she was the wife of the debtor. Where the husband contracts to sell to the wife, or conveys property to her in payment of an alleged debt, or for an alleged money consideration paid by her, the burden is upon her to show the *bona fides* of the transaction. State v. Mitchell, supra. But, where she claims under a sheriff's deed and an execution sale, there is no such presumption as would arise from a direct sale and conveyance by him to her. The subsequent payment of the whole debt, due the plaintiff in execution, by some one, and the fact that the husband was the defendant in execution, were the circumstances relied on, in connection with the inadequacy of price, to establish the alleged fraud. If these, standing alone, were sufficient to be submitted, as the judge did, to the jury, to show a fraudulent combination, it will not be insisted that they are strong enough to raise such a presumption of fraud as would, without explanation, justify the court in instructing the jury to respond "Yes" to the fourth issue. We are aware that there is some apparent conflict of authority in those cases where the property has been sold at judicial sale, as to the weight of certain evidence tending to establish fraud, but it is now settled that, since separate courts of equity were abolished, the judge has no right to instruct the jury as to the weight of evidence, when it is not

sufficient to raise a presumption of the truth of the allegation of fraud. Berry v. Hall, supra; Ferrall v. Broadway, 95 N. C. 551. Under our present Code a married woman may purchase property and carry on business on her separate account, and through her husband as agent. The fact that she employs him and supports him does not raise a presumption of fraud, though it is competent in trying the issue to show his manner of conducting the business. State v. Mitchell, supra; Abbott's Tr. Ev. 171, 172; Rankin v. West, 25 Mich. 195; Kluender v. Lynch, *43 N. Y. 363. Her title to the property is not impaired, nor do his creditors acquire any interest in the profits because he gives his services without other compensation than an indefinite allowance applied by her permission to the payment of his expenses. Abbey v. Deyo, 44 N. Y. 345; Knapp v. Smith, supra; Gage v. Dauchy, 34 N. Y. 293; Buckley v. Wells, 33 N. Y. 518. In Manning v. Manning, 79 N. C. 293, the right of the wife to hold the husband, as her agent, to account for the rents and profits of her land, though received by him without objection, was distinctly recognized.

While creditors may subject one's choses in action, including even a claim for compensation due him for his services under an express or implied contract in a supplementary proceeding, they have no lien upon his skill or attainments, nor can they compel him to exact compensation for managing his wife's property, or collect from her as on a *quantum meruit* what his services were reasonably worth. 2 Bish. Mar. Wom. §§ 299, 300, 453, 454. She may remunerate him by furnishing him a support. He may, if he choose, serve her without compensation. Id. § 439; Corning v. Flower, 24 Iowa, 584. Indeed, a creditor cannot collect from any person compensation for service rendered by his debtor with the understanding that it was gratuitous. 2 Bish. Mar. Wom. supra. We think, therefore, that there was no error in the refusal of the court to give the plaintiff's instruction numbered 4, nor in the amendments made to those numbered, respectively, 5 and 13. The plaintiff certainly has no just ground to complain of the charge given upon that point, and the defendants, in view of the verdict rendered, have no reason for objecting.

In the trial of issues like those submitted in our case, where so many competent circumstances are adduced as badges of fraud, it necessarily opens the door quite as wide for the introduction of evidence in rebuttal. When so much testimony had been offered for the purpose of showing an intent on the part of Wilkes and his wife to evade the payment of the debt to Coates Bros., it was competent to show in rebuttal that with full knowledge that the judgment was barred by the statute of limitations he had voluntarily allowed them to renew it. The *feme* defendant was not a party to the suit brought in the superior court of Rowan county by Coates Bros. on the 20th of March, 1874, and in which judgment was recovered and proceedings supplementary to execution were instituted. The affidavit, which was the basis of the supplementary proceedings, was dated September 7, 1874. In obedience to an order dated September 24, 1874, the defendant John Wilkes appeared before J. M. Horah, clerk of said court, during the same month, and was examined. No further action was taken till the 21st of April, 1883, when another order was issued upon a similar affidavit, in obedience to which John Wilkes was again summoned before said clerk and examined, first on the 8th of May, 1883. John Wilkes again appeared, on notice, December 17, 1883, when he and F. W. Hall and others were examined before said Horah, clerk. The deposition of George M. Coates, Jr., was taken before a commissioner of affidavits on the 3d of January, 1884, to be read in said proceeding. From an order of GRAVES, Judge, refusing a motion to appoint a receiver upon the testimony of the witnesses examined, and to compel the defendant John Wilkes to produce the books of the Mecklenburg Iron-Works, kept by or under the direction of John Wilkes, for his wife, Mrs. Jane Wilkes, the plaintiff appealed, and the judgment below was reversed. Osborne v. Wilkes, 92 N. C. 376. From an order made by MONTGOMERY, Judge, at August term, 1885, and subsequently amended, appointing the plaintiff, Osborne, receiver, and empowering him to bring suit, etc., and restraining Mrs. Wilkes, who was not a party, from disposing of or transferring certain property, the defendant John Wilkes appealed. Coates v. Wilkes, 94 N. C. 174. This court declared that it was error to order that she be restrained from transferring property claimed by her, when she was not a party, and had not been ordered to appear for examination, or otherwise notified of the decree, though in other respects the judgment of the lower court was affirmed. Accordingly the plaintiff, as receiver, caused the summons in this action to be issued against the defendants, John Wilkes and his wife, on the 20th day of August, 1886. The exceptions to the charge given by the court at the request of the defendants raised the question whether what was called the first cause of action, brought for the recovery of the Mecklenburg foundry property, had been barred by the lapse of time since the right of action accrued. The plaintiff in his complaint demanded judgment that the deed conveying the Mecklenburg foundry property to the defendant Jane Wilkes be declared void, and that she be declared a trustee of said property for the benefit of the creditors of John Wilkes, and that she be required "to surrender to said lot, buildings, machinery, and all things thereunto belonging or used in said foundry and shops to the plaintiff as receiver," etc., and that she and John Wilkes be "decreed to account with the plaintiff for use and occupation, rents," etc. The case was one solely cognisable in a court of equity, and therefore, without regard to the amendment of 1889, the plaintiff's right to have the defendant Jane Wilkes declared a trustee for Coates Bros. was barred three years after the discovery of the fraud by Coates Bros., or three years after, by

the exercise of reasonable diligence, they might have discovered it. Code, § 155, subsec. 9; Day v. Day, 84 N. C. 408; Lanning v. Commissioners, 106 N. C. 511, 11 S. E. Rep. 622; Hurlbert v. Douglas, 94 N. C. 122; Jaffrey v. Bear, 103 N. C. 165, 9 S. E. Rep. 382. This action is brought with the special view of declaring Mrs. Wilkes, who was not a party to the former action or proceeding, a trustee, and therefore to her plea of the statute of limitations it is not sufficient to reply that this action (as in Hughes v. Whitaker, 84 N. C. 640) was brought in aid of the former suit. The right of action accrued as to her when the fraud was or might by due diligence have been discovered. If the testimony of George M. Coates, Jr., a member of the firm of Coates Bros., be taken as true, John Wilkes told him in the year 1871 that he conducted the business in his wife's name "because his creditors would hamper him," if he conducted it otherwise. If Coates Bros. had notice that Wilkes used his wife's name in 1871 to avoid embarrassment on account of his debts, being then creditors, a cause of action accrued at that time in their favor. After their right to equitable relief was barred by the lapse of time, a receiver appointed at their instance could not recover when the statute was pleaded by Mrs. Wilkes.

In so far as the action was prosecuted for the purpose of recovering from the feme defendant the possession of specific articles of personal property, or of compelling her to account for the use of the personal property or the rent of real property, it was clearly barred after the three years from the time when the right of action accrued. Code, § 155, subsec. 4. If the first cause of action had not been barred in three years, under the subsections of section 155 of the Code, as to Mrs. Wilkes, she might clearly have availed herself of the general provision, (Code, § 158,) and therefore it was not error to tell the jury that the first cause of action was barred within ten years after the right to bring it accrued. The cases of Dobson v. Erwin, 1 Dev. & B. 569, Bridges v. Moye, Busb. Eq. 170, and others cited, were decided long before either of the three statutes upon which the rulings of his honor below rested were enacted as a part of the Code of Civil Procedure in 1868. Before that time there was no limit short of 20 years to the right to follow the funds of a debtor fraudulently invested in the name of another, except where the statute in relation to the abandonment of an equity (Rev. Code, c. 65, § 19; Laws 1826, c. 28, § 2) applied. With full and fair instruction the jury, as it was their province to do, passed upon the good faith of the parties interested in the transactions in reference to the sale of the "Navy Yard Property" and the lot on which the Mecklenburg foundry is located, as well as in the purchase of the Capps mine. There was testimony tending to throw a cloud of suspicion over the treaties that culminated in the conveyance of each of the three tracts of land to the feme defendant; but this may always be expected where the wife purchases property, making little, if any, outlay of money, and, after placing her husband, as agent,

In charge of it, realizes a large profit, or receives an extraordinary income. There was no testimony offered by the plaintiff that raised a presumption of fraud in either purchase, so as to shift the burden of proof to the defendants. We have not adverted to the large number of cases cited, and for the most part decided by the supreme court of Pennsylvania, in which a different view is taken as to the right of married women to acquire property by purchase during coverture, and in reference to the weight of evidence bearing upon issues of fraud. We must be governed by our own constitution and laws, and by the construction given to them by this court. The adoption of our constitution embodying especially article 10, § 6, and the enactment immediately thereafter of chapter 42 of the Code, (Laws 1868-69, c. 122,) marked a new era in our law affecting the rights of married women. Having thus disposed of all of the assignments of error that were insisted on here, we conclude that the judgment of the court below must be affirmed.

DAVIS, J., dissents.

SHEPHERD, J. I dissent from that part of the opinion which declares that the three-years statute of limitations (Code, § 155, subsec. 9) applies to this case.

WOOL v. SAUNDERS, Secretary of State.

(*Supreme Court of North Carolina.* May 12, 1891.)

GRANTS OF STATE LAND—EVIDENCE—PROCEDURE.

1. The secretary of state cannot consider evidence outside the papers filed by a claimant for a grant of vacant and unappropriated land belonging to the state, under Code N. C. c. 17.

2. Where it clearly appears on the face of the warrant and survey that the land is not subject to entry, or is subject to entry only on conditions which have not been complied with, the secretary may refuse to issue a grant therefor.

3. Where on the face of the papers the claimant has a right to the grant, the court will not refuse to require its issue on account of extraneous communications, which may be incorrect or susceptible of explanation.

AVERY, J., dissenting.

Appeal from superior court, Wake county; E. T. BOYKIN, Judge.

Controversy submitted without action. *The Attorney General,* for appellant. *C. M. Busbee,* for appellee.

SHEPHERD, J. Two questions must be determined before we enter upon the consideration of the facts of this particular case.

First, whether the secretary of state has a right to receive and act upon testimony outside of the papers filed by a claimant for the purpose of obtaining a grant for vacant and unappropriated land belonging to the state? We are of the opinion that the question must be answered in the negative. The law has carefully prescribed how vacant lands may be entered, and in what cases the secretary of state may issue grants. Chapter 17, Code. The entry takers and surveyors of the several counties are sworn officers charged with important duties in respect to the subject; and

if it appears from the warrant and survey that they have discharged these duties, and if the claimant has in all other respects complied with the law, the secretary has no discretion, and must issue the grant. To permit or require the secretary to go behind the *prima facie* right of the claimant, and determine whether the land is subject to entry, would necessarily involve an inquiry into the legal or equitable rights of other parties claiming under prior entries or grants, or by adverse possession, and thus a new tribunal, unknown to the constitution and laws, would be erected for the investigation of titles to real estate, the practical workings of which would be productive of inestimable conflict, uncertainty, and confusion. The trial of such questions is wisely left to the courts after the grant is issued; the grant being voidable if irregularly issued, and void if the land is not subject to entry. Strother v. Cathey, 1 Murph. 162; Harshaw v. Taylor, 8 Jones, (N. C.) 514; State v. Bevers, 86 N. C. 591; Brem v. Houck, 101 N. C. 627, 8 S. E. Rep. 365.

2. The *second* question is whether the secretary of state may refuse to issue a grant when, upon the face of the claimant's papers, (that is the warrant and survey,) it clearly appears that the land is not subject to entry, or subject to entry only upon certain conditions which are not shown to exist? The power of the secretary as to issuing grants is a limited one, and extends only to those lands which by statute are subject to entry. When, therefore, he issues a grant of lands which are not subject to entry, the grant is void in a court of law, because he has exceeded the authority delegated to him, and his act has no more validity than that of any private citizen. Strother v. Cathey, supra. This being so, it would seem exceedingly plain that no court ought to compel him to perform such an unauthorized act where the want of the authority appears upon the face of the claimant's papers.

3. The application of these principles to the case before us is free from difficulty. Excluding from our view, for the foregoing reasons, the communication of Mr. Bond and its accompanying exhibits, and looking only at the papers of the claimant, we find upon an examination of entry No. 39 that the land described is covered by navigable water, and in front of an incorporated town. Such land is not the subject of entry except under the conditions prescribed in Code, § 2751, subsec. 1, one of which is that "the town corporation shall regulate the line on deep water to which entries may be made." It seems to be conceded (and we think very properly) that until the town authorities have acted the land is not the subject of entry. The language of the statute clearly implies this, and there are obvious reasons why it should be so. If, as suggested, the town authorities refuse to act, the courts may compel them to discharge their duty in this respect, and in no event can our construction result in one party's getting an undue priority over the other by any possible collusion with the town authorities, since only one person (the owner of the adjacent land) has a right to

make such an entry. It affirmatively appearing, then, that the land is covered by water in front of an incorporated town, and such land not being subject to entry until the town authorities have acted, and this not being shown, we are of the opinion that the secretary of state had a right to decline issuing a grant for the same. As to entry No. 38, we think it sufficiently appears from the face of the papers presented by the claimant that the town authorities had designated the line on deep water to which the entry could be made, and that the boundaries indicated are in conformity therewith. We conclude, therefore, that as to this entry a grant should be issued by the secretary.

It has been suggested that although upon the face of the papers the claimant has a right to have a grant issued, and although the secretary cannot consider the communication of Mr. Bond and its exhibits, still, the court being possessed of this information, we should not require the defendant to do a vain thing. To this it may be answered that the court cannot act upon such information, as it may be incorrect or susceptible of explanation, and the claimant ought not to be precluded in this "short hand" way of asserting his alleged rights in "a due and orderly course of procedure." The judgment must be modified to conform to this opinion.

AVERY, J., (dissenting.) I do not concur in the opinion of the court. I do not think that the secretary of state "had a right to decline issuing" either of the grants applied for by the plaintiff. On the contrary, he is a mere ministerial officer, acting under the positive mandate of the law, that he "shall make out grants for all surveys returned to his office, which grants shall be authenticated by the governor, countersigned by the secretary, and recorded in his office." Code, § 2779. The same section provides further that "no grant shall issue upon any survey unless the same be signed by the surveyor of the county." The requirement that he shall make out and deliver the patent upon every warrant and survey authenticated by the surveyor is mandatory. The implication arising out of this command of the law, subject to but a single limitation, is that the certificate of the surveyor, and nothing short of that, is to be considered by the secretary as ample evidence not only of the number of acres embraced within the boundaries, but of the proper and lawful location of the land. A surveyor is required to give bond conditioned for the faithful discharge of his duties, and when he has been inducted into office the law presumes that he has a knowledge of the art of surveying. Lawson, Pres. Ev. p. 57; Ashe v. Lanham, 5 Ind. 434. Our statute recognizes this principle by thus requiring the secretary to issue grants in all cases where the survey bears upon its face his certificate that he made it in accordance with the law.

I concur with the majority of the court in the opinion that the secretary of state cannot assume judicial functions, and hear evidence *dehors* the warrant and survey as to the conflicting contentions of claimants. But it seems to me to be equally without warrant of law to constitute the secretary of state a judicial officer clothed with the power to pronounce an entry void upon its face for failure to comply with the law. I find the peremptory requirement that the grant shall issue to the claimant when he presents certain papers, but the most minute search and critical examination of chapter 17 and of our statutes generally does not lead to the discovery of any clause or section under which explicitly, or by implication of the law, the judicial power to pass upon the sufficiency of an entry is given to any officer or tribunal other than courts erected for the purpose of passing upon such issues of law as well as the facts. The constitution (article 4, § 2) declares that "the judicial power of the state shall be vested in a court for the trial of impeachments, a supreme court, superior courts, and such other courts inferior to the supreme court as may be established by law." If we concede the soundness of the abstract proposition that when the secretary refuses to issue a grant upon an entry void upon its face the courts will not use the writ of *mandamus* to do a vain thing, by requiring him to issue it, I seriously doubt whether since the enactment, by the provincial legislature of 1777, of the first laws authorizing the conveyance of public lands by patent in the name of the state, a single entry or warrant has ever been forwarded to the secretary which upon its face appeared to cover land not subject to entry. The judicial annals of the state for over 100 years show no instance where the secretary of the state has refused to issue for any such reason, and no entry, upon its face appearing to cover land, that could not by law be conveyed by grant. The ruling of the court in this case is an innovation certainly upon the established practice, and, in my opinion, is such a departure from an important principle as will lead to confusion, and give rise to unnecessary litigation. A vague entry was declared not to be void against the state nor against a subsequent purchaser with notice, because the location is made certain by the survey, and because it was and is deemed public policy to have our vacant lands appropriated by our people, and made a source of income to the owners as well as the state. Harris v. Ewing, 1 Dev. & Bat. Eq. 374; Bryson v. Dobson, 3 Ired. Eq. 138. Where persons have chosen to enter and obtain grants for land not subject by law to entry, the secretary has been accustomed to act without question upon the certificate of the surveyor, leaving the courts to determine what interest passed by the conveyance as against the state, or against other persons claiming under the state through other patents. The persistent efforts of owners of large bodies of land to establish some tribunal empowered to pass upon the validity of entries have proven unavailing because of the popular opposition to imposing any restriction that might postpone the making out of grants. The code commissioners reported a provision, which was enacted as a part of section 2765 of the Code, for allowing interested parties to show cause why a warrant of survey should not issue; but at the very next session of the general assembly an amendment was passed striking out that provision, and inserting in lieu the words, "the entry taker shall issue and deliver to the surveyor or enterer a proper warrant of survey, in which shall be copied such entry, with its true number and date." The same unequivocal language is applied to the issue of the warrant by the entry taker as that used in reference to the issue of the grant. If the secretary of state has "the right" to refuse to issue the patent because, according to his own view of the law, the entry, as incorporated in the warrant, appears *prima facie* to cover land they cannot pass by grant, what is to prevent the entry taker from constituting himself a court with jurisdiction of the single question whether the entry is not upon its face void because it covers land that under a proper construction of some statute is not subject to grant? We will search in vain for any legal warrant for vesting one of these officers with a discretionary right to disobey a positive mandate of the law because he is a high official of the executive department of the state, while the lower official is denied the right to disregard a similar requirement for the same reason. If we arbitrarily establish the right of both to disregard the peremptory requirement of the law, then we will erect two petty tribunals, not heretofore known to our law, for construing all statutes authorizing the entering and granting of lands.

It seems to me manifest that the secretary of state is a ministerial officer, bound to obey the law and issue grants upon all surveys signed by the surveyor of the county, (or deputy when he is authorized by the law to act for him,) and that he has no right to pass upon the question whether the entry is void upon its face. If we concede, however, that, whatever may be the extent of his power, the courts are not required to compel him to issue a void grant, I maintain that there is nothing upon the face of the entry numbered 39 that would justify this court in pronouncing it void. The statute, (section 2765, Code,) as amended, provides that "the claimant of land shall produce to the entry taker a writing, signed by such claimant, setting forth where the land is situated, the nearest water-courses, mountains, and remarkable places, and such water-courses and remarkable places as may be therein, the natural boundaries and lines of any other person, if any, which divide it from other lands, and every such writing shall be on one quarter sheet of paper, at least, and indorsed by the entry taker with the name of the claimant, the number of acres claimed, the date of the entry, and a copy thereof shall be entered in a book well bound and ruled, with a large margin in spaces of equal distance, each space to contain one entry, and every entry to be made in the order of time in which it shall be received and numbered in the margin." This is all of the statutory provision as to the form of entries, and its requirements are declared to be largely directory, it being deemed

sufficient if the survey contain a specific description, though the entry may be a "floating one," not upon its face definitely located. Harris v. Ewing, supra; Currie v. Gibson, 4 Jones, Eq. 25; Munroe v. McCormick, 6 Ired. Eq. 85. The effect of the ruling in this case is to superadd a proviso not only that it shall appear affirmatively, when land covered by water is entered in front of an incorporated town, that the authorities have marked out the line of navigable water as the statute prescribes, but that this new requirement shall be considered mandatory, so that without previous compliance on the part of the corporation the entry shall be declared void, and even a specific survey shall not be sufficient to make it effective as the basis of a grant from the state.

The material portion of the entry declared void in this case is the following description: "The land covered by water in part of Jacob Wool's wood-yard wharf in the town of Edenton, running out from the foot of said wharf, south between lines parallel and distant one from the other sixty-four and one-half feet, so far as the channel, a distance of one hundred and forty-five feet, containing —— acres." The entry which is declared by the court to be upon its face valid is in the following form: "Jacob Wool, a resident of Chowan county, and a citizen of the state of North Carolina, makes an entry of the following described and unappropriated lands to such marks and lines on deep water and at the channel as may have been heretofore indicated by the board of councilmen of the town of Edenton, in front Jacob Wool's John M. Jones lot, bounded on the north by Blount street, on the east by lot No. 187, south by creek and arm of Edenton bay, and on the west by lot of D. W. Roper, containing —— acres, more or less, to-wit, lands covered by water in front of the land of the said Wool, above described, running south from the front of said Wool to deep water at the channel in lines parallel and confined to straight lines, including only the said water-front and the land covered by water within the said lines to deep water on the channel. This entry is made for the purpose of erecting a wharf and other purposes incident thereto." The Code, § 2751, provides generally that all unappropriated lands belonging to the state shall be subject to entry, but excepts land covered by navigable water, with swamp lands and land covered by the waters of lakes. The exception to the first exception is that littoral and riparian owners may for the purpose of erecting wharves enter the land, in which they before had a qualified property by the common law, as far as the deep water, which of course means the margin of the navigable water. Bond v. Wool, 107 N. C. 139, 12 S. E. Rep. 281. When such entries are made in front of a town, the corporate authorities are required to "regulate the line on deep water to which entries may be made." It will be conceded that if Jacob Wool's wood-yard was located on Edenton bay, beyond the limits of an incorporated town, he would have the right to a grant for the land covered by the water in his front as far as the channel or margin of the navigable water and an entry calling for the channel or for navigable water would be valid, the surveyor being of necessity at liberty to locate the line of the channel. There is nothing in entry No. 39 except the expression "in front of Jacob Wool's wood-yard in the town of Edenton" to indicate that the land lies in front of an incorporated town. As the secretary cannot look beyond the particular entry in passing upon its validity (according to the view taken by the court) I respectfully insist that neither the secretary of state nor this court has the right to draw the inference, from the fact that Edenton is called a town in the entry, that it is an incorporated town, when the act incorporating it is not in evidence. Durham, etc., R. v. North Carolina R. Co., 12 S. E. Rep. 963, (decided at this term.) The law recognizes the fact that a town or city may exist with known limits and streets admitted to be highways, but without corporate existence. Meriwether v. Garrett, 10 Myer's Fed. Dec. tit. "Corporations," § 2224. The opinion of the court rests upon the idea that not only is the marking of the line by the authorities of the town or city a condition precedent to the acquisition of the right by the riparian proprietor to convert his qualified ownership into an absolute property, but that even where such line has been marked, and in the absence of any prescribed statutory form except the general one, declared by this court to be merely directory, the entry must be pronounced void because it does not affirmatively appear that the corporation has taken action. I do not think that either proposition is supported by reason or authority; but, were we to concede that any grant issued to the applicant would be void unless the corporation had previously fixed its outer limit, even in this extreme view of the case I contend that the presumption of law would be that the officials named had discharged the duty required of them, and in the proper manner, this being one of the many cases in which "acts of executive officers of the government (e. g., sheriffs, registers, treasurers, surveyors) are presumed to be regular so far as to throw the burden of proof on the party collaterally assailing such act on the ground of irregularity." 2 Whart. Ev. §§ 1297-1318; Best, Ev. § 300; U. S. v. Ross, 92 U. S. 284. Entry No. 39 extended as far as "the channel," that word being used to designate the nearest portion of the bay where vessels could pass. The term "deep water" is used in the statute to denote precisely the same thing. I think that the presumption of law is that the lines mentioned in entry No. 39 extended to the channel or deep-water mark, as that had been indicated by the officers authorized to mark such lines.

But I further maintain that it is not essential to the validity of a grant to a riparian proprietor of his own water-front that the corporation should fix the line of the channel before the entry is made. It has been decided by this court, and settled by the leading courts of the country, that littoral and riparian owners have as an incident to their ownership of their adjacent land a qualified property in that covered by water on their front extending to navigable water or to the channel or deep water. Bond v. Wool, 107 N. C. 150, 12 S. E. Rep. 281. "It does not seem that the general assembly intended, if it had the power to do so, to wrest [Code, § 2751] from the riparian proprietors any rights that they already held, but simply to allow them, at a fair price, to acquire an absolute instead of a qualified property." 107 N. C. 154, 12 S. E. Rep. 285. This court has held that the plaintiff had the right to erect a wharf at the channel on the margin of navigable water in his own front, and that he is not bound to await the action of a corporation in whose limits his land lies before building it, though he erects it subject to the risk of losing it, if located outside of the high-water mark subsequently made by the corporate authorities. When a person had erected a wharf before the passage of the act of 1854, (Code, § 2751,) the legislature in that statute recognized his qualified property and right to erect it "under the restrictions and the terms" prescribed in that act, viz., provided it should fall inside the deep-water line in front of any town when established in the manner indicated by the laws, (Code, § 2751.) Even the entry (No. 38) declared to be valid in this case calls for "such marks and lines on deep water and at the channel as may have been heretofore indicated," etc., not that have been designated; and it is not positively asserted either in the entry or the survey that such line has been established, though the high-water mark and the line of deep water are called for. But the law recognizes the existence of a line of deep navigable water to which the qualified property of the riparian owner extended before the act of 1854 was passed; and, if it should affirmatively appear that the line has been marked, it must be essential to state it more explicitly than it is stated either in entry No. 38 or the survey of it. If we are permitted to infer from the language used in No. 38 that the line has been actually marked, and is the deep-water line called for in the survey, I can see no sufficient reason why the channel called for in No. 39 should not be presumed to have been indicated by the proper officials of the town.

The opinion of the court rests upon the ground that it appears affirmatively from the language of entry No. 39 that the land entered is covered by navigable water, and that "such land is not the subject of entry except under conditions prescribed in the Code, § 2751 (1,) one of which is "that the town corporation shall regulate the line on deep water to which entries may be made." When the colony of North Carolina joined the other colonies in declaring its independence, all vacant lands were held to rest *ipso facto* in the sovereign state, instead of in the British king, or the single lord proprietor who claimed a portion of it under a grant from the crown. The act of 1777 first gave to the citizen the right of making entries upon certain conditions. One of these conditions was that the lands entered must not cover any portion of the territory set apart to the Cherokee Indians. Yet, when grants were made for land along the line of the Cherokee Nation, it was never thought necessary to set forth in an entry that it was located east of said line. Where entries were made and grants were issued after the line was established by treaty still further to the west, it was held by this court repeatedly that an entry and grant located on the Indian boundary line, and covering land partly within and partly outside of the prohibited territory, were only void as to the portion within the Cherokee boundaries. Brown v. Brown, 106 N. C. 451, 11 S. E. Rep. 647. I do not see the obvious reason why, when a riparian proprietor, in attempting to acquire the absolute property in land covered by water in his front co-extensive with his qualified property, mistakes the line of the channel as subsequently marked out by the proper officers, he should not be treated in the same way as one who by mistake has located his entry and grant so as to extend beyond the Meigs and Freeman line, or beyond the boundary of the county in which the entry was recorded. It is difficult to understand how the rights of any individual would be imperiled if only so much of the land granted as should lie inside of the line ultimately marked by the town authorities should pass by the grant. It is certain that the state has no ground of complaint if the result of this mistake be to place in her coffers for the benefit of the public schools the purchase money for so much of the land covered by water as extends beyond the established high water mark, just as he acquires no title for so much of the land embraced in his grant as laps upon the older grant. It seems to me, therefore, that the rule laid down by this court in this case is arbitrary, not in harmony with previous adjudications construing analogous provisions of statutes in relation to entries and grants, and is not supported by reason.

TUCKER v. COMMONWEALTH.

(Supreme Court of Appeals of Virginia.　June 18, 1891.)

MURDER—SUFFICIENCY OF EVIDENCE.

In a murder trial the evidence showed that defendant went with his gun to a certain orchard, of which he and deceased each occupied a part, to gather apples, accompanied by his two children, aged 10 and 12 years. Deceased, also carrying a gun, followed not far behind. An animosity had existed for some time between them, and each had threatened to kill the other. A few hours later the dead body of deceased was found in the highway, near the orchard fence, with the top of his head crushed, a bullet wound in his back, and his gun lying near broken and empty. A witness for the prosecution testified that, from a mountain three-fourths of a mile away, he heard defendant swearing, then two reports of a gun, and saw a man run and disappear in the orchard. The children both testified that they were with their father, and that he did not shoot, but that two shots were fired at him by some unseen person. *Held*, that the evidence was insufficient to warrant a verdict of murder in the second degree, and a new trial will be granted.

Appeal from circuit court, Craig county.

Mr. Skeen, for appellant. *The Attorney General*, for the Commonwealth.

LEWIS, P. The prisoner was indicted in the county court of Craig county, and tried in the circuit court of that county, for the murder of Strodder Helms. He was found guilty of murder in the second degree, and sentenced, in accordance with the verdict, to confinement in the penitentiary for the term of 10 years. There was a motion for a new trial on the ground that the verdict was contrary to the law and the evidence, which motion was overruled. To this ruling the prisoner excepted, and the evidence is certified in the bill of exceptions. The single question to be determined is whether there was error in overruling the motion for a new trial. The case briefly stated, is substantially as follows: The dead body of the deceased was found in the highway on the 13th of August, 1889, with the top of his head crushed, and a bullet wound in the back. His gun was found lying near the body, empty and broken. Both the prisoner and the deceased were seen going that morning in the direction of an orchard some distance from their respective residences, a portion of which belonged to the former, and another portion, called "the dower interest," was in the possession of the latter. There had existed for some time previous to the homicide an animosity between them, and each had been heard to threaten to kill the other. The prisoner was accompanied by his two children, aged respectively 10 and 12 years, going to the orchard, with a horse and sled, for apples. He also carried his gun. The deceased, who likewise carried a gun, followed not a great distance behind. The dead body was found a few hours afterwards near the orchard fence.

A witness, W. E. Starks, testified that the same morning he was on a mountain about three-quarters of a mile from the orchard, and in view of it, "coursing bees;" that while there he heard the prisoner's voice at the orchard, "swearing, rearing, and charging;" that he "saw a person" in the orchard, and soon after heard the report of a gun, and then a second report, and "saw smoke rise up;" that "immediately after the second shot a man ran and disappeared in the orchard, and then all became quiet." On the other hand, both of the prisoner's children testified, as witnesses for the defense, that they were with their father all the time, and that he did not shoot that morning, while he was absent from home. The body was first discovered between 10 and 11 o'clock A. M. They also testified that the prisoner knew nothing of the homicide until several hours after it had been committed, and that, before hearing of it, he started to get a warrant from a justice of the peace for the arrest of Helms, the deceased. They further testified that, while the prisoner was in the orchard gathering apples two shots were fired at him,—they did not see by whom,—and that one ball passed through his hat and the other through his shirt. And as this evidence is not in conflict with the commonwealth's evidence, or with any inference that the jury could have reasonably drawn therefrom, it is not waived by the demurrer to evidence. We say demurrer to evidence, because, the evidence (not the facts) being certified, the case is to be considered in the appellate court as if there had been a demurrer to evidence, according to the rule of decision prescribed by section 3484 of the Code. These are the salient points in the evidence, and we are constrained to the conclusion that the case of the commonwealth is not made out. A dreadful crime, undoubtedly, has been committed, but that the prisoner committed it is not shown by this record. Every man, in the eye of the law, is innocent until he is proven guilty; and not only is the burden of proving the guilt of a person charged with crime on the commonwealth, but, to warrant a conviction, his guilt must be proven to the exclusion of every rational hypothesis consistent with his innocence. Circumstances of mere suspicion are not sufficient. In other words, the rule, as often stated, is that before the jury can convict they must be satisfied, not only that the circumstances are consistent with the prisoner's having committed the crime charged, but they must also be satisfied that the facts are such as to be inconsistent with any other rational conclusion than that he is guilty. "To doubt," it has been said, "is to acquit." Applying this elementary test to the present case, it is obvious, without the least discussion of the evidence, that the judgment must be reversed, and the case remanded for a new trial.

MARKS' ADM'R v. PETERSBURG R. Co.

(Supreme Court of Appeals of Virginia. June 11, 1891.)

RAILROAD COMPANIES — ACCIDENT AT CROSSING — CONTRIBUTORY NEGLIGENCE.

1. A person who, after standing near a railroad crossing, towards which a train has commenced to back in obedience to the signal of a brakeman in full view from where she stood, attempts to cross the track when the train is but seven feet from, and moving towards, her is guilty of contributory negligence, and cannot recover for the injuries she receives, though the railroad company is guilty of negligence in backing the train.

2. The fact that such person is blind in one eye will not excuse her, but only imposes the duty of a higher degree of care to avoid danger.

Error to judgment of the hustings court of the city of Petersburg, rendered on the 15th of November, 1889, in an action of trespass on the case, wherein W. R. McKenney, administrator of Elmira V. Marks, deceased, was plaintiff, and the Petersburg Railroad Company was defendant. The action was brought to recover damages for the alleged negligent killing of the plaintiff's intestate by the defendant company, at the intersection of its road with Market street, in the city of Petersburg, on the 27th of May, 1889. The deceased, a woman 53 years of age, was killed by being run over by a backing freight train, as she was crossing the railroad. There was a flagman at the crossing, but no lookout on the leading car, although an ordinance of the city provides that, "when a train of cars is moving back-

wards on any railroad within the corporate limits, said railroad company shall be required to keep a person on the leading car of such train to give proper warning to persons in the act of crossing the track in front of said train of cars." The evidence was conflicting as to whether the bell on the locomotive was being rung at the time. The defendant's track extends for some distance in Washington street, which intersects Market street at the place of the accident. The latter street, at that point, is "a much-traveled street, both by vehicles and pedestrians," and much shifting of the trains is done there; there being a side track also in Washington street, and a switch on either side of Market street. The railroad, like Washington street, runs east and west, and intersects Market street at right angles. The accident occurred a short while before sundown. At the trial the defendant demurred to the evidence, and the jury conditionally assessed the damages at $5,790. The court sustained the demurrer, and gave judgment for the defendant, to which judgment the plaintiff obtained a writ of error and *supersedeas* from one of the judges of this court.

W. R. McKenney, for plaintiff in error. *Alexander Hamilton* and *R. B. Davis,* for defendant in error.

LEWIS, P., (*after stating the facts as above.*) The principles of law which govern the case are well settled. A railroad company, undoubtedly, is bound to exercise care to avoid a collision where its road crosses a public highway, and the greater the danger the greater is the vigilance required. It has accordingly been held in numerous cases, independently of any statute or ordinance on the subject, that, when a train is backed over a crossing in a frequented street, a lookout must be employed; that merely ringing the bell or sounding the whistle on the engine, when the train is standing near, with its rear to the crossing, is not sufficient warning to passers-by of an intention to back the train, and that without other notice the company will be negligent. The rights and duties, however, of the company and of the public are reciprocal, and hence no greater degree of care is required of the one than of the other. Both the company and the traveler on the highway are charged with the mutual duty of keeping a careful lookout for danger, and the degree of diligence required is such as a prudent man would exercise, under the circumstances of the case, in endeavoring to fairly perform his duty. The traveler on the highway, when he approaches a crossing, must assume that there is danger, and act accordingly. The existence of the track is a warning of danger. He must therefore be vigilant. He must look and listen. He has no right to close his eyes and ears to the danger he is liable to incur; and if he does, and injury results, he must bear the consequences of his folly or carelessness. In such a case he is the author of his own misfortune. Beach, Contrib. Neg. § 65; Improvement Co. v. Stead, 95 U. S. 161; Nash v. Railroad Co., 82 Va. 55; Railroad Co. v. Burge, 84 Va.

68, 4 S. E. Rep. 21; 4 Amer. & Eng. Enc. Law, 68, and cases cited. In Railroad Co. v. Kellam's Adm'r, 83 Va. 851, 3 S. E. Rep. 703, where the subject is considered, it was held that a traveler on an intersecting highway, before crossing the railroad, must use his senses of sight and hearing; that he must look in every direction that the rails run, to make sure that the crossing is safe; and that his failure to do so will, as a general rule, be deemed culpable negligence. The only exceptions to the rule have been stated to be these, viz.: (1) Where the view of the track is obstructed, and hence where the injured party, not being able to see, is obliged to act upon his judgment at the time,—in other words, where compliance with the rule would be impracticable or unavailing; (2) where the injured person was a passenger going to or alighting from a train, and hence under an implied invitation and assurance by the company to cross the track in safety; and (3) where the direct act of some agent of the company had put the person off his guard, and induced him to cross the track without precaution. 2 Wood, Ry. Law, § 323, and cases cited. In the present case the negligence of the defendant company is conceded. There was no lookout on the leading car of the backing train, as the city ordinance in such cases requires, nor were such precautions of any kind taken as were necessary to duly warn the deceased of the approaching danger.

But the question arises, was that the cause of her death, or was she guilty of such contributory negligence as to defeat the action? For, unless the negligence of the defendant was the immediate and proximate cause of the injury, the plaintiff is not entitled to recover. Railroad Co. v. Anderson, 31 Grat. 812; Dun v. Railroad Co., 78 Va. 645. The case, viewed in the light of the rule applicable to a demurrer to evidence, is substantially as follows: A few minutes before the accident occurred the deceased passed up Washington street, going west, in the direction of Market street. When she reached the intersection of those streets, she turned to the left, (i. e., to the south,) and started to cross the street. When within four feet of the railroad crossing, she stopped on the walk-way to wait for a freight train to pass, which was moving westwardly. This train, which consisted of an engine and three box-cars, was operated by an engineer and a fireman, who were on the engine, and a brakeman, who was riding on the rear car. Just before the rear of the train reached the crossing, the brakeman jumped off the car, and ran to a switch, about 15 feet east of the crossing, to turn the switch for the train to back on the side track at that point. The train passed over the crossing, where the deceased was standing, and stopped before its rear end had gotten half-way across Market street, which is less than 60 feet wide. The switch in the mean time having been turned, the brakeman at the switch signaled the engineer to back. One of the witnesses says he turned his face in the direction of the engineer, and "hallooed to him to come back;" another says he blew his whistle for him to come back; but both

say that with his hand he also waved or beckoned him back. This was within 20 feet of the deceased. The signal was promptly obeyed, and the train moved slowly backward, but without a lookout on the leading car, as already stated. There was, however, a flagman at the crossing. The deceased meanwhile was standing on the granite walk-way, between the brakeman and the train, with an unobstructed view of both. After signaling the engineer, the brakeman turned his back to the crossing, and walked in the opposite direction, to couple the train, when it should get there, to a car standing on the side track. The deceased did not move from her position above mentioned until after the train had commenced to back, nor until the leading car had gotten within "two or three steps" from her, when she started across the track. But, just as she had gotten her left foot over the last or southern rail, she was struck by the train, knocked down, and run over. The point at which she fell was several feet east of the walk-way, where blood and particles of human flesh were afterwards found on the track. In the collision she received injuries which caused her death within an hour afterwards.

The plaintiff's contention, in answer to the defense of contributory negligence, is (1) that the deceased was not conscious of the reverse movement of the train before she was struck; and (2) that, under the circumstances, she was not bound to have seen it. But can this position be maintained? We think not.

As to the first point, two of the defendant's witnesses, who were eye-witnesses of the occurrence, testify that, when the train commenced to back, she was standing on the granite crossing, close to the track. They say, further, that when she started to cross the track she stepped to the left, "as if to walk around the train," and the place where she fell, and the blood and flesh on the track, tend to sustain this view; that is, that she saw the train approaching her, and attempted to avoid it. If this evidence be in conflict with the plaintiff's evidence, or any reasonable inferences from that evidence, it was, of course, waived by the demurrer to the evidence. But we perceive no such conflict. Neither Jennie Davis nor Lemme Starke, the two principal witnesses for the plaintiff, testify to the contrary, nor does any one else. The former, in answer to the direct question whether the deceased, in crossing the track, moved in a straight line, or swerved to the left, as if to avoid the train, said she did not know; and Starke merely says, in a general way, that she was crossing on the cross-way. He does not say positively, however, that she was "on the cross-way" when she was struck. But, waiving the defendant's evidence on this point, the result is the same. If the deceased did not see the backing train, she ought to have seen it, for had she looked, or, in other words, had she exercised ordinary care, she could not have failed to see it. It was her duty, as we have seen, to be vigilant, and the train was only a few feet from her, with nothing to obstruct her view of it, when.

she stepped in front of it. The locality, moreover, is an especially dangerous one, because it is much frequented, and many trains daily pass over it. Much shifting of cars is also done there. This was presumably known to the deceased, as she had long been a resident of the city. Yet, without taking ordinary precautions for her safety, she stepped in front of the train, and was killed. It would be strange if, under the circumstances of the case, the action could be maintained, notwithstanding the negligence of the defendant, for the defendant's negligence was no excuse for her want of care. The language of the supreme court in Railroad Co. v. Houston, 95 U. S. 697, is very pertinent to the present case. In that case it was said: "The negligence of the company's employes [in failing to give proper signals] was no excuse for negligence on the part of the deceased. She was bound to listen and to look, before attempting to cross the railroad track, in order to avoid an approaching train, and not to walk carelessly into the place of possible danger. Had she used her senses, she could not have failed both to hear and to see the train which was coming. If she omitted to use them, and walked thoughtlessly upon the track, she was guilty of culpable negligence, and so far contributed to her injuries as to deprive her of any right to complain of others. If, using them, she saw the train coming, and yet undertook to cross the track, instead of waiting for the train to pass, and was injured, the consequences of her mistake and temerity cannot be cast upon the defendant." The fact, not before mentioned, that the deceased was blind in her right eye, does not affect the case; for that, instead of relieving her from the duty of ordinary care, imposed upon her the duty of greater precaution to avoid injury. 4 Amer. & Eng. Enc. Law, 80; Beach, Contrib. Neg. § 147.

The plaintiff, however, contends that the case is not within the general rule to which we have alluded, because, he says, the deceased had the right to act upon the presumption that the train that had just passed her would not be backed without proper warning; and for this proposition he relies upon Duame v. Railroad Co., 72 Wis. 523, 40 N. W. Rep. 394, and French v. Railroad Co., 116 Mass. 537. As to these cases, it is enough to say that, in their facts and circumstances, they widely differ from the case at bar. In the first case, as the deceased was approaching the crossing in a buggy, a train passed over it and out of sight, the view at that point being obstructed. It then, without any warning whatever, immediately backed towards the crossing, struck the deceased, and killed him. After the train passed, the deceased kept straight on, driving in a trot, and neither looked nor listened. The court recognised the general rule that a person approaching a railroad crossing must look and listen, but held that, under the peculiar circumstances of that case, the deceased was evidently surprised and thrown off his guard, and that the question of contributory negligence ought, therefore, to have been left to the jury. It accordingly reversed the action of the trial court directing a verdict for the defendant. In the Massachusetts case, as the plaintiff approached the crossing in a light, open carriage, a train passed, and immediately afterwards she attempted to cross. There was no warning given that other cars were approaching, and she did not look in the direction from which the train had come, and gave as a reason that she did not suppose one train would follow another so closely. In crossing the track, she was struck and injured by a car that had been detached from the train for the purpose of making a flying switch, and it was held, as in the Wisconsin case, that the question of contributory negligence was for the jury. This case was criticised and disapproved of by the supreme court of Rhode Island in the recent and well-considered case of Ormsbee v. Railroad Corp., 14 R. I. 102, and held to be in conflict with both the earlier and later Massachusetts decisions. In the Ormsbee Case the plaintiff's intestate, a deaf mute, was struck and killed by a train of cars which was making a flying switch at a highway crossing. The engine passed the crossing towards the south, and then backed towards it on another track. As the engine was backing, the deceased, looking towards it, stepped upon the track without looking north, whence the detached cars were approaching, and as he did so he was struck by the forward car, and killed. The plaintiff contended that the passing and backing of the engine diverted the attention of the deceased, and excused his not looking both ways. But the court, overruling this view, held that the failure of the deceased to look both ways was negligence as a matter of law, and therefore precluded a recovery, whatever may have been the defendant's negligence. After examining many authorities, it was said: "This review of the cases is sufficient to show the rule to be uniform and unquestionable that a traveler, in crossing a railroad, even in the absence of ordinary signals, must look up and down the track, except where he is unable to do so, or where, as a passenger or otherwise, he has an assurance of safety from the company which excuses him. Indeed, it is quite unusual to find so little difference in so many cases, and it must be for the reason that the rule is founded, not in opinion or judgment, but in common prudence and experience, to such an extent that courts can declare it as law." The rule, as we understand it, stated a little differently and more fully, is this: If a person attempts to cross a railroad at a highway crossing, without using his senses of sight and hearing, even though the company be negligent, the law, as well as common prudence, condemns his act as careless. But this is a mere presumption, which may be repelled by evidence, showing that the case is within one or more of the exceptions to the general rule before mentioned. In the absence of such evidence, however, the contributory negligence of such person, when injured, will preclude a recovery, unless the company might, by the exercise of ordinary care on its part, have avoided the consequences of the plaintiff's negligence. This qualification of the doctrine of contributory negligence is that laid down in the leading case of Tuff v. Warman, 2 C. B. (N. S.) 740, and so often recognized by this court. Railroad Co. v. Anderson, 31 Grat. 812; Dun v. Railroad Co., 78 Va. 645; Railroad Co. v. Moose, 83 Va. 827, 3 S. E. Rep. 796; Railroad Co. v. White, 84 Va. 498, 5 S. E. Rep. 573; Railroad Co. v. Pickleseimer, 85 Va. 798, 10 S. E. Rep. 44. Applying this test to the present case, we are of the opinion that the plaintiff is not entitled to recover; for it is manifest that ordinary care on the part of the defendant could not have discovered the negligence of the deceased in time to avoid the accident. When the train began to back, she was in a place of safety, apparently waiting for the train to pass, and remained in that position until the train was within about seven feet from where she stood. It was then too late to have stopped the train in time to avoid the effects of her own careless, not to say reckless, act, even had there been a lookout on the leading car, and everything done which ought to have been done in the exercise of ordinary care. Our conclusion, therefore, is that the judgment of the hustings court is right, and that the same must be affirmed.

RICHARDSON and HINTON, JJ., concur in the opinion. LACY and FAUNTLEROY, concur in the result.

MUSICK v. MUSICK.

(*Supreme Court of Appeals of Virginia.* June 11, 1891.)

DIVORCE—ADULTERY—CIRCUMSTANTIAL EVIDENCE.

In a suit for divorce *a vinculo*, on the ground of adultery, where the evidence shows that defendant had seduced plaintiff before he married her, and that he deserted her immediately after the marriage, and consorted with lewd women, with whom he was frequently found in compromising situations, a decree for plaintiff is warranted, though both the husband and the alleged *particeps criminis* deny the adultery.

J. C. Gent, for appellant. Routh & Stuart, for appellee.

LACY, J. This is an appeal from a decree of the circuit court of Russell county, rendered on the 14th day of March, 1888. The bill was filed in this case by the appellee, Bessie Musick, against her husband, the appellant, Elexions Musick, seeking an absolute divorce a vinculo matrimonii, an allowance of alimony, and also the allowance of an attorney's fee against the defendant. The grounds alleged in the bill were adultery and desertion. The facts alleged therein are, briefly, that she was a female infant of tender years, living at her father's house, of pure and chaste character, life, and repute, when the defendant, a young man of good standing, resident in the neighborhood, sought and obtained an engagement of marriage with her, and, suiting his movements to his opportunities, under promise of marriage seduced and ruined her; that he then, dreading the consequences, and fearing punishment for his crime, sought and obtained from her father and herself consent to an immediate marriage, as the best and

only means of such atonement as was possible under the circumstances; that the marriage having been solemnized, and the prosecution for seduction thus barred, he lived with her only a few days as her husband, and then, without the slightest cause, abandoned her, and took up with, and kept openly, lewdly, and lasciviously, the company of fallen women, and contributed nothing in attention or care, nor otherwise, to the support of his said wife and their infant child, issue of the marriage. The defendant answered admitting the marriage, the seduction, and the desertion, but says the plaintiff offered opportunities which led him astray. He denies, however, the adultery charged in the bill, subsequent to his marriage; admitting the association with the fallen woman in question, claiming to be ignorant of her character as such. Depositions were taken by the plaintiff, proving the lewd character of the women in question, two in number, and the association with them in public and private by the defendant. The defendant took and filed the depositions of the two fallen women in question, each of whom denied all knowledge of any adultery committed by the defendant with any person subsequent to his marriage. The circuit court by its decree of March 14, 1888, being of the opinion that the plaintiff, Bessie Musick, had shown herself entitled to a divorce from the defendant, Elexions Musick, her husband, a vinculo matrimonii, and that she was entitled to alimony, and to the care and custody of her infant child, issue of the marriage, decreed the said divorce, and restrained the defendant from marrying again without the further order of the court; and referred it to a commissioner to report upon the proper alimony to be allowed the plaintiff for the support of herself and her infant child. From this decree the defendant appealed to this court. The errors assigned here are as follows, to-wit: First. It was error in the court below to dissolve the bonds of matrimony in this case upon the charge of adultery upon circumstantial evidence, the adultery having been emphatically and clearly denied in the answer. Secondly, it was error in the court, under the circumstances, to prohibit the defendant husband from marrying again, as being against public policy, and contrary to the spirit of the constitution of Virginia, and detrimental to society. The evidence as to the adultery is that he paid open and marked attention to Diely, a young unmarried woman whose reputation in the neighborhood is that of an unchaste and lewd woman; one witness proving that he surprised them on horseback in a compromising attitude, and also on a log; other witnesses proved the character of the woman, and the intimate character of her association with the defendant; but no one proves the act of unlawful sexual intercourse between these two. As to another woman shown to be of evil life, the defendant is shown by the evidence to have sought her, and procured liquor, and to have brought her out on the road, and gone off in the woods or bushes with her alone, and to have remained alone with her a considerable time, in the night-time. There is a denial of the adultery charged, as has been stated, by the alleged *particeps criminis*.

The circuit court held that the crime of adultery had been proved, and the first question we must determine is whether this action was erroneous or otherwise. In the recent work of Mr. William Hardcastle Browne, of the Philadelphia bar, on Divorce and Alimony, it is said, (page 54:) "If a married man, without justifiable cause appearing, visits a house of ill fame, he must have gone there for an improper purpose, and it is universally held as a proof of adultery. So, also, when he has been shut up alone with an unchaste woman." Citing Evans v. Evans, 41 Cal. 103; Van Epps v. Van Epps, 6 Barb. 320; Langstaff v. Langstaff, Wright, (Ohio,) 148. The same learned author also remarks that criminal desires may be inferred from consorting with prostitutes, entertaining persons known to be dissolute, or intimacy of any kind with such after knowledge of their immoral reputation. Id. p. 55. Mr. Greenleaf says, (Ev. vol. 2 § 44:) "A married man going into a known brothel raises a suspicion of adultery, to be rebutted only by the very best evidence. His going there, and remaining there alone for some time in a room with a common prostitute, is sufficient proof of the crime." Mr. Bishop, in his work on Marriage and Divorce, says, (volume 2, § 613:) "Adultery is peculiarly a crime of darkness and secrecy; parties are rarely surprised in it; and so it not only may, but ordinarily must, be established by circumstantial evidence. The testimony must convince the judicial mind affirmatively that actual adultery was committed, since nothing short of the carnal act can lay a foundation for a divorce. That is, generally speaking, necessary to prove that the parties were in some place together where the adultery might probably be committed." Citing Lord STOWELL as saying: "Courts of justice must not be duped. They will judge of facts, as other men of discernment, exercising a sound and sober judgment, on circumstances that are duly proved, judge of them. The only general rule that can be laid down upon the subject is that the circumstances must be such as would lead the guarded discretion of a reasonable and just man to the conclusion; for it is not to lead a harsh and intemperate judgment, moving upon appearances that are equally capable of two interpretations; neither is it to be a matter of artificial reasoning, judging upon such things differently from what would strike the careful and cautious consideration of a discreet man. The facts are not of a technical nature; they are facts determinable upon common grounds of reason; and courts of justice would wander very much from their proper office of giving protection to the rights of mankind, if they let themselves loose to subtleties, and remote and artificial reasonings upon such subjects. Upon such subjects the rational and legal interpretation must be the same."

Upon the consideration of precedents, carefully considering the evidence in this case, can we say that the crime of adultery has been proved? Let us glance at the evidence. It is proved that the defendant husband had, under promise of marriage, seduced the plaintiff wife, a woman of chaste character; that, to prevent exposure and prosecution, he hurried her into a hasty marriage, under many protestations; that, this accomplished, he in a day or two deserted his wife, a girl of tender years, and it was given out that he had left the country. It is further proved that he has been since notoriously attentive, in public and in private, first with one unchaste female, being surprised, when alone with her, in kisses and embraces. That this woman is unchaste, and that these things are true, he, the defendant, has not denied. He denies nothing but the adulterous cohabitation, and claims that the act cannot be established by circumstantial evidence. It is further proved that he subsequently went to a house of ill fame, and brought hence another unchaste woman, and, getting whisky, went off with her along the highway, and into the forest with her, and remained all night thus associated, lugging along with them an infant bastard child, which was called by his name by the mother in his presence. For a married man thus to act, after he has thrown off all the safeguard of association with and regard for his wife and his legitimate child, and has deserted her finally and without reserve, leaves no rational doubt as to what his acts were. The guilty desire on his part, and of the *particeps criminis*, and the concurrence of ample opportunity thus sought and obtained, prove the crime. Mr. Browne cites the familiar case of Latham v. Latham, 30 Grat. 307, when the visit to the brothel was successfully explained, the visit being then established to be accidental and innocent. But what explanation have we here on the part of her husband? None whatever. He takes the depositions of Diely and Sal, and they testify that they have no knowledge of any adultery committed by him. What weight can properly be given to their denials, under the uncontradicted circumstances set forth in the evidence in this cause? I think there is no doubt as to the commission of the act of adultery.

The only remaining question to be considered is as to the action of the circuit court in prohibiting the defendant and guilty husband from marrying again. Mr. Browne, in his work mentioned above, says as to this: "It is difficult to understand how a marriage can be dissolved as to one of the parties without being equally dissolved as to the other, and it is certain that no court can impose a restriction on the marriage of a divorced party without statutory grant of power. A prohibition to the guilty party to marry a second time, after the entry of a decree of divorce *a vinculo*, may be contained in a statute, or may be entered by a court under the authority of a statute. In either case the effect would be the same. Statutes imposing such restrictions are constitutional." Page 41; citing Barber v. Barber, 16 Cal. 378; Elliott v. Elliott, 38 Md. 357; Sparhawk v. Sparhawk, 114

Mass. 355. In this state the question is regulated by the statute. Section 2265 of the Code provides that, "in granting a divorce for adultery, the court may decree that the guilty party shall not marry again; in which case the bond of matrimony shall be deemed not to be dissolved as to any future marriage of such party, or in any prosecution on account thereof; but, for good cause shown, so much of the decree as prohibits the guilty party from marrying again may be revoked and annulled, at any time after such decree, by the same court by which it was pronounced." In the decree complained of and appealed from here, as we have already seen, the provision on this subject is: "But the defendant is restrained from marrying again till the further order of the court." The authority of the statute has been followed; the discretion of the court has been exercised, in the mean time, and not finally. The decree settling the principles of the cause, and therefore appealable, is interlocutory only, and not final; an account having been ordered as to the proper amount of alimony which should be granted to this plaintiff wife and her infant child. The defendant is not barred by a final decree from marrying again, which decree might be revoked by the same court by which it was rendered. But, an account having been ordered, the court restrains the defendant from marrying again until the further order of the court. When the unsettled questions in the cause have been determined, and the final decree rendered, the defendant may or may not be decreed not to marry again. I am clearly of the opinion that the circuit court did not err in restraining the defendant from marrying again until the further order of the court; and, if the decree in question could be construed to be a disposition of that question, I think the action of the court is authorized by the law, and that this subject is essentially one to be regulated by law, and that, if there can be any case in which this discretion vested by law in the courts can be wisely exercised in restraint of marriage, this is such a case. The decree against remarrying may be revoked when it appears proper to the court to do so; but if the evidence in this case is to be believed,—and the defendant does not deny it,—then the court could not but consider this defendant as he now appears an unsuitable person to enter into the marriage relation. We perceive no error in the decree appealed from and the same will be affirmed, without in any degree intending to interfere with the future exercise by the court of its discretion upon this question of the refusal of the court to permit the defendant, the guilty party, to remarry.

THOMPSON v. COMMONWEALTH.

(Supreme Court of Appeals of Virginia. June 18, 1891.)

ROBBERY—COMPETENCY OF JURORS—EVIDENCE—WITNESSES—INSTRUCTIONS.

1. On a trial for robbing a woman at 10:30 o'clock at night, as she was on her way from a depot carrying her valise, the testimony of a policeman, offered by the defense, that he had seen a colored man in the yard of the railroad at 3 o'clock on the following morning, was irrelevant, and properly excluded.

2. Where the jury were instructed to find for defendant, unless the state proved everything essential to the establishment of the charge to the exclusion of a reasonable doubt, it was not error to charge, immediately afterwards, that "the burden rests upon the commonwealth to make out its case, * * * to the exclusion of a reasonable doubt, but, where the accused * * * attempts to prove an *alibi*, * * * the burden of proving the *alibi* rests upon him."

3. Having subpœnaed a witness who did not appear, defendant, on the court's suggestion, obtained a rule against him, but the officer returned that the witness was sick. Defendant's motion to adjourn was overruled, on the ground, as stated by the judge, that when the case was called in the morning no motion for continuance was made because of the absence of such witness. Defendant made no objection to this statement, nor did he show that the evidence of such witness would not be merely cumulative. *Held,* the court was justified in proceeding with the trial.

4. The persons filling the offices of treasurer and councilman of a city are not disqualified to serve in the Hustings court thereof, in a criminal case.

5. Code Va. 1887, § 3991, providing that, "in a prosecution for a misdemeanor, the name of the prosecutor, if there be one, * * * shall be written at the foot of the presentment, indictment, or information," does not apply to an indictment for a felony found by the grand jury.

6. It is in the discretion of the court to limit the argument to two hours upon each side.

Error to Hustings court of Bristol; RHEA, Judge.

One Thompson was convicted of robbery. Code Va. 1887, § 3991, provides that, "in a prosecution for a misdemeanor, the name of the prosecutor, if there be one, * * * shall be written at the foot of the presentment, indictment, or information."

Paul, Peters, Wood & Sutherland, for plaintiff in error. The Attorney General, for the Commonwealth.

FAUNTLEROY, J. The plaintiff in error was indicted, tried, convicted, and sentenced in the hustings court of the city of Bristol for the crime of felonious assault and robbery; and the judgment of the said court was in accordance with the verdict of the jury, which fixed the term of his confinement in the penitentiary for eight years. The record of the proceedings upon the trial presents several bills of exception taken by the accused, Thompson. The first bill of exceptions objects to the refusal of the court to exclude from the *venire* and from the jury J. L. C. Smith and George W Wolfe, who were duly summoned as venire-men, upon the ground that the said Smith was treasurer of the city of Bristol, and the said Wolfe was a member of the council of the city of Bristol. There is nothing in this objection, and the trial court did not err in overruling the motion to exclude them. They were qualified jurors, and the record shows that they were selected according to law.

The second bill of exceptions objects to the ruling of the trial court as to the relevancy of the evidence of H. S. Price. Thompson, the accused, was charged with the assault and robbery of one Mary Abrahams, on the night of her arrival at the depot of the Norfolk & Western Railroad passenger train, in the city of Bristol, at 10:30 o'clock that night, at a place about one-half a mile from the depot, as she was on her way, carrying her valise, to her brother's house, upon a dark and rainy night; and the commonwealth's attorney objected to the introduction of the fact that the policeman Price had seen a colored man in the yard of the Norfolk & Western Railroad at 8 o'clock in the morning succeeding the night of the alleged robbery; which objection the court sustained, and excluded the statement. It could have, so far as the exception discloses, no bearing or relevancy upon the issue to be tried by the jury, and it was properly excluded.

The bill of exceptions No. 8 states the objection of the accused to the giving of the following instruction by the court at the request of the attorney for the commonwealth: "The burden rests upon the commonwealth to make out its case against the accused to the exclusion of a reasonable doubt, but, where the accused relies upon or attempts to prove an *alibi* in his defense, the burden of proving the *alibi* rests upon him; but upon other questions in the case the burden still rests upon the commonwealth." The court gave the foregoing instruction after, and in sequence to, the instruction which it had given at the request of the accused, as follows: "The court instructs the jury that the commonwealth must prove everything essential to the establishment of the charge in the indictment, to the exclusion of a reasonable doubt; and, if it fails to do so, then they must find for the defendant." There was no error in giving the instruction objected to.

The fourth bill of exceptions states that "when the evidence was all in, the court stated to the counsel that the court deemed two hours upon each side would be reasonable and sufficient for the argument of the case, and so limited the argument to two hours upon each side; to which action of the court the defendant excepted." This court, in the case of Jones v. Com., reported in 12 S. E. Rep. 226, decided that it is in the discretionary competency of the trial court to restrict the argument of counsel to reasonable limits; and though it was held in that case that the peremptory restriction of counsel to only 20 minutes, where there were numerous and conflicting witnesses and circumstances, was an arbitrary abuse of the power, we are at a loss to conceive how two whole hours could be reasonably consumed in the argument of this case. There was no abuse of the court's discretion in this case.

The fifth bill of exceptions says that, upon the calling of the case for trial on the 6th day of October, 1890, the defendant moved the court to continue the case because of the absence of three of his witnesses, viz., Maria Martin, Lizzie Nowlin, and Mary Isabell, but the said three witnesses did appear and testified in the case in behalf of the defendant. No motion was made for the continuance of the cause because of the absence of any other witness, or upon any other ground. When the commonwealth had about closed the tes-

timony upon its part, the attorney for the commonwealth moved the court for a rule against one T. P. Owen to appear and testify in behalf of the commonwealth, which motion the court overruled, because no subpœna had been issued by the commonwealth for said witness, but stated that the defense would be entitled to a rule, if they desired it, as said witness had previously been summoned for the defense; and thereupon the defendant moved the court for a rule against the said witness, which was granted, and the officer returned the said rule, "Executed," but stated, in open court, that he found the said witness sick in bed. Whereupon the defendant moved the court to adjourn said case until the following day, so that, if said witness was able, his attendance might be secured, as he was a material witness for the defense; which motion was objected to by the attorney for the commonwealth, and said objection sustained by the court, for the reason, as stated at the time by the court, that the defendant, when the case was called for trial in the morning, had made no motion for a continuance of the case because of the absence of said witness Owen; to which statement of the court there was no objection by the defendant or his counsel, and the court directed the trial to proceed, etc. We think that the trial having progressed thus far, and the defendant not stating anything by which the court could be informed that the witness Owen could or was expected to give any evidence which would be not merely cumulative upon the testimony already given for the accused by his three witnesses, Maria, Martin, Lizzie Nowlin, and Mary Isabell, and the silence of the defendant and his counsel when the court made the statement of its reason for proceeding with the trial, justified the proceeding, and was proper.

The indictment was demurred to on the ground that it is vague, uncertain, and indefinite, and that no witness' name was appended to it. The indictment is clear, pointed, and pithy, and distinctly charges a felonious assault and robbery,—a felony. It is the act of a grand jury, and not that of a personal prosecutor; and section 3991, Code 1887, applies only to misdemeanors. See the case of Com. v. Dever, 10 Leigh, 685. The court did not err in overruling the motion for a new trial, on the ground that the verdict is contrary to the evidence, or of surprise to the defendant. The evidence is full, clear, explicit, and positive to prove the guilt of the accused, and the judgment of the court is to affirm the judgment of the trial court. Affirmed.

HUNTER v. HUME.

(*Supreme Court of Appeals of Virginia.* June 18, 1891.)

DEEDS—DESCRIPTION—BOUNDARIES.

1. The W. turnpike ran in a northerly and southerly direction through plaintiff's plantation. West of this turnpike, also running north and south, was the A. canal. A road, known as the "Old Military Road," running nearly easterly and westerly, intersected the canal. A trust-deed executed by plaintiff on part of his planta-

tion described the mortgaged land as being west of the W. turnpike, and then specifically bounded it, but by mistake the A. canal was given as the southern boundary instead of the eastern, and the old military road as the eastern, instead of the southern. *Held* that, as the parties could not reasonably have intended to locate the canal on the south when it was actually on the east, the true eastern boundary of the mortgaged land should be regarded as the canal, and that the land lying between it and the W. turnpike did not pass by the deed of trust.

2. The fact that the quantity of land stated in the deed falls short in actual measurement by taking the A. canal as the eastern boundary, instead of the W. turnpike, is immaterial, since words indicating quantity must yield to descriptions by boundary.

J. K. M. *Norton*, for appellant. *James R. Caton* and *E. S. Brent*, for appellee.

LACY, J. This is a writ of error to a judgment of the circuit court of Alexandria county, rendered at the May term, 1890. The action is ejectment, brought by the plaintiff in error, Hunter, to recover a parcel of land lying between the parallel lines of the Alexandria canal on the west, and the Alexandria and Washington turnpike on the east. By trust-deed of October 4, 1871, the plaintiff in error, Hunter, conveyed a part of his Abingdon plantation to a trustee, one Wattles, to secure a debt due to W. D. Mitchell. Wattles sold under this deed on the 1st day of June, 1882, and conveyed by the deed executed by him the land in the identical terms used to describe it in the deed from Hunter to him of October 4, 1871, and by successive alienations this land has passed to the defendant in error, Hume. The said descriptive terms used in the first deed mentioned above, and in the second deed, June 1, 1872, having been departed from so as to conform the descriptions in the latter deeds to the contention of the defendant in error, Hume, the question is whether the land between the western boundary of the Alexandria canal and the Alexandria and Washington turnpike passed by the deed of Hunter to Wattles of October, 1871, and so, through successive alienations, to the defendant in error. The following plat exhibited with the record shows the true situation of the land;

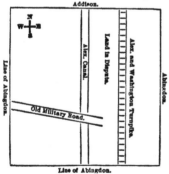

The description of this land, contained in the deed of October 4, 1871, is as follows:

"A certain tract of land situate, lying, and being in Alexandria county, Virginia, containing 280 acres, more or less, on the west side of the Washington and Alexandria turnpike, and bounded as follows: (1) On the north and west by the lands of Addison; (2) on the south by the Alexandria canal; (3) and on the east by the old military road." By consulting the plat above it will be perceived that by the contention of both parties to this controversy the land in question—the part of Abingdon conveyed to Wattles—is situated west of the Alexandria and Washington turnpike, and is the western part of the Abingdon plantation; and it also appears that the land is included within the designated boundaries set forth in the deed, as is contended for by the appellant, Hunter. But the Alexandria canal is on the east, and not on the south, and the old military road is on the south, and not on the east, as stated in the deed, except that the old military road running south of the Abingdon plantation cuts off a part of the land conveyed to Wattles; but there is no denial that this triangular piece cut off by the line of the old military road passed under the deed of October 4, 1871. In October, 1871, the Alexandria canal was full of water, and in use, but is now abandoned. Hunter had the land between the canal and the turnpike held by a different tenant in October, 1871, and has held it and paid taxes up to this time upon it, and claims that his purpose was to convey the land included between the particular boundaries set forth in the deed, which at that time was cut off from the residue of his plantation by the waters of the canal; and that he conveyed the land bounded by this Alexandria canal, the old military road, and the Addison lands, it being that part of the Abingdon tract lying west of the Alexandria canal. A jury being waived, and the whole matter of law and fact being submitted to the court, the court decided that the strip of land between the Alexandria and Washington turnpike passed by the deed of October 4, 1871, to the grantee, Wattles, and has passed by successive alienations to the defendant in error, Hume, the defendant below, and gave judgment accordingly; whereupon the plaintiff, Hunter, applied for and obtained a writ of error to this court.

The general description in the deed in question is that the land conveyed is situated in Alexandria county, and contains 280 acres, more or less, on the west side of the Washington and Alexandria turnpike. The turnpike is not stated there nor elsewhere in the deed to be a boundary; but this inference is excluded by setting forth as one of the boundaries the Alexandria canal, which runs between the body of the land granted and the turnpike throughout its whole extent. The only difficulty in the question of boundary grows out of the misplacing of the points of the compass, stating south for east and east for south. This error in description is not unusual, and has often occurred, and has often been the subject of litigation, and has been as often reformed and corrected by the courts. And when this error is corrected according to the plain intention of the parties, the Alexandria canal being put where it really is, on the east, and not on the south, where it really is not, and the old military road being stated on the south, where it really is, and not on the east, where it is not, everything is plain. The parties could not reasonably be held to have intended to locate the canal on the south, because it was actually on the east; and the same may be said of the old military road. In other words, substitute "east" and "south," one for the other, so that the true description may appear, and we have a tract of land bounded by the lands of Addison on the north and west, and on the east by the Alexandria canal, and on the south by the old military road, part of Abingdon, and west of the turnpike, but not bounded by the turnpike. There is nothing in the deed to indicate the turnpike as one of the boundaries, but in fact other and different boundaries are given, one of which excludes the turnpike as a boundary. It is well settled that when a general description of the land intended to be conveyed is given in a deed, and also the particular boundaries, the latter are to govern; and we do not understand that this is denied by either side to this dispute. Numerous authorities are cited thereto by the learned counsel of the appellee. Tyl. Bound. p. 180; Thorndike v. Richards, 13 Me. 430; Woodman v. Lane, 7 N. H. 241; Makepeace v. Bancroft, 12 Mass. 469; 1 Greenl. Ev. § 301. The last-named author, speaking upon this subject, said: "There is another class of cases, so nearly allied to these (*ambiquitas patens*) as to require mention in this place, namely, those in which, upon applying the instrument to its subject-matter, it appears that in relation to the subject, whether person or thing, the description in it is true in part, but not true in every particular. The rule in such cases is derived from the maxim: *Falsa demonstratio non nocet, cum de corpore constat.* Here so much of the description as is false is rejected; and the instrument will take effect if a sufficient description remains to ascertain its application. It is essential that enough remains to show plainly the intent. 'The rule,' said Mr. Justice PARKER, 'is clearly settled, that when there is a sufficient description set forth of premises by giving the particular name of a close, or otherwise, we may reject a false demonstration; but that, if the premises be described in general terms, and a particular description be added, the latter controls the former.' It is not, however, because one part of the description is placed first and the other last in the sentence; but because, taking the whole together, that intention is manifest. For, indeed, it is vain to imagine one part before another; for, though words can neither be spoken nor written at once, yet the mind of the author comprehends them at once, which gives *vitam et modum* to the sentence." And if the language of the instrument is susceptible of more than one construction the intent of the parties to be collected from the whole instrument must govern; and, in order to ascertain that intent, the court may take into consideration the extrinsic circumstances authorizing the transaction, the situation of the parties, and the subject-matter of the instrument. This is the established rule of the common law. Tyl. Bound. p. 131. The quantity of land stated in the deed appears to have fallen short in actual measurement, but that cannot alter the question of boundary as set forth in the deed. Words indicating quantity in the descriptive part of the deed, when conflicting with words of a more accurate description, yield. Quantity is regarded as the least certain mode of describing land, and hence must yield to description by boundaries and distances. Id. 131. Extrinsic evidence, it is said, is always admissible to explain the calls of a deed for the purpose of their application to the subject-matter, and thus to give effect to the deed. And when the true location of the land in dispute has been ascertained, parol evidence is admissible to show the proper location of all the descriptive locations and calls of the deed, to the end of determining whether or not the land in dispute passed by it, and thus give effect to the true intent of the parties. Reamer v. Nesmith, 34 Cal. 674; Broom, Leg. Max. 269. These principles are well settled by the decision of this court. In the case of Herbert v. Wise, 3 Call, 209, it was shown that such mistakes as leaving out lines, putting north for south, and east for west, were to be corrected by parol evidence of the true intent of the parties. See, also, Shaw v. Clements, 1 Call, 873; Preston's Heirs v. Bowman, 6 Wheat. 582; Newsom v. Pryor, 7 Wheat. 10; Elliott v. Horton, 28 Grat. 766; Baker v. Seekright, 1 Hen. & M. 177; Dogan v. Seekright, 4 Hen. & M. 125; Pasley v. English, 5 Grat. 141. Mr. Minor says the two rules of most general application in construing writings are: (1) That they shall, if possible, be so interpreted *ut res majis valeat quam pereat,* so that they shall have some effect, rather than none; and (2) that such meaning shall be given to them as may carry out and make effectual the intention of the parties. 2 Minor, Inst. 948; Herrick v. Hopkins, 28 Me. 217; Peaslee v. Gee, 19 N. H. 278; Inge v. Garrett, 38 Ind. 96; Yoder v. Swope, 3 Bibb, 204; Gano v. Aldridge, 27 Ind. 294; Doe v. Porter, 3 Ark. 18; Jones v. Smith, 73 N. Y. 205; Tatum v. Smith, 2 Hawks, 226; Bell v. Hickman, 6 Humph. 398; Koenigheim v. Miles, 67 Tex, 113, 2 S. W. Rep. 81; Schoenewald v. Rosenstein, 5 N. Y. Supp. 766. The plaintiff in error, Hunter, conveyed the land west of the canal, and the grantee took nothing more by the deed of October 4, 1871, and the plaintiff was entitled to a judgment in his favor for the premises described in the declaration, and the circuit court of Alexandria county erred in rendering judgment in favor of the defendant, and the same will be reversed and annulled, and such judgment rendered here as the said circuit ought to have rendered.

ORDER.

This case, which is pending in this court at its place of session at Richmond having been heard, but not determined, at said place of session, this day came here the parties, by their counsel, and the court, having maturely considered the transcript of the record of the judgment and the arguments of counsel, is of opinion, for reasons stated in writing and filed with the record, that the circuit court of Alexandria county erred in its judgment rendered herein on the 30th day of May, 1890; that the plaintiff is not entitled to recover of the defendant the land in the declaration described and set out; and that the said judgment is wholly erroneous. It is therefore considered by the court that the said judgment be reversed and annulled, and that the plaintiff in error, Alexander Hunter, do recover of the defendant in error, Frank Hume, his costs by him expended in the prosecution of his writ of error aforesaid here. And this court, proceeding to render such judgment as the said circuit court ought to have rendered, it is considered by the court that the plaintiff, Alexander Hunter, recover of the defendant, Frank Hume, the land and the premises in the declaration described and set forth, and that the plaintiff in error do also recover of the defendant in error his costs by him expended in the prosecution of his action in the said circuit court. And it is further ordered that this order be entered by the clerk of this court on the order-book here, and forthwith certified to the clerk of this court at its place of session at Richmond, and entered by him on the order-book there, and certified to the clerk of the circuit court of Alexandria county.

MARSHALL'S ADM'R v. CHEATHAM.

(Supreme Court of Appeals of Virginia. June 18, 1891.)

COMMISSIONER TO ASCERTAIN DEBTS OF DECEDENT—SCALING JUDGMENT AS CONFEDERATE TRANSACTION.

1. A commissioner appointed to ascertain the debts of a decedent, and their order of priority, has no authority to go behind a judgment rendered against the decedent in his life-time; and since Acts Va. 1865-66, c. 171, §§ 1, 2, provide for setting up the fact of a Confederate transaction only as a defense to a suit while pending, so as to reduce the judgment to be rendered, the action of the commissioner in scaling the judgment as a Confederate transaction will not affect the judgment creditor, who was no party to and had no notice of the proceedings.

2. Code Va. 1873, c. 177, which provides for corrections of mistakes, errors in calculation, and misrecitals in judgments, within five years after their rendition, does not apply to the scaling of a judgment as a Confederate transaction, since this fact might have been interposed as a defense to the suit; and hence the action of the commissioner in scaling such a judgment seven years after its rendition cannot be justified under this chapter.

RICHARDSON and HINTON, JJ., dissenting.

Wm. H. Mann, for appellant. *R. Turnbull* and *J. B. Bell,* for appellees.

FAUNTLEROY, J. The petition of J. J. Parrish, administrator upon the estate of W. J. Marshall, deceased, complains of a decree of the circuit court of Lunenburg county, pronounced on the 24th day of May, 1889, in the chancery cause in the said court pending, under the short style of "Cheatham, for, etc., against Love's

Administrator, etc." It is shown by the record that on the 11th day of November, 1863, A. H. Love and H. H. Love executed and delivered to John J. Parrish, administrator of W. J. Marshall, deceased, their bond under seal, in words and figures following, viz.: "Lunenburg, Nov. 11th, 1863. $810.00. Six months after date we promise to pay to John J. Parrish, administrator of Wm. J. Marshall, deceased, the sum of eight hundred and ten dollars, current money of Virginia, for value received. Given under our hands and seals this date above. A. H. LOVE. [Seal.] H. H. LOVE. [Seal.]" Suit was instituted on this said bond, and at the April term, 1867, of the circuit court of Lunenburg there was judgment by default thereon in favor of the said Parrish, administrator of W. J. Marshall, deceased, for the full amount of the said bond, viz., $810, with interest from May 11, 1864, and $7.42 costs, against the said A. H. Love and H. H. Love, which said judgment was duly docketed in the said clerk's office in April, 1864. In 1871, the said H. H. Love having died, Thomas Cheatham instituted a creditor's suit for himself and others against the executors of the said H. H. Love, deceased, and his widow and children, to ascertain the debts against the estate of the said H. H. Love, deceased, and their order of priority, the assets, real and personal, and to settle the estate accounts of his executors and to enforce payment of his debts. Pending this suit, the powers of the executors of H. H. Love, deceased, were revoked, and the estate was committed to J. W. Ellis, as sheriff administrator *de bonis non;* and on the 13th of May, 1872, there was a decree for an account and a reference to a master commissioner in the cause. Under the said decree H. E. Boswell, commissioner, gave notice by personal service to the parties named in the proceedings, (plaintiffs and defendants;) and he states in his report that he published notice in the Southside Sentinel, a newspaper printed in Burkeville, in Nottoway county. But there is no proof of this, nor is there order for notice by publication. Parrish, administrator of W. J. Marshall, was not a party to the suit. The commissioner, Boswell, returned his report November 15, 1872, in which he reported this judgment from the record as a debt of the first class, as for $810, with interest and costs as aforesaid; but he, of his own motion, scaled it, at 22 for 1, as a Confederate transaction, thus reducing the debt ascertained by the judgment from $810 to $36.84, with interest and costs. On the 17th of November, 1875, the court rendered a decree confirming the said report of Commissioner Boswell, and approving the scaling of the said debt as ascertained by the said judgment, and for payment of the amount, as scaled. Parrish, administrator of W. J. Marshall, deceased, who was not a party to the suit, filed his petition, in which he deposes that he was utterly ignorant of the said suit, and of all the proceedings therein, until 1885, and prays to have the said confirmation of the said report of Commissioner Boswell and the scaling of the said judgment set aside; and by leave he amended his petition, asking to be allowed to prove his judgment. J. W. Ellis, sheriff administrator *de bonis non* of H. H. Love, deceased, answered both the original and amended petitions. The court, by its decree, refused the prayers of Parrish in both petitions, and refused to set aside the confirmation of the report of Boswell, commissioner, and decreed that the scaling of Parrish's judgment was proper, and should stand. From this decree Parrish has appealed.

The only question for this court to pass upon, presented by the record, is, was the scaling of appellant's judgment by the commissioner a valid act, which he was authorized to do, or was it simply void? We are of the opinion that it was unauthorized, invalid, and void. A judgment in an action of debt by a competent court is a judicial ascertainment of the debt demanded, or of so much thereof as is set out in the judgment. It is a final adjudication, which no court or officer can go behind or set aside or change, except by procedure prescribed by rules of law or equity; and by those only who are by said rules and methods invested with jurisdiction so to do. A commissioner taking accounts should take evidence and inquire as to unascertained open accounts and other debts; but he has no authority or power to make any change in a judgment, nor to make any alteration or abatement in it, for reasons or causes arising at or prior to its rendition. His duty is to take the judgment as recorded, and to report it. If there be legal evidence of payments on it since its rendition he cannot, even then, reduce the said recorded judgment by the said subsequent payments without notice to the owner of the said judgment. There is but one statutory provision by which any debt can be scaled as a Confederate transaction, and that is found in the first and second sections of chapter 71, p. 185, Acts 1865–66, enacted March 3, 1866, which act provides only for setting up the fact of Confederate transaction by defense to a suit while pending, and before judgment, so as to reduce the judgment to be rendered. If no such defense be made, and judgment be rendered for full amount of the face of the obligation, the defense of "Confederate transaction" cannot be made afterwards. It is true that the third section of the said act of March 3, 1866, attempts to give a remedy, by the court, on motion, after 10 days' notice. If this were law, it would not give the power to a commissioner, nor validate the act of Commissioner Boswell. The remedy is extraordinary and statutory, and the statute must be strictly followed. But even this remedy is not law. The third section of the act of March 3, 1866, was amended and re-enacted by the act of March 25, 1873. Chapter 219, p. 197, acts 1872–73. The amendment makes no change in the language of the amended section, but adopts it word for word, with an addition which in no degree changes its character. In the case of Ratcliffe v. Anderson, 31 Grat. 105, in an elaborate opinion delivered by Judge CHRISTIAN, decided that this amended statute is unconstitutional, upon grounds including the original section, and holding it as objectionable, unconstitutional, and void as that of March 25, 1873. And the case of Marpole v. Cather, 78 Va. 239, approves this decision in the opinion delivered by the judge. These cases settle the law of this case, which comes wholly within their terms and ruling. The appellant's judgment, duly obtained and recorded in 1867, could not be scaled by the unauthorized, *ex mero motu*, act of the commissioner in 1872, and that, too, without notice to the owner of the judgment, and in a report in a cause in which he was not a party. He could not go behind the judgment in favor of Parrish, nor abate it, nor inquire into the kind or character of the transaction. The Code of 1873, c. 177, provides for corrections of mistakes, errors in calculations, and misrecitals, and that only within five years after the date of the judgment; and it cannot apply to the scaling of a judgment upon a ground which would have been an admissible defense under the special law for Confederate transactions if set up before the judgment, but which was not so set up or pleaded. It is plain from the record that Parrish had no notice or knowledge of the suit of Cheatham, nor of the proceedings in it. He accounts for his delay. It is not objected to by any one, or in any form, that the judgment is reported as a debt of the first class. It was so reported in 1872, and this would preclude the issue of any execution after that, and repels any operation of the statute of limitations. See Omohundro v. Crump, 18 Grat. 705, and Hansbrough v. Uts, 75 Va. 962. The circuit court erred in confirming the act of Commissioner Boswell scaling the judgment, which was not a claim to be proved, but the record of which proved itself. The question of scaling could have been raised only on the trial of the action of debt on the bond. It cannot be raised after the adjudication. The appellant is entitled to have his judgment enforced as first lien for $810, with interest from May 11, 1864, and the costs, and to recover his costs in the circuit court and in this court. The decree appealed from is wholly erroneous, and must be reversed and annulled.

RICHARDSON and HINTON, JJ., dissent.

***

CUNNINGHAM v. COMMONWEALTH.

(*Supreme Court of Appeals of Virginia.* June 18, 1891.)

ASSAULT WITH INTENT TO RAPE—INDICTMENT—EVIDENCE.

1. Under Code Va. § 3888, which provides that every person who attempts to commit an offense, "and in such attempt does any act towards its commission," shall be punished, etc., an indictment for an attempt to commit a rape must aver the act or acts done by defendant towards the commission of the crime.

2. An indictment for an assault with intent to rape, which alleges that defendant violently and feloniously made an assault on a female, and feloniously did attempt to ravish her and carnally know her, against her will and by force, sufficiently charges an act done towards the commission of the offense.

3. The commonwealth's evidence showed that the prosecutrix and defendant were employed as

cooks at the same hotel. Defendant made an indecent proposal to her, which she rejected. A few nights thereafter she was awakened by a man in her room, who put his hand on her person, and who said he was going to do what he came to do. The prosecutrix recognized defendant, and began to scream, when defendant choked her. Her screams aroused another servant in the same room, who lit a lamp, when defendant escaped. *Held,* that the evidence was sufficient to support a verdict of guilty, though defendant and several of his witnesses testified to an *alibi.*

4. The fact that the court limited the argument of counsel to an hour and a half on a side is no ground for reversal, where defendant made no objection until after the commonwealth's attorney had concluded his opening argument, and the witnesses were few, and the facts very limited in their range.

Mr. Blanchard, for appellant. *The Attorney General,* for the Commonwealth.

LACY, J. This is a writ of error to a judgment of the corporation court of the city of Bristol, rendered on the 2d day of September, 1890. The case is a prosecution for an attempt to commit a rape. The charge is that defendant, with force and arms, in and upon one Martha Hartsock, violently and feloniously made an assault; and her, the said Martha Hartsock, feloniously did attempt to ravish and carnally know, against her will and by force. To the indictment the plaintiff in error demurred, and, the demurrer being overruled, he pleaded not guilty. Upon the trial, witnesses were examined on both sides, and, the argument of counsel being about to commence, the court limited the counsel in their arguments to one hour and a half on a side, and the plaintiff in error excepted because the court limited the time to be consumed by the counsel in argument; and, the argument of counsel being concluded, the jury rendered a verdict as follows: "We, the jury, find the defendant guilty as charged in the indictment, and fix the term of his imprisonment in the penitentiary at three years." Whereupon the prisoner moved the court to set aside the verdict of the jury as being contrary to the law and the evidence, and grant him a new trial, which motion the court overruled; and the prisoner excepted; and judgment was therefore rendered by the court in accordance with the verdict. Whereupon the prisoner applied for and obtained a writ of error to this court.

The first assignment of error here is as to the action of the court in overruling the demurrer to the indictment. His ground of objection to the indictment is that, as the indictment is for an attempt to commit a felony, under section 3888 of the Code of Virginia, it was necessary that the indictment should set out the overt acts done by the accused towards the commission of the offense. Section 3888 is as follows, so far as it affects this question: "Every person who attempts to commit an offense, and in such attempt does any act towards its commission, shall, when not otherwise provided, be punished as follows: If the offense attempted be punishable with death, the person making such attempt shall be confined in the penitentiary not less than two nor more than five years, except that, in

case of an attempt to commit rape, the term of confinement in the penitentiary shall not be less than three nor more than eighteen years." The contention of the plaintiff in error is that the indictment must set out the act done in the attempt to commit the felony charged to have been committed. Section 3888 provides, as we have seen, that every person who attempts to commit an offense, and in such attempt does any act towards its commission, shall be punished, etc. This is an indictment for an attempt to commit a rape, and it is necessary, to constitute the crime, that the accused should have done some act towards the commission of the said rape. This is an element of the offense,—an essential element of the offense.—and without its existence the crime does not exist. Being, therefore, an essential part of the offense, which is not complete without it, it must be averred and proved. In the case of Com. v. Clark, 6 Grat. 675, Judge LEIGH said, for the general court, that the indictment ought to have alleged some act done by the defendant of such a nature as to constitute an attempt to commit the offense mentioned in the indictment; it having been adjourned to the general court, among others, this question: "Whether the said indictment should not allege that the defendant did some act towards the commission of the offense with the attempt to do which he is charged in the indictment." In the subsequent case of Uhl v. Com., Id. 706, on an indictment for an attempt to burn a barn, it was held that an indictment charging that the defendants "did, about 12 o'clock of the night of the said day, attempt to set fire to the said barn, * * * by then and there carrying live coals of fire in a certain tin cup, then and there held by them, * * * and then and there putting and placing the said live coals of fire, which they * * * then and there had in their possession, in manner aforesaid, to, at, and against the straw, chaff, and other combustible matter, in, about, and against said barn, with a wicked intention, by means thereof, unlawfully, wilfully, and maliciously to burn and consume said barn," was a good indictment under this statute; and held, further, that, according to the true intent and meaning of the law, an attempt can only be made by an actual ineffectual deed done in pursuance of, and in furtherance of, the design to commit the offense. Com. v. Nutter, 8 Grat. 699; Hicks v. Com., 86 Va. 223, 9 S. E. Rep. 1024; Glover v. Com., 86 Va. 882, 10 S. E. Rep. 420; Whart. Crim. Law, § 192, and case cited.

The indictment in this case is for an attempt to commit rape, under section 3888, supra, and the charge is in the words of the statute charging the attempt. The act done towards the commission of the offense—that is, not of rape, but of an attempt to commit rape—is that the defendant did, with force and arms, in and upon Martha Hartsock, then being over the age of 12 years, to-wit, of the age of 50 years, violently and feloniously make an assault, and her, the said Martha Hartsock, then and there, to-wit, on the day

and year aforesaid, feloniously did attempt to ravish and carnally know,
against her will, and by force, etc. The
plaintiff in error complains that this indictment did not charge or aver an act
done in the attempt to commit the offense,
and so that he is surprised when the evidence was offered to show that in the night-
time, while the said Martha Hartsock was
in bed and asleep, he, the said plaintiff in
error, laid his hands upon her and declared his purpose, and, when she called
for help, threatened to choke her, and
seized her by the shoulders to that end,
when, help arriving in response to calls,
the said plaintiff in error fled. The indictment distinctly charges the violent and felonious assault, and the attempt to rape.
If this be true, then an act was done by
him in the attempt to commit the offense.
He made a violent assault, and attempted to commit rape. To charge this, is to
charge and aver an act done towards the
commission of the offense. An assault is
an act; no mere words can constitute an
assault. The demurrer to the indictment
was properly overruled. There was no
error in that action of the corporation
court of Bristol.

Upon the question as to the action of
the trial court, the court limited the argument to one hour and a half to a side, and
this was not objected to at the time, but
only after the attorney for the commonwealth had concluded his opening argument. Under the circumstances of this
case, this does not appear to be an
abridgment of the right of the accused to
be fully heard, and was not an undue exercise of that superintending control which
is the province of the trial court, and constitutes no ground of reversal. The witnesses were few, and the facts very limited in their range. See Jones v. Com., 12
S. E. Rep. 226, and the cases cited.

It remains to consider whether the court
erred in refusing to set aside the verdict
and grant a new trial to the accused in
this case, upon the ground that the verdict was contrary to the law and the evidence. The evidence is certified, and must,
under our law, be considered here as upon
a demurrer to evidence. The evidence of
the commonwealth is that Martha Hartsock, a white woman, and a widow of 50
years of age, was employed in the kitchen
of the Hamilton House, of the city of Bristol, as assistant cook; and the accused
was an unmarried colored man, who was
employed on Tuesday, the 17th of June,
1890, as assistant meat cook in the same
kitchen. In a day or two after his arrival
and employment the accused, while engaged about his work, as was Mrs. Hartsock, sitting fronting each other, said to
her: "I like your look mighty well; let's
you and me live together, and be as one."
That he was promptly repulsed, Mrs.
Hartsock saying she had not got low
enough yet to live that way with white
men, let alone with negroes. On the following Saturday night, after her work
was done, Mrs. Hartsock went to her
room, and went to bed, in a house in the
same yard as the Hamilton House kitchen
was situated. At about 2 o'clock in the
night she was awakened by a man put-

ting his cold hand upon her leg. When
she awoke, she said it was Mann Cunningham, the prisoner. He told her he came
there to do something with her, and he
was going to do what he came to do.
She cried for help, and tried to arouse a
woman sleeping in the same room,—the
witness Retty Scott; but she did not answer, and the prisoner said, "Damn you,
if you don't stop hollowing I'll choke
you;" and, suiting his action to the word,
grabbed her by the shoulders as if he was
going to put the threat in execution; that
he came there to do something, and was
not going away until he did it; and she
screamed, and then Retty Scott answered,
and struck a match, and lit the lamp; and
the prisoner turned around, looked at her,
and went out of the room the way he
came in, through the window, and went
pretty fast. That she recognized the prisoner as soon as she opened her eyes. That
the light from an electric lamp was shining through the window into the room.
That the next morning, when the prisoner
came to work, he passed Mrs. Hartsock,
and dropped his eyes. That immediately
outcry was made, and Retty Scott went
to call help from the other servants, and
Mrs. Hartsock's brother-in-law and Mr.
Hamilton, of the Hamilton House, were
notified, and some of the servants came
to her room that night. Retty Scott says
that when sufficiently aroused she jumped
out of bed, and lit the lamp, and opened
the door, and it was "sorter dark" in the
room, but she could tell that there was
something in the house. It was a short,
dusky-looking object, and she took it to be
a man, and that when she opened the
door he went out of the door, and she
went out and called for Mrs. Dingo, one of
the employes of the house.

The prisoner denied on the witness stand
having done any of the things charged
against him, and his sister and his
brother-in-law endeavored to set up an
alibi, claiming that he slept in their house,
and they did not know of his going out
during the night, and did not think he
could have gone out without their knowledge, as the door was fastened with a
poker which rattled in the latch, and made
a noise when the door was opened, and
they were frequently up that night giving
medicine to the husband, who was sick to
some degree; and some other witnesses
attempted the same thing,—to establish an
alibi,—by showing that the accused went
to bed at 10 o'clock, and did not get up
any more. The jury, however, upon the
facts, found the accused guilty, and the
trial court rendered judgment upon the
verdict, overruling the motion for a new
trial by the prisoner. And, if we consider
the case upon the principles of a demurrer
to the evidence, there is no way that we
can disturb the verdict of the jury. The
proof is direct that the accused committed
the crime. The evidence for the defendant
attempts to contradict this by proving an
alibi, but the jury has considered and decided this. In this court the exception
must be held to admit as true the evidence
of the commonwealth, and all just inferences that may flow from it, and waive
all of his own evidence in conflict there-

with. Apply this rule, and the case is distinctly proved for the commonwealth, and there is nothing to the contrary. As far as the alleged conflict between the commonwealth's witnesses is concerned, one woman said the prisoner jumped out of the window, and the other that she thought she saw a short, dusky object, and that it went out of the door when she opened it. One said there was light in the room from the electric lamp outside somewhere, and the other said it was "sorter dark" in the room, while the witnesses for the defense say that the electric light could not shine through this window. Whatever conflict there is in this had to be determined by the jury, the proper triers of the fact, and they have done so. It is probable that, while the electric light could not shine directly through the window, when lighted outside some light, by reflection, found its way through the open window. The witness Retty Scott does not say the room was absolutely dark, but "sorter dark;" and that would indicate some light, enough perhaps to enable the startled woman to identify her assailant, who was so close to her as to have laid hold on her, and who was helping the recognition by speaking to her in a voice which she had become acquainted with during the few days she had served with the prisoner. I do not think this court can properly disturb this verdict upon the ground that it is contrary to the evidence. And, under the law, the term of confinement fixed for this crime is not less than 3 nor more than 18 years. In accordance with the law the term is fixed, and it is tempered with mercy, as the lowest time allowed by the law is fixed for the period of the punishment. This answers also the complaint of the counsel for the prisoner, who claims that the jury was actuated by prejudice against the negro because he assaulted a white woman. Upon the whole case there is no error in the action of the corporation court of Bristol, and the same should be affirmed.

MACON & A. RY. CO. v. RIGGS et al.

(Supreme Court of Georgia. April 30, 1891.)

EMINENT DOMAIN — CONDEMNATION OF CHURCH PROPERTY—DEED FROM MEMBERS OF SOCIETY.

1. Church property is private property, and is subject to condemnation according to law for railway purposes.

2. A deed from certain members of a church, who had no authority to make the same, purporting to convey to a railway company a right of way over land belonging to the church, does not authorize the company to take such land for the purpose designated in said deed.

(Syllabus by the Court.)

Error from superior court, Bullock county; JAMES K. HINES, Judge.

Gustin, Guerry & Hall, for plaintiff in error. Brannen & Brannen, for defendants in error.

LUMPKIN, J. 1. The judge below held that the property of a church was not subject to condemnation for railway purposes. It has been settled by this court that church property is private property,

and it follows that land belonging to a church may be condemned for public use, such as the building of a railway thereon, just as the property of an individual may be. City of Atlanta v. First Presbyterian Church, 13 S. E. Rep. 252, (this term.) See, also, Lyons v. Bank, (Ga.) 12 S. E. Rep. 882.

2. The railway company obtained from five members of the church, including a deacon, a deed conveying to it the right to construct its track across the land of the church, and delivered, in payment for said land, a draft for $175. These members of the church did not own the land, and had no right to make said deed. Afterwards the church deliberately repudiated this action on the part of said members, and returned the draft to the company. The company, nevertheless, was about to proceed to build its railway across the land of the church, having no authority or right so to do except such as may have been conferred by said deed; whereupon Riggs and a number of others, members of the church, and representing it, filed their petition for an injunction against the company to restrain it from encroaching upon the land of the church, and upon the hearing thereof the court granted the injunction. We think the judge did right, because, under the facts disclosed, the company had no right, title, or authority whatever to use this land. We affirm the judgment of the court below, but this ruling must not be so construed as to prevent the railway company, if it sees proper so to do, from instituting condemnation proceedings according to law.

Judgment affirmed.

KEA et al. v. EPSTEIN et al.

(Supreme Court of Georgia. April 20, 1891.)

FRAUDULENT CONVEYANCES — CONSIDERATION— VALIDITY OF CHATTEL MORTGAGE.

1. The evidence warranted the jury in finding that a large part of the debt secured by the mortgage was fictitious, and therefore that the mortgage was tainted with actual fraud; also that the assignment was tainted with like fraud, because it made the mortgagee one of the preferred creditors to the full amount of the mortgage.

2. A mortgage upon a stock of goods as a whole, and to secure a single debt as a whole, if void as to a large part of the debt by reason of a contemplated fraud upon other credits, designed to be perpetrated by the execution and use of the mortgage, is void as to the whole debt.

(Syllabus by the Court.)

Error from superior court, Emanuel county; JAMES K. HINES, Judge.

Williams, Brannon, Hines & Felder, for plaintiffs in error. Alfred Herrington and T. H. Potter, for defendants in error.

BLECKLEY, C. J. 1. If the mortgage was tainted with fraud, it was with actual, not constructive, fraud. As to the existence of a large part of the debt which purported to be secured, there was no evidence, outside of the mortgage and the note described by it, except the testimony of the mortgagee; and he entered into no particulars as to time or place, but said that he had advanced or loaned to the mortgagor, before the mortgage was executed, about $600. He did not show how or where he obtained the means to do this, and, according to the tax-books adduced in evidence, he possessed nothing taxable but his own head, the year before or the year after the mortgage was executed. The amount secured was $1,200, and when the mortgage was taken the stock of goods embraced in it was valued by the mortgagee himself at that amount. Thus, according to his testimony, he added to a loan of about $600, previously made, a further loan of $400 when the mortgage was executed, with the understanding that more was still to be advanced to make up the sum secured by the mortgage, and this was advanced afterwards. The jury could well believe that he would not hazard $1,200 upon a stock of goods worth no more than that sum, especially when by other evidence it appeared that the value of the stock was in fact only $800. Furthermore, the mortgage was kept off the records for nearly 12 months, and for more than 2 months after the mortgagor had made an assignment. Indeed, it was not recorded until after the bill to set it aside had been filed. Another fact of some moment is that the note for $1,200, secured by the mortgage, was not to become due until nine months and a half after its date, but contained no stipulation that it was to commence bearing interest until after maturity. There is no explanation in the evidence of why the mortgagee would or should allow the use of his money by the mortgagor for such a length of time, and on such security, without compensation. The jury, it seems to us, were entitled to conclude, if they thought proper to do so, that about one-half of the debt covered by the note and mortgage was fictitious. True, in arriving at this conclusion, they would have to discredit the mortgagee as a witness, but this, in view of his interest, would be allowable. They must be supposed to know whether his oath, or the circumstances militating against his veracity, should be preferred as a guide to truth. If so large a proportion of the debt was fabricated, some actual fraud upon other creditors must have been intended by both the mortgagor and mortgagee; and, if the mortgage was fraudulent, the assignment must also have been fraudulent; for it makes the mortgagee one of the preferred creditors to the extent of the whole amount of the mortgage debt, to-wit, $1,200. Besides this, the assignment has another infirmity. One of the creditors was omitted from the schedule, and certain assets with which to pay him were left out of the assignment. This was done, not inadvertently, but by design, the intent being that the assets should afterwards be applied to the satisfaction of that creditor's demand, which was done.

2. It is contended, however, that the mortgage would not be void because a part of the debt was fictitious, but would be good as to so much as was real and genuine. We think this position is not sustainable, if actual fraud was contemplated in fixing the amount of the debt or pretended debt to be secured by the mortgage. Baldwin v. Short. (N. Y., Feb., 1891,) 26 N. E. Rep. 928. Says Chancellor KENT: "A deed fraudulent in fact is absolutely void, and is not permitted to stand as a security for any purpose of reimbursement or indemnity." Boyd v. Dunlap, 1 Johns. Ch. 482. In Allen v. Brown, 43 Ga. 305, a decision of doubtful correctness, the parties, at the time the deed was executed, made separate stipulations as to each half of the lot covered by the deed. Here, on the contrary, there was no division of the property covered by the mortgage contemplated or agreed upon. All of it was devoted alike to the legal and to the illegal object sought to be subserved by the execution of the mortgage. What the parties joined together for the consummation of a fraud, the court and jury called upon to defeat the fraud were not bound to put asunder. Judgment affirmed.

PENDLETON v. HOOPER.

(Supreme Court of Georgia. April 20, 1891.)

CLAIM OF HOMESTEAD EXEMPTION — ESTATE REQUIRED.

The head of a family who, after judgment for a debt has been rendered against him, has parted with the title to his land by deed of gift, but has never parted with possession, may still assert the exemption allowed by section 2040 of the Code to arrest a sale of the land by virtue of the judgment. No present interest or estate in land beyond that implied in the fact of possession is requisite to sustain the claim of exemption, as against a debt or lien inferior to the exemption right.

(Syllabus by the Court.)

Error from superior court, De Kalb county; RICHARD H. CLARK, Judge.

Rosser & Carter, for plaintiff in error. H. C. Jones and J. N. Glenn, for defendant in error.

BLECKLEY, C. J. The premises in controversy consist of six acres, and are of the estimated value of $400. Hooper was in possession when the judgment against him was rendered, and has remained in possession ever since. He parted with the paper title by a voluntary conveyance made to several persons, some of them minors, on the day the judgment was rendered, and at an hour subsequent to its rendition. The lien of the judgment was made neither better nor worse by this conveyance. Had he parted also with possession, and never resumed the same, his ownership of the property would have been at an end; but, as he retained possession, he is still the owner against all the world except his donees. They may choose never to disturb him, or assert any title against him. That possession of itself imports ownership is familiar law. 2 Bl. Comm. 196; English v. Register, 7 Ga. 391. Naked possession is the lowest and most imperfect degree of title, but it is nevertheless enough to hold off creditors, where exemption is claimed under section 2040 of the Code, and where the terms prescribed in section 2041 are complied with. Here there was a compliance with these terms pending the levy, and while Hooper was in possession. It is not disputed that he was the head of a family, or that he would be entitled to the exemption, if he had not divested himself of all title except possession. But he retained the very thing which the law of exemption is solicitous to protect. It cares not how little interest the debtor may have, so long as he remains in its actual enjoyment. The exempt land is "for the use and benefit of the family of the debtor;" so says the Code. The exemption does not depend on the quality or duration of the estate which the debtor has in the land. A tenancy at will or at sufferance will protect it from levy and sale as his property, equally with an estate in fee-simple. The exemption attaches to the land, not merely to his estate in it. Our exemption laws do not cut up exempt property into divers estates, but protect the physical thing as a whole from levy and sale, so long as the exemption continues. Van Horn v. McNeill, 79 Ga. 122, 123, 4 S. E. Rep. 111. Of course, it is not meant to say that, if others have an interest in the property as well as the debtor who has claimed the exemption, the property would not be subject to sale, so far as their interest is concerned. But a forced sale of an exempt thing, whether it be land or personalty, cannot be made as the property of the debtor against his claim of exemption, while he is the head of a family, and holds possession, unless the debt be one which for some reason overrides the exemption. The law devotes the thing to the use and benefit of the family, as against the ordinary rights of his creditors. Some debts are superior to the exemption right, but the one involved in this case is not of that class. How, then, can the land be consistently treated as the property of the debtor for the purpose of subjecting it to sale, and not so treated for the purpose of exempting it? The creditor's lien being inferior to the debtor's right to have the enforcement of the lien suspended, of what concern to the creditor is it that the debtor has no title to the land, as against third persons to whom he has conveyed it by a deed of gift? Even were he a trespasser relatively to his donees, he would, while in possession, be owner relatively to his creditors. The court below decided the case correctly. Judgment affirmed.

PARKER et al. v. BELCHER et al.

(*Supreme Court of Georgia.* April 20, 1891.)

VACATING JUDGMENT—ABSENCE OF PARTY—JURISDICTION.

1. The plaintiff in a pending suit having two counsel employed to represent him, the absence of himself without leave of the court, and of his leading counsel with leave, when the case was regularly called for trial, will not entitle him to have the verdict and judgment set aside at a subsequent term; one of his counsel having been present when the case was called and disposed of, and having made no motion for a continuance because the leading counsel was absent, or upon any other ground.

2. A verdict and judgment for costs alone against the plaintiff will not be set aside upon the ground that the court in which his action was brought had no jurisdiction of the subject-matter of the suit.

(*Syllabus by the Court.*)

Error from superior court, Clayton county; RICHARD H. CLARK, Judge.

J. A. Anderson, J. B. Hatcheson, and *T. P. Westmoreland,* for plaintiffs in error. *Stewart & Daniel* and *E. T. Dorsey,* for defendants in error.

BLECKLEY, C. J. 1. A suitor in the superior court has no right to consult the judge while off the bench for his opinion as to when the case will come on for trial, or as to what will be done with it when it does come on. The sayings and doings of the judge in such an interview are extra judicial, and cannot be treated as announcements or rulings of the court. It is manifest that Mr. Parker had no leave of absence. Not only so, but he was expressly warned by one of his counsel not to absent himself. He nevertheless went home, and thus failed to be present when his case was called and brought on for trial. The counsel present made no motion for a continuance, on the ground that associate counsel was absent with leave of the court, or on any other ground; but finding himself abandoned, as he supposed, by his clients, consented that a verdict might be taken in favor of the opposite party, the defendants in the action. The sole question of any difficulty presented by the evidence adduced on the hearing of the petition to set aside this verdict, and the judgment for costs founded thereon, is whether the agreement of the opposite party or counsel to pay the fees of the plaintiffs' counsel tainted the consent with fraud as against the plaintiffs. But this question is not covered by the petition. The petition does not rest on the ground of fraud, but expressly alleges "that said case was called, and the verdict rendered therein, through inadvertence, and after petitioners had been discharged from further attendance on said court." According to the facts in evidence, this allegation is simply untrue. There was no inadvertence, but average attention to everything that was done, and the plaintiffs had not been discharged from further attendance on the court. That one of their counsel was absent with leave of the court, though he was the leading counsel and the one mainly relied on, was no reason for granting a continuance not applied for in due time and manner, there being one counsel present and undertaking to conduct the cause. A proper showing has to be made, where the leading counsel is absent, even though his absence be occasioned by providential cause. Code, § 3525.

2. It can hardly be seriously contended that a verdict and judgment for costs only should be set aside merely because rendered against the plaintiffs in a suit brought by them in a court having no jurisdiction of the subject-matter. If they are not liable for the costs of their own action, who is liable? Their redress, if any, is against their attorney for bringing action in the wrong court. We do not say that this was done, but simply rule on the question as made. Indeed, this ground is not only without affirmative merit, but, assuming it to be true in fact, its effect would be to negative or neutral-

ise any reason whatsoever for reinstating the case. Why should the court resume the exercise of jurisdiction, if it had no jurisdiction at first? There was no error in denying the prayer of the petition to set aside the verdict and judgment. Judgment affirmed.

McLEOD et al. v. SWAIN.

(*Supreme Court of Georgia.* April 20, 1891.)

EJECTMENT—EVIDENCE—DECLARATIONS.

Declarations of a deceased person in disparagement of his title to land, made while in possession thereof, are admissible in evidence, not only against the declarant and those claiming under him, but also for or against strangers.

(*Syllabus by the Court.*)

Error from superior court, Emanuel county; JAMES K. HINES, Judge.

Williams & Brannen, Saffold & Warren, and *Rogers & Potter,* for plaintiffs in error. *Twiggs & Verdery* and *H. R. Daniel,* for defendant in error.

LUMPKIN, J. Mrs. Swain brought an action of ejectment against McLeod et al. for the recovery of a tract of land in Emanuel county. The evidence was conflicting, and sufficient to sustain a verdict for either side. The jury found for the plaintiff. After Mrs. Swain had proved by her own testimony that a certain Mrs. Wiggins, who at one time was in possession of the land and remained in possession for many years, until her death, was her tenant, the court, over defendants' objection, admitted proof of declarations made by Mrs. Wiggins, while in possession of the land, to the effect that she held it as the tenant of plaintiff, and that it was the land of plaintiff. The only question of law presented in this case for our determination is whether or not this testimony was properly admitted. Section 3776 of the Code declares that "the declarations and entries of a person, since deceased, against his interest, and not made with a view to pending litigation, are admissible in evidence in any case." It was contended in the argument that such declarations should be received only against the declarant, and those in privity with or claiming under him; but this view does not seem to be sustained by the authorities. It was held in the case of Peaceable v. Watson, 4 Taunt. 16, that "the declarations of a deceased occupier of land of whom he held the land are evidence of the seisin of that person;" and in Davies v. Pierce, 2 Term R. 53, that "declarations by tenants are admissible evidence after their death to show that a certain piece of land is parcel of the estate which they occupied." In both these cases the declarations admitted were made by persons not in privity with any of the parties to the record, nor did any of such parties in any way claim title through or under the declarants. Again: "Statements of a deceased occupier touching his title are admissible in evidence generally, without reference to the particular effect they may produce in the cause." Carne v. Nicoll, 27 E. C. L. 707. See, also, Barry v. Bebbington, 4 Term R. 514. We find the following in 1 Taylor, Ev. § 684: "Under the head of declarations against proprietary interest may be classed the statements made by persons while in possession of land, explanatory of the character of their possession; and it is now well settled that such declarations, if made in disparagement of the declarant's title, are receivable, not only as original admissions against himself and all persons who claim title through him, but also as evidence for or against strangers. Whether in this latter event they are admissible in the life-time of the declarant, or only in cases where his death can be proved, is a point which does not appear to have been distinctly decided. In most of the cases where the evidence has been received, the declarant was dead; but on two occasions, at least, the evidence was admitted, though the declarant was living." Wharton also lays down the rule that such evidence is admissible, not only against privies, but strangers. "The reason for this conclusion is that possession implies, *prima facie,* an absolute interest, and any statement which would tend to limit it to a less interest is self-disserving." 2 Whart. Ev. § 1156. The same principle is stated in 1 Greenl. Ev. § 109, and the same reason for the admissibility of such declarations is there given. These authorities abundantly sustain the correctness of the ruling made by the court below, and its judgment is therefore affirmed. Judgment affirmed.

ALFORD v. HAYS et al.

(*Supreme Court of Georgia.* April 20, 1891.)

RECOVERY OF LAND — ADVERSE POSSESSION—LACHES.

Where a husband brought suit against his divorced wife to recover an undivided half interest in certain land, alleging in his declaration that she had been in the exclusive and adverse possession of this land, without interruption, for more than 15 years, holding under a deed fraudulently made to her and her children, which should have been made to herself and him, and it further appears from the declaration that he had actual knowledge of the alleged fraud from the time her adverse possession began, but failed sooner to bring his suit because of ignorance of his legal rights, and the testimony substantially sustains the allegations of the declaration, a nonsuit was properly awarded.

(*Syllabus by Lumpkin, J.*)

Error from superior court, Washington county; J. K. HINES, Judge.

Rogers & Potter and *Harris & Rawlings,* for plaintiff in error. *J. C. Harman* and *H. D. D. Twiggs,* for defendants in error.

PER CURIAM. Judgment affirmed.

STATE v. BRADLEY.

(*Supreme Court of South Carolina.* June 17, 1891.)

MURDER—DYING DECLARATIONS—EXPERT EVIDENCE.

1. Dying declarations are admissible on an indictment for murder, where they indicate that deceased fully expected to die, and where he in fact did die a few hours after making them.

2. A question put to a physician examined as an expert, whether it was possible for deceased

to have inflicted on himself, in a scuffle with defendant, the knife wound of which he died, is properly excluded, as it calls for the opinion of a witness in a matter requiring no special skill or knowledge.

Appeal from common pleas circuit court of Aiken county; HUDSON, Judge.

Henderson Bros. and *O. C. Jordon*, for appellant. *W. Perry Murphy*, for the State.

McIVER, J. Under an indictment for the murder of Jasper Craig, the appellant was convicted of manslaughter, and sentenced to confinement in the penitentiary for the term of three years. From this judgment he appeals upon the several grounds set out in the record. It appeared that, in an altercation between these parties which took place in the yard of the deceased about dark in the evening, the deceased received a mortal wound inflicted by a knife, and was soon after carried into his house, where he died, some time near the middle of the next day. One witness, the son of the deceased, testified that he saw the prisoner strike the mortal blow, while other by-standers testified that they did not see prisoner strike any blow, but that they saw or heard deceased fall. All the parties were drinking more or less, and the defense was that the deceased, being much under the influence of liquor, in striking at the prisoner fell upon his own knife, and thus received the mortal wound. The first, second, and third grounds of appeal impute error to the circuit judge in his rulings as to the admissibility of certain testimony, while the fourth ground, which has very properly been abandoned, as it manifestly could not be sustained, complains of error in the charge to the jury. The testimony alleged to have been erroneously admitted by the first and second grounds of appeal was as to what passed between the deceased and the prisoner, shortly after the wound had been inflicted, and after deceased had been carried into his house, and the prisoner had been brought in. When this testimony was first offered, the judge, conceiving that the proper foundation had not been laid for the admission of such testimony as a dying declaration, declined to receive it as such, but ruled that it was competent as a conversation between the deceased and the prisoner; and it is to this ruling that exception is taken by the first ground of appeal. Afterwards, however, when the circuit judge considered that a proper foundation had been laid, he ruled such testimony competent as a dying declaration; and to this ruling the second ground of appeal is directed. If, therefore, this testimony was admissible as a dying declaration, it is unimportant to consider whether it was competent as a conversation between the parties. We will therefore confine our attention to the question whether the testimony in question was admissible as a dying declaration. The rules upon this subject are so well settled that we need not do more than state them briefly: (1) Death must be imminent at the time the declaration is made. (2) The declarant must be so fully aware of this as to be

without hope of life. (3) The subject of the charge must be the death of the declarant, and the circumstances of the death must be the subject of the declaration. State v. Johnson, 26 S. C. 152, 1 S. E. Rep. 510, and the cases therein cited. That death was imminent in this case is demonstrated by the fact that it followed within 24 hours after the declaration in question was made. When the deceased was carried into the house a little after dark he fainted, and, when he regained consciousness temporarily, the declaration in question was made, and but a few hours afterwards—about midnight—he became speechless, and remained in that condition until he died, about the middle of the next day. Next, was the declarant so fully aware of his condition as to be without hope of life? The language of the declaration itself shows this,—"Angus has killed me." State v. Quick, 15 Rich. Law, 342. But, in addition to this, he not only expressed no hope of living, but said "that he had to die; that Angus had killed him." State v. McEvoy, 9 S. C. 212. The fact that the attending physician says, in his testimony, that, after examining the wound, he did not think it would be "necessarily fatal; didn't think he would die,"—cannot affect this question, unless it had appeared that he had expressed such opinion to the deceased. The deceased manifestly believed that he was about to die of that wound, and it does not appear that the doctor either said or did anything calculated to remove, or even shake, that belief. As to the third requirement of the rule, it is too clear for argument that it was fully met. It is clear, therefore, that there was no error in admitting the testimony in question as the dying declaration of the deceased as to who killed him, on the trial of a case for the murder of deceased. The third ground of appeal complains of error in ruling out the following hypothetical question propounded to Dr. E. F. Wyman, "an expert surgeon." "If, in a particular case, the facts be as follows: Two men, say Craig and Bradley, are seen very near each other, both with drawn knives. Craig, being very drunk, cuts at Bradley, but misses him, whereupon with his left hand he seizes Craig's right arm, and pushes it from him towards Craig, and at the same time with his right hand seizes Craig's left shoulder, and gives him a severe blow, which fells him to the ground. Afterwards it is found that Craig has a knife wound about two and a half inches long below, and to the left of, the left nipple, which enters the cavity and touches the heart, and passes out, ranging to the right, so much so that the shirt is cut in that direction: Is it probable and possible, from this state of facts, that Craig was wounded by the knife he held in his own hand." To say nothing of any other objection to the proposed question, we think the question was properly ruled out upon the ground that it required no special knowledge, skill, or experience to enable one to give an opinion as to the matter inquired about, and hence was not a proper subject for expert testimony. In 7 Amer. & Eng. Enc. Law, 491, it is said.

"Expert evidence is that given by one especially skilled in the subject to which it is applicable, concerning information beyond the range of ordinary observation and intelligence. And again, on the same page of that very valuable and useful compendium of the law, it is said: "An expert is one who has made the subject upon which he gives opinion a matter of particular study, practice, or observation, and he must have a particular and special knowledge on the subject." Now, however expert and skillful Dr. Wyman may be as a surgeon, and however competent he may be to express an opinion upon a subject involving a knowledge of anatomy, we can hardly suppose that either he, or any one for him, would claim that he had ever given the subject inquired about any special study, practice, or observation, or that he had any special knowledge on the subject. On the contrary, we would suppose that any intelligent person, of ordinary experience, would be quite as competent to express an opinion as to whether, under a given state of facts, it would be probable or possible for Craig to have inflicted the wound from which he died by falling upon his own knife, as the most learned and experienced surgeon could be. The question, therefore, was calculated to elicit an opinion from the witness as to a matter involving no special knowledge or skill, which the jury was quite as competent to form as the witness, and it was therefore clearly incompetent. The judgment of this court is that the judgment of the circuit court be affirmed.

McGowan, J., concurs.

STATE v. CHAVIS.

(Supreme Court of South Carolina. June 17, 1891.)

Stealing from the Person—New Trial—Chambers.

1. On an indictment for privily stealing from the person, where the jury has been instructed that the taking must have been secret in order to make out the offense, it is not error to add that it is not necessary for the state to prove that no force was used.

2. In South Carolina, a judge in chambers has no power to grant a new trial in a criminal case on the ground of newly-discovered evidence.

Appeal from common pleas circuit court of Orangeburg county; Izlar, Judge.

Raysor & Summers and Izlar, Glaze & Herbert, for appellant. W. St. Julien Jervey, for the State.

McIver, J. In this case the defendant was indicted for and convicted of the offense of privily stealing from the person of another. Upon the rendition of the verdict a motion for a new trial on the minutes of the court was made and refused; whereupon the defendant was sentenced to 15 months' imprisonment in the penitentiary. After the adjournment of the court, a motion was made before his honor, Judge Izlar, at chambers, who had presided at the trial, for a new trial upon the ground of after-discovered evidence, who held that he had no jurisdiction to hear such a motion at chambers, and there-

fore declined to consider the motion on its merits. Defendant appeals upon the several grounds set out in the record. The first ground, having very properly been abandoned, need not be stated. The second imputes error to the circuit judge in charging the jury that, "in matters of proof of this kind, it would not be necessary for the state to show that there was no force used." The third and fourth grounds raise, in different forms, the question whether the circuit judge erred in holding that he had no jurisdiction, at chambers, to hear a motion for new trial upon the ground of after-discovered evidence. In considering the second ground of appeal, it would be well to understand exactly what the circuit judge did say to the jury; and for this purpose we extract from his charge, as set out in the "case," the following language: "First, the stealing must be done secretly; and, secondly, the property stolen must be taken from the person of the party at the time. Now, I charge you that the statute would not be violated in a case of this kind where force was used, as where money is forcibly taken from a person. Nor would the statute be violated if it was taken with the knowledge of the prosecutor. The property must be secretly and privately taken from the person of the prosecutor to bring the offense within the terms of the statute However, in matters of proof of this kind, it would not be necessary for the state to show that there was no force used. The value of the property stolen is not material, if it be of some value. The gravamen of this offense consists in secretly taking from the person." It seems to us that this charge is not open to any valid exception The error imputed seems to be in instructing the jury that it was not necessary for the state to prove that no force was used. This rests upon the assumption that, contrary to the general rule, the state was bound to prove a negative, by direct testimony, for it seems to us that if the jury were satisfied, as the judge instructed them that they must be before they could convict, that the property was taken secretly and privately from the person of the prosecutor, that carried with it the idea that it was not taken forcibly. There are several different species of larceny, made up of different elements, and we see no reason why the state should be required to offer evidence ignoring one element more than another; and the logical result of the view contended for by appellant would be that an indictment for any given species of larceny could not be sustained unless the state offered evidence negativing the existence of the elements necessary to constitute every other species of larceny. Such a view cannot be accepted. All that is necessary for the state to prove, under an indictment for any offense, is the existence of all the facts necessary to constitute such offense, and, if it is claimed that other facts exist which would show that the offense is really of a different character from that charged, that is a matter to be shown by the defense, and need not be negatived by the state, unless the statute creating the offense shall so require; and certainly there is no such requirement in the statute under which this prosecution was brought. This view is illustrated by the case of Genning v. State, 1 McCord, 573, recognized in Information v. Oliver, 21 S. C., at page 324, where it was held that, under an indictment for retailing spirituous liquors without a license, the state need not prove that the defendant had no license, as that was a matter of defense to be proved by defendant. For a much stronger reason it was clearly unnecessary for the state to prove that there was no force in taking the property alleged to have been privily stolen from the person of the prosecutor. The third and fourth grounds raise the single question whether a judge at chambers has jurisdiction to hear and determine a motion for a new trial in a criminal case, upon the ground of after-discovered evidence. So far as we know, there is no authority to show that a judge at chambers has any such jurisdiction by virtue of any powers inherent in his office. If, therefore, such a power exists, it must be derived either from the constitution or some statute, and no provision of the constitution, nor has any statute, been cited conferring such a power. It cannot be derived from the act of 1868, now incorporated in Gen. St. § 2113, for there the power is conferred upon the circuit courts, not upon the judges, and the distinction between the powers of the circuit court and a judge at chambers is well recognized, especially in regard to motions for a new trial. Clawson v. Hutchinson, 14 S. C. 517; State v. David, Id. 428. These cases also show that such a power cannot be derived from the act of 1869, for the reasons therein stated, and we may add for the additional reason that such act has been expressly repealed by the act of 1880, (17 St. 341.) It is clear, therefore, that there was no error on the part of Judge Izlar in declining to take jurisdiction of the motion at chambers It seems to be supposed that the practical result would be to deprive a party, who had been convicted in the court of sessions and sentenced, of the privilege of moving for a new trial upon the ground of after-discovered evidence, where the discovery was not made until after judgment rendered. But this is a mistake, as shown by State v. David, supra, where such a motion was made and granted long after judgment had been rendered against him. But in that case the motion was made to the court of sessions, not to a judge at chambers. The judgment of this court is that the judgment of the circuit court be affirmed, without prejudice to the right of the defendant to move for a new trial upon the ground of after-discovered evidence, before the proper jurisdiction, if he shall be so advised.

McGOWAN, J., concurs.

HILL v. LAURENS COUNTY.

(Supreme Court of South Carolina. June 17, 1891.)

DEFECTIVE HIGHWAYS—LIABILITY OF COUNTY.

Where one receives injuries from defects in a road which is a deviation from the regular highway laid out by the overseer of the road-hands at the suggestion of the neighbors, and without the authority of the county commissioners, who alone are empowered by law to alter highways, he cannot recover against the county under Gen. St. S. C. § 1087, which provides that "any person who shall receive bodily injury * * * through a defect in the repair of a highway * * * may recover in an action against the county," etc.

Appeal from common pleas circuit court of Laurens county; WALLACE, Judge.

Benet & McGowan and Haskell & Dial, for appellant. H. Y. Simpson, for respondent.

McIVER, J. This was an action to recover damages for an injury sustained by plaintiff while traveling along an alleged public highway in Laurens county, leading from the town of Laurens to the town of Hamburg. It seems that the recognized public highway between those two points, after the construction of the Port Royal & W. C. Railroad, in 1884, passed under a trestle on said railroad, and that, the highway at that point becoming very rough, in the summer of 1886 a new road was cut out, at the suggestion of the neighbors, which left the public highway some 75 yards before reaching the trestle, and, passing under the trestle at a point some 25 or 30 yards below, again joined the public highway about 75 yards beyond the trestle; and that in passing under the trestle by this new road a very sharp turn had to be made, which seems to have been, in large part at least, the main cause of the accident complained of. There was no evidence that this new road was opened by any authority from the county commissioners, or that it was ever known to them. No special commissioners were appointed, as required by the act of 1883, which will hereinafter be referred to, and no notice given to the railroad company or to any one else that such new road was to be opened, or that such change was to be made in the recognized public highway. But the overseer of the road-hands, at the instance of the neighbors, undertook to make this change in the public highway without any authority; so far as appears. It does appear, however, that in 1888, after the accident complained of had occurred, the public highway was changed by the authority of the board of county commissioners, which, it seems, avoided the difficulty of passing under the trestle. At the close of plaintiff's testimony defendant moved for a nonsuit upon the ground that there was no evidence that the road upon which the accident occurred was a highway. The motion was granted by his honor, Judge WALLACE, and the plaintiff appealed upon the several grounds set out in the record.

Under the view which we take of this case it will not be necessary to consider in detail the several grounds of appeal. Inasmuch as it is well settled, in this state at least, that a municipal corporation is not liable to a civil action for damages sustained by reason of its failure to perform any of the duties imposed upon it by law, in the absence of a statute imposing such liability, (Young v. City of Charleston, 20 S. C. 116; Chick v. Newberry Co.,

27 S. C. 419, 3 S. E. Rep. 787,) it is quite clear that we must look alone to the statute to ascertain whether such a corporation is liable in a given case. Our statute upon this subject is to be found in section 1087, Gen. St., which reads as follows: "Any person who shall receive bodily injury or damage in his person or property through a defect in the repair of a highway, causeway, or bridge, may recover, in an action against the county, the amount of damages fixed by the finding of a jury." It is very obvious, therefore, that the plaintiff could not recover in this case unless he showed that the injury of which he complains occurred "through a defect in the repair of a highway." We agree with the circuit judge that the plaintiff not only failed to offer any evidence tending to show this, but, on the contrary, his own evidence shows that the injury was caused by a defect in a road which was not a highway,—a road which was not laid out by any competent authority, and over which the defendant corporation, through its recognized agents, the county commissioners, could exercise no control,—and hence the corporation cannot be held responsible for any defects in its condition. The act of 1888, above alluded to, (18 St. 631,) expressly provides "that the board of county commissioners of the several counties in this state be, and the same are hereby, authorized and empowered, upon the petition of twenty freeholders interested therein, to appoint three special commissioners and employ a surveyor, whose duty it shall be to lay out or change the location of public highways in those cases where said county commissioners shall be satisfied that the road applied for is important for the convenience of travel and benefit of commerce." This act, after prescribing the mode of proceeding, etc., concludes with a section expressly repealing all acts and parts of acts inconsistent therewith. This, so far as we are informed, is now the only law prescribing the mode of laying out a new highway, or changing the location of one previously laid out. Hence, where any one undertakes to change the location of an existing highway without conforming to the mode prescribed by law, such change is not only illegal and without authority, but by the provision of section 1070 of the General Statutes he subjects himself to a suit at the instance of the county commissioners. It is clear, therefore, that when Moore, the overseer of the road-hands, at the instance of some of the neighbors, undertook to change the location of the previously existing highway, his act was not only without lawful authority, but subjected him to a penalty. There is not only no evidence tending to show that the county commissioners either knew of or much less approved the change in the location of the existing highway, but the contrary may be inferred from the fact that when the location was changed, in 1888, by their authority, a different route was selected from that which had been adopted by Mr. Moore. But, even if it could be assumed that the county commissioners knew and approved the change made by

Moore, that would not make it lawful, unless it also appeared that the mode prescribed by the act of 1888 had been pursued. The position taken by the appellant's counsel, that the defendant is estopped by the act of Moore, certainly cannot be sustained; for, even if Moore could be regarded as the agent of the defendant corporation, it is quite clear from the case of Chick v. Newberry Co., supra, that no estoppel would arise. We agree, therefore, with the circuit judge that, the injury sustained by plaintiff having occurred from an alleged defect in a road which was not a highway, he has no cause of action against the defendant. The judgment of this court is that the judgment of the circuit court be affirmed.

McGOWAN, J., concurs.

STATE v LEVELLE.

(*Supreme Court of South Carolina.* June 17, 1891.)

HOMICIDE—MALICE—PROVOCATION — SUICIDE—INSTRUCTIONS.

1. On an indictment for murder it is not error to charge that the law infers malice from the unlawful use of a deadly weapon resulting in death.

2. No words, however opprobrious, furnish sufficient provocation to reduce a killing with a deadly weapon from murder to manslaughter.

3. Nor is it error to charge that suicide is an unlawful act, and that when one, in attempting to commit suicide, takes the life of another, that is murder.

Appeal from common pleas circuit court of Charleston county; ALDRICH, Judge.

Clement S. Bissell, for appellant. W. St. Julien Jervey, for the State.

McIVER, J. The defendant was indicted for and convicted of the murder of his wife, and, judgment having been entered on the verdict, he appeals upon the following grounds: "(1) Because his honor erred in charging the jury that 'malice will also be inferred from the use of a deadly weapon;' and that intent and malice are one and the same thing, when there is no presumption or inference of law, unless it is a natural and reasonable presumption from the facts proved. (2) Because the charge of his honor 'that no words, however cruel, and the man, no matter how great the heat and passion may be, who slays his fellow-man upon no other provocation than mere words, is guilty of murder,' is not in accordance with the modern doctrine of our law, was not applicable to the case, and was very misleading to the jury. (3) Because his honor erred in charging the jury that every death that results from the unlawful act of another is murder. (4) Because the charge of his honor was otherwise contrary to law." The charge of Judge ALDRICH, before whom the prisoner was tried, is set out in the "case," and should be incorporated in the report of this case. We will therefore proceed to consider the several grounds of appeal in their order as stated, only referring to such portions of the charge as will be necessary for a proper understanding of the questions raised and considered.

The first ground presents two questions: (1) Whether there was any error in saying to the jury that "malice will be inferred from the use of a deadly weapon." (2) Whether intent and malice are one and the same thing, provided it shall first appear that the judge so instructed the jury. As to the first question, it will be observed that the words then quoted were not used by the circuit judge, but are taken from the language of the solicitor's ninth request, to which the judge responded in these words: "That is a presumption or rule, not so much of law as of common sense. Ordinarily, if a man, in his senses, uses a deadly weapon in a way calculated to do great harm to another person, the law and common sense says that he intended the result which his act brought about." The rule is well settled that every sane man is presumed to intend the ordinary and probable consequences of any act which he purposely does, and this rule is applied even in capital cases. 3 Greenl. Ev. §§ 13, 14. This is plainly what the judge meant by the language he used, and therefore there was no error in this respect. But, even if it be assumed that the judge must be regarded as adopting the language used in the solicitor's ninth request, quoted above, we still think there was no error. In 2 Bish. Crim. Law, § 680, it is said: "As general doctrine, subject, we shall see, to some qualification, the malice of murder is conclusively inferred from the unlawful use of a deadly weapon, resulting in death." And to the same effect, see 3 Greenl. Ev. §§ 145, 147. This doctrine has also been recognized in this state. See State v. Toohey, 2 Rice, Dig. 105; State v. Ferguson, 2 Hill, (S. C.) 619; State v. Smith, 2 Strob. 77. It is true that the inference of malice drawn from the use of a deadly weapon may be rebutted by testimony, but, in the absence of any such testimony, malice may be and is inferred from the use of a deadly weapon causing death. The second inquiry arising under the first ground of appeal is as to the identity of intent with malice. But we do not find anything in the charge of the judge which warrants the idea that any such instruction was given to the jury. The jury were instructed that, if the act which produced death be attended with such circumstances as indicate a wicked, depraved, and malignant spirit, the law will imply malice, without reference to what was passing in the prisoner's mind at the time, and this was good law, as it was taken, word for word, from the opinion of the court in State v. Smith, supra.

The second ground of appeal likewise presents three inquiries: (1) Whether provocation by words only will be sufficient to reduce a killing from murder to manslaughter; (2) whether the language complained of in this ground was applicable to the case; (3) whether it was misleading to the jury. We will first consider the last two questions, which are really one, for we suppose that the language objected to as misleading is thought to be so because not applicable to the case as made by the testimony. But as none of the testimony is incorporated in the case, and the record does not furnish us with even a

general outline of the circumstances attending this deplorable tragedy, it is impossible for us to say that these remarks were either inapplicable to the case made or calculated to mislead the jury. On the contrary, we are bound to assume that they were applicable, as we cannot suppose that the circuit judge, in instructing the jury as to their duties in so grave a case, would allow himself to indulge in general observations that had no application to the case, and might, therefore, tend to distract the minds of the jury from the real issues they were to pass upon. Turning, then, to the first inquiry, it will be observed that the judge, after explaining to the jury the difference between murder and manslaughter, used the language objected to, probably for the purpose of disabusing their minds of what seems to be a popular impression, that, where the killing is done in sudden heat and passion, the crime will be manslaughter, and not murder, without reference to the provocation received. It was then very natural for him to go on and explain the nature of such provocation as would or would not be sufficient to reduce the killing from murder to manslaughter. It was in this connection that the jury were instructed, correctly as we think, that provocation by words only, no matter how opprobrious, would not be sufficient. That this has been the law of this state from time immemorial cannot be questioned, and we are not aware that any such modern doctrine as that contended for has ever been recognized in this state. On the contrary, one of the recent decisions of this court (State v. Jacobs, 28 S. C. 29, 4 S. E. Rep. 799) expressly holds the contrary. This broad statement of the doctrine must be understood as applying to a case where the death was caused by the use of a deadly weapon, as it may be different where the death results from the use of some agency not likely to produce death, as, for example, from a blow with the fist. But although, as we have said, there is nothing in the record furnished us to show the circumstances attending the homicide, yet the fact that the death, in this instance, was caused by the use of a deadly weapon sufficiently appears, as well from the judge's charge as from the agreement to amend the brief made at the hearing, by stating that the prisoner fired two shots. We do not think, therefore, that the second ground of appeal can be sustained.

The third ground of appeal rests upon a misconception of the judge's charge. Indeed, it seems to be conceded, in the argument of appellant's counsel, that the judge did not state in terms to the jury the proposition there excepted to, but that such is the inference to be drawn from the language used by him. We do not think that any such inference could properly be drawn from the language used. On the contrary, as it seems to us, the plain meaning of the proposition stated to the jury was that the law will imply that a person who does an unlawful act intended the natural and probable consequences of his unlawful act, and is therefore responsible therefor; and, when read in connection with the illustration given of A., intending to shoot B., fires upon him, intending to murder him, but misses B. and kills C., then A. would be guilty of murder, although he may not have had the slightest intention of killing C. or even injuring him in any way, the jury could not possibly have had a doubt as to the meaning of the proposition, which was clearly correct, as was held in State v. Smith, supra. The other illustration given by the judge of one killing another in an attempt to commit suicide, and commented on by counsel for appellant in his argument here, as presenting an incorrect view of the law, will be considered, though the case as prepared for argument here contains nothing from which it can be inferred that there was any evidence out of which such a question could be raised. It is true that counsel in his argument does say that, according to the evidence, the defendant attempted to kill himself, and in doing so unfortunately killed his wife, who was attempting to prevent the suicidal act. But as we have often held that we cannot decide a case upon any testimony, stated only in argument, and not appearing in the case prepared for a hearing in this court, this matter is not properly before us. Inasmuch, however, as this is a case involving such grave consequences, we are not unwilling to depart from the well-settled rule, and consider the propriety of what was said to the jury upon the subject of suicide, although there is no exception to that part of the charge. The judge used this language in his charge: "In the eye of the law, self-destruction—suicide—is an offense; it is an unlawful act; and, if a man with a deadly weapon undertakes to take his own life, he is doing an unlawful act; and if in the commission, or attempted commission, of that act, he takes the life of an innocent party standing by, then, in the eye of the law, that is murder." To this instruction there is no well-founded exception. In 1 Russ. Crimes, (3d Amer. Ed.) 424, it is said: "Whenever an unlawful act, an act *malum in se*, is done in prosecution of a felonious intention, and death ensues, it will be murder." Now, as suicide is an unlawful act, *malum in se*, and is a felony, (1 Bish. Crim. Law, §§ 511-615,) there can be no doubt that the proposition laid down by the judge is correct. We have carefully examined the case of Com. v. Mink, 123 Mass. 422, cited by counsel for appellant, on this point and we do not think it is applicable, for the reason that in the state of Massachusetts they have a statute providing that "any crime punishable by death or imprisonment in the state-prison is a felony, and no other crime shall be so considered." Suicide therefore is not a felony in that state, as, from the very nature of the case, it cannot be punishable by death or imprisonment in the state-prison;" and yet, in that very case, GRAY, C. J., in delivering the opinion of the court, intimates pretty plainly that one who, in an unsuccessful attempt to commit suicide, unintentionally kills another, who is endeavoring to prevent it, is guilty of murder. But in this state we have no such statute, and, on the contrary, section 2678 of the General Statutes prescribing the form of the verdict of a coroner's inquest, in a case of suicide, by the use of the term "feloniously" expressly recognizes it as retaining its common-law character as a felony.

The fourth ground of appeal is too general to require attention. Nevertheless, in favorem vitæ, we will not decline to consider such questions as we can gather from the argument were intended to be raised by that ground. The first is as to the doctrine of "moral insanity," as it is sometimes called, or uncontrollable impulse. While it is not to be denied that there are cases in some of the states which recognize this doctrine as a defense against a charge of crime, yet it never has and we trust never will obtain a foothold in this state; for we agree with Judge SHERWOOD, when he said in the recent case of State v. Pagels, 92 Mo. 300, 4 S. W. Rep. 931: "It will be a sad day for this state when uncontrollable impulse shall dictate a rule of action to our courts." It is a matter that is not susceptible of proof, and to allow a person to escape the consequences of his criminal act by asserting that he acted under an impulse which he could not restrain, although he knew his act to be unlawful, would be dangerous, if not destructive, to the peace of society. See State v. Bundy, 24 S. C. 444, 445; State v. Alexander, 30 S. C. 74, 8 S. E. Rep. 440. See, also, Leache v. State, 22 Tex. App. 279, 3 S. W. Rep. 539, where the question is ably and elaborately discussed, and the ruling was in conformity to the view we have adopted. In Parsons v. State, 81 Ala. 577, 2 South. Rep. 854, the whole subject of insanity as a defense is most ably and elaborately discussed, and both sides of the question more immediately presented will be found fully presented in the opinion of the court delivered by SOMERVILLE, J., and the dissenting opinion by STONE, C. J.

Under this ground, the appellant's counsel further objects to the definition of "malice" as given by the circuit judge, because it omits the word "intentionally," and claims that a correct definition should read: "'Malice' means the doing of an unlawful act intentionally, without justification or excuse." Perhaps this criticism might be well founded if we confined our attention solely to the particular sentence upon which it is based; but when the whole charge is considered together, as the rule requires it to be, there is plainly no foundation for the exception. From what we can discover as to the nature of the case in which this charge was made, as well from the record as the argument here, it does not seem to us that the omission of this qualifying word in defining the term "malice" could possibly have prejudiced the prisoner. As we have seen, the law presumes that a person intends the natural and probable consequences of his own act, and it is for the party charged to show the absence of intention. Hence, when it is shown that one has taken the life of another, without justification or excuse, the law will imply malice, without reference to what was actually passing in the prisoner's mind at the time he committed the homicide. The judgment of this court is that the judgment of the circuit court he affirmed, and that the case be remanded to that court for the purpose of having a new day assigned for the execution of the sentence heretofore imposed.

McGOWAN, J., concurs.

CUNNINGHAM et al. v. CAUTHEN.

(Supreme Court of South Carolina. June 17, 1891.)

APPEAL—FILING EXCEPTIONS—DISMISSAL — REINSTATEMENT.

Though Act S. C. Dec. 24, 1889, § 2, (30 St. 356,) requires appellant to serve his case with exceptions on the opposite party or his attorney within 30 days after service of the notice of appeal, the trial judge may extend his time; and when he has done so, and the clerk, without knowledge of the extension, has dismissed the appeal, under supreme court rule No. 1, the appeal will be reinstated.

Appeal from common pleas circuit court of Lancaster county; WITHERSPOON, Judge.

This is a motion in behalf of defendant (appellant) to reinstate his appeal, dismissed by the clerk under rule 1 of this court. The petition of the defendant (appellant) represents as follows: "(1) That in the above-stated case the defendant, on the 28th day of January, 1891, gave in good faith regular notice of appeal from the circuit decree in said action, and the said notice, with certain exceptions, was on the same day regularly served on plaintiffs' attorneys, the right to serve other exceptions being therein reserved. The circuit decree was made after term-time, and was filed on the 19th day of January, 1891; and the settled determination of defendant and his attorneys was then, and is still, to prosecute the appeal, with all convenient speed and dispatch. (2) That on account of the magnitude of the work in the preparation of the case, and the lack of time, with other pressing business, to do the same properly, defendant, by his attorneys, gave written notice to plaintiffs' attorneys, on the 11th day of February, 1891, that he would apply to the judge (WITHERSPOON) who heard the cause and filed the decree for an extension of time in which to serve his case with exceptions, whereupon Judge WITHERSPOON, at chambers, on the 23d day of February, 1891, at the time and place designated in the notice, made an order extending the time within which to serve the case with exceptions until the 1st day of June next, (1891,) which order thus extending the time was filed in the clerk's office at Lancaster C. H., on the 26th day of February, 1891, and the said plaintiffs and their attorneys had notice thereof on the same day. (3) That Ernest Moore, one of the plaintiffs' attorneys, who had express notice of the order aforesaid, on the 11th day of March, 1891, on his own affidavit, moved before A. M. Boozer, Esq., clerk of the supreme court in Columbia, for a dismissal of said appeal, to which said affidavit petitioner craves reference; and thereupon the said clerk did sign an order dismissing

the appeal of defendant, on the alleged ground, as defendant is informed, that defendant had failed to make to the said clerk the return provided for in the first and second rules of the supreme court. (4) That at the time the said clerk, A. M. Boozer, signed the said order dismissing the said appeal, the record constituting the said return had not been completed, and it cannot be completed, as defendant respectfully submits, until defendant has served his case, with exceptions, under the order aforesaid, extending the time until the 1st day of June next. (5) That, if there be no error in the order of the said clerk dismissing said appeal, (which the undersigned do not admit,) then defendant's attorneys have made a mistake inadvertently, in construing the act of 1889, in relation to appeals, in connection with the rules of court, and he respectfully prays the court to restore and reinstate his appeal on the following grounds: First. Because the said clerk acted in ignorance of the fact that the record constituting the return had not been completed, and his order is erroneous. Second. Because, since the passage of the act of 1889, (page 356,) on the subject of appeals, no return under rules 1 and 2 of the supreme court can be filed with the clerk of this court until the case and exceptions are served upon the opposing attorneys. Third. Because the time for filing said return in this appeal had not expired, and the clerk erred in determining otherwise. Fourth. Because, if the clerk was right in dismissing the appeal, (which is not conceded,) then defendant's attorneys made a mistake in their construction of the act of 1889, in connection with the rules of the supreme court and its decisions, and on that account the defendant should have had his appeal restored and reinstated, according to the practice of this court. Fifth. Because the appeal, in the judgment of defendant's counsel, has great merit in it, and, if the order dismissing the same is allowed to stand, the estate of A. J. Kibler, deceased, will suffer great and implorable detriment. And your petitioner further prays that the order of 11th day of March, 1891, be repealed, and that plaintiffs pay the costs of this proceeding so unjustly and unrighteously imposed on the defendant."

The following is plaintiffs' (respondents') answer thereto: "That at the time of the motion to dismiss the appeal of the defendant herein this deponent did not inform the clerk of the supreme court of the granting of an order prior to that date extending the time for service of defendant's 'proposed case,' for the reason that he did not then, nor does he now, regard that fact as at all material. That, at the time of the motion to dismiss the appeal of the defendant herein, this deponent thought, and he still thinks, that the attorneys for the defendant were not making any serious effort to advance the hearing of the appeal of the defendant herein; and that, if the said attorneys had desired an early hearing of the appeal, they could easily have prepared their 'case' for the supreme court, as well as the 'return' within the time allowed by law. That deponent does not doubt that the attorneys for the defendant believe it to be true, as stated by them in the affidavits herein, that the said attorneys have been endeavoring to carry on their appeal 'in good faith,' but deponent believes that said attorneys grievously deceive themselves in such belief that, they are prosecuting their appeal in good faith and without unnecessary delay. Deponent denies the charge of illiberality in practice, brought against himself and his colleague herein, and avers that the liberality of the attorneys for the plaintiffs herein has for so many years been exercised in this case that it has ceased to be a virtue. Deponent further avers that for more than seven years the attorneys for the plaintiffs have been endeavoring to force this cause to final judgment; and that, unless they can obtain the aid of the courts in the enforcement of the rules made to expedite the trial of causes, the plaintiffs' attorneys greatly fear that yet another seven years will have passed before the final judgment herein. Deponent further says that the plaintiffs also duly gave notice of appeals herein, with exceptions fully as numerous and important as those of the defendant, to the said circuit decree, and, within the time required by law, caused to be filed in the office of the clerk of the said supreme court the 'return' upon the said appeal, and also, within the time required by law, served upon the attorneys for the defendant their 'proposed case,' as required by the rules of court; that said 'return' and said 'case' were fully as voluminous as would have been the return and 'case' for the hearing of the appeal of the defendant herein; and that proper effort on the part of the attorneys for the defendant would easily have enabled them in like manner to have served their 'case' and filed their 'return,' within the time required by law."

Giles J. Patterson and *R. E. Allison,* for appellant. *Ernest Moore,* for respondents.

PER CURIAM. The facts in this case are undisputed. We assume the counsel on both sides acted in good faith, and the question is narrowed down to a question of law. In this case proper notice of appeal was given, which was accompanied with certain exceptions, appellant's attorneys reserving the right to file additional exceptions. The law is plain as to what the returns shall consist of, to- wit, copies of the judgment roll, notice of appeal, and exceptions. The return is not complete without these. Section 2 of the act of December 24, 1889, (20 St. 356,) provides as follows: "Sec. 2. That section 345 of the Code of Civil Procedure be, and the same is hereby, amended by striking out subdivision 1, and by amending subdivision 2. so as to read as follows: '(1) In every appeal to the supreme court from an order, decree, or judgment granted or rendered at chambers, from which an appeal may be taken to the supreme court, the appellant or his attorney shall, within ten days after written notice that such order has been granted, or decree or judgment rendered, give notice to the opposite party or his attorney of his intention to appeal; and in all other appeals to the supreme court the appellant or his attorney shall, within ten days after the rising of the circuit court, give like notice of his intention to appeal to the opposite party or his attorney, and within thirty days after such notice the appellant or his attorney shall prepare a case with exceptions, and serve them on the opposite party or his attorney. The respondent, within ten days after service of such case, may propose any objection thereto or alteration thereof, and the case shall be settled in such mode as may be provided in the rules of the supreme court.'" Under this act appellants are allowed 30 days after the notice of appeal to serve exceptions. The appellant in this case, when he served his notice of appeal, filed certain exceptions; but he reserved the right to file additional exceptions. Before the 30 days had expired, on application to a circuit judge, ne was allowed further time to file his exceptions. Under the law the circuit judge had a right to extend this time. The appellant therefore is not in default. There was no fault on the part of the clerk in dismissing the appeal as the facts were not all before him. Under the facts as they came before him he was right in dismissing the appeal. Under the facts, however, as developed, the dismissal was erroneous, and the appellant is entitled to have his appeal reinstated. The court therefore granted the following order: "On hearing the notice of motion of defendant herein, dated 16th April, 1891, and the petition and accompanying papers, and the answer of plaintiff, with accompanying papers, and argument in favor of the motion by defendant's attorneys and of plaintiffs' attorney in opposition, it is ordered that the order of the clerk of this court of 11th March, 1891, be set aside, and the defendant's appeal be reinstated.

ELDER *et al.* v. GREENE *et al.*

(*Supreme Court of South Carolina.* June 17, 1891.)

BREACH OF REPLEVIN BOND.

After a court has adjudged, without appeal being taken, that it had no jurisdiction of a replevin suit, its order that the property replevied be returned is void, and non-compliance therewith constitutes no breach of the bond conditioned for a return of the property if a return be adjudged.

Appeal from common pleas circuit court of Spartanburg county; WALLACE, Judge.

Bomar & Simpson, for appellants. *Stanyarne Wilson,* for respondents.

MCIVER, J. It appears in this case that the defendants herein had brought an action in the trial justice court against the plaintiffs herein of claim and delivery, to recover possession of a certain horse, and that, having given the required undertaking, the horse was seized by the constable, and delivered to the defendants herein, who were the plaintiffs in the action before the trial justice. When the original case came on for trial before the trial justice, the defendants therein, who are now the plaintiffs herein, moved to dismiss that action on the ground that the trial justice had no jurisdiction. That motion was granted, and the case was dismissed, and the horse ordered to be returned to the defendants in that action. This order not having been complied with, the plaintiffs herein made a demand on the defendants herein for the horse, with which demand the defendants refused to comply. Whereupon this action was commenced, in which the plaintiffs, after setting out the facts in detail, which have been substantially stated above in a more condensed form, alleges "that, by the aforesaid wrongful seizure, conversion, and disposition of said horse, and by the said failure of these defendants to comply with said judgment of the trial justice, and by their refusal to accede to the said demand of these plaintiffs, they have caused plaintiffs damage in the sum of one hundred and thirty-five dollars;" for which sum, besides costs, judgment is demanded. The defendants answered, setting up title in themselves to said horse, and that they had acquired possession from the former owner, and denying that plaintiffs had any interest in or right to the possession of said horse. At the trial, when defendants offered to introduce testimony to support their defense, the same was, upon objection, ruled inadmissible, and defendants duly excepted. The circuit judge charged the jury, among other things, that the action was on the bond or undertaking, and therefore the question as to the ownership of the horse, or the right to the possession thereof, was not in issue in this case, and for that reason all the testimony as to that had been ruled out, and the only issue was whether defendants had complied with the condition of the bond. The jury rendered their verdict in the following form: "We find for plaintiff a verdict of one hundred dollars, and costs." Whereupon a motion for a new trial was made upon the grounds, among others, that defendants were not bound to return the horse, as required by the order of the trial justice, because the same was void for the want of jurisdiction, and because the judgment of the trial justice, not being in the alternative, was not in the form required by law, which motion was refused. Thereupon the defendants gave due notice of appeal upon the several grounds set out in the record, which need not be specifically repeated here. The frame of the complaint, a copy of which is set out in the "case," might possibly leave it doubtful whether the action was based upon trespass committed by the alleged wrongful and unlawful seizure of the horse under the proceedings before the trial justice, or upon the bond or undertaking given by the defendants under that proceeding. If it should be regarded as an action for the trespass alleged to have been committed, then it is quite clear that there was error in excluding the testimony which was offered for the purpose of showing that the plaintiffs had no title or right to the possession of the horse. But the action seems to have been treated below as an action on the bond or undertaking. The circuit judge so charged the jury, and counsel for respondents in his argument here has insisted that such was the true character of the action; and, if so, then it is equally clear that there was no error in excluding the testimony as to title or right to possession, for the reason that in such case the only issue would be whether there had been a breach of the condition of the bond or undertaking, and the testimony as to title would be wholly irrelevant. Such testimony, however, would not be incompetent, as seems to have been supposed by the court below, because the issue as to title had been disposed of in the trial justice court, and therefore could not be renewed here; for if, as was ruled, the trial justice had no jurisdiction, then no issue, except that of jurisdiction, was or could be heard or determined by him.

Looking at the case, then, as an action on the bond or undertaking, the question presented is whether the circuit judge erred "in refusing to hold that the judgment of the trial justice court ordering the return of the horse was irregular and void, because not in legal form, and because [that] court was without jurisdiction." Under the view which we take of the matter of the jurisdiction, the alleged irregularity in the form of the judgment cannot properly arise, and therefore need not be considered. The undertaking or bond, as it is called, is set out in the case, and, after the proper recitals, is conditioned "for the return to the defendants [the plaintiffs herein] of the said property, or so much thereof as shall be taken by virtue of the said affidavit and requisition thereupon indorsed, if a return thereof shall be adjudged." Of course, a court is bound to construe this as meaning, if the return of the property in question be adjudged by any competent authority; and hence, until that appeared, there was no breach of the condition of the bond. The real question in the case being whether there had been a breach of the condition of the bond, which was more a question of law than of fact, dependent, as it was, upon a construction of the terms of the bond, and the legal effect of the judgment which the trial justice undertook to render, it seems to us that the circuit judge erred in refusing to hold that the judgment of the trial justice ordering a return of the property was absolutely void for want of jurisdiction, and hence, legally speaking, the return of the property never had been adjudged, and consequently there was no breach of the condition of the bond. After it had been adjudged, without appeal, in a case between these same parties, that the trial justice had no jurisdiction of the case in which the bond was taken, he, of course, could render no valid judgment for the return of the property, or for anything else, except to dismiss the case for want of jurisdiction. His effort to do so was a mere nullity, and amounted to no more than if he had not undertaken to render any judgment at all or pass any order, either for the return or retention of the property. Having no jurisdiction of the case, he had no authority to try or determine any of the issues raised therein, and, until such issues were tried and determined, he could not lawfully render any judgment or pass any order with respect to such issues. He did not have any authority to try the issue as to which of the parties was entitled to the possession of the horse, and he did not undertake to do so; and, surely, until that issue was tried and determined, he had no authority to order the return of the horse; and his so-called order or judgment to that effect was entitled to have no more effect than if passed or rendered by a private individual. Any other view would completely deprive the defendants of the opportunity of having the title to, or the right to the possession of, the horse in question tried at all. It was not and could not have been tried in the trial justice court, for want of jurisdiction in that court; and it could not, as we have seen, be tried in this action upon the bond.

It will be observed that the point of objection raised by this appeal is not, as in the case of Cavender v. Ward, 28 S. C. 470, 6 S. E. Rep. 302, because the bond sued on, being taken in a case of which the court in which it was instituted had no jurisdiction, was illegal; but the point made here does not rest upon any illegality in the bond, but rests solely upon the ground that there has been no breach of the condition of the bond, because what is claimed to have been a judgment for the return of the property is a mere nullity, for want of jurisdiction in the court undertaking to render it; and hence the case must be considered as if there never had been any such judgment, and, if so, then, clearly, there was no breach of the condition of the bond. It is plain, therefore, that the case of Cavender v. Ward, and the authorities therein cited, have no application to the question raised here. Although this action, as we have seen, cannot be maintained as an action on the bond or undertaking, yet, as it may be possible that the complaint can be regarded as containing sufficient allegations to sustain an action for trespass, or, if not, that it may be possible to so amend it as to give it that character, in which the parties will have an opportunity, which they have not yet had, of having the question of title to, or right to the possession of, the horse tried and determined, we think that the case should be remanded to the circuit court for a new trial, with leave to plaintiffs to apply to that court for such amendments as may be deemed proper to effect the end indicated, if they shall be so advised. The judgment of this court is that the judgment of the circuit court be reversed, and that the case be remanded for a new trial, with leave to the plaintiffs, if they shall be so advised, to apply for such amendment of the complaint as may be deemed proper by the circuit court.

McGOWAN, J., concurs.

STATE v. JAMES.

(Supreme Court of South Carolina.   June 17, 1891.)

HOMICIDE—JURORS—CONSPIRACY.

1. A juror in a capital case, who swears on his *voir dire* that he is opposed to capital punishment, is properly rejected.

2. The impressions of a juror as to defendant's guilt, based on what he "had heard," does not disqualify him, where he states on his *voir dire* that he can render a fair and impartial judgment according to the law and the evidence.

3. One of the conspirators, who has turned state's evidence, and who, on his cross-examination, has denied that he had ever told his attorney that a confession of the crime had been procured from him by the threats of the sheriff, does not thereby waive the privileged character of his communications to the attorney, and the latter cannot be compelled to disclose them for the purpose of impeaching the witness.

Affirming 12 S. E. Rep. 657.

On rehearing.

To the Honorable Supreme Court: The appellant respectfully asks for a rehearing of the above-entitled cause on the following grounds: (1) That the court overlooked the fact that the juror Best, notwithstanding his opposition to capital punishment, found a verdict of guilty against Lewis Williams, charged with murder, as a co-defendant of the appellant, thereby conclusively demonstrating that his declared opposition was not of such a fixed and unalterable character as would have disqualified him from serving in this case. (2) That in overruling the appellant's exceptions to the competency of the juror Hurle the court overlooked the fact that the juror had formed and expressed an opinion as to the guilt of the appellant on evidence which he had heard in court as well as outside; but they overlooked the further fact that no decided case sustains the competency of a juror who had formed and expressed an opinion of the guilt of the defendant on evidence which he had heard in court on the preceding day on the trial of a co-defendant, charged with the murder of the same person, under the same indictment as the defendant. Further, that they overlooked the distinction between this case and Coleman's, where the opinion expressed by the juror was hypothetical; whereas, in appellant's case, it was categorical, and positive, pointing directly to a belief of the prisoner's guilt. (3) That in holding that Scott was an "ordinary witness" the court overlooked the fact that he was jointly indicted for the same crime with the appellant; that he not only admitted his own guilt, but that he was captain of the band, and made all the arrangements; that he occupied the position, both as regards the state and the appellant, of an accomplice who had turned state's evidence; that his act in testifying for the state, was voluntary, and under the expectation of saving his own life by swearing away the life of another.

PER CURIAM. The court, after a careful examination and consideration of this petition, has reached the conclusion that no material fact or principle of law was overlooked or misunderstood in preparing the opinion heretofore filed, and therefore there is no ground for the rehearing asked for. It is ordered that this petition be dismissed, and that the stay of the remittitur heretofore granted be revoked.

McGEE v. JONES *et al.*

(*Supreme Court of South Carolina.* June 17, 1891.)

FRAUDULENT CONVEYANCES — SETTING ASIDE—
BONA FIDE PURCHASERS—NOTICE—LIMITATION.

1. The purchaser at execution sale of land of which there has been a voluntary conveyance by the judgment debtor since the debt was contracted may sue to set aside such conveyance, though he had actual notice thereof when he purchased, where the judgment creditor in whose behalf the land was sold had no notice thereof.

2. Though a third person has actual notice of the fraud infecting a conveyance, his right of action to set it aside only accrues upon his purchase of the land, and the statute does not begin to run against his action until then.

Appeal from common pleas circuit court of Abbeville county; JAMES F. IZLAR, Judge.

Graydon & Graydon, for appellants. *Benet & Cason,* for respondent.

McIVER, J. On the 1st day of January, 1878, the defendant David S. Jones, being indebted at the time to one Ezekiel Rasor, conveyed, by a deed in which the consideration stated was $650, to his father-in-law, Mason C. Henderson, the tract of land which is the subject of this action. Jones retained the possession of this land, paying the taxes thereon, up to the time when it was sold by the sheriff, as will be hereinafter stated, and still retains such possession. After the death of said Ezekiel Rasor his executors recovered a judgment on said debt against David S. Jones, in March, 1882, and under that judgment the land was sold by the sheriff on the 4th day of February, 1884, and bid off by said executors, who transferred their bid to the plaintiff in this action, and he, having paid the same, took title from the sheriff, and an assignment of the judgment from said executors, which was not paid in full by the proceeds of the sale. In the mean time, however, Mason C. Henderson, a day or two before his death, to-wit, on 16th of October, 1882, conveyed the said land to the defendant Nancy R. Jones, the second wife of David S. Jones, who does not appear to have been in any way related to said Mason C. Henderson, and to the children of David S. Jones by his first wife, who was the daughter of said Mason C. Henderson, all of whom are parties defendant to this action. At the sheriff's sale the attorneys for defendants gave public notice of these conveyances, which had been put on record on the 26th day of January, 1884, a few days before the sale, and forbade the sale upon the ground that the land did not belong to the judgment debtor, David S. Jones, but belonged to his wife, Nancy, and the children of his first marriage. The plaintiff, in his complaint, alleges that these conveyances were really without any consideration, and were made with intent to hinder, delay, and defraud the creditors of said David S. Jones in the enforcement of their claims, especially the Rasor claim, above mentioned; that the said David S. Jones had no other property except the land in question out of which his creditors could obtain satisfaction of their claims: and that said David S. Jones is still unlawfully

in possession of said land, and unlawfully withholds the same from plaintiff; wherefore he demands judgment that the said conveyances be declared fraudulent and void as to the plaintiff, and that the same be set aside and canceled, and that plaintiff may recover possession of said land.

The defendants answered, denying all fraud, alleging that plaintiff knew all the facts and circumstances connected with said conveyances long before the sale by the sheriff, and he took his title with full knowledge thereof, and that they, together with Mason C. Henderson, have had peaceable and quiet possession of said land for more than nine years next preceding the commencement of this action. It is very singular, however, that, although the statute of limitations is relied upon as one of the defenses to this action, we have been unable to find anything whatever in the "case" to show, or even indicate, when this action was commenced; and surely this is material to the determination of such a defense. It is true that the appellants do, in their argument, say that the action was commenced on the 5th of February, 1887, but this, as we have often had occasion to say, is not sufficient. But inasmuch as the respondent's counsel, in their argument, do say that the action was commenced in 1887, we suppose we may regard this as an admission that the action was commenced some time during that year. But we must again take the occasion to call the attention of the bar to the importance of this matter, and urge the necessity, imperatively required, that every fact deemed material shall appear in the "case," as otherwise it cannot be considered, unless admitted in the argument here. This court is very averse to being compelled to decide a case without considering some material fact which, however well known to counsel, cannot be noticed by the court unless brought to its attention in the manner prescribed by well-settled rules. The testimony in the case was taken and reported by the master, and the case was heard by his honor Judge IZLAR upon the pleadings, the testimony so reported, and the argument of counsel, who rendered his decree, finding, as matter of fact that David S. Jones was insolvent at the time he made the conveyance to Mason C. Henderson, and is now unable to pay his debts, having no property subject to levy and sale; that said conveyance was without consideration, and made with intent to defraud the creditors of said David S. Jones, especially the Rasors; that the deed of Mason C. Henderson to the other defendants was intended for the same purpose, and was fraudulent; and as matter of law he found that plaintiff could maintain this action, and that the deeds above mentioned should be set aside and canceled, and that the clerk be required to cancel the same, as well as the records thereof. From this judgment defendants appeal upon the several grounds set out in the record, which substantially impute error to the circuit judge—*First,* in his findings of fact above stated; *second,* in his conclusion of law that one who purchases land with notice of a prior voluntary deed has the right to bring an action to set aside such deed; *third*, in finding that the plaintiff purchased at the sale of Rasor, who had no notice, when the evidence was that the deeds were recorded before the sale, and express notice was given at the sale, and that the same was made by the sheriff, and not by Rasor; *fifth*, in disregarding or overruling the plea of the statute of limitations. So far as the errors assigned in the findings of fact are concerned, they may be disposed of by the single remark that where, as in this case, there was a conflict of testimony, this court rarely, if ever, interferes with the findings of fact by the circuit judge, even where the testimony is taken and reported by a referee or the master. Gary v. Burnett, 16 S. C. 632.

We do not understand that the circuit judge held in broad terms, as stated in the assignment of error, that one who purchases land with notice of a prior voluntary conveyance has the right to bring an action to set aside such conveyance. On the contrary, as we understand the decree, the judge held that, notwithstanding the fact that plaintiff had notice, yet, as the Rasors had no notice except that derived from the recording of the deeds a few days before the sale, and that given at the sale, the plaintiff occupied their position, and, if they had no such notice as would be sufficient to defeat them, the plaintiff would be protected by their want of notice; and in this, we think, there was no error. It is well settled that if one, with notice, purchased from another, who had no notice, he succeeds to all the rights of his grantor, and is protected. See 2 Pom. Eq. Jur. § 754; Jones v. Hudson, 23 S. C 494, recognized in London v. Youmans, 31 S. C. 147, 9 S. E. Rep. 775. As it is well expressed by JOHNSTON, Ch., in his circuit decree in Dopson v. Harley, reported in a note to Brown v. Wood, 6 Rich. Eq. 176: "When, in tracing a title in defendants, you come upon an innocent purchaser having no notice, from that moment the title is secure in equity; under which principle a purchaser with notice from one without notice is protected in this court." The reason of this rule is "to prevent a stagnation of property, and because the first purchaser, being entitled to hold and enjoy, must be equally entitled to sell." Per KENT, Ch., in Bumpus v. Platner, 1 Johns. Ch. 220. For if a person with notice could not safely buy from an innocent purchaser without notice, it is very obvious that, to borrow the idea of KENT, Ch., supra, the property would be stagnant in the hands of such innocent purchaser, who could not exercise one of the rights of ownership,—that of sale; for when he offered it for sale, especially at public outcry, all that would be necessary to drive off purchasers would be to give notice at such sale, and this would effectually defeat the attempt to sell. This principle, by which purchasers are protected, may be, and has been, applied in the case of Massey v. McIlwaine, 2 Hill, Eq. 421, to the protection of creditors, for, as was said by JOHNSTON, Ch., in his circuit decree: "If the creditors had the sale of the land in their power, a sale

by them to a person infected with notice was as good as if made to one who had no notice at all. To say otherwise would put it in the power of one first to obtain credit, and then, by giving general notice, to defeat the creditor of his remedy by cutting off all purchasers under the creditor's execution. The well-known principle that one infected with notice may safely purchase from and protect himself under another destitute of notice is of easy application to this case." It is true that this circuit decree was reversed by the court of appeals, but it was on another wholly different ground, and the court of appeals, so far from indicating any dissatisfaction with the doctrine as stated in the quotation from the circuit decree above, expressly approve it.

From what has been said above it is very manifest that the fact, relied upon by appellants' counsel, that the Rasors, as well as the plaintiff, had notice, at the time of the sale, by the recording of the deeds a few days before the sale, and by the public notice given at the sale, is of no consequence whatever. David S. Jones acquired credit from Rasor upon the faith of this land, and his subsequent conveyance, intended to hinder, delay, and defraud his creditors, certainly would not prevent his creditors from following the land into the hands of his fraudulent grantee; and when the same is offered for sale under the execution of the creditors, no notice given at or before such sale can affect the validity of such sale even to one who had full notice. As is said in the opinion of the court of appeals in Massey v. McIlwaine, supra, the purchasers at such execution sale "are not only invested, under their purchase, with all the rights of King, [the judgment debtor,] but they are also clothed with the rights of his creditor, at whose instance the land was sold. The creditor has the right to have his debt satisfied out of the property of his debtor, and, if it is sold under execution for that purpose, the purchaser is invested not only with the rights of the debtor, but those of the creditor also, which is in some degree peculiar. If, for example, the debtor convey lands after judgment signed against him, or even before, when he conspires with the purchaser to defraud his creditors, a purchaser at sheriff's sale, at the instance of the creditor, is entitled to prevail against the voluntary alienee of the debtor, notwithstanding the legal estate of the debtor had been before divested by his voluntary alienation; and in that case the rights of the purchaser are derived from the creditor."

It only remains to consider whether there was any error in disregarding or overruling the plea of the statute of limitations. If this case be regarded simply as an action to recover the possession of the land in question, which, it would seem, would have been the proper action, then it is clear, under the recent case of Amaker v. New, (S. C.) 11 S. E. Rep. 386, that the plea of the statute would be of no avail to the defendants. But as the action seems to have been treated below, and in the argument here, as an action to set aside fraudulent deeds, we will consider the question under that aspect. It is settled by the case of Suber v. Chandler, 18 S. C. 526, that the statute runs from the discovery of the fraud only where a right of action also then exists; so that, granting that the plaintiff here had notice of the fraud for a longer period than six years before the commencement of the action, that would not be sufficient to bar his right of action unless such right of action then existed. Now, it is quite clear that the plaintiff never had any right of action until his purchase in 1884, and, as the action was commenced within three years thereafter, it follows that the bar of the statute does not apply. Furthermore, there is no evidence that the Rasors had any notice whatever until the sale in 1884, and hence the statute would not bar their right of action, and, regarding the plaintiff as standing in their shoes, he would not, as holding their rights, be barred. The judgment of this court is that the judgment of the circuit court be affirmed.

McGOWAN, J., concurs.

STATE v. MERRIMAN.

(*Supreme Court of South Carolina.* June 17, 1891.)

HOMICIDE—EVIDENCE—CHARACTER—CROSS-EXAMINATION.

1. It is competent, on cross-examination, for the purpose of attacking the witness' credibility, to ask him whether he has ever been convicted of larceny.

2. A witness for the defense, who testifies that defendant is of a peaceable character, may be asked, on cross-examination, if he knows of certain particular acts of violence committed by defendant, for the purpose of showing that he gives defendant a character inconsistent with that inferable from facts known to him.

3. An accused person who becomes a witness in his own behalf assumes the position of an ordinary witness; and where he has put his character for peaceableness in issue he may be cross-examined as to particular acts of violence which he is alleged to have committed.

4. He may also be asked whether he ever told persons named of an act of violence which he at one time purposed, but was prevented from consummating, with a view to contradicting him by the evidence of the persons named.

Affirming 12 S. E. Rep. 619.

On rehearing.

To the Honorable Supreme Court:

The appellant respectfully asks for a rehearing of the above-entitled cause upon the following grounds:

First. That character alone is admissible, and the court overlooked the fact that individual acts do not establish character.

Second. That the court overlooked the fact that, in proof of character, general reputation alone is admissible, and that specific and particular acts of violence do not make general reputation, and are never admissible to establish character, or to rebut proof of it.

Third. That the court overlooked the distinction of the law that a witness cannot be cross-examined in a matter irrelevant and collateral to the issue for the purpose of laying the foundation to contradict him in reply, and thereby impeach his testimony. State v. Alexander, 2 Mill, Const. 174 The defendant was cross-examined as to a matter irrelevant and collateral to the issue. Whether the defendant did lie in ambush to shoot Gardner three or four years before the trial of this case was wholly irrelevant to the issues tried. The proof about defendant's trouble with Gardner had not the remotest connection with any of the issues in this cause.

Fourth. That the court overlooked the fact that the defendant was not examined in his own behalf to establish his own character, and that to cross-examine him as to whether he lay in ambush to shoot Gardner was to cross-examine him upon a matter wholly irrelevant and collateral to the issues, and greatly to his prejudice.

Fifth. That the court overlooked the fact and distinction of law that to cross-examine the defendant as to whether he lay in ambush to shoot Gardner, when he had not been examined in chief on that subject, was like the state putting up a witness in reply to prove that fact in rebuttal of the evidence of general reputation offered by the defendant to establish his good character for peaceableness.

Sixth. That the court has overlooked the fact that the state could not have proved in reply, by witnesses of its own, that defendant lay in ambush to shoot Gardner in order to rebut the evidence given by him of good character. Was it not in principle precisely the same to cross-examine the defendant, and then put up Hunt, Huggins, and Cassidy to contradict him, as if the state had been allowed to put up witnesses of its own to testify of their own knowledge as to the difficulty with Gardner? The defendant was not cross-examined to test his knowledge of his own reputation, or to show his bias in his own favor. In every case where the least departure from the general rule has been allowed, it has been only upon the cross-examination, and the courts have in every case put this right of cross-examination upon the sole ground that it was only allowed for the purpose of testing the knowledge of the witness as to the reputation to which he had testified, or to show his bias in favor of the party that called him. The evidence of Hunt, Huggins, and Cassidy could not have been offered for any other purpose than to rebut the evidence of good character offered by the defense. It could not have been offered to simply contradict the defendant, because, as a witness, he could not be contradicted upon a collateral and irrelevant issue. As to whether the defendant lay in ambush or in wait to shoot Gardner three or four years before the homicide was certainly a collateral and irrelevant issue to the trial of the defendant for the killing of Archibald I. Douglass.

Seventh. That while the real character of the defendant did become a "material inquiry," the court overlooked the fact that the defendant was cross-examined, and Hunt, Huggins, and Cassidy were examined in reply for the sole purpose of establishing an act of violence on the part of the defendant wholly unconnected with the case on trial, to-wit, that defendant lay in ambush to shoot one Gardner three or four years previous to the homicide.

Eighth. That the court has overlooked the fact that every case (and they are very few; they make a very small exception, and not the rule) which seems to contravene the general rule, that evidence of general reputation alone can be offered to establish character, is a case where the witnesses were cross-examined only for the purpose of testing their knowledge of the reputation which they were called to prove, or their bias in favor of the party calling them, and that in none of those cases was the cross-examination for the purpose of proving an independent act of violence against the prisoner.

Ninth. That the court has overlooked the fact that the evidence of Hunt, Huggins, and Cassidy was in reply, and that there is no decided case to be found where a specific act of violence is allowed to be proved in reply to rebut the evidence of general reputation by the defense, but in every decided case where such evidence has been allowed in the court below the appellate court has never failed to reverse the lower court's ruling, and State v. Merriman, 12 S. E. Rep. 619, is the sole authority allowing such evidence to be received.

Tenth. That the court overlooked the fact that the section of volume 3 of the American and English Encyclopedia of Law, on pages 115 and 116, cited by the court lays down the rule broadly that character can only be proved by general reputation, and that evidence "in rebuttal must be of the same kind, whether by cross-examination or by independent testimony."

Eleventh. That the court overlooked the fact that the testimony of Hunt, Huggins, and Cassidy was offered, not for the purpose of establishing the general reputation of the prisoner, but to prove against the prisoner a specific act of violence wholly unconnected with the cause for which he was on trial.

Twelfth. That the court has overlooked the reason of the rule that general reputation alone is admissible to establish character, or rebut proof given of it, to-wit: *First,* that one particular act does not make character; *second,* that if such evidence be allowed, there is no possible chance of meeting it. The defendant Merriman could not possibly have anticipated the attack made upon him by the witnesses Hunt, Huggins, and Cassidy, and could not possibly have been prepared to meet it. The defendant is always presumed to be prepared to defend his general character, but not his individual acts.

Thirteenth. That the court has overlooked the distinction of law that in proving character, and in rebutting proof of it, neither good nor bad acts are admissible. The state could not prove any particular bad act, to rebut the proof given by the defense; and the defendant had no right to prove particular acts of his good conduct to establish his character when it had been assailed.

Fourteenth. That the court has overlooked the fact that the case of Oliver v.

Pate, 43 Ind. 132, cited in the notes to 3 Amer. & Eng. Enc. Law, 116, to sustain the position that the defendant and other witnesses may be cross-examined as to the particular acts of violence of the defendant for the purpose of rebutting proof of general reputation given by the defense, and to sustain the further position that particular acts of violence may be proved in reply by contradicting the defendant, does not sustain that position, but holds precisely the contrary doctrine. The case was an action for damages for malicious prosecution. Verdict for plaintiff. The defendant on the trial offered evidence to impeach the character of the plaintiff. Plaintiff then offered evidence in reply to sustain it. The defendant offered to prove by the cross-examination of these witnesses that the sheriff had once arrested the plaintiff for larceny. The court refused to allow the cross-examination upon this matter, and the supreme court of Indiana sustained the ruling.

Fifteenth. That the court has overlooked the fact that the case of Abernethy v. Com., 101 Pa. St. 322, cited in the notes to 3 Amer. & Eng. Enc. Law, 116, to sustain the position that the defendant and other witnesses may be cross-examined as to particular acts of violence of the defendant for the purpose of rebutting proof of general reputation given by the defense, and to sustain the further position that particular acts of violence may be proved in reply by contradicting the defendant, does not sustain the proposition, but holds the contrary doctrine. That case was an indictment for murder. A witness for defense was offered to prove his good character. "Without objection," the commonwealth was allowed to cross-examine the witness to show that at one time defendant had been in the "reform school." The defendant then offered a witness to prove that defendant, when a boy, went voluntarily to the reform school to procure a maintenance and education, he having been abandoned by his father. The commonwealth's attorney objected, and the courts below rejected the evidence on the ground that the defendant did not object to the cross-examination, and, if he had, the court would have ruled it out. The appellate court reversed this ruling, holding that the evidence was in explanation of what the state had been allowed to prove without objection.

Sixteenth. That the court has overlooked the fact that the cases of Gulerette v. McKinley, 27 Hun, 320, cited in the notes to the same authority, and for the same purpose, does not sustain the position. Neither does the case of People v. Clark, 1 Wheeler, Crim. Cas. 292, cited by the same authority for the same purpose. The first of the above cases was an action for damages for an assault with an attempt to ravish. The defendant offered evidence of the general bad character of the plaintiff. One witness was asked on cross-examination whom he had heard speak of her. He answered, her father. Another witness testified on the cross-examination that he had heard stories about the plaintiff's bad character, but did not tell what they were. Upon the re-examination in reply of these witnesses, the defense proposed to go into particulars, and ask the witnesses what they had heard the parties say about plaintiff. The plaintiff objected. The court sustained the objection, and the appellate court affirmed the ruling. The other case was an indictment for forgery. Witnesses were called to prove good character of defendant. The district attorney offered evidence in rebuttal of good character. The witness said it was had, "and was proceeding to relate the particular facts upon which his opinion was grounded," when the defense objected, and the objection was sustained.

Seventeenth. That the court has overlooked the fact that the very few cases that might seem to be in conflict with the general rule are cases where witnesses were cross-examined to test their knowledge of reputation, and to show their bias, and that in all these cases, even on the cross-examination, the witnesses were confined to general reputation,—what they had heard, not what they themselves knew. It seems to us that such is the rule laid down in the few cases to be found where it was allowed on the cross-examination. Of this class is the case of Leonard v. Allen, 11 Cush. 241, cited in the note to page 116 of 3 Amer. & Eng. Enc. Law, cited by the court. That case was an action for damage for slander. In mitigation of damages, defendant offered evidence (general reputation) to impeach plaintiff's good character. A witness for the defense testified that the plaintiff's character for "moral worth was not good." On the cross-examination by the plaintiff the witness was asked, "What immorality was imputed to him?" and objection was allowed. Another witness, one called by the plaintiff in reply, testified that the community was about equally divided; some speaking well, and some evil, of the plaintiff. The plaintiff, over objection, was then allowed to ask "in what particulars the people spoke against them." It seems to us that the witness in this matter was confined to what the people said, —general reputation; not what one or two or any number said, but "the people." The case of People v. Annis, 13 Mich. 511, cited in the same note, was a prosecution for larceny. Defense offered evidence to impeach character of witness for prosecution. Evidence was given that character of witness for prosecution was "bad." The prosecuting attorney then was allowed, on cross-examination, to inquire of the witness as to whom he heard speak evil of the witness, and what he had heard him say. It seems to us that the inquiry here was confined to what the witness had heard, and, so far as we can see, to what he had generally heard,— reputation. There is nothing in the case to show that the witness testified of his own knowledge. It is perfectly apparent that these witnesses were examined to test their knowledge of reputation, bias, etc., and that it was not for the purpose of proving a specific and particular offense against the party to the record. There are two or three other cases cited in the same note, and they are of the same character. In every case where such cross-examina-

tion has been allowed, the court has placed it in every instance upon the ground that it was for the purpose of testing the knowledge or bias of the witness.

Eighteenth. That the court has overlooked the fact that the overwhelming weight of the decided cases cited in the section on character in 3 Amer. & Eng. Enc. Law, as well as all approved text-writers on the subject, lay down the rule broadly that evidence of particular acts is inadmissible to rebut proof of good character, even when elicited on the cross-examination. Of such is the case of Brownell v. People, 38 Mich. 736. Chief Justice Campbell, delivering the opinion, says: "It was entirely inadmissible, in answer to good general reputation of the prisoner, to receive evidence of an alleged act of violence against another person than Bailey at a former time and different place. The prisoner could not be prepared to meet any such testimony or explain it. and its introduction might seriously prejudice the jury." Of such, too, is the case of Engleman v. State, 2 Ind. 91. The court says: "On the trial the defendant called witnesses to his general good character. The state was permitted on cross-examination, over the objection of the defendant, to prove particular acts of his bad conduct. This was wrong. The defendant could not prove particular acts of his good, nor the state of his bad, conduct." Of such, also, is the case of State v. Gordon, 3 Iowa, 415. Chief Justice Wright says: "It only remains to inquire whether it was correct to permit the state, on cross-examination of a witness who was called as to the good character of the defendant, to go into proof of particular acts or difficulties on his part: and in permitting this, we think, the court erred. It is true that in the cross-examination of witnesses the court, in the exercise of its discretion, may permit great latitude; but we apprehend that it cannot be so far extended as to allow the introduction of illegal and improper testimony. The rule permitting this latitude is rather for the purpose of testing the memory and credibility of the witness than to enable the party to get before the jury testimony which would be inadmissible if offered in direct examination of his own witness. In this case it appears that the defendant sought to prove his general good character as a quiet and peaceable citizen. This he had a right to do. The prosecution then, against his objection, asked the witness if he knew of instances in which defendant had been engaged in difficulties with individuals, and the state was permitted to go into an examination of particular instances of difficulties with others. This would have been clearly improper if offered by the state as direct testimony, and we cannot conceive it to be any less so from the fact that it was drawn out on cross-examination. It is evidence of character which is admissible, which of course is to be confined to the trial of character that is in issue. But the examination must be confined to the general character or reputation, and neither can ask questions as to particular facts or difficulties." Of this kind of cases the law books and reports of the state and England contain many.

Nineteenth. That the court has overlooked the fact that the testimony of the witness A. J. Smith, which was ruled out on the trial, was in direct reply and explanation of the testimony of this witness brought out by the state.

PER CURIAM. The court, after a careful examination and consideration of this petition, has reached the conclusion that no material fact or principle of law was overlooked or misunderstood in preparing the opinion heretofore filed, and therefore there is no ground for the rehearing asked for. It is ordered that this petition be dismissed, and that the stay of the *remittitur* heretofore granted be revoked.

BURNS v. GOWER.

(Supreme Court of South Carolina. June 17, 1891.)

APPEAL FROM JUSTICE OF THE PEACE—QUESTIONS RAISED BY EXCEPTIONS.

Code S. C. § 358, providing that appeals from trial justices to the circuit court shall be heard upon all the papers in the case, including testimony taken in writing on the trial, "and the grounds of exception made," confines the circuit court, on the hearing, to the consideration of such questions only as are raised by the exceptions.

Appeal from common pleas circuit court of Greenville county; JAMES F. IZLAR, Judge.

Action by Amanda Burns against T. C. Gower. Judgment for plaintiff. Defendant appeals.

Shuman & Mayfield and *Wells & Orr,* for appellants. *Nix, Dill & Nix,* for respondent.

McIVER, J. The plaintiff brought this action before a trial justice to recover the value of certain articles of personal property which she alleged had unlawfully been taken from her by defendant. The defense was that the articles in question had been seized under a distress warrant issued to enforce the payment of rent in arrear of a certain dwelling-house in the city of Greenville, which defendant alleged had been leased from him by the plaintiff. But two questions seem to have been raised at the trial before the trial justice: (1) Whether the plaintiff had in fact made the agreement; (2) whether she had the power to make such a contract, she being a married woman at the time. The trial justice found, as a matter of fact, that the alleged contract was made by the plaintiff; but he held, as matter of law, that she, being a married woman, had no power to make the contract, and he therefore rendered judgment in favor of the plaintiff. From this judgment the defendant appealed to the circuit court upon numerous grounds set out in the "case," all of which, however, so far as this appeal is concerned, substantially make the single question whether the trial justice erred in holding that the plaintiff had no power to make the contract in question. This appeal was heard by his honor, Judge IZLAR, upon the testimony taken by the trial justice, his report of the case, (all of which is set out in the "case,") and the defendant's exceptions, there being no exception by either party to the finding of fact by the trial justice that the agreement for the rent of the premises was made by the plaintiff. Upon the hearing of this appeal the judge granted an order in these words: "That the finding of the trial justice be confirmed, and that the appeal be dismissed." The defendant, supposing, as he says, that the circuit judge had affirmed the findings of the trial justice, both of fact and law, gave notice of appeal to this court, upon numerous grounds set out in the record, which, however, practically make the same question raised by his appeal from the judgment of the trial justice. But, when the case was submitted to the circuit judge for settlement, he incorporated therein certain amendments, which showed that the views of the circuit judge had been entirely misapprehended by the appellant, and that the circuit judge, while holding that the contract was such a one as the plaintiff, though a married woman, was capable of making, yet, at the same time, he was satisfied that the testimony failed to show that the contract was made by the plaintiff, and for that reason only he had affirmed the judgment of the trial justice, while not concurring in the views taken by that officer. When this amendment was made, defendant applied to and obtained from this court leave to file additional exceptions, upon the ground that the case, as amended, presented different questions from those which arose out of the case as originally proposed. These additional exceptions are set out in the record, but, as they practically present only two questions, they need not be repeated here. These questions are (1) whether the circuit judge erred in reversing the finding of fact by the trial justice that the agreement for renting the premises was made by the plaintiff, and not by her husband; (2) whether the circuit judge erred in considering that question of fact at all, in the absence of any exception to such finding, or any ground of appeal from the judgment of the trial justice, raising that question.

We will consider the second question first, for, if there was error on the part of the circuit judge in considering whether the testimony was sufficient to sustain the finding of the trial justice that the agreement for renting was in fact made by the plaintiff, then the first question cannot arise. Section 358 of the Code, as adopted in 1882, provides: "When a judgment is rendered by a trial justice, * * * the appeal shall be to the circuit court of the county wherein the judgment was rendered. The said appeal shall be heard by the circuit court upon all the papers in the case, including the testimony on the trial, which shall be taken down in writing, and signed by the witnesses, and the grounds of exception made, without the examination of witnesses in court." It will be observed that the Code of 1882 makes a very different provision, in the section just quoted, for the hearing of an appeal from the judgment of a trial justice by the circuit court from that prescribed by the Code as originally adopted, which practically provided that upon such appeal the case should be tried *de novo* by the circuit court, and therefore, under that system, the question now presented could not arise. Now, however, such an appeal must be heard "upon all the papers in the case, including the testimony on the trial, which shall be taken down in writing, and signed by the witnesses, *and the grounds of exception made.*" The practical question, therefore, is whether the words italicized in the clause just quoted have the effect of confining the circuit court, in hearing such an appeal, to the consideration of such questions as are raised by the exceptions. If that is not the effect of those words, it is difficult, if not impossible, to conceive of any reason for the insertion of those words; and under the well-settled rule of statutory construction, that a court is bound, if possible, to give some place and effect to every word found in a statute, the conclusion must be that the words in question were intended to limit the power of the circuit court to the consideration of such questions as are presented by the exceptions. It is manifest that the legislature, in adopting the section as it now stands, intended to provide a different system for the hearing of appeals from an inferior court by the circuit court from that previously established by the Code as originally adopted. If the only change intended was that in hearing such an appeal the testimony taken down in writing at the trial before the inferior court should be used, instead of examining the witnesses in the circuit court, as in a trial *de novo*, then the provision that the appeal shall be heard, among other things, upon "the grounds of exception made," becomes absolutely meaningless, and those words would have no force or effect whatever. In effect, the present provision is that the appeal "shall be heard" upon three things: (1) All the papers in the case; (2) the testimony taken in writing at the trial below; (3) the grounds of exception made. Hence it seems to us that it would be just as admissible for the circuit court, in hearing the appeal, to use papers other than those in the case, or to hear other testimony than that taken at the trial, as to consider questions other than those made by the exceptions.

It is true that section 363 of the Code does provide that, "upon hearing the appeal, the appellate court shall give judgment according to the justice of the case, without regard to technical errors and effects" which do not affect the merits;" but we cannot regard this matter as technical. It is certainly a very material matter that parties should be advised of the nature of the case which the court is called upon to determine, and of the questions therein involved. In an appeal, those questions are presented by the exceptions, and in this case it is manifest that the only question presented by the defendant's appeal from the judgment of the trial justice was the legal question as to the power of the plaintiff to make the contract of lease. Neither party had any reason to suppose that any other question would be considered by the court, and, for all that we know,

neither party was prepared to discuss, or did discuss, any other question. So that, if the appellate court should undertake to decide the case upon any other question, both parties would be taken by surprise, and the losing party would have just cause to complain that he had been condemned without an opportunity of being heard. It is true that neither party was in a condition to raise by appeal the question whether the trial justice had erred in his finding of fact as to who made the contract of lease. The defendant could not do so, because the decision of that question was in his favor; and the plaintiff could not, because the judgment was in her favor; but, in analogy to the well-settled practice in appeals to this court, (Weinges v. Cash, 15 S. C. 44,) she might, if she had so desired, have raised the question by giving the notice indicated in that case; but she was not bound to do so. That not having been done, it seems to us that the only question before the circuit judge was as to whether the trial justice had erred in his conclusion of law that the contract of lease was not such a contract as a married woman had the power to make, and having determined that there was error in such conclusion, his only course was either to reverse the judgment absolutely, or to order a new trial, if he thought, as he manifestly did, that there was also error in the finding of fact to which the trial justice had applied what he regarded an erroneous principle of law, as that seems to be the only legal mode by which a judgment could be rendered "according to the justice of the case." Believing, as we do, that the only proper solution of this somewhat anomalous case is to order a new trial, without prejudice, we have been careful to avoid any indication of opinion as to either of the questions mentioned above; for it is quite clear that, under the case as amended, the question of law does not properly arise, under this appeal, as the amendment shows that the circuit judge decided that question in favor of appellant; and, as we have seen, the question of fact was not properly before the circuit judge, and certainly is not before us, even if we assume that we could take jurisdiction of such a question in a case like this. The judgment of this court is that the judgment of the circuit court be reversed, without prejudice, and that the case be remanded to that court, with instructions to order a new trial of all the issues, both of law and fact, in the trial justice court.

McGowan, J., concurs.

FERGUSON *et al.* v. HARRISON *et al.*

(*Supreme Court of South Carolina.* June 17, 1891.)

REFERENCE — WHEN MAY BE ORDERED — PRESUMPTIONS — APPEALABLE ORDER.

1. Code Civil Proc. S. C. § 293, provides that the court may, upon application, or of its own motion, except where the investigation will require the decision of difficult questions of law, direct a reference, "where the trial of an issue of fact shall require the examination of a long account on either side." *Held* that, in an action to set aside a deed and mortgage upon the grounds of fraud, where the court heard statements of

counsel upon the nature of the case, which statements are not in the record, and made an order of reference, it will be presumed, upon appeal, that the statements showed that there was a long account involved.

2. Code Civil Proc. S. C. § 11, provides that the supreme court shall have exclusive jurisdiction to review upon appeal "any intermediate judgment, order, or decree involving the merits in actions commenced in the courts of common pleas and general sessions." *Held*, that an order of reference, in an action to set aside a deed and mortgage upon the ground of fraud, is not appealable, when the pleadings show that the questions raised were purely equitable in character, and it appears that the order was made after full statements by counsel.

Appeal from common pleas circuit court of Greenville county; JAMES ALDRICH, Judge.

Perry & Heyward and *Westmoreland & Haynsworth*, for appellants. *Wells & Orr*, for respondents.

McIVER, J. The plaintiffs, as existing creditors of the defendant John H. Harrison, brought this action to set aside an alleged voluntary deed to his wife, and also certain mortgages made by the wife to the defendants Samuel E. Harrison and Richard Harrison, brothers of said John H. Harrison, under the allegation that the same were made with intent to hinder, delay, and defraud the creditors of John H. Harrison. The defendants answered, denying all fraud, and alleging that the deed to the wife was made upon the understanding that she would secure the two brothers in the claims they held against her husband, and was not, in fact, without consideration, and the mortgagees demanded that their mortgages should be foreclosed. The case being at issue and on the docket for three terms, when it was called for trial, at the third term, the defendants John H. Harrison and his wife moved for a continuance, upon the ground of the sickness of some of their children, though no affidavits to that effect were presented. The motion to continue was resisted by the plaintiffs, who insisted "that some progress should be made, as this was the third term on the calendar, and these defendants were destroying the value of the mortgaged premises, already scant security, by cutting, sawing, and selling off the lumber." An order of reference was then suggested by plaintiffs' attorneys. The questions involved were then stated by the respective counsel. Plaintiffs moved for an order of reference. No written notice of this motion or affidavit in support thereof was submitted, the motion being based upon what was stated in open court. The counsel for John H. and Nannie E. Harrison stated that they objected to a reference. The attorneys for Samuel E. and Richard Harrison neither consented nor objected to the order of reference, but stated that they were willing to unite with the other defendants in any course they might pursue. Judge ALDRICH stated that it was such a case as was referable under the Code; that the plaintiffs were entitled to a trial, but, under the circumstances, he would not force them to an immediate trial; that he would, during the term, either try the case himself, or re-

fer it, if these defendants did not wish to leave their children. The attorneys for John H. and Nannie E. Harrison said that their clients did not wish to come away from their children again, again urged a continuance, and refused to consent to a reference. Thereupon the judge stated that he would not continue the case, and passed an order of reference in the following words: "On hearing the pleadings in this case, it is ordered that it be referred to the master to take the testimony in this case, and report the same to the court, together with his conclusions of law and fact."

From this order defendants appeal, upon the several grounds set out in the record, which impute error to the circuit judge in granting this order, for the several reasons suggested therein, which will be hereinafter stated and considered. While there is no such statement in the record as prepared for argument here, yet the fact is conceded, in the brief presented by appellants' counsel, that respondents' counsel served on appellants a notice "that they will ask the court to sustain the order upon the ground that the same is not appealable," and hence we are at liberty, as we would not otherwise be, to consider that question.

Section 11 of the Code specifies the cases in which an appeal may be taken to this court, as well from a final judgment as an intermediate order. It is very clear that the order under consideration is not appealable under subdivision 3 of that section, for that relates to an order made in a special proceeding. It is equally clear that it does not fall under subdivision 2, for that relates to orders which must not only affect a substantial right, but must, in effect, determine the action, etc., and, as no such effect can be attributed to the order in question, it certainly cannot be appealable under that subdivision. Carlington v. Copeland, 25 S. C. 41. If, therefore, it is appealable at all, it must be under subdivision 1 of that section, which gives the right of appeal from an intermediate order "involving the merits." What is the precise meaning of the words just quoted has never, so far as we know, been distinctly determined. But in the case of Blakeley v. Frazier, 11 S. C. 122, it was held that whenever a substantial right of a party to an action, material to obtaining a judgment, is denied, this subdivision of section 11 secures the right of appeal to this court, and, as we suppose the mode of trial, whether by the court, by a referee or master, or by a jury, is a matter material to obtaining a judgment, it follows that, where a party is denied the mode of trial to which he is entitled by law, and required by an order to submit to some other mode of trial, such order is appealable. While, therefore, every order of reference is not appealable, yet there are some which are. To determine, therefore, whether the order in question is appealable, it is necessary to inquire, as in Du Pont v. Du Bos, (S. C.) 11 S. E. Rep. 1073, whether any substantial, legal right of the appellants has been denied by referring all the issues in the action to the master. The first objection to the order raised by the grounds of appeal is that it was granted without previous notice that such order would be applied for. We have not been cited to any law, and we do not know of any, which requires notice in a case like the present.

The second objection is that "no sufficient showing was made as to whether or no it was such a cause as could be referred to the master without consent of all parties." The circuit judge had before him the pleadings in the cause, copies of which are set out in the "case," and they were quite sufficient to show what was the nature of the case,—that it was one of purely equitable cognisance, involving no issues which either party had the right to try by jury; and hence we see nothing in this objection. Bouland v. Carpin, 27 S. C. 235, 3 S. E. Rep. 219. Besides, it is stated in the case that the questions involved were stated by the respective counsel; and, surely, with the pleadings before him, and these statements of counsel, the circuit judge had the fullest means of ascertaining the nature of the case, and the character of the issues involved.

The next objection seems to be that the judge erred in referring the issues of law as well as of fact to the master, even if it were a proper case for reference without consent. The Code certainly contains no such limitation on the right to order a reference. On the contrary, section 292 expressly provides that "all or any of the issues in the action, whether of fact or law or both, may be referred," etc., where the parties consent, or, in certain specified cases, presently to be considered, when the parties do not consent. We suppose, therefore, that the real point of this objection will be found in the third ground of appeal, where it is claimed that, inasmuch as the trial would "require the decision of difficult questions of law," the circuit judge had no power to refer any of the issues under the special exception contained in section 293. But whether the decision of difficult questions of law would be required was a matter for the circuit judge to determine, and which we must assume he did determine, before granting the order. Assuming, then, that he did determine that there was no such difficult questions of law to be decided as would bring the case within the exception contained in section 293, we must say that we see no error in such determination. So far as we can perceive, from an examination of the pleadings, the issues presented are mainly issues of fact.

It is contended, however, that a circuit judge has no right to order a reference of any case to the master or referee without the consent of the parties, except in two specified cases: "(1) Where the trial of an issue of fact shall require the examination of a long account on either side, in which case the referee may be directed to hear and decide the whole issue, or to report upon any specific question of fact involved therein. (2) Where the taking of an account shall be necessary for the information of the court, before judgment, or for carrying a judgment or order into effect," etc. Code, § 293. And it is insisted that no such accounting was necessary

in this case. Whether such was the fact was a matter necessarily to be determined by the circuit judge, in the first instance, at least; and if necessary we would assume in the absence of any evidence to the contrary that the circuit judge had before him enough to satisfy him of that fact. Cartee v. Spence, 24 S. C. 550. Now, he had before him not only the pleadings, which we also have, but, in addition thereto, the statements of the respective counsel as to the questions involved, which statements are not before us; and it may be that they, in connection with the pleadings, were sufficient to satisfy him that the taking of a long account would be necessary to ascertain the true state of the indebtedness alleged to exist on the part of John H. Harrison to his two brothers. At all events, we could not undertake to say that such was not the fact. This case is distinguished from Smith v. Bryce, 17 S. C. 588; for there the action was upon a plain money demand, in which the parties were clearly entitled to a trial by jury, while here the action is one of purely equitable cognisance, in which the right of trial by jury is not and cannot be claimed. While, therefore, we are of opinion that, even in an equity cause, the circuit judge has no power, without the consent of the parties, to refer the issues to a master or referee for trial, (though he may order the testimony taken and reported by a referee,—McSween v. McCown, 21 S. C. 371,) unless the case falls under subdivision 1 or 2 or 3 of section 293 of the Code, yet in this case we must assume that the circuit judge had before him sufficient to show that the case did fall under one of those subdivisions. It is true that the case of Pelzer v. Hughes, 27 S. C. 418, 3 S. E. Rep. 781, does contain some expressions which, unless read in connection with the point there made, might imply that the issues in any equity cause may be referred to the master, without the consent of the parties; but when read in connection with the point there made, as they should be, there is no room for any such implication. The only point made there was as to whether the defendant was entitled to a trial by jury, and can have no reference to his right to a trial by the court. Here, however, appellants insist upon their right to a trial by the court, and do not claim a right to a trial by a jury; and hence we do not think that case applies to the present.

But, in addition to what we have said, it seems to us that the order of reference appealed from may well be regarded as an order by consent. For this reason we have been careful to copy in full from the case the statement of what occurred in the court below just before the order in question was passed. From that statement it seems to us that defendants were offered the alternative either to go to trial at once or accept a reference. The motion to continue was addressed to the discretion of the court, which could have either refused it absolutely, or granted it upon terms; and, practically, it was granted upon the condition that the case should be referred to the master. The fact that the attorneys for appellants, after being offered the alternative, still "urged a continuance, and refused to consent to a reference," cannot avail them; for, after having accepted a continuance, which was only granted upon a condition, they cannot now be permitted to repudiate the condition upon which their motion was granted. It seems to us, therefore, that we cannot, in any view of the case, say that there was any error in granting the order of reference. The judgment of this court is that the order appealed from be affirmed.

McGOWAN, J., concurs.

LANE v. LANE.

(Supreme Court of Georgia. May 27, 1891.)

LIMITATION OF ACTIONS—SUIT AGAINST GUARDIAN —FRAUD.

1. An action against one formerly plaintiff's guardian, and administrator of his father, for alleged fraudulent misappropriation of money received in such capacities, is barred by limitations where the administration was closed 26 years, and plaintiff reached his majority 18 years, prior to the commencement thereof.

2. Plaintiff can recover lands not administered, but fraudulently merged into the administrator's estate, and mesne profits thereon, since no prescriptive title can ripen from a possession originating in fraud.

Error from superior court, Emanuel county; ROGER GAMBLE, Judge.

Bill by E. L. Lane against B. S. Lane to recover money and land alleged to have been misappropriated by the latter as administrator and guardian.

Williams & Brennan, T. H. Potter, and *Dell & Wade,* for plaintiff in error. *Twiggs & Verdery* and *Edward Hunter,* for defendant in error.

SIMMONS, J. Before the passage of the procedure act of 1887, E. S. Lane filed a bill in the superior court of Emanuel county against B. L. Lane, making, in brief, the following case: About May 22, 1854, complainant's father died intestate, leaving as his sole heirs complainant and his mother. Defendant qualified as administrator of the estate, and was also appointed guardian of complainant. The estate consisted of a large amount of personal property, and various tracts of land situate in Emanuel and other counties. Defendant realized large sums of money from the proceeds of the personalty and the sales and hire of slaves, and made false and fraudulent returns to the court of ordinary as to his disposition of the same. At the September term, 1861, of the court of ordinary, he obtained a letter of dismission as administrator of the estate, but procured the same by reason of said fraudulent returns and other gross misrepresentations of fact to said court of ordinary. Some of the tracts of land belonging to the estate of complainant's father, and mentioned in the bill, were never sold or otherwise administered by defendant, but he merged them into his own estate, converted them to his own use, and is now in the possession and enjoyment of the same. In January, 1873, when complainant was within one year of his majority, he had an interview with defendant, who was his uncle, and for whom he entertained the utmost veneration and

love. In this interview, defendant falsely told him that the estate of his father was overwhelmingly in debt; that there was nothing coming to him from the estate; and that the court-house of Emanuel county was burned during the war, and all the records destroyed. Complainant was raised on the farm of his step-father, had very few educational advantages, and grew up in profound ignorance of his rights. Having the utmost confidence in the integrity and truthfulness of defendant, complainant believed his statements, and did not, until the early part of the year 1887, learn the true history of the administration and guardianship, or have any knowledge of the gross frauds and deception practiced upon him by defendant. The bill prays that the judgment of the court of ordinary, granting defendant a discharge as administrator, be annulled and set aside; that defendant be compelled to come to a just accounting with complainant concerning all matters involved, both in the administration and guardianship; that complainant have a decree in his favor for large sums of money due to him by defendant in both capacities; and that defendant be compelled to restore to complainant his undivided half interest in all the lands of the estate converted by defendant to his own use, together with the rents thereof. A motion to dismiss the bill, on the ground "that no legal cause of action under the law was set forth," was sustained by the court below; and this is the error complained of. Strictly construed, the terms of this motion would not cover the statute of limitations; but in the argument here counsel for both parties treated it as embracing that defense, and we rule on it accordingly.

1. So far as this bill seeks to bring defendant to account for his actings and doings as administrator and guardian, and to recover money alleged to be due to complainant by the defendant in both or either of these capacities, the case is hopelessly barred by the statute of limitations. Complainant attained his majority in the year 1874, but waited about 13 years before making a demand on defendant either for information or a settlement, or bringing his suit. It is manifest, from the allegations of the bill itself, that complainant has been guilty of the grossest negligence and inattention in looking after his rights. The exercise of the slightest diligence would have enabled him to discover at any time the existence of the frauds alleged to have been perpetrated by the defendant; and no sufficient reason appears in the bill why he could not and should not have long since ascertained the truth and brought his suit. We deem the proposition that complainant is barred by the statute of limitations, so far as this branch of the case is concerned, too plain to require further argument or elucidation.

2. Although the lands alleged to have been converted by the defendant to his own use are very loosely described, yet, taking all the allegations of the bill and exhibits thereto together, the description is sufficient to identify them, and, by amendment, this description may be made

more full and complete. There was no special demurrer to so much of the bill as seeks a recovery of the land on the ground that complainant had a remedy by suit at law, or for any other reason, but only a general motion to dismiss, as above stated; and there is enough in the bill, we think, to retain it in court as an action for the recovery of complainant's interest in such of these lands as are situate in Emanuel county, and are still in defendant's possession, together with mesne profits. If defendant's possession originated in fraud, as the bill alleges, no prescriptive title could ripen in his favor against the complainant; and, while the bill does not purport to be an action of ejectment, the allegations and prayers thereof are broad enough, in our judgment, to allow the case to proceed for the purpose indicated.

We reverse the judgment of the court below dismissing the bill, with directions that leave be granted to complainant to so amend his bill as to make it complete in all respects necessary to recover a half interest in the unadministered lands of his father's estate lying in Emanuel county and still in defendant's possession, as well as such rents for the same as he could recover in an action of ejectment. Judgment reversed, with directions.

BRITT v. RAWLINGS.

(Supreme Court of Georgia. April 20, 1891.)

CONSTRUCTION OF WILL — NATURE OF ESTATE.

Code Ga. § 2454, provides that the word "lend," when occurring in a will, must be construed to mean "give," unless the context requires its restricted meaning. *Held,* that the words, "I loan to my wife" certain land "in lieu of dower," convey only a life-estate, when occurring in an item wherein testator also "gives and bequeaths" certain slaves to his wife, "to her and her heirs forever," and "gives and bequeaths" to her certain perishable property "in fee-simple."

Error from superior court, Washington county; JAMES K. HINES, Judge.

Rogers & Porter, for plaintiff in error. *Harris & Rawlings, A. F. Daly,* and *Evans & Evans,* for defendant in error.

SIMMONS, J. The third item of the will of William Tanner was as follows: "I give and bequeath to my beloved wife, Louise Tanner, one negro woman, Elcy, and her five children, Malinda, Jincy, Isaiah, Eady, and Sarah Ella, and their future increase, to her and her heirs forever. I also loan to my said wife all that portion of my land, embracing my homestead, lying between the creek by William Whiddon to the Fenn's Bridge road from Sandersville, containing about three hundred acres, more or less. This land I loan her in lieu of a dower. I also give and bequeath to my said wife, in fee simple, an equal portion of my perishable property with my children, to her and her heirs forever." Upon the trial of this case below, the court held that this item conveyed an absolute fee-simple estate in the lands therein described to Mrs. Tanner, the testator's widow, and accordingly directed a verdict for the plaintiff, who was an heir of Mrs. Tanner, and claimed under her by virtue of

this will. A new trial was granted, for the reason, no doubt, that the court's construction of the will was wrong. We think the court erred in his ruling at the trial, and did right in recalling the same. Section 2454 of the Code provides that the word "lend," when occurring in a will, will be construed to mean "give," unless the context requires its restricted meaning. We have no difficulty in arriving at the conclusion that in this particular will the context does require that the word "loan" should be held not to mean "give." It is a cardinal and familiar doctrine that, in the interpretation of wills, the "intention of the testator shall be diligently sought for, and effect given to the same so far as may be consistent with the rules of law." Code, § 2456; Weed v. Knorr, 77 Ga. 644, 1 S. E. Rep. 167, and cases there cited. It will be observed that, in disposing of the slaves mentioned in the item of the will above quoted, the testator gave and bequeathed them to his wife, "to her and her heirs forever." In the same item he also gave and bequeathed to his wife a share of his perishable property in fee-simple. It appears, then, that the gifts of the slaves and the share in the perishable property were plainly and unequivocally absolute; but in this same item, in disposing of his land, the testator uses the word "loan," and expressly says that the land is loaned to his wife in lieu of a dower, which he unquestionably knew was only a life-estate. It is difficult to conceive why he should have used these different expressions in relation to the several kinds of property disposed of by this item, unless he intended that his wife should have the slaves and other personalty absolutely, and the land only for life. We are entirely satisfied that this was the intention of the testator, and that such intention is easily and unmistakably to be gathered from the will itself. It follows that the heirs of Mrs. Tanner had no title to the land in dispute, but that the title to the same was in the defendant, who bought the land at a public sale, lawfully and regularly made by the administrator *cum testamento annexo* of William Tanner's estate, after Mrs. Tanner's death. The judgment of the court below is therefore affirmed.

BERNSTEIN v. CLARK.

(Supreme Court of Georgia. April 20, 1891.)

CERTIORARI TO JUSTICE—APPEAL.

Where there are issues of fact, and the amount involved is less than $50, *certiorari* will not lie to a judgment of a justice of the peace. Appeal is the proper remedy.

Error from superior court, De Kalb county; RICHARD H. CLARK, Judge.

J. N. Glenn, for plaintiff in error. *John S. Candler,* for defendant in error.

LUMPKIN, J. From the judgment of a justice of the peace, rendered in a suit upon an account for less than $50, there being issues of fact involved, a *certiorari* will not lie, but there should be an appeal to a jury in the justice's court. Thompson v. Dodd, 84 Ga. 264, 10 S. E. Rep. 739; Greenwood v. Furniture Factory, 13 S. E. Rep. 128, (last term.) Judgment reversed.

MILLER v. MANN et al.

(Supreme Court of Appeals of Virginia. July
2, 1891.)

SALE UNDER TRUST-DEED—VALIDITY.

Code Va. § 2442, provides that the trustee
in a deed given to secure debts shall, when required by any creditor secured, after the debt
due him has become payable and default has
been made, sell the property, or so much thereof
as may be necessary, at public auction, having
first given reasonable notice, etc. *Held,* that a
sale made as thus required is valid, and the fact
that the trustee sold only half of the land will
not be presumed to be an abuse of discretion,
when it was sufficient to satisfy the debt, and
the debtor made no request that he sell a greater
amount.

Action for partition by J. M. Miller,
against Henry A. Mann and Milton G.
Mann and others. From a decree for defendants, plaintiff appeals.

Routh & Stuart and *F. S. Blair,* for
appellant. *Dan'l Trigg,* for appellees.

LACY, J. This is an appeal from a decree of the circuit court of Washington
county, rendered on the 26th day of February, 1889. The bill was filed in this
cause by the appellant, J. M. Miller, in
June, 1885, representing that he had become the purchaser of a tract of land at
a sale thereof by a trustee, regularly and
duly made after due notice and due advertisement; that the land was conveyed
in trust to the trustee to secure the payment of a bond of $600, duly executed by
Henry A. Mann (the father) and Milton
G. Mann (the son) to Henry Roberts, their
creditor, and L. T. Cosby was named
trustee therein, and duly accepted the
trust, and signed the deed as trustee;
and that there was also a second tract of
land conveyed in the said deed to secure
the said debt, about which there appears
to be no controversy here. The tract of
land situated in Poor valley, in the county of Washington, was sold under the
trust-deed, and purchased by the said appellant. The bill sets forth that this tract
of land, which contained 300 acres, was
formerly the property of Charles Mann,
deceased, who was the father of the said
Henry A. Mann and the grandfather of
the said Milton G. Mann. That there
were eight devisees of the said Charles
Mann, deceased, and that Henry A. Mann
purchased the interest of all of them except
a grandchild, one Pattie Lucenda Mann,
but that, being about to go into bankruptcy at that time, the said Henry A.
Mann caused the said land to be by his
brothers and sisters (he himself joining
therein) conveyed by deed to his son, Milton G. Mann. That said deed was not recorded, but held subject to the order of
Henry A. Mann, duly acknowledged by a
third person. That both Henry A. Mann
and Milton G. Mann executed the deed to
the trustee, Cosby, to secure the debt due
to Roberts. That after he had become
the purchaser of this land he received a
deed from the trustee, having paid the
purchase money down, which was $600,
the amount of the Roberts debt secured
therein. That it had not been necessary
to sell the whole tract of land to pay the
$600 due thereon, but that the trustee had

v.13s.E.no.13—22

divided the same, and he had become the
purchaser of one piece of the land. That
he had received and held possession of the
deed from the children of Charles Mann,
deceased, to Milton G. Mann; it having
been delivered to him by Henry A. Mann,
who had retained control of it, as the sale
to Milton G. Mann was merely formal.
That both of these, Henry A. Mann and
Milton G. Mann, were now demanding
this deed, and both claiming to be the
owner of the land in question, whereas
this constituted a cloud upon his title, and,
moreover, the said Pattie Lucenda Mann,
having never parted with her interest in
the said land, was the owner of one-eighth
of the same, whereas he, as the purchaser
under the aforesaid trust-deed, was the
owner of one-half of the whole; and prayed
that the land might be partitioned between him, giving him his one-half, according to his purchase, and to Pattie Lucenda Mann her one-eighth out of the
residue, and the rest allotted to Henry A.
Mann or to Milton G. Mann, as the right
might appear. Milton G. Mann answered
this bill, and set forth that the facts in the
bill detailed leading up to the sale by the
trustee, Cosby, to Miller were true, and
adding that when the deed was made to
him he executed and delivered to Henry A.
Mann his note for $1.600, which had been
given by his father to Miller along with
the deed. In his answer he contended
that the sale was made on a most inclement day, at the court-house of the county, remote from the land sold, and but
few persons were present at the sale;
charged that the land had been divided
by the trustee, at the suggestion of Miller,
who had then become the purchaser of the
best part of the farm, and had left only
what was worthless for him, and that
this was a fraud upon his rights: he denied any fraudulent intent on the part of
either Henry A. Mann or himself; and
prayed that the sale to Miller, as set forth
above, might be set aside as fraudulent
and unfair; that inquiries be made about
title, and priorities of liens ascertained,
before any future sale. Lucenda Mann,
being an infant, answered by guardian *ad
litem;* and on the 14th of May, 1886, the
court rendered a decree in the cause to the
following effect, after bringing the cause
on upon what has been mentioned, and
the order of publication, duly published
and posted against Lucenda Mann, as
follows, to-wit: "On consideration whereof, the court doth adjudge that complainant, Miller, under purchase from trustee,
Cosby, acquired any title held by H. A.
Mann and Milton G. Mann to the land so
purchased by him; and it is further adjudged, ordered, and decreed that L. T.
Cosby do, as special commissioner, hear
proof of and report to court whether or
not the deed from Charles Mann's devisees
to M. G. Mann was delivered to M. G.
Mann as and for his deed." The commissioner reported that "your commissioner
is of opinion that said deed was delivered
to M. G. Mann as and for his deed," and
returned the deposition upon which his report was based. In October following, a
petition was filed in the cause, by leave of
the court, praying for a rehearing of the

decree rendered at the May term, aforesaid; which objected to the trustee, Cosby, as a suitable person to take the account ordered; that the bill was demurrable; and suggesting various defects in the bill and in the proceedings. The answer to this bill set forth, among other things, that the special commissioner, Cosby, was not only not objected to, but that his appointment was consented to, and that he was never objected to until he made his report against the defendant. On the 22d day of February, 1887, another decree was rendered in the cause, by which Cosby was set aside as commissioner, and the deposition taken by him suppressed, and the same ordered to be retaken, and referred it to F. T. Barr, who was appointed a commissioner to ascertain who has been in possession of the land devised by Charles Mann, deceased, since his death, and who is chargeable with rents to plaintiff, Pattie L. Mann, and for what time, and what amount of rents, and if those in possession thereof have placed permanent improvements thereon; what these improvements now add to the value of the land, and by whom they were placed there; what waste or injury, if any, has been done to the same by those in possession, and by whom the damages were caused thereby. And the commissioner will ascertain whether land has advanced in value since the 30th of April, 1881, and, if so, what is the extent of said advance. And the commissioner will also ascertain whether or not the deed of said devisees of said Charles Mann to said Milton G. Mann was ever consummated by delivery. Said commissioner to make report to court. And leave was given to the defendants to file a cross-bill against the plaintiff, James M. Miller, to set up any fraud or any other matter going to the validity of the deed of Cosby, trustee, to said Miller, under which said Miller claims. This cross-bill was filed accordingly, set up substantially what has gone before, and bringing out the fact that James M. Miller was the son-in-law of Henry A. Mann, and had lived as a tenant on a part of this land, and had been put there by Henry A. Mann with the consent of Milton G. Mann. And to this Miller made answer, denying all fraud or collusion on his part with Cosby or anybody else. As to the sale, he said that the beneficiary required the trustee to sell under the deed. The land was advertised for two courts, being at one court adjourned over, to gratify the debtor; to the next court, to give him the opportunity to raise money to pay the debt. That on the second court-day the debtors, neither of them, paid any part of the debt, nor did they put in an appearance. That complainant's son was in town, and yet absented himself from the court-house and from the sale. That a large crowd was present, and the day not specially inclement for the winter season. That since his purchase he has improved his land a good deal by honest toil, fencing, clearing, and building some, and it is more productive; whereas the residue of the land has been left severely alone, and his land, being thus improved, is much sought after by his

generous relatives, "who toil not, neither do they spin." The commissioner, Barr, on the 16th of May, 1888, made his report, and returned the accounts ordered. "*First.* Since the death of Charles Mann, in 1866, the lands have been in the possession, first, of H. A. Mann down to May 6, 1872, when M. G. Mann, by virtue of his deed, came into possession of these lands, except that Miller has since his purchase held possession of the lands he purchased from Cosby, trustee. *Secondly.* That H. A. Mann and M. G. Mann and J. M. Miller are severally liable for rents to Pattie L. Mann, and returned an account of this. *Thirdly.* That the improvements put on the land by Miller on his portion constitute the only improvements that add materially to the value of the land; that these add $250.00 to the value of the land; that the waste on the H. A. & M. G. Mann part of the land, when taken together, counterbalances, when the whole tract is considered, the improvements put by Miller; and that the deed of the lands by the devisees of Charles Mann, dec'd, to M. G. Mann was consummated by delivery." To this report H. A. and M. G. Mann excepted, in seven exceptions, all pointed to and against the account for rents. On the 26th day of February, 1889, the decree complained of and appealed from here was rendered, in which the sale to Miller by Cosby was set aside and annulled, and Mann, the plaintiff in the cross-bill,—that is, M. G. Mann,—was required to pay to the purchaser $797.33, with interest of $654, part thereof, from 26th day of February, being the amount of the purchase money with interest, and the value of improvements, from which rents were deducted, and in default of this payment a resale was ordered; and, default being made in this payment, the commissioner named in the decree for the purpose, made the sale ordered, and reported the sale May 7, 1889, when it was bought by N. W. Mann, when it was sold at $833.22. The court, by decree in the cause, on the 25th day of May, 1889, confirmed this report, decreed that the money be distributed, costs first, and Miller's purchase money next, from which was to be deducted one-third of the cost of Commissioner Barr's report. It is assigned as error here that this decree—that is, the decree of February 26, 1889—is erroneous because it annulled the sale made by the trustee, Cosby, to Miller, and in disturbing the decree of May 14, 1886.

It is difficult to discover from this decree the reason which moved the court to set aside and annul this sale made by this trustee. No reason is given. The commissioner in each case, Commissioner Barr as well as the first, reports otherwise, and the court had by its decree of May 14, 1886, ratified the sale. One ground upon which it is attacked is that more time was not given the debtor to pay the debt secured by the said trust-deed; another is that the trustee sold a part of the land, instead of the whole of it; and still another is that the sale was made of the best part. The evidence shows that every opportunity was afforded to the debtor to pay the debt; that, upon his assurance that he had $200 he could and would pay on the debt of $600, it was postponed a month, from one court-day to another, but this he did not pay, as we have seen; and on the day of sale, fixed upon by his request, he was absent because of bad weather, but a large crowd was present of other people. He did not have the money to pay, and after three years and more of postponement by this litigation he was still unable to pay it or to borrow it upon the condition of having the land back; and the claim of inadequacy of price is shown of any force by the circumstance that after all this delay, and notwithstanding Miller's permanent and substantial improvements, the land did not bring enough to pay the costs and Miller's debt for the purchase money he had paid. The sale was made after due advertisement, and full notice to the debtor and the general public. The sale was completed, the money paid down by the purchaser, and a deed made by the trustee to him. And upon the faith of his purchase he had built upon the land, and made fences, and cleaned up rugged places, and improved the land for agriculture; whereas the other half of the land had been allowed to go to waste by the other parties, while they clamored for this, which had been adorned by the fruits of Miller's toil and industry. It would be a hard case if a purchaser in the market overt from the holder of the legal title, and acting according to the authority of the deed under which he held it, could by any rule of law be made thus to suffer. The trustee certainly did not err in selling so much of the land as was sufficient to pay the debt. A trustee, in any such deed, unless the deed otherwise provide, shall, whenever required by any creditor secured, or any surety indemnified by the deed, or the personal representatives of any such creditor, or for which such surety may be liable, shall have become payable, and default shall have been made in the payment thereof, or any part thereof, by the grantor, sell the property conveyed by the deed, or so much thereof as may be necessary, at public auction, for cash, having first given reasonable notice of the time and place of sale; and shall apply the proceeds of sale, first, to the payment of expenses attending the execution of the court, including a payment to the trustee of 5 per cent. on the first $300, and 2 per cent. on the residue of the proceeds, and then *pro rata* (or in the order of priority, if any is prescribed in the deed) to the payment of the debts secured, and the indemnity of the sureties indemnified by the deed, and shall pay the surplus, if any, to the grantor, his heirs, personal representatives, or assigns. Code Va. § 2442. The trustee was vested with clear and distinct powers under this statute, by virtue of this deed, subject to the right of the debtor to deprive him of all power and control over the subject by payment of the debt. The debtor had himself clothed him with this power, and procured his acceptance thereof, by causing him to sign the deed along with himself. Having thus undertaken the trust, the trustee was liable if he failed faithfully to perform the trust. Every opportunity was given the debtor to pay the debt, and thus extinguish the powers of the trustee, but this he failed and neglected to do; and the execution of the power of sale in the deed conveyed the title to the purchaser, and deprived the debtor of all interest in the premises. The purchaser's title, if the power has been properly and regularly executed, is absolute and irredeemable. Irregularities, if taken advantage of promptly, may be corrected in a court of equity; and it is said that any conduct of the debtor that would render it inequitable for him to take advantage of such defects would debar him from setting them up; as, if the debtor has acquiesced for a long time, and has seen valuable improvements made upon the land, or has been guilty of laches or negligence in claiming his rights, equity will not interfere in his favor. 2 Perry, Trusts, §§ 602*bb*, 602*f*, 602*ee*. But equity will not interfere to give the debtor further time to pay the debt.' Mr. Perry further says, the trust of a creditor under his deed or mortgage, if not otherwise expressed in the deed, is to sell the property, and, after deducting the amount of his debt and the expenses of the sale, to pay the balance, if any, to the debtor, his heirs, assigns, etc. As to the complaint that the trustee did not sell the whole tract, that was unnecessary, as a part of it paid the debt, and it was his duty only to sell so much of the land as would satisfy the debt. In doing this he must exercise a reasonable discretion, and act as the agent of both parties, and, if the debtor so request, it might become his duty to sell more of this land than was necessary to satisfy the trust, to prevent injury to the residue of the tract; but in this case the debtor made no such request, and left the trustee to the exercise of his discretion, which in this case he has not abused. There was no ground to set aside this sale. It was in all respects regularly and properly done; and the cross-bill of the defendant Mann should have been dismissed, with costs. The court had no power, under the circumstances, to disturb this sale; and this is apparently recognized in the decree of the 14th May, 1886, when it ratified and held the sale binding. We are referred to several decisions limiting the power of a commissioner to disturb a sale once confirmed by the court. These cases have no application. In this case the trustee was the vendor, and the sale was complete and binding and final without the aid of a court, to be disturbed only for causes which we have considered. None of these exist in this case. The suit was not brought for that purpose, and under the circumstances of this case could not properly be entertained for that purpose. The suit was brought for the settlement of disputes growing out of the transactions between the said Henry A. and M. G. Mann, and to settle the dispute as to whether the deed to M. G. Mann could be recorded, and to have partition between Lucenda and the said Henry A. and M. G. Mann. The said M. G. Mann, as well as the said Henry A. Mann, had signed the bond and the deed, and it was not material to Miller to whom the title should finally accrue; but the sale had been of only one-half to pay the debt of both, whereas Lucenda Mann claimed one-eighth of the land, which should, as against Miller, be assigned to her in the one-half remaining; and upon them also is the burden of paying the rents due upon the one-eighth. The decree appealed from, as we have seen, is widely at variance with these well-settled principles, and the same must be reversed and annulled, and the cause remanded for further proceedings to be had in the said cause, in order to a final decree in the cause in accordance with the foregoing opinion of this court.

NORFOLK & W. R. CO. v. COMMONWEALTH

(*Supreme Court of Appeals of Virginia.* June 25, 1891.)

CONSTITUTIONAL LAW — INTERSTATE COMMERCE—RAILROAD COMPANIES—SUNDAY TRAINS.

Code Va. § 3801, forbidding the running of trains on Sunday between sunrise and sunset, except wrecking, passenger, stock, and United States mail trains, conflicts with Const. U. S. art. 1, § 8, providing that congress shall have power to regulate commerce among the several states, and is void as to trains running between points in different states. LACY, J., dissenting.

Error to judgment of the circuit court of Pulaski county, rendered March 25, 1891, affirming a judgment of the county court of that county against the Norfolk & Western Railroad Company in a prosecution for a misdemeanor. The indictment was for running a train of cars on Sunday, contrary to the act of March 19, 1884, now carried into section 3801 of the Code. That act forbids the running of trains between sunrise and sunset on a Sunday, except such as are used exclusively for the relief of wrecked or disabled trains, or for the transportation of the United States mails, passengers, live-stock, or articles of such perishable nature as would be necessarily impaired in value by one day's delay in their passage. Section 5258, Rev. St. U. S., however, (not noted in the indictment,) makes every railroad in the country, operated by steam, an agency of commerce for the transportation, among other things, of "freights on their way from one state to another state." There was a motion to quash the indictment, on the ground that it was not sufficiently certain,—that is to say, that, even admitting the charge in the indictment to be true, the defendant was not necessarily guilty of any offense under the laws of the land; which motion was overruled, whereupon the defendant pleaded not guilty. The facts were argued on the trial, and are as follows: That on Sunday, the 21st day of September, 1890, the defendant, by its agents and employes, ran over the New River Division of its road, in Pulaski county, after 9 o'clock in the morning, and before sunset, a train of cars loaded with coal and coke, which was being transported from Bluefield, a station on defendant's road, in the state of West Virginia, into and through Virginia, and that said train was being run only for the transportation of said coal and coke. The defendant demurred to the evidence, whereupon the jury conditionally assessed the fine of $50. The county court overruled the demurrer,

and rendered a judgment for the fine assessed, which judgment was afterwards affirmed by the circuit court.

Phlegar & Johnson and *Brown & Moore,* for plaintiff in error. *The Attorney General,* for the Commonwealth.

LEWIS, P., (*after stating the facts as above.*) The defendant's contention on the merits in the trial court, and here, is that the statute upon which the indictment was founded is, so far as it applies to a case like the present, repugnant to the constitution of the United States, which gives to congress the power to regulate commerce among the several states. The precise propositions contended for on this point are: (1) That the act of transportation mentioned in the proceedings was commerce between the states; (2) that such commerce is, as to all matters that admit of uniformity of regulation, subject only to congressional regulation; (3) that section 3801 of the Code is a regulation of commerce; and (4) that, as such, it cannot be applied to interstate commerce, or to the train in question. It is an historical fact, well known, that to secure uniformity and freedom in commercial intercourse, and, with that view, to establish a single government empowered to regulate commerce, was the chief consideration that led to the formation and adoption of the federal constitution. Accordingly, that instrument ordains that "congress shall have power to regulate commerce with foreign nations, and among the several states, and with the Indian tribes." Article 1, § 8. The power thus conferred, as the supreme court of the United States has repeatedly decided, is complete and exclusive. It is the unlimited power, in other words, to prescribe rules by which commerce shall be governed, and to determine how far it shall be free and untrammeled. Any attempt, therefore, by a state to regulate foreign or interstate commerce is the attempted exercise of a power which has been surrendered by the states, and granted exclusively to the national government. It is an attempt to do that which congress alone is authorized to do, and hence is a nullity. As was said in Railroad Co. v. Husen, 95 U. S. 465: "Whatever may be the power of a state over commerce that is completely internal, it can no more prohibit or regulate that which is interstate than it can that which is with foreign nations. Power over one is given by the constitution to congress in the same words in which it is given over the other, and in both cases it is necessarily exclusive." And in a subsequent part of the same opinion it was said that transportation is not only essential to commerce, but that it is commerce itself, and that every obstacle to it, or burden laid upon it, by legislative authority is regulation. See, also, County of Mobile v. Kimball, 102 U. S. 691; McCall v. California, 136 U. S. 104, 10 Sup. Ct. Rep. 881. "It cannot be too strongly insisted upon," said the court in Wabash, etc., R. Co. v. Illinois, 118 U. S. 557, 7 Sup. Ct. Rep. 4, "that the right of continuous transportation from one end of the country to the other is essential, in modern times, to that freedom of commerce from the restraints which the states might choose to impose upon it that the commerce clause of the constitution was intended to secure; and it would be a very feeble and almost useless provision, but poorly adapted to secure the entire freedom of commerce among the states, which was deemed essential to a more perfect union by the framers of the constitution, if, at every stage of the transportation of goods and chattels through the country, the state within whose limits a part of the transportation must be done could impose regulations concerning the price, compensation, or taxation, or any other restrictive regulation interfering with and seriously embarrassing this commerce." And in a still more recent case it was remarked that in the matter of interstate commerce the United States are but one country, and are and must be subject to one system of regulations, and not to a multitude of systems. Robbins v. Taxing Dist. 120 U. S. 489, 7 Sup. Ct. Rep. 592. There is, indeed, what has been termed a kind of neutral ground which may be constitutionally occupied by the state, so long as it interferes with no act of congress. Thus, where the subject is local in its nature or sphere of operation, such as the establishment of highways, the construction of bridges over navigable streams, the regulation of harbor pilotage, the erection of wharves, piers, and docks, in these and other like cases, which are considered as mere aids rather than regulations of commerce, the state may act until congress supersedes its authority; but where the subject is national in its character, admitting of uniformity of regulation, such as the transportation and exchange of commodities between the states, congress alone can act upon it. The case of Cooley v. Port Wardens, 12 How. 299, is sometimes cited as an authority to the contrary; that is, for the proposition that, in the absence of congressional action, a state may regulate interstate commerce within its own territorial limits. But this statement is broader than the decision justifies; for it was expressly said in that case that "whatever subjects of this power are in their nature national, or admit of only one uniform system or plan of regulation, may be justly said to be of such a nature as to require exclusive legislation by congress." And in the very recent case of Leisy v. Hardin, 135 U. S. 100, 10 Sup. Ct. Rep. 681, known as the "Original Package Case," where the subject is fully considered, Mr. Chief Justice FULLER, in delivering the opinion of the court, used the following language: "The power to regulate commerce among the states is a unit, but, if particular subjects within its operation do not require the application of a general or uniform system, the states may legislate in regard to them with a view to local needs and circumstances until congress otherwise directs; but the power thus exercised by the states is not identical in its extent with the power to regulate commerce among the states. The power to pass laws in respect to internal commerce, inspection laws, quarantine laws, health laws, and laws in relation to bridges, ferries, and highways, belong to the class of powers pertaining to locality, essential to local intercommunication, to the progress and development of local prosperity, and to the protection, the safety, and welfare of society, originally necessarily belonging to, and upon the adoption of the constitution reserved by, the states, except so far as falling within the scope of a power confided to the general government." But these powers, it was said, "though they may be said to partake of the nature of the power granted to the general government, are strictly not such, but are simply local powers, which have full operation until or unless circumscribed by the action of congress in effectuation of the general power." And in the same case the principle was again announced, as it had often been before, that the transportation of passengers or of merchandise from one state to another is in its nature not local, but national, and therefore admitting of but one regulating power.

These authorities, which are only a few of many that might be cited to the same effect, are sufficient to show the invalidity of legislation by the states in regard to subjects of commerce which are in their nature national, no matter what may be the avowed object of such legislation, and that nothing is gained by calling it the "police power." The subject was elaborately discussed, and with his accustomed force, by Mr. Justice MILLER in Henderson v. Mayor, 92 U. S. 259, where it was declared that, however difficult it may often be to distinguish between one class of legislation and another, it is clear, from our complex form of government, that whenever the statute of a state invades the domain of legislation which belongs exclusively to congress it is void, no matter under what class of powers it may fall, or how closely allied to powers conceded to belong to the states. In Railroad Co. v. Husen, supra, it was said: "We admit that the deposit in congress of the power to regulate foreign commerce, and commerce among the states, was not a surrender of that which may properly be denominated 'police power.' What that power is, it is difficult to define with sharp precision. It is generally said to extend to making regulations promotive of domestic order, morals, health, and safety. * * * But whatever may be the nature and reach of that power," it was added, "it cannot be exercised over a subject confided exclusively to congress by the federal constitution. It cannot invade the domain of the national government." Nor does it matter, in such a case, that congress has not acted; for it is now settled that the silence of congress is not only not a concession that the powers reserved by the states may be exerted as if the specific power had not been elsewhere reposed, but, on the contrary, the only legitimate conclusion is that the general government intended that power should not be affirmatively exercised, and the action of the states cannot be permitted to effect that which would be incompatible with such intention. "Hence," as was decided in Leisy

v. Hardin, following many previous decisions, "inasmuch as interstate commerce, consisting in the transportation, purchase, sale, and exchange of commodities, is national in its character, and must be governed by a uniform system, so long as congress does not pass any law to regulate it, or allowing the states so to do, it thereby indicates its will that such commerce shall be free and untrammeled." In Railroad Co. v. Pennsylvania, 136 U. S. 114, 10 Sup. Ct. Rep. 958, the court, in an opinion by Mr. Justice LAMAR, said: "Whenever a commodity has begun to move as an article of trade from one state to another, commerce in that commodity between the states has commenced. The fact that several different and independent agencies are employed in transporting the commodity, some acting entirely in one state, and some acting through two or more states, does in no respect affect the character of the transaction. To the extent in which each agency acts in that transaction, it is subject to the regulation of congress." It is also a well-established principle that an article of commerce transported from one state to another is protected by the constitution against interfering state legislation until it has mingled with, and become a part of, the common mass of property within the latter state; and, if this be so, *a fortiori* is it protected while *in transitu.* Brown v. Maryland, 12 Wheat. 419; Welton v. Missouri, 91 U. S. 275; Leisy v. Hardin, 135 U. S. 100, 10 Sup. Ct. Rep. 681. Tested by these principles, which are axiomatic, it is clear that the judgment complained of is erroneous.

That the transportation of the coal and coke mentioned in the proceedings was an act of commerce, national in its character, is too plain to admit of doubt; and it is equally clear that the legislation in question, in so far as it extends to a case like the present, is unwarranted and void. A statute which forbids the running of interstate freight trains between sunrise and sunset on a Sunday is by its necessary operation, no matter what its professed object may be, a regulation of commerce. At all events, it is an obstruction to interstate commerce, which for the purposes of the present case amounts to the same thing; for, in any view, it is an invasion of the exclusive domain of congress, and therefore void. To say that the state may, in the exercise of her police powers, enforce by statute the observance of the Sabbath, not as a religious duty, but as a day of rest, is no answer to the constitutional objection here raised. The validity of such legislation, when not in conflict with a higher law, is acknowledged by all, and its wisdom and propriety denied by none, certainly not by this court. But when, in a case like the present, it contravenes the constitution of the United States, the latter must prevail, because it is "the supreme law" in all matters relating to the regulation of interstate commerce. Such a statute, if passed by congress, so far as it concerns foreign or interstate commerce, would be valid, not, however, as the exercise of police power, but as a regulation of commerce; and the

reason which would make such legislation valid as an act of congress makes it invalid as an act of a state legislature. As to the effect of the statute in question, if sustained, upon the commercial interests of the country, we need not stop to inquire. It is enough to say that, to the extent indicated, it is not valid. In Henderson v. Mayor, supra, it was decided that, whatever may be the nature and extent of the police power of the state, "no definition of it, and no urgency for its use, can authorize a state to exercise it in regard to a subject-matter which has been confined exclusively to the discretion of congress by the constitution." This principle was reaffirmed in Leisy v. Hardin, where it is said that such a subject-matter is not within the police power of a state, unless placed there by congressional action; and the observations of Mr. Justice MATTHEWS in Bowman v. Railway Co., 125 U. S. 465, 8 Sup. Ct. Rep. 689, 1062, were quoted in the opinion, to the effect that, in view of the commercial anarchy and confusion that would result from the diverse exertions of power by the several states of the union, it cannot be supposed that the constitution or congress have intended to limit the freedom of commercial intercourse among the people of the several states. The fact, if it be a fact, that the statute in question was not intended as a regulation of commerce, does not, we repeat, affect the case. There may be no purpose, it has been held, upon the part of a legislature, to violate the constitution, and yet a statute, enacted under the forms of law, may, by its necessary operation, injuriously affect rights secured by the constitution, in which case the statute, to that extent, must be declared void. Brimmer v. Rebman, 138 U. S. 78, 11 Sup. Ct. Rep. 213. This is merely stating in different form the proposition affirmed in the Henderson Case, namely, that, in whatever language a statute may be framed, its constitutional validity must be determined by its natural and reasonable effect,—a proposition that would seem to be incontrovertible. In the last-mentioned case, a statute of New York which required the master or owner of every vessel landing passengers at the port of New York from a foreign country to give a bond in a prescribed penalty for each passenger so landed, as an indemnity against any expense to be incurred by the state or city for the support of such passengers, was held void, as being a regulation of commerce, although it was sought to be sustained as a police regulation to protect the state against the influx of paupers; the practical result of the statute being to impose a burden upon all passengers so landed from a foreign country. So, in the case of Chy Lung v. Freeman, 92 U. S. 275, a similar statute of California, intended to prevent the introduction of lewd women into that state, was held void, as going beyond the necessity of the case, and amounting, in its practical operation, to a regulation of foreign commerce. Upon the same principle, statutes prohibiting the introduction of intoxicating liquors into the state enacting them have been held to be infringements of the commerce clause of the constitution, and not valid police regulations to guard against the evils of intemperance. And numerous illustrations of the same principles are to be found, in the adjudged cases, all of which show that when, in the attempted exercise of the police power, no matter upon what grounds it is sought to be exercised, the action of a state comes in conflict with a power vested exclusively by constitution in congress, such attempt is a nullity; and the present case comes within this principle.

The power of the state to enforce observance of the Sabbath as a police regulation stands upon no higher footing than her power to guard against the evils of vice or intemperance, or of imported pauperism, or infectious diseases. In either case the nature and extent of the power is exactly the same, and there is no principle for holding otherwise. Our attention has been called, in this connection, to State v. Railroad Co., 24 W. Va. 783, wherein a "Sunday law," so called, similar to the one we are considering, was upheld, under circumstances resembling those of the present case. The court in that case admitted that the transportation between the states is commerce between the states, and that such commerce is necessarily under the exclusive control of congress; but it denied that non-action by congress is equivalent to a declaration that such commerce shall be free and untrammeled, and upon that ground sustained the statute *in toto.* As to the last proposition, we have already shown by the cases referred to—some of them decided since that case was decided—that the rule is otherwise, and, after a careful examination of the case, we find nothing in it to raise a doubt that the rule has been rightly settled. The judgment must therefore be reversed, and the defendant discharged from further prosecution under this indictment, which ought to have been quashed.

LACY, J., (*dissenting.*) This is a writ of error to a judgment of the circuit court of Pulaski county, rendered at the March term, 1891, when the circuit court affirmed the judgment of the county court, rendered at the February term, 1891, of said county court, where the plaintiff in error was convicted for a violation of the Sunday laws of this commonwealth, and adjudged to pay a fine of $50. It is admitted that the said plaintiff in error openly violated the law of the state, upon the ground that it is in violation of the constitution of the United States, because it is an interference by the state with the subject of commerce among the states; that the constitution of the United States provides (article 1, § 8) that the congress shall have power to regulate commerce with foreign nations, and among the states, and with the Indian tribes. Our Code provides that "if a person, on a Sabbath day, be found laboring at any trade or calling, or employ his apprentices or servants in labor or other business, except in household or other work of necessity or charity, he shall forfeit two dollars for each offense. Every day any servant

or apprentice is so employed shall constitute a distinct offense." Code Va. § 3799. This plaintiff in error is a domestic corporation, domiciled within the state of Virginia, holding its chartered rights under the grant of the state, whose charter, by its express terms, provides that it may be altered, modified, or repealed by any future legislature as may think proper. Id. § 1240. The absolute prohibition against laboring at its calling being, in the legislative mind, inexpedient in its application to this or other domestic corporations, the legislature, in 1884, enacted a statute which modified the general law, and excepted such trains as were loaded with passengers and perishable freight, and which suffer injury by delay, and provided as follows: "No railroad company, receiver, or trustee controlling or operating a railroad shall, by any agent or employe, load, unload, run, or transport upon such road on a Sunday any car, train of cars, or locomotive, nor permit the same to be done by any such agent or employe, except when such cars, trains, or locomotives are used exclusively for the use of wrecked trains, or trains so disabled as to obstruct the main track of the railroad, or for the transportation of the United States mail, or for the transportation of passengers and their baggage, or for the transportation of live-stock, or for the transportation of articles of such perishable nature as would be necessarily impaired in value by one day's delay in their passage: provided, however, that, if it should be necessary to transport live-stock or perishable articles on a Sunday to an extent not sufficient to make a whole train-load, such train-load may be made up with cars loaded with ordinary freight." Section 3802 provides that "the word 'Sunday,' in the preceding section, shall be construed to embrace only that portion of the day between sunrise and sunset; and trains *in transitu* having started prior to twelve o'clock on Saturday night may, in order to reach the terminus or shops of the railroad, run until nine o'clock the following Sunday morning, but not later." Section 3803 provides the penalty, which is immaterial in this case; the fine assessed not being in violation thereof. These sections constitute our Sunday laws, not very stringent, it must be admitted, as far as railroads are concerned; its extreme liberality in the privileges to labor on the Sabbath accorded therein suggesting the thought that, when the law was drawn, the railroads in some form stood by consenting; but how this is I have no information. However that may be, the law is now obnoxious to the railroad in question, and in some localities the lower courts have refused to enforce the law.

The question now to be inquired into is, what is the nature of this law? Is it an act to regulate commerce with foreign nations, or among the states, or with the Indian tribes? And does it thus invade the granted powers of the congress, under the constitution of the United States, and conflict with them? If so, it cannot be upheld. It certainly was not so intended. Nothing is said about commerce nor about transportation between the states. It is absolutely limited in its operation to the state of Virginia. It is to be found in the chapter of our Code entitled "Of offenses against morality or decency; protection of religious meetings." The section which precedes it is entitled "Profane swearing and drunkenness, how punished." The section which succeeds it is entitled "Sale of intoxicating liquors on Sunday, how punished." The next is, "Disturbance of religious worship, how punished." It is intended as an exercise of the police power of the state, in the interest of morality and decency, and that is what I think it is. It is no part of the province of congress, under its granted powers, to enact police laws for the regulation of such affairs within a state; and if this state may not enact, for the protection of its citizens, police laws for the observance of the Sabbath day, we must ever remain practically without such. I think I am sustained in this view by the decision of the courts of this country, both state and federal; and I will briefly proceed to consider this. Commerce consists of the various agreements which have for their object facilitating the exchange of the products of the earth, or the industry of man, with the intent to realize a profit. Commerce with foreign countries and among the states, strictly considered, consists in intercourse and traffic, including in these terms navigation, and the transportation of persons and property, as well as the purchase, sale, and exchange of commodities. The power conferred upon the congress by the above clause is exclusive, so far as it relates to matters within its purview which are material in their character, and admit of a requisite uniformity of regulation affecting all the states. That clause was adopted in order to secure uniformity against discriminating state legislation. State legislation is not forbidden in matters either local in their operation, or intended to be mere aids to commerce, for which special regulations can more effectually provide, such as harbors, pilotage, beacons, buoys, and other improvements of harbors, bays, and rivers within a state, if their free navigation be not thereby impaired. Congress, by its inaction in such matters, virtually declares that until it deems best to act they may be controlled by the state. County of Mobile v. Kimball, 102 U. S. 691, (opinion of Mr. Justice FIELD.) In the case of Sherlock v. Alling, 93 U. S. 99, the same learned justice said: "In supposed support of this position, numerous decisions of this court are cited by counsel to the effect that the states cannot by legislation place burdens upon commerce with foreign nations or among the several states." Upon an examination of these cases, it will be found that the legislation adjudged invalid imposed a tax upon some instrument or subject of commerce, or exacted a license fee from parties engaged in commercial pursuits, or created an impediment to the free navigation of some public waters, or prescribed conditions in accordance with which commerce in particular articles or between places was required to be conducted. In all the cases the legislation condemned operated directly upon commerce, either by way of tax upon its business, license upon its pursuits in particular channels, or conditions for carrying it on. Thus, in the Passenger Cases, reported in 7 How. 445, the laws of New York and Massachusetts exacted a tax from the captains of vessels bringing passengers from foreign ports for every passenger landed. In Pennsylvania v. Wheeling, etc., Bridge Co., reported in 13 How. 518, the statute of Virginia authorized the erection of a bridge which was held to obstruct the free navigation of the river Ohio. And in all the other cases, when legislation of a state has been held to be null for interfering with the commercial power of congress,—as in Brown v. Maryland, 12 Wheat. 425; Tax Cases, 12 Wall. 204; and in Welton v. Missouri, 91 U. S. 275,—the legislation created in the way of tax, license, or condition a direct burden upon commerce, or in some way directly interfered with its freedom; and it may be said generally that the legislation of a state not directed against commerce or any of its regulations, but relating to the rights, duties, and liabilities of citizens, and only indirectly and remotely affecting the operations of commerce, is of obligatory force upon citizens within its territorial jurisdiction, whether on land, or engaged in commerce, foreign or interstate, or in any other pursuit. Judge Cooley says, in his work on Constitutional Limitations, (page 722:) "The line of distinction between that which constitutes an interference with commerce and that which is a mere police regulation is sometimes dim and shadowy, and it is not to be wondered at that learned jurists differ when endeavoring to classify the cases which arise. It is not doubted that congress has the power to go beyond the general regulations of commerce which it is accustomed to establish, and to descend to the most minute directions, if it shall be deemed advisable; and that to whatever extent ground shall be covered by these directions the exercise of state power is excluded. Congress may establish police regulations as well as the states, confining their operations to the subjects over which it is given control by the constitution. But as the general police power can better be exercised under the supervision of the local authorities, and mischiefs are not likely to spring therefrom so long as the power to arrest collision resides in the national courts, the regulations that are made by congress do not often exclude the establishment of others by the state covering very many particulars. Moreover, the regulations of commerce are usually, and in some cases must be, general and uniform for the whole country; while in some localities state and local policy will demand peculiar regulations with reference to special and peculiar circumstances." In the late case of Cardwell v. Bridge Co., 113 U. S. 205, 5 Sup. Ct. Rep. 423, after citing the earlier cases, the court said that they illustrate the general doctrine, now fully recognized, that the commercial power of congress is exclusive of state authority only when the subjects upon which it is exerted are national in their character, and admit and require uniformity of regulations affecting all the states; and that when the subjects within that power are local in their nature or operation, or constitute mere aids to commerce, the states may provide for their regulation and management until congress interferes and supersedes their action. I will cite as an illustration of my view of this subject yet another decision of the supreme court of the United States upon this subject, which applies to a through line of railway, and is much in point. In the case of Stone v. Trust Co., 116 U. S. 307, 6 Sup. Ct. Rep. 334, 388, 1191, (one of the Railroad Commission Cases,) that court said: "There can be no doubt that each of the states through which the Mobile & Ohio R. R. passes incorporated the company for the purpose of securing the construction of a continuous line of interstate communication between the Gulf of Mexico, in the south, and the Great Lakes, in the north. It is equally certain that congress aided in the construction of parts of this line of road, so as to establish such a route of travel and transportation; but it is none the less true that the corporation created by each state is, for the purposes of local government, a domestic corporation, and that its railroad within the state is a matter of domestic concern. Mississippi may govern this corporation as it does all domestic corporations, in respect to every act, and everything within the state which is the lawful subject of state government. It may, beyond all question, by the settled rule of decision of this court, regulate freights and fares for business done exclusively within the state; and it would seem to be a matter of domestic concern to prevent the company from discriminating against persons and places in Mississippi. So it may make all needful regulations of a police character for the government of the company while operating its road in that jurisdiction. In this way it may certainly require the company to fence, etc., as much of its road as lies within the state, to stop its trains at railroad crossings, to slacken speed while running in a crowded thoroughfare, to put its tariffs and time-tables at proper places, etc. This company is not entirely relieved from state control in Mississippi, simply because it has been incorporated by, and is carrying on business in, the other states through which its road runs. While in Mississippi it can be governed by Mississippi in respect to all things which have not been placed by the constitution of the United States within the exclusive jurisdiction of congress. It is not enough to prevent the state from acting that the road in Mississippi is used in aid of interstate commerce. Legislation of this kind, to be unconstitutional, must be such as will necessarily amount to or operate as a regulation of business without the state as well as within." See, also, Smith v. Alabama, 124 U. S. 465, 8 Sup. Ct. Rep. 564; Railroad Co. v. Alabama, 128 U. S. 96, 9 Sup. Ct. Rep. 28; Railroad Co. v. People, 105 Ill. 657; Rae v. Railroad Co., 14 Fed. Rep. 401; Iowa v. Railroad Co., 33 Fed. Rep. 391; Railroad Co. v. Becker, 32 Fed.

Rep. 849. And as to the right of the state to regulate the charge for taking on through cars—"switching," as it is called —by a state commission it was held to have no reference to interstate commerce, in the case of Railroad Co. v. Becker, supra. And again it was held in the state of Iowa v. Railroad Co., 33 Fed. Rep. 391, that, even if such switching be an act of interstate commerce, such regulation is valid, as it does not refer to the carriage of freight outside the state. And, again, it was said by the supreme court of the United States in Ferry Co. v. Pennsylvania, 114 U. S. 196, 5 Sup. Ct. Rep. 826, that the power to prescribe regulations to protect the health of the community, and to prevent the spread of disease, is incident to all local municipal authority, however much such regulations may interfere with interstate commerce. The interstate commerce act itself, passed February 4, 1887, and amended March 2, 1889, when congress subjected to its control all common carriers engaged in continuous interstate or international transportation of passengers or property, was held not to include the carriage or handling of passengers, by rail or otherwise, when such carriage or handling is performed wholly within a state. Ex parte Koehler, 30 Fed. Rep. 887. This is the result of all the decisions of the federal courts. If the act in question only applies to and operates upon transportation within the state, it is immaterial that the company operated on is part of an interstate line. It must not only affect commerce, but it must affect commerce with foreign nations, or among the states, or with the Indian tribes. But, if the act is one done in the exercise of a police power, it is within the legitimate and unchallenged domain of the state; such as to regulate concerning the public health, public peace, and morality and decency.

Now, what is this police power, and where does it reside? It is defined to be the authority to establish, for the intercourse of the several members of the body politic with each other, those rules of good conduct and good neighborhood which are calculated to prevent a conflict of rights, and to insure to each the uninterrupted enjoyment of his own, so far as is reasonably consistent with a corresponding enjoyment by others, and is usually spoken of as the authority or power of police. This is a most comprehensive branch of sovereignty, extending, as it does, to every person, every public and private right, everything in the nature of property, every relation in the state, in society, and in private life. The power vested in the legislature to make, ordain, and establish all manner of wholesome and reasonable laws, statutes, and ordinances as they shall judge to be for the good and welfare of the commonwealth, and for the subjects of the same. The exercise of this power, at least, has been left with the individual states, and cannot be taken from them, and exercised wholly or in part under legislation of congress. Cooley, Const. Lim. 715; U. S. v. Dewitt, 9 Wall. 41. Quarantine and health laws of every description, proper regulations for the use of highways, and the general right to control and regulate the public use of navigable waters are unquestionably with the state under the police power. Indeed, the police power of a state, in a comprehensive sense, embraces its whole system of internal regulations by which the state seeks, not only to preserve the public order, and to prevent offenses against the state, but also to establish for the intercourse of citizen with citizen those rules of good manners which are calculated to prevent a conflict of rights. Judge Cooley says, in the American constitutional system the power to establish the ordinary regulations of police has been left with the states individually, and it cannot be taken from them, either wholly or in part, and exercised under legislation of congress; so decided, as we have seen, in U. S. v. Dewitt, 9 Wall. 41. Neither can the national government, through any of its departments or officers, assume any supervision of the police regulations of the states. The state may also, under this power, says the same learned author, regulate the grade of railways, and prescribe how and upon what grade railway tracks may cross each other; and it may apportion the cost of making the necessary crossings between the corporations owning the roads; and it may establish regulations requiring existing railways to ring the bell or blow the whistle of their engines immediately before passing highways at grade, or other places when their approach might be dangerous to travel, or to station flagmen at such or any other dangerous places. The legislature has power by general laws, from time to time, as the public exigencies may require, to regulate corporations in their franchises so as to provide for the public safety. This is held to be a mere police regulation. Railroad Co. v. Loomis, 13 Ill. 548. But certain powers directly affecting commerce may sometimes be exercised, when the purpose is not to interfere with congressional legislation, but merely to regulate the time and manner of transacting business with a view to facilitate trade, secure order, and prevent confusion. Vanderbilt v. Adams, 7 Cow. 351, where Woodworth, J., states very clearly the principles on which police regulations are sustained in such cases.

We have said that the laws to prevent the desecration of the Sabbath came properly under the police power of the state. Judge Cooley says, on this subject, the statute for the punishment of public profanity requires no further justification than the natural impulses of every man who believes in a supreme being, and recognizes his right to the reverence of his creatures. The laws against the desecration of the Christian Sabbath by labor or sports are not so readily defensible by arguments, the force of which will be admitted by all. The laws which prohibit ordinary employments are to be defended either on the same ground which justifies the punishment of profanity, or as establishing sanitary regulations, based upon the demonstration of experience that one day's rest in seven is needful to recuperate the exhausted energies of body and mind. Judge Cooley, speaking

of those laws enacted to prevent desecration of the Sabbath, says they are not unconstitutional as a restraint upon trade and commerce. There can no longer be any question, if any there ever was, that such laws may be supported as regulations of police. Specht v. Com., 8 Pa. St. 312; Bloom v. Richards, 2 Ohio St. 387; Ex parte Andrews, 18 Cal. 678; Ex parte Bird, 19 Cal. 130. Upon this subject of the Sabbath day observance, I have found none but state decisions in a great multitude of cited cases. It does not appear to have been ever, so far as my investigation has gone,—which has been somewhat limited, and not thorough,—a matter of decision with the federal courts, so far as the states are concerned. And I believe there is no probability that congress will ever assume the right to regulate the observance of the Sabbath day in the states. If, however, it should ever do so, I do not doubt that the American congress will protect the American Sabbath day from unnecessary desecration, by whomsoever it is essayed. Nor do I doubt that, if the supreme court of the United States should have this question under consideration, it would hold, as my view is, that the Sunday laws of this commonwealth are within the police powers of the state, and, moreover, that they in no wise affect interstate commerce, but, being limited in their operations to the state, whatever effect they have upon the through line of transportation outside of the state, it is no more than is proper, and in no way an interference with the granted power of the congress. It is to be regretted, as it is a federal question, that it cannot go up to the supreme court of the United States, and be settled there. Holding the views I do, I am constrained to dissent from the opinion of the majority.

Meyers v. Meyers' Ex'r et al.

(*Supreme Court of Appeals of Virginia.* June 25, 1891.)

Wills—General and Demonstrative Legacies.

A testator provided for the sale of certain land and of his personal property to pay debts and a bequest of $700 to one of his seven children, "which should be his entire portion." The homestead was devised to another son, who was executor, to be cultivated by him during the widowhood of testator's wife, one-fourth of the proceeds thus arising to be paid to the widow. and the remainder to be divided among the six heirs. At the death or marriage of the widow, the executor was to elect to take the homestead at $40 per acre, or to sell it at auction, and divide the proceeds equally among the six heirs. At the death of the widow, the homestead was sold at auction. The proceeds of the personalty and of the land were insufficient to pay the debts and the legacy of $700, without resorting to the proceeds of the sale of the homestead. *Held,* that the devise to the six heirs was a demonstrative legacy, while the $700 bequest was a general legacy, and hence the latter must abate to pay debts before the former could be touched.

Appeal from circuit court, Roanoke county; Henry Blair, Judge.

B. Haden, for appellant. Hansbrough & Hansbrough, for appellees.

Hinton, J. This suit was instituted by the appellant, George G. Meyers, to enforce the payment of a legacy of $700 left him in the will of his father, the late David Meyers. The assets of the estate being insufficient to discharge the debts and all the legacies, the question to be decided is whether there is any property other than that subjected by the decree of the circuit court which is liable for the payment of said legacy,—an inquiry which obviously depends upon the construction to be placed upon the other bequests. For this purpose it is only necessary for the court to consider the following provisions of the will, which, being holograph, shows that the testator was a plain and illiterate man: "My last will an testament I appoint John O. Meyers my Exator after my diseas, sale mate all my personel property sold an one hundred an Sixty acres of mountain land in Carvens Cove atjoining the lands of Wats an others, an my depts paid I then give an bequate to my son George G. Meyers, three hundred dollars twelve months after my diseas twelve months thereafter four hundred dollars which shel be his intire porshone of my estate, John O. Meyers to live an remain on my home place so long as my witte remains to be my witte, to cultivate it an keep it in good order an pay one-fourth of the proceeds thereof in rent for the support of my witte, if there be serples after her support, that serples be divited equil between my six hairs, after my witte ceases to be my witte then John O. Meyers takes the home place at forty dollars per acre, an if he thinks in his judgment he can he can do better then hold the farm at forty dollars per acre he can put it up to the highest bidder an devide the proceds thereof equilly between my six hairs," etc. The testator had seven children, including the appellant. His personal property at the time of his death consisted of four cattle, a few farming utensils, and household and kitchen furniture, valued at $162.50. He had not farmed during the latter years of his life, and kept no horses or stock; and as John O. Meyers had to remain on and cultivate the home place during his mother's widowhood, which terminated with her life in 1888, and she remained there also with the right to her support out of the products, these articles were retained for her use, and at her death such of them as had not been worn out in the use were sold and accounted for by him. The Carvin Cove tract of 160 acres of mountain land was appraised at $80, and afterwards sold for $72; but this sale was set aside by the decree complained of. The home place was not taken by the executor, John O. Meyers at $40 per acre, as he was authorized by the will to do, but was sold at auction, and bought by a third party for $25 per acre, who subsequently sold it to the said John O. Meyers at the same price. The circuit court, by the decree complained of, adjudged that the appellant "is entitled under the said will," meaning the will of David Meyers, to be paid out of the assets of the testator's estate the legacy of $700 given him by the testator, out of any assets of said estate which may remain after the payment of all the debts of the estate, including the expenses of his burial

and the administration of the estate, and the payment of the specific or demonstrative legacy out of the proceeds of the sale of the testator's farm, called in the will his "Home Place," to his six children and heirs at law other than the complainant; but that the complainant is not entitled to receive any portion of his said legacy out of the proceeds of the sale of said "Home Place," and has no pecuniary interest therein whatever. This decree seems to us to be plainly right. The legacy to George G. Meyers is clearly a general or pecuniary legacy, which, of course, cannot be paid until the debts have been discharged, and which, according to all the authorities, must abate for the payment of debts before specific or demonstrative legacies. On this head says Mr. Minor, "general legacies (sometimes inaptly styled 'pecuniary legacies') are legacies of money, or of chattels which may be satisfied by the delivery of anything of that kind. Thus the legacy of 'my usual riding horse' is specific, whilst one of 'a riding horse' is general. A legacy of $1,000 is general, whilst one out of the money owing me by Z. is demonstrative." And "general legacies," he then goes on to say, "abate ratably amongst themselves for the payment of debts, first of all, before either specific or demonstrative legacies, but they are not liable to be adeemed as specific legacies are." 3 Minor, Inst. (Lith. Ed.) 201; 2 Lomax, Ex'rs p. 75; Skipwith v. Cabell, 19 Grat. 789; Robinson v. Mills, Id. 468–472; 3 Lomax, Dig. top p. 392; 3 Jarm. Wills, p. 449. Now, in this case, as the proceeds of personalty are less than $200, while the record shows the debts to amount to more than $3,200, it is manifest that the legacy to George G. Meyers must abate, unless the Carvin Cove tract, which is ordered by the decree aforesaid to be resold, shall bring an excess over the sum of $72, for which it first sold, and which has been accounted for, sufficient to discharge the balance of debts and the said legacy, or unless it can be charged upon the home place, which is all that is left of the testator's estate. But the direction in the will of David Meyers that John O. Meyers, his executor, should take the home place at $40 an acre, or put it up to the highest bidder, and divide the proceeds thereof equally between his six children, is a demonstrative legacy. A demonstrative legacy, says this court in a noted case, is a legacy of quantity, with a particular fund pointed out for its satisfaction, and it is so far general, and differs so much from one properly specific, that, if the fund be called in or fail, the legatee will not be deprived of his legacy, but be permitted to receive it out of the general assets, yet is so far specific that it is not liable to abate with general legacies upon a deficiency of assets. 2 Lomax, Ex'rs, 70; 2 Williams, Ex'rs, 1252; 2 Redf. Wills, 465; Corbin v. Mills, 19 Grat. 470; 3 Pom. Eq. Jur. § 1133; Morriss, etc., v. Garland's Adm'r, 78 Va. 223, 3 Minor, Inst. p. 200. And these "legacies, so far as the fund to which they are referred will suffice for payment, are preferred to general legacies, because it is to be inferred that, by referring to specific parts of the estate for their payment, the testator intended them to be preferred to other legacies, which he had not so secured." 13 Amer. & Eng. Enc. Law, p. 146, note; Williams, Ex'rs, (7th Eng. Ed.) 1371. Such being the relative characters of these two different legacies, and the rule being that a demonstrative legacy is preferred to a general legacy, in the case at bar, inasmuch as the assets of the testator are insufficient to pay his debts and his legacies too, the general legacy of $700 to the appellant has to abate to pay the debts before the demonstrative legacy to the remaining six children can be touched. This is the view taken by the circuit court in its decree, and, for the reasons just stated, we concur in that view. The decree appealed from is right, and must be affirmed.

KENEFICK v. CAULFIELD.

(Supreme Court of Appeals of Virginia. June 25, 1891.)

ATTACHMENT—BOND—REVIEW ON APPEAL.

1. Under Code Va. § 2968, providing that in attachments, if the plaintiff shall file a bond, etc., the sheriff shall take the property attached into his possession, a bond is not required unless the sheriff is directed to take the property into his possession.

2. When no motion to vacate an attachment was made, exceptions thereto, not raised below, will not be considered on appeal.

Action in *assumpsit* by Patrick Caulfield against William Kenefick. From a judgment for plaintiff, defendant appeals. *Holdway & Ewing* and *J. J. H. Rowell,* for plaintiff in error. *Hoge & Green,* for defendant in error.

LACY, J. This is a writ of error to a judgment of the circuit court of Scott county rendered on the 25th day of June, 1890. The action was *assumpsit,* and when the summons was issued an attachment was sued out by plaintiff against the estate or effects of the defendant situated within the jurisdiction of the court. The summons was returned, "Not found." Upon affidavit that the defendant was justly indebted to the plaintiff in the sum demanded, which was due and payable, and that the defendant was a non-resident of this state, but had estate in the county in which the suit was brought, the attachment issued; but no bond was given so as to enable the sheriff to take the property into his possession; and the said attachment was levied on 12 head of mules belonging to William Kenefick, the defendant; and there was at the same time an order of publication which was issued in a newspaper published in the county, which is certified to by the manager of the company by which the paper was published. The declaration was in the usual form, containing the common counts in *assumpsit,* and an account of the claim was filed with the declaration. The defendant demurred to the declaration, and the demurrer was overruled, non *assumpsit* pleaded by the defendant, a jury impaneled and sworn, and upon the trial, after hearing the evidence, the jury rendered a verdict for the plaintiff for

$637.46. Whereupon the plaintiff applied for and obtained a writ of error to this court.

The first error assigned here is that the court erred in overruling the demurrer to the declaration. The declaration is in the usual form, and is without defect. The next is that the court refused to continue the case because of the absence of a material witness. If this be a fact, the record does not disclose it. The next is that the court overruled the motion of the defendant to set aside the verdict and grant the defendant a new trial upon the ground "because the court overruled the demurrer to the indictment, because the return of the sheriff was insufficient, and because the levy of the attachment and the return thereon was irregular and insufficient, there and then being no bond given when the attachment issued, and because the account filed with the declaration had no date." As to the demurrer, we have said that there was no error of the court in overruling that. There is no defect in the return of the sheriff, which is sufficient. As to the assignment that no bond was given by the plaintiff when the attachment was issued, none is required by our statute, unless the sheriff is directed to take the property into his possession, which was not done in this case. Section 2968, Code Va. As to the date of the account, the date of the account was stated in the declaration with which it was filed, and it was presented as debt due at the date of the suit, and the verdict was rendered accordingly. Again, that the declaration does not allege any promise to pay the debt. This is a mistake of fact; the declaration does so allege a promise to pay the debt.

Exceptions are set forth here to the attachment, but in the court below there was no exception taken to the attachment, and no motion to abate the attachment, but the defendant appeared, and pleaded to the action. The objection comes too late here. There is no exception in the record, and no bill of exceptions taken, and neither facts proved nor evidence certified, and, in the absence of anything appearing to the contrary, the judgment must be here held to be right. We discover no ground of error in the record, and the judgment of the circuit court is right, and will be affirmed.

REYNOLDS v. NECESSARY.

(Supreme Court of Appeals of Virginia. June 25, 1891.)

SPECIFIC PERFORMANCE — RECEIVING PART PAYMENT OF PRICE—DELIVERY OF POSSESSION.

Plaintiff made an oral agreement to sell and immediately deliver certain land to defendant for a fixed sum, in consideration of his taking up and delivering two notes which were a lien upon said lands, and paying the balance at stated times. Defendant bought the notes, and delivered one, and offered to perform the remaining conditions of the contract, and went into possession, and cut logs from the land. Plaintiff refused to further perform the contract, obtained an injunction, and sought to recover the logs, still, however, retaining the note. *Held,* that specific performance of the contract will be decreed.

Action by Nancy Reynolds against Joel F. Necessary for an injunction and the appointment of a receiver. From a judgment in favor of defendant, plaintiff appeals.

J. H. Wood, for appellant. *A. L. Pridemore* and *J. B. Richmond*, for appellee.

LACY, J. This is an appeal from a decree of the circuit court of Scott county, rendered on the 28th day of March, 1889. The bill was filed by the appellant against the appellee to enjoin and restrain him, his agents, etc., from cutting timber from the land of the plaintiff in the bill mentioned, and praying the appointment of a receiver to take charge of such logs as had been already cut. The injunction was granted pursuant to the prayer of the bill. The defendant answered. He admitted that the plaintiff had purchased the land from H. J. Carter and wife, as shown by the deed filed with the bill, and supposed it to be true that the purchase money had been paid, except $167, as stated by complainant. And the defendant, in his answer, set up a parol purchase of the land by him from the plaintiff, and payment to her of one of the notes due on the land *instanter*, and at her request the payment of the other notes due on the land by her to John Fickle, the then owner of the note for $87.58, and that on the day of the said purchase the possession of the land was delivered to him, and that he had held the possession of it ever since; that the defendant agreed to meet the plaintiff at Ira P. Robinett's to pay to her the said note of $87.58, and execute his notes for the deferred payments according to their agreement; that the plaintiff, after making the sale, and receiving a part of the purchase money, and placing the defendant in possession of the land, refused to accept the note for $87.58 after he had at her request purchased it, and sought to rescind the agreement, but he claimed under the said contract, and sought to have the agreement performed by the decree of the court. On the 26th of March, 1889, the court rendered its decree upon the pleadings and the depositions of witnesses taken in the cause. And the court being of opinion that the plaintiff sold to the defendant, and agreed for the defendant to have possession, in pursuance of the said agreement; that the defendant took possession of the tract of land in the bill mentioned, at the price of $1,000; and that the defendant, in pursuance of his contract, paid to the plaintiff in hand her own note for $80, and proceeded and tendered to her the John Fickle note for $87.58; and, in further pursuance of the said contract, tendered, at the time agreed upon, the cash payment provided for by said contract; thus performing the contract on his part as far as he could, and that while so performing the said contract the defendant cut and removed a large lot of logs from the said land. The court was therefore of opinion that it would now be inequitable to rescind the same, dissolved the injunction, and decreed specific performance of the contract, and directed the defendant to deposit the purchase money with the clerk, and the plaintiff to file with the clerk a good and sufficient deed, and thereupon to be paid the money by the clerk. The plaintiff thereupon applied for and obtained an appeal to this court. The evidence in the case shows that the plaintiff, Nancy C. Reynolds, was the owner of the land in dispute, and owed two notes,—one of $80, and another of $87.58,—which were liens upon the said land; that on the 14th day of January, 1887, she was pressed to pay the first-named note by a man named Wells, who held it by assignment; that, in default of the money to pay this note, a negotiation was commenced between them for the sale of enough timber on the land to pay this, and the other also; that the plaintiff expressed her unwillingness to sell off her timber, if it could be prevented, as that would render the land unsalable, and she desired to sell the land upon which she did not reside. Wells informed the defendant, Joel F. Necessary, that the plaintiff was disposed to sell the land, and suggested to him to buy it; and together they sought the plaintiff, and the defendant offered to buy the land. The plaintiff fixed the price at $1,000, and the defendant agreed to buy at that price if the terms could be agreed on. After a good deal of talk on the subject, the defendant offered to take up the two notes above mentioned without delay, and to pay her $100 when Owen Franklin came back from his stock sale, and $100 more when the defendant sold his logs, and $632.42 in twelve months from date; possession of the land to be given at once. To this she agreed, and the defendant then and there obtained the $80 note, and delivered it to the plaintiff, and the parties separated, agreeing to meet the next Monday at Ira P. Robinett's, a relation of the plaintiff, selected by her to draw the several papers required in full execution of their agreement. The defendant attended at the time and place named, and purchased and brought with him the $87.58 note above mentioned; but the plaintiff absented herself, and did not appear, as she had agreed to do. The defendant, however, procured the services of the said Robinett, and had all the papers required written, and sought for and found the plaintiff, and offered them to her, together with the note for $87.58; but the plaintiff, having been made to believe that she could get more for the land, and having possession of the $80 note, which had been pressing upon her, refused to comply with her bargain, and refused to give up the note, relying on the fact that no writing had been signed by her, and believing that the parol sale of the land was not binding on her. The object of the bill, as we have said, was to restrain and enjoin a trespass, and to prevent irreparable injury to the property of the plaintiff. The answer set up a parol agreement for the sale of the land, delivery of possession, and part performance by the purchaser, and sought specific performance of this contract; and while, according to the strict rules of pleading, this relief should have been sought by a cross-bill filed for that purpose by the defendant, the answer of the defendant may be so treated for that purpose.

Courts of equity treat such contracts, when there has been part performance, as valid and as effectual as those evidenced by the most solemn instruments in writing. In order to prevent the possibility of fraud, however, in engrafting this exception upon the statute of frauds, it is settled that the parol agreement relied on must be certain and definite in its terms; the acts proved in part performance must refer to, result from, or be done in pursuance of, the agreement; and the agreement must have been so far executed that a refusal of full execution will operate as a fraud upon the party, and place him in a situation which does not lie in compensation. Opinion of Judge STAPLES in Floyd v. Harding, 28 Grat. 406, citing Wright v. Pucket, 22 Grat. 370; 2 White & T. Lead. Cas. 1052. The learned judge says, further, when these circumstances concur it is as much a matter of course for the equity courts to decree a specific execution as for the common-law courts to award damages for the breach of a written contract. The purchaser is regarded as the real beneficial owner of the estate, and the vendor as the mere trustee of the legal title for his benefit. Whatever loss may fall on the estate is the loss of the purchaser; whatever advantage may accrue to it is his gain. This doctrine is now too firmly established ever to be changed by anything short of a legislative enactment. It is, to every intent, a law of property, as much so as if the exception had been engrafted in the statute of frauds. Upon the faith of its existence, purchases of valuable estates have been made and held throughout this commonwealth. There can be no grounds of controversy upon these points. It may be further affirmed that the title thus vesting in the purchaser under a valid parol contract is good against all the world, except subsequent purchasers of the legal title for valuable consideration without notice. That the equitable estate of the purchaser is good against creditors of the vendor is incontrovertible. Hicks v. Riddick, 28 Grat. 418. Specific performance cannot be considered as a matter of right, however, in either party. It does not proceed *ex debito justitiæ*, but as a matter of sound and reasonable discretion, which governs itself by general rules and principles, but withholds or grants relief according to the circumstances of each particular case, when these general rules and principles will not furnish any exact measure of justice between the parties. All applications to the court to decree specific performance must depend upon the circumstances of each case governed by the established principles of the court. The contract must be clear and distinct; it must be mutual. If specific performance would work injustice, a party will be left to his action for damages. It is a general rule that the party seeking specific performance should not have been backward. As equity is never bound to give this relief, so it never will, unless the justice of the case, as drawn from all the facts, demands it. 3 Pars. Cont. 416; 2 Minor, Inst. 808, 809; St. John v. Benedict, 6 Johns. Ch. 111; Long. Dig. 72, 100; Ford v. Euker, 86 Va.

76, 9 S. E. Rep. 500. In this case, the plaintiff, being in trouble about a lien on her land which was very urgent, made her contract to sell to the defendant on terms stated and clearly proved, and indeed evasively, but substantially, admitted by her; received a part of the purchase price, and obtained relief against her pressing necessity; delivered possession of the land; and, being thus relieved of this debt, and also of another which, though not large, was more than she could pay without selling her land or the wood on it, and having gained this advantage, recanted and refused to do more, held the note, and sought to regain possession of the land also. To have upheld her in this pretension would have been to enable her to defraud the defendant, and the circuit court properly decreed that her contract be specifically performed; and we perceive no error in the said decree, and are of opinion to affirm the same.

HINTON, J., absent.

VIRGINIA COAL & IRON CO. *et al.* v. ROBERSON *et ux*.

(Supreme Court of Appeals of Virginia. June 25, 1891.)

WIFE'S SEPARATE ESTATE—CONTRACT TO CONVEY.

Act Va. April 4, 1876, provides that a married woman shall have power to make a contract for the disposition of her separate estate, provided her husband shall join therein. The law in force March 1, 1880, provided that if the wife, "on being examined privily and apart from her husband, and having the writing fully explained to her, acknowledged the same to be her act, and declared that she had willingly executed it, and does not retract it, such privy examination, acknowledgment, and declaration shall thereupon be recorded," etc. *Held*, that a certificate reciting that a husband and wife, who executed a deed, "personally appeared before the undersigned, * * * and acknowledged the same to be their act and deed, the said" wife "being examined separate and apart from her husband, to the effect that she signed the said deed willingly, and that she does not wish to retract from it," though insufficient to render the deed a valid instrument of conveyance, still renders it a valid executory contract of sale.

Bullitt & McDowell and *E. M. Fulton*, for appellants. *Duncan & Mathews* and *Richmond & Sewell*, for appellees.

LACY, J. This is an appeal from a decree of the circuit court of Wise county, rendered on the 19th day of September, 1890. The bill was filed in this cause by the Virginia Coal & Iron Company and the Big Stone Gap Improvement Company in December, 1889, against the appellees, J. M. Roberson and wife, having for its object the specific performance of an alleged contract for sale of certain lands in the bill mentioned, and to compel the said J. M. Roberson and Letitia D. Roberson, his wife, to convey to the plaintiffs the land described in the said alleged contract. This alleged contract for the sale of this land was a deed made by the said defendants for the land in question to one Charles W. Kilgore, which by successive conveyances had passed to the plaintiffs. The deed was made on the 1st day of

March, 1880; and the certificate of acknowledgment was signed the same day, and the writing was admitted to record. The appellants, regarding the certificate of acknowledgment as insufficient to authorize the recordation of the deed as to the married woman so as to pass her right therein, brought this suit to compel a conveyance in due form, having first applied to the parties to make the said deed without suit, and said request refused. The land in dispute is the land of the wife, and is her separate estate, under the act of assembly of April 4, 1876. The law in force March 1, 1880, provided that if the wife, "on being examined privily and apart from her husband, and having the writing fully explained to her, acknowledged the same to be her act, and declared that she had willingly executed it, and does not wish to retract it, such privy examination, acknowledgment, and declaration shall thereupon be recorded," etc. The certificate to the deed in question was: "J. M. Roberson and L. D. Roberson, his wife, whose names are signed to the foregoing deed for land, personally appeared before the undersigned justice of the peace for Wise county, Va., and acknowledged the same to be their act and deed; the said L. D. Roberson being examined separate and apart from her husband, to the effect that she signed the said deed willingly, and that she does not wish to retract it." This certificate is admitted on both sides to be defective, and it clearly does not conform to the statute; it nowhere appearing that the writing was first explained to her, and her acknowledgment appearing to be jointly with her husband, and before her alleged privy examination.

While it is well settled by our decisions that a literal compliance with the statute is not necessary, and that when there has been a substantial compliance therewith it is sufficient, (Langhorne v. Hobson, 4 Leigh. 225; Tod v. Baylor, Id. 498; Siter v. McClanachan, 2 Grat. 280; Dennis v. Tarpenny, 20 Barb. 371; Dundas v. Hitchcock, 12 How. 256; Deery v. Cray, 5 Wall. 795, and Hockman v. McClannahan, [Va.] 12 S. E. Rep. 230,) yet the result of the authorities is, as was said in the last-named case, that, while a substantial compliance with the statute will suffice, it must be a substantial compliance with every requisite of the statute. None of these requirements can be dispensed with, and a compliance with some of them will not be held to contain the substance of them all. This subject was fully considered in the case of Hockman v. McClannahan, supra, and it is sufficient to refer to that case and the authorities there cited. In the light of these decisions, the counsel are right on both sides in conceding that the said certificate is defective. The counsel for the appellees insist that the certificate being insufficient to pass the wife's right, the conveyance is a nullity, and the land is still the property of the wife; and the counsel for the appellants, conceding that the deed is insufficient to pass the wife's right, claim, further, that the deed, though not duly acknowledged as to the wife, and not properly recorded as to her, and not sufficient to convey her land, is yet a contract in writing by the wife to convey, is executory, and should be by the court specifically enforced against the wife, notwithstanding the coverture.

The appellees insist that the executory contract of a married woman to convey her land cannot be enforced against her, because of the coverture. If the contract had been made since the adoption of the Code of Virginia in force May, 1888, it is conceded that the executory contract of a married woman may now in this state be enforced against her, if made since the adoption of the new Code, supra, by authority of sections 2286, 2288, and 2289, as was held by this court in the case of Gentry v. Gentry, (Va.) 12 S. E. Rep. 966, where the statutes are set forth in full. If, however, the deed had been executed before the passage of the act of April 4, 1876, supra, it is equally clear, and is likewise conceded, that specific performance could not be enforced against the married woman as the law then stood because of her coverture. Iron Co. v. Gardiner, 79 Va. 305, and authorities cited; also Railroad Co. v. Dunlop, 86 Va. 349, 10 S. E. Rep. 239. The writing in question was a writing signed and delivered by a married woman purporting to convey her real estate, which by law was her separate estate. If any contract comes within the well-settled rule as to specific performance generally, this is such; for here the entire purchase money has been paid, and possession delivered. The question in this case, however, is, can the married woman's contract for the sale of her separate estate be enforced against her? If there is any authority for this, it must be found in the act of April 4, 1876. That act provides that the real and personal property of any female who may hereafter marry, and which she shall own at the time of her marriage, and the rents, issues, and profits thereof, and any property, real or personal, acquired by a married woman as a separate and sole trader, shall not be subject to the disposal of her husband, nor be liable for his debts, and shall be and continue her separate and sole property; and any such married woman shall have power to contract in relation thereto, or for the disposal thereof, and may sue and be sued as if she was a *feme sole:* provided, that her husband shall join in any contract in reference to her real and personal property, other than such as she may acquire as a sole trader, and shall be joined with her in any action by or against her. This property in question is the separate estate of a married woman under this act. The act expressly grants to her the power to contract in relation thereto, or for the disposal thereof; and she is authorized to sue and may be sued as if she were a *feme sole.* If a *feme sole* had made this contract, no question could have been raised of this sort. The law provides that the married woman may sue and be sued concerning her contract concerning this separate estate as if she were a *feme sole.* She has made a valid contract, which she could have enforced against the other contracting parties; and I feel no hesitation in holding, and perceive no difficulty in arriving at the conclusion, that it may be equally enforced against her. She has made the contract concerning her separate estate, and her husband has united with her in said contract, and the statute has been complied with. It was said by this court in a late case, arising upon this act, after reciting the act in full, (Crockett v. Dorlot, 85 Va. 243, 3 S. E. Rep. 128:) "This act must be construed according to its terms. They alone justify the court in departing from the rule heretofore existing. By the act in question the said separate estate is created, and the power is granted to her 'to contract in relation thereto, or for the disposal thereof; and she may sue and be sued as a *feme sole*, provided that her husband shall join in any contract in reference to her real or personal property,' etc. If this power to contract is to be restricted to the terms of the act, then the power to contract which is granted is to contract in relation to her said estate, or for the disposal thereof, in which her husband is required to join. * * * Though a wife may by a contract bind her property, she cannot in any way bind her person. It is only in consequence of the existence of her separate estate that this statute authorizes her to make the contract." In that case it was sought to enforce against the wife a contract not made with reference to or concerning her separate estate, and in which her husband did not join. This could not be done under that act, for reasons there stated. But this is a very different case. The contract is for the disposal of her separate estate, and the husband has joined with her in making the contract. It comes within the express terms of the statute, and is a valid and binding contract, clearly enforceable against the married woman and her separate estate. This, I think, is clearly the true construction of our statute upon this subject; and we will say in this case as we said in the last-mentioned case, we have rested our decision in this case upon the terms of our own statute. While many cases have been cited in the argument, they all proceed upon the statutes of other states, in some respects unlike our own; and we think the conclusion we have reached is clearly the true construction of the statute in question. The circuit court decided otherwise, and we are of opinion that the said decree is plainly erroneous, and must be reversed and annulled, and the cause remanded to the said circuit court, with directions to proceed in the cause to grant the relief prayed for in the bill, by causing a proper and sufficient deed to be made to the plaintiff by the said defendant married woman, or by causing the same to be executed by a commissioner of the court in this cause, so as to conclude the rights of all the parties hereto.

CARTER'S HEIRS v. EDWARDS et al.

(*Supreme Court of Appeals of Virginia.* July 2, 1891.)

EJECTMENT — EVIDENCE — PATENTS — CODIFICATION — REPEAL.

1. In an ejectment suit by heirs, a patent to the land in controversy, issued to their ancestor by the state, lacking the state seal, was excluded until the plaintiffs introduced evidence that the seal was upon it when issued. The court then allowed it to go to the jury, but required a finding as to whether or not the seal had been attached. *Held* error, since the patent should have gone to the jury with an instruction that its validity depended upon its legal execution.

2. The exclusion of a copy of the patent, duly signed, sealed, and verified, was error.

3. Act Va. March 9, 1880, providing that "in all cases of ejectment * * *" in the counties of Buchanan, Dickenson, and Wise the plaintiff shall file with his declaration, 30 days before trial, the written and record evidence on which he relies, and unless he does so the defendant may have a continuation," etc., is a "general" law, within Code Va. 1887, § 4202, which provides that upon the adoption of the Code all acts of a "general" nature shall be repealed.

LEWIS, P., dissenting.

Action in ejectment by Dale Carter's heirs against James T. Edwards and others. From a verdict and judgment for defendants, plaintiffs bring error.

Burns & Fulton and *Routh & Stuart*, for plaintiffs in error. *Kilgore & Miller* and *Mr. Hagan*, for defendants in error.

LACY, J. This is a writ of error to a judgment of the circuit court of Wise county, rendered on the 22d of April, 1889. The action is ejectment, brought in December, 1878, by Dale Carter against the defendants in error, to recover 55,000 acres of land situated in the said county of Wise. At the trial the verdict and judgment were for the defendants; and the plaintiffs, having excepted to various rulings of the court against them, and having moved to set aside the verdict, which was likewise decided against them, and the decision of the court excepted to, applied for and obtained a writ of error to this court.

The first assignment of error here is that, after the jury had been sworn in the cause, the plaintiffs, to maintain the issue on their part, offered to read in evidence to the jury a paper purporting to be a patent which purported to have been issued by the commonwealth of Virginia to Dale Carter on the —— day of July, 1856, for 18,157 acres of land. The said patent was signed with the genuine signature of the governor of Virginia, the late Hon. Henry A. Wise; and on the left-hand side, while the seal was not thereon, there was an appearance of abrasion which it was claimed showed where the seal had been. But upon the ground that the law required that a patent from the commonwealth of Virginia should have upon it when issued, not only the signature of the governor, but also the lesser seal of the commonwealth, the court excluded the patent from going to the jury. The plaintiffs offered to show that the said patent had a seal upon it when issued, and in rough use by surveyors and others the seal appended to the patent had become broken off. A surveyor who had used it said that when in his possession, when making a survey by it in 1879, to the best of his recollection the patent had a seal on it, which was of wax or wafer, and the said seal was red. The clerk of the court said that he had made an official copy of this patent in 1880, and marked the seal on the left-hand corner of it with "L. S.," and that he did not think that he would have marked the seal on the left-hand lower corner in the copy unless the original had been sealed, and to the best of his recollection the said patent had the seal of the commonwealth on it when he made the copy. And the witness further said that the writing on the left-hand side of the patent, at the bottom, was in the handwriting of Dale Carter. This writing was as follows: "Note. The beginning corner of this survey is N., 67 E., 800 p. from the mouth of Big Thoru's creek." And he also said that he might have so certified the copy by reason of the impression which appears on the lower left-hand corner of the said patent. Whereupon the court permitted the patent to go to the jury, and that the jury should pass upon the question as to whether or not the seal of the commonwealth had been attached to said patent; to which last action of the court, requiring the jury to pass upon the question as to whether or not the said seal had been attached to the said patent, the plaintiffs excepted, and this is the second assignment of error; and the third is that after the court had refused to allow the said patent to go before the jury, and had referred the question as to the missing seal to the jury, the plaintiffs offered to read to the jury the certified copy of the patent mentioned above; but this was overruled, and the copy of the patent, duly signed and sealed, and duly certified, was not allowed to be read to the jury; and the plaintiff again excepted, and this is the third assignment of error. Upon consideration of which said assignments of error, we think the circuit court plainly erred in excluding from the jury the defaced patent. That should have gone before the jury for what it was worth, with an instruction that its validity depended upon its legal and due execution, signed and sealed by the governor, signed with his signature, and sealed with the lesser seal of the commonwealth, at the time of its issuance. The course pursued was to exclude it till the jury should determine that it had been duly sealed, and then exclude from their consideration the most important, and indeed conclusive, proof showing that it had been sealed. The ground for this ruling of the court is accounted for by the circumstance that this copy of the patent was not filed by the plaintiff in the clerk's office 30 days before the trial.

The act of assembly approved March 9, 1880, provides "that in all cases of ejectment now pending or hereafter brought in the counties of Buchanan, Dickenson, and Wise the plaintiff shall file with his declaration, thirty days before trial, the written and record evidence on which he relies, and unless he does so the defendant may have a continuance of the case at the cost of the plaintiff; and, if the said case shall be so continued for two terms consecutively, the court may, in its discretion, enter judgment for the defendant." As to this act, we will remark—*First.* That, while it requires the plaintiff's written and record evidence on which he relies

v.13s.e.no.13--23

to be filed 30 days before the trial, it does not provide that if he shall not file this thirty days before the trial he shall thereupon lose the benefit of it, and forfeit his property right thereby. The provision of the law is that if the defendant so desires, and so moves the court, he shall have a continuance, for which the plaintiffs shall pay. So that the court did not administer this law, but this action was supported by no law whatever. The motion was to exclude this written evidence because it had not been filed in the clerk's office 30 days before the trial. There was and is no law for this, and the action was clearly erroneous. *Secondly.* This law was enacted in 1880. The laws since then have been codified, and this act left out of the Code. Section 4202 of the Code of Virginia, in force, provides that upon the adoption of that Code, which was done on the 1st day of May, 1888, all acts of a general nature should be repealed; and it is insisted that this section repeals this act. If the law was a special law, as contradistinguished from a general law, the adoption of the Code did not affect it, and it was not necessary that it should appear in the Code to prevent its repeal, and consequently laws of such a nature are left out of the Code, and are nevertheless still in force. Let us consider whether this law is a general law, within the meaning of section 4202 of the Code. It is a law which provides a different rule of procedure in ejectment trial in three counties of this state. We have a law which provides for a different limitation as to actions for land in many counties of this state,—all counties west of the Alleghany mountains, including the county of Carrol. This is a comparatively small section of the state, and yet it cannot be called a special law any more than the different limitations east of the Alleghany mountains. They are both general laws, and, if they had been left out of the Code, would have been repealed. They are re-enacted in Code, § 2915. Section 848 of the Code provides a different compensation for the members of the board of supervisors of the counties of Lee, Scott, Wise, Buchanan, Floyd, Russell, and Bland from that provided as to other counties. Why was not this omitted from the Code? Section 1004 of the Code re-enacts provisions of the road law, to apply specifically to Wise, Dickenson, and other counties. And all over the Code are to be found acts comparatively local in their character, applying to sections of the state more or less limited, and not applying to the whole state, but affecting portions thereof only, as to roads, fences, water-courses, fishing, hunting, proceedings in the courts, etc., all in existence and upon the statute-book at the time the Code was adopted; and if they had not been general laws, within the meaning of section 4202, supra, might have been left out of the Code without being affected. But it is clear that they are general laws, within the meaning of that section, and so had to be codified or repealed. They are general laws, applying to all the people of this commonwealth, limited to designated territorial application. For example, the general laws of this commonwealth provide a close season as to hunting. It, however, varies as to different localities; and so as to fishing, catching oysters, terrapins, etc. In the wide extent of the state, they vary as to section, necessarily. They are nevertheless parts of the general law of the state, applicable to all the people thereof. So this law in question is a general law of this state, within the meaning of section 4202 of the Code, applicable to all the people thereof who shall be plaintiffs in actions of ejectment in the section of the state to which it applies,—not only to all the people of Virginia, but the people of all the world who shall occupy that position in the section designated,—just as much so as this section 2915, supra, providing a limitation of entry on or action for land; and it has been repealed by the adoption of the present Code, and the mode of procedure in ejectment trials, so far as the introduction of the plaintiff's evidence, is the same in Wise county as elsewhere in this commonwealth; and the ruling of the court complained of in these assignments is erroneous.

The fourth assignment of error, relating to the introduction of evidence after the argument had been partly heard, is immaterial, as a new trial will be ordered, when this is not likely to arise.

The fifth is the exclusion of the plaintiffs' remaining evidence, because it did not show title in Dale Carter till after the day laid in the declaration as the day on which his title accrued, and after this suit was instituted, and refused to allow them to be read to the jury. It was sufficient if the plaintiffs could show a right to the possession of the premises at the time of the commencement of the suit. Section 2735, Code. It does not appear that the papers referred to covered the whole tract of land, and there appeared to be a compromise of an adverse claim of title in another, which, being abandoned, tended to show that the right was in the plaintiff from the beginning,—a question for the jury to determine, whether it was or was not so, and was undoubtedly a question of fact.

As to the sixth assignment of error,—the action of the circuit court in overruling the motion to set aside the verdict, and grant the plaintiffs a new trial,—this was erroneous, as appears from what has gone before. Upon the whole case we are of opinion to reverse, and remand the case for a new trial to be had therein in accordance to the foregoing views.

LEWIS, P., (dissenting.) It is clear to my mind that independently of the ruling of the circuit court as to the admissibility of the patent of 1856, or the construction and effect of the act of March 9, 1880, the judgment ought to be affirmed; for upon the merits the case is with the defendants. If, therefore, there is any error in those preliminary rulings, such error, as is apparent from a survey of the whole record, has not operated to the prejudice of the plaintiffs. This court has decided in numerous cases that, if it can be clearly seen from the whole record that a preliminary ruling of the lower court did not affect the actual merits of the case, the erroneousness of the ruling is no ground for a reversal of the final judgment, if that be substantially right. Now, in the present case, the defendants, to maintain the issue on their part, introduced in evidence several patents issued to one Richard Smith by the commonwealth in the latter part of the last century, and then proved that the land in controversy was embraced in those patents; the effect of which was to show that the patent of 1856 amounted to nothing, as the land had already been granted. Hannon v. Hannah, 9 Grat. 146. The plaintiffs, therefore, in rebuttal, offered evidence to show that the title of Richard Smith under those patents had been vested in Dale Carter. This they undertook to show in part by the record of a chancery suit in the circuit court of Russell county, in which suit one James Campbell was plaintiff, and the unknown heirs of the said Richard Smith, deceased, were defendants. The suit was brought to obtain the legal title of those defendants, and in the progress of the suit a decree was rendered in March, 1880, appointing a commissioner to convey the title to Campbell, which was done. Dale Carter, the ancestor of the plaintiffs, claimed through Campbell. But the commissioner's deed to Campbell was not made until April, 1880, which was nearly two years after the commencement of this action. The circuit court accordingly rejected the evidence, and, as I think, correctly. If there had been no dealings between Carter and Campbell, and this were an action by Campbell, he would not be entitled to recover, because, aside from any other consideration, the legal title was not in him, and there is nothing to show a right on his part to the possession of the premises in controversy at the time of the commencement of the action. Nor is it pretended that there has ever been any conveyance by Campbell to Carter. The compromise agreement, moreover, between Campbell and Carter, which was offered in evidence along with the record in the chancery suit, merely stipulated that in a certain action of ejectment, pending at the time between the parties, the defendant, Campbell, would withdraw his pleas, and allow Carter to obtain a judgment for the land embraced in the patent of 1856. This agreement was entered into in 1871, and there was no evidence offered even tending to show that Carter ever had, or that he was ever entitled to, possession of the land in controversy, except by virtue of the patent of 1856, and that agreement. "The rule at common law," says Tyler, "and in all the states which have preserved the distinction between legal and equitable title to land, is that the plaintiff in ejectment must show a legal title in himself to the land he claims, and the right to possession under it, at the time of the demise laid in the declaration, and at the time of the trial. He cannot support the action upon an equitable title, however clear and indisputable it may be, but must seek his remedy in chancery." Hence, as he says in the same connection, a title acquired after the commencement of the action will in no case entitle the plaintiff to recover. Tyler, Ej. 75. In McCool v. Smith, 1 Black, 459, the court says: "The rule of the common law is inflexible that a party can recover in ejectment only upon a title which subsisted in him at the time of the commencement of the suit." Therefore, although it was conceded in that case that the plaintiff had acquired a valid title, yet, inasmuch as it was acquired after the commencement of the action, it was held that the action could not be maintained. If the plaintiff can recover at all, said the court, it must be in an action brought after the date at which the title was acquired. In Tapscott v. Cobbs, 11 Grat. 172, although it was held that, where an intruder ousts a party in peaceable possession of land, the latter may recover the premises in ejectment upon his possession merely, yet the general rule was recognised that a plaintiff in ejectment must recover, if at all, upon the strength of his own title, and that the defendant may maintain his defense by simply showing that the title is in some one else than the plaintiff. And the statute itself provides that a plaintiff in such an action must show "a right to the possession of the premises at the time of the commencement of the suit." Code, § 2735. There is no evidence in this record, and none was offered, tending to show any such right in the plaintiff when this suit was commenced. It is not even shown that either Campbell or Dale Carter has ever at any time been in possession of the premises. It is shown, however, as I have already said, that the legal title was not acquired by Campbell until after the commencement of the action, and that neither Dale Carter nor those claiming under him have ever acquired it at all. How, then, this judgment, consistently with the established principles I have indicated, can be rightly reversed, I must confess my inability to understand. I think it ought to be affirmed. For, to summarise what has been said, conceding (for the sake of the argument) that the court erred in its ruling in respect to the patent of 1856, and conceding that the act of March 9, 1880, has been repealed by the new Code, still the judgment ought not to be reversed, because the records show that that patent conferred no title, and the plaintiffs have shown no right to recover the premises at the time the action was commenced. It is proper to add that counsel for the defendants in error deny that Campbell acquired the legal title in the Russell suit, and insist that it is outstanding in another. I do not wish to be understood, therefore, as the case is to go back for a new trial, as expressing any opinion on that point.

BURROWS v. FRENCH.

(*Supreme Court of South Carolina.* June 17, 1891.)

STATUTE OF LIMITATIONS—DISABILITIES—ABSENCE FROM STATE—NON-RESIDENT—"RETURN."

Code Proc. S. C. § 121, providing that, if any person be out of the state when a cause of action accrues against him, such action may be commenced within a specified time after his "return," applies not only to a resident of the state who has gone abroad temporarily, and then returns, but also to one who has never been a resident, and who comes for the first time within its limits.

Appeal from common pleas circuit court of Greenville county; JAMES F. IZLAR, Judge.

Action by Lewis P. Burrows against A. H. French on a promissory note. Judgment for defendant. Plaintiff appeals.

Perry & Heyward, for appellant. *Westmoreland & Haynsworth*, for respondent.

MCIVER, J. In this case there is no controversy as to the facts, and the single question presented is whether the plaintiff's action, under the conceded facts, was barred by the statute of limitations. The action was on a note dated 20th of March, 1874, payable on demand, with interest annually, with a payment indorsed thereon, dated 14th of December, 1879. At the time of the making of this note, both payee and maker were citizens of the state of New Hampshire, and the payee still resides there. The maker, however, some time after the execution of the note, (but when, precisely, is not stated,) left that state, and eventually settled in this state, where he has been residing for a period of less than six years before the commencement of this action. This action was commenced on the 10th of June, 1890, and, the plea of the statute having been interposed and sustained by the circuit judge, judgment was rendered in favor of defendant, and plaintiff appeals, alleging error in holding that the action was barred by the statute of limitation. Inasmuch as it is apparent from this statement that, upon the face of the papers, the action would be barred by the statute of limitations, unless it falls within some one of the exceptions provided for in the statute, the only question is whether it does come within any one of those exceptions. The only one which, it is suggested, covers this case is that found in section 131 of the Code of Procedure, which reads as follows: "If, when the cause of action shall accrue against any person, he shall be out of the state, such action may be commenced within the terms herein respectively limited after the return of such person into this state; and if, after such cause of action shall have accrued, such person shall depart from and reside out of this state, or remain continuously absent therefrom for the space of one year or more, the time of his absence shall not be deemed or taken as any part of the time limited for the commencement of such action." Inasmuch as it is not pretended that the defendant, after the accrual of plaintiff's cause of action, departed from this state, it is very clear that the second clause of the section just quoted has no application, and it only remains to consider whether the first clause applies, and what is its effect. It being conceded that the defendant was out of the state when the cause of action accrued, the inquiry is narrowed down to the question whether the plaintiff can avail himself of the privilege conferred by the latter part of the first clause, allowing the action to be brought within six years (that being the period limited by the Code within which an action like this may be brought) "after the return of such person into this state;" and that turns upon the construction proper to be given to the word "return," as used in the section.

On the one hand, the appellant contends that this word, as there used, should be so construed as to embrace a person who never was a resident of this state before, but for the first time comes within its limits, and takes up his residence here; while the respondent contends that it must be confined to persons who, having once resided here, have gone abroad for a time, and have come back to the state. It is very obvious that, if the construction contended for by appellant can be sustained, that there was error in the ruling below, as it is conceded that the action was commenced within six years after the defendant came into this state. But, on the other hand, if the construction contended for by respondent be the correct one, then it is equally clear that there was no error in the ruling below, for it is not claimed that the defendant ever did "return" to this state, in the strict sense of that word. While it is true, so far as we are informed, that there is no decision in this state construing this particular section of the Code, as no case involving the question has ever come before this court since the adoption of the Code, yet we are not without authority here upon the subject. In the case of Alexander v. Burnet, 5 Rich. Law, 189, (decided in 1851,) a similar question to that now presented, involving the construction of very similar language, was considered by the former court of appeals; and it was there held that the provision of the statute of Anne allowing a creditor to bring an action against his debtor, who was "beyond seas," (which, it is well settled, means beyond the limits of the state,) at the time the cause of action accrued, at any time within a specified period after his return to the state, applies as well to foreigners residing abroad as to persons who, having once resided here, had gone abroad, and then returned to this state. In that case EVANS, J., in delivering the opinion of the court, used this language: "It has been agreed that the statute of Anne has no application to the case, because Alexander, being a citizen of another state, cannot be said to have returned to the state, and therefore the statute must relate only to the case of citizens who are absent for a time, and then return. This may be the literal import of the words, but, where the words of a statute have received a uniform construction, it is always safe to adhere to it. In 6 Bac. Abr. 392, (Bouv. Ed.,) it is said: 'The exceptions in the statutes of James and Anne, as to persons beyond seas, are not confined to Englishmen, who may occasionally go beyond seas, but is general, and extends to foreigners who are constantly resident abroad.' Strithorst v. Graeme, 3 Wils. 145. This is clearly the English law, and the same construction, I believe, has been uniformly put on the same or similar words in most, or all, the states." The same view was manifestly entertained by the court in Lavasseur v.

Lignies, 1 Strob. 326, though the precise question here presented was not decided in that case. In Ruggles v. Keeler, 3 Johns. 263, the same construction was adopted, and KENT, C. J., in delivering the opinion of the court, used these words: "Whether the defendant be a resident of this state, and only absent for a time, or whether he resides altogether out of the state, is immaterial. He is equally within the proviso. If the cause of action arose out of the state, it is sufficient to save the statute from running in favor of the party to be charged until it comes within our jurisdiction. This has been the uniform construction of the English statutes, which also speak of the return from beyond seas of the party so absent. The word 'return' has never been construed to confine the proviso to Englishmen who went abroad occasionally." So, also, the same doctrine was declared in Fowler v. Hunt, 10 Johns. 464, where it is said: "The word 'return' applies as well to persons coming from abroad, where they had resided, as to citizens of this state going abroad for a temporary purpose, and then returning;" and the case of Ruggles v. Keeler, supra, is cited with approval. While it may be true that different views have prevailed in some of the states, yet we prefer to adopt the construction of our own court of appeals, indorsed by the great name of KENT, and in conformity to the uniform construction given to the English statutes of similar import. This, too, seems to be in conformity to the evident intention of the legislature; for it is manifest that the purpose was to declare the limitations of time within which the doors of our courts should be open for the enforcement of the several causes of action mentioned in the statute, and, as the doors of the court are practically not open for that purpose until the person to be charged comes within the jurisdiction, provision has been made that the time of such limitation shall not commence to run until the courts are practically open for the enforcement of a given cause of action against the particular person sought to be charged thereby; and the statute even goes further, and provides, by the second clause of section 121 of the Code, that "if after such cause of action shall have accrued such person shall depart from and reside out of this state, or remain continuously absent therefrom for the space of one year or more, the time of his absence shall not be deemed or taken as any part of the time limited for the commencement of such action." This shows that the legislature intended that a creditor should have the full period of six years, in a case like this, while his debtor was within reach of the process of the court, to bring his action, except where his temporary absence was for a period less than one year. It seems to us, therefore, that the circuit judge erred in sustaining the plea of the statute of limitations. The judgment of this court is that the judgment of the circuit court be reversed, and the case be remanded to that court for a new trial.

MCGOWAN, J., concurs.

HIBERNIA SAV. INST. v. LUHN.

(Supreme Court of South Carolina.　June 17, 1891.)

WIFE'S SEPARATE ESTATE — HUSBAND AS AGENT
TO SECURE LOAN—PRESUMPTIONS.

1. A husband, representing himself as agent of his wife, made an application in the name of the wife for a loan to be secured by a bond and mortgage upon her property, which were accordingly delivered to the lender by the husband, who received the money. The wife admitted the execution of the bond and mortgage. *Held,* that the husband was acting as agent for his wife, and the lender was justified in presuming that the loan was for the benefit of her separate estate.

2. Where a married woman, either directly or through her agent, borrows money, the money so borrowed becomes at once a part of her separate estate, and her contract to repay the same is a contract with reference to her separate estate, which may be enforced, unless it is shown that the lender had notice that the money was not for her use.

Appeal from common pleas circuit court of Charleston county; T. B. FRASER, Judge.

This was an action brought to foreclose a mortgage given by defendant, Josephine S. Luhn, to the Hibernia Savings Institution of Charleston, plaintiff. The cause was referred, and the master's report is as follows: "To the Honorable the Presiding Judge: This case was referred to me by an order of the court filed July 5, 1889, to inquire into and report upon the issues of law and fact therein involved, with leave to report any special matter. I have held references, have been attended by the solicitors of the parties, have taken testimony, which is hereto attached, and have heard arguments upon the issues involved. I submit the following report: The complaint in this action is brought for the foreclosure of a mortgage executed by the defendant to the plaintiff, under date of 23d January, 1885, to secure her bond of even date, conditioned for the payment of $1,800 on the 18th January, 1886, with interest after maturity at the rate of 7 per cent. per annum payable semi-yearly in advance. The complaint alleges simply: (1) That the plaintiff is a corporation, chartered under the laws of this state. (2) That the bond and mortgage were duly made, executed, and delivered by the defendant to the plaintiff, as above stated; describing the property mortgaged. (3) That the mortgage was duly recorded. (4) That the condition of the bond has been broken, and that there is due thereon the sum of $1,989. And then follows the prayer of judgment of foreclosure and sale. The answer of defendant admits all the allegations of the complaint, but alleges 'that at the time of the execution and delivery of the bond and mortgage mentioned this defendant was a married woman; that the money received from plaintiff corporation was not used for the benefit of this defendant, or for the benefit of her separate estate. Wherefore defendant prays that the said bond and mortgage be declared null and void, and that the complaint be dismissed.' After the testimony had been closed, and the plaintiff had made his argument in chief, the attorney for the de-

fendant moved for leave to amend the answer by striking out the words, 'that the money received from plaintiff corporation was not used for the benefit of this defendant, or for the benefit of her separate estate,' and substituting the words, 'that said bond and mortgage were not made for the benefit of her separate estate.' The motion was opposed by plaintiff, but I granted the amendment, as it does not seem to me to change materially the defense, and it was represented to me by defendant's counsel that, owing to his sickness at the time. the answer had not been drawn according to his instruction. Plaintiff excepted to this order. The case therefore came up upon the complaint and the amended answer. A great deal of testimony offered was excepted to on both sides on the grounds of irrelevancy and incompetency, and by consent of counsel for both parties it was all taken subject to any legal exception that may be urged against it, whether stated specifically in the minutes of reference or not. After a careful examination and weighing of evidence, I find the following facts: On January 16, 1885, the late Dr. G. J. Luhn, the husband of defendant, applied to the Hibernia Savings Institution, the plaintiff herein, for a loan on behalf of his wife, representing himself as her agent. The application was made to F. J. McGarey, the cashier of the bank, at the banking-house. The application was made in writing upon a printed slip of paper, and the original application is in existence. (Ex. A.) It reads as follows: 'To the President and Board of Directors of the Hibernia Savings Institution. Charleston, S. C., January 16, 1885. Gentlemen: I ask for a loan of $1,800, @ 7 % per annum, for which offer as security one new two-story frame house, Smith street, just below Vanderhorst street, lot 40x133. Respectfully, JOSEPHINE S. LUHN, per G. J. LUHN.' On Mr. McGarey's examination. he was asked by plaintiff's attorney, 'At the time Dr. Luhn was negotiating for the loan, and at the delivery of the bond and mortgage, as the agent for his wife, what purpose did he state the money would be used for by her?' I ruled this question out as incompetent. The answer of the witness thereto was however taken, subject to exception, and will be found in the appendix to the testimony. The application was referred to the board of directors. They employed Capt. James F. Redding to examine the property. Redding made the examination, found that the buildings on the premises 'were nearing completion,' and made the following indorsement in writing upon the original application: 'Approved. J. F. REDDING, Committee, January 19th, 1885.' On January 24, 1885, Dr. Luhn presented himself at the bank with the bond and mortgage, (Exhibits B and C,) which are dated 23d January, 1885, the mortgage being probated January 24, 1885, and received the money. Eight hundred dollars was paid him in cash, and one thousand in check No. 160 on the Bank of Charleston, N. B. A., to the order of 160, which check is in evidence. (Ex. D.) It is indorsed, 'G. J. Luhn.' No further inquiry was made by the bank. The title seems to have been examined by their solicitor, but no written opinion was furnished, and no abstract of title has been offered in evidence. There are no payments indorsed upon the bond. Mr. McGarey testifies that the loan was charged on the books of the bank against Mrs. Josephine S. Luhn. Dr. Luhn is dead. The defendant being a married woman, the burden of proof is upon the plaintiff to show that the contract was made with reference to the separate estate of Mrs. Luhn. The mortgage is of property which is conceded to be Mrs. Luhn's separate estate. As I understand the law, however, the mortgage is only the security for the debt; the debt or contract being the bond. If the contract represented by the bond was made with reference to the separate estate, then it was competent for Mrs. Luhn to mortgage the separate estate to secure the bond; otherwise, the contract and the mortgage securing it are both void. Mrs. Luhn has testified to a state of facts tending to show that she never intended to sign any bond and mortgage at all; that she never authorized her husband to borrow money for her, as her agent, upon the security of her separate estate; and that she was in fact overreached by her husband in the matter; and that she signed the bond and mortgage under a misapprehension of their purport. Inasmuch as the bond and mortgage is admitted by the answer, I do not consider the testimony competent, not being pertinent to any issue raised in the pleadings. See McGrath v. Barnes, 18 S. C. 606; Mitchell v. De Graffenreid, Harp. 451. Discarding Mrs. Luhn's testimony upon this point, therefore, from consideration, there remains, however, sufficient evidence to satisfy me of the following facts: That the lot in Smith street was given by Dr. Luhn to his wife, the conveyance being dated July 23, 1884, and that he proceeded to erect upon it a house for her. That he employed a builder, F. Lucas, to erect the house, made the contracts himself individually, with said builder, paid the bills regularly every week, and purchased and paid for the lumber which went into the house. That the house was begun in October, 1884, and was finished by the 1st of February, 1885, or a few days after. That immediately after the completion of the house the same builder went on with the work of erecting other houses for Dr. Luhn upon the adjoining lots owned by him. That on the 26th of January, 1885, there were issued from the office of the city assessor several building permits. One of these was issued to Mrs. Josephine S. Luhn, upon the application of the builder, F. Lucas, for the erection of a two-story wooden building on the lot on the east side of Smith street, between Calhoun and Vanderhorst streets, at an estimated cost of $1.800. On the same day, permits were taken out by G. J. Luhn for various other buildings on adjacent lots. That on the 26th January, 1885, when this permit was issued to Mrs. Luhn, upon the application of the builder, the buildings on the said lot were almost completed, and they were in fact completed a few days later. That

Mrs. Luhn had no money of her own to pay for the erection of said buildings, and that the cost of the same had been, by weekly payments, defrayed by Dr. Luhn. While it is of course possible that Dr. Luhn may have intended to reimburse himself for the cost of the house from the $1,800 raised upon the bond, there is no proof whatever that the money was obtained for that specific purpose or was so applied. I find that Mrs. Luhn did not receive the money raised upon the bond and mortgage, and that the plaintiff has failed to show by satisfactory proof that the contract sued upon was made with reference to Mrs. Luhn's separate estate. On the contrary, I hold that the transaction was in substance a borrowing of money for the husband's benefit, upon the credit of the wife's separate estate. The plaintiff was dealing with a married woman, —a person with a limited power,—and is bound to show, therefore, by a preponderance of legal proof, that the contract was made within the scope of that power. This the plaintiff, in my judgment, has failed to do; and therefore, under the settled law of this state, I hold, as conclusion of law, that the bond and mortgage sued upon must be declared null and void. I recommend, therefore, that said bond and mortgage be adjudged to be null and void, and that the complaint be dismissed, with costs. Respectfully submitted, G. H. SASS, Master. October 8, 1889."

Decree, Filed 20th April, 1890: "This case came before me at the term of the court held in March, 1890, on a report of the master, and exceptions thereto on the part of the plaintiff. The action has been brought to foreclose a mortgage executed by the defendant to the plaintiff to secure the payment of a bond of the same date given by the defendant to the plaintiff, to pay the sum of ($1,800) eighteen hundred dollars, on the 18th January, 1888, with interest after maturity, at the rate of seven per cent., payable semi-annually in advance. The mortgage covers a lot in the city of Charleston, the property and separate estate of the defendant, a married woman. The answer of the defendant admits the execution of the bond and mortgage, but sets up as a defense that she was at the time of the execution 'a married woman, and that the said bond and mortgage were not given for the benefit of her separate estate.' The master recommends that the bond and mortgage be adjudged null and void, and that the complaint be dismissed, with costs. I do not consider it necessary to take up the exceptions seriatim, and I will announce my conclusions briefly, endeavoring to conform as near as I can to the rulings of the supreme court on this subject. I am inclined to think that the admissions in the answer, that the bond and mortgage were duly executed are in accordance with the testimony, but after the admission in the pleadings it is too late now to claim that there was any defect which could affect the plaintiff. After the execution of the bond and mortgage, the defendant, to put it no stronger, allowed her husband to take them to the plaintiff's officers and agents, where they were discounted. The plaintiff had a right to act on the assumption that the husband was the agent of the defendant for the purpose of having the bond discounted and receiving the money. The money was loaned to her, and the payment to the husband and agent was a payment to her. And I see no reason why a married woman should not be held bound by such a transaction as well as any other person. To allow her now to set up as a defense that her husband had been guilty of a fraud on her rights would operate as a greater fraud on the plaintiff, whom she permitted to be misled by the execution of the bond and mortgage, and delivering them to her husband under circumstances which held him out to plaintiff as her agent for this business. I hold that this was a lending of the money to her, and that she is estopped from denying it, unless it shall affirmatively appear that in some way it was brought home to the notice of plaintiff's agent or officers that the money was for the use of her husband, or some other person besides herself, and of which there was not the slightest evidence. I confess that I see no good reason why she should not be bound by her bond and mortgage, even if she had communicated the fact to the plaintiffs that she intended to give the money to her husband. In the light of recent decisions of the supreme court, I do not regard it as at all important whether any statement was made to the plaintiff that the money was borrowed for her own use or not, or as to what use was in fact made of it. If she borrowed the money, it was not necessary for it to be for the benefit of her separate estate. See Association v. Jones, 10 S. E. Rep. 1079, (S. C. March, 1890.) It is ordered and adjudged that the report of the master be overruled. The interest is payable semi-annually in advance, and bears interest. The last payment of interest was due 18th January, 1890. I have allowed two months and twenty-two days interest on the principal instead of six months, for this last payment of interest, and have calculated interest on all these sums of unpaid interest to date. The amount now due is ($2,106.30) two thousand one hundred and six 30-100 dollars. It is therefore ordered and adjudged that the mortgaged premises be sold by the master on some convenient sales day, after due advertisement in one of the newspapers published in the city of Charleston, for one-third cash, and the balance on a credit of one and two years, with interest from the day of sale, to be secured by the bond of the purchaser and mortgage of the premises, and a policy of insurance on the buildings on the lot to the full extent of their insurance value, to be assigned to the master; the purchaser to have the right to pay all cash, and either party to have the right to purchase at the sale. It is ordered that out of the proceeds of the sale the master do pay the costs and expenses of the sale, and then the plaintiff's costs, including officers of the court, attorneys and witnesses; then the amount of the mortgage debt and interest thereon; if there be any surplus, the same to be paid to the defendant;

and if there be any deficiency on the coming in of the master's report on sale, the plaintiff shall have the right to move for leave to enter judgment and issue execution for the same. It is ordered that in compliance with the terms of sale the master shall execute and deliver to the purchaser title to the property so sold, and that he be let into possession thereof, and that the defendant, and all persons claiming under her since the filing of the notice of lis pendens in this case, be forever barred and foreclosed of all right and equity of redemption in the mortgaged premises so sold and conveyed. T. B. FRASER, Presiding Judge. 10th April, 1890."

Defendant appeals from the decree.

Lord & Hyde, for appellants. *C. A. Mc-Hugh*, for respondent.

McIVER, J. This was an action to foreclose a mortgage, and the defense was that the defendant, being a married woman at the time, had no power to make the contract evidenced by the bond and mortgage upon which the action was based. In the complaint it is alleged that the defendant made and executed the bond and mortgage in question to the plaintiff, and in the original answer defendant admits this allegation, "but alleges that at the time of the execution and delivery of the bond and mortgage mentioned this defendant was a married woman; that the money received from the plaintiff corporation was not used for the benefit of this defendant, or for the benefit of her separate estate." And in her amended answer she makes the same admission, "but alleges that, at the time of the execution and delivery of the bond and mortgage mentioned, this defendant was a married woman, and that said bond and mortgage were not made for the benefit of her separate estate." The undisputed facts are that Dr. G. J. Luhn, the husband of defendant, representing himself as agent of his wife, made an application in writing to the plaintiff for the loan of the money mentioned in the bond, to be secured by a mortgage on a lot, owned by defendant, on Smith street, which application was signed, "Josephine S. Luhn, per G. J. Luhn;" and that a few days afterwards, when the loan had been approved by the board of directors of the plaintiff bank, Dr. Luhn delivered to the bank the bond and mortgage, and obtained the money, and the loan was charged on the books of the bank against Mrs. Josephine S. Luhn.

The issues were referred to Master Sass, who made his report, wherein, after narrating the facts which he considered as established by the evidence, which is set out in the "case," concluded, as matter of fact, "that Mrs. Luhn did not receive the money raised upon the bond and mortgage, and that the plaintiff has failed to show, by satisfactory proof, that the contract sued upon was made with reference to Mrs. Luhn's separate estate;" and, as matter of law, "that the bond and mortgage sued upon must be declared null and void." To this report the plaintiff filed numerous exceptions, and the case was heard by his honor, Judge FRASER, upon the report and exceptions, who rendered his decree (which, together with the master's report, should be incorporated in the report of this case) overruling the conclusions reached by the master, for the reasons therein stated, and rendering judgment in favor of plaintiff. From this judgment defendant appeals upon the several grounds set out in the record, which, under the view we take of this case, need not be specifically stated here. In Association v. Jones, 32 S. C. 313, 10 S. E. Rep. 1079, the following language was used by the court: "Since the decisions in the cases of Greig v. Smith, 29 S. C. 426, 7 S. E. Rep. 610; Brown v. Thomson, 31 S. C. 436, 10 S. E. Rep. 95; Gwynn v. Gwynn, 31 S. C. 482, 10 S. E. Rep. 221; Howard v. Kitchens, 31 S. C. 490, 10 S. E. Rep. 224; Law v. Lipscomb, 31 S. C. 504, 10 S. E. Rep. 226, 1104; and Schmidt v. Dean, 31 S. C. 498, 10 S. E. Rep. 228, 1104,—it must be regarded as settled, that where a married woman, either directly or through her agent, borrows money from another, the money so borrowed becomes at once a part of her separate estate, and her contract to repay the same is a contract with reference to her separate estate, which may be enforced against her; and that the lender, in the absence of notice to the contrary, has a right to assume that the money was borrowed for the use of the married woman; and she is estopped from denying that fact, unless it is shown that the lender had notice to the contrary. These cases furthermore determine that the husband may, if so authorized by the wife, act as her agent, and that the disposition which may be made of the money after it has been borrowed cannot affect the question. See, also, McCord v. Blackwell, 31 S. C. 125, 9 S. E. Rep. 777."

In view of this deliberate statement of what must be considered as the settled law of this state in regard to the contracts of married women entered into after the adoption of Gen. St. 1882, and prior to the amendment of 1887, it seems to us that the material questions raised by this appeal are: (1) Whether the money secured by the bond and mortgage was borrowed for the use of the defendant; (2) if not, whether the plaintiff had any notice that it was borrowed for the use of her husband. While there is no evidence that the money was borrowed by defendant in person, we think the evidence does show that it was borrowed by her through her agent. It is true that there is no direct evidence that the defendant had ever constituted her husband her agent, yet agency may be, and often is, established by circumstances. There can be no doubt that in this instance the husband assumed to act as agent for his wife in effecting this loan, and so represented himself to the plaintiff; for the application was in writing to which the name of the defendant was signed by the husband as her agent; and though this would not be sufficient, of itself, to establish the agency, yet, taken in connection with the other circumstances, we think the agency is clearly established. The defendant admits in her answer the execution of the bond

and mortgage, which necessarily involved the delivery of those papers; and as it is not pretended that she delivered them in person to the plaintiff, but they were delivered by the husband, her admission, connected with this act of the husband, shows that they were delivered by him as her agent, unless we should assume, in the absence of any evidence to that effect, that this husband, who the defendant's own witness, her mother, says was "a kind husband,—all that could be desired as a husband and father,"—had practiced a deliberate fraud on his wife. If, then, the husband, as the agent of his wife, made this application in his wife's name for the loan of the money, promising to deliver, and actually delivering, his wife's bond and mortgage, the execution of which is admitted by her, to secure the repayment of the money borrowed, surely the plaintiff had a right to assume, in the absence of any evidence whatever to the contrary, that the money was being borrowed for the wife's own use, upon the plain, common-sense view that where one person applies to another for the loan of money the lender has a right to assume, in the absence of anything being said or intimated to the contrary, that the borrower wants the money for his own use. It is contended, however, that this doctrine, which it is claimed was for the first time laid down in Association v. Jones, supra, is in conflict with the rule laid down in Taylor v. Barker, 30 S. C. 242, 9 S. E. Rep. 115; McCord v. Blackwell, 31 S. C. 135, 9 S. E. Rep. 777; Brown v. Thomson, 31 S. C. 442, 10 S. E. Rep. 95; and Gwynn v. Gwynn, 31 S. C. 482, 10 S. E. Rep. 221. But a careful examination of those cases will show that there is no such conflict. While it is true that, inasmuch as a married woman has but a limited power to contract, a person dealing with her must take notice of such disability, and when he seeks to enforce his contract the burden is upon him to show that the contract is one which a married woman is capable of making, yet how this may be shown is an altogether different question. Like every other fact necessary to be established in the trial of a case in court, it may be shown as well by circumstances as by direct evidence.

The question in every case like the present is, first, a question of fact,—whether the contract in question was a contract as to the separate estate of the wife. If it is, then the law declares that she is liable; but if it is not, then she is not liable, no matter how clearly she may have expressed her intention to make her separate estate liable. For, after the fact is ascertained that the contract was not in reference to the separate estate of the wife, the question becomes a legal question of power, not of intention. Applying this doctrine to the case of a contract to secure the payment of money borrowed, the first inquiry is whether the money was borrowed for her own use; for if it was, then she would be liable; but if not, then she would not be liable even though she may have expressly declared her intention to bind her separate estate, in the obligation given to secure the repayment of the money borrowed, for the simple reason that in the latter case she had no power to make such a contract, and her intention to do that which she has no power to do is wholly insufficient to bind her legally. Where, however, a married woman borrows money or buys a horse from another, and by her conduct or representations induces the lender or the vendor, as the case may be, to suppose that she is borrowing the money or buying the horse for her own use, when in fact her real purpose, unknown to the party with whom she is dealing, is to obtain the money or the horse for her husband or some one else, she will be estopped from denying that what she herself had induced the lender or vendor to believe was true, upon the ground that it would be a fraud to allow her to repudiate a contract which she had induced the person with whom she dealt to believe she had the power to make, when as a matter of fact she had no such power. She is estopped from disputing that the fact is as she represented it to be. But when it is once ascertained as a matter of fact that the contract in question was not made in reference to her separate estate, then nothing that she may do or say will estop her from denying her legal liability under the fact as thus ascertained. If, however, the person with whom she deals, notwithstanding her representation to the contrary, has notice that the contract is not a contract as to her separate estate, but is for the benefit of another, then no estoppel will arise, for the obvious reason that he has not been misled as to the fact, and he is bound to take notice of the legal disability of the married woman under the facts of which he has notice. The following language, used by this court in the case of Gwynn v. Gwynn, as reported in 27 S. C., at page 542, 4 S. E. Rep. 229, is quoted and relied upon by counsel for appellant: "It does not seem to us that there is any room for any estoppel. As we have seen, the question is one of power, not of intention; and in the absence of any allegation and proof of fraud we do not see how any representations, either by word or act, could affect the inquiry." But it will be observed that this language was used after it had been ascertained that the contract there in question was not such a contract as a married woman was capable of making; and hence, while that language was entirely appropriate to the case then under consideration, it has no application to the present case. There it was sought to make a married woman liable under a contract of partnership, and there was no question of fact there as to the nature of the contract; while here the primary question is of fact. In that case, after reaching the conclusion that a married woman had no power to enter into a contract of partnership, it followed necessarily, as we have said above, that nothing which she may have afterwards said or done could affect the inquiry. It seems to us, therefore, that there was no error on the part of the circuit judge in holding that the testimony was sufficient to show that the money was borrowed by the defendant through her husband, as her agent, for her

own use, and that she is therefore liable, unless it further appears that the plaintiff had notice, at the time, that the money was borrowed for the use of the husband. This brings us to the second question in the case. There is certainly no direct evidence of any such notice to the plaintiff. On the contrary, all the circumstances show that the plaintiff had every reason to believe that the money was wanted for the use of the wife. The application for the loan was made, in writing, in her name, and her separate property was offered as security. Her bond and mortgage were delivered by one manifestly clothed with her authority as agent; for, as we have said, the admission in her answer of the execution of these papers necessarily implies, in view of the undisputed fact that they were delivered by her husband, and not by herself in person, that he was her agent in making such delivery. The loan was charged on the books of the bank against Mrs. Luhn, and not against her husband; and this tends to show that the bank then regarded the transaction as a loan to her. But when to this is added the testimony of the cashier that Dr. Luhn stated at the time that the money was to be used in the erection of a building by Mrs. Luhn, we do not see how it is possible to doubt that, so far from the bank having any notice that the money was borrowed for the use of the husband, there was every reason to believe that it was borrowed for the use of the wife. The fact that the money was delivered to the husband cannot affect the question; for this was manifestly done because the bank regarded him as her agent, and had every reason to so treat him. While, therefore, we are not prepared to indorse the remark of the circuit judge to the effect that she would be liable "even if she had communicated the fact to the plaintiff that she intended to give the money to her husband," yet we think the conclusion which he reached was correct, for the reasons stated above. The judgment of this court is that the judgment of the circuit court be affirmed.

McGOWAN, J., concurs in the result.

STATE ex rel. CANADAY v. BLACK, Sheriff.

(*Supreme Court of South Carolina.* June 17, 1891.)

MANDAMUS TO SHERIFF—RECOVERY OF POSSESSION OF LAND—JURISDICTION IN CERTIORARI.

1. Gen. St. S. C. § 1817, provides that, on the determination of a lease of lands, when the lessee shall hold over, any two justices in the county may, on proof by the lessor, summon a jury to try the case, and, if they shall find that the lessor is entitled to the possession of the premises, the justices shall thereupon issue their warrant, commanding the sheriff to deliver to such lessor full possession of the premises. *Held,* that where, on verdict against the lessee and one holding under him, the justices have issued the proper warrant to the sheriff, *mandamus* will lie to compel him to execute same; and the fact that *certiorari* proceedings are pending before a judge of another circuit is immaterial, when such proceedings are void for lack of jurisdiction.

2. Under sections 2116, 2117, relative to the functions of circuit judges, which provide that a

circuit judge shall have jurisdiction to discharge all the duties of his office within the circuit where he resides, except the holding of circuit courts therein, when some other circuit judge shall be engaged in holding said courts, a judge has no jurisdiction to grant a writ of *certiorari* in a case tried in another circuit, while the judge thereof is holding court therein.

Petition for *mandamus*.
Original petition for *mandamus* by State ex rel. J. I. Canaday. Gen. St. S. C. §§ 2116, 2117, relative to the functions of circuit judges, provide that a circuit judge shall have jurisdiction to discharge all the duties of his office within the circuit where he resides, except the holding of circuit courts therein, when some other circuit judge shall be engaged in holding said courts.

Howell, Murphy & Farrow, for petitioner. *Tracy & Klein*, for defendant.

McIVER, J. This was a petition addressed to this court in the exercise of its original jurisdiction, for the purpose of obtaining a writ of *mandamus* directing the respondent "to forthwith put your petitioner into possession of the lands hereinbefore mentioned and described." In the petition, which was verified, it is alleged that the petitioner is the owner of and entitled to the immediate possession of a certain tract of land situate in the county of Colleton, particularly described therein. (2) That on the 11th of October, 1890, he made an affidavit (a copy of which is filed with the petition as an exhibit) before a trial justice of said county, that one Phillip Loyd was in possession of the said premises as a tenant, and, though his lease had expired, had refused to surrender possession to the petitioner. (3) That the said trial justice, together with another trial justice of said county, took the necessary proceedings (copies of which accompany the petition as exhibits) under section 1817 of the General Statutes to eject the said Philip Loyd and one James Sanders, who, it was alleged, was also in possession under the said Phillip Loyd and by his consent. (4) That as the result of such proceedings, and in conformity with the verdict of the jury, the said trial justices issued their warrant addressed to the said Robert Black, as sheriff of Colleton county, commanding him "forthwith to deliver to the said J. I. Canaday full possession of the premises as hereinafter described, and to levy expenses incurred of the goods and chattels of Mrs. L. C. Campbell." A copy of this warrant, containing a description of the premises, is likewise filed as an exhibit with the petition. (5) That the respondent, Robert Black, has refused to execute the warrant of the said trial justices requiring him to deliver possession of the said premises to the petitioner, basing his refusal upon an order, set out in the petition, granted by his honor, Judge IZLAR, judge of the first judicial circuit, at his chambers in Mt. Pleasant, in Berkeley county, a county which is not embraced within the limits of the second circuit, wherein the land in question is situate, and wherein the cause of action arose. (6) That this order was based upon an *ex parte* unverified petition,

presented by the said James Sanders, (a copy of which is filed as an exhibit,) praying that a writ of *certiorari* might be issued, directed to the said trial justices, requiring them to certify their proceedings to the next term of the circuit court for Colleton county, and that in the mean time further proceedings in said cause be stayed; and that upon this petition Judge IZLAR, without notice to the relator, indorsed the following order: "On filing and reading the foregoing petition, and on application of W. E. Klein, attorney for petitioner, I allow the writ of *certiorari* herein prayed for, and order that all further proceedings in said action be stayed." (7) Relator submits that, inasmuch as his honor, Judge ALDRICH, judge of the second circuit, was then in said circuit, holding court therein, his honor, Judge IZLAR, had no jurisdiction to grant the order allowing the writ of *certiorari*, and staying the proceedings. It will be noted that, in stating the substance of this petition, we have not followed the numbering of the paragraphs as found in the petition, and this statement is made simply to avoid confusion or misapprehension.

Upon hearing this petition, the usual rule to show cause was issued, to which the respondent has made return, in which, while not controverting any of the facts stated in the petition, he states additional facts which are not traversed by the relator, to-wit, that on the 1st of November, 1890, the order of Judge IZLAR "came up for a hearing before his honor, Judge ALDRICH, at Walterboro, when the return of the said trial justices was read, and objection to the authority of Judge IZLAR was then made as to his right to grant the same; that such hearing was postponed, and, owing to the indisposition of Judge ALDRICH, was not heard during the October term of court for Colleton county, and the cause was continued;" and files as exhibits copies of said return, etc. Respondent submits "that it is not his plain ministerial duty to obey an order of ejectment unless the same be regular in form, and directed solely against the parties to the proceeding, and unless the same issue from a court of record or other competent authority;" and that it is not his plain ministerial duty to disobey the order of a circuit judge, regular on its face.

The first ground relied upon by the respondent clearly cannot be sustained. It is conceded that the proceeding which culminated in the warrant was instituted under section 1817 of the General Statutes, and that section expressly declares that "if, upon hearing the case, the jury shall be satisfied that the complainant is entitled to the premises in question, they shall so find; whereof the justices shall make a record, and shall thereupon issue their warrant, directed to the sheriff of the county wherein the lands are situated, commanding him forthwith to deliver to such lessee, his heirs or assigns, full possession of the premises, and to levy all expenses incurred of the goods and chattels of the lessee, or the person in possession as aforesaid." Here was a plain ministerial duty imposed upon the sheriff, which he was bound to perform. He had no authority to inquire into the regularity of the proceedings before the trial justices, or whether they had committed any errors in performing the duties required of them by the statute. Whether all the proper parties had been made was not for him to inquire about. His duty was simply to execute the warrant as it came to him. See Bragg v. Thompson, 19 S. C. 576; Goodgoin v Gilreath, 32 S. C. 391, 11 S. E. Rep. 207, Rogers v. Marlboro Co., 32 S. C. 561, 11 S. E. Rep. 383. If the trial justices committed any errors of law, either in the institution or conduct of the proceedings, the law affords a remedy for the correction of such errors; but it is not to be found in the refusal of the sheriff to execute the warrant. If, for example, the trial justices improperly incorporated in the warrant a mandate to levy the expenses out of the property of Mrs. Campbell, (as to which, however, we adjudge nothing, as she is not a party to this case,) she will have her remedy, if the sheriff undertakes to make such levy. But that matter is not before us, as the only question presented for our decision is whether the relator is entitled to a writ of *mandamus* requiring the respondent forthwith to deliver possession of the premises to the petitioner.

The only real question in the case is whether the respondent bases his refusal, to-wit, the order of Judge IZLAR, can be sustained. There can be no doubt that, if Judge IZLAR had jurisdiction to grant such order, this would afford ample excuse to the respondent for refusing to obey the mandate of the trial justices. But if, on the other hand, he had no such jurisdiction, then it is obvious that the order is a nullity, and affords no excuse whatever to respondent. If the order was a nullity, then it is the same, legally, as if no such order had ever been signed; in which case respondent would stand without any excuse whatever for refusing to obey the mandate of the trial justices, and the appropriate remedy would be by *mandamus*. The vital question, then, is whether Judge IZLAR had any jurisdiction to grant the order in question. His jurisdiction is assailed upon two grounds: (1) Because the order was granted at chambers; (2) because it was in a cause arising in the second circuit, and only triable there, by the judge of the first circuit, while holding the courts of that circuit; the resident judge of the second circuit being at the time in the second circuit, and engaged in holding the courts of that circuit.

First, there can be no doubt, since the case of State v. Senft, 2 Hill, (S. C.) 370, that the writ of *certiorari*, at common law, could only be granted in open court, in term-time; and hence, if the writ can be granted by a judge at chambers, the power must be derived either from the constitution or from some statute. It is very obvious that this power is not conferred upon a judge at chambers by any provision of the constitution, and hence it must be looked for in some statute. Section 2115 of the General Statutes, the object of which seems to have been to confer upon the circuit judges at chambers the power

to grant certain specified writs, and to hear certain cases therein mentioned, as it was originally adopted, did not mention writs of *certiorari* as one of the writs which might be granted at chambers; but, at the very next session of the general assembly, the act of 21st of December, 1882, (18 St. 38,) was passed, manifestly for the purpose of supplying this omission, for the amendment was simply that the section be amended so as to read as follows; repeating the language, *in totidem verbis*, of the section as originally adopted, with the single addition of writ of *certiorari* to the writs named in this section as it originally read. So that it is plain that the sole object of the act of 1882, above cited, was to confer upon a circuit judge at chambers the power to grant writs of *certiorari*, as well as writs of prohibition and *mandamus*, mentioned in the section as originally adopted. As long as the statute law remained in this condition, there could be no doubt as to the power of a circuit judge, at chambers, in a proper case, to grant a writ of *certiorari*. But by the act of 1887 (19 St. 812) section 2115 of the General Statutes was again amended, and the form of this amendment gives rise to the difficulty in this case; for the legislature, doubtless overlooking the fact that the section had been previously amended by the act of 1882, so as to insert therein writs of *certiorari*, after specifying the amendments then proposed to be made, used these words: "So that said section, when so amended, shall read as follows;" repeating the language of the section as it originally appeared in the General Statutes with such additions as were then made, but omitting the addition of writs of *certiorari*, made by the act of 1882. The result is that if the section is read as it appears in the act of 1887, it contains no provision conferring upon a judge at chambers the power to grant writs of *certiorari*. From this it is argued, by counsel for relator, with much force and ingenuity, that the practical effect is that the provision of section 2115, as declared by the act of 1882, giving this power to judges at chambers, has been repealed. This presents a grave and important question, which, as it is not necessary to the determination of the present case, we do not propose to decide, in the present condition of the court, but think it should be reserved for the consideration of a full bench. There may be, and doubtless are, other instances of a like kind, some of which may be far more important than the present. We will therefore, without deciding the question, simply throw out some suggestions which have occurred to us. While we do not doubt that this omission was a clear oversight upon the part of the legislature in 1887, yet it is a very delicate, and perhaps dangerous, thing for the court to undertake to supply what it supposes to be omissions on the part of the legislature, and we have no disposition whatever to usurp the functions of another department of the government. It may be, however, that where the supposed omission does not rest upon conjecture merely, but may be implied from the language used by the legislature itself, that a court would be warranted in supplying an omission which the language used by the legislature shows was unintentional. Authority for this may be found in End. Interp. St. §§ 39, 203, 298, 317. In this case the language used by the legislature in the act of 1887 might possibly be regarded as negativing any intent to repeal or drop that provision in section 2115, as amended by the act of 1882, conferring the power in question; for it does not, as in the act of 1882, simply declare that the section "shall be amended so as to read as follows;" but it first declares what amendments are intended to be made by the insertion of certain words, in the places specified, none of which indicate any intention to drop the provision previously inserted as to writs of *certiorari*, and then proceeds as follows: "So that said section, when so amended, shall read as follows;" giving the language originally used in this section, which did not contain the provision in regard to writs of *certiorari*. It may, therefore, be possible that the proper construction, as derived from the language used in the act of 1887, is that the purpose of the legislature was to make no other alteration in the section, as it then read, except those specially indicated. But, as we have said, we do not propose now to decide this question.

We come, then, to the consideration of the second ground of objection to the jurisdiction of Judge IZLAR to grant the order in question. Assuming, for the purposes of this case only, that a circuit judge has, at chambers, the power to grant a writ of *certiorari*, it seems clear, from the express terms of the section claimed to confer the power, that he can only exercise such power in the same manner, in every respect, as if the court was actually sitting; in other words, that a judge at chambers has the same power—no less and no more—than the court itself would have if it were sitting at the time. So that the practical question is whether the court of common pleas, while sitting in the first circuit, would have the power to grant the writ of *certiorari*, in a case arising in another circuit, and there triable. Upon this question we do not see how there can be two opinions. It seems to us that sections 13 and 14 of article 4 of the constitution, read in connection with sections 2116 and 2117 of the General Statutes, together with the case of Ex parte Parker, 6 S. C. 472, point to but one conclusion; and that is that the court of common pleas, while sitting in one circuit, has no jurisdiction over a case pending in another circuit. It follows, therefore, that even if section 2115 of the General Statutes can be regarded as conferring the power, upon a circuit judge at chambers, to grant a writ of *certiorari*, yet Judge IZLAR had no jurisdiction to grant the order under the provisions of that section. Nor can his power to do so ..e derived from subdivision 3 of section 402 of the Code of Civil Procedure, which reads as follows: "Orders made out of court, without notice, may be made by the judge of the court in any part of the state." In the first place, it

is more than doubtful whether this provision has any application to the granting of a writ of *certiorari*, which cannot be regarded as an order, but is rather in the nature of a judgment. But, in addition to this, that provision only applies to an order made "without notice," which, of course, means an order which can properly be made without notice. Now, inasmuch as the Code makes no provision in regard to proceedings to obtain a writ of *certiorari*, and does provide, in section 449, that where that is the case "the practice heretofore in use may be adopted, so far as necessary to prevent a failure of justice," and inasmuch as it was settled by the case of State v. Senft, supra, that "the writ can in no case be granted only on cause shown," it seems clear that an application for a writ of *certiorari* does not fall within the provisions of subdivision 3 of section 402 of the Code. Again, that section only permits an order without notice to be made, not by a judge of the court, but the language is, "by the judge of the court having jurisdiction of the case in which the order is applied for." We have not deemed it necessary to make any reference to those special statutory provisions which permit a judge of one circuit to grant certain orders in cases pending in another circuit, where the judge of such circuit is absent or unable to act; for it is conceded here that the judge of the second circuit was actually holding court in that circuit when the order in question was granted by Judge IZLAR. Consequently those provisions, having no application to the case as presented here, have not been considered. We must, therefore, conclude that the order of Judge IZLAR, granting the writ of *certiorari*, and staying proceedings in the case, was a mere nullity; we have no jurisdiction in the matter; and consequently such order affords no excuse for the refusal of respondent to execute the warrant of the said trial justices.

It is argued, however, by respondent's counsel, that the relator is not entitled to the writ of *mandamus* prayed for, because he has another plain and adequate remedy; and, if this be so, then, of course, the application for *mandamus* should be refused. We must therefore consider next whether the relator has another plain and adequate remedy. The only one suggested is under the proceedings in *certiorari* now alleged to be pending before Judge ALDRICH. Without stopping to inquire whether such proceedings would afford to the relator such a plain and adequate remedy as would defeat his right to *mandamus*, it is sufficient to say that, having determined that those proceedings are based upon an alleged order which is a mere nullity, it cannot be properly said that any such proceedings are now pending. The foundation being taken away, the superstructure must fall. We think, therefore, that the relator is entitled to the writ of *mandamus* as prayed for. The judgment of this court is that a writ of *mandamus* do forthwith issue out of, and under the seal of, this court, directed to the respondent, Robert Black, as sheriff of Colleton county, requiring him forthwith to deliver to the petitioner full possession of the premises described in the petition.

McGOWAN, J., concurs.

JEFFERIES et al. v. ALLEN et al.

(Supreme Court of South Carolina. June 17, 1891.)

RIGHT TO DOWER — ESTOPPEL — ALLOTMENT — INTEREST.

1. Where a widow is estopped from claiming certain land, originally belonging to her, by reason of acquiescence in a judicial sale thereof as her husband's property, she is nevertheless entitled to dower in such land.

2. Failure of the widow to object to parol evidence that such land belonged to her, on a reference held after it had been adjudged to belong to the husband, does not constitute a waiver of her right to claim dower in such land.

3. A creditor, in whose favor a judgment has been passed that such land belonged to the husband, is estopped from afterwards claiming that it was not the property of the husband, and that therefore the widow is not entitled to dower therein.

4. Under Act S. C. 1883, (18 St. 453,) which provides "that, on all assessments of dower in lands of which the husband died seised, the value * * * at the death of the husband, with interest from the accrual of the right of dower, shall be taken and received by the courts * * * as the true value on which to assess said dower," the value of the lands at the time of the husband's death will be ascertained without reference to any subsequent improvements, and interest will be added, and the widow allowed one-sixth of the total amount.

Appeal from common pleas circuit court of Spartanburg county; HUDSON, Judge.

Action by John R. Jefferies and Eber C. Allen, executors of Woodward Allen, and others, against Harriet Allen, R. C. Oliver and others. Defendant R. C. Oliver brings this appeal. For further statement of facts, see 7 S. E. Rep. 828 and 11 S. E. Rep. 764, where the case was before this court on prior appeals.

C. P. Sanders and D. E. Hydrick, for appellants. Nicholls & Moore and W. S. Thompson, for respondents.

McIVER, J. This being the third appeal in this case, it will not be necessary to make any further statement of the facts than may be found in 29 S. C. 501, 7 S. E. Rep. 828, and 11 S. E. Rep. 764, except such as are necessary for a proper understanding of the points raised by the present appeal. The attorneys for the respondent Harriet Allen, who alone is interested in resisting this appeal, having consented, in the record, that the judgment appealed from shall be modified as claimed in the several grounds of appeal indicated in such consent, except upon a contingency which will not arise under the view we take of the case, there are but two questions left for us to determine: (1) Whether the circuit judge erred in allowing Mrs. Harriet Allen dower out of the 82-acre tract of land mentioned in the proceedings; (2) whether there was error in adjudging that she was entitled to interest on the amounts assessed to her in lieu of her dower from the time of the death of her husband.

1. As we understand it, this 82-acre tract of land constituted a part of a tract which, in fact, belonged to Harriet Allen, and not to her husband; but inasmuch as she had assented to, or rather acquiesced in, an order for the sale of this land as a part of the estate of her husband, and all of it except the 82 acres had been sold as such, it had been previously adjudged in these proceedings that Harriet Allen was estopped from claiming the said tract of land as her separate estate. If this were all, there could be no doubt as to the right of Mrs. Allen to claim dower therein. But it appears that, after the termination of the action brought by Mrs. Moss to recover the 82-acre tract of land, the pendency of which had prevented the sale of that tract and the admeasurement of dower therein, an order was passed by his honor, Judge IZLAR, referring two questions to the master: (1) Whether Woodward Allen was seised in fee, during coverture, of the 82-acre tract; (2) whether Harriet Allen was entitled to dower therein. The testimony taken at the reference held in pursuance of this order is set out in the "case" as prepared for the argument of this appeal. The master made his report, finding that Woodward Allen was not seised in fee during coverture of the 82-acre tract of land, and consequently that Mrs. Allen was not entitled to dower therein. To this report the respondent Harriet Allen excepted; and the same, together with other matters not necessary to be adverted to here, came before his honor, Judge NORTON, for hearing. It is stated in the "case," and there does not seem to have been any objection interposed by the appellant herein, that "the entire record, with all of the testimony at the various references, was before his honor." Judge NORTON, among other things, rendered judgment overruling the report of the referee finding that Woodward Allen had not been seised in fee, during coverture, of the 82-acre tract, and consequently that Mrs. Allen was not entitled to dower therein, and, on the contrary, adjudged that she was entitled to dower, and that the sums of money assessed in lieu of dower should bear interest from the time of the death of Woodward Allen. From this judgment R. C. Oliver appeals, whereby the two questions above stated are presented for our determination. We agree with the circuit judge that Mrs. Allen is entitled to dower in the 82-acre tract. After it had been adjudged in this very case that Mrs. Allen was precluded from setting up a claim to this land, on the ground that it had already been determined to be the land of her husband, it would be strange, indeed, for the court to adjudge, in the same case, that the widow was not entitled to dower because her husband had never been seised in fee. To use the language of the circuit judge: "It would be a reproach to the law if the widow should be prevented from setting up her fee in the land because it had been adjudged to be the land of her husband, and at the same time prevented from setting up the judgment that the land was her husband's because witness testified that it belonged to her in fee." It is urged, however, that this anomalous result must be accepted, because the

widow failed to object to the parol evidence before the referee, and failed to introduce the record showing that the matter of the title to the land was *res adjudicata*. We suppose, however, that the referee had, or had the right to have, the whole record of the case, in which he was appointed, before him, and, in the absence of evidence to the contrary, we would assume that such was the fact. At all events, it does appear that the circuit judge, while hearing the exceptions to the referee's report, had "the entire record" before him; and to this no objection was interposed. So that we see no reason why the circuit judge could not look into the record, and, if he found that one of the questions presented for his determination had already been adjudged, he was bound to so hold. This case differs very materially from the case of Griffin v. Griffin, 20 S. C. 490, relied on by counsel for appellant; for there the circuit judge, of his own motion, against the objection of counsel, called for and obtained a paper, constituting a part of the record of another case in another court, which he used as evidence in considering the exceptions to the report of the referee, then under consideration, which paper had not been in evidence before the referee, and did not constitute any part of the record of the case under consideration. Again, it is urged by appellant that Oliver is not estopped from denying seisin in the husband by reason of the previous adjudication in this case that the land did belong to the husband, and, as such, was liable to be sold for the benefit of his creditors, of whom Oliver was one. It will be observed, however, that the estoppel here relied on is that the matter is *res adjudicata*, and does not arise from any privity of estate between the husband and the defendant in dower. Hence the authorities cited for the purpose of showing that, where the defendant in dower holds under a conveyance from the husband, that is only *prima facie* evidence of the husband's seisin, and the defendant is not precluded from showing that the husband's seisin was of such a character—as would not give rise to the right of dower. Here, however, the adjudication that the land in question was the husband's, and, as such, liable to be sold for the payment of his debts, one of which was held by the appellant, amounting to a judgment that the husband's seisin was of such a character as would support the claim of dower, and the appellant being a party to the case in which such adjudication was made, partly at least, in his interest, he is estopped, under the doctrine of *res adjudicata*, from again raising the question, when it becomes important to his interest to obtain a different adjudication from that already made in his own interest.

2. The question as to the time from which interest should be allowed will next be considered. It is claimed by respondent that this question had been previously determined in accordance with the view taken by Judge NORTON, and that this court sustained this ruling of Judge FRASER, by implication, at least, if not

directly. It is true that Judge FRASER did hold that the widow was entitled to interest from the death of her husband; but his judgment was appealed from, and exception, in several forms, was taken to that, among other provisions of his decree. But it is a mistake to suppose that his judgment was affirmed, even impliedly, by this court; for by reference to the case as reported in 11 S. E. Rep. 764, it will be seen that Mr. Justice McGOWAN, in delivering the opinion of this court, near its close used this language: "This makes it unnecessary to consider the grounds of appeal from the order of Judge FRASER confirming the return of the commissioners." It is clear, therefore, that the question is still open for consideration. The act of 1824, as amended by the act of 1825, now incorporated in Gen. St. as section 2289, with an additional provision in regard to improvements, while making specific provision as to the mode of making the assessment, and the time from which interest on the same should be allowed, where the land, out of which dower is claimed, had been alienated by the husband, omitted any provision of that kind where the land had not been alienated. To supply this omission, probably, the act of 1883 (18 St. 453) was passed, which act seems to have been overlooked in the many discussions to which this case has been subjected. That act provides as follows: "That, on all assessments of dower in lands of which the husband died seised, the value of the lands at the time of the death of the husband, with interest from the accrual of the right of dower, shall be taken and received by the courts of this state as the true value on which to assess said dower." Under this explicit rule established by the law-making department of the government, we do not see how a court can undertake to deprive the widow of the right to interest from the time of the death of her husband, which, of course, is the time when the right of dower accrued. Under this express statutory rule, the proper mode of arriving at the amount to be allowed a widow for her dower would be to ascertain the value of the lands at the time of the death of the husband, without reference to any improvements which may have been subsequently put upon them, (proviso to section 2289, supra,) and adding the interest thereon from the time of his death, and allowing the widow one-sixth of the amount thus ascertained, which will produce the same result as if one-sixth of the value be first ascertained, and then the interest be added to the amount thus ascertained. It is true that taking the amount which the lands brought at a sale made several years after the death of the husband may seem to be a departure from the rule prescribed by the statute above cited, unless the result of such sale should be regarded as the best test of the value of the land at the time of the death of the husband; yet that provision of the judgment is not excepted to or appealed from, and, indeed, could not well be under the previous adjudications in this case; and that matter is not now before us, but has passed beyond our control. The judgment of this court is that the judgment of the circuit court be affirmed, except as modified by the agreement set out in the record.

McGowan, J., concurs.

STATE v. HUDKINS.

(Supreme Court of Appeals of West Virginia.
June 20, 1891.)

JURY—CRIMINAL LAW—FORMER ACQUITTAL—
TRIAL.

1. Where the record shows that the prisoner was tried by a jury of 13 jurymen, instead of 12, the verdict should be set aside and a new trial awarded.

2. When the plea of not guilty, and a special plea of *autrefois acquit*, are pleaded at the same time, the law and practice in this state do not imperatively require two trials by separate juries, but the matter is within the sound legal discretion of the judge before whom the trial is conducted; but in all cases when both issues are tried by a single jury the verdict must respond to both issues separately.

3. In all criminal trials in this state, the attorney for the commonwealth is entitled to open and conclude before the jury.

4. Under a plea of former acquittal, parol or extrinsic evidence may be admitted to establish or disprove the identity of the offense or of the person. These are matters of fact, to be established *dehors* the record. But as to the form or substance of the indictment, or exceptions thereto, the record alone can be vouched or received as evidence. If it appears to have been sufficient on the former trial, neither the prisoner nor the state can be heard to say that it was otherwise. The record, when produced, proves itself, and is conclusive of all matters provable thereby, and cannot be contradicted, amended, nor supplemented by parol testimony of what took place at the trial.

(Syllabus by the Court.)

Error to circuit court, Ritchie county; THOMAS P. JACOBS, Judge.

R. S. Blair & Son, for plaintiff in error. *Alfred Caldwell,* Atty. Gen., for the State.

LUCAS, P. This was an indictment in the circuit court of Ritchie county against the defendant for throwing stones and other dangerous missiles into a passenger-car of the Baltimore & Ohio Railroad Company. The indictment was framed under our statute upon the subject, and conformed substantially to the language of the statute. See Code, c. 145. There was a motion to quash, which was overruled. The prisoner then pleaded not guilty; also filed a special plea setting up the fact of a former acquittal. In addition to the general issue, the state filed a special replication, which sets up that the defendant on the former trial was not acquitted by the jury upon the facts and merits, but that he was acquitted upon exceptions to the form and substance of the former indictment. The prisoner demanded a separate trial upon the plea of *autrefois acquit,* but the court refused to impanel a separate jury, and proceeded to try the prisoner upon both pleas by the regular jury, which is assigned as error. The prisoner further demanded that he was entitled to conclude the argument upon the special plea before the jury, but the court overruled his claim. Upon the trial the prisoner was found guilty by the jury, and the court gave judgment

sentencing him to confinement in the penitentiary for two years. It appears by the record, and it is assigned as error, that 13 jurors were impaneled, and rendered the verdict of which the prisoner complains. The state asked the court to give an instruction in the language of section 15, c. 152, of the Code, but the court declined to do so, and in lieu thereof gave two instructions as follows: "No. 1. If the jury believe from the evidence that Thomas Hudkins was acquitted at the October term, 1888, of this court of the offense with which he is now charged, upon an exception to the form or substance of the indictment on which he was then tried, and not upon the facts and merits, then such acquittal is no bar to the present prosecution. No. 2. If the jury believe from the evidence that Thomas Hudkins, at the October term, 1888, was acquitted by the jury for the same offense with which he is now charged on the facts and merits, then he is entitled to be acquitted, notwithstanding the indictment on which he was then tried may have been defective." The giving of these two instructions is assigned as error in the third bill of exceptions, but we see no error in them. After verdict of guilty, the prisoner moved the court to set aside the verdict and grant him a new trial, to which action of the court the prisoner excepted, and the evidence taken on the trial is set out in full.

The first difficulty which arises in this case is easily disposed of. It seems to be conceded by the attorney general that in a felony case a verdict by 13 jurors against the prisoner cannot be sustained. Section 14 of the bill of rights provides: "Trials of crimes and misdemeanors, unless herein otherwise provided, shall be by a jury of twelve men, public, without unreasonable delay, and in the county where the alleged offense was committed, unless for good cause shown it shall be removed to some other county." Even if the benefit of this provision could be waived by the prisoner in a felony case, such waiver would have to appear clearly and affirmatively by the record. In the case of Younger v. State it was so held by this court. 2 W. Va. 569. For this cause, therefore, the judgment of the circuit court must be reversed and set aside.

The further assignment of error is that the court below declined to permit a separate jury to be impaneled for the purpose of trying the issue raised upon the plea of a former acquittal. There can be no doubt that the practice in England, as laid down by Mr. Bishop, is to require this issue of a former acquittal to be tried by a separate jury, and, if found against the prisoner, he is permitted to plead over to the indictment. As to the American practice, however, in section 812 of his work on Criminal Procedure, (vol. 1,) Mr. Bishop adds: "Where the special plea and not guilty are pleaded together, the better practice is not to try them together, but to submit the former to the jury first. Still, some American courts appear to allow it, when accompanied by the instruction to the jury to pass on the former first, and disregard the latter if they find on the former for the defendant. But, even then, a verdict of guilty, with no response to the special plea, will be erroneous." This appears to be the practice in this state and in the state of Virginia; that is to say, there is no imperative rule requiring the issue upon a special plea of a former acquittal to be tried by a separate jury. Our Code, in a chapter devoted to the trial of criminal cases, felonies, and misdemeanors, does not provide for a separate issue, except in cases where insanity has been suggested. Had it been intended that special pleas in bar should be tried by a separate jury as an imperative rule, the legislature, no doubt, would have so provided. It is a fair inference, we think, that it was the intention of the legislature to leave this matter to the sound legal discretion of the judge who decides the case. In the case of Vaughan v. Com., 2 Va. Cas. 273, the plea of not guilty and the plea of *autrefois acquit* were tried at one and the same time by the same jury, and the verdict found distinctly upon both issues; and this seems not to have been considered error. In Page's Case, 27 Grat. 954, the issue on the plea of *autrefois acquit* was tried first, and the general issue of not guilty was tried by a separate jury. It is to be observed, however, that in that case eight of the jurors who had tried the special plea were included in the new panel that tried the general issue; and this was not considered error. I think it quite clear, however, as insisted upon by Mr. Bishop, that the jury should respond separately to both issues. In the absence of legislation on the subject, and in view of the precedents in Virginia and this state, the better rule may be stated to be that it is not imperative to have two juries, but that this matter is within the sound legal discretion of the trial judge before whom the trial is conducted.

A further error assigned by the prisoner is that his counsel was not given the conclusion upon the issue made up on the special plea. This exception is disposed of at once by the authority and ruling of this court in State v. Schnelle, 24 W. Va. 767, in which it was held that in all criminal trials the state was entitled to open and conclude.

We come now to consider the verdict of the jury, and the motion to set it aside and grant a new trial. Independently of the fatal error which the record discloses that there were 13 jurors, we cannot resist the conclusion that the verdict was erroneous in form, and the finding itself contrary to the law and evidence. The jury, as we have said, should have found distinctly upon both issues, which they failed to do. The special plea sets out in full the record of the former trial, and avers, moreover, that the cause was heard and determined on its merits, and a verdict of acquittal rendered. To this plea the state replied specially, "that the state ought not to be barred from further prosecuting the said indictment, because it says that the defendant, Thomas Hudkins, was not acquitted by the jury upon the facts and merits on a former trial on this indictment, but that he was acquitted thereon upon exceptions to the form and substance

of said former indictment." It will be observed that the plea concedes the identity of the offense and the identity of the person, but denies that the acquittal was upon the merits, and avers that it was upon exceptions to the indictment. The provision of the Code upon this subject is as follows: "(14) A person acquitted by the jury upon the facts and merits on a former trial may plead such acquittal in bar of a second prosecution for the same offense, notwithstanding any defect in the form or substance of the indictment or accusation on which he was acquitted. (15) A person acquitted of an offense on the ground of a variance between the allegations and the proof of the indictment or other accusation, or upon an exception to the form or substance thereof, may be arraigned again upon a new indictment or other proper accusation, and tried and convicted of the same offense, notwithstanding such former acquittal." It is important to consider how far parol testimony may be admitted to sustain an issue made up under either or both of these two sections. It is quite clear that parol or extrinsic testimony may be given to establish the identity of either the person of the prisoner or the identity of the offense. These are matters of fact, to be established *dehors* the record; but as to the form or substance of the indictment or exceptions thereto the record alone can be vouched or received as evidence. If it appears to have been sufficient on a former trial, neither the prisoner nor the state can be heard to say that it was otherwise. If it be said that although the indictment is on its face sufficient, yet the presiding judge at the former trial decided otherwise, and directed an acquittal after the jury was sworn, all this must be proved by the record, or, at all events, no extrinsic or parol testimony can be received to contradict the record. In Adcock's Case, 8 Grat. 661, it was alleged by the prisoner that three terms had intervened without an indictment, and be moved for his discharge upon this ground. The attorney for the commonwealth opposed the prisoner's motion, and offered to introduce the record of the proceedings of the circuit court upon the first indictment, showing, or purporting to show, that the prisoner had not only been indicted, but tried upon the indictment in due time, and found guilty by the verdict of the jury. To the introduction of this evidence the prisoner objected, and, his objection being overruled, the question was certified to the general court, as follows: "Ought the court, on the said motion of the prisoner to be discharged, to receive and consider the record and proceedings offered by the attorney of the commonwealth?" To this the general court replied: "The first question is free of all doubt and difficulty, admitting of a prompt and easy solution. We are all agreed that the evidence objected to ought to be received and considered; indeed, it is the only evidence admissible or competent on such an issue." 8 Grat. 668. This is in accordance with the general principle that matter of record can only be proved by the introduction of the record itself, and, when introduced, it can neither be contradicted, supplemented, nor amended by extrinsic testimony. In Powell's Case, 11 Grat. 822, an application was made, on the part of the prisoner, to the judge in vacation, to amend the record; and the judge made an order directing that the record should be amended so as to show that, upon the arraignment of the prisoner for the offense aforesaid, he, by his counsel, moved the court to quash the indictment, and each count thereof, which motion was overruled, but was omitted to be entered upon the record. When the case came to the court of appeals the amendment was disregarded, and it was held that nothing could be introduced into the record as a part thereof not before found therein, depending on the recollection of the judge, or upon proofs to be submitted to him. In the present case the former indictment was as follows: "It was presented that the said Thomas Hudkins on the —— day of ——, 1886, in the county aforesaid, unlawfully and feloniously did throw stones and other dangerous missiles at and into a certain passenger-car and other railroad cars, used for carrying passengers and other persons, while such passengers and other persons were within the same, against the peace and dignity of the state." This is the exact language of the statute, (see Code, c. 145, § 31,) and it appears to be sufficient. The record discloses that no exceptions were taken to this indictment, although the replication in this case alleges that the former acquittal was founded upon exceptions to the form and substance of the indictment. The state attempted to supplement and contradict the record on this point by parol testimony, but this was clearly inadmissible. Again, the record says that the jury was "selected, tried, and sworn to well and truly try and true deliverance make between the state of West Virginia and Thomas Hudkins, the prisoner at the bar, and a true verdict render according to the law and the evidence; who, after hearing the evidence and argument of counsel, were sent to their chamber to consider of their verdict, and after some time returned into court, and upon their oaths did say: 'We, the jury, find the defendant, Thomas Hudkins, not guilty as charged in the within indictment.'" Nevertheless, the state undertook to prove by oral evidence that the testimony on the former trial was excluded by the court. This was in plain contradiction of the record, and in manifest violation of the rules of evidence upon this subject. Mr. Bishop, in his work on Criminal Procedure, (vol. 1, section 816,) says: "The former record is produced, and for what is provable thereby it is conclusive. Nor can the matter of the record be proved otherwise than by itself. There must be no variance between it and the plea. The identity of the parties and of the offense is established by parol testimony." "If the identity alike of the parties and of the offense is conceded, it becomes a question for the court, whether or not there has been a previous conviction or acquittal." This is in entire accord with the Virginia decisions

and the ancient common-law authorities. 2 Hale, P. C. 241; Rex v. Sheen, 2 Car. & P. 635. We are of opinion, therefore, that the court below erred in not directing an acquittal, or in not setting aside the verdict, and discharging the prisoner (who, it seems, is already in the penitentiary upon conviction of a distinct felony) from further prosecution upon the charge for which he stood indicted. For these reasons, therefore, the judgment of the circuit court must be reversed, the verdict set aside, and a new trial awarded.

WHEELING BRIDGE & T. RY. CO. v. CAMDEN CONSOLIDATED OIL CO.

(Supreme Court of Appeals of West Virginia. June 13, 1891.)

RAILROAD COMPANIES — CONSTRUCTION OF ROAD — EMINENT DOMAIN.

1. A railroad company chartered under the general law of the state may complete and operate a part of its railroad, and, as to the part so completed and operated, retain its corporate existence, franchise, and powers. Chapter 54, § 66, Code, (Ed. 1887.)

2. A railroad company organized under such general law may build and construct lateral and branch roads not exceeding 50 miles in length, and use and operate any part or portion of their main line and branch or branches when completed, the same as though the whole of the proposed railroad were fully completed. Chapter 54, § 69, Code 1887.

3. Such branches may have, in part, a common stem leading from the main line,—that is, there may be a branch from a branch,—provided the limit as to length is not exceeded.

4. Under the provisions of the general law of this state, the filing of the map and profile of the location of the railroad in the office of the secretary of state, and in the office of the clerk of the county court of each county in which any part of the road is located, is not in law a condition precedent to the appointment of commissioners to ascertain a just compensation to the owners of the real estate proposed to be lawfully taken for the purpose of such road; but the circuit court may, in its discretion, require such map and profile, or such part as may be needed, to be filed or produced before appointing such commissioners.

5. The delivery of the certificate of incorporation of such company, or of a copy thereof properly certified, to the clerk of the county court for record in the county in which the principal office or place of business of such company is, is not a condition precedent to the proper and lawful exercise of the right to condemn.

(Syllabus by the Court.)

Error to circuit court, Ohio county; JOSEPH R. PAULL, Judge.

J. J. Jacob and H. M. Russell, for plaintiff in error. Ewing, Melvin & Riley and W. P. Hubbard, for defendant in error.

HOLT, J. This is a writ of error to the judgment and rulings of the circuit court of Ohio county in a proceeding by way of petition on the part of the railway company to condemn certain real estate belonging to the Camden Consolidated Oil Company. The constitution of the state of West Virginia requires that "the legislature shall provide for the organization of all corporations hereafter to be created by general laws uniform as to the class to which they relate; but no corporation shall be created by special law." Const. W. Va. art 11, § 1; Code W. Va. (Warth's

Ed.) p. 40. In pursuance of this requirement, the legislature has from time to time enacted the law as we now find it in chapters 52-55, pp. 484-559, Code W. Va. Under this law the railway company became incorporated and received its charter on the 6th day of March, 1882, but by the name of the "Wheeling & Harrisburg Railway Company of West Virginia." On the 12th day of September, 1889, the name was changed to the present one, "Wheeling Bridge & Terminal Railway Company." The railroad which this corporation proposed to build commences at the west corporation line of the city of Wheeling, in Ohio county, on the line between the state of Ohio and the state of West Virginia, and is to run thence by the most practicable route to a point in Marshall county, at or near where the line between the state of West Virginia and the state of Pennsylvania is crossed by Wheeling creek. The city of Wheeling, by ordinance of its council passed February 28, 1888, which took effect May 28, 1888, gave its consent that this railway company might construct, maintain, and operate a branch railroad for terminal and connecting tracks and facilities in the city of Wheeling, subject to certain restrictions and conditions which need not here be mentioned; and on the 18th day of January, 1889, the city passed another ordinance on the subject. This railroad company has already built along its main line a double-track railroad bridge across the Ohio river, two double-track tunnels,—one 557 feet long; the other 1,203 feet long,—to a point called the "Peninsula," in the valley of Wheeling creek, and a branch from that point down Wheeling creek, on the south side, thence through Chapline hill, a double-track tunnel 2,460 feet long, to the lower end of the city of Wheeling, on the Ohio river. The railway company has found it necessary for its legitimate purpose to have a freight station near the northern portal of its Chapline-Hill tunnel; but there is no room on the south side of Wheeling creek. Therefore it is compelled to build a switch or branch across Wheeling creek to the north side for that purpose; and this proceeding has been instituted for the condemnation of the land in question, lying on the north side, belonging to the oil company. The oil company appeared in the court below, and resisted such condemnation, putting its objections in the form of seven common-law pleas, which it tendered and offered to file, to each of which the plaintiff objected. The court rejected pleas numbered 1, 2, 4, and 5, but permitted numbers 3, 6, and 7 to be filed, on which issues were made up, and tried by a jury. During the trial the court gave at the instance of plaintiff, and against the objection of defendant, seven several instructions. The defendant then moved that the jury be directed to find in writing upon three several questions of fact written out for the purpose, (see section 5, c. 131, Code, p. 813;) but the court refused, and, the case being submitted to the jury, they returned for plaintiff a general verdict on the issues joined, also a special finding for plaintiff on each of the issues joined on the three pleas filed. Thereupon

the defendant moved the court to set aside the verdict, and grant it a new trial; but the court overruled the motion and proceeded to appoint five commissioners, in accordance with section 10, c. 42, p. 312, of the Code, to ascertain what would be a just compensation to defendant for each parcel of real estate proposed to be taken. To all these rulings against defendant it excepted, the evidence being certified, and the cause is now here for review.

The serious question intended to be presented by this record grows out of the rejection of pleas Nos. 1 and 2. Section 65, c. 54, p. 525, Code, (Warth's 2d Ed.,) reads: "Every such corporation shall, within a reasonable time after its railroad is located, cause to be made a map and profile thereof, with the names of the owners of the lands through which it runs, and of the noted places along the same stated thereon, and file the same in the office of the secretary of state, and in the office of the clerk of the county court of each county in which any part of said road is located." Plea No. 1 avers, in substance, that plaintiff had failed to comply with this section as to its main line, although a portion of such road had been located for the space of one year before the beginning of this proceeding. Plea No. 2 makes the same averment as to the lateral or branch railroad mentioned in plaintiff's petition. Is the filing of such map and profile of location a condition precedent to the right to condemn land? It is not in express terms made a condition precedent to the exercise of such right, and, if it be such, it must arise from an implication reasonably necessary. By chapter 54, § 34, p. 512, Code, when the certificate of incorporation shall have been issued and delivered as provided, "the corporators named in the articles of incorporation recited therein, and who have signed the same, and their successors and assigns, shall from the date of said certificate become and be a body corporate, as therein stated, and, as such, authorized to proceed to carry into effect the object set forth in said articles of incorporation, in accordance with the provisions of this chapter." Chapter 42 of the Code confers upon railroad companies, among others, the right to take private property for the construction of their roads, and prescribes the prerequisites and the method of procedure, and among them is the requirement that the application be in writing, "describing with reasonable certainty the real estate proposed to be taken;" so that to give a particular and certain description to the owner of the land proposed to be taken cannot be the sole purpose of requiring the map and profile to be filed, but rather that its location as a whole may be accessible to the public, and a description of the extent and limits of the real estate owned by the railway company may be preserved. And the court below has the right to require that the description of the land proposed to be taken be made certain and definite, and, if deemed necessary to that end, to require a map and profile of the location, as far as it has been made, to be filed or produced; for the law contemplates that construction of the road may be commenced, and therefore, if necessary, condemnation of the land be had, before a final location of the whole road, as intended and set out, has been made; for section 69 of chapter 54 provides that "any railroad company organized under this chapter may build and construct lateral and branch roads or tramways, and of any gauge whatever, not exceeding fifty miles in length; and it may build planes and gravity roads, use and operate any part or portion of their main line and branch or branches, when completed, the same as though the whole of their said proposed railway was fully completed." So, again, our statute contemplates, in fact requires, in this particular, as a necessary prerequisite to the right of condemnation, that the railroad corporation shall acquire such real estate by purchase, if it can agree with the owners. Section 48, c. 54, p. 518, Code. And in this instance the railway company appears to have acquired its real estate for the most part in that way, and to have already occupied such part with the bridges, tunnels, and road-ways of a railway well nigh to that extent completed. Our lack and need of railroads is thought to be great; hence our general law upon the subject is broad and liberal, perhaps beyond precedent. The railway company has been unable to agree with the defendant for the purchase of its part of the real estate needed. Can it be that under such a statute it can interpose as a plea in bar to the awarding of a commission of condemnation the fact that the map and profile of location has not been filed as required by law. How are we to say that one year is a reasonable time in this particular case? The evidence shows that the difficulties and perplexities of location, as well as of construction, have been great to an extraordinary degree,—so much so that it has had to feel its way, as it were, with great caution and circumspection,—and it might have been highly inconvenient and embarrassing to commit itself at once to a definite location throughout. The main line, with its bridges and tunnels and the rest of its track, is about complete from the Ohio state line into the valley of Wheeling creek; and it seems to be the purpose of the company to stop there in the construction of the main line until the more pressing need of branches and terminals in the city is supplied. The branch that runs down Wheeling creek, on the south side, by the land in question, and thence through the Chapline-Hill tunnel to Lower Wheeling, is well nigh complete; certainly, far enough to show its location. There is no complaint that the petition does not designate with sufficient certainty the real estate proposed to be taken. If there had been for the purpose of this proceeding any need of such map and profile, the court below could and would have required its production; but we do not think that the failure to file it in the proper offices could be pleaded in bar of the right to have the commission awarded; and therefore we think that pleas Nos. 1 and 2 were properly rejected. Besides, it appears that this land is needed only for a station and a switch to connect it with the branch on the south side of the creek.

Plea No. 4 avers that the land sought to be condemned was so situated that it could not be used until the street had first been occupied, and that no permission to occupy the street had been obtained. This plea was properly rejected. The city of Wheeling may give its consent but, if this property cannot be obtained, it is not worth while to ask such consent. If the property is obtained, and no consent by the city be given, the property owner is not hurt, because the land condemned would then revert to the original owner. Chapter 54, § 69a, par. 9. The company cannot do everything at once; and if each condemnation or permission on the part of the city is made a condition precedent to every other one, then no property could be condemned at all. Besides, that is a matter between the city and the railway company, and does not directly enter into this controversy. Plea No. 5 avers that the railway company did not, within three months after its certificate of incorporation had been issued, cause the same, or a certified copy thereof, to be delivered for record to the clerk of the county court of Ohio county, in which its principal office and place of business is kept, as required by section 20, c. 54, Code, p. 508. This plea also was properly rejected; such recordation, for the reasons given in considering pleas Nos. 1 and 2, not being a condition precedent to the right to condemn, and for the additional reason that the same section provides that, "if such company fail therein, it shall be fined not exceeding $1,000." Lumber Co. v. Thomas, 33 W. Va. 566, 11 S. E. Rep. 37. Plea No. 6 "denies that the railroad, for the purposes for which the land is sought to be condemned, is a branch or lateral road, as stated in the petition." This plea is obscure and uncertain in meaning; but, taking it to aver with sufficient certainty what defendant claims it is intended to aver,—that it is a branch of a branch, and therefore not a branch of a main line,—it should have been rejected as immaterial; for nothing is clearer under our statute than that the railway company may legally construct a branch of a branch, or that two branches may have a common stem leading into the main line, provided neither exceeds 50 miles in length from such main line. Plea No. 7 alleges, in brief, that the plaintiff has abandoned the line which it was chartered to build, and has begun to build an entirely different line, for which it sought to condemn the property in controversy, without authority of law. Plea No. 8 avers that the said parcels of land in said petition mentioned, and sought to be condemned, are not, nor is either of them, necessary for the purposes of the petitioner's railroad. These pleas, Nos. 3, 6, and 7, were admitted, issues were made and joined thereon, and the jury found generally for the plaintiff, and specifically on each one of these three pleas. It was proved that the road along the main line from the west bank of the Ohio river to a point in the Wheeling Creek valley, called the "Peninsula," had been built, and there the company proposed to stop until, by the building of a branch line down Wheeling creek, it had made terminal facilities for the city of Wheeling; ther-fore it was not material to this inquiry where or how the main line was to run on from that point east, and it was not error to exclude such evidence. Again, the chief engineer of the railway company was asked by plaintiff why the work had been mainly done upon the line from the western boundary of the state to the peninsula, and from the peninsula, with the creek, southward. To this question defendant objected, but its objection was overruled. The answer was material under plea No. 7, as tending to show that the further extension of the main line was not abandoned, but only, for the reasons given, deferred until the terminal facilities in the city of Wheeling were practicable by actual construction, and the road thus put upon a solid and paying basis. It also tended to show that the one was a part of the main line, and the other going down the creek was a branch.

It is admitted by counsel that all the instructions given to the jury do not appear in the record; therefore the court cannot say to what extent, if any, the instructions given and set out in the record were qualified by those given, but not set out. Seven instructions were on motion of plaintiff, and against the objection of the defendant, given to the jury, which are a part of this record, and are as follows. (1) If the jury believe from the evidence that the petitioner built and constructed its main line of railroad as designated and contemplated by its charter from the western boundary of the city of Wheeling to a point on the peninsula, it had and has the right to construct a branch or lateral line of railroad connecting with the main line at such point; and this, although the jury may further believe from the evidence that it ceased further work on the main line, and abandoned all intention of building and constructing further in an easterly direction, or towards the Pennsylvania state line. (2) If the jury find from the evidence that the line of railroad constructed from the Ohio river near the Top mill to the peninsula is a portion of the main line of petitioner's railroad, as contemplated by its charter, they are instructed that the length of the line connecting with such main line at the peninsula, and running thence southwardly, is not decisive of the question whether such second line is or is not a branch or lateral road. Neither length nor direction enters into the definition of a 'branch or lateral' railroad. The only limit in this state as to length is the statutory one of 50 miles. (3) If the jury find from the evidence that any substantial portion of the main line of the railroad contemplated by the charter of the Wheeling & Harrisburg Railroad Company has been built or constructed by the petitioner, their verdict should be in its favor upon the issue raised by the 7th plea. (4) If the jury find from the evidence that so much of the petitioner's railroad as has been constructed from the Ohio river near the Top mill to a point on the peninsula is a portion of the main line of such railroad, as designated and contemplated by the charter of the Wheeling & Harrisburg Railroad Com-

pany, then their verdict should be for the petitioner, the Wheeling Bridge and Terminal Railway Company, on the issue presented by the 7th plea filed by the defendant. (5) Even if the jury should believe from the evidence that so much of the petitioner's railroad as crosses Wheeling creek near the Whitaker mill is a branch railroad or a branch railroad, this will not warrant a finding to that effect, or for the defendant, on the issue raised by the 6th plea of the defendant. (6) While it is incumbent on the petitioner to show by a preponderance of the evidence that a necessity exists for the taking of the property described in the petition, such necessity is not to be regarded and treated as an imperative, but a reasonable, one, looking to the proper discharge by the petitioner of its duties to the public; and if the jury believe from the evidence that such a necessity exists, taking into consideration the present, and also the prospective, needs of the petitioner, within a reasonable time, and that it has not in this instance unreasonably exercised the discretion it possesses in locating its tracks, buildings, etc., then the verdict should be in its favor upon the issue presented by the 3d plea filed herein. (7) Railroad companies possess a large discretion as to the location of their tracks and buildings; and this discretion is not to be controlled if it has not been exercised unreasonably. And in this case, even if the jury should believe that lands other than those in question might or could have been found and acquired suitable for the petitioner's purposes, that fact would constitute no defense or objection to the present claim." In view of our statute on the subject, especially sections 66 and 69 of chapter 54, pp. 526, 527, instruction No. 1 propounds the law correctly as applicable to this proceeding; because under chapter 54, section 50. par. 9, p. 520, Code, plaintiff "has the right to erect and maintain all necessary and convenient buildings and stations, fixtures and machinery, for such connections, constructions transfer accommodation, and use of passengers freights, and business interest, or which may be necessary for the construction or operation and repair of said railroad, its track, road-way, and machinery, for the purposes of that part of the main line and branch already built," and to condemn such land as may be necessary for such purposes, within the limits as to quantity and distance as are prescribed by statute. The effect of the abandonment of construction of the residue of the main line in other respects need not be here discussed; it cannot avail to defeat, this proceeding. Instruction No. 2 states the law correctly as given by our statute, and has been already discussed. Instruction No. 3 has already been discussed, and is substantially correct. Instruction No. 4 is also correct for reasons already given. Instruction No. 5 was in effect the rejection of plea No. 6. Instructions Nos. 6 and 7 propound the law correctly.

Under section 5, c. 131, p. 813, Code, the defendant moved the court to direct the jury to find in writing upon particular questions of fact, as follows: "(1) Is the line of road with which, at a point near

Whitaker's mill, the road for which the property is sought connects, the main line of the petitioner? (2) Is the line of road with which, at a point near Whitaker's mill, the road for which the property sought connects, a branch or lateral road? (3) Is the line of road which crosses the defendant's property a branch or lateral road?" This the court refused to do, and properly, because, on motion of defendants, it had already directed the jury to find separate verdicts on the issues joined on the three pleas, in addition to a general verdict, and pleas Nos. 6 and 7 cover the same ground. Wheeling Bridge Co. v. Wheeling & Belmont Bridge Co., 11 S. E. Rep. 1009, (decided by this court, 13th September, 1890,)

In conclusion, did the court err in overruling defendant's motion for a new trial? The evidence in this case shows without contradiction in any essential particular, and by a clear and decided preponderance in all matters of inference, that this railway company, acting under our general law, has, at an expense of millions, built in good faith some 3,000 feet of its road along its charter line from the west bank of the Ohio river to the peninsula, in the valley of Wheeling creek, made up for the most part of double-track bridges and double-track tunnels; that the financial success and public usefulness of the road, as a whole, depended almost entirely, as far as the facts proven now enable us to see, upon the feasibility of making by various branches what the experts call a "terminal system,"—"a railroad funnel," one witness calls it—in and around the city of Wheeling, by which the raw material may be easily and abundantly brought in, and the manufactured products taken out; that the making of this terminal system was confronted with so great and so many physical difficulties, not to speak of difficulties of other kinds, that capitalists who were to furnish the money could only be convinced that the thing could be done by the doing of it; hence the expensive and difficult branch down Wheeling creek on the south side, and through Chapline hill by a long double-track tunnel, and hence the necessity of the land in question, in connection with contiguous tracts, above and below, already acquired for station and side tracks, for heavy freight, and for the switch leading from the branch line by bridge across the creek thereto. The evidence makes the necessity for taking it for this purpose palpably plain. The defendant, apart from the question of filing map and profile and certificate of incorporation, resists the condemnation on two grounds: (1) It suggests a conjecture that the plaintiff may never complete any more of its charter line; that therefore its present branch line down the creek is not a branch in fact, but a part of the main line, perverted from its lawful course under the guise of a branch. (2) That this switch, driven across the track as a physical necessity to reach the station and track-yard on the north side, is not a switch, but a branch in the guise of a switch, and that there cannot be a branch of a branch, and therefore the making of it is without warrant of law, as if two

branches could not lead back to the trunk part way along a common stem. The court below overruled this motion for a new trial, and, in pursuance of the statute, directed and appointed a commission to view, appraise, and report. We think the merits on all material points are with the plaintiff, and therefore affirmed.

TOWN OF MOUNDSVILLE v. VELTON.

*(Supreme Court of Appeals of West Virginia.
June 13, 1891.)*

JUDICIAL NOTICE—ORDINANCES—VIOLATION — APPEAL.

1. Courts of a municipal corporation will take judicial notice of its ordinances without allegation or proof of their existence.

2. Where, upon conviction of a violation of an ordinance of a municipal corporation before its mayor, an appeal is taken to the circuit court, under section 230, c. 50, and section 39, c. 47, Code 1887, on the trial of such appeal the circuit court will take judicial notice of such ordinance.

3. Where such appeal is tried by a court in lieu of a jury, upon a review of the case upon the evidence by this court it will be treated as upon a demurrer to the evidence, and the appellant regarded as a demurrant to evidence.

4. A conviction for a violation of an ordinance of a municipal corporation will not be reversed for want of a plea by the defendant.

(Syllabus by the Court.)

Error to circuit court, Marshall county; JOSEPH R. PAULL, Judge.

J. B. McLure and *D. B. Evans*, for plaintiff in error. *Ewing, Melvin & Riley*, for defendant in error.

BRANNON, J. L. E. Velton was convicted before the mayor of the town of Moundsville upon a warrant for selling spirituous liquors without license, in violation of an ordinance of said town, and fined, and upon an appeal to the circuit court of Marshall he was again convicted and fined, and he has come to this court upon a writ of error.

We are asked to reverse the circuit court's judgment, first, on the ground that the ordinance on which the prosecution rests was not given in evidence. It is well settled that courts do not judicially notice the ordinances of a municipal corporation unless directed by charter or statute to do so, but they must be pleaded and proven as facts. 1 Dill. Mun. Corp. § 413. But it is equally well settled that the courts of the municipality will take judicial notice of such ordinances without pleading or proof. Wheeling v. Black, 25 W. Va. 266; 1 Dill. Mun. Corp. § 413. Therefore it was not necessary to prove such ordinance on the trial before the mayor. Then, is it necessary, when an appeal is taken to the circuit court and a new trial is there had, that proof must be given of such ordinance on such new trial? Clearly it is not necessary to allege in the complaint or warrant the existence of such ordinance. Then, is it necessary when the case goes to the circuit court to amend the warrant or complaint, or file any pleading alleging the existence of the ordinance? In an action brought in the circuit court it would be necessary to allege the ordinance; but I think no one would venture the proposition that on such appeal the pleading must be changed to make such allegation. Why not? Because the case started in the municipal court. If the papers do not, and need not, allege the existence of the ordinance, why require proof of it? If the law excuses the absence of an allegation of such ordinance, why will it not excuse evidence of it? Again, shall it be said that when we are in the municipal court we need not prove the ordinance, but that when the case is transferred to the circuit court such proof must be given, though it is only a retrial of identically the same matter? This, it seems to me, would be an unreasonable anomaly. I think the rule of reason and common sense is that, as the law does not require such allegation or proof of the ordinance in the municipal court, neither does it require it on appeal to the circuit court; that the circuit court is only substituted for the municipal court in this case. And so it was held in City of Solomon v. Hughes, 24 Kan. 211.

The second ground on which reversal is asked is that the case was commenced in 1888, and was pending on February 18, 1889, when the town of Moundsville was by an act of legislature rechartered under the name of the city of Moundsville, which provided that proceedings then pending in the name of the town of Moundsville should be proceeded with, tried, and determined in the name of the city of Moundsville; and there was no order that the case proceed in the name of the city of Moundsville until after the trial on the evidence, and the finding of the defendant guilty. After the judge, who tried the case in place of a jury, had heard the evidence and adjudged the defendant guilty, the defendant for this cause moved in arrest of judgment; and then the court changed the style of the case from that of "The Town of Moundsville v. L. E. Velton," to that of "The City of Moundsville v. L. E. Velton," and then rendered judgment. The municipality had for years been a corporate entity under the name of the town of Moundsville, and its corporate entity never ceased for a moment, for there was no hiatus or break in its corporate existence under the former charter and the new charter; the only change under the new charter being the substitution of the word "city" for the word "town," —the same corporation, under a changed name only. Is it possible that these facts can reverse this judgment? Is not the objection unsubstantial? How does it prejudice the defendant? There is no change of the subject-matter in issue. The most that might be said is that there is a change of party; but that is only in name. The action and the cause of action were certainly kept alive by the letter of the statute. The judgment is in the proper name. The only vice is the immaterial one of the judge's hearing the evidence, and adjudging the defendant guilty, before changing the title of the proceeding.

Another point made against the finding is that there was no evidence of a sale of the ale; that the witness' opinion that it was a sale is not evidence of a sale. The witness stated that the defendant kept a saloon. When asked whether he pur- chased any liquors of defendant, he answered that he got a glass of ale of defendant; that he asked for beer, but defendant said that he had no beer, but would give witness a glass of ale; that he got the ale, but did not pay for it. When asked why he did not pay for it, he answered: "Well, I don't know why I didn't pay for it, unless it was because he was up before the town." When asked whether he had been in the habit of buying liquor there before or since, he answered: "I had been in the habit of going; yes, sir." When asked whether he bought any before that time, he answered: "I may have, but I don't remember of it." When asked whether it was a sale or gift of the ale, he answered: "Well, I regarded it as a sale at the time then." The witness was evidently unwilling. The judge saw and heard him. We cannot say that his finding is erroneous. The witness' statement that he regarded it as a sale is admissible. Cannot one of the contracting parties state his intent in the purchase? Intention of the parties is an important element in a sale, and it is not merely opinion evidence for a party to a sale to say in what light he regarded it, for it reflects the intent of himself, at least, if not both parties. A saloon-keeper, presumably, does not intend to give away liquors. Unless shown to be a gift, the fair implication would be one of sale. To say the least, there was some evidence to sustain the finding. And we must remember that, where a case is tried by a court in lieu of a jury, in this court the case will be regarded as on a demurrer to evidence, placing the appellant under the disadvantage borne by a demurrant to evidence. State v. Miller, 26 W. Va. 106.

The next point made against the conviction is that the defendant was convicted before the mayor on a sale to one person, and before the circuit court on a sale to another person. There is no need to detail evidence as to this point. Suffice it to say that it must affirmatively appear that the conviction before the mayor was for one sale, and that before the court on another, and that it does not so appear here. For anything appearing, the conviction before the mayor may have been, as it was in the circuit court, for a sale to James Burley.

The last point against the judgment is that there was no issue joined. Were this an indictment, certainly a plea would be indispensable. But formal pleadings are not necessary in proceedings before justices. No provision of chapter 50, Code 1887, requires such a plea. After providing in section 223 that the warrant shall describe the offense, section 225 provides that, "on the appearance of the accused, the justice may proceed to try the case." It is not supposed that the charge can be taken for confessed, but that the prosecution must prove its case, though there be no plea of denial. The plea would simply be, "Not guilty." And if we see that the town was required to prove its case as if such plea had been entered, how does the defendant suffer for want of the plea? In Lexington v. Curtin, 69 Mo. 626, and St. Louis v. Knox, 74 Mo. 79, it was held that in proceedings to recover penalties under city ordinances there need be no plea, as in criminal proceedings on indictments. Moreover, there may have been a plea before the mayor. There is no full transcript of his proceedings before us. The judgment is affirmed.

HARTLEY et al. v. HENRETTA et al. LUTES et al. v. RILEY et al. STIDGER et al. v. KEILEY et al. DICK et al. v. KULL et al.

(Supreme Court of Appeals of West Virginia. June 15, 1891.)

INTOXICATING LIQUORS—NUISANCE—ABATEMENT—INJUNCTION.

Under section 18 of chapter 32 of the Code, a court of equity cannot restrain by injunction a party charged with selling intoxicating liquors contrary to law, or abate the house, building, or place where such intoxicating liquors are alleged to be sold contrary to law, until the owner or keeper of such house or place has been convicted of such unlawful selling at the place named in the bill. HOLT and BRANNON, JJ., dissenting.

(Syllabus by the Court.)

Appeals from circuit court, Marshall county; JOSEPH R. PAULL, Judge.

J. B. McLure and J. J. Jacob, for appellant. J. A. Ewing, D. B. Evans, J. Howard Holt, and T. J. Parsons, for appellees.

ENGLISH, J. On the 12th day of December, 1890, D. J. Hartley, R. S. McConnell, S. A. Walton, T. D. Cheadle, Thomas Gatts, and W. L. Edwards, citizens of the county of Marshall, who sued in their own behalf and in behalf of all other citizens of the state of West Virginia, presented a bill to the judge of the circuit court of Marshall county in which they alleged that Patrick Henretta was the owner in fee of a certain lot or parcel of ground on which stands a certain house known as the "Henretta Hotel," fronting on the south side of Tenth street, between Thompson avenue and the Ohio River Railroad track, in the Second ward of the city of Moundsville, Marshall county, and state aforesaid, and filed a copy of his deed as an exhibit with said bill. They further alleged that in said house on said lot or parcel of land intoxicating liquors—whisky, wine, porter, ale, beer, and drinks of like nature—for a long time had been sold and vended by John Henretta, contrary to law, and without a state license therefor, to the great and irreparable injury of the plaintiffs and all other citizens of the state, and that said John Henretta had been selling and vending said liquors in said house contrary to law, and without a state license therefor, for a long space of time, to-wit, since the 1st day of May, 1890; so that by reason of said intoxicating liquors being sold contrary to law, and without a state license therefor, in said house, the said house had become and was a common and public nuisance, and they charge the truth to be that the said Patrick Henretta had been for a long time, and was then, knowingly permitting the said John Henretta to sell and vend in said house said intoxicating liquors contrary to law, and without a state license therefor, and had so permitted him (the said John Henretta) to sell and vend said liquors therein contrary to law, and without a state license therefor, for a long time, to-wit, since the 1st day of May, 1890; and they pray that the said John Henretta be enjoined and restrained from either selling or vending intoxicating liquors—whisky, wine, ale, porter, beer, and drinks of like nature—in said house contrary to law, and that said Patrick Henretta be enjoined and restrained from knowingly permitting said liquors to be either sold or vended in said house contrary to law, and without a state license therefor, and that said nuisance be abated. An injunction was granted as prayed for by said judge in vacation, restraining said Patrick Henretta from knowingly permitting intoxicating liquors to be sold and vended contrary to law in the following-named house, to-wit, a certain house known as the "Henretta Hotel," fronting on the south side of Tenth street, between Thompson avenue and the Ohio River Railroad track, in the Second ward in the city of Moundsville, W. Va., being the same property conveyed to said Patrick Henretta by Charles Thompson by deed bearing date March 13, 1882, and enjoining and restraining John Henretta from selling and vending intoxicating liquors in said house contrary to law. On the 25th day of December, 1890, the defendants appeared before said judge in vacation, and moved to dissolve said injunction; which motion was overruled, and from this ruling said John Henretta applied for and obtained this appeal.

The first error assigned by the appellant is that the judge had no jurisdiction to award the injunction in vacation, because, under section 18 of chapter 32 of the Code, an injunction must be awarded by a court, and not by a judge in vacation. Said section 18 reads as follows: "All houses, buildings, and places of every description where intoxicating liquors are sold or vended contrary to law shall be held, taken, and deemed to be common and public nuisances, and may be abated as such upon the conviction of the owner or keeper thereof, as hereinafter provided; and courts of equity shall have jurisdiction by injunction to restrain and abate any such nuisance upon bill filed by any citizen." Now, while it is true that circuit courts in term-time exercise the power of awarding injunctions, yet the power of awarding injunctions is also conferred upon judges in vacation, and they are perhaps more frequently granted in vacation than by the court in term-time, and, when granted in vacation, process is awarded, and the case is regularly matured for a hearing, like any other chancery suit. It is true, a motion to dissolve may be made in vacation before the case reaches the court docket; but this result is caused by the defendant giving notice, and moving to dissolve, before the case is matured. After an injunction has been awarded and process has issued, we must consider that a suit has been instituted in a court of equity, and that a court of equity has taken jurisdiction of the matters alleged in the bill, notwithstanding the order of injunction may have been awarded by the judge in vacation, which action of the judge must be regarded as an initiatory proceeding incident to the suit. The language of the statute is: "Courts of equity shall have jurisdiction by injunction to restrain and abate any such nuisance upon bill filed by any citizen;" and while we readily concede that a judge in vacation is not a court of equity, yet when he has, upon a bill presented to him in vacation, awarded an injunction, the injunction bond has been executed, and process awarded, the suit must be considered as pending in a court of equity. Section 6 of chapter 133 of the Code provides that "every judge of a circuit court shall have general jurisdiction in awarding injunctions;" and section 4 of the same chapter provides that "jurisdiction of a bill for an injunction to any judgment, act, or proceeding shall be in the circuit court of the county in which the judgment is rendered, or the act or proceeding is to be done or is doing, or is apprehended," etc.; showing, as I construe the statutes, that wheter the injunction is awarded in court or in vacation, it is considered, when awarded, as falling within the jurisdiction of a court of equity, and the subsequent procedure is controlled by the practice and rules prevailing in a court of equity. I therefore conclude that the judge had jurisdiction to award the injunction in vacation, if the bill filed presented such a case as entitled the plaintiffs to the injunction prayed for. We understand the expression used in section 18 of chapter 32, "courts of equity shall have jurisdiction by injunction," etc., as merely conferring equity jurisdiction in restraining or abating the nuisance complained of.

The next assignment of error relied upon is that "an injunction under said section 18 cannot be awarded until after the conviction of the party or parties creating the nuisance." This section authorizes any citizen to file a bill to abate what is declared by the section to be a common or public nuisance; and it is contended by counsel for the appellant that conviction of the offense, to-wit, selling intoxicating liquors contrary to law at the house or place alleged or designated in the bill, must precede the abatement of such house as a nuisance. It would hardly be seriously contended that a court of equity could make up an issue and try tne question as to the guilt or innocence of the defendant or defendants upon the charge of selling intoxicating liquors at any designated place. Upon a trial of that kind the accused would be entitled to all the presumptions prevailing in criminal cases, or where parties are charged with the violation of a penal statute. If the party charged is found guilty, section 19 provides that he shall be fined not less than $20 nor more than $100, and, at the discretion of the court, imprisoned in the county jail not less than 10 nor more than 30 days. This clearly defines and characterizes the offense, and we at once conclude that such an issue cannot be determined in a court of equity. It is, however, contended that any citizen may proceed at once, in the first instance, in a court of equity, to restrain and abate such nuisance. This statute is exceedingly broad

in its terms, and in its absence it is clear that no citizen could maintain a bill to abate such a nuisance, in the absence of some peculiar or special injury to themselves. High, Inj. § 762, reads as follows: "No principle of the law of injunctions is more clearly established than that private persons seeking the aid of equity to restrain a public nuisance must show some special injury peculiar to themselves, aside from and independent of the general injury to the public," etc. Jurisdiction, however, by this statute, is conferred upon a court of equity to award an injunction at the relation of any citizen. The right to go into a court of equity, then, to abate such a nuisance is conferred upon any citizen by this section of the statute, and we must look to the same statute to ascertain what is necessary to authorize any citizen to abate such nuisance; and we find the statute says that "all houses, buildings, and places of every description where intoxicating liquors are sold or vended contrary to law shall be held, taken, and deemed to be common and public nuisances, and may be abated, as such, upon the conviction of the owner or keeper thereof as hereinafter provided." Under this section, most assuredly no such house or place could be abated without a conviction of the owner or keeper thereof, as thereinafter provided, whether the same was abated by a decree in equity or by a judgment at law, under the nineteenth section. Webster defines "conviction" to be "the act of proving, finding, or determining to be guilty of an offense charged against a person before a legal tribunal, as by confession, by the verdict of a jury, or by the sentence of other tribunal," etc.; and the definition found in Bouvier's Law Dictionary is as follows: "In practice, that legal proceeding of record which ascertains the guilt of the party, and upon which the sentence or judgment is founded, finding a person guilty by verdict of a jury," etc. In order that the house mentioned in the plaintiff's bill may be declared a nuisance, the owner or keeper thereof must be convicted of selling intoxicating liquors at that particular house. Until that conviction takes place it remains undetermined whether a nuisance exists or not; and a court of equity will never undertake to determine the guilt or innocence of a party charged with selling intoxicating liquors contrary to law. Such a trial would be at war with every rule of practice upon the subject in this country and in England. Wood on the Law of Nuisance (page 928, § 807) says: "In this country as well as in England, unless the party has done something to deprive himself of an equitable remedy to restrain a continuous nuisance after the question of nuisance has been determined in a court of law, an injunction will be granted, even though no actual damage results therefrom." Under the section of our statute which we are considering, the question of nuisance must be determined by ascertaining the guilt or innocence of the party accused of selling intoxicating liquors at the place named in the bill contrary to law; and the section just quoted from Wood on Nuisance shows that the practice is to determine such questions in a court of law, before a court of equity will interfere by injunction. The bill filed in this case merely alleges that intoxicating liquors — whisky, wine, porter, ale, beer, and drinks of like nature—for a long time have been, and are now, being sold and vended by John Henretta contrary to law, and without a state license therefor, to the great and irreparable injury of plaintiffs and all other citizens of the state, and that Patrick Henretta, the owner of the house, is knowingly permitting said John Henretta to make such unlawful sales in said house. To these charges the defendants are entitled to plead not guilty, and a trial of the issue thus made before a jury, since a conviction results, under the nineteenth section of said statute, in a fine of not less than $20 nor more than $100, and imprisonment may be added for not less than 10 nor more than 30 days, and the building or other place shall be abated or closed up as a place of sale, etc. We cannot construe the sections of our statute under consideration so as to determine that a court of equity would be thereby clothed with power to abate the defendant's place of business without first being satisfied of his guilt by proper legal investigation, or that it was the intention of the legislature to take from the defendant his liberty or his property without a trial by jury. In the case of Slack v. Jacob, 8 W. Va. 612, this court held: "(1) It is the duty of the court to uphold a statute when the conflict between it and the constitution is not clear; and the implication which must always exist, that no violation has been intended by the legislature, may require in some cases, where the meaning of the constitution is in doubt, to lean in favor of such a construction of the statute as might at first view seem most obvious and natural. Where the meaning of the constitution is clear, the court, if possible, must give the statute such a construction as will enable it to have effect. (2) It is always to be presumed that the legislature designed the statute to take effect, and not to be a nullity. (3) Wherever an act of the legislature can be so construed and applied as to avoid a conflict with the constitution, and give it the force of law, such construction will be adopted by the courts." The case of Mugler v. Kansas, 8 Sup. Ct. Rep. 275, (decided by the supreme court of the United States on December 5, 1887,) in which the opinion was prepared by Justice Harlan, is relied upon to show that no conviction is necessary before any citizen may proceed in equity, and not only restrain the sale of intoxicating liquors, which the plaintiff alleges are being sold in violation of law, but abate the house at which such sales are being made as a nuisance; but it will be found upon examination that the Kansas statute is very different from our own. The thirteenth section of the Kansas statute declares, among other things, all places where intoxicating liquors are manufactured, sold, bartered, or given away, or are kept for sale, barter, or use, in violation of the act, to be common nuisances; and provides that, upon the judgment of any

court having jurisdiction finding such place to be a nuisance, the proper officer shall be directed to shut up and abate the same. Our statute, however, provides that "all houses, buildings, and places of every description where intoxicating liquors are sold or vended contrary to law * * * may be abated as such upon the conviction of the owner or keeper thereof," as thereinafter provided, and not, as under the Kansas statute, upon the judgment of any court having jurisdiction. As I understand our statute, a conviction must precede an abatement, whether such abatement is directed by a decree in equity or a common-law order; while in Kansas the abatement is preceded by the judgment of a court of competent jurisdiction. Justice Harlan, in the course of his opinion, says: "As to the objection that the statute makes no provision for a jury trial in cases like this one, it is sufficient to say that such a mode of trial is not required in suits in equity, brought to abate a public nuisance;" and it is for that very reason that our statute, not intending to deprive the accused of a trial by jury, provides that the nuisance may be abated upon the conviction of the owner or keeper. Proceeding, Judge Harlan says: "The statutory direction that an injunction issue at the commencement of the action is not to be construed as dispensing with such preliminary proof as is necessary to authorize an injunction pending the suit. The court is not to issue an injunction simply because one is asked, or because the charge is made that a common nuisance is maintained in violation of law. The statute leaves the court at liberty to give effect to the principle that an injunction will not be granted to restrain a nuisance except upon clear and satisfactory evidence that one exists." This is true, because the statute provides that the judgment of a court of competent jurisdiction must find the place to be a nuisance before it can be abated. In that state they have a Code practice, while here the distinctions between courts of law and courts of equity are maintained, and their separate powers and jurisdiction are well defined; and we do not understand that a conviction of an offense of this character can be obtained in a court of equity. After a conviction in a court of law, however, a court of equity might better provide for restraining a repetition of the offense and an abatement of the nuisance, although it is clear that under our statute it may be done by either. The cases of Littleton v. Fritz, 65 Iowa, 488, 22 N. W. Rep. 641, and Applegate v. Winebrenner, 66 Iowa, 67, 23 N. W. Rep. 267, are also relied upon by counsel for the appellees. It will be found by reference to the statutes of Iowa, however, that the sale of intoxicating liquors is prohibited except for mechanical, medicinal, culinary, and sacramental purposes, and that parties who are licensed to retail liquors for those purposes are required to obtain a license therefor, and to keep an accurate account of all liquors purchased, the names of the persons from whom purchased, and the amount, also an accurate account of the sales, and to whom sold, which accounts shall be open to the inspection of the prosecuting attorney, the grand jury, and the judge; and a person selling liquors otherwise is regarded as guilty of a nuisance; and, under said statutes, proof of the manufacture, sale, or keeping with intent to sell intoxicating liquors in violation of the provisions of said act is deemed sufficient presumptive evidence of the offense, and, upon affidavit made by three residents of the county, the nuisance may be abated by order of a justice of the peace. In that state they have a Code practice which is very different from ours, so that their rulings in regard to jurisdiction and practice should have little or no influence in determining a question of practice or jurisdiction in this state.

High on Injunctions, (section 762,) as before stated, asserts the doctrine as follows: "No principle of the law of injunctions is more clearly established than that private persons seeking the aid of equity to restrain a public nuisance must show some special injury peculiar to themselves, and independent of the general injury to the public, and in the absence of such special and peculiar injury sustained by a private citizen he will be denied an injunction, leaving the public injury to be redressed upon information or other suitable proceedings by the attorney general in behalf of the public;" and there can be no doubt that this is the general rule. The same author, in section 20, says: "The subject-matter of the jurisdiction of equity being the protection of private property and of civil rights, courts of equity will not interfere for the punishment or prevention of merely criminal or immoral acts, unconnected with violations of private rights. Equity has no jurisdiction to restrain the commission of crimes, or to enforce moral obligations and the performance of moral duties; nor will it interfere for the prevention of an illegal act merely because it is illegal." But when these general rules are altered by statute we must look to the statute, and construe it, in order to restrain or abate a nuisance. And, returning again to said section 18, the question presents itself, when shall houses, buildings, and places of every description where intoxicating liquors are sold or vended contrary to law be abated as nuisances? and the answer is apparent in said section, to-wit, upon the conviction of the owner or keeper thereof, as is hereinafter provided. Courts of equity, as we have seen, had general jurisdiction to abate nuisances without the aid of that statute, when a proper case was presented; but until this statute was enacted it was not any and every citizen that could maintain a bill for the purpose, but in order to do so they must show some peculiar damage or special injury; so that the whole statute must be taken together to ascertain when any citizen may file such bill; and again we find the statute answers, upon conviction. And here it is pertinent to inquire how such conviction is to be obtained. Section 14 of our bill of rights reads as follows: "Trials of crimes and of misdemeanors, unless herein otherwise

provided, shall be by a jury of twelve men, public, without unreasonable delay, and in the county where the alleged offense was committed, unless upon petition of the accused, and for good cause shown, it is removed to some other county," etc.; and section 1 of chapter 158 of the Code provides that "prosecutions for offenses against the state, unless otherwise provided, shall be by presentment or indictment." We deem it unnecessary to quote our statute to show that the sale of intoxicating liquors contrary to law is a misdemeanor, and we have seen how convictions for misdemeanors must be obtained under the constitution and statute, and we therefore conclude that such conviction cannot be obtained in a court of equity; and surely no court would either fine or imprison a defendant or abate his property as a nuisance until he was properly ascertained to be guilty of the charge which would render his place of business a nuisance. Again, we find in High on Injunctions (section 744) the author says: "In cases of conflicting evidence as to the fact of a nuisance, it is proper to refuse an injunction in limine until the question of nuisance can be finally determined by a verdict." Now, the property that is sought to be abated in this suit is described in the bill as a certain lot or parcel of ground on which stands a certain house known as the "Henretta Hotel," fronting on the south side of Tenth street, between Thompson avenue and the Ohio River Railroad track, in the Second ward of the city of Moundsville, Marshall county, W. Va., and a copy of the deed of Patrick Henretta is exhibited with said bill, and prayed to be considered as part thereof, and in said exhibit the property is described as a certain lot of ground situated in Moundsville, Marshall county, W. Va. Said lot fronts 60 feet on Mound street, and runs back south with Mechanics street 120 feet, and being on the corner of said streets; and in proceeding to abate property as a nuisance it must be conceded that the property must be described with convenient certainty, as the defendant may own several lots in the same town, and great damage and injustice may be done in an extraordinary proceeding of this character; and it occurs to me it would be extremely difficult to find any similarity in the description of the lot described in the bill and the one described in the exhibit which is alleged to evidence the title of the defendant. To say the least of it, the description is too uncertain to enable a court to abate the alleged nuisance, even if the defendant had been convicted. For these reasons the decree complained of must be reversed, with costs; and, this court proceeding to render such decree as should have been rendered, it is ordered that the plaintiff's bill be dismissed.

LUCAS, P., concurs.

HOLT, J. I concur in the decree, but not in the syllabus. The bill must allege conviction of unlawful selling by defendant at the place, and continuance of unlawful selling thereafter at the place, to the annoyance of the plaintiffs and the public;

but it is not necessary to allege or prove that the house has been adjudged a nuisance. Or it must allege the nuisance by reason of unlawful selling at the place, and give some good reason for urgency of the need for preliminary restraint until the question of nuisance can be determined by some proper and legal method, or some other good reason why the procedure at law under the statute is not adequate. It was not the intention of the law-maker, by adding this short and very general supplementary clause, to take this whole subject out of the hands of the proper officers, whose special duty it is to look after this matter, and to put it in the power of any citizen of the state, no matter where living, or how extreme his views on the subject, to conduct it to suit himself for the public interests according to his peculiar notions, with the real purpose, perhaps, of letting the business go on; for it must be remembered that it might be very embarrassing to have a house pronounced not a nuisance, by the connivance of the plaintiff, when it was flagrantly so in fact. Surely it was not the intention of the legislature, when providing this very efficient remedy, to put the whole matter in the hands of any private citizen, whether friend in fact or enemy in disguise, and to thus embarrass the state, counties, and municipal corporations. We have not as yet, to any great extent, a state policy on the subject, but leave it by way of local self-government to counties and towns.

BRANNON, J., (dissenting.) I regret to differ in opinion with three brother judges, but my opinion is so decided that I am compelled to do so. The majority hold that equity has no jurisdiction under the statute involved in the case until after conviction upon indictment,—a position in which I cannot unite. I hold that the words "upon conviction" apply only as a precedent condition to abatement upon indictment. In 1877 the legislature amended and re-enacted chapter 32 of the Code, regulating licenses, making sections 14 and 15 read as follows: "(14) All houses, buildings, and places of every description where intoxicating liquors are sold or vended contrary to law shall be held, taken, and deemed to be common and public nuisances, and may be abated as such upon conviction of the owner or keeper thereof, as hereinafter provided. (15) The owner of any house, building, or other place mentioned in the next preceding section, who sells or knowingly permits intoxicating liquor to be sold or vended therein contrary to law, and every person engaged in any such unlawful sale in any such house, building, or place, may be indicted for keeping and maintaining a common and public nuisance, and upon conviction thereof he shall be fined not less than twenty nor more than one hundred dollars, and, at the discretion of the court, imprisoned in the county jail not less than ten nor more than thirty days; and judgment shall be given that such house, building, or other place be abated or closed up as a place for the sale of such liquors contrary to law, as the court may determine." Here buildings where intoxicating liquors are sold contrary to law are stamped as nuisances, and persons carrying on such nuisances are subjected to the personal punishment of fine and imprisonment, and remedy against such nuisance is made in a twofold character of personal punishment and abatement of the nuisance upon the conviction of the party, but both upon an indictment only, and no other remedy is prescribed. In 1887, however, section 14 was amended by adding at its close the words, "and courts of equity shall have jurisdiction by injunction to restrain and abate any such nuisance upon bill filed by any citizen." By this amendment equity is called into service as a remedy against the evil declared by the statute. How does it come into this service at the bidding of the legislature? Does it come as a separate, independent, vigorous remedy, exercising the full powers it had always exercised when dealing with public nuisances, or only as an ancillary or auxiliary remedy, powerless until conviction upon an indictment? The authorities which I shall cite will show that it comes in the former garb. Let me ask, why did the legislature call into requisition this additional remedy? Because after 10 years' experience it had found the remedy by the tedious process of indictment, trial, and verdict of guilty, to be found by 12 men, inefficient and slow. Why call in this additional remedy if it was to be only ancillary to the law jurisdiction? The statute as it was before amendment gave the law court ample power to abate the nuisance after conviction. It needed no aid from an injunction after conviction. The law jurisdiction could only abate after conviction; but equity is by the statute given power to "restrain and abate,"—to abate when the fact of the existence of the nuisance should be finally fixed according to equity practice, and in the mean time, pending the investigation, to restrain it. This fact—that it need not await the final decision, but could act in restraint at once—is the reason the legislature had recourse to it, and a reason why we should not give it this secondary import. And we are to give to equity this subordinate role under a statute made to protect the public revenue, and the well-being of society, and those who do pay license taxes for the privilege granted them, when that very statute declares that the provisions referred to "shall in all cases be construed as remedial, and not penal;" that is, not rigidly, to the protection of the evil designed to be remedied, but liberally, so as to suppress the evil, and advance the remedies which the legislature directed against it. The decision in this case emasculates the statute of its strength, and defeats the legislative design; and not only that, but it denies to equity the force it has always had under the general principles of equity jurisprudence when dealing with public nuisances. If it is true that equity, for centuries, has wielded an original independent jurisdiction as to public nuisances, may I not ask, can it possibly be conceived that the legislature intended to lessen its efficacy? Rather did it not intend, by express provision, to declare the acts de nounced nuisances, and to expressly apply the remedy by injunction so as to leave no question as to jurisdiction, and to widen its scope by putting that remedy in the hands of any citizen? Such are both the letter and spirit of the statute. It is said that such a construction of the act, giving equity jurisdiction before conviction at law, deprives a party of a jury trial, and is not due process of law. There are two answers to that. (1) An injunction is not a criminal prosecution. In the language of the opinion in Carleton v. Rugg, 149 Mass. 550, 22 N. E. Rep. 55, the fallacy of the argument lies in disregarding the distinction between a proceeding to abate a nuisance, which looks only to the property that in the use made of it constitutes the nuisance, and a proceeding to punish the offender for the crime of maintaining a nuisance. These two proceedings are entirely unlike. The latter is conducted under the provision of the criminal law, and deals only with the person who has violated the law; the former is governed only by the rules which relate to property, and its only connection with persons is through property in which they may be interested. That which is declared by a valid statute to be a nuisance is deemed in law to be a nuisance in fact, and should be dealt with as such. The people, speaking through their representatives, have proclaimed it to be offensive and injurious to the public, and the law will not tolerate it. The fact that keeping a nuisance is a crime does not deprive a court of equity of the power to abate a nuisance. Attorney General v. Hunter, 1 Dev. Eq. 12; People v. City of St. Louis, 5 Gilman, 351; Ewell v. Greenwood, 26 Iowa. 377; Minke v. Hopeman, 87 Ill. 450." See Cherry v. Com., 78 Va. 375. In Minke v. Hopeman, supra, it was held that they are so far distinct that an acquittal on an indictment for maintaining a nuisance will not bar equitable relief, and that equity need not wait until the fact of the nuisance be settled at law. (2) No jury right is violated, because equity has long had jurisdiction in public nuisance matters, and had it before our constitutions, and that mode of trial is unknown to equity. This doctrine, as well as other principles pertinent to this case, is well stated in the cases of Mugler v. Kansas, and Kansas v. Ziebold, quoted below; also in Kansas v. Crawford, 28 Kan. 726, citing many authorities. See, also, opinion, page 515, in 25 W. Va., in Barlow v. Daniels. A Kansas statute provided that all places where intoxicating liquors were sold in violation of the act should be deemed nuisances; and upon judgment of any court having jurisdiction, finding such place to be a nuisance, the sheriff should be directed to shut up and abate the place by taking possession, and destroying all liquors there found, and that the owner should, on conviction be guilty of maintaining a nuisance, and punished by fine and imprisonment; and the attorney general, county attorney, or any citizen were given the right to an action to abate or enjoin the same. In the United States supreme court, in Kansas v. Ziebold, 123 U. S. 623, 8 Sup. Ct. Rep. 273, Mr. Justice HARLAN, in delivering the opinion, said: "Equally untenable is the proposition that the proceedings in equity for the purposes indicated in the thirteenth section of the statute are inconsistent with due process of law. In regard to public nuisances, Mr. Justice STORY says: 'The jurisdiction of courts of equity seems to be of a very ancient date, and has been traced back distinctly to the reign of Queen Elizabeth. The jurisdiction is applicable not only to public nuisances, strictly so called, but also to purprestures upon public rights and property. * * * In case of public nuisances, properly so called, an indictment lies to abate them, and to punish the offenders; but an information also lies in equity to redress the grievance by way of injunction.' 2 Story, Eq. Jur. §§ 921, 922. The ground of this jurisdiction in cases of purpresture, as well as of public nuisances, is the ability of courts of equity to give a more speedy, effectual, and permanent remedy than can be had at law. They cannot only prevent nuisances that are threatened, and before irreparable mischief ensues, but arrest or abate those in progress, and by perpetual injunction protect the public against them in future; whereas courts of law can only reach existing nuisances, leaving future acts to be the subject of new prosecutions or proceedings. This is a salutary jurisdiction, especially where a nuisance affects the health, morals, or safety of the community. Though not frequently exercised, the power undoubtedly exists in courts of equity thus to protect the public against injury. District Attorney v. Railroad Co., 16 Gray, 245; Attorney General v. Railroad Co., 3 N. J. Eq. 139; Attorney General v. Ice Co., 104 Mass. 244; State v. Mobile, 5 Port. (Ala.) 279, 294; Hoole v. Attorney General, 22 Ala. 194; Attorney General v. Hunter, 1 Dev. Eq. 13; Attorney General v. Forbes, 2 Mylne & C. 123; Attorney General v. Railroad Co., 1 Drew. & S. 161; Eden, Inj. 259; Kerr, Inj. (2d Ed.) 168. As to the objection that the statute makes no provision for a jury trial in cases like this one, it is sufficient to say that such a mode of trial is not required in suits in equity to be brought to abate a public nuisance." That there is general equity jurisdiction as to public nuisances has been recognized by our own courts. Beveridge v. Lacey. 3 Rand. (Va.) 63; Bridge Co. v. Summers, 13 W. Va. 484. That no jury right is invaded in such cases has also been held in Carleton v. Rugg, supra; Littleton v. Fritz, 65 Iowa, 488, 22 N. W. Rep. 641; Kansas v. Crawford, 28 Kan. 726. In Eilenbecker v. District Court, 134 U. S. 31, 10 Sup. Ct. Rep. 424, Justice MILLER said, as to the point that the Iowa act gave equity jurisdiction, and thus took away trial by jury: "So far as at present advised, it appears to us that all the powers of a court, whether at common law or in chancery, may be called into operation by the legislative body for the purpose of suppressing this objectionable traffic, and we know of no hindrance in the constitution of the United States to the form of proceeding, or to the court in which this remedy can be had. Certainly, it seems to us to be quite as wise to use the processes of the law and the powers of the court to prevent the evil as to punish the offense as a crime after it has been committed." That the legislature, under its police power, may constitutionally declare places where intoxicating liquors are sold contrary to law to be nuisances is abundantly settled. Mugler v. Kansas, and Kansas v. Ziebold, 123 U. S. 623, 8 Sup. Ct. Rep. 273; Fisher v. McGirr, 1 Gray, 1; State v. Thomas, 47 Conn. 546; McLaughlin v. State, 45 Ind. 338; State v. Waynick, 45 Iowa, 516; Streetor v. People, 69 Ill. 595; Bish. St. Crimes, § 1068. And outside the statute it seems that by common law a building where sales of liquor are habitually made contrary to law is a public nuisance. Bish. St. Crimes, § 1068; Howard v. State, 6 Ind. 444; Meyer v. State, 42 N. J. Law, 145; Meyer v. State, 41 N. J. Law, 6; Kansas v. Crawford, 28 Kan. 726. It is true that though equity has jurisdiction against public nuisances, yet, to enable a private individual to call it into exercise, he must show that the nuisance works a special and peculiar injury to him. Beveridge v. Lacey, 3 Rand. (Va.) 63; Bridge Co. v. Summers, 13 W. Va. 484; Talbott v. King, 32 W. Va. 6, 9 S. E. Rep. 48. But the statute changes that general rule as to this particular class of cases, as it declares that any citizen may obtain an injunction. The legislature may authorize any citizen to sue to abate a public nuisance. The citizen in such case represents the public. Littleton v. Frits, 65 Iowa, 488, 22 N. W. Rep. 641; Carleton v. Rugg, 22 N. E. Rep. 55; Applegate v. Winebrenner, 66 Iowa, 67, 23 N. W. Rep. 267. I have discussed only the question of equity jurisdiction. I do not express any opinion as to what quantity of selling is necessary, or whether the selling must be done habitually, to make a place a nuisance.

JANESVILLE HAY TOOL CO. et al. v. BOYD et al.

(Supreme Court of Appeals of West Virginia. June 18, 1891.)

DEEDS—ACKNOWLEDGMENT—RECORDING—CLERK OF COURT.

1. A court of equity has jurisdiction to pass upon the validity and regularity of the record of a deed in the office of the clerk of the county court in cases where the jurisdiction of the court has attached upon independent and equitable grounds.

2. The clerk of a county court has power to take the acknowledgment of the parties signing a deed, within his county, elsewhere than in his office.

3. Our recording statutes are remedial, and should be construed to advance the remedy, rather than to invalidate a record upon narrow and technical grounds.

4. All the provisions of the Code and general acts prescribing the duties and powers of the clerks of county courts in this state as to recording and preservation of deeds are applicable to the clerk of the county court of Ohio county.

(Syllabus by the Court.)

Appeal from circuit court, Ohio county.

White & Allen and W. P. Hubbard, for appellants. A. J. Clarke and J. J. Jacob, for appellees.

LUCAS, P. The appellants instituted this suit for the purpose of enforcing cer-

tain judgments against the real estate of S. E. Boyd, one of the appellees. As incidental to this relief, they set out that said Boyd gave a deed of trust upon all of her real estate to one J. B. Sommerville as trustee, dated the 3d day of December, 1888. An office copy of the deed is filed as an exhibit with the bill, and the acknowledgment and certificate of registration as indorsed upon the deed are set out in full as follows: "State of West Virginia, county of Ohio, to-wit: I, George Hook, clerk of the county court of said county, do hereby certify that S. E. Boyd, whose name is signed to the writing hereto annexed, bearing date the 3rd day of December, 1888, has this day acknowledged the same before me in my said county. Given under my hand this 3rd day of December, 1888. GEORGE HOOK, Clerk." "West Virginia, Ohio county, ss.: I, George Hook, clerk of the county court of said county, do certify that the foregoing (or annexed) writing, bearing date the 3rd day of December, 1888, with the certificate of acknowledgment thereto annexed, was presented for, and by me admitted to, record in my office, as to the party therein named, this 4th day of December, 1888, at 9.20 A. M. Teste: GEORGE HOOK, Clerk."

It is charged that this certificate, as a record, is defective in not showing that the acknowledgment was taken by the clerk of the county court in his office. They further charge that the acknowledgment was not taken, as a matter of fact, in his office, but was taken elsewhere in the body of the county. The registration being thus, as they charge, invalid, the deed itself is to be treated as void as to their judgments which have been duly placed upon the judgment lien docket. The plaintiffs pray that said deed of trust may be set aside so far as their judgments are concerned, and that the real and personal estate of said S. E. Boyd, and the proceeds thereof, be subjected and applied to the payment of their judgments, according to their respective priorities. To this bill there was no answer filed, but Mary E. Boyd and others demurred to so much of the bill as set out the defects in the registration of the deed, and the prayer that priority be given, over the debts therein secured, to the plaintiffs' judgments. Upon this state of the pleadings, on the 3d of April, 1890, the court entered a decree sustaining the demurrer, and dismissing the bill, and awarding costs to the defendants.

The first question which confronts us in this case is the question of jurisdiction. We have here an independent and original ground of equitable jurisdiction, the suit having been instituted to enforce the liens of sundry judgments against real estate. The bill is in fact in the nature of a creditors' bill, and the attack upon the validity of the deed in question, though made directly, and not collaterally, is an incident to the main object of the suit. In such a suit one creditor may assail the validity of a judgment claimed by a creditor of a prior class, and seek to set it aside. This is as far as we need to go upon the subject of jurisdiction in the present case. Were there no such ground of original equitable jurisdiction, it would be necessary to consider whether, under our comprehensive acts defining the functions of prohibition and *certiorari*, the remedy at law might not be considered complete and adequate, and the court of equity might not be compelled to decline to interfere; for, as the court said in Carper v. McDowell, "if there was a want of authority in the officer to take the acknowledgment out of his office, how can that give jurisdiction to a court of equity over the subject?" 5 Grat. 236. But in the present case this difficulty is eliminated by the fact that we here find an original and independent ground of chancery jurisdiction. The material question to be decided is whether the clerk could take the acknowledgment within his county elsewhere than in his office. If so, there will exist in this case no variance between the actual facts and the certificate, and hence no ground to interpose the doctrine of estoppel as against parol testimony. It is even doubtful whether an estoppel is not waived by the form of the demurrer to the bill, as, in general, an estoppel must be pleaded. Herm. Estop. §§ 581, 582.

We come, then, to discuss the material question in the case as stated above. Chapter 73 of the Code, which treats of "the authentication and record of deeds," provides as follows: "(2) The clerk of the county court of any county in which any deed, contract, power of attorney, or other writing is to be, or may be, recorded, shall admit the same to record in his office, as to any person whose name is signed thereto, when it shall have been acknowledged by him, or proved by two witnesses as to him, before such clerk of the county court. (3) Such clerk of the county court shall also admit any writing to record, as to any person whose name is signed thereto, upon the request of any person interested therein, upon a certificate of his acknowledgment before a justice, notary public, recorder, prothonotary, or clerk of any court within the United States, or a commissioner appointed within the same by the governor of this state, written or annexed to the same, to the following effect." Here follows a form of acknowledgment substantially the same as that attached to the deed we are now considering. See Code, p. 627. Both of these sections would seem to authorize a clerk of a county court to take the acknowledgment of any one signing a deed. Section 2 says he shall admit to record when it has been acknowledged before him; and section 3 provides, in general terms, that the clerk of any court in the United States may certify the acknowledgment. No good reason can be assigned why this language (which is sufficiently comprehensive to embrace any clerk of a county court in West Virginia) should be given a forced and narrow construction for the purpose of excluding the clerk of that county court whose duty it is to receive and record the deed. Upon the contrary, we should say that the recording statutes are remedial, and should be construed to advance the remedy, rather than to invalidate a record upon narrow

and technical grounds. The second section, as it stood in the Code of Virginia of 1849 and 1860, did distinctly provide that the acknowledgment or proof, if taken by the county clerk, should be so taken "in his office." The provision was as follows: "The clerk of any such court, in his office, shall admit to record any such writing as to any person whose name is signed thereto, when it shall have been acknowledged by him, or proved by two witnesses as to him, in such court, or before such clerk in his office." Code 1849, c. 121. By comparing this section with our own act, above quoted, which was passed (re-enacted) March 27, 1882, it will be found that we have stricken out the concluding words, "in his office," thus leaving us to infer by an irresistible inference that the legislature intended to abolish the restriction, and to clothe the clerk with power to hear proof and take acknowledgment, under this section, anywhere within the limits of the county which bounds his territorial jurisdiction, for which he was elected. But it is urged that our act, as above quoted, does not apply to Ohio county, for the supposed reason that she has now, strictly speaking, no county court, that institution having been abolished, as it is argued, by the amendment to the eighth article of the constitution, adopted in 1880. Conceding this to be true, Ohio county has nevertheless a clerk of the county court, recognized as such by said amendment, and his duties defined generally by the twenty-sixth section thereof, as follows: "The voters of each county shall elect a clerk of the county court, whose term of office shall be six years. His duties and compensation, and the manner of his removal, shall be prescribed by law." Const. W. Va. art. 8, § 26; Code p. 37. The voters of Ohio county have elected a county clerk under this provision, and all the general acts prescribing the duties and powers of clerks of county courts apply as much to the county clerk of Ohio as to any other county. Consequently sections 2 and 3 in the act of 1882 must define his powers and duties as to recording and taking acknowledgment. This view is not weakened, but confirmed, by a consideration of our legislation especially applicable to Ohio and other counties, which had availed themselves of the thirty-fourth section of the eighth article of the constitution of 1872 to establish separate tribunals for judicial and probate matters, and for the police and fiscal affairs of the county. Ohio county had established by the act of December 1, 1872, for judicial and probate purposes, a county court with a single judge, and a county clerk, upon whom devolved the duties pertaining to the county clerk in other counties except as to police and fiscal matters. The county court thus established and its clerks were, of course, embraced in subsequent legislation, so far as such legislation was applicable. By an act passed December 21, 1875, the seventy-third chapter of the Code was amended and re-enacted, and we find embraced therein the second section precisely in the language of the same section in our present Code, passed and re-enacted in 1882;

while the third section conferred specific-ally upon the clerk of a county court the power to take acknowledgments. It follows, therefore, that when the amendment to the constitution was enacted in 1880 there had been conferred by the act of 1875 on the clerk of the county court of Ohio county power to take acknowledgments out of his office and within his county. Neither the amendment to the constitution of 1880, nor the subsequent act of the legislature, "Concerning county courts and their jurisdictions and power," (see Acts 1881, c. 5,) did in the slightest degree curtail the power of the clerk of the county court of Ohio county with respect to the recording of deeds, but confirmed such as he already possessed, and super-added thereto all the probate jurisdiction which had theretofore pertained to the court itself. The act of February 11, 1881, provided in its ninth section as follows: "And until otherwise provided by law such clerk as is mentioned in thirty-sixth section of the eighth article of the constitution, as amended, shall exercise any powers and discharge any duties heretofore conferred on, or required of any court or tribunal, established for judicial purposes, under the said article and section of the constitution of 1872, or the clerk of such court or tribunal, respectively, respecting the recording and preservation of deeds and other papers presented for record." This is almost the exact language of the amendment to the constitution itself, and it is quite obvious that it was the intention to preserve to the clerk of the county court of Ohio county (and other counties similarly situated) all of the powers pertaining to the recording of deeds which they then already possessed. And, as the power to take acknowledgments in the manner prescribed by section 2 already belonged to the clerk of the county court of Ohio county, nothing but the most narrow and illiberal construction of the language of the constitutional amendment could deprive him thereof. As we have seen, such a construction ought not to be, and will not be, resorted to.

For these reasons we find no error in the action of the circuit court in sustaining the demurrer to the bill. As the demurrer did not extend to the whole bill, but only to so much thereof as related to the registration of this deed, and the prayer to set it aside, it would, under ordinary circumstances, have been error to have dismissed the bill. As the plaintiffs were obviously entitled to have their debts audited and paid out of any surplus which might remain after discharging the prior liens, their bill should not have been dismissed. The decree complained of, therefore, so far as it sustained the demurrer to that charge in the bill whereby it was sought to set aside the deed to J. B. Sommerville, trustee, and awarded to S. E. Boyd her costs, must be affirmed; also so much as orders a sale, being based on consent and agreement; but for the error of dismissing the plaintiff's bill it must be reversed, and the cause remanded to the circuit court, to be there proceeded in according to the principles set out in this opinion, and further in accordance with the principles of courts of equity. The appellees having substantially prevailed in this appeal, it is ordered that their costs in this court be recovered by them against the appellants.

BROWN MANUF'G CO. v. WILLIAM DEERING & CO.

(Supreme Court of Appeals of West Virginia. June 20, 1891.)

PRINCIPAL AND AGENT—GOODS IN POSSESSION OF AGENT—EXECUTION.

A party whose entire business consists in selling agricultural implements, wagons, etc., as agent for the manufacturer thereof, receiving a commission for his services in disposing of the same, cannot be regarded either as a trader or commission merchant; and although his name, with the addition of the words "Mfrs.' Agent," be on a sign nailed on the outside of the building in which he does business, in a conspicuous place, farming implements which he has on sale as an agent for the manufacturer are not liable to execution and sale as his property, under the provisions of section 13 of chapter 100 of the Code of West Virginia.

(Syllabus by the Court.)

Error to circuit court, Wood County; A. Q. BOREMAN, Judge.

V. B. Archer, for plaintiff in error. Merrick & Smith, for defendant in error.

ENGLISH, J. On the 4th day of October, 1887, the Brown Manufacturing Company sued out of the clerk's office of the circuit court of Wood county two writs of fieri facias against the goods and chattels of one Warren Morehead, which two writs were issued upon two certain judgments which had been recovered in said court against said Morehead, one of which writs was for the sum of $131.30, with interest from the 18th day of April, 1879, and $29.45 costs, and the other was for the sum of $393.90, with interest from the 18th day of April, 1879, and $30.55 costs. These writs were on the 4th day of October, 1887, levied upon certain personal property, to-wit, one binder and four mowers, as the property of said Warren Morehead. Deering & Co. asserted a claim to the ownership of said property so levied upon, and on the 14th of November, 1887, the Brown Manufacturing Company filed in said circuit court its petition for the trial of the right of property to the binder and four mowers which had been levied on, as aforesaid, as the property of said Warren Morehead. An issue was made up; the parties waived a jury; and the court in lieu of a jury, having heard the evidence, rendered a judgment on the 8th of March, 1890, holding said property liable to sale by virtue of said executions; and to this judgment the said William Deering & Co. objected and excepted, and moved that the same be set aside as contrary to law and the evidence and otherwise improper, and that a new trial be awarded, which motions were overruled, to which ruling and judgment of said court the said William Deering & Co. applied for and obtained this writ of error. The court certified that all the evidence and facts read, heard, and considered by the court on the trial of said issue were set forth in the agreement of facts, which was in writing and signed by the plaintiffs and defendants by their counsel, which was made part of the record in the cause, which facts are substantially as follows: First, that the date and amount of said writs of *fieri facias*, and the time and manner of their levy, and the property levied upon, are in accordance with what has been stated; that the binder and four mowers so levied upon were claimed by said William Deering & Co. as their property at the time of said levy, and as not being subject to said executions; that an indemnifying bond was required by the sheriff, and given by said Brown Manufacturing Company; that said binder and four mowers were found in the building occupied by said Morehead, situated on the east side of Court square in Parkersburg, where said Morehead was carrying on business as manufacturers' agent, selling agricultural implements and machinery, vehicles, and other merchandise, having a sign nailed on the outside of said building, in a conspicuous place, in the words following: "Warren Morehead, Mfrs.' Agent;" and that no other sign (except one so placed with the letters thereon stating "Studebaker's Wagons") appeared on said building; that no notice was ever published by said Warren Morehead, as provided by section 13, c. 100, Code W. Va., and that said Morehead had been so engaged in said business for a number of years prior to said levies; that said binder was claimed by said William Deering & Co. to be of the value of not less than $130, and the said mowers to be not less than $180 in value. It was further agreed that said binder and four mowers were shipped from Columbus, Ohio, by said William Deering & Co. (which is an Illinois corporation, created by the state of Illinois) to said Warren Morehead, upon the terms and conditions mentioned and set forth in a contract in writing signed by said Deering & Co. and said Morehead, dated January 18, 1887, which contract is set forth *in hæc verba* in said agreement of facts; and said contract in substance authorizes said Morehead to receive said binders and mowers, to sell the same for said Deering & Co., and to receive commissions for so doing, providing that where they are sold on credit the notes for deferred installments to be made payable to the order of William Deering & Co. It was further agreed that for several years previous to the year 1887, and immediately preceding that year, the said Morehead had a license as broker and commission merchant, and that for the year 1887, while said Morehead was doing business as aforesaid, the city authorities informed him that it did not grant or impose any tax or license to brokers or commission merchants; and it was further agreed that said Morehead claimed to be and was carrying on the same business at the same place from the 1st day of January, 1887, to the 4th day of October, 1887, and still is carrying on the same. It was further agreed that the said William Deering & Co. claimed to own and have title to the said binder and four mowers by virtue of the terms and conditions of said contract of January 18, 1887; and it was

further agreed that the said Morehead had no other right to the possession of said binder and mowers than that which is shown on the face of said contract, and with the power to sell the property as therein provided, and that said binder is sometimes called a "harvester," and that said goods were shipped to said Morehead by the agent of said William Deering & Co. in pursuance of said contract, as is shown by the letter accompanying said goods at the time they were shipped, and a copy of which letter is made part of said statement of facts.

The questions presented for our consideration in this case involve a proper construction of section 13 of chapter 100 of the Code of West Virginia, p. 704, which reads as follows: "If any person shall transact business as a trader with the addition of the words 'factor,' 'agent,' 'and company,' or 'and Co.,' and fail to disclose the name of his principal or partner by a sign in letters easy to be read, placed conspicuously at the house wherein such business is transacted, and also by a notice published for two weeks in a newspaper (if any) printed in the town or county wherein the same is transacted, or if any person transact such business in his own name without any such addition, all the property, stock, choses in action acquired or used in such business shall, as to the creditors of such person, be liable for the debts of such person. This section shall not apply to a person transacting such business under a license to him as an auctioneer or commission merchant." And in construing this section properly the first question which presents itself is, what is the true definition of the word "trader," and who in a legal point of view are included within the word "trader?" One of the definitions given by Webster, and I think the true one, is "a dealer in buying and selling or barter;" and Bouvier in his Law Dictionary defines "trader:" "One who makes it his business to buy merchandise or goods and chattels, and to sell the same for the purpose of making a profit. The quantum of dealing is immaterial when an intention to deal generally exists. (2) Questions as to who is a trader most frequently arise under the bankrupt laws, and the most difficult among them are those cases where the party follows a business which is not that of buying and selling principally, but in which he is occasionally engaged in purchases and sales." In 3 Pars. Cont. (5th Ed.) p. 461, and note, we find it is said: "The meaning of the word 'trader' was well set forth by Mr. Justice THOMPSON, in the circuit court of the United States. Wakeman v. Hoyt, 5 Law Rep. 310. The doctrine of the court was that any person engaged in business requiring the purchase of articles to be sold again, either in the same or in an improved shape, must be regarded as using the trade of merchandise, within the intent of the bankrupt law." The law seems to contemplate buying and selling, and that both must concur in order to constitute a trader. In the American and English Encyclopedia of Law, (volume 2,) under the head of "Bankruptcy," note

2, under the heading, "Who is a Trader," it is said the commercial definition of a trader is one who makes it his business to buy and sell merchandise or other things ordinarily the subject of traffic. Love v. Love, 2 Pittsb. Leg. J. 101. Now, in order that the binder and mowers levied upon as aforesaid should be liable to sale for the satisfaction of said executions against the goods and chattels of said Morehead, it is necessary, in the first place, that the said Morehead must have been transacting business as a trader; but under the facts agreed in this case, considered in the light of the legal definitions and rulings which we have quoted and cited, said Morehead could not at the time said levy was made be regarded as a trader. There is no fact in the case which indicates that he was then engaged in buying and selling goods of any character; on the contrary, it is clearly manifest from the agreed statement of facts that the business of said Morehead was confined to selling entirely, and for this reason he cannot be regarded as falling within the definition of a commission merchant; for it will be found that Webster defines "commission merchant" as follows: "A merchant who transacts business as the agent of another man in buying and selling, and receives a rate per cent. as his commission or reward." It is not pretended that said Morehead was engaged in buying any merchandise of any character from any person or for any person on commission. The said Morehead, then, being neither a trader nor commission merchant, either with or without license, according to the legal definition or common acceptation of said terms, and the business he was engaged in not having the distinguishing features which would cause him to be classed either as a trader or as a commission merchant, it follows that he could not be considered as transacting business either as a trader or commission merchant; and we must conclude that said binder and four mowers were not, under the circumstances of this case, subject to levy and sale under executions sued out upon judgments against the goods and chattels of said Morehead, and the judgment complained of must be reversed at the costs of the defendant in error.

STATE v. MORGAN.

(Supreme Court of Appeals of West Virginia. June 30, 1891.)

JURY—MURDER—INDICTMENT—EVIDENCE—INSTRUCTIONS.

1. The record shows that Jeremiah S. Peirpoint is one of the jury sworn in the case, and the verdict is signed by J. S. Peirpoint. This will not affect the verdict.

2. An order to separate witnesses during a trial should always be granted, unless there be very strong reason against it, which can rarely exist; but it is not so far matter of right as to call for the reversal of a judgment where it has been refused unless it affirmatively appear that the party suffered injury from its refusal.

3. An exclamation made by a person at night, while in bed, not addressed to any one, is offered against her in evidence on trial for murder, and objected to, because made in sleep. It does not appear whether the person was asleep or awake. It was properly allowed to go to the jury.

4. To exclude a confession, it must not only be made under inducement of favor or fear, but such inducements must come from one in authority.

5. Motive in the commission of a crime is a material element for a jury in considering it, but it is not indispensable that it should be apparent to sustain a conviction. An instruction telling a jury that, if they find that no motive on the part of the prisoner existed for the commission of the crime, that itself is sufficient to raise a reasonable doubt of guilt, is bad.

6. An instruction should not single out one fact or element of the case, and make the case turn entirely on it, by telling the jury to find according to the hypothesis of that fact or element, ignoring all other material facts or elements.

7. The state is not bound to call all the witnesses present at the commission of the offense, nor a person so present who appears to be the only one present save the prisoner. It is the province of the prosecuting officer, not the court, to determine who shall be examined as witnesses for the state.

8. Upon an indictment in the form prescribed by section 1, c. 144, Code 1887, for murder, the state may prove any manner of killing or different manners of killing.

9. Discussion of principles on application in an appellate court to set aside a verdict on the ground that the evidence is not sufficient to warrant it.

(Syllabus by the Court.)

Error to circuit court, Tyler county; THOMAS P. JACOBS, Judge.

R. S. Blair & Son, for plaintiff in error. Alfred Caldwell, Atty. Gen., for the State.

BRANNON, J. On the 15th day of September, 1890, in the circuit court of Tyler county, Mary Jane Morgan was sentenced to the penitentiary during her natural life for the murder of her husband, Jacob Morgan, and she has come to this court praying relief from her sentence.

The first ground assigned for reversal of the sentence is that the verdict finding the prisoner guilty is signed by J. S. Peirpoint, whereas the list of jurors sworn in the case does not show any juror of that name, and thus an unsworn juror tried the prisoner. The record does show in the panel a juror named "Jeremiah S. Peirpoint." Clearly, we ought to say that this juror, Jeremiah S. Peirpoint, wrote only the initials of his Christian name, as is very common, and that the juror sworn on the panel and the one signing the verdict are one and the same. Are we to say that while the jury was in custody of the sheriff, and kept together and secured, one of them escaped, and another man was substituted, or that another man got into the case? We think not, especially when an explanation of the apparent discrepancy so readily presents itself. Younger's Case, 2 W. Va. 581, does not compel us to such an unreasonable decision, which would bring the administration of criminal justice into ridicule; for there the juror signing the verdict was P. B. Shively, while the sworn panel showed no such name, the nearest approach to it being P. B. Smith.

The second ground on which we are asked to reverse the sentence is that the court refused to separate the witnesses on the prisoner's motion. 1 Bish. Crim. Proc. §§ 1188, 1189, lays down the law on the subject thus: "Justice will sometimes be promoted, and seldom hindered, by causing witnesses to be examined apart from one another. Therefore, almost as of course, yet not as of strict right or necessarily, the court, on motion of either party, will direct the retirement of witnesses to a separate room, to return and testify, one by one, as called." "The making or refusing of the order, and the form of it when made, are alike within the discretion of the presiding judge, not generally subject to revision by a higher tribunal." Whart. Crim. Pl. § 569, states the law thus: "It is within the power of the court to order that the witnesses should be excluded from the court-room. At the same time, the action of the court trying the case will not be revised in this respect in error, unless it appear that manifest injustice has been done." In 1 Thomp. Trials, §§ 275, 276, it is said that in civil and criminal trials it is a rule of practice for the judge, on motion of either party, to direct that the witnesses shall be examined out of the hearing of each other, and such an order is rarely withheld, but that "by the weight of authority the party does not seem entitled to it as a matter of right." In section 276, Thompson says: "According to a much prevailing view, whether the court will thus sequester witnesses, or, as it is sometimes called, ' put them under the rule,' is a matter of sound judicial discretion, which discretion will not be revised on error or appeal, in the absence of an appearance of abuse." 1 Greenl. Ev. § 432, states that the order of separation "is rarely withheld; but, by the weight of authority, the party does not seem entitled to it as a matter of right." Old English authorities cited by Greenleaf hold that the matter is one of discretion, not of strict right. From these great text-writers, and an examination of many of the authorities which they cite, I conclude that the separation of witnesses ought, on the motion of either party, to be granted in the interest of the discovery of truth, and the detection and exposure of falsehood, unless strong reason be shown against it, which rarely occurs; but that it is not strictly matter of right, so that its refusal shall be ground for reversal, in the absence of the appearance of prejudice to the party. If the order were a matter of right, and not of discretion, then, from its refusal, the law would infer prejudice to the party; but, it not being a matter of right, it must in some way affirmatively appear that the party was in fact injured. It does not so appear in this case. Why this order, almost universally accorded, especially in grave criminal trials, was in this case refused, does not appear; but it does not appear that it worked harm to the prisoner. The cases are numerous holding that a witness remaining in court in violation of an order of separation may nevertheless be examined, his conduct bearing only on his credit, and subjecting him to proceedings for contempt. Hopper v. Com., 6 Grat. 684; Hey's Case, 32 Grat. 946, and citations; Gregg's Case, 3 W. Va. 705. The Case of Gregg, just cited, is urged upon us as ground for reversal. The syllabus there states that "it is the duty of the

courts to separate witnesses, either in civil or criminal cases, if asked by either party." The constitution did not then, as now, require that the syllabus should be prepared by the court. The language is that of Judge MAXWELL in delivering the opinion, and is not at all objectionable, as a general statement of the duty of the trial court; but Judge MAXWELL did not mean to say that the non-observance of that duty would reverse a judgment, and, if he did, the expression is *obiter dictum*, because the question did not arise in the case; for in that case the court did make an order of separation, but, a witness having remained in the room, the question was whether he could be examined. Baron ALDERSON once said that it was the right of either party to require such separation; but, as the author of Thompson on Trials (section 277) says, "this was very different from holding that a judgment would be reversed because the trial court had refused to grant such an application." Not a single case or text-writer has been cited as squarely holding that a refusal to separate the witnesses is ground for reversal.

The third ground assigned for the reversal of the sentence is the admission in evidence of a certain ejaculation or exclamation of the prisoner, which it is claimed is not admissible, because made by the prisoner in sleep. Lottie Callahan, the prisoner, and a little girl were sleeping together in one bed, the little girl in the middle, and in the room were two other beds occupied by others; and about 12 or 1 o'clock at night Lottie Callahan heard the prisoner exclaim: "They have deviled me so much about this that I don't care how it goes; I only consented to his death, and gave him the poison." One case (People v. Robinson, 19 Cal. 40) has been cited holding it error to admit declarations or talk of a defendant while in sleep, the court holding that if he was in sleep the inference is that he was not conscious of what he was saying. In the present case it does not appear whether or not the prisoner was asleep when this exclamation escaped from her, the witness saying that she could not say whether she was asleep or awake. A question occurred to my mind whether it was incumbent on the state to show that the prisoner was not asleep as a condition precedent to the introduction of the exclamation, in analogy to the law that it is a condition precedent to the admissibility of a confession that it be voluntary, and that the burden of showing it to be voluntary is upon the state, and that before admitting it the court must find it to be voluntary, (Thompson's Case, 20 Grat. 724;) but we conclude that the action of the court, in laying it before the jury, to have such weight as they thought proper to accord to it, was proper. It was a question of fact, which the jury was competent to decide, whether the prisoner was awake or asleep when the ejaculation was made. We must assume that it was discussed before the jury in lights applicable to the subject, to enable the jury to make an intelligent estimate of its weight. It was with them to say whether it was made in sleep, and was therefore worthless, or whether, though in sleep, it was but the divulgence of truth, springing from guilt which rested heavy on the soul, and broke forth through voice and lips, the half conscious man revealing secrets indelibly impressed on the memory, which, if fully awake, he would fain have suppressed. It was with the jury to say whether she was fully awake, and forgot herself, and in this soliloquy spoke out the truth. The operation of the human mind is an enigma, and its expressions in the unconsciousness of sleep are frequently vagaries and fictions, but sometimes born of reality. In this connection there is a somewhat notable coincidence. It is beyond question that Jacob Morgan died of a shot entering his back, passing through liver and lungs, and coming out in the breast, a deep stab in the side, and a cut or cuts on his throat severing his jugular vein, and cutting out the root of his tongue, and not at all from poison. The prisoner in this midnight exclamation said: "I only consented to his death, and gave him the poison." When the neighbors, after dark, went into the murdered man's house in answer to the alarm which the prisoner had spread among her neighbors, she having, as she said, left her husband struggling with two murderers, who were shooting and cutting him to death, and run to give alarm, they found the supper table spread; and on the table was a tea-cup with tea and bread in it, and she, returning to the house with these neighbors, at once took this tea-cup and threw its contents out, saying that the murderers might have put poison in it. She told a witness that when her husband returned from town that evening she had supper ready, but he declined eating, saying he had had supper, but that she urged him to take a cup of tea with her. Had she designed and prepared his murder by poison, and, this failing, resorted to other means? There is something of mysterious import in this matter. If there was poison in the cup, who put it there? Not the unknown strangers. It would tell strongly the murderous intent. It is urged in argument that, the state having relied on death by other means than poison, this ejaculation was not admissible, because it tended to prove death by poison; but a theory of the state, prominent in the case, was that the prisoner was a party to a plot and conspiracy with paramours or others to murder her husband, and that that part of this exclamation which makes her say, "I only consented to his death," corroborates and sustains that theory; and therefore, if the exclamation be at all admissible, that part of it would meet and answer the point of objection to it just stated. It does not appear that when this exclamation was made the prisoner was asleep, and, if that fact would exclude it, for its want we cannot hold that it was error to place it before the jury.

The fourth ground assigned for the reversal of the sentence is that the court refused to exclude confessional statements of the prisoner made to Christa Craig. It is clearly true that it was under the promise of Craig, who stated to her that he had discovered circumstances strongly implicating her, that he would favor her, and suppress the evidence which he claimed to have, that she made these statements; and clearly, if Craig had been a person in authority, the evidence would be rejected. But Craig was only a detective, ferreting out the crime, who interviewed the prisoner in jail. Though perhaps admitted to the jail by the jailer, he was not a person in authority. The only reason suggested for deeming him a person in authority is that presumably he was admitted to the jail by the jailer, and that the statements were made under his apparent sanction. It is so well settled that, to exclude confessions, they must be made, not only under inducements, but under inducements held out by persons in authority, that I shall not discuss the subject, but simply refer to Smith's Case, 10 Grat. 734; Shifflet's Case, 14 Grat. 659; Thompson's Case, 20 Grat. 734; Venable's Case, 24 Grat. 643; Page's Case, 27 Grat. 930; Mitchell's Case, 33 Grat. 845.

The fifth objection to the sentence is that the court refused the prisoner's instructions Nos. 5, 6, 7, 8, 9, 12, 13, 14, and 15, and substituted and gave one numbered 26 in lieu of No. 13. No. 5 is as follows: "The jury is instructed that, if they find from the evidence in this cause that no motive existed in the mind of the defendant to commit the crime wherewith she is charged in the indictment, that is sufficient, within itself, to be taken into their consideration, upon which to predicate a reasonable doubt." This instruction is bad, because it tells the jury that, if no motive was apparent to commit the crime, that is itself sufficient to inspire a reasonable doubt, in effect, to acquit; for, if there be reasonable doubt, acquittal must follow. It would have been, perhaps, proper to tell the jury to take into consideration a want of motive, along with other features of the case, for that is an item in the process of weighing evidence and reaching a conclusion; but this instruction singles out that single fact, and forgets all other facts in the case, and tells the jury, in effect, to acquit, and invades the right of the jury to weigh all the evidence. Want of apparent motive is not all-controlling in a trial, as this instruction would make it. It may be true that crime is never committed without a motive, but that motive may be beyond the reach of evidence, or even conjecture and therefore proof of motive is not indispensable to conviction. 1 Bish. Crim. Proc. § 1107. Dean's Case, 32 Grat. 912, by no means asserts that, to warrant a conviction upon circumstantial evidence, time, place, motive, means, and conduct must each and all concur in pointing out the prisoner as the guilty agent, and that, if one of those elements be wanting, there can be no conviction. It only says that, when all these elements do concur, a strong case is made against him.

No. 6 is as follows: "The jury is instructed that, before the defendant can be convicted as an accessory before the fact, they must be satisfied from the evidence beyond a reasonable doubt that the defendant was not only present at the time, but also they must be satisfied from t' evidence beyond a reasonable doubt that she was aiding and abetting the perpetrator." This instruction was irrelevant, as the prisoner was not indicted as an accessory, but as principal. Also, though based on the theory of an accessory before the fact, it supposes evidence which does not suit that theory, but would make the party a principal. Besides, it cannot be harmonized with No. 7 in its legal proposition.

No. 7 is as follows: "The jury is instructed that an accessory before the fact is one who, being absent at the time the felony was committed, does yet procure, counsel, or command another to commit a felony, and words amounting to bare permission will not alone constitute this offense, nor concealment of a design to commit it." As the prisoner was not indicted as an accessory, what relation to the case has this instruction? If it was intended to tell the jury that, as the prisoner was indicted as a principal, she could not be convicted ·if the evidence showed her to be an accessory, it was irrelevant, for, if guilty, she was a principal, and there was no evidence tending to show that she was only an accessory. It may be questionable whether the words "bare permission" reflect the law, or, at least, whether a permission on the part of the wife to the murder of a husband would not make her participation sufficiently active as an encouragement to the actors to make her an accessory. Hawkins' Pleas of the Crown, cited by Mayo's Guide as authority for this language "bare permission," may not sustain it, as it says, (volume 2, c. 29, § 16:) "As to the second point, viz., in what case a man shall be adjudged an accessary before, it seems to be agreed that those who by hire, command, counsel, or conspiracy, and it seems to be generally holden that those who, by showing an express liking, ·approbation, or *assent to another's felonious design of committing a felony*, abet and encourage him to commit it, but are so far absent when he actually commits it that he could not be encouraged by the hopes of any immediate help or assistance from them, are all of them accessories before the fact, both to the felony intended, and to all other felonies which shall happen in and by the execution of it, if they do not expressly retract and countermand their encouragement before it is actually committed." The italics are mine. But I do not deem it necessary to pursue this feature of instruction 7. Instructions 6 and 7 are not urged in the brief of prisoner's counsel.

No. 8 is as follows: "The jury is instructed that, if they believe from the evidence in this cause that Clarissa Morgan was present, and saw the act committed with which this defendant is charged, it is incumbent upon the state to have produced the said Clarissa Morgan as a witness (if she be living under jurisdiction and within reach of the process of this court) in behalf of the state, and it cannot substitute circumstantial evidence in lieu of positive evidence." No. 9 is as follows: "The jury is instructed that it devolves upon the state to produce, if it is

in her power, in all criminal cases of this kind, the very best evidence that can be obtained. Therefore, if the jury believe from the evidence in this cause that the crime wherewith the defendant is charged was committed openly and not secretly, and in the presence of Clarissa Morgan, who is now living and within the jurisdiction of the court and subject to its process, it was the duty of the state to have procured her upon trial, and its failure to do so raises the presumption of law that, if she had been so produced, her evidence would have been adverse to the state, and that that in itself is sufficient to raise a rational doubt as to the guilt of the defendant; therefore you must acquit." I shall not discuss the principles involved in these two instructions, because this court in Cain's Case, 20 W. Va. 679, elaborately discussed them, and held that it is not the duty of the state to examine all the witnesses present at the commission of an offense, and that it is the province of the prosecuting officer, and not the court, to determine who shall be examined for the state. The fact that the state fails to call a witness present at the fact may be considered by the jury, but is not a ground of error. This child, Clarissa Morgan, is the granddaughter of the prisoner, and was of tender years, and raised by the prisoner. We do not know, even, that she knew the obligation of an oath, or was at all competent, if the law were that the state was bound to call her. Evidence in the case tends to show that on one occasion, after the murder, the child said she wanted to go to her Uncle Bas. Morris' house, and said she was afraid to stay with her grandmother, and her grandmother called her a "dirty little thing;" and the child persisted in going, and said, "I am going to tell;" and her grandmother said, "Tell what?" and added, "I'll cut your throat, if you tell that." Under these circumstances, it is not surprising that the state exercised its right of not calling her as a witness. The prisoner could have called her.

No. 12 is as follows: "The jury is instructed that if they believe from the evidence in this cause, beyond any reasonable doubt, that the decedent came to his death by poison, then no conviction can be had under this indictment, and it will be your duty to acquit." This instruction is not insisted upon in the brief, and does not propound the law correctly, for, the indictment being the general form prescribed by Code 1887, c. 144, § 1, which does not specify any mode of killing, any mode or manner of killing may be proves under it. No. 13 is as follows: "The jury is instructed that extrajudicial confessions should be received with great caution. Therefore, if you believe from the evidence in this cause that the confessions claimed to have been made by the defendant are inconsistent, improbable, incredible, contradictory, or discredited by other evidence, or were the emanations of a weak or excited state of the mind, the jury may exercise their discretion in rejecting them, either wholly or in part; and, if you have any reasonable doubt as to the probability, consistency, or credibility of such confessions, or that they emanated from an unexcited mind, then it is your duty to acquit." This instruction is bad. It makes the case of the state rest solely on the prisoner's confession, telling the jury that, if they find the confession to be circumstanced as set forth in it, they should disregard it, and acquit the prisoner, thus ignoring all other evidence in the case criminating the prisoner, and there was a very considerable quantity of it, and thus withdrawing every other feature of the case from the jury; thus making the court say that, in its opinion, if the confession of the prisoner were so circumstanced, the balance of the evidence was inadequate to sustain a conviction, and so making the court usurp the province of the jury; and the theory that, if the confession emanate from an excited mind, it should be disregarded, is untenable. That was a matter to be weighed by the jury. The fact that parties were under fear and excitement did not exclude their confessions in Smith's Case, 10 Grat. 734, and Venable's Case, 24 Grat. 639. Speaking for myself, while the circumstances of inconsistency, improbability, etc., supposed in the instruction, were entirely proper to be considered by the jury in weighing the confession, and the court might properly have told the jury that it should consider those circumstances, yet it could not, as proposed by this instruction, invade the province of the jury, and tell them absolutely that, if the confession were so circumstanced, they must throw it away. In short, the instruction infringed upon the province of the jury, and was very properly refused. The court, in lieu of the last instruction, (13,) gave an instruction, No. 26, as follows, and we think there is no error in substituting it for No. 13, and that it was fair to the prisoner, and all she could ask on the subject of which it treated. Instruction No. 26: "The jury are instructed that, in considering extra-judicial confessions, they have the right to take into consideration the circumstances under which they were made, the credibility of the witness or witnesses by whom they are detailed, the condition and circumstances of the party alleged to have made them, the probability or improbability of such confessions, and that you have the right to consider the same in connection with all the evidence in the case; that you are the sole judges of the credibility of all the witnesses and the weight of the evidence, and you may give to the evidence of the witnesses just such weight as you think it entitled to under the circumstances of the case." The prisoner complains of the refusal of instruction No. 14, which is as follows: "The jury is instructed that, if they believe from the evidence in this cause that the confessions detailed by C. Craig, as having been made to him by defendant, were extorted from her by false representations of apparently strong and incontrovertible evidence of guilt which he claimed to have in his possession, then such confessions should be received by you with extreme caution, and you may reject or receive them either in whole or in part." I think it trenched upon the jury's right to weigh and consider the confession, without any discounting of its effect by the court, as a legal proposition. As to these instructions, in effect, telling the jury how to treat the confession, I would apply the language used by Judge JOHNSON in State v. Betsall, 11 W. Va., on page 740, that "in Virginia and this state the juries are the judges of the law as well as the facts in a criminal case; and while the court may charge the jury as to the law of the case, yet the court is not permitted to charge the jury as to the weight of the evidence. Our courts are somewhat peculiar in this respect; but the law has been so held in Virginia from the earliest history of its jurisprudence, and we think it constitutes one of the brightest ornaments thereof." In Ross v. Gill, 1 Wash. (Va.) 88, Pres. PENDLETON said: "If the question depends on the weight of the testimony, the jury, not the court, are exclusively and uncontrollably the judge." See Hurst's Case, 11 W. Va. 75. In Betsall's Case, while the practice stated in all the books justified, nay, made it the duty of, the judge to advise the jury not to convict on the uncorroborated testimony of an accomplice, and that its omission is error, (1 Greenl. Ev. § 380,) it was there held that a verdict might rest solely on his testimony, and that "in this state it is not proper for the court to give any instructions to the jury as to the weight of such or any other evidence." And besides, I think that instruction 26, given in lieu of 13, was all that the prisoner was entitled to on the matters contained in No. 14 as well as 13.

Instruction No. 15 refused the prisoner is as follows: "The jury is instructed that, if they believe from the evidence in this cause that a conspiracy was formed by the defendant and others associated with her for the purpose of murdering Jacob Morgan, the decedent named in the indictment in this prosecution, then no conviction can be had of the defendant under this indictment." It is plainly bad. Why could she not be convicted under this indictment, though she had entered into a conspiracy? If the instruction had said that if she entered into such a conspiracy, but was not present aiding and abetting at a murder, it would have been proper. The theory of the state was, and it gave evidence tending to show, that the prisoner had confederated with others to murder her husband, and was present aiding and encouraging the bloody and atrocious deed; and she admitted to different persons, at different times, she was present, and there was no evidence of her absence; and the instruction was improper and irrelevant.

The court gave the following instruction, on the state's motion: "If the jury believe from the evidence, beyond any reasonable doubt, that a conspiracy was formed between the prisoner, Mary Jane Morgan, and other persons, whose names are unknown, that the purpose of that conspiracy was to murder Jacob Morgan, and that, pursuant to that conspiracy, the unknown members of the conspiracy, or some of them, killed Jacob Morgan, and that the killing was done with malice aforethought, either expressed or implied.

and that the prisoner, Mary Jane Morgan, was present at the time Jacob Morgan was killed, and aided by acts, or encouraged by words or gestures, those actually engaged in said killing, then said prisoner was a principal in the killing and murder." It does not seem to be assigned as error, but it is urged in the brief of prisoner's counsel as error, because it is said that, while it states the law correctly, there was no evidence tending to prove such a conspiracy, and that the prisoner aided in the murder. Christa Craig stated, in effect, that the prisoner, on being told that he had evidence implicating her, asked him how he got it; that he showed her some statements implicating her, when she again asked how he got the information, and asked Craig if he could not help her, when he told her that he could, on condition that she would tell him if there was not a plot to murder Morgan, and she admitted there had been, and that it was formed on a Sunday, not on a Wednesday, and she promised to tell him who was in the plot, but did not, though requested by him several times to do so after she had been released from jail; that he asked her what was the inducement to kill Morgan, and she said she cared nothing for him; that he did not please her any too well; that there were other men she could enjoy herself with. Craig also stated that he asked her what they did with the blood on the floor, and she said she had scrubbed it up. He also stated that he told her that on the night of the murder he was about the house for a bad purpose, at a certain time and place, and told her the number of times she had come out of the house, and she exclaimed, "My God, you know it." She gave Craig her note for $100 for his services and favor. There was evidence that she was anxious to have her husband convey her his farm; that she said if Morgan were dead she would draw a pension, and asked whether she would, and was informed that she would; that she was discontented, and lived unhappily with her husband; and said she had been "haggared to death," and would rather die than live in that way; and that she would have things carried to her own notion. On one occasion, when mad, she said she would be God damned if she was going to live there another year longer. She said she did not think hard of the men that murdered him, and that he was better off. She told several shortly before the murder that she had a dream that two or three men had come there to murder her husband, and said she knew he would be murdered. On one occasion, when the conversation was about her husband's going west when he should receive his pension, she said that it would do him no good, for some one would kill him for his money; and, some one saying that he reckoned not, she said, "You will see." After his murder she still talked of this dream, saying that she knew he would be killed from that dream; that "she dreamed it was done, and her dream turned out just the same men she saw in her dream." She uniformly and frequently stated that, while she and her husband were at supper after dark, an unknown

man came to the house, and asked supper for three, and then the man shot her husband in the breast, and they engaged in a scuffle around the room, and her husband, though she did not lift a finger to help him, was getting the better of this man, when another man appeared on the scene and commenced cutting the throat of her husband, whereupon she fled. The room was found in order, the table set, giving no evidence of a scuffle. The physicians who made the post mortem examination say that the deadly shot through liver and lungs would have instantly paralyzed Morgan so that he could not scuffle, tending to show the utter improbability of any such scuffle as she narrated. She told that he was shot in the breast, while it is certain it was in the back. In one of his garments was found $3.29, in another $11. The prisoner had on her person $110 of his money after the murder, which she asked a party to conceal. If strangers murdered him for money, it is strange that they left any money. There was evidence tending to show that a skirt of the prisoner's, found hidden in a barrel of feathers in the loft, and thence moved and hidden under the hearth, had blood on it. This short statement is enough, I think, to show that there was evidence tending to show such conspiracy, that she was a party to it, and that she was present at the murder, encouraging it, if not committing it alone and unaided, so as to render the instruction asked by the state relevant. The evidence in the record is very detailed and voluminous, showing many more circumstances bearing on this instruction and on the general phase of the case than I have given.

The sixth and last ground relied upon for reversing the sentence is that the evidence did not warrant the verdict. I shall not detail the evidence under this head. As no two cases are alike in facts, such detail would be no precedent for future cases, and is not necessary for the purposes of our decision. I have stated under other heads only a fraction of the many facts and circumstances appearing in the many pages of the evidence. Enough has been indicated, however, to show that there was some evidence—a great deal of evidence—tending to sustain the verdict. In the first place, as to the motion for a new trial, I remark that the record certifies, not the facts, but the evidence, and therefore we are to apply the well-established rule, acted on in Flanagan's Case, 26 W. Va. 116, and Baker's Case, 33 W. Va. 319, 10 S. E. Rep. 639, that, in such case, this court will not reverse the judgment unless, after rejecting all the conflicting parol evidence of the exceptor, and giving full faith and credit to that of the adverse party, the decision of the trial court still appears to be wrong. Assault is made in argument on the credit of witnesses Callahan and Craig, but, under the rule just stated, they are to be given en credit. The evidence of Craig is very material in this case, the case turning largely, but by no means entirely, upon it. A jury is uncontrollably the judges of the credit of witnesses, and, where a case turns solely or materially on the credit of witnesses, a new trial will not be granted by this court. Patteson v. Ford, 2 Grat. 19; Proctor v. Spratley, 78 Va. 254. A misconception of the functions of this court, as to setting aside a verdict, seems to prevail quite widely. It seems to be considered that this court can take the place, not only of a circuit judge, but also that of a jury, and enter upon the process of weighing evidence, and, if it should think the evidence short, or such as, had its members been of the jury, they would not have found the verdict, then the verdict should be set aside. This is by no means the function of this court. This would be for this court to usurp the province, not only of the trial judge, but that of the jury, who are peculiarly the triers of fact under our system. The circuit judge and the jury see and hear the witnesses, their words, their demeanor, their countenances, the true and actual features of the case, while we see only the evidence on paper, and are at this distance much less competent to weigh evidence. Why have a jury and circuit judge, 18 in number, if their verdicts are to be reversed by 4 appellate judges, because they happen to think their decision erroneous on the evidence? In Lawrence's Case, 30 Grat. 845, the judges said they would have acquitted the prisoner if they had been on the jury, or granted a new trial had they presided at the trial, but as an appellate court they could not do so. Same principle in McCune's Case, 2 Rob. (Va.) 771; Sheff v. Huntington, 16 W. Va. 307. I am aware that cases in Virginia and this state are to be found granting new trials where there was evidence tending to sustain the verdict, but the appellate court undertook to weigh the evidence, and grant new trials, with perhaps doubtful propriety, and seemingly not in harmony with the principles they themselves laid down. The principles on which an appellate court will act in this matter have been stated in differing language, on different occasions, and the exact rule is somewhat hard to define. In Hill's Case, 2 Grat. 594, and Grayson's Case, 6 Grat. 712, it is said that it is only where a verdict is "plainly against the evidence, or without sufficient evidence;" so in Smith's Case, 24 W. Va. 815; but different men, under this rule, would differ. In Miller v. Insurance Co., 12 W. Va. 116, and Sheff v. Huntington, 16 W. Va. 308, it is said a new trial should be "only in a case of plain deviation from right and justice, not in a doubtful case, merely because the court, if on the jury, would have given a different verdict;" that the verdict "ought not to be interfered with * * * unless manifest wrong and injustice have been done, or unless the verdict is plainly not warranted by the evidence or facts." Other cases phrase it in different language. A criminal case in a circuit court, and in this court on an overruled motion for a new trial, occupies a vastly different place. I might almost say that in the circuit court the question is whether the prisoner is guilty beyond a reasonable doubt, whereas, after a verdict of guilt and its approval by the circuit court, the situation is reversed, and the question here is whether it appears that

he is innocent. I think that an appellate court enters on dangerous ground when it assumes the role of a jury, and enters upon the process of accurately weighing evidence. I think that, when there is some evidence to sustain a verdict, it is dangerous to overthrow it. It seems to me that, where the question is whether there is sufficient evidence to sustain a verdict, the language used in several cases, so far as language can express a general rule aptly, reflects the true principle, and that is that "where some evidence has been given which tends to prove the facts in issue, or the evidence consists of circumstances and presumptions, a new trial will not be granted " by an appellate court. Grayson's Case, 6 Grat. 712; Sheff v. Huntington, 16 W. Va. 307; Miller v. Insurance Co., 12 W. Va. 116. I strongly approve the aptness and force of Judge SNYDER's language in Cooper's Case, 26 W. Va. 338: " In Virginia and this state the courts have always guarded with jealous care the province of a jury. If the question depends on the weight of testimony, or inferences and deductions from facts proved, the jury, not the court, are exclusively and uncontrollably the judges. This conclusion is based upon the well-established rule that the jury are the sole judges of the evidence, the credibility of all admissible testimony, and the inferences from the facts and circumstances proved." In Betsall's Case, on p. 743 of 11 W. Va., Judge JOHNSON said that, where a jury has found a party guilty in a criminal case, and a new trial is asked on the ground that the evidence is insufficient to sustain the verdict, the appellate court will not grant a new trial, unless it is "irresistibly clear that the conviction was wrong." We cannot say that it is thus clear that the verdict in this case is wrong; indeed, grave and solemn as is this verdict, we do not see that it is unjust. It seems to me, after reading all the evidence, that time, place, motive, and conduct point to the accused as the guilty agent in this horrible murder, and this circumstance, under Dean's Case, 32 Grat. 912, makes a strong case against her. It is a most solemn duty, that of confirming a sentence condemning a woman to the penitentiary as long as life shall last. Let us hope that no mistake has been committed. It is a terrible crime of which the prisoner has been convicted, the murder of a husband, and the deed done in so cruel and revolting a manner as to make us shudder. If guilty, the prisoner meets a well-deserved punishment; and her conviction is but another of the many instances to show that the law, "Thou shalt do no murder," is yet as vital and instinct with life, as when it was delivered by the great Law-Giver, and follows the guilty one with unerring eye and unfaltering step. The judgment is affirmed.

LUCAS, P., and ENGLISH, J., concur.

HOLT, J., is of opinion that the record shows a case in which the prisoner's motion to separate the witnesses should have been granted.

FERGUSON'S ADM'R v. WILLS.

(Supreme Court of Appeals of Virginia. July 2, 1891.)

ADMINISTRATORS — CONTRACT OF DECEASED — NOTICE—BILL OF EXCEPTIONS.

1. Where one contracted with a person since deceased to build a church, the fact that the administrator, shortly after the work was commenced, gave notice not to proceed therewith, and that the estate would not be responsible therefor, was no bar to a recovery for work afterwards done, when the church was completed according to the contract.

2. The fact that, before proceeding, the contractor secured the guaranty of the church trustees that he should be paid the contract price, and as much in excess of it as the work should cost, and that he then sublet the work to another did not bar a recovery against the estate on the original contract.

3. The action of the trial court in amending a requested instruction cannot be reviewed when the instruction itself is not embodied in the bill of exceptions. The fact that the clerk copied it into the transcript made it no part of the record.

4. Alleged error in overruling a motion for a new trial, on the ground that the verdict was contrary to the law and the evidence, cannot be considered, when the bill of exceptions shows that all the evidence is not certified.

5. Where an instruction covering the law of the case has been given, it is not error to refuse to give another, though it state the law correctly in a different manner.

Error to circuit court, Roanoke county; HENRY E. BLAIR, Judge.

Mr. Griffin, for plaintiff in error. Hansbrough, Penn & Cocke, for defendant in error.

LEWIS, P. This was an action of covenant in the circuit court of Roanoke county, wherein W. L. Wills was plaintiff, and Henry S. Trout, administrator of I. M. Ferguson, deceased, was defendant. The action was upon a sealed contract, entered into on the 5th day of March, 1881, between the defendant's intestate and Wills, for the erection of a church, in the then town of Big Lick, on a lot thereafter to be selected by the congregation or trustees of the church. The stipulated price for the work was $1,962.70. Ferguson died about the 1st of April thereafter, and the defendant qualified as his administrator. The site was not selected until nearly a year after the date of the contract, soon after which the work was commenced. Shortly thereafter, to-wit, on the 4th of April, 1882, the administrator notified Wills in writing not to build the church under the contract, and saying further that, if he did so, it would be at his own risk, and that payment would be contested. Wills was by trade a carpenter, and for some time had been in the employ of John Kefauver & Son, house-builders and contractors. He was a man of limited means, and was consequently unable, without the aid of others, to perform the contract. Accordingly he proposed to Kefauver & Son to turn over the contract to them, which they declined, on the ground that they were not willing to undertake the work for the price. He was then told by the trustees to go on with the work, and that they would not only guaranty him his money, but that he would be paid for the work the difference between the contract price and the cost of the work when completed. Kefauver & Son thereupon agreed with Wills to do the work for him, and employed him as their foreman to do it, paying him for his services two dollars a day; and they were subsequently paid for the work by "Wills' check on the bank." From what source Wills got the money does not distinctly appear, but the presumption is he got it from the trustees. The work was completed about the 1st of September, 1882. A witness for the plaintiff, Rev. L. L. Loyd, who was in charge of the church, testifies that he overlooked the work, and that it was done by Wills under the contract with the defendant's intestate; that he heard of no other contract; and that the work was done in accordance with the specifications of that contract. The jury found a verdict for the plaintiff, upon which judgment was entered, which is the judgment complained of. The question is whether there is any liability on the part of Fergusons' estate to the plaintiff by reason of the contract aforesaid, or whether that contract was abrogated or abandoned, and the work done, not by the plaintiff, but by other parties under a different contract. That the obligation of the contract was not affected by the notice served by the administrator on the plaintiff, above mentioned, is too plain for discussion. If it was, then all that a party to a contract has to do who wishes to rid himself of its obligations is to notify the other party not to perform his part of it, and the contract is at an end. But such a proposition is not sanctioned by any principle, either of law or justice, and cannot seriously be contended for. The circuit court did not err, therefore, in refusing to instruct the jury, on the motion of the defendant, that if the said notice was given before work under the alleged contract was commenced, and if the plaintiff thereafter did the work relying on the alleged contract, he could only recover the profits that he might show himself entitled to for doing his work under the contract. In short, the notice was without any legal effect whatever, and the court did not err in refusing to give any of the instructions offered by the defendant, which, if given, would have told the jury otherwise. Nor is there anything to show that the contract was abandoned by the plaintiff. The case, so far as it is disclosed by the record, is simply this: The plaintiff, being without means of his own to fulfill the contract, arranged with Kefauver & Son to do the work for him. They did it, and he paid them for it with money, no doubt received from the trustees, but that is immaterial. They simply verbally guarantied that, if he would go on and complete the contract entered into by him with Ferguson, he should lose nothing by it. That contract was completed, not by turning it over to Kefauver & Son, but through their aid or instrumentality, and, so far as Ferguson's estate is concerned, their work was the plaintiffs' work. Such being the tendency of the evidence, the circuit court properly submitted the case to the jury in giving the following instruction at the instance of the plaintiff: "The court instructs the jury that, if they believed from the evidence that the plaintiff, either himself or through others employed by him, constructed the building in the declaration mentioned, in accordance with the specifications in said agreement set forth, and relying upon the contract in the declaration mentioned, then the jury shall find for the plaintiff the price therefor in said agreement stipulated to be paid by Isham M. Ferguson to the plaintiff, although from the evidence the jury may believe that outside parties by parol agreement guarantied that the plaintiff should lose nothing by his construction of said building under said agreement, and actually advanced to the plaintiff the money necessary to pay for the material and labor employed in the construction of the said building." This instruction covers the entire case as shown by the record. Hence there was no error in the refusal of the court to instruct the jury that if they should believe from the evidence that the plaintiff did not construct the church under the contract in question, but that it was erected by other parties, not under that contract, and relying on the promises of other persons to pay for the building when completed, then the plaintiff was not entitled to recover in this action. If it can be fairly said that this instruction is relevant to the evidence, the refusal to give it, we repeat, was not a reversible error, because the point is sufficiently presented in the instruction given to the plaintiff, and the settled rule is that, when an instruction is given which covers the entire case, and properly submits it to the jury, it is not error to refuse to give another, even though in point of law it is correct.

The next objection relates to the action of the court in amending the second instruction offered by the defendant. But the instruction itself is not set out in the bill of exceptions, and therefore, although copied into the transcript by the clerk, it is not a part of the record proper, and cannot be considered here.

The next and last assignment of error is that the court erred in overruling the motion for a new trial, which motion was based on the ground that the verdict was contrary to the law and the evidence. It appears, however, from the bill of exceptions, that all the evidence before the jury is not certified, and hence the objection is unavailing. In such a case the appellate court cannot know the grounds of the action of the trial court, and must presume that it was right. The judgment is affirmed.

FARRIER v. REYNOLDS.

(Supreme Court of Appeals of Virginia.　July 2, 1891.)

CONTRACT FOR SALE OF LANDS — HAZARD AS TO QUANTITY—SPECIFIC PERFORMANCE—RECEIPT.

1. A contract for the sale of land, described as "all that parcel or tract of land situate on the waters of Sinking creek, in the county of Craig, state of Virginia, known as the 'C. B. Duncan Farm,' containing fifty-six acres, more or less," is a contract of hazard as to quantity, and the vendee cannot claim a corresponding reduction in the price, especially when he is well acquainted with the land.

2. The fact that the vendor signed a receipt for the purchase money prepared by the vendee, and stating that the land contained 56 acres, which latter provision he did not read, cannot control the interpretation of the contract in an action by the vendor for specific performance.

Hansbrough & Hansbrough, for appellant. *J. W. Marshall*, for appellee.

PER CURIAM. This is an appeal from a decree of the circuit court of Craig county, rendered on the 17th day of October, 1890. The bill in this cause was filed in February, 1890, by the appellant, R. W. Farrier, against the appellee, R. C. Reynolds, and others, to compel the specific performance by the said appellee of a contract made by him for the purchase of the land of the appellant known as the "Duncan Farm" at the price of $1,800. The appellee answered, admitting the purchase of this land at the price stated, but alleging that the land had fallen off more than one-fourth in quantity upon a survey, and claiming an abatement of the purchase price on that account; and, as the tract was without buildings, claiming that the average price per acre of the whole tract, under the purchase price agreed, should be applied to the deficiency, and tendering, as he had done before suit was brought, the balance of the purchase money still due, upon this basis of 38¾ acres instead of 56 acres, adding 2 acres to the 38¾ acres, making 40¾. The appellant, upon the other hand, insists that it was a contract of hazard, and a sale in gross of a tract of inclosed land by its well-known name in the neighborhood, and by its known boundaries, made to a person well acquainted with it, living close by. The depositions were taken on both sides, and the plaintiff, the appellant here, testified that the purchaser, the appellee, expressly took upon himself the hazard, and agreed to purchase without reference to the number of acres, and signed a written contract stating that the land contained "fifty-six acres, more or less;" and, upon making a payment afterwards, had drawn a receipt setting forth the purchase of 56 acres, which he had signed without reading carefully; that, suspecting no trap, he had merely looked at it, and, seeing the amount paid was correctly stated, he had signed it. The appellee, on the other hand, said that there was nothing said about the acreage more than was expressed in the contract. At the hearing, the circuit court being of opinion that the sale in question was a sale by the acre, and not a sale in gross and at hazard, abated the purchase price accordingly; from which decree the plaintiff applied for and obtained an appeal to this court.

The agreement between the parties on this point was as follows: "All that parcel or tract of land situated on the waters of Sinking creek, in the county of Craig and state of Virginia, known as the 'C. B. Duncan Farm,' containing fifty-six acres, more or less." The evidence shows that the tract of land in question was inclosed by a fence, and well-known to the purchaser, who resided in the immediate neighborhood, and owned land close by; that the vendor intended to sell by the tract, and would not have taken the hazard on himself; that, pending the negotiations between the appellant, Farrier, (when he was about to become the purchaser of this land,) and Duncan, the then owner, finding that the deed had not yet been made, the appellee, Reynolds, sent an emissary to Duncan, and called him out, and said, "I am too late, I reckon, but R. C. Reynolds (the appellee) will pay one hundred dollars more for the land in question;" Duncan replied scornfully that he did not do business that way; that then this same appellee, Reynolds, procured the father of Mrs. Duncan to go to her, and offer $100 to her to refuse to release her dower interest in this land, and so to defeat the sale to Farrier, but this failed also, and Farrier became the purchaser; whereupon the appellee, Reynolds, exacted of Farrier a promise that, if he ever sold this land, he should have the refusal; that Farrier was offered $1,300 for this land by the witness Gorman, but, mindful of his promise to Reynolds, he felt obliged to offer the land to him at that price first, when Reynolds first declined to go above $1,200, then above $1,250, and finally agreed to give $1,300 only when he heard that Gorman was about to buy it. The receipt in question was drawn ready for a casual meeting long after the purchase when the idea of finding a shortage had been conceived. The proof is clear that this was the object of the receipt, and the appellee admitted in the presence of witnesses that he knew the appellant did not know what was in the receipt. When the complaint was first made of this shortage in the acreage, the vendor promptly offered to pay back all the money that had been paid, and take back the land, and informed the vendee that there was the same party ready now to give $1,300 for it as a whole, just as he had sold it to him; but the appellee, although able to reimburse himself, and be rid of the bargain if it did not suit him, insisted upon what he conceived to be his legal rights, and kept the land and claimed the reduction,—the abatement of the purchase money.

The question we have to decide is this a sale in gross of a tract of land by the boundaries, at a hazard as to quantity, or was it, as the circuit court decided, a contract for a sale by the acre? It is evident that there was no agreement to buy by the acre, and the purchase price cannot be evenly divided by the number of acres. It is proved that there is a deficiency. If it is a sale by the acre, then the purchaser is clearly entitled to an abatement. In the recent case of Trinkle v. Jackson, 86 Va. 241, 9 S. E. Rep. 986, this branch of the subject is considered, and the authorities cited. Then it is—and so, too, when the land is neither bought nor sold expressly by the acre, but both parties, in fixing the price for the land, have regard to the quantity which they supposed the estate to consist of—the same rule as to liability for deficiency will prevail. Yost v. Mallicote, 77 Va. 610, and cases cited. But when the lands in a con-

veyance are mentioned to contain so many acres by estimation, or the words "more or less" added, if there be a small portion more than the quantity the vendor cannot recover it; and, if there be a small quantity less, the purchaser cannot obtain any compensation in respect to the deficiency; and even a large excess or deficiency has not been considered a ground for relieving a vendor or purchaser. And, although the contract states the property to contain a given quantity, yet the purchaser must be content with a much less quantity, if it be stipulated that the quantity shall be taken as stated, whether more or less. When the real contract is to sell a tract of land, as it may contain more or less, fully understood to be so, the purchaser takes the tract at the risk of gain or loss by deficiency or excess, in the number of acres contemplated, and neither can resort to the other for compensation on the grounds of deficiency. Jolliffe v. Hite, 1 Call, 284, and Hull v. Cunningham, 1 Munf. 335. It was said here the words of the bond do not amount to a warranty of the quantity, inasmuch as, in speaking thereof, there is this caution used: "Said to contain 370 acres, be it more or less, to-wit, all that tract left him by his father, John Cunningham, deceased." These circumstances indicate a contract in gross, and not by the specific number of acres.

In Keytons v. Brawford, 5 Leigh, 48, it was said of such a controversy: "This depends upon the question whether the sale was in gross or by the acre; for if it was a contract of hazard, in which each party took upon himself the risk of excess or deficiency, there can be no relief afforded to either, whatever may be the actual quantity in the tract sold. Questions of this character have frequently been before this court, and nothing is better established than the law of the subject, when the real intention of the parties in the contract is once clearly established. But this intention it is sometimes difficult to discover, from the carelessness of the parties, from the use of equivocal expressions, and from the glosses which are given to the transaction by the testimony of witnesses. Contracts of hazard, such as those we are now considering, never have been discountenanced by our law. Where they are clearly established, they are valid. * * * It is not readily to be presumed that the parties designed to enter into such a contract, unless it is clearly sustained by the facts." In the case of Russell v. Keeran, 8 Leigh, 18, it is declared that every sale of land in gross or by the tract is ex vi termini a sale of hazard as to quantity; the vendor being debarred from claiming any addition to the purchase money, in case the real quantity of land shall be found to exceed the estimated quantity, and the vendee being debarred from claiming any diminution of the purchase money, in case the real quantity shall fall short of the estimated quantity. In that case the deficiency was more than one-fourth of the entire tract,—the stated quantity being 405½, "be the same more or less," the actual quantity 289½, acres. The question depends upon the intention of the parties as expressed in the contract by the words "more or less," and the evidence of witnesses as to the true intention of the parties; the latter being held admissible because of the ambiguity in these words, (Russell v. Keeran, supra,) and not upon the quantity of deficiency. In Caldwell v. Craig, 21 Grat. 132, there was a deficiency of 200 acres,—one-fifth. In Tucker v. Cocke, 2 Rand. (Va.) 51, there was a deficiency of 2,000 acres in a large tract. In the case of Jones v. Tatum, 19 Grat. 720, 90 acres, more or less, were sold, at the price of $4,750. Judge Moncure said, upon a claim for diminution of purchase price for a small deficiency: "I think the land was not sold by the acre, but that it was sold by the tract for $4,750, which is far from being an equimultiple of the supposed number of acres. The boundaries of the land were well defined, and are minutely set out in the deed of trust. There appears to have been no doubt or difficulty as to any of the corners or lines. The purchaser no doubt viewed every part of it. Being a small tract, he could probably stand in the center of it, and see all of it in one view."

These remarks are appropriate to this case. It is clearly, in this case, not a sale by the acre. The purchase price and the number of acres clearly show this. The contract excludes the idea by the words "more or less." The vendor testified that it was expressly agreed to be a sale by the acre, quantity not to be considered, as forming any part of the sale. The vendee says there was nothing said about this, but he impliedly confesses the contrary, by the circumstance that, instead of standing by the contract of sale mutually agreed to at the time of the sale, he prepares a receipt for some of the money, and inserts in that, not "fifty-six, more or less," but fifty-six acres absolutely; and when, by casual meeting, as appears, the same was carelessly signed by the vendor, holding this as a sort of sealed-up mystery, approaching the vendor in the field at his work, and threatening him with a receipt which he had, and which he did not know the contents of, and crowning the whole with the boast, "and I am going to use it against you, too;" and when, upon reading the receipt, the vendor said he certainly had not known what it contained, the vendee replied, "I knew you did not," as if he would now make no more defense against the claim. But certainly the contract between the parties cannot be set aside or construed by any such transaction as this. The question is what the parties intended at the time, as shown by the contemporaneous circumstances, and I think in this case the purchase was of a tract of land as such, by boundaries, and by name, and the number of acres did not enter into the consideration of the parties at all. Another party stood by ready to give, and is ready to give now, $1,300 for this land, and the vendor promptly, upon complaint made, offered to refund the money, and take back the land, which the other refused. It is evident that he is not damaged in any degree, as he can rid himself of the purchase, and receive back the money, and this without any outlay by him. The circuit court

having decided otherwise, I am of opinion to reverse and annul the decree complained of here.

REYNOLDS v. REYNOLDS' EX'R.[1]

(Supreme Court of Appeals of Virginia. July 2, 1891.)

VENDOR AND VENDEE—SALE IN GROSS—BILL OF REVIEW—AFTER-DISCOVERED EVIDENCE.

Where a sale was made of "one-half" of a certain tract of land in gross, and a deed executed based upon a subsequent survey which so defined the boundaries as to inclose 109 acres less than the parties supposed the one-half contained, a bill of review of a judgment for the balance of the purchase money recovered by the grantor's executor should be granted, where it was discovered after judgment that the surveyor acted fraudulently as to both parties in so defining the boundaries, and that upon discovering that fact the grantor avowed his purpose to correct the injustice thus done, although in the main action the mistake had been alleged by the grantee as ground for an equitable abatement of the purchase money, and the judgment had been affirmed on appeal. LACY, J., dissenting.

Appeal from circuit court, Floyd county; HENRY E. BLAIR, Judge.

Phlegar & Johnson, for appellant. *Dennis Tompkins*, for appellee.

FAUNTLEROY, J. This is an appeal from a final decree of the circuit court of Floyd county, rendered on the 19th day of September, 1887, on a bill of review filed by Harvey A. Reynolds, appellant, by leave of the said court, in the original cause in said court pending, of Stephen Watts in his own right, and as executor of Charles B. Reynolds, deceased, complainant, against Harvey A. Reynolds, defendant. A transcript of the record of the said bill of review, and a transcript of the record in the original cause in which the said bill of review was filed, show the following case: In September, 1882, Stephen Watts, as executor of Charles B. Reynolds, deceased, and in his own right, filed his original bill in the circuit court of Floyd county against Harvey A. Reynolds, charging that the said Harvey A. Reynolds was indebted to C. B. Reynolds, deceased, in the sum of $1,600, due by four bonds, filed with the bill, of $400 each, for unpaid purchase money for land sold and conveyed by said C. B. Reynolds, in 1869, to the said Harvey A. Reynolds, for which a vendor's lien was reserved in the deed filed with the bill, which he prayed to enforce. Harvey A. Reynolds answered the bill, setting out that he had bought of Charles B. Reynolds, in 1869, 30 or 40 acres of a tract of "Wiley" land, and one-half of the "Guerrant" land, owned by the said C. B. Reynolds, and had paid all of the said purchase money except the four bonds filed with the bill; that no lines or boundaries for the division of the "Guerrant" land were pointed out, mentioned, fixed, or agreed to at the time of the said sale in 1869; and that it was not divided, and no division was marked across it, until 1872, when Charles B. Reynolds instructed a surveyor, Stephen Guerrant, to lay off to Harvey A. Reynolds one-half of the Guerrant land, telling him that he had sold to him one-half of the said tract of Guerrant land; that the said surveyor,

---

[1] For dissenting opinion, see 13 S. E. Rep. 596.

Stephen Guerrant, reported to the said C. B. Reynolds that he had laid off by boundaries in a deed which he had prepared, one-half of the said land to the said Harvey A. Reynolds, and that the said boundaries in the said deed mentioned did embrace one-half of the said Guerrant tract of land; that this deed, prepared by the said Stephen Guerrant, was executed and delivered by Charles B. Reynolds, and accepted by the said Harvey A. Reynolds, in absolute and undoubting faith in the integrity and competency of the said Stephen Guerrant, entertained at that time by both the said grantor and grantee in the said deed; that the truth was only revealed by a survey ordered and made in the original cause in 1884; that the boundaries specified in the said deed did not embrace, and did not convey to the said Harvey A. Reynolds, one-half of the Guerrant land by a deficiency of 102 acres, for which large deficiency the said defendant prayed for an equitable abatement of the purchase money. The court below, by its decree of May, 1884, was of opinion that the contract between C. B. Reynolds and Harvey A. Reynolds was a contract of hazard, according to the boundaries in the deed, and refused to allow any abatement of the purchase money on account of the loss of the 102 acres less than one-half of the Guerrant land. From this decree of the circuit court of Floyd county an appeal was allowed to this court; and this court, by its decree of June 25, 1885, affirmed the said decree of the circuit court of Floyd.[1] After the cause went back to the court below for further proceedings, and the land of the appellant was sold under the decree of May, 1884, but the purchase money not collected, the defendant Harvey A. Reynolds, at the November term, 1886, by leave of the said circuit court of Floyd county, filed his bill of review in the cause, founded upon after-discovered evidence, material and sufficient to change the decrees of the circuit court and of this court, and which he never knew of before, and could not have known of by due diligence. Watts answered this bill, and the evidence was taken on both sides, whereupon the circuit court, by its decree of September 19, 1887, refused to correct the decrees of May, 1884, and the decree of this court of June 25, 1885, and dismissed the bill of review. The complainant thereupon appealed from this decree; and the question presented for the decision of this court now is, did the circuit court err in denying the relief prayed for in the bill of review, and in dismissing the bill?

In the case of Connolly v. Connolly, 32 Grat. 657, Judge BURKS delivered the opinion of this court, in which, after stating the requisites of a bill of review based upon the ground of after-discovered evidence, it is decided that "a bill founded on after-discovered evidence, with the requisites just stated, may be filed to review a decree even after it has been affirmed by an appellate court,"—citing Campbell's Ex'rs v. Campbell's Ex'r, 22 Grat. 649, and cases cited; Singleton v. Singleton, 8 B. Mon. 340. In the case of Campbell's Ex'rs

v. Campbell's Ex'r, supra, MONCURE, P., delivered the opinion of the court, in which it is said, (on page 673:) "That a decree of the court of appeals which has been certified to and entered as the decree of the court below may be reviewed and corrected, or reversed, on a bill of review filed in the latter court, founded on new matter, seems to be true." "But, while it is no doubt true that a bill of review may be allowed in such a case, * * * the new matter, to be sufficient ground for the reversal of the decree, ought to be very material, and newly discovered, and unknown to the party seeking relief at the time the decree was rendered, and such as he could not then have discovered by the use of reasonable diligence. This is necessary even in an ordinary case of a bill of review of a decree of the same court in which the bill is filed, on the ground of new matter. A fortiori, it must be necessary when the object is to reverse a decree of the court of appeals, in favor of the finality of which there are so many reasons founded on public policy and convenience." Upon the pleadings and proofs in the original cause, the question was whether C. B. Reynolds had sold to Harvey A. Reynolds one-half of the Guerrant tract of land, or only so much thereof as was embraced in the boundaries of the deed. The circuit court decreed that the boundaries in the deed, which was accepted by Harvey A. Reynolds, made it a contract of hazard and a sale in gross: and this construction was affirmed by the decree of this court upon the record then presented. The counsel for the appellees, commenting upon the newly-discovered testimony presented by the bill of review, asks: "Would it have produced a different result on the first trial, or is it of a different character and kind from that taken on the first trial to overthrow the words of the deed from C. B. Reynolds to Harvey A. Reynolds?" We answer this question with an emphatic affirmative. All the characteristics of after-discovered evidence as a basis of a bill of review obtain in the evidence presented by the record now under review: It was discovered after the decree was rendered in the circuit court, and after it was affirmed by this court; it could not have been discovered before by the exercise of reasonable diligence; it is material, and such as, if true, ought to produce on the trial of the issue a different result, and one in consonance with the demands of justice; and it is not merely cumulative. It consists of the full, clear, and positive testimony of the Reverend James M. Price, Capt. William P. Thompson, Mr. M. G. Angel, and Mr. Aaron Beckner, all highly respectable white men of Franklin county, the life-long friends and neighbors of C. B. Reynolds, who all swear that the facts within their knowledge were never made known by them to Harvey Reynolds until after the decision of the case in the supreme court of appeals, and the discussion in the neighborhood about the suit, and the sale of Harvey A. Reynolds' land to satisfy the decree against him; and neither of these gentlemen testified in the original cause. The evidence in the record shows that

C. B. Reynolds was a wealthy land-owner in Franklin and Floyd counties who had no wife or children or descendants living; that Harvey A. Reynolds who had been his former slave, and up to his death, in 1875, his trusted friend and business manager, was an illiterate, but industrious, thrifty, and worthy, colored man, between whom and C. B. Reynolds there existed kindness, affection, and perfect confidence. In January, 1869, C. B. Reynolds sold to Harvey A. Reynolds, upon long time and easy terms, one-half of the Peter Guerrant tract of land in Floyd county, with 80 acres of his Wiley tract adjoining, for $5,000. At the time of the said sale it was not known how many acres were contained in the Guerrant tract; and the evidence is cleared and conclusive that the boundaries of the land sold, simply by the designation of "one-half of the Guerrant tract," were not then named, referred to, or fixed, nor was even any division line indicated or agreed upon. More than two years after, to-wit, in February, 1872, C. B. Reynolds instructed Stephen Guerrant, a surveyor, to go upon the land, and survey and lay off the one-half of the Guerrant land to Harvey A. Reynolds, to whom he told the said Stephen Guerrant he had sold it. Guerrant reported to C. B. Reynolds that he had surveyed and laid off one-half of the Guerrant tract, and that the lines or boundaries indicated and expressed in the deed which he prepared would give to Harvey A. Reynolds one-half of the Guerrant tract. This he expressly said and assured to Harvey A. Reynolds, who, under that information and belief, accepted the deed which C. B. Reynolds had executed under the same information and belief in the competency and integrity of the said Stephen Guerrant, surveyor,—a mutual mistake, into which both the grantor and grantee in the said deed were deceived by the statements and misrepresentations made by the said Stephen Guerrant, who had, as the event and the evidence disclose, designedly so expressed the boundaries in the deed as to convey to the said Harvey A. Reynolds less than one-half of the Guerrant tract by the deficiency of 102 acres,—nearly one-fourth of what he was entitled to. This mistake, or, more accurately speaking, this imposition upon both C. B. Reynolds and Harvey Reynolds, was never known to or discovered by either C. B. Reynolds or Harvey A. Reynolds until C. B. Reynolds sold the residue, one-half of his Guerrant tract, to one W. H. Poff, who refused to buy it except by the acre, and C. B. Reynolds had it surveyed by the said Stephen Guerrant, and found that it contained 562 acres. This disclosure of the fact that the deed which he had made to Harvey A. Reynolds, as prepared by Stephen Guerrant, did not convey to him one-half of the Guerrant tract, greatly surprised and distressed him; and he expressed, openly and frequently, his purpose to repair the injustice done to Harvey A. Reynolds, but which he did not do because of extreme ill health, suffering, and death away from his home, in Lynchburg, whither he had gone for treatment.

It will not be possible to extend in this opinion, without swelling it to unnecessary length, all the evidence newly discovered, and presented under the bill of review; but the testimony of W. P. Thompson (which is only a sample of the others) will fully expose the action and motive of the fraud and abuse of confidence practiced by Stephen Guerrant upon both the grantor and grantee in the deed which he imposed upon them, and of which he subsequently took his own advantage. W. P. Thompson says: "I knew Charles B. Reynolds for many years,—in fact, from my childhood,—until he went to Lynchburg, in 1875, where he died. When I first knew him he lived in Floyd county. About the year 1842 he fixed his residence in Franklin county, in my immediate neighborhood, where he remained until shortly before his death. Before the war he was a man of large property, consisting mostly of land and slaves; and even after the war he had a good estate. After he removed to Franklin I visited and saw him frequently, and he talked with me familiarly. He lived, for years before his death, by himself; his wife and children having been dead for years. About the year 1869 or 1870 he told me, in the course of conversation, that he had sold one-half of a tract of land which he owned in Floyd, called the 'Guerrant Place,' estimated to contain about 800 acres, to Harvey Reynolds, a former slave of his. I asked him if he did not think that this was too large a contract for a person in Harvey's condition to carry out. He replied that he thought not; that Harvey was an industrious, energetic man; and that he had so arranged the payments that he thought he would be able to meet them. Again, during the year 1875, and but a short time before Mr. Reynolds went to Lynchburg, I fell in company with him, and we talked some time. In the course of the conversation Mr. Reynolds adverted to and dwelt at some length on a controversy which he had nearly had with one Stephen Guerrant. He went on to say that not long previously one Poff had proposed to purchase from him the part of his Guerrant tract in Floyd county left to him after his previous sale of one-half to Harvey Reynolds; that he had offered to sell it to Poff at 400 acres in the lump, as he had originally purchased the tract at 800 acres, and had sold only one-half to H. Reynolds; but that Poff would only buy by the acre, and required a survey should be made to ascertain the number of acres, and that he accordingly made the sale to Poff in this way. He said he spoke to Stephen Guerrant to make the survey; that he had some time before got Guerrant to cut off one-half the tract to Harvey Reynolds; and, under the belief and assurance that he had done so properly, he had conveyed the land to Harvey, who was under the same belief. He said he told Guerrant of his attempt to sell the land to Poff at 400 acres, and he was satisfied that it contained that much, but that Poff refused to take it at that; that Guerrant thereupon offered to guaranty that it would hold out 400 acres if he (Mr. Reynolds) would agree to let him have all over that amount; that he consented to do this, and upon Guerrant's suggestion this agreement was reduced to writing; that Guerrant thereupon made a survey of the land, and reported that the original tract contained more than 900 acres, instead of 800 acres, and that the part left to him contained greatly more than 400 acres; while the part he had conveyed to Harvey Reynolds, by deed based upon the reported representations of Guerrant, and which he thought was one-half of the tract, was many acres less than half. He said that Guerrant had sued him on his contract for a large amount,—the value of the land in excess of 400 acres,—and that he had been compelled to compromise the matter by paying $300. He spoke very bitterly about the manner in which Guerrant had acted; said he had fraudulently misled him and Harvey Reynolds into making a deed which conveyed far less than one-half the land, when it was his intention to convey Harvey, and he thought he had conveyed him, the full half which he had contracted to sell him; but that he had only become aware of this mistake and injustice to Harvey after Guerrant made his report of the survey of the land sold to Poff." The testimony of the three other after-discovered witnesses is as full and clear, and as positive and direct, on all points, as that of the witness W. P. Thompson, above detailed; and they all say that C. B. Reynolds expressed his surprise and indignation at the fraud practiced upon both him and Harvey Reynolds by Stephen Guerrant, and asseverated his desire and purpose to redress the injustice done to Harvey Reynolds, by giving him credit for the value of the land he did not get upon his purchase-money bonds; that, having sold the land to Poff, this was the only way in which he could correct the wrong. We are of opinion that the after-discovered evidence which was before the circuit court under the bill of review entitled the appellant, Harvey A. Reynolds, to the relief prayed for in his bill; and that the decree of the said court of the 19th of September, 1887, appealed from, is wholly erroneous, and must be reversed and annulled; and the order of this court is to send the cause back to the circuit court of Floyd county, with instructions to reinstate the bill of review, and to enter a decree reversing the decree of that court entered at the May term, 1884, and the decree of affirmance of that decree by this court at the June term, (twenty-fifth day,) 1885; and granting the relief prayed for in the bill of review. Reversed.

HASH v. COMMONWEALTH.

(Supreme Court of Appeals of Virginia. July 2, 1891.)

MURDER—INDICTMENT—SELF-DEFENSE—EVIDENCE
—INSTRUCTIONS.

1. On a murder trial it appeared that defendant was engaged in building a fence on his land, which he had removed from the line between him and deceased, contrary to the prohibition of the latter, although the fence was owned by defendant. Deceased's son testified for the state that deceased came up to the draw-bars, and an altercation occurred, in which the lie was given and returned, and that thereupon defendant drew his pistol, and shot deceased, who was unarmed and standing still. The defense proved that, as soon as the lie was passed, deceased assaulted defendant, inflicting injuries upon him with a knife, and that he retreated, when thus attacked, about nine steps from the draw-bars to a fence, and, while warding blows from the knife, drew his pistol, and fired the fatal shot. *Held* error to instruct th. defendant was guilty of murder if deceased was going from the draw-bars towards his home, and defendant advancing towards him, drew a pistol, which he had concealed about his person, and shot him, he neither making nor attempting to make an assault, since there was no evidence that defendant either pursued the deceased, or had concealed the pistol.

2. A charge which is based upon and recites the evidence for the state is erroneous in failing to recite that of the defense also, and to give an hypothetical alternative instruction based thereon.

3. The removal of the fence, notwithstanding the prohibition of deceased, was not an unlawful act; and it was error to charge that if defendant built it upon the line, so that it rested partly on the land of each, and it had been used as a line fence for a number of years, and deceased had notified defendant not to remove it, and that defendant, arming himself with a pistol, went to the fence to remove it by force, if necessary, and did remove it, he was guilty of an unlawful act, and if, while removing it, a conflict arose on account thereof, in which defendant killed deceased, then defendant cannot avail himself of the plea of necessary self-defense.

4. It is error to charge that "a man cannot in any case justify the killing of another upon the pretense of self-defense unless he be without fault in bringing the necessity of so doing upon himself," since the instruction does not distinguish between controversies provoked in order to furnish a pretext for killing and those provoked without such felonious intent.

5. It was error to refuse to charge that the accused must have been without fault in bringing on the combat, and must not have provoked it, or produced the occasion for the killing of deceased; but if he was so at fault, or provoked the combat or produced the occasion in order to have a pretext for the killing, yet, if he fairly declined the combat by retreating as far as he could, and then killed deceased in self-defense, he is not guilty.

6. Where deceased's son testifies that he knew the hour at which the assault occurred, because he looked at a clock in the house, and his sisters testify that there was no clock, the value of his evidence is for the jury, and an instruction is properly refused declaring that, if the witness falsely testified in this respect, his whole testimony is destroyed, and should be disregarded.

7. A joint indictment for murder is sufficiently definite as to the persons charged with the crime where a comma is inserted between the names of defendants, although the word "and" is omitted.

Error to circuit court, Grayson county; JOHN A. KELLEY, Judge.

Hackler & Robt. Crockett, for plaintiff in error. *The Attorney General,* for the Commonwealth.

RICHARDSON, J. On the 3d day of June, 1890, the plaintiff in error, Columbus Hash, and Rowan Hash were jointly indicted in the county court of Grayson county for the murder of Anderson Rutherford in said county; and, on their arraignment in said county court, the prisoner, Columbus Hash, demanded to be tried in the circuit court of said county, whereupon he was remanded for trial in the said court, and the proceedings had in said county court were duly certified to said circuit court. The prisoner, by his counsel, moved that court to quash the indictment, but the court overruled the motion. At the trial the attorney for the commonwealth asked the court to give to the jury six instructions, the first, second, third, and fourth of which were given without objection, but the court refused the fifth and sixth of the same, and gave in lieu thereof two others, of its own motion, which in the record are designated by corresponding numbers; to the giving of which two instructions the prisoner, by his counsel, excepted. And the prisoner, by his counsel, asked the court to give the jury ten instructions, to the seventh and eighth of which the attorney for the commonwealth objected; which objection the court sustained, and refused to give said seventh and eighth instructions, but gave all the others so asked for by the prisoner; and to the action of the court refusing said seventh and eighth instructions the prisoner, by his counsel, also excepted. All the instructions asked for on both sides, as well as those given by the court in lieu of instructions 5 and 6 asked for by the attorney for the commonwealth, and instructions 7 and 8 asked for by the prisoner and refused by the court, are set forth in the one bill of exceptions taken by the prisoner to the rulings of the court objected to; and in the same bill of exceptions the court certifies all the evidence adduced at the trial. The jury returned the following verdict: "We, the jury, find the accused, Columbus Hash, guilty of murder in the second degree, and fix his confinement in the state penitentiary for a term of six years." And thereupon the prisoner, by his counsel, moved the court to set aside the verdict and grant him a new trial, upon the ground that the same was contrary to the law and the evidence, and for other causes; but the court overruled the motion, and refused to set aside the verdict and grant a new trial, and thereupon proceeded to pronounce sentence upon the accused in accordance with the verdict of the jury; and to such ruling and judgment the prisoner, by his counsel, also excepted, and, on application, obtained from one of the judges of this court a writ of error and *supersedeas* to said judgment. The several objections taken by the plaintiff in error to certain rulings of the trial court are comprehended in the one question, did the court correctly propound the law, as applicable to the evidence in the case, as respects the rulings complained of?

The first assignment of error is to the action of the court overruling the prisoner's motion to quash the indictment. The objection to the indictment is that it is insensible and uncertain as to the number of persons charged with the offense set forth. The record, aside from the indictment itself, shows that the indictment was a joint indictment against Columbus Hash and Rowan Hash for a felony; but on looking to the indictment itself we find that it charges that the offense was committed by "Columbus Hash, Rowan Hash," omitting the copulative conjunction "and." After the usual formula, the indictment sets forth "that Columbus Hash, Rowan Hash, on the —— day of May, 1890, in the said county of Grayson,

and in the jurisdiction of said court, with force and arms in and upon the body of one Anderson Rutherford, in the peace of said commonwealth then and there being, feloniously, willfully, and of their malice aforethought, did make an assault, and the said Columbus Hash, Rowan Hash, a certain pistol of the value of two dollars, then and there charged with gunpowder and leaden bullets, which said pistol they, the said Columbus Hash, Rowan Hash, in their right hands then and there had and held, then and there feloniously, willfully, and of their malice aforethought, did discharge and shoot off, to, against, and upon the said Anderson Rutherford, and that the said Columbus Hash, Rowan Hash, with the leaden bullets aforesaid, out of the pistol by the said Columous Hash, Rowan Hash, discharged, and shot off as aforesaid, then and there feloniously, willfully, and of their malice aforethought, did strike, prostrate, and wound the said Anderson Rutherford in and upon the head of him, the said Anderson Rutherford, giving to him, the said Anderson Rutherford, then and there, with the leaden bullets aforesaid, so as aforesaid discharged and shot out of the pistol aforesaid by the said Columbus Hash, Rowan Hash, in and upon the head of him, the said Anderson Rutherford, one mortal wound, of which mortal wound he, the said Anderson Rutherford, from the —— hour of the evening of the —— day of May, 1890, to the —— hour of the evening of that day, in the year aforesaid, did languish, and languishing, did live, on which said evening of the —— day of May, in the year aforesaid, the said Anderson Rutherford, in the county aforesaid, of the said mortal wound died; and so the jurors aforesaid, upon their oaths aforesaid, do say that the said Columbus Hash, Rowan Hash, the said Anderson Rutherford, in manner and form aforesaid, feloniously, willfully, and of their malice aforethought, did kill and murder, against the peace and dignity of the commonwealth of Virginia." The insistence is that the indictment is insensible and uncertain as to the number of persons charged, by reason of the absence of the conjunction "and" whenever the words "Columbus Hash, Rowan Hash," occur in the indictment. We are, however, clearly of the opinion that the objection is not well taken. It will be observed that, in every instance in which the expression occurs in the indictment, the words "Columbus Hash" are followed by a comma, and then come the words "Rowan Hash." The use of the comma clearly indicates that the words "Columbus Hash" represent the name of one of the two persons jointly indicted, and that the words "Rowan Hash" represent the name of the other, and that by necessary intendment, the meaning is the same as if the expression had been written "Columbus Hash and Rowan Hash." It is true that, in speaking of the pistol from which the fatal shot was fired, the indictment proceeds, "which said pistol they, the said Columbus Hash, Rowan Hash, in their right hands then and there had and held," etc. If we take but a superficial view of the thing, we are almost irresistibly led to the conclusion that it is senseless to say that, in the midst of a heated and deadly conflict, two persons could at the same time hold in their right hands and fire the same pistol; but, however improbable such an occurrence may be, it cannot be said to be impossible. Bishop says: "Where the indictment is against more defendants than one for an offense committed by them jointly, it need not employ the word 'jointly' in describing the offense. According to the forms generally used, it simply means the defendants, and says they did so and so. Offenses are in law several, even when jointly committed; and such an allegation, therefore, is equivalent to saying that each defendant did the criminal act." 1 Bish. Crim. Proc. § 471. We are therefore of opinion that, while the indictment is awkwardly drawn, it is nevertheless sufficient. It with sufficient certainty charges that Columbus Hash and Rowan Hash committed the criminal act therein set forth. Hence, if the proof sustains the charge in the indictment, they are both guilty, no matter which of them fired the fatal shot.

The real questions presented by the record arise upon certain instructions given by the court on behalf of the commonwealth, and on certain others asked for by the prisoner, but refused by the court; but before considering these questions it is necessary to call attention to the material evidence in the cause, so as to test, in the light of legal principles applicable thereto, the correctness of the instructions in question. The plaintiff in error, Columbus Hash, and the deceased, Anderson Rutherford, lived within a few hundred yards of each other in the county of Grayson, were adjoining land-owners, and got at outs about a division fence which had been recognized as the line fence between them. In the evidence certified by the court it is distinctly stated, in the testimony of Isham Rutherford, a son of the deceased, and the only person that testified on behalf of the commonwealth, who was an eye-witness to the homicide, that the fence was built by the plaintiff in error, and that the deceased had no interest in the fence. The plaintiff in error determined to move this fence a short distance on his side, and he forbade the deceased from joining his fence thereto; and, in turn, the deceased forbade the removal of said fence. The plaintiff in error, with his two brothers, on the Thursday preceding the Saturday on which the homicide occurred, proceeded to move the fence; and on Saturday, the day of the homicide, the work was complete, except the erection of a pair of draw-bars, for which a space remained open. On the last-named day (Saturday) the deceased and his son Isham came to the open space in the fence where the plaintiff in error, aided by his said two brothers, was about to erect the draw-bars, and very soon the deadly conflict arose which resulted in the death of the deceased, Anderson Rutherford. Only three persons were present. They were Isham Rutherford, the son of the deceased, and Seabart Hash and Rowan Hash, brothers of the plaintiff in error.

At the risk of tediousness, we will give their evidence in full, as certified by the trial court.

Isham Rutherford, the son of the deceased, testified as follows: "That he is a son of Anderson Rutherford, and that he was present when his father, the said Anderson Rutherford, was killed. Just after 12 M. we passed out to see if any stock was in our field. Mr. Hash and his two brothers were fencing. Father says, 'I see you are building some fence.' My 'ould' Pa studied a little while, and said, 'I will build me a piece of fence.' They then came up to us. Columbus Hash said to my old Pa, 'What made you present your gun on me this morning?' My poor old Pa told him he was a liar: he never drew it. The prisoner said, 'You are a G——d d——n liar.' Prisoner then drew his pistol. My poor old Pa says, 'I have no weapons.' Prisoner then shot him, and in a minute Rowan Hash drew a pistol. The ball struck my father in the head. He (A. Rutherford) fell with his head to the N. E. I then ran home to tell my folks. When I got back my poor old Pa was lying on the side of the road, 22 steps from where he was shot; was lying on his back. He lived till after dark. The tragedy occurred about 1 P. M. Rowan Hash, Seabert Hash, deceased, the prisoner, and myself were present. They were propping up the fence down at the lower end of the fence they had moved. My poor old Pa said, 'I will get me two or three hands, and build me a fence.' Prisoner said nothing to that, but went to driving stakes, then threw his axe down, and started at Pa. Hash says to my poor old Pa, 'What made you draw your gun on me this morning?' Pa told him he was a liar; he never drew it. Prisoner replied, 'You are a G——d d——n liar.' Prisoner drew his pistol. My poor old Pa said he had no weapons, and just stood there. There was a gum-stump where he (deceased) fell, and open woods around. When the conversation commenced, my poor old Pa and myself were at the draw-bars, close to the road. They were fifty yards north of us. When we went up there, we went the path to the bars. The chestnut tree was 22 steps from where my poor old Pa was shot. When we left the tree, we started towards home, and went a little above the path. We were near the Hashs, above the path. They were below us. We first went above it. After a while my sister Tinsey and myself came back. Father was on bank of the road near the bars. I don't know how he got there. Aunt Peggy Rutherford and Wm. Lovelace came next. My sister and myself came back to where my Pa was, together. We walked back. I had to run about 200 yards to tell my folks my poor old Pa was killed. I saw my sister Tinsey coming walking. After she came up, we walked back together. My father had no interest in the fence. Mr. Hash built the fence. The fence was to the lower side of the draw-bars. My father had no weapon except a little old knife. I never saw the knife. He had nothing in his hand when the prisoner shot him." On cross-examination, this witness testified in the remarkable manner following: "My father and myself started about one P. M. to where the tragedy occurred. We were one half hour going. We had a clock at our house. It is 250 yards from our house to where my poor old Pa was killed. We went up the hill from our house to top of the hill, and then went the old path. The first place we stopped at was the draw-bars, near the chestnut tree. The way I know it was 1 o'clock when my poor old Pa was killed was because I looked at our clock, for we owned one, and had it in our house on the day of the killing. I know it was 22 steps to where my poor old Pa fell, for I stepped it. When I stepped it I only stepped a foot at a time. I don't know how many feet there are in a yard, but they tell me there are three feet in a yard. I don't know how many yards it takes to make a foot, but they tell me it takes three feet to make a yard. When I went home, after the pistol-shot, I was gone but a minute or two. I then went back in company with my sister Tinsey, and I got there first, and she was just behind me. I do not know why I passed the gum-stump and went to the road, but he was shot at the gum-stump. My Pa was 57 years of age. No one told me to call him 'my old Pa.'" Such is the incredible story told by Isham Rutherford, the son of the deceased, and the only witness for the commonwealth who was present at the time of the tragedy. It is, on its face, unnatural, senseless, self-contradictory, and unworthy of credit; and is, in material particulars, flatly contradicted, not only by his two sisters, Tinsey Rutherford and Nellie Rutherford, who testified on behalf of the commonwealth, but by other witnesses, and by the surrounding circumstances. There is but little in the evidence of Tinsey and Nellie Rutherford that is material; and, in this connection, it need only be referred to in so far as it contradicts a material statement made by their brother Isham as to the time of day when the homicide occurred. His statement, substantially, is that he and his father started out about half past 12 to see if there was any stock in the field; that they went by the path leading from the house to the draw-bars, near which the killing occurred; and then, after giving his account of how the conflict came about, he adds that his father was killed about 1 o'clock P. M. and in his cross-examination he says: "The first place we stopped at was the draw-bars, near the chestnut tree. The way I know it was 1 o'clock when my poor old Pa was killed was because I looked at our clock, for we owned one, and had it in our house on the day of the killing." But both Tinsey and Nellie Rutherford testify that there was no clock in the house on the day of killing; the latter stating that they never had one.

The theory of the defense was that at the time the fatal shot was fired by the accused the deceased was making a sudden, fierce, and murderous assault upon him with a dangerous and deadly weapon, and that the killing was done in necessary self-defense; and, from the evidence

v.13s.E.no.15—26

disclosed by the record, such theory was supported by an overwhelming preponderance of evidence. It was, then, of the utmost importance for the commonwealth to show both the time and manner of the killing; and this was attempted by her chief witness, Isham Rutherford, who fixed the time at about 1 o'clock, and to support his accuracy he says that, on leaving the house with his father, he looked at the clock; that it was then half past 12; that it took them a half hour to walk to the draw-bars, where they first stopped; and that the killing occurred at about 1 o'clock; when his two sisters, Tinsey and Nellie, both testify that there was no clock in the house on the day of the homicide, and Nellie says they never had one; and the undisputed evidence is that the homicide occurred near 4 o'clock in the afternoon. Again, this witness testifies positively, in his examination in chief, that his father the deceased, was shot and fell at the gum-stump, 22 steps from the draw-bars, and in the direction of his house; that he (witness) "ran to the top of the hill to tell his folks that poor old Pa was killed;" that he was gone only a "minute or two:" and that on his return he found his father, the deceased, lying near the road, 22 steps from the gum-stump. For some unexplained reason, this witness thus sought to create the impression that the accused had, after shooting the deceased, moved his body back to the road-side, near the draw-bars; the obvious purpose being to show that the deceased had been pursued to the gum-stump, and there shot. The story is a most improbable one. Its ready refutation is found in the witness himself. He says he was gone only a minute or two, in which time it is not reasonable to believe that the body could have been moved, if, indeed, the thought of doing so could have occurred to the accused under the circumstances. Moreover, there was direct, independent, and uncontradicted evidence that this witness was, for only some 50 yards of the distance traversed by him in going to tell what had occurred, out of view of the gum-stump; and from his own statement, that he was gone only a minute or two, he could not have been out of sight of the gum-stump for as much as a half minute. And yet, after making this incredible statement that the deceased was shot and fell at the gum-stump, and that the body was moved back to the road-side, 22 steps distant, this same witness, in his cross-examination, says: "I know it was 22 steps from the gum stump to where my poor old Pa fell, for I stepped it. When I stepped it I only stepped a foot at a time," etc. Obviously, this witness was either a part simpleton, or one wholly incompetent to testify; and it would seem that but little credit could be given to his statement by any upright judge presiding at a trial involving the life of a human being.

Seabert Hash and Rowan Hash, brothers of the plaintiff in error, were the only other witnesses to the deadly conflict. Seabert Hash is certified as saying: "I am 16 years old. I remember the day deceased was killed. I was there. I went there to help Col.; help fix up his fence. As we got done, A. Rutherford came up on hill near a ches. tree. Rutherford came to the bars, and asked bro. if he was going to put up bars; told him that he would not do it; that he would build a fence. Rutherford came to the chestnut tree, and was sighting down the fence, and, as the accused passed through the draw-bar place, Rutherford said to him, 'Are you going to put up draw-bars here?' Accused said, 'Yes.' Rutherford said, 'You need not do it; I will get some hands and build me a fence.' Accused said, 'Build as much as you please, but build it outside of the row of stakes which you see I have driven in the ground.' Rutherford replied, 'I will build it where I d——d please, and I am going to have this line run.' Accused said, 'Run it as much as you please, so you pay for it.' Rutherford said, 'I will make you help pay for it.' Accused said, 'Did I not offer you everything fair, even after you drew your gun twice on me this morning?' Rutherford said, 'You are a d——d liar. I didn't draw my gun on you.' Accused said, 'You are another.' Rutherford said, 'You are a d——d liar, G——d d——n you,' and here drew his knife, open, from his right pants pocket, and struck the accused, cutting his pants and drawers about the waistband, and cutting his left arm between the elbow and shoulder; and the accused retreated from the time the knife was first drawn until he was down to a fence, when he raised up his left hand to ward off another blow of said Rutherford, and caught said blow, with his arm and hand raised, between the thumb and first finger; and at this time the accused had drawn his pistol, raised it, and fired, and the ball took effect in the forehead, above the left eye, of Rutherford, and he fell to the ground; and the accused received a severe cut between the thumb and forefinger just before or about the time Rutherford was shot. Rutherford fell, and we left. I went after our coats, Rowan after axe, and Columbus went on down the road. Isom R. was near deceased when shot. He went off towards home. None of us touched the body after it fell. The deceased was shot right by the side of the road, and was left lying there. The body was lying on its back. Saw no one about the gum-stump. Didn't see deceased's hat after he was shot. Don't know how long R. had been there before difficulty. R. first asked Col. if he was going to build a pair of bars there. Defendant replied, 'Yes.' Deceased said, 'If you do, build it on yours.' We went out there, just after 12 o'clock, to fix up fence. From Hash's to where the difficulty occurred was about 100 yards. There were 31 panels of fence. Had knife in his hand when he fell. I saw knife after he fell. Stakes were put there by Columbus on the line. Deceased cut Hash three times,—across body, on arm, and on hand." On cross-examination, this witness said, in substance: "I and my brother were helping Columbus make fence. I was twenty steps behind when difficulty began, and heard what was said. Accused asked deceased if he (Hash) had not offered to do all that was fair and right, even after he (Rutherford) drew his gun on him. That deceased drew the knife out of his pocket. I saw him. I saw part of the handle and the blade, and can swear that it was the knife exhibited in court. He had cut my brother three times when he shot him." Rowan Hash, in his account of how the homicide occurred, said: "Rutherford came to the chestnut tree, and was sighting down the fence, and, as the accused passed through the draw-bar place, Rutherford said to him, 'Are you going to put up draw-bars here?' Accused said, 'Yes.' Rutherford said, 'You need not do it. I will get me some hands, and build me a fence.' Accused said, 'Build as much as you please, but build it outside of the row of stakes which you see I have driven in the ground.' Rutherford replied, 'I will build it where I d——d please, and I am going to have this line run.' Accused said, 'Run it as much as you please, so you pay for it.' Rutherford said, 'I will make you help pay for it.' Accused said, 'Did I not offer you everything fair, even after you drew your gun twice on me this morning?' Rutherford said, 'You are a d——d liar. I didn't draw my gun on you.' Accused said, 'You are another.' Rutherford said, 'You are a d——d liar, G——d d——n you,' and here drew his knife, open, from his right pants pocket, and struck the accused, cutting his pants and drawers about the waistband, and cutting his left arm between the elbow and shoulder; and the accused retreated from the time the knife was first drawn until he was down to a fence, when he raised up his left hand to ward off another blow of said Rutherford, and caught said blow, with his arm and hand raised, between the thumb and first finger; and at this time the accused had drawn his pistol, raised it, and fired; the ball took effect in the forehead, above the left eye, of Rutherford, and he fell to the ground; and the accused received a severe cut between the thumb and forefinger just before or about the time Rutherford was shot." He further testified, in substance, that he (Rowan Hash) had no pistol; that the body of deceased was not moved after he fell, and that he fell near the road, about nine steps from the new draw-bar place; that accused gave back when deceased was striking at him. He further says that he saw deceased draw the knife from his right pocket; that it was a large knife, with buck-horn handle, and that the knife was gripped in the hand of deceased after he fell: that deceased did not cut accused to the hide on the body, but cut his arm, and it bled freely; that he (witness) was not about the gum-stump that day, and that the stump was about 30 steps from draw-bars; that there was no difficulty at the stump, and that witness did not see the accused there that day; and that the chestnut tree is about 3 or 4 panels of fence from the bars. These two witnesses, who were introduced on behalf of the accused, substantially agree in their statements as to how and where the homicide occurred. They both testify that the deceased was shot and fell at or near the draw-bars.

The accused also testified, and his statement agrees substantially with that of Seabert and Rowan Hash. And all these concur in saying that the deceased came first to the chestnut tree, from which point he was sighting down the fence; that he then came to the draw-bars, where the conversation was commenced by him with the accused, and near which point he was shot and fell.

Such being the theory of the defense, what was that of the prosecution? Briefly recapitulated, it may be stated thus: Isham Rutherford, the son of the deceased, and only witness introduced for the commonwealth who was present and saw what occurred, says that he and the deceased went by the path from the house to the draw-bars; that they first stopped at the bars, near the chestnut tree. This was said on his cross-examination. He had on his examination in chief made this statement: "They [meaning the accused and his two brothers] were propping up the fence down at the lower end of the fence they had moved. My poor old Pa said, 'I will get me two or three hands, and build me a fence.' Prisoner said nothing to that, but went to driving stakes, then threw his axe down, and started at Pa. Hash says to my poor old Pa, 'What made you draw your gun on me this morning?' Pa told him he was a liar; he never done it. Prisoner replied, 'You are a G——d d——n liar.' Prisoner drew his pistol. My poor old Pa said he had no weapons, and just stood there. There was a gum-stump where he (deceased) fell, and open woods around. When the conversation commenced, my poor old Pa and myself were at the draw-bars, close to the road. They were 50 yards north of us. When we went up there, we went the path to the bars. The chestnut tree was 22 steps from where my poor old Pa was shot. When we left the tree, we started towards home," etc. He (Isham Rutherford) had just previously, in his statement in chief, made a less circumstantial, but much clearer, statement, in which he said: "Mr. Hash and his two brothers were fencing. Father says, 'I see you are building some fence.' My poor old Pa studied a little while, and said, 'I will build me a piece of fence.' They then came up to us. Columbus Hash said to my old Pa, 'What made you present your gun on me this morning?' My poor old Pa told him he was a liar; he never drew it. The prisoner said, 'You are a G——d d——n liar.' The prisoner then drew his pistol. My poor old Pa says, 'I have no weapons.' Prisoner then shot him, and in a minute Rowan Hash drew a pistol," etc. Take all the variant statements of this witness together, and it is impossible to extract from them any meaning other than that the fatal rencounter occurred at the draw-bars, and that the deceased was there shot and there fell. He distinctly states that the conversation which led up to the conflict of blood was commenced by his father, the deceased, at the draw-bars. He does not intimate that there was any lull in the conversation from its commencement until the fatal shot was fired and the deceased fell. Nor is it possible, from his statement,

that the deceased ever, of his own volition, left the draw-bars, where, according to this witness, he stood unarmed and was shot. He nowhere speaks of the deceased going from the draw-bars to the chestnut tree, nor does he intimate that the deceased was either pursued or intercepted and shot; but, after showing that the deceased must have been shot at or near the draw-bars, he does say that, when deceased left the tree, (chestnut tree,) "we started towards home," and that "there was a gum-stump where deceased fell."

In this state of the testimony, the trial judge, by certain instructions given or refused, propounded the law in the remarkable manner now to be inquired into. As already stated, of the six instructions offered by the commonwealth the court gave the first four, to which there was no objection; but in lieu of the last two it gave two others, of which the first is as follows: "(5) If the jury believe from the evidence that deceased was going from draw bars towards his home, and had got to a point at which a gum-stump stands, and the accused advanced towards and came near to him, and drew from his person a pistol, and that the pistol up to that time had been concealed, and that the accused then and there, with a willful, deliberate, and premeditated intent to kill deceased, shot him fatally with the pistol, and that the deceased was making no assault, nor doing any overt act indicative of any intention to make an assault, on the accused, then the accused would be guilty of murder in the first degree." In the light of the evidence contained in the record, this instruction is pregnant with error, there being at least two sound objections thereto: *First.* There is no evidence in the record which tends to establish the main proposition contained in the instruction. The only facts testified to by Isham Rutherford, the only witness introduced by the commonwealth who was present when the homicide occurred, tending to that result, is the fact that the accused drew his pistol and shot the deceased, and that he fell at the gum-stump. There is no evidence that the deceased, after the commencement of the conversation at the draw-bars, was going home, and had got to the gum-stump, and that the accused advanced towards and came near to him, and then drew from his person a pistol, and that the pistol up to that time had been concealed. On the contrary, as already shown, this witness testified that, when the conversation commenced, "we were at the draw-bars;" that the deceased addressed a remark to the accused and his brothers; that they then came up to us; that then the lie was given and returned; and that the accused then drew his pistol, and shot the deceased. There is nothing whatever even tending to show that the deceased was either pursued or intercepted by the accused, and was shot by him with a pistol which, up to the time of his overtaking the deceased, had been concealed, as is erroneously assumed in the instruction. Hence the instruction was irrelevant, well calculated to mislead the jury, and doubtless did mislead them. *Second.* The instruction, in effect, supposes the evidence tending to support the theory of defense set up by the accused. It is a rule too well settled to need the citation of authorities, that, where an instruction undertakes to recite the evidence, it must not garble the same by giving a portion of it, and withholding the rest; the well-established principle being that the accused has a right to a full and correct statement by the court of the law applicable to the evidence in his case, and that any misdirection by the court, in point of law, on matters material to the issue, is ground for a new trial. Whart. Crim. Pl. §§ 709, 710; Rea v. Trotter, 26 Grat. 585; Honesty's Case, 81 Va. 283. In the present case there were other persons present at the homicide, and who testified at the trial. The court should not have based its instruction, as it did, upon the testimony of the only witness whom the attorney for the commonwealth saw fit to introduce. It should have recited the testimony of Seabert Hash, Rowan Hash, and the accused, and have based an hypothetical alternative instruction upon their testimony, and thus have presented the theory of the defense as well as that of the prosecution, so that the jury might be enabled to have before it the whole case, and to adopt the one theory or the other, according to their opinion as to the credibility of the respective witnesses.

In lieu of the sixth instruction asked for by the attorney for the commonwealth, the court, of its own motion, gave the following: "The court instructs the jury that a man cannot in any case justify the killing of another upon the pretense of self-defense, unless he be without fault in bringing the necessity of so doing upon himself. Therefore, if the jury believe from the evidence that the accused built the fence spoken of by the witnesses, running north from the draw-bars mentioned by the witnesses, upon the line between himself and the deceased, so that it rested partly on the land of each, and that the deceased joined to the same at the draw-bars, thereby inclosing his premises, and that said fence had been used as a line fence between the accused and deceased for a number of years, and that deceased had notified accused not to remove said fence, and that the accused afterwards, on the day of the homicide, armed himself with a pistol, and, in company with two brothers, went to the fence with intent to remove the same with force, if necessary, and did remove said fence, then he was guilty of an unlawful act; and if the deceased came upon the premises while the unlawful act was being committed, and then and there, on account thereof, a conflict arose, in which the accused killed the deceased, then the accused cannot avail himself of the plea of necessary self-defense. But the court instructs the jury, further, that if they believe from the evidence that the accused had reasonable ground to fear that deceased might kill him, or do him some great bodily harm, while he was engaged in the exercise of his lawful right of removing said fence, then the accused might lawfully arm himself for the purpose, if it became necessary, of protecting his life and person; and if the accused did,

after being notified by the deceased not to remove said fence, on the day of the homicide, and in company with two brothers, after arming himself with a pistol, proceed to remove said fence, with no intent to use said pistol, except only to protect his life and person while engaged in the exercise of his lawful right, then the accused was not engaged in an unlawful act; and if the deceased came upon the premises while the accused was so engaged in removing the fence, or after its removal, and on account thereof a conflict arose, then the accused would not be precluded from availing himself of the plea of self-defense, if the conflict was of such a character, and the conduct of the accused in the conflict was such, as to make the killing of deceased by the accused excusable homicide." This instruction is palpably erroneous in several respects. The law, under circumstances such as characterize the present case, asserts no such cruel and inhuman doctrine.

(1) The word "pretense" in the first paragraph of the instruction, implies sham, falsity, and groundlessness; and now as it is, in the outset of the instruction, it gives color to all that follows, and in effect says to the jury that the defense set up by the accused is a mere false pretense, and could but prejudice the minds of the jury against the theory of necessary self-defense relied on by the accused. Instead of the word "pretense," thus employed in the introductory sentence of the instruction, the word "plea" should have been used. It is often the case that the circumstances attending a homicide are such that the court may, in an instruction to the jury, based on the evidence adduced at the trial, properly employ the word "pretense;" as, for instance, where the evidence strongly tends to show that the accused sought and brought about the deadly conflict in order to have a pretext for killing his adversary, or doing him great bodily harm. In such case it would not only be the right but the duty of the court to propound to the jury an hypothetical case based upon such evidence, and to say to them that if, from the evidence, they believe the case supposed in the instruction to be true, then the accused is guilty of murder, and that he cannot justify such killing under the "pretense" of necessary self-defense. But this is widely different from saying, as the court did in the paragraph under consideration, that "a man cannot in any case justify the killing of another upon the pretense of self-defense unless he be without fault in bringing the necessity of so doing upon himself." Not only does this part of the instruction assert a proposition that cannot be maintained, as will presently be shown, but in its frame and structure it is paradoxical and absurd. It asserts in one sentence two irreconcilable propositions: *First*, that no man can justify the killing of another upon the pretense of self-defense unless he be without fault in bringing the necessity of so doing upon himself; and, *second*, by necessary implication, that a man may in any case justify the killing of another upon the pretense of self-defense if he be without fault in bring-

ing the necessity of so doing upon himself. Obviously, no question could arise in either case as to pretense. The absurdity is too palpable to need comment.

But the paragraph in question goes further, and asserts a proposition which, in effect, strikes at some of the most vital principles of criminal jurisprudence touching the law of self-defense. In discussing the question when killing in self-defense is permissible, Bishop says: "The rule is commonly stated in the American cases thus: If the individual assaulted, being himself without fault, reasonably apprehends death or great bodily harm to himself unless he kills his assailant, the killing is justifiable." 1 Bish. Crim. Law, (6th Ed.) § 865. "There are two kinds of permissible defense of person or property. The one extends, when necessary, to the taking of the aggressor's life; and this is called the 'perfect' defense. The other, or 'imperfect,' defense does not permit him who employs it to go so far; but he may resist trespassers on his person or property to an extent not exactly the same in all circumstances, yet not involving the life of the trespasser; and this is called the 'imperfect' defense." Id. §§ 840, 841. The same eminent author says: "The right to defend one's person or property proceeds from necessity; and however complete this right may be, or however far the law permits it to be carried, it stops where necessity ends. The party making the defense may use no instrument and no power beyond what will simply prove effectual. Thus, though it is lawful for one to oppose another who is committing a felony, even to the taking of his life, yet, if there is no obstacle to his arrest, the shooting of him in the felonious act, instead of having him arrested, is a felonious homicide; and, while it is lawful to kill a man in self-defense, still his mere assault with the fist will not justify the instant taking of his life by a stab, and to thus resort to a defense wholly unnecessary is murder. It is not lawful to kill another, who even meditates the taking of one's life, till some overt act is done in pursuance of the meditation; in other words, till the danger becomes immediate. The steps necessary may be taken, and no more. Thus, again, a man who expects to be attacked should first employ the means in his power to avert the necessity of self-defense; and until he has done this his right of self-defense does not arise. Nor can a man avail himself of a necessity which he has knowingly and willfully brought upon himself. Yet one assaulted by another, who has threatened to kill him, is not bound to run in the particular instant; thus increasing his danger by encouraging the assailant to repeat the attempt when he will be less prepared to resist." Id. §§ 842-844. In support of these propositions, which are founded in reason, justice, and humanity, the author cites very numerous authorities. In the above summary we have a clear statement of the law with respect to one's right to defend his person, and how far that right may be carried. Elsewhere the same author gives a summary showing the right to defend one's property. He says: "One

in defense of his property must not commit a forcible detainer, a riot, or any like crime. He must not kill the aggressor; but, if the question comes to this, he must find his redress in the courts. If the wrongful act is proceeding to a felony on the property, he may then kill the doer to prevent the felony, if there is no other way; otherwise, this extreme measure is not lawful. And the defense may be such, and such only, as necessity requires; of course, within the limits which forbids the taking of life. Therefore a man commits a felonious homicide who inflicts death in opposing an unlawful endeavor to carry away his property. There is here the right to resist, but not to the taking of life. In the above formula we have the doctrine concisely stated in respect to both the perfect and the imperfect right of self-defense, and we have also a clear recognition of the essential distinction between the two. The perfect right of self-defense extends, when necessary, to the taking of the aggressor's life, but it cannot be resorted to for the protection of property, except where it consists of the castle, or a felony is being committed on it; while, on the other hand, the imperfect right of defense is permitted as well of the property as the person. Hence a man may lawfully defend his property in possession by any degree of force, short of the taking of life, necessary to make the defense effectual, unless it amounts to a riot, a forcible detainer, or some other like crime. Yet he cannot proceed therein beyond what necessity requires." 1 Bish. Crim. Law, §§ 860, 861. This doctrine of perfect and imperfect defense is well illustrated by Bishop, as follows: "If, without provocation, a man draws his sword upon another, who draws in defense, whereupon they fight, and the first slays his adversary, his crime is murder, for he who seeks and brings on a quarrel cannot, in general, avail himself of his own wrong in defense. But, where an assault which is neither calculated nor intended to kill is returned by violence beyond what is proportionate to the aggression, the character of the combat is changed; and if, without time for his passion to cool, the assailant kills the other, he commits only manslaughter." Horrigan and Thompson, in their cases in self-defense, p. 227, in a note to Stoffer v. State, 15 Ohio St. 47, cited in State v. Partlow, 90 Mo. 608, 4 S. W. Rep. 14, give an admirable summary of the authorities on this subject, as follows: "If he [the slayer] provoked the combat or produced the occasion in order to have a pretext for killing his adversary, or doing him great bodily harm, the killing will be murder, no matter to what extremity he may have been reduced in the combat. But if he provoked the combat or produced the occasion without any felonious intent, intending, for instance, an ordinary battery merely, the final killing in self-defense will be manslaughter only." Here is a clear recognition of the doctrine that, although the slayer provoked the combat or produced the occasion, yet, if it was done without any felonious intent, the party may avail himself of the plea of self-defense. In the case of State v. Partlow, supra, the learned judge delivering the opinion cites, in support of this doctrine: State v. Lane, 4 Ired. 113; Reg. v. Smith, 8 Car. & P. 160; Slaughter's Case, 11 Leigh, 680; Murphy v. State, 37 Ala. 142; Adams v. People, 47 Ill. 376; State v. Hildreth, 9 Ired. 429; State v. Hogue, 6 Jones, (N. C.) 381; State v. Martin, 2 Ired. 101; Atkins v. State, 16 Ark. 568; Cotton v. State, 31 Miss. 504; Stewart v. State, 1 Ohio St. 66; State v. Hill, 4 Dev. & B. 491; and 2 Bish. Crim. Law, § 702, supra,—and, by way of enforcing this well-settled legal principle, the learned judge makes this remark: "Indeed, the assertion that one who begins a quarrel or brings on a difficulty with the felonious purpose to kill the person assaulted, and accomplishes such purpose, is guilty of murder, and cannot avail himself of the doctrine of self-defense, carries with it in its very bosom the inevitable corollary that if the quarrel be begun without a felonious purpose, then the homicidal act will not be murder. To deny this obvious deduction is equivalent to the anomalous assertion that there can be a felony without a felonious intent; that the act done characterizes the intent, and not the intent the act. The bare statement of such a doctrine accomplishes its own ample refutation,—a doctrine inconsistent with its premises, and illogical in its conclusion. In the light of this well-settled doctrine, it is manifest that the trial court erred egregiously in saying to the jury that "a man cannot in any case justify the killing of another upon the pretense of self-defense unless he be without fault in bringing the necessity of so doing upon himself." Recurring now to the rule laid down by Bishop,—that if the individual assaulted, being himself without fault, reasonably apprehends death or great bodily injury to himself unless he kills the assailant, the killing is justifiable,—the inquiry presents itself, what "fault" is it that will deprive a man of his plea of justifiable self-defense? This question has already been answered by the authorities cited. It is the "fault" of seeking and directly bringing about the occasion for the killing; limited, however, by the intention with which the occasion was brought about. Inasmuch, therefore, as the right of a party, accused of a felonious homicide, to avail himself of the plea of justifiable self-defense depends upon the intent with which he provoked the difficulty, and inasmuch as it is the doctrine of the law that no man is to be punished as a criminal unless his intent is wrong, and as the intent is a fact to be found by the jury, then in every case where the evidence creates any doubt as to the character of the intent the court should instruct the jury as to the distinction between perfect and imperfect defense, as applicable to the particular circumstances attending the homicidal act of the accused. Meuly's Case, (Tex.) 9 S. W. Rep. 563, and authorities cited.

(2) The second paragraph of said sixth instruction is to the effect that if the jury should believe that the accused had built the fence on the line between his land and that of the deceased, and that said fence had been used as a line fence for a number of years, and deceased had notified the accused not to remove it, then the removal of the fence by the accused, under the circumstances, was an unlawful act, and that if the accused killed the deceased in a conflict on account thereof, then the accused could not avail himself of the plea of necessary self-defense. This is unquestionably a misstatement of the law. Such removal of the fence could have amounted to nothing more than a mere trespass, if that; and if, to prevent such trespass, the deceased had made an attack on the accused with a deadly weapon, under circumstances calculated to excite in the mind of the latter a reasonable apprehension of death or great bodily injury to himself, can it be possible that to kill his assailant under such circumstances would deprive him of the right to avail himself of the plea of self-defense? Certainly not, as is shown by the authorities already referred to. A man may even draw his sword in a quarrel with his adversary; then, on reflection, may decline the fight and withdraw; but, on being pursued, may turn, and, if necessary, may slay his pursuer in self-defense. But while there was evidence tending to prove that the fence was on the land of the deceased, and was recognized and used as the line fence, the overwhelming preponderance of evidence was to the effect that it was not on the line, but was removed therefrom; that it was built by the accused, and that deceased had no interest in it. Under such circumstances, was the removal of the fence a tortious act? We think not. In 2 Wat. Tresp. § 714, (Real Estate,) it is said, in respect to property in fences, that "fences are a part of the freehold, and the fact that the material of which they are composed are accidentally or temporarily detached, without any intent in the owner to divert them from their use as a part of the fence, works no change in their nature. If I build a fence on my neighbor's land, it is his, not mine; and the dominion which any man has over his own property gives him a right to remove it whenever he pleases. If it be useful to me as well as to him, and if I build it in consideration of his promise that it shall stand there permanently, and he removes it in violation of that promise, I may recover, in an action on the contract, the value of my labor, and perhaps for the consequential injury; but I cannot maintain trespass." In a note the author cites Burrell v. Burrell, 11 Mass. 294, which was an action of trespass for entering on the plaintiff's land, and taking away a fence on the dividing line between premises owned by the parties respectively. The part of the fence removed by the defendant was made of rails, and he proved that he built it 23 years previously, and had ever since kept it in repair; and that at the time of the alleged trespass he took away the rails, in order to replace the fence by a stone wall, which he built the following year, putting it nearer his own land than the place where the rail fence stood. A verdict was found for the defendant in the court below; and the supreme court, in sustaining it, said: "The only question which could exist at the trial was wheth-

er the facts there testified were true; and, the jury having decided that they were, the verdict was a necessary legal consequence. There is nothing in the report from which an entry on the plaintiff's land can be inferred, unless such entry was necessary for the purpose of taking down the fence in order to rebuild it, which would not be tortious. The part of the fence assigned to the defendant to keep in repair was his property, so far, at least, that the removal of it for lawful purposes could not make him a trespasser; and we do not think there was any joint tenancy or tenancy in common of the materials of which the fence was composed." That case, in its facts, as to the erection, ownership, and use of the fence, was almost precisely like the case here. If we apply to the evidence in the present case the principles applied under similar circumstances in that case, it is plain that the accused, in removing the fence in question, did no legal wrong to the deceased, and that there was nothing in the evidence upon which to base the direction to the jury contained in the second paragraph of said sixth instruction, and the jury should not have been so instructed.

(3) The third paragraph of said sixth instruction, taken in connection with the second, was well calculated to mislead the jury, and induce them to make the conviction or acquittal of the accused depend upon the decision of the question whether the accused had or had not the right to remove the fence; whereas such right was wholly immaterial in considering his guilt or innocence, the undisputed testimony being that the fence had been removed before the deceased went to the scene of the conflict which resulted in his death, and the clear preponderance of evidence being to the effect that the deceased sought, and without any sufficient provocation brought about, the conflict which resulted so fatally to him, and made a fierce and murderous assault upon the accused with a deadly weapon,—a knife suddenly drawn, open, from his right pants pocket.

(4) The fourth and last paragraph of the said sixth instruction is amenable to the same criticism, and should not have been given.

On behalf of the accused, 10 instructions were asked for, all of which the court gave except the seventh and eighth. The seventh instruction asked for by the accused, and refused by the court, is as follows: "The jury are further instructed that the accused must have been without fault in bringing on the combat, and that he must not have provoked the combat, or produced the occasion for killing the said Anderson Rutherford, or doing him some great bodily harm. But if they shall also believe that, even if the accused was not without fault in bringing on the combat, or that he provoked the same, or produced the occasion in order to have a pretext for killing said Rutherford, or doing him some great bodily harm, yet if they shall also believe that the accused fairly declined said contest by retreating as far as he could, and then killed said Rutherford in self-defense, the

killing was excusable, and they should acquit the accused." We are of opinion that this instruction correctly propounds the law, and there was evidence in the case tending to establish the proposition contained therein, and that the court erred in refusing to give it.

The eighth instruction asked for by the accused, and refused by the court, is as follows: "If the jury shall believe from the evidence that Isham Rutherford, a witness called on by the prosecution, and sworn in court to give evidence in this case, testified that he knew that the difficulty occurred between Anderson Rutherford, the deceased, and the accused between the hours of 12 and 1 o'clock on the day that said Anderson Rutherford was killed, and if they shall also believe that Isham Rutherford gave, as the reason why he knew that the said difficulty occurred at the time so testified by him, was that his father, the said Anderson Rutherford, owned a clock, and that it was in the house at that time, and that he looked at the clock before he started with his father to the place of said difficulty, and if they shall also believe that said witness willfully swore falsely in this behalf, then such false testimony or swearing of said witness vitiated and destroyed the whole of his evidence, and the same should be disregarded by the jury." We are of opinion that this instruction does not correctly propound the law, and that the court did not err in refusing it. The jury is the sole judge of the credibility of witnesses, and to have given the instruction would have been to invade the rightful province of the jury.

For the errors hereinbefore pointed out, the judgment of the circuit court must be reversed and annulled, the verdict of the jury set aside, and the cause remanded to said circuit court for a new trial to be had therein in accordance with the views expressed in this opinion.

STOCKHOLDERS OF BANK OF ABINGDON v. BOARD OF SUPERVISORS OF WASHINGTON COUNTY.

(Supreme Court of Appeals of Virginia. July 16, 1891.)

BANK-STOCK—TAXATION OF—RESIDENCE OF STOCK-HOLDERS.

Under Acts Va. 1883–84, § 17, p. 568, providing for a state tax on the assessed market value of the shares of banks located in the state, regardless of the residence of the stockholders, and Code Va. § 833, cl. 2, providing that the board of supervisors of each county shall order a levy on all property assessed with a state tax within the county, the board has power to levy a tax for county purposes on the shares of stock of a bank located in the county, although some of its stockholders are non-residents of the state. HINTON and LACY, JJ., dissenting.

Error to circuit court, Washington county; JOHN A. KELLY, Judge.

Bill by Ernest Middleton and others against board of supervisors of Washington county and S. M. Withers, treasurer, to restrain the collection of a tax. Decree for defendants, and plaintiff appeals. Affirmed.

Fulkerson, Page & Hurt, for plaintiffs

in error. *White & Buchanan,* for defendants in error.

FAUNTLEROY, J. The appellants, Ernest Middleton and others, some of whom are residents and others of whom are non-residents of Virginia, stockholders in the Bank of Abingdon, in Washington county, Va., in January, 1889, filed their bill in chancery in the circuit court of Washington county against the board of supervisors of said county and Salmon M. Withers, treasurer of said county, praying for an injunction to restrain the collection of a certain county levy made by the said board of supervisors against the appellants as stockholders in the Bank of Abingdon, upon their respective shares of stock in the said bank, the collection of which the said Withers, treasurer as aforesaid, was then seeking to enforce. An injunction was granted January 5, 1889, according to the prayer of the bill; and at the May term, 1889, a decree was entered dissolving the said injunction.

The only question presented by this appeal is whether a county in this state has the right to levy and collect a tax for county purposes upon the shares of stock of a bank located in the county. The state, without regard to the residence of stockholders, levies for state purposes a tax on the assessed market value of their shares of stock, as it does upon other moneyed capital. Acts 1883–84, p. 568, § 17. This assessment is directed to be made annually in the month of May by each commissioner of the revenue on the shares of stock in each bank or banking association in his district, and to be reported to the auditor of public accounts; and the tax so assessed is required to be paid by the cashier of each bank to the auditor of public accounts on or before the 1st of June following. The board of supervisors of each county is required to fix the amount of the county levy, for county purposes, annually, and to order the levy "on all property assessed with state taxes within the county." Code 1887, § 833. The assessment on the shares of stock of the appellants in the said Bank of Abingdon for taxation for state purposes was made by the commissioner of revenue for the district in which the said bank is situated, and a copy of the said assessment was furnished by the said commissioner of the revenue to the treasurer of Washington county; and, according to the said assessment upon the said shares of stock for state tax, the board of supervisors made the levy of a tax for county purposes upon the assessed market value of the said shares of stock, as prescribed by the statute. The said shares of stock were duly and regularly assessed for state taxes, and that assessment was made within the county by the commissioner of the revenue of the county in which the bank is located. The right of the board of supervisors of Washington county to levy the tax complained of is palpable and unquestionable. At common law, the *situs* of the stock, for purposes of taxation, is with the stockholders, and not with the bank; but by the statute of the state the stock, no matter where the

stockholder lives, is assessed and taxed in the county and district where the bank is located. Acts 1883–84, p. 568, § 17. Chief Justice WAITE, in the case of Tappan v. Bank, 19 Wall. 490, says: "The state, therefore, within which a national bank is situated, has jurisdiction for the purposes of taxation of all the shareholders of the bank, both resident and non-resident, and of all its shares, and may legislate accordingly." If a state may do this as to stock and stockholders created by the congress of the United States, a *fortiori,* it may legislate (as it has done) to authorize a county to levy a tax for county purposes upon the shares of stock of a bank located within the county, where the property is protected by the county. The decree of the circuit court of Washington county, appealed from, is clearly right, and the judgment of this court is to affirm it. Affirmed.

LEWIS, P., and RICHARDSON, J., concur.

PEYTON v. STUART.

(Supreme Court of Appeals of Virginia. June 18, 1891.)

CONTRIBUTION BETWEEN SURETIES.

Plaintiff, defendant, and another, stockholders of a corporation, jointly indorsed its notes as accommodation indorsers, the proceeds being used in betterments of its property, and additional stock being issued upon the basis of such improvements. By agreement between plaintiff and defendant the latter sold to the former all his stock and interest in the company, and obtained a release of all his liability upon the notes, which plaintiff afterwards paid. *Held,* that defendant was not liable to plaintiff for contribution. LEWIS, P., and FAUNTLEROY, J., dissenting.

Bill in chancery by William A. Stuart, stockholder of the Greenbrier White Sulphur Springs Company, and joint accommodation indorser of its notes, against George L. Peyton, another stockholder and indorser, for contribution upon the notes paid by plaintiff. Decree for plaintiff. Reversed.

W. W. Gordon and *James Bumgardner,* for plaintiff in error. *W. J. Robertson* and *Geo. M. Harrison.* for defendant in error.

LACY, J. This is an appeal from a decree of the circuit court of Augusta county, rendered on the 3d day of July, 1889. The bill was filed by the appellee, William A. Stuart, on the 28th day of December, 1886, wherein it is set forth that on the 14th day of September, 1882, the Greenbrier White Sulphur Springs Company, a corporation duly incorporated under the laws of the state of West Virginia, made its certain negotiable note in writing, by which it promised to pay, 30 days after the date thereof, at the bank of Lewisburg, West Va., the sum of $4,000, to William A. Stuart, George L. Peyton, and H. M. Mathews, as joint indorsers. That said note was duly protested for non-payment when due, according to law. Another note like the foregoing, for $2,000; another for $7,500, like the foregoing, curtail and discount on this note of $2,605; another note for $5,000, curtail and discount on this of $995.43, and $4,148.05 paid on this note. That all these notes were protested, and not paid by the said the Greenbrier White Sulphur Springs Company, nor by George L. Peyton, nor by the said H. M. Mathews, but by the said William A. Stuart. That the maker of these notes, the said the Greenbrier White Sulphur Springs Company, is insolvent, and so is H. M. Mathews; and that George L. Peyton is, as joint indorser with him, bound to pay to him one-half of the money so paid by him, the said William A. Stuart; and that, when judgment has been obtained on this indebtedness, and liens secured on the lands of the said George L. Peyton, that he, the said William A. Stuart, is entitled to be subrogated to the rights of the creditor as against the said George L. Peyton. On the 7th of December, 1886, the circuit court of Augusta rendered a decree for the following account: (1) As to the solvency or insolvency of the Greenbrier White Sulphur Springs Company. (2) As to the solvency or insolvency of the estate of Henry M. Mathews, deceased. (3) What amount is due the plaintiff from his joint indorsers for contribution upon the notes filed with the bill, or upon said judgment filed with the bill, or is due said plaintiff from such of said indorsers as may be found to be solvent. And leave was given the said George L. Peyton to file his answer in this cause in 60 days thereafter, which was done accordingly.

The said George L. Peyton filed his answer, saying that, while he had no independent recollection on the subject, he supposes it is true that the notes described in the bill were executed by the said the Greenbrier White Sulphur Springs Company, and indorsed jointly by the complainant, the said respondent, George L. Peyton, and the said H. M. Mathews, as alleged, and that originally said Stuart, Mathews, and respondent were jointly and equally bound by said indorsement. Respondent did not know, and called for proof, of any alleged payments made on these by said William A. Stuart. That it is admitted that H. M. Mathews is dead and insolvent. But the respondent denies the insolvency of the said the Greenbrier White Sulphur Springs Company, and the statement that nothing can be made out of it. That, so far from being insolvent, it is possessed of a large amount of good and solvent assets, sufficient to pay all, or within a small fraction of, its liabilities. That these assets consist of unpaid stock subscriptions, the purchase price of mortgage bonds sold, and of unincumbered real estate, personal property, etc., and that said complainant is himself indebted to the said company in a sum not less than $94,000 for unpaid stock subscription and for bonds of the company bought and not paid for, and that the charge of insolvency comes with a bad grace from him, the said William A. Stuart. That the said Stuart had not been compelled to pay these notes held by him as security for the maker, but had acquired them by purchase at a discount of 50 per cent., and that at the time of the purchase he was legally indebted to the company; and when he acquired the note the debt became extinguished. That the said Stuart

cannot call on the respondent for contribution, because payment has been provided for by placing 190 of the mortgage bonds at the par value of $500 that have been deposited with the cashier of the creditor bank as collateral security therefor, and that the said collateral should be exhausted before one of the securities should be held liable for them. That, independently of the question whether the Greenbrier White Sulphur Springs Company is or is not solvent, and of the question whether the said notes or a part of them are or are not secured in other ways, to the exoneration of the said George L. Peyton, the said George L. Peyton denies that there is now any liability on him to the said William A. Stuart on account of the said note in the said bill described. On the contrary, he claims that on account of a contract and agreement to that end made by the said William A. Stuart he has been released from all liability for these joint indorsements. That the notes in question were given by the said company for the purpose of raising money to make improvements on the property owned by it; and, when indorsed by the said William A. Stuart, Henry M. Mathews, and George L. Peyton, as accommodation indorsers, they being all large and equal stockholders in said company, the money so obtained was used in the improvement and in the furnishing of the property of the said company, and on the basis of the improvements so made a large amount of the stock of the company was issued as full-paid stock. On the 4th day of November, 1882, George L. Peyton held $37,500 of the stock of the said company, for which he paid in cash the sum of $17,500; the balance of it being issued in consideration of betterments and improvements placed on the property, and for the payment of which notes of the company were outstanding and unpaid, indorsed by the parties interested in the company. In this state of affairs, and on the said 4th day of November, 1882, George L. Peyton sold to William A. Stuart all of his said stock on the distinct understanding and agreement that said stock was sold on the basis of cost, and that the said George L. Peyton was to be relieved of all liability as indorser or otherwise for the debts of the said company; said Stuart agreeing to return to Peyton all of his paper, including interest and discount paid. That said agreement was reduced to writing, as follows: "Richmond, Va., Nov. 4th, 1882. I have this day bought of George L. Peyton his stock on the basis of cost and $5,000.00. I am to give him up his paper, including discount and interest paid, and pay Dr. Moorman about $4,000.00, and enough in addition to make $5,000.00. Said Peyton is to have his salary on the first of January so far as it has not been realized from the company, after taking from his account, and charging back to said Stuart, any board-bill to said Stuart or his family which has been charged to said Peyton. Said Peyton is to throw no obstacle in the way of said company regaining or holding possession of their property, and release any claim I have to any of his salary. And any amount I pay said Peyton on his salary I am to hold as a debt against the White Sulphur. [Signed] WILLIAM A. STUART." That the stock sold as set forth above on the 4th day of November, 1882, to said William A. Stuart, was delivered to him, and has been converted to his own use. That under this agreement it was the duty of the said William A. Stuart to pay and take up the said notes on which Peyton was an indorser to the exoneration of said Peyton, and that there is no liability on said Peyton on account of any of the said notes in the hands of the said Stuart, and the said Stuart has no just demands against the said Peyton for contribution on account of their joint indorsement of the same.

Under the decree of December 7, 1886, J. W. Green Smith, one of the commissioners of the circuit court of Augusta county, undertook to take the testimony, state the account, and make the report required by the said decree. His report is returned on the 16th day of April, 1889. He says that he gave notice as required by the decree, and on Saturday, the 5th day of February, 1887, at his office in the city of Staunton, being the time and place fixed by said notice, he proceeded to take the account ordered by the decree, but that, not being completed on that day, he adjourned the taking of the same from day to day, from that day to the day of making his report; that is, from the 5th day of February, 1887, to the 16th day of April, 1889, he adjourned the account from day to day; so that for more than two years he adjourned this account from day to day. On the first account he reported that the White Sulphur Springs Company was insolvent. On the second, that the estate of Henry M. Mathews, deceased, is insolvent. On the third branch of the decree, as to what amount is due the plaintiff from his joint indorsers for contribution, he has much to say, which must, under the contention here involved, be carefully considered. He says on the threshold that before proceeding further "commissioner would here state that there are now pending before him for settlement and report four several cases,—three chancery and one common law,—instituted by William A. Stuart against George L. Peyton, in which said Peyton sets up a line of defense common to all four of said cases, which, if sustained, will defeat the said Stuart out and out as to the said Peyton; and it has therefore been agreed between counsel of said Stuart and Peyton, respectively, that your commissioner in order to save time, repetition, and expense, may in this one suit of William A. Stuart vs. George L. Peyton dispose of all matters as between Stuart and Peyton, making mere naked findings as to Peyton in the other three cases, and referring to this report for his reasons therefor." So that by agreement of the parties by counsel this suit was considered and heard by the commissioner and by the court, which approved and ratified this report in all respects, together with three others, all four depending upon the same question, so that the decision of one is the decision of all four.

We will now, from the said report, see what these four cases are. The first named is the one we have already stated at considerable length. The second suit is, as the commissioner, Smith, states in this report by the agreement aforesaid, as follows: In the chancery cause of William A. Stuart vs. Lancaster & Co. the plaintiff, Stuart, set up for contribution as against the defendant George L. Peyton ("to say nothing here," says the commissioner, "of any contention from his codefendant, R. A. Lancaster") two negotiable notes executed by said corporation the Greenbrier or White Sulphur Springs Company, duly organized December 29, 1880, under its charter granted on the 6th day of December, 1880: First, a negotiable note of $10,000, due four months after date, dated August 16, 1881, payable at the bank of Lewisburg, W. Va., executed by the said corporation the Greenbrier White Sulphur Springs Company, and jointly indorsed by the said William A. Stuart, George L. Peyton, Henry M. Mathews, and R. A. Lancaster, who signs himself "R. A. Lancaster & Co.," the same having been duly protested according to law at maturity for non-payment, and afterwards paid alone by the said William A. Stuart, one of the indorsers thereof. Second, another negotiable note of $6,550.83, of date of August 9, 1881, due at four months after date, payable at the office of P. C. Barber & Co., Baltimore, Md., executed by said corporation the Greenbrier White Sulphur Springs Company, and jointly indorsed by the said William A. Stuart, George L. Peyton, H. M. Mathews, and R. A. Lancaster, who signed himself "R. A. Lancaster & Co.," duly protested according to law at maturity for non-payment, and afterwards paid in full by the said Stuart alone. The third case: A case at common law, pending in the circuit court of Augusta, under the style of William A. Stuart vs. George L. Peyton, wherein the said Stuart sues the said Peyton as first indorser on a certain negotiable note in the amount of $5,000, due November 15, 1881, payable at the bank of Lewisburg, W. Va., executed by the said the Greenbrier White Sulphur Springs Company, severally indorsed first by George L. Peyton, second by said William A. Stuart, third by R. A. Lancaster & Co., and which was duly protested, to which Peyton filed $5,000 as offset, and Stuart files counter-offsets as follows, $20,000, as to which $20,000 Peyton contends the proceeds, to the extent of every dollar, was expended in improving the property of the White Sulphur Springs Company. Fourth suit is that of William A. Stuart vs. George L. Peyton, seeking by creditors' bill to set up a lien on Peyton's real estate, one-third of $27,519.30, the amount of the recovery, by J. Fred Effinger, etc., vs. Stuart, Peyton, Camden, and Thompson; said liability having arisen out of a purchase made by said Stuart for himself and his associates of certain furniture, live-stock, etc., from George L. Peyton & Co., composed of J. Fred Effinger, R. H. Catlett, George L. Peyton, and others, which is defended by said Peyton upon the ground that it formed a part of the cost of his stock, and discovered and indicated by the words "basis of cost" in the contract of November 4, 1882.

The said commissioner, Smith, having thus stated in detail the grounds and causes of the several actions brought by the said William A. Stuart, proceeds to state the relations of the parties previous to the commencement of this litigation. He says that in 1879, and for several years previously, the White Sulphur Springs realty was in litigation, under the control and custody of the courts of West Virginia. That the partnership firm of George L. Peyton & Co., composed of R. H. Catlett, J. Fred Effinger, George L. Peyton, and others, were lessees of that property from the court, their lease to expire on the confirmation of a sale thereof, which had been decreed to take place on the 30th day of March, 1880. That William A. Stuart was a large incumbrancer of the said realty, and interested in a profitable management of the property, and agreed with George L. Peyton and J. N. Camden that the three would form a joint-stock company upon the basis of one-half to be held by Camden, who was to take in H. M. Mathews to share with him when it could be done, H. M. Mathews not to be known in the purchase which was to be made on behalf of the said joint-stock company; but there was a side contract between Camden and Mathews by which this was agreed between them: That Stuart was to hold one-fourth of the stock, and George L. Peyton one-fourth; that Stuart was to buy at the price of $340,000 for himself and his associates. That this arrangement was perfected, and Stuart became the purchaser; and Camden turned over to H. M. Mathews a one-fourth interest in the stock, and subsequently assigned to one W. P. Thompson one-eighth interest, or one-half of his one-fourth. On the 1st day of May following, R. H. Catlett, acting for himself and his other partners, Effinger, Peyton, etc., sold the personalty belonging to them to the said William A. Stuart, who was acting for himself and his associates, at the price of $35,000, and this furniture was taken and used and contributed to the production of the alleged $56,488.91 net profits of the springs during the summer of 1880, and formed a part of the basis on which the $150,000 of the stock was issued as full paid up. The commissioner then says as to the contract of purchase by Stuart of Peyton's interest in the springs, made on the 4th day of November, 1882, as this is a common defense against all the other claims set up by Stuart in these four several suits, on the grounds of said Peyton's indorsement of the several negotiable notes of the Greenbrier White Sulphur Springs Company, commissioner will take up all of the said claims, and discuss them simply in the light of the paper claimed and filed by Peyton as the original contract of sale of his stock, November 4, 1882. He says that Peyton claims that every dollar realized by the corporation the said the Greenbrier White Sulphur Springs Company on discount by the banks of its sundry notes indorsed by Peyton, in all but one instance jointly with other company stockholders,

and now asserted in the plaintiff Stuart's bill, went into the improvement and furnishing of the springs property; that the stock was issued on the basis of these improvements; that the liability assumed by Peyton in indorsing these notes was assumed by reason of his being a stockholder, and as a part of the stock transaction; that, had the notes been paid by the company out of its profits, he, as a stockholder, would have contributed his part of the profits, and, if he had to pay individually, the payment would be on account of the stock, and that the terms of the sale "on the basis of cost" would naturally and by ordinary interpretation include all these asserted liabilities, thereby relieving Peyton therefrom, independently of the verbal agreement at the time. The commissioner found against Peyton in all the cases, made an elaborate report in this case, to be applied in its effects to all the cases, and made formal findings in the other cases, and the circuit court sustained the commissioner in all his findings. When the commissioner's report was filed in April, (as has been stated,) 1889, Judge Sheffey, the able and leading and managing counsel for Peyton, had just died, and the court met in 20 days, and the defendant was not able to supply the place of Judge Sheffey with a lawyer who could give sufficient attention to the case, as the circuit court was then in session, and all the lawyers were full of their cases in which they had been already retained; and moved the court for a continuance, but the court overruled the motion, and ruled that the case must be tried at that term. An able lawyer was then retained, who moved for a continuance, and assured the court that in view of the immense record to be studied it would be impossible for him to do justice to his client or to himself; but the court insisted that the case must be heard at that term, and gave an indulgence of a few weeks, to which refusal to continue the case the defendant refers as error in this court. The case being submitted, the circuit court decreed against Peyton in all the cases, and he applied for and obtained an appeal to this court.

The question as to a continuance of the cases under the circumstances lies at the threshold of the cases here, but for the present it will be waived, and we will consider first the main question which affects and controls not only this case, but the other three set forth in the commissioner's report; the agreement of the parties being that to save expense and delay all the cases should be considered and determined along with this. The defense set up in each case being the same, and the evidence in each case being the same, there is no controverted fact not common to them all. And it was competent for the parties plaintiff and defendant to agree, as they did agree, to make no contest except in this case, and the result of this must therefore determine them all. The findings in the other cases being merely formal, no formal appeals have been taken in them, and none could be taken, as there were none but formal findings therein, and so no error is apparent on the face of the record. But this appeal, when decided, will decide them all, as the contract between the parties on the subject is a valid and binding one, and will be enforced for or against either party, as the result may determine. And, if the circuit court's decree in this case be affirmed, the findings in all the cases will stand affirmed; whereas, if the decree of the circuit court shall be reversed in this case, by agreement of the parties the formal findings in the other cases will be annulled by proper order in this court in these causes.

We will now consider the main, indeed the only, defense set up by Peyton, which is relied on to defeat all of the said actions. We have said enough to make it clear that the execution of the notes of the said the White Sulphur Springs Company and their indorsements are not denied. It appears, however, that they were executed for the common benefit of all of the incorporators of the said company, and the money raised upon them applied likewise to the common benefit; that Stuart and Peyton were, with others, stockholders in large amounts of the stock of this company, which owned the White Sulphur Springs property; that there were debts due by the company; that the property was valuable, and its future believed to be promising, the net profits for a single season being stated on the books of the concern at $56,000. The debts of the old concern, still unpaid, gave trouble to the management, and the matter was still in litigation and in the hands of the court. In this state of affairs, Peyton, the owner of 410 shares of the company's stock, was appointed by the court the court's custodian, and it was expected that at the next term of the court he would be appointed receiver of the property; and he was also the manager of the business, being a practical hotel man. Stuart was a large incumbrancer of the property, and anxious to formulate some plan by which he could make the place more profitable. He turned his eyes now to the wealthy and skillful architect of the Hygeia Hotel at Old Point, Harrison Phœbus; the extension of the Chesapeake & Ohio Railroad line to Newport News and to Old Point, where the Hygeia Hotel stood, having connected these two great rival public resorts by a continuous all-rail line. He procured the presence of Henry M. Mathews and of Mr. Phœbus at the Exchange Hotel in Richmond, and opened negotiations to lease the White Sulphur to Phœbus. Pending these negotiations, which were conducted without notice to Peyton, by accident Peyton visited the Exchange Hotel, and came upon them. Henry M. Mathews, soon after Peyton's arrival, told him it was proposed to lease the springs to Phœbus. Peyton forthwith announced his purpose to lease them himself. The next morning Stuart announced to Peyton that, to be frank with him, they had already agreed with Phœbus, and he was to be there that day to close the matter. Peyton objected now in earnest, and announced his purpose of striking for control of the property by securing the aid of the creditors, some of whom were already with him. (This to Gov. Mathews, who told Stuart, and returned to Peyton with the information that Stu-

art would buy him out, and negotiations to that end at once began in earnest.) And Stuart asked Peyton if he would sell out, as he had said he would, what terms would he make? Peyton replied that if Stuart would pay him $5,000 bonus, and release him from all responsibility for the company, and all responsibility and liability to him, he would close with him. Stuart, having planned to substitute Mr. Phœbus for Peyton, asked Peyton to give him an option, and wanted 10 days. Peyton told him he could have until 12 o'clock that day. Stuart objected to the shortness of the time, and Peyton agreed to extend it to 3 o'clock of that day. Stuart then commenced to prepare the option proposition, which is exhibited with the deposition of Stuart, and is as follows:

"I, George L. Peyton, do hereby sell to W. A. Stuart my stock in the Greenbrier White Sulphur Springs Company, of West Va., on the basis of cost, which cost is represented by my notes in the hands of the said Stuart, and the matters of discount and interest paid for me by said Stuart. These notes are to be returned to me as paid out. In addition to the above, said Stuart is to pay my debt to Dr. Moorman, (of about $4,000.00,) and enough in addition to make the sum of $5,000.00 within ten or fifteen days. This contract is binding on me until 3 o'clock this P. M., between now and which time Stuart is .to accept the same in writing, if he so elects, and place said writing of acceptance in my hands. [A line appearing, run through the words, "in addition to the above said Stuart is to bear said Peyton's share of his liability." The whole of this paper is written in the handwriting of said William A. Stuart, and the word "liability" is followed by a full stop, or period, showing that the sentence was completed. In addition to the above, it further agrees that said Stuart will pay to said Peyton the amount of his, Peyton's, (uncollected) salary for the present year up to the 1st day of January, including the amount of board-bill for Stuart and family at the W. S. Springs, during the past summer, which was paid by said Peyton for Stuart, and credited to the one-fourth of the superintendent's salary, to which the said Stuart was by contract entitled.] Witness my hand and seal, Nov. 4th, 1882. GEO. L. PEYTON. [Seal.]

"I further agree to put no obstacles in the way of said Stuart and his associates in their efforts to regain and hold the control of the said Greenbrier White Sulphur Springs. GEO. L. PEYTON.

"I accept the above. W. A. STUART. Nov. 4th, 1882.

"Above acceptance in time. GEO. L. PEYTON."

The defendant, George L. Peyton, gives his version as to the erased words inserted above with a line drawn through them, "in addition to the above, said Stuart is to bear said Peyton's share of his liabilities," as follows: "Stuart was writing, and when he got there he said, 'If we refer to the indebtedness of our company, Phœbus is very scary; and, if he should find out about the large indebtedness of the company, it might defeat my agree-

ment with him.' We then discussed the
matter verbally, and he agreed to give me
the protection from the debts of the company as I had proposed. He then erased
from the option proposition as he had
written it the provision releasing me from
the debts of the company, but it was distinctly understood and agreed between us
that I was to be protected by him from
all liability for said debts. A very short
time after I had given him this option paper, I thought it would be safer for me to
have our verbal understanding in writing, and I had another paper prepared,
protecting me on the line on which we had
agreed. He declined to sign the paper,
and we did not discuss it at all. I then
made up my mind that we could not
trade, and went to work on my plan of
securing the creditors' debts. Some hours
after the time had passed limited for the
acceptance of my option, he came to me,
and said that he was behind time, but
proposed that we go to a room, and have
some talk. We did so, and after very little
talk we agreed on the contract of November 4, 1882, filed with my answer; and I
accepted it as a clear acquittal, believing
that it would, as it was intended to do,
protect me from all liability for the debts
of the company and to Mr. Stuart. The
term 'basis of cost,' as used in that contract, was used, and was intended to
mean, and was claimed by me and admitted by him to mean, to release me from
all responsibility for the company and to
Mr. Stuart. These were the only terms
on which I would agree to sell out. and
this was the distinct agreement and understanding between us at the time of the
execution of that paper. He says further
that all the proceeds of the notes he had
indorsed for the company were used for
the improving and furnishing the springs
property, and were partly the basis for
issuing the stock which I held and sold
to Mr. Stuart on the basis of cost, and
it was so understood and agreed at the
time. At the time we traded, I held Mr.
Stuart's receipt for 375 shares of the stock,
and was besides entitled to 35 additional
shares; making in all 410 shares, worth
at par $41,000.00. Mr. Stuart had ad-
vanced for me, as part payment of this
stock, the sum of $17,500.00, and held my
notes for that amount and the interest
and discount he had paid on it. This
was all I owed him at the time, except my
notes of the company indorsed by me,
which he had before that time paid, and
then held. The trade was intended to be
a complete settlement of all matters between us, and left me without any interest in or liability for the company, or responsibility to him. It is not reasonable
that I would have surrendered my rights
in the company and still left myself liable
for the notes of the company I had indorsed. The agreement was that I was
to be paid the $5,000.00 in cash. And
when he found I was going to pay Dr.
Moorman this debt, he suggested the provision as to Dr. Moorman, because he
thought he could get indulgence from the
doctor. On the 18th of the same month
Stuart wrote to me, and asked indulgence on the money he was to pay me

until the 1st of January following. This
letter asking indulgence at my hands was
written fourteen days after his contract,
at a time when he had in his hands notes
of the company indorsed by me, and which
he had paid, and would have been an offset as well then as now. Since the 4th of
November, 1882, Peyton never indorsed
any renewal of any note, nor had any
business transaction with Stuart."

This is Peyton's version of the agreed
meaning of the words "basis of cost" at
the time. Stuart now denies this, and contends that he only agreed to give Peyton for
his stock what he had paid for him on the
stock,—about $17,500. This term "basis of
cost" has had a construction put upon it
by Stuart in the progress of these transactions. Mr. Stuart testifies that early
in 1881 Camden & Thompson sold their
stock to R. A. Lancaster on the basis of
cost. Upon turning to that sale by Camden & Thompson of their stock in this
company, which Stuart says was upon
the basis of cost, we find what Mr. Stuart's definition of this term is when it
does not affect him. It is, in part, as follows: "The object of this agreement being
to substitute the said R. A. Lancaster to
all the rights of said Camden and Camden
and Thompson in said contract and in the
company formed under the same, as if
the said R. A. Lancaster had been in it
from the beginning, and the said Robert A.
Lancaster on his part agreeing and hereby obligating himself to protect and fulfil
all the obligations of the said Camden and
Camden and Thompson, and to save them
harmless, and acquit from all liability, as
fully as if the said Robert A. Lancaster
had been the original party to the said
contract, instead of the said Camden."
Mr. Stuart used this language when he
traded with Col. Peyton, and this is the
meaning which Peyton says Stuart put
upon the words at the time. But Stuart
says he meant nothing of the sort. That
when he was trading with Peyton, "basis
of cost" meant what Peyton's stock had
cost Stuart in the way of loans; and that
he received Peyton's stock, worth $40,000,
and all of Peyton's interest in the White
Sulphur Springs Company, of which he
was one-fourth owner, and superintendent, with a large salary, for $17,500, and
$5,000 more, and, while Peyton gave up
all interest in the springs, and all hope of
ever making anything out of them, yet he
stood sponsor for the company's debts created for betterments on the springs for the
amount set forth in his several suits, and
stated above. But when "basis of cost"
was used between Lancaster and Camden
it meant "basis of cost." But again Mr.
Stuart has put his own interpretation in
writing upon this term within a few days
after he made the purchase of Peyton and
made the sale to Mr. Phœbus. Here is
the letter of Stuart to Peyton, written
shortly after he agreed to buy Col. Peyton's stock on the basis of cost: "Nov.
18th, 1882. Col. Geo. L. Peyton—Dear Sir:
I have seen Dr. Moorman, and told him of
our trade. He does not care to have his
money just now; and hope it will be
agreeable to you to let it stand till next
fall, unless the Dr. desires it sooner. I

would like you also to indulge me a little on the balance that will be due you, say till Jan. 1st. I know you would have done this if I had asked it in Richmond, but after I had sold the interest to Phœbus, I was too much hurried to ask you. Phœbus had to leave at 4 o'clock and I had to see him again. I get nothing from him under a year. [Signed] W. A. STUART." Wants time then on the Moorman debt. In these proceedings(and there have been no subsequent transactions between him and Peyton) he repudiates it altogether. Politely asks for indulgence on the $1,000 due Peyton,—asks indulgence for a short time, say till January 1st. He now offsets Peyton's offset of this $2,000 with a counter-offset of more than $20,000, due to him from Peyton, by his insistance in this suit at this very time, when, if he is right now, Peyton should have begged indulgence from him for more than $70,000. The short indulgence asked was granted, and, the time running out, and 30 days more, Peyton drafted on Stuart for $300, a part of what was due him; but Stuart refused payment, and spoke of these notes. Peyton promptly replied: "As to the claims of which you speak, they were all in existence at the time our contract was made, and you had paid some of them at that time, as I understood. And I suppose, moreover, that the claims are amply secured, and you yourself hold indemnity in your own hands in the greater part of them, if not for the whole. It is a matter of inconvenience to me to go without the money due me, small as the sum may be regarded. I will remind you of the fact that 190 bonds of $500.00 each are held by Alex. F. Mathews [the bank cashier] as collateral security for the notes you refer to. [Signed] GEO. L. PEYTON. Feb. 23rd, 1883."

The learned counsel for the appellant has referred us to many circumstances which show in the record that Stuart's memory was very frail, and where he appears to be contradicted by incontrovertible circumstances, and indeed by his own admissions. We have given these careful examination and consideration, and we find them in every case sustained by the record; but we cannot follow that line of discussion further within the reasonable limits of an opinion already too long. But upon consideration of the whole record, we find no difficulty in arriving at our conclusions. Stuart had seen Camden and Camden & Thompson bought out by Lancaster upon the basis of cost, Lancaster stepping into the shoes of Camden and Camden & Thompson, receiving their share of the stock and of the property, and assuming all the liabilities of the company so far as Camden and Camden & Thompson had done so, letting out the latter, who transferred to Lancaster, as the contract states, "without recourse or future liability in any form;" and, being dissatisfied with Peyton, who was the superintendent upon a large salary, and who had the authority of a sort of receiver from the court holding the property in litigation, and not being able otherwise to get him out and substitute in his stead a famous hotel man, Mr. Harrison

Phœbus, who had developed the Hygeia Hotel, and with it an immense fortune, proposed to buy Peyton out upon the basis of cost, as was understood between them, in the light of the Camden and Lancaster trade, for Peyton of course knew as much about this contract as Stuart did. He entered into the contract, the subject of this controversy, by which he not only secured one-fourth interest in the stock and the springs property, but made vacant the place of superintendent and receiver, and opened the way to lease the property to Mr. Phœbus, which was accomplished. On November 18th, when he so politely asked indulgence of Peyton, Peyton's time was not out, and January 1st was named. When that time came he took no notice of Peyton, nor of his contract; but when, after waiting 30 days, Peyton drafted for $300, he dishonored the draft, and began this controversy, by which he has caused all of his contracts with Peyton to be set at naught, not only not paying Dr. Moorman, not only not paying Peyton, not only not returning to Peyton his paper, with interest and discount as paid, but, sweeping away every defense set up by Peyton, he has overwhelmed him, by the help of the commissioner and the circuit court, under a load of debt of $70,000 and more on account of these very debts of the company which passed under his control into his hands, and which he agreed to pay with the property Peyton turned over to him. He has all of Peyton's interest in the springs property, and holds Peyton bound for the debts contracted by the company in making the springs property what it is, has Peyton's $35,000 worth of furniture (by his own valuation) for nothing. This is the result of the court's decrees and orders in these four suits. We are of opinion that they are wholly unsustained by the facts in this record. Peyton's defense, as we have seen, is set up against, and is a valid defense to, each and every of these four suits, and as such will be upheld by proper orders here, and will be enforced against the said Stuart in each suit; and as Stuart has not paid, but repudiated his obligation to pay, Dr. Moorman the $4,000 which Peyton owed him, and which he agreed to pay him, Peyton being left to take care of that himself, a decree will be rendered here against said Stuart for the $5,000 due Peyton, with interest, and the other suits ordered to be dismissed. And the decrees and orders appealed from here are wholly erroneous, and must be reversed and annulled.

RICHARDSON and HINTON, JJ., concur.

JONES v. RICHMOND.

(Supreme Court of Appeals of Virginia. July 9, 1891.)

BREACH OF COVENANT—TITLE PARAMOUNT — PARTIES.

1. An action for breach of covenant cannot be maintained upon the mere claim of title paramount by another, where no disturbance of possession is shown.

2. Such action cannot be maintained by one who has parted with the title conveyed by the

deed the covenants of which are alleged to have been broken.

Error to circuit court, Wise county; H. K. MORRISON, Judge.

Action of covenant by D. C. Jones against J. C. Richmond. Judgment for defendant, and plaintiff brings error. Affirmed.

Bullitt & McDowell, for plaintiff in error. *A. L. Pridemore* and *J. B. Richmond,* for defendant in error.

LACY, J. This is a writ of error to a judgment of the circuit court of Wise county, rendered on the 16th day of September, 1890. The action is covenant, and the complaint of the plaintiff, in the circuit court, the plaintiff in error here, is that the defendant conveyed to him, for a valuable consideration, a certain lot of land in the town of Big Stone Gap, in the said county of Wise; and that the said defendant, by his deed to the said plaintiff, covenanted, for himself and his heirs, with the said plaintiff and his heirs, that the said defendant and his heirs would warrant and forever defend, to the said plaintiff, his heirs and assigns, the title to the said lot of land, against all persons whomsoever, as by the said deed referred to would appear; but that the defendant had broken this covenant, in that, at the time of making said deed, one Rachel S. Gibson and C. A. Gibson, her husband, had lawful title to said land, and afterwards sold said lands to I. F. Necessary, who thereupon acquired title to said land; that, prior to this sale to Necessary, Gibson and wife threatened to bring suit against the plaintiff and his grantees for possession and title of said land; and the said Necessary, as soon as he purchased the said land, made the same threats, and was about to proceed at once to carry said threats into execution, and to oust plaintiff and his grantees from the possession of the said land; that all of this said defendant had full notice, but refused to take any steps to prevent the plaintiff and his grantees from being ousted from the said land; that the plaintiff was bound to protect the persons to whom he had sold in the quiet enjoyment thereof; that nevertheless two of the persons, to-wit, W. E. Harris and R. H. Jones, who held said land under the plaintiff, agreed to pay a part of such sum as might be necessary to purchase the said claim of said Necessary, and plaintiff agreed to pay the residue; that they purchased the claim of said Necessary at $975, and were unable to get it for any less, and that it was reasonably worth as much as that; and the plaintiff paid $500 of this amount; and that then Necessary conveyed the said land to W. E. Harris, and claimed $1,000 damages. To this declaration the defendant demurred, and the circuit court, by the order in the case of the 16th of September, 1890, sustained the said demurrer, and gave judgment for the defendant, and his costs. Whereupon the said plaintiff applied for and obtained a writ of error to this court. The grounds of the demurrer were (1) that the declaration did not set forth an eviction nor disturbance of his possession; (2) that the declaration showed that the plaintiff had parted with and disposed of by grant to another the land in question, and had therefore no right to maintain the suit, no breach having occurred in his time.

First. The declaration sets forth the existence of an adverse and paramount claim of title by another against the land, which was asserted only, but which proceeded to no entry or dispossession of the grantee in possession of the land, nor was there any assertion of a surrender of the possession to the rightful owner by legal process. But the eviction set forth is by an adverse assertion of a paramount title. It is conceded by the declaration that there has been no actual eviction or disturbance of the possession by ouster, because the possession of the grantee of the plaintiff is distinctly averred. But the assertion of a title paramount by a third person is held and claimed to be an eviction. It is said by Mr. Rawle (Rawle, Cov. p. 144) that nothing is more generally or truly said than that an eviction is necessary to a breach of the covenants for quiet enjoyment or of warranty. A covenant for quiet enjoyment, says Mr. Chief Justice GIBSON in Stewart v. West, 14 Pa. St. 338, which resembles the modern covenant of warranty, differs from it in this: that the former is broken by the very commencement of an action on the better title; and any entry and dispossession adversely and lawfully made under paramount title will be an eviction, and whenever such a right is exercised it is considered to have all the force and effect of a dispossession under legal process. Mr. Minor says, as to the covenant of title, (2 Int. 720,) it is supposed to be in fact and in essence substantially the same as a covenant or quiet enjoyment, and it is believed that no action lies upon it until actual eviction, or at least disturbance of the possession. 2 Lomax, Dig. 355, 356; Emerson v. Proprietors, 1 Mass. 464; Findlay v. Toucray, 2 Rob. (Va.) 374, 379; Rawle, Cov. 210, 211; Marbury v. Thornton, 82 Va. 702, 1 S. E. Rep. 909. "The existence of an incumbrance, or the mere recovery in a possessory action under which the bargain has not been actually disturbed, are held, for technical reasons, not to be breaches of a covenant for quiet possession, or, in other words, upon warranties." An adversary dispossession or a compulsory yielding up of the possession constitutes an actual eviction. A constructive eviction is illustrated by the case in which the eviction is deemed to be caused by the inability of the purchaser to obtain possession by reason of the paramount title. Thus, as was tersely said by Chief Justice RUFFIN, (Grist v. Hodges, 3 Dev. 200,) the existence of a better title, with an actual possession under it in another, is of itself a breach of the covenant. It is manifestly just that it should be so considered; for otherwise the covenantee would have no redress but by making himself a trespasser by an actual entry which the law requires of nobody, or by bringing an unnecessary suit, for the event of that suit proves nothing in the action on the covenant. But upon purely legal grounds it is so; for, as between the bargainor and the bargainee, the legal estate is acquired by the deed. * * * As between the parties, the bargainee is on strict principles in; but, if there be in reality an adverse possession, he can only be held to being in for an instant, for there will be no implication against the truth, further than is necessary to make the deed effectual for its purposes. If such adverse possession be upon paramount title, then there is an eviction of the bargainee *eo instanti* that the possession takes place, and the eviction need not be by process. And Mr. Rawle says, (Rawle, Cov. 154:) "The rule, therefore, as best supported by reason and authority, would seem to be this: where, at the time of the conveyance, the grantee finds the premises in possession of one claiming under a paramount title, the covenant for quiet enjoyment or of warranty will be held to be broken, without any other act on the part of either the grantee or the claimant; for the latter can do no more towards the assertion of his title, and as to the former the law will compel no one to commit a trespass in order to establish a lawful right in another action." The declaration, as we have seen, does not set forth such an eviction, but avers the undisturbed possession of the grantee. There is no allegation of an eviction, and, upon the first ground of demurrer stated, the demurrer was properly sustained.

As to the *second* ground, we will remark, briefly, that such a covenant as this passes with the land, and is binding on the land, and in favor of assignees although assigns are not expressly named; but the liability of the assignee is confined to the period of his occupancy, or of his interests in the land; and it is said that no covenant which is broken is capable of being assigned at law. When, therefore, a covenant is violated, the suit must be brought by the party at that time interested, and not by one to whom the land may afterwards come by assignment. The second ground of demurrer is therefore fatal, also, to the declaration, which distinctly avers the conveyance to and possession of another under the plaintiff. The result is that the demurrer was properly sustained to the declaration, and, as the suit could not be maintained by the plaintiff, judgment was rightly rendered for the defendant, and there is no error in the said judgment, and the same must be affirmed.

WHITE *et al.* v. TOWN COUNCIL OF ROCK HILL.

(*Supreme Court of South Carolina.* July 21, 1891.)

MUNICIPAL CORPORATIONS—TAXATION—LICENSE TO MERCHANTS.

Under an ordinance providing "that all persons coming into the town of Rock Hill to engage therein in the business of a merchant for a shorter period than one year shall pay a license tax of $50," a tax is invalid which is assessed upon a merchant who, having conducted a dry goods store for 75 days, changes his business to that of selling produce, where the evidence shows that he had leased his store building for one year, with the privilege of two years.

Appeal from common pleas circuit court of York county.

Action by F. H. White & Co. against the town council of Rock Hill to recover taxes paid under protest. Judgment for plaintiffs, and defendant appeals. Affirmed.

W. J. Cherry, for appellant. Wilson & Wilson, for respondents.

MCIVER, J. By the act of 1887, (19 St. 1163,) the town council of Rock Hill is, among other things, invested with power "to require all insurance, telegraph, and express companies, doing business in said town, and also all transient persons, companies, or corporations of any kind whatsoever, engaged temporarily in any business, profession, or occupation in said town, except such as are engaged as teachers or as ministers of the gospel, to pay to said town such sum or sums of money as a license tax as said town council may by ordinance direct: provided, said license tax shall not exceed the sum of one hundred dollars per annum." On the 6th of February, 1888, an ordinance was adopted by the said town council, portions of which are set out in the "case," for the purpose of fixing the amount of licenses and special taxes imposed for the year commencing 20th January, 1888, and ending January 20, 1889, the fifth section of which reads as follows: "That all persons coming into the town of Rock Hill within said year to engage therein in the business of a merchant, for a shorter period than one year, shall severally pay into the treasury of said town a license tax of fifty dollars." The following somewhat equivocal statement is made in the case: "The plaintiffs engaged in the business of merchants in the town of Rock Hill commencing about June 30, 1888, and continuing for about seventy-five days, when they sold out *or changed their business from dry goods to produce store*. Thereupon, demand being made upon them for the license fee of fifty dollars, according to the requirements of the said ordinance, they paid the same under protest, and commenced this action before a trial justice to recover back the same." The case was first heard by a jury, which failing to agree, a mistrial was ordered, and it was again heard by the trial justice, who rendered judgment for the defendant, which, upon appeal to the circuit court, was reversed, and judgment rendered in favor of plaintiffs. From this last-mentioned judgment defendant appeals to this court upon the several grounds set out in the record. The words which we have italicised in the quotation from the case above render it doubtful, to say the least of it, whether the plaintiffs were amenable to the tax; for, if they simply changed their business from dry goods to groceries, they were still engaged in the business of a merchant, and until it was shown that they were engaged in that business for a shorter period than one year they did not come within the provisions of the ordinance. The circuit judge simply reversed the judgment of the trial justice, by a short order, without assigning any reasons; and we are not informed of the grounds upon which he based his conclusion. If he concluded as matter of fact that the evidence was not sufficient to show that the plaintiff had been engaged in business as a merchant for a less period than one year, then we have no jurisdiction to review such finding; and, as there is evidence set out in the case which tends to support that conclusion, we cannot say that there was any error in his judgment. In addition to this, it is at least doubtful whether the tax imposed in this case was legal. Two things are essential to the validity of any tax imposed by a municipal corporation: (1) The power to do so must be conferred upon such corporation by an act of the legislature, that body having been intrusted with the taxing power by the people through the constitution, which contains a provision (section 8, art. 9) authorizing the delegation of that high power to the corporate authorities of towns for certain purposes, etc. See Floyd v. Perrin, 30 S. C. at page 15, 8 S. E. Rep. 14. (2) The power thus conferred must be exercised by the municipal authorities in conformity with the terms of the grant. In this case it appears that the town council of Rock Hill has been invested by the legislature with power to require "all transient persons, * * * engaged temporarily in any business," to pay a certain license tax, and the said town council has undertaken to exercise this power by passing an ordinance to impose license and special taxes for the year commencing 20th January, 1888, in which it is provided "that all persons coming into the town of Rock Hill within said year, to engage therein in the business of merchant for a shorter period than one year," shall pay the tax in question. Now, whether the power conferred has been exercised in conformity to the terms of the grant; whether the power to impose such a tax as the one in question upon transient persons, engaged temporarily in business, is properly exercised by imposing such tax upon any person coming into the town to engage in the business of a merchant for a less period than one year,—is a question which may admit of some doubt. But waiving that, and assuming that the power was properly exercised, yet, inasmuch as there was no evidence that the plaintiffs went to Rock Hill to engage in business as merchants for a less period than one year, and, on the contrary, there was evidence derived from the terms of the written agreement for the rent of the store for one year, with the privilege of two years, tending to show that the plaintiffs came to Rock Hill to engage in business for at least a year, if not longer, the circuit judge was fully justified in reaching the conclusion that the plaintiffs were entitled to judgment. The judgment of this court is that the judgment of the circuit court be affirmed.

McGowan, J., concurs.

ELLIS v. SANDERS et al.

(*Supreme Court of South Carolina.* July 31, 1891.)

FORECLOSURE — PENALTY OF BOND — REVIEW ON SECOND APPEAL.

1. Where any portion of the debt, for the payment of which a bond is conditioned, is unpaid,

the obligee may recover to the full extent of the penalty of the bond, although the unpaid balance, together with payments previously made, would exceed the penalty.

2. Where a report of a referee upon foreclosure of a mortgage was excepted to only upon one ground, and an appeal therefrom taken, the parties, upon a second appeal from a report made in conformity with the decision of the supreme court, cannot allege exceptions to the report in regard to matters not excepted to upon the first trial.

Appeal from common pleas circuit court of Hampton county; J. B. KERSHAW and T. B. FRASER, Judges.

The following statement was agreed on by counsel: "We agree that the following papers shall constitute the two several cases and returns herein: (1) Exceptions of defendants, appellants, and plaintiff, appellant. (2) Report of referee, and portion of first report, showing calculation of interest. (3) Exceptions of plaintiff to first report of referee. (4) Order of Judge Kershaw. (5) Order of Judge Fraser. (6) Statement that penalty of the bond is nineteen hundred and thirty-six dollars, and that thirteen hundred and sixty dollars has been paid before the commencement of this action. The service of exceptions on Judge Fraser, printing the notices of appeal, which we admit to have been served, filing copy of return with clerk of the circuit court, waived." The substance of the referee's report, and of the orders of Judges KERSHAW and FRASER, is stated in the opinion below.

E. F. Warren, for appellant. W. S. Tillinghast, for respondents.

McIVER, J. While the foregoing statement, taken from the "case" as prepared for argument here, would indicate that there were two cases to be heard together, yet there is, in fact, but one case, in which both parties have appealed. This is the second appeal in the case, and reference may be had to the case as published in 10 S. E. Rep. 824—where it is more fully reported than in the "Notes of Unreported Cases," in 32 S. C. 584,—for a more detailed statement of the facts than it is deemed necessary to make here. The general question involved is as to the amount due on a bond secured by a mortgage on real estate, which this action was brought to foreclose, which depends upon the proper mode of calculating the interest on the bond, and consequent thereupon another question is presented, as to whether judgment can be rendered for an amount which, with the payments made, will exceed the penalty of the bond. The referee to whom it was referred to compute the amount still due upon the bond, in his first report, made a statement showing that he had calculated the interest on the balance of the total amount of the debt, after deducting the cash payment made on the bond at its date, at the rate of 18 per cent. per annum, the rate specified in the bond, up to the dates of the several payments; and, after deducting each payment at the date on which it was made, computed the interest at the same rate up to the time of the maturity of the last installment, after which he made the calculation at the reduced rate of 7 per cent. per annum, and recommended judgment for the amount thus ascertained. To that report the only exception taken was by the plaintiff upon the ground that the referee had erred in reducing the rate of interest to 7 per cent. after the maturity of the last installment, and claiming that interest should have been calculated at the rate of 18 per cent. until the bond was fully paid. That report, with that single exception, was heard by his honor, Judge KERSHAW, who sustained the exception, and recommitted the report to the referee, with directions "to compute the amount due on the bond and mortgage at the rate of interest as specified in the bond, to-wit, eighteen per cent. per annum, or one and one-half per cent per month, after maturity of the last installment." From that judgment the defendants appealed solely upon the ground that Judge KERSHAW had erred in holding that the bond continued to draw interest, after the maturity of the last installment, at the rate of 18 per cent., and this court affirmed that judgment. Accordingly the referee has reformed his calculation precisely in accordance with the directions of Judge KERSHAW, affirmed by this court, by continuing the calculation of interest at 18 per cent. after as well as before the maturity of the last installment, and has made a second report ascertaining the balance due on the bond, on the 18th of April, 1890, to be $700.22. To this last report the defendants seem to have excepted, but upon what grounds does not appear in the "case," and the report and exceptions were heard by his honor, Judge FRASER, who overruled the exceptions, and directed the referee "to ascertain and report amount paid on said bond; it being the judgment of this court that plaintiff cannot recover more than the penalty of the bond in excess of the payments." From that judgment both parties appeal,—the defendants upon the ground that the report of the referee "is contrary to the order of Judge KERSHAW previously made in the cause, and the decree of the supreme court thereon, in this: that said order of Judge KERSHAW recommitted the cause to the referee to calculate the interest on the bond at 18 per cent. 'from the maturity of the last installment,' and the supreme court confirmed same; and the referee allowed and reported interest at 18 per cent. on the condition of the bond from its date, regardless of the installments, which was confirmed by Judge FRASER, although the supreme court declares in said judgment that the interest prior to the maturity of the last installment had already been incorporated in the installments, 'and it would be manifestly improper to allow it again.'" The plaintiff's appeal is based upon the ground that Judge FRASER erred in holding that plaintiff could not recover the amount found due by the referee on the bond, ($700.22,) although the penalty of the bond is $1,936.

It seems to us that the exception of defendants is based upon a misconception both of Judge KERSHAW's judgment and the former decision of this court in this case. The only question presented for the decision of Judge KERSHAW, and the only one which he decided, was whether the referee had erred in reducing the rate of interest from 18 per cent. to 7 per cent. after the

maturity of the last installment; and the only question before this court was whether Judge KERSHAW had erred in deciding that single question. No exception was taken to the mode adopted by the referee in making the calculation of interest up to the maturity of the last installment, and hence neither Judge KERSHAW nor this court had any authority to determine whether his mode of calculation up to that point was correct or not, and neither undertook to do so. Perhaps the strictly accurate mode of making the calculation would have been to compute the interest on each installment from the day it became payable, at the rate of 18 per cent., allowing credit for the several payments at their respective dates, instead of calculating the interest on the amount of the condition of the bond, after deducting the cash payment from the date of the bond; but, as that would have produced a result much more unfavorable to the defendants than that obtained by the mode adopted by the referee, they have no right to complain. Indeed, the result of that mode of calculation would have been to compound the interest to a certain extent, at least; for, in order to account for the anomaly presented by a bond conditioned for the payment of a certain sum of money in four installments, the aggregate of which exceeds the amount of the condition, the theory was suggested that this discrepancy could and should be accounted for by assuming that the amount of each installment was fixed by adding thereto the interest thereon at the rate of 18 per cent. from the date of the bond to the day at which each installment became payable. If this be the correct theory, then it is manifest that the interest on each installment from the date of the bond to the day when the installment became payable would bear interest from that day, and thus the interest, to that extent at least, would be compounded. It was in reference to that view of the matter that the remark quoted from the former opinion of this court in defendant's ground of appeal was made. But, be all this as it may, it is sufficient in this case that, neither party having excepted to the mode of calculating the interest adopted by the referee in his first report, except as to the reduction of the rate of interest after the maturity of the last installment, both parties must be regarded as having acquiesced in the report in every other respect. We do not think, therefore, that defendant's exception can be sustained.

It only remains to consider the exception taken by the plaintiff. We must confess that we do not exactly understand the latter part of Judge FRASER's order upon which this exception is based, and must suppose that there is some misprint or clerical error. It certainly cannot be understood as simply announcing the general proposition that, in an action on a bond, the plaintiff cannot recover judgment for more than the penalty; for the amount for which the referee recommended judgment ($700.22) is much less than the penalty; and, indeed, that proposition is not disputed, and is fully supported by Bonsall v. Taylor, 1 McCord, 503, recognized and affirmed in Stroble v. Large, 3 McCord, 112, and by at least two cases decided by the former court of equity, (Cruger v. Daniel, McMul. Eq. 197 et seq., and Harper v. Barsh, 10 Rich. Eq. 155,) and by the present supreme court in Dial v. Gary, 27 S. C. 177, 3 S. E. Rep. 84. But as it appears from the report of the referee that the aggregate of the payments credited on the bond, together with the cash payment made on the original debt, which is stated as the condition of the bond at the date of the bond, added to the amount for which judgment was recommended, would exceed the amount of the penalty named in the bond, we suppose the question intended to be made is whether the plaintiff can recover the balance of the condition remaining unpaid after the application of the payments at their several dates, when such balance, added to the payments already made, exceeds the penalty of the bond; or must the recovery be limited to an amount which, added to the sum of the payments, will not exceed the penalty? The question thus stated has been distinctly decided in the case of Smith v. Macon, 1 Hill, Eq. 339, where it was held that, as long as any portion of the condition of the bond remained unpaid, the plaintiff could recover to the full extent of the penalty, if necessary, even though such unpaid balance, when added to the payments previously made, would exceed the penalty. That decision is conclusive of the question. It is true that Mr. Hill, the reporter, in a note to that case, does cite the case of Bonsall v. Taylor, 1 McCord, 503, above referred to by its correct title, as in conflict with the decision in Smith v. Macon; but an examination of the case so cited will show that to be a mistake, as it did not appear in the case of Bonsall v. Taylor that any payment had been made on the bond, and therefore that case does not touch the present question, and only decides the general proposition that, in an action upon a bond, judgment cannot be rendered for an amount exceeding the penalty of the bond. But here it is not asked that judgment shall be rendered for an amount exceeding the penalty, but only for the balance due, which is less than the penalty of the bond. As is said by O'Neall, J., in delivering the opinion of the court in Smith v. Macon, supra: "The penalty is to secure the payment of the whole condition; any part of it remaining unpaid is a forfeiture of the penalty, which is the debt at law. The party to be relieved against it, in equity, must pay the amount really due on the condition. What is the amount due on it? The balance of the debt specified in the condition, after applying the payment, at the time it was made, to the extinguishment of the interest to that time, and the residue to the principal, with interest on the balance to the present time. If this is less than the penalty, (as it is admitted to be,) the defendant can only claim to be relieved from the penalty by paying such balance." This language is directly applicable to the question under consideration, and concludes the inquiry. We are unable, therefore, to perceive any necessity for the further inquiry, directed by the circuit judge, as to the amount paid on the bond, as that already appears from the report of the referee, and, as the balance left unpaid also appears from the report of the referee to be less than the penalty, we see no reason why judgment cannot be rendered for such balance. The judgment of this court is that the judgment of the circuit court, as herein construed, be so modified as to conform to the views above announced, and that the case be remanded to the circuit court for the purpose of such further proceedings as may be necessary to carry out such views.

McGowan, J., concurs.

CARTER v. OLIVER OIL CO.

(*Supreme Court of South Carolina.* July 18, 1891.)

Master and Servant—Dangerous Machinery—Evidence of Negligence—Nonsuit.

1. In an action to recover for personal injuries it appeared that plaintiff was employed to operate a machine in defendant's oil-mill; that while so doing he was required to do very rapid work, and that he was supplied with bags, which were placed on top of the machine by other employes; that it was necessary, for the safety of the machine operator, that these bags should be free from holes; that, if the operator discovered any hole in a bag, he would throw it out; and that the injury resulted from the use of a bag with a hole in it. *Held* error to nonsuit plaintiff upon the ground that no negligence was shown. Distinguishing Davis v. Railroad Co., 21 S. C. 93.

2. In South Carolina the question of contributory negligence cannot be considered on motion for nonsuit.

Appeal from common pleas circuit court of Richland county; W. H. Wallace, Judge.

Action by Richard Carter against the Oliver Oil Company to recover for personal injuries. Judgment for defendant. Plaintiff appeals. Reversed.

Melton & Melton, for appellant. *John C. Haskell,* for respondent.

McIver, J. The plaintiff brought this action to recover damages for injuries sustained while in the employment of the defendant company, under the allegation that the injuries sustained resulted from the negligence of the company in not furnishing the plaintiff with safe and suitable appliances to do the work for which he was employed. The testimony tends to show that plaintiff was employed by defendant to operate a machine in their oil-mill, called a "former," whereby the cotton-seed meal was pressed into cakes; and that the work required of the plaintiff had to be done rapidly, to prevent the meal from burning; that the plaintiff, standing at the machine, was supplied by other servants of the defendant company with bags or sacks, which plaintiff, with the assistance of another, had to place in the machine; that these bags or sacks were placed in a pile on the top of the machine, and, when one was wanted, the plaintiff reached up and took one off the pile, which had to be done with rapidity; that it was very necessary for the safety of the person operating the machine that these bags or sacks should be free from holes or rents, and therefore another person was employed to repair any torn sacks; that the disaster which gave rise to this action probably resulted from the use of a sack with a hole in it, whereby plaintiff's finger became entangled in it, and his hand was crushed. There was also some testimony tending to show that if the person operating the machine discovered any hole or rent in the sack when taken off the pile, he would throw it over his shoulder, when it would be taken to the person charged with the duty of repairing the sacks. Upon the testimony thus briefly outlined, his honor Judge WALLACE held that there was an entire absence of any testimony tending to show any negligence on the part of the defendant company, and therefore rendered a judgment of nonsuit, from which the plaintiff appeals upon the grounds set out in the record, which make the single question whether there was such an entire absence of testimony tending to show negligence on the part of the defendant as would warrant the granting of a nonsuit.

The rule is well settled that it is the duty of the master to furnish safe and suitable appliances for the performance of the work required of the servant, and also to see that the same are kept in proper repair; and hence, where either of these duties have not been performed, there is an omission of duty on the part of the master which affords at least *prima facie* evidence of negligence on his part; for these duties cannot be delegated to another, so as to relieve the master from liability to another for injuries sustained by reason of a failure to perform them properly. Gunter v. Manufacturing Co., 18 S. C. 262. This general statement of the rule is not to be construed as implying that the master is bound to provide appliances which shall prove to be absolutely safe under all contingencies, or even such as are of the best and most approved description, but, as said in the case cited, "only such as a reasonable and prudent person would ordinarily have used under similar circumstances." In other words, the rule does not require of the master the greatest care possible, but only such as prudent persons usually exercise under similar circumstances. This being the rule, the inquiry is whether there was in this case any evidence tending to show an absence of such care on the part of the defendant, not whether the testimony adduced was sufficient to prove negligence, as that is a matter exclusively for the jury, and we have neither the power nor the disposition to consider that question. It seems to us that there was some testimony tending to show an omission of duty on the part of the master in furnishing the plaintiff with safe appliances to do the work required of him, for there is some testimony tending to show that the injury complained of resulted from the fact that the plaintiff was furnished with a torn sack, and also some testimony to show that the use of such a sack was dangerous. It is true that there is also testimony tending to show that the defendant had employed another person, charged with the special duty of repairing the sacks; yet, if it shall appear that this duty was negligently performed, such negligence would be imputable to the master, under the rule above stated, which requires that

the master shall not only provide safe and suitable appliances in the first instance, but also see that the same are kept in repair, and the delegation of this duty to another cannot relieve the master from responsibility. The circuit judge seemed to base his conclusion upon the fact that the testimony not only did not tend to show that the defective sack which was used was the only one furnished, but, on the contrary, there was evidence tending to show that a number of other sacks were furnished, some of which he assumed were free from any defect, and hence no negligence could be imputed to defendant, causing the injury complained of, as plaintiff had been furnished with good sacks, and it was his own act to use one that was defective; citing and relying on the case of Davis v. Railroad Co., 21 S. C. 93. Before proceeding to point out the distinction between this case and that of Davis, we may remark that the view taken of the circuit judge seems to be based upon the idea that Carter, the plaintiff, was guilty of contributory negligence, and therefore could not maintain his action. It may be that such was the fact, but it is well settled in this state, at least, that the question of contributory negligence cannot be considered under a motion for a nonsuit.

But, again, the rule is that it is the duty of the master, and not of the servant, to exercise due care and diligence to ascertain whether the appliances furnished are safe and suitable; and a servant has a right to assume, without inquiry or examination, that the appliances furnished him are safe and suitable. Lasure v. Manufacturing Co., 18 S. C. 281. Of course, if he uses a machine or other appliance, knowing at the time that it is out of repair to such an extent as to render it unsafe, then another rule applies, with certain qualifications, which it is needless to state here. It does not seem to us that the case of Davis v. Railroad Co., supra, relied upon by the circuit judge, applies. In that case the plaintiff was on the top of the train, waving his lantern as a signal to an approaching train, when the cup of his lantern fell out. The plaintiff, however, did not then sustain the injury complained of; but by reason of the loss of the cup of his lantern he had to descend into the cab to procure another, and in returning to his post on the top of the train was struck by the projecting timbers of a tank while ascending the ladder leading to the top of the car. The question whether there was any negligence on the part of the company in furnishing the plaintiff with a defective lantern was decided upon the ground that there was really no evidence that the lantern from which the cup dropped was defective, except the simple expression of opinion by one of the witnesses that the cup dropped out because of a defect in the lantern. That might very well have happened from some other cause than a defect in the lantern, and no witness testified that he had ever examined or even seen the lantern in question. It is true that the late chief justice, in delivering the opinion of the court, after commenting on the fact that there was no evidence tending to show any defect in the lantern, does use this language: "We find not a word in the testimony on that subject, at least none to the precise point necessary to inculpate the defendant, to-wit, that the deceased was using a defective lantern because of the fact that defendant had negligently furnished him with such; on the contrary, it appears that the deceased procured another from the cab, which we suppose was safe and perfect, as there is no testimony to the contrary. He might have taken that one at the first. That he did not was perhaps his own negligence, rather than that of the company. We think there was an entire absence of all testimony directed to the negligence of the company as to the lantern." It is obvious that this language was not used for the purpose of laying down the doctrine that it was the duty of the servant to examine the appliances provided by the master for his use, as that would be inconsistent with the decision in Lasure's Case, supra, and certainly not for the purpose of indicating that the doctrine of contributory negligence could be considered on a motion for nonsuit, as that would have been in conflict with numerous cases there recently decided; but it was only designed to show that, in addition to the fact that there was no evidence to show that the defendant company had furnished the defendant with a defective lantern, the evidence, on the contrary, tended to show that safe and suitable lanterns had been furnished by the company for the use of its servants, and, if there was any fault at all, it lay with the plaintiff, rather than the defendant. Besides, in this case, the testimony tended to show that the work required of the plaintiff had to be done so quickly as to afford no time or opportunity for him to examine the sacks furnished him, whereas it was not so in the case of the lanterns. The judgment of this court is that the judgment of the circuit court be reversed, and that the case be remanded to that court for a new trial.

McGOWAN, J., concurs.

BOWEN v. CAROLINA, C. G. & C. R. Co.

(*Supreme Court of South Carolina.* June 18, 1891.)

CORPORATIONS—ACTION FOR PRESIDENT'S SALARY—EVIDENCE—INSTRUCTIONS.

1. Where, in an action to recover salary by a railroad president, it is claimed that his services were gratuitous, and that he did not intend to charge therefor at the time they were rendered, it is not error to charge that "the position of the defense is that the president did not intend to charge, * * * and that he never thought about charging till he got out of office."

2. In an action to recover for such services upon a *quantum meruit*, a charge that "the salaries of railway presidents are very high, and much higher than that of state officials, and are made so because of the great responsibility attached to the office, and the high order of ability required," is not erroneous as violating the constitutional provision prohibiting a charge upon the facts.

3. One who, against objection, introduces testimony upon a point not raised by the pleadings, cannot object to the giving of a charge based upon such testimony.

4. The fact that a construction company agreed with a railway company to pay the salaries of its officers does not relieve the latter from liability in the absence of an agreement to that effect.

5. A misstatement of the testimony in the charge to the jury is a cause for a new trial, and cannot be presented for the first time in the supreme court.

6. The supreme court will not consider a matter not shown by the record to have been presented to the lower court for determination.

Appeal from common pleas circuit court of Aiken county; HUDSON, Judge.

Action by R. E. Bowen against Carolina, Cumberland Gap & Chicago Railroad Company to recover salary. Judgment for plaintiff. Defendant appealed. Affirmed.

The court gave the following charge:
"The plaintiff, R. E. Bowen, brings this action against the Carolina, Cumberland Gap & Chicago Railroad Company to recover of that company five thousand dollars, the amount claimed to be due him for his salary as president of that road from the 27th day of November, 1887, to the 27th day of November, 1888,—one year's salary. The complaint has two counts, so to speak, or causes of action. The first lays claim to this salary upon a promise,—contract express; and then, in the second count, upon an implied contract, commonly called in law-books, 'quantum meruit,' claiming that his services were well worth $5,000.00, and that the defendants are bound in law to pay it. The answer of the defendant is that there was no contract; and, in the next place, his services were not worth $5,000.00. It devolves upon the plaintiff to make out his case by the preponderance of evidence. In this court you are governed by a more moderate rule than in the court of general sessions, and you have been sitting in both courts; and in that court you cannot convict unless you are satisfied beyond a reasonable doubt, but in the court of common pleas you render your verdict according to the preponderance of evidence, so that, if the evidence in favor of the plaintiff is sufficient to establish his claim by preponderating over the evidence of the defendant, why, the plaintiff is entitled to a verdict.

"The first question you are to determine is whether the office to which he was elected had not had affixed to it a salary of five thousand dollars. If that was the case, and he was elected to the office,—if that was the contract between the parties (the company and the president,)—as matter of course he should be paid the salary of $5,000.00. If that was affixed to the office, —if it was a five thousand dollars salaried office,—and he was elected to fill it, and did fill it for the space of the year for which he sued, he would be entitled to recover. Well, in order to show that such was the fact, the plaintiff introduced a contract that was made before President Hagood was elected. (I believe it was before or during his term of office.) It was a contract made between the company and a construction company,—the Atlantic and Northwestern Construction Company. It was signed by the railroad company as well as by the construction company. In that contract this railroad company stipulates that this Atlantic and

Northwestern Construction Company is to build the entire road, and that construction company also stipulates to pay the officers' salaries of the president and officers of the company—the railroad company—and characterizes them; and the president's salary is fixed at $5,000.00; and then there is evidence introduced to show that the salary of President Hagood, who served for three years, was $5,000.00,—he so testified himself; and there is evidence to show that his salary quarterly was audited at $1,250.00 for one quarter,—four hundred and sixteen and something for one month,—and then the testimony in regard to the payment,—so much of it as was paid, and so much as was not. In addition to that, he has introduced the evidence that that executive committee during the presidency of Mr. Bowen audited his salary account at $5,000.00. It is claimed upon this testimony that five thousand dollars was the recognized compensation for the president of this company, and the company had committed itself—contracted—in this way to pay five thousand dollars to the president. Against this the defense has introduced testimony; for instance, some testimony from President Hagood that some years he did not intend to charge, and that some of the other officers did not, and that, after Presiden. Bowen went out of office, the present board disapproved of the auditing of his account for his salary of five thousand dollars; and it is contended by the defense that he didn't intend to charge the road any fixed salary or regular salary; that his services were, in other words, gratuitous; and that he could not convert into a charge that which he intended as a gratuity. Now, I charge you, gentlemen of the jury, that, if you find—and you have heard all the papers read; I cannot recite them—if you find from the testimony, written and oral, the documentary writing from the company, contracts, and so forth,—if you find that to this office was attached a salary of five thousand dollars; that it was recognized by the company,—then the present plaintiff is entitled to his services for one year to five thousand dollars, unless there is something else to prevent him from recovering. In other words, if you find that five thousand dollars was his salary, you will have one difficulty removed. But it is further contended by the defense that the railroad company was not responsible because it made a contract with the Atlantic and Northwestern Construction Company to pay this salary, and therefore, when the plaintiff took his office, he knew of that contract, and it was implied by his so doing that he was to look to the construction company for his salary, and not to the railroad company. I charge you that it does not absolve the railroad company from liability to its own officers. It merely binds the construction company to pay these salaries. It creates an obligation on the part of the construction company to pay the officers of the railroad company; and the officers, in order to be bound by that, would have to be a party to the contract, and when they took office it would have to be made to show that they took the

offices with that understanding. But the contract does not show that. It only shows that the construction company undertook to help the railroad company pay its officers, and the officers taking office afterwards would not be bound to look to it. They would really have two sources to look to. They would have the construction company to look to, and, if it did not pay, they could fall back upon the railroad company, unless there was some further consideration by which they would discharge, either expressly or by implication, the railroad company from that liability to them. Well, then, it is conceded furthermore by the defense that the president, as a member of that executive committee, was in possession of certain assets for the purpose of paying off the floating indebtedness of the company and all the salaries that he would have a right to pay, and that, he being in possession of these assets, it should be considered that he was paid. That is the substance of the contention, and the object of introducing that testimony. But this testimony, so far as I remember it, (your recollection must be better than mine,) shows that that stipulation was made by the railroad company at the time that the contractor Potts took charge of this short end, and that it was necessary that an arrangement of that sort should be made before Potts would undertake the work, and that it only referred to the debts existing at that time, but not to any subsequently contracted; and the president's salary was a subsequent debt. Such, gentlemen, must be the interpretation of that contract. All that stipulation of 'the floating indebtedness' should be applied to the debts existing at that time and before the executing of that contract,—a debt or debts then existing; so that Potts would not be interfered with, so as not to have the obligation of the company to him hampered by the existence of the floating indebtedness.

"Well, now, if you find that five thousand dollars was the salary contracted by the company to the president, the plaintiff here, and if you should find from the testimony that there was nothing in these other stipulations or from the facts proven that would deprive him of his salary, your verdict would have to be for the plaintiff for five thousand dollars; but if you find that there was no fixed salary, but that the plaintiff is willing to recover only what his services are worth, then you have another and different question before you,—one, which probably will be attended with some difficulty on your part in arriving at a correct conclusion,—and that is the quantum meruit count in the complaint. Now, in regard to that, gentlemen, there is evidence that the services of a railroad president are to be estimated from various circumstances, various elements entering into the services of a railroad president going to show what salary he should have. A man may be elected, and is generally elected,—ought to be elected,—with a view to his services to be rendered to the company in its then condition: and when he is elected president of a railroad company, the railroad of which is then only in process of construction, you have heard from the testimony its many things to look after, and you have got to take into consideration the time it is necessary, when away from home, the various matters he has to look after, the energy and zeal with which he should push the work, and the responsibility that rests upon him as the head and guide and leader of the men for the time being. All these matters are to be taken into consideration, his personal address, his standing in the country through which the road is to run, his influence, judgment, education, his experience in railroading, railroad matters, experience in business,—all these are to be taken into consideration in fixing the value of his services; and you will observe from the testimony in this case that the salaries of railroad presidents in the land are very high, much higher than the salaries of the officers of the state, who are put in office by the people. There is no office in the state of South Carolina which would begin to reach the salaries of presidents of long lines of railroads. Those salaries run— I forget from the testimony what amounts are spoken of, but some are very large, and I suppose, if we were correctly informed, you might find the salary of some president equal to the salary of the president of the United States; I don't pretend to tell you what, but I tell you these salaries are large, and are made so because of the great responsibility attached to the office, and ardent, laborious, and constant duties attached to the office, for the exercise of which, with proper energy and attention to business, it takes a great deal of his time, and requires a high order of ability, executive and administrative, to fill the office; so that, if you find that the salary was not fixed by the company at five thousand dollars, and you must look to the testimony as to the value of his salary to see what it ought to be, then you will take all these things into consideration, and on which sidesoever the preponderance of testimony is you will find your verdict.

"I will now read the requests to charge in behalf of the defense.

"'(1) If the jury find that the plaintiff participated in the proceedings of the executive committee on the 27th day of November, 1888, at which time the resolution fixing his salary was passed, then such resolution is null and void, and does not bind the defendant company.' I charge you that my understanding of that resolution— I don't understand that the resolution fixes the salary. Mr. Henderson, (interrupting:) 'It audited it.' Mr. Croft: 'That is what I call "fixing it." It is the only time it is mentioned in the minutes.' (Mr. Croft reads the resolution beginning: 'The following resolution was adopted: Resolved, that the purchase of land in the town of Edgefield, * * * the account of R. E. Bowen for salary, $5,000.00, from November the 27th, 1887, to November the 27th, 1888, was audited, allowed, and ordered to be paid, and so forth.' Question by the foreman of the jury: 'Who was present? Answer. R. E. Bowen, Dr. T. G. Croft, and J. S. Cothran.'. The Court, (continuing:) I, gentlemen, will instruct you that that was not a making of any contract with the president, by the committee, but the resolution shows merely that his account as claimed was audited and allowed; and I don't interpret this resolution to mean that that committee for the first time fixed his salary, but that he put in his claim for his salary of five thousand dollars, and they audited it, and allowed it, so that I charge you that this first proposition has no application to the case, unless you should find that it undertook to enter into a contract with him for that salary, and that he, as a member of that committee, participated and did participate. That contract, under those circumstances, ought not to stand; but to audit an account, or being a member of the auditing committee, ought not to invalidate it.

"'(2) That the resolution of the executive committee fixing the salary of the plaintiff is not binding upon the defendant company, unless such resolution was afterwards approved by the board of directors. And if the jury find that the board of directors have not approved the action of the executive committee in passing such resolution, then the plaintiff cannot recover upon his first cause of action.' This is a sound proposition, if that was a resolution fixing the salary, or, in other words, making a contract with the president as to what his salary should be; but, if the resolution which was passed there was merely the auditing of his account, then this proposition has no application.

"'(3) That under the by-laws of the defendant company it is the province of the board of directors to fix the salaries of the officers of the company, and no independent action of the executive committee fixing such salaries can bind the defendant company.' Yes, that is correct. I don't think the executive committee, as an independent committee, would have the power, outside of the board of directors, or meeting of the stockholders, and so forth, to fix the salary of the president, unless the board of directors would approve of it; but the interpretation I made of that resolution.—it was merely passing upon what they recognized as his salary.

"'(4) Under the undisputed evidence in this case the resolution passed by the executive committee fixing the salary of the plaintiff as president is not binding upon the defendant company.' That is a correct proposition, if they did then and there fix the salary as a matter of original contract with him; but that, as I charged you, is not my interpretation.

"'(5) That, under the contract between the defendant company and the Atlantic and Northwestern Construction Company, it was agreed that the said Atlantic and Northwestern Construction Company should pay the salary of the president of the defendant company, and, if the jury find that the plaintiff accepted office knowing of such agreement, he is bound to look to the said Atlantic and Northwestern Construction Company for such salary, and could not, under such circumstances, claim the same of the defendant.' I cannot charge that request, because, as I told you, gentlemen of the jury, taking that contract, standing as it does, and it merely giving an officer of the company two companies to look to for his pay, the company of which he was the officer, a railroad officer, why, ultimately the railroad company was bound, and the railroad company's duty would be, to make the construction company pay the salary; and if it did not or could not, why, the officer should not lose his salary, and the railroad company is responsible for it, and the officer could look to it for his pay, and, unless he has made a contract with the company, either expressly or by the necessary implication, that he would not look to the railroad company, but look to the Atlantic and Northwestern Construction Company, the railroad company would be responsible. The railroad company is responsible primarily to its officers for their pay when it employs them or elects them; but the railroad company might and could under that contract call upon the construction company to pay its officers, and, if the construction company violated its contract with the railroad company, and did not pay its officers, the officers could go upon the railroad company; and, so far as the officer is concerned, there is nothing in the contract to prevent him from suing the railroad company in the first instance. That is the view I take of the contract. Now, when President Bowen took office, if he knew of the existence of this contract, that of itself did not make him a party to it. He was not bound by it. Not at all. There would have to be some further evidence going to show that he made a further contract with the railroad company not to look to it, but to look to the construction company. Now, if there is any evidence of that fact, you would have no trouble at all in saying, 'Go to the construction company;' but you have no evidence of that fact, as I remember; but if you remember any you can be governed by it.

"'(6) That, if the plaintiff intended to look to the defendant for his salary for the year commencing November the 27th, 1887, then it was his duty to notify the board of directors of the defendant company of such intent, and, if he failed to do so, and acted in such a manner as to lead the directors to believe that he would make no charge for such services, but would continue to serve from that time as president without compensation, as he had done in the past, then he cannot now legally demand compensation for such service.' The request is a long one, and, to be correctly disposed of, it will have to be reviewed in detail. 'That, if the plaintiff intended to look to the defendant for his salary for the year commencing November the 27th, 1887, then it was his duty to notify the board of directors of defendant company of such intent.' Not at all. A man is not bound to notify any board of directors that he is going to look for pay, because this is the contract. If there is any salary fixed at all in the contract when he is elected or made an officer, the contract is implied, if not express. When he wants his pay he is bound to call upon them for it; and, if they do not pay it, he can institute his action. 'And if he failed to do so, and acted in such a manner as to lead the directors to expect that he would make no charge for such services, but would continue from that time to serve as presi-

dent without compensation, as he had done in the past, then he cannot now legally demand compensation for such services.' Here is an assertion. I could not instruct you that 'he had in the past' served as president gratuitously. 'He cannot legally demand compensation for such services,'—meaning that, if one undertakes to render services gratuitously, that is without compensation, if he intends to make no charge, and acts in such a manner as to show that he did not intend to make any claim, but that he gave his services free, then he could not afterwards make a charge; that is the meaning of that request and if that be the real meaning that is good law, but in order to apply it to this case you would have to find that President Bowen entered upon that office with the understanding that he was to get no pay; that his services were to be gratuitous; or that he was to perform all his services for nothing, making a gift of them, of all his labor; and so, now, if the evidence shows that, why, after he comes out of office he could not make any charge; but you must find that that was his intent from the evidence.

"'(7) If the jury believe that the plaintiff did not intend to exact compensation at the time he rendered such service, he could not afterwards change his mind, and make a charge for the same.' That is a repetition,—really what is meant by the latter part of the preceding request, as I understand it; and it is good law if the jury find from the evidence that such is the fact; but as I said, if there is no evidence to show it, then the request would have no application. The position of the defense is that the president did not intend to charge; that his services were rendered gratuitously; and that he never thought about charging till he got out of office. If that is a fact, he cannot recover; but, if it is not a fact, then he is entitled to his salary.

"Another thing: There is evidence as to the small earnings of the company, its straitened circumstances, and inability to pay. Why, with that you have nothing to do. If you had a case against one of your fellow-citizens for a thousand dollars, and you were to sue him here in court, it would not be a good defense that he had no property, was not doing business, was not getting along well, and could not pay. A long, that would not justify a jury in giving him a verdict. Whether the railroad company can pay or not is not the question, and has nothing to do with the issue. The only thing you have to do is to say whether or not this plaintiff is entitled to the verdict. You have nothing to do with those other questions. They rest with the railroad company.

"First, if you find that his office when he took it was attached a salary of five thousand dollars by the company, fixed previously or during Gov. Hagood's presidency, and that was the existing salary, he ought to recover his five thousand dollars, because there is no going outside of the testimony to say that he ought not to recover. If there is no fixed salary, then you have got to fix one according to what you think his services are worth. If you find that the company contracted to pay the sum of five thousand dollars, you will have to find for him five thousand dollars. If you find that the company did not contract to pay him five thousand dollars, but he was to be paid whatever his services were worth, fix his salary, and give him whatever it is worth. If you find that he was to get nothing, you will find for the defendant. If you find for the plaintiff, say, 'We find for the plaintiff' so many dollars. But if you find that he is entitled to nothing, and you find for the defendant, say, 'We find for the defendant.'"

Defendant took the following exceptions, among others, to the charge:

"(2) Because his honor, the presiding judge, charged the jury that in ascertaining whether the office of president of the defendant company had a fixed salary attached to such office they were to consider the fact of the Atlantic and Northwestern Construction Company having agreed with the defendant company to pay the salary of such office at $5,000 per year, and had characterized 'the president's salary as fixed at $5,000;' and that the jury were also to consider that during the plaintiff's administration the executive committee had audited his salary account at $5,000. It is respectfully submitted that such charge was erroneous, for it allowed the jury to find that the defendant company was bound by the rate of salary agreed upon by the construction company, where his honor should have charged that, as between the president and the railway company, the salary was regulated by the by-laws of the railway company, and could only be fixed by the directors of said company."

"(4) Because his honor, the presiding judge, erred in charging the jury that the officers of the railroad company would have two sources to look to for their salaries: First, to the construction company, and, if that company failed to pay the same, then such officers could fall back on the railway company. It is submitted that such charge was erroneous, for it assumed that the railway company was bound to pay the $5,000 to the president if the construction company failed to pay. Such charge fixed $5,000 absolutely as the amount to be paid by the railway company, and made the company's liability to depend solely upon the fact that the construction company had failed to meet its obligation. (5) Because his honor, the presiding judge, charged the jury that 'the salaries of railway presidents in the land are very high, much higher than the salaries of the officers of the state, who are put in office by the people. There is no office in the state of South Carolina which would begin to reach the salaries of presidents of long lines of railroads. Those salaries run,—I forget from the testimony what amounts are spoken of, but some are very large; and I suppose, if we were correctly informed, you might find the salary of some presidents equal to the salary of the president of the United States. I don't pretend to tell you what, but I tell you their salaries are large, and are made so because of the great responsibility attached to the office, and ardent and laborious and constant duties attached to the office, for the exercise of which with proper energy and attention to business it takes a great deal of his time, and requires a high order of ability, executive and administrative, to fill the office; so that, if you find that the salary was not fixed by the company at five thousand dollars,—and you must look to the testimony as to the value of his salary to see what it ought to be,—then you will take all things into consideration, and, on which side soever the preponderance of testimony is, you will find your verdict;' and in this it is submitted that his honor erred, for such charge was upon the facts, and also upon facts which were not relevant to the issue, and was calculated to confuse, and did confuse, the jury in reaching a verdict."

"(10) That his honor, the presiding judge, erred in refusing to charge the defendant's fifth and sixth requests. (11) That the comments of the presiding judge upon the defendant's seventh request were calculated to confuse the jury, in that his honor attributed a position to the defendant they never contended for, namely, that the plaintiff did not think of charging for his services until he got out of office. The position taken by the defendant was that the plaintiff did not intend to charge for his services at the time they were performed, and that his honor charged in such manner as to lead the jury to believe that, in order to find for the defendant, they must have express evidence that the plaintiff intended to serve gratuitously; and such charge precluded the jury from arriving at such a conclusion by a proper inference which would arise from the circumstances and the conduct of the plaintiff in this case. (12) That it appears from the whole case that there was no evidence showing that a salary had been fixed to the office of president previous to or during the administration of Gov. Hagood as president, and his honor erred in submitting such a question to the jury. His honor also erred in charging the jury that, 'if there is no fixed salary, then you have got to fix one according to what you think his services are worth.' Such instruction amounted to a positive direction to the jury to find for the plaintiff, and deprived the defendant of all chances of the jury finding in its favor."

Croft & Chafee, for appellant. *Henderson Bros.,* for respondent.

McIver, J. This action was brought by the plaintiff to recover the sum of $5,000, alleged to be due him for his salary as president of said company from the 27th of November, 1887, to the 27th of November, 1888. In this complaint the plaintiff states as his first cause of action a special contract on the part of the defendant company to pay him the said sum of money as his salary for the year mentioned, and his second cause of action is based upon a *quantum meruit.* The defendant answered, setting up as its first defense a general denial; and for a further defense alleges that, though the plaintiff was president of said company for the year mentioned in the complaint, yet that for a part of that time the railway was in the course of construction, and was not completed until November, 1888, and that plaintiff never had charge of or operated said railway, but that it was under construction by the contractor, George Potts; and that under the contract for the construction of said railway it was expressly stipulated that the Atlantic & Northwestern Construction Company was to pay the salary of the president of defendant company; and that plaintiff accepted the office of president, knowing of such stipulation, and is therefore estopped from claiming his salary from defendant company. The records of the defendant company, the contract with the construction company, and the contract with Potts, together with the verbal testimony of witnesses taken in court and by commission, were all offered in evidence. There was also some testimony adduced by defendant, and received against the objection of plaintiff, tending to show that certain assets of the defendant company had been placed in the hands of the plaintiff for the purpose of paying off its debts at the time the contract was entered into with Potts for the construction of that portion of the road lying between Aiken and Edgefield. The charge of his honor, Judge HUDSON, is set out in full in the "case," and should be embraced in the report of the case; and under that charge the jury found a verdict in favor of the plaintiff for the full amount of his claim, and, judgment being entered thereon, the defendant appeals upon the several grounds set out in the record.

The first exception imputes error to the circuit judge in not requiring the plaintiff, on the application of defendant, to elect upon which of the two causes of action stated in the complaint he rested his case. To dispose of this exception it is sufficient to say that the "case" as prepared for argument here fails to show that any such application was made to the circuit judge. We can discover nothing in the record that indicates that this matter was ever brought to the attention of the judge, or that he made any ruling in reference thereto. There is nothing, therefore, in the record for this court, as an appellate tribunal, to review.

The second and fourth exceptions may be considered together. These two exceptions are based upon a misconception of the judge's charge in reference to the matter therein referred to. His honor merely called the attention of the jury to the contract between the railway company and the construction company, in which the latter had assumed the payment of the president's salary at the rate of $5,000 a year as one of the circumstances which they might consider in determining the question whether the railway company had agreed to pay that salary to the plaintiff when he was elected president; but he did not say, nor could it be implied from anything he did say, that the defendant company was thereby bound to pay that salary to the plaintiff. He did say, however,—and in this we think he was right,—that the fact that the construction company had in that contract, to which the plaintiff was not a party, assumed the payment of the president's salary, would not relieve the defendant company from liability therefor, provided they had received the services of the plaintiff as president, under an agreement, either express or implied, to pay him, in the one case, the amount agreed upon, or, in the other, the amount which his services were reasonably worth. That contract did not bind the plaintiff to look alone to the construction company for the payment of his salary. There was nothing in it which forbade the plaintiff from holding the defendant company liable for the salary, if any was due, in case the construction company failed to comply with its agreement with the railway company to pay the salary.

The third exception alleges error on the part of the circuit judge in charging the jury that the defendant company set up as a defense that the plaintiff had received certain assets of the railway company at the making of the contract with Potts, out of which the plaintiff was to pay the debts of the company, including his own salary, and that such stipulation only applied to the debts existing at the date of the Potts contract. While it is true that no such defense was set up in the answer, yet the defendant insisted, against plaintiff's objection, upon introducing testimony to that effect, which could have been for no other purpose than to show that plaintiff had been provided with means out of which he could and should have paid himself whatever was due on his salary, if anything, and all that the circuit judge said to the jury was, not that such a defense was set up in the answer, but that it was contended by defendant that, plaintiff having been furnished with these assets, any claim that he may have had should be considered as paid; and he then went on to construe the contract, which, being in writing, it was his province to do, and properly held that the stipulation in that contract only related to debts then existing, and had no reference to any that might afterwards be incurred. As this Potts contract bears date 25th of November, 1887, it manifestly could have no application to the plaintiff's claim for salary from the 27th day of November, 1887, to the 27th of November, 1888. There is therefore no foundation for the third exception.

The sixth, seventh, eighth, and ninth exceptions may be considered together, as they all relate to what was said to the jury in reference to the action of the executive committee in auditing the salary of the plaintiff. We do not see that we can add anything to what was said to the jury by the circuit judge in reference to this matter. The jury were distinctly told that the executive committee had no authority to fix the salary of the president, and we think it was correctly added that, according to the proper construction of the resolution adopted by them, and offered in evidence, from the minutes, they did not undertake to do so; and, furthermore, we do not see how the defendant could have possibly been prejudiced by anything said to them on this subject.

The tenth exception imputes error to the

circuit judge in refusing defendant's fifth and sixth requests to charge. These requests called upon the judge to instruct the jury that under the contract with the construction company, by which it assumed the payment of the president's salary, the plaintiff, if cognizant of such agreement, at the time he accepted the office of president, was bound to look to the construction company for his salary, and could not hold the defendant company liable therefor, unless he had given notice to the defendant company at the time he accepted office of his intention to look to the railway company for payment of his salary; or, if he acted in such a way as to lead the directors of the railway company to believe that he intended to make no charge against the defendant company, then he cannot now be permitted to make a charge. So much of these requests as relates to the service by plaintiff being gratuitous will be passed over until we come to the eleventh exception, with which it is more properly connected. As we have already indicated, we do not see how the contract between the defendant company and the construction company, whereby the latter undertook to pay the salary of the president, can affect the question in this case. The plaintiff was no party to that contract, which was made long before the plaintiff was elected president, and, though he doubtless knew of that contract, he, as an individual, was in no way bound by its terms, and could not be, unless it was shown that he had agreed to look to the construction company alone for his salary, which is not pretended. If he accepted the office of president, either under a special contract as to his salary or under an implied agreement that he was to be paid whatever his services might be reasonably worth, he certainly has a right to recover from the company which employed him either the amount stipulated for or the amount which his services were reasonably worth, as the case might be. Surely the fact that his employer had obtained from another an obligation to pay such amount could not possibly affect the plaintiff's right to recover from the party who employed him. The utmost effect that contract could have would be to give the railway company a claim against the construction company for any amount which the former might have to pay its president for his salary in case of the failure of the latter to pay the same; but it certainly cannot have the effect of relieving the railway company from liability to pay its president's salary, unless there was some agreement to that effect with the president.

The eleventh exception complains that the comments of the circuit judge upon defendant's seventh request were calculated to confuse the jury. That request, just referred to, relates to the question whether plaintiff's services were gratuitous at the time they were rendered. An examination of the judge's charge will show that his remarks to the jury upon this subject were free from exception. He did not instruct the jury that there must be "express evidence" that plaintiff intended to serve the

defendant company gratuitously, and it does not seem to us that there is anything in the language used which would properly warrant, or even would be likely to lead the jury to such an inference.

The first part of the twelfth exception complains that the circuit judge erred in submitting to the jury the question whether the amount of the salary of the president was fixed previous to or during the administration of Gov. Hagood, the predecessor of plaintiff, when there was no evidence to that effect. In the first place, we do not see that any such question was left to the jury, as the judge simply called the attention of the jury to the testimony as to what occurred in reference to the payment of the president's salary during the administration of Gov. Hagood, which had been relied on by plaintiff as a circumstance tending to show the amount fixed as the salary of that office. And, in the second place, if the judge misstated the testimony to the jury, the remedy was by a motion for a new trial before the circuit court, and not by appeal to this court. State v. Jones, 21 S. C. 596.

The only remaining question is that raised by the fifth and the latter part of the twelfth exception, as to whether the circuit judge violated the constitutional provision prohibiting a charge upon the facts. The specifications of the particular portion of the charge in the fifth exception do not show that the judge either expressed or intimated any opinion as to any question of fact which the jury were called upon to determine. There was some testimony tending to show that the salaries of railway presidents were sometimes high, and what was said upon this subject was more by way of illustration than as indicating any opinion on the part of the judge. Fitzsimons v. Guanahani Co., 16 S. C. 192; Rembert v. Railway Co., 31 S. C. 309, 9 S. E. Rep. 968. The specification contained in the latter part of the twelfth exception is a sentence extracted from the charge, which, when read in its proper connection, as it should be, affords no ground whatever for the complaint made. The judgment of this court is that the judgment of the circuit court be affirmed.

McGOWAN, J., concurs.

DRAFFIN v. CHARLESTON, C. & C. R. Co.

(*Supreme Court of South Carolina.* July 21, 1891.)

CONTRACTS TO FURNISH CROSS-TIES — BURDEN TO SHOW DEFECT—ADMISSIONS—ESTOPPEL.

1. Where a contract with a railroad company for furnishing ties provided that they should be accepted or rejected by the company's inspector, the burden of proof is on the company to show that ties, used by it without such inspection, were defective.

2. In an action on contract for furnishing ties, the court charged that the defendant had set up admissions of plaintiff that a very large amount of ties had been paid for, which was a question for the jury to determine. He then charged that such admissions must be received and weighed with great care, and would not estop plaintiff, "unless defendant has done some-

thing or in some way acted upon them." Held not erroneous, as invading the province of the jury, nor as inapplicable to the case.

Appeal from common pleas circuit court of Lancaster county; J. J. NORTON, Judge.

Action by R. W. Draffin against the Charleston, Cincinnati & Chicago Railroad Company for ties furnished on contract. Verdict and judgment for plaintiff, and defendant appeals. Affirmed.

J. F. Hart and R. E. & R. B. Allison, for appellant. Jones & Williams, for respondent.

McIVER, J. This was an action to recover a balance alleged to be due plaintiff under a written contract with the defendant company for the delivery of a large number of railroad cross-ties, according to certain specifications contained in the contract. The plaintiff having recovered a verdict for $600, the defendant moved for a new trial on the minutes, which being refused, judgment was entered on the verdict, from which defendant appeals upon the several grounds set out in the record.

The third, fourth, sixth, and seventh grounds raise questions of fact only, and this being an action at law, pure and simple, it is very obvious that we have no jurisdiction to consider such questions. The first ground imputes error to the circuit judge in charging the jury "that, if the defendant, the railroad company, took up and used the cross-ties of plaintiff, whether they had been accepted or rejected by the inspector of the company, under the contract between the parties, the onus rested on the defendant to show that said cross-ties were defective." We do not see any error in this. The contract provided that the cross-ties to be delivered by plaintiff were to be inspected by an officer or agent of the company, and those which came up to the specifications were to be accepted and paid for at the stipulated price, while those which did not come up to the specifications were to be rejected. Hence the natural inference would be, and the jury would have the perfect right to assume, in the absence of any evidence to the contrary, that all the cross-ties accepted and used by the company came up to the contract, and were to be paid for accordingly. But this natural, and we may say necessary, inference was susceptible of being rebutted by testimony showing that, although the cross-ties were received, yet in fact some of them did not come up to contract; and this was what the jury were told, in effect, when they were instructed that the onus of proof would be upon the defendant to show that, although the cross-ties were received and used by the company, yet in fact some of them were defective. The second ground of appeal does not correctly represent the charge of the circuit judge, and for this reason, if there were no other, cannot be sustained; for the jury were not charged that the defendant would be chargeable as for good ties at the rate stipulated for in the contract, if the defendant used the cross-ties of plaintiff, whether they had been inspected and received or rejected by the inspector, but

the charge was that the company would be presumably chargeable, in such case, for good cross-ties. This was but saying, in a different form, the same thing which is made the subject of the first ground of appeal already considered.

The fifth ground complains that the circuit judge "invaded the province of the jury in charging that they must receive and weigh the admissions of the plaintiff with great care, and that, unless the defendant was misled by them, the plaintiff is not now bound by them." The circuit judge did not use the language here attributed to him, but what he did say was "that you must receive and weigh these admissions of the plaintiff with great care; unless the defendant had done something, or had in some way acted upon them, they cannot have effect as estoppels against his claim now." This remark was immediately after the judge had stated that the defendant had set up as a defense the admission of the plaintiff that a very large amount of the cross-ties had been paid for, which the jury were told was a question of fact for them to determine, and then followed the charge excepted to as to the law of estoppel; which, as we learn from the argument, was not objected to as presenting an incorrect proposition as to the law of estoppel, but as inapplicable to the case. And the case of Thomson v. Sexton, 15 S. C. 95, where this court said: "Error may be committed, not only by laying down to the jury incorrect general principles of law, but also by applying correct principles of law to cases in which they are not properly applicable." The defendant manifestly relied, as a part, at least, of its defense, upon certain admissions alleged to have been made by the plaintiff, and it is very obvious that such a defense might raise both questions of fact and law. The questions of fact would be whether such admissions were in fact made, and, if so, whether they were true, or made under a mistake, and these would be questions for the jury. The question of law, however, would be whether such admissions, whether true or false, or made under a mistake, would amount to an estoppel. It seems to us that the practical effect of the judge's charge was to leave the questions of fact to the jury without any intimation whatever as to his own opinion, and then to lay down the law of estoppel, in which we see no error. The judgment of this court is that the judgment of the circuit court be affirmed.

McGOWAN, J., concurs.

BOYD v. WILSON.

(Supreme Court of Georgia. Jan. 17, 1891.)

EXECUTION FOR TAXES—DEBTOR'S RIGHT TO POINT OUT PROPERTY.

Code Ga. § 3641, providing that, when a defendant in fi. fa. shall point out any property on which to levy, which is in the hands of a person not a party to the judgment, the officer shall not levy thereon, applies only to executions on judgments, and not to fi. fas. issued by a tax collector under section 891, which provides that defendant "shall have the privilege of pointing out property," but that the execution may be levied upon any property when the collector deems it necessary; and in the latter case the officer may levy on lands in the possession of another claiming title, although defendant possesses other property subject to levy. Affirming Wilson v. Boyd, 10 S. E. Rep. 499.

On rehearing.

For former reports, see 10 S. E. Rep. 499, and 12 S. E. Rep. 744. Code Ga. § 3641, provides that, when a defendant in *fi. fa.* shall point out any property on which to levy which is in the hands of a person not a party to the judgment, the officer shall not levy thereon. Section 891 provides that the defendant in *fi. fa.* issued by a tax collector for taxes shall have the privilege of pointing out property, but it shall be within the discretion of the collector to have the officer levy the same upon any other property, when he deems it necessary.

PER CURIAM. Petition for rehearing denied, this court having already decided in the same case that section 891 of the Code applies to pointing out property under tax executions. See 84 Ga. 36, 10 S. E. Rep. 499. Section 8641 of the Code applies, not to tax executions, but to executions founded on judgments.

RICHMOND & D. R. CO. v. GEORGE.

(Supreme Court of Appeals of Virginia. July 9, 1891.)

INJURIES TO EMPLOYE—DEFECTIVE CARS — NEGLIGENCE OF FELLOW-SERVANT — OBJECTION NOT RAISED BELOW.

1. In an action for personal injuries by a brakeman against a railroad company, it appeared that plaintiff, on a car on the front end of the train, attempted to descend to uncouple the engine. The bottom rung of the car ladder was missing, and, while feeling for it with his foot, the engineer, without the customary signal, suddenly backed the engine against plaintiff and injured him. The night was dark, and the bumper on the end of the car was broken off, so that the tender came up close to it. Plaintiff did not know the bumper had been broken off, and it was shown that the train was made up under the supervision of the regular car inspector, who was not called as a witness by the company. *Held,* the defective condition of the car was the proximate cause of the injury, and defendant was liable, although the negligence of a fellow-servant, the engineer, contributed to the injury.

2. The objection that the damages are excessive cannot first be made in the supreme court.

Error to circuit court, Franklin county; S. G. WHITTLE, Judge.

Action by George against Richmond & Danville Railway Company for personal injuries. Verdict and judgment for plaintiff, and defendant brings error. Affirmed.

Mr. Blackford, for plaintiff in error. *Green & Miller,* for defendant in error.

LEWIS, P. The real merits of the case in this court lie within a narrow compass. The action was for injuries received by the plaintiff while in the employ of the defendant company as a brakeman. The charge in the declaration was that the injuries were caused by the negligence of the defendant in failing to provide suitable and safe cars and other appliances for the performance of the work required of

the plaintiff in the course of the employment. The jury found accordingly, and, judgment having been entered in conformity with the verdict, the defendant obtained a writ of error.

The accident occurred between 10 and 11 o'clock in the night, on the 12th of March, 1889. At that time the plaintiff was employed as front brakeman on a "mixed train," running between Elba Junction and Rocky Mount, a distance of about 35 miles. When the train, on the occasion in question, arrived at Rocky Mount, the plaintiff was riding on top of the front car, which was a box-car. It was his duty to descend from the train, upon its arrival at that point, and with his lantern to signal the engineer to "give slack," by which is meant to slightly reverse the engine, in order to "slack the coupling," that the pin may be "lifted," and the front car uncoupled from the tender. The engine is then put away for the night in a house provided for the purpose. The evidence of the plaintiff was that in descending the ladder of the car next to the engine, to signal the engineer, he for the first time discovered that the bottom rung of the ladder was missing. "And in reaching down with my left leg," he says, "trying to find the missing rung, which had been broken off, I brought my right thigh in a horizontal position," when the engineer suddenly, without a signal, backed the engine. The result was that the plaintiff was caught between the tender and the car and very seriously and permanently crippled. It was customary for the engineer, and the rules of the company require him, to wait for the signal before backing. An examination of the car, immediately after the accident, disclosed the fact that not only was the front ladder defective, but that the car was otherwise unsafe, in that it was provided with a defective and inadequate bumper on the end next to the engine. "The bumper on a car," says one of the defendant's witnesses, "is simply to give brakemen a chance to couple or uncouple," by which was meant to enable the brakeman to go between the cars to couple or uncouple them with safety. Speaking of the car in question, the plaintiff testifies: "This car had no platform, and I do not think it had a good bumper. If it had had a bumper like the others, I would not have got mashed, because the distance between the tender and the car would then have been longer than my thigh, and I could not have been hurt." One of the defendant's witnesses, the engineer of the train, testified that there would still be room enough to couple or uncouple with two or three inches off the bumper, but that if the whole bumper was off it would be different. A witness for the plaintiff, however, who was present when the accident occurred, and whose evidence is uncontradicted, says he noticed a piece of the bumper was off, and that, when he saw it, he remarked it was a wonder the plaintiff had not been killed. "It looked to me," he says, "as if there was five or six inches of the bumper broken off. It looked shivered, not square off." The plaintiff also testified that Orange, one of the brakemen on the train, told him shortly after the accident that he examined the car the next day, and that about four inches of the bumper were missing. This, Orange, as a witness for the defendant, denied; but in the course of his examination he admitted he could not tell how much was missing. There is other evidence to the same effect. But, without stopping to review it, it is enough to say that, viewing the case as we must, in the light of the familiar rule applicable to a demurrer to evidence,—the evidence, not the facts, being certified,—it is established that not only was the car defective, but that but for these defects the misfortune could not have happened.

Contributory negligence on the part of the plaintiff is not shown. Indeed, it is hardly contended for. His uncontradicted testimony is that he was not aware of the dangerous condition of the car before he started in the dark to descend the ladder to signal the engineer. It is not disputed that an employe must be reasonably observant of the machinery he operates, but in the present case there is nothing to show that reasonable diligence on the part of the plaintiff would have sooner discovered the danger of the situation. The train, which consisted of several freight-cars and caboose or passenger car, was made up in the evening at the junction, and while the plaintiff was stationed as a flagman, about a quarter of a mile away, on the main track of the Midland road, nor was he "called in" from that position until the train was ready to start. "I had nothing to do," he testified, "with making up the train. I did not know, when we stated from the junction, the condition of the car. I took it to be a sound car. Before reaching Rocky Mount I had no occasion to descend the ladder. The car was loaded for Rocky Mount; it had no local freight at all. The rear freight-car, next to the caboose, had the local freight, and if I was on the front car when a station was reached I went back over the cars to the one we had to unload, and then got on the caboose, and got back over the train. I did not notice the bumper on the car. I was not so I could throw the light from my lantern on it. I did not know the condition of the ladder or the bumper before I was hurt." It is true the engineer of the train testified that the plaintiff "passed the engine several times that night." But this the plaintiff denies. He said: "I did not go by the engine after we left the junction. I looked at the car all I could. It was a very dark night." And it is needless to say that so much of the defendant's evidence as is in conflict with this statement must, according to the rule above mentioned, be considered as waived.

It appears, moreover, that the train was made up under the supervision of a regular car inspector. Yet the inspector was not examined as a witness, and no explanation of the failure to examine him was offered; nor was any witness called by the defendant, who testified positively as to the condition of the car before the accident happened. The conductor of the train, although he testified in chief that, if there was any defect, it happened after leaving the junction, admitted, on cross-examination, that he had no recollection of "this particular car," and that he made no special examination of any of the cars before leaving the junction. In this state of evidence the plaintiff's right to recover is clear. The doctrine of fellow-servant has no application to the case. It is immaterial, therefore, whether the engineer, in backing the engine without a signal, was negligent or not. Nor is it necessary to inquire whether, upon the facts of the case, the engineer and the plaintiff were fellow-servants; for, be that as it may, the defective condition of the car was the proximate cause of the injury complained of, and for that the company is responsible. It was undoubtedly negligence on the part of the agents of the company, who were charged with the duty of inspecting the car, to send it out in that condition, and their negligence was the company's negligence. It is the universally recognized duty, as well of a railroad company as of any other employer, to provide suitable appliances for the conduct of its business, and to keep them in repair, and if, in consequence of its failure to do so, a servant in its employ is injured, without fault on his part, it cannot successfully defend on the ground of the negligence of a fellow-servant. The servant, although he assumed the ordinary risks of business, including the negligence of fellow-servants, does not contract against the combined negligence of a fellow-servant and of his employer. "To say," said the court in Cayzer v. Taylor, 10 Gray, 274, "that the master should not be responsible [to his servants] for an injury which would not have happened had a safeguard required by law been used, because the engineer was negligent, would be to say, in substance and effect, that he should not be liable at all for an injury resulting from the failure to use it." In the analogous case of Railway Co. v. Cummings, 106 U. S. 700, 1 Sup. Ct. Rep. 493, the court, in approving an instruction given by the trial court, used this language: "We find no error in the instruction. It was, in effect, that if the negligence of the defendant company contributed to—that is to say, had a share in producing—the injury, the company was liable, even though the negligence of a fellow-servant of the plaintiff was contributory also. If the negligence of the company contributed to, it must necessarily have been an immediate cause of, the accident; and it is no defense that another was likewise guilty of wrong." Contributory negligence to defeat the right of action in such a case must be negligence of the party injured. Paulmier v. Railroad Co., 34 N. J. Law, 151. The doctrine that the master is bound to use ordinary care in supplying and maintaining adequately safe instrumentalities for the performance of the work required, and then, if he fail in the performance of this duty, he is as liable to the servant as he would be to a stranger, has been so often asserted by courts of the highest character as to be no longer an open question,—certainly not in this court. As was said in Railroad v. Norment, 84 Va. 167, 4 S. E. Rep. 211: "It is a cruel and inhuman doctrine that the employer, though he is aware that his own neglect to furnish the proper safeguard for the lives and limbs of those in his employment puts them in constant hazard of injury, is not to be held accountable to those employes who, serving him under such circumstances, are injured by his negligent acts and omissions." And to the same effect are Moon's Adm'r v. Railroad Co., 78 Va. 745; Railroad Co. v. Moore's Adm'r, Id. 93; Railroad Co. v. McKenzie, 81 Va. 71, and other cases.

This sufficiently disposes of the case, except the point made in the brief of appellant's counsel, that the damages awarded are excessive. As to this, it is enough to say that the objection, made as it is for the first time in this court, comes too late. The bill of exceptions states that a motion for a new trial was made, but the motion was in general terms. It was not put upon the ground, specifically, that the damages were excessive. The established rule in this state is that, if no objection appear by the bill of exception taken to the overruling of a motion for a new trial to have been made in the trial court to the excessiveness of damages, such objection cannot afterwards be made in the appellate court. And the reason is that, upon a motion to grant a new trial for this cause, the court may impose upon the successful party the alternative of remitting such portion of the damages as justice may require, or submitting to a new trial. 4 Minor, Inst. 557, 872; Law v. Law, 2 Grat. 366. The judgment is affirmed.

WESTERN UNION TEL. CO. v. PETTYJOHN.

(Supreme Court of Appeals of Virginia. July 16, 1891.)

JUSTICE OF THE PEACE—JURISDICTION—TELEGRAPH COMPANIES—FAILURE TO DELIVER DISPATCH.

Under Code Va. § 2989, providing, among other things, that a justice of the peace shall have jurisdiction of any claim to any fine if the amount thereof does not exceed $20, and of other claims where the amount does not exceed $100, a justice has no jurisdiction of an action for the $100 penalty imposed by section 1292 upon telegraph companies for failure to deliver a dispatch, since such penalty is a fine within the meaning of the statute.

Action by J. W. Pettyjohn against the Western Union Telegraph Company for $100 penalty for failure to deliver a telegraph message. Judgment for plaintiff, and defendant brings error. Reversed.

Code Va. § 1292, provides, among other things, that "it shall be the duty of every telegraph or telephone company, upon the arrival of a dispatch at destination, to deliver it promptly to the addressee, where the regulations of the company require such delivery. For every failure to deliver a dispatch as promptly as practicable the company shall forfeit $100 to the sender or to the addressee."

A. S. Holladay, for plaintiff in error. *W. S. Hamilton*, for defendant in error.

LACY, J. This is a writ of error to a judgment of the corporation court of the city of Bristol, rendered on the 14th day of July, 1890. The case is as follows: On the 25th day of July, 1890, a warrant was

issued by a justice of the peace, commanding a constable of Washington county, Va., to summon the petitioner to appear at the mayor's office in the town of Goodson, situated in said county of Washington, on the 15th day of February, 1890, to answer the complaint of said John W. Pettyjohn upon a claim of $100 as a forfeiture under section 1292 of the Code of Virginia for a failure to deliver a telegraphic message sent from Bristol, Tenn., to Radford, Va., which was executed by serving a copy of the warrant on an agent of the said company at Abingdon, in Washington, Va. And on the said 15th day of February, 1890, the said justice of the peace rendered a judgment against the defendant for $100 and costs, which was carried by writ of error to the corporation court of Bristol City, such being the designation of the town of Goodson, now a city, upon the grounds: *First*, that the said justice of the peace of Washington county did not have jurisdiction of the action to recover the penalty, and upon other grounds; *secondly*, that the statute of the state of Virginia (section 1292 of the Code) is repugnant to the constitution of the United States, (article 1, § 8,) and therefore void. The judgment of the justice was affirmed by the corporation court of Bristol City, whereupon the defendant brought the case to this court by writ of error.

As to the first question involved, did the said tribunal rendering the judgment have jurisdiction in the premises? Let us consider. The said justice did not have jurisdiction to try "this claim for a fine amounting to one hundred dollars" under any aspect under which this case can be considered. He did not have jurisdiction under section 4106 of the Code, giving him jurisdiction of certain offenses, occurring within his jurisdiction, (1) because this offense charged is not charged to have occurred within the district where he had jurisdiction; (2) because this offense, if any, is not enumerated in the said section where he is clothed with jurisdiction as to certain offenses occurring within his jurisdiction. The said justice did not have jurisdiction under the said section 1292, providing the penalty in question, no tribunal being there prescribed. And he did not have jurisdiction under section 2939 of the Code of Virginia, prescribing for what a justice has jurisdiction, which is as follows: "Any claim to specific personal property, or to any debt, fine, or other money, or to damages for any breach of contract, or for any injury done to property, real or personal, would be recoverable by action at law or suit in equity, shall, when the claim is to a fine, or damages for breach of any contract, or for injury to property real or personal, if the amount of such claim do not exceed twenty dollars, (exclusive of interest,) and in other cases, if the claim do not exceed one hundred dollars, (exclusive of interest,) be cognizable by a justice." This is a claim to a fine, and does exceed $20. The jurisdiction of the justice is therefore expressly excluded, and this assignment of error is fatal to the pretensions of the plaintiff below, the defendant in error; and the said judgment is a nullity. The court which rendered it being without jurisdiction in the premises, and as this question lies *in limine*, and the court under review is without jurisdiction. that ends the case, and there is nothing more before the court. Any act of a tribunal beyond its jurisdiction is null and void, and of no effect whatever, whether without its territorial jurisdiction or beyond its powers. When want of jurisdiction arises from formal defects in the process, or when the want of jurisdiction is over the person, it must be taken advantage of in the early stages of a cause. But when the cause of action is not within the jurisdiction granted by law to the tribunal, the court will dismiss the suit at any time when the fact is brought to its notice; and a court of limited jurisdiction, or a court acting under special powers, has only the jurisdiction expressly delegated, and it must appear from the record that its acts are within its jurisdiction. For this reason the judgment appealed from must be reversed and annulled, and an order will be entered here dismissing the action.

NORFOLK & W. R. CO. v. STONE'S ADM'R.

(Supreme Court of Appeals of Virginia. July 23, 1891.)

ACCIDENT AT RAILROAD CROSSING—CONTRIBUTORY NEGLIGENCE.

Where a boy of 13 years, familiar with a railroad crossing at which, on account of a deep cut, a train could not be seen until one was on the track, drives upon it with his ears covered up on account of the cold, though he had just been told at the post office that the train was late, and would probably reach the crossing at about the same time he did, he is guilty of contributory negligence which will prevent recovery for his death, though the train was running at a high rate of speed, and the whistle was not blown.

Error to circuit court, Smythe county; JOHN A. KELLY, Judge.

Action by A. S. Stone, administrator of S. H. Stone, deceased, against the Norfolk & Western Railroad Company to recover damages for the death of his intestate. Judgment for plaintiff, and defendant brings error. Reversed.

W. H. Bolling, for plaintiff in error. *Sheffy & Richardson* and *F. S. Blair,* for defendant in error.

FAUNTLEROY, J. The petition of the Norfolk & Western Railroad Company complains of a final judgment rendered on the 11th day of December, 1890, by the circuit court of Smythe county in an action of trespass on the case, in which A. S. Stone, administrator of Samuel Hall Stone, deceased, is plaintiff, and the said petitioner is defendant. The action is for damages for the alleged negligent killing of the plaintiff's son and intestate, a boy 13 or 14 years old, by the defendant's passenger train, on the 9th day of March, 1889, at or near the Mt. Carmel mills, in Smythe county, Va., when the said intestate was driving a one-horse wagon across the track of the said defendant's railroad at a highway crossing. The jury rendered a verdict for $8,000

damages, whereupon the defendant moved the court to set aside the verdict, and grant to it a new trial, on the ground that the testimony failed to prove negligence on the part of the defendant company, its agents and employes, to warrant the finding of the jury; that the testimony plainly shows such contributory negligence on the part of the plaintiff's intestate as to prevent a recovery; and that the amount of the verdict is excessive. But the court overruled the defendant's said motion, and entered judgment upon the said verdict that the plaintiff recover against the defendant $8,000, with legal interest thereon from the 11th day of December, 1890, till paid, and the costs. The case is here upon a writ of error awarded to the said judgment. The record presenting only a certificate of the evidence, and not the facts, we must consider the case here under the statutory rule fixed by the Code of 1887, § 3484, as upon a demurrer to evidence. But, so reviewing the case presented by the record, we are of opinion that the plaintiff's testimony, considered with that part of the defendant's which is not contradictory nor inconsistent with that of the plaintiff, shows a clear case of contributory negligence on the part of the plaintiff's intestate, without which the accident by which he met his death would not have occurred. The facts of this case, which will be presently detailed, bring it directly and squarely within the reasoning and the rule laid down by this court, in the case of Improvement Co. v. Andrew, 86 Va. 279, 9 S. E. Rep. 1015, and in the case of Marks' Adm'r v. Railroad Co., 13 S. E. Rep. 299, decided at this term, and not yet officially reported. In this last-mentioned case the following propositions of law are settled: "A railroad company undoubtedly is bound to exercise care to avoid a collision where it crosses a public highway; and, the greater the danger, the greater is the vigilance required. The rights and duties, however, of the company and of the public are reciprocal; and hence no greater degree of care is required of the one than of the other. Both the company and the traveler on the highway are charged with the mutual duty of keeping a careful lookout for danger. The traveler on the highway, when he approaches a crossing, must assume that there is danger, and act accordingly. The existence of the track is a warning of danger. He must therefore be vigilant; be must look and listen; he has no right to close his eyes and ears to the danger he is liable to incur; and if he does, and an injury results, he must bear the consequences of his folly or carelessness. In such a case he is the author of his own misfortune." In the case of Railroad Co. v. Kellam's Adm'r, 83 Va. 851, 3 S. E. Rep. 703, it was held that a traveler on an intersecting highway, before crossing the railroad, must use his senses of hearing and sight; that he must look in every direction that the rails run, to make sure that the crossing is safe; and that his failure to do so will, as a general rule, be deemed culpable negligence." See Railroad Co. v. Anderson, 31 Grat. 812; Dun

v. Railroad Co., 78 Va. 645. In the case of Railroad Co. v. Houston, 95 U. S. 697, it is said by the supreme court of the United States that "the negligence of the company's employes in failing to give proper signals was no excuse for negligence on the part of the deceased. She was bound to listen and look before attempting to cross the railroad track, in order to avoid an approaching train, and not to walk carelessly into the place of possible danger. Had she used her senses, she could not have failed both to hear and see the train which was coming. If she omitted to use them, and walked thoughtlessly upon the track, she was guilty of culpable negligence, and so far contributed to her injuries as to deprive her of any right to complain of others. If, using them, she saw the train coming, and yet undertook to cross the track, instead of waiting for the train to pass, and was injured, the consequence of her mistake and temerity cannot be cast upon the defendant." Now, the facts presented by the record, to which the foregoing explicit and well-settled law of contributory negligence is to be applied as the rule of decision in this case, are as follows: On the 9th day of March, 1889, a passenger and mail train upon the Norfolk & Western Railroad, which was 5 hours and 30 minutes behind time, and which was running at a speed of 40 or 45 miles an hour, going west, collided with the wagon and horse driven by the plaintiff's son and intestate, Samuel Hall Stone, a boy between 13 and 14 years of age, upon a public crossing over the said railroad track called "Stone's Crossing," at "Mount Carmel Mills," a short distance —2½ miles—east of Marion, in Smythe county, Va., by which collision the said Samuel Hall Stone was killed, having his head torn from his body. The horse was killed, and the wagon smashed to pieces. The plaintiff alleges, and by numerous witnesses who swear that they live near by the said crossing, and did not hear, proves, that no signal whistle was blown by the said train as it passed the "whistling post," 440 yards east of the said "Stone's Crossing," which omission or neglect, together with the high rate of speed at which the train was going, he contends was the proximate cause of the accident and death of the plaintiff's son and intestate. Under the rule which excludes from consideration here all the testimony of the appellant upon this point, it boots nothing that the numerous and respectable and unimpeached witnesses of the appellant swear positively that the usual, appointed, and proper signal was given, by blowing the whistle for the approach of the train to Stone's crossing. Yet, though this must, under the rule, be held to be proved neglect of duty by the defendant company, the plaintiff's own witnesses prove that they did hear the whistle blown by the train at Scott's crossing, which is less than a mile east from Stone's crossing. This crossing is described by the plaintiff's witnesses as being "right in front of the mill. It was a dangerous crossing; heavy grade from the macadam road to the railroad." "A man in a wagon cannot see the train east

or west until he gets on the track. A man going in a wagon down to the crossing to the mill cannot see a train coming either way until you get to the track." "The road leading down to the crossing slopes a portion of the way. The bluff, ten feet high, does not continue all the way down to the railroad track." "The road leading down from the macadam road to the railroad crossing is down grade. The grade measures about 108 feet from the railroad to the top of the grade. It is about a sixteen or eighteen feet fall in that distance,—that is, the road the little boy was driving down." "It is a steep incline there." "A steep descent for 112 feet to the railroad of 17¼ feet fall. Just before you get to the crossing the descent is not so steep. It is a little level just before you get on the railroad." This crossing was within a few yards of the mill owned and occupied by the father of Samuel Hall Stone, and about the same distance from their dwelling. He was perfectly familiar with it; and had been, for a year previous to the accident, systematically employed by his father in driving his delivery wagon and thoroughly trained horse across this crossing, and up and down this steep cut, back and forth, with mill supplies for customers in Marion and at the asylum, making frequently as many as four trips, or eight passages, a day. And on the fatal 9th day of March, 1889, he had driven over it to Marion and back to the mill; and gone again to Marion, where, at the post-office, when he inquired for his mail, as his custom was, he was informed by the postmaster that the west-bound mail train was behind time, and would be passing in a little while, and would most probably pass "Stone's Crossing" at the mill just as he would reach there with his wagon on his return home, and that he should be on his guard against the imminency of the danger of being hurt by it. The day was very cold and windy; and he was wrapped in his overcoat and a comfort around his neck and over his head and ears, with his cap drawn down. Thus equipped, he drove his horse and wagon down the steep cut in the bluff or bank, onto the crossing, where he was struck and instantly killed by the train, which he had been expressly and officially informed by the postmaster at Marion he should expect and look out for at that crossing. If he could not hear the rumbling thunder of the on-rushing train, it may have been because of the wrapping over his ears; and if, as the plaintiff's own witnesses prove, he could not see the train until he emerged from the defile of the road onto the track itself, it is made equally manifest and certain by the same testimony that the engineer of the train could not by any possibility see him till he so emerged from the cut, and attempted to pass the crossing just under the flying train. They, by their own testimony, prove the engineer of the train, Pile, (who is proved to be a skilled, expert, and first-class engineer,) to have expressed, on the spot and moment of the disaster, his deep regret and utter inability to have prevented or avoided the poor boy's death; declaring that he did not see the situation until so close upon the boy and wagon and horse as to be powerless to save them. The boy was of great activity, industry, intelligence, and practiced skill, and was perfectly familiar with the danger of the locality; and, melancholy as his fate was, we think it was the result of his own fault or misfortune, and without the possibility of prevention or avoidance by the defendant company. His own contributory negligence bars any right of recovery, and the circuit court erred in not setting aside the verdict. The judgment of this court is to set the verdict aside, and to remand the case with directions to grant new trial. Reversed.

TRIGG et al. v. CLAY et al.

(Supreme Court of Appeals of Virginia. July 28, 1891.)

BREACH OF CONTRACT—PROFITS AS DAMAGES.

Where lumber dealers purchase and pay for lumber to be delivered at a future time, and then resell it, the measure of damages for breach of the contract and failure to deliver is, in the absence of a market at or near the place of delivery, the amount paid, together with the profits which would have arisen from the resale. LEWIS, P., and HINTON, J., dissenting.

Danl. Trigg, for appellants. *Holdway & Ewing* and *J. J. A. Powell,* for appellees.

LACY, J. This is an appeal from a decree of the circuit court of Scott county rendered on the 27th day of March, 1890. The suit is a foreign attachment in equity, brought to attach the property situated within the jurisdiction of the court belonging to the non-resident defendants, and subject the same to the satisfaction of the debt of the plaintiffs. The case is briefly as follows. The appellants, a firm of lumber merchants resident at Abingdon, in Virginia, made a contract by which they agreed to buy, at a stated price, lumber of agreed dimensions from the appellees, a firm of lumber getters, resident at Rogersville, in the state of Tennessee; the lumber to be delivered at Clinchport, in Scott county, in Virginia, from 500,000 feet to 700,000 feet thereof; and the plaintiffs agreed to accept the drafts of the said appellees to the amount of $3,000. And on the 28th day of November, 1888, the date of the contract, the appellee H. B. Clay, Jr., of the said firm, represented to the appellants that 300,000 to 400,000 feet was already cut and dry or drying; and that the residue, necessary to compensate for the $3,000 in drafts to be accepted at 60 days, should be delivered at Clinchport at the maturity of the drafts. The drafts were all made in the first week in December, 1888, a few days after the contract was made, which was on the 28th day of November, as has been stated. The lumber was not delivered,—not a foot of it,—and the drafts were neglected and allowed to fall upon the hands of the plaintiffs, when the lumber had not yet been delivered, and the drafts had been paid. So the plaintiffs, as had been agreed between them in case the said contingency should arise that the drafts should have to be paid before the lumber in sufficient quantity had arrived, drafted back

upon the defendants for the money thus paid out; but this action was treated with derision by the appellee, and the draft dishonored. Upon the hearing, the circuit court decreed in favor of the plaintiffs for the $3,000 paid on the draft and the costs of protest, etc., and referred it to a commission to ascertain what damages the plaintiffs had sustained. It was proved that the defendants had absolutely refused to fulfill the contract upon the ground that the lumber had been priced too low by them, and also refused to refund the money paid them under the contract. The plaintiffs proved that they were lumber merchants, and, as was known to the defendants, purchased the lumber for sale; and they proved that they had actually placed this lumber to their customers at a profit which amounted to $1,000, but which they were made to lose by the wrongful act and fraudulent conduct of the defendants; and the commissioner reported that the said plaintiffs were entitled to this sum of actual damages incurred by them, estimating the profits on the maximum amount of the lumber to be delivered under the contract. But the defendants excepted to this report, "because the damage allowed is excessive, and not supported by law; because the commissioner had based his damages on supposed profits, instead of the market value of the lumber at the places of delivery." The circuit court by its decree of March 27, 1890, sustained these exceptions, and held that the plaintiffs were entitled to no specific damages for the non-performance of the contract set out in the plaintiffs' bill, and rested the matter where it had been placed by the former decree, which decreed in favor of the plaintiffs for the amount paid on the said drafts. From this decree the appeal is here. The idea of the circuit court was that the general rule applied which fixed the difference between the market price at the place of delivery and the contract price agreed to be paid. Upon the principle that the buyer could supply himself in the market overt, and when he had been compensated for the excess in the cost, over and above what his cost would have been under the contract, he had nothing more to complain of. But this case does not come within that principle, (1) because there is no market at that place from which, or in which, the plaintiffs could supply their need; (2) because there is no other market practically near enough to purchase the lumber and add transportation to the market price; (3) because the plaintiffs, relying on the promises and good faith of their bargainers, as they had a right to do, when they had themselves fully complied on their part by paying the purchase money therefor, had contracted to sell this lumber at a profit, which profit is the basis on which the commissioner assessed his damages.

In a case like this, with such circumstances as we have here, the case where there had been a contract to resell them at an agreed price, and when there is no market to afford a surer test, the price at which they were bargained to a purchaser affords the best and indeed very satisfactory evidence of their value. This was a purchase in that market, and there was no more for sale. In a case of such actual sale, why should the court go into conjecture as to what the goods were there worth? And again, if lumber could have been purchased and brought there at a lower price, there is not only no proof of it, but we have satisfactory proof to the contrary, because the defendants had the lumber, and were by their solemn contract under the highest obligations to deliver it; to say nothing of the requirement of common honesty, when they had agreed to do it, and had collected the purchase price. And yet they preferred to break their contract, and dishonored their bank obligation, rather than deliver this lumber at the agreed price, which they declared had been bargained at too low a price. In Wood's Mayne on Damages, § 22, it is said: "But, if they [the goods] cannot be purchased for want of a market, they must be estimated in some other way. If there had been a contract to resell them, the price at which such contract was made will be evidence of their value." In the American and English Encyclopædia of Law it is said: "Where there is no market at the place of delivery, the price of the goods in the nearest market, with the cost of transportation added, determines their value." Ice Co. v. Webster, 68 Me. 463; Griffin v. Colver, 16 N. Y. 489. In the case of Culin v. Glass-Works, 108 Pa. St. 220, it is said: "Upon the breach of a contract to furnish goods, when similar goods cannot be purchased in the market, the measure of damages is the actual loss sustained by the purchaser by reason of the non-delivery." A distinction is drawn in some of the cases between a resale made at an advance subsequent to a contract of purchase and a resale made at an advance before the contract of purchase, which was known to the seller of the goods. Carpenter v. Bank, 119 Ill. 354, 10 N. E. Rep. 18. This is rather a fanciful distinction. It is not in accord with the ordinary usages of trade that a dealer, a man buying to sell again, should disclose his dealings with the same goods at a profit to his vendor. But, if there were any sound principle upon which this could rest, if the seller could be supposed to enter into his contract upon the basis of a resale in which he had no interest, still, in this case, it is reasonable to suppose that a lumber getter selling 700,000 feet of lumber to a dealer in lumber should know (1) that it was for a resale, (2) that this resale was to be on a profit, and (3) that he should know that his vendee would be damaged to the amount of his profit, if the vendor should prove faithless. But the true basis of the general rule is that when there is a market, the vendee cannot be damaged, except in the difference between what the lumber did actually cost him and what he had purchased it at from the seller to him. But this rule can have, upon reason, no application whatever to a case where there is no market, (1) because the disappointed purchaser cannot buy in that market when there is no market to buy in, and (2) because the market price cannot be ascertained when there is no market.

Under the circumstances of this case, the commissioner ascertained the true and just amount of the damages. It has been often held that profits which are the direct and immediate fruits of the contract are recoverable. There are many cases in which the profit to be made by the bargain is the only thing purchased, and in such cases the amount of such profit is strictly the measure of damages. Wood's Mayne, Dam. p. 82. It has been held that, when the defendant refused to allow the contracts to be executed, the jury should allow the plaintiffs as much as the contract would have benefited them,—profits or advantages which are the direct and immediate fruits of the contract, entered into between the parties, and part and parcel of the contract itself, entering into and constituting a portion of its every elements, something stipulated for, and the right to the enjoyment of which is just as clear and plain as to the fulfillment of any other stipulation. They are presumed to have been taken into consideration and deliberated upon before the contract was made, and formed, perhaps, the only inducement to the arrangement. If the inducement to the plaintiffs to buy this lumber, they being lumber dealers, and trading in lumber, was not the profits they were to make by a resale, what was their inducement? And if the sellers did not understand and contemplate this resale on a profit, what contemplation on the subject can be reasonably ascribed to them? See Masterton v. Mayor, etc., 7 Hill, 62; Morrison v. Lovejoy, 6 Minn. 319, (Gil. 224;) Fox v. Harding, 7 Cush. 516; Devlin v. Mayor, etc., 63 N. Y. 8; McAndrews v. Tippett, 39 N. J. Law, 105; Kendall Bank Note Co. v. Commissioners of the Sinking Fund, 79 Va. 563; Bell v. Reynolds, 78 Ala. 511. An examination of the cases will show that the courts have been endeavoring to establish rules by the application of which a party will be compensated for the loss sustained by the breach of contract; in other words, for the benefits and gain he would have realized from its performance, and nothing more. It is sometimes said that the profit that would have been derived from performance cannot be recovered; but this is only true of such as are contingent upon some other operation. Profits which certainly would have been realized but for the defendant's default are recoverable. It is not an uncertainty as to the value of the benefit or gain to be derived from performance, but an uncertainty or contingency whether such gain or benefit can be derived at all. It is sometimes said that speculative damages cannot be recovered because the amount is uncertain, but such remarks will generally be found applicable to such damages as it is uncertain whether sustained at all from the breach. Sometimes the claim is rejected as being too remote. This is another mode of saying that it is uncertain whether such damages resulted necessarily and immediately from the breach complained of. The general rule is that all damages resulting necessarily and immediately and directly from the breach are recoverable, and not those that are contingent and uncertain. The latter description embraces, as I think, such only as are not the certain result of the breach, and does not embrace such as are the certain result of the breach, but uncertain in amount, for which the plaintiff will be fully compensated by recovering the value of his bargain. He ought not to have more, and I think he is not precluded from recovering this by any infirmity in the law in ascertaining the amount. Wakeman v. Manufacturing Co., 101 N. Y. 205, 4 N. E. Rep. 264; Taylor v. Bradley, 4 Abb. Dec. 366; Bell v. Reynolds, 78 Ala. 511. In this case this report of the commissioner was upon the correct principle, and the circuit court erred in sustaining the defendants' exception to the said report; for said exceptions should have been overruled, and the commissioner's report confirmed. The decree of the circuit court appealed from here is therefore erroneous, and the same will be reversed and annulled, and this court will render such decree as the said circuit court ought to have rendered.

HINTON, J., dissents.

LEWIS, P., (dissenting.) In this case I dissent from the opinion of the court and am for affirming the decree of the circuit court. The case is narrowed down by the exception to the commissioner's report to the simple question of the measure of damages. The rule adopted by this court is, in my opinion, not only unjust, but contrary to the long-settled rule which governs in such cases. Here the measure of damages is held to be the loss sustained by the appellants by reason of their inability, on account of the default of the appellees, to fulfill certain contracts made by them for the sale and delivery of lumber to other parties. But those contracts were collateral to the contract between the parties to this appeal, and were, in point of time, subsequent thereto. They could not, therefore, have been in the contemplation of the parties when the contract was made, the breach of which is the subject of this controversy.

HUDSON v. YOST.

(Supreme Court of Appeals of Virginia. June 23, 1891.)

INJUNCTION—SALE ON EXECUTION—DESTRUCTION OF RECORDS—REVIEW.

1. Code Va. § 3376, provides that, if the original papers in any cause be lost or destroyed, the court wherein the case is may docket the same; and, "on affidavit of such loss or destruction," the case may be proceeded in upon an authenticated copy of what is lost or destroyed, or proof of the contents thereof, or so much of the contents thereof as may enable the court to determine the case, as if the papers had not been lost or destroyed. Held, that where, after a decree directing a sale of certain lands has been rendered, the original papers have been burned, and a complete certified office copy thereof obtained from the supreme court, to which the case was taken on appeal, an injunction will not lie to enjoin such sale, on the ground that no "affidavit of the loss or destruction" was filed, where the destruction was alleged in complainant's bill, supported by his affidavit, and admitted in defendant's answer, supported by his affidavit.

2. In such action, a contention that there is a defect in the title will not be considered, where the original case was fully investigated by a referee, and his report confirmed by the circuit

court, and an appeal to the supreme court dismissed.

Bill for an injunction by one Hudson against W. L. Yost, commissioner. Decree for defendant. Plaintiff appeals. Affirmed.

Mr. Blair, for appellant. Williams Bros., W. L. Yost, and D. S. Pierce, for appellee.

LACY, J. This is an appeal from a decree of the circuit court of Bland county, rendered on the 30th day of September, 1889. The bill was filed to injoin the appellee from selling under a decree of said court a tract of land decreed to be sold by the said court, upon the ground that, since the decree was rendered, the court-house of Bland county had been destroyed by fire, and all of the court papers destroyed, and among them the records of the suit in which the said decree had been rendered; and praying that no sale be allowed to take place until the proof had been taken to supply the lost record, and to restrain the sale until the title could be perfected. The decree under which this sale was proposed to be made was rendered at the April term, 1887, and an appeal had been taken to this court, which had been subsequently dismissed. The defendant answered, admitting and setting forth the destruction of the records in Bland county clerk's office, and among them the original papers in this case; but asserting that, the case having been appealed to the supreme court of appeals, a certified office copy of the said record was thus preserved; and it was obtained, after some delay, having been for some time stolen and concealed. But, it being obtained, a certified transcript of the original papers was presented to the court, and taken and held as a sufficient record, being in fact complete in all its parts; when, the cause coming on to be heard upon the said bill and answer, the circuit court of Bland county dissolved the injunction September 30, 1889, and at the April term, 1890, dismissed the bill of the plaintiff, with costs; and from these decrees the plaintiff appealed. The ground of the appeal is that the record of the case has been destroyed by fire, and the same has not been set up by legal and proper proof, and that there is a defect in the title. As to the second assignment, it is sufficient to say that this question has been put to rest by the former trial. The case having been fully investigated upon a reference to the commissioner, and his report, and confirmation thereof by the court in a decree which had been brought to this court by appeal, and the appeal dismissed, it is too late to discuss that.

As to the first ground, that the lost record had not been set up in the mode required by law, we will cite the statute, (section 3376 of the Code of Virginia,) which is as follows: "If, in any cause, the original papers therein, or any of them, or the record for or in an appellate court, or any paper filed or connected with such record, be lost or destroyed, the court wherein the case is, or in which it would or ought to be, but for such loss or destruction, may docket the same; and, on affidavit of such loss or destruction, the case may be proceeded in, heard, and determined upon an authenticated copy of what is lost or destroyed, or proof of the contents thereof, or upon proof of so much of the contents thereof as may enable the court to proceed in, hear, and determine the case, and make such entry, order, or decree therein as if the papers, or any of them, had not been lost or destroyed." Upon consideration of this statute, the question is divested of any difficulty or doubt whatever; the case in hand being expressly and distinctly provided for. But it is said the statute has not been complied with, because the record does not disclose an affidavit as to the loss of the original papers. This affidavit is intended by the law to prove the loss of the original papers. But, in this case the bill alleges the loss of all the originals, and is supported by the affidavit of the plaintiff. The answer admits the loss of the original papers, and alleges the fact, and the answer is supported by the affidavit of the defendant. This is a compliance with the law, and the said certified copies of the original papers were properly admitted by the court, and the case was properly proceeded in, heard, and determined as if the papers therein had not been lost or destroyed. And there was no error in the said decree, and the same will be affirmed.

SHANNON et al. v. HANKS.

(Supreme Court of Appeals of Virginia. June 25, 1891.)

APPOINTMENT OF RECEIVER—RIGHT TO APPEAL—DISCRETION OF COURT.

1. Code Va. § 3454, provides that an appeal may be allowed in any case in chancery wherein there is a decree or order requiring the possession of the property to be changed. Held, that a decree of the circuit court in equity, appointing a receiver, is appealable.

2. After a decree in an action to subject property fraudulently conveyed, a receiver may be appointed, though not prayed in the bill, where the circumstances justify it.

3. The fact appearing from the commissioner's report that, independent of the land sought to be subjected, the annual value of defendant's real estate is only about $200, and the liens thereon amount to about $20,000, justifies the appointment of a receiver.

4. Where the court appointed two receivers, the mere fact that one of them was attorney for complainant will not be deemed an abuse of discretion, where the other was attorney for defendant.

Appeal from circuit court, Bland county; D. W. BOLEN, Judge.

Bill in equity by one Hanks against Samuel B. Shannon and others to subject certain property. Decree for plaintiff. Defendants appeal. Affirmed.

Mr. Harman, for appellants. Williams Bros. and Mr. Pierce, for appellee.

LEWIS, P. This was a suit in equity in the circuit court of Giles county by the appellee, Hanks, against Samuel B. Shannon and others, to subject the real estate of the defendant Shannon to the satisfaction of two judgments recovered by the plaintiff against the firm of Compton & Shannon, of which firm the defendant Shannon was a member. The real estate sought to be subjected consisted of several tracts of land situate in Giles county, one of which was conveyed by the defendant, prior to the recovery of the plaintiff's judgments, to Isaac Hudson, trustee, for the benefit of Alice R. Gish, in consideration of her intended marriage with the defendant, which marriage was soon after solemnized. It appears from the commissioner's report that, independent of the land conveyed to Hudson, trustee, for the benefit of Mrs. Shannon, which is not involved in this appeal, the annual value of the defendant's real estate is only $200, whereas the liens thereupon amount in the aggregate to about $20,000. Upon the coming in of the commissioner's amended report the plaintiff moved for the appointment of a receiver, which motion was granted by the decree complained of. The appellee has moved to dismiss the appeal as having been improvidently allowed, on the ground that an appeal will not lie from a decree appointing a receiver. But we are of opinion that this objection cannot be sustained. An order appointing a receiver in a case like this changes the possession as well as the control of the property, and is therefore embraced within the provision of section 3454 of the Code, which enacts expressly that an appeal may be allowed in any case in chancery wherein there is a decree or order requiring the possession of the property to be changed. And so it was decided in Smith v. Butcher, 28 Grat. 144, in which case it was held that an order appointing a receiver is an appealable order, although made in vacation. The same case is also an authority for the action of the circuit court in appointing a receiver in the present case, although there is no specific prayer for a receiver in the bill. The general rule is that, when there is no such prayer in the bill, and the application for a receiver is made before a decree, it will not be granted. But at the hearing, or at any time after a decree, a receiver may be appointed, though not prayed in the bill, if the circumstances of the case require it. 1 Bart. Ch. Pr. 486. The appointment of a receiver is a matter resting in the discretion of the court, although it is a power to be cautiously exercised. Where, however, as in the present case, the lien far exceeds the value of the property, an order appointing a receiver will not be reversed by an appellate court. It is objected that the application was not supported by affidavits, and that there is nothing to show that the property is in danger of being wasted or injured during the progress of the suit, in case a receiver should not be appointed. But it was not necessary that the application should have been supported by affidavit, nor was it essential that the court should have been satisfied that the property was in danger of being wasted or injured. The undisputed facts appearing from the commissioner's report, than which there could be no more satisfactory evidence, were ample, as in Smith v. Butcher, to justify the appointment of a receiver to collect the rents and profits of the land, to be applied pro tanto to the payment of the debts, in order to prevent to that extent the swelling of the debts by the accumulation of interest. In Smith v. Butcher not only was there nothing to show that the appointment of a receiver was necessary to prevent injury to the property *pendente lite*, but, on the contrary, it was proved by the defendant, in opposition to the appointment of a receiver, that he had improved the land, and enhanced its value by the judicious system with which he was managing it. Yet this court, in passing upon the objections to the order appointing a receiver, used this language: "Under all the circumstances disclosed by the record, the probably protracted litigation, the insufficiency of the property of the defendant to pay his debts, and the just claim of the creditors to have the rents and profits applied first to keep down the interest, and then to the reduction of the principal, the case is one eminently proper for a receiver." In the present case it appears that all the judgments reported against the appellant Shannon are judgments against him as a member of the firm of Compton & Shannon, and that a suit for the settlement of the partnership debts is pending in the circuit court of Bland county, in which suit the property of Compton is sought to be subjected to the payment of those debts. Accordingly, the circuit court, in its order appointing a receiver, very properly removed the case to the Bland circuit court, to be there heard together with the suit pending in that court. It would seem, however, from what appears in the record, that the property of both partners will not be sufficient to pay all the debts in full. But, be that as it may, enough appears to justify beyond doubt the appointment of a receiver in the present case. The court in fact appointed two receivers,—one the attorney of the plaintiff, the other the attorney of the defendant,—and the appointment of the plaintiff's attorney constitutes another ground of objection to the action of the lower court. This objection, however, is not only made for the first time in this court, but there is nothing in the record to sustain it. The general rule undoubtedly is that a receiver ought to be an indifferent person between the parties. But the selection of a proper person is very much a matter within the discretion of the court, and hence will very rarely be interfered with by an appellate court. 1 Bart. Ch. Pr. 495; High, Rec. § 65. In Cookes v. Cookes, 2 De Gex J. & S. 526, Lord Justice KNIGHT-BRUCE observed that to induce an appellate court to act against the decision of the lower judge in the selection of a receiver, it is necessary to find some overwhelming objection in point of propriety of choice, or some objection fatal in principle; and certainly no such objection is found in the present case, in view of the fact that of the two receivers one is the appellant's own attorney. We are therefore of opinion to affirm the decree.

STUART et al. v. HURT.

(*Supreme Court of Appeals of Virginia.* June 24, 1891.)

DECREE FOR INTEREST—DAMAGES FOR DETENTION.

In an action of debt on a decree for the payment of a certain amount of interest, interest on the amount of the decree can be recovered in the shape of damages for its detention.

Error to circuit court, Washington county; JOHN A. KELLY, Judge.

Routh & Stuart, for plaintiffs in error. White & Buchanan, for defendant in error.

HINTON, J. The case is as follows: The circuit court of Washington county, at its January term, 1880, rendered a decree in the chancery cause of J. D. Mitchel et als. against A. McCall et als., directing one of its commissioners to take an account charging Stuart, Buchanan & Co. with the annual rent of $2,500 on the one-eighth of the King salt-works, with or without interest, as the circumstances shown might warrant, and allowing credits for all payments made to the receiver for years 1864, 1865, 1866, 1867, 1868, and to show the balance, if any, due the receiver. From the report of the commissioner it appeared that there was a balance due the receiver on the 2d of April, 1869, of $1,500, and that the interest on said balance from April 2, 1869, to May 2, 1882, was $1,177.50. At the hearing the court decreed in favor of Samuel F. Hurt, receiver of the circuit court of the United States for the western district of Virginia in the case of John Vints, Administrator, vs. The Heirs of John Allen and Hannah Allen for the aforesaid sum of $1,500 and costs, subject to a credit of one-sixth part of the principal sum, which it was admitted that Mrs. A. E. T. Campbell, who was entitled thereto, had settled with Messrs. Stuart and Palmer by some arrangement among themselves. The decree, however, recites: "And, it appearing to the court that the said sum [meaning the $1,177.50] is for interest upon unpaid rent, the court doth therefore decline to allow interest upon the sum hereinbefore decreed," manifestly referring to the sum of $1,177.50 of interest mentioned above. On this decree the defendant in error instituted an action of debt in the court below against the plaintiffs in error, and, a jury being waived, the said court rendered at its October term, 1890, the judgment which is the subject of this writ of error, for the amount of the decree, to-wit, $1,250, with interest thereon from the date of said judgment until paid, and costs, and for $631.25 damages for the detention of the said debt from the 12th day of May, 1882, the date of the decree sued on. Now, it is insisted on behalf of the plaintiffs in error that the court below erred in allowing said damages for the detention of the debt in lieu of interest. The theory of the plaintiffs in error seems to be that the decree was rendered for a balance, no part of which was principal, but all of which was interest; and that, as the general rule of law is that interest shall not bear interest, (see Pindall's Ex'x v. Bank, 10 Leigh, 506,) interest cannot be recovered in the shape of damages. The vice in this argument, however, is that it overlooks the fact that the decree changed the character of the interest, and converted it into a debt, which carried with it the incidents of costs, lien, etc. Such a debt is due presently, and we can perceive no good reason why, if it should not be paid, damages should not be recovered for its detention. "It is natural justice," says Judge PENDLETON in Jones' Ex'r v. Williams, 2 Call, 102, "that he who has the use of another's money should pay interest on it;" and this seems to be the policy of the legislature, if anything can be gathered from the statutes fixing the period for the commencement of interest where the verdict fixes none, and providing that the judgment or decree may be rendered for interest on the principal sum recovered until such judgment be paid, where no jury is impaneled. See sections 3390, 3391, Code 1887. In Tazewell v. Saunders, 13 Grat. 368, Judge MONCURE says: "In this state interest is generally recoverable on a judgment, both at law and in equity." He then adds: "But if the judgment does not carry interest on its face, it can only be recovered by action or suit upon the judgment." In Mercer's Adm'r v. Beale, 4 Leigh, 189, Judge TUCKER said: "That in an action of debt upon a judgment, the plaintiff may, in the shape of damages, recover interest upon his demands, is a proposition too plain to have required proof;" although he subsequently says that, while interest on a judgment not carrying interest may be given, it is not a matter of course. And that such an action lies, and that the same judgment can be rendered upon a decree of a court of chancery as upon a judgment at law, see 2 Rob. Pr. (New Ed.) 124; Pennington v. Gibson, 16 How. 76; 2 Bart. Ch. Pr. 827. It seems to be supposed, however, by the plaintiff in error that the question of interest is adjudged in his favor by the decree of the circuit court. We do not so understand the language of the decree. The chancellor was acting upon the report of the commissioner, which showed the interest on the balance of money ascertained to be due down to the time of the rendering of the decree; and that is the interest which we understand that the court refused to allow. We find no error in the decree of the circuit court, and it must be affirmed.

BOON v. SIMMONS.

(*Supreme Court of Appeals of Virginia.* July 9, 1891.)

TAX-SALE—CONFIRMATION—TAX-DEED.

Act Va. Feb. 26, 1886, § 5, provides that within 30 days after a tax-sale the treasurer shall report same to the county court if in session, and, if not in session, at its next term, and record the return of the report thereof, and "continue the matter until the next term, for exceptions to be filed by any person affected by such report;" and, if the proceedings appear regular, the court "shall confirm said sale." A sale was made under such act, but the county court failed to confirm the treasurer's report thereof then or at any subsequent term, or to give a deed, and the purchaser never took possession. Six months later the same property was regularly sold under attachment proceedings to a purchaser without notice, actual or constructive, who held possession for about three years, when the court endeavored to confirm the former tax-sale, and executed a deed, which conveyed, not the land described in the treasurer's report as "two acres and forty poles, near S.," but "the following described real estate, situated in * * *, consisting of lots * * * on the survey of * * * of lots of the D. estate." *Held* that, on suit by the purchaser at the attachment sale to remove a cloud

from his title, the tax-deed will be declared void.

Appeal from circuit court, Roanoke county; H. E. BLAIR, Judge.

Action by Sparrel F. Simmons against Walter Z. Boon to remove a cloud from title. Decree for plaintiff. Defendant appeals. Affirmed.

Penn & Cocke, for appellant. *Hansbrough & Hansbrough*, for appellee.

FAUNTLEROY, J. The appellant, Walter Z. Boon, complains of a decree of the circuit court of Roanoke county, pronounced on the 6th day of April, 1891, in a cause therein pending, in which Sparrel F. Simmons is complainant and the said Walter Z. Boon is defendant. The record discloses the following case: On the 19th day of December, 1887, W. W. Brand, treasurer of Roanoke county, sold a certain tract or parcel of land described as "two acres and forty poles, near Salem," assessed in the names of J. W. Shell, T. D. Shell, and E. A. Shell, as delinquent for payment of taxes due and unpaid for the year 1886, to the amount of $2.47, which said lands at said sale were purchased by Walter Z. Boon, appellant, for the sum of $2.72. This sale and all the proceedings were under an act of the general assembly, passed February 26, 1886. Acts 1885–86, p. 280. The list of the sales made December 19, 1887, by the said treasurer, (of which this sale of the said two acres and forty poles was one,) was returned to the county court of Roanoke county at its January term, 1888, and there was made and entered by and in the said court at its said January term, 1888, the following order, viz.: "This day W. W. Brand, treasurer of this county, returned to this court a list of real estate within the county of Roanoke, sold in the month of December, 1887, for the non-payment of taxes thereon for the year 1886; and, the court seeing no cause to doubt the correctness of the said list, it is ordered that a copy thereof be certified to the auditor of public accounts, and that the original be recorded in a well-bound book, properly indexed, to be preserved in the clerk's office of this court." No other order concerning the said sale to Boon was made by the said county court until the January term, 1890, when the court made the following order: "This day Walter Z. Boon, who was the purchaser of a tract of two acres and forty poles, lying near Salem in this county, and assessed in the names of J. W., T. D., and E. A. Shell, at a sale of lands delinquent for taxes for the year 1886, made by W. W. Brand, treasurer of Roanoke county, on the 19th day of December, 1887, returned to the court a plat and certificate of survey of said land made by the surveyor of this county, which the court, upon examination, finds to be in conformity to the law, and orders the same to be recorded, and that the clerk do make the necessary deed conveying the said tract to the said purchaser." In pursuance of the foregoing order, the clerk of the said county court, by a deed dated February 13, 1890, conveyed to the said Walter Z. Boon, not the land described on the list returned by the treasurer aforesaid to the county court at the January term, 1888, as "two acres forty poles, near Salem," but "the following described real estate, situated in the town of Salem, Roanoke county, Va., near the depot of the Norfolk and Western Railroad," within certain metes and bounds, and "consisting of lots 119, 120, 121, 122, 123, 54, 55, 56, 57, and 58, on the survey of John Snyder of lots of the Dupmore estate." It appears from the copy of the record of the circuit court of Roanoke county that, under attachment proceedings in the said court against the said Shells, owners of the said lots, they, the said lots, were sold, and purchased on the 22d day of May, 1888, by Sparrel F. Simmons, the appellee, for the sum of $801, which he paid, and the sale was confirmed, and a deed was made to the said Simmons, in pursuance of the order of the said court, by F. C. Shell, J. W. Shell, T. D. Shell, and W. Lee Brand, deputy-sheriff of Roanoke county, and the said Simmons was put into possession of the said lots, which possession he has held uninterruptedly to this time. It nowhere appears that the said Boon has ever had possession of any part of the said lots in controversy. In May, 1890, Sparrel T. Simmons (the appellee) instituted this suit in the circuit court of Roanoke county to have the aforesaid sale of the said lots made December 19, 1887, by the said treasurer, W. W. Brand, and the deed for the same, made to the said Walter Z. Boon by the aforesaid McCauley, clerk of the county court of Roanoke county, February 13, 1890, declared to be illegal, null, and void, and to vacate the same, as a cloud upon his title to the aforesaid land in controversy; and the said circuit court rendered the decree of April 6, 1891, declaring the said sale to be illegal, null, and void, and vacating and annulling the said deed of February 13, 1890, made by the said clerk, McCauley, of the county court of Roanoke county, to the said Walter Z. Boon, the appellee. We are of opinion to affirm the said decree appealed from, for the reasons given in writing by the judge of the circuit court, filed with the decree, and made part of the record, in an elaborate opinion.

The record shows sundry defects and irregularities in the proceedings attending the sale of the real estate in controversy, and in the deed itself, sufficient to warrant the annulment of the said sale and deed. Section 5 of the act of February 26, 1886, under which the sale was made, and all the proceedings were had, is as follows: "(5) Within thirty days after the sales have been completed the treasurer shall report all the sales to the county court of his county, or corporation court of his city, * * * the court is in session, and, if not in session, at its next term, shall enter on record the fact of the return of the report of said sale, and shall continue the matter until the next term, for exceptions to be filed by any person affected by such report; and, if no cause be hown to the contrary, or in so far as the said report appears to be proper, and the sales to have been regularly made, the court shall confirm said sale, and make the same binding upon the parties in interest, subject to the limitations and exceptions

hereinafter described; and writs of possession may in all cases be granted to the said purchasers during term, or at any time thereafter on demand, whether said purchaser shall be a person, company, firm, or corporation, or the auditor of the state." Though positively and peremptorily commanded to continue the matter reported at the January term, of the sale made of this land in controversy by the treasurer, until the next term, for exceptions to be filed by any person affected by the said report and proceedings of the treasurer, and thereafter at the next succeeding February term, or at some subsequent term, to confirm the said sales, and make the same binding upon the parties in interest, the county court failed to continue the matter of the treasurer's report of the said sale, at its January term, 1888, and did not make an order confirming the sale of the land in controversy to Boon, to make it binding upon the parties in interest, at that January term, nor at any subsequent term, of the said court. Without such order of confirmation, the sale to Boon was null and void; the essential requirement of the fifth section of the act of February 26, 1886, under which the sale was made and the proceedings subsequent were had, being that the report of the sale by the treasurer shall be continued for one term, for a most positive and provident reason given, and that then, this having been done, "the court shall confirm the said sale, and make the same binding upon the parties in interest." It is well established by the decisions of this court that, whenever it is necessary for a court to confirm a sale, there is no sale until the order of confirmation is made. "Judicial confirmation of the sale, when required by law, is essential to a valid title, but no confirmation can aid a void title." 2 Blackw. Tax-Titles, § 674; 2 Minor, Inst. p. 322. "The power to sell land for non-payment of taxes is not a common-law power, but arises entirely from the statutes, and therefore exists only when the conditions prescribed by the statute are fulfilled; and, since these statutes are penal, and the proceedings under them ex parte, summary, executive, rather than judicial, and an infringement of the rights of property, only tolerated by reason of necessity, great strictness and exactness in following the law is required in favor of the land-owner. All acts prescribed by the statute must be performed in the place, manner, form, and time therein named; every provision in which the owner can possibly have an interest must be strictly obeyed, or the resulting tax-title will be void." 1 Blackw. Tax-Titles, § 121. In section 126 the same writer says: "The proceedings are adverse, ex parte, * * * and statutory, and have nothing to stand upon but the statute, from which, if they vary, they can lay no claim to its support, and are therefore wholly without support. The purchaser claims under the statute; by that let his pretensions be judged. The consideration is grossly inadequate. The maxim caveat emptor applies with great force to the purchaser. If the forms of law can be departed from at all, a dangerous power is put in the hands of the officers, and great difficulty will be found in deciding how far departure may go. If at all, why not any distance? The officer sells what he does not own, and has no interest in and no authority over, except as agent of the law. He is made agent for this purpose by certain prescribed steps, and, if a single condition is absent, his agency fails. Moreover, the law is penal in its nature, and must be strictly construed." And in section 127 the same writer quotes the words of Chief Justice MARSHALL in the case of Thatcher v. Powell, 6 Wheat. 119: "That no individual or public officer can sell and convey a good title to the land of another, unless authorized to do so by express law, is one of those self-evident propositions to which the mind assents without hesitation; and that the person invested with such a power must pursue with precision the course prescribed by law, or his act is invalid, is a principle which has been repeatedly recognized in this court." In Wilsons v. Bell, 7 Leigh, 22, this court said: "It is the well-settled law that he that claims under a forfeiture must show that the law has been exactly complied with." See, also, Yancey v. Hopkins, 1 Munf. 419; Nalle v. Fenwick, 4 Rand. (Va.) 585; Allen v. Smith, 1 Leigh, 231, 248; Jesse v. Preston, 5 Grat. 120. The record shows that the sale made and reported by the treasurer to the January term, 1888, of the county court of Roanoke county, of "two acres and forty poles, near Salem," to the appellant, Boon, was not continued as the law required; that no order of confirmation by the said court of the said sale was ever made, so as to make the same binding upon the parties in interest; and that Boon never sued out a writ of possession, or took possession, of the land in controversy, which he was reported to have bought at a sale of land delinquent for taxes for $2.72, but which sale was never confirmed so as to consummate his tax-title, or to bind or divest the title of the owners of the land delinquent. The appellee, Simmons, is not a delinquent owner failing to pay the taxes on his land, but an innocent purchaser for value,—$801 cash,—without notice, actual or constructive, of the claims of the tax-sale purchaser. Under a decree in a suit in chancery and an order in attachment proceedings, which were pending in the circuit court of Roanoke county at the time of the sale, December 19, 1887, to Boon, the sheriff of Roanoke county sold the land in controversy to the appellee, Simmons, who paid the price, $801 cash, reported the sale to the circuit court, which was approved and confirmed, and a deed of conveyance made to Simmons as said purchaser at the said judicial sale, July 7, 1888, which was united in both by the said officer of the circuit court and the Shells, the assessed owners of the land, and on that day admitted to record. Possession of the land was delivered to the appellee immediately by virtue of his said purchase, and actual possession thereof he has retained ever since. This is not a suit for the possession of the land, but is a suit by the purchaser at a judicial sale, who has paid the purchase money, and been in possession since July 7, 1888, under a decree of the circuit court of Roanoke county, to remove the cloud upon his title by the tax-title claim of the appellant as purchaser at a sale made by the treasurer of Roanoke for delinquent taxes on the 19th day of December, 1887, which sale was never confirmed or consummated according to law. The deed of February 13, 1890, from the clerk of the county court of Roanoke county was illegal and void, because the county court had never confirmed the sale, nor in other essential and material prescriptions of law proceeded properly and regularly; and, while the sale reported described the land sold as "two acres and forty poles, near Salem," the deed describes and conveys "ten lots in the town of Salem, near the depot of the Norfolk and Western Railroad." *Non constat* that it is the same land. For the foregoing reasons we are of opinion that there is no error in the decree of the circuit court of Roanoke appealed from, and that the same must be affirmed.

HUBBLE v. COLE.

(Supreme Court of Appeals of Virginia. July 9, 1891.)

REMEDIES OF TENANT—BREACH OF COVENANT.

Where a lessor prevents the lessee from enjoying the leased property by a preliminary injunction, which is afterwards dissolved, the fact that the lessee has a right of action on the injunction bond will not bar his action of covenant.

Action for breach of covenant by one Hubble against one Cole. Judgment for defendant. Plaintiff appeals. Reversed and remanded.

F. S. Blair, for plaintiff in error. *Buchanan & Buchanan* and *St. John,* for defendant in error.

LACY, J. This is a writ of error to a judgment of the circuit court of Smythe county, rendered at the March term, 1890. The action is covenant, and the declaration set forth that on the 30th day of December, 1881, in the county of Smythe, the defendant leased for the term of five years to the plaintiff, in consideration of the sum of $3,000, to be paid to her as stated in the deed of lease executed by them, certain real estate situated in the said county, with conditions stated and set forth in said deed; that the plaintiff performed all the covenants of the said deed on his part, but that the defendant did not perform on her part, setting forth the breaches, and by injunction prevented the plaintiff from cultivating the land, etc., and deprived him of the use and profit of the said land mentioned in the declaration from the 28th day of November, 1883, until after the expiration of the lease; that the said injunction was by decree of the supreme court of appeals of Virginia dissolved, and the bill dismissed; and laid his damages at $4,500. The defendant demurred to the declaration, which demurrer the court sustained, and rendered judgment for the defendant, from which judgment the plaintiff applied for and obtained a writ of error to this court. The ground of the court's decision is that the common-law action of covenant will not lie when the alleged breach was by legal process, as by injunction; that, when damage was caused, and the injunction not sustained, the injunction bond furnished the only remedy, all others being merged therein. Mr. High says, (High, Inj. § 1648:) "Some conflict of authority exists as to whether a defendant in an injunction suit may, by an action on the case, recover damages for having been enjoined without cause; and the rule has been broadly stated that no such right of action exists. The better doctrine, however, seems to be that defendant's right of action at common law is not merged in the remedy upon the bond, and that an action in the case wil lie;" citing Cox v. Taylor, 10 B. Mon. 17. Mr. Barton says, in his Chancery Practice, (page 478:) "The right to damages upon the dissolution of an injunction is independent of any statutory provision upon the subject, and amid some conflict of the decided cases it is said that this right is cumulative of, and in addition to, the right of action at law upon the injunction bond. While the court decrees damages upon the dissolution, it cannot go beyond the injunction bond, so far as the penalty is fixed therein, and, when damages have been thus awarded, the decree of the court is conclusive as to the amount which can be recovered in an action on the bond; but not so the right of action on the contract, whose covenants have been broken." Mr. Lawson says, (Lawson, Rights, Rem. & Pr. § 3704:) "It is now held that the defendant in an injunction suit has a common-law right of action to recover damages for having been improperly enjoined, in addition to his remedy upon the bond." Mitchell v. Railroad Co., 75 Ga. 398; Manlove v. Vick, 55 Miss. 567; Gorton v. Brown, 27 Ill. 489; Iron Mountain Bank v. Mercantile Bank, 4 Mo. App. 505; Hayden v. Keith, 32 Minn. 277, 20 N. W. Rep. 195. In some of the states this matter is regulated by statute, and it is provided by law that before decree defendant may file his account for all damages, and have them in that suit allowed; but when there is no specific mode prescribed by the statute of assessing damages, and no such provision exists by statute, the right of action at law is in addition to the remedy upon the bond. The declaration states a good cause of action, and the demurrer should have been overruled. The defendant was undoubtedly bound by her deed; and if, without sufficient cause, (and the dissolution of the injunction and dismissal of the bill is conclusive of that,) the defendant deprived the plaintiff of the benefits and profits accruing to him thereunder, she should undoubtedly respond in damages. The judgment appealed from is erroneous, and the same will be reversed and annulled, and the cause remanded for a new trial to be had therein, when the demurrer must be overruled, and the case proceeded in to final judgment upon the merits.

WELLS et al. v. MAYOR, ETC., OF CITY OF SAVANNAH et al.

(Supreme Court of Georgia. July 20, 1891.)

TAXATION—TAXABLE PROPERTY—INJUNCTION.

1. Real estate in Savannah, held by purchase from the city, the terms of purchase being the payment of an annual ground-rent forever, or, at the election of the purchaser, his heirs, executors, administrators, or assigns, the payment in full of the stipulated purchase money at any time, is taxable by the municipal government as the property of the purchaser or his successor in the title.

2. There was no error in denying the injunction prayed for to restrain the collection of the tax.

(Syllabus by the Court.)

Error from superior court, Chatham county; R. FALLIGANT, Judge.

J. R. Saussy, for plaintiffs in error. S. B. Adams, for defendants in error.

BLECKLEY, C. J. Some cases task the anxious diligence of a court, not by their difficulty, but their simplicity. This is one of them. Because the case seemed too plain for controversy, we have had some apprehension that we might decide it incorrectly. Impressed always by the ability and learning, the wide research, and earnest advocacy of the distinguished counsel for the plaintiffs, we have experienced a vague dread that we might stumble over legal obstacles which, if they exist, a treacherous darkness conceals. In order to examine the ground thoroughly, we have held up the case for months, read authorities cited and not cited, perused books before unknown to us, deliberated, meditated, considered, and reconsidered. But to the last hour we have discovered nothing debatable in the controlling question raised for our decision, fringed though it certainly is with technical niceties of great delicacy and much interest. To which side the artificial logic of these niceties would incline the scale is immaterial, for the solid practical subject of taxation must be dealt with on broader principles. The value of property consists in its use, and he who owns the use forever, though it be on condition subsequent, is the true owner of the property for the time being. This holds equally of a city lot or of all the land in the world. Where taxation is *ad valorem*, values are the ultimate objects of taxation, and they to whom the values belong should pay the taxes. Land sold, or by a contract of bargain and sale demised, forever subject to a perpetual rent, is taxable as corporeal property; and in private hands the rent also is taxable as an incorporeal hereditament. The tax on the former is chargeable to the purchaser or perpetual tenant, and on the latter to the owner of the rent. The corporeal property in such case is at the direct risk of the purchaser; he alone sustains the losses of depreciation in value, and he alone takes the benefit of appreciation. The vendor risks only the fixed rent, or the fixed purchase money, and neither of these will ever become more or less by anything which may happen to the premises. Only his security, not his property, will be affected thereby. It is to be assumed that the whole contract between the parties will be observed, not broken, and their true relation to the property is to be determined on that assumption. Possession of real estate, attended with an indefeasible right to occupy in perpetuity, and also with an indefeasible right to be clothed with the fee upon the voluntary payment of a fixed sum as purchase money, will constitute the purchaser the substantial owner of the property. So long as his possession, supplemented with these rights, continues, he is not a mere lessee, but a purchaser admitted into possession on the faith of his contract of purchase. Such were the contracts involved in the present case, and under them the purchasers have the actual possession and use of the premises, with the right to hold forever, on condition of paying up the purchase money whenever they please, and until that time an annual ground rent due by quarterly installments, the amount of which is fixed by contract, and is the equivalent of interest at a moderate rate per annum on the unpaid purchase money. In all essential respects, so far as liability for taxes is concerned, these purchasers are in the position of ordinary purchasers in possession under a bond for title, and these last are chargeable with accruing taxes on land so held. Denning v. Danforth, 80 Ga. 55, 7 S. E. Rep. 546. Not an iota of beneficial ownership in the city lots now in question abides in the municipality. The city but retained a qualified and wholly unproductive title as security for the purchase money, and, until that shall be paid, as security also for the annually accruing compensation under the name of "ground-rents" in lieu of interest on that money. If the municipal government held all the values in the city as trustee for the owners, or as security for purchase money, these values would be none the less taxable for that reason. The constitution of the state requires that taxes on property shall be ad valorem, and that when any part is taxed all shall be taxed which is subject, for the time being to the taxing power in the given locality. This rule is without exception. It prevails in Savannah. Mayor, etc., v. Weed, 84 Ga. 683, 11 S. E. Rep. 235. The property in question is situate in that city, and, as already said, its beneficial ownership is not in the municipality, but in those who long ago purchased it from the city or who hold under such purchasers by succession to their title. Relatively to the question of taxation, it makes no substantial difference whether the estate or property of beneficial owners be classed as realty or personalty; whatever property of either kind belongs to them is taxable ad valorem. That the so-called ground-rent lots, as long as the conditions of sale are unbroken, are the property of the purchasers, follows from what was decided by this court in Laurence v. Mayor, etc., 71 Ga. 392; and that case shows that, even after condition broken, the limit of the city's rights would generally be to have all arrearages cleared and discharged, the surplus proceeds realized by a sale of the property being payable to the real owner. Our reasons for the conclusion at which we have arrived need not be further elaborated. The constitution is imperative that property is to be taxed ad valorem. The foundation principle of such a system is that those who own and enjoy values are to pay the taxes. The real owners of the money which these lots would now sell for on the market are the persons whom we have designated as owners, and it is upon the cash market value that taxes are assessable. If that value is any less, on account of the subjection of the property to ground rents or unpaid purchase money, than it otherwise would be, that fact would no doubt be taken into consideration in making the assessment. The market value, whatever that may be, is the proper basis.

2. There was no error, either of practice or decision, in denying the injunction. Whatever the expectation of purchasers or the unbroken practice of the city hitherto may have been, the mandate of the constitution of 1877 is to tax all property, save that expressly exempted by the legislature under constitutional authority, if any is taxed. That this mandate may have heretofore been disregarded is no reason why it should not be obeyed now.

Judgment affirmed.

PENDLY et al. v. STATE, (two cases.)

(Supreme Court of Georgia. May 6, 1891.)

JURISDICTION OF SUPREME COURT — WRIT OF ERROR — BILL OF EXCEPTIONS.

1. The constitution confers no jurisdiction upon the supreme court, save for the trial and determination of writs of error from the superior and city courts. The writ of error provided for by statute prior to the act of 1889 was abolished by that act, and a new and different one prescribed, an essential part of which is a clause in the judge's certificate showing that the bill of exceptions specifies all of the record material to a clear understanding of the errors complained of, or else that none of the record is material.

2. Though the sole error complained of be the denial of a motion in arrest of judgment, a legal writ of error is requisite to bring up any part of the record below, and to give this court jurisdiction to entertain the case.

3. It is not the duty of the judges of the superior or city courts to prepare or correct certificates to bills of exceptions, but only to sign such as are presented to them when they are in the form prescribed by statute. The remedy to have the certificate signed when it is both true and in proper form is by mandamus. Any other certificate may be treated as none at all.

(Syllabus by the Court.)

Error from superior court, Pickens county; GEORGE F. GOBER, Judge

W. T. Day, E. L. Darnell, and Glenn & Maddox, for plaintiff in error. Geo. R. Brown, Sol. Gen., and Harrison & Peeples, for the State.

BLECKLEY, C. J. 1. The motion to dismiss the writ of error in each of these cases must be granted. By the constitution this court is one "for the trial and determination of writs of error from said superior and city courts." Code, § 5133. Save by writ of error, it has no jurisdiction whatever. The act of 1889 (pamphlet p. 114) declares "that no case shall be taken to the supreme court by bill of exceptions except in the following manner." It proceeds to specify the manner, and in so doing says that the judge "shall require the clerk to send up only so much of the record as he may certify is material." It prescribes the form of the certificate, and according to that form one of the facts to which the judge must certify is that the bill of exceptions "specifies all of the record material to a clear understanding of the errors complained of." The order which is to be given to the clerk in the certificate is "to make out a complete copy of such parts of the record in said case as are in this bill of exceptions specified, and certify the same as such, and cause the same to be transmitted," etc. The certificate of the judge to the bill of exceptions is the only writ of error provided for by the law, and consequently, if the certificate does not substantially comply with the requirements of the statute, there is no writ of error at all, and this court has no jurisdiction of the case unless defects in the writ are waived either expressly or by acquiescence. In each of these cases the certificate is in the form prescribed in section 4252 of the Code; that is, it would have been a good statutory writ of error under the law as it stood prior to the act of 1889. Tested by that act, it has two defects: It fails to certify that the bill of exceptions specifies all of the record material to a clear understanding of the errors complained of, and, instead of ordering the clerk to make out and transmit a copy of such parts of the record as are in the bill of exceptions specified, it orders him to make out and transmit "a complete copy of the record of said case." The statute contemplates that the judge shall consider and decide the question as to what parts of the record are material, and that he shall limit his direction to the clerk to such parts only. It is enough to say that by the act of 1889 the legislature has abolished such writs of error as have been sued out and issued in the two cases now before us, and in prescribing an exclusive mode of bringing cases to this court has ordained a writ of error substantially different. Without first determining that the bill of exceptions specifies all of the record material to a clear understanding of the errors complained of, or that none of it is material, the judge has no authority to issue a writ of error. The judge has no legal authority for ordering the clerk to send up more or less of the record than he himself certifies to be material, and the clerk has no authority to send up more or less than the judge orders him to send. In these cases the clerk has not attempted to comply with the judge's order, but has undertaken to overleap that order, and guide himself independently of it by the specifications in the bill of exceptions, his certificate being in each case "that the above and foregoing is a true and correct transcript of the record in the above-stated case, as asked for by bill of exceptions filed by defendant's counsel." The clerk does not assure us, as he was commanded by the judge's order to do, that we have "a complete copy of the record of said case," and the judge does not assure us that what the clerk has sent up is all of the record material to a clear understand-

ing of the errors complained of. As verification of this latter proposition we have only the specifications made by counsel in the bill of exceptions. The counsel and the clerk have worked in harmony, but without any co-operation of the judge, in verifying the accuracy or exhaustiveness of their selection.

2. In the argument of the motion to dismiss, counsel sought to draw a distinction between the two cases as to the materiality of the judge's certificate in respect to its compliance with the requirements of the statute. One of the bills of exceptions being founded on the denial of a motion for a new trial, and the other on the denial of a motion in arrest of judgment, it was contended that the certificate to the latter was sufficient because this court could and would know judicially that the parts of the record specified in the bill of exceptions, to-wit, the bill of indictment, the verdict, the motion in arrest, with the entries thereon, and the order overruling the motion, are all the parts of the record that could be material to a clear understanding of the error complained of. To this we reply that, until jurisdiction is acquired by this court through a legal writ of error, we can take no judicial notice of any record whatever or of its contents. Without a writ of error the clerk had no authority for sending to this court anything as a copy of the indictment, verdict, motion in arrest, or judgment on that motion. The writ of error is a jurisdictional writ, and when the attention of this court, by a motion to dismiss, is called to the fact that no legal writ has been issued, and we find that suggestion to be true, it is the right of the defendant in error to have the defective writ dismissed. That is the limit of any proper authority which this court has to deal with the case.

3. Another contention of counsel, applicable alike to both cases, was that the failure of the judge to certify in conformity to the statute was the default of a public officer, for which the plaintiffs in error were in no respect responsible, and that they ought not to suffer for his misfeasance. Two sufficient answers may be made to this contention. The first is that no court can exercise jurisdiction over a case in the absence of a necessary writ because some other court or officer should have issued it but did not; and the second is that, according to the regular course of practice in this state, it is not the duty of a judge who certifies a bill of exceptions to prepare the certificate, but the duty of counsel to prepare it and present it to him for signature. The manual labor of writing out the certificate is not cast upon the judge, and he could not be compelled, by *mandamus* or otherwise, to perform it. But if counsel should present to him for signature a proper certificate annexed to a true and correct bill of exceptions, the judge could be compelled to sign it, or, at all events, his refusal to sign in obedience to a *mandamus* applied for and issued in due time would not be allowed to work any prejudice to the party. Code, § 4258. And a signing by the judge of a certificate not authorized by law is the same as signing none. If he has done this at the

instance of counsel for the plaintiffs in error, the judge is in no fault except that of doing officially a vain and idle act. If, on the other hand, he does it, not at the instance of counsel or client, but of his own motion, the counsel may treat it as equivalent to not signing at all, and resort to *mandamus*, the same as if signature had been withheld or refused. Anderson v. Faw, 79 Ga. 558, 4 S. E. Rep. 920. Writs of error dismissed.

ELLISON *et al.* v. LUCAS *et al.*

(*Supreme Court of Georgia.* May 8, 1891.)

SALE OF PARTNERSHIP ASSETS—FRAUDULENT CONVEYANCES.

1. Two members composing a partnership may unite in selling the entire assets thereof in payment of debts due individually by such members, and the sale, if made in good faith and without fraud, will be valid against creditors of the firm, notwithstanding the insolvency of the partnership; provided the transaction is not, as to any one of the partners, obnoxious to the statute against voluntary conveyances by insolvent debtors. If the value of one partner's share in the partnership property considerably exceeds in amount his individual debts settled by the sale, it amounts in law to a donation by him of such excess to his partner.

2. Where it appeared that two partners composing a firm conveyed all the property of the firm to a third person in satisfaction of their individual debts, the consideration being recited as a given sum of money, and it being admitted that the purchaser paid full value for the property, these facts are *prima facie* evidence that the consideration named is the actual value of the property, and a verdict, in effect, finding to the contrary, should be set aside.

(*Syllabus by the Court.*)

Error from superior court, Clark county; N. L. HUTCHINS, Judge.

Barrow & Thomas, for plaintiffs in error. *T. W. Reed, T. W. Rucker, A. J. Cobb,* and *Lumpkin & Burnett,* for defendants in error.

LUMPKIN, J. 1. It was held by this court in the case of Veal v. Veal, (Ga.) 12 S. E. Rep. 297, that a mortgage given by a partnership on partnership property to secure a debt due by one of the partners was valid against creditors of the firm, and that this was especially true when the debt due by the individual member had, by consent of the partners, been made a debt of the firm. This doctrine, irrespective of the qualification as to making the debt that of the firm, is supported by Jones on Chattel Mortgages, § 44, there cited. In Veal's Case, the question as to how the solvency or insolvency of the partnership would affect the transaction was not made or considered. Our Code, § 1953, gives every debtor the right to prefer one creditor to another, and to that end he may give liens or sell property in payment of the debt. No distinction is made as to the kind of creditors who may be preferred, or as to the kind of property which may be used for this purpose. In this case, it appears that the transfer of the partnership property to Cohen was signed by Lucas and McDuffie as a firm, and by each of the members individually. We think, under the section of the Code cited, and under the law generally, each of

these members had the right, with the consent of his partner, to sell his share in the firm assets in payment of his individual indebtedness. As stated in the section above cited from Jones on Chattel Mortgages: "The rule preferring partnership property for the payment of partnership debts is for the benefit of the partners, and they may waive it. * * * The partners, while the partnership property is still under their control, have power to appropriate it to secure their individual debts. The mere preference of individual debts * * * over partnership debts is not such a fraud upon partnership creditors that a court of equity will set it aside. The partnership creditors have no lien on the property of the partnership, if the partners themselves have none." See, also, Story, Partn. § 358. It must not be overlooked that, under our own statute, the right to prefer creditors is secured as well to insolvent as to solvent debtors; provided, of course, they exercise this right in good faith, and without fraud on the rights of others. The doctrine is laid down in Bates on Partnership that it is not uncommon for a partnership to use the right of absolute disposition of its property by employing firm funds to pay the separate debt of a single partner; and it is said, in effect, that this right is unlimited, except as controlled by statutes against voluntary conveyances in fraud of creditors and the similar provisions of the bankrupt law. Of course, where this right is exercised for fraudulent purposes, the transaction will be void. Bates Partn. §§ 565, 566. In Marks v. Hill, 15 Grat. 400, it was held that "partnership effects may be applied, by the concurrence of the partners, to pay an individual debt of one of them, if the other receives a sufficient consideration therefor, though they may be unable to pay all their partnership debts." In Woodmansie v. Holcomb, 34 Kan. 35, 7 Pac. Rep. 603, it was held that while the partnership remains in existence, and in a solvent condition, it may, with the consent of all the partners, transfer firm property in payment of the individual debt of one of its members; and in the opinion, on page 38, 34 Kan., and page 605, 7 Pac. Rep., JOHNSTON, J., says: "The decisions of the courts have gone further than this, and, although not unanimous, the weight of authority seems to be that mere insolvency, where no actual fraud intervenes, will not deprive the partners of their legal control over the property and of the right to dispose of the same as they may choose; and where the separate creditor purchases from the firm in good faith, and the individual indebtedness is a fair price for the property purchased, such purchase cannot of itself be held fraudulent as against the general creditors of the firm." The following cases are there cited in support of this assertion: Sigler v. Bank, 8 Ohio St. 511; Schmidlapp v. Currie, 55 Miss. 597; Case v. Beauregard, 99 U. S. 119; Bank v. Sprague, 20 N. J. Eq. 13; Wilcox v. Kellogg, 11 Ohio, 394; Gwin v. Sedley, 5 Ohio St. 97; Allen v. Center Valley Co., 21 Conn. 130; Rice v. Barnard, 20 Vt. 479; Haben v. Harshaw, 49 Wis. 379, 5 N. W. Rep. 872; White v. Parrish, 20

Tex. 688; Schaefer v. Fithian, 17 Ind. 463; McDonald v. Beach, 2 Blackf. 55; Ex parte Ruffin, 6 Ves. 119; Whitton v. Smith, 1 Freem. Ch. (Miss.) 231; Freeman v. Stewart, 41 Miss. 138; Potts v. Blackwell, 4 Jones, Eq. 58. See, also, the notes to the case of Schmidlapp v. Currie, in 30 Amer. Rep. 533, in which reference to many cases bearing on this subject will be found, and among them that of Sigler v. Bank, 8 Ohio St. 511, above cited, in which it was held that, where a creditor of a firm and one of its members, with the assent of all the partners, bought of the firm in good faith, and at a fair price, goods to the amount of such joint and separate indebtedness, though with knowledge that the firm was insolvent in the popular sense of the term, such purchase was not fraudulent, as against other creditors of the partnership. As will be seen above, in the quotation from the opinion of Johnston, J., in the case cited from 34 Kan., and 7 Pac. Rep., he remarks that the decisions are not unanimous in holding "that mere insolvency, where no actual fraud intervenes, will not deprive the partners of their legal control over the property," etc. Accordingly, we have found, in support of the contrary doctrine, the following cases: Wilson v. Robertson, 21 N. Y. 591; Menagh v. Whitwell, 52 N. Y. 146; Clements v. Jessup, 36 N. J. Eq. 572; Arnold v. Hagerman, 45 N. J. Eq. 186, 17 Atl. Rep. 93; and Phelps v. McNeely, 66 Mo. 554. See, also, Davies v. Atkinson, 124 Ill. 474, 16 N. E. Rep. 899, and 2 Story, Eq. Jur. § 1253. Nevertheless, we are of the opinion that the true law of the case is as stated in the language taken from page 38 of 34 Kan., and page 605, 7 Pac. Rep., and that the current of authority is in that direction. Indeed, this doctrine was recognized by the learned counsel who argued this case for the plaintiff in error, who conceded that, if the value of Lucas' share in the partnership assets was not materially greater than the amount of his individual indebtedness to Cohen, the transaction would be legal and valid. He rested his case upon the law that a voluntary deed or conveyance by an insolvent debtor is void as to his creditors, and contended that, under the agreed statement of facts, it appeared that Lucas' half of the partnership assets, which he transferred to Cohen, was actually worth about $500 more than the amount Lucas owed Cohen, and consequently that Lucas had donated to his partner, McDuffie, without any valuable consideration therefor, about $500 worth of the property. We will now consider whether this position has merit in it.

2. The assignment of Lucas & McDuffie to Cohen recites that it is made for and in consideration of the sum of $4,331¾, and in the agreed statement of facts it appears that full value was paid by Cohen for the property. Lucas' debt to Cohen was $1,-600, and some interest thereon. McDuffie's debt to Mrs. Reese, assumed by Cohen, was $2,625, and interest. These sums, added together, make the consideration expressed in the assignment. The facts stated amount to prima facie proof that this consideration was the actual value of the property sold to Cohen. From no

other source in the record is any light thrown upon this question, except the statement that all these parties acted in perfect honesty and without fraud. These things being true, the presumption arises that the goods were bought at a fair price. To assume otherwise, in the light of the facts, would be mere conjecture. Moreover, if Cohen actually paid more for the goods than they were worth, it is quite certain he would have taken pains to make this exceedingly important fact appear. Taking the case, therefore, as it stands, it seems that Lucas parted with his half of the firm assets for a consideration materially less than its actual value; and, to the extent of the difference between such value and the amount of the debt he owed Cohen, this action on his part amounted in law to a donation of so much of his property to his partner, McDuffie, and was void as to creditors. The entire record of the case was not sent up, and we are therefore unable to ascertain what the pleadings contain; but, for the reasons stated above, we think the verdict was wrong, and that the court erred in refusing a new trial. Judgment reversed

---

SIMPSON v. EARLE.

(Supreme Court of Georgia. May 8, 1891.)

LANDLORD AND TENANT — ACTION ON NOTE FOR RENT—PLEADING.

An action by the payee against the makers of a promissory note which states on its face that it was given for rent, is in order for judgment at the first term of the court; and, in declaring upon such a note, it is not essential to the validity of the action that the declaration should expressly aver the relation of landlord and tenant, more especially where no motion to set aside the judgment was made until after the lapse of more than seven years.

(Syllabus by the Court.)

Error from superior court, Cobb county; George F. Gober, Judge.

J. E. Moseley and Richd. H. Earle, for plaintiff in error. Saml. Earle and Clay & Blair for defendant in error.

SIMMONS, J. In November, 1882, a judgment was rendered in favor of John W. Hill against W. R. Root, E. P. Earle, and J. H. Simpson, as the joint and several makers of a promissory note which recited that it was given by them to the plaintiff in consideration of house rent. The record shows that each of the defendants was duly served, but that they failed to defend, and judgment was rendered against them at the return term of the court. In March, 1890, in an affidavit of illegality filed by Simpson, one of the defendants, to an execution issued upon this judgment, he set up that the court had no jurisdiction to render judgment at the first term after the suit was brought, it not appearing from the record that the relation of landlord and tenant existed between the parties; and because, as a matter of fact, the affiant and E. P. Earle were merely securities for their co-defendant, Root, for a debt contracted prior to the signing of the note; and, upon the trial of the illegality, parol testimony was offered to establish this fact. The trial judge ruled that the testimony was inadmissible, in so far as it contradicted the note or contract sued on; and also held that the record introduced in evidence was of a suit for rent, and a judgment could be rendered therein at the first term. These rulings are the grounds of error insisted upon here. It is contended that, in a suit for rent, the declaration should in express terms aver the relation of landlord and tenant. We do not think this was essential to the validity of the action. The jurisdiction of the court to render this judgment at the first term sufficiently appeared when it was shown that the suit was for rent. The language of the Code is that "judgments upon suits for rent may be rendered at the first term." Section 2289. And the fact that this was a suit for rent appeared, both from the declaration which stated that the debt was for rent, and from the note, a copy of which was annexed to the declaration, and which, as we have seen, recited that it was given "in consideration of house rent." The testimony offered to show that the relation of landlord and tenant did not exist between the defendant, Simpson, and the plaintiff, and that he was merely a security upon the note, was properly rejected. The note upon its face showed that the defendants were jointly and severally liable as makers. They were sued as such, and, after due and legal notice, judgment was rendered against them as such. They had three years in which to move to set aside this judgment, (Code, § 2914:) but, so far as appears. no attack was made upon it until more than seven years had elapsed. It is clear that, after the lapse of this time, the defendant could not, upon an affidavit of illegality, come into court, and by parol testimony contradict or vary the terms of his written contract, and go behind a judgment thereon in all respects valid on its face. Judgment affirmed.

HARRIS v. BRATTON *et al.* DE LOACH *et ux.* v. SAME. WILLIAMS v. SAME.

(Supreme Court of South Carolina. July 28, 1891.)

PAROL TRUST—EVIDENCE TO ESTABLISH—LAPSE OF TIME.

In an action to establish a parol trust in personal property it appeared that 23 years prior to the suit, plaintiffs' mother, desiring to divide a sum of money among her children, delivered certain portions of it to some of them in person, and directed defendant to take the shares of plaintiffs, invest it for them, and pay them only the interest. No demand was made by plaintiffs upon defendant for the principal or interest of their shares for a series of years, although two of them were in needy circumstances, and had frequently requested pecuniary assistance from defendant. The testimony of the plaintiffs was vague and uncertain, and the details of the original transaction were stated in three different ways. *Held,* that the evidence was insufficient to establish the trust.

Appeal from common pleas circuit court of York county; W. H. WALLACE, Judge.

Separate actions by Agnes B. Harris and Jane Williams and James E. De Loach and wife against Harriet J. Bratton, administratrix of John S. Bratton,

Sr., deceased, and others, his heirs and distributees, to establish a trust in personal property. Decrees for plaintiffs, and defendants appeal. Reversed.

C. E. *Spencer, Wilson & Wilson & McDow* and *Hart & Hart,* for appellants. *McCan & McDonald,* for respondents.

McIVER, J. These three cases, involving substantially the same facts and same legal principles, were heard and will be considered together. The plaintiffs claim that as far back as 1867 the intestate, John S. Bratton, Sr., was constituted their trustee of certain personal property, to-wit, money, by their mother, Mrs. Harriet Bratton, for which he never accounted; and now, he being dead, the object of these actions is to obtain from his administratrix, as well as from his heirs at law and distributees, among whom his estate has been distributed, an account of their several alleged trust funds, as well as judgment for the amounts found due upon such accounting. The defendants set up several defenses: (1) A denial that any trust had ever been created; (2) that such alleged trust, if ever created, has been discharged by settlement, which should be presumed from lapse of time; (3) the statute of limitations; (4) actual payment; (5) that before any notice of plaintiffs' claim came to the defendants the estate of said John S. Bratton, Sr., had been fully settled, and the several parties interested had gone into the exclusive possession of their respective shares. The circuit judge, without passing upon the fourth and fifth defenses, overruled all the others, and rendered judgment that plaintiffs had established the alleged trusts, and that the defendant Harriet J. Bratton, as administratrix of the personal estate of said John S. Bratton, Sr., should account for the several trust funds, as well as for her administration of the estate of her intestate, and that she, with the other heirs and distributees of said John S. Bratton, Sr., should account for the assets to them descended. From this judgment the defendants appeal upon the several grounds set out in the record, which it is unnecessary to repeat here, as we think the whole case turns upon the question made by the first defense above stated.

For a proper understanding of this question a brief outline of the facts will be necessary. It appears that old Mrs. Bratton, the mother of these plaintiffs, as well as of the legal trustee, John S. Bratton, Sr., had, through her said son, who had for several years been acting as her agent in the management of her property, sold a large quantity of cotton, whereby she became possessed of quite a large sum of money, a very considerable portion of which she determined to divide among her eleven children and two grand-children. This division was made at her house, in the parlor, some time in the year 1867,—when is not precisely stated, though it is probable that it was prior to the 17th of November of that year,—three of the sons and a son-in-law being in the room where the money was divided. The share of each was $892, and each of the sons present received their respective shares; but the plaintiffs not being in the room at the time, their shares were counted out, and each package labeled with their names. John S. Bratton, Sr., then gathered up the packages of money which had not been delivered to the respective children, and carried them into the bedchamber of his mother, when, according to the testimony of the plaintiff Jane Williams, who was then living with her mother, and who was the only witness as to what then occurred, the following took place: "Question. Just state what happened in your presence between your mother and your brother John on that occasion. Answer. Brother John handed me the money, and said it was our trust money; and mother told me not to take it; that she was not satisfied to keep the money in the house, and she wished him to take it, and invest it for our benefit. Q. For the benefit of those four girls? A. Yes, sir. Q. Did John take the money? (Defendant's counsel object to the case of this plaintiff under section 400 of the Code. The court: Any conversation between Mrs. Harriet Bratton and John Bratton she can testify to.) Q. Did your mother tell him anything about paying the girls interest? A. Yes, sir. She said she didn't want us to use the principal, but to use the interest. Q. And your brother, in your presence, did take those four shares? A. Yes, sir." This witness, on her cross-examination, having stated that her mother had insured her life, was asked whether the premiums on the life policy were to be paid by her mother out of her own money, or out of this package set apart for her on the division above referred to, and testified as follows: "She insured our lives, and of course she was to pay the money. Question. You can't say whether or not it was to be taken out of this $892? Answer. No, sir; it was not to be taken out of that. Q. How do you know it was not to be taken out of that? A. Because mother told brother John to invest that money for the benefit of our children, and she insured our lives." Again, when this witness was examined in reply, she was asked by the court as to what occurred in the bed-chamber of her mother, when her brother John brought the packages of money into that room, and, after stating that there were three packages,—one for witness, one for Mrs. Harris, and one for Mrs. DeLoach, with their names indorsed on the slip of paper in which the packages of money were wrapped,—she was asked: "Question. Was that money given to your mother? Answer. No, sir; that was the time mother said she didn't want them to have it; she wanted him to keep it for them. Q. Did he say anything? A. He said he would take it, and do the best he could with it." It also appears that John S. Bratton, Sr., became an exile from the state on account of the Ku-Klux prosecutions, some time in the year 1871, and did not return to this state until some time in the year 1873, where he continued to reside up to the time of his death, 21st January, 1888. His mother died in 1874, and these actions were commenced 21st

February, 1890. There was also some testimony which is relied upon as tending to show a recognition of the trust alleged by John S. Bratton, Sr., which will be more particularly stated in the progress of the discussion, and need not, therefore, be specifically set forth here.

It is very obvious that the fundamental question presented by this appeal is whether any express trust ever was created, for until that is determined the other question cannot arise. While there is no doubt that a trust in personal property may be proved, as well as created, by parol evidence, there is as little doubt that the evidence relied upon for that purpose must amount to a clear and explicit declaration of trust. As is said in Hill on Trustees, p. 59: "In order to fasten a trust on property of any kind by means of parol declarations, the expressions used must amount to a clear and explicit declaration of trust. They must also point out with certainty the subject-matter of the trust, and the person who is to take the beneficial interest. Loose and indefinite expressions, and such as indicate only an incomplete and executory intention are insufficient for this purpose." And, as is said in 2 Pom. Eq. Jur. § 1008: "The consensus of authorities demands clear and unequivocal evidence." The reason of this well-settled rule is obvious; for, while the terms and objects of a trust declared or established by some writing can and must be ascertained from the language used in the writing, yet, where a trust is raised by parol evidence, it is absolutely essential that such evidence should be clear and explicit, for otherwise a court would not be able to enforce the trust, the terms and objects of which were left by the evidence in confusion or uncertainty. In the light of these well-settled principles, let us examine the question whether the evidence adduced was sufficient to show that any express trust had ever been created in favor of these plaintiffs. The only testimony which we have been able to discover in regard to the creation of the alleged trust comes from a party interested, who is testifying as to a conversation which she heard about 23 years before she was examined; and we find that she gives three different versions of this conversation. In her first examination in chief, when asked to state what occurred when it is claimed that this trust was originally created, she said: "Brother handed me the money, and said it was our trust money; and mother told me not to take it; that she was not satisfied to keep the money in the house; and she wished him to take it, and invest it for our benefit." Now, it is perfectly certain that the witness is mistaken in saying that her brother "said it was our trust money," for it cannot be pretended that up to that time any trust had been created, or even thought of; certainly none had been mentioned. Now, if she had said simply that her brother, when he came into the bedchamber, handed her the trust money, it might possibly be argued that she characterized it as trust money, because she so regarded it from what afterwards occurred; but how she could have said that her brother, who, so far as the evidence discloses, had never received the slightest intimation up to that time that there was any intention to impress it with any trust, "said it was our trust money," it is absolutely impossible to conceive. But, in addition to this, the language of the mother, italicised above,—that she was not satisfied to keep the money in the house,—shows anything else but an intention to constitute John S. Bratton, Sr., a trustee of the money; and, on the contrary, rather tends to show that the old lady's idea was to keep the money herself for the benefit of her daughters, but, not deeming it safe to keep that amount in her house, requested her son, as her agent, to invest the money for the benefit of her daughters. Then take her statement on the cross-examination as to what occurred, where she gives as a reason why her mother did not intend to pay the premiums on the life insurance out of this alleged trust money, the fact that her mother told her brother John "to invest that money for the benefit of our children." This, it is claimed in the argument, was a mere *lapsus linguæ* on the part of this good lady; but while there might possibly be some ground for such a claim if the witness had simply stated that her mother told her brother to invest the money "for the benefit of our children," whereas she really meant to say "for the benefit of her mother's children," we do not see how it is possible to suppose that it was a mere "slip of the tongue" when the statement was made *as a reason why the fund could not be used in paying premiums on the life policy,"* for, if the investment was to be made for the benefit of the children of the witness, then, of course, it could not be used for any other purpose, but if for her own benefit, then it could be. But when this witness is recalled, in the reply, she for the first time speaks of this transaction between her mother and brother John, in a way that might possibly tend to show that there was an intention to create some kind of a trust; but what was its nature or terms is still left in obscurity, for all that she says then is that her mother, speaking to her son in regard to the three packages of money intended for these plaintiffs, said, "She didn't want them to have it; she wanted him to keep it for them;" to which he replied, "He would take it, and do the best he could with it."

It may be contended, however, that the testimony of Mrs. Williams, relied upon to establish the creation of the trust, is confirmed by certain alleged admissions of John S. Bratton, Sr., as derived from his letter to his mother, written during his exile from "Dark Corner," bearing no date, and set out in the "case" as "Exhibit D" of the testimony, as well as from certain alleged declarations made by his wife, as to what he had said to her. These statements attributed to the wife, which, however, she denies, were plainly incompetent as mere hearsay, even taking the testimony on the part of the plaintiff as true, and rejecting altogether the testimony of the wife. They certainly do not fix upon

John S. Bratton, Sr., any admission of the trust by any competent testimony. And as to the letter to his mother, so far from its affording any evidence that he admitted the trust, it rather tends to show what we are inclined to think was the true character of the relation of John S. Bratton, Sr., to this money which his mother intended to give these plaintiffs, viz., that of agent of his mother; for there is nothing in the letter which even indicates that he regarded himself as trustee for his sisters. The word "trust" or "trustee" is not found in it; but, on the contrary, he seems to speak of himself only as the agent of his mother, and bound only to account to her as such. He says: "When I left home it was so sudden and unexpected to me that I had no time to make preparations, or even bid you farewell. I left my business matters all in black and white, [which can be readily comprehended,] and filed them in safety, which I did not desire to be handled until I returned. You have requested of Harriet [his wife] your notes and land papers; also your will, made and written at your request, and approved by you. I have informed her where she can find them, and return them to you. I knew that there must be some dissatisfaction about the will; and when it is returned to you, I hope that you will read it over to all the family, and see if it was made out for my benefit. Your eight hundred dollars in gold, left in my possession, I was necessarily forced to use four hundred dollars of when I left home, as I could not get it from the store. You recollect that I informed you more than once that I paid Jane and Aggie's [plaintiffs Mrs. Williams and Mrs. Harris] insurance premiums, and you requested me to pay myself out of your gold, and at your request I used four hundred dollars, which did not pay me the amount I paid out for them. I can show what has been paid in black and white, and will show their accounts to your satisfaction when I return home." And then he goes on to speak of the disposition to be made of certain notes of his mother's. It seems that, so far from there being anything whatever in this letter which in the remotest degree recognizes any liability to any of his sisters, or that he held any funds of theirs in his hands, its whole tenor shows that he was only referring to his business relations with his mother, of whom he had for a long time been the agent; and his only anxiety was to satisfy her that his dealings with her were correct, and that he would be able to show that fact to her satisfaction. His only allusion to his sisters—two of the plaintiffs—is in reference to the payment of the premiums upon their life-policies, which it is not claimed were to be paid out of this alleged trust fund, but were to be paid by the mother; and it is in this connection he says: "I can show what has been paid in black and white, and will show their accounts to your satisfaction when I return home;" not to the satisfaction of his sisters, as he would have said if he had been alluding to their so-called "trust funds," but to the satisfaction of his mother, who would have had nothing to do with any trust fund that might have been created, but did have something to do with the use of her money,—her gold,—used in the payment of the insurance premiums. It seems to us, therefore, that, even considering the case upon the testimony as adduced by the plaintiffs only, it is altogether insufficient to establish the creation of any trust by that "clear and unequivocal evidence" which the rule of law above stated requires, and that the circuit judge erred in holding otherwise. In cases like this the burden of proof to establish the trust is upon the plaintiff; and where the plaintiff fails to furnish such evidence as the rule of law requires he cannot recover.

This conclusion, which has been reached from a consideration of the testimony on the part of the plaintiffs alone, is confirmed and strengthened by the facts and circumstances brought out in the defense. In the first place, the lapse of time between the alleged origin of this trust and any attempt to enforce it—about 23 years—is a circumstance entitled to great consideration, for, while it is true that mere lapse of time will not bar an express trust, after it has once been established, yet it is entitled to great weight in considering the parol evidence relied on to establish the trust. As is said in 2 Story, Eq. Jur. § 1520a: "It is often suggested that lapse of time constitutes no bar in cases of trust; but this proposition must be received with its appropriate qualifications. As long as the relation of trustee and *cestui que trust* is acknowledged to exist between the parties, and the trust is continued, lapse of time can constitute no bar to an account or other proper relief for the *cestui que trust.* But where this relation is no longer admitted to exist, or time and long acquiescence have obscured the nature and character of the trust, or the acts of the parties or other circumstances give rise to presumptions unfavorable to its continuance, in all such cases a court of equity will refuse relief upon the ground of lapse of time, and its inability to do complete justice. This doctrine will apply even to cases of express trust, and, *a fortiori,* it will apply with increased strength to cases of implied or constructive trusts." See, also, the remarks of Lord COTTENHAM in Attorney General v. Fishmongers' Co., 5 Mylne & C. 16, where, among other things, he said: "If there be no doubt as to the origin and existence of a trust, the principles of justice and the interests of mankind require that the lapse of time should not enable those who are mere trustees to appropriate to themselves that which is the property of others; but in questions of doubt whether any trust exists, and whether those in possession are not entitled to the property for their own benefit, the principles of justice and the interests of mankind require that the utmost regard should be paid to the length of time during which there has been enjoyment inconsistent with the existence of the supposed trust." And, without incumbering this opinion with further quotations, see Prevost v. Gratz, 6 Wheat. 481; Badger v. Badger, 2 Wall. 87. Now, in this case there is not only great lapse of time,

but we fail to find any evidence of any admission or acknowledgment by the alleged trustee of the trust now claimed to be established by mere parol evidence of a single interested witness of a conversation which she heard about 23 years previously, which she narrates in three different forms, leaving not only the nature and character of the alleged trust in obscurity, but, to say the least of it, leaving it doubtful whether any trust was in fact created. On the contrary, the evidence shows that the alleged trustee lived for about 11 years after his return from exile, and yet during all that time no claim or demand was ever made upon him by either of these plaintiffs, even for the interest of the alleged trust fund, although the evidence also shows that during that time at least two of the plaintiffs were in needy circumstances, and one of them made repeated demands upon the alleged trustee by letter for pecuniary assistance, which letters contain no intimation whatever of the trust now sought to be set up, after the death of old Mrs. Bratton, who, it is claimed, created the trust, and after the death of the alleged trustee, who died leaving quite a handsome estate, which was divided among his heirs at law before these actions were instituted. It seems to us that, in view of these circumstances, it would be extremely unsafe to allow a parol trust to be established by parol evidence of "loose and indefinite expressions" which a witness claims to have heard in a conversation between parties, both of whom are dead, about 23 years before such evidence was taken, especially when her statement as to such conversation contains a mistake palpable on its face, and varies in its terms on each occasion when she is asked to state what occurred; for, without intending to impute the slightest intentional wrong to the witness, the frailty of human memory is such as to render it unsafe, after such a lapse of time, for a court to base a decree upon such evidence, where it is not only not corroborated by the other circumstances, but, in our judgment, is altogether inconsistent with them. Having reached the conclusion that the plaintiffs have failed to establish the alleged trust upon which these actions are founded, the other questions presented cannot arise, and need not, therefore, be considered. The judgment of this court is that the judgment of the circuit court in each of the cases above stated be reversed, and that the complaints in said cases be dismissed.

McGOWAN, J., concurs.

In re KIRKPATRICK'S ESTATE.

(*Supreme Court of South Carolina.* July 28, 1891.)

PARENT AND CHILD—COMPENSATION FOR SERVICES —PRESUMPTIONS.

On a trial to recover for services rendered for defendant's decedent by his daughter, two witnesses testified that they had heard the father say the daughter ought to be paid for her services. Another testified that she had heard him say that she ought to have "extra pay for her services to him." *Held* insufficient to create a legal obligation, as in such cases the presumption is that the services were gratuitous, which must be overcome by proof of an express agreement to pay.

Appeal from common pleas circuit court of York county; W. H. WALLACE, Judge.

S. E. Aycock filed a claim against the estate of J. J. Kirkpatrick, deceased. From an order disallowing her claim she appeals. Affirmed.

Wilson & Wilson & McDow, for appellant. *Hart & Hart*, for respondents.

MCIVER, J. Under proceedings to marshal the assets of the estate of J. J. Kirkpatrick, deceased, his creditors were called in to establish their claims. Among the claims presented was one in favor of the appellant, who was the daughter of the deceased, for services rendered by her to her father during his life-time. To this claim the administrator presented two defenses: (1) A general denial; (2) the statute of limitations. The clerk of the court, to whom it was referred to take proof of claims, reported that a part of the claim was barred by the statute of limitations, and established the claim of the remaining part. To this report both parties excepted; the appellant alleging error in sustaining the plea of the statute to any part of the claim, and the administrator contending that there was no evidence of any contract, either express or implied, to pay for the service rendered by appellant to her father, and hence there was error in allowing any part of the claim. Upon this report and the exceptions thereto the case was heard by his honor, Judge WALLACE, who sustained the exception filed by the administrator and rendered judgment disallowing the entire claim. From this judgment Mrs. Aycock appeals. The testimony is all set out in the "case," and the only question is whether it is sufficient to establish any contract, either express or implied, on the part of the deceased to pay the appellant anything for her services.

The general rule is that, where one, who is under no legal or moral obligation to do so, renders service to another, at his request or with his knowledge and acquiescence, the law raises an implied promise on the part of the person receiving the services to pay what they are reasonably worth; but where there is a legal or moral obligation on the part of one to render service to another, no such promise can be implied from the mere rendition and acceptance of such service. In the former case, there being nothing else to which the rendition of the services can be referred, the inference is that they were rendered upon an implied understanding that compensation was to be made; but in the latter case the rendition of the services can be and is referred to a desire to comply with the legal or moral obligation, unless the testimony shows that such was not the consideration upon which the services were rendered; or, to use the language of GIBSON, C. J., in Bash v. Bash, 9 *Pa.* St. 260, unless there is "direct and positive" evidence that the services were rendered under a contract for compensation. In 3 Amer. & Eng. Enc. Law, 861, it is said: "Between parent and child there can be no recovery for board or wages in the absence of an express agreement." In Dodson v. McAdams, (N. C.) 2 S. E. Rep. 453, where the rule was held to apply, as between grandfather and grandchild, it was held that in such a case there was not only no presumption of a promise to pay, but the presumption was the other way; and the burden is on the claimant to rebut such presumption, which cannot be done by showing casual declarations of the grandfather that his granddaughter ought to be paid for her work. See, also, Young v. Herman, (N. C.) 1 S. E. Rep. 792. In Hall v. Finch, 29 Wis. 278, where the rule was applied as between brother and sister, it was said: "The relation existing between the parties * * * is itself strong negative proof, and raises a presumption that no payment or compensation was to be made beyond that received by claimant at the time, (in the way of board, clothing, etc.,) which can only be overcome by clear and unequivocal proof to the contrary. The evidence must be clear, direct, and positive that the relation between the parties was not the ordinary one of parent and child, or of brother and sister, but that of debtor and creditor, or of master and servant;" and, further, quoting with approval the language of Judge STRONG in Hartman's Appeal, 3 Grant, Cas. 276: "Loose declarations, made to others, or even to the claimant himself, will not answer. That which is only an expression of intention is inadequate for the purpose. It must have been the purpose of the deceased to assume a legal obligation, capable of being enforced against him. The ordinary expressions of gratitude for kindness to old age, weakness, and suffering, are not to be tortured into contract obligations." See, also, Miller's Appeal, 100 Pa. St. 568, where it is said: "The question always is whether the parties contemplated payment and dealt with each other as debtor and creditor. A son who takes his decrepit parents into his house and supports them is presumed to do so from the promptings of natural affection. No contract is implied. But if the father, before they go and afterwards, repeatedly declares that he was to pay for their board, such declarations are evidence, and, with the circumstances, may be so direct and strong as to compel belief that he expressly agreed to pay for it. Loose declarations, made to the son or others, will not answer. That which may be only the expression of an intention to compensate is not evidence of an agreement to compensate. If he intended to pay, and often said so to others, he was not bound. It must appear that he purposed to assume a legal obligation capable of being enforced against him." It seems to us that the true rule upon the subject is that, where a child renders service to his parents, the presumption is that such service was rendered in obedience to the promptings of natural affection, and not with a view to compensation; but that such presumption may be rebutted by positive and direct evidence that such is not the fact, and that mere loose declarations on the part of the parent that the child ought to be paid for his services, or that he intended or wished him to be paid, will not be sufficient to rebut the presumption. It must appear either that there was an express agreement between the parties providing for specific or reasonable compensation, or that the circumstances should show clearly that the parent had not only intended to pay something, but had assumed a legal obligation to do so. Applying this rule to the case under consideration, it is very clear that there is no error in the judgment of the circuit court. It is not pretended that there was any evidence whatever of any express agreement between the parties, and the testimony adduced is wholly insufficient to rebut the presumption that the services rendered by appellant to her aged father were gratuitous. While the testimony does show that the appellant rendered faithful service to her father, for which she is entitled to commendation, we are unable to discover any evidence which even tends to show that such services were rendered under a contract for compensation, either express or implied. One witness says that he heard the father say "that Mrs. Aycock had too much to do, and that she ought to be paid, but that he had no money." Another witness testified that she had heard the father say "that Em [meaning appellant] had a hard time, and she ought to have pay for it." And another says "that she has heard her grandfather say that Mrs. Aycock ought to have extra pay for her services to him." This is all that is relied upon to rebut the presumption, arising from the relationship of the parties, that the services were intended at the time as a gratuity, prompted by feelings of natural affection; and, under the authorities cited, such testimony is clearly insufficient to create any legal obligation. Under this view of the case it was not necessary either for the circuit court or this court to consider the question as to the statute of limitations. The judgment of this court is that the judgment of the circuit court be affirmed.

McGOWAN, J., concurs.

BERTHA ZINC CO. v. BLACK'S ADM'R.

(Supreme Court of Appeals of Virginia. July 23, 1891.)

WRONGFUL DEATH — EXCESSIVE DAMAGES — NEW TRIAL.

A cut 18 feet deep and 12 feet wide was being driven through the side of a mountain in a strata of thin layers of slate rock, with loose slip clay between, with no artificial support. Plaintiff's intestate was at work in the bottom of the cut, and was killed by a slide from the side covering him. He was a new man, and had no knowledge of the treachery of the dirt. Defendant thoroughly understood the dangerous character of the place, and regarded it as a question of profit against risk to put in supports. Held error to set aside a verdict of $10,000 as excessive, under Code Va. § 2903, which provides that in case of wrongful death damages may be assessed not to exceed $10,000.

Action by Michael Black's administrator, against the Bertha Zinc Company, to recover damages for negligently killing plaintiff's intestate. Judgment for plaintiff. New trial granted. Plaintiff assigns error. Reversed.

Brown, Moor & Blair, for plaintiff in error. J. A. Walker, for defendant in error.

LACY, J. This is a writ of error to a judgment of the circuit court of Wythe county, rendered at the March term, 1890. The action is trespass on the case by the defendant in error against the plaintiff in error, the Bertha Zinc Company, on account of the killing by the defendant, the said Bertha Zinc Company, of the plaintiff's intestate, through the negligence of the said defendant and its agents. At the trial the evidence on both sides was heard, certain instructions given and others refused by the court, when the jury rendered a verdict for $10,000 damages against the defendant, whereupon the defendant moved the court to set aside the said verdict and grant it a new trial, upon the ground that the said verdict was contrary to the law and the evidence, on account of the misdirection by the court to the jury as to the law of the case, and because the damages were excessive. The court did set aside the verdict, on the ground that the damages were excessive, and overruled all other grounds of exception, to which action of the court, in setting aside the verdict because the damages were excessive, the plaintiff excepted and filed his bill of exception, which was duly signed and made a part of the record, and all the evidence was certified. A new trial was thereupon had, when the jury found a verdict for the plaintiff, and assessed his damages at $9,166. The defendant again moved the court to set aside the verdict and grant to it a new trial, upon the ground that the verdict was contrary to the law and the evidence. But the circuit court overruled this motion, and rendered a final judgment in the cause, whereupon the defendant applied for and obtained a writ of error to this court.

The plaintiff in error assigns various alleged errors, but the defendant in error assigns as error, to his prejudice, the action of the court in setting aside the first verdict, because the damages assessed by the jury were deemed excessive; and we will consider this assignment first, as it stands, in point of time, prior to all others.

The circuit court refused expressly to disturb this the first verdict, because of all grounds of exception alleged by the defendant except that which concerned the amount of the damage, but the defendant did not except. The first matter for inquiry in this case is whether the circuit court erred in granting a new trial, and in not rendering judgment upon the first verdict. The verdict in question was set aside because the damages allowed by the jury were, in the opinion of the trial judge, excessive. How far, and when, may a judge review the action of the jury in fixing the amount of damages? In this state, by our statute law, it is provided that "the jury, in any such action, may award such damages as to it may seem fair and just, not exceeding $10,000, and, may direct in what proportion they may be distributed, etc. "But nothing in this section shall be construed to deprive the court of the power to grant new trials, as in other cases." Code Va. § 2908. This section refers to cases mentioned in the preceding section, where death is caused by the wrongful act of another. In personal torts and actions, generally sounding in damages, it being within the strict province of the jury to estimate the injury, unless there be a manifest abuse, the court will not interfere. In its general acceptation this rule applies equally to an unjust assessing of the damages as to an intemperate excess. Justice BUTLER says, (Bull, N. P. 327:) "In actions grounded upon torts the jury are the sole judges of the damages, and therefore the court, in such cases, will not grant a new trial on account of the damages being trifling or excessive. This was the common-law rule, and was followed in this state until changed by statute." 1 Rev. Code, p. 510, §§ 96, 97; Code 1877, c. 173, § 15; Code Va. § 3392. "In any civil case or proceeding, the court before which a trial by jury is had may grant a new trial, unless it is otherwise specially provided. A new trial may be granted as well where the damages awarded are too small as where they are excessive." While the law thus expressly leaves the question under the control of the court, the jury is nevertheless the proper tribunal for the assessment of damages in cases like the present, and, as was said by Judge STAPLES, in Borland v. Barrett, 76 Va. 137, their verdict will not be disturbed unless it shows that the jury were actuated by passion, prejudice, or undue influence, or unless the amount is grossly excessive upon any just view of the evidence which might have been taken by the jury. Citing Peshine v. Shepperson, 17 Grat. 488; Treanor v. Donahoe, 9 Cush. 228; 2 Sedg. Dam. 334; Moak, Underh. Torts, 72, 226. In Dangerfield v. Thompson, 33 Grat. 136, it was said by this court: "The question of what damages the plaintiff sustained was a question for the jury to determine. The appellate court will not interfere with such a verdict unless it appears that the verdict is plainly extravagant and excessive." And, as has been often said, the reason for holding parties so tenaciously to the damages found by the jury in personal torts is that in cases of this class there is no scale by which damages are to be graduated with certainty. They admit of no other test than the intelligence of the jury, governed by a sense of justice. It is, indeed, one of the principal causes in which the trial by jury has originated. From the prolific fountain of litigation numerous cases must daily spring up calling for adjudication for alleged injuries, accompanied with facts and circumstances affording no definite standard by which these alleged wrongs can be measured, and which, from the necessity of the case, must be judged of and appreciated by the views which may be taken of them by impartial men. To the jury, therefore, as a favorite and almost sacred tribunal, is committed by unanimous consent the exclusive task of examining those facts and circumstances, and valuing the injury, and awarding compensation in the shape of damages. The law which confers on them this power, and exacts of them the performance of this

solemn trust, favors the presumption that they are actuated by pure motives. It therefore makes every allowance for different dispositions, capacities, views, and even frailties, in the examination of heterogeneous matters of fact when no criterion can be supplied. And it is not until the result of the deliberations of the jury appears in a form calculated to shock the understanding, and impress no dubious conviction of their prejudice and passion, that courts have found themselves compelled to interfere. Grah. & W. New Trial, 452.

In this case the negligence of the defendant is clearly established. The defendant company was engaged in cutting through the side of the mountain a horizontal opening, in which they intended to lay a railroad track to reach the zinc mines to be opened in the mountain. This cut was opened 18 feet deep and 12 feet wide, with the banks perpendicular, and not propped nor boarded up, nor supplied with any support. It was cut in what is called three benches, the first bench being cut four feet deep, and in advance of the second, which followed with a depth of four feet more, and that by the third, which was still behind the second, and was opened four feet more; and the first and second benches had a floor laid behind, over which the dirt was carried off as it was dug, in wheelbarrows. The third or bottom cut had a dirt floor, which was the bottom of the cut, over which the wheelbarrows were rolled. The deceased was a new man, and was employed on the top bench. But, a noon-day shower having driven off the hands, a good many did not return in the afternoon, and among them the wheelbarrow men, for whom he had been digging dirt in the morning at the top bench, and he, desiring to make a full day's work, and receive a full day's pay, asked to be assigned to work elsewhere, there being nobody to haul off the dirt upon his bench. He was set to work in the bottom of the cut on the ground floor, where he was very soon killed by a slide from the side of the cut which covered him up in clay, and injured several others. The evidence shows that the earth at this point was very treacherous, being composed in a large degree of what is termed "slip clay," or "block clay," which was liable to sudden slides, which came without warning, with great suddenness, being described as, "as quick as lightning," the cut being driven through slanting strata of thin layers of slate rock, with this loose clay lying between, which, when deprived of support at the base, slipped through between the strata, to which it was not adherent, and into which it was loosely deposited. The evidence shows, further, that the company knew of the dangerous character of this formation, and it shows, further, that the attention of its agents was called to the dangerous character of the cut, and that they admitted it, and, when urged to slant the sides so as to leave a support for this slip clay, they declined, saying that they would hurry through to the zinc, and then slope the sides, and, when warned that supports ought to be put up for the protection of human life, said it was a question of risk against profit, and they would not do it, and directed that nothing be said about it whatever. It is also found that the deceased had no notice or knowledge of the danger, and that when down under the two floors it was too dark to see much about it. It was necessary, to avoid this danger, only to slant the sides on one side, that being the side from which, by the formation of the seams, the base was removed from the clay; on the other side the top sections being removed. This was a precaution which had to be taken before the cut could be used for the purpose for which it was made, and it was against the advice of the "boss of the cut," as he is termed, that the manager compelled the cut to be driven in with perpendicular sides. It was negligence to so unnecessarily expose the lives of the workmen. The sides were sloped after the accident. · This should have been done in the first instance, and this life would then have been spared. It was negligence to go on with the work in the afternoon, after the rain, as the rain greatly increased the danger. The negligence of the company is clearly established; but it is sought to condone this by a charge of negligence on the part of the deceased to go in the cut at the bottom, when his work was on the top, and that, being thus guilty of contributory negligence which was the proximate cause of the injury which he sustained, he cannot, therefore, recover. But the record furnishes no support for this whatever. The deceased, a new man, and uninformed about the business, worked where he was put to work by the person in charge. He was put to work in the top in the morning; and in the evening, there being no work for him to do there, he was put to work on the bottom. There is nothing to show that he knew anything about the danger then; while, on the other hand, it is abundantly shown that the defendant did thoroughly understand the dangerous character of the place, and regarded it as a question of profit against risk. It is a case in which the verdict of the jury should not have been disturbed, and judgment should have been rendered on the first verdict. The circuit court erred in setting aside the verdict of the jury on the first trial, and for that cause the judgment of the said circuit court will be reversed and annulled here, and judgment rendered here on the first verdict; and it thus becomes unnecessary to notice any of the proceedings on the second trial.

NORFOLK & W. R. CO. v. GROSECLOSE'S ADM'R.

(Supreme Court of Appeals of Virginia. July 16, 1891.)

INJURY TO PASSENGERS—REVIEW ON APPEAL.

1. A freight train, with caboose for passengers, stopped at a certain station, and the conductor, though he saw several persons approaching with baggage, ordered the engineer to back the train. Without warning, the train was violently backed while the passengers were boarding it, fatally injuring a boy between five and six years old, standing on the ends of the ties,

and about to get on. *Held,* that the railroad was negligent.

2. Where the evidence, and not the facts, are certified to the supreme court, the case will be treated as on a demurrer to evidence; and evidence for the defendant that the child was standing behind the car, between the rails, and attempting to climb upon the bumper, will be rejected.

3. In a suit by the administrator of such infant, the contributory negligence of the parents cannot be imputed to him, and is therefore immaterial.

4. Although the railroad required fare for all children over five years old, the fact that the father purchased no ticket for such child will not bar recovery, and whether or not he knew that a ticket was required is immaterial.

5. Where the mother is not a party to the suit, and is in no way interested therein, her declarations, made immediately after the accident, are immaterial.

Error to circuit court, Washington county; JOHN A. KELLY, Judge.

Action by the administrator of one Groseclose, an infant, against the Norfolk & Western Railroad Company, for the negligent killing of the deceased. Judgment for plaintiff. Defendant brings error. Affirmed.

Fulkersons, Page & Hart, for plaintiff in error. *F. S. Blair* and *D. Trigg,* for defendant in error.

LEWIS, P. The action was to recover damages for the alleged negligent killing of the plaintiff's intestate, a child five years and one month of age. On the 9th of February, 1888, M. L. Groseclose, accompanied by his wife and five children, went to Meadow View, a station on the defendant road, in Washington county, to take a train for Rural Retreat, in Wythe county. He purchased of the defendant's agent at Meadow View two whole tickets and two half tickets for himself and family. Of the five children, two were under five years of age; the other three were over that age, but under twelve. Before the arrival of the train at the station, the father asked and secured the assistance of three gentlemen, who were present, in getting the children on the car. The train was a local freight train, having at its rear end a caboose for passengers. Upon the arrival of the train, and after it had stopped, the children and their adult attendants left the depot platform, and started for the train. Several passengers alighted from the caboose car, when Groseclose, the father, with one of the children, went up the steps, and into the car. He was followed by Mr. Naff, who carried another child. Following Naff was Mrs. Groseclose, but, just as she had gotten up the steps, the train, with a violent and sudden jerk, started backward, the steps of the caboose striking the deceased, who was standing on the end of the ties, and throwing him under the wheels of the train, which passed over and crushed his left leg, and inflicted other injuries, which caused his death the same day. The conductor of the train saw the party approaching the caboose, with their luggage, but paid no attention to them. In fact, he went in another direction, to see, as he says, about the freight. And, not only this, but he deliberately ordered a brakeman to signal the engineer to back the train when he knew, or ought to have known, that passengers were in the act of getting on, to whom no warning whatever was given. The whistle on the engine was not sounded, nor the bell rung, and the only signal to the engineer was a slight wave of the brakeman's hand. Under these circumstances, a clearer case of culpable negligence, or the violation of the duty of a railroad company, as a part of the implied contract to carry safely, to give its passengers time to get off and on in safety, could hardly be imagined. Whart. Neg. § 648; Railroad Co. v. Prinnell, (Va.) 3 S. E. Rep. 95.

The company, however, contends that it was negligence on the part of the parents to allow the deceased to stand at the place he was when struck, and their contributory negligence bars a recovery. It is conceded that the deceased himself, by reason of his tender years, was *non sui juris,* and therefore incapable of contributory negligence. There was evidence for the company, on the question of the parents' negligence, tending to show that the deceased, when struck, was standing behind the car, between the rails, apparently attempting to climb upon the bumper. But this evidence must be rejected, because it is in conflict with the plaintiff's evidence, which shows that he was not between the rails, but was standing near the car on the ends of the ties. We say the evidence must be rejected, inasmuch as the evidence, not the facts, being certified, the case stands in this court as on a demurrer to evidence; and, viewing the case in this light, the charge of contributory negligence is not sustained.

But that is a wholly immaterial question in this action. When the suit is by a parent for the loss of service caused by an injury to the child, the contributory negligence of the plaintiff is a good defense; but such negligence is not imputable to the child, and is consequently not to be considered when the suit is by the child or its personal representative. Shear. & R. Neg. § 48a; Glassey v. Railroad Co., 57 Pa. St. 172; Huff v. Ames, 16 Neb. 139, 19 N. W. Rep. 623. The doctrine of Hartfield v. Roper, 21 Wend. 615, has been repudiated in this state, as in many other states of the Union, and the doctrine established as just stated. Beach, Contrib. Neg. § 42; Railroad Co. v. Ormsby, 27 Grat. 455; Railroad Co. v. Snyder, 18 Ohio St. 408; Railway Co. v. Moore, 59 Tex. 64; Railway Co. v. Schuster, 113 Pa. St. 412, 6 Atl. Rep. 269; Robinson v. Cone, 22 Vt. 214; Daley v. Railroad Co., 26 Conn. 591; Smith v. Railway Co., 92 Pa. St. 450; Coal Co. v. Brawley, 83 Ala. 371, 3 South. Rep. 555; Wymore v. Mahaska Co., 78 Iowa, 396, 43 N. W. Rep. 264; Railroad Co. v. Stout, 17 Wall. 657; 4 Amer. & Eng. Enc. Law, 88, and cases cited. Hence, when the facts are such that the child could have recovered had his injuries not been fatal, his administrator may recover, without regard to the negligence or presence of the parents at the time the injuries were received, and although the estate is inherited by the parents. Of course, it is essential to a recovery in any case that negligence on the

part of the defendant be shown. But, when that is proven in a suit by the child, the parents' negligence is no defense, because it is regarded, not as a proximate, but as a remote, cause of the injury. And the reason lies in the irresponsibility of the child, who, itself being incapable of negligence, cannot authorize it in another. It is not correct to say that the parent is the agent of the child, for the latter cannot appoint an agent. The law confides the care and custody of a child *non sui juris* to the parents, but, if this duty be not performed, the fault is the parents', not the child's. There is no principle, then, in our opinion, upon which the fault of the parent can be imputed to the child. To do so is to deny to the child the protection of the law. Whart. Neg. § 312; Patt. Ry. Acc. Law, 93; Wymore v. Mahaska Co., supra. In the last-mentioned case, which was an action by the administrator of a deceased child, two years of age, whose death was caused by the breaking of a bridge upon which the child was driven in a carriage by its parents, the supreme court of Iowa, after announcing the same doctrine, adds: "Some authorities seem to make a distinction between cases where the contributory negligence of the parent occurs while he has the child under his immediate control, and other cases which occur when the child is away from the parent; but we are of opinion that there is no sufficient ground for the distinction claimed. The authority of the parent does not depend upon the proximity of the child." This view seems to us correct in principle, and is undoubtedly supported by the great weight of authority. In a recent work, wherein the subject is discussed and the cases are collected, the learned author says: "A doctrine formerly obtained in some courts of this country called 'imputed negligence,' under the operation of which, if a child, of such tender age as not to be capable of caring for its own safety, was negligently exposed to danger by its parent or guardian, and injured, the negligence of the parent or guardian would be imputed to the child, and the child could not recover damages for the injury." But this rule, he adds, "though approved at one time in several American jurisdictions, has been denied in others, and seems fast going by the board." 2 Thomp. Trials, § 1687.

Another point made by the company is, and the court at the trial was asked, in effect, to instruct the jury, that if the father of the child, at the time of the accident, was endeavoring to take it on the train without paying fare, then he could not be considered a passenger, and the liability of the company was not to be determined by the law relating to carriers and passengers. This instruction was rightly refused. The purchase of a ticket, before entering a railroad train, is not necessary to constitute a person a passenger, nor is there any evidence in the case tending to show that the father was attempting to defraud the company, or was not acting in perfect good faith. It does not appear, moreover, that he knew a ticket for the deceased was required. The conductor of the train, a witness for the company, testified that tickets for children under six years of age were not required. In point of fact, however, the regulations of the company require half-rate tickets for children between the ages of five and twelve years. But, if the conductor of the train was ignorant of that requirement, would it be strange if the father of the deceased was, also? This is a matter, however, of no importance whatever. The deceased undoubtedly was a passenger, and as such entitled to the utmost degree of diligence and care on the part of the company in looking out for his safety. 2 Walt. Act. & Def. 65; Railroad Co. v. Noell, 32 Grat. 394; Railroad Co. v. Moose, 83 Va. 827, 3 S. E. Rep. 796.

Complaint is also made of the action of the circuit court in refusing to permit the defendant to prove the declarations of the mother of the child immediately after the accident. The assignment of error on this point is general in its terms, and no reasons are urged in support of it, nor are we aware of any principle upon which the declarations were admissible. The mother is not a party to the suit, nor interested in the result. Her declarations were merely hearsay, and no more bind the estate of the deceased than would the declaration of any stranger. There was no error, therefore, in excluding them. In short, we find no error in the record, and the judgment must be affirmed.

RICHARDSON, J., concurs in the result.

BAILEY CONST. Co. et al. v. PURCELL.

(Supreme Court of Appeals of Virginia. July 23, 1891.)

MECHANICS' LIENS—FORECLOSURE—APPEAL—EVIDENCE.

1. A proceeding to foreclose a subcontractor's lien is a suit in equity.

2. Where, in a suit to foreclose a subcontractor's lien, a cross-bill is filed, and all the evidence brought into the record, the supreme court will review the action of the lower court, and order a decree in accordance with equity and justice.

Appeal from circuit court, Washington county; JOHN A. KELLEY, Judge.

A bill by Edward Purcell, Jr., against the Bailey Construction Company, the South Atlantic & Ohio Railroad Company, and others, to foreclose a subcontractor's lien. Decree for plaintiff. Defendants appeal.

J. B. Richmond and J. H. Wood, for appellant. Mr. Blanchard, for appellee.

LEWIS, P. This was a suit in equity in the circuit court of Washington county, by the appellee, Purcell, against the Bailey Construction Company, the South Atlantic & Ohio Railroad Company, and others. The construction company was the general contractor to construct the South Atlantic & Ohio Railroad Company, and employed the plaintiff to do certain work as a subcontractor. The work was completed about the 1st of December, 1887, whereupon the plaintiff duly recorded in the proper clerk's office his mechanic's lien for an alleged balance due him, amounting to about $9,000. The object of the suit was to enforce the mechanic's lien, and to

recover that amount. A copy of the original contract between the parties is exhibited with the bill, wherein it was stipulated that for the work done and materials furnished under the contract payment should be made on or about the 20th of each month, upon estimates to be approved by the appellant's engineer. Before the completion of the work, however, the parties entered into a new contract, dated November 17, 1887, whereby it was agreed that the first contract should terminate on the 30th of the same month, and that the work done by the plaintiff should be measured upon or before the 1st day of December of that year, and paid for as soon as the final estimates were finished. The bill charges that the work done by the plaintiff amounted to about $37,000, according to the estimates of one Charles K. Moore, who, it is alleged, was the chief engineer of the construction company. But the company, both in its answer and cross-bill, denies that Moore was, at any time, its chief engineer; and avers, moreover, that the estimates made by him were not only inaccurate and excessive, but that the final estimates, upon which the plaintiff's claim is based, were made after he had been discharged from the company's service, which was on the 19th of October, 1887. It is averred that he was merely employed to do work as an engineer along with others, and that the company relied on its engineers, Jones and Hodge, in whose skill and competency it had entire confidence. The evidence in the cause is voluminous, and we do not deem it necessary to review it. It is enough to say that we have examined it carefully, and are satisfied that the principal contention of the company, the appellant here, is supported by the record. It appears that, after the completion of the work done by the appellee, it was measured up by Jones and Hodge, whose competency and integrity is not assailed, and that they estimated the whole at $24,690.-67. These estimates, however, are less by several thousand dollars than those made by Rollins, another of the company's engineers, whose estimates amounted to $28,327.40, the reasons for which difference are stated in the record. Taking Rollins' estimate as the proper basis for a settlement between the parties,—and the appellant does not contend to the contrary,—then there would be a balance due the appellant of $1,493.85, as overpaid, it appearing that there has been paid to the plaintiff various sums, at different times, on account of the work, aggregating $29,821.-25. The decree against the appellant, and of which it complains, must therefore be reversed, and a decree entered in its favor for the sum of $1,493.85 and costs.

It is proper to add that there was no error in overruling the demurrer to the bill. The appellant's contention was that the case presented a simple question of quantum meruit, which, upon the authority of Morgan v. Carson, 7 Leigh, 238, and other cases, belonged, properly, to a court of law, and not to a court of equity. But a sufficient answer to this position is that the object of the suit was to enforce an alleged mechanic's lien, and hence the case

is one of equitable jurisdiction. Code, §
2484. Upon the merits, however, the case
is with the appellant, as we have said.

GRAYSON v. BUCHANAN.

*(Supreme Court of Appeals of Virginia. July
9, 1891.)*

SALE OF LANDS — CONSTRUCTION OF CONTRACT—
PRESUMPTIONS—SET-OFF—PLEADING—DUPLICITY
—PAROL EVIDENCE.

1. A contract for the sale of lands, described
as "containing 140 acres, more or less, and known
as the 'Kelly Tract,'" will be presumed to be a
sale by the acre, in the absence of proof that it
was a sale in gross.

2. When the vendor represented that the tract
contained 140 acres, and included within its
boundaries one-half of a certain spring, when in
fact it only contained 196 acres, and did not include the spring, the vendee is entitled to an
abatement of the purchase price, to the extent
that the tract was damaged by loss of the spring,
as well as the proportionate loss of the 14 acres.

3. In such case, a verdict assessing defendant's damages at $600 for loss of one-half of the
spring, and $540 for the loss of 14 acres of land,
and directing the manner in which this sum
shall be applied towards the purchase price, is
not vague and uncertain.

4. It was proper to refuse to grant a new
trial upon the ground of newly-discovered evidence when the affidavit in support thereof does
not give the date or details of a conversation between affiant and defendant, which is made the
basis of the motion, as in such case the relevancy
of the testimony does not appear.

5. Code Va. § 3299, provides that, "in any action
on a contract, the defendant may file a plea, alleging any such failure in the consideration of
the contract * * * as would entitle him to recover damages at law, * * * or to relief in
equity, * * * alleging any such matter arising under the contract, existing before its execution, as would entitle him to relief in equity."
Held that, in an action to recover the purchase
price of land, the vendee may plead, by way of
set-off, and prove by parol, that the vendor falsely represented that a certain spring was upon the
land, although such spring was not mentioned in
the contract of sale.

6. A plea of set-off, showing that there was a
partial failure of consideration, in that a spring
was represented to be on the land, when in fact
it was not, and that there was a deficiency of 14
acres in the tract, is not double.

Error to circuit court, Smythe county;
JOHN A. KELLY, Judge.

Action by Grayson against Thomas M.
Buchanan on two bonds given to secure the purchase price of lands. Judgment
allowing a set-off. Plaintiff appeals. This
action was on two bonds, for $1,000 each,
executed by the defendant to the plaintiff,
Grayson, for the last two deferred payments of purchase money for a certain
tract of land situated in that county. In
the written contract between the parties
for the land, the tract is described as the
"Kelly Tract," and "containing one hundred and forty acres, more or less," for
which the defendant agreed to pay the
sum of $6,000. It does not appear that a
deed to the land has ever been delivered
to the defendant. The defendant offered
a special plea of set off, averring that the
tract was represented by the vendor, at
the time of the purchase, to contain 140
acres, and that it included within its limits one-half of a spring on the north-east-
ern portion of the tract, which was the
only running water on the entire tract,

except a small spring on the opposite side
of the tract, and that, relying upon these
representations, he contracted to purchase
the land. The plea then goes on to aver
that the tract did not, in fact, contain as
much as 140 acres, as represented, but only
126 acres, and that the said spring is not
included within the tract, nor any part
thereof. Wherefore it is further averred
there had been a failure of consideration
to the extent of 14 acres of land and one-
half of the said spring, and that the defendant has been thereby damaged to the
extent of $3,000. The plaintiff objected to
the plea, and moved the court to reject it,
which motion was overruled. The defendant offered evidence before the jury, which
was not excepted to, tending to support
the averments of the plea, and the plaintiff introduced evidence tending to support
the contrary view; that is, that the sale
was in gross, and that there was no representation on his part that the tract included any part of the spring. The verdict
of the jury was as follows: "We, the jury, find for the plaintiff $2,000, the debt in
the declaration mentioned, with interest
on $1,000, part thereof, from January 1,
1879, and on $1,000, the residue thereof,
from January 1, 1880, subject to a credit
of $398.38, as of October 11, 1882, and $613.-
79, as of October 22, 1883. And we further
find for the defendant as offsets to said
debt, $600 damages for the loss of one-half
of the spring in controversy, and $540 as
an abatement for deficit of fourteen acres
of the land, to be applied to said bonds in
the order in which they fall due." The
court overruled a motion for a new trial,
and gave judgment on the verdict; whereupon the plaintiff applied for and obtained a writ of error.

S. W. *Williams*, for plaintiff in error.
Sheffy, Buchanan & Buchanan, for defendant in error.

LEWIS, P., *(after stating the facts.)* The
doctrine is established by numerous decisions of this court that the use of the
words "more or less," or "supposed to
contain so many acres, more or less," in
a deed or contract for land, will not relieve the vendor or vendee, as the case
may be, from the obligation to make
compensation for an excess or deficiency
beyond what may be reasonably attributed to small errors from variations of instruments or otherwise, unless, indeed, a
contract of hazard was intended. But, in
the absence of proof that it was, the presumption is that it was not; that is, that
the parties contracted with reference to
quantity, which influenced the price. In
other words, that the sale was by the
acre, and not in gross. It is equally well
settled that contracts of hazard, though
not void, are yet not regarded with favor.
The presumption, as we have said, is
against them, and this presumption can
be repelled only by clear and convincing
proof. Caldwell v. Craig, 21 Grat. 132;
Watson v. Hoy, 28 Grat. 698; Benson v.
Humphreys, 75 Va. 196; Trinkle v. Jackson, 86 Va. 238, 9 S. E. Rep. 986. In the present case the parties contracted for the
payment of the gross sum of $6,000 for the
land, which in the written contract is de-

scribed as "containing one hundred and forty acres, more or less, and known as the 'Kelly Tract.'" The presumption, therefore, is that the quantity influenced the price, and that the sale was by the acre.

The defendant, however, not only sets up in the special plea a deficiency of 14 acres in quantity, but avers that the tract does not include within its boundaries one-half of a certain spring, which the vendor represented it to include, and with reference to which, it is averred, the contract was made; and to this extent he claims there has been a failure of consideration, and that he is entitled to an abatement of the purchase money accordingly. The general rule of compensation, in a case of deficiency in quantity within the boundaries of the land contracted for, is according to the average value of the whole tract; and this was the rule applied by the jury, under an instruction from the court, in the present case, so far as the deficiency in the land, independently of one-half of the spring, was concerned, there being no peculiar circumstances to take the case out of the general rule. But, as to the loss of one-half of the spring, a different rule necessarily applies. As to that the jury, being of the opinion that the defendant had been damaged $600, found accordingly. Upon this point the instruction was that if the jury should believe from the evidence that the plaintiff represented to the defendant, at the time of the sale, that one-half of the spring in the pleadings mentioned was on the Kelly tract, and that the defendant relied upon the representations, and if they should believe, further, that the half of said spring was not on the Kelly tract, then that the defendant was entitled to an abatement of the purchase price to the extent to which the tract was damaged by the loss of the half of said spring, estimating the price of the land, including half of the spring, at $6,000. The case was thus properly submitted to the jury on the question of failure of consideration, and the jury, upon the evidence, which was conflicting as to what the real contract between the parties was, having found for the defendant, its finding, approved as it was by the trial judge, ought not to be disturbed by this court. Caldwell v. Craig, 21 Grat. 132.

The appellant, however, contends that the defense set up in the special plea was not a proper one for a court of law, because it seeks to contradict the written contract, and to incorporate into it extraneous matter, by parol evidence. There is no mention of the spring in the written contract, and the point of the objection is that, if there was any mistake in that particular, the proper remedy was in equity to reform the contract. If this were a suit for that purpose, there is no doubt that parol evidence would be admissible to show what the true agreement was; that is to say, whether the contract was in gross or by the acre, and also whether or not the parties contracted for one-half of the spring, as alleged in the plea. "In all such cases," says Judge Story, "if the mistake is clearly made out by proofs entirely satisfactory, equity will reform the

contract so as to make it conformable to the precise intent of the parties." 1 Story, Eq. Jur. § 152. And to the same effect is Mauzy v. Sellars, 26 Grat. 641, where it was distinctly held, in conformity with all the authorities, that the mistake may be shown by parol proof, and that relief will be granted, whether the mistake is set up by bill or as a defense. In all such cases, however, where mistake alone is set up as a ground for relief, the mistake must be mutual. But the same relief is afforded where there has been a mistake on one side, accompanied by fraud or other inequitable conduct on the other. Railroad Co. v Dunlop, 86 Va. 346, 10 S. E. Rep. 239. In the present case the jury, on this branch of the case, found for the defendant; so that, whether the plaintiff was mistaken in representing that the land included one-half of the spring, or whether he fraudulently made such representation, is immaterial; for, in either case, the defendant, in good faith, relied upon that representation, and in either case he would be entitled, upon the state of facts found by the jury, to relief in equity.

Why, then, under the comprehensive terms of the statute relating to the special plea of set-off, is he not entitled to relief in this action? That statute, now carried into section 3299 of the Code, enacts as follows: "In any action on a contract, the defendant may file a plea, alleging any such failure in the consideration of the contract, or fraud in its procurement, or any such breach of any warranty to him of the title or the soundness of personal property, for the price or value whereof he entered into the contract, or any other, as would entitle him to recover damages at law from the plaintiff, or the person under whom the plaintiff claims, or to relief in equity, in whole or in part, against the obligation of the contract; or, if the contract be by deed, alleging any such matter arising under the contract, existing before its execution, or any such mistake therein, or in the execution thereof, or any such other matter as would entitle him to such relief in equity, and in either case alleging the amount to which he is entitled by reason of the matters contained in the plea. Every such plea shall be verified by affidavit." The plea in the present case sufficiently conforms to this statute, except that it was not sworn to. It does not affirmatively appear, however, that the omission to swear to it was a subject of objection in the lower court. But, be that as it may, the defect is not one for which the judgment will be reversed, inasmuch as, upon a survey of the whole record, the judgment appears to be substantially right. The case was fully gone into before the jury, and its merits ascertained. The material averments of the plea were found to be true, and hence the omission to swear to it does not warrant a reversal of the judgment. Fleming v. Toler, 7 Grat. 310; Bank v. Waddill, 27 Grat. 448; Payne v. Grant, 81 Va. 165; 4 Minor, Inst. 870, 874, and cases cited.

The contention that the plea is bad for duplicity is met by a twofold answer, viz.: (1) That objection to a plea on that ground can be taken, at common law, only by special demurrer, which is not now available in Virginia, except as to dilatory pleas, (4 Minor, Inst. 939;) and (2) that the plea in setting up, as it does, a partial failure of consideration, as well on the ground of a deficiency of 14 acres of the land as of the loss of one-half of the spring, is not double because the matters alleged constitute but one connected proposition or entire point As well might it be contended that a separate plea ought to have been filed for each one of the 14 acres.

It is also insisted that the verdict ought to have been set aside for vagueness and uncertainty. The verdict assesses the defendant's damages at $600 for the loss of one-half of the spring, and $540 for the loss of 14 acres of the land, and directs that these sums "be applied to said bonds in the order in which they fall due." The declaration itself states when the bonds, respectively, fell due, and we see no difficulty in applying the credits as the verdict directs; that is, as of the date of the maturity of the bonds, respectively.

Lastly, it is contended that a new trial ought to have been granted for after-discovered evidence. An affidavit of one John M. Humphreys was filed, to the effect that several years before the trial, and after the purchase of the land by the defendant, the latter admitted to the affiant that he had no interest in the spring. And there was also an affidavit by the plaintiff that the evidence had been discovered since the trial, and that reasonable diligence could not have secured it at the trial. The affidavit of Humphreys, however, does not give the details of the conversation between the defendant and himself, nor does it state when the admission was made. And if it was made after the defendant discovered by the survey, made subsequent to the sale, that he had no interest in the spring,—and *non constat* it was not,—then the admission was not material, because since that dicovery the the defendant has made no claim to the spring, but only to an abatement of the purchase money. If, on the other hand, it was made before the survey, then the evidence was collateral, and could not avail as ground for a new trial, inasmuch as it would only tend to contradict the defendant, and discredit him as an opposing witness. Read's Case, 22 Grat. 946; 4 Minor, Inst. 759, and cases cited. Upon the whole, without going more fully into the case, we are of opinion that the judgment is right, and that the same must be affirmed.

MAYFIELD v. SAVANNAH, G. & N. A. R. Co.

(*Supreme Court of Georgia.* July 13, 1891.)

RAILROAD COMPANIES — NEGLIGENCE — EVIDENCE.

1. The locomotive engineer, from whose negligent act the injury complained of was sustained, is an agent of the corporation within the meaning of the statute of October 29, 1889, and, he being dead, the person injured is an incompetent witness to testify in his own behalf to such negligent act, it not appearing that any surviving officer or agent of the corporation was present.

2. A custom or usage, obviously dangerous, and the facts alleged in the plaintiff's declaration showing that it would be dangerous, is not admissible to excuse contributory negligence by the plaintiff, more especially where it did not appear that such custom or usage had been adopted by the defendant, or that it prevailed at the place or on the particular railway concerned.

3. That the plaintiff acted cautiously is a conclusion, not a mere fact, and he is not competent to testify in general terms that he so acted.

4. Where an employe of a railroad engages another person to work in his place, private instructions, given by the former to the latter, as to how the work should be executed, are not competent evidence to affect the company.

5. There was no error in granting a nonsuit.

(*Syllabus by the Court.*)

Error from superior court, Spalding county; JAMES S. BOYNTON, Judge.

Geo. W. Austin, Bryan & Dicken, and *Cobb & Walker,* for plaintiff in error. *Hall & Hammond,* for defendant in error.

SIMMONS, J. Mayfield sued the railroad company for damages for a personal injury, which he alleged was sustained by him while in the discharge of his duty as an employe of the company, in attempting to couple the engine to a car. The declaration alleged, among other things, that the injury was caused by the careless and negligent jerking and driving of the engine, and that the machinery was defective, in that the foot-board or rim around the pilot, on which plaintiff stepped to make the coupling, was too narrow to make a secure footing at such a point of danger. The plaintiff was introduced as a witness in his own behalf, and, being asked how he came to be hurt, said: "As I went to get upon the cow-catcher, the engineer put on steam, which caused the engine to jerk violently forward, and my foot to slip." Defendant objected to this testimony, on the ground that Carroll, the engineer, was dead, and plaintiff, under the act of 1889, could not testify in his own favor. The objection was sustained, and the plaintiff excepted. Being asked by counsel, "What was the usual custom in making such couplings of such engines and cars?" defendant's counsel objected to the proof of "usual custom." The court sustained the objection, and plaintiff excepted. Plaintiff also testified that, in order to make the coupling, he had to get upon the rim of the pilot, which was about one and a half inches broad. It is broad enough to be safe by practice and by being careful. He had always done it with safety before. He was very cautious in getting on there. Defendant's counsel moved to rule out the witness' answer that he got on there very cautiously. The court sustained the motion, and ruled out the answer, to which plaintiff excepted. Plaintiff also testified that he was working that day for the company in the place of Robinson, and that Robinson told him to get upon the pilot, as he himself had always done. Defendant moved to rule out this answer, which motion was granted, and plaintiff excepted. Plaintiff having closed his case, on motion of defendant's counsel the court granted a nonsuit, to which plaintiff excepted. These are the questions made in this bill of exceptions for decision by this court.

1. Was the court right in ruling that

the plaintiff could not testify as to any transaction that occurred with Carroll, the engineer, he being dead at the time of the trial? The act approved October 29, 1889, (Pamphlet, p. 85,) declares: "Where any suit is instituted or defended by a corporation, the opposite party shall not be admitted to testify in his own behalf to transactions or communications solely with a deceased or insane officer, or agent of the corporation, and not also with surviving and sane persons, officers, or agents of said corporation." It was contended by counsel for plaintiff in error that the deceased engineer was neither an officer nor an agent of the corporation within the meaning of this section of the act, but was a mere servant of the company, and that therefore the court erred in not allowing plaintiff to testify to what the engineer did at the time plaintiff was injured. "While the line of demarkation between the relation of principal and agent and that of master and servant is exceedingly difficult to define," we are inclined to think, under our Code, that the engineer was such an agent as was contemplated by this act. Section 2202 of the Code declares that "the principal is not liable to one agent for injuries arising from the negligence or misconduct of other agents about the same business." Section 3033 declares that "a railroad company shall be liable for any damage done to persons * * * by the running of the locomotives or cars, * * * unless the company shall make it appear that their agents have exercised all ordinary and reasonable care and diligence." Section 3034 declares that "no person shall recover damage from a railroad company for injury to himself. * * * If the complainant and the agents of the company are both at fault, the former may recover." These sections seem to us to treat employes of corporations as agents thereof in their particular lines of duty, and this court, in construing these different sections, has frequently treated them as agents. The legislature, knowing of these sections of the Code and the construction placed upon them by this court, must have used the words in the act under consideration in the same sense; and when they provided that the opposite party shall not testify in his own behalf to transactions or communications solely with a deceased or insane officer or agent of the corporation, they meant, in our opinion, to include employes of the corporation as agents thereof. And there is good reason for putting this construction upon this section of the act. The case now under consideration shows the necessity of such a construction. We gather from the bill of exceptions and the argument of counsel that the purpose was to prove by this witness that, just as he had put one foot upon the rim of the pilot, the engineer put on steam, and this caused a jerk by the engine. If the engineer saw him attempting to mount the rim of the pilot, and put on the steam, thus causing the engine to jerk, it would have been a negligent act on his part, and the jury would likely have found a verdict for the plaintiff, if nothing else had appeared to show that the plaintiff was not entitled to recover. The engineer, being dead, could not contradict or answer the plaintiff's evidence if it was untrue; and the company on this vital point would have been at the mercy of the plaintiff. It is argued, also, that this was not a transaction between the plaintiff and the engineer, but a single act on the part of the engineer himself, and therefore did not come within the terms and meaning of the statute. We think the act of the engineer is covered by the word "transaction" used in this section. The plaintiff was attempting to mount the pilot. The engineer put on the steam causing the engine to jerk; and the plaintiff was injured. This was a transaction about which one party is forbidden to testify, the agent of the opposite party being dead. There was no error, therefore, in ruling out plaintiff's testimony upon this point.

2. There was no error in ruling that the usual custom in making car-couplings was not admissible. It will be observed that the witness was not asked as to the custom of this particular railroad, nor as to the custom of the railroads at the particular place where he was injured, but was asked as to the usual custom of making car-couplings on such engines. We do not think that this was sufficient to bind the company; the custom, if it existed, being obviously dangerous, and the declaration alleging that "the machinery was defective, in that the foot-board or rim around the pilot, on which plaintiff stepped to make the coupling, was too narrow to make a secure footing at such a point of danger." As to inadmissibility of usage or custom to excuse negligence, see Deer. Neg. § 9; Bailey v. New Haven, etc., Co., 107 Mass. 496; Hill v. Railroad Co., 55 Me. 438; Hamilton v. Railroad Co., 36 Iowa, 32; Cleveland v. Steam-Boat Co., 5 Hun, 523; Miller v. Pendleton, 8 Gray, 547; Kuhns v. Railroad Co., (Iowa,) 31 N. W. Rep. 868; Larson v. Tobin, (Minn.) 44 N. W. Rep. 1078; Whitsett v. Railroad Co., (Iowa,) 25 N. W. Rep. 104; Railroad v. De Bray, 71 Ga. 407, and cases cited in Railway Co. v. Flannagan, 82 Ga. 589, 9 S. E. Rep. 471.

3. There was no error in ruling out plaintiff's answer that he got on the pilot very cautiously. A witness may state facts, but not his own conclusion from those facts. This was a conclusion of the witness, and was the very question which the jury was to decide,—whether he had got upon the pilot cautiously or carelessly. It was the same as if he had said that he was not negligent in getting upon the pilot. He might have stated whether he attempted to mount hurriedly or slowly; how far he was from the engine when he raised his foot to make the attempt; where he placed his foot; and things of that sort, leaving the jury to say from these facts whether it was done cautiously or carelessly.

4. Nor was there error in ruling out plaintiff's answer to the question of defendant's counsel that Robinson told him to get upon the pilot as he himself had always done. It appears from the evidence that Robinson was a car-coupler himself,

and had hired this plaintiff for that day
to work in his place. We do not think
that any instruction which Robinson may
have given him when he hired him to
work in his place would be admissible to
bind the company.

5. The next exception complains that
the court erred in granting a nonsuit under the evidence in the case. We do not
think so. The evidence shows that the
engine was moving at the rate of four or
five miles an hour; that there was a rim
one and a half inches broad around the
pilot; and that the plaintiff undertook to
mount this rim, and stand on a space only
an inch and a half broad, while the engine
was in motion at that rate of speed. It
seems to us that this was clearly an act of
negligence, if not gross negligence. This
act was as negligent as the act in the case
of Roul v. Railway Co., (Ga.) 11 S. E.
Rep. 558, if not more so. There the plaintiff undertook to mount the engine by the
steps, and was injured, and we held that
he could not recover. Here he undertook
to jump from the ground, and light upon
a rim only an inch and a half broad, without anything to hold to, so far as appears
from anything in this record, after he had
got upon the rim. Judgment affirmed.

PERSEVERANCE MIN. CO. v. BISANER.

(*Supreme Court of Georgia.* May 6, 1891.)

REFERENCE TO AUDITOR — POWERS — PLACE OF
HEARING — JURISDICTION — WAIVER OF OBJEC-
TIONS—FINDINGS—EVIDENCE.

1. Where one appears before an auditor at
the time and place fixed for a hearing, and moves
to continue the same, which is granted, he cannot thereafter at the hearing object for the first
time to the auditor taking the testimony upon the
ground that the place fixed was outside of the
county where the suit was pending.

2. Where one files a plea to the merits he
thereby waives the question of jurisdiction of
the person.

3. An auditor cannot hear and determine a
demurrer to the declaration. Such pleading can
only be filed in the court where the cause is pending.

4. Where a suit is brought against a corporation, and it files its pleas as such, it is not reversible error to admit parol evidence that it is
a corporation.

5. It was proper for the auditor to refuse to
suspend the hearing until the evidence of plaintiff was transcribed, so that defendant might
make a motion of nonsuit, as an auditor cannot
grant a nonsuit.

6. An auditor's finding that the court had jurisdiction is immaterial when no such issue is
raised by the pleadings in the superior court.

7. A finding that memoranda and evidence
introduced by defendant in connection therewith
were not sufficient to charge plaintiff with the
money thereby charged to him, will not be disturbed when it was not shown that plaintiff had
knowledge of such memoranda, and received the
money.

8. Plaintiff testified that he was employed
by defendant, and went to work in April. Other
witnesses testified that he was attending to such
duties in April. Defendant claimed and introduced
testimony that he was not employed until July,
although on the premises. The auditor found that
he was employed and went to work in April,
which finding was confirmed by the trial court.
Held, that such finding would not be disturbed,
although it seemed against the preponderance of
the evidence.

Error from superior court, Pickens
county; JAMES S. BOYNTON, Judge.

Action by J. A. Bisaner against the
Perseverance Mining Company on an account. Judgment for plaintiff on an auditor's report. Defendant brings error.
Affirmed.

J. H. Lumpkin, C. D. Phillips, and H. C.
Peeples, for plaintiff in error. Clay & Blair,
for defendant in error.

SIMMONS, J. Bisaner sued the Perseve-
ance Mining Company in the superior
court of Pickens county upon an account
for 12 months' services rendered the company as superintendent in the year 1885 and
the month of January, 1886. The suit was
filed on the 5th day of April, 1887. On the
28th day of April, 1887, the company filed
the plea of the general issue, and a special
plea that the plaintiff had failed to account
for $1,000 which had been sent him to ex-
pend for the company. At the April term,
1889, upon motion of the defendant, and
by consent of counsel for the plaintiff, the
case was referred to an auditor, with
power given to the auditor to fix a time
and place of hearing. In pursuance of this
order, the auditor fixed as the time of
hearing June 27th, and as the place, Marietta, in Cobb county. On the day fixed for
the hearing the counsel for both parties
were present, and, on motion of the defendant, the case was continued until July
thereafter, and the order recited that it
was to be heard in Marietta, Ga. On July 10th counsel for the defendant appeared,
and objected to proceeding with the trial,
except upon condition that, should they
desire to controvert any of the evidence
that might be introduced for the plaintiff
by witnesses residing in Pickens county,
the trial should be transferred to that
county for the purpose of obtaining the
testimony of such witnesses. This objection was made upon the ground that
the auditor could have no authority to
sit outside of Pickens county, except by
the consent of counsel. The objection was
overruled, and this is the ground of the
first exception to the auditor's report.
Without deciding now whether, without
consent of parties, an auditor appointed
by the court can sit outside of the county
where the case is pending, to hear and determine the case, it is sufficient to say
that we think the objection came too late.
The order gave the auditor power to fix
the time and place of hearing. He fixed
the time, and appointed as the place, Marietta, Ga., outside of Pickens county,
where the suit was pending. Counsel for
the defendant appeared at that time and
place, and made no objection, but moved
to continue the case, which was done;
and the time and place was again fixed by
the auditor, without objection on the part
of the defendant or its counsel. If the defendant intended to make this point, it
should have done so at that time, and
not moved to continue the case and put
the plaintiff and his counsel to the trouble
and expense of again attending at Marietta. By not objecting at the proper time,
we think he waived it, and it was too late
at the next meeting to make the objection.
When this motion was overruled counsel

for the defendant objected to proceeding with the trial, and moved to dismiss the case for want of jurisdiction, on the ground that the act incorporating the Perseverance Mining Company provides that for all judicial purposes the location of said company shall be in Paulding county. This motion was also overruled, and this is made the ground of the second exception to the auditor's report. The trial judge did not err in disallowing this exception. The above recital of facts shows that the defendant had not filed any plea to the jurisdiction in the superior court, but had filed a plea to the merits of the case, and thereby waived the jurisdiction.

Before the introduction of any evidence, counsel for the defendant demurred to the declaration filed in the case, and the demurrer was overruled. This made the ground of the third exception to the auditor's report. We know of no law authorizing an auditor to hear and determine a demurrer to the declaration. If the declaration was insufficient, the demurrer should have been made to the superior court, before a reference to an auditor was applied for. If this declaration had been good in law, the judge would have sustained it, and dismissed the case, and saved the trouble and expense of a hearing before an auditor. Ayers v. Daly, 56 Ga. 119; White v. Reviere, 57 Ga. 386.

After these preliminary motions were disposed of as above stated, the plaintiff introduced his testimony, and was allowed to testify that the Perseverance Mining Company was a corporation. This was objected to by the defendant, and the objection was overruled, and this is made the ground of the fourth exception to the auditor's report. The trial judge also disallowed this exception, holding that it was immaterial, and could not affect the final result. We agree with him in this view of the case. It could not possibly have damaged the defendant. The suit was brought against it as a corporation, and it filed its pleas as a corporation; and while it may have been improper to allow the plaintiff to prove by parol that it was a corporation, and such testimony should have been ruled out, it was not such an error as to prejudice any of the defendant's rights, and therefore should not result in a reversal.

At the close of the plaintiff's testimony, the defendant's counsel moved that the hearing be suspended until the evidence introduced by the plaintiff could be written out, in order that the same might be used in a motion to nonsuit the plaintiff, which motion the defendant's counsel desired to make; and the refusal of the auditor to suspend the case for this purpose is made the ground of the fifth exception. The defendant then moved for a nonsuit on the ground that the plaintiff had failed to show that the defendant was a corporation, or that the contract sued on was made by an agent or officer authorized to contract for the defendant; and the overruling of this motion is made the ground of the sixth exception to the auditor's report. To move to suspend a case that the evidence might be written out, so that

the defendant could use it in making a motion for a nonsuit, was rather an extraordinary motion, and we doubt that any such motion was ever made before, and are sure that such a motion was never granted by a court at the request of counsel. Nor do we suppose any auditor ever granted a nonsuit on motion of the defendant's counsel. An auditor would have no more right or power to grant a nonsuit than to sustain a demurrer to the declaration. His duty is to take the testimony, and report to the court his conclusions thereon and his views of the law governing the case.

The seventh exception complains that the auditor erred in deciding that the declaration in the case sufficiently set forth the allegations. This was an immaterial and irrelevant finding. As we have just shown, the sufficiency of the pleadings was not referred to the auditor, and any finding or conclusion that he made concerning the same was immaterial and irrelevant.

It is complained in the eighth ground that the auditor erred in finding that the superior court of Pickens county had jurisdiction both of the parties and the subject-matter. This was also an immaterial and irrelevant finding. There was no plea filed to the jurisdiction of the court, but, as we have before remarked, a plea to the merits was filed. There being no plea to the jurisdiction of the court, the finding of the auditor that the superior court of Pickens county had jurisdiction was immaterial.

The ninth exception complains that the auditor found that the memoranda of the defendant were not sufficient, under the evidence in connection therewith, to fix liability on the plaintiff for money received by him. This exception was disallowed by the trial judge as an exception of fact. After reading the memoranda of Harrison, we think the auditor was right in holding that they were not sufficient to bind the plaintiff. They were memoranda made by Harrison, and kept by him; and it is not shown that the plaintiff knew of them, or ever received the money charged to him thereby; and we cannot say that the auditor erred in not charging the plaintiff with the amounts set out in the memoranda, or that the trial judge erred in disallowing this exception.

The other grounds in the original and amended exceptions, not herein discussed, are all questions of fact.

The main point insisted upon here by counsel for the plaintiff in error was that Bisaner was not employed by the company until July, 1885, and that the auditor found that he was employed from the 1st of April of that year. We have read the evidence carefully, and, while it is conflicting upon this point, and while the weight of the testimony seems to be in favor of the contention of the plaintiff in error, yet there is evidence on the part of the defendant in error tending to show that he was employed by the company for the time allowed by the auditor. He testifies that Harrison was vice-president of the company before its reorganization, and employed him at $75 per month as superintendent of the mining company. He shows by his own testimony and that of others that he was at the place of business of the company in April, and was attending to the duties of superintendent. The testimony of the defendant also shows that he was there, but denies that he was employed by the company. The auditor found that he was so employed in April. The evidence was reported to the court, and submitted to the judge to pass on without the intervention of a jury, and the judge found the same as the auditor did. We cannot say, therefore, that there was no evidence to sustain their finding upon this or the other questions of fact made in the exceptions. We therefore affirm the judgment.

MORTON *et al.* v. FRICK CO.

(Supreme Court of Georgia.　May 8, 1891.)

CONDITIONAL SALES — DEFECTIVE RECORDING OF NOTES—TROVER—JUDGMENT.

1. In an action of trover, where no plea was filed save that of the general issue, and on the trial there was no evidence as to the value of the property, and the plaintiff, who was the seller, elected, under section 3564 of the Code, to take a verdict for the property and its hire, defendants were entitled to no deduction from the amount of hire on account of partial payments made to the plaintiff by them or by their predecessor in the purchase, the plaintiff having retained title in himself as security for the payment of the purchase money.

2. Although notes embracing a contract of conditional sale may not have been legally recorded, yet, if the defendants, before they became interested in the property by purchase from one who bought from the plaintiff, had actual notice of the retention of the title by the plaintiff, and that some of the notes were unpaid, the defective recording is of no consequence as to them.

3. When personal property has been sold for $375, and $250 thereof has been paid to the seller, who, having retained the title to the property to secure the purchase money, recovers in an action of trover the property itself and $100 for its hire, this court will direct that the judgment in favor of the plaintiff may be discharged by defendants' paying the plaintiff the balance of the purchase money and the interest thereon, to-wit, $125, with interest at the rate of 8 per cent. per annum from January 18, 1887, as well as all costs of the case, within 10 days from the time the *remittitur* from this court is made the judgment of the court below; and, if not so paid, then the original judgment in favor of the plaintiff to stand of full force.

(Syllabus by the Court.)

Error from superior court, Milton county; GEORGE F. GOBER, Judge.

H. L. Patterson and T. L. Lewis, for plaintiff in error. J. P. Brooke, for defendant in error.

LUMPKIN, J. The Frick Company sold a saw-mill and saw to T. D. Terry and T. F. Abbott for $375, taking therefor seven promissory notes, in all of which it reserved title till such notes were paid. Five of these notes, for $50 each, were signed by both Terry and Abbott. The remaining two—one for $25, and the other for $100—were signed by Abbott alone. The testimony is conflicting as to whether Terry signed as surety for Abbott, or Abbott as surety for him. The five notes signed by both were paid by Terry before

their maturity, and were transferred to him by the Frick Company, without recourse on it or on the property for which they were given until after the company was paid in full. Whatever interest Terry had in the property was sold by him to the defendants below, Louis and M. M. Morton; and Terry also transferred to them the five notes above mentioned. The Mortons thereupon took possession of the property. The evidence tended to show, and the jury so found, that the Mortons, at the time they bought from Terry, knew that Abbott's notes were still outstanding and unpaid, and that they contained a reservation of title in the Frick Company. There was no evidence at all as to the actual value of the property at the time of the trial. The plaintiff recovered from the Mortons the property itself and $100 for the hire thereof.

1. The plaintiff having elected, as was its right under section 3564 of the Code, to demand a verdict for the property itself and the hire thereof, and the title still being in it, a verdict in its favor was inevitable. The only plea filed was that of the general issue, and there was no evidence at all as to the value of the property at the time of the trial. In this state of the pleadings and evidence, there could be no deduction from the amount of hire proved on account of the partial payments of the purchase money which had been made. The plaintiff was standing upon its strict legal rights, and defendants interposed no legal defense to the enforcement of the same. If, by a proper plea, they had set forth their true equities in the case, and tendered to the plaintiff the balance of the purchase money, with interest thereon; or if they had shown by evidence that the property was still worth as much as such balance,—no doubt the proper relief could and would have been afforded them. In the absence of such pleadings or proof, neither the jury nor the court could assume that a recovery of the property alone, without hire, would have done full justice to the plaintiff; nor could it be determined what apportionment, if any, of the hire would accomplish this purpose. We are therefore constrained to hold that, taking the case as it stood, the jury were bound to find in favor of the plaintiff the property and its hire, without deduction.

2. There was some dispute as to whether or not the purchase-money notes given to the Frick Company were legally recorded. It is unnecessary to decide whether they were or not, because the Mortons, before their transaction with Terry, had actual notice of the fact that the notes made by Abbott were outstanding and unpaid, and that the title to the property remained in the plaintiff till these notes were paid. Section 1955a of the Code, in regard to recording such contracts, distinctly provides that the existing statutes and laws of this state in relation to the registration and record of mortgages on personal property shall apply to and affect all conditional sales of personal property, as defined in that section. A purchaser who takes personalty with actual knowledge of the existence of a mortgage thereon, takes subject thereto, and this rule, by the section

cited, is applied to purchasers of personalty of which the seller has reserved the title.

8. In strict justice, and in accordance with the principles ruled in Bradley v. Burkett, 82 Ga. 255, 11 S. E. Rep. 492, and the cases there cited, the recovery of the plaintiff in this case, if the defense had been properly conducted, ought not to have exceeded in value the amount remaining due upon the purchase price of the property, with interest thereon. Exercising the authority conferred upon us by statute, we affirm the judgment of the court below, with the directions set forth in the third head-note. Judgment affirmed, with directions.

PONDER v. STATE.

(*Supreme Court of Georgia.* May 27, 1891.)

HOMICIDE—SELF-DEFENSE—EVIDENCE.

In a trial for murder, verbal directions given by the deceased to his brother to follow the accused, and see that he did not leave the road in which the homicide shortly afterwards occurred, and over which the deceased and his brother were about to pass, being in evidence, the state, in order to show that this request was probably meant as a precaution for defense, and not as a measure of attack, may prove that it followed and was connected with a suggestion made by a third person that the accused would "waylay the boys to-night," although the accused was not present, and did not hear the conversation, or any part of the same.

(*Syllabus by the Court.*)

Error from superior court, Cherokee county; GEORGE F. GOBER, Judge.

Clay & Blair, *C. D. Phillips*, *H. W. Newman*, and *Thomas Hutcherson*, for plaintiff in error. *Geo. R. Brown*, Sol. Gen., for the State.

BLECKLEY, C. J. Ponder and the two brothers Reese were together at the house of Seabolt until late in the night. The same road, for some distance, was the way home for all three. Ponder and Aaron Reese were unfriendly, and each of them had a gun. Ponder left for home first, and, as the Reese brothers were about leaving, some conversation took place in which Seabolt and wife participated. Mrs. Seabolt said, "Ponder will waylay the boys to-night." Aaron Reese told his brother to go on and watch Ponder, and see that he staid in the road. The brother then set out, and not long afterwards was joined by Aaron. Ponder was not far ahead, and the two brothers soon overtook him, and Aaron was shot and killed by him in the road. At the trial, counsel for Ponder insisted upon having before the jury what Aaron, the deceased, said to his brother, but objected to what Mrs. Seabolt said. The court ruled, in effect, that both might be excluded, but that if one was received the other should be also. Without the suggestion to the mind of Aaron Reese which was made by the remark of Mrs. Seabolt, his own words might never have been uttered. Her remark tends, not only to account for their origin, but to explain their real object and purpose. He directed his brother to go ahead, watch Ponder, and see that he remained in the road. Why?

Was it as a precaution against ambush, or as a preliminary to contemplated attack? Standing alone, the words are ambiguous as to their motive and end. With the remark of Mrs. Seabolt to illustrate them, they indicate a defensive rather than offensive purpose. This being so, the fact that Ponder was not present, and heard no part of the conversation in which the remark of Mrs. Seabolt occurred, does not affect its admissibility for the sole purpose of accounting for and explaining what was said immediately afterwards by the deceased. Of course, the evidence would have no relevancy for any other purpose. Brown v. Matthews, 79 Ga. 2, 4, 4 S. E. Rep. 13. The other grounds in the motion for a new trial were all waived by the learned counsel for the plaintiff in error on the argument in this court. Judgment affirmed.

MOORE v. O'BARR.

(*Supreme Court of Georgia.* May 8, 1891.)

LEVY — EXECUTION — AFFIDAVIT OF ILLEGALITY—RETURN—HOMESTEAD EXEMPTION.

1. Code Ga. § 3666, provides that where an execution is levied and an affidavit of illegality is filed thereto, the officer shall return the execution, affidavit, and bond to "the court from which the execution issued," and the issue of illegality shall be tried in that court. *Held*, that an execution issued from a justice court should be returned to such court, and not to the superior court, for trial of the issue of exemption of the land as a homestead.

2. An issue as to whether land is exempt from levy and sale under an execution as a homestead does not bring the title of the land in question.

3. Where both husband and wife were defendants in *fi. fa.*, the fact that the husband made an affidavit of illegality, claiming the property levied upon as a homestead, which was determined in a court which had no jurisdiction, does not bind the wife, and she may thereafter make an affidavit claiming the land upon the same ground, and have it determined by a court of competent jurisdiction.

Error from superior court, Franklin county; N. L. HUTCHINS, Judge.

Affidavit of illegality of E. E. O'Barr to try the issue of homestead exemption upon execution issued in favor of J. B. Moore against her and Asa O'Barr, her husband. Judgment for affiant. Moore brings error. Affirmed.

McCurry & Proffitt, for plaintiff in error. *J. B. Parks*, for defendant in error.

SIMMONS, J. The record in this case discloses that Moore obtained a judgment against Asa O'Barr and E. E. O'Barr in a justice's court. Execution was issued thereon, and levied on a certain tract of land. Asa O'Barr filed an affidavit of illegality to this execution, upon the ground that the land had been set apart to him as a homestead. The affidavit of illegality was returned to the superior court of the county, and on the trial thereof in that court the jury returned a verdict in favor of the plaintiff in *fi. fa.*, and the judge entered a judgment ordering the *fi. fa.* to proceed. The land was again advertised for sale, and Mrs. E. E. O'Barr, the wife of Asa O'Barr, filed her claim thereto, on the ground that it had been set apart as a homestead to her husband, for the benefit of her and her minor children, and was therefore exempt from levy and sale. This claim was returned to the superior court of the county, and the plaintiff in fl. fa. tendered issue thereon, and insisted that "the issue raised by said claim was fully adjudicated and passed upon by a court of competent jurisdiction, to-wit, the superior court of said county, at the September term, 1889 under an affidavit of illegality filed to the same levy by Asa O'Barr, one of the defendants, * * * in which he alleged and undertook to prove that the land levied upon had on the 16th of November, 1878, been set apart to himself and family as a homestead, and that under the issue made upon said affidavit of illegality the same was fully investigated and decided adversely to said Asa O'Barr and his family, by a verdict of the jury, and upon said verdict a judgment was entered, which verdict and judgment have never been excepted to or set aside. * * * Said adjudication is a complete bar to the present claim; and of this he puts himself upon the country." In reply to this issue the plaintiff insisted that she was not bound by said former adjudication, for the reason that the court trying the same had no jurisdiction, and that the claimant's husband could not waive the jurisdiction, and the claimant was not bound by any election of the remedy by him, unless tried by a court having jurisdiction. The trial judge ruled that the claimant was not bound by the former adjudication, because the court rendering the judgment upon the illegality had no jurisdiction to try the same. The case was then submitted to the jury, and under the charge of the court they returned a verdict for the claimant. The plaintiff made a motion for a new trial, on the ground that the judge erred in holding that the claimant was not bound by the former adjudication, which motion was overruled, and the plaintiff excepted.

We think the court was right in refusing to grant a new trial on this ground. Code, § 3666, requires that when an execution is levied and illegality filed thereto the officer shall return the execution, affidavit, and bond to "the next term of the court from which the execution issued," and the issue raised by the illegality shall be tried in that court. This execution was issued from a justice's court, and when the illegality was filed by Asa O'Barr, the officer levying the same should have returned it to the justice's court, and it should have been tried in that court.

It was argued, however, that the illegality made an issue respecting the title to the land, and that the superior court was the proper court to which it ought to have been returned, because that court had exclusive jurisdiction to try titles to land, and therefore the judgment was not a nullity, but was legal and binding upon the claimant. We do not think this was a suit or issue of which the superior court had exclusive jurisdiction. While the superior court has exclusive jurisdiction to try titles to land, that is, of all suits brought for the purpose of trying title, it does not have exclusive jurisdiction

in suits where the title is only incidentally or collaterally involved. The issue made by the illegality was not an issue involving the title to the land levied upon, but was an issue as to whether the land was exempt from levy and sale under the execution. There was no dispute as to the title of the land. The plaintiff asserted in his levy that the title was in the defendant, and the defendant did not deny it, but insisted that, although the title was in him, it was exempt, under the homestead law, from levy and sale. The title to the land, therefore, was not involved, and the illegality should have been returned to the justice's court from whence it was issued.

It was also insisted that while it might be true that the superior court did not have exclusive jurisdiction to try this case, and that the case might have been returned to the justice's court for trial, the defendants in fl. fa. waived the jurisdiction by appearing in the superior court, and participating in the trial there of the illegality. We have shown that, under the Code, the execution should have been returned to the justice's court, that court alone having jurisdiction of the parties and subject-matter of the case. The superior court had no jurisdiction of the parties or subject-matter, because there was no law authorising an officer to return the case to that court. It had no more jurisdiction of this case than it would have had of the original case begun in the justice's court by Moore against the defendants upon the contract, if the constable had returned the summons to the superior court, when required by law to return it to the justice's court. The superior court, in the latter case, would have had no jurisdiction of the parties or the subject-matter of the suit, and if it had rendered a judgment therein it would have been void. "Parties, by consent, express or implied, cannot give jurisdiction to the court as to the person or subject-matter of the suit. It may, however, be waived, so far as the rights of the parties are concerned, but not so as to prejudice third persons." Code, § 3466. We do not think, therefore, that the participation of one of the defendants on the trial of the illegality in the superior court gave that court jurisdiction, or that his wife, the other defendant in the execution, and the present claimant, is estopped from making the question. Bostwick v. Perkins, 4 Ga. 48; Yon v. Baldwin, 76 Ga. 769. Judgment affirmed.

BURNSIDE, Judge, v. DONNON et al.

(*Supreme Court of South Carolina.* Aug. 11, 1891.)

ACTION AGAINST TRUSTEE—LIMITATION.

1. The rendition of a judgment against an administratrix, trustee of a continuing trust, and her failure to appeal therefrom, do not evidence a purpose on her part to throw off the trust; and the statute of limitations does not then begin to run against an action by the probate court against her sureties.

2. In an action against the sureties, the presumption that the administratrix has discharged her liability, if it arises from the fact that more than 20 years have elapsed since the execution of the administration bond, is rebutted by the collection, subsequent to the commencement of

the action, of a judgment in favor of the estate against one of the sureties.

Appeal from common pleas circuit court of Laurens county; JAMES IZLAR, Judge.

Action by A. W. Burnside, as judge of probate, against James M. Donnon and another upon an administration bond. Judgment for plaintiff. Defendants appeal. Affirmed.

B. W. Ball, for appellants. H. Y. Simpson and J. W. Ferguson, for respondent.

MCIVER, J. The action was brought by plaintiff to recover from defendants as sureties on the administration bond of Sophia M. Langston as administratrix of John Langston, deceased, the balance found to be due by the administratrix upon an accounting had for that purpose in the court of probate. It appears that the administration bond was given on the 31st of August, 1863; that the accounting above referred to was had on the 6th of April, 1880, when all the creditors of John Langston were called in, among whom was the defendant, James M. Donnon, and who established claims against the intestate. In the balance there found due by the administratrix was included the amount of a judgment which she had previously recovered, viz., on the 2d of October, 1875, against the said James M. Donnon and his wife for a debt due her intestate's estate. The administratrix having refused to enforce this judgment, (which was against her son-in-law and daughter,) the judge of probate was directed by the court to institute proper proceedings to revive the judgment and enforce its collection. The defense made by said James M. Donnon was payment, which being found against him by the jury, the judgment was revived, and the amount thereof was collected by the judge of probate subsequent to the commencement of this action, and applied to the balance found due by the administratrix, which still left a balance due by her, for which judgment was rendered in this action, which was commenced 31st December, 1886. From this judgment the defendant James M. Donnon alone appeals (the other defendant, Clark, having made default) upon the several grounds set out in the record. The appeal raises but two questions: First, whether the action is barred by the statute of limitations; second, whether the claim of the plaintiff is to be presumed paid by lapse of time.

As to the first question, it seems to us clear that the plea of the statute cannot be sustained. In this case the administratrix was trustee of an express and continuing trust, and the sureties upon the bond had bound themselves to make good any loss which might result from her failure to perform her duties as such trustee. In such a case the statute of limitations has no application, unless the trustee has done some act evidencing a purpose to throw off the trust, which would give currency to the statute from the time when such act was done, provided the cestui que trust has actual or pre-

sumptive notice of such act. In this case the only thing relied upon as throwing off the trust is the decree made against the administratrix by the judge of probate on the 6th of April, 1880. As was well said by the master in his report, this, so far from showing or purporting to show that the trust was terminated, shows just the contrary. It was an admission, implied, at least, from the acquiescence of the administratrix in that decree, (for it does not appear that she appealed from it,) that she still had in her hands a trust fund to the amount of such decree, for which she was still liable as trustee to pay over to the parties entitled, according to the terms of her bond. The remarks made by his honor, Judge FRASER, in delivering the opinion of this court in Langston v. Shands, 23 S. C., at page 153, are directly applicable to and conclusive of this case; for, although those remarks were applied to a guardianship bond, yet, so far as this question is concerned, there is no difference between such a bond and an administration bond. The difference between this case and that of State v. Lake, 30 S. C. 43, 8 S. E. Rep. 322, cited by appellants' counsel, is clearly pointed out by the late chief justice at page 52, 30 S. C., and page 325, 8 S. E. Rep.

As to the second question, it seems to us that there is as little doubt. Even if it be assumed that the fact that more than 20 years had elapsed after the execution of the administration bond before the commencement of this action would raise a presumption that all the conditions of the bond had been fully complied with, (which, however, we do not propose to decide in this case,) yet such a presumption may be rebutted, and we think would be fully overcome by the facts and circumstances developed in this case. It would seem that at least one of the reasons of the delay in setting up the estate of the intestate was the refusal of the appellant to pay a debt due by him to the estate, even if it had been reduced to judgment by the administratrix; but when his liability to pay such debt was judicially ascertained, it was then practically determined that he had had all the time in his hands a part of the assets of the intestate's estate, which it was the duty of the administratrix to have collected and administered,— a duty the performance of which he had guarantied when he signed the administration bond. This, to say nothing of any other fact or circumstance, would be amply sufficient to rebut the presumption arising from lapse of time, relied on by appellant; for if he had all the time a portion of the assets belonging to intestate's estate in his hands, which he neglected or refused to pay over to the administratrix, it was manifestly impossible for her to have complied with the condition of the bond, and hence any presumption, arising from lapse of time, that she had done so, is effectually overcome. The judgment of this court is that the judgment of the circuit court be affirmed.

MCGOWAN, J. I concur.

ORR *et al.* v. ORR *et al.*

(*Supreme Court of South Carolina.* Aug. 11, 1891.)

EXECUTORS — COLLECTION OF ASSETS — EVIDENCE.

1. The mere fact that an executor made no attempt to collect the unsecured note of a solvent person will not render him liable to the remainder-men for loss occasioned by the unforeseen failure of such person, especially when the executor was deterred from suing by the express objections of the life-tenant.

2. The testimony of the executor that his mother, the life-tenant, objected to his suing upon such note, was competent as bearing upon his *bona fides.*

3. The executor's testimony that the life-tenant told him that testator requested her not to sue on such notes was hearsay.

4. It was also incompetent on the ground that the will alone should determine testator's wishes.

Appeal from common pleas circuit court of Union county; IZLAR, Judge.

Action for an accounting by David Orr, Archie Orr, and James Orr against Thomas J. Orr, as executor of James Orr, deceased, and in his own right, George Orr, William Orr, John Orr, Mary Orr, Jane Williams, Robert Orr, Walter G. Orr, and Violet Martin. Judgment for plaintiffs. Defendants appeal. Reversed.

J. C. Wallace, for plaintiffs. *I. G. Mc-Kissick,* for defendants.

McIVER, J. James Orr, having duly made his last will and testament, departed this life some time in the year 1876, and the appellant Thomas J. Orr was appointed executor thereof, who, on the 20th of December, 1876, duly qualified and entered upon the discharge of his duties as such. There is no copy of the will set out in the "case," but it is therein stated that "the testator devised and bequeathed to his wife, Martha Orr, all his real and personal estate, of every kind and description whatsoever, to have, to hold, and enjoy during her natural life, with remainder after his death of his whole estate, real and personal, to his children, to be equally divided, share and share alike." On the 22d of April, 1884, the life-tenant departed this life, and on the 29th of June, 1886, this action was commenced, in which an account of the testator's estate was demanded of the appellant, as executor as aforesaid. Among the assets of the testator's estate was a note of B. B. Foster for $400, dated 9th of December, 1875, and payable to the testator. This note has never been collected, and, the maker having become insolvent, the amount thereof has been lost to the estate; and the only question in the case is whether the appellant, as executor, is chargeable with the amount due on the note. The executor, being examined as a witness, testified that the note came into his hands as executor after the death of his mother, the life-tenant; that his mother, being an old lady, unable to attend to any business, gave witness all the papers to keep for her during her life; that she never would let witness collect any money on the notes, especially the Foster note, saying it was the testator's wish that Foster's note should stand as long as she lived, unless she actually needed the money; and, although advised by the appellant several times to

collect some of the money, she always objected. After the death of the life-tenant appellant received a payment of $10 on the note, to bring the note within date. Counsel for respondents objected to the witness testifying "as to any transaction between witness and his mother in regard to this note; and, furthermore, what his mother said would be hearsay." So far as we can discover, there was no ruling, either by the master or the circuit judge, as to the competency of the testimony objected to, and no exception seems to raise this point. The defendant Mary Orr, the daughter of testator and the life-tenant, testified that she lived with her mother up to the time of her death, and also corroborated the testimony of the executor as to the wish expressed by the testator that the notes should not be collected until after the death of the old lady, unless actually needed, as well as to the unwillingness of the mother to have the notes—particularly the Foster note—sued. This testimony was also objected to, but there does not appear to have been any ruling as to such objection. There was also testimony tending to show that the note of Foster was at one time collectible, as other claims against him had been enforced by third persons, after the death of the testator. The master found as matter of law "that it was the duty of the executor to have collected and invested the securities, or at least to have kept the same active and secured;" and as matter of fact that the Foster note was good and collectible, and that the debt secured thereby was lost by the failure of the executor to collect the same; and he therefore charged the executor with the amount due thereon. This report, upon exceptions thereto, was confirmed by the circuit judge, and from his judgment the executor Thomas J. Orr appeals upon the single ground that there was error in holding the executor liable for the Foster note.

While, as we have said, there does not appear to have been any ruling by the court below as to the competency of the testimony objected to as above, yet in a case of this kind we do not see how we can avoid a consideration of the competency of such testimony, bearing so directly as it does upon one of the vital questions in the case,—as to the good faith with which the executor has acted. We do not see any valid ground of objection to the testimony as to what passed between the executor and the life-tenant, except that portion of it which undertook to state the wishes of the testator in regard to the collection of the note in question, which is objectionable upon two grounds: *First,* because it was hearsay; and, *second,* because we must look alone to the will for the purpose of ascertaining the wishes of the testator, without regard to any verbal directions which he may have undertaken to give either as to the disposition or management of his estate after his death. But the appellant was not the executor of the life-tenant, and hence the testimony as to any transaction or conversation with her would not be incompetent under section 400 of the Code; and, while it is true that the respondents not claiming under her would not ordinarily be bound by anything she may have said, yet her expressed wishes as to the management of property in which she had the more immediate interest would seem to be competent as throwing light upon the question of good faith on the part of the executor. Assuming for the present that, although the Foster note constituted a part of the residue of the estate which was given in mass to the life-tenant, still it was the duty of the executor to look after it, and see that the principal sum secured thereby was preserved for the remainder-men, yet it never was supposed that an executor was bound to insure the absolute safety of all the assets committed to his care. On the contrary, he is only required to exercise such care and diligence as prudent persons usually do in the management of their own affairs. Now, while ordinarily it is the duty of an executor or administrator to collect in the choses in action due the testator or intestate, and, after providing for the debts, distribute the surplus among the several parties entitled under the terms of the will or the provisions of the law, in reference to the distribution of intestate estates, yet even in such a case, if the parties interested prefer to receive their portions in the form in which their ancestor has seen fit to invest his property, whether by loans on notes or bonds, or in bank-stock, or otherwise, we do not see how the executor would be chargeable with any breach of duty in omitting to collect such notes and bonds, and turning them over *in specie* to the parties interested. But where, as in this case, the choses in action, if collected, would have to be reinvested and held for an uncertain time,—the life of the life-tenant,—there would be still greater reason for the executor omitting to call in an investment made by the testator, simply for the purpose of reinvesting the amount in some other form. In such a case the court would, and has in the case of Pope v. Mathews, 18 S. C. 444, sanctioned the conduct of the executor in pursuing such a course. It is true that the case just cited was decided by a divided court, of which the writer of this opinion constituted the minority; but, in the first place, there was no division in the court as to the non-liability of the executor for Judge O'Neall's individual note, in which the testator had allowed a portion of his estate to remain invested, just as the testator had here invested a portion of his funds in the Foster note; and, in the second place, although the writer did not then, and does not now, approve of all that was decided in that case, yet it is an authoritative decision of the court of last resort, and no one, whatever may be his official station, has the right to disregard it. It is also true that in that case the loss resulted from the general disasters which followed the war between the states, while the loss here cannot be attributed to any such cause. But the case does decide that, while it is the duty of an executor or other trustee having funds in his hands to invest to require good and sufficient security, yet, where funds of the tes-

tator have been invested by him in his lifetime in the note of a solvent person, without security, the simple fact that he allows the fund to remain in the form in which his testator saw fit to invest it will not render the executor liable, in case of unforeseen loss, unless such loss has been occasioned by some other fault on the part of the executor than that of allowing the fund to remain in the form in which the testator left it. It is clear, therefore, that the simple fact that the executor allowed the money due on the Foster note to remain invested in the same form in which it was left by the testator would not render him liable; and, to make him so, some fault on his part should be shown, from which the eventual loss resulted. The fault claimed in this case was in not suing the note in time to get ahead of other creditors of Foster, for all the claims which exhausted Foster's estate seen to have been sued. Whether the executor could by the use of proper diligence have succeeded in getting ahead of the other creditors is not shown by the testimony in this case. Foster might, by giving voluntary liens upon his property, as he seems to have done, in one instance at least, have defeated any effort upon the part of the executor to secure this debt. But, more than this, the testimony shows that the executor was deterred from suing by the express and earnest objections of the life-tenant,—the party more immediately interested. This possibly may have rendered the estate of the life-tenant liable to the remainder-men, just as if she failed or refused to take proper measures for the preservation of any other portion of the property given to her for life; but it seems to us it would be a hard measure of justice to hold the executor liable under all the circumstances.

There is also another view of this case, which we will present without intending to decide anything definitely, as it was not argued. As we understand the decisions in this state, it seems to be settled that where property, real and personal, is given to one in mass, for life, with remainder over, the whole mass is to be placed in the hands of the life-tenant to be used as a whole during life, with a liability to account for and turn over to the remainder-men the whole mass, not in precisely the same plight and condition in which it was received, but in as good a plight and condition, allowing for the necessary "wear and tear" of imperishable articles,—for example, plate, furniture, etc. See Patterson v. Devlin, McMul. Eq. 459; Robertson v. Collier, 1 Hill, Eq. 373; Calhoun v. Furgeson, 3 Rich. Eq. 160; Glover v. Hearst, 10 Rich. Eq. 329; Brooks v. Brooks, 12 S. C. 422. Under this rule it might well be argued that, where an estate, consisting of various kinds of property, one of which is a chose in action, is given as a whole to one for life with remainder over, the life-tenant being entitled to the possession of the entire estate, when the executor has delivered the same to the life-tenant in accordance with the directions of the will his liability ceases, and the remainder-men can look alone to the estate of the life-tenant, who, in a proper case, may be required to give security for the forthcoming of the estate at the termination of the life-estate, in as good, though not in the same, condition in which it was received, the proper allowance, above indicated, being made. If this view be adopted, then it is clear the executor would not be liable for the Foster note, as he seems, from the testimony, to have turned over that note, along with all the rest of the property, to the life-tenant, who exercised absolute control over it during life. The judgment of this court is that the judgment of the circuit court, in so far as it makes the executor liable for the amount of the Foster note, be reversed, and that the case be remanded to that court for such further proceedings as may be necessary to carry out the views herein announced.

McGOWAN, J. I concur.

WESTLAKE et al. v. FARROW.

(Supreme Court of South Carolina. Aug. 11, 1891.)

COMPLAINT—SINGLE CAUSE OF ACTION—COURT OF COMMON PLEAS.

1. A complaint which alleges ownership of certain lands, and that defendant is in possession, claiming to have some interest, and wrongfully withholds the same from plaintiffs, and that they own no other land in common with defendant, contains but one cause of action, namely to recover land, though the prayer of judgment is for an accounting and partition, as the prayer is no part of the cause of action.

2. Since the court of equity in South Carolina, as a separate tribunal, has been abolished, and its jurisdiction vested in the court of common pleas, the common pleas may take jurisdiction of an action to recover possession of land, for the purpose of partition among plaintiffs.

Appeal from common pleas circuit court of Spartanburg county; NORTON, Judge.

Action by O. D. Westlake and others against Abner T. Farrow, to recover possession of land. Demurrer to the complaint overruled. Defendant appeals. Affirmed.

Duncan & Sanders and Bomar & Simpson, for appellant. F. M. Ansel and Arch. B. Calvert, for respondents.

McIVER, J. The question presented by this appeal having arisen under a demurrer, it will be necessary to set forth, substantially, the allegations of the complaint, as follows: First, that one Thomas Rhodes died intestate, seised and possessed of the tract of land which is the subject of the action; second, that the said land descended to the four plaintiffs, naming them, as the heirs at law of said intestate; third, that said plaintiffs are each entitled to one undivided fourth part of said premises; fourth, that defendant "is in possession of said premises, claiming to have some interest in same, and wrongfully withholds same from these plaintiffs;" fifth, that plaintiffs "own no other land in this state in common with the defendant;" sixth, that the intestate left no debts. The only judgment demanded is for an accounting and for partition. To this complaint the defendant filed a written demurrer: (1) "That several causes of action have been improperly united, one being for partition of a tract of land between the plaintiffs, and the other being to recover the possession of said tract from the defendant." (2) "That the court of equity has no jurisdiction to hear and determine the issues between the plaintiffs and the defendant." The case came on for hearing before his honor, Judge NORTON, who overruled the demurrer, and ordered the cause to be transferred to calendar 1. From this ruling defendant appeals upon the several grounds set out in the record, which raise but two questions: (1) Whether there was an improper joinder of causes of action; (2) whether the court had jurisdiction to try the case. We infer that the case was originally docketed on calendar 2, as it involved an issue of law raised by the demurrer to be tried by the court, and when that issue was determined by the court by overruling the demurrer, upon the ground, as we suppose, that the only cause of action stated in the complaint against the defendant was that for the recovery of the possession of real estate, the case was very properly transferred to calendar 1, in order that the only issue raised between the parties, which was triable by a jury, should be tried in that way. The case does not show that the defendant was allowed to answer, but, as that is conceded in the statement submitted by counsel for respondents, we see no necessity for this court to make any provision for that effect.

Taking up the second question first, we are unable to discover any ground for the proposition that the court had no jurisdiction to try the cause. While it is quite true that as long as the court of equity was a separate tribunal, invested with jurisdiction of equity matters, it could not take jurisdiction of a cause of action purely legal in its character; and hence, as was held in Albergottie v. Chaplin, 10 Rich. Eq. 428, that court could not take jurisdiction of a case in which the demand was for the recovery of real estate from one or more of the defendants, in order that it might be partitioned among the plaintiffs and the other defendants. But since the court of equity, as a separate tribunal, has been abolished, and the jurisdiction formerly belonging to it has been vested in the court of common pleas, it is very manifest that there is no objection, on jurisdictional grounds, to the maintenance of such an action. McGee v. Hall, 23 S. C. 388.

The only remaining inquiry is whether two causes of action—one for partition and the other for the recovery of real estate—were improperly joined. Whether two such causes of action can be properly joined may admit of some question, though there are at least two cases. (McGee v. Hall, supra, and Reams v. Spann, 28 S. C 530, 6 S. E. Rep. 325,) in which actions based upon these two causes of action have been maintained; but, as the question presented here does not seem to have been raised in either of those cases, they cannot be regarded as decisive of the point. Nor, under the view which we take of the complaint in this case, is it necessary now to decide the point. It seems to us that the complaint, properly construed, really states one cause of action against the defendant, to-wit, for the recovery of real estate. It is true that, at first blush, the action would seem to be for partition; and judging from some of the allegations, —the fifth and sixth,—together with the demand for relief, it would seem that the object of the action was partition among the plaintiffs, but there is an absence of any allegation necessary to connect the defendant with such a cause of action; and as it is well settled that the demand for relief constitutes no part of the cause of action, (Balle v. Moseley, 13 S. C. 439; Levi v. Legg, 23 S. C. 282;) and as is said in Pom. Rem. p. 630, § 580: "The prayer for relief is generally regarded as forming no part of the cause of action, and as having no effect upon it, and as furnishing no test or criterion by which its nature may be determined;" and, to use the language of Mr. Justice McGowan in Hellams v. Switzer, 24 S. C., at page 44, "one of the standing admonitions of text-writers on the Code is not to confound the cause of action with the nature of the relief sought," —it is very obvious that the prayer for relief should have no influence in determining the nature of the cause of action set forth in the complaint. Looking, then, solely to the allegations in the complaint, and disregarding the demand for relief, it seems to us clear that, while it is very possible that the pleader may have intended to set forth two causes of action,—one for the recovery of real estate and the other for partition,—yet he has, in fact, set forth but one cause of action, and his intention to set forth a cause of action for partition was not carried out by making the necessary allegations for that purpose. This being so, it follows that the demurrer for misjoinder of causes of action cannot be sustained; for, as is said in Jenkins v. Thomason, 32 S. C., at page 258, 10 S. E. Rep. 963, quoting from Pom. Rem. p. 484, § 448: "To sustain a demurrer for this reason, however, the complaint must contain two or more good grounds of suit, which cannot be properly joined in the same action. When a complaint, therefore, consists of two or more counts, and one sets forth a good cause of action, and another does not, although it attempts to do so, the pleading is not demurrable on the ground of misjoinder, even though the causes of action could not have been united had they been sufficiently and properly alleged." If this be so where the complaint purports to set forth two causes of action separately, as the rules of good pleading require, it is more especially so where, as in this case, the complaint purports to contain two causes of action, "mingled and combined in the same allegations;" for, as is said by that standard author just quoted from in section 451: "If the averments are found sufficient to express one cause of action, it may generally be said that the other averments are mere surplusage, which should be rejected on a motion made for that purpose." Indeed, that distinguished author, while admitting that the decisions in several of the states are the other way, suggests as the

proper practice in such a case, for the reasons stated in the section just quoted from, a motion in the first instance to make the pleading more certain and definite by arranging it into distinct causes of action stated separately, or a motion to strike out the redundant matter as surplusage, and thus reduce it to a single, definite cause of action. Inasmuch as we are not hampered by any authority here, and are not bound to follow the decisions elsewhere, we are disposed to adopt the suggestion of Mr. Pomeroy, and to hold, where a complaint, in a single count, (so to speak,) contains several allegations, some of which are appropriate to one cause of action and some to another, which it is claimed cannot be properly joined in the same action, that the remedy, in the first instance, is not by demurrer, but by a motion to make the pleading more definite by arranging the two causes of action separately, after which demurrer may be interposed, or by a motion to strike out as surplusage such of the allegations as may be appropriate to one cause of action, and not to the other, with the right to the plaintiff to elect which cause of action shall be retained. It seems to us, therefore, that, in any view of the case, the demurrer was properly overruled, and the judgment of this court is that the judgment of the circuit court be affirmed.

McGowan, J., concurs.

FISHER v. FAIR et al.[1]

(Supreme Court of South Carolina. July 18, 1891.)

RIGHT TO CONVEY EASEMENT.

Where the owner of a lot grants the use of a private alley-way, entirely upon his lot, to an adjoining property owner, his heirs and assigns, and provides that the grantee shall have the right to convey the privilege granted to certain persons named, the grant is one in gross, and does not become appurtenant to the land of the grantee, and he cannot convey the easement thereby obtained to persons other than those named in the grant, and he cannot invest others with the powers conferred upon him by deed of indenture.

Appeal from common pleas circuit court of Richland county; WALLACE, Judge.

Action by W. C. Fisher against Mary D. Fair and J. Q. Marshall, to recover damages for obstructing an alley-way, etc. Judgment for defendants. Plaintiff appeals. Affirmed.

Allen J. Green, for appellant. F. H. Weston and Lyles & Haynesworth, for respondents.

McIVER, J. This was an action to recover damages for the obstruction of an alleged right of way over the lands of defendants, and to perpetually enjoin the defendants from obstructing the same. The diagram annexed to the "case" shows distinctly the situation of the premises, and the course of the way claimed by the plaintiff, and should be incorporated in the report of this case.

It is sufficient to state generally that the

---

[1] Rehearing denied, 13 S. E. Rep. 858.

alleged way is an alley between adjacent lots in the city of Columbia, plaintiff being the owner of the two lots designated on the diagram as the "Black Lots," and defendants being the owners—the one for life and the other the remainder in fee—of the lot designated the "Fair Lot," which was originally owned by Dr. Samuel Fair; Thomas Davis having been formerly the owner of the other lots adjoining the alley on the west, designated as the Davis property, a part or the whole of which is now owned by the Central Bank. The evidence tends to show that originally Davis was in some way entitled to a right of way through and along the alley separating the Davis property from the Fair lot, 10 feet wide, up to a point where it intersected an alley running east from Richardson street, and separating the Davis property from the Black lots. So that Davis had a right of way, but whether in gross or appurtenant does not appear, all around his property, by an alley beginning on Plain street, and running north to the point where it intersected

TAYLOR STREET.

the alley running west into Richardson street. While things were in this situation, to-wit, on the 29th of February, 1856, Dr. Fair and Davis executed a deed of indenture, whereby, in consideration of certain covenants therein stated on the part of Davis, Dr. Fair, acknowledging the right of way of Davis through the alley leading from Plain street north to the point where it intersected the alley running from Richardson street above mentioned, conveyed to said Davis a further right of way through an alley running from Sumter street west over the northern edge of the Fair lot, and agreed to extend the right of way already owned by Davis north to the alley leading from Sumter street west; the practical result being to give Davis a right of way from Plain street around the western and northern sides of the Fair lot to Sumter street. This conveyance of the right of way was to Thomas Davis, his heirs and assigns, forever; and the deed of indenture contains the following clause: "And the said Samuel Fair further agrees to allow the said Thomas Davis, and his

heirs and assigns, to have the right, at his or their discretion, of conveying to Charles H. Black, and his heirs and assigns, or to the owners for the time being of the lot adjoining the lot of Thomas Davis (which lies on the west side of, the above described lot of Samuel Fair) on the north, the right of way through the two alleys running into Plain and Sumter streets, to be enjoyed as fully as by the said Thomas Davis, his heirs and assigns." In March, 1872, Thomas Davis conveyed to the Central Bank the property designated as his on the diagram, together with the right of way secured to Davis by the deed of indenture above mentioned. This conveyance contains the following clause: "The unobstructed use and right of way of these two alleys last mentioned, to be held and used in common by the heirs, successors, and assigns of the said Dr. Fair, and of said Central National Bank, and also by the said Charles H. Black, his heirs and assigns, who may be the owner of the said lot on Richardson street adjoining the alley on the north of the lot herein conveyed. This limitation of the use of said alley, which runs around two sides of said Dr. Fair's lot, on the part of the said Charles H. Black, his heirs and assigns, is herein specified, upon the supposition that I may have heretofore granted to them this right of way. But, if I have not granted to them this right by deed, the right is not herein confirmed by me, but is especially reserved to the said Central National Bank, which is hereby invested with all the rights I hold in and by reason of an agreement entered into between Dr. Samuel Fair, and myself, February 29, 1856, which said agreement is duly recorded in the office of the register of mesne conveyances for Richland county." The conveyance also contains a clause forbidding the bank from violating the covenants on the part of Davis contained in the deed of indenture of 29th February, 1856. On the 23d of July, 1889, the Central National Bank conveyed to the plaintiff and another the right of way, through the two alleys above mentioned, secured to Davis by the deed or indenture aforesaid; and the plaintiff, having become the owner of the Black lots, bases his claim to the right of way upon the several conveyances above stated; there being no evidence that Davis had ever conveyed to Black the said right of way, as he supposed he might have done. It further appears that on the 16th of June, 1863, Dr. Fair executed a paper, which was adjudged by this court in Brazel v. Fair, 26 S. C. 370, 2 S. E. Rep. 293, to take the absolute title to the Fair lot out of Dr. Fair, and vest it in a trustee for the benefit of the defendants herein. At the close of plaintiff's testimony, a nonsuit was moved for and granted; the circuit judge holding that the right of way conveyed to Davis by Dr. Fair was not a right of way appurtenant to any tenement owned by Thomas Davis, "and that the power conferred upon Thomas Davis to grant the right of way to the owner of the lot now owned by the plaintiff was a mere naked power, not coupled with an interest in the land, and that it was not exercised by Thomas Davis in his life-time, or by any one in the life-time of the said Dr. Fair," and therefore plaintiff's claim of a right of way could not be sustained. From this judgment plaintiff appeals upon the several grounds set out in the record, which need not be repeated here, as we propose to consider the several points which we understand to be raised thereby.

The first, and perhaps the most material, question in the case is as to the character of the right of way in question.—whether it was a right of way appurtenant to the premises of the original grantee, Davis, or whether it was a right of way in gross. In the case of Whaley v. Stevens, 21 S. C. 221, it was held that a right of way appurtenant is a right which inheres in the land to which it appurtenant, is necessary to its enjoyment, and passes with the land, while a right of way in gross is a mere personal privilege, which dies with the person who may have acquired it; and the same doctrine was reaffirmed in the same case, (27 S. C. 549, 4 S. E. Rep. 145,) when it was again before this court, the chief justice in delivering the opinion quoting the following language from Washburn on Easements, (chapter 2, par. 5, p. 257:) "Ways are said to be appendant or appurtenant when they are incident to an estate, one terminus being on the land of the party claiming. They must inhere in the land, concern the premises, and be essentially necessary to their enjoyment." In view of these authoritative declarations as to what is requisite to constitute a right of way appurtenant, it seems to us very clear that the right of way secured to Davis by the deed of indenture above mentioned cannot be regarded as a right of way appurtenant to any premises owned by Davis. It does not appear that it had either of its termini on such premises, nor that it was essentially necessary to their enjoyment. On the contrary, it was a right of way in gross, a mere privilege personal to him, and incapable of transfer by him; for, as is said in Washb. Easem. c. 1, par. 2, p. 2: "A man may have a way in gross over another's land, but it must, from its nature, be a personal right, not assignable nor inheritable; nor can it be made so by any terms in the grant." Hence, though by the indenture Fair "agrees to allow Thomas Davis to have for himself, and his heirs and assigns, forever, a right of way," etc., the same not being appurtenant to any premises then owned by Davis, the right secured is a right of way in gross, a mere personal privilege, which is not assignable, and dies with the person. It follows, therefore, that the attempt of Davis to convey this right of way to the bank was futile, and transferred no right.

It is urged, however, that, even if this be so, yet, as the deed of indenture invested Davis with power to convey this right of way "to Charles H. Black, and his heirs and assigns, or to the owners for the time being of the lot adjoining the lot of Thomas Davis (which lies on the west side of the above-described lot of Samuel Fair) on the north," Davis could, by virtue of this power, convey the right of way to the bank, as he undertook to do, and the bank could convey the same to the plaintiff, by virtue of a similar power contained in its deed from Davis. There are several objections to this view: (1) Davis is only invested with power to convey to Black, his heirs or assigns, or to the owners of the Black lots, and we are unable to find any evidence that the bank ever was the owner of those lots; and therefore, when Davis undertook to invest the bank with the power conferred upon him to convey the right of way to one who was not the owner of the Black lots, he exceeded the terms of his power. But we do not rest our decision upon this point, inasmuch as by the indenture the power to convey was vested in Davis, and his heirs and assigns; and it may be that after the bank became the assignee (so to speak) of Davis, it would have had the power to convey to the plaintiff, who was then the owner of the Black lots. But, in the second place, we agree with the circuit judge that the power conferred upon Davis, not being coupled with an interest, could not survive, and could not be exercised after the donor of the power had parted with his title to the land over which the power was to be exercised. While, therefore, the circuit judge may possibly have erred in assigning as the reason for his conclusion that the power of conveying to the plaintiff was not exercised during the life-time either of Davis or Fair, inasmuch as the "case" fails to contain any evidence as to the death of either of those persons, yet, as it does show that the power was never exercised until after Fair had parted with his title to the land over which the right of way was to be enjoyed, the conclusion reached by the circuit judge was undoubtedly correct. Assuming that the owner of land having the right to convey to another a right of way in gross over his land may invest a third person with power to make such conveyance, yet such a power, when not coupled with an interest, does not survive, nor can it be exercised after the donor of the power parts with his title to the land to be subjected to such easement. In such a case the donee of the power acts as a mere attorney in fact, and must convey in the name of his principal. Hence when the principal is dead, or has parted with his title to the land, neither he nor his attorney in fact can fix any burden or servitude upon the land. That the power in this case was not coupled with an interest is abundantly shown by the definition of that phrase as given by MARSHALL, C. J., in Hunt v. Rousmanier, 8 Wheat. 205, quoted with approval by Mr. Justice McGOWAN in Johnson v. Johnson, 27 S. C., at page 316, 3 S. E. Rep. 606. The equitable right which appellant sets up in his argument presents a question which does not appear to have been presented to or considered by the court below, nor is it mentioned in the exceptions, and therefore that matter is not properly before us. We may add, however, that the case, as made by the plaintiff, does not seem to us sufficient to warrant the court in extending to him the equitable relief demanded. The judgment of this court is that the judgment of the circuit court be affirmed.

McGOWAN, J., concurs.

GRIFFIN v. EARLE.

(Supreme Court of South Carolina. July 28, 1891.)

SEPARATE ESTATE OF MARRIED WOMEN — POWER TO CHARGE FOR LOAN TO HUSBAND — TRANSACTIONS WITH DECEDENTS—EVIDENCE.

1. A bond given by a married woman to secure the payment of money borrowed by the husband for his own use is void, and cannot be enforced as against her separate estate.

2. The fact that the bond was given in 1884, and thereafter assigned to defendant, who sought to foreclose in 1889, and that plaintiff had not claimed that the money was not borrowed for her use, will not operate as an estoppel, especially when she did nothing to induce the defendant to take the assignment.

3. Under Code S. C. § 400, which provides "that no * * * person who has a legal or equitable interest which may be affected by the event of the action * * * shall be examined in regard to any transaction * * * between such witness and a person at the time of such examination deceased," a husband may testify as to conversations had with a deceased mortgagee who held a mortgage upon the separate property of the wife, when she seeks to enjoin the sale of the premises upon the ground that the husband received the benefits of the mortgage.

4. The wife was competent to testify that she had no conversations with the deceased in regard to the transaction.

5. It was proper to exclude evidence as to conversations between the attorney for the mortgagee and plaintiff's husband, when it did not appear that he was acting as her agent.

Appeal from common pleas circuit court of Richland county; W. H. WALLACE, Judge.

Action by Emma Griffin against Caroline L. Earle, to enjoin the sale of mortgaged premises. Judgment for plaintiff. Defendant appeals. Affirmed.

John T. Sloan, Jr., and *Lyles & Haynsworth*, for appellant. *Melton & Melton* and *Bachman & Youmans*, for respondent.

McIVER, J. On the 20th of February, 1884, Emma Griffin, then being the wife of B. F. Griffin, made and executed a bond, secured by a mortgage on her house and lot in the city of Columbia, payable to S. L. Leapheart, which bond and mortgage was duly assigned by the executors of Leapheart, who had died in the mean time, to the defendant. On the 12th of April, 1889, the assignee, Mrs. Earle, under a power contained in the mortgage, advertised the mortgaged premises for sale; whereupon this action was commenced to enjoin the sale, and to have said bond and mortgage declared null and void, upon the ground that plaintiff, being a married woman at the time, had no power to make the contract evidenced by the bond and mortgage, alleging that the contract was not in reference to her separate estate, but that the same was to secure the repayment of money borrowed from Leapheart by her husband for his own use, and so applied by him. B. F. Griffin, the husband, was called as a witness for plaintiff, and, when asked to state the transaction between himself and Leapheart, objection was interposed upon the ground that such testimony was incompetent, under section 400 of the Code. The objection was overruled, and this ruling constitutes the basis of the first ground of appeal. When the plaintiff was examined as a witness, and asked whether she had ever had any conversation or transaction with Leapheart in regard to the loan of this money, objection was interposed upon a similar ground; and, this objection being overruled, such ruling constitutes the basis of the second ground of appeal. The defendant offered to prove by the testimony of Col. John T. Sloan, Jr., what passed between himself, as the attorney of Leapheart, and B. F. Griffin, when the loan was negotiated, which, upon objection being interposed by plaintiff, was ruled to be inadmissible, and this is the basis of the third ground of appeal.

The case was heard by his honor, Judge WALLACE, who, among other things, found, as matter of fact, that B. F. Griffin borrowed from Leapheart the money which the bond and mortgage purports to secure "for the purposes of his own business as a merchant, and not in any wise as agent of the plaintiff, and afterwards expended the same therefor;" and, further, "that said loan was not made to the plaintiff, or for the benefit of her separate estate; that the proceeds thereof were not expended, in whole or in part, for the same; that the debt evidenced by the bond and mortgage, and said bond and mortgage, were not contracted as to the separate property of the plaintiff." As matter of law, he found that the bond and mortgage were null and void, and that plaintiff is entitled to the relief demanded. Judgment having been rendered in accordance with these findings, the defendant appeals upon the several grounds set out in the record. The first, second, and third grounds have already been sufficiently indicated. The fourth and fifth raise only a question of fact, as to whether the circuit judge erred in his finding that the money was borrowed by B. F. Griffin for his own use, and that his wife had nothing to do with the use or use of the money. The sixth ground is general in its character, and simply imputes error to the finding that plaintiff was entitled to the relief demanded. The seventh and eighth grounds allege error in not finding that the action was barred by the laches of the plaintiff, and that she was estopped. The plaintiff having died pending this appeal, the action has been continued in the name of W. H. Griffin as her administrator by a proper order to that effect.

The first ground of appeal cannot be sustained. As was said in Boykin v. Watts, 6 S. C. at page 82, and quoted with approval in Robinson v. Robinson, 20 S. C. 572, in speaking of the proviso to section 400 of the Code: "The obvious purpose and intent of the proviso * * * is to exclude the evidence, by a party interested in the event of the suit, of any transaction or communication with a deceased by which such event may be determined in favor of such witness." To same effect, see Moffatt v. Hardin, 22 S. C. 25. B. F.

Griffin not being a party to the action, his testimony as to conversations and transactions with Leapheart could be excluded only upon the ground that he had some "legal or equitable interest which may be affected by the event of the action or proceeding," or because his "examination, or any judgment or determination in such action," could, "in any manner," affect his interest, which the cases above cited show means, "be calculated to promote his interest." Now, even if it be conceded that B. F. Griffin had such a legal or equitable interest as is contemplated by the statute, (which, however, we are not to be understood as saying, except for the purposes of this case,) we do not see how his testimony could possibly promote his interest, which, if he had any, was equally balanced; for if, by his testimony, the plaintiff would be relieved from liability on the bond, then B. F. Griffin would be clearly liable to Leapheart for the money which he got from him and used for his own purposes. The suggestion that the statute of limitations would protect him from such liability will not avail, for, as was said in Roe v. Harrison, 9 S. C. 280, "a question of fact * * * could not be determined as an incident merely to the question of the interest of the witness in the event of the suit. Such a proceeding would be without precedent, and incompatible with orderly procedure in trials of issues of fact, and it is not to be assumed that the legislature intended such a qualification of its language." It would therefore have been "incompatible with orderly procedure" for the court to have turned aside from the issues of the case on trial, for the purpose of determining whether the statute of limitations would have protected B. F. Griffin from liability to Leapheart, or whether the plea of the statute could not have been successfully met by proof of subsequent aknowledgments, or otherwise, before it could determine what interest B. F. Griffin may have had in the event of the suit. On the other hand, if the liability of the plaintiff to Leapheart could be fixed, then B. F. Griffin would be liable to the plaintiff for having used her money. It seems to us clear that there was no error in admitting the testimony of B. F. Griffin as to his conversations and transactions with Leapheart.

The second ground is equally untenable. The plaintiff was not called upon to testify, nor did she testify, to any conversation or transaction with Leapheart. She simply said that she never had any communication or transaction with Leapheart, and this was clearly competent, under the cases of Brown v. Moore, 26 S. C. 163, 2 S. E. Rep. 9, and Richards v. Munro, 30 S. C. 284, 9 S. E. Rep. 108, cited by counsel for respondent.

As to the third ground, there can be no doubt that Sloan's testimony as to what passed between him and B. F. Griffin was clearly incompetent, as mere hearsay evidence, unless it had been shown that B. F. Griffin was acting as the agent of the plaintiff, which was not only not shown, but the contrary was abundantly proved.

The fourth and fifth grounds raise simply a question of fact as to who borrowed the money from Leapheart, and, as the conclusion reached by the circuit judge is fully sustained by the evidence, these grounds need not be further considered.

In view of these findings of fact, there can be no doubt that there was no error on the part of the circuit judge in holding that the bond of a married woman, not given with reference to, or for the benefit of, her separate estate, but, on the contrary, to secure the repayment of money borrowed by her husband and used for his own purposes, was an absolute nullity, on the ground that, under the law as it stood at the making of the bond, a married woman had no power to enter into such a contract. In view of the cases which have recently been decided by this court, in reference to the power of a married woman to contract, it surely cannot be necessary to enter again into the discussion. The cases may be found extremely well classified in the argument of respondent's counsel.

It remains only to consider the question of laches and estoppel raised by the seventh and eighth grounds of appeal. So far as we can discover, there is nothing whatever in the case upon which the charge of laches can be based. The bond was given in 1884, but it does not appear when it was transferred to the defendant. There is no evidence tending to show that the plaintiff ever did or said anything to induce the defendant to take an assignment of the bond. Indeed, it does not appear that plaintiff ever even knew that defendant held the bond until the advertisement of the sale, and this action was brought very soon afterwards. As to the estoppel, we can discover nothing in the testimony to support it. There is no evidence that the plaintiff ever represented to Leapheart or to the defendant that the money was borrowed for her own use, and nothing whatever to induce the defendant to suppose that such was the fact. It may be as well for us to add that we do not understand the question of jurisdiction, as it is termed,—that is, the right of the court to grant the relief demanded in case the conclusion was reached that the plaintiff was not liable on the bond and mortgage,—as being made in this case, and therefore that question has not been considered. It is not raised by any exception, nor does it appear that the circuit judge made, or was requested to make, any ruling upon the subject. It is not presented in the argument of appellant, and, on the contrary, it is stated in respondent's argument that the jurisdiction was conceded by defendant. Under these circumstances, we have not felt at liberty to consider it, and do not desire to be regarded as intimating any opinion, either one way or the other, as to that question. The judgment of this court is that the judgment of the circuit court be affirmed.

McGowan, J., concurs.

HUGHEY v. KELLAR.

(*Supreme Court of South Carolina.* Aug. 11,
1891.)

ANSWER—NEW MATTER.

In an action to recover damages for an alleged assault and battery, an affirmative answer
which alleges that plaintiff first assaulted defendant, who committed the acts complained of
in self-defense, is sufficient on demurrer, under
Code S. C. § 170, which provides that the defendant may set up any matter which will constitute a
defense to the action.

Appeal from common pleas circuit court
of Abbeville county; JAMES ALDRICH,
Judge.

Action by Thornton Hughey against J.
Frank Kellar, to recover damages for an
alleged assault and battery. Judgment
for defendant. Plaintiff appeals. Affirmed.

Graydon & Graydon, for appellant.
Parker & McGowan, for appellee.

McIVER, J. The action in this case
was brought by plaintiff against the defendant to recover damages for an alleged assault and battery committed upon him by the defendant. In his complaint
the plaintiff alleges "that, on the 31st day
of May, 1888, the defendant committed a
violent assault and battery upon him by
shooting him with a double-barreled
shotgun loaded with bird-shot;" and goes
on to state the injury sustained by him,
as well as the amount of damages which
he claimed. The answer was in the following words: "That the plaintiff and his
wife first assaulted the defendant, who
thereupon necessarily committed the acts
complained of in self-defense." To this
answer the plaintiff interposed an oral
demurrer, upon the ground that it does
not state facts sufficient to constitute
a defense. The circuit judge overruled the
demurrer, and the trial proceeded, and
resulted in a verdict for the defendant,
and, judgment having been entered thereon, the plaintiff appeals upon the several
grounds set out in the record, which substantially make the single question whether the demurrer was properly overruled.
Section 170 of the Code provides that the
answer must contain a general or specific
denial of each material allegation controverted by the defendant; and section 189
declares that every material allegation of
the complaint, not controverted by the
answer in the manner prescribed, "shall,
for the purpose of the action, be taken as
true." These sections also provide that the
answer may, in cases where the facts warrant it, contain "a statement of any new
matter, constituting a defense or counter-
claim, in ordinary and concise language,
without repetition;" and in a case where
this is done, unless the new matter pleaded as a defense amounts to a counter-
claim, the allegation of such new matter
shall be deemed controverted by the plaintiff as upon a direct denial. Looking at
the pleadings in this case in the light of
these provisions of the Code, it seems to
us plain that the allegation in the complaint that the defendant had committed
a violent assault and battery upon the
plaintiff was admitted by the omission of
the defendant in his answer to deny such
allegation; and that the only issue presented by the pleadings was whether the
statement of the new matter by way of
defense, which must have been deemed
controverted by the plaintiff, was true.
The only question, therefore, was whether
the new matter stated in the answer was
sufficient, if established to the satisfaction
of the jury, to constitute a defense of the
acts admitted by defendant to have been
done by him, upon which the plaintiff
bases his cause of action. As to this,
we cannot see how there can be a doubt.
If the defendant was first assaulted by
the plaintiff, and in self-defense necessarily
committed the acts complained of by
plaintiff, it seems to us too clear for ar
gument that the defendant had committed
no violation of law; certainly none
which would render him liable in damages
to the plaintiff. There was no error in
overruling the demurrer. The judgment
of this court is that the judgment of the
circuit court be affirmed.

McGOWAN, J., concurs.

NORFOLK & W. R. Co. v. GILMAN'S ADM'X.

(*Supreme Court of Appeals of Virginia.* July
9, 1891.)

MASTER AND SERVANT — RAILROAD BRAKEMEN—
DEFECTIVE STRUCTURE — NEGLIGENCE — PLEAD-
ING.

1. In an action to recover damages for wrongful death, the evidence showed that a train of
six cars was being run along a coal wharf, upon
a wooden structure 25 feet high, and about 300
feet long. The only obstruction on the end of the
structure was a log chained to the wharf. The
chain gave way, and let the cars pass over the
end thereof, killing plaintiff's intestate, who was
a brakeman. It further appeared that the company had ordered timbers four years before, intending to build a dead-block, but the same was
not built. *Held* sufficient to show negligence on
the part of the company.

2. Where the declaration charges that the
damages were occasioned by the negligence of
the defendant, it is sufficient on demurrer, although there is no denial of contributory negligence.

Error to circuit court, Smythe county;
JOHN A. KELLEY, Judge.

Action by J. S. Gilman's administratrix
against Norfolk & Western Railroad Company. Judgment for plaintiff. Defendant
brings the case for review upon writ of error. Affirmed.

W. H. Bolling, for plaintiff in error.
Blair & Dickenson, for defendant in error.

LACY, J. This is a writ of error to a
judgment of the circuit court of Smythe
county, rendered on the 24th day of December, 1889. The action is trespass on
the case by the defendant in error against
the plaintiff in error, the Norfolk & Western Railroad Company, for the alleged
negligent killing of her intestate, J. S. Gilman, deceased. The said J. S. Gilman was
a brakeman in the employment of the
plaintiff in error, the Norfolk & Western
Railroad Company, when the injury was
inflicted upon him of which he died. An
engine pushing six loaded coal-cars up a
steep ascent which led up to the top of an
elevated structure, called a "coal wharf,"
was run up to the top of the ascent, or

nearly so, with two brakemen to man the brakes upon the coal-cars. This coal wharf was 25 feet high and on the level 800 feet long. When some of these cars had been pushed over the ascent, and upon the level wharf, the engineer shut off steam, sounded for brakes, and upon the evidence, as we must regard it, reversed his engine. The strain thus thrown upon the coupling, by the sudden halt of the engine when fastened to six loaded cars, moving with considerable impetus imparted by the rapid motion of the engine up the ascent, caused the coupling-pin to break, and the cars and the engine parted company. The object the engine-man had in halting and reversing the engine was to hold the cars, so that they would remain on the wharf, and not run off at the far end, which was high from the ground, and presented a danger point. But either the pin was defective, or the halt too sudden, and, the engine no longer holding the cars, they rolled on to the end of the wharf, and, pushing off a temporary obstruction placed there to check them, fell over the end. One brakeman jumped off when the engine broke loose, upon a gang-plank, which ran along the side, and then, by another jump, landed on the coal-heap, and thus saved his life; but the said J. S. Gilman, now deserted by his co-laborer and fellow-servant, manfully stuck to his post, and pursued the only possible course to save the company, his employer, from loss, and put the brakes down on his car, the first, and ran upon the second, put the brakes on that, and upon the third also, and was in the act of manning the brakes upon the fourth, when he went down bravely turning the brakes on that. His life was forfeited under circumstances which all must respect. He was killed at the post of duty. His wife qualified as his administratrix, and instituted this suit for damages against the said railroad company because of the alleged negligence which had caused the injury. At the trial the jury rendered a verdict for the plaintiff in the sum of a thousand dollars. The defendant moved the court to set aside the verdict, and grant a new trial. The grounds of the motion are not stated in the bill of exceptions, but this motion the court overruled, and the defendant having excepted to the ruling of the court in giving and in refusing certain instructions, and all the evidence having been certified, the said defendant applied for and obtained a writ of error to this court.

The first error assigned here by the plaintiff in error is to the action of the circuit court in overruling the defendant's demurrer to the plaintiff's declaration; the ground of the demurrer being that the declaration does not deny that the plaintiff was guilty of contributory negligence. In an action for damages occasioned by the negligence or misconduct of the defendant, it is not necessary for the plaintiff to allege and prove the existence of due care on his part to enable him to recover. If the defendant relies upon contributory negligence of the plaintiff to defeat the action, he must prove it, unless, indeed, the fact is discovered by the evidence of the plaintiff, or may be fairly inferred from all the circumstances. As proof of due care on his part is not a part of the plaintiff's case, it is, of course, not necessary that he should aver it in his declaration. If the defendant relied on the contributory negligence of the plaintiff, it is matter of proof for him, either by testimony adduced by him, or as matter of inference deducible from the evidence of the plaintiff. But it is not the duty of the plaintiff to negative it by proof, and no part of his case to deny it in his declaration. Shear. & R. Neg. § 43; Railroad Co. v. Gladmon, 15 Wall. 401; Railroad Co. v. Whittington, 30 Grat. 809. In Improvement Co. v. Andrew, 86 Va. 273, 9 S. E. Rep. 1015, this court said as to this: "It is true that some of the courts, in some of the states, have thrown this subject into some obscurity by 'conflicting and evasive decisions,' as they are termed by Shearman and Redfield." And an interesting discussion of the subject and comparison of decisions may be found in their work on Negligence, § 43. But we do not consider it necessary to cite nor to discuss them. The subject is well settled here in this state upon what we consider the correct principle,—that negligence on the part of the plaintiff is a mere matter of defense, to be proved affirmatively by the defendant, though, of course, it might be inferred from the circumstances proved by the plaintiff. This was the view held by Duer, J., in Johnson v. Railroad Co., 5 Duer, 21, when he pointed out that parties were never required to prove negative matters of this kind, and that it had never been held necessary, in a complaint upon negligence, to aver that the plaintiff had taken due care. The error assigned as to the instructions given by the court to the plaintiff are rather as to abstract question of law than statements of the law applicable to this particular case, and is not pressed nor insisted on here, the instructions being drawn to meet phases of the case not now relied on; there being no insistence that the plaintiff, by standing by the brakes and going down to death, rooted to his post of duty, was thereby guilty of contributory negligence which caused his death, or contributed approximately thereto. Nor does the question as to whether the engineer and the jumping brakeman were fellow-servants play any part in the controversy here. It is not necessary, therefore, to review at length the instructions, the question having been narrowed here to the single inquiry whether the injury to the plaintiff was caused by the negligence and want of due and proper care on the part of the defendant company.

And for the due consideration of this question, bearing in mind the well-established rule of evidence, that, where the evidence is certified as in this case, the case must stand as upon a demurrer to evidence, let us turn to a brief review of the evidence of the plaintiff, and such evidence of the defendant as is not in conflict therewith. And we find this case: The cars were pushed up this ascent, and run upon a wharf high above the ground,—a wooden structure raised 25 feet. They were then and always were loaded with coal when going up. Six cars loaded with coal, and in motion upon a level 800 feet long, left but little margin for them to be stopped in by the brakes, and, if anything should happen to the engine so that they should become detached the brakes were the only hope, unless some obstruction was placed on the end of the wharf. It was proved in the evidence that the company had fastened a log at the end or near the end of the wharf by a chain attached to the middle of the log by a hook. The defendant's own witness states that the cars, as they passed along on this wharf, were not going faster than a man walks, their speed having been so far checked by the engine before they parted with it by the breaking of the pin, and by the brakes which had been set. But nevertheless they snapped this chain, and went over. They came against a log not bolted down, but tied with a chain in the middle, and it furnished no better safeguard than a fence-rail would have done. That the company had ordered heavy pieces of timber 45 feet long, 14 inches square at one end, and 12 inches square at the other end, these to be set in the ground, and bolted to heavy timbers placed in upright position on the wharf track, so as to prop the upright pieces with the long pieces 45 feet in length. That at the time the wharf constructor said that these timbers were wanted, as he regarded the chained log as only temporary. That the witness Sprinkle had declined to furnish these timbers; and, although four years had elapsed, they had not been furnished to the company, which had continued to use the temporary contrivance, until at last it gave way before the strain we have mentioned. If the stout battery indicated above had been furnished, there is no reason to believe that these cars, heavy as they were, would have broken it down. Was it not the duty of the company to have furnished a safe and suitable structure at the end of this wharf, so as to have guarded as far as possible against injury to its employes engaged in this truly perilous employment of riding up this steep place before an engine struggling with its immense burden to such a height. What is the law? The defendant company was bound to use ordinary care; that is to say, such care as reasonable and prudent men use, under like circumstances, in selecting competent servants, and in supplying and maintaining suitable and safe appliances for the work so to be performed, and in providing generally for the safety of the servant in the course of his employment, regard being had to the work, and to the difficulties and dangers attending,—for what would be ordinary care in one case may be gross negligence in another. Beach, Contrib. Neg. 22; Thomp. Neg. 962.

And, as has been often said here, nothing is better settled than that the employe takes upon himself all the natural risks and perils incident to the service, and this grows out of the contract which the law implies from the engagement of the parties. When a servant enters upon an employment, he accepts the service, subject to the risk incident to it. An employe who contracts for the performance of hazardous duties assumes such risks as are incident to their discharge from causes open and obvious, the dangerous character of which causes he had opportunity to ascertain. If a man chooses to accept employment, or continue in it, with the knowledge of the danger, he must abide the consequences, so far as any claim against his employer is concerned. On the other hand, it is the duty of the company to exercise all reasonable care to provide and to maintain safe, sound, and suitable machinery, road-way, structures, and instrumentality; and it must not expose its employes to risks beyond those which are incident to the employment, and were in contemplation at the time of contract of service; and the employe has the right to presume these duties have been performed. Here we have six cars under brakes as to three, and also checked up; that they were proceeding on a level at a rate of speed at which a man commonly walks; and as they were on a level, and not on a down grade, their speed was decreasing, because their tendency, on a level, was to come to a stand-still. And yet so inadequate was the "dead-block," as it is called here, that the cars were not only not stopped by it at this slow rate of speed, but checked by it so little that they rolled on over the brink, and were piled up in a mass of ruins, with fatal result to the faithful brakeman. None can doubt that, if these heavy timbers had been planted there, resting in the solid earth, the accident would have been prevented. Did not the company know they were necessary? Clearly so, because the record shows that they were ordered, and, when one man declined to furnish them, the evidence does not disclose any further effort to procure them, simple as the matter was, and easy of adjustment; as it is not to be doubted that timbers of that or similar size are in frequent use by the company in its structures. The company declared this chained log to be a temporary expedient; but yet four years passed, and this temporary contrivance was allowed to become permanent, and was allowed to remain there until the injury happened. Was not this negligence? The structure was temporary only, and not safe. This was known to the company, as better timbers were ordered, and yet knowing the danger, and advised of the need, days were allowed to run into weeks, weeks into months, months into years, and still the temporary and unsafe structure had not been replaced by the permanent and substantial contrivance in use elsewhere and which if it had been in place on this wharf would have arrested without danger these slowly moving cars. This was negligence beyond question, and this was the negligence in this case which caused the injury, and without which it would probably not have happened. Of course we understand that no dead-blocks and no battery, however substantial, could prevent disaster, when brought into collision with an escaped, or otherwise rapidly moving, train, beyond control; but an elevated coal wharf can never, under ordinary conditions, be submitted to any such catastrophe; trains pushed up a very steep ascent can never retain any very great velocity, and there is no reason why this obstruction at the end should not be made substantial and safe. It is clear that the injury was caused by the negligence of the company as indicated, to which the injured party in no degree contributed, and the plaintiff was entitled to recover. There is no complaint as to the amount of the damages. The jury fixed these at a thousand dollars, and they cannot be considered excessive. We perceive no error in the judgment complained of, and the same must be affirmed.

GARLAND'S ADM'R v. GARLAND'S ADM'R et al.

(Supreme Court of Appeals of Virginia. April 30, 1891.)

WILL—TRUSTS—UNEXPENDED PROFITS — REMAINDER.

A testator set apart in trust in the hands of his executor, for the benefit of his brother, certain plantations and personal property, and provided that "the profits of the estate is set apart for his use, under his superintendence; but neither the estate nor profits shall be bound for his past debts, or for future debts or liabilities, other than decent and comfortable support. At his death, all the said property is to pass to a trustee, in trust for certain other devisees." *Held,* that the brother took only a qualified right to support from the profits, subject to no debts except to those who furnished him supplies, and that unexpended profits passed at his death to the remainder-man.

Appeal from circuit court of city of Lynchburg.

Action by John F. Slaughter, administrator *d. b. n. c. t. a.* of Samuel Garland, Sr., against Charles. Y. Morriss, administrator *c. t. a.* of B. Garland, and others, to enforce a decree rendered in the state of Mississippi, and for distribution thereunder. Decree for plaintiff, and defendants appeal. Reversed.

W. J. Robertson and E. S. Brown, for appellants. J. S. Diggs, R. G. H. Kean, and E. C. Burks, for appellee.

HINTON, J. This is the sequel to the case of Garland's Adm'r v. Garland's Adm'r, reported in 84 Va. at page 181, 4 S. E. Rep. 334. As the case was then presented, it appeared that William H. Garland, executor of Burr Garland, deceased, had brought a suit in the proper court in Mississippi to settle the administration accounts of his testator as administrator *c. t. a.* of Samuel Garland, Sr., deceased; that the court in Mississippi ascertained the amount due to be $64,130.88, and decreed that the domiciliary executor, the said William H. Garland, should pay the same to John F. Slaughter, who had qualified in Virginia as administrator *de bonis non c. t. a.* of the said Samuel Garland, Sr. Burr Garland died in Virginia in December, 1869. On his death there was found in the hands of John T. Murrell, in Lynchburg, Va., the sum of $1,421.52, which was the remains of a sum of money said Burr Garland had deposited with him on call, and subject to his (Burr Garland's) order. It also appeared that when Burr Garland died he was in possession of certain conveyances or assignments to himself from several legatees of the said Samuel Garland, Sr., who were children of Nicholas Garland, a brother of the testator, of the legacies given to them in the will of Samuel Garland, Sr. Slaughter being unable, by reason of Burr Garland's insolvency, to make the money decreed by the Mississippi court in that state, and finding these assets in Virginia, brought suit in Virginia to enforce the Mississippi decree. To that suit Charles Y. Morriss, administrator with the will annexed of Burr Garland, deceased, and Mary Garland, his surety, were made defendants. Upon this state of facts, this court held that the decree of the Mississippi court must be accepted as final and conclusive evidence of the fact and amount of indebtedness by Burr Garland, the Mississippi administrator of Samuel Garland, to Samuel Garland's estate. And, further, that the decree of that court did not undertake to distribute it, nor to determine who are entitled to receive it, under Samuel Garland's will, but decreed it to be paid over to the Virginia domiciliary executor, to be by him distributed to those entitled, according to the declared intention of the testator; "but this decision is without prejudice to any right of action which Paulina B. Morriss may have in this or in an independent suit." When the case got back to the circuit court, the plaintiff filed his amended bill, making Paulina B. Morriss and her children parties.

After the case had been matured for hearing, on application for an order directing accounts, the court proceeded to construe the ninth clause of the will of Samuel Garland, Sr., upon the true construction of which the present controversy must turn. That clause is in these words: "(9) My favorite brother, B. Garland, raised by me, and long a resident of Mississippi, is, and has for a long time past been, embarrassed in debt by losses of trade in 1837, and liabilities as surety for others. It might be unsafe to devise property to him absolutely. I therefore set apart in trust in the hands of my executor for the benefit of my said brother, either of my plantations in Hinds county, called 'Barrens' or 'Tudor Hall,' whichever he may choose, and forty slaves in families,—say about twenty-five hands, balance heads of families, children, and house-servants,—to be selected out of the stocks in both places; mules, horses, stock, etc., sufficient for the cultivation of the place so selected by him, with provisions, house and kitchen furniture, plantation tools, etc., oxen, hogs, etc., to make a complete estate. The profits of the estate is set apart for his (B. Garland's) use, under his superintendence. But neither the estate or profits shall be bound for his past debts, or for future debts and liabilities other than decent and comfortable support. At his death all the property in this clause is to pass to Charles Y. Morriss, in trust, to the separate use of his wife, Paulina B. Morriss, and her children." The circuit court was of opinion and decreed "that the estate of the said Burr Garland, in the profits set apart by the said clause for the use of the said Burr Garland, became and was, under the law, and by virtue of said will, his absolute estate, and, as such, liable not only for such debts as might be contracted for his decent and comfortable support, but for all his debts; and the said profits did not, nor did any part thereof, pass under the said will to the said Charles Y. Morriss, in trust for the separate use of the said Paulina B. Morriss and her children, nor did they, or either of them, acquire any estate or interest therein under the said will."

This, however, is not, in our opinion, the interpretation to be put upon the clause of the will now under review. Burr Garland, as the very first words of this clause of the will says, was the favorite brother of the testator, by whom he had been reared. He had become so involved in debt, by reason of losses in business, doubtless occasioned by the financial panic of 1837, and by liabilities incurred as surety for others, that it appeared to the testator practically impossible for him ever to free himself from this load of debt. In this condition, the testator saw that an absolute gift or devise of property to him would be of no service to him, but would, in effect, be a gift of so much property to his creditors, who had not the slightest claim upon the testator. He therefore endeavored, by a carefully-devised trust, to protect his brother in his declining years from penury and want, by giving him the mere right to "a decent and comfortable support" out of the profits of an estate, the legal title to which, as well as to the profits, he is careful to confer upon the trustee. And, having made this provision for his brother,—a provision strictly limited to the use of so much of the profits as was necessary for "a decent and comfortable support,"—and having declared that neither the estate or profits shall be bound for his past debts or liabilities, or for future debts incurred on any other account, he gives all the property in this clause (clearly meaning the estate and any surplus profits) over to Charles Y. Morriss, in trust to the separate use of his wife, Paulina B. Morriss, and her children.

Now, this being the purpose of the testator, too clearly manifested to require any verbal criticism upon the mere words of the will, the only remaining inquiry is whether this intention shall be allowed to prevail; or, to express the same idea differently, whether there is any rule of the court of chancery in this state which defeats it. On behalf of the appellees, it is insisted that the testator, by his will, gave to Burr Garland the profits therein mentioned absolutely, and that the exemption of the profits from liability for Burr Garland's debts is void, because they say that it is a fundamental doctrine of the English chancery, and that the same rule prevails in America, that no such estate can be deprived of the incident of alienability or liability for the debts of the owner. But this argument seems to me to be beside the mark. In this case the devisee and legatee, Burr Garland, did not take any absolute property in the profits of the estate which he might have assigned or aliened; but, on the contrary,

he acquired the mere, although exclusive, right to a reception of so much of said profits as would furnish a decent and comfortable support for himself, and this was so qualified and limited as to fence out all his creditors, except those who furnished him supplies for his support. Had he undertaken to expend these profits in any other way, he would have been guilty of a breach of trust, for there was, in the eye of a court of equity, as complete a trust in him to apply these profits in this one direction as there was in the trustee to hold the legal title. And while he (Burr Garland) took this qualified right, which we think it is a misnomer to call property, the remainder-men took a vested remainder in all the surplus or unexpended profits. It is admitted that this exact question has never been decided in Virginia, although several cases have arisen in this state, where the trusts were held to be blended, and therefore that donee had no interest that was divisible from the other cestuis que trustent, and therefore no property that could be subjected to his debts. But in Nickell v. Handly, 10 Grat. 336, Judge Samuels, delivering the opinion of the court, said: "There is nothing in the nature or law of property which could prevent the testatrix, when about to die, from appropriating her property to the support of her poor and helpless relations; nothing to prevent her from charging her property with the expense of food, raiment, and shelter for such relations. There is nothing in law or reason, I conceive, which should prevent her from appointing an agent or trustee to administer her bounty." But the question has been carefully considered by the supreme court of the United States in the case of Nichols v. Eaton, 91 U. S. 716, and by the supreme court of Massachusetts in the case of Bank v. Adams, 133 Mass. 170, and in each case it was held that there was nothing in the doctrines of the American chancery which prohibits a trust like the present. The reasoning of these cases commends itself to our judgment, and fully establishes the validity of this trust. The decree of the court below being in conflict with these views, must be reversed, and the cause must be remanded for further proceedings to be had in accordance with this opinion. Decree reversed.

FRENCH v. CHAPMAN.

(*Supreme Court of Appeals of Virginia.* July 23, 1891.)

REFORMATION OF DEED—MUTUAL MISTAKE—BURDEN OF PROOF—HEARSAY.

1. In an action to reform a deed plaintiff testified that his written contract with defendant provided for the mutual exchange of all their lands, but that by mistake defendant's deed omitted one 50-acre tract. Defendant denied that the contract included his tract, and that there was any mistake in the deed. It appeared that the contract was written by plaintiff, and had been lost. The deed was drawn under plaintiff's directions, and in his presence, defendant being absent, and was, after execution, accepted and placed on record by plaintiff. Plaintiff's witnesses testified merely that, in conversations with defendant, he had said nothing about receiving this tract. When defendant moved, he left his

mother in possession of it, and at his instance she forbade defendant to remove a house therefrom. *Held*, that the burden of proof was on plaintiff, and that the mistake was not clearly established by the evidence.

2. Declarations by his mother, in defendant's absence, that the contract embraced the land in controversy, was inadmissible as hearsay.

Appeal from circuit court, Giles county; D. W. BOLEN, Judge.

Bill by William H. French against James W. Chapman to reform a deed. Decree for defendant, and plaintiff appeals. Affirmed.

Mr. Blair and *Williams Bros.*, for appellant. *Phlegar & Johnson*, for appellee.

RICHARDSON, J. This was a suit in chancery brought in the circuit court of Giles county in 1877, by William H. French, plaintiff, v. James W. Chapman, defendant. The object of the suit was to have a certain deed from the said Chapman and wife to said French, dated 27th day of April, 1872, so reformed as to embrace one moiety of a certain 50-acre tract of land alleged to have been omitted, by mistake or otherwise, in drawing said deed. The case, as made by this bill, answer, and exhibit is as follows: The bill alleges that on the 27th day of April, 1872, mutual deeds were executed by and between the said William H. French and wife and said James W. Chapman and wife, which were intended to carry into effect and to perfect an exchange of lands before that time made between them, the said French giving in exchange to said Chapman his tract of about 400 acres on Wolf creek, in Bland county, for all the lands owned by said Chapman on Wolf creek, in Giles county; and with his bill the complainant exhibits a copy of said deed, marked "A." But the bill sets forth that there is a mistake in said deed, greatly to the prejudice of said complainant, French, the effect of which, if not corrected, will deprive him of title to the most valuable portion of the land which he was to receive in said exchange from said Chapman; that by the terms of his contract he was to receive from said Chapman a deed conveying to him all the land owned by Chapman on Wolf creek, in Giles county, and that said deed was intended by both parties to embrace all of said lands. The bill then sets forth that said Chapman, at the time of said contract for exchange, and at the time of execution of said deed, was the owner of an undivided moiety in three tracts of land which he owned jointly with his sister, one Sarah L. Chapman, two of which, to-wit, a tract of 84 acres and a tract of 1,350 acres, descended to them from their grandfather, James Chapman, through their father, John W. Chapman, who was the only child and heir at law expectant of said James Chapman, and who died before his father, the said James Chapman, leaving said James W. and Sarah L. Chapman as the only heirs at law of their said grandfather, James Chapman; and that said James W. Chapman owned an undivided moiety in another tract of 50 acres, contiguous to said other two tracts, and upon which is situate a mansion-house and other valuable buildings

and improvements, which said tract, it is alleged, is by far the most valuable part of said land, and is also jointly owned by said James W. and Sarah L. Chapman, and was inherited by them from their great-grandfather, John Chapman, deceased, through their father, the said John W. Chapman, as follows: The said John Chapman, by his will, a copy of which is filed with the bill, and was probated in Giles county in 1847, devised said 50-acre tract to said James Chapman for life, with the remainder in fee, after his death, to his said son, John W. Chapman, who died before his father, James Chapman, the life-tenant, and at the death of said life-tenant the fee-simple vested in said James W. and Sarah L. Chapman; and that the said James W. was the owner of an undivided moiety thereof at the date of said deed made from him to the complainant, William H. French, his grandfather, the said James, being then dead. And the bill then sets forth that the language of said deed only conveys to the complainant the land descended to the defendant, James W. Chapman, from his grandfather, the said James Chapman, deceased, but omitting the moiety owned by him in said 50-acre tract, which, it is alleged, constituted one of the chief inducements to the complainant to make said exchange; that the omission was the result of mistake, and that the mistake was recently discovered, when the complainant, French, immediately called upon the defendant, Chapman, to correct it, but that he fraudulently declines and refuses to do so. And the prayer of the bill is that said James W. Chapman be made a party defendant thereto, and required to answer its allegations on oath; that said omissions and mistake in said deed be corrected, and said Chapman required to convey said moiety of said 50-acre tract to complainant, and for general relief, etc.

The defendant, James W. Chapman, answered the bill, and denied most emphatically that there is any mistake in his deed to complainant, referred to in and exhibited with the bill, and says that the deed was prepared according to, and in exact conformity to, the contract between complainant and himself. And he says that he has complied fully with the terms of his contract, by the execution of the deed conveying the land which descended to him from his grandfather, James Chapman, deceased. He denies that he ever agreed to convey to complainant all the land owned by him (respondent) which lies in Giles county, on Wolf creek, and he denies that said deed was intended to convey any more land than is described therein. He denies that he fraudulently declined and refused to correct the deed referred to in complainant's bill, because, he says, no correction was necessary or due to complainant, the deed being in perfect conformity with the agreement between the parties; that the deed was accepted and placed on record by the complainant; and that respondent is advised that complainant is estopped from denying its correctness, or varying the terms thereof; and he denies that he ever sold to complainant his moiety in the land which descended to him from John Chapman, deceased, or that it was intended to be embraced in the deed.

Numerous depositions were taken in the case by both parties, and the same came on and was heard at the November term, 1887, when, after bringing the cause on to be heard upon the bill of complainant and exhibits therewith filed, the demurrer of respondent to complainant's bill and rejoinder in said demurrer, the answer of James W. Chapman, and replication thereto, depositions of witnesses theretofore filed in the cause, the decrees and orders theretofore entered therein, together with all the papers formerly read, and arguments of counsel, the court entered its decree, as follows: "On consideration whereof the court doth overrule said demurrer; and the court being of opinion that complainant, William H. French, under the pleadings and evidence in the cause, has failed to sustain the allegation contained in his bill, that the evidence does not establish any mistake in the deed from James W. Chapman to William H. French, bearing date the 27th day of April, 1872, it is therefore adjudged, ordered, and decreed that the complainant's bill be dismissed, and that the respondent, James W. Chapman, recover the said William H. French his costs," etc. From this decree the case is here on appeal.

The simple question for the decision by this court is, did the circuit court err in holding, as it did by its decree, that the complainant, William H. French, failed to sustain the allegations in his bill; that the evidence did not establish any mistake in the deed from James W. Chapman to said French, bearing date the 27th day of April, 1872; and in dismissing said complainant's bill? After a most careful scrutiny of all the facts disclosed by the record, we are clearly of the opinion that said decree is without error. The contest here is between the parties to the contract exclusively; the one seeking to reform the deed of April 27, 1872, by parol proof of mistake, and the other resisting it upon the ground that there was no mistake. It will not be denied that it is entirely competent for a court of equity to correct a mistake in a deed or other writing upon parol evidence. Hence, in Mauzy v. Sellars, 26 Grat. 641, Judge STAPLES, quoting with approbation the language of Chancellor KENT in Gillespie v. Moon, 2 Johns. Ch. 585, 596, says: "I have looked into most, if not all, of the cases on this branch of equity jurisdiction, and it appears to me to be established, and on great and essential grounds of justice, that relief can be had against any deed or contract in writing founded on mistake or fraud. The mistake may be shown by parol proof, and the relief granted to the injured party, whether he sets up the mistake affirmatively by bill or as a defense." So in 3 Pom. Eq. Jur. §1376, p. 413, it is said: "Equity has jurisdiction to reform written instruments in but two well-defined cases: (1) Where there is a mutual mistake,—that is, where there has been a meeting of minds, an agreement actually

entered into, but the contract, deed, settlement, or other instrument, in its written form, does not express what was really intended by the parties thereto; and (2) where there has been a mistake of one party, accompanied by fraud or other inequitable conduct of the remaining party. In such cases the instrument may be made to conform to the agreement or transaction entered into, according to the intention of the parties." But, while the jurisdiction of a court of equity to reform written instruments is thus clearly established, there are certain requisites with which the party invoking this power of a court of equity must comply, or else the relief sought will not be granted: (1) It must appear that the mistake was mutual. This proposition is too well established to be now questioned. 3 Pom. Eq. Jur. p. 413; 5 Wait, Act. & Def. 441, 443; 7 Wait, Act. & Def. 328; Hoback v. Kilgores, 26 Grat. 442; Massie's Adm'r v. Heiskell's Trustee, 80 Va. 801. (2) The evidence of the mistake "must be clear and satisfactory, leaving but little, if any, doubt of the mistake." 7 Wait, Act. & Def. p. 327. It "must be made out by the clearest and most satisfactory testimony." 2 Minor, Inst. p. 701, (side page 625.) "The evidence in all such cases must be very strong and clear," such as to leave no fair and reasonable doubt on the mind that the writing does not correctly embody the real intention of the parties." Mauzy v. Sellars, supra; 2 Pom. Eq. Jur. § 859, p. 325; Carter v. McArtor, 28 Grat. 360. (3) The burden of proof is on the appellant, and mere preponderance of evidence will not suffice. Carter v. McArtor, supra; 2 Minor, Inst. p. 701, (side page 625;) 5 Wait, Act. & Def. p. 442. In the light of these well-established principles, let us turn to the evidence, and see whether it meets the requirement of the rules above stated; and in doing so let it be kept in view that a mere preponderance of evidence is not sufficient to justify the court in reforming the deed in question.

The bill calls for an answer on oath, and the defendant so answered, denying every material allegation in the bill. Neither the bill nor the answer mentions specifically that there was, at the time of the agreement for the exchange of land, a written agreement; but it turns out in evidence that the agreement, which was prior to the deed in question, was reduced to writing, and was not only written by the complainant, William H. French, himself, but was, with the assent of the defendant, Chapman, placed in the hands of one Joshua G. French, for safe-keeping. This Joshua G. French was introduced as a witness for the complainant, but he deposes that he never read the paper; that it was lost; and that he knows nothing of its contents. The complainant, French, testifies that that paper included the land in controversy; but the defendant, Chapman, in his answer and in his deposition, swears positively that it was not so included, and was never intended to be. This is all the evidence in respect to the contents of the original written agreement, and thus far the complainant signally failed to prove his case

Moreover it appears in evidence—indeed, it is not disputed—that the deed in question was written by George W. Easley, the clerk of Giles county, at the instance, by the direction, and in the presence of the complainant, French, the defendant, Chapman, being absent, and knowing nothing about it until it was presented to him by the complaniant, and he executed and acknowledged it, and delivered it to complainant, who accepted it, and placed it on record. Is it credible that a deed thus prepared, in the presence and by the direction of the complainant, varied in any particular from the original agreement, which was written by the complainant himself? We think not. But, in the face of these potent facts and circumstances, the complainant (appellant here) seeks to establish that there was mutual mistake, and strives to uphold this contention by the testimony of the scrivener, and some 19 other witnesses, to whom it is claimed the appellee made certain declarations, amounting to admissions by the appellee that, in the contract for exchange of lands, the land in controversy was included. But in this contention the appellant is not sustained. Judge Easley, the scrivener, who was then the clerk of the county, and not a lawyer, does not sustain him, but only gives his thoughts and impressions, which must have been acquired from the appellant himself, as he does not pretend to have learned anything from the appellee, who was not present when the deed was written, and gave no directions touching the matter. As to the other witnesses who testify as to conversation with the appellee in respect to the exchange of lands, it is only necessary to say that their testimony is simply negative in character. In other words, they respectively testify that, while they had frequent conversations with the appellee, they never heard him say anything about reserving any land; and such is the testimony of the great bulk of the witnesses introduced on behalf of the appellant. Such testimony by no means comes up to the reasonable and just requirements of the rule above laid down. It cannot be said that such evidence establishes that there was a mutual mistake, much less that it is strong and clear evidence that there was such mistake,—so strong and clear as to leave no fair and reasonable doubt of the fact. It must therefore be discarded as worthless.

Among the large number of witnesses examined on behalf of the appellant are Alexander Cooper and his son, Lewis Cooper. Alexander Cooper is asked this question: "You will please state if you lived near the William H. French land, in Bland, to which J. W. Chapman removed, at the time of his removal, and some time afterwards. If so, please state what, if anything, you heard the said Chapman say about what land he had sold to William H. French, in Giles, and fully what he said about it." He answered: "I lived in about 500 yards of J. W. Chapman. I lived there two years after he moved to Bland. I heard him say that he traded his interest in that land his mother lived on. He went on and talked

a good deal, and appeared to be dissatisfied for some time after. Sometimes he appeared to get perfectly satisfied, and said he was, at least, and said he would not swap back, even with Mr. French." Second question: "In your conversation with said Chapman, did he say he had reserved any of said land on Wolfcreek, in Giles county, in his trade with French? Answer. Not that I heard, at all." This is the entire deposition of Alexander Cooper. It is composed of two questions and answers. The same two questions and similar answers constitute the deposition of Lewis Cooper. It will be seen that neither of these witnesses refer in any way to the interest of James W. Chapman in the 84-acre tract, and the 1,350-acre tract embraced in the deed from him to French, but both of them confined themselves to the interest of James W. Chapman in the 50-acre tract in controversy; so that their statement, taken literally, confines the agreement for exchange of lands to the 50-acre tract alone as the land which Chapman gave in exchange for French's land in Bland county. It will be observed, too, that Alexander Cooper says, in substance, that he had repeated conversations with the appellee, Chapman, but he details nothing except the pretended declaration of Chapman that his interest in the 50-acre tract in controversy was the land given in exchange for the land of French in Bland county. The statement is fragmentary, irrelevant, and of no value. No man's property right would be secure if such lame, disjointed, and selected parts of conversations could be taken as sufficient to reform and insert into a solemn deed betwen contracting parties new provisions working a vital change in the contract; and especially when the deed was written by the direction and under the supervision of the party seeking to reform the instrument, and when there is no satisfactory evidence that the deed is not in strict conformity with the original agreement.

Again, the appellee's mother, Rhoda, during her widowhood, intermarried with one Isaac French, and she was entitled to dower in the 50-acre tract in controversy, and lived thereon with her son, the appellee, up to the time that he exchanged his other land with the appellant for his land in Bland county; and when the appellee moved to the French land he left Isaac French, his step-father, and his mother, Rhoda, in possession of the 50 acres in controversy; and the appellant in his own deposition states that when he moved to Giles he moved into a house near the land he got in exchange from the appellee. Yet the appellant introduced as a witness on his behalf, one James F. Hare, who deposed as to declarations made to him by Mrs. Rhoda French, the mother of the appellee, to the effect that the interest of her son, the appellee, in the 50-acre tract, was embraced in the contract of exchange. It is not pretended that such declarations by Mrs. Rhoda French were made in the presence of her son, the appellee. Her testimony was mere hearsay, and inadmissible. Doubtless the court disregarded or rejected it, and properly so. Moreover, Mrs. Rhoda French was living, and gave her deposition in this cause; so that, if she had said to James F. Hare what he testifies to, the matter could have been establishd by her rather than in the illegal way resorted to. But Mrs. Rhoda French acts an important part in this controversy, but not in accord with the appellant's claim. It appears in evidence that the appellant, after the exchange of land, moved a house from the 50-acre tract in controversy, and at the instance of the appellee, her son, she (Mrs. Rhoda French) forbade the removal of the house. There is some other evidence intended to show that appellant took and held undisputed possession of the land in controversy from the time of the exchange of land between him and the appellee, but a careful examination shows that this insistence is not upheld by the evidence. Taken all together, there is not even a preponderance of evidence in favor of the appellant's claim, and, if there was only a preponderance, it would not suffice under the rule applicable in such cases. The evidence would not justify the rescission of the contract, much less the reformation of the deed in question. The circuit court was therefore clearly right in holding that the appellant had failed to sustain the allegations of his bill, and in dismissing the same. For these reasons we are of opinion to affirm the decree of the court below.

WILDER et al. v. KELLEY, Judge.

(*Supreme Court of Appeals of Virginia.* July 16, 1891.)

INJUNCTION — APPLICATION TO COURT OF APPEALS — MANDAMUS TO CIRCUIT JUDGE.

Code Va. § 3438, provides that, where a circuit judge refuses to award an injunction, a copy of the proceedings may be presented to a judge of the court of appeals, who may award the injunction. Held, that where a circuit judge has denied a petition for an injunction, and the appointment of a receiver, and a judge of the court of appeals has granted same, the circuit judge has no right to refuse to enforce his order; and the fact that the petition was a second and supplemental one is immaterial, and *mandamus* will lie to compel him to carry out the order of the appellate judge. LEWIS, P., and FAUNTLE-ROY, J., dissenting.

Petition for *mandamus* by Jonas Wilder, John M. Bailey, W. G. Sheen, John L. Wellington, T. S. Hawkins, and A. B. Wilder against John A. Kelley, judge of the circuit court of Washington county.

W. W. Gordon and *R. M. Brown,* for petitioners. *R. W. Robertson* and *R. A. Ayres,* for respondent.

LACY, J. On a petition for a writ of *mandamus* by the petitioners, Wilder and others, it appears that on the 6th day of August, 1890, an injunction was granted by the circuit court of Russell, sitting in the county of Russell, to the petitioners, on their bill praying the same, and a receiver appointed in accordance therewith, for the Virginia, Tennessee & Carolina Steel & Iron Company, the South Atlantic & Ohio Railroad Company, the Bailey Construction

Company, and the Bristol Land Company, and others; and these companies, their agents, etc., were enjoined from all further interference with the said receiver, and the affairs, property, and effects and management of these companies. Under this order, the receiver qualified, as was required; but circumstances not now necessary to set forth so hindered the execution of this order, by conflicting orders of the circuit court judges, one sitting and acting in a circuit court, not his own, by authority of law, during the illness of the incumbent judge on the one hand, and *ex parte* orders by the sick judge in his bed-chamber on the other hand, that the same plaintiffs prepared a supplemental bill of injunction, and asking the appointment of a receiver, and set forth therein the substance of the original bill, and a narrative of the subsequent new facts, and presented it to the incumbent judge, the respondent herein, and prayed for an injunction. Upon this bill the respondent made an indorsement, as follows: "Injunction refused. JNO. A. KELLEY, Judge of the 16th Judicial Circuit of Virginia." Whereupon the complainants, as authorized by section 3438 of the Code of Virginia, by which it is provided that, "when a circuit or corporation court, or a judge thereof, shall refuse to award an injunction, a copy of the proceedings in court, or the original papers presented to a judge in vacation, with his order of refusal, may be presented to a judge of the court of appeals, who may thereupon award the injunction," presented the said bill, etc., and the order of refusal of the circuit court judge endorsed thereon, to one of the judges of this court, and by him, as his order states, upon consideration of the bill, exhibits, affidavits, and order of refusal, an injunction was awarded according to the prayer of the bill, restraining the defendants, their agents, etc., from in any manner interfering with the said properties and effects of the said companies, and restraining the directors of these companies from acting as such until the further order of the court; and as incident to the injunction order, and for the purpose of preserving the property affected thereby, and for protecting the rights and interests of all parties interested, and that the court may hold the property subject to the litigation pending, and administer to the parties their rights, respectively, it was ordered that upon the perfection of the injunction awarded, by the execution of the required bond, etc., John M. Bailey be appointed a receiver in this cause, and as such receiver to take charge and possession of the property and assets of the companies named above. The receiver was required to execute bond in the penalty of $20,000, whereupon the said receiver was to be put into possession by writ to that end directed by the clerk to the sheriff, etc.

This order was in part executed, when before its complete execution the United States marshal, under an *ex parte* order of the federal circuit court judge, rescued the property from the hands of the sheriff, put him out before he had gotten full possession, and prevented him from completing the same. This interference was of short duration, the said order of the federal circuit court being shortly thereafter annulled by the order in the case of the chief justice of the United States, by which the whole subject was remitted to the circuit court of the state of Virginia, John A. Kelley, the respondent, being the judge thereof, of Washington county. Whereupon the sheriff again attempted to enforce the order of the judge of this court, referred to above, but, as is stated, he was resisted by an armed force, and prevented thereby from an execution of the said order. The plaintiffs applied to the respondent judge of the circuit court, as aforesaid, to enforce the said order of the appellate judge by proper directions to the sheriff. But the respondent refused to enter and enforce this order, but took the case up upon a motion to dissolve the injunction of the appellate judge, and upon a motion to enjoin and restrain the order of Judge Richardson, and also to hear rules for contempt, and decided that there was no jurisdiction in a single judge of the supreme court of appeals to control by vacation orders the action of a circuit court in its direction to its receiver, or in enforcing injunctions pending in the circuit court, and that such appellate judge had no jurisdiction to modify, alter, or otherwise control the same, nor had he power to enter orders enforcing the same; and that the order of the appellate judge was null and void, and the partial possession obtained under it was unlawful and dismissed the proceedings for contempt for disobedience thereto, and, without otherwise disposing of the case on its merits, continued the same, possession of the property, assets, etc., to remain in the hands of the defendants, until the 25th day of July, 1891. Whereupon, after giving due notice, as required by the statute, the plaintiffs applied for the peremptory writ of *mandamus* from this court, to compel the said John A. Kelley, judge, to enter and enforce the order aforesaid of the appellate judge. The said John A. Kelley, judge, answers, and says that the acts complained of were judicial acts, and submits that, although they should be held erroneous, they cannot be corrected by *mandamus.* And further stated that Joseph L. Kelley never appeared as counsel in the case, and in a written statement of considerable length reiterated his refusal to enter and enforce the order of the appellate judge, and declares the same null and void; and that when the receiver undertook, under the order of the appellate judge, to take possession as there authorized, in contravention of the order of respondent, he was guilty of an unlawful act, and in contempt.

It will thus be seen that Judge John A. Kelley, a judge of an inferior court, has refused an injunction and indorsed his refusal on the bill praying the same; that then, as authorized by the law of this state, as above cited, the plaintiffs in the said bill had presented the bill, with the order of refusal of the said circuit court judge entered thereon, to one of the judges of this court, by whom the injunction was awarded, and a receiver appointed, and directed to take possession of the property;

and that, passing by intervening interruptions, as narrated above, the said order was presented by the plaintiffs to the circuit court judge, who declined to enter and enforce the same, and declared the same null and void, issued without authority of law, and any act done thereunder in contempt of that court.

Now let us briefly consider what is the law.

The statute confers upon the appellate judge authority to render such order. What is the character of this duty? It cannot be declined by the appellate judge; he must act; and, when he does act, is it the action of an inferior judge, subject to the review of the circuit court judge, who, when it is presented to him, may enter and enforce it if he approves it, or annul it if he does not approve it? This is obviously not so. It is not only not in contemplation of law that the appellate judge is to do and act subject to the approval of the circuit court judge, as his superior, but he is authorized by the law to act only when he has refused his action, and in contravention and review thereof. It is an appellate action, and an appellate power conferred on one of the judges of the supreme court of appeals to annul an action of the circuit court judge, which appears to him to be improper and erroneous; and, if the pretension of the respondent is correct, then, as soon as he has been, to this extent, reviewed and reversed, he is immediately transferred from his inferior station, and made an appellate judge of an appellate judge, on whose action he may in turn sit with appellate power; and, as the appellate judge has declared his action erroneous, so now he will declare the act of the appellate judge null and void, and hold all acts done under it in contempt of his superior authority. This is the *reductio ad absurdum,* and not only declares the action of the appellate judge null and void, but annuls the law itself, because, if the order of the appellate judge was in contemplation of the law to be by leave of the circuit court judge, whom he overruled, then none can discern the object of the law.

But this contention of the circuit court judge is not only not the law, but is sustained by no opinion of any court, nor of any jurist, ever delivered. The law of this state is that this order, which comes to the inferior judge, made over his head by the law's prescript, must be by him entered and enforced. There is no other rational construction to be placed upon the statute itself. Decided cases upon this subject are therefore not frequent. It was settled early in this century that when an injunction had been refused by a circuit judge, and afterwards awarded by an appellate judge, it was the province of the inferior judge to enforce the same, and restrain any disobedience to the same, by attachment or other proper process; and this compelled the chancellor, sitting in review of the order of his superior, to enforce the same by effectual measures. Tollbridge v. Freebridge, 1 Rand. (Va.) 206. But the respondent insists, further, that the act in question has no application to this case, because the injunction in question was the second and a supplemental bill for an injunction; but there, again, he is plainly at fault. Long ago (1823) that question, also, was put to rest by this court, when this court held that a motion to reinstate the injunction on additional evidence tendered by the complainant was in the nature of an original application for an injunction, and that on the refusal of the chancellor to reinstate the injunction, an application to the judges of this court, or any of them, (under the act of Rev. Code, 1819; vol. 1, p. 205. art. 44,) was proper under that act, and was not to be discharged by the chancellor, (or inferior judge.) Gilliam v. Allen, 1 Rand. (Va.) 414. And so the law has remained to the present time. The respondent cites the late case of Fredenheim v. Rohr, reported in 13 S. E. Rep. 193, as sustaining his view; but there, again, he is at fault. In that case the order of the appellate judge was not set aside and annulled by the chancellor, but by him entered and enforced, and the receiver put in possession by the court's mandate to the sergeant directed.

The order of the appellate judge was annulled in that case, and the receiver set aside, but not by the chancellor. This was done by the court of appeals, under the sanction of a majority of the judges. The mistake this circuit judge has made is in installing himself into the prerogative of sitting in appeal upon the order of his superior. That the court of appeals may annul such an order, none will deny, but that is a different matter from the inferior judge undertaking the appellate role. It is clear—too clear for further argument—that the respondent, an inferior judge, had no right, nor power, to annul this order. But it remains yet to consider whether mandamus is the proper remedy to compel this judge to obey the law, or if he may annul the order, and by dilatory orders and continuances, under the guise of exercising judicial discretion, reviewable by appeal only, entirely defeat the same.

Without entering at length into a discussion of the nature and origin of the writ of mandamus, it is sufficient to say it is an extraordinary remedy, in cases where the usual and ordinary modes of proceeding are powerless to afford remedies to the parties aggrieved, and when without its aid there would be a failure of justice. It is said to be a high prerogative writ, usually issuing out of the highest court of general jurisdiction in a state, in the name of the sovereignty, directed to any natural person, corporation, or inferior court of judicature within its jurisdiction, requiring them to do some particular thing therein specified, and which appertains to their office or duty. 3 Bl. Comm. 110; 4 Bac. Abr. 495; Marbury v. Madison, 1 Cranch. 137, 168. It was introduced to prevent disorder from a failure of justice and a defeat of police. Therefore it ought to be used upon all occasions where the law has established no specific remedy, and when in justice and good government there ought to be one. Lord MANSFIELD in Rex v. Barker, 3 Burrows, 1265: Lord ELLENBOROUGH in Rex v. Archbishop of

Canterbury, 8 East, 219. But the party must have a perfect legal right, and the remedy extends to the control of all inferior tribunals, corporations, and public officers, and even private individuals, in some cases. Ang. & A. Corp. 761. It is the proper remedy to compel the performance of a specific act, when the act is ministerial in its character; but when the act is of a discretionary character, or of a judicial nature, it will lie only to compel action generally. The general rule on this subject is that if the inferior tribunal or corporate body has a discretion, and exercises it, this discretion cannot be controlled by mandamus; but if the inferior tribunals refuse when the law requires them to act, and the party has no other adequate legal remedy, and when in justice there ought to be one, mandamus will lie to set them in motion, to compel action, and in proper cases the court will settle the legal principle which should govern, but without controlling the discretion of the subordinate jurisdiction. Mandamus, of course, will not lie to compel a judicial tribunal to decide any question submitted to its discretion in any particular way; and I will go further, and say that, while it will lie to compel the inferior tribunal to act, speaking generally, if to act or not to act is matter submitted by law to the court's discretion, it will not lie.

Now, let us inquire what discretion is vested in an inferior tribunal, when it receives the mandate of a superior court, which by lawful authority has reversed its action. If the circuit court of Washington county renders an erroneous decision, and the case is brought here by an appeal or writ of error, and the erroneous decision is reversed, and mandate of this court is sent down, must that judicial tribunal review and revise, or reverse and annul in its turn, at its discretion? Can it exercise any discretion, or must it implicitly obey the mandate as it is written? It obviously can have and may exercise no discretion, but it must enter and enforce the same, and, if it fails or refuses, mandamus would lie to compel obedience and compliance. If it may with impunity refuse to enter and enforce such order, to what end is an appellate tribunal established? Back and forth from one court to the other orders go and come, each in turn reversing the other, and each powerless to enforce any order. Such is not the law.

When a mandamus goes down from the appellate tribunal to the inferior tribunal, whose action has been reviewed and reversed, there is no discretion; that has been exercised, and in the exercise been exhausted so far as it has been established by the law, and the simple province of the inferior tribunal is to obey the command of the superior. Now let us see: The circuit court judge is vested by law with a discretion to grant or to refuse to grant an injunction when the bill is presented to him, and mandamus will not lie to compel him to grant, nor compel him to refuse to grant, the injunction. But when he has exercised his discretion, and refused to grant the injunction, and the law provides that, in the discretion of the appellate judge upon application, he may exercise his discretion, and refuse to grant or grant the injunction, which is to be certified to the inferior court, what discretion further has the inferior court in the premises? None whatever. The lower court has been in so far reversed by the appellate court judge by lawful authority, and the lower judge must enter and enforce the same, and he has no discretion in the premises. This being so, why should not *mandamus* issue to compel the court to act? It is settled law that when this order from an appellate court or appellate judge, made in review of the order of an inferior court, comes down, the lower court must enter and enforce it. It is an order in his court in the latter case, and it is an order in his court in the former case, but it is there in each case for him to enter and obey. He may not set aside and annul it upon any pretext whatever. That may be done in a proper case by the court of appeals when in the latter case it reaches that tribunal, but it is not the province of the lower court to do this. Being then a matter of plain duty, and in no wise dependent upon any discretion of any sort, it must be entered and enforced as made, and *mandamus* will lie to enforce the performance of this plain legal duty. We have said nothing concerning the merits of the case. They are in no wise involved and do not affect this decision in any degree. Whether the order was a proper one cannot, in this proceeding, be considered by this court. That the case is exceptional in character, as the respondent declares, and whether, as is freely asserted, armed resistance is made, and may again be made, by organized bands of lawless men, armed and banded to defy the law, is not now the question. When this order here made goes down, it will be obeyed by the judge below; and when the mandate issues accordingly the law will be enforced, and the mandate of the courts executed. It may be safely considered that the orders of the judiciary will be enforced in this case, as in all others in this state. The *mandamus* will issue as prayed for. .

LEWIS, P., (*dissenting.*) The judgment awarding a *mandamus* in this case is, in my opinion, so extraordinary and unprecedented that I deem it proper to state the reasons that constrain me to dissent from it. The history of the controversy, briefly stated, is as follows: In July, 1890, John N. Bailey and others filed their bill in the circuit court of the United States for the western district of Virginia, against the Virginia, Tennessee & Carolina Steel & Iron Company, the South Atlantic & Ohio Railroad Company, the Bailey Construction Company, and the Bristol Land Company, praying an injunction and the appointment of a receiver. The Hon. John Paul, one of the judges of the said court, refused, upon the presentation of the bill to him, to grant the prayer of the bill, without notice to the defendants. Notice was therefore given, but, before any further action was taken, the bill was dismissed by the complainants. On the same day, to-wit, on the 6th of August, 1890,

the same complainants, and one or two others, presented a substantially similar bill against the same defendants, to the Honorable D. W. Bolen, judge of the fifteenth judicial circuit of Virginia. The latter at the time was holding a court in Russell county, in the sixteenth circuit, for the respondent, the Honorable John A. Kelley, to whom the bill was addressed as the judge of the circuit court of Washington county. Upon the presentation of the bill, Judge Bolen, without any notice to the defendants, granted an injunction, and appointed the said Bailey, one of the complainants, and a non-resident of the state, receiver of all the property of the defendant corporations, aggregating several millions of dollars in value, and required an injunction bond in the penalty of $500, and a receiver's bond in the penalty of $10,000. The order, however, was expressly made subject to "the further order of the court or the judge thereof in vacation." As can readily be imagined, the proper officers of the defendant corporations, upon learning that such an order had been made, lost no time in applying to the judge of the court to vacate it; and an order was promptly made by Judge Kelley, suspending its operations for 20 days, in order to afford the defendants an opportunity to give notice of a motion to dissolve the injunction. Notice was accordingly given, but, before the day fixed for the hearing of the motion, the case was removed by the defendants to the circuit court of the United States. In this posture of the case, the complainants, on the 16th day of August, 1890, presented what they termed a "supplemental bill" to Judge Kelley, almost identical in its terms with that upon which Judge Bolen had acted, and containing the same prayer. Upon this bill the judge indorsed the words, "Injunction refused;" whereupon the same day, without notice to the defendants, it was presented to the Honorable Robert A. Richardson, a judge of this court, who awarded an injunction, and appointed the said Bailey receiver, requiring a receiver's bond in penalty of $20,000. The order of Judge Richardson was directed to the clerk of the circuit court of Washington county, and, in pursuance of its mandates, the sheriff of the county put the receiver into possession of all the defendants' property in that county, as appears by the return on the process issued by the clerk of the circuit court, which is made part of the record before us. It seems, however, that on the same day, or soon afterwards, possession of the property was restored to the defendants by the United States marshal, in obedience to an order of the federal court. Some months afterwards the case was removed from the last-mentioned court to the state court, soon after which application was made by the complainants to Judge Kelley to enforce the order made by Judge Richardson. They averred in their petition that, after the case had been remanded, the officers of the defendant corporations forcibly resisted the sheriff in his attempt to again put the receiver into possession, and had thus put themselves in contempt. About the same time the defendants gave notice that, on the 11th of June, 1891, they would move Judge Kelley to dissolve as well the injunction awarded by Judge Richardson as that previously awarded by Judge Bolen. This motion was opposed by the complainants, who contended that the duty of Judge Kelley to enforce "the order of Judge Richardson" was purely ministerial, that it was therefore his duty to enforce it at once; and that he had no discretion in the matter. This view, however, was not sustained by Judge Kelley, who decided (1) that the order made by Judge Richardson was void; (2) that the defendants were not in contempt; and (3) that he would postpone the hearing of the motion to dissolve until the 25th of July. The complainants thereupon presented a petition to this court for a *mandamus* to compel Judge Kelley to enforce the order made by Judges Richardson and Bolen, "before allowing the defendants to invoke the jurisdiction of the circuit court of Washington county." To this petition Judge Kelley filed an answer, and, the case having been fully argued by counsel, the judgment of this court is to award the *mandamus*, requiring the "order of Judge Richardson" to be forthwith carried into execution.

But, in legal contemplation, is there any such order? Section 3438 of the Code provides that when a circuit or corporation court, or a judge thereof, shall refuse to award an injunction, a judge of this court may award it. But did Judge Richardson have the authority, under the circumstances of the present case, to make the order that he did? I think not. When the order was made, the injunction awarded by Judge Bolen was still in force, or, at least, had not been dissolved, although its operations had for 20 days been suspended. Hence there is no authority on the part of Judge Richardson to act, inasmuch as it is only when an injunction is refused by an inferior court or judge that a judge of this court is authorized to award it. Judge Kelley's indorsement on the supplemental bill, "so called," as he says in his answer, was misleading. An injunction in the cause having been already awarded, which had not been dissolved, he had no power, as he expressed it, to award "an injunction on an injunction." "Though called a bill for an injunction," the answer avers, "it was in effect a motion in disguise to dissolve the suspending order, with intent to take the chances, in the event of a refusal, of applying to another judge. So apparent, indeed, was this," the answer further states, "that respondent promptly refused to consider it. Being in great affliction and seriously ill at the time, respondent yielded to pressure, and made the indorsement, 'Injunction refused.' This was hastily done, and in form it no doubt diverted Judge Richardson's mind from the fact that the bill was merely an indirect mode of getting rid of the suspending order. Respondent ought to have indorsed that he declined to act for want of notice to the adverse side, regarding it as a mere motion to dissolve the suspending order." And I fully concur in the further averment in the answer that, in any view,

Judge Richardson had no power to act in the premises, and that his order was simply void.

But let it be supposed that it was valid. It was directed to the clerk of the circuit court of Washington county, by whom, as the record shows, it was entered; and in point of fact, as we have seen, it was enforced by the sheriff's putting the receiver into possession, although that possession, without any fault on the part of the sheriff, was of short duration. But when entered, whose order did it become? This the statute answers by providing that, when in such a case an injunction is awarded, the proceedings thereupon shall be as if the order had been made by the court, or the judge thereof, to whose clerk the order is directed. Code, § 3439.

The order, then, made by Judge Richardson, became, in contemplation of the statute, as much the order of the circuit court of Washington county as if it had been signed by Judge Kelley, or entered by him in open court, and hence was no less subject to his control. What authority, then, is there for now calling it "the order of Judge Richardson?" None, I think, whatever. Upon its receipt by the clerk of the circuit court, it was as much an interlocutory decree of that court as the previous order made by Judge Bolen; and whoever heard of a chancellor sitting to hear a motion to enforce one of his own interlocutory decrees, or to dissolve an injunction, who was not acting judicially? There is nothing ministerial about it. It is purely a judicial function, *i. e.*, a duty calling for the exercise of judicial discretion, and nothing else. The proposition, to my mind, is so plain that nothing can make it plainer than the mere statement of it. To argue it is like arguing that two and two make four. The idea that in making the order Judge Richardson was exercising an appellate power is, I think, a mistaken view. When a judge of this court awards an injunction, he exercises a special original jurisdiction, with which he is clothed by the statute. At all events, his act, when completed, is as if the order had been made by an inferior court or judge; nothing more. The statute upon this point is too plain to be misunderstood.

And here it is pertinent to inquire, if a circuit court or judge, to whose clerk an order awarding an injunction by a judge of this court is directed, has no discretion respecting it, but must literally enforce it, as a ministerial duty, how is such an order to be dissolved or gotten rid of at all? Are the parties aggrieved by it remediless until a final or other appealable decree has been entered? Could that have been the intention of the legislature? And yet such is the case if the theory of the majority of the court be correct. Meanwhile, to whose orders is the receiver appointed by such an order subject? And can he be removed for misconduct or other cause? These are important questions, which will no doubt arise in the future, and as to which we can now only conjecture.

As to the question of the alleged contempt, little need be said: *First*, because it is clear that there has been no contempt; and, *secondly*, because, if there had been, that could not affect the application for a *mandamus*. The alleged contempt consists in the refusal of the defendants' agents to surrender possession of the property to the sheriff, to be by him again turned over to the receiver, after the case was remanded from the federal court. And the contention is that the defendants are not entitled to be heard, either to move for a dissolution of the injunction, or for any other relief, in the circuit court, until they shall have purged themselves of their contempt. But what authority had the sheriff to act in the matter? He had executed the process that promptly issued on the order made by Judge Richardson, and his authority, without a further order from the court, was at an end. The possession which, under that process, he delivered to the receiver, had been restored to the defendants by an order of the federal court; and when the case was remanded to the state court, the sheriff, as the case then stood, had no more authority to act than any private individual. But suppose he had, and that the defendants were in contempt. Is the circuit court, in the exercise of its judgment or discretion in dealing with that question, to be controlled by *mandamus?* This can hardly be seriously contended for, although much was said about it in the argument at the bar.

To enter into a discussion of the nature and office of the writ of *mandamus* is wholly unnecessary. There is nothing more familiar to the profession. The writ is never available where there is another adequate remedy, and hence will not lie in any case where the alleged error may be corrected on a writ of error or appeal. Neither does it lie to control the exercise of judgment or discretion. The only acts that can be rightfully controlled by it are such as are purely ministerial. As was said in Wise v. Bigger, 79 Va. 269, while the writ lies to compel the performance of a purely ministerial duty, so clear and specific that no element of discretion enters into it, yet, as to all acts or duties calling for the exercise of judgment or discretion on the part of the officer or body sought to be coerced, it will not lie. The application of this test to the present case shows, I think, that the writ ought not to be awarded. If it ought, then I see no reason why the execution of any interlocutory decree in a chancery cause in this state may not be compelled by *mandamus.* The majority of the court is, I think, not only without a precedent, but without any correct foundation whatever. If Judge Kelley has erred, it has been in the exercise of his judicial discretion, and the law has provided an ample remedy by which, at the proper time, those errors may be corrected, which remedy is by appeal. I deem it not improper, however, to add that, if the whole case were now before us on appeal, there is nothing in the action of Judge Kelley which, in my judgment, is open to criticism. It is apparent that in his course he has been actuated throughout by a desire to exercise his judgment

rightly. The record, I think, bristles with reasons which justified him in stopping to look carefully into the case, after hearing counsel, before proceeding to further carry out the interlocutory order granting an injunction and appointing a receiver,—an order made without any notice to the defendants, and requiring property, worth millions of dollars, to be turned over to a non-resident plaintiff as receiver, upon his executing a bond, the inadequacy of which as a security is simply amazing. I refer now to the order of Judge Bolen, for I consider, as Judge Kelley did, that the order made by Judge Richardson is out of the case. But, if it were not, the result would be the same.

In their petition addressed to Judge Kelley, praying him to dissolve the injunction awarded by Judges Bolen and Richardson, and to hear all the matters together which had been brought to his attention, the defendants, among other things, aver: "Your petitioners [defendants] do not owe the complainants anything. Their claims are false and fabricated. Your petitioners charge that complainants entered into a conspiracy to wreck and loot the defendant corporations, and that, pursuant to the conspiracy, their claims were trumped up for the purpose; and that they imposed upon and induced Judges Bolen and Richardson to grant the orders before mentioned, requiring only nominal bond. Your petitioners further charge that the object of the conspirators is to get possession of the properties of the said corporation, and as much money belonging thereto as possible; to pay themselves large salaries for services performed for the railroad; and thus loot and consume all of the substance of the company before they can be gotten rid of by due course of law. Your petitioners further charge that the said conspirators intend, if they can get possession of the properties of the defendant companies, to pay out of the money belonging to them large sums which they have contracted to pay in their efforts to enforce their fraudulent and fictitious claims. And your petitioners further charge that, unless restrained, these conspirators, who are insolvent, will, if they get possession of the funds of the defendant companies, thus squander and waste the same, and, when after the properties are restored to the companies, they will be found to have been despoiled and damaged irreparably." There is much more to the same effect, all of which is supported by affidavit, although it is but just to say there are counter-affidavits. But enough appears to vindicate the propriety of Judge Kelley's action in deciding to pause and to hear counsel on all the questions brought before him, before taking action on the order made by Judge Bolen. But be that as it may, he was acting judicially, and that ought to end the case, so far as this proceeding is concerned. And now, having said this much, I will only add that I can but deplore the action of this court. It not only does, in my opinion, manifest injustice in the present case; but violating, as I think it does, rules of law that have been settled for centuries, it is likely, if adhered to, to be productive of infinite mischief in the future. If this is a proper case for a *mandamus*, it will be difficult to determine hereafter what functions of the judiciary in Virginia are judicial and what are ministerial, and thus confusion will inevitably result. At all events, with my views of the case, I would be untrue to myself and to my official trust did I not enter my emphatic dissent from the opinion of the court and the order to be entered.

FAUNTLEROY, J., concurred in the opinion of LEWIS, P.

O'CONNELL v. EAST TENNESSEE, V. & G. RY. CO.

(*Supreme Court of Georgia.* May 27, 1891.)

WATER-COURSES — OBSTRUCTIONS — ACTION FOR DAMAGES.

When a railway company erects an embankment for its track along the margin of a river, the accumulated waters of which, in times of flood, had previously escaped on that side, it being lower than the other, but which thereafter, and because of the embankment, overflowed the opposite side more than it had done before, and thus injured land there situate, the owner has a right of action against the company; or if, by the erection of such embankment, the river was deflected from its natural course, or deposits were made therein so as to raise its bottom, and from either of these causes such land was injured by the river when swollen, a recovery may be had for the damages thereby occasioned.

(*Syllabus by the Court.*)

Error from superior court, Bibb county; A. L. MILLER, Judge.

Gustin, Guerry & Hall, for plaintiff in error.   *Bacon & Rutherford,* for defendant in error.

LUMPKIN, J. The precise question in this case is whether the owner of land on the bank of a river can without liability erect on his own land an embankment which increases the overflow in times of flood upon the lands of the opposite proprietor, to the injury thereof; or is there any duty for each owner to receive upon his land the share allotted it by nature of the flood-waters of the river. It is contended by defendant's counsel that the overflow from a river in time of flood or freshet is surface water, against which, by the common law, a man may protect himself without regard to the consequences to his neighbor. Many cases cited by him make a distinction between the common law and the civil law as to surface water; the former allowing the land-owner to dispose of it in any way, the latter restraining him from so using it as to injure his neighbor's tenement. There is authority to show that there is no difference between the common and the civil law in this respect, but that the common follows the civil law. Gillham v. Railroad Co., 49 Ill. 484; Gormley v. Sanford, 52 Ill. 158; and the able opinion in Boyd v. Conklin, 54 Mich. 583, 20 N. W. Rep. 595. There is much conflict in the American cases, (Washb. Easem. p. 485, *353, et seq.,) the majority of the states seeming to follow the so-called "civil law rule." Thus it is material to consider

whether the overflow, as above stated, is properly classed with surface water. This depends upon the configuration of the country, and the relative position of the water after it has gone beyond the usual channel. If the flood-water becomes severed from the main current, or leaves the stream, never to return, and spreads out over the lower ground, it has become surface water; but if it forms a continuous body with the water flowing in the ordinary channel, or if it departs from such channel *animo revertendi*, presently to return, as by the recession of the waters, it is to be regarded as still a part of the river. The identity of a river does not depend upon the volume of water which may happen to flow down its course at any particular season. The authorities hold that a stream may be wholly dry at times without losing the character of a water-course. So, on the other hand, it may have a "flood channel," to retain the surplus waters until they can be discharged by the natural flow. The low places on a river act as natural safety-valves in times of freshet; and the defendant claims the right to stop up one of these without liability for ensuing damage.

The English cases on the question are not numerous, though from the decisions and *dicta* of the judges the law appears to be well understood and settled. In Rex v. Commissioners, etc., of Pagham, 8 Barn. & C. 355, it was held that an owner of land on the seashore could erect works to protect his land from encroachments by the sea, without liability for damage inflicted on his neighbor. The sea was called a "common enemy," against which each might fortify at will. It appeared in Rex v. Trafford, 1 Barn. & Adol. 874, that a canal had been built by authority of parliament, and carried across a river and the adjoining valley by means of an aqueduct and an embankment containing several arches. A brook fell into the river above its point of intersection with the canal. In times of flood the water, which was then penned back into the brook, overflowed its banks, and was carried, by the natural level of the country, through the arches into the river, doing much mischief to the lands over which it passed. The aqueduct was sufficiently wide for the passage of the river at all times but those of high flood. The occupiers of the injured lands adjoining the river and brook, for the protection thereof, erected banks, (called "fenders,") so as to prevent the flood-water from escaping; consequently the water, in time of flood, came down in so large a body against the aqueduct and canal as to endanger them, and obstruct the navigation. The fenders were not unnecessarily high, and without them many hundred acres of land would be exposed to inundation. It was held that the defendants were not justified, under these circumstances, in altering for their own benefit the course in which the flood-water had been accustomed to run; that there was no difference in this respect between flood-water and an ordinary stream; that an action would have lain at the suit of an individual; and, consequently, that an indictment lay where the act affected the public.

The conviction was accordingly sustained. The doctrine of Rex v. Commissioners, etc., of Pagham, supra, was sought to be extended to this case, but TENTERDEN, C. J., who had rendered the decision in that case, said: "It has long been established that the ordinary course of water cannot be lawfully changed or obstructed for the benefit of one class of persons, to the injury of another. Unless, therefore, a sound distinction can be made between the ordinary course of water flowing in a bounded channel at all usual seasons, and the extraordinary course which its superabundant quantity has been accustomed to take at particular seasons, the creation and continuance of these fenders cannot be justified. No case was cited or has been found that will support such a distinction. The Pagham Case * * * is of a very different kind. * * * In the one case the water is prevented from coming where, within time of memory at least, it never had come; in the other it is prevented from passing in the way in which, when the occasion happened, it had been always accustomed to pass." This seems to be an authoritative enunciation of the common law. Menzies v. Breadalbane, 3 Bligh, (N. S.) 414, is directly in point, but was determined by the law of Scotland. Yet the lord chancellor said: "It is clear beyond the possibility of a doubt that by the law of England such an operation could not be carried on. The old course of the flood stream being along certain lands, it is not competent for the proprietors of those lands to obstruct that old course by a sort of new water-way, to the prejudice of the proprietor on the other side." In Attorney General v. Earl of Lonsdale, L. R. 7 Eq. 387, 20 Law T. 64, it was attempted to extend the sea doctrine to the case of a tidal river, but Vice-Chancellor MALINS refused to so extend it on the authority of Menzies v. Breadalbane, supra, saying that Lord ELDON put that case upon the general law of England. In Mason v. Railway Co., L. R. 6 Q. B. 581, we find a *dictum* by BLACKBURN, J., as follows: "Before the canal was made, the person whose estate the plaintiff now has, had the ordinary rights and liabilities of a riparian owner on the banks of a natural stream. He was entitled to have the water flow to him in its natural state, so far as that was a benefit,—as, for instance, to turn his mill, or water his cattle; and he was bound to submit to receive the water, so far as it was a nuisance, as by its tendency to flood his lands." Lawrence v. Railroad Co., 4 Eng. Law & Eq. 265, 16 Q. B. 643, is considerably in point. A railway was constructed across certain low lands adjoining a river, over which the flood-waters used to spread themselves. These low lands were separated from the plaintiff's lands by a bank, constructed under certain drainage acts, which protected the plaintiff's lands from floods. By the construction of the railway the flood-waters could not spread themselves as formerly, but were penned up and flowed over the bank upon the plaintiff's lands. It was held that an action would lie against the company for the injury. PATTESON, J., said: "*Prima facie* this would give the plaintiff a cause of action, and the question is whether the company are protected by their act;" a question which cannot arise in our law. In connection with the cases of Rex v. Trafford and Lawrence v. Railway Co., supra, it must be borne in mind that the first obstruction of the flood-waters there mentioned is, in England, justified by the statute authorizing it, and therefore stands on much the same footing as a natural obstruction; but the liability of the other party, who erected the second obstruction without statute authority, springs from the common law. No English authority has been found to controvert these principles, but the text-writers recognize them as settled law. Woolr. Waters, 213, (78 Law Lib. 212;) Crabb, Real Prop. 420, (54 Law Lib. 263;) Michael & W. Gas. & Water, (London Ed. 1884,) pp. 213, 214, 666; Ang. Water-Courses, §§ 333, 334; Gould, Waters, §§ 160, 209.

In grouping the American cases, those tending to sustain the contention of the defendant in error will first be stated. Taylor v. Fickas, 64 Ind. 167, was much relied upon. There the injury was caused by the obstruction of the passage of drift-wood, both owners being on the same side of the river, and the lower owner having planted a row of trees along the dividing line. The opinion, it is true, treats overflow in flood times as surface water, but it will be noticed that nothing is said or decided about changing the course of the water. The facts are obviously different from those in the present case. In Railroad Co. v. Stevens, 73 Ind. 278, the plaintiff's land was between the river and the railroad embankment. The overflow is treated as surface water, and the road held not liable; but it would seem that the water doing the damage had left the river, never to return. Turnpike Co. v. Green, 99 Ind. 205, follows the last case. The turnpike was flooded because of an embankment erected by Green to protect his land from overflow, both parties being on the same side. It was held that the company could not recover. But note that the court adverts to the fact that the company did not own the soil over which the pike ran, but merely had an easement therein. McCormick v. Railroad Co., 57 Mo. 433, can also be distinguished. Here the overflowing water left the stream permanently, and entered a pond formed thereby and by other surface water, the draining of which pond caused the injury sued for. In Shane v. Railroad Co., 71 Mo. 237, the overflow is apparently treated as surface water, although it had a way, through a slough, back into the stream. But the court applied the civil law, and held the railroad liable. This case, together with that of McCormick v. Railroad Co., 70 Mo. 359, is overruled, in so far as the civil law was followed, by Abbott v. Railroad Co., 20 Amer. & Eng. R. Cas. 103, and the common law as to surface water returned to. In this last case it is said that the court in the Shane Case treated the overflow as part of the stream, and, therefore, that the decision was correct on common law principles. In the Abbott Case, the court expressly assumes the waters to be surface waters. It seems they escaped from the bed of the creek, and flowed over the lands without any return. Lamb v. Reclamation Dist., (Cal.) 14 Pac. Rep. 625, is not much in point. The defendant was a public corporation for the purpose of reclaiming the low lands protected by the embankment, which closed up a slough through which an inconsiderable part of the flood-waters escaped into a natural basin. The plaintiff's land lay two miles below, on the opposite side. The court applied the sea doctrine of the common law, and held the company not liable; but the decision is mainly rested on another ground, namely, that the corporation was not liable as for exercising the right of eminent domain; and in view also of the concurring opinions, the case is weak on the question involved in the case at bar. See below for an earlier decision by the same court looking another way, not noticed in the case above. In Hoard v. City of Des Moines, 62 Iowa, 326, 17 N. W. Rep. 527, the plaintiff's land was between the river and the embankment, and it was held that the plaintiff had no right to have the flood-waters from the river pass over his land onto that of another, although they finally joined the river again at a point further down. At first view, Moyer v. Railroad Co., 88 N. Y. 351, seems to support the defendant's position; but a close examination shows otherwise. The complaint averred that the damage was caused by the railroad building an embankment on the opposite side of the river. Evidence was offered and objected to, to show damage caused by raising the tracks. It was admitted; the railroad excepting. The referee included in his finding for the plaintiff the damages caused by raising the tracks, as to which the complaint alleged nothing; thus tainting the whole finding with illegality. The judgment was reversed for the error in admitting said evidence and in said finding. The court say the defendant, as a matter of law, would not be liable for consequential damages caused by the raising of the embankment on the company's own land in a proper and workman-like manner; citing Bellinger v. Railroad, 23 N. Y. 47. This case bases the freedom from liability upon the legislative authority, but concedes that a private individual would be liable under the same conditions. In our law the railroad occupies no better position in this respect than the private individual.

Now will be stated the American cases going to show that the defendant is liable if it has erected the obstruction to the flood-waters of the river, as complained of in this case. The surplus waters do not cease to be part of the river when they spread over the adjacent low grounds, without well-defined banks or channel, so long as they form with it one body of water, eventually to be discharged through the channel proper. Thus it is held, where the waters of a stream disperse themselves over low ground, without any well-marked course, but gather up lower down into a defined channel, they are not surface water while in the dispersed state, and interference with them then gives the injured party a right of action. Macomber v. Godfrey, 108 Mass. 219; Gillett v. Johnson, 30 Conn. 180; Briscoe v. Drought, 11 Ir. C. L. 250; West v. Taylor, 16 Or. 165, 13 Pac. Rep. 665. But if it were conceded that the overflow is surface water, it would certainly cease to be such when turned back into the stream by the defendant's obstruction. Sullens v. Railroad Co., 74 Iowa, 659, 38 N. W. Rep. 545; Moore v. Same, 75 Iowa, 263, 39 N. W. Rep. 390; Jones v. Hannovan, 55 Mo. 462; Railroad Co. v. Archibald, (Miss.) 7 South. Rep. 212. Under these authorities, this declaration might be sustained as complaining that the defendant prevented the flood-waters from becoming surface waters, and threw them back across the river upon plaintiff's land. See, further, as to surface water, 17 Cent. Law J. 42, 62; Aug. Water-Courses, § 108a et seq.; Gould, Waters, § 263 et seq. But it is not necessary to take this view, as the following authorities show the defendant to be liable under the alleged facts: Where the effect of the defendant's dike was to retain on the land of the plaintiff flood-waters from the river longer than they would otherwise remain, the injury was held actionable, and the demurrer overruled. Montgomery v. Locke, (Cal.) 11 Pac. Rep. 874. Where, in a freshet, the stream broke over one of its banks, carrying a part of it away, it was held that the owner might replace the bank with a dam, provided he did not build higher than the original bank, or otherwise cause the water to flow differently from the natural flow. Pierce v. Kinney, 59 Barb. 56. "It is well settled that every person through whose land a stream of water flows may construct embankments and other guards on the bank to prevent the stream washing the bank away, and overflowing and injuring his land. But in doing this he must be careful so to construct them as not to throw the water upon his neighbor's lands, where it would not otherwise go in ordinary floods. If he does, he will be liable for the injury." Wallace v. Drew, 59 Barb. 413. There is no distinction in principle or authority between obstructing the flow of a stream at its ordinary level and in time of flood. Burwell v. Hobson, 12 Grat. 322. This case is in point, and holds the defendant liable. Another case in point is Crawford v. Rambo, 44 Ohio St. 279, 7 N. E. Rep. 429, holding that flood-water is not surface water, and that interference therewith gives a right of action. So Byrne v. Railroad Co. (Minn.) 36 N. W. Rep. 339, holds that overflow in times of high water is not surface water, and the railroad is liable for obstruction of such water by an embankment erected on its own land. See, also, Rau v. Railroad Co., 13 Minn. 442, (Gil. 407,) where the railroad made an extensive excavation on its own land, into which overflow waters from the Mississippi river entered, to the damage of an adjoining owner. The railroad was liable. Gerrish v. Clough, 48 N. H. 9, 97 Amer. Dec. 561, and notes, and Tuthill v. Scott, 43 Vt. 525, seem not to involve the question as to the action of the water in times of flood, but are adverse to defendant as far as they go. In

Carriger v. Railroad Co., 7 Lea, 888, the railroad embankment did not affect the usual flow of the streams, but obstructed the flood channel, and threw the excessive waters upon the plaintiff's lands. This same defendant contended that they were surface waters, which it had a right to obstruct. The trial court gave judgment for the defendant, holding "that the overflow in question resulted from accumulations of surface water caused by extraordinary rains, and that the law relating to surface water, and not that of running streams, governs the case." The supreme court said: "The question to be determined is, is this such surface water as to relieve the defendant? * * * The springs and their branches are never-failing, and flow off in a northward direction, towards the farm of plaintiff. In ordinary times they find outlets through the caverns or sinks in the earth. In extraordinary times their volumes are too great for the usual place of discharge. These springs and branches are sometimes large and sometimes small; still they are the same springs and branches, requiring, as all running streams do, sometimes less and at other times more surface for their escape. * * * If the embankment had been erected in a valley, near a low bank of the river, which overflowed at high tide, but escaped in one passage, so as not to materially injure adjoining lands, but, if obstructed by the embankment, would overflow and damage, as in this case, we think it would not be insisted that it was not obligatory on the defendant to build a culvert to prevent damage that must certainly come with the high tide. Is there a difference in reason as to the case put and the one at bar? We think not. While they may not be so frequent, the overflows from the branches are as certain as those from the river; one is as certainly a constant running stream as the other. * * * It is no defense for it to say that it was only in extraordinary times the injuries now complained of could result. The rises in the waters had for all time occurred at intervals before the building of the road, and it was to be conclusively presumed they would occur afterwards from similar causes." The court entered judgment for the plaintiff. This is a stronger case than the one now to be decided.

Counsel for defendant ably and strenuously insist that the common, and not the civil, law be applied to this case. The above authorities prove that the common law does not regard the waters here complained of as mere surface water, but as a part of the river. The civil law might be more favorable to the defendant's case; for it seems to regard the flood-waters of a river as a common enemy, against which each riparian owner may build defenses with impunity. Mailhot v. Pugh, 30 La. Ann. 1859, citing authorities. The defendant also claims that the question is settled by an act of the legislature, and cites section 2232 of the Code. That section says: "All persons owning, or who may hereafter own, lands on any water-courses in this state, are authorized and empowered to ditch and embank their lands, so as to protect the same from freshets and overflows in said water-courses: provided, always, that the said ditching and embanking does not divert said water-course from its ordinary channel: but nothing shall be so construed as to prevent the owners of land from diverting unnavigable water-courses through their own lands." This contention may be answered in three ways: *First.* The declaration in this case distinctly alleges that the defendant did divert the river from its ordinary channel, for which act the statute affords no shadow of protection. *Secondly.* The allegations of the declaration do not show that defendant embanked its land "so as to protect the same," but constructed an embankment on which to lay its track, without regard to any consequences of benefit or injury to the contiguous country. *Thirdly.* The construction long ago and repeatedly put by this court on the last part of the section, which says, "Nothing shall be so construed as to prevent the owners of land from diverting unnavigable water-courses through their own lands," necessitates the conclusion that this whole statute is not alterative, but only declaratory, of the common law. In other words, the legislature did not intend to give riparian owners the privilege of ditching or embanking their lands, or of diverting unnavigable water-courses, so as to injure neighboring proprietors, without liability therefor. Indeed, the power of the legislature so to alter the common law is expressly denied in Persons v. Hill, 33 Ga. Supp. 143. And in Cheeves v. Danielly, 80 Ga. 118, 4 S. E. Rep. 902, the same view is taken as to the intention of the legislature in passing this act. It is true, these cases deal with the diversion of an unnavigable stream, but it would be absurd to impute to the legislature two conflicting intentions in the same act; and the ground taken in Persons v. Hill will equally well support the same rule of construction as to the other branch of the statute. The facts in Persons v. Hill require notice. The owners were on the same side of the Flint river, into which Beaver creek emptied after passing through the defendant's land. By mutual agreement between the upper owner (plaintiff) and the lower owner, (defendant,) the expense being also shared, an embankment was erected along the river to keep back the flood-waters which, from the facts of the case, seemed to have this course,—that is to say, coming out on plaintiff's land, they flowed across the same over defendant's land into the creek, by which they would empty back into the river. The embankment not being kept up according to the agreement, defendant proposed to protect himself by diverting the creek through a canal on his own land to the river and building an embankment along his side of the canal. This canal would make an opening through the high bank of the river, and, with the embankment, would allow and cause the high waters to back up on the plaintiff's land. This court granted an injunction against the construction of the canal, but allowed the defendant to continue the embankment. One great difference from the present case might be found in the agreement for consideration to have the common protection of the first embankment. See Railway v. Lawton, 75 Ga. 192. But at any rate the decision does not contemplate that defendant's individual embankment would injure the plaintiff's land, such an inference being inconsistent with the plain language of the opinion on page 197.

There is another section of the Code, not cited or discussed in the argument, which deserves mention in this connection: "No person shall be permitted to make or keep up any dam to stop the natural course of any water, so as to overflow the lands of any other person, without his consent; nor shall any person stop or prevent any water from running off of any person's field, whereby such person may be prevented from planting in season, or receive any other injury thereby; nor so as to turn the natural course of any water from one channel or swamp to another, to the prejudice of any person." Code, § 1607. This statute was passed September 29, 1773, and apparently revived by the act of February 25, 1784, (Marbury & C. Dig. p. 404,) being recognized by subsequent amendments and by the Codes, (Acts 1855-56, p. 12; Acts 1865-66, p. 27.) It is put in the Code under the head "Cultivation of Rice," but from reading the original act (Marbury & C. p. 178) it is by no means clear that it was intended to apply only on rice farms. Neither the title nor the body of the act contains the slightest intimation to that effect. Its terms are as broad and general as they well could be. The preamble, it is true, in stating the mischiefs to be remedied, describes such as probably were common in the localities where rice was cultivated, though even here there is no distinct allusion to rice culture. These mischiefs may, as a matter of history, have occasioned the enactment of the statute. But might not the legislature have deemed it wise to pass a general law, applicable in all portions of the state where similar mischiefs were likely to happen? It is not inconsistent with the purpose of an act for curing a special class of mischiefs to provide therein a remedy at the same time for all mischiefs of that genus. On the contrary, that would be a highly proper mode of legislation. If the preamble is not to be given a controlling and restrictive effect, this act alone would completely and effectually dispose of the present case, as the declaration alleges acts by the defendant which violate the law in question if it was intended to have a general application. But, since it is unnecessary for the purposes of this case to measure the extent of this statute, the question is not decided, especially as it deserves more argument and consideration. It was urged in the argument that the law ought to encourage the reclaiming and improvement of lands which are subject to injury from the natural action of floods and surface water, and it is surprising to find this argument unquestioningly relied upon in many cases which are supposed to follow the common law of surface water. The error therein is easily exposed, for to the same extent as the land of an adjoining owner is damaged by the improvement on the defendant's land, so far exactly is the development of the damaged land set back and retarded. The defendant might bring his land to perfection for his uses, and then have all that good work ruined by the first measures of improvement adopted by his less progressive neighbor. The rule contended for by the defendant would be a poor encouragement to painstaking labor engaged in reclaiming unprofitable land. Every one is charged with notice of nature's operations; but who can tell when a man will build his bulwarks against the flood? There is no public policy to allow one land-owner to improve his condition at the cost of his neighbor; but the improver must, at his peril, see to it that the benefit to himself is large enough to pay both him and his neighbor's damage, if any. The law does not look to the interest of one individual, but recognizes and enforces the duties implied in his relation to others. Of course, for these principles to apply, there must be, as in this case, an invasion of some tangible right. Peel v. City of Atlanta, 85 Ga. 138, 11 S. E. Rep. 582. And it must not be understood that this discussion rules anything beyond the questions contained in this particular case. Undoubtedly there is a class of rare cases not within the general rule, as indicated by the eloquent language of AGNEW, J., in Railroad Co. v. Gilleland, 56 Pa. St. 452, where he says: "There is, therefore, no liability for extraordinary floods,—those unexpected visitations whose comings are not foreshadowed by the usual course of nature, and must be laid to the account of Providence, whose dealings, though they may afflict, wrong no one." But such is not the case made by this declaration. For the foregoing reasons it is evident that the court erred in sustaining the demurrer to the declaration. Judgment reversed.

PRITCHARD v. SAVANNAH ST. & R. R. R. Co.

(Supreme Court of Georgia. May 27, 1891.)

ACTION FOR PERSONAL INJURIES—ABATEMENT.

An action against a railroad company for personal injuries, pending when the act of November 12, 1889, amending section 2967 of the Code, was passed, was not abated by the death of the plaintiff; nor is that act, as applicable to actions pending at the time of its passage, unconstitutional.

(Syllabus by the Court.)

Error from superior court, Chatham county; R. FALLIGANT, Judge.

Jackson & Whatley and A. C. Wright, for plaintiff in error. Lawton & Cunningham, for defendant in error.

LUMPKIN, J. The first proposition stated in the above head-note was settled by this court in the case of Johnson v. Bradstreet Co., 13 S. E. Rep. 250, (decided at the present term.) In that case, however, the main question was whether or not the above-mentioned section of the Code applied to actions for libel, and no question was raised in the argument as to the applicability of the amending act to pending suits, or its constitutionality as to them. If held applicable. This court, in the case just mentioned, considered the first of these questions, and decided that the act did apply to actions pending at the time of its passage, but did not discuss it in extenso in the opinion. The constitutional question was not considered or decided in that case. We will now examine both of them.

As stated in the case above cited, the language of the act seems sufficiently broad and comprehensive to include pending actions. The law, as amended, reads: "Nor shall any action of tort for the recovery," etc., "abate by the death of either party." The words "any action" may as well mean any action now in existence as any action hereafter commenced, and it is not straining to give them this interpretation. In Bailey v. State, 20 Ga. 742, very similar reasoning is used. The legislature had passed an act declaring "who are qualified to serve as jurors in criminal cases," and its first section enacted that certain described persons shall be "liable to serve as jurors upon the trial of all criminal cases." The second section began: "When any person stands indicted," etc. Judge BENNING said: "'Criminal cases' is an expression that includes criminal cases of every sort." "'All criminal cases' includes criminal cases of every kind." "'Any person' is a universal term." The act in question was accordingly held applicable to cases happening before its passage. A Vermont act, providing that in case of the removal of sheriff or high bailiff from the state an action of scire facias may be brought directly upon the recognizance of such officer, was held to apply to all causes of action, whether existing at the time it took effect or accruing thereafter, although the act contained no provision expressly applying it to pending actions. Hine v. Pomeroy, 39 Vt. 211. In Kimbray v. Draper, L. R. 3 Q. B. 160, it was held that a statute requiring plaintiffs to give security for costs in certain cases applied to such cases then pending; citing Wright v. Hale, 6 Hurl. & N. 227, in which it was held that when the plaintiff in any action recovers less than five pounds, he shall not be entitled to any costs if the judge certifies to deprive him of them, and the judge may so certify in an action commenced before the passage of the act. In Hepburn v. Curts, 7 Watts, 300, it was held that the legislature may pass laws affecting "suits pending, and give to a party a remedy which he did not previously possess, or modify an existing remedy, or remove an impediment in the way of recovering redress by legal proceedings." An action of assumpsit was proceeding in the name of a firm, which included among its members one Samuel Hepburn, against another firm of which the same man was also a member. Defendants insisted that the suit could not be maintained, because the same person was among both the plaintiffs and the defendants. The objection was sustained, and a bill of exceptions taken. While these proceedings were pending, the legislature passed an act providing in effect that an action brought by one firm against another should not abate by reason of one individual being a member of both firms, and it was held that this act applied to the case then pending. A married woman sued alone for personal injuries to herself, when she had no right to bring such action without being joined therein by her husband. While her case was pending, the legislature of Wisconsin passed an act authorizing married women to bring such suits alone, and it was held that this act applied to her pending suit, and made it good, even though it must have been abated if a motion to that effect had been made before the passage of the act. McLimans v. City of Lancaster, 63 Wis. 596, 23 N. W. Rep. 689. This act was also distinctly held not to be unconstitutional, although retroactive as to the case pending, because it affected only the remedy. In Weldon v. Winslow, 13 Q. B. Div. 784, it was held that a married woman might, by virtue of the married woman's property act of 1882, sue alone for a tort committed before the act came into operation, the law, before the passage of that act, being that she could not sue without joining her husband with her in the action.

Being satisfied that our act of 1889, now under consideration, was intended to, and does, apply to pending actions, we will now inquire into its constitutionality. It will be noticed that some of the following authorities are also applicable to the question just disposed of. Section 6 of the Code provides that "laws looking only to the remedy or mode of trial, may apply to contracts, rights, and offenses entered into, or accrued or committed prior to their passage." The constitution of 1865 forbade the passage of "retroactive laws, injuriously affecting any right of the citizen." No provision against retroactive legislation appears in the constitution of 1868. That of 1877 forbids the passage of a "retroactive law." Construing together the above constitutional provisions in connection with the section of the Code cited, we take it that they all amount to substantially the same thing, and mean that retroactive laws, which do not injuriously affect any right of the citizen, that is to say, laws curing defects in the remedy, or confirming rights already existing, or adding to the means of securing and enforcing the same, may be passed. In Bouton v. Cummins, 16 Ga. 102, it was held that "retrospective laws often operate for the benefit of society, and to repudiate them altogether would be to obliterate a large portion of the statute law of the state;" and accordingly it was ruled that a registry act, requiring deeds to be recorded within a limited time, applied to deeds executed before the passage of the act. In the same volume, in Knight v. Lasseter, 151, it was held that an act operating only on the remedy, though retrospective, was not unconstitutional. The legislature of Mississippi passed an act authorizing a court of chancery to refuse confirmation of a sale, provided the party objecting to the confirmation would make a certain bond, and it was held that the provisions of this act applied to a sale made under a mortgage executed prior to the passage of the act, and that as the act affected the remedy only, and not the mortgagee's contract rights, it was not, therefore, unconstitutional. Before the passage of this act the power of a chancery court to set aside a sale was much more limited. Chaffe v. Aaron, 62 Miss. 29. It is not unconstitutional for the legislature to take away a right which is not vested, but contingent upon some event subsequent to the date of the statute. Before the occurrence transpires upon which an inchoate right is to become vested and unalterable, a law may be passed providing, in effect, that the happening of such occurrence shall not make that right complete. Thus, a joint tenancy may be converted into a tenancy in common, thereby destroying the right of survivorship, and the statute will apply to estates already vested at the time of its enactment. Burghardt v. Turner, 12 Pick. 538; Bambaugh v. Bambaugh, 11 Serg. & R. 191. So an estate tail may be changed into a fee-simple, and thereby destroy a remainder limited upon the fee-tail. De Mill v. Lockwood, 3 Blatchf. 56. It has been often held that the right of dower, before it becomes consummated by the death of the husband, may be taken away or changed at the pleasure of the legislature. Lucas v. Sawyer, 17 Iowa, 517; Noel v. Ewing, 9 Ind. 37; Hamilton v. Hirsch, 2 Wash. T. 2231; Morrison v. Rice, 35 Minn. 436, 29 N. W. Rep. 168; Henson v. Moore, 104 Ill. 403; Barbour v. Barbour, 46 Me. 9; 7 Lawson, Rights, Rem. & Pr. § 3867; 1 Shars. & B. Lead. Cas. Real Prop. 300, and cases cited; 2 Hare, Const. Law, 824; Cooley, Const. Lim. (6th Ed.) 440 et seq. In Wilbur v. Gilmore, 21 Pick. 250, it was held that an act allowing an action to be brought by an executor for an injury in the life-time of his testator was not unconstitutional, even when applied to a trespass committed before this act went into operation, inasmuch as it affected the remedy only. "The presumption against a retrospective construction has no application to enactments which affect only the procedure and practice of the courts, even where the alteration which the statutes make has been disadvantageous to one of the parties. * * * A law which merely alters the procedure may, with perfect propriety, be made applicable to past as well as future transactions. * * * No person has a vested right in any course of procedure, nor in the power of delaying justice, nor of deriving benefit from technical and formal matters of pleading. He has only the right of prosecution or defense in the manner prescribed, for the time being, by or for the court in which he sues; and if a statute alters that mode of procedure, he has no other right than to proceed according to the altered mode. The remedy does not alter the contract or the tort. It takes away no vested right, for the defaulter can have no vested right in a state of the law which left the injured party without, or with only a defective, remedy." End. Interp. St. § 285, and cases cited. See, also, sections 286, 287. "No person can claim a vested right in any particular mode of procedure for the enforcement or defence of his rights. * * * A remedy may be provided for existing rights, and new remedies added to or sub-

stituted for those which exist." See Suth. St. Const. § 482, and cases there cited. Judge Cooley lays it down as a rule that "a party has no vested right in a defense based upon an informality not affecting his substantial equities." Cooley, Const. Lim. 454. In New Orleans v. Clark, 95 U. S. 644, the court held: "It is competent for the legislature to impose upon a city the payment of claims just in themselves, for which an equivalent has been received, but which, from some irregularity or omission in the proceedings creating them, cannot be enforced at law." This legislation was held not to be within the provision of the constitution of Louisiana, inhibiting the passage of a retroactive law. The constitution of Louisiana contains a provision similar, in effect, to that of our own. "The best general rule laid down touching the validity of such statutes is given in 1 Kent, Com. 456, where it is stated that statutes which go to confirm existing rights, and in furtherance of the remedy by curing defects, and adding to the means of enforcing existing obligations, are clearly valid." See notes to Goshen v. Stonington, 10 Amer. Dec., beginning on page 131. "Any statute which changes or affects the remedy merely, and does not destroy or impair vested rights, is not unconstitutional, though it be retrospective, and although, in changing or affecting the remedy, the rights of parties may be incidentally affected." Rich v. Flanders, 39 N. H. 304. The decision in this case was made in construing a statute making competent as witnesses persons who were not so before, and it was held applicable to pending suits, the act expressly so declaring. SARGENT, J., who delivered the opinion, quotes and adopts the following language of Daniel Webster in his argument in the case of Foster v. Essex Bank, 16 Mass. 245: "A distinction must be made between acts which affect existing rights, or impose new obligations, and acts which give new remedies for existing rights, and enforce the performance of previous obligations." See, also, cases cited in Rich v. Flanders, supra. In California it was held that an act requiring a purchaser of property sold for delinquent taxes to give notice of the expiration of the time of redemption was constitutional, and applied to sales previously made. Oullahan v. Sweeney, (Cal.) 21 Pac. Rep. 960. "A statute altering the mode of proceeding in point of form, in a suit pending when the act passed, so as to prevent a delay and hasten the time of trial, is not unconstitutional. Such an act will be construed liberally, and general words, not expressly prospective, will be applied to a pending proceeding. The rule that a statute should not be so construed as to affect vested rights does not apply to a statute which alters the form of the remedy merely." People v. Tibbets, 4 Cow. 384.

We have quoted copiously from the numerous authorities above cited, making little comment thereon, because they seem to be strongly in point, and sustain the doctrine sought to be established more forcibly than would perhaps any language of our own. The case of Wilder v. Lumpkin, 4 Ga. 208, cited by counsel for the de-

---

[1] 5 Pac. Rep. 315.

fendant in error, is not in conflict with our conclusions in the case at bar, either as to the applicability of the act of 1889 to pending actions, or to its constitutionality. That case was ruled mainly upon the ground that the act of 1847, providing "it shall not be necessary to make securities on appeal and injunction bonds parties to writs of error," was not intended to apply to cases pending at the time of its passage. Judge NISBET says, in effect, that the legislature did not contemplate that the act should have retrospective operation, because, by its own terms, it is made to take effect from and after its passage. No such language appears in the act of 1889. This great and learned judge then proceeds to discuss the question of the constitutionality of the act of 1847 as to its applicability to pending cases, and concluded that, so applied, it would not be constitutional. It appears that the rights of Lumpkin, the defendant in error, had been fixed by a judgment, and a subsequent statute affecting the manner in which that judgment might be set aside affected, not merely the remedy, but the right itself. Judge NISBET lays great stress upon this idea, and, after referring to Lumpkin's rights under the judgment in his favor, remarks that "to give the law a retrospective operation would be to divest rights which had already vested in the defendant in error." We will not follow him further through the opinion delivered in this case. It evidences considerable research, great ability, and much learning, and has become celebrated. Of the correctness of the decision, in so far as it holds that the act was not intended to be applicable to pending cases, there can be no doubt; and if a distinction between that case and the one at bar, on the constitutional question, cannot be soundly rested on the fact that Lumpkin's rights were vested because fixed by a judgment, we will only add that we do not feel constrained to adopt every assertion made in the splendid argument of our illustrious predecessor. The act of the legislature of Tennessee, construed in the case of Railroad Co. v. Pounds, which case was relied on by counsel for the defendant in error, as will be seen by an examination of the same, not only affected the remedy, but gave a new, distinct, and additional cause of action, which, of course, could not constitutionally be done. 15 Amer. & Eng. R. Cas. 510. The same criticism is applicable to the case of Osborne v. City of Detroit, 32 Fed. Rep. 36. In the latter case an act limiting the amount of recovery to be had for injuries occasioned by a defective sidewalk was held not applicable to pending suits. So it appears in that case that not only was the plaintiff's remedy affected, but also the measure of his damages a substantial matter. After a careful consideration of the questions involved in this case, and in view of the authorities cited, we affirm the ruling made by this court in the case of Johnson v. Bradstreet Co., that the act of 1889 is applicable to actions pending at the time of its passage; and we rule in the present case that this act, when so applied, is not unconstitutional. Judgment reversed.

SMITH et al. v. DOBBINS et al.

(Supreme Court of Georgia. May 27, 1891.)

EXECUTION — EQUITY — MULTIPLICITY OF SUITS—FRAUD OF DEBTOR—SALE.

1. Where several executions in favor of different plaintiffs have been levied on the same property, and one person has filed in resistance to each levy a separate claim, and the claim cases thus made are pending in court, all involving the same question, and it being one upon the decision of which the subjection or non-subjection of the property to all the executions depends, an equitable petition will lie in favor of the claimant against all the plaintiffs, jointly, to bring to trial all of the claims together, and dispose of them by one verdict and judgment.

2. An agreement between an insolvent debtor, whose land is about to be sold at sheriff's sale under execution, and another not a party to the same, to the effect that the latter will purchase the land and give the former a year's time to refund the purchase money with interest, and thereupon convey to him the land, the plaintiff in fi. fa., not participating in the agreement, is not per se fraudulent as against the debtor's creditors. Nor is such agreement rendered fraudulent by a stipulation that the debtor should have the crop then upon the land without paying for it, nor by a stipulation that the succeeding year's crop should be the property of the purchaser at the sheriff's sale in case the debtor failed to take the land, and pay for it within the time agreed upon.

3. After the purchase of the land at the sheriff's sale, in pursuance of the agreement above set forth, the purchaser was the exclusive owner thereof, and the debtor had no interest in it subject to levy and sale. That the purchaser extinguished the debtor's right to pay for and take the land by paying him, or his assigns, a consideration for such extinguishment, was not a fraud upon his creditors, the debtor having paid nothing whatever for such right, nor upon the agreement out of which it sprang.

(Syllabus by the Court.)

Error from superior court, Bartow county; THOMAS W. MILNER, Judge.

The following is the official report referred to in the opinion:

Dobbins, by his bill, alleged the following: Some time previous to the first Tuesday in October, 1881, one Burkhalter had bargained with W. T. Wofford. then in life, to sell Wofford certain land, describing it, and for the purchase price of the land Wofford had given Burkhalter his promissory notes, taking Burkhalter's bond for titles. Wofford paid a part of the purchase money, and, having failed to pay the balance, Burkhalter brought suit therefor, and obtained judgment for the amount of the balance, and had execution issued upon the judgment, and levied upon the land, after filing his deed to Wofford in the office of the clerk of the superior court. After due advertisement, the land was sold by the sheriff, under the levy, on the first Tuesday in October, 1881, at public outcry, to the highest bidder, and was knocked off to complainant for $4,150, which he paid, and the sheriff made him a deed. On the same day, and after the sale, Wofford asked him for a chance to buy the land back, and he agreed with Wofford to allow him to do so at the amount of his (complainant's) bid, and 8 per cent. interest per annum, to be paid by October 4th following; which agreement was reduced to writing, and a copy of it is annexed to the bill. Shortly before the last-named date, Wofford found he was unable to pay, and transferred all his rights under the contract to T. R. Jones, who was Wofford's creditor, the consideration of the transfer being the settlement of a note for $800 held by Jones against Wofford, and the payment of $800 by Jones to Wofford. On September 23, 1882, Jones presented to complainant the writing obtained by him from Wofford and complainant, desiring to hold the place, paid Jones $1,200 for the relinquishment of all Jones' rights under the writing, and took a transfer of it. All the transactions above mentioned were in good faith, and with no intention on complainant's part to wrong any one, and he believed and believes neither Wofford nor Jones had any intention to wrong any one. Complainant had gone into possession shortly after the sheriff's sale, was in possession when he purchased Jones' rights, and from that time on has so remained. After he had been in possession over two years, and had made valuable improvements, J. M. Smith, having on January 11, 1883, obtained a judgment against Wofford, had a fi. fa. issued and levied on a portion of the land, to which complainant filed his claim, which claim was tried, and a portion of the property was found subject, and complainant moved for a new trial, which was granted. Afterwards, on September 1, 1886, a fi. fa. in favor of M. L. Johnson against the executrix of Wofford, one in favor of the same person against Wofford, and one in favor of the same person as guardian against Wofford, were levied on the land; and complainant filed separate claims, which were returned to court, and are now pending. On January 24, 1887, a fi. fa. in favor of Satterfield against Wofford as principal, and J. C. Wofford as indorser, was levied upon the same land, and to this complainant filed his claim, which was returned to court, where it is now pending; but since the claim was filed Satterfield has died intestate, and there is no administration on his estate, for which reason his estate is not made a party defendant. Plaintiffs in these various fi. fas. claim that complainant procured his title in fraud of the rights of creditors of W. T. Wofford, who died in May, 1884, leaving his estate utterly insolvent, and besides the fi. fas. named there are a number of others which will probably be levied so as to put complainant to the annoyance and expense of a number of trials, unless this bill is sustained compelling all of the issues to be tried and disposed of therein. All the charges of fraud are denied by complainant. He has every reason to believe and did believe that the sheriff's sale was fair and open, and nothing done to deter any one from bidding. He entered into his agreement with Wofford after the sale, being moved by appeals being made to him by Wofford, and out of kind feelings excited by these appeals, and without any hint from Wofford that he desired or intended by such arrangement to hinder, delay, or defraud his creditors, nor was the true status of the matter sought to be kept secret but it was all done honestly, that Wofford might, if he could, procure

the money to buy the land back, which, if he had done so, would have been to the benefit of his creditors. The land brought its full cash value at the sheriff's sale, and since he bought it complainant has put valuable improvements upon it, to the extent of about $5,000, nearly all of which were made before the above-mentioned levies, and without notice on his part that any one would or could question the validity of his title. He charged that said creditors had conspired for the purpose of annoying and harassing him, hoping to induce him to pay them considerable sums of money to buy his peace. As his remedy is less adequate at law than in equity, and in order to avoid the delay, expense, and trouble of a multiplicity of suits, and so many separate trials involving the same issues, he prayed that each of the plaintiffs in fi. fa. be enjoined from proceeding with the claim cases, and compelled to submit their alleged rights to adjudication under this bill, and that the rights of all parties be settled by final decree under it. He further prayed that, so soon as the estate of Satterfield was represented, he have leave to amend his bill by making the administrator a party defendant, for temporary restraining order, perpetual injunction, general relief, etc. He waived discovery. Attached to the bill as an exhibit was a copy of the agreement made between Dobbins and Wofford, the transfer to Jones, and the transfer by Jones to Dobbins. The agreement was signed by Dobbins, dated October 4, 1881, and recited that Dobbins that day had bought the land, which contained 1,200 acres, more or less, and that day went into possession of it, "but except the present crops, with the understanding that any tenant I may rent to have the right to sow grain and grass of any kind, and make any other improvements I, the said Dobbins, may think proper for the preparation of crops for the ensuing year;" and that should Wofford pay to Dobbins, or his legal representatives, $4,-150, with interest from date at 8 per cent. per annum, on or before October 4, 1882, the crops then on the lands being reserved to Dobbins with the right to remove them, Dobbins would make to Wofford, or to his legal representatives or assigns, quit-claim deed to the land. Upon this agreement was an order from Wofford to Dobbins to make a deed to Jones to the land, on Jones paying Dobbins the $4,150 and interest. This was dated September 23, 1882; also the transfer by Jones to Dobbins, which was "for value received," and was dated September 23, 1882. The bill was filed June 11, 1887.

The defendants demurred on the grounds that there was no equity in the bill; that it was multifarious; that complainant had a full, adequate, and complete remedy at law, and the facts alleged showed that a court of law had already taken jurisdiction of the cases, and the case of Smith was pending on writ of error in the supreme court, so that of that case the superior court had no longer jurisdiction; and that the bill was filed since 1885, and under the law as it stood when it was filed and now, even if complainant were entitled to relief, he could have obtained it by proper pleadings in any one of the claim cases. Defendants answered in brief as follows: The alleged judgment of Burkhalter was a nullity, because it was granted by the court without a verdict, when an issuable plea under oath was on file, and all sales or proceedings under it are void, and did not divest Wofford's title. The lands were bid off at the sheriff's sale by Dobbins for $4,000, and he paid $4,150, under the fraudulent scheme. The agreement between Dobbins and Wofford was made before the sale, though it may have been put in writing afterwards. Jones did relinquish his rights to Dobbins, but on the basis of $1,600 instead of $1,200, and Dobbins did not act in good faith in this matter. When the bill was filed the grant of a new trial in the case of Smith against Dobbins, claimant, had been excepted to, and the case was pending in the supreme court, and therefore the superior court had no jurisdiction of that case. The estate of Satterfield has no interest in the Satterfield fi. fa., as J. C. Wofford, before Satterfield's death, as indorser, paid Satterfield the money due on the fi. fa., and it is now proceeding for the benefit of J. C. Wofford. W. T. Wofford is dead, and his estate is insolvent, and he was insolvent October 4, 1881. The land did not bring its value at the sheriff's sale by $2,000 or more. If Dobbins made improvements on it, he did not make them in good faith, as he had full notice of the worthlessness of his title. There has been no conspiracy among defendants, but they antagonized each other, each claiming priority if the property is subjected. Before the sheriff's sale Dobbins, Burkhalter, and W. T. Wofford agreed, in fraud of all other creditors of Wofford, that the land be sold; that Dobbins should bid it off, and, whatever his bid might be, he should pay Burkhalter his debt, and give Wofford 12 months in which to redeem the land, both Dobbins and Burkhalter knowing at the time that Wofford was insolvent, and that the land was worth $7,000. This combination was not only known and rumored among the by-standers at the sale, but Burkhalter told several persons that the sale would be for Wofford's best interest, and Wofford, before the sale, told others that the arraugement had been made. By this means bidding was depressed, there being only one bid made, which was Dobbins', at $4,000; and while the sheriff was crying this, Dobbins, Wofford, and Burkhalter, a few feet off, had a consultation, in which the latter complained that the bid was not enough to pay his debt; and the two former both assured him that, if the property was knocked off to Dobbins at that bid, his debt should be paid in full, and Burkhalter allowed the sale to proceed, which he would not have done but for this assurance, which was simply carrying out the fraudulent scheme; and in further pursuance of it, on October 4, 1881, Dobbins paid Burkhalter $150 in addition to the bid of $4,000, and gave Wofford the writing. While the sheriff's deed was recorded the right of redemption left in Wofford, which was worth $1,600, has never been recorded, which was a fraud on Wofford's

creditors. The scheme did hinder, delay, and defraud the creditors of at least $800, which went into Wofford's pocket, and which they could not reach, so that the scheme is a fraud and void as to the whole property, and as against the creditors Dobbins cannot hold it. Defendants prayed that the sheriff's deed should be canceled, and the property ordered to be sold, and the proceeds distributed among the creditors of Wofford, according to their priority. They further alleged that Dobbins, and since his death his estate, was liable to them for rents and profits of the land, amounting to $500 a year, and prayed that an accounting be had as to the amount thereof, which should be decreed to be a lien upon the lands.

The case made by the bill and answer was referred to a master, who reported in brief as follows: He overruled the demurrer. There were proven before him the judgments of M. L. Johnson, both individually and as guardian of Satterfield now J. C. Wofford's, and of Smith. The judgment of Johnson, as guardian, was rendered October 3, 1881; of Johnson individually, August 10, 1881; of Satterfield, November 23, 1881; and of Smith, January 11, 1883. These judgments now amount to $5,649.92. The testimony failed to establish an intention on the part of either Wofford or Dobbins to defraud Wofford's creditors. The estimates of all the witnesses, reduced to an average, would put the value of the property, at the time Dobbins bought it, at a little less than $5,000, so that it may be seriously doubted whether Dobbins did not pay full value. The agreement between Wofford and Dobbins was made before the sale, and by reason of it Dobbins paid, at the end of the 12 months, $1,200, in addition to what he had before paid on the land, making the cost of the land to him $5,350, which was its full value. The agreement allowing Wofford to redeem the property did not render the sale void, there being no intention upon Wofford's part to defraud his creditors, known to or participated in by Dobbins. Wofford tried to get others of his creditors to pay off the purchase money before the sale, and take the land on their claims against him. He made no secret of the agreement, but after the sale told it to different creditors of his, among them J. C. Wofford, and tried to get them to furnish the money to redeem the land, and take it on their debts, and finally did procure one of them, Jones, to do so. While the agreement to redeem was not put on record, there is no law authorizing such record, and there is little probability that if it had been put on record it would have done any good. Wofford did nothing that could be construed into a want of good faith, and was moved, both before the sale and afterwards, by a desire to prevent the sacrifice of his property, so far as he lawfully could, and the fact that $800 was paid him by Jones, in cash, does not affect the transaction. No person was prevented from bidding, either from sympathy with Wofford or any other reason. That Wofford realized $1,600, by sale of his right to redeem, would not warrant a decree to that extent, or to the extent of $1,200, the amount paid by Dobbins for the transfer to himself of that right in favor of the creditors, since the judgments of the defendants were no lien on the interest of Wofford under his agreement with Dobbins. Wofford's rights were simply an option on the property. He was not liable to be called on to pay anything, and could pay or not as he chose, and had paid nothing on the purchase or option price at all; hence his equity was a naked equity, upon which a judgment against him took no lien, and there was nothing to prevent his selling the equity, as he might have sold a promissory note, and the purchaser got it free from any lien or incumbrance in favor of judgment creditors. The trade with Jones was a fair and honest transaction, and he got all Wofford's right free from any incumbrance, and could and did convey the same to Dobbins for value. If the sale by Wofford to Dobbins were but a private sale, yet, if it were an honest sale, and the purchase of Dobbins were in good faith, the land would not be subject to defendants' judgments. There was nothing in Dobbins' conduct inconsistent with entire good faith under the law. The fact that he may have got the land at less than its value, and knew Wofford's insolvency, and expected to get the land at the price he bid, would not invalidate his purchase. If a private sale were made, those having judgments against the seller would have four years in which to levy their executions or lose their liens; hence, if this were a private sale, these judgment creditors lost such rights as they had by failure to levy on the property for more than four years after it went into the hands of Dobbins; and, if the purchase was in good faith, it would be difficult to find a reason why the land should be subject to the judgment of Smith, the sale having been made before Smith began suit against Wofford. The deed of Dobbins is not void for usury; the fact that Dobbins, under the contract with Wofford, was to be repaid his money with 8 per cent. interest, and in addition to have the crops grown on the land for 1882, not making it so.

All the testimony which was introduced before the master seems not to have been sent up in the record. The deed by the sheriff to Dobbins was an ordinary sheriff's deed, and recited a consideration of $4,000. It was made October 4, 1881, and recorded October 5, 1881. Burkhalter's deed to Wofford was made May 3, 1881, and recorded May 4, 1881. The contract between Dobbins and Wofford was put in evidence. Dobbins testified, in brief, that the bidding at the sheriff's sale commenced at about $2,000, and witness ran the property up to $4,150, and it was knocked off to him at that sum, and he paid the money, and the sheriff made him a deed; that no arrangement about the land was made between him and Wofford before the sale, and that he never saw Wofford at the sale at all; that he never had any conference before the sale with Wofford or Burkhalter about buying the land in for Wofford, and never heard that such a thing was claimed to be true until

after the levy of the Smith *fi. fa.*; that he never did or said anything, or heard anything said by anybody, or saw anything done by anybody, to deter bidders or depress the bidding; that after the sheriff had made him the deed Wofford came and asked him for a chance to get the property back, and get more for it if he could, and he told Wofford that he would let him pay the purchase money, $4,150, back, with 8 per cent. interest per annum, if he would do so by the 4th of the following October, and would make him a quitclaim deed to the land, but he (Dobbins) was to have the crop to be grown on the land for that year, and the right to take it away, to which Wofford agreed and the writing was executed; that, just before the time for Wofford to redeem had expired, Jones came to witness with the paper witness had given Wofford, with the written request on it from Wofford that Jones be allowed to pay the money, and for Dobbins to make the deed to Jones; that Jones did not pay the $4,150 with interest, nor tender it, nor offer to pay it, but witness proposed to give Jones $1,200 for such rights as might be secured to Wofford by the paper, and he did pay Jones that sum, and Jones transferred the paper to him; that witness thought the land brought its value at the sale, but after the sale Burkhalter said he had lost $150 by not having run the land high enough to cover his debt, but witness would not have bid any more, and said so at the time; that witness has improved the land to the extent of about $5,000. It appeared from the documentary evidence that the bid made by Dobbins and the amount paid by him to the sheriff was $4,000, but that Burkhalter bid $150 in addition on the day of the sheriff's sale. There was further evidence tending to show that $4,000 was full value for the property at the time of the sale, for a cash sale; that persons were not deterred from bidding; that the character of Wofford and Dobbins for honesty was good; that Dobbins' improvements to the place would amount to about $5,000; that the rent of the place at present is worth $500 a year, but was only worth $200 to $300 in 1881; that the only plea filed in the suit of Burkhalter against Wofford was that the note on which Burkhalter sued would not draw more than 7 per cent., after its maturity, as matter of law; that Wofford tried to get one Veach, who was a creditor of his, to buy the land to make his (Veach's) money, but Veach would not have given $4,000 for it, the place being in bad condition; that Wofford said nothing to Veach about depressing the bidding at the sale; that the farm was advertised for sale under the Burkhalter *fi. fa.*, when Wofford tried to get Veach to buy it, and, while Wofford's plan was not fully unfolded to Veach, if he had any other plan than to enable Veach to save his debt Veach did not remember it; that he had before that time solicited Veach to furnish him money to pay his debts, giving him an inventory of his assets; that in 1881 Wofford was very much embarrassed, but thought he was solvent, and, if his property had been worth as much as he estimated it at, he could have paid his debts, and had property left; that Veach thought then he was solvent, but from what he learned afterwards changed his opinion. From the testimony of Jones it appeared that the consideration of the transfer to him by Wofford of the written agreement between Dobbins and Wofford was $6,000, of which he was to pay Dobbins $4,400, the amount Wofford then owed Dobbins for the property, and the balance of $1,-600 was made up of two items, $800 in money, which he paid Wofford, and $800, which he paid Wofford in a note Wofford owed him. On the day after the transfer was made to him he, Jones, transferred the writing and all his interest to Dobbins for $5,600; that is, for the difference between the $4,400, which he owed Dobbins, and $5,600, which Dobbins gave him; in other words, $1,200 was paid in cash by Dobbins. The Smith fi. fa. was levied on the property March 26, 1884, the fi. fas. of Johnson, and Johnson, guardian, on September 1, 1886, and the Satterfield fi. fa. on January 24, 1887.

The defendants excepted to the master's report on the following grounds: (1) The master erred in overruling the demurrer. (2) The master did not decide on all the issues made in the answer, one of the issues made being that the property, or a sufficiency thereof, should be found subject to raise the sum of $800, which was paid to Wofford, and that the action of Dobbins was withdrawn from Wofford's creditors, Dobbins having put it into the power of Wofford to withhold said sum from his creditors. (3) The master erred in holding that the making of the agreement before the sale was not a fraud in law and fact on the then existing creditors of Wofford. (4) He erred in not holding that, under the circumstances under which the contract was made and the rumors of the contract among the bystanders, and that the sale was being had for Wofford's benefit, the sale was fraudulent and void, and the whole of the land subject as to the existing creditors of Wofford. (5) He erred in holding that the contract did not give Wofford such an interest in the land as was subject to levy and sale, but only gave him a naked equity, and in not finding that the contract gave to Wofford the crop then on the land, which was worth at least $250. (6) Because he did not find on the issue as to whether or not Dobbins was liable to the creditors of Wofford for the value of said crop, Dobbins having put it into the power of Wofford so to defraud his creditors. (7) Because he did not find that the land was subject to the executions of defendants to the extent of the value of the contract or equity of redemption as proven, $1,600, or at least to the value of $1,-200. (8) Because the master found that the sale of October 4, 1881, was not a private sale and void on account of usury. (9) Because he reports that the bar of four years would have 'precluded defendant Johnson, even if it had been a private sale. As an exception of fact, they excepted on the ground that the master found that the contract was a naked equi-

ty, when the only evidence on the question was by the contract itself, which conveyed the crop then on the land, which, as the master reports, was worth $250; and the testimony of Jones shows that it was worth $1,200 or $1,600, and that Dobbins paid him $1,200 cash, and $400 being the interest due from Wofford to Dobbins, and Dobbins himself so swore. The exceptions were overruled, and the master's report confirmed, to which the defendants excepted.

Albert S. Johnson, for plaintiffs in error.
M. R. Stansell, for defendants in error.

LUMPKIN, J. The facts of this case are set forth in the reporter's statement.

1. The doctrine is well established that equity will interfere to restrain the bringing of a multiplicity of suits when the rights of all concerned may be adjudicated without prejudice to any in a single proceeding, and there is no reason in principle why this rule should not be applied to cases already brought and pending by consolidating them into a single case. In 1 High on Injunctions, § 12, we find the following: "Where there is one common right in controversy which is to be established by or against several persons, one person asserting the right against many, or many against one, equity may interfere and, instead of permitting the parties to be harassed by a multiplicity of suits, determine the whole matter in one action." See, also, 2 High. Inj. § 1406; Story, Eq. Pl. § 286, and Wait, Fraud. Conv. §§ 151, 152, and cases there cited. The doctrine is fully discussed in 1 Pom. Eq. Jur. § 255 et seq. In section 269 is the following: "Under the greatest diversity of circumstances, and the greatest variety of claims arising from unauthorized public acts, private tortious acts, invasion of property rights, violation of contract obligations, and notwithstanding the positive denials by some American courts, the weight of authority is simply overwhelming that the jurisdiction may and should be exercised either on behalf of a numerous body of separate claimants against a single party, or on behalf of a single party against such a numerous body, although there is no 'common title,' nor 'community of right,' or of 'interest in the subject-matter,' among these individuals; but where there is, and because there is, merely a community of interest among them in the questions of law and fact involved in the general controversy, or in the kind and form of relief demanded and obtained by or against each individual member of the numerous body." See, also, section 274. In Orton v. Madden, 75 Ga. 83, it was held that equity "will entertain a bill to avoid a multitude of suits by establishing a right in favor of or against several persons which is likely to be the subject of legal controversy, or in similar cases." And see Johnson v. O'Donnell, Id. 453. In the case of McHenry v. Hazard, 45 N. Y. 580, it appeared that an obligation was obtained from the plaintiff by fraudulent representations. A. and B. both claimed to own it by assignment. Each commenced an action against him, and claimed in hostility to each other; and it was held that he might,

during the pendency of the actions against him, bring a separate suit against both claimants to be relieved from the contract on the ground of fraud therein. ANDREWS, J., delivering the opinion of the court, observed that "it was a prominent motive, in constituting a single court, having jurisdiction in law and equity, to remedy the inconvenience which existed, when legal and equitable remedies were administered by separate tribunals, of obliging parties to resort to two courts to determine rights connected with a single transaction;" and that conferring such power upon the court was "designed to prevent unnecessary litigation, and to enable parties to bring into one suit all the elements of the controversy for the purpose of a complete and final adjudication." Again, in the case of Board v. Deyoe, 77 N. Y. 219, it appeared that a county treasurer, under authority to issue notes for money advanced to the county for a certain amount, had fraudulently issued notes for a much larger amount. Some of the claims against the county were valid, while others were not. Thirty-one persons holding these notes had brought separate actions thereon against the county, and others intended to do so. The petition brought at the instance of the county alleged that it could not be ascertained who were the rightful owners of the debt owing by the county, or how much thereof was due to either of the holders of the notes, and that separate litigation with each would subject the plaintiff to great expense. Upon demurrer to the complaint, it was held that the plaintiff was entitled, upon equitable principles, to implead the holders of the notes for the purpose of having their respective rights and the liability of the county determined in one action; that the claims were of the same general character; and the action was maintainable for the purpose of preventing a multiplicity of suits. In reply to the suggestion that the plaintiff in the present case should not be allowed to consolidate all these claim cases into one, because he himself was responsible for their existence, in having filed his claim to the property in every instance where a levy thereon was made, which he was not absolutely compelled to do, it may be said that in filing such claims he only availed himself of one of the methods which the law gave him for the protection of his alleged rights. The fact that he resorted to a statutory remedy in each case should not, we think, deprive him of the more valuable remedy in equity of having all this litigation terminated by a single verdict and judgment, the more especially as so doing could in no way injure any of the parties. Whether or not the agreement between him and Wofford constituted such a fraud upon the creditors of Wofford as would invalidate Dobbins' title to the land was a question involved in all the claim cases, and was a vital one in each. Upon its determination depended, in every one of these cases, the subjection or non-subjection of the property; and we are unable to perceive why, in justice and upon principle, this question should not be determined once for all, and thus finally settle in one judgment, without having numerous, tedious, and expensive trials, the rights of all these parties.

2. We do not think that such an agreement as is set forth in the second headnote was necessarily fraudulent as against the creditors of Wofford. It was not shown that Burkhalter, the plaintiff in execution, participated therein. There was no binding obligation on Wofford's part to redeem the land by paying back the purchase money with interest, and Dobbins would have had no power to compel a performance of this agreement by Wofford. It was simply a privilege of which the latter might, or might not, avail himself, as he chose. Considered even as a bond for titles, no part of the purchase money was paid by Wofford, and he therefore had no leviable interest in the land. To make such an agreement fraudulent on the creditors, it must have been intended to defraud them, the object, and not the effect, of the agreement, being the true test of its validity. Upon this question the master reports that Wofford's whole conduct was a laudable effort to cause his property to bring full value for the benefit of his creditors, and he further reports that there was no fraud whatever throughout the entire transaction in the conduct of Dobbins. The fact that Dobbins agreed that Wofford should have the crop upon the land at the time of the sale could not invalidate his title to the land itself; and if, by this arrangement, the title to the crop passed into Wofford, it was subject to executions against him, and the creditors could have had it levied upon. The agreement that, in case Wofford failed to redeem the land within the time agreed upon, the succeeding year's crop should be the property of Dobbins, was entirely immaterial, because the same would have been his, as the owner of the land, without any such agreement.

3. The master having found that the title of Dobbins to the land in controversy was wholly free from fraud, such finding negatives the liability of the property to be subjected to any part of the debts of the plaintiffs in fi. fa., or any of them. The fact that Wofford transferred his right to pay for and redeem the land to another, to whom Dobbins paid a valuable consideration for the extinguishment of this right, could not, under the facts of this case, be a fraud upon the creditors of Wofford. He had paid nothing whatever for this right, and it appears to have been a mere gratuity to him on the part of Dobbins. In the absence of actual fraud, and of any intention on the part of Dobbins, Wofford, or Burkhalter to injure the several plaintiffs in execution who sought to subject this land as the property of Wofford, the fact that Dobbins donated, without valuable consideration, a privilege to Wofford, which the latter afterwards sold for money, and which Dobbins purchased from Wofford's transferee, does not, in our opinion, affect the honesty or legality of Dobbins' title to the land. Judgment affirmed.

CENTRAL RAILROAD & BANKING CO. v. KENT.

(Supreme Court of Georgia. July 20, 1891.)

MASTER AND SERVANT—NEGLIGENCE—ACTION FOR INJURIES—JURY—INSTRUCTIONS.

1. A railroad company which has performed the duty of inspecting and keeping in safe condition its track and road-bed, with that degree of diligence which the law requires of it, is not liable in damages to one of its engineers for injuries occasioned by running his engine into a washout or chasm caused by a sudden, most violent, and unprecedented rain-fall, such as the oldest inhabitants of the neighborhood had never before witnessed; the calamity being directly attributable to the act of God, for which no individual or corporation is ever held responsible.

2. After a jury has been stricken to try a cause, it is not error to refuse to allow a restriking because counsel for one of the parties simply states in his place that he had by oversight left on the jury a man who, for reasons alleged, would, in his opinion, be partial and prejudiced against his client; it not appearing that, even if these things were true, any diligence had been shown to ascertain the same, or that they might not easily have been known by proper and timely inquiry.

3. Upon the trial of an action for personal injuries against a railroad company by one of its engineers, after admitting evidence tending to show that such engineer was experienced and reliable, it was error to charge that, as throwing light on the question whether or not he was to blame, the jury might consider his character as an experienced and reliable engineer, if such character had been shown by the testimony, the evidence mentioned not being relevant upon this particular issue.

4. Whether or not an engineer exercised proper diligence in looking out for defects in the track is a question for the jury, in determining which they should take into consideration the various other duties which he was required to perform in managing and running his engine.

5. When, in its charge, the court mentions and emphasizes a certain issue, and informs the jury that the pressure of the case is upon that issue, it should be careful not to use in this connection language which may confine the jury, in the determination of this important issue, to a portion only of the facts and circumstances pertinent thereto; but, on the contrary, should so frame its instructions that they may, in arriving at the truth, have in mind and give proper weight to the theories of both sides, and the proof offered in support thereof. Hence where the court, in charging upon a vital question, as above set forth, calls attention in detail to particular facts favorable to one side, it would be better to call attention in like manner to the facts favorable to the other side, instead of using, as to them, general terms which, however intelligible to a trained legal mind, may not impress as intended the minds of jurors, who are non-professional men.

BLECKLEY, C. J., dissenting.

(Syllabus by the Court.)

Error from superior court, Bibb county; A. L. MILLER, Judge.

R. F. *Lyon*, for plaintiff in error. *Depau & Bartlett*, for defendant in error.

LUMPKIN, J. 1. The testimony in this case was quite voluminous. After a careful examination of it, we find that the following facts indisputably appeared: The culvert under the embankment where the washout occurred, which was near the 126th mile-post from Macon, was constructed in 1858, was properly built, was sufficient in all ordinary storms and freshets to carry off all the water which had

to pass through it, had withstood the storms of nearly 30 years, and immediately preceding the great rain-storm which caused the washout was apparently in a perfectly safe condition. That rain-storm was sudden, violent, and unprecedented. The oldest inhabitants of the neighborhood had never before witnessed one like it, and the culvert had never been subjected to such a flood as this storm caused. One Jordan, who was then a section-master of the railroad, having charge of the section on which this accident occurred, saw this culvert about 12 o'clock on the day the washout occurred. It was then apparently in good condition, and he examined it sufficiently to satisfy himself there was no reason to apprehend any danger at this point. At the time he made this examination the barrel of the culvert was not half full of water, and the rain was falling lightly. Being satisfied that the culvert was in its usual good condition, and perfectly safe, he went to another place on the railroad, near the 122d mile-post, known as "The Slide," where he apprehended there might be danger, as an accident had occurred there before. While Jordan and his hands were at "The Slide," which was the place on this section at which there was more likely to be danger than anywhere else, the rain was falling very lightly, and there was nothing to indicate that such a thing as a waterspout had occurred, or would be likely to occur, four miles below, where the culvert was situated. Besides the above facts, concerning which we think there can be no dispute, we desire to allude briefly to some other portions of the testimony. Mr. Kent, the engineer, himself testified that he had never recognized the place where this culvert was located as a dangerous one, and that it was as safe here as any place on the road, according to his knowledge. The train was due at the place where the accident occurred about 3 o'clock in the afternoon, but probably reached there a little after that time. The evidence does not accurately show what time elapsed between the washout and the arrival of the train. This time, as we gather from a consideration of the testimony of all the witnesses whose evidence bore upon this question, was somewhere between 30 minutes and two hours and a half. This case was before this court at the October term, 1889, and is reported in 84 Ga. 351, 10 S. E. Rep. 965. The last head-note of that decision is in the following language: "The pressure of the case is upon the question whether the company was negligent in not knowing of the washout, so as to have given the plaintiff due notice and warning; and this is a question for the jury, under proper instructions by the court." In the opinion, delivered by Justice BLANDFORD, we find the following words on page 356, 84 Ga., and page 966, 10 S. E. Rep.: "The question is, was the railroad company negligent in not knowing of the washout, so as to have given the plaintiff due notice and warning? This was a question of fact for the jury. Did the railroad company have time to know the washout had occurred, so that it would be chargeable with notice thereof? If the company knew, or could have known, of this washout by the exercise of ordinary and reasonable care and diligence, it would seem from the authorities that it would be liable to the plaintiff for the damage he sustained. But if it did not know of it, and if there was no negligence on the part of the company's servants in not knowing, or trying to know, the company would not be liable. It seems to us the pressure of the whole case is upon this point, and, in the charge of the court as contained in the record, we do not think that this point was prominently brought to the attention of the jury. This is a matter for the jury to pass upon on another trial of the case."

Trying the case by the test thus made, we are of the opinion that the railroad company has conclusively shown it exercised all that ordinary and reasonable care and diligence required of it by law. The question propounded by Justice BLAND-FORD, "Did the railroad company have time to know the washout had occurred, so that it would be chargeable with notice thereof?" must be decided in the light of the established facts of the case. In determining whether the defendant, after the washout occurred, had sufficient time before the accident to have discovered the danger, and to have given warning to those in charge of the approaching train, reference must be had to something more than the mere lapse of minutes and hours between the two events. If a servant of the company had been at or near the culvert exactly at the time the washout occurred, doubtless he could have gone forward, and met the train in time to warn the engineer of the danger he was approaching. Indeed, it may be true that, after the washout actually occurred, there may have been sufficient time for an employe of the company at "The Slide," or anywhere else within the limits of the section, to have gone to the scene of the washout, and then to have given notice to the engineer in time to avert the accident. But it seems to us that there are other questions which ought to be considered and determined in this same connection. What was the character of this culvert? What had been its condition for more than a quarter of a century, and how had it withstood storms and carried off their angry waters during all these years? What was its condition on the very day of this unfortunate accident, but a short time before the accident occurred? What examination had been made of it by the section-master just preceding the washout, and what conclusion had he reached upon the question of its safety? Was his conclusion justified by the attending facts and circumstances? Did the light rain which was falling at "The Slide," where the section-master was engaged in the discharge of his duty, give any premonition that a waterspout had occurred, or was likely to occur, at the culvert, four miles below? If the answers to all these questions, and others of like kind which might be suggested, establish the fact that there was no good reason to expect a washout at this point at all, then it was not legally necessary for the company to keep this place under constant watch. We think, in view of all the testimony contained in the record, that no such necessity reasonably appeared to exist. There was far more reason to carefully guard the other place designated as "The Slide," and this, it seems, was being faithfully done. In the light of many years' experience, and in view of the almost numberless tests of strength, durability, and security to which this culvert had been subjected, we think the company was justified in concluding on this particular day that it was in safe condition and would remain so. Of course, if the company, by its servants, had actually known of the washout; or the circumstances were such that it ought to have known of it in time to warn the approaching train; or if the facts showed that the company had any reason to apprehend danger at this point, and failed to provide against the same,—then undoubtedly it would have been a case of such negligence on the part of defendant as would entitle the plaintiff to recover. But we do not think this negligence on the part of the company existed, and are of the opinion that the proof shows to the contrary. Railroad companies are under legal duty, both as to passengers and their own employes, to keep their tracks and road-beds in a safe condition, and every engineer has the right to assume that this duty will be observed. The facts in this case, however, show that the defendant complied with its duty in these respects, at least to the extent of exercising all "ordinary and reasonable care and diligence." The simple truth is, this calamity was occasioned by an unusual and unexpected cause, so awful in its nature, and so disastrous in its consequences, that no human being could have foreseen it, or ought, in justice, to be chargeable with negligence for having failed to provide against it. It was the act of God, and the authorities holding that no individual or corporation is, or ever ought to be, held responsible for His acts, are so strong, so numerous, and so well recognized, it is unnecessary to cite them. Our conclusion, therefore, is that, even upon the line suggested for a proper solution of this case in the opinion delivered by Justice BLANDFORD, above quoted, the verdict was unwarranted by the evidence, and ought not to stand.

2. The correctness of the proposition announced in the second head-note is sufficiently apparent without discussion.

3, 4. It was contended by defendant upon the trial that plaintiff, by exercising proper care in looking out for dangerous places in the track, might have seen the washout in time to stop his engine before running into it, and thus have averted the terrible calamity which occurred. Whether or not this contention of defendant was well founded was one of the questions to be passed upon by the jury, and, in determining it, it was, of course, proper for them to take into consideration, not only the duty which devolved upon the engineer of looking out, but also the various other duties it was necessary for him to perform in managing and running his engine, the state of the weather, and all other pertinent facts shown by the testimony. But, in solving the question whether or not the engineer was negligent, the facts that he was experienced, and had previously been reliable, were not pertinent. These facts may have been relevant, and proper to be considered by the jury with reference to other questions involved in the case, but they were not so as to the particular issue with which we are now dealing. Hence it was error for the court to charge the jury they might consider them, if shown, as throwing light on the question whether or not the engineer was to blame. In the case of Railroad Co. v. Newton, 85 Ga. 517, 11 S. E. Rep. 776, substantially the same question was passed upon by this court. That was a suit by a widow for the homicide of her husband, alleged to have been occasioned by the negligence of the railroad. The deceased was not an employe of the company, but nevertheless one of the defenses was that he could have avoided the injury by the exercise of ordinary care and diligence, and this court held that upon this issue it was not admissible to show his character was that of a prudent and cautious man. The authorities there cited, on page 526, 85 Ga., and page 777, 11 S. E. Rep., sustain the ruling then made by this court, and are, we think, in point upon this particular branch of the case at bar.

5. The charge of the able and learned judge who tried this case in the court below was clear, comprehensive, and in the main a correct exposition of the law applicable; but in certain particulars, to which we shall presently refer, it did not present as fully as it might have done the defense of the railroad upon the most vital and important issue in the case. To explain our meaning, we make the following extract from the charge in reference to the question whether or not the railroad company was negligent in not knowing of the washout, so as to give Kent warning: "Now, the jury will observe that right here is the main contention of the railroad company, if Kent, the plaintiff, was not at fault on his part; for, if you should find Kent free from blame or negligence in this occurrence, the pressure of the case would be upon this issue: Was the railroad company negligent in not knowing of the washout, so as to have given Kent, the plaintiff, due notice and warning? This, gentlemen, is a question of fact for you. It is for you, and you alone, to decide, after a careful study and examination of all the testimony bearing upon that point. At what hour did the rain-fall occur that caused the washout? At what point on the road was the train at that hour? How far was the train at that time from the place where the washout occurred? And how long a period of time was consumed by the train in traversing the intervening distance? Find out from the testimony, as nearly as you can, how long that period of time was. Was that period of time sufficiently long for the railroad company, by the exercise of ordinary and reasonable care and diligence, to have discovered the washout, and given Kent due notice and warning of its existence? If you find from the evidence that a sufficient length of time intervened between the hour the washout occurred and the time of the accident, so that, by the exercise of ordinary and reasonable care and diligence, the railroad company could have discovered the washout and given notice to the plaintiff, then they would be chargeable with notice of the existence of the washout. But if sufficient time had not elapsed so that, by the exercise of ordinary and reasonable care and diligence, the railroad company could have discovered the washout, then they would not be chargeable with that notice. So you will see, gentlemen of the jury, a great deal depends right there on your finding as to the amount of time that intervened; and whether the amount of time was sufficient for the railroad company, by the exercise of ordinary care and diligence, to have discovered that washout and given warning." The objection to this charge is that it lays great stress upon the amount of time elapsing between the washout and the accident, without calling attention to other facts and circumstances, which were of as great importance as the mere length of time intervening between these two events. We have already intimated in the first division of this opinion what some of these facts and circumstances were, and will again refer to them in suggesting what, in our opinion, would have been a proper addition to the charge. The effect of the charge quoted was, we fear, to exclude from the consideration of the jury the real defense of the railroad upon this most important branch of the case. It is true the charge does, in effect, say in more than one place that if the railroad did not have time, "by the exercise of ordinary and reasonable care and diligence," to discover the washout and give notice of its existence, it would not be liable; but the use of these general terms last above quoted was not sufficient to properly direct the minds of the jury to the facts they ought to consider in determining whether or not the company did observe due diligence in this respect. It is more than likely the jury understood the court to mean that, if the employes of the company had time to go from where they were to the washout after it occurred, discover its existence, and then go back and stop the approaching train, the company was liable; and, as he had already instructed the jury that the pressure of the case would be upon this issue, the charge, taken as a whole, was not sufficiently full to do the railroad company justice. It would have been better, we think, if the judge had added to this charge some such language as the following: "In deciding whether or not the railroad company exercised reasonable care and diligence in discovering the washout, you may take into consideration the character of the culvert, the length of time it had stood, its condition on the day of the accident, the examination (if any) made by the section-master, and the character of the rain-fall at 'The Slide' on the day of the calamity; and in this connection you may determine whether or not there was sufficient reason for the company's servants to apprehend a washout would occur at this point, or

to require the company to keep this culvert under special watch during that day." The charge given, with some such addition as this, would have required the jury, as was proper, to consider the proof offered by both sides upon the controlling issue in the case, and would have enabled them to fairly determine whether or not the company had established the defense it relied upon, viz., that the attendant circumstances were not such as to indicate that a washout was to be apprehended at this point, and consequently that due care and diligence did not require of the railroad company any further inspection or watch over the culvert than was actually given. Rule 9 of the railroad company, which was put in evidence by the plaintiff, is as follows: "Should a section-master have reason to apprehend washes or injury to the track, bridges, or culverts, by rain or storm or flood, he must, whether by day or night, pass over his section fully one hour preceding the passage of any regular train, or repair to the place known to be in the most danger." Under this rule, the section-master is only required to pass over his section one hour preceding the passage of trains, when he has "reason to apprehend washes or injury to the track, bridges, or culverts, by rain or storm or flood." Holding the company by its own rule, and taking into consideration the real contest in this case as made by the pleadings and the evidence, it becomes apparent that the most important question to be determined was whether or not there was reason to apprehend that this washout would occur. We think, for the reasons above given, this question was not properly submitted to the jury. A ruling of the supreme court of Minnesota, in the case of Gates v. Railway Co., 28 Minn. 110, 9 N. W. Rep. 579, so aptly concurs with and illustrates the views we have above endeavored to express that we quote, though somewhat lengthy, the charge given by the trial judge, and the remarks concerning it made by the reviewing court. The charge given was as follows: "It is the duty of those who use hazardous agencies and instrumentalities to control them carefully, and to adopt every ordinary known and usually approved invention to lessen the danger, and to guard against every ordinary probable danger by such means as ordinary prudence would suggest or dictate. Railroad companies are bound to take notice of the topography of the country along their lines of road, and to take notice of the climate in which their roads are, and about the storms and floods that annually occur in those localities, and make all necessary guards against danger caused by ordinary and usually severe storms of the locality where the road is located. It was the duty of defendant to so construct its road as to make it reasonably safe and to guard against washouts, land-slides, and obstructions, which endanger the lives of the passengers and employes passing over the same; and any neglect of the defendant in that behalf would make it liable to the plaintiff, if such neglect caused the injury. It was the duty of the defendant to keep its road in suitable and safe repair, and keep and maintain suitable ditches and culverts, at suitable and proper places, to carry off the surplus water running down upon the track or road of the defendant company; and the neglect of the defendant to perform that duty, if such neglect was the cause of the accident, will make the defendant liable." Referring to this charge, the supreme court held that, "notwithstanding the court also in general terms charged the jury that the degree of care and prudence required of the defendant in the case was 'due and ordinary care,' 'reasonable care,' and 'ordinary prudence,' the charge, as a whole, was erroneous; for the jury may have understood from it that it was the absolute duty of the defendant, without regard to the degree of care used by it to effect the purpose, to make all necessary guards against danger caused by ordinary storms, and to guard against land-slides, washouts, and obstructions which might endanger the lives of passengers and employes, and to keep its road in suitable and safe repair." In addition to what appears in the head-note just quoted, GILFILLAN, C. J., in the opinion, observes, in effect, that, under this charge, no amount of care and prudence in guarding against storms and keeping its road in suitable and safe repair would relieve the defendant from liability if the ends aimed at were not accomplished. The views herein expressed, and supported by the above authority, will make apparent to us, we think, the correctness of the proposition announced in the fifth head-note. Judgment reversed.

BLECKLEY, C. J., (dissenting.) On a previous writ of error, (see 84 Ga. 351, 10 S. E. Rep. 965,) the right of the plaintiff to recover was resolved, and as I think correctly, into a question of fact for decision by the jury. Upon the second trial, the court committed no error of law which affected that question on its substantial merits, and, while the verdict may or may not be correct, there was evidence to support it. I believe the presiding judge did not abuse his discretion in denying a new trial. For this reason I dissent from the judgment of reversal.

AMERICAN EXCHANGE NAT. BANK v. GEORGIA CONSTRUCTION & INVESTMENT CO. et al.

(Supreme Court of Georgia. July 20, 1891.)

NEGOTIABLE INSTRUMENTS—INDORSEMENT FOR DISCOUNT — POWER OF PARTNER TO BIND FIRM—RATIFICATION.

1. Where, in order to have a note discounted at bank, a partner indorsed it in his own name, and also in the partnership name, and the undisputed evidence shows that the bank would not make the discount and advance the money without the latter indorsement, there was no ground in the evidence for charging the jury as to what was the effect of the transaction, if it was based on the credit of the one partner only; and this is so, although the bank knew that, before the partnership indorsement would be binding on the firm, ratification by the other partner would be essential.

2. An indorsement in the partnership name to raise funds for the indorsing partner or for a third person will not bind the partnership without ratification, (the bank discounting the paper

knowing such ratification to be necessary,) although the funds be entered in the bank-books to the credit of the partnership, and afterwards drawn out on checks of the partnership signed by the partner not privy to the transaction. The execution of such checks without notice that the funds were raised on the partnership credit, or by an indorsement in the partnership name, will not amount to a ratification. But if the proceeds of such checks, or some of them, be used for the benefit of the partnership, and any of them be retained after notice of the material facts has been acquired, this will be a ratification, no offer being made to return them.

3. If, after acquiring such notice and after a dissolution of the partnership, the partner informs the bank in writing that he has bought out his copartner's interest, and will pay the notes of the firm, as he has assumed the firm's liabilities, the *prima facie* effect of such writing is to ratify the indorsement; but the writing is ambiguous, and is open to explanation by extrinsic evidence as to whether there was an intention to ratify the indorsement or not.

(Syllabus by the Court.)

Error from city court of Richmond; W. F. EVE, Judge.

Jos. B. Cumming and *Bryan Cumming,* for plaintiff in error. *J. R. Lamar,* for defendants in error.

BLECKLEY, C. J. 1. The charge of the court excepted to in the third and fourth grounds of the motion for a new trial was based on the hypothesis that the money might have been loaned on the credit of R. P. Sibley. No such hypothesis arises out of the evidence. On the contrary, the only testimony on the subject, that of the vice-president of the bank, was express that the bank refused to discount the note unless it was first indorsed by the firm of R. P. & G. T. Sibley, and passed through their regular account; that the note was discounted upon the credit of the indorsements, and the bonds deposited as collateral security; that, when first offered for discount, the indorsement of R. P. & G. T. Sibley was not on the note; and that the bank never agreed to discount it until their name was indorsed on it, but expressly refused to do so, in consequence of which refusal the note was indorsed by R. P. Sibley in their name. Moreover, the money was entered to their credit in the books of the bank, and so stood until it was drawn out on checks signed in the firm name by G. T. Sibley. True, the bank knew that the indorsement of the firm was an accommodation indorsement, and that the ratification of it by G. T. Sibley was necessary, but it was expected that such ratification would take place and the indorsement be made effectual. This being so, the charge of the court was error, and, while this error might have been harmless, it may, on the other hand, have been hurtful. In view of all the facts of the case and the finding of the jury, we consider it cause for granting a new trial.

2. Uncle and nephew were copartners, under the name of R. P. & G. T. Sibley, as cotton factors, in Augusta, Ga. The partnership did business with the American Exchange National Bank of New York, and its dealings with that bank ran through a considerable time and embraced many transactions. R. P. Sibley, the senior partner, was president of the

Georgia Construction & Improvement Company. That company, by him as president, executed a promissory note for $5,000, dated Augusta, Ga., August 15, 1888. It was payable at the American Exchange National Bank, New York, to the order of W. H. Penland, and due December 1st after its date. This note, bearing the indorsement of the payee and several others, the last of whom was R. P. Sibley, indorsing as an individual, was offered by him to the bank for discount. The bank declined to discount it without the partnership indorsement also, and even with that indorsement would discount it only upon condition that the money should be entered to the credit of the partnership, and pass through its account on the books of the bank. The bank officer knew that the indorsement was for accommodation, and that, to render it binding on the partnership, the ratification of the junior partner would be necessary. This ratification the uncle promised to procure, and the bank discounted the paper on the 24th of August, 1888. By letter addressed to the partnership at Augusta, the bank communicated information at once that the note of the construction and investment company had been discounted and the firm credited with the proceeds. R. P. Sibley, also as president, by a letter similarly addressed, gave information to the firm that the bank had discounted the note, "and placed to your" credit. Both of these letters disclosed the amount of the note, and the name of the maker, but neither of them gave any further description of the instrument, or mentioned any of the indorsements or indorsers. It is altogether improbable that any fraud was intended by the partnership. It expected actual knowledge of the indorsement to be communicated by the partner who was present to the one who was absent. Moreover, it refused to subject the avails of the indorsement to the order of anyone save the partnership. It retained the fund as partnership assets entered to the credit of the partnership in the partnership account with the bank, and did not afterwards pay out the money, except on checks of the partnership; all of them, so far as appears, were signed by the absent partner. No copy of any of the checks is in the record, but presumably they were not drawn upon any particular fund. They were some 20 in number, and the aggregate amount covered by them was about $100,000; the balance to the credit of the partnership, at one time after this fund was entered to its credit, being run down to less than $20. It is manifest, also, that the avails of this indorsement passed through the partnership books as well as the books of the bank; for it appears that, at the time the above-mentioned small balance was stricken, the state of the account as kept by the parties, respectively, was the same; that is, the books of the partnership correspond with the books of the bank. On this state of facts, did the checking of the money out of the bank by the partnership, the checks being signed by the junior partner, constitute a ratification of the indorsement, irrespective of whether the partnership received the actual benefit of the fund, or whether that benefit was realized alone by the maker of the note, the Georgia Construction & Investment Company? Inasmuch as the bank was aware that the partnership indorsement was for accommodation, and that the junior partner was ignorant of it when it was made, the burden of proving that he afterwards assented to it would be upon the bank. Doubtless the fact that he checked out the money would be strong evidence of such assent; indeed quite enough evidence to charge him and the partnership with the indorsement. But if his own testimony is to be credited in opposition to the circumstantial evidence, (and there is no legal reason why it might not be,) it affirmatively appears that, at the time the money was checked out, he did not know of the indorsement. If he was then ignorant of it, and believed that the credit of the firm had in no way been engaged to raise the money, it would seem that his ignorant co-operation in effectuating an arrangement beween his copartner and the bank to transfer the money from the possession of the bank to that of the party for whose accommodation the indorsement, when made, was intended, ought not to render himself or the partnership liable. True, the bank, before parting with the money, had fortified itself with a firm indorsement executed by one partner, and with firm checks executed by the other. But if these checks were issued by the junior partner without any knowledge or information of the indorsement, or any sufficient ground for believing that the note had been discounted on the credit of the firm, no assent to or ratification of the indorsement could fairly be imputed to him. Whether, according to commercial usage and the general understanding of business men, the letter of the bank, and that of the senior partner, written to the firm on the day the note was discounted, would communicate notice that the credit of the firm had been engaged in procuring the discount, would probably be a subject for expert testimony; but no such testimony appears in the record before us. In its absence, our conclusion is that checking out the money would not make the indorsement effective, unless the partnership received the benefit of it, either in whole or in part. But the receiving such benefit before notice, and retaining it after notice, would operate as a ratification of the indorsement, whether so intended or not; for this would be a ratification by conduct,—that is, by checking out the money under a misapprehension, and failing to relinquish the fruits of the mistake after full discovery of all the means by which they were obtained. Whether by reason alone of checking out the money the indorsement should be operative or not ought to depend, in a large degree, upon the equities between the parties. To put the matter in a condensed form, let the partnership element be eliminated. If A., without authority from B., executes a promissory note in the name of the latter, sells it to C., (who has notice of such want of authority at the time, but expects it to be supplied,) and deposits the proceeds with C. to the credit of B., and afterwards B., believing that the money had been rasied by A. on his own credit, checks it out and applied it to the use of A., it is clear that B. is not bound to pay the note. But suppose B. checks out the money, and keeps it in his own pocket, or appropriates it to his own use, he cannot hold on to the money and repudiate the note, assuming the transaction to be free throughout from any intention on the part of C. to defraud. By retaining the money after knowledge that it was raised on his credit by an assumption of authority, B. ratifies the act irrespective of whether he intends to ratify it or not; and, as he cannot ratify it in part and repudiate it in part, such ratification will result from retaining any of the money with no offer to return the amount retained, although he may have paid out the residue for A.'s benefit before acquiring knowledge of all the material facts.

That the bank did not intend to perpetrate, or aid in the perpetration of, an actual fraud on the partnership, is fairly inferable; for it was understood that the senior partner was to inform his copartner of the transaction, and that the proceeds of the indorsement should be entered in the partnership account. This was equivalent to putting the title to these proceeds in the partnership, there to remain until the partnership itself should draft them out of the bank, and thus control their disposition. This afterwards took place, with what result on the finances of the partnership the record before us does not fully disclose. The state of the account between the firm and the Georgia Construction & Investment Company does not appear. As the firm actually drew this money from the bank on its checks, the junior member representing it in drawing the checks, it is *prima facie* chargeable with the whole sum. This partner says in his testimony that he "paid out some money for the Georgia Construction & Improvement Company," and the brief of evidence contains this statement: "Agreed that the money was paid out a few days after August 24th, without communicating with the bank." Whether this means that all the money produced by the indorsement was so paid out, or whether it means that so much of it as the witness had previously referred to was so paid, we cannot determine. This is a matter which seems to need explanation.

3. The firm of R. P. & G. T. Sibley was dissolved by mutual consent on or about the 6th of September, 1888. Between that time and the 10th of September, probably on the 8th or 9th, G. T. Sibley, the junior member, received notice of the dishonor of this note. The notice, though expressed in very brief terms, sufficiently indicated that the firm of R. P. & G. T. Sibley was an indorser upon the instrument. On the 10th of September he wrote the bank that he had bought out the interest of R. P. Sibley in the firm, and would continue the business in all its branches, adding these words: "The notes of R. P. & G. T. Sibley that you hold will be paid by me, as I have assumed the lia-

bilities of R. P. & G. T. Sibley." As we understand the evidence, this letter was written and sent after notice to the firm had reached the writer that the note now in question was dishonored. He testified that he did not have, when he wrote this letter, "any actual knowledge of R. P. & G. T. Sibley's indorsement on the note," but he does not deny that he had such information as the notice of dishonor communicated. Actual knowledge was not requisite to render the ratification of the indorsement resulting from his promise to pay the note effective. It was enough if he had such information as would raise the belief in his mind, or in the mind of a reasonable man, that the bank regarded the firm as an indorser upon the note, and sought to hold the partnership liable as such. The phraseology of the letter is somewhat ambiguous, for the terms, "the notes of R. P. & G. T. Sibley," may be restricted to notes of which they were the makers, or these terms may comprehend all notes held by the bank on which the firm name appeared, whether as makers or indorsers. Inasmuch as the letter states that the writer had assumed the liabilities of R. P. & G. T. Sibley, we think this more comprehensive sense is apparently the true signification of the doubtful words. But under the rule of our Code as to allowing all ambiguities, whether latent or patent, to be explained, extrinsic evidence is no doubt receivable as to whether there was any intention to ratify this indorsement or not. The *prima facie* import of the latter is to recognize this note as one of the liabilities of the firm. While we rest the grant of a new trial directly on the third and fourth grounds of the motion, we think the general substance of the case calls for a more thorough and sifting investigation than appears to have been had. We have ruled upon the controlling questions indicated in the motion for a new trial; and, as the evidence on the next trial may be materially different, we deem it unnecessary to deal more specifically than we have done with the several grounds of the motion. Judgment reversed.

GEORGIA RAILROAD & BANKING CO. v. CRAWLEY.

(Supreme Court of Georgia. May 6, 1891.)

EXCESSIVE VERDICT—REMITTITUR—INTEREST.

Where the verdict is for a larger sum than is sued for, and no amendment covering the excess is offered, the court should set it aside or require a *remittitur*, though interest added to the damages proved would equal the verdict.

Error from superior court, McDuffie county; H. C. RONEY, Judge.

Action by W. J. Crawley against the Georgia Railroad & Banking Company for injuries to stock. Verdict and judgment for plaintiff, and defendant brings error. Reversed.

J. B. Cumming, Bryan Cumming, and *M. P. Reese,* for plaintiff in error. *Thos. E. Watson,* for defendant in error.

SIMMONS, J. Crawley sued the railroad company for the killing of two mules, alleging in his declaration that the defend-

ant had damaged him $200. The jury found in his favor $278.25. The defendant made a motion for a new trial, on the grounds that the verdict was contrary to the evidence; that the evidence showed that the defendant exercised all ordinary and reasonable care at the time the mules were killed; that the verdict was for a larger sum than that sued for; and that no amendment was made covering the excess, and no order passed requiring the plaintiff to write it off. The trial judge refused to grant the motion upon either or any of the grounds, and the defendant excepted.

We think the court erred in refusing a new trial. The declaration alleged that the plaintiff had been damaged in the sum of $200 by the negligent killing of the mules by the defendant, and the jury by their verdict gave him a larger sum than he claimed in the declaration. The amount of damages claimed in the declaration is the limit of the plaintiff's recovery, and, where the verdict is rendered for a greater sum, the court should set it aside, unless the plaintiff amends his declaration to cover the excess. In this case there was no amendment, and no offer to amend, either before or after the verdict, to cover this excess of damages; nor did the court require the plaintiff to write off the excess, as he should have done if he was otherwise satisfied with the verdict. Giles v. Spinks, 64 Ga. 205; 2 Sedg. Dam. (7th Ed.) 614; 5 Amer. & Eng. Enc. Law, 53; 3 Estee, Pl. & Pr. § 4909; 1 Tidd, Pr. 697; Decker v. Parsons, 11 Hun, 295; Corning v. Corning, 6 N. Y. 97; Manson v. Robinson, 37 Wis. 339; Kelley v. Third Nat. Bank, 64 Ill. 541. It is claimed, however, by counsel for the defendant in error, that this case has been pending nearly 10 years; that the proven value of the mules was $175; and that interest on this amount up to the time of the verdict, at 7 per cent., would make the sum found by the jury; that the jury did not find as the principal debt more than the amount laid in the declaration, but added the $78.25 as interest, and therefore the verdict was for more than was claimed in the declaration. While the jury in a case like this may add interest to the value of the property which has been injured, if they do so it is really not interest, but damages. They cannot find so much principal and so much interest, as they could upon a promissory note, but their verdict must be for so much damages, although it may include interest, against the defendant; and, if the amount thus found is in excess of the amount claimed in the declaration, the verdict is illegal, and should be set aside, unless the declaration is amended, or the court requires the excess to be written off. The court, therefore, should have granted a new trial upon this ground; and we will say that, if he had granted it upon the other grounds set out in the motion, we would have sustained his judgment in so doing. The evidence upon the last trial was not materially different from what it was when this case was here before, (82 Ga. 190, 8 S. E. Rep. 417,) and it was then held that a verdict against the defendant was contrary to the evidence, and the grant of a new trial by the court below was approved on this ground. We reverse the judgment, with directions that the case be tried again in the court below, unless the plaintiff should elect to dismiss his action. Judgment reversed.

CHARLOTTE, C. & A. R. CO. v. WOOTEN et al.

(*Supreme Court of Georgia.* May 8, 1891.)

CARRIERS OF GOODS—LOSS—DAMAGES.

Though goods saved by a common carrier from the perils of a freshet were damaged by passing through the freshet, yet if some not saved are unaccounted for, and it is not shown that the freshet caused their loss, or what their condition was when they disappeared, a recovery for their value may be had against the carrier without deducting anything for conjectural damage which they may have sustained by reason of the freshet before the loss occurred.

(*Syllabus by the Court.*)

Error from city court of Richmond; W. F. EVE, Judge.

Pope Barrow, for plaintiff in error. *Fleming & Alexander,* for defendants in error.

BLECKLEY, C. J. The question is whether the goods lost by the carrier, and never delivered, should be paid for as sound or as damaged goods. If they were damaged, it was by a freshet, and without fault of the carrier. The goods not lost or stolen were damaged, but there is no direct evidence that those which disappeared were damaged, or, if so, to what extent. So far as appears, they were never seen during or after the freshet, and consequently to say that they were damaged when the carrier lost possession of them would be a mere conjecture. They might or might not have been stolen during the confusion in business occasioned by the freshet, and when stolen they may or may not have been damaged. It seems that the burden of proof on this subject must necessarily rest upon the carrier. It had the custody of the property, and that custody has been lost, exactly when does not appear. We can discover no reason for holding that, under the evidence, the jury made any mistake in finding the value of the goods as proved, irrespective of the mere chance that their value may have been impaired before they were lost. There was no error in denying a new trial. Judgment affirmed.

McCORD et al. v. LAIDLEY et al.

(*Supreme Court of Georgia.* May 8, 1891.)

SALES—REFUSAL TO ACCEPT—DAMAGES.

Laidley & Co. sold to McCord & Son a car-load of bacon, to be shipped to Augusta and paid for on delivery. They shipped the bacon, and drew on McCord & Son a draft payable on demand, which was presented before the arrival of the bacon. McCord & Son refused to pay the draft, and directed the bank to which it was sent for collection to return it to Laidley & Co., stating at the time that they would refuse to accept the bacon because the sellers had violated their contract in demanding payment before the money was due. Afterwards the bacon arrived, and the agent of Laidley & Co. tendered it to McCord & Son, and gave them an opportunity to accept and pay for it, which they declined to do. The bacon was then sold by Laidley & Co.'s agent for the best price that could be obtained in the Augusta market, but, bacon having declined in price, it brought less than McCord & Son had agreed to pay. *Held,* that McCord & Son were liable to Laidley & Co. for the difference between the contract price and the net proceeds of the sale of the bacon.

(*Syllabus by the Court.*)

Error from city court of Richmond; W. F. EVE, Judge.

Charles Z. McCord and *Harrison & Peeples,* for plaintiffs in error. *F. W. Capers, Jr.,* for defendants in error.

LUMPKIN, J. The substantial facts of this case are stated in the head-note. The draft which Laidley & Co. drew on McCord & Son for the price of the car-load of bacon was payable on demand. This was entirely consistent with the contract between the parties that the bacon was to be paid for on arrival, and the draft, therefore, was not improperly drawn. The only mistake about it was that it was presented for payment before the bacon arrived, and was therefore presented too soon; but certainly this fact did not give to McCord & Son the right to repudiate the entire contract, and refuse to accept and pay for the bacon when it did arrive. If a note payable at a future day should be given for the purchase of personal property to be delivered when the note was paid, and by mistake or inadvertence payment of the note was demanded before its maturity, all that the maker need do would be to decline payment, and notify the other party that he must wait until the note became due before demanding payment, thereof. The present case seems to be one entirely analogous to the one supposed. There is ample evidence to sustain the conclusion that, simply because the draft was presented to McCord & Son before the bacon reached Augusta, they sought to repudiate and cancel the entire transaction; and also that, when the bacon did arrive, and they were afforded an opportunity to accept and pay for it, which they refused to do. We see no reason, in view of these facts, for setting aside this transaction, or denying to Laidley & Co. their right to recover what they lost by reason of the decline in bacon, and the refusal of McCord & Son to comply with their contract. The motion for a new trial contains various exceptions to the charges and refusals to charge of the court, but in none of them do we find any error requiring a new trial. It seems quite plain, from a careful examination of the record, that exact justice has been done in this case. Judgment affirmed.

WHITE et al. v. MAGARAHAN et al.

(*Supreme Court of Georgia.* May 8, 1891.)

DEEDS—RECORDING—RIGHTS OF GRANTOR'S CREDITORS.

1. A voluntary deed from a husband to his wife dated November 19, 1887, and witnessed by two unofficial persons, was handed by the maker to the clerk for record, February 9, 1888. The latter refused to record it for want of legal attestation. Whereupon the maker acknowledged it was his deed, and the clerk signed his name officially under the usual attestation clause, "signed, sealed, and delivered in presence of us," and

recorded it. *Held*, that this record was not notice of the execution of the deed at the time it bears date to a creditor of the maker, who extended credit on the faith of the property covered by the deed after its execution, and before record.

2. When a course of dealings begins between parties, and credit is extended by one to the other on the faith of particular property, the legal presumption is that this property is relied on for all credit given while the dealings continued, until there is some notice or agreement to the contrary, such dealings covering a period of only a few months.

3. The verdict being inevitably right in any view of the case as presented, it was error to grant a new trial.

(Syllabus by the Court.)

Error from superior court, Richmond county; H. C. RONEY, Judge.

J. R. Lamar, for plaintiffs in error. Salem Dutcher, for defendants in error.

LUMPKIN, J. The firm of Durst, Shea & Co., of which Magarahan was a member, obtained credit from White & Co. upon the faith of a statement made for the purpose of obtaining the credit to the Bradstreet Mercantile Agency, dated October 4, 1887, and signed by the firm and Magarahan individually, in which it was represented that the latter owned real estate to the value of $16,000. White & Co. sold various bills of goods to Durst, Shea & Co., the last credit being given in January, 1888. November 19, 1887, Magarahan, by a voluntary deed, conveyed to his wife for life the land referred to in said statement, with remainder to his children by her in life at the time of her death, and, if none, the property to revert to himself. The deed was witnessed by two unofficial persons. February 9, 1888, Magarahan carried it to the clerk of the superior court, and requested him to record it. The latter refused to do so, remarking, in substance, that it must have an officer as a witness, whereupon Magarahan acknowledged that it was his deed, and the clerk signed his name officially as a witness under the usual attestation clause, and then took the deed and recorded it. According to the testimony of Magarahan, all the indebtedness of his firm to White & Co. up to the date of the deed was actually paid. Assuming this to be true, the debt for the payment of which White & Co. now seek to subject the land was for goods sold and delivered after the execution of the deed, and before its record. White & Co. had no notice of the existence of this deed until after it was recorded. By making the deed, Magarahan left himself practically insolvent.

1. The counsel for Mrs. Magarahan, who claimed the property levied on for the benefit of herself and children, insisted that the deed of Magarahan was legally recorded, and was therefore constructive notice to White & Co. of its existence from the time it bore date, because it was actually recorded in accordance with the provisions of section 1778 of the Code within three months after the execution thereof. In our opinion, the deed was not legally recorded. Section 2706 of the Code provides that, in order to authorize the record of a deed executed in this state, it must be attested by one of certain mentioned officers, including the clerk of the superior court; or, subsequent to its execution, acknowledged in the presence of one of these officers. The section further provides that the fact of such acknowledgment must be certified on the deed by the officer in order to entitle it to be recorded. The provisions of this section were not observed as to the deed before us. It was not signed, sealed, and delivered in the presence of the clerk, and therefore what appears to be an attestation of witnessing the deed by him does not set forth the truth. What transpired between the maker of the deed and the clerk may have amounted to an acknowledgment of the deed by the former, but the fact of such acknowledgment is not certified on the deed by the officer as the law requires. A statement in the attestation clause of the deed that it was executed in the presence of the clerk is not a statement that it was acknowledged before him. Attestation and acknowledgment are different acts. Attestation is the act of witnessing the actual execution of a paper, and subscribing one's name as a witness to that fact. Acknowledgment is the act of a grantor in going before some competent officer and declaring the paper to be his deed; and, to make such acknowledgment good in law, it must be accompanied by the certificate of the officer that it has been made. In Webb on Record of Title, § 69, the author says the certificate should state the fact of the acknowledgment, and by whom made, using substantially, at least, the statutory language in stating these matters; and also the certificate must show a compliance with the law by a specific statement of the facts constituting a valid acknowledgment. See, also, 1 Amer. & Eng. Enc. Law, tit. "Acknowledgment," and Bouv. Law Dict., same title. It is immaterial whether the record of the deed conveyed notice to White & Co. from February 9, 1888, or not, because the transactions between them and Durst, Shea & Co., so far as extending credit to the latter is concerned, had all ended before the actual record of the deed. The law at that time being that, if this deed was legally recorded within three months from its execution, the record should be constructive notice to all parties, taking effect from the date of the deed itself, it appears that claimant's rights, as asserted by her, are based upon a mere technical rule of the law. To enforce alleged rights resting on this foundation against one who extended credit upon the faith of this very property, it is incumbent upon the claimant to show that she has strictly complied with the law itself. This, we have seen, she failed to do, because it is clear that this deed was neither attested nor acknowledged in such manner as to entitle it to be placed on record. It therefore certainly was no notice to White & Co. prior to the time of its actual record, and they in justice, and by strict law, should be protected, and payment to them secured for all goods sold and delivered on the faith of this property after the execution of the deed and before its record.

2. It is quite apparent from the testimony in this case that White & Co. extended credit to Magarahan's firm on the faith of the property set forth in the statement made to the Bradstreet Agency, and mainly upon the real estate referred to therein. The statement was made for this very purpose. Having no knowledge that the deed had been executed, they continued to extend credit undoubtedly on the faith of the same property, only a few months elapsing between the beginning and end of the dealings between these firms. This is a common-sense view of the matter, is the legal presumption in such cases, and is the only reasonable conclusion to be gathered from the testimony in the case. If Magarahan wished White & Co. to understand that this property should no longer be the basis of credit in their dealings with his firm, he ought to have given them distinct notice of the fact, or, at least, to have so executed his deed that the record thereof would be notice to them according to law. Having failed to do either, the presumption remains that White & Co. continued to sell on the faith of this property, and there is no reason appearing in the record to conclude otherwise.

3. Under the facts of this case, and in view of the illegal record of the deed, but one legal conclusion could result, viz., a verdict finding the property subject; section 1778 of the Code providing that such a deed shall not be of any force against a creditor who in good faith, and without notice, may become such before the actual recording of the same. Various charges and rulings of the court are complained of in the motion for a new trial, but we have not scrutinised them closely to ascertain whether they were erroneous or not. It is unnecessary to do so, because, the verdict being inevitably right for the reasons already stated in this opinion, it was error to set it aside, and grant a new trial. Judgment reversed.

GEORGIA RAILROAD & BANKING CO. v. WALKER.

(Supreme Court of Georgia. May 8, 1891.)

REPEAL OF STOCK LAW — KILLING STOCK — EVIDENCE.

1. The fact that the people of a certain section had held a mass-meeting, and agreed to disregard the "stock law," does not repeal the law, and evidence of such fact should not have been admitted.

2. In an action against a railroad company for the negligent killing of a cow, evidence that the company had at different times paid other persons for cattle killed by its trains at the same place was irrelevant and inadmissible.

3. When the evidence shows conclusively that the servants of a railroad company used all ordinary and reasonable care and diligence to prevent the killing of a certain cow, a verdict in favor of the owner for the value of the animal is contrary to law and the evidence, and should be set aside.

(Syllabus by Simmons, J.)

Error from superior court, McDuffie county; H. C. RONEY, Judge.

W. B. Cumming and *Bryan Cumming*, for

plaintiff in error. *S. A. Walker*, for defendant in error.

Judgment reversed.

THOMPSON v. EASLEY.

(Supreme Court of Georgia. May 27, 1891.)

HIGHWAYS — DEDICATION — REMOVING OBSTRUCTIONS — JURISDICTION OF ORDINARY.

1. Though a lane established by two coterminous proprietors, and embracing an equal strip from the land of each, was originally intended only as a way for cattle, yet, if used for more than seven years as a general way by both proprietors and those to whom they conveyed the land, the successors of neither could close up the lane, or the part taken from his own land, as against the successors of the other.

2. In such case, the ordinary has jurisdiction, under section 788 of the Code, to remove the obstruction.

(Syllabus by the Court.)

Error from superior court, Whitfield county; THOMAS W. MILNER, Judge.

W. K. Moore, J. R. McCamy, and *W. C. Glenn,* for plaintiff in error. *McCutchen & Shumate,* for defendant in error.

LUMPKIN, J. 1. In 1856 or 1857 Haynes and Burns were adjoining land-owners. There being no way for their cattle to get to the range except by a circuitous route, they agreed, in 1858, to open a lane between them 14 feet wide, each giving half of the way, and building his fence in accordance with their agreement. Haynes sold his land to Johnson in 1863, who held possession until he sold to Easley, in 1884. Thompson was the successor in title of Burns. It appears from the evidence that this lane, though originally intended only for the passage of cattle, was for many years used by the owners of the land on both sides of it as a general way, and that it was so used by any one who had occasion, and was a general public convenience. This state of things continued for perhaps 20 or more years, certainly for a much longer time than 7 years, and the evidence discloses that at various times work was done upon the lane so as to make it suitable for hauling wood and rails, and for traveling on horseback or otherwise. While the various persons who held under Haynes testified that they had never "claimed" any right of way over this lane, a fair construction of their testimony leads to the conclusion that they certainly understood they had this right, but simply did not assert the same in words, because, in fact, there was no denial of it; the use of the land as a general way being well known to Thompson, and he having for long years acquiesced therein. Finally Thompson moved his fence out to the middle of the lane, thus retaking possession of so much thereof as came originally from his side. It was to remove the obstruction thus made by Thompson that proceedings were instituted by Easley before the ordinary. In the case of Craven v. Rose, 8 Rich. 72, the supreme court of South Carolina went so far as to hold that, where proprietors of adjoining lots contribute strips of land to form a lane common for the use of both, and one, after he has acquired a right of way by prescription over the other's strip, puts an obstruction on his own strip, even that does not destroy his right of way over the other's land. In Townsend v. Bissell, 4 Hun, 297, the doctrine was recognized that successors in title derive from their grantors all their rights to the use of a way established by agreement between coterminous proprietors, and it was held therein that, "when the owners of adjoining lots make a way between them, each setting off an equal portion of land for that purpose, and they and their grantees continue to use it in common as a way for a period of twenty years, the inference is that such use was under a claim of right and adverse." The same case is reported in 6 Thomp. & C. 565. If the lane in controversy in the present case had never been used for any purpose except as a way for cattle, no right of prescription to it as a general way could have arisen; but as it was not confined to the use originally intended, and for more than seven years had been used by the owners of the adjoining lots, their tenants and other persons, as a general way, we are of the opinion that section 731 of the Code is applicable. The general use of this land, as stated, was practically a denial that it was only a way for cattle, and an assertion of a right to use it for other purposes, and therefore such general use grew into a prescriptive right. In answer to the argument that, under section 728 of the Code, providing for the opening of a private way by agreement among land-owners, no right of way could arise in favor of vendees of the original owners, unless the fact of the opening of such private way was entered on the road-book, it may be said that this section does not refer to the right of prescription, but under it such vendees may acquire a right of way irrespective of the time the way may have been used by them, and this section does not interfere with the acquirement of a right of way by prescription, under section 731 of the Code.

2. It follows, from what has been said, that the ordinary had jurisdiction, under section 738 of the Code, to cause the obstructions placed in this lane by Thompson to be removed. Judgment affirmed.

ELECTRIC RY. CO. OF SAVANNAH v. SAVANNAH, F. & W. RY. CO.

(*Supreme Court of Georgia.* May 27, 1891.)

TEMPORARY INJUNCTION—NEWLY-DISCOVERED EVIDENCE—REOPENING CASE.

1. The controversy involving disputed facts as well as grave questions of law, there was no abuse of discretion in granting an injunction until a trial can be had upon the merits of the cause.

2. It is discretionary with the judge sitting at chambers, upon an application for injunction, to reopen the case for more testimony, upon the discovery of additional witnesses by one of the parties after argument, and while holding up the matter for decision. Warren v. Bunch, 80 Ga. 134, 7 S. E. Rep. 270. Nothing to the contrary was decided in Huff v. Markham, 70 Ga. 284, or in Boyce v. Burchard, 21 Ga. 74.

(*Syllabus by Blockley, C. J.*)

Error from superior court, Chatham county; ROBERT FALLIGANT, Judge.

Charlton & Mackall, for plaintiff in error. *Erwin du Bignon & Chisholm,* for defendant in error.

Judgment affirmed.

FOOTE v. GORDON, Governor.

(*Supreme Court of Georgia.* May 27, 1891.)

CRIMINAL LAW—BAIL—FORFEITURE.

1. A recognizance for the appearance of the accused to answer to an indictment for the offense of larceny will cover larceny from the house, and is not restricted to simple larceny.

2. An indictment charging burglary, and also larceny from the house, will serve as a basis for forfeiting a recognizance binding the party to appear and answer for larceny.

(*Syllabus by the Court.*)

Error from superior court, Whitfield county; T. W. MILNER, Judge.

Maddox & Longley and *R. J. & J. Mc-Camy,* for plaintiff in error. *A. W. Fite,* Sol. Gen., for defendant in error.

SIMMONS, J. Nettie McAfee entered into a recognizance with Foote, the plaintiff in error, as one of her sureties, whereby she bound herself "to be and appear at the next superior court of said county to be held on the first Monday in October next, from day to day, and from term to term, then and there to answer to a bill of indictment for the offense of larceny, with which she stands charged, and shall not depart thence without the leave of said court," etc. At the October term of the court the grand jury returned a true bill against her for burglary, and for larceny from the house. Upon her failure to appear, after being duly called, a judgment *nisi* was taken, and a *scire facias* issued calling upon her and her securities to show cause at the next term of the court why final judgment should not be entered up against them. Foote, one of the sureties, showed for cause, in substance, that he agreed to be bound for the appearance of Nettie McAfee at the October term of the court to answer to a bill of indictment charging her with the offense of larceny, but that the indictment which was afterwards found charged her with the offense of burglary; that he thought the offense of which she stood charged was a misdemeanor; but that being indicted for the offense of burglary, as to which the punishment is greater than for larceny, to-wit, imprisonment in the penitentiary, the risk was much greater than he had agreed to assume. Upon demurrer, this plea was stricken for insufficiency, and Foote excepted. It was contended here by counsel for the plaintiff in error that the offense being mentioned in the recognizance as larceny, it meant simple larceny; and, as the principal was indicted for larceny from the house, a different kind of larceny from that mentioned in the recognizance, the sureties were not bound to produce her to answer either for burglary, or larceny from the house. We think that when the sureties bound themselves for the appearance of their principal to answer for the offense of larceny, larceny from the house was included as well as simple larceny. The word "larceny" in a recognizance is not restricted to simple larceny. People v. Dennis, 4 Mich. 616.

2. It was also argued by counsel for the plaintiff in error that, inasmuch as the indictment charged the principal with burglary, which is a higher and graver offense than larceny, it would increase his risk if he were bound to produce her to answer for the offense of burglary. As the plaintiff in error, in bringing up the record material to a clear understanding of the errors complained of in this case, failed to bring up the judgment *nisi* forfeiting the recognizance, we cannot know whether the recognizance was forfeited because the principal failed to appear and answer to the charge of burglary, or because she failed to appear and answer to the charge of larceny from the house. The judgment of the court recites that the defendant was also charged in the indictment with larceny from the house, which would indicate that the judgment *nisi* recited that she was called to answer for that offense. The judgment *nisi* not being before us, we are authorized to presume it does recite that she was called to answer for larceny from the house, and, if so, the sureties were bound to produce her to answer for that offense, as we have shown above. For authorities holding that the condition of the recognizance is broken when the indictment charges a greater offense than that named in the recognizance, see Crutchfield v. State, 24 Ga. 335; Adams v. State, 22 Ga. 417; also Brandt, Sur. § 436; State v. Tennant, 30 La. Ann. 852; State v. Cole, 12 La. Ann. 471; State v. Cunningham, 10 La. Ann. 393; Pack v. State, 28 Ark. 235. Judgment affirmed.

ERWIN v. HARRIS.

(Supreme Court of Georgia. July 8, 1891.)

SALES BY SAMPLE—DELIVERY—RIGHT TO INSPECT —WAIVER—DAMAGES.

1. The evidence introduced by the defendant himself showing that the contract and the terms of it were in writing, by means of correspondence, the defense that the contract was void for the want of writing is overcome by the proof.

2. A contract for the sale of five car-loads of oats, at a stipulated price per bushel, f. o. b. cars at a given point, does not contemplate that delivery on the cars to the carrier at that point should be a delivery to the purchaser, where the seller takes the bill of lading to his own order, and attaches it to a draft drawn on the buyer, transmitting the draft and bill of lading to a banker of the city of the buyer's residence. Under such circumstances, the fair inference would be that both parties contemplated delivery at such city, and payment of the price upon delivery.

3. The sale being made by sample, the buyer was entitled to inspect the oats before paying the draft drawn for the price, and where the shipment embraced two car-loads only, and the buyer refused to pay the draft covering the price of these, upon the ground that the cars had not arrived, and he had no opportunity to inspect, and thereupon the banker caused the draft to be protested for non-payment, this did not justify the seller in not sending forward the other three cars according to contract.

4. A subsequent purchase of the same two car-loads of oats by the same purchaser from the broker of the seller, after the seller had declined to forward the other three car-loads, was no waiver of the right of action for a breach of contract in failing or refusing to forward them.

5. The contract contemplating delivery by the seller to the buyer at the city of the latter's residence, the measure of damages for failing to deliver the three car-loads was the difference between the stipulated price and the market price at that city when the delivery ought to have been made, less the freight.

(Syllabus by the Court.)

Error from city court of Macon; C. J. HARRIS, Judge.

S. A. Reid, for plaintiff in error. *M. W. Harris,* for defendant in error.

SIMMONS, J. 1. Erwin, the plaintiff in error, pleaded, among other things, the statute of frauds. One of his assignments of error in the motion for a new trial was that the verdict was in favor of Harris, and contrary to the charge of the court; the court having charged, in substance, that if the buyer bought of the defendants the five car-loads of oats f. o. b., at 21 cents, the contract would be void under the statute of frauds, if the oats were worth more than $50, and the contract was not in writing, and if the buyer had accepted none of the goods, nor given anything in earnest to bind the bargain or in payment. The testimony of Erwin, the defendant in the court below and plaintiff in error here, shows that there was a correspondence between him and Harris by mail and by telegraph, the letters and telegrams showing the price of the oats and the terms of the contract agreed upon. This evidence of the plaintiff in error shows that the contract was in writing, and was not void because in violation of the statute of frauds.

2. Erwin wrote Harris from Pilot Point, Tex., that he had five car-loads of oats, which he wished to sell, and sent Harris a sample, naming his price for the oats. Harris telegraphed him that he would take the five car-loads at 21 cents per bushel, free on board cars at Pilot Point. This offer was accepted by Erwin by telegram. Erwin shipped promptly two car-loads of the oats, sending drafts with the bill of lading attached. The oats were consigned to Harris, at Macon, Ga., and the bill of lading attached to the drafts was taken by Erwin to his own order, and sent by him to a bank in Macon. The bank presented the draft to Harris, and he refused to pay, on the ground that he had a right to inspect the oats before paying, and on the trial urged the further ground that he had purchased five car-loads, and Erwin had only sent two. It was contended by counsel for the plaintiff in error that when Harris made the offer of 21 cents, and it was accepted by Erwin in Texas, and Erwin placed the two car-loads of oats free on board the cars, that amounted to a delivery of the oats to Harris, in Texas. The general rule is that when one orders goods from a distant place to be shipped by a common carrier, and the order is accepted and the goods shipped, the delivery to the common carrier is a delivery to the purchaser, the common carrier being the agent of the purchaser to receive them; and when this is done the title, without more, passes from the vendor to the vendee. If, however, the vendor of the goods

is not satisfied of the solvency of the purchaser, or is doubtful thereof, or wishes to retain the title in himself, he may vary this rule, when he makes the consignment and delivers the goods to the carrier, by taking a bill of lading from the carrier to his own order. When the vendor does this, it is evidence that he does not part with the title of the goods shipped, but retains the same until the draft which he sends with the bill of lading is accepted or paid; and, when the title is thus reserved in the vendor or consignor, the carrier is his agent, and not the agent of the consignee, and the risk is the consignor's, and not the consignee's. Erwin, the consignor, having taken the bill of lading to his own order, and attached it to the drafts drawn on Harris, and sent them to the bank in Macon, Ga., delivery to the carrier in Texas was not a delivery to Harris. Under these facts, the title remained in Erwin, the consignor, and the delivery to Harris was contemplated to be at his residence in Macon, payment of the price to be made by him there on delivery. See Bennett's Benj. Sales, (1888,) § 381; 2 Schouler, Pers. Prop. § 391; Blackb. Sales, (2 Eng. Ed.) 162; Newmark, Sales, § 147 et seq.; Dows v. Bank, 91 U. S. 618; Bank v. Wright, 48 N. Y. 1; Bank v. Jones, 4 N. Y. 497; Bank v. Logan, 74 N. Y. 568; Bank v. Bangs, 102 Mass. 291; Bank v. Crocker, 111 Mass. 163; Bank v. Dearborn, 115 Mass. 219.

3. The court charged the jury, in substance, that, if the oats were sold by sample, the buyer had a right to examine and inspect them in bulk before paying for them, and the denial of this right would be a reason for non-payment of the draft; that the contract sued on was an entire contract; and that if they found that Erwin did ship two of the five cars of oats, and demanded pay for the two cars as soon as shipped, and the buyer refused payment, he had a right to refuse, and his refusal did not excuse the shipper from sending the balance. There was no error in either of the propositions submitted to the jury in this charge. Where a vendor sells goods by sample, and draws a draft on the vendee for the purchase price thereof, the vendee certainly has a right, before paying the draft, to inspect the bulk of the goods purchased. When goods are sold by sample, there is an implied warranty on the part of the seller that the bulk of the goods will come up to the standard of the sample. It was contended by counsel for the plaintiff in error that, although there might be an implied warranty that the goods were equal to the sample, still Harris should have paid the drafts, and, if the oats when they arrived did not equal the sample which had been sent to him, he could sue Erwin for breach of warranty. Harris might have done this if Erwin had lived in the same county or state, but, as Erwin resided in the distant state of Texas, a suit against him there would have cost more, perhaps, than the difference would have amounted to between the price of oats of the grade contained in the sample, and the price of inferior oats in bulk. The better rule and practice is to allow the purchaser to inspect the bulk before requiring him to pay. On the right of the purchaser to inspect before payment, see 2 Schouler, Pers. Prop. § 406; Newmark Sales, § 260; Bennett's Benj. Sales, § 699. The second proposition contained in this extract from the charge, in our opinion, was also sound. The contract for the purchase of the oats was entire. Harris had a right to insist that all the five cars should be delivered to him, and be inspected by him, before he paid for any of them. He purchased five cars, and Erwin agreed to sell and deliver him five cars at his place of residence, as we have heretofore shown. Erwin, therefore, had no right to deliver two cars at a time and draw drafts on Harris for the purchase price. When, therefore, he delivered or proposed to deliver a quantity less than he sold, Harris had a right to refuse it. There is no indication in the record that any specified quantity was to be delivered in car-loads from time to time. Nor was there any proof that there was a general custom of the trade authorizing Erwin to deliver at different times a less quantity than the entire contract called for, and draw drafts for the same before his contract was completed. See Benj. Sales, (Bennett's,) § 690; Newmark, Sales, § 35 et seq.; 2 Schouler, Pers. Prop. § 388. The case of Branch v. Palmer, 65 Ga. 210, was relied on by counsel for the plaintiff in error; but, while this court there held that the contract was an entire one, that case is different in its facts from this. The facts of that case show that Palmer was to purchase 600 bales of cotton for Branch, to be delivered in different lots and at different times, and that the custom of the trade was that he had a right to draw for the amount due on each lot as it was shipped. This court held, upon these facts, that, when Branch refused to pay the drafts thus drawn, Palmer was not bound to carry out and complete the contract. A contract may be an entire one, and yet contain stipulations for a delivery by installments, as in the contract between Branch and Palmer; but in the contract under consideration, as we have before remarked, there was no understanding or agreement that the five cars were to be delivered by installments, nor was there any custom proved which would authorize Erwin to draw on Harris before the completion of the entire contract. The court was right, therefore, in instructing the jury that the refusal of Harris to pay for the two cars of oats did not relieve Erwin from sending the other three cars.

4. After Harris had refused to accept or pay the draft drawn for the two car-loads of oats, and Erwin had declined to forward the other three car-loads, and had turned over the two car-loads to a broker to be sold on his account, Harris purchased these oats from the broker. It was contended by counsel for the plaintiff in error that, when he purchased the identical car-loads of oats from Erwin's broker, he waived his right of action for a breach of the contract in failing to forward the other three cars. We do not think Harris waived his right of action by purchasing the two car-loads from the

broker. The broker had them for sale, and Harris had the same right to purchase them that any one else had. The contract was abrogated by the failure of Erwin to perform his part of it. There was no reason to forbid Harris from going into the market and purchasing the oats.

5. The court charged the jury, in substance, as to the measure of damages, that, if they found for the plaintiff, they could find the difference between the price contracted for and the market value at the time of the failure of the defendant to ship the oats. Counsel for the plaintiff in error contended that, if Harris was entitled to recover, he would only be entitled to recover the difference between the cost of the oats in Texas when the contract was made and the price at the same point when Erwin refused to deliver them, because, he claimed, the point of delivery was in Texas. We have shown in the former part of this opinion that the point of delivery under this contract was not in Texas, but in Georgia, and therefore the measure of damages for failure to deliver the three car-loads was the difference between the stipulated price and the market price in Macon when delivery ought to have been made, less the freight. Judgment affirmed.

GEORGIA S. & F. R. Co. v. SMALL et al.

(*Supreme Court of Georgia.* July 8, 1891.)

EMINENT DOMAIN—FAILURE TO TENDER COMPENSATION—APPEAL.

There being no tender made by the company on the basis of the first verdict or award in the condemnation proceedings, there was no taking by the company for public use on that basis, and it was not error on the trial of an appeal to admit evidence of the value of the property at the time of the appeal trial, and to instruct the jury to assess compensation accordingly.

(*Syllabus by the Court.*)

Error from superior court, Bibb county; A. L. MILLER, Judge.

Gustin, Guerry & Hall and *Dessau & Bartlett*, for plaintiff in error. *R. W. Paterson* and *Robt. Hodges*, for defendants in error.

SIMMONS, J. This bill of exceptions recites "that, during the April term of the superior court of Bibb county, there came on to be heard a certain cause, wherein A. B. Small, trustee, was complainant, and the Georgia Southern & Florida Railroad Company was defendant, the same being an action to enjoin the said railroad company from the further prosecution of condemnation proceedings to condemn certain lands in the city of Macon belonging to said complainant, which condemnation proceedings had been instituted under the charter of said railroad company; and also the case of the Georgia Southern & Florida Railroad Company v. A. B. Small, trustee, said last-mentioned case being a statutory proceeding to condemn the property of said Small, trustee, for the use of said railroad company, and then and there pending upon appeal from the verdict of the jury in said condemnation proceedings; both of which cases were by the order of the court consolidated and tried together; and, both parties having announced ready in both cases, a jury was impaneled to try the same." The bill of exceptions then goes on to recite that, pending the trial, the court allowed certain witnesses to testify as to the value of the property at the time of the trial. This was objected to upon the ground that the testimony sought to be elicited was illegal, for the reason that the value of the property to be submitted to the jury was the value at the time of the condemnation proceedings in July of the preceding year and not its value at the time of the pending trial, (May, 1890;) which objection was overruled by the court, and the witnesses allowed to answer the questions. The company excepted, and assigned error thereon. The judge charged the jury as follows: "The sole issue for the jury, on this branch of the case, is to determine the present value of the property, located as it is in the city of Macon, at the present time, and for that purpose may be used all the testimony that throws any light upon that question of the present value of the property." To this charge the company also excepted, and assigned the same as error. The constitution of the state declares (Code, § 5024) that "private property shall not be taken or damaged for public purposes without just and adequate compensation being first paid." It appears from the above recital of facts set out in the bill of exceptions that the railroad company had, under its charter, in July, 1888, instituted condemnation proceedings for the purpose of taking this land from Small for its use. A jury had been summoned by the sheriff in accordance with the provisions of the charter, and they had assessed the value of the land. Small, being dissatisfied with the verdict, appealed to the superior court, and at the same time filed a bill seeking to enjoin the railroad company from condemning the land. The only question made by this record is whether, on the trial of the appeal in the superior court, the value to be assessed by the jury should be the value of the land at the time of the condemnation proceedings in July, 1888, or its value at the time of the trial of the appeal, May, 1890. This question depends upon what time the taking is complete, so as to authorize the railroad company to take possession of the land. Under the clause of the constitution above quoted, the land-owner must first be paid, before the railroad company is entitled to take his property and go into possession of it. If both parties are satisfied with the award of the jury summoned to assess the value of the property, the railroad company must pay the amount assessed before it can take possession. If the owner is dissatisfied, and appeals to the superior court, and the railroad desires immediate possession, it must tender the amount assessed by the jury before it can go into possession. In the case of Oliver v. Railroad Co., 83 Ga. 257, 9 S. E. Rep. 1086, this court held that the tender of the sum assessed and awarded, duly made and continued, but refused, is the equivalent of actual payment of the awa in its effects on the right of the corp tion to enter upon the land and prosecute the work of construction. If this company had tendered to Small the amount assessed by the jury in the condemnation proceeding, it might have had the right at the time to take possession of the property, and a tender, properly made and continued, would have been equivalent to an actual payment. It is not necessary, however, to decide definitely this particular question. We have carefully scrutinized this record, and there is no indication or intimation therein that any tender of the amount assessed was made by the company to Small. There was consequently no taking by the company for public use, and it was no error on the trial of the appeal to admit evidence of the value of the property at the time of the trial; nor was there any error in the charge of the court above recited. If a tender had been made and continued, then the value of the property at the time it was assessed in the condemnation proceeding might have been the proper basis for estimating its value at the appeal trial; but, inasmuch as the record does not show that tender was made, there was no taking, and no right of possession, and the value at the time of that trial was the proper basis. Judgment affirmed.

LOGAN v. WESTERN & A. R. CO.

(Supreme Court of Georgia. July 13, 1891.)

CORPORATIONS—EXPIRATION OF CHARTER—RIGHT OF LEGISLATURE TO CONTINUE CHARTER IN FORCE.

1. When not checked by contract, the legislature may vary by a special law any of the privileges, powers, rights, duties, or obligations of a particular corporation, except such as by an existing general law are common to all corporations; but provisions applicable alike to all must remain applicable to each until they are changed by a general law. Hence with section 1679 of the Code in full force, which declares that all corporations have the right to sue and be sued, to have and use a common seal, to make by-laws, to receive donations, to purchase and hold property necessary for the purpose of their organization, and to do all acts necessary for the legitimate execution of this purpose, the legislature cannot hinder the charter of a business corporation from expiring, and the corporation from being dissolved, by enacting a special law declaring that the charter be continued in force for the purpose of terminating suits and litigation pending against the corporation at the time of the expiration of its charter, and forbidding that the corporate existence should be construed as extended for any other purpose. A legal entity, with no right or power but that of defending itself against pending actions, is not a living corporation.

2. By an existing general law, (Code, § 1684,) every corporation is dissolved by expiration of its charter. As the constitution declares that laws general in their nature shall have uniform operation throughout the state, the Western & Atlantic Railroad Company was dissolved when its charter expired.

3. Existing general laws provide for enforcing the rights of creditors against corporations both before and after dissolution, and the constitution inhibits the enactment of any special law in a case provided for by an existing general law.

4. A writ of error pending in the supreme court against a corporation when its charter expires will be dismissed on motion.

(Syllabus by the Court.)

Error from superior court, Gordon county; THOMAS W. MILNER, Judge.

J. M. Neal, T. C. Milner, and Glenn & Maddox, for plaintiff in error. O. N. Starr and R. J. McCamy, for defendant in error.

SIMMONS, J. When this case was called, a motion was made to dismiss it on the ground that the charter of the Western & Atlantic Railroad Company had expired on the 27th of December, 1890. The motion was resisted, because, it was said, the legislature had passed an act which was approved December 26, 1890, continuing the charter in force for the purpose of terminating suits and litigation pending against the corporation at the time of the expiration of its charter. Counsel for the movant contended that the act was unconstitutional. The head-notes in this case will fully explain the views of the court, and are so full and exhaustive that I deem further elaboration unnecessary. All that need be added, for a clear understanding of the case, is the language of the Code, (sections 1679, 1684, 1688,) and of the act of 1890. Section 1679 is as follows: "All corporations have the right to sue and be sued; to have and use a common seal; to make by-laws binding on their own members, not inconsistent with the laws of this state and of the United States; to receive donations by gift or will; to purchase and hold such property, real or personal, as is necessary to the purpose of their organization; and to do all such acts as are necessary for the legitimate execution of this purpose." Section 1684 is as follows: "Every corporation is dissolved (1) by expiration of its charter; (2) by forfeiture of its charter; (3) by a surrender of its franchises; (4) by the death of all its members without providing for a succession." Section 1688 is as follows: "Upon the dissolution of a corporation, for any cause, all of the property and assets of every description belonging to the corporation shall constitute a fund, first, for the payment of its debts, and then for equal distribution among its members. To this end the superior court of the county where such corporation was located shall have power to appoint a receiver, under proper restrictions, properly to administer such assets under its direction." The act of 1890 is as follows: "An act to extend the charter of the Western & Atlantic Railroad Company for purposes of litigation. Section 1. Be it enacted," etc., "that the charter of the Western & Atlantic Railroad Company, approved October 24, 1870, shall be continued of full force and effect as to such suits and litigation as may be pending against it at the time of its expiration, as though such expiration had not occurred, and the assets of the company shall be subject to such final judgment as may be recovered in such litigation, and the Western & Atlantic Railroad Company is empowered to make any and all the defenses to such litigation as it might have made before such expiration; that nothing in this act shall be construed to extend the existence of said corporation for any other purpose than that of continuing till its close the litigation referred to in this section. Sec. 2. Be it further enacted that all laws and parts of laws in conflict with this act be, and the same are hereby, repealed." Writ of error dismissed.

LATHROP et al. v. ADKINSON.

(Supreme Court of Georgia. July 8, 1891.)

DESCENT AND DISTRIBUTION — ACTION BY HEIR — AMENDMENT OF PLEADINGS — PARTIES — EVIDENCE.

1. The amendment did not introduce a new cause of action; nor was it improper because one of the defendants resided in another county; nor did it render necessary the making of other parties defendant.

2. An agreed synopsis of the evidence of a deceased witness, together with the stenographer's report in full of said evidence, was not objectionable on either of the two grounds presented.

3. A nonsuit was properly denied.

4. Heirs at law of a deceased partner take no better title on division of the assets than the partner himself or the partnership had.

5. No special rule of evidence, with respect to force and clearness, is applicable to the facts of this case.

6. Where an agreement is relevant merely as evidence of intention, it matters not whether one of the parties was legally competent to represent a third person in making it or not.

7. The charge requested in the fifth subdivision of the fourth ground of the motion was properly refused.

8. According to the decision of this court on the former writ of error, the charge set forth in the seventh ground of the motion was correct.

9. The verdict was warranted by the evidence, and not contrary to law.

10. The defendants not having severed in their defense as to mesne profits, and there being nothing in the record to show that the question as to what each severally was liable for was presented to or passed upon by the court below, the question as to such several liability is not for adjudication by this court.

(Syllabus by the Court.)

Error from superior court, Houston county; A. L. MILLER, Judge.

W. L. Grice, for plaintiffs in error. Hardeman, Davis & Turner, for defendant in error.

SIMMONS, J. The pleadings and evidence in this case, with the exception of an amendment to the pleadings hereinafter noticed, will be found reported in the case of Lathrop v. White, 81 Ga. 29, 6 S. E. Rep. 834. The judgment was then reversed, and the theory made by the evidence which had not been submitted to the jury was directed to be submitted to them on the next trial. To meet this suggestion or direction, when the case came on for a second trial in the superior court, the plaintiff offered an amendment to her declaration, alleging, in substance, that her guardian, George H. White, had died pending the suit; that her father, W. T. White, having become indebted to Lathrop & Co., moved to Louisiana without having paid the debt, and there died; that after his death George H. White, her guardian, made an arrangement with Lathrop & Co. that the rents, issues, and profits of the land should go to Lathrop & Co. until said indebtedness of W. T. White was paid; and that under said arrangement White, the guardian, paid out of the rents, issues,

and profits of said land $785, up to and including the year 1879; that during that time said guardian remained in possession of the land, paying taxes on it; that in the year 1879 said guardian removed from Houston county to Pulaski county; that he rented the land to Parker before removing, having appointed Houser to collect the rents and turn them over to Lathrop & Co.; that in that way Houser got possession of the land, and collected and paid sums aggregating $1,806.50, for the years 1880 to 1887, inclusive; that said sums largely overpaid the indebtedness due to Lathrop & Co.; that the plaintiff was entitled to recover said lands, and "the rents thereof, for four years prior to the bringing of said suit, and reasonable rents during said time;" that she had attained her majority since the filing of the suit; and she prayed that the suit might proceed in her own name. To this amendment the defendants objected (1) because it introduced a new cause of action; (2) that Mrs. Lathrop was the only real claimant to the land, and that she lived in Chatham, and not in Houston, county, where the suit was pending; and (3) that Lathrop & Co., through their surviving partner, Warren, should be made a party defendant. All of said objections were overruled, and the amendment was allowed.

1. There was no error in allowing this amendment. It did not introduce a new cause of action. The evidence on the former trial made the same questions that the amendment now makes, and it was upon this evidence that the direction was given in the former case that the question should be submitted to the jury. The allegations in the amendment were therefore made to correspond to the proof in the case. Nor was it improper to allow the amendment because the real defendant resided in a different county. She had been made a party in the original declaration, and was properly served, and had appeared and pleaded, and the court thereby obtained jurisdiction of her person. This having been done, any proper amendment could be made to the declaration, although she resided out of the county where the suit was pending. She was the real claimant of the land, and the other defendants named in the original declaration were the tenants in possession. The action was complaint, seeking to recover the land and mesne profits. It was therefore unnecessary to make Lathrop & Co. or the surviving partner parties to the action. If there were equities between Mrs. Lathrop and the partnership or the surviving partner, the plaintiff in this action was not interested therein, and these equities should be determined between them in another action, to which this plaintiff would not be a necessary party.

2. When this case was brought here before, counsel for both sides agreed on a brief of evidence, which was approved by the court. In making this agreement they took the report as written out by the official stenographer, and struck therefrom the questions and other irrelevant matter, and filed in the clerk's office the brief thus agreed upon and approved. On the sec-

ond trial, George H. White, the guardian, having died, his testimony on the former trial, which had been agreed upon in the brief of evidence and approved, was offered by the plaintiff. The defendant objected to the testimony being read, because, under the amendment which was allowed, the issues were not substantially the same as on the former trial, and because the brief as offered showed that it did not contain the whole of White's testimony, much of what purported to be his testimony having been expunged and otherwise altered before approval. When this objection was made, counsel for the plaintiff offered the whole of White's testimony as it appeared in the stenographer's report before the alterations were made, and the court admitted it over objection. The court did right in overruling the objections. The amendment allowed, as before remarked, did not change the issues in the case. They were substantially the same, and the parties to the action were the same. Code, § 3782. We think the testimony of this witness in the brief of evidence agreed upon on the former trial was admissible by itself. The defendants and their counsel brought the case here when their motion for a new trial was overruled, and their counsel must have made out the brief of evidence. He was not likely to put anything in the brief that was not true, or to leave out anything that would illustrate the issues in the case; and when both counsel agree to a brief of the evidence, and it is approved by the court, testimony of a witness since deceased or inaccessible, contained therein, is admissible. Adair v. Adair, 39 Ga. 75; Smith v. State, 28 Ga. 23. In the case last cited it is said: "The test surely ought to be no more than this: Is it probable that the admission admits only what is true, that the judgment (of approval) sanctions only what is true. For the truth is all that justice requires; and, taking this as the test, the paper in question would, it is certain, be admissible. Is it likely that the parties agreed to anything as proved that was not proved, even though the only purpose of this agreement was to comply with the requisitions of the law as to new trials, and the law as to writs of error? Is it likely that the court would have approved as true anything that was not true, even though the purpose of the approval was merely to comply with the requisitions of these same laws? Certainly it is not. Surely, all will agree that a paper thus agreed to by the parties, and approved by the court, will be more trustworthy on the question, what was the evidence delivered on the trial, than the daily fading recollection of persons who happened to hear the evidence when it was so delivered." Of course, if there was anything material of the deceased witness' testimony left out of the agreed brief by mistake or inadvertence, or because at that time it was not deemed material, it could be supplied by either party; and this was done when the court allowed the whole testimony of the deceased witness, as taken down by the stenographer, to be read to the jury.

3. At the conclusion of the testimony of the plaintiff, the defendant moved for a nonsuit, and the motion was overruled by the court. The court did not err in refusing to grant the motion. There was sufficient evidence to authorize him to submit it to the jury.

4. Counsel for the defendant in error requested the court to charge as follows: "If you believe that upon the death of J. W. Lathrop, Sr. and Jr., and the dissolution of the partnership of J. W. Lathrop & Co., the effects of the late firm were divided out by agreement among the heirs at law and the surviving partner, and that in this division one-third fell to Mrs. M. A. Lathrop, and she took this land as part of her share, and took a conveyance for it from the other parties, and, in consideration of what she got in this division, she gave up to the other two parties her interest in the other assets about whose title there was no dispute, this made her a *bona fide* purchaser for value; and if this division took place after the alleged arrangement between Geo. H. White and J. W. Lathrop & Co., referred to in the amendment, her right to this land could not be affected by such an arrangement, unless she had notice of it, and the burden of proof is on the plaintiff to show that she had such notice."

If all the facts set out in this request were true, the court should not have given it in charge to the jury. The main question in issue between the parties on this trial was, to whom did the land belong,—in whom was the legal title? If, therefore, Mrs. Lathrop had no legal title to the land, it was immaterial and irrelevant in what manner she procured the title under which she claimed. If Lathrop & Co. had no title to the land, and she procured the title under which she claimed by the division of the assets of the firm, she got no better title than the firm had. Nor did she get any better title than her deceased husband would have had if the assets had been divided during his life; and if, in taking this land as part of her portion of the assets of the firm and of her deceased husband, she gave up other assets about the title of which there was no dispute, the interest of the plaintiff in the court below should not be affected thereby; nor would these facts make Mrs. Lathrop a *bona fide* purchaser, so far as the rights of Mrs. Adkinson, the plaintiff, were concerned. Both parties stood in relation to each other upon their respective titles. If Mrs. Lathrop had the legal title, she would have been entitled to retain the land. If she did not have the legal title, and the plaintiff did, the plaintiff would be entitled to recover the whole land, and not merely one-third, as the court was requested to charge in the second subdivision of the request.

5. The court was also requested to charge that, "when an attempt is made to set up a parol agreement concerning land, like the one referred to in the amendment, the proof of the agreement should be clear and satisfactory." Under the facts of this case, no special rule of evidence with respect to force and clearness was applicable. The agreement set up in the amendment was not concerning the title

to land, but was only as to how the rents should be disposed of.

6. The court was requested to charge as follows: "If George H. White was not at that time guardian, and had no interest in this land, he had no right to bind anybody by any such agreement, and it could not be enforced, even if proved." "If Lathrop & Co. received from Boon a transfer of the bond for titles, and Boon was not a party to the agreement referred to in the amendment, but the agreement was made between George White and Lathrop & Co., and no money or other thing of value was paid or expected to be paid to Lathrop & Co., and no improvements were made or to be made by Geo. White or the plaintiff, and the agreement was simply that Lathrop & Co. should have the use or rents of the land till the debt due them by W. T. White was paid in rents, such an agreement, if made, was a *nudum pactum*, and cannot be enforced." In the former decision of this case, on the question of this contract or agreement, this court said: "White, the guardian, however, contends that Lathrop & Co. never went into possession of this land. He claims that when Boon surrendered the possession he surrendered it to him, and that he and Warren, one of the partners of Lathrop & Co., made a verbal contract, whereby it was agreed that White should take the land and rent it, and pay the debt of his brother, and when that was done the land should belong to his ward. This Warren denies. The court below seemed to take a different view of the case from what we have taken, and failed to submit this matter to the jury. We think that, if White made this contract with Warren, that he was to take the land and rent it, and pay the debt of his brother, and after the debt was paid the land was to go to his ward and niece, then, if the debt was paid, she would be entitled to it. But if there was no such contract as that made, and Warren only gave him twelve months in which to redeem the land, and he failed to redeem it, then, of course, she cannot recover. This is a matter entirely for the jury, as to which theory they will adopt after hearing the evidence. If the case should be tried again in the court below, we presume that the court will submit this matter to the jury, under proper instructions."

According to this ruling, the trial judge submitted the question to the jury, and by their verdict they must have found that White's theory was true. The request recited above was that the court should charge that, if White's testimony was true, White was not authorized to make such an agreement, and it could not be enforced, and was a *nudum pactum*. We still think, if such an agreement was made by White with Warren, one of the firm of Lathrop & Co., the plaintiff would be entitled to recover. It does not matter, under the facts of the case, whether White had authority to make the agreement or not, or whether the agreement by itself could be enforced in a court of law: the great and controlling fact which the agreement demonstrates is the inten-

tion of Warren as to the capacity in which the firm would hold the land. If White's testimony is true,—and the jury has so found,—Warren never intended to assert title to the land. He only intended to hold it under the bond for titles of Boon until the debt due his firm was paid from the rents. Other facts in the case tend to confirm the testimony of White. A very important fact was that several years after the contract was made with Boon, and the agreement with George White, Lathrop & Co. sent George White a statement of the balance due on the deceased White's account. This shows that Lathrop & Co. did not consider their debt against W. T. White paid by their surrender of the notes and judgment against Boon. W. T. White, the father of the plaintiff, being thus indebted to Warren's firm, and having given it the two notes of Boon for $500 each for the balance of the unpaid purchase money, as collateral security for his debt to the firm, the firm sued Boon on the notes and obtained judgment. Whereupon Boon agreed with the firm to surrender the land to it, and the firm agreed to cancel his notes. He transferred his bond for titles to the firm of Lathrop & Co. Lathrop & Co. did not pay a dollar of their own money to Boon or to White for the land. All they paid Boon for the land was the assets which they had received from W. T. White, their debtor, as collateral security. When they canceled their notes and the judgment thereon against Boon, and he agreed to surrender the land, and transferred his bond for titles, it did not amount to placing the title to the land in Lathrop & Co., but was only an exchange of collaterals. Lathrop & Co. gave up their notes and judgment, and took in lieu thereof the land as collateral. The agreement with Boon did not pass the title, because the title was still in W. T. White, or in the plaintiff as his sole heir at law, he being dead. When a pledgee with whom collaterals have been placed as security for an antecedent debt changes the character of collaterals upon a note or mortgage to land or other property without the consent of the pledgeor, it does not amount to a payment of the debt, but the pledgee holds the new collateral upon the same terms and conditions as he held the old. And while the new collateral is thus held by the pledgee, if any rents or profits are made by him, he must account therefor to the pledgeor; and if the rents or profits are sufficient to pay the debt, the debt becomes canceled, and the pledgeor is entitled to recover the collateral. Coleb. Coll. Sec. §§ 182, 183; Jones, Pledges, §§ 659, 660; Story, Bailm. § 343; Brown v. Tyler, 8 Gray, 139; Montague v. Railroad Co., 124 Mass. 242; Dalton v. Smith, 86 N. Y. 176–183; Depuy v. Clark, 12 Ind. 427; Gage v. Punchard, 6 Daly, 229; Hoyt v. Martense, 16 N. Y. 231; Diller v. Brubaker. 91 Amer. Dec. 177; Richardson v. Mann, 30 La. Ann. 1060; Conyngham's Appeal, 57 Pa. St. 474. As before remarked, Lathrop & Co. did not obtain the title to this land, because a the time the contract between t' Boon was made W. T. White ' and the title, never having p him, was in his estate. Nor did he or his legal representative agree to the change of the collateral to be made by Lathrop & Co. The agreement shows that, according to the real intention of the firm as expressed by Warren at the time, this holding was to be in conformity with the general rule of law applicable to such a case, and was not treated as an adverse holding to the estate of W. T. White. For these reasons the court did not err in refusing to give the requests above copied.

7. The court charged the rule as laid down by this court in that part of the opinion above quoted, to which charge the defendant excepted, making it the seventh ground of his motion for a new trial. There was no error in giving this charge.

8. The verdict was warranted by the evidence.

9. It was claimed by counsel for the plaintiff in error that that verdict was contrary to law, "for the reason that mesne profits were found not only against Mrs. Lathrop, the owner of the land, but also against Houser, the agent, and against the tenants, all of whom were moving for a new trial; that some of these tenants did not rent the place for more than two or three years, and all of them paid a stipulated rent to Houser, who forwarded it to Lathrop & Co.; that Houser was the agent to collect these rents; and having done this, as both parties admit, the tenants were discharged from any further liability." Upon the trial of the case the tenants did not sever in their defense as to the mesne profits. The record does not show that any question was made or presented to the court as to what each was severally liable for, nor did the court pass upon the question. It not having been made before the trial judge, and ruled upon by him, it is not for adjudication here. Judgment affirmed.

CENTRAL RAILROAD & BANKING CO. v. BRUNSWICK & W. R. CO.

(Supreme Court of Georgia.   July 13, 1891.)

RAILROAD COMPANIES — COLLISIONS — ORDINANCE REGULATING SPEED — ACTION FOR DAMAGES— EVIDENCE.

1. Where a railroad company and its employe are both injured by the same negligence of another railroad company, the first company has no right, in an action for its own damages against the second, to sue also for the use of its employe to recover the damages sustained by him in excess of those already paid to him by the plaintiff in the action.

2. Railroad companies and their employes using railways in a city must take notice of all valid city ordinances duly promulgated.

3. Where a collision between the plaintiff's train and the defendant's train occurred on a track used by them in common, while the plaintiff or its agent was engaged in the violation of a valid city ordinance limiting the rate of speed in the running of trains in the city, and the jury believed from the evidence that the collision would not have occurred but for such violation, the plaintiff could not recover; but not appearing that the defendant could have avoided the consequences of the plaintiff's negligence after becoming aware of the same.

4. If a city ordinance regulating the speed of trains embrace in its language the whole area of the city, and is reasonable in itself, the court may submit to the jury the question as to whether, on account of the special local conditions and surroundings, it would or would not reasonably apply to the particular locality in question, that locality being just inside of the city limits.

5. The verdict was warranted by the evidence.

(Syllabus by the Court.)

Error from superior court, Dougherty county; ALLEN FORT, Judge.

Lawton & Cunningham and *R. F. Lyon,* for plaintiff in error. *D. H. Pope,* for defendant in error.

SIMMONS, J. 1. The Central Railroad & Banking Company brought an action against the Brunswick & Western Railroad Company, alleging that an engine belonging to plaintiff had been damaged to the amount of $1,000, and its engineer, Scoville, had been seriously injured by a collision between said engine and a train of defendant, which resulted from the negligence of the latter. The declaration set forth in detail the injuries alleged to have been sustained by the engineer. It also alleged that plaintiff had paid out large sums of money, specifying the amounts, for expenses incurred in the nursing of the engineer, physicians' and druggists' bills, and also that plaintiff had compromised and settled the claim of said Scoville against it for the injuries he had sustained by paying the sum of $2,000, which was inadequate and insufficient to compensate him for the damage he had sustained. The declaration prayed a recovery against defendant, not only for the damage to its property and the sums paid out for and to Scoville, as aforesaid, but also for the damages sustained by him in the personal injuries he had received in excess of the amount paid him therefor by plaintiff, the latter alleging that it sued for this last-named item for the use of the said Scoville. Upon demurrer, the court below struck out of the declaration all parts thereof that sought a recovery for the use and benefit of Scoville, and this ruling is assigned as error.

There can be no question that plaintiff had the right to sue for any injuries to its own property, or for any injury it may have sustained in the loss of its engineer's services, and expenses flowing directly therefrom, which may have been caused by defendant's negligence. But we are at a loss to perceive how the plaintiff can maintain an action for personal injuries received by Scoville for any amount exceeding what it had actually paid him on this account. For injuries received by him, and for which no compensation had been made to him by plaintiff, he, and he alone, in our opinion, would be entitled to sue the defendant. It is not alleged in the declaration that Scoville assigned to the plaintiff any right of action he may have had against the defendant, and certainly plaintiff is in no better position to bring suit for his use than it would have been to sue in its own right if such assignment had been made. If it be alleged in reply that plaintiff was seeking this particular recovery, not for its own benefit, but for the use and benefit of Scoville himself, the answer is that Scoville was competent to bring suit in his own name and right, and no

reason appears why he should not do so.
Even if he had attempted to assign his
claim against the defendant to the plaintiff, we do not think this could have been
done. In Comegys v. Vasse, 1 Pet. 212, it
was held that a right of action for mere
personal torts was not assignable; and to
this effect, see Gardner v. Adams, 12 Wend.
297, and Rice v. Stone, 1 Allen, 566. A
right of action is not assignable "if it does
not directly or indirectly involve a right
of property;" and hence an assignee's
claim of a right to sue for fraud to his assignor cannot be enforced. Dayton v.
Fargo, 45 Mich. 153, 7 N. W. Rep. 758. This
same question has been frequently passed
upon in cases where disputes arose as to
what rights of bankrupts passed to their
assignees, and in such cases it has generally been held that such assignees could
not maintain actions for injuries to the
person of the bankrupt. 2 Add. Torts,
§ 1300, and cases cited. Among the latter
is that of Howard v. Crowther, 8 Mees. &
W. 601, in which Lord ABINGER held that
causes of action purely personal do not
pass to the assignee, but the right to sue
remains in the bankrupt. In Marshall v.
Means, 12 Ga. 67, Judge LUMPKIN quotes
approvingly another opinion of Lord AB-
INGER, delivered in the case of Prosser v.
Edmonds, 1 Younge & C. 481, sustaining
the doctrine that a bare right to file a bill
or maintain a suit is not assignable. Says
the opinion referred to: "It is a rule, not
of our law alone, but that of all countries,
that the mere right of purchase shall not
give a man a right to legal remedies. The
contrary doctrine is nowhere tolerated,
and is against good policy. All our cases
of maintenance and champerty are founded on the principle that no encouragement
should be given to litigation by the introduction of parties to enforce those rights
which others are not disposed to enforce."
No doubt authorities in conflict with those
above cited may be found, but our own
Code, at least by implication, seems to
settle the question that causes of action
arising from torts are not assignable.
Section 2243 classes such rights as choses
in action, but the next section provides
expressly that choses in action arising upon contract may be assigned, and is silent
as to the assignment of choses in action
arising upon tort. It would seem. therefore, under the rule, *expressio unius ex-
clusio alterius*, that the latter are not assignable in this state. Such was the ruling
of this court, and we think it sound, in
Gamble v. Banking Co., 80 Ga. 599, 600, 7
S. E. Rep. 315. The court, therefore, did
not err in sustaining the demurrer to so
much of the declaration as sought a recovery for the use of Scoville.

2. Valid ordinances ordained by the
mayor and council of a city are binding
upon all persons who come within the
scope of their operation, and no reason
occurs to us why railroads and their employes should not be thus bound. It
would be something quite unusual, and
not justified by any precedent of which
we are aware, if special notice had to be
given to these corporations, or their servants, of the existence of such ordinances.

3. The evidence shows that the collision
took place on a track used in common by
the two railroad companies. The court,
in effect, charged the jury that defendant,
when using this track, would have the
right to suppose that the plaintiff, coming in with its train, would run in accordance with the provisions of a valid ordinance of the city of Albany; and further
instructed them that, in case they believed
there would have been no collision if the
plaintiff had observed that ordinance,
then the plaintiff would not be entitled to
recover. In the same connection he left
the jury to determine whether or not the
ordinance in question was reasonable in
its application to the locality where the
accident occurred. Upon this portion of
the charge comment will be more particularly made in the next division of this
opinion. Under the facts of this case,
there was no error in the charge given.
It was equivalent to instructing the jury
that running a train within the limits of
a city, at a speed prohibited by a valid
ordinance, would be negligence on the part
of the plaintiff. This is certainly a correct statement of the law; and, inasmuch
as the evidence shows conclusively that
defendant, after becoming aware of this
negligence on the part of the plaintiff,
could not have avoided the consequences
of it, it follows plainly that the plaintiff
ought not to recover. Even if the defendant was to some extent negligent, the
above assertion remains true, because it
is equivalent to stating in other language
the provision contained in section 2972 of
the Code, viz.: "If the plaintiff, by ordinary care, could have avoided the consequences to himself caused by defendant's
negligence, he is not entitled to recover."
The court's language meant that, if the
jury found that defendant was negligent,
yet if plaintiff, by ordinary care,—that is,
by obeying the city ordinance,—could have
escaped injury notwithstanding defendant's negligence, it could not recover, and
this is our understanding of the law.

4. It was contended by counsel for
plaintiff in error that the city ordinance
was unreasonable in its application to
the particular locality where this accident
occurred; and the assignment of error upon the charge given in reference to this
subject implies that the court ought to
have so declared. Instead of doing so,
the court left the jury to determine, in
view of all the facts and circumstances
of the case, whether there was a necessity
for the ordinance in this particular locality,
and whether or not the operation of it
at this place was reasonable. This was a
very fair and proper method of disposing
of this question. The jury, with all the
facts before them, were competent to decide it fairly. The charge submitted to
them impartially the contentions of both
sides as to the necessity and reasonableness of the ordinance, and they were, perhaps, better qualified to reach a just conclusion on the subject than the judge himself. At any rate, he saw proper to submit
this question to them, and we are unable
to see that in so doing he committed any
error. To justify courts in declaring void
an ordinance limiting the speed of trains
within a city, its unreasonableness, or

want of necessity as a police regulation for the protection of life and property, must be clear, manifest, and undoubted. Knobloch v. Railway Co., 31 Minn. 402, 18 N. W. Rep. 106. In the case just cited, the crossing at which a cow was killed was in the plat of the city, but the surrounding country was similar to the open country outside of the city, and the street similar to a common country road, there being no graded streets within three-quarters of mile, and no houses within a quarter of a mile, in the direction of the built-up portion of the city, but the street seems to have been a good deal traveled. GILFILLAN, C. J., remarked: "While it may be true that a higher rate of speed through the portion of the city in question would be consistent with the public safety, we cannot say it is so clearly and manifestly the case that we can hold the passage of the ordinance an abuse of discretion on the part of the common council." The fact that the railroad owned the land on which the injury occurred did not relieve it from the operation of the ordinance. Whitson v. City of Franklin, 34 Ind. 397; Mers v. Railway Co., 88 Mo. 677, 1 S. W. Rep. 382; Crowley v. Railroad Co., 65 Iowa, 658, 20 N. W. Rep. 467, and 22 N. W. Rep. 918; Green v. Canal Co., 38 Hun, 51; Horr & B. Mun. Ord. §§ 239, 145. As to reasonableness of ordinance generally, and rule as to pronouncing void, see Horr & B. Mun. Ord. § 188 et seq.; Meyers v. Railroad Co., 57 Iowa, 555, 10 N. W. Rep. 896; Railroad Co. v. State, 19 Amer. & Eng. R. Cas. 83. The rule is laid down in Horr & Bemis, supra, that the question whether an ordinance regulating the speed of trains in a city is reasonable, or unreasonable and void, is for the court. In this case the court ruled that the ordinance was, in itself, valid and reasonable, but held that the application of it to the particular locality in question was reasonable or otherwise according as certain facts were or were not established, and left it to the jury to determine whether or not these facts existed. We think that in thus acting the court disposed of both questions in the proper manner.

5. The verdict was warranted by the evidence, and, having been approved by the trial judge, will not be disturbed. Judgment affirmed.

WEED v. MAYOR, ETC., OF CITY OF SAVANNAH.

(Supreme Court of Georgia. July 13, 1891.)

MUNICIPAL CORPORATIONS—STREET IMPROVEMENTS —CONSTITUTIONAL LAW.

1. The special acts of September 5, 1885, and October 1, 1887, empowering the mayor and aldermen of Savannah to improve the streets and levy local assessments therefor, are not unconstitutional as special laws, or for any other reason brought to the attention of this court.

2. There was no abuse of discretion in denying the temporary injunction prayed for.

(Syllabus by the Court.)

Error from superior court, Chatham county; ROBERT FALLIGANT, Judge.

Chas. N. West, for plaintiff in error.
Saml. B. Adams, for defendants in error.

LUMPKIN, J. In 1885 the general assembly passed an act authorizing the mayor and aldermen of Savannah to pave, and otherwise improve, the streets of said city, and providing for the assessment of a portion of the cost of such improvements upon real estate abutting on the street improved, etc. In 1887 another act was passed authorizing said mayor and aldermen to require paving and otherwise improving the streets of said city, and to levy and collect assessments for the same. The plaintiff in error insists that these acts are violative of paragraph 1, § 4, art. 1, of the constitution. (Code, § 5027.) That paragraph provides that "no special law shall be enacted in any case for which provision has been made by an existing general law;" and, further, that "no general law affecting private rights shall be varied in any particular case, by special legislation, except with the free consent, in writing, of all persons to be affected thereby." No provision has ever been made by any general statute of this state as to how municipalities shall cause or require the paving of streets to be done, or other local improvements to be made therein, nor for collecting the cost thereof. An act, therefore, which empowers a particular city to make such improvements, or require the same to be made, and to collect a portion of the cost thereof by assessment upon the property abutting on such streets, is not a special law infringing that clause of the constitution first above quoted. This proposition, to our minds, is so clear and plain that simply stating it is sufficient, without argument. Again, there is no general statute of which we are aware exempting the citizens of the cities and towns in this state from imposition of assessments for improving public streets on which their property abuts; hence there are no "private rights" in the nature of such exemption which would be varied by the passage of an act authorizing a particular city to make such improvements in its streets, and to levy assessments therefor. It seems equally clear, therefore, that the acts above mentioned do not vary any "general law affecting private rights," and we make the same remark with reference to the second paragraph of the constitution, above quoted, as we did concerning the first. We have given the interesting and ingenious argument of the learned and gifted counsel who presented this case for the plaintiff in error our most careful attention and thorough consideration, but it fails to convince us of any fallacy or error in the simple statements we make above as to the constitutional questions presented in this case. If his views prevailed, improvements in the streets of our cities and towns could never be made at all upon the assessment plan, unless the legislature should see proper to pass a general law on the subject applicable alike to every city and town in the state, which would certainly be exceedingly inconvenient to many, if not most, of them. Indeed, the opposition to such a law would be so great we doubt the possibility of its enactment. Be this as it may, we cannot think either that the framers of the constitution intended to make the passage of such a law necessary in order that paving and other like work in cities and towns, where expedient or desirable, might be carried on, or that such a conclusion is fairly deducible from any language in that instrument itself. To press the argument of counsel for plaintiff in error to one extreme to which it might lead, it would follow that all municipal charters in this state must be in all respects identical, a result manifestly undesirable and altogether impracticable. In our judgment the acts recited are not unconstitutional for the reasons assigned, or for any other reason to which our attention has been called, either by the record or the argument submitted. The trial judge did not abuse his discretion in denying the temporary injunction.

Judgment affirmed.

TRIPPE v. McLAIN et al.

(Supreme Court of Georgia.   July 13, 1891.)

SALES—BREACH OF WARRANTY—RIGHTS OF SELLER.

Although it may be true that machinery purchased at the price of $600 is, in its present condition, inefficient and worthless, yet where, by undisputed testimony, it appears that, by the expenditure of $50, it could be repaired and made to perform good work, it is not worthless so as to entitle the purchaser to keep it without paying for it.

(Syllabus by the Court.)

Error from city court of Cartersville; SHELBY ATTAWAY, Judge.

J. B. Conyers, for plaintiff in error.   J. A. Baker, for defendants in error.

BLECKLEY, C. J.   Under the evidence in the record, the trial of this case in the court below had an improper result. The machinery was purchased at the price of $600, and, by the undisputed testimony, an expenditure of $50 would be sufficient to repair it and make it perform good work. It is therefore not worthless so as to entitle the purchaser to keep it without paying for it, although in its present condition it may be inefficient, and, if left in that condition always, would be worthless. Granting that there was no substantial error committed by the court in its charge to the jury, or otherwise during the progress of the trial, the verdict is not sustainable, and a new trial should be had for that reason. The court erred in not granting it.   Judgment reversed.

LAMPKIN v. STATE.

(Supreme Court of Georgia.   July 13, 1891.)

ROBBERY—INDICTMENT—EVIDENCE.

1. The misjoinder of offenses in the same count of an indictment is matter of form, and, under the Code of Georgia, is no ground for arresting judgment upon a verdict finding the accused guilty in express terms of one of the offenses so charged.

2. Robbery by force and robbery by intimidation are not two offenses, but different grades of the same offense, and both may be charged in the same count.

3. Robbery by intimidation was a felony prior to the act of March 20, 1866, and was not reduced to a misdemeanor by that act. Consequently it is still a felony. Where a bill, as passed by the general assembly, applies by number to one section of the Code, and, as enrolled, signed by the presiding officers of the two houses and approved by the governor, the completed act applies by number to another section of the Code, and the two sections relate to different offenses, the first to robbery and the second to rape, and where a subsequent act recognizes the law of rape as changed, but not the law of robbery, the result is that no change is effected in the law of robbery.

4. On a trial for robbery committed in a certain hotel, it is competent for the state to prove by the prosecutor that he hurried down from the hotel, and met a policeman on the street, to whom he made complaint that he had been robbed, and by the policeman that the prosecutor came down to him on the street, and said that he had been robbed at the hotel, that a certain named person had taken his money, and that the accused was present. The evidence indicating that all this took place immediately after the criminal act, and as a natural and probable consequence therefrom, it was admissible as a part of the *res gestæ*.

5. Although the prosecutor was intoxicated when he was robbed, it was not competent evidence for the accused that three nights previous thereto he was in a certain saloon intoxicated, and complained that two men were trying to rob him, but that he was prepared for them, and only carried two or three dollars with him. This was immaterial to the issue on trial, and was not admissible to discredit the prosecutor, who had testified that he did not go to the saloon, and had not made the statements attributed to him. Nor was it admissible because tending to show that he was in a state of drunkenness for several days prior to the alleged robbery, and while in that state was under the delusion that he was being robbed.

6. The presiding judge was warranted in finding, upon the affidavits adduced, construing them all together, that the juror alleged to be incompetent had not heard any of the evidence at the preliminary trial in the justice's court, and consequently that, whether he had formed and expressed an opinion or not, he might be a competent juror, his apparent incompetency, as indicated by some of the affidavits taken separately, being answered and explained by the others and the attendant circumstances.

7. When facts, and a witness by whom they can be proved, to manifest the incompetency of a juror, come to the knowledge of counsel for the accused, after the jury are sworn, but before any further step in the trial has been taken, the question of the juror's competency should then be raised and submitted to the court. It is not sound practice for counsel to remain silent, take the chances of acquittal for his client, and then, after conviction, urge the juror's incompetency as a ground for setting the verdict aside.

8. There was evidence to support the finding, and the newly-discovered evidence is not such as to require a new trial.

(Syllabus by the Court.)

Error from superior court, Clark county; N. L. HUTCHINS, Judge.

Barrow & Thomas, for plaintiff in error. R. B. Russell, Sol. Gen., for the State.

BLECKLEY, C. J.   1. The first ground of the motion in arrest of judgment attacks the verdict as founded upon an indictment which attempts to charge the accused in one count with two offenses, to-wit, robbery by force and robbery by intimidation. Were this ground true in fact, it would be no cause for arresting the judgment. It would render the indictment bad in form, but not in substance. Code, § 4628, declares that "every indictment or accusation of the grand jury shall be deemed sufficiently technical and correct which states the offense in the terms and language of this Code, or so plainly that the nature of the offense charged may be easily understood by the jury." And the next section declares that "all exceptions which go merely to the form of an indictment shall be made before trial, and no motion in arrest of judgment shall be sustained for any matter not affecting the real merits of the offense charged in such indictment." That two offenses are charged in the same count will not hinder the charging of either of them in the terms and language of the Code, and the jury may as easily understand the nature of each as if they were set forth in separate counts. It is true that the Code recognizes as a rule of good pleading that separate counts ought sometimes to be used, for it says, in laying down the form of an indictment: "If there should be more than one count, each additional count shall commence in the following form," etc. Section 4628, supra. But it fails to exact as necessary to the substance of an indictment more than one count. On the contrary, it prescribes, as the only test of substance, that the indictment shall state the offense in the terms and language of the Code, or so plainly that the nature of the offense charged may be easily understood by the jury. When an indictment should contain more than one count, and contains one only, it is bad in form, and is subject to exception before trial. But no motion in arrest of judgment can be sustained for any matter not affecting the real merits of the offense charged. Dividing the indictment into several counts has no effect whatever on the real merits of the offense or offenses charged. Such a defect has relation alone to the manner and form of setting forth the offense or the several offenses. It is a defect in the mode of pleading, and not in the substance or real merits of the matter pleaded. If the accused is unwilling to go to trial upon an indictment defective in form only, his remedy is to demur, or except in due time and manner. If upon being arraigned he shall demur to the indictment, his demurrer must be made in writing; and one object of the arraignment is to afford him an opportunity to demur to the indictment before trial. Code, § 4639. If he insists upon it, he has a right to be tried upon an indictment good in form as well as in substance. But if he neglects matters of form until after verdict, he is then too late. If he is found guilty in express terms of one of the offenses charged in the indictment, he may be sentenced for that offense, irrespective of whether it is charged alone or in conjunction with others in the same count. Since the language which we have quoted from the Code first came into our law, there have been several cases ruled by this court, in which it has been treated as law that two distinct offenses cannot be joined in the same count in an indictment. But there is no affirmative ruling that such joinder would be cause for arresting the judgment, though several adjudications, as we have just said, pronounce the practice bad pleading. We concur in this view, and would not hesitate to declare an overloaded count bad on exception or demurrer taken before trial. In dealing with such defects, the distinction we now make has not always been noticed, but it should have been. It was fully brought out in Williams v. State, 60 Ga. 88, in which case the indictment charged, in the same count, two felonies, to-wit, burglary in the night-time and larceny from the house. After a verdict of guilty of larceny from the house, a motion in arrest of judgment was made and overruled. This judgment was affirmed.

2. But the indictment in the present case does not charge two distinct offenses. Robbery by force and robbery by intimidation are two grades of the same offense, and both grades may be charged in the same count. This was expressly ruled in Long v. State, 12 Ga. 293.

3-8. The other questions involved in the case are carefully and explicitly dealt with in the head-notes. Judgment affirmed.

BAKER et al. v. DOBBINS.

(*Supreme Court of Georgia.* July 13, 1891.)

ORDERS—CONDITIONAL ACCEPTANCE.

1. When an order is drawn by the surviving member of a firm of contractors for a specific sum, with direction to "charge the same to firm on account of work done and to be done on your building now in process of erection," and the same is accepted in these terms, "I agree to pay the within order when the building is finished and received by Messrs. Bruce & Morgan," the acceptance is conditional upon the completion of the building by the drawer; and if, without fault of the acceptor, he fails to complete it, and the acceptor has it completed by others at his own expense, there can be no recovery in an action on the acceptance.

2. With or without the parol evidence brought out from the plaintiffs' witness on cross-examination, the judgment of nonsuit was correct.

(*Syllabus by the Court.*)

Error from city court of Cartersville; SHELBY ATTAWAY, Judge.

J. A. Baker, W. I. Heyward, and Harrison & Peeples, for plaintiffs in error. J. M. Neel, for defendant in error.

SIMMONS, J. Wallace & Collins made a contract with Dobbins whereby the former agreed to build a house for the latter. They were indebted to Baker & Hall, and, Wallace having died, Collins, the survivor of the firm, gave the following draft or order on Dobbins: "$300. Mr. Miles G. Dobbins: Please pay to Mess. Baker & Hall three hundred dollars, ($300,) and charge the same to firm of Wallace & Collins on account of work done and to be done on your building now in process of erection. This Decr. 24th, 1888. A. J. COLLINS, Survivor." On the back of this order was written as follows, to-wit: "I agree to pay the within order when the building is finished and received by Messrs. Bruce & Morgan. Dec. 24th, 1888. MILES G. DOBBINS." The evidence shows that Wallace & Collins failed to complete the building, and turn it over to Bruce & Morgan. Dobbins had advanced to Wallace & Collins the full amount for the work they had actually performed, and, when they failed to complete the house, he employed hands at his own expense, and had it completed. He refused to pay the draft, and Baker & Hall brought suit upon it, and the above-recited facts were put in evidence before the court and jury, and the plaintiffs closed their case. The court, on motion of the defendant's counsel, granted a nonsuit, to which the plaintiffs excepted. The draft or order was accepted by Dobbins on the condition that Wallace & Collins should complete the house, and that it should be received by Bruce & Morgan, who seem to have been the architects of Dobbins. He only agreed to pay the draft upon the completion of the building. The evidence does not show that the failure to complete it was on account of any fault of Dobbins. The building never having been completed by Wallace & Collins, the time of payment never arrived. Moreover, he agreed to pay it out of a fund of Wallace & Collins, to accrue to them by the performance of the contract, which, never being performed, the fund out of which the draft was to be paid never existed. 2 Rand. Com. Pap. § 522; Newhall v. Clark, 56 Amer. Dec. 741; Linnehan v. Matthews, (Mass.) 20 N. E. Rep. 433. The court was right, therefore, in granting a nonsuit. Judgment affirmed.

CENTRAL RAILROAD & BANKING CO. v. PATTERSON.

(*Supreme Court of Georgia.* July 20, 1891.)

PLEADING—AMENDMENT.

After a general demurrer to a declaration has been sustained, and the cause dismissed, by the superior court, and that judgment affirmed in the supreme court without condition or direction, the declaration is not amendable. The case of King v. King, 45 Ga. 195, is rested upon a misconception of two preceding cases, and is not authority, or, if authority, the same is hereby overruled.

(*Syllabus by the Court.*)

Error from superior court, Burke county; H. C. Roney, Judge.

Lawton & Cunningham, for plaintiff in error. *Twiggs & Verdery* and *Phil P. Johnston,* for defendant in error.

LUMPKIN, J. Patterson brought an action against the Central Railroad & Banking Company for personal injuries. Defendant demurred to the declaration, and the judgment of the superior court sustaining this demurrer was affirmed by this court, without condition or direction. 85 Ga. 653, 11 S. E. Rep. 872. When the *remittitur* was returned to the court below, and before defendant moved to make the same the judgment thereof, plaintiff moved to amend his declaration, which the court allowed him to do, over defendant's objection. We think the court erred. When the demurrer to plaintiff's original declaration was sustained, and that ruling was affirmed by this court, the plaintiff's case was entirely out of court, and there was nothing to amend by. An examination of the case of King v. King, 45 Ga. 195, will show that the ruling of this court therein was based upon an entire misconception of the two cases cited to sustain it, viz.: Sullivan v. Railroad Co., 28 Ga. 29, and Cothran v. Scanlan, 34 Ga.

555. In the former, a nonsuit was refused by the circuit court, and the judgment reversed by this court; and when the case went back the plaintiff, before the *remittitur* was entered, moved to amend his declaration so as to make it correspond with his proof. This court held the amendment should have been allowed. In the latter case complainant's bill was demurred to generally for want of equity, and the court below overruled the demurrer. That judgment was reversed by this court, and at the conclusion of the opinion WALKER, J., remarked: "As to the proposition to amend the bill, we apprehend that is a matter we had better let the court below pass upon, as was done in the case of Sullivan v. Railroad Co., 28 Ga. 29." As will be seen, the action of the court below in the two cases cited did not finally dispose of them. The judgments of this court, without more, would have so disposed of them; but suppose, in the first case, the judge below should have been disposed to grant a nonsuit, and had so announced, he certainly would have been authorized to allow the plaintiff to amend his declaration, so as to conform to his proof, before making the nonsuit final; and in the latter case Judge WALKER probably meant to suggest that the court below could allow complainant to amend his bill, upon the return of the case to that court, so as to state a cause of action, before finally dismissing the bill, but left this question open to be determined by the superior court. At any rate, the above statement will suffice to show that these cases were entirely different from the King Case. In Wynne v. Alford, 29 Ga. 694, the court below sustained a demurrer to complainant's bill, and ordered it dismissed; but this court, in affirming that judgment, granted leave to complainants to amend their bill. It was not, therefore, an absolute affirmance of the judgment below, which would take the case entirely out of court, but the leave to amend left it in such condition that the amendment could still be made. We think the correctness of our ruling, as stated in the head-note, is sufficiently apparent, without further discussion of the cases above cited. Judgment reversed.

FISHBURNE v. SMITH et al.

(*Supreme Court of South Carolina.* Aug. 12, 1891.)

JUDICIAL SALE—WITHDRAWAL OF BID—SALE FOR LESS THAN HIGHEST BID—EVIDENCE—APPEAL.

1. An agreement was made between a mortgagor and mortgagee that proceedings to foreclose the mortgage, which were then pending, should be withdrawn, and the land conveyed to trustees, who were authorized to sell the land, if the mortgage debt should not be paid on a certain day A sale by the trustees was set aside in an action brought by the mortgagor, and a resale was ordered to be made by the master. Held, that it was error to order the sale without a formal discontinuance of the foreclosure suit, as the pendency of such suit was a cloud on the title, and deterred bidding at the sale.

2. Where an agreement for the sale of mortgaged premises by trustees provided that the surplus, after paying expenses and the debt, should be paid to the mortgagor, the tender of the mortgagor's receipt on account of the surplus was not equivalent to a tender of the cash payment required by the terms of the sale.

3. Where the mortgagee bid a certain sum at the trustee's sale, but withdrew the bid at the suggestion of the trustee, and afterwards bid in the property for a much smaller sum, the sale was void.

4. The agreement requiring that expenses should be first paid, failure to make the cash payment required avoided the sale, although the mortgagee was the purchaser.

5. The mortgagee, having ignored the mortgagor's bid, cannot insist that, on failure to comply therewith, the mortgagor should forfeit all interest in the property, and that the mortgagee should be entitled to it on compliance with his own bid

6. Evidence of negotiations between the parties which culminated in a written agreement was incompetent.

7. Where no motion to suppress testimony was made at the trial, an exception that the court erred in not suppressing it will not be considered on appeal.

8. Where particular instances of misconduct are not specified, an exception that the court erred in not holding that the mortgagor, by improper conduct, had lost his right to object to the sale, will not be considered on appeal.

Appeal from common pleas circuit court of Colleton county; T. B. FRASER, Judge.

Action by Julian Fishburne against H. A. M. Smith and others to set aside a trustee's sale of mortgaged premises. Decree annulling the sale and granting other relief. Both parties appeal. Modified and affirmed.

After hearing the testimony, the court rendered the following decree: "This case is before me for a hearing on the merits in pursuance of an order made by consent at the term of court held in June, 1890. It has been heard on the pleading, and testimony taken out of court on notice in pursuance of the act. The parties were represented by counsel, and the cause fully argued; several exceptions to the testimony were noted: but I think it necessary to say only that I regard all testimony as to matters which occurred previous to the execution by plaintiff, 6th November, 1889, of the deed to H. A. M. Smith and A. M. Lee, as incompetent. Julian Fishburne, the plaintiff in this case, had given to H. A. M. Smith, one of the defendants in this case, a mortgage of a tract of land mentioned in the complaint, and known as 'Hoats,' to secure bonds, payable to Mrs. Lowndes and others, one of which, and the one first payable, had been assigned to C. C. Pinckney, Jr. Fishburne having made default in payment, action was commenced against him by Mr. Smith for foreclosure. A. M. Lee was one of the attorneys for the plaintiff in this action in that suit for foreclosure, while this action was pending; and, for the purpose of meeting the issues involved and paying the debt, the deed of 6th November, 1889, and the paper expressing the trust on which the conveyance was made, were executed. In an order overruling a demurrer to the answer of some of the defendants I have indicated my opinion that the formal discontinuance of the action for foreclosure was not a condition precedent to the right of Mr. Smith and Mr. Lee to execute the trusts created by the within instrument. I have not changed

the opinion therein expressed, that the tender of his receipt for one thousand dollars by the plaintiff in this action was not the equivalent of the tender of one thousand dollars in money, because the first money received by the trustees was applicable to certain expenses and the debt, and not to the surplus, in which alone he had any interest. The next question is whether Mr. Elliott is entitled to have a conveyance of the bond at his bid, $44,000, at the sale which the two trustees attempted to make in pursuance of the power vested in them. By an arrangement made by the two trustees, the land had been duly advertised and offered for sale by Mr. T. Pinckney Lowndes. The property was bid off for plaintiff at $44,000, and, he having tendered only the receipt above referred to instead of $1,000 in money, the property was again put up. At this second offering the property was run up by Mr. Elliott to $39,950, and, at the suggestion of Mr. Smith, this bid was withdrawn, and the property again was bid off for plaintiff for $36,000. He tendered the same or a similar receipt in place of the cash, and it was again refused, and the property put up a third time, and bid off by Henry D. Elliott, who did not pay or tender the one thousand dollars required by the published terms of sale. This last bid of Elliott was at $30,000, as heretofore stated. Mr. Lee was not present at the sale, but was absent from the state. Mr. Smith was attorney for all the holders of the bonds, and was the trustee to whom the mortgage was made. At the same time he and Mr. Lee were trustees, to make the sale for the benefit of the bondholders, and for the plaintiff as to the surplus. He occupied a double relation to the property, and represented conflicting interests. Now, this seems to me to involve the same principle as was involved in the case of Anderson v. Butler, 31 S. C. 183, 9 S. E. Rep. 797. While in that case the court recognized the right of such a trustee to purchase at a judicial sale, it suggested as to other property, which the trustees had a right to sell without the intervention of the court, that a partition would most likely give satisfaction; and it seems to me that this advice was given for the same reason which had induced the circuit judge in that case to order a sale by the master, with an express provision that the trustee might protect himself at the sale by bidding on the property, which he would not have a right to do at a sale made by himself. Ex parte Wiggins, 1 Hill, Eq. 353; also McCelvey v. Thomson, 7 S. C. 201. Mr. Elliott in this whole matter acted under the advice and instruction of Mr. Smith, and on behalf of the creditors, and I think that the withdrawal of the bid for $39,950, under his advice, rendered void the subsequent sale to him at $30,000. In such cases the court cannot consider the question whether the amount bid was or was not a fair price. If, however, you admit this bid to have been regular and valid, it has not been complied with. I am satisfied that a creditor who bids at such sales is not bound to pay in any money which is coming to him, and that it is not necessary even to tender a receipt for it. In this case certain expenses provided for in the mortgage and bill of sale were first payable out of any money realized from this sale, and the creditors were not entitled to anything until these were paid. This was a joint power of sale, and one of the trustees was absent. And, even if the two had a right to waive the cash, or any part of it, it seems to me to be clear that one trustee had no such right in the absence of the other. For these reasons I do not regard the sale to Mr. Elliott as valid, and another sale will be necessary. The time fixed by the deeds for the sale has passed, and an order from the court will be necessary. I understand that the trustees prefer that the sale shall be made by the master, if to be made at all. It is therefore ordered and adjudged that the master for Colleton county, after due advertisement in some newspaper published in said county, and one in the city of Charleston, do sell the premises described in the complaint on sales-day in October next, or on some subsequent sales-day, for $5,000 in cash, and the balance on a credit of one or two years, with interest from day of sale, payable annually, until the whole is paid; to be secured by a bond of the purchaser and a mortgage of the premises. It is ordered that, if the creditors, or any of them, should become purchasers at the said sale, the receipt for so much of the proceeds as may be coming to said purchaser, as due on the bond or bonds, shall be regarded as so much cash. By consent in writing, filed with the record in this case, the master is authorized to make the sale in the city of Charleston. It is ordered that the expenses of sale, and the costs and fees of the master and other officers of this court, be paid out of the cash proceeds of sale, and the balance of the cash paid to C. C. Pinckney on his bond, and that the master do hold the bond and mortgage taken by him subject to the further order of the court, to be paid out to the parties entitled to the same on the coming in of the report of the master on the matters hereinafter referred to him. There is testimony which satisfies me that there is more due to C. C. Pinckney than will be paid out of the cash, but the precise amount of the debt due on the several bonds cannot be ascertained without a reference to the master, and other amounts may be chargeable on the bond. It is therefore ordered that it be referred to the master to inquire and report what is the amount due on the several bonds secured by the mortgage, and also to inquire and report on all claims on the fund arising from said sale, including all legitimate expenses covered by the mortgage, or incurred by the trustees, H. A. M. Smith and A. M. Lee, and amounts due them. It is ordered that all the costs not hereinbefore provided for be paid by the parties, respectively, incurring them. Ordered that parties may apply at the foot of this decree for any order proper to carry out the same."

Bryan & Bryan, for plaintiff. *A. T. Smythe*, for defendants Smith and Elliott. *Julian Mitchell*, for defendant Lee.

McIver, J. The defendant Smith, as the attorney of Mrs. Lowndes, Mrs. Minott, and Mrs. Elliott, sold and conveyed to the plaintiff herein a certain tract of land in Colleton, known as "Hoats," belonging to the three ladies named, for the sum of $36,-000, a portion of which was paid in cash, and the balance secured by several bonds, payable at different dates, together with a mortgage, which bonds were payable to Smith as trustee of the ladies above named. Default having been made in the payment of the bond first maturing, Smith commenced an action to foreclose the mortgage, to which Fishburne appeared by his attorneys, Smythe & Lee. While this action was pending, an agreement was entered into on the 6th of November, 1889, by Fishburne, Smith, and the defendant A. M. Lee, a member of the firm of Smythe & Lee, containing the following stipulations: "*First.* The present proceedings to be withdrawn, Mr. Fishburne paying all costs. *Second.* Mr. Fishburne to execute and deliver to A. M. Lee and H. A. M. Smith a deed of conveyance of the property. This deed not to be recorded before the 17th day of February, 1890, unless some proceedings or liens are threatened against Mr. Fishburne. *Third.* If Mr. Fishburne does not settle, on the 17th of February, 1890, all amounts then due, the property to be advertised and sold at Charleston on the first Monday in April by Messrs. Lee and Smith, on terms one-third cash, balance in one and two years with annual interest secured by mortgage; Messrs. Lee and Smith to adopt such measures as they may think proper to secure sale to a responsible bidder. *Fourth.* Proceeds to be applied to all costs and expenses provided for in this mortgage, and of the sale, and then to the mortgage debt, and balance to Julian Fishburne." The amount due not having been settled on the day appointed by this agreement, the property was advertised for sale by Lee and Smith on the 7th of April, 1890, on the following "Terms: One-third (⅓) cash, viz., one thousand dollars, when the property is knocked down, and the rest in twenty days from the day of sale; balance in one and two years, with interest at 7 per cent. per annum, payable annually, secured by bond of the purchaser and mortgage of the purchased premises."

It appears that within a very short time before the sale—perhaps an hour—Fishburne had spoken to a broker, Hyde, to attend the sale, and bid on the property for him up to a specified amount; and, finding that there was some doubt whether Hyde would be able to attend the sale, he made a similar arrangement with another broker, Marshall; but it turned out that both of these gentlemen attended, neither knowing that the other had been employed by Fishburne. When the property was first offered for sale, Marshall being the highest and last bidder, at the sum of $44,000, the property was knocked down, when he gave the name of Fishburne as purchaser; and a paper signed by Fishburne, acknowledging the receipt by him from Smith and Lee of the sum of $1,000, on account of the surplus proceeds of sale coming to him, was tendered to the auc tioneer, as the cash payment required by the advertisement to be made when the property was knocked down. This receipt was referred to Smith, who was directing the sale, Lee being then absent from the state, and he declined to receive it, and directed the auctioneer to proceed with the sale. When the property was offered the second time, it was run up by the defendant Elliott, who claims to have been acting as the agent of the ladies to whom the debt was really due, to the sum of $39,950, when that bid was withdrawn by Elliott, at the suggestion of Smith, and the property was finally knocked down to Hyde at the sum of $36,000, who gave the name of Fishburne as the purchaser, when the same receipt was again offered and refused, and the auctioneer was again directed to proceed. The property was then offered a third time, and bid off by Elliott for the sum of $30,000, but no cash or receipt was offered by him, in compliance with the requirement that $1,000 should be paid; Mr. Smith saying, in response to the demand of Mr. Fishburne that this requirement should be complied with, that he knew Elliott to be the representative of the parties really entitled to the proceeds of the sale, and his bid was therefore practically a cash bid, and that he would be personally responsible for the credit on Fishburne's bond of the $1,000. A few days after the property was thus offered for sale Fishburne addressed a note to Smith, asking for a statement "showing amount of costs and expenses provided for in mortgage, and of the sale, and amount of the mortgage debt;" saying he wished to provide for a prompt settlement of his bid of $44,000. To this Smith replied, saying that the property "was sold on 7th April, 1890, to Mr. Henry D. Elliott at public auction. To him, as the purchaser, will the title be made." Thereupon this action was commenced, in which the plaintiff demands judgment that the sale made on the 7th of April, 1890, together with all proceedings thereunder, be declared null and void, and that a resale may be made under the direction of the court, for the purpose of carrying out the true intent and meaning of the agreement of 6th of November, 1889, and requiring that the proceedings therein mentioned be withdrawn as covenanted therein. And, as alternative relief, that plaintiff have a decree for the specific performance of the contract of sale made with him on the 7th of April, 1890, at the sum of $44,000; that the proceedings referred to in the agreement of 6th of November, 1889, be withdrawn; that the defendants Smith and Lee may account to him for any surplus that may remain after providing for the payment of all costs and expenses provided for in the mortgage, and of the sale, as well as the mortgage debt; and that the alleged sale to Elliott be declared null and void. The case was heard by his honor, Judge FRASER, who held that there was no necessity for any formal discontinuance of the proceedings commenced by Smith as trustee against Fishburne, for the foreclosure of the mortgage above referred to, as a condition precedent to the right of Smith and Lee to make the sale, under the agree-

ment of 6th of November, 1889, but that in fact there had been no valid sale; that the alleged sale to Elliott could not be sustained, because he had withdrawn a bid made by him higher than that at which the property was knocked down to him, and this was done "at the suggestion of Mr. Smith," as well as because he never complied with the terms of the sale by paying or tendering the $1,000 cash required to be paid when the property was knocked down; that the alleged sale to the plaintiff could not be sustained, because he did not comply with that requirement; that another sale should be made, and, it being understood that the trustees (Smith and Lee) preferred that it should be made by the master, he ordered that officer to make the sale after due advertisement, at a time specified, on the following terms, viz., $5,000 cash and the balance on a credit of one and two years. He further ordered that, after paying the costs and expenses of the sale, the balance of the cash payment be applied to the bond held by C. C. Pinckney, Jr., (the bond first maturing having, as it seems, been transferred to him;) the circuit judge being satisfied from the testimony that there is more due on Pinckney's bond than will be paid out of the cash; but, as the precise amount due on the other bonds had not been ascertained, a reference was ordered for that purpose, and in the mean time the master is to hold the bond and mortgage subject to the further orders of the court. This statement of the provisions of the decree will be sufficient to indicate the questions raised by this appeal; but for a more complete statement reference may be had to the decree as set out in the "case," which should be incorporated in the report of this case. From this decree the plaintiff, as well as the defendants Smith and Elliott, appeal, upon the several grounds set out in the record.

The plaintiff, in his first exception, imputes error to the circuit judge "in not striking out and suppressing the deposition of defendant Smith for his refusal to answer questions on the cross-examination." In this connection we will also consider defendant's second exception, presenting a similar question in regard to the suppression of the plaintiff's testimony on the same ground. Without entering into any discussion as to the merits of the questions raised by these exceptions, it is sufficient to say that, so far as we can discover, the record does not show that any motion to suppress the testimony of either of these witnesses was ever presented to or passed upon by the circuit judge, and there is therefore nothing for this court, as an appellate tribunal, to review.

The second exception of plaintiff charges error in not requiring a formal discontinuance of the action for foreclosure instituted by Smith, as trustee, against the plaintiff herein, before the resale ordered by the decree. This exception is, we think, well taken. While it may be true that, so far as the parties to this record are concerned, no formal discontinuance of that action may be necessary, inasmuch as they have full knowledge of the agreement to that effect, yet, as the purpose of the resale is that the property shall bring its full value, any cloud on the title, even though apparent only, arising from the pendency of that action, and the filing of the notice of *lis pendens* therein, should be removed, in order that outsiders who may know nothing of this agreement be not deterred from bidding by this apparent cloud, and that there may be full and free competition. It seems to us, therefore, that the circuit decree should, in this respect, be modified by providing for a formal discontinuance to be entered on the record of that action.

The third exception, in regard to the application of the cash payment to the Pinckney bond before due proof of the amount due thereon, is also well taken. While it may be, and no doubt is, quite true that the testimony was sufficient to show that more was due on this bond than could be paid out of the cash payment of $5,000, required by the decree, yet, as we think defendants' thirteenth exception to this provision of the circuit decree is well taken, inasmuch as the resale should be made on the same terms stipulated for in the agreement of 6th of November, 1889, it will be necessary to modify the decree to conform to this view; for until the sale is made it cannot be ascertained whether the cash payment of one-third which should be required will be more or less than sufficient to pay the amount due on the Pinckney bond, and hence such amount must first be ascertained before any order as to the application of the cash proceeds, except so far as costs and expenses are concerned, can properly be made.

Plaintiff's fourth exception cannot be sustained, for the reasons stated by the circuit judge. The plaintiff was only entitled to any surplus over and above the amount of costs and expenses, and the amount due on the mortgage debt, which unquestionably were all entitled to be paid in full before the plaintiff could be entitled to receive a dollar. To allow his receipt for $1,000 out of the surplus, if there should prove to be any, to be received as cash, would practically give him the first proceeds of the sale, whereas, in fact, he was the last to be paid. It is true that the testimony does seem to show that the mortgage debt, together with all costs and expenses, would not exceed the sum of $40,000, which would leave a surplus of about $4,000 out of the bid of $44,000, made by plaintiff; but, granting this to be so, he could not be entitled to any portion of the $4,000 until the claims having precedence were fully provided for; and hence his receipt for a portion of a sum which might be coming to him in the future could not be treated as cash.

Turning to defendants' exceptions, we will take up first the third exception, which imputes to the circuit judge error in holding "that all testimony as to matters which occurred previous to the execution by plaintiff of the deed of 6th of November, 1889, was incompetent." Defendants had offered testimony as to the various negotiations and transactions between Smith and Fishburne, as to the original sale of the land, and the reasons which prompted it, as well as to what passed between

these parties on the failure of Fishburne to meet the first payment, and as to Fishburne's course in defending the action for foreclosure brought against him by Smith as trustee, with a view to show that Fishburne had not acted in good faith, and was resorting to all practicable means to obstruct Smith in collecting the debt due to him as trustee. It appears, however, that all these matters culminated in the execution of the agreement of 6th of November, 1889, and when Fishburne, in pursuance of one of the terms of that agreement, conveyed the land to Smith and Lee, they assumed the duty of selling the land to the best advantage of all parties concerned; and the only question here, or rather the primary inquiry here, is whether that duty has been properly performed, and, if not, whether the court shall now require its proper performance. We do not see, therefore, what these prior negotiations and transactions have to do with our present inquiry; and we do not think that there was any error on the part of the circuit judge in holding that all the testimony as to matters which occurred prior to the execution of the agreement of 6th November, 1889, was incompetent.

The 1st, 4th, 5th, 6th, 7th, and 8th exceptions, relating to the ruling of the circuit judge that the alleged sale to Elliott was invalid, and could not be sustained, may be considered together. It seems to us that the reasons given by his honor are amply sufficient to vindicate his conclusion. Under the agreement of 6th of November, 1889, there can be no doubt that it became the duty of Smith and Lee, as trustees, to that extent, at least, to sell the property to the best advantage; and, Lee being absent from the state at the time of the sale, that duty was devolved upon Smith, and there is as little doubt that the property could have been sold to Elliott for a sum much larger than that at which it is now claimed that he bought it; for Elliott himself testifies that he went to the sale with the intention of bidding, in good faith, as high as $40,000, and the undisputed fact is that he did actually bid $39,950. When, therefore, a sale at those figures was prevented by the suggestion of Smith to withdraw that bid, upon which suggestion Elliott acted, we do not see how a court of equity can sustain a sale for a much less sum to the same person, who had publicly proclaimed his willingness to bid a much larger sum, and had been deterred therefrom by the trustee whose duty it was to obtain the highest price for the property. It may be, and doubtless was, the fact that Mr. Smith acted in entire good faith, and honestly believed that Elliott was induced to raise his bid as high as the amount above stated by puffing bids, which were not made in good faith. But such suspicion, or even belief, would not, in our judgment, justify his course (occupying the position of trustee, as he did,) in defeating a sale at the higher price, even though he was also in the position of attorney for the bidder. His proper course, as it seems to us, was to allow the sale to proceed, and, when the property was knocked down to Elliott, let him make the question, if he so desired, whether he could be relieved upon the ground of the alleged puffing bids made at the sale.

But, in addition to this, when the property was offered a third time, and was bid off by Elliott for $30,000, he never complied with the terms of the sale by either paying or tendering the $1,000 in cash, as required. Even assuming that Elliott was bidding as the agent of the bondholders, though there might be a question whether he had any sufficient legal authority to do so, this would not relieve him from the necessity of making the cash payment required; for, although it may be true that one who is entitled to the proceeds of a sale may not be required to comply with that term of the sale providing for the payment of so much cash, as his receipt may be taken as such, yet the proceeds of this sale were first to be applied to the payment of certain costs and expenses; and therefore, even if the holder or holders of the bonds had in person bid off the property, the cash payment would have had to be made, or at least so much thereof as would be necessary to pay such costs and expenses; and in this case it is not pretended that Elliott either paid or tendered any cash at all. It is clear, therefore, that in no view of the case can the alleged sale to Elliott be supported.

The ninth and tenth exceptions, alleging, in general terms, that the plaintiff, by his improper conduct, caused the alleged failure of the sale, and therefore has no right to complain of the same, or to demand any relief on account thereof, cannot be sustained. These exceptions do not specify any particular instances of alleged misconduct on the part of the plaintiff, and we find nothing in the circuit decree upon which they can be based, nor do we think that they can be sustained by the testimony.

The eleventh and twelfth exceptions may be considered together, as they both are based upon the ground that the circuit judge erred in not requiring the plaintiff to comply with his bid of $44,000, the former insisting that, upon his failure to do so, he should "lose all right to the property;" and the latter that, upon the failure of the plaintiff to comply, the defendant Elliott should be entitled to take the property at his bid of $30,000. From what has already been said, it is clear that neither of these exceptions can be sustained. Even assuming that the plaintiff could have been required to comply with his bid, in this form of proceeding, the defendants, by their course in ignoring the plaintiff's bid, have precluded themselves from demanding that relief, and, as we have seen, the other alternative suggested cannot be adopted, because Elliott never complied with his bid. Under these circumstances, there was no other alternative, except to order a resale of the property. The judgment of this court is that the judgment of the circuit court, as modified herein, be affirmed, and that the case be remanded to that court for the purpose of such further proceedings as may be necessary to carry out the views herein announced.

McGowan, J., concurs.

Sease v. Dobson et al.

(Supreme Court of South Carolina. Aug. 12, 1891.)

Res Judicata—Agricultural Lien — Equitable Chattel Mortgage—Injunction—Appeal.

1. A judgment for the rent only in what was essentially a special proceeding to establish an agricultural lien on crops for rent and advances, but which in form was an action by summons and complaint, in which an agreement for a lien was held invalid as an agricultural lien, because not signed by both parties, is not a bar to an action in equity to declare the agreement an equitable chattel mortgage on the crop, and for an accounting of the amount due thereon for the advances.

2. Error cannot be predicated on an order in chambers refusing an injunction which does not decide the merits of the main case, though the reason for the refusal was that, according to the court's view of the merits, there was no ground for the injunction.

3. A hearing on the merits was properly refused, where it would require the decision of a material question involved in a pending appeal from an order in the case refusing an injunction.

Appeal from common pleas circuit court of Barnwell county; T. B. Fraser, Judge.

Action in equity by Alfred Sease against Joseph and Henry Dobson, S. L. Knopf, intervenor, to establish an equitable mortgage upon crops, and for an accounting. An injunction asked by plaintiff was refused, and he appeals. The action was afterwards brought on for hearing in the trial court, which refused to entertain it while the first appeal was pending, and from this order plaintiff appeals. Reversed on first appeal, and affirmed on second appeal.

W. A. Holman, (Bates & Sims, of counsel,) for plaintiff. J. J. Brown, for defendants.

McIver, J. The controversy between these parties had its origin in two papers bearing date 12th November, 1888, copies of which are set out in the "case," both of which were signed by the two Dobsons, Joseph and Henry, defendants herein, purporting to give to the plaintiff liens on the crops of the two Dobsons raised during the year 1889, on certain land of the plaintiff rented to the defendants, for the purpose of securing the payment of advances to an amount stated in each paper, as well as the rent of said land. Each of these papers contains a clause giving to the plaintiff a mortgage on a horse as further security. These papers, however, were not signed by the plaintiff, and for that reason they have heretofore been held by this court not to be agricultural liens on the advances claimed to have been made, and enforceable as such, under the provisions of the statute in reference to that subject. See Sease v. Dobson, (S. C.) 11 S. E. Rep. 728. Some time in the fall of the year 1889 the plaintiff applied for and obtained from the clerk of the court a warrant for the enforcement of the papers as agricultural liens, which was placed in the hands of the sheriff, who at the same time was appointed agent of the plaintiff under the mortgage clause in the papers. By virtue of this warrant, and his appointment as agent as aforesaid, the sheriff seized the crops of the defendants, and the two horses mortgaged, and, having sold the crops, an arrangement was made for the release of the horses by the deposit with the sheriff of an amount sufficient, with the proceeds of the sale of the crops, to pay the claims of the plaintiff, amounting in all to the sum of $683.70, which was left in the hands of the sheriff to await the result of the proceedings. This deposit was made by the defendant S. L. Knopf, who claimed to hold valid liens on the property of the defendants, and who was permitted to intervene as one of the parties to the proceedings in order to sustain his claims. After the sale of the crops by the sheriff, and within the time prescribed by the statute, the Dobsons filed their affidavit, accompanied with a notice to the effect that the amount claimed by plaintiff, under his alleged agricultural liens, was not justly due; but instead of proceeding, under the issue thus made up, to have the question of the amount due determined, it now appears that the plaintiff commenced what, on its face, appears to be a formal action, by summons and complaint, against the Dobsons, to which the sheriff was made a party, in which, after alleging that the plaintiff had rented the land to the Dobsons, and also made advances to them, in consideration whereof they had agreed to pay to the plaintiff a specified sum of money, and to secure such payment had given plaintiff a lien on their crops, and after further alleging the seizure and sale of said crops by the sheriff, who continued to hold the proceeds under a notice from the Dobsons not to pay the same to the plaintiff, notwithstanding the same was justly due, they demanded judgment against the Dobsons for the sum of $683.70, and that the sheriff be required to pay the same to the plaintiff out of the proceeds of the sale in his hands. This summons and complaint was served on the attorney for the defendants; but it appears that the defendants, the Dobsons, answered the complaint, admitting so much of the claim as was for rent, ($200,) but denying the claim for advances, and setting up a counter-claim. Under these pleadings, the case was heard by his honor, Judge HUDSON, who manifestly was induced to suppose that he was simply trying an issue under the statute as to the amount due under an agricultural lien; for, after having held that the papers relied on as agricultural liens could not be so regarded, for the reason that they were not signed by both parties thereto, he refused to allow the plaintiff to offer any evidence as to the amount which he claimed to have advanced to the Dobsons, inasmuch as the only question presented by the issue then on trial was whether anything, and, if so, how much, had been advanced under the alleged liens; and, having determined that the papers offered were not liens, of course nothing could be due under them; and hence evidence as to what the Dobsons may have been owing the plaintiff, by open account or otherwise, was wholly irrelevant to the issue on trial. But as the lien for rent arose by virtue of the statute, and did not require any agreement in writing, he instructed the jury that the plaintiff might recover to that extent. Accordingly the

jury rendered their verdict in the following form: "We find for the plaintiff two hundred (200) dollars for rent." Judgment having been entered upon this verdict, the plaintiff appealed, making three questions: (1) Whether there was error in holding that the papers relied on as such could not be regarded as agricultural liens, under the statute, because not signed by the plaintiff; (2) whether there was error in refusing to allow plaintiff to offer evidence tending to show that he had made the advances as claimed. The third question, not being pertinent to the present inquiry, need not be stated. This court affirmed the rulings of Judge HUDSON, as may be seen by reference to 11 S. E. Rep. 728.

After the judgment of this court was rendered, the plaintiff commenced a formal action against the Dobsons and the sheriff, to which the other defendant, Knopf, became a party defendant, as above indicated, in which, after narrating the facts above stated more fully and at greater detail than we have deemed it necessary to do, and after alleging that Judge HUDSON had, upon the notice of appeal from his rulings, granted an order directing the sheriff to retain in his hands until the further order of the court the entire sum of $683.70, which included the amount found due for rent, as well as the amount deposited to secure the release of the horses seized under the mortgage, he demands judgment (1) that the sheriff pay over to the plaintiff the sum of $200, found due for rent; (2) that the papers above referred to, and originally relied on as agricultural liens, be declared equitable mortgages on the crops, and that an accounting be had of the amount due thereon; (3) that the sheriff, after paying the amount found due for rent, be required to apply the balance of the fund in his hands to the amount found due on such accounting; (4) for such other and further relief as may be just and equitable, and that, in the mean time, the sheriff be enjoined from paying out any of the fund in his hands except the amount found due for rent. Upon the filing of this complaint, an application was made to his honor, Judge FRASER, at chambers, for an injunction in conformity to the prayer of the complaint, who granted a rule requiring the defendants to show cause why the injunction demanded should not be granted, and in the mean time restraining the sheriff from paying out the money. Upon hearing the return to this rule, Judge FRASER rescinded the restraining order, and refused the motion for injunction, upon the ground that the whole matter was res adjudicata. From this order the plaintiff appealed, substantially making two questions: (1) Whether the judge erred in considering the merits on a motion for injunction at chambers; (2) whether there was error in holding the matter to be res adjudicata. This appeal having been perfected, the plaintiff applied for and obtained from Mr. Justice McGowan an order requiring the sheriff to retain in his hands the fund until the cause should be heard and determined by the supreme court. Subsequently the case, upon its merits, was submitted to his honor, Judge ALDRICH, who declined to consider any of the questions involved, upon the ground that, the case having been carried by appeal to the supreme court from an order of Judge FRASER determining one of the main issues in the action, the court of common pleas could not exercise any jurisdiction therein while it was pending in the supreme court. From this plaintiff also appeals, alleging error in such ruling.

From the foregoing statement it is very manifest that the plaintiff has never yet been allowed the opportunity of proving, if he can, his claim for supplies alleged to have been furnished the Dobsons; nor have they ever been permitted to prove, if they can, their demands against the plaintiff, set up in their counter-claim; and, if they are now precluded from doing so, the result would indeed be most unfortunate. It is true that parties may, and sometimes do, fail to obtain that justice which the real facts entitle them to, by the manner in which their cases are presented to the court; but such an unhappy result ought always to be avoided, if it is practicable to do so without infringing settled rules of law which it is essential to the welfare of the commonwealth to preserve in their fullest integrity, for, being established for the guidance and control of the whole community, they should never be disturbed or strained to suit the fancied justice of a particular case. Guided, or rather restrained, by these principles, we will proceed to consider the questions involved in these two appeals.

The first question presented is whether Judge FRASER erred in considering the merits of the case upon an application for an injunction made to him at chambers. We do not understand that the judge undertook to decide any of the merits of the case on which the application was made, but he simply gave, as his reason for refusing the motion, that, according to his view of the merits, the plaintiff had no ground for his motion; and in this we think there was no error. After Judge FRASER had refused the motion, there was nothing to prevent the plaintiff from proceeding to have the merits of his case decided by the proper tribunal having jurisdiction to do so, and this shows conclusively that the judge did not decide anything as to the merits; for, if he had, the matter would have been *res adjudicata*, which is not and cannot be pretended. As we understand it, all that Judge FRASER undertook to say was that the case as presented to him was not sufficient, in his judgment, to entitle the plaintiff to the order asked for; and this he, unquestionably, had a right to say. If, however, the reason upon which his conclusion was based, rested upon an erroneous proposition of law, then the plaintiff's remedy was that to which he has properly resorted, by appeal.

This brings us to the next question, whether there was error in holding that the whole matter was *res adjudicata*. There can be no doubt that the case before Judge HUDSON was treated by the court and by the parties on both sides simply as an issue, under the statute, to try the question whether anything, and, if so, how much, was justly due under the alleged liens, and not as an ordinary action to recover money alleged to be due by the defendants to the plaintiff; whether properly or not, we will consider hereafter. This is manifest from the ruling of Judge HUDSON, and is made more manifest by the "agreed case," upon which the former appeal was heard, a copy of which is in the present record, and is perfectly obvious from the language used by the late chief justice in delivering the opinion of this court upon that appeal. The reasons given by Judge HUDSON for his rulings show, beyond dispute, that he so regarded the issue he was trying. It is so expressly stated in the "agreed case," above referred to. The opening sentence of the opinion of this court is in these words: "This was a proceeding commenced by the plaintiff to enforce an alleged agricultural lien on the crops of the defendants;" and, after stating the seizure and sale of the crops, these words follow: "The proceeds were held subject to the decision of the court upon an issue raised by the defendants, 'that the amount claimed by the plaintiff was not justly due him in accordance with the latter part of section 2398, Gen. St.' This was tried before his honor, Judge HUDSON," etc. And again, in considering the second point raised by the former appeal,—that there was error in refusing to admit testimony as to the amount advanced by plaintiff to the defendants,—the chief justice used this language: "Had this been an action to recover a debt contracted by the defendant for goods and supplies furnished, such evidence would have been relevant and competent, but such was not the character of the action. On the contrary, it was a special proceeding provided by statute for the recovery of a debt of a certain character, and the plaintiff was confined to that proceeding." In the face of this, we do not see how it is possible to doubt that the former proceeding was treated by all parties, as well as by both the courts before which it was heard, as a special proceeding under the agricultural lien law, wherein the only issue would be whether anything, and, if so, how much, was justly due under the alleged liens, and the question whether anything was due to the plaintiff on any other account would have been wholly irrelevant. This being so, it would certainly be very extraordinary, to say the least of it, to permit either party now to claim that the court, which had been induced, by the act of the parties themselves, to try one issue arising under a special statutory proceeding, had in fact determined other and altogether foreign issues to that raised by such special proceeding. It will be noted that the "case" agreed upon for the hearing of the former appeal contained no hint even that the proceeding was an ordinary action for the recovery, but, on the contrary, specially characterized it as a special proceeding under the statute, and this "case" was in express terms consented to by defendants' attorney, who in his argument of the present appeal admits that what he now claims to have been the real nature of the former proceeding was not made made known to the court. But, more than this, when, in the trial of the issue before Judge HUDSON, counsel objected to the introduction of any testimony tending to show that the plaintiff had made advances to the defendants, who thereby became indebted to the plaintiff in the amount of such advances, he thereby necessarily assumed that the issue on trial was simply an issue under the special proceeding provided for by the statute to determine whether anything was justly due under the liens; and, when the circuit court sustained such objection, it necessarily adjudged that such was the character of the proceeding, and that it was not an ordinary action for the recovery of money, for, if so, then plainly there would have been no foundation whatever for such objection. From this adjudication necessarily implied in the ruling of Judge HUDSON, there was no appeal, and hence it was conclusive. But, even if it was not, yet when this court expressly declared (italics ours) that the former proceeding was not an ordinary action for the recovery of money, but, "*on the contrary, it was a special proceeding provided by statute* for the recovery of a debt *of a certain character, and the plaintiff was confined to that proceeding,*" that, surely, was conclusive, and fixed beyond dispute the character of the former proceeding. We are quite sure that Judge FRASER could not have had the former decision of this court before him when he heard the motion; indeed, it was scarcely possible that he could have had, for the opinion of this court was filed 2d of July, 1890, and Judge FRASER probably heard the motion on the 18th of that month,—the day on which the rule was returnable,—and rendered his decision on the 23d of July, 1890; and, after allowing for the 10 days during which the *remittitur* is retained, it would not have been more than barely possible for him to have had the opinion before him on the day fixed for the hearing, and scarcely within the bounds of probability that he could have had it when he rendered his decision.

But in addition to this, inasmuch as the statute prescribes no form in which the issue therein provided for to determine whether the amount claimed is justly due shall be framed, and, so far as we know, there being no rule of court or of practice prescribing such form, we do not see why the parties may not resort to any form which will present the issue to be tried. Johnstone v. Manigault, 13 S. C. 403. If they choose the more cumbrous form of a formal complaint, instead of adopting some more simple form, we do not see why they may not do so; especially when, as in this case, it is perfectly manifest that neither party was misled, and, on the contrary, both parties fully acquiesced in the adoption of the more cumbrous form, a complaint and answer to raise the issue provided for by the statute. The case of Cheatham v. Morrison, 31 S. C. 326, 9 S. E. Rep. 964, relied on by defendant's counsel, is not in point. In that case certain crops of one Seawright had been seized under a warrant to enforce an agricultural lien, and the same were replevied by him, he giving an undertaking, with the defendants as sureties, under the provisions of the amendment to the lien law, conditioned for the delivery of the property, in case such delivery should be adjudged, and for the payment of any sum of money that the plaintiff might in that action recover, and at the same time Seawright gave the necessary notice required by the statute to raise the issue as to whether anything was justly due under the lien. At that point that proceeding was stopped. Some time afterwards Cheatham commenced a formal action by summons and complaint against Seawright to recover a specified sum of money, which proceeded regularly to judgment against Seawright, and, when the execution issued to enforce such judgment was returned *nulla bona,* an action was commenced against Morrison and others, as sureties of Seawright, on the undertaking above mentioned. The court held that the two proceedings were separate and distinct, and that the sureties had a right to stand upon the contract as they made it, which bound them to pay any sum that might be recovered against Seawright in the proceeding under which the undertaking had been entered into, and, as nothing had ever been recovered in that proceeding, the sureties were not liable. They had no connection whatever with the subsequent action brought by Cheatham v. Seawright, and were in no way liable for the judgment recovered therein. It is plain that that decision has no application to the present case. There the court, both circuit and supreme, as well as the parties, treated the two proceedings as entirely distinct and separate, while here precisely the reverse is the case. It seems to us, therefore, that there was error, on the part of Judge FRASER, arising doubtless from the fact that the case was not fully presented to him, in holding that the matter was *res adjudicata;* and for this reason his order refusing the motion for injunction must be reversed, with leave to the plaintiff to apply again for such injunction, as soon as the *remittitur* is sent down to the circuit court, and that in the mean time the restraining order granted by Mr. Justice McGOWAN be continued.

It remains only to consider the appeal from the order of Judge ALDRICH refusing to entertain the case for want of jurisdiction, pending the appeal from the order of Judge FRASER. This appeal cannot be sustained. The appeal from the order of Judge FRASER involved a question which lay at the threshold of the case, and, while that question was pending in the supreme court, the circuit court could not assume jurisdiction, as that would have involved the necessity of determining the same question which was then pending in the supreme court. The cases cited by the circuit judge are amply sufficient to vindicate his conclusion. The judgment of this court is that the order of Judge ALDRICH be affirmed, but that the ruling of Judge FRASER, that the whole matter is *res adjudicata,* be reversed, and that the case be remanded to the circuit court for such further proceedings as may be necessary to carry out the views herein announced, so that both parties may have a full oppor-

tunity of establishing their several claims,
—the one against the other,—if they can.

McGOWAN, J., concurs.

McMAKIN v. FOWLER.

*(Supreme Court of South Carolina. Aug. 11,
1891.)*

RES JUDICATA—PAROL EVIDENCE.

1. Five notes were given under a contract in
payment of personal property of the value of
$9,500 each, to be paid at a specified time by de-
livering a certain number of brick to the payee.
The first two payments were not made as agreed,
and, before maturity of the last three, suit was
brought to recover the value of the brick which
should have been delivered on the first two notes,
alleging that the notes were two of the five given,
and laying the damages at $3,055. The maker filed
a counter-claim. Judgment was rendered for
$1,186.07. Afterwards suit was brought on the
last three of the five notes, and the maker filed a
plea of *res judicata. Held* proper, in the second suit, to admit parol evidence to prove the issues presented to the jury in the first suit.

2. The trial judge in the first case testified
in the second suit that only two of the notes
were involved, and submitted to the jury that it
appeared during the trial that other notes existed
between the parties in relation to the same contract, which had not matured, and that he instructed that the jury were only to consider the
first two notes. *Held* sufficient to show that the
recovery in the first suit was limited to the first
two notes.

Appeal from common pleas circuit court
of Spartanburg county; HUDSON and IZ-
LAR, Judges.

Action by James McMakin against W. D.
Fowler to recover on notes. Judgment
for plaintiff. Defendant appeals. Affirmed.

Nicholls & Moore, for appellant. *Duncan & Sanders* and *Carlisle & Hydrick,* for
respondent.

McIVER, J. On the 6th day of November, 1884, the defendant executed five obligations, in the form of promissory notes,
whereby he promised "to pay" to the
plaintiff good brick in the kiln at McMakin's brick-yard, as follows, viz., 100,000 on
the 1st May, 1885; the same number on 1st
October, 1885; the same number on 1st
May, 1886; the same number on the 1st
October, 1886; and 50,000 on the 1st October, 1887. These obligations, though
lacking one of the essential features of a
promissory note, will, for convenience
merely, be designated as "notes" in the
further consideration of this case. On or
about the 10th of February, 1886, after the
first two of these notes had matured,
and before the remaining three had been
payable, the plaintiff commenced an action against the defendant, alleging in his
complaint—*First,* the making of the two
notes set out in the complaint by the defendant; *second,* "that the consideration
of said contract was the sale by the plaintiff to the defendant of certain personal
property of the value of two thousand
and fifty-five dollars;" *third,* "that at the
time the defendant gave to the plaintiff
three other contracts of a similar character, which make up the amount of the purchase money;" *fourth,* "that the value of
the said brick is five dollars per thousand;"

fifth, "that the plaintiff has delivered to
the defendant the property aforesaid, and
the defendant has refused, although often
requested so to do, to deliver to the plaintiff the brick mentioned in the contract
aforesaid;" *sixth,* "that, in consequence
of the failure of the defendant to perform
his part of the contract, the plaintiff has
been damaged in the sum of two thousand
and fifty-five dollars; wherefore judgment was demanded for that sum, besides
costs and disbursements." To this complaint defendant answered, setting out
specifically the terms of the trade with the
plaintiff, whereby plaintiff sold to the defendant his brick-yard, and also the engine, brick-machine, and other machinery
and tools used there in the making of
brick, under the representation that the
clay was 10 feet thick over all of the land,
and that said engine and machinery were
as good as new; that in consideration
thereof he gave to plaintiff the two notes
set out in the complaint, and also the
other three notes mentioned in the foregoing statement, "it being well understood
that the brick therein referred to was un-
burned brick,"—but alleging that by reason of the delay in putting him in possession of the brick-yard, and by reason of
the failure of the property purchased to
come up to the terms of the warranty, he
had sustained damages for which he set
up a counter-claim. He also alleged that
ever since he obtained possession of the
brick-yard he was always ready to deliver the brick according to the contract, as
he claimed it to have been understood by
both parties, but that plaintiff refused to
receive anything but burned brick. To
this answer, or so much thereof as set up
a counter-claim, plaintiff filed a reply denying each and every allegation upon
which such claim was based. The case,
being thus at issue, came on for trial before his honor, Judge WALLACE, and a jury, on the 27th of March, 1888, when a verdict was rendered in favor of plaintiff for
$1,186.07, upon which judgment was duly
entered. In the mean time, the other
three notes having matured, the present
action was commenced on the 16th of February, 1888, a short time before the previous case was tried; and in his complaint the plaintiff alleges as his first cause
of action the making for valuable consideration by the defendant of the obligation
(which for convenience we designate as a
"note") payable 1st October, 1888, setting
out a copy thereof, and that defendant,
although often requested so to do, has
refused and neglected to deliver to the
plaintiff the brick mentioned in said contract, to the damage of the plaintiff $700;
and as a second and third cause of action
sets out the other two notes, with similar
allegations, and demands judgment for
the aggregate sum of these three notes.
To this complaint the defendant answered, admitting the execution of the
three notes set out in the complaint, but
denying each and every other allegation
therein contained. As a further defense, he
pleads the judgment recovered in a former
action as a bar to this. From the fact
that the plea is a former recovery, and not
the pendency of another action for the

same cause, we infer that, although the present action was commenced before the recovery of judgment in the previous case, the answer was filed after such judgment was recovered; and while it is possible that a point might be raised as to whether the plea should not have been pendency of another action rather than of a former recovery, yet as no such point was suggested, and as it would be purely technical, we will ignore it altogether in the consideration of the present appeal. The case first came on for hearing before his honor, Judge Hudson, when the counsel for defendant moved to dismiss the complaint upon the ground that the matters now sought to be brought in issue were *res adjudicata*, as shown by the record of the former case filed as an exhibit to the answer in this case. Thereupon plaintiff's counsel asked leave to introduce parol testimony for the purpose of showing that the issues involved in the present action were not submitted to the jury in the former action, reading from the stenographic notes of the charge of Judge Wallace in the former case, wherein it appeared "that, at the request of the attorney for the defendant on the trial of that action," the jury were instructed "that only two of the contracts mentioned in the complaint in that action, to-wit, those that were due at the time of the commencement of that action, were in issue, and were submitted to them." After hearing argument, an order was passed sustaining the plea of former recovery, and dismissing the complaint herein. But during the same term the matter was, at the request of Judge Hudson, reconsidered, and, after more full argument, another order was passed rescinding the previous order, restoring the case to the docket, "and that the plaintiff have leave to introduce testimony to show what issues were submitted to the jury" on the trial of the former action. To this order defendant duly excepted for the purpose of an appeal, after final judgment was rendered. The case was then continued, as we suppose, and at a subsequent term came on for trial before his honor, Judge Izlar, and a jury, when a similar motion to that presented to Judge Hudson, was submitted, which was overruled by Judge Izlar upon two grounds: (1) Because he had no right to review or disregard the order of Judge Hudson; (2) because, even if the matter were *res integra*, he thought the plaintiff was entitled to show by parol what were the issues submitted to and passed upon by the jury in the former action. Accordingly, the testimony of Judge Wallace, which is set out in the "case," was received against the objections of defendant. From that testimony it is very clear that the issues in the present action were neither submitted to nor passed upon by the jury in the former trial. On the contrary, the judge not only says, "Only the two agreements above referred to were involved in the trial of that action and submitted to the jury," but he adds: "In the course of the trial it was developed that there were other instruments in relation to the same contract between the parties, but they

had not matured at the time of the commencement of that action. I instructed that they were only to pass upon the two instruments above described, and that these latter were not to be considered by them." And, further, in reference to the counter-claim, "the defendant requested that the jury should be charged that only the matured agreements upon which the action had been brought could be set off against this counter-claim, and they were so charged." The plaintiff having recovered a verdict, defendant appeals from the judgment entered thereon, upon the grounds set out in the record.

These grounds really raise but three questions: (1) Whether his honor, Judge Izlar, erred in holding that he was bound by the order of his honor, Judge Hudson; (2) whether there was error in overruling the plea in bar; and this involves the question (3) whether it was competent to show, by parol evidence, what were the issues really submitted to and determined by the jury in the former action. Under the view which we take of the second and third questions, the first question becomes wholly immaterial. If the plea in bar was properly overruled, then, of course, it matters not what may have been the reasons assigned by Judge Izlar for his ruling; for, even if he erred in holding that he was bound by the order of his predecessor, (which, however, we are not to be understood as saying,) yet if he was right in admitting the parol evidence objected to, and holding that the plea of a former recovery could not be sustained under that evidence, it is of no consequence that he assigned an additional reason for his ruling, which, possibly, might not have been well founded. Indeed, there is but one real question in the case, and that is whether the parol evidence of Judge Wallace was admissible; for, if it was, there could not be a question that the issues in the present action were not submitted to or decided in the former action; but, on the contrary, they were expressly withdrawn from the jury, and that, too, at the request of defendant; and the jury were distinctly instructed that they could only consider and pass upon the two notes which had matured, which are in no way involved in the present action.

We proceed, then, to consider the question whether parol evidence was admissible in this case to show what were the issues passed upon in the former action. While it is undoubtedly true that a verdict, with the judgment entered thereon, is conclusive, so far as the parties to the record and their privies are concerned, as to all matters or issues decided by it, yet the question often arises as to what issues were decided, and when this is the case, while we must look, primarily, to the pleadings to ascertain what were the issues thereby made and decided, yet they are not necessarily conclusive; for, as is said by Evans, J., in Henderson v. Kenner, 1 Rich., at page 479: "If these [the pleadings] make single questions, to which the verdict directly applies, then the parties are concluded, and the same matter can never, as between them, be inquired into again." But on the same page he adds: "Where the pleadings are general, and there is more than a single proposition to be decided, and the verdict may be equally applied to both or all, in such case a verdict has not that conclusiveness which belongs to it when applied to a single proposition stated in the pleadings." And on the next page that eminent judge states, as the rule resulting from all the authorities on the subject, "that where the pleadings present two distinct propositions, and the verdict may be referred to either, it is conclusive, because there is no precise issue made by the pleadings, and the verdict wants that certainty which is necessary to give it the effect of an estoppel. In such case, as the jury may have decided on both questions, the verdict is *prima facie* evidence, but it is not conclusive, and may be rebutted by evidence *aliunde*. Such evidence is not resorted to, to contradict or explain the verdict by any direct evidence of intention, but to give it application by showing what were the facts to which it applied, and upon which the jury passed in rendering it. There are many cases in which parol and extrinsic evidence may be resorted to, to show the effect of a verdict." And he cites the case of Seddon v. Tutop, 6 Term R. 607, in which the plaintiff sued on a note and an open account, and, failing to give any evidence to prove the account, took a verdict for the amount of the note only. In a subsequent action on the account, it was held that the record in the former action was not conclusive; and as the fact that no evidence was offered to prove the account in the former action, and therefore that the jury did not pass upon it, could not appear from the record, it might be shown by parol. The rule, as established by this case from which we have so liberally quoted, is fully sustained by the authorities here and elsewhere. See Shettlesworth v. Hughey, 9 Rich. 387, where the parol evidence adduced to show what was the issue passed upon in the former action was very much like that resorted to in the present case, and the case of Henderson v. Kenner was distinctly recognized as authority for the admissibility of such testimony. See, also, Hart v. Bates, 17 S. C. 35; Ex parte Roberts, 19 S. C. 150,—where the same doctrine is recognized. In Eason v. Miller, 15 S. C. 194, though that case is not directly in point, the right to resort to the charge of the judge to ascertain what issues were submitted to and passed upon by the jury was distinctly recognised. The same doctrine was recognized elsewhere, as may be seen by reference to the following cases, with the authorities therein cited: Steam-Packet Co. v. Sickles, 24 How. 333; Davis v. Brown, 94 U. S. 423; Russell v. Place, Id. 606; Campbell v. Rankin, 99 U. S. 261; Cromwell v. County of Sac, 94 U. S. 351; Bissell v. Spring Valley Tp., 124 U. S. 225, 8 Sup. Ct. Rep. 495.

It being thus settled that there are cases in which parol or extrinsic evidence may be resorted to for the purpose of showing what were the issues determined in a former action, it only remains to determine whether the present case falls under that class. It seems to us that the bare inspection of the pleadings is sufficient to show that the issues presented by the pleadings in the two actions were not the same; and, if so, then it is conceded that the plea in bar was properly overruled. In the former case the two notes which had matured at the time of the commencement of that action are set out as the plaintiff's cause of action, and the mere fact that the other three notes, which had not then matured, are casually mentioned as going to make up the amount of the purchase money of the property for which the two notes actually sued upon were given in part of such amount, does not warrant the inference that the three notes, which had not then matured, and which, therefore, were not then suable, except under the special provisions of the statute, which should have been set forth, if the purpose was to embrace them in that action, constituted any part of the cause of action in the former case. Anderson v. Pilgram, 30 S. C. 499, 9 S. E. Rep. 587. So that we are not prepared to admit that the record in the former action of itself is sufficient to show that the issues presented by the complaint in the present action were the same as those presented by the former complaint, or were even necessarily involved therein. But, under the authorities above cited, it is quite sufficient to show that the record relied on as a bar leaves it doubtful as to what issues were therein determined. The contention of the appellant that the former action may and should be regarded as an action to rescind the original contract for the sale of the property, and to recover the property sold, or its value, from the defendant, upon the ground that he had failed to comply with his part of the original contract, cannot be sustained. It seems to us that the original complaint is conspicuously wanting in the necessary allegations for that purpose. On the contrary, the allegations of the complaint, as well as the answer in the first action, show that the defendant had fully complied with the terms of the original contract for the sale of the property. The sale of the property was on a credit, and, in compliance with the terms of the sale, the defendant had executed the obligations to the plaintiff stipulated for, and had received possession of the property. So that the only ground of complaint which the plaintiff had or could have had against the defendant was his failure to meet those obligations as they became due; and this, as we understand it, was the only demand made upon the defendant in the former action, and did not and could not involve any demand for a failure to meet obligations which had not then matured. The fact that the plaintiff demanded, in his previous complaint, damages to an amount much larger than those which would have ensued from the breach of the first two contracts, (the only ones which had then matured,) which amount seems to have been very nearly the same as the amount of the purchase money of the property sold, is of no consequence whatever; for nothing is better settled than that the demand for relief constitutes no part of the cause of action, and cannot give character to it. Balle v. Moseley, 13 S. C. 439; Levi v. Legg. 23 S. C. 282. The judgment of this court is that the judgment of the circuit court be affirmed.

McGOWAN, J., concurs.

HALE v. COLUMBIA & G. R. Co.

(Supreme Court of South Carolina. Aug. 11, 1891.)

RAILROAD COMPANIES — INJURIES TO PERSONS ON TRACK.

1. In an action against a railroad company to recover damages for the negligent killing of plaintiff's decedent, it appeared that deceased was a jeweler, and often went to defendant's office to obtain the correct time; that it was not necessary for him to cross the track, but that on the day of the accident he went to see an engine which was being repaired on the side track, and while standing between the tracks (there being a space of about 10 to 15 feet between them) he was struck by the steps of a passing coach, and thrown under the wheels. The accident occurred in the yard while the switch-engine was shifting cars, and running at the rate of about 10 miles per hour. The yard was surrounded by public streets. No signals were given of the approaching train. *Held*, that the company was not liable.

2. Gen. St. S. C. § 1483, required railway corporations to ring a bell or sound a whistle at a distance of 500 yards from all public crossings. Section 1529 makes a railway corporation liable for injuries to persons resulting from collisions at such crossings for failure to give the signals, unless the person injured was guilty of gross negligence. *Held*, that one injured, while standing in the switch-yard of the railroad company, and not passing over a crossing, could not recover under the above statutes, though the yard was surrounded by streets, and the required signals were not given by the company. Following Neely v. Railroad Co., 11 S. E. Rep. 636.

Appeal from common pleas circuit court of Greenville county; ALDRICH, Judge.

Action by William R. Hale, administrator of B. Werle, deceased, against the Columbia & Greenville Railroad Company, to recover damages for the negligent killing of plaintiff's decedent. Judgment for defendant. Plaintiff appeals. Affirmed.

Westmoreland & Haynsworth, for appellant. *Wells & Orr* and *J. S. Cothran,* for respondent.

McIVER, J. This was an action brought by the plaintiff, as administrator of Berthold Werle, deceased, against the defendant company, to recover damages for the killing of the deceased by the alleged negligence of the defendant company in moving its train, for the benefit of the wife of the deceased. The plaintiff offered testimony tending to show that the deceased was a watch-repairer, living in the city of Greenville, and was accustomed to go to the telegraph office of the defendant company, which was located near the railroad track, on the side next the city, for the purpose of obtaining the correct time as transmitted daily from Washington, so that it was not necessary for the deceased to cross the track or go on it for the purpose of reaching the telegraph office; that, on the occasion when the unfortunate disaster occurred, the curiosity of deceased to see certain work which was being done on a freight-engine standing on the side track

induced him to cross the side track, and, while standing between the side track and the main line, separated by a distance of some 10 or 15 feet, he was struck by the steps of a passenger-car, which "jutted out about six inches from the body of the coach," whereby he was thrown under the wheels of the coach, and the whole train ran over his leg, crushing it to such an extent as to cause his death within the ensuing 24 hours; that this passenger-car was being pushed back by a shifting-engine used for the purpose, which was moving at a speed of about 10 miles an hour; that the accident occurred in the railroad yard, through and along which persons were accustomed to pass for their own convenience, though the whole yard was surrounded by public streets, and that those in charge of the shifting-engine gave no signal of their approach, either by ringing the bell or blowing the whistle, or otherwise, and that no person was at the rear of the backing train as a lookout; that, when the deceased was struck, the engineer of the freight engine shouted to the engineer of the shifting-engine, and the deceased cried out in distress three times, but the moving train was not stopped until after it had passed over the leg of deceased. At the close of the testimony adduced by the plaintiff the defendant made a motion for a nonsuit, which was granted upon the ground that the plaintiff had failed to offer any evidence tending to show negligence upon the part of the defendant company, or of its agents or servants; and, judgment having been entered accordingly, the plaintiff appeals upon the several grounds set out in the record. Without considering these grounds in detail, we propose to consider and determine the fundamental question whether his honor, Judge ALDRICH, erred in holding that there was no evidence tending to show negligence. It seems that while the judge granted the motion in a short order without assigning any reasons, yet he did so, verbally, before signing the order, and his remarks seem to have been taken down by the stenographer, and are incorporated in the "case." An examination of those remarks will show that there is not the slightest foundation for such of the grounds of appeal as impute error in granting the motion upon the ground of contributory negligence on the part of the deceased. On the contrary, the circuit judge, in express terms, declared that he could not consider the question of contributory negligence on a motion for a nonsuit, and expressly recognized the rule laid down in several cases recently decided, that the only question for him to determine was whether there was an entire absence of testimony to support all or any of the necessary and material allegations in the complaint, and reached the conclusion that there was no evidence to support the averment that the death of the deceased was caused by any negligence on the part of the defendant company, its servants or agents. So that the only practical question in this case is whether there was any error on the part of the circuit judge in reaching this conclusion, for there can be no doubt that the allegation of negligence was a necessary and material allegation, and, unless some evidence was offered to sustain it, the nonsuit was properly granted. It is true that the circuit judge also held that the place where the injury complained of was received was not a "traveled place," and hence the provisions of Gen. St. §§ 1483, 1529,[1] did not apply; and that this also is made the basis of one of the other grounds of appeal; but the correctness of the judge's ruling is so completely vindicated by the recent decision of this court in the case of Neely v. Railroad Co., 33 S. C. 136, 11 S. E. Rep. 636, that it cannot be necessary to say more upon the subject. In the first place, we agree with the circuit judge that the point where the disaster occurred was not a "traveled place," in the sense of these words as used in the statute, which manifestly contemplates a way along which persons are not only accustomed, but have a right, to travel, and certainly does not include a railroad yard; and in the second place the deceased was not injured while crossing, or attempting or intending to cross, the railroad track, and therefore the provisions of the statute do not apply; for, as is said by the late chief justice in the case just cited: "There can be no doubt but that the object of these sections [1483 and 1529] was to prevent collisions which might occur between persons attempting to cross the track of the railroad and the locomotive and cars approaching at the same moment, and the provisions of the act did not include, nor was the act intended to include, injuries inflicted upon by-standers not intending to cross."

The only remaining question, therefore, is whether there was error in holding that there was an absence of any testimony tending to show negligence on the part of defendant. After a careful examination of the testimony, as set out in the case, we must say that we have failed to discover any evidence tending to show negligence. We do not see that the defendant either did anything which, under the circumstances, it ought not to have done, or that it omitted to do anything which it ought to have done. It appears that the defendant was shifting its train, in its own yard, in the usual way, and that the deceased was where he had no legal right to be, and where the servants of the company had no reason to suppose he would be, and hence there was no occasion for them to keep a lookout, or give signals that a train was approaching. We suppose they were doing what was probably done every day in the same way, and doubtless many times a day. But even if those in charge of the shifting-engine saw, or ought to

have seen, the deceased standing between the main line and the side track where the freight engine which he was watching stood, they would have had no reason to apprehend that he was within reach of the shifting train, as there was ample room for him to stand there in safety, as the evidence was that the two tracks were some 10 or 15 feet apart. Even if he had been standing on the track, where he had no right to be, and where defendant did have a right to move its train, accustomed as he was to visit the depot and telegraph office, he must have known that the tracks were used for shifting trains daily, and the engineer in charge of the shifting-engine would naturally assume that he would get out of the way. But, more than this, one of the plaintiff's witnesses, who was within 20 feet of deceased when he was struck, though he saw the shifting train approaching, gave no warning to the deceased, for the reason that he did not see that he was in any danger, and yet the plaintiff asks that the court shall assume that those in charge of the shifting-train saw, or ought to have seen, that deceased was in a position of danger. The eighth ground of appeal is based upon a misrepresentation of the testimony in that it exaggerates the distance which the steps of the passenger-car extended beyond the body of the coach, and assumes that this projection was unusual, and was the cause of the injury. There was absolutely no testimony that this projection was the cause of the injury, as it was possible, from the evidence, that the car might have struck the deceased, standing within two feet of the main line, even if there had been no steps to the car; and we think there was no evidence that the steps were of an unusual kind, for the only witness who speaks upon this subject is Garrett, who does not even claim to have been an expert, and all that even he says is in answer to the question: "Have you ever seen any other coach that way?" "I have never noticed one, if they did." This it seems to us is very far from affording any evidence that there was anything peculiar or unusual in the steps of that particular car. It is, however, contended that the failure to stop the shifting train after the hind wheels of the passenger coach had passed over the leg of the deceased, before the other wheels of the coach, and those of the tender and engine could reach the unfortunate man, affords evidence of negligence on the part of those in charge of the shifting-engine. But there is not the slightest evidence that the train could have been stopped in so short a distance, even by the exercise of the utmost effort and skill; and surely it is not to be inferred, without evidence, that those in charge of the shifting-train would be guilty of so barbarous and cruel an act as to wantonly run over a human being incapable of moving out of the way. The judgment of this court is that the judgment of the circuit court be affirmed. .

McGowan, J., concurs.

[1] Gen. St. S. C. § 1483, requires railway corporations to ring a bell or sound a whistle at a distance of 500 yards from all public crossings. Section 1529 makes a railway corporation liable for injuries to persons, resulting from collision at such crossings for failure to give the signals, unless the person injured was guilty of gross negligence.

ATLANTIC PHOSPHATE CO. v. SULLIVAN.

(Supreme Court of South Carolina. Aug. 11, 1891.)

CONTRACT OF SALE — WHAT CONSTITUTES — EVIDENCE—REPLY.

1. A written offer to sell defendant 100 tons of fertilizer, "with the privilege of 200 tons more at the same price if in stock unsold or when wanted" by defendant, was made by plaintiff's salesman, subject to approval by plaintiff's general agent, and was returned, indorsed "Approved" by the general agent, with a letter, written by his direction, stating that the contract for 100 tons was approved, but that plaintiff could not now promise to supply more than that. *Held,* that the court properly charged, in an action for the price of the 100 tons, that, if the offer was approved by the general agent, and the letter written by his direction, and the two were sent together to defendant, the original offer and the letter constituted the contract between the parties.

2. The court properly refused to charge at defendant's request that, if plaintiff had on hand or could have shipped when demanded the 200 tons, and failed to do so, plaintiff was responsible for damages sustained by defendant because of such failure.

3. The letter, being a part of the contract, was competent evidence.

4. The allegations of a counter-claim are sufficiently put in issue by a reply stating that plaintiff, "replying to the counter-claim, denies the same."

Appeal from common pleas circuit court of Greenville county; IZLAR, Judge.

Action by Atlantic Phosphate Company against John D. Sullivan for goods sold and delivered to defendant under a written contract. A counter-claim was pleaded by defendant. Verdict and judgment for plaintiff, and defendant appeals. Affirmed.

The plaintiff introduced in evidence a written offer by his agent as follows: "Mr. John D. Sullivan—Dear Sir: I hereby offer to sell you for account of the Atlantic Phosphate Company, of Charleston, S. C., the following fertilizers, at their works on Ashley river, on the terms and at the prices hereinafter named, subject to the approval of the general agents at Charleston: (100 tons of fertilizer,) with privilege of two hundred tons more at same prices, if in stock unsold when wanted, or when you notify us you will want it. * * * G. W. McIVER, Traveling Agent. Accepted in duplicate, January 12, 1888. JOHN D. SULLIVAN. Approved January 16, 1888. PELZER, RODGERS & Co., General Agents." After the introduction of the testimony the court charged the jury as follows: "This action was brought by the plaintiff to recover the value of one hundred tons of fertilizers alleged to have been sold and delivered by the plaintiff to Mr. John D. Sullivan, the defendant, and for which, it is alleged, he has not paid. The defendant admits the corporation of the plaintiff. But while he admits that he received the one hundred tons of fertilizers, he sets it up, by way of defense, that he was induced by the plaintiff to get two hundred additional tons, and that the plaintiff having failed to deliver the two hundred additional tons, that he had to get guano elsewhere, and that he was damaged by this breach of the contract entered into between the defendant and the plaintiff for the two hundred additional tons, and he sets up a counter-claim for damages for that breach of contract. Now, a counter-claim is in the nature of a cross-action. The defendant sets up these facts as a counter-claim, by which he says he was damaged by that failure to deliver to the extent of $2,000. Now, I charge you in reference to this contract: The construction of this contract is a matter of law for the court, and I charge you that this offer to sell by the traveling agent, Mr. McIver, to Mr. Sullivan, on the 12th of January, 1888, did not become a complete contract until it was submitted to Pelzer, Rodgers & Co., in Charleston, for their approval. That up to that time no party was bound by the contract, and when it was submitted to Pelzer, Rodgers & Co., in Charleston, if they had approved of that contract, then it would have become a binding contract upon all of the parties here, and Pelzer, Rodgers & Co. would have been bound to have complied with the terms of that contract; and also the defendant would have been bound by the terms of it. Now, you have heard the testimony of Mr. McIver that these duplicates were to be sent to Charleston, to be submitted to Pelzer, Rodgers & Co., and that it was returned to Mr. Sullivan, together with this letter. If you believe from the testimony that this contract was signed by Pelzer, Rodgers & Co., and that this letter was written by their direction, and that the two were sent together to Mr. John D. Sullivan, then this original offer for sale and the letter together, I charge you, made the contract between the parties. If this paper had stood alone, and no letter had been sent, I charge you that this would have been the contract; and before Mr. Sullivan could have recovered he would have to show that the Atlantic Phosphate Company had in stock and unsold at the time he ordered the same the two hundred tons additional. Now, if this paper had stood by itself it would have shown that, for it says: 'With the privilege of two hundred tons if, when ordered, the plaintiff had the same in stock and unsold.' Defendant would have had to show that they had that much in stock and unsold when he ordered. I call your attention to that in case you should come to the conclusion that these two papers did not go together and did not make up the contract. For, taking that as the contract alone, then I say, that the testimony would have to show that Mr. Sullivan had ordered his two hundred tons, and that they had in stock at that time, unsold, two hundred tons. Now, the letter which was written by Mr. Freeman, you will recollect, was written on the 24th of February, which was eight days after this offer was made, and I do not recollect the testimony whether in that eight days Mr. Sullivan had demanded these two hundred tons or not. Now, I say that the traveling agent, Mr. McIver, could not act outside of the authority which was given him, and if he did, it would not bind Pelzer, Rodgers & Co., because he could not make a contract binding Pelzer, Rodgers & Co. until the offer was sent in for approval.

Now, if you come to the conclusion that this paper was sent alone, and that Mr. Sullivan demanded the two hundred additional tons, and that they had two hundred tons in stock, and it was unsold at the time,—I say if he was standing on this paper alone,—why Pelzer, Rodgers & Co. would be liable for such damages as you think he has sustained by reason of plaintiff's failure to keep the contract. But if you come to the conclusion that this letter was written by direction of Pelzer, Rodgers & Co., and was sent with this contract to defendant, and that this paper was signed by Pelzer, Rodgers & Co., then it was not any more than a contract for the sale of one hundred tons of guano, and you will ascertain from the testimony whether it has been paid for or not. If you come to the conclusion that the contract was only for one hundred tons, and that that one hundred tons was not paid for, it would be your duty to find your verdict for the plaintiff for $1,300, or whatever the balance is, with interest from May 1, 1889. On the other hand, if you come to the conclusion that they approved for the whole amount, and they had it on hand and unsold when ordered by defendant, and did not ship it, why then you will ascertain what damages, if any, Mr. Sullivan has suffered, and your verdict will then be for the difference between the damages Mr. Sullivan claims and what he owes. I have been requested by the defendant to charge you: 'First. That the plaintiff is bound by the contract as signed and approved by Pelzer, Rodgers & Co., and its terms are not affected by the letter written by Mr. G. W. McIver and addressed to the defendant.' I refuse to charge you that. 'Second. That if the jury believe from the evidence that the plaintiff had on hand, or could have shipped to the defendant when demanded, the two hundred tons of fertilizer referred to in the contract, or any part thereof, and failed so to ship the same, then the plaintiff is responsible for any damage sustained by the defendant by reason of such failure.' I charge you that that is a good proposition if the evidence satisfies you that the plaintiff had two hundred tons on hand and unsold, and refused to ship it, if they were bound under the contract to ship it. Take the record."

Perry & Heyward, for appellant. *Wells & Orr*, for respondent.

McIVER, J. The action in this case was to recover from defendant the amount claimed to be due plaintiff for 100 tons of commercial fertilizers, alleged to have been sold and delivered by plaintiff to defendant. The complaint, among other things, contains an allegation that this sale was made under a written agreement, a copy of which is set out in the "case." This agreement was executed by the traveling agent of the plaintiff, G. Walter McIver, and the defendant, on the 12th of January, 1888, the terms of which will be hereinafter more specifically stated. Defendant answered, admitting the execution of an agreement for the sale by plaintiff to defendant of certain fertilizers at the stipulated prices therein stated, but denying all the other allegations of the complaint, except as afterwards admitted in the answer; "that by the terms of the agreement made between the plaintiff and defendant the plaintiff bound itself to ship to defendant one hundred tons of fertilizers, as specified in said agreement, and two hundred tons more at the same prices, if in stock unsold, when ordered by defendant, or when notified by defendant that he, defendant, would want it;" that defendant, relying upon this stipulation for the delivery of the additional 200 tons when wanted, with which the agent of plaintiff represented that plaintiff would be able to comply, entered into engagements with others to furnish them with said fertilizers, and for this purpose ordered from plaintiff said additional 200 tons, but the plaintiff failed and refused to ship the same to defendant, although the plaintiff then had the same in stock unsold; that in the mean time the price of fertilizers had advanced rapidly, and defendant, in order to comply with his engagements to others, was compelled to buy fertilizers elsewhere, at an advanced price, which occasioned him much damage and expense, which he sets up as a counter-claim to plaintiff's alleged cause of action. The plaintiff filed a reply in these words: "The plaintiff, replying to the counter-claim set up in the answer of the defendant herein, denies the same." At the trial defendant's counsel moved for judgment upon the ground that the reply contained no sufficient denial of the counter-claim. This motion was refused, and defendant excepted, whereupon the plaintiff proceeded to offer testimony in support of its claim. The written agreement above referred to was offered in evidence, and contains, among other things, an offer by the traveling agent, McIver, to sell to defendant the fertilizers sued for, "subject to the approval of the general agents at Charleston, * * * with privilege of two hundred tons more at same prices, if in stock unsold, when wanted, or when you notify us you will want it;" and this paper, bearing date 12th January, 1888, is signed by McIver, as traveling agent, with these words appended: "Accepted in duplicate. JOHN D. SULLIVAN," —with these words following: "Approved January 16th, 1888. PELZER, RODGERS & Co., General Agents." This agreement was signed by McIver and Sullivan on the day of its date, 12th January, 1888, in duplicate; and both copies were on the same day forwarded to Pelzer, Rodgers & Co., who were to be the general agents of plaintiff, in Charleston. On the 16th of January, 1888, McIver, who had in the mean time returned to Charleston, after conference with the general agents, wrote a letter to defendant, by their directions, in which, among other things, he says: "I inclose your contract of one hundred tons, duly approved. The sales made by the company have been so large in the past ten days (something like twelve thousand tons) that they cannot now promise to supply more than the one hundred tons for which your contract calls. Later on we may be able to let you have some ammoniated goods, but we have to go into the market and buy more materials, and the prices will be higher. At present our contracts foot up as much as we can manufacture to 1st April." To this letter, inclosing duplicate of the agreement, which was mailed on the 16th of January, 1888, and would have been received by defendant, in due course of mail, on the next day, and which was in fact received by him, but when, precisely, does not appear, though it was about the time it was due in Greenville, there does not seem to have been any reply. There is testimony, however, tending to show that the 100 tons were shipped to defendant, and received and used by him. The defendant offered testimony tending to show that one of the inducements for him to enter into this agreement was the assurance of the traveling agent that plaintiff would be able to supply the additional 200 tons which he ordered, and, failing to get, had to go into the market, and supply himself at higher prices, and otherwise incurred expense in traveling and hotel bills, etc.; but the only evidence adduced by defendant for the purpose of showing that plaintiff had "in stock, unsold," at the time defendant ordered the additional 200 tons, which tim the testimony does not fix, is that of his witness, Freeman, who says that, in reply to a letter from him to Pelzer, Rodgers & Co., written at the instance of d fendant, asking them "to quote acid phosphates," they answered under date of 24th January, 1888, offering to sell the witness "fifty tons pure acid phosphate, in dissolved bone bags, at $11.00 per ton, spot cash, F. O. B. cars here, in car-load lots," which price was somewhat higher than that stipulated for in the agreement with defendant. The case having been submitted to the j ury under the charge of the circuit judge, a verdict was rendered in favor of the plaintiff for the whole amount claimed, and, judgment having been entered thereon, defendant appeals upon the several grounds set out in the record.

The first ground, alleging error in the ruling that there was a sufficient denial of the counter-claim in plaintiff's reply, cannot be sustained. It seems to us that the form of the denial adopted in the reply was quite sufficient to put in issue all the allegations upon which the counter-claim rested.

The second and third grounds impute error to the circuit judge in holding that the letter of McIver to defendant constituted any part of the contract, or could have any effect upon it. The charge of the judge seems to be set out in full in the "case," and should be incorporated in the report of this case; and in our judgment it fully and clearly sets forth the law applicable to this case. In the first place, the judge did not instruct the jury that the letter constituted a part of the contract, but his instruction practically was this: That the paper called the "agreement," when executed in Greenville by the traveling agent of the plaintiff and the defendant, amounted to nothing more than an offer by the former to sell the goods in question to the defendant, provided the general agents in Charleston approved; and that until such approval there was

no contract binding on the plaintiff at all. That this was correct is manifest from the express terms of the paper: "I hereby offer to sell you, for account of the Atlantic Phosphate Company of Charleston, S. C., the following fertilizers, * * * subject to the approval of the general agents at Charleston." The paper, then, not being a contract until it was so approved, the jury were instructed that: "If you believe from the testimony that this contract was signed by Pelzer, Rodgers & Co., and that this letter was written by their direction, and that the two were sent together to Mr. John D. Sullivan, then this original offer for sale and the letter together, I charge you, made the contract between the parties." This is very different from saying in broad and unqualified terms that the letter constituted a part of the contract. The paper, as originally signed, being nothing more than a proposal by a subagent to sell on certain terms, subject to the approval of the general agents, could only become a contract by such approval, which might be absolute or qualified; and such qualification might be indicated either by alterations in the paper as originally written, or by any accompanying writing,—by letter, as in this case,—written by or under the direction of the general agents, and transmitted along with the paper containing the offer to sell, to the defendant, who was thereby fully informed of what the parties authorized to contract were willing to do; and, if he was unwilling to accept the qualifications contained in the accompanying letter, all he had to do was to withdraw from the contract as thus qualified; for, having accepted the offer upon the terms originally proposed, he would have had a perfect right to withdraw when he was notified of an alteration in the terms; but, not having done so, he cannot now insist upon terms which he was informed by the agent of the persons competent to contract they could not agree to. Having received and used the 100 tons of fertilizers, he cannot escape from his obligation to pay for the same according to the terms of the contract, by insisting upon other terms originally embraced in the offer to sell, but practically erased therefrom by the letter accompanying the contract when it was returned to him. It can scarcely be necessary to cite authority to show that the terms of a contract may be contained in several instruments of writing, which, as is said in 2 Pars. Cont. 503, "if made at the same time, between the same parties, and in relation to the same subject, will be held to constitute but one contract, and the court will read them in such order of time and priority as will carry into effect the intention of the parties, as the same may be gathered from all the instruments taken together." The same doctrine is frequently exemplified in cases arising under the statute of frauds, as may be seen by reference to the case of Varnish Co. *v*. Lorick, 29 S. C. 533, 8 S. E. Rep. 8, and the cases therein cited.

The fourth ground of appeal imputes error on the part of the circuit judge in refusing to charge the jury "that if the jury believe from the evidence that the plaintiff had on hand, or could have shipped to the defendant, when demanded, the two hundred tons of fertilizers referred to in the contract, or any part thereof, and failed so to ship the same, then the plaintiff is responsible for any damages sustained by the defendant by reason of such failure." The "case" does not show that such request was refused. On the contrary, the language used by the judge was this: "I charge you that that is a good proposition, if the evidence satisfies you that the plaintiff had two hundred tons on hand and unsold, and refused to ship it, if they were bound under the contract to ship it;" plainly meaning that, if they should come to the conclusion that the letter had not been written under the direction of Pelzer, Rodgers & Co., or had not been transmitted to defendant along with the duplicate copy of the contract when returned to him, as the previous part of the charge most clearly shows. But, even if the request had been refused outright, there would have been no error, for by incorporating in the request the words, "or could have shipped to the defendant, when demanded, the two hundred tons," etc., the whole request was vitiated; for there was no such provision in the paper containing the original offer to sell. The provision there found was, "if in stock unsold."—a very different thing from that embraced in the request, for, even if the plaintiff did not have "in stock and unsold" the additional number of tons when ordered, the plaintiff might still have shipped them to defendant, by going into the market and buying from others. It is very clear, therefore, that this request, as presented, could not properly have been charged, and that the judge's remark when it was submitted was entirely correct.

The fifth ground—"that his honor erred in allowing the letter of G. W. McIver to be put in evidence for the purpose of contradicting the written contract of the plaintiff"—cannot be sustained. In the first place, we do not see that any such objection was interposed when the letter was offered in evidence. But, waiving that, it is quite certain that the letter was neither offered nor received for the purpose of contradicting any written contract. On the contrary, it was offered as a part of the contract, and for this purpose was clearly competent.

The only remaining ground of appeal, imputing error to the circuit judge "in charging the jury in respect to matters of fact," is couched in such general terms as would justify us in disregarding it altogether, for in the exception there is no specification of any instance in which the clause of the constitution upon which this exception is based has been violated. But, waiving this, we do not find anything in the charge to sustain the exception. In the folios of the "case," to which we are referred in appellant's argument as indicating that the judge charged upon matters of fact, we do not see that there was any expression, or even indication of opinion, on the part of the circuit judge as to any question of fact; and, on the contrary, all such questions seem to have been fairly and fully submitted to the jury. The judgment of this court is that the judgment of the circuit court be affirmed.

McGOWAN, J., concurs.

DUCKETT v. POOL.

(Supreme Court of South Carolina. Aug. 11, 1891.)

ENTICING AWAY SERVANT—EVIDENCE—EXEMPLARY DAMAGES—HARMLESS ERROR.

1. Where defendant, in an action for enticing a servant from his employer, offers the servant to prove there was no contract of employment, plaintiff, having laid the foundation on cross-examination, may prove in reply that the servant had admitted the contract to others, for the purpose of discrediting the testimony of the servant.

2. An instruction, asked by defendant, that to constitute the relation of master and servant the terms of the employment must bind the servant to give his exclusive personal service to the master for the whole time agreed, was properly modified to the effect that the relation existed if the servant was bound to render services for such time as was usual and necessary in the work for which he was engaged.

3. One who entices away a servant being liable to the master in damages by the common law, it was harmless error to charge that such enticement was a "violation of our statute for which damages could be recovered," though no such statute existed.

4. An instruction that if defendant, knowing that the servant was under contract with plaintiff, induced him to leave plaintiff's employ before the contract was terminated, defendant would be liable unless the servant voluntarily left before the inducement was offered, is not objectionable as not stating the time when the inducement was made, and when it contemplated the servant's abandoning his employment.

5. Where the testimony showed that defendant acted maliciously or in wanton disregard of plaintiff's rights in enticing away his servant, the court properly charged that exemplary damages could be awarded.

Appeal from common pleas circuit court of Laurens county; WALLACE, Judge.

Action by Thomas J. Duckett against Martin B. Pool for damages for enticing away a servant. Verdict and judgment for plaintiff, and defendant appeals. Affirmed.

After introduction of the testimony, the court charged the jury as follows:

"Counsel on either side have submitted what are called 'requests to charge.' They are always statements of what, in the opinion of counsel, are legal principles that arise out of the case. I will read them to you, and, after that, I will, in a more connected form, undertake to explain to you what the principles involved in this case are. They are, as presented by this case, a little intricate, and it is important that they should be understood. The plaintiff asks me to charge: 'First. That if the jury believe from the evidence that the man Murrell was under contract with the plaintiff, Duckett, and under said contract was to work plaintiff's land under his (plaintiff's) direction and control, and to receive as compensation therefor one-half of the crops, then said Murrell was plaintiff's servant.' Well, as a general statement, that is true, and I charge you that. 'Second. That if the defendant, Pool, with a knowledge of the said contract, induced or caused the man Murrell to leave plaintiff's employment or violate his contract, he committed a wrong, and is liable to plaintiff for such damages as he (plaintiff) sustained by reason of the said Murrell leaving plaintiff's premises.' I charge you that. 'Third. That, so far as the rights of the plaintiff and defendant are concerned, it was not necessary that the contract between Duckett and Murrell should be in writing.' I charge you that. 'Fourth. That if the jury believe from the evidence that the defendant, Pool, induced or caused Murrell to leave plaintiff's employment, and in so doing knew of the contract and acted willfully, then he is liable to plaintiff, not only for actual damages, but exemplary damages as well. Hiring one's servant after notice of the contract is prima facie evidence of enticement.' I charge you that. I will have more to say to you about all of these things when we get through.

"The defendant asks me to charge you as follows: 'First. If Mr. Duckett, the plaintiff, made a verbal contract with Henry Murrell, by the terms of which he was to live on his (Duckett's) farm and work for him for the year of 1889, the terms of that contract must also be such as bound Murrell to give his exclusive personal service to Duckett for the whole period of time agreed upon, and under his (Duckett's) direction, or he cannot recover any damages against Mr. Pool in this action, and you must find a verdict for the defendant; because it is necessary that the testimony establish the relation of master and servant before the plaintiff can recover any damages; and in order to do so, when one receives a portion of the crops he produces in lieu of wages, he must be bound to give his exclusive personal services to his employer, under his direction, or the relationship of master and servant does not exist, and this action cannot be maintained.' I will charge you that; but before I get through I will suggest some explanations and modifications of it. 'Second. If, however, you find that there was verbal contract between Duckett and the man Murrell, by the terms of which Murrell was bound to render to Duckett his exclusive personal service under his direction for the year of 1889, and that this contract was made or agreed upon by Duckett and Murrell in November, 1888, or at any time previous to the last of December, 1888, and there seems there was no question that if made at all it was in November, 1888, I charge you, as matter of law, that such a contract was not binding on Murrell, and he could of his own volition leave the place or employment of Mr. Duckett, either after he had entered his service under the contract for 1889, or before he had done so, and enter the employment of Pool, and he would not be liable to Mr. Duckett for any damages he may have sustained by reason of Murrell's refusing to remain and carry out his part of the contract alleged to have been made for the year 1889.' I charge you that; and I will explain it to you more fully before I get through. 'Third. If Pool did induce or entice the man Murrell to leave Duck-

ett's place and employment, and those inducements only contemplated his doing so after his time of service under his contract with Duckett for 1888 had expired, and before he had entered upon his alleged contract for 1889, Pool is not liable to Duckett for any damages he may have sustained by reason of Murrell's abandoning his alleged contract with Duckett for 1889, even though, except for his employment by Pool, he had no intention of leaving Duckett's service upon the expiration of his term for 1888.' I charge you that, with the modification that I will state in my general charge. I charge you what is asked by both sides.

"Of course, you all understand that this is an action by Mr. Duckett against Mr. Pool to recover damages from Mr. Pool, because, as is alleged, Mr. Pool enticed Mr. Duckett's servant away from him, and thereby injured him, and he therefore brings his action to be reimbursed for any injury he has sustained by reason of such alleged enticement, and, for what are called 'exemplary damages;' because, as he alleges, Mr. Pool willfully did him this wrong. He must be punished for it by being compelled to pay exemplary damages, which is more and which is above what would be necessary to remunerate Mr. Duckett for any loss that he had sustained by his being induced away. That is the action. Now, to enable you to apply the testimony to the issues involved, you must know what a servant is, as that term is contemplated by the law. What is a servant? Now, everybody has a general idea what a servant is. In legal contemplation, a man is a servant who enters the employment of another, and agrees to act under the direction and control of the master, generally for compensation, or to do some specific thing under the control and direction of the master for compensation; whenever any one does that he sustains the relation of servant to his employer, and his employer sustains to him the relation of master. They are master and servant. Now, in some cases decided by our own supreme court, —a case reverted to in argument of counsel, one called Huff v. Watkins, 25 S. C. 243, down here in Newberry; another one of Daniel v. Swearengen, 6 S. C. 297, over here in Abbeville,—this question as to what was a servant arose, and whether or not an agricultural laborer who worked for a part of the crop upon the land of the landlord was a servant. Now, in those two cases, the court held that such a person was a servant, although he worked for a part of the crop, and not for what is called 'wages;' that is, payment in money. But if he worked for a compensation, or agreed to work under the direction of his employer in the cultivation of a crop, for which he was to receive a part of the crop produced by his labor, then he was an agricultural laborer.—not only an agricultural laborer, but a servant; and to entice him away from his employer, from his master, was a violation of our statute, for which damages could be recovered. So now the first question you will have to settle in this case, as matter of law and fact,—does the testimony satisfy you, from what I have stated to you, that this man Murrell was the servant of Mr. Duckett? Was he employed by Mr. Duckett for a part of the crop to work certain lands of Mr. Duckett under Mr. Duckett's direction and control? If he was, he was Mr. Duckett's servant, and to entice him away was a violation of the law. Now, in order to constitute a servant, even an agricultural servant, it is not necessary that he should work the whole year, but the time he should work is to be limited and described by the contract, and for the time limited in the contract he is to be under the control of his employer, and under his direction.

"Now, if he is employed to do certain work upon the farm, and that is the contract, and he is to do it under the direction of his employer, all the time that is necessary to do that work,—to perform his contract,—why that time belongs to the master,—to the employer. The time outside of that is not embraced in the contract, does not belong to the employer, and for another to employ him during that time is not a violation of the employer's rights, or a violation of our statute. Now, just to give a simple illustration: Suppose a servant was hired by somebody here in town to attend to his horse, and somebody who sleeps to himself hires him at night to cut up wood, too. That is no violation of the contract with the employer, because for all time that is not necessary in the performance of the duties of the contract, the labor incidental to the relation that he sustains to his employer, that time is his own. That is not under contract. He is not bound to render that, or to give an account of that to his employer. So, now, in the cultivation of a crop for a part of the crop under the direction of the employer, all the time that is necessary to perform that contract belongs to the employer; all the time outside of that belongs to the employe. So much for the servant. Now, what is enticement? Enticement is inducing him to break the contract, no matter what form it takes. If he breaks his contract on account of the conduct of somebody else, why, that somebody else violates the rights of the employer, and is liable to all the penalties and consequences of our statute upon the subject. Now, if you should find here as a matter of fact and of law, that Murrell was the servant of Mr. Duckett, and that in consequence of any conduct to that end by Mr. Pool, Mr. Pool knowing of the relation of Murrell to Mr. Duckett, why, then, he has enticed his servant away, and must take the consequences of his act. Now, it is alleged here, and was argued to you by counsel, that if this contract was made in November, 1888, that it related to the year 1889, that, therefore, it was a verbal contract not to be performed within a year, and therefore, under a statute that we call the 'statutes of frauds,' it was not binding upon the parties. That is so. If a contract is made in this state, and rests only in parol,—I mean a verbal contract,—that is not to be performed within a year, it does not bind the parties. They are not bound by it. And if Mr.

Duckett and this man Murrell made a contract for 1889 by word of mouth in November, 1888, it did not bind Murrell, and it did not bind Mr. Duckett. Either one of them could disregard it, without the other having any right to have damages or to compel its performance; and that is the law with regard to all verbal contracts, contracts of master and servant, or any other contract. When any verbal contract now, a contract resting in parol, is made, if it is not to be performed within a year, that contract does not bind the parties to it. Neither has any legal right under it. Now, you see, this was made in November, and it was to relate to 1889, and that was not to be performed within a year from the date of the contract. It was in November; the year would run out in November, 1889; and this was not to be performed until the expiration of the year 1889. Now, while neither of the parties to contracts like that have any enforceable legal right under it, still they can go on and perform it if they want to. It is a violation of no law for them to go on and perform the contract if they want to. It is done, and men do it every day. Men make contracts of that sort, and, while neither are bound by it, still they both go on and perform. And if there was a contract or hiring, a contract intended to establish the relation of master and servant, of that sort which is not binding upon either party, still both can go on and perform, and a stranger must not interfere to prevent the performance.

"So, now, if you find that there was a contract of this sort betwixt Mr. Duckett and Murrell, neither was bound by it, and both can go on and perform it; and if Mr. Pool comes in and interferes, and by his interference and on account of his interference Murrell jumps his contract, and goes and lives with him, Mr. Pool is just as responsible for his act as if Murrell had been bound by the contract that he had made with Mr. Duckett. Just the same exactly, notwithstanding Murrell was not bound to perform it; notwithstanding he might voluntarily abandon Mr. Duckett's plantation whenever he saw fit; still neither Pool, nor anybody else, had a right to induce him to do it by any act upon his part; and if you find that, in consequence of anything that Mr. Pool did, Murrell left and violated a contract that did not bind him, still Pool is just as liable as if Murrell was bound. But now you see Murrell had a right to go if he wanted to, notwithstanding the contract, because it was a verbal contract, not to be performed within a year. He had a right to go, and, if Murrell went away or out of his own head determined that he would not perform that contract, no matter what he did as evidence of his determination, if he determined that out of his own head that he would not perform that contract, and voluntarily sought other employment, his other employer, if he employed him without any inducement on his part to get Murrell to violate his agreement with Mr. Duckett, then his employer is not responsible, because the violation of the contract was voluntary upon the part of Murrell, upon the supposition that nobody could be liable for hiring Murrell under those circumstances, when no act that the employer had done had induced Murrell's act or actions in violating his contract with Mr. Duckett. You see the difference, Mr. Foreman.

"Now, in order to make this plain: Murrell had a right to go away whenever he wanted to, because the contract did not bind him; because Mr. Duckett says that the contract was made in November, and was to be performed throughout the year 1889. That did not bind Mr. Duckett, and did not bind Murrell, and Murrell had a right to go away. He had a right to hire himself to somebody else. He had a right, out of his own head, to conclude and determine, 'I will not perform that contract; I will not stick to it;' and if he did that out of his own head, and went and hired to somebody else, the other employer has committed no offense against the statute of this state, or against the common law. Murrell had a right to go, and his employer had a right to hire him. But if Murrell's determination to renounce his contract with Mr. Duckett was induced by the conduct of Pool, and then Pool hires him, Pool is responsible. You see the difference. If the hiring was done upon Murrell's own motion and action, and Mr. Pool had nothing to do with Murrell's determination in violating his contract with Mr. Duckett, then Pool is not liable. If Murrell's conduct in renouncing his contract with Mr. Duckett was induced by any action upon the part of Pool, then Pool is liable. If Pool interfered he is liable. If Pool did not interfere, and Murrell, out of his own head, went to Mr. Pool, and said, 'I am not going to live with Mr. Duckett; I have made up my mind to that, and I want to hire to somebody else;' and upon that Pool hired him,—Pool is not responsible. I do not know, gentlemen, that there is any other legal principle that it is necessary that I should state to you. If you think on the law and the facts that the plaintiff is entitled to recover damages, then he is entitled to recover such damages as it has been proven to your satisfaction he has sustained by reason of Mr. Pool's conduct. And if you think that Mr. Pool, knowing of Duckett's rights, willfully violated them, then it is competent for jury, if they think proper, to award a larger sum than mere remuneration for the damages that Mr. Duckett has sustained, and that sum, in addition to the amount of injury that Mr. Duckett has sustained, is called 'punitive damages;' it has got several names,—'exemplary damages,' 'vindictive damages.' That is intended by way of punishment to Mr. Pool for willfully violating the law, and for willfully violating another man's rights. That is a matter that is left to the jury. It is more largely perhaps in the discretion of the jury than any other matter that is submitted to their consideration. If you do not think that Mr. Duckett is entitled to any damages on the law and the facts, then you simply say, 'We find for the defendant.' If you find for the plaintiff, then you say, 'We find for the plaintiff so many dollars and cents,' Mr. Foreman, writing

v.18s.e.no.23—35

out the amount in words, and not stating it in figures. You can retire."

W. H. Martin, for appellant. Ferguson & Featherstone, for respondent.

McIVER, J. The action in this case was commenced on the 9th of January, 1889, and its purpose was to recover damages from the defendant under the allegation that he had enticed an alleged servant of plaintiff, one Henry Murrell, to violate his contract with plaintiff, by leaving his service during the time he had contracted to serve the plaintiff, and taking service with the defendant, who knew at the time that said Henry Murrell was under a contract to serve plaintiff as an agricultural laborer for the year 1889. This being the second appeal in this case, reference may be had to the case as reported in 33 S. C. 238, 11 S. E. Rep. 689, for a fuller statement of the pleadings and testimony than it is deemed necessary to make here. The case was heard before his honor, Judge WALLACE, and a jury, when a verdict in favor of plaintiff for $200 having been rendered, and judgment having been entered thereon, defendant appealed upon the following grounds: (1) Because of error in admitting the declarations of Henry Murrell as to having entered into a contract with plaintiff; (2) because of error in instructing the jury "that it was not necessary, in order to create the relationship of master and servant, that one receiving a share of the crops produced in lieu of wages should be bound, under his contract, to render his exclusive personal service to his employer;" (3) because of error in instructing the jury "that to entice a servant to leave his employer was a violation of our statutes, for which damages could be recovered;" (4) because of error in instructing the jury "that if, in consequence of anything Mr. Pool did, Murrell left and violated his contract that did not bind him, still Pool is liable, unless his honor had qualified this statement by stating the time when the inducements must have been offered, and when they contemplated Murrell leaving Duckett's employ;" (5) because the jury were instructed "that they could award to the plaintiff punitive or exemplary damages;" (6) because the jury were instructed "that they could award to the plaintiff damages against the defendant by way of punishment."

The first ground of appeal is manifestly misleading, as it seems to be based upon the assumption that the plaintiff was permitted, against the objection of defendant, to offer in evidence the declarations of Henry Murrell to show that he was under contract with the plaintiff when he left and took service with defendant, which is shown by the "case" to be an entirely unfounded assumption, for, on the contrary, it there appears that when the plaintiff, in the development of his testimony in chief, undertook to prove the declarations of Murrell in regard to the alleged contract, the question was objected to by defendant's counsel, and his objection was sustained. Afterwards, when the defendant had offered Murrell as a witness to show that he had made no contract with plaintiff for the year 1889, and on the cross-examination he had been asked if he had not admitted the contract in a conversation with two specified persons, at a place and time designated, the plaintiff was very properly, in reply, permitted to prove by the persons thus specified that he had made such admissions; for the plaintiff, having laid the necessary foundation, in the cross-examination of Murrell, was clearly entitled to offer, in reply, evidence to contradict him, and thus discredit his testimony, as to one of the material issues in the case. Whether there was a contract between plaintiff and Murrell was certainly a material issue in the case,—in fact, was the primal inquiry; and certainly the plaintiff, in reply, had a right to resort to any of the recognized modes of discrediting the testimony adduced by defendant as to this material issue. This is plainly what was done, and hence the first ground of appeal cannot be sustained.

All of the other grounds impute error to the circuit judge, in his several instructions to the jury, and it is therefore but fair to the judge that his charge, which is set out in full in the "case," should be incorporated by the reporter in his report of the case; especially when, as it seems to us, that, with the exception of the fifth and sixth grounds of appeal, which raise the same question, all of the other grounds, unless perhaps it be the third, are based upon a misconception of the charge, which in fact recognizes substantially the positions contended for by appellant in his second and fourth grounds of appeal. It will be observed that each of the requests to charge submitted by both parties were first set out by the circuit judge *in hæc verba*, and that every one of them were charged, with certain amplifications, explanations, and modifications given in the general charge all of which we fully approve. For instance, take the second ground of appeal, which seems to rest upon the idea that to constitute the relation of master and servant it is necessary that the latter shall be bound by his contract to render his exclusive personal service to his employer. Now, the request upon which this ground is based was charged with "some explanations and modifications of it." And these explanations and modifications simply amount to this: that the term "exclusive," upon which stress seems to be laid by appellant, is not to be construed as preventing the servant from devoting a part of the time covered by his contract to his own purposes, or even to the service of another, provided he is under an obligation to devote so much of that time as may be necessary to perform properly, and in the usual way, the service for which he is employed by the master. For example, to vary the illustration used by the circuit judge, one who is employed to serve another, even under a written contract, as a farm laborer, for a given period of time, is not debarred from making baskets for his own use or profit at night, when his services as a farm laborer are not expected or required, and his doing so would be no violation

of his contract with his master; the test being that he is required to render such service and devote such time as is usual and necessary to perform the work for which he is employed to the master exclusively, and he cannot, without a breach of his contract, devote any of the time, in which he ought to be engaged in the service for which he is employed, to the service of any one else. This is the only explanation or modification of defendant's second request, and it is plainly warranted both by law and common sense.

The third ground of appeal cannot be sustained; for, even conceding that the judge may have erred, technically, in saying to the jury that to entice a servant to leave the employment of his master "was a violation of our statute for which damages could be recovered," inasmuch as no statute giving an action for damages in such a case has been brought to our attention, yet it was such an error as could not possibly have prejudiced appellant, and therefore affords no ground for the reversal of the judgment. It was wholly immaterial whether defendant's liability arose by statute or at common law, so far as this case is concerned; and it is not questioned that the act with which defendant was charged rendered one liable, at common law, to an action for damages.

It is somewhat difficult to understand the precise point intended to be raised by the fourth ground of appeal. This ground seems to impute an error of omission rather than of commission, and it would be sufficient to dispose of it by saying that there was no distinct request to charge the special proposition there presented. But, reading this ground in the light of the argument presented by counsel for appellant, the contention seems to be that the proposition submitted to the jury was erroneous, because it was not accompanied with the qualification contended for. It seems to us, however, that the whole tenor of the charge plainly recognizes this so-called qualification. It is impossible to conceive that the jury should have been led to suppose, from anything contained in the charge, that the defendant would have been liable if he had induced Murrell to enter his employment before he had contracted with plaintiff, or after such contract had terminated. On the contrary, the idea plainly presented by the charge was that, if the defendant, knowing that Murrell was under contract with the plaintiff, induced Murrell to disregard such contract, and leave plaintiff's employment before the termination of such contract, the defendant would be liable, unless the contract was terminated by Murrell of his own free will and accord, before any inducement was offered him by the defendant to enter his service. The contract not being in writing, and being an agreement not to be performed within a year, was not, under the statute of frauds, legally binding upon Murrell; and hence he could, without legal fault, abandon it at any time. But still, as was held under the former appeal in this case, if Murrell was induced by defendant to abandon the contract and enter into the service of defendant, he would be liable; and all this was plainly laid before the jury by his honor, Judge WALLACE. We do not think, therefore, that the fourth ground of appeal can be sustained.

It only remains to consider the question presented by the fifth and sixth grounds of appeal, viz., whether, in a case of this kind, the jury is at liberty to award punitive or exemplary damages, by way of punishment to the wrong-doer, where the testimony shows that the defendant acted maliciously, or in wanton disregard of the rights of the plaintiff. It is not to be denied that there is much conflict of authority elsewhere as to this question.—so much so as to lead to quite a celebrated controversy between two eminent text-writers, Sedgwick and Greenleaf, which may be found fully set forth in 7 Amer. & Eng. Enc. Law, 450–477, together with the comments of Mr. Justice GREEN of the supreme court of West Virginia, favoring the view contended for by Greenleaf. But, in that same valuable publication (5 Amer. & Eng. Enc. Law, 21–28) the other view is presented as best sustained by the authorities. Now, while the writer of this opinion is disposed to think that the weight of the argument is in favor of the view contended for by Greenleaf.—that in no case should damages be awarded against a defendant, in a civil action, by way of punishment,—and that, if the question were entirely an open one, he would be disposed to adopt that view, yet, as it requires that the terms "exemplary," "vindictive," or "punitive" should be given a signification entirely different from that which they usually and properly bear, it would be a grave question whether a court should take such liberties with the language, for the purpose of protecting a wrong-doer. But, without going into a discussion of this question, it is quite sufficient for us to say that in this state, at least, the doctrine is settled, by a long line of unbroken authority, that in an action of tort, where the testimony satisfies the jury that the defendant acted maliciously, willfully, or in wanton disregard of the rights of the defendant, the jury may, in addition to such damages as will compensate the plaintiff for any loss or injury which he may have sustained by the wrongful act of the defendant, either in person, property, or feelings, award other damages, called, indifferently, "exemplary," "vindictive," or "punitive," by way of punishment to the defendant, and as a means of deterring him and others from committing like wrongful and wanton acts. Johnson v. Hannahan, 3 Strob. 432, where the idea of punishment of the defendant is plainly recognized as one of the elements entering into the assessment of damages: Spikes v. English, 4 Strob. 37, where the same idea is distinctly presented; Hamilton v. Feemster, 4 Rich. 573; Wolff v. Cohen, 8 Rich. 144; Rowe v. Moses, 9 Rich. 423, where the case of Chanellor v. Vaughn, 2 Bay, 416, in which it was distinctly held that the jury were at liberty, after considering all the circumstances of the case, to award such damages "as they thought would be commensurate with the nature of the injury, *and such as would effectually check such evil,*" (italics ours,) was quoted with approval; and O'NEALL, J., in delivering the opinion of the court of appeals, adds: "This direction has been, in all subsequent cases, followed; and it may be here remarked that, although the party defendant, in assault and battery, may be liable both civilly and criminally, yet the damages found on the civil side of the court, if they are regarded as a sufficient punishment, uniformly make the punishment criminally nominal." In Windham v. Rhame, 11 Rich. 283, which was an action on the case for obstructing a way, the jury were instructed on circuit that "punitive damages might be found in the sound discretion of the jury, if evil motive or unworthy conduct, deserving punishment, had been established against the defendant;" and, in response to an exception to this instruction, the court of appeals expressly affirm the right of a jury, in such a case, to give damages "by way of punishment." In Jefcoat v. Knotts, 11 Rich. 649, the same doctrine was held, and the case just cited was expressly approved. So, also, in Railroad Co. v. Partlow, 14 Rich. 237, the same doctrine was recognized, the court citing with approval the cases of Rowe v. Moses and Chanellor v. Vaughn, supra. In Burckhalter v. Coward, 16 S. C. 435, which was an action of slander, the jury were instructed that the damages "should be sufficient to compensate the plaintiff for the injury done him, and to punish the defendant for his wrongful act;" and, in response to an exception to this part of the charge, Mr. Justice McGOWAN, as the organ of the supreme court, after stating the general proposition that, in actions of the kind under consideration, the jury were authorized "to give what is called 'exemplary' or 'vindictive' damages," uses this language: "The primary object in such cases is to obtain such a verdict as will compensate the plaintiff for the injury done him, and [to?] operate as an example to others, but it is also allowable to add something by way of punishment to the defendant." To same effect, see Epstein v. Brown, 21 S. C. 599, and Hall v. Railway Co., 28 S. C. 261, 5 S. E. Rep. 623. In view of this array of authoritative decisions, we have no hesitation in sustaining the instructions to the jury upon the subject of damages. The judgment of this court is that the judgment of the circuit court be affirmed.

McGOWAN, J., concurs.

TISDALE v. KINGMAN *et al.*

(*Supreme Court of South Carolina.* Aug. 12, 1891.)

MALICIOUS PROSECUTION — SUFFICIENCY OF COMPLAINT—TERMINATION OF PROSECUTION.

1. In an action for malicious prosecution of a civil action by attachment, the complaint does not state a cause of action, where it fails to allege that such attachment terminated in plaintiff's favor.

2. The complaint, in an action for malicious prosecution of an attachment, alleged that the sheriff seized and sold all the crop remaining in the possession of plaintiff. The action was com-

menced before an issue could be raised to try the question whether anything was due in the attachment case. *Held*, that the complaint did not show that the attachment proceeding had terminated in favor of plaintiff.

3. The allegation in a complaint for malicious prosecution of a civil attachment that the claim for which the attachment was made was paid before the warrant was issued is not sufficient to show that such warrant should be vacated.

Appeal from common pleas circuit court of Sumter county; T. B. FRASER, Judge.

Action by George W. Tisdale against Kingman & Co. for malicious prosecution of a civil action by attachment. Order sustaining demurrer. Plaintiff appeals. Affirmed.

Lee & Moise, for appellant. *C. C. Manning*, for respondents.

McIVER, J. This being an appeal from an order of his honor, Judge FRASER, sustaining a demurrer upon the ground that the complaint fails to state facts sufficient to constitute a cause of action, it is proper to state, first, the substantial allegations of the complaint. The first allegation is as to the copartnership of defendants. (2) That plaintiff gave to defendants an agricultural lien on his crops to secure the payment of supplies to be advanced to him to an amount not exceeding the sum of $225. (3) That plaintiff has paid the full amount advanced to him under said lien. (4) Is practically a repetition of the preceding allegation. (5) That plaintiff demanded of defendants an itemized account of the advances, which demand was refused. (6) That defendants demanded of plaintiff that he pay them the further sum of $125, which they claimed as the purchase money of a horse; but plaintiff, stating his inability to pay the same, offered to return the horse, and pay a reasonable sum for the hire thereof, which offer was not accepted; whereupon defendants applied for and obtained from the clerk of the court a warrant to enforce the lien, "wrongfully and maliciously, and without probable cause," making oath that plaintiff was about to sell and dispose of his crop subject to the lien and to defeat the same, and did "wrongfully, maliciously, and without probable cause, and with intent to injure and oppress the plaintiff," cause said warrant to be placed in the hands of the sheriff, who seized and sold all of plaintiff's remaining crops on sales-day in January, 1890. (7) That, by reason of the wrongful and malicious acts of the defendants, the plaintiff has been damaged to the extent of $1,000, for which sum, as well as costs, he demands judgment. The complaint is dated 27th of January, 1890, and is sworn to on the next day, so that the action must have been commenced within less than 30 days after the sale by the sheriff. The circuit judge held "that this was an action for the malicious prosecution of a warrant of attachment," and that, the complaint having failed to state "the termination or discharge of said warrant in favor of the plaintiff," the demurrer must be sustained. The plaintiff appeals upon two grounds: (1) That there was error in holding that it was necessary to state in the complaint the termination or discharge of said warrant in favor of plain-

tiff; (2) that there was error in holding that there was no such statement in the complaint. This case having been held by the circuit judge to be an action for malicious prosecution, and no exception having been taken to such ruling, but, on the contrary, the appellant having so treated it in his argument here, the question is whether in such an action it is necessary to allege that the action or proceeding claimed to have been maliciously instituted has terminated in favor of the plaintiff. There can be no doubt that in such an action, based upon a criminal prosecution, it is necessary to allege and prove that such prosecution has been terminated; and this is conceded by the appellant in his argument here; but he contends that such an allegation is not necessary where the action is for the malicious prosecution of a civil action or proceeding. It is difficult to perceive any good reason for the distinction contended for. Until the civil action or proceeding has terminated, at least one, if not more, of the material issues involved therein would again be presented by the action for malicious prosecution, and there would be the anomaly of two actions between the same parties, pending at the same time, perhaps before different tribunals, involving some, if not all, of the same issues. This, as we understand it, is one, if not the main, reason for the rule requiring that the action or proceeding upon which the case for malicious prosecution is based, shall be terminated before any action for malicious prosecution can be commenced; and this reason applies as well where the action is based upon a civil action or proceeding as where it is based upon a criminal prosecution. It is true that in the case of a criminal prosecution there is an additional reason, based upon considerations of public policy, but that does not weaken or destroy the other reason for the rule. For all that appears in this case, there may have been, at the time this action was commenced, another proceeding pending to vacate the warrant issued to enforce the agricultural lien, and, if so, then it might have happened that in that proceeding the warrant would be held valid, while, if this case is allowed to go on, a different result might be reached. While this may not be at all likely, yet it is sufficient to illustrate the propriety of the rule as above announced. These views are supported by authority. See 14 Amer. & Eng. Enc. Law, 43, where the cases are cited. We are not aware of any case in this state in which the question under consideration has been directly decided, but we think our view is recognized in the case of Hogg v. Pinckney, 16 S. C. 387, in which the action was for malicious arrest, where it was held that while it was not necessary either to allege or prove the termination of the action in which the provisional remedy, by arrest and bid, was resorted to, yet it seemed to be recognized that it was necessary to allege and prove the termination of the proceedings under the provisional remedy, which, in that case, was alleged and proved. So here we think it was necessary to allege and prove that the proceedings under the provisional remedy, by attachment, had terminated in favor of the plaintiff before the commencement of this action.

It is contended, however, under the second ground of appeal, that this allegation was substantially made in the sixth paragraph of the complaint stated above. We cannot so construe the language of that paragraph. There is no intimation there that any proceeding whatever had been instituted to vacate the warrant of attachment, and certainly none that it terminated in favor of the plaintiff. The inference from what is there stated would be just the contrary, and that the warrant of attachment was still in process of execution at the time of the commencement of the action. Before the 30 days had expired within which an issue could be raised to try the question whether there was anything justly due, this action was commenced, and hence we do not see how it could be said that the proceeding under the warrant had terminated. As was suggested in the argument of respondent's counsel, there being no allegation in the complaint that the proceeds of the sale made by the sheriff were sufficient to satisfy the claim under the lien, there was no reason why the sheriff might not have seized and sold any other crops of the plaintiff, if he could find any; and this is sufficient to show that the proceedings under the warrant had not terminated. It is true that it is stated in the sixth paragraph that the sheriff "did seize and sell all of the crops *remaining in plaintiff's possession*," (italics ours,) but that did not preclude the sheriff from levying the warrant upon any other crops which he could find not in the possession of plaintiff subject to the lien. Nor do we think that the allegation in the complaint that the debt secured by the lien had been fully paid was sufficient to show that the warrant should be vacated; for it was held by the majority of the court in the case of Baum v. Bell, 28 S. C. 201, 5 S. E. Rep. 485, that, on a motion to vacate a warrant of this kind, the question whether anything was due under the lien was not a pertinent inquiry. The judgment of this court is that the order of the circuit court sustaining the demurrer be affirmed.

McGowan, J., concurs.

ALLISON v. ALLISON.

(*Supreme Court of Appeals of Virginia.*   July 23, 1891.)

JUDICIAL SALE — INADEQUATE PRICE — NOTICE OF MOTION TO CONFIRM SALE.

1. The confirmation of a judicial sale for about $4,000 will not be vacated on the ground that the price was grossly inadequate, when, on two prior sales within two years preceding such sale, the land, after wide advertisements, brought $1,560 and $2,650, respectively; and the purchaser at the last sale agreed to sell the land to a third person for $5,000.

2. The fact that the attorney of the owner of land sold at a judicial sale died about two weeks before the confirmation of the sale, and that the owner had notice of motion for confirmation only from Saturday until Monday, are not sufficient grounds for vacating such confirmation, when the owner had several days' notice of the death of his attorney, and lived only three or four hours' ride from the place where the motion was made.

Appeal from circuit court, Wythe county; D. W. Bolen, Judge.

Suit in equity by C. H. Allison and others against W. R. Allison, to subject defendant's land to the payment of his debts. Decree for plaintiffs. Defendant appeals. Affirmed.

Mr. Blair, for appellant. *Mr. Caldwell, J. W. Walker,* and *J. A. & Robt. Crockett,* for appellees.

HINTON, J. This appeal cannot be sustained. A decree of confirmation is a judgment of the court determining the rights of the parties, and such a decree possesses the same force and effect as any other adjudication by a court of competent jurisdiction. Such a decree will not be set aside except for fraud, mistake, surprise, or other cause, for which equity would give like relief if the sale had been made by parties in interest, instead of by the court. Brock v. Rice, 27 Grat. 812; Berlin v. Melhorn, 75 Va. 639; Coles' Heirs v. Coles' Ex'r, 83 Va. 529, 5 S. E. Rep. 673. In the present case none of these circumstances appear. The price cannot be said to be grossly inadequate, even if that by itself be admitted to be a ground for setting aside a sale duly made and confirmed, which I very much doubt. As the record shows, there have been three sales of this property, after a wide advertisement, and within less than a year of each other. At the first sale the property brought $1,560; at the second sale, $2,650; and at the third sale, if a debt of about $500 due the purchaser, and which cannot be reached, be included, about $4,000; and the record shows that the purchaser evidently did not consider that he had gotten a wonderful bargain, for he has agreed to sell it for $5,000. There is therefore nothing in this objection.

There is less, if that be possible, in the appellant's second point, namely, that he did not have time between the 5th and the 27th September to prepare himself to oppose the confirmation. He lived only three or four hours' ride from the place where the motion was to be made, and had known of the death of his counsel several days before the motion was made, and ought to have provided himself with counsel in time to oppose the confirmation, although the actual notice given him, from Saturday to Monday, was somewhat short. The decree of the circuit court is right, and must be affirmed.

CHAPMAN et al. v. PERSINGER'S EX'X.

(*Supreme Court of Appeals of Virginia.* March 26, 1891.)

RESCISSION OF CONTRACTS — MISTAKE—ESTOPPEL.

1. In an action by an executrix to recover on three bonds of $917, $1,250, and $2,493.81, respectively, executed to testator by his daughter and her husband, the only competent witness of a settlement had between them, on the day when the last bond was signed, was the daughter's attorney, who testified that testator presented a claim for several thousand dollars paid for the daughter's husband; that the latter and testator had small memorandum books, and pieces of

paper with memoranda on them; that the "$1,250 note" was not executed at this time; that, as to the bond for $917; "there was no dispute over this debt;" that the bond of a third person for $3,900, which he thought, from the testimony of another witness, may have been erroneously charged against the daughter, "entered into the result which was arrived at;" that testator contended that the daughter's husband owed the bond under some agreement they had made; and that he had no recollection of the various items, which amounted to a considerable sum. Testator's will gave none of his estate to the daughter, reciting that he had already given considerable property to her and her husband. *Held* insufficient to prove that the bonds were executed under a mistake of fact.

2. The signers of a bond are estopped, after the death of the obligee, to aver that they were induced to sign it by his promise to give it to them.

RICHARDSON, J., dissenting.

Appeal from circuit court, Roanoke county.

Mary E. Persinger, executrix of James S. Persinger, brought an action at law to collect two bonds, and a suit in equity to collect another, against Clementine P. Chapman, F. J. Chapman, and others. Decree for plaintiff. Defendants appeal. Reversed.

G. W. & L. C. Hansbrough, for appellants.

HINTON, J. James S. Persinger was the father of the appellant Clementine P. Chapman. He was a man of considerable means, and during his life had many transactions of a business character with his son in law, the appellant F. J. Chapman, and had paid for him at various times divers sums of money amounting in the aggregate to many thousands of dollars. At the death of the said James S. Persinger, which occurred in September, 1884, there were found among his papers three bonds, viz.: (1) A bond of F. J. Chapman and F. Rorer, dated February 13, 1883, for $1,250, payable at six months; (2) a bond of F. J. Chapman for $917, dated February 14, 1883; and (3) a bond of C. P. Chapman and F. J. Chapman for $2,492.81, at 12 months, with interest from its date, to-wit, February 14, 1883. On the two first-named bonds Mary E. Persinger, the widow and executrix of James S. Persinger, instituted actions at law in the circuit court of Roanoke county, on its common-law side. On the third bond she brought this suit on the chancery side of said court, in order to charge the property of the obligor, Clementine P. Chapman, who was a married woman.

In this cause the defendants filed their answer, which they asked to be taken as a cross-bill, alleging that this third bond was executed "under a mistake as to the indebtedness between the obligor, F. J. Chapman, * * * and the testator, who kept in view chiefly what he had paid out for F. J. Chapman, and overlooked, not only that he had made the payments with the latter's funds, but that the latter had paid much for him;" charging, also, that the bond for $1,250 was executed under a mutual mistake of fact; and alleging, also, that the deceased, James S. Persinger, had assured the respondent "he would never require them to pay, but would sur-

render and give" the three above-mentioned bonds "to the female respondent, as and for her portion of" his estate; "and that by such assurance the testator induced them to execute the bond [meaning the third bond] in the bill mentioned." James S. Persinger left a will, the third item of which reads as follows: "I have already given and paid for my three daughters, Clementine, the wife of F J. Chapman, Elizabeth, wife of Samuel Nowlin, who is now dead, leaving children, and Mary, wife of C. I. Preston, and their husbands, considerable amounts of property and money; and it is my will, and hereby expressly provided, that neither of my said daughters, or either of their husbands, or the children of my deceased daughter, Elizabeth Nowlin, shall have any portion of my estate." It is shown that the bond for $2,492.81, in the bill mentioned, was given as the result of a settlement of accounts had between the said F. J. Chapman and the said James S. Persinger on the day of its date, *i. e.,* on the 14th day of February, 1883, and that at that settlement there was present, besides these parties, but one witness, Major Ballard, the friend and counsel of Chapman. This witness testifies, among other things, that "Mr. Persinger presented an account for claims which he had paid for Chapman, including judgments and some notes on which he was security, amounting to several thousand dollars; I don't recollect the amount;" that "Mr. Persinger had a small memorandum book; Chapman also had a small pocket memorandum book; Mr. Persinger also had two or three small pieces of paper with memorandums on them, and a receipt for money he had paid for Nowlin;" that "the $1,250 note * * * was not executed at this time;" that, as to the bond for $917, "there was no dispute over this debt; Mr. Chapman never objected to it when we were considering the item;" that "the bond of John A. Persinger for $2,900, which he now thinks, from the testimony of Logan, may have been erroneously charged against Chapman, "entered into the result which was arrived at on that occasion;" and that "Mr. Persinger contended that Chapman owed the bond under some agreement they had made," but that he had "no recollection of the various items, outside of the judgments and the Persinger and Nowlin bonds;" and that "the items between them were numerous, and amounted to a considerable sum," and that he did not attempt to charge his memory with them. With these statements from the only witness who could testify as to the settlement before it, and in despite of the statement of the commissioner that the evidence was not sufficiently full and direct for him to make a statement "with much"—he might, with equal propriety, have said "with any"—confidence in its accuracy, the learned judge of the circuit court held that the bond for $2,492.81 was executed under a mutual mistake of fact, directed various accounts, decreed in favor of the appellee for only $1,461.59, and directed a cancellation of the bonds for $917 and $1,-250.

In entering this decree the circuit court manifestly erred, to the prejudice of the appellee, for the following patent reasons:

First. The testimony shows beyond all question that the bond for $2,492.81, far from being executed under a mistake of fact, was the result of deliberation and discussion, in which some of the most important factors were considered item by item; and that, while possibly Chapman may have been finally induced to execute the bond from a desire to have Mr. Persinger pacified as to the settlement, or, in the language of the answer, that both of the defendants were induced by the assurance of the testator that he would surrender and give them to the female respondent to execute the same, yet that it was done by them with their eyes open, and with a full knowledge of all the facts.

Secondly. Because the appellants cannot be permitted under the law, to set up and prove such a promise as the one last referred to, in avoidance of their solemn obligation. See the cases of Towner v. Lucas, 13 Grat. 705, 722; Harris v. Harris, 23 Grat. 766.

Thirdly. Because, while equity will reform instruments executed in mutual mistake, yet that this can never be done unless the true state of the case can be established. In this case any account that may be stated must be purely conjectural. In such a case, equity always withholds its hand. In Foster v. Rison, 17 Grat. 340, MONCURE, P., says: "It is possible, after all, that the account given of this matter in the examination of William Rison is the true one, and that the credit of $975, given to J. W. F. in the settlement, was, in fact, given by mistake. But whether the fact be so or not, I think it is not proved by that degree and amount of evidence which ought to be required under the circumstances, and that, in attempting to correct such supposed mistake, there would be danger of doing injustice to the estate of J. W. F." White v. Campbell, 80 Va. 181.

Fourthly. Because the circuit court erred in directing a cancellation of the bonds for $917 and $1,250; for, as to the first of these bonds, Major Ballard's testimony proves, if it proves anything on the point, that there was no dispute over this bond, and that it was executed on the same day with the $2,492.81 bond, and presumptively, therefore, was given for some additional amount due from Chapman to Persinger; and, as to the $1,250 bond, it is proven by Ballard that it did not enter into the final settlement, and it was error in the court to cancel that bond by making it a part of that settlement. For these reasons the decree of the circuit court must be reversed in favor of the appellee, and a decree must be entered here in conformity with this opinion.

RICHARDSON, J., dissenting.

SIMS et al. v. STATE.

(Supreme Court of Georgia.　July 13, 1891.)

CRIMINAL LAW—JOINT VERDICT — SETTING ASIDE AS TO SAME DEFENDANTS.

1. Four persons, indicted together for riot, having been put upon trial, and the state having announced that it would claim no conviction as to two of them, and then having examined these two as witnesses against the other two, a verdict of guilty as to all was not void, and might be set aside as to two and left to stand as to the other two. The grant of a new trial as to the former will not work a new trial as to the latter.

2. There being no objection to the examination of two of the accused as witnesses when their evidence was offered because no *nolle prosequi* as to them was entered, the objection comes too late after verdict.

3. The verdict was warranted by the evidence.

(Syllabus by the Court.)

Error from superior court, Rockdale county; JAMES K. HINES, Judge.

Geo. W. Gleaton, for plaintiffs in error. E. Womack, Sol. Gen., for the State.

Judgment affirmed.

BLALOCK v. MILAND.

(Supreme Court of Georgia.　July 13, 1891.)

RECORDING DEED—GIFT—LOSS OF DEED—SECONDARY EVIDENCE—NOTICE TO PRODUCE—DELIVERY—DECLARATIONS OF DONOR—INSTRUCTIONS.

1. A deed saying nothing of delivery in the attestation clause is nevertheless prepared for record if attested by two witnesses, one of whom was the clerk of the superior court, who signed the attestation in his official character.

2. In order for the heir of a deceased donee to set up a deed of gift made to her by her father it is not necessary that it should appear that the donee or her heir ever had possession of the premises, or that either of them ever had actual custody of the deed.

3. When it appears that an original deed of gift by a father to his daughter was never in the actual custody of the daughter; that the father is dead; and that the deed was not among the papers left by him,—the loss of the original is sufficiently accounted for to admit a copy taken from the record.

4. The donor, after making a deed of gift, having sold and conveyed the premises to other persons, there is no presumption that the deed of gift, which was adverse to their title, ever went into their possession; and consequently, whether a notice to one of them was properly directed, or a subpoena *duces tecum* to the other was properly served, is immaterial, there being no diligence to inquire of them incumbent upon the party now claiming under the deed of gift.

5. Declarations of a vendor, now deceased, made at the time of conveying to his vendee, that a previous deed of gift executed by the vendor to his daughter had never been delivered, and that he had destroyed the same, are not admissible in evidence in favor of the vendee against the heir of the daughter claiming under the deed of gift; nor are declarations of a third person, now deceased, that he knew the deed had not been delivered, and that the donor destroyed it.

6. A written declaration, made by the donor, and recorded in the record of deeds, to the effect that he had not delivered to his daughter the deed of gift, and that he revoked and annulled the deed, is not admissible in evidence in favor of his vendee of the premises, the same being made several years after the deed of gift was executed and recorded.

7. It is not incumbent upon the court to specify in his charge to the jury what facts and circumstances would negative the presumption that a duly recorded deed was delivered, or to go over the various facts and circumstances in the evidence tending to negative that presumption, there being no request so to do so, and the court referring the jury in general terms to the evidence on the subject.

8. The evidence warranted the verdict.

(Syllabus by the Court.)

Error from superior court, Pike county; JAMES S. BOYNTON, Judge.

S. N. Woodward, for plaintiff in error. Claude Worrill and B. F. McLaughlin, for defendant in error.

Judgment affirmed.

GREER v. STATE.

(Supreme Court of Georgia. July 13, 1891.)

NEW TRIAL—NEWLY-DISCOVERED EVIDENCE—PRACTICE—HEARING ARGUMENT.

1. The evidence warranted the verdict.

2. The newly-discovered evidence was cumulative, and by due diligence could, in all probability, have been discovered before the trial. See Rosch v. State, 63 Ga. 362.

3. The court did not abuse its discretion as to the length of time allowed for preparing to argue the motion for a new trial and bringing the same to a hearing. The time allowed was seven days, one of which was Sunday, and another Saturday of a term of court in which all the counsel were practitioners.

(Syllabus by the Court.)

Error from superior court, Butts county; JAMES S. BOYNTON, Judge.

Anderson, Wright & Beck, for plaintiff in error. E. Womack, Sol. Gen., for the State.

Judgment affirmed.

COLLINS v. POWELL et al.

(Supreme Court of Georgia. July 13, 1891.)

ASSUMPSIT—RECOVERY OF OVERPAYMENT—MONEY HAD AND RECEIVED.

Where husband and wife paid their joint money for land conveyed to the wife alone, and it turned out there was an overpayment, the sum so overpaid may be recovered back in a joint action by them as money had and received for their use. So much of the payment as was due for the land was applied for the wife's use, but the excess was held for the use of the owners of the fund, and not for that of the wife alone.

(Syllabus by the Court.)

Error from superior court, Rockdale county: JAMES S. BOYNTON, Judge.

J. R. Irwin and A. C. McCalla, for plaintiff in error. Geo. W. Gleaton, for defendants in error.

Judgment affirmed.

JORDAN v. GROGAN.

(Supreme Court of Georgia. July 13, 1891.)

LEVY OF EXECUTION—CLAIMS OF THIRD PERSONS—DISMISSAL.

Although it may be irregular to dismiss a claim for want of any evidence to support it, yet if the claimant, after admitting possession in the defendant in fi. fa. at the time of the levy, thus making a prima facie case for the plaintiff, closes his evidence without showing anything to overcome the effect of his admission, the error is immaterial, and the judgment will not be reversed.

(Syllabus by the Court.)

Error from superior court, Cherokee county; GEORGE F. GOBER, Judge.

C. D. Maddox, for plaintiff in error. W. H. Simmons and C. D. Phillips, for defendant in error.

Judgment affirmed.

STARLING v. THORNE et al.

(Supreme Court of Georgia. July 13, 1891.)

NEW TRIAL—STRANGER IN JURY-ROOM — BILL OF EXCEPTIONS.

1. The losing party is entitled to a new trial where it appears that a man who was not a member of the jury, and whose name was not on the list, did, without the knowledge or consent of such party or his counsel, accompany the jury to their room, remain there with them, and participate in the formation and rendition of the verdict. 1 Thomp. Trials, §§ 3, 4, and cases cited.

2. The recital of facts in a motion for a new trial is verified where the bill of exceptions sets forth in detail all the grounds, and adds: "The recitals of fact contained in the motion for new trial, and in each of the foregoing six grounds thereof, are true and correct."

(Syllabus by the Court.)

Error from superior court, Bulloch county; JAMES K. HINES, Judge.

J. G. & D. H. Clark, for plaintiff in error. D. R. Groover, for defendants in error.

Judgment reversed.

BURNETT v. STATE.

(Supreme Court of Georgia. July 13, 1891.)

CRIMINAL LAW—CONTINUANCE—EVIDENCE ON FORMER TRIAL—ADMISSIONS.

1. A showing for a continuance on the ground of the absence and illness of leading counsel is not complete, under section 3525 of the Code, without a statement on oath that the application is not made for delay only. Where the showing was thus deficient, and the presiding judge had given notice to both the leading and associate counsel a month before the trial that the case would not again be continued for illness of the former, it having been previously continued on the same ground, there was no abuse of discretion in overruling the motion.

2. The Code, § 4696, requires the evidence given in on the trial of a felony to be taken down; and by section 4096a the official stenographic reporter is the officer to perform this duty. His report, proved by him to be correct, although he may not remember the testimony, is competent evidence in another case of what a witness swore upon the trial at which the report was made, in so far as the same may be pertinent and otherwise competent.

3. The state may read in evidence a part of such report without putting in the whole, the other party being at liberty to introduce the balance, or so much thereof as is pertinent. Pound v. State, 43 Ga. 89.

4. What a witness voluntarily testified at a former trial of another party for the homicide is not privileged on a trial of the witness himself for the same homicide. It may be given in evidence against him as an admission.

5. It does not legally appear to this court that the verdict was not warranted by the evidence.

(Syllabus by the Court.)

Error from superior court, Crawford county; A. L. MILLER, Judge.

M. G. Bayne, R. D. Smith, and A. O. Bacon, for plaintiff in error. W. H. Felton, Sol. Gen., and R. W. Patterson, for the State.

Judgment affirmed.

STEWART et al. v. CRANE et al.

(Supreme Court of Georgia. May 27, 1891.)

MASTER'S REPORT—FILING EXCEPTIONS.

1. When, under section 4208 of the Code, the superior court in term has passed an order fixing the time within which exceptions to a master's

report may be filed, the judge of that court has no authority of law to pass at chambers an *ex parte* order extending the time for filing such exceptions.

2. When exceptions to a master's report have not been filed within the time allowed by the court for that purpose, it is within the discretion of the court to allow them to be filed thereafter upon proper cause shown.

(*Syllabus by the Court.*)

Error from superior court, Polk county; GEORGE F. GOBER, Judge.

Action by Crane, Boylston & Co. and another against Stewart, administrator, and another. Judgment for plaintiffs. Defendants bring error. Affirmed.

Blance & Noyes and *Broyles & Sons*, for plaintiffs in error. *I. F. Thompson, J. M. Neel, Dean & Smith, W. C. Bunn,* and *Jones & Richardson,* for defendants in error.

LUMPKIN, J. The case of Crane, Boylston & Co. *et al.* v. Stewart, Administrator, *et al.*, was referred to a special master. November 22, 1882, his report was filed, and on the same day, during an adjourned term of Polk superior court, an order was passed allowing all parties 30 days within which to file thereto exceptions of law and fact. December 21, 1888, counsel for Stewart, without notice to the other side, applied to and obtained from the judge at chambers an order allowing further time to file such exceptions, which the judge granted for certain providential reasons stated. A similar order, still further extending the time, was in like manner granted by the judge at chambers, January 21, 1889, and the exceptions were filed within the time allowed by the last order. At the August term, 1890, of the superior court, the case was reached in its order, and a motion was made to dismiss the exceptions upon the ground that they were not filed within the time originally fixed by the order of the court, and that the judge at chambers had no authority to modify the order made in term, and extend the time for filing exceptions. The granting of this motion is one of the errors assigned. During the same term a motion was made to refile the identical exceptions which had already been dismissed. The court was then in the midst of another case, and passed no order on this latter motion except to make it returnable before the judge of the circuit, who was not then presiding; and error is assigned upon the refusal of the court to allow the defendants to then file these exceptions. After dismissing the exceptions, the court passed an order approving the report of the master, and directing that a verdict be had in accordance therewith. No error is assigned upon this action of the court.

1. While it may be true that a court of equity is always open, and that the judge accordingly may, at chambers, pass all proper orders in an equity cause, we are of the opinion that the language of section 4203 of the Code restricts the authority of the court as to master's reports to such things only as may be done in term-time. The section provides that the master's report, "when returned to court, shall be subject to exceptions for such

time as the court may allow." The word "court," as first above used, evidently cannot mean the judge. We presume it was never contemplated that the report should be filed with him, but that it must be filed with the clerk. The word "court," where it appears the second time in the section, is used, we think, in the same sense as in the first place; that is, it means the superior court, and not the judge thereof. Moreover, when the court does in term pass an order fixing the time within which exceptions may be filed, or at a subsequent term passes another order allowing further time to file exceptions, the time designated may, so far as the particular case is concerned, be regarded as a part of section 4203, and the section may be held to mean that a particular report will be subject to exceptions for the period of time specified by the court. No provision is made by law for obtaining from a judge at chambers an order allowing further time within which to file exceptions to a master's report, or for giving notice thereof to the opposite side, or for entering any such order upon the minutes. With a report as filed one side might be satisfied if the other made no objection thereto; but it not unfrequently happens that a party so satisfied would himself desire to file exceptions if the other side did so, and yet an order at chambers, although it gave the right to all parties to file exceptions, and extended the time for so doing, would be valueless to one who had no notice thereof until the extended time had itself expired. This result would be manifestly unfair and unjust, and, irrespective of the construction we have placed upon the above-mentioned section of the Code, we think it unwise to establish a precedent allowing such orders to be granted at chambers.

2. As already intimated, we do not mean to hold that under no circumstances will a party be allowed to file exceptions to a master's report after his failure to do so within the time originally allowed for that purpose by an order of the court. In the case of Cook v. Commissioners, 62 GA. 228, Judge McCUTCHEN, then presiding in the place of Chief Justice JACKSON, who was disqualified, said: "The order of reference had fixed the time within which the parties should file their exceptions to the report, as hereinbefore fully set forth. The time limited having expired without any exceptions being filed, the plaintiff in error could not legally file his exceptions afterwards without obtaining leave of the court for this purpose. In matters resting in legal discretion, the courts favor the diligent, but not the negligent. Where parties are prevented by good cause from filing their exceptions within the time fixed for that purpose, they should see to it that they are guilty of no unreasonable delay in applying to the court for an extension of time. If delay having the effect to protract the litigation exists before the application is made, some reasonable excuse for this delay must be shown to the court, as well as the excuse for the original failure, before any extension of time should be granted. The application should be made

at the first term at which it could be done." It will be seen from the language just quoted that the entire matter is in the discretion of the court, and we approve the rule as above laid down. Judgment affirmed.

NOLEN v. HEARD et al.

(Supreme Court of Georgia. May 27, 1891.)

JUSTICE OF THE PEACE—CONDUCT OF JURY—VERDICT.

1. The evidence being in direct conflict, and the jury having credited a single witness in opposition to two others, the verdict was not without evidence to support it.

2. The verdict of a jury in a justice's court is not vitiated because the jury, after deliberating for some hours, came into court, announced that they could not agree unless they could have before them a certain cash book, and, upon being informed by the presiding justice that the book was not legal evidence, returned to their room, under the direction of the justice, to resume their deliberations, and in a few minutes brought in a verdict. Though it was irregular for the jury to call for more evidence, it was not such misconduct as to render their subsequent finding illegal.

(Syllabus by Simmons, J.)

Error from superior court, Newton county; JAMES S. BOYNTON, Judge.
E. F. Edwards, for plaintiff in error. *J. F. Rogers,* for defendants in error.
Judgment affirmed.

JONES v. FARMER et al.

(Supreme Court of Georgia. May 27, 1891.)

APPEAL—SUFFICIENCY OF EVIDENCE.

The evidence being irreconcilable, and this being a second verdict for the same party, and the trial judge having refused a new trial on condition that a part of the recovery be written off, and this condition being complied with, the supreme court will not interfere. The case, on a previous writ of error, is reported in 84 Ga. 296, 10 S. E. Rep. 626.

(Syllabus by Bleckley, C. J.)

Error from superior court, Newton county; JAMES S. BOYNTON, Judge.
E. F. Edwards and *J. M. Pace,* for plaintiff in error. *L. L. Middlebrook,* for defendants in error.
Judgment affirmed.

BRYANS v. ALMAND.

(Supreme Court of Georgia. July 13, 1891.)

HIGHWAYS — REMOVAL OF OBSTRUCTIONS FROM STREET.

While the municipal authorities of a city or town may, on complaint of a citizen, cause an obstruction to be removed from any public street in actual use by the public, yet where a street exists only in the plan of such city or town, and has not been actually opened, worked by the municipal authorities, and used by the public, but, on the contrary, has been in private occupation for 30 or 40 years, this mode of procedure is not available. Parsons v. Trustees, 44 Ga. 529.

(Syllabus by the Court.)

Error from superior court, Butts county; JAMES S. BOYNTON, Judge.
Wright & Beck and *Hall & Hammond,* for plaintiff in error. *W. W. Anderson* and *L. L. Ray,* for defendant in error.
Judgment reversed.

GRANT v. STATE.

(Supreme Court of Georgia. May 27, 1891.)

INTOXICATING LIQUORS—ILLEGAL SALES.

In a prohibition county, a person who receives money from another with a request to procure whisky, and who shortly afterwards delivers the whisky, may be treated as the seller if no other person filling that character appears, and if it is not shown where, how, or from whom the whisky was obtained. This case is controlled in principle by Paschal v. State, 84 Ga. 326, 10 S. E. Rep. 821.

(Syllabus by Bleckley, C. J.)

Error from superior court, Henry county; JAMES S. BOYNTON, Judge.
Bryan & Dicken, for plaintiff in error. *W. A. Browe,* opposed.
Judgment affirmed.

KENNY v. WALLACE.

(Supreme Court of Georgia. July 13, 1891.)

ATTACHMENT—DISSOLUTION—APPEAL.

If a writ of error lies at all to a decision of the judge of the superior court dissolving an attachment issued against a fraudulent debtor under sections 3297, 3298, of the Code, it is an ordinary, not a "fast," writ. Consequently this case, if it can be entertained, is returnable to the next term. Ordered, that it be entered on the docket of that term, to be properly disposed of in its order.

(Syllabus by the Court.)

Error from superior court, Fulton county; MARSHALL J. CLARKE, Judge.
R. J. Jordan, for plaintiff in error. *Broyles & Sons,* for defendant in error.

HYFIELD v. SIMS et al.

(Supreme Court of Georgia. May 27, 1891.)

MOTION FOR NEW TRIAL—MOTION TO DISMISS—EXCEPTIONS.

1. Where a motion was made at one term of the court to dismiss a motion for a new trial, and was overruled, it was too late at the next term to assign error thereon in a bill of exceptions to the final judgment of the court granting a new trial in the case, no exceptions *pendente lite* having been taken and filed at the term when the rulings complained of were made.

2. When a case is submitted to the judge upon the law and the facts, to be tried by him without the intervention of a jury, and he finds upon the facts and decides the questions of law, the losing party may either move for a new trial or file his bill of exceptions, as he may see proper. In this case, however, a verdict was taken in accordance with the judge's finding, and to review it a motion for new trial was indispensable.

3. Where the judge grants a new trial in an illegality case, and it does not appear from the bill of exceptions or the transcript of the record what the ground or grounds of the illegality were, the judgment granting the new trial will be affirmed.

(Syllabus by the Court.)

Error from superior court, Floyd county; JOHN W. MADDOX, Judge.
Execution by W. L. Sims & Co. against Robert Hyfield from a justice's court. Defendant appealed to the superior court. Judgment for defendant. Motion for new trial granted. Defendant excepted. Affirmed.
Wright & Harris, for plaintiff in error. *Junius F. Hillyer,* for defendants in error.

SIMMONS, J. An execution from a justice's court in favor of Sims & Co. against Hyfield was levied upon certain property, and Hyfield interposed an illegality. The case was taken by appeal to the superior court, where, on April 14, 1890, at the spring term of the court, all the questions of fact and law involved, by agreement of counsel, were submitted to the presiding judge, and it was agreed by counsel that a verdict should be taken in accordance with the finding of the judge. A verdict was so taken on the day named, sustaining the illegality, and judgment thereon was rendered. On April 23d thereafter the plaintiffs in fi. fa. filed a motion for a new trial, and a correct brief of the evidence. On May 19th counsel for the defendant in fi. fa. moved to dismiss the motion for a new trial because it did not show that it was filed within 30 days after the trial, because the grounds had not been certified by the judge, and because no service had been perfected on the defendant in fi. fa.; all of which motions the court overruled, allowed movant to amend, certified the grounds, and granted the rule. The motion for a new trial was then argued, and the court held up its decision until December 4, 1890, at the fall term of the court, when counsel for the defendant in fi. fa. again moved to dismiss it on the ground that, both law and facts having been originally submitted to the judge, and a verdict having been rendered under instructions from the court, a bill of exceptions, and not a motion for a new trial, was the proper remedy. The motion also was overruled, and the defendant excepted. The court then granted a new trial, and the defendant excepted.

1. It appears that the motion to dismiss the motion for a new trial on the ground that it did not show that it was made within 30 days, that the judge had not approved the grounds, and that no rule nisi had been granted, etc., was made at the spring term of the court, and no exceptions pendente lite were filed and approved at that term of the court. It was too late, therefore, to except to this ruling at the fall term of the court, more than six months after the ruling had been made. City of Waycross v. Youmans, 85 Ga. 708, 11 S. E. Rep. 865. This disposes of this exception.

2. On December 4, 1890, at the fall term of the court, the defendant in fi. fa. called the attention of the judge to the motion, and moved to dismiss it, on the ground that, both law and facts having been originally submitted to the judge, and a verdict rendered under instructions from the court, a bill of exceptions, and not a motion for a new trial, was the proper remedy. This motion the court overruled, and to this ruling the defendant excepted. When a case is submitted to the judge upon the law and the facts, to be tried by him without the intervention of a jury, and he finds upon the facts, and decides the question of law against one of the parties, the losing party may either move for a new trial, as if the case had been tried by a jury, or file his bill of exceptions, as he may see proper. Of course there must be a motion for a new trial when there is

an actual verdict, as in this case. We are inclined to think that where issues of fact are involved, and the judge, by agreement of the parties, passes upon them, the better practice is to make a motion for a new trial, so that the judge may have an opportunity to review his finding on the facts. 2 Thomp. Trials, § 2713.

3. When this last motion was overruled the court granted an order sustaining the motion for a new trial, and to this ruling the defendant excepted. The plaintiff in error seems to have been very particular and full in specifying in the bill of exceptions the parts of the record necessary for a clear understanding of his case, but with all his particularity, he omitted the main part of the record which would enable us to determine whether the trial judge erred in the grant of a new trial or not. The defense to the execution was made by an affidavit of illegality, and the judge granted a new trial because he had erred in finding in favor of the illegality; but what the grounds of that affidavit of illegality were we have been unable to ascertain from this record. The affidavit was not specified in the bill of exceptions as material, and consequently was not embodied in the record sent up by the clerk. Without knowing what the grounds of illegality were, we cannot decide whether the grant of a new trial was erroneous or not. We therefore affirm the judgment of the court below. Judgment affirmed.

REEDY v. EAST TENNESSEE, V. & G. RY. CO.

(Supreme Court of Georgia. May 27, 1891.)

MASTER AND SERVANT — NEGLIGENCE — QUESTION FOR THE JURY.

Under the facts of this case it was error to grant a nonsuit.

(Syllabus by the Court.)

Error from superior court, Floyd county; JOHN W. MADDOX, Judge.

W. J. Reedy sued the East Tennessee, Virginia & Georgia Railway Company to recover damages for personal injuries. Plaintiff was nonsuited, and brings error. Reversed.

Wright & Harris, for plaintiff in error. W. T. Turnbull, Dorsey & Howell, and A. O. Bacon, for defendant in error.

LUMPKIN, J. The evidence for the plaintiff made in brief the following case: One Wood was in the employment of defendant, and Reedy, who had been employed by him as a laborer in transferring freight, was instructed by Wood to assist in putting up some wires for defendant. This instruction had been given at the request of a line repairer, to whom Wood was informed defendant's superintendent had directed he should furnish a couple of hands. There was evidence to authorize the inference that this repairer was the servant of the defendant. A ladder was placed against the depot wall, and extended some eight feet above the roof. The line repairer directed Reedy to take some wire and carry it up, which Reedy did, but only went part of the way and stopped. He was then ordered to go to the top of the ladder with the wire, but refused to do so. The repairer, who had been holding the ladder, then let it loose, ran up it, passed Reedy, taking the wire from him as he did so, and sprang upon the roof, doing so in such a manner as to make the ladder fall with Reedy to the ground, and he was thus injured. Under these facts we think a jury should determine whether or not Reedy was injured by the negligence of a co-employe in the service of defendant; whether or not by his own negligence he contributed to the injury; and whether or not, by the exercise of ordinary care, he could have prevented it. Judgment reversed.

CAMPBELL v. HIGGINBOTHAM.

(Supreme Court of Georgia. May 27, 1891.)

EXECUTION OF DEED—DURESS—INSTRUCTIONS.

1. The evidence being entirely insufficient to authorize the verdict, it should be set aside.

2. The evidence showing that the deed in question was executed freely and voluntarily, and there being no testimony from which the jury could rightly infer that it was the result of duress or fraud, there was nothing to warrant the court in charging upon these subjects.

(Syllabus by Lumpkin, J.)

Error from superior court, Floyd county; JOHN W. MADDOX, Judge.

Wright & Alexander and *Dabney & Fouché*, for plaintiff in error. *Dean & Smith*, for defendant in error.

Judgment reversed.

MEEKS v. STATE.

(Supreme Court of Georgia. May 27, 1891.)

BILL OF EXCEPTIONS—SERVICE ON ATTORNEY GENERAL.

The bill of exceptions in this case having been served upon counsel employed to assist the solicitor general, and not upon the latter, as the law requires, the writ of error is dismissed. Code, § 4261; Oliver v. State, 66 Ga. 243.

(Syllabus by Lumpkin, J.)

Error from superior court, Paulding county; JOHN W. MADDOX, Judge.

C. D. Phillips and *C. D. McGregor*, by *G. P. Roberts*, for plaintiff in error. *A. Richardson*, Sol. Gen., and *Thompson Spinks*, for the State.

Writ of error dismissed.

CORLEY v. STATE.

(Supreme Court of Georgia. May 27, 1891.)

INTOXICATING LIQUORS—ILLEGAL SALES—NEW TRIAL.

1. Newly-discovered evidence to discredit the only witness for the state is not cause for granting a new trial over the refusal of the trial judge.

2. That the accused refused to sell liquor to another is not admissible evidence to show that he did not sell to a particular person on a different occasion.

(Syllabus by Lumpkin, J.)

Error from superior court, Rockdale county; JAMES K. HINES, Judge.

J. R. Irwin and *A. C. McCalla*, for plaintiff in error. *E. Womack*, Sol. Gen., for the State.

Judgment affirmed.

POOL v. STATE.

(Supreme Court of Georgia. July 13, 1891.)

HOMICIDE—INSTRUCTIONS—EVIDENCE—MOTION FOR NEW TRIAL.

1. The jury having found a verdict for the offense of murder, and desiring to recommend imprisonment in the penitentiary for life, it was proper for the court, in the presence of the jury, and at their request, to allow this recommendation to be put in proper form by the solicitor general, and thus prepare the verdict for signature by the foreman.

2. A request to charge with reference to doubt, with no qualification as to the doubt being reasonable, was properly refused.

3. One of the questions in grading the homicide being as to whether the pistol was recklessly fired, with criminal indifference to the consequences, it was not necessary, in order to constitute the offense of murder, that the accused should have been engaged in an unlawful act at the time of firing it. A request to charge the jury, the whole of which is not pertinent and legal, should be declined.

4. The court is not bound to instruct the jury that, when the proof in favor of the accused is stronger and more direct than the evidence against him, there is room for doubt, and he ought not to be convicted.

5. Under the evidence it was not error to decline a request to charge section 4309 of the Code, in the language of that section, on the subject of homicide by misadventure. The pistol was handled in a way to make it dangerous to bystanders, and so handling it was culpable negligence.

6. It was not error to decline to charge the abstract proposition that when the conduct of the accused is equally susceptible of two constructions the one in favor of the hypothesis of innocence is the one that ought to be adopted, there being no conduct in evidence specially requiring the application of this principle.

7. A statement in the motion for a new trial that the court allowed evidence to go to the jury, over objection of defendant's counsel, relating to a subsequent difficulty with another party, without specifying what the evidence was, is not sufficiently full and certain as a basis for assigning error; more especially where, according to the testimony of one of the state's witnesses as set forth in the brief of evidence, the difficulty with the third person was apparently a part of the *res gestæ* of the homicide, and material in determining whether the shooting was willful or accidental.

8. Though one may have a pistol at a church in violation of the statute prohibiting the bearing of arms at such a place, and though he may handle the pistol negligently and discharge it intentionally, thereby committing accidentally a homicide, yet this is not necessarily murder. It may be involuntary manslaughter in the commission of an unlawful act. The question would depend upon whether it was a reckless or only a negligent shooting.

9. When the court fails to charge fully, to the satisfaction of counsel for the accused, on the prisoner's statement, attention should be called to the omission.

10. Grounds of objection to testimony must be stated.

11. No error as to other grounds of the motion for a new trial.

(Syllabus by the Court.)

Error from superior court, Hall county; CARLTON J. WELLBORN, Judge.

Indictment of Jesse Pool. Verdict of murder in the first degree. Defendant brings error. Reversed.

Fletcher M. Johnson, for plaintiff in error. *Howard Thompson*, Sol. Gen., for the State.

LUMPKIN, J. 1. When it is thoroughly understood what verdict the jury desire to find, there can be no possible error or injury to any one in allowing the solicitor general, in open court, at their request, to put the verdict in such form as will legally express the finding they wish and intend to make. Brantley v. State, (Ga.) 13 S. E. Rep. 257.

2. In criminal cases the jury must be satisfied beyond a reasonable doubt of defendant's guilt before he can be legally convicted; and a request to charge, "If there is any doubt as to whether the defendant is guilty, it is the duty of the jury to acquit,"—was properly refused. It is not necessary that the jury should be satisfied beyond all doubt of defendant's guilt; and this, in effect, is the meaning of the charge requested. With doubts about the law juries are not concerned.

3. It has been frequently ruled by this court that, unless a request to charge the jury is in all respects pertinent and legal, it should be declined. Where a request is in part proper and in part improper, the court cannot give it as a whole, and is not bound to separate the legal portions of it from those which are not so. The law infers guilty intention from reckless conduct; and where the recklessness is of such character as to justify this inference, it is the same as if defendant had deliberately intended the act committed. When, therefore, one recklessly fires a pistol with criminal indifference as to the consequences, and another is killed, it is not necessary, in order to constitute this killing murder, that the accused should at the time of firing have been engaged in the commission of some unlawful act, independent of and in addition to the reckless firing itself. The above remarks will, we think, be sufficient to show that the following request was properly refused: "If the defendant, when his pistol went off and killed deceased, had abandoned or was free from all evil intent, it could not be that at that time he was engaged in the commission of any unlawful act; but, unless at the time of the killing he was engaged in the commission of an unlawful act, he could not be guilty of murder, or of involuntary manslaughter, in the commission of an unlawful act. If a man, though intending to commit an unlawful act, abandons his intent to do so, and afterwards by accident kills a man, the killing is not murder; nor is it involuntary manslaughter in the commission of an unlawful act." Under this request the jury might have acquitted defendant, although satisfied by the evidence that he was guilty of criminal negligence in firing the pistol at the time it went off and killed deceased.

4. When the court properly charges concerning the law of reasonable doubt, as was done in this case, it is not bound to instruct the jury as indicated in the fourth head-note. It is for the jury to determine when there is reasonable doubt of defendant's guilt, and not for the court to inform them under what circumstances there is or is not room for such doubt.

5. When the evidence shows conclusively that the defendant handled his pistol in such a reckless manner as to make it dangerous to by-standers, the court properly refused to charge section 4302 of the Code, relating to the law of homicide by misadventure.

6. The observations made above in reference to the fourth head-note are also applicable here, the more especially as the evidence fails to show any conduct on the part of defendant which would make the request referred to in the sixth head-note appropriate.

7. One ground of the motion for a new trial assigns as error the court's allowing evidence to go to the jury relating to a subsequent difficulty between defendant and another party, but does not specify what this evidence was. We are therefore unable to determine whether the admission of this evidence was such error as would require a new trial or not. It appears from the testimony of one of the state's witnesses that after the killing defendant did have a difficulty with another person. It occurred so soon after the homicide as to be apparently a part of the *res gestæ* of the killing, and may have been material in determining whether the shooting was willful or accidental. The evidence just referred to was to the effect that defendant struck and shot at a by-stander, who appears to have done nothing but reproach him for having killed deceased.

8. The court, in effect, charged the jury that having a pistol at church would be an unlawful act, and then added: "But if you believe he had a pistol under such circumstances as rendered it unlawful to have it, and that he fired it off voluntarily, intending to fire it, and in such firing it hit Moon and killed him, then he would be guilty of murder." This charge, we think, was error. It amounted to instructing the jury that unlawfully having a pistol at a church, and there killing another with it, would necessarily be murder if the firing was voluntary. This, in our opinion, was stating the law too strongly against the defendant. If the shooting was intentional, but simply negligent, and resulted in the death of another, which was not intended, it could not be more than involuntary manslaughter. On the other hand, if the shooting was intentional, and was done so carelessly and recklessly that the law would imply an actual intention to kill from the mere wantonness of the act, and death resulted, it would be murder. This question was not properly submitted to the jury, and for this reason a new trial will be ordered.

9, 10, 11. The head-notes state all that need be said concerning these grounds of the motion for a new trial. Judgment reversed.

MORRISON *et al.* v. COHEN.

(*Supreme Court of Georgia.* July 20, 1891.)

Error from superior court, Fulton county; MARSHALL J. CLARKE, Judge.

C. T. Ladson and *Hulsey & Bateman,* for plaintiff in error. *Simmons & Corrigan,* for defendants in error.

PER CURIAM. There was no abuse of discretion by the court in granting a first new trial in this case. Judgment affirmed.

FOSTER et al. v. FOSTER et al., Commissioners.

(Supreme Court of Georgia. May 27, 1891.)

COUNTY BOARD—CORRECTION OF RECORD.

1. When the records of the board of county commissioners fail to speak the truth, they may be corrected by an order *nunc pro tunc.* Code, § 206.

2. This case is controlled by Hillaman v. Harris, 84 Ga. 482, 11 S. E. Rep. 400

(Syllabus by Simmons, J.)

Error from superior court, Floyd county; JOHN W. MADDOX, Judge.

Wright & Harris, for plaintiffs in error. *Dean & Smith* and *Seaborn Wright,* for defendants in error.

Judgment affirmed.

MANGUM v. STATE.

(Supreme Court of Georgia. July 13, 1891.)

BURGLARY—POSSESSION OF STOLEN PROPERTY—VERDICT.

1. Recent possession, not satisfactorily explained, of goods stolen from the house at the time the alleged burglary was committed, may be sufficient as a basis of conviction of burglary, where the burglary has been established, and the jury believe from all the evidence beyond a reasonable doubt that the accused is the guilty party.

2. On a trial for burglary it is not error to refuse to receive a verdict of "guilty of receiving stolen goods," and to direct the jury that they would have to find a verdict of guilty or not guilty.

3. The evidence was sufficient, and there was no error in refusing a new trial.

(Syllabus by the Court.)

Error from superior court, Troup county; SAMPSON W. HARRIS, Judge.

Indictment of Taylor Mangum for burglary. Verdict of guilty. Defendant brings error. Affirmed.

H. E. Ware, T. H. Whitaker, and *D. J. Gaffney,* for plaintiff in error. *T. W. Atkinson,* Sol. Gen., for the State.

BLECKLEY, C. J. 1. The grounds on which the motion for a new trial were rested appear in the reporter's statement. The substance of that part of the charge of the court complained of is that recent possession of the stolen goods, not satisfactorily explained, may be sufficient to convict of burglary if the burglary is otherwise proved, and the jury believe from all the evidence beyond a reasonable doubt that the accused is the guilty party. As the court distinctly stated in connection with this proposition that mere "naked unexplained possession of stolen goods alone will not authorize a conviction of burglary," the request to charge that "unexplained possession of stolen goods does not of itself authorize a conviction, but is a circumstance for the jury to consider," was virtually complied with. The truth is that what would or ought to be the effect of unexplained possession, standing alone, is a question in the nature of an empty abstraction, for in practice the fact of possession is usually connected with other facts throwing more or less light on the general question of the prisoner's guilt or innocence. In one case the possession may count for much more than in another. Speaking generally, if it is recent and unexplained, or falsely explained, the jury may treat it as sufficient to identify the guilty party. But to do this they must be convinced from other evidence that a burglary has been committed, and the whole evidence taken together must leave no reasonable doubt upon their minds that the person on trial was the burglar, or one of the burglars, if the offense was committed by several. As we construe the charge given in this case, it was in harmony with this view. It left to the jury the valuation of the fact of possession in the particular case, and in its true relation to the evidence as a whole. The same legal thought may be expressed in many shades and variations of language, and we think what the court said in this instance is not in conflict with the meaning, properly understood, of any previous decision of this court. Falvey v. State, 85 Ga. 157, 11 S. E. Rep. 607; Harris v. State, 84 Ga. 269, 10 S. E. Rep. 742; Wynn v. State, 81 Ga. 744, 7 S. E. Rep. 689; Grimes v. State, 77 Ga. 762; Davis v. State, 76 Ga. 16; Harrison v. State, 74 Ga. 802; Lundy v. State, 71 Ga. 360; McGruder v. State, Id. 864; Bryan v. State, 62 Ga. 179; Phillips v. State, 56 Ga. 28; Wilson v. State, 55 Ga. 324.

2. It is not contended that a verdict of guilty of receiving stolen goods was a finding upon any issue involved in the indictment; but the motion for a new trial suggests that, as the indictment charged larceny from the house as well as burglary, the direction of the court to find a verdict of guilty or not guilty was improper. It does not appear, however, that the attention of the court was called to the double aspect of the indictment, or that an appropriate charge with respect to each of the offenses it alleged had not been given. The brief of counsel says, "A question possibly arises whether bringing in a verdict of guilty of receiving stolen goods was not an acquittal of the charge of burglary;" and Jordan v. State, 22 Ga. 558, is cited. But in that case the verdict found voluntary manslaughter on an indictment for murder. The offense found was covered by the indictment, and the verdict was received. Here, on the contrary, the offense which the jury attempted to find in the first instance was not covered by the indictment, and the improper finding was rejected by the court as unwarranted by law. There is thus nothing analogous in the two cases.

3. The statement of the accused, as it comes to us in the record, though probably false in some respects, and not a full disclosure of the whole truth, makes on our minds a strong impression that this man, even if guilty of some offense, may not be guilty of burglary. But the jury did not credit his statement, and they are made by law the exclusive judges of its credibility. Besides, it is altogether probable on general principles that their estimate of it is much more reliable than

our own. With the statement discredited there was evidence to warrant the verdict, and the court did not err in refusing a new trial. Judgment affirmed.

STAFFORD v. MADDOX.

(Supreme Court of Georgia. July 13, 1891.)

WATER-COURSES—RIGHT TO BACK WATER — CONTRACT—RES ADJUDICATA.

1. A finding in a former suit for the plaintiff, though for nominal damages only, is not conclusive in favor of the defendant as to anything involved in the present controversy.

2. A right established by contract to back water in a stream to the height which an existing dam would raise it does not necessarily confer a right to back the water as high as a subsequent dam, located higher up the stream, will back it, although the top of the subsequent dam may be on a level with the top of the former dam. The width of the two dams, and the conformation of the land on the shore lines, may cause inequality in the effect of the dams in backing the water.

(Syllabus by the Court.)

Error from superior court, Whitfield county; THOMAS W. MILNER, Judge.

Action for damages by Henry M. Stafford against Martha H. Maddox. Judgment for plaintiff. Defendant brings error. Reversed.

McCutchen & Shumate, for plaintiff in error. *Thos. R. Jones* and *R. J. & J. McCamy,* for defendant in error.

BLECKLEY, C. J. 1. It was error for the court to charge the jury, in effect, that, if the recovery by the plaintiff in a former suit was for nominal damages only, then the verdict in that case would be conclusive that there was no substantial damage at any time, and the jury should find for the defendant. The present action was brought seven or eight years after the former one. Why should the failure of the plaintiff to prove any actual damage on the trial of his first action cut him off from showing that he sustained such damage afterwards, and before instituting the second? The second action does not apply to the same period of time involved in the first; and, as the first resulted in a finding for the plaintiff, that finding surely could not be conclusive in favor of the defendant as to anything involved in the present controversy. It seems to us that its conclusiveness, if it has any which affects this case, would all be in favor of the plaintiff, and would extend to the right of recovery, leaving the quantum of damages dependent entirely upon other evidence and the doctrine of punitive damages. 1 Hill. Torts, 608. For the jury to find for the defendant in a second action for a continuous tort because only nominal damages were found in the first action would be very remarkable. Why not find at least nominal damages again and again, so long as the plaintiff by successive actions seeks to vindicate his right, though he may fail to prove actual damage? Nothing is needed but a right in the plaintiff, and some invasion of that right by the defendant. Code, §§ 2243, 3065, 3070; 1 Sedg. Dam. §§ 97–99.

2. As the dam now complained of is neither the same dam by which the water-rights of the defendant were measured in the several deeds of conveyance, nor located at the same place, but is altogether a different dam, and located higher up the stream, perhaps the actual performance of the first dam in the way of backing water would be the safer limit of the defendant's right to back the water by the second dam. What would be the capacity of the first, had it been made tight, would necessarily be more or less matter of conjecture; but what it actually did while in its best condition would be susceptible of proof. It may be that there was a right to improve and tighten that dam, or to build a new and better one in the same place; but that right was never exercised, nor can it be certainly known what increase in the height of the water would have resulted from all the favorable changes in that dam which were practicable, such changes never having been made. But conceding that the new dam might, though located higher up the stream, be allowed to raise the water not only as high as the water had ever been raised by the old, but as high as the old dam would have been capable of raising it had it been put in the best possible condition, it was error for the court, in its charge to the jury, to assume that if the new dam was only of the same height as the old one the two would be equally capable of affecting the lands above by overflow. Two dams, themselves equal in height, located at different places on the same stream, would not necessarily equally retard the escape of water. The difference in their width and in the conformation of the land on the shore lines, and various other local conditions, might cause inequality in their capacity for detaining and backing water, and for injuring thereby the lands above. Instead of assuming equality as matter of law, the question whether there would be equality or inequality in the given instance is one of fact for determination by the jury. Where the old dam and the new are on the same ground, and other conditions are equal, the rule announced by the court would probably be correct. Baker v. McGuire, 53 Ga. 245; Maguire v. Baker, 57 Ga. 109; Manufacturing Co. v. Neese, 54 Ga. 459. The court erred in not granting a new trial. Judgment reversed.

MADDOX v. STATE.

(Supreme Court of Georgia. July 8, 1891.)

FORGERY OF LICENSE AS TEACHER.

No provision of the Penal Code of this state makes it an offense to utter and publish as true a false and fraudulent certificate or license issued by the county school commissioner to a teacher.

(Syllabus by the Court.)

Error from superior court, Houston county; A. L. MILLER, Judge.

Indictment of J. W. Maddox, *alias* W. J. Maddox, for forgery. Verdict of guilty. Defendant brings error. Reversed.

L. J. Gartrell, J. T. Spence, C. H. Brand, and *Harrison & Peeples,* for plaintiff in error. *W. H. Felton, Jr.,* Sol. Gen., for the State.

BLECKLEY, C. J. The first section of the seventh division of the Penal Code enumerates certain instruments of writing, and deals with falsely and fraudulently making, forging, altering, or counterfeiting the same, causing or procuring it to be done, or willingly aiding or assisting in the doing thereof, by any person or persons, and proceeds as follows: "Or shall utter or publish as true any false, fraudulent, forged, altered, or counterfeited audited certificate, governor's, president's, speaker's, public officer's, court's, or other duly-authorized person's certificate, draft, warrant, or order, so as aforesaid issued, or purporting to have been issued, or any deed, will, testament, bond, writing obligatory, bill of exchange, promissory note, or order for money or goods, or other thing or things of value, or any acquittance or receipt for money or goods, or other thing or things of value, or any indorsement or assignment of any bond, writing obligatory, bill of exchange, promissory note, or order for money or goods, or other thing or things of value, with intent to defraud the said state, public officers, courts, or persons authorized as aforesaid, or any other person or persons whatsoever, knowing the same to be so falsely and fraudulently made, forged, altered, or counterfeited. Every such person so offending, and being thereof lawfully convicted, shall be punished by imprisonment and labor in the penitentiary for any time not less than four years nor longer than ten years." Code, § 4442. By the act of October 27, 1887, relating to common schools, the county board of education are authorized, upon the report and recommendation of the county school commissioner, to grant to applicants licenses as teachers. Acts 1887, p. 76, § 29. In practice it would seem that the issuing of licenses granted by the board devolves upon the county school commissioner as their secretary and executive officer. No form appears to be prescribed by statute, the whole subject of prescribing forms being committed by the sixth section of the above-cited act to the state school commissioner; but it may be assumed that the form rightly in use is that of a certificate signed by the county commissioner. Penal laws are to be construed strictly, and we think it would be too great a strain to bring an instrument which the statute denominates a "license" under a penal law relating to certificates, merely because the form in which the license happens to be cast is that of a certificate made by a public officer. Besides, reading the language which we have quoted above from the Penal Code, and construing it by its context, we think the certificates therein referred to are such as relate to money, property, or things of value. None of the enumerated instruments are of like genus or species with licenses, which are issued, not as evidence of a right to money or property, but as evidence of competency or qualification to engage in the business of instruction. The mere absence of any other provision from the statute-book which will reach the nefarious practice of uttering or publishing as true an altered license will not authorize an extension by construction of the provision quoted, in order to make it comprehend such a case. Perhaps it is a casual omission in section 4451 of the Code that it does not provide for forging or publishing as true, as well as for forging or altering, any writing whatever, not elsewhere enumerated. If this indictment had been for altering the license, it would doubtless have been good under this section, but we know of no statute which makes it penal to utter or publish as true an altered teacher's license issued by the county school commissioner or by any other person. The court erred in not sustaining the demurrer to the indictment. Judgment reversed.

LUMPKIN, J., not presiding.

FARMERS' LOAN & TRUST CO. v. CANDLER et al.

(Supreme Court of Georgia. May 8, 1891.)

CONSTRUCTION OF RAILROAD—CONTRACTORS' LIENS —PROCEEDINGS TO PERFECT.

1. By section 1979 of the Code, contractors to build railroads are entitled to liens upon such railroads, but each lien is upon the whole railroad to which it applies. There is no provision of law allowing a contractor to set up and enforce a lien upon a part of any railroad, though such part may be all of the road which he constructed or aided to construct.

2. As, under section 1990 of the Code, the verdict must set forth the lien allowed, and the judgment and execution must be awarded accordingly, a verdict and judgment which attempt to set up and enforce a lien upon a specified portion of a railroad are void upon their face, so far as the contractor's special lien is concerned.

3. A verdict describing the lien intended to be allowed thereby in these terms: "That the plaintiff have a lien as a contractor to build railroads upon that part of the Gainesville and Dahlonega Railroad from its terminus, in the city of Gainesville, to the Chattahoochee river, in Hall county, including its right of way, roadbed, depot grounds, and all other property belonging to said railroad company, for the sum aforesaid," etc.,—does not set up a lien upon the whole railroad referred to, but only attempts to do so upon the part extending from Gainesville to the Chattahoochee river.

(Syllabus by the Court.)

Error from superior court, Hall county; G. H. PRIOR, Judge *pro hac vice.*

Contest between the Farmers' Loan & Trust Company and Allen D. Candler and another to establish priority of claims against the Gainesville & Dahlonega Railroad Company. Judgment for Candler. The trust company brings error. Reversed.

Calhoun, King & Spalding, Reid & Stewart, and *H. H. Dean,* for plaintiff in error. *R. H. Baker, W. P. Price, J. B. Estes,* and *S. C. Dunlap,* for defendants in error.

LUMPKIN, J. The Gainesville & Dahlonega Railroad, including its right of way, franchises, and all other property, was sold as a whole by a receiver duly appointed. A contest arose over the proceeds of the sale. A. D. Candler claimed the same upon a judgment foreclosing a contractor's lien, and his right thereto was contested by the Farmers' Loan & Trust Company, who claimed under a mortgage or deed of trust securing certain bonds which had been issued by the railroad company. The fund was not sufficient to satisfy the claims of both. The case was submitted to the decision of the court upon the finding of a jury on certain questions of fact and a statement of facts agreed upon by the parties. The result was a decision in favor of Candler. The controlling questions made by the record are those set forth and adjudicated in the head-notes.

1. An examination of section 1979 of the Code will show that it does not contemplate a lien upon a portion of a railroad. The language plainly and unmistakably means that the lien thereby given to a contractor to build railroads must be upon the whole road. If the law were otherwise on this subject, it would be impolitic and impracticable, and would often lead to disastrous consequences. To sell a railroad in detached portions would utterly destroy, or greatly diminish, the value of the entire property; and yet this would inevitably result if a contractor could have a lien upon a part only of a railroad, and enforce the same by judgment and sale. We quote the following apt language from Knapp v. Railway Co., 7 Amer. & Eng. R. Cas. 395: "A railroad, with its depots, bridges, and other appurtenances, is no less an entirety than a dwelling-house, with its kitchen, its chimneys, and its door-steps; and yet no one has ever supposed that a mechanic's lien could be enforced against the door-steps or chimneys of a dwelling-house, or that they could be sold and removed, to the utter destruction of the whole property." The suit brought by Candler for the foreclosure of his lien contemplated a judgment of foreclosure against the whole road, but the verdict and judgment thereon covered only that part of the railroad lying between Gainesville and the Chattahoochee river.

2. Section 1990 of the Code, providing for the foreclosure of liens on real property, declares that, if the lien is allowed, the verdict shall set it forth, and the judgment and execution be awarded accordingly. It follows from what has already been said that a verdict and judgment attempting to set up and enforce a lien upon a specified portion of a railroad are void upon their face, so far as the special lien is concerned; and therefore the money in court could not legally be awarded to Candler upon his judgment, considered as a special lien.

3. It was contended that the language of the verdict and judgment purporting to establish Candler's special lien extended to and covered the entire railroad and its property. This language is quoted in the third head-note, and we think a fair construction of it leads to the conclusion that it covers only that part of the railroad situated between Gainesville and the Chattahoochee river, and the property immediately therewith connected. The words, "including its right of way, roadbed, depot grounds, and all other property belonging to said railroad," must be construed with the words preceding them, viz., "that part of the Gainesville and Dahlonega Railroad," etc.; and the obvious meaning is that the items of property following the word "including" are those only which are situated within the limits designated.

The court below did not consider or determine whether or not Candler's judgment, considered merely as a general lien on the railroad's property, was superior to the mortgage, but adjudged that his special lien as a contractor to build railroads was lawfully foreclosed, and that his judgment was valid, as such, against the property, and entitled to take the money. This ruling, we think, was error, and the judgment of the court below is therefore reversed. Judgment reversed.

CRAYTON et al. v. SPULLOCK et al.

(Supreme Court of Georgia. May 27, 1891.)

ATTORNEY AND CLIENT—DUTIES AND LIABILITIES.

An attorney who brings an equitable petition to marshal and administer the assets of a corporation, and who, by a consent decree, is paid for his services by the corporation, so far represents it that he cannot purchase its property for himself at a receiver's sale at a grossly inadequate price.

(Syllabus by the Court.)

Error from superior court, Floyd county; JOHN W. MADDOX, Judge.

Action by J. R. Crayton and another against James H. Spullock, receiver, and another, to set aside a receiver's sale. Judgment for defendants. Plaintiffs bring error. Reversed.

Nunnally & Neel, for plaintiffs in error. Wright & Harris, for defendants in error.

LUMPKIN, J. Messrs. Wright & Harris, as attorneys for one Latiner, for the use of Kohn et al., filed an equitable petition against the Rome Nail Manufacturing Company, praying for a judgment against the corporation, and also for the appointment of a receiver to take charge of and sell its assets. No resistance was made to the appointment of a receiver, and afterwards a consent decree was rendered in the case, directing the sale of the property of the corporation by the receiver, and also providing that the firm of Wright & Harris be paid out of the proceeds of the sale $150 for their services in bringing the petition, etc. Afterwards the receiver sold the property in gross, including all its real and personal assets, to H. M. Wright, one of the firm, for $250, his being the only bid. The evidence is somewhat conflicting as to the actual value of the property, but it was undoubtedly worth at least $1,500, and probably much more. After the sale, Crayton, as president of the company, and others, directors and stockholders therein, filed their motion to set aside the sale made by the receiver, alleging, among other things, that they understood that the proceedings instituted by Wright & Harris were intended for the benefit of all parties interested, and that these attorneys really represented therein the corporation and all others concerned; that for these reasons no objection had been made to the appointment of a receiver or the sale of the property; and that they failed to attend the sale, fully believing that their rights would be protected in all respects by Messrs. Wright & Harris. In their answer respondents denied that Wright & Harris were attorneys for movants or the corporation, or that they were under any obligation to protect their interests; and alleged that they represented Lattner, for the use of Kohn *et al.*, and none others, in bringing the petition, and in the proceedings had thereunder. On the hearing the evidence was voluminous and quite conflicting as to the relations existing between Messrs. Wright & Harris and the corporation, or the movants in the present case, with respect to the petition for receiver, etc. In the view we take of this case, it is unnecessary to determine the issues of fact made by the motion and answer, and the evidence offered in support of each. One undisputed fact appears, viz., that Messrs. Wright & Harris obtained a decree, to which all persons interested consented, and of which they accepted the benefit, providing that they should be paid for their services out of the proceeds of the sale of the property of this corporation to be made by the receiver whose appointment they had obtained. This fact established such a fiduciary relation between them and all the stockholders as will preclude one of these attorneys from buying the property for himself at the receiver's sale at a price which represented but a small per cent. of its actual value. An unbroken line of authorities, both in England and in America, establishes beyond question the doctrine that when an attorney is intrusted with litigation, the conduct of proceedings, or the management of any business in which he is under the slightest obligation to look after and protect the interests of others, he will not be permitted to derive therefrom any personal benefit which conflicts in the least degree with that obligation and the protection of those interests. Without discussing the other questions made by the record, we are entirely satisfied that, for the reason stated above, the court erred in confirming this sale and in refusing to grant an order setting it aside. The judgment is reversed, with direction that the sale be set aside upon the amount paid by Mr. Wright under his bid being refunded to him. Judgment reversed, with direction.

GRAY v. WESTERN UNION TEL. CO.

(*Supreme Court of Georgia.* July 8, 1891.)

TELEGRAPH COMPANIES — ACTION FOR DELAY IN DELIVERING MESSAGE.

After receiving a telegram for transmission, and accepting payment for the same, the company cannot defend an action for the statutory penalty incurred by failure to deliver it with due promptness, on the ground that the contents of the telegram related to a sale of futures, and consequently to an illegal transaction.

(*Syllabus by the Court.*)

Error from superior court, Houston county; A. L. MILLER, Judge.

Action by J. M. Gray against the Western Union Telegraph Company for delay in delivering a message. Judgment for defendant. Plaintiff brings error. Reversed.

W. C. Winslow and Hardeman, Davis & Turner, for plaintiff in error. Gustin, Guerry & Hall, for defendant in error.

BLECKLEY, C. J. That the United States mail might lawfully carry either a sealed letter or an open circular from Ft. Valley to Macon, though the contents of the document related to the purchase and sale of futures, is certain. Equally certain is it that a common carrier between these points might innocently transport a passenger whose known business was to make a trip for the exclusive purpose of buying or selling futures, or might carry and deliver a bundle of stationery intended by the consignee for use in his business as a dealer in futures. In each of these cases the object sought to be subserved by the writer, the passenger, or the consignee would simply be irrelevant. To consider it would be to introduce moral distinctions not pertinent to the function which the mail or the carrier was designed to perform. In like manner, under the statute on which the present action is founded the moral purpose of a telegram is immaterial, provided it is not designed to prompt or promote the commission of a crime or a tort. Telegraph companies, like common carriers, are voluntary servants of the general public. They exercise a public employment, and offer themselves for the transaction of business in behalf of every person who seeks to engage their skill and their special facilities for a peculiar class of work. Their relation to the public imposes upon them the duty of undertaking as well as the duty of performing, and the violation of either duty is a misfeasance,—a tort. It is the equivalent, therefore, of an affirmative interference by a mere private person to hinder or obstruct communication. For one of these companies not to receive or not to transmit and deliver a dispatch when it ought to do so, is more than a refusal to contract, or than the breach of a contract; it is a wrong as pronounced as would be that of a person who should forcibly exclude another from the telegraph office, and prevent him from handing in a dispatch which he desired to lodge for transmission. In dealing with the wrong as such, the element of contract is not involved. Why should this company not have transmitted and delivered the reply which the plaintiff sent to his correspondent in answer to a dispatch from the latter which the company had brought to him by telegraph? The dispatch was: "Shall I draw for more bonus? Answer quick." The reply was: "If necessary, draw for more bonus." It is admitted that the subject of this correspondence was a transaction in futures,—a species of gambling of the worst description.—and it is on this ground that the failure of the company is sought to be justified. But the statute which we are considering makes by its letter no exception. It declares that every company of this description "shall, during the usual office hours, receive dispatches, whether from other telegraphic lines or from individuals; and on payment or tender of the usual charge, according to the regulations of such com-

pany, shall transmit and deliver the same
with impartiality and good faith, and
with due diligence, under penalty of $100,"
etc. Acts 1887, p. 111. In construing and
administering the statute, what exceptions can the courts make by implication?
Doubtless a dispatch, to be entitled to
transmission, must be free from open in-
decency or profanity, and perhaps other
vices of language might condemn it, but,
supposing it to be proper in tone and expression, we should say that the company
would have no concern with its import
unless it sought to subserve either crime
or tort. If it disclosed either of these objects, it seems to us that the company,
for its own protection, might and should
refuse to handle it. It would be unreasonable to suppose that the legislature
intended telegraph companies to aid in
the perpetration of crimes or actionable
wrongs, for this would be to constrain
them to do by legislative mandate what
they would have no right to do by their
own choice. But, on the other hand, any
dispatch which a company could lawfully
transmit by its own choice the statute
obliges it to transmit and deliver. The
power of voluntary selection is denied, for
every company is required to transmit
and deliver "with impartiality and good
faith." A dispatch cannot be rejected on
account of its subject-matter, unless by
sending it the company would or might
subject itself or its servants either to indictment or a civil action. This is a rational test, and one that may fairly be
presumed to coincide with legislative intention. If, before the statute was enacted, a telegraph company could at its own
will serve one customer and decline to
serve another, the dispatches of the two
being exactly similar, this option no longer
exists. All customers are now to be treated alike. If one can correspond by telegraph touching his speculations in futures, all may do so. There can be no discrimination, no favoritism. The company cannot waive morality for one, and
stand on it against another. Now, in
this state, it is neither a crime nor a tort
to speculate in futures. It is gross immorality, and conflicts with public policy,
but it is not indictable nor actionable.
On the contrary, by a recent statute dealers are recognised and tolerated on condition of registering themselves and paying
a fixed tax. Acts 1888, p. 22. It was certainly the legal right of the company to
transmit and deliver the dispatch sent by
the plaintiff if it had elected to do so. It
would have incurred no penalty, subjected itself to no action or indictment. Moreover, it actually undertook to do it, and
received pay for the service; and it had
already transmitted and delivered the dispatch to which this was a reply. Why
serve one of the parties and not the other?
But we hold that it was bound to serve
both, for the reason that the law leaves it
free to serve them. Where there is such a
statute as we are construing, it cannot be
a matter of option to obey or disobey.
On the contrary, unless some other law
forbids what the letter of the statute commands, the letter must prevail. In adjudicating upon a like statute, the supreme
court of Indiana, in Telegraph Co. v. Ferguson, 57 Ind. 495, held that the company,
when sued for the penalty incurred by
failing and refusing to transmit a dispatch
expressed in these terms: "Send me four
girls, on first train to Francisville, to tend
fair,"—could not defend by setting up that
the dispatch was ambiguous, and that,
on account of certain extrinsic facts, the
company had reasonable cause to believe
and did believe that the girls wanted were
prostitutes, and that the object of the
message was to draw prostitutes to the
fair. It seems to us that this decision was
correct. It did not appear that the company or its servants would have been subject either to indictment or to action if
the girls called for had been sent and had
attended the fair. When a dispatch is
ambiguous, the law would give the benefit of the ambiguity to the company dealing with it either civilly or criminally for
transmitting the dispatch; and hence it
would be the duty of the company, in deciding whether to transmit or not, to
give the benefit of the doubt to the sender.
On no other rule would it be practicable
for telegraph companies to perform their
legitimate functions as servants of the
general public. They could not wait to
question and investigate the motives of
those who offer ambiguous dispatches for
transmission. Indeed, in this state they
are required by the same statute we are
now discussing to forward dispatches
written in cipher, and this enables the
sender not only to conceal his motives
partially, but to conceal them altogether.
This may serve to suggest how little the
company is concerned with unlawful or
improper motives, unless they are plainly
disclosed on the face of the dispatch. The
cases of Bryant v. Telegraph Co., 17 Fed.
Rep. 825, and Smith v. Same, 84 Ky. 664,
2 S. W. Rep. 483, were not ruled upon any
statute, but upon principles of general
law. Doubtless it is true that a telegraph
company is not bound, even when it contracts to do so, to furnish to "bucket-
shops" reports of the market prices of
stock and provisions, nor to allow "tickers" for the purpose to remain in the offices of these immoral establishments. But
were the supplying of market reports and
"tickers" for all applicants, "with impartiality and good faith," enjoined by statute, a different question, and one more
germane to the present case, might arise.
The Sunday messages adjudicated upon
in some of the cases are also without relevancy, for the statute does not purport
to prescribe duties except as to dispatches
offered "during the usual office hours,"—
meaning, of course, legal office hours. So
far as we are aware, no decision of any
court is to be found which holds it illegal
for a telegraph company to receive and
transmit messages relating to speculative
transactions in futures, where that class
of business has not been made penal by
statute. That damages for the breach of
a contract to correctly transmit a message of that nature cannot be measured by
the results of such dealings was decided
in Cothran v. Telegraph Co., 83 Ga. 25, 9
S. E. Rep. 836, but there is no suggestion
in that decision that the broken contract

was unlawful. On the contrary, this language will be found in the opinion: "We think this standard cannot be invoked, for the reason that contracts relating to 'futures' are illegal; and we see not how an illegal contract can be called in to measure the damages sustained by reason of the breach of a legal contract." There may be strong reasons of public policy why legislation ought to prohibit all dealings in futures, and all communication by telegraph tending to foster or facilitate such dealings; but in the present state of the law, no matter how reluctant telegraph companies may be to transmit and deliver messages of this class, especially if their reluctance arises after they have accepted pay for doing it, they have no option but to perform the service or pay the penalty. Judgment reversed.

LUMPKIN, J., not presiding.

WRIGHT v. SUPREME COMMANDERY OF GOLDEN RULE.

(*Supreme Court of Georgia.* July 8, 1891.)

MUTUAL BENEFIT INSURANCE—ACTION ON CERTIFICATE—FORFEITURE—PLEADING.

The terms of the certificate of membership binding the assured to pay such assessment as should be levied and required by the supreme commandery, and the declaration alleging that the assessment not paid was one of which the assured had no notice whatever, and also that under the charter and by-laws of the association 30 days after the assessment is due were allowed holders of certificates and beneficiaries thereof to pay such assessment, that the assured died within the 30 days, and that before the 30 days had expired the beneficiaries tendered the unpaid assessment, and the association refused to receive it, there was enough in the declaration to show *prima facie* that no forfeiture of the policy resulted from the non-payment of the assessment, more especially as the declaration also alleged that the association continued to treat the assured as a member in good standing, by making a subsequent assessment against him.

(*Syllabus by the Court.*)

Error from superior court, Bibb county; A. L. MILLER, Judge.

Action by Mary F. Wright against the supreme commandery of the Knights of the Golden Rule to recover on a contract of insurance. Dismissed. Plaintiff brings error. Reversed.

Lanier & Anderson, for plaintiff in error. J. G. Chandler and A. A. Dozier, for defendant in error.

BLECKLEY, C. J. A useful collection of authorities on the general subject-matter may be seen in 33 Cent. Law J. 42, 65, 87. The contract of insurance declared upon stipulated for the payment "of all assessments levied and required by the supreme commandery," and provided that "any violation of the above-mentioned conditions, or of the requirements of the laws now in force or hereafter enacted governing the order of this class, shall render this certificate and all claims under it or upon the order null and void." The certificate says nothing of giving notice of assessments, and nothing with regard to the time at or within which assessments had to be paid. They were to be paid "as levied and required by the supreme commandery." The declaration, as it stood at first, alleged that Wright, the assured, had no notice whatever, up to the time of his death, of the making of the unpaid assessment, or that any assessment against him remained unpaid. In the case of ordinary life policies, the successive premiums or installments of premium are uniform in amount, and mature at fixed times. No occasion for notice, therefore, exists, unless it shall be created by custom or course of dealing between the parties. But a different rule prevails touching contingent and irregular assessments made by mutual aid associations upon their members. Unless notice is dispensed with by the contract, no liability to pay an assessment becomes fixed until notice has been given. Bac. Ben. Soc. § 379. If any special law applicable to the given association, or any by-law, dispenses with notice, this is matter of defense, unless it is disclosed in the pleadings of the plaintiff. Here no such disclosure is made. By an amendment to the declaration it was alleged that within less than 30 days after the unpaid assessment was due, the full amount of it was tendered to the defendant, but was refused, "although, under the charter and by-laws of the said defendant, thirty days after an assessment was due were allowed holders of insurance certificates and the beneficiaries thereof * * * in which to pay an assessment past due, and such payment relieves from any default or suspension caused by failure to pay an assessment when due." The demurrer to the declaration as amended admits this allegation to be true. It will be noticed that it is alleged that the by-laws allow the beneficiaries to make payment within 30 days after an assessment becomes due. We think this implies, if nothing to the contrary appears in the by-laws, that the assured can make this payment though the assured be dead. In this instance he was dead, but his death occurred within the 30 days, and therefore before the time allowed by the by-laws for payment of the assessment had expired. Perhaps the declaration is also somewhat aided by another allegation in the amendment, to the effect that the association continued to treat the assured as a member in good standing by making a subsequent assessment against him. Nibl. Mut. Ben. Soc. § 345. At all events, taking the declaration as it stood after amendment, it set forth a cause of action sufficiently to put the defendant on pleading anything contained in its by-laws, or any extrinsic facts tending to negative its liability. We do not at present see what the promise of Adams, the agent, had to do with the merits of the case. But this, though a seeming irrelevancy, would not vitiate the declaration. The court erred in sustaining the demurrer and in dismissing the action. Judgment reversed.

LUMPKIN, J., not presiding.

ALLEN et al. v. GLENN.

(Supreme Court of Georgia. July 8, 1891.)

LIMITATION OF ACTIONS — COVENANTS IN MORT-
GAGE.

Though the plaintiff, by his declaration,
attempts to found his action on two separate and
distinct instruments, the first a promissory note
not under seal, and the second a mortgage under
seal upon real estate to secure the note, which
mortgage contains a covenant binding the mortgagor to pay all reasonable attorney's fees of collecting said note if not paid at maturity, the action is barred upon its face by the statute of limitations. The covenant in the mortgage is to be
construed as applying to attorney's fees incurred
in proceedings to collect the note, commenced
while it was collectible by law, and not after
the bar of the statute had attached. The action
was commenced more than six years after the
maturity of the note.

(Syllabus by the Court.)

Error from superior court, Bibb county;
A. L. MILLER, Judge.

Action by John C. Allen and another,
executors, against J. R. Glenn, to recover
on a note and mortgage. Judgment for
defendant. Plaintiffs appeal. Affirmed.

S. A. Reid, for plaintiffs in error. Hardeman, Davis & Turner, for defendant in
error.

BLECKLEY, C. J. The promissory note
was not under seal, and the action upon
it was commenced more than six years
after it became due. Confessedly the bar
of the statute had attached if this result
was not prevented by suing also upon the
mortgage, which was under seal, and contained a covenant binding the mortgagor
to pay all reasonable attorney's fees of
collecting the note if the note was not
paid at maturity. The two instruments
were separate and distinct, and founding
the action upon both did not aid one of
them to uphold or extend the other. This
court has ruled that the bar of the statute
might attach upon a promissory note secured by mortgage, and the mortgage itself be still enforceable against the specific
property, the proceeding to foreclose being commenced before the mortgage also
was barred. Elkins v. Edwards, 8 Ga. 325.
This implies that each instrument will go
out of date when the period of time has
elapsed fixed by the statute for bringing
actions upon instruments of its own class.
Let it be conceded that the covenant in
the mortgage to pay attorney's fees would
run and retain vitality as long as the lien
which the mortgage creates, still the declaration does not disclose that any attorney's fees have been incurred in any proceeding to collect the note, commenced
while the note was collectible by law.
Surely the covenant is not susceptible of
the construction that attorney's fees are
to be paid for an ineffectual attempt to
collect the note, made in this present suit,
—a suit begun after the bar of the statute
had attached. No breach of the covenant
would or could result from the non-payment of counsel fees for commencing and
prosecuting an ineffectual action on a
barred debt, and it is this covenant alone
that connects the mortgage with the purpose of the action, for the judgment sought
is a judgment in personam, and no other.
There is no prayer to foreclose the mort-

gage; and indeed, under the statute applicable to ordinary foreclosure proceedings, the superior court of Bibb county
would have no jurisdiction for that purpose, the mortgaged property being land
situate in Putnam county. Code, § 3962;
Hackenhull v. Westbrook, 53 Ga. 285. It
might be otherwise if foreclosure were
sought in equity. Code, § 3979a. There
was no error in dismissing the action.
Judgment affirmed.

LUMPKIN, J., not presiding.

LOWE et al. v. SUGGS.

(Supreme Court of Georgia. July 13, 1891.)

PLEADING AND PROOF—VARIANCE.

Two lessors alleging a joint title, and the
title proved, if any, being several in one, there
can be no recovery. De Vaughn v. McLeroy, 82
Ga. 713, 10 S. E. Rep. 211, and cases cited.

(Syllabus by the Court.)

Error from superior court, Upson county; JAMES S. BOYNTON, Judge.

Action by Mollie E. and James R. Lowe
against J. W. Suggs to recover land.
Judgment for defendant. Plaintiffs bring
error. Affirmed.

Ben H. Walton, Thornton & Cameron,
and Morgan McMichael, for plaintiffs in error. M. H. Sandwich and Hall & Hammond, for defendant in error.

LUMPKIN, J. Benjamin H. Lowe, in
July, 1866, made a deed conveying the
premises in dispute to one Heard, in trust
for the grantor's wife, Emma R. Lowe,
for her life, with remainder to her children.
This deed gave to the trustee power to
sell the property thereby conveyed, and to
reinvest the proceeds in such manner as
Mrs. Lowe might designate, her consent
to be manifested in writing, and indorsed
upon the deed. Heard, the trustee, died;
and upon the petition of Mrs. Lowe to the
judge of the superior court her husband
was appointed trustee in his stead. At
that time she had only two children, Mollie E., of full age, and James R., a minor.
The latter was not a party to the proceeding for the appointment of a new trustee.
The former, while not formally a party,
joined in an affidavit attached to the petition, wherein she swore that Lowe was
a suitable person to be appointed trustee.
This action on her part was sufficient,
we think, to make binding upon her the
appointment of Lowe as trustee. At any
rate, she was thereby estopped from denying the regularity or legality of his appointment. After this, Lowe, as trustee,
sold the trust property to Suggs, Mrs.
Lowe expressing her consent thereto in
the manner prescribed by the original
trust-deed. The plaintiffs in this action,
Mollie E. and James R., sought to recover
the property from Suggs, upon the idea
that the appointment of Lowe as trustee
was void as to them, and consequently
any sale by him as trustee could not divest their title in remainder to the land
after the death of their mother. From
the above statement of facts it will appear that Mary E. was bound by this appointment; that the sale by Lowe, as

trustee, was good as against her; and consequently there can be no recovery in her favor. This being true, the correctness of the proposition set forth in the head-note, supported by the authority there cited, is manifest. Judgment affirmed.

WILSON v. STATE.

(Supreme Court of Georgia. July 13, 1891.)

HOMICIDE — PRESENCE OF PRISONER — DUTY OF JUDGE.

On a trial for murder it is the right of the accused to be present at all stages of the proceeding, and it is the duty of the court to see that he is present when any charge is delivered to the jury. If the judge recharges the jury without verifying for himself the prisoner's presence, and it afterwards appears that the prisoner was not present, but was in an adjoining room, in the custody of an officer, and did not know that the jury was being recharged, and knowledge did not come to him until after such recharge was concluded, it is cause for a new trial.

(Syllabus by the Court.)

Error from superior court, Monroe county; JAMES S. BOYNTON, Judge.

Indictment of S. F. Wilson for murder. Verdict of guilty. Defendant brings error. Reversed.

A. D. Hammond, for plaintiff in error. E. Womack, Sol. Gen., for the State.

BLECKLEY, C. J. The sixth ground of the motion for a new trial complains that the court recharged the jury without notifying defendant, and in his absence, although his counsel was present. It appears from the record that the judge did not know whether the accused was present in the court-room or not, when the recharge was delivered, and that the fact was that he was in an adjoining room, in the custody of an officer, not knowing that the jury was being recharged, and knowledge did not come to him until after the recharge was concluded. Whether his absence from the room was voluntary or by compulsion, we think the court should not have recharged the jury in his absence. He was in the custody of an officer, and whether the officer took him to the adjoining room with or without his consent, it seems to us, made no difference. There is nothing to indicate that it was his intention to be absent when any material step was to be taken in the trial; and before taking such a material step as recharging the jury we are of opinion that the court should have seen and known that he was present, verifying the fact, if necessary, by ocular demonstration. The presence of the counsel was no substitute for that of the man on trial. Both should have been present. Bonner v. State, 67 Ga. 510; Wade v. State, 12 Ga. 25; Martin v. State, 51 Ga. 567. There was error in not granting a new trial on this ground of the motion. Judgment reversed.

REBB v. EAST TENNESSEE, V. & G. R. Co.

(Supreme Court of Georgia. July 20, 1891.)

INJURIES TO SERVANT COUPLING CARS — CONTRIBUTORY NEGLIGENCE.

Though attempting to couple cars when the engine is running at a speed of 15 miles an hour is apparently not only dangerous, but reckless, yet if it be true in the experience of engineers and railroad men that it is safe, provided the engine is properly managed, and if the failure in question resulted solely from the fault of the engineer in manipulating the engine, the high speed will be no obstacle to a recovery by the car-coupler for a personal injury sustained by him in making the attempt. Though to non-experts its truth would seem in a high degree improbable, if not impossible, yet, there being direct and positive evidence tending to support the theory of safety, the court erred in granting a nonsuit.

(Syllabus by the Court.)

Error from city court of Atlanta; HOWARD VAN EPPS, Judge.

Hoke & Burton Smith and Simmons & Corrigan, for plaintiff in error. Dorsey, Brewster & Howell and A. O. Bacon, for defendant in error.

PER CURIAM. Judgment reversed.

SIMMONS, J., concurring *dubitante*.

FINCH v. BARCLAY.

(Supreme Court of Georgia. July 13, 1891.)

WIFE'S POWER TO CONTRACT — WEIGHTS AND MEASURES — WITNESS — REFRESHING MEMORY.

1. Under the rule that all public officers are presumed to do their duty, the ordinaries, who are required by section 1592 of the Code to give notice by publication and otherwise when standard weights and measures are obtained by them, will be presumed to have given such notice. Nor would a failure to give such notice relieve the citizen from his obligation to have his weights and measures duly marked.

2. The Code, § 1559, requires all persons engaged in selling by weights and measures to have the same properly marked by the ordinary, and declares that in default thereof they shall not collect any account, note, or other writing, the consideration of which is any commodity sold by their weights and measures. Whether, under this provision, taken in connection with section 3745 of the Code, the note and mortgage are void only for so much of their consideration as arose from sales of goods weighed and measured by unmarked instruments, or for the whole amount thereof, some of the consideration being other dealings, was not decided by the court below, and is left an open question for determination in this case on the new trial.

3. A married woman is liable for goods bought on her sole credit for the use of her son. If her undertaking was not primary, but as surety for him, she is not liable. Her separate note and mortgage would be *prima facie*, but not conclusive, evidence of her actual relation to the debt.

4. A witness may refresh his memory by a memorandum taken from his books if, after so refreshing it, he can and does testify to the facts from his own recollection.

(Syllabus by the Court.)

Error from superior court, Twiggs county; D. M. ROBERTS, Judge.

Action by J. A. Barclay against Mary A. Finch. Judgment for plaintiff. Defendant brings error. Reversed.

L. D. Moore, for plaintiff in error. Bacon & Rutherford, for defendant in error.

BLECKLEY, C. J. 1. The court erred in withholding from the jury so much of the defense as related to selling by weights and measures not duly marked. True, the Code, § 1592, directs that "when such standards are obtained it is the duty of such ordinary to give sixty days' written notice thereof at the door of the court-house and in the public gazette where the sheriff of the county advertises his sales;" and there was no affirmative evidence that such notice had been given. But the law presumes that a public officer performs all his official duties, and the effect of this presumption is to dispense with proving the fact otherwise when it comes collaterally in question. Moreover, this provision of the Code is simply directory to the officer, and failure to comply with it would not relieve the citizen from his express statutory obligation to have his weights and measures duly marked before proceeding to make sales by them.

2. Section 1589 of the Code is in these words: "All persons engaged in selling by weights and measures shall apply to the ordinaries of their respective counties, and have their weights and measures so marked; and in default thereof shall not collect any account, note, or other writing, the consideration of which is any commodity sold by their weights and measures." It was affirmatively proved in this case that the creditor sold by his weights and measures, and that they were not marked as required. That this was a good defense to so much of the action as sought a recovery for the price of the commodities so sold there can be no doubt. It admits of grave question, however, whether such an infirmity as to a part of the consideration of the note and mortgage will vitiate the whole, or whether there may be a recovery for so much of the consideration as arose out of other dealings between the parties. This question was not passed upon by the superior court, nor was it argued here in a way to enable us to settle it satisfactorily without further argument. Section 2745 of the Code declares that: "If the consideration be good in part and void in part, the promise will be sustained or not, according as it is entire or severable, as hereinafter prescribed; but, if the consideration be illegal in whole or in part, the whole promise fails." Ought the consideration of a promissory note, in so far as it embraces the price of goods or commodities sold by unmarked weights and measures, to be treated as merely void, or should it be treated as illegal? If the former, the balance of the note would be collectible; if the latter, such balance would probably not be collectible by an action on the note itself, but only by an action upon the original promise or contract apart from the note. Some of the authorities which will serve to throw light on the subject are the following, the cases more specially applicable being these: Scott v. Gillmore, 3 Taunt. 226; Cotten v. McKenzie, 57 Miss. 418; Sheerman v. Thompson, 11 Adol. & E. 1027; Sawyer v. Smith, 109 Mass. 220; Eaton v. Kegan, 114 Mass. 433; Wheeler v. Russell, 17 Mass. 258; Miller v. Post, 1 Allen, 434; Hewes v. Piatts, 12 Gray, 143; Spencer v. Smith, 3 Camp. 9. On the general subject, see Tied. Com. Paper, § 179; 2 Rand. Com. Paper, § 537; 1 Daniel, Neg. Inst. 204; Wood's Byles, Bills, *746; Benn. Benj. Sales, § 538; Pollock, Cont. p. 321; 1 Add. Cont. § 300;

In re Stowe, 6 N. B. R. 429; Corbett v. Woodward, 5 Sawy. 404; Feldman v. Gamble, 26 N. J. Eq. 494; Chandler v. Johnson, 39 Ga. 85; O'Byrne v. Mayor, etc., of Savannah, 41 Ga. 331; Taliaferro v. Moffett, 54 Ga. 150; Allen v. Pearce, 84 Ga. 606, 10 S. E. Rep. 1015; Bishop v. Palmer, 146 Mass. 469, 16 N. E. Rep. 299.

3. A married woman cannot make any valid contract of suretyship, but she can enter into an original undertaking to pay for the goods bought on her own credit for the use of her son. Freeman v. Coleman, 86 Ga. 590, 12 S. E. Rep. 1064. Her separate note and mortgage would be prima facie, but not conclusive, evidence that her relation to the debt is that of a principal and not that of a surety.

4. There surely can be no doubt that a witness may refresh his memory by a memorandum taken from his books, if, after so refreshing it, he can and does testify to the facts from his own recollection. The court erred in not granting a new trial. Judgment reversed.

DAVIS v. EAST TENNESSEE, V. & G. RY. CO.

(Supreme Court of Georgia. July 13, 1891.)

RAILROAD COMPANIES — CONSTRUCTION OF ROAD — DAMAGES FOR USING STREET.

1. Neither by express grant nor by necessary implication has the E. T., V. & G. Ry. Co. any authority to construct and operate its railway longitudinally upon the public streets of the city of Macon.

2. In an action by the owner of abutting property against the company for damage to the freehold and for diminishing the annual value of the premises for use there can be no recovery as to the freehold where the market value has been increased, but as to the latter there may be a recovery, notwithstanding such increase in the market value. A wrong-doer cannot set off increase of market value, caused by his wrongful act, against loss of rents and profits occasioned thereby.

3. Evidence as to a matter not covered by the declaration is not admissible.

(Syllabus by the Court.)

Error from superior court, Bibb county; A. L. MILLER, Judge.

Action by Ellen Davis against the East Tennessee, Virginia & Georgia Railway Company to recover damages. Judgment for defendant. Plaintiff brings error. Reversed.

Gustin, Guerry & Hall, for plaintiff in error. Bacon & Rutherford, for defendant in error.

BLECKLEY, C. J. 1. The Macon & Brunswick Railroad, extending from Macon to Brunswick, was the property of the state. By virtue of certain acts passed in 1879 it was first leased and then sold to a company which one of these acts incorporated by the name of the "Macon & Brunswick Railroad Company." See Acts 1878–79, pp. 115–122. The twelfth section of that act contains these clauses: That the lessee company which the act provides for "shall have full power and authority to survey, lay out, construct, equip, use, and enjoy a railroad from the city of Macon to the city of Atlanta," and divers others; "and shall further have power and authority to connect said roads, or either of them, at each terminus, with the roads of other companies constructed to said terminus, or which may hereafter be constructed to the said terminus." The thirteenth section requires the company or the lessees to "proceed, within one year or less time after the date of the execution of said lease, to build and put in good running order a railroad of five-feet guage, or the same guage with the Macon and Brunswick Railroad, between the city of Macon, in the county of Bibb, and the city of Atlanta, in the county of Fulton, and finish the same within five years from the execution of said lease; with the right to unite their tracks with the tracks of the roads now built or that may hereafter be built into said cities, by which cars may be transferred, without breaking bulk or detention, from road to road, at said cities." The evidence in the record indicates that the railroad from Macon to Atlanta was constructed by the Macon & Brunswick Railroad Company under and by virtue of these statutory provisions, and that, with the consent of the municipal government of the city of Macon, a part of the line was located and constructed along Wharf street, one of the public streets of the city. This occupation of the street was in pusuance of a contract between the company and the city authorities, by which the company agreed to pay to the city $2,000 per annum for the privilege; and this payment has been regularly made from year to year. The main line along the street had already been constructed and was in use when the plaintiff, Mrs. Davis, in 1884, purchased two city lots abutting on the street. These lots she improved by erecting upon them a dwelling-house and a blacksmith, carriage, and paint shop, afterwards used for carrying on a carriage and wagon manufacturing and repairing business. The evidence indicates that, after the plaintiff purchased, and her occupancy commenced, the main track was removed from its original position, and placed several feet nearer to her property; and also that a second side track was constructed in front of her premises. The defendant is the successor of the Macon & Brunswick Railroad Company, and has all its rights and privileges, including the right, if any, to occupy and use the street in question as a location for its line of railway. The first question is whether its occupation of this street is lawful or unlawful. It was settled by the decision of this court in the case of Daly v. Railroad Co., 80 Ga. 793, 7 S. E. Rep. 146, that power to authorize the public streets of the city of Macon to be occupied and used as the route of a steam railway resides exclusively in the legislature of the state, and that the municipal government is without authority to grant such a privilege to a railway company. No express grant by the legislature to the defendant or to any of its predecessors has been produced. The Code declares in section 719: "Public highways, bridges, or ferries cannot be appropriated to railroads, plankroads, or any other species of road, unless express authority is granted by some constitutional provision of their charter." Highways, in the broad sense, include streets. Elliott, Roads & St. 1, 2, 12, 13;

1 Abb. Law Dict. 562; 1 Bouv. Law Dict. 750; 2 Bouv. Law Dict. 672; And. Law Dict. 981; 9 Amer. & Eng. Enc. Law, 362. This section of the Code had its origin in the Code of 1863, and was of force when the above-quoted legislation was enacted in 1879. Construing it as applying to streets as well as to public roads in the country, it would be decisive against any implied grant of authority to build a railroad along Wharf street in the city of Macon, however strong any implication of such authority might be. This court, in Railroad Co. v. Mann, 43 Ga. 200, appears to have treated the matter of the section as probably applying to the streets of a town; but, without ruling definitely on this question, we can rest our decision in the present case on the general doctrine that no authority not granted in express terms would exist unless it arose by necessary implication. "Though 'the grant of land for one public use must yield to that of another more urgent,' and though 'every grant of power is intended to be efficacious and beneficial, and to accomplish its declared object, and carries with it such incidental powers as are requisite to its exercise,' yet 'when it is the intention of the legislature to grant a power to take land already appropriated to another public use, such intention must be shown by express words, or by necessary implication.' Therefore the mere grant of a charter right to build a railroad between two points does not carry with it, by necessary implication, the right to occupy longitudinally a highway lying in the general route contemplated, unless the topography of the ground be such (as, for instance, the notch of the White mountains) as to physically preclude a location, by reasonable intendment, to have been designed on any other line." Ror. R. R. 502. See, also, Daly v. Railroad Co., supra. Nothing appears on the face of the legislation itself, nor from any evidence in the record before us, tending to show that it would be necessary to use any public street in order to construct a railroad from the city of Macon to the city of Atlanta; or to connect it with any other road at Macon, including the road from Macon to Brunswick; or to unite its tracks with that and other roads terminating in said city, so that cars could be transferred from road to road, without detention or breaking bulk. That to accomplish these objects some, and perhaps many, of the streets would have to be crossed, is a necessary implication; and the presence of that serves to furnish a good example of what a necessary implication is. Authority to run a railroad through a city involves in its terms the privilege of crossing the streets, but not of occupying them longitudinally. The act of 1850 conferred upon the Central Railroad and the Macon & Western Railroad authority to unite their tracks in one common depot within the city of Macon; but, as construed by this court in Daly's Case, supra, the act did not by implication grant any right of using the public streets for the purpose. Indeed, nothing is more manifest than that, under ordinary conditions, roads may pass through cities and make connections, one line with an-

other, without appropriating to themselves any of the streets used by the public. The only necessary encroachments upon the streets would be to cross and recross them; sometimes at one angle, and sometimes at another. When it is the intention of the legislature to allow steam railways to occupy or appropriate the public streets or highways, it is easy to say so; and where the intention is left the least doubtful, the doubt must be given in favor of the general public and against the railway corporation. There is always a strong presumption that public property, or property already devoted to public use, is intended to remain intact, and not be converted, in whole or in part, to another public use. Mayor of Atlanta v. Railroad, etc., Co., 53 Ga. 120. The case of Wood v. Railroad Co., 68 Ga. 539, involved no question as to the appropriation of highways or streets. It concerned the location of the railway along the river bank, through a plat of ground to which the city had title, and which the city, not the state, had dedicated to public use as a cemetery. The ruling of this court was that the city, without express authority from the legislature, could devote a part of the ground not actually used for burial, nor adapted to that use, to another public purpose, to-wit, the location of the track and road-way of this railroad. The court also held, in effect, that, construing the legislation which we have quoted above in the light of the special facts disclosed in the record of that case, that legislation conferred the requisite authority by necessary implication, so far as any authority was needed from the legislature. The title to the public streets of Macon is not in the city, but in the state; the state, not the city, has dedicated them to public use; and that part of Wharf street now in question was, it may be assumed, in actual use by the public as a highway both in 1879, when this legislation took place, and afterwards, when the city undertook to change the original dedication in part by consenting to the occupation of the street as the route of a steam railway. Had Wood's Case related to one of the streets of the city instead of to the river margin of the cemetery grounds, the decision would doubtless have been different. Indeed, it must have been different if streets are highways within the meaning and intent of section 719 of the Code. It follows from what we have said that the defendant must be treated as occupying Wharf street with its railway without legal authority; and, consequently, that the law of nuisance, and not the law of assessment for property taken or damaged by the exercise of the right of eminent domain, applies between the parties in the present controversy.

2. The scope of the plaintiff's action embraces two classes of damage,—damage to the *corpus* or freehold, and damage by diminishing the annual value of the premises for use. The evidence shows very conclusively that the market value of the property was increased, rather than diminished, by the location and use of the railroad in the street. The plaintiff can recover nothing on that score, for the reason, if for no other, that she proved no damage of that class. But the evidence did tend to show that she had sustained damage by the diminished annual value of the premises for use in their present condition. The court, in its charge to the jury, seems not to have recognised this element as a basis for recovery. We think this was error. A wrong-doer cannot set off increase of market value, caused by his unlawful act, against loss of rents and profits occasioned thereby. Marcy v. Fries, 18 Kan. 353; Francis v. Schoellkopf, 53 N. Y. 153; Gerrish v. Manufacturing Co., 30 N. H. 478. Injury to rental value is or may be separate and distinct from injury to market value. The measure of damages in an action for a nuisance affecting real estate is not simply the depreciation of the property. Baltimore & P. R. Co. v. Fifth Baptist Church, 108 U. S. 317, 2 Sup. Ct. Rep. 719. The owner of property is entitled to use it in its present condition, and one who unlawfully hinders, obstructs, or interferes with such use, cannot appeal to the increased market value which might be realised if the property were devoted to other purposes, and take credit for such increase by way of indirect set-off against the direct loss or injury which he has occasioned. Nor would the purchase of the premises by the plaintiff after the road was located and constructed in the street be any reason why she might not recover damages of this class which she has actually sustained. Glover v. Railroad Co., 51 N. Y. Super. Ct. 1; Werfelman v. Railroad Co., 11 N. Y. Supp. 66.

3. Under the declaration, as we construe it, there was no error in excluding evidence "that the means of ingress to and egress from the property of plaintiff by a street on which said property is situated had been, by the construction of the railroad of defendant in said street, interfered with at a point 200 feet, and that by reason of such interference the property of plaintiff had been damaged." This is a somewhat obscure statement of what was offered to be proved; but if it means what we suppose, namely, that ingress and egress were impeded by an obstruction 200 feet distant from the plaintiff's premises, the declaration seems to us not to cover it. The court erred in not granting a new trial. Judgment reversed.

ALLGOOD v. STATE.

(Supreme Court of Georgia. July 20, 1891.)

FORGERY—INDICTMENT—EVIDENCE—WITNESS.

1. It is no cause for quashing an indictment that the prosecutor in a former indictment was not the same as the prosecutor in the pending indictment.

2. A question to a witness, which is not necessarily leading, will not be held by a reviewing court to be objectionable as a leading question.

3. It is not admissible evidence, to discredit the prosecutrix as a witness, that some one else induced her to commence the prosecution.

4. Small variances in the spelling of some of the words used in the forged instrument will not vitiate an indictment for the forgery, nor prevent the introduction of the instrument in evidence.

5. The making of the forged deed by the accused is established by proof that the signatures of the maker and witnesses were in his hand-

writing, that he deposited the deed in the clerk's office to be recorded, and that the maker and witnesses did not authorize the signing of their names.

6. A deed purporting to be executed in one county cannot be legally recorded upon the attestation of a notary public of another county, together with that of an unofficial witness. A certified copy, taken from a record so made, is no evidence of the execution of an original deed corresponding with it, and is not admissible in evidence in lieu of such original without further proof.

7. Though a deed may be without formal words of conveyance, yet if a valuable consideration, and the names of a vendor and a vendee, appear in the instrument, and there is a warranty of title, the legal effect would be to pass title if the instrument were genuine, and consequently, if spurious, it may be a subject of prosecution for forgery.

(*Syllabus by the Court.*)

Error from superior court, Carroll county; SAMPSON W. HARRIS, Judge.

Indictment of J. N. Allgood for forgery. Verdict of guilty. Defendant brings error. Reversed.

O. L. Reese and *W. F. Brown*, for plaintiff in error. *Sol. Gen. Atkinson* and *W. C. Adamson*, for the State.

SIMMONS, J. 1. Allgood was indicted and tried for the offense of forgery, and was convicted. He made a motion for a new trial, which was overruled, and he excepted. At the trial the defendant moved to quash the indictment, on the ground that in a former indictment for the same offense Reagan was the prosecutor and in the present indictment Mrs. Russell was the prosecutor. This motion was overruled by the court, and was made the basis of the fourth ground of the motion for a new trial. The court did not err in overruling this motion. The ground stated is not sufficient to authorize a court to quash an indictment. If the first indictment was quashed or *nol. pros'd*, and Reagan's name was written thereon as prosecutor, the solicitor general was not compelled by law, when he presented the next indictment before the grand jury, to place Reagan's name upon that indictment. Any person has the right to prosecute for a violation of the criminal laws of the state. After the first indictment was disposed of, if Reagan was not the real prosecutor, the solicitor general had the right to put upon the indictment the name of Mrs. Russell, who seems to have been the person aggrieved by the forgery, and the real prosecutrix in the case.

2. The fifth ground complains that the court erred in overruling the objection of defendant's counsel to the following question addressed to a witness by the solicitor general, the objection being that the question was leading: "What did he [meaning the defendant] say to you about testifying that he was authorized to sign your name to the deed?" While this question, taken by itself, appears to be leading, yet, when we take it in connection with the previous question asked the witness, it is not leading. The brief of evidence shows that the witness was first asked if he had a conversation with the defendant about signing his (witness') name to the deed, and he replied that he

did, and then followed the question objected to. Taking the question objected to with the other question asked the witness, the court did not err in overruling the objection.

3. There was no error in refusing to allow the defendant to ask the prosecutrix if Reagan did not induce her to prosecute this case, as complained of in the sixth ground. It was insisted that the evidence was material to show what influence was brought to bear upon the witness, and to illustrate what credit the jury should attach to her evidence. The evidence was not admissible for that purpose, and, if it had been admitted, it should not have affected the credit of the prosecutrix. If the criminal law has been violated, it is a duty of the citizen to prosecute the criminal, and it is the right of any citizen to advise and induce the party aggrieved to prosecute; and the fact that a person was induced by others to prosecute for the criminal offense should not discredit his testimony before the jury, nor should the trial judge allow the fact to be proven for that purpose.

4. The seventh ground complains of two rulings as erroneous: (1) That the court admitted the alleged forged deed in evidence, over the objection of the defendant that its execution had not been sufficiently proven. We presume this means that it had not been sufficiently proven that the defendant signed the name of Mrs. Russell to the deed, and the names of the witnesses thereto. The evidence shows that Mrs. Russell, whose name was signed as the maker of the deed, did not sign it, and did not authorize any one to sign it for her. It further shows that the persons whose names were affixed to the deed as witnesses did not sign, nor authorize any one to sign, their names as witnesses thereto. It was further shown that the signatures to the deed were in the handwriting of the defendant, and that he carried it to the clerk of the superior court, and left it with him for record. We think this was sufficient proof that the defendant signed the names of Mrs. Russell and the witnesses to the deed. (2) The next ground of objection to the admissibility of the forged deed in evidence was that it did not correspond with the one set out in the indictment, the variances being as follows: In the first line of the second page of the indictment was the word "hereby," and the deed offered in evidence had the word "hereby" in the third line; the indictment had the word "parcel," and the deed the word "parsel;" the indictment had the word "heirs," and the deed the word "hears;" the indictment had the word "warrant," and the deed the word "warrent." We do not think these small variances in spelling are sufficient to vitiate an indictment for forgery, nor to prevent the introduction of the forged deed in evidence. The principal reason of the strictness required by the rule of pleading in the setting out of the forged instrument is that the court may be able to judge whether it is an instrument whereof forgery may be committed. The misspelling of words, therefore, unless the misspelling changes the sense of the word,

will not vitiate the indictment, nor prevent the introduction of the deed set out therein as evidence. 1 Bish. Crim. Proc. § 562; 2 Russ. Crimes, (9th Ed.) 799; 8 Amer. & Eng. Enc. Law, 512. It does not appear that the dislocation of the word "hereby" altered the sense of the instrument or affected its validity.

5. The record shows that the forged deed conveyed certain lots of land from Mrs. Russell to Allgood, the defendant; and that Allgood borrowed a certain sum of money from one Bethune, and made him a deed to the same land, signed by himself and his wife. This deed from Allgood was headed "Georgia, Carroll county," and the copy-deed put in evidence shows that it was attested by A. J. Hansell, and by J. H. Jones, notary public of Fulton county, Georgia. It was recorded in Carroll county. A subpœna duces tecum was issued to the attorneys of Bethune to produce the original deed from Allgood to Bethune, but they declined to do so, claiming their privilege as attorneys. A copy from the record in Carroll county was then introduced in evidence, over the objection of defendant's counsel, and this is excepted to in the eighth ground of the motion for a new trial. We do not think that a copy made from the record in Carroll county, without further proof of execution of the original than the fact of its being recorded, was admissible as evidence. Under the facts above stated the clerk of the superior court of Carroll county was not authorized to admit the deed to record. It purported to have been made in Carroll county, and was attested by another witness and an officer of Fulton county. If it was executed in Carroll county, the notary public in Fulton county had no authority to act officially in Carroll county, and his attestation as notary public of Fulton county would not authorize the recording of the deed in Carroll county. The Code, § 2706, says that, if a deed is executed in this state, "it must be attested by a judge of a court of record of this state, or a justice of the peace, or notary public, or clerk of the superior court in the county in which the three last-mentioned officers, respectively, hold their appointments." A notary public of Fulton county, therefore, has no right to attest a deed officially in Carroll county, and the clerk in Carroll county had no right to put the deed on record; and if it was not recorded properly in Carroll county a certified copy thereof was not admissible in evidence without proof of an original, and of its execution, and that this was a copy thereof. There was proof that there was an original, but no proof of its proper execution; nor was there any proof that the copy offered was a copy of the original. The court, therefore, erred in admitting this copy-deed in evidence over the objection of the defendant. See Fain v. Garthright, 5 Ga. 12; Hammond v. Wilcher, 79 Ga. 424, 5 S. E. Rep. 118.

6. The next ground we will notice complains that the verdict is illegal "for the reason that the alleged forged deed conveys nothing to any person or by any person;" that "there is neither grantor nor grantee in said deed." It is true, this deed does not contain the usual and formal words of conveyance; but it sets out the names of the vendor and vendee, and a valuable consideration, and contains a warranty of title. Our Code declares (section 2692) that "no prescribed form is essential to the validity of a deed to lands or personalty. If sufficient in itself to make known the transaction between the parties, no want of form will invalidate it." We think this deed is sufficient to make known the transaction between the parties; and the legal effect of it, if genuine, would be to pass the title from Russell to Allgood; and, if a forgery, it may be the subject of a prosecution for forgery. In the case of Newton v. McKay, 39 Mich. 1, a deed similar to the one before us was objected to on the ground that no grantee was named or sufficiently described; but the court held that it was a valid conveyance. The reasoning of GRAVES, C. J., in that case, will apply to the present deed. It is not necessary that the forged paper should be shown to be a perfect instrument. It is sufficient if the indictment shows that it is one which, if genuine, is capable of having some legal effect. Amer. & Eng. Enc. Law, 512, 513. Judgment reversed.

CHISHOLM v. SPULLOCK.

(Supreme Court of Georgia. July 20, 1891.)

DEEDS—CONSTRUCTION—RENTS.

Where a will has been admitted to probate in solemn form by the court of ordinary, and an appeal has been entered to the superior court, during the pendency of which legatees to whom real estate was devised by the will made a compromise of the litigation over it with the administrator *cum testamento annexo*, and, in pursuance thereof, conveyed to him individually "all right, title, interest, and claim, vested or contingent, which [they] have or may have in the future unto and to [said real estate] under and by virtue of [said will,] directly or indirectly," *held*, that this deed conveyed to the grantee therein all rents which up to this date had accrued upon the real estate mentioned, and which had never been paid over to said legatees, the title to the rents being dependent upon the interest devised in the realty. SIMMONS, J., dissenting.

(Syllabus by the Court.)

Error from superior court, Floyd county; JOHN W. MADDOX, Judge.

Action by J. P. Chisholm, administrator, against E. A. Spullock, to foreclose a mortgage. Judgment for defendant. Plaintiff brings error. Reversed.

Dabney & Fouché, for plaintiff in error. *Wright & Harris,* for defendant in error.

LUMPKIN, J. Mrs. Martha B. Chisholm died, leaving a paper which purported to be her last will and testament. It devised a one-third interest in a store-house in the city of Atlanta to her mother, Mrs. Spullock, for life, and at her death to the heirs of the latter. With this exception the will provided that all the property of the testatrix should be equally divided between her daughter, such other children as she might have by her then husband, and the husband himself; the portion of the latter to go to him for life, with remainder over to the children of the testatrix. This will was offered for probate in solemn form by Mrs. Spullock and others, and a *caveat* was interposed. It was admitted to probate by the court of ordinary, and an appeal entered to the superior court. Willis P. Chisholm, the husband of the testatrix, after having been appointed administrator *cum testamento annexo* on her estate, died, and his brother, J. P. Chisholm, became administrator in his stead. While the litigation over the will was pending in the superior court, and for the purpose of effecting a compromise thereof, Mrs. Spullock and her children, who were remainder-men under the will as to the store-house property, in consideration of $10,000 sold and conveyed to J. P. Chisholm, by the deed referred to in the head-note, all their rights under the will to the realty therein devised to them. It appears that Mrs. Spullock was indebted to her daughter, Martha B., $526.25, besides interest, on two promissory notes, secured by a mortgage on real estate in the city of Rome. J. P. Chisholm, as administrator, sought to foreclose this mortgage, and as a defense thereto Mrs. Spullock filed a set-off, claiming therein one-third of the rents which had accrued upon the Atlanta real estate up to the time the deed above mentioned was made. The question, therefore, presented for our adjudication is whether or not she was entitled to her alleged share in these rents. We do not think she was. The title to the realty upon which these rents accrued had never vested in Mrs. Spullock. The very issue to be determined in the controversy over the will was whether or not the title to a one-third of this realty should vest in her. That issue was never finally determined in her favor, and by her own deed she forever conveyed all her interest in the realty to another. The executor had never assented to the legacy to Mrs. Spullock and her children, and this, under section 2451 of the Code, was necessary before the title could pass to them. Instead of assenting to the legacy, the executor was resisting it,—in fact, was contesting the will itself. The appeal from the judgment of the court of ordinary suspended that judgment, and while the controversy was still pending Mrs. Spullock and her children sold out their interest in the Atlanta realty, and abandoned their effort to set up the will. Hence there can never be an assent by the executor to this legacy. The title to this Atlanta realty can never vest in Mrs. Spullock or her children, nor can the judgment of the court of ordinary ever have any force or effect. In view of these facts, it must inevitably result that the purchase by J. P. Chisholm of all the right, title, and interest of Mrs. Spullock and her children in the Atlanta realty under Mrs. Chisholm's will, made in compromise of litigation touching the validity of the will, related back to the death of the testatrix, and passed to the purchaser any interest in uncollected rents accruing from the realty mentioned which the devisee or devisees had, because the interest in the rents was dependent upon the interest devised in the realty. We are satisfied that the purpose and effect of the compromise had between Mrs. Spullock and her children on the one side and J. P.

Chisholm on the other were to settle finally and definitely all controversy over the will, and that by its terms every right of Mrs. Spullock under the will was disposed of. The rents could not belong to her, nor had she any right to demand the same, until her title to an interest in the realty was established. This, we have shown, was never done; and, further, that it never can be done. Necessarily, therefore, the rents followed the realty into the hands of its real owner. We think the court erred in holding that the deed above recited passed to J. P. Chisholm only the right that Mrs. Spullock had in the real estate, and that her claim for rent was a separate and distinct matter, and did not pass thereby. The verdict, having allowed the defendant's set-off, was, in our opinion, wrong, and a new trial should therefore have been granted. Judgment reversed.

McMAHON et al. v. PARIS et al.

(Supreme Court of Georgia. July 20, 1891.)

ACTION ON ADMINISTRATOR'S BOND—LIABILITY OF SURETIES—EXCEPTION TO AUDITOR'S REPORT.

1. Where the suit was against two sureties upon an administrator's bond, and both of them excepted to the first report made by an auditor, and only one excepted to the second report, the other surety could be allowed to join him in these latter exceptions, it not affirmatively appearing that the time fixed by the court for excepting had expired.

2. According to the transcript of the record, there was no authority for the auditor to investigate, at his second sitting, the question of the administrator's solvency or insolvency, or of the time when he became insolvent.

3. The duty of administering the estate of an intestate is devolved by law upon the administrator, not on the heirs and distributees, who have a right to act for the protection of their own interests, and in doing so to invoke and accept the co-operation of the administrator in resisting creditors by all lawful means; and, if creditors are thus defeated, and the estate is saved to the heirs and distributees, though in the mean time wasted by the administrator, and he becomes insolvent, the sureties on his administration bond are not discharged.

(Syllabus by the Court.)

Error from superior court, Dade county; THOMAS W. MILNER, Judge.

Action by Jane McMahon and another against R. M. Paris and others. Judgment for defendants. Plaintiffs bring error. Reversed.

W. U. & J. P. Jacoway, E. J. & J. McCamy, and *W. K. Moore,* for plaintiffs in error. *McCutchen & Shumate* and *Dabney & Fouché,* for defendants in error.

SIMMONS, J. This was a suit by the ordinary of Dade county for the use of the heirs at law of Milton Derrybery, upon the administration bond of Graham, the principal, and Paris, Cureton et al., sureties. The case was referred to an auditor, who, after taking testimony, filed his report. To this report Paris and the heirs of Cureton, who were made parties defendant, filed exceptions. One of the exceptions, it seems, was that the report was not full enough upon certain points, and the court re-referred the matter to the auditor. The auditor made and filed another report, to which Paris filed exceptions and the Curetons did not. The case coming on for trial, the Curetons asked leave to consolidate their exceptions to the original report with those of Paris, and to adopt the exceptions filed by Paris to the supplemental report. This motion was objected to by the plaintiffs on the ground that it was too late for the Curetons to file exceptions; that "they had filed no exceptions within sixty days, nor even up to the September term, 1800, of said court;" and that, as they had "failed to file any exceptions to the supplemental report, as required by the order of the court, they could not now do so." The court overruled the objection, and allowed the exceptions to be consolidated, and the Curetons to join in the exceptions to the supplemental report. This is excepted to as error.

1. As before stated, this was a suit against the principal and the sureties on Graham's bond. Both of the sureties excepted to the original report of the auditor, and only one to the supplemental report. We think the court was right in allowing the Curetons to join in the exceptions filed by Paris to the supplemental report. Their defenses were the same; and, if the facts stated by Paris in his exceptions were sufficient to discharge him, they would also discharge the Curetons. Besides, it does not appear from the record within what time the defendants were required to file exceptions. What the order of the court was as to the filing of the exceptions, or the time of filing, is not stated. The order of the court, if there was an order, stating in what time exceptions might be filed, is not in the record, and therefore it does not appear to us but that the Curetons were in time to join in the exceptions filed by Paris. The report of an auditor is subject to exceptions for such time as the court may allow, (Code, § 4205,) and the time may be extended within the discretion of the court. The court having allowed the exceptions, and it not appearing from the record that they were improperly allowed, it is to be presumed that they were in time.

2. At the rehearing by the auditor the defendants offered testimony as to the solvency or insolvency of Graham, their principal, and as to the time when he became insolvent. This testimony was objected to by the plaintiffs on the ground that the auditor had no authority to take testimony on that question. On the trial of the case the defendants offered to read this testimony to the jury, and the plaintiffs again objected, "on the ground that the auditor had no authority to hear and report upon this question, as it was closed by the first hearing before the auditor, and this question was not re-referred to the auditor." The objection was overruled, and the evidence admitted, and to this ruling the plaintiffs excepted. The bill of exceptions states that the case was re-referred to the auditor, and he was directed "to hear testimony, and find and report who were and are the heirs of Milton Derrybery, whether John McMahon is an heir or not, and what relation Nancy Derrybery sustained to said deceased, if

any; and to this end the auditor shall hold another sitting, and give previous notice to the parties or their attorneys of such sitting and further hearing, and shall then take and report any testimony offered by either party on the question here referred to him in relation to said alleged mistake in his former report." The order of re-reference is not in the record, and this quotation from it in the bill of exceptions is all that appears in the entire record. Whether the quotation contains all of the order we do not know. If it does, then it is clear that the auditor had no authority to hear and determine any other question than the one submitted in the order, and the court therefore erred in admitting testimony taken and reported by the auditor as to the question of Graham's solvency or insolvency, because he had not been directed to take such testimony at the rehearing.

3. The exceptions filed by the defendants were, in substance, that the auditor erred in not finding and reporting that there was an understanding and agreement between Graham, the administrator, and Nancy Derrybery and the children of the deceased that Graham should hold all the money and effects of said estate, and not pay the same over to the creditors, and should delay making returns, and should fight off and delay the creditors in the collection of their debts, under the various laws made after the war in relation to old and ante-war debts; that this understanding was unknown to the sureties of Graham; and that, in pursuance of the understanding, Graham failed to make regular returns, and refused to pay out the money in his hands to the creditors, but took advantage of the several laws aforesaid to delay and fight off creditors through the space of many years; that the valid debts of the deceased were more than sufficient to consume the whole estate at the time said agreement was made; that at that time Graham was solvent, and able to account for the whole amount of the estate, but afterwards, while carrying out said undertaking, he became insolvent, and that the sureties of Graham were injured and damaged, and their risks increased, by reason of the understanding between Graham and the heirs aforesaid. The judge charged the jury that, if they found from the evidence the facts as contended for by the sureties, then they would be discharged from liability upon Graham's bond as administrator, and they should find the exceptions covering this issue in favor of the defendants. To this charge the plaintiffs excepted, and assign error thereon. We think this exception is well taken. If all the facts alleged in the exceptions to the auditor's report were true, we do not think they would be sufficient to discharge the sureties of the administrator. Under the law it is the duty of the administrator to administer the estate of the deceased. He, and not the heirs and distributees, represents the estate. It is his duty to collect the assets and pay all just debts of his intestate. If a debt is presented to him which, under the law existing at the time the debt was contracted, is not bind-

ing upon the estate, he has the right to litigate with the creditor, and to get rid of it, if the law will allow. The heirs and distributees have the right to protect their own interests in the estate, and they also have the right to invoke the aid of the administrator in resisting creditors by all lawful means; and, if they can defeat the creditors with the aid and assistance of the administrator, by lawful means, and the estate is saved to them, they can sue and recover from the administrator, or his sureties, in case the administrator has wasted the estate pending such litigation. If creditors are lawfully defeated in their claims against the estate, the heirs are entitled to such benefit as may be derived therefrom. The fact that the heirs cooperated with the administrator in defeating the creditors by lawful means, and the further fact that the administrator, with their consent, held the assets pending litigation, and afterwards wasted them and became insolvent, will not discharge the sureties. The sureties, in their bond, guarantied that the administrator would faithfully administer the assets of the estate, and that, if he failed to do so, they would be responsible. It was therefore their duty to look after the administrator, and to see that he regularly made his returns to the court of ordinary, and generally to see that he faithfully administered his trust; and, if they failed to do this, they became liable, as his sureties, for his waste or mismanagement. Judgment reversed.

VAN PELT v. HOME BUILDING & LOAN ASS'N.

(Supreme Court of Georgia. July 13, 1891.)

BUILDING AND LOAN ASSOCIATIONS — DISSOLUTION — ACTIONS — EXCEPTIONS TO AUDITOR'S REPORT.

1. A judgment overruling exceptions to an auditor's report, and not excepted to *pendente lite*, or otherwise, within 60 days after its rendition, is not open to review and reversal by the supreme court.

2. Where a building and loan association sells out, and assigns in writing all its claims for unpaid loans, thereby realizing a fund sufficient to raise the value of its stock to the maximum fixed by the constitution or the by-laws, and with this fund, in connection with other assets, pays off and satisfies all its stockholders, and entirely ceases to transact business, it is virtually dissolved, and is incapable of further prosecuting a pending action founded upon a bond so transferred and assigned after the action was brought.

(Syllabus by the Court.)

Error from superior court, Fulton county; MARSHALL J. CLARKE, Judge.

Action by the Home Building & Loan Association against F. M. Van Pelt. Judgment for plaintiff. Defendant brings error. Reversed.

John A. Wimpy, for plaintiff in error. S. Barnett and W. S. Thomson, for defendant in error.

BLECKLEY, C. J. 1. The exceptions to the auditor's report were overruled on March 25th. No exception was entered *pendente lite*. On April 1st thereafter the case came on for final hearing and trial, and the trial terminated on that day in a final judgment for the plaintiff below.

The bill of exceptions was certified on the 31st of May, which was within 60 days after the trial and judgment, but was more than 60 days after the exceptions to the auditor's report were overruled. The bill of exceptions was too late to reach any alleged error committed by the court in overruling the exceptions. In order to preserve the right to have that decision reviewed it was necessary that exceptions should have been entered *pendente lite*, under section 4254 of the Code. City of Waycross v. Youmans, 85 Ga. 708, 11 S. E. Rep. 865. The longest time allowed by the statute for signing a bill of exceptions is 60 days from the date of the decision complained of. Code, § 4252.

2. The court erred in striking the amended pleas filed by the defendant below on the day of the trial. If the facts set forth in these pleas be true, the association was virtually dissolved pending the suit. It not only had transferred and assigned in writing the subject-matter of the present action, but had virtually gone out of existence. If it had paid off and satisfied all its stockholders, and ceased to transact business, it was incapable of further prosecuting a pending action founded upon a bond which it transferred and assigned after the action was brought. It might admit of some question—indeed, very considerable question under the authorities—whether it could proceed to recover on a cause of action after parting with title, both legal and equitable, although it had not parted with its own legal existence as well; but we are clear that, taking the matter of these pleas as true, the association could not prosecute this action, or any other. Judgment reversed.

FLEETWOOD v. LORD et al.

(Supreme Court of Georgia. July 13, 1891.)

HOMESTEAD — SALE — TITLE OF PURCHASERS — EVIDENCE.

1. A widow, as the head of a family consisting of herself and a minor child, having had a homestead set apart to her in 1873 out of the lands of her deceased husband's estate, and the adult heirs having acquiesced in the same, and the lands so set apart having been subsequently sold by order of the judge in conformity to section 2025 of the Code, the purchaser at such sale acquired, not only the title of the beneficiaries, but that of the estate, so as to bar the rights of the adult heirs and all persons claiming under them, their rights being transferred to the property in which the proceeds of the sale were invested.

2. The homestead not having been taken by the widow in her own individual share of the realty belonging to her husband's estate, the indebtedness of the estate, the value of its assets, etc., were inadmissible for the purpose of showing that the homestead was not more than her own interest in the lands would have amounted to.

(Syllabus by the Court.)

Error from superior court, Wilkinson county; W. F. JENKINS, Judge.

Petition by Mrs. S. J. Fleetwood against James Lord and others. Judgment for defendants. Plaintiff brings error. Reversed.

Hardeman & Davis and Whitefield & Allen, for plaintiff in error. M. W. Harris and J. W. Hall, for defendants in error.

SIMMONS, J. In 1871, Joel Dees died intestate, leaving a large estate of lands and other property. All the property went into the hands of the administrators, Duggan and Freeman, who were appointed in 1872. Dees left as his heirs at law his widow, Nancy, and three children, to-wit, Mrs. Fleetwood, Lizzie Dees, and his minor son, Joel T. Dees. In November, 1872, the ordinary of Wilkinson county set apart to the widow, for herself and her minor son, a homestead out of the estate, consisting of 450 acres of land, and the widow went immediately into the possession of the same. The administrators retained possession of the property until 1875, without paying the debts or making distribution. James Lord and H. A. Hall were the neighbors and friends and confidential advisers of the family, and in 1875 advised the heirs that the administrators were mismanaging the estate; and that, if it were not got out of their hands, it would be sacrificed; and the only way to get it out of their hand was to raise money and pay the debts, or sell their interest to some one who could control the administrators; and, the heirs being unable to raise the money, Lord and Hall said they could find a purchaser, and in a few days proposed to purchase themselves. They were allowed to name their own price, and agreed to pay all the debts and pay each heir $1,800 for all the estate except the homestead. In 1883 the widow petitioned the judge of the superior court for leave to sell the homestead. All the heirs of the intestate were made parties. The judge granted the order authorizing the widow to sell the homestead, and Mrs. Fleetwood, one of the heirs, purchased it from the widow, paying her $2,500, and taking her deed in fee-simple. This sale was afterwards ratified by the judge, who ordered the money to be reinvested. Subsequently Lord and Hall set up a claim to Lizzie's part of the homestead, which they alleged would accrue to her after the death of the widow, Lord and Hall alleging that they had purchased it from Lizzie, and Lizzie claiming that her interest in the homestead was excepted, and that, while it did not appear in the deed from her to Lord and Hall, it was the understanding and agreement that it should be excepted, and that Lord and Hall agreed to make the exception in the deed. A great deal of testimony was taken upon this point, which, in the view we take of the case, it is unnecessary to detail. Mrs. Fleetwood filed her petition setting out these facts and a great many others which need not be mentioned, and prayed for a decree against Lord and Hall, canceling as much of the deed from Lizzie Dees to them as conveyed to them any interest in the homestead, and reforming the deed and the records thereof so as to exempt from the operation thereof all interest in the homestead lands, and that she might recover damages for the slander of her title, and for perpetual injunction against defendants. Lord and Hall answered the petition, and denied all the material allegations therein, and set up a claim to Lizzie's interest in the homestead property after the death of the widow. On the trial of the case the jury found in favor of Lord and Hall. The plaintiff moved for a new trial, and the motion was overruled by the court.

1. Plaintiff's counsel requested the court to charge the jury that "the order of said court authorizing Nancy Dees to make a sale of the homestead, and the purchase by plaintiff of said homestead lands under said order, divested all claim or interest of the heirs at law, or the purchasers from them, in and to said land, and transferred said interest or claim to the proceeds of said sale." Also that, "if the widow, in such a case, under an order of court, sells said homestead, the fee would pass to the purchaser, to the exclusion of said adult heirs or purchasers from them." Also that plaintiff obtained by her purchase from Mrs. Dees, under the order of the court, the absolute fee-simple in the lands. These charges the court refused to give, and error is assigned thereon in the sixth, seventh, and eighth grounds of the motion. We think the court should have given these instructions to the jury. The Code, § 2025, declares that the sale of the homestead property in compliance with the order of the court "shall operate to pass to the purchaser the entire interest and title of the beneficiaries in the exempted property, and also the entire interest and title owned before the exemption was made by the party out of whose estate the property was so exempted." So it would seem that the purchaser of this homestead property under the order of the judge obtained the absolute fee therein, and all the interest and title of the beneficiaries passed to her. This being true, it did not matter, so far as the purchaser was concerned, whether the interest of Lizzie in the homestead was excepted in her deed to Lord and Hall or not. If Lizzie had any interest, it was transferred from the homestead property to the property purchased with the proceeds of the sale thereof. She is therefore barred from claiming any interest in the homestead property so sold, and Lord and Hall, who claim under her, are also barred from claiming any interest in the land sold under the order of the court. When a widow takes a homestead out of her husbands' estate with the acquiescence of the adult heirs, and a sale thereof is duly made under the above cited section, this is an administration by competent authority of so much of her deceased husband's estate as against all persons not having liens thereon to be enforced after the homestead expires.

2. During the trial the plaintiff proposed to prove by Mrs. Dees, the widow, the value of the estate, of its assets, etc., for the purpose of showing that the homestead was worth no more than her own interest in the land would have amounted to. The record shows that the widow did not take this homestead in her own individual share of the realty belonging to her husband's estate, but took it as the head of a family, for herself and her minor son, out of the estate. The evidence, therefore, of the value of the estate, its assets, etc., was inadmissible for the purpose offered, and the court did not err in excluding it. As this decision will finally

settle the controversy, it is unnecessary to notice the other grounds of the motion for a new trial. Judgment reversed.

MOORE v. GARLAND et al.

(Supreme Court of Georgia. July 13, 1891.)

NEGOTIABLE INSTRUMENTS — CONSIDERATION — LICENSE TO SELL PATENTED ARTICLE.

1. The charge of the court that Garland's assignment was sufficient, and that Moore could not go behind it, was not error, under the facts of this case.

2. It appears from the evidence that what Moore bought was a license to use and sell in Crawford county, and the evidence shows that he got what he bought.

3. It further appears from the evidence that Shellnut, the patentee, reserved the exclusive right to make the machines; and also that he acquiesced in the license to Moore to use and sell.

(Syllabus by the Court.)

Error from superior court, Crawford county; A. L. MILLER, Judge.

Action by M. J. Moore against R. H. Garland and others. Judgment for defendants. Plaintiff brings error. Affirmed.

L. D. Moore, for plaintiff in error. W. S. Wallace, for defendants in error.

LUMPKIN, J. A case between these same parties, from which the litigation between them in the present case evolved, was before this court at March term, 1887, and is reported in 78 Ga. 764, 3 S. E. Rep. 654. It was then held it was no sufficient defense to plaintiff's action that no assignment of the patent-right had been made to defendant before demanding payment of his note, there being no evidence to show that defendant was to have such assignment before paying the note; and that, in the absence of such proof, the presumption from the note itself would be, he was entitled to such assignment when he paid the note. The judgment of the court below in favor of the plaintiff was then affirmed, and, in our opinion, this ought to have finally ended the controversy. In delivering the opinion, however, Justice BLANDFORD remarked that the defendant "could yet defend the case, after judgment, by tendering the money and demanding the assignment; and, upon the refusal to assign this right, a court of equity would not hesitate to enjoin the collection of the judgment." In our opinion, the words quoted were used rather *arguendo*, in giving a reason for the conclusion reached, than as being really necessary to a disposition of the case as it then stood. Treating these words, however, as properly a part of the adjudication then made, we are nevertheless of the opinion that the judgment of the court below upon the last trial was correct. The complainant, Moore, who sought to enjoin the collection of the judgment Garland had obtained against him, himself introduced an assignment from Garland, which conveyed to him the right "to use and to sell said patent within the limits of Crawford county, Georgia." Upon the authority of Rice v. Boss, 46 Fed. Rep. 195, and the cases there cited, this instrument conveyed to Moore only a license to use and to sell the "Shellnut water-engine" in Crawford county. The original note was not introduced in

evidence or considered by the jury whose verdict is now under review; and, if it would have proved that Moore was entitled to an assignment of the patent-right itself upon paying the note, this proof was wanting at the last trial, at which the evidence established that what he bought was only the license above mentioned. It was shown that Shellnut, the original patentee, had never parted with, but expressly reserved, the right to manufacture the engines. This reservation made all the subsequent transactions hereinafter mentioned in connection with said patent-right amount in law to nothing more than licenses, under which the licensee's rights were limited to what they actually purchased. The first of these transactions was one by which Shellnut authorized one Sims to use and sell these engines in the state of Georgia on certain conditions, with which Sims failed to comply, and in consequence thereof Shellnut, about July 1, 1886, again became the proprietor of such rights as Sims had in all the counties in Georgia which he had failed to dispose of. While Sims was operating under his contract with Shellnut, he bargained the right to use and sell these engines throughout the state of Georgia to one Holland, who afterwards received back the notes he had given for his purchase, and abandoned all claims thereunder. Before doing so, however, Garland, as his agent, on April 19, 1885, had made the contract with Moore, which amounted, as we have shown, to only a license to the latter to use and to sell these engines in the county of Crawford. The assignment of this license, which was made by Garland after the rendition of the judgment of this court upon the former trial, was ratified by Holland by a written instrument reciting that on the 27th day of March, 1885, he was the owner of this patent-right for the entire state of Georgia, and as such owner had authorized Garland to sell the right in certain counties of the state, including the county of Crawford. It further appears from the evidence that Sims "made arrangements with Garland to sell counties in south Georgia," and that Shellnut himself acquiesced in the transaction between Garland and Moore. In view of these facts, and the authority cited above, it seems clear that neither Sims nor Holland nor Garland ever had the right to sell, nor Moore the right to expect that he was purchasing, anything more than a mere license, and it is quite apparent that no person in any way connected with or interested in this patent-right could by any possibility dispute or interfere with his right to exercise his license in Crawford county; nor does it appear that any one has ever sought to do so, or desires to do so. Hence we say that, under the above-recited facts, the charge of the court that Garland's assignment to Moore was sufficient, and that Moore could not go behind it, was not erroneous; and, further, that Moore now has what he bought, and no legal reason appears why he should not pay for it. On none of the other grounds of the motion, all of which we have carefully considered, was Moore entitled to a new trial. Judgment affirmed.

AUGUSTA FACTORY v. DAVIS.

(Supreme Court of Georgia. July 20, 1891.)

PARENT AND CHILD—ACTION FOR DEATH OF CHILD —DAMAGES—PRACTICE.

1. There is no duty upon the judge of the superior court, after overruling a demurrer to the declaration, to suspend or postpone a trial of the case by the jury on issues of fact. The defendant may either except *pendente lite* to the judgment overruling the demurrer, or wait until after the trial is concluded, and make that judgment a subject of exception in a regular bill of exceptions.

2. A father may recover damages against the wrong-doer for loss of labor and services of his minor child, and for burial and other expenses incurred on account of the negligent homicide of the child, such child being old enough to perform labor, and having lived for several days after the infliction of the injury resulting in death.

3. It would seem that the damages recoverable for loss of labor and services might be computed for the whole remnant of minority, though the mother of the child be living, and might, under the act of October 27, 1887, have a right of action for the homicide; the father's action not being brought for the homicide, but for the loss of labor and services, caused by the wrongful negligence of which death was one of the consequences.

(Syllabus by the Court.)

Error from superior court, Richmond county; H. C. RONEY, Judge.

Action by John H. Davis against the Augusta Factory for damages for the negligent killing of a daughter. Judgment for plaintiff. Defendant brings error. Affirmed.

J. B. Cumming and *Bryan Cumming,* for plaintiff in error. *Twiggs & Verdery,* for defendant in error.

BLECKLEY, C. J. After overruling the demurrer to the declaration, the judge, in the exercise of his discretion, and having doubts in his own mind of the correctness of his ruling on the demurrer, ordered the case to be withdrawn from the jury. This was done for the avowed purpose of giving the defendant an opportunity to bring the case to this court on writ of error in advance of a trial by jury on the issue of fact. Though it was in the power of the court to suspend the trial, there was no duty incumbent upon it to do so. The defendant might have entered exceptions *pendente lite* to the decision overruling the demurrer, (Bradley v. Saddler, 54 Ga. 681;) or, without excepting *pendente lite,* the question on the demurrer alone could have been brought here by regular bill of exceptions, after the trial was over, and a recovery had by the plaintiff, (Lowe v. Burke, 79 Ga. 164, 3 S. E. Rep. 449, and see Kitchens v. State, 80 Ga. 810, 7 S. E. Rep. 209;) or after a mistrial, (Railroad Co. v. Denson, 83 Ga. 267, 9 S. E. Rep. 788;) but it was not necessary that the trial should proceed any further after the demurrer was overruled, in order to render the judgment on the demurrer reviewable here, (City Council v. Lombard, 86 Ga. 165, 12 S. E. Rep. 212.)

2. The plaintiff's daughter was 15 years of age, and was injured on the 8th day of January, 1890. She survived until the

24th day of the same month, when she died of her injuries. The action is for the loss of her labor and services, and for expenses incurred in her last illness, death, and burial. The negligence of the defendant which caused the injury and consequent death was in furnishing unsafe machinery for the child to work with, she being in the employment of the defendant as a laborer in its cotton-mill. This negligence was a tort, and the death resulted from it. The plaintiff, according to all the better authorities, would be entitled to recover the necessary expenses incurred by him in consequence of it, and also compensation for the loss of the labor and services of his minor daughter from the time she was disabled by the injury until she died. 3 Thomp. Neg. 1272, and notes; 3 Lawson, Rights, Rem. & Pr. § 1016.

3. This action not being for the homicide of the daughter, but for the tort of which the homicide was only a consequence, and the gist of the suit being the loss of labor and services, the right of action was altogether independent of the act of October 27, 1887, and the recovery would embrace damages for the loss of services of the daughter from the time of the injury until she would have been 21 years of age, according to the ruling of this court in McDowell v. Railroad Co., 60 Ga. 320. Inasmuch as one and the same tortious act may cause separate and distinct damage to two persons,—as, for instance, to master and servant, (Smith, Mast. & S. *178,)—it is not easy to see how the scope of the father's damage, as recognised prior to the act of 1887, would be contracted by the right of action given by that act to the mother, even where the conditions are such as to entitle the mother to sue and recover for the homicide. Her damages are arbitrarily measured by the statute at the full value of the life of the child; but this is not necessarily inconsistent with the duty on the part of the wrong-doer of compensating the father, on the basis of the prior law, for the damages sustained by him in the loss of the child's services up to the period of majority, in so far as those services would have been of value to him. The tort, with the homicide as an incident, might be treated as furnishing a cause of action to the father, and the homicide itself as furnishing a cause of action in behalf of the mother. In prescribing a measure of recovery for the latter, the legislature could make the value of the life the standard, without changing or intending to change the measure of recovery for the former. It does not appear, however, that the child now in question left any mother; nor was it needful that the declaration should disclose anything on that subject, the present action not being founded on the act of 1887, but on the prior law. The contention that the prior law has been abrogated by implication is not sustainable, though it is doubtless true that a father, when himself entitled to sue under the new act, would have to elect between the remedy which it affords and the more restricted remedy afforded by the law as it stood before the act was passed. He could not sue severally for the homicide and for the orig-

inal tort from which the homicide resulted, and recover in both actions. Judgment affirmed.

JONES et al. v. LEWIS et al.

(Supreme Court of Georgia. July 8, 1891.)

PRINCIPAL AND SURETY—JUDGMENT AGAINST SURETIES.

In an action at law upon a joint promissory note, all the makers except one being sureties, a verdict against some of the sureties for the whole amount of the note, and against one of them for half that amount, is contrary to law. The plaintiff may, however, enter judgment against all the sureties for the lesser sum, and direction is given accordingly.

(Syllabus by the Court.)

Error from superior court, Macon county; ALLEN FORT, Judge.

Action on a promissory note, by John F. Lewis and son against William Jones and another. Verdict and judgment for plaintiffs. Defendants bring error. Affirmed.

John. W. Haygood, for plaintiffs in error. *J. M. Du Pree,* for defendants in error.

SIMMONS, J. Lewis sued Stubbs as principal, and J. F. Barfield, Jones, and Jesse Barfield, as sureties, on a joint promissory note for $115.98, with interest from maturity at 8 per cent., and attorney's fees. The sureties pleaded that Stubbs was the principal upon the note, and they were only sureties, which the plaintiff knew at the time, and before he advanced the money; that they only agreed to stand security for $50, and that they signed the note in blank, no amount whatever being on its face when they signed; that they never signed or agreed to sign the note sued on, and authorized no one else to do so for them; that one of them told the plaintiff before he signed that he would only be responsible for Stubbs for $50, and that he never consented to be surety for him for any other sum; that the note was filled out by the plaintiff without the authority of these defendants, but they did authorize Stubbs to have the plaintiff fill it out for $50 only. The proof showed, and so the jury found, that one of the sureties notified the plaintiff before the note was filled out that he would only be bound for $50; but the proof fails to sustain the plea of the other sureties that they had agreed to sign only for $50, and that the plaintiff had notice thereof. The court instructed the jury, in substance, that, if they believed the note was signed in blank, but that Jesse Barfield, one of the sureties, notified Lewis that he would only be bound for $50, they could only find a verdict against him for that sum; and if the other sureties also signed in blank, but did not notify Lewis that they would be bound for $50 only, they would be authorized to find against them for the principal and interest on the note. Under this instruction the jury returned a verdict in favor of the plaintiff for $50 against Jesse Barfield, and against the principal and the other sureties for the whole amount of the note. This charge was error. This was an action at law, and upon a joint

promissory note. There was nothing on the face of the note to show that the sureties agreed to be severally bound for different amounts. When Lewis filled up the blank in the note for $115, after notice from one of the sureties that he would be bound only for $50, he could not recover from that surety more than $50. Clower v. Wynn, 59 Ga. 246; Johnson v. Blasdale, 40 Amer. Dec. 85; Gess v. Whitehead, 33 Miss. 213. And, the note being a joint one, in our opinion, the plaintiff could not recover more than that amount from the other sureties who had given no notice. The obligation was joint, and not joint and several; and the law will not allow the plaintiff to recover on a joint contract more from one surety than from another. The sureties have a right to contribution among themselves; and if one of them, against whom there is a verdict for $115, should pay it off, he would be entitled to equal contribution from his co-sureties, where the contract shows no different liability; and, if the judgment is only $50 against one and is $115 against another, there cannot be equal contribution. We direct, therefore, that the judgment be amended by entering up judgment against all the sureties for $50 principal, with interest thereon, and 10 per cent. attorneys' fees, and costs.

Judgment affirmed, with direction.

LUMPKIN, J., not presiding.

ATLANTA & F. R. Co. v. WRIGHT, Comptroller General.

(Supreme Court of Georgia. July 13, 1891.)

TAXATION OF RAILROADS.

1. That some of the railroads cannot constitutionally be taxed upon their property beyond a specified percentage upon their annual income does not hinder the legislature from taxing all other railroad companies *ad valorem* upon their property, the former being also taxed up to the limit established by their charters.

2. Under the constitution, which requires taxes to be levied and collected under general laws, the legislature has no power to impose a pecuniary penalty for non-payment upon one class of tax-payers exclusively, leaving all other classes exempt from any penalty whatever.

3. Nor can the legislature subject one class of tax-payers to execution for taxes on the 1st of October when the great mass of the tax-payers are exempt until the 20th of December.

(Syllabus by the Court.)

Error from superior court, Fulton county; MARSHALL J. CLARKE, Judge.

Execution for delinquent taxes issued by W. A. Wright, as comptroller general, against the Atlanta & Florida Railroad Company. Defendant's affidavit of illegality dismissed. Defendant brings error. Reversed.

P. L. Mynatt & Son, for plaintiff in error. *Geo. N. Lester,* Atty. Gen., and *Clifford Anderson,* for defendant in error.

SIMMONS, J. The general tax act of 1888 declares that "all the property of railroad companies doing business in this state shall be taxed at the same rate as property of natural persons is taxed, except * * * that portion of the property of each railroad company that is exempt by its charter from taxation," etc. In 1889 the legislature passed an act which declares that, "if any railroad company or companies doing business in this state shall fail or neglect to pay to the state all the taxes which such company or companies may be due and owing to the state for taxes by the first day of October in each year, then such railroad company or companies shall incur a penalty therefor of five hundred dollars; and the comptroller general shall immediately issue execution against such company or companies for the same, and collect the same." Acts, p. 130. The Atlanta & Florida Railroad Company neglected and failed to pay the taxes levied and assessed against it by the 1st day of October, 1889; whereupon W. A. Wright, the comptroller general, in compliance with the terms of the last-recited act, issued his execution for the sum of $2,412.96 taxes due by said company, and also for the further sum of $500 as penalty for failure to pay the taxes. This execution was levied upon certain property of the company on December 13, 1889. On the 15th of January, 1890, R. F. Maddox, president of the company, filed an affidavit of illegality, upon the grounds: (1) That the Southwestern Railroad Company, the Central Railroad Company, the Augusta & Savannah Railroad Company, the Georgia Railroad & Banking Company, and the Western & Atlantic Railroad Company are each taxed one-half of one per cent. upon their net income, while the tax *fi. fa.* mentioned above is an *ad valorem* tax upon the property of the defendant railroad company, which is a greater tax than that levied upon the roads above mentioned, and which violates the provision of the constitution that all taxation shall be uniform upon the same class of subjects, and *ad valorem* on all property subject to be taxed within the territorial limits of the authority levying the tax, and shall be levied and collected under general law. (2) Said *fi. fa.* is proceeding for the sum of $500 as penalty for the failure to pay the *ad valorem* tax assessed against said company by said comptroller general on or before the 1st of October of the year 1889. This tax is illegal, because the constitution provides that all taxation shall be levied under a general law, but one applicable to railroads alone, and therefore it violates the meaning of the constitution. The case coming on to be heard before the trial judge, the attorney general moved to dismiss the affidavit of illegality upon the ground that the same presented no legal defense to the *fi. fa.* and the penalty. The court granted the motion, and dismissed the affidavit of illegality, and ordered the execution to proceed; and to this ruling the railroad company excepted.

1. We think the trial judge was right in holding that the first ground of illegality presented no legal defense to the *fi. fa.* The constitution of 1877 (Code, § 5181) declares that "all taxation shall be uniform upon the same class of subjects, and *ad valorem* on all property subject to be taxed within the territorial limits of the

authority levying the tax, and shall be levied and collected under general laws." The legislature, in granting charters to five railroad companies mentioned in the first ground of the affidavit of illegality, long prior to the adoption of this constitution limited the taxation on the property of these companies to a certain per cent. on their net income. Their charters have been construed to be contracts which the state could not violate. The partial exemption of their property from taxation being legal, and binding upon the state, it was therefore not "subject to be taxed" beyond the rate fixed in their charters. The legislature did right in observing the contract limit in taxing the property of these companies in the general tax of 1888. The fact that the property had been partially exempted from taxation in the charter of the companies, and the fact that the legislature, in the general tax act, recognized the limitation, did not prevent the legislature from levying an *ad valorem* tax upon all other railroads in this state which had no such exemption. The general tax act levies a tax on all property in the state "subject to be taxed." The fact that there was some property in the state which the legislature had only a limited power or authority to tax did not make the act void for want of uniformity. It was uniform upon all property subject to be taxed *ad valorem*.

2, 3. We think the trial judge erred in holding that the second ground of the affidavit of illegality presented no defense to the execution. The same paragraph of the constitution above quoted declares that taxes shall be levied and collected under general laws. We think that this means that the laws for the levying and collecting of taxes shall be substantially the same for all classes of property; that, if a pecuniary penalty is put upon delinquent tax-payers, it shall affect all alike; that the legislature cannot impose one penalty upon a railroad company for its failure to pay taxes upon its property, and another penalty upon an individual for his failure to pay taxes upon his property. If any pecuniary penalty for failure to pay taxes upon property is exacted, there must be such a penalty upon all taxpayers who fail to pay. The general law requires that each and every tax-payer shall pay his taxes by the 20th of December in each year, and in case of default it is made the duty of the tax-collector to issue execution. Acts 1885, p. 66. The general law, therefore, being that taxes shall be paid by the 20th of December, and, if not paid, that an execution shall issue upon that day, the legislature had no power to prescribe for railroad companies exclusively a different day of payment, and a different day for the issuance of the execution, and a penalty not imposed upon other classes of tax-payers. We do not mean to suggest that the legislature may not prescribe penalties for failure to pay taxes promptly, or that they must be equal in amount upon all; for, doubtless, they may be graduated according to the amount due from each tax-payer. Judgment reversed.

GEORGIA MIDLAND & G. R. CO. v. EVANS.

(Supreme Court of Georgia. July 20, 1891.)

RAILROAD COMPANIES—NEGLIGENCE — PLEADING—
EVIDENCE—NEW TRIAL.

1. Under our Code, negligence of a railroad company being presumed when injury by the running of its train is shown, it is not necessary for a father, suing for loss of the services of his minor son, not an employe of the company, who was killed on a public crossing, to allege in his declaration either that he or the son was in the exercise of due care or was without fault.

2. Ordinary care for his own safety is not necessarily the measure of diligence incumbent upon a child under 14 years of age; nor is such child bound, as matter of law, to anticipate negligence by others. The evidence showing that the boy in question was under 14 years of age, a request to charge the jury, which assumed him to be of the age of 14, was properly declined.

3. A locomotive engineer is not entitled to assume in all cases that persons on a public crossing will get off in time to save themselves. In running a train at a public crossing in a city he is bound to observe reasonable diligence, before he discovers peril as well as afterwards; and the company is responsible for his negligent errors of judgment.

4. A request to charge in terms not applicable to the facts in evidence, or which in laying down a proposition omits some of the material elements to be considered, is properly refused.

5. The deceased not having been killed while jumping on or off cars, his previous habit of doing so at the public crossing where he was killed is not relevant evidence.

6. It is improper for counsel, on a motion to reopen the case for more evidence, made while the argument is in progress, to give the names of witnesses, and state what their evidence would be, without first requesting the court to cause the jury to retire. But the impropriety will not necessarily work a new trial, it not appearing that counsel acted in bad faith, or with any purpose to get facts before the jury by artful practice.

7. The evidence warranted the verdict, and there was no error in denying a new trial.

(Syllabus by the Court.)

Error from superior court, Spalding county; JAMES S. BOYNTON, Judge.

Action by A. M. H. Evans against the Georgia Midland & Gulf Railroad Company for the negligent killing of a minor son. Judgment for plaintiff. Defendant brings error. Affirmed.

Goetchius & Chappell, for plaintiff in error. *J. B. Stewart* and *E. W. Hammond,* for defendant in error.

LUMPKIN, J. 1. Where a father sues a railroad company for loss of services of his son, alleged to have been occasioned by the negligent killing of the latter by the company, the declaration not affirmatively disclosing any negligence or want of care on the part of either the father or deceased, it is not necessary for the plaintiff to allege that he had exercised ordinary care and diligence to avoid the injury to his son. Nor is it necessary, where the declaration alleges that the son was killed by the negligence of the railroad company, and specifies the negligent acts complained of, to further allege that deceased himself exercised all ordinary care and diligence to prevent the injury, and that the homicide was without fault on his part. If the deceased was in fault, or could by the exercise of reasonable care have avoided the injury, these were matters of defense. Deer. Neg. § 400; 3 Lawson, Rights, Rem.

& Pr. § 1216; Pierce, R. R. 322. The foregoing authorities sustain the above rulings, though they show also that, if the declaration itself alleges facts from which consent to the injury, negligence on the part of the person injured, or failure on his part to exercise due care to avoid the consequences of defendant's negligence may be inferred, then the declaration must go further, and avoid or explain such facts, and make defendant's liability appear notwithstanding the same. The presumption under our Code being against the railroad, if injury and negligence by defendant are clearly set forth, the declaration is sufficient, as to these points, and need not, when the plaintiff or person injured is not an employe of the company, further allege diligence or freedom from negligence on the part of such plaintiff or person injured, unless the declaration itself contains averments tending to relieve defendant of the legal presumption against it.

2. The measure of diligence required of a child under the age of 14 years is not the same as that required of an adult. It follows that such a child is not bound, as matter of law, to anticipate negligence on the part of others. Railroad Co. v. Young, 83 Ga. 512, 10 S. E. Rep. 197; Rhodes v. Railroad, etc., Co., 84 Ga. 320, 10 S. E. Rep. 922. It was manifestly proper to decline to charge a request which assumed the boy in question to be 14 years old, when the evidence shows conclusively he was under that age.

3. While it is generally true that a locomotive engineer may assume that a person on a railroad track in front of an approaching engine will get off in time to save himself, he is not entitled to act upon this assumption at all times and under all circumstances. The public have a right to go upon the track of a railroad at public crossings, and our statute requires railroad engineers to have their engines under such control that they can be stopped at such crossings, whenever necessary, to prevent injury. It is especially incumbent upon engineers to observe this requirement of the law in approaching public crossings in cities and towns, where it is so much more likely that people will be upon the crossings than in the country. In such places engineers should be extremely careful, as well before as after discovering persons upon the track; and railroad companies are responsible, not only for actual negligence, but also for negligent errors of judgment on the part of their engineers. Any other rule on this subject would expose the people of our crowded cities and towns to constant dangers and great injuries, for which they would have no adequate remedy. Of course, people who cross railroad tracks even at public crossings must observe the ordinary rules of prudence and common sense, and exercise due caution in protecting themselves. These duties between the public and the railroads are mutual, and should be carefully observed on both sides.

4. No comment is necessary upon the proposition stated in the fourth head-note.

5. It may have been pertinent in this case to show that the deceased was familiar with the locality and the movements

of trains at and near the place where he was killed. This could have been done by proving he was frequently there; but it was not competent, in establishing this relevant fact, to go further, and prove he was in the habit of jumping on and off the cars at this place. Evidence of this latter fact was, therefore, properly rejected by the court, his death not having been caused in consequence of such habit.

6. Complaint is made in the motion for a new trial that, after one of plaintiff's counsel had addressed the jury, and in the midst of the argument of counsel for defendant, one of plaintiff's counsel interrupted the speaker, and moved the court to allow him to introduce further testimony, stating the names of two witnesses, and very important facts which he could prove by them. This certainly was an impropriety. Under such circumstances, it would be a much better and fairer practice to request the court to cause the jury to retire, and not to state in their presence and hearing the facts sought to be proved, and the names of the witnesses by whom it was expected the same could be established. If it appeared that this conduct on the part of plaintiff's counsel was willful, and that it was deliberately intended to thus take an unfair advantage of the defendant before the jury, we would unhesitatingly order a new trial upon this ground alone. But it does not appear from the record that the counsel referred to acted in bad faith, or with any improper purpose to get facts before the jury by an artful practice. For aught that appears to us, it was simply an honest effort to get the court to allow him to place before the jury facts just discovered, which he considered of great importance to plaintiff's case. As above indicated, we do not think this effort was made in the proper manner; but, in our opinion, a new trial should not be granted solely on account of this impropriety.

7. The verdict being warranted by the evidence, and the trial judge being satisfied therewith, we will not disturb the finding of the jury. Judgment affirmed.

STAFFORD et al. v. THOMAS.

(Supreme Court of Georgia. July 18, 1891.)

MARRIAGE SETTLEMENTS—CONSTRUCTION.

The court construed the marriage settlement correctly.

(Syllabus by the Court.)

Error from superior court, Pike county; JAMES S. BOYNTON, Judge.

Petition by J. A. and J. W. Stafford, administrators, against James M. Thomas, administrator. Judgment for plaintiffs. Defendant brings error. Affirmed.

James S. Pope and Hall & Hammond, for plaintiff in error. I. B. Cabaniss, A. D. Hammond, and J. F. Redding, for defendants in error.

LUMPKIN, J. Alvis Stafford, in consideration of a marriage about to be solemnized between himself and Mrs. Lucy McKenzie, made a deed conveying to J. A. Stafford, as trustee, certain property, the terms of the conveyance being as follows:

"In trust for the use and benefit of her, the said Lucy McKenzie, for and during her natural life, and reserving to myself the use of the same during my natural life. And after my death the same to be held, used, and controlled for the benefit of the said Lucy during her natural life. And after the death of myself and the said Lucy, or the death of myself and the marriage again of the said Lucy, then the house and lot to be by the said J. A. Stafford divided between [two granddaughters, naming them,] to them one-half, and the other half to the said Lucy McKenzie, including the household and kitchen furniture." It was admitted that Mrs. Stafford never married after the death of Alvis Stafford, and that she died leaving no lineal heirs. The administrator of the deceased, Mrs. Stafford, filed a petition against the administrators of Alvis Stafford for a partition of the house and lot mentioned in the above deed. The defense was that the plaintiff could not recover, because his intestate took only a life-estate under the deed. The court held that Mrs. Stafford took a fee in an undivided half interest in the property, and this decision is the error complained of. In our opinion, the court correctly construed the marriage settlement. The deed, after reserving to Mr. Stafford the use of the property during his life, conveyed to Mrs. Stafford, after his death, the entire use of it while she lived. It seems the grantor expected that Mrs. Stafford would survive him, because he provided for her a trustee, who was to act as such after his death. In the next place, the deed provided that after the death of the grantor and Mrs. Stafford, or after his death and her marriage, upon the happening of either of these events, the property was to be divided, one-half going to grantor's granddaughters, and the other half to Mrs. Stafford. To adopt the plain and grammatical construction of this clause of the deed, when the grantor and Mrs. Stafford were both dead the absolute title to one-half of the property was to go to Mrs. Stafford; and, as she would then be dead, that half would necessarily go to her heirs. If, however, she again married after the death of the grantor, the title to one-half would vest immediately in her. Counsel for plaintiff in error contended that the proper construction of this deed would give to the wife a life-estate after grantor's death, with remainder to the granddaughters named, provided she died without marrying again; but, in the event of her so doing, the property would be equally divided, one-half to her and one-half to the granddaughters. To adopt this construction would lead to the strained and unnatural conclusion that the grantor meant to offer a premium to his wife to marry again after his death, which, in our opinion, certainly never was his intention. If so, it is the first instance of the kind of which we have any knowledge. The difficulty suggested by counsel for plaintiff in error as to the disposition of the property in case of the death of both Mr. and Mrs. Stafford, to-wit, that Mrs. Stafford, being dead, could not take, can be obviated by adopting the construction that the grantor intended that after his death, and during Mrs. Stafford's life, the property was to be managed for her by the trustee, and upon her death her half was to go as she might direct by will, or to her heirs. Again, the deed nowhere gives to the granddaughters any more than one-half of the property, and we are at a loss to perceive how, under it, they could in any event take more than one-half. It cannot be doubted that the instrument intended to make a disposition of all the property; and, as no distinction whatever is made by the grantor as to the division to be made upon the death of himself and his wife, or the death of himself and the marriage again of his wife, we are strengthened in our conclusion that he intended in either of these events that the granddaughters should have one-half, and the wife, or her estate, the other. It should also be borne in mind that, the consideration of this deed being marriage, it is more than likely the lady stipulated that she was in any event to have an absolute half interest in this property, and that this was understood by the contracting parties. Judgment affirmed.

AYCOCK et al. v. AUSTIN, Sheriff.

(Supreme Court of Georgia. July 13, 1891.)

FORTHCOMING BONDS—ACTIONS ON.

1. Two bonds for the forthcoming of personal property levied upon by the sheriff by virtue of two executions in favor of the same plaintiff against the same defendant (one of them being also against another defendant) may, after breach thereof, be sued upon in one action, the makers of both bonds being the same persons, and the sheriff being the obligee in both. All causes of action of like kind between the same parties may be joined. Code, § 3261.

2. Where the defendant in fi. fa. gives to the sheriff a forthcoming bond for the production of the property at the time and place of sale, and afterwards the levy is duly advertised and the property not produced, the bond is broken, notwithstanding a third person may, on the day of sale, interpose a claim thereto, and the sheriff accepts a claim affidavit and bond. A recovery may be had on the forthcoming bond pending such claim, and the sheriff will hold the money collected in the suit upon the forthcoming bond for whom it may concern. That the suit is brought for the use of the plaintiff in execution will not hinder a recovery, such recovery being allowable only for the purpose of indemnifying the sheriff.

3. Whether interest is recoverable or not on the forthcoming bond is not a question for adjudication by the supreme court, when it does not appear that the attention of the trial court was ever called to the same.

(Syllabus by the Court.)

Error from superior court, Rockdale county; JAMES S. BOYNTON, Judge.

Action by W. H. Austin, sheriff, to use, etc., against W. T. Aycock and another. Judgment for plaintiff. Defendants bring error. Affirmed.

A. C. McCalla and A. C. Perry, for plaintiffs in error. J. N. Glenn, for defendant in error.

SIMMONS, J. It appears from the record that Reynolds obtained a judgment against W. T. Aycock, and also a judgment against W. T. Aycock and his wife, L. F. Aycock. Upon these judgments executions were issued and levied upon 3,000 pounds of seed cotton in the field. Aycock, desiring to keep possession of the cotton, gave the sheriff two bonds, with Almand as security, for the forthcoming of the property on the day of sale. The sheriff advertised the cotton for sale, and on the day of sale Aycock failed to produce the cotton. On the same day two claim affidavits were filed by Almand and George, in which they alleged that the cotton was not the property of Aycock, but their property. These claims the sheriff accepted, and returned to the proper court. The cotton not having been produced by Aycock as agreed in his bonds, the sheriff brought suit on the bonds for the use of Reynolds, the plaintiff in execution. On the trial of the case the jury returned a verdict for the plaintiff, and the defendant made a motion for a new trial, which was overruled, and he excepted. There are several grounds in the motion complaining that the court admitted evidence over the objection of the defendants, but the grounds of objection are not stated in any of them, and we therefore decline to notice them.

1. One of the grounds relied upon by the plaintiffs in error for a reversal of the judgment of the court below was that the court erred in admitting the two fi. fas. in evidence, because there was a misjoinder of causes of action. There was no error in overruling the motion for a new trial upon this ground. Aycock and Almand signed both bonds, and both were made payable to Austin. They were therefore two contracts between the same parties. The Code, § 3261, allows all causes of action of a like kind between the same parties to be joined in one action.

2. The defendant requested the court to charge that, "if the jury believes from the evidence that the sheriff, Austin, received claims filed to the levies made by him to the property described in the levies, as shown by the entries on the fi. fas., and returned the same to the court for trial of the rights of property, then plaintiff cannot recover in this action, and it will be your duty to find for the defendants." The refusal of the court to give this in charge is one of the grounds of the motion for a new trial. The court did right in refusing to instruct the jury as requested. The defendants obligated themselves to deliver the cotton to the sheriff on the day of sale. When that day arrived, and they failed or refused to deliver the cotton, there was a breach of the bonds. The fact that a third party on the same day filed a claim to the cotton did not release Aycock and Almand from their obligation to deliver the cotton to the sheriff on that day, nor did the fact that the sheriff accepted the claims, and returned them to court, release them. When the condition of the bonds was broken, the sheriff had the right to commence his action thereon, and to recover the value of the cotton for the use of the plaintiff in fi. fa. When he recovers the money, it will be his duty to hold the same until the claim cases are disposed of.

3. It was argued before us that the plaintiff could not recover interest on the forth-

coming bond. Whether that is so or not we will not decide, because it does not appear that the attention of the trial judge was called to this question. Judgment affirmed.

HUDSON v. HUDSON.

(Supreme Court of Georgia.   July 20, 1891.)

CONTRACTS—CARE OF FATHER BY SON—EVIDENCE.

1. A son, breaking up at home, and removing himself and family to the residence of his infirm father, upon an express promise by the latter to will him his home place if he would attend to and take care of him for life, and performance by the son but failure to perform by the father, who became and died insane, would entitle the son to recover of the father's administrator upon a *quantum meruit.*

2. No change in the original contract would result from an agreement made by the children after the father became insane.

3. The son is a competent witness in his own favor to answer the testimony of the administrator (his brother) as to what occurred between them before the death of their father.

4. The evidence not being full and specific as to rents, etc., for which the plaintiff ought to account, there was no error in granting a new trial.

(Syllabus by the Court.)

Error from superior court, Rockdale county; JAMES S. BOYNTON, Judge.

Action by D. J. Hudson against D. N. Hudson, administrator. Judgment for plaintiff. Defendant's motion for new trial granted. Plaintiff brings error. Affirmed.

Geo. W. Gleaton, for plaintiff in error. *A. C. McCalla* and *J. N. Glenn,* for defendant in error.

LUMPKIN, J. 1. An old and infirm father proposed to one of his sons that if the latter would remove from his own home to that of the former, and attend to and take care of him during his life-time, he would will to the son his home place. The son accepted this offer, and, according to the evidence, complied faithfully with his part of the contract. Some time after his removal to his father's place, the old man became insane, and remained in that condition until his death, so that it was impossible for him to make the promised will. Nevertheless the son continued his ministrations until the father's death. The old man required constant nursing and attention. Most of the time he was altogether as helpless as an infant, and the care of him involved considerable time, watchfulness, and labor, and the performance of services menial and disagreeable in the highest degree. From all the circumstances shown by the proof it is perfectly manifest that when the arrangement between the father and son was originally entered into both parties contemplated that the son would be entitled to and should receive compensation for his services, and it was not a case in which it was expected that the services would be performed on account of mere filial duty and affection. It also appears that the son received $96 per year, which came to the father as a pension from the government, and that he received and used the rents, issues, and profits of the father's land and stock thereon, in excess of what was required for the father's support. It was certainly not incumbent on the son, after the father became insane, and consequently incapable of making the promised will, to abandon his part of the contract; but he had the right, and it was his duty, to continue taking care of his father as he had agreed to do. The latter having become unable to comply with his part of the contract, the son had a right to regard it as one that never could be literally performed; and the existing circumstances were such as to justify him in continuing to render the necessary services to his father, with the right to be paid for the same. Indeed, it was held in Link v. Sherman, 25 Barb. 433, a case very similar to this, that the plaintiff was entitled to recover only the actual intrinsic value of the services rendered for the time they were rendered, and according to their kind and character, without reference to the contract or the value of the property which deceased had agreed to leave him as compensation for such services. Again, in Graham v. Graham's Ex'rs, 34 Pa. St. 475, it was held that a parol contract of a decedent to give to the plaintiff a certain portion of his estate in consideration of services rendered could only be enforced when clearly proved, and when its terms were distinct and certain; and also, that the measure of damages for the breach of such a promise was the value of the services rendered, and not the proportion of decedent's estate promised to be given. See, also, Thompson v. Stevens, 71 Pa. St. 161. If, by a proceeding in the nature of a bill to compel a specific performance of the father's contract the plaintiff would be entitled to recover the home place from the administrator of his father, he would, of course, be obliged to account for what he had already received in money, rents, etc., during the life-time of the deceased. This being true, and it being manifest from the evidence that the son is undoubtedly entitled to compensation in some way for his services, it seems the fairest and best way of adjusting these matters is to allow the son to recover of the administrator, upon a *quantum meruit,* the actual value of his services; but the amount must in no event exceed the value of the home place, and he must account for and have deducted from the full amount he is entitled to all he has received from the property of the father over and above what was necessary for the support and maintenance of the latter during his life-time. The above authorities sustain the propriety of giving this direction to the case. By his declaration, as amended, the plaintiff simply seeks to recover what his services were worth, and after much consideration we regard this as the proper and legal way to solve the problem, and accordingly so direct.

2. It is manifest, without discussion, that whatever may have been the original contract between the father and son, it could not be changed by any agreement or understanding, if there were such, made by the children after the father became insane.

3. The plaintiff was a competent witness in his own favor to answer the testimony

of the administrator concerning matters which occurred between them before the death of the father, not in the presence of the latter, and in which he did not in any way participate.

4. On the trial the jury returned the following verdict: "We, the jury, find for the plaintiff, above what he has already received from all sources, the sum of $600 principal, and interest, $119." The court set this verdict aside and granted a new trial. The evidence does not accurately disclose what the rents, etc., which the plaintiff had received amounted to, and it is therefore impossible to determine from the record upon what basis of calculation the jury arrived at the amount they found in favor of the plaintiff. For this reason we will not interfere with the discretion of the trial judge in granting a new trial, but will allow the judgment of the court below to stand, and the case to be again tried, with such light thrown upon the law of it as may be gathered from the head-notes and this opinion. Judgment affirmed.

CENTRAL RAILROAD & BANKING CO. v. RYLES.

(Supreme Court of Georgia. July 13, 1891.)

RAILROAD COMPANIES—NEGLIGENCE—INJURIES TO PERSONS ON TRACK—INSTRUCTIONS.

1. A deed made in 1869 to the defendant company, or its predecessor, conveying the land on which the yard of the company is located, was irrelevant. An exception in the warranty of title which that deed contained would be no evidence that the public or any individual had a right of way or used the premises as a pass-way at the time the accident occurred, the exception merely excluding from the warranty rights, if any, that may have grown up previous to the execution of the deed. Other evidence tending to show how the premises were used before they became the railroad yard of the company was irrelevant, and therefore inadmissible.

2. Though the analogies of criminal law touching presumptions as to the age of discretion are properly regarded by a court in ruling upon a demurrer where contributory negligence by an infant is involved, (as was decided by this court in Rhodes v. Railroad, etc., Co., 84 Ga. 890, 10 S. E. Rep. 922,) it is doubtful whether these analogies have any relevancy on the trial of the case before the jury. It would seem the better rule would be for the jury to deal with each case on its own facts, unhampered by presumptions of law either for or against the competency of the child. In the present case, however, the charge of the court on this subject, if erroneous, was harmless.

3. Only express consent would serve to license a thoroughfare under stationary cars. Mere knowledge by a railroad company or its servants that numerous persons, including children, without any public or private right of way, passed daily and hourly through its yard, situate in or near a populous part of the city, and crawled under stationary cars occupying its tracks, will not render it liable for an injury accruing to a child by a sudden and involuntary movement of a long line of such cars, resulting from the negligence of the company's servants in handling other cars several hundred yards distant from the scene of the accident, such other cars rolling against the standing cars and setting them in motion while the child was passing under one of them.

4. The other grounds of the motion are not cause for a new trial.

(Syllabus by the Court.)

Error from city court of Atlanta; HOWARD VAN EPPS, Judge.

Action by Maud Ryles, by next friend, against the Central Railroad & Banking Company of Georgia, for personal injuries. Judgment for plaintiff. Defendant appeals. Reversed.

Calhoun, King & Spalding and *J. T. Pendleton,* for plaintiff in error. *Hoke & Burton Smith,* for defendant in error.

SIMMONS, J. Maud Ryles, by her next friend, brought her action against the defendant for damages. So far as specifically enumerated, the facts in the declaration (excluding certain mere conclusions therein stated, and which, in connection with the specific facts alleged, made the declaration good against a demurrer) were substantially proved, and were as follows: The defendant company had a yard in which it left stationary cars. Two streets ended at this yard, but there was a pass-way from one of these streets to the shops of another railroad company; and this pass-way was used by men, women, and children at all hours of the day, and was so used with the knowledge of the defendant. The places at which the people were accustomed to pass were, at the time of the injury, occupied by stationary cars, and "the line of cars stretched as far as the eye could see." The plaintiff was under nine years of age, and was going to the shops of another railroad, to carry a meal to one of the employes. When she reached the place where people usually crossed, she found it occupied by these stationary cars. There was no way for her to cross except by passing under the cars. Children in the neighborhood were in the habit of passing beneath the cars while stationary at the place. In attempting to pass under one of the stationary cars she was injured. The injury was occasioned by the employes of the defendant "kicking" other cars from a quarter of a mile above where the child was, and out of sight, and these cars ran down and "kicked" the stationary cars, so as to cause them to move, and the one under which the child was ran over her leg. The plaintiff further proved that people were in the habit of crossing at this place before the railroad company established its yard. The plaintiff also introduced the deed by which the defendant company obtained title to this property, dated in 1869, in which it was recited that the company then claimed and had possession of the premises therein described, which were also claimed by the vendors, who had brought ejectment against the company, which, to settle the action, and to obtain an undisputed warranty title to the premises in fee-simple, had, by way of compromise, and without surrendering its former claim or conceding the invalidity thereof, agreed to pay the vendors $2,000, for which consideration the vendors warranted the title to the premises against the claims of all persons whatsoever; but this warranty was not to extend to any right the Western & Atlantic Railroad and certain other named persons might have to remove the buildings, tracks, or other structures erected by them on the premises, "nor to any right of way the public may have acquired in streets, ways, or roads over, across, or upon said premises." The defendant objected to the admission of this deed in evidence, "because it showed no use by the public of a pass-way across its tracks, and because, if it did, it showed a right to use by the public, whereas this suit is to recover on the ground of permissive use by the defendant." The objection was overruled, and the defendant excepted. A witness for the plaintiff testified that he had lived on Mechanic street since 1863; that it was a common wagon way until about 1870. From 1855 to 1860 there was no obstruction across the old Monroe track. "We passed on just as though it continued a street. We walked on it, and drove on it, and rode on it." The defendant moved to rule this out, because it did not show a permissive use by the defendant to pass over its tracks, but referred to a use at a time prior to the occupancy of the place by tracks, and before its ownership by the defendant. This objection was overruled, and the defendant assigns error thereon.

1. Counsel for the plaintiff in error insisted that the deed was admissible because the exception in the warranty showed that at the time the railroad company bought the land people were using the place as a pass-way, and thus brought home knowledge to the company of this fact. The deed was clearly inadmissible and irrelevant. While the warranty in the deed was a limited one, it was not the purpose of the grantors in making the limitation to assert or to give notice to the grantee that the public had acquired the right to pass over the land. The grantors only intended to limit their liability in case it should subsequently appear that the public asserted a right to use the land as a pass-way. The limitation in the warranty does not give notice, nor was it intended to give notice, to the grantee that the public had acquired or were exercising the right of passage over the land. The other evidence tending to show how the premises were used before they became the railroad yard of the company was also irrelevant and inadmissible. The company could not be bound by the use made of the premises by the permission or acquiescence of its former owner. The company purchased it for the purpose of laying tracks and running cars thereon, and for the purpose of keeping other cars standing on it when not in use,—a purpose totally inconsistent with the former use by the public. The purpose for which the company purchased the land, to-wit, to lay tracks, and keep standing cars thereon, destroyed the former use by the public. It was, in effect, a notice to the public that the land could not be used longer as a pass-way. It seems, therefore, it would be absurd to hold that the company was bound to recognize the former use made of this land by the public.

2. The judge charged the jury that "the law declares that an infant under the age of 10 years *prima facie* does not have sufficient capacity and discretion and knowledge of right and wrong to make her responsible for her conduct and acts,

unless it is clearly shown that she had such capacity and discretion. The presumption is that she did not have sufficient capacity to be sensible of danger, and to have the power to avoid it, and this presumption continues until overcome by proof showing the contrary." This charge was excepted to by the defendant, and assigned as error in its motion for a new trial. Where a child under 14 years of age is injured, and brings his action for the injury, and there is a demurrer to the declaration on the ground that the allegations therein show that the child did not observe due care, or could have avoided the injury by the observance of such care, the court may overrule the demurrer, on the ground that *prima facie* the child did not have sufficient knowledge or capacity to know what was due care, or sufficient capacity to have avoided the injury by its observance, and may invoke the analogy of the criminal law, and hold that the presumption is that the child did not know or did not have sufficient capacity, as was held in the case of Rhodes v. Railroad, etc., Co., 84 Ga. 390, 10 S. E. Rep. 922. But where there is no demurrer, and the case is submitted to the jury, there is no presumption one way or the other, and the jury must find from the evidence whether the child had sufficient capacity at the time of the accident to know the danger, and to observe due care for its own protection. If it has such capacity, and voluntarily goes into danger or to a dangerous place, it cannot recover; otherwise it can. Railroad Co. v. Young, 81 Ga. 397, 7 S. E. Rep. 912, 83 Ga. 512, 10 S. E. Rep. 197. It depends altogether upon the capacity of the child at the time of the injury. The better rule would be for the jury to deal with each case upon its own facts, unhampered by presumptions of law either for or against the competency of the child. In the present case, however, the charge of the court on this subject, if erroneous, was harmless.

3. It was argued by counsel for the defendant in error that the fact that the people were allowed to use this place as a pass-way to go under these cars when they were stationed upon the track was a license by the company for them to do so, and the company was therefore bound, before it moved the stationary cars, to give the public notice; and, not having done so in this instance, it was guilty of such negligence as would authorize the plaintiff to recover. It is such gross negligence and want of care and so reckless an act for persons to attempt to pass under cars which are left standing upon the track and are liable to be moved at any moment, that we do not think a license can be implied from the fact that the company had knowledge that people were in the habit of passing under the cars there. Where, under such circumstances, a person attempts to pass under the cars and is injured, before he can recover upon the theory that he had a license to pass under the cars, he must prove to the satisfaction of the jury an express license from the company. It would be unreasonable to hold the company bound by an implied license or permission when the act is of such a

negligent character. It would be unreasonable to hold the company bound by an implied license when it is occupying the track with its own cars. It would be unreasonable to hold that it had agreed that others might have a joint occupancy of the tracks at the time the company was using them for its own purposes. The joint use by the company and by the public of the tracks at the same time would be so inconsistent and so dangerous that the law will not imply a license from the company to the public for such joint use. The placing of stationary cars in its yard on the tracks where people are accustomed to pass is notice to the public not to attempt to pass while the cars remain, and if a person undertakes to pass under the cars he does so at his peril. It is different where the public pass over a track which is occupied by a railroad company with its cars only a few times a day, and then when the track is not being used by the company. In a case of that kind, where the railroad company permits people to pass over its track when not in use by the company, the permission may amount to an implied license; but where the company is in continuous occupation of its tracks, either in runing its cars or in keeping stationary cars thereon, a license will not be implied. The facts of this case show that the cars constantly occupied these tracks; that this stationary train was more than a quarter of a mile long; and that at the upper end of the train the servants of the company, negligently perhaps, kicked another train of cars against the stationary train and set it in motion, and thus injured the plaintiff. We do not think the mere knowledge by the company or its servants that numerous persons passed daily and hourly through its yard, situated in a populous part of the city, and that they crawled under these stationary cars, will render the company liable for an injury occurring to this child, under the facts above stated.

4. The other grounds of the motion are not cause for a new trial. Judgment reversed.

FIRST NAT. BANK OF CHATTANOOGA v. HARTMAN STEEL CO., Limited, et al.

(Supreme Court of Georgia. July 8, 1891.)

ASSIGNMENT OF ACCOUNT—EVIDENCE.

Under the special facts of this case, the account in controversy was assigned to the bank, and the assignee is entitled to the fund over the garnishing creditor.

(Syllabus by the Court.)

Error from superior court, Muscogee county; JAMES M. SMITH, Judge.

Action by the Hartman Steel Company, Limited, against the First National Bank of Chattanooga and the Columbus Water-Works Company. Verdict for plaintiff. The bank brings error. Reversed.

Francis D. Peabody, for plaintiff in error. Winbish & Gilbert and Peabody, Brannon & Hatcher, for defendants in error.

SIMMONS, J. The Union Iron-Works Company of Chattanooga was under contract with the Columbus Water-Works company to build a stand-pipe for $8,783,

$6,000 of which had been paid, and the balance was to be paid when the whole work was completed and accepted by the water-works company or its representative. On November 12, 1888, the iron-works company made a draft on the water-works company for $2,783, payable 15 days after date, "as advised," and indorsed it to the First National Bank of Chattanooga, which, on November 13, 1888, the day it received the draft, credited the iron-works company with the same; and on the same day the iron-works company checked out of the bank $3,308, which sum included the proceeds of the draft. On that day the iron-works company sent a letter to the water-works company, from which the following are extracts: "We have to-day made draft on you at 15 days, for balance of contract on stand-pipe at Columbus, $2,783.00. This draft, of course, we would like for you to accept, but it is not absolutely necessary if, for any reason, you prefer not doing so. We make the draft, however, inasmuch as we have gotten some money from the First National Bank here on this work, and simply want to transfer this balance to them. In other words, we wish the draft paid whenever the amount is due, either by taking up the draft or remitting to the First National Bank here, as you see fit. * * * It would be quite an accommodation to us if you would transfer this amount in the manner indicated." The remaining parts of the letter relate to certain details about completing the stand-pipe, which are immaterial. The words "as advised" in the draft were intended to refer to this letter. The letter was received by the water-works company, and the next day thereafter the draft was presented for acceptance, which was refused, the water-works company informing the iron-works company by telegraph that it could not accept the draft till the work was satisfactory to Mr. Hill, who was the representative of the water-works company. At the time the draft was received by the bank it was agreed between it and the treasurer of the iron-works company that the latter would notify the water-works company of the transfer to the bank of the balance due on the contract. The president of the bank knew that the letter above mentioned had been written, and relied upon it as effecting such transfer, believing that the water-works company would respect the request of the iron-works company, and would recognize the transfer thus made and pay the draft for $2,783. After delivery of the draft to the bank and the forwarding of the letter of advice, neither the bank nor the iron-works company regarded the latter as having or retaining any further interest in the debt due by the water-works company. It also appears that the treasurer of the iron-works company not only notified the bank of having written the letter of advice, but delivered to its president the contract he had made with the water-works company, informed him the amount due thereon was then $2,783, and assured him that, even if the draft was not accepted when presented, the amount would nevertheless be remitted to the bank. It was the intention of this treasurer, by the transactions abovestated, to sell and convey to the bank the indebtedness due by the water-works company to the iron-works company, and the bank so understood the matter, and parted with its money on the faith of this understanding. On December 12, 1888, the Hartman Steel Company, a creditor of the iron-works company, sued out an attachment, and caused a garnishment to be served on the water-works company, which answered, setting forth the above-stated facts, and admitting an indebtedness of $2,672.68, which amount it offered to pay into court. The bank was made a party to this proceeding, and the contest in the court below was between the bank and the steel company as to which was entitled to this fund. The plaintiff in attachment contended that the draft did not operate, nor was it intended, as an assignment to the bank of the fund in controversy; that it was merely placed with the bank for collection for the account of the drawer, and was designed merely as collateral security for a pre-existing indebtedness of the drawer to the bank. On the other hand, the bank contended that the draft was drawn, and the letter of advice written, in pursuance of a *bona fide* transaction for value, and that the two instruments, construed together or separately, constituted a good and valid assignment to the bank of the balance in the hands of the water-works company, due or to become due to the iron-works company on the contract; and that it was immaterial whether the draft was accepted or not, the latter expressly dispensing with the necessity of a formal acceptance by the water-works company. All matters and questions both of law and of fact were, by consent of the parties, submitted to the determination of the presiding judge, without the intervention of a jury. The judge rendered a decision in favor of the steel company, and a judgment was entered accordingly. Upon a motion for a new trial this judgment was adhered to, and the refusal of a new trial is the main error assigned in the bill of exceptions. The contract between the iron-works company and the bank was made in the state of Tennessee. Under the statutes and decisions of that state, so far as we have been able to acquaint ourselves with the same, it is not necessary to the validity of an assignment of a chose in action that the same should be in writing, but, as far as we are informed, the common-law rule on this subject prevails in Tennessee. Under the law of Georgia, in order to vest the legal title to a chose in action in the assignee, the contract must be in writing. Code, § 2244; Turk v. Cook. 63 Ga. 681, Bank v. Prater, 64 Ga. 613. In the view we take of this case, however, it is immaterial to determine whether the law of Tennessee or of this state should control, because, in our opinion, under the facts proved, the account was assigned to the bank in writing; and whether this assignment vested in the bank the legal or only an equitable title to the account, the result, we think, should be the same. The following au-

thorities sustain our conclusion that the draft and the letter, when considered in connection with the other facts set forth in the foregoing statement, amounted to a transfer of the account to the bank: Ex parte Imbert, 1 De Gex & J. 152; Frith v. Forbes, 4 De Gex F. & J. 409; Ranken v. Alfaro, 5 Ch. Div. 786; McWilliams v. Webb, 32 Iowa, 577; Bank v. Bogy, 44 Mo. 13; Risley v. Bank, 83 N. Y. 318; Schmittler v. Simon, (N. Y.) 21 N. E Rep. 162; Moore v. Davis, 57 Mich. 251, 23 N. W. Rep 800; Gardner v. Bank, 39 Ohio St. 600; Burn v. Carvalho, 4 Mylne & C. 690. Of course we do not mean to assert that all the cases above cited cover precisely the question now under consideration, but a careful examination of them establishes, we think, the correctness of our ruling in this case, that the account was assigned to the bank. It will be observed that in many of these authorities great stress is laid upon the question whether or not, by the several transactions therein stated, the parties actually intended a transfer or assignment of the claims or funds to which these transactions related; and the courts have held with great uniformity that, where such intention appears, effect should be given to it. Indeed, this idea is given a controlling prominence and influence in most of the adjudications made on this subject. In Stanford v. Connery, 84 Ga. 731, 11 S. E. Rep. 507, it was held that a letter from one May, the plaintiff in *fi: fa.*, as usee, to his attorney, Guerard, stating that the execution was the property of Dillon, "and is subject to his control and direction, and you are hereby authorized to pay the amount over to him when collected, or assign him the execution if he requires it," was an assignment thereof to Dillon, and that said usee could not afterwards transfer the execution to another. A similar ruling was made in Dugas v. Mathews, 9 Ga. 510. If the legal title to the account was passed to the bank by the draft and letter, it would follow beyond question that the latter would be entitled to the fund in court in preference to the steel company. But suppose only the equitable title to this account passed to the bank, then, under the following authorities, it will also appear that the bank would still be entitled to the money. 2 Wade, Attachm. §§ 437, 438; Drake, Attachm. § 604. "A valid assignment by the defendant, which transfers either the legal or equitable title to the assignee, of property in the hands of a garnishee, or debts owing by him to such defendant, is sufficient to discharge the garnishee from liability for such property or upon such obligation." 8 Amer. & Eng Enc. Law, tit "Garnishment," p. 1179, and cases cited. We are the better satisfied with the conclusion we have reached in this case because, in our opinion, it is in perfect harmony with what we regard as exact justice between these contesting parties.

One special assignment in the bill of exceptions alleges that the court erred in adjudging that the bank should pay interest on the fund in dispute from May 13, 1889, the day the answer of the garnishee was filed, instead of from the 5th day of July, 1890, when the garnishment was dissolved by the bank, and the money paid over to it. It is unnecessary to decide this question, however, because, under the judgment we now render, the bank is entitled to the entire fund in controversy, and the question made concerning interest is, therefore, out of the case. Judgment reversed.

Lumpkin, J., not presiding.

Lewis et al. v. Hill.

(Supreme Court of Georgia. July 8, 1891.)

Judgment—Res Judicata—Marshaling Assets.

1. This case is *res judicata* by the decision in 80 Ga. 402, 7 S. E. Rep. 114, except as to the amount of Ray's property that was subject to be applied to the judgment and execution in favor of Armstrong, the direction given being to determine how much thereof was released by the plaintiff, and to credit the defendants (the heirs of Lewis) with whatever amount was released.

2. Under the evidence adduced at the last trial it is manifest that the heirs of Ray, by some arrangement among themselves, received all the property, real and personal, of Ray, the intestate. They were liable to Armstrong for the same at its real value, less the debts of higher dignity, and less also the *pro rata* of other debts of Ray's estate of equal dignity with the bond from Ray to Armstrong, its dignity being that of promissory notes and debts ranked by the Code with promissory notes. The $1,000 paid on compromise is to be counted as if paid out of Ray's estate.

(Syllabus by the Court.)

Error from superior court, Dougherty county; B. B. Bower, Judge.

D. H. Pope, for plaintiffs in error. W. D. Hill and R. Hobbs, for defendant in error.

Simmons, J. The facts of this case will be found reported in the case of Lewis v. Armstrong, 80 Ga. 402, 7 S. E. Rep. 114. The decision, as announced in that case, covers all the points of law made in the present bill of exception, and they are *res adjudicata,* so far as the present case is concerned. At the conclusion of the opinion the following direction was given: "The court should ascertain upon the next trial the amount of Ray's property that was subject to this judgment and execution, and determine how much thereof was released by the plaintiff, and credit whatever amount was released to the heirs of Lewis." The court, on the last trial, undertook to carry out this direction, but erred in crediting to the Lewises the amount only which Ray's property brought at the administrator's sale. Under the evidence adduced at the last trial it is manifest that the heirs of Ray, by some arrangement among themselves, received all the property, real and personal, of their intestate. The evidence shows that the widow of Ray purchased all the real estate at the sale. She had no separate estate, and there was no bid other than hers at the sale. Her two sons, the administrators, testified upon this trial, by interrogatories, that the real estate bought by their mother was worth $2,500 more than she gave for it at the sale; and that they would not have allowed it to be sold to an outside party for the same

amount. Coney, another witness, testifies that the real estate was worth about $2,500 more than it sold for at the sale; that he was one of the appraisers of the intestate's estate, and that the inventory and appraisement were correct, and that the estate was worth the amount it was appraised at, to-wit, $11,703. The value of the estate, as returned by the administrators after the sale, was less than $5,000. Another witness testified that he was intimate with the Ray boys, the administrators, and that they knew their father had signed the injunction bond, and were uneasy about it, and they said they were anxious to wind up their father's estate as soon as possible, to avoid the bond if they could; that he knew the value of Ray's estate when Ray died, and there was no change in values until after it was wound up, and the railroad came through the county; that T. J. Ray, one of the administrators, told him he sold the property for less than it was worth, to make the estate as small as possible, to avoid the bond; and he further testified that Mrs. Ray had no separate estate; that she continued to live on the estate, and was supported from the place by her sons. They all lived on the place. This evidence shows that the real value of the real estate was much more than the widow gave for it at the administrator's sale; and the court should have found the true market value of Ray's estate, instead of being governed by the amount which the widow bid at the sale, and should have given the Lewises credit for the true value. The Rays were liable to Armstrong for the real value of the estate, less the debts of higher dignity, and less also the *pro rata* of other debts of Ray's estate of equal dignity with the bond from Ray to Armstrong, the dignity of the bond from Ray to Armstrong being that of promissory notes and debts ranked by the Code with promissory notes. Section 2533, par. 7. Of course the $1,000 paid by T. J. Ray to Armstrong as a compromise and settlement of his father's liability on the bond will be counted as if paid out of Ray's estate. Judgment reversed on the main bill of exceptions, and affirmed as to the cross-bill.

Lumpkin, J., not presiding.

Central Railroad & Banking Co. v. Summerford.

(Supreme Court of Georgia. July 18, 1891.)

Railroad Companies—Stock-Killing Cases—Instructions.

1. Though the existence of the stock law is pertinent, and may be material on the question of ordinary and reasonable care and diligence in guarding against killing stock by the running of trains, yet a request to charge in general terms that a less degree of diligence is required in a county where that law prevails than in a county where it does not may be declined. The court may also decline a request to charge that a less degree of diligence in looking out for stock is required while running through a field than while running through lands uninclosed.

2. The evidence warranted the verdict.

(Syllabus by the Court.)

Error from superior court, Lee county; ALLEN FORT, Judge.

Action by J. D. Summerford against the Central Railroad & Banking Company for killing stock. Judgment for plaintiff. Defendant brings error. Affirmed.

G. W. Warwick and *R. F. Lyon*, for plaintiff in error. *C. B. Wooten* and *H. L. Long*, for defendant in error.

BLECKLEY, C. J. 1. The Code, in section 3033, declares that a railroad company shall be liable for any damage done to stock or other property by the running of the locomotives or cars, unless the company shall make it appear that their agents have exercised all ordinary and reasonable care and diligence, the presumption in all cases being against the company. This rule of diligence was not modified or altered by subsequent legislation known as the "stock law." Railroad v. Hamilton, 71 Ga. 461. With or without the stock law, the degree of diligence required of railroad companies is one and the same; it is "ordinary and reasonable." What would amount to that degree of diligence in each particular case under all the circumstances, including the application or non-application of the stock law at the particular locality, and including also the scene of the occurrence, whether in an inclosed field or upon uninclosed lands outside, is a question for the jury. The jury can and should take into consideration all the pertinent and material facts, and in the light of the whole determine whether the care and diligence observed in the particular instance came up to the degree of ordinary and reasonable, or fell below it. The instructions requested and refused in this case sought to relieve the company, or to authorize the jury to relieve it, from as high a degree of care at the place of this occurrence as might be due from it at some other place. This is not allowable, for one and the same degree of care is due alike at all times and places; but what conduct will come up to that standard may not, and indeed would not, be alike at all places. To tell the jury that the degree of care and diligence might be varied is a very different thing from instructing them that, while ordinary and reasonable care and diligence would be always required, the requirement might be met. if in their opinion it could be done, under all the circumstances, by using less vigilance or watchfulness at one place than at another, always, however, keeping such lookout as would be reasonably necessary at the time and place in question to avoid coming in contact with animals that might happen to be at large and stray upon the track of the railway. Of course it would be reasonable for the lookout to be less strict according to the less probability of such accidents, and more strict where the probability was greater. While this, perhaps, may have been the distinction intended by counsel in submitting the request to charge, yet, as the language used was susceptible of another construction, the court was justified in declining the request, and committed no error in so doing. The principle of discrimination in adapting conduct to conditions, while adhering to

a single standard of diligence, was recognised in Railroad, etc., Co. v. Ryles, 84 Ga. 420, 11 S. E. Rep. 499.

2. It might have been more satisfactory to us if the verdict had been the other way; but the evidence warranted the finding, and, the presiding judge being satisfied, we have neither the right nor the will to interfere. Judgment affirmed.

LUMPKIN, J., not presiding.

SMALL v. WILLIAMS.

(Supreme Court of Georgia. July 20, 1891.)

MORTGAGES—PROCUREMENT BY FRAUD OR DURESS —AGENCY — EVIDENCE — INSTRUCTIONS — NEW TRIAL.

1. Pertinent declarations, made by a person while on his way to procure the execution of a mortgage to secure an antecedent debt or liability, the expedition having resulted in its procurement, are admissible in evidence against the mortgagee on the question whether the mortgage was procured by fraud or duress. They are a part of the *res gestæ* of the transaction, and consequently are admissible in evidence, irrespective of the relation of agency between the mortgagee and the person who procured for him the execution of the mortgage.

2. The sayings of an alleged agent *dum fervet opus*, while not evidence to prove his agency, may be looked to on the question whether he was acting as agent, there being other sufficient evidence to establish the agency.

3. If the matter of a lengthy extract from the charge of the court is sound in part, any unsound part should be specifically pointed out in the motion for a new trial.

4. If declarations which require some answer or contradiction are made in one's hearing, and he remains silent, his silence may be treated as signifying his assent to the truth or correctness of the statement.

5. A note and mortgage, given in whole or in part upon an agreement, express or implied, to settle or prevent a criminal prosecution are void, unless the case falls within some express statute authorizing settlement. The statement of a legal proposition favorable to one party, if fairly given in charge, need not be in immediate connection with the alternative in favor of the other party.

6. No request being made to charge as to the burden of proof or the preponderance of evidence, mere failure to charge on these topics will not require a new trial.

7. The evidence warranted the verdict.

(Syllabus by the Court.)

Error from superior court, Bibb county; A. L. MILLER, Judge.

Bill by J. W. Williams against A. B. Small to set aside a mortgage and note. Judgment for plaintiff. Defendant brings error. Affirmed.

R. W. Patterson and *R. Hodges*, for plaintiff in error. *Dessau & Bartlett*, for defendant in error.

SIMMONS, J. Williams filed his bill in equity to set aside and cancel a mortgage and note given by him to Small, on the ground that they had been procured from him by duress and fraud. It seems that Williams' son John, at the time of the transaction, was an agent or drummer for Small, and had lost some eight or nine hundred dollars of Small's money at Reynolds, Ga. He telegraphed his loss to Small, and Small employed Shackleford, a detective, to go to Reynolds, and find the money or the thief. Shackleford and young Williams returned to Macon in the afternoon of the same day, and young Williams said to Small that the money was lost through his negligence, and proposed to secure Small by giving him his note, with his father-in-law as surety. Failing to get his father-in-law to sign the note as surety, he and Shackleford went to J. W. Williams, his father, and procured him to sign the note. When it was delivered to Small he declined to accept it, on the ground that he had no knowledge of J. W. Williams' solvency. Young Williams then proposed to have his father secure the note by a mortgage on his farm, which Small said he would accept. The mortgage was prepared by Small's bookkeeper, in Small's presence, and handed to Shackleford, the detective, and he and John Williams, the son, and De Lane, one of Shackleford's assistants, procured a carriage, and started to the home of J. W. Williams, which was three miles in the country. On the way to the latter place Shackleford called at the house of Subers, a magistrate, and got him to accompany them for the purpose of officially attesting the mortgage. Subers entered the carriage with Shackleford and the others, and while going to the house of J. W. Williams, Shackleford, in explanation of his reason for requiring the presence of Subers, said to him that Small had had young Williams arrested for embezzlement; that he had done away with some of his money at Reynolds; that he had applied to his father-in-law to stand his bond, and that he declined to do it, etc.; saying this in an undertone, so that Williams could not hear it. After arriving at the house of the elder Williams, and after he had signed the mortgage, Shackleford made other declarations. Counsel for Small objected to proof of the conversation between Shackleford and Subers, and the other declarations made at the house, (1) because they were irrelevant, and (2) because the declarations of Shackleford were inadmissible for the purpose of proving his agency.

1, 2. Under the facts above recited we think the declarations of Shackleford were admissible for the purpose of illustrating the question of fraud or duress, which had been charged in the bill. Small would not take the note of the elder Williams without a mortgage. He had it written, and delivered it to Shackleford, the detective. It seems to have been a part of Shackleford's business to procure the signature of the elder Williams to the mortgage; and, whether he was the agent of Small or not for this purpose, whatever he said in carrying out his object in procuring the signature to the mortgage was admissible. If he had been a mere volunteer to procure Williams to sign the mortgage, and did procure him to sign it, his declarations would be admissible to illustrate the question whether he procured it by duress or fraud. It was a part of the *res gestæ* of the transaction. Taken in connection with the fact that young Williams told his father, in the presence of Shackleford, that if he did not sign the mortgage he would have to go to jail that

night, it tended to show that Shackleford wished to produce the impression on the young man and the father that the former was charged with embezzlement, and would be put in jail unless the mortgage were signed.

(a) What Shackleford said at the time the mortgage was being executed, or shortly thereafter, while not admissible to prove his agency, may be looked to on the question whether he was acting as agent, especially when there is other sufficient evidence to establish the agency.

3. The fourth and fifth grounds of the motion contain long extracts from the charge of the court, but no particular specifications of error are assigned thereon; there is simply a general assignment that the court erred in giving these charges. Where long extracts from the charge of the court are copied in the motion, and no particular part of the charge is specified as error, it is not our duty to hunt for errors in the charge. The rule is that these long extracts will not be considered unless the whole be erroneous. If the extract is sound in part, any unsound part should be specifically pointed out in the motion.

4. The attention of counsel for the plaintiff in error having been called to this rule by counsel for the defendant in error during the argument, he undertook to show that the latter part of the extract from the charge contained in the fifth ground was erroneous. That part of the charge, in substance, is that, if the jury believe that Shackleford was in the position of a detective, and representing Small, and that the young man, about the time the papers were signed, said to his father that if the latter did not sign the mortgage he (the son) would have to go to jail, and Shackleford was present and heard the words and made no reply, the old man had a right to believe from his silence that the son's statement was true. Instead of this being error, we think it sound law. If Shackleford was the agent of Small to procure this mortgage,—as the evidence indicates he was,—and this declaration was made by the young man in his presence, it required an answer or contradiction from him. The evidence shows that the old man was very much excited by the appeal of his son. He was trembling and shedding tears, and he testifies that he signed the mortgage to keep his son from going to jail. Shackleford saw his excitement, and must have known the object of the father in signing the mortgage, and if he did not have the young man under arrest it was his duty to so inform the father. He did not do this, but kept silent; and the court was right in instructing the jury that the father had the right to believe from his silence that the son's statement was true. Code, § 3790.

5. The court charged the jury in substance that, if the mortgage was given partly to settle the criminal prosecution, and also to pay Small for the alleged shortage in the son's account, it would still be void. There was no error in this charge. A note or mortgage, given in whole or in part upon an agreement, express or implied, to settle or prevent a

criminal prosecution, is void unless the case falls within some express statute authorizing settlement. If a part of the consideration of the contract is legal and the other part illegal, it renders the whole contract void. If, therefore, the mortgage was given partly upon an agreement to settle a criminal prosecution, whether that agreement was express or implied, and given partly to settle the debt of the son, it was illegal, and could not be enforced by the mortgagee against the father. Code, § 2745. The agreement to settle the criminal prosecution, the act charged being a felony, was illegal; and, if such settlement entered into the consideration of the contract, it rendered the whole contract void. It is complained also in this ground that the court failed to put the alternative proposition to the jury. While the charge, as sent up in the record, shows that the court did not put the alternative in immediate connection with this part of the charge, it is shown that the alternative was put subsequently. The alternative of a legal proposition favorable to one party, if fairly given in charge, need not be in immediate connection with the alternative in favor of the other party.

6. It is also complained that the court failed to charge as to the preponderance of testimony in civil cases, and to charge that the burden of proof was upon the plaintiff. No request having been made to charge as to the burden of proof or the preponderance of evidence, a mere failure to charge on these topics will not require a new trial.

The other grounds of the motion are the usual ones that the verdict is contrary to evidence, etc. We think the evidence warranted the verdict. Judgment affirmed.

LUMPKIN, J., not presiding.

JONES v. STATE.

(Supreme Court of Georgia. July 13, 1891.)

HOMICIDE—INSTRUCTIONS—EVIDENCE.

1. Under the evidence, it is not cause for granting a new trial that the court charged the jury on the law of voluntary manslaughter, and submitted that grade of homicide as a question before the jury for their finding.

2. Though there was much conflict in the evidence, the verdict is supported, and is not contrary to law.

3. The newly-discovered evidence is not such as to require a new trial.

(Syllabus by the Court.)

Error from superior court, Oconee county; N. L. HUTCHINS, Judge.

Indictment of Percy Jones for murder. Verdict of voluntary manslaughter. Defendant brings error. Affirmed.

The fatal trouble arose at a dance. The evidence for the state made a case of murder. The evidence for defendant tended to show that two men, while disputing about dancing, ran over defendant, who told them to watch out, or he would cripple somebody. One Sophie Carithers said, "You talk about killing my husband," (who, according to the evidence, was not one of the two above mentioned, and with whom defendant had had no difficulty,)

and struck defendant with a torch two or three times. Defendant made a motion as if to strike her, when Scott Long, the deceased, came up with a pistol, and said he would take her part. Defendant hit Long with a little stick he had in his hand, and ran off. Long snapped his pistol at him, and, after defendant got into the yard, shot twice at him. Defendant came back into the house, but Long advanced on him with pistol in hand, when defendant dropped on his knees, and said, "Lord have mercy!" and shot Long, killing him. There was evidence for the state that defendant shot twice at deceased, only one ball striking him; but the evidence for defendant tended to show that he fired only once. The newly-discovered evidence, on which a new trial was asked, consisted of the affidavits of three persons that they had thoroughly examined the house in which the killing was done, and found no hole nor impression of a pistol ball on the wall or roof, and that the house appeared to have undergone no change; also the affidavit of defendant that the facts stated in those affidavits were unknown to him at the time of the trial, and that he had used due diligence to discover evidence and prepare for the trial.

B. E. Thrasher, E. T. Brown, and J. H. Lumpkin, for plaintiff in error. R. B. Russell, Sol. Gen., for the State.

PER CURIAM. Judgment affirmed.

BEACH v. ATKINSON.

(Supreme Court of Georgia. May 27, 1891.)

COLLUSIVE JUDGMENTS—SUFFICIENCY OF EVIDENCE—JUSTICE'S JURISDICTION—NOTES PROVIDING FOR ATTORNEYS' FEES.

1. H. lived in Texas, and owed plaintiffs, who lived there, $1,470, and gave a bill of sale of his interest in his father's estate in Georgia. The bill of sale was sent to an attorney there, to collect the legacy; but before it reached him the administrator had been garnished by A., another of H.'s creditors, whereupon the attorney returned the bill, with instructions to get small notes to be sued in justice court. Plaintiffs obtained 24 notes,—17 for $95 and upwards, the other 7 for less than $90,—all providing for 10 per cent. attorneys' fees. The notes were dated in April and November, 1887, due in 30 days, but were executed after February 1, 1888, and were immediately sent to the attorney, and suit was commenced February 20th. The attorney then had H. come to Georgia, ostensibly to attend to a guardianship matter, when summonses in justice court were served on him in the actions. H. then left for Texas the same day, without doing anything in the guardianship matter. Judgments were rendered on the notes March 26th thereafter. H. made no objection to the actions being commenced before he reached Georgia. Held sufficient evidence to support a finding that the judgments were obtained by collusion to defeat the rights of A., and were therefore invalid.

2. The 10 per cent. attorneys' fees was a part of the principal of the other 17 notes, and, added to the specified amounts therein, made the amounts more than $100, which is the amount of a justice's jurisdiction; and the judgments entered thereon were void. Following Hill v. Haas, 73 Ga. 129, and Bell v. Rich, Id. 240.

3. The notes being executed in February, 1888, they were not due until 30 days thereafter, notwithstanding that they bore date in 1887. Following Raefle v. Moore, 58 Ga. 94.

4. Under Code Ga. § 3460, which declares that "parties by consent, express or implied, cannot give jurisdiction to the court as to the person or subject-matter of the suit, * * * so as to prejudice third parties," the maker of the notes, by not objecting to the commencement of the suits before his arrival in Georgia, or before the notes were due, could not waive jurisdiction to the prejudice of the creditor proceeding by garnishment.

Error from superior court, Coweta county: SAMPSON W. HARRIS, Judge.

Rule against I. A. Atkinson to show cause why certain money should not be paid to Beach, and Frank & Divine. Judgment for defendant. Plaintiffs bring error. Affirmed.

P. F. Smith, for plaintiffs in error. T. A. Atkinson, for defendant in error.

SIMMONS, J. Hindsman was a resident of Texas, and was entitled to a legacy in his father's estate in Georgia. Brunswig had obtained a judgment against Hindsman, and sued out garnishment against the administrator of Hindsman's father, in Meriwether county, Ga. Hindsman seems to have been indebted to one Beach, who also resided in Texas, for borrowed money, eleven or twelve hundred dollars, and to Frank & Divine, a firm of attorneys in Texas, for counsel fees, $470. Hindsman gave to Beach and Frank & Divine a bill of sale to his interest in his father's estate in Georgia, and this was sent to an attorney in Georgia, with instructions to collect the legacy money thereon, and transmit to Beach and Frank & Divine. Garnishment proceedings having been commenced against the administrator before the attorney in Georgia received the bill of sale, he returned it to Texas, and instructed his Texas clients to obtain from Hindsman small promissory notes which could be sued in a justice's court in Georgia. They obtained from Hindsman 24 promissory notes, 17 of which were for $95 and upwards, besides 10 per cent. attorneys' fees, and 7 for less than $90, also besides 10 per cent. attorneys' fees. These notes were executed, Frank & Divine say in their testimony, in January or February, 1888. Beach says positively that they were executed after the 1st of February, 1888. They were dated in April and November, 1887, and made payable 30 days after date. Immediately after their execution they were sent to their attorney in Georgia, who placed them in the hands of a justice of the peace for suit, and the suit was commenced on the 20th of February, 1888. The attorney in Georgia wrote a letter to Hindsman, in which he stated it was necessary for him to come to Georgia to look after the matter of the guardianship of a younger brother. Hindsman came, and when he arrived at the office of the Georgia attorney there appeared and served him with the summonses issued by the justice of the peace in the suits on the notes which he had executed a few days before in the state of Texas to Beach and Frank & Divine. He arrived at Newnan, was served by the constable, and left for Texas on the same day. The attorney testified that he had no previous understanding with Hindsman that he should come to Georgia to be served, but

that it is true he wrote him to come in the guardianship matter, in order to serve him in the cases, and that nothing was done in the guardianship matter after he was served; that he left on the same day for Texas because he had been threatened with prosecution for some offense. These suits against Hindsman in the justice's court proceeded, and judgment was rendered therein on the 26th of March, 1888. The administrator answered the garnishment, and admitted that he had in his hands $1,450, the interest of Hindsman in his father's estate. This money was paid over to Atkinson, the attorney for Brunswig, with the understanding that he would hold it until it was legally ascertained whether Brunswig was entitled to it, or Beach and Frank & Divine on their justice's court judgments; whereupon a rule was issued against Atkinson, at the instance of Beach and Frank & Divine, requiring Atkinson to show cause why the money should not be paid over to them on their judgments, their judgments being of older date than the judgment of Brunswig in his garnishment proceeding. Atkinson answered, in substance denying the validity of the judgments issued by the justice's court against Hindsman, on the grounds that they were collusive between Hindsman and the plaintiffs, and made for the purpose of defeating, delaying, and hindering Brunswig; that the service made upon Hindsman was not sufficient to give the court jurisdiction; and that, although the notes were dated in the year 1887, they were really not executed until after the 1st of February, 1888, and were not payable until 30 days after that date; and that suit was commenced thereon before the notes were due, to-wit, on the 20th of February, 1888. It was agreed between the parties that the judge might try the issue thus formed without the intervention of a jury. On the trial before him the foregoing facts were shown, and the judge held that the judgments on the 17 notes for $95 and upwards, with 10 per cent. additional for attorneys' fees, were void, because they exceeded $100, the amount of a justice's jurisdiction, and that the judgments on the seven notes which were within the jurisdiction as to amount were invalid under the facts above set forth; and he awarded the money to Brunswig's judgment. Beach and Frank & Divine excepted to this finding and judgment, and brought the case here for review.

1. Under the rulings of this court in Hill v. Haas, 78 Ga. 122, and Bell v. Rich, Id. 240, the trial judge did not err in excluding the 17 judgments and holding them void on the ground that they exceeded the jurisdiction of the justice's court. All the notes on which these judgments were predicated were given for $95 or more, with 10 per cent. attorneys' fees. This court held in the two cases above cited that the 10 per cent. for attorneys' fees was a part of the principal of the notes, and if the addition of 10 per cent. to the amount specified in the note made the amount more than $100, a justice's court had no jurisdiction, and any judgment entered thereon was a nullity.

2. We think the facts above recited are sufficient to authorise the judge as a jury to find that the other seven judgments were invalid and collusive between the parties thereto. The fact that the plaintiffs and the defendant resided in the same town in Texas; that the debts evidenced by the notes were all incurred in Texas, and some time prior to the execution of the notes; that this large indebtedness was divided into small notes for the purpose of being sued in Georgia, and judgments obtained thereon, before Brunswig could obtain his judgment; that Hindsman was induced to come to Georgia ostensibly for the purpose of removing the guardianship of his younger brother from Georgia to Texas, but really to be served with summonses in the suits commenced in the justice's court before his arrival, and on the same day returned to Texas without saying or doing anything about the guardianship matter; and the fact that he made no objection to the suits having been commenced before his arrival in the state and before the notes had matured,—all go to show that there was collusion between him and the plaintiffs to obtain these judgments before Brunswig could obtain his. Although these notes, upon their face, were past due at the time the suits were commenced, it was shown on the trial that they were ante-dated, being in fact executed after the 1st of February, 1888; and they were not due until 30 days after their execution. In the case of Raefie v. Moore, 58 Ga. 94, this court held "that a note payable one day after date, which was not made on the day it purported to have been made, became due on the day after it was in fact made, and could not be sued until the next succeeding day." The evidence shows that these suits were commenced on the notes on the 20th of February, though the notes were in fact executed after the 1st of the same month. Under the above ruling this could not be done. It may be argued, however, that this was a personal matter to Hindsman, the defendant, and he therefore waived jurisdiction of the court, which he had a right to do; and that, if he does not object, other parties cannot. Section 3460 of the Code declares: "Parties, by consent, express or implied, cannot give jurisdiction to the court as to the person or subject-matter of the suit. It may, however, be waived, so far as the rights of the parties are concerned, but not so as to prejudice third persons." While the judgments, under this section, might be good against Hindsman, his waiver of the jurisdiction of the court could not prejudice his creditors. If the judgments prejudiced Brunswig's rights as a creditor, he can take advantage of the want of jurisdiction, and have the judgments declared void so far as they affect him; as was done in the case of Suydam v. Palmer, 63 Ga. 546. In that case the executor agreed that a suit should be brought against him in a county other than that of his residence. Judgment was rendered thereon for the plaintiff, and execution issued and was levied upon certain property, which was claimed by Palmer et al., and on motion of the claimants the levy was dismissed on

v.13s.e.no.24—38

the ground that the judgment was void for want of jurisdiction in the court which rendered it. See, also, Railroad, etc., Co. v. Harris, 5 Ga. 527; Bank v. Gibson, 11 Ga. 453; Raney v. McRae, 14 Ga. 589. Judgment affirmed.

CALHOUN *v.* PHILLIPS.

(Supreme Court of Georgia. July 8, 1891.)

SUNDAY CONTRACT—RATIFICATION.

A contract of sale made on Sunday, with no delivery of the property then or afterwards, is void, although the parties intended to waive delivery. Ratification by the vendee alone, made by allowing a credit on the vendor's account, it not appearing that the vendor ever took or claimed the benefit of such credit, will not suffice to validate the sale.

(Syllabus by the Court.)

Error from superior court, Montgomery county; D. M. ROBERTS, Judge.

Action of trover by Dempsey Phillips against James Calhoun. Judgment for plaintiff. Defendant brings error. Reversed.

Clark & Norman and *Martin & Smith,* for plaintiff in error. *Chas. D. Loud,* for defendant in error.

SIMMONS, J. Dempsey Phillips brought trover against James Calhoun for the recovery of a certain pair of oxen. The plaintiff testified that the oxen sued for were his; that he bought them from Prince Mosely, for $20; that Mosely owed him for some timber money that he had kept and used, and he was to allow Mosely $20 on the account, and take the oxen as they ran in the woods, the oxen not being present and actually delivered; that the sale was on the 6th of February, 1887; and that he afterwards allowed the credit of the $20 on the money Mosely was due him. The calendar showed that the 6th of February was Sunday. Hammond, Hull & Co. obtained a judgment against Mosely on the 11th of February, 1887, and had it levied on the oxen as the property of Mosely. The property was advertised for sale, and on the day of sale was bought by Calhoun, the defendant. He took possession of it, and the action of trover was brought against him as before stated. On this state of facts the court charged as follows: "If the contract of sale between Dempsey Phillips and Prince Mosely for the oxen in dispute was made on Sunday, and the trade was not annulled, but Mosely allowed it to stand, and received and retained the benefits of the trade, the trade, although made on Sunday, is not void, but the sale would be a good one and hold the property, if made before the rendition of the judgment in favor of Hammond, Hull & Co. against Prince Mosely and Joseph Phillips,—the judgment on which *fi. fa.* issued and sale was made under the *fi. fa.* under which defendant claims title to the property,—unless the sale was made by Mosely to plaintiff for the purpose of defeating his creditors, and this was known to plaintiff at the time of the sale, or plaintiff did not buy the oxen in good faith." This charge was erroneous. In order for Phillips to recover in this action he must prove his title to the oxen. It not appearing that he ever had possession of them. I.. attempting to prove his title, he showed that the contract under which he claimed title was made on Sunday. Under our Code, §§ 2749, 4579, this contract was illegal and void, and the courts will not assist him to set up such an illegal and void contract. Ellis v. Hammond, 57 Ga. 179; Morgan v. Bailey, 59 Ga. 685; Finn v. Donahue, 35 Conn. 216; Pope v. Linn, 50 Me. 83; Block v. McMurry, 56 Miss. 219; 5 Lawson, Rights, Rem. & Pr. § 2411. The evidence shows that the contract was not executed, because there was no delivery of the oxen by Mosely to Phillips; and, although it could be inferred that delivery was waived, the contract would still be illegal, because, if under the law they could not make a valid contract on Sunday, they could not on Sunday agree to waive the delivery of the oxen. It was claimed, however, that the contract was ratified on a week-day, because Phillips allowed Mosely the credit of $20—the price agreed to be paid for the oxen—on a day other than Sunday. The courts in different states differ as to whether a contract made on Sunday can be subsequently ratified. 5 Lawson, Rights, Rem. & Pr. § 2414. Whether such a contract can be ratified or not it is unnecessary to decide here, as the evidence shows that this contract was not ratified. While it is true that Phillips testified that "he afterwards allowed the credit," it is not shown that Mosely ever agreed to ratify the contract; it is not shown that he knew the credit had been allowed him, or that he accepted any benefit from it; the record is silent as to whether Mosely agreed with Phillips upon a ratification. Ratification by Phillips alone would not be sufficient to render an illegal contract legal. Judgment reversed.

HARALSON v. McARTHUR.

(Supreme Court of Georgia. July 8, 1891.)

SETTING ASIDE JUDGMENT—ABSENCE OF COUNSEL.

1. The defendant's attorney being absent with leave of the court on account of sickness, his relationship to the case being known to counsel for the plaintiff, although his name was not marked on the docket, his leave of absence applied to the case; and, if his client was also absent on account of a public announcement made by the judge in open court (she being then present and hearing it) that no case would be taken up in which the absent counsel was concerned, the judgment against such defendant ought to be set aside upon application made at the same term, supported by an affidavit of a meritorious defense.

2. A joint verdict and judgment against several defendants, some of whom were never served, and had not waived service by appearance, should be set aside on motion made at the same term.

(Syllabus by the Court.)

Error from superior court, Montgomery county; D. M. ROBERTS, Judge.

Action by W. I. McArthur against Elizabeth Haralson and others. Judgment for plaintiff. Defendant Haralson brings error. Reversed.

Martin & Smith and H. W. Carswell, for plaintiff in error. E. A. Smith, D. C. McLennan, and De Lacy & Bishop, for defendant in error.

SIMMONS, J. 1. At the time the judgment was rendered in this case in the court below, Mr. Stanley, the attorney of Mrs. Haralson, one of the defendants, was absent from the court under a leave granted on account of sickness. This providential cause would have been a sufficient excuse for his absence without any leave from the court. It was known to plaintiff's counsel that he had been employed in this case, although his name was not marked on the docket. Mrs. Haralson heard the judge announce in open court that no case in which Mr. Stanley was concerned as counsel would be taken up. For this reason she was not present when the case was called, and, doubtless for the same reason, made no arrangement to be represented by other counsel. She ascertained during the term that a judgment had been rendered against her, and immediately, before the expiration of the term, moved to set the same aside, which the court declined to do. This decision, in our opinion, was erroneous. Although Mr. Stanley had neither filed a plea for defendant nor caused his name to be marked on the docket, his client should not, in our opinion, suffer on account of his failure to do these things, because at the time the case was called and disposed of he was at home sick, and unable to attend to any business. If his leave of absence had been obtained for any other cause, he could at least have done what was necessary to inform the court what cases were to be affected by the leave granted. This he could have accomplished by furnishing the court with a list of his cases, or by seeing to it that his name was marked on the docket in all of them. Where an attorney is well, and gets a leave of absence from the court for his own convenience, it would be negligence to allow a case he was employed to defend to stand on the docket till called for a final disposition, without having previously done anything whatever to inform the court the case was to be contested, and that he represented the defendant. There seems to be no good reason, other than sickness or some other providential cause, why an attorney could not do this much, in person or otherwise, before the case was reached in its order for a hearing; and, unless prevented by such cause, he would have until then to protect his cases under his leave of absence; but where he is sick his opportunity to do so does not extend up to that time, and for this reason we think the rule above indicated should be modified in a case like this, where providential interference cuts an attorney off from the full exercise of his rights and privileges. In the case of Bentley v. Finch, (Ga.) 13 S. E. Rep. 155, the record shows that the judge stated to Mr. Humphreys, counsel for defendant, who was present in court, he would not try that day any case in which he was employed, yet nevertheless, on the same day, did render judgment against his client in a case wherein Mr. Humphreys' name was not marked on the docket, the judge not knowing he was employed therein. The court below afterwards set that judgment aside, and was, we think, properly reversed by this court for so doing. The suit was upon an unconditional written contract, and was in default, no plea having been filed, and no counsel's name having been marked for defendant on the docket. Mr. Humphreys' client relied upon the clerk to enter his name, and, this being at his own risk. he could take nothing by the clerk's failure to comply with his request. Again, Mr. Humphreys was present in court when the judge made the announcement as to his cases, and there is no reason why he could not have then had his name marked in the cases he defended, or at least have informed the judge what his cases were. Nothing of the sort was done, and under these facts we thought no sufficient reason appeared for setting the judgment aside. In the Bently Case, the motion to set aside the judgment was not made at the term at which it was rendered, as was done in the case at bar; nor does the record in the former allege that defendant or his counsel were ignorant, till after the term closed, of the rendition of the judgment, or state any reason whatever why the motion to set aside was not made during the term. These two cases differ in many respects, but the controlling distinction between them is that in one the defendant's counsel was prevented by providential interference from giving all needed attention to his client's interests, and in the other he was not, but had ample and sufficient opportunity to do so, and by availing himself thereof could have prevented the rendition of the judgment.

2. This was an action against several defendants, including the plaintiff in error, some of whom were not served at all, and never had their day in court. The verdict and judgment, being a joint one in favor of the plaintiff against all the defendants, ought not to stand. Those who were not served, of course, are not bound by it; and this fact would effectually prevent the plaintiff in error, in case she satisfied the judgment, from having her right to contribution from all her co-defendants. In the event she should demand such contribution, they would only have to reply they were not bound by the judgment at all, and that it established no right against them in favor of any one. If the plaintiff had obtained judgment against those defendants only who were served, it may have been valid as to them; but inasmuch as the judgment is against all the defendants, including those not served, we are clear it should be set aside for the reason above stated. Judgment reversed.

LUMPKIN, J., not presiding.

WOOTEN v. WILCOX et al.

(*Supreme Court of Georgia.* July 8, 1891.)

STATUTE OF FRAUDS—DEBT OF ANOTHER.

Where one has a statutory lien for supplies upon personal property belonging to a firm, which property is sold to another firm, composed in part of the same members, and thereupon the purchasing firm, to prevent a foreclosure and sale under the lien, agree with the creditor to pay the debt if he will grant certain indulgence and furnish other like supplies to them for their use, and the creditor complies with his undertaking,

the case is not within the statute of frauds, and he may recover of the second firm upon their contract to pay the debt of the first firm.

(*Syllabus by the Court.*)

Error from superior court, Dodge county; D. M. ROBERTS, Judge.

Action by A. H. Wooten against Wilcox, Stilson & Co. to enforce a lien on logs. A demurrer to the declaration was sustained in the court below, and plaintiff brings error. Reversed.

De Lacy & Bishop and *D. C. McLennan,* for plaintiff in error. *E. A. Smith,* for defendants in error.

BLECKLEY, C. J. According to the declaration, the plaintiff had a statutory lien upon a saw-mill of Wilcox & Cleland, for logs and timber, amounting to $463.70. With notice of that lien, Wilcox, Stilson & Co. purchased the mill, after which the plaintiff was about to proceed to foreclose and enforce his lien, but was prevented from so doing by the undertaking of the latter firm, who promised and agreed with the plaintiff that they would pay him the sum due from the former if he would indulge them a few days, and not proceed at once to foreclose and enforce his lien, and if he would continue under a similar contract with them to furnish logs and timber to the mill. They thus became indebted to him in the sum of $55 for logs and timber furnished to them under this contract, in addition to the amount assumed by them for the previous firm, making a total of $518.70. The declaration was demurred to on the general ground that there was no cause of action alleged against the defendants, and the demurrer was sustained so far as it related to the antecedent debt, the court basing its decision partly upon the specific ground that the "declaration did not clearly allege that the plaintiff had released the original debtor." The defendants were a partnership, which had purchased the property of another firm and continued as successors in the same business, one of the old firm having retired, and his associate, with two others, composing the new partnership. The question is as to the liability of the new firm upon its promise to a creditor to pay the latter a debt of the original firm, this promise not appearing to have been made in writing. The rule of our Code is that a promise to answer for the debt of another must be in writing, signed by the party to be charged therewith, or some person by him lawfully authorized; otherwise it is not obligatory. An exception to the rule exists, however, "where there has been performance on one side, accepted by the other, in accordance with the contract." Code, §§ 1950, 1951. Here the plaintiff alleges full performance on his part. He gave the stipulated indulgence, and continued to furnish logs and timber so long as the defendants continued in the business, and until they dissolved partnership. They took the benefit of the plaintiff's performance; and, having done so, they are not in a condition to allege the statute of frauds, modified as it has been by our Code, as a defense to an action which seeks to compel them to perform the contract on their part. Indeed, we are inclined to think that, irrespective of the express exception contained in the Code, this contract is enforceable as an original undertaking by the new firm, made on a valuable consideration moving to them, and entered into to serve their own interest as a leading object, and to protect property which had become theirs, subject to the plaintiff's lien, from being subjected to that lien at once. According to the declaration, the lien was ripe for immediate enforcement, and it was to prevent that enforcement that the defendants stipulated for indulgence and obtained it. The plaintiff tied his hands, bound himself by contract to allow the indulgence asked for, and did in fact allow it. To suspend the enforcement of the lien for the stipulated time was, or might have been, beneficial to the defendants. It left them in the possession and use of the property, and, while it may have been less valuable to them than an extinction of the lien would have been, it fulfilled all the requisites of a valid consideration as defined by the Code. "A consideration is valid if any benefit accrues to him who makes the promise, or any injury to him who receives the promise." Code, § 2740. The fulfillment of their promise by the defendants would discharge the lien, and that seems all that the true principle of the authorities on the subject would require. Throop, Verb. Agr. § 573. Moreover, coupled with the consideration to forbear was the agreement by the plaintiff to continue to furnish logs and timber to the defendants. This part of his contract he also performed, and it is to be presumed that the defendants were benefited thereby. The case is thus within the principle of many authorities which tend to uphold the contract, though not in writing, as an original undertaking on the part of defendants to make the debt their own. Young v. French, 35 Wis. 111; Weisel v. Spence, 59 Wis. 301, 18 N. W. Rep. 165; Fitzgerald v. Morrissey, 14 Neb. 198, 15 N. W. Rep. 233; Muller v. Riviere, 59 Tex. 640, 46 Amer. Rep. 291, notes; Throop, Verb. Agr. § 647; Browne. St. Frauds, § 200a; 1 Reed, St. Frauds, §§ 72, 143; Phil. Mech. Liens, §§ 213, 505. The court erred in sustaining the demurrer; consequently a new trial is necessary. Judgment reversed.

LUMPKIN, J., not presiding.

LASLIE et al. v. LASLIE.

(Supreme Court of Georgia. July 8, 1891.)

YEAR'S ALLOWANCE TO WIDOW — FILING OBJECTIONS.

The question involved in this case, respecting the time of filing objections to the allowance of a year's support to a widow, is decided in Parks v. Johnson, 79 Ga. 567, 5 S. E. Rep. 243.

(Syllabus by the Court.)

Error from superior court, Dodge county; D. M. ROBERTS, Judge.
De Lacy & Bishop, for plaintiff in error. *Smith & Clements*, for defendants in error.
Judgment reversed.

LUMPKIN, J., not presiding.

DAVIS v. MOBLEY.

(Supreme Court of Georgia. July 8, 1891.)

JUSTICE OF THE PEACE—TRIAL OF APPEAL.

1. On the trial of an appeal in a justice's court it is not error in the magistrate to allow a promissory note, the foundation of the action, to be read in evidence pending the argument to the jury. Such allowance is virtually reopening the case for that purpose, and the opposite party, if desirous of doing so, would be permitted to introduce further evidence also.

2. The other grounds in the petition are not sufficient to require a new trial in the magistrate's court.

(Syllabus by the Court.)

Error from superior court, Montgomery county; D. M. ROBERTS, Judge.
D. C. McLennan and *De Lacy & Bishop*, for plaintiff in error. *C. H. Mann*, for defendant in error.
Judgment reversed.

LUMPKIN, J., not presiding.

McDUFFIE v. STATE.

(Supreme Court of Georgia. July 20, 1891.)

INTOXICATING LIQUORS — ILLEGAL SALE — INDICTMENT—TITLE OF STATUTE.

1. Some intoxicating liquors are not comprehended in the descriptive term "spirituous liquors." Consequently a statute enacting that it shall be unlawful for any person to sell intoxicating liquors contains matter different from what is expressed in the title thereof, the title being "An act to prohibit the sale of spirituous liquors."

2. An indictment founded upon such statute, which charges in general terms the sale of intoxicating liquors, without alleging that they were spirituous liquors, does not set forth any offense with requisite certainty.

(Syllabus by the Court.)

Error from superior court, Wilcox county; D. M. ROBERTS, Judge.
Indictment of D. L. McDuffie for selling intoxicating liquors contrary to Act Ga. Feb. 22, 1877. Verdict of guilty. Defendant brings error. Reversed.
Martin & Smith, for plaintiff in error. *Tom Eason*, Sol. Gen., by *Hines & Felder*, for the State.

SIMMONS, J. 1. McDuffie was indicted for selling intoxicating liquors, under the special act passed for Wilcox county, approved February 22, 1877. The title of that act is as follows: "An act to prohibit the sale of spirituous liquors within the limits of Wilcox county." The first section of the act makes it "unlawful for any person or persons to sell, barter, or in any other way dispose of, for value, intoxicating liquors of any kind or quality within the limits of Wilcox county." The indictment under this act charged McDuffie" with the offense of misdemeanor in selling intoxicating liquors, for that the said D. S. McDuffie, on the 5th day of March, in the year 1890, in the county aforesaid, did then and there unlawfully, and with force and arms, within the limits of said county, and not within the corporate limits of any town or city whereby authority to issue license is vested in the corporate authorities, for a valuable consideration, sell, barter, or otherwise dispose of a quantity of intoxicating liquors, contrary to the laws of said state," etc. One of the special demurrers made to this indictment was that the act above cited was unconstitutional, having in its body matter different from its title, the title prohibiting the sale of "spirituous" liquors, and the act prohibiting the sale of "intoxicating" liquors. The demurrer was overruled by the court, and defendant excepted. The court should have sustained this special demurrer. The title of the act prohibits the sale of spirituous liquors, while the body of the act makes it unlawful for any one to sell intoxicating liquors. The act, therefore, contains matter different from what is expressed in the title. "All spirituous liquors are intoxicating, but all intoxicating liquors are not spirituous." "Spirituous liquor means distilled liquor." "Fermented liquor, though intoxicating, is not spirituous." Com. v. Grey, 61 Amer. Dec. 476; State v. Oliver, 26 W. Va. 422, 11 Amer. & Eng. Enc. Law, 571; And. Law Dict. 565; 1 Abb. Law Dict. 641.

2. It will be seen from the above quotation made from the indictment that it charges in general terms the sale of intoxicating liquors, without alleging that they were spirituous liquors. If it had alleged that the intoxicating liquor sold was spirituous liquor, the indictment, so far as this question is concerned, would have been sufficient; but, having alleged generally the sale of intoxicating liquors, it did not set forth any offense with requisite certainty. Judgment reversed.

LUMPKIN, J., not presiding.

FULGHAM v. CARRUTHERS.

(Supreme Court of Georgia. July 8, 1891.)

ACTION AGAINST EXECUTOR — OFFICIAL DESIGNATION.

In strict law, where a plaintiff has a suit pending against the defendant in the character of executor, all proceedings in other courts intended to create evidence to be used in such suit should be against him in the same character, and not in the character of administrator, inasmuch as an executor represents primarily the devisees and legatees, and the administrator represents the heirs at law. This court will not reverse the judgment of nonsuit, it not appearing that the plaintiff would be remediless by bringing another action.

(Syllabus by the Court.)

Error from superior court, Pulaski county; D. M. ROBERTS, Judge.

Action of ejectment by Fulgham against J. W. Carruthers. Judgment for defendant. Plaintiff brings error. Affirmed.

Jordan & Watson and Pate & Warren, for plaintiff in error. L. C. Ryan and Martin & Smith, for defendant in error.

SIMMONS, J. Fulgham brought ejectment against J. W. Carruthers for a lot of land in Pulaski county. After the suit was bought Carruthers died. T. L. Carruthers was appointed his executor, and as such was, by consent of the parties, made defendant in place of his testator. It seems that the lot of land formerly belonged to one Rainey, of Merriwether county, and William Boyd, as administrator of Rainey, had sold the land as wild land at private sale, professing to have an order of the ordinary of Merriwether county authorizing him so to do. But the order authorizing Boyd, the administrator, to sell was not upon the minutes of the court of ordinary of Merriwether county. It was necessary to have a certified copy of this order before the plaintiff could introduce his deed in evidence. After the plaintiff's counsel had agreed to make T. L. Carruthers a party defendant as executor, they petitioned the ordinary of Merriwether county, asking the entry nunc pro tunc of a certain order alleged to have been granted by the ordinary to Boyd to sell the wild lands of Rainey's estate. To this petition was attached a copy of the alleged order, bearing date October 4, 1869. It was filed with the ordinary on April 7, 1890, and he granted an order citing T. L. Carruthers, as administrator, to appear before him on the first Monday in May, to show cause why the petition of Fulgham should not be granted, and this petition was served on T. L. Carruthers as administrator of J. W. Carruthers, on the 14th of April, 1890. At the May term, 1890, of the court of ordinary of Merriwether county an order was granted entering the alleged order on the minutes nunc pro tunc. Certified copies of all the above proceedings accompanied the deed, and were tendered in evidence with it; and, on objection by the defendant, the court rejected the deed and certified transcript of the record as evidence. The plaintiff introducing no further testimony, the court granted a nonsuit. The rejection of the tendered evidence is the only question involved. It was not error to reject the evidence offered. The plaintiff commenced his suit against J. W. Carruthers, and consented, after his death, that his son should be made a party defendant as executor. After this consent he commenced proceedings in the court of ordinary of another county to create evidence to be used on the trial of the ejectment case in Pulaski county. Instead of the proceedings against Carruthers in the court of ordinary being commenced against him as executor, they were commenced against him as administrator. Where a party commences suit in one county against a person in the capacity of executor, and wishes to create evidence by having a judgment in a court of another county entered nunc pro tunc to be used in the former suit, he should proceed against him in the same capacity in which he was made defendant to the original suit. The suit in Pulaski was against him as executor; the judgment granting the order nunc pro tunc in the court of ordinary of Merriwether county was against him as administrator. The suit in ejectment being against him as executor, the evidence offered, showing that he was administrator, was not admissible. The office of executor is different from that of administrator. The executor represents the devisees and legatees, and the administrator represents the heirs at law. Fulgham and his counsel agreed to make the defendant a party as executor, and it seems to have been negligence on their part that the evidence was procured against him as administrator. We therefore will not reverse the judgment granting a nonsuit, especially as it does not appear that Fulgham would be remediless by bringing another action. Judgment affirmed.

REYNOLDS v. REYNOLDS' EX'R.

(Supreme Court of Appeals of Virginia. Aug. 18, 1891.)

VENDOR AND VENDEE — SALE IN GROSS — BILL OF REVIEW — AFTER-DISCOVERED EVIDENCE.

Where a sale was made of "one-half" of a certain tract of land in gross, and a deed executed, based upon a subsequent survey, which so defined the boundaries as to inclose 102 acres less than the parties supposed the one-half to contain, a bill of review of a judgment for the balance of the purchase money, on the ground of newly-discovered evidence, should be dismissed where it appeared that the evidence was merely cumulative to the effect that the grantor had intended to sell one-half the land, that a large number of witnesses had testified to the same thing at the former trial, and that the grantee had failed to claim any deficiency when pressed for the purchase money in the life-time of the grantor. By LACY, J., dissenting.

Action by Charles B. Reynolds' executor against Harvey Reynolds to charge defendant's lands with the balance of purchase money due and unpaid. A judgment for plaintiff was affirmed. Defendant then filed a bill of review, which was dismissed in the lower court, and reinstated in this court. For majority opinion, see 13 S. E. Rep. 395.

LACY, J. (*dissenting.*) This is the same case which was decided at the June term of this court, 1885, under the name of Reynolds against Watts, etc., Watts being the executor of Charles B. Reynolds, deceased; the appellee then and the appellee now. The case as it is stated in the opinion of the court at that term is as follows:

"LACY, J. This is an appeal from a decree of the circuit court of Floyd county, rendered at the May term, 1884. In October, 1882, the appellee, Watts, executor of Chas. B. Reynolds, deceased, instituted this suit against the appellant, seeking to charge the lands of the appellant to the payment of the residue of the purchase money due and unpaid thereon to the said Chas. B. Reynolds, deceased. The said land having been sold to the said appellant by the said Reynolds, deceased, a lien was retained in the deed to secure the payment of the purchase money unpaid, being evidenced by the four bonds of the purchaser, two of which had been assigned to the appellee, Watts, and two of which were due to the estate of the said Chas. B. Reynolds, deceased. The appellant answered, setting forth that the land had been purchased in 1869, and that the unpaid purchase money claimed in the bill had never been paid, but that he was entitled to an abatement in the purchase money because of a falling off in the quantity of land of one hundred and fifty-five acres, which, at $11.19 per acre, would be $1,734. That the bonds sued for only amounted to $1,600 in the aggregate, upon one of which a credit of $81 appeared;

and that the estate of Chas. B. Reynolds was indebted to him for overpayment in the sum of $215; and filed set-offs in addition to the amount of $500 and $31.09, without interest, and asked for a decree against the estate of Chas. B. Reynolds. That Chas. B. Reynolds had sold to him one-half of what was known as his 'Guerrant Land,' which contained eight hundred and fifteen acres, from which four acres had been sold off. That he was thus entitled to have over four hundred acres of this land; and that subsequently he had bought of Chas. B. Reynolds another tract of land of one hundred and fifty-four acres, out of the other half of the Guerrant land, at $7.50 per acre. The deeds in question, and the other deeds conveying other portions of the Guerrant land, are exhibited, and the testimony of numerous witnesses filed in the record. The land was surveyed, and the report of a commissioner filed to whom it had been referred for an account of the purchase money remaining unpaid, etc. And on the 1st day of May, 1884, a decree was rendered in the cause, in which the circuit court, allowing the offsets claimed and proved, decreed against the appellant for the balance due to the estate of Chas. B. Reynolds, deceased, and for the balance due on the assigned bonds, and held the same to be a charge upon the land, and decreed a sale of the land to pay the same, unless the said appellant should pay the said balances within ninety days from the rising of the court, and refused to make any deduction for the alleged loss of land. From this decree an appeal was allowed to this court. There are no disputed questions of law in the case, the principle upon which the case must be decided being well settled and conceded on both sides.

"The whole case depends on the disputed question of fact as to whether the sale of the land was a sale in gross, and in so far a contract of hazard,—that is, a tract of land within designated boundaries, as to which a falling short in quantity will be no ground for relief,—or whether it was a sale of land at gross price, upon estimate of quantity influencing price, when a mistake has occurred, which, if understood, would probably have prevented the sale, or varied its terms, which, upon well-settled principles, would have been ground for relief in equity. The appellant claims to have bought one-half of the Guerrant land—about 400 acres—and 30 acres of another tract in 1869, boundary to be afterwards ascertained; that in 1872 line was run, deed made, and bonds executed, the price in gross being $5,000; that he was put in possession of the land at once, and so remained. His vendor died in 1876, and this suit, as has been said, was instituted in October, 1882. The last bond fell due in January, 1882, when, four bonds remaining unpaid, suit was instituted in the month of October of that year. The deed by which this land was conveyed described it 'as a certain tract of land containing a supposed boundary of three hundred and fifty acres, be the same more or less, and bounded as follows,' setting out the boundary lines with great minuteness, giving courses and distances, with the words added, 'it being about one-half of the said C. B. Reynolds Guerrant land,' and to the deed was appended this memorandum: 'N. B. All the land is sold in the boundaries, except four acres, which was sold to I. Huff before this deed was made.' It is clear from the evidence that at the time this sale was made the Guerrant land had not been surveyed and was only known by the boundaries. Soon after the land not sold to appellant was surveyed, and turned out to contain 563 acres. This fact was then known to the appellant, and yet he never said anything about having bought by the acre, or with reference to the number of acres, until the vendor was dead,—indeed, had been dead six years,—and not until suit was brought to compel payment of the unpaid purchase money. And, although the land conveyed to appellant as about half of the Guerrant tract contained, in accordance with the contract, 30 or 40 acres of the Wiley tract, no mention whatever is made of the 30 or 40 acres in the deed, but the two pieces are conveyed together, without distinction by metes and bounds, as included within a boundary containing 350 acres, more or less. If only bought as one-half of the Guerrant tract, why was this 30 or 40 acres included? The evidence shows that, while the original agreement was for these two pieces of land, there was no deed made until the line was run and the boundaries laid off. The sale was for the gross sum of $5,000 for this marked and designated tract of land, and there was not a word said about the price per acre, and where the quantity is mentioned it is as 350 acres, more or less, within certain boundaries. There is no ground to suppose that the sale was other than a sale in gross of a designated piece of land at an agreed price. The estimation of the quantity, so far as it went, was made by both parties, upon the same facts, which were equally known to both. The vendor did not take upon himself to make any affirmation or representations in respect to quantity. The vendee knew as much about the land as the vendor, having resided upon it and known it just as long. The vendor spoke his real opinion founded upon the very same information which his vendee had, and in which the latter concurred with him, without being influenced by it, so far as the evidence shows. The vendor concealed no fact within his knowledge which could in any degree influence the opinion. The sale was a sale in gross, within ascertained boundaries, and consummated without a survey, by mutual agreement,—was a contract of hazard, without any fraud, concealment, misrepresentation, or negligence on the part of the vendor. The error in the quantity, if there was any such, was mutual, and was not in relation to the substance of the thing contracted for, but in relation to the very hazard contemplated by the parties,—a contract in which the purchaser took the risk of quantity upon himself. This court has uniformly recognized the validity and obligation of such a contract, and in all cases where relief has been given it has been founded on

circumstances either of fraud, misrepresentation, or concealment, or mistake in whole or in part as to the substance of the thing contracted for.

"It is not deemed necessary to review the evidence in detail. It is immaterial whether the reference to the one-half part of the Guerrant land in the deed is as to quantity or as to value in this case. It is sufficiently clear from the deed and the admitted facts that the sale was for the land within certain boundaries, uninfluenced by the estimate in the deed; that it was a contract for a sale in gross; and a contract of hazard. And the circuit court of Floyd having so held in the decree complained of, the same must be affirmed."

At this hearing one of the judges of this court dissented in the following language, which states his views at that time:

"I dissent from the opinion which has just been read. In my judgment the decree appealed from is plainly wrong and ought to be reversed. I think it fails to give effect to the intention of the parties, and in consequence does great injustice to the appellant here. That parol evidence is admissible in cases like the present to explain the true understanding of the parties is not only well established, but undisputed. As was said by this court in Mauzy v. Sellars, 26 Grat. 641: 'That it is competent for a court of equity to correct a mistake in a deed or other writing upon parol evidence cannot now be questioned. No branch of equity jurisdiction is more fully established than this; none is sustained by a greater array of authorities, English and American.' The application of this principle to the present case leaves no room for doubt in my judgment that the decree should be reversed. The bill was filed to enforce a vendor's lien on the defendant's land, and the single question is whether the latter is entitled to an abatement of the purchase money as claimed in his answer. The original contract to convey the land was by parol. The deed was executed several years thereafter. That at the time the contract of sale was entered into neither party knew the exact quantity of land in respect of which they were contracting there can be no doubt. The Guerrant land, of which the land he sold to the appellant was a part, had not then been conveyed to the vendor, but was supposed to contain about 800 acres. The deed to the latter, subsequently made, describes it as containing about 815 acres; and to my mind the evidence is conclusive that the parties contracted with reference to about one-half of that tract of land. Then, did the deed to the appellant convey the land for which he contracted? If it did not, then clearly we have here presented the ordinary case of a mutual mistake, which calls for correction in a court of equity. But what says the deed? It purports to convey 'a certain tract of land containing a supposed boundary of 350 acres, be the same more or less.' But it does not stop here. It gives the boundaries, as best the parties could, and then concluded as follows: 'It being about one-half of the said C. B. Reynolds' part of the Guerrant tract.' Now, if these two statements of the deed are conflicting, then upon the familiar rule of construction that must be taken which is most strongly against the grantor. In point of fact, the deed conveyed, as was afterwards ascertained, less than one-half of Reynolds' part of the Guerrant tract by one hundred and two acres, and this the appellant contends is contrary to the intention of both parties to that instrument. In support of this contention many witnesses were examined, whose testimony is unimpeached; and if their statements are to be taken as true, as I think they must be, then the case of the appellant is established beyond a doubt. The witness Enoch Reynolds testifies that he was present when the contract was made, and heard the conversation between the parties. It was agreed, he says, that the appellant was to pay $5,000, and was to have one-half of Reynolds' part of the Guerrant tract, and 35 or 40 acres of the Wiley tract; and he further says that Reynolds, the vendor, expressed the belief that his part of the Guerrant tract contained about 800 acres. After the land to the appellant was sold, the residue of the tract was sold by Reynolds to one Chas. Craig; and the latter testified that Reynolds represented to him that he had sold one-half of the tract to the appellant. Subsequently the land thus sold to Craig was again acquired by Reynolds, who offered to sell it to various persons as containing 400 acres, and at a much less sum than he obtained for the land he had sold the appellant. The witness Robt. P. Craig testifies that he repeatedly heard Reynolds say that he had sold the appellant one-half of his part of the Guerrant land. And to the same effect is the testimony of other witnesses. The witness Buckner testifies that, in a conversation with Reynolds, after the sale to the appellant, he informed him that he had instructed the surveyor to run off to the appellant all the Guerrant land but 400 acres. And various witnesses testify that after the sale to the appellant Reynolds offered to sell to them the residue of the tract, and represented it to contain 400 acres. I am at a loss to imagine how stronger evidence than this could be adduced to show the real intention of the parties in respect to the transactions in question, when taken in connection with the expressed object of the deed to convey 'about one-half of Reynolds' part of the Guerrant tract.' In opposition to this testimony are the depositions of four witnesses, one of whom is Mrs. Mary Jack, and another, Chas. W. Aldrige. These witnesses testify to vague and loose conversations with the appellant and admissions by him, which at the most are entitled to little weight, if any at all, as against the clear and positive evidence which was taken for the appellant. It appears, moreover, that Mrs. Jack and Aldrige are the wife and step-son, respectively, of one John O. Jack, who, apart from his hostility to the appellant, appears in no enviable light in the present controversy, if the uncontradicted testimony is to be taken as true. The witness S. L. Walton testifies that in a conversation with Jack, while the depositions in the suit were being taken, the latter said

to him that if he (Jack) and his wife and her son (Aldrige) were summoned, Harvey Reynolds (the appellant) would be thrown; and further said that they 'might make some money, probably a hundred or two,' if Mr. Watts, the plaintiff, were informed, and would summon them. Prudently enough Jack himself was not summoned, and I deem it unnecessary to further comment upon the testimony of his wife and her son, who were.

"Now, in view of the language of the deed, already quoted, construed, as it must be, in the light of the parol evidence in the case, I cannot hesitate to say that, in my judgment, this appellant, whom the record shows to be an ignorant, old, colored man, of exceptional merit, and who, in the life-time of his 'old master,' the appellee's testator, was the object of his confidence and affection, and but for whose death this controversy most probably would never have arisen, has been most grievously wronged by the decree complained of. By that decree, now affirmed by this court, he is required to pay the sum of nearly $2,000; or, in default thereof, his land to be sold, when, according to the evidence in the case, and the well-established law of this state, as I understand it, he justly owes not one cent. A late case on the subject is Yost v. Mallicote's Adm'r, 77 Va. 610. In that case the vendee purchased and took a deed for a tract of land within certain metes and bounds, which was verbally represented to contain a certain number of acres, and probably more. Afterwards it was ascertained that the quantity of land within the boundaries was less than had thus been represented. It was held, upon the evidence in that case, that the vendee was entitled to an abatement of the purchase money on the ground of mistake, although judgments on the bonds for the purchase money had been obtained at law. The present case, it seems to me, is equally strong for the appellant. The contract was entered into for the purchase of about one-half of the Guerrant land, as shown by the deed itself and the evidence of the witnesses. It is not denied that the land fell short more than 100 acres of that quantity. It is equally certain that the price contracted to be paid was an adequate consideration for the one-half of the tract the appellant supposed he was buying, and therefore a much larger sum than the quantity of land he actually got was worth. Why, then, should he not be entitled to an abatement of the purchase money when summoned to answer in a court of equity? The deed says he was to have about one-half of the land. Three witnesses heard the vendor say he had sold him one-half of the land, and five witnesses (all white men) heard him say, after the sale was made, that he had but four hundred acres left; and the evidence shows that he actually agreed to give all over four hundred acres in the residue of the tract to the man who would insure that it contained as much as four hundred acres. The fact is that, owing to the mistake of the parties, it really contained five hundred and sixty-two acres. And the result is that vendor not only retained more than one hundred acres of land justly belonging to the appellant, but that now his executor, under what seems to me a mistaken view of the law and the facts of the case, is decreed to be entitled to recover a large sum of money besides. I had omitted to refer to the memorandum at the end of the deed, to which much weight seems to be attached in the opinion of the court. Its object and effect was simply to exclude from the operation of the conveyance four acres of the land which had previously been sold to another party, and nothing more. Its language is as follows: 'All the land is sold in the boundaries except four acres, which was sold to I. Huff before this deed was made.' And that this is the correct view is conclusively shown, I think, not only by the evidence already referred to, but by the deposition of a witness who says the vendor informed him that the land had cost the appellant about $12 per acre. I have thus, in great haste and very imperfectly, expressed my views in this case. I have endeavored to present it fairly and impartially, and am satisfied that the case, as shown by the record, is even stronger for the appellant than I have presented it. But enough has been said, I think, to show that the decree is erroneous and ought to be reversed."

After the rendition of this decision a rehearing was applied for and refused by this court. Subsequently a bill of review was filed in the circuit court of Floyd county, having for its object a review and reversal of the decree of the said court above mentioned, and the decree of this court affirming the same. The ground was newly-discovered evidence, which could not with reasonable diligence have been discovered by the plaintiff in said bill before the first trial, to the effect that C. B. Reynolds "had admitted on four different occasions, to four different persons, just precisely what your orator contended for in the original cause, to-wit, that he sold your orator, in 1869, the Wiley land, and one-half of the Peter Guerrant tract, for $5,000; that C. B. Reynolds found out that he had made a mistake and intended to correct it; that these facts, within the knowledge of Rev. James M. Price, Capt. Wm. P. Thompson, Mr. M. J. Angell, and Mr. Aaron Beckner, all highly respected white men of Franklin county, and friends and neighbors of Mr. C. B. Reynolds, never became known to plaintiff till decision of case in supreme court of appeals." Alleging further that "plaintiff knew nothing of these admissions, and there was nothing to suggest itself to him before trial to go to said witnesses, or either of them, and ask them of such admissions, or whether they had any knowledge of said case." What this newly discovered evidence was is set forth in the opinion of the majority on page 397 of the thirteenth volume of the Southeastern Reporter (July 2, 1891) to some extent as to the testimony of Capt. Wm. P. Thompson. "He [C. B. Reynolds] told me that he had sold one-half of a tract of land which he owned in Floyd, called the 'Guerrant place,' estimated to contain about 800 acres, to Harvey Reynolds, a former slave of his." This

in 1869 or 1870. In 1875 he fell in with him, and he dwelt some time on a controversy he had with Guerrant. On cross-examination this witness was asked: "Didn't Harvey go to see you when he was first sued by Reynolds, executor, about the matter in controversy in this suit?" He answered: "I don't remember that he did. He might have said something to me on that subject." He was also asked if, in giving his answers to questions asked by plaintiff's counsel, he did not copy from a memorandum in writing, which he had before him; and he answered: "Yes, that memorandum was made after due reflection." The witness Angell says: "He [C. B. Reynolds] told me he had sold half of the Guerrant tract of land to Harvey Reynolds. I don't think he said at what time. That he had employed Stephen Guerrant to survey one-half to Harvey Reynolds, and in the survey he had fallen short a large number of acres of giving him one-half." The old man, Charles B. Reynolds, went on to say that Harvey Reynolds owed him a considerable amount, and this survey being short, it would make him safe in the deferred payments. The witness Price says that Mr. Reynolds had told him that said plaintiff had complained to him about not getting the number of acres, and that he could not make up to Harvey then; that the land had been sold, and he was going to pay him back, etc. It was proved in the cause that the plaintiff lived in the neighbourhood of these new witnesses, and when he was hunting evidence before the first trial he went to the house of the newly-discovered witness Thompson. The appellee, Watts, testified that he had talked with the plaintiff, Harvey Reynolds, about these bonds during the life-time of C. B. Reynolds, and he never heard any claim as to any deficiency in this land until after the death of C. B. Reynolds; and numerous witnesses testify that they talked with C. B. Reynolds about this land sold to Harvey Reynolds, and never heard from him a suggestion that Harvey Reynolds was in any way dissatisfied with his purchase; and, indeed, that the sale to Harvey was so liberal in terms that it amounted to a rental of 10 years and then a gift of the land.

There are filed 15 letters, written by Harvey Reynolds to C. B. Reynolds in his life-time, and to J. R. Reynolds acting for him, and to Watts, his executor, after his death, in which this indebtedness is the topic, and in which he sets forth in detail his offsets against this debt, and promises payment, they being applied, and for years begs indulgence, pleading poor crops, and hard work, and yet not one word is said about any falling short in the number of acres, nor one word of any dissatisfaction as to the contract of purchase. I am satisfied that this defense now set up is an afterthought conceived only after the death of Charles B. Reynolds; and this record demonstrates that, if sooner conceived, it was never disclosed until Charles B. Reynolds' lips had been closed by death. Harvey Reynolds bought a part of two tracts of land by metes and bounds, and agreed to pay a sum agreed on, which had no reference whatever to the number of acres nor to the question whether it was half or less than half of the Guerrant land; and, indeed, it was not all a part of the Guerrant land, but was in part made up out of the Wiley tract. But, in any event, according to the heretofore unbroken line of decisions of this court on this subject, the bill of review was properly dismissed by the learned judge of the circuit court. The evidence was merely cumulative, and was just as well known to the purchaser before the first trial, as said. That it was cumulative only the first record abundantly shows. From what has gone before concerning this bill of review, it appears that the newly-discovered evidence was to the effect that C. B. Reynolds had sold to Harvey Reynolds, his former slave, one-half of the lands belonging to him known as the "Guerrant Land," and that Harvey Reynolds did not get this. In the first record it appears that at the first trial the witness Enoch Reynolds testified that C. B. Reynolds had admitted that he had sold to Harvey "half of Reynolds' part of the Guerrant tract." Charles Craig said, in answer to the question, "Did you hear Mr. C. B. Reynolds say how much of the Guerrant land he had sold to Harvey Reynolds?"—"Well, sir, I never heard him say how many acres, but that he had sold to Harvey Reynolds half of the Guerrant land." The witness Price says: "Mr. Reynolds told me Guerrant had made a mistake; that he only claimed 400 acres." The witness Marshall Reynolds says in reply to the question, "State what you heard Mr. Reynolds tell Mr. Armistead Burwell about what part of the Guerrant land he had sold to Harvey Reynolds,"—"I heard him tell Mr. Armistead Burwell that he sold half of his part of the Guerrant land to Harvey Reynolds." The witness Robert Craig says: "I have often heard him say that he had sold to Harvey Reynolds half of his part of the Guerrant land." What is the law upon the subject of new trials to be granted upon the ground of new evidence? It has been often stated thus: (1) The evidence must have been discovered since the trial. (2) It must be evidence that could not have been discovered before the trial by the plaintiff or defendant, as the case may be, by the exercise of reasonable diligence. (3) It must be material in its object, and such as ought on another trial to produce an opposite result on the merits. (4) It must not be merely cumulative, corroborative, or collateral. Opinion of BURKS, J., in Wynne v. Newman, 75 Va. 817; 4 Minor, Inst. pt. 1, pp. 758, 759, and cases cited; St. John's Ex'rs v. Alderson, 32 Grat. 140, 143. Judge BURKS says in Wynne v. Newman, supra: "Evidence newly discovered is said to be cumulative in its relation to the evidence on the trial when it is of the same kind and character;" citing Chief Justice SAVAGE as saying in People v. Superior Court, 10 Wend. 285, 294: "According to my understanding of cumulative evidence it means additional evidence to support the same point, which is of the same character with evidence already produced." The evidence introduced to sustain the bill of review was cumulative

only, a large number of witnesses had testified to the same thing on the former trial. At both trials it was stated by witnesses for Harvey Reynolds that C. B. Reynolds had in his life-time said these things; but during his life-time, and after he had assigned some of these bonds, neither to him nor to his assignee would Harvey Reynolds assert any such thing; but, although pressed hard for this money, he never hinted at such a defense, but wrote many letters, admitting his liability, and begging for time. Yet he did not then know, or, if he knew, he did not then state, any such defense, although the other half of the Guerrant land had been surveyed and sold to others under his eyes, and had amounted to a good many acres more than he had gotten by his actual survey and deed. And even when he was urging his offsets and payments, and having them allowed to him, he did not claim this, nor make any hint of any such deficiency. I think the ase was decided rightly by the circuit court on both trials, and by this court on the first hearing here, six years ago, and that the decision at this hearing cannot be sustained upon any sound principle. I therefore dissent from the opinion of the majority.

CLARK v. CROUT et al.

(Supreme Court of South Carolina. Sept. 14, 1891.)

RES JUDICATA—ACTION BY NEXT FRIEND—COMPROMISE — ESTOPPEL — LACHES — INVESTMENT IN CONFEDERATE BONDS — PLEA OF PLENE ADMINISTRAVIT PRÆTER.

1. An agreement in compromise of an action brought by the next friend of a lunatic against his committee for an accounting of the trust-estate, which was not submitted to and approved by the court, is not a bar to an action by the administrator of the lunatic against the administrator of the committee involving the same matter.

2. The next friend, being one of the heirs of the lunatic, should have been made a party to the action, since the amount of the recovery would be affected by the construction of the agreement as an estoppel against him.

3. Laches will not be attributed to the heirs of the lunatic for failure to bring an action to prevent waste during his life, where it appears that his administrator brought suit for an accounting against the committee shortly after the lunatic's death.

4. Where the committee received the trust fund in gold or its equivalent in 1857, and retained it in his possession, he thereby became a debtor of the estate, and could not allege, in defense to an action for accounting, that a portion of it was lost by an investment in Confederate bonds in 1864, although at that time such bonds were current in the community.

5. Where it appeared that the trust fund was not exhausted, a counter-claim for the lunatic's support was properly disallowed.

6. Where the evidence was conflicting as to the value of the maintenance of the lunatic, a conclusion concurred in by both referee and circuit judge will not be disturbed on appeal.

7. It is error to disregard a plea of plene administravit præter in an action against an administrator, since any recovery would be subject to such plea, if sustained.

Appeal from common pleas circuit court of Lexington county; WITHERSPOON, Judge.

Action for accounting by H. A. Clark,

administrator of Charles Banks, against M. A. Crout and Alice Assman, administratrices of Uriah Crout. Decree for plaintiff, and defendants appeal. Modified and affirmed.

A reference was ordered, and the report of the referee was as follows:

"This is an action instituted on the —— day of ——, 188N, by B. F. Banks and H. A. Clark, as administrators of the estate of Charles Banks, deceased, against M. A. Crout and Alice E. Assman, administratrices of the estate of Uriah Crout, deceased, for an account of the administration by defendants' testator, the duly-appointed committee of the lunatic's estate of plaintiffs' intestate, from the 1st day of February, 1856, until the death of Uriah Crout, alleging that such lunatic's estate consisted of two thousand nine hundred and twenty-six sixty-four one hundredth dollars, received by said committee on or about January 1, 1857, and that the labor performed by said lunatic for his committee, and his services rendered, were reasonably worth the further sum of two hundred dollars a year. The complaint also called in question the reasonableness of the charges made by the committee for the support and maintenance of the lunatic, and demanded an accounting. The answer of the defendants admit the receipt of money as charged in the complaint, but deny that any services rendered by Charles Banks to Uriah Crout were of pecuniary value, or that the credits claimed by the committee for the support of the lunatic were unreasonable. The defendants also alleged as affirmative defenses, (1) that a large part of the corpus of the lunatic's estate had perished in the form of Confederate bonds, into which Confederate money of the lunatic, properly in the hands of his committee, had been converted; (2) that the remaining part of such corpus had been necessarily expended for the lunatic's support during the war and immediately thereafter, under the sanction of the court of equity; (3) that all matters here brought into controversy had been compromised and settled under an agreement entered into in 1870 between Charles Banks, by his next friend, and Uriah Crout, in a cause then pending between them in the court of equity; (4) that defendants had fully administered, with the exception of one asset, their testator's estate, without any notice of plaintiffs' claim; and defendants asserted as a counter-claim a demand for the lunatic's support from 1864 to the date of his death, and for burial expenses." Plaintiffs' reply denied this counter-claim. After the adjournment of the first reference, and before the date of the second, B. F. Banks, one of the plaintiffs, died. The fact being brought to the attention of the referee, he noted it on the record, and thereafter the cause proceeded in the name of H. A. Clark, as sole surviving administrator of Charles Banks. To the issues, briefly outlined above, the evidence was directed, and from that evidence I find the facts to be as follows:

"Charles Banks, the son of Amos Banks, was a person of very weak understanding, of unsound mind, or, in popular language, an idiot, from his birth until his death.

When Charles was about twenty-five years of age, (in 1844,) his father being dead, and he entitled to an estate of inheritance from his father and grandmother, his brother-in-law, Uriah Inabinet, filed a petition in the court of equity for Edgefield district praying to be appointed committee of Charles' estate. By proceedings duly taken under this petition, Charles Banks was judicially declared to be an idiot, and his person and estate were committed to the custody and charge of Uriah Inabinet. In 1855, Inabinet died intestate, and letters of administration on his estate were granted to Levi Shealy on November 16th of that year. Under petition of Uriah Crout to be appointed committee of the person and estate of Charles Banks in the place of Uriah Inabinet, deceased, Uriah Crout was so appointed by Chancellor F. H. WARDLAW on February 1, 1856, such appointment to take effect upon his executing a bond in the penal sum of eight thousand dollars conditioned for the faithful discharge of his trust. This bond was executed on April 22, 1856. By an order of Chancellor WARDLAW of June 27, 1856, passed upon the ex parte petition of Uriah Crout, committee, all papers relating to the appointment of Crout, as committee, were transferred to the county of Lexington, and all returns by this committee were ordered to be made to the commissioner in equity for Lexington county. In both of these proceedings, instituted by Uriah Crout, he was represented by Messrs. Carroll & Bacon, attorneys at law. In 1856, Charles Banks was taken to the home of Uriah Crout, in Lexington county. Charles was then about thirty-seven years of age, of large frame and good physique, but afflicted with a sore right leg, which incapacitated him for such work as is ordinarily done about a farm and around a farm-house. And, moreover, his mental unsoundness was such that no work at his hands could be counted on or relied on, and therefore no services rendered by him were of any pecuniary value to Uriah Crout, or to the family, or to anybody else. The evidence shows that he did little jobs of work about the stock-yard and farm, but he did only what it pleased him to do and when it suited him. It was not required of him by Uriah Crout or the members of Mr. Crout's family; it was not enforced by Mr. Crout or anybody else. Charles probably had a melon patch in which at times he essayed to plow and hoe and in which he gathered. He was sometimes in the fields where the hands were at work, and as it pleased him, and for such length of time as it amused him, he would do the work assigned to the negroes for their day's task. When it suited him, he cut wood, carried it into the house, made fires, picked cotton, rode to the beef club and beef market for the family meat, fed and watered the stock, drove cattle to pasture and back, went to mill, brought fish home from the neighboring ponds and creeks, and when it did not please him to do so he did not do it. What he thus did had often to be done over again, and often not, but it was fitful, irregular, unreliable, 'done more for the occupation of his mind than anything else,' and of no value to any one. It was purely voluntary on his part, not enforced. What he did might sometimes have otherwise required other hands to do, but the other hands were there to do it, kept by their master or hired by their employer for the purpose; and sometimes extra work was required to undo and do over what Charles had wrongly done. Comparing the testimony of the several witnesses, it is manifest that the life of this poor afflicted man was of no possible pecuniary value to Uriah Crout or to his family, and that he did as he pleased, and very frequently, if asked to render assistance in any way, he complied only for a compensation,—a nickle, a dime, or a piece of tobacco. In this connection, it is proper that this report should make some response to the mass of testimony bearing upon the treatment of Charles Banks in the house of his committee. Uriah Crout took Charles to his house at Holley's creek in 1856; then with him to the Edmunds place, in 1857 or '58; and then to Leesville in 1879; and Charles remained an inmate of his committee's house, and a member of his committee's family, from 1856 until the death of Uriah Crout, on January 1, 1886. During all this time Uriah Crout and his first wife, Sophy, treated their unfortunate charge with all the consideration that could have been shown to one of their own children, similarly afflicted, and they required their own children to do likewise. Charles was ordinarily of good temper and good behavior, so much so as to gain the affection of those with whom he was thrown, notwithstanding the many circumstances of frequent occurrence which tended to make him a repulsive object. But he was not always amiable. His temper, ordinarily placid, was unrestrained by a sound mind, and so became at times disagreeable and violent, even to the extent, on one or two occasions, of rendering him dangerous. When thus yielding to his animal instincts he was hard to control, and offensive,—a sore trial to those who were about him. He was at all times self-willed and wayward; to cross him was to irritate him. His clothing was such as it was proper for him to have. If occasionally clad insufficiently, it was the result of his own waywardness; if sometimes filthy, it was not the fault of the Crout family. His lodgings were in no sense inferior to that of the committee's own children. No difference was made between him and them, and when put into a room, specially built for him, it was a necessity caused by the mental and physical condition of the poor idiot. What the Crout family ate, he ate. He sat at the same table when he would, was fed from the same dishes, helped by the same hand, and had as much as any one else in that household, his plate being sometimes the first supplied,—the difference, if any, between him and the children of Mr. Crout being in his favor. His appetite not being regulated by any judgment on his part, and not always under the observation or control of the older members of the family, his habits were sometimes disgustingly filthy. To remedy this evil, attention was given, such as babies require at the hands of their nurses; and the testimony shows that often Mrs. Sophy Crout and others performed for him the most menial and disgusting offices. For the same reason his washing bill was large, and his supply of clothing greater than would have been otherwise necessary. Charles Banks was also afflicted physically. On his right leg was a running sore, sometimes worse and sometimes better, but never healed. This sore caused his leg and foot to swell, affected his gait, and weakened his muscles. It had to be nursed and tended, washed and dressed, and all this was done. Its offensiveness to the smell was so great as to be often apparent to mere visitors at the house and to passers-by on the road-side. The maintenance and support of Chas. Banks required food, lodging, fuel, washing, clothing, medicine, doctors' attention, and other incidentals. These were all paid for by Uriah Crout during his life-time and out of his estate after his death. It thus appears, and I so find, that Chas. Banks received at the hands of Uriah Crout and his two wives, and his children, the most considerate, kind, and humane treatment, far beyond the requirements of mere duty. To Mrs. Sophy Crout, particularly, was this poor imbecile indebted for many an act of attention and care which must have roused, even in his weak mind, if he was capable of entertaining any mental emotions, a feeling of profound gratitude.

"On January 1, 1857, Uriah Crout, as committee, received from Levi Shealy, administrator of the estate of Uriah Inabinet, former committee, the sum of two thousand nine hundred and twenty-six sixty-four one-hundredth dollars belonging to Charles Banks. What was done with the money does not appear. There was some testimony on the part of the plaintiff looking to a charge that Uriah Crout had used a large part of this money in purchasing a tract of land from Dr. Edmunds, but such was not the fact, as is conclusively shown by the testimony of Dr. Edmunds, from whom this tract of land was purchased. Mr. Crout paid Dr. Edmunds for this land in October, 1856, partly in paper of Dr. Edmunds bought up for the purpose, and the balance in cash, three months before any money of the lunatic's estate was received by Mr. Crout. Uriah Crout was a man of large means and of the highest integrity of character. There is no testimony to show that Crout used this money for his own purposes. But whether he invested it, and, if so, how he invested it, and, if lent out, to whom it was lent and when, and for what time, does not appear. All this was many years ago, and the evidence is, perhaps, not now to be had. At any rate, no evidence has been produced. We must necessarily be governed by his returns made under the requirements of the law, and it may be that he has suffered in failing to show what was done with this estate. Regular returns were made by Uriah Crout down to the year 1868, inclusive. Of these returns, those for the years 1857 and 1858, have been lost through the casualties of war. Turning to the returns for 1859, filed January 12, 1860, we find that the committee charges himself with a principal sum of only $2,575.95, which is $350.69 less than the sum received on January 1, 1857. How this amount out of the *corpus* was consumed does not appear with certainty, but, under the circumstances, the right to charge commissions, the probability of a counsel fee having been paid to Messrs. Carroll & Bacon, the returns having been made to the proper office and since lost, and the commissioner in equity having approved the returns of 1859, I find as a fact that this amount of $350.69 was expended for such items as were properly chargeable to the *corpus* of the estate, and that on January 1, 1859, the true *corpus* was $2,575.95, together with interest, $51.72, up to that date. The committee expended for his *cestui que trust* the following sums: $150.47 in 1859, $178.28 in 1860, $177.79 in 1861, $245.89 in 1862, $467 in 1863, $778.28 in 1864, $287.96 in 1865, $171.25 in 1866, $132.40 in 1867,—all of which expenditures were reasonable and necessary to the proper support and maintenance of the idiot. But the expenditures of 1863 and 1864, and $130.50 of the expenditures of 1865, had relation to Confederate money, which amounts in excess of the interest received, when scaled according to Corbin's bill, were equivalent to $231.66 for 1863, $266.32 for 1864, and $162.62 for 1865. The credits claimed in the returns of 1863 and 1864 include $600 for board of the idiot at the house of his committee. For the years 1868 to 1857, both inclusive, we have no testimony as to what was actually expended, and the witnesses differ in their estimates. But, from the preponderance of the evidence based upon estimates, $195 a year for the idiot's support during the years 1868 to 1897, both inclusive, was reasonable. This is slightly in excess of the annual income on the then reduced *corpus*, and is about $33 a year in excess of the average for the five years of 1859, 1860, 1861, 1866, and 1867, and nearly $17 in excess of the largest expenditures of any year in which Confederate prices did not prevail. There is no testimony to the point that living was higher after 1867 than before the war, or during the years 1866 and 1867, or of additional expenditures then. Under these circumstances, the committee should not be allowed credit for more than the annual income, this credit to include all expenditures and charges. I further find that Confederate money was the only currency in this state from January 1, 1862, to May 1, 1865; that it was freely taken and freely paid by all; that officers of the court received it with the sanction of the court; that it was regarded in the community as unpatriotic to refuse it; that prior to 1864 it was received by everybody, with very few exceptions; that Confederate money in hand in 1864 was enormously taxed if not funded; that Confederate bonds were generally regarded as government securities, and a desirable investment. Uriah Crout made provision in his will for the support of Charles Banks. Charles Banks died January 1, 1868, and his burial expenses amounted to $60. On the *ex parte* petition of Uriah Crout, an order was passed by Chancellor CARROLL on June 27, 1864,

permitting said Crout to charge $300 a year for the board of Charles Banks during the years 1863 and 1864, this sum and necessary expenditures to be deducted from the *corpus* after exhausting the interest account. On July 1, 1864, Charles Banks, by his next friend, George L. Banks, (his brother,) filed his bill in equity, calling Uriah Crout to account for his administration of the trust-estate. Uriah Crout answered, claiming that by investment of $1,500 of the idiot's money in Confederate bonds, (which were produced,) and by his large expenditures during the years 1862 to 1865, inclusive, the entire estate of the idiot had been exhausted. After testimony taken in that suit, a compromise was agreed upon between the solicitors and signed by George L. Banks and Uriah Crout, to the effect that the action should be discontinued, Uriah Crout to be discharged from all accountability for the lunatic's estate, and to support him for the remainder of his life. An order or decree approving this arrangement was prepared and consented to, but never presented to the judge for signature, probably, because the then judge of this circuit had been of counsel in the cause. Some of the family of Charles Banks knew of this suit. George L. Banks is a distributee of Charles' estate.

"Uriah Crout made an investment of $1,500 in Confederate bonds in 1864. It does not appear that Crout then had properly in hand $1,500 of the idiot's estate in Confederate money.

"From the facts as thus found, the following are my conclusions of law: (1) That Uriah Crout is chargeable with twenty-five hundred and seventy-five ninety-five one-hundredth dollars principal, and fifty-one seventy-two one-hundredth dollars interest, on January 1, 1859, properly reduced to twenty-four hundred and seventy-four forty-four one-hundredth dollars principal on January 1, 1865, with interest thereafter on said principal sum; but he is not chargeable with anything on account of the labor or services of his idiot charge. (2) That said committee is entitled to credit on his account for the several items mentioned in Exhibit V, herewith filed as a part of this report. (3) The proceeding entitled 'Ex parte Banks' is admissible in evidence in this case to the point that the committee was authorized to use a part of the principal of the trust-estate, and the decree in that proceeding authorizes an encroachment on the *corpus* of Charles Banks' estate so far as necessary. (4) That the cause entitled 'Charles Banks, by next friend, George L. Banks, against Uriah Crout,' does not operate as an estoppel by record or *in pais* upon the plaintiff in this action. (5) That the answer of Uriah Crout in said last-mentioned cause is not evidence in this case against the plaintiff here of any matters of fact alleged in said answer. (6) That the effect of the agreement between George L. Banks and Uriah Crout upon the rights of George L. Banks cannot be determined in this action. (7) That the administrators of Charles Banks are not chargeable with laches in instituting this action, nor are the distributees of his eslate chargeable with laches in failing at an earlier day to come into court as next friend of Charles Banks, and in his name demand an accounting from Uriah Crout of an estate in which they or their children would some day probably acquire an interest. (8) That there being no evidence that Confederate money belonging to the estate of Charles Banks, beyond the annual collections of interest, was properly in the hands of Uriah Crout, either by having been collected for the necessity of the idiot or received from the outstanding securities which afterwards became worthless, and there being no evidence as to how the idiot's money was invested, it cannot be assumed that the securities called in were mere notes of hand, upon which the committee realized only par in Confederate money, and therefore the payment in 1863 in excess of the interest received should be scaled as of the value of Confederate money on July 1, 1863; the payment in 1864, in excess of the interest received, should be scaled as of the value of Confederate money on July 1, 1864; and the payments during the first four months of 1865, according to the average value of Confederate money during that period. (9) That for the same reason the investment of fifteen hundred dollars in Confederate States bonds in 1864 cannot be sustained. (10) That the plaintiff is entitled to judgment against the defendants as administratrices of Uriah Crout for two thousand eight hundred and forty-six seventy-five one-hundredth dollars, together with interest on two thousand four hundred and seventy-four forty-four one-hundredth dollars from May 1, 1890, until judgment entered, and for costs as per statement herewith filed as Exhibit Y to this report. (11) That the defendants are entitled to nothing on their counter-claim.

"I will briefly state the reasons which have induced the above conclusions of law, or such of them as were seriously contested in the arguments made before me: A lunatic or an idiot is incapable of conducting or directing a suit, and, if he sues at all, it must be by his next friend, upon whom the court will rely for assistance in the action, and to whom resource may be had for the payment of the costs. But, in such case the court itself will look to the interests of the idiot, and decree what is to his best advantage without regard to the next friend's consent. The right of a next friend to appear in court as the representative of a lunatic gives the next friend no authority to make contracts for the lunatic, or enter into compromises affecting his estate. Only the court of equity could do that. If the proposed consent decree in Banks v. Crout had been presented to the judges of the circuit court, it might have been signed or it might not. Not having been signed it comes before us with no assent of the lunatic, or of the court acting for him, and no individual was clothed with power to bind the lunatic. A fortiori, the answer of Uriah Crout, in that action, cannot be introduced as evidence against the personal representative of Charles Banks in this action, even as to the points upon which the allegations of the answer were strictly responsive to the

charges of the bill. It seems to me that George L. Banks should be excluded from recovering, directly or indirectly, from Uriah Crout any portion of the estate of Charles Banks, and, if George was a party to this action, I would have reported that defendants were entitled to receive credit for the share of George L. Banks in the net estate of Charles; but, as he is not a party, his rights cannot be concluded now. It was earnestly contended before me that this plaintiff and the distributees of Charles Banks' intestate estate are barred by laches from now presenting this demand. But in view of the fact that none of the distributees had any interest in Charles Banks' estate prior to January 1, 1888, and that this action was instituted within a few months thereafter, this defense cannot be sustained. The fact that any one of these distributees would have been permitted to act as next friend for Charles Banks, and in his name call upon Uriah Crout for an accounting and discovery of the trust-estate, did not so impose such a proceeding upon them as a duty as to subject them to the charges of laches for not having done it. In an accounting by a committee of his lunatic's estate, the burden is upon the committee to make a full disclosure. If his returns make such a disclosure, they will be evidence in his behalf, after the lapse of years and the losses of time. If he fails to make a full exhibit of his administration annually to the court of equity, the time may come when he will have to suffer for the want of evidence to prove the legal management of the trust. In this case, Mr. Crout was an upright, honest man, but, when he took possession of this money of Charles Banks, the then latest utterance of the highest court in South Carolina justified the belief that it was not improper for a trustee to use for his own purposes, and, under the securities of his own bond, the money of his *cestui que trust.* Sweet v. Sweet, Speer, Eq. 311. Mr. Crout's high character cannot, therefore, as matter of law, raise a presumption that he did not use Charley's money for his own purposes. Or, if it be conceded that this money was invested, there being not a tittle of testimony to show in what securities, the burden imposed by law upon the trustee cannot be relieved by mere inference that he invested it by lending it to his neighbors on well-secured notes. Why may it not have been invested in state bonds or stock, railroad mortgage bonds, or other securities? Pope v. Mathews, 18 S. C. 458. In the absence of all testimony—all showing by the committee in his returns—as to the *status* of the *corpus* of the idiot's estate, it cannot be assumed that the securities converted into the money, in 1863 and 1864, were not securities which felt the appreciation of values then prevailing as to all articles of commerce or exchange. To give committee credit for the full amount in good money of all his payments during those years would be to assume that he had previously invested the idiot's money, and that the securities in which he had so invested could be converted into currency only at their face value, an assumption not inconsistent with his returns or the testimony, but not supported by such evidence. It would be changing the burden of proof as fixed by the law. To the extent of the interest received, which must have been in Confederate money, I have given him full credit; only the balance has been scaled. As these payments cover the period of a year, without more specific date in most instances, I have taken the 1st day of July as the average date of them all. As to the Confederate investment. This question has surely perplexed the southern courts since the war. Even in our own state the decisions are not in accord. In Womack v. Austin, 1 S. C. 440, Moses, C. J., characterizes Confederate bonds as 'the issues not of a recognized government, but of one endeavoring to assert and maintain its independence by waging war against the United States.' This may be a correct *post bellum* view of the matter, but in 1864 they were regarded throughout the south, as the securities of an established government, which was sure to succeed in driving off a foreign invader then waging a war against her or on her own soil. When the case of Koon v. Munro, 11 S. C. 139, was brought before the court, a careful consideration was given to the question, and rules laid down which have since been adhered to. In the subsequent cases of Wilson v. Braddy, 16 S. C. 520; Hyatt v. McBurney, 18 S. C. 213; and Brabham v. Crosland, 25 S. C. 585, 1 S. E. Rep. 33,— the court have clearly and strongly declared the sound equitable principle that the conduct of trustees in accepting Confederate money in payment of *ante bellum* securities must be determined in the light of that time, and not in the light of subsequent events. Some of these conditions have been as strongly stated in those cases as they have been strongly stated in the testimony taken by me in this case; but there are some other facts, not stated in those cases, nor in this testimony, but matters of history, which, it seems to me, have been overlooked, or not given their due weight. Those facts are: (1) That our courts have always regarded government securities as the most approved fund for the investment of trust funds, so that the conversion of personal notes, secured by solvent securities, or mortgages of land, into government securities, would not be considered a breach of trust. (2) That Confederate bonds were the securities of a government then recognized by the legislature and courts of this state, and regarded by our people as established, and whose independence, it was confidently believed, would surely be acknowledged at some future day by the United States and all other nations of the earth. The mere suggestion of a doubt upon this point aroused a wave of indignation against a distinguished member of the Confederate congress from South Carolina, late in 1864. (3) That no one knew or could possibly foretell, even as late as 1864, whether the war would last one year, five years, or ten years longer. And yet it was in the light of these facts that trustees received Confederate money and invested in Confederate bonds. Nevertheless, the parties

to this cause are entitled to my judgment upon the law as it is. And my judgment is that, under the law of this state, a trustee will be sustained in an investment of trust money in Confederate bonds only where he rightfully had Confederate money in hand for investment, and that such money was rightfully in hand only where it was received in payment for a Confederate contract, in the collection of doubtful securities, or to meet the necessities of the trust-estate, or for the payment of such claims against the estate as could be liquidated with that currency. Finding no evidence to bring the receipt of Confederate money by Uriah Crout for Charles Banks' estate under these exceptions, I have been forced to find, as matter of law, that the interest receipts of Uriah Crout in 1863 and 1864 were the only Confederate money rightfully in his hands as trustee, and that, therefore, his investment in Confederate bonds must be disallowed."

Exceptions being filed to the report, the court, after argument thereon, rendered the following decree:

"This is one of the many cases arising since the war involving the liability of trustees for investments during the war in Confederate bonds. Uriah Crout was duly appointed committee of Charles Banks, a lunatic, in 1856, and on the 1st of January, 1857, he received $2,926.64, as the *corpus* of the estate of Charles Banks. Uriah Crout died testate in January, 1886, and the defendants administered upon his estate *cum testamento annexo*. Charles Banks, the lunatic, died intestate in January, 1888. This action was instituted during the year 1888, by the plaintiffs, as administrators of Charles Banks, against the defendants, as administratrices of Uriah Crout, for an account by defendants of the estate of Charles Banks received by Uriah Crout as committee. The complaint questions the reasonableness of the charges made by the committee for the maintenance of Charles Banks. The plaintiffs further allege that Charles Banks performed services for his committee from the date of his appointment to the date of the death of the committee which were reasonably worth the sum of $200 per annum, for which amounts plaintiffs also demand judgment against the defendants. The defendants admit in their answer that their testator, Uriah Crout, received the amount alleged in the complaint as committee of Charles Banks, but they deny that Charles Banks rendered any service to said committee of pecuniary value, or that the credits claimed by the said committee for the maintenance of Charles Banks were unreasonable. Defendants further allege, as affirmative defense, (1) that a large part of the *corpus* of the lunatic's estate has perished in the form of Confederate bonds in the hands of Uriah Crout, the committee; (2) that the remaining portion of the estate of Charles Banks during the war, and immediately thereafter, was used under the direction of the court of equity; (3) that all matters brought into controversy in this action have been compromised and settled under agreement entered into July 11, 1870, between Charles Banks, by his next friend, George L. Banks, and Uriah Crout, as committee, in a cause filed July 1, 1869, and then pending in the court of equity for Lexington county; (4) that defendants have fully administered their testator's estate with the exception of one asset, amounting to $1,000, without any notice of plaintiffs' claim. By way of counter-claim, defendants set up a demand for the support of Charles Banks from the date of the committee's last return, in 1864, to the date of his death, in 1868, and for burial expenses. Plaintiffs, in reply, deny the defendants' counter-claim. It was referred to R. W. Shand, as referee, to take the testimony and to hear and determine all of the issues raised by the pleadings. B F. Banks, one of the plaintiffs, died after the first reference, and the action thereafter proceeded in the name of H. A. Clark, as surviving administrator. The referee finds, as matter of fact, that Charles Banks did not render services of any pecuniary value to Uriah Crout, committee, and there is no exception to said finding by the referee. The defendants claimed credit for $1,500 of Charles Banks' estate alleged to have been invested in 1864 by the committee in Confederate bonds. The referee reports that it does not appear that the committee then properly had $1,500 of Confederate money of the lunatic's estate in his hands, and concludes that the defendants are not entitled to credit for $1,-500 in the accounting. To this the defendants have excepted. It appears that upon the ex parte petition of Uriah Crout, on the 27th of June, 1864, the court passed an order permitting said Crout, as committee, to charge $300 per annum for the board of Charles Banks for the years 1863 and 1864, which, with other necessary expenditures, were to be deducted from the corpus of the trust-estate, after exhausting the interest account. The referee concludes that this proceeding is only admissible as evidence in this case to show the authority of the committee for applying a portion of the corpus of the estate to the maintenance of the lunatic. It appears that on July 1, 1869, Charles Banks, by his next friend, George L. Banks, (his brother,) filed a bill in the court of equity for Lexington district against Uriah Crout, committee, calling upon said committee to account for the administration of the estate of Charles Banks, in which suit the issues raised were substantially the same as those raised in this action. Uriah Crout, in his answer to said bill, alleged that the estate of Charles Banks had become exhausted by an investment of $1,-500 in Confederate funds, (which were produced,) and by expenditures on behalf of said Charles Banks from 1862 to 1865 inclusive. After the reference and the taking of testimony in said cause said suit was compromised and settled under an agreement signed by George L. Banks and Uriah Crout, to the effect that Uriah Crout would support Charles Banks during the remainder of his life, and that he (Uriah Crout) was therefore to be discharged from liability on account of his trust. An order or decree approving of said settlement was prepared and consented to, but was

never signed by the court, owing probably to the fact that the then judge of the fifth circuit (S. W. Melton) was of counsel for the plaintiffs in said cause. It further appears that, in pursuance of said agreement for the settlement of said suit, Uriah Crout up to his death maintained Charles Banks, and in his will provided for such maintenance thereafter during the life-time of Charles Banks. The referee concluded that the answer of Uriah Crout in said former action is not evidence against the plaintiff in this action, and that the former action does not operate as an estoppel by record or in pais upon the plaintiffs in this action. To this the defendants have excepted. The referee further concluded that the effect of the agreement between George L. Banks and Uriah Crout under the settlement of the former action, upon the rights of George L. Banks, as a distributee of Charles Banks, cannot be determined in this action. To this conclusion defendants have excepted. The referee further concludes that neither the administrator nor the distributees of Charles Banks are chargeable with laches. To this conclusion defendants have excepted. The referee applied the scale according to the Corbin bill to payments by the committee in excess of the interest received for the years 1863 and 1864, and during the first four months of 1865. To this defendants have excepted. From 1868 to 1887, inclusive, the referee allowed credit for the maintenance of Charles Banks at the rate of $195 per annum. To this defendants have excepted. The referee finds that defendants are not entitled to anything on their counter-claim. The referee finally concludes that the plaintiff is entitled to judgment against the defendants, as administratrices of Uriah Crout, for $2,846.70 with interest on $2,470.44 from May 1, 1890, and for costs as per statement filed with the report as Exhibit Y. To this conclusion defendants have excepted.

"The cause came on to be heard upon the referee's report and defendants' exceptions to said report. Before considering the defendants' exceptions, it is proper to refer briefly to the enviable reputation for integrity sustained by the committee up to his death, the nature of the unfortunate lunatic's afflictions, as well as to the exceptionally humane treatment of the lunatic by the deceased committee and the members of his family. From 1856 up to the close of the war, Uriah Crout, the deceased committee, was regarded as one of the wealthiest citizens of Lexington district, and up to his death, in 1886, he enjoyed a reputation for scrupulous honesty in all his business transactions. According to one of the witnesses, 'his honesty was his religion.' At the time that Uriah Crout was appointed the committee of Charles Banks (1856) he took the said Charles Banks to his home, and continued to maintain and care for this poor unfortunate lunatic, as a member of his family, up to the period of his (Crout's) death, in 1886. Uriah Crout also provided in his will for the comfortable maintenance of Charles Banks after his (Crout's) death. Charles Banks had been adjudged a lunatic, but in point of fact was more of an idiot, when taken charge of by Uriah Crout. He was about 37 years of age, of a large frame, and was afflicted with a sore leg. Having no reason to control his appetite, Charles Banks was, at times, disgustingly filthy in his habits. His helpless and offensive condition frequently demanded the most menial attention. These disagreeable services were rendered by Uriah Crout and his family from 1856 up to the death of Uriah Crout, in 1896. The referee finds that during all of this period, and under such trying circumstances, this unfortunate creature was treated with the most humane consideration by Uriah Crout and the members of his family. The evidence shows that Uriah Crout exhibited a tender consideration for the comfort of his unfortunate *cestui que trust*, far beyond that usually manifested by a committee who is not related to his *cestui que trust*. Some of the defendants' exceptions merely allege that the referee erred in ascertaining the balance reported to be due on the accounting, without indicating any specific error in said accounting. The specific errors alleged in the exceptions to the accounting are (1) the failure of the referee to allow credit for the $1,500 invested in 1864 by the committee in Confederate bonds; (2) the scaling of certain payments made by the committee in the years 1863 and 1864 and 1865; and (8) as to the amount of compensation allowed the committee by the referee for the maintenance of Charles Banks. Did the referee err in not allowing the deceased committee credit for $1,500 invested in 1864 in Confederate bonds? It appears that Uriah Crout, as committee, made annual returns to the commissioner in equity for Lexington district. In his return for 1864, filed February 10, 1865, is the following entry. 'Invested in 7 per cent. Confederate bonds, Nos. 17.515, 18,499,—$1,500.' It also appears that two Confederate bonds, one for $1,000 and the other for $500, were produced and the commissioner in equity signed on each of said bonds the following indorsement: 'Entered in return of Uriah Crout, committee of Charles Banks, in 1865.' It appears that the two confederate bonds, indorsed by the commissioner as aforesaid, were produced in the former suit of Charles Banks, by next friend, v. Uriah Crout, committee, filed July 1, 1869, as aforesaid, and were found in the record in the said suit. Under these facts and circumstances, and in consideration of the well-established reputation of Uriah Crout for integrity and uprightness in his business transactions, I am satisfied that Uriah Crout held in good faith the two Confederate bonds, as committee for Charles Banks. To hold otherwise would cast a reflection upon the memory of Uriah Crout that could not be justified under the facts and circumstances developed by the evidence in this case. But, as I understand the rule established in this state, relating to investments by trustees in Confederate bonds, it must not only appear that the trustee acted in good faith, but it must also appear that the money alleged to have been so invested was at the time of said investment act-

ually and 'rightfully' in the hands of the trustee. Koon v. Munro, 11 S. C. 140; Finch v. Finch, 28 S. C. 165.[1] The investment is set up in this case by way of affirmative defense, and the burden is upon the defendants to show the circumstances under which the trustee came into possession of the fund alleged to have been invested in 1864, to enable the court to determine whether the investment can be sustained under the established rule as above cited. The evidence fails to show that the deceased committee ever invested the *corpus* of Charles Banks' estate received January 1, 1857.

"It does not appear that the deceased committee 'rightfully' had any of the *corpus* in his hands in 1864. This defect in the evidence cannot be supplied by legal presumption in favor of the deceased trustee on account of lapse of time. It is probable that, if Uriah Crout was alive, he could furnish evidence that defendants cannot produce. The rigid application of the above rule, with reference to Confederate investments, to this case may appear harsh. But the rule was established for the guidance of this court, and as stated in Finch v. Finch, supra, must be regarded as the law, until reversed. Under the authority above cited, the referee in the accounting did not err in refusing to allow defendants credit for the $1,500 Confederate bonds. I do not think the referee erred in applying the Corbin bill to payments made by the committee in 1863 and 1864, and during the first four months of 1865. In addition to the reason given by the referee on this point, it appears that the *ex parte* petition of the committee in 1863, for leave of court to encroach upon the *corpus* of the estate, is based upon the 'high prices then prevailing.' The $300 per annum that the court allowed for the board of Charles Banks for the period to which the Corbin bill was applied, as well as the prices paid for the articles furnished by the committee during that period, show that the prices charged had reference to Confederate money. The charges by the committee in his returns, for the support of Charles Banks up to the 1st of January, 1868, were regarded by the committee as sufficient, and were approved by the commissioner in equity. No charges were made for the support of Charles Banks subsequent to the 1st of January, 1868, and up to 1st of January, 1888, (when Charles Banks died,) as he was then being maintained by Uriah Crout, under the agreement for the settlement of the former suit instituted July 1, 1869. The evidence is conflicting as to what would be a proper compensation for the maintenance of Charles Banks from January 1, 1868, to January 1, 1888. The referee found from the preponderance of the evidence that $195 a year would be a reasonable compensation to be allowed for the maintenance of Charles Banks from 1868 to 1887, both inclusive. It was argued that, in view of the facts and circumstances connected with the case, the court should allow more liberally for the maintenance of the *non compos* than

---

[1] 5 S. E. Rep. 848.

the charges made by the committee or the amount allowed by the referee, even to the extent of encroaching upon the *corpus* of the estate of the *non compos*. It seems to me that the defendants are concluded by the committee's own estimate as to what was a reasonable compensation, and I do not think that the referee's finding upon conflicting evidence, as to the period between 1868 and 1887, inclusive, should be disturbed. Defendants' other exceptions cannot, in my opinion, be sustained. It is therefore ordered, adjudged, and decreed that the defendants' exceptions to the referee's report in the above-entitled case be overruled, and the report of the referee be confirmed and made the judgment of this court, except in so far as the said report provides for the payment of the costs of this action. In equity, the payment of costs is in the discretion of the court. The complaint in this action not only seeks an accounting for the estate received by the deceased committee, but also seeks an accounting for services alleged to have been rendered the deceased committee by Charles Banks for nearly 30 years, at the rate of $200 per annum. The referee finds and the evidence shows that the deceased committee is not chargeable for any services rendered by Charles Banks. A considerable proportion of the testimony was introduced, and much of the cost of this action has been incurred, upon the issues raised by plaintiff as to compensation for the services of the *non compos*, which issue has been decided in defendants' favor. Under these circumstances, it would not be just to charge the defendants with the payment of all the cost of this action. It is ordered and adjudged that plaintiff do pay one-half of the cost of this action, to be taxed by the clerk, and the defendants pay the other half of said cost, and to this extent the referee's report is hereby modified. In all other respects the referee's report is confirmed."

Meetse & Mullee and *Melton & Melton*, for appellants. *Sheppard Bros.*, for respondent.

McIver, J. This was an action brought by the plaintiff, as administrator of Charles Banks, a deceased lunatic, against the defendants, as administratrices of Uriah Crout, the duly-appointed committee of said lunatic, for an account of the administration of the estate of the lunatic, as well as for his services. The facts of the case are so fully and clearly stated in the report of the referee, which, together with the decree of the circuit judge, should be incorporated in the report of the case, as to render it unnecessary to make any further statement. We will therefore proceed at once to the consideration of the several questions presented by this appeal, stating only such facts as are necessary to a proper understanding of such questions.

It is conceded that Uriah Crout, after having qualified as committee on or about the 1st of January, 1857, received from the estate of the former committee the sum of $2,926.64 for the lunatic, and this appeal concerns only the administration of that fund. The defendants by their answer set up several defenses: (1) That a large portion of the fund was properly invested in Confederate bonds in 1864, which, of course, became worthless at the close of the war between the states, and that the balance of it was exhausted in the proper maintenance and support of the lunatic. (2) That all the matters here brought into controversy had been compromised and settled by an agreement entered into in 1870, between Charles Banks, by his next friend, George L. Banks, and Uriah Crout, in an action then pending in the court of equity between them. (3) That the defendants had fully administered the estate of Uriah Crout before notice of the claim set up herein, except one bond held by them due to said estate for about the sum of $1,000. The defendants also set up, as a counter-claim, a demand for the maintenance and support of the lunatic after his funds were exhausted up to the time of his death, and for burial expenses. The referee disallowed the investment in Confederate bonds, overruled the defense resting on the compromise of the former suit, and after stating the account, as set forth in Exhibit Y to his report, recommended that the plaintiff have judgment against the defendants as administratrices of Uriah Crout for the balance therein shown, and for the costs of this case; but it does not appear that any notice was taken of defendants' plea of *plene administravit præter*. To this report defendants filed numerous exceptions, and the case was heard by his honor, Judge Witherspoon, who rendered judgment overruling all of the exceptions, and confirming the report except as to costs, which he adjudged should be paid, one-half by the plaintiff, and the other half by the defendants. From this judgment defendants appeal upon the several grounds set out in the record, which, as stated in appellants' argument, present the following matters for the consideration of this court: "(1) The effect of the former suit and the agreement therein upon this action, and upon the heirs of Charles Banks, especially George L. Banks, the next friend, and his heirs. (2) The laches of Charles Banks and of other parties now interested in this action. (3) The validity of the investment in Confederate bonds; and herein the competency, as evidence in this action, of the answer of the committee in the former suit, touching this subject. (4) The statement of the account; and herein of Exhibit Y to referee's report, the scaling of the expenditures during the war, and the value of the maintenance of the *non compos* since the war. (5) The counter-claim. (6) The plea of *plene administravit præter*."

First, then, as to whether the former suit, and the compromise thereof, can operate as a bar to this action. It seems that on the 1st of July, 1869, Charles Banks, by his next friend, George L. Banks, who was his brother, filed a bill in the court of equity against Uriah Crout, as committee, calling on him to account for his administration of the funds belonging to the estate of the lunatic. After the pleadings in that case (copies of which are embraced in the "case" as prepared for argument here) were made up, and after some testimony had been taken therein, an agreement was made for the compromise of that suit, whereby the same was to be discontinued, and Uriah Crout on his part agreed to supply the lunatic, for and during his natural life, with good and comfortable clothing and wholesome food, and such necessary care and attention as his situation required; whereupon the said Uriah was to be discharged from any further liability on account of the funds received by him on account of the lunatic. The terms of this agreement were reduced to writing, and signed by George L. Banks and Uriah Crout in July and August, 1870, and an order was prepared, to be submitted to the court, confirming such agreement, to which was appended the written consent of the complainant's solicitor; but the order was never signed, never having been presented to the court, probably because the judge of the circuit had been of counsel in the cause. The lunatic himself being incapable of contracting, neither he nor his distributees can be affected by such agreement, unless it could be shown that his next friend had authority to contract for him. We are not aware of any authority which recognizes the power of one who has assumed the office of next friend of a lunatic to enter into any contract or agreement binding upon the lunatic. He may institute suit for the benefit of the lunatic, but the court before which suit is pending is charged with the protection of the interests of the lunatic, and it alone could authorise any compromise of his legal rights; and this the court would never sanction unless, after full inquiry, it was satisfied that such a course was best for the interests of the lunatic. This view was manifestly recognized by the parties to the former suit, as well as their counsel, for they prepared and agreed upon an order sanctioning the compromise, but, unfortunately for the defendants in this action, such order never was signed. Whether it would or would not have been signed by the court we cannot now know with any degree of certainty, as all the testimony in that case is not before us. But from what is before us we think the action of the court would have depended largely, if not entirely, upon the view which it might take of the Confederate transactions of the committee; especially of the propriety of the investment of a large portion of the lunatic's estate in Confederate bonds. Our remark made above, that neither the lunatic nor his distributees can be affected by such agreement, is not to be understood as prejudging the question whether George L. Banks, or rather his representatives, he having died since the commencement of this action, is estopped, by his being a party to said agreement, from sharing in any recovery that may be had against the defendants, or even as indicating any opinion whatever as to that question. Until his representatives are made parties, that question cannot properly be considered; and, as we think that question should be determined in this action, provision should

be made to bring them in as parties. For if it should eventually be determined that George L. Banks, by signing that agreement, is estopped from making any claim against the estate of the committee, then, clearly, whatever would otherwise be his share of the recovery should first be deducted from any amount that may be established in this action before any judgment is rendered against the defendants herein. It is stated in the "case" that this point was made in the court below, but, so far as we can discover, it was not distinctly passed upon, and the failure to do so is made one of the grounds of exception to the circuit decree. It seems to us, therefore, that the decree should be modified in this respect, and that the pleadings should be so amended as to bring before the court the parties necessary to a proper determination of this question. It is contended, however, that, Uriah Crout having performed his part of the agreement by providing for the comfortable support of the lunatic during his life, his estate has a right to claim, in equity and good conscience, that the entire agreement shall now be carried out by a discharge of the estate of the committee from any further liability. But it will be observed that, until it is made to appear that such support was provided for out of the committee's own funds, which involves the question whether the lunatic's estate had been exhausted, Uriah Crout was doing no more than what his duty as committee required of him; and, as we shall presently see, the lunatic's estate had not been exhausted, this ground cannot, for this reason, be sustained.

As to the defense of laches, we agree with the referee and the circuit judge. To say nothing of the fact that this defense is not set up in the answer, we see nothing in the case to sustain it. Charles Banks died in January, 1888, and this action was commenced within a few months thereafter, and certainly there was no unreasonable delay in instituting this action. It is true that the parties who might ultimately be entitled to an interest in the lunatic's estate might possibly have instituted an action against Uriah Crout to save the estate of the lunatic from waste or destruction, or to enforce its application to the support of the lunatic, as required by the terms of the trust which Crout had assumed; but this could only have been done under proper allegations and proofs. So far as we can see, there were no grounds upon which such allegations could have been made. The testimony shows that Crout continued to discharge his duties faithfully up to the time of his own death, and made provision in his will for the support of the lunatic as long as he might live, which seems to have been faithfully carried out. There is no testimony that the security given by him had become impaired by the sureties on his bond becoming insolvent, and his own estate seems to have been sufficient to enable him to meet any balance that might remain of the trust fund, after the trust terminated by the death of the lunatic. There was nothing to call for the bringing of such an action as is suggested, except the fact that Crout claimed by his returns to have invested $1,500 of the trust fund in Confederate bonds in 1864, and this we do not regard as sufficient to require that an action should have been brought within a reasonable time thereafter, by parties who might or might not be ultimately interested in whatever balance of the lunatic's estate might remain after his death, at the peril of being charged with laches, when they brought their action, after their rights had become vested. But, in addition to this, the referee finds as matter of fact that Crout continued to make regular returns down to and including the year 1868, copies of which are set out in the "case," from which it appears that he claimed a balance due him in the return for 1865; nor can the fact that an agreement of compromise herein before referred to had been entered into between George L. Banks and Uriah Crout, in 1870, have any effect; for this, if known to the parties ultimately interested, would be accompanied with the knowledge that such agreement had never been sanctioned by the court, and was therefore not binding.

Next, as to the validity of the investment in Confederate bonds, and, as preliminary or incidental thereto, the question as to the competency of the answer of Crout in the former case as evidence in this case. While we agree with the view taken of this question by the referee and the circuit judge, yet we regard it as scarcely a practical question in this case; for it seems to us that all the evidence furnished by the answer, so far as this investment is concerned, is contained in the returns of Crout, which were received without objection. Recurring, then, to the main question, we do not think this investment can be approved. Crout received the money of his ward on or about the 1st of January, 1857, and, in the absence of any testimony whatever tending to show that he ever invested it in any way prior to 1864, we are bound to conclude that he retained it in his own hands. This, though a technical breach of trust, as it is termed by WARDLAW, C., in his circuit decree in Spear v. Spear, 9 Rich. Eq., at page 188, did not necessarily involve any moral delinquency whatever. Indeed, under the then latest utterance of the highest judicial tribunal in this state, in the case of Sweet v. Sweet, Speer, Eq. 309, such a course was not only approved, but rather recommended. It is true that the reasoning of that case was disapproved in the subsequent case of Spear v. Spear, supra, which, however, was not heard until January, 1857, but when decided does not appear, as it was not customary at that time to give the dates of the filing of opinions. It does appear, however, that the volume containing the last-mentioned case was not published until 1858. It is very obvious, therefore, that Crout could not possibly have been influenced by what was said in the last case, in the disposition of the money when he received it. At all events, the undisputed facts remain that he received the money in January, 1857, and he never claimed to have invested it in any way until 1864,

Even in his answer to the former case, he makes no such claim. In the face of the fact that there is no evidence whatever that Crout had ever made any other investment, and in view of the further fact that although he made regular returns he never even claimed that he had made any investment of his ward's funds until 1864, and that he entered the investment now in question upon his next return, we do not see how it is possible to doubt that the trust fund had been retained in his own hands up to that time. This being so, when Crout received the trust fund in January, 1857, he became a debtor to the estate of the lunatic, and continued to be so until such debt was properly discharged. The practical question, therefore, is whether a trustee, becoming indebted to the trust-estate, in gold or its equivalent, in 1857, could properly discharge such indebtedness, by paying the amount thereof to himself in 1864, in a depreciated currency. To the question thus stated there can be but one answer. Confederate treasury notes, though used as money, never really acquired a legal character as such. Such a debt, therefore, could not legally be discharged with Confederate treasury notes, except by the creditor consenting to receive them as money, when, upon the principle that anything received by the creditor as payment shall operate as such, the debt might be thus discharged. But this principle cannot be applied to the present case, for the committee occupied the position of both debtor and creditor, and, as the principle really rests upon the agreement to receive such depreciated currency as payment, it could not apply in a case where no such agreement was possible, for the reason that the two parties necessary to make an agreement were wanting,—the committee could not, as debtor, make such agreement with himself as creditor. While, therefore, we can very readily understand how a trustee might be justified, under proper circumstances, in receiving from another Confederate treasury notes in payment of a debt due to the trust-estate, even when contracted on a gold basis, we do not see how he could be justified in receiving from himself payment of such a debt in that kind of currency, further than what was necessary for the immediate exigencies of the trust-estate. While, therefore, the committee may be justified in receiving, even from himself, so much as was necessary for the comfortable support of the lunatic, in Confederate currency, from the necessity of the case, inasmuch as the evidence shows, and the referee so finds, that such currency was the only one in use in this state from 1st January, 1862, to 1st of May, 1865; yet there was no such necessity to justify the receipt of anything more. We agree, therefore, with the referee and circuit judge that the alleged investment in Confederate bonds cannot be sustained.

The fourth matter presented by the counsel in behalf of appellants for the consideration of this court involves three inquiries: (1) As to the correctness of the figures in the account as stated by the referee, and the alleged omission to allow commisions on the expenditures for 1863, and on the interest which accrued to date of report. (2) As to scaling the expenditures during the war. (3) As to the value of the maintenance of the lunatic since the war. As to the first, we find it difficult to ascertain with certainty whether there is any error in the figures or in the omission of credit for commissions, owing to the condensed form in which the account is stated, and, as the case will be recommitted to the referee for another purpose, the parties will be allowed to show, if they can, any errors in the figures or any omissions of credit for commissions. As to the second inquiry, it seems that the referee only scaled the excess of the disbursements in 1863, 1864, and the first four months of the year 1865, over and above the interest for those periods, and in this we do not see that there was any error. These disbursements were made in Confederate currency, and the prices paid for articles furnished the lunatic, as shown by the returns of the committee, are quite sufficient to justify the course which the referee pursued. The third inquiry presents only a question of fact, upon which there was conflicting testimony, and, under the well-settled rule, the conclusion adopted by the referee, and concurred in by the circuit judge, cannot be disturbed. As to the counter-claim, it follows necessarily, from what has been said, that there was no error in disallowing it, except so far as the burial expenses are concerned, and they are more properly allowed by the referee as a credit on the account as stated by him.

The only remaining inquiry is as to the plea of *plene administravit præter.* So far as we can discover, this matter has not been distinctly passed upon either by the referee or the circuit judge. In this we think there was error; for, if the defendants can sustain this plea, any judgment which may be rendered against them should be subject to such plea. It seems to us, therefore, that the case should be recommitted to the referee for the purpose of having the issues raised by that plea passed upon. The judgment of this court is that the judgment of the circuit court, except as modified herein, be affirmed, and that the case be remanded to that court for the purpose of such further proceedings as may be necessary to carry out the views herein announced.

McGOWAN, J. I concur.

EBAUGH v. MULLINAX.

(*Supreme Court of South Carolina. Sept. 19, 1891.*)

TAXATION — SALE OF LAND FOR NON-PAYMENT— PREREQUISITES — EXECUTION AGAINST PERSONALTY.

Act S. C. 1890, (17 St. 880, §§ 9, 10,) providing that, when the "taxes charged against any property" shall not be paid on a certain day, the county treasurer shall collect the same by distress or otherwise, and that, if such taxes shall not be paid or collected on a certain other day, "then the same shall be treated as delinquent taxes on such real and personal property," and shall be collected by sale of such property as hereinafter prescribed; and providing that "all

personal property subject to taxation shall be liable to distress for the payment of taxes hereunder;" and that, after any taxes become due, the county treasurer may distrain sufficient personal property to pay the same,—requires the issuance of an execution against the personal property of a defaulting tax-payer, and a return of *nulla bona,* as an essential prerequisite to the sale of land.

Appeal from common pleas circuit court of Berkeley county; WALLACE, Judge.

Trespass by D. C. Ebaugh against A. J. Mullinax. There was judgment for defendant, and plaintiff appeals. Reversed.

Robert J. Kirk, for appellant. *L. Moultrie Mordecai* and *Burke* for respondent.

McIVER, J The plaintiff brought this action against the defendant to recover damages for certain trespasses alleged to have been committed by him on a tract of land claimed by the plaintiff. The defendant, in addition to a general denial, set up title in himself to said land, acquired at a tax-sale made on 6th February, 1882. At the trial it was admitted that plaintiff had title up to the time of the tax-sale, and it was "proved that every step required to be taken by the various acts of the general assembly of the state for the proper carrying out of delinquent land sales was, in this instance, strictly complied with, the only exception thereto claimed by the plaintiff being that there was no issuance of the tax execution, nor a return of *nulla bona* thereon,—the defendant claiming that neither was necessary, and that, even if it were, the testimony showed that the same had been practically complied with." The foregoing extract from the "case" is followed by the testimony relied on to show that the alleged requirement in reference to the issuing and return of the execution had been practically complied with. But as the circuit judge held, and so instructed the jury, that the issuing of an execution was not necessary to the validity of the title set up by defendant, he made no ruling, and submitted no question to the jury, as to whether the alleged requirement of an execution and return thereon had been practically complied with, and, therefore, that matter cannot be considered. The circuit judge having instructed the jury as above indicated, they found a verdict in favor of defendant, and plaintiff appeals upon the several grounds set out in the record, which practically make but two questions: (1) Whether the judge erred in charging the jury upon the facts; (2) whether there was error in holding that the issuing and return of an execution was an essential prerequisite to the validity of the tax-sale.

The first question presents but little difficulty, and, indeed, was not discussed in the argument here by appellant's counsel. It is very manifest from a consideration of the whole charge that the constitutional provision was not violated, but, on the contrary, every question of fact was fully and fairly left to the jury. The utmost that can be said is that, in those portions of the charge in which error is imputed by the exceptions, the judge simply repeated to the jury certain undisputed facts, and this certainly was no violation, either in spirit or letter, of the constitutional provision.

The real controversy arises under the second question. There can be no doubt that, before a man's land can be lawfully sold for the non-payment of taxes, every step required to be taken by the law authorizing such sale must be shown to have been taken; in other words, the mode prescribed by the statute must be followed in every particular. This, indeed, is conceded, and therefore the practical question in this case is whether the issuing of an execution or warrant against the personal property of the defaulting taxpayer and a return of *nulla bona* thereon is an essential prerequisite to the exercise of the right to sell land or offer it for sale at a delinquent land sale. This depends upon the construction which should be given to the terms of the act of 1880, (17 St. 380,) under which the tax in this case was levied, more especially the ninth and tenth sections of that act. Section 9 provides, so far as the matter under consideration is concerned: "That when the taxes and assessments, or any portion thereof, charged against any property * * * shall not be paid on or before the 31st day of October, 1881, the county treasurer shall proceed to collect the same by distress or otherwise, as now prescribed by law; * * * and if the amount of such delinquent taxes, assessments, and penalties shall not be paid on or before the fifteenth day of November, 1881, or be collected by distress or otherwise, then the same shall be treated as delinquent taxes on such real and personal property, and shall be collected by sale of such real and personal property, as hereinafter prescribed." So much of section 10 as is applicable to the present case reads as follows: "All personal property subject to taxation shall be liable to distress and sale for the payment of taxes and assessments hereunder; and at any time after any taxes or assessments shall become due, according to the provisions of this act, the county treasurer, by himself or deputy, may distrain sufficient personal property of the party against whom such taxes or assessments are charged, if the same can be found in his county, to pay the taxes or assessments, so due, with any penalty charged or chargeable thereupon, and the costs that may accrue;" and, after advertising the same for the time and in the manner prescribed, proceed to sell the same, or so much thereof as may be necessary, unless said taxes, assessments, penalties, and costs are paid before the day appointed for the sale. From an examination of these two sections it seems to us that before any real estate can be sold at a delinquent land sale, besides other requirements, which may not be mentioned here, as it is conceded that all the other requirements were complied with, an unsuccessful effort must have been made to enforce the payment of the taxes on the land by distress and sale of the personal property of the defaulting tax-payer; and this can be best evidenced by issuing an execution against the personal property, and showing that it had been returned *nulla bona*.

It will be observed that **section 9** provides that when the taxes "charged against *any* property" (which includes *real* as well as personal property) shall not be paid on the day specified, the county treasurer is imperatively required to proceed to collect the same, by distress or otherwise, as now prescribed by law. The language is "*shall* proceed to collect the same, by distress," etc.; and the section proceeds to declare that, if such taxes shall not be paid, "or be collected by distress or otherwise," on or before a certain other time specified, "*then* the same shall be treated as delinquent taxes on such real and personal property, and shall be collected by sale of such real and personal property, as hereinafter prescribed." The use of the word "*then*" italicized in the extract of the section just quoted is very significant, for it necessarily implies that the legislature intended that when taxes were unpaid upon "*any* property," whether real or personal, the first step which the county treasurer was required to take was by distress, and if that failed, *then* (not before) the land could be placed on the delinquent list, and offered for sale as delinquent land. It is true that there is an omission in this section to declare in express terms that personal property, and not real estate, shall be distrained, but this omission, more apparent than real, is supplied by the terms of the very next section, which authorizes the county treasurer to distrain sufficient *personal* property to pay the taxes and assessments levied under that act; and there is no provision, either in this section or in any other act, so far as we are informed, passed since the adoption of the present system, which authorizes a distraint of *real* estate, if, indeed, such a term can be properly applicable to that species of property. So much of section 10 as relates to this matter reads as follows: "All personal property subject to taxation shall be liable to distress and sale for the payment of taxes and assessments *hereunder*; and at any time after *any* taxes or assessments shall become due according to the provisions of this act, the county treasurer, by himself or deputy, may distrain sufficient personal property of the party against whom *such* taxes or assessments are charged, if the same can be found in his county, to pay the taxes or assessments so due," etc.; going on to provide how and when the personal property distrained may be sold. It seems to us that the words "hereunder," "any," and "such," which we have italicized in this quotation from the section, show very clearly that the intention was to authorize the enforcement of the payment of *any* taxes levied under that act, whether upon real or personal property, by distress and sale of *personal* property. The explicit declaration contained in the section is that *all* personal property, except such as may be exempt from taxation, shall be liable to distress and sale for the payment of taxes and assessments *hereunder;* which must necessarily mean either under that section, or under the act in which the section is embraced. It cannot mean the former, for there are no taxes or assessments levied by that section; and therefore it must mean the latter, as there are taxes and assessments levied under the act. But the language following makes this more plain, where it is provided that "after any taxes or assessments" shall become *due according to the provisions of this act,* the county treasurer * * * may distrain sufficient *personal* property of the party against whom *such* taxes or assessments are charged "to pay the same, —shows beyond all dispute that the purpose was, not to make the personal property of the defaulting tax-payer liable only for the taxes on that species of property, but to make it liable for *any* taxes assessed under the provisions of the act, which embraced real as well as personal property as subjects of taxation. It seems to us that the true construction of the ninth section of the act is that, when taxes upon *any* property, either real or personal, are unpaid on the day appointed for that purpose, the county treasurer must first proceed to enforce payment by distress, and, if that mode proves unavailing by a day specified, *then,* and not before, the land may be placed on the delinquent land list, and disposed of as provided by law, and that the purpose of section 10 was to declare what kind of property—personal property—should be liable to distress and sale for the non-payment of taxes, whether assessed upon either real or personal property. The scheme of the tax laws seems to be that, in enforcing the payment of taxes upon any species of property, the personal property of the defaulting tax-payer must first be exhausted before the sovereign right to sell the land—perhaps the homestead—can be exercised. This does not in any way interfere with the statutory provision that taxes shall be a first lien upon the property taxed, for without impairing the force and effect of such lien it is entirely competent for the legislature to require that resort shall first be had to the personal property. It is well settled that, while it is the duty of executors or administrators to pay a mortgage debt out of the personal property,—that being the primary fund for the payment of debts,—to the relief of the mortgaged premises, yet that does not impair the lien of the mortgage on the land covered by it, which may still be resorted to if the primary fund be insufficient. See Wilson v. McConnell, 9 Rich. Eq. 500, and the cases therein cited, as well as Henagan v. Hurllee, 10 Rich. Eq. 285. So here, while section 170 of the General Statutes gives the state a lien on the property for the taxes assessed upon it, yet the law, as we have seen, providing that resort must first be had to the personal property, does not impair the lien on the particular property upon which the taxes are assessed, which may still be enforced if the primary fund shall prove insufficient. It seems to us, therefore, that the circuit judge erred in instructing the jury that the issuing of an execution was not an essential prerequisite, and thus practically withdrawing from the jury the question whether this requirement had been complied with. The judgment of this court is that the judg-

ment of the circuit court be reversed, and that the case be remanded to that court for a new trial.

McGowan, J. I concur.

___

McLURE v. MELTON et al.

In re HARDIN.

(*Supreme Court of South Carolina.* Sept. 14, 1891.)

SUBROGATION — LIMITATION OF ACTIONS — CLAIMS AGAINST DECEDENTS.

1. A. sold real estate to B., with general warranty, receiving therefor four sealed notes, secured by mortgage. At maturity A. surrendered the notes and mortgage in consideration of B.'s unsealed agreement to pay a judgment against A., which was a lien on the land when sold. B. did not pay the judgment, and afterwards made a voluntary conveyance, with warranty, to trustees for the benefit of his wife and children. The trustees conveyed without warranty to plaintiff, who in turn sold the premises with warranty, and afterwards paid the judgment in exoneration of his covenants. *Held,* that plaintiff was not entitled to be subrogated to the rights of the judgment creditor against B.'s estate, nor to the rights of A.'s estate against it, since he did not pay the judgment for the benefit of A.'s estate, but in performance of his own covenants.

2. Nor could he set up the mortgage against B.'s estate, since it was a lien only on the particular property it covered.

3. Plaintiff had no claim under the agreement between A. and B. for the payment of the judgment, since he was neither the assignee of A. nor the holder of the judgment.

4. An order enjoining creditors from prosecuting actions at law against an estate, and fixing a time for proving their claims in the action in which the injunction was granted, will not suspend the running of the statute of limitations against a creditor who brings suit on a simple contract claim more than six years after the time so fixed.

Appeal from common pleas circuit court of Chester county; WALLACE, Judge.

Action by John J. McLure, administrator of George W. Melton, against Margaret A. Melton and others to marshal the assets of the estate. W. Holmes Hardin afterwards filed a petition in the cause, setting up a claim against the estate. The court dismissed his petition, and Hardin appeals. Affirmed.

After hearing the evidence the court rendered the following decree: "The cause entitled J. J. McLure, administrator of George W. Melton, was instituted by the administrator against M. A. Melton and others to facilitate the settlement of the estate of G. W. Melton, which was insolvent. Creditors of the estate were enjoined from proceeding against it save through that action, and were required to establish their demands in it. W. Holmes Hardin claims to be a creditor of the estate, and seeks by this petition to be allowed to establish his demand. The facts upon which petitioner supports his demands are as follows: On the 25th November, 1867, C. D. Melton sold and conveyed to G. W. Melton a dwelling-house and land adjacent for a large sum of money. Notes were executed by G. W. Melton to C. D. Melton for the purchase price, and these notes secured by a mortgage of the premises. When the note which had the longest time to run matured C. D. and G. W. Melton had a settlement on 25th November, 1871. It was agreed that G. W. Melton should assume the payment of several judgments, which had been obtained against C. D. Melton prior to the conveyance of the house and land to G. W. Melton, and which were liens upon the property, and which in the aggregate were about equal in amount to the aggregate sum due upon G. W. Melton's notes. Upon this understanding the notes and mortgage of G. W. Melton were canceled and given up to him. G. W. Melton, in pursuance of this agreement, paid all the judgments which were liens upon the land save one, known as the 'Wright judgment.' That judgment, at the time the others were paid, was in litigation, its validity as a lien being in controvery. Its validity as a lien was finally established. It was obtained 15th November, 1867. In the mean time the house and land had been conveyed by G. W. Melton to trustees, with warranty, in trust for his wife and children. G. W. Melton died insolvent, and had not paid the Wright judgment. The trustees who had the title to the property asked and obtained leave of the court to sell it with a view of making a more advantageous investment for the *cestuis que trustent.* At the sale thus ordered the petitioner here, W. Holmes Hardin, became the purchaser for the sum of $5,000. In a little more than a year after his purchase he sold to another for the sum of $6,000. All this while the Wright judgment was in litigation, and, as before said, its validity and as a lien upon this house and land was finally established. All the time of these transfers this judgment had been of record in the register's office of Chester county, and upon the final determination of the contest as to it W. Holmes Hardin's vendee, James C. Hardin, (who had it under a warranty deed from W. Holmes Hardin,) was in possession. After further litigation, which need not be set out here, the Wright judgment was levied upon the house and land. W. Holmes Hardin was informed by his vendee that he rested upon his warranty; and because there was no further ground of resistance W. Holmes Hardin paid to the sheriff of Chester county the amount, principal, interest, and costs, of the Wright judgment, and thus made good his warranty to James C. Hardin. W. Holmes Hardin claims upon this state of facts that he is a creditor of the estate of G. W. Melton, and that he should be allowed to set up both the mortgage of G. W. Melton to C. D. Melton and the Wright judgment, which he has paid. The force of the mortgage of G. W. Melton to C. D. Melton related only to the house and land upon which it was a lien. To restore to it now all the force it ever had would not aid petitioner in the collection of a claim against G. W. Melton's estate, for it would not constitute a lien upon any property of that estate. The same may be said of the Wright judgment. That was a judgment against C. D. Melton, obtained in a proceeding to which G. W. Melton was not a party. The doctrine of subrogation cannot im-

part new and enlarged scope to instruments, but only prevent extinguishment in support of an equity. It is the relegation to another's right; nor is the right enlarged by the transfer. If, therefore, the mortgage and judgment were both restored to their original vigor, they could have no relation to the estate of G. W. Melton. G. W. Melton promised to pay the Wright judgment, and reserved money due C. D. Melton with which to do so. This promise did not make him liable on the judgment. The ground of his liability was his promise. This promise was made in November, 1871, and of course has been long since barred by the statute of limitations. It is therefore ordered that the prayer of the petitioner be denied."

Thereupon Hardin filed the following exceptions: "(1) Because his honor erred in holding that the petitioner had no right to prove the amount paid by him in satisfaction of the Wright judgment against the estate of George W. Melton, when the petitioner was the assignee of the covenant of warranty of George W. Melton against incumbrances and for quiet enjoyment, and said covenant was broken by the levy of the execution issued on said judgment on the Chester property and the payment of the same by the petitioner, and he was entitled to prove the same according to the rank of his said debt under the statute. (2) Because, the case of J. J. McLure, administrator, vs. M. A. Melton and others, being still before the referee, the fund still in court arising from the sale of the real estate of the intestate, the administrator not having accounted for his administration, and there being a large sum of money in his hands undistributed, it was error in his honor not to allow the petitioner to prove in this action the breach of the covenant of warranty of George W. Melton, of which the petitioner was the assignee, and his payment of the Wright judgment, as a debt against the estate of the said G. W. Melton. (3) Because his honor erred in not holding that when W. Holmes Hardin paid the Wright judgment he was entitled to be subrogated to all the rights which the estate of C. D. Melton had in the agreement between C. D. and G. W. Melton of November 25, 1871, and through that instrument to prove it as a judgment debt against the estate of George W Melton. (4) Because, when W. Holmes Hardin paid the Wright judgment, he paid the unpaid part of the purchase money of the Chester real estate, on which C. D. Melton held a mortgage of G. W. Melton, and Hardin is entitled to be subrogated to all the rights of the former in said mortgage, and has a right to have it kept alive for his benefit, so that he may prove it against the estate of George W. Melton as a mortgage debt; and his honor erred in not so finding. (5) That his honor erred in holding that the petitioner's claim was in any sense barred by the statute of limitations."

L. P. Hamilton, for appellant. *G. W. S. Hart, G. J. Patterson,* and *J. & J. Hemphill,* for respondent.

McIVER, J. The principal case in which the petition of appellant has been filed was an action brought by the plaintiff, as administrator of George W. Melton, deceased, against his heirs and creditors, to marshal the assets of the estate of said George W. Melton, which is insolvent, and it was commenced on the 17th of July, 1877. On the 24th of August, 1877, an order was passed in said case enjoining all creditors of George W. Melton "from suing on said claims, or prosecuting their actions at law thereon against said administrator, until the further order of this court." On the 13th of October, 1877, another order was passed, whereby, among other things, all creditors were required to prove their demands before the clerk on or before the 15th of January, 1878; and on the 14th of November, 1881, A. G. Brice was substituted as referee in place of the clerk, who, after holding several references, made his report on the 1st of February, 1884, ascertaining the debts proved, and classifying them according to their legal priorities. To this report some of the creditors filed exceptions to the classifications adopted by the referee, and his report with the exceptions thereto came before his honor Judge WALLACE, who, on the 20th of May, 1885, rendered judgment sustaining the exceptions, but in all other respects confirming the report of the referee. From that judgment some of the mortgage creditors appealed, and on the 22d of April, 1886, the supreme court rendered judgment affirming the judgment of Judge WALLACE. 24 S. C. 559. The case was then carried by writ of error to the supreme court of the United States, where the writ of error was dismissed, (10 Sup. Ct. Rep. 407,) and the mandate from that court, together with the *remittitur* from the supreme court of this state, was filed in the circuit court on the 4th of June, 1890. In the mean time the real estate of the said George W. Melton had been sold, and a considerable portion of the proceeds of such sale remain in the hands of the clerk; and it is conceded that there are assets yet in the hands of the administrator, who has not yet formally accounted.

On the 25th of June, 1890, the appellant filed his petition in the cause, praying for leave to come in and prove his alleged claim against the estate of George W. Melton. His claim is based upon the following allegations contained in his petition: That Mrs. Wright, on the 15th of November, 1867, recovered a judgment against C. D. Melton, which became a lien on certain real estate in and adjoining the town of Chester; that on the 25th of November, 1867, C. D. Melton conveyed said real estate to his brother, George W. Melton, with general warranty, and received from his brother four notes under seal, bearing that date, and secured by a mortgage of the premises; that when the last of these notes became payable, to-wit, on the 25th of November, 1871, an agreement in writing, not under seal, was entered into by the Melton brothers, whereby George W. Melton assumed the payment of certain specified judgments, including that in favor of Mrs. Wright, which had been previously obtained against C. D. Melton, and were liens upon said real estate, and thereupon the said C. D. Melton canceled and surrendered the said four notes, together with the mortgage to secure the payment of the same, to the said George W. Melton, but the record of said mortgage still remains uncanceled; that thereafter, to-wit, in August, 1875, the said George W. Melton conveyed the said real estate, with the usual covenants of warranty, to certain trustees for the benefit of his wife and children; that in January, 1880, the said trustees, being duly authorized so to do, sold and conveyed the said real estate to the appellant, who bought in entire ignorance of the agreement above mentioned between the Melton brothers; that in April, 1881, the said appellant sold and conveyed the said real estate to James C. Hardin, with the usual covenants of warranty; that on the 13th of July, 1886, the Wright judgment, which had not been paid by George W. Melton in his life-time or by any one since his death, was levied upon the real estate in the possession of James C. Hardin, and the appellant, in exoneration of his covenant of warranty, having no defense to an action thereon, paid up the Wright judgment; wherefore the appellant claims that by the payment of said judgment he became the assignee of the covenant of warranty in the deed of George W. Melton to the said trustees; and that, having been compelled to pay the Wright judgment, which George W. Melton had undertaken to pay by his agreement of the 25th of November, 1871, the appellant stands as a surety to George W. Melton's estate, "and is entitled to set up said judgment in equity in his own favor in the marshaling of the assets of the estate of the intestate." Again, appellant claims that by the payment of the Wright judgment he in effect paid the balance of the purchase money due by George W. Melton for the said real estate, over which C. D. Melton held a mortgage, and appellant "is entitled to have the benefit of said mortgage as against the estate of George W. Melton, and to have leave to set it up as a mortgage debt against his estate, and to be subrogated to all the rights of the estate of C. D. Melton in said mortgage." To this petition the creditors of George W. Melton who have heretofore established their claims filed an answer, admitting all of the allegations of the petition except the following, which they deny: That appellant has become a creditor of the estate of George W. Melton; that appellant bought the real estate "in entire ignorance of the agreement" set forth in the petition; that petitioner had no defense to an action on the covenant of warranty contained in his deed to James C. Hardin; and that appellant, by the payment of the Wright judgment, became an assignee of the covenant of warranty in the deed from George W. Melton to the trustees. They also plead the statute of limitations.

It is conceded that the deed from George W. Melton to the trustees was a voluntary deed, based upon the consideration of natural love and affection only; and we presume that the deed from the trustees to the appellant contained no warranty. The testimony adduced on the part of the appellant was that of Maj.

Hamilton, who stated that he was the attorney of George W. Melton, and as such drew the deed to the trustees, as well as the proceedings under which the trustees obtained leave to sell, and conducted the sale made by them to appellant, and that at that time the Wright judgment was supposed by all parties to be no judgment and no lien upon the property sold, and that the agreement between the Melton brothers, of the 25th of November, 1871, was not known to witness or any one engaged in the case until it was produced in evidence by W. A. Clark in 1884. G. W. S. Hart, a witness examined for respondents, testified that he, with his partner, were the attorneys of Mrs. Wright, and they first learned that George W. Melton had assumed the payment of the Wright judgment some time in the latter part of 1881 or early part of 1882, prior to July, 1882; but the appellant, it is admitted, had no personal knowledge of such assumption at the time he purchased. It appears from the statements made in the case that C. D. Melton died in December, 1875, and George W. Melton in July, 1876, both being insolvent. The case was heard by his honor Judge WALLACE, who rendered judgment dismissing the petition, and from his judgment the petitioner appeals upon the several grounds set out in the record. Inasmuch as the decree of the circuit judge, together with appellant's exceptions thereto, should be incorporated in the report of the case, it is unnecessary for us to state them particularly here.

The fundamental inquiry in the case is whether the appellant has any such claim against the estate of George W. Melton as entitled him to the aid of the court in enforcing it. Whatever claim he may have is unquestionably based upon the fact that he has paid the Wright judgment, the payment of which was assumed by George W. Melton by the agreement of 25th of November, 1871; but, as such payment was not made for the purpose of relieving the estate of C. D. Melton, but solely for the purpose of relieving the property from the lien of said judgment, which the appellant had bought with notice of the judgment, and conveyed with warranty to another, in order to perform his covenant of warranty, it is difficult for us to understand what equity he has to be subrogated to the rights which the holder of that judgment, or to the rights which C. D. Melton's estate may have had against the estate of George W. Melton. There was no privity whatsoever between the appellant and C. D. Melton. He was not a surety of C. D. Melton, and in no way bound to pay said judgment for him. Indeed, practically, he paid no debt for which the estate of C. D. Melton was in equity and good conscience liable; for, though such estate was legally liable to pay such judgment, yet in equity and good conscience it was really payable out of the property which the appellant saw fit to buy with notice that it was subject to such lien. But, in addition to this, as the circuit judge well says, the judgment was against C. D. Melton and not against George W. Melton, who was never liable

to pay the amount thereof as a judgment, but only liable by reason of his agreement of 25th of November, 1871, which was a mere simple contract obligation, and hence we do not see how it is possible, under any view of the case, for the Wright judgment to be set up as a judgment against the estate of George W. Melton.

As to appellant's claim to set up the mortgage originally given by George W. Melton to C. D. Melton to secure the payment of the purchase money of the Chester property, the same remark as that just made in reference to the Wright judgment may be made. That mortgage never was a lien on anything but the Chester property, and did not cover any other portion of the property belonging to the estate of George W. Melton; and hence it could not be proved as a mortgage debt against the assets of the estate of George W. Melton, under the principle decided in McLure v. Melton, 24 S. C. 559; but, if set up at all, it must take the same rank as the debt which it was given to secure, to-wit, that of a sealed note.

It is necessary, therefore, to inquire whether the appellant can set up the sealed notes as a claim of that rank against the estate of George W. Melton. These notes were extinguished by the arrangement between the Melton brothers of the 25th of November, 1871, when they were canceled and surrendered to George W. Melton, and they cannot now constitute any legal cause of action against the estate of George W. Melton; and whatever equities C. D. Melton or his estate may have had, as intimated in the case of Hardin v. Clark, 32 S. C., at pages 485, 486, 11 S. E. Rep. 304, the appellant has no connection with, so far as we as we can see. He cannot claim as assignee of the covenant of warranty contained in the deed from C. D. Melton to George W. Melton, as was held in the case just cited, and we do not see what claim he could have against the estate of George W. Melton, as assignee of the covenant of warranty contained in the deed from George W. Melton to the trustees, for, that being a voluntary deed, and the measure of damages for breach of a covenant of warranty being fixed by statute at the amount of the purchase money paid, with interest from the time of the alienation, where there was nothing paid, nothing could have been recovered. If the trustees had been evicted they certainly could have recovered nothing from the estate of George W. Melton for the breach of the covenant of warranty contained in the voluntary deed under which they held; and the appellant, as their assignee could have no higher rights than his assignors. If, therefore, the appellant has any claim at all upon the estate of George W. Melton, it must arise from the agreement of 25th of November, 1871, whereby George W. Melton assumed the payment of the Wright judgment. But how can the appellant connect himself with that agreement? That was made for the benefit of C. D. Melton, and possibly might have inured to the benefit of the holder of the Wright judgment; but appellant is neither the assignee of C. D. Melton nor of the holder of the Wright judgment. It seems to us that the true position of the appellant is that of a purchaser of real estate under a quitclaim deed, without warranty, upon which there rested the lien of a judgment, of which he had not only constructive notice unquestionably, arising from the record, which would have been sufficient, but also, as it would seem, actual notice, if we are at liberty to refer to the decision in Hardin v. Clark, supra, offered in evidence in this case, at the time he purchased, and has seen fit to remove such lien by payment in order to protect himself against an action for breach of his covenant of warranty in his deed to his vendee. If this be so, then it is plain that he has no cause of action against the estate of George W. Melton; for, if so, then, in every case where a person who sells real estate covered by a judgment or other lien, of which his vendee has notice, and conveys the same without warranty, the vendor would be liable for any amount which the vendee might be called upon to pay for the purpose of removing such lien; and this could hardly be pretended, as it would destroy all distinctions between a quitclaim deed and a warranty deed. The fact that the vendor may have assumed the payment of such lien by a contract with a third person, with whom the vendee has not been able to connect himself, cannot alter the case, as such third person might at any time he saw fit release the vendor from the performance of such contract. But, even if appellant could connect himself with the agreement of 25th of November, 1871, that would create a simple contract obligation, which could not be enforced by action after the lapse of six years,—not four, as contended by one of the counsel for respondents, as the change in the statutory period was effected by the Code, which was adopted 1st March, 1870, and not by the Revised Statutes of 1872. So that it is clear that C. D. Melton or his administrator would have been barred of their action on such promise long before the petition in this case was filed, unless protected by the order of injunction; and the appellant, who certainly could not claim any higher rights, would be in like condition.

We must consider, then, the effect of the order of injunction, which was granted before the expiration of the six years. It will be observed that this order only restrained creditors from prosecuting their actions at law and did not prevent them from coming in and proving their demands in the case in which the order of injunction was granted. On the contrary, they were called upon to do so by a time fixed for that purpose,—15th of January, 1873. But the appellant not only failed to come in within six years from that date and present his demand, but he failed to do so within six years from the filing of the report on claims,—1st February, 1884; so that, even if appellant ever had any claim against the estate of George W. Melton growing out of his promise to C. D. Melton to pay the Wright judgment, it was barred by the statute before he filed his petition or presented his claim, which, according to what was held in Warren

v. Raymond, 17 S. C., at pages 203, 204, must be regarded as the time when he commenced his action. The fact that the appellant filed his petition—commenced his action—within six years after he paid the judgment cannot affect the question, for, without considering the question whether he could have brought his action before making such payment, it is sufficient to say that he can claim no higher rights than C. D. Melton, and certainly he and his administrator were barred long before the appellant instituted this proceeding. The judgment of this court is that the judgment of the circuit court be affirmed.

McGOWAN, J. I concur.

TRUSTEES OF WADSWORTHVILLE POOR SCHOOL v. BRYSON et al.

(*Supreme Court of South Carolina.* Sept. 14, 1891.)

WIFE'S SEPARATE ESTATE—CONVEYANCE TO WIFE —SETTLEMENT—BADGE OF FRAUD—SEAL.

1. A sealed instrument, executed in 1862 by a husband to an administrator acknowledging the receipt of money as his wife's share of her parents' estate, which he bound himself to return to her to dispose of as she saw fit, sufficiently shows an intent to create a separate estate in the money in his wife, and his marital rights do not attach thereto.

2. A conveyance of his land to her in consideration of such sum is valid as a settlement on her, and not fraudulent as to creditors, and will be sustained in equity as such, though they were incapable of contracting with each other.

3. The fact that the husband retained possession of the land so conveyed until his death, being consistent with the nature of the marriage relation, is not a badge of fraud.

4. Where it appears that the grantor intended to make an actual conveyance, and that the seal was omitted by mistake, a court of equity will regard the instrument as a deed, and supply a seal.

Appeal from common pleas circuit court of Laurens county; NORTON, Judge.

Action by the trustees of the Wadsworthville Poor School against W. H. Bryson, administrator of Samuel Bryson, and others, to subject to their claims certain real estate transferred by intestate to his wife and children. Decree for plaintiffs, and defendant Tabitha Bryson appeals. Reversed.

The case was referred to a master, who filed the following report:

"This cause was referred to me to hear and determine the issues of law and fact involved 'and to report my findings to the court, with leave to report any special matter.' This action is to have deeds made by Samuel Bryson in his life-time of all his real estate, to his wife and sons, declared void for fraud as to creditors, and to subject the said real estate to the payment of the indebtedness of the said Samuel Bryson. It appears that on the 2d January, 1846, Samuel Bryson and Mathew Bryson made their joint and several sealed note, whereby they, or either of them, covenanted under their hands and seals to pay, on the 1st January next after date, to Edmund Pasley, as treasurer of the Wadsworthville Poor School, or his successors in office, two hundred and forty-seven dollars and fifty-one cents, for value received of him, with interest from 1st January, 1846, to be paid annually. Numerous payments were made on this note, and credited thereon; the last one having been made on the 20th of March, 1884. That on the 28th of December, 1849, James Leaman and Samuel Bryson made their joint and several sealed note, whereby they, or either of them, covenanted under their hands and seals to pay, twelve months after date, to Edmund Pasley, as treasurer of the Wadsworthville Poor School, or his successors in office, two hundred and seventy-six dollars, for value received, with interest from date, to be paid annually. Several payments were made and credited on this note,—the last one having been made on the 7th January, 1883. That on the 10th of February, 1877, the said Samuel Bryson made, executed, and delivered to his sons William H. and William W. Bryson three separate deeds to three separate tracts of land, containing, respectively, one hundred and four acres, fifty-six acres, and twenty-four and three-fourths acres, more or less, the consideration expressed in said deeds, respectively, being seven hundred and fifty dollars, three hundred and ninety-two dollars, and one hundred and seventy-five dollars. These deeds were filed and recorded in the office of the register of mesne conveyance for said county on the 31st January, 1879, and embraced all the land owned by the said Samuel Bryson, except one tract hereinafter mentioned. That on the 16th day of June, 1862, the said Samuel Bryson made a receipt under his hand and seal, of which the following is a copy: 'Received of James McDowell, Jr., administrator of the estate of James McDowell, Sr., deceased, eleven hundred and five dollars, which was my wife, Tabitha Bryson, share of her father and mother's estate, which I do here bind myself to return to her to dispose of as she sees proper to do, without interest. Given under my hand and seal, this 16th day of June, 1862. SAMUEL BRYSON. [Seal.] Witness: THOMAS McDOWELL. WILLIAM H. BRYSON.' That on the 15th December, 1879, the said Samuel Bryson signed in the presence of two witnesses a paper purporting to be a deed to his wife, Tabitha Bryson, for the only remaining tract of land in his possession and ownership after the conveyance aforesaid to his sons—the said tract containing one hundred and seventeen acres, more or less, and being worth some $6.00 or $8.00 an acre. The said paper begins as follows: 'Whereas, on the 16th day of June, A. D. 1862, I, Samuel Bryson, under my hand and seal, acknowledged the receipt of eleven hundred and five dollars of James McDowell, Jr., of the share of my wife in the estates of her father and mother, which by said receipt I agreed to return, to be disposed of as she might choose, now, in pursuance of said receipt and the agreement thereunder, and in consideration of the said sum of eleven hundred and five dollars, the said receipt being witnessed by W. H. Bryson and Thomas McDowell, know all men by these presents, that I, Samuel Bryson, of said county, in consideration of the premises and one dollar to me in hand paid by Tabitha Bryson, my wife, as aforesaid, of said

county in the state aforesaid, have granted,' etc. The signature of Samuel Bryson to this paper has no seal affixed to it, but it was filed and recorded in the office of the register of mesne conveyances for said county on the 12th January, 1880. That the said Samuel Bryson continued to live on the said land with his wife, and 'farmed the place,' as the witnesses say, until his death, which occurred on the —— day of February, 1885. That the defendants W. H. Bryson and S. W. Bryson were duly appointed the administrators of the personal estate of Samuel Bryson, and on the 11th May, 1887, made a final accounting in the court of probate, when all creditors were called in to establish their claims; and among others, the aforesaid notes were established as subsisting debts against the estate; and it was found by that court that there was then due on the note first mentioned above the sum of $521.88, and on the other note the sum of $468.48. That accounting developed the fact that the personal estate was altogether insufficient to pay debts, the administrators having applied all the money which came to their hands to the payment of a certain judgment against the estate, and their action in so doing was confirmed by the probate court, so that nothing was left for the claims herein sought to be collected and other claims established at that accounting. This action was commenced in May, 1888.

"As to the deeds made by Samuel Bryson to his sons, there is not sufficient proof to warrant the finding that they were made in fraud of the rights of creditors. They cannot, therefore, be declared void. As to the paper made by him to his wife, it is claimed that the plaintiffs must have a nulla bona return upon an execution issued on their judgment obtained in the probate court if the establishment of their claims there amounts to a judgment, —which is questioned. Upon the showing made I do not think that the question as to nulla bona return arises or need be considered, for the attempted deed to Mrs. Bryson is practically and technically not a deed. It is fatally defective in its execution, having no seal affixed; and is therefore ineffectual to convey the fee to her. The fee then remained with Samuel Bryson, and at his death the land descended to his heirs at law, the defendants here, subject to his debts. But it is agreed that this was in fact a bona fide purchase by Mrs. Bryson of her husband with her patrimony from the estates of her father and mother, and that the paper may be regarded as an equitable assignment giving Mrs. Bryson a higher right to ask and require the other heirs at law of Samuel Bryson to make her a deed to the land than creditors have to subject the land to the payment of debts. That the husband's receipt in 1862 for the money paid to him by the administrator of McDowell, and his agreement therein set forth to return the money to Mrs. Bryson, was a waiver of his marital rights, and he had a right to do so, at that time. I do not think the position can be maintained. While it may be true, as shown by the testimony, that Samuel Bryson owned in 1862 property amply sufficient to pay his indebtedness, and that he was then able to give this money, or property to the value of it, to his wife, without furnishing his creditors reason to complain, yet he did not at that time give it to her, but bound himself to do so at some future time. I think his marital rights did attach, and that at the time he attempted to make a voluntary conveyance of this land in lieu of returning the money itself to his wife he was not in a condition to do so. It is said that this action is barred by the statute of limitations, because it was not commenced within six years from the accrual of the right of action. But the right of action on the part of a creditor to subject lands descended to the payment of his debt is not barred short of ten years, provided his right of action on the debt itself is not barred. Samuel Bryson died in February, 1885, and this action was commenced in May, 1888,—a little over three years. At the time of the execution of these sealed notes there was no statute of limitations applicable to such contracts, but they could only have been presumed paid by the lapse of twenty years. This presumption did not arise because payments were made on the notes almost every year down to 1888 and 1884. Besides, they were established in the probate court in a proceeding to which these defendants were parties in May, 1887, about a year previous to the commencement of this action. I do not see that the action is barred by the statute. I recommend that the plaintiffs have the decree of this court directing a sale of the 117-acre tract of land, and the application of the proceeds of sale to the expenses thereof and the costs of these proceedings, and then to the plaintiffs' claims as established at the accounting in the probate court, with interest from that time, and to other claims as established at that accounting, with interest according to the rank of all said claims. All objections to testimony inconsistent with the conclusions herein announced are overruled, otherwise they are sustained. My notes of testimony are herewith filed as a part of this report. All of which is respectfully submitted."

Thereupon Tabitha Bryson filed exceptions to the report as follows: "(1) Because the master erred in holding that it was not necessary for plaintiff to have a judgment and execution thereon, and a return of *nulla bona*, before it could maintain this action against the defendant. (2) Because he erred in holding that the claims of plaintiff were established against the estate of Samuel Bryson in the accounting had in the probate court. (3) Because he erred in holding that the marital rights of Samuel Bryson attached to the money received by him from James McDowell, Jr., and for that reason the promise on the part of the said Samuel Bryson to pay said money to the defendant was without consideration. (4) Because he erred in not holding that the paper given by Samuel Bryson to the defendant when he received the money that she was entitled to from her father's estate was such a promise as would be enforced by a court of equity, and as made her his

creditor. (5) Because he erred in holding that Samuel Bryson had a right to prefer her to the balance of his creditors, and that the paper executed by him to her with the view of conveying the tract of land therein described amounts to an equitable assignment or mortgage, and will be enforced by a court of equity. (6) Because he erred in not holding that it was the intention of Samuel Bryson to convey the fee in the said tract of land to the defendant, and in not ordering a seal put to the paper, so as to carry out the intention of the parties. (7) Because he erred in not holding that the arrangement entered into by Samuel Bryson, James McDowell, Jr., and the defendant amounted to a settlement upon the defendant such as a court of equity would have made if called upon. (8) Because he erred in not holding that plaintiff's claims have been paid. (9) Because he erred in not holding that plaintiff's action is barred by the statute of limitations. (10) Because he erred in ordering the land sold for the benefit of creditors."

Ferguson & Featherstone, for appellants. *N. S. Harris* and *L. W. Simkins*, for respondents.

McIVER, J. The plaintiffs bring this action in the nature of a creditors' bill against the administrators and heirs at law of Samuel Bryson, deceased, to subject certain real estate, originally belonging to the intestate, to the payment of their debts. It appears that the intestate executed two notes under seal, payable to the treasurer of plaintiffs,—one dated 2d January, 1846, and payable on the 1st of January following; and the other dated 28th December, 1849, and payable 12 months after its date; and that upon each of these notes numerous payments are credited,—on the first note the payments beginning in 1847, and the last bearing date 20th March, 1884; and on the other the first payment being credited 5th January, 1852, and the last 7th January, 1888,—there not being an interval of twenty years between any of the credits indorsed upon either of the notes On the 16th of June, 1862, the intestate, Samuel Bryson, received from the administrator of his wife's father the sum of $1,105, when he executed, under his hand and seal, in the presence of two subscribing witnesses, a paper of which the following is a copy: "Received of James McDowell, Jr., administrator of the estate of James McDowell, Sr., deceased, eleven hundred and five dollars,' which was my wife, Tabitha Bryson, share of her father and mother's estate, which I do here bind myself to return to her to dispose of as she sees proper to do, without interest. Given under my hand and seal, this 16th day of June, 1862. SAMUEL BRYSON. [Seal.] Witness: THOMAS McDOWELL, WILLIAM H. BRYSON." On the 10th of February, 1877, the said Samuel Bryson executed three deeds to his sons, defendants herein, for three separate tracts of land, containing, respectively, 104 acres, 56 acres, and 24¾ acres; the consideration expressed in said deeds, respectively, being $750, $392, and $175. These deeds were recorded on the 31st January, 1879. On the

15th December, 1879, he signed a paper, purporting to be a deed, in the presence of two subscribing witnesses, conveying to his wife, Tabitha, his only remaining tract of land, containing about 117 acres, the value of which seems to have been from $6 to $8 per acre. This paper begins with a recital of the terms of the receipt and agreement of the 16th of June, 1862, hereinabove copied, and proceeds in these words: "Now, in pursuance of said receipt and the agreement thereunder, and in consideration of the said sum of eleven hundred and five dollars, the said receipt being witnessed by W. H. Bryson and Thomas McDowell, know all men by these presents that I, Samuel Bryson, of said county and state, in consideration of the premises and one dollar to me in hand paid by Tabitha Bryson, my wife, as aforesaid, of said county in the state aforesaid, have granted," etc., following the usual form of an ordinary deed, and containing the words: "Witness my hand and seal," and the words, "signed, sealed, and delivered in the presence of" the two subscribing witnesses; but it contains no seal opposite the name of the said Samuel Bryson. The usual probate was indorsed, in which, in the ordinary form, one of the subscribing witnesses deposes "that he saw the within-named Samuel Bryson sign, seal, and as his act and deed deliver, the within written deed; and that he, with W. R. Crisp, [the other subscribing witness,] witnessed the execution thereof." This being sworn to before the clerk of the court, the paper was spread upon the records of the office of the register of mesne conveyances on the 12th of January, 1880. Some time in February, 1885, Samuel Bryson died intestate, and administration of his personal estate was duly committed to the two defendants hereinabove named as his administrators, who made a final accounting in the probate court on the 11th of May, 1887, to which all the parties to the present case, except, perhaps, the grandchild of intestate, Mattie Young, were parties; when the plaintiffs' claims were established, and the amount due thereon ascertained. From this accounting it appeared that the personal estate of intestate was wholly insufficient for the payment of his debts,—the whole amount thereof being applied to a judgment, leaving nothing applicable to the payment of the claims of plaintiffs.

In May, 1888, this action was commenced for the purpose of subjecting the several tracts of land conveyed by the intestate to his two sons and his wife to the payment of said claims, upon the allegations that these conveyances were voluntary, and in fraud of the rights of creditors. The defendants answered, setting up several defenses, which need not be fully stated here, as they will sufficiently appear in the progress of the discussion. The issues both of law and fact were referred to the master, who, after hearing the testimony set out in the "case," made his report, which should be incorporated in the report of the case, wherein he found that there was no sufficient proof to warrant the finding that the deeds to the two sons were made in fraud of the rights of creditors,

and they could not therefore be declared void; but that the attempted conveyance to the wife failed for want of a seal, and, the marital rights of the husband having attached upon the money received by the intestate from the administrator of her father's estate, and he being insolvent at the time, his attempt to convey the land to his wife by a voluntary deed could not be upheld in equity; and, having overruled the plea of the statute of limitations as well as the plea of payment, together with the defense set up that plaintiffs could not maintain this action without showing a return of *nulla bona* on an execution issued to enforce their claims, recommended that plaintiffs have judgment for the sale of the 117-acre tract of land, and the application of the proceeds thereof, after providing for the costs and expenses of the case, to the claims established according to their rank. To this report the defendant Tabitha Bryson filed numerous exceptions, set out in the "case," and, the case being heard by his honor, Judge NORTON, upon this report and the exceptions thereto, he rendered judgment overruling all the exceptions and confirming the master's report, which he made the decree of the court. From this judgment defendant Tabitha Bryson appeals upon the several grounds set out in the record, the material points of which we will proceed to consider. Inasmuch as there was no finding of any actual or intentional fraud, and, we may add, no evidence which would warrant such a finding, the judgment appealed from must be considered as resting upon constructive fraud only, arising from a voluntary conveyance made by a person in insolvent circumstances, whereby the claims of his creditors were defeated.

Those of the grounds of appeal which make the questions as to the necessity for a return of *nulla bona*, as to the sufficiency of the evidence to establish plaintiffs' claims, as to the plea of payment, and as to the statute of limitations, while not distinctly abandoned, were not pressed in the argument here, and, as they manifestly cannot be sustained, need not be further considered. The real question is as to the nature and effect of the paper purporting to be a conveyance of the tract of land in question to the appellant, Tabitha Bryson, by the intestate, Samuel Bryson, and this depends largely upon the question whether the marital rights of the intestate ever attached upon the money received by him from the administrator of his wife's deceased father under the receipt and agreement of 16th of June, 1862, a copy of which is set out above. This transaction, having occurred prior to the adoption of the constitution of 1868, whereby such radical changes were effected in the relations of husband and wife in relation to the property of the latter, must be viewed in the light of the law as it stood prior to the adoption of the present constitution. Under that law it was well settled that the husband acquired by the marriage the absolute legal title to all of his wife's personal property so soon as the same was reduced to possession by him; but there was much conflict of opinion as to what would amount to such a reduction into possession as would invest the husband with a legal title. See Verdier v. Hyrne, 4 Strob. 463, where the authorities were elaborately reviewed. It was, however, universally conceded that the marital rights did not attach upon the wife's choses in action until actually collected, or reduced to judgment in favor of the husband. Hence, where the wife became entitled to a legacy in the hands of an executor, or to a distributive share of a deceased ancestor's estate in the hands of an administrator, the marital rights would not have attached upon such legacy or distributive share, even where a decree had been obtained, unless there was an order of payment to the husband. Muse v. Edgerton, Dud. Eq. 179; Reese v. Holmes, 5 Rich. Eq. 531. It is clear, therefore, that the share of appellant in the estate of her deceased father, while in the hands of his administrator, being a mere chose in action, the marital rights of her husband, the intestate, could not have attached thereon until he reduced the same into possession. Now, upon familiar principles, if he had invoked the aid of a court of equity in enforcing payment by the administrator of this distributive share of his wife, that court might, and probably would, have required a settlement upon her of the fund sought to be obtained by the husband. Clancy, Mar. Wom. 441-443; Heath v. Heath, 2 Hill, Eq. 104. As is said in Bouknight v. Epting, 11 S. C., at page 77: "The rule on the subject of the wife's equity to a settlement is that, whenever the wife's property is under the jurisdiction of the court of chancery in such a manner that it requires a decree or order of the court to put a party rightfully into possession of it, the court will not deliver it over except upon terms of a settlement being made, unless the wife has been sufficiently provided for out of other property, or unless the wife, upon a private examination, shall waive her right to such settlement;" citing the authorities. Now, if the court would have ordered a settlement upon the wife in this case, if applied to for that purpose, it will undoubtedly sanction and sustain a settlement voluntarily made by the parties. Clancy, Mar. Wom. p. 446; Perryclear v. Jacobs, 2 Hill, Eq. 504; Ryan v. Bull, 3 Strob. Eq. 91. These principles being settled, our next inquiry is whether the receipt and agreement of the 16th of June, 1862, set out above, can be regarded as a settlement of the principal sum of the amount received by the husband from the administrator as the distributive share of his wife in her deceased father's estate. It is undoubtedly true that, if the husband had received this money from the administrator unconditionally, and without any qualification, his marital rights would have attached, and the money would have become absolutely his, without any liability on his part to account to her for the same, and therefore he could not have given his wife the money or property bought with it, to the prejudice of his creditors. But, as is said in Jackson v. McAliley, Speer, Eq., at page 307, "in order that the marital rights may attach, at

all events in this court, it is necessary that the husband should take possession as husband, and as of his own property, and not as trustee." To the same effect, see Medaker v. Bonebrake, 108 U. S. 66, 2 Sup. Ct. Rep. 351; Higgenbottom v. Peyton, 3 Rich. Eq. 398. The fact, therefore, which is undisputed, that the husband did actually receive this money from the administrator of his wife's deceased father, is not conclusive; but the inquiry still remains whether he received it as his own or as trustee for his wife. This depends largely upon the intention of the husband, as expressed at the time. 2 Perry on Trusts, § 639; McCampbell v. McCampbell, 2 Lea, 661. If when he received the money he declared that he did so simply as the agent of his wife, and assumed an obligation to repay it to her, this would negative any intention to receive or hold it by virtue of his marital rights, and a court of equity will hold him to his declared intention; for it might be that the administrator would have refused to pay him but for such declared intention, in which case he would have had to invoke the aid of the court, when a settlement would have been required. Now, in this case the terms of the receipt and agreement leave no doubt as to his intention at the time, for in it he says, not only that the money is his wife's share of her deceased father's estate, but he adds: "Which I do hereby bind myself to return to her, to dispose of as she sees proper to do, without interest." This completely negatives the idea that he received the money by virtue of his marital rights as husband, and, on the contrary, clearly recognizes his liability to account to his wife for the same. Practically this paper made him a trustee for his wife, so far as this money was concerned. It is true that the paper was informal, but it is well settled that no particular form is essential to the creation of a separate estate in a married woman. As is said in 3 Pom. Eq. Jur. § 1102: "No particular form of words is necessary in order to vest property in a married woman for her separate use, and thus to create a separate estate." It is a question of intent. Charles v. Coker, 2 S. C. 133. The paper containing an obligation on the part of the husband to return the money to the wife, "to dispose of as she sees proper to do," sufficiently shows an intent to create a separate estate in the wife. Wilson v. Bailer, 3 Strob. Eq. 258; Ellis v. Woods, 9 Rich. Eq. 19. The fact that no person is named as trustee is of no consequence, for in such a case a court of equity will regard the husband as trustee. See 3 Pom. Eq. Jur. § 1100, where the rationale of this rule is fully and clearly explained. See, also, Boykin v. Ciples, 2 Hill, Eq. 200.

It seems to us that the case now under consideration cannot be distinguished in principle from that of Banks v. Brown, 2 Hill, Eq. 558. There a husband, being in debt at the time, by a deed expressed to be in consideration of love and affection settled property, both real and personal, upon his wife. He was at that time negotiating a sale of a large estate which he had acquired by the marriage, which sale was subsequently effected, and the real inducement for the renunciation of the wife's inheritance in the real estate sold was the deed of settlement first mentioned. Upon a bill filed by the creditors of the husband to set aside the deed of settlement as voluntary, it was held that parol evidence was admissible to show that the real consideration of the deed of settlement, which, on its face, appeared to be voluntary, was the renunciation by the wife of her inheritance in the real estate subsequently sold by her husband, and that such consideration was sufficient to support the deed of settlement against the creditors of the husband. This case, therefore, is stronger than that, for here the valuable consideration of the conveyance to the wife, which plaintiffs now seek to set aside,—the wife's distributive share of her father's estate, received by the husband from the administrator of her father,—is stated in the deed itself, while there the only consideration stated in the deed was love and affection, and the valuable consideration—the renunciation of the wife's inheritance in the real estate sold by the husband—was allowed to be proved by parol evidence. Here, also, the consideration was received by the husband before the execution of the deed to the wife, while there the valuable consideration did not inure to the husband until after the execution of the deed of settlement upon the wife. In this case the husband received the wife's money under a promise to return it to her, to be disposed of by her as she might think proper; and, if she chose to receive it in the shape of land instead of money, as she did, we do not see why this would not constitute just as valid a consideration for the deed to her as the renunciation of the wife's inheritance in the case of Banks v. Brown, supra. It is contended, however, that this promise on the part of the husband to return the money to his wife was a mere nullity, on account of their marital relations, husband and wife being incapable of contracting with each other. It is true that, according to the principles of the common law, such incapacity did exist; but a court of equity would, under certain circumstances, recognize and uphold such a contract. 2 Story, Eq. Jur. § 1372 et seq. As is said in section 1377a: "If a husband should voluntarily enter into a contract to make a settlement, or should actually make a settlement, upon his wife and children, in consideration of personal property coming by distribution or bequest from her relatives, to no greater extent than what a court of equity would upon a suitable application by bill direct him to make, in such a case the post-nuptial contract or settlement will not only be held valid and obligatory upon him and his representatives, but equally so against his creditors." This case falls within the principle thus stated by this eminent author; for here the money came to the husband as the distributive share of his wife in the estate of her deceased father, and he received it under a promise to return it to her, to be disposed of as she might think fit, thus negativing the idea that he took it by virtue of his marital rights, and plainly recognizing her

right to it, as well as her absolute dominion over it. The amount was about one-tenth of the value of the property then owned by him; and it cannot be doubted that a court of equity, if appealed to, would have made just such a settlement as was practically made by the husband voluntarily. The fact that in the event the husband proved to be insolvent cannot affect the question, for there was in fact a valuable consideration for the deed to the wife, and there is no valid pretense that any actual fraud was intended. The manifest object was simply to secure to the wife her money, which had been received by the husband under a promise to return it to her; and the conveyance of the land, which the testimony shows was less in value than the amount received, cannot in any aspect be regarded as a fraud upon his creditors. Taylor v. Heriot, 4 Desaus. Eq. 227. The debts due plaintiffs were contracted long before the money was received, and, therefore, it cannot be said that the husband obtained credit on the faith of this money being his. If it should be said that this attempted conveyance by the husband to the wife, being at most a post-nuptial settlement, is void for want of registry in the office of secretary of state, inasmuch as it rested upon the receipt and agreement of 16th of June, 1862, executed prior to the change in the registry law, the answer is found in the case of Banks v. Brown, supra, where it is shown that the terms of the marriage settlement act apply only to settlements founded upon the consideration of marriage; and could not, therefore, directly apply to settlements entered into after the marriage, unless made in pursuance of articles previously entered into. This case practically overrules the case of Price v. White, Bailey, Eq. 236. so far as this point is concerned. See the reporter's note to Price v. White, at page 237 of the last edition of Bailey's Equity Reports.

But it is contended that the paper purporting to be a conveyance of the land in question to the appellant lacks a seal, and therefore could not operate as a transfer of the legal title; that, a most, the appellant has only an equity which must yield to the alleged superior equity of the plaintiffs. It will be observed that the terms of the paper itself show conclusively that it was not intended as a mere agreement to convey, but as an actual conveyance. It has all the essential elements of a conveyance of real estate, except the seal; and its omission was clearly accidental, and certainly not intentional. It concludes with the words, "Witness my hand and seal;" and purports to have been "signed, sealed, and delivered" in the presence of two subscribing witnesses, one of whom goes before the proper officer and makes affidavit that he saw the grantor "sign, seal, and as his act and deed deliver, the within written deed," and the paper is spread upon the records of the proper office as a deed; so that there cannot be a doubt that the intention was to execute a formal deed, and the parties, as well as the witnesses, together with the recording officer, manifestly supposed that the paper was what it was intended to be,—a valid deed. This being the case, a court of equity will regard the paper as a deed, and will supply this accidental omission of the seal. 1 Pom. Eq. Jur. § 833; Wadsworth v. Wendell, 5 Johns. Ch. 224; Bernards Tp. v. Stebbins, 109 U. S. 341, 3 Sup. Ct. Rep. 252; Pope v. Montgomery, 24 S. C. 595.

Finally, it is urged that the retention of the possession of the land which Samuel Bryson undertook to convey to his wife up to the time of his death is sufficient to establish the fraudulent character of such attempted conveyance; but, as was said by Desaussure, in Taylor v. Heriot, 4 Desaus. Eq. at page 234: "It was consistent with the deed and with the nature of the connection between the husband and wife, and therefore does not furnish that evidence of fraud which possession retained by the person conveying usually does." See, also, Pregnall v. Miller, 21 S. C.385, and the cases therein reviewed. The judgment of this court is that the judgment of the circuit court be reversed, and that the complaint be dismissed.

McGowan, J. I concur.

GARVIN v. GARVIN.

(Supreme Court of South Carolina. Sept. 14, 1891.)

JUDGMENT LIEN — FILING TRANSCRIPT — DIVISION OF COUNTY—EXECUTION.

1. A judgment rendered in 1866 against a debtor in L. county became, by the law then in force, a lien on the debtor's land in that county, and an execution was issued and returned unsatisfied. In 1871, A. county was created (14 St. S. C. 685) out of a portion of L. county, including the land which was subject to the judgment rendered in 1866. The act creating A. county contained no provision affecting the lien on lands within each county of judgments theretofore rendered. In 1874 the judgment debtor sold the land (then in A. county) to defendant. In 1875 the judgment creditor filed in A. county a transcript of his judgment, as authorized by Act S. C. 1873, § 14, (15 St. 499,) which provides that "from the date of the filing of such transcript it shall have the same force and effect as if the judgment had been originally entered in the county in which said transcript is filed." Held, under Code Proc. S. C. 306, (the original Code,) which provides that "the party in whose favor judgment has been heretofore or shall hereafter be given * * * may, at any time within five years after the entry of judgment, proceed to enforce the same, as prescribed by this title," that an execution issued on the judgment in question, immediately on filing the transcript thereof in A. county, was valid as against the land in defendant's hands, and authorized the sheriff to sell such land under a judgment rendered in A. county against the same judgment debtor after the conveyance by the debtor to defendant; and the purchaser at such sale acquired a title superior to that of defendant.

2. Where a new county is created out of a portion of an existing county, the lien of judgments theretofore rendered is not affected as to lands included within the new county, where the act creating it contains no retroactive provisions relating to such judgments.

3. Code Proc. S. C. 306, (the original Code,) provided that "the party in whose favor judgment has been heretofore or shall hereafter be given * * * may, at any time within five years after the entry of judgment, proceed to enforce the same, as prescribed by this title." Section

v. 13s. E.no.25—40

307 provided that, "after the lapse of five years from the entry of judgment, an execution can only be issued by leave of court. * * * But the leave shall not be necessary when execution has been issued on the judgment within the five years, and returned unsatisfied, in whole or in part." Section 315 provided that, "if the first execution is returned unsatisfied, in whole or in part, another execution, as of course, may be issued at any time within the period limited by this act for issuing executions." Held, that the issuance of a second execution at any time within five years from the return, unsatisfied, of the first execution was not authorized by the statute, but a second execution, as of course, must be issued within five years from the entry of the judgment.

4. Under Gen. St. S. C. § 665, providing that "the sheriff shall pay over the proceeds of sale of any real estate sold by him to any judgment having prior lien thereon," the title of a purchaser at a sale under an execution, junior to a conveyance made by the debtor, may be referred to and supported by a judgment senior to the conveyance, though no valid execution thereon had been issued.

5. The fact that defendant, in an action to recover land, has held adverse possession of the land for the period of limitation, cannot be urged on appeal as an additional reason to support the judgment of the trial court in his favor, since that is a question for the jury.

Appeal from common pleas circuit court of Aiken county; Hudson, Judge.

Action by John Garvin against R. C. Garvin to recover possession of real estate. A nonsuit was granted, and plaintiff appeals. Reversed.

Croft & Chafee and Henderson Bros., for appellant. Islar, Glass & Harbert and G. C. Jordan, for respondent.

McIver, J. This case having been several times before this court under previous appeals, it will not be necessary to give any detailed statement of the facts presented in its various phases, as these may be ascertained by reference to the former adjudications in 27 S. C. 472, 4 S. E. Rep. 148, and 31 S. C. 581, 10 S. E. Rep. 507. We will therefore confine ourselves to a general statement of the nature of the case, together with such facts as are pertinent to the questions raised by the present appeal. The action was brought to recover possession of a tract of land, now included within the boundaries of Aiken county, but which formerly constituted a part of Lexington county, from which it was cut off when Aiken county was established by the act of 1871, (14 St. 695.) The plaintiff claims under a deed made by the sheriff of Aiken, dated 7th January, 1878, by virtue of a sale made under certain executions obtained against Robert Garvin, the former owner of the land, while the defendant claims under a deed dated 15th April, 1874, from said Robert Garvin to himself. It seems that there were two judgments obtained against Robert Garvin, the first of which, designated as the "Fox judgment," was entered in the clerk's office of Lexington county, on the 6th of April, 1868, and execution duly issued thereon, at which time the land in question was embraced within the boundaries of Lexington county, where Robert Garvin then resided. That execution was returned to the clerk's office on the 4th of April, 1872, "unsatisfied and for renewal," by the sheriff of Lexington county. On the 5th of August, 1875, Aiken county in the mean time having been established, and the land in question having thereby been embraced within the boundaries of that county, a transcript of said judgment was filed in the office of the clerk of the court of common pleas for Aiken county, and on the same day an execution was issued thereon by the said clerk, which, for convenience, will be designated as the "Quash execution," that being the name of the clerk who issued it. The second judgment, which will be designated herein as the "Garvin judgment," was obtained in Aiken county, in September, 1877, and execution to enforce the same was duly lodged with the sheriff of that county on the 10th of December, 1877. Under this last-mentioned execution the land was levied on and sold by the sheriff to the plaintiff, as hereinbefore stated, on the 7th of January, 1878. It seems, however, that the land in question had been previously levied on under the Quash execution, though the date of such levy is not given, but the sale under that levy was enjoined until the determination of the issues in the case in which the Garvin judgment was obtained. Under this state of facts, as presented in the development of the plaintiff's case, (he having offered in evidence the deed from Robert Garvin to the defendant herein for the purpose of showing that both parties claimed from a common source of title,) a motion for a nonsuit was made and granted by his honor, Judge Hudson, who held that, the plaintiff having shown that the defendant held the land under a deed executed prior to the recovery of the judgment under which the sale was made to the plaintiff by the sheriff, the plaintiff had proved himself out of court, by showing that defendant held under a superior title; for he held that plaintiff could not avail himself of the lien of the Fox judgment, which was anterior in date to the defendant's deed, because there was not, at the time of the sheriff's sale, any execution on that judgment in the sheriff's office having active energy, and hence there was no other authority for the sheriff to make the sale except the execution issued to enforce the Garvin judgment. The circuit judge further held that the question now presented had not been adjudicated by any former decision in this case, as was claimed by plaintiff. From this judgment of nonsuit plaintiff appeals upon the several grounds set out in the record, which substantially make three questions: (1) Whether the point now presented has been already adjudicated by any former decision in this case; (2) whether there was, at the time of the sheriff's sale, any valid execution in his office, having active energy, from which his authority to make the sale could be derived; (3) if not, whether the lien of the Fox judgment was not sufficient of itself to constitute authority for the sheriff to make the sale under the execution junior to defendant's deed.

As to the first question, we agree with the circuit judge that the point now raised has never been adjudicated by any former decision in this case. In the case

as reported in 27 S. C. 472, 4 S. E. Rep. 148, which is relied upon by plaintiff as sustaining his view of this question, the only point really decided was that the Fox judgment was not merged in the Garvin judgment, and therefore plaintiff could claim the benefit of the lien of the former; but whether he could enforce such claim without showing a live execution issued on such judgment was neither considered nor determined. His right to the benefit of the lien of the Fox judgment was recognized, but how he should make such right available was not a question in the case. We have looked carefully through all the former decisions in this case, and we have been unable to find that the question now presented has ever before been decided, or that its decision was necessarily involved in any adjudication heretofore made.

As to the second question, we are unable to agree with the circuit judge. The Fox judgment was recovered in Lexington county prior to the enactment of the Code, and as the land then was embraced within the limits of that county, where the judgment debtor then resided, it unquestionably then became a lien upon the land, which continued until the debt was paid either in fact or by operation of law. The fact that the land was afterwards cut off from Lexington county, and embraced within the boundaries of the new county of Aiken, established by the act of 1871, hereinbefore cited, could not affect this lien, for there is nothing in that act which indicates any intention to give to it any retroactive operation, and hence, under the well-settled rule, no such operation can be given to it. Indeed, the terms of the act, so far from showing any intention to give to it a retroactive operation as to judgments already recovered, indicates precisely the contrary; for, while provision is made for the transfer of all papers and records in pending suits, etc., nothing of the kind is said in reference to cases already determined. But, in addition to this, counsel for appellant has furnished this court with two cases from other states which distinctly decide the point in accordance with the conclusion which we have adopted. Davidson v. Root, 11 Ohio, 98; Bowman v. Hovious, 17 Cal. 471.

The lien of the Fox judgment thus continuing on the land after it was cut off from the county of Lexington, where the judgment had been originally entered, and embraced within the limits of the new county of Aiken, the question is whether there was at the time of the sheriff's sale any execution in the sheriff's office of Aiken having active energy, under which such lien could be enforced. By section 306 of the original Code of Procedure it was provided that "writs of execution for the enforcement of judgments, as now used, are modified in conformity to this title, and the party in whose favor judgment has been heretofore or shall hereafter be given * * * may, at any time within five years after the entry of judgment, proceed to enforce the same, as prescribed by this title." And the next section (307) provides that, "after the lapse of five years from the entry of judgment, an execution can only be issued by leave of the court. * * * But the leave shall not be necessary when execution has been issued on the judgment within the five years, and returned unsatisfied, in whole or in part." And section 315, in the same title, provides that, "if the first execution is returned unsatisfied, in whole or in part, another execution, as of course, may be issued at any time within the period limited by this act for issuing executions." It will be observed that these provisions, with respect to the enforcement of judgments by execution, are made retrospective in express terms, and apply as well to executions issued to enforce judgments previously as well as subsequently rendered; while the provisions in section 313, with respect to the lien of judgments, are, in like express terms, prospective only,—"final judgments hereafter rendered," etc. It is therefore contended by counsel for appellant that, as the provisions above quoted are applicable to the issuing of execution to enforce the Fox judgment, although it was recovered prior to the Code, they warranted the issuing of the Quash execution on the 5th of August, 1875, as that was within 5 years after the return of the first execution unsatisfied on the 4th of April, 1872, though not within 5 years from the original entry of the judgment in Lexington county. This view proceeds upon the assumption that the provision above quoted from section 315 authorizes the issue of a second execution as of course at any time within 5 years from the return of the first execution. But, in the first place, we do not think that is a proper construction of section 315; for by the preceding part of that section, not quoted above, it is provided that executions shall be returnable within 60 days, and it seems to us that the proper construction of the words quoted is that, though an execution must be returned within 60 days, yet it may be renewed at any time within 5 years from the entry of the judgment, as of course, not at any time within 5 years from the return of the execution. But, in the second place, section 315 of the Code was stricken out by the act of 25th of November, 1873, (15 St. 499,) and the provisions inserted in lieu thereof contained no such provision as that quoted above from section 315 of the Code. So that, even if the construction of section 315 contended for by the appellant could be adopted, yet, as the plaintiff did not undertake to avail himself of that construction until after that section had been repealed, he cannot claim any benefit thereunder.

The act of 1873, just referred to, does, however, contain another provision, which, as it seems to us, will warrant the issuing of the Quash execution on the 5th of August, 1875, which was within three years before the sheriff's sale. Section 14 of that act, after providing for the filing of a transcript of a judgment obtained in one county in another county, contains this language: "And from the date of the filing of such transcript it shall have the same force and effect as if the judgment had been originally entered in the county in which said transcript is filed." Now, if the Fox judgment had been originally en-

tered in the county of Aiken on the 5th of August, 1875, one of the effects which it would have had would have been to authorise the issuing of an execution thereon at any time within five years from that date; for it will be observed that section 306 of the original Code is not repealed by the act of 1873, or by any other act, so far as we are informed. The fact that the Fox judgment may have had the additional force and effect of fixing a lien on the land from the date of its entry in Lexington county, as we have seen, instead of from the date of the filing of the transcript thereof in Aiken county, cannot deprive it of the further effect, under this provision of the act of 1873, of authorizing the issue of an execution thereon at any time within five years after the filing of the transcript in Aiken county. And as the lien on real estate is derived from the judgment, and not from the execution, which only serves as authority to the sheriff to enforce it, we do not see why the Quash execution, which was issued within five years after the filing of the transcript, did not furnish authority to the sheriff to enforce the previously existing lien of the judgment arising from, and at the time of, the original entry of the judgment in Lexington county. It seems to us, therefore, that though the execution issued on the Garvin judgment, under which the sheriff made the sale, was not sufficient authority to enable him to do so, inasmuch as that judgment was not entered until after the land was conveyed by the judgment debtor to the defendant herein, yet there being at the time in the office of the sheriff another execution,—the Quash execution,—which would furnish such authority, his act in making the sale may, under the well-settled doctrine, (Agnew v. Adams, 17 S. C. 364,) be referred to that authority; and, as the Quash execution was issued to enforce the lien of a judgment which antedated the conveyance under which the defendant claims, the purchaser at such sale took a title superior to that of the defendant. We have not deemed it necessary to consider the effect of the act of 1884, (18 St. 749,) and the act of 1885, (19 St. 229,) amending the Code, as it had been previously altered by the act of 1873, above referred to, because both of those amendatory acts expressly provide that nothing therein contained shall be construed to affect the lien of judgments or executions thereunder entered prior to the 1st of March, 1870, and hence their provisions cannot affect this ante Code judgment, or any execution issued thereunder.

It is contended, however, by counsel for defendant, that while it is true that where a sheriff sells under an execution which has been satisfied, or has lost its active energy, and he has, at the time, another valid execution in his office, having active energy, the sale may be supported by referring it to the latter execution, yet, where the execution under which the sheriff sells is unsatisfied, and, having active energy, furnishes authority to make the sale, that the sale must be referred to it, and the sale cannot be supported by referring it to another valid, enforceable execution then in the sheriff's office; and hence it is claimed that as the sale in this case was made under the Garvin execution, which was a valid execution, having active energy, it cannot be supported by referring to any other execution which may have been in the sheriff's office at the time. This view cannot be sustained for two reasons. In the first place, the Garvin execution having been issued to enforce a judgment obtained after the land had been conveyed away by the judgment debtor, that judgment never was a lien upon the land, and, of course, the execution issued upon it furnished no authority whatever for the sale,—no more than if the execution had, for some reason, been absolutely void, or had been fully satisfied. In the second place, the view contended for is in direct conflict with a recent decision of this court in the case of Henderson v. Trimmier, 32 S. C. 269, 11 S. E. Rep. 540. In that case there were three liens on the land—*First*, the Cooley judgment; *second*, the mortgage in favor of Trimmier; and, *third*, the Matthis judgment. The land was sold under the junior judgment, and it was held that the lien of the mortgage was divested thereby, although the execution on the Cooley judgment had lost its active energy. In that case, though the Matthis execution was held to furnish sufficient authority to make the sale, inasmuch as the judgment upon which it was issued was a lien, though subject to the prior lien of the mortgage, yet the sale was supported, and it was held to vest a good title in the purchaser, free from the lien of the mortgage, by virtue of the senior lien of the Cooley judgment. As it is well expressed by his honor, Judge FRASER, in his circuit decree in that case: "The sale being for the benefit of the older judgment lien, the title under such sale is necessarily sustained by such older lien." So that, even if we are in error in holding that the Quash execution was a valid execution, having active energy, which, being in the hands of the sheriff at the time, would have furnished him with authority to make the sale, yet, under the case just cited, the title of the plaintiff, who purchased at the sheriff's sale, may be supported by the lien of the Fox judgment, even though no valid execution on that judgment may have been in the sheriff's hands at the time of the sale. There can be no doubt that, where a sheriff makes a sale of real estate under an execution, he is bound to apply the proceeds of such sale to any judgment senior to that under which the sale is made, for such is the express provision of the statute. "The sheriff shall pay over the proceeds of sale of any real estate sold by him to any judgment having prior lien thereon." Gen. St. 685. This provision is even more stringent than that found in section 60 of the sheriff's act of 1839, from which the present section seems to have been taken, for there the requirement was to pay over the proceeds of sale to any judgment having prior lien: provided, notice of such judgment be given to the sheriff before the proceeds have been otherwise applied. But there is no such proviso in the sec-

tion as incorporated in the General Statutes, and hence it would seem to be necessary for the sheriff to examine the clerk's office to see if there is any judgment having prior lien before he can safely apply the proceeds of the sale of real estate. If, therefore, the holder of a senior judgment is entitled to receive the proceeds of the sale of his judgment debtor's real estate when made under a junior judgment, it would seem to be nothing but right and proper that the purchaser, whose money has been applied to the senior lien, should be protected under such lien. This doctrine seems to have been settled by the case of Vance v. Red, 2 Speer, 90, which has been recognized and followed in a number of subsequent cases. This disposes of the third question made by the plaintiff's grounds of appeal.

The defendant has, however, according to the proper practice, given notice that he will ask this court to sustain the judgment below, upon a ground other than those upon which it was based by the circuit judge. This ground, as stated in the notice, is because "it appears by the evidence introduced by the plaintiff that the defendant has been holding this land in dispute adversely to the plaintiff and all the world, more than ten years last past before the commencement of this action." To dispose of this ground, it is sufficient to say that whether a party has been in adverse possession of a tract of land for the prescribed time presents a question of fact, which the circuit judge would have had no authority to determine, as that was a matter for the jury. The judgment of this court is that the judgment of the circuit court be reversed, and that the case be remanded to that court for a new trial.

McGOWAN, J. I concur.

CITY COUNCIL OF CHARLESTON v. WELLER.

(*Supreme Court of South Carolina.* Sept. 12, 1891.)

JURISDICTION OF SUPREME COURT—APPEALS FROM CITY COURT OF CHARLESTON.

1. Gen. St. S. C. § 2134, concerning the city court of Charleston, provides that "all parties shall have the same right of appeal to the supreme court from the decisions of the said city court," in the same manner as parties in the circuit court in like cases. Code S. C. § 356, provides that when a judgment is rendered by a trial justice's court, by the county commissioners, or any inferior court save the probate court, the appeal shall be to the circuit court of the county wherein the judgment was rendered. *Held*, that appeals lie from the city court to the supreme court, notwithstanding the city court is an inferior court.

2. The jurisdiction of the supreme court over appeals from the city court is exclusive.

3. Code S. C. § 11, provides that the supreme court shall have exclusive jurisdiction to review upon appeal any judgments, orders, or decrees entered by the "courts of common pleas and general sessions." *Held*, that the absence of a provision conferring jurisdiction to review appeals from the city court did not affect the jurisdiction of the supreme court, specially given by Gen. St. § 2134, which provides that the supreme court "shall hear and determine such appeals."

Appeal from common pleas circuit court of Charleston county; IZLAR, Judge.

Action by the city council of Charleston against J. C. H. Weller. Judgment for plaintiff. Defendant appealed to the circuit court of Charleston county. Appeal dismissed. Appellant appeals from the order of dismissal. Affirmed.

Trenholm & Rhett, for appellant. *Charles Inglesby*, Corp. Counsel, for respondent.

McIVER, J. The sole question presented by this record is whether, in a case heard by the city court of Charleston, the appeal is to the circuit court of the county of Charleston or to the supreme court. Section 2134, found in chapter 81 of the General Statutes, entitled "Of the City Court of Charleston," provides as follows: "All parties shall have the same right of appeal to the supreme court from the decisions of the said city court, in the same form which is now or may be lawful for parties in the circuit courts in like cases, and the supreme court shall hear and determine such appeals in the same manner as appeals from the circuit court of Charleston county." Under that section, expressly giving to all parties in the city court the right of appeal to the supreme court, and requiring that court to hear and determine such appeal in imperative terms, ("shall hear and determine such appeals,") and placing appeals from the city court in all respects upon the same footing as appeals from the circuit court, there could be no possible doubt as to the proper response to the question above stated if there were nothing more. But it is contended by the appellant that, since it has been determined in the case of City of Charleston v. Phosphate Co., 11 S. E. Rep. 386, that the city court has no jurisdiction in cases involving more than $100, it must be regarded as one of the inferior courts, which the general assembly is authorised to establish by section 1 of article 4 of the constitution; and, being an inferior court, an appeal from its decision must be to the circuit court of the county wherein it is rendered, under the provisions of section 358 of the Code of Procedure. The decision in the case referred to was based upon the ground that the constitution in section 15 of article 4, having conferred on the court of common pleas exclusive jurisdiction in all civil cases "which shall not be cognisable before justices of the peace," and the jurisdiction of such justices being limited by section 22 of the same article to cases "where the amount claimed does not exceed one hundred dollars," the general assembly would not have the power to confer upon the city court jurisdiction of any civil case where the amount claimed exceeded $100, as that would conflict with the exclusive jurisdiction conferred by the constitution on the court of common pleas in such cases. So that the necessary conclusion was that the general assembly, in conferring upon the city court jurisdiction for the trial of causes arising under the ordinances of the city council, intended to confer such jurisdiction only in cases where the amount claimed did not exceed $100. While, therefore, the city court of Charleston was not declared in terms by that

case to be an inferior court, yet we think that such is the necessary inference from that decision.

Assuming, then, that the city court is an inferior court, the precise question here presented is whether the right of appeal to the supreme court from the decisions of the city court, expressly conferred by section 2134, above quoted, is abrogated by the more general provisions contained in section 358 of the Code, which, so far as this question is concerned, reads as follows: "When a judgment is rendered by a trial justice's court, by the county commissioners, or any other inferior court or jurisdiction save the probate court, heretofore provided for in this Code of Procedure, the appeal shall be to the circuit court of the county wherein the judgment was rendered." Upon this section it is first to be remarked that the saving clause in reference to the probate court was manifestly not intended to except that court from the list of those courts or jurisdictions from whose decisions appeals should be to the circuit court, for in preceding sections of the Code, dealing specially with the probate court, express provision had been made for appeals from that court to the circuit court. That saving clause was doubtless designed simply to except appeals from the probate court from the operation of the regulations as to appeals from inferior courts generally in respect to the time within which they must be taken, and other like details. It is next to be observed that the provisions of this section, while specially designating the trial justice's court and the county commissioners, are general, as to the other courts and jurisdictions referred to, under which alone could the city court be placed, if referred to at all. But, on the other hand, the provisions of section 2134 of the General Statutes relate only to a single tribunal, specifically designated by name. It is understood that the General Statutes of 1882, embracing the Code of Procedure, constituted a single act, all of which was passed at the same time; and it is claimed, whether correctly or not we are not informed, that section 358 of the Code is in a subsequent portion of the general act to that in which section 2134 above referred to is found, and is therefore the latest expression of the legislative will. Assuming this to be so for the purposes of the present discussion, the question is presented whether these two apparently conflicting provisions in the same act can be reconciled? If so, how? And if not, which is to control? It is very obvious that if the view advocated by the appellant shall prevail, then the provisions of section 2134 of the General Statutes will become absolutely nugatory. No court will readily adopt the conclusion that the legislature has deliberately inserted in a statute a provision which becomes utterly useless and unmeaning because of an inconsistency with some subsequent provision in the same statute. On the contrary, the well-settled rule is that in construing an act it must be considered as a whole, and such a construction must be adopted, if possible, as will give full force and effect to each one of its provisions. If they are apparently inconsistent with each other, such inconsistency must, if possible, be reconciled, in order to give full force and effect to the legislative will as expressed by the words they have used. So that the practical question here is whether it is possible to reconcile the particular intention, explicitly declared in section 2134, of securing the right of appeal to the supreme court from the decisions of the city court of Charleston, with the general intention declared in equally explicit terms in section 358 of the Code, that all appeals from inferior courts (to which class, as we have seen, the city court belongs) shall be heard by the circuit court. It seems to us this can be, and ought to be, done in order to avoid imputing to the legislature an intention of inserting in an act a perfectly useless and nugatory provision by reading the particular provision as an exception to the general provision; that while, as a general rule, appeals from the decisions of an inferior court are to the circuit court, yet the city court constitutes an exception, and an appeal from that court is to be heard and determined by the supreme court. This mode of construction has been approved and resorted to in at least two cases in this state involving the construction of two apparently inconsistent provisions in the constitution, (State v. Shaw, 9 S. C. 94, and State v. McDaniel, 19 S. C. 114,) where, in the former, the special provision requiring circuit judges to be elected by ballot was read as an exception to the general provision that in all elections by the general assembly the members shall vote *viva voce;* and in the latter the provision of section 3 of article 5 requiring a revision and arrangement of the statutes was held to constitute an exception to the general provision contained in section 20 of article 2, requiring that every act or joint resolution shall relate to but one subject, which shall be expressed in the title. So in Ex parte Turner, 24 S. C. 214, the same mode was resorted to for the purpose of reconciling two apparently inconsistent provisions in the General Statutes of 1882. See, also, Endlich on the Interpretation of Statutes, (section 215,) where it is said: "If there are two acts or two provisions on the same act, of which one is special and particular, and clearly includes the matter in controversy, while the other is general, and would, if standing alone, include it also, and if, reading the general provision side by side with the particular one, the inclusion of that matter in the former would produce a conflict between it and the special provision, it must be taken that the latter was designed as an exception to the general provision." This language is directly apposite to the case in hand, and fully supports the view which we have adopted.

It is contended, however, that the supreme court has never been invested with jurisdiction to hear appeals from the judgments of the city court, and section 11 of the Code is cited to show that such appeals are not embraced within those mentioned in that section. Granting this to be so, there can be no doubt that un-

der the provisions of section 2134 such jurisdiction is not only expressly conferred upon the supreme court, but it is imperatively required to exercise such jurisdiction,—"shall hear and determine such appeals." Again it is urged that the provision for appeals to the supreme court in section 2134 from the decisions of the city court is permissive only, ("all parties shall have the same right of appeal," etc.,) while the provision in section 358 of the Code is imperative, ("the appeal shall be to the circuit court," etc.,) and from this it is argued that the losing party to a case in the city court may appeal either to the circuit court or supreme court, as he may prefer; and hence that, for this reason, if for no other, the circuit judge erred in dismissing this case for want of jurisdiction to hear this appeal. We cannot adopt such a view. We cannot think that there is anything in either of the sections which warrants the idea that the legislature intended to give to a party to a cause in the city court the right to select the tribunal to which his appeal should be addressed. On the contrary, we are of opinion that the proper construction of the statute is that the only right of appeal secured to a party to a cause in the city court was a right to appeal to the supreme court, and there was no error on the part of the circuit judge in declining to hear this appeal for want of jurisdiction. The judgment of this court is that the judgment or order of the circuit court be affirmed.

McGowan, J. I concur in the result upon the ground that the law expressly gives the appeal to the supreme court.

Barber v. Richmond & D. R. Co.

(Supreme Court of South Carolina. Sept. 18, 1891.)

Accident at Crossing—Failure to Signal—Construction of Track.

1. Gen. St. S. C. § 1483, requires locomotive engineers and firemen on trains, when approaching any public highway or "traveled place," to signal, either by a bell or whistle. *Held,* that "a traveled place" means a place where the public have a legal right to cross the track, and not a place where people are accustomed to cross to reach a store and post-office, where such crossing was not a public one, and the railroad company did not know of or acquiesce in such crossing.

2. Defendant's failure to give the required notice of its approaching train will not give plaintiff a right of recovery when he knew of its approach without any signal being given.

3. Negligence cannot be imputed to defendant by reason of its track being within three feet of the platform in front of the store where the accident occurred, when it owned only the roadbed at that point, and had no interest in or control over either the platform or the ground upon which it rested.

Appeal from common pleas circuit court of Chester county; Norton, Judge.

Action by William S. Barber, by his guardian *ad litem,* James G. Barber, against the Richmond & Danville Railroad Company for personal injuries. Judgment of nonsuit, from which plaintiff appeals. Affirmed.

Henry & Gage, for appellant. *B. L. Abney,* for defendant.

McIVER, J. This was an action to re-over damages for injuries sustained by the minor, William S. Barber, through the alleged negligence of the defendant company. In the complaint the negligence complained of is stated as follows: That at a station on the railroad called "Bascomville" "the said William S. Barber was crossing the track of the railroad, well knowing that the locomotive and cars thereof, then about due, would stop to discharge passengers at the said station; but the defendant carelessly and recklessly caused its locomotive and cars to pass rapidly over the track at said station, and negligently omitted to slow up, or give a signal by bell or whistle, while so approaching, though then crossing a public highway, by reason whereof the said William S. Barber was unaware of the approach, and by reason of the said negligence, and without any fault or negligence of the said William S. Barber, the locomotive struck him and threw him with great violence to the ground," whereby he sustained the serious injuries for which damages are claimed. The plaintiff introduced testimony tending to show that the place at which the disaster occurred was not a regular, but a flag, station, where the trains did not usually stop except upon signal, unless they had passengers to discharge at that point; that on the day when the accident occurred there was a passenger on the east-bound train to be put off at Bascomville, which was known to William S. Barber; that young Barber, a youth of 15 years of age, had gone to the station that morning, driving a team of mules, which he left in the open space between the public road to Rocky Mount and the railroad track, where persons visiting the station were accustomed to leave their teams, and had gone into the back part of the store of Hafner & Howze, in which the post-office was kept, for the purpose of warming his feet; that the railroad track runs immediately in front of said store, within about three feet of the piazza or platform of the store; that while at the fire young Barber heard the train approaching, and, fearing that his mules would become frightened, started, with a companion, on a run, intending, as he said, to jump from the platform across the track,—the road being narrow gauge,—three feet, so as to reach his team before the train came up; that when he reached the door of the store opening on the platform he saw the train abreast of the platform, and tried to stop, attempting to catch hold of a post, but, missing the post, he fell against the tender of the engine, and the train passed over one of his feet, injuring it so severely as to render amputation necessary. For a proper understanding of the location the diagram found in the "case" should be embraced in the report of the case, from which it appears that the train had already crossed the public road leading to Rock Hill before the disaster occurred, and that it did not cross the public road leading to Rocky Mount at all, at least near the Bascomville station, and that there was no public highway or street at the point where young Barber undertook to cross the railroad track. The plaintiff also introduced testimony tending to show that the engineer in charge of the train failed to give the signals required by section 1483 when approaching the place where a railroad track crosses "any public highway or street or traveled place;" the whistle not having been blown until the engine was abreast of Cousar's store, about 28 steps distant from the platform above mentioned. There was also testimony tending to show that persons were in the habit of stopping and hitching their teams in the open space in front of the stores of Hafner & Howze and Cousar, between the railroad track and the public road

leading to Rocky Mount, and crossing the railroad track to reach those stores, in one of which the post-office was kept; but there was no evidence that the defendant company either knew of or acquiesced in this habit of crossing its track at that place. The plaintiff also offered testimony, without objection, tending to show that since the accident occurred the defendant company had cut off three feet from the platforms both of Hafner & Howze and of Cousar, making the distance now between the edges of the platforms and the railroad track six feet instead of three feet, but it also appeared from the testimony of the same witness that the defendant company owned only the road-bed at that point, and had nothing to do with erecting or maintaining those platforms within three feet of their track, and had to obtain permission from the owners to cut them off as above stated. At the close of plaintiff's testimony defendant's counsel moved for a nonsuit, which was granted upon the ground that there was an entire absence of any testimony tending to show negligence on the part of the defendant company.

The plaintiff appealed upon the several grounds set out in the record. It seems to be conceded, and properly so, that the failure of the defendant to give the signals required by the section of the General Statutes above cited cannot avail the plaintiff unless it appears that the disaster occurred at a point where the railroad track crosses a public highway or street or traveled place. Neely v. Railroad Co., 33 S. C. 136, 11 S. E. Rep. 636; Hale v. Railroad Co., 13 S. E. Rep. 637, (decided at the present term.) But it is contended that, while the disaster did not occur at a public highway or street, yet it did occur at a "traveled place," and exception is taken to the construction placed upon those words by the circuit judge,—that it must be a place where the public are authorized to travel, and that, although persons were accustomed to cross the track for the purpose of reaching the stores and post-office, this would not constitute "a traveled place," in the sense of those terms as used in the statute, unless it was shown that the railroad company knew of and acquiesced in this use of its track. We do not think there was any error in the view taken by the circuit judge, unless, indeed, he went too far in favor of the plaintiff. It seems to us that the object of the statute was to protect persons in crossing railroad tracks at points where they had a right to do so, and not at points where they had no legal right to cross. We are not prepared, therefore, to admit that the mere fact that persons were in the habit of crossing a railroad track with the knowledge of and without objection from the company would constitute such a traveled place as is contemplated by the statute, unless the public had in some way acquired the legal right to cross at such point. See Hale v. Railroad Co., referred to above.

But there is another view upon which the ruling of the circuit judge might be sustained. In Glenn v. Railroad Co., 21 S. C. 470, it was held that it was not sufficient to sustain a case of this kind to show negligence, but there must be also some evidence showing that the injury complained of was the result of such negligence; and the same doctrine was recognized in the case of Petrie v. Railroad Co., 29 S. C. at page 318, 7 S. E. Rep. 515. Now, in this case, while there was evidence of negligence in failing to give the statutory signals, which would have made the defendant liable if the disaster had occurred at a public highway or street or traveled place, provided it had been shown that the injury complained of resulted from such negligence, yet, as we have said, the disaster did not occur at any such place, and, if it had, how could it be said that the injury was the result of such negligence, in face of the admitted fact, testi-

fied to both by the party injured and by his companion, that young Barber knew the train was not only approaching, but was near at hand, before he started from the fire? The manifest object of requiring the signals is to give notice to persons crossing or wishing to cross a railroad track, in order that they may keep out of the way of an approaching train; but if they know of the approach of the train without any signal being given, where is the necessity for such signals, and how could it be said with any propriety that the failure to give them contributed in any way to the disaster? The fact that the train was running rapidly—from 20 to 25 miles an hour—is no evidence of negligence in the absence of other circumstances. Zeigler v. Railroad Co., 7 S. C. 402.

The fact that the platform from which young Barber fell was within three feet of the railroad track cannot be a ground of imputing negligence to the defendant, for there is not only no testimony tending to show that the platform was either erected or maintained by the railroad company, but, on the contrary, plaintiff's own testimony shows that such was not the fact, —that the company had nothing to do either with the construction or the maintenance of the platform; that it only owned the road-bed at that point, and had no control over the ground upon which the platform rested. When, therefore, the company, probably with the view to prevent similar disasters, desired to cut off the platforms so as to increase the distance between the track and the outer edge of the platforms, permission had first to be obtained from those who own and control the platforms. To avoid misapprehension, we desire to add that we have considered the question whether there was any evidence of negligence on the part of the company in allowing the platform to remain so near the track, although the complaint contains no allegation of negligence in that respect, because evidence was received without objection, as to that point, and therefore, under the liberal provisions of the Code, it is possible that the complaint might be amended, even after verdict, so as to conform to the facts proved, by inserting an allegation to that effect. But we are not to be understood as disregarding the rule implied by the case of Fell v. Railroad Co., 33 S. C. 198, 11 S. E. Rep. 691. The judgment of this court is that the judgment of the circuit court be affirmed.

McGowan, J.: I concur.

LORENTZ et al. v. ALEXANDER.

(Supreme Court of Georgia. July 8, 1891.)

CONSTITUTIONAL LAW—SPECIAL ACTS—ESTABLISHMENT OF COUNTY COURT.

1. In so far as the act of 1879 is a law for the establishment of county courts, it is not a general law, inasmuch as it excepts by name the county of Walton, and also excepts all counties having a city court, and all county courts then existing.

2. There being no general law, having operation throughout the state, providing for the establishment of county courts, the local law of

1887, touching the establishment of a county court for Early county, is not unconstitutional.

3. The act of 1879 (Code, 279 et seq.) establishes uniformity as to jurisdiction, powers, proceedings, and practice of all county courts, and, in so far as any local or special law on the subject conflicts with the same, such local or special law is unconstitutional; but this does not vitiate any such act in so far as it establishes a county court, and ordains jurisdiction, powers, proceedings, and practice in conformity to the general law.

(Syllabus by the Court.)

Error from superior court, Early county; J. H. GUERRY, Judge.

H. C. Sheffield and J. H. Lumpkin, for plaintiffs in error. R. H. Powell, for defendant in error.

SIMMONS, J. Lorentz & Rittler brought suit against Alexander in the county court of Early county, and obtained a judgment. Alexander appealed to the superior court. The case coming on to be tried there, Alexander moved to dismiss it on the ground that the law organizing the county court was unconstitutional. This motion was granted, and the plaintiff excepted. The county court of Early county was organized under a special act passed by the legislature in 1887. It was contended here by counsel for the defendant in error that the legislature had no authority under the constitution to pass a special act establishing a county court, inasmuch as by the act of 1872, amended by the act of 1879, a general law was already upon the statute-book, providing for the establishment of county courts. The constitutional provision relied on is as follows: "Laws of a general nature shall have uniform operation throughout the state, and no special law shall be enacted in any case for which provision has been made by an existing general law." Article 1, § 4, par. 1, (Code, § 5027.)

1. The act of 1872, which first provided for the establishment of county courts, was not a general law having uniform operation throughout the state, for the act itself excepted 46 counties from its operation. The act of 1879, which amended the prior act, was not a general law, for the same reason. It excepted Walton county by name, and all counties in which a city court had been established, and all counties in which county courts were then existing. A law, to be general, under this section of the constitution, must operate uniformly throughout the whole state upon the subject or class of subjects with which it purposes to deal. The act under consideration deals with the establishment of county courts. In order for it to be general and have uniform operation throughout the state it must affect each county in the state. If it except one or several, it is not general, and cannot have this uniform operation in all counties of the state. It follows, therefore, that the act in question is not a general law, under this clause of the constitution. Where the legislature has not passed a general law upon a subject of a local nature, the constitution does not prohibit it from passing special laws for any particular locality upon that subject; but, if there is a general law upon the subject, it is prohibited

by the constitution from passing special laws for particular localities, changing that general law.

2. The legislature not having passed any general law having operation throughout the state providing for the establishment of county courts, the act of 1887 establishing a county court for the county of Early is not unconstitutional.

3. It was contended, however, by counsel for the defendant in error that the special act for Early county is different in some respects, as to jurisdiction, powers, proceedings, and practice, from the act of 1879, which establishes uniformity in jurisdiction, powers, etc., for all counties. If it be true that the special act is different in these respects, it is unconstitutional and void so far as these differences are concerned; but the fact that the special act gives more or less jurisdiction, and establishes different proceedings or practice, does not render the whole act unconstitutional. So far as the act established a county court and ordained jurisdiction, powers, proceedings, and practice in conformity to the general law, it was constitutional, and the court thus established must be governed by the act making the practice uniform in all county courts. If there is a difference in these respects, the special act must yield to the general law.

Judgment reversed.

COBB et al. v. HOGUE et al.

(Supreme Court of Georgia.　July 8, 1891.)

APPLICATION FOR INJUNCTION—ANSWER—DENIAL OF PETITION.

1. One against whom an injunction is prayed may in his answer set up that he did the acts complained of as agent for another, and this is no cause for striking his answer.

2. There was no abuse of discretion in refusing the injunction prayed for as to any of the defendants in the proceeding, notwithstanding some of them failed to answer.

(Syllabus by the Court.)

Error from superior court, Sumter county; ALLEN FORT, Judge.

Simmons & Kimbrough and Hudson & Blalock, for plaintiffs in error. Hinton, Cutts & Tyson, for defendants in error.

Judgment affirmed.

LUMPKIN, J., not presiding.

HORNE v. JOHNSON.

(Supreme Court of Georgia.　July 8, 1891.)

EJECTMENT BY EXECUTOR—EVIDENCE—TRANSFER OF TAX EXECUTION.

1. According to the cases of Sorrell v. Ham, 9 Ga. 55, and Mays v. Killen, 56 Ga. 537, an executor cannot recover in ejectment without introducing the will.

2. As to the question relating to the transfer of a tax execution by the comptroller general, this case is controlled by Scott v. Stewart, 84 Ga. 772, 11 S. E. Rep. 397.

(Syllabus by the Court.)

Error from superior court, Dooley county; ALLEN FORT, Judge.

Martin & Smith, for plaintiff in error.

J. W. Haygood and *B. P. Hollis*, for defendant in error.

Judgment reversed.

LUMPKIN, J., not presiding.

HOUSTON et al. v. LADIES' UNION BRANCH ASS'N.

(Supreme Court of Georgia. May 6, 1891.)

INSTRUCTIONS—RIGHT TO SET-OFF—CERTAINTY OF VERDICT.

1. The verdict being manifestly right, and the only one that could result from the pleadings and evidence, it was not error for the court, when the jury were about to consider of their verdict, to say, "You can retire if you wish to do so," nor to send an officer to them a few minutes after they had retired with instructions to inquire "what was the difficulty."

2. Where an association sues its former treasurer and her attorney for money due it, the treasurer cannot set off against the plaintiff's demand damages and expenses resulting from a malicious prosecution for embezzling the funds in her hands; nor can such attorney set off against the plaintiff's demand his claim for fees for services rendered in defending the treasurer, either in the prosecution or the action for the money, there being no allegation that the association was insolvent.

3. In an action against two defendants sued jointly, a general verdict for the plaintiff is a finding against both, and is sufficiently certain.

(Syllabus by Lumpkin, J.)

Error from city court of Savannah; W. D. HARDEN, Judge.

Garrard & Meldrim, for plaintiff in error. *Geo. W. Owens*, for defendants in error.

Judgment affirmed.

BAXTER v. WINN.

(Supreme Court of Georgia. May 8, 1891.)

CONSTRUCTION OF WILLS—"HEIRS."

The cardinal rule in the construction of wills is to ascertain the intention of the testator. The court below rightly held that the word "heirs," as used in the will construed in this case, meant "children."

(Syllabus by the Court.)

Error from superior court, Gwinnett county; N. L. HUTCHINS, Judge.

Juhan & McDonald, for plaintiff in error. *T. M. Peeples* and *S. J. Winn*, for defendant in error.

LUMPKIN, J. The will of John Morrow was, substantially, as follows: It gave to D. W. Spence, in trust for Moriah Morrow and Warren Henry Morrow, a lot of land in Gwinnett county, together with the household and kitchen furniture, farming implements, and all testator's stock. It further directed that Moriah and Warren Henry should live in the house then occupied by testator as a dwelling, and that they should not, in any event, bring any one else to live in the house with them; that they should not have any right to trade or sell the place, but through their trustee should enjoy the proceeds, profits, rents, and increase of the property, share and share alike; that the executor should sell testator's farm in Mississippi, and purchase with the money arising therefrom Georgia railroad stock, which he should hold as trustee for Moriah and Warren Henry Morrow, allowing them to receive the interest or dividends arising from it; that, after the executor should pay his just debts and burial expenses, whatever money came into his hands belonging to testator's estate, from collections of debts, rents, or sales of property, he should invest in Georgia railroad stock, as directed above; that, if Wiley H. Baxter remained on the place, he was to have no control of any part of the property, and his property was to be kept separate from Moriah's and Warren Henry's; that, in the event Moriah or Warren Henry should die leaving no heirs, the survivor should have the whole interest arising under the will, and, on the death of the survivor, testator directed that he or she might will it to whom he or she pleased, but that during the lives of Moriah and Warren Henry they were never to have or dispose of any part of the land, stock, or railroad stock, outside of the rents and interest. We think it obvious, without discussion, that the court below rightly construed this will as stated in the headnote. Judgment affirmed.

HALL v. STATE.

(Supreme Court of Georgia. May 8, 1891.)

INTOXICATING LIQUORS—ILLEGAL SALES.

1. On an indictment charging the sale of whisky to two named persons, proof of a sale to either of them will warrant a conviction.

2. An indictment, charging a sale as made to a person named, will be supported by evidence that it was made to him through his servant or messenger, and the latter need not be mentioned by name or otherwise in the indictment.

(Syllabus by the Court.)

Error from superior court, Elbert county; SAMUEL LUMPKIN, Judge.

Indictment of James N. Hall for illegal sale of whisky. Verdict of guilty. Defendant brings error. Affirmed.

John P. Shannon, for plaintiff in error. *W. M. Howard*, Sol. Gen., for the State.

BLECKLEY, C. J. 1. The indictment charged the sale of whisky to two named persons. The evidence showed a sale to one of them, not made to him directly, but through the medium of his servant or messenger, the person himself paying for the article on the next day, which payment was accepted by the accused. The evidence was certainly admissible. Did it warrant a conviction? In Moore v. State, 79 Ga. 498, 5 S. E. Rep. 51, it was ruled that an accusation alleging a sale to a named person and other persons unknown would be supported by proving either a joint or a several sale. And in Dukes v. State, 79 Ga. 795, 4 S. E. Rep. 876, a sale to one minor was held to warrant conviction on an indictment charging a sale to two. The principle of these decisions controls this case in so far as the question of a several sale is concerned.

2. It was contended in the argument that as the servant or messenger of the purchaser was not named or referred to in the indictment, and as there was no sale except the one effected to or through him, the transaction which actually took place

was not covered by the indictment. We think otherwise. According to the evidence, the servant was not the purchaser, but the agent or instrument through which the purchase was made and the whisky delivered. If the transaction had been effected through a common carrier, it certainly would not have been necessary to name the carrier in the indictment. Why, then, should it be requisite to name the servant? Had it appeared that the sale was made to an agent for an unknown principal, there might be good reason for holding that the indictment should set forth the agent's name; but here the principal sent for the whisky, received it, and paid for it in person next day. If the sale was made at all, the accused knew from the indictment what sale was referred to. In his statement he denied the whole business, but the jury believed the testimony, and thought it more credible than the statement. Judgment affirmed.

LUMPKIN, J., not presiding.

MILLIKEN et al. v. KENNEDY.
(*Supreme Court of Georgia.* July 8, 1891.)

ADVERSE POSSESSION.

Title to land acquired by prescription is not lost by ceasing to hold actual possession for 12 months or more, the *animus revertendi* existing.

(*Syllabus by the Court.*)

Error from superior court, Worth county; B. B. BOWER, Judge.
D. H. Pope, for plaintiff in error   W. A. Harris, Richd. Hobbs, and Harrison & Peeples, for defendants in error.
Judgment affirmed.

LUMPKIN, J., not presiding.

ALLEN v. NUSSBAUM et al.
(*Supreme Court of Georgia.* July 8, 1891.)

CONSTITUTIONAL LAW — APPOINTMENT OF RECEIVERS.

1. Act 1881, (Code, § 3149a et seq.,) for putting the assets of insolvent traders into the hands of a receiver, is a general law, and is constitutional.
2. The evidence being conflicting, the judge did not abuse his discretion in appointing a receiver.

(*Syllabus by the Court.*)

Error from superior court, Calhoun county; B. B BOWER, Judge.
C. J. Thornton, for plaintiff in error. H. C. Sheffield, J. J. Beck, and J. H. Lumpkin, for defendants in error.
Judgment affirmed.

LUMPKIN, J., not presiding.

MILLER et al. v. MILLER.
(*Supreme Court of Georgia.* July 13, 1891.)

NEW TRIAL—CONFLICTING EVIDENCE.

There was no abuse of discretion in refusing a new trial, the evidence upon the main issue being conflicting.

(*Syllabus by the Court.*)

Error from superior court, Baldwin county; W. F. JENKINS, Judge.

C. P. Crawford, for plaintiffs in error. Whitfield & Allen, for defendant in error.
Judgment affirmed.

FULLER et al. v. VINING.
(*Supreme Court of Georgia.* July 13, 1891.)

RENEWAL OF JUDGMENT — AFFIDAVIT OF ILLEGALITY.

Defendant in a fi. fa. issued upon a revived judgment, after litigating the legality of a levy, and after final judgment that the levy proceed, cannot raise the question, by a subsequent affidavit of illegality, of proper service upon him in the proceedings to revive the judgment before the fi. fa. issued.

(*Syllabus by the Court.*)

Error from superior court, Morgan county; W. F. JENKINS, Judge.
Action by Fuller and Oglesby against D. M. Vining. Judgment for defendant. Plaintiffs bring error. Reversed.
Foster & Butler, for plaintiffs in error. Calvin George, for defendant in error.

LUMPKIN, J. The fi. fa. referred to in the head-note was, in June, 1888, levied upon certain property of D. M. Vining, the plaintiff's attorney having placed in the sheriff's hands an affidavit to the effect that the property was subject, although covered by a homestead. Vining filed a counter-affidavit, to the effect that the property had been regularly and legally set apart as a homestead, and denying that it was subject to this fi. fa. The final verdict in this case was against the counter-affidavit, and a judgment was rendered ordering the fi. fa. to proceed. The same fi. fa. was afterwards levied upon property of D. M. Vining, and he filed an affidavit of illegality, alleging that he was not personally served with a copy of the scire facias to revive the dormant judgment. He was served with a copy thereof by leaving the same at his residence. It is unnecessary to decide whether the service actually made was legally sufficient or not, because it was adjudicated between these parties that the fi. fa. was a valid one against D. M. Vining. This ruling disposes of the case, but we may remark that the counter-affidavit originally filed by this defendant was substantially an affidavit of illegality, and, so regarding it, rule 81 of the superior courts would be applicable. That rule provides that a second affidavit of illegality cannot be filed for "causes which existed and were known, or in the exercise of reasonable diligence might have been known, at the time of filing the first." If the ground of the second illegality was true in fact, it must have been known to defendant when he filed the first. Manifestly, therefore, the judgment of the court below in sustaining this last affidavit of illegality was wrong.
Judgment reversed.

CUNNINGHAM v. SCOTT et al.
(*Supreme Court of Georgia.* July 13, 1891.)

DISMISSAL OF APPEAL—FAILURE TO FILE RECORD—TIME OF FILING.

1. On a review of the case of Markham v. Huff, 72 Ga. 106, holding that, "where the record and bill of exceptions in an injunction case were

not transmitted to the clerk of the supreme court by the clerk below within fifteen days from the service, the case must be dismissed," the same is affirmed.

2. The service the date of which is to be counted in estimating the 15 days for transmission is the service upon the opposite party in the case brought up, and not a later voluntary service on a co-party with the plaintiff in error, on whom the law requires no service to be made.

3. In this case, the date of service on the defendant in error being the 4th day of the month, and the date of the clerk's certificate to the transcript of the record being the 21st of the month, the transmission was too late, and the writ of error is dismissed.

(Syllabus by the Court.)

Error from superior court, Fulton county; MARSHALL J. CLARKE, Judge.

Thos. W. Latham and Thos. J. Lettwich, for plaintiff in error. J. H. Lumpkin, N. J. & T. A. Hammond, Ellis & Gray, Will Haight, and Rosser & Carter, for defendants in error.

Writ of error dismissed.

GEORGIA, C. & N. RY. CO. v. ARCHER et al.

(Supreme Court of Georgia. May 8, 1891.)

WILLS—ESTATE CONVEYED—EMINENT DOMAIN— COMPENSATION.

1. A devise of the testator's home place to A. and B. and their heirs forever, followed immediately by these words: "It is my will and desire that the said A. and B. shall enjoy and own my home place equally and jointly, and at their death to go to their heirs,"—construed in the light of the parol evidence submitted in this case, vests a fee-simple title in A. and B., the testator having died in 1888, and consequently the provisions of the Code being applicable.

2. The judge did not err in granting a temporary injunction restraining the railroad company from appropriating, under the right of eminent domain, a portion of the lands included in said devise, without first making compensation to the prima facie owners of said land.

3. This adjudication is not meant to include or affect the rights of persons not parties to this case.

(Syllabus by the Court.)

Error from superior court, Clarke county; N. L. HUTCHINS, Judge.

Suit for an injunction by C. S. Archer and J. A. Fowler against the Georgia, Carolina & Northern Railway Company. Temporary injunction granted. Defendant brings error. Affirmed.

Barrow & Thomas and A. J. Cobb, for plaintiff in error. Lumpkin & Burnett, for defendants in error.

SIMMONS, J. The only question in this case is the proper construction of the third item of the will. It reads as follows: "Item 3. I give, will, and bequeath to my nephews Cicero S. Archer and Livingstone H. Weir my home place where I now reside, together with all the rights, members, and appurtenances thereunto appertaining or belonging; to belong to them, the said Cicero S. Archer and Livingstone H. Weir, and their heirs, forever. It is my will and desire that the said Cicero S. Archer and Livingstone H. Weir shall enjoy and own my said home place equally and jointly, and at their death to go to their heirs." In the construction of wills, the great thing to be sought for is the intention of the testator. If the intention is not clearly expressed, if it is obscure or ambiguous, Code, 2457, declares that "the court may hear parol evidence of the circumstances surrounding the testator at the time of its execution," and "may hear parol evidence to explain all ambiguities, both latent and patent." Under this section, the court below, in construing this item, heard parol testimony as to the intention of the testator and his surroundings at the time of the execution of the will. That testimony shows, in substance, that the testator was a man advanced in years, with no immediate family, and that he had never married; that he desired to make a final disposition of all his property; that he had a number of brothers and sisters and nieces and nephews; that as to a certain number of them he entertained no kindly feelings, and had nothing to do with them; that Cicero Archer and Livingstone Weir were his favorite nephews and lived about half of the time with him; that they were both middle-aged men, and had never married, and were not likely to marry; that Livingstone Weir was a paralytic, and incapable of marriage, and that the testator knew this; and that he stated, at or about the time of the execution of the will, that he did not desire those of his kindred with whom he was unfriendly to have any of his property. The property bequeathed to these favorite nephews by the item above quoted constitutes the bulk of the estate. The fourth item gives to the same nephews all of his personal property, and the fifth item gives to six other nephews 330 acres of land. The testator died in 1888. Construing these items of the will in the light of the facts now before us, we think it vested a fee-simple title in Cicero Archer and Livingstone Weir. The court, therefore, did not err in granting a temporary injunction restraining the railroad company from appropriating, under the right of eminent domain, a portion of the lands included in the third item of the will, without first making compensation to the prima facie owners thereof. This decision, of course, applies only to the parties now before the court. If other parties should be made to the case hereafter, the latter would not be bound thereby; or if upon the trial of the case the facts should be materially different from the facts now before us, as to the intention and surroundings of the testator at the time of the execution of the will, our construction of the will would perhaps be different.

Judgment affirmed.

BRYANT v. JONES.

(Supreme Court of Georgia. July 8, 1891.)

DISMISSAL OF BILL—INJUNCTION.

1. After a full hearing and investigation on an application for temporary injunction, and after the judge has announced his purpose to deny the injunction, the plaintiff still has the right to dismiss his bill; but it is discretionary with the judge whether he will reduce his judgment to writing, and make it a part of the case, or not.

2. On the facts in evidence, there was no abuse of discretion in refusing the injunction prayed for.

(Syllabus by the Court.)

Error from superior court, Sumter county; ALLEN FORT, Judge.
Clarke & Hooper, for plaintiff in error.
Whatley & Fitzgerald and *L. J. Blalock*, for defendant in error.
Judgment affirmed.

LUMPKIN, J., not presiding.

SLOAT et al. v. ROUNTREE.

(Supreme Court of Georgia. July 8, 1891.)

HOLDING OVER—CONSENT OF TENANT—LANDLORD
—NOTICE—DAMAGES.

1. Where one gives another permission to occupy a house until a tenant is obtained for the year, the occupant is entitled to reasonable notice that a tenant has been obtained.

2. Where the suit is against the tenant for holding over after the expiration of a definite term, a sufficient reply to it is that the landlord consented for him to hold over. If the real cause of action be damages resulting from the violation of the terms of this consent, that cause should be alleged in the declaration.

(Syllabus by the Court.)

Error from superior court, Lowndes county; A. H. HANSELL, Judge.
Action by A. J. Rountree against Sloat Bros. for holding over a tenancy. Judgment for plaintiff. Defendants bring error. Reversed.
J. R. Slater and *W. H. Ramsey*, for plaintiffs in error. *D. W. Rountree* and *Wilkinson & Ashley*, for defendant in error.

BLECKLEY, C. J. 1. As the landlord consented that his tenants might hold over after the expiration of their term until he found another tenant for the new year, some reasonable notice that a tenant was found ought to have been given before the new tenant attempted to move in. It could not be expected that an occupant having permission to remain for an indefinite time would hold himself ready to vacate at any and every moment. Certainly a few hours', if not a few days', warning might reasonably be expected in such a case. Here the evidence indicated that the new tenant appeared at the house with some of his goods to enter immediately, and that, failing to be admitted, he claimed and exercised the right of canceling his contract with the landlord.

2. But the decisive point in the case is that the evidence does not support the declaration. The declaration complains of holding over after the expiration of the original term of renting. The proof shows that the landlord consented to this, and that consent is certainly a sufficient reply to the holding over complained of. The real cause of action, if any, is a violation of the terms of this consent, and neither the consent nor the violation is referred to in the declaration. They should both have been alleged in order to recover. Certainly, according to the evidence, the defendants were entitled to hold over beyond the expiration of the original term. They were in no default, on any view of the case, until after the new tenant was found, and that new tenant did not make his appearance until three days after the definite term mentioned in the declaration had run out. At that time

the defendants were in possession under a new agreement, which agreement is not mentioned in the declaration. The action as brought was well defended. The court erred in not granting a new trial. Judgment reversed.

LUMPKIN, J., not presiding.

GEORGIA RAILROAD & BANKING CO. v. RHODES.

(Supreme Court of Georgia. July 13, 1891.)

NEW TRIAL—WEIGHT OF EVIDENCE.

This court having ruled that a cause of action was set forth in the declaration, and the evidence adduced at the trial being sufficient to support the declaration, the court did not err in refusing to grant a new trial.

(Syllabus by the Court.)

Error from superior court, Morgan county; W. F. JENKINS, Judge.
Action by John Rhodes against the Georgia Railroad & Banking Company for the negligent killing of plaintiff's son. Demurrer to plaintiff's declaration sustained. Plaintiff brought error. Reversed. On retrial there was judgment for plaintiff. Defendant brings error. Affirmed. For prior report, see 10 S. E. Rep. 922.
J. B. Cumming, *J. A. Billups*, and *Bryan Cumming*, for plaintiff in error. *Foster & Butler*, for defendant in error.
Judgment affirmed.

JOHNSON v. PALMOUR et al.

(Supreme Court of Georgia. May 8, 1891.)

TRIAL—RIGHT TO OPEN AND CLOSE—NEW TRIAL.

1. On the trial of a claim case, the claimant demanded the right to assume the burden of proof, and to open and conclude the argument, but made no offer to admit any particular fact or facts. It appeared that claimant was in possession of a portion of the property levied on, and the defendant in *fi. fa.* was in possession of the remaining portion thereof. *Held*, there was no error in refusing to allow this demand of claimant.

2. The evidence was sufficient to warrant the verdict; and the newly-discovered evidence, being cumulative, or only tending to discredit a witness, is not cause for a new trial.

(Syllabus by the Court.)

Error from superior court, Hall county; C. J. WELLBORN, Judge.
Intervention of Mary J. Johnson against Palmour and Smith. Claim refused. Claimant brings error. Affirmed.
J. M. Towry, *G. H. Pryor*, and *W. I. Pike*, for plaintiff in error. *H. H. Dean*, for defendants in error.

LUMPKIN, J. 1. In order to authorize the claimant to demand the right to open and conclude, she should have admitted facts amounting to a *prima facie* case for the plaintiff in *fi. fa.* This she did not offer to do. She could not admit that defendants in *fi. fa.* were in possession of the property, because, in fact, she herself was in possession of a portion of it, and therefore, even had she attempted to make this admission, simply to obtain the right to open and conclude, the court should not have allowed it for this purpose. See

Royce v. Gazan, 76 Ga. 79. In view of the facts stated, we can see no error in the court's refusal to allow the demand made by the claimant.

2. The remaining points made by the motion for a new trial are disposed of in the second head-note. Judgment affirmed.

HAWKS *et al.* v. SAILORS.

(*Supreme Court of Georgia.* May 8, 1891.)

CONSTRUCTION OF DEED—EVIDENCE IN EJECTMENT.

A deed from a father-in-law, made in consideration of $500, "less $200 for the love and affection the said White bears to his daughter, Martha A. Sailors, donated out of the $500 at and before the sealing and delivery of these presents," and conveying the premises to the son-in-law with warranty title, vests the title in him for his own use, no other use being declared. No trust results in favor of the daughter, and, while parol evidence would be admissible in a proceeding to reform the deed if it does not execute the intention of the parties, such evidence is not admissible upon the trial of an action of ejectment brought by the daughter against a person in possession of the land.

(*Syllabus by the Court.*)

Error from superior court, Jackson county; N. L. HUTCHINS, Judge.

Action in ejectment by Martha A. Sailors against Henry Hawks and another. Judgment for defendants. Plaintiff brings error. Reversed.

D. W. Meadow and *Barrow & Thomas,* for plaintiff in error. *Thomas & Strickland,* for defendants in error.

SIMMONS, J. We think the court erred in refusing to grant a new trial in this case. The deed put in evidence by Mrs. Sailors, the plaintiff in the court below, upon which to predicate a recovery, shows that the whole title to the land was in her husband, and not in her. It conveys the title to C. C. Sailors, the husband, and warrants the same to him. The use is also declared "to him and their heirs, to his and their own proper use, benefit, and behoof forever, in fee-simple." It is true that, in stating the consideration, it declares that "said White has, for and in consideration of the sum of $500 to him in hand paid by said Sailors, less $200 for the love and affection the said White bears to his daughter, Martha A. Sailors, donated out of the $500, at and before the sealing and delivery of these presents, * * * hath bargained and sold," etc. But we do not think this clause is inconsistent with the intention of the grantor to place the title to the land in his son-in-law, Sailors. The love and affection which he bore to his daughter was a sufficient consideration to donate to the son-in-law the $200. Whether the grantor intended to donate the $200 to his daughter or to his son-in-law makes no difference in this suit, because, as we have before remarked, the deed clearly puts the title in the son-in-law, and for his own use, and fails to declare any other use to the son-in-law. Nor do we think that under the terms of this deed any trust resulted in favor of the daughter, or that the husband was trustee for her for two-fifths of the land described in the deed. This was a suit in ejectment, where the daughter sought to recover two-fifths of the land. Under this deed, we do not think she was entitled to do so. In a suit in ejectment, she could not ingraft upon the deed by parol testimony new terms and conditions, and the court, therefore, erred in allowing the parol testimony which is set out in the amended motion for a new trial. If the suit had been to reform the deed, and make it declare the true intention of the parties at the time it was made, parol testimony would have been admissible for that purpose, but in this form of action it was not admissible. Judgment reversed.

MAYOR, ETC., OF MILLEDGEVILLE v. BROWN.

(*Supreme Court of Georgia.* July 18, 1891.)

MUNICIPAL CORPORATIONS—DEFECTIVE STREETS—PERSONAL INJURIES—EVIDENCE.

There was no error in refusing a nonsuit, and the verdict was warranted by the evidence, the jury having inspected the premises.

(*Syllabus by the Court.*)

Error from superior court, Baldwin county; W. F. JENKINS, Judge.

Action by Lucy M. Brown against the mayor, etc., of Milledgeville, for personal injuries. Judgment for plaintiff. Defendant brings error. Affirmed.

The following is the official report:

Action for damages by Miss Lucy M. Brown against the mayor and aldermen of the city of Milledgeville. The evidence showed as follows: Between 7 and 8 o'clock in the evening of the 31st of January, 1886, the plaintiff and Miss Stanley started from the house of Mrs. Garrett, on the south side of Hancock street, in Milledgeville, to go to the house of Mrs. Crawford, on the north side of that street, and just opposite the end of Liberty street where it intersects Hancock. They went east down the sidewalk to the middle of Liberty street, a point nearly opposite Mrs. Crawford's. Did so to get the benefit of the lamp at the south-east corner of Hancock and Liberty streets, which was the nearest lamp to the mouth of the culvert to be referred to. When they reached the middle of Liberty street they turned and started across Hancock street, the plaintiff a little in advance, going towards the light they saw in Mrs. Crawford's house. There was no crossing at this place. The sidewalks did not extend across. When near the north side of Hancock street, at a point between the road-bed and the sidewalk, the plaintiff fell four or five feet from the top of a culvert into a sewer. It had been raining, and was cloudy, and the streets were muddy. The culvert was a covered drain, about three feet high and four feet wide, under Hancock street, connecting the under-drain north with that south of Hancock street. The bottom of the culvert was about five feet below the surface-bed of the street. A semi-circular brick wall four feet high, its top flush with the street, protected the mouth of the culvert, holding up the earth of the street, and facing towards the north sidewalk. A surface drain 1½ to 2 feet deep and 6 to 15 feet wide, sloping to the middle, separated the street from the sidewalk, and emptied into the culvert over a convex funnel of brick and cement descending to its mouth. It was upon this funnel, four feet lower than the wall, that plaintiff fell. The culvert is in line with the surface drain of Liberty street; and Mrs. Crawford's gate is west of the culvert, and opposite the south-west corner of Liberty and Hancock streets. The culvert is an excellent piece of work, and has been in its present condition for many years. It carries off a great deal of water. The city is built on very broken and precipitous ground, there being necessarily many abrupt places, banks, etc., where one might fall and be hurt. The plaintiff was 24 years old, and was acquainted with the place in question, knew it was there, and was looking out for it when she fell. She was under the impression that the wall or end of the culvert over which she fell projected a few inches above the ground, and expected to feel that with her feet and be warned of the danger. Very little or no light from the lamp across the street shone on this sewer. For two years she had been living in Macon, and was back to Milledgeville on a visit. The last time she remembered to have seen the culvert before she fell the bricks were elevated above the ground, and she was feeling for them when she fell. There are no foot crossings over Hancock street nearer than the two streets parallel to Liberty which intersect Hancock. To go from Mrs. Garrett's by one of these crossings would require a walk of nearly 500 yards; by the other, 250 yards; while it was but about 80 yards the way plaintiff went. By going directly across the street from Mrs. Garrett's, she would have avoided the culvert, and would have had to walk no further than she did. She might have crossed safely a few feet east or west from where she fell. The surface drain on the north side of Hancock street is broad and shallow, bad for crossing, though wood wagons do cross it with safety. A female witness fell at the same place some time after plaintiff did, but from the opposite side,—from the sidewalk, and before she reached the masonry leading to the mouth of the sewer. She was not injured from this fall. The plaintiff was badly hurt, and she testified that she was permanently injured. She suffered great pain, and was confined to her bed four or five weeks, and it was still longer before she could leave her room. Her hip was dislocated by the fall, and was replaced by a physician. She was a strong and healthy woman before the fall. Has to work for her living, but cannot do half as much as she could before. Her father was an old man, and she rendered material aid to him in his work. At the time of the injury she was making eight to ten dollars per week: but afterwards, on account of her health, she was forced to decline to do work she had been doing before. Her physician did not know that she received any permanent injuries. About two years after the accident he treated her with electricity for pains in hip and back. He could not say that these pains were the result of the fall into the sewer; they may have been; he could not tell; he had known such pains so produced. No bones were broken by the fall,

"only a tendon that held the joint in place." The defendant moved for a nonsuit, which was refused. At the instance of counsel, assented to by both sides, the court permitted the jury, before argument was begun, to view and examine the place where the injury occurred. They found for the plaintiff, $500. The trial took place on the 28th of January, 1890. The defendant moved for a new trial, on the ground that the verdict was against the law and the evidence. To the overruling of this motion and of the motion for a nonsuit exceptions were taken.

C. P. Crawford and *R. W. Roberts,* for plaintiff in error. *W. A. Lofton,* for defendant in error

LUMPKIN, J. The only question to be determined in this case is whether or not the verdict was authorized by the evidence. The facts will appear in the reporter's statement. Among other things, it was proved that the city authorities of Milledgeville permitted a sewer to remain open for years on one of the principal streets, and in a neighborhood lighted so dimly and imperfectly that the light was of little benefit to any one passing that way at night. The jury, with the consent of counsel for both sides, were permitted by the court to visit the scene of the accident, and make a personal inspection of the same for themselves. We think this was a good practice, as it must undoubtedly have materially aided them in arriving at a correct conclusion as to whether the city authorities were negligent or not. In view of the testimony, and of this personal examination by the jury of the open sewer, we cannot say they erroneously found that defendant was negligent, or that the court abused its discretion in allowing their verdict to stand. There was evidence to show that the plaintiff was familiar with the locality, and it was contended that by reason of this familiarity she could, by exercising proper diligence, have avoided the injury. But there was also evidence to show that since the last time she saw the place of the accident there had been a change in the condition of the open sewer. She had been absent from Milledgeville two years. At the time she left, the brick-work of the sewer projected some inches above the ground, but when she was injured it was on a level with the surface of the ground,—a circumstance which misled her, and to some extent contributed to the injury. Doubtless the court charged the jury upon the law of contributory negligence, and the amount of the verdict would seem to indicate that the jury considered this in making their finding. In view of all the facts, we see no reason to interfere with the discretion of the court below in upholding this verdict. The judgment is therefore affirmed.

MOORE v. WESTERN UNION TEL. CO.

(Supreme Court of Georgia. July 18, 1891.)

TELEGRAPH COMPANY—FAILURE TO DELIVER MESSAGE—RIGHT OF ACTION.

A transient visitor to a town or city, who furnishes to the company no definite address, is not a person residing in the same or within one mile of the station, in contemplation of the act of 1887, subjecting telegraph companies to a forfeiture for failing to deliver dispatches to residents.

(Syllabus by the Court.)

Error from superior court, Crawford county; A. L. MILLER, Judge.

Action by L. D. Moore against the Western Union Telegraph Company for failure to deliver a message. Nonsuit granted. Plaintiff brings error. Affirmed.

The following is the official report:

Moore sued the telegraph company for damages in the sum of $100 for failure to deliver to him at Knoxville, Crawford county, Ga., where he was temporarily, a message sent to him from Macon, Ga. By another count in his declaration he alleged that he had been damaged by such failure to deliver, $125, by being deprived of certain business. Upon the trial of the case plaintiff introduced the telegraphic dispatch. It was admitted that it was delivered to defendant at its office in Macon at 11 o'clock A. M., on June 3, 1889, and that the charges for sending it to Knoxville, Ga., were prepaid by the sender to defendant at the time. There was evidence for plaintiff that he came to Knoxville from Macon on the day before the message was sent; that he saw the telegraph operator at the depot, the place where the telegraph office is kept, and told him that, if any message should come for him, to send it over to Knoxville; that he remained in Knoxville until about sunset of the evening of June 3d, and then went out into the country, and returned on the evening of the 4th, and went back to his home in Macon, on the railroad; that he stayed on and around the courthouse square the most of the time while in Knoxville; that he spent the night of the 3d at a Mr. Wright's; that everybody in Knoxville knew him, and he could have been easily found; that the telegram has never been delivered to him; that the telegraph office is within less than one mile of Knoxville and of Wright's house; that the telegraph operator told Wright he received the message about 2 o'clock on June 3d, and, being busy, gave it to one Harris to carry to Knoxville to Moore. At the close of the evidence for plaintiff defendant moved for a nonsuit, on the grounds that plaintiff was not entitled to recover, in that, as he permanently resided in Macon, and not in Knoxville, defendant did not incur any penalty for a failure to deliver the telegram. This motion was sustained, to which plaintiff excepted.

W. S. Wallace, L. D. Moore, and Hardeman, Davis & Turner, for plaintiff in error. Gustin, Guerry & Hull, for defendant in error.

SIMMONS, J. The facts will be found in the official report. Under these facts the grant of a nonsuit was right. By the express terms of the statute (Acts 1887, p. 112) the penalty is imposed upon these companies for failure to deliver messages to persons to whom they are addressed who at the time reside within one mile of the telegraph office, or within the town or city in which the office is. The act is clearly intended to apply to only a part of the public, and it imposes this duty on the company, under this penalty, when it is dealing with that class which come within the strict letter of the act. The act is a penal one, and must be strictly construed. Any other construction placed upon it would work great hardship upon the telegraph companies. It would subject them to this penalty in many cases where from the very nature of things it would be impossible for them to avoid the penalty. The legislature evidently designed to limit the operation of the law to that class of persons who come within the proviso of the second section of the act. Moore was residing in the city of Macon, and was merely a transient visitor to the town of Knoxville; and, although he requested the telegraph operator at the station near Knoxville to send him any message that might be received for him there, he gave no definite address. If, after notifying the operator that he would be in Knoxville, and to send the messages to him there, he had given him a definite address, such as a given street and number, or the name of the owner of a particular house where the message should be delivered, perhaps he would have come within the spirit of the law, if not the letter of it. But it would be unreasonable to hold telegraph companies bound to deliver messages to strangers in a town or city when they have no means of knowing the place at which the message can be received. If the person to whom the message is sent resides in a town or city, or within one mile of the station, then it is the duty of the telegraph company to ascertain where he resides; but if he is a transient visitor or a stranger, with no fixed abode, it might be impracticable for the company or its agents to ascertain the place where the message could be delivered. 2. The action was also for damages in the loss of certain business by the nondelivery of the dispatch. There was no proof submitted to the court and jury upon this question, and the court did not err in granting a nonsuit upon both counts in the declaration. Judgment affirmed.

MCNEIL et al. v. HAMMOND et al.

(Supreme Court of Georgia. July 13, 1891.)

CONSTRUCTION OF WILL—ADVANCEMENTS.

The will is not ambiguous. Its provision in respect to advancements relates only to a particular part of the testator's property, not to the whole estate, and is confined to a distribution of one-sixth of that part between the two granddaughters named in the sixteenth item. No scheme of accounting for advancements was contemplated as between the legatees of the other five-sixths and the two granddaughters who took the one-sixth.

(Syllabus by the Court.)

Error from superior court, Bibb county; A. L. MILLER, Judge.

Petition for the construction of a will, etc., by Viola McNeil and Irene Petty against A. D. Hammond and another, executors. Decree for respondents. Petitioners bring error. Reversed.

The following is the official report:

The contention of the petitioners was

that an undivided one-sixth part of the estate of testator as mentioned in the sixteenth item of the will was to be given to them jointly, and that they were to account between themselves,—that is to say, that Mrs. McNeil should first receive as much more of this one-sixth part as would first make her equal with her sister, Mrs. Petty, and then the balance of this one-sixth share should be equally divided between them. To this petition the defendants filed an answer, in which they admitted the allegations in the petition, except that they contended that under a proper construction of the sixteenth item, when taken in connection with the seventh item of the will, and the entries of the testator made in a book, which were copied as exhibits to their answer, the petitioners should first account to the estate for the advancements mentioned under the sixteenth item, and should first pay these sums into the estate before they were allowed to participate in the distribution of the estate. Under an agreement of parties the cause was submitted to the judge below for decision without the intervention of a jury. The petitioners introduced the will. By it the testator bequeathed to his wife a certain amount to be paid her in cash; to his son, A. D. Hammond, and one of his (testator's) daughters, certain other amounts, to be paid them in cash; to another daughter an amount in cash, which he desired to be retained by his wife as trustee for this daughter; and to the four children of a deceased daughter another amount in cash, to be equally divided between them. By the seventh item of his will he bequeathed to the two children of his deceased daughter Mrs. Johns, to-wit, to "Viola McNeil $100, and to Irene Petty no money, as she [Irene] has recently, as she has at times before, received from me several hundred dollars in money." He further bequeathed to the children of another deceased daughter a sum to be held by his wife as trustee for them. By the ninth item of his will he directed that all the remainder of his estate should remain under the control of his wife during her life or widowhood, etc. By the tenth item he devised to his wife absolutely certain property. By the eleventh item he directed that at the death of his wife all the property remaining in her control be sold, and the proceeds of the sale, together with the cash in hand, be divided equally between his children and grandchildren in six parts, as follows: By the twelfth item, one undivided sixth part to his son, in trust for the use of his son's wife and their children; by the thirteenth item, another undivided sixth part to one of his daughters; by the fourteenth item, another undivided sixth part to another daughter, to be held for her in trust by his (testator's) wife; by the fifteenth item, another undivided sixth part to the children of a deceased daughter. The sixteenth item was as follows: ["Another undivided sixth part thereof I give to my grandchildren, Viola McNeil and Irene Petty, the children of my deceased daughter, Mary E. Johns, to be equally divided between them, after each of them shall account for the respective sums of money I

have heretofore advanced to each, to-wit, to Viola McNeil three hundred and twenty-five dollars, and to Irene Petty seven hundred dollars, (in fact more, but I charge her now with that sum;) I mean that Viola McNeil is to receive more of the said sixth share in proportion as she has received less of the said advances mentioned in this item. The proportion thus given each to be paid over to each of them directly as the separate property of each, and free from the debts or control of the present or any future husband of each."] By the seventeenth item he gave another undivided sixth part in trust to the children of another deceased daughter. By the eighteenth item he provided that in case the cash in hand at his death "has diminished in amount from that now in hand, in view of which the foregoing legacies are given," his wife was still to have the amount in cash before mentioned, and Nettie and Mamie Barnes, the children of one of his deceased daughters, were to have the sum in cash which had been bequeathed them, but the other legatees were to share the deficit between them in proportion to the amount of their several legacies, and, if the cash in hand had increased in amount, each of the legatees might receive more in proportion, in the discretion of his wife, not interfering with any other provision in the will as to the surplus cash. By another item he provided that in case his wife should marry again all of his property remaining undisposed of after paying debts, expenses, and legacies should be converted into money, and this divided into seven equal shares, one of which was to go to his wife, and the other six shares divided as provided hereinbefore in the will.

In rebuttal of evidence put in by respondents, to the introduction of which petitioners objected, the petitioners put in evidence an affidavit of Mrs. Petty to the effect that her grandfather (testator) raised her; that he made advancements of equal amounts at the marriage of each of his children; that, in addition thereto, since her mother's death, he made large advancements to each of his children, though living separately from him; that he for years aided A. D. Hammond in the support of his family, advancing him money, and, just before A. D. Hammond's son arrived at age, also made advances to start the son off in life; and also a mortgage given by Mrs. McNeil to the testator, dated November 9, 1877, to secure the payment of a note for $325 on a house and lot in the town of Quitman. On the back of this mortgage was an entry dated April 28, 1883, signed by the testator, to the effect that, the note to secure which this mortgage was given having been fully paid off and settled, the mortgage was discharged, released, and canceled. The respondents offered the book above referred to in evidence, containing the entries, of which the following are copies:

"1885. Viola McNeil. To loaned money, $325.00; when she located in Quitman, Ga., several years ago.

"Macon, Dec. 7th, 1885. I make the above charge for the purpose of having it understood that if I leave her anything at my death, that the above amount, $325, is to be deducted from whatever may be coming to her from my estate. I raised her, and educated her in Macon and at Salem, North Carolina, which me at Salem $400 or $500. Kept her about eighteen years, and gave a good outfit at her marriage, which is more than I ever done for any of my grandchildren, with the exception of her sister, Irene. I merely mention this to show what I have done for her without making any charge for the same. It might be proper to mention that her father was insolvent. I paid for her and sister Irene over $5,-000 to raise and educate them, which will appear on the books of the ordinary book of the county. It must have cost me to raise and school them over $10,000.

[Signed]　　　"D. W. HAMMOND.

1885.　　　Irene Petty.

Loaned money	$325 00
Loaned her to pay her board	40 00
1885. Do	25 00
Sent Petty check, N. Y	300 00
	$690 00
Gave $100 when she was burnt out Kimbal House; will only charge her	10 00
	$700 00

"I make the above charge for the purpose of having it understood that if I leave her any property at my death that the above amount, $500, is to be deducted from whatever may be coming to her from my estate. I raised and educated her, and kept her about twenty years, and furnished her a good outfit of clothing at her marriage, which is more than I done for any of my grandchildren, etc. I thought it might be proper to mention, although I do not make any extra charge for it, but only expect the money loaned to be paid back, or deducted from any legacy that may be coming to her at my death, etc.

[Signed.]　　　"D. W. HAMMOND. "December 7th, 1885.

"1886. Brought over, so at my death I will expect to deduct $700 from what legacy may be coming to her (if any at all.) Mention this in my will.

[Signed]　　　"D. W. HAMMOND. "30th January, 1886."

To the introduction of this evidence petitioners objected, on the ground that the sixteenth item of the will was not ambiguous, but was plain in its terms, and, being so, this evidence was not admissible for explaining an ambiguity, or showing the circumstances under which the will was made; and for the further reason that the will was the highest evidence of the testator's intention. These objections were overruled, and the evidence admitted. The court, then, over the objection of petitioners, permitted read in evidence a former will made by testator, the seventh and sixteenth items of which were identical with those in the will introduced by petitioners; and also permitted A. D. Hammond, over the objection of petitioners, to testify that he wrote the will, copying it largely, and especially this section, from a former will made by his father; that at the time of the marriage of each of his children his father advanced to

them about equal; that since the death of petitioners' mother he had made other advancements to living children, but witness could not say that they got more advances than he had in her life-time given them; that during a long spell of sickness witness had his father give him $200, and when his oldest son was 17 or 18 years of age, his father gave him $100 or $125; that one of testator's daughters, Mrs. Lockett, is married, and his father helped her, paid her board, and made various advances to her; that he advanced to Mrs. Thomas, another daughter, as much as any of them; that he never did for any of his grandchildren as much as he did for plaintiffs, raised them from infancy, and educated them, etc. The objections to the introduction of the former will, which was dated January 31, 1886, and to the testimony of A. D. Hammond, were upon the same grounds as those made to the introduction of the entries from the book above mentioned, but these objections were also overruled. The court held that there was such an ambiguity in the sixteenth item of the will, when read in connection with the seventh item, as would authorize the introduction of testimony to explain the intention of the testator, and that the testimony concerning the entries in the book, the entries themselves, and the other testimony concerning the testator's estate and advancements to the beneficiaries, was competent and admissible; and that, construing the will in the light of the testimony, the petitioners should account to the estate for the respective sums of money advanced to them, before receiving their part of the estate,—that is, Mrs. McNeil should account for $325, and Mrs. Petty for $700, before receiving the shares allotted to each, and should then also account as between themselves, ratably, as provided in the sixteenth item, and the executors should proceed in accordance with this finding in the distribution of the estate. To this decision the petitioners excepted, alleging that the court erred in deciding that there was such an ambiguity in the sixteenth item, when read in connection with the seventh item, as would authorize the introduction of testimony to explain the testator's intention, in admitting the testimony mentioned, in construing the will in the light thereof, and in the construction made by the court.

Hardeman, Davis & Turner, for plaintiffs in error. *A. D. Hammond* and *Hill, Harris & Birch,* for defendants in error.

LUMPKIN, J. The sixteenth item of the will of D. W. Hammond was as follows: "Another undivided sixth part thereof [meaning all that part of testator's estate which he had devised to his wife and on hand at her death] I give to my grandchildren, Viola McNeil and Irene Petty, the children of my deceased daughter Mary E. Johns, to be equally divided between them, after each of them shall account for the respective sums of money I have heretofore advanced to each, to-wit: To Viola McNeil, three hundred and twenty-five dollars, and to Irene Petty, seven hundred dollars, (in fact more, but I charge her with that sum.) I mean that

Viola McNeil is to receive more of the said sixth share in proportion as she has received less of the said advances mentioned in this item. The proportion thus given each to be paid over to each of them directly as the separate property of each, and free from the debts or control of the present or any future husband of each." The other parts of the will material to a proper construction of the item quoted will be found in the reporter's statement. Considering together all the provisions of this will, it will be plainly apparent that it contained no general scheme of accounting for advancements by the legatees therein named, and certainly there was no such scheme as between the legatees of the five-sixths of that part of the estate disposed of by the sixteenth item and the two granddaughters, to whom the other sixth thereof was given. It was the obvious intention of the testator to equalise his granddaughters, Viola McNeil and Irene Petty, in the division between them of the sixth of the specified portion of his estate which they were to receive; and we think the meaning of the testator to this effect is clearly and plainly expressed in the above-quoted item of his will, the more especially as the only provision anywhere made in the will in reference to advancements is that contained in said item. That item, by its express terms, limits and confines the matter of accounting for advancements to the division between the two granddaughters of their share of the estate. The court held that there was such an ambiguity in the sixteenth item of the will, when read in connection with the other parts of it, as would authorise the introduction of extrinsic testimony to explain the intention of the testator. We think the court erred in admitting this outside testimony, and, after so doing, in holding that Mrs. McNeil and Mrs. Petty, before receiving their part of the estate, should account to the other legatees for the sums of money respectively advanced to them by the testator. As already shown, these ladies are entitled to one-sixth of that portion of the estate devised to testator's wife for life and remaining on hand at her death, in the division of which between themselves each must account to the other for the amount she has already received from the testator, as directed by the will, so that their shares may be equalised as therein contemplated. Judgment reversed.

SWIFT SPECIFIC CO. v. JACOBS et al.

(Supreme Court of Georgia. July 13, 1891.)

INJUNCTION—PLEADING.

Where a petition by the manufacturer of a certain medicine to enjoin a person who owned a large quantity thereof, which had been in a burned building, alleged that the medicine had a large sale; that it was composed of vegetable substances, and that, by reason of the great heat to which it had been subjected, its medicinal properties were dissipated, and that the sale thereof under petitioner's trade-mark would cause great damage to petitioner's business; but failed to allege that defendant was insolvent, or to show wherein petitioner would suffer irreparable injury, or wherein the medicine had lost its virtue,—there was no abuse of discretion in denying the injunction.

Error from superior court, Fulton county; MARSHALL J. CLARKE, Judge.

Petition for an injunction by the Swift Specific Company against Joseph Jacobs and the Jacobs Pharmacy Company. Denied. Petitioner brings error. Affirmed.

The following is the official report:

The Swift Specific Company, by its equitable petition, made, in brief, the following allegations: Petitioner manufactures a blood medicine, popularly called "S. S. S.," the medicine being put up in packages and bottles bearing a particular label, on which is the name of petitioner as manufacturer and the said "S. S. S.," which is both the trade-name and a trade-mark. The medicine is of great reputation and wide sale. Its composition is a trade secret. Petitioner has spared no pains in the manufacture of the medicine to give it the greatest possible virtue, and to keep it at a high standard of purity, and for many years has spent in preparing it, and in advertising and selling it, a very large amount of money. The property in the medicine is of great value,—a value especially dependent upon the high reputation which the efforts of petitioner have given the medicine. Some time during the present year a fire occurred in the warehouse of Henry J. Lamar & Sons, and, in settlement of policies covering the loss by the fire, some insurance companies took possession of all the burned goods in the warehouse covered by the policies, and among these goods were about 451 cases of S. S. S., the same being in bottles, and bearing the label, trade-mark, and trade-name aforesaid, with the name of petitioner as the manufacturer. The medicine was exposed in the fire to such a degree of heat that its medicinal qualities, which are mainly vegetable, were dissipated, and thereby all of its virtue was lost; and defendants, petitioner believing that they were aware of the effect of the fire upon the medicine, purchased it from the insurance companies, and are now attempting to sell it as genuine, unadulterated, and good medicine; and they offer it for sale under the trade-mark, label, and name of petitioner. By reason of the facts above mentioned, all of the medicine so purchased by defendants, or much the larger part of it, is not really the medicine manufactured by petitioner, but it has lost all its virtue, and for defendants to sell it as the medicine of petitioner is to palm off upon the public a spurious substance, under the name of petitioner's medicine, to the irreparable damage and injury of petitioner. Each of the cases of the medicine mentioned above contained a dozen bottles, and each case, if uninjured, was of the value of $8 or $10. The sale of said burned medicine by defendants will be an infringement of the exclusive right of petitioner to the use of its packages, label, trade-name, trade-mark. and its own name, to designate its manufacture as its real, and not a spurious, medicine. Petitioner prayed that defendants (Joseph Jacobs and the Jacobs Pharmacy Company) be restrained from selling, or offering to sell, any of the medicine which was injured as aforesaid in the cases, in the bottles, under the label, trade-mark, trade-name, or name of petitioner as manufacturer, and be especially restrained from selling any of the burned medicine as the manufacture of petitioner. The defendants demurred upon the grounds: The petition contains no cause of action against defendants, and the allegations in it are insufficient to authorize injunction or other relief against defendants. If plaintiff has suffered, or should suffer, injury because of the things complained of, it would have ample remedy, if any remedy, by action for damages against defendants, and no insolvency of defendants is alleged. The petition does not show wherein the medicine purchased by defendants is spurious or injurious, nor does it show the qualities, properties, quantities, or ingredients of the medicine manufactured by petitioner, from which the charge made by petitioner might be fully investigated, but withholds the character and quality of the medicine, and states that the medicine is a trade secret. The petition does not allege or show that any person or the public will be injured by the selling of the medicine, and plaintiff has no rights in this case, because of any claim to trade-mark or label, or both, by the medicine, because plaintiff had manufactured and sold the medicine, and, having done so, the medicine passed completely out of its control; and the petition does not set out any facts showing how or in what way petitioner would suffer irreparable damage and injury. Defendants answered, in brief: The purchase of the medicine was by the defendant the Jacobs Pharmacy Company. About February 14, 1891, its representative, Joseph Jacobs, was approached by insurance agents concerning a lot of S. S. S. that was in the then recent fire of H. J. Lamar & Sons, they stating that they were unable to get a satisfactory understanding with Lamar & Sons, and wished defendant to make them an offer. Jacobs went and examined a great many of the cases of the medicine, particularly those that seemed to be most charred on the outside, and found them all in good condition, except a few loose bottles that were on the floor, and which were not included in the sale, of S. S. S. made to defendant. Defendant, knowing that S. S. S. was made in Atlanta by steam percolation, and that it contained sufficient alcohol to preserve it, felt safe in making an offer for the goods, knowing that heat sufficient to injure a medicine thus prepared would either break the bottle or blow out the cork, neither of which had been done. Defendant finally purchased the goods. The lot of S. S. S. which he purchased was free from injury by the fire, and is the same kind of medicine as is manufactured and sold throughout the country by plaintiff. The insurance companies had, by agreement with Lamar & Sons, acquired the title to the medicine, and had the legal right to sell it to defendant. Defendant in making the purchase did so after careful and diligent examination, acted in entire good faith in the transaction, and paid for it $1,994.50. Defendant has had samples of the medicine bought as aforesaid, as also samples of the medicine as sold generally by plaintiff, and

which had never been about the fire, analyzed and examined by capable experts, and all of the samples were of the same quality and value. Defendant denied that the medicine had been damaged by fire, had lost any of its virtue, or is a spurious substance, and alleged that it is of the same quality, virtue, and substance as the other medicine manufactured by plaintiff, whatever that may be. H. J. Lamar, the senior member of the firm of H. J. Lamar & Sons, is a large stockholder and the president of the plaintiff, and that firm was willing to purchase or retain the S. S. S. which defendant purchased from the insurance companies, but were not willing to give the price for it that defendant paid, which defendant believes was on account of the superior advantages enjoyed by H. J. Lamar & Sons in obtaining the medicine from plaintiff, by reason of the interest and official connection of H. J. Lamar with plaintiff, and his connection with the firm. Much testimony was introduced on the hearing for injunction by both plaintiff and defendants. The evidence was conflicting, and the judge below refused to grant the injunction prayed for, to which decision the petitioner excepted.

John C. Reed and Hopkins & Son, for plaintiff in error. Weil & Goodwin, for defendants in error.

PER CURIAM. There was no abuse of discretion in denying the injunction. Judgment affirmed.

PHILLIPS et al. v. EAST TENNESSEE, V. & G. RY. Co.

(Supreme Court of Georgia. May 27, 1891.)

ACCIDENT ON RAILROAD TRESTLE — NONSUIT.

Deceased was killed by a train at the north end of a trestle 150 yards long and from 12 to 15 feet high. She and another woman had been to a water-tank at the other end of the trestle, and were on their way back. They did not commence to run until the train had passed the water-tank, where they thought it would stop. Deceased fell, and her companion tried to help her up, but before she could do so she was hit by the train, and thrown from the track, and deceased was run over and killed. The train stopped with the front driving-wheels on her. Held, that a nonsuit was properly granted, as it was gross negligence for them to go on the trestle about the time when a train was due, and where all that was possible was done to stop the train after they were discovered.

Error from superior court, Gordon county; THOMAS W. MILNER, Judge.

Action by Callie C. Phillips and another against the East Tennessee, Virginia & Georgia Railway Company for the killing of plaintiffs' mother by defendant's train. A nonsuit was granted, and plaintiffs appeal. Affirmed.

The following is the official report:

The suit was by the minor children of Mrs. Phillips, by their guardian, against the railway company, for the homicide of their mother by the running of its trains. After the introduction of the evidence for the plaintiff the court granted a nonsuit, which is assigned as error.

The principal witness for plaintiff was a Mrs. Craig, whose testimony was, in brief, as follows: Mrs. Phillips was run over and killed by the train of defendant at the north end of a trestle on its road at about 10 o'clock in the morning. Witness and Mrs. Phillips had been at the water-tank at the south end of the trestle, and had started back home across the trestle. When they first heard the train they were not frightened, as they thought it would stop for water. When they saw it pass the tank they were not walking very fast, but commenced running. As they were nearing the north end of the trestle Mrs. Phillips fell, and witness tried to assist her to rise, but before she could do so was herself thrown from the track by the locomotive and Mrs. Phillips was run over and killed. The railroad is straight at the place where the killing occurred, and the two could have been seen about one-half mile. The train was running very fast, and no warning was given or whistle blown, except that the bell was rung as the engine passed the tank. It was customary for this train to stop and take water at the tank. Mrs. Phillips was killed about 100 yards north of the tank, and would not have been hurt if the train had stopped at the tank. The people of the neighborhood were in the habit, and had been for a number of years, of using the trestle as a footway, with the knowledge of the railroad authorities, and without objection. Mrs. Phillips and witness took the precaution to listen before they got on the track, but could not see or hear any train. When they became aware of the approach of the train they ran as fast as they could, and made every effort to get off the trestle. They thought the train would stop at the tank, because it usually did. They did all they could to save themselves. "They saw her in time to stop the train before she was killed." Witness and Mrs. P. could have gone to the tank by another way. The former lived near the railroad, and the latter lived in Chattanooga, but was at the former's house on a visit. Witness did not know how often trains passed on the road. They did not consider themselves in danger, as they had been on the trestle often before. Mrs. P. had the same chance witness had to get off the trestle, if she had not fallen. Witness does not remember how far the engine ran after it struck Mrs. Phillips, and does not know that she did not hear the train coming, from the fact of water running over the dam, and the noise the tank-engine was making. They were going in the same direction as the train, and had their backs to it; and she does not remember how far the train was from them when she first saw it. Does not think it was down grade. At the time of and before this accident there were no notices put up by defendant forbidding people to walk along its road. Witness had Mrs. Phillips by the hand, and she did not get loose from witness until she fell at the end of the trestle, nor did she stoop down or stop until she fell. They were probably half-way on the trestle when they first saw and heard the train coming. Did not have any thought of a train coming on the road so soon. Believed they had plenty of time to cross

the trestle before the coming of the train. The reason they thought it would be safe for them to pass over the trestle was, they did not see or hear any train approaching. They did not know what time the train was due at Sugar Valley,—a station near by,—and did not know that it was behind time. The trestle is a long one, and is about 15 feet high. The ground is not soft and marshy along the trestle. There was some grass growing there. They did not have plenty of time to get off the trestle after they first heard the train. Witness supposed the train did not at all times stop at that tank, but she had seen it stop there often. Does not think the train rolled far after striking Mrs. P.

From the testimony of other witnesses the following, in substance, appeared: The people of the neighborhood, and the public generally, have been in the habit of using the road and trestle as a footway for a number of years, with the knowledge of and without objection by the defendant. The trestle is about 300 or 400 feet long, and about 12 or 15 feet high. The ground under the east side of it is in grass, and on the west side there are rocks, timber, etc. The creek comes near the trestle at the north end, and turns and runs nearly parallel with the track nearly all the way to the tank at the south end; and there is a dam across the creek, and water is pumped into the tank, the water running over the dam and the pumping making, when the pump is in motion, a considerable noise. The road is straight, south of the trestle, for about half a mile, and a person on an engine could see a person on the trestle for that distance. It is a little up grade where Mrs. P. was killed. One witness testified that the pump runs constantly. That the water running over the dam made so much noise that when he went across the trestle he could not hear the roar of a train, and never depended on his hearing for trains, but kept a lookout. That he did not know whether he could have heard this train or not, (it was a passenger train, making less noise than a freight train.) That he could hear a whistle, but did not depend on the sound of the train at all. That at the north end the trestle is 8 or 10 feet high, and on the east side it is tolerably smooth with grass. That a person on the trestle could see an engine as soon as the engineer could see him; and that the ground is smooth under the north end, and a wagon road passes under the trestle at that end. There was testimony, further, by a witness who saw the killing, that he was 100 or 150 yards "on the rise" above Mrs. Phillips, and saw the train when it first came in sight. That he reckoned it was about a quarter of a mile from where it first came in sight to where Mrs. Phillips was killed, but could not say how far. That Mrs. Phillips was on the right-hand side of the trestle, going north, when killed at the north end. That he saw her running before she was killed, but did not know how long she had been running before the train struck her; it hit her so quick. That the train was running pretty fast, and came along until it got from 45 to 75 feet of her, and then it went "who-ye-who-ye," and ran right upon her. That he did not hear the whistle blow. That he saw the two ladies break and run as hard as they could, and the train caught them. That the trestle was 450 feet long. He measured it. That Mrs. P. was behind, and Mrs. Craig caught her, to pull her up when she fell down, but could not do so, for the train knocked her off. That he saw the train before the ladies saw it, may be a minute. Was looking at them, and one of them looked back, and just as quick as she did she started to run, and both ran as fast as they could. That he did not think they saw the train before they began to run, because they were walking slowly. Thinks the train was about 200 yards from them when they looked back and began to run. They were then about the middle of the trestle. That when they looked back the train was about the north end of a little trestle which is about 60 or 100 yards south of the·trestle on which the killing occurred. That it might be that the speed of the train was checked before he heard the noise mentioned above, but he did not know that it was. That noise was caused by the wheels turning backwards. That he reckoned Mrs. P. would have gotten off if she had not fallen down. That the front driving-wheel stopped right on her. That he was higher up than the ladies, and could have seen further. That it is about a quarter of a mile from where they could have seen it if they had been looking, but does not know whether they could have seen the engine before the person on the engine could have seen them. That, if they had been looking, they probably could have seen the smoke-stack before the engineer could have seen them. That he never saw any slowing up of the train before the noise mentioned above. That he did not know whether Mrs. Phillips could have gotten off if she had not fallen down or not. That the ladies had run about one-third of the way before she fell down, and when she fell Mrs. Craig pulled her up, and when she got up the train knocked Mrs. C. loose and ran over Mrs. P. That the engine was about 40 feet from Mrs. P. when the wheels were running backwards, and the fuss commenced just as she fell, and the engineer put his head out of the window. That he never heard the bell ring. That the pumping-engine was making a great deal of noise, but he does not know whether the noise of the pump and the running water would keep the ladies from hearing the train or not, though he thinks it would have prevented their hearing as soon as he did. That he heard the engine, and looked around and saw it. Does not know that he heard it before he saw it. Heard it, and looked right around, and it was in sight. That the wind was blowing from the south, etc. Another witness who saw the train testified, in brief, that it was running fast, perhaps 30 miles an hour, when it passed him; and he heard a noise when it got about the tank, which supposes was the reversal of the en-   ). That it was a half mile from the   ·re of the road to the south end of the

trestle. That the train had air-brakes on it, and·could have been stopped before it got to the ladies. That he did not notice any noise from the brakes being on when it passed him, and he was right at the tank. That he did not know whether it checked up any before it got to the trestle. That a person on the trestle, and in proximity of the pump and water, could not hear a train as soon as one away from it; and a passenger train makes less noise than a freight train. That he could probably have seen the train before he heard it. That a person on the engine could see one on the track as soon as he turned the curve, and, if a person on the trestle were looking, he could see the engine as soon. That there was a public road crossing about a mile from the tank, and that the whistle was blown there. There was also evidence that Mrs. Phillips was a widow, leaving surviving her the two minor children, for whom the suit was brought; and that she supported them by her labor; and testimony as to her age, earnings, etc.

Dabney & Fouché, for plaintiffs in error. *Dorsey & Howell, S. P. Maddox,* and *A. O. Bacon,* for defendant in error.

SIMMONS, J. The facts of this case will be found in the official report. Under these facts the court did right in granting a nonsuit in the case. It was gross negligence on the part of two females to attempt to walk upon a trestle 150 yards long and from 12 to 15 feet high, near the time when a train was due; it further appearing that the servants of the railroad company did all that was possible to be done after they discovered the females on the trestle. Judgment affirmed.

BARNETT v. NORTHEASTERN R. CO.

(Supreme Court of Georgia. May 6, 1891.)

RAILROAD COMPANIES — OPERATION BY ANOTHER ROAD — INJURY TO BRAKEMAN — NEGLIGENCE — LIABILITY.

1. In an action against a railroad company for personal injuries, plaintiff, a brakeman, testified that he went below the engine to uncouple it; that it was standing still at the time, but afterwards, without any signal from him, backed up, and caused him to catch his hand between the bumpers; and that he would not have been hurt but for its unexpected movement. He knew it was an ordinary coupling, and that the drag-bar, which they generally used, had been broken a day or two before; and did not think the engine and car could have come together if the drag-bar had been in position. He further testified, on cross-examination, that to the best of his recollection he had uncoupled the link before he was hurt, and that in that case the cars would have come together even if the drag-bar had been there. *Held,* that the evidence of the company's negligence was sufficient to go to the jury, and that it was error to grant a nonsuit.

2. In an action against a railroad company for personal injuries the contention was that plaintiff had sued the defendant, when he should have sued the company which operated the road. Plaintiff testified that he kept the books at one of defendant's stations for a short time; that he made his remittances to the operating company, and may possibly have been paid by it, but that he did not know it was operating the road; that he afterwards became a brakeman on the train of a conductor who had been for a long time in defendant's employ; that the cars were marked with the name of that company, and that the su-

perintendent to whom he applied for the position was the superintendent of both companies. The time schedules published in a newspaper were headed by the name of the defendant, and were separate from those of the operating company. The proprietor of the newspaper received separate passes for their publication. The name of the operating company appeared on the books of the station. *Held,* that the testimony as to which company was the employer was sufficient to go to the jury, and that it was error to grant a nonsuit.

Error from superior court, Clarke county; N. L. HUTCHINS, Judge.

Action by W. B. Barnett against the Northeastern Railroad Company to recover for personal injuries. There was a judgment for defendant, and plaintiff appeals. Reversed.

The following is the official report:

The main exception in this case is to the granting of a nonsuit, which was moved for on the grounds that the plaintiff was guilty of contributory negligence, and that he had sued the Northeastern Railroad, when he should have sued the Richmond & Danville. It is stated in the bill of exceptions that the nonsuit was granted on the first ground, though the order passed by the court was a general one. It is also alleged that the court erred in allowing defendant's counsel, in cross-examining the plaintiff, to read from and state the contents of the pay-rolls, cash-books, and other books, which he presented to the witness, and in forcing him to state what these books, pay-rolls, and other papers contained, such as their caption, what they purported to be, etc. It is alleged that this was error, because the papers and books themselves were the best evidence of their contents, and, if their contents were desired, should have been introduced in evidence by defendant; and that they were not first submitted to plaintiff's counsel for inspection, and there was no evidence that they were what they purported to be. It is stated that plaintiff objected to this action of defendant's counsel; but what the objection made was is not stated. The plaintiff testified: "The injuries were received at the depot yard of the Northeastern Railroad in Athens. I was train-hand and car-coupler on the Northeastern Railroad. Was employed by the Northeastern Railroad Company. It was my duty to make up a train. I went in to pull pin to uncouple a flat-car from the tender, and the engine came back on me, and caught my right hand. When I went in, the car and engine were standing still. The engine headed towards town, and the train was behind it. It was my duty to uncouple that car. There was nothing that I could do to avoid the injury. I did all I could to prevent it. At the time I was hurt they were using an ordinary coupling between the engine and the first car. They had been using what is known as a 'drag-bar,' which is four or five inches longer than a coupling. I knew it was a coupling when I went in, but not whether it was a short link, or what it was. I knew the drag-bar had been broken. We had made a trip to Tallulah Falls and back without it. I do not reckon the engine and car could have come together with the drag-

bar in there. In September, 1886, was employed by Capt. Cox to work with him on the train of which he was conductor on the Northeastern Railroad. Knew he was working on the Northeastern. He did not say what company he was conductor for. Bernard was superintendent. Berkely is superintendent now. I do not know when the change was made. I think Berkely is also connected with the Richmond & Danville. I am not sure he was superintendent at that time. Wrote to him after he was superintendent of the Northeastern, in July, 1886, asking him to give me a place on that road. When Cox employed me he had been conductor on the Northeastern for a long while. Did not say he had authority from Berkely. It was after I wrote to Berkely. Cheney was the agent. I think I helped him in the office. I wrote those pages, which are shown to me, in the railroad book kept at Harmony Grove. That is the record of the freight received in Harmony Grove in 1886. Do not know that I knew the Richmond & Danville was operating the Northeastern. Entries shown me in the cash-book are in my handwriting. The cash I remitted to the treasurer of Richmond & Danville, I think. It is the cash-book of the agent at Harmony Grove. They are in my handwriting from the 2d of August to the 14th of August. That is my signature to the pay-roll for fourteen days' work as acting agent at Harmony Grove. I may have been paid by check on Richmond & Danville; I do not recollect. When I went to uncouple that train it was standing still. The engine came back, I am positive, I think. I think the car remained stationary. I am certain it was the engine and tender that came back. My hand was caught between the bumper and the tender. Think they were very nearly the same height. I was just about to pull the pin. It was not necessary to put my hand between bumpers to get the pin; the head of it is on top of one of the bumpers. The thing moved, and my hand got caught between the bumpers. If it had stood still I would not have got caught. I do not think I pulled the pin. If it had not moved I would have got the pin, instead of getting my hand between the bumpers. The drag-bar had been broken a day or two. It is five or six inches longer than the link."

Among other things, on cross-examination, the witness was asked the following questions, which are given with the answers: "Question. Here are your entries for fourteen days on these Richmond & Danville books. Do you say now that you were working for the Northeastern Railroad Company or the Richmond & Danville Railroad Company? Answer. It would seem from these books that I was working for the Richmond & Danville. Q. Will you be good enough now to say which you were working for? A. It was my understanding that I was working for the Northeastern Railroad Company. Q. Do you think now you were working for the Northeastern Railroad Company? A. It seems now I was working for the Richmond & Danville Railroad Company, from those books. Q. Don't these papers show, and ain't it your recollection, that you were employed by the Richmond & Danville to work on the Northeastern Railroad? These papers show that you were working for the Richmond & Danville Railroad Company, don't they? A. It seems so. Q. What is your testimony as to which company you were working for? A. I was working on the Northeastern Railroad. Q. Do you say that you do not know whether you were working for the Northeastern Railroad Company or the Richmond & Danville Railroad Company? A. I do not know. I do know I was working on the Northeastern Railroad, and it was my impression that I was working for the Northeastern Railroad Company. Such was my impression until these books were brought up. Q. That letter to Mr. Berkely was written July 22, 1886. It did not say he was superintendent of the Richmond & Danville. You simply said 'superintendent.' Were you applying for the position on the Northeastern Railroad? A. Yes, sir. Q. You swear you did not know Mr. Berkely was superintendent of the Richmond & Danville? Did you know he was superintendent of the Northeastern R. R. at the time you wrote the letter? A. Yes, sir. Q. These books show they are Richmond & Danville books, don't they? A. Yes, it seems so. Q. After having your recollection refreshed by looking at your letter to Berkely, your entries in freight and cash books of August, 1886, the signature to these pay-rolls of R. & D. R. R., and Cox's signature, [conductor for that company,] state what company you were employed by. A. It was always known as the 'Northeastern.' I was employed by Mr. Cox, conductor of Northeastern R. R."

He further testified, if the drag-bar had been there, and if it was not uncoupled, and if the bar was long enough to prevent the bumpers from coming together, it would have kept the bumpers apart; but if it was uncoupled, and he thinks it was, it would have come together any way. From his best recollection of how it occurred, he thinks it was caused by the engine coming back on him, and pushing him and causing him to stumble, and catching his hand; and thinks he would have been hurt even if the drag-bar had been there. It would have made no difference. The only drag-bar the road had was broken, and they furnished the coupling for use. The train which hurt him started from Athens and went to Tallulah Falls, part of the way being over the track of the Richmond & Danville, and from Tallulah Falls back to Athens. It had been running that way for several years. It was called the "Northeastern Railroad." Cheney had been working for the same Northeastern Railroad since 1876. Cox had been working several years as conductor of the Northeastern Railroad Company. The car and engines were marked "Northeastern." If the Richmond & Danville began operating that road he did not know it; was not informed of any change. When he wrote the letter, Berkely was superintendent of the Northeastern, and also the Richmond & Danville.

When he signed the pay-rolls he did not read them, and his attention was not called to the top of them. The engine came back and caught witness. The best of his recollection is, when he was in there it came back,—sort of pushed him down to the car, and he may have stumbled. It is his impression that he did, and, as he threw out his hand to keep from falling, it got caught between the bumpers, and got crushed. Won't say positively that it made him stumble. The best of his recollection is, he 'had uncoupled the link. When the engine came back it pushed him, and he kind of stumbled, and, as he tried to save himself, his hand got in between the bumpers and was crushed. The motion of the tender coming back caused him to stumble. He thinks he had fully uncoupled the cars; that is the best of his recollection. Supposes the pin had dropped down, or lay on the coupling. If he had got the pin out in uncoupling the cars there would not be anything to hold them apart. Does not know that the drag-bar would have held them apart if it had been there, and does not think it would. It might have done so if it had never been taken out of position. Does not know whether the drag-bar was long enough to keep the cars from coming together. It could not have gotten out from between the bumpers unless the space between the cars was widened, and he does not recollect positively whether the space was widened or not, nor remember whether the link was long enough to keep them from coming together or not. The bumpers did come together. Some bumpers are hollow and some not; and it is possible, if the bumpers are hollow, for the link to get out of the bumpers without the space being widened. He has seen a tender pushing a car without a drag-bar being put in. He was to give the signal for the train to move, and they had no right to move until he gave the signal. He had the right to rely on it that the engine or train would not move until he gave the signal. If the engine had stood still he would not and could not have gotten hurt. He does not know that that special link was used before. They had been using a link. It was all the road gave them. Either Kane or witness put the link there; and he does not remember which. It was necessary for the train to go, and they had to use the link. Links are frequently used in place of the drag-bar, because more convenient in making coupling where the bumpers are of unequal heights, not because it is less dangerous. He would have been hurt even if the drag-bar had been there. It would have made no difference. The engine's moving was what caused him to get hurt.

Further testimony for plaintiff tended to show that certain advertisements of the schedule of the Northeastern Railroad were published in a newspaper at Athens on November 23, 1886, and December 14, 1886, and were put in by authority of the Northeastern Railroad. Two of them were dated June 21, 1886, and one November 15, 1886. These schedules were put in evidence. They were headed, "Northeastern

Railroad. Superintendent's Office;" and were signed, "H. R. Bernard, Superintendent." In the same paper were published schedules of the Piedmont Air-Line Railroad. The schedules were separate and distinct, having no connection with each other as advertisements. The employe of the newspaper, who testified as to these schedules, testified that he did not remember who authorized them to be printed. They generally came through the mails; but they would not have been put in unless sent to the paper. That they ran for months, and a copy of the paper was taken at the railroad office regularly. Witness got a pass on the 31st of June, and another the last of September, from the Northeastern Railroad, as a courtesy on account of the advertisements; and had separate passes over the Northeastern and Richmond & Danville during the year 1886. Bernard testified, among other things, that he thought he quit the Northeastern Railroad the 1st of July, 1887; that Berkely succeeded him as superintendent of that railroad, and he became general agent; that he was general agent after July, 1886, and was appointed such by the general manager of the Richmond & Danville system; that he had no authority in the running of trains on the Northeastern Railroad after July, 1886, nor in the employment of men, nor with the making and publishing of schedules, and had no recollection of furnishing any schedules; that he did not know who employed these men; they were in the employment of the Northeastern when he was superintendent; that where the accident occurred was down grade, and if a car or engine was standing there without a brake on, and got a very slight momentum, if there was no obstruction on the track, a slight push or jar would move it off; that, if the track had been perfectly level there, it could not roll; that the cars frequently stood there without brakes. The plaintiff then introduced certain reports of officers of the Northeastern Railroad Company for the year ending September 30, 1887. These reports indicated a separate existence of the Northeastern Railroad Company, with a full board of officers, Berkely being superintendent; and consisted of a report by the president to the stockholders of the company, accompanied by reports to the president by the superintendent. There was also much evidence introduced by plaintiff on the subject of the nature and extent of his injuries, showing that they were quite serious.

E. T. Brown and *Lumpkin & Burnett,* for plaintiff in error. *Barrow & Thomas* and *J. T. Pendleton,* for defendant in error.

SIMMONS, J. Under the facts, as disclosed by the record, the court erred in granting a nonsuit in this case. The testimony introduced by the plaintiff as to the negligence of the company was, in our judgment, sufficient to put the defendant upon his defense, and to require it to explain the acts complained of by the plaintiff. The testimony as to who was the employer of the plaintiff was also sufficient to require it to be submitted to the jury. Judgment reversed.

ALABAMA G. S. R. CO. v. FULGHAM.
(*Supreme Court of Georgia.* May 27, 1891.)

CONSTRUCTION OF RAILROAD BY FOREIGN CORPORATION — SERVICE OF PROCESS — CONFLICT OF LAWS—LIABILITIES OF PURCHASER.

1. Acts Ga. 1853-54, p. 464, authorizing a foreign corporation to build a railroad in Georgia, and declaring that it shall be subject to suit by citizens of the state, in the county in which it is located, allows service of process to be made as upon a domestic corporation; and a brakeman who is a citizen and runs upon one train, partly in Georgia and partly in Alabama, is entitled to maintain an action in Georgia for an injury sustained in Alabama.

2. A foreign corporation, which acquires the franchises of the said corporation, is subject to whatever suits could have been maintained against that company.

Error from superior court, Dade county, THOMAS W. MILNER, Judge.

Action by George L. Fulgham against the Alabama Great Southern Railroad Company to recover for personal injuries. There was judgment for plaintiff, and defendant appeals. Affirmed.

The following is the official report:

The error assigned in this case is the overruling a demurrer to the plaintiff's declaration. The declaration was for damages for personal injuries alleged to have been sustained by Fulgham, in the state of Alabama, while he, as a brakeman of defendant, was endeavoring to uncouple cars. It alleged, among other things, that plaintiff was at the time he sustained the injuries, and still is, a citizen of Georgia, and of Dade county, where the suit was brought; that the defendant is running and operating a railroad through that county, and into and through the state of Alabama, and has a place of business in Dade county; that the defendant owns and operates the railroad through that county, formerly known as the "Wills Valley Railroad," which was built through the county under an act of the legislature of Georgia approved 1853, and the defendant is subject to all the liabilities and obligations, and has all the rights and privileges, by that act conferred and imposed upon the Wills Valley Railroad Company; and that the train upon which plaintiff was employed and engaged while injured was a train running though the county on said railroad, and on the trip on which he was injured ran through the county. The demurrer was upon the ground that the cause of action did not arise in Dade county, nor within the state of Georgia, but did arise, if there be any, in Alabama, and so the court has no jurisdiction, but jurisdiction to try the cause is in the courts of Alabama; and it is not alleged in the declaration, nor is it the fact, that defendant has ever been incorporated under the laws of Georgia, but is a body politic, incorporated under the laws of Alabama.

W. U. & J. P. Jacoway and *R. J. & J. McCamy,* for plaintiff in error. *T. J. Lumpkin* and *McCutchen & Shumate,* for defendant in error.

BLECKLEY, C. J. 1. A railroad corporation, whether *de facto* or *de jure,* and whether foreign or domestic, is subject to suit in this state *in personam* by a citizen thereof, if it owns and operates a railroad in this state which was built by virtue of an act of the legislature authorizing another corporation, chartered by an adjoining state, to build and operate said railroad, and which act declared the corporation so building and operating it subject to suit by citizens of this state in the county in which the road is located. A corporation, in the actual use and exercise of all the rights and privileges of another corporation, is subject to its burdens, and, among them, to suit for like causes of action for which suits could be maintained against such other corporation were it in possession of the franchises which have been acquired from it, or else usurped.

2. Under the act of 1853, (Acts 1853–54, p. 464,) in relation to the Wills Valley Railroad Company of Alabama, an employe (a brakeman) whose business was upon one and the same train running over the line of road, partly in Georgia and partly in Alabama, can maintain an action in Georgia for a personal injury sustained in Alabama, service of process being made as upon a domestic railway corporation. 2 Redf. R. R. 633, and notes; 1 Ror. R. R. 677; 1 Beach, R. R. 54; Railroad Co. v. Harris, 12 Wall. 65; Railroad Co. v. Wightman's Adm'r, 29 Grat. 431; Railroad Co. v. Noell's Adm'r, 32 Grat. 394; Graham v. Railroad Co., 118 U. S. 161, 6 Sup. Ct. Rep. 1009. The facts are stated in the official report. Judgment affirmed.

BANK OF STATE OF GEORGIA v. PORTER.

(*Supreme Court of Georgia.* July 18, 1891.)

INJUNCTION—CONFLICTING EVIDENCE.

A petition, asking that the erection of a stairway be enjoined, alleged that it would occupy 8 feet on the north side of an alley 20 feet wide, on the south side of which petitioner owned a lot and house. Defendant alleged that the alley was only 12 feet wide, and the stairway was wholly on his own lot. His deed called for a lot 127 feet deep, on an alley 12 feet wide. *Held* that, the evidence being conflicting, there was no abuse of discretion in denying the injunction, on the ground that it had not been shown that the ground on which the stairway was being erected had ever been dedicated to the public use as a public alley.

Error from superior court, Fulton county; MARSHALL J. CLARKE, Judge.

Action by the Bank of the State of Georgia to enjoin J. H. Porter from erecting a certain stairway. Injunction was denied, and petitioner excepted. Affirmed.

The following is the official report:

The Bank of the State of Georgia, by its petition, alleged that it was the owner of the city lot on the south side of Kenny's alley, a public alley in Atlanta, adjacent to said alley, and fronting on the west side of Loyd street; that J. H. Porter was having a stairway built about 4 feet wide, and extending at the base about 8 feet in the alley on the north side thereof, just opposite the property of petitioner; that petitioner's property has on it a house, with windows opening on the alley, just opposite said stairway; that the alley where the stairway and platform are being erected is 20 feet wide, and extends up to the rear of the building of Porter, against which the stairway and

platform are being constructed; that the stairway and platform are entirely within the alley, and will constitute an obstruction in the same, if allowed to be completed; that special damage will result from the erection of the obstruction to petitioner's property because of the fact that the width of the alley will be thereby materially reduced, and the means of egress and ingress to and from petitioner's building will be reduced, and the staircase and platform will necessarily be an unsightly object in the alley. Wherefore petitioner prayed for injunction restraining Porter from further proceeding with the erection of the staircase and platform. Porter answered that it was not true that he was building, or attempting to build, a stairway on the alley, or any part thereof. The alley is not 20 feet wide, but is only 12 feet wide, on no part of which was defendant building, or attempting to build, but he is building on his own land, to which he has perfect title, and which has been in his continuous possession for years, and never used except as a convenience to his store, the same being left vacant for his own convenience, and not for the public use, or as a part of a public alley. He denied that any damage would result to plaintiff on account of building the stairway, and alleged that it would be a great convenience to him, (defendant,) and add to the value of his property. On the hearing for injunction, it was admitted that petitioner had title to the city lot on the south side of the alley. The deed under which defendant claimed title to the lot on the opposite side of the alley was dated December 10, 1877, and purported to convey to him a tract of land, fronting 24 feet on Alabama street, running back parallel with and fronting on Loyd street, 127 feet, to a "12-foot alley;" and it appeared from testimony for defendant that a lot beginning at the corner of Alabama and Loyd street, and running back 127 feet, would leave an alley but 12 feet wide between such a lot and the property of petitioner. The evidence adduced before the judge below was conflicting, and he denied the injunction asked for, on the ground that it had not been shown that the ground on which defendant was erecting the stairway had ever been dedicated to public use as a public alley. To the decision refusing the injunction petitioner excepted.

Hall & Hammond, for plaintiff in error. *A. A. Murphy*, for defendant in error.

PER CURIAM. There was no abuse of discretion in denying the injunction. Judgment affirmed.

CROCKER v. ALLEN.

(*Supreme Court of South Carolina.* Sept. 18, 1891.)

ENFORCEMENT OF JUDGMENT—EQUITABLE RELIEF.

1. A court of equity will not restrain the enforcement of a judgment on the ground that defendant was never served with process, where the record shows no flaw or defect in the service, and where defendant does not state any facts imparting to the case some feature of equitable cognizance, such as fraud, accident, or mistake; defendant having a plain, speedy, and adequate

remedy by a motion to vacate the judgment in the court, and in the action wherein it was rendered. 2. The mere fact that the judgment was recovered on the equity side of the court will not authorize the maintenance of the separate equitable action to set the judgment aside. 3. The fact that an injunction may be necessary to make the relief on the motion for the vacation of the judgment effectual is not sufficient to give a court of equity jurisdiction, since that relief was always obtainable by a motion to stay the execution, even before the enactment of Gen. St. S. C. § 2115, expressly conferring such power on a circuit judge in chambers.

Appeal from common pleas circuit court of Spartanburg county; Izlar, Judge.

Action by R. F. Crocker against Anna G. Allen to set aside a judgment. Suit dismissed, and plaintiff appeals. Affirmed.

The complaint was as follows: "That heretofore, on the ——— day of February, 1888, the defendant herein attempted to institute an action against her and a co-defendant, J. J. Lipscomb, by the service upon him and an attempted service upon her of a summons and complaint therein, which complaint alleged: (1) That on the 9th of March, 1886, they (the said defendants) executed to her their joint and several note wherein they promised to pay her, twelve months after date, the sum of seven hundred dollars, with interest from date, at ten per cent. per annum, until paid, payable semi-annually, and, if not paid, to bear same rate as principal, and also to pay all costs and expenses, including ten per cent. attorney's commissions. (2) That the said defendant, R. F. Crocker, to secure the payment of the said note, executed to her on same day a mortgage upon two tracts of land in said county, known as 'Lots Nos. 5 and 6 of the estate of Gullie Crocker, deceased,'—lot No. 5 being bounded by lands of Madison Lee, C. B. Hammett, Elisa Lee, and others, and No. 6 being bound by lands of J. W. Wilkins, Mrs. E. M. Wilkins, Mrs. E. M. Lipscomb, and others; containing together two hundred and forty-five acres, more or less, —and that the mortgage was duly recorded in Book 8, p. 140. (3) That the condition of the note and mortgage had been broken, and that there was due thereon the sum of seven hundred dollars, with interest from the 9th of September, 1887, and the further sum of seventy dollars attorney's commissions. Judgment was asked for foreclosure of mortgage, and execution for balance of debt remaining due after exhausting mortgaged lands. (4) That on the 3d day of April, 1888, a decree was rendered in said action by his honor, Judge W. H. Wallace, wherein he ordered that the said mortgaged premises, or so much thereof as should be necessary, be sold at public auction at Spartanburg C. H., by the sheriff on sales-day in October, or some convenient sales-day thereafter, on terms of one-half cash and balance on credit of six months, and provided for the application of the proceeds of such sale in accordance with the allegation and prayer of the complaint, and rendering judgment against both defendants for any balance that might be found due, after exhausting the proceeds of such sale; also ordering that the said R. F. Crocker, and all persons claiming under her, be forever

barred and foreclosed of all right, title, interest, and equity of redemption in the said premises so sold. (5) That the said decree was on the 4th day of April, 1888, duly filed with the clerk of court of said county, and on the 12th of same month the costs in said action were by him duly taxed and approved, and, along with the decree, entered and signed in judgment and recorded; all of which will more fully appear by reference to the judgment roll in said action, No. 9,172. (6) That the said decree was rendered by default, notwithstanding it appears from said judgment roll that there was no affidavit of plaintiff or her attorney that no answer, demurrer, or notice of appearance had been served or received therein. (7) That plaintiff has never at any time been served with a summons or complaint in said action, and that the first information she had of her having been sued therein was the advertisement of her aforesaid land for sale under said decree. (8) That, in accordance with the terms of said decree, the sheriff has advertised the said premises for sale on sales-day of November next, and that they will be sold unless prevented by this court. (9) That the said decree and all proceedings thereunder are null and void as to this plaintiff. Wherefore plaintiff asks judgment (1) that the sheriff of said county, the defendant, her agents or servants, be restrained from advertising and selling said land, and from otherwise attempting to enforce said decree as against plaintiff; (2) that said decree be set aside and vacated as to her; (3) for the costs of this action, and such other relief as may be just."

Stanyarne Wilson, for appellant. *Bomar & Simpson,* for respondent.

McIver, J. This was an action brought by the plaintiff herein to set aside a judgment previously obtained against her by the defendant herein, and to obtain an injunction to restrain the enforcement of the execution issued on said judgment, solely upon the ground that she was never served with the summons in the former action, and had no knowledge of any such proceedings against her until her land was advertised for sale under said execution. In her complaint—a copy of which is set out in the "case," and which should be incorporated in the report of this case—she makes no allegation of fraud, and states no fact imparting an equitable feature to her case; and her demand for an injunction is not sufficient to give it such a character, for two reasons: (1) Because, as we have held in the case of Westlake v. Farrow, 13 S. E. Rep. 469, (decided at the present term,) the demand for relief cannot be looked to as giving character to the cause of action; and (2) because she states no case entitling her to an injunction. Gillam v. Arnold, 32 S. C. 503, 11 S. E. Rep. 331. The circuit judge held, among other things, which, under the view we take of the case, need not be stated, that the complaint failed to state facts sufficient to constitute a cause of action, and therefore rendered judgment dismissing the complaint. From this judgment plaintiff appeals upon the several grounds set out in the record; but as the fundamental question in the case, superseding all others, is whether the circuit judge erred in his ruling as above stated, we shall confine ourselves to that question.

In the case of Manufacturing Co. v. Thew, 5 S. C. 5, the action was brought to set aside a judgment confessed by the president of the plaintiff company to the defendant, upon the allegation that the judgment was null and void for three reasons, substantially: (1) Because the confession, not being under the corporate seal, was not legal or binding upon the plaintiff; (2) because the debt admitted by the plaintiff was not the legal obligation of the plaintiff corporation; (3) that the confession was signed by a person having no authority whatever to do so. It was held that these averments, standing by themselves, would neither support an action at law nor a bill in equity under the former procedure; but that the remedy was by motion in the court in which the judgment was rendered, if the same was insufficient in form, or for any reason void. In that case it is said: "An action under the Code of Procedure only lies where the subject-matter of such action furnished ground previous to the adoption of the Code for the maintenance of either an action at law or a bill in equity," or in certain other cases not applicable to the present inquiry. "What rights shall be enforced, and what wrongs shall be redressed, by a civil action is not determined by the Code, except in the case of proceedings formerly taken by *sci. e facias, quo warranto*," etc. "These matters are therefore to be determined according to the law as it stood previous to the adoption of the Code. In order, then, to ascertain whether a complaint under the Code sets forth a sufficient cause of action, except in the special cases above enumerated, the inquiry must be whether, under the former practice of this state, the matters set forth were sufficient either to support an action at law or a bill in equity."

Now, as it was well settled that a court of equity would not entertain a case asking for relief where the party complaining had a plain, adequate, and complete remedy at law, the practical inquiry in this case is whether, under the former practice, the plaintiff would have had a plain and adequate remedy for the wrong of which she complains by motion to the court and in the cause in which the judgment in question was rendered. If she had, then she cannot maintain an action on the equity side of the court to obtain the redress sought, but must resort to the simpler and less expensive remedy by motion. A review of the authorities will show beyond dispute that the court of common pleas has always claimed and exercised the power to entertain such a motion. In Mooney v. Welsh, 1 Mill, Const. 133, the motion was to set aside a judgment on the ground that the verdict and judgment exceeded the damages laid in the writ; and it was held that the court of common pleas has always exercised the power of looking into its own records, and, on motion, affording the remedy which is obtained by writ of error in England. In

Barns v. Branch, 3 McCord, 19, a motion was entertained to set aside proceedings for partition in the law court upon the ground of want of notice to the guardian *ad litem* of the infant defendants, although such want of notice did not appear on the record. In that case, NOTT, J., expresses the opinion that a court of equity could not afford relief. In Wotton v. Parsons, 4 McCord, 368, the motion was to set aside a judgment upon the same ground as that upon which the plaintiff in the case now under consideration bases her action, to-wit, want of service of the process; and it was held that while a judge at chambers could not grant such a motion, yet he might order a stay of execution until the motion could be heard and determined by the court. In Poscy v. Underwood, 1 Hill, (S. C.) 263, O'NEALL, J., uses this language: "Generally, there can be no doubt that a court of law possesses exclusive jurisdiction over the amendment or vacation of its own judgments. This power applies most usually to matters of form or substance apparent on the face of the record. Sometimes, however, it is exercised, as between the parties, on matters out of, and beyond, the record;" and he goes on to prescribe the mode of proceeding in such cases. To the same effect is Dial v. Farrow, 1 McMul. 292, in which Judge O'NEALL, in terms, recognizes the doctrine that a judgment may be set aside, on a motion, upon the ground that defendant had not been served with process In Haigler v. Way, 2 Rich. 324, it was held that the proper mode of proceeding to set aside a judgment irregularly obtained against an infant, there having been no guardian *ad litem* appointed, and no appearance having been entered, was by a motion in the case. In Williams v. Lanneau, 4 Strob. 27, a judgment for the amount assessed in lieu of dower was set aside, on motion, upon the ground that the defendant had not been served with a copy of the summons on which the subsequent proceedings were based; the court recognizing several of the preceding cases, especially Wotton v. Parsons, and citing another very similar case, (O'Neall v. Wright,) which does not seem to have been reported. To same effect, see Crane v Martin, 4 Rich. 251; Mills v. Dickson, 6 Rich. 487; and Stenhouse v. Bonum, 12 Rich. 620, in which last-named case the judgment was set aside on motion upon the ground of want of jurisdiction in the court which undertook to render said judgment. The case of Townsend v. Meetse, 4 Rich. 510, is not in conflict with the foregoing cases; on the contrary, the practice of proceeding by motion was distinctly recognized, and the only reason why the motion was refused in that case was because a discovery was demanded and was necessary, which could only have been obtained in a court of equity. These cases unquestionably establish the doctrine that the proper mode of proceeding to set aside a judgment prior to the abolition of the court of equity was by motion to the court and in the cause wherein the judgment was rendered; and therefore a bill in equity for that purpose would not be entertained by the court of equity unless it contained allegations imputing to the case some features of equitable cognizance,—such, for example, as fraud, accident, or mistake,—or unless a discovery was demanded. See Attorney General v. Baker, 9 Rich. Eq. 530, 531; McDowall v. McDowall, Bailey, Eq. 325. That the same practice has been recognised and followed since the court of equity was abolished as a separate tribunal may be seen by reference to the cases of Manufacturing Co. v. Thew, supra; Clark v. Manufacturing Co., 8 S. C. 22; Ex parte Carroll, 17 S. C. 446; Ferguson v. Gilbert, Id. 26; Darby v. Shannon, 19 S. C. 533; Turner v. Malone, 24 S. C. 398. To these authorities in our own state may be added that of the supreme court of the United States in the case of Walker v. Robbins, 14 How. 584. In that case a bill in equity was filed in the circuit court of the United States for the district of Mississippi praying a perpetual injunction against a judgment recovered in an action at law in the same court upon the ground, among others, that Walker had not been served with process in the action at law, though the record of such judgment showed on its face that Walker had been duly served. It was held that the bill could not be maintained; the court using this language: "Assuming the fact to be that Walker was not served with process, (that being the undisputed evidence in the case,) and that the marshal's return is false, can the bill, in this event, be maintained? The respondents did no act that can connect them with the false return. It was the sole act of the marshal, through his deputy, for which he was responsible to the complainant, Walker, for any damages that were sustained by him in consequence of the false return. This is free from controversy; still the marshal's responsibility does not settle the question made by the bill, which is, in general terms, whether a court of equity has jurisdiction to regulate proceedings and to afford relief at law, where there has been abuse in the various details arising on execution of process, original, mesne, and final. If a court of chancery can be called on to correct one abuse, so it may be to correct another, and, in effect, to vacate judgments where the tribunal rendering the same would refuse relief either on motion, or on a proceeding by audita querela, where this mode of redress is in use. In cases of false returns affecting the defendant, where the plaintiff at law is not in fault, redress can only be had in the court of law where the record was made, and, if relief cannot be had there, the party injured must seek his remedy against the marshal." It is true that in that case the court does go on to assign another reason for the conclusion reached,—that the appellant, Walker, though not served with process, had really appeared by counsel in the action at law; but this does not weaken the force and effect of the first reason assigned in the words above quoted.

It seems to us clear, therefore, that this action on the equity side of the court cannot be sustained, where, as in this case, the complaint contains no allegations imputing to the case any features of equi-

table cognizance, but rests solely upon the allegation that plaintiff was never served with process in the action in which the judgment in question was recovered. The fact that such judgment was recovered in an action on the equity side of the court to foreclose a mortgage cannot affect the question. The record of the case in which the judgment is sought to be set aside is complete in itself, and shows no flaw or defect. It does not show that the defendant therein (the plaintiff here) was not served, but shows the contrary; and if it is proposed to show that the return of the sheriff was false, by evidence dehors the record, it should be done by a motion in that case, for while it stands as it is it must be regarded as a valid judgment in any other action or proceeding. In this respect the present case differs radically from Finley v. Robertson, 17 S. C 439, and Genobles v. West, 23 S. C. 160; for there the jurisdictional defect—for want of proper service—appeared upon the face of the record, while here the contrary is the case.

It cannot be said that the necessity for an injunction would be sufficient to give the court of equity jurisdiction; for that relief was always obtainable by a motion to stay the execution, which the authorities above cited show could have been granted by a circuit judge at chambers, even before the enactment of the statute expressly conferring such power, now incorporated in General Statutes as section 2115.

There is another view which would be sufficient to show that this action on the equity side of the court cannot be maintained under the allegations made in the complaint. In Freeman on Judgments, § 498, the author, while admitting that there are decisions in some of the states to the contrary, says: "The better established rule undoubtedly is that, notwithstanding an alleged want of service of process, a court of equity will not interfere to set aside a judgment until it appears that the 'result will be other or different from that already reached.'" This, we suppose, rests upon the elementary doctrine that he who seeks equity must do equity. Where, therefore, a party invokes the aid of the court of equity to be relieved from a judgment obtained against him for a debt which is neither alleged nor shown to be unjust, simply on the ground of some error in the proceedings, not affecting the merits, the court of equity may very properly refuse its aid in enabling a party to escape the payment of what appears to be a just debt, and which is neither alleged nor shown to be otherwise, and leave the party to his remedy at law, if he has any. As is said by Curtis, J., in Hendrickson v. Hinckley, 17 How. 443: "A court of equity does not interfere with judgments at law unless the complainant has an equitable defense of which he could not avail himself at law, because it did not amount to a legal defense, or had a good defense at law which he was prevented from availing himself of by fraud or accident, unmixed with negligence of himself or his agents;" citing Walker v. Robbins, supra, and also Insurance Co. v. Hodgson, 7

Cranch, 333, in which that great judge, MARSHALL, C. J., said: "Without attempting to draw any precise line to which courts of equity will advance, and which they cannot pass, in restraining parties from availing themselves of judgments obtained at law, it may safely be said that any fact which clearly proves it to be against conscience to execute a judgment, and of which the injured party could not have availed himself in a court of law, or of which he might have availed himself at law, but was prevented by fraud or accident, unmixed with any fault or negligence in himself or his agents, will justify an application to a court of chancery." It seems to us, therefore, that in no view of the case could the action be maintained, and that there was no error in dismissing the complaint. The judgment of this court is that the judgment of the circuit court be affirmed.

McGOWAN, J., concurs.

STATE v. McCLUNG.

(Supreme Court of Appeals of West Virginia Sept. 10, 1891.)

BURGLARY—INDICTMENT—CHARGING LARCENY AND BURGLARY—SENTENCE.

1. A count of an indictment alleging a breaking and entering into a dwelling with intent to steal goods therein, and actual larceny therein, is not bad as a count for burglary, because that part charging larceny is not drawn with sufficient precision to support a conviction of larceny. As the breaking and entering are charged to have been done with intent to commit larceny, a charge of actual larceny is not necessary, and may be rejected as surplusage.

2. To support a conviction of larceny, the charge of it in such count must be well laid, as in an indictment for larceny.

3. Upon a count properly alleging both burglary and larceny, there may be a conviction of either, but not of both.

4. Upon a general verdict of guilty on such a count, the sentence would be for burglary, not for both larceny and burglary, or for larceny.

5. Each count in an indictment must have the conclusion, "Against the peace and dignity of the state," else it is fatally defective. Advantage of the defect may be taken for the first time in this court.

(Syllabus by the Court.)

Error to circuit court, Clay county; V. S. ARMSTRONG, Judge.

Indictment of Frank McClung, *alias* Frank McAllister, *alias* Frank McClintock, for burglary. Verdict of guilty. Defendant brings error. Reversed.

E. R. Andrews, for plaintiff in error. *Alfred Caldwell,* Atty. Gen., for the State.

BRANNON, J. The following indictment was found in the circuit court of Clay county: "The grand jurors of the state of West Virginia in and for the body of the county of Clay, and now attending the said court, upon their oaths present that Frank McClung, *alias* Frank McAllister, *alias* Frank McClintock, on the —— day of ——, 1890, about the hour of —— o'clock, in the night-time of that day, feloniously and burglariously did break and enter into the dwelling-house of one Lewis Kyer, situated in said county, with intent the goods and chattels of him, the said Lewis Kyer, in the said dwelling-house then and there being, then and there feloniously and burglariously to steal, take, and carry away, and one pair of pants or pantaloons, and other goods and chattels, of the value of $24, of the goods and chattels of the said Lewis Kyer, in the said dwelling-house, in the county aforesaid, then and there being found, then and there feloniously and burglariously did steal, take, and carry away. And the grand jurors aforesaid, upon their oaths aforesaid, present that the said Frank McClung, *alias* Frank McAllister, *alias* Frank McClintock, on the —— day of ——, 1890, in the county aforesaid, did feloniously and burglariously take, steal, and carry away goods and chattels belonging to one Lewis Kyer of the value of $24, and one pair of pants of the value of $5, and he, the said McClung, *alias* McAllister, *alias* McClintock, did then and there break and enter the dwelling-house of the said Lewis Kyer in the night-time, with intent to commit larceny and burglary, and did then and there feloniously and burglariously take, steal, and carry away household goods of the value of $24, against the peace and dignity of the state." The defendant, having been convicted of burglary, and sentenced to the penitentiary for five years, has come to this court upon a writ of error. When application for this writ of error was made, I observed but one point of reversible error, nor do I now see any other; and perhaps that was inadvertently overlooked in the circuit court; and that is the want of the constitutional conclusion to the first count.

The first error assigned is the overruling of a demurrer to the indictment. That demurrer was not to each count, or to the indictment and each count, but was general to the indictment; and therefore, if either of its two counts be good, there is no error in overruling the demurrer; for where the indictment contains more than one count, and the demurrer is general, and one count is found good, the demurrer must be overruled. State v. Cartright. 20 W. Va. 32; Hendricks' Case, 75 Va. 934; Whart. Crim. Pl. § 401; 1 Bish. Crim. Proc. § 449. For this purpose and generally, each count is regarded as a separate indictment, and as presenting a separate offense. State v. Smith, 24 W. Va. 814. Then let us see whether either of the counts of this indictment is good. Except for want of a conclusion, the first count is good for burglary. If counsel specifies any defect in this count, it is that the charge of larceny is bad. I think that feature is bad,—that is, to support a verdict of guilty of larceny,—because it specifies only one article of the things stolen, the pantaloons, and alleges that "other goods and chattels" were stolen, without specifying them, and gives a value of $24 to all of them together. But the fact that the charge of larceny is bad, by no means vitiates the count regarded as a count for burglary, because, if we reject the larceny feature, there remains the charge of burglary. It is common and better practice to allege in one count both the burglary and the larceny. (1 Hale, P. C. 560; Speer's Case, 17 Grat. 572;) and under such count there may be a conviction of the one or the other of those offenses, (Reece's Case,

27 W. Va. 375; Clarke's Case, 25 Grat. 908; 1 Hale, P. C. 559; Rosc. Crim. Ev. 847; Whart. Crim. Pl. § 244.) In Vaughan's Case, 17 Grat. 576, where there was a count charging both burglary and larceny, Judge JOYNES said: "The allegation of actual larceny is only in aid of the intent. If that allegation were struck out altogether, enough would remain to describe the offense of which the prisoner has been convicted. Such being the object for which the charge of an actual larceny is introduced, it need not be laid with the same formality as in an indictment for the larceny itself. Larned v. Com., 12 Metc. (Mass.) 240; Com. v. Doherty, 10 Cush. 52; and see Regina v. Clarke, 1 Car. & K. 421, (47 E. C. L.) It is always better, however, to lay the charge of larceny in proper form to avoid objection in case the prisoner should, as he may, on such a count as this, be found not guilty of breaking and entering, but guilty of larceny." In Josslyn v. Com., 6 Metc. (Mass.) 236, the count charged the breaking and entering of the shop of Charles W. Fogg, "with intent the goods and chattels of said Fogg, then and there in said shop being found, feloniously to steal, take, and carry away." Chief Justice SHAW said: "Nor is it necessary to describe the goods intended to be stolen. A general intent to steal goods would complete the offense, and therefore the averment of such intent, without more, is sufficient to charge it, and the rule would be the same if there were no goods or no goods of Fogg in the shop. The crime was complete by the breaking and entering with intent to steal goods." In Larned v. Com., 12 Metc. (Mass.) 240, to the objection that the charge of larceny was defective in an indictment for burglary, the court said that the charge of actual larceny was not necessary to constitute the burglary; that the mere intent to commit larceny was sufficient; and the allegation was only to be taken in aid of the charge of intent, and, if a conviction was had, the punishment would be for burglary, not a distinct sentence for larceny. The court held the specific charge of larceny surplusage, and that, if wholly defective, there would still remain sufficient to sustain a conviction. It might be supposed that, as on a count charging both burglary and larceny there may be a conviction of either, there could also, if both offenses were proven, be a conviction of both, followed by the separate penalty for each; but this is not so, for, if there be a general verdict of guilty on such a count, it is deemed a conviction of burglary only, and the sentence is for burglary, not for both, or for larceny. Speer's Case, 17 Grat. 570; 1 Hale, P. C. 559. In Com. v. Hope, 22 Pick. 1, it was held that, on a general verdict of guilty on a count charging both offenses, the sentence must be for burglary, and not for a distinct sentence for larceny, and Chief Justice SHAW said no case could be found where there were two punishments on such an indictment. In Kite v. Com., 11 Metc. (Mass.) 581, it was held that in such case the conviction is of burglary, the larceny being larceny. In Breese v. State, 12 Ohio St. 146, it was held that the sentence must be for burg-

lary, not larceny. The case of State v. Henley, 30 Mo. 509, cited in 1 Whart. Crim. Law, § 819, as sustaining double sentence, was on a statute expressly authorizing it, and does not oppose the proposition above stated; and Kite v. Com., supra, cited by Wharton to same effect, is just to the reverse. On separate counts there can be convictions of both burglary and larceny. 1 Bish. Crim. Law, § 893; Speer's Case, 17 Grat. 570. The reason for thus framing an indictment in a dual form, as stated in East's Pleas of the Crown, note to page 520, is that the definition of "burglary" is breaking and entering with intent to commit an offense, of which intent the actual commission is so strong evidence that the law has adopted it, and admits it to be equivalent to a charge of intent in the indictment, and therefore the charge of the intent is supported by proof of the fact, though the reverse would not be true, This would account for the anomaly in inserting two offenses in one count, apparently violating the rule against duplicity, and the rule against joining different offenses, especially in the same count. Anyhow, the exception exists.

But, though this first count is not bad for the reason above suggested by counsel, it is bad because it wants the conclusion, "against the peace and dignity of the state," required by Const. art. 2, § 8. Lemon's Case, 4 W. Va. 755, holds that there must be a literal compliance with this requirement. All authorities agree that, where there is a total want of this conclusion, the indictment is bad. 1 Bish. Crim. Proc. § 159; Whart. Crim. Pl. § 279. Each count is as to this point to be regarded a separate indictment, and each must have the conclusion, and the conclusion found in one count, though the last, will not cure its absence from another count. Carney's Case, 4 Grat. 546; Thompson's Case, 20 Grat. 724; 1 Bish. Crim. Proc. § 185. Next, as to the second count. It is bad, as a count for burglary, because it omits as to that charge the words "feloniously and burglariously." McDonald's Case, 9 W. Va. 456; Vest's Case, 21 W. Va. 796; Meadow's Case, 22 W. Va. 766. Verdict does not cure this defect. Randall's Case, 24 Grat. 644. As a count to support a conviction of grand larceny, it is not sufficient, because it alleges the larceny of "goods and chattels," but does not specify them. It does, however, allege the larceny of one pair of pantaloons, of the value of five dollars, and is thus good for petit larceny. It is clear that, upon an indictment for grand larceny there can be a conviction of petit larceny, as the major includes the minor offense,—plainly so in the instance of grand and petit larceny. Howes' Case, 26 W. Va. 110; Whart. Crim. Pl. § 246; Hardy and Curry's Case, 17 Grat 592; Canda's Case, 22 Grat. 899; Code, § 18, c. 159. Striking out other goods than the pantaloons, the count is one for petit larceny, and the court could not hold it bad on demurrer. Thus, the conclusion is that, as the demurrer was general, and one count charges an offense, there is no error in the overruling of the demurrer. What then? The verdict found the prisoner guilty of burglary. The second count could not support that finding, as it is not good for burglary, and, though otherwise good for burglary, the first count cannot support it, because it is bad for want of conclusion. Thus neither count is good for burglary. But there was, in effect, no demurrer to this count. Can the defendant have the advantage of this defect in the appellate court? Had he made a motion in arrest of judgment, the circuit court ought to have sustained it, because of such defect in the first count. In Randall's Case, supra, the indictment being bad, it was held that the judgment should be reversed, though no motion in arrest had been made. In Matthew's Case, 18 Grat. 989, it was held that "anything which is good cause for arresting a judgment is good cause for reversing it, though no motion in arrest be made;" and in Lemons' Case, 4 W. Va., where there was no demurrer or motion in arrest of judgment, yet the court held that the prisoner had not waived his right to ask a reversal for want of the constitutional conclusion to the indictment, and might make it for the first time in this court, it being a requirement of the constitution. As the verdict stands alone on the bad first count, we must set it aside. There can be no further trial for burglary or grand larceny on this indictment, and resort for that purpose must be had to a new indictment. Though three bills of exception are copied into the transcript, but one is noted in the record. The record says that the bill which it notes was for the refusal of the court to set aside the verdict as contrary to the evidence, and refers to it as No. 1; but the bill numbered 1 is one relating to the admission of evidence, and that relating to the refusal of a new trial and certifying the evidence is numbered 2. We think that we must consider the latter bill as the one referred to in the record, and that it is simply misnumbered. As the case may be tried again, we shall express no opinion as to the facts, and we cannot consider the matters contained in the two other bills of exception, as the record makes no note of them. Wickes v. Railroad Co., 14 W. Va. 157; Bank v. Showacre, 26 W. Va. 49. Therefore the judgment is reversed, the verdict set aside, and the cause is remanded, to be acted upon in accordance with principles above indicated.

DUNLAP v. HEDGES et al.

(Supreme Court of Appeals of West Virginia. Sept. 10, 1891.)

APPOINTMENT OF RECEIVER — WASTE BY MORTGAGOR.

W. sold and conveyed a tract of land to H., and took a deed of trust to secure certain notes given for the purchase money. After a portion of said notes were paid, a second deed of trust was given on the same property to secure the notes remaining unpaid. Default was made in the payment of one of these notes, and the trustee was requested to sell under said last-named deed of trust, which he proceeded to do by advertising the same, and, during the pendency of said advertisement, H. confessed a judgment to his father for something over $3,000, which judgment was docketed. On the day of

sale his said father was present, and publicly announced, through his attorney, that his said judgment was a lien upon said property, and entitled to priority; and when, in the afternoon of that day, said trustee proceeded to sell said property, the same was bid off by the father of said H. for the sum of $4,900, but failed to comply with the terms of sale by paying the purchase money, claiming that he was entitled to it by virtue of said judgment. Upon a bill filed by the trustee setting forth these facts, and alleging that H. was insolvent, and had been allowing said farm to run down, and was cultivating said land in a wasteful and destructive manner, supported by affidavits, a proper case was presented for the appointment of a special receiver to take charge of said land, to rent and preserve the same until the conflicting claims asserted could be adjusted.

(Syllabus by the Court.)

Appeal from circuit court, Ohio county.

Application by William M. Dunlap, trustee, against Burton Hedges and Ellen Hedges, his wife, C. B. Hedges, the McCormick Harvesting Machine Company, and Robert B. Wayt, for the appointment of a receiver. Decree for plaintiff. Defendant C. B. Hedges appeals. Affirmed.

J. B. Sommerville, for appellant. Erskine & Allison, for appellee.

ENGLISH, J. On the 24th day of May, 1890, William M. Dunlap, trustee, by leave of the court, filed in the circuit court of Ohio county, in open court, his bill of complaint, verified by affidavit, against Burton Hedges and Ellen Hedges, his wife, C. B. Hedges, the McCormick Harvesting Machine Company, and Robert B. Wayt, together with certain exhibits, accompanied with proof of service of the notices upon the defendants Burton Hedges and C. B. Hedges as to the time of filing said bill, and that the appointment of a special receiver would be applied for as soon as the application could be heard for the purposes prayed for in the bill. The defendants upon whom said notice was served appeared by counsel, and the hearing of said application was fixed for Monday, May 26, 1890. The plaintiff in said bill alleged, among other things, that on the 4th day of December, 1883, said Robert B. Wayt sold, and he and his wife conveyed, to said Burton Hedges, a farm in Ohio county, containing 170 39-100 acres; and on the same day said Burton Hedges and wife executed a deed of trust on said premises to secure the purchase money therefor, evidenced by 9 promissory notes of the said Burton Hedges, all bearing date on the 4th day of December, 1883, and payable to the order of the defendant Robert B. Wayt, the first 8 of which notes were for the sum of $800, each, and were payable, respectively, with interest from date, in 1, 2, 3, 4, 5, 6, 7, and 8 years from the date thereof. The ninth note was for the sum of $823.40, payable, with interest, 9 years from the said date, which deed of trust was duly admitted to record. That some time after making said deed of trust it was discovered that the same was defective, by reason of the omission of an attesting clause at the conclusion thereof, and to remedy said defect a new deed of trust was executed by the same grantors to J. S. Cochran, trustee, upon the same property, dated April 13, 1885, to secure said notes; which last-named deed of trust showed on its face that it was executed for the purpose of correcting said mistake, and that it was to stand in lieu of said former defective deed of trust, which last-named deed of trust was duly recorded. That on the 12th day of January, 1889, three of said promissory notes that had become due had been paid, and a fourth was subject to a credit of $447 as of the 22d day of December, 1886, and a further credit of $47.75 as of September 15, 1888. Another of said notes that had become due was held in a bank in Wheeling, and in order to give the note that was in bank and the note that was partly paid a preference in the order of security, and because the said J. S. Cochran, trustee in the two deeds of trust aforesaid, had removed from the state of West Virginia, a new deed of trust was made and executed by said Burton Hedges and wife to the plaintiff, William M. Dunlap, as trustee, dated on the 12th day of January, 1889, conveying the same property, with the exception of three parcels thereof, containing about 11 acres in all, which had been sold and conveyed by said Burton Hedges and wife to other persons; which last-mentioned deed of trust was to secure the last 5 of the notes above described, and the unpaid portion of another of said notes, but was so drawn as to give the preference first to the note held in bank, then the preference to the note that was partly paid, and, as to the four notes which were last to become due, they were placed on an equality with each other; and it was provided that said last-named trust-deed, when properly signed, acknowledged, and admitted to record, was intended to take the place of a deed of trust made by Burton Hedges and wife to J. S. Cochran, trustee, dated April 3, 1883; and the plaintiff alleged that it was the agreement of parties and intention of the grantors that said deed of trust to him should, when so executed and recorded, take the place of said deed of trust dated April 3, 1885, and that the date April 3, 1883, was written in said deed of trust by mistake, instead of April 3, 1885. That said deed of trust to plaintiff as trustee, dated January 12, 1889, was duly executed and acknowledged, and was duly admitted to record on the 28th day of January, 1889. That after the making of said last-mentioned trust-deed, the two notes which were given the preference therein were paid, and when the next of said promissory notes became due, to-wit, on December 4, 1889, it was not paid; and afterwards the plaintiff, having been requested by the defendant Robert B. Wayt, the holder of said note, to proceed to collect the same by means of a sale of the property under said deed of trust, advertised the same for sale on the 8th of April, 1890; and after the commencement of the publication of said advertisement, to-wit, on the 15th day of March, 1890, the defendant Burton Hedges confessed a judgment in favor of his father, C. B. Hedges, for the sum of $8,337.86, with interest thereon from the 15th day of March, 1890, until payment, which judgment was docketed the 8th of April, 1890, and was predicated

upon a promissory note of said Burton Hedges dated January 7, 1890, for the sum of $8,248.50, payable one day after date, to the order of C. B. Hedges; and that on the 6th day of December, 1889, the defendant the McCormick Harvesting Machine Company obtained a judgment against the said Burton Hedges before a justice for the sum of $53.75, and costs, $5.30, which judgment was docketed on the 6th day of December, 1889. On the 8th of April, 1890, before the commencement of the sale, the said Robert B. Wayt executed, acknowledged, and filed for record in the county clerk's office of said county two deeds of release, releasing said two first-mentioned deeds of trust, and on the same day said property was offered for sale at auction in pursuance of said advertisement. That soon after the beginning of the auction J. B. Sommerville, an attorney at law practicing at that bar, publicly announced to the persons in attendance at said sale that there was a judgment of about $9,000 which was a lien upon the property, and he claimed that it was the first lien upon the property, and that he desired to give notice of the fact so that purchasers might not get into trouble. That he did not announce who his client, the judgment creditor, was, but he afterwards informed the plaintiff that he referred to the said judgment in favor of C. B. Hedges for the sum of $8,337.86. The plaintiff, believing his trust-deed was the first lien, continued to receive bids for the farm, the sale was continued until the afternoon of the same day, when the defendant C. B. Hedges appeared as a bidder, and, being the highest bidder, became the purchaser at the price of $4,900, but failed to comply with the terms of sale by paying any portion of the purchase money, but claimed, through his attorney, that he was entitled to the first lien on the property, and that none of the purchase money was payable to the plaintiff as trustee, except so much as would pay the expenses of advertising and making said sale. That the defendant Burton Hedges is still occupying and using said farm, which at the time it was sold to him, in 1883, was in good condition and repair; but that he has suffered it to go down, the buildings and fences have been neglected, and his manner of cultivating said land has been very wasteful and destructive, so that the fields have been badly washed and otherwise injured. That said Burton Hedges has no more personal property than he could successfully claim as exempt from execution. That the price for which the said farm was sold at said auction to said C. B. Hedges is sufficient to pay the debt secured by said deed of trust, but that if the said farm is allowed to remain in the charge of said Burton Hedges, and he is allowed to have the profits from it, and to continue the destructive use of it, it will, as he believes, soon become of too little value to be safe security for the said debt, considering it the first lien. That there is no reasonable ground for considering said judgment as prior or superior to the lien of said deed of trust under which said sale was made. That the assertion of said claim casts a cloud upon the title to said land, and by the further claim that said purchase money need not be paid the said C. B. Hedges and Burton Hedges will he able, unless prevented by the order of the court, to deprive the said Robert B. Wayt, the *cestui que trust* under said deed of trust, of the money, or a large portion of the money, owing to him from said Burton Hedges, and secured by said deed of trust. That if he should treat the said purchaser, C. B. Hedges, as having forfeited his rights as a purchaser by reason of his non-compliance with the terms of said sale, and should again advertise the property for sale, the said Robert B. Wayt would be injured and deprived of his rights by the continuance of the said Burton Hedges in the possession of the property for an indefinite length of time, because the said claim that the lien of the said judgment in favor of C. B. Hedges is superior to that of said deed of trust would still be asserted, and so the title would be clouded, and a fair and reasonable sale would be prevented. The plaintiff charges that the said claim of Robert B. Wayt for the amount of said last four notes constitutes the first lien on said property; the said judgment of the McCormick Harvesting Machine Company for $53.75, with interest and costs, constitutes the second lien on said property; and the said judgment of C. B. Hedges for $8,337.86, with interest and costs, if it be a valid lien at all, is the third and last lien thereon; and he prayed that a special receiver might be appointed to take charge of the said property, to care for, rent out, and protect the same, and to collect, receive, and preserve the rents and profits thereof until said property should be sold by order of the court. That the claim and pretension of the said C. B. Hedges, in regard to the superiority of the lien of his said judgment, might be considered and determined; and that the said C. B. Hedges, his agents and attorneys, might be perpetually enjoined from setting up the said claim in any way to the injury of the plaintiff as trustee, or of his *cestui que trust,* the said Robert B. Wayt; and that if the said property should, at any sale that might thereafter be made by order of the court, not bring enough money to pay in full the claim of R. B Wayt, with the interest thereon, a decree might be entered requiring the said C. B. Hedges to pay the deficiency. This bill was verified by affidavit, but neither of the defendants ever tendered or filed an answer denying its allegations. On the 30th day of May, 1890, the plaintiff moved the court, after giving notice, for the appointment of a receiver, and supported his motion by affidavits, which were replied to by counter-affidavits; and, after taking time to consider, the court, on the 24th day of June, 1890, appointed William J. W. Cowden special receiver, who was required, after giving bond in the penalty of $3,000, conditioned for the faithful performance of his duties, to take charge of the farm described in said deed of trust, and to rent out the same for a period ending April 1, 1891, upon the terms therein set forth, and directing said Burton Hedges to deliver possession of said property to said receiver; and from this decree the defendant C. B. Hedges applied for and obtained this appeal.

The first error assigned and relied upon by the appellant, C. B. Hedges, is that the plaintiff's bill, and the affidavits of appellant and Burton Hedges, filed in said cause, show that the plaintiff sold the real estate mentioned and described in the bill and exhibits in said cause to appellant on the 8th day of April, 1890, and that at or shortly after said date appellant took possession of said real estate, and leased the same to said Burton Hedges, who was occupying the same under said lease when said receiver was appointed, thus leaving nothing for said plaintiff to do but to collect the purchase money for said real estate. It is true the plaintiff, as trustee, on the 8th day of April, 1890, sold said land at public auction to the appellant; but it is also true that, but for the failure and refusal of the appellant to comply with the terms of the sale by paying the purchase money, and by the assertion on his part of a claim that his judgment lien was entitled to priority over the trust lien under which said sale was made and under which he purchased, the intervention of a receiver would not have been necessary, and his appointment would not have been assigned as error by the appellant. The facts set forth by the plaintiff in his bill, and which are not controverted by any answer, seem to me to present a case which peculiarly calls for the appointment of a receiver. In the case of Beverley v. Brooke, 4 Grat. 208, Judge BALDWIN, in delivering the opinion of the court, discusses elaborately the appointment, powers, and duties of receivers. He says: "By means of the appointment of a receiver, a court of equity takes possession of the property which is the subject of the suit, preserves it from waste or destruction, secures and collects the proceeds or profits, and ultimately disposes of them according to the rights and priorities of those entitled. * * * The receiver appointed is the officer and representative of the court, subject to its orders, accountable in such manner and to such persons as the court may direct, and having in his character of receiver no personal interest but that arising out of his responsibility for the correct and faithful discharge of his duties. * * * The order of appointment is in the nature, not of an attachment, but a sequestration; it gives in itself no advantage to the party applying for it over other claimants, and operates prospectively upon rents and profits which may come to the hands of the receiver as a lien in favor of those interested, according to their rights and priorities in or to the principal subject out of which those rents and profits issue." Barton, in his Chancery Practice, (volume 1, p. 480,) says: "The object of the appointment of a receiver is to preserve the *status* of the property until there can be an adjudication of conflicting claims to or interest in it;" and on page 482 he says: "The immediate moving cause for the appointment of a receiver is that the subject of litigation may be preserved from waste, loss, or destruction, so that there may be some harvest, some fruits to gather, after the labors of the controversy are over."

In the case under consideration, the appellant, by claiming to be entitled to the entire proceeds of said sale by reason of his judgment, created the controversy in reference to the priorities of the lienholders, and necessitated the action of the court of which he complains. In the case of Fleming v. Holt, 12 W. Va. 149, point 4 of the syllabus, the court held that such a suit (meaning a suit in equity for specific performance) may be brought against the purchaser of land sold at public auction by the trustee, on the refusal of the purchaser to comply with the terms of sale, without the trustee selling the land again at auction, and, if the trustee made a second sale, no such suit would lie against the first purchaser. The object of the bill filed in this case by said trustee was the appointment of a receiver to take charge of said property, and to rent and receive the rents, and preserve the same until the property could be properly sold by the order of the court, and until the claim of said C. B. Hedges in regard to the superiority of the lien of his said judgment could be heard and determined. By asserting that claim, the said C. B. Hedges proclaimed to those present at the sale the existence of a controversy between the owners of said respective liens; and as men, as a general rule, are averse to purchasing litigation, said claim had a tendency to deter others from bidding, and thereby to prevent the property from bringing what it would under different circumstances; and, although it may be said that those wishing to purchase had the opportunity of resorting to the records and making the examination for themselves as to the validity and priority of said trust and judgment liens, yet, if the time had been allowed for such an examination in this instance, the records would have disclosed that the trust lien was the oldest in point of time, and apparently entitled to the priority, and the party would have been left to conjecture and uncertainty as to the grounds upon which the claim of priority was asserted by said C. B. Hedges,—all of which would have a tendency to depress the price, and deter bidders. In the disposition of property at public auction, equity always discountenances anything that has a tendency to prevent a fair sale, and will not, as a general rule, allow a purchaser to obtain the title to property for less than its value by resorting to unfair means or representations; but, as the property at this sale appears to have brought a sufficient amount to pay off and discharge said trust lien which said trustee claims is entitled to priority, he does not formally ask in his bill that said sale may be treated as a nullity, or that the same may be rescinded, but, without praying a specific execution of the contract between himself and C. B. Hedges as purchaser at said sale, he merely asks that a special receiver be appointed to care for the property and collect the rents until the priority of the liens can be determined,

and until the property shall be sold by order of the court. Said trustee was proceeding, in pursuance of the request of his cestui que trust, to make sale of the said real estate under said trust-deed as the property of Burton Hedges, and, when it was knocked off to C. B. Hedges at a sum sufficient to pay off and discharge said trust debt, the said purchaser claimed that he was entitled to the entire purchase money, and refused for that reason to comply with the terms of the sale. Under these circumstances, it is manifest that the trustee still retained the legal title to the land described in said trust, and has not in any manner released said trust lien, but still had the right to look to the land of said Burton Hedges for satisfaction of the debt secured in said deed of trust. This being the case, and it having been alleged that said Burton Hedges is the owner of no property that can be reached and subjected by execution, which allegation is not contradicted either by answer or affidavit filed in the cause, and it being further shown by the allegations of the bill, supported by affidavits, that said Burton Hedges was suffering said real estate to deteriorate in value by allowing the fences to go down, and that his manner of cultivating the same was wasteful and destructive, a case is presented which would authorize the appointment of a receiver to take charge of the property, and to rent the same, and receive the rents, until such time as the priorities of the liens asserted could be ascertained and determined. The duty of the trustee, under these circumstances, is plainly defined in 2 Minor, Inst. p. 286, where it is said: "It is the trustee's duty to forbear to sell, and to ask the aid and instructions of a court of equity, in all cases where the amount of the debt is unliquidated or in good faith disputed, where any cloud rests upon the title, where a reasonable price cannot be obtained, or where, for any reason, a sale is likely to be accompanied by a sacrifice of the property, which, at the cost of some delay, may be obviated." Bryan v. Stump, 8 Grat. 247. It may be true that the defendant C. B. Hedges is worth, as he alleges, five or six times the amount of the plaintiff's claim; but he denies that he is liable for any portion of the purchase money, or that said trustee is entitled to receive any portion of the amount he bid for said property, because, as he asserts, he is entitled to the amount by reason of his judgment; thus raising a question as to the priority of the liens as aforesaid, the determination of which question is peculiarly within the province of a court of equity; and during the delay occasioned by the determination of this question it was the plain duty of the court, under the circumstances of the case, to appoint a receiver to take charge of the property, to rent the same, and receive the rents, as provided in said decree complained of. For these reasons we are of opinion that the court below committed no error in the appointment of the receiver, with the powers and authority conferred upon him by the decree complained of, and said decree must be affirmed, with costs.

BREWSTER v. HAMILTON *et al.*

(*Supreme Court of Georgia.* July 13, 1891.)

JUDGMENT BY DEFAULT — PLEADING — WANT OF VERIFICATION.

A note for a stated sum, with interest from maturity, provided that, if placed in the hands of an attorney for collection, the maker would pay 10 per cent. of the attorney's fees, and that it might be assigned without notice. The recited consideration was the price of certain machinery which the vendors had sold on condition that the title should remain in them till the purchase price was paid. On default, the vendor could take possession of the machinery, the maker to pay all damage for such default, and waive all equities. *Held*, that where, in an action on this note, no pleas on oath or affirmation were filed, judgment was properly rendered for the payee, under Code Ga. 1882, § 5145, which provides that "the court shall render judgment without the verdict of a jury, in all civil cases founded on unconditional contracts in writing, where an issuable defense is not filed under oath or affirmation."

Error from superior court, Polk county; JOHN W. MADDOX, Judge.

Action by Hamilton & Co. against R. B. Brewster, on two notes. Judgment for plaintiffs. Defendant brings error. Affirmed.

The following is the official report:

Hamilton & Co. sued Brewster on two promissory notes. Before the last day of the appearance term of the case defendant appeared, and filed the plea of the general issue. The appearance docket was not called for the term to which the case was filed, and no entry of default was made. The names of counsel were marked opposite defendant's name in the case on the issue docket. At the trial term, on August 22, 1890, defendant, by his counsel, filed an amendment, which amendment was a plea of partial payment. On the last-named day the judge presiding, on motion of plaintiffs' counsel and over objection of defendant's counsel, before the case was regularly reached on the docket, called it up for the purpose of entering judgment therein as in default. Defendant was not present when the case was so called or during the trial of the case, but resides within the limits of the county, at a place connected by railroad with the county-site, and the court gave defendant's counsel a day to send for him before entering the judgment hereafter to be mentioned, which judgment was entered up on the — day of the term, which had been held for two weeks. The court dismissed both of the pleas, on the ground that they were not verified by the oath of defendant. Plaintiffs introduced the notes sued on, and the court thereupon entered up judgment as in cases of default upon unconditional contracts in writing. Defendant excepted, and says that the judgment was illegal, in that the case was based on a conditional contract, and in that it was rendered in a case which was taken up out of its order on the docket, and which was not in default, and not so marked on the docket. Defendant also excepted to the ruling of the court in striking out the pleas, and says that they presented an issuable defense, and it was not necessary that they should be verified by the oath of defendant, because the debt

sued on was not an unconditional contract in writing. These notes were each signed by Brewster, and each payable to the order of Battey & Hamilton. They were each for $145, with interest from maturity. Each provided that if, after maturity, it was placed in the hands of an attorney for collection, the maker agreed to pay 10 per cent. upon the amount due for attorney's fees, and that it might be transferred or assigned without notice. Each recited that its consideration was the purchase money of a gin, feeder, and condenser, the vendors selling and delivering said property with the condition that the title thereto was to remain in them until the purchase price should be paid in full and all expenses on account of the sale; that if default was made in the payment of the indebtedness, or any part thereof, the said firm, as survivors, attorney, agent, or assigns, at any time might take possession of the property, or any part thereof, and, if any part of the purchase money were paid before this was done, the firm or their assigns might sell the property at public or private sale, at such prices and on such terms as they might deem advisable; and the maker of the note bound himself to pay all loss or damage which might be caused by his failure to pay the indebtedness when due, and waived any equities he might have, and directed that the property be sold to ascertain what loss or damage had been sustained. One of these notes contained credits, and each contained an entry of transfer by Battey & Hamilton to Hamilton & Co.

Blance & Noyes, for plaintiff in error.
Joy F. Thompson, for defendants in error.

PER CURIAM. This case is controlled, with reference to attorney's fees, by Coleman v. Slade, 75 Ga. 61; and as to other question, by Craig v. Herring, 80 Ga. 709, 6 S. E. Rep. 283; Mosely v. Walker, 84 Ga. 274, 10 S. E. Rep. 623, and cases cited. Judgment affirmed.

WOODS *et al.* v. CRAMER *et al.*

(*Supreme Court of South Carolina.* Sept. 26, 1891.)

SALES—REFUSAL TO ACCEPT—DAMAGES—INTEREST.

1. Where the purchaser of grain by sample, after refusing to accept on the ground that it was not up to sample, agrees to accept it without any new arrangement as to price, he becomes liable for the contract price, and, if he afterwards fails to accept, and the seller has to sell the grain at auction, he is liable to the seller for the difference between the contract price and the price realized at such sale, together with costs of storage and other expenses necessitated by his failure to accept.

2. In such action, plaintiffs are entitled to interest on the amount fixed as the measure of damages, and it may be incorporated in the aggregate sum of damages found.

3. In an action for breach of a contract to accept grain which plaintiffs sold defendants, and which defendants refused to accept because not up to sample, but which they did afterwards accept, an exception that the court charged that the measure of damages was the difference between the contract price and the net proceeds realized by plaintiffs at an auction sale, whereas it should have been the difference between such

net proceeds and the price at the time of such acceptance, could not be sustained, even if well taken, if defendants offered no proof of the price of such grain at the time of acceptance.

Appeal from common pleas circuit court of Charleston county; FRASER, Judge.

Action by Robert J. Woods and another against Adolph F. C. Cramer and another, to recover the difference between the contract price of oats sold defendants by plaintiffs, but which defendants failed to accept, and the price at which plaintiffs afterwards sold the same at auction. Judgment for plaintiffs. Defendants appeal. Affirmed.

The charge of the court, and defendants' exceptions thereto, were as follows:

"This is an action to recover damages which the plaintiffs allege they have sustained by breach of a contract. The contract is alleged to be for the sale of certain car-loads of oats said to have been sold by sample. The question for you is whether those goods came up to sample, or whether, if they did not come up to sample, he nevertheless accepted them. If he accepted them, notwithstanding that they did not come up to sample, he is liable to take them and liable for the damages. The amount sued for is the difference between the amount which the oats sold for originally and the amount they sold for at auction, together with the expenses. That is the case before you, and I propose now to charge you upon these requests to charge, and to confine myself to them. The plaintiffs request me to charge: '(1) This is an action brought to recover damages for the breach of two contracts made by Kracke & Janssen, as brokers of the plaintiffs, for the delivery of certain rust-proof oats, and, if the jury believe that the plaintiffs tendered to the defendants the oats required by sample, and the defendants refused to accept the same, then the plaintiffs are entitled to recover the loss sustained by them.' I think that is correct. '(2) The measure of damages in case the jury find for the plaintiffs is the difference between the contract price and the price for which the goods were afterwards sold, and also all charges attending said sale and storage, and other expenses after the goods should have been received by the defendants, and before the sale.' I think that is right. '(3) In a contract for sale for the price of $50. or upwards, made by brokers, to satisfy the statute of frauds, the memorandum must be in writing, and may be proved by a note of sale handed by the brokers to the seller, and a note of purchase handed by the brokers to the buyer, and, therefore, both the letters of Kracke & Janssen to the plaintiffs and defendants in this case are evidence of the contract.' I charge you that. '(4) It is a question for the jury whether the oats shipped by the plaintiffs to Charleston were accepted by the defendants on the 18th day of October, 1886, and if the same were then accepted, they must find for the plaintiffs.' There must have been an acceptance, not merely an agreement to accept. An acceptance must be some exercise of ownership, and some definite action to show that they were

accepted. If the jury come to the conclusion that there was only an agreement to accept, then that agreement to accept, in order to amount to a new contract, must be evidenced either by writing, or be accompanied by all the evidence and formalities which are necessary to create an original contract. But, if there was an actual acceptance, that would alter the case. If the goods were in a house, and a man takes the key, that would be an acceptance. To take possession of a watch, a man would have to take the watch in his hand. To take possession of a horse, he would have to turn him into his lot, or take the bridle, or have him hitched somewhere. Acceptance is taking possession and control of property. 'Question, by a juror: Suppose Mr. Blohme, in his office on the 13th October, told Miller he would take the drafts up, wasn't that tantamount to an acceptance?' By the Court: I don't think it would, unless he was bound to take them because they were up to sample. If he told the agent, "I will take the goods; you go away,"—that would be tantamount to his accepting it. But an agreement to accept is not an acceptance.' The defendants ask me to charge: '(1) That, where goods are sold by sample, the seller is held to warrant that the goods shall correspond with the sample, both in kind and quality.' I charge you that. '(2) That, where one has a general agency to sell goods for another, he may sell by sample, and this is a warranty that the goods shall come up to the sample, binding on the principal.' I charge you that in that shape. '(3) Under the contract offered in evidence in this case, the defendants were not required to notify the plaintiffs of their refusal of the oats; notice to their agents, Kracke & Janssen, was sufficient.' That is correct. '(4) That, under the contract in this case, the rise or fall of oats is immaterial, and should not be considered by the jury.' I think it is immaterial whether the oats rose or fell in the market. The question is, did the parties fulfill their contract? A mere agreement to accept the oats, without some act amounting either to symbolical or actual possession, would not be acceptance. If he put the plaintiffs in position to be injured by saying, 'I will take the goods, you go off,' then he would be estopped from saying he had not accepted them. 'Question, by Mr. Buist: Will your honor charge the jury on the matter of interest? By the Court: I think the plaintiffs would be entitled to interest, if you find for the plaintiffs.' "

Defendants' exceptions to the charge were as follows:

"First. Because his honor erred in saying to them: 'The question for you is whether these goods came up to sample, or whether, if they did not come up to sample, he nevertheless accepted them.' The judge thus changes the issues from those made by the parties themselves; the plaintiffs' case being that the goods were not accepted, but that they did come up to contract, and should have been accepted; also, that there was an agreement to accept, which was not performed; and so the jury were prevented from properly considering and passing upon the real issues in the cause, or were misled as to the same. *Second.* Because his honor erred in charging that, 'if he accepted them, notwithstanding that they did not come up to sample, he is liable to take them and liable for the damages.' (*a*) For that the expression 'liable for the damages,' in the connection in which it occurs, means the damages sued for,—that is, the difference between the amount which the oats sold for originally and the net amount that they brought on the resale; whereas, if the oats were accepted, yet, if they did not come up to sample, the damages would be the difference between the real value of the oats at the time of acceptance and the net amount realized by plaintiffs upon the resale. (*b*) For that in so charging the defendants were precluded from any benefit of this defense, that the goods did not come up to sample, in the event that the jury should consider that they had accepted them; whereas, notwithstanding such acceptance, damages for the breach of the warranty of quality in the sale by sample, was a proper subject for consideration and allowance by the jury. (*c*) For that in so charging the judge implied a distinction between an acceptance and a taking of the goods; whereas, if there was an acceptance, the title passed and the goods were taken; and as said charge was calculated to mislead the jury in finding whether or not there was an acceptance. (*d*) For that in so charging the judge drew a distinction between an acceptance and the taking of the goods, which was calculated to mislead the jury, inasmuch as an acceptance involves the ownership and custody of the goods, and to suggest that there might be an acceptance without the control and custody of the goods was calculated to prevent the jury from considering the acts of plaintiffs in maintaining control and custody of the goods, and reselling the same, upon the question whether or not there was an acceptance. *Third.* Because his honor erred in charging that 'the measure of damages, in case the jury find for the plaintiffs, is the difference between the contract price and the price for which the goods were afterwards sold, and also all charges,' etc. (*a*) For that such charge was erroneous in case the jury should have found that the oats were not up to sample, but that defendants had accepted them, in which case they might have found for plaintiffs, if the application of the measure of damages required it, and the measure of damages in such case would have been the difference between the value of the goods so falling below sample at the time of acceptance and the net amount realized by vendors on resale. (*b*) For that said charge withdrew from the jury all consideration of damage to defendants upon a breach of the warranty implied in the sale by sample, in the case of the acceptance of the goods by the defendants. *Fourth.* Because his honor erred in charging upon the fourth instruction prayed for by plaintiffs in such manner as to approve the said instruction, subject only to his explanation of the meaning of

acceptance; whereas, even if the goods were accepted by defendants, it did not follow that plaintiffs must recover, for, if they were not up to sample, the difference in value between them and the contract price would have been a good offset, and in this case might have prevented any recovery by plaintiffs at all. *Fifth.* Because his honor erred in charging, 'if he told the agent, "I will take the goods; you go away,"—that would be tantamount to his accepting it;' whereas, an acceptance could only have been made by taking control of the property, and said charge was calculated to prevent the jury from considering, upon the question of acceptance, the force and effect of plaintiffs' own allegations, and proves that defendants never accepted, but that plaintiffs stored and resold the goods. Further, that, considered as an agreement to accept, such words do not amount to a valid agreement to accept. *Sixth.* Because his honor erred in charging that, 'if be put the plaintiffs in position to be injured by saying, "I will take the goods: you go off,"—then he would be estopped from saying he had not accepted them;' for that such a state of facts presents an entirely different case from a case of acceptance. *Seventh.* Because his honor erred in charging that the plaintiffs would be entitled to interest."

Simons & Cappelmann and *J. E. Burke*, for appellants. *Bulst & Bulst* and *John Wingate*, for respondents.

McIVER, J. This was an action to recover damages for breach of contract. The plaintiffs claim that on the 11th of September, 1886, through the brokers, Kracke & Janssen, mentioned in the complaint, they made a contract with defendants for the sale and delivery to them of 10 car-loads of oats, according to the sample then delivered to them, at the price of 55 cents per bushel; that the 10 car-loads of oats, corresponding with said sample, were forwarded to defendants in Charleston, and tendered to them, who thereupon accepted and paid for three car-loads, but refused to accept and pay for the other seven car-loads; that on the 15th of September, 1886, plaintiffs made another contract with defendants, through said brokers, for the sale of three car-loads of oats, according to the sample furnished, at the price of 51½ cents per bushel, and that said three car-loads were forwarded to defendants in Charleston, and tendered to them, who thereupon accepted and paid for one of the car-loads, but refused to accept and pay for the other two car-loads; that thereafter, on the 18th of October, 1886, the said nine car-loads of oats which had previously been rejected by defendants were again tendered to them, and the defendants thereupon agreed to accept and pay for the same according to the terms of said contracts, but that, notwithstanding such agreement, the defendants wholly neglected and refused to comply with the same; that, in consequence of said refusal, on the 4th of December, 1886, after due notice to defendants, and after due advertisement, the said nine car-loads of oats were sold at public auction, at the risk of defendants, for a sum much less than the contract price, and the plaintiffs claim as their damages the difference between said sum and the contract price, together with the expenses of sale and storage. The defendants, in their answer, admit the contracts for the sale of the oats, the tender of the same, the acceptance of a portion of each lot, and the refusal to accept and pay for the balance, which was done because they allege that the rejected car-loads did not correspond with the samples furnished, but were much inferior in grade; but they deny the allegation that they had agreed, on the 18th of October, 1886, to accept and pay for the oats previously rejected, and they deny any knowledge or information sufficient to form a belief as to the allegations in reference to the sale of the rejected oats at public auction at their risk. While there was a conflict of testimony as to some of the facts involved, which will be more specifically stated hereinafter, there seems to have been no dispute that the oats were duly shipped by plaintiffs, and reached Charleston by rail in due course of transportation, when they were examined by defendants, and a portion thereof rejected, as above stated, of which due notice was given to the said brokers; nor is there any dispute that after all negotiations for the settlement of the matter had failed, that the rejected oats, after due notice to defendants, and after advertisement in the public prints, were sold at public auction for the amount stated in the complaint, and that the difference between the amount realized at such sale, together with the costs and expenses, and the contract price, are correctly stated in the complaint. It seems that, when plaintiffs learned that defendants had declined to accept a portion of the oats, they sent their confidential clerk or agent to Charleston, to inquire into the matter, who reached that city on the 9th of October, 1886, but was unable to procure an interview with defendants until the 13th of that month. As to what occurred at that interview there is a direct conflict of testimony,—the testimony on the part of plaintiffs being that defendants then agreed to accept and pay for the oats according to the terms of the contracts, and that plaintiffs' agent, relying upon that agreement, immediately left Charleston, understanding that the drafts drawn by plaintiffs on the defendants would be paid on the next day; but the testimony on the part of the defendants is directly the reverse, they denying that any such agreement was made, or any such understanding entered into. The plaintiffs, being notified that the drafts were not paid, again sent their agent to Charleston, who, after remaining there some time engaged in a fruitless effort to settle the matter, had the oats advertised and sold, as above stated.

The charge of his honor, Judge FRASER, before whom the case was tried, is very brief, and seems to be set out fully in the case, and should, together with defendants' exceptions, be incorporated in the report of the case. The jury found a verdict in favor of the plaintiffs for the differ-

ence in the contract price of the oats and the amount realized at the auction sale, after deducting therefrom the expenses; and, judgment having been entered, defendants appeal upon the several grounds set out in the record.

The charge of the circuit judge is very brief, comprehensive, and to the point, and, so far as we can perceive, is free from any just exception. There can be no doubt that, under the contracts, the making of which is admitted, the real question for the jury was whether the goods tendered came up to the samples by which they were sold; and that was purely a question of fact for the jury. If they did, there can be no doubt that defendants were liable. We think there is as little doubt that, even if the goods did not in fact correspond with the sample, yet if the defendants accepted them, they would be liable for the contract price; for, while the defendants would have had the right to reject the oats if they did not substantially correspond with the samples by which they were sold, yet if they nevertheless chose to accept them, that would be a waiver of their right of rejection, and they would be bound to perform their contract to pay the stipulated price. They certainly could not take the oats, after they had discovered, as they say, that they did not come up to sample, at any less price than that stipulated for in the contracts, for that would be allowing them to change one of the essential terms of the contracts, without the consent of the other contracting party. We say nothing here as to what would be the effect if the defect in the article sold was discovered after acceptance, for there is nothing in the testimony which would present the case in that aspect.

If the defendants were liable, the next inquiry would be as to the measure of damages, which the jury were instructed was the difference between the contract price and the amount for which the oats were sold at auction, less the expenses of sale and storage. This was undoubtedly the correct measure of the damages, for that unquestionably represented the amount of the loss to which plaintiffs were subjected by reason of the failure of the defendants to comply with the contracts. If the contract had been fully performed, the plaintiffs would have been entitled to receive, and would have received, the amount of money which the oats at the contract price would have brought, and of course their loss is the difference between that amount and the amount which they actually received, to-wit, the net proceeds of the sale at auction, after deducting the expenses of storage to which they had been subjected by reason of the failure of the defendants to perform their part of the contract. This seems to be in accordance with the well-settled rule of law. Benj. Sales, § 788; Sands v. Taylor, 5 Johns. 395; Jackson v. Watts, 1 McCord, 288; Millar v. Hilliard, Cheves, 149; Stack v. Railroad Co., 10 S. C. 91. The general charge of the circuit judge was in conformity to these views, and all the rest of the charge was simply an adoption of the several requests to charge submitted by both parties, which, in the main, covered the foregoing principles.

In the exceptions complaint is made that the minds of the jury were diverted from the real issue in the case by what was said in relation to the acceptance of the oats by the defendants, and a good deal has been said in the argument as to the difference between the acceptance and actual receipt of an article alleged to have been sold in a case like this. Inasmuch as there was no pretense, and could not have been, that there was any invalidity in either of the contracts under the statute of frauds, (both of the contracts having been in writing,) we are at a loss to appreciate much that has been said upon the subject. If the effort had been to take the case out of the operation of the statute of frauds by showing that there had been both an acceptance and receipt of the goods alleged to have been sold, such remarks might have been quite pertinent. Here, however, there was no dispute as to the making or the validity of the contracts which lie at the foundation of this action, and the only question was whether such contracts had been performed; and, as we understand it, all that was said to the jury upon the subject of the acceptance by the defendants of the oats shipped to them by the plaintiffs was simply for the purpose of indicating to the jury that the acceptance of the oats, or a declaration to that effect, whereby the plaintiffs were misled to their prejudice, would be a circumstance to be considered in determining whether the defendants had not thereby admitted that the goods sold were up to the sample by which they were sold. The exception to the measure of damages given to the jury by the circuit judge, in which it is contended that the defendants, even if they accepted the goods notwithstanding they were not up to sample, would only be liable for the difference between the market value of the goods so falling below the sample at the time of the acceptance and the net amount realised by the sale at auction, cannot be sustained, not only for the reason, as above indicated, that this would be allowing one of the parties to a contract to change one of its essential terms without the consent of the other, but also for the further reason that the defendants furnished no testimony for the application of such a measure of damages, as they offered no evidence as to the market value of such defective oats as they claimed the rejected oats to be; and, on the contrary, by their objection to the seventh interrogatory propounded to R. J. Woods, which was sustained, they expressly admitted the correctness of the measure of damages applied by the circuit judge.

The only remaining inquiry is whether there was any error on the part of the circuit judge in instructing the jury that, if they found for the plaintiffs, they would be entitled to interest on the amount fixed as the measure of the damages. That there was no error in this instruction may be seen by reference to the cases of Davis v. Richardson's Ex'rs, 1 Bay, 105; Price v. Justrobe, Harp. 111; and Wilson v. Railroad Co., 16 S. C. 592, cited by counsel for re-

spondents, to which may be added Blackwood v. Leman, Harp. 219; Wolfe v. Sharp, 10 Rich. Law, 64; and Kyle v. Railroad Co., Id. 382. See, also, Goddard v. Bulow, 1 Nott. & McC. 45; Holmes v. Mixroon, 1 Tread. Const. 21; Ancrum v. Slone, 2 Speer, 594,—where the question in what cases interest is recoverable is fully discussed, and where the distinction between a finding of interest *eo nomine* and incorporating the interest in the aggregate sum of damages found, as seems to have been done in the present case, is discussed and recognised. The judgment of this court is that the judgment of the circuit court be affirmed.

McGowan, J., concurs.

Curtis v. Renneker *et al.*

(*Supreme Court of South Carolina.* Sept. 19, 1891.)

Mortgages—Duration of Lien—Effect of Assignment—Foreclosure—Judgment on Bond—Tax-Sale.

1. Gen. St. S. C. 1882, § 1831, passed in 1879, provides that no mortgage, judgment, decree, or other lien on real estate shall constitute a lien on any real estate after the lapse of 20 years from the date of the creation of the same, provided that, if the holder thereof shall, at any time during the continuance of such lien, cause to be recorded upon the record of such mortgage, etc., or file with the record thereof, a "note of some payment on account," or some written "acknowledgment of the debt," such mortgage, etc., shall continue to be a lien for 20 years from the date of the record of such payment or acknowledgment. *Held,* that the recording of an assignment of a mortgage before the expiration of the 20 years was neither a "note of some payment on account," or an "acknowledgment of the debt," within the statute.

2. Such section does not apply to mortgages executed prior to its passage. Henry v. Henry, 31 S. C. 1, 9 S. E. Rep. 726, distinguished.

3. The fact that the obligee on a bond secured by a mortgage has recovered judgment on the bond does not invalidate a subsequent judgment in his favor foreclosing the mortgage, where the mortgagor failed to interpose the prior judgment as a defense; and the judgment of foreclosure constitutes a valid lien from its rendition upon the property of the mortgagor.

4. The laws relative to the sale of land for delinquent taxes in South Carolina in 1877 required the issuance of an execution against the personal property of a defaulting tax-payer, and a return of *nulla bona,* as an essential prerequisite of the sale of land. Ebaugh v. Mullinax, (S. C.) 13 S. E. Rep. 613, followed.

Appeal from common pleas circuit court of Charleston county; Fraser, Judge.

Action by J. Alice Curtis against Louisa E. Renneker, T. W. Bacot, assignee of John H. Renneker, and others, to establish the priority of certain liens upon the proceeds of a sale of land. Judgment for certain defendants. Plaintiff and defendant T. W. Bacot appeal. Reversed in part, and affirmed in part. Following are the master's reports:

"FIRST REPORT OF MASTER.

"By order of his honor, Judge Norton, filed 12th June, 1888, this case was referred to me to hear and determine all the issues therein, and to report my conclusions thereon, with leave to report any special matter. I have been attended by the solicitors of the parties, and have taken testimony, as hereinafter stated. The original complaint (filed 15th March, 1888) was for the foreclosure of a mortgage of a lot of land and buildings at the south-east corner of King and Queen streets, in the city of Charleston. The said mortgage is dated 27th March, 1867, and was given by John H. Renneker and Adam B. Glover to L. E. Amsinck & Co., to secure their joint and several bond conditioned for the payment of $3,084.38. A payment of $1,500 having been made on said bond and mortgage on 7th April, 1868, the said bond and mortgage were, on 6th January, 1882, assigned by L. E. Amsinck & Co. to John H. Renneker, (then John H. Renneker, Jr.,) and on 9th January, 1882, assigned by the said John H. Renneker, Jr., to the plaintiff, J. Alice Curtis.

"The complaint states the deaths of John H. Renneker and Adam B. Glover, and the devolution of title. Joseph W. Harrisson, who recovered judgment 16th July, 1869, against Annie B. Glover, as administratrix of Adam B. Glover, and William E. Butler, as executor of Hannah Enston, who recovered judgment 16th May, 1872, (decree enrolled 15th July, 1881,) against John H. Renneker; and John H. Renneker, Jr., claiming a lien under deed from the city council of Charleston, (dated 10th January, 1882,)—were made parties defendant. At a reference held on 6th July, 1888, the plaintiff proposed to produce in evidence certain testimony discovered subsequent to the filing of the complaint, viz., the proceedings in the court of common pleas, Charleston, in the case of John H. Renneker, survivor of the firm of Renneker & Glover, vs. Annie B. Glover et al., filed 18th March, 1868, under which proceedings the lot at the corner of King and Queen streets was sold and conveyed to John H. Renneker, surviving partner, in severalty. (Deed dated 24th March, 1871.) The solicitor for the defendants Harrisson and Butler, executor, judgment creditors, objected to the competency of this evidence, because inconsistent with the allegations of the complaint as to the title of the mortgaged property. On the 10th September, 1888, a motion, upon notice to the solicitors in the cause, was made before me for leave to amend the complaint in accordance with the facts shown by the testimony discovered after filing the complaint. I granted an order to amend the complaint upon payment of the costs of the answers of the defendants Harrisson and Butler, executor, by the plaintiff, at the termination of the suit. I also granted an order that the complaint be dismissed as against the defendant John B. Glover, with costs to be paid by the plaintiff at the termination of the suit, and as against the defendants Annie Hughes and Samuel Hughes without costs, the said defendants not having answered and being in default. The amended complaint was filed 1st October, 1888. The defendants Harrisson and Butler, executor, filed answers to the amended complaint, 24th October, 1888, asserting their liens on the mortgaged property, and denying the right of plaintiff to the amount claimed to be due to her under the mortgage. By decree of his honor, Judge WALLACE, made with consent of all parties, (none of whom are minors,) filed 6th December, 1888, it was ordered that I, as master, without waiting to make and file a report, proceed to sell the mortgaged premises, free and discharged from all incumbrances, at public auction, after due advertisement, upon the terms therein prescribed; one of said terms being that the purchaser have the option to pay all cash, the purchaser to pay all taxes payable in 1889. In conformity with this decree, after due advertisement, as therein directed, I sold the mortgaged premises described in the pleadings and decree, at public auction, on the 10th day of January, 1889, to Samuel B. Renneker, for the sum of $1,700, he being, at that price, the highest bidder for the same. Samuel B. Renneker, in writing, transferred his bid to Edward J. Lewith. The said Edward J. Lewith, on 9th August, 1889, complied with the terms of sale by paying to me the entire purchase money in cash,—$1,700.00,—and I have executed and delivered to him a conveyance of the property.

"I have, in accordance with said decree, from the proceeds of sale as above stated—

		$1,700 00
Paid 'the expenses of said sale,' viz., News and Courier, advertising...................	$22 20	
And for 'taxes which were a lien on said property at time of sale (excepting the taxes payable in 1889, to be paid by purchaser,)' viz.:		
City taxes for 1887...... $23 20		
City taxes for 1888...... 28 59		
	51 79	
		73 99
		$1,627 01

—Leaving $1,627.01 in my hands, which, under said decree, I hold subject to the further order of the court.

"By order of his honor, Judge PRESSLEY, filed 23d August, 1889, Edward McCrady, Jr., Esq., was substituted as plaintiff's attorney in place of T. W. Bacot, Esq., and J. M. Bacot, Esq., was substituted as attorney for the defendants Louisa E. Renneker and Kate H. Schirmer, in place of Edward McCrady, Jr., Esq.

"Thomas W. Bacot, assignee of John H. Renneker, one of the defendants, on 4th September, 1889, filed his petition for leave to intervene in the cause, and his honor, Judge KERSHAW, by order filed 4th September, 1889, granted leave to the said T. W. Bacot, assignee, to intervene for the rights and interests which he represents, and that the plaintiff make him a party, with leave to said assignee to contest the claims of the judgment creditors, and to establish his rights; the petition of the said T. W. Bacot, assignee, to be held and taken as his answer to the complaint herein from the date of the filing of the same; and that any party to the cause have leave to reply to the same; and that the master proceed under the order of reference heretofore made to inquire into and report upon the issues raised by said petition or answer.

"I respectfully recommend that the sale

to Edward J. Lewith be confirmed; and that, all rights and equities of the parties being transferred to the funds in my hands as herein reported, I proceed to hold references and to make further reports as directed by the orders in the cause.

"Respectfully reported,

"CH. RICHARDSON MILES, Master.

"26th October, 1889."

"SECOND REPORT OF MASTER.

"For a statement of the pleadings, of the sale under the decree filed 6th December, 1888, of the payments made by me thereunder, and of the balance remaining in my hands subject to the further order of the court, to-wit, $1,627.01, I respectfully ask leave to refer to my report in this case dated and filed 26th October, 1889, which report was in all respects confirmed by the order of his honor, Judge HUDSON, filed 29th November, 1889. By the said decree of sale any and all claims or liens on the premises sold of the parties to the action were transferred from said premises to the proceeds in the hands of the master, after payment thereout of the expenses of such sale and any taxes which may be a lien on said premises at the time of such sale. My report shows that out of the proceeds of sale I paid the expenses of sale and such taxes as were a lien, but did not pay any costs of these proceedings, which should be provided for in the final decree which shall be made in the cause. The claimants of the fund in my hands are:

"(1) The plaintiff, J. Alice Curtis, the assignee and holder and owner of a mortgage from John H. Renneker and Adam B. Glover, copartners under the firm name of Renneker & Glover, for the foreclosure of which this action is brought.

"(2) Joseph W. Harrisson, who recovered judgment against Annie B. Glover, administratrix of Adam B. Glover, for $177.91, on the individual debt of said Adam B. Glover, on 16th July, 1869.

"(3) The estate of Hannah Enston, deceased, based upon a judgment in the court of common pleas for Charleston county, recovered by said Hannah Enston against John H. Renneker, survivor of Renneker & Glover, for $7,588.72, on 16th day of May, 1872, and a judgment and money decree against John H. Renneker, survivor of Renneker & Glover, for $4,-714.68, with interest from 26th March, 1878, entered on 15th day of July, 1881, in a suit for foreclosure of a mortgage which secured the bond upon which the above judgment was recovered, this decree being for the deficiency after applying the proceeds of sale of the mortgaged premises to the mortgage debt. This suit was instituted on 12th May, 1877. John H. Renneker was a party defendant, and answered. This claim is set up by William Enston Butler, executor of Hannah Enston. All the above claimants are parties to this action.

"(4) Thomas W. Bacot, assignee of John H. Renneker, the younger, who, upon his petition to intervene, was by order of his honor, Judge KERSHAW, filed 4th September, 1889, made a party defendant, with leave to contest the claims of the judgment creditors, and by all lawful means to establish his rights, who claims

under a conveyance of the premises made to him by the city council of Charleston, dated 10th January, 1882, and a conveyance of the same lot to the city council of Charleston by the commissioners of the sinking fund of the state of South Carolina, dated 20th July, 1881.

"I have held frequent references and taken the testimony which is herewith filed. The case has been presented and argued by the solicitors representing the several interests with great care and ability. I will not undertake to follow the several arguments in detail, but will endeavor to state clearly the positions taken and my conclusions thereon, so as to enable the court to understand and decide them.

"First. The mortgage debt. The original bond and mortgage of J. H. Renneker and Adam B. Glover to L. E. Amsinck & Co. have been produced and proved, and are herewith filed. They are dated 27th day of March, 1867. The condition of the bond is for the payment of $3,084.38 in three equal successive installments, payable in six, nine, and twelve months from date, together with interest at the rate of 7 per cent. per annum from 22d January, 1867, on the whole amount of the indebtedness, payable at the date of the payment of each installment.' The mortgage recites the condition of the bond in full. It was duly proved and recorded in mesne conveyance office, Charleston, Book C, No. 15, p. 119, on 29th March, 1867. Upon the original bond is indorsed a receipt, dated 7th April, 1868, by the mortgagees, through their attorney, W. Alston Pringle, from J. H. Renneker, of $1,500 on account of the bond. (This payment is also proved by the testimony herewith filed.) On the original bond is also indorsed an assignment by the mortgagees, L. E. Amsinck & Co., for valuable consideration, to J. H. Renneker, Jr., dated the 6th day of January, A. D. 1882. The evidence herewith filed proves that this assignment was made to John H. Renneker, Jr., (the son of the mortgagor J. H. Renneker,) in consideration of the sum of $700 cash paid by him; and that the said John H. Renneker, Jr., took and held possession of this lot, receiving the rents upon it up to the time of his failure, when, on 9th January, A. D. 1882, he assigned it bona fide and for valuable consideration to Mrs. J. Alice Curtis, the plaintiff. This assignment is also indorsed on the original bond. The assignment by L. E. Amsinck & Co. to J. H. Renneker, Jr., dated the 6th day of January, 1882, is indorsed upon the record of the mortgage in mesne conveyance office. The receipt on the bond for $1,500 on account, dated 7th April, 1868, does not appear on the record of the mortgage. The solicitor for the judgment creditors contends that this mortgage ceased to constitute a lien on the mortgage property on 27th March, 1887,—20 years having then elapsed from the date of its creation, and there being no note of any payment on account or written acknowledgment of the debt secured thereby having been recorded upon the record of such mortgage, (the original complaint for the foreclosure of said mortgage and lis pendens not having been filed until 15th March, 1888,)—under the provisions of the act of 1879, now section 1831 of the General Statutes. The section is as follows: 'No mortgage or deed having the effect of a mortgage, no judgment, decree, or other lien on real estate, shall constitute a lien upon any real estate after the lapse of twenty years from the date of the creation of the same: provided, that if the holder of any such lien or liens aforesaid shall, at any time during the continuance of such lien, cause to be recorded upon the record of such mortgage, deed having the effect of a mortgage, or shall file with the record of such judgment, decree, or other lien, a note of some payment on account, or some written acknowledgment of the debt secured thereby, with the date of such payment or acknowledgment, such mortgage, deed having the effect of a mortgage, judgment, decree, or other lien shall be and continue to be a lien for twenty years from the date of the record of any such payment on account or acknowledgment: provided, further, that nothing herein contained shall be construed to affect the duration of the liens of judgments as prescribed by section 310 of the Code of Procedure.'

"In the case of Henry v. Henry, (April 15, 1889,) 9 S. E. Rep. 726, the supreme court of the state held in relation to the lien of a judgment that this act was retroactive, but was nevertheless not unconstitutional. The court (SIMPSON, C. J., dissenting) held that the act must necessarily be implied to have a retroactive effect as to judgments, for it could not otherwise have any effect at all; for the only judgments which could be affected by it were those recovered prior to that act, and it would be wholly inoperative unless held to be applicable to such judgments. The court held the act in that case not to be unconstitutional, because it does not impair the obligation of a contract, or divest vested rights resting on contract or vested rights of property, but as only the alteration in a rule of evidence, not in any wise affecting any previously existing right. They considered the scope, purport, and object of the act, and what was the old law which the act was designed to amend. Under the old law, neither a judgment nor a mortgage, after the lapse of 20 years, constituted a lien, because of the presumption of payment, which, though susceptible of being rebutted by evidence, the nature and kind of the evidence was not distinctly defined, and the object and effect of the act was to declare what should be, after the passage of the act, the kind of evidence necessary to rebut the presumption of payment. They further held that, conceding that such legislation cannot be applied to a pre-existing contract, unless a reasonable time has been afforded the party affected thereby to conform to the requirements of the new law, there was nothing to prevent its application in that case, for the appellant had a reasonable time to conform to the new law, for the act was passed in 1879, upwards of 7 years before the expiration of the 20 years from the entry of his judgment in 1867.

"There are important differences between this case and the case of Henry v. Henry. In that case the question was as to a judgment; in this case it is as to a mortgage. A judgment is always payable at its date, while a mortgage is always payable at a subsequent date. The act is not in express terms retroactive, but the court held it was by necessary implication intended to be retroactive as to judgments, because otherwise it would be wholly inoperative, there being no judgments to which it could be applied except to those existing before its passage. But there is no such necessary implication as to mortgages, and the act can be construed to apply only to the lien of mortgages created after its passage. A judgment creates a lien only by operation of law, and is not strictly a contract protected by the constitution, (In re Kennedy, 2 S. C. 226;) but a mortgage is, and the duration of its lien under the laws existing at the time of its creation is a 'right resting on contract, which would be affected and limited if this act is held to be applicable to it. In the case of Henry v. Henry, the court say that, under the view of the case taken by them, 'the important and interesting question (as to which a good deal might be said) whether an act limiting the duration of the lien of a judgment can be applied to pre-existing judgments without a violation of the constitution does not arise.' But that question is involved if the act is applied to a pre-existing mortgage, as to which, as in this case, there is no presumption of payment arising from the lapse of 20 years.

"In this case the bond is dated 27th March, 1867. The last installment was payable on the 27th March, 1868. A payment on account was made on 7th April, 1868. When this action for the foreclosure of the mortgage securing payment of the said bond was commenced—15th March, 1888—20 years had not elapsed from the date at which the last installment was payable, nor from the date of the payment on account from which date the presumption commenced. The mortgage sets out in full the condition of the bond, showing the dates of payment; and the mortgage was recorded. To adopt the language of the court of errors in the case of Wright v. Eaves, 10 Rich. Eq. 595: 'There is no doubt that the debt to secure which the mortgage was given remains. * * * As a general rule the security [the mortgage] ought to be regarded as co-existent with the debt,'—and in Nichols v. Briggs, 18 S. C. 484, 'the lien lasts as long as the debt.' Under the circumstances and facts of this case, it seems to me that there is in the act in question neither an expressed purpose nor 'an unequivocal and unavoidable implication from the words of the statute, taken by themselves, and in connection with the subject-matter and the occasion of the enactment, admitting of no reasonable doubt, but precluding all question as to such intention,' (End. Interp. St. § 271,) which makes the act retroactive in its application to mortgages; and that, therefore, it should not be so construed, and should not be held to apply in this case. For authorities in our state on this point, see, among others, Ex parte Graham, 13 Rich. Law, 283, in which it was said 'that statutes are not to be construed retrospectively, or so as to have a retroactive effect, unless it shall clearly appear that it was so intended by the leg islature; and not even then if by such construction the act would divest vested rights.' Nichols v. Briggs, 18 S. C. 481; State v. Pinckney, 22 S. C. 504. To hold that the act has such retroactive effect as to mortgages executed before its passage would, I think, 'affect a vested right rest ing in contract,' by 'limiting the duration of the lien of such mortgage' as fixed by the law at the time the contract was en tered into, which would not be constitu tional. In the case of Henry v. Henry the court held 'that the object of the act was not to limit the duration of such liens, but simply to declare [and it is noticeable that such was the word used in the title] what should be the evidence of such pay ment or new promise as would be sufficient to rebut the presumption of payment,' and on this ground held it not to be uncon stitutional. A judgment being payable at its date, the presumption of payment arises 20 years after its entry; but a mort gage secures a debt payable after its date, and the presumption of payment does not arise until 20 years after the date at which the debt is payable. But if this was 'the object' of the act, how can the act apply in a case like this, in which there is no pre sumption of payment to be rebutted? Other arguments were urged by the solic itor for the plaintiff, but I think it unneces sary to go further into the argument, or to do more than state the conclusion at which I have arrived,—that the plaintiff's mortgage constitutes the first lien, to be first paid out of the funds in my hands, and I so recommend.

"*Second.* The judgment of Joseph W. Harrisson. The evidence herewith filed shows that this judgment was for the in dividual debt of Adam B. Glover, who died 28th May, 1867, and was entered up against Annie B. Glover, his widow and administratrix, on 16th July, 1869, for $177.81. John H. Renneker, the survivor of Renneker & Glover, instituted proceed ings in the court of common pleas, 18th March, 1868, to which the administratrix and heirs and distributees of Adam B. Glover were parties, for the settlement of the affairs of the partnership of Renneker & Glover. Under and in pursuance of a de cree in said cause, filed 23d January, 1871, William J. Gayer, special referee, conveyed a lot at the corner of Concord and Inspec tion streets, part of the partnership prop erty, to Mrs. Annie B. Glover, widow of said Adam B. Glover, and their children, freed and discharged from all partnership debts, and the remaining real estate of the partnership, including the lot at the corner of King and Queen streets, mort gaged by Renneker & Glover to Amsinck & Co., (and which has been sold under the order in this case,) to John H. Renneker, the surviving partner, subject to all part nership debts of Renneker & Glover. I am of opinion that the lien of this judgment was transferred from the property con veyed to John H. Renneker, subject to the partnership debts, to the lot conveyed to

Mrs. Annie B. Glover and children, freed and discharged from the partnership debts, (Riley v. Gaines, 14 S. C. 457,) and that this judgment creditor is not entitled to re ceive any part of the fund in my hands, and I so respectfully recommend.

"*Third.* The estate of Hannah Enston. The judgment recovered by Hannah En ston on 16th May, 1872, upon the bond of Renneker & Glover did not, in my opinion, constitute a lien upon the lot, the pro ceeds of which are to be now apportioned. Subsequently, on 12th May, 1877, Hannah Enston instituted proceedings in this court against John H. Renneker, survivor, to foreclose the mortgage of a lot on the west side of King street, given by Ren neker & Glover to secure the same bond upon which the above-mentioned judg ment was recovered in 1872. To this ac tion Joseph W. Harrisson, as a judgment creditor, was a party. The mortgage property was sold, the proceeds applied to the debt, and on the 15th July, 1881, a judgment and money decree for the de ficiency, viz., $4,714.68, with interest from 26th March, 1878, was entered and en rolled. It has been contended before me that this decree for the deficiency, enrolled 15th July, 1881, is void because of the judg ment upon the bond secured by the mort gage recovered in 1872, and the case of An derson v. Pilgram, 30 S. C. 499, 9 S. E. Rep. 587, is relied upon in support of the position. In that case it was held that 'a mortgagee cannot maintain an action at law on his debt while at the same time he is prosecuting an action in chancery for the foreclosure of his mortgage and for judgment for deficiency.' 'The mortgagee 'should not be permitted to harass his debtor by two suits at the same time, both tending to the same result.' But the defendant Renneker, who was a party to and filed an answer in the foreclosure suit, set up no such ground of objection, and, it being a privilege of the debtor which should be pleaded, (as it was in Anderson v. Pilgram,) and which he waived, I do not see that it can be set up by a third person against the validity of the judg ment and decree. It was urged that the court was without jurisdiction to make the decree, but I do not consider that the case of Anderson v. Pilgram sustains that position. I therefore consider that the money decree enrolled on 15th July, 1881, constituted a valid lien upon the lot sold in this case, which was subsisting when this action was instituted, (15th March, 1888,) and would be entitled to receive any portion of the proceeds of the sale of said lot which might remain after the mortgage debt of the plaintiff, which I consider a prior lien, unless the claimant under the tax-title is held to have a prior claim.

"*Fourth.* T. W. Bacot, assignee of John H. Renneker, Jr. As before stated, the as signee, made a party defendant by order in this case, with leave to contest the claims of the judgment creditors, claims under a tax-title. John H. Renneker, Jr., held under a conveyance from the city council of Charleston, dated 10th January, 1882, (and by his assignment for benefit of creditors, dated 30th June, 1888, conveyed to T. W. Bacot, assignee.) The city council of Charleston held under deed from the commissioners of the sinking fund of the state of South Carolina, dated 20th July, 1881. These two several deeds have been produced and proved, and are filed with the testimony. The question, upon whom rested the burden of proof as to the validity of the tax-title? was elaborately and ably argued; the solicitor for the judgment creditors contending that the claimant under the deed from the commissioners of the sinking fund must show the validity by proving that all the requirements of the tax laws were duly complied with, as held in State v Thompson, 18 S. C. 538, while the solicitor for the assignee contended that this rule is confined to contests between the holder of the tax-title and the original owner, or one who claims under him, and that a judgment creditor whose claim is adverse to the original owner has upon him the burden of proof that the tax-title is invalid. I do not think it necessary, in this case, to make a ruling upon the point, because the evidence has been produced before me as to all the steps taken upon which the tax-title rests, and it is not material by whom it was offered. If the evidence shows that all the requirements of the law were complied with, the tax-title is good; if that such requirements have not been complied with, the tax-title is not good. This report has been necessarily so long that I must confine it, so far as relates to 'the tax-title,' to such facts and conclusions of law as are sufficient, in my opinion, to decide the question of its validity, although the entire testimony offered on both sides is herewith filed. The lot covered by the tax-title was charged with $13.56 for taxes (this, apparently, including costs and penalties) for the fiscal year commencing 1st November, 1877, in name of John H. Renneker. These taxes, not having been paid, were advertised as 'delinquent' by the county auditor for sale on 6th day of January, 1879. The advertisement was headed thus: 'In accordance with instructions from the comptroller general, I hereby publish the list of delinquent lands of Charleston county for the tax year 1877, as reported to me by the county treasurer.' This advertisement was dated 26th December, 1878, and was published on 28th December, 1878, and on 4th January, 1879. The sale took place on 6th January, 1879, and the property, for want of bidders, was knocked down to the state. The same property was advertised for sale as 'forfeited land,'—the advertisement, being dated 20th August, 1879, was published on 21st August, 1879, —and in accordance with said advertisement was offered for sale on 21st October, 1879, as 'under section 3 of an act entitled "An act to determine the manner of disposing of lands purchased by the state for taxes," approved 23d September, 1868.' At the time advertised the lot was offered for sale, and for want of bidders it was knocked down to the estate, entered on the books of the county auditor, and was turned over to the sinking fund commission 5th April, 1881. Upon the legality and sufficiency of these several proceedings, an-

terior to the conveyance by the commissioners of the sinking fund to the city council of Charleston, (20th July, 1881,) the validity of the tax-title depends.

"The testimony shows that no execution or distress warrant to collect the tax from personal property was ever issued in this case; the reason assigned by the officials being that the owner of the lot, John H. Renneker, made no return of personal property for the fiscal year 1877, and that it was not customary to issue executions where there was real estate charged with the taxes, and no return of personal property. The laws governing the assessment and collection of taxes for the fiscal year 1877, by which this tax-title must be tested, were Rev. St. 1873, tit. 3, c. 13, (General Tax Act of 1874, 15 Sess. Laws, p. 731;) the act to amend the same, (15 Sess. Laws, 979;) act to raise supplies for the fiscal year 1877, approved March 22, 1878, (16 Sess. Laws, 549;) and the act to amend the general tax law, approved March 22, 1878, (16 Sess. Laws, 559.) The evidence further shows that the 'delinquent land sale' for the taxes of 1877 did not take place on the day fixed by statute, viz., first Monday in December, 1878, but on 6th January, 1879. Section 9 of the act of March 22, 1878, provides: 'If any of the duties herein required to be performed on or before certain days, by any officers herein named, cannot, for want of proper time or other causes, be so performed, the comptroller general, with the approval of the governor, may extend the time for the performance of the same,' etc. The testimony of W. G. Eason, county auditor, shows that 'the sale of delinquent lands on 6th January, 1879, was in pursuance of instructions of the comptroller general, in a letter addressed to him, dated 18th December, 1878, as follows: "In regard to delinquent lands, if you have not already done so, you had best proceed to give the notice of sale two weeks, as required by law. Make the sale for a period not later than first Monday in January, or earlier, if you can comply with the law." Signed, 'Winthrop Williams, for Comptroller General,"—written on official paper of the comptroller general's office. There is no indorsement on the paper by the governor.' Mr. Eason further testifies that 'Winthrop Williams is, and was on 18th December, 1878, clerk of the comptroller general, in charge of the tax department. I frequently received instructions from the comptroller general signed by the clerk.'

"I am of opinion that the laws under which the taxes for 1877 were levied required the county treasurer to first endeavor to collect said taxes from personal property, and that, having failed to comply with this requirement of the law, the proceedings by which the property was offered for sale as delinquent lands were illegal and void, and the alleged forfeiture to the state was without authority. It is conceded that the delinquent land sale for the taxes of 1877 did not take place on the day fixed by statute, but it is contended that the sale was nevertheless valid by reason of the order of the comptroller general to the county auditor, before stated. Even assuming that the section of the act of 1878 before quoted was applicable to the proceedings for the collection of the taxes of the fiscal year commencing 1st November, 1877, and that the approval of the governor is to be presumed in the absence of testimony on the subject, (neither of which is admitted by the solicitor for the judgment creditors,) I do not think that the comptroller general had the authority to order this sale after the time for the sale fixed by statute had passed. His authority was only to extend the time for the performance of the duties of certain officers where they cannot be performed on the days required to be performed for want of proper time or other causes; and the direction to sell on a different day, given after the day fixed by law had passed, cannot, I think, be properly considered as an extension of the time, and therefore not authorized by the act. I think the auditor's duty, under the circumstances of the case, was to have carried forward the delinquent lands to the delinquent land list of the next fiscal year. Section 112, Act Sept. 15, 1868, (14 Sess. Laws, p. 60;) section 105, Act March 19, 1874, (15 Sess. Laws, p. 769.) See, also, Roddy v. Purdy, 10 S. C. 137, and Dougherty v. Crawford. 14 S. C. 629.

"Several other grounds of objection to the validity of the tax-title were urged by the solicitor for the judgment creditors: (1) That the requirements of the law in relation to the county board of equalization had not been complied with. (2) That the advertisement of the delinquent land sale was published on two successive weeks, less than fourteen days, and not for two weeks, as required by law. (3) That the sale by the sinking fund commission to the city council was not made at auction. (4) That the conveyance by the commissioners of the sinking fund to the city of Charleston was signed by only three of the five commissioners. (5) That said deed was not under the great seal of the state. Being of opinion that for the reasons hereinbefore given the property in question was never legally forfeited to the state, and that all the subsequent steps were therefore inoperative, and the tax-title void, it is not, I think, necessary to pass upon these objections; but, that the solicitor presenting them may have the most convenient mode of bringing them to the attention of the court by exceptions stated in my report, I report that, in my judgment, none of the five grounds above stated are sufficient to make the tax-title void. I respectfully recommend that the balance in my hands subject to the order of the court—$1,627.01—be applied first to the payment of such costs of the action as determined by the court to be so payable except the costs of the answers of the defendants Joseph W. Harrisson and W. E. Butler, executor of Hannah Enston, to the original complaint, which are to be paid by the plaintiff in accordance with the order giving leave to the plaintiff to amend the complaint, filed 10th September, 1888, and the costs of the defendant John B. Glover, which are to be paid by the plaintiff in accordance with the order dismissing the complaint as against the said John B. Glover, filed 10th September, 1888.

The amount due upon the bond secured by the mortgage, with interest to date, is $4,240.97 as appears by a statement herewith filed, and I respectfully recommend that the balance in my hands, after payment of costs, be paid to the plaintiff on account of said debt."

T. W. Bacot, for appellant. L. de B. McCrady, for claimant under tax-title, appellant. J. F. Ficken, for judgment creditors, respondents.

McIver, J. The full and clear statement of the facts in this case by Mr. Miles, the master, in his two reports, which should be embraced in the report of the case, relieves us of the necessity of going into any detailed statement of the facts, and we will therefore confine ourselves to a consideration of the questions raised by this appeal, calling attention to such facts only as are necessary to a proper understanding of the points now involved. The general question involved is as to the priority of the liens or claims of the several parties upon a certain lot in the city of Charleston, or, rather, the proceeds of the sale thereof in the hands of the master. The plaintiff claims the first lien under a mortgage executed on the 27th of March. 1867, given to secure the payment of a bond of like date, payable in three installments, at six, nine, and twelve months from the date thereof, upon which a payment was indorsed on the 7th of April, 1868. This mortgage was duly recorded, and is now held by the plaintiff under successive assignments from the original mortgagees and their assignee; the first bearing date 6th of January, 1882, and the second, 9th of January, 1882. The defendant William E. Butler, as executor of Hannah Enston, denying the lien of the said mortgage, claims the first lien under two judgments recovered by said Hannah against the mortgagor, one entered 16th of May, 1872, and the other 15th of July, 1881. The defendant T. W. Bacot, as assignee as aforesaid, recognizing the priority of the plaintiff's mortgage, claims under a tax-title, derived, as he alleges, through regular proceedings to sell the property for the non-payment of taxes assessed thereon for the fiscal year 1877, which, being subsequent to the lien of the mortgage, its precedence must be acquiesced in, but, being prior to the entry of the second judgment recovered by Mrs. Enston, (it being conceded that the first judgment never had a lien,) the tax-title takes precedence of the judgment. The validity of the lien of the mortgage is assailed upon the ground that more than 20 years having elapsed after its date before this action was commenced (15th of March, 1888) to foreclose this mortgage, and neither the original mortgagees nor the assignees having caused "to be recorded upon the record of such mortgage * * * a note of some payment on account, or some written acknowledgment of the debt secured thereby," the lien had expired under the provisions of the act of 1879, now incorporated in the General Statutes as section 1831. It is claimed, however, on behalf of the plaintiff, that the requirement of this statute that some note of payment on account or written acknowledgment of the debt should be recorded upon the record of the mortgage was substantially complied with by the recording of the assignment from the original mortgagees to Renneker, the intermediate holder, upon the record of the mortgage, before the expiration of the 20 years from the date of the mortgage. But we cannot accept that view. That assignment was, certainly, neither a note of payment nor a written acknowledgment of the debt. It was the act of the assignee merely, and, so far as appears, the mortgagor knew nothing about it; while the statute manifestly contemplates that the record of the mortgage should show some act of the mortgagor recognizing the continual validity of the mortgage. Assuming, then, as we must assume, that this provision of the statute was not complied with, the real question is whether this statute was intended to apply to mortgages executed prior to the enactment of that law; and, if so, whether it was competent for the legislature to pass such an act. This is a very important question, and far-reaching in its effects: for, as was suggested in the argument for plaintiff, if the view taken by the circuit court should prevail, then it would be possible, and perhaps not improbable, that a mortgage might lose its lien before any right of action to enforce it could arise. If a mortgage debt should be made payable more than 20 years after the date of the mortgage, as is known to be the case with mortgages on railroads, then the lien would be lost before any right of action could arise, unless, perhaps, there had been default in the payment of interest in the mean time.

Our first inquiry is whether the legislature intended this statute to have a retroactive operation, so far as mortgages are concerned. The rule that a statute will never be given such a construction, unless it is required by the express words of the statute or must necessarily be implied from such words, is too well settled to need the citation of any authority to support it. Now, it is quite certain that there are no express words in the statute evidencing an intention that it should be retroactive, and we are unable to discover anything in the language used necessarily implying such an intention, so far as mortgages are concerned. It is true that in the case of Henry v. Henry, 31 S. C., 1, 9 S. E. Rep. 726, it was held that such an intention was necessarily implied, so far as judgments were concerned; but that was solely because it was absolutely necessary to give the act such a construction as to judgments, as otherwise the act would have been entirely nugatory in that respect; for the legislature manifestly intended to make some alteration in the previously existing law as to the lien of judgments, by the statute in question; and, as the second proviso expressly forbade its application to the lien of judgments recovered since the adoption of the Code by the express declaration "that nothing herein contained shall be construed to affect the duration of the liens of judgments as prescribed by section 310 of the Code of Procedure," it was absolutely necessary, in order to give the statute, so far as judgments were concerned, any effect at all, to apply its provisions to antecedent judgments. But no such necessity arises in the case of mortgages, and therefore there is no warrant for giving the statute a retroactive operation as to them. At first view, it may seem inconsistent to give a section of a statute a retroactive operation as to one of the subjects mentioned therein, and deny a similar operation as to another subject, mentioned in the same section. But the inconsistency is seeming, rather than real. There can be no doubt that it is entirely competent for the court to declare one portion of a statute unconstitutional, and at the same time recognize the constitutionality of that portion of the same statute which does not conflict with any constitutional provision. Wardlaw v. Bussard, 15 Rich. Law, 158; State v. Carew, 13 Rich. Law, 498. So, also, a statute which in general terms refers to all contracts may be declared unconstitutional as to certain contracts, while its constitutionality as to other contracts may be recognized. Barry v. Iseman, 14 Rich. Law, 129, heard by the court of errors in connection with State v. Carew, supra. In State v. Platt, 2 S. C. 150, it was held that one portion of a section of an act might be declared unconstitutional, while another portion of the same section may be held free from all constitutional objection; and the same doctrine was recognized, though the point was not distinctly decided, in State v. Hagood, 13 S. C., at page 56. The test, according to these two cases last cited, seems to be whether the unconstitutional provision relates to an independent matter which can be separated from the rest of the section without impairing its efficiency or altering its terms,—whether the portion declared unconstitutional was capable of being the subject of a separate, independent act. In this connection a remark made by DAWKINS, J., in delivering the opinion of the court in Wardlaw v. Bussard, supra, seems quite pertinent: "It was not conteded seriously that if one part of an act was unconstitutional it vitiated the whole, *or that the same section might not be unconstitutional as affecting any [one?] class of cases, and constitutional as to others.*" (Italics ours.) Upon the same principle we see no reason why one portion of a section of a statute dealing with one subject may not be declared retroactive, from the necessity of the case, while another portion of the same section, dealing with a distinct and different subject, as to which no such necessity arises, may not be construed as prospective only. It is manifest that this section was dealing with two entirely distinct and different subjects, either one of which might have been omitted or obliterated without in any way affecting the efficiency of the provisions of the statute as to the other. Either might have been made the subject of a separate act. There was no such connection between them as required that the statute should be construed alike as to both. For example, there was nothing to prevent the statute from being construed constitutional as to judgments, and unconstitutional as to mortgages, or *vice versa.* And so we think there is nothing to prevent the statute from being construed retrospectively as to judgments, especially when such a construction is demanded by the necessity of the case, and prospectively as to mortgages, where no such necessity exists. It seems to us, therefore, that the act of 1879, now incorporated in the General Statutes as section 1831, cannot be construed as applying to a mortgage executed anterior to the date of that act, and that the circuit judge erred in holding otherwise.

Under this view, the question whether it was competent for the general assembly to pass such an act giving to it a retroactive operation cannot arise, and will not be considered; for it is a delicate matter for the court to declare an act of the legislature void for unconstitutionality, and it should not be done unless necessary to the decision of a case. We therefore must decline to express, or even intimate, any opinion upon this grave question. Having reached this conclusion, the other questions raised are, practically, of no importance, for it is manifest that the fund in controversy will not be sufficient to satisfy the mortgage debt, which we hold is the first lien thereon; but as these questions have been made and may be regarded as important, we will proceed to dispose of them.

First, as to the Enston judgment. It seems that the debt upon which this judgment was recovered was evidenced by a bond secured by a mortgage on property other than that now in question, and that an ordinary action at law on the bond was brought, which culminated in a judgment, entered 16th of May, 1872, which, under the provisions of the Code, had no lien; and no steps appear to have been taken to give it a lien. Subsequently, however, Mrs. Enston commenced proceedings to foreclose the mortgage, which resulted in a judgment of foreclosure, under which the mortgaged premises were sold, and, after applying the proceeds of sale to the mortgage debt, there remained a balance due thereon, and a judgment for the deficiency was entered 15th of July, 1881. It being conceded that the judgment on the bond, obtained in the action at law, and entered 16th of May, 1872, never had a lien, the only question is as to the validity of the judgment obtained in the proceedings to foreclose the mortgage for the balance left unpaid by the proceeds of the sale of the mortgaged premises, which was entered 15th of July, 1881, after the lien for the unpaid taxes of 1877 had been fixed upon the property, as claimed by the holder of the tax-title. It is contended that the judgment of 15th of July, 1881, was void, because Mrs. Enston, the plaintiff in that judgment, had previously obtained a judgment for the same debt in the action at law on the bond; and the case of Anderson v. Pilgram, 30 S. C. 499, 9 S. E. Rep. 587, is relied on to sustain this proposition. All that case holds is that a mortgagee cannot maintain an action at law on his debt, while at the same time he is prosecuting an action in chancery for the foreclosure of his mortgage, and claiming judgment for any deficiency that may arise from the insufficiency of the proceeds of the sale of the mortgaged premises to pay the mortgage debt. But the pendency of another action, or the previous recovery of judgment, for the same debt is a defense which must be pleaded and proved, like any other defense, and if it is not so pleaded and proved there is nothing to prevent the court from rendering judgment in the second action. If one is sued upon a note to which his name has been forged, or which has been paid, and he fails to set up and prove the forgery or payment, whereby judgment is recovered against him, neither he nor any one else can afterwards assail such judgment upon the ground that the note was forged, or had been paid. Fraser v. City Council, 19 S. C. 384. It is not, as seems to be supposed, a matter of jurisdiction; and there is nothing in the case of Anderson v. Pilgram, supra, to warrant such an idea. It is a mere matter of defense, and, if not pleaded and proved at the proper time, it cannot be urged afterwards, either by the defendant in the case or any one else; for the judgment is conclusive. Even, therefore, if it should be conceded (as to which, however, we express no opinion) that the mortgagor could have successfully defended himself in the action for foreclosure from a judgment for the deficiency, yet, not having done so when he had the opportunity, he cannot do so now, as he is concluded by the judgment, which became a valid lien from the date of its entry, as to him as well as all others.

It only remains to consider the question as to the tax-title. It being conceded that no execution or distress warrant had ever been issued to enforce payment of the taxes in arrear out of the personal property of the tax-payer, we think the question is concluded by our decision in Ebaugh v. Mullinax, 18 S. E. Rep. 613, (at the present term,) and we refer to that case for the reasons upon which we rest our conclusion. It is true that in that case the question arose out of the failure to pay the taxes for the year 1880, while here the taxes in arrear were those for the year 1877; but, as it is conceded that the terms of the two acts under which the taxes for those two years were levied are identical, so far as this matter is concerned, the reasoning in that case is applicable here. Without considering any of the other alleged defects in the tax-title, we think the failure to issue the execution against personal property was fatal.

The judgment of this court is that the judgment of the circuit court, in so far as it adjudges that the lien of the plaintiff's mortgage has been destroyed by the act of 1879, be reversed, but that in all other respects it be affirmed, and that the case be remanded to the circuit court for such further proceedings as may be necessary.

McGOWAN, J., concurs.

WHEELER v. ALDERMAN.

(*Supreme Court of South Carolina.* Sept. 28, 1891.)

ENJOINING ENFORCEMENT OF EXECUTION—FRAUD
—AUTHORITY OF ATTORNEY.

1. In an action to enjoin the sale of land on execution the complaint alleged fraud and collusion. It appeared that the owner of certain land confessed judgment in favor of his brother, the defendant; that he and the attorney who acted in taking the judgment represented to one who was about to advance money upon a mortgage on the land that the judgment had been paid, and the attorney then entered a satisfaction of record as attorney of defendant; that, relying upon such representations and satisfaction, the money was loaned on the mortgage; that plaintiff afterwards purchased the land at a sale under a foreclosure of the mortgage, and had no notice of defendant's claim; that defendant afterwards, without notice to plaintiff, had the satisfaction of his judgment set aside, and sought to sell the land on execution. *Held,* that the facts entitled plaintiff to equitable relief.

2. Although there was no direct evidence that the attorney was authorized to satisfy the judgment, yet, as defendant claimed through the act of that attorney in procuring the judgment, it will be presumed, so far as plaintiff is concerned, that the attorney was authorized to satisfy the judgment.

3. The finding of the master that there was no fraud or collusion is not conclusive, even though the trial court did not disturb such finding.

Appeal from common pleas circuit court of Barnwell county; J. H. HUDSON, Judge.

Action by W. G. Wheeler against H. S. Alderman to enjoin the sale of certain land on execution. Judgment for plaintiff. Defendant appeals. Affirmed.

J. O. Patterson and *Mr. Moorman,* for appellant. *J. J. Brown,* for respondent.

McIVER, J. The facts out of which the controversy in this case has arisen are substantially as follows: One Owen Alderman, the brother of the defendant herein, confessed a judgment to him for the sum of upwards of $500, which was duly entered in the proper office of Aiken county on the 12th of March, 1885, and a transcript thereof was duly filed in the proper office of Barnwell county, where the land which constitutes the subject of this litigation is located, on the 23d of November, 1885. Upon the back of this transcript the following indorsement, without date, appears: "Received of the judgment debtor herein the full amount of the within judgment, with the cost and the interest thereon, which is full satisfaction of the same. [Signed] H. S. ALDERMAN. Per JAS. E. DAVIS, Plaintiff's Atty." On the 28th of December, 1885, the said Owen Alderman executed a mortgage on the land in question to the American Freehold Land Mortgage Company of London to secure the payment of money then borrowed by him from said company; and, upon default in the payment of the same, the said land, on the 5th of December, 1887, was sold under the power contained in the said mortgage, and bought by W. G. Wheeler, the plaintiff herein. On the 11th of June, 1888, the said H. S. Alderman, the defendant herein, but the plaintiff in said judgment, moved for and obtained from his honor, Judge A. P. ALDRICH, an order vacating the entry of satisfaction above copied, with leave to issue execution on said judgment. This motion was made without notice to the plaintiff herein, or any one else, except the said Owen Alderman, and was based upon the affidavit of said H. S. Alderman that the entry was made without his authority or knowledge, and that nothing had, in fact, been paid on said judgment. Under the execution thus authorised to be issued to enforce said judgment, the sheriff of Barnwell county levied upon the said land, and advertised the same for sale on sales-day in July, 1888, as the land of said Owen Alderman. Thereupon the plaintiff commenced this action to perpetually enjoin said sale. In his complaint, among other appropriate allegations, the plaintiff alleges that he has paid the whole amount of the purchase money bid at the sale under the mortgage, and that the subsequent proceedings to open the judgment were intended as a fraud upon him, and will operate as such, unless he obtains the relief demanded. The defendant answered, denying all fraud and collusion on his part, and denying that the said James E. Davis ever was his attorney, or ever had any authority to receive the money due upon said judgment, or to enter satisfaction thereon. The testimony adduced on the part of the plaintiff tends to show that the transcript of judgment was entered in Barnwell county after the negotiations for the loan of the money by the mortgage company had been completed; but before the money was made over to Owen Alderman the agent of the company made a final search of the records, which revealed the fact that the transcript of judgment had been entered a short time before, whereupon this fact was brought to the attention of Owen Alderman, who said the judgment had been paid, and should so appear upon the record; and the said James E. Davis, one of the attorneys of record in the said judgment, informed said agent that the judgment was actually paid, and had already been marked satisfied upon the back of the transcript in the clerk's office, and that he would also make the entry of satisfaction upon the abstract of judgments, which he subsequently did, to-wit, on the 5th of April, 1886.

The testimony on the part of the defendant tended to show that James E. Davis, the attorney who took the confession of judgment, and who indorsed the entry of satisfaction on the record thereof, was not the attorney of H. S. Alderman, who had never seen or had any communication with him, but acted entirely at the request and under the direction of Owen Alderman, who was his brother-in-law; and the defendant, in his testimony, says that his brother, Owen, owed him $500, besides interest, for money loaned him on the 24th of February, 1888, for which a note was then given. That the said Owen promised to secure him. "He confessed judgment in my favor voluntarily, to make me secure for my money; and told me he had confessed the judgment for that purpose." That no part thereof has ever been paid, either to defendant or to any one for him within his knowledge; and that he never authorized any one to collect or satisfy said judgment until he employed Mr. Patterson, some time in the spring of 1888, to collect the judgment; and that he had never employed James E. Davis, "did not know him, and had never had any business transaction with him." The issues in the action having been referred to the master, he made his report, finding the facts, substantially, as we have stated them in the outset of this opinion, and finding as matter of fact "that there was no fraud or collusion on the part of H. S. Alderman, the defendant herein." He found as matter of law that the plaintiff is not entitled to any equitable relief upon the ground of fraud, and "that plaintiff is not entitled to equitable interposition by injunction on the ground that the judgment has been satisfied." Upon this report, and the exceptions thereto filed by the plaintiff, the case was heard by his honor, Judge HUDSON, who held "that, while there may have been no collusion on the part of the Aldermans, or corrupt purpose in their transactions, at the same time the loan was made to Owen Alderman upon the faith of the statements of the said Owen Alderman and James E. Davis, who acted as attorney for both parties in obtaining the judgment; and, while the satisfaction made and acknowledged by said James E. Davis on the records of the county may be incorrect, its effect was to induce the lender of the money to make the loan, and W. G. Wheeler, the plaintiff, to become the purchaser of the land. To allow a sale under such circumstances would operate as a fraud upon the rights of the party who made the loan, and upon the rights also of the plaintiff, who claims under the lender of the money." He further held that a court of equity "will enjoin a sale under execution, although the purchaser acquires no title, where the effect of such sale is to cloud the title of one who, like this plaintiff, occupies the position of an innocent purchaser for value without notice." Judgment was accordingly rendered, perpetually enjoining the enforcement of said judgment against the land in question. From this judgment defendant appeals upon the several grounds set out in the record, which impute error to the circuit judge in holding (1) that the case made by the plaintiff entitled him to "equitable interference;" (2) that Davis acted as attorney for both parties in obtaining the judgment, and that H. S. Alderman was bound by the statements made by Davis and Owen Alderman; (3) that, while the satisfaction entered upon the record of the judgment may be incorrect, yet, as it induced plaintiff to become the purchaser of the land, the defendant is thereby estopped by said entry, although said Davis acted without authority, and without receiving the money; (4) in perpetually enjoining the enforcement of the execution against the land in question.

The first ground raises the question of the jurisdiction of the court, and, therefore, lies at the very foundation of the case. That the court of equity has jurisdiction to prevent or remove a cloud up-

on the title to land in certain cases cannot be questioned. 2 Pom. Eq. Jur. § 783; 3 Pom. Eq. Jur. §§ 1398, 1399; High, Inj. §§ 269–273. The inquiry, then, is whether this is one of the cases in which such jurisdiction can be exercised. It will be observed that the plaintiff in this case bases his claim for protection upon the ground that he is an innocent purchaser for valuable consideration without notice, which is peculiarly an equity doctrine, (2 Pom. Eq. Jur. § 788;) and also charges fraud and collusion between the creditor, against whose judgment he is seeking protection, and his judgment debtor. It is therefore clearly distinguishable from the cases of Green v. Bank, 10 Rich. Eq. 27; Brown v. Dickinson, Id. 408; Wilson v. Hyatt, 4 S. C. 369; and Gillam v. Arnold, 32 S. C. 503, 11 S. E. Rep. 831,—relied upon by appellant. The plaintiff here does not rely upon a mere legal right which he does not need the aid of a court of equity to enforce, as in the cases just mentioned; but his reliance here is upon a pure equity, which does require the aid of a court of equity to enforce. The present case is more analogous, though not strictly so, to the case of Martin v. Martin, 24 S. C. 446, where a purchaser of land, with covenant of warranty, was allowed to invoke the aid of equity to protect himself from a prior mortgage held by his grantor. The fact that the master has found that there was no fraud or collusion on the part of H. S. Alderman, which finding has not been disturbed by the circuit judge, is not conclusive; for, though there was no actual fraud upon the part of H. S. Alderman, yet, as the circuit judge well says, it would certainly operate as a fraud upon the plaintiff, whether so intended or not, to allow a sale of the land under a judgment which, at the time of plaintiff's purchase, bore upon the face of the record evidence that it was satisfied, even though it should afterwards be made to appear that the entry of satisfaction was without authority.

The second ground of appeal incorrectly represents the circuit judge as holding that the defendant herein "was bound by the statements made by Mr. James E. Davis and Owen Alderman, the judgment debtor." We do not understand the decree of the circuit judge as being based upon any "statements" made either by Davis or the judgment debtor, but upon the fact that Davis, who acted as the attorney for both parties in obtaining the judgment, had acknowledged satisfaction on the record. That Davis acted as the attorney for both parties cannot well be disputed in the face of the uncontradicted testimony that he prepared the papers, and indorsed the name of his firm thereon, as attorney for the plaintiff in said judgment, and advised the filing of the transcript of the judgment; and, what is much more significant, signed the name of H. S. Alderman to the entry of satisfaction. "per Jas. E. Davis, Plaintiff's Atty.;" and the real question is that which the third ground of appeal was doubtless intended to raise,—whether he had any authority so to act for H. S. Alderman. While it is quite true that there is no direct evidence that Davis was ever employed as an attorney by H. S. Alderman, yet the fact of his having so acted, and that H. S. Alderman is now claiming the benefit of his act, together with other circumstances presently to be alluded to, is sufficient, in our judgment, to establish that relation between Davis and H. S. Alderman. If the confession of judgment had never been taken, or if, after it was taken in the county of Aiken, the transcript thereof had never been filed in Barnwell county, it is very obvious that H. S. Alderman would have had no pretense of a lien upon the plaintiff's land; and hence, if he has any such lien, he must claim it through the judgment which was prepared by Davis, acting as his attorney; and he cannot now claim the benefit without assuming the corresponding burden, at least so far as the rights of subsequent innocent purchasers are concerned. As is said in 1 Pars. Cont. § 51: "An adoption of the agency in part adopts it in the whole, because a principal is not permitted to accept and confirm so much of a contract, made by one purporting to be his agent, as he shall think beneficial to himself, and reject the remainder." Upon this principle, H. S. Alderman cannot be permitted to claim the benefit of the act done by Davis as his attorney, and at the same time repudiate his attorneyship. In addition to this, it appears from the defendant's own testimony that when the money was loaned for which the judgment was taken it was on the promise of the borrower to secure or make safe the lender, and that the judgment was voluntarily confessed by Owen Alderman to H. S. Alderman for that purpose, and H. S. Alderman was told by Owen that he had confessed the judgment in accordance with his promise. It would seem, therefore, that H. S. Alderman, when he loaned the money to his brother, Owen, relied upon him to secure the same, and when Owen employed Davis to take the confession for the purpose of carrying out his promise he was really acting for the benefit of H. S. Alderman, who cannot now be permitted to avail himself of such benefit, and at the same time repudiate the agency through which it was secured. It seems to us, therefore, that Davis must be regarded as the attorney of H. S. Alderman in taking the confession of judgment. If so, then he had authority to receive the money due thereon, and enter satisfaction on the judgment. Poole v. Gist, 4 McCord,259; Treasurers v. McDowell,1 Hill, (S.C.) 184; Taylor v. Easterling,1 Rich. Law, 310. It is very true that an attorney has no authority to enter satisfaction without the actual receipt of the money, and, as between the parties, such an entry of satisfaction without the actual receipt of the money may be vacated upon a showing to that effect. But where the rights of third persons intervene the question of estoppel comes in, as it would operate a fraud upon an innocent purchaser without notice to allow a judgment which, when he purchased, bore upon its face the evidence that it was satisfied, to be opened and used as a lien upon the property purchased, even though it should be after-

wards made to appear that the satisfaction was improperly entered. See City Council v. Ryan, 22 S. C. 339. In the present case it appears that when the money was loaned upon the mortgage under which the land was sold, and when the plaintiff purchased, the judgment which is now sought to be set up as a lien on the land bore upon its face not only an entry of satisfaction, but also a declaration of the receipt of the money due, so that the records, which purchasers are invited and expected to examine before purchasing, showed that there was no lien upon the land; and it would be a palpable fraud upon the plaintiff herein to allow the judgment to be set up as a lien upon the land because it has been subsequently made to appear that no money was in fact received, and the entry of satisfaction was made without authority. Any other view would shake confidence in the public records, and jeopardize many titles acquired upon the faith of what such records show, and cannot for a moment be entertained.

The fourth ground is too general in its character to call for further notice than what it has incidentally received in considering the other grounds. The judgment of this court is that the judgment of the circuit court is affirmed.

McGOWAN, J. I concur.

GRANTHAM v. GRANTHAM et al.

(Supreme Court of South Carolina. Sept. 19, 1891.)

HUSBAND AND WIFE — GIFT OF WIFE'S EARNINGS —PURCHASE OF LAND—PARTITION.

Where a wife's earnings were allowed to accumulate with her employer for the express purpose of providing a fund for the purchase of a home for her, and the husband, both before and after the purchase, always spoke of the money as hers, and never on any occasion as his own, the inference is irresistible that he had given it to her, though, under the law as it then stood, it could not have become hers in any other way; and the fact that the property purchased with such earnings was taken in the husband's name is not sufficient to overcome the undisputed evidence of his declarations that it was paid for with his wife's money.

Appeal from common pleas circuit court of Sumter county; T. B. FRASER, Judge.

Action by Elizabeth Grantham against James Grantham and others for partition of real estate. There was a judgment for plaintiff, and defendants appeal. Affirmed.

Blanding & Wilson, for appellants. Haynsworth & Cooper, for respondent.

McIVER, J. James Grantham, the elder, died some time in 1881, intestate, seised and possessed of some real estate, leaving as his heirs at law his widow, the plaintiff herein, and two children, James Grantham, one of the defendants herein, and Julia Ann Diggs, who died in 1887, leaving 11 children, who are the other defendants herein; and this action was commenced in May, 1890, for the partition of said real estate. The only question presented by this appeal is as to whether a certain lot in the city of Sumter, described in the complaint, constituted a part of the real estate of the said intestate; the plaintiff claiming that it belongs to her individually, and the defendants claiming that it constituted part of the real estate of intestate, and as such is subject to partition among his heirs at law. The facts seem to be undisputed, and are substantially as follows: The intestate, James Grantham, and his wife, Elizabeth, were both in the employment of late Judge Moses, and, while the intestate was in the habit of drawing his own wages, those of his wife were allowed to remain in the hands of the judge. On the 3d of May, 1873, Martha E. McCoy executed a conveyance of the lot in question to the intestate, wherein it was recited that it was in consideration of the sum of $45 paid by him to her; but the plaintiff claims that this money was hers, and therefore contends that there is a resulting trust in her favor in the said lot. The testimony leaves but little, if any, doubt that the lot was paid for with the wages of the wife, which had been allowed to accumulate in the hands of Judge Moses, and drawn from him by the intestate for the purpose of paying for the lot, and, but for the marital relation existing between the parties, these facts would be sufficient to raise a resulting trust in favor of the plaintiff. It is contended, however, that under the law as it then stood, the earnings of the wife belonged to the husband, and therefore, though the money used in paying for the lot was derived from the wages of the wife, it was in law the money of the husband, and hence there was no resulting trust. While it is quite true that, as the law then stood, the earnings of a married woman, derived from her personal services, belonged exclusively to the husband, yet there was nothing to prevent the husband from making a gift to his wife of her earnings, provided this was done without detriment to the claims of the husband's creditors, of whom there does not appear to be any in this case. So that the real inquiry in this case is whether the intestate had given his wife's wages to her, and whether when he drew them he was not acting simply as her agent. This is a question of fact which has been determined adversely to the appellants by the circuit judge, and we think his conclusion is most abundantly sustained by the testimony set out in the "case." From that it appears that the wife's wages were allowed to accumulate in the hands of her employer for the express purpose of providing a fund for the purchase of a home for her. The intestate, both before and after the purchase, always spoke of the money as his wife's, and never upon any occasion spoke of it or claimed it as his own; and it could not have been hers except by a gift from her husband, and hence the inference that he had given it to her is irresistible. As the counsel for respondent well puts it, suppose he had drawn his wife's wages every month, and deposited the money in bank to her credit, what higher evidence would be needed of a gift from him to her?" And when, instead of doing this, he left her wages from month to month in the hands of Judge Moses, declaring his purpose in doing so, he practically deposited his wife's monthly wages from time to time with the judge for her benefit, instead of drawing them every month for his own use, as he might have done, and he thereby just as unmistakably made a gift to his wife as if he had drawn the money and deposited it in bank to her credit. The fact that when the purchase was made the title was taken in the name of the husband is not sufficient to overcome the undisputed evidence of his declarations, made both before and after the purchase, that the property was paid for with his wife's money; for, in the first place, that might have arisen from ignorance or some other cause; and, in the second place, if he had already given the money to his wife, he could not afterwards recall the gift without her consent, of which there is not the slightest evidence. We do not think, therefore, that there was any error on the part of the circuit judge in concluding that the property was paid for with the money of the wife, and hence a resulting trust arose in her favor. The judgment of this court is that the judgment of the circuit court be affirmed.

McGowan, J. I concur.

RHODE et al. v. TUTEN et al.

(Supreme Court of South Carolina. Sept. 19, 1891.)

SUPPORT OF INFANTS—LIABILITY OF MOTHER—APPEAL.

1. A widow, who has not sufficient property of her own to support minor children, may resort to the children's property for that purpose; and therefore, where she arranges with her father to furnish the support, agreeing to allow him as consideration the use of the children's land, from which he derives an income less in value than the support, neither she nor they have any claim against his estate.

2. The existence of a contract is a question of fact, and, under the well-settled rule, is concluded by the concurrent findings of a referee and circuit judge.

3. A question as to the effect of the statute of frauds on a contract, when not raised below, nor by any exception to the judgment, is not determinable on appeal.

Appeal from common pleas circuit court of Hampton county; J. D. WITHERSPOON, Judge.

Action by Mary E. Rhode and others against W. H. and G. W. Tuten, as executors of W. R. Tuten, to recover for the rent of land alleged to have been received by their testator. There was judgment for defendants, and plaintiffs appeal. Affirmed.

Howell, Murphy & Farrow, for appellants. James W. Moore, for respondents.

McIver, J. On the 10th of July, 1867, James E. Altman departed this life intestate, leaving as his heirs at law his widow, Mary E., who subsequently intermarried with J. A. Rhode, and his three children, Mary Ella, who has since intermarried with Morgan Pye, Ada E., who died intestate on the 21st of June, 1877, and William G. Altman. All of these children at the time of the death of their father were minors,—Ada E. having been born on the 22d of April, 1860; Mary Ella, on the 27th of January, 1863; and William G., on the 13th of December, 1866. The intestate James E. Altman was at the time of his death seised and possessed of a tract of land in Hampton county, which descended to and vested in his heirs at law, named above. The widow of the intestate, soon after the death of her husband, and before her second marriage, with her minor children went to reside with her father, W. R. Tuten, where she remained, with her children, until after her second marriage with Rhode, the date of which is not specifically stated, though it seems, from the circuit judge's decree, to have been some time in 1872. The said W. R. Tuten went into possession of the said tract of land, and rented out the same for the years 1869, 1870, 1871, and 1872, receiving as rent for the first two years $200 for each year, and for the last two years $150 for each year. At the expiration of the year 1872 the land was surrendered to Rhode and wife, at their request, and they have since been in possession. On the 24th of February, 1885, the said W. R. Tuten died, leaving a last will and testament, of which the defendants are the duly-qualified executors. On the 1st of July, 1887, this action was commenced by the plaintiffs, as heirs at law of said James E. Altman, to recover from the defendants, as executors as aforesaid, the amount alleged to have been received to the use of the plaintiffs for the rent of said land by their testator, W. R. Tuten. The defendants answered, saying, among other things, that the said James E. Altman was at the time of his death indebted to their testator, as well as to other parties, and that in the year 1868 the plaintiff Mary E., "in behalf of herself and her infant children, entered into a contract with the said William R. Tuten, by which it was agreed that, in consideration of the said indebtedness of the said James E. Altman to the said William R. Tuten, and that William R. Tuten should pay the other creditors aforesaid, and in the mean time support the said Mary E. Rhode and her children, (the plaintiffs,) the said William R. Tuten should take the said land and rent it out for five years, and during that period receive the rents and profits to his own use." And the defendants allege that in pursuance of said agreement the said W. R. Tuten did rent out the land for the years 1869-1872, inclusive, for the amounts above stated, and faithfully carried out his part of the said contract; but that, at the end of the said four years, the said Mary E., having intermarried with Rhode, desired possession of the said land, and the same was surrendered to them by said W. R. Tuten, he losing the rent for the fifth year, to which he was entitled under the terms of the contract. The defendants also pleaded the statute of limitations. The issues in the action were referred to a referee, who heard the testimony adduced, and made his report, rejecting the claim of the plaintiffs; and his report, with the exceptions thereto, came before his honor, Judge WITHER-

SPOON, who rendered judgment confirming the report, and that the complaint be dismissed. From this judgment plaintiffs appeal upon the several grounds set out in the record, which need not be set out here, as, according to the view which we take of the case, there are really but two questions in the case: *First.* Was there such a contract as that set up in the defendants' answer? *Second.* If so, what was its effect, so far as the rights of the minors are concerned? For the third question—as to the statute of limitations—is superseded by the conclusion which we have reached as to the other two questions.

Whether there was such a contract as that set up in the answer is a question of fact, and, under the well-settled rule, is concluded by the concurrent finding of the referee and the circuit judge; for there certainly was testimony tending to support the conclusion which they reached, and surely the simple denial of Mrs. Rhode would not be sufficient to warrant us in saying that the conclusion reached was contrary to the manifest weight of the testimony. Indeed, as the circuit judge well remarks, the fact that when the land was surrendered by the old man after his daughter's second marriage, nothing whatever, so far as the testimony discloses, was said about the rents, which they knew W. R. Tuten had been receiving for the previous years, is a pregnant circumstance to show that some such arrangement about the rents had been made; and when to this is added the fact that, though William R. Tuten lived for some 13 years afterwards, no claim was made upon him, and that this action was commenced soon after his lips were closed by death, there can be but little doubt that the conclusion reached by the referee and concurred in by the circuit judge was correct. If, then, such an arrangement was made by the mother with her father for the support and maintenance of herself and her minor children, and the same was faithfully carried out by the old gentleman,—as the evidence and the findings below show to have been the fact,—the only remaining inquiry is, what was its effect, so far as the rights of the minors are concerned? It will be observed that when Altman died he left three children of tender years,—the eldest being then only about seven years of age, and the youngest "an infant in the arms;" and the estate which he left seems from the evidence to have been small, barely sufficient to afford his family a scanty support. What, then, was the widow to do in order to provide for these children, who were then, all of them, unquestionably unable to provide for themselves? What better arrangement could she have made than that which she did make with her father, whereby she and her children were provided with a comfortable support and maintenance, without any encroachment upon the capital of the estate left by her husband and their father? Whether a widowed mother is under a legal obligation to support her minor children, even where her own estate is sufficient for the purpose, has not, so far as we are informed, been distinctly decided in this state, and elsewhere there is a conflict of authority. See Railway Co. v. Stutler, 93 Amer. Dec. 714; Reeve, Dom. Rel. c. 9, p. 350, and the authorities cited in notes; also, chapter 11, p. 369, and notes. In Kerr v. Butler, 2 Desaus. Eq. 279, where a testator gave the profits of his whole estate to his wife for life, and to his son afterwards, it was held that the mother was bound to maintain the son during his minority and until her death; but that decision was not based upon the idea that a widowed mother was under any legal obligation to maintain her minor son, but upon the construction given to the will: "The court will not suppose on the part of the testator an intention so extraordinary as leaving his infant son for a series of years without the means of maintenance or education, or that an account of these purposes was to be kept until the son came into possession of his fortune, and then to be paid out of the capital thereof; but the court will rather suppose the testator intended his wife to take the profits of his estate as well for the support of his son as for her own use." That case, therefore, does not decide that there was any legal obligation on the widowed mother to support her infant child. On the contrary, the implication is that the court did not hold to any such doctrine, for, if it had, then there would have been no necessity to place the decision upon the ground of intention. In Cudworth v. Thompson, 3 Desaus. Eq. 256, it was held that minor children must be supported out of their own property where the mother has insufficient means to enable her to do so. Here the implication seems to be the reverse of what it was in the preceding case, and that the allowance made to the mother out of the estate of her minor children for their support would not have been made if the mother's estate had been sufficient. In Heyward v. Heyward's Ex'r, 4 Desaus. Eq. 445, a mother who had only a bare competence for herself, and had minor children living with her, was granted an allowance out of their estates for their support. In Teague v. Dendy, 2 McCord, Eq. 207, it seems to have been conceded that minor distributees of an estate were entitled to an allowance out of the income of the estate for their support, although their mother was living, and entitled to her distributive share of the estate. In Ellerbe v. Ellerbe, Speer, Eq. 328, the question was as to the construction of a will of the grandfather, providing that his wife, together with his daughter and grandson, should have a reasonable and competent support out of the proceeds of his estate until his just debts were paid, and during the life of his wife. It was held that, as the daughter had a sufficient property of her own for the support of herself and child, though the child had none, the provision could not take effect, and the claim of the daughter to be reimbursed the expense which she had incurred in supporting her child was rejected. HARPER, C., in delivering the opinion of the court, plainly intimates his opinion that a mother who has sufficient means of her own to maintain her children as well as herself is

bound to do so. In Buck v. Martin, 21 S. C. 590, one of the questions was whether the mother (who had married a second time) was liable to her infant children, who lived with her, for the rents and profits of the common property, and the court held she was not. Mr. Justice McGOWAN, in delivering the opinion of the court, used this language: "It was not the legal duty of the mother or her [second] husband to support the children without the use of their shares. The possession of the mother was also the possession of the children living with her, and of course they have no just claim for rents and profits which they consumed themselves."

From this review of the authorities in this state we think it is safe to conclude that, whatever may be the rule as to the legal obligation of a mother, possessed of sufficient means for the purpose, to support her minor children, no such obligation exists where the mother has not sufficient means of her own, but that in such case the property of the minors may be resorted to for the purpose of providing them with a proper support, at least so far as the income of their property extends; and that even an encroachment upon the capital may be made, provided a proper application is made to the court to allow such encroachment. Now, in this case, the evidence shows that the property of the mother was insufficient for the support of herself and her children, and hence resort must have been had to their property for that purpose. It will be remembered that these children had no guardian, and there was no one but the mother to provide for them, and, as was said in Connolly v. Hull, 3 McCord, 9, she, as their natural guardian, was "the fittest judge" of what was necessary for them; and, as we have said, she seems to have made the best practicable arrangement for their support, without using anything but the income of their property. If the family had continued to live together on the land they would have derived their support from the rents and profits of the land, or from its cultivation; and, as was said in Buck v. Martin, supra, in such a case "the possession of the mother was also the possession of the children living with her, and of course they have no just claim for rents and profits which they consumed themselves." But, instead of doing this, she made a better arrangement with her father, whereby the children doubtless received a better support, with some education, than it was at all likely they would have received if the family had continued to occupy the land and use it for their joint support. Having thus practically enjoyed the benefits of the rents and profits of the land, neither she nor her children can have any just claim on the estate of W. R. Tuten for the rents which he received in consideration of furnishing a support for the family, as the evidence shows that the amount of such rents was not equal to the value of the support furnished.

The question raised in the argument as to the effect of the statute of frauds upon the alleged contract, not having been raised in the court below, nor by any exception to the judgment appealed from, is not properly before us. But we may see that, even if it were before us, the point raised could not avail the plaintiffs, for there is no attempt here to enforce an executory contract, but reliance is placed upon an executed contract. The provision, therefore, of the statute that no action shall be commenced upon a contract falling within the statute of frauds would have no application. Under the view which we have taken of the case the question as to whether all or any of the parties are barred of their action by the statute of limitations cannot arise, and, therefore, need not be considered. The judgment of this court is that the judgment of the circuit court be affirmed.

McGowan, J. I concur.

DOBSON v. COTHRAN et al.

(*Supreme Court of South Carolina.* Sept. 28, 1891.)

ACTION FOR ABDUCTION.

1. In an action by a father for damages for the abduction of his daughter for immoral purposes, it is no answer that she, as well as plaintiff's whole family, was of a loose and immoral character.

2. Where on demurrer allegations of such immoral character were stricken out of the answer, but all the evidence offered to prove the same was received. defendants were not prejudiced, even though the allegations were material.

3. The family Bible, containing an entry of the daughter's age, was not the best evidence of her age, and it was not error to allow plaintiff to prove her age by his own testimony as to the date of her birth, and to refuse to require the production of the Bible.

4. The daughter not being a party to the action, it was not competent for defendants to prove by plaintiff declarations made by the daughter while he was carrying her home.

5. Where the daughter was examined as to declarations made to her father while he was carrying her home, and witnesses were afterwards examined to contradict her testimony, defendants were not prejudiced by not allowing them to examine plaintiff as to such declarations.

6. Where the daughter was intoxicated and much excited when taken by plaintiff out of a wardrobe at defendants' house, and had no recollection of seeing plaintiff on that occasion, it was not error to rule out a question put to her as to whether she did not tell him that she would not go home until she got the money she made at defendants' house.

7. The daughter not being a party to the action, it was not competent for defendants to show that she said plaintiff made declarations as to his motives in commencing this action.

8. It was no abuse of discretion for the court to not allow a Bible to be exhibited in evidence after the testimony was closed, and argument by counsel commenced.

9. Where an exception charges error in giving an instruction, but contains no specifications as to what the error was, the exception will not be sustained.

10. Where an exception to the charge was based upon the assumption that defendants pleaded separate defenses, when the record shows that they did not, the exception will not be sustained.

11. Where, if defendants had pleaded separately, the charge correctly laid down the law as to what facts would implicate one or more of them, and left it to the jury to say whether such facts were established, the charge was not erroneous.

12. Although defendants did not entice the daughter from home, if they persuaded her, after she came to their house, to lead a life of shame,

and when plaintiff came for her hid her from him, he was entitled to recover.

13. An exception, "because the finding of the jury was contrary to the clear preponderance of the testimony," is insufficient.

14. An exception based upon the allegation that the damages found by the jury are excessive cannot be considered by this court. Steele v. Railroad Co., 11 S. C. 589; Petrie v. Railroad Co., 29 S. C. 303, 7 S. E. Rep. 515,—followed.

Appeal from common pleas circuit court of Greenville county; IzLAR, Judge.

Action by William A. Dobson against Elisabeth Cothran, Emma Cothran, and Lucie Anderson, for damages for abducting plaintiff's daughter for immoral purposes. Verdict and judgment for plaintiff. Defendant Elisabeth Cothran appeals. Affirmed.

At the close of the arguments the judge delivered the following charge:

"This action is brought by the plaintiff against the defendants to recover damages for the abduction of a female child of twelve years of age, the daughter of the plaintiff, and for procuring said child to be debauched. The complaint alleges that the defendants are women of notoriously bad character and ill repute, and are engaged in the business of keeping and occupying a house of ill fame in the city of Greenville, in this state, and that on or about the 31st of March, 1889, the defendants did maliciously, wrongfully, and unlawfully, by messages, allurements, promises, and inducements, prevail upon Susie Dobson, the female child of the plaintiff, of tender years, to be enticed and abducted from the presence, home, care, control, and protection of the plaintiff, for bad, wicked, and unlawful purposes, and harbored and concealed said child, and refused to give her up to the plaintiff. And that while the said child was in the wrongful keeping of the defendants, and while being unlawfully harbored by them, to-wit, from March 31, 1889, to April 1, 1889, they caused, persuaded, and influenced the said child to be drugged, debauched, deflowered, and ravished, and to commit fornication or adultery, and to be otherwise injured, by some man or men unknown to the plaintiff, who at the time aforesaid were patronising their wicked establishment. And by reason of the wicked, malicious, wrongful, and unlawful conduct of the defendants towards said infant child, the plaintiff was deprived of the services of his child, was outraged and aggrieved in his feelings, and endured great mental anguish and suffering, and has thereby been injured ten thousand dollars. The defendants answer separately, but substantially the same. They say that they have no knowledge or information sufficient to form a belief whether the plaintiff is the father of Susie Dobson, an infant female child of the age of twelve years, and was reared by him, and has always lived with him, and been in his service, and under his care, protection, and control, as alleged in the first paragraph of his complaint, and deny all the other allegations of the complaint. Now, that is the case that is presented for your consideration. Now, you are to decide this case according to the testimony that you have heard on the stand, and the law as I shall give it to you The facts are for you, and you will have to pass upon them. I cannot aid you in regard to the facts, but will only state to you the law as I understand it. It is incumbent upon the plaintiff, of course, to establish the allegations in the complaint by the preponderance of the evidence. In this court you have to decide according to the preponderance of the evidence, and not be satisfied beyond a reasonable doubt, as in the court of general sessions. Now, this action, as I understand, is brought not for seduction. This could not be. But the allegation is that these defendants procured and persuaded this child to commit adultery or fornication. This, as I understand, is not the gist of the present action, but only intended to show the aggravation of the injury to the plaintiff. As has been very properly said, an action could not be maintained against a female for seducing a female child. But, as I understand this case, it is for abduction; that is, for persuading away a child for bad, wicked, and unlawful purposes; and that, after that was done, by their promises and persuasions, the female child was debauched and deflowered. It is not for seduction. Now, I charge you that, where several persons unite in an act which constitutes a wrong to another, they intending at the time to commit such wrong, the reasonable and just rule of the law compels each of the parties to bear the misconduct of all. The law does not require the party injured to point out how much of the injury was done by the one and how much was done by another, or what share of responsibility is fairly attributable to each, as between themselves, and leave it to the jury to apportion the responsibility among them according to the mischief done by each. If this was the rule, it would be a practical denial of justice in many cases. But all concerned in the injury are to be treated as constituting one party, by reason of their joint co-operation, and all are liable to respond in a gross sum as damages. The law permits the party injured to proceed against any one of the joint wrong-doers, or any number less than the whole, and to enforce his remedy, regardless of the participation of the others; for, while the wrong is joint, it is, in contemplation of law, several, and there cannot be any apportionment of responsibility, whether the action be against one or against all. Each is responsible for the whole, and the degree of blamableness as between herself and her associates is wholly immaterial when the action of all contributes to the result. I charge you that it is unimportant to the party injured that one contributed much and another little. The one least guilty is as much liable as the one most guilty, all having aided in accomplishing the result.

"The facts alleged in the complaint set forth a good cause of action. A father can maintain an action for the abduction of his daughter who is under twenty-one years of age. The father has such property in his infant child as will enable him to maintain an action for injury done him, by depriving him of the society of his child, and defeating the education of his child, etc. The true ground of the action, as I understand the law, is not so much the loss of the services of the child, but the outrage and deprivation, the injury the father sustains in the loss of his child, the insult offered his feelings, the agony in the destruction of his hopes concerning his child, and the irreparable loss of that comfort and society which may be the only solace of his declining years; and I hold that this action is maintainable, although the evidence does not show a forcible taking or abduction. An infant child is not able to consent, and the law therefore implies force, as the taking is unlawful. As a general rule, in cases of abduction of this kind, even if no actual force be shown, yet the action may be maintained. Now, the child may be under the age of consent,—I mean at that age when the child is not able to consent to going away from the parent's home. As was said in a case of this kind where the child was under twelve years, the mere fact of the taking away being unlawful would imply force, and would be sufficient to maintain this action. Now, that is all that I have to say in regard to the nature of this action, and the law governing that part of the case. The most serious part of this case for your consideration is the part with reference to damages, and all I would say is that, if the defendants enticed or persuaded Susie Dobson to leave the home of her father, and enter upon a life of shame and disgrace, in the bawdy-house of the defendants, the mere fact that Susie Dobson had had sexual intercourse with other men before she went would not be a defense against the action brought by the father for the injury of taking his child away, but such fact would have weight in fixing the amount of damages sustained by the father. Now, if these defendants enticed and persuaded Susie Dobson to leave and remain away from her father, even after she got to the house, and to hide in the wardrobe in order to keep her from being found by the father, this would be an unlawful act, and it would be sufficient to maintain this action, and would amount to sufficient force, even if the defendants did not persuade her by promises or entice her to leave her father's house. If they did persuade her to pursue this life of shame after she went to their house of ill fame, and when her father came for her she was hid by them in the wardrobe, I think there would be sufficient force in that to maintain the action. Now, in an action of this kind. I charge you that, in case you come to the conclusion that the plaintiff is entitled to recover, you will have to consider the question of damages before you can make up your verdict. If you come to the conclusion that the plaintiff is not entitled to recover, you will not consider the question of damages; but, if you come to the conclusion that the plaintiff is entitled to recover anything, I charge you that he is entitled to recover such damages as will compensate him for taking away his child to this place of ill fame, and procuring her to be debauched. (If you come to the conclusion that that was so,) and that she was induced to have sexual intercourse with men. These are all matters which would come in in aggravation of the damages which the plaintiff is entitled to recover; and, if you think he is entitled to recover anything, you can give him a verdict for any amount, from one cent up to ten thousand dollars. But, in considering these damages, you will consider Susie Dobson's character before she went there,—whether she was a virtuous girl, whether she was properly raised up; because, if she was a pure, innocent, and virtuous little girl before she went there, and she was enticed away from home, and carried to this house of ill fame, it would be a very different thing from a girl who had been improperly brought up, and who had previously lost her virtue. You will consider all that in making up your verdict, if you find for the plaintiff. You will consider whether or not she was brought up properly, and whether the father countenanced such things in his family. You are to consider all of these questions in making up your verdict. And I charge you that acts of this kind before this should have more weight with you than acts committed afterwards. All testimony as to the character and conduct of Susie Dobson, and as to the action of the father in countenancing improper conduct of his daughters, should be considered in determining the question of damages. But subsequent acts of the child Susie Dobson are not entitled to as much weight as her previous conduct, for, if she had lived a pure and virtuous life up to the time of the alleged abduction, her subsequent conduct might have been influenced by reason of the fact that she had lost her virtue, and become reckless as to her subsequent conduct. Now, that is my idea of the rule as to damages by which you should be governed in making up your verdict.

"Now, I charge you further: A great many questions were propounded to this little girl as to her course of life previous to her going to this house of Bettie Cothran's, and as to her intercourse with men, which she answered in the negative, stating that they were not so. Witnesses were afterwards put upon the stand to prove the contrary. That does not make the statements and acts about which she was asked, in order to contradict her, evidence. Gentlemen, it only affects her credibility; it weakens the force of her testimony, but it does not make it evidence. But where she has voluntarily confessed it, or it was testified to by other witnesses, or where acts have been proven by other witnesses which would lead you to the conclusion that she had done so, why of course that is evidence. There was a witness who testified that she made the remark in the house of Bettie Cothran that she had made money by having intercourse with men, and then it was testified to that she had remained at the house of other people with men. That is all for you to consider, and I only want to call your attention to this other matter, for where the questions were put to her, and she was contradicted, I charge you that

that is not testimony. It only goes to weaken her testimony. Now, I trust you will find no difficulty in coming to a conclusion in this case. I have tried to explain the law to you as I understand it. If you come to the conclusion that this child was enticed and persuaded away by Bettie Cothran, and she was persuaded afterwards, by promises or force, to have sexual intercourse with men,—I say if you come to that conclusion, the plaintiff would be entitled to a verdict. It may be for any amount from one cent up to ten thousand dollars. And, if you find for the plaintiff, your verdict will be for so many dollars, writing it out in words, not in figures. And if you come to the conclusion that she was not persuaded to go there, or that she was not by promises and persuasion induced to remain, and have sexual intercourse with men, the plaintiff would not be entitled to recover a verdict, and you would say, 'We find for the defendants.' Take the record."

James I. Earle and *Wells & Orr*, for appellant. *W. A. Williams* and *Cothran & Ansel*, for respondent.

McIVER, J. The plaintiff brings this action to recover damages from the defendants, who are alleged to be keepers of a bawdy-house, for enticing and abducting from the home of her parents Susie Dobson, an infant child of plaintiff, of the age of 12 years, and causing her to be debauched in the said bawdy-house. The allegations of the complaint are so fully and clearly set forth in the charge of his honor, Judge IZLAR, which for this and other reasons should be incorporated in the report of this case, as to supersede the necessity for anything more than the general statement which we have made as to the nature of the action. The defendants filed separate answers, only one of which, that of the appellant, Elizabeth Cothran, is set out in the case, from which we infer that the answers of the other two defendants were of the same general character; at all events, there is nothing in the case to indicate that the defendants relied upon different defenses. The first defense set up in appellant's answer amounts simply to a general denial of all the material allegations of the complaint. For a second defense she alleges (1) that another and older daughter of plaintiff was, for a period of three years, and up to a short time before the alleged abduction of the said Susie Dobson, with the knowledge and consent of plaintiff, an inmate of said bawdy-house, and that during the whole of that period the said Susie was a frequent visitor there, with the consent and approval of plaintiff; (2) that during the whole of said period the plaintiff and his wife, the mother of Susie, frequently visited said house for improper and immoral purposes; (3) that another sister of Susie, with the knowledge of plaintiff, and without objection from him, made application to be allowed to become an inmate of said house, and was refused; (4) that the said Susie Dobson is, and has been for a year last past, a person of "loose character;" (5) that the said elder sister of Susie is now living in plaintiff's house, receiving, without objection from him, "the promiscuous and indiscriminate visits of men for improper purposes;" (6) that the appellant has not the control and management of the house referred to in the complaint, "but only the use and occupation of two rooms therein;" (7) that at the time of the alleged occurrences mentioned in the complaint the appellant was sick in bed, and had nothing to do with said occurrences, if any such took place; (8) that all the females of plaintiff's immediate family are persons of bad character for chastity. When the case was called for trial, counsel for plaintiff interposed an oral demurrer to the second defense set up in appellant's answer, which was sustained, and defendants excepted. All the testimony is set out in the case, and it is manifestly very conflicting as to many material matters of fact. The jury, however, rendered a verdict against all of the defendants for $1,000, and, judgment being entered thereon, the defendant Elizabeth Cothran alone appeals, upon the several grounds set out in the record.

The first ground questions the correctness of the ruling sustaining the demurrer to the second defense, whereby the eight paragraphs of that defense, stated substantially above, were stricken out. The ground upon which the circuit judge sustained the demurrer is not stated in the case, though we infer, from what subsequently occurred, that his honor was of opinion that the allegations contained in those eight paragraphs did not amount to such a defense as would, if true, constitute a bar to the action, but were more properly circumstances in aid of the general denial, or in mitigation of damages; for we find that much testimony, indeed all that was offered tending to show the truth of such allegations, was received during the progress of the trial. So that, even if there was technical error in the ruling complained of, the defendants sustained no damage thereby, as they obtained all the benefit which they could have derived if these allegations in the answer had not been stricken out. We are not prepared to admit, however, that there was even technical error in the ruling, for the fact that the plaintiff and every member of his family had been persons of bad character and loose habits in respect to chastity would not constitute a defense to an action of this kind, no more than the fact that a female upon whom a rape has been committed is a person of dissolute character would constitute a defense to an indictment for the rape. It would be no bar to an action of this kind to show that the girl whom defendants are charged with having enticed from the paternal roof, and induced to become an inmate of a den of infamy, was not a person of chastity, and that her domestic surroundings were not favorable to the cultivation of that virtue. That would not justify the act of defendants inducing her to enter a bawdy-house, where her previous bad habits would be intensified and fixed. It is very true that such allegations as are contained in the second defense set up in the answer, if established, would tend to shake confidence in the charge upon which the action was based, and aid materially the first defense under the general denial, and would also have an important bearing upon the question of damages. But, as we have said, the record shows that the defendants were allowed the full benefit to which they were entitled in these respects by being permitted to offer such testimony as they desired, tending to show the bad habits of the plaintiff and other members of his family.

The second ground of appeal is in these words: "There being a family Bible in the court-house having the record of the age of Susie Dobson, it should have been submitted, instead of parol testimony." This ground is based upon the unfounded assumption that the entry in a family Bible is the best evidence of the age of a person, the date of whose birth is there entered. Such evidence, however, is in fact secondary, and is only permitted where better evidence cannot be obtained. It is really nothing more than the written declaration of the person who made the entry, and is admissible in cases of pedigree, as an exception to the general rule upon the subject. But it is useless for us to pursue the inquiry, as the question has been distinctly decided in this state in the case of Taylor v. Hawkins, 1 McCord, 164, where it was held that the entry in a family Bible of the date of a person's birth was not the best evidence of the age of such person, but that it might be proved by a person who testified from mere recollection of the fact and time of the birth of the person whose age was in question. In delivering the opinion of the court, Colcock, J., used this language: "In this case, the witness may have proved the age of the defendant, although (such entry existed) from mere recollection of the fact of his birth. In short, it is the very best evidence which the nature of the case admits. If no other evidence could have been had, the memorandum, upon proof of the handwriting, may have been admitted." The same doctrine is recognised in Robinson v. Blakely, 4 Rich. Law, 586; and in Wilson v. Railroad Co., 16 S. C. 587, the general proposition, which would conclude the question under consideration, is laid down that entries in a book need not be produced to prove a fact within witness' own knowledge. It was therefore clearly competent for the plaintiff to prove the age of his own daughter by his own testimony as to the date of her birth, as well as by the testimony of the child's mother to the same effect, and there was no error in refusing to require the production of the entry in the family Bible.

The third, fourth, and fifth exceptions impute error to the circuit judge in refusing to allow certain questions to be put to plaintiff as to what his daughter said after she had been found in the bawdy-house and was being carried home by her father. Susie Dobson not being a party to this action, her declarations, under the general rule, would be incompetent. She could have been, and was in fact, examined as a witness, and there was therefore no occasion for asking another witness what she had said. But, more than this, when she was on the stand as a witness, she was asked what she said to her father, as well in the house as on her way home, and subsequently witnesses were examined for the purpose of contradicting her, and thus the defendants had before the jury all the facts which they complain were excluded. So that in no point of view can these exceptions be sustained.

The sixth exception imputes error in ruling out the following question propounded to Susie Dobson while on the stand as a witness: "That night when you were taken out of the wardrobe, didn't you tell your father that you were not going home until you had got your money you had made there?" What relevancy such a question had to the issue which the jury were called upon to determine it is somewhat difficult to say; but, in view of the undisputed testimony that Susie Dobson was very much intoxicated and quite excited when taken out of the wardrobe, and in view of the further fact that she had testified that she had no recollection whatever of having seen her father on that occasion, we cannot say that there was any error in excluding the question.

The seventh exception complains of error in excluding testimony as to what Susie Dobson was supposed to have said to Mrs. Fletcher she heard her father say was his motive for bringing this action. This question was so plainly incompetent as an effort to elicit declarations of persons not parties to the case that we need not say more.

The eighth exception is in the following words: "Plaintiff's counsel, during the closing argument, having exhibited to the jury the Dobson family Bible, and stated that the age was there recorded, the judge should have either directed the jury that they must not consider that fact, or granted defendants' motion to submit the Bible to the court and jury, that they might see that the date of Susie Dobson's birth had been changed therein." This exception, if for no other reason, cannot be sustained, because it does not correctly represent the occurrence upon which it is based. The case, by which alone are we to be governed, shows that "during the argument" one of defendants' counsel "stated to the jury that no family Bible showing the age of Susie Dobson had been produced or offered in evidence," and that one of the counsel for plaintiff in reply "stated that the judge had not ruled that it was necessary to produce a family Bible to prove age; that there was nothing in the evidence to show that any record was made by either the father or mother of Susie Dobson; that the family Bible was in court, and could have been produced if the judge had ruled it was necessary. The Bible was not exhibited to the jury, but was taken out of the desk drawer by Mr. Ansel, at the request of Mr. Williams, both of whom were counsel for plaintiff, and was laid on the desk. It was then taken up by Mr. Orr, one of the counsel for defendants, who stated, in the presence and hearing of the jury, that the date had been altered, and he then asked the consent of Mr. Williams that the Bible be shown to the jury. Mr. Williams objected, saying the judge had ruled it out. Mr. Orr then asked that the Bible be shown to the court and jury," which was objected to, and the objection was sustained. But, even if we take the representation as made in the exception to be correct, we do not see any foundation for the exception. All this occurred while the argument was in progress, and after the testimony on both sides had been closed; and the rule is well settled that a motion to receive further testimony at that stage of the case is addressed to the discretion of the circuit judge, with which this court will rarely interfere, (Kairson v. Puckhaber, 14 S. C. 627; State v. Clyburn, 16 S. C. 375, and the cases there cited;) especially where, as in this case, we think his discretion was properly exercised.

The ninth exception—"because the judge's charge clearly indicated to the jury his opinion on the facts of the case" —is too general in its terms to require consideration at our hands, as it contains no specification of any instance in which the constitutional provision is supposed to have been violated. But we may add that it seems to us that the charge is singularly free from any such exception.

The tenth exception is based upon the assumption, for which we find no support in the case, that the defendants pleaded separate defenses, and cannot therefore be sustained. But, even were it otherwise, we see nothing in the charge which would warrant the assertion that the judge "led the jury to believe that they must find for or against all of the defendants." On the contrary, we think he correctly laid down the law as to what facts would implicate one or more of the defendants, and left it to the jury to determine whether such facts were established.

The eleventh exception complains of error "in charging the jury that, even if the defendants did not persuade her by promises, or entice her, to leave her father's house, if they did persuade her to pursue this life of shame after she went to their house of ill fame, and after her father came for her she was hid by them in that wardrobe, I think there would be sufficient force in that to maintain this action." The cases of Kirkpatrick v. Lockhart, 2 Brev. 276, and Vaughan v. Rhodes, 2 McCord, 227, cited by counsel for respondent, are sufficient to vindicate the instruction complained of.

The twelfth exception—"because the finding of the jury was contrary to the clear preponderance of the testimony"— has been so often ruled to be insufficient as to require no further notice.

The thirteenth and fourteenth exceptions, based upon the allegation that the damages found by the jury are excessive, it is well settled cannot be considered by this court. Steele v. Railroad Co., 11 S. C. 589; Petrie v. Railroad Co., 29 S. C. 303, 7 S. E. Rep. 515. The judgment of this court is that the judgment of the circuit court be affirmed.

McGowan, J., concurs.

BUENA VISTA MANUF'G CO. *et al.* v. CHAT-
TANOOGA DOOR & SASH CO. *et al.*

(*Supreme Court of Georgia.* July 20, 1891.)

INJUNCTION—DISCRETION OF TRIAL COURT.

It not appearing that there was any abuse
of discretion by the court below in granting an
injunction and appointing a receiver, the judgment is affirmed.

(*Syllabus by the Court.*)

Error from superior court, Marion county; ALLEN FORT, Judge.

Petition by the Chattanooga Door &
Sash Company, Wallace McPherson, and
D. C. Jones, against the Buena Vista Manufacturing Company and others, for a receiver and an injunction. Petition granted, and defendants bring error. Affirmed.

The official report is as follows:

The exception in this case is to the
granting of an injunction against the defendants, and the appointment of a receiver of the property of the Buena Vista
Manufacturing Company. Complainants
were the Chattanooga Door & Sash Company, Wallace McPherson, and D. C. Jones.
By their petition they alleged that the
Buena Vista Manufacturing Company, a
corporation, owed the Chattanooga Door
& Sash Company $1,369.49, on two promis-
sory notes, neither of which was due when
the petition was presented. These notes
were secured by a mortgage on the land
of the manufacturing company, describing
it, together with the buildings on said
land, and its machinery, lumber, sash,
doors, blinds, etc. The manufacturing
company is indebted to McPherson $400,
due and unpaid, and owes Jones ——
dollars upon open account, which is overdue and unpaid. On April 16, 1891, the
manufacturing company made to M. R.
Edwards a deed of assignment of all of
its property. Under this deed of assignment there are certain preferred creditors,
to-wit: (1) The attorney of the corporation, whose claim is not set out, and is
unliquidated, and other employes and
agents of the corporation, whose names
are not set out, and whose demands are
not liquidated. (2) The Americus Iron-
Works, in the sum of $2,000, upon ten notes,
already secured by mortgage. (4) The
Planters' Bank of Ellaville, $515, upon an
unsecured note, and M. R. Edwards $408.80,
upon an unsecured note. (5) The Buena
Vista Loan & Savings Bank $800, upon four
unsecured notes. Under the deed of assignment the property mortgaged to the
Chattanooga Door & Sash Company is
conveyed to the assignee, and he is empowered and authorized to convert it into
money, and pay the money arising from
the sale on the preferred claims in the deed
of assignment, and the assignee is endeavoring to sell the property at private sale.
If he is allowed to sell the property, most
of which is personalty and portable, and
a portion of which is perishable, it can
and will be moved, and thereby the door
and sash company will be defeated in the
collection of its claim and the enforcement
of its lien. The assignee will sell the
property unless enjoined. The mortgage
of the door and sash company on the real
estate of the corporation is not valid
against innocent purchasers for value, be-

cause it was only attested by one witness; but it is a valid subsisting lien
against the assignor and assignee, and, if
the assignee is allowed to sell the land to
an innocent purchaser, the right of petitioner would be jeopardized and defeated.
The assignee is about to sell all of the property in bulk, and is directed in the assignment to pay the proceeds to the preferred
creditors, one of whom (the Americus
Iron-Works) is preferred both by mortgage on a portion of the property embraced in the mortgage of petitioner and
by the assignment; and it would be inequitable and unjust to allow the assignee
to convert all the property into cash, and
give the preferred creditors the benefit of
a fund arising from the sale of property
upon which petitioner had a legal subsisting lien before the execution of the assignment. By selling the property in bulk, petitioner would be deprived of the right to
foreclose its mortgage, and recover the
amount due thereon. The property assigned is not of sufficient value to cover
the preferred claims and the claim of this
petitioner. The assignment is void for
the following reasons: The Planters'
Bank of Ellaville is not a creditor of the
assignor in any sum whatever. A full and
complete schedule of the liabilities of the
corporation is not set out, in that the assignor failed to set out a list of the stockholders in the corporation; it failed to set
out the true amount due by the corporation on open account to the Americus
Iron-Works, the true amount being $23,
and the amount set out being $10. The
assignor undertakes to make preferred
creditors of the attorney and of the employes, whose names are not set out, nor
is any indebtedness to them shown. The
corporation is hopelessly insolvent, and
was so when it executed the deed of assignment. The assignment is also void
because W. C. Singleton owes the assignor
$500, which indebtedness is not set out or
disclosed in the deed of assignment and
schedule annexed, and there are other
creditors of the corporation whose names
are not set out, nor the amount due them.
The property of the assignor consists
largely of buildings, machinery, lumber,
and the like, near to the railroad, and liable to be destroyed by fire at any time,
and there is very little or no insurance on
it, and the assignee is unable to get insurance, not being authorized so to do in the
deed of assignment, so that the creditors
are in danger of losing their claims altogether. The assignment should be set
aside for the following additional reasons:
The schedule of liabilities filed in connection with it fails to set out an indebtedness of $280 by note to M. R. Edwards, or
bearer, executed by S. N. Rushin, and
indorsed by the assignor, by its president;
and a note for $700 to the same payee, and
with the same indorsement, executed by
W. R. Hair as maker; and a note for $168,
with the same payee and indorsement, executed by J. R. Little as maker; and a
note for $112, with the same payee and in-
dorsement, executed by W. H. Crawford
as maker. The makers of these notes
were stockholders and directors of the assignor, and the amounts expressed in the

notes, less certain interest, were due by them to the assignor for their unpaid subscriptions to the capital stock of said corporation. Being unable to pay the sums, they executed and delivered to the assignor these notes, and its president, in order to realize upon them, procured Edwards to discount them, and, in pursuance of this agreement, the corporation authorized its president to indorse the notes, whereby it became indebted to Edwards $1,271.20. The schedule of liabilities fails to set out as creditors certain other persons mentioned, to whom it was indebted. The assignor was also indebted to its president $412.73 for salary as such, which debt is not set out in the schedule. The schedule sets out an indebtedness of $309.32 to one Little, when the corporation only owed him $179. The assignment is void, also, because it was executed and delivered by the president of the corporation without authority of the stockholders or board of directors, and without authority of law. Petitioners prayed that the assignor and assignee and the preferred cerditors be made parties defendant; that the deed of assignment be set aside; for injunction, receiver, etc. The petition was presented, and a temporary restraining order granted, and a temporary receiver appointed, and rule to show cause issued on May 2, 1891. The deed of assignment was executed April 16, 1891.

Defendants, by way of demurrer and answer, alleged: The manufacturing company ceased to do business on April 16, 1891, and when the petition was presented were not manufacturers and traders, within the meaning of section 3149f of the Code of 1882, and during the continuance of the company it did not at any time manufacture articles to the extent of $5,000. Its indebtedness to the door and sash company is secured, and not due. Its indebtedness to McPherson and Jones is only $675, which is not one-third of the unsecured liabilities of the assignor, as shown by the deed of assignment. It is not true that the Planters' Bank of Ellaville is not a creditor of the assignor. The deed of assignment was executed and delivered under the direction and by authority of the officers, directors, and stockholders of the assignor, and was full and complete of all the property of the assignor, they making no claim, as stockholders or otherwise, to the same. The assignment sets out in full a list of all the creditors, with the amounts due them, so far as the same was known, or could be ascertained, at the time it was made. The names of the employes and the amounts due them at the time of the assignment are set forth therein, and, as to the attorney and other employes, there was no sum due them when the assignment was made; the preference given them being for any services which they might hereafter render by way of current expenses for services or wages in running, shaping up, and putting in order the machinery or other property of the assignor. The deed of assignment was made in good faith, without any intention to hinder, delay, or defraud creditors. W. C. Singleton does not owe defendant $500,

or any amount whatever, except that set forth in the assignment. The property is insured to the extent that insurance could be procured, and the assignee has given good and valid bond in the sum of $12,000. It is not true that Rushin, Hair, and Little executed their notes to the assignor, which were afterwards discounted by it to Edwards, and which were indorsed by it. Hair, Crawford, Rushin, and Little were stockholders in the corporation, and owed it, for unpaid stock subscriptions, an amount equal to the notes referred to; and, desiring to pay the indebtedness, negotiated with Edwards through Singleton, the president of the corporation, for a loan of money wherewith to pay up the stock, and Edwards made the loan to them for that purpose, taking their promissory notes, which notes were indorsed by Singleton, president. Hair, Crawford, Little, and Rushin are all solvent, and able to pay their notes promptly, and no liabilities will accrue to the corporation by reason of the indorsement, and, if it is liable at all on the notes, it is only as surety. The corporation is not now, and was not when the deed of assignment was made, indebted to Singleton $412.73. It does owe Little $309.32.

Upon the hearing for injunction and receiver, much testimony was introduced. It was admitted that the copy deed of assignment attached to the answer of defendant was correct, and that the manufacturing company had, by its president, indorsed the notes of Crawford, Rushin, Hair, and Little, which was an accommodation indorsement, and without any consideration. Briefly stated, the testimony for petitioners was to the following effect: The indebtedness of the manufacturing company to the door and sash company is as has been stated above, and was secured as stated. The assignee was endeavoring to sell all the assets of the assignor after the assignment was made, and most of the property upon which the door and sash company had a mortgage was personal and portable, and a portion of it was perishable. The assignee stated at first that there was no insurance on the property, and that he could procure none, but afterwards said there was insurance on the property to the amount of $1,500, but he refused to exhibit the policy to an officer of the door and sash company. The manufacturing company is insolvent, and was when the assignment was made, and Singleton stated on April 4, 1891, that he owed it $500, unpaid subscription to the capital stock. On April 16, 1891, J. J. Kemp was a creditor to the amount of $7.50 for labor performed; J. H. Wall to the amount of $5.50; F. M. Orr to the amount of $17.00; C. H. Willis to the amount of $7.50; Robert Heard to the amount of $6.50; Jesse Wilcher to the amount of $12; Irwin Smith to the amount of $5.50; and W. B. Short, clerk of the superior court, $6.00. These debts are not set forth in the schedule to the deed of assignment. S. H. Christopher does not owe the assignor $134, as stated in the deed of assignment, but only $105. When the assignment was made, S. N. Rushin owned stock which was paid up, and the corporation owed him $10.20. Singleton owed the corporation $500 upon stock subscription, which was to be settled by the amount due him for salary, and a resolution to that effect was passed by the directors. The notes above mentioned of Rushin, Crawford, and others were indorsed by Singleton, as president, by authority of the board of directors of the corporation, and they are unpaid. The temporary receiver called on the assignee, and requested him to deliver the assets, and the assignee turned over certain money and books, but has failed to turn over the book of minutes belonging to the corporation, or the minutes in any other form, and diligent search in its safe for evidence of minutes upon sheets of paper, or in any form, has failed to discover them. The temporary receiver has had the property of the company insured for $7,500. A. J. Taylor did not owe the assignor $184.91, but only owed $54.20, while it owed him a much larger sum, to-wit, $70.-50, by way of damages for violation of contract. The indebtedness of Taylor is stated in the schedule attached to the assignment to be $84.91. In the schedule Mrs. Thorpe is stated as indebted $476, when in truth she was only indebted $225. W. H. Carr was indebted only $200, or thereabouts, instead of $350. (In the schedule, as transmitted in the record, Carr's name does not appear.) J. B. Johnson was only indebted $90.63, instead of $103.95, as stated in the assignment. W. D. Benson was not a creditor of the assignor $163, as set out in the assignment, but it only owed him $10 or $12.

The evidence for defendants was in brief: The assignor does owe the Planters' Bank of Ellaville $515.45, by a promissory note, for loaned money. The stockholders and directors of the assignor never kept a book of minutes. Its secretary often requested its president to furnish a book, but it was never done, and the minutes were kept only in an informal way, on loose sheets of paper, which were left in the safe of the assignor, and the safe, including books and papers of all kinds, the secretary is informed and believes, has been turned over to the temporary receiver by the assignee. The secretary, as book-keeper of the assignor, was called upon by the officers, at the time the assignment was made, to make out and furnish to the attorney who drew the deed of assignment a complete list of the creditors, with the amounts due them, which he earnestly endeavored to do, and believes he did do. He represented to the attorney that the assignor owed the American Iron-Works $10.50, which was the amount of the purchases made by the assignor of it on open account, as by statement rendered by it to the assignor, and, if a mistake was made in not setting forth the correct amount, it was the fault of the iron-works company, and not of defendant. The deed of assignment sets forth the names and amounts due to the employes by the assignor, so far as was possible for the book-keeper, or any of the officers of the assignor, to have ascertained the same. The book-keeper was called upon, on or before the 16th day of April, which was

Thursday, to furnish a statement of the indebtedness, and at that time did furnish a correct statement of all the existing liabilities of the defendant. It employed its hands by the day and week, to be paid off each Saturday afternoon, and some of the employes would lose time during the week, a record of which was kept by the superintendent, and turned over to the book-keeper each Saturday afternoon, that he might settle with them according to the time they had worked. On the Thursday the assignment was made, the book-keeper had no knowledge of how much was due the employes in the way of current expenses, and could not have known, but they were few in number, and the total amount accruing to and due them on the last week of their work was not over $60, and provision is made for their payment in the deed of assignment as well as it was possible to have done. The difference between the amount set out in the assignment as due to Benson and the amount really due him was caused by the fact that just prior to the assignment he collected some money for the corporation with which he credited his account, and Singleton gave him an order for $175, which facts were unknown to the secretary of the company, who made out the schedules, and Benson is satisfied with the assignment. So are Wall, Johnson, Kemp, and Wilcher, employes of the company. Crawford, Hair, and Rushin are each perfectly solvent, and have sufficient property to insure the payment of the debt they owe Edwards, and for which the assignor is security or indorser. The debt of $6 due to Short, the clerk of the superior court, is due him as a fee for recording the deed of assignment. The assignee has never seen the book of minutes of the assignor, and it has never been in his custody, power, or control.

M. H. Blandford, W. D. Crawford, and *Thornton & McMichael,* for plaintiffs in error. *Clark & Hooper, B. P. Hollis,* and *Butt & Lumpkin,* for defendants in error.

Judgment affirmed.

HOBBS et al. v. SHEFFIELD et al.

(Supreme Court of Georgia. July 8, 1891.)

INSOLVENCY—RECEIVERS — INJUNCTION—TRADERS.

1. Under the facts of this case, the defendant Odom was not a trader at the time the suit praying for injunction and receiver was brought. Comer v. Coates, 69 Ga. 491; Blanchard v. Vansyckle, 70 Ga. 278; Coates v. Allen, 71 Ga. 787; Scott v. Jones, 74 Ga. 762; Kimbrell v. Walters, (Ga.) 12 S. E. Rep. 305.

2. The judgment enjoining the mortgage *fi. fas.,* and appointing a receiver as to the property levied upon and advertised for sale, is reversed, with direction that, in case the proceeds of sale should yield to Hobbs and Tucker more than $4,900, with interest and attorney's fees thereon, the excess be held up to await the result of this litigation; and the judgment appointing a receiver as to the other effects in controversy is affirmed.

(Syllabus by the Court.)

Error from superior court, Lee county; ALLEN FORT, Judge.

This bill of exceptions was taken by Hobbs et al., preferred mortgage creditors of Odom, a merchant, to the grant of as injunction and the appointment of a receiver upon the petition of Sheffield and six other unsecured creditors, to which petition were filed answers by Odom and by the plaintiffs in error, and an answer in the nature of a cross-petition by Weston et al., second mortgage creditors. It appears that on April 8th Odom made four mortgages: (1) To Lucy A. Odom, covering other property than his stock of goods, such as real estate, cows, horses, etc., to secure notes due one day after date for the sum total of $2,000; (2) to Hobbs and eleven other creditors, to secure them in the aggregate sum of $7,850 and 10 per cent. attorney's fees, covering his entire stock of goods, wares, merchandise, books, notes, and accounts, his storehouse and two vacant lots, but not covering the same realty and personalty described in the mortgage to Lucy A. Odom; (3) to Randall and five others, to secure them in the aggregate sum of $400 clerk hire and 10 per cent. attorney's fees, covering the same property described in the Hobbs mortgage, and to be equal in dignity to it and superior to the one about to be mentioned; (4) to Weston and nine others, to secure them in the aggregate sum of $8,942.69 and 10 per cent. attorney's fees, due the day of its date, covering the same property described in the Hobbs mortgage, and known as the "second mortgage." On April 9th, the Hobbs and Weston mortgages were foreclosed on the personalty described therein, by separate affidavits of ten of the mortgagees in the Hobbs mortgage, and of four of the mortgagees in the Weston mortgage. The other two mortgagees in the Hobbs mortgage made affidavits to foreclose on the personalty on April 10th and 16th, respectively, and on April 14th one of the other five mortgagees in the Weston mortgage made a similar affidavit. All these affidavits were attached to the mortgages to which they related, and were filed in the clerk's office, and executions were issued and levied. The petition of Sheffield et al. was presented on April 18th, and it contained these allegations: The sheriff, acting under an order of the ordinary, advertised the stock of goods for sale on April 20th, and would on that day proceed to sell the same, unless restrained. Odom's assets consist of the stock of goods of the nominal value of fifteen or twenty thousand dollars, and about the same amount of notes and accounts; and his liabilities amount to something over $40,000. It is his manifest intention to have the stock of goods sold at a sacrifice. His purpose is to hinder, delay, and defraud his creditors; and the creditors named in the Hobbs mortgage are aiding him in his efforts to have said property sold. Many of the creditors live at a distance, and have had no time to investigate the condition of his affairs, or to arrange to be present at the sale so as to make the property bring its value. If the sale is allowed to proceed, the property will not bring half its value. Odom executed mortgages on other property in favor of his wife and his mother-in-law, and these mortgages are fraudulent and void. In the present situation it is impossible for petitioners or any unsecured creditor to gain any information as to the true *status* of Odom's business; and a receiver could sell the stock of goods to much better advantage than the sheriff, could more readily collect and preserve the assets belonging to Odom, and could, by authority of the court, compel him to pay over any moneys in his possession. He fraudulently procured the goods for which he owes one of the petitioners about ten days before the failure, by a statement that he had in value two dollars for every one he owed. Said goods were to be paid for in cash as soon as delivered. Odom answered, admitting the indebtedness claimed by the petitioners and his insolvency. He alleged that he executed the mortgages in good faith, to secure the several parties *bona fide* debts which he owed them. All of his property was included in the mortgages. Not one dollar was reserved. Everything that he could think of was included, so that his creditors could have the benefit of the same. It is not true that he is attempting to hinder or delay any of his creditors, but he has done, and is willing to do, anything in his power to enable them to get their money. Nor is it true that the mortgage creditors are aiding and abetting him in any such arrangement or efforts. There is no combination, agreement, or understanding between him and the mortgagees. He made the mortgages to secure the payment of just and *bona fide* debts. The after-action of the mortgagees was not precipitated or instigated, or even suggested, by him, and he had nothing to do with having the mortgages foreclosed. The mortgagees had a careful inventory of the whole stock made, divided it into desirable lots, and advertised the sale freely, which brought a large number of merchants from neighboring towns; and if the property had been sold as advertised, it would have sold well and for its full market value. The mortgages to secure respondent's wife and mother-in-law were for money paid to him in good faith, and used by him in his business; and he was bound in honor to secure the same. There was no fraud or intention of fraud about it. He denies that he has any moneys in his hands, or reserved or held back anything of value which he has not turned over to the sheriff or included in the mortgages. He bought the goods referred to at the close of the petition on thirty days' time; and he positively denies that he made a statement to the effect that he had in value two dollars for every one he owed, because there was no occasion to make the statement, the creditor not objecting to sell him the goods at the time. He bought them in good faith, expecting to pay for them; but afterwards, when pressed by a Savannah firm on some guano debts, he investigated his affairs, and, finding himself badly embarrassed, secured the creditors set forth in the mortgages in the utmost good faith, and without any fraudulent intent whatever. Hobbs et al. made similar allegations as to the good faith and absence of fraud or of any combination between them and Odom. They foreclosed their mortgages for the purpose of collecting their claims, and had the *fi. fas.* put into the sheriff's hands for enforcement. If he had been allowed to proceed with the sale as advertised, they believe the property would have sold for its full market value. They object to the appointment of a receiver because the sheriff is both competent and efficient, and as well qualified to sell the property levied on as any one else. A receiver will result in additional fees and expenses, amounting to deducting from their already insufficient security a large sum of money which should go to their claims. It is their good fortune to be secured by Odom without any undue influence or improper conduct on their part; and that the petitioners were left out of the mortgage is no reason why respondents should be damaged by them by delay, expenses of receivership, etc. Respondents are amply solvent, and able to respond to any suit or judgment petitioners may obtain against them; and they do not wish any assistance to collect their debts other than from the attorneys whom they have employed and by the process of foreclosure they instituted. The personalty levied on is not sufficient to pay the debts included in the mortgages, and therefore the petitioners can have no interest in it. The petitioners filed an amendment alleging as follows: In December, 1890, Odom, his book-keeper, and one Bridler, carefully went over Odom's books to ascertain the amount of his indebtedness; and it amounted to $17,-013.26. He has not bought since that time more than $2,000 worth of goods, and has borrowed about $14,000, besides such amounts as have been received from sales of goods. Petitioners believe he has been receiving all the cash he could from every source, and that a small amount of the same has been paid on his liabilities, and the balance is now in his hands, or those of some one for him, and ought to be paid to his creditors. On the 8th and 9th of April he removed from his store dry goods and groceries to the amount of twelve or fifteen hundred dollars, all of which should be appropriated to his creditors, and is now in his power, custody, and control. A few days before the mortgages were given he stated that he did not owe Hobbs and Tucker anything, but had paid them all he owed, and they would not loan him any money; and since the 9th of April he has stated that his creditors thought he was a fool, for he was fixed all right, and was able to go into business again. Petitioners believe that the amounts represented by the mortgages are not just and *bona fide.* The whole transaction is in such shape that it is impossible to get at the truth of it without the appointment of a receiver with power to make a thorough investigation of the matter.

The answer and cross-petition of Weston et al. alleges as follows: The amount due them by Odom, with interest, aggregates the sum of $9,750.69. On April 8th, Odom, finding himself unable to proceed in business, and feeling under special obligations to respondents, and to Hobbs & Tucker, and others mentioned in the mortgage, expressed his desire to prefer his creditors, and with that intention conferred with his attorney, Hobbs, who is a member of the firm of Hobbs & Tucker, the principal creditors of Odom. He stated to Hobbs that he was in a failing condition, owed more than he could pay, and desired to make an assignment; that he could not pay all his debts, but felt particularly bound to Hobbs & Tucker and to respondents; that he desired to put them on an equal footing; and that to this end he wished to make an assignment, giving preference as stated. Hobbs advised him that it was difficult to make an assignment that would stand the test, and that it would be better and simpler for him to prefer his creditors by mortgage. To this advice Odom yielded, yet declaring his intention to put the creditors mentioned on an equal footing of preference. When the mortgage was about to be written, it was suggested by some one present that, as there would be enough to pay all the creditors mentioned, it would be less complicated (or something to that effect) to have two mortgages; that it would amount to the same thing. Odom replied that he was willing any way, so that the creditors mentioned were made safe and preferred alike. Though none of respondents were present or cognizant of what was going on, still they were made beneficiaries of one of the mortgages, all of which they ratified on the assurance that there would be enough to pay both mortgages, and that both sets of mortgagees should fare alike and be paid alike. Respondents deny any fraud, combination, or complicity with Odom or any one else in the procurement of the mortgages. Aside from the money received by Odom in the regular line of his business, there have, since January 1, 1891, come into his hands about $15,000, consisting of $4,000 from Hobbs & Tucker, $5,050 from two of respondents, and the balance from the Commercial Bank in Albany; but the most rigid and exhaustive search fails to show any trace or entry on his books showing what became of said money, or any part of it, nor has he given respondents any satisfaction or information with regard to it. Since the making of the mortgages, and his declaration of his failure, he entered into a conspiracy whereby more than $1,000 worth of goods were taken from his store at night and carried away. It was his intention to make an assignment or such instrument as would put respondents on the same footing with Hobbs & Tucker; and he persisted in that intention, and was only prevented from carrying it into effect by the influence of Hobbs & Tucker. In the light of the confidential relations between the parties, this was a legal wrong, especially since it turns out that the assets are barely sufficient to pay the amounts named in the Hobbs mortgage; and especially will this be true if the amounts are permitted to stand as therein named, for the amounts which Hobbs & Tucker held against Odom did not exceed $4,200, which was not to become due until next fall, as respondents are advised. Yet Hobbs & Tucker have taken their mortgage for $5,000, besides attorney's fees, which is unjust to respondents. They pray that Odom be required to pay over to the receiver said $15,000 so received by him, and to turn over to the receiver all the goods which he caused or permitted to be taken from the store after making the mortgages; and that, upon final hearing, the court will decree that the so-called distinction between the two mortgages in question be abolished, and respondents be placed on the same footing with Hobbs & Tucker, and that the claim of the latter, and all other claims, be reduced to proper amounts.

At the hearing there were affidavits tending to sustain the allegations of the amended petition, except as to Odom's saying that his creditors thought he was a fool, and that he did not owe Hobbs & Tucker anything. His book-keeper testified that, in his opinion, if the goods had been sold as advertised by the sheriff, they would not have brought more than 25 cents on the dollar; that, in his opinion, a receiver with authority to find purchasers could make the stock net 75 or 80 cents on the dollar; and that the stock invoiced over $16,000. Affidavits of respondents tended to show that the mortgages were drafted in strict accordance with Odom's instructions; that he called out the names and amounts that were put in the first mortgage, and so as to the second; that all were written exactly as he indicated they should be; that the roll of creditors was called, and he dictated in which mortgage the different creditors were placed, and the number 1 or 2 was placed opposite the several names as he called them out, and the mortgages were carefully read over to him before they were signed; and that Hobbs used no influence, directly or indirectly, to have him make the mortgages as he did, and explained to him that to make them as he did would be simpler than to make an assignment.

The points made by the exceptions are as follows: (1) Under the law and evidence, the judge should not have enjoined the fi. fas. from proceeding, and should not have put the property in the hands of a receiver. (2) The evidence shows that plaintiffs in error are amply solvent; that Odom is insolvent; that the stock of goods would not bring more than sufficient to pay their mortgage claims and those of others; and that no good can come to the unsecured creditors by receiver and injunction, as they will get nothing from the stock of goods in any event. (3) The order of the judge gives to the receiver power to run and continue the business of Odom, which has proved a failure in Odom's hands, and in this particular the order is improvident, and an abuse of discretion. (4) The evidence shows that plaintiffs in error are bona fide creditors and mortgagees; that their mortgages were properly foreclosed; and that the fi. fas. were properly issued, and legally proceeding against an insolvent; and that there was no defense against them, and none suggested by the defendants in error. (5) Odom had ceased to be a trader several days before the petition for receiver was filed, the sheriff having closed him up and taken possession of his

v.13s.e.no.28—44

stock under levy of the mortgage fi. fas. In connection with the third point, it may be stated that the judge's order requires the receiver to maintain policies of insurance on the stock of goods; to take notes and mortgages from the debtors of Odom where such notes and mortgages were to have been given; to do and perform all acts necessary for the collection and preservation of the assets of Odom; and to proceed to sell the stock of goods and other property for cash, either at public outcry or privately, and in such quantities as in his discretion may be to the interest of the parties. In the matter of sale he is given full discretion to the end that the property may be sold to the best possible advantage, and he is expected to exercise the discretion wisely, and to adopt such plans as will realize the best possible prices for the property in his hands.

R. Hobbs and W. I. Jones, for plaintiffs in error. J. W. Walters, B. P. Hollis, Wooten & Wooten, Simmons & Kimbrough, and Harrison & Peeples, for defendants in error.

Reversed in part; affirmed in part.

LUMPKIN, J., not presiding.

JACKSON v. STATE.

(Supreme Court of Georgia. July 8, 1891.)

DISTURBING PUBLIC WORSHIP—JOINT INDICTMENT —EVIDENCE.

Where two are charged in one count of the same indictment with a misdemeanor committed by disturbing a congregation of persons assembled for divine service, in order to convict both, the evidence of guilt must apply to one and the same transaction. Two separate and independent transactions on the same day, at the same church, will not support the indictment; one of the accused having disturbed the congregation at 12 o'clock and the other at 1 o'clock, and there being no concert or connection between the two offenders.

(Syllabus by the Court.)

Error from superior court, Houston county; GEORGE F. GOBER, Judge.

Prosecution against Jackson, Lane, Pattishall, Haywood Glenn, and Cameron Glenn, jointly, for disturbing a religious meeting. The Glenns were granted a severance, and the others were tried jointly. Lane was acquitted, and Pattishall and Jackson convicted, and judgment entered. Jackson brings error. Reversed.

The official report is as follows:

Jackson, Lane, Pattishall, and Haywood and Cameron Glenn were accused, jointly, of the offense of disturbing a congregation of persons lawfully assembled for divine service at Green Grove Baptist Church, Houston county, "by cursing, or using profane or obscene language, or by being intoxicated, or otherwise indecently acting." The case was called for trial in the county court of Houston county, and all of the defendants pleaded not guilty. The two Glenns were granted a severance, and the other defendants were put on trial under the accusation. Jackson and Pattishall were found guilty, and Lane not guilty. Jackson took the case by certiorari to the superior court, alleging that the evidence failed to show that the congregation assembled for divine service at Green Grove Baptist Church were disturbed and interrupted, as set out in the accusation, or that Richard Jackson so interrupted and disturbed the congregation, because Richard Jackson was accused jointly with the others, and the evidence failed to show that in any manner, in connection with, or jointly with, any or all of the others, were any of the things charged in the accusation against them done by defendant; but the evidence showed that, if he did anything that interrupted and disturbed the congregation, it was done by himself alone, not jointly or in connection with either or all of the other defendants, but at a different time and place from any act or deed proven or charged against either, any or all of the defendants; because the evidence showed that, if he did any act to disturb the congregation, it was an act separate and distinct from that charged against him in the accusation, and for which he cannot be legally adjudged guilty under the accusation; because the verdict and judgment are contrary to law, evidence, etc.; and because the fine of $100 imposed upon him was excessive. The *certiorari* was overruled, to which he excepted. The evidence introduced by the state in the county court was in substance as follows: There were a great many people assembled at divine services at Green Grove Baptist Church. The church was crowded, there being many outside of the church, standing near it, and near the windows of the church, to hear the sermon, and others were scattered around. About 12 o'clock, while preaching was going on, Jackson was standing about 56 steps from the church, and a big crowd was around him, and one Parker, who was not in the church, but outside, having been appointed to keep order among those on the grounds, heard him cursing. Parker was near the church, and did not see or hear Jackson until Parker's wife, who had been to the spring, and come back by Jackson, came to Parker, and told him to go down and quiet Jackson. Parker went down where Jackson was, and was about 12 yards from him, and heard him cursing terribly. Parker did not know who he was cursing. The people were trying to get him off home. He cursed loud enough to be heard twice as far as the church, and disturbed the people in the church. Some of the people came out of the church, and came down there. The people were going in and out of the church all the time. No one was then making any disturbance but Jackson. One of the deacons, who was sitting on the bench near the pulpit, heard Jackson cursing, and he testified that it disturbed the congregation, and some of them went out. About 1 o'clock, and before the close of the services, this deacon heard Pattishall cursing. Pattishall was about 10 steps from the door of the church, and, as Haywood Glenn passed by with a plate, put his hand in the plate to take some of the provisions, and Haywood spoke to him about it, and Pattishall cursed him. This cursing disturbed the congregation, several getting up and coming to the door, and

looking out, to see what was the matter. What Jackson was cursing about was that he had ridden one of Alfred Lane's mules from the spring to the church, and, while he was sitting on the mule, Alfred told him to go and tie it. He did not go right off, and Alfred untied one side of the bridle rein, which made Jackson mad, and he cursed, and told Alfred to show him where he wanted the mule tied, and he would tie it, and Alfred tied the rein again, and went off, and Jackson rode the mule a few yards, and tied it; got off the mule, and went to cursing. He was not cursing any one, but was just mad, and cursing. Alfred Lane was not present, and made no disturbance. One of the state's witnesses testified that he was in the church, on the seats near the pulpit, and did not hear any disturbance. Evidence was introduced by the defendant, and Jackson and Pattishall both made statements not necessary to be reported.

R. N. Holtzclaw, for plaintiff in error. *W. C. Davis,* and *W. H. Felton, Jr.,* Sol. Gen., for the State.

SIMMONS, J. The facts will be found in the official report. The opinion of the court is fully set out in the head-note. For a full discussion of the principle announced, see the following authorities. Some of them go beyond what we think is the true law: Stephens v. State, 14 Ohio, 386; Elliott v. State, 26 Ala. 78; Lindsey v. State, 48 Ala. 169; Johnson v. State, 13 Ark. 684; Com. v. McChord, 2 Dana, 242; 1 Bish. Crim. Proc. §§ 470, 473; Whart. Crim. Pl. §§ 302, 307. 315, 874; Lewellen v. State, 18 Tex. 538; Com. v. Cobb, 14 Gray, 57; 1 Bish. Crim. Law, § 802; Rex v. Messingham, 1 Moody. Cr. Cas. 257; Reg. v. Dovey, 2 Eng. Law & Eq. 532; Reg. v. Barber, 1 Car. & K. 442; Rex v. Hempstead, 1 Russ. & R. 343; 2 Rosc. Crim. Ev. 916 et seq.; 1 Chit. Crim. Law, *270. Judgment reversed.

LUMPKIN, J., not presiding.

BERRY v. STATE.

(Supreme Court of Georgia. July 13, 1891.)

RAPE—EVIDENCE—NEW TRIAL—APPEAL.

1. No ground of objection to evidence being stated, the alleged error in admitting it is not examinable.

2. The evidence as to the identity of the accused was sufficient, notwithstanding it was possible for the prosecutrix to have been mistaken.

3. As the evidence showed the consummation of the offense of rape, it was not incumbent upon the court to charge the jury on the minor offense of an assault with intent to rape.

4. The so-called newly-discovered evidence was not newly-discovered; and that the accused did not know of its materiality, and his counsel were ignorant of it as a fact, is not cause for a new trial.

(Syllabus by the Court.)

Error from superior court, Henry county; J. S. BOYNTON, Judge.

Prosecution against John Berry for rape. Defendant was convicted and sentenced to death, and, his motion for a new trial being denied, he brings error. Affirmed.

The official report is as follows:

Berry was convicted of rape, and was sentenced to death. He excepted to the denial of a new trial, the grounds of his motion being as follows: (1) Verdict contrary to law. (2) Verdict contrary to evidence and law, in that the evidence does not sufficiently identify the defendant as the person who committed the crime. (3) Error in admitting the following testimony of Glass: "Arrested persons on a description given me by Miss Dunn; Miss Dunn gave me the description,"—the effect of which testimony was to put before the jury declarations made by Miss Dunn the next day after the alleged rape was committed. (4) Error in failing to charge the jury on the law of an attempt to commit a rape. (5) Newly-discovered evidence.

Ann Dunn testified that the crime was committed in the county and in the month charged in the indictment. That the defendant came to her house in that month. "He came to the door, and tried to get it open. This waked me up. I struck a match, and light a torch or splinter. He then came round to the other door, and broke it open, and come in, and grabbed me by the throat, and told me if I hollowed he would kill me. He dragged me out of the door. I saw he was going to kill me. He choked me down,—choked me to death. I did not know anything until I got back into the house. He done what he wanted to. He choked me down, and first I knew he was getting up. He raped me. I examined myself. He entered my person. I could tell by my feelings when I got up. He was down on the ground choking me. He got my clothes up. Don't have any idea how long he was on me. He helped me up, and carried me back into the house, and left me lying there. He hurt my throat. No one else was in the house. In about fifteen minutes I got to Mr. Moore's house. It was about twelve o'clock at night. It was about twelve o'clock the next day before I saw him again. I saw him by a light that night. I never saw him before that night." Cross-examined: "I am not married. I live at Tunis station, on the East Tennessee road. I live about 50 yards from the railroad. It is about 50 yards from the railroad. It is about 50 yards to the public road. I work for Mr. Moore for a living, and live about 50 yards from him. I went to Mr. Moore, and told him what had happened that night after the defendant left. There are some negroes living on Mr. Moore's place. I think the time the thing occurred was at night, between ten and twelve o'clock. * * * My attention was first aroused by the door opening. I got up, struck a match, and he broke open the other door. When he tried to open the front door a button fell, and I got up and struck a match and light a splinter. I was excited. Just as I lit the splinter he grabbed me. While I was striking a light he went around to the other door, and broke it open. I held the splinter in my hand. The defendant was about two steps from me when I first saw him. He just made two steps, and grabbed me. It was a moderately dark night. I did not see him any more that night. * * * He was dressed in a blue coat and pants and a cap. * * * He said, 'I am going to kill you.' I saw the defendant next day at Tunis. He was then in charge of Mr. Glass. When Mr. Glass brought him up, I said, 'That is the negro.' He had on the same clothes I saw that night. There was no peculiarity about the negro that differed from other negroes. * * * When the negro left me he went on up the railroad towards Atlanta. He was walking." Moore testified that about 10 o'clock that night, or between 9 and 10, Ann Dunn came to his house, scared nearly to death, and said a negro had committed rape on her; that her throat was bruised like she had been choked; that the defendant, when he left her house, went across the railroad track in direction of Jonesboro, and he did not go in direction of McDonough, where he was arrested; that it is five miles from Tunis to McDonough, and two miles from Tunis to rock-quarry; and that there were a number of hands employed there at the time of the crime. Glass, the sheriff, testified: "I arrested John Berry next morning after the night the rape was committed. Arrested him here in the depot at McDonough. Several loungers sitting around. I arrested him on the description given me by Miss Dunn. He did not have on a cap when I arrested him. He had on a hat. He had a cap in his bundle when I carried him to Tunis. I searched his bundle. He had an old valise, and the cap fell out a pair of pants legs that were in the valise. I put the cap on his head. Miss Dunn said he was the right negro. When I arrested him he said he had been at work at the rock-quarry. The rock-quarry is about three miles above Tunis. It was about eight or nine o'clock when I arrested him. He said he was waiting to take the freight-train to Juliette. * * * He never made any effort or attempt to escape. Miss Dunn did not recognize the defendant at first; but when I put the cap on his head she then said he was the man. Passengers then sitting around. His cap was in the valise in a pair of pants. There were a great many negroes employed at the rock-quarry; some of them were bad characters. I suppose he said he had been up there at work, and had been there to get his money." Prisoner's statement: "My home is down at Juliette, about 4 miles from Juliette. I had been at work up at the rock-quarry, and went up there to get my money from Mr. Hall. I could not see the boss man, and I went back the next day. Then he said would not pay off till the end of the quarter; said next Wednesday or Thursday the pay-train would come along. The cap I had I got from one of the hands. I worked for it. All the hands wore caps. This woman I never saw before. I did not know nobody up here. I passed Tunis that evening about sundown, and went right on down the railroad track to near the water-tank, and laid down and went to sleep above the depot. We hands all rides on the local, and I was waiting there to take it home. I never saw this woman before. I have got a family in Monroe. I am a farmer, and live in Dillard's district,—

think that's what they call it. Mr. John Chamlin and George Taylor live there." The newly-discovered evidence was by the justice of the peace who presided on the preliminary trial of the defendant. He made affidavit that when he, as a court, was examining Ann Dunn as a witness, he put this question to her: "When John Berry had you down, did he do what he wanted to?" to which she replied, "He tried to;" and that this was all she swore to on said trial in regard to the defendant entering her person or having any sexual intercourse with her. The defendant's counsel represented him by appointment made on the afternoon of the day before the trial. They did not know of this testimony of the justice; and, though they called for the testimony before the committing court, they were informed that it had not been reduced to writing, as in fact it had not been. The defendant made affidavit that it was not on account of diligence that he did not inform his counsel as to what was sworn on the committing trial, but because, owing to his want of education and ignorance, he did not understand or comprehend the nature or effect of said evidence, and because he did not know that it would have any effect or weight on the trial in the superior court.

Lloyd Cleveland, J. H. Turner, and *Bryan & Dicken,* for plaintiff in error. *Emmett Womack,* Sol. Gen., for the State.

Judgment affirmed.

WOODS et al. v. WOODS et al.

(*Supreme Court of Georgia. July 13, 1891.*)

DEED—DEFEASIBLE FEE.

A conveyance to a trustee by a husband forever in fee-simple for the use of his wife and her children by him, born and to be born, with a condition in the *habendum* that, if he should survive her, the whole property should revert to him free from the trust, conveyed to the trustee a fee defeasible upon the contingency specified; and, on the happening of that contingency, the title revested in the husband, and thenceforth the property was his absolutely.

(*Syllabus by the Court.*)

Error from superior court, Henry county; J. S. BOYNTON, Judge.

Petition of John L. G. Woods, Joshua A. P. Woods, L. C. Woods, Jr., and Georgia Miller against A. H. Woods and others for the sale of lands, and a distribution of the proceeds among plaintiffs. Defendants demurred, and from an order sustaining the demurrer plaintiffs bring error. Affirmed.

The error assigned is the ruling of the court sustaining the demurrer to plaintiffs' petition. The petitioners were John L. G., Joshua A. P., and L. C. Woods, Jr., and Georgia Miller, formerly Woods. They alleged that they were the children and heirs of William Woods, deceased, and his wife, Martha C. Woods, L. C. Woods, Jr., being the only child of L. C. Woods, Sr., a son of William and Martha C. Woods; that, before the marriage of William and Martha C., William had no property, and all the property the two had was brought into the coverture by their mother; that on September 2, 1847, their father, William, made to one Harvey, as trustee, a deed in trust for their mother, Martha C., the child she then had, petitioner John L. G., and the children she might thereafter have by said William, to all the property he then owned, consisting of houses and lots, notes, etc., providing that it should be free from his debts, liabilities, etc., and that the rents, interest, and profits thereof should be applied by the trustee to the maintenance, support, and education of Martha C. and the children, without using any of the *corpus;* that the trustee managed the property as required by the deed until he was relieved of the trusteeship, and William Woods was himself appointed trustee in 1854; that the property mentioned in the deed was disposed of, and by William Woods invested in other property, (describing it,) which was afterwards sold by him, and the proceeds finally invested in other property owned and controlled by him long before and at the time of his death; that he died in March, 1889, leaving property, describing it, into which the trust funds were put; that Martha C. Woods died in 1861, and William married a second time, having by the second marriage three children, who are of age and living; that William was caused to make a will, by which he gave to his second wife and his children by her all of the property, except 100 acres. They prayed that they might have a judgment or decree for the property, or that it might be sold, and the proceeds paid over to them, or that at least four-fifths of the property or its proceeds might be so paid over to them, according to their several shares as they might appear entitled, with the rents, issues, and profits thereof; and they also prayed for subpœna to the widow and her children. A copy of the deed was attached to the petition. By it William Woods conveyed to Harvey, in trust for Mrs. Martha C. Woods, the child she then had, and such other children as she might thereafter have by the grantor, free from the control or disposition of the grantor, or any future husband she might have, except as afterwards provided in the deed, a number of pieces of realty and certain promissory notes. The deed further provided that the property should be held in trust free from the debts, liabilities, and control of William Woods; that the trustee was authorized to rent the realty, and collect the notes, and invest the proceeds, and to make sale of all or any of the pieces of realty with the consent of Martha C. as he might deem most advantageous to her and her children, reinvest the proceeds in other property, and, without using any part of the *corpus,* apply the income of the property to the support and maintenance of Mrs. Woods and her child or children, and for the education of the child or children, all sums above an amount sufficient for such purpose arising from the income to be paid over to William Woods. But it was provided in the deed that, in the event artha C. should die leaving William Woods surviving her, then all the property conveyed should revert back to William Woods, in as full and ample a manner as if the deed had not been executed, etc. There was also attached to the petition a copy of the decree changing the trusteeship, and of the will of William Woods. The demurrer was upon the grounds that the deed provided that, if Martha C. Woods should die leaving William Woods surviving her, then all the property should revert back to William Woods, and, the petition showing that Martha C. did die leaving William Woods surviving her, the property, and all interest and title therein, reverted to him, and became his individual property, as though the deed had never been executed; that the action was improperly brought, in that subpœna was prayed for and attached when it should have been process; and that there was no law or equity in the cause of action.

Bryan & Dicken, for plaintiffs in error. *Payne & Tye* and *E. J. Reagan*, for defendants in error.

Judgment affirmed.

LEWIS et al. v. CLEGG.

(*Supreme Court of Georgia.* July 8, 1891.)

BILL OF EXCEPTIONS—CONTENTS—TRANSCRIPT ON APPEAL.

1. It is not the office of the bill of exceptions to verify and bring up a transcript of the record. The transcript is to be certified and sent up by the clerk. The bill of exceptions should deal with the record no further than to specify such parts thereof as are material.

2. Although the bill of exceptions sets out what purport to be copies of the various parts of the record, and the judge certifies in the usual form, this does not verify the record, or dispense with a certified transcript by the clerk, the judge not certifying that no transcript is necessary.

3. Where no transcript is sent up by the clerk, and no steps are taken by plaintiff in error to cause this to be done on the call of the case for argument or before, the writ of error will be dismissed.

(*Syllabus by the Court.*)

Error from superior court, Schley county; ALLEN FORT, Judge.

A mortgage execution in favor of John F. Lewis & Son against T. B. Clegg was levied upon two mules and a mare, to which a claim was interposed by T. B. Clegg as the head of a family, alleging that the property had been duly set apart to the family as a homestead exemption by the ordinary. At the trial, before joining issue, counsel for the claimant moved to dismiss the levy, because there were no legal parties plaintiff to the proceeding; there being no such firm in existence as John F. Lewis & Son, said John F. Lewis being dead before the giving of the note and mortgage upon which the execution was founded. Counsel for the plaintiff admitted that John F. Lewis was dead before the note and mortgage were given, and moved to amend the foreclosure proceedings by striking the name of John F. Lewis & Son, and inserting the name of E. B. Lewis, the sole member of the firm of John F. Lewis & Son. The motion to amend was overruled, and the motion to dismiss the levy was sustained, and upon each ruling the plaintiff assigns error. The bill of exceptions shows that the note to secure which the mortgage was given, was payable to "John F. Lewis & Son or bearer," while the mortgage was made to "John F. Lewis & Son, their assigns."

The foreclosure was by affidavit of the attorney for "John F. Lewis & Son, a firm composed of E. B. Lewis," doing business under the firm name of "John F. Lewis & Son." The above appears from copies of the papers constituting the record, set out in full in the bill of exceptions. There is no specification of the part or parts of the record material. The judge's certificate is in the prescribed form, except that it directs the clerk "to make out a complete of such parts of the record," etc. There is no transcript of the record accompanying the bill of exceptions.

J. M. Du Pree, C. R. McCrory, and *Harrison & Peeples*, for plaintiffs in error. *W. H. McCurry* and *E. A. Hawkins*, for defendant in error.

Writ of error dismissed.

LUMPKIN J., not presiding.

HARVEY v. WEST.

(*Supreme Court of Georgia.* July 13, 1891.)

EXECUTION—PROPERTY SUBJECT TO—EQUITABLE INTEREST IN LAND—EVIDENCE—ADMISSIONS.

1. Land held by a son for less than seven years under a parol gift from his father is not subject to execution in favor of the son's creditor against the claim of the father, though the son may have erected valuable improvements on the faith of the gift. The legal title remaining in the father, and the son's remedy being by a suit for specific performance of the voluntary agreement, his creditor must resort to a like remedy.

2. Admissions against one's title to land, and in favor of the title of a third person, will be no estoppel in behalf of one to whom they were not made, and who has merely heard of them, it not appearing that they were made for the purpose of being acted upon, or with any design or intention that they should be acted upon.

3. Though evidence be improperly rejected, if the verdict is correct, and the excluded evidence could not properly have changed it, the error is immaterial.

(*Syllabus by the Court.*)

Error from superior court, Fayette county; S. W. HARRIS, Judge.

Action by W. H. West against M. P. Harvey. Judgment for plaintiff. Defendant brings error. Affirmed.

R. T. Dorsey and *Roan & Golightly*, for plaintiff in error. *Thomas W. Latham*, for defendant in error.

BLECKLEY, C. J. 1. In Georgia, title to land is not acquired or lost by parol, but passes from one person to another by writing. This is the general rule, but to this rule there are some exceptions. One exception is, after a child is allowed to hold a father's land under certain conditions for seven years, the law conclusively presumes a gift. Code, § 2664. And a child, or any other donee within the range of a meritorious consideration, may compel the specific performance of a voluntary agreement if possession has been given under the agreement, and the donee has made valuable improvements upon the faith thereof. Code, § 3189. A parol gift of land not yet rendered complete by lapse of time, under the first of these citations, nor established by a decree or judgment for specific performance, under the second, is inchoate, and therefore not sufficient to divest the donor of ownership, and clothe the donee with title. Hughes v. Clark, 67 Ga. 19; Howell v. Ellsberry, 79 Ga. 475, 5 S. E. Rep. 96; Hughes v. Berrien, 70 Ga. 273. If the donee is not in a condition, without first enforcing specific performance, to assert and vindicate his right as against the claim of the donor, neither is the donee's creditor in such condition. The creditor may be treated as in a situation as good as that of his debtor, but not in a better. If the latter would have to establish his inchoate title by suit for specific performance, it would be inconsistent not to require the former to resort to a like proceeding. In this case the legal title was in the claimant, the father of the defendant in execution, at the time of the levy and at the time the claim case was tried. That fact was decisive of the controversy. Taking as true all the evidence favorable to the plaintiff, including that which the court rejected, nothing beyond a parol gift, followed by possession and the making of valuable improvements, was established; and the possession shown was for a much shorter period than seven years.

2. It is insisted that the father was estopped from asserting his title as against the plaintiff in execution, because the plaintiff gave credit to the son while the son was in possession of the land now under levy, and because the father admitted before the credit was given that the land was not his property, but belonged to the son. But the admissions relied upon were not made to the plaintiff, nor were they made, so far as appears, for the purpose of having them acted upon by him or any other person, or with any design or intention that they should be used as a basis of credit to the son, or to influence any one to extend such credit. If the plaintiff, by reason of hearing of the admissions from one or more persons to whom they were made, was induced to give the son credit, he volunteered to act upon something which was not addressed to him; and there is no evidence that any of the admissions were communicated to him by the order or direction, or even the permission, of the speaker. Surely, mere loose talk in the neighborhood, uttered when no particular transaction is in progress or in contemplation, cannot be seized upon by dealers eager for trade who happen to hear of it, and be made a basis for extending credit to their customers, and afterwards for enforcing collections out of property to which their customers have no title. This would be a very dangerous and pernicious extension of the law of estoppel. The admissions evidently related to the parol gift. They were evidence for what they were worth as admissions, but they certainly did not come with the irresistible force of an estoppel. This being so, it was immaterial whether the plaintiff had heard of them or not, or whether, after taking them at second hand, he acted upon them in extending credit.

3. Some of the rejected evidence may have been admissible, but, treating it as admitted, the verdict must have been as it was; that is, in favor of the claimant. It was correct, and the excluded evidence could not have changed it without illegally sacrificing the substantial merits of the case. In none of the grounds of the motion is there any cause for a new trial It is needless to discuss them severally.

Judgment affirmed.

SMALL v. GEORGIA, S. & F. R. Co.

(Supreme Court of Georgia. July 13, 1891.)

EMINENT DOMAIN—PARTIES—TRUSTEES.

1. In condemnation proceedings to subject trust property to public use in the exercise of the right of eminent domain, the trustee is the proper party to represent the trust-estate, and it is not necessary that the beneficiaries should be parties to the proceeding.

2. Under the charter of the G., S. & F. R. Co. and the amendments thereto, including the act of 1888, the company may condemn private property in the city of Macon for depot grounds and other necessary terminal facilities.

3. There was no error committed by the court on the trial, and the verdict was warranted by the evidence, under the law.

(Syllabus by the Court.)

Error from superior court, Bibb county; A. L. MILLER, Judge.

R. W. Patterson and R. Hodges, for plaintiff in error. Depau & Bartlett and Gustin, Guerry & Hall, for defendant in error.

Judgment affirmed.

Ex parte CALHOUN, Ordinary.

(Supreme Court of Georgia. July 13, 1891.)

ESTABLISHMENT OF LOST RECORDS — PRODUCTION OF PRIVATE PAPERS.

A witness cannot, under Act Oct. 22, 1887, be compelled, by a *subpoena duces tecum*, to make discovery of the contents of lost public records in a proceeding to establish a copy of such records, where the pleadings for the purpose do not allege or set out anything whatever as the specific contents to be proved. The production of books and writings which are the private property of the witness will not be compelled for the information of the public, where such information is valuable, and where its disclosure is not sought as testimony for the proof of any alleged fact, but as a substitute in the first instance for the allegation of facts unknown, or not known sufficiently to enable the plaintiff to set them forth conformably to general laws applicable to pleading.

(Syllabus by the Court.)

Error from superior court, Fulton county; MARSHALL J. CLARKE, Judge.

Hall & Hammond, for plaintiff in error. Abbott & Smith, for defendant in error.

BLECKLEY, C. J. Each county is the owner of the public records appertaining to the several courts thereof, and, upon the loss or destruction of any book of that description, the county owning it would have, as such owner, a right, irrespective of the act of 1887, to have a copy of the same established if the requisite service could be effected on all parties interested. The act of 1887 takes the right for granted, and attempts to provide machinery for exercising it. It authorizes the ordinary to proceed by petition in the superior court, which petition must set forth the fact of stealing, loss, or destruction, specify the book as near as may be, and pray for the establishment thereof. Upon the hearing of the petition, the court may, in its discretion, grant or deny it, as the public interest may require. In case the petition is granted, the court is to pass an order establishing a copy, or substantial copy, as near as may be; and, after its establishment, this copy is to be in all respects evidence, just as the original would have been. The provisions for taking evidence in aid of the petition, and reporting thereon, are contained in the fourth section of the act, which reads as follows: "It shall be lawful for said court, or the judge thereof, in vacation, in all cases where he shall deem it proper and necessary so to do, to appoint an auditor whose duty it shall be to hear evidence, and who shall have power to summon witnesses and compel the production of books and papers, under such rules and regulations as are now practiced in courts of law in this state; and he snall make his report to the court of such copies of such lost, stolen, mutilated, or destroyed copies; and such report, when filed, shall be acted on by the court, and made the judgment, unless objection be filed to the same, or some part thereof, as being incorrect, which objection, if any, shall be heard and determined by the court without the intervention of a jury." Acts 1887, pp. 112, 113.

It will be observed that the power to compel the production of books and papers conferred upon the auditor is to be exercised, not according to any novel or arbitrary method of procedure, but "under such rules and regulations as are now practiced in courts of law in this state." The prescribed standard to which the auditor must conform is the practice of the courts. What a court of law could do without deviating from the rules and regulations which govern and control its practice the auditor can do. The auditor must guide his conduct by the rules and regulations applicable to courts. Where the person called upon is not a party to the cause, he can be reached by a *subpœna duces tecum*. Code, § 3514. The subpœna, after due service, must be complied with, or certain acts must be done by the witness in lieu of literal compliance, or a sufficient excuse for non-compliance must be rendered; otherwise an attachment will issue on motion, and a fine be imposed for the default. Id. § 3515. The letter of the statute seems to contemplate that the time for rendering excuses is after attachment has issued, but no doubt this extension of the time is intended as an indulgence to the witness. Where he is not wholly disobedient, but appears as the writ of subpœna commanded him to do, there can be no reason why his excuse for not producing the books or documents called for should not be heard at once if the court is ready and willing to hear him. When he is already present, no attachment is needed to bring him into court; and if his excuse, on hearing the same, should prove to be good, it would necessarily show that he ought not to be dealt with by attachment or otherwise. What shall constitute a sufficient excuse the statute makes no attempt to specify or define. It leaves each case to be deter-

mined on its own facts. All it says on the subject is that the excuse is "to be judged of by the court." Whatsoever the court, in the exercise of a sound discretion, ought to deem satisfactory, should be recognized and accepted as sufficient. The excuse rendered to the auditor in the present instance was at bottom a claim of privilege. It challenged the power of the auditor. What it was in detail may be seen by consulting the official report. Resolved into its legal essence, it was that, consistently with the rules and regulations observed by the courts of law of this state, the witness could not be compelled to make discovery by *subpœna duces tecum*. So far as appears, there had been no other writ or process issued in the case. There was no party defendant to the petition. The suit was *ex parte*. It might be considered a proceeding *in rem*, the *res* being books which had not been seized, and could not be seized, because they were stolen, lost, or destroyed. The whole object of the suit was to generate other books to supply their place, and stand in their stead as a part of the public records. Nothing whatever was alleged in the petition as to the specific contents of the books, or any of them, the different volumes being described simply in terms like the following: "Deed-Book B, covering a period of time from about June 5, 1855, to about January 10, 1856; Mortgage Book E, covering a period of time from about February 18, 1874, to about May 8, 1876." The contents of the books were, doubtless, unknown to the petitioner, and most probably he could not ascertain them with any degree of fullness or accuracy by mere inquiry, or by any means in his power, personally or officially, to command. He needed compulsory discovery from one or more persons who had or could furnish the information. But, according to the methods of procedure known to courts of justice, in order for a plaintiff to obtain discovery, either to enable him to plead, or to assist him in establishing the truth of what he has pleaded, he must make the person from whom the discovery is to come a party to the cause. He must sue that person for something, and ask for discovery as an incident, or sue for discovery alone. And a suit *in personam* requires process and service thereof on the defendant. A *subpœna duces tecum* is not process by which to inaugurate a suit, or by which to connect a new party with a pending suit. Such use of it is unheard of in the practice and procedure of courts. Nor, under our Code, does that kind of subpœna ever issue to any one who is a party to the cause, the mode of compelling the production of books and papers when they are in the power or possession of a party being by the service of written notice. Code, § 3508. A *subpœra duces tecum* is not mentioned by the act of 1887, and, of course, that act cannot be invoked to render it available for any purpose which it would not subserve under the prior law. Most certainly there was no warrant in the prior law for using it as a means to compel discovery of the contents of books or documents, with a view to establish copies of them to stand in lieu of the originals. It could be used to bring in evidence to show that an alleged copy was a true copy; that is, it could be used to obtain evidence as contradistinguished from discovery. To verify what is alleged is a legitimate use of the subpœna, but, without anything for verification being alleged, to employ it for ascertaining what is to be verified, and at the same time for verifying the matter thus discovered, is giving it a double operation, the first half of which is illegitimate. The difference is that between making a statement and then fishing with the subpœna for proof of it, and fishing in silence for proof, treating the proof itself as supplying the statement to be established. Should it be said, in reply, that if the contents of the lost books were already known, so that they could be alleged, there might be no use for the evidence now sought, the answer is that there would still be all the use for it which can be considered in dealing with it under a subpœna duces tecum. It would contribute none the less towards proving the contents of the books, and, in order to establish a copy of them, their contents, after being alleged, would have to be proved. The evidence might be less material or indispensable if the contents of the books were otherwise known sufficiently to enable the petitioner to allege them specifically beforehand, but the use or availability of a subpœna duces tecum does not depend in any degree upon the scarcity or abundance of the means of proof which may happen to be accessible. The rule is the same whether the evidence called for by the subpœna is all that is within reach, or only a small part of it. To prevent misconception, it may be well to observe that it is not meant to intimate that it would be necessary that the contents should be proved to be exactly, or even substantially, as at first alleged. No doubt the copy offered to be established could be varied by amendment, under the general law applicable to pleadings, as might be needful to make it conform ultimately to the evidence. What we decide is that something must be presented in the petition, or annexed to it, which is claimed to be a copy, in substance, of the lost volume or document. This is the scheme of the general law of the state applicable to the establishment of writings which have been lost or destroyed. Code, §§ 3982-3985. In proceedings between party and party, to establish a copy of a lost deed or other document, no court, we suppose, would think of compelling the production of evidence without seeing something in the petition, taken as a whole, (including, of course, the exhibits,) to which the evidence wanted could be applied, and which that evidence would or might prove true, or, at least, tend to prove true. A petition stating that a particular deed, of a given kind and date, was lost or destroyed, but wholly silent as to the contents, would not serve as a basis for coercing the production of evidence to verify its contents, and enable the court to formulate by the evidence a copy of the instrument. True it is that gener-

ally, in such a case, the court might treat the deficiency in the pleading as waived unless it was insisted upon by the defendant; but the present case was ex parte, and had no defendant to speak on the subject. Besides, in any case, the witness ought to be heard in behalf of his own interest when it appears that he is actuated by a bona fide regard for that interest, and is not influenced by contumacy or mere caprice. Here the witness urged the interest of the corporation of which he was the proper representative, a private corporation of which he was official secretary, and of whose books he was the custodian. The subpœna was addressed to him as secretary and treasurer; and the books called for were described therein as "all the abstract-books of the Land Title Warranty & Safe Deposit Company, in which appear the abstracts of the following lost records of said county, to-wit: Deed-Books, B, F, and H, and Mortgage Book E, of the superior court of Fulton county." These abstract-books called for by the subpœna came into existence as the result of private enterprise and labor, and were afterwards purchased by this private corporation at great expense. They are its private property, and are used by it in the conduct of its corporate business. They have never been published. Their contents are kept secret, except as disclosed, piecemeal, in furnishing to applicants therefor abstracts of title relating to specified parcels of real estate; and the furnishing of such abstracts is carried on as a business for pay and profit. The value of the books consists mainly in the secrecy of their contents.. Were the information which they afford rendered accessible to the public by other means, the demand for it through the one source now available would be diminished, if not destroyed. The monopoly enjoyed by a closely sealed intelligence office would be broken, and the losses inflicted by free competition would be instantly felt in the exchequer of the establishment. There can be no doubt that the corporation has a vital interest in maintaining the secrecy of these books as a repository of valuable information. And certainly its secretary is under a duty, both legal and moral, not to aid in killing the goose that lays the golden egg if he can help it. His claim of privilege is therefore as meritorious as if his own personal interest were involved. We think the claim protects him, and that the auditor ruled correctly in so holding. It follows that the court committed no error in sustaining the auditor's report, and overruling the exceptions thereto which were on file in behalf of the ordinary. Judgment affirmed.

ROBERTSON v. STATE.

(Supreme Court of Georgia. May 8, 1891.)

VOLUNTARY MANSLAUGHTER—EVIDENCE— MOTION FOR NEW TRIAL—REVIEW.

1. Defendant and deceased met after work hours to fight in accordance with an agreement made earlier in the day, when deceased had dunned defendant for money and cursed him. The wound from which deceased died was a cut in the bowels. Besides this, he received a cut in the right shoulder, and one in the left arm,

all made with a knife. Defendant received some bruises, and had the skin on his head torn somewhat, but was not severely injured. There was no witness at the commencement of the fight, which started behind a shed. The evidence for the state was that when first seen deceased was running with nothing in his hands, and defendant was running after him with a knife in his hand; that when defendant overtook deceased the latter picked up a stone, and threw it at defendant; that deceased slipped and fell, and defendant jumped on him and cut him. Defendant testified that when they met for the fight deceased hit him on the head with a plow-point, and he fell, and deceased got on him, and he then cut deceased; that he then ran, and deceased threatened to knock his brains out if he made another move; that deceased hit him on the shoulder with a rock, knocking him down; and that he then cut deceased in the bowels, as the latter reached for some other implement; and that he then got up and ran with deceased after him. *Held,* that the evidence was sufficient to sustain a verdict of voluntary manslaughter.

2. On appeal from the denial of a motion for a new trial, the ground of the motion that the court erred in admitting certain evidence cannot be considered, where the motion does not set out what, if any, objection was made to the evidence when introduced.

Error from superior court, Oconee county: N. L. HUTCHINS, Judge.

Lon Robertson was convicted of voluntary manslaughter, and appeals. Affirmed.

The following is the official report:

Lon Robertson was indicted for the murder of John Owens. The evidence for the state tended to show the following: Owens was killed by Robertson in November, 1889. About the first of that year they had had "a little scrimmage," but it did not appear what their difficulty was about. On the day of the killing John had gone with an axe up to a wagon where Lon was, had dunned him for money, and cursed him. They agreed to fight after working hours. After working hours, and about dark, John sought Lon, found him behind a buggy-house, and there the fatal difficulty began None of the witnesses saw what occurred there. When they were first seen after the encounter there, John was running, and Lon after him. John had nothing in his hands, but, according to one witness, Lon was running after John with a knife, and, when Lon overtook John, John turned around, and threw at him a rock which John had picked up, and after he threw the rock John had a pole; but this witness did not see John strike Lon, and did not see him hit Lon with a plow-point. When Lon overtook John he cut John in the shoulder. John slipped up, and then Lon jumped on him. It was after the quarrel, on the day of the fatal difficulty, when Lon got the knife. He borrowed it from another. Said he wanted to make some fiddlescrews, and went and sat down, and was whittling. Another witness testified that he did not see Lon do anything to John; that John was running, and Lon was after him; that they ran 100 yards, he reckoned; that he did not know whether John fell down or not,—when he saw them they were together, and Lon was on top; that Lon hit John three times in the face with his fist, at that time having his knife in his hand; that John was begging Lon to get off of him, and begged witness once to take him off; that John did not have anything in his hands; that shortly before the difficulty John had asked witness where Lon was, but did not say what he wanted with him, and witness told him that Lon went towards the buggy-house, and John went right on down that way, and went behind the buggy-house; that witness did not see anything like the plow-point or pole or rock in John's hands. A physician testified that John Owens was wounded in three places,—one cut in his right shoulder, one in his left arm, and one in his bowels,—all of which seemed to have been made with a knife, the last being the fatal one. He lived four or five days after witness was called to see him. The stab in the shoulder could possibly have been made while John was on top of Lon. This witness also treated Lon. Dressed a cut on his head, which was a lacerated wound, requiring four stitches. The skin looked like it had been torn; was more of a bruise than anything else, and appeared to have been made with a dull instrument. The skull was not fractured, and the wound seemed to have been made by two licks. Witness did not know whether it could have been made with an instrument like a plow-point with a piece or wing, but thought not. It looked like it was made with a curved instrument. If a rock, the size of one shown to him, had been thrown at Lon by John, and had struck Lon, it would be likely to produce death. A pole (the one in court) in John's hands would be a weapon likely to produce death. The two men were very nearly the same size. John seemed to be a very stout man. After Lon was brought to jail the physician found a wound on his shoulder, which seemed to be from a glancing lick, and could have been made with a rock or some hard instrument. This wound he did not see the night Lon was hurt, and when he saw it there was a scab on it, showing that it had been a considerable bruise. It looked more like there had been several scratches together than anything else he could think of There appeared to be no bruised blood there. The wound on Lon's head was not such a wound as you would expect from a rock. It would take a large rock to make it. It could be done by a sharp rock. Witness did not know whether the wound in John's stomach could have been made while John was on Lon or not. Before the coroner's jury Lon made a statement in which he said they had had some trouble out at a new ground before the fight. and cursed each other, and that they then came home, and that John Owens came to the buggy-house, and John took him by the collar, and he cut him. The coroner told Lon to make such statement as he saw proper, and the statement was taken down and read to Lon, and he said it was correct.

The testimony for defendant tended to show that John was the better man physically. Only one of defendant's witnesses saw anything of the difficulty, and he only saw the latter part of it. When he got to them, John had a rail in his hand, and hit Lon over the head with it; and said to witness, who was their employer, he would give witness five dollars to let him whip the "damn nigger." Witness told him they could fight, if they would fight fair, and asked John where was his money. John said he did not have any money, but would work for witness 25 years if he would let him kill "that damn nigger." Lon did not show any disposition to fight. All at once John gathered him and threw him under the buggy-shelter, and witness saw then that John was cut. John and Lon were friendly before this difficulty, but afterwards John's brother told witness of a former fight in the woods, and said they both quit laughing. Up to the 12th of July that year Lon had stayed at John's house, slept there every night, and John's wife did his washing for him. The night John died he sent for witness, and said he was going to die, and told his wife he was going home; that he did not want her or any of her folks to do anything with Lon; that he brought it on himself. Witness did not know whether he realized that he was in a dying condition or not, but he died in 20 or 30 minutes, and witness thinks he thought he was going to die. Lon was smaller than John. Witness did not see John with a plow-point or rock in his hands. The rail with which John struck Lon might have caused the wound on Lon's head, and that wound might have been made after the cutting. John had no knife, and Lon gave up his knife to witness. The plow-point in court witness picked up at the corner of the buggy-house where they had the fight. There was no blood on it when he found it. It had been raining. The next morning there was blood where they fought. The night he died, and while he was in a dying condition, and knew the fact, John told another witness that he was to blame in the whole matter; that he brought the difficulty on with Lon, and that if he had listened to his wife that night he would not have gone up there to hunt Lon. He told this witness and others this several times the night before he died. About half an hour before he died he sent for Lon, and told Lon that the Lord had forgiven him, and that he had nothing against Lon; that he brought the whole trouble on himself; and he told his wife not to do anything with Lon, for he was to blame in the whole matter. The defendant made a statement to the following effect: That afternoon he was getting wood, and went by John, who called him, and he did not answer; and John asked him why in the hell he did not answer, and kept on cursing defendant. He walked up to defendant, and said his wife wanted some money. Defendant said he had none, and John said he was going to have it. Defendant went on getting his wood. John came up with his axe on his shoulder, and another, who was present, said they had better not have any fuss, as he would tell the boss. Then defendant said he would not have any fuss now, and John said he would get him to-night, and went on back. Defendant carried his wood to the house, put up and fed the mules, unloaded the wood, and went to cutting wood. John took in his wood. Defendant went

behind the buggy-house, and was fixing a peg, when John came up, and said he would whip defendant or defendant would whip him, and cursed defendant, using very opprobrious language, to which defendant replied similarly. John grabbed a plow-point about the size of the one in court, and hit defendant on the head; and defendant fell, and John got on him, and defendant cut him. Then defendant went on around the lot, and dodged behind the bars, and John ran up and said if he made another move he would knock his brains out. About that time John struck him on the shoulder with a rock, and he fell to his knees, and cut John in the bowels just as John reached for something else. He got up and, ran, and John ran after him. The boss came up, and John said he would work for him 20 years if he would let him knock defendant's brains out. The boss took the piece of rail from John, and said, "Quit:" and then John ran defendant under the buggy-shelter, and when he got up hit him with a stick; and then the boss stopped John. The defendant was found guilty of voluntary manslaughter. He moved for a new trial, on the grounds that the verdict was contrary to law, evidence, etc., and because the court allowed proof of confessions that were in the statement he made before the coroner's inquest. The motion was overruled, and defendant excepted.

B. E. Thrasher and *Thomas & Strickland,* for defendant in error. *R. B. Russell,* Sol. Gen., by *Harrison & Peeples,* for the State.

SIMMONS, J. The evidence in this case, which will be found in the official report, was sufficient to sustain the verdict of voluntary manslaughter found by the jury, and the court did not err in refusing to grant a new trial on the ground that the verdict was contrary to the evidence. The other ground of the motion, that the court erred in admitting the defendant's statement at the coroner's inquest, cannot be considered by us, because the motion did not set out what objection was made to the evidence at the time it was introduced, or that any objection was made at that time. Judgment affirmed.

JAMESVILLE & W. R. CO. v. FISHER.

(Supreme Court of North Carolina. Oct. 13, 1891.)

SHERIFFS—AGE OF DEPUTIES.

In the absence of any statute making a deputy-sheriff an officer or making provisions as to his age, a minor may be appointed deputy, though Const. N. C. art. 6, §§ 4, 5, provide that an officer shall be 21 years old.

Appeal from superior court, Beaufort county; SPIER WHITAKER, Judge.

Action by the Jamesville & Washington Railroad Company against A. Fisher. From a judgment dismissing the action for want of service plaintiff appeals. Reversed.

This was a civil action originally instituted before a justice of the peace, and brought by appeal to the superior court of Beaufort county, in which court it was

tried at the May term, 1890, before WHITA-
KER, Judge. The return of the officer upon the summons was as follows: "Received March 24th, 1890. Served March
24th, 1890, by reading the within summons
to A. Fisher. R. T. HODGES, Sheriff. By
J. H. HODGES, D. S." Both in the court
of the justice of the peace and in the superior court the defendant entered a special appearance, and moved to dismiss for
want of service, because James H. Hodges,
who actually served the summons as deputy for R. T. Hodges, was at the time of
serving it under the age of 21 years. It
was admitted in both courts that he
(James H.) was not 21 years old on said
24th March, 1890, when said summons was
served by him. From the judgment of the
court dismissing the action the plaintiff
appealed.

John H. Small, for appellant. *Chas. F.
Warren,* for appellee.

AVERY, J., (*after stating the facts.*) A
sheriff is liable to answer in damages for
any wrongful act of his deputy done under
color of his office, for which the sheriff
would have incurred such liability had he
done the act himself, and in all such cases
he and his deputy are, in contemplation
of law, one person. Murfree, Sher. §§ 20,
59, 60, 62. So far has this doctrine, as to all
wrongful acts of the deputy done *colore
officii,* been carried by this court, that a
demand on a defaulting deputy for money
collected by him in that capacity has been
declared equivalent to a demand on the
sheriff. Lyle v. Wilson, 4 Ired. 226. While
a deputy is professing to act, and inducing
others to believe that he is acting, under
color of his office, his personality, like that
of other agents, seems to be merged, in
legal contemplation, in the person of the
sheriff under whose directions, as principal, he is supposed to act. Murfree, Sher.
§§ 20, 61. The service of the summons is a
mere ministerial duty which can be performed by a deputy, where the law gives
the right to appoint one, and even as between him and third persons his official acts
are considered those of the sheriff, done by
his lawfully constituted agent. The right
to appoint under-sheriffs or bailiffs and
deputies is not always, if generally, regulated by statute. These subordinates are
the servants and agents of the sheriff, and
his responsibility for them and relations
with them are controlled generally by the
law governing the relation of principal
and agent. Id. §§ 16, 60. While policy
may have induced the courts to hold his
responsibility in some instances to be
greater, never less, than that of a principal for the acts of his agent within the
scope of the agency, our Code is still silent as to the manner of appointment or
the distinct duties of both general and
special deputies, while this court has declared that there is no provision of the
common law which requires the deputa-
tion of a sheriff to be in writing, and that,
in any action against a sheriff for the misconduct of a person alleged to be his deputy, it is not necessary to prove a deputa-
tion, but it is sufficient simply to show
that the person acted as deputy with the
consent or privity of the sheriff. State v.

Allen, 5 Ired. 36; State v. McIntosh, 2 Ired.
53. In some of the states statutes have
been enacted providing for the appointment of general deputies and bailiffs, and
prescribing certain duties and liabilities
arising out of the position; and the interpretations of these laws have given rise
to some confusion, and apparent conflict,
in the decisions of different states. In
some of these states we find distinctions
drawn by the courts as to the duties,
powers, and liabilities of general deputies,
coming within the provisions of their
statutes, and special deputies, who are
left as at common law to be treated as
the trusted servants or agents of the sheriff. Proctor v. Walker, 12 Ind. 660. In
North Carolina, both general and special
deputies may be appointed by the sheriff
without writing, and, when they act with
his assent or privity, they are either his
general or special agents as to the discharge of his ministerial duties, and are
accountable to him as such. An individual can unquestionably constitute an infant his agent, and subject himself to responsibility for all acts of the latter within the scope of the agency. Whart. Ag. §§
15, 16; 1 Lawson, Rights, Rem. & Pr. § 6;
Story, Ag. § 7. In the absence of statutory
restrictions, we see no reason why a
minor, appointed by the sheriff as his general or special deputy, should not have
the power to perform a mere ministerial
duty of his office, such as serving a summons issued in a civil action. Murfree,
Sher. § 71; McGee v. Eastis, 3 Stew. (Ala.)
307.; Barrett v. Seward, 22 Vt. 176; Miller
v. McMillan, 4 Ala. 530; Ewell Evans Ag.
*40, *41. Indeed, Judge Story says, (in a
note to section 149 of his work on Agency:)
"There is a distinction between doing
an act by an agent and doing an act by a
deputy, whom the law deems such. An
agent can only bind his principal when he
does the act in the name of his principal.
But a deputy may do the act and sign his
own name, and it binds the principal; for
the deputy, in law, has the whole power
of the principal." This citation is made
not to give approval to the distinction
drawn by him, but to show that the
learned jurist considered a deputy as sustaining the relation of an agent to the
officer who appoints him. If a deputy-
sheriff were, by law, constituted an officer, and the mode of appointing him and in-
ducting him into office were prescribed, as
in some of the states, our view of this case
might be materially different. Guyman
v. Burlingame, 36 Ill. 203; Murfree, Sher.
§ 72. The qualifications of an officer are
clearly set forth in sections 4 and 5 of article 6 of the constitution, and it is declared essential that he should be "twenty-
one years old;" but we find no provision
in our constitution or laws which restricts
the right to appoint agents on the one
hand, or the liability for their acts on the
other. In Yeargin v. Siler, 83 N. C. 348,
Justice DILLARD, for the court, says:
"The rule in matters judicial is *delegatus
non potest delegare;* but in duties ministerial the officer may act in person or by
deputy, of his own choice and appointment." We think that, in the absence of
any statutory restriction, the sheriff has

the power to appoint a minor his general, as well as his special, deputy, and clothe him with the power of a bailiff, as to his ministerial duties, as effectually as he could constitute him his agent to attend to private business for him as an individual. Broom, Leg. Max. 619. The current of authority in this country sustains this view. It is true that in the English case cited by counsel (Cuckson v. Winter, 17 E. C. L. 713) the court held that it was highly improper for a sheriff to intrust the service of a warrant in replevin to an infant, because the deputy was authorized to take possession of the goods, and was responsible for the custody of them, and that service of the warrant by the infant was illegal. The learned judge who tried the case below was doubtless influenced by this authority in holding the service void in our case. But the conclusion of the court in Cuckson v. Winter seems to be based upon the idea that a defendant, whose goods were taken for rent, had no remedy for an unlawful seizure except against the deputy. That difficulty is met by holding that the sheriff is civilly responsible for the unlawful acts of his deputy to the extent to which he would be liable if he had acted in his own proper person; and that he selects and appoints his agents at his own hazard, third parties having no interest in the security he may exact from them. Murfree, Sher. §§ 20, 59, 60, 64. Thus in every way the courts of this country have, in the absence of specific statutory provisions, adjusted the powers of sheriffs and their deputies, and their liabilities to the public and to each other, according to the rules which determine the duties and responsibility of principal and agent, and have recognized the right of the sheriff to select such agents for the discharge of mere ministerial duties, as an individual could appoint and constitute for the transaction of private business, even though he might intrust the duty to a person not sui juris. Id. §§ 71, 75, and references; Yeargin v. Siler, supra. Mr. Wharton says, in substance, that the only qualification of the rule that infants may act as agents, and bind their principals, is that the infant agent must not be very deficient in mental capacity. Whart. Ag. § 15. We think that the judge below erred in sustaining the demurrer, and the judgment is therefore reversed. The cause will be remanded, to the end that the defendant may be allowed to answer if he be so advised. Judgment reversed.

WARDENS OF ST. PETER'S EPISCOPAL CHURCH v. TOWN OF WASHINGTON.

(Supreme Court of North Carolina. Oct. 13, 1891.)

EQUITY JURISDICTION—UNLAWFUL ORDINANCE— INJUNCTION.

An injunction will not lie to prevent the enforcement of an alleged unlawful ordinance, even to prevent an apprehended breach of the peace and arrest, in case of a violation of the ordinance, there being adequate remedy at law.

Appeal from superior court, Beaufort county; HENRY R. BRYAN, Judge.

Action by the wardens of St. Peter's Episcopal Church against the town of Washington to have an ordinance declared void and its enforcement enjoined. From a judgment sustaining a demurrer to the complaint, plaintiffs appeal. Action dismissed.

W. B. Rodman & Son, for appellants. Chas. F. Warren and John H. Small, for appellee.

CLARK, J.. The plaintiffs in this action seek to have a town ordinance declared void, and an injunction against enforcing the same. The ordinance in question had been authorized in terms by an act of the legislature, (Priv. Acts 1876-77, c. 34,) and has since been recited and declared "valid and legal" by two acts, (Priv. Laws 1891. cc. 110, 223.) It is unnecessary, however, that we pass upon the question debated before us as to the competency of the legislature to authorize or to validate the ordinance in the exercise of the police power inherent in the state, for we have an express authority, if one were needed, that an injunction does not lie to prevent the enforcement of an alleged unlawful town ordinance. Should the plaintiff be injured by its enforcement, he has a redress at law by an action for damages. Cohen v. Commissioners, 77 N. C. 2, in which READE, J., says: "We are aware of no principle or precedent for the interposition of a court of equity in such cases." Nor can there be any for the proposition that the court should declare void an unenforced municipal ordinance. To do so would be to pass upon a mere abstraction. If the plaintiffs, or any one else, should violate the ordinance upon a criminal prosecution for such violation, the validity of the ordinance, and of the acts of the legislature authorizing and validating it, would come directly and properly before the courts; or if the town, by arrest or otherwise, should prevent the attempted violation, an action for damages, as in the case cited, or an indictment, would equally present the question. Indeed, the allegations of the plaintiffs that, if they should violate the ordinance, they fear an arrest and a breach of the peace, and their application for an injunction to prevent such consequences, though made in good faith, will not warrant the court in departing from settled authority. As was said in Busbee v. Lewis, 85 N. C. 332, "a court of equity will never interpose its jurisdiction in the way of a mere protective relief [there, by a decree to remove a cloud upon a title] when the party has an adequate and effectual remedy at law." To same purport, Busbee v. Macy, 85 N. C. 329; Pearson v. Boyden, 86 N. C. 585. But the learning is familiar, and the principle well settled by authority and reason. The complaint does not set out facts sufficient to constitute a cause of action; therefore let it be entered, action dismissed.

STATE v. POPE.

(Supreme Court of North Carolina. Oct. 13, 1891.)

ADULTERY—SUFFICIENCY OF EVIDENCE.

Where, on the trial of a man for fornication and adultery with a woman who lived at his house, it does not appear that the woman was single, or that she was not defendant's wife, or that her child, born while she lived at defendant's house, was a bastard, there is insufficient evidence to go to the jury.

Indictment against K. C. Pope and Nettie Dunn for fornication and adultery, tried before CONNOR, J., at April term, 1891, of Edgecombe superior court. The defendant Pope alone was on trial. There was a verdict of guilty, and judgment, from which he appealed to this court. The case on appeal is as follows: Walter Pope, a witness for the state, testified as follows: "I lived in the house with the defendant up to about a year ago. There were four or five rooms in the house. The defendant Pope occupied a room by himself. The woman occupied a room connected with the house, but under a different roof. I lived there all the time the woman did, except the last year. I never saw the defendant Pope in the woman's room, nor the woman in Pope's room. Never saw anything suspicious between them, —no intimate relations between them. I never noticed any favor in the children. Never heard Pope claim them, or say whose they were. The woman had two children when she went there to live, and has given birth to one since she has been living there,—at present, a child in arms. She washed and cooked and did other work. Pope has no family, and is sixty-seven years of age." The witness, the defendant Pope, the woman, and her older children all ate at the same table. Joseph Hopgood, a witness for the state, testified: "Pope lives in Battleboro. I have been there several times to see him on business. I don't know anything about his living in fornication and adultery with Nettie Dunn." At this point his honor took charge of the witness' examination, and asked this question: "Did you notice the favor of this woman's children to any one?" To which witness replied: "There are several sets of children there." His honor then asked the witness: "What do you mean by 'several sets of children?'" Witness answered: "I mean children gotten by Pope on women who lived there before this woman." Counsel for defendant objected to this testimony, saying: "I did not interrupt your honor in the course of your examination of the witness regarding his adulterous relations with other women to interpose an objection to such testimony. I desire now to interpose an objection to that testimony, and to move your honor to exclude the same." His honor replied: "Certainly, I will give you the benefit of the objection, and will instruct the jury as to its incompetency." This was said to counsel in the presence of the jury, but it is not certain that the jury heard and understood the same. The defendant demurred to the evidence, for that there was no evidence of his guilt to go to the jury. His honor submitted the case to the jury, and the defendant excepted. His honor omitted to charge the jury that the testimony of Hopgood above set out and objected to was incompetent, and was not to be considered by them in investigating the guilt of defendant. Exception. Verdict of

guilty. Judgment of the court that the defendant pay a fine of $500, and be imprisoned six months in the county jail. Motion before judgment for new trial for errors above assigned. Motion denied. Defendant appealed from the judgment. The statement of the case on appeal was duly served on G. H. White, solicitor second judicial district.

Batchelor & Devereux, for appellant. *The Attorney General,* for the State.

DAVIS, J., (*after stating the facts as above.*) The defendant demurred to the evidence, and insisted that there was no evidence of guilt sufficient to go to the jury. There was no evidence in the case on appeal that the woman was a single woman; nor was there any evidence that her child, born while she lived at the house of defendant Pope, was a bastard child; nor was there any evidence, other than indirect and inferential, that the defendants were not husband and wife. There was no evidence sufficient to go to the jury, and the defendant is entitled to a new trial. It is but just and due to the able, accurate, and conscientious judge before whom the case was tried to say that the defendant's case on appeal was served upon the solicitor for the state, and no amendments were suggested or objections made by him. It did not appear in evidence in the case on appeal that the woman was unmarried, or that the child born at defendant's house was a bastard. The solicitor may have overlooked or failed to advert to the evidence, but, if he had no evidence other than that set out in the case on appeal, he ought not to have prosecuted the defendant; but we will not do the learned judge who tried the case the injustice to suppose that the case contained all the evidence, or that he would have permitted a verdict of guilty only upon the evidence set out.

Error. New trial.

LEWIS v. ROPER LUMBER CO.

(*Supreme Court of North Carolina.* Oct. 13, 1891.)

COLOR OF TITLE — DEED OF LAND LYING IN TWO COUNTIES—WHAT PROBATE SUFFICES.

Where, in an action of trespass for cutting timber from certain land, plaintiff's title is brought in issue, but it is proved that he or his grantors have been in continuous possession for more than seven years, a deed to land lying in two counties, including the *locus in quo* and constituting a link in plaintiff's title, though properly proved and registered only in one county, is admissible to show color of title, under Code N. C. § 1248, which provides that, where real estate is situate in two or more counties, probate of the deed conveying same, made before the clerk of the superior court of either county, is sufficient.

Appeal from superior court, Washington county; HENRY R. BRYAN, Judge.

This was an action by W. W. Lewis against the John L. Roper Lumber Company to recover damages for an alleged trespass on land, and cutting and taking timber therefrom. The defendant denies the allegations of the complaint, and says that the defendant was the owner in fee of the land upon which the trespass is alleged to have been committed. There was a verdict and judgment for the plaintiff, and the defendant appealed. Reversed.

C. L. Pettigrew and *W. D. Pruden*, for appellant. *S. B. Spruill*, for appellee.

DAVIS, J., (*after stating the facts.*) Among other questions presented by the case on appeal is the following: "The defendant offered, as a link in his chain of title, a deed for land lying in Washington and Tyrrell counties, including the *locus in quo*. This deed had been properly proved and registered in the county of Tyrrell, but had not been registered in Washington county. This deed defendant also offered as color of title. Plaintiff objected to the introduction of this deed, because it had not been registered in Washington county, unless the execution of the same should be proved. The court excluded the deed, and the defendant excepted." There was evidence tending to show that the defendant, and those under whom he claims, had been in the continuous possession of the land in controversy for more than seven years. We think the deed offered in evidence constituted color of title, and that there was error in excluding it. The deed had been properly proven and registered in Tyrrell county, the land in both Tyrrell and Washington counties, and Code, § 1248, provides that, "where real estate is situate in two or more counties, probate of the deed or other instrument conveying or concerning the same, made before the clerk of the superior court of either of said counties, is sufficient." It is the continuous possession of land under color of title for the statutory period that confers title, and not the validity or genuineness of the instrument constituting color of title. The possession puts everybody upon notice as to the possessor's title, or claims of title, whether legal or equitable, registered or unregistered; and it is well settled that a deed, whether registered or not, is good as color of title. Campbell v. McArthur, 2 Hawks, 33; Hardin v. Barrett, 6 Jones, (N. C.) 159; Brown v. Brown, 106 N. C. 451, 11 S. E. Rep. 647. The deed had been proved in a court of original and competent jurisdiction, and the defendant was entitled to the benefit of it as evidence in making out his chain of title to the land in controversy. Edwards v. Cobb, 95 N. C. 4; Evans v. Ethridge, 99 N. C. 43, 5 S. E. Rep. 386, and cases there cited. There were other exceptions presented in the case on appeal, but we deem it unnecessary to consider them. There was error in excluding the deed offered as color of title, and the defendant is entitled to a new trial. There is error.

THORP v. MINOR *et al.*

(*Supreme Court of North Carolina. Oct. 13, 1891.*)

NEGLIGENCE — RUNAWAY HORSE — LIABILITY OF MINOR.

1. The owner of a horse, having rented a warehouse to a certain firm, left the horse with them, and used the horse in common with the firm. A clerk of the firm obtained the horse from the firm without the knowledge of the owner, to drive to a picnic, the firm telling him to send the horse back if he had opportunity, which he did by a minor not in the employ of the firm or of the owner. The minor left the horse standing in the street, and it ran away, and killed plaintiff's horse. *Held,* that the minor was not liable, since no guardian *ad litem* had been appointed.

2. The clerk was not liable, because there were no allegations against him in the complaint.

3. The firm were not liable, because the minor was not in their employ, and the clerk, as to the use of the horse, was not acting in the scope of his employment.

4. The facts fail to show any negligence on the part of the owner.

Appeal from superior court, Granville county; EDWIN T. BOYKIN, Judge.

Action for negligence by Gilbert Thorp against R. V. Minor and others. The defendant Minor was the owner of a horse which he permitted to remain with the defendants Meadows & Wilkerson, when he rented his warehouse to them, and all three occasionally used the horse. On the day in question W. A. Wilkerson, who was a clerk in the employ of the firm, obtained the use of the horse by permission of Meadows (without the knowledge or authority of Minor, the owner of the horse) to drive to a picnic; and Meadows told him to send the horse back if he had an opportunity to do so, which he did by the defendant Hester, a boy of 18 or 19 years of age, and who was not in the employ of Meadows & Wilkerson or of Minor. It was further in evidence that the defendant Hester left the horse standing in the street unhitched, under charge of no one; that the horse ran away, and ran violently against plaintiff's horse, in spite of his efforts to prevent it, and damaged plaintiff's horse by running the buggy-shaft into his shoulder, so that he died. The court intimated an opinion that plaintiff could not recover of Hester, because he was a minor, and no guardian *ad litem* had been appointed, nor against Meadows & Wilkerson, because there was no evidence that Hester was in their employ. The plaintiff, in deference to the intimation of the court, took a nonsuit, and appealed. Affirmed.

Battle & Mordecai and *A. W. Graham,* for appellant. *T. T. Hicks,* for appellees.

CLARK, J., (*after stating the facts as above.*) We concur with his honor.

1. The plaintiff could not recover against the defendant Hester, because he was an infant, and no guardian *ad litem* had been appointed.

2. Nor against the clerk, W. A. Wilkerson, for there is no allegation of any kind against him in the complaint, his name not being so much as mentioned therein. There must be *allegata* as well as *probata.*

3. Nor against Meadows & Wilkerson, as the evidence did not disclose that Hester was in their employ. The clerk, (W. A. Wilkerson,) as to the use of the horse, was not acting in the scope of his employment, and it was as if the horse had been loaned or hired to any one else. The mere request to the clerk to send the horse back would not have made the firm responsible for the pay of the person who brought the horse back if he charged for such service, and, of course, would not,

therefore, have made them responsible for his negligence. Whether the clerk borrowed or hired the horse, it was an implied part of the hiring or borrowing that he should return the horse, and, if he chose to send him back by another, such other was his servant, and not the servant of the firm. If the clerk had driven the horse back himself, the firm would not have been responsible for his negligence, nor can they be made liable because he chose to send him back by a substitute.

4. Nor is there any evidence to charge the owner, Minor, with negligence or liability in any respect. No error.

BROWNE et al. v. DAVIS.

(Supreme Court of North Carolina.　Oct. 13, 1891.)

RELEASE OF TRUST-DEED — LIEN OF PURCHASER— ALLOWANCE FOR PERMANENT IMPROVEMENTS.

1. The grantees of land, as part of the purchase transaction, conveyed the land in trust to secure the grantors, but afterwards, without authority from the grantors, conveyed a portion thereof to a stranger, who had notice that the trust had not been satisfied. The register recorded in the margin of the record of the trust-deed a memorandum, not under seal, reciting that the trustee, for value received, thereby released from the trust said portion of land, and this entry was signed by the trustee. Held, that where the trustee, though agent for the grantors, had no authority to make such entry, it did not divest him of his title, under Code N. C. § 1271, which provides that a trustee may acknowledge the "satisfaction of the provisions" of a trust, in the presence of the register of deeds, whose duty it shall be to make, upon the margin of the record of such trust, an entry of such acknowledgment, which shall be witnessed by the register, and this entry shall operate to discharge all interest of the mortgagee.

2. In a decree awarding to the grantors the portion of land attempted to be sold by the trustee, it was proper to charge the land with the amount paid therefor to the grantors through the trustee, since a person cannot repudiate a transaction made in his behalf, and retain the fruits thereof.

3. Code N. C. § 473, provides that any defendant against whom a judgment shall be rendered for land may present a petition stating that, "while holding the premises under a color of title believed by him * * * to be good," he has made valuable improvements thereon; and the court may, if satisfied of the probable truth of the allegation, impanel a jury to assess the allowance to defendant for such improvements. Section 481 provides that nothing herein shall apply to any suit brought by a mortgagee, or his heirs or assigns, against a mortgagor, or his heirs or assigns, for the recovery of the mortgaged premises. Held, that though the purchaser of said portion did not hold the premises "under a color of title believed by him * * * to be good," and was therefore not entitled to betterments, yet the suit was within the spirit of section 481, and, in assessing the grantor's damages for the use and detention of the land, it was proper to make allowance to said purchaser for permanent improvements thereon.

Appeal from superior court, Pasquotank county; HENRY R. BRYAN, Judge.

Action by S. C. Browne, M. F. Browne, M. L. Browne, and R. M. Browne against John T. Davis, to recover certain land. The plaintiffs had conveyed the land to W. O. Temple, who, as part of the transaction, conveyed it in trust to E. F. Lamb to secure to plaintiffs the purchase money. A portion of the land was subsequently conveyed by Temple to defendant. Judgment for plaintiffs. Plaintiffs appeal. Modified and affirmed.

J. H. Sawyer, for appellants. Grandy & Aydlett, for appellee.

SHEPHERD, J. The trustor conveyed a part of the land included in the deed of trust to the defendant for the sum of $450, and at the same time the trustee made the following entry on the margin of the record of the said trust: "For value received, I hereby release from the operation of this deed of trust that portion of the within described tract of land which was sold by W. O. Temple and wife to John T. Davis by deed dated February 7th, 1888. Witness my hand and seal. [Signed] E. F. LAMB, Trustee. Witness: T. P. WILCOX, R. of D." There was in fact no seal attached, and therefore the entry could not, under the most liberal construction, be considered as a deed of release, divesting the title of the trustee. Linker v. Long, 64 N. C. 296; Wharton v. Moore, 84 N. C 479. We are also of the opinion that the said entry, under the circumstances, was not warranted by section 1271 of the Code.[1] That statute only authorizes the trustee to "acknowledge the satisfaction of the provisions of such trust," etc., in which case the entry operates as a reconveyance. It was never contemplated that the trustee could, by this means, release from an unsatisfied trust specific parts of the land; and it is entirely clear that this cannot be done, where, as in the present case, the purchaser had actual knowledge that the large indebtedness secured by trust had not been satisfied. It is true that the jury found that the trustee was "the agent of the plaintiffs, [the cestuis que trustent,] and acting as such at the time he made the entry;" but it is also expressly found that this agency did not authorize him to make such entry; that the land was sold to the defendant without the knowledge or consent of the plaintiffs; and that there was no agreement on their part that any portion of it should be discharged from the indebtedness. What effect is ordinarily to be given, by way of estoppel, to the reception of the purchase money, in cases like the present, need not be considered at this time, as there is nothing to show (and proof of this is incumbent on the defendant) that the plaintiffs received the money from the trustee with knowledge of the sale and entry of record. On the contrary, it appears that very soon thereafter they caused the trustee to sell the entire tract, which proved insufficient in value to satisfy their demands. The plaintiffs becoming the purchasers at the said sale, we think that his honor was correct in holding that they acquired the legal title and were entitled to recover.

---

[1] This section provides that a trustee may acknowledge the "satisfaction of the provisions" of a trust in the presence of the register of deeds, whose duty it shall be to make, upon the margin of the record of such trust, an entry of such acknowledgment, which shall be witnessed by the register, and this entry shall operate to discharge all interest of the mortgagee.

We also concur in the ruling of the court in charging the land with the amount paid by the defendant to the plaintiffs through the trustee. There is nothing in the cases cited by the appellants' counsel which conflicts with the principle so often laid down by this court that one cannot repudiate a transaction made in his behalf, and at the same time retain the fruits thereof. Walker v. Brooks, 99 N. C. 207, 6 S. E. Rep. 63; Burns v. McGregor, 90 N. C. 225; Boyd v. Turpin, 94 N. C. 137. The action of his honor, however, is clearly sustained upon the principle of subrogation, and the cases cited in Sheldon on Subrogation (section 30 et seq.) seem directly in point.

In respect to the question of improvements, we think there was error. We have seen that the entry made on the record by the trustee did not divest his title: but granting that it had this effect, or that the trustee, without the consent of the *cestuis que trustent*, had executed a formal deed of release to the defendant, the latter, affected, as he was, with actual as well as constructive notice that the indebtedness was still existing, would have taken subject to the trust; and, so far from "holding the premises under a color of title believed by him to be good," (section 473, Code,)[1] the law would have implied that he had knowledge of the infirmity of his claim. Scott v. Battle, 85 N. C. 192, and the authorities there cited. Moreover, our case is excepted from the provision above mentioned by section 481;[2] and in Wharton v. Moore, 84 N. C. 479, it is held that improvements put upon the land by a purchaser from the mortgagor become additional security for the debt. Our case, we think, very plainly falls within the spirit of both the excepting statute and the decision just referred to.

While we are of the opinion that the defendant is not entitled to betterments, still, when the jury come to inquire into the plaintiffs' damages on account of the use and detention of the lands, "they will be at liberty, and, indeed, in duty bound, to make a fair allowance out of the same for improvements of a permanent character, and such as [plaintiffs] will have the actual enjoyment of. That such an allowance could properly be made by the jury was said in Dowd v. Faucett, 4 Dev. 92; notwithstanding it was at the same time adjudged that the defendant's claim for improvements, as such, would not be recognized by the court." Scott v. Battle, supra. Modified and affirmed.

[1] Section 473 provides that any defendant against whom a judgment shall be rendered for land may present a petition stating that, "while holding the premises under a color of title believed by him * * * to be good," he has made valuable improvements thereon; and the court may, if satisfied of the probable truth of the allegation, impanel a jury to assess the allowance to defendant for such improvements.

[2] Section 481 provides that nothing herein shall apply to any suit brought by a mortgagee, or his heirs or assigns, against a mortgagor, or his heirs or assigns, for the recovery of the mortgaged premises.

SPENCER v. BELL et al.

(*Supreme Court of North Carolina.* Oct. 13, 1891.)

CLAIM AND DELIVERY—AFFIDAVIT—BOND—WAIVER—INSTRUCTIONS—JUDGMENT.

1. In a claim and delivery action instituted by "J. M. S.," an affidavit of claim signed, "J. M. S., per D. M. S.," is sufficient, under Code N. C. § 322, which provides that such affidavit shall be made "by the plaintiff or some one in his behalf."

2. In such action, an undertaking of plaintiff for delivery of the property, which is signed by neither plaintiff nor his sureties, but which contains a justification signed by each surety, in which he makes oath that he is worth a certain sum above his liabilities and exemptions, cannot be objected to on the trial, under Code N. C. § 325, which provides that if the defendant fail, within three days after the service of the affidavit and undertaking, to give notice that he excepts to the sufficiency of the sureties, he shall be deemed to have waived all objection to them.

3. Where only one witness testified as to the value of the property claimed, it was error to refuse to charge that, if the jury believed the testimony of that witness, they should accept his valuation.

4. Code N. C. § 431, provides that, in an action for the recovery of personal property, judgment for the plaintiff may be for the recovery of possession, or for the value thereof, in case a delivery cannot be had, and the damages for the detention. *Held*, in an action to recover certain corn, alleged to be worth $45, that a judgment, decreeing that "plaintiff recover of the defendants the sum of $50, the value of said corn, to be discharged upon the payment by the defendants to the plaintiff of the sum of $36.36, with interest thereon," was unauthorized, where the only finding of fact by the jury was that the corn was worth $50.

Appeal from superior court, Beaufort county; HENRY R. BRYAN, Judge.

This is an action of claim and delivery by J. N. Spencer against Bell and Bishop to recover "one certain lot of corn, in the barn on the Bell farm," of the alleged value of $45, originally commenced before a justice of the peace in the county of Beaufort, and carried by appeal to the superior court of said county, and tried before BRYAN, J., at the February term, 1891, of said court. The affidavit required in the application for the delivery of the possession of the corn is signed as follows: "J. M. SPENCER. Per D. M. SPENCER. Sworn before me this 1st day of February, 1889. W. D. SADDLER, J. P." In the transcript of the justice of the peace it is stated: "The plaintiff appeared by his agent, D. M. Spencer." There is what purports to be an undertaking of the plaintiff for delivery of property as required by section 324 of the Code, with two sureties, but it is not signed by either the plaintiff or the sureties; but there is a justification, signed by each surety, in which he makes oath that he "is worth, over and above his liabilities and his property exempted by law, the sum of $——." In the superior court, before the trial, defendants moved to dismiss the claim and delivery proceedings upon the following grounds: *First*, because the affidavit purported to have been made by plaintiff J. M. Spencer, per D. M. Spencer; *second*, because the plaintiff gave no bond before the issuing of the order to seize the property, as required by law. Motion denied, and defendants excepted. The plaintiff moved and the court granted him leave to amend his summons so as to demand therein a certain lot of corn, of the value of $45, for advances. In the trial in the superior court plaintiff claimed the possession of a certain lot of corn cultivated by and in the possession of defendant Bell, by reason of certain advances made to defendant Bell by plaintiff as landlord. Defendant Bishop claimed the corn in controversy as mortgagee of Bell. The issues hereinafter recited were framed by the judge without objection by defendants. Defendant Bell denied that plaintiff was his landlord, or made any advances to him for the year 1888, in which year the corn was cultivated. The plaintiff testified: "I rented the land to Bell in 1888, the year in which the corn was cultivated. Defendant Bell gave me a mortgage, in 1887, upon his crop of 1888, which mortgage was not paid in full. In first part of 1888 defendant Bell told me he could not pay the mortgage of 1887 and have enough to farm on in 1888. Defendant Bishop had a second mortgage on his crop of 1887. Defendant Bell told me if both Bishop and myself closed down on him, and took his corn, he could not farm that year, but if we did not he could do so. I told him, as far as I was concerned, I would advance balance he owed me on next crop if defendant Bishop would agree not to shove him and take what he had. Afterwards we saw Bishop, and he agreed to indulge his mortgage also." Plaintiff claimed balance due upon this mortgage as advances to cultivate the crop of 1888, which balance was admitted to be $17.74 by the plaintiff. Plaintiff further claimed as advances certain sacks sold to defendant Bell, valued at $2.22, and also the use of a cart, valued at $1; all other claims of the plaintiff were abandoned. The defendants denied all the above testimony. The evidence as to the value of the corn in controversy was that of defendant Bell, who testified that it was worth $55, and defendant Bishop, who testified: "I got the money for the corn. I got $50 out of the corn. I do not know how much there was." The defendants requested the judge to charge the jury "that, if the jury believed the testimony of defendant Bell, they will find the value of the property to be $55, and answer the second issue accordingly." Refused. Defendants excepted. The jury responded to the issues as follows: "(1) Is the plaintiff the owner and entitled to the possession of the corn mentioned in the affidavit? Answer. Yes. (2) What is the value of the said corn? A. $50." The defendants moved for a new trial, and assigned the following grounds of error: "(1) For that the court refused to dismiss the claim and delivery proceedings, as hereinbefore set forth. (2) For that the court refused to instruct the jury as prayed by defendants. (3) For that the issues were not complete, and no judgment could be rendered thereon, in that the plaintiff claimed a lien upon the crop in controversy by reason of advances as landlord, and the amount of indebtedness due by defendant Bell to plaintiff for such advances was not ascer-

v.13s.E.no.29—45

tained." There was a judgment for the plaintiff, and appeal by the defendants.

John H. Small and Chas. F. Warren, for appellants.

DAVIS, J., (after stating the facts as above.) The first exception is to the refusal of his honor to dismiss the claim and delivery proceeding because the affidavit purported to have been made by the plaintiff, J. M. Spencer, per D. M. Spencer. Code, § 322, provides that the requisite affidavit shall be made "by the plaintiff or some one in his behalf." The essential requisite is that an affidavit shall be made by the plaintiff, or some one on his behalf; that the facts on which the application is based are true; and while the affidavit should have been signed by D. M. Spencer, agent for or on behalf of J. M. Spencer, it sufficiently appears that the affidavit was made for the plaintiff, and the exception cannot be sustained.

The second exception is to the refusal to dismiss because the plaintiff gave no bond. There was what purported to be an undertaking, with two sureties, and if the defendants excepted to its sufficiency, they should, within three days after the service of a copy of the affidavit and undertaking, proceeded as required by Code, § 325,[1] or they shall be deemed to have waived all objection to the sufficiency of the sureties. We think the objection on account of the insufficiency of the bond and surety came too late, and this exception cannot be sustained.

The next exception is to the refusal of the court to instruct the jury, as requested, that, if they believed the testimony of the witness Bell, they will find the value of the property to be $55, and answer the second issue accordingly. Bell was the only witness who testified as to the value of the property, and he said it was worth $55. It is true the witness Bishop testified that he "got $50 out of the corn," but he said he did not know how much corn there was, and did not testify as to its value, nor does it appear that he got all of the corn. The only evidence as to the value of the property was that of the witness Bell, who said it was worth $55, and the defendants were entitled to the instruction asked, and there was error in refusing it.

The last exception is to the judgment. The court adjudged "that the plaintiff recover of the defendants the sum of $50, the value of the said corn, to be discharged upon the payment by the defendants to the plaintiff the sum of $20.96, with interest thereon," etc. There were no findings of fact upon which such a judgment could be rendered. It is true the plaintiff claimed a balance of $17.74 on advances to cultivate the crop of 1888, and he also claimed the value of some sacks, and the use of a cart, amounting to $3.22, which, added to the $17.74, would make $20.96; but this was denied by the defend-

[1] This section provides that if the defendant fail, within three days after the service of the affidavit and undertaking, to give notice that he excepts to the sufficiency of the sureties, he shall be deemed to have waived all objection to them.

ants, and it was not within the province of his honor to say how the fact was,—only a jury could decide and say how the fact was. Besides, the action was to recover the possession of a certain lot of corn alleged to have been worth $45, and upon no state of facts, even if it had been found by the jury that the defendants were indebted to the plaintiff in the sum of $20.86, as assumed by his honor, would the plaintiff have been entitled to the judgment as rendered. Section 431[1] of the Code prescribes clearly and distinctly the manner in which judgment in an action for the recovery of personal property shall be rendered. Horton v. Horne, 99 N. C. 219, 5 S. E. Rep. 927; Taylor v. Hodges, 105 N. C. 344, 11 S. E. Rep. 156, and cases cited. There is error.

NORFOLK & W. R. Co. v. McDONALD'S ADM'R.

(Supreme Court of Appeals of Virginia. Sept. 10, 1891.)

MASTER AND SERVANT—ASSUMPTION OF RISK— CONTRIBUTORY NEGLIGENCE.

1. A brakeman, who enters into the employ of a railroad company owning cars, the couplings of which are mismatched, and who continues to use such couplings for over a year without any promise by the company to change them, assumes the extra hazard incident to the use of the mismatched couplings; and no recovery can be had from the company for his death resulting from their use.

2. A railroad brakeman, who, in coupling cars, with knowledge that the couplings are mismatched, places the pin in the moving car, and remains between the two cars to shake the pin into position, when he might have safely made the coupling by placing the pin in the standing car and permitting it to be shaken into position by the concussion of the two cars, is guilty of negligence, and no recovery can be had for his death resulting from being crushed between the two cars.

Error to circuit court, Pulaski county; D. W. BOLEN, Judge.

Action by Robert M. Chumbly, administrator of Charles O. McDonald, deceased, against the Norfolk & Western Railroad Company, for the death of plaintiff's intestate. There was a judgment for plaintiff, and defendant brings error. Reversed.

Phlegar & Johnson and *Moore & Brown*, for plaintiff in error. *Mr. Wysor*, for defendant in error.

LEWIS, P. This was an action of trespass on the case, wherein Robert M. Chumbly, administrator of Charles O. McDonald, deceased, was plaintiff, and the Norfolk & Western Railroad Company was defendant. The action was brought to recover damages for the alleged negligent killing of the plaintiff's intestate while coupling cars as a brakeman on a passenger train in the defendant's employ. The charge in the declaration was that the defendant company, at the time the deceased entered its service, was using self-coupling cars, and that the continued use of such cars was contemplated in the contract of

service, but that the defendant violated its contract in this particular, and, at the time the deceased was killed, was using mismatched couplings, which, although apparently self-coupling and safe, were, in fact, not so, in consequence of which the deceased was killed. There was a verdict for the plaintiff for $10,000 damages, which the defendant moved the court to set aside, as being contrary to the law and the evidence; but the motion was overruled by the judgment complained of.

The case is a simple one, and may be briefly disposed of. It belongs to a numerous class of cases, that of late years have come to this court, involving the correlative duties of master and servant, and as to which the law, so far as a case like the present is concerned, is too well settled and familiar to require a citation of the authorities in this opinion. The plaintiff relies upon the undisputed rule that the master must observe ordinary care in supplying and maintaining adequately safe machinery and other appliances for the work required of the servant, which rule, it is contended, has not been observed in the present case. On the other hand, the company insists that there has been no violation of duty on its part, and that the death of the deceased was caused by his own negligence, and this position is well taken. The charge in the declaration, that self-coupling cars, exclusively, were used by the company at the time the deceased entered its service, is not supported by the evidence. It appears that at one time it had, in use on its passenger trains, what were known as the "Miller Couplers," but that when the deceased entered the service they were being gradually replaced by other self-couplers, known as the "Janney Coupler;" that this change was commenced several months before that time, and was known to the deceased, who continued in the service for a year or more before his death. The deceased was killed while attempting to couple two cars, upon one of which was a Miller coupler, and on the other a Janney coupler. These couplings being mismatched, the consequence was that, when the cars came together, the couplers passed each other, and the deceased was caught between the cars, and crushed to death. When self-couplers of the same kind are used, the coupling is effected without the use of link and pin. But with mismatched couplers a link and pin are essential, and the coupling is then made by a person on the ground. The latter mode of coupling is more dangerous than the former, which renders a greater degree of care and caution necessary in making it. The brakeman or other person making it should not go between the cars, but stand outside the rail, after adjusting the link in one coupler and the pin in the other. When a Miller and Janney coupler are used, the link ought to be adjusted in the former, and the pin in the latter, so that when the cars come together the pin, by force of the concussion, will drop into the link. It appears, moreover, that the mismatched couplers in question had been in use, on the train upon which the deceased was employed, some time before he entered the service, and that after his employment he often used them. He was presumably aware of the extra hazard incident to their use, and there was no promise on the part of the company to use other couplers. This brings the case within the principle that when the servant voluntarily enters upon the employment knowing that the machinery he is required to operate is defective or unsuitable, and continues in the service without any promise by the master to render the same less dangerous, he assumes the risk, and must abide the consequences, so far as any claim against the master is concerned. Darracott v. Railroad Co., 83 Va. 288, 2 S. E. Rep. 511; Tuttle v. Railway, 122 U. S. 189, 7 Sup. Ct. Rep. 1166. In the present case the danger of the coupling was not only known to the deceased, but it was open and obvious; yet, with reckless disregard of his safety, he went between the cars and was killed. Moreover, instead of fastening the link in the Miller coupler, and placing the pin in the Janney coupler on the standing car, he did exactly the reverse; and then remained between the cars, "to shake the pin in," instead of taking position outside the rail, as he ought to have done. It is clear, therefore, that, even if negligence could be rightly imputed to the company on any ground, the deceased was guilty of such contributory negligence as to defeat the action. The judgment approving the verdict must therefore be reversed, and the case remanded for a new trial.

PENN'S EX'R v. PENN et al.

*(Supreme Court of Appeals of Virginia.
Sept. 10, 1891.)*

ESTOPPEL — ALLEGATIONS IN ANOTHER ACTION.

A debtor conveyed certain land to a person who, in consideration thereof, agreed to pay certain of the former's debts, and subsequently conveyed a portion to the debtor's mother in satisfaction of a judgment. P. and another, creditors of the debtor, filed a petition in bankruptcy, seeking to set aside the original conveyances as made to defraud creditors. A compromise was effected, wherein the bankruptcy proceedings were abandoned, and the mother gave her notes to P. and the other creditor, and placed the land in trust as security. Another creditor sued, and the trust property was sold, under decree of court, to satisfy his claim, and P. became one of the purchasers. *Held,* in an action by another creditor of the debtor to set aside all these conveyances as in fraud of creditors, that the allegations of fraud in the bankruptcy proceedings instituted by P. did not estop him to maintain that he was an innocent purchaser.

Appeal from circuit court, Roanoke county; BLAIR, Judge.

Suit in equity by the executors of Thomas G. Penn against James A. Penn and others to set aside certain conveyances of land on the ground of fraud. Dismissed. Plaintiffs appeal. Affirmed.

Anderson, Staples & Mullins, for appellant. *Penn & Cocke,* for appellee.

LEWIS, P. This was a suit in equity, commenced in the circuit court of Patrick county, and afterwards removed to the circuit court of Roanoke county, wherein the executors of Thomas G. Penn, deceased, were plaintiffs, and James A. Penn and others were defendants. The suit was brought to set aside three deeds to a tract of land in the first mentioned county, and also a judicial sale thereof, made under a decree of the circuit court of that county. The bill charges that the deeds were made with intent to hinder and delay the creditors of James A. Penn, the owner of the land, and the grantor in the first deed, and that the same are therefore fraudulent and void. The first deed is from James A. Penn to William C. Staples, and bears date October 30, 1867; the second deed is from Staples to Mary Penn, and bears date July 26, 1870; and the third is a deed of trust from Mary Penn to George W. Hylton, trustee, to secure certain debts of James A. Penn, and bears date February 7, 1871. The recited consideration in the deed from Penn to Staples is $7,000. It appears, however, that on the same day the deed was executed the parties entered into a written agreement, whereby it was stipulated that, in consideration of the conveyance, the grantee, Staples, would pay certain debts of the grantor, Penn, amounting in the aggregate to a sum exceeding $7,000. Among these debts was a judgment in favor of Mary Penn for something over $4,000, which it was agreed should be satisfied by Staples conveying to her one of the two tracts of land conveyed to him by James A. Penn, known as the "Home Place," and which is the land involved in this controversy. The second deed was made in pursuance of this agreement. Shortly after the date of the first deed F. R. Penn and Green Penn, creditors of the grantor, James A. Penn, filed a petition in involuntary bankruptcy in the United States district court against him, in which they attacked the deed on the ground that it was made with intent to give preferences among his creditors, in violation of the provisions of the then bankrupt law. They also charged that it was made with intent to defraud his creditors. A compromise was thereupon effected, whereby Mary Penn agreed to give her notes for certain enumerated debts of her son, the said James A. Penn, and to secure the same by a deed of trust on the "Home Place," and in execution of this agreement the trust-deed to Hylton was executed. The bankruptcy proceedings were thereupon abandoned. After the execution of the trust-deed a suit was instituted by Jesse Fry, a creditor of James A. Penn, against Mary Penn and others, to subject the land to the payment of his debt, and in that suit the land was decreed to be sold. The land was accordingly sold under the decree, and was purchased by F. R. Penn and James P. Crits, which sale was confirmed. The charge in the bill is that, not only were the deeds in question fraudulent and void, but that the beneficiaries in the trust-deed and the purchasers at the judicial sale had notice of the fraud, and were therefore affected by it. The answers, however, deny these charges, and the circuit court of Roanoke county, when the cause came on to be finally heard, dismissed the bill, on the ground that, even if there was fraud in the first and second deeds, the trustee and beneficiaries in the trust-deed were innocent purchasers for value, and that their claims were valid against all other creditors of James A. Penn. In this decree, which is the decree complained of, there is no error. The *bona fides* of the appellees' debts, secured in the trust-deed, if it can be said to be questioned at all in the bill, is clearly proven, and if there was fraud in the transactions assailed, or any of them, it was incumbent on the plaintiffs to show by clear and convincing evidence that the appellees participated in or had notice of it. This they have not done. It is true that two of the appellees, Frank R. and Green Penn, in their petition in bankruptcy, charged in general terms that the deed from James A. Penn to Staples was not only an unlawful preference under the bankrupt act, but that it was made with intent to hinder, delay, and defraud the creditors of the grantor. But this latter averment, of which there was no proof, can be taken, in the present case, merely as an admission, which is not conclusive. 1 Greenl. Ev. § 212. The bill calls for answers on oath, and in the answers of the defendants the charges of fraud are distinctly denied, as also the charge that the defendants had notice of the alleged fraud. The only evidence is that taken by the defendants, and, looking to the whole case, we are of opinion, without stopping to review the evidence, that the decree dismissing the bill must be affirmed.

SAWYERS v. COMMONWEALTH.

(Supreme Court of Appeals of Virginia. Sept. 17, 1891.)

CRIMINAL LAW—RIGHT TO CLOSE—REMARKS OF COUNSEL—ARSON.

1. In a criminal prosecution, where counsel is employed by a private person to assist the commonwealth's attorney, the question whether or not defendant is entitled to the closing argument before the jury rests in the sound discretion of the trial court, and its ruling against defendant is not subject to review, except for abuse of discretion.

2. In a criminal case, a remark by the commonwealth's attorney that, though he had no right to swear any man accused of crime, he had the right to prove the latter's statements, does not violate Code Va. § 3897, which provides that the failure of accused to testify shall not be the subject of comment before the court or jury.

3. In a prosecution for setting fire to an unoccupied dwelling-house, which was only partially completed when burned, the evidence showed that when the fire was discovered, the flames were bursting out at every opening, and that the fire appeared to have been set in several places. It was also shown that defendant entertained hostile feelings towards the owner of the building; that he had repeatedly threatened to burn it; that, after the fire, he was seen to stand on the site of the house, and hold up his hands, and yell as if in delight; and that he had admitted to several witnesses that he had burned the house. *Held,* that the evidence so clearly established defendant's guilt that an erroneous ruling by the court, excluding evidence offered to impeach one of the commonwealth's witnesses, was no ground for reversal, since such exclusion could not have harmed defendant.

Defendant Sawyers was indicted for maliciously and feloniously burning the building of another. He was convicted, and now brings error. Affirmed.

Marshall & Bowller, for plaintiff in error. The *Attorney General,* for the Commonwealth.

LEWIS, P. This is a writ of error and *supersedeas* to a judgment of the circuit court of Alleghany county, affirming a judgment of the county court of that county, whereby the prisoner was sentenced, in accordance with the verdict of the jury, to three years' imprisonment in the penitentiary for the felonious and malicious burning of a certain building, the property of one John W. Jennings.

The first assignment of error that we will consider raises the question whether or not the county court erred in permitting the argument before the jury to be concluded (against the prisoner's objection) by R. L. Parrish, an attorney employed by Jennings to aid the attorney for the commonwealth. It is contended that in a criminal prosecution, wherein counsel are employed by private parties to prosecute, the accused has the right to answer any argument that may be made to the jury by such counsel, and that it was error in the present case to permit the case before the jury to be concluded by Parrish; but we do not concur in this view. It was a matter to be determined by the trial court, in the exercise of a sound discretion; and there is nothing in the record to show that this discretion had been abused. Hopper's Case, 6 Grat. 684; 3 Rob. Pr. (Old.) 227; 1 Bish. Crim. Proc. (3d Ed.) § 282.

The subject of the next assignment of error is a remark made by Parrish in the closing argument, which was as follows: "Although I have no right to swear any man who is accused of crime, I have the right to prove his statements." The prisoner objected to the remark at the time, as he does now, claiming that it was in violation of section 3897 of the Code, which provides that the failure of the accused to testify shall create no presumption against him, nor be the subject of any comment before the court or jury by the prosecuting attorney. There was certainly no direct reference in the remark to the failure of the accused to testify, and it would be a strained and unwarranted construction to hold it to be an indirect or implied comment on that subject. The objection is, therefore, not well taken. Sutton's Case, 85 Va. 128, 7 S. E. Rep. 323.

The next point is as to the exclusion of certain evidence at the trial. The commonwealth, to maintain the issue on her part, introduced a witness, Ledford Sawyers, who, on cross-examination, was asked by the prisoner whether, in a conversation, after the burning, with Mrs. Sawyers, he had not admitted that he did the burning, to which the witness, without objecting to the question, answered that he had no such conversation. The prisoner then called Mrs. Sawyers as a witness, and asked her the following question: "Did or did not Ledford Sawyers, in a conversation with you, say that if you were true in your declaration that you would not tell, if you knew, who burned Jennings' house, he would tell you who did it; and did he not say, when you told him you were, 'Well, then, I will tell you. I did?'"—to which question the attorney for the commonwealth objected, and the objection was sustained. It is contended that the question was relevant, and therefore admissible to impeach the credit of Ledford Sawyers as a witness. But, be that as it may, it is clear from the evidence certified in the fourth bill of exceptions (which was taken to the refusal of the court to grant a new trial) that the jury could not have rightly found otherwise than that the prisoner was guilty; and hence, in any view, he has not been prejudiced by the ruling of the court. The established rule is that when the question in the appellate court is as to an erroneous ruling at the trial in admitting or excluding evidence, or in the giving or refusing an instruction, and the accused may have been prejudiced by such ruling, even though it be doubtful whether he was or not, the judgment will be reversed; but when, from a survey of the whole record, it is manifest that he has not been so prejudiced, the judgment will be affirmed, the rule in this respect being the same in criminal as in civil cases. Payne's Case, 81 Grat. 855; Vaughan's Case, 85 Va. 671, 8 S. E. Rep. 584; Bank v. Waddill, 27 Grat. 448. In the present case the evidence is clear and satisfactory, leaving no room for a rational doubt as to the prisoner's guilt. It was proved by Jennings, the owner, of the building, that it was burned between 8 and 9 o'clock at night, on the 25th of April, 1888; that he lived about 400 yards from it, and passed near it on his way to supper, about 35 or 40 minutes before the fire was discovered; that at that time there was no fire in or near it; that the building was a dwelling-house, but was not completed, and was unoccupied. When the fire was discovered, he says, the flames were bursting out at every opening, and the house appeared to have been set on fire in several places. As tending to fix guilt upon the prisoner, it was further proven that he had long entertained feelings of hostility towards Jennings, originating in the fact that the farm upon which the house was built formerly belonged to the prisoner's father, and had been purchased by Jennings, several years before the burning, at a judicial sale. Only a week before the burning, he (the prisoner) declared to one of the witnesses his intention to burn the house, and to make Jennings a pauper; and several months previously he remarked to another witness, who mentioned that Jennings was building a new house, that if he built it, it would not stand 12 months. On two occasions soon after the burning, when passing the standing chimneys where the house had stood, he was seen to "hold up his hands, and yell as if in delight;" and, on another occasion, he said to one of the witnesses that only a few persons knew he burned the house, and they would not tell. He made substantially the same statement to another witness at a different time, and he repeatedly threatened, before the burning, to make Jennings a

pauper. Among the chief *indiciæ* which go to substantiate at once *corpus delicti* and the guilt of the prisoner in a case like this, say the authorities, are the circumstances that the fire broke out suddenly in an uninhabited house, or in different parts of the same building, and that the accused had a cause of ill will against the sufferer, or had been heard to threaten him. In the present case, not only do all these circumstances concur, but others, as we have seen, were established, which make a clear case for the commonwealth,—a case so strong and clear as to make it apparent that the jury could not have rightly found for the prisoner had the court permitted the question propounded to Mrs. Sawyers, above quoted, to be answered, and the answer had been favorable to the prisoner; nor even if the testimony of the witness Ledford Sawyers had been discarded altogether. It is true, the bill of exceptions embodies only the evidence for the commonwealth, the court deeming it unnecessary, as the bill states, to certify the evidence introduced by the prisoner; but, inasmuch as the court was not asked to certify the latter, and as no point was made either in the trial court or in the circuit court (nor has any been made in this court) as to the failure to certify it, the prisoner must be taken to have acquiesced in the view that it was not essential to his case in the appellate court. The judgment is therefore affirmed.

NORFOLK & W. R. CO. v. PENDLETON.

(Supreme Court of Appeals of Virginia. Sept. 10, 1891.)

RAILROAD COMPANIES — OVERCHARGES — CONSTITUTIONAL LAW.

A railroad company organized in 1848, and exempted by its charter from legislative regulation as to tolls until it should become able to pay dividends of more than 15 per cent. on its capital stock, was acquired by another company organized in 1870 under a charter investing it with all the rights and franchises of the first company, but containing a provision that it should be subject to all the laws applying to railroad companies generally. *Held*, the latter company and its successors were subject to the general act of 1858, prescribing certain maximum rates of toll, and a penalty for overcharges. Railroad Co. v. Pendleton, 11 S. E. Rep. 1062, followed.

Error to circuit court, Wythe county; D. W. BOLEN, Judge.

Mr. Bolling, for plaintiff in error. *Mr. Pierce*, for defendant in error.

LEWIS, P. This was an action of debt in the circuit court of Wythe county by Edmund Pendleton against the Norfolk & Western Railroad Company, to recover penalties for alleged overcharges for the transportation of certain fertilizers. There was a judgment for the plaintiff for $400 and costs. The case, except as to the amount involved, is like the case of Railroad Co. v. Pendleton, 86 Va. 1004, 11 S. E. Rep. 1062, in which case a judgment in favor of the same plaintiff was affirmed. It is useless to repeat what was there said. It is enough to say that, upon consideration, we adhere to the ruling in that case, and are therefore of opinion, for the reasons given in that case, to affirm the judgment in the present case.

MORGAN et al. v. HARROLD et al.

(Supreme Court of Georgia. July 13, 1891.)

COMPETENCY OF WITNESS — TRANSACTIONS WITH DECEDENT.

1. In an action against surviving partners brought by the beneficiaries of a trust fund, the trustee is *prima facie* incompetent as a witness for the plaintiffs to affect the partnership with notice of the trust, by means of a transaction or communication between himself and a member of the partnership now deceased, the evidence act of 1889 declaring that "where a person not a party, but a person interested in the result of the suit, is offered as a witness, he shall not be competent to testify, if, as a party to the cause, he would for any cause be incompetent."

2. There was no error in granting a nonsuit.

(Syllabus by the Court.)

Error from superior court, Sumter county; ALLEN FORT, Judge.

Suit by Russell Morgan and others against N. B. Harrold and others, survivors, to recover trust funds. Nonsuit granted. Plaintiffs bring error. Affirmed.

Hinton & Cutts, for plaintiffs in error. B. P. Hollis and E. A. Hawkins, by Harrison & Peeples, for defendants in error.

BLECKLEY, C. J. 1. The suit was by the children of Morgan against the surviving partners of the firm of Harrold, Johnson & Co. and others. It involved the tracing of a trust fund which Morgan had held as trustee for the plaintiffs, and which he had wasted. A portion of this fund had been invested by him in certain realty, which was paid for in part with his own money and in part with the trust money. He took the title to this property in his own name, with no declaration or disclosure of any trust upon the face of the conveyance. He afterwards sold and conveyed it as his own to Harrold, Johnson & Co., and they paid him for it. The plaintiffs by this action to assert their rights as beneficiaries of the trust, and to charge Harrold, Johnson & Co. with their equitable interest in the realty thus acquired by the firm from their trustee. To affect the firm with notice of the trust, they offered at the trial to prove by their father, the trustee, conversations which he had with Thomas Harrold, (a member of the firm since deceased,) in which he informed him (Harrold) that some of the trust money was invested in this land. These conversations were prior to and at the time of the execution of his deed to the firm. There was no suggestion that any other member of the firm was present at or privy to the conversations or any of them. The court ruled the witness incompetent to give the evidence offered, because Thomas Harrold was dead. The witness act of 1889, in clause b, declares that "where any suit is instituted or defended by partners, persons jointly liable, or interested, the opposite party shall not be admitted to testify in his own favor as to transactions or communications solely with an insane or deceased partner, or person jointly liable or interested, and not also with a survivor thereof." Under this provision, if one or all of the plaintiffs had been present at the alleged conversations with Harrold, and had heard notice of the

trust communicated to him, they would have been incompetent to so testify at the trial, Harrold being then dead. Thus, the plaintiffs themselves were not competent witnesses to prove what they sought to prove by their trustee. In clause d the act declares that "where a person not a party, but a person interested in the result of the suit, is offered as a witness, he shall not be competent to testify if, as a party to the cause, he would for any cause be incompetent." The trustee was not a party to this suit. If he had been a party, that is, if he had brought the suit as trustee to recover the trust fund or trust property which he had parted with to Harrold, Johnson & Co., he would have been incompetent to testify in the cause in his own favor as to his conversations with Harrold, for the reason that Harrold is dead. Thus he certainly has two of the three marks of an incompetent witness which are specified in clause d, the clause last above quoted. Has he the third and most important mark,—was he interested in the result of the suit?

"The predicaments in which a witness may be incompetent in respect of the result admit of three varieties: (1) Where actual gain or loss would result simply and immediately from the verdict and judgment; (2) where the witness is so situated that a legal right or liability would immediately result from the verdict and judgment; (3) where the witness would be liable over to the party calling him in respect to some breach of contract or duty on the part of the witness involved in the issue." 1 Starkie, Ev. (7th Amer. Ed., from 3d London Ed. 1842,) pp. 106, 107. "It seems that, in general, where a witness is *prima facie* liable to the plaintiff in respect of the cause for which he sues, he is not a competent witness for the plaintiff to prove the defendant's liability; for his evidence tends to produce payment or satisfaction to the plaintiff at another's expense, and the proceeding and recovering against another would afford strong, if not conclusive, evidence against the plaintiff in an action against the witness." 1 Starkie Ev. supra, 112. There can be no doubt that a trustee who has wasted the fund is liable to answer for it to the beneficiary of the trust; and it is manifest that if the beneficiary follows the fund, and recovers it from a third person to whom the trustee has parted with it, the liability of the trustee to his *cestui que trust* is thereby discharged. The trustee is consequently as much interested in aiding the beneficiary in maintaining a suit to recover the fund from a third person as he would be were the suit his own. Nothing, therefore, can be more clear than that Morgan, the trustee, was interested in the result of this suit; and *prima facie* his whole interest was on the side of the plaintiffs, the party calling him to testify. What effect the warranty of title in his deed as an individual to Harrold, Johnson & Co. may have had in balancing his interest is not now for consideration; for that warranty, so far as appears, was not before the court, or brought to its attention, when the competency of the witness was under adjudication. According to the order of statement in the bill of exceptions, the deed was not put in evidence until after the decision on the competency of the witness was pronounced; and it is nowhere intimated that the witness or the rejected testimony was again offered after the deed was introduced. Ignoring the warranty as a factor in the question, we hold simply that, on the facts presented, the court did not err in ruling the witness incompetent, and excluding his testimony.

2. Nor was it error to order a nonsuit. There being no evidence of any notice to Harrold, Johnson & Co., the purchasers from Morgan, that a trust fund or estate was in any way involved in their purchase or the subject-matter of it, they stand on the footing of *bona fide* purchasers for value and are protected; and, they being protected, there was no basis for a recovery against the survivors of that firm or any of the defendants in the action. Judgment affirmed.

WARD v. STATE.

(Supreme Court of Georgia. April 22, 1891.)

PRACTICE IN SUPREME COURT—BILL OF EXCEPTIONS—CONTINUANCE.

Where a bill of exceptions is not signed as required by Code Ga. § 4251, and there is no entry or other evidence of service, an application for continuance in the supreme court, based upon the certificate of a physician, and the letters and affidavit of appellant's senior counsel, showing the sickness of the latter, and his consequent inability to attend court or prepare briefs, will not be granted, and the writ of error will be dismissed.

(Syllabus by the Court.)

Error from superior court, Liberty county.

Rosa Ward was indicted for fornication. She was found guilty, whereupon she took this writ. Judgment affirmed, and writ dismissed.

J. T. Jordan and *E. M. Hewlett,* for plaintiff in error. *W. W. Fraser,* Sol. Gen., for the State.

BLECKLEY, C. J. On the call of this case in its regular order, there was no appearance for the plaintiff in error; but the attention of the court was called to documents on file in the clerk's office, consisting of two letters from E. M. Hewlett, two letters from J. Parker Jordan, an affidavit of the latter purporting to have been sworn to in the District of Columbia before a notary public, and a medical certificate signed, A. A. Marsteller, M. D. The purpose indicated by these documents was to apply for a continuance in behalf of the plaintiff in error, and show cause for granting the same; the cause alleged being the indisposition of the said J. Parker Jordan, and his consequent inability to attend the court at the present term, or even to prepare briefs, etc., for use in argument, he being the senior counsel and the one relied upon for services in this court. After these documents were read, the solicitor general, representing the state, objected to any continuance being granted, and moved to dismiss the writ of error because the bill of exceptions had not been signed as required by section 4251 of

the Code. The court thereupon inspected the bill of exceptions, and the entries thereon; and seeing that the bill was unsigned, and that there was no entry or other evidence of service, decided that the case was not legally in this court so as to give the court jurisdiction of the same. Whereupon it was ordered and adjudged that a continuance be denied, the writ of error be dismissed, and the judgment of the court below stand affirmed. Writ of error dismissed.

TUTTY v. STATE.

(Supreme Court of Georgia. April 22, 1891.)

Error from superior court, Liberty county. *J. T. Jordan* and *E. M. Hewlett,* for plaintiff in error. *W. W. Fraser,* Sol. Gen., for the State.

BLECKLEY, C. J. The facts recited in the final order made in the case of Ward v. State, ubi supra, being true of this case also, it was ordered and adjudged that a continuance be denied, the writ of error be dismissed, and the judgment of the court below stand affirmed. Writ of error dismissed.

SIBLEY v. OBER & SONS CO.

(Supreme Court of Georgia. May 8, 1891.)

TRIAL BY COURT—DECISION ON RECOLLECTION OF EVIDENCE—ACCOUNTING OF AGENT.

1. Where notes held by a creditor as collateral security are in the hands of the principal debtor for collection, with the understanding that the proceeds are to be and remain the property of the creditor until the principal debt is paid, cotton received in payment of the collateral notes, and sent to an agent of the creditor for sale, must be accounted for by such agent to the creditor as property belonging to the latter.

2. There was evidence from which the trial judge, acting as a jury by the consent of parties, could find that the cotton in question belonged to the creditor, and that the agent was affected with notice of his title.

3. Where the judge, acting as a jury, decides the case long after hearing the evidence and argument, he may act upon his recollection of the written evidence without having it in his possession at the time of deciding, provided he is satisfied that he remembers it, and especially if he remains of the same opinion as to the effect of it after reviewing it upon a motion for a new trial, in deciding which motion the evidence was all put before him again and re-examined.

(Syllabus by Simmons, J.)

Error from superior court, Richmond county.

J. R. Lamar, for plaintiff in error. *Harper & Bro.,* for defendant in error.

Judgment affirmed.

BOAZ et al. v. CENTRAL RAILROAD & BANKING CO.

(Supreme Court of Georgia. July 8, 1891.)

LIVE-STOCK SHIPMENT—FEEDING AND WATERING—SPECIAL CONTRACT.

1. The shipper of live-stock by railway, under a special contract in which he agrees that, "in case of accidents to or delays of train from any cause whatever," he "is to feed, water, and take proper care of the stock at his own expense," cannot recover damages resulting from his own failure to perform his part of the contract, although the company may have consumed more time than necessary in effecting the transportation. There might be damage from such delay

by increasing the expense of the shipper, or by some loss to him in consequence of the change of market value, but the deterioration in the condition of the animals from lack of food, water, and attention would not result from the delay, but from the negligence of the shipper.

2. Where there is a special contract varying the liability of the carrier, the action is properly brought on the special contract, and not on the general liability.

(Syllabus by the Court.)

Error from superior court, Dougherty county; B. B. Bower, Judge.

Action by G. R. Boaz & Co. against the Central Railroad & Banking Company, to recover damages for delay in shipping cattle. Judgment for defendant. Plaintiffs bring error. Affirmed.

D. H. Pope, for plaintiffs in error. R. F. Lyon and W. T. Jones, for defendant in error.

BLECKLEY, C. J. 1. Where parties dealing with each other enter into a lawful contract touching a given transaction, the terms of that contract are the law of the transaction, as between themselves. Their rights and obligations are measured by their own stipulations. Here there was a written contract; the animals were shipped at a reduced rate; the owner was allowed free transportation for himself or his agent; and the owner or shipper agreed on his part to assume all risk incident to railroad transportation not occasioned by negligence of the company; and, "in case of accidents to or delays of train from any cause whatever, to feed, water, and take proper care of the stock at his own expense." According to the evidence, there was delay from some cause not explained, and the deterioration of the animals in condition and value resulted chiefly, if not exclusively, from lack of food, water, and due attention pending this delay. The owner or shipper did not go along with the stock, or upon the same train, nor send an agent. The contract obligation to "feed, water, and take proper care of the stock" was wholly disregarded, and yet the complaint is that the animals suffered for the want of food, water, and attention, and were thereby damaged. The theory of the plaintiff seems to be that, if there had been no delay, there would have been no need for food and water en route, and consequently no damage from his failure to furnish the same. But it was foreseen that there might be delay, and the contingency was provided for by mutual agreement, the terms of which cast the duty on the owner or shipper to feed and water in case of delay from any cause. Manifestly, the non-performance of this duty was the proximate cause of the damage.

2. As there was a special contract substituting a conventional for the ordinary liability of the carrier, the action, as ultimately shaped by amendment to the declaration, was properly rested on the special contract. After the plaintiffs' evidence disclosed that the shipment in question was not made under the general law applicable to common carriers, it would be obviously unjust to measure the duty and obligations of the carrier by that law instead of by the stipulations of the parties embodied in their express contract. Had the plaintiffs refused to amend, and stood upon their declaration as originally framed, counting in tort upon the public duty of the carrier, they could have pursued that course; but the defendant would have been allowed to set up the special contract, and take the benefit of it in that way. Railroad Co. v. Thornton, 71 Ga. 61. Bliss, Code Pl. § 14; 2 Amer. & Eng. Enc. Law, 903; 1 Bates, Partn. 872; Oxley v. Railway Co., 65 Mo. 629. Judgment affirmed.

LUMPKIN, J., not presiding.

BROOKS v. WOODSON et al.

(Supreme Court of Georgia. July 8, 1891.)

EXECUTION OF WILL — ATTESTING WITNESSES.

According to the doctrine of Duffie v. Corridon, 40 Ga. 122, the witnesses to a will must subscribe their names as witnesses after the will is signed by the testator, there being nothing to attest until his signature has been annexed. It makes no difference that the signing and attestation are each a part of one and the same transaction.

(Syllabus by the Court.)

Error from superior court, Bibb county; A. L. Miller, Judge.

Action by John W. Brooks against Lula Woodson and another. Judgment for defendants. Plaintiff brings error. Affirmed.

Hill & Harris, for plaintiff in error. Hardeman & Davis, Turner & Willingham, and Dessau & Bartlett, for defendants in error.

BLECKLEY, C. J. There is nothing to distinguish this case from Duffie v. Corridon, 40 Ga. 122, except that in the execution and attestation of this will there was but one transaction, the witnesses all subscribing the unsigned will in the presence of the testator, and he, at the same time and place, and immediately after they affixed their signatures, signing the document in their presence. In Duffie v. Corridon there were two interviews, at the first of which two of the witnesses (togther with another who was not afterwards present) subscribed, and at the second the testator and the third witness. But is this difference in the facts of the two cases material? The doctrine distinctly held by the court in ruling Duffie v. Corridon is that, until the testator signs, there is nothing to attest; the signature of the testator being the principal, if not the only, matter to which the attestation contemplated by law applies. It is obvious that, if this be the true reason why the witnesses cannot subscribe their names until after the testator has signed his, it is of no consequence, when the form of attesting an unsigned will is gone through with, whether on the same occasion of the testator's added signature or on a previous occasion. In either case, the attesting act would be performed when there was no signature in existence to be attested, and therefore no subject-matter to which the act could apply. To witness a future event is equally impossible, whether it occur the next moment or the next week. We rule the present case on the authority of the prior one above cited; being satisfied, after careful examination, that to abide by the principle of that decision we must regard the order of time in which the respective signatures occur, rather than the interval of time by which they are separated. The manifest teaching of Duffie v. Corridon is that the testator must sign first. That teaching is not followed, but directly violated, when the witnesses sign first. Judgment affirmed.

LUMPKIN, J., not presiding.

NOTE. Where signing by one or more of the witnesses precedes that of the testator, and is on a different occasion, the will is not validly attested. Reed v. Watson, 27 Ind. 443; Hindmarsh v. Carlton, 8 H. L. Cas. 160. But when all (witnesses and testator) sign on the same occasion, authorities differ. The will is held not good in Olding's Case, 2 Curt. Ecc. 865; Byrd's Case, 3 Curt. Ecc. 117; Cooper v. Bockett, Id. 648; Shaw v. Neville, 1 Jur. (N. S.) 408; Ragland v. Huntingdon, 1 Ired. 563; Jackson v. Jackson, 39 N. Y. 153; Sisters of Charity v. Kelly, 67 N. Y. 409; McMulkin's Case, 6 Dem. Sur. 347. And see Pearson v. Pearson, L. R. 2 Prob. & Div. 451; Fischer v. Popham, L. R. 3 Prob. & Div. 246. In the following cases the attestation had an additional element of invalidity, namely, as not being done in testator's presence: Cox's Will, 1 Jones, (N. C.) 321; Boldry v. Parris, 2 Cush. 433; Chase v. Kittredge, 11 Allen, 49, (cases reviewed.) The will is held good in O'Brien v. Galagher, 25 Conn. 229, and in Miller v. McNeill, 35 Pa. St. 217. But, in connection with this latter case, it must be observed that the Pennsylvania law does not require subscribing witnesses. Statute quoted and cases cited in Frew v. Clarke, 80 Pa. St. 178, 179. In Swift v. Wiley, 1 B. Mon. 114, the decision rests partly upon acknowledgment of signatures by the witnesses. It is miscited in Chisholm v. Ben, 7 B. Mon. 410, but followed in Sechrest v. Edwards, 4 Metc. (Ky.) 163. The case of Vaughan v. Burford, 3 Bradf. Sur. 78, is overruled by the New York cases cited supra. Rosser v. Franklin, 6 Grat. 1, rests partly on the fact that the signature of the testator was by his request affixed before attestation. In Virginia, too, witness may acknowledge signature. Sturdivant v. Birchett, 10 Grat. 67. And see Pollock v. Glassell, 2 Grat. 439. In general, see 1 Jarm. Wills, 110; Schouler, Wills, § 328; Beach, Wills, § 43.

ALBERTSON et al. v. TERRY et al.

(Supreme Court of North Carolina.　Oct. 13, 1891.)

REFUSAL OF CHANGE OF VENUE — REVIEW ON APPEAL — NONSUIT — PROSECUTION BONDS — LIMITATIONS — INSTRUCTIONS.

1. Under Code N. C. §§ 196, 197, which forbid a judge to remove a cause on an allegation that a fair trial cannot be had in the county where pending, unless satisfied, after thorough examination of the evidence, that the ends of justice demand a removal, a finding that a party can secure a fair trial in the county where pending is conclusive, and cannot be reviewed on appeal.

2. After the jury is impaneled, a motion to nonsuit plaintiffs, on the ground that the prosecution bond is improperly executed, will be denied where plaintiffs offer to perfect the bond.

3. Under Code, § 413, which provides that no judge, in giving an instruction to the petit jury, shall give an opinion whether a fact is fully or sufficiently proven, an instruction that no charge in the bill of particulars appears against one of the defendants which is not paid, as shown by copies of receipts filed, was properly refused, as invading the province of the jury.

4. The statute of limitations is not available where not pleaded, and it is proper to refuse to charge that items of indebtedness accruing more than three years before suit brought are barred, where the trial is an inquiry on a judgment by default.

Appeal from superior court, Pasquotank county; HENRY R. BRYAN, Judge.

Action by J. W. Albertson & Son against Harvey Terry and Timothy Ely to recover attorney's fees. Verdict and judgment for plaintiffs. Defendants appeal. Affirmed.

H. Terry, for appellants. Grandy & Aydlett, for appellee.

CLARK, J. The case on appeal presents four exceptions for review:

1. The denial of the motion to remove. The statute (Code, §§ 196, 197) forbids the judge to remove a cause on an allegation that a fair trial cannot be had in the county where pending, unless satisfied, after thorough examination of the evidence, that the ends of justice demand a removal. Here the judge finds as a fact that the defendants could secure a fair trial in said county. Such finding is conclusive, and, besides, the granting or refusal of such motion is not reviewable. State v. Duncan, 28 N. C. 98; State v. Hildreth, 31 N. C. 429; State v. Hill, 72 N. C. 345; State v. Hall, 73 N. C. 134; State v. Johnson, 104 N. C. 780, 10 S. E. Rep. 257.

2. After the jury was impaneled the defendants moved to nonsuit the plaintiffs because the prosecution bond was improperly executed. The plaintiffs asked leave to perfect the bond, which was granted, and defendants' motion denied. The objection came too late. Brittain v. Howell, 19 N. C. 107; Russell v. Saunders, 48 N. C. 432; Hughes v. Hodges, 94 N. C. 56.

3. After argument by counsel to the jury, the defendants asked the court to charge the jury that "no charge in the bill of particulars against Terry is shown that is not paid in full to plaintiffs, as shown by copies of receipts filed; therefore Terry is not liable for the debts of Ely." The court declined to give the instruction, and charged the jury that it was a question of fact for them, in passing upon which they were to be guided by the evidence submitted to them. Had the judge granted the prayer, it would have been a palpable violation of the act of 1796, (Code, § 413.[1]) The question of payment was an issue of fact for the jury.

4. Because the court declined to charge, as requested, that all items of charges made by plaintiffs more than three years before suit brought were barred by the statute of limitations. The trial was an inquiry instituted upon a judgment by default for want of an answer taken at the previous term. It is familiar learning that the statute of limitations is not available unless pleaded. (Guthrie v. Bacon, 107 N. C. 337, 12 S. E. Rep. 204; Randolph v. Randolph, 107 N. C. 506, 12 S. E. Rep. 874;) and this is required by the statute, (Code, § 138.) No error.

---

[1] This section provides that "no judge, in giving a charge to the petit jury, either in a civil or a criminal action, shall give an opinion whether a fact is fully or sufficiently proven, such matter being the true office and province of the jury."

STATE v. HADDOCK.

(Supreme Court of North Carolina. Oct. 20, 1891.)

DESTROYING REPUTATION OF INNOCENT WOMAN —INDICTMENT.

An indictment which, in the language of Code N. C. § 1113, creating the offense, charges that defendant, attempting wantonly and maliciously to injure and destroy the reputation of L. B., an innocent and virtuous woman, did, by words spoken, declare, in substance, that she was an incontinent woman, is sufficient, without setting forth the words by which the attempt was made.

Criminal action tried before WHITAKER, Judge, at the June term, 1891, of the superior court of Pitt county. The defendant was indicted for attempting to injure and destroy the reputation of an innocent woman, under section 1113 of the Code. The indictment was as follows: "The jurors for the state upon their oaths present that Spencer Haddock, late of the county of Pitt, on the 26th day of May, in the year of our Lord one thousand eight hundred and ninety-one, at and in the county of Pitt, attempting, wantonly and maliciously, to injure and destroy the reputation of one Lany Booth, being an innocent and virtuous woman, did, by words spoken, declare, in substance, that the said Lany Booth was an incontinent woman, against the form of the statute in such case made and provided, and against the peace and dignity of the state." The counsel for defendant moved to quash the bill of indictment, which motion was allowed, and the state appealed. Reversed.

The Attorney General, for the State.

DAVIS, J., *(after stating the facts.)* By section 1113 of the Code it is made a misdemeanor for any one to "attempt, in a wanton and malicious manner, to destroy the reputation of an innocent woman, by words written or spoken, which amount to a charge of incontinency." The defendant is indicted under this section, and the only question presented for our consideration is, does the indictment "express the charge against the defendant in a plain, intelligible, and explicit manner?" If it does, it is sufficient. See Code, § 1183. The indictment follows the very language of the statute; but it is said that the indictment should set forth the words "spoken," and the circumstances under which they were spoken, in order to enable the court to see whether they amount to a charge of incontinency, and to enable the defendant to know what he is to answer. The charge is clearly and distinctly made, in the very language of the statute, that he wantonly and maliciously attempted to injure and destroy the character of Lany Booth, an innocent and virtuous woman. Whether she is an innocent and virtuous woman, and whether he has attempted, by words spoken, to injure and destroy her character, are matters for proof. It is not necessary to set forth the words by which the attempt was made. The offense is created by statute, and it is sufficient if the indictment follows the words of the statute. State v. George, 93 N. C. 568, and cases cited. The legislature has thought wise to relax the stringency of the common-law requirements in indictments under which defendants frequently escape trial and punishment upon informalities and refinements. Code, § 1183, supra. In the case of State v. Edens, 95 N. C. 693, an indictment, in form precisely like this, was before this court, in which there was a motion in arrest of judgment. That was the defendant's appeal, and a new trial was awarded because of error in instructions to the jury upon the evidence, but the court refused to arrest the judgment. It is true that the form of the indictment was not passed on; but SMITH, C. J., said: "We do not find it necessary to pass upon the form of the indictment, * * * since we propose to dispose of the appeal upon the ruling to which the first exception is taken, with the remark that similar forms of indictment have been heretofore before this court, and acted on without objection, for these alleged defects." State v. Edens, 95 N. C. 693, and cases there cited. There is error. Let this be certified.

CUNNINGGIM et al. v. PETERSON et al.

(Supreme Court of North Carolina. Oct. 13, 1891.)

DEEDS—REGISTRATION—WHAT CONSTITUTES—FILING.

In an action to recover land, the issue was as to whether a certain deed was filed for registration before December 30, 1889, and the deed contained an indorsement by the register that it was "filed for registration at 12 o'clock M., July 27, 1889, subject to the annexed facts;" that, no fees having been paid, it was left open to the inspection of the public until December 30, 1889, when the fees were paid, and it was duly filed and recorded. The register and others testified that he expressly refused to receive the deed till the fees were paid. *Held* that, under Code N. C. § 3654, which requires the register to "indorse on each deed in trust and mortgage the day on which it is presented to him for registration," and section 3758, which provides that he shall not be compelled to perform any service, unless his fee be paid or tendered, except in criminal actions, it was error to refuse to charge that, if the jury believed the evidence, they should find that the deed had not been "filed for registration" prior to December 30, 1889.

Appeal from superior court, Beaufort county; HENRY R. BRYAN, Judge.

Action by W. H. Cunninggim and another against W. H. Peterson and another to recover land. The following is so much of the case settled on appeal as need be reported:

Plaintiffs offered this evidence: (1) A deed from L. H. Cunninggim and wife to W. H. Peterson, dated July 12, 1891, and recorded in Book 72, p. 223, register's office of Beaufort county. This deed was received by the register at 10 A. M., on July 27, 1889, and recorded July 29, 1889. This deed conveys *locus in quo.* (2) Mortgage from W. H. Peterson and wife to L. H. Cunninggim, dated July 27, 1889, and recorded in Book 73, p. 227, register's office of Beaufort county. The original of this mortgage is attached to the complaint herein as a part of the same. This mortgage was proved before B. F. Mayo, a justice of the peace for Beaufort county, on July 17, 1889, and the privy examination of Julia Peterson taken on July 27, 1889. The clerk of the superior court of Beaufort county placed his certificate upon the said mortgage, and ordered its registration. Upon this mortgage and upon the record is the following indorsement: "Filed for registration at 12 o'clock M., July 27, 1889, subject to the annexed facts indorsed, and registered in the office of the register of deeds for Beaufort Co. in Book 73, page 227. January 1, 1890." Upon the said mortgage and record is the further indorsement: "This mortgage was brought into this office by G. Wilkens, clerk of the superior court, July 27, 1889. No fees having been paid, the same was left in the office, open to the inspection of the public, until December 30, 1889, at 10 A. M., when H. H. Broome paid fees, and the same was duly filed and recorded in Book 73, p. 227, register's office of Beaufort county. M. F. WILLIAMSON, Register." M. F. Williamson testified: "I am the register of deeds for this county." The original mortgage was handed the witness, and the question asked, "When did you first see this mortgage?" Witness testified: "On July 26, 1889, Mr. Bonner sent me two mortgages, of which this is one." Witness testified that "Bonner stated in the letter that he wished me to distinctly understand that he was not responsible for the fees, and that I would have to look to Mr. Cunninggim for them. I then took the mortgages, and carried them to the clerk; and on July 27, 1889, the clerk carried them back into my office, and handed me this mortgage." The witness testified the clerk said he would not be responsible for the fees. "He threw it down on my desk. I told him I would not receive it. I took the paper, and put it in a box where there were a number of others sent for registration without fees. On December 30, 1889, H. H. Broome paid the fees, and I immediately filed the paper. I made the indorsement on the mortgage, December 30, 1889. I kept this mortgage in a separate box from the one in which I keep deeds filed for registration." Upon cross-examination, witness testified: "The clerk collects my fees sometimes and sometimes he does not. I receive instruments sometimes without fees. Sometimes the clerk collects and pays me, and at times I collect and pay the clerk. The box in which I put this mortgage is open to the public. Mr. Jacobson came, and I told him the mortgage was there. I do not recollect any other indorsement made by me upon any other instrument." G. Wilkens testified: "I am clerk of the superior court of Beaufort county." The question was asked, "State what took place when you carried this mortgage in the office of the register of deeds. Answer. The register brought me several papers for probate, among them two mortgages of Mr. Cunninggim, of which this was one, and also a letter from Mr. Bonner, in which he stated that he (Bonner) would not pay the fees. The register told me he would not receive the paper without the fees, and that I might keep them in my office. When I probated the other papers I also probated these mortgages, and carried all to the register for registration. The register objected to

receiving the Cunninggim papers. I pointed out to him that his predecessor used to have a box in which he filed any papers upon which the fees had not been paid, and that he could put them in the box, and that Mr. Cunnluggim would probably write soon, and send the fees, when he could file and register the papers. I then left him. I saw the papers afterwards, and, before it was recorded on the day when Broome paid the fees, there was no indorsement on it by the register. I do not know what day this was. I do not know when the deed from Peterson was recorded." W. K. Jacobson testified: "Mrs. Chapin is my sister. The deed from Peterson to her was sent to me, with a letter instructing me to have the deed registered. The next morning I took the deed over to the register's office, and while there the subject of the mortgage was brought up. The register stated that there was such a mortgage. I asked the register what he was going to do, and whether he considered it filed. He said he did not consider it filed, as he had no fees, and he would not register it without the fees. I did not see the mortgage. I never saw it until after the entry was made on it." The first issue submitted to the jury was this: "Was the mortgage from W. H. Peterson to L. H. Cunninggim filed for registration on July 27, 1889, or any day prior to December 28, 1889?" The jury responded, "Yes." The appellants requested the court to instruct the jury: "If you believe the evidence, [that above recited,] or any part thereof, you will answer the first issue, 'No.'" The court declined to give this instruction or the substance thereof, and the defendants excepted. Reversed.

W. B. Rodman & Son and *John H. Small,* for appellants. *Chas. F. Warren,* for appellees.

MERRIMON, C. J., (*after stating the facts as above.*) We are of opinion that, in any just view of all the evidence produced on the trial bearing upon and pertinent to the first issue submitted to the jury as to the time when the mortgage deed mentioned in the pleadings was delivered to the register for registration, it went to prove, and only to prove, that this deed was not so delivered to him as required by the statute (Code, § 3654) prior to the 30th day of December, 1889, and that the court should so have instructed the jury, as it was requested by the appellants to do, but which it declined to do. The register and other witnesses examined, who testified as to the pertinent facts, stated, in substance, that the register expressly refused to receive the deed for registration until his fees were paid. It was insisted on the argument here that the entry on the deed, "Filed for registration at 12 o'clock M., July 27, 1889," made by the register, was evidence to the contrary, and that it had technical meaning and effect, because the statute requires the register to "indorse on each deed in trust and mortgage the day on which it is presented to him for registration." But the statute does not make such indorsement essential to the validity of the registration. Metts

v. Bright, 4 Dev. & B. 173. When made, it is *prima facie* true, but it is not conclusive. In a proper case, it would be competent to show that it was not true in fact; that by inadvertence, mistake, or for some fraudulent purpose, it was not made truly and in accordance with the facts. Otherwise such indorsement might, in some instances, work wrong and injury without remedy. The statute does not so intend, nor is there reason why it should. Such indorsements must also be taken and treated as a whole, especially when it appears from its terms to be explanatory, and to have intentionally a qualified meaning and purpose. In this case the indorsement upon the mortgage was not simply, "Filed for registration at 12 o'clock M., July 27, 1889." It went materially further, reciting and explaining that such statement was made "subject to the annexed facts indorsed, and registered in the office of register of deeds for Beaufort county, in Book 73, page 227, January 1, 1890. This mortgage was brought in this office for registration by G. Wilkens, clerk of the superior court, July 27, 1889. No fees having been paid, the same was left in the office, open to the inspection of the public, until December 30, 1889, at 10 A. M. H. H. Broome paid fees, and the same was duly filed and recorded in Book 73, page 227, register's office, Beaufort county, January 1, 1890. [Signed] M. F. WILLIAMSON, Register." This indorsement plainly implies that the mortgage was "filed," in the sense of presented for registration, on the 27th of July, 1889; but the register refused to accept it as delivered to him because his fees had not been paid. Hence it is stated that it "was duly filed and recorded" on the 30th of December, 1889. The register intentionally refused, as he had the right to do, (Code, § 3758,)[1] to treat the mortgage as delivered to him for registration until his fees in that respect had been paid. His fees were paid on the last-mentioned day, and he then recognised and treated the mortgage as "delivered to him for registration." It was then "delivered," in the sense of the statute. There is no evidence in the indorsement nor of any witness examined that tends to prove that it was so "delivered" on the 27th of July, 1889, or at any time prior to the 30th of December, 1889. The indorsement is not materially inconsistent with the evidence of the register and others; the latter only recites the facts more fully and in detail. The mere fact that the mortgage was left in the office of the register, and with his knowledge, did not imply necessarily that it was delivered to him. It must have been delivered to him in such way, and with such accompaniments, as made it his duty to receive it for registration. There is error. The appellants are entitled to a new trial, and we so adjudge. To that end the judgment must be reversed, and the case disposed of according to law. Let this opinion be certified to the superior court. It is so ordered.

[1] Section 3758 provides that the register of deeds shall not be compelled to perform any service, unless his fee shall be paid or tendered, except in criminal actions.

CARTER v. ROUNTREE et al.

(Supreme Court of North Carolina. Oct. 13, 1891.)

SETTING ASIDE ORDER OF SALE OF DECEDENT'S LAND — FRAUD — PROCEDURE — FINDINGS OF FACTS.

1. After the termination of a special proceeding, wherein a sale of a testator's lands was ordered for the payment of his debts, a motion in the cause is not the proper remedy for setting aside for fraud the orders directing the sale, but this can be done only by an independent action.

2. But such motion, if made within a reasonable time, is the proper remedy for setting the orders aside for irregularities; and the fact that the motion alleges fraud in addition to the irregularities is immaterial, since such allegations will be treated as surplusage.

3. The failure of the record to show that the court made specific findings of fact will not invalidate its reversal of the former orders, where it does not appear that findings were requested.

4. Code N. C. § 217, provides that a summons, if against a minor under the age of 14 years, shall be served on the minor personally, and also on his father, mother, or guardian. Held, that where, in a special proceeding to sell a testator's lands for the payment of his debts, service of summons was had on the mother of a minor defendant, failure to serve him personally was cured by section 387, which provides that in all civil actions and special proceedings pending on the 14th day of March, 1879, or theretofore determined, wherein any of the defendants were infants, on whom there was no personal service of the summons, the proceedings and judgments shall be valid, except that they may be impeached and set aside for fraud.

Appeal from superior court, Hertford county; HENRY R. BRYAN, Judge.

This is a motion in a special proceeding, by J. E. Carter, administrator, against A. J. Rountree and another, to set aside, for alleged irregularity and fraud, the orders directing a sale of the land therein specified, to make assets to pay debts of a testator, the proceeding having been determined before the motion was made. The court heard the motion, and gave judgment setting the orders complained of aside. The plaintiff and defendants filed affidavits in support of and against the motion, but it does not appear affirmatively that the court found the facts or based its judgment upon any finding of fact. The appellants assigned as error— First, that a motion in the cause was not a proper remedy; secondly, that the court failed to find the facts on which its judgment was based. Reversed.

R. B. Peebles, for appellants. B. B. Winborne, for appellee.

MERRIMON, C. J., (after stating the facts as above.) A motion in the cause is the proper remedy, whether the action be ended or not, for mere irregularities in the course of the action, and it may be made at any time within a reasonable period. This is settled by many decisions of this court. Williamson v. Hartman, 92 N. C. 239; Fowler v. Poor, 93 N. C. 466; Morris v. White, 96 N. C. 93, 2 S. E. Rep. 254; Syme v. Trice, 96 N. C. 243, 1 S. E. Rep. 480; Smith v. Fort, 105 N. C. 452, 10 S. E. Rep. 914; McLaurin v. McLaurin, 106 N. C. 331, 10 S. E. Rep. 1056; and there are other cases. It is as well settled that, pending an action before the final judgment, an interlocutory order or judgment may be attacked for fraud by a motion or proceeding in the action; but after the final judgment the remedy for fraud is by an independent action brought for the purpose. See the cases cited supra, and other cases cited in Seymour's Digest, (7th Ed.) p. 281 et seq. The motion in this case is made in the form of a petition setting forth specifically the grounds thereof. The form does not change or at all affect its nature and purpose. Indeed, in some cases of complication it would be well to specify and set forth the grounds thereof. The motion is summary, and to specify the grounds would give it greater certainty, and render it more intelligible. As to the alleged irregularities complained of here, the motion in the proceeding is the appropriate and proper remedy. Inasmuch as the proceeding is ended, as to the alleged fraud, the remedy is not by such motion, but by an independent action, as clearly pointed out in the cases cited supra. The motion need not fail, however, because of the allegations of fraud. These may be treated as surplusage, and it may be upheld as sufficient as to the alleged irregularities.

It does not appear from the record that the court below found the facts from the evidence submitted to it in support of and against the motion. It may have done so, and probably did, without setting forth its findings in the record. It was competent for it to omit entering them, unless it had been requested by a party to so set them forth, so as to enable the party to take exception with a view to an appeal to this court. In such case it would be the duty of the court to comply with the request, and to refuse to do so would be error. Millhiser v. Balsley, 106 N. C. 433, 11 S. E. Rep. 314; Holden v. Purefoy, 108 N. C. 163, 12 S. E. Rep. 848. It does not appear affirmatively that the court failed to find the facts, nor did the appellants request it to enter its findings on the record. The second exception cannot, therefore, be sustained.

It is our duty, however, to look through the record proper, and to see whether it warrants the judgment appealed from, although no exception appears. Thornton v. Brady, 100 N. C. 38, 5 S. E. Rep. 910; Bush v. Hall, 95 N. C. 82; and other like cases. We have examined the record, and are of opinion that it does not. The evidence produced tended to prove that the order of sale and the sale of the land complained of were fraudulent, and the court may have founded its judgment upon the ground that they were so. That it did, does not, however, appear. If it did, the judgment was not warranted, because the orders complained of could not be attacked for fraud by a motion in the cause. The court ought not to have received evidence of such fraud, nor ought it to have based its judgment upon such ground. As we have seen, the orders could be attacked for fraud, only by an independent action. Judgments may be void, irregular, or erroneous. A void judgment is one that has merely semblance, without some essential

e'ement or elements, as where the court purporting to render it has not jurisdiction. An irregular judgment is one entered contrary to the course of the court, —contrary to the method of procedure and practice under it allowed by law in some material respect; as if the court gave judgment without the intervention of a jury, in a case where the party complaining was entitled to a jury trial, and did not waive his right to the same. Vass v Association, 91 N. C. 55; McKee v. Angel, 90 N. C. 60. An erroneous judgment is one rendered contrary to law. The latter cannot be attacked collaterally at all, but it must remain, and have effect, until by appeal to a court of errors it shall be reversed or modified. An irregular judgment may ordinarily and generally be set aside by a motion for the purpose in the action. This is so, because in such case the judgment was entered contrary to the course of the court, by inadvertence, mistake, or the like. A void judgment is without life or force, and the court will quash it on motion, or ex mero motu. Indeed, when it appears to be void, it may and will be ignored everywhere, and treated as a mere nullity. In this case the court had jurisdiction of the parties and the subject-matter of the proceeding. The defendant was a minor, and there was no service of the summons upon him personally, but service thereof was made upon his mother, as allowed by the statute, (Code, § 217;)[1] and a guardian ad litem was appointed for him, who filed an answer for the infant defendant. The record shows that the order of sale was entered, the land was sold, and the sale confirmed. Regularly, the infant defendant ought to have been served personally with process. The land specified in the petition was not very definitely described, but it was designated so as to be ascertained, and the report of the commissioner who sold it described it with more definiteness. Granting that there was irregularity, in that the summons was not served upon the infant defendant personally, the same was cured by the statute. Code, § 387;[2] Stancill v. Gay, 92 N. C. 464; Cates v. Pickett, 97 N. C. 21, 1 S. E. Rep. 763. We are clearly of opinion that there was not such irregularity as warranted the judgment setting the order complained of aside. It may be that these orders were tainted with fraud, but, as we have seen, the remedy for that is by an independent action. There is error. The judgment must be reversed, and the motion in the cause denied. To that end let this opinion be certified to the superior court. It is so ordered.

---

[1] Code N. C. § 217, provides that a summons, if against a minor under the age of 14 years, shall be served on the minor personally, and also on his father, mother, or guardian.

[2] Section 387 provides that, in all civil actions and special proceedings pending on the 14th day of March, 1879, or theretofore determined, wherein any of the defendants were infants, on whom there was no personal service of the summons, the proceedings and judgments shall be valid, except that they may be impeached and set aside for fraud.

GRANT et al. v. HARRELL et al.

(Supreme Court of North Carolina. Oct. 18, 1891.)

SETTING ASIDE JUDGMENT—PROCEDURE.

An independent action is not the proper remedy for setting aside a judgment, entered in a special proceeding, on the ground that a summons, necessary to give the court jurisdiction, was not served; but relief can be obtained only by a motion in the cause.

Appeal from superior court, Northampton county, HENRY G. CONNOR, Judge.

Action by James W. Grant against Paul Harrell. In a special proceeding specified in the complaint in this action, it appears by the return of the summons in that proceeding that the same was duly served upon the defendants therein named; whereas in fact, as the plaintiffs allege, that summons never was served. In that special proceeding a final judgment was entered, of which the plaintiffs complain, and the purpose of this action is to have the same set aside and declared void, upon the ground that the summons mentioned was never served, and hence the court had no jurisdiction of the parties named therein as defendants. The court below, "being of opinion that a motion in the cause is the proper remedy for the plaintiffs' alleged grievance," gave judgment dismissing the action, and both parties, having excepted, appealed to this court.

Thos. W. Mason and *R. B. Peebles*, for plaintiffs. *Robt. O. Burton*, for defendants.

MERRIMON, C. J., *(after stating the facts.)* In view of a multitude of decisions of this court it is too clear to admit of serious question that the court properly dismissed the action upon the ground that the plaintiffs' remedy is by a motion in the cause. Carter v. Rountree, 13 S. E. Rep. 716, (decided at this term.) Judgment affirmed.

MERRIMON, C. J. This, the defendants' appeal, is in effect disposed of by what we have said at the present term in the plaintiffs' appeal, in the same case. Judgment affirmed.

STATE v. FLOWERS.

(Supreme Court of North Carolina. Oct. 27, 1891.)

PERJURY—INDICTMENT—JUSTICES OF THE PEACE—JURISDICTION IN CRIMINAL CASES.

1. Under Acts N. C. 1889, c. 83, prescribing a form for indictments for perjury, and requiring them to state the court in which the perjury was committed, it is not error, in an indictment for perjury committed at a trial in a justice's court, to give, in addition to the name of the court, the names of the justices who sat at the trial.

2. An indictment for perjury under Acts N. C. 1889, c. 83, which fails to allege that defendant knew the false statement alleged to have been made by him to be false, or that he was ignorant whether or not the statement was true, is defective, since the act specially requires such allegations; but such defect is not ground for quashing the indictment, the proper action being for the court to hold the prisoner, and permit the solicitor to send a new bill curing the defect.

3. Code N. C. § 1159, authorizing two justices of the peace to sit together in criminal proceedings, and giving them the same powers and duties as are given to any justice sitting alone, was authorized by Const. N. C. art. 4, § 12, empowering the general assembly to allot and distribute the judicial power and jurisdiction which does not pertain to the supreme court in such manner as they may deem best.

Appeal from superior court, Wake county; SPIER WHITAKER, Judge.

Indictment of D. L. Flowers for perjury. Defendant's motion to quash the indictment was allowed, and the state appeals. Reversed.

The Attorney General, for the State. *F. H. Busbee*, for appellee.

CLARK, J. The indictment is drawn under chapter 83, Acts 1889, which provides a simple form of indictment for perjury. A motion to quash below was allowed, which action defendant's counsel seeks to sustain on the ground that the indictment charges the perjury to have been committed upon the trial of an action "in the court of ROBERT SANDERS and W. R. CREECH, justices of the peace" in and for said county, acting and sitting together, etc. We fail to see the force of the objection. If the names of the justices had been left out, the charge of the commission of the perjury "in a court of a justice of the peace" would have been a compliance with the statute. The addition of the names of the justices could not possibly prejudice the defendant in any manner, and really gave him additional information. Indeed, it is probably better, and certainly is fairer to the defendant, that, when the perjury is alleged to have been committed on a trial before a justice, the name of such justice should be charged. At the most, though the names of the justices were not required to be charged, their use was mere harmless surplusage.

Nor can there be more force in the argument that a court of two justices of the peace is a tribunal unknown to our constitution. Code, § 1159, authorizes two justices to sit together in criminal proceedings, and gives them the same "powers and duties" as are given to any justice sitting alone. The constitution, art. 4, § 12, empowers the general assembly to "allot and distribute" the judicial power and jurisdiction which does not pertain to the supreme court "in such manner as they may deem best." It was therefore competent for the legislature to thus bestow the "powers and duties" mentioned on two justices, as in like manner they have bestowed prescribed powers and duties on three or five justices by the title of inferior courts, or on one judge in a criminal court. It sufficiently appears in the indictment that the action in which the perjury is alleged to have been committed was a criminal proceeding, and of such the two justices, "acting and sitting together," as charged in the indictment, had as full jurisdiction as one justice sitting alone.

To quash the indictment for the harmless and really advisable addition of the names of the justices would contravene the explicit prohibition contained in Code, § 1183, that no criminal proceeding, whether "by warrant, indictment, information, or impeachment," shall be "quashed, or judgment stayed, by reason of any informality or refinement, if in the bill or proceeding sufficient matter appears to enable the court to proceed to judgment." State v. Burke, 108 N. C. 750, 12 S. E. Rep. 1000; State v. Haddock, (at this term,) 13 S. E. Rep. 714. The form of indictment provided by the act in question has been sustained by this court in State v. Gates, 107 N. C. 832, 12 S. E. Rep. 319, and State v. Peters, 107 N. C. 876, 12 S. E. Rep. 74. The effect of the act is not to change in any respect the constituent elements of perjury, nor the nature or mode of proof. It only relieves the state from charging in the indictment the details, or rather the definition, of the offense, and makes it sufficient to allege that the defendant unlawfully committed perjury, charging the name of the action and of the court in which committed, setting out the matter alleged to have been falsely sworn, and averring, further, that the defendant knew such statement to be false, or that he was ignorant whether or not it was true. Upon an inspection of the record, we find that the indictment is in fact defective, in that it does not, as required by said act, (1889, c. 83,) allege either that the defendant "knew said statement to be false," or that he was "ignorant whether or not said statement was true." But such defect would not warrant the court below in quashing the indictment. In State v. Colbert, 75 N. C. 368, which was an indictment for perjury, the court say, (READE, J.:) "Quashing indictments is not favored. It releases recognizances, and sets the defendant at large where it may be he ought to be held to answer upon a better indictment," though "allowable," he goes on to say, "where it will put an end to the prosecution altogether, and advisable where it appears that the court has not jurisdiction, or where the matter charged is not indictable in any form. * * * It is therefore a general rule that no indictment which charges the higher offenses, as treason or felony, or those crimes which immediately affect the public at large, as perjury, forgery, etc., will be thus summarily dealt with. * * * The example is a bad one, and the effect upon the public injurious, to allow the defendant to escape upon matters of form. * * * The indictment is very informal, and probably no judgment could be pronounced; but still the court had jurisdiction, and the matter intended to be charged is a crime which greatly concerns the public, and therefore the defendant ought to have been held and tried upon a sufficient indictment. * * * There was abundant cause for his honor's declaring the indictment informal and insufficient, but not for quashing." We have quoted at some length from the eminent judge who was easily master of his profession, as he states clearly the reasons which govern the administration of justice in such cases. This case is cited and approved by ASHE, J., in State v. Knight, 84 N. C. 789, in which, though the supreme court arrests the judgment, it is held that the court below properly refused to quash. To the same effect are the best authorities. State

v. Harper, 94 N. C. 936; 2 Hawk. P. C. c. 25, § 146; 1 Chit. Crim. Law, 300; 1 Bish. Crim. Proc. § 452; Whart. Crim. Pl. 386, 387; Archb. Crim. Pl. 66; Rex v. Belton, 1 Salk. 372. Indeed, quashing an indictment, however defective, is never a matter of right. "The judges are in no case bound, ex debito justitiæ, to quash an indictment, but may oblige the defendant either to plead or demur to it; and this they generally do, where it is for a crime of an enormous or public nature, as perjury, forgery, and like offenses." 2 Hawk. P. C. c. 25, § 146. In such cases, if the bill is defective, the court does not quash, but holds the prisoner, and permits the solicitor to send a new bill.

We are not inadvertent to the fact that this action was removed from another county, and though the record does not state that the plea of not guilty was entered, presumably such was the case, as in criminal actions an order of removal can only be made after issue joined. State v. Reid, 1 Dev. & B. 377; State v. Swepson, 81 N. C. 571; State v. Haywood, 94 N. C. 947. But it is, in the present instance, immaterial, for though, after issue joined, it is too late for the defendant, as a matter of right, to move to quash, the court in its discretion can permit the motion (in proper cases) to be made. State v. Esson, 70 N. C. 88; State v. Miller, 100 N. C. 543, 5 S. E. Rep. 925; State v. Sheppard, 97 N. C. 401, 1 S. E. Rep. 879.

There was error in quashing the indictment, and this must be certified, that further proceedings may be had according to law. The solicitor can, if so advised, send a better bill curing the defect above pointed out. State v. Colbert, supra.   Error.

STATE v. ROANOKE RAILROAD & LUMBER CO.

(Supreme Court of North Carolina. Oct. 13, 1891.)

OBSTRUCTING HIGHWAY — VARIANCE — RAILROAD CROSSING—ARREST OF JUDGMENT.

1. An indictment against a railroad company charged it with obstructing a public highway by placing in and across the highway certain plank. The evidence showed that the company's road where it crossed the highway was about 10 inches above the highway, and that one of the planks used to raise the highway to a level with the railroad had slid down, leaving a hole about eight inches deep. Held, that the variance was fatal.

2. Code N. C. §§ 1710, 1957, par. 5, provide that where a railroad crosses a highway it must do so in a way not to impede public travel, and that the company must restore the crossing to such a state as not to unnecessarily impair its usefulness. Held, that the company may use plank in restoring a highway to a level with the railroad at one of its crossings.

3. Where the indictment did not show in what way the plank was misused or misapplied at the crossing, or that defendant allowed the plank to become out of repair, and in such improper condition as to obstruct the highway, it failed to appropriately charge a nuisance.

4. Though a motion in arrest of judgment was not made in the court below, the supreme court of North Carolina will entertain such a motion when the whole record is before the court, and it appears that the judgment was unwarranted.

Appeal from superior court, Beaufort county; HENRY R. BRYAN, Judge.

Prosecution against the Roanoke Railroad & Lumber Company for obstructing a public highway. The indictment charges "that he unlawfully and willfully did obstruct said public road by placing in and across it certain plank where the road of said corporation (the defendant) crossed the said public road, so that the good citizens of the state could not nor cannot now cross and recross over said public road with their teams, as they were accustomed to pass and repass, and so continues to impede and obstruct said road, to the common nuisance," etc. The defendant pleaded not guilty. On the trial, but one witness was examined, and the material parts of his testimony were that "the defendant's road crosses this public road. The company did not have enough plank. It was elevated 8 or 10 inches above the public road. Between the track of the defendant's road and the platform which sloped to the track was a hole. This hole was 8 to 10 inches deep from top to bottom. It was not safe for teams. I think the elevation above the public road was 8 or 10 inches; might have been less. The hole was on the north side of defendant's road. The hole was there about April or May, 1890. The plank had slipped down, leaving the hole. The plank was well up to the railroad when I first saw it. The lumber road was not down there more than two or three months before I saw it. It was there some time before there was any hole. The hole was as much as four inches wide." There was a verdict of guilty, and judgment for the state. The defendant, having excepted, appealed to this court. Reversed.

John H. Small, for appellant. *The Attorney General* and *C. F. Warren*, for the State.

MERRIMON, C. J., (*after stating the facts.*) Accepting the evidence of the single witness for the state as true, there was a substantial variance between the charge as laid and the proof. The charge was the obstruction of the public road mentioned "by placing in and across it certain plank" at the place specified. The proof was, in substance, that a dangerous hole in the crossing was permitted to be and continued for a week or two, occasioned by the slipping down of a plank, from its place. The constituent facts charged were widely different in their substance and meaning from those proven. The indictment charged one offense; that proven was in substance, as to the constituent facts, a distinct and different one. In such case, the court should direct the jury to render a verdict of not guilty.

We are further of opinion that no offense is sufficiently charged in the indictment. The defendant is a railroad company, and constructed its railroad across the public road specified in the indictment. This it had the right to do in such way and manner "as not to impede the passage or transportation of persons or property along the same," restoring such road so crossed "to its former state, or to such state as not unnecessarily to have impaired its usefulness." Code, §§ 1710, 1957, par. 5. In constructing such crossing, it might appropriately and reasonably use plank, timber, earth, etc., to make the same such as the statute allows and intends, and as the public ease, convenience, and safety require. It might lawfully use such things in forming and securing the incline on each side of the railroad track so as to provide an easy and safe passway across it for carriages, wagons, horses, etc.

It was not, therefore, unlawful *per se* for the defendant to use plank about the crossing in question. Hence the indictment ought to charge appropriately the misuse or misapplication of the plank in placing it across the public road at and about the crossing in such way and manner as to constitute the offense of obstructing the public road, or that the same was allowed by the defendant to become ruinous, out of repair, and in such unlawful condition as to constitute the offense. The material facts should be charged with such fullness as to show the complete offense. In this case the offense is not so charged. Indeed, no offense is sufficiently charged. How the plank was misused or misapplied at the crossing does not appear, nor is it charged that the defendant suffered it to become ruinous, out of repair, and in such improper condition as to obstruct the public road. The court ought, therefore, to have quashed the indictment before the defendant pleaded; or, failing to do that, it should, after verdict, have arrested the judgment. The counsel of the defendant in this court insists that the judgment of the court below should be reversed, and judgment there arrested. We are of that opinion, and so direct. The court seeing the whole record, including the indictment, should have entered such judgment as in law ought to have been rendered thereon. That it did not is error.

Although a motion in arrest of judgment was not made in the court below, it may be made here, because this court sees the whole record, and takes notice of errors appearing in the record proper, though not regularly assigned in the court below. It must appear from the record that, in some aspect of it, the judgment rendered is warranted. Here it does not appear that any offense is charged. The trial and verdict were immaterial and nugatory. There is error. Let this opinion be certified to the superior court according to law.

It is so ordered.

HURDLE v. STALLINGS.

(*Supreme Court of North Carolina. Oct. 13, 1891.*)

SETTING ASIDE AWARD — FAILURE TO RECEIVE EVIDENCE.

By the terms of a submission of a controversy relating to party lines, the arbitrators were to settle the lines between plaintiff and defendant, and all matters of difference in relation thereto. Plaintiff offered in evidence certain deeds and plats for the purpose of showing his lines. *Held*, that the award should be set aside for the refusal of the arbitrators to consider such evidence.

Appeal from superior court, Perquimans county; HENRY R. BRYAN, Judge.

Cuntroversy between Richard Hurdle,
plaintiff, and Reuben Stalling, defendant,
to settle party lines. The matter was
submitted to arbitration, and an award
was had for defendant. Plaintiff moved
to set aside the award, and from an order of the court denying the motion he
appeals. Reversed.

F. Picard, for appellant.

SHEPHERD, J. By consent of the parties
it was ordered by the presiding judge that
the award of the arbitrators should be a
rule of the court. The terms of the submission were that the arbitrators were to
"go upon the land in controversy, and settle the lines between the lands of the plaintiff and the defendant, and settle all matters of difference in relation thereto." It
appears from the uncontroverted testimony of the plaintiff and the witness Harrell that, when the arbitrators met, the
plaintiff offered his deeds, plats, etc., relating to the lands in controversy, and
that the arbitrators refused to receive or
examine them. Harrell also states that
the evidence was offered for the purpose of
fixing the lines, and, none of this testimony being disputed, we must assume
that the papers offered were relevant to
the questions which were about to be
passed upon. The settlement of controversies by arbitration is looked upon with
great favor by the courts, and, ordinarily,
if the award be within the power of the
arbitrators, "and unaffected by fraud,
mistake, or irregularity, the judge has no
power over it, except to make it a rule
of court, and enforce it according to the
course of the court." Lusk v Clayton, 70
N. C. 184. Even where they decide erroneously, the error will not vitiate the award
"unless it appears that the arbitrators
intended to decide according to law,"
(Jones v. Frazier, 1 Hawks, 379;) and it is
said by SHAW, C. J., in Water-Power Co. v.
Gray, 6 Metc. (Mass.) 131, that, "as incident to the decision of the questions of
fact, [the arbitrators] have power to decide all questions as to the admission and
rejection of evidence, as well as the credit
due to evidence, and the inferences of fact
to be drawn from it." So, also, arbitrators have some power within their discretion to determine how much evidence they
will hear, (Nickalls v. Warren, 6 Q. B. 615,
per Lord DENMAN, C. J.,) but it is their
general duty to hear all evidence material
to the case which is offered, (Morse, Arb.
142;) and Russell, in his work on Arbitration, (3d Ed. 178,) says that "declining
to receive evidence on any matter is, under
ordinary circumstances, a delicate step to
take; for the refusal to receive proof
where proof is necessary is fatal to the
award." In this case the arbitrators
were to settle the lines between the parties and all matters of difference in relation thereto. The evidence, according to
the affidavits of the plaintiff, was offered
for that purpose, and there is no attempt
whatever to show that it was immaterial.
Without undertaking to lay down any
rule, beyond the general principles indicated, as to how far arbitrators may go in
the rejection of testimony, we are clearly
of the opinion that they have no power

to arbitrarily decline to receive or examine
any testimony whatever. For this reason
we think that the award should have been
set aside. Error.

HORNTHALL *et al.* v. BURWELL *et al.*

*(Supreme Court of North Carolina. Oct. 20,
1891.)*

LIEN OF CHATTEL MORTGAGE—REMOVAL OF PROP-
ERTY TO ANOTHER STATE.

Plaintiffs held a chattel mortgage on certain horses and other personal property, which
were in the possession of the mortgagor, in
North Carolina. The mortgage was duly recorded in the county where the property was situated,
and also in the county where the mortgagor resided. While the mortgage debt was unpaid, the
mortgagor took the property into Virginia, where
it was seized and sold on attachment by defendants, who were creditors of the mortgagor, and
the proceeds were applied in part payment of
their judgments against him. Plaintiffs brought
an action against defendants to recover the debt
secured by such mortgage. *Held,* that they
were entitled to recover, though the mortgage
was not recorded in Virginia.

Appeal from superior court, Washington
county; HENRY R. BRYAN, Judge.

Action by Hornthall & Bro. against D.
S. Burwell and others to recover a debt
secured by mortgage on certain horses
and other personal property, where the
property had been seized and sold on attachment proceedings against the mortgagor on a debt due defendants. Defendants
demurred to plaintiffs' complaint. The
demurrer was overruled, and, on defendants' refusal to plead over, judgment was
entered for plaintiffs. Defendants appeal.
Affirmed.

The complaint alleged that one Moore
was owner of and had in his possession
in Washington county, N. C., certain
horses, mules, oxen, and log wagons, and
to secure a debt due from him to plaintiffs conveyed the same to plaintiffs by
mortgage with power of sale; that the
mortgage was duly recorded in said
Washington county, and also in the county of Hartford, where Moore resided; that
Moore afterwards took the property
across the state line, into Southampton
county, Va., where it was seized and sold
on attachment by defendants, and the
proceeds applied on debts due from Moore
to defendants; that the mortgage was
not recorded in Southampton county, Va.
Defendants demurred to the complaint on
two grounds, one of which was that the
mortgage had not been recorded in Virginia, which was necessary under the laws
of that state. The other ground was
that, the property having been regularly
taken on attachment in Virginia, plaintiffs
were precluded by the judgment in that
action. The demurrer being overruled,
and defendants refusing to answer, judgment was rendered for plaintiffs, and defendants appealed.

B. B. Winborne, for appellants. *C. L.
Pettigrew* and *Pruden & Vann,* for appellees.

SHEPHERD, J. The principle embodied
in the maxim *mobilia sequuntur personam* is generally recognized in all civilised
countries, and it follows as a natural con-

sequence, says Story, (Confl. Laws, 383,) that "the laws of the owner's domicile (or the *lex loci contractus*) should in all cases determine the validity of every transfer, alienation, or disposition made by the owner, whether it be *inter vivos* or be *post mortem*." The authority of such laws, however, is admitted in other states, not *ex proprio vigore*, but *ex comitate*, and hence it is now very generally held that when they "clash with and interfere with the rights of the citizens of the countries where the parties to the contract seek to enforce it, as one or the other of them must give way, those prevailing where the relief is sought must have the preference." Olivier v. Townes, 2 Mart. (N. S.) 93; 2 Kent, Comm. 458; Moye v. May, 8 Ired. Eq. 131. This is illustrated by the leading case first cited, where a ship sold in Virginia was before delivery attached by creditors at New Orleans. The court held the sale void as to the attaching creditors, because the law of the *situs* required an actual delivery to pass the title. So, in the case of Green v. Van Buskirk, 7 Wall. 139, an attachment in Illinois was sustained as against a mortgage executed by the owner in New York, but not registered in Illinois, where the property was situated. The laws of that state provided that the mortgage should be "void as against third persons unless acknowledged and registered, and unless the property be delivered to and remain with the mortgagee." This principle, however, has no application to a case like ours, where the mortgage was executed and duly registered according to both the law of the domicile and the law of the *situs*. The property was situated in this state, and the title of the mortgagees perfected here. This being so, we think it quite clear that the removal of the property to another state could not deprive the mortgagees of their rights. In support of this position there seems to be a *consensus* of judicial opinion. Even in Louisiana (whose courts were, perhaps, among the most prominent in giving effect to the law of the *situs*, as above explained) there has never been any doubt upon this question. On the contrary, in Thuret v. Jenkins, 7 Mart. (La.) 318, it was held that, where the title had passed, "the circumstance of the chattel being afterwards brought into a country, according to the law of which the sale would be invalid, would not affect it." The doctrine of this case has since been affirmed in Bank v. Wood, 14 La. Ann. 554. To the same effect is Langworthy v. Little, 12 Cush. 109, where Shaw, C. J., says that "a party who obtains a good title to property, absolute, or qualified by the laws of a sister state, is entitled to maintain and enforce those rights in this state." The property was attached in Massachusetts as the property of the mortgagor, and the sheriff was held liable for its conversion. So in Jones, Chat. Mortg. 301, it is said that, "although the mortgage be not executed in conformity with the laws of the state to which the property is afterwards removed, if executed and recorded according to the laws of the state or country of its execution, it is effectual to hold the

property in the state to which it is removed." So in Ballard v. Winter the supreme court of Connecticut sustained an action of trover against one of its own citizens for suing out attachment proceedings against property which had been mortgaged according to the law of Massachusetts, but which had been subsequently removed to the former state. The court said: "By the general rules of law, title thus perfected in one state is respected in all other states and countries into which the property may come. * * * It would certainly be very inconvenient if such mortgages, fairly made in Massachusetts, should be held invalid in Connecticut in respect to movable property, which may be daily passing to and fro along the dividing lines between the states." This case is reported in 12 Amer. Law Reg. (N. S.) 759, and is highly approved by the annotator, who cites several authorities in its support. The same point was decided by the supreme court of the United States in Bank v. Lee, 13 Pet. 107. There certain property, being in Virginia, was conveyed in trust to Richard Bland Lee, for the benefit of Mrs. Lee. The title passed according to the Virginia law, but, the property being subsequently removed to the District of Columbia, where, under a prevailing Maryland statute, such a transfer would not be good except upon certain conditions, which had not been complied with, the court (CATRON, J.,) said that "the statute had no reference to a case where the title has been vested by the laws of another state, but operates only on sales, mortgages, and gifts made in Maryland." The following authorities are also directly in point: Hil. Mortg. 412; Keenan v. Stimson, 32 Minn. 377, 20 N. W. Rep. 364; Ferguson v. Clifford, 37 N. H. 86; Jones v. Taylor, 30 Vt. 42; Bank v. Danforth, 14 Gray, 123; Martin v. Hill, 12 Barb. 631; Kanaga v. Taylor, 7 Ohio St. 134; Wilson v. Carson, 12 Md. 54; Smith v. McLean, 24 Iowa, 322; Hicks v. Skinner. 71 N. C. 539; Barker v. Stacy, 25 Miss. 477; Feurt v. Rowell, 62 Mo. 524.

The defendants, however, contend that they are protected by the sale under the attachment proceedings in the Virginia court. They rely upon the case of Green v. Van Buskirk, supra, and insist that under the act of congress full faith and credit must be given to the judgments of the courts of a sister state. It is true that the decision referred to was chiefly based upon that statute, but it must be observed that the record of such an adjudication has only (we quote from the opinion) "the same faith and credit as it has in the state court from which it is taken," and that, "in order to give due force and effect to a judicial proceeding, it is often necessary to show by evidence outside of the record the predicament of the property on which it operated." Such was the course pursued by the court in that case; and, as we have seen that the title to the property had not passed according to the law of the *situs*, the attachment proceedings were sustained. If, however, it had appeared that at the time of the execution of the mortgage in New York the property was also there, but had been afterwards removed to Illinois, it cannot be doubted that the decision would have been otherwise. Happily we have a case directly in point from the supreme court of Illinois,—Mumford v. Canty, 50 Ill. 370. It is there distinctly held that, "where personal property was mortgaged in the state of Missouri, and permitted to remain with the mortgagor (contrary to the law of Illinois) after the maturity of the debt to secure which the mortgage was given, and, upon being subsequently brought into Illinois, was seized under an attachment in favor of a *bona fide* creditor of the mortgagor, the rights of the mortgagee [would] be determined by the law of Missouri;" and the mortgagee was permitted to recover the property of the purchaser. Here, then, we have an express decision as to the effect which is to be given to such a judgment in the state in which it is rendered, and it is only to this extent, and no further, that the judgment is conclusive in a sister state. To hold otherwise would go beyond what the statute requires, and give the same effect to an attachment proceeding which generally follows a proceeding which is strictly and technically *in rem*. Such is not the law. An attachment proceeding, though often spoken of as a proceeding *in rem*, "cannot be admitted to come within the strict meaning of that term; the judgment is conclusive only upon the actual parties to the litigation and those in privity with them, * * * and they use the hold obtained by the seizure of specific property merely as a means of reaching and giving effect to the rights of parties, and neither claim nor exercise any controlling authority over the title of strangers. The same remark applies to replevin." 2 Black, Judgm. § 801; Duchess of Kingston's Case. 3 Smith, Lead. Cas. 2011; Drake, Attachm. § 245. In his notes to the latter case Judge HARE cites with entire approval the opinion of HALL, J., in Woodruff v. Taylor, 20 Vt. 65, in which it is said that the operation of such a proceeding "must be limited to the parties to it, and cannot in any manner affect the right or interest of any other person having an independent and adverse claim to the goods," etc. Having shown, we think, that the title, perfected here, was not lost by the removal of the property to Virginia, and that the record of the judgment in the attachment proceedings is only to be respected in so far as effect is given to it in that state, we cannot but assume, in the absence of any decision to the contrary, that the same principle of comity so universally recognized and acted upon likewise prevails in Virginia, and that, even if these plaintiffs were suing in that jurisdiction, they would be permitted to recover. This would seem all the more reasonable, as we have extended this very comity to a citizen of our sister state in a case precisely similar to the one under consideration. Anderson v. Doak, 10 Ired. 295. There, a slave, being in Virginia, was mortgaged by its owner, and the mortgage duly registered in Carroll county. It was never registered in this state, nor was it executed according to its laws.

The slave came to this state, and was attached by a creditor of the mortgagor. In an action of trover, brought by the mortgagee against the sheriff, the plaintiff was permitted to recover. It will be noted that we have discussed this question as if the plaintiff were seeking redress in the courts of Virginia. If we have shown that, according to what appears to be the entire course of judicial opinion, they would be entitled to recover there, *a fortiori* can they recover in the courts of this state when they have acquired jurisdiction over the parties. To the foregoing authorities we will add a recent decision of the court of appeals of New York. In that case (Edgerly v. Bush, 81 N. Y. 199) B. executed to plaintiff a chattel mortgage upon a span of horses. Both parties were then residents of New York. B. subsequently took them to Canada, where they were sold by a regular trader dealing in horses, the purchaser buying in good faith. Under the laws of Canada property cannot be reclaimed from one so purchasing without refunding the price paid. Defendant, a resident of this state, bought the horses in Canada from such purchaser, and they were left in Canada. Upon refusal of defendant to deliver them, the plaintiff sued for their conversion. The court held (FOLGER, C. J., delivering an elaborate opinion) that the plaintiff was entitled to recover. We are of the opinion that his honor very properly overruled the demurrer, but he should have given the defendant an opportunity to answer. Code, § 272; Moore v. Hobbs, 77 N. C. 65; Bronson v. Insurance Co., 85 N. C. 411. Affirmed.

BRAY v. CREEKMORE.

(*Supreme Court of North Carolina.* Oct. 20, 1891.)

APPEALABLE ORDERS—AMENDMENT OF PLEADINGS —LIMITATION.

1. Where the words, "State on the relation of," precede plaintiff's name in the summons and complaint, an amendment striking out such words is in the discretion of the court, and is not appealable. State v. Mitchell, 102 N. C. 347, 9 S. E. Rep. 702, and Maggett v. Roberts, 108 N. C. 174, 12 S. E. Rep. 890, followed.

2. Though the amendment was not made within a year, yet being merely as to the name of a party, and not the insertion of a new cause of action, it did not come within the statute of limitations, which required the action to be commenced within a year.

3. Where the amendment was formal, and defendant could derive no benefit from a service of the summons and complaint as amended, such service is unnecessary.

4. The action of the court in allowing plaintiff to file a new complaint in the place of one that was lost is discretionary, and cannot be reviewed on appeal.

Appeal from superior court, Currituck county; GEORGE H. BROWN, Judge.

Action by William H. Bray against W. P. Creekmore. Judgment for plaintiff. Defendant appeals. Affirmed.

Pittman & Shaw, for appellant. *Grandy & Aydlett,* for appellee.

CLARK, J. 1. The action was brought, "State on the relation of W. H. Bray" against the defendant. On motion, the words. "State on relation of," were stricken out of summons and complaint, and defendant excepted. Such amendment rested in the discretion of the trial judge, and is not appealable. State v. Mitchell, 102 N. C. 347, 9 S. E. Rep. 702; Maggett v. Roberts, 108 N. C. 174, 12 S. E. Rep. 890. In both these cases the amendment was identical with that here objected to.

2. The complaint having been lost, the defendant asked that the action be dismissed. The plaintiff asked to file another complaint in lieu of that which had been lost. The court refused defendant's motion, and granted the motion of the plaintiff. The defendant excepted. The action of the judge in allowing new pleadings to be filed in place of those lost is not reviewable.

3. The facts alleged in sections 5 and 7 of the complaint were not denied, and subjected the defendant to the penalties sued for. Code, § 711.

By consent the order was made in vacation, as of fall term, 1890, which was within less than a year after those causes of action accrued, (Code, § 156, subd. 2;) but, were it otherwise, the amendment was merely of the name of the party, not the insertion of a new cause of action, as was the case in Hester v. Mullen, 107 N. C. 724, 12 S. E. Rep. 447; and therefore, unlike the latter case, the statute of limitations is not affected by the amendment.

We may also note that when the amendment is merely formal, as here, no necessity arises for the service of the amended summons or complaint. If the amended summons adds a new defendant, it must be served on such defendant, (Plemmons v. Improvement Co., 108 N. C. 614, 13 S. E. Rep. 188;) and, where the amended complaint touches a matter of substance, the judge may order it to be served on the defendant. Here the motion disclosed the nature and extent of the amendment asked, and when granted the defendant could derive no benefit from service anew of the summons and complaint, with merely the words, "State on relation of," stricken out of them. No error.

BALTZER v. STATE.

(Supreme Court of North Carolina. Oct. 20, 1891.)

CONSTITUTIONAL LAW—OBLIGATION OF CONTRACTS —LIABILITIES OF STATE.

Const. N. C. 1868, art. 4, § 9, provides that the supreme court shall have original jurisdiction of claims against the state, but that its decisions shall be merely recommendatory, and shall be reported to the legislature for action. Held, that Const. 1880, art. 1, § 6, amendatory thereto, which provides that the legislature shall not pay, "either directly or indirectly," any debt or bond incurred or issued by the convention of 1868, or by the legislature of that year, with certain exceptions, unless the proposition therefor be submitted to the voters of the state, is not obnoxious to Const. U. S. art. 1, § 10, in impairing the obligation of contracts, since no one has any right of action against the state except as given by its constitution and laws. Baltzer v. State, 104 N. C. 265, 10 S. E. Rep. 153, followed.

Original action by Herman R. Baltzer against the state of North Carolina to recover on certain bonds issued by the state. Dismissed.

E. C. Smith and Kingsbury Curtis, for plaintiff. The Attorney General, for the State.

MERRIMON, C. J. We cannot hesitate to decide that this court has no jurisdiction of the cause of action alleged in the complaint. It plainly comes within what was said in Horne v. State, 84 N. C. 362, and Baltzer v. State, 104 N. C. 265, 10 S. E. Rep. 153, cases very thoroughly argued and decided by the court after much earnest consideration. We are called upon to overrule those cases, and proceed to consider the case upon its merits, and determine the important questions presented by the pleadings. Nothing appears from the brief of the learned counsel for the plaintiff, nor can we conceive of any adequate reason, that ought to prompt us to do so. For the reasons sufficiently stated in the cases cited supra, the motion of the attorney general to dismiss the action must be allowed. Action dismissed.

BOONE v. DRAKE.

(Supreme Court of North Carolina. Oct. 13, 1891.)

JURISDICTION OF JUSTICE — CONTRACT TO CONVEY LAND—SILENCE AS ESTOPPEL.

1. Under Code N. C. § 834, which provides that justices of the peace shall have exclusive original jurisdiction of all civil actions founded on contracts, except where the demand exceeds $200, or the title to real estate is in controversy, a justice has no jurisdiction in ejectment, where the issue is whether a contract to purchase the land was abandoned by defendant, and a suit for specific performance of the contract, instituted by defendant, is pending in the superior court.

2. The mere fact that defendant neither objected nor consented while a third person, under the direction of plaintiff, destroyed the written contract, is insufficient to divest defendant of his equity therein, where there was evidence that the parties had entered into a parol modification of the contract.

This was a summary proceeding by Walter Boone against John C. Drake to eject defendant, brought before a justice of the peace, and tried on appeal at the spring term, 1891, of the superior court of Northampton county, before CONNOR, Judge.

The defendant failed to appear before the justice of the peace, but appealed and filed, by leave of the court, his answer to the superior court. There was evidence on the part of the plaintiff tending to show that in January, 1889, there was an oral agreement between the plaintiff and defendant for the sale of the land in controversy to the defendant for $4,500 cash; that defendant moved some of his goods on the place; that early in February, 1889, he came to plaintiff, and told him he was unable to raise the money, and the contract was rescinded, and defendant agreed to rent for 1889, and that one Everett should fix the amount of rent, which he afterwards did at $600; that defendant then moved his family upon the land, and raised a crop on it in 1889; that in October, 1889, a written contract was entered into between the plaintiff and one Jenkins, under the firm name of Boone & Jenkins, and defendant, as follows: "We have sold to Mr. J. C. Drake the J. W. Hill farm for five thousand dollars, with interest at the rate of eight per cent. from 1st day of January, 1889. He is to pay us fourteen hundred dollars, if possible, by the 1st day of January, 1890, and if he fails to raise this amount by the shipment of three hundred bags of peanuts, then he is to pay us twelve hundred dollars and execute a note for two hundred dollars. After making this payment of twelve or fourteen hundred dollars, then Mr. J. C. Drake is to execute his four notes, at one, two, three, and four years, for one thousand dollars each, with interest at the rate of eight (8) per cent. October 17th, 1889. BOONE & JENKINS. Witness: J. E. EVERETT." Nothing was ever paid under said contract, nor any condition thereof performed by Drake. That about the 1st of December, 1889, Drake expressed his inability to carry out said written contract, and his dissatisfaction therewith, and the same was canceled, and a new parol contract was then entered into, by which Drake agreed to pay $5,000 for the land, of which he should pay $1,400 cash by the 20th of December, 1889, and to execute his notes at one and two years for the residue, with interest from date; that in case he failed to make the cash payment by said 20th of December, 1889, then the contract should be at an end; that the 20th December was fixed upon in order to enable the plaintiff to get a tenant if Drake failed to comply; that nothing was ever paid by Drake, nor notes executed. The defendant, Drake, on the other hand, denied that the written contract was canceled, but admitted that its terms were changed as above set out. It appeared to the court by the record that at the time of the trial there was pending in this court an action brought by the said Drake against the said Boone & Jenkins to compel specific performance of the said contract of October 17, 1889, the summons in which was issued on the 16th day of January, 1890, and served on the 18th day of January, 1890. Plaintiff testified to the mutilation of the original contract which had been deposited with Everett for safe-keeping, and the paper was produced with the names torn or cut through; Everett stating that Boone so directed him, and Drake saying nothing. There was evidence tending to show that Drake, about the 30th of December, 1889, offered to comply with the said written contract. At the close of the evidence the defendant's counsel moved to dismiss for want of jurisdiction. His honor, being of opinion that the justice was not competent to try the question of surrender and cancellation of the contract, allowed the motion and dismissed the action. Appeal by plaintiff. Affirmed.

R. O. Burton, for appellant. B. B. Winborne and R. B. Peebles, for appellee.

AVERY, J., (after stating the facts as above.) The testimony was conflicting upon the question whether the defendant agreed to abandon his rights acquired under the contract of October 17, 1889. The witness who seems to have had the custody of the writing testifies that he mutilated it by direction of Boone, the defendant saying nothing, neither objecting nor consenting. That paper constituted Drake a vendee; and if, according to his contention, he did not surrender it, and all rights secured to him under it, so as to constitute an abandonment, there is no admitted phase of the facts in which the relation of vendor and vendee can be held to have ceased, and that of landlord and tenant to have begun. Acts relied upon as constituting an abandonment must be "positive, unequivocal, and inconsistent with the contract." Faw v. Whittington, 72 N. C. 324; Miller v. Pierce, 104 N. C. 389, 10 S. E. Rep. 554. The fact, if established, that the defendant remained silent, when the witness Everett, under the direction of the plaintiff, mutilated the contract, is not necessarily inconsistent with the claim of an equity under it, much less a positive and affirmative surrender of his interest acquired under it. White v. Butcher, 6 Jones, Eq. 231. It is familiar learning that, in equity, time is not of the essence of the contract, and, notwithstanding the default in paying the purchase money, the vendee, if he had not formally or unequivocally abandoned his rights, was the owner in equity, the vendor holding the legal title merely as security for the purchase money. Scarlett v. Hunter, 3 Jones, Eq. 84; Faw v. Whittington, supra; Falls v. Carpenter, 1 Dev. & B. Eq. 237. The defendant Drake denies the allegation that he expressed dissatisfaction with the contract, or asked that it be amended, but insists that the parties entered into a parol agreement merely for the modification of its terms. To maintain his claim he had brought his suit for specific performance, and it was then pending in the superior court.

If, in any view of the testimony, the relation subsisting between the plaintiff and defendant was, when the action began, that of vendor and vendee, and not that of lessor and lessee, there was such a controversy as to the title as would oust the jurisdiction of the justice of the peace. The superior court, in the exercise of its powers as a court of equity, has the exclusive right to adjust the equities growing out of a contract of purchase, if it is still subsisting. Parker v. Allen, 84 N. C. 466; Hughes v. Mason, Id. 472. The issue raised by the evidence is whether the defendant abandoned the contract of purchase. Of that question a court of equity formerly had exclusive jurisdiction, and now the material facts, being in dispute, must be passed upon by a jury in the superior court. There is a controversy about the title, bringing the case clearly within the provisions of subsection 2, § 834, Code.[1] The action was properly dismissed. There is no error.

---

[1] This section provides that justices of the peace shall have exclusive original jurisdiction of all civil actions founded on contracts except where the demand exceeds $200 or the title to real estate is in controversy.

STATE v. WHITFIELD.

(Supreme Court of North Carolina. Oct. 20, 1891.)

CRIMINAL LAW—VOLUNTARY DECLARATIONS WHILE UNDER ARREST.

The facts that a defendant was in arrest and secured by a hand-cuff placed on one hand, and connected by a chain with the buggy in which he was riding, in company with an officer who had in his pocket the warrant under which he had been committed on a charge of larceny, do not of themselves constitute duress, so as to exclude any material declaration made to the officer in reference to the crime; and, unless it appears that the defendant was induced to make the declaration by some advantageous offer, or by threats, or actual force, arousing hope or exciting fear in his mind, it is not error to admit the officer's testimony.

Indictment against Whitfield for larceny. There was judgment of conviction, and defendant appeals. Affirmed.

This was an indictment for larceny of two oxen, tried at the fall term, 1891, of the superior court of Pitt county, before CONNOR, Judge. Other testimony having been offered tending to prove the guilt of defendant, the solicitor was allowed to show that, after the defendant had been arrested on a justice's warrant, and committed to jail to await a trial upon the charge upon which he was then arraigned, he was taken by virtue of a writ of *habeas corpus ad testificandum* under custody, to Williamston, to testify in the superior court of Martin county. R. W. King, the sheriff's deputy, who took defendant in custody to Williamston, testified as follows: "I was conveying defendant from Greenville to Williamston under an order from Judge CONNOR to testify in a case from Martin. He was in custody, charged with the offense for which he is now being tried. I offered him no inducement to talk about it, nor said to him that it would be better for him to tell about it. I was riding along the road in a buggy with him. He had one hand-cuff on, and was tied to the buggy. I had the warrant upon which he had formerly been arrested in my pocket. I did not tell him that I had the warrant. He knew that I was going to bring him back. He said to me that he bought the steers from a man by the name of Sam Sheppard, near Great Swamp, for $20, and offered to sell them for $22. He said that his mother had given him thirty dollars to trade upon. I asked him why he did not try to get his cattle back after he got out of jail. He said that his friends advised him not to do so, and that he had learned that it might give him some trouble. He said that he went to Roper City and Baltimore, and then came back to Martin. He was arrested by the sheriff of Martin." To these declarations the defendant objected, for that he was under arrest and hand-cuffed at the time. The court overruled the objection, for that it appeared from the statement of the deputy-sheriff, without contradiction, that the said declarations were voluntary. Defendant excepted. Defendant testified and introduced evidence to show that he bought the oxen from Samuel Sheppard along the public road at Great Swamp, and that he used money loaned him by his mother. There was evidence, both corroborative and contradictory, of the defendant's statements. Verdict. Motion for new trial for error in admitting testimony of King overruled. Appeal.

The Attorney General, for the State.

AVERY, J., *(after stating the facts.)* The facts that a defendant was in arrest, and secured by a hand-cuff placed on one hand, and connected by a chain with a buggy in which he was riding in company with the officer who had in his pocket the warrant under which he had been committed to jail on a charge of larceny, do not of themselves constitute duress, so as to exclude any material declaration made to the officer in reference to the commission of the crime of which he is accused. Unless, in such a case, it appeared to the court that the defendant was induced to make the confession or declaration by some advantageous offer, or by threats or actual force, by arousing hope or exciting fear in his mind, it was not error to admit the testimony of the officer. State v. Sanders, 84 N. C. 728; State v. Bishop, 98 N. C. 773; 4 S. E. Rep. 357; State v. Graham, 74 N. C. 646; State v. Efler, 85 N. C. 585; State v. Howard, 92 N. C. 772. There was no error. The judgment below must be affirmed.

STATE v. TELFAIR.

(Supreme Court of North Carolina. Oct. 20, 1891.)

SECRET ASSAULT—EVIDENCE—IDENTITY.

In a prosecution for a secret assault, the prosecutor testified that he was fired on in the evening by some one standing behind a fence six feet distant, whose size, height, complexion, and appearance were those of defendant; that at the time of the shooting it was possible for witness to see a man plainly 50 yards distant; and that the shirt worn by his assailant was the same as that worn by defendant at the preliminary hearing, two days afterwards. It was also shown that the tracks made by the assailant corresponded with the shoes worn by defendant. *Held,* that the evidence identifying defendant was sufficient to warrant its submission to the jury, and that a verdict of guilty would not be disturbed.

This was an indictment for a secret assault, (drawn under chapter 32, Laws 1887,) tried at the fall term, 1891, of the superior court of Pitt county, before CONNOR, Judge. The prosecutor testified, among other things, that the defendant lived near to him in the same township, in Pitt county, was known to him, and had traded at his store; and that on the 26th of May previous he was going from his home to his store, about 7:30 P. M., when some one, who was standing behind a fence, fired a gun loaded with BB and buckshot, one of the shot striking witness, others passing through his clothes, and still others lodging in the trees near by the witness. The person did not move till the witness inquired who it was, and then he ran off. The witness stated that he recognized a dark checked shirt which the person was wearing; that he saw he was a colored boy, of about the size and height of the defendant, and clean shaven; and that on the second morning afterwards, when the defendant was brought to trial, he was wearing a dark checked shirt, exactly like the one worn by the person who shot him; and that the gun used was a single-barreled musket. As soon as the justice of the peace, Mr. Laughinghouse, could be found on the next day, the prosecutor procured a warrant for the arrest of defendant, and then examined the track, and found it was made by a No. 7 shoe that had been run down. The shoe worn by the defendant at the trial was run down. On cross-examination the prosecutor stated that he could have seen a man 100 yards away when he was shot; that the defendant was about six steps from him when the shot was fired; and he could see at that place 50 yards, and he saw the defendant as he started to run. The witness testified also that a shoe exhibited to him on the trial was the one he saw next day. Mr. Laughinghouse, the justice of the peace, testified that he asked the prosecutor the next day why he thought that the defendant shot him, and he replied that he knew it by his size, and the color of his shirt, which the prosecutor described to him. The witness also testified that he placed the shoe given him by the officer in one of the tracks near the alleged place of shooting, and it fitted the track exactly, and he afterwards tried it on defendant's foot, and it was of the same size that he wore. Mr. Holliday testified that the track where the person appeared to be standing was 11 inches long, where he was running 11¼ inches long, (it being in evidence that defendant wore a No. 7 shoe, and that the length of that number was 11 inches.) That witness further testified that the defendant was working in a field, where he could see him, on the day before the shooting, and left the field a considerable time before the usual hour of quitting work. The witness stated that he recognized the shoe exhibited at the trial as the one worn by the defendant the day before the shooting. The shoe which the defendant used in chopping cotton was run down. The shoe shown on the trial was cut across the toe, (the prosecutor having testified that the cut across the toe appeared at the trial to be fresh.) The defendant's counsel offered no testimony, and asked the court to instruct the jury that the evidence makes at best nothing more than a weak probability of defendant's identity as the person who committed the assault. To the refusal so to charge defendant excepted. Verdict of guilty. Defendant appealed. Affirmed.

The Attorney General, for the State.

AVERY, J., (*after stating the facts.*) The defendant's request for instruction was equivalent to a demurrer to the strongest phase of the testimony which is presented in the foregoing summary of those facts tending to establish his guilt. This evidence, together with other testimony tending to explain or contradict it, which it is not necessary to set forth here, should unquestionably have been submitted to the jury, to determine whether they entertained any reasonable doubt of the defendant's guilt. There is no exception to the terms of the charge, which seems to

have been conceived in a spirit of fairness, if not of liberality, towards the prisoner. The testimony of the prosecutor, if not sufficient of itself to go to the jury on the question of identity, is strengthened by proof that the defendant's shoes, which had been run down, fitted in the tracks made by the person who committed the assault, and also on the foot of defendant. Besides, one witness (Holliday) swore to the absolute identity of the shoes worn by the defendant on the afternoon just before the shooting, when he left the field at an unusual hour, and the shoes exhibited on the trial, and which the officer making the arrest testified that he found in the defendant's house. The prosecutor testified that the size, height, complexion, and appearance of the man who shot were those of the defendant, according to his best judgment, and that the shirt worn by the person who shot him at a distance of six steps was in his opinion that worn by the defendant on the preliminary trial two days after, it being possible for the witness to see a man plainly 50 yards, looking from his stand-point when shot, in the direction in which his assailant stood, and subsequently ran. These facts, admitted by the request in the nature of a demurrer, were sufficiently strong to make it the duty of the judge to submit them to the jury, and to warrant the verdict of guilty returned by them. The contradictory and explanatory testimony elicited from the witnesses was presented, or might have been presented, to the jury on the argument by counsel in their bearings upon the question of guilt. It was the province of the jury to weigh all of the evidence, which we assume that they did.

A review of the testimony, (which, as it is insisted, is insufficient to justify the verdict,) and a comparison of it with that held to be sufficient to go to the jury in other cases, will show that testimony not so satisfactory has been held sufficient to sustain a verdict of guilty. State v. Whitfield, 93 N. C. 519; State v. Powell, 94 N. C. 965; State v. McBryde, 97 N. C. 393, 1 S. E. Rep. 925; State v. Christmas, 101 N. C. 749, 8 S. E. Rep. 361. Placing the most liberal construction upon the evidence, the prosecutor testified to the positive identity of the shirt worn by the prisoner at the trial, two days after the shooting, with that worn by the person who shot him, and corroborated this opinion by the statement that his assailant was about the same height, size, and complexion, and, like the prisoner, was clean shaven, and that he made the track subsequently examined by the witness with what appeared to be a run-down shoe. The identification of the shoe worn by him on the previous afternoon, and fitting it in the track by other witnesses, form, together with the prosecutor's evidence, a net-work of circumstances so strong as to leave no room for question as to the correctness of his honor's holding that there was testimony which it was his duty to submit to the jury. We have not construed the language used by the prosecutor on his cross-examination according to its literal meaning, but have interpreted his whole statement together. Stokes said, among other things: "I could see fifty yards at that place. Defendant was about six steps from me when he shot. I saw him as he started to run." Taking this detached statement literally, and construing it without reference to the qualifying language used by the witness, it is an absolute assertion that he recognized the defendant when he started to run, immediately after firing the gun. Whether the prosecutor claimed to have identified the defendant at that moment, and gave the description of the dress, size, and complexion solely for the purpose of corroborating his positive claim of recognition, or whether his opinion of the identity of his assailant and the accused was founded upon, instead of being justified by, the description he has given, in either view there was testimony which took the case beyond that pale within which the court could discuss its weight. State v. Perkins, 104 N. C. 710, 10 S. E. Rep. 175. The evidence was not clearly inconclusive as to the defendant's guilt, and it would have been error to have so held, and to have withdrawn the case from the consideration of the jury. State v. Dixon, 104 N. C. 704, 10 S. E. Rep. 74. There was no error.

BOONE v. DARDEN et al.

(*Supreme Court of North Carolina. Oct. 20, 1891.*)

LANDLORD'S LIEN ON CROPS — CLAIM AND DELIVERY.

Under Code N. C. § 1754, giving a landlord a lien on the whole of the tenant's crop for the rent, and providing that the crop is "held to be vested in possession of the lessor" until the rent is paid, and giving the landlord an action of claim and delivery if the crop, or any part thereof, shall be removed from the land without the consent of the lessor, the landlord may maintain the action for a certain part only of the crop, though all of it has been delivered to a third person.

Action of claim and delivery by Walter Boone against James P. Darden and John Drake. Judgment for plaintiff, and defendants appeal. Affirmed.

Civil action tried before CONNOR, Judge, at the spring term, 1891, of the superior court of Northampton county. The plaintiff alleged, in substance, that he rented a plantation, described in the complaint, to John Drake for the year 1889, for which Drake was to pay $600 rent; that said Drake raised, upon the said plantation, peanuts and other crops; that the rent was due and unpaid; and that the defendant Drake had removed the peanuts produced on the said plantation, and placed them in the hands of the defendant Darden for shipment; and he demands possession of said peanuts, or their value, if possession cannot be recovered. At the time of issuing the summons the plaintiff, as provided by chapter 2, § 321 et seq., Code, made claim to the immediate possession of 150 bags of peanuts, alleging that he was the owner and entitled to the immediate possession of the same, and that they were wrongfully detained by the defendant Darden. In obedience to the clerk's fiat, the sheriff seized 150 bags of peanuts, being a portion of the peanuts in the hands of the defendant Darden. The defendant Drake denied the plaintiff's claim, alleged that he was the owner of the peanuts, gave the undertaking requisite to retain the possession of property thus seized, and retained the possession of the peanuts. "By consent, the case was tried by his honor (a jury trial being waived) on the following admitted facts: The defendant Darden was agent for the R. & T. Railroad at Severn; that the peanuts in controversy were raised by the defendant Drake on the plaintiff's farm, in Northampton county, in the year 1889; that Drake was a tenant of plaintiff at the annual rental of $600, no part of which has been paid; that Drake had carried the peanuts to Severn for shipment, and plaintiff had enough thereof seized to pay his rent; that the sheriff took 150 bags of peanuts from the pile, and seized them under the order of court. The defendants relied on the point of law that there was no lien on any specific number of bags, and the action could not be maintained. His honor ruled otherwise, and refused to dismiss the action, and defendants excepted. Upon the admitted facts, his honor gave judgment for the plaintiff. Defendants appealed."

B. B. Winborne, for appellants. R. O. Burton, for appellee.

DAVIS, J., (*after stating the facts.*) It is insisted for the defendants that there were more than 150 bags of peanuts in the possession of the defendants, and "the interest of the plaintiff is not properly described, so that the officer can measure it out to him." By the provisions of Code, § 1754, the entire crop of peanuts raised on the land of the plaintiff, landlord, was vested in possession of the lessor until the rent for the land was paid. This is conceded, but the defendants insist that the plaintiff has no lien on any specific number of bags. We are unable to see how, if the plaintiff had a lien upon, and was entitled to the possession of, the whole number of bags, he was not entitled to the possession of a portion of them, nor can we see that any division was to be made by the officer. Code, § 1754, gives the landlord a lien upon the whole of the tenant's crop to secure the payment of the rent, and, to make the lien more effectual, the crop is "held to be vested in possession of the lessor" until the rents are paid; and, if the crop or any part thereof shall be removed from the land without the consent of the lessor, the statute gives him the remedies provided in an action upon claim for the delivery of personal property. The lessor's vested right to the possession of the crop is coupled with a lien upon the crop to secure the payment of rent or the compliance with stipulations contained in the lease. It is not an unqualified right to dispose of the crop as he pleases, but when the rents are paid, and the stipulations of the lease complied with, the right to the surplus passes to the lessee or his assigns, and the lessor has no further right to it. The law is founded on reason, and to say that, because the plaintiff is entitled to the possession of the entire bulk of 400 bags to secure his rent, therefore he is not entitled to the possession of 150 bags, a part of the 400 sufficient to secure his rent, is as shocking to reason as it would be to say that the whole of a thing does not include all its parts, or that a part is greater than the whole. The plaintiff is entitled to the possession of the whole 400 bags of peanuts to secure the payment of his rent, and the defendant's mistake is in confounding his right to have 150 bags of it seized in an action for the claim and delivery with his right to seize 150 bags to which he might be entitled out of a mass of 400 bags, 250 of which belonged to some one else, to which he had no right or claim. Counsel for the defendants admit that an action of replevin (in the case before us, claim and delivery) "can be maintained for a part of property in mass, such as oats, corn, etc.; but the interest sued for should be described as so many pounds or bushels, so as to enable the officer to make proper division;" and he cites Blakely v. Patrick, 67 N. C. 40; McDaniel v. Allen, 99 N. C. 135, 5 S. E. Rep. 737; Cobbey, Repl. §§ 78, 400–402; Low v. Martin, 18 Ill. 286; Piassek v. White, 23 Kan. 621. Upon an examination of these authorities, it will be seen that they bear no analogy to the case before us. In the case of Blakely v. Patrick, known as the "Buggy Case," the action was "for damages for the conversion of 10 new buggies by the defendant." The court said that the mortgage under which the plaintiff claimed did not pass the title to 10 new buggies as an executed contract, but only had the effect of an agreement to sell 10 new buggies, for a breach of which damages may be recovered. In the case before us, both the legal title and the right of possession to all the peanuts were by statute vested in the plaintiff. So, in the case of McDaniel v. Allen, the plaintiff was not the owner, entitled to the possession, of the three bags of cotton sued for, but his remedy was for a breach of contract for refusal to comply. The other cases cited relate to property in mass belonging to different parties, and in which the property is so commingled that each owner cannot identify and show what part of the property so mixed belongs to him; but even then, "if a division can be made of equal value," says Cobbey, "as in the case of corn, oats, and wheat, the law will give to each owner his just proportion, and each owner may recover his share by replevin." If the plaintiff had been the owner and entitled to the possession of only 150 bags of the peanuts, and they had, without any fault of his, been mixed with 250 bags belonging to the defendants, we are unable to see why, upon the authority cited by the defendants, this action could not be maintained. The plaintiff was entitled to enough of the crop to pay the rent due, and after his claim was satisfied the defendants were entitled to the balance discharged of the lien. If the plaintiff had seized more than enough to satisfy his lien, and refused "to make a fair division of the crop," the defendants could have compelled him to do so in the manner prescribed in section 1755 of the Code; and we are unable to see upon what ground they can complain that the plaintiff, who was entitled to the possession of the whole crop to secure his rent, took only enough for that purpose, and left them in possession of the balance, to which they were entitled, after, and not until after, the rent was paid. There is no error.

BRAY v. BARNARD.

(*Supreme Court of North Carolina.* Oct. 20, 1891.)

COUNTY COMMISSIONERS—NEGLECT OF DUTY—PENALTIES.

1. Under Code N. C. § 711, making a county commissioner liable to a penalty of $200 if he neglect to perform any duty required of him by law as a member of the board, where a sheriff fails both to make an annual renewal of his bonds and to produce receipts, failure to do either of which creates a vacancy in the office by the provisions of section 2070, but one penalty can be recovered against a commissioner for failure to declare the office vacant, and to fill the same by appointment, though section 720 provides that, whenever a vacancy shall occur in the office of sheriff, the board of county commissioners shall fill it by appointment; and section 1875 provides that, on failure of any such officer to make an annual renewal of his bond, it shall be the duty of the board of commissioners to declare his office vacant, and to appoint a successor; the duties of the commissioners prescribed by the several sections being substantially the same.

2. Under Code N. C. § 775, providing that, for failure of the sheriff to perform certain duty, the board of county commissioners "may forthwith" bring suit on his official bond in an action against a commissioner to recover the penalty prescribed by section 711 for failure to perform any duty required of him by law, it is not enough that the complaint allege that the sheriff failed to perform the duty, and the commissioners failed to sue on his bond, as the statute leaves it to their sound discretion whether they will sue or not, and therefore the complaint should at least allege facts showing negligent failure or willful refusal of the commissioners to exercise their authority.

Appeal from superior court, Currituck county; HENRY G. CONNOR, Judge.

Action by W. H. Bray against W. D. Barnard to recover penalties incurred by defendant by failure to perform his duty as county commissioner. Recovery was allowed in a single instance only, and plaintiff appeals. Affirmed.

This action is brought by the plaintiff to recover from the defendant divers penalties, which the complaint alleges he incurred as a member of the board of commissioners of the county of Currituck by neglecting to perform his duty in numerous respects as such commissioner. Among other things it is alleged as follows: "(5) That said Barnard, sheriff as aforesaid, was required to renew his bonds annually, and on the 1st day of December, 1889, and produce his receipts as set out in section 2070 of the Code of North Carolina, which he failed to do, thereby creating a vacancy in said office of sheriff of said county by act and operation of law; and the said board of commissioners, and the defendant as a member thereof, was required to fill said vacancy by appointment, as required by section 720 of the Code of North Carolina, which said board, and this defendant as a member thereof, failed and neglected to do, in violation of said section 720 of said Code; and this defendant thereby became liable for the penalty of two hundred dollars, and indebted to this plaintiff for same, he having brought suit for same according to section 711 of the Code aforesaid." "(8) That said John E. Barnard failed and neglected to make and renew his official bonds as sheriff as aforesaid on the 1st Monday in December, 1889, as required by section 2070 of the Code of North Carolina, and the said board, and the defendant as a member thereof, failed and neglected to declare his office vacant and appoint his successor, as required by section 1875 of the Code of North Carolina; and, by reason of said failure and negligence, the defendant has become liable to a penalty of two hundred dollars, and indebted to plaintiff in said amount, as provided by section 711 of said Code. (9) That said John E. Barnard, sheriff as aforesaid, failed and refused to settle the taxes collected for the year 1888, and the finance committee of said county so reported to the treasurer of said county and to said board of commissioners that said sheriff was in arrears the sum of $1,759.94, and that said board, and this defendant as a member thereof, failed and neglected to institute suit against said Barnard, sheriff as aforesaid, and his bondsmen, as they were required to do, in violation of section 775 of the Code aforesaid, and thereby became liable to a penalty of two hundred dollars, and same is due this plaintiff according to the provisions of section 711 of the Code of North Carolina." The plaintiff moved for judgment upon the pleadings. The court denied this motion for judgment for the penalties alleged and specified in paragraphs 8 and 9 of the complaint above set forth upon the ground that the penalty alleged in paragraph 8 is substantially that alleged in paragraph 5 thereof; and upon the further ground that paragraph 9, above set forth, does not state facts sufficient to constitute a cause of action. The plaintiff excepted. As to these penalties, the court gave judgment for the defendant, and the plaintiff appealed to this court.

J. H. Blount and Grandy & Aydlett, for appellant. Pittman & Shaw, for appellee.

Merrimon, C. J., (after stating the facts.) The statute (Code, § 711) prescribes that "any [county] commissioner who shall neglect to perform any duty required of him by law as a member of the board shall be guilty of a misdemeanor, and shall also be liable to a penalty of two hundred dollars for each offense, to be paid to any person who shall sue for the same." The plaintiff contends—First, that the defendant incurred a penalty under this statutory provision, because the sheriff mentioned failed for the year specified in the fifth paragraph of the complaint to file the annual bonds required of him, and to produce receipts for moneys that he had collected, or ought to have collected, whereby his office became vacant, as prescribed by the statute, (Id. § 2070,) and the defendant neglected to perform his duty as commissioner, in that he and his associates did not proceed to fill the vacancy so occasioned by appointment, as prescribed and required by the statute, (Id. § 720,) which provides that "whenever

a vacancy shall occur in the office of sheriff, constable, register of deeds, county treasurer, or county surveyor, the board of commissioners of the county shall fill the same by appointment." He contends, secondly, that the defendant incurred another penalty, as alleged in the eighth paragraph of the complaint, because the board of commissioners — the defendant joining them—failed to declare the office of the sheriff vacant for the causes alleged, as required by the statute, (Id. § 1875,) which prescribes that "upon the failure of any such officer (including sheriffs) to make such regular annual renewal of his bond it is the duty of the board of commissioners, by an order to be entered of record, to declare his office vacant, and to proceed forthwith to appoint a successor," etc. The court below was of opinion and held that the duties of the board of commissioners of the county, prescribed by the statutory provision just cited, were substantially the same as those prescribed in the other statutory provision, (Id. § 2070,) cited supra. In this we think the court was correct, in so far as these sections affect this case. They, as to the sheriff, are intended to secure the same purpose, except that section 2070 enlarges the purpose, so as to require the sheriff, in addition to the renewal of his bonds, annually to "produce the receipts in full from the state treasurer, county treasurer, and other persons, of all moneys by him collected, or which ought to have been by him collected, for the use of the state and county, and for which he shall have become accountable," etc. As to the sheriff, in respect to the annual renewal of his bonds, the sections are in pari materia, and must be taken together; they are intended to effectuate the same purpose. It is not to be presumed that the legislature intended to impose double penalties for the same failure of duty in a public officer. If it had so intended, it would have said so in explicit terms. The duty of the board of commissioners was to declare the office of sheriff vacant, and to fill the vacancy, when and if he failed to renew his bonds annually. The same duty is prescribed by the two sections of the Code just recited. In one of these sections the same duty arises if the sheriff shall fail to produce the receipts mentioned as required. Under this section, if the sheriff should fail to renew his bonds, it would be the duty of the board of commissioners to declare his office vacant. If he renewed his bonds, and failed to produce the receipts mentioned, it would be their like duty. It would be their like duty if he failed to renew his bonds and to produce the receipts required; but in the latter case they would not be liable to two penalties. The purpose of the sections cited of the statute is to compel the board of commissioners to perform their duty in declaring the office of sheriff vacant, and filling the vacancy in any one or more or all of the contingencies specified therein. Only one penalty is given against each commissioner composing the board if he fails to perform his duty in such respect. That penalty, in this case, the plaintiff recovered under and in pursuance of the allegations contained in the fifth paragraph of his complaint.

We are also of opinion that the court properly decided that the ninth paragraph of the complaint set forth above fails to state facts sufficient to constitute a cause of action. The statute (Code, § 775) certainly does not make it the imperative duty of the board of commissioners of the county to "bring suit on the official bond of the sheriff or other officer." It provides that they "may forthwith" do so. It is thus left to their sound discretion whether they will or not. There might be substantial reasons why they would not, and, moreover, they might be content to leave it to the county treasurer to bring such suit, especially as, regularly, he is the proper officer to do so. Hewlett v. Nutt, 79 N. C. 263. The plaintiff, claiming under this statutory provision, should at least allege facts showing that the board of commissioners had negligently failed or willfully refused to exercise their authority, and hence they had neglected to perform their duty as required by law. In such case it may be that each of them participating in such neglect would incur the penalty prescribed. Judgment affirmed.

JOHNSTON v. WHITEHEAD et al.

(Supreme Court of North Carolina. Oct. 20, 1891.)

DISMISSAL OF APPEAL—NOTICE—MOTION TO REINSTATE.

1. Under Sup. Ct. N. C. rule 17, providing that, if an appeal be not docketed before the call of the district to which it belongs, the appellee may have it dismissed, and that if improperly dismissed the motion to reinstate should be made "during the term," an agreement of counsel to give until January 31, 1891, to perfect an appeal, while ground to resist a motion to dismiss if made at the fall term of 1890, when the appeal should in due course have been docketed, was no excuse for the appeal not being docketed or a *certiorari* applied for at the spring term of 1891, and a motion to reinstate at the next term thereafter was too late.

2. Notice of the motion to dismiss was not required.

Petition by Johnston to reinstate an appeal. Denied.

C. M. Bernard, for appellant.

CLARK, J. This action was tried in the superior court of Pitt at June term, 1890. At spring term, 1891, of this court, the transcript on appeal not having been brought up, the appellees filed their requisite certificate, and had the appeal dismissed, under rule 17. At this term (fall, 1891) the appellant moved to reinstate, and as cause therefor files an agreement of counsel, made in September, 1890, that time till 31st of January, 1891, should be allowed the appellant "to perfect case on appeal;" and also urges that the motion to dismiss was made without notice. The agreement to give time till 31st of January, 1891, to perfect appeal, would have been ground to resist a motion to dismiss, if made at fall term, 1890, when the appeal should in due course have been docketed, but was no excuse for the transcript not being on file when the district to which it belongs was called at spring

term, 1891, or for a *certiorari* not being applied for if the appellant was in no default. Pittman v. Kimberly, 92 N. C. 562. Besides, if the appeal was improperly dismissed, the motion to reinstate by the rule (17) should have been made "during the term" at which it was dismissed, and, if granted, the cause would have stood for argument at this term. To permit the cause to be reinstated now is not only not authorized by the rules, but contrary to the rights of the appellees, as it would put off the argument and decision of the appeal till spring term, 1892, which regularly should have stood for argument at fall term, 1890, and that, too, when, by appellant's own showing, the agreement for delay only postponed the hearing till spring term, 1891. If the case on appeal was lost or mislaid, the remedy of appellant was by a *certiorari* at the first term of this court. Pittman v. Kimberly, supra; Bailey v. Brown, 105 N. C. 126, 10 S. E. Rep. 1054; Porter v. Railroad Co., 106 N. C. 478, 11 S. E. Rep. 515; Mitchell v. Tedder, 108 N. C. 226, 12 S. E. Rep. 1044.

The objection that the motion to dismiss was granted without notice is without force. Notice of such motion is not required. Appellants are too often prone to forget that appellees have rights. The "law's delay" is assigned by Hamlet as one of the great evils of life, and the barons at Runnymede thought it so great a one that they exacted the insertion of a guaranty against it in *Magna Charta*,—a guaranty that has been copied into the constitution probably of every American state, and which is to be found in section 35 of our own declaration of rights. This guaranty, so notably won, so carefully continued for so many centuries, and still incorporated in our organic law, that "justice shall be administered without delay," is not a mere rhetorical flourish. It is a constitutional right. The party who seeks delay must show good cause why the other party should be subjected to it, and the burden is on him to show that he himself is without laches. The appellant has shown no cause why the appeal was not docketed here, or a *certiorari* applied for, at the spring term, 1891, and none why this motion to reinstate, if there had been ground for it, was not made "during the term" at which the appeal was dismissed. Motion denied.

TURNER v. HOLDEN.

(Supreme Court of North Carolina. Oct. 27, 1891.)

SUPPLEMENTAL PROCEEDINGS—NOTICE—RETURN—AMENDMENT—APPEALABLE ORDER.

1. Leaving a copy of an order on a judgment debtor to appear and answer in supplemental proceedings with the debtor's wife was a sufficient service.

2. Where the sheriff's return on the notice did not show that the person with whom it was left was defendant's wife, and a person of suitable age and discretion, it was proper to allow an amendment so as to show such facts.

3. On a hearing before him the clerk of the court denied defendant's motion for a special appearance for the purpose of a motion to dismiss, whereupon defendant appealed to the judge, who ordered that the motion to dismiss be overruled. *Held,* that such order was not appealable.

Appeal from superior court, Wake county; ROBERT W. WINSTON, Judge.

Proceeding supplemental to execution instituted by Josiah Turner against W. W. Holden. Defendant moved to dismiss the proceeding for want of sufficient service. The motion was overruled, and defendant appealed. Appeal dismissed.

It appears that the plaintiff had obtained his judgment against the defendant in the superior court of Wake county, and that the same was duly docketed; that afterwards, on the 20th day of April, 1891, the plaintiff began this proceeding supplementary to the execution, and obtained from the court (the clerk) an order requiring the defendant to appear and answer concerning his property, at a time and place specified, as allowed by the statute in such cases. A copy of this order was placed in the hands of the sheriff of said county to be served upon the defendant. The sheriff made return thereof as follows: "Received April 25, 1891. Executed by delivering a copy and exhibiting the original of the within order and affidavit to Mrs. L. V. Holden, and also left a copy of order and affidavit with Mrs. L. V. Holden, for W. W. Holden, the 29th day of April, 1891, at 4 o'clock P. M. M. W. PAGE, Sheriff Wake County. By C. M. WALTERS, Deputy." Sheriff, by leave of court, makes the following amended return: "Received April 25, 1891. Executed by delivering a copy and exhibiting the original of the within order and affidavit to Mrs. L. V. Holden, and also by leaving a copy of order and affidavit with Mrs. L. V. Holden, wife of W. W. Holden, for said W. W. Holden, at his residence in the city of Raleigh, at the hour of 4 o'clock P. M., on the 29th day of April, 1891, the said L. V. Holden being a person of suitable age and discretion with whom to leave such papers. M. W. PAGE. Sheriff. Per C. M. WALTERS, D. S." The defendant contended that the copy of the order and notice was not properly and duly served upon him, and his counsel contended, further, that they had the right to appear for the purpose simply of a motion to dismiss the proceeding on the ground that notice had not been served. They moved that the record be so amended as to show that they appeared, and only for such purpose. The court (the clerk) denied this motion, and the defendant appealed to the judge. The clerk refused to certify the record, etc., to the judge. Thereupon the defendant applied to the judge for the writ of certiorari, requiring the clerk to certify the record, etc., to him. The judge granted the writ, and due return thereof was made.

The court (the judge) upon consideration, made its order, whereof the following is a copy: "This cause coming on to be heard this day before ROBERT W. WINSTON, judge, the plaintiff, represented by John Devereux, Jr., and Chester Turner, and the defendant by Thos. C. Fuller and W. R. Henry, who enter a special appearance in writing, and move to dismiss upon the return of John W. Thompson, C. S. C. of Wake county, to the order to him to certify the record of his proceedings ᵗᵒ the court, and having been heard up-

on the argument of counsel for both sides, the defendant's counsel state that they do not appear generally in this action, but specially in order to move to dismiss the proceedings, and insist that the same ought to be dismissed for the reason that W. W. Holden has not been properly served with process, in that for this proceeding to be begun by process the same should have been read to him in person; that the clerk ought to have permitted an amendment of the record, so as to show that the appearance of Messrs. Fuller and Hinsdale, on the 11th of May, 1891, was a special appearance, and not general. The court, being of opinion that the notice of this supplemental proceeding had been properly served, and also that the clerk's finding and ruling that the said attorneys appeared generally on said 11th of May, 1891, was final and conclusive, and that such general appearance cured any defect in serving said process or notice, if such defect ever existed, overruled the motion to dismiss, from which order and ruling the defendant took an appeal to supreme court, notice of appeal waived, bond of $15 adjudged sufficient, and this statement to be case on appeal to the supreme court."

J. W. Hinsdale, for appellant. C. D. Turner, W. W Fuller, and Batchelor & Devereux, for appellee.

MERRIMON, C. J., (after stating the facts.) The court had jurisdiction of the defendant by virtue of the service of the summons,—the original process,—and his appearance in the action. The action was not ended for all purposes when the plaintiff obtained his judgment. It remained and remains current for all proper purposes in the enforcement of the judgment by the ordinary execution and other appropriate means, including proceedings supplementary to the execution. The latter are not separate from and independent of the action; they are incident to and part of it; they constitute and are no more than a means allowed by the statute in the action whereby to reach the property of the defendant and enforce satisfaction of the judgment. Hence they are not begun by original process,—a summons. The statute does not so provide. It (Code, § 488) prescribes that the judgment creditor, "at any time after such return made, [return of the ordinary execution,] and within three years from the time of issuing the execution, is entitled to an order from the court to which the execution is returned, or from the judge thereof, requiring such debtor to appear and answer concerning his property before such court or judge at a time and place specified in the order, within the county to which the execution was issued." Although the statute does not in terms prescribe that notice of such order shall be given, still its nature, purpose, practice, and justice require that notice shall be given for such time as the court shall deem just. Weiller v. Lawrence, 81 N. C. 65. Such notice must be so given and served upon the party to be notified in the way prescribed for giving and serving notices in actions. The statute (Code, § 597) provides that "notices shall be in writing. Notices and other papers may be served on the party or his attorney personally, where not otherwise provided in this chapter." One of the methods provided (the same section, par. 2) prescribes that "if [service] upon a party, it may be made by leaving the paper at his residence, between the hours of six in the morning and nine in the evening, with some person of suitable age and discretion." Service thus made is sufficient. The court has jurisdiction in cases like this of the party to the action, and it is deemed sufficient to give him notice, in the way prescribed, of any motion or proceeding in the action. It is the duty of parties to actions to be on the alert at all times until the same shall be completely ended. If it should turn out that a party was prejudiced in that he did not actually get the notice, the court would, in a proper case, afford relief. In the present case, the order, so far as appears, was regularly granted, and the service of notice thereof on the defendant was sufficient.

The court clearly had power to allow the sheriff to amend his return, and the return, as amended, shows that the notice to the defendant was served by leaving a copy of the order for him at his residence at the hour specified; that it was left with his wife. She, surely, was a person of "suitable age and discretion" to deliver the notice to him, (her husband,) and the inference is that she did so. If he did not in fact get the notice, then his remedy is not to move to dismiss the proceeding, but to ask for reasonable time to answer as the law requires. As the court had jurisdiction of the defendant, and the notice had been duly served, the motion of his counsel to be allowed to appear for the purpose of a motion to dismiss the proceeding was not pertinent, and was properly denied. No question is presented here as to the sufficiency of service of notice upon an attorney.

The court held properly that the notice had been duly served. This was sufficient. It did not need to further state as a ground of its order that "the clerk's finding and ruling that the said attorneys appeared generally on said 11th of May, 1891, was final and conclusive," etc. The action of the clerk was not final and conclusive. In a proper case, on appeal to him, it would be the duty of the court to review the findings of fact by the clerk, and correct his errors of law. He was no more than the servant of the court, and subject to its supervision in the way prescribed by the statute. Code, § 251 et seq.; Bank v. Burns, 107 N. C. 465, 12 S. E. Rep. 252. The court (the judge) did not need to grant the writ of certiorari to compel the clerk to state the case on appeal, as allowed by the statute. Code, § 254. He might have directed the clerk to do so by mere order. The plaintiff moved to dismiss the appeal to this court, and we are of opinion that the motion must be allowed. The order appealed from was incidental, and no more, at most, than interlocutory. To deny the defendant's motion could not seriously prejudice him, or impair any substantial right he might have. The court simply decided that he had been duly served with notice, and was before it for pertinent and proper purposes. If the notice had not been properly served, the court would simply have directed a reasonable delay of proceedings, or that a new notice issue forthwith to be served within a day specified. Weiller v. Lawrence, supra. Appeals to this court do not lie from every order in the course of an action. This has been decided in many cases, and the court has repeatedly pointed out when an appeal does and does not lie. Appeal dismissed.

STATE v. NASH.

(Supreme Court of North Carolina. Oct. 27, 1891.)

APPEAL IN CRIMINAL CASES—PAYMENT FOR TRANSCRIPT IN ADVANCE.

Under Code N. C. § 3758, which provides that no officer shall be compelled to perform any services unless his fees be paid or tendered, "except in criminal actions," where defendant had executed his bond on appeal in a criminal proceeding against him he was entitled to have the transcript on appeal sent up without paying or tendering to the clerk his fees for making such transcript.

Motion by H. A. Nash for certiorari to bring up the transcript of a criminal proceeding against him to the supreme court on appeal. Motion allowed.

The Attorney General, for the State. *T. M. Argo,* for defendant.

CLARK, J. The defendant, who did not appeal in forma pauperis, but has executed his appeal-bond, refused to pay the costs of the transcript of the record on appeal. The clerk thereupon declined to send it up. The application for certiorari, therefore, presents the question whether, in criminal actions, the clerk can require the cost of the transcript to be paid in advance. It is settled that in civil cases he can. Andrews v. Whisnant, 83 N. C. 446; Bailey v. Brown, 105 N. C. 127, 10 S. E. Rep. 1054. But in criminal actions it is otherwise. Code, § 3758, provides: "No officer shall be compelled to perform any services, unless his fee be paid or tendered, except in criminal actions." This inhibition against requiring payment of fees in advance in criminal actions, we think, embraces all services, including that in question. We are strengthened in this view by the fact that it has been held that the appeal-bond secures only the costs of the appellee, and not of the appellant, (Morris v. Morris, 92 N. C. 142, and cases cited;) and hence that, when such bond is dispensed with in civil cases by leave to appeal in forma pauperis, the appellant may still be required by the clerk to pay for the cost of the transcript on appeal and cost in this court as well, (Martin v. Chasteen, 75 N. C. 96; Andrews v. Whisnant and Bailey v. Brown, supra.) The reason of this distinction is that section 212, allowing a party to sue as a pauper, exempts him from paying fees to any officer; but section 553, allowing an appeal in forma pauperis, is more restricted, and only exempts the appellant from giving bond to secure the appellee's costs, leaving him to pay his own costs, if exacted, if he chooses to appeal to another tribunal after having had gratuitous services from all officers in the lower courts. If the same rule prevailed in criminal actions, it would follow that all appellants in such cases, as well those appealing *in forma pauperis* as others, would be compelled to prepay the costs of the transcript and the costs in this court, if demanded. 'Such is not our understanding of the statute. Code, § 3758. An *instanter certiorari* should issue to bring up the transcript. Motion allowed.

LIVERMON v. ROANOKE & T. R. R. Co.

(*Supreme Court of North Carolina.* Oct. 27, 1891.)

EMINENT DOMAIN — DEED FROM MORTGAGOR— RIGHT OF MORTGAGEE TO COMPENSATION—LIMITATION OF ACTIONS.

1. Since Code N. C. § 701, provides that the general railroad act (Code, c. 49) shall apply to railroad corporations created by special act of assembly, and shall govern and control, anything in the special act to the contrary notwithstanding, unless in such special act the sections of the general act intended to be repealed shall be specially referred to, and as such specially repealed, the provision in the charter of the Roanoke & Tar River Railroad Company, by which it is granted "the powers and incidents of the North Carolina Railroad Company, and other corporations of like nature created by the laws of the state," does not make applicable the provision in the charter of the North Carolina Railroad Company, that two years shall bar the claim for damages or compensation by the owner of land over which it has constructed its road, nor prevent the application of the general railroad act, under which a railroad company can only acquire title to a right of way by purchase or condemnation, and under which, so long as the company occupies the land without title, the owner is not barred unless its possession has been adverse for a length of time sufficient to mature title.

2. Since, under the general railroad act, a railroad company can only acquire title to a right of way by purchase or condemnation, if it constructs its road over land without so acquiring title, and the owner of the land subsequently sells and conveys it, the purchaser may sue the company for compensation.

3. Where the mortgagor of land grants a right of way to a railroad company without the consent of the mortgagee, and without any proceeding against the mortgagee to condemn the land, the mortgagee's interest is not affected, and the purchaser at a foreclosure sale under the mortgage, or his grantee, may sue the company for compensation, though he cannot recover damages incident to the entry before he acquired title.

Appeal from superior court, Bertie county; HENRY G. CONNOR, Judge.

Action by Martha A. Livermon against the Roanoke & Tar River Railroad Company to recover compensation for land of plaintiff taken by defendant for its right of way. Judgment for defendant. Plaintiff appeals. Reversed.

Plaintiff had title to the land under the foreclosure of a mortgage. Defendant claimed title to the right of way by virtue of a deed from the mortgagors before the foreclosure, the road having also been constructed before the foreclosure. No consent to the right of way was obtained from the mortgagees. Defendant contended that the action was barred by the statute of limitations, in that it had not been brought within two years from the accruing of the cause of action, and relied on its charter, (Act N. C. 1885, c. 218,) which granted to it "the powers and incidents of the North Carolina Railroad Company, and other corporations of like nature created by the laws of the state." The charter of the North Carolina Railroad Company provided that the owners of land over which its road should be constructed should apply within two years next after such part of the road should be finished, or should be barred from recovering said land, or compensation therefor. Defendant also contended that plaintiff could not maintain the action because she was not the owner of the land at the time of defendant's entry thereon, and that the deed from the mortgagors gave them title to the right of way.

Winston & Williams, for appellant. *Martin & Peebles,* for appellee.

SHEPHERD, J. 1. The plea of the statute of limitations cannot be sustained. It is true that the charter of the defendant provides that it shall have "the powers and incidents of the North Carolina Railroad Company and other corporations of like nature created by the laws of the state," but this language is exceedingly indefinite upon the question under consideration, as the charters of some of these corporations contain provisions barring the owner's claim for damages or compensation after a certain period, while others provide for no such limitation whatever. Land v. Railroad Co., 107 N. C. 72, 12 S. E. Rep. 125. Even had the charter of the North Carolina Railroad Company been particularly referred to, the two-years bar therein prescribed would not have prevented the application of the general railroad act, (chapter 49, Code,) which was enacted prior to the granting of the defendant's charter. Under the general act, as construed by this court in Land v. Railroad Co., supra, the defendant can only acquire title to the right of way by purchase or by proceedings to condemn, and so long as it occupies the land without title the owner is not barred, unless the defendant's possession has been adverse, and for such length of time as to mature title, as in ordinary cases. Thus it appears that there is a very great difference between the charter of the North Carolina Railroad Company and the general act, and it was clearly the policy of the legislature that the provisions of the latter should not in any material particular be repealed by implication. Hence it was enacted (Code, § 701) that the general act "should govern and control, anything in the special act of assembly to the contrary notwithstanding, unless in the act of assembly creating the corporation the section or sections [of the general act which are intended to be excluded] shall be specially referred to by number, and as such specially repealed." See Durham & N. R. Co. v. Richmond & D. R. Co., 106 N. C. 16, 10 S. E. Rep. 1041, which is conclusive upon this point.

2. It is insisted, however, that, as the plaintiff was not the owner of the land at the time of the entry and the completion of the road, she is not entitled to main-

tain this proceeding. The cases from other states, cited by the defendant's counsel, sustain this view so far as the recovery of mere damages, incident to the unlawful entry, is concerned. They may also be applicable where the railroad company acquires a right by a simple entry, leaving the damages and compensation to be subsequently assessed. In such cases the claim of the owner is said to be personal, and does not pass to a purchaser by an ordinary conveyance of the land. The principle does not apply where, as in our case, (under the general act,) the railroad company acquires no right whatever until, either at its instance or that of the owner, proceedings have been instituted to condemn the property. Until this is done the company occupies the land without title. (Land v. Railroad Co., supra,) and it would seem quite plain that the occupation of a trespasser ought not to take away the owner's power of alienation. In our case the only authority to enter was given by the mortgagor, and it is admitted that the consent of the mortgagee has never been obtained. It is well settled that "a deed from a mortgagor conveys only his interest, and is subject to the mortgage." Lewis, Em. Dom. § 289. To the same effect is Mills, Em. Dom. § 74, from which work we extract the following: "In the case of Wade v. Hennessy, 55 Vt. 207, in which the company, instead of condemning the land by due process, took a deed from the mortgagor, a mortgage having previously been given by the grantor, and recorded, it was held that the fact that the railroad company, under the exercise of the right of eminent domain, might have taken the mortgagee's interest in the mortgaged premises, and thereby have obtained an unimpeachable title, did not vary the relations of the railroad company to the holder of the mortgage, as it did not exercise that right, but contented itself with the right it acquired by said deed. To the proper exercise of the right of eminent domain it is indispensable that compensation be made to the owner of the property taken by the payment of an equivalent in money. The railroad company must make all parties claiming the title parties to the proceedings. * * * If this is not done the railroad must either redeem or seek protection by the exercise of the right of eminent domain, under the statute against the mortgagee." See, also, Wilson v. Railroad Co., 67 Mo. 358; Beck v. Railroad Co., 65 Miss. 172, 3 South. Rep. 252; 2 Wood, Ry. Laws, § 244. The mortgagee's interest, then, not having been affected by the deed of the mortgagor, and the mortgage having been foreclosed, it would seem very clear that the title passed to the plaintiff, who purchased the entire tract under the foreclosure sale. It seems equally clear that, while she cannot recover damages incident to the entry made before she acquired the title, she may recover compensation for the land, the title to which can only vest in the defendant by virtue of this proceeding. The defendant has been content to occupy the land without title, and it was charged with notice of the mortgage. Mills, Em. Dom. § 103. It did not offer to redeem, as it might

have done, but suffered the title to pass to the plaintiff. We are of the opinion that the plaintiff is entitled to compensation for the land, the title to which is to be vested in the defendant by virtue of this proceeding. Error.

SMITH v. YOUNG et al.

(Supreme Court of North Carolina. Oct. 27, 1891.)

COUNTER-CLAIM—ACTION FOR CONVERSION.

Code N. C. § 244, provides that in an action arising on contract any other cause of action arising on contract, and existing at the commencement of the action, may be set up as a counter claim. Plaintiff sold to defendants cotton, and received from their agent a ticket on defendants for the cash, which ticket was presented for payment, but defendants refused to pay the cash, and against plaintiff's consent they applied the amount on a balance due them from plaintiff on notes given about two years previous. Plaintiff sued them for conversion, and defendants set up the old debt as a counterclaim. *Held* that, as the action was one for tort, the counter-claim did not come within the statute.

Action by M. R. Smith against Young Bros., to recover for the conversion of a bale of cotton. Defendants set up as a counter-claim growing out of a contract. The counter-claim was overruled, and judgment given for plaintiff. Defendants appeal. Affirmed.

This was an action commenced before a justice of the peace, and tried on appeal before WINSTON, J., at the February term, 1891, of Harnet superior court. During the year 1888 the plaintiff gave the defendants two promissory notes, secured by liens on his crop of 1888, for provisions, etc., for that year, and failed to fully pay off said notes, but at the commencement of this action there was a balance still due on said notes of $96. In the fall of 1890 the plaintiff carried a bale of cotton to the town of Dunn, in which place defendants were doing business as general merchants and cotton buyers, and offered said cotton for sale, it being a part of his crop of 1890, and the defendants' agent, being on the market, bought the cotton as agent of defendants, weighed the same, and gave the plaintiff a ticket to the defendants for the money for said cotton, amounting to $47.32. When the plaintiff presented his ticket to the defendants for his money, the pay for said cotton, the defendants refused to pay the plaintiff any money for said cotton, but against the consent of the plaintiff the defendants applied the cotton as a payment to the balance due of $96 on the notes of the preceding year. The plaintiff then, in a few days, began his action before a justice of the peace for the value of said cotton, alleging that the defendants had unlawfully converted the same to their use. The justice decided that the defendants hold only a part of the cotton, and both sides appealed to the superior court. On the hearing, the defendants, having set up their counter-claim of $96, denied that there was any unlawful conversion. The defendants contended that there was no unlawful conversion, and that they were entitled as a matter of right to their counter-claim, $96, with interest on the same, and that the price of said cotton should go as a payment on said counter-claim, and that they have judgment against the plaintiff for the remainder of said counter-claim. His honor held that there was an unlawful conversion, and that that was a tort, and that the defendants could not set up their counter-claim, and were not entitled to the same in this action, and overruled the defendants' contentions, and gave judgment overruling the defendants' counter-claim, and judgment for the full amount of the cotton, together with the costs of this action, to which the defendants excepted and appealed.

F. P. Jones, for appellants.

AVERY, J., (after stating the facts.) In furtherance of the general purpose pervading the Code system of pleading to prevent a multiplicity of actions, when the controversies between the parties can be settled without the expense and delay incident to the old practice, the language of our statute (section 244 of the Code, with subsections 1, 2)[1] was made very comprehensive, and, interpreting it in the spirit that animated those who enacted it, we should certainly be slow to restrict its operation so as to prevent the pleading as a counter-claim of any demand within the statutory definition liberally construed. Subsection 1 embraces, first, causes of action arising either out of the contract or transaction set forth in the complaint as the foundation of the action, and in giving effect to this clause it has been held not only that the defendant could plead a counter-claim growing out of the contract sued on, but that where action is brought for what would have been formerly denominated a tort the defendant may set up a claim arising out of contract, if it also arises out of the same transaction, or vice versa. Bitting v Thaxton, 72 N. C. 541; Walsh v. Hall, 66 N. C. 233. But the last clause of the subsection is even broader,—permitting the party brought into court to meet a demand, whether purporting to arise out of contract or tort, by setting up as a counter-claim any state of facts "connected with the subject of the action," which would constitute sufficient ground for an independent action by the plaintiff against the defendant. But it cannot be maintained that dealings between the same parties, culminating in a settlement, in which notes and mortgages on the crops of previous years were executed by the plaintiff, have any remote connection with the sale of the particular cotton out of which the controversy arose. When the agent of the defendants weighed the cotton, and gave the plaintiff a statement of the number of pounds to be taken to the defendants, as evidence of the amount of cash due, which he agreed to pay, and by such promise induced the plaintiff to give up his cotton, the refusal of the defendants to pay, and their retention of the

cotton after demand, was a wrongful conversion of the property to their use, and the plaintiff had the right to recover its value, $47.32, in the action before the justice of the peace. Carraway v. Burbank, 1 Dev. 306; Ragsdale v. Williams, 8 Ired. 498. The defendants bought for cash, and were bound to pay the money or return the cotton. A man cannot take property wrongfully, and apply the value of it rightfully, even in discharge of a just debt due him from the owner. If tolerated it would prove a dangerous and demoralizing method of collecting debts. The sale was properly treated as a nullity by the court upon the general principle that a purchase made with the intent to get the property without paying for it is fraudulent, and voidable at the instance of the seller. 1 Benj. Sales, § 656, and note 18; Donaldson v. Farwell, 93 U. S. 631. If a suit in the nature of an action for conversion is brought, and can be maintained, then a defendant will not be allowed to set up a debt as a counter-claim under subsection 2, because that, by its express terms, applies only where the action is brought to enforce a contract, and here the defendants did not elect to waive the tort. For the reasons given we think that the judgment of the court below should be affirmed.

TAYLOR v. RICHMOND & D. R. Co.

(Supreme Court of North Carolina. Oct. 27, 1891.)

INJURIES TO RAILROAD LABORER — CONTRIBUTORY NEGLIGENCE.

1. Plaintiff, an experienced railroad laborer on defendant's road, who knew that it was rough and crooked, was riding on a material train running very rapidly. He was in a closed car, having a large opening in one of its sides, and moved from the rear of the car, where he was protected, towards the stove, located in the center; and as he passed by the opening the train made a swift curve, which threw him out of the car. Held, that plaintiff was guilty of contributory negligence in passing by the opening without supporting himself, when he might have reached the place he intended to occupy by passing along the side of the car opposite to the opening.

2. The fact that plaintiff left his position of safety in the rear of the car through fear of an accident, and to be near the opening, so that he might jump off the car in case of an emergency, does not relieve him from negligence in passing unsupported by the opening, when he might have safely reached the position he intended to occupy by passing along the opposite side of the car.

Appeal from superior court, Wayne county; ROBERT W. WINSTON, Judge.

This action is brought to recover damages occasioned by the alleged negligence of the defendant. The latter, in its answer, denies the material allegations of the complaint, and alleges contributory negligence on the part of the plaintiff, which directly brought about the injuries complained of. The court submitted the following issues to the jury: "(1) Was the plaintiff injured by the negligence of the defendant? (2) Was the plaintiff guilty of contributory negligence? (3) What damage, if any, is the plaintiff entitled to recover?" To the first of these issues, the jury responded "No." There was no response to the second and third.

---

[1] Section 244, subsec. 2, provides that in an action arising on contract any other cause of action arising on contract, and existing at the commencement of the action, may be set up as a counter-claim.

On the trial the plaintiff was examined as a witness in his own behalf, and testified as follows: "I was injured on the railroad from Winston to Wilkesboro, in October, 1890. I had been working for defendant since July 7, 1890, and had been a railroad hand for seven years. I do not know the rate of speed of the train on which I was at the time, but it was very fast,—faster than mail trains run. Looked like the world was turning round. It was an awful crooked road; not one-half mile of it straight. It ran with the Yadkin river. It was a mountainous, hilly country, and it was a new road. The track was pretty rough. I was thrown off the train. The train went to Elkin, and laid over. There was a side track there long enough to hold the train, but the conductor came out, and we went on. The train ran fast. It was a material train made up of flat-cars and a shanty-car. I was employed on the train as a laborer. I was at the rear end of the shanty-car, near my bunk on the inside of the car. I got scared and uneasy, and came to stove in middle of car. There were two other men in the car, sitting on seats, blocks of wood, on either side of the door, which was open. The door was on the side of the car. The right-hand man got up, and I went to take his seat, and as I raised my foot the train made a swift curve, and switched me out of the door. I moved from the end of the car because I was afraid; and if she jumped the track I could jump out. I thought it would turn over because the road was rough, crooked, and the train running fast. I was flung down a fill in the weeds and stunned for a few minutes. Broke my arm and hurt me inside. Hurt me for life-time, I think. Two doors to shanty, one on each side. Window in each end of car. One door was open and the other closed. Flat-cars were in front of the shanty-car." On cross-examination the witness said: "I had been over that road often. Knew that it was pretty rough and had short curves. Had been over that curve often, and knew it well. Was sitting between the bunks on block of wood, near rear of car. Nelson Smith and Martin Holt were in the car with me. The left-hand door was partly open, and they were sitting on blocks of wood near the door. Blocks were not fastened. I went to the open door to get out if she slacked up. Martin Holt got up from his seat. Nelson Smith did not get up. There was a stove in the middle of the car between the doors. I went to take Martin Holt's seat. Went on side of stove next to open door. Right-hand door was shut. I tried to get hold of the stovepipe as I was falling. I could have gone by the closed door and reached the block if I had thought of it. That was the safest way, and if I had thought it was going to jerk I would have done it. The train came back and took me up. I did not tell Dr. Dalton at the depot in Winston, on October 29, 1890, that the train was running twenty-five miles an hour." There was other evidence that need not be reported. There were divers exceptions to the instructions the court gave and others it refused to give at the instance of the plain-

v.13s.e.no.30—47

tiff. These need not be reported, for reasons stated in the opinion of the court. There was judgment for the defendant, and the plaintiff appealed to this court. Affirmed.

W. C. Munroe and *W. R. Allen*, for appellant. *F. H. Busbee*, for appellee.

MERRIMON, C. J., (*after stating the facts.*) When the plaintiff brings his action to recover damages for injuries sustained by him, occasioned by the alleged negligence of the defendant, he cannot recover if the defendant alleges and proves contributory negligence on the part of the plaintiff, which was the direct, proximate cause of such injuries. To make such defense effective, it must appear that the negligence of the plaintiff was concurrent with that of the defendant, and directly contributed to the injuries complained of. The contributory negligence is direct, proximate, when the concurrent negligence of the parties, respectively, at once produces such injuries. Duggett v. Railroad Co., 78 N. C. 305; Gunter v. Wicker, 85 N. C. 310; Farmer v. Railroad Co., 88 N. C. 564; Troy v. Railroad Co., 99 N. C. 298, 6 S. E. Rep. 77. Now, accepting the evidence of the plaintiff, and all the evidence produced on the trial favorable to him, as true, and granting, for the present purpose, that the defendant was negligent as alleged in the complaint, we are of opinion that he is not entitled to recover. He was himself negligent, and his negligence contributed directly and proximately to the injuries of which he complains. He was an experienced railroad laborer; was familiar with the defendant's road; had been a laborer on it for several months; had frequently passed over it; knew that it was new and rough, and had many short curves. At the time of the accident in question he was on a material train, which was running very rapidly. He was in the rear of the "shanty-car." It was a closed car, having an opening (a large one) on each side of it. One of them was closed and the other was open. A person standing unsupported in front of that opening would be very subject to be thrown out by a sudden jerk or rocking motion of the car while the train of which it was part was running rapidly over the rough and crooked road. This was obvious to any person of ordinary intelligence, and especially to one familiar with railroads and moving trains, as was the plaintiff. Nevertheless the plaintiff left the rear of the car, where he was seated, and protected, and walked towards the stove located in the center of the car, and between it and the open door on the side of the car, the space between being about two or three feet. He did not support himself by holding fast with his hands to anything, or otherwise he might safely have passed between the stove and the closed door. He did not do so. He was unnecessarily passing the plainly perilous place without any support or protection, when he might have avoided it, and as he raised his foot, moving towards a seat he intended to reach and occupy, "the train made a swift curve, and switched me [him] out of the door." As a consequence he was stunned, and his arm broken. It was gross negligence on his part thus to expose himself to imminent peril. He thereby clearly contributed directly to the injuries he sustained, and must suffer the misfortune he so helped to bring upon himself. This is a much stronger case against the plaintiff than that of Smith v. Railroad Co., 99 N. C. 241, 5 S. E. Rep. 896, in which the plaintiff was held to have contributed to his injury. The appellant's counsel insisted on the argument that the plaintiff was not chargeable with contributory negligence because he was frightened, and moved by fear of impending danger to go to the open door, so that in case of emergency he might jump off the car. It is not necessary to determine or inquire here to what extent sudden fright or well-grounded fear, occasioned by the negligence of the defendant. might in possible cases relieve or excuse a party as to contributory negligence. In this case the plaintiff did not through fear jump, or attempt to jump, off the car. He did not intend to do so unless in case of emergency. He was only apprehensive of danger, and intended to be where he could promptly get off the car. if need be. In so doing he was careless and grossly negligent. Instead of going the safer way, as he admitted he might and would have done if he had been more circumspect, he attempted to pass, without support or protection, almost immediately in front of the open door; a place, under the circumstances, of much danger. The mere fact that a person is alarmed, and seeks to place himself where he may the more readily relieve himself from danger, does not excuse him from reasonable care and prudence in his efforts to do so. It is unnecessary to consider and pass upon the several assignments of error, because, as we have said before, granting that the defendant was negligent as alleged in the complaint, and accepting all the evidence favorable to the plaintiff as true, the latter could not recover, inasmuch as he contributed directly, by his own negligence, to the injuries he sustained. This court sees that according to the plaintiff's own showing he is not entitled to judgment; that the court properly entered judgment for the defendant. The plaintiff cannot, therefore, be heard to complain that the court possibly erred in some respect in the course of reaching a proper conclusion, and entering judgment accordingly.

Judgment affirmed.

BOTTOMS v. SEABOARD & R. R. Co.

(*Supreme Court of North Carolina. Oct. 27, 1891.*)

INSTRUCTIONS—VERDICT—CONFLICTING FINDINGS.

1. Since, under the procedure in North Carolina, issues are submitted to the jury, and on their findings the court adjudges the recovery, it was not error in the court to refuse defendant's request to instruct the jury that upon the evidence plaintiff could not recover.

2. An exception "to the charge as given" is too vague and indefinite to be considered on appeal.

3. In an action by plaintiff against a railroad company for injury to his child the following issues were submitted to the jury: "(2) Was the

defendant guilty of negligence in respect to the injury of plaintiff's child? Answer. Yes. (3) Was the plaintiff guilty of contributory negligence in respect to the injury of his child? A. Yes. (4) Was the plaintiff's child injured by defendant's negligence? A. Yes." *Held* that, as the material facts found are confused, a new trial will be ordered.

Appeal from superior court, Northampton county; HENRY G. CONNOR, Judge.

Action by Turner B. Bottoms against the Seaboard & Roanoke Railroad Company to recover for injuries to his child. Verdict for plaintiff. Defendant moved for a new trial, which was denied, and judgment entered against it. Defendant appeals. New trial ordered.

W. H. Day and *J. W. Hinsdale*, for appellant. *W. W. Peebles & Son* and *R. B. Peebles*, for appellee.

CLARK, J. The defendant's counsel requested the court to charge (1) that upon the evidence offered by the plaintiff, he could not recover; (2) that upon the whole evidence the plaintiff could not recover,—and excepted to the refusal of the same. As the verdict, under the present procedure, is never that the plaintiffs do or do not recover, but the jury respond to issues submitted to them, and on their findings the court adjudges the recovery, such prayers are not proper, and it is not error to refuse them. Farrell v. Railroad Co., 102 N. C. 390, 9 S. E. Rep. 302; McDonald v. Carson, 94 N. C. 497.

The exception "to the charge as given" furnishes no information to the appellee or to the court, and has been repeatedly held too vague to be considered. McKinnon v. Morrison, 104 N. C. 354, 10 S. E. Rep. 513.

The following issues were submitted to the jury, to which they responded, as appears by the record: "(1) Was the plaintiff's child injured by the defendant? Answer. Yes. (2) Was the defendant guilty of negligence in respect to the injury of plaintiff's child? A. Yes. (3) Was the plaintiff guilty of contributory negligence in respect to the injury of his child? A. Yes. (4) Was the plaintiff's child injured by defendant's negligence? A. Yes. (5) What damage has plaintiff sustained? A. $750." The defendant moves here for judgment upon these findings, on the ground that the fourth issue is the same as the second, and that the substance of all the findings is that the defendant was guilty of negligence and the plaintiff was guilty of contributory negligence. But the form of the fourth issue differs somewhat from the second, and, taken in connection with the charge, it is extremely probable that the court meant by the fourth issue to submit to the jury an issue as suggested by the court in Denmark v. Railroad Co., 107 N. C. 185, 12 S. E. Rep. 54, whether, notwithstanding the contributory negligence of the plaintiff, the defendant could have avoided the accident by proper care on his part. But it is not clear that the jury so understood it, and on their face the second and fourth issues are so nearly alike that the jury may well have been misled; indeed, the issues are framed in such a manner that the material facts as found by the jury are confused and unsatisfactory. Under such circumstances, the settled practice is to order a new trial. Allen v. Sullinger, 105 N. C. 333, 10 S. E. Rep. 1020. A case almost exactly "on all fours" with that before us is Turrentine v. Railroad Co., 92 N. C. 638. New trial.

DIBBRELL v. GEORGIA HOME INS. CO.

(Supreme Court of North Carolina. Oct. 27, 1891.)

HEARING ON APPEAL—CONTINUANCE.

When a printed brief is filed under rule 12 the party filing it is to be taken as asking a decision at such term, and as opposing a continuance, and a motion by the opposite party to continue the case till next term will not be granted unless expressly assented to or for good cause shown.

(Syllabus by the Court.)

Motion of plaintiff to strike out order of continuance.

A. C. Zollicoffer, for plaintiff. *J. W. Hinsdale,* for defendant.

CLARK, J. Rule 12 of this court provides: "When a case is reached on the regular call of the docket, and a printed brief or argument shall be filed for either party, the case shall stand on the same footing as if there were an appearance by counsel." When this cause was reached in the regular call of the docket there was a printed brief on file for plaintiff's counsel, who was not present. The defendant's counsel, who was in court, moved for a continuance, which was granted, not for any good cause, but because unopposed. The plaintiff's counsel moves to strike out the continuance, and that the cause stand for decision at this term. His contention is that by going to the expense of printing and filing a brief he gave notice that he desired and expected the cause to be disposed of at this term, and that the rule would be of practically little benefit to non-resident counsel if, notwithstanding, they must attend in person to prevent the continuance of their cases at the mere motion of the opposite party. It seems to us that this contention is just, and is based on the proper construction of the rule. When the counsel files his printed brief, that is his argument submitted to the court, and the case stands for decision without further argument unless he shall see fit to also aid us with an oral argument, or the other side shall present an oral or printed argument when the cause is called. When good cause is shown in support of a motion for continuance the court will grant it, whether the opposite party is represented by counsel in person or by brief; but such was not the case here. The motion for a continuance was improvidently granted, and must be stricken out. The counsel for defendant did not submit an oral argument when he had the opportunity, and he cannot do so now, as the district has been passed. The plaintiff, is, however, not to be deprived of his right to have the case disposed of at this term, and the defendant will be allowed 10 days from the filing of this opinion to submit a printed brief. This is the first occasion on which the construction of this rule has been be-

fore the court, and the embarrassment arising as to the conflicting rights of the parties consequent upon the improper granting of the continuance cannot again occur. Motion allowed.

FINLAYSON v. AMERICAN ACC. CO.

(Supreme Court of North Carolina. Oct. 27, 1891.)

VACATING JUDGMENT—EXCUSABLE NEGLECT—EVIDENCE.

1. The fact that a letter to counsel to appear in a case reached him a half-hour after the case was set for trial furnished no ground for opening the judgment, there having been plenty of time to secure counsel by telegraphing, and it being negligence not to do so.

2. Where an attorney is engaged simply to employ counsel to appear at another place, he is a mere agent, and his negligence to employ the counsel is the negligence of his principal.

Appeal from superior court, Wayne county; SPIER WHITAKER, Judge.

Action by H. J. Finlayson against the American Accident Company of Louisville, Ky. Judgment was rendered for plaintiff on his evidence, defendant not being present or represented by counsel. From a judgment of the superior court, affirming the refusal of the justice to reopen the case, defendant appeals. Affirmed.

Allen & Dortch, for appellant. *W. C. Munroe,* for appellee.

CLARK, J. The defendant, who was not present at the trial before the justice of the peace "in person or by attorney," moved within 10 days to set aside the judgment for excusable neglect, under section 845 of the Code. The justice found as a fact there was no excusable neglect or mistake on the part of the defendant, who thereupon excepted and appealed. In the superior court the judge found the facts as sent up in the case on appeal, and affirmed the ruling of the justice. The findings of fact by the justice are reviewable by the judge of the superior court on appeal, while findings of fact by the judge (except in injunctions and in similar cases) are not subject to review by this court. The reason for the distinction is pointed out in Deaton's Case, 105 N. C. 59, 11 S. E. Rep. 244. We are therefore bound by his honor's findings of fact, and can only consider whether in law they constitute excusable neglect. Clegg v. Stone Co., 66 N. C. 391; Powell v. Weith, Id. 423; Jones v. Swepson, 79 N. C. 510. In this case it was found as a fact that on the return-day of the summons the defendant's local agent appeared and procured a continuance for 10 days, but notwithstanding it did not employ counsel till so late that, though he "immediately wrote to local counsel in Goldsborough," (where the cause was tried,) the letter was received a half-hour after the time set for the trial. This was inexcusable neglect. Nor is there any force in the objection that the judge declined to find that the general agents of the defendant company understood that they had retained said counsel a week previously, for, even if it be admissible for such an excuse to be set up, they certainly knew of the misunderstanding when they had the second interview with their counsel, and it was negligence not then to telegraph, which would have secured local counsel in ample time, instead of trusting to the slower movement of the mails. Then, too, the local agent in Goldsborough, who appeared on the return-day, and procured the continuance when he found his company unrepresented at the trial, should have employed counsel, or at least have asked a short delay to telegraph the general agents. Besides, take it most strongly for the defendant, that the agents in Raleigh not only understood they had, but actually had, employed counsel in Raleigh a week before, as he was not to appear in the case himself, but merely to employ local counsel in Goldsborough, the scope of his employment *pro hac vice* was not professional, but that of a mere agent, being a duty which they could have performed themselves, and his negligence was the negligence of the company, (Churchill v. Insurance Co., 92 N. C. 485; Griffin v. Nelson, 106 N. C. 235, 11 S. E. Rep. 414,) and would not excuse. In fact, however, the judge does find that subsequent to the alleged first interview with counsel in Raleigh, and three days before the trial, one of defendant's general agents saw the plaintiff, mentioned the date set for the trial, and stated that they themselves would write to counsel in Goldsborough to represent the defendant. Litigation is a serious matter. When a party has a case in court, the best thing he can do is to attend to it. The very perfunctory attention which was given by the defendant or its agents in the present case is not of such a nature as to call for the interposition of a court.

The point is also suggested that the defendant appealed from the judgment on the merits, as well as from the judgment refusing the motion to set aside the judgment; but, if so, it should be made to appear that the appeal was taken within the 10 days after such judgment was rendered. The record does not disclose such fact, but merely that the motion to set aside the judgment was refused, and an appeal taken,—presumably from the judgment refusing the motion. If in fact the appeal was from the judgment on the merits, the appellant should have applied to the justice to have had it so stated, or have served his notice of appeal stating it, and within the time prescribed by law, and the burden was on him to show this. On the contrary, it appears from "the case on appeal" that the appeal was treated in the superior court solely as an appeal from the refusal of the motion to set aside, and it recites the judgment before the justice, the motion to set it aside and reopen the case, its refusal, and that "from the refusal to reopen said case the defendant appealed to the superior court." Had there been an appeal within 10 days on the merits, the trial in that court would have been *de novo*, and there would have been no point in the contest whether the justice should have set aside the judgment. While in case of a disagreement between the record proper and the "case on appeal" the former governs, (State v. Keeter, 80 N. C. 472; Adrian v. Shaw, 84 N. C. 832,) there is, as we have said, nothing in the record to show clearly that there was an appeal from the judgment on the

merits, and nothing at all to indicate that if it was such appeal was taken within the prescribed time. Code, § 876. However the fact may be, we are restricted to what appears in the transcript. The presumption is always in favor of the correctness of the judgment below, and the burden is on the appellant to show error. This we do not think he has done. No error.

BERTHA ZINC Co. *et al.* v. BOARD OF SUPERVISORS OF PULASKI COUNTY.

(*Supreme Court of Appeals of Virginia.* Sept. 10, 1891.)

ROAD-TAX—AUTHORITY TO LEVY.

Under the general law of Virginia, the board of supervisors of Pulaski county were given authority to assess and levy a road-tax on property in the county, including the town of Pulaski, not only on the fourth Monday of July, but, if not done then, as soon thereafter as practicable during the tax year. Act of February 22, 1890, which took effect from its passage, made the town a separate and distinct road-district of the county, and provided that no road-tax should be levied on the property within the limits of the town, except by the town council, which tax should be expended on streets and roads within the limits of the town, under the direction and supervision of the council. *Held*, that the act of February, 1890, repealed the general law in so far as the latter authorized the board of supervisors to levy a road-tax on property in the town, and after its passage they had no authority to levy such tax for the tax year beginning on the first Monday of July, 1889, and ending the first Monday of July, 1890.

Suit by the Bertha Zinc Company and others against the board of supervisors of Pulaski county, to enjoin the collection of a road-tax. Decree for defendant. Complainants appeal. Reversed.

Brown & Moore, for plaintiff in error.
Mr. Pollock, for defendant in error.

LACY, J. This is an appeal from a decree of the circuit court of Pulaski county rendered on the 3d day of April, 1891. The bill was filed by the Bertha Zinc Company, L. S. Calfee, M. H. Calfee, Thomas Jones, James W. Lyons, J. R. Moore, and R. M. Brown, citizens and tax-payers of the town of Pulaski, Pulaski county, Va., in behalf of themselves and the other tax-payers of the said town who are similarly aggrieved, setting forth that, in the month of May, 1890, the board of supervisors of said county made an assessment and levy of 15 cents on the $100 of property—on the $100 in value of all the real estate and personal property of all the tax-payers of said town—for road purposes; and that on the 5th day of April, 1890, the town council of the town of Pulaski enacted an ordinance making an assessment of 10 cents on the $100 of personal property for road purposes; that the county of Pulaski, in May, 1890, levied this tax for road purposes upon the property holders of Pulaski town, as a part of the Dublin magisterial district of said county, and on the 5th day of April, 1890, the town of Pulaski levied a tax for road purposes upon the property holders of the town; that this tax, levied by the board of supervisors of Pulaski county for road purposes.—that is, for working and keeping in repair the roads of Dublin magisterial district of said county,—was illegal, and in violation of law so far as it was levied upon the property holders of the town of Pulaski as a part of said road-district of said county, because, before the assessment and levy of the said tax upon the property holders of the said town, the legislature had taken the said town out of the said road-district, and by an act approved February 22, 1890, and in force from its passage, among other things, had provided that "the corporate limits of said town are hereby created and declared to be a separate and distinct road-district of Pulaski county, and no road-tax shall be levied on any property within said limits except by the council of the town of Pulaski, which tax shall be expended within the limits of the corporation, on the streets and roads therein, and under the direction and supervision of said council." Acts 1889–90, c. 336, pp. 570, 572, § 9. The board of supervisors of said county demurred and answered, alleging that in the month of May, 1890, it did make an assessment and levy of 15 cents on the $100 in value of all real and personal property of the county, including the tax-payers of the Dublin magisterial district, of which the town of Pulaski formed a part, as a road-tax, to be applied to the said district road purposes for the year 1890, and that under said assessment and levy complainants were assessed, and levies extended upon the land and property books of the said county, and tax-tickets issued therefor, as set out in complainants' bill; but denying that said assessment and levies for a road-tax, as to the tax-payers of the town of Pulaski, are illegal and void, or that the town of Pulaski was not in the Dublin magisterial district, as asserted in the complainants' bill; that the said act of February 22, 1890, did not apply to the assessment and levy authorized by law to be made by the board of supervisors annually on the fourth Monday in July of each year, or as soon thereafter as practicable, for the ensuing tax year, beginning on the fourth Monday in July; that the assessment for the tax year beginning on the fourth Monday in July, 1889, and ending on the fourth Monday in July, 1890, could not be made on the fourth Monday in July, 1889, but was made as soon thereafter as practicable, to-wit, in the month of May, 1890; and that, although the said act was passed on the 22d day of February, 1890, and was in force from its passage, yet that it was not the intention of the general assembly to take away respondent's right, already accrued, to make said assessment and levy for the tax year beginning on the fourth Monday in July, 1889; and that the intention of said act was only to deprive respondent of the right to assess and levy a road-tax on the property in the town of Pulaski for any tax year ensuing after its passage.

At the hearing the circuit court dissolved the injunction which had been awarded on the bill of the plaintiffs, and dismissed the bill, with costs. Whereupon the plaintiffs applied for and obtained an appeal to this court.

There is but one question in this case,

and that is, when did the act of February, 1890, become effectual to erect the corporate limits of the town of Pulaski into a separate and distinct road-district of Pulaski county, in which no taxes for road purposes, except by the town council of the said town of Pulaski should be assessed and levied. It is conceded on both sides, of course, that the act in question was in force from its passage. But the controversy is as to its effect when applied to the subject which it concerns. The appellee contends that, as the measure was enacted in the midst of the tax year, and that the authority of the board of supervisors having attached for that year, the said board having lawful authority to act on the fourth Monday of July, 1889, or as soon thereafter as practicable, it was competent for the said board to act on the first day when the authority began, or on any subsequent day of the year; and that, when that action was had at any time during the year, when it might lawfully be had, it related back and was effectual from the first day; and so that, in contemplation of the law, when the act of February, 1890, was enacted it was subject to this action of the board of supervisors already had under the law; and a number of cases are cited by the learned counsel of this county to support this view. Railroad Co. v. Koontz, 77 Va. 698; Prince George Co. v. Railroad Co., (Va.) 12 S. E. Rep. 667. It is conceded by the appellants that the power existed by the general law to assess and levy, not only on the fourth Monday in July, but, not being done then, as soon thereafter as practicable, during the tax year. But their contention is that this power to assess and levy taxes upon the property in the corporate limits of the town of Pulaski, as a part of the Dublin magisterial district of Pulaski county, under the general law, was taken away on the day the act of February 22, 1890, became a law; that the power of the board derived under the general law, as to this town, was extinguished by the new law, which repealed, as to that, the former law; and that on the 17th day of May, 1890, when the board of supervisors of the county assessed and levied a road-tax upon the property of the town, there was in force in Virginia no law under which the act could be held to be lawful; that this act might have been performed at any time during the tax year when it might lawfully be done, and it would be valid as if done on the fourth Monday in July.

I think the latter is the correct view. Under our constitution, the legislature is vested with all legislative authority. The law under which the board of supervisors make their assessments and lay their levies is of force and effect because it is the expression of the legislative will. It was enacted by the legislature, and is in force so long as it is unrepealed. The act of February 22, 1890, repeals the former law so far as it applies to the subject in hand. Its provisions are plain and explicit; the effect of construction has no place in the matter. It leaves no room for doubt. It divests the county board of supervisors of all power in the premises, and provides a tribunal to lay the tax and to disburse it. What the board did, or may have done, before the passage of the act, or what would have been the effect of an act done before its passage, is not the question arising for decision here.

The question raised is whether the board of supervisors could lawfully assess and levy a tax upon this property, situated in this town, after an act of assembly had gone into effect depriving them of the power. It was the duty of the board, on the fourth Monday in July, or as soon thereafter as practicable, to assess and levy this tax; and if from any cause it was not or could not be done on the fourth Monday in July, 1889, their duty remained to do so as soon thereafter as practicable, because the law so commanded; but when the law ceased to exist their power in the premises ceased to exist also. There is nothing in this in conflict with the cases of Railroad Co. v. Supervisors of Clarke Co., 78 Va. 269; Prince George Co. v. Railroad Co., supra; nor in the case of Railroad Co. v. Supervisors of Smyth Co., (Va.) 12 S. E. Rep. 1009; nor in the case of Railroad Co. v. Koontz, 77 Va. 698. These cases are clearly right. There the assessment and levy was made under a law in full force and effect, and which had not been repealed. In this case the distinction is obvious. The board of supervisors of Pulaski county, at the time of the action complained of, had no lawful authority to act in the premises. So far as they had acted while the power remained in them, under the law, there is no objection taken, as in those cases. But the complaint here is not of their action under the law, but of their action without the authority of law, and, moreover, in direct contravention of the law; and at the time the act in question was done the law plainly prescribed that such action should not be taken by them, because their authority extended to Dublin magisterial district, as one of the road-districts of Pulaski county, and on the 17th day of May, 1890, the corporate limits of the town of Pulaski had ceased to be part of that district by the law of the land. The circuit court of Pulaski county held otherwise, and its action in so holding and dissolving the injunction, and in dismissing the bill of the plaintiffs, was plainly erroneous, and must be reversed and annulled.

BELL v. COMMONWEALTH.

(Supreme Court of Appeals of Virginia. Sept. 17, 1891.)

POISON—ATTEMPT TO MURDER—EVIDENCE.

On the trial of a husband, a day-laborer, for attempting to poison his wife, it appeared that he had at one time abandoned his family, but was then living with them; that he and his wife had been at enmity for a long time, and he was enamored of another woman. On the day of the alleged poisoning the daughter had prepared dinner. While he and the children were eating, the wife came in and went into the sitting-room. The children soon after followed her, leaving the husband alone at the table. When the wife came to dinner he brought her some bread. Presently she called out that the gravy was "awful bit-

ter," and spit out what she had taken. The children said there was nothing the matter with it; that they had all eaten of it; but when they came to taste it again they too pronounced it bitter. The son gave it to the dog, and, the mother feeling sick, they gave her some milk as an antidote. The husband said, if milk was good for her to give some to the dog, which was in great suffering, and died shortly after. The doctor found her suffering with some of the symptoms of strychnine poison. No analysis was made of the gravy or of the stomach of the dog; and the husband gave no explanation as to where the poison came from, or who put it in the gravy. Many witnesses testified to his steady habits and previous good character. *Held*, that a conviction would not be disturbed.

Indictment against James F. Bell for attempt to commit murder by poison. From a judgment of conviction defendant appeals. Affirmed.

O. B. Roller and *W. L. Yancey*, for appellant. *The Attorney General*, for the Commonwealth.

LACY, J. This is a writ of error to a judgment of the circuit court of Rockingham county, rendered on the 18th day of April, 1891, affirming a judgment of the county court of said county, rendered on the 25th day of March, 1891, whereby the plaintiff in error, James F. Bell, was convicted of an attempt to commit murder by poison, and sentenced to imprisonment in the penitentiary for three years. The only assignment of error is that the trial court erred in overruling the prisoner's motion for a new trial, on the ground that the verdict of the jury was contrary to the law and the evidence. The evidence certified is that the plaintiff in error and his wife had had four children, and had been married 19 years. The ages of the children were from 17 to 5 years. That for 6 years all marital relations had been abandoned. That they had long been at enmity, and that he had at one time abandoned his family altogether, and had moved into his present abode, where he had remained without them for about one year, when the family had come to him, and he had rented the house, and they lived in it. The evidence shows that the plaintiff in error was a hard-working day-laborer, without a trade, and that he devoted his wages, as such, to the support of his family; but a mutual antipathy existed between the two,—the wife sometimes speaking of leaving her husband altogether, and the husband charging his wife with unchastity, which greatly offended her, and, it seems, gave some currency to injurious reports concerning her; he often, and to various witnesses, announcing his purpose to get rid of her in some way, so that he could be a happier man. His son, grown to be 17 years old, and a stout laborer, worked out on his own account, and his wages became a new element of discord in the family; his father claiming the right to collect them, and the son denying it. About this time the husband and father became enamored of a young woman in the neighborhood; so much so that he said he intended to get rid of her, (not calling his wife's name;) that he loved the ground on which the new inamorata walked. On the 13th day of December, 1890, the following incidents occurred in this family: The wife was absent from home, and dinner had been prepared by the daughter, 14 years of age. The husband and father and the other three children were called in to dinner at the usual hour by the daughter, and while they were at dinner the wife, who had been to the house of a neighbor to borrow a pattern to make some garment for the eldest son, returned, and passed through the dining-room or kitchen into the adjoining room, and returned and procured a smoothing-iron from the cooking-stove, and went back into the sitting-room adjoining, and proceeded to smooth out the wrinkles in the pattern, and when the eldest son finished eating his dinner he came into the room,.and the mother was trying the pattern on him, when the other children finished their dinner and came out of the dining-room, leaving the father still eating his dinner, sitting at the table. When the wife came in to get her dinner, and took her seat at the table, the plaintiff in error got up and went to the stove, and brought some bread therefrom, and handed it to his wife, and seated himself at the stove, and put his feet inside, with his back to his wife. She took some gravy out of a bowl on the table, and mixed some corn-bread with it, and proceeded to eat. With the first mouthful she halloed out "This is awful bitter," and ran to the door and spit out what she had in her mouth, and called out to the children, to know what was the matter with the gravy; They replied, "Nothing;" that they had all eaten of it at dinner. The mother tasted it again, and again spit it out, and taking up the bowl of gravy, carried it towards the sitting-room, and her son met her, and, perceiving a lot of white particles in it, took off a white speck with a slate pencil, and tasted it, and said it was bitter, and one of the other children tasted with like result, and the son said, "Give it to the dog," which they did; and the mother, feeling a stiffening of the jaws, and jerking of the limbs, and a cramp in her fingers, and a burning in her stomach, became alarmed, and they sent for the doctor, and gave her some sweet milk as an antidote; and the plaintiff in error, who had taken no part, up to this time, in what was going on, said, "If sweet milk is good for her, give me some to give the dog,"—the dog at the time manifesting symptoms of great suffering. The dog died shortly,—in about 20 minutes. The doctor came, and found the wife suffering with some of the symptoms of strychnine poison, caused by the absorption through the mucous membrane of the mouth, none having been swallowed. He thought her case not very serious, the burning in the stomach being no symptom of strychnine poison, though the others were; gave her the best antidote he had, not saying what it was; inserted morphine after a while, and she became quiet. No analysis was made of the stomach of the dog, nor of the remnant of the gravy and the bread bottled up and sealed by the doctor. And the accused, when questioned about this poison, said he could not have gotten it from a store without giving his name, and having that and the quantity and the

date recorded, and gave no other explanation as to where the poison came from, or who put it in the gravy. After he and the children had eaten, and while he was alone in the room, before his wife came in, he was in this room all the time, and no one else came in. The door between the dining-room and sitting-room was all the time open, so that persons passed through without disturbing it. It is clear that poison was put in this gravy while he sat alone at the table on which it was sitting; that no other person was in the room, and no other person had the opportunity to place the poison until his wife came in. He certainly had the opportunity, and he is proved to have had a motive to destroy his wife. He had indulged, to persons with whom he talked, in threats to that end; and his actions at the time.—handing his wife the bread, notwithstanding their bad relations, and then seating himself with his back to her, and sticking his feet in the oven of the stove, still hot, while he had been in the house a considerable time. His posture was one of waiting and expectancy, and the act of putting his feet in the warm oven of the stove was doubtless suggested by that chilliness of the extremities incident to his surroundings. His conduct afterwards was suspicious. He said he could not have gotten the poison without giving his name, etc. Under what circumstances had he found this out? When he saw what was supposed to be an antidote for his wife he asked for some for the dog, he doubtless was fully impressed with the deadly character of the white powder in the gravy. He was tried by a jury of his neighbors and former friends and associates. He was ably defended by skillful counsel. His steady habits and general good character were spread before the jury and the trial court by a host of good men, who cheerfully so testified; and upon their oaths the jurors have passed between him and the commonwealth, and have found him guilty of attempting to poison his wife. In mercy they have fixed the period of his incarceration at three years,—the shortest time allowed under the law. The trial judge has heard all the testimony, and has refused to disturb the verdict so found. We must, under our law, consider the case as upon a demurrer to evidence; that is, we must admit the truth of the commonwealth's evidence, and all just inferences flowing therefrom, and reject all the parol evidence of the accused in conflict therewith; and we cannot disturb the verdict unless it appears to be, when thus considered, plainly wrong. We cannot say that this conviction is without evidence, or against the evidence. It appears to be warranted by the evidence. There is no reasonable hypothesis consistent with his innocence. The contention of the counsel for the plaintiff in error that it was possible for the wife to have dropped this poison out of her sleeve, in order to poison herself, to get her husband into the penitentiary, and so be rid of him, is unreasonable, and unsupported by any evidence in the case to any degree whatever. We perceive no error in the judgment appealed from, and the same must be affirmed.

KENNY v. WALLACE.

(*Supreme Court of Georgia.* Oct. 19, 1891.)

ATTACHMENT—BURDEN OF PROOF—DISSOLUTION.

1. Where the affidavit supporting the petition for an attachment issued on the ground of fraud is not positive, but only "to the best of affiant's knowledge and belief," the burden of proof on the hearing of an application to dissolve the attachment is upon the plaintiff.

2. On the facts in evidence there was no abuse of discretion by the presiding judge in dissolving the attachment.

(*Syllabus by the Court.*)

Error from superior court, Fulton county; MARSHALL J. CLARKE, Judge.

Petition for attachment by P. J. Kenny against P. J. Wallace. Judgment for defendant. Plaintiff brings error. Affirmed.

The following is the official report:

The exceptions in this case are that the judge below erred in removing an attachment which had been issued on the petition of Kenny against P. J Wallace upon an allegation of fraudulent sale by P. J. Wallace to his brother, F. M. Wallace, and in requiring the plaintiff in attachment to assume the burden of proof upon the hearing of the petition of P. J. Wallace to remove the attachment. The petition for the attachment alleged that P. J. Wallace owed the petitioner $651.75, and for the purpose of avoiding the payment of his debts had fraudulently sold out his entire stock of liquors, etc., to his brother, F. M. Wallace, who knew that P. J. Wallace was insolvent, and that the sale was for the purpose of defrauding creditors, and that the price paid was less than the value of the property sold. The attachment issued under this petition was levied on a stock of whisky, etc., as the property of the defendant; and the defendant, by his petition for the removal of this attachment, made the following averments: He denied that the sale was a fraudulent one, and alleged that it was in good faith, and to pay his debts so far as he could. At the time of the sale he owed one Redwine $2,038.30 for borrowed money, one Vaughn $1,600 borrowed money, J. H. & A. L. James $85.37 borrowed money, and F. M. Wallace $1,065.25 borrowed money. The indebtedness due Redwine and Vaughn was evidenced by promissory notes, and the Vaughn notes secured by mortgage on the property sold, and $1,000 of the amount due F. M. Wallace was evidenced by notes secured by mortgage on the same property. The consideration for the sale to F. M. was the payment of the amount due F. M., and the undertaking by F. M. to pay the amounts due Redwine, James, and Vaughn, making a total consideration of $4,788.92, which was the full value of the property conveyed. He, P. J. Wallace, was not able to pay his debts when they fell due, and Redwine was urging payment of his claim, and threatening to close up his business, and, if he had done so, the amount that could have been realized by forced sale would not have been enough to pay off the mortgage of Vaughn and the claims of Redwine and Wallace; and, to avoid being closed up and prevent the sacrifice of his goods, he made the arrangement with F. M. Wallace, with the consent of Redwine and Vaughn. At the

hearing of the petition for removal of the attachment, affidavits were produced by plaintiff in attachment, from which the following appeared: P. J. Wallace was largely indebted in addition to the indebtedness already mentioned, of which fact F. M. Wallace knew. F. M. Wallace had previously been in the bar-room business, and had sold out, (he said,) because he wanted to quit that business, or because his wife opposed his being in it. On the morning of February 7, 1891, F. M. Wallace was in charge of P. J. Wallace's bar-room, and for several days previously seemed to be exercising the same control over the property that he was on the 7th inst., and never mentioned to Kenny, who had been going during the time mentioned to the bar-room for the purpose of collecting the indebtedness of P. J. Wallace to him, that he, F. M., had bought out P. J. Wallace. Kenny informed F. M. Wallace that the notes of P. J. Wallace to Kenny were past due; and when Kenny went to the bar-room, on February 7th, and asked F. M. why F. M. did not tell him when he was there with the notes that he, F. M., had bought out his brother, F. M. replied that he thought Kenny knew it, and told Kenny that the transfer took place on the 5th of February. Kenny asked him to let him see the papers relating to the trade, and F. M. agreed to do it at 2 o'clock that day,—the 7th,—but at 2 o'clock informed Kenny that he did not bring up the papers, and referred him to Redwine. The indebtedness of P. J. Wallace to Redwine was as stated, and was for money loaned. Redwine believed him to be solvent until after the sale, and knew nothing about his indebtedness. F. M. Wallace paid Redwine $402.75, and this was voluntary on the part of F. M., there being no agreement at all, except that F. M. told Redwine, after the sale, that he would pay Redwine first of all. Since February 6, 1891, F. M. Wallace gave his individual notes to Redwine,—some of them being dated February 7, 1891, some February 5, 1891, some January 28, 1891, and some January 30, 1891. Some of these notes were signed also by P. J. Wallace. Redwine kept P. J. on the notes because he never liked to release any body except for cash. The notes dated February 5th were not signed until February 7th. They were given for indebtedness of P. J. Wallace to Redwine, which fell due on the 5th, and for that reason were dated February 5th. The bill of sale was drawn on February 6th by Redwine in the presence of both the Wallaces, and at their joint request. The mortgages of Vaughn and F. M. Wallace are not of record. The evidence introduced on behalf of the defendant in attachment tended to sustain the allegations of his petition, and to show that the indebtedness to Redwine, Vaughn, and F. M. Wallace was *bona fide;* that the sale was made in good faith, without knowledge on the part of F. M., or reason to suspect, that P. J. Wallace in making the sale was acting fraudulently; that the consideration for the sale was full and adequate; that F. M. agreed to pay the indebtedness due to Redwine, Vaughn, and to the Jameses; that an inventory of the stock and appurtenances of the business footed up $3,285.10, which amount was expressed as the consideration for the bill of sale in that instrument, but Redwine, who drew the bill of sale, overlooked at the time the further condition that F. M. Wallace was to pay the Vaughn mortgage.

R. J. Jordan, for plaintiff in error. *Broyles & Sons*, for defendant in error.

Judgment affirmed.

McDANIEL *et al.* v. MAYOR, ETC., OF CITY OF COLUMBUS.

(Supreme Court of Georgia. July 8, 1891.)

INJUNCTION—CONSTRUCTION OF SEWERS—EVIDENCE.

In a suit to enjoin a city from constructing a sewer through plaintiffs' residence lot, it appeared from defendants' affidavits that, on petition of some of the residents of the block, who agreed to pay the costs, the city council ordered the sewer to be built, and that it could only be constructed by crossing part of plaintiffs' lot. The affidavits on behalf of plaintiffs showed that there was no necessity for the sewer, that it would be of benefit only to a few individuals, and that it would injure plaintiffs' lot for residence purposes. The affidavits for defendants showed the sewer was necessary to the health of the public generally; that it would be constructed in such a manner as not to injure plaintiffs; that defendants had offered plaintiffs $200 for a right of way, but they demanded $650; and that defendants had selected an arbitrator, and requested plaintiffs to select another, as provided by law, to assess the compensation to be paid, but that plaintiffs failed to select one. *Held*, that there was no error in refusing an injunction.

Error from superior court, Muscogee county; J. H. MARTIN, Judge.

Suit by Juliette McDaniel and others against the mayor and council of the city of Columbus, to restrain defendants from constructing a sewer across plaintiffs' lot. The injunction was refused. Plaintiffs appeal. Affirmed.

The petition alleged that the mayor and council were seeking to condemn plaintiffs' lot for the purpose of laying thereon sewers and drainage-pipes, by which a large excavation would be made across their lot, and in their yard and garden, wherein the sewer and pipes would be placed, and there would be left open on the lot, and near plaintiffs' dwelling, eyes or openings to the sewer, wherefrom would arise foul and noxious vapors and odors, thereby endangering plaintiffs' health, and rendering their lot unfit for dwelling purposes, the same being in the residence portion of the city; that the mayor and council were proceeding to appropriate the property for this purpose without having first paid therefor, and without first making reparation for the damage they would cause to it; that the taking of it for this purpose would not be for the welfare and benefit of the public at large, but only for the accommodation and benefit of a few adjoining lot-owners, who had proposed to pay the expense incurred in constructing the sewer; and that the damage caused thereby would be irreparable to plaintiffs, as it would ruin their lot and home. Defendants answered that they were seeking to condemn so much of the lot as might be necessary to lay a sanitary sewer for the purpose of draining a certain block, as a protection to the citizens residing therein and to the public at large; that they had the right, under the charter of the city, to condemn any land whenever, in their judgment, it should be necessary to construct a sewer on the same; and, if the land-owner should object to the sewer being built, the charter provided that defendants should select one arbitrator, and the land-owner another, and these two should select a third, and the three should estimate the damage done to the land by the construction of the sewer; that, in pursuance of this power, defendants selected an arbitrator for the city, and notified plaintiffs in writing of such selection, and asked them to select an arbitrator for themselves, in order that the damage might be ascertained and estimated, and that plaintiffs might be paid for the same, they having previously refused to permit the sewer to be built unless they were paid $650; that to construct the sewer across their land it would not be necessary to make a large excavation, but only a small portion of their lot would be used; that the sewer would be under the ground, entirely covered with dirt; and that no eyes or openings would be left, nor any foul and noxious vapors and odors arise; and that, instead of injuring the health of plaintiffs and other citizens, it would be a benefit thereto, and would improve the lot for dwelling purposes; that it would be not only for the welfare and benefit of the citizens residing in the immediate vicinity, but for that of the public at large; that it would not ruin or damage either the lot or the home of the plaintiffs, but would be beneficial to both, and, if any damage to the lot should be caused by its construction, the same could be easily ascertained and fixed; that the amount could only be ascertained by arbitrators; and the defendants are ready and willing to pay plaintiffs whatever amount the arbitrators legally selected may assess. The answer further alleged that, owing to the topography of the land, to make the sewer effectual, it was necessary to construct it through plaintiffs' land; that the lots on this block were in a dreadful condition, because there were no sewers to convey the storm-water falling thereon, and for this reason it would be necessary to construct, not only a sanitary sewer, but also a sewer to convey the storm-water from the block to the main sewer; that these two sewers were located immediately in the center of the block, or as near the center as it was possible to locate in order to give proper fall at the point near it adjoining the main sewer; that, unless the sanitary sewer should be constructed on its located route, the vast quantity of garbage, night-soil, and other things injurious to health would be left standing on the block, and would produce disease, and cause an epidemic endangering the health of the citizens, not only in the neighborhood, but of the entire city. Defendants denied that the sewer was to be constructed for the welfare of a few individuals, and alleged that the public at large would be benefited thereby, and that twice during the year they sought to purchase of plaintiffs the right of way over their land, and offered them $200 for the same, but that they asked $650.

On the hearing it appeared that on January 7, 1891, the mayor and council received a petition signed by seven persons, stating that they were property owners on the block containing the plaintiffs' lot, and asking for the construction of a sewer of suitable dimensions for sanitary drainage of said block, "agreeing to pay in full *pro rata* for the construction of the sewer as per services rendered the property of each property owner signing this petition;" together with the written recommendation of the city sanitary inspector that the sewer be built. The council thereupon ordered this to be done, its minutes reciting that the board of health also recommended the same. The affidavits in behalf of plaintiffs tended to show, in brief, that the construction of the sewer, as proposed by the city council, would not be of public benefit to the city at large, but only for the benefit and convenience of three or four adjoining lot-owners by carrying off the excrement from their water-closets; and that this was not at all necessary, because for 20 years the inhabitants of the block had done without this convenience, and could continue to do without it; that the health of the residents of this block and the vicinity was unusually good, as good as in other portions of the city; that the sewer would be short and private in its nature; that at the point of entrance to the street sewer there was then an eye, and if all the excrement from this block should be emptied into the street sewer at this eye, as was planned by the mayor and council, the fumes arising therefrom would be unpleasant and unwholesome, and would greatly depreciate the value of plaintiffs' lot, and render it undesirable as a residence lot; that for years privies had been located in the gardens attached to these lots in the block, and by the use of disinfectants and the burning of the excrement no unpleasant or unwholesome odors had arisen; that one of the signers of the petition to the mayor and council for the sewer was a partner in business with the mayor, and the sewer would be primarily for the benefit of this petitioner; that the mayor and council have not tried satisfactorily to settle with plaintiffs for the damage they would do to their property, and had made no effort to pay plaintiffs the value of their lot, or for the full damage they would do to it. The affidavits for defendants tended to show that the construction of the sewer would be for the good of the public generally, and that it was a necessity for the health of the citizens of that portion of the city; that a sewer which would accomplish the purpose intended to be served could not be built through any other lot, in consequence of the topography of the adjacent streets and lots; that the president of the board of health of the city recommended the construction of the sewer as proposed; that its construction was determined by the council independently of the act of the mayor, who had no voice or vote in the matter; that it would not be for the

benefit of the mayor's partner in business or of any other individual, but for the benefit of the aggregate number of the citizens of the whole city as well as of that portion of it; that the mayor and the chairman of the street committee of the council had each sought of the plaintiffs permission to construct the sewer, and, failing to obtain it, in behalf of the city offered plaintiffs $200 for the right of way over their lot; that they refused to take this, but asked $650; and the action of the council in selecting an arbitrator was based on the fact that an agreement with plaintiffs could not be reached; that on several occasions the mayor had stated to plaintiffs that the sewer which the city desired to construct through their lot should not have an eye, and that every precaution should be taken to protect them in their health and convenience.

Thornton & McMichael and *Peabody, Brannan & Hatcher*, for plaintiffs in error. J. H. Worrill, for defendants in error.

Judgment affirmed.

LUMPKIN, J., not presiding.

McGEE et al. v. POTTS et al.

(*Supreme Court of Georgia.* July 13, 1891.)

NEW TRIAL—CONFLICTING EVIDENCE.

1. The evidence being conflicting, and that for the plaintiff warranting the verdict, there was no error in refusing a new trial.

2. The charge requested excluded the element of ratification, and moreover was not adapted to the evidence, there being no evidence that, if a dissolution of the partnership was contemplated at the time the goods were ordered, the plaintiffs knew they were to be delivered after the dissolution, the evidence showing that, if the plaintiffs knew of any dissolution at all, it was of one which had already taken place.

(*Syllabus by the Court.*)

Error from superior court, Crawford county; A. L. MILLER, Judge.

Action by Potts & Potts against Jeff D. McGee and Julius S. McGee, as partners under the firm name of McGee Bros., for goods sold defendants. Judgment for plaintiffs. Julius S. McGee appeals. Affirmed.

The evidence on behalf of plaintiffs, as shown by the official report, was briefly stated, as follows: One Dorsett sold the goods for plaintiffs on December 2, 1888, without information as to the dissolution of the firm of McGee Bros., though they told him they expected to dissolve. He met them the morning he sold the goods to J. D. McGee, and the latter told him that Julius S. McGee was going into business at Musella, and would want some liquor. He (Dorsett) remained there until evening, and sold a bill to J. D. McGee, to be delivered about January 20th. Dorsett did not come back to that neighborhood until February. Julius S. McGee paid Dorsett $181.25, on the account, having at the time the bill of plaintiffs, the same account sued on, in his possession, (this payment being one of the credits upon the account as sued on.) This payment was made at Julius McGee's store at Musella, and J. D. McGee was not there. A bill, hereafter to be mentioned, to which J. D. McGee called

Dorsett's attention as being billed to McGee Bros., instead of J. D. McGee, was not the bill sued on, but another. Neither J. D. nor Julius told Dorsett that McGee Bros. had dissolved, but said they were going to dissolve. Dorsett thought the store Julius was building at Musella was to be his private enterprise, apart from the business of McGee Bros. The goods sued for were shipped in the name of McGee Bros., and delivered to the wagon of J. D. McGee on an order signed by McGee Bros. The evidence for defendants was: The firm of McGee Bros. dissolved about December 1, 1888. On the day the bill sued on was made the firm had dissolved, and J. D. McGee, who bought the bill of goods, so informed Dorsett, and told him that Julius was building a house at Musella, and was going to open there soon, and would want some liquors; and Dorsett told Julius that J. D. had so told him, and sold Julius a bill of goods to be delivered in January. The fact of the firm's dissolution was discussed by all three of them. A week or two afterwards Julius bought out a store in Bibb county, and needed some liquor, and his brother, J. D., agree to let him have the three last items in the bill bought by him from plaintiffs, (the account sued on;) and Julius got this, and paid Dorsett for it $181.25. J. D. gave Julius the bill, so that Julius would know how to settle with Dorsett. Some time after December 31, 1888, Dorsett came into the store of J. D. McGee, who got after him about billing goods to McGee Bros. that had been bought by J. D., and Dorsett said it was a mistake of the book-keeper. In addition to the contention that a verdict for plaintiffs was contrary to the law and the evidence, appellant excepted to the court's refusal to instruct the jury that "if the goods were bought by J. D. McGee before the dissolution, and were to be delivered to him after the dissolution, and plaintiffs knew it, they would not be entitled to recover against J. S. McGee."

Smith & Blasslugame, for plaintiff in error. *O. P. Wright*, for defendants in error.

Judgment affirmed.

DEES v. FREEMAN et al.

(Supreme Court of Georgia. July 13, 1891.)

CONVERSION OF ESTATE BY ADMINISTRATORS—
RIGHTS OF HEIR—PETITION.

In an action by an heir against the administrator of the estate and others, the petition alleged that, though the administrators had ample personalty to pay decedent's debts, they mismanaged the estate so as to procure an order for the sale of the larger part of the realty, in pursuance of a conspiracy between themselves and their co-defendants to convert the estate to their own use; that petitioner was then a minor; that the other heirs were women, unused to business; that the co-defendants, who were the persons on whom petitioner's mother chiefly relied, represented to her that the administrators had so mismanaged the estate as to prevent bidding at the sale; that, relying on such representations, the heirs sold their interest in the land to the co-defendants for $5,400; that petitioner was represented in this transaction by his mother as guardian; that his share of the price was only $1,800, though his interest in the land was well worth $20,000; and that the lands or their proceeds were divided between the administrators and their co-defendants. The petition also alleged

that the administrators had permitted another tract of land to be recovered from the estate on a fraudulent title set up thereto; that they had sold the balance of the lands to their co-defendants for a grossly inadequate price; that they had turned over all the personalty of the estate, worth $10,000, to their co-defendants; and that they had then procured themselves to be discharged. The petition prayed that all the various sales be set aside; that petitioner be permitted to recover a one-fourth interest in the lands or their proceeds; and that the administrators be compelled to account for the rents and profits of the lands, and also for the personal estate. *Held*, that the petitioner set forth a cause of action, and that it was error to dismiss the case on demurrer.

Error from superior court, Wilkinson county; W. F. JENKINS, Judge.

Action by Joel T. Dees against T. M. Freeman and others. Plaintiff's petition was dismissed on demurrer, and he brings error. Reversed.

The official report is as follows:

Petition to Wilkinson superior court for equitable relief, by Dees against Lord, Hall, Freeman, and Duggan, alleging as follows: He attained his majority in 1888, and is the only son of Joel Dees, who died intestate on the 30th of September, 1871, leaving petitioner, his mother, Nancy Dees, and his sisters, Lizzie Dees and Mrs. Fleetwood, his heirs at law. He then owned and possessed a large estate, worth $40,000 or other large sum, consisting in lands, personalty, notes, choses in action, money, etc. His widow, Nancy Dees, took for herself and petitioner a homestead in 450 acres of land in Wilkinson county. On October 5, 1871, the court of ordinary of that county appointed defendants Freeman and Duggan temporary administrators upon said estate, and at the December term of that court they were appointed and qualified as permanent administrators on said estate, and as such took possession of the whole estate of their intestate, whose debts were few, and not exceeding $5,000. Yet the administrators, having only to deal with women who were unused to business, and petitioner, who was then a child of few years, conspired to convert a large part or the whole of said estate to their personal profit; and though the personal property, money, and choses in action were nearly sufficient to pay all the debts of the intestate, and there was no necessity to sell more than a small part (if any) of the real estate, yet they began systematically to mismanage said estate so as to render an excuse to get an order to sell the whole, so that they and their confederates (the other defendants) might become the purchasers thereof at a mere song. They failed and refused to collect the choses in action due their intestate, and, when collected, failed and refused to pay the same on the debts, allowed judgment to be obtained against them on fictitious claims, and especially allowed fictitious titles to be set up in certain of the property of their intestate, including a lot in Wilkinson county, which is well worth $3,000, and which they allowed to be recovered through their fraud, negligence, and failure to properly defend the suit,—all of which misfeasance renders them liable to petitioner. This misfeasance was in pursuance of the conspiracy to bring the lands to sale; and at the October term, 1872, they applied to the ordinary for leave to sell all of the lands of their intestate, without setting out where said lands were situate or of what they consisted, and at the same term obtained an order of sale. For the above reasons said order was void, and no title passed thereunder. Thereafter defendants Lord and Hall represented to the mother and sisters of petitioner that, unless they sold their interest in the estate to some person who could cope with the administrators, they would be defrauded out of their whole interest. Lord was a relative, and he and Hall were near neighbors and the chief advisers, the persons on whom his mother and sisters chiefly relied to advise them in all business affairs: and they, having implicit confidence in them, in January, 1875, being frightened by said representations, commissioned them to obtain a purchaser. In a few days they returned, and reported they could find no one to buy on account of the manner in which the administrators had systematically confused matters of said estate so as to prevent purchasers from knowing its affairs and condition, but that they would become the purchasers of all the heirs at $5,400, which they admitted was much less than its true value, but, owing to the way the administrators had complicated it, was all they could offer. His relatives, being much alarmed by their representations, agreed to sell them then and there all the claim in and to all the estate, except the homestead, at said price. At the same time, January 18, 1875, said defendants, in pursuance of said conspiracy, procured Nancy Dees, who claimed to be acting as petitioner's natural guardian, to make to them a private bargain and sale of all his interest in said estate of his father, at the price of $1,800, though this interest was well worth $20,000. Immediately afterwards Lord and Hall had the administrators make a public sale of the estate, so as to convey the legal title in them; said sale being fraudulent, and its sole purpose being to carry out said private sale. The property sold and bid in by Lord and Hall or their agents for the sum of $5,200 was well worth $20,-000, "and consisted of the following lands, to-wit: Nos. 222, 223, 224, 225, 228, 199, 125 acres of lot No. 229, 28 acres of No. 251, in 3d district of Wilkinson county; Nos. 251, 278, 279, 101 acres of No. 248, in 2d district of said county; No. 287, and 147 acres of No. 294, in 2d district of originally Wilkinson, now Laurens, Co.; 25 acres No. 6, 5th dist. of Pulaski Co.; 40 acres No. 647, of 1st dist., 3d sec.; 40 acres No. 216, 7th dist., 2d sec.; 40 acres No. 284, 26th dist., 3d sec.; 10 acres No. 153, 11th dist., 1st sec.; 10 acres No. 251, 3d dist.. 4th sec.,—in originally Cherokee Co." Though these lands were so bid in by Lord and Hall, and titles were made to them, yet the same, or the proceeds thereof, were divided between all of said defendants. The remainder of said lands, consisting of about 1,000 acres and some town lots, of the value of $5,000,

were sold to other persons unknown for about $1,000 to cover up their fraud. The administrators also turned over to Hall and Lord all the personalty, choses in action, money, etc., worth about $10,000. All this was done to so cover up the property that, when petitioner came of age, he would not be able to discover the fraudulent dealings and obtain his rights. Shortly after said transaction, the administrators, representing that they fully administered said estate, procured letters of dismission from their trust. All of said defendants had been in the continuous enjoyment of said property or its proceeds; and they are still in possession of a large part of said lands, which are worth $3,000 per annum as rent. All said transactions, for reasons as aforesaid, were fraudulent and voidable. Waiving discovery, the petitioner prays that he may have a verdict and decree setting aside all of said sales, and the titles thereunder; that he may recover from defendants one-fourth of all the lands that are still in their possession, or have not been sold to bona fide purchasers, and the rents or profits thereon from the time defendants have had them; that he may recover his interest in the proceeds of those sold off, with interest on the sums received, and the profit thereon while enjoyed by defendants; that defendants be required to account for all the notes, moneys, choses in action, and personal property belonging to the estate of Joel Dees that went or ought to have gone into their hands as administrators, and all moneys, choses in action, and property said administrators turned over to the other defendants; and that he may have verdict, judgment, and decree against said defendants for all of said sums, with interest thereon; and for general relief. The defendants demurred on the following grounds: (1) "No equity in complainant's bill;" (2) "Freeman and Duggan, as administrators, fully administered said estate, and have been discharged from the same;" (3) "the complainant was represented by his guardian at all times, and he has no cause of complaint then." They demurred also on the grounds "that the land sought to be recovered is not specially described in complainant's bill," and because "part of the lands sought to be named lies in counties other than Wilkinson, as shown by the allegations in complainant's bill, and therefore the court has no jurisdiction." The demurrer was sustained, and the case dismissed, and the plaintiff excepted. He "specially assigns as error—First, that the court erred in not specifying on which ground of the demurrer he based the judgment dismissing said suit; second, in entering up a judgment at all sustaining said demurrer and dismissing said suit."

Hardeman & Davis and *Whitfield & Allen*, for plaintiff in error. *J. H. Hall*, for defendants in error.

PER CURIAM. On the facts alleged in the petition, a cause of action was set forth, and the court erred in dismissing the case on demurrer. Judgment reversed.

BROOME v. DAVIS.

(Supreme Court of Georgia. July 13, 1891.)

HOMESTEAD—PROPERTY IN WIFE'S NAME—RIGHTS
OF HER CREDITORS.

1. Land paid for with homestead land is
homestead property, though the deed be taken in
the name of the wife when it should have been
taken in the name of the husband.

2. Possession by the husband with the wife,
he being the head of the family, is presumptively
his possession; and, if the premises occupied be
homestead property, the creditor of the wife is
chargeable with constructive notice of its homestead character, though the formal paper title be
in the wife.

(Syllabus by the Court.)

Error from superior court, Greene county; SAM'L LUMPKIN, Judge.

Claim by L. C. Broome, as trustee for
his wife and children, against C. A. Davis,
to set aside certain property as a homestead. Judgment for defendant. Motion
for new trial by claimant denied, and
claimant brings error. Reversed.

The following is the official report:

On February 26, 1870, a homestead was
duly set apart, under the constitution of
1868, to L. C. Broome, as head of a family,
consisting of his wife and three minor
children. The homestead consisted of
167 acres of land in Greene county. On
July 19, 1870, this homestead was exchanged, with the approval of the ordinary, under the laws then in force, to A. B.
Tappan, for a tract of land in the same
county, containing 128.6 acres, and the
deed from Tappan was made to Mrs.
Broome. On February 2, 1882, she executed a mortgage on the last-named tract
to C. A. Davis, Sr., to secure a note given
by her on February 2, 1882, to Davis, due
October 1, 1882. At the time of the exchange mentioned Broome went into possession of the 128.6 acres as trustee for
his wife and minor children, and has remained in possession ever since. Mr.
Broome is still living, and some of the
children are still minors. At the time of
the exchange the approval of the ordinary
was indorsed on the deed to the 167 acres.
Davis had no actual notice of the homestead in the 128.6 acres, outside of the fact
that both Broome and his wife lived on
the place of 128 acres; and, though the
approval of the ordinary allowing the exchange was indorsed on the deed from
Broome to Tappan, Davis had no knowledge of this fact. The mortgage of Davis
was regularly foreclosed and levied on the
128 acres, and the same was claimed by
Broome as trustee of his wife and minor
children. The case was submitted to the
presiding judge for trial without a jury
upon the above, as an agreed statement
of facts. He held the property subject,
and claimant moved for a new trial on
the grounds that the verdict is contrary
to law and evidence, etc.

Jas. B. Park, for plaintiff in error. *W.
H. Branch,* for defendant in error.

BLECKLEY, C. J. Before the translation of
our Brother LUMPKIN to this bench, though
his judicial accuracy was remarkable, he
shared in the fallibility which is inherent
in all courts except those of last resort.
In some rare instances he committed error, and the very last of his errors is now
before us for correction. The facts of the
case are correctly set forth in the reporter's statement.

1. It is settled law that property paid
for in full with other property previously
set apart, in due and proper manner, under the homestead and exemption laws,
takes the place of the latter, and is impressed with the homestead character.
Mitchell v. Prater, 78 Ga. 767, 3 S. E. Rep.
658; Murray v. Sells, 53 Ga. 257; Cheney
v. Rodgers, 54 Ga. 168, 59 Ga. 861; Morris
v. Tennent, 56 Ga. 577; Dodd v. Thompson,
63 Ga. 393. This is true, though the conveyance of the new property be made to
the wife, (supra, 78 Ga., 3 S. E. Rep., and
53 Ga.;) or to the husband and wife, (supra, 54 Ga.;) and the homestead right can
be asserted against a purchaser with notice, (supra, 53 and 54 Ga.) A mortgagee
stands on the same plane with a purchaser. Lane v. Partee, 41 Ga. 202.

2. Could the creditor and mortgagee of
the wife, his rights having attached while
the paper title to the land in controversy
was in her, stand upon that title, and
claim protection as a mortgagee without
notice, notwithstanding the husband was
at the same time in actual possession of
the premises? Possession of land is notice to the world of whatever right or title
the occupant has. Cogan v. Christie, 48
Ga. 585; Sewell v. Holland, 61 Ga. 608; Atkins v. Paul, 67 Ga. 97; Finch v. Beal, 68
Ga. 594; Association v. Atlanta, 77 Ga. 496.
In this state, notwithstanding his reduced
importance as a domestic factor, the husband is still the head of his family, and,
though his wife may reside with him, she
does not thereby divest his possession of
the homestead, and make the possession
her own. Presumptively he is the owner.
Primrose v. Browning, 59 Ga. 69; Neal v.
Perkerson, 61 Ga. 346; City of Atlanta v.
Word, 78 Ga. 276. While for most purposes this presumption would be rebutted
by the mere production of a conveyance
from a third person to the wife, yet this
alone should not excuse a stranger, about
to give her credit on the faith of the premises, from consulting the husband touching his rights as the actual occupant. His
possession, to be of any force at all as notice, must be treated as directing inquiry
to be made of himself, and not as a suggestion to go to his wife and deal with
her upon what she might say, fortified by
documents in her possession. So long as a
man clings to his home in person, he has
a right to be treated by strangers as the
head of the family, and as entitled to answer for it and himself touching his right
to be there and remain. If the true title
to the property is in him, though the apparent title be in his wife, he cannot be
driven out as the result of contracts of
sale or mortgage made by her without
his consent, and with persons who have
not consulted him. Indeed, he would be
incapable of effectually consenting to any
sale or mortgage of homestead property,
except with the approbation of the proper
judicial officer. Code, §§ 2025, 5212, 5218.

The judgment is reversed.

LUMPKIN, J., not presiding.

CENTRAL RAILROAD & BANKING CO. v.
PICKETT et al.

(Supreme Court of Georgia. Oct. 19, 1891.)

ACTIONS—ELECTION—VENUE—LIABILITY OF CARRIERS—SHIPMENT OF LIVE-STOCK.

1. Where a declaration against a common carrier is susceptible of being construed equally as an action upon contract or an action of tort based upon an alleged violation of a public duty by the carrier, and the same is not demurred to, the plaintiff at the trial may, at his option, elect to treat it as either species of action.

2. The superior court of the county in which delivery was made to the common carrier, and in which the violation of the carrier's duty commenced, has jurisdiction of the action, although the tort may have been only partially completed in that county, and its full completion took place in another county.

3. That the name of a partnership was inverted in making a written contract will not defeat an action brought in tort against the carrier by the partnership in its proper name.

4. If the live-stock delivered to the carrier consisted of both cattle and hogs, it is not a material variance that they are described in the written contract as one car-load of cattle, the action being treated as one of tort, and not as founded upon the contract.

5. There was no error in denying a nonsuit, nor in overruling the motion for a new trial.

(Syllabus by the Court.)

Error from superior court, Fulton county; MARSHALL J. CLARKE, Judge.

Action by Pickett & Blair against the Central Railroad & Banking Company of Georgia. Judgment for plaintiffs. Defendant brings error. Affirmed.

Calhoun, King & Spalding and *J. T. Pendleton,* for plaintiff in error. *E. M. Mitchell,* for defendants in error.

LUMPKIN, J. 1. It does not clearly appear from the declaration in this case whether the cause of action intended to be set forth therein was founded upon an alleged breach of a contract between the plaintiffs and defendant, or upon an alleged violation of a public duty by the defendant as a common carrier. In this respect the declaration is at least ambiguous, and is susceptible of being construed as an action of either kind. Undoubtedly defendant was entitled to be distinctly informed of the nature of the complaint made against it, in order that it might have a fair opportunity to make its defense; but it neglected taking the proper step to secure this important right by failing to demur to the declaration. Had it done so, the court below would either have dismissed the cause for duplicity, or required the plaintiffs to so shape their allegations as to leave no doubt of the manner in which they sought to hold defendant liable. No demurrer having been made, and the declaration containing enough to make it good either as an action upon contract or upon tort, it follows, we think, that plaintiffs were left free to treat it as they deemed proper. They elected to proceed with the action as one of tort, and our rulings in this case are therefore made accordingly.

2. Under section 3406 of the Code, railroad companies are liable to be sued for injuries to person or property in any county in which the cause of action originated. It appears unmistakably from the evidence in this case that the injury to plaintiffs' stock began in Fulton county, before the train upon which they were loaded left the city of Atlanta; and it is more than probable this injury materially contributed to, if it did not actually cause, the further damage to the stock which occurred during the journey. It does not appear in what county or counties these further injuries to the stock took place; but, as the perpetration of the tort began in Fulton county, it seems entirely consistent both with law and common justice that the action may be maintained in that county, although the tort may not have been fully completed before the train had passed its limits. Unquestionably plaintiffs can sue in Fulton county for any injury to their property actually occasioned therein, and this they might do in each county through which the train passed for injuries in such county sustained; but what would be the sense or propriety of thus cutting up into several actions a cause or causes of complaint which might as well be included in one, even if plaintiffs could know and prove what injury or injuries their property sustained at particular points along the journey, and in what county or counties these points were located? As so doing would be exceedingly difficult, if not altogether impossible, we see no reason why plaintiffs should be subjected to such unnecessary hardships, especially as it could result in no fair or proper advantage to defendant. Treating the action as one for a tort, we may safely say, under the facts of this case, it originated and was properly brought, in Fulton county.

3. The firm of Pickett & Blair shipped over defendant's road the stock that were injured, and made a written contract with defendant concerning this shipment. This contract was signed, "Blair & Pickett," but there is no doubt that the same firm shipped the stock and made the contract. It requires no argument to show that the inversion of the name and style of the firm is entirely immaterial, especially when it appears, as has been shown, that the action proceeded as one for a tort.

4. For the reason last stated, it is equally clear that, although the stock delivered to the carrier consisted of both cattle and hogs, it was immaterial that they were described in the written contract above referred to as one car-load of cattle.

5. No railroad company can lawfully contract against liability for injuries caused by its own negligence, and defendant did not attempt to do so in this case. That it was negligent was proved beyond doubt, and the recovery by plaintiffs was both lawful and just. Notwithstanding the stipulation in the written contract that "the owner or person in charge of stock shall give notice in writing of his claim thereof to some officer of said Central Railroad or connections, or its nearest station agent, before said stock is removed from the place of destination above mentioned, or from the place of delivery of the same, and before such stock is mingled with other stock," the plaintiffs, under the facts presented, even if they had

sued upon the written contract, would still be entitled to recover, because the stock never reached Savannah, the place of destination contemplated by the contract, and the defendant had actual knowledge of the injury from the very beginning of the journey; and, further, the car containing the stock was side-tracked, and the animals taken therefrom, in Macon, with defendant's express consent, thus rendering the notice, etc., mentioned in the contract unnecessary. The nonsuit was properly refused, and the motion for a new trial rightly denied. Judgment affirmed.

ATLANTA & W. P. R. CO. v. HOLCOMBE.

(Supreme Court of Georgia.   Oct. 19, 1891.)

BEST AND SECONDARY EVIDENCE — CUSTOM — INSTRUCTIONS.

1. Where the employe whose business it was to place a stool used for the purpose of assisting lady passengers to enter the train was not produced or accounted for, there was no error in rejecting evidence that it was the custom and habit of the company to have the stool in its proper place up to the time of the starting of the train, there being positive evidence in behalf of the plaintiff that it was out of place when he was injured, and only negative evidence to the contrary in behalf of the defendant.

2. It not appearing that the witness who would ordinarily know the fact in question, and who was one of the employes of the company at the time the cause of action arose, was inaccessible, or that the defendant was ready to produce him, there was no error in calling attention to his absence or non-production in charging the jury as a fact to be considered by them in connection with the case.

3. There was no error in denying a new trial.

(Syllabus by the Court.)

Error from superior court, Fulton county; MARSHALL J. CLARKE, Judge.

Action by S. L. Holcombe against the Atlanta & West Point Railroad Company for personal injuries. Judgment for plaintiff. Defendant brings error. Affirmed.

Calhoun, King & Spalding and J. T. Pendleton, for plaintiff in error. S. N. Connally and Cox & Reed, for defendant in error.

LUMPKIN, J. 1. The main question in this case is not whether the railroad company had a custom and habit of keeping at its proper place, up to the time a train was ready to leave the depot, a stool used for assisting lady passengers to enter the train, but whether, on the occasion when the plaintiff below was injured, the stool caused the injury by being in the wrong place. It appears from the evidence that the proper use of such a stool would require its being kept on the ground or floor at the foot of the steps of the car until the train was about to depart; and the fact that such use was generally made of it would be almost, if not quite, as apparent from the other circumstances in proof as if defendant's witness had been permitted to swear the company did have such a custom. Testimony, therefore, to the effect that it was the custom and habit of defendant's servants to take up the stool just as the train was ready to pull out of the depot, and not 10 minutes before, would, of itself, be of but little probative value upon the real question at issue. Doubtless the jury understood, without such testimony, what was usually the company's habit as to this stool; and the chief thing for their determination was, not the existence or non-existence of such a habit, but whether or not the stool was where it ought to be when the plaintiff was hurt. If the servant of the company whose duty it was to look after this stool had been sworn as a witness, and had testified that when the plaintiff fell the stool was where it should be, we think it would have been proper to allow him to strengthen his testimony by stating, if he could, that he knew the stool was in its proper place on this particular occasion because it was his invariable habit and custom to keep it where it belonged, and not to take it up till the train was about to start. No such witness was offered, and defendant's witnesses, who swore concerning the location of the stool, did not positively say it was not on the platform between the cars. Their testimony was, at best, only negative on this point, while the testimony for plaintiff was positive that the stool was on such platform, and that he fell over it. We think that, while a witness may testify to the existence of a custom or habit concerning which he has personal knowledge, and with which he had personal connection, by way of strengthening his statement that this custom or habit was observed on a particular occasion, it would not be proper, as a general rule, to admit independent testimony as to what was or was not the habit of a person or corporation with reference to a given subject. See Hardeman v. English, 79 Ga. 387, 5 S. E. Rep. 70, and Mayfield v. Railroad Co., (Ga.) 13 S. E. Rep. 459. These authorities and the cases therein cited not only sustain the above view, but an examination of them will show that a manifest distinction exists between customs which, by reason of their general operation, have the force and effect of law, and the mere habit of one individual or corporation. Of course, a custom so well known and recognized within the sphere of its operation as to become a part of the law of contracts or other transactions made in a particular locality may be proved by witnesses familiar with the existence of the same; but the rule is different in reference to the particular way or manner in which a single corporation or person transacts a specific kind of business. With reference to the latter, we have above stated to what extent proof should be allowed.

2. In view of the repeated rulings of this court, we see no reason why there should be any impropriety in the court's calling the attention of the jury to the absence or non-production of a witness who ought to have special knowledge concerning the particular fact under investigation. It appears by an affidavit attached to the motion for a new trial that the witness who ought to have known about the location of this stool at the time of the injury had been subpoenaed by both sides, and was actually in court; but, this fact not being known to the court, its charge on this subject was properly given. The de-

fendant could easily, during the trial, have informed the court of the presence of the witness; and, if this had been done, the charge complained of would doubtless have been omitted.

3. The jury found from the testimony that the stool was in an improper place, and was the occasion of the injury. The evidence sustaining such finding was ample, and we will not, therefore, interfere with the discretion of the court below in refusing a new trial. Judgment affirmed.

GRESHAM v. EQUITABLE LIFE & ACC. INS. CO.

(Supreme Court of Georgia.   July 13, 1891.)

ACCIDENT INSURANCE—MUTUAL COMBAT.

If both parties engage willingly in a personal rencounter, it is a mutual combat or fight, and death resulting therefrom is not included in a policy of accident insurance which excepts from the risk death or injury which may have been caused by fighting. It makes no difference, in such case, whether the slayer was sane or insane.

(Syllabus by the Court.)

Error from superior court, Fulton county; MARSHALL J. CLARKE, Judge.

Action by Mattie E. Gresham against the Equitable Life & Accident Insurance Company to recover on an insurance policy. Nonsuit granted. Plaintiff brings error. Affirmed.

J. D. Cunningham, J. A. Austin, and *Broyles & Sons,* for plaintiff in error. *Candler & Thomson,* for defendant in error.

BLECKLEY, C. J. The policy covered bodily injuries inflicted by external, violent, and accidental means. It excepted, however, various classes of accidental injuries which might be embraced in these general terms,—among them, those caused by dueling, fighting, wrestling, etc., and those happening in consequence of voluntary exposure to unnecessary danger, hazard, or perilous adventure, or while engaged in, or in consequence of, any unlawful act, and all injuries, the result of design, either on the part of the claimant or any other person. It may be conceded that the homicide was accidental, within the meaning of the policy, as such policies have generally been construed by the courts. Ripley v. Railway Co., 2 Bigelow, Ins. Cas. 738; Hutchcraft's Ex'r v. Insurance Co., 87 Ky. 300, 8 S, W. Rep. 570; Phelan v. Insurance Co., 38 Mo. App. 640; Richards v. Insurance Co., (Cal., May, 1891,) 26 Pac. Rep. 762; Supreme Council v. Garrigus, 104 Ind. 133, 3 N. E. Rep. 818; notes to Paul v. Insurance Co., 8 Amer. St. Rep. 763; Bliss, Ins. §§ 396, 397; 5 Lawson, Rights, Rem. & Pr. § 2140 et seq.; 1 Amer. & Eng. Enc. Law, 87 et seq.; 7 Amer. Law Rev. 585; same article, 8 Alb. Law J. 85. It may be conceded also that, though the killing was manifestly willful on the part of the slayer, it was open to question whether it was the result of design,—that is, of rational design,—inasmuch as there was some evidence tending to show that the slayer might have been insane. It may likewise be conceded that, had the case turned alone on the question whether at the time the insured was shot he was en-

gaged in an unlawful act, there was some evidence for consideration by the jury. The evidence as a whole might warrant a negative finding on this point, according to some of the authorities, though not so, perhaps, according to the spirit of others. Cluff v. Insurance Co., 13 Allen, 308; Bradley v. Insurance Co., 45 N. Y. 422; Harper v. Insurance Co., 19 Mo. 506; Insurance Co. v. Seaver, 19 Wall. 532; Bloom v. Insurance Co., 97 Ind. 478. But, if the view we entertain of the law is correct, the matter on which after close study there could be no two opinions, no reasonable doubt in impartial and intelligent minds, is that the injury which resulted in death was caused by fighting. Shooting caused the injury, and fighting caused the shooting. The cause of the cause was the real cause of the event. Fighting may cause death by causing a contemporaneous act which causes death. In such case, the first causal agency is not too remote, though the event be related to it only in the second degree of lineal descent. It is not every fight, however, in or from which a mortal injury might be received by the insured, which could be regarded as the cause of the injury or of death resulting therefrom. A faultless and unwilling conflict by the insured—one which he neither provoked nor invited, one which he did not accept when formally or informally tendered, one in which he was forced to engage for self-defense alone, and from which he withdrew, or endeavored in good faith to withdraw, when his defense was accomplished—ought not to, and would not, be treated as a causative fight on his part, within the meaning and intent of the policy, but would be regarded as right and proper resistance to aggressive or offensive violence. To protect his life from destruction or his person from injury might be as much a matter of duty to the insurance company as of interest to himself. Means of resistance which it would be reasonable for him to employ for his own safety, he could not be excused for neglecting, if an efficient use of them were shown to be within his power. It would be no objection to their use that they involved "fighting back" in order to repel the violence of an assailant. The stipulation against liability for injuries caused by fighting refers to voluntary fighting by the insured, or involuntary fighting brought on wholly or partially by his fault or temerity,—fighting for which he is partly responsible, either as a volunteer or as a rash speaker or wrong-doer. It could not be the purpose of the stipulation to cut off the right of self-defense by the use of force,—the right to repel violence with violence of like nature. The exercise of this right might be mutually beneficial to both of the contracting parties, and that either of them had any purpose to restrict a fair and reasonable exercise of it is in the highest degree improbable.

In order to attribute to the insured anything caused by the fight, he must have some voluntary agency in causing the fight itself. If he had such agency, if by improper speech or voluntary conduct he was a material factor in bringing on the fight, he was, as between himself or his wife and the insurance company, chargeable with the consequences. If the fight was the cause of the mortal injury, and he was the cause of the fight, whether in whole or in part, he was, to that extent, the cause of his own death. If he begat the fight, and the fight begat the shooting, and the shooting begat the injury, he bore an ancestral relation to the last offspring as well as to the first. At all events, being father to the fight, neither he nor his wife, under the terms of this policy, could profit by the fight or by what it brought forth. That, according to the evidence in this case, there was a fight, admits of no possible question. There was hostile contact, physical collision, an attempt by each combatant to hurt the other; blows were given by one, which took effect; strokes were made by the other, which missed their aim. The origin of the fight is equally manifest. It was not born of the passion of one of the parties, but of a conjunction of the passions of both. It proceeded from an altercation in which each party used rash and insulting language; language calculated to excite anger and provoke conflict. Both being in the same room, but some distance—say 20 feet—apart, the other party spoke abusively of secret societies and their members, referring to them in general terms; no particular society or member (so far as appears) being mentioned. This speech was made in the hearing of the insured and several others, but was not addressed to him. Some of the others, who were nearer to the speaker, remonstrated with him upon the impropriety of his animadversions. Shortly afterwards, as the speaker was passing by the insured on his way out, the latter, without rising from his seat, said to him mildly, in a tone of mortified resentment: "I heard all you said about secret societies; that no gentleman would belong to a secret society." The other answered: "Yes, I said it; and, by G—d, it is true. Do you want to take it up?" The insured replied, "Well, it's a lie," or "a damned lie;" adding, "Yes, I do." Then followed a blow from one of them, probably the former, and the latter "tumbled off his seat," possibly as the result of receiving the blow. They backed towards one of the entrances to the room, several feet, and the insured was stricken by his antagonist several times with a small walking cane, which was broken over his shoulders. The insured struck back with his hands without effect, several of his blows missing their aim. Then, while the other maintained his position close to where the fight took place, the insured moved back 10 or 12 feet to the seat which he had occupied, and looked for and inquired after his hat, which had fallen or been knocked from his head. The other combatant, without changing his position, then drew a pistol, and fired the fatal shot. Before anything above referred to was said or done, the parties were aware of each other's presence in the room; they had spoken together in a friendly way, each calling the other by his first, or Christian, name. In substance, this is the whole story of the quarrel, the fight, and the homicide,

v.18s.r.no.31—48

as told by the testimony. The first insult came from the slayer, attended with a challenge to fight. The question, "Do you want to take it up?" propounded in anger, does not, according to the common understanding of it in Georgia, import a proposal to debate or discuss, but a challenge to the arbitrament of force, or a trial of the issue by the personal prowess of the disputants. It is the end, not the beginning, of argument. It is no less significant of defiance than was the ceremony of throwing down the glove as a preliminary to trial by battle. The insult was returned by the insured by responding in words of foul opprobrium,—words so irritating that gentlemen rarely address them to their equals, except when they intend to back them with their courage; and, to make the intent clear in this instance, the challenge was accepted in the superadded phrase, "Yes, I do." Instantly active hostilities commenced, each party having thus declared his willingness to champion his side of the trivial and needless quarrel. Had not both of them acted with hot-headed rashness in passing insults, there would have been no fight. Had the insured squarely objected to fighting, and tried to keep out of it, there is no reason to suppose he would have failed of success. Instead of so doing, he provoked his adversary by giving him the lie, most probably with a profane prefix to the offensive imputation; and, instead of pursuing a pacific policy, he accepted what he must have understood as a challenge to fight. No doubt he was under the influence of strong passion, but this is no excuse for him in the present litigation. The fighting was in a public place,—that is, a place to which a portion of the public habitually resorted. It was in a room occupied and used as a saloon and restaurant, in the city of Atlanta. The fight, merely as such, was a joint offense, and would be classified, under our Code, as an affray. Code, § 4515. This is true, notwithstanding the evidence indicates none of the blows dealt by the insured took effect, and that the first blow, as well as all others which reached their object, came from his antagonist. In so far as the constituents of a fight are concerned, the consent of both parties makes the consequent violence of either chargeable to both. "We think the judge was in error in saying there must be mutual blows to constitute a mutual combat. There must be a mutual intent to fight. But we think, if this exists, and but one blow be stricken, that the mutual combat exists, even though the first blow kills or disables one of the parties." Tate v. State, 46 Ga. 157, 158, (McCay, J.) To the like effect is a *dictum* by Chief Justice Pearson, of North Carolina, who says: "Is it necessary that both parties should give and take blows, or is it sufficient that both parties should voluntarily put their bodies in a position to give and take blows, and with that intent? To illustrate: Suppose Rippy had not been killed. Upon an indictment for an affray, would he not have been convicted? Two men go out to fight. One is knocked down on the 'first pass,' and that is the end of it. Are they not both guilty of an affray?—

that is, 'a fight by mutual consent.'" State v. Gladden, 73 N. C. 155. We are no less certain that the fight was a mutual combat, in the legal sense, than if it had been so found by the verdict of a jury under a full and proper charge from the presiding judge; and the palpable truth that fighting caused the shooting, and therefore the injury, needs confirmation by verdict just as little. The evidence is all one way; but one rational inference is possible. The shooting is accounted for easily and naturally by ascribing it to the fight. This is the proper explanation of it, whether it be regarded as a part of the fight proper or as a sequel to it. It was certainly embraced within the *res gestæ* of the combat. It took place on the same stage and within the atmosphere of the antecedent performance. The homicide could well be treated as the culmination of the final scene,—the catastrophe of the drama. At the very least it was a bloody epilogue, and not an independent afterpiece. Nor is it material that it was not down on the bill, but was wholly unexpected by one or both of the actors. Rarely, if ever, can the incidents or the result of a personal encounter be foreseen. A deadly weapon may make its appearance at the last moment, and a homicide be the result, although the fight intended and begun was one with "fist and scull" only. To fight at all is dangerous. When the combative passions are aroused and get a taste of gratification, what momentum they will acquire, and to what extremes it will carry them in their lust for more, is always uncertain. Even friendly wrestling is a door by which anger and a mortal wound may come in. Knowing the hazards attendant on physical competition and contention, this insurance company declined to assume the risk of accidental injury or death caused by fighting or wrestling. The insured might fight if he pleased, but he was not allowed to indulge his combative propensities at the expense of the company; that kind of indulgence was to be at his own risk. Not that the company might not have borne the risk for him if it had chosen to do so. In the language of Judge SCOTT, in Harper v. Insurance Co., 19 Mo. 509, supra: "Unless it is otherwise stipulated, the insurer takes the subject insured, with his flesh and blood and passions. The dangers to which the lives of men are exposed from sudden ebullitions of feeling are a lawful matter of insurance." But in the policy before us the company had "otherwise stipulated." By so doing it has narrowed the range of the policy over the emotions so as to shut out all those of a pugnacious character. If both combatants contributed to bring on the fight, their relative blame or guilt has nothing to do with the relation of cause and effect between it and the homicide. Nor is it of any moment to consider whether the offense committed in the end was murder or manslaughter. With or without malice, in the technical sense of criminal law, the homicide was caused by the fight, as causation is understood and regarded in the law of contracts. The fight occasioned it, for the fight produced the shooting as a direct and immediate consequence. Who can doubt that the shooting grew out of the fight,—sprang from it directly and immediately? Had there been no fight, there would have been no shooting and no killing. It was the fight that excited the homicidal impulse, generated the desire and the purpose to kill. There was nothing else to do it. Even if the slayer was insane, or subject to homicidal mania, the mania alone was harmless; it required the superadded excitement of the fight to render it destructive. Had the insured abstained from provoking the fight or accepting a challenge, had he contributed nothing towards bringing on a useless combat, there is no probability whatever that he would have been slain. And he could no more provoke a crazy man, or accept his challenge, at the expense of the insurance company, than he could so deal with a sane man at the company's expense. Indeed, it would be more hazardous to engage in an affray with a madman than with a rational being; and any reason for protecting the company against the consequences of the less dangerous fighting will apply with increased force to the more dangerous. Injuries caused by rash or needless fighting with any description of combatant are excluded from the scope of the policy. The nonsuit was properly awarded, and we have stated our reasons very fully for so deciding. Judgment affirmed.

SELLERS' EX'R v. REED et al.

(Supreme Court of Appeals of Virginia. Nov. 5, 1891.)

WILLS—CONSTRUCTION—NATURE OF ESTATE—APPEAL—JURISDICTION.

1. Testator gave his wife all his property, both real and personal, "until" their youngest child should reach the age of 17 years, his wife to board, clothe, and educate all the children until that time; and further provided that, "when the younger child becomes 17 years of age, I will and bequeath to my wife the one-third of my estate, both real and personal; the remainder to my children equally." *Held,* that each child took a vested interest, which, on his death before the youngest child reached the age of 17, passed to his personal representatives.

2. In a suit to administer the estate of a deceased remainder-man under a will, leaving real property, the object of which is to subject his interest to a deed of trust given thereon by him, the question being whether such remainder-man, who died before the time provided for the payment of his interest, took a vested or contingent estate, the controversy concerns the title to land, and the supreme court of appeals, under Code Va. § 3455, has jurisdiction, though the amount secured by the deed of trust, and sought to be collected, is less than $500.

Appeal from circuit court, Rockingham county.

Bill by Jacob S. Sellers, as executor of Reuben Sellers, for the administration of the estate of Patrick H. Reed, deceased, a beneficiary under the will of Gideon B. Reed, deceased. The will provided: "I will and bequeath to my wife, Mildred Reed, all my property, both real and personal, until the youngest of our children shall arrive at the age of 17 years, she to board, clothe, and educate all of our children until that time. * * * When the younger child becomes 17 years of age, I will and bequeath to my wife, Mildred Reed, the one-third of my estate, both real and personal; the remainder to my children equally." Patrick H. Reed, one of the adult children, gave a deed of trust on his interest, and died before the youngest child reached the age of 17 years. and the question arose whether he took a vested interest under the will, which went to his personal representative, or a contingent interest, which lapsed at his death. The court held that he took a contingent interest, and so decreed. Jacob S. Sellers, trustee in the deed of trust, and executor of the beneficiary therein, appeals. Reversed.

Sipe & Harris, for appellant. *John E. Roller* and *Strayer & Liggett*, for appellees.

LEWIS, P. Whether a legacy which is directed to be paid at a future time is vested or contingent depends on the meaning of the testator (to be gathered from the whole will) to annex the time to the payment or possession only, or to the gift itself. In the former case the legacy vests immediately; in the latter it is contingent. The rules upon this subject were fully stated in Major v. Major, 32 Grat. 819, and need not be here repeated at large. According to those rules, the word "when," like "at," "if," "provided," etc., in a testamentary gift of personalty, is a word of condition, denoting, unless qualified by the context, the time when the gift is to take effect in substance; so that, if the legatee die before the period specified, the legacy is lapsed. Hence, while a legacy payable to the legatee at 21, or any other age, is vested,—*i. e., debitum in præsenti, solvendum in futuro*,—a legacy to one, generally, at 21 or when he attains 21, is contingent. But to the latter rule there are some exceptions, one of which is that if the intermediate interest is given to the legatee, or is directed to be applied for his benefit, the legacy is *prima facie* vested, this circumstance being considered as an indication of the testator's intention that the legatee shall have the principal at all events. 1 Rop. Leg. 572; Hoath v. Hoath, 2 Brown, Ch. 4; Fonereau v. Fonereau, 3 Atk. 645; Hannon v. Graham, 6 Ves. 239; Cropley v. Cooper, 19 Wall. 167.

These rules as to legacies, however, which were borrowed from the civil law, do not altogether apply to devises of realty; and in a case, like the present, of a mixed gift of realty and personalty, the rules relating to devises control. Collier's Will, 40 Mo. 287; Raney v. Heath, 2 Pat. & H. 207. In both classes of cases the rule is observed that the law favors the vesting of estates, as also the rule that the intention of the testator will prevail over merely technical words or expressions. The courts, however, lean even more strongly in favor of the vesting of devises than of legacies. The former are always held to be vested, except estates in the devise of which a condition precedent is so clearly expressed that to treat them as vested would be to decide in direct opposition to the intention of the testator. Hence words of seeming condition, as "when," "upon," etc., are, if possible, held to have only the effect of postponing the right of possession. And even though the devise be clearly conditional, yet the condition will be construed, if possible, as a condition subsequent, so as to confer an immediately vested estate, subject to be divested on the happening of the contingency. Hawk, Wills, 228, 237; 2 Minor, Inst. 357. Boraston's Case, 3 Coke, 19, is an instance of the first sort. There the devise was to A. and B. for the term of eight years, with remainder to the testator's executors until such time as H. B. should arrive at 21 years, and, when he should come of age, then to him in fee. H. B. died under age, and it was contended that the remainder did not vest in him, because he did not live to attain 21 years. But it was determined otherwise; that is, that the world "when" in the devise applied only to the time of enjoyment, and not to the vesting of the estate. This, and other like cases, were followed by Lord MANSFIELD in Goodtitle v. Whitby, 1 Burrows, 228. That was a devise to trustees to lay out the rents and profits of the devised premises for the maintenance and education of the testator's two nephews during their minorities, and when and as they should respectively attain the age of 21, then to them equally. Lord MANSFIELD, in delivering judgment, said he would lay down two rules, which were these, viz.: (1) That wherever the whole property is devised, with a particular interest given out of it, it operates, by way of exception, out of the absolute property; and (2) that where an absolute property is given, and a particular interest given in the mean time, as until, or when, the devisee shall come of age, then to him, that that does not operate as a condition precedent, but as a description of the time when the remainder-man is to take in possession. Accordingly, he held that the devise to the trustees was only an exception out of the absolute property given to the nephews, and that they took vested interests at the testator's death. This was so plain, he said, that it would be a shame to cite cases upon it. In Doe v. Lea, 3 Term R. 41, the devise was to trustees, and when M. L. should attain the age of 24, then to him, etc. The devisee died under 24, and it was contended in that case, also, that the word "when" operated as a condition precedent. But the whole court were of opinion that it did not, Lord KENYON remarking that the question had been settled ever since Boraston's Case; and the subsequent cases to the same effect are very numerous.

In the light of these principles, when applied to the will before us, the case is free from difficulty. Here the testator devises the whole property, real and personal, to his wife, charged with a trust for the benefit of all the children, until the youngest child shall attain the age of 17 years. He then, in effect, directs that, upon the happening of that event, the absolute property shall go, one-third to the wife, and the rest to the children equally. His purpose evidently was to provide a home and support for the family until such time as, in his judgment, a division of the estate would be expedient, which time be specifies. There is nothing in the will to show that he intended to give anything contingently. All the children—certainly in respect to the ulterior estate—are put upon a footing of exact equality, nor is there anything indicating an intention to disinherit the offspring of any of them in any event. Yet such would be the consequence of sustaining the appellees' view, if any one of the children should marry and die, leaving issue, before the determination of the trust-estate. This consideration had weight with Lord MANSFIELD in Goodtitle v. Whitby, where he said: "Here, upon the reason of the thing, the infant is the object of the testator's bounty, and the testator does not mean to deprive him of it in any event. Now, suppose this object of the testator's bounty marries and dies before his age of twenty-one, leaving children, could the testator intend, in such event, to disinherit him? Certainly he could not."

The appellees rely upon the third sentence in the first clause of the will, which is in these words: "When the younger child becomes seventeen years of age, I will and bequeath to my wife, Mildred Reed, the one-third of my estate, both real and personal; the remainder to my children equally." Particular stress is laid upon the first word, "when," in the sentence, as importing a condition precedent; and the repetition of the words, "I will and bequeath," it is contended, virtually amounts to "a new devise." But the sentence must be construed in connection with what immediately precedes it, and, so construing it, it is merely descriptive of the event upon the happening of which the particular (or trust) estate is to determine, and the absolute estate is to take effect in possession. This construction is in harmony no less with what seems to us the apparent intention of the testator than the established rule of construction in such cases. "Where a testator creates a particular estate," says Jarman in stating the rule, "and then goes on to dispose of the ulterior interest, expressly in an event which will determine the prior estate, the words descriptive of such event, occurring in the latter devise, will be construed as referring merely to the period of the determination of the possession or enjoyment under the prior gift, and not as designed to postpone the vesting." 2 Jarm. Wills, (5th Amer. Ed.) c. 25. This is but stating in slightly different language the rule laid down by Lord MANSFIELD in Goodtitle v. Whitby, and which has since been the universally accepted canon of construction. The case of Major v. Major, 82 Grat. 819, wherein the word "when" was construed as a word of condition, is not in point, because that was not only, in effect, a gift of personalty, as the will directed the real estate to be converted into money, (Cropley v. Cooper, 19 Wall. 167,) but the context showed that the word was annexed to the substance of the gift, which rendered the gift contingent. We hold, therefore, that Patrick H. Reed took a vested interest in the estate, real and personal, at the testator's death, which, at his death, passed to his representatives.

The only other question in the case is one of jurisdiction. The appellant's debt being less than $500, the appellees contend that the case is not within the jurisdiction of this court. But this position is untenable, because the question being whether Patrick H. Reed, the grantor in the deed of trust, took an immediate vested, descendible interest under the testator's will, the controversy concerns the title to land, which gives this court jurisdiction, independently of the amount of the debt secured in the deed. Code, § 3455; Pannill v. Coles, 81 Va. 380. The decree will therefore be reversed, and an order entered here in conformity with this opinion.

OBERDORFER et al. v. MEYER et al.

(Supreme Court of Appeals of Virginia. Nov. 5, 1891.)

FRAUDULENT CONVEYANCE — RIGHTS OF CREDITORS—KNOWLEDGE OF FRAUD.

A deed of trust, given to secure creditors of the grantor, who act in good faith, and without notice either to them or the trustee that the goods conveyed by the deed were obtained by the grantor by fraud, will not be set aside at the suit of the creditors from whom the goods were so obtained.

Appeal from hustings court of Staunton.

Bill by Meyer, Reinhardt & Co. against M. B. Oberdorfer and others for an injunction and the appointment of a receiver, and to set aside as fraudulent a deed of trust given by said Oberdorfer to secure certain debts specified therein. Among the goods covered by the deed of trust were some which Oberdorfer had a short time before obtained from complainants on credit, by false and fraudulent representations. A commissioner, to whom the cause was referred, reported that the deed of trust was valid, and the debts therein secured bona fide. The court, however, on complainants' exception to the commissioners' report, held the deed of trust invalid. Defendants appeal. Reversed.

A. C. Gordon, for appellants. A. C. Braxton and Geo. M. Cochran, for appellees.

LEWIS, P. It is clear from the evidence that the complainants' goods were obtained by fraud, as charged in the bill; and, if this were a contest between them and the fraudulent buyer alone, their right to reclaim the goods would be unquestionable. But, unfortunately for them, rights of third persons have intervened, which presents a very different case; for the doctrine is now established, both in England and Virginia, that a sale of goods, although the owner has been fraudulently induced to make it, passes the title to the vendee. The contract, however, in such a case is voidable, at the election of the vendor, as against the vendee, but not a subsequent bona fide purchaser for value; that is to say, the vendor, on discovery of the fraud, may disaffirm the contract, and reclaim the goods, provided they have not passed into the hands of a bona fide purchaser. The latter, buying, as he does, without notice of the fraud, is protected on the principle that when one of two innocent persons must suffer by the fraud of a third the loss shall fall on him who has enabled such third person to do the wrong. 1 Benj. Sales, (6th Amer. Ed.) § 648; Williams v. Given, 6 Grat. 268; Wickham v. Martin, 13 Grat. 427; Steam-Ship Co. v. Burckhardt, 31 Grat. 664; Donaldson v. Farwell, 93 U. S. 631. The case of Wickham v. Martin is much like the present. There an insolvent merchant, fraudulently misrepresenting his pecuniary condition, purchased goods, not intending to pay for them, and afterwards conveyed them in trust for the benefit of creditors, the trustee and beneficiaries in the deed having no notice of the fraud. This court decided that the trustee, as an innocent purchaser, took an indefeasible title, which entitled him to recover the value of the goods in an action of trover against the original vendors, who, after the date of the deed, had obtained possession of the goods. This principle is decisive here, for there is no proof, nor is it even charged, that the trustee or beneficiaries in the deed had notice of the fraud by which the purchase of the goods was effected; nor is it proved that they were privy to or colluded with the grantor in accomplishing a fraud, if in fact there was any such design on his part when the deed was executed. So that the case is not within the condemnation of the statute of fraudulent conveyances, which enacts expressly that nothing therein shall affect the title of a purchaser for valuable consideration unless it appear that he had notice of the fraudulent intent of his immediate grantor, or of the fraud rendering void the title of such grantor. Code, § 2458; 2 Minor, Inst. 602; Paul v. Baugh, 85 Va. 955, 9 S. E. Rep. 329; Jones v. Christian, 86 Va. 1017, 11 S. E. Rep. 984. It is true the deed was drawn by Craig, the trustee therein, and after, as counsel of the grantor, he had made an examination into his affairs; but nothing, for aught the record shows, was disclosed by that examination sufficient to charge him with notice of any fraudulent intent, if any such existed. He soon discovered, as he testifies, that the grantor was, and for some time had been, insolvent; but that circumstance was in itself no bar to a valid assignment, with preferences as between creditors. He also knew, when he drew the deed, that the remnant of the goods which had shortly before been purchased from the complainants was embraced in the assignment, and that the goods had not been paid for. But that circumstance does not vitiate the deed, especially as he knew nothing of the circumstances under which the goods had been purchased. Nor was there anything to justly awaken suspicion, or to put a reasonably prudent man on further inquiry as to the bona fides of the debts due the grantor's father and brother-in-law, respectively, and which were put in a preferred class. In fact, they have since been reported by the commissioner as bona fide, and the question has not as yet been passed on by the lower court. The trustee, moreover, testifies that the grantor was averse to making an assignment; that he tried, but without success, to borrow money with which to tide over his embarrassment; and that he consented to make an assignment only after his real situa-

tion had been fully explained to him. He says further that, the season being late, cold, and wet, he (the grantor) was disappointed in making sales sufficient to meet his obligations, which were then about to fall due, for goods purchased the previous year, and that he advised him that, unless an assignment was made, his friends who had loaned him money would be "left out in the cold," and that he ought to protect them in preference to other creditors. Pursuant to this advice, he says, the assignment was made. In short, we are of opinion that the alleged invalidity of the deed is not established by the evidence, and that, to this extent, the decree must be reversed.

CENTRAL RAILROAD & BANKING CO. v. CURTIS.

CURTIS v. CENTRAL RAILROAD & BANKING CO.

(Supreme Court of Georgia. July 3, 1891.)

FILING BRIEF OF EVIDENCE — CONTINUANCE — NEWLY-DISCOVERED EVIDENCE—INJURY AT RAILROAD CROSSING.

1. The court has power to pass an order during term allowing until the hearing of the motion to file the brief of evidence; and if the hearing by subsequent order be regularly continued from one time in vacation to another, the case having in term been set down for hearing in vacation, the judge may approve and allow the brief of evidence to be filed at or before the hearing, though he may not be absolutely bound to do so. But *quære*, where the act of 1889 is applicable and insisted upon, must not all briefs of evidence be filed within 30 days after the trial?

2. There was no abuse of discretion in denying a continuance on account of the discovery of evidence pending the trial, it not appearing then or afterwards, otherwise than by hearsay, that the newly-discovered witness could or would testify to any material fact whatever, the party or his counsel not having had any personal communication with him.

3. It is discretionary with the court to reopen a case for the re-examination of a witness.

4. It is negligence *per se* for a railroad company, in violation of a valid municipal ordinance, to obstruct with standing cars or locomotives a public street or space in actual daily use by the public; and that the municipality may have acquiesced passively in violations of the ordinance will not excuse such negligence.

5. The various rulings complained of in other grounds of the motion are not cause for a new trial.

(Syllabus by the Court.)

Cross-errors from superior court, Houston county; A. L. MILLER, Judge.

C. M. Curtis sued the Central Railroad & Banking Company of Georgia for damages for personal injuries. Judgment for plaintiff. Both parties excepted, and brought error. Affirmed.

The following is the official report:

Curtis brought his action for damages for personal injuries against the railroad company, alleging, in brief: He was traveling along a public street in the town of Ft. Valley, driving a horse hitched to his buggy or cart and leading another horse, and as he neared the public crossing where the railway crossed the street, it being the principal crossing in the town and in the business part thereof, a train of cars was standing completely obstructing the crossing, which compelled him to stop and wait; that while so waiting the train was divided, the engine moving from the train, leaving a car towards the left of the street, near to and just missing the usual wagon route, and extending into the street, the engine moving just to the right of the wagon-way, but stopping in the street, leaving only a narrow way for vehicles to pass through, and obstructing much of the street, in violation of the town ordinances, which made it unlawful for any train, engine, or cars to obstruct any street for longer than five minutes; that this obstruction was maintained for more than ten minutes, which petitioner knew; that seeing this way open, and not knowing when the locomotive or car would be moved, and having waited, and knowing from the nature of his horses, which were of ordinary gentleness, that he could safely pass between the car and the locomotive, he began to drive along the highway across the crossing, and when he had reached the track, and was between the car and the locomotive, the employes of defendant, without using all ordinary and reasonable care and diligence, suddenly, and without warning, let off steam from the locomotive, (which was standing with the pilot towards the opening,) and it began puffing, which, together with the close proximity of the locomotive and car, frightened his horses, causing one or both of them to rear and plunge, and the led horse became entangled in the vehicle, and from the fright and unmanageableness of his horses, from which he was then and there thrown and injured, etc. No plea of defendant appears in the record. The jury found for the plaintiff, and during the term at which the verdict was rendered defendant moved for a new trial on various grounds. The judge presiding passed an order that plaintiff or his counsel show cause, during the term or as soon as counsel could be heard, why the motion should not be granted, and that defendant have until the hearing to perfect and amend the motion by adding other grounds if it desired, and that defendant have until the hearing to make out and perfect brief of evidence in the case. Afterwards, during the same term, the defendant applied for and obtained an order from the judge then presiding (a different judge from the judge before whom the case was tried) that, it appearing that the motion could not be heard during the term, it was ordered that it be continued to November 15th, to be then heard before him; that plaintiff or his counsel show cause before him on that date why the new trial should not be granted, and in the mean time this order to operate as a supersedeas. On November 15th, at chambers, the hearing of the cause was continued until November 22d, by order of the judge, and it was ordered that movant have until that time to complete and perfect the motion for new trial and brief of evidence, and to give notice of this hearing to counsel for defendant. It was recited in this order that the brief of evidence and motion for new trial had been already prepared and put in the

hands of the judge who presided in the cause for approval, and that this continuance was made because of inability of counsel for defendant to be present on account of engagements in other courts. The hearing was again continued from the 22d of November until the 6th day of December, and in the order of continuance it was ordered that the movant have until the 5th day of December to perfect the motion and brief of evidence. On the 6th of December it was again continued to the 20th of December, and it was ordered that the parties have until that time to agree on or perfect the motion and brief of evidence. On December 20th the hearing was again continued to the 3d day of January, 1891. The brief of evidence was agreed to by counsel on November 19, 1890, and was approved, at chambers, December 20, 1890, and ordered filed in the clerk's office as the brief of evidence. All of the above continuances were made at chambers, except the first mentioned. The continuances, except the first named, were by consent of counsel, counsel for Curtis reserving the right to take exceptions to any defects in the proceedings. When the motion came on to be heard on January 3d, counsel for Curtis moved to dismiss it, on the ground that the order continuing the cause to a hearing in vacation had never been agreed to by Curtis or his counsel, nor had they been served in any manner when that order was signed, and that said order gave no right or privilege to movant to file a brief of evidence during vacation, which brief was never perfected or filed until after the adjournment of the court. The judge overruled both the motion to dismiss and the motion for new trial. The railroad company excepted to the overruling its motion, and Curtis, by cross-bill, excepted to the overruling his motion to dismiss.

In the motion for new trial, in addition to the usual grounds, that the verdict was contrary to law, evidence, etc., it was alleged that the court erred in refusing to continue the case, on the motion of defendant's counsel, made after the evidence had been closed on both sides, and after one of the counsel for plaintiff had made his opening argument to the jury. In making the motion counsel for defendant said that he had on that morning discovered a witness whose evidence would be, in his opinion, material, and that he did not know or hear of it until that morning; that the witness' name was Eb Everett; and from what Everett's uncle told counsel that morning Everett would swear, from what Everett told his uncle, that the way and track were entirely open and unobstructed when Curtis attempted to cross; that when he got nearly across, his horse hesitated for some cause, and he struck him with his whip, and the horse jumped, and that jerked him back, and the other horse commenced rearing, and got excited, and that was the way it happened; that this witness was not present, but counsel thought his uncle stated that he was employed by the S. A. & M. R. R.; that counsel had no knowledge of the existence of this witness himself; that the management and preparation of the case had been entirely in the hands of himself and the local counsel, and he had had no communication whatever from the officers or employes that would lead them to expect the existence of this witness, the only information he had about it being what Everett's uncle told him, and he could have the uncle brought in and sworn if desired. The local counsel stated that he had no knowledge of what Everett would swear, and did not know that he was a witness; that it was his (local counsel's) business to look up the witnesses, and prepare the case, but Everett was not in the town at the time the case was prepared. He had gone to Americus, and no one else had had charge of the case but the local counsel. After hearing these statements, and there being no dispute as to the facts stated, the court refused to continue, and went on with the case. In connection with the ground of the motion as to the refusal to continue the case, the presiding judge states that counsel stated that their informant was in town, or was near, that morning, but made no effort to produce him, though the court had him called; and, in an affidavit produced at the hearing of the motion, counsel for the defendant stated that after he had moved for the continuance, and after his informant had been called, he (counsel) ran out of the court-house, and made most diligent search for his informant, so as to produce him in court, but could not find him, and did not until the trial was over. It was also alleged that the court erred in refusing to allow defendant to reopen the case, after both sides had announced closed, and counsel for plaintiff had made the opening argument, to question one of plaintiff's witnesses as to the distance of the locomotive from the crossing, stating that the witness would testify that the locomotive was some distance from the crossing; that he wanted to show that the engine was not near the track, but was some 50 yards away; and that there was no such obstruction as claimed. Counsel also stated that he, or his associate counsel, he thought, knew of this fact, and that it could have been proved by this witness when this witness was on the stand, but his associate had neglected to call his attention to it, and he had omitted to ask the question, if he had known it. In connection with this ground, it is stated that this witness was subpœnaed and put upon the stand by defendant, and examined as to what he knew in the matter, and as to what he saw in connection with it, and that a night had intervened between the time the case was announced closed and the time when counsel asked to reopen the case and examine this witness.

It was also alleged that the court erred in refusing to charge, as requested by defendant: "If the defendant left enough of the street open and unobstructed to give plaintiff a safe crossing, and in attempting to cross was injured by no act or fault of defendant, he is not entitled to recover." "If the corporation permitted the defendant to occupy all of the street, except the road that was usually traveled, notwithstanding the ordinance, such permission operated as a license." It was also al-

leged that the court erred in charging: "The defendant denies its liability, and says by its plea it is guilty of no act of negligence, and this, under our procedure, makes the issue which you are to pass on;" the error assigned being that the effect of this charge was to imply that any act of negligence by the defendant would render it liable, without reference to any negligent conduct on the part of the plaintiff. Also that the court erred in charging the language of section 3033 of the Code; the error assigned being that the damage suffered by plaintiff was shown by the evidence to be not the result of the running of the locomotive, etc., of the company, but of plaintiff's own careless and imprudent conduct. Also that the court erred in charging: "It would be negligence, as matter of law, for the defendant to disregard a requirement of a valid municipal ordinance of the town of Ft. Valley as to obstructing the public crossway of that town. If the defendant was negligent in this respect, and if such negligence was the cause of the plaintiff's injuries, and if the plaintiff could not, by ordinary care and diligence, have avoided the consequences to himself caused by defendant's negligence, the plaintiff would be entitled to recover." "If the jury believe the plaintiff's act in attempting to cross was the act of a prudent man, and plaintiff endeavored prudently to cross said crossing, and sustained injuries while crossing, which were the result of defendant's failing to comply with a valid municipal ordinance passed by the municipal authorities, and by ordinary care could not have avoided the consequences of defendant's negligence, then I charge you plaintiff would be entitled to recover;" the error assigned being that there was no evidence that the violation of any ordinance of the town was the cause of plaintiff's damage. Also that the court erred in stating to the jury in the opening of his charge the following, as the case upon which plaintiff relied to recover: "The plaintiff sought to cross this road, the defendant's road, at Ft. Valley, at the public crossing in this county, and while endeavoring to cross, they not having complied with the regulations made by the town of Ft. Valley, for the crossing was blocked, he sustained certain injuries;" the error assigned being that this was an incorrect statement of the case as made by the declaration. And that the court in the same connection erred in stating the defense as follows: "The defendant denies any liability, and says by its plea it is not guilty of negligence, and this, under our proceeding, makes the issue which you are to try and determine." It is alleged in this ground of the motion that defendant claimed that the ordinance had nothing to do with plaintiff's recovery, and that the street was not so obstructed but that he could have passed with safety had he exercised ordinary care; and that while he was crossing he struck his horse, which caused the horse to jump, and the other horse, which he was leading, to plunge, and together they threw the buggy over, and knocked plaintiff out; and, further, that if the crossing, under the circumstances, was dangerous, it was gross carelessness on plaintiff's part to attempt to cross, driving one horse and leading another; that this was the defendant's reply, which was before the jury, and not put in by the court, and the court misstated the issues, and in doing so misled the jury, placing the whole stress of the case on the violation of the ordinance, and not as to the real issue made by the pleadings; also, that the court erred in not stating the defense, it not being true that the defense was put solely upon the ground that defendant was not guilty of negligence, but it was put also upon the ground that, if it were guilty of negligence, plaintiff might have avoided the result of that negligence by the exercise of ordinary care and diligence on his part, which he had not done, and that plaintiff's injury was the result of his own negligence. Also that the court erred in charging: "It is the province of the jury to pass upon the question of negligence, and say whether defendant's servants or agents have been negligent or not, and say whether the defendant has been negligent." It is alleged that this was error, in that it did not fairly and fully state the issue on which the jury was to pass in this connection. Also that the court erred in charging that it would be negligence as matter of law for defendant to disregard a requirement of a valid municipal ordinance of the town of Ft. Valley as to obstructing the public crossings of the town; and that the court, after thus charging, erred in not qualifying the charge, to the effect that if defendant had not obstructed the whole of the street so as to prevent a crossing at that place, and the city of Ft. Valley had, by acquiescence, permitted the railroad to occupy a part of the street longer than five minutes, notwithstanding the existence of that ordinance, and requiring it only to keep open enough of the street to enable persons to cross at that point, then partially obstructing the street would not be negligence as a matter of law. Also that the court erred in charging: "If, in crossing the track at the public crossing, the jury believe the plaintiff's act in attempting to cross was the act of a prudent man, and plaintiff endeavored prudently to cross said crossing, and sustained injuries while crossing, which were the result of defendant's failing to comply with a valid municipal ordinance passed by the municipal authorities, and by ordinary care could not have avoided the consequences of defendant's negligence, then I charge you plaintiff would be entitled to recover;" it being alleged that this was error, because not authorized by any evidence, because containing an intimation of an opinion as to the evidence, because the court took it for granted that the defendant was guilty of negligence; and the charge was calculated to mislead the jury, was one-sided, giving the case to the plaintiff, and took away from the jury the right to determine whether the facts amounted to negligence, and whether it was such negligence as gave plaintiff the right to recover. In the main bill of exceptions it is stated that the brief of evidence was agreed on, approved, and ordered of file in the clerk's office, and that plaintiff in error prayed that the court cause to be sent up as parts of the record, which were necessary to a clear understanding of the errors complained of, with other things specified, the whole of the brief of evidence as agreed upon and approved by the court. The judge's certificate to this bill of exceptions is in the usual form, except that it does not state that the bill of exceptions contains or specifies all of the evidence material to a clear understanding of the errors complained of. In the cross-bill of exceptions it is alleged that the plaintiff in error in the main bill of exceptions had specially set out the motion for new trial, the different orders of the court setting the motion and continuing the same, and the judgment of the court overruling the motion, and that plaintiff in the cross-bill simply prayed reference thereto. The certificate of the judge to the cross-bill of exceptions was similar to his certificate to the main bill.

R. F. Lyon, for plaintiff. W. C. Winslow and Hardeman & Nottingham, for defendant.

BLECKLEY, C. J. 1. Under the orders taken in this case, (for the substance of which see the official report,) the judge who heard the motion for a new trial had power to approve the brief of evidence, and allow it to be filed at or before the hearing. He may not have been bound to do so after the lapse of so long a time since the trial, for in such matters a judge may, in the exercise of a sound discretion, construe the terms of an order strictly or liberally, adopting the one construction or the other according as the ends of justice may require, in the light of all the attendant circumstances. Independently of the orders made in this particular case, the time of filing the brief would be governed by the forty-ninth rule of practice in the superior courts, (Code, p. 1352,) which reads thus: "In every application for a new trial, a brief of the testimony in the cause shall be filed by the party applying for such new trial, under the revision and approval of the court. If, pending the motion, the presiding judge shall die, or a vacancy otherwise occur, then his successor shall hear and determine the motion from the best evidence at his command." It will be observed that the rule does not expressly designate or fix any time, but the practice under it has usually been to file the brief with the motion, or during the same term of the court, unless further time be granted by special order. The power to regulate the time by such orders, according to the discretion of the court, has been considered as unlimited. Whether a limit of 30 days after the trial has not been imposed by the act of November 12, 1889, (Acts 1889, p. 83,) as to all cases to which that act applies, need not be discussed, for the present is one of the cases pending when it was passed, and is consequently not within its operation. Very probably, under that statute, as perfect a brief as can be gotten ready within the 30 days must, in each case, be approved and filed before that period has elapsed, leaving the necessary additions to be made by subsequent amendment. Only in rare instances will diligent counsel need to invoke the aid of the amending power. But the proper construction of the new statute has now no immediate relevancy, and is not meant to be dealt with further than to indicate a query.

2, 3. There was no abuse of discretion in denying the motion for a continuance, nor in declining to reopen the case for a further examination of one of the defendant's witnesses after the evidence had been closed and the opening argument made by counsel for the plaintiff. It is needless to amplify the head-notes on these topics.

4. The ordinance of Ft. Valley made it unlawful to obstruct any public street of the town for more than five minutes by any engine, car, or train of cars. We can perceive no reason why this ordinance was not valid and obligatory. The violation of it was negligence *per se*, and the charge of the court on that subject was correct. We agree with the court in thinking the ordinance had something to do with the case, and that the evidence warranted its consideration by the jury. It was not for the railway company or its servants to determine how wide the street on which this disaster occurred ought to be, or how much of it ought to be left open and unobstructed. That was a question for decision by the town council in the enactment of the ordinance. The ordinance, by its terms, applies to the whole street; and the street certainly includes all the space that was in actual, daily use as a passway by the public. Nor would mere passive acquiescence of the municipality in violations of the ordinance furnish any excuse for continuing to violate it, or for the negligence involved in so doing In the face of such an ordinance, the company cannot justify itself by showing that it left room enough in the street for vehicles to pass, and that it had frequently or habitually occupied the street in the same way without remonstrance from the town authorities, and without being prosecuted or otherwise proceeded against for its conduct. Forbearance to enforce a law neither repeals it, nor confers a license to break it with impunity. If the public street was unlawfully obstructed, and if that obstruction was the proximate cause of the plaintiff's injury, why should he not have redress? The question of negligence on his part, and of his power to shun the injury by the exercise of ordinary care, was fairly submitted for determination by the jury.

5. There are many grounds in the motion for a new trial, but in view of the evidence, and of the full charge of the court, a copy of which is in the record, we discover no cause for reversing the judgment. The "air" of the movant's case being out of harmony with the law, it would be a needless consumption of time to follow all the variations, some of them very minute, which ramify through the motion. The verdict was warranted, and should not be set aside. Judgment affirmed.

LUMPKIN, J., not presiding.

WEIL et al. v. FLOWERS.

(*Supreme Court of North Carolina.* Oct. 27, 1891.)

CHATTEL MORTGAGE ON CROP—DESCRIPTION—APPLICATION OF PAYMENTS.

1. A chattel mortgage on "all my entire crop, now growing or to be grown the present year on my own land," describes with sufficient certainty the property intended to be mortgaged; but a further description, covering the crop which the mortgagor might raise on "any other land," is too indefinite, because it points to no particular land.

2. A chattel mortgage on a growing crop and other property, given to secure a note executed by the mortgagor and future advances to be made on the crop, empowered the mortgagees to sell the crop, and apply the proceeds in payment of the advances and the note. Held, that the acceptance by the mortgagees of a second mortgage, covering property already embraced in the first mortgage, as security for another debt, did not modify the provision in the first mortgage as to the application of payments; and a direction by the mortgagor that the mortgagees apply the proceeds of the crop to the payment of the debt secured by the second mortgage was not binding on them.

Appeal from superior court, Wayne county; ROBERT W. WINSTON, Judge.

This action is brought to recover the personal property specified in the complaint, the plaintiffs availing themselves of the provisional remedy of claim and delivery. The plaintiffs allege their title to and right to have possession of the property particularly specified. The defendant in his answer denies the material allegations of the complaint. The court submitted to the jury, among others, this issue, to which they responded, "No:" "(1) Are the plaintiffs owners of the property in dispute, or any part thereof?" On the trial the plaintiffs put in evidence a paper writing, whereof the following is a copy: "Know all men by these presents, that I, R. B. Flowers, (farmer,) of Wayne county and state of North Carolina, for and in consideration of the sum of five dollars, to me advanced by H. Weil & Bros., (merchants of said county,) and in consideration of further advances promised to be made by said H. Weil & Bros. during the year, from time to time, not to exceed the sum of two hundred dollars, the better to enable me to make a crop the present year, have bargained, sold, and assigned, and by these presents do bargain, sell, and assign, unto said H. Weil & Bros., all my entire crop now growing or to be grown the present year, on my own land, or on any other land I may cultivate the present year, of cotton, corn, fodder, peas, rice, and other agricultural products, and hereby promise, covenant, and agree to transfer, set over, and deliver the same, or as much thereof as may be necessary to pay for said advances, on or by the 15th day of October, 1888, to said H. Weil & Bros., to be by them sold for cash, and the proceeds of such sale to be applied to the payment of such advances, and any balance remaining they are to apply to a note of $876, given H. Weil & Bros., January 1, 1885. And the said R. B. Flowers, in consideration of the premises above set forth, hereby sells and conveys to said H. Weil & Bros. the following articles of personal property, to-wit, one black mare mule 12 years old, one cow and two heifers, three sows and three pigs and their increase, one wagon, two carts, one buggy and harness, and my entire interest in the crops of my tenants, renters, and croppers for the year 1888, either for rent or guano or supplies I may furnish them, and one cotton-gin and press, —all of which the party of the first part represents to be his own right and property, and that no other person has any claim on the same; with the agreement, nevertheless, that if the said R. B. Flowers shall pay said H. Weil & Bros. for all such advances as they may make said R. B. Flowers in pursuance of this agreement, on or by the 15th day of October, 1888, as aforesaid, then this agreement, and every part thereof, to be void; and, on failure of the said R. B. Flowers to pay said H. Weil & Bros. by the said 15th day of October, they are hereby authorised and empowered to take possession of said crops and personal property, and sell the same, or so much thereof as will satisfy said debt and all necessary expenses, and the balance, if any, apply to said note of $876. It is further agreed and understood that if the party of the first part should from any cause fail to cultivate said crops, or do any act, the effect of which would defeat the objects of this conveyance, then the party of the second part shall not be obliged to make any further advances, and the indebtedness already incurred shall become due and collectible at once, in the manner hereinbefore provided. In witness whereof the said R. B. Flowers hath hereunto set his hand and seal this 13th day of February, 1888. [Signed] R. B. FLOWERS. [Seal.] Witness: JOHN H. POWELL." The defendant objected "to so much of the crop lien or chattel mortgage [that just recited] as refers to the crops, on the ground that no sufficient description of the crop is given. Objection sustained, and the plaintiffs except." The plaintiffs then put in evidence a note of defendant to them for $876, dated January 1, 1885, and due November 1, 1885. They also put in evidence the defendant's other note to them for $135, to be due on the 15th day of November, 1888, which was secured by a chattel mortgage executed on the 17th of February, 1888. This mortgage purported to convey to the plaintiffs certain property therein described, as follows: "One mouse-colored horse mule and one black mare mule, and all my crop of cotton, corn, fodder, peas, etc., to be raised or grown by me the present year, 1888; also all the interest I have or may have in the crops of my tenants for the year 1888." The defendant contended that he had paid for all advancements made to him in pursuance of the above set forth agricultural lien, and likewise the debt secured by the last-mentioned chattel mortgage. The plaintiffs contended, on the other hand, that the last-mentioned note had not been paid; that the payments made by the defendant with proceeds of cotton embraced by the agricultural lien had been applied, and properly, to the payment of advancements made under the lien, and to payment in part of the note therein mentioned for $876. The

defendant testified that he had instructed the plaintiffs to apply the payments made by him to the discharge of debt for advancements and the note for $135 secured by the chattel mortgage.

The court, among other things, instructed the jury as follows: "That the inquiry was whether the $135 note had been paid. (1) A debtor owing several debts has a right to apply the payments to any one of them, but this right must be exercised when the money is paid; otherwise the creditor has the right to make the application. (2) If the jury believe that at the time R. B. Flowers made these different payments which the plaintiffs admit he made he directed the plaintiffs to apply the same to the mule note, they ought to have been so applied." The plaintiffs requested the court to charge: "(1) That in the absence of a special agreement at the time of the payments spoken of or thereafter to apply them differently, the law would apply them to the $876 note. (2) That there could be no agreement to apply said payments differently unless assented to by the plaintiffs, and there is no evidence of such assent." The first of the foregoing instructions was given by his honor, and the second refused, and the plaintiffs excepted. Plaintiffs excepted: "(1) To the first instruction given by his honor, upon the ground that it was inconsistent with the special instruction prayed for by the plaintiffs and given by his honor; and, further, upon the ground that said instruction, while true as an abstract proposition of law, was not applicable to the facts in the case." There was a verdict for defendant. The plaintiffs appealed to this court. Reversed.

Allen & Dortch, for appellants. *W. C. Munroe,* for appellee.

MERRIMON, C. J., *(after stating the facts.)* The first exception must be sustained. The description of the crops in the agricultural lien as "all my entire crop now growing or to be grown the present year on my own land," designated with sufficient certainty the land and also the crops intended to be conveyed. They could by such description be ascertained. The other words, "or on any other land," were too indefinite, because they pointed to no particular lands. The lands of the maker of the lien, at the time he executed it, could be seen and known; those that he might cultivate could not. Woodlief v. Harris, 95 N. C. 211; Gwathney v. Etheridge, 99 N. C. 571, 6 S. E. Rep. 411; State v. Logan, 100 N. C. 454, 6 S. E. Rep. 898; Brown v. Miller, 108 N. C. 395, 13 S. E. Rep. 167; Rountree v. Britt, 94 N. C. 104.

We are also of opinion that the court should have instructed the jury that the plaintiffs had the right, by virtue of provisions of the agricultural lien, to apply the money, the proceeds of the cotton or other property embraced by it, after paying the debt for advancements, to the payment of the note therein specified. The agricultural lien was not simply such. It took on and possessed the qualities of a chattel mortgage as to the note, and expressly provided that any surplus above the payment for advancements should be applied to the payment of the note so far as the same might be adequate. Such provision might be made in such lien. An agricultural lien may contain a mortgage provision. Rawlings v. Hunt, 90 N. C. 270. The subsequent chattel mortgage to secure the note for $130 mentioned did not have the effect to change or modify the provision for paying the note above referred to. Though this mortgage embraced the same property that the lien embraced, it was made subsequent and subject to the lien, and all the provisions therein contained, in the absence of any modifying provision. It did not, in terms or by implication, modify the lien. As to the large note specified in the latter, it was a second mortgage subject to the first. The mere fact that the plaintiffs took the second mortgage did not, in legal effect, modify the provision for the large note in the first one. There is nothing in the second mortgage that shows such purpose; nor was there any evidence of agreement, by parol or otherwise, to modify the first mortgage provision in the lien. The court ought not, therefore, to have told the jury that the defendant had the right to direct the application of the money to the note embraced by the second mortgage, and they might find that he gave such instruction to the plaintiffs. The evidence went to prove that the plaintiffs had the right to apply the payment made as above stated, and there was no evidence to the contrary. There is therefore error. The plaintiffs are entitled to a new trial. To that end let this opinion be certified to the superior court. It is so ordered.

BENTON v. TOLER.

(*Supreme Court of North Carolina.* Oct. 27, 1891.)

EVIDENCE OF PAYMENT—QUESTION FOR JURY.

In an action against defendant for $354 due plaintiff's intestate, where there was evidence tending to show that defendant had nearly paid the whole claim during the life-time of deceased, the jury were the judges as to the amount paid, and it was error for the court to instruct them that they could not find that defendant had paid more than $96.

Appeal from superior court, Johnston county; SPIER WHITAKER, Judge.

Action by J. H. Benton, administrator, against Toler, to recover money alleged to be due plaintiff's intestate. Verdict for plaintiff. Defendant moved for a new trial, which was denied, and he appealed. Reversed.

STATEMENT BY THE COURT. The plaintiff alleges, in substance, that the defendant executed to his intestate four several bonds set out in the complaint amounting in the aggregate to $254.45, with interest from the date mentioned, and that at the death of his intestate said bonds were found among his valuable papers, with no payments or credits indorsed on either of them, and he demands judgment for payment of said debt and interest. The defendant answers, and admits the execution of the notes, but says all except the note for $25 has been paid; and the following was the only issue submitted to the jury: What amount, if any, has the defendant paid on the notes set out in the complaint? The following evidence is material to the question on appeal: William Stafford, a witness for the defendant, testified that he had a conversation with plaintiff's intestate the August before he died; that he told him to tell Toler (the defendant) to come to see him; that he (Toler) had about paid for his land, and that he wanted to cancel and give up to Toler his papers; that he knew of Toler's paying intestate one bag of cotton that brought $51. D. W. Fuller, a witness for defendant, testified that, some time before the death of the intestate, the intestate told him that Toler had nearly paid for his land. Witness had a mortgage on Toler's crop and personal property. J. E. Thornton, a witness for defendant, testified that he had a conversation with the intestate shortly before his death, in which he said Toler had nearly paid him for his land. D. B. Lanham, a witness for the defendant, testified that he saw Toler pay intestate $9 on December 24, 1885, from the sale of two hogs. John B. Parish testified that the average weight of a bale of cotton was 440 pounds, and the average price for the years 1885, 1886, and 1887 was 9½ cents per pound. N. B. Smith testified that Toler came to him since Benton's death, and swore to his account against Benton, amounting to about $200. S. A. Smith testified that Toler, in a conversation with him about his land, said he could not settle with Benton until he had sworn to his account; that he had paid upwards of $200, and was sorry he had paid anything, as he was afraid he would lose it. The plaintiff introduced the notes mentioned in the complaints. They had no credits on them. V. A. Benton, the widow of the intestate, testified, so far as material to the question before this court, that the defendant paid one bale of cotton in 1879; that he sometimes sold her husband chickens, for which he was paid cash, as he said the chickens belonged to his wife; that he brought pork three times, but none since the beginning of 1883; that the defendant brought cotton one time only, and that was in 1879; that in January, in 1887, the first note had not been paid, or she never knew of any payment; that the pork went on the note, also the lard, some hams in 1882 and 1883, and two cows, at $18 each, or $36 for the two, in 1882-83. "His honor instructed the jury that the burden was on the defendant, and having pleaded payment, it was necessary for him to prove it; that in answering the issue submitted to them they might say as much as $96, that is, the $9 as testified to by the witness Lanham, the one bale of cotton at $57 as testified to by the witness Stafford, and the two cows at $18 each, if they were so satisfied by the evidence, but they could not find any greater payment than $96, to which the defendant excepted." The jury responded to the issue, "$96." The defendant moved for a new trial, on the ground of error in his honor's instruction as above stated. The motion was refused, and the defendant appealed.

Pou & Pou, for appellant.

DAVIS, J. The burden of proof of payment was on the defendant, and his honor instructed the jury that "they could not find any greater payment than $96." If there was any evidence, in the most favorable view of it for the defendant, that more than $96 had been paid, it was a question for the jury, and not for the court, to say how much had been paid. It was in evidence that the intestate, the August before he died, sent word to the defendant to come to see him; that he, the defendant, had about paid for his land, and he wanted to cancel and give up Toler his papers. Fuller testified that some time before the intestate's death, he told him that the defendant had nearly paid for his land. Thornton testified that the intestate, shortly before his death, said that Toler had nearly paid for his land. The witness Stafford testified to the delivery of one bale of cotton, and the widow of the intestate testified to the delivery of one bale in 1879. Whether there was only one bale delivered was a question for the jury. The widow of the intestate testified that the defendant brought pork three times, and that the pork went on the note; also the lard and some hams. It was in evidence, without objection, that Toler said Benton, the plaintiff, would not settle until he swore to his account; that he said that his account against the intestate was upwards of $200, and that he swore to his account. There was evidence, taking it in its most favorable aspect for the defendant, tending to show that more than $96 had been paid by him, and, though it may be difficult to say just how much was paid, that difficulty is for the jury, and not for the court. The court cannot weigh the evidence, and declare the result as a matter of law to the jury. State v. Locke, 77 N. C. 481. It is too well settled to need citation of authority that, if there was any evidence of a greater payment than $96, it should be left to the jury. Besides competent evidence, the declaration of the deceased was before the jury without objection, and, for the purpose of deciding the question before us, it must be taken as competent and true. Gibbs v. Lyon, 95 N. C. 147. The defendant was illiterate, as it appears upon the face of the record that he used a mark in signing his name. He had executed to the plaintiff's intestate four notes, aggregating $254.48, two of them for $100 each, on the 9th day of February, 1878, for land, payable, respectively, January 1, 1880 and 1881. It is in evidence, and not controverted, that the defendant made payments from time to time in cotton, pork, lard, hams, and cows, for none of which was credit indorsed on the note; and, if the witnesses are to be believed, the plaintiff's intestate himself said, more than once, shortly before his death, that the defendant had nearly paid for his land, for which the bulk of the debt was created. If it be said that the defendant ought to have taken receipts, may it not be as truly said that the creditor, in whom it is to be presumed from the facts he confided, ought to have given credit? If it appear that the debt was nearly all paid, can the debtor get credit for no payment, unless he can show just how many dollars and cents were paid, and when? His honor should have left the question of payment to the jury upon the whole evidence, with proper instructions, and there was error in telling them that they could find a payment of $96, and no more. Error.

McMILLAN et al. v. PARKER et al.

(Supreme Court of North Carolina. Oct. 27, 1891.)

EXECUTION SALE OF HOMESTEAD — ENFORCEMENT OF MECHANIC'S LIEN — ALLOTMENT OF HOMESTEAD.

1. A purchaser at execution sale of land which the judgment debtor claims exempt as his homestead has the burden of showing that he is within Const. N. C. art. 10, § 4, which permits the sale of a homestead to satisfy a mechanic's lien; and where the record of the action in which the execution was issued shows that the action was brought for work and labor, and the judgment itself contains nothing showing that it was obtained in proceedings to enforce a mechanic's lien, a recital in the execution, commanding the officer to sell the property owned by the judgment debtor at the time plaintiffs "filed their lien," is not sufficient to show that the sale took place to enforce a mechanic's lien.

2. A homestead may lawfully be assigned to a partner out of partnership property; and, where all the partners gave their assent at the time of the allotment, a creditor of the partnership cannot attack the validity of the proceedings, and subject the land assigned to a judgment in his favor.

Appeal from superior court, Harnett county; EDWIN T. BOYKIN, Judge.

Civil action by McMillan Bros. against Parker & Williams for the possession of land. Judgment for defendants, and plaintiffs appeal. Affirmed.

STATEMENT BY THE COURT. The plaintiffs relied upon a sheriff's deed for the land in dispute, and offered the record of a civil action before a justice of the peace in which the judgment was obtained, which was afterwards docketed in the superior court, and with it the execution issued thereon, levy, and sale, by virtue of which the sheriff executed the deed. The account declared upon before the justice of the peace was as follows: "For labor done in November, December, and January in the years 1887 and 1888, to the amount of $128.82. The defendant appears in court and confesses judgment, and the court adjudges that the defendant pay to the plaintiff the sum of $128.82, and the further sum of all costs," etc. Signed, "B. F. Smith, J. P." The plaintiffs relied upon a laborer's lien to authorize the sale of the land without allotting the homestead. The lien filed was in the following form:

"The said McMillan Bros. file this lien against the said C. T. Williams and S. W. Parker, in the office of the clerk of the superior court of Harnett county, N. C., in and for said county. Said lien is for work and labor on the two houses of C. T. Williams and S. W. Parker, as per bill of particulars herewith filed; the said houses, two in number, being situate in the county of Harnett in the town of Dunn, in said county of Harnett; and upon the said two houses where the said C. T. Williams and S. W. Parker now reside, in said town of Dunn, Harnett county, N. C., the said

McMillan Bros. claim their lien. This, the 6th day of June, 1888. McMILLAN BROS., Claimants."

"Bill of particulars: C. T. Williams and S. W. Parker, owners, to McMillan Bros., claimants, Dr. Dated Jany. 3, 1888. To roofing, guttering, spouting, etc., on the house where said C. T. Williams and S. W. Parker now live, in the town of Dunn, Harnett Co., N. C., bal. due, $137.82."

The itemized account was as follows:

1887.		
Nov. 29.	630 ft. tin roof, plain..	$34 65
	481 ft. tin roof, dark ..	38 67
	300 sqr. feet cornice gutter..............	30 00
	98 ft. spouting........	8 90
	R. Rd. fare for hands up................	1 40
Dec. 16.	78 ft. Valley tin......	6 24
1888.		
Jan. 3.	1,001 feet tin roof.....	55 05
	37 feet dark roof......	2 59
	370 sqr. feet cornice gutter..............	37 00
	97 feet pipe spouting..	7 70
	R. Rd. fare hands up and return.........	2 80
		$210 00
1888.	Cr.	
March 17.	By bal. of Cr. of $75.00 draft, after paying store acc't..........	$32 18
April 26.	By draft..............	40 00
		72 18
		$137 82

T. H. Sutton and *Armistead Jones*, for appellants. *F. P. Jones*, for appellees.

AVERY, J. The record of a judgment, execution, levy, and sale of a tract of land as the property of a defendant in an action for possession, the sheriff's deed to the plaintiff, or to one with whom the plaintiff connects himself, by mesne conveyances, together with evidence or admission of the identity of the land conveyed by the sheriff with that declared for in the complaint, and of the actual possession of some portion of said land by the defendant when the action was brought, will, nothing more appearing, constitute a *prima facie* proof of title in the plaintiff. Mobley v. Griffin, 104 N. C. 112, 10 S. E. Rep. 142. But where it is admitted, as in this case, that the sale under the execution was made to satisfy a debt contracted since the homestead provision of the constitution became operative, and without assigning a homestead to the defendant in execution, when he did not hold one under a previous allotment, the burden of proof is shifted, and the *onus* is on the plaintiff to show the liability of the land to be sold to satisfy the debt. Mobley v. Griffin, supra; Long v. Walker, 105 N. C. 90, 10 S. E. Rep. 858; McCracken v. Adler, 98 N. C. 400, 4 S. E. Rep. 138. The plaintiffs in this case have taken up this burden, and attempted to bring themselves within the exception, (contained in article 10, § 4, of the constitution,[1] and provided for in chapter 41 of the Code,) by showing that the sale was made to satisfy a subsisting mechanic's lien upon the

land. They offered the record of the action before the justice of the peace, from which it appeared that the plaintiffs complained for "an account for labor done in November, December, and January in the years 1887 and 1888 to the amount of $128.89." The judgment was entered on the judgment docket in the following form, after entitling the case: "Judgment by confession in J. P. court of Harnett county on the 13th of July, 1888, in favor of plaintiff and against defendant for $128.82, and the further sum of costs in this action. Docketed Aug. 23, 1888, 10 A. M. J. P. costs, 80 cents; C. S. C. costs, $1.05." On the 6th of June, 1888, the plaintiffs had filed a lien, the form of which we need not discuss, with an account for furnishing and putting tin on a roof, amounting to the sum of $137.82. In Boyle v. Robbins, 71 N. C. 133, the act of 1868-69, c. 117, § 9, (which has been brought forward and reenacted in the Code, § 1791,) was construed to require, at least by implication, that the justice of the peace should set forth in the judgment the date of the lien, and that it should also embody a general description of the property which the plaintiff seeks to subject to primary liability under it. If only personal property be bound by the lien, the justice must insert in his execution a requirement that the specific property subject to the lien shall be first sold before seizing other goods or chattels, while, if the property described in the notice be land, the justice's judgment must be docketed in the superior court, and the clerk must incorporate in the execution a similar direction as to the order of selling. So that the judgment cannot be enforced in strict compliance with the law unless the officer whose duty it is to issue execution has gotten such information from the record in his court as will satisfy him that some property, described with reasonable certainty, is subject to the lien, and consequently to a primary liability for the debt. The most convenient method of recording the date of the lien and the description of the property bound by it is to embody it in the judgment, which will constitute a part of the record in either court, no matter which officer may find it necessary to insert the date and description in the execution. The case at bar illustrates the importance of adhering to this rule for another reason. It is essential that the judgment should be identified as that brought within the period prescribed in the statute (Code, § 1790) to enforce the lien. The defendants in the answers deny that this judgment was rendered upon the account, filed as a lien, and, while some circumstances tend to show that the same claim was or may have been the subject both of the lien and the action, we have no evidence sufficient to establish absolutely the identity of the two accounts. The burden being on the plaintiffs to bring the judgment within the exception, under section 4, art. 10, of the constitution, before he can establish the validity of the sale of the defendant's homestead, we think that in failing to connect the judgment and execution with the lien filed they have failed to adduce testimony that is essential to show their

---

[1] This section permits the sale of a homestead to satisfy a mechanic's lien.

title. The words inserted in the execution after the words, "You are commanded to satisfy said judgment," and before the words, "Out of the personal property of the defendant within your county, to-wit, by first selling the right, title, and interest which the said owners had in the property at the time of filing their lien, and next"—do not answer the purpose of connecting the lien with the judgment. If it were true that the plaintiffs recovered two judgments against the defendants for sums nearly the same as that claimed in the lien, neither being for an identical amount, he might issue on either, selecting that one not secured by some other means than the lien. The land sold has been allotted to the defendant S. W. Parker as his homestead, and, though the deed for it may have been executed to the firm of Parker & Williams, (composed of the defendant, C. T. Williams, and himself,) he might lawfully have it assigned out of partnership property, with the assent of Williams. Scott v. Kenan, 94 N. C. 296; Burns v. Harris, 67 N. C. 140; Stout v. McNeill, 98 N. C. 1, 3 S. E. Rep. 915. The right to lay off the exemption of either out of the fund or joint property by consent of the other partner cannot be questioned by a creditor. Scott v. Kenan, supra. While a partner cannot, as a right, demand that his homestead shall be allotted out of the partnership lands, yet, if all of the other partners give their assent up to the time of allotment, a creditor cannot attack the validity of the proceeding and subject the land assigned to the satisfaction of a judgment in his favor. Though the defendants filed separate answers, there is nothing inconsistent in the answer of Williams with the claim set up on the part of the defendant Parker to the land as an allotted homestead, and we must assume, if his allegation be true, that the former assented to the assignment made, and now acquiesces in its consequences. In a controversy between partners or their assignees the assent must appear to have been positive and voluntary, but even a partner cannot withdraw such assent after the allotment. Stout v. McNeill, supra. There is no error, and the judgment is affirmed.

BRYAN v. SPIVEY et al.

(Supreme Court of North Carolina. Oct. 27, 1891.)

ADVERSE POSSESSION—EVIDENCE—COLOR OF TITLE.

1. The direct testimony of a witness that a certain person was in possession of land is the statement of a simple fact, and, as such, evidence of actual possession and occupation, for the purpose of establishing adverse possession.

2. Testimony that a certain person, and those claiming under him, had certain land in possession during a certain period, immediately followed by testimony of the same witness giving the names of the heirs and devisees of such person, and the successive descents and devises down to the date of the conveyance of the property to plaintiff, warranted a finding that these were the persons claiming under such person, and that they were in possession as stated by witness.

3. Plaintiff's admission that defendants were for a certain time in adverse possession of certain land, claiming in the same manner as a certain witness, is not an admission that they were claiming under color of title,—the testimony of said witness being, first, that he claimed under a deed to one S. in trust for the people of J.; and, next, that he claimed his lot in severalty, though under such deed the beneficiaries would take as tenants in common; and, next, that he claimed in the same way he did when he first went on the land, though the deed was executed several years thereafter.

4. Though defendants' adverse possession is admitted, proof of the deed to S. in trust raises no presumption that they claimed under it, none of them being grantees therein, or named in it as cestuis que trustent.

Appeal from superior court, Craven county; HENRY G. CONNOR, Judge.

Ejectment by James A. Bryan against Washington Spivey and others. Judgment for plaintiff, and defendants appeal. Affirmed.

M. de W. Stevenson, O. H. Guion, and J. W. Hinsdale, for appellants.

SHEPHERD, J. The exceptions addressed to the admission of the documentary evidence of the plaintiff having been abandoned, the only questions which remain for our consideration are whether the testimony adduced upon the trial was legally sufficient to sustain the findings of fact, and whether these findings warrant the conclusions of law as declared by the court below.

1. It is first insisted by the defendants that upon the whole testimony the plaintiff has failed to show that the title has passed out of the state, and that, granting that the title is out of the state, there is nothing to support the presumption of a conveyance to the plaintiff, or those under whom she claims. It is well settled that an adverse possession of land for 30 years raises a presumption of a grant from the state, "and that it is not necessary even that there should be a privity or connection among the successive tenants." Davis v. McArthur, 78 N. C. 357; Reed v. Earnhart, 10 Ired. 516; Wallace v. Maxwell, Id. 110; Fitzrandolph v. Norman, Tayl. (N. C.) 127. "This presumption," says SMITH, C. J., in the case first cited, "arises at common law, and without the aid of the act of 1791, and it is the duty of the court to instruct the jury to act upon it as a rule of the law of evidence. Simpson v. Hyatt, 1 Jones, (N. C.) 517." Now if, as found by his honor, the land in controversy was "in the possession of the children and devisees of Richard D. Speight and those claiming through them," from 1829 to 1858, (a period of 29 years,) and that from that date until 1862 it was occupied by Peter G. Evans, the law would raise a presumption that the title had passed out of the state, and this without reference to whether the said Evans was claiming jointly with Richard S. Donnell, and regardless of any privity between him and the preceding occupants. If the title was out of the state, the law would also presume that a deed had been executed by the true owner to the parties under whom the plaintiff claims, they having had continuous adverse possession of the same, succeeding each other as privies, for 29

years. Hill v. Overton, 81 N. C. 895; Sea-well v. Bunch, 6 Jones, (N. C.) 195; Taylor v. Gooch, 3 Jones, (N. C.) 467; Davis v. McArthur, supra; Melvin v. Waddell, 75 N. C. 361. These propositions do not seem to be seriously controverted by the counsel for the defendants, but they insist that the testimony is not sufficient to show any possession whatever from which his honor could find, as a legal inference or otherwise, that there was an adverse occupation as claimed by the plaintiff. In support of this position, they say "that the testimony of W. H. Marshall [the only witness introduced by the plaintiff] in regard to possession was insufficient; too uncertain and indefinite; that possession is a question of fact and law, and that plaintiff must show that the land was used and occupied by showing what was done on it, and by whom." It cannot be doubted that what constitutes adverse possession is a mixed question of law and fact, and the same may be said of a possession that is not adverse, where the evidence shows that the possession claimed is constructive only, or in other instances where it depends upon the application of legal principles. Where, however, a witness testifies that a certain person is in possession of land, and where, as in the present case, there is nothing in his or any other testimony to indicate that the possession was a conflicting one, or that the witness intended that his language should be understood in any other than its ordinary sense among laymen, to-wit, actual possession or occupation, we cannot but treat it as the statement of a simple fact, and as such a proper subject for the consideration of a jury, or the court, when a jury trial has been waived. That such is the ordinary meaning of the language is manifest from the following authorities: "Possession expresses the closest relation of fact that can exist between a corporeal thing and the person who possesses it, implying either (according to its strictest etymology) an actual physical contact, as by sitting, or (as some would have it) standing, upon a thing." Burrill, Law Dict. 313. "A witness may testify directly in the first instance to the fact of possession if he can do so positively, subject, of course, to cross-examination." Abb. Tr. Ev. 590–622. In Rand v. Freeman, 1 Allen, 517, a witness was asked, "Did you take possession of the property?" The question was objected to as incompetent to prove possession. The court said: "It is objected that the question was illegal, because possession consists partly of law and partly of fact. But it is a sufficient answer to this to say that the word is often used merely in reference to the fact, and the defendant could have protected himself from all prejudice by cross-examination." In Lansingburgh v. Crary, 1 Barb. 542, the court, in reference to a similar question, said: "It might involve the necessity of further questions, and perhaps of a rigid cross-examination; but this last [we] think was the true remedy, and not an objection to the question itself. It belongs to that class of facts of which there are many in the law, seemingly involving,

to some extent, the expression of an opinion, or a conclusion from other particular facts as to which, from the necessity of the case, the law tolerates a direct and comprehensive question." Our conclusion, therefore, is that the testimony of the witness Marshall was evidence of actual possession and occupation, and, as such, was proper to be considered by the court.

It is further objected that the testimony of the said witness that "Richard D. Speight, and those claiming under him, had it [the land] in possession from 1829 to 1858," was "insufficient, uncertain, and improper, unless the names of the persons referred to were given, and evidence of the manner of their claims under him was shown." The witness, after testifying as above, immediately proceeded to state with much particularity the names of the heirs and devisees of the said Speight, and the successive descents and devises down to the date of the conveyance of the property in question to the plaintiff. His honor finds, in substance, that these were the persons who were claiming under the said Speight, and were in possession, as stated by the said witness. We think that a fair construction of the testimony warranted the finding. This being so, we have but to apply the presumption of the adverse character of the holding arising from the unexplained fact of actual occupation, and the conclusion of the court that those under whom the plaintiff claims were the owners of the property is fully vindicated. Ruffin v. Overby, 88 N. C. 369. The case just cited is fully sustained by Jackson v. Commissioners, 1 Dev. & B. 177, in which it is said (RUFFIN, C. J., delivering the opinion) that "every possession is taken to be on the possessor's own title, until the contrary appears, as the possession is in itself the strongest evidence of the claim of title, and, when long continued, of the title also. Leaving the possession to the jury as a ground of presumption, left it as evidence both of the right and the claim of right; and it cannot be doubted that the jury must have understood that, to authorize the presumption, they must believe that Brooks occupied and used the ground as his own. To establish such claim did [not] require express evidence of it, independent of the possession itself."

2. It is further contended that, admitting that the title was in the persons above named, the defendants are protected by their adverse possession under color of title for seven years. This defense is an affirmative one, and the onus probandi is, of course, upon the defendants to establish it. Ruffin v. Overby, 105 N. C. 78, 11 S. E. Rep. 251. It is admitted by the plaintiff that the defendants have been in the adverse possession of the several parts of the property (James City) since 1863, "claiming the same as the witness Wm. Benbury." It is denied, however, that they claim under color of title; and his honor finds that they entered without such color in 1863, and that after the execution of the deed by Hunter and others to James Salter in 1867, the defendants "continued to occupy their several lots inclosed by them in the same manner as before, and [that] the

character of their possession was not thereby changed." "This finding," says his honor, "is based upon the fact that the testimony in respect thereto is conflicting; and, taken in connection with the answer of November 11, 1890, the court is unable to find that they were holding under the provisions of said deed for seven years prior to the commencement of this action." It is insisted that this finding was unauthorized by the testimony, and especially by reason of the admission of plaintiff. It will be observed that the admission was not that the defendants were holding under color of title, but that they were claiming in the same manner as the witness Benbury. The testimony of this witness, as his honor says, is conflicting. The witness says, first, that he claims under the deed to Salter. This deed, it will be noticed, is in trust for "the people of James City;" by which we must understand (nothing further appearing) they are to take as tenants in common. He then states, in effect, that he claims his lot in severalty, and further remarks, "I claim it in the same way I did when I first went there." Eliminating even the answer above mentioned, which claims in severalty and makes no mention of the deed, we are not surprised at the inability of his honor to find that Benbury was claiming under color of the deed to Salter; and surely his statement referred to in the admission of plaintiff cannot, even in the absence of the finding, be construed into the concession insisted upon. Appreciating the force of this reasoning, the counsel for defendants very earnestly contend that the possession being admittedly adverse, and the deed to Salter having been proved and introduced in evidence, the law raises a presumption that the defendants claim under it, and that, therefore, the burden of proof is shifted, and it is incumbent on the plaintiff to rebut such presumption. Register v. Rowell, 3 Jones, (N. C.) 312. To this it may be answered that the supposed presumption is already rebutted by the finding of the court, and that we cannot review its conclusion of fact when there is any evidence tending to sustain it. Treating the finding, however, as negative in its character, (which is not the case,) and conceding that, in order to raise the presumption, it is unnecessary that the color of title should have been executed contemporaneously with the entry, an insuperable objection to the defendants' contention is encountered in the fact that none of these defendants are grantees in the deed, nor are they named therein as *cestuis que trustent*. Graybeal v. Davis, 95 N. C. 508, and the cases cited. This is an indispensable requisite to the presumption insisted upon. Such being the case, the burden continued upon the defendants to connect themselves with the said deed, and to show that they claimed under the same. Having failed to show this to the satisfaction of the court, and indeed, it having been affirmatively found to the contrary, we are unable to see any ground for reversing the judgment, and it must therefore be affirmed.

MOORE v. GARNER.

(*Supreme Court of North Carolina.* Nov. 3, 1891.)

APPEALS FROM INFERIOR COURTS—PLEADING—RES JUDICATA.

1. On appeals from justice court, under Code N. C. §§ 875, 880, 881, when the return fails to show the pleadings before the justice, the superior court may allow all pleas to be filed to which either party might have been entitled.

2. In an action to recover amount realized from sale of property placed in the hands of a judgment creditor to be sold and applied on the judgment, which plaintiff claimed was not so applied, it appeared that prior to this action plaintiff was cited to show cause why execution should not issue on said judgment, and in that proceeding alleged that the execution was paid by the proceeds of the property, which question was then adjudicated. *Held*, that plaintiff was estopped from again trying the issue.

Appeal from superior court, Granville county; EDWIN T. BOYKIN, Judge.

Action in *assumpsit* by James I. Moore against W. H. Garner, administrator. From a judgment for defendant, plaintiff appeals. Affirmed.

N. Y. Gulley, for appellant. *A. W. Graham* and *John W. Graham,* for appellee.

MERRIMON, C. J. This action began in the court of a justice of the peace, and the pleadings there were oral. The plaintiff appealed to the superior court from a judgment adverse to him. In the latter court, "it did not appear what pleas were put in before the justice of the peace, and counsel could not agree as to the matter," and the court hence allowed "all pleas to which either party might have been entitled." The plaintiff assigned this as error. The plaintiff had the right to appeal, and the superior court, upon the appeal, had complete jurisdiction of the action for all the purposes of "a new trial of the whole matter at the ensuing term of said court," the appeal to "be heard on the original papers." Code, §§ 875, 890, 881. The action thus in the superior court was to be tried *de novo,* and the court had ample power to amend the pleadings, and to allow new pleas or matters of defense to be alleged, including matters of estoppel, whether such defense had been allowed in the court below or not, and the exercise of its discretion by the court in allowing new and additional defenses is not ordinarily reviewable here. Poston v. Rose, 87 N. C. 279; Johnson v. Rowland, 80 N. C. 1; Hinton v. Deans, 75 N. C. 18; Thomas v. Simpson, 80 N. C. 4; Falson v. Johnson, 78 N. C. 78; Dobson v. Chambers, Id. 334. The plaintiff brings this action to recover from the defendant $164.14, with interest, which he alleges the intestate of the defendant realized from the sale of certain property of the plaintiff, and agreed to apply to the payment of certain judgments against the plaintiff that belonged to the intestate, which the latter failed to do. The defendant, by permission of the court, alleged as a defense that the plaintiff's alleged claim and cause of action had been litigated and determined adversely to him in another proceeding, wherein the present defendant was the interested plaintiff, and the present plaintiff was defendant. That proceeding was a rule upon the defendant (the present plaintiff) to show cause why an execution should not issue to enforce the judgments above mentioned. The defendant insisted that, therefore, the plaintiff was estopped as to his alleged cause of action, and the court so decided. This decision is assigned as error. The record is confused, and not very intelligible. It was the duty of the appellant to show the alleged error, if he could. If he failed because of his laches, it is his fault, not that of the court. We cannot see that there is error. It appears from the evidence, accepted as true, (and the court so treated it,) that the plaintiff's alleged cause of action was litigated and determined against him in the proceeding above mentioned and referred to. That it was contested and determined in an application for leave to issue an execution to enforce a judgment is no reason why the plaintiff should not be estopped. The whole matter embraced properly by such application became and remains *res adjudicata*. In disposing of the application, it was pertinent and proper for the present plaintiff to show that he had paid the judgment, and he did allege and contend that it was paid by the proceeds of the sale of his property realised by the intestate, the very money he seeks by this action to recover. In another proper proceeding between the plaintiff and the defendant, the present alleged cause of action was litigated, and its merits adjudicated. The defendant clearly has the right to avail himself of the defense the court allowed him to allege and establish. Sanderson v. Daily, 83 N. C. 67; Tuttle v. Harrill, 85 N. C. 456; Warden v. McKinnon, 99 N. C. 251, 5 S. E. Rep. 917; Temple v Williams, 91 N. C. 82; McElwee v. Blackwell, 101 N. C. 196, 7 S. E. Rep. 893. Judgment affirmed.

PHILLIPS et al. v. HODGES.

(*Supreme Court of North Carolina.* Oct. 27, 1891.)

ESTOPPEL IN PAIS—JOINT TENANCY—DEED TO HUSBAND AND WIFE — FAILURE TO RECORD — BONA FIDE PURCHASER.

1. A husband and wife took a deed of land on April 2, 1852, but did not record it until January 11, 1886. April 28, 1852, the husband alone deeded back to their grantor, S., who reconveyed the same, and his grantee died in 1880, and the land was sold to defendant at administrator's sale. S. publicly stated at the sale, in presence of the husband and wife, that the title was perfect, and they made no objection. The husband acted as auctioneer. Defendant had no notice of the deed to the husband and wife, and went into possession, and in 1884 recorded his deed. *Held*, that the wife's conduct at the sale did not estop her from asserting her right of survivorship to the land.

2. Code N. C. § 1326, which abolishes survivorship in joint tenancies, does not apply to conveyances to husband and wife.

3. Under Act N. C. 1885, c. 147, which provided that no deed of conveyance then executed should be valid as against an innocent purchaser for value unless recorded prior to January 1, 1886, no claim could be asserted under the deed to the husband and wife, which was not recorded until January 11, 1886.

4. The unrecorded deed to the husband and wife passed only an equitable title, to be perfected by registration.

5. Where defendant had no source of information to which he could more reasonably resort than to the husband to ascertain how the husband acquired the title which he conveyed in 1852, the husband's conduct at such auction sale excused defendant from making any inquiry as to such title.

Appeal from superior court, Harnett county; EDWIN T. BOYKIN, Judge.

Action by W. P. Phillips' heirs against H. A. Hodges to recover land. Judgment for defendant on nonsuit. Plaintiffs appeal. Affirmed.

STATEMENT BY THE COURT. The action was commenced 8th June, 1888, by W. P. Phillips, who afterwards died, and the present plaintiffs were made parties. It was admitted that prior to April 2, 1852, one W. B. Surles owned the land, and on that day conveyed it by deed to N. L. Phillips and Patience W. Phillips, his wife, which deed was registered 11th January, 1886. On 28th April, 1852, Nathan L. Phillips alone executed a deed back to W. B. Surles, which was registered 10th April, 1854. W. B. Surles continued in possession until the 7th February, 1859, when he sold and conveyed the land for a valuable consideration to James C. Surles, who immediately entered and remained in possession until his death, in 1880. His family continued in possession until, under special proceedings to make real-estate assets, the land was sold by Daniel Stewart, his administrator and commissioner, at public sale, to H. A. Hodges, the defendant, to whom, after confirmation of sale and payment of the purchase money, the said Stewart, by order of the court, executed a deed for the land, dated 7th April, 1884, and registered 23d April, 1884. At the public sale W. B. Surles was present, and at the request of the administrator, Daniel Stewart, got up and publicly stated that the title was perfectly good. This statement was made in the presence of N. L. Phillips and wife, Patience W. Phillips, neither of whom interposed any objection, and N. L. Phillips assisted at the sale by acting as auctioneer. H. A. Hodges immediately took possession, and has remained in possession ever since. A year or two after H. A. Hodges had paid for the land, obtained his deed, and taken possession, N. L. Phillips showed him the old deed to himself and wife from W. B. Surles, dated 2d April, 1852, then unregistered, and told him that, although he had been paid for the land, he could hold it under that deed, but would surrender the deed to him for $25, to which Hodges remarked that he would not give him 25 cents for it. This was the first notice Hodges had of the deed. On 12th November, 1887, N. L. Phillips and wife made a deed of gift for the land to their son, W. P. Phillips, the original plaintiff, who instituted this suit 8th June, 1888. N. L. Phillips died in 1889, leaving his wife, Patience W. Phillips, surviving him, who is still living, and was present at the trial of this cause, but not examined. The defendant asked the following special instructions in writing: "That the deed from W. B. Surles to N. L. Phillips and wife, dated 2d April, 1852, not having been registered until 11th January, 1886, passed no title as against J. C. Surles or the defendant, H. A. Hodges, under Acts 1885, c. 147, § 1." His honor having intimated that such was his opinion, and that he would so charge the jury, the plaintiffs excepted to the ruling of the court, and in deference thereto submitted to a nonsuit, and appealed. Judgment accordingly.

F. P. Jones, for appellants. *R. P. Buxton,* for appellee.

DAVIS, J. The foregoing is the full statement of the case on appeal, from which it will be seen at a glance that there is not a shadow of merit or equity in the plaintiffs' claim to the land in controversy, and we shall see, upon an examination of the law upon which they rely, that it is equally without foundation in law. It will be conceded, as insisted for the plaintiff, that by the deed of April 2, 1852, from W. B. Surles to N. L. Phillips and Patience W. Phillips, his wife, the husband and wife took the land *per my et per tout;* and the act of 1784, (Code, § 1326,) abolishing survivorship in joint tenancies, does not apply to conveyances to husband and wife, for the reason assigned by GASTON, J., in Motley v. Whitemore, 2 Dev. & B. 537, that, "being in law but one person, they have each the whole estate as one person, and on the death of either of them the whole estate continues in the survivor." Long v. Barnes, 87 N. C. 329, and cases cited. It will be conceded, too, that the subsequent reconveyance by N. L. Phillips alone to W. B. Surles could not deprive the wife, Patience W. Phillips, of the right of survivorship. Simonton v. Cornelius, 98 N. C. 433, 4 S. E. Rep. 38, and cases cited.

It is insisted for the defendant that the conduct of N. L. Phillips and his wife at the sale was a fraud upon the purchaser for value and without notice, and that they are thereby estopped from asserting title to the land. That is true as to N. L. Phillips; but the wife, by reason of her presence at the sale with her husband, and her silence when he stated publicly in her hearing that the "title was perfectly good," was not by that alone estopped. While the reason for this may not be entirely satisfactory, it is well settled by authority; though, speaking for myself, and yielding to settled judicial precedent, I am unable to see why it was not as much a fraud in the wife—who, it appears, had sufficient interest to attend the sale—to stand by and hear the husband make the statement that estopped him as a fraud upon an innocent purchaser, as it was in him to make the statement. It is not easy to conceive of any honest purpose in withholding from registration and publicity for more than 30 years the deed to N. L. Phillips and wife, through whom the plaintiffs claim. The statute of presumptions had commenced to run more than a quarter of a century before this action was instituted; and, though unlike the statute of limitations, which is a complete bar as to all persons not under disabilities, it is so emphatically a statute of repose that no saving is made in it of the rights of infants *femes covert* or persons *non compos mentis.* Headen v. Womack, 88 N. C. 468, and cases cited. But the learned counsel for the defendant was content, as he might well be, to rely upon the act of 1885, c. 147, which made the deed of no avail against creditors or innocent purchasers for value unless registered prior to January 1, 1886, whereas it was registered after that time. The unregistered deed did not pass the legal title, but only an equitable title, to be perfected by registration. Davis v. Inscoe, 84 N. C. 396, and cases cited. Counsel, in his brief, says: "Would it not have been prudent for a purchaser to have inquired as to how N. L. Phillips acquired his title? Such inquiry would have disclosed the fact that he held only a joint estate with his wife," etc., which would bring the case within the proviso of the act of 1885. This contention might perhaps be made with some force, but for the fact that the purchaser had no source of information to which he could more reasonably resort than to N. L. Phillips, who, in the presence of his wife, with the deed under which they claimed in his possession, gave the fraudulent assurance that the title was perfect. The counsel for the plaintiffs says the deed, when registered, related back to its execution; and "the act of 1885 would be unconstitutional if the effect of it would be to divest from P. W. Phillips in 1885 an estate which vested in her by deed in 1852." The error of counsel is in overlooking the fact that but for the act of 1885, and the various successive acts after two years from April, 1852, extending the time for registration, the deed to Phillips and wife would have conveyed no legal title unless registered within two years from April 2, 1852. Registration is required for the protection of innocent purchasers for value, and creditors, and to prevent frauds; and the legislature did not think it wise to extend the time for registration after January 1, 1886, so as to give legal validity to deeds, as against innocent purchasers and creditors; and the case before us illustrates the wisdom of the law-makers. There is no error, and the judgment is affirmed.

KORNEGAY v. KORNEGAY.

(*Supreme Court of North Carolina.* Oct. 27. 1891.)

CONDITIONAL SALES — REGISTRY — INCONSISTENT FINDINGS—OWNERSHIP OF PROPERTY.

1. Code N. C. § 1275, requiring conditional sales of personal property to be reduced to writing and registered, does not render such sales invalid as between the parties, nor affect the remedies of the parties against each other, unless it is complied with; and, in an action by the seller against the buyer, a note for the purchase money may be put in evidence, although it has not been registered.

2. Plaintiff sued on a note given in part payment for a horse, which he claimed was to remain his until the note was paid. Defendant alleged that he bought the horse, paying part cash, and giving his note for $45 for the balance; that plaintiff warranted the horse to be sound, whereas in fact it was unsound; and claimed damages for breach of warranty. The jury found that plaintiff was not the owner of the horse; that defendant owed him for the same $45; that his

representations in regard to its soundness were
false; and that the defendant was entitled to
$22.50 damages. *Held*, that the finding in regard
to ownership was material, and not inconsistent
with the other findings or with the general verdict, and that the court erred in adjudging that it
was mere surplusage and that the plaintiff was
the owner.

8. The findings that defendant owed plaintiff
$45, and that he was entitled to $22.50 damages,
were not sufficiently intelligible to warrant a judgment, for the reason that it could not be determined with certainty whether the jury meant to
find that defendant owed plaintiff $45 and that
his damages should be deducted from that sum,
or whether the damages should be recovered by
defendant and plaintiff should recover nothing,
or that defendant was damaged $45, and in addi-
tion $22.50.

Appeal from superior court, Wayne
county; ROBERT W. WINSTON, Judge.

Action by Robert Kornegay against J.
F. Kornegay to recover on a promissory
note given in part payment for the purchase of a horse. There was judgment
for plaintiff, and defendant appeals. Reversed.

STATEMENT BY THE COURT. The complaint alleges, in substance, that the plaintiff is the owner of the horse specified
therein, and entitled to have possession
thereof; that the defendant has possession of the horse, and refuses to surrender the same, etc. The defendant denies
the material allegations of the complaint,
and alleges that the plaintiff sold him the
horse for $95; that he paid $50 of this
price, and gave the plaintiff his note for
the balance, $45, to be due on the 1st day
of November, 1888; that the plaintiff warranted the horse to be sound, whereas he
was unsound, and he was greatly endangered by such unsoundness; thereby he alleges his counter-claim for damages, etc.
The reply puts in issue the allegation of
the answer. The court submitted to the
jury the following issues, to which they
responded as indicated at the end of each:
"(1) Is the plaintiff the owner of the property in controversy? Answer. No. (2)
What, if anything, does the defendant
owe the plaintiff? A. $45 and interest.
(3) Did plaintiff represent that the mare
in controversy was sound? A. Yes. (4)
Was said representation false, and was
it relied upon as a material inducement
to the trade? A. Yes. (5) What damage, if any, is defendant entitled to recover? A. $22.50." On the trial the plain-
tiff put in evidence a note, whereof the following is a copy: "Mt. Olive, N. C., February 18, 1888. On the first day of November, 1888, I promise to pay Robert
Kornegay or order the sum of forty five
dollars, for value received, balance due on
horse, said horse to remain R. Kornegay's
property until this note is paid. Witness
my hand and seal. [Signed] J. F. KOR-
NEGAY. [Seal.]" Said note had not been
registered, and the defendant objected
to the introduction of the same on the
ground that it had not been registered.
Objection overruled, and note admitted,
and defendant excepted. Upon the return
of the verdict by the jury as above set
out, defendant moved to set aside the
verdict as inconsistent. Motion refused,
and defendant excepted. The defendant

then moved for judgment adjudging him
to be the owner of the mare in controversy. The court refused to give such
judgment, and defendant excepted. The
defendant then asked the court to allow
him costs, insisting that the question of
costs was in the discretion of the court.
The court stated that it was disposed to
allow defendant costs if it had the power,
but that it had not such power, and
thereupon gave the judgment set out in
the record, and defendant excepted. Defendant excepted to the said judgment,
for that it adjudged that said mare be
sold, and that she was the property of
the plaintiff, and for that it awarded costs
against the defendant. The defendant,
having excepted, appealed to this court.

W. C. Munroe, for appellant. *Allen &
Dortch*, for appellee.

MERRIMON, C. J. The purpose of the
statute (Code, § 1275) requiring all conditional sales of personal property to be reduced to writing and registered, is to
protect creditors and purchasers for value.
It is no part of its purpose to render
such sales, whether in writing or not, invalid as between the parties to it. As between them such sale has the same qualities, and is just as effectual, as it would
have been, and may be proven by the like
evidence, as before the statute was enacted, and the parties may have the like remedies against each other. Brem v. Lockhart. 93 N. C. 191; Drill Co. v. Allison, 94
N. C. 548; Butts v. Screws, 95 N. C. 215.
This controversy is between the parties
to the conditional sale in question, and
hence the court properly allowed the note
for part of the price of the horse to be put
in evidence, although it had not been registered. The plaintiff alleged in his complaint that he had title to the horse in
question. This the defendant broadly denied, and thus the first issue submitted to
the jury—a very material one—was raised
by the pleadings. The jury found by
their verdict that the plaintiff was not
the owner. Nevertheless, "the court, being of opinion that the first of said issues
is a general finding, controlled by the findings upon the other issues, and may be
treated as surplusage, * * * adjudged
that the plaintiff is the owner of said
horse, and entitled to retain the possession thereof," etc. We are unable to see
upon what ground the court treated the
finding of the jury upon the first issue as
immaterial, or how this finding was rendered so by the other findings of the jury.
The latter may have been proper, but they
were not necessarily inconsistent with the
first one. The plaintiff may not have been
the owner of the horse, and the defendant
may have owed him for the same $45. The
plaintiff may have falsely represented to
the defendant that the horse was "sound;"
the defendant may have relied upon such
representation, and been endamaged as a
consequence; and yet the plaintiff might
not be the owner of the horse. There are
no special findings of fact inconsistent
with the general verdict. The findings
may all be true,—certainly, they are not
necessarily inconsistent. The finding in response to the first issue was very materi-

al, and, if it was unwarranted by the evidence, the court should have set the verdict aside, and directed a new trial. In view of the verdict, the court erred in adjudging that the plaintiff was the owner of the horse, and that the same be sold by a commissioner. The findings of the jury, in response to the second and fifth issues, are not sufficiently intelligible; they leave the matter to which they refer too vague and uncertain to warrant a judgment based upon them. It cannot be determined with reasonable certainty whether the jury simply meant to find that the defendant owes the plaintiff $45, with interest, and that the damages allowed the defendant shall be subtracted from that sum, or whether the damages so allowed shall be recovered by the defendant, and the plaintiff shall recover nothing. It may be the jury meant to find that the defendant was endamaged $45, with interest, and, in addition, $22.50. It is so contended. It is contended as earnestly otherwise. In such a state of uncertainty, the verdict must be treated as void, and a new trial directed to be had. We do not intend to be understood as condemning the practice of submitting issues for the purpose of ascertaining damages in favor of the defendant in cases where he pleads a counter-claim. There is error. To the end that there may be a new trial, let this opinion be certified to the superior court.

SCOTT v. LANE.

(Supreme Court of North Carolina. Nov. 3, 1891.)

FORECLOSURE OF MORTGAGE—RIGHTS OF PURCHASER.

The purchaser of land on foreclosure of a mortgage, made by the owner alone, acquires title thereto, subject only to the wife's right of dower, where it does not appear that the mortgagor was in debt at the time of executing the same, or the land had been allotted as a homestead. Hughes v. Hodges, (N. C.) 9 S. E. Rep. 437, followed.

Appeal from superior court, Guilford county; JAMES C. MACRAE, Judge.

Ejectment brought by L. M. Scott against George D. Lane. Plaintiff claims title by commissioners' deeds on foreclosure of two mortgages executed by defendant, and not signed by his wife. Judgment was directed for defendant by the court, and plaintiff appeals. Reversed.

L. M. Scott, for appellant.

CLARK, J. According to the defendant's testimony, he was indebted to no one else when he executed the mortgage, and there is nothing in the pleadings and evidence to indicate that the mortgaged property had theretofore been allotted as a homestead. There was no restriction, therefore, upon the owner's *jus disponendi*, and the purchaser at the sale under the mortgage acquired a good title as against the defendant mortgagor, subject to the contingent right of dower of the wife if she should survive him. A case exactly in point is Hughes v. Hodges, 102 N. C. 236, 262, 9 S. E. Rep. 437, 442. Upon the evidence, the court should have instructed the jury to return a verdict for the plaintiff. Error.

MOORE v. GOODWIN et al.

(Supreme Court of North Carolina. Nov. 3, 1891.)

LIMITATIONS OF ACTIONS—PAYMENT ON ACCOUNT —EFFECT ON SURETY.

Under Code N. C. § 172, providing that the requirement that an acknowledgment or promise shall be in writing to remove the bar of the statute of limitations "shall not alter the affect of any payment of principal or interest," and section 171, providing that no act or admission of the maker of a bond, after it is barred, shall be received in evidence to repel the bar, except against him, the payment of interest on a bond by the maker, before it is barred, renews the running of the statute as to a surety.

Appeal from superior court, Wake county; ROBERT W. WINSTON, Judge.

Action by James Moore against H. J. Goodwin et al. as sureties on a bond. The plaintiff alleges that on the 6th day of February, 1886, one Colin Campbell, as principal, and the defendants H. J. Goodwin and C. E. J. Goodwin as sureties, covenanted under their hands and seals to pay the plaintiff, 12 months after date, $300, with interest at 8 per cent. from date, for money borrowed; and that no part of said debt has been paid, except $24, interest to January, 1887, and $24, interest to January 9, 1888, both of which payments were indorsed as credits on the bond. The defendants answer, and admit the execution of the bond, but they say that it was executed by them, as was well known to the plaintiff, as sureties, and that the same was payable more than three years prior to the bringing of this action. They further say that they are informed and believe that said note has been paid by the principal, Campbell, in a settlement with the plaintiff. The only evidence offered to prove a payment was that of the defendants, who said that Campbell told them that he was square with Moore; that Moore was not present; and that one of them told the plaintiff, in 1887, that he must collect the note, to which plaintiff replied, "All right." His honor excluded this evidence, but stated that he would admit it if the defendants would offer substantive proof of a settlement of the note in controversy between the plaintiff and Campbell. The defendants' counsel stated that they had no substantive evidence of such a settlement. Defendants excepted. Affirmed.

S. G. Ryan, for appellants. Battle & Mordecai, for appellee.

DAVIS, J., (after stating the facts as above.) The evidence was properly excluded by the court. In fact, counsel for defendants in this court did not urge the exclusion as error, but earnestly insisted that the statute of limitations was a bar to the collection of the debt, as against the sureties. Code, §§ 155, 171. Section 155 bars a recovery, as to sureties, unless the action is brought within three years; and section 171 provides that "no act, admission, or acknowledgment, * * * by any of the makers of a promissory note or bond after the statute of limitations shall have barred the same, shall be received in evidence to repel the statute," etc., except against the party making the admission or acknowledgment. Section 172 requires the acknowledgment or promise to be in writing to remove the bar, but this shall not "alter the effect of any payment of principal or interest." In the case before us the payments were made before the statute had barred, and his honor held that this repelled the bar. That this was correct is too well settled by the decisions of this court to admit of doubt: Bank v. Harris, 96 N. C. 118, 1 S. E. Rep. 459, and the cases there cited. We are earnestly asked by counsel to review and reverse this ruling, and we are referred to many adjudications in other states; but, upon examination, we have no doubt of the correctness of the construction placed upon our statute, and reaffirm it. Counsel says that if several co-obligors owe a debt of $1,000, under this ruling, if the note or bond shall be credited with the pitiful sum of 10 cents within every three years, the debt may be kept in force against the sureties for a century. The hardship and injustice, so eloquently portrayed by counsel, are without force, in view of the facts that the payment must be honestly made, and the credit not falsely or fraudulently given, and the surety or indorser, if he shall consider himself in danger of being held liable for a century, or for a longer time than he may wish, can easily and safely protect himself against such hardship by giving the notice prescribed in section 2097 of the Code. There is no error.

LAMBE et al. v. LOVE.

(Supreme Court of North Carolina. Nov. 3, 1891.)

ESTABLISHMENT OF HIGHWAY — APPEAL FROM ORDER OF COMMISSIONERS—TIME OF TAKING.

1. An appeal from an order of the county commissioners establishing a public road, and directing a jury to be summoned to lay it out and assess damages, may be taken as well after the confirmation of the report of the jury as before.

2. An appeal will not lie to the supreme court from a decision of the superior court refusing to dismiss, during the trial, an appeal from an order of the county commissioners opening a public road; but the appellant, in such a case, should have assigned error in the record to be considered on appeal from the final judgment.

Appeal from superior court, Chatham county; JAMES D. MCIVER, Judge.

This was a petition to have a public road and ferry established. The prayer of the petitioner was allowed. The jury laid out the road, assessed damages, and made their report to the county commissioners, who confirmed the same. Thereupon the respondent appealed to the superior court. In the latter court, the appellants (petitioners) moved to dismiss the appeal, "upon the ground that the defendant (respondent) should have appealed from the order of the commissioners establishing the public road, fixing the termini, and directing the sheriff to summon a jury of freeholders to lay off said road, and that the defendant could not appeal from the order confirming the report of the jurors." The court denied the motion, and the petitioners, having excepted, appealed to this court. Affirmed.

John Manning and J. S. Manning, for appellants. T. B. Womack, for appellee.

MERRIMON, C. J., (after stating the facts as above.) It may be that the respondent was satisfied with the order of the county commissioners directing the laying out of the public road, and he did not desire to appeal from such order; but he may have been dissatisfied, for good cause, with the action of the jury in some material respect, and that of the county commissioners in confirming their report. The jury may not have been a lawful one. They may have proceeded improperly in the execution of the order, or in assessing damages, to the prejudice of the respondent. If so, and their report was improperly confirmed, he had the right to appeal, and it was the duty of the superior court to hear and determine the matter according to law. What we have said is in no sense in conflict with what is said and decided in McDowell v. Insane Asylum, 101 N. C. 656, 8 S. E. Rep. 118. It may, and frequently does, happen that the principal, and, in a legal sense, final, judgment or order in an action or proceeding is erroneously executed. In such case, the complaining party has the right to appeal, certainly when and as soon as the execution of the order or judgment is completed and acted upon by the court. The court, therefore, properly denied the motion. Moreover, an appeal did not lie from the denial of a motion to dismiss the appeal. The appellants should have assigned error in the record to be considered on appeal from the final judgment. Wilson v. Lineberger, 82 N. C. 412; Railroad v. Richardson, Id. 343; West v. Reynolds, 94 N. C. 333; Davis v. Ely, 100 N. C. 283, 5 S. E. Rep. 239; State v. Warren, 100 N. C. 489, 5 S. E. Rep. 662. Judgment affirmed.

WEIR v. PAGE et al.

(Supreme Court of North Carolina. Nov. 3, 1891.)

LIABILITIES OF MARRIED WOMAN — CONTRACT BY HUSBAND.

Under Code N. C. § 1826, providing that no woman during her coverture shall, without her husband's written consent, make any contract to affect her real estate, except for her necessary personal expenses, etc., unless she be a free trader, a married woman is not liable for labor and material furnished for her real estate under her husband's contract, although the evidence tends to show that she was aware of said contract, and ratified and approved it. Farthing v. Shields, 106 N. C. 289, 10 S. E. Rep. 998, followed.

Appeal from superior court, Wake county; ROBERT W. WINSTON, Judge.

The action was originally brought by W. J. Weir against Rufus H. Page and Sallie E. Page, his wife, but Rufus H. Page died before the complaint was filed, and his personal representative has never been made a party, and the action is prosecuted against Sallie E. Page alone. The plaintiff seeks to enforce a claim and lien for work and labor done and material furnished on the property of Rufus H. Page and the separate property of the feme defendant, as set out in the complaint. The defendant, in her answer, says that she was informed by her husband, now deceased, that he had contracted with the plaintiff, or the firm of Hammill & Weir, to do some work ou the property mentioned in the complaint, some of which was her separate property, and that the same was to be paid for in the manner set out in the answer; but she denies that said contract was for or on her behalf, and she denies that her said husband had any power or authority to bind her by said contract, but that her said husband was to be solely responsible for the same, and to pay in the manner particularly stated in the answer. She denies that any one had any authority from her to make the contract alleged in the complaint. W. J. Weir testified in his own behalf that he had a contract with Rufus H. Page to do the brick-work and plastering on two houses on Saunders street; that he made the contract with Rufus H. Page, and never had a word of conversation with Sallie E. Page about the houses; that Ellington lives in one and Mrs. Page in the other; that the value of the work done ou the property of Rufus H. Page was $5.87, and the residue, amounting to $1,571.11, was done on the property of Mrs. Page; that $771.11 has been paid on the claim, and no other sum; that he owed Page only a small sum when the work was begun; that Rufus H. Page gave his individual note for the amount due in settlement of the whole claim upon which the suit is brought. The defendant, Mrs. Sallie E. Page, introduced as a witness for the plaintiff, testified that she owned the wood-yard lot, and described it from the complaint; that she had bargained to buy two lots on Saunders street, adjoining R. W. Best and others, and described it fully from the complaint; that she knew that work was being done on both the Saunders-Street lots and on the wood-yard lot at the time, and went around several times and saw the work going on; that she did not authorise her husband to contract for any work on these houses; that she knew who did the work; that Stanley and Thomas were the carpenters, and Hammill & Weir were the contractors for the brick and plaster work; that she raised no objection to the work that the plaintiff did on the place. The plaintiff proposed to ask this witness what was her husband's pecuniary condition in 1877; asked to show that the plaintiff did not rely on the husband for payment, but relied on his lien, and also to corroborate Weir's statement to this effect. This was objected to by the defendant, and excluded by the court, and the plaintiff excepted. This witness further testified that she did not direct or authorize any change in the buildings; that she expected to rent the places out; that in 1877 Mr. Page was operating with money borrowed on the wood-yard property; that the wood-yard property was under mortgage when she took it. The defendant offered in evidence an account rendered by the plaintiff, at the foot of which was the following: "Settled by due-bill. Raleigh, N. C., Jan. 17th, 1878;" and signed by W. J Weir. The plaintiff was recalled, and testified, after objection from the defendant, that he did not give the paper referred to in lieu of his lien, but told Rufus

H. Page that he would rely on the statutory lien. The court charged the jury that there was no evidence of any contract to bind the separate property of the feme defendant, and that her property cannot be subjected to the lien of the plaintiff's claim. To this charge the plaintiff excepted, and assigned the same as error. The plaintiff insisted that the husband was agent for his wife, and, besides, that the separate estate was bound under the whole evidence. The court, being of contrary opinion, so held, and plaintiff excepted. Case on appeal settled at Oxford, 29th August, 1891, by consent. Affirmed.

S. G. Ryan, for appellant. *Batchelor & Devereux,* for appellees.

DAVIS, J., (*after stating the facts as above.*) The plaintiff bases his claim and lien for work and labor done and material furnished upon a contract made with Rufus H. Page, the deceased husband of the defendant. It is well settled that unless a married woman be a free trader, as prescribed by statute, (Code, §§ 1827, 1828, et seq.,) she is incapable of making any executory contract affecting her real or personal estate, except as allowed in section 1826 of the Code. We deem it sufficient to refer to these sections of the Code, and to Farthing v. Shields, 106 N. C. 289, 10 S. E. Rep. 998, and the authorities there cited, in which the subject is considered, as conclusive of the correctness of the ruling of his honor below.[1] But counsel for the plaintiff says the defendant's property has been greatly enhanced in value by the work and labor done and material furnished, and that she enjoys the benefit of this increased value at the expense of the plaintiff, and upon broad principles of equity —ex æquo et bono—he is entitled to compensation, and ought to be paid by the defendant, who enjoys the benefit of the increased value. The only answer to this —and, so far as this court is concerned or has power, it is conclusive—is that the law to which reference has been made clearly and explicitly declares otherwise, unless the work and labor had been done and the material furnished under a contract allowed by law. It is the duty of this court to construe and declare the law, and it is not within its province to make or alter it. The constitution of North Carolina secures to every married woman the sole and separate estate in her real and personal property, independent of her husband, as if she were a *feme sole.* Having in relation to her separate estate all the rights of a *feme sole,* whether and to what extent her protecting disabilities ought to be removed, and her liabilities, in dealing with her separate estate, as to all persons other than her husband, made commensurate with her rights, and whether such alterations in the law would not pre-

[1] Code N. C. § 1826, provides that "no woman during her coverture shall be capable of making any contract to affect her real or personal estate, except for her necessary personal expenses, as for the support of the family, or such as may be necessary in order to pay her debts existing before marriage, without the written consent of her husband, unless she be a free trader, as hereinafter allowed."

vent much injustice and many frauds, are questions to be addressed to the wise consideration and sound discretion of the law-making power, and not to the court. No error.

RAMSEY v. CHEEK.

(Supreme Court of North Carolina. Nov. 8, 1891.)

LIBEL— PRIVILEGED COMMUNICATIONS — CHARGES AGAINST PUBLIC OFFICER.

An alleged libel consisted in a letter written by the defendant to the superintendent of the United States census, wherein it was stated that the defendant thought himself entitled to recommend some of his political friends in the district in which he lived, and have them appointed as enumerators; that the supervisor, however, had paid no attention to his recommendations, but had appointed the plaintiff, a man who had since the war murdered two Union soldiers, and been instrumental also in defrauding the defendant out of his election to the legislature. There was evidence that the charges were untrue, and that the character of the plaintiff was good. There was no evidence in reply, and the answer admitted that the object of the defendant was to secure plaintiff's removal from office. Held, that the communication was one only of qualified privilege, and that, as there was evidence tending to show malice, the case should have been submitted to the jury.

Appeal from superior court, Durham county; EDWIN T. BOYKIN, Judge.

This was an action for libel, brought by N. A. Ramsey against James A. Cheek. The alleged libel consisted of the following letter, written by the defendant, concerning the plaintiff and others, and was addressed to the Honorable Robert Porter, superintendent of the Eleventh United States census: "Hillsboro, N. C., June 10th, 1890. Hon. Robert Porter, Washington, D. C.—Dear Sir: In this district, Mr. Hawkins [the supervisor] appointed a large majority of enumerators, extreme Democrats, ballot-box stuffers, among them murderers and drunkards. I, having represented the county and Durham in the state legislature, having been the Republican candidate for the state senate last election, thought that I was entitled to recommend and get a part of my Republican friends appointed enumerators, but instead of this Hawkins pays no attention to me and friends, but appoints in Durham a man named Ramsey, who murdered, since the war, over two Union soldiers while they were asleep. This same man was the leader in defrauding me and Mr. Nichols out of our election last election. Another of his appointees, * * *. The above characters is a sample of the kind of men Hawkins appointed. We do not know, or can we understand, such work coming from a Republican. Some good men say he has boodled out the places to Democrats to injure the Republican cause in the future. Whoever has control or recommends the appointments in North Carolina, does not care for the interest of the Republican party in this section. * * * Respectfully, JAMES A. CHEEK." The court held, as a matter of law, that the communication was privileged, and that, as there was no evidence of express malice, plaintiff could not recover. From

an order taking the case from the jury plaintiff appeals. Reversed.

W. A. Guthrie and J. S. Manning, for appellant. J. W. Graham and Boone & Parker, for appellee.

CLARK, J. The words used charged the plaintiff with an indictable offense, and also were calculated to disparage him in his office. They were actionable per se. The defendant introduced no evidence, neither to prove the truth of the allegations, nor to show that he had written the letter for an honest, bona fide purpose; but contended that the letter was a privileged communication, and that the burden was on the plaintiff to show express malice, which he had failed to do. The court being of opinion with the defendant, the plaintiff took a nonsuit and appealed. Ordinarily, in libel and slander, if the words are actionable per se, the law presumes malice, and the burden is on the defendant to show that the charge is true. It is otherwise if the communication is privileged. Privileged communications are of two kinds: (1) Absolutely privileged,—which are restricted to cases in which it is so much to the public interest that the defendant should speak out his mind fully and freely that all actions in respect to the words used are absolutely forbidden, even though it be alleged that they were used falsely, knowingly, and with express malice. This complete immunity obtains only where the public service or the due administration of justice requires it, e. g., words used in debate in congress and the state legislatures, reports of military or other officers to their superiors in the line of their duty, everything said by a judge on the bench, by a witness in the box, and the like. In these cases the action is absolutely barred. 13 Amer. & Eng. Enc. Law, 406. (2) Qualified privilege. In less important matters, where the public interest does not require such absolute immunity, the plaintiff will recover in spite of the privilege if he can prove that the words were not used bona fide, but that the defendant used the privileged occasion artfully and knowingly to falsely defame the plaintiff. Odger, Sland. & L. 184. In this class of cases an action will lie only where the party is guilty of falsehood and express malice. 13 Amer. & Eng. Enc. Law, supra. Express malice is malice in fact, as distinguished from implied malice, which is raised as a matter of law by the use of words libelous per se, when the occasion is not privileged. Whether the occasion is privileged is a question of law for the court, subject to review, and not for the jury, unless the circumstances of the publication are in dispute, when it is a mixed question of law and fact. The present case is one of qualified privilege. The plaintiff was not in government employ under Porter. He was not called upon by any moral or legal obligation to make the report, and it was not made in the line of official duty. It was not absolutely privileged. But he was an American citizen, interested in the proper and efficient administration of the public service. He had, therefore, the right to criticise public officers; and if he honestly and *bona fide* believed and had probable cause to believe that the character and conduct of the plaintiff were such that the public interest demanded his removal, he had a right to make the communication in question, giving his reasons therefor, to the head of the department. The presumption of law is that he acted *bona fide*, and the burden was on the plaintiff to show that he wrote the letter with malice or without probable cause. Briggs v Garrett, 111 Pa. St. 404, 2 Atl. Rep. 513; Bodwell v. Osgood, 3 Pick. 379. "Malice," in this connection, is defined as "any indirect and wicked motive, which induces the defendant to defame the plaintiff. If malice be proved, the privilege attaching to the occasion is lost at once." Odger, Sland. & L. 267; Clark v. Molyneux, 3 Q. B. Div. 246; Bromage v. Prosser, 4 Barn. & C. 247; Hooper v. Truscott, 2 Bing. N. C. 457; Dickson v. Earl of Wilton, 1 Fost. & F. 419. The rules applicable to an ordinary action for libel apply in such cases whenever malice is proved. Proof that the words are false is not sufficient evidence of malice, unless there is evidence that the defendant knew at the time of using them that they were false. Fountain v. Boodle, 43 E. C. L. 605; Odger, Sland. & L. 275. That the defendant was mistaken in the words used by him on such confidential or privileged occasion is, taken alone, no evidence of malice. Kent v. Bongarts, 15 R. I. 72, 23 Atl. Rep. —, and cases cited.

We do not assent to the opposite doctrine, which would seem to be laid down by PEARSON, J., in Wakefield v. Smithwick, 49 N. C. 327, which is not supported by the authority he cites and doubtless intended to follow; for, if the words are true, a defendant does not need the protection of privilege. It is when they are false that he claims it. To strip him of such protection there must be both falsehood and malice. To hold that falsehood is itself proof of malice in such cases reduces the protection to defend on the presumption of the truth of the charges. If, however, there were means at hand for ascertaining the truth of the matter, of which the defendant neglects to avail himself, and chooses rather to remain in ignorance when he might have obtained full information, there will be no pretense for any claim of privilege. Odger Sland. & L. 199. 'To entitle matter otherwise libelous to the protection [of qualified privilege] which attaches to communications made in the fulfillment of duty, *bona fides*, or, to use our own equivalent, honesty of purpose, is essential; and to this again two things are necessary' (1) That it be made not merely on an occasion which would justify making it, but also from a sense of duty; (2) that it be made with a belief of its truth." COCKBURN, C. J., in Dawkins v. Lord Paulet, L. R. 5 Q. B. at page 102. The malice may be proved by some extrinsic evidence, such as ill feeling, or personal hostility, or threats, and the like, on the part of the defendant towards the plaintiff; but the plaintiff is not bound to prove malice by extrinsic evidence. He may rely on the words of the libel itself, and on the circumstances attending its

publication, as affording evidence of malice. Odger Sland. & L. 277–288; 13 Amer. & Eng. Enc. Law, 431.

In the present case, the letter charged the defendant with murder, and with having cheated the plaintiff out of his election. There was evidence tending to prove that these charges were untrue, and that the character of plaintiff was good. There was no evidence in reply, and the answer admits that the object of the communication was to secure the removal of plaintiff from the office he held. There was evidence on the face of the letter tending to show that the motive of the plaintiff was ill will to the plaintiff by reason of his alleged action in defrauding defendant of his election, and spleen on account of his (the defendant's) not having had his recommendation more considered, and his friends appointed to the offices to which Ramsey and others, named in the letter, had been appointed. There being evidence tending to prove malice as above defined, (which need not be personal ill will to the plaintiff,) his honor erred in not submitting the case to the jury. If the defendant made the communication, not recklessly or maliciously, but *bona fide*, and out of a desire to benefit the public service, the plaintiff cannot recover, though the charges made by the defendant may be untrue. That the plaintiff was of a different political party from himself gave him, however, no license to make to the appointing power false and defamatory charges against him maliciously or without probable cause, simply to secure his removal from office. If the defendant thought the plaintiff should be removed from office because belonging to a different political party, and therefore, in his judgment, unsuitable or unfit to hold the office, he should have put his letter on that ground, and there could have been no complaint. He had no right to make defamatory charges, if false, to secure defendant's removal, the motive not being a *bona fide* one to purge the public service of a felon and ballot-box stuffer, but merely to remove one who was objectionable to him either as being of an opposite party or by having injured him personally, or from having been appointed instead of his own recommendee for the place. If the defendant's motive was to injure Hawkins, and to do that he recklessly made false and defamatory allegations against the plaintiff, that is malice which would entitle the plaintiff to damages. It is to the public interest that the unfitness or derelictions of public officials should be reported to the authority having the power of removal, and any citizen *bona fide* making such report does no more than his duty, and is protected by public policy against the recovery of damages, even though the charge should prove to be false. But public justice will not permit the government archives to be made with impunity the receptacle of false and defamatory charges, made to secure the removal of an officer, whereby the malice of the party making such charge may be gratified, or that some benefit or advantage, direct or indirect, may come to him. Proctor v. Webster, 16 Q. B. Div. 112, (1885.) If the party knows the charge to be false, or makes it without probable cause, this is evidence of malice. Wakefield v. Smithwick, 49 N. C. 327. If the charge in such cases is false, the law looks to the motive. If the defendant, not moved by the public welfare, but by some wicked and indirect motive, such as to gratify his malice, or his love of patronage, to assert his own influence, or the like, by false charges has willfully or recklessly defamed the plaintiff, the later is entitled to recover damages at the hands of the jury. Error.

BRADSHER v. CHEEK.

(Supreme Court of North Carolina. Nov. 3, 1891.)

Appeal from superior court, Durham county; EDWIN T. BOYKIN, Judge.

Action for libel by W. C. Bradsher against James A. Cheek. Defendant wrote a letter to the United States census supervisor, charging the plaintiff with an attempt to murder. At the close of plaintiff's testimony the court said that it would charge the jury that the letter was a privileged communication, and that there was no evidence of malice. Plaintiff submitted to a nonsuit, and appealed. Reversed.

W. W. Fuller, for appellant. *Boone & Parker* and *J. W. Graham,* for appellee.

CLARK, J. This action is brought against the same defendant and upon the same letter as in the case of Ramsey v. Cheek, 13 S. E. Rep. 775. The only difference is that the charge made against this plaintiff in the letter is of an attempt to murder instead of murder, and there is no allegation of personal injury to the defendant by this plaintiff having defrauded him out of his election. But from the letter itself there was evidence to go to the jury tending to show express malice, as stated in our opinion in that case. The defendant may have made the communication, as the law presumes, with a *bona fide* and patriotic motive to secure the removal from office of a man whom he deemed unfit to fill it by reason of his having attempted to commit a felony, or it may be that his motive was wounded self-love in not having those recommended by himself appointed, or to obtain the removal of the plaintiff and Ramsey on false allegations, and the securing the nomination of their successors for his own friends. This was a matter for the jury to pass upon, and they had a right to consider the paper itself, there being on its face, taken altogether, and with the circumstances surrounding, some evidence of express malice, as is more fully pointed out in the foregoing case. Error.

MᴄNAMEE v. COKE, Secretary of State, et al.

(Supreme Court of North Carolina. Nov 3, 1891.)

PUBLIC LANDS — TITLES DERIVED FROM STATES— VOID ENTRIES—REMEDIES—INJUNCTION.

1. The claimant of title to several contiguous tracts of land cannot enjoin the secretary of state from issuing grants thereto upon void entries, on the ground that they will prove a cloud upon his title, because he is not entitled to such relief unless in rightful possession, in which case his remedy at law is adequate, as under Code N. C. § 1277, by recording surveys of their outer lines, so as to exhibit their outer boundaries as if the whole territory were one tract, his possession of one is possession of all, enabling him to redress an invasion of any of them; in addition to which he may under Code N. C. § 2786, bring an action in the superior court of the county in which the land lies to repeal and vacate grants issued "against law," or obtained "by false suggestion, surprise, or fraud."

2. An act of the legislature curing the grantee's title as to the state would in no wise affect plaintiff's title.

Appeal from superior court, Wake county; ROBERT W. WINSTON, Judge.

Suit in equity by Charles McNamee for an injunction to restrain Octavius Coke, secretary of state, from issuing to B. J. Alexander grants of land from the state. Injunction dissolved. Plaintiff appeals. Affirmed.

STATEMENT BY THE COURT. The plaintiff set forth in his complaint that the defendant B. J. Alexander had entered and caused to be surveyed a portion of the bed of the French Broad river, in Buncombe county, for all of which land the plaintiff had title through mesne conveyances connecting him with grants from the state, some of which crossed the river so as to include the whole bed, and others of which extended to the middle of the stream from each side. The plaintiff alleged that the said entries, on account of the form and the manner of recording them upon the books of the entry-taker, and the mistakes made by the surveyor in locating them, were void; but that the evidence showing them to be void for irregularity might be lost by lapse of time. The plaintiff prayed judgment that the entries be declared void; that the secretary of state be enjoined from issuing, and the defendant Alexander from receiving, or putting on record, grants issued upon said entries. It was contended that the grants, if issued, would prove a cloud upon the title of the plaintiff, among others, for the reason that the legislature might cure the defects in the entries by statute. The judge below, after granting a temporary restraining order, dissolved it, and gave judgment that the defendant go without day, and for costs. The plaintiff appealed from the judgment.

F. H. Busbee, for appellant. *Strong & Stronach, F. A. Scuddley,* and *A. W. Graham,* for appellee.

AVERY, J. If the plaintiff, by means of some grants from the state, covering the whole bed of the French Broad river, by crossing the stream, and others extending *ad filum aquæ* from each side, together with mesne conveyances connecting him with all of such grants, could, as he alleges, show title to the whole of the bed of said river from Smith's bridge to the mouth of Avery's creek, being the portion of the river bed covered by the entries and surveys of the defendant Alexander, and for which the latter is asking that grants be issued, it would follow, according to his own statement of the facts, that for any conceivable injury that the plaintiff may hereafter sustain on account of the issuing of the grants applied for he would have a full and complete remedy by an action of law. If this proposition can be sustained, it is familiar learning that he is not entitled to extraordinary relief by injunction. Should the defendant obtain his grant, enter upon the bed of the river, and erect a fish-trap, as suggested by counsel, then the plaintiff, having the older and better title, as he alleges, could bring the proper action, and recover possession, and such damages as he may have sustained on account of the trespass. Meantime, if the plaintiff is in the actual possession of any part of the land covered by one of the grants through which he claims title, his constructive possession extends over the whole boundary of such grant, either across the bed of the stream or *ad filum aquæ*, according to the nature of the particular patent; and until the defendant Alexander shall enter the plaintiff cannot maintain an action at law, even on account of location of the entry on, or the issuance of the grant for, his land. Pearson v. Boyden, 86 N. C. 585; Kitchen v. Wilson, 80 N. C. 191; Staton v. Mullis, 92 N. C. 623; Davis v. Higgins, 91 N. C. 382; Ruffin v. Overby, 105 N. C. 78, 11 S. E. Rep. 251. By recording and registering a survey of the outer lines of several contiguous tracts so as to exhibit their outer boundaries, as if the whole territory had been covered by one tract, a possession at any point on either of the separate tracts will become equivalent in law to a possession of "the whole and every part." Code, § 1277. It is therefore in the power of the plaintiff to make an actual possession on one of his tracts,—a constructive possession of all of his contiguous tracts. If the plaintiff, therefore, has shown himself to be in the rightful possession of the land in controversy, he cannot maintain the action in this case to remove a cloud upon his title, because, nothing more appearing, he has an adequate remedy by action at law in case of any wrongful invasion of the premises. On the other hand, an action brought for the purpose of removing a cloud upon the title cannot be maintained at all, unless it appears affirmatively that the plaintiff is in the rightful possession. Peacock v. Scott, 104 N. C. 154, 10 S. E. Rep. 456. If it be admitted that the plaintiff is holding rightfully under each and every grant, through which he claims, his remedy at law is adequate, unless it can be made to appear that proofs upon which the plaintiff would now recover in a controversy at law, despite grants issued to defendant on his entries, may be lost by the lapse of time, and that by such loss the defendant may be enabled to prevail in such action hereafter, whereas the plaintiff can show the better title now. Browning v. Lavender, 104 N. C. 69, 10 S. E. Rep. 77; Busbee v. Macy, 85 N. C. 329; Busbee v. Lewis, Id. 332; Murray v. Hazell, 99 N. C. 168, 5 S. E. Rep. 428. If the plaintiff had, when this action was brought, a perfect title, as he alleges and contends, to the whole of that portion of the bed of the river in dispute, then he would have the right to recover in an action for possession, as against the defendant Alexander, claiming under a junior grant, whether valid or void. If the plaintiff cannot connect himself with older grants or good title covering the land in dispute, then he is not aggrieved, and has no *status* in the court; for even an entry located by him so as to cover the *locus in quo* would be but an inchoate equity, which would not be enforced by an action. Featherston v. Mills, 4 Dev. 596; Plemmons v. Fore, 2 Ired. Eq. 312. If the plaintiff can show title through older grants, though it be admitted that,

as between the defendant Alexander and the state, a grant which when issued was void for failure to comply with the entry laws, could be made valid by a curative act of the legislature, still no remedial statute could be construed to divest an interest in land, acquired by the plaintiff before its passage, out of him, and vest it in Alexander. No law, which transfers the property of one person to another for his own private purposes, without the consent of the owner, has ever been held a constitutional exercise of legislative power in any state in the Union. Cooley, Const. Lim. *165; Wilkinson v. Leland, 2 Pet. 627; Hoke v. Henderson, 4 Dev. 4; King v. Hunter, 65 N. C. 603; Stanmire v. Powell, 13 Ired. 312; Sedgwick, St. & Const. Law, pp. 195, 368, and Suth. St. Const. § 480; Westervelt v. Gregg, 12 N. Y. 202; Eakin v. Raub, 12 Serg. & R. 340; Alter's Appeal, 67 Pa. St. 341; Hasbrouck v. Milwaukee, 13 Wis. 37; White Mts. Railroad v. White Mts. (N. H.) Railroad, 50 N. H. 50. We have discussed *seriatim* the questions raised by the plaintiff's assignment of errors, because they may hereafter arise again. But the plaintiff cannot maintain this action brought in the superior court of Wake county, to enjoin the secretary of state, the defendant Octavius Coke, from issuing grants to the defendant Alexander, for the reason that our statute (Code, § 2786) provides a remedy at law, to be prosecuted in the superior court of Buncombe county, where the land lies, against the defendant Alexander, if he shall hereafter obtain, or has since this action was brought obtained, a grant from the state "by false suggestion, surprise, or fraud," or "against law," to the injury of the plaintiff. Carter v. White, 101 N. C. 31, 7 S. E. Rep. 473; Crow v. Holland, 4 Dev. 417; Miller v. Twitty, 3 Dev. & B. 14. If the plaintiff can hereafter make it appear before the proper tribunal that a junior grant has been issued contrary to law for the land which he holds, as he alleges, under older patents, then he can find redress for any grievance shown under the plain provisions of the statute. It is unnecessary, therefore, to discuss the other question, so elaborately presented by the able counsel for the plaintiff. The secretary of state has not refused to issue the grants to Alexander, as in case of Wool v. Saunders, 108 N. C. 729, 13 S. E. Rep. 294, and he has not raised the question, whether the entry is void upon its face, and, if not, whether he shall be compelled to issue the grants applied for. If the plaintiff can connect himself with older grants covering all of the lands embraced by defendant's entries, as surveyed, or could have shown a perfect title to the land in controversy in any way, when the entries were made by the defendant Alexander, then, in case the latter should enter upon it claiming under a junior grant, the plaintiff could bring his action for possession in the superior court of Buncombe county, and put him out, or, if the junior grant has been or should hereafter be issued contrary to law, a party aggrieved thereby could proceed under the statute, (Code, § 2786,) though no trespass may have been committed. Meantime, if the entries appeared from a bare inspection to be manifestly void, the courts would neither interpose to restrain the secretary of state from issuing grants upon them, nor compel him by *mandamus* to issue them. Wool v. Saunders, supra. We concur with the judge who tried the case below in the opinion that the law has provided a full and adequate remedy for the plaintiff, and that he has failed to show that the grants, if issued to the defendant, would prove a cloud upon his title. There is error. Judgment must be affirmed, except as to the order of dismissal. It was error to order that the case be dismissed, but as that does not affect the merits, and the only material question was whether the secretary of state should be restrained from issuing a grant, the plaintiff must pay the costs incurred in this court.

Judgment modified and affirmed.

———

WYATT v. LYNCHBURG & D. R. Co. *et al.*

(*Supreme Court of North Carolina.* Nov. 8, 1891.)

APPEAL—INSUFFICIENT RECORD—REMAND.

Where the transcript on appeal merely shows process, a reference to arbitration, an award, exception thereto, the action of the court below thereon, and an appeal, but there are no pleadings, nor an agreed statement of facts, so that the supreme court can see the contention of the parties, and that the court below had jurisdiction, and where both parties are not able to file the pleadings *nunc pro tunc* in the supreme court, the cause will be remanded.

Appeal from superior court, Durham county.

Action by W. J. Wyatt against the Lynchburg & Durham Railroad Company and others. Judgment for plaintiff. Defendants appeal. Remanded.

Wm. A. Guthrie, for appellants. *Boone & Parker, J. S. Manning,* and *John W. Graham,* for appellee.

CLARK, J. The transcript shows process, a reference to arbitration, an award, exception thereto, the action of the court below thereon, and an appeal; but there are no pleadings, nor an agreed statement of facts in lieu thereof, that we might see the contention of the parties, and that the court below had jurisdiction of the cause of action. The court would permit the pleadings to be filed in this court *nunc pro tunc,* (Sup. Ct. Rule 26, 12 S. E. Rep. vii.,) so as not to delay the hearing, but, as both parties are not able to do this, the cause must be remanded. The case is substantially the same as Daniel v. Rogers, 95 N. C. 134; Rowland v. Mitchell, 90 N. C. 649. Remanded.

———

EDWARDS v. TOWN OF HENDERSON.

(*Supreme Court of North Carolina.* Nov. 12, 1891.)

APPEAL—FAILURE TO PRINT RECORD—NEGLECT OF COUNSEL.

The duty of having the record printed, as required by Sup. Ct. N. C. rules 28–30, is not a professional duty of counsel, and if they assume to discharge it, they are *pro hac vice* agents of appellant, who will be bound by their neglect.

Motion to reinstate appeal dismissed for failure to print record.

A. C. Zollicoffer and *T. T. Hicks,* for appellant. *Batchelor & Devereux,* for appellee.

CLARK, J. This is a motion to reinstate an appeal which was dismissed for failure to print the record, as required by rules 28–30, (12 S. E. Rep. viii.) The appellant says that he intrusted the duty of causing the record to be printed to his counsel. Counsel offer no excuse, except that they were busy, and forgot to have it done. The duty of having the record printed is not a professional one, since the client can attend to it himself, and might easily have it printed below and sent up with the transcript. Hence, if counsel assume to discharge such duty, they are *pro hac vice* agents, not counsel, and their neglect is the neglect of the party himself, as was held in Griffin v. Nelson, 106 N. C. 235, 11 S. E. Rep. 414, which has been cited with approval at this term in Finlayson v. Accident Co., 18 S. E. Rep. 789. The duty of printing the record is not a mere formality. It is a necessity, that the increasing volume of business in the court of last resort may be more easily understood on the argument, and that each of the judges may not only then, but afterwards, have each case before him. When there is but one record, and that in manuscript, the disadvantage is seriously felt. The court, like the supreme courts (it is believed) of every other state, several years since adopted this rule. This was not lightly done, but after full consideration. This court has ever since felt the necessity for a strict adherence to the rule. Rencher v. Anderson, 93 N. C. 105; Witt v. Long, Id. 388; Horton v. Green, 104 N. C. 400, 10 S. E. Rep. 470; Whitehurst v. Pettipher, 105 N. C. 39, 10 S. E. Rep. 857; Griffin v. Nelson, 106 N. C. 235, 11 S. E. Rep. 414; Stephens v. Koonce, 106 N. C. 255, 11 S. E. Rep. 282; Hunt v. Railroad Co., 107 N. C. 447, 12 S. E. Rep. 378; Roberts v. Lewald, 108 N. C. 405, 12 S. E. Rep. 1028. To permit an appellant to obtain a delay of six months by his negligence in not complying with this requirement would convert a rule which was adopted as a means for the speedier and better consideration of causes into a fruitful source of delay. Rather than that, appellees would prefer to argue their causes without the printed record, which the court, in justice to itself and the litigants, cannot permit. Appellants might as well fail to send up the transcript as not to have it in a condition to be heard by failing to have the "case and exceptions" printed. No sufficient cause has been shown, and the motion to reinstate must be denied.

———

SPRUILL *et al.* v. ARRINGTON *et al.*

(*Supreme Court of North Carolina.* Oct. 20, 1891.)

LANDLORD'S LIEN ON CROPS — RIGHTS OF PURCHASERS AT FORECLOSURE SALE — APPORTIONMENT OF RENT—COSTS.

1. Code N. C. § 1754, provides that the landlord shall have a lien on crops which shall "be preferred to all other liens," and that the crops

shall be "vested in possession of the lessor" until the rents are paid. Section 1800 provides that the lien in favor of those making advances on crops "shall not affect the rights of the landlords to their proper share of rents." *Held*, that a purchaser at foreclosure sale who enters upon the land before the crop is planted, and rents it to the mortgagor in possession, is entitled to all the rights of a landlord, notwithstanding that at the time of the sale considerable advances have been made upon the crop. Killebrew v. Hines, 104 N. C. 182, 10 S. E. Rep. 159, 251, distinguished.

2. Code N. C. § 1748, provides that, when rents are payable to successive owners, and the right of any owner is terminable by death or other uncertain event, the payment following shall be apportioned among the said owners. Section 1749 provides that when a farm lease determines by the happening of an uncertain event, determining the estate of the lessor, the tenant shall continue to the end of the year, and shall pay to the succeeding owner a proportionate part of the rent. *Held*, that a foreclosure is not such an uncertain event as to entitle one to the apportionment of a crop which is planted after the sale, and on which he has made advances with knowledge of the foreclosure decree.

3. Under Code N. C. § 525, plaintiff is entitled to costs of course upon recovery in an action for the possession of personal property; and where other defendants intervene in such a case, and file a joint answer with the original defendant, and make a joint defense, the costs which occur after the intervention should be taxed, not merely against the interveners, but against all the defendants.

Appeal from superior court, Nash county; Spier Whitaker, Judge.

Action by W. T. Spruill and others against M. T. Arrington and others to recover the possession of crops. There was judgment for plaintiffs, and defendants appeal. Affirmed.

Bunn & Battle and *Batchelor & Devereux*, for appellants. *F. A. Woodard*, for appellees.

Davis, J. In September, 1880, the defendant M. T. Arrington contracted to purchase of C. M. Cooke the land on which the cotton which is the subject of this controversy was produced. All the purchase money was not paid, and on the 28th day of April, 1889, the said land was sold under a judgment and decree of foreclosure in an action properly instituted for that purpose, to pay the purchase money therefor, and the *feme* plaintiff became the purchaser, and the next day rented the same to the defendant M. T. Arrington, who had previously been in possession under the contract of purchase from C. M. Cooke. It was in evidence, and not controverted, that the day after the plaintiff purchased the land her husband went on it, that it was unoccupied, and no cotton had been planted. It is admitted that the defendant Arrington rented the land from the *feme* plaintiff for the balance of the year after the 30th of April, 1889, and was to pay $120 rent. On the 28th day of January, 1889, the defendant Arrington executed an agricultural lien upon the crop to be raised on said land in the year 1889 to the defendants Boddie, Ward & Co. to secure advances, etc.; and that they furnished the said Arrington supplies, etc., for agricultural purposes, amounting to $292.18 up to the 18th day of April, 1889, and after that to the 16th of October, 1889, to the amount

of $202.18. There is much irrelevant matter sent up with the transcript, but the material question presented for our determination is whether the plaintiff landlord, who purchased the land on the 28th day of April, 1889, and rented it to the defendant Arrington for the balance of the year, was entitled to a preferred lien on the crop produced this year to secure the rent; or are the defendants Boddie, Ward & Co. entitled to the crop under the lien executed to them by M. T. Arrington on the 28th of January, prior to the purchase by the plaintiff?

Code, § 1754, not only gives to the landlord or lessor a lien on all crops raised on the land rented, which shall "be preferred to all other liens, but the crop is vested in possession of the lessor" until the rents are paid, and all stipulations contained in the lease or agreement are complied with, whether the land be rented by written or oral agreement; and it is provided in section 1800 that the lien in favor of those making advances on crops "shall not affect the rights of the landlords to their proper share of rents." The lien in aid of advances is in preference to all other liens except that of the landlord for rents. Wooten v. Hill, 98 N. C. 48, 3 S. E. Rep. 846, and cases cited and relied on by counsel for defendant. The relation between the plaintiff and defendant M. T. Arrington was that of landlord and tenant, and not that of vendor and vendee. But it is insisted by counsel for defendants that when the lien was executed in January, 1889, Arrington was the vendee of C. M. Cooke, and entitled to all the crops made upon the land as vendee in possession, and not a lessee; and, if the lien upon the crop to be made was a preferred lien to them, it could not be defeated by any arrangement between the plaintiff, who succeeded to the rights of the vendor, and the said Arrington, in respect to his paying rent, to which Boddie, Ward & Co. were in no way parties. How it might be between a mortgagor and mortgagee, or between a vendor and vendee, when there was no change in the possession, we need not consider; but the purchaser of the land, whether under a foreclosure, or from the vendor or mortgagee, who takes possession and rents the land, whether to the vendee or mortgagor or to any other person, occupies the position and is entitled to the rights of a landlord; and that is the case before us. The counsel for the defendants says: "Unless possession has been taken of the premises, or a receiver has been appointed, the mortgagor is the owner as to all the world, and is entitled to all the profit made." And for this he cites Killebrew v. Hines, 104 N. C. 182, 10 S. E. Rep. 159, 251. This is true, but there is a marked difference between the case before us and that of Killebrew v. Hines. In that case the cotton was made by the vendees in possession, and it was not until after it was severed and baled that the vendor asserted his claim to it; and it was properly held "that, if there be no entry or equitable proceeding by which the crops are sequestered, the mortgagee [vendor] has no lien upon and cannot recover them in an action in the nature of replevin." In the case before us the purchaser at the sale for the foreclosure took possession of the land, as she had the undoubted right to do, before the cotton was planted, and rented it to Arrington. Suppose, instead of renting it to him, she had cultivated it herself, or rented it to some one else, as she had the right to do, what would have become of the claim of Boddie, Ward & Co. under their lien? Noting the distinction between the cases, we refer to the able discussion of the questions in Killebrew v. Hines, and the cases there cited, as settling the claim of priority in favor of the plaintiffs.

But it is said that the plaintiffs had no interest in the land prior to the purchase in April, and Boddie, Ward & Co. had then made considerable advances under their agricultural lien. They had notice of the decree of foreclosure, and the crop was not planted when the plaintiffs purchased, nor does it appear that the advances were used in preparing the land for the crop; and, even if it did, they could not claim an apportionment of the crop under sections 1748 and 1749 of the Code,[1] for Arrington would have been entitled to no such apportionment. The lien executed by Arrington gave them no title to what did not belong to him. There was some discussion upon the question of the sufficiency of the description of the property in the lien of January 28, 1889, to which the plaintiffs objected, but they did not appeal; and that question is not before us, and is immaterial, if it were. We can see no force in the defendants' objection to the form in which the issues were submitted. They presented clearly and fairly the questions raised by the pleadings.

The only remaining objection is to the judgment because it taxes the costs against the defendants, whereas Boddie, Ward & Co. ought to have been charged with the costs that accrued after they intervened. The defendants Boddie, Ward & Co. intervened, and filed a joint answer with their co-defendant, M. T. Arrington, and they made a joint defense, and the judgment is for the plaintiffs against all the defendants for the recovery and for costs. The plaintiffs are entitled to the costs. Code, § 525, subsec. 2.[2] Having joined in the controversy, and made common cause in the defense, the interveners must abide the result. There is no error.

---

[1] Code N. C. § 1748, provides that when rents are payable to successive owners, and the right of any owner is terminable by death or other uncertain event during a period in which a payment is growing due, the next payment shall be apportioned among the successive owners according to the parts of such periods elapsing before and after the terminating event. Section 1749 provides that, where a lease of farming land determines by the happening of any uncertain event determining the estate of the lessor, the tenant, in lieu of emblements, shall continue to the end of the year, and shall pay to the succeeding owner a proportionate part of the rent, and be entitled to a reasonable compensation for the tillage.

[2] Code N. C. § 525, provides that costs shall be allowed of course to the plaintiff upon recovery in any action to recover the possession of personal property.

TRUSTEES OF GOLDSBOROUGH GRADED SCHOOL v. BROADHURST.

(Supreme Court of North Carolina. Nov. 12, 189*.)

SCHOOLS — TAXATION FOR THEIR ERECTION AND SUPPORT—LIABILITY OF TOWNSHIP.

1. Acts N. C. 1881, c. 189, and Acts 1887, c. 882, authorizing the levy of taxes on the taxable property and polls of Goldsborough township for the purpose of establishing and for the annual support of graded schools in that township, do not, either in terms or by implication, authorize the board of county commissioners to levy taxes to pay the interest or principal of any debt created for that purpose.

2. Acts N. C. 1891, c. 906, authorized the school trustees to issue bonds, secured by a mortgage, and sell them; to take up other bonds previously issued for the purpose of paying for and repairing graded schools in a certain township; and, to raise a fund to pay the interest, and provide a sinking fund to pay the principal, allowed said trustees to appropriate annually a sufficient amount of the school fund going into their hands; and then provided that if they failed to do so the county commissioners should levy a tax on the taxable property and polls of the township for such purpose. Held, that the purpose of the act, in directing the county commissioners to levy a tax on the township property to pay the bonds in case the trustees should not do so, was to make the township assume and pay a debt other than for its necessary expenses, and, not having been sanctioned by a majority of the voters of the township, was to that extent in violation of Const. N. C. art. 7, § 7, which provides that no municipal corporation shall contract any debt, nor shall any tax be levied or collected by any officers of the same, except for the necessary expenses thereof, unless by a vote of a majority of the qualified voters therein.

Appeal from superior court, Wayne county; SPIER WHITAKER, Judge.

Action by board of trustees of the Goldsborough graded school against D. J. Broadhurst to recover the price of certain school bonds sold defendant. Judgment for plaintiffs. Defendant appeals. Reversed.

STATEMENT BY THE COURT. In pursuance of the statute (Acts 1881, c. 189) an election was held in Goldsborough township in the county of Wayne on the fourth Monday in May, 1881, to take the sense of the voters therein as to establishing therein graded schools, as contemplated by that statute, and at that election a majority of the qualified voters of the township voted in favor of establishing such schools, and to levy the tax to support the same. Afterwards the statute (Acts 1887, c. 882) amended and modified, as therein provided, the above-cited statute, and under and in pursuance of its provisions, as alleged, an election was held in said township on the first Monday in May, 1887, at which a majority of the qualified voters thereof approved of the levy and collection of the annual tax in the statute allowed and provided for. The money raised by levy of taxes and constituting the school fund, as intended by the last-mentioned statute, was applied by the board of trustees of such graded schools to supplying such schools and the payment of the debt incurred for the purchase of grounds and the construction of the buildings for the colored school. The trustees mentioned, at the time they purchased the grounds and buildings for white children, executed bonds to the amount of $10,000, and, to secure the payment of the same, executed a mortgage on the said grounds and buildings, which bonds are yet unpaid. The said grounds and buildings are necessary to the said schools. The statute (Acts 1891, c. 206) prescribes that for the purpose of paying for and repairing the school buildings and grounds of the said graded schools for white children the said trustees shall have power and they are authorized to issue bonds of the denomination of $100 to an amount not exceeding $15,000, bearing interest at a rate not exceeding 6 per cent. per annum, and running to maturity at a period not exceeding 30 years. The trustees are allowed to sell said bonds at not less than par of their face value, or exchange them for the bonds above mentioned. To raise a fund to pay the interest and provide a sinking fund to pay the principal on said bonds, the trustees are allowed to appropriate annually a sufficient amount from the school fund going into their hands; and, if they fail to do so, the county commissioners of said county are required to levy a tax on the taxable property and polls of said township for the purpose as prescribed. To secure the payment of said bonds the said trustees are empowered to execute a mortgage of the said school property. Accordingly the said trustees have executed bonds and a mortgage of the property referred to, to secure the same, as allowed by the statute last cited, and sold and delivered to the defendant three of them, representing to him that they were valid, and a charge upon the taxable property of said township. It is alleged that he agreed and promised to pay for the bonds so delivered to him $300, and he refuses now to pay the same. This action is brought to recover that sum. The defendant alleges that the bonds are not a charge upon the taxable property and polls of the township, because the proposition to make such charge has not been submitted to and voted for by a majority of the qualified voters of said township. The court held otherwise, and gave judgment for the plaintiffs, and the defendant, having excepted, appealed to this court.

W. C. Munroe, for appellees.

MERRIMON, C. J. The single distinct question raised by the assignment of error for our decision is: "Are the board of commissioners of the county of Wayne charged and required by the statutes, (Acts 1881, c. 189; Acts 1887, c. 382; Acts 1891, c. 206,) all or any one of them, to annually levy a tax, as prescribed, upon the taxable property and polls of Goldsborough township in said county to pay the interest as the same shall come due, and to provide a sinking fund to pay the principal, when the same shall mature, of the bonds in question?" It is insisted that this question must be decided in the negative, because a majority of the qualified voters of the township named have not voted to create the mortgage debt of which such bonds are a part, nor have

they voted in favor of the levy of such tax. The first and second of the statutes cited above authorize the levy of taxes on the taxable property and polls of Goldsborough township for the purpose of establishing and the annual support of graded schools in that township, but they do not—certainly they do not in terms—authorize the trustees of these schools to create a debt secured by the mortgage of the school property, nor do they in terms or by implication authorize the board of commissioners of the county to levy taxes to pay the interest or principal of any debt for any purpose.

The statute of 1891 expressly authorized the trustees of the schools to issue their bonds to the amount of $15,000, and exchange them for those bonds first mentioned, unpaid and outstanding, and to sell the same, and to annually apply so much of the taxes levied for the support of the schools as may be necessary to pay the interest on such bonds, and to provide a sinking fund for the payment of the principal of the debt at its maturity. It is further provided that, "if the said board of trustees shall fail to provide for the payment of the interest or for the establishment of the sinking fund hereinbefore provided for, it shall be the duty of the board of county commissioners of Wayne county to levy a tax upon the property and polls in Goldsborough township in said county annually for the payment of said interest and the establishment of said sinking fund," etc. Thus, plainly, the debt last mentioned is sought to be made that of the township, and taxes are to be levied to pay it by the board of commissioners of the county in the way and to the extent prescribed. The obvious purpose is to have the township assume and pay the debt secured by the bonds and mortgage if the trustees fail to provide for its payment. The township, with corporate entity conferred upon it, is, in an important sense, a municipal corporation, exercising such corporate powers and functions as may be conferred upon it by statute. Code, § 707, par. 14; Brown v. Commissioners, 100 N. C. 92, 5 S. E. Rep. 178; Wallace v. Trustees, 84 N. C. 164. Here the clear purpose was to confer upon the township as a corporate entity capacity, power, and authority to assume a debt of the trustees of the graded schools. Whether this is sufficiently done or not is a question we need not now decide. It is not necessary to do so, because, granting for the present purpose that it is, we are clearly of opinion that the tax cannot be levied as prescribed for the conclusive reason that a majority of the qualified voters of the township have not voted in favor of assuming the debt of the trustees, nor in favor of the levy of a tax for the purpose. The constitution (article 7, § 7) expressly provides that "no county, city, town, or other municipal corporation shall contract any debt, pledge its faith, or loan its credit, nor shall any tax be levied or collected by any officers of the same, except for the necessary expenses thereof, unless by a vote of the majority of the qualified voters therein." No vote was taken to ascertain the will of a majority of such voters. It cannot be said properly that the debt authorised by the last-mentioned statute, or the other debt at first created by the trustees of the graded schools for the purchase of lands and the erection of appropriate school buildings, are debts created to pay "necessary expenses" of the township. Expenses incurred in establishing and supporting graded schools are not part of such "necessary expenses," because such schools do not pertain to or constitute part of the organization, or come within the ordinary purposes of townships, any more than colleges or the like institutions or particular enterprises or undertakings that are intended specially to promote the convenience or advantage of the people of a particular locality. Such things are exceptional in townships, and not necessary for their ordinary purposes. The very purpose of the constitutional inhibition is to prevent the creation of debts for such exceptional purposes without the sanction of a majority of the qualified voters of the township, city, or town. Important as are public schools, and graded schools as well, it is not the purpose of townships as such to establish and support them. Under the constitution and appropriate legislation in pursuance thereof. schools are otherwise provided for. Hence, when it is deemed expedient and desirable that a graded school shall be established in a particular township, a debt for the purpose can be created only with the sanction of a majority of the qualified voters thereof. Lane v. Stanly, 65 N. C. 153. This case is in no sense like that of Blanton v. Commissioners, 101 N. C. 532, 8 S. E. Rep. 162. There no new debt was in question or to be paid. The statute simply allowed the board of commissioners to issue new bonds in lieu of or to pay the old ones maturing. Here there was no old or prior debt of the township to be paid; the purpose is to pay a new debt. There is error. The judgment must be reversed, and the case disposed of according to law. To that end let this opinion be certified to the superior court. It is so ordered.

LYNCHBURG & D. R. CO. v. BOARD OF COMMISSIONERS OF PERSON COUNTY, (two cases.)

(*Supreme Court of North Carolina.* Nov. 3, 1891.)

RAILROAD AID BONDS—ACTION TO COMPEL ISSUANCE—SUBSCRIPTION—AUTHORITY OF AGENTS.

1. Under Const. N. C. art. 7, § 7, prohibiting a municipal corporation from contracting any debt unless authorized by a majority of its qualified voters, the issuance of township bonds will not be compelled when plaintiff alleges that it was authorized by "a majority of the votes cast."

2. In the absence of such authority, a township is not bound by the appointment of agents by the county commissioners and township justices to subscribe for stock on behalf of the township, and to represent it and vote at meetings of stockholders, and by the exercise of such authority by said agents. Jones v. Commissioners, 107 N. C. 248, 12 S. E. Rep. 69, distinguished.

Appeal from superior court, Person county; EDWIN T. BOYKIN, Judge.

Application by the Lynchburg & Durham Railroad Company for writ of *mandamus* to compel the board of comissioners of Person county to issue bonds for Mount Tirzah township. From a judgment for plaintiff defendant appeals. Judgment reversed, and writ denied.

W. W. Kitchin, for appellant. *W. A. Guthrie* and *A. W. Nowlin*, for appellee.

CLARK, J. It has been settled in this state by numerous decisions that a majority of the qualified or registered voters, and not merely of those voting, is necessary to enable a municipal corporation to loan its credit or contract a debt, under the provisions of article 7, § 7, Const. Southerland v. City of Goldsboro, 96 N. C. 49, 1 S. E. Rep. 760; Duke v. Brown, 96 N. C. 127, 1 S. E. Rep. 873; Markham v. Manning, 96 N. C. 132, 2 S. E. Rep. 40; McDowell v. Construction Co., 96 N. C. 514, 2 S. E. Rep. 351; Wood v. Town of Oxford, 97 N. C. 227, 2 S. E. Rep. 653; Rigsbee v. Durham, 98 N. C. 81, 3 S. E. Rep. 749, 99 N. C. 341, 6 S. E. Rep. 64. The plaintiff, who applies for a *mandamus* to compel the county commissioners to issue bonds for Mount Tirzah township, does not allege an adjudication or declaration by the county commissioners on a canvass of the returns that the subscription had been carried by a majority of the qualified voters of said township. Nor does it aver that in fact it was so carried. The complaint alleges that "the returns showed that a majority of the votes cast were in favor of subscription," and a declaration of the result to that effect by the commissioners on a canvass of the vote and a copy of such is set out. The basis of authority to issue the bonds—the vote of a majority of the qualified voters—is wanting, and the *mandamus* must be denied. Had the plaintiff averred that, though not so declared by the canvassing board, a majority of the qualified voters of said township in fact voted in favor of subscription, the proceedings, if brought to impeach the decision of the canvassing board, would be too late, the election having been held August 7, 1886, and this action not instituted till December 31, 1890. Jones v. Commissioners, 107 N. C. 248, 12 S. E. Rep. 69. In fact, however, the proceeding is not to impeach the declaration of the result as declared; and it is alleged in the answer, and it was not controverted in the argument, that a majority of the qualified voters of said township did not vote in favor of the subscription.

The plaintiff, however, claims that the defendants are estopped by the fact that they appointed an agent to subscribe the amount of the subscription on behalf of said township, who did so subscribe for it on behalf of the township on the books of the plaintiff company, and that said township has been represented in the meetings of the stockholders of the company by an agent appointed by the justices of the peace of the township, who has voted in such meetings; and that the plaintiff has made contracts relying upon the validity of such subscription. These allegations are denied in the answer, and it is alleged that the plaintiff well knew that such election did not authorize the issuance of the bonds, and this before making the contracts referred to. The judge found the facts on this contention as claimed by the plaintiff. The only authority that can fasten upon the township an obligation to pay a subscription is the duly-ascertained vote of a majority of its qualified voters. Without it any action of the county commissioners or 'township justices appointing agents to subscribe for and to represent or vote for said township in the stockholders' meetings of the plaintiff company was a nullity and *ultra vires*. The life-giving power required by the constitution—the expression of the popular will at the ballot-box—being lacking, if the commissioners had gone still further, and actually issued the bonds, they would have been invalid even in the hands of innocent purchasers. Duke v. Brown, 96 N. C. 127, 1 S. E. Rep. 873. Jones v. Commissioners, 107 N. C. 248, 12 S. E. Rep. 69, differs from this case. There the townships named voted the same day as those in this case, but as to them the county commissioners, on a canvass of the vote, declared that a majority of the qualified voters duly registered had voted in favor of the subscription. Afterwards the bonds were issued, and taxes levied to pay the interest. After the lapse of more than three years the plaintiff there, a tax-payer, sought to impeach the result, alleging, among other things, that a majority of the qualified voters had not in fact voted in favor of such subscription. The court, while adhering to the precedents that such proceedings were admissible if made in reasonable time, held that the delay was unreasonable, and the proceeding was barred. It is unnecessary to consider the exception that the summons was returnable at chambers and not to term. The complaint fails to state a cause of action, therefore let it be entered, action dismissed.

This opinion and decision applies also to 179 "A," between the same parties.

STATE v. NEAL.

(Supreme Court of North Carolina. Nov. 3, 1891.)

ROAD-TAX—SUFFICIENCY OF WARRANT.

A warrant simply charged that defendant willfully refused to attend and work on the public road after being lawfully warned, contrary to the statute, etc., but did not negative the payment of one dollar in discharge of his liability to perform the labor. *Held,* that a motion in arrest of judgment should have been allowed.

Appeal from superior court, Orange county; ROBERT W. WINSTON, Judge.

Prosecution against John W. Neal for refusing to work on a public road. Verdict of guilty. Defendant moved in arrest of judgment, which motion being denied, he appeals. Reversed.

W. A. Guthrie, for appellant. *The Attorney General,* for the State.

SHEPHERD, J. The warrant simply charges that the defendant "willfully refused to attend and work on the public road after being lawfully warned, contrary to the form of the statute," etc. There is nothing to negative the payment

of one dollar, in discharge of the defendant's liability to perform the labor required of him. No amendment was asked at any stage of the trial, either before or after verdict, and upon conviction the defendant moved in arrest of judgment. It is expressly decided that the motion should have been allowed. State v. Pool, 106 N. C. 698, 10 S. E. Rep. 1083; State v. Baker, 106 N. C. 758, 11 S. E. Rep. 360. The insufficiency of the warrant was not, we presume, called to the attention of his honor, the argument before him being addressed to the constitutionality of the act under which the defendant was prosecuted.

There is error.

COLTRANE v. LAMB.

(Supreme Court of North Carolina. Nov. 3, 1891.)

PUBLIC LANDS—GRANT FROM STATE—ACKNOWLEDGMENT — DEED PROVED BEFORE CLERK OF COURT.

1. A grant from the state of North Carolina, made in 1787, and registered in the county where the land was situated, is admissible in evidence without any acknowledgment or order of registration thereon, as is required by statute in the case of other conveyances. Ray v. Stewart, (N. C.) 11 S. E. Rep. 182, followed.

2. Under Rev. St. N. C. c. 37, § 25, which provided that deputy-clerks of the court of pleas and quarter sessions may prove and order registered conveyances of land, which was in force up to and including 1867, deeds so proven and ordered registered, and registered in 1867, were properly admitted in evidence.

3. Where the deeds were so proven and ordered registered by a deputy-clerk in 1867, nothing to the contrary appearing, it will be presumed such deputy was a deputy-clerk of such court of pleas and quarter sessions, and that he was duly qualified as such.

Appeal from superior court, Guilford county; JAMES C. MACRAE, Judge.

Proceeding by Lindsay Coltrane against T. C. Lamb to settle a boundary line. Verdict and judgment for plaintiff. Rule for a new trial denied. Defendant appeals. Affirmed.

L. M. Scott, for appellee.

MERRIMON, C. J. The plaintiff and defendant are the owners of adjoining tracts of land, and the purpose of this action is to settle the line that divides their property. On the trial, for the purpose of locating the line in question, the plaintiff was allowed to put in evidence, the defendant objecting, a grant from the state of date the 16th of May, 1787, which was registered in the county of Guilford. The ground of objection was that there did not appear any acknowledgment or order of registration thereon. The court, upon inspection of the registration, found that the grant had been so registered more than 100 years. The objection is without force. For the reasons well stated in Ray v. Stewart, 105 N. C. 472, 11 S. E. Rep. 182, the ruling of the court must be sustained. See, also, Freeman v. Hatley, 3 Jones, (N. C.) 115.

For the like purpose, the plaintiff was allowed, the defendant objecting, to put in evidence a deed dated December 1, 1848, which was proven and ordered to be registered, and registered in 1867; and also another deed, dated 27th of May, 1856, which was proven and ordered to be registered, and registered in 1867. The defendant's objection to these deeds was that they were proven before and ordered to be registered by a deputy-clerk. The objection cannot be sustained. Nothing to the contrary appearing, it must be taken that the deputy-clerk who took the proof of the deeds, and ordered the same to be registered, was the deputy of a clerk of the late court of pleas and quarter sessions, and that he was duly qualified as such. The objection is that such officer could not take proof and make such order of a deed. The statute pertinent (Rev. St. c. 37, § 25; Rev. Code, c. 37, § 2) expressly provides otherwise, and that the deputy may take probate of deeds, etc., of instruments and papers required to be registered. That statute was in force during and long before the year 1867, when the deeds referred to were proven and registered. Suddereth v. Smyth, 13 Ired. 452.

The defendant also excepted upon the ground that the court failed to give the jury a particular instruction specified. It does not appear that it was error not to give the same. So far as appears, there was no evidence that warranted such instruction, nor does it appear that the nature of the contention of the parties rendered it pertinent. So much of the evidence should always be stated in the case settled or stated for this court as to show the pertinency and purpose of the exception; otherwise it must be disregarded. This court cannot see that the instruction should have been given.

Moreover, it does not appear that the defendant requested the court to give the same in addition to others that it gave in varying aspects of the case. Judgment affirmed.

AVERITT v. ELLIOT.

(Supreme Court of North Carolina. Nov. 12, 1891.)

MORTGAGE FORECLOSURE — PURCHASE BY MORTGAGEE — VALIDITY.

The fact that plaintiff claims title to land as the grantee of a mortgagee, who procured it to be bid in and conveyed to himself, is not a defense to an action against the mortgagor for possession, unless pleaded, since plaintiff's title is not void, but merely voidable.

Appeal from superior court, Cumberland county; JAMES C. MACRAE, Judge.

Action by Deceyrus Averitt against Jacob Elliot to recover possession of land. Judgment for defendant. Plaintiff appealed. New trial ordered.

STATEMENT BY THE COURT. The complaint was in the usual form adopted in such cases, and the answer contained only a general denial of the allegations of title and right to possession and damages for detention. In addition to the three issues involving these denials, the following was submitted by the court, numbered 4, viz.: "(4) Was the sale by John Averitt under the mortgage, and the bidding in by Nimocks, and assignment of the bid to the plaintiff, an arrangement by which the land was bid in for John Averitt?" The plaintiff offered in evidence: (1) A deed from Jacob Elliot and wife to James A. Gainey, agent, March 7, 1883, and a

v.13s.E.no.32—50

note secured thereby, and an assignment of the same to John Averitt, February 2, 1884. This deed and assignment covered the land in the complaint. (2) A deed from John Averitt and wife to Deceyrus Averitt, the plaintiff, executed 1st February, 1886, reciting sale, etc., under the mortgage. Plaintiff rested. The defendant offered in evidence a deed for the same land from Deceyrus Averitt to George A. Guy, 29th September, 1888. Jacob Elliot, the defendant, testified at great length, admitting that he had bought the land in controversy from Gainey, and given the mortgage to secure the payment of the purchase money; that he had paid a large part of the same, some to Gainey and some to John Averitt, (in money and cotton;) that he had no notice of the sale under the mortgage; that he had never paid any of the money or cotton as rent for the land, but always to be applied upon the mortgage debt. And other testimony was offered by defendant, tending to corroborate him. The plaintiff, in reply, offered a deed from George A. Guy and wife to Deceyrus Averitt, 19th of December, 1888, prior to the beginning of this action for the same land. The judge instructed the jury: "This action is brought by Deceyrus Averitt to recover the possession of a tract of land in the county which he claims to own by virtue of a deed from John Averitt and wife, dated 1st of February, 1886, which recites a sale of the land under a power granted in a mortgage made by the defendant Jacob Elliot and wife to James A. Gainey, and an assignment of the mortgage and debt secured thereby by Gainey to John Averitt; the purchase by Nimocks; a transfer of his bid to the plaintiff, and payment of the purchase money by him to the defendant, admitting that he executed the mortgage to Gainey, and that the debt secured in said mortgage has not been paid in full; says that the plaintiff has no right to recover the land from him, because there never has been a fair sale of the land under the mortgage; and therefore that the deed from John Averitt and wife to plaintiff conveys no title to the land." The presiding judge then went on at length, and instructed the jury upon the law governing the case. The plaintiff excepted to that portion of the charge which has been set out. The jury responded to the first and second issues, "No," and to the fourth issue, "Yes." Rule for new trial, for errors alleged. Rule discharged. Judgment for defendant.

John W. Hinsdale, for appellant. Sutton & Cook, for appellee.

AVERY, J. Where a mortgagee of land purchases at his own sale directly or by an agent, though he may convey to the agent and have the latter reconvey to him, the effect is to vest the legal estate in the mortgagee in the same plight and condition as he held it under the mortgage, subject to the right of the mortgagor to redeem. Joyner v. Farmer, 78 N. C. 198. The sale by the mortgagee is not void, but only voidable. Joyner v. Farmer, supra. The mortgagee has the right to recover possession at any time as against the defaulting mortgagor in an action brought for that purpose, whether he has fraudulently put forward an agent to buy at his own sale or not. Wittkowski v. Watkins, 84 N. C. 458. If John Averitt bought at his own sale, and then conveyed to the plaintiff, Deceyrus Averitt, the legal estate passed to the latter, upon which he was entitled to recover in an action involving title and right to possession only. Joyner v. Farmer, supra. If the mortgagor wished to avoid the sale on the ground of fraud, he ought to have alleged the fraud in his answer. It was not sufficient simply to prove it. It is essential that there shall be *allegata* in the answer as well as *probata* on the trial in order to make available an equitable right or other new matter as a defense. Willis v. Branch, 94 N. C. 142; Rountree v. Brinson, 98 N. C. 107, 8 S. E. Rep. 747; Montague v. Brown, 104 N. C. 165, 10 S. E. Rep. 186; Ellison v. Rix, 85 N. C. 77. As the issue was submitted to the jury, the defendant might have been allowed, in the progress of the trial, to amend his answer, and set up the fraudulent purchase as a defense. The court will doubtless permit him to amend before another trial, so that with due notice the facts may be fully developed by both parties. Willis v. Branch, supra. But as the plaintiff has excepted to that portion of the charge in reference to the fourth issue, and as it appears that the defendant has relied solely upon the inability of the plaintiff to show the legal title in himself, a new trial must be awarded. This is in accordance with the uniform rule adopted by this court. It is true, as suggested by counsel, that a deed may be directly attacked on trial of an action for possession for incapacity in the maker, fraud in the *factum*, because void under 13 & 27 Eliz., or because it was executed in the face of a statutory prohibition. Mobley v. Griffin, 104 N. C. 112, 10 S. E. Rep. 142; Gilchrist v. Middleton, 107 N. C. 679, 12 S. E. Rep. 85; Helms v. Green, 105 N. C. 259, 11 S. E. Rep. 470. But the deed offered by the plaintiff was not void, but voidable. It left in the defendant an equitable right, which could have been avoided only by the mortgagor and his heirs, and which might be confirmed by the mortgagor by release, or conduct amounting to an abandonment, or working an estoppel *in pais.* Joyner v. Farmer, supra. For want of specific allegations, setting up the defense that the plaintiff claimed under a fraudulent conveyance, a new trial will be awarded.

BLAKE et al. v. BLACKLEY.

(*Supreme Court of North Carolina.* Oct. 27, 1891.)

RESCISSION OF SALE—FRAUD OF PURCHASER—EVIDENCE—ACTION BY MARRIED WOMAN.

1. In an action by a husband and wife and W. to recover certain horses, the property of the wife and W., it appeared that W. sold them to defendant, to be paid for in cash on delivery; that by exhibiting a check, which he claimed he would get cashed as soon as a bank was open, and would pay for the property, defendant got possession of the horses, and when W. demanded payment therefor defendant tendered a note which he held against W., who refused to accept

it. *Held,* that this rendered the contract voidable at the instance of the owners.

2. The *gravamen* of the fraud was in impressing W. with the idea that defendant would procure the money by means of the check, and pay for the horses, when in fact he intended to acquire possession of them and credit their value on the note; and it is immaterial whether his language was such as to convey the idea that his money was on deposit in a bank in R. or elsewhere.

3. Defendant's representation that he wished to start the horses early in the morning, his transferring them from the road ordinarily traveled to his home to another road not so well known, and his declaration before he acquired possession that he intended to play a trick on W., were sufficient to warrant a verdict for plaintiffs.

4. It was immaterial whether the property belonged to the wife, or to her and W. as partners, or to W. individually.

5. The statutes of North Carolina only operate to restrain a married woman from disposing of her separate property by contract, and do not prevent the wife from joining with her husband in an action for the conversion of the horses.

Appeal from superior court, Wake county; ROBERT WINSTON, Judge.

Action by Joseph Blake, Lucy Blake, his wife, and George W. Wynne against J. C. Blackley to recover possession of certain horses and harness wrongfully taken. Verdict and judgment for plaintiffs. Motion for a new trial denied. Defendant appeals. Affirmed.

STATEMENT BY THE COURT. The plaintiffs brought their action to recover two horses and one set of harness, valued at $300, and by claim and delivery proceedings took possession of the property sued for soon after the action was brought, in June, 1890. The testimony was as follows:

Geo. W. Wynne: "Knew defendant in 1890. Was selling horses for Mrs. B. in 1890; she to furnish money, I to sell and buy horses in my judgment, and have one-half the clear profits. Sold defendant pair of horses in June, 1890,—one bay, and other brown. B. came in and wanted to buy horses for some one in Henderson. Said he had the money. Showed him the two horses. Told him to wait, and, if I did not trade with Burwell, I would sell to him. Late in the evening he come,—evening before he said he had the money; had a check. Went to bank. Said bank was closed, and he would settle next morning, after bank opened. At night said he wanted to start very early next morning, as it was hot,—6 o'clock. Wanted to carry them that night to another stable; but I said, 'No,' I wouldn't charge board. Next morning, when I come back, the horses were gone, and I told him to pay me, and he offered me a note that was no account. I would not accept it. Went to stable, and he pulled out the note. Never offered to pay me the cash. Under the contract was to pay me cash. I didn't see horses again till brought back stables. That morning I went off ou road a mile or so, but didn't find horses. Arrested B. in Franklin at Franklinton. Blake told Blackley wanted horses. He said they were where he (Blake) couldn't get them. We sent after the horses, and got back the same horses he carried away. Sold harness at $25 to be paid for in cash, with horses. and have been paid for neither.

Harness he expressed to Franklinton. Blackley showed me a check the day he was trading for the horses. I saw it was a check, but could not see the writing. Blackley's brother was there with B., but not when trade was made." Cross-examination: "Thirty years horse trader in many counties and states. 15,000 or 20,000 traded. At time we rented Parham's stables four months. Sold out before to Jones & Powell. Name had been Geo. W. Wynne & ·Co. Yancey had been partner. After Christmas,—February or March, 1890,—Mrs. Blake and I made the arrangement, but the name continued Geo. W. Wynne. Opened no new books. Trade in June. Up to transaction had bought and sold some 25 horses, and the proceeds of all sales were simply worked into the business. Mrs. Blake paid for feed and rent. Mrs. Blake's check was the first money we got. She handed me check. Blackley and I had traded, and Blackley had been agent for my son. We had swapped horses. Traded always on my own judgment. No sign up at all. I told Blackley when he come in that these were my horses, but I had told him Mrs. Blake had an interest in the horses; had told him often before, and he knew all about it. I did not say anything about Mrs. Blake's owning any horses that day, or her having any interest in the two particular horses that day. But at Jones & Powell's, the brown horse was in the stable, and then I told Blackley that Mrs. Blake had an interest in him. This was between February and June, 1890. Told him Mrs. B. furnished the money. I have said this before at the other trials. Had loaned the brown horse to Stronach. I told B. the horses were mine, —bay and brown. Trade not made till after supper. Don't think that price was fixed till after Blackley left that evening, and till Burwell was seen. Blackley said he would pay cash if he bought the horses. Day that Col. Anderson was buried—at 3 o'clock—he went to the bank. Dark when Blackley came back, and we traded two horses at $275, harness, $25. Blackley had swapped horses next morning, and got $20 or $25 to boot. We got in his buggy, and went back to my stables. I told him to settle. He pulled out a note for $250 of mine (not sealed) and some money. I told him the note was no account. I would not take it, and said, 'Get out, you thieving rascal,' and he ran for the door. I didn't tell him next morning that the horses were Mrs. Blake's." Redirect: "Told Blackley not to trade for note; it was no account, and I would not pay it. Six months after date I had written Leach, if certain things were done, would pay note."

Jos. Blake, husband plaintiff feme: "Blackley is a horse-trader. In June, 1890, Mrs. B. had some horses that were purchased with some money that Mrs. B. let W. have. Real estate left to Mrs. B by her father. The land was sold. I drew the money out of bank and gave it to W. Horses bought with the money by W., and he drew on me, and I paid draft with her money. Also I paid rent and expenses with her money. If we made anything he was to have one-half net profits. Saw Blackley 10 next day. Said, 'Blackley, those my horses, and you know it.' He: 'Don't know so much about that; will see lawyer.' In February, '90, he was in stable, looking at horses, and talking to me, and I told him they were my horses, and Mr. W. was the salesman. One horse on hand at that time. After trade I went to Franklinton, and met Blackley. Asked him where horses. He said, where I could not get 'em. He said he'd run 'em out of my reach. I told him better not. Young man stepped up, and said he ought not to have told me. Same two horses that the suit is about. Harness was bought with wife's money, too. Heard Blackley say it was a trick, fixed up to get horses away from me. Married in 1860, (20th September.) Arrangement with Wynne in February, 1890. Brown horse got in February 1st lot. Bay horse got in April. (Land sold after 1868.) After sale with Blackley was advertisement, but before then there was none. Another man's stables, and we used Jones & Powell's license."

Ives Brooks: "June, 1890, tending horses at Parham's for Blake. Knew Mr. Blackley. Saw him in June. 11 o'clock Blackley come down. Wynne had not come. Next time B. and W. together. Wynne said, 'Good horse,' and he drove him. Blackley got out at corner. Then drove the other horse. Blackley wanted him to decide. Said could not do it then, but would after a while. Never decided till near sunset what they would do. After supper, come down. Blackley said, 'I got cash to pay for them.' After supper they talked, and Blackley said, 'I will take 'em.' B. wanted to carry them away that night, but W. said he would feed them next morning. Very soon they come in with lantern. Delivered horses to Blackley. Got back the same horses in Franklin. No one with Blackley the evening before but Wynne. After horses gone one-half hour, saw Mr. Blackley, and he had gone off after his brother on horseback; and Blackley told me he had forgot something, the reason he went."

Mr. Holder: "Working June, 1889, with Jones & Powell, about 40 yards from Parham's stables. Saw Blackley in June, 1890. It was in evening or night. He told me that he wanted to buy horses, and then afterwards said bought of Wynne. Said was going to pay for 'em with Wynne's note. I said, 'Blake's horses.' He said, 'Wynne said were his.' He also said he was going to work a little scheme, if I would not say anything about it. Next morning saw Blackley. Blackley had rode off Jones & Powell's horse. B. said that 'saw Mr. Wynne drive out, and thought Wynne would suspicion something, or found out about trade;' and he drove out to change the horses on another road. B. said he had bought horses from W., and was going to pay for 'em in his own note."

It is admitted that Blackley had no money in the banks of Raleigh in June, 1890. The plaintiffs rest, and the defendant offers no evidence. At the close of the evidence and before his honor charged the jury, the defendant, in writing, prayed for the following instruction: "Upon the whole evidence the plaintiffs are not entitled to recover," which his honor refused to give, and defendant excepted. His honor charged the jury as follows: "If Geo. W. Wynne was drawn in to part with the property described by fraudulent misrepresentations or concealments of facts on the part of Blackley, material to the contract, and operating as inducements thereto, and they were such as a man of ordinary sagacity might reasonably rely on and be influenced by, and such owner or owners did rely on and were influenced by them in making said contract, then such trade was voidable, and the owner or owners of the property have the right to annul the contract, and sue for the recovery of the same. Now, if the jury believe that the defendant on the 7th of June, 1890, went to Wynne and falsely and fraudulently represented to him that he had the money with which to pay for the horses and harness, and would pay cash for the same, when in truth and in fact he did not have such money, and did not intend to pay cash for the same; and if the jury believe further that the defendant went to the bank to collect money, intending thereby to deceive the said Wynne, and to lead him to believe that he would pay for said horses with money drawn from said bank, when in truth he did not intend at said time to use such money to pay cash for said horses; and if the jury believe from all the other facts and circumstances of this case that the intent of Blackley was to deceive said Wynne, and to fraudulently induce him to part with the possession of said property by making false statements, or by concealing facts, and because of such false and fraudulent representations and concealments said Wynne did part with said horses,—then in law such a fraud would have been perpetrated on said Wynne that no title passed to Blackley, and you will answer the second issue, 'Yes.' The jury will consider in this connection all the evidence as you remember it,—the early departure next morning, and the argument of defendant's counsel that this was because of hot weather; changing the direction that the horses had started; the declarations made to Holder that he intended to work a trick on Wynne, and Holder's reply that Mrs. Blake owned the horses, and all the other evidence in the case. On the other hand, if the evidence has not led your minds to the conclusion that Blackley did falsely and fraudulently represent that he had the cash with which to pay for said horses and with which he would pay for same, and that his intention was to defraud and deceive said Wynne, then you will answer the second issue, 'No.' On the first issue the court charges: That, if Mrs. Blake furnished the money with which to buy the horses and with which the horses were bought, Mrs. Blake to pay the expense of feeding, and also the rent, Wynne to buy any horses in his own judgment, and also to sell the same, and Wynne to have one-half the profits, then you will answer issue, 'Yes;' but if Mrs. Blake did not furnish such money, and if the said horses really belonged to Wynne, then you will answer

the first issue, 'G. W. Wynne alone.' Third issue: If evidence is believed, you will answer, '$300.' It is the province of the jury and not of the court to pass on the credibility of witnesses."

The issues and responses were as follows: "(1) Were the plaintiffs Lucy W. Blake and George W. Wynne entitled to the possession of the horses and harness mentioned in the complaint on 7th July, 1890? Yes. (2) Did the defendant, J. W. Blackley, obtain possession of the horses and harness by false and fraudulent representations? Yes. (3) What damage did Lucy Blake and G. W. Wynne sustain by the taking of the horses and harness? $300."

The defendant moved for a new trial, and assigned as grounds therefor: (1) The refusal of his honor to give the instruction prayed for. (2) A variance in the allegations in the amended complaint and the evidence, the complaint setting up a co-ownership in the property in the plaintiffs Lucy A. Blake and George W. Wynne, and the evidence showing that said parties were copartners. (3) That from the evidence it appeared that Mrs. Lucy A. Blake was a married woman at the commencement and trial of this action, and that the business connection between herself and George W. Wynne was formed and conducted for the sole purpose of trading in horses. Such business connection, defendant contended, was contrary to the policy of the law. (4) That there was no evidence to show that defendant, Blackley, did not have money with which to pay for the property mentioned in the complaint, the evidence being (by admission) that he had no money deposited in any bank in Raleigh to his credit, but it being proved that he had in his possession a check for money, which he showed to Wynne, when he said he was going to the bank to get money. Motion for new trial refused. Defendant excepted and appealed.

N. Y. Gulley, for appellant. *Batchelor & Devereux* and *A. G. Ryan*, for appellees.

AVERY, J. The main question raised by the appeal is whether, upon the whole of the evidence, in any phase of it, and in the particular aspects presented by the judge below to the jury, the plaintiffs were entitled to recover. The mere fact, if admitted, that the defendant told a falsehood, or made a promise to pay at a time when he knew he would not, in all reasonable probability, be able to pay, would not invalidate the sale. But if one induces another to part with his goods by a promise to pay cash for them on the same day, showing a check to inspire confidence in his engagement, when in fact he does not intend at the moment of making the representation to pay for the property in money at any time, but purposes, after getting possession of it by holding out the hope of the immediate receipt of ready cash, to credit its value on a claim held by him against the owner or one of the owners of it, the contract is fraudulent and voidable at the instance of the original owner, and where the owner has been induced to surrender the possession he may maintain an action in the nature of detinue, and recover the specific property, if to be found, or in the nature of trover for the wrongful conversion consummated by the refusal to surrender it on demand. Bish. Cont. § 667; Benj. Sales, § 656, and note 18; Smith v. Young, 13 S. E. Rep. 735, (at this term;) 8 Amer. & Eng. Enc. Law, 650; Donaldson v. Farwell, 98 U. S. 631.

The representation of the defendant, if the testimony was believed, that he wished to start the horses in the early morning, while it was cool, and transferring them from the road ordinarily traveled to his home from the place of purchase to another way not so well known, in connection with the declaration made to a witness before he acquired possession of them, that he intended to play a trick on Wynne, were sufficient to warrant the verdict. It was the duty of the judge to submit this testimony with all of the circumstances, and let the jury pass upon the intent of the defendant; and the defendant has no just ground to complain that the language in which his honor couched the proposition was such as might have misled the jury to his prejudice.

Whether the declaration of the defendant was drawn out by a direct question, or whether made gratuitously, the object in telling Wynne that he had money in the bank and exhibiting a check was to induce Wynne to surrender the property before it was paid for, and ultimately to avoid paying for it; and therefore the false representation, which the jury find misled Wynne, and caused him to part with the horses before receiving the purchase money, vitiated the contract *ab initio* at the option of the injured party, to be exercised within a reasonable time. Wilson v. White, 80 N. C. 280; Donaldson v. Farwell, supra. In this view of the case it is immaterial whether the property belonged to the *feme* plaintiff, or to her and Wynne as partners, or to Wynne individually. A creditor is not allowed, by practicing a fraud, to acquire title to the property of his debtor, even with the purpose of crediting its value on a just debt. Smith v. Young, supra. If the law should give its sanction to the wrongful conversion of property, whether by force or fraud, for the purpose of collecting even undisputed debts, the end would not justify the means, either legally or morally. There was evidence tending to show that the defendant exhibited a check, for which he declared that he could not get the cash in the afternoon or evening before, because the banks of the city of Raleigh were closed, and that he would get the cash for it on the morning following, so soon as the banks should be opened.

It was not material whether his language was such as to convey the idea that his money was on deposit in a Raleigh bank or elsewhere. The *gravamen* of the fraud was in falsely and willfully creating the impression on the mind of Wynne that he had money which could be procured by means of a check, and which he would apply in payment for the horses, when in fact the defendant's purpose was to acquire possession of the horses, and to credit the value, with or without the assent of Wynne, on a debt which Wynne owed him.

Another exception made by the defendant seems to be founded upon the theory that because a married woman is not a free trader, and has no power to bind her separate property by a contract, she has no right to acquire property by purchase, or to maintain (even when her husband is joined) an action for the wrongful withholding of it after she has acquired it. "It is settled law in North Carolina that our statutes (Code, c. 37) impose no limit upon the wife's power to acquire property by contracting with her husband or any other person, but only operate to restrain her from or protect her in disposing of property already acquired by her." Osborne v. Wilkes, 108 N. C. 667, 13 S. E. Rep. 285; Battle v. Mayo, 102 N. C. 489, 9 S E. Rep. 384; George v. High, 85 N. C. 99; Kirkman v. Bank, 77 N. C. 394; Dula v. Young, 70 N. C. 450; Stephenson v. Felton, 106 N. C. 121, 11 S. E. Rep. 255. For the reasons given we think there was no error in the rulings of the court below which constitute the grounds of exception, and the judgment must be affirmed. No error.

DAVIS, J., did not sit on the hearing of this case.

GLASCOCK v. HAZELL.

(*Supreme Court of North Carolina.* Nov. 8, 1891.)

SALES ON APPROVAL—MONEY HAD AND RECEIVED.

1. Where one who has bought a water-wheel on trial sells both it and the mill with which it is connected for a gross sum, and there is nothing to show the amount obtained for the wheel, the seller is not entitled to recover from the second purchaser upon an implied contract as for money had and received.

2. Where property is not sold absolutely, but only delivered on approval, and the buyer fails to signify his approval, or make the payments required by the contract, the title still remains in the seller.

Appeal from superior court, Guilford county; JESSE F. GRAVES, Judge.

This was an action by G. T. Glascock to recover of G. M. Hazell the price of a water-wheel. Plaintiff shipped the wheel to Holden & Hill on trial, and the latter sold both it and the mill with which it was connected to the defendant for $1,300. Defendant afterwards sold the wheel and mill for $1,800. There was judgment for defendant, and plaintiff appeals. Reversed.

J. T. Morehead, for appellant. *Dillard & King* and *Jas. E. Boyd,* for appellee.

SHEPHERD, J. As the plaintiff does not sue for the specific property, and as the amount claimed by him is over $50, he can only recover before a justice of the peace upon a contract, either express or implied. We concur with his honor that the plaintiff could not recover upon the implied contract,—that is, for money had and received,—as there was no testimony to show the amount obtained for the wheel by the defendant. Rand v. Nesmith, 61 Me. 111; Pearsoll v. Chapin, 44 Pa. St. 9. We think, however, that there was some testimony of an express agreement to pay for the wheel if it was the property of the plaintiff, and neither this testimony nor that bearing upon the title of the plaintiff was submitted to the jury. The court seems to have treated the action as if brought for money had and received,—the tort being waived,—but we are of the opinion that the informal complaint filed before the justice was broad enough to have warranted a recovery upon an express promise. The authorities cited by the defendant do not satisfy us that the plaintiff was precluded from asserting title to the property. The plaintiff testified that Hill & Holden did not buy the wheel, but that it was delivered to them upon the understanding that they might purchase, after testing it, upon paying $50 cash, and securing the balance. These terms do not seem to have been complied with, and we do not see, under these circumstances, how the title passed out of the plaintiff. If the jury, however, should believe that it was a conditional sale, (and of this, there was some evidence,) then the plaintiff must fail in this action, as there was no registration, and the condition would be void as to purchasers. Brem v. Lockhart, 93 N. C. 191; Code, § 1275. There is error.

BRUCE *et al.* v. SUGG *et al.*

(*Supreme Court of North Carolina.* Nov. 3, 1891.)

HUSBAND AND WIFE—SALE OF LAND—JUDGMENT AGAINST HUSBAND—INTEREST OF WIFE—FORECLOSURE OF MORTGAGE — RIGHTS OF JUDGMENT CREDITORS.

1. Under Code N. C. § 1840, which provides that no land belonging to the wife shall be disposed of by the husband for his own life or any less term without her assent, and that no interest of the husband shall be subject to sale to satisfy any execution obtained against him, a tract of land held by the husband and wife by entireties cannot be sold on execution against the husband so as to pass any title during their joint lives, or as against the wife if she survives.

2. The husband's curtesy initiate in his wife's land is not such an interest as under said section 1840 can be subjected to sale to satisfy a judgment against the husband.

3. Code N. C. § 435, providing that a judgment shall be a lien on the real property of every person against whom it shall be rendered, and which the said person may then have or shall thereafter acquire at any time during 10 years, does not vest in the judgment creditor any estate or interest in the land, but only secures his right to have the judgment satisfied out of the proceeds of a sale made under an ordinary process of execution; and the lien in such a case embraces only such estate, legal or equitable, as may be sold at the time it attaches.

4. Judgment creditors are not entitled to be made party defendants in foreclosure proceedings for the purpose of proving collusion between the mortgagor and mortgagee to the prejudice of themselves and other creditors, and to contest the validity of the mortgage, but the proper remedy is by an independent action for that purpose.

Appeal from superior court, Pitt county; SPIER WHITAKER, Judge.

The following is so much of the case stated on appeal as need be reported: "The plaintiff, in his complaint, recited two mortgages of land, executed by defendants (Sugg and wife) to plaintiff, (the one on December 7, 1883, and the other on December 1, 1886,) and a certain judgment rendered in favor of one W. S. Rawls against said defendant at March term, 1889, which had been purchased by plaintiff for a valuable consideration, and duly assigned to him. Among the tracts conveyed by the mortgages was one which Sugg and wife held under a deed executed to them jointly by Charles D. Rountree and wife. The action is to foreclose the mortgage, etc. No answer was filed. Service of summons was accepted by the defendants. J. J. Nicholson & Sons, judgment creditors of the defendant Isaac Sugg, by virtue of a certain judgment rendered at June term, 1886, of said court, caused a notice of motion in this cause to be served on the parties, and at the present term, upon affidavits filed, they moved for leave to come in and be made party defendant for the reasons set forth in the affidavit, to the end that they may have their rights as judgment creditors duly protected. A counter-affidavit, made by defendant Isaac Sugg, was filed by plaintiff. The court refused the application of Nicholson to be made party defendant, for the reason that he had no interest in the land sought to be sold, and the court found that the land covered by the mortgage is the sole property of the *feme* defendant, except one tract, and that this tract is the property of Sugg and his wife, holding by entireties. Nicholson, the appellant, excepted. Thereupon a judgment by consent of plaintiff and defendant Sugg and wife was rendered, and Nicholson appealed."

C. M. Bernard, for appellants. T. F. Davidson, for appellees.

MERRIMON, C. J., (*after stating the facts as above.*) The appellants' judgment is not against the *feme* defendant, who is the wife of her co-defendant, nor do they seek to have her property — land — devoted to its satisfaction. It is against the defendant husband. The land, except a small tract of four acres, embraced by the mortgages of the plaintiffs, which they seek by this action to foreclose, is that of the defendant wife. The court so expressly finds and declares. The husband has no such interest in her land as is subject to levy and sale to satisfy the appellants' judgment. It does not appear that he is tenant by the curtesy initiate, and, if it did so appear, such interest could not be sold to satisfy the judgment. The statute (Code, § 1840)[1] so expressly provides. Code, § 1838. As to this land, the appellant has no judgment lien to be enforced in or by this action.

The defendants, husband and wife, held the small tract of land conveyed to them, not as joint tenants or tenants in common, but by entireties. In contemplation of law they were, for such purpose, but one person, and each had the whole estate as one person; and when one of them

---

[1] This section provides that no land belonging to the wife shall be disposed of by the husband for his own life or any less term without her assent, and that no interest of the husband shall be subject to levy and sale to satisfy any execution obtained against the husband.

should die the whole estate would continue in the survivor. They, by reason of these relations to each other, could not take the fee-simple estate conveyed to them by moieties, but both were seised of the entirety *per tout et non per my*. This is so by the common law, and is the settled law of this state. Motley v. Whitemore, 2 Dev. & B. 537; Long v. Barnes, 87 N. C. 329; Todd v. Zachary, Busb. Eq. 286; Simonton v. Cornelius, 98 N. C. 433, 4 S. E. Rep. 38; Harrison v. Ray, 108 N. C. 215, 12 S. E. Rep. 993; 2 Bl. Comm. 182. The nature of this estate forbids and prevents the sale or disposal of it or any part of it by the husband or wife without the assent of both; the whole must remain to the survivor. The husband cannot convey, incumber, or at all prejudice such estate to any greater extent than if it rested in the wife exclusively in her own right. He has no such estate as he can dispose of to the prejudice of the wife's estate. The unity of the husband and wife as one person, and the ownership of the estate by that person, prevents the disposition of it otherwise than jointly. As a consequence, neither the interest of the husband nor that of the wife can be sold on execution so as to pass away title during their joint lives, or as against the survivor after the death of one of them. It is said in Rorer on Judicial Sales that "no proceeding against one of them during their joint lives will by sale affect the title to the property as against the other one as survivor, or as against the two during their joint lives. Neither party to such tenancy can sell or convey their [his] interest, for it is incapable of being separated." He cites many authorities to support what he thus says. Indeed, it seems that the estate is not that of the husband or the wife; it belongs to that third person recognized by the law,—the husband and the wife. It requires the co-operation of both to dispose of it effectually. Ror. Jud. Sales, § 549; Freem. Co-Ton. §§ 73, 74; 4 Kent, Comm. 362; Simonton v. Cornelius, supra.

The statute (Code, § 435) prescribes that a docketed judgment directing the payment of money "shall be a lien on the real property, in the county where the same is docketed, of every person against whom any such judgment shall be rendered, and which he may have at the time of the docketing thereof in the county in which such real property is situated, or which he shall acquire at any time thereafter for ten years from the date of the rendition of the judgment." The lien thus intended and created does not vest in the judgment creditor any estate or interest in the real property subject to it. It only creates and secures the right of the creditor to have the judgment debt paid out of the proceeds of the sale of the property made under the ordinary process of execution or other proper process or order of the court. The lien extends to and embraces only such estate, legal and equitable, in the real property of the judgment debtor as may be sold or disposed of at the time it attached. In Bristol v. Hallyburton, 93 N. C. 384, Justice ASHE, for the court, said: "A sale under an execution upon a judg-

ment which is a general lien on all the property of the debtor vests only the interest of the debtor at the time the judgment lien attaches, or such as the debtor might have conveyed by suitable instrument for a valuable consideration. It is limited to, and can rise no higher than, that [the interest] of [the] debtor. A stream cannot rise higher than its fountain. A purchaser under an execution takes all that belongs to the debtor, and nothing more." It was hence said in that case that a vested remainder in land might be sold under execution, but a contingent remainder could not. McKelthan v. Walker, 66 N. C. 95; Hoppock v. Shober, 69 N. C. 153; Dixon v. Dixon, 81 N. C. 323; Dail v. Freeman, 92 N. C. 351. The statute contemplates and intends a lien upon some present subsisting estate, legal or equitable, in the real property of the judgment debtor, that may be enforced in some proper way. It would be idle and absurd to intend a lien that could not be made effectual. Freem. Judgm. § 357; Ror. Jud. Sales, § 557, and note. As we have seen, the husband, who is the judgment debtor in this case, had no interest in the land that he could dispose of, nor that was subject to sale under execution or any legal process. A sale would be ineffectual. The possibility that the husband might survive his wife, and thus become the sole owner of the property, was not the subject of sale or lien. This did not constitute or create any present estate, legal or equitable, any more than a contingent remainder, or any other mere prospective possibility. Bristol v. Hallyburton, supra. It seems that at the common law the husband, by virtue of his marital rights, could dispose of the possession of real estate held by entireties. But, however this may be, the statute (Code, § 1840) expressly provides that he shall not have power to dispose of his wife's land for his own life or any less term of years without her assent, nor can the same be subject to sale to satisfy any execution obtained against him. The appellants, therefore, had no lien upon the land or any part of or interest in it, so far as appears, and the court properly denied their motion to be made parties defendant. It appears from the affidavit upon which the appellants based their motion, and from the brief of their counsel, that they did not ask to be made a party defendant in the action for the purpose of enforcing their supposed lien and sharing in the funds, the proceeds of the sale of the land, according to their alleged right, but for the purpose of alleging collusion between the plaintiffs and defendants to the prejudice of themselves and other creditors, and to contest the validity of the plaintiffs' mortgages and debts secured by them. The court might properly have denied the motion upon the ground that a party would not be allowed to come into the action for such purpose. The effect of such suggested procedure and practice would be, not to completely determine the action and administer the rights of divers persons who had mortgages and liens upon the property to be sold, etc., but to allow a party to come into the action and allege a distinct and different cause of action against the plaintiffs and defendants, and litigate the same. Such practice is unwarranted, and cannot be tolerated. In such case the remedy of the complaining party is by an independent action, brought for the purpose, against the plaintiffs and defendants. Judgment affirmed.

BARBEE et al. v. BARBEE et al.

(Supreme Court of North Carolina. Nov. 10, 1891.)

CONSIDERATION OF DEED—PAROL EVIDENCE.

Where defendant's father, in his life-time, conveyed to defendant land worth $1,200, reciting in the deed as the consideration $400, which was paid, it may be shown by parol evidence, after the father's death, that the excess was intended as an advancement from his estate. 13 S. E. Rep. 215, affirmed.

Appeal from superior court, Durham county; EDWIN T. BOYKIN, Judge.

Action for partition by W. R. Barbee et al. against B. W. Barbee et al. From a judgment for plaintiffs, defendants appeal. Affirmed.

STATEMENT BY THE COURT. The following is so much of the case stated on appeal as need be reported: "In 1872, Gray Barbee, the ancestor of the parties, and who subsequently died intestate, conveyed to his son, B. W. Barbee, a tract of land by a deed of bargain and sale in fee, regular in form and with usual covenants of warranty. The consideration expressed in said deed was $400, and this was actually paid by said grantee, $100 to the grantor, and $100, according to his direction, to each of three other children of said grantor. The land was worth $1,200, and this amount, deducting the $400 which the land actually cost him, made the said B. W. Barbee share in the advantage of the partition of some of his lands made by the said Gray Barbee, equally with his brothers and sisters, who were advanced. The referee, who found as facts that the price paid by said B. W. Barbee was $400, and the actual value of the land conveyed was $1,200, found also, as a fact, that the said Gray Barbee intended the $800 excess of value over price paid as an advancement to said B. W. Barbee. Upon a consideration of the report of the referee, finding the facts as just stated, and the opinion of the supreme court filed in this case, his honor, Judge BOYKIN, held that the grantee (appellant) was chargeable with $800, the difference between the price paid for said land and the value of said land as an advancement, and rendered the judgment set out in the record. Appellant insisted that as it was found as a fact, and undisputed, that he had paid $400 for the land, the same (the land) could not be charged to him as an advancement, nor could any part of it, though its actual value was $1,200. This objection was overruled, and the defendant excepted, and appealed to this court from so much of the judgment only as charged him with said $800, he being charged in said judgment with $1,137.50 for land, while, as he insisted, he should only have been charged with $337.50. The defendant (appellant) B. W. Barbee contended that there was no evidence to sustain the referee's finding as to the intent of Gray Barbee that the land conveyed should be an advancement. Plaintiffs contend that there was."

W. W. Fuller and J. W. Graham, for appellants. Boone & Parker and W. A. Guthrie, for appellees.

MERRIMON, C. J. This case has been before this court by a former appeal, disposed of at the last term. In that appeal (see Barbee v. Barbee, 108 N. C. 581, 13 S. E. Rep. 215) it was decided that the recital in the deed of the payment of the consideration therein specified for the land referred to, conveyed by the appellant's father to him, did not preclude and estop the plaintiffs from showing, by parol evidence, that the real value of the land was not the consideration recited in the deed, but was in fact $1,200, and that the father intended that the appellant should account for $800 of that sum as an advancement in the division of his estate among his children after his death. It appears from exceptions to evidence that one purpose of this appeal is to ask the court to overrule or modify that decision. If the appellant was dissatisfied with it, he should have made his application to rehear. That would have been the orderly and regular course to pursue. Perhaps we have the power to overrule the decision, but we are entirely satisfied with its correctness, and are not in the least inclined to disturb it. The mere fact that the appellant's father in his life-time conveyed to him a tract of land worth $1,200, and recited in the deed of conveyance the consideration for it of $400, could not prevent the father from charging the appellant with the value of the land above and beyond the consideration recited in the deed as an advancement, if he saw fit and really intended to do so. The father might find it convenient to do so, and there is no rule of justice, nor principle nor statute, nor reason of policy, that forbids it to be done. It might be better and safer to explain in the deed such purpose, but it is not at all necessary that this shall be done. The purpose to treat a part of the value of the land as an advancement may be proven by parol evidence, whether the same be in writing or not. The cases of Harper v. Harper, 92 N. C. 300, and Barbee v. Barbee, supra, in effect sustain the view just expressed. It is difficult to conceive of a just reason why a father shall not have the right to require his son to pay part of the value of a tract of land he conveys to the latter and charge him with the remaining part as an advancement. Meeker v. Meeker, 16 Conn. 383; Speer v. Speer, 14 N. J. Eq. 240. The evidence is voluminous, and it would serve no useful purpose to recite and advert to it here in detail. It is sufficient to say that we have examined it, and cannot hesitate to decide that there was competent evidence before the referee from which he might find that the father of the appellant intended to charge the latter with $800 of the value of the land referred to, not as a gift, but as an advancement. The objections and exceptions to the admission of evidence before the referee do not appear to have been passed upon by the court below, and hence they are not before us for review. It seems that it was not intended that we should consider them. Judgment affirmed.

HUMPHREY et al. v. BOARD OF TRUSTEES OF M. E. CHURCH.

(Supreme Court of North Carolina. Nov. 10, 1891.)

CONSTITUTIONAL LAW—MUNICIPAL CONTROL OF CEMETERIES—INSTRUCTIONS.

1. The ownership of a lot in a cemetery, or license to inter therein, is subject to the police power of the state, and interments may be forbidden, and bodies already interred removed, by ordinance of the city, if authorized by act of the legislature.

2. Where there is no evidence in support of requests to charge, they are properly refused.

3. A verdict of a jury will not be disturbed on appeal on the ground that it is contrary to the weight of evidence.

Appeal from superior court, New Hanover county; JESSE F. GRAVES, Judge.

Action by H. W. Humphrey and others against trustees of Methodist Episcopal Church for damage in removing the remains of plaintiffs' father from its cemetery. From a judgment for defendant, and refusal to grant a new trial, plaintiffs appeal. Affirmed.

STATEMENT BY THE COURT. The plaintiffs proposed these issues: (1) Did ancestors of plaintiffs purchase from the defendant corporation the vault described in the pleadings? (2) Did the defendant corporation convey by deed to the ancestors of plaintiffs the property described in the pleadings? (3) How long have the plaintiffs, and those under whom the plaintiffs claim, been in the possession of said vault, and the land on which it was built, and used the same as a place of interment? (4) Has such use given to the plaintiffs an easement in the lands of defendant corporation over which said vault was constructed? (5) Did the defendant corporation, by its agents, enter upon and tear down said vault, against the will of the plaintiffs, and without a license from the plaintiffs? The defendant, before the issues were settled, admitted that the plaintiffs were the heirs at law of Bryan L. Koonce; that defendant was a corporation, and that by its proper officers it had executed a paper writing, which had been duly registered in 1854, whereby it acknowledges the receipt of $100 from Bryan L. Koonce and his heirs, in full payment for one vault constructed in the burying-ground back of the brick church on the corner of Front and Walnut streets, in the town of Wilmington, and numbered 21, the numbers commencing with 1 on Walnut street, extending northwardly successively to 24; the said Bryan L. Koonce, his heirs, administrators, and assigns, to have full and exclusive right to inter in said vault as long as it should be used for the purpose of interment, and have free and perpetual privilege of entering upon the church land for that purpose. The court was of opinion that an easement was granted to Bryan L. Koonce which descended to plaintiffs, his admitted heirs.

There seemed to the court that there was no necessity for the first, second, third, and fourth issues proposed by the plaintiffs; declined to submit them to the jury; and, not being satisfied with form of the fifth issue, it was not submitted in the precise words asked for by plaintiffs. The court settled these issues: (1) Did the defendant corporation, by its agents or servants, wrongfully tear down and destroy said vault? (2) What amount of damages have plaintiffs sustained thereby? And plaintiffs excepted.

There was much evidence offered by plaintiffs tending to show that the corporation desired to erect a church building at some other point in the city of Wilmington, and to change the burying-ground, and with that purpose agents of defendant were requested to treat with plaintiffs for the cession of their rights of property in said vault. (The judge did not wish to incumber the case unnecessarily, and did not think it material to set out the evidence in detail, but directed that if appellant desired, at the risk of costs, to have the letters set out in his statement go up, the clerk might copy them as a part of the case.) There was evidence that Bryan L. Koonce was buried in that vault, and this was not denied. There was evidence tending to show that the other vaults had been removed, and the remains interred in them removed, by the defendant or friends of the deceased; and that the remains of Bryan L. Koonce were removed without the consent of plaintiffs, and that the remains had been removed against their will; and there was testimony as to the costs incurred by the plaintiffs by reason of the removal, and that the vault had been torn down without their consent. The defendant admitted that the vault had been opened, and the remains of the deceased, Bryan L. Koonce, had been removed; and offered evidence tending to show that the vault had been opened, and the remains removed, with the consent of plaintiffs, and that one of plaintiffs was present and assisted in removal. The defendant offered in evidence the act of general assembly in relation to the town of Wilmington, 1854–55, (charter,) and the ordinances of the city of Wilmington passed June 11, 1858, and April, 1861, prohibiting interments within certain bounds, and there was testimony to show that the vault was inside the boundary named in the ordinances in which interments were prohibited. The plaintiffs asked the court to instruct the jury "that, if the plaintiffs removed said remains from the said vault involuntarily, the plaintiffs are entitled to recover." This was refused, and plaintiffs excepted. The plaintiffs asked the court to further instruct the jury that, if the plaintiffs removed said remains from said vault influenced by the promises or threats of the defendant in making such said removal, the plaintiffs are entitled to recover; and this was refused, and the plaintiffs excepted.

The court instructed the jury: "The deed or paper writing made by the defendant to Bryan L. Koonce and his heirs is sufficient in form, and passed by grant an easement to use the land described, a vault for burial, which descended to his heirs, the plaintiffs. That easement became an inherent right, which the defendant was bound to recognize. But, although the grant was an executed contract, the right of the public is superior to the right of any private person; and where there arises a public necessity for it on account of public convenience, or to protect public health, the law allows private rights to be subjected to such restrictions as are for the common good, so that if the issue read, purporting to be acts of the general assembly, were really passed and became law, they conferred power on the proper authorities of the city of Wilmington to pass ordinances to regulate the burial of the dead in the city; and if you find that the ordinances offered in evidence have been adopted by the proper authority, and if you find that the vault described in this action was in the boundaries in which burials were prohibited, then the plaintiffs had no right to use the vault as a place of further burial, but they did have the right to continue to enjoy the easement so far as to have the bodies which had been deposited there remain unmolested. The plaintiffs, then, are entitled to recover if the defendant broke down the vault or removed the remains of Bryan L. Koonce, by its agents or officers, wrongfully; and if the defendants removed the remains or broke down the vault and removed it without the consent of the plaintiffs, such removal of the remains or breaking down or removing the vault was wrongful, and the plaintiffs would be entitled to recover. If the remains of Bryan L. Koonce were removed with consent of plaintiffs, then such removing the remains was not wrongful, and plaintiffs could not recover for that; or, if the vault was opened by plaintiffs' consent, such act was not wrongful as to defendant, and plaintiffs could not recover for that. If defendant wrongfully removed remains in vault, your answer to first issue should be, 'Yes;' but if the vault or remains were removed with plaintiffs' consent, your answer should be, 'No.' If you answer first issue, 'No,' it is not necessary to pass on the question of owner." The court also instructed the jury as to the measure of damages, and called their attention to the evidence, and pointed out the bearing of the evidence on each of the issues, and plaintiffs made no exception on that account. There was a motion for a new trial, which was overruled, and the plaintiffs appealed to the this court from the rulings and judgment, and assigned as error: (1) The verdict is against the weight of the evidence, and is contrary to the justice and equity of the cause. (2) The legal effect and consequence of the verdict of the jury would be to deprive the plaintiffs of a vested right created by deed, which can only be done by a deed from them, or by a release in writing; and this, being a grant by a corporation of a freehold interest in the nature of an easement, and being made by deed, cannot be revoked nor extinguished nor conveyed in any other way than by a deed, or by a voluntary abandonment for

such a length of time as would raise the presumption of a grant. (3) The grant of an easement for an indefinite period amounts in law to the grant of a freehold interest, and a deed is necessary for creating or conferring an easement if the interest is freehold, and such interest cannot be conveyed in any way but by a deed, nor extinguished in any way but by non-user for such a length of time as would raise the presumption of a grant.

S. W. Isler, for appellants. *E. S. Martin,* for appellee.

CLARK, J. There is no just ground for the exception to the issues. It is settled by repeated decisions of this court that, while the issues must arise upon the pleadings, the trial judge may, in his discretion, submit either one or many, subject only to the restriction that sufficient facts shall be found to enable the court to proceed to judgment, and that neither party shall be denied the opportunity to present any view of the law arising upon the evidence through the medium of pertinent instructions. McAdoo v. Railroad Co., 105 N. C. 140, 11 S. E. Rep. 316; Denmark v. Railroad Co., 107 N. C. 187, 12 S. E. Rep. 54; Leach v. Linde, 108 N. C. 547, 13 S. E. Rep. 212. The issues submitted were in compliance with these requirements, especially after the admissions made by the defendant. The fewer the issues, if sufficient to develop the case, the better, as a jury may be confused by a multiplicity of issues. The two prayers for instructions were properly not given, as they were not applicable to any evidence sent up, nor to any issue, either those asked by plaintiffs or those submitted, and the court was not called upon to charge as to abstract propositions of law. While there was conflicting evidence whether the remains of Bryan L. Koonce were removed with the consent of the plaintiffs, there appears no evidence that the plaintiffs removed them involuntarily, or induced by threats or promises. It seems from the evidence that the remains were removed by the defendant, and the finding of the jury, construed in connection with the charge, was that such removal, and the incident damage to the vault, were with the consent of the plaintiffs; for the court told the jury, "if the vault or remains were removed with plaintiffs' consent, to answer the first issue, 'No;'" but, if defendant wrongfully removed the remains, to respond "Yes" to such issue. The jury responded to the issue "No." Whether plaintiff had an easement or a mere license, (as was held in Kincaid's Appeal, 66 Pa. St. 411,) it is subject to the police power of the state, which by act of assembly has authorized the ordinance of the city forbidding interments at that spot. This is inherent power in the state, and is very generally exercised with the growth of towns, by forbidding further interments within city limits after a given date; otherwise a burial-ground which, in the infancy of a town may be outside the limits, might continue a place of interment, to the nuisance of the city, after the cemetery has become the central point of population, and surrounded on all sides by dwellings

and places of business, (Presbyterian
Church v. New York, 5 Cow. 538; Wood-
lawn Cemetery v. Everett, 118 Mass. 354;
City Council v. Baptist Church, 4 Strob.
306; Coates v. New York, 7 Cow. 585;
Cooley, Const. Law, 595;) and the legislative discretion even· extends to the
power to authorize the removal of bodies
already interred, (Kincaid's Appeal, 66
Pa. St. 411; Richards v. Dutch Church,
32 Barb. 42; Page v. Symonds, 63 N. H.
17; 3 Lawson, Rights, Rem. & Pr. §
1343; 3 Amer. & Eng. Enc. Law, 53, and
numerous cases there cited:) though usually, as in this case, the legislature restricts the authority conferred to the prohibition of future interments. Besides, the
conveyance under which the easement is
claimed only grants "the right to inter in
said vault so long as it shall be used for
the purpose of interment." By virtue of
the burning of the church, and its subsequent removal to another lot, as well as
by the city ordinance forbidding interments within city limits, the lot in question has ceased to be used for interments,
and the easement granted has ceased certainly as to future interments by its own
terms. There is no question arising, therefore, whether an easement could be surrendered or extinguished otherwise than
by deed. The *gravamen*, however, of
plaintiffs' action, is as to removal of the
remains of the plaintiffs' ancestor heretofore interred. As to that, the jury has
found that such removal was with plaintiffs' consent. They have, therefore, no
ground of complaint in that respect. As
to the first error assigned as ground for a
new trial, "that the verdict was against
the weight of the evidence," that was a
matter with the judge below, and not reviewable. Whitehurst v. Pettipher, 105
N. C. 40, 11 S. E. Rep. 369; High v. Bailey,
107 N. C. 70, 12 S. E. Rep. 45; Redmond v.
Stepp, 100 N. C. 212, 6 S. E. Rep. 727; Mc-
Kinnon v. Morrison, 104 N. C. 354, 10 S. E.
Rep. 513. No error.

ISLEY v. BOON et al.

(*Supreme Court of North Carolina.* Nov. 10,
1891.)

LOST RECORDS—SECONDARY EVIDENCE.

Where it becomes essential on the trial of
a cause to produce in evidence the record of another proceeding, and the clerk of the court, after
diligent search, is unable to find certain material
parts of the said record, secondary evidence is
admissible to prove the loss or destruction of
such parts, as also their contents.

Appeal from superior court, Alamance
county; EDWIN T. BOYKIN, Judge.

This was an action by Christian Isley
against John Boon and others to try title
to land. There was judgment for defendants, and plaintiff appeals. Reversed.

STATEMENT BY THE COURT. On the trial
it became material for the plaintiff to produce in evidence the record of a special
proceeding, and the following is so much
of the case stated on appeal for this court
in respect thereto as need be reported:

"The plaintiff then introduced the letters of administration issued to E. S.
Parker upon the estate of Samuel Adams,
deceased, issued by the clerk of the superi-

or court of Alamance county, under his
official seal of the 8th day of November,
1875. The plaintiff then proposed to show
a sale of the land in controversy, by E. S.
Parker, administrator of Samuel Adams,
deceased, on the 3d day of April, 1876, (under special proceeding taken by him in the
superior court of Alamance county, for the
purpose of creating assets for the payment
of debts of his intestate,) to John Ireland,
the last and highest bidder, and a deed
made on the 5th of January, 1881, to the
heirs at law of the said John Ireland, who
had theretofore died intestate, after having paid the whole of the purchase money
for said land to the administrator, Parker. To establish such special proceedings
the plaintiff put in evidence two summons
issued by the clerk of the superior court
of Alamance county under his official seal,
bearing date of November 27, 1875, entitled
'E. S. Parker, as administrator of Samuel
Adams, against John Adams, John Boon
and wife, Robena, Jacob Hicks and wife,
Piety,' commanding the sheriff to summon
the defendants to appear at the office of
the clerk of the superior court of said county within twenty-one days after the service of summons on them, to answer the
complaint to be therein filed, one of which
summons was directed to the sheriff of
Alamance county, and was returned by
the sheriff of said county as served upon
John Boon and wife, Robena, on the 24th
of January, 1876. The other was directed
to the sheriff of Forsyth county, and was
returned by the sheriff of said county on
the 24th of January, 1876, as served on Jacob Hicks and wife, Piety; also the petition of E. S. Parker, administrator of
Samuel Adams, deceased, against John
Adams, John Boon and wife, Robena, Jacob Hicks and wife, Piety, filed in said
court, praying for a license to sell the real
estate described in the petition, the same
being the land in controversy in this action, as the property of Samuel Adams,
deceased, to create assets for the payment
of the debts of his intestate, subject to the
right of the dower of the widow of said
deceased, which said petition was verified
before the clerk of said court on the 20th
day of January, 1876. Plaintiff also introduced an order directing publication to be
made in the Alamance Gleaner, a paper
published in Alamance county, for six
weeks.

"The plaintiff introduced A. Tate, and
showed by him that he was the clerk of
the superior court of Alamance county
from 1878 to the first Monday in December,
1890, who testified that the two summons,
together with the petition of E. S. Parker,
administrator of Samuel Adams, deceased,
and the order of publication, which were
introduced by the plaintiff, were (records) found by him in the office of the superior court of Alamance county. He also
proved that W. A. Albright was his immediate predecessor in the clerk's office of
said county, and that he well knew his
handwriting, and that the signature to
the two summons, and also to the verification to the petition and the signature
to the order for publication, were his handwriting. Witness also testified that the
case of E. S. Parker, administrator of Sam-

uel Adams, deceased, against John Adams, John Boon and wife, Robena, Jacob Hicks and wife, Piety, appeared in the summons docket of said superior court; and, further, that he had made diligent search in his office for the order of sale, the report of sale, the decree confirming the sale by E. S. Parker as administrator to John Ireland, or any other papers or records belonging to said case in said office, but was unable to find such. Witness testified that he found no other entry of the case upon docket or records than the statement of the case and the issuing of the summons. He stated that he found no minutes, or memorandum, or order upon said records.

"The plaintiff then introduced E. S. Parker, the administrator of Samuel Adams, deceased, and, after exhibiting a written notice to the defendants that the plaintiff would offer parol evidence of the existence of the records and orders and proceedings in the special proceeding for the sale of the land of the said Samuel Adams, deceased, and the loss or destruction of said records, and of the plaintiff's purpose to show the contents thereof by parol, proposed to prove by him the issuing of the summons hereinbefore mentioned and the fact of the filing by himself, in the office of the clerk of the superior court, of the petition, hereinbefore mentioned, for the sale of land to make assets, and an order for publication, and that the said petition and order were in his handwriting, and signed by him as attorney and petitioner, and were the original papers they purported to be. Plaintiff further proposed to prove by said witness the existence of an order adjudging that publication had been made for the defendant John Adams, a non-resident, and of a decree of the said court in the said special proceeding directing him, as the administrator of Samuel Adams, to sell the land described in his petition at public auction at the court-house in Graham, to the highest bidder, for cash, after duly advertising the same, and that the proceeds of the sale be assets in his hands for the payment of debts; it being adjudged that there was no personal estate of said intestate with which to pay debts; also that he made said sale, after due advertisement, on the 3d day of April, 1876, at the court-house in Graham, when and where John Ireland became the purchaser at the price of $50.50, and paid the purchase money down, and that he made no report of said sale to the court; also a decree of the court made, confirming said report and sale, and directing the administrator to make title in fee to the purchaser; and further proposed to prove by said witness that, the said John Ireland having died soon thereafter, after having paid for said land, he made and executed a title deed to the heirs at law of the said John Ireland, deceased, being the grantors named in the said administrator's deed, which deed was made on the 5th day of January, 1881. And plaintiff further proposed to prove by said Parker that he afterwards saw on several occasions said special proceeding, petition, and other orders, order of sale, report of sale, and decree confirming said sale, etc., in the clerk's office as records of said court, and knew that all of said orders did exist and were on file in said office, and that diligent search has been made since in said office for them. Upon objection by the defendants to the proposed evidence of the witness E. S. Parker, as hereinbefore set forth, the court sustained the said objection, and refused the proposed evidence, to which ruling of the court the plaintiff excepted. The plaintiff then proposed to introduce in evidence the deed executed by E. S. Parker, administrator of Samuel Adams, to J. R. Ireland, W. F. Ireland, Samuel Ireland, W. S. Caffey and wife, Caroline, C. Isley and wife, Louisa, for the land in controversy, bearing date 5th day of January, 1881, which deed has been duly proven and registered, and insisted upon the title derived from said deed, as well as recitals contained therein, as evidence of the existence of the record and other proceedings recited in said deed under the law and the maxim, 'omnia praesumuntur rite esse acta.' The court, upon objection of the defendants, refused to admit the evidence offered, and the plaintiff excepted. Upon the intimation of the court the plaintiff submitted to a nonsuit and appealed."

L. M. Scott, for appellant.   J. A. Long, W. P. Bynum, Jr., and Batchelor & Devereux, for appellees.

MERRIMON, C. J. The evidence proposed and rejected on the trial must be accepted for the present purpose as true, because it was material; and, if it had been submitted to the jury, they might have believed and so treated it. The facts showed that material parts of the record of the special proceeding referred to had been lost or destroyed. The clerk of the court, the proper custodian of the record, made diligent search in his office for such parts of it as were alleged to have been lost, and he was unable to find them. It must be taken that he made such search where, regularly, they ought to be, and generally through his office, where he might hope to find them. He failed to find them, if they ever existed. They were lost or destroyed. It is not suggested that they were not, nor did the court found its opinion upon such supposition. Then, if the parts of the record specified were lost or destroyed, it was clearly competent to prove on the trial by secondary evidence such loss or destruction, and also what the nature, meaning, and purport of such lost parts were. It has been so expressly decided. In Mobley v. Watts, 98 N. C. 284, 3 S. E. Rep. 677, Justice Davis said: "If the record is lost, and is ancient, its existence and contents may sometimes be presumed; but, whether it be ancient or recent, after proof of the loss its contents may be proved, like any other document, by secondary evidence, where the case does not from its nature disclose the existence of other and better evidence." This case, it seems to us, plainly comes within what is said and decided in the case just cited. Indeed, it is well settled that where the record is lost, that it existed, and its purpose and contents, may be proven, on the trial of any action where it becomes n...

terial, by secondary evidence. The loss or destruction of the record should, however, be made to appear clearly before receiving such secondary evidence. Stanly v: Massingill, 63 N. C. 558; Yount v. Miller, 91 N. C. 331; Hare v. Holloman, 94 N. C. 14. There is error. The judgment of nonsuit must be set aside, and the case disposed of according to law. To that end let this opinion be certified to the superior court. It is so ordered.

BROWN et ux. v. BROWN.

(Supreme Court of North Carolina. Nov. 10, 1891.)

LANDLORD'S LIEN ON CROPS—ADVANCEMENTS.

Code N. C. § 1754, provides that crops raised on leased land shall, unless otherwise agreed, be deemed vested in possession of the lessor until the rent is paid, and the lessor reimbursed for all "advancements" in making and saving said crops. *Held,* that where the lessor furnishes table board to the lessee and his family, in order that the latter may make and save his crops, such board at once becomes an advancement, and the lessor is not required to prove an express agreement showing that it was to be so considered between the parties.

Appeal from superior court, Duplin county; EDWIN T. BOYKIN, Judge.

This was an action by D. D. Brown and wife, Adeline E. Brown, against Jonas H. Brown, a tenant on plaintiffs' land, to recover for advancements in making and saving crops. Judgment for defendant. Plaintiffs appeal. Reversed.

W. R. Allen, for appellants. *B. L. Stevens* and *H. R. Kornegay,* for appellee.

MERRIMON, C. J. The statute (Code, § 1754) prescribes that "when lands shall be rented or leased by agreement, written or oral, for agricultural purposes, or shall be cultivated by a cropper, unless otherwise agreed between the parties to the lease or agreement, any and all crops raised on said lands shall be deemed and held to be vested in possession of the lessor or his assigns at all times until the rent for said lands shall be paid, and until all the stipulations contained in the lease or agreement shall be performed, or damages in lieu thereof shall be paid to the lessor or his assigns, and until said party or his assigns shall be paid for all advancements made and expenses incurred in making and saving said crops." The agreement for the purposes thus prescribed having been made, this statutory provision at once gives and secures the lien upon the crops in favor of the landlord without any stipulation for that purpose between the parties. The lien is a legal incident to the agreement, and it attaches not only to secure the rents, but as well to secure "all advancements made and expenses incurred in making and saving said crops." The intention of the parties to create the lien is implied by the agreement, unless otherwise agreed between them. A leading purpose of the statute is to secure the landlord as to the rents and advancements made by him in making and saving the crops. To that end the lien is given, and it is expressly provided that it "shall be preferred to all other liens." An advance-

ment, in the sense of the statute, is anything of value pertinent for the purpose to be used directly or indirectly in making and saving the crops, supplied in good faith to the lessee by the landlord. Many things are in their nature and adaptation *per se* pertinent for such purpose, and presumptively constitute advancements whenever so supplied. Thus, subsistence for the tenant and his employee and work animals, appropriate farming implements, and the like, are advancements when so supplied. These and other like things are directly appropriate for such purpose, and when supplied to that end make advancements. They are presumed to be such. There are other things not directly so appropriate, such as shoes, tobacco, dry goods, groceries, and the like, which the landlord may supply to the lessee to pay his laborers. When such supplies are made, whether they make advancements or not depends on whether they were supplied for the purpose specified. It must appear affirmatively that they were. That the lessee diverts such things from the purpose contemplated cannot change their nature and the purpose of them. Womble v. Leach, 83 N. C. 84; Ledbetter v. Quick, 90 N. C. 276. If here the plaintiff had supplied the defendant as his tenant with meal, meat, sugar, and coffee in reasonable quantities, or appropriate farming tools, to make and save his crop, such things, in the nature of the matter, would have been directly appropriate for the purpose, and the presumption would have been that they were advancements. That the plaintiff supplied subsistence from his own table to the defendant for such purpose could make no substantial or legal difference, because he supplied that which was in its nature, and that of the whole matter, essential to make and save the crops; and the relations of the parties raised the presumption that such supplies were advancements. The plaintiff, as he alleges, supplied the defendant, in his own house, with subsistence, to the end he might make his crops. That the defendant's wife shared in the subsistence so supplied cannot alter the case. It was his duty to feed and care for her. To feed his family proper was a burden incident to making and saving the crops. The court should therefore have instructed the jury substantially, in submitting the view of the case insisted upon by the plaintiff, that, if the latter supplied the defendant with board, to the end he might make and save his crops, then he was entitled to recover the reasonable value of the board, and the same would (nothing to the contrary appearing) constitute an advancement, and therefore a lien upon the crops. The plaintiff was not required, as the court said he was, to prove an express contract that the board of defendant and his wife should be an advancement, because, if the plaintiff leased the lands to the defendant, (and that he did was not controverted,) and supplied him with board, to the end he might make and save his crops at once, such supplies, perforce of the statute, became advancements, in the absence of agreement to the contrary, and a lien upon the crops. There is, therefore, error, and the plaintiff is entitled to a new trial. To that end let this opinion be certified to the superior court. It is so ordered.

FOLB et al. v. PHŒNIX INS. CO.

(Supreme Court of North Carolina. Nov. 12, 1891.)

ACTION ON POLICY—OTHER INSURANCE—BREACH OF CONDITIONS.

A policy of fire insurance provided that in the event of other insurance without the consent of defendant the policy should be void. In an action thereon defendant's agent testified that he had written a second policy for plaintiff, in another company, on the same property; had tendered the policy, and demanded the premium, which they promised to pay, but that they had failed to do so, and the policy was not delivered. It did not appear that they had requested him to write such second policy. Defendant offered to show that it was customary to write policies and hold them until the premiums were paid; that the second policy was regularly issued, and that after the fire plaintiffs had demanded the policy. *Held* not sufficient to show a contract for such second policy of insurance.

Appeal from superior court, Cumberland county; R. F. ARMFIELD, Judge.

Action by M. Folb and Louis Folb against the Phœnix Insurance Company on a policy of fire insurance. Verdict and judgment for plaintiffs. Defendant appeals. Affirmed.

STATEMENT BY THE COURT. The plaintiffs brought this action to recover the sum of $1,500, which the defendant, by its policy of insurance, agreed and promised to pay them in case of the loss of their goods therein specified by fire, in the contingency and as therein provided and stipulated. The policy contained, among others, a clause in these words: "Or if the assured shall have or shall hereafter make any other insurance (whether void or not) on the property herein specified, or any part thereof, without the consent of the company written hereon, then and in every such case this policy is void." In the answer the defendant alleged as a defense, among other things, "that after the issuing of the policy of insurance set out in the complaint the plaintiffs made other insurance on the property specified, without the consent of the defendant written upon the said policy, and in violation of its express terms, and thereby rendered said policy void." On the trial the defendant introduced a witness, who testified in its behalf as follows: "I am an insurance agent. As such, I wrote a policy for plaintiffs on the goods destroyed and the subject of this suit in the Continental Fire Insurance Company, dated November 8, 1889." Witness further testified that he tendered this policy to the plaintiffs both before and after the fire which consumed the goods, and demanded the payment of the first premium specified in said policy; that the plaintiffs promised to pay, but did not do so, and witness never delivered this policy to plaintiffs, and that, after these tenders, witness received a telegram from his company instructing him not to deliver this policy to plaintiffs. Defendant then offered to prove by that witness that the books of his company, which he had with him in court, showed that this policy had been

regularly issued, and a record made on said book. Upon objection by the plaintiffs' counsel, this evidence was excluded by the court, and the defendant excepted. Defendant then offered to prove that it was the custom of insurance companies to write policies and hold them for the convenience of the assured until the premiums were paid. On objection of plaintiffs' counsel this was excluded, and defendant excepted. Defendant then offered to prove that after the fire which destroyed the goods the plaintiffs demanded of this company (the Continental) the amount of this last policy, to cover the loss. Upon objection by plaintiffs' counsel, this testimony was excluded by the court, and the defendant excepted. This was all the evidence in the case tending to show that plaintiffs had taken out other insurance on the property in violation of the terms of the policy sued on. His honor submitted to the jury the first issue upon the evidence as to the value of the goods, with instructions to which there were no exceptions. As to the second issue, "Did the plaintiffs, after issuance of the policy sued on, take out other insurance on said stock of goods without the consent of the defendant indorsed on the said policy?" his honor instructed the jury that there was not sufficient evidence to justify them in finding this issue in favor of the defendant, and directed them to answer this issue "No," which they did. Defendant excepted. There was a verdict for plaintiffs on the first issue. The court gave judgment for plaintiffs, and the defendant appealed to the supreme court.

John W. Hinsdale, for appellant. *Thos. H. Sutton,* for appellees.

MERRIMON, C. J. It seems to us very clear that there was no sufficient evidence produced on the trial to go to the jury to prove that the plaintiffs did "make any other insurance, whether valid or not, on the property" specified in the policy sued upon, subsequent to the date of its execution. Accepting the evidence produced as true, it does not appear from it, unless by mere vague inference, that the plaintiffs, before the loss by fire, requested the defendant's agent to supply them with such subsequent insurance; nor does it appear that it was agreed between the parties that the defendant should do so. At most it appears only that the plaintiffs thought of getting additional insurance, and that the defendant's agent was zealously trying to induce them to do so. It does not, however, appear affirmatively that they did not receive the policy tendered them, and that they did not pay the premium demanded. If such arrangement had been feasible, the agent of the defendant did not agree that the policy tendered by him should become the property of the plaintiffs, and he would hold it for them until they should pay the premium. It does not appear that there was any purpose of the parties to observe a very unbusinesslike and unreasonable "custom of insurance companies to write policies and hold them for the convenience of the insured until the premiums were paid." The mere fact that defendant's books "showed that this policy had been regularly issued, and a record made in said book," was not evidence to prove a contract of insurance; nor was the mere fact that the plaintiffs demanded of the company the payment of the supposed additional insurance evidence of such contract. The evidence went to prove that the contract of insurance contemplated (talked about,—thought of) was to be made in the ordinary way by executing a proper policy. There was not the slightest evidence of a purpose to make a merely verbal contract. The alleged contract, behind which the defendant seeks to find shelter, was never consummated; nor was what was said as to it in any sense binding upon any party; nor did it come within the meaning or purpose of the clause of the policy sued upon, and relied on as a defense by the defendant. Judgment affirmed.

McPHAIL et al. v. JOHNSON.

(*Supreme Court of North Carolina.* Nov. 12, 1891.)

SPLITTING CAUSE OF ACTION.

Where plaintiffs' contract provided for furnishing defendant with certain lumber, and on a performance of their contract the amount due them exceeded the jurisdiction of a justice of the peace, they could not split the amount so as to bring three actions within such jurisdiction, though the lumber had been delivered by installments.

Appeal from superior court, Cumberland county; R. F. ARMFIELD, Judge.

Action by McPhail Bros. against James H. Johnson on a contract for lumber furnished. Judgment for defendant on nonsuit. Plaintiffs appeal. Affirmed.

STATEMENT BY THE COURT. This was one of three civil actions commenced and tried at the same time in the court of a justice of the peace of Cumberland county, in all of which plaintiffs recovered judgment, and the defendant appealed to the superior court; and this action came on for trial by a jury, before Judge ARMFIELD, at May term, 1891, of Cumberland superior court. The said actions were founded upon a written contract between the defendant and the firm of H. Wade & Co., the latter firm having assigned their interest in said contract to plaintiffs. Plaintiffs alleged that the whole of said contract had been performed before the bringing of the said three actions in the justice's court, and that there was then due to plaintiffs on said contract, or for work done thereunder, a sum largely in excess of $200; but as the contract had been performed by several deliveries of lumber at different times, which several deliveries were, respectively, under $200, that they had a right to split up their account, and bring their several actions for sums, respectively, less than $200, though aggregating more than $200, in the court of a justice of the peace. The following is a copy of the part of the contract material here: "(4) The said James H. Johnson is to receive the entire output of said mill, and pay the said H. Wade & Co. the sum of two dollars and fifty cents per thousand feet for any and all lumber so sawed as it is taken from the saw and sawed ac-

cording to bills furnished, in a workmanlike manner." "His honor intimated that, as the whole amount claimed by plaintiffs was due when these three actions were commenced, the plaintiffs could not split up their cause of action as they had attempted to do, so as to give jurisdiction to the justice. In deference to this opinion of his honor, plaintiffs took a nonsuit, and appealed to the supreme court."

Thos. H. Sutton and John G. Shaw, for appellants. Geo. M. Rose, for appellee.

MERRIMON, C. J. The alleged indebtedness of the defendant to the plaintiffs accrued from time to time, and at divers times, under and by virtue of a single contract, whereby H. Wade & Co. agreed to supply the defendant with "the entire output" of a lumber-mill, and they completely performed their part of such contract. The sum of money demanded by the plaintiffs was much more than $200, and, to facilitate the collection of their debt, they subdivided their claim, so as to bring each part of it within the jurisdiction of a justice of the peace. They contend that they had the right to do so, because they supplied the lumber from the mill at divers times and on various accounts. This contention is not well founded. The indebtedness, having accrued, was single,—a whole, one debt,—arising out of a single contract, that possessed a single purpose, —the supply of lumber. This case clearly comes within what is said and decided in Jarrett v. Self, 90 N. C. 478; Moore v. Nowell, 94 N. C. 268; Kearns v. Heitman, 104 N. C. 332, 10 S. E. Rep. 467. If, however, the delivery under the contract as made by distinct installments, an action would lie for the amount due for the same at once. But when more than one such installment has been delivered, but one action lies for the whole amount due on account of the same. Judgment affirmed.

FISHER v. BULLARD.

(*Supreme Court of North Carolina.* Nov. 12, 1891.)

JUSTICE OF THE PEACE—JURISDICTION—PENALTIES.

Under Code N. C. § 871, forbidding a justice of the peace to issue process to any county other than his own where there is only one defendant, and section 191, (applicable to proceedings in superior courts,) providing that an action for the recovery of a penalty must be brought in the county where the cause arose, a justice has jurisdiction of an action against a resident of his county for a penalty incurred in another county, in the absence of any provision extending the provision of section 191 to justices' courts.

Appeal from superior court, Cumberland county; R. F. ARMFIELD, Judge.

Action by John Fisher against Henry Bullard to recover the statutory penalty for setting fire to woods. From an order dismissing the action on the ground that the justice of the peace before whom it was brought, and who rendered judgment against defendant, had no jurisdiction, plaintiff appeals. Reversed.

F. R. Cooper, for appellant.

CLARK, J. This was a civil action, begun before a justice of the peace in Cumberland county against a defendant residing in said county, to recover the penalty of $50, incurred under Code, §§ 52, 53, by any one setting fire to any woods not his own property. The woods burned lay wholly in Sampson. The defendant moved to dismiss for want of jurisdiction, which was refused, and judgment given against him. On appeal to the superior court, the motion was renewed in that court on the same ground, and allowed. The Code, § 871, forbids a justice to issue process to any county other than his own unless there is more than one *bona fide* defendant, and one of them shall reside in another county. That not being the case here, a justice of the peace in Sampson could not reach the defendant, so that the case might be tried there, unless he happened to be caught in Sampson. The provision for indorsing warrants issued in another county (Code, § 1136) is restricted to criminal cases. The justice of the peace in Cumberland, having jurisdiction of the person of the defendant, by service of process upon him, and of the subject-matter,—a penalty of fifty dollars,—was the proper officer before whom to bring the action, unless there is some statute forbidding it. It is claimed that this is done by Code, § 191, which provides that an action for the recovery of a penalty must be brought in the county where the cause of action arose. But it must be noted that section 191 is in the Code, chapter 10, (commonly known as the "Code of Civil Procedure,") which is applicable to proceedings in the superior courts. Section 871, supra, is in chapter 22 of the Code, which relates to justices' courts. By section 840, rule 15, the Code of Civil Procedure, respecting forms of action, parties to actions, times of commencing actions, and service of process, is made applicable to justices' courts. By sections 849, 853, and 889, the provisions of Code Civil Proc. as to arrests and bail, attachments, and claim and delivery, were made applicable to such proceedings in the justice's court, but we do not find any statute making the provisions of Code Civil Proc. as to place of trial, (in which is the above section 191,) applicable to trials before a justice. The justice of the peace in Cumberland county therefore had jurisdiction, and in granting the motion to dismiss there was error.

BEVILLE v. COX.

(Supreme Court of North Carolina. Nov. 10, 1891.)

PROCEEDINGS AFTER REMAND — AMENDMENT OF PLEADINGS—ADDITIONAL RETURN OF JUSTICE OF THE PEACE — LIABILITY OF MARRIED WOMAN'S ESTATE.

1. After remand for a new trial, the refusal to allow further pleadings is within the discretion of the trial court, and not reviewable, unless the refusal is based on want of power.

2. On appeal from a justice of the peace, an additional return will not be recognized, unless filed by consent of parties, or made pursuant to a *recordari.*

3. The coverture of plaintiff, which does not appear in the complaint, cannot be raised on a plea of the general issue.

4. Where a *feme sole* employed plaintiff, and

after her marriage died, plaintiff has an action against her estate before a justice of the peace for services rendered before the marriage.

Appeal from superior court, Guilford county; BOYKIN, Judge.

Action by Mary E. Beville against H. S. Cox, administrator of the estate of Joanna Cox, deceased, to recover compensation for services by plaintiff to the intestate of defendant, first tried on appeal from justice's court, before MACRAE, J., at August term, 1890, upon the issue, "Is the defendant indebted to the plaintiff as alleged, and, if so, how much?" and from the judgment at that term there was an appeal to the supreme court, and new trial granted. 12 S. E. Rep. 52. And afterwards, at the May term, 1891, of the superior court of Guilford, the case came on again to be tried before BOYKIN, J., upon the same issue aforesaid. Upon the call of the cause, and after the jury was impaneled, the plaintiff tendered the same issue on which the case had been tried before MACRAE, J., and then and thereupon the defendant tendered the following additional issues, to-wit: Is the plaintiff a married woman? Did plaintiff's cause of action, if any she has, accrue within three years before the beginning of this action? Is the action barred by the statute of limitations? To the submission of these issues tendered by defendant the plaintiff objected, on the ground that defendant had offered to plead the same matters before MACRAE, J., who declined them, to which refusal of the judge no exception was taken by defendant; and on the further ground that the paper writing filed in the papers, and marked by the clerk as filed the 19th of November, 1890, and called a supplemental return of the justice of the peace, had been procured from the justice without an order of the superior court therefor, and put into the papers without notice to plaintiff, and therefore did not constitute a part of the record. On this objection, on inquiry of the judge as to whether these matters embraced by said issues had been discussed before MACRAE, J., and ruled upon by him, the defendant admitted they had been; and thereupon BOYKIN, J., rejected the said issues, and ordered the trial to proceed upon the issue tendered by the plaintiff, which was the same on which the trial was had before MACRAE, J. To this refusal of defendant's issues by the judge the defendant excepted. In the statement of plaintiff's case, plaintiff announced to the court that plaintiff claimed to recover in this action in conformity with the decision of the supreme court in the case, supra, only for her services to intestate of defendant, under contract with her, from February, 1885, to August, 1886, at which last date she had intermarried with the defendant, H. S. Cox. In support of the issue on plaintiff's part, she introduced testimony tending to show that she lived with the defendant's intestate, her aunt, from February, 1885, to August, 1886, at which last date she married H. S. Cox, under a contract with said intestate to pay her for her services, such as cooking, washing, etc., and also tending to show that her services were reasonably worth one dollar per week, and that during all the time the intestate of defendant was a *feme sole*. To support the contention of defendant under the issue submitted, there was testimony tending to show that plaintiff was living with the intestate of the defendant as a member of her family, without any contract for or expectation of pay; and defendant proposed to ask of the plaintiff whether she was or was not, at the date of her alleged contract and during her services to defendant's intestate, the wife of a man by name of Smith, which was objected to as not pertinent to and embraced in the issue submitted to the jury, which was ruled as irrelevant by the court, and excluded by the court. Defendant excepted. The defendant moved to dismiss the action for want of jurisdiction in justice's court, which the court refused to do. The court instructed the jury that, if the testimony satisfied them that plaintiff rendered the services as alleged under a contract to be paid for the same, she was entitled to recover such amount as from the testimony they should find such services were reasonably worth from February, 1885, to August, 1886, the date of intestate's marriage with the defendant, Cox, and that she could not recover for services rendered since said marriage. There was verdict for plaintiff for services up to August, 1886. Plaintiff moved for judgment, and defendant moved for new trial, for errors, to-wit, the refusal of the court to submit the issues tendered by defendant, and exclusion of testimony as excepted to, and so much of the charge to the jury as instructed them that plaintiff could recover. The court declined to give a new trial, and signed judgment for plaintiff. Defendant appealed. Affirmed.

J. T. Morehead, for appellant. *J. E. Boyd* and *Dillard & King*, for appellee.

CLARK, J. When this case went back for a new trial, it was competent to admit additional evidence, or further pleadings and issues. Ashby v. Page, 108 N. C. 6, 13 S. E. Rep. 90. A new trial is on the whole merits, (unless it is restricted to certain issues,) and the court below can proceed as if no former trial had taken place. McMillan v. Baker, 92 N. C. 110; Jones v. Swepson, 94 N. C. 700. Whether, however, the court would permit the additional pleas asked by defendant, was in its discretion, and not reviewable, (Hinton v. Deans, 75 N. C. 18; Johnson v. Rowland, 80 N. C. ? ,) unless the court put the refusal upon a want of power, which was not done. The inquiry by the court as to the action of the preceding judge seems to have been to aid himself in the exercise of his discretion. At least, we are not to presume error when it is not affirmatively stated that the refusal was on the ground of a want of power. Besides, the additional issues asked and refused did not arise upon the pleadings or the magistrate's return. We know of no practice which would require the judge to recognize the additional returns voluntarily sent up since the former trial by the justice of the

v.13s.e.no.33—51

peace. Why the justice did not amend his return earlier, or why a *recordari* was not issued to have the additional matter sent up, does not appear. Doubtless the judge, if the parties consented, or without their consent, might permit the supplementary returns to be filed, but he did not do so. If a *recordari* had been applied for, the adverse party would have had notice, and been put on inquiry, of which benefit he was deprived by the volunteered action of the justice. It is clear that, under both the old practice and the new, advantage cannot be taken of the coverture of the plaintiff under the plea of the general issue. That plea controverts the allegations of the plaintiff. It does not admit of proof of matter in avoidance, such as the coverture of plaintiff. Gould, Pl. 531. A married woman may sue alone on a contract to pay her for her services rendered, subject to the non-joinder of the husband being pleaded in abatement. Morgan v. Cubitt, 3 Exch. 611; Bendix v. Wakeman, 12 Mees. & W. 97; Dalton v. Railroad Co., 22 L. R. (N. S.) 177. If a married woman sues alone, and the disability does not appear upon the face of the complaint, the defendant can only avail himself of the coverture by specially pleading it. The objection is waived by a general denial. Dillaye v. Parks, 31 Barb. 132. The plea of the general issue is a waiver of all objections to the person of the plaintiff, and admits his capacity to sue. Brown v. Illius, 27 Conn. 84; Bank v. Curtis, 14 Conn. 437. In our own state it is held that, if the subject-matter is within the jurisdiction, "any peculiar circumstance excluding the plaintiff or exempting the defendant must be brought forward by a plea to the jurisdiction. Otherwise there is an implied waiver of the objection, and the court goes on in the exercise of its ordinary jurisdiction." Blackwell v. Dibbrell, 103 N. C. 270, 9 S. E. Rep. 192, citing PEARSON, J., in Branch v. Houston, Busb. 85. The court, therefore, properly excluded evidence which would only have been competent to support a plea in abatement, not pleaded. If the contract had been a continuing one, the plaintiff could have recovered before the justice of the peace for the entire services, (not exceeding $200,) as was pointed out in this case, (107 N. C. 175, 12 S. E. Rep. 52,) as well for those rendered after marriage of defendant's intestate as before. But if, in her complaint before the justice, the plaintiff joined in the account charges for services rendered after the marriage of such intestate as well as those before, and on appeal only recovered for those rendered before the marriage, we do not see how the defendant can complain. Deloatch v. Coman, 90 N. C. 186; Ashe v. Gray, 88 N. C. 190. In any aspect of the case the coverture of the defendant's intestate could not defeat the recovery before a justice for at least the services rendered before her marriage. Code, § 1823; Hodges v. Hill, 105 N. C. 130, 10 S. E. Rep. 916; Neville v. Pope, 95 N. C. 346. No error.

LYLES v. COMMONWEALTH.

(Supreme Court of Appeals of Virginia. Nov. 12, 1891.)

CRIMINAL LAW—GRAND JURIES—INDICTMENT FOR MURDER—COMPETENCY OF JURORS—VENIRE FACIAS—EVIDENCE—CREDIBILITY OF WITNESS.

1. Under Acts Va. 1889-90, p. 91, providing that at least seven of a regular grand jury must concur in finding an indictment in any case, while in the case of a special grand jury only five of its members need concur, there is no ground for holding that an indictment for a capital felony can be found only by a regular grand jury.

2. Objection to the competency of a juror is properly overruled where he states that he is impartial, and can give the prisoner a fair trial, and that he has no opinion about the case, though he had previously stated that at the time of its commission he heard some talk about it, and might then have had some opinion about it, but did not remember whether he had or not.

3. The irregularity in a *venire facias* ordered in vacation, that it commands the summoning of 40 persons for the trial of two persons and others charged with felony, but not jointly indicted with the two, not being prejudicial, cannot, by the provisions of Acts Va. 1887-88, p. 18, for the first time be objected to after verdict.

4. The credibility of a witness, on whose testimony a conviction for murder rests, and who admitted having made different statements, is a matter for the determination of the jury.

5. Where, on error to a conviction for murder, the evidence (not the facts) is certified, the evidence for the state must be considered as admitted, and that for defendant waived, in determining whether it sustains the conviction.

Error to corporation court of Danville. James Lyles was convicted of murder, and brings error. Affirmed.

John D. Blackwell and *J. T. Smith,* for plaintiff in error. *R. Taylor Scott,* Atty. Gen., for the Commonwealth.

LEWIS, P. The prisoner, James Lyles, and Margaret Lashley, were jointly indicted in the corporation court of Danville for the murder of George Lashley. He was tried separately, found guilty, and sentenced to be hanged.

The first error assigned for the refusal of the lower court to quash the indictment, on the ground that it was found by a special grand jury composed of seven jurors only. It is contended that an indictment for a capital felony can be lawfully found only by a regular grand jury, which consists of not less than nine nor more than twelve persons; but no such distinction between the powers of a regular and special grand jury is made by the statute, and for the courts to do so would be to assume legislative authority. All that the statute provides on the subject is that at least seven of a regular grand jury must concur in finding an indictment in any case, whereas an indictment may be found by a special grand jury upon the concurring votes of five of its members. Acts 1889-90, p. 91.

The next question relates to the competency of the juror McGuire. Upon this point the bill of exceptions states that upon his *voir dire* the juror said he had heard some talk about the case at the time the alleged offense was committed, and that he might have had some opinion about it at that time, but did not recollect whether he had nor not. He stated

further, however, that he had no opinion on the subject then; that he stood impartial, and could give the prisoner a fair trial. Under these circumstances, an objection to his competency was overruled by the trial court, and, as we think, correctly. Clore's Case, 8 Grat. 606; Smith's Case, 7 Grat. 593; Wormeley's Case, 10 Grat. 658.

Objection was also made to the *venire facias* ordered in vacation, on the ground that it commanded the officer to summon 40 persons, whose names were upon a list furnished by the judge, for the trial of the prisoner and Margaret Lashley and others, charged with felony, but not jointly indicted with the prisoner and Margaret Lashley; but, as the objection was not made until after verdict, and as the irregularity was not to the prejudice of the prisoner, the objection came too late. Acts 1887-88, p. 18; Vawter's Case, (Va.) 12 S. E. Rep. 339.

There was also a motion for a new trial on the ground that the verdict was contrary to the law and the evidence, which motion was overruled; and this ruling is the subject of the next and last assignment of error. The principal witness for the commonwealth was Mary Darkins, who, as an eye-witness of the occurrence, gave the details of the shooting by which the deceased was killed. She testified that on the night of the homicide Margaret Lashley, the wife of the deceased, and the prisoner, by clandestine appointment, attended a dance in the neighborhood, leaving the deceased at home, and that they did not return until about 2 or 3 o'clock in the morning. It was also proven by the same witness and other witnesses for the commonwealth that the prisoner and the deceased, for some time prior to the homicide, had been on bad terms, growing out of the intimacy, it would seem, that existed between the wife of the deceased and the prisoner. It appears that they quarreled, and that the prisoner on several occasions threatened to kill the deceased. The latter was much of the time absent from home, working on a railroad, and during his absence the prisoner often visited his house at night, although he had been forbidden to do so. While returning from the dance the prisoner was heard to say that he had just one bullet left in his pistol, and that he intended to put that into the deceased before morning. The witness Mary Darkins also testified that when the prisoner and the wife of the deceased returned from the dance they stopped at the gate in front of the house of the deceased, and stood there talking for some time; that when Margaret went into the house the deceased, who was sitting on the bedside, said to her: "When did I ever treat you this way?" To which she replied: "Don't let us have a quarrel." At the same time she asked him to go out of doors, and, taking him by the hand, led him out of the back door. As they got to the corner of the house, the prisoner, who in the mean time had gone around the house and into the garden, raised his pistol and fired, inflicting upon the deceased a wound which caused his death a few minutes afterwards. The witness said she witnessed the shooting from a window, where she was standing at the time. On cross-examination, however, she admitted that immediately after the shooting she stated to a Mrs. Brown, who lived near by, that the deceased had "accidentally shot himself while fooling with a pistol," and that she afterwards made a similar statement as a witness before the coroner's jury; but she explained, in her re-examination, that she said to Mrs. Brown what she did because Margaret Lashley told her to do so, and that she was influenced to repeat the statement at the inquest by the threats of the prisoner and Margaret to kill her if she did not stick to her statement made to Mrs. Brown. It is not disputed that her evidence establishes a clear case for the commonwealth, if she was a credible witness; but the question of her credibility was a matter peculiarly for the jury, and upon this point they have found for the commonwealth. Moreover, the evidence (not the facts) being certified, the case stands in this court as on a demurrer to evidence,—that is to say, the prisoner must be considered as admitting the truth of the commonwealth's evidence, and as waiving all his own evidence which conflicts therewith; and, viewing the case in the light of this familiar rule, the judgment approving the verdict must be affirmed.

LASHLEY v. COMMONWEALTH.

(*Supreme Court of Appeals of Virginia.* Nov. 13, 1891.)

MURDER—EVIDENCE.

One witness testified that on the return of defendant, the wife of defendant, with one L., from a dance, where they had clandestinely gone, defendant induced her husband to go to the door, where L. shot him. Another witness testified that defendant told her that she got L. to kill her husband. There was evidence that L. had threatened to kill deceased, with whom he had been on bad terms, growing out of the intimacy of L. and defendant. *Held*, that the evidence warranted a conviction.

Error to corporation court of Danville.

Margaret Lashley was convicted of murder, and brings error. Affirmed.

John D. Blackwell and *J. T. Smith*, for plaintiff in error. *R. Taylor Scott*, Atty. Gen., for the Commonwealth.

LEWIS, P. The only question in this case not disposed of by what was said in the Lyles Case, 13 S. E. Rep. 802, (just decided,) is as to the overruling by the lower court of the motion for a new trial. The evidence is substantially the same as that in the Lyles Case, with this important addition: That the witness Mollie Wright testified that, as she was returning from the dance, about 3 o'clock in the morning, soon after the prisoner and Lyles had left, she met the prisoner on the street, who said she was going for a doctor; that George Lashley (the deceased) had shot himself; that she (the witness) accompanied the prisoner to the house of the deceased, where his dead body lay on the floor; and that soon after arriving there the prisoner asked her to go with her for a policeman. To this the witness assent-

ed, and, as they were on their way, she says they met Lyles, who inquired: "Is the d——d son of a b—— dead?" To which the prisoner replied: "Yes, and gone to hell." Continuing on their way the prisoner remarked that Lyles had killed her husband, and that she had gotten him to do it; that she loved him better than her husband, who had been "as mean as hell" to her. The jury returned a verdict of guilty, upon which the prisoner was sentenced to be hanged. We think the evidence warranted the verdict. At all events, there is nothing in the record to justify this court in setting it aside and awarding a new trial.

CONWAY v. GRANT.

(*Supreme Court of Georgia.* Nov. 10, 1891.)

ANIMALS—VICIOUS DOGS.

One who, in a city, enters the back-yard of another through an open gate on lawful business, and is bitten by ferocious dogs running loose in the yard, of which he has no notice, has a right of action against the owner if the latter knew that the dogs were accustomed to bite, and nevertheless permitted them to run loose in such yard, with the gate of the same standing open.

(*Syllabus by the Court.*)

Error from city court of Atlanta; How-ARD VAN EPPS, Judge.

Action by Edward S. Conway against Martha Grant. Judgment for defendant. Plaintiff brings error. Reversed.

John A. Wimpy, for plaintiff in error. *John T. Glenn*, for defendant in error.

BLECKLEY, C. J. The ferocious character of the dogs and the knowledge of the owner are sufficiently alleged. The only matter of controversy is touching the fault of the plaintiff in exposing himself to attack by entering the premises of the defendant where the dogs were kept. There was an open gate in rear of the premises, and the plaintiff, according to his declaration, was on lawful business. Being in search of employment as a carpenter, and seeing indications that such work was probably carried on in a certain house, he entered the premises for the purpose of making engagement or to work, having no notice or knowledge of the dogs. In this way he became exposed and was bitten. We think a cause of action is substantially set forth. Code, § 2964, declares: "A person who owns or keeps a vicious or dangerous animal of any kind, and, by the careless management of the same, or by allowing the same to go at liberty, another, without fault on his part, is injured thereby, such owner or keeper shall be liable in damages for such injury." The fault here referred to is not that of being a trespasser, but that of being in some way instrumental in provoking or bringing on the attack complained of. "It must, at the same time, be understood that the right of redress of the injured person will be defeated if the injury was caused by his own fault. A person who irritates an animal, and is bitten or kicked in turn, is deemed in law to have consented to the damage sustained, and cannot recover. But if the fault of the injured party had no necessary or natural and usual connection with the injury, operating to produce the injury as cause produces effect, the owner of the animal will be liable. For example, the defendant keeps upon his premises a ferocious dog, and the plaintiff, having no notice that such dog is there, trespasses in the day-time upon the premises, and the dog rushes upon him and bites him. The defendant is liable, since it is not the necessary or natural and usual consequence of a person's trespassing upon a man's premises by day that he should be attacked by a savage dog." Bigelow, Torts, pp. 249, 250. Though the gate was open, and the plaintiff was on lawful business, it may be that he had no strict legal right to enter the premises from the rear. But this would be no justification for leaving dangerous dogs loose on the premises to bite him or others that might so intrude. Such dangerous means of defense against mere trespassers the law will not countenance. As general authorities on the subject, see Brock v. Copeland, 1 Esp. 203; Sarch v. Blackburn, 4 Car. & P. 297; Curtis v. Mills, 5 Car. & P. 489; Loomis v. Terry, 17 Wend. 496; Pierret v. Moller, 3 E. D. Smith, 574; Kelly v. Tilton, *42 N. Y. 263; Sherley v. Bartley, 4 Sneed, 58; Woolf v. Chalker, 31 Conn. 121; Laverone v. Mangiante, 41 Cal. 138; notes to Knowles v. Mulder, (Mich.) 41 N W. Rep. 896; Cooley, Torts, *345; Bish. Non-Cont. Law, 1235 et seq.; 1 Thomp. Neg. p. 220, § 34; Muller v. McKesson, 73 N. Y. 195; Rider v. White, 65 N. Y. 54. It will be observed that the most that could possibly be said against the plaintiff is that he trespassed by going upon the premises. This is a milder fault than going there to commit a trespass. If his purpose had been to commit a crime, the dogs would have been properly employed in resisting him. But he seems to have had a virtuous and worthy object, although his mode of executing it was doubtless injudicious. It was not lawful to bite him by the instrumentality of dogs or other dangerous animals. The court erred in dismissing the action. Judgment reversed.

LA MOTTE v. HARPER et al

(Supreme Court of Georgia. Nov. 2, 1891.)

GARNISHMENT—RES ADJUDICATA.

Where wages are garnished, and the garnishee, in discharge of a judgment against him rendered by a justice's court, pays the money to the constable, and afterwards the laborer claims the fund as exempt, and such claim is adjudicated against him in the justice's court, he cannot maintain a rule against the constable in the superior court for the money, founded on his exemption right. The matter is res adjudicata by the result of the claim in the justice's court.

(Syllabus by the Court.)

Error from superior court, Fulton county; MARSHALL J. CLARKE, Judge.

L. F. La Motte obtained a rule nisi against J. W. Harper, a constable, and from an order discharging the same he brings error. Affirmed.

The following is the official report:

La Motte obtained a rule nisi against Harper, constable, and one Litchenstadt was made a party defendant. Harper answered, but Litchenstadt did not. It was agreed by counsel that all the allegations in the petition at variance with the answer should be withdrawn, and that the case should be decided by the presiding judge. He ordered that the rule be discharged, and to this La Motte excepted. The petition was to the following effect, in substance: Petitioner is an employe and laborer for the R. L. Polk & Co. Publishing House, and as such labored for his living and the living of his family, working for wages which were and have been payable monthly at the end of each month, and his earnings in this way are necessary to the support of himself and family. Polk & Co. are represented in Georgia by one Saunders as manager, and petitioner is employed under Saunders. Litchenstadt sued out summons of garnishment against Polk & Co., and Saunders, as manager, on a suit against petitioner, and a judgment was rendered in a magistrate's court against the garnishees, the summons not having been answered by them. Petitioner has been informed by Saunders that no summons of garnishment was ever served upon him for Polk & Co., nor as their manager, and that Saunders did not know of any such proceedings until the constable came with the fi. fa. issued upon the garnishment judgment. Upon such a demand for the amount of the judgment and fi. fa. against the garnishee, Saunders paid them off to the constable, Harper, taking his receipt therefor; the amount paid being $36.20. The money which was thus paid out was the wages of petitioner, and the same amount has been charged to him and deducted out of his wages due him from Polk & Co. through Saunders, and he has been compelled to do without this sum as portion of his wages, due each week, as before related. Neither Polk & Co., nor Saunders, as manager or personally, owed petitioner any other debt or liability than for his wages, and an answer to the garnishment could not have made any other debt, nor developed any other fact. These wages were not then, and are not now, subject to process of garnishment, and petitioner has a right to them, whether in the name of his employer or any other person, and Harper has no right to receive or withhold the money. In addition to the $32.30 paid the constable by check of Saunders, $3.90 was afterwards paid out of money which petitioner had collected for Saunders. When the check was given the constable, petitioner notified him that it was his wages, and then made demand on Harper for the money, and Harper then and has ever since refused to pay it over, etc. This petition was supported by evidence as to the payment of the money, and its being on account of wages due La Motte, which was charged to La Motte in settlement with him by Saunders. The answer of Harper was to the following effect: The summons of garnishment was by respondent in person duly served upon Saunders personally. The money paid respondent was paid for Polk & Co. as settlement in full of the fi. fa. against them, and, in accordance with the payment, the judgment against them was marked "Satisfied," and claimant cannot go behind the judgment. La Motte, immediately after the payment was, filed in the magistrate's office a claim for the money in dispute, upon which claim an issue was made which was heard by the magistrate, and decided in favor of the plaintiff in fi. fa. From this judgment claimant appealed to a jury in the magistrate's court, and a verdict was rendered by the jury finding the fund subject to the judgment, which verdict and judgment still stand.

R. L. Rodgers, for plaintiff in error.
Blalock & Birney, for defendant in error.

PER CURIAM. Judgment affirmed.

CITY OF ATLANTA v. MARTIN *et ux.*

(Supreme Court of Georgia.　Nov. 2, 1891.)

MUNICIPAL CORPORATIONS—DEFECTIVE SIDEWALKS—DAMAGES FOR PERSONAL INJURIES.

The evidence warranted the verdict, and the damages are not so excessive as to require the supreme court to interfere.

(Syllabus by the Court.)

Error from superior court, Fulton county; MARSHALL J. CLARKE, Judge.

Action by J. B. Martin and wife against the city of Atlanta. Judgment for plaintiffs. Defendant brings error. Affirmed.

The following is the official report:

Mrs. Martin sued the city of Atlanta for damages for personal injuries sustained by her, alleged to have been caused by the negligence of the city in failing to keep in repair a sidewalk on Luckie street. Her husband also sued the city for loss of services, expenses for medicine, medical attention, etc., growing out of the injuries. By consent of parties the cases were consolidated. A verdict was rendered in favor of the plaintiffs for $1,000. Defendant moved for a new trial, which motion was overruled, and to this it excepted. The grounds of the motion were that the verdict was contrary to law, evidence, etc., contrary to the charge of the court on the subject of plaintiffs' right of recovery being defeated if Mrs. Martin could have avoided the injury by the exercise of ordinary diligence on her part; and because if, under the facts of the case, there ought to have been any recovery, the verdict was excessive, because, according to the testimony of plaintiffs as to their knowledge of the defective condition of the sidewalk, and according to their testimony as to their neglect and delay in calling a physician to treat the injuries, and the medical testimony as to the effects of this delay in securing proper medical treatment promptly, the damages should have been apportioned according to law and the charge of the court on that subject, and when so apportioned the amount of the verdict complained of could not, in justice and good conscience, have been awarded to plaintiffs, under the facts of the case. The testimony was to the effect: On the night of March 15, 1888, Mrs. Martin went with her husband to the corner of Luckie and Hunnicutt streets, where there was a church. Her husband went into the church, and she started to the parsonage behind it. On her way there the sidewalk

gave way, or crumbled off, and she fell into a ditch between the sidewalk and the street. She managed to get to the parsonage, where her foot was bathed, and where she staid until about 11 o'clock at night, when she was carried home. Her foot was sore and swollen, and she could not walk nor put on her shoe. She then had several hard chills, and her foot was poulticed by her sister with clay and vinegar. She still suffers with the injury. It was seven months before she could walk without a crutch. Her foot is still swollen. During a part of the seven months when she was not suffering so much she could sew when work was handed her. Before she was injured she, with the assistance of a little girl, did all her domestic work, which now costs from ten to fifteen dollars per month, and was a dress-maker. After the first seven months she tried to move about the house and do some work, and supposes she could do one-half as much as before she was hurt for a year and a half after the injury. Before she was hurt she could and did work all day and part of the night, and now her ankle begins to pain her about 11 o'clock, and she has to stop. She has suffered greatly. She is 40 years old. Before she was hurt she made a dollar a day, "and other days more or less," sewing and dress-making. She can do half as much dress-making now as before. It was four weeks after she was hurt before she had a physician. When she was hurt she did not know her leg was broken, but thought it was a bad sprain, and so her husband thought. During the four weeks before getting a doctor it kept getting worse and worse. It did look as if she would have had it examined earlier, but she had done a good deal of nursing, and thought herself and sister could get along with it without a doctor. She had never nursed any one with a broken limb. She had a book in which she could read about sprains, and would do what the book said. A small bone of her leg was broken just above the ankle. There was more pain than usual in such fractures, because it was so near the joint, and of such long standing before given the attention of a physician. Usually the bone would have united in four weeks with one of her age, but it took a longer time to unite because not promptly treated by a physician. The bone is now united, and there is no evidence of an unsound bone, though the limb is not perfectly sound, and she has not full use of it, which condition may be permanent. If the limb had been properly set immediately after the injury, it would have reunited in from four to six weeks, and there would have been much less pain and loss of time. The physician's bills were about $110, and need not have been so large if a physician had been sooner secured. A physician of ordinary capacity, if there had been prompt treatment, could have detected the condition of the limb so that in the course of two or three months she ought to have been as well as ever. The sidewalk was in a bad condition at the time of the injury. It was a dirt sidewalk, about two feet in width, and sloping towards the ditch. Some complaint had been made to the city authorities before this injury occurred, and in November before some work had been done, but the wet weather and freezes in the winter and early spring made the sidewalk crumble and wash. Mrs. Martin testified, among other things: She had been at the place before, but did not know much about its condition. Knew it was not a paved street, and not a very good street, but did not know it was so dangerous or she would not have gone there. She had been a member of the church for a number of years, and a regular attendant there, but when walking to the church it was the custom of herself and husband to come up the other side of Luckie street. She had not been a frequent visitor of the parsonage since the August before she was hurt. She was careful in walking, and is always careful. She did not know that it was so narrow, nor that it was dangerous. Knew there was a gully there, but did not know the ground was crumbling. By coming there to church she knew that the gully was by the side of the sidewalk, but did not know the sidewalk was dangerously narrow. Never noticed or thought of it. The night was fair. There was a lamp on the street corner, but she did not remember whether it was lighted. She could see the parsonage very well all along. The sidewalk has since been paved with brick, and there has been a general improvement of the neighboring streets. Her husband testified, among other things: In walking along this sidewalk one had to be very careful, even in the day-time, especially in wet weather. One could walk on this sidewalk if on the alert, all the time looking out and watching. The place where his wife fell was in plain view of the corner by the church in day-light, but not so at night. He let his wife go by herself along there that night. He offered to go with her, thinking she was scared in the dark, but had no idea about her falling, and she told him she was not afraid to go to the parsonage. There was a tolerably good sidewalk on the other side of the street, and witness knew that it was better than the sidewalk where his wife was hurt, and reckons his wife knew it. She can see pretty well. Coming along on one side one could see the other side. He knew all the time that the sidewalk was a desperate place; knew it when he let his wife walk along there that night; and below where she got hurt knew it was worse than where she got hurt, etc.

J. B. Goodwin and *J. A. Anderson*, for plaintiffs in error. *Cox & Reed*, for defendant in error.

PER CURIAM. Judgment affirmed.

HADDEN v. LARNED.

(Supreme Court of Georgia. July 20, 1891.)

EXECUTION—CLAIMS OF THIRD PARTIES—HUSBAND AND WIFE—DEED OF GIFT—RATIFICATION — ESTOPPEL—EVIDENCE.

1. Where all the pertinent facts on behalf of the claimant are admissible in evidence in a claim case, and actually admitted, the refusal of the court to allow an amendment to the claim affidavit, setting out these facts in detail, is of no consequence.

2. For the purpose of admitting to record a deed executed in another state, the attestation of a commissioner of deeds for Georgia, in that state, is sufficient, without a certificate verifying his identity and official character; and that printed words describing him were erased, and the same words interlined in their proper place, without explanation of the erasure, will not vitiate the attestation.

3. That the official seal of the commissioner attached to or impressed upon the original deed was not copied or referred to in the record will not affect the sufficiency or validity of the recording.

4. A deed of gift from wife to husband, duly recorded, is admissible in evidence in favor of a third person who has loaned money on the faith of it, without affirmative proof that the deed was freely and voluntarily executed, and not obtained by undue influence, persuasion, or fraud.

5. Though a *fi. fa.* appear on its face to carry interest upon interest accrued up to the time of judgment, yet this may be the result of contract, and will not render the *fi. fa.* inadmissible in evidence.

6. Instruments acknowledging or ratifying a deed previously made are not required to be of the same formality as the deed itself, or to have more than one witness.

7. Though the charge of the court was in part not strictly accurate, yet, in view of the substantial merits of the case, the inaccuracy did no harm, and is not cause for a new trial.

8. Where money is loaned on security of land, conveyed by deed of gift from wife to husband, which deed she has ratified before delivery of the money, that the deed or the ratification was obtained by him under undue influence or other improper means will not vitiate the security, unless the lender had notice of the same; and where there is no proof of notice to the lender's agent, it is not error to refuse to charge that notice to the agent as such would be notice to the principal.

9. Ratification of a deed of gift may operate as an estoppel, and not merely as an admission, after it has been acted upon as affording security for money advanced upon the faith of it.

10. As against one who has loaned money upon the faith of a wife's deed of gift to her husband, and her formal ratification of the same, she knowing when she ratified that the loan had been negotiated for, and that her ratification was necessary, the gift is not subject to be set aside for undue influence of the husband in procuring it, of which the lender had no notice or information.

(Syllabus by the Court.)

Error from superior court, Screven county; JAMES K. HINES, Judge.

Charles Larned levied on property under a judgment against one Hadden. Clarissa Hadden, the wife of defendant, intervened as claimant. Judgment for plaintiff, and claimant brings error. Affirmed.

W. Hobby and *Dell & Wade*, for plaintiff in error. *Barrow & Thomas*, for defendant in error.

BLECKLEY, C. J. 1. In the trial of a case in which property has been levied upon as that of the defendant in execution, and a third person has intervened as claimant, the claim affidavit, expressed in the usual form, is generally the only pleading necessary to admit whatever evidence the claimant may have to offer to uphold his or her own title, or to disparage that of the defendant as a competing title. Here this privilege was allowed in its full extent; and consequently, whether the affidavit was amendable or not in the manner proposed, the refusal to allow the amendment worked no prejudice. The court treated all the pertinent facts as admissible under the affidavit as it stood, and admitted them with as little stint as if they had been set out in detail upon the face of the affidavit.

2. One of the deeds introduced in evidence was executed in the state of Massachusetts before two subscribing witnesses, one of whom attested the execution as a commissioner of deeds for Georgia in Massachusetts, affixing to his attestation his seal of office. It is contended that to prepare the deed for record, and to render it admissible in evidence as a recorded deed, without further proof of its execution, it was necessary that the attesting commissioner should have certified to his own identity and official character. His attesting signature was followed by words describing him as a commissioner of deeds 'or Georgia in Massachusetts, and, to avouch his identity and the genuineness of the transaction, his official seal was added. The statute applicable to the question reads as follows: "To authorize the record of a deed to realty or personalty it must be attested, if executed out of this state, by a commissioner of deeds for the state of Georgia, or a consul or vice-consul of the United States, (the certificate of these officers, under their seals, being evidence of the fact,) or by a judge of a court of record in the state where executed, with a certificate of the clerk, under the seal of such court, of the genuineness of the signature of such judge." Code, § 2706. The words in parentheses would seem to contemplate a certificate in every instance as evidence of some fact. But what fact? Not the fact merely that the person purporting to be the attesting officer is such officer, but the whole complex fact of execution and attestation of the deed, including the identity and official character of the attesting witness. To make the certificate, together with the seal, evidence of the whole of this complex fact, it is not necessary that the commissioner shall certify in express terms that he is a commissioner in addition to describing himself as such. Whether he is truly a commissioner or not can, when it is disputed, be made to appear by resort to the minutes of the executive department; for such commissioners can be appointed only by the governor. Code, § 59. The certificate in the instance now before us was the usual attesting clause of a deed, its words being, "Signed, sealed and delivered, in presence of." We think this was sufficient. It was certainly not a full and formal certificate, but it was the "attesting" certificate usually subscribed by all public officers in witnessing deeds executed in this state. We think the Code does not contemplate as indispensable a more formal certificate of attestation by a commissioner of deeds acting for Georgia in another state than is requisite from a home magistrate acting here. The difference is that the attestation of the former must be verified by his seal, a verification not needed to authenticate an attestation by the latter.

Another point made upon the attesting act of the commissioner was that the description of his office was interlined between his own signature and that of the other witness, and printed words the same as the written words so interlined were erased or stricken out, the place of the printed words being immediately after the name of the other witness. It seems to us these alterations explained themselves, if they were free from special marks of suspicion, and no such marks are suggested. So far from violating the attestation, the official seal of the commissioner shows that they were necessary in order to render the attesting act complete, and put the document in proper condition for use. Had the printed words been left to stand, the office of commissioner would have been erroneously attributed to the second witness, and by interlining them at the proper place, in writing, the office was correctly attributed to the first witness.

3. It seems that in recording the deed the clerk omitted to copy or otherwise indicate the seal of the commissioner which was affixed to the certificate of attestation. This was an imperfection in the recording, but not such as to vitiate it. The deed itself was recorded, and so was the attestation. It was only an adjunct of the attestation that was omitted. No doubt some note or indication of the seal, such as "L. S.," should have appeared in order to make the record complete and perfect, but to pronounce the recording fatally defective for so slight a blemish would be overtechnical. A ruling so strict would be out of harmony with the general spirit of our law touching the requisite accuracy of clerical work. A substantial compliance in the performance of such duties is sufficient. Code, § 4, subd. 6.

4. The deed of gift from Mrs. Hadden to her husband had been used by the latter to obtain a loan of money from Larned, who parted with his money on the faith of it. It was duly recorded, and was admissible in evidence in behalf of Larned to show title in Hadden, without affirmative proof that it was freely and voluntarily executed by Mrs. Hadden, and not obtained from her by undue influence, persuasion, or fraud. True it is that the relation of husband and wife is one of the confidential relations. Code, § 3177; 1 Story, Eq. Jur. § 218, 2 Lawson, Rights, Rem. & Pr. § 759; Bisp. Eq § 237; 1 Bigelow, Frauds, p. 353; 2 Pom. Eq. Jur. § 963. Many authorities treat the relation alone as generating a presumption of undue influence. See Smyley v. Reese, 53 Ala. 89; McRae v. Battle, 69 N. C. 98; Converse v. Converse, 9 Rich. Eq. 567; Shipman v. Furniss, 69 Ala. 555; Boyd v. De la Montagnie, 73 N. Y. 498; Stiles v. Stiles, 14 Mich. 72. But our Code says: "Fraud may not be presumed, but, being in itself subtle, slight circumstances may be sufficient to carry conviction of its existence." Section 2751. And section 2666 is in these words: "A gift by any person just arriving at majority, or otherwise peculiarly subject to be affected by such influences, to his parent, guardian, trustee, attorney, or other person standing in a similar relationship of confidence, shall be scrutinized with great jealousy, and, upon the slight-

est evidence of persuasion or influence towards this object, shall be declared void, at the instance of the donor or his legal representative, at any time within five years after the making of such gift." The rule of decision fairly deducible from these provisions of the Code is that a gift from wife to husband is, in this state, *prima facie* pure; but that it is to be scrutinized with great jealousy, and will, at her instance, be declared void upon the slightest evidence of persuasion or influence used by him in its procurement. Did the Code intend that such conveyances are to be treated as void, at any time within five years after their execution, without some evidence to impeach them, why should it require any evidence, even the slightest, to set them aside? Why not declare them subject to be set aside or held void, unless supported by evidence showing they were not the offspring of persuasion or influence? It seems to us clear that the Code throws the weight of the legal presumption in favor of the gift, and not against it; and, notwithstanding the strong current of authorities to the contrary, we deem this treatment of the presumption as sound and philosophic on general principles. That, in the present state of the law, a wife is legally competent to make a gift to her husband is not questionable. Cain v. Ligon, 71 Ga. 692; White v. Stocker, 85 Ga. 200, 11 S. E. Rep. 604. When she exercises this power by a solemn deed of conveyance, would it not conflict with all the analogies of the law to treat the deed as *prima facie* void, and require it to be upheld by extrinsic evidence before any fact whatever tending to impeach it has been adduced? Is it not the settled habit of the law to regard as effective all deeds between competent parties and embracing an appropriate subject-matter? The presumption which it raises in their favor may, in some instances, be very slight; but for the law to presume a certain class of allowable deeds vicious, and require them to be shown by extrinsic evidence to be free from taint before recognising them as having operation, would be very anomalous. We think no such anomaly is to be found in the law of this state, and there are authorities tending to prove that it ought not to be recognized elsewhere. Scarborough v. Watkins, 9 B. Mon. 540; Golding v. Golding, 82 Ky. 51. See Sharpe v. McPike, 62 Mo. 300; Waddell v. Lanier, 62 Ala. 347; Bancroft v. Otis, (Ala.) 8 South. Rep. 286; Parfitt v. Lawless, L. R. 2 Prob. & Div. 462; Schouler, Husb. & Wife, §§ 218, 248, 249, 283, 290. Thus far the discussion relates to the rule of evidence as between the direct parties to the deed, but the actual case before us is much stronger. Hollis v. Francois, 5 Tex. 195.

5. The *fi. fa.* under which the land in controversy was levied upon was for a certain amount as principal, a certain amount as interest up to a given day prior to the rendition of judgment, "with interest on the principal and interest * * * until paid." The presumption is that the *fi. fa.* followed the judgment; and it was legally possible for the judgment to be correct, although requiring interest to

be computed on the interest which had accrued and become due prior to the time when the judgment was rendered. This could have been stipulated for as matter of express contract, and no doubt such was the stipulation in the contract on which this judgment was based. It has become usual, in borrowing money on long time, to make the interest payable annually or semi-annually, and agree that matured interest in arrears shall bear interest until paid. Such a stipulation is enforceable. Tillman v. Morton, 65 Ga. 386; Merck v. Mortgage Co., 79 Ga. 213, 7 S. E. Rep. 265; Calhoun v. Marshall, 61 Ga. 275.

6. The claimant, Mrs. Hadden, sought to avoid the deed of gift by which she conveyed the premises in controversy, to her husband on several grounds, one of which was that she was *non compos mentis* at the time of its execution. Besides contesting the truth of this ground as matter of fact, the plaintiff met it with subsequent instruments purporting to acknowledge the deed as hers, and ratifying it, all of them executed by her before the plaintiff parted with the money which he loaned to her husband on the faith of the land as security. These instruments did not have the same formality as the deed itself, nor was each of them attested by more than one witness. They were, however, sufficiently full and formal to show a distinct purpose on the part of Mrs. Hadden to treat the deed as her act and to abide by it. We think this was sufficient. At the worst, the deed was not void, but only voidable. It was susceptible of ratification after her restoration to sanity. Martind. Conv. § 26; Devl. Deeds, §§ 73, 77; Busw. Insan. §§ 395, 396, 404, et seq.; 2 Field, Briefs, § 532; Howe v. Howe, 99 Mass. 88. There is no rule of law which requires an instrument ratifying a prior one to have attesting witnesses, or to be cast into any particular form. Its substance, not form, is the material thing.

7. In charging the jury as set out in the eleventh ground of the motion for a new trial, the court was not quite accurate. Merely signing the ratifying instruments, one or all of them, after her restoration to sanity, would not estop Mrs. Hadden, unless her so signing was a part of the means by which Hadden obtained the plaintiff's money. But the evidence clearly shows that this was the fact, and so the inaccuracy in the charge could not have been prejudicial to the claimant on the substantial merits of her case.

8. If any infirmity of Mrs. Hadden's deed to her husband was not attributable to her want of capacity, but solely to undue influence or other improper means used by him in procuring it, or if the subsequent ratification was procured by such influence or improper means, and if the plaintiff, in making the loan to Hadden, parted with his money on the faith of the land as security, and without notice of the misconduct on the part of her husband which induced Mrs. Hadden to execute the deed or ratify it, the plaintiff would not be affected by such misconduct, and the security for the loan afforded by Hadden's deed to him would not be vitiated. If Mrs.

Hadden was imposed upon or defrauded by her husband, and if a subsequent creditor who contracted with him for this specific security was not aware of any imposition or fraud, it is much more equitable that she should lose her land than that the innocent creditor should lose his security. For this reason, the charge of the court complained of in the twelfth ground of the motion was correct. It was not contended that the plaintiff himself had any notice, but it was sought to affect him with such notice as Mathews, the agent of Hadden, may have had, on the theory that he (Mathews) was not the agent of Hadden alone, but also of the plaintiff. This theory, on the state of facts in the record, is of doubtful correctness. But, granting it to be correct, there was no evidence that Mathews had any notice of any improper conduct by Hadden towards his wife, or that Mathews thought, or had reason to think, she was not acting freely and voluntarily in facilitating the procurement of this loan. If he had advanced his own money on the faith of what he saw and heard, taking the same security which the plaintiff accepted, it is manifest that he would have been protected. Looking at the transaction from this standpoint, it must have appeared to him that Hadden and wife were acting together in harmonious co-operation to invest Hadden with title to the premises as a free gift, and enable him to borrow money on the same as security. There was nothing, so far as we can discover, to suggest to him a different hypothesis. It would be a gross outrage upon justice to make the plaintiff lose his money by reason of some conjectural or imaginary notice to Mathews, who was the agent of the borrower, and had with the lender no relation of agency, except for the one purpose of holding the money intended to be loaned until certain papers were executed, and then delivering it to the borrower. If we are correct in this view, it was not error to decline the request to charge set out in the thirteenth ground of the motion.

9. Nor was the request embraced in the fourteenth ground of the motion a legal one. The ratification of a deed of gift may operate as more than a mere admission; it may operate as an estoppel, after it has been acted upon by advancing money upon the faith of it as a link in the security of the loan.

10. The matter of the twelfth ground of the motion is again complained of in the fifteenth ground, and it is insisted that notice that the deed was voluntary was notice that under section 2666 of the Code it was subject, for five years from the date of its execution, to be set aside at the wife's instance for undue influence, persuasion, or other improper practice by the husband in procuring it, and that the omission so to charge was error. We think otherwise. The ratification was with knowledge by the wife that the loan had been negotiated for, and all the facts indicated that she was aware that the property was to be pledged to secure the loan, and that ratification of her prior conveyance was deemed necessary to complete the transaction. It is of great importance to protect wives against being impoverished by the arts, importunities, and undue influence of their husbands; but it is of equal importance to protect honest creditors against being defrauded by wily husbands, who first induce their devoted wives to aid them in getting money, and then, after the money has been enjoyed by the family, aid their devoted wives to repudiate their acts on the ground that these acts were prompted by wifely affection and confidence, and were therefore not free and voluntary. There is no combination of any two average, every-day people so powerful for good or evil as that of husband and wife; and if one spouse is angelic, it seems not to cripple the combination, provided the other is intensely human. This remark is general, and no special application of it to the character or conduct of any particular couple is intended. The evidence warranted the verdict, and there was no error in denying a new trial. Judgment affirmed.

ELLISON v. GEORGIA RAILROAD & BANKING CO.

GEORGIA RAILROAD & BANKING CO. v. ELLISON.

(*Supreme Court of Georgia.* Oct. 19, 1891.)

RAILROAD COMPANIES—INJURY TO EMPLOYE—NEGLIGENCE—PLEADING—AMENDMENT—APPEAL.

1. Courts of final review are bound by the rule of *stare decisis*, both as a canon of public good and a law of self-preservation. Nevertheless, where a grave and palpable error, widely affecting the administration of justice, must either be solemnly sanctioned or repudiated, the maxim which applies is *fiat justitia ruat coelum.*

2. Amendment is a resource against waste. It proceeds on the principle that it is better to preserve what has been done, and improve it, than to throw it away. There is as much reason for correcting important defects as the less important, and those of substance as those of form.

3. Amendment of substance at an early stage has always been allowable as matter of judicial discretion. The act of 1854 made it matter of right at any stage. The Code does the same, "provided there is enough to amend by," and with a further restriction against adding new parties or a new cause of action. The act made the right at law as broad as in equity, and *vice versa,* and this feature is retained by the Code.

4. As a declaration must contain all the substance requisite to enable the plaintiff to recover, no amendment of its form would be of any value without a complete cause of action in substance. Hence, in order for a declaration to be amendable in form, a substantial cause of action must appear; otherwise there is not enough to amend by.

5. But when the amendment needed is one of substance itself, "enough to amend by" does not mean the same as "enough to be good in substance without amendment." On the contrary, failing to be good in substance is generally the reason why amendment of substance is needed. "Enough to amend by" is to be determined by what is enough relatively to the particular amendment needed and offered. There may be enough to amend by in one respect, though not in another. The Code does not make the standard for form and substance the same. In this regard it has been misconstrued, and the case of *Martin v. Railroad,* 78 Ga. 307, based upon such misconstruction, is hereby overruled.

6. Enough to amend by in matter of substance, in aid of an incomplete cause of action, is the least amount of substance in a declaration which will serve to show that, according to the

original design of the pleader, what is offered to be added rightly belongs to the cause of action which he meant to assert, and that the addition proposed would make the cause of action complete. There must be a plaintiff, a defendant, jurisdiction of the court, and facts enough to indicate and identify some particular cause of action as the one intended to be declared upon, so as to enable the court to determine whether the facts proposed to be introduced by the amendment are part and parcel of that same cause. Any amendment whatever which, if allowed, would leave the cause of action incomplete, should be rejected.

7. Under the Code, a declaration which has all the requisites to make it good and sufficient in substance, save that it omits to allege some fact essential to raise the duty involved in the cause of action which the pleader evidently intended to declare upon, is amendable by supplying the omitted fact at any stage of the case. Thus, where the duty claimed was the duty of forbearing to obstruct a sewer-pipe which conveyed waste-water from the plaintiff's premises and discharge the same on the defendant's land, the declaration was amendable by alleging an easement subjecting his land to the burden of receiving the water so discharged. Also, in an action by a mother suing for the homicide of her son, where the fact omitted from the declaration was that she was dependent upon him for a support, the declaration was amendable by alleging that fact.

8. Where two railway companies, each under its own franchise, use the track of one of them in common, at a terminal point, the one owning the track is responsible for the consequences of its negligence in failing to render harmless to the employes of the other company a low bridge spanning the track, if the duty of taking proper precautions for that purpose was upon it, and it alone. The mother of an employe of the other company, if otherwise in a situation to sue, may recover for the homicide of her son, caused by such negligence. In such case, though it be not alleged that the company not owning the track (that is, the master of the employe) was ignorant of the danger or of the conditions which caused it, it will not be assumed, in deciding upon a demurrer to the declaration, that it was negligent in running the train to which the employe was attached when injured; consequently the question whether any negligence of that company could be imputed to the employe, so as to render him chargeable with contributory negligence, is not now for decision.

(Syllabus by the Court.)

Cross-errors from superior court, Fulton county; MARSHALL J. CLARKE, Judge.

Action by M. E. Ellison against the Georgia Railroad & Banking Company. Judgment for defendant. Both parties bring error. Judgment reversed on plaintiff's assignment of error.

W. M. Bray, E. M. Mitchell, and John T. Glenn, for Ellison. J. B. Cumming, Bryan Cumming, and Hillyer & Bro., for Georgia Railroad & Banking Company.

BLECKLEY, C. J. 1. Some courts live by correcting the errors of others and adhering to their own. On these terms courts of final review hold their existence, or those of them which are strictly and exclusively courts of review, without any original jurisdiction, and with no direct function but to find fault, or see that none can be found. With these exalted tribunals, who live only to judge the judges, the rule of *stare decisis* is not only a canon of the public good, but a law of self-preservation. At the peril of their lives they must discover error abroad, and be discreetly blind to its commission at home. Were they as ready to correct themselves as others, they could no longer speak as absolute oracles of legal truth; the reason for their existence would disappear, and their destruction would speedily supervene. Nevertheless, without serious detriment to the public or peril to themselves, they can and do admit now and then, with cautious reserve, that they have made a mistake. Their rigid dogma of infallibility allows of this much relaxation in favor of truth unwittingly forsaken. Indeed, reversion to truth, in some rare instances, is highly necessary to their permanent well-being. Though it is a temporary degradation from the type of judicial perfection, it has to be endured, to keep the type itself respectable. Minor errors, even if quite obvious, or important errors, if their existence be fairly doubtful, may be adhered to, and repeated indefinitely; but the only treatment for a great and glaring error affecting the current administration of justice in all courts of original jurisdiction is to correct it. When an error of this magnitude, and which moves in so wide an orbit, competes with truth in the struggle for existence, the maxim for a supreme court,—supreme in the majesty of duty as well as in the majesty of power.—is not *stare decisis*, but *fiat justitia ruat cœlum.*

2. Scarcely any right of procedure is more important to suitors or more frequently called into exercise in actual practice than that of amending their pleadings. Amendment is a resource against waste. In pleading, as in every art, the philosophy of amendment, or of bettering the results of work imperfectly executed, is comprehended in the frank recognition of two things, both of which are made manifest by actual experience. The first is that, in the practice of any art, it is generally better to preserve what has been done, improving it, and taking some benefit from it, than to throw it away, and begin over. The second is that, in the practice of any art, save by the most finished and accomplished experts, many errors and mistakes will be committed; some by reason of ignorance or other incompetency; some by reason of haste or carelessness; and some by reason of inherent difficulty and uncertainty as to what is exactly the right thing to do, the right manner of doing it, or the right materials to be used. Carried out consistently to its rational limits, the principle of amendment applies to both substance and form, and with quite as much force to the important as to the less important. No sensible builder discards what he has done, and goes back to the first block and the first blow, unless he has utterly failed in his foundation. If he has used too much material, or not enough, or some of an improper kind, or has put together his materials, or some of them, informally or unskillfully, he corrects his mistake with the least sacrifice possible, and retains everything which he can render useful in completing the structure which he intended and endeavored to build. The law has all the wisdom and prudence of all the trades. When practicable, it will conserve its own work, the

work of its magistrates and ministers, and that of suitors in its courts, and their counsel.

3. There never was a time when pleadings were not amendable. Both form and substance were amendable at common law; certainly so by leave of the court in the exercise of its discretion in the early stages of the suit. To the English statutes of force in Georgia relative to disregarding or amending defects of form, passed for the purpose of preventing the miscarriage of justice in consequence of such defects, and found in Schley, Dig. 196, 223, 231, 244, 326, were added by state legislation the acts of 1799 and 1818, (Cobb, Dig. 486, 488.) But as in England, so with us, the amendment of substance was left chiefly to the discretion of the court down to the passage of the act of 1854, save that by a standing rule of the superior courts, after an appeal was entered, either party might amend at will. 2 Kelly, 466, rule 5. The act of 1854 took away from the courts all discretion by expressly declaring both species of amendment to be matter of right. Acts 1853–54, p. 48. This act was reproduced, almost *verbatim,* by the Code, but with a proviso requiring "enough to amend by," and with an added limitation forbidding the introduction of new parties, or a new cause of action. Code, §§ 3479, 3480, 3482. The three sections here cited read thus: "All parties, whether plaintiffs or defendants, in the superior or other courts, (except the supreme court,) whether at law or in equity, may, at any stage of the cause, as matter of right, amend their pleadings in all respects, whether in matter of form or of substance, provided there is enough in the pleadings to amend by." "No amendment adding a new and distinct cause of action, or new and distinct parties, shall be allowed, unless expressly provided for by law." "In case the party applying for leave to amend the pleadings or other proceedings shall have been guilty of negligence in respect to the matter of amendment, the court may compel him to pay his adversary the cost of the proceedings for which he moves, and may force reasonable and equitable terms upon him at discretion, not touching the real merits of the cause in controversy." It will be observed that the rule for amending at law is as broad as for amending in equity. Certainly courts of equity have always been liberal in allowing substantial amendment where facts additional to those alleged in the bill were needed to make a complete case for relief. Construing these provisions of the Code, it has been directly decided in one case, on a state of facts presenting the point squarely for decision, and suggested or assumed in some other cases, that a plaintiff has no right to amend his declaration in matter of substance, unless the declaration, as it stands, sets forth in substance a full and complete cause of action. Shall we abide by this construction or overrule it?

4. Relatively to the law of pleading, a cause of action is some particular legal duty of the defendant to the plaintiff, together with some definite breach of that duty which occasions loss or damage. Though it is the breach, and not the duty

itself, which justifies the action, or causes it to be brought, yet every breach involves a duty, and, in order to make the breach appear, it is indispensable that the duty also should appear. In so far as the duty in question can be known to the court by taking notice of any matter of public law, its creation or origin need not be pleaded; but in so far as it derives its origin from any special state of facts, whether relating to persons, events, time, place, or anything whatsoever, the essential facts must be pleaded. Some negative duties, such as not to beat, wound, libel, etc., are practically universal, and no special facts are needed to occasion them to exist or to verify their existence. Under ordinary circumstances, the law treats them as permanent relations between any and every two persons. Such duties, until denied, are taken for granted. Consequently, in a suit for the breach of a duty of this class, the breach may be described, and damage therefrom alleged, without more. But much the larger number of duties arise under the law out of particular conditions or events, such as this or that contract, the ownership of this or that property, etc.; and very many of them cannot arise save between some person in general, on the one side, and a person of this or that class, on the other. Frequently both parties must be of the same class, and not infrequently each must be of some class to which the other does not belong. In many cases of tort a proper classification of the parties respectively is all the pleading of specific facts which is requisite in order that the existence of the duty may appear, the law raising the duty being noticed judicially as soon as the parties are classified in the declaration; but in every case of contract the fact of contract, or the facts from which it will be implied, must be alleged. It is hardly needful to say that every duty is attended with a correlative right. A cause of action may be defined from the stand-point of rights, with exactly the same result as when it is defined from the stand-point of duties. Thus the precise equivalent of the definition given above would be this: Relatively to the law of pleading, a cause of action is some particular legal right of the plaintiff against the defendant, together with some definite violation thereof, which occasions loss or damage. It may be well to observe that the word "duty" is used throughout this opinion in its broad sense, as including every species of legal obligation between party and party,—the sense referred to in Patterson on Railway Law, 386, citing Treatise on the Law of Negligence, by Robert Campbell, p. 12.

The outcome, under the law, of any state of facts whatever which will embrace a cause of action, may be expressed as follows,—the first proposition affirming the duty, the second the breach, and the conclusion the right to recover: It was the defendant's legal duty to the plaintiff to do so and so, (or not to do so and so, as the case may be.) He did not do so and so, (or he did do so and so, as the case may be,) and thereby caused the plaintiff such and such loss or damage. Therefore the plaintiff is entitled to recover for the reparation of his loss, or for his proper compensation in damages. The office of the declaration is to state or describe the material out of which, viewed in the light of the law applicable to the case, a logical syllabus like this can be constructed in advance of the trial for justification by evidence when the trial takes place. Unless the plaintiff can and will allege beforehand that such material exists, no trial ought to be had, for it would be useless. The direct end, both of pleading and verification, so far as the plaintiff is concerned, is to obtain a valid and final judgment. Substance and form are alike worthless, unless, on the showing of the plaintiff himself, this result can be reached. He can verify no fact of substance unless his pleading covers it, and it is useless for him to verify anything unless he can verify all the facts which are necessary to enable him to recover. For this reason his declaration must show on its face a cause of action. The business of the declaration is to tell what the plaintiff proposes to verify. The manner of telling it, and the words and sentences employed in the story, together with all mere technical requisites, are form; the material facts told are substance. If the declaration is deficient by reason of the omission of any material fact whatever which is absolutely necessary to give it full and complete substance, it is not amendable *in form.* Why? The answer is conclusive,—the amendment would do no good; the declaration would still be fatally defective, and to obtain a valid judgment upon it would be no less impossible than before. To challenge form by a demurrer always directs attention to substance likewise, for every special demurrer brings substance under review, and enables the party to take advantage of any substantial defect, though the same be not specified. Hence it may be said that every special demurrer is also a general demurrer. Gould, Pl. p. 485, c. 9, §§ 19, 20; Steph. Pl. 141; 1 Chit. Pl. 664. Where defects of substance are urged and insisted upon, a special demurrer is not answered by bettering form. The true and correct test, therefore, of the right to amend in matter of form, is completeness of a cause of action in all the essential elements of substance. The most perfect form, without sufficient substance, would be mere waste. To add waste to waste—more waste-work to that already done—would be to violate the fundamental principle on which the privilege of amendment is founded.

5. But is the same quantitative test applicable to the amendment of substance? This court has decided that it is. Can we, on solemn review, after hearing and rehearing able and exhaustive argument, and after deliberate and protracted study of the question, adhere to that decision? We think not. What is "enough to amend by" in matter of substance will be shown under the next head of this opinion. For the present, the inquiry is not what the phrase "enough to amend by" truly means in its relation to substance, but whether this court has not gravely erred by adopting a construction which

requires as much to amend by in matter of substance as in matter of form. Is it a true interpretation of the phrase "enough to amend by," to say that it always includes in its signification "enough to be good in substance without amendment?" Are these two expressions so nearly identical in meaning? It is impossible to study them with the slightest attention without seeing that they are not. The latter expression marks out the lowest measure of substance which will suffice to render a declaration amendable in matter of form. Unless there is sufficient substance, no improvement of form would be of the least service to the declaration. It might as well have no substance as not enough. Deformity is of no consequence if the misshapen substance would be worthless after its deformity was corrected. The law never does a vain and idle thing, nor provides for having it done. The amendment of mere form is never in order unless the substance is complete. Form can wait until substance is made sufficient; or both may become good together, at the same time, and by the same amendment or series of amendments. For the statute to say that a declaration is amendable in all respects, provided there is enough in it to amend by, carries no implication or suggestion that enough to amend by in one respect is enough to amend by in every other respect. The true sense of proviso requires us to take the words "in all respects" distributively, and understand them as making proper allowance for the nature of the defect and the kind of amendment requisite for its cure, so that each respect may have its own proper measure of "enough." To be amendable at all, a declaration must contain some substance; how much, we shall see hereafter. Unless it comes up to some rational standard, it is not amendable in any respect, whether in form or substance. But to raise the standard as high for substantial as for formal amendments would be to treat all declarations which are deficient in substance as not amendable for the sole reason that they stand in need of amendment. Is it supposable that any system of amendment deliberately devised would declare in one breath that in all respects declarations are amendable in matter of substance if they contain enough to amend by, and in the next that, unless they contain enough to be good in substance without amendment, there is not enough to amend by? Is no declaration which is not good in substance amendable in matter of substance? Must it first appear that no amendment is necessary, before any can be received? If the action cannot be maintained without it, must the amendment be rejected for that reason? Who would imagine that the test of a sufficient declaration and of an amendable declaration would ever come to be the same, under the liberal law of amendment embraced in the Code? The rule of the Code is that at any stage of the case every declaration is amendable in substance in all respects, provided there is already in it enough to amend by. The construction we are combating holds this to mean that, if a declaration lacks any part of a cause of action,—that is, anything which is necessary to make up enough substance to resist a general demurrer,—it lacks having enough to amend by, and is not amendable. It holds, in effect, that a general demurrer is not to be "spoiled" by putting more substance into a declaration, but only by taking some out when it has an excess. You may empty by one-half if the declaration is too full; but if it is half empty you can never fill it. Nay, if it lacks anything whatever of being full, what it wants can never be supplied, though the means of supply may exist in abundant measure. Under this singular construction, a declaration too strong in substance—as, for instance, if it sets forth two causes of action which cannot be joined because one originated in tort, the other in contract—may be weakened down; but, if it is too weak already, it cannot be strengthened. A declaration may take an emetic, but not more food. Curative treatment is restricted to depletion; all tonics are prohibited. We are reminded of that tender regard for a demurrer insinuated from the bench nearly 200 years ago, in Fox v. Wilbraham, 1 Ld. Raym. 668, Lord HOLT saying: "It would be hard to spoil the defendant's demurrer." But is not a general demurrer too diabolical to have any claim upon modern emotion? Stated in the most partial terms, its merits would seem to stand thus: "Demurrer is the only legal devil always present and always ready. Every logical universe requires one such character. Some destructive work has to be done; and how can it be done if there is only resistance, no co-operation; not even sympathy?" But the spirit of modern procedure is altogether constructive and conservative, and, though it gives the devil his due, it takes care to restrict his dues as much as possible. Any declaration is amendable in all respects, provided it contains enough to amend by in all respects. If it contains enough to amend by in any one respect, it is amendable in that respect, though it may lack enough to amend by in some other. If it does not contain enough to amend by in respect to form, it may be amendable in respect to substance, and will be whenever it contains enough to amend by in respect to substance. In two general respects touching substance may a declaration be defective and stand in need of amendment,—it may be defective in respect to the quantity of substance or in respect to the substantial particulars entering into that quantity. A defect of quantity may be in respect of deficiency or in respect of excess,—there may be too little or too much. In either of these respects a declaration is amendable, in the one equally with the other. In respect to particulars, also, the declaration is amendable whenever it is already sufficient in quantity, or when it becomes sufficient by adding the particulars brought in by the amendment. But whether the question be on form or substance, and whether on quantity or particulars, the amendment is to be allowed if the declaration has in it enough to amend by in respect to the nature and contents of the amendment offered, but not otherwise. That the declaration is amendable in one respect is of itself no warrant for amending it in another. The particular respect to which the proposed amendment appertains is the one to be regarded, and others are material only as they throw light on that in its relation to the question of enough to amend by. A declaration which is amendable in form is always amendable in substance; and one not full enough to be amendable in form may be amendable in substance, and, when made full enough, will be amendable in form also. Substance and form may both be perfected by one and the same amendment or series of amendments. That the Code does not confound all distinction between substance and form, nor make one and the same test of the amendable applicable to both, is so obvious that it could never have escaped our attention or that of our predecessors, were it not that truth on the surface is often more difficult to discern than if it lay deeper. Sometimes it is more out of sight at the top of the well than at the bottom. The very brightness of the light which shines upon it serves to conceal it. The case of Martin v. Railroad, 78 Ga. 307, is overruled; and so in any and every other case, in so far as the judgment of affirmance or reversal rests upon the construction herein reviewed and disapproved. This repudiates for the court, as now constituted, much that has been said *arguendo* by a single justice in writing out opinions, but probably very little, if any, save as to the case here mentioned by name, which has been actually and necessarily adjudicated. A careful examination of each case in the light of its facts will usually reconcile the judgment with the principles of this opinion.

6. Having freed the court from its own misconstruction of the Code in relation to the amendment of substance, we are now ready for a new and true construction; and to find it is one of those difficult easy things which so frequently present themselves in the law. When the right point of view is discovered, the problem is more than half solved. With reference to deficient substance, enough to amend by in substance is something incomplete in substance, something less than enough to be good in and of itself, something that would not be good without amendment. The object of amending it is to make it good. Some "enough" which is not good, and another "enough" to make it good, put together, would accomplish the object. The problem is, from two quantities, one given in the declaration, the other in the law, as an ultimate standard, to ascertain a third which will represent the exact difference between them. The solution will determine what amendment is needed; and there is enough to amend by if that particular amendment is offered, but not enough if any other is offered. In every suit there must be three classes of substance,—parties, subject-matter, and jurisdiction. By express provision of the Code, § 3488, the facts necessary to show jurisdiction may be brought into the declaration by amendment; so that enough

to amend by, in respect to this class of substance, is the mere presence of the other two classes in their minimum quantity. A declaration having parties and a subject-matter is amendable so as to show that the court has jurisdiction over both. Parties cannot be supplied without express permission of law, (Code, § 3480,) and there is no such permission, save in some cases for increasing the number, or in some other cases for the substitution of one plaintiff for another. In every action *in personam* there must be at least one plaintiff and one defendant to start with. Without these there is no case, and nothing to amend by in any respect. Neither is there any permission of law for supplying the declaration with a subject-matter. The declaration must contain enough from the beginning to indicate a subject-matter for adjudication, and to classify it as tort, contract, or something over which the court has jurisdiction. But the subject-matter need not, as first described in the declaration, be a complete cause of action, though it must be some kind of subject-matter of which a cause of action, if fully developed, would or might consist. And it must go further than this,—the declaration must enable the court to see both the terms of comparison to be used in ascertaining the exact difference between what is in it and what would under the law be good. With both these terms the amendment offered must be compared, and, if it would fill the gap, there is, so far as mere quantity is concerned, enough to amend by; otherwise there is not. The declaration must show what the design of the pleader was, and that his design was such that, if filled out and completed, a cause of action might appear. But in looking for his design by the light of the imperfect declaration, no test of full certainty, but only the test of probability, is to be applied. If enough is alleged to render it fairly and reasonably probable that the plaintiff claims to have a cause of action of the kind indicated, and that it was his design, or that of his pleader, to declare upon it, this probability is to be accepted for the purpose of allowing amendment, just as though his design were known with full certainty; for it is only when a party stops pleading and stands upon the result that certainty is the guide and measure of construction. So long as he proposes to amend, he is still endeavoring to plead; and if he reaches the requisite certainty by the amendment and the original pleading together he will be excused for any want of certainty before, higher than that of reasonable probability. When the declaration is indistinct, some light in aid of its own may be derived from the nature and contents of the amendment offered. The contents of the amendment, as compared with what is already in the declaration, may tend to show either that the plaintiff is endeavoring to follow up a cause of action, or supposed cause, which he had in view when the declaration was prepared and filed, ~ that, having since discovered that no :h cause exists or is maintainable, he s concluded to shift his ground, and

bring in surreptitiously a new and distinct cause of action in violation of one of the limitations upon his right to amend. In consequence of this limitation—the one which excludes any new cause of action—a test of quality is added to that of quantity. It is requisite that, in order to have enough in his declaration to amend by in respect to the cause of action, the plaintiff must go still further than to indicate a subject-matter and some cause of action of a particular kind. His declaration must indicate what particular individual cause of action the design of the suit embraces; and to render the amendment offered admissible, it must contain, not merely the quantity and general quality of matter requisite to fill out the declaration, but its matter must be the residue of the identical cause of action of which a part is already described in the declaration. The identity may be disclosed through the duty element alone, or through the breach element alone, or partly through each. Some transaction must be indicated, and some particular duty and breach in respect to that transaction must apparently be asserted by the declaration, and must be shown to exist by the amendment.

If the plaintiff has two causes of action of the same class, though the same facts may, in part, be common to both of them, he is not allowed to declare upon one, and afterwards abandon it, and substitute the other by amendment; and this is so whether he has made his declaration perfect as to the one covered by his original design or left it imperfect. He must abide by his design, and, in order that the court may see that he does abide by it, he must disclose it in the first instance; not, as we have already said, with certainty, but with reasonable probability. Any cause of action whatever would be new and distinct if no trace of it could be found in the declaration. There must be some trace of a particular cause of action in the declaration in order that it may contain enough to amend by; and, as the original cause must be adhered to, and no other substituted in its place, the trace furnished must be sufficiently plain and distinct to identify the particular cause of action to which the declaration points or refers. If it points to no one cause more than to any other, it will be too indefinite, and should be treated as nothing better than a blank. As a cause of action consists of duty and breach, these two questions should be asked and answered in the joint light of the declaration and the proposed amendment: Did the design of the pleader embrace a real duty and breach, or only something which he supposed by mistake of law to be such? If real, and not merely supposed, what particular duty and breach did he intend to declare upon? The correct answer to these questions will govern his right to amend in the given instance. No right to amend in aid of a fanciful design, or of a true design which cannot be definitely ascertained, exists. An example of a fanciful duty and breach would be the supposed legal duty of the defendant not to kill the plaintiff's infant child, and a breach by killing it. This, as between party and party, would be a moral, not a legal, duty, and the breach of it would be no cause of action. Allen v. Railroad Co., 54 Ga. 503. An example of a real duty and breach would be the duty of not depriving the plaintiff of the services of his minor child, able to render service, and the breach of that duty by wounding such child so that he died. This would be cause of action. Chick v. Railroad Co., 57 Ga. 357. In order to understand clearly why, on principle, a cause of action not completely set forth, but merely indicated or suggested, in a declaration, may be brought fully within it by amendment, it should be noticed that a cause of action, being compounded of duty and breach, is not, like plaintiff or defendant, a simple indivisible unit without parts, but that it consists of parts, some of which may by description be in the declaration and others out. The declaration may, therefore, lay hold upon it, as it were, by one or more of its parts, and this hold may serve, with the aid of a proper amendment, for drawing in a description of the entire body. Every proposition to amend by adding to an incomplete cause of action is, in reality, only a proposition to add descriptive matter enough to finish an incomplete description; and it involves a comparison of what is already within the declaration with what is sought to be brought in. Nothing can be admitted from the outside unless, on comparison, it matches with something inside, and goes to make up the identical organism to which they both belong. There is no actual disruption or dismemberment of the cause of action by failing to describe it all at first, but the process which takes place in amending the description may be conceived of as one of restoration and reconstruction, much like that conducted by a zoölogist when, from a few bones, or perhaps a single one, he draws or describes the whole skeleton. There is this difference, however: The zoölogist undertakes only to find an individual which will represent the species to which the specimen belongs, whereas reconstruction by amendment must result in covering with the declaration as amended the identical individual case embraced originally in the design of the pleader, and of which each essential fragment of the restored whole formed a part. If the original design of the pleader, carried out in full, would embrace no cause of action, the declaration is not amendable. That which would be no cause of action when fully stated has no parts of any cause. A legal nonentity is as destitute of parts as of wholeness. When a cause of action appears in the declaration, that, and that only, is the one which the pleader is supposed to have designed. When none appears, the design is to be sought in the light of what is alleged in the declaration compared with what is alleged in the proposed amendment. If the two sets of allegations harmonize so as to be parts of one and the same sufficient design, and so as to fill out that design, and render it as complete on paper as the law requires it to be, the amendment is germane, and must be allowed. In looking for the design of the pleader, he is to be judged by his work, not by his testimony. The search is for something outside of the pleading, at least not wholly inside of it; but in conducting the search the court must look through the pleading as far as completed, and through that which is offered by way of amendment for making it complete. Through these alone the search must be carried on, in the light of the law, and with the aid of common sense, and sound inference acccording to probability. The pleader is a builder who has a right to go on and finish from any beginning whatever, provided he can show his original plan by what he has done and what he proposes to do, and provided he will confine himself to that plan, and provided the plan is one which, when fully executed, will result in a real edifice, and not a mere castle in the air. Anything is a castle in the air which lacks the support of a complete cause of action in the plan of it as that plan would appear if all of it were finally registered in the declaration. The plan is to be considered as fully formed before any of it was registered; and amending the declaration is simply completing the registry, no substantial change of plan being allowable. The builder must construct at least a slight foundation, using proper materials, and go far enough in the development of his plan to show not merely the kind of structure, but the particular edifice, he designed to erect. Then he may go on and complete it. But he will not be allowed to reject either his foundation or his plan, and substitute another. He may repair the foundation, or vary the plan in some of its particulars, but must preserve the identity of both. The outcome must be the identical edifice designed in the beginning, and not substantially a different one. To amend substance in respect to the cause of action there must be within the declaration a substantial part of some particular cause of action. It will not suffice to have a part which identifies only a given class of cases. There must be complete differentiation; not with full certainty, but with fair probability. There must be means of identifying the particular individual cause, so as to adhere to one and the same cause, and guard against the substitution of any other in its place. What proportion of the whole substance will suffice for individualising the particular cause of action embraced in the pleader's design is not a fixed quantity. It is variable, and in one instance will be more, in another less. A few characteristic fragments might serve the purpose, or it might require a considerable number. If we could be sure that only a single fragment is inside, and if, by it, the rest could all be identified, they might be brought in. However numerous the fragments, if they can each be recognised as belonging to one and the same whole, they may be recombined. It is needful to observe further that, in order to render appropriate any particular amendment or series of amendments offered to complete substance, it must not stop with partial completion, but must contain all that is necessary to make the cause of action full and entire in the amended statement, when read in connection with the original declaration. Nothing is enough to amend by when the cause of action is incomplete, if the amendment offered would not complete it. Merely improving substance without making it good, or increasing it without adding enough, has no value. When nothing less than four can win, one is equal to three, for each of them counts for naught. Waste will not be added to waste in amending substance, any more than by amending form to no purpose. An amendment which does not amend is not better, but somewhat worse, than none.

From what has been said, it is apparent that nothing less is enough to amend by, in matter of substance in respect to the cause of action, than a plaintiff, a defendant, jurisdiction of the court, and facts enough to indicate and identify some particular cause of action as the one intended to be declared upon, so as to enable the court to determine whether the facts proposed to be introduced by the amendment are part and parcel of that same cause; and that, when all these elements are in the declaration, there is enough to amend by. The least amount of substance in a declaration which will serve to show that what is offered to be added rightly belongs there is enough to amend by if the addition proposed would make the cause of action complete. On the other hand, there is not enough to amend by if what is already in will not suffice to identify the now-coming matter as rightly belonging there, or if receiving the latter would not make the cause of action complete, but would leave it still incomplete. The test here proposed would apply in principle to all pleadings with reference to the amendment of substance. See that the new-comer would be at home in the pleading, and that, with it admitted, there would be no material absentee, and the question is settled. It has been suggested that an incomplete cause of action has no life in it, and, consequently, that a complete cause is necessary in order to render the declaration amendable, a dead thing not being susceptible of any amendment whatever; but this begs the question. It assumes by the use of a simile that life, or something analogous to it, is necessary to a legal document which is used by the law as mere means to span the chasm between process and judgment; and it assumes that life is in a cause of action when the whole of it is in the document, but not when less than the whole is in. The first assumption may be granted, but half of the second is unwarrantable. A cause of action, if alive at all, is alive all over. Each fragment is living matter, and has neither more nor less vitality in consequence of being put in or left out of the declaration. The pleader does not slaughter his cause of action by the way he deals with it in pleading. In point of fact, pleading merely describes it, and failing to mention some of its parts is only omitting to tell the whole truth about it. It might as well be said that a man or an animal is killed by a deficient description. A cause of action is indestructible by any means as incomplete description. On the contrary, it remains so absolutely alive

that, without the least change in itself, a proper supplement to the description will set the whole business right. Used merely for illustration, figures are often helpful, and the life-simile may be helpfully employed in the present discussion. Amendment being a resource against waste, and waste in pleading being, according to common sense and sound economic principles, no more justifiable than waste in anything else, no pleading, especially no declaration, (that on which the existence of the whole case depends,) should be cast out as worthless if it can be saved by a fair and reasonable use of the amending power. That power neither creates nor raises from the dead. Its function is neither generation nor resurrection, but is rather one of development, nutrition, and medication. If the legal case which the pleader intended to make has been so far developed and differentiated in design that the court can recognize it as probably fit to become a member of the case family, though it may still be in the womb, and deficient in vigor, or not fully developed in some of the essential parts or organs which would enable it to live as an independent being, indeed, if it be little more than a mere germ, the law has quickened it, and it is within the reach of amendment. Life, in the law of amendment, means mere quickening, ante-natal life, that which is sufficient to start with, though it may be much less than is requisite to support existence against the most feeble attack if the amending power be not invoked. Altogether a different and higher measure of life is contemplated in the law as a basis for amending form. In order that form may be amended there must be vitality of substance sufficient to burst from the womb, pass through all the stages of being until final judgment is rendered, and endure perpetually in the judgment itself. The reason for this difference is that amendment of substance is capable of increasing vitality and raising it to any required standard of vigor and durability, whereas by amending form the quantity of life is not varied, the whole of life being lodged in substance, none of it in mere form. Amendment of substance aids a declaration to live and augment its life, and not merely to exert the vital force which it already possesses.

7. We are now ready to apply the doctrines of the foregoing discussion first to the case which we have just overruled, and next to the case at bar. The declaration in the former sought to lay down this scheme of action, or supply the materials for its construction: It was the defendant's legal duty to the plaintiff not to obstruct a certain sewer-pipe, which conveyed waste-water from the plaintiff's premises, and discharged the same on the defendant's land. The defendant did obstruct it, to the plaintiff's damage; therefore, a right to recover, etc. It was manifest from the original declaration that this was the particular duty and the actual breach comprehended in the pleader's design. 78 Ga. 307. The breach was fully described, but the duty was apparently assumed to exist, for nothing from which it could be rightly inferred was alleged. By

reason of this omission no duty of forbearance to obstruct the pipe appeared, and consequently no cause of action was set forth, although a good and sufficient one was evidently embraced in the design of the pleader. He had a complete design. The duty and breach he intended to declare upon would, if they existed, constitute a real cause of action, and only one fact requisite to show their existence was omitted. By amendment in the court below, made in response to a demurrer, this omission was supplied. The plaintiff pleaded an easement subjecting the defendant's land to the burden of receiving the water discharged from the pipe. The moment this fact was added to what the declaration already contained a complete cause of action was stated. But this court held that it was error to allow the amendment, the declaration not being amendable, for the reason that no cause of action was set forth at first. We have already seen that this reason was the very one why the declaration should have been amended, because, but for it, no amendment would have been needed. And there was certainly enough to amend by, even if we are to attribute to the pleader the absurd intention of treating it as the legal duty of one man to allow another at will and without permission to conduct his waste water to his premises in an artificial drain, and discharge it thereon. If it was the pleader's real purpose to propound this theory of a legal duty, we could still be in no doubt as to what duty he meant to assert and insist upon. It seems much more probable, however, that he intended to rely upon the easement which he afterwards alleged by way of amendment, and that on account of inadvertence, haste, or carelessness, he failed to plead it in the beginning. It was apparently very gross negligence not to plead it, but the right to amend, given by statute, is not lost by any negligence whatever. The court may, by virtue of section 3482 of the Code, impose terms upon its exercise, but cannot for any reason wholly deny the right to amend if there is enough in the declaration to amend by. No false theory of the pleader as to what facts will suffice to raise the duty covered by his design will count against the right to amend, provided the design itself is disclosed, and is one which, when filled out by all the necessary facts, will embrace a cause of action,—the identical cause on which the suit was commenced. If the plaintiff really has the identical cause of action which he has endeavored to plead, why should the mistake of his pleader in leaving out one of its necessary constituents, because he supposed it need not go in, be any bar to amending? Is not the chief object of amendment the correction of mistakes? Mistakes occasioned by error of judgment or opinion are quite as open to correction as any other. Indeed, were counsel of purpose and by intention to leave a declaration incomplete after so far developing the design and the identity of his cause of action as to furnish enough to amend by, he would not thereby forfeit the statutory right of his client to amend. The statute,

v.13s.e.no.33—52

except as a guide to the court in imposing terms, cares not what occasions the amendment to be needed. The right to amend is granted irrespective of any and every consideration as to whether there was fault or not in failing to have the pleading sufficient at first. In the case at bar, also, the declaration was ample—more than ample—in its supply of matter to amend by. Its theory of duty, breach, and right to recover may be formulated thus: It was the defendant's duty to the plaintiff not to cause the death of her son by negligence; the defendant did by negligence cause his death, to the plaintiff's damage, etc.; therefore, the right to recover, etc. The breach and the manner of it were set out with much particularity, and all the facts needful to raise the duty under the act of 1887 appeared, except the one fact that the plaintiff was dependent upon her son for support. Misled by the previous misconstruction of the Code by this court, the presiding judge refused to allow the plaintiff to amend by supplying this omitted fact, the amendment being offered as soon as the judge announced his opinion in favor of sustaining the defendant's demurrer, and before any judgment to that effect was written out or entered. The statute giving the right of action to the mother in such cases was not pleaded or referred to in the declaration; but so full was the declaration that any one of average intelligence, whether learned in the law or not, on hearing it read in connection with the statute, could not fail to understand that the design of the pleader was to base his action on that statute. In administering the law of amendment courts cannot afford to be less astute than ordinary by-standers who may happen to be present at their proceedings. We have no doubt that the able and learned judge who presided in this case well knew what duty of the defendant towards the plaintiff was meant to be asserted; and, had he been at liberty to follow his own convictions as to the true law, it is very probable he would have allowed the amendment. This is the second instance in which we have been constrained to reverse him as a consequence of correcting a misleading decision of this court. His willingness to abide by authority which ought to control him for the time being is not the least conspicuous of his many judicial virtues.

8. The cross-bill of exceptions complains of error in not sustaining the demurrer on another ground in addition to that just considered. This ground asserts, in substance, that for the time being the track was that of the Central Company,—the employer of the plaintiff's son, —which company was using it under its own franchise, and, therefore, that the defendant was under no duty to a servant of the Central Company. But according to the declaration the track belonged to the defendant, and all duties relating either to it or to the bridge were its duties exclusively. It was the lord paramount, and was in possession and use of the track in common with its tenant or licensee, the other company. There is no hint in the declaration of any undertaking by the latter to

keep either the track or the bridge in proper condition. On the contrary, it is alleged that the defendant owed to that company, as well as to the plaintiff's son, the duty of keeping the track and the bridge safe for use. In connection with this ground of demurrer was urged in the argument the doctrine of imputed negligence, a doctrine which is of doubtful standing in the law, and which, if recognized, is to be cautiously applied. The application of it sought to be made here is this: According to the declaration the plaintiff's son was in the employment, not of the defendant, but of the Central Company. By some arrangement between the two companies the latter acquired the right to run its trains over a portion of defendant's track in the city of Atlanta. The track was spanned by a bridge, which it was the defendant's duty to keep lighted at night, and in safe condition, and, the bridge being low, to keep ropes adjusted in proper position and at a proper elevation so that persons on top of the cars approaching the bridge would come in contact with the ropes, and thus receive warning of danger in time to shun it by bowing down low enough to pass under the bridge without injury. The defendant was negligent in maintaining too low a bridge, in not lighting it at night, in allowing the ropes to decay or be out of place, and in not keeping them up so as to give the necessary warning; also in allowing dangerous timbers to project from the bottom of the bridge downwards. In consequence of this negligence, of which the plaintiff's son was ignorant, he, during a dark night, while on top of a moving train of cars of the Central Company, and engaged in the line of his duty, struck against the bridge and was killed. There was no allegation that the Central Company was ignorant of the defendant's negligence and the danger occasioned thereby, and the contention is that, as there was no privity between the defendant and the plaintiff's son, the duty of the defendant in regard to the bridge and the ropes was not directly to him, but was to the Central Company; and that, if the latter company knew of the danger, and nevertheless ran into it, this was contributory negligence by the master, which is to be imputed to the servant who suffered or was killed by the joint negligence of the master and the defendant. There is an answer to this contention, dependent on the rules of pleading, which answer we shall make presently, but we may suggest in passing what might be said were that response not at hand. One who engages with a master to furnish a safe way for the passage of the latter and his servants, and allows them to enter upon and use the way accordingly, is to be understood as holding it out to the servants, as well as to the master, as fit for safe use, and as inviting the servants to use it in the due course of transacting the master's business. This puts him in a relation of duty towards the servants no less direct than that which he bears to the master; but a duty governed by the law of tort, instead of the law of contract. For the violation of this duty, by which one of the servants is

injured, it is no answer to say that the master aided in the violation, or was instrumental in causing injury to be sustained by reason thereof, or that he was negligent in not protecting the servant against the consequences of the defendant's negligence, if the defendant's negligence was in part the proximate cause of the injury. The rule of our law (Code, § 2972) is that, if the person injured could, by the use of ordinary diligence, have protected himself against the consequences of the defendant's negligence, there can be no recovery; but, we apprehend, he is not to lose his action if some one else could have protected him, and negligently failed to do it. Far more reasonable would it be to treat both the negligent parties as wrong-doers, and make them both answerable for the result to which they mutually contributed, than to excuse one of them because the other also was at fault. Be this as it may, there was no error in overruling this ground of demurrer to the plaintiff's declaration, because it does not appear that the Central Company was negligent or at fault in any way whatever. On the contrary, the death of the plaintiff's son is attributed in the declaration wholly to the negligence of the defendant. If in this respect the declaration is not true, its want of truth is matter of defensive pleading by direct denial or otherwise. The mere failure to allege that the Central Company was ignorant of the danger, or of the conditions which caused the danger, is no warrant for assuming contributory negligence on the part of that company. Kentucky & I. B. Co. v. Hall, 125 Ind. 220, 25 N. E. Rep. 219; Railroad Co. v. Evans, (Ga.) 13 S. E. Rep. 580. Judgment reversed. On cross-bill of exceptions, affirmed.

NOTE.

Authorities, besides cases in the Georgia Reports, which may be consulted in connection with the foregoing opinion: Pleading at common law was originally *ore tenus* at the bar, and defects were cured *instanter*. 2 Reeves, Hist. Com. Law, (Ed 1880,) 569. Afterwards, when they came to be written, either party could amend in form or substance, so long as the proceedings were in paper,—that is, before the record was made up. 1 Bac. Abr. 224; 2 Vin. Abr. 291; 1 Petersd. Abr. (503) et seq.; 1 Tidd Pr. 694 et seq.; 1 Har. Dig. 124; Mans. Dem., 149 et seq., "The Compleat Attorney and Solicitor," 309 et seq.; Anon., 1 Salk. 47; Anon., 2 Salk. 520; Walker v. Laughton. Fortes. 277; Bonfield v. Milner, 2 Burrows, 1098; 1 Amer. & Eng. Enc. Law, p. 546; Queen v. Inhabitants, Sid. 107 It is not too late to amend the declaration after demurrer, joinder, and argument. Taylor v. Bramble, Barnes, 6; Farmer v. Burton, Id. 9; Pool v. Hamerton, 2 Barnard. 65; Hardy v. Gilding, 3 Lev. 39; Jones v. Edwards, 3 Mees. & W. 215; Goodwin v. Hannah, 5 Strob. 157. See King v. Ellames, Hardw. Cas. Temp. 49, 2 Strange, 976; Anon., 2 Mod. 167; Queen v. Inhabitants, supra; 1 Bac. Abr. 296; 2 Vin. Abr. (317;) 1 Petersd. Abr. (529;) 1 Tidd, Pr. 709; 3 Chit. Pr. 761. Penal actions are amendable at common law, the same as ordinary actions. 1 Tidd, Pr. 711, King v. Ellames, supra; Jones v. Edwards, supra. Something to "amend by." 1 Tidd, Pr. 713; King v. Ellames, Hardw. Cas. Temp. 42; Woodman v. Inwen, Barnes, 9; Giddens v. Mirk, 4 Ga. 364; Christian v. Penn, 5 Ga. 482; Ledsingor v. Central Line Steamers, 75 Ga. 567; Smets v. Weathersbee, R. M. Charlt. 537. Declarations setting out no cause of action amendable. Skinner v. Grant, 12 Vt. 456; Pullen v. Hutchinson, 25 Me. 249; King v. Railway Co., 79 Mo. 328; Manz v. Railway Co., 87 Mo. 278; Railway Co. v. Piper, 26 Kan. 58. But see Hobby v. Mead, 1 Day, 205. Leave to amend. Creel v. Brown, 1 Rob, (Va.) 265; Strange v. Floyd, 9 Grat. 474; Trumbo v. Finley, 18 S. C. 305; Bischoff v. Blease, 20 S. C. 460; Miller v. Stark, (S. C.) 7 S. E. Rep. 501; Stovall v. Bowers, 10 Humph. 560; Gammon v. Schmoll, 5 Taunt. 344. Not allowed after dismissal on general demurrer. Hart v. Bowie, 34 La. Ann. 323. "Cause of action." Colby Pr. p. 166 et seq.; 3 Amer. & Eng. Enc. Law, 46; Petre v. Craft, 4 East, 433; Stevenson v. Mudgett, 10 N. H. 338; Merrill v. Russell, 12 N. H. 79; Cabarga v. Seeger, 17 Pa. St. 514; Jackson v. Spittall, L. R. 5 C. P. 552; Cooke v. Gill, L. R. 8 C. P 107; Durham v. Spence, L. R. 6 Exch. 46; Cherry v. Thompson, L. R. 7 Q. B. 573; President, etc., v. Railroad Co., 10 How. Pr. 1, Veeder v. Baker, 83 N. Y. 160; Hill v. Smith, 34 Vt. 535; Rodgers v. Association, 17 S. C. 410. Amendment of bills in equity. Story, Eq. Pl. § 883 et seq.; Mitf. Eq. Pl. by Tyler, 309, 413, 418, 419; 1 Daniell, Ch. Pr. 401 et seq. Substance and form distinguished. Gould, Pl. p. 485, c. 9, § 18.

JOHNSON v. CUMMINGS.

(Supreme Court of Georgia. Oct. 19, 1891.)

CERTIORARI—WHEN LIES.

One of the errors assigned in the *certiorari* being that the magistrate rendered judgment for the plaintiff's debt, and the action being based upon an account, there was a question of fact involved, and consequently the remedy in the first instance was not by *certiorari*, but by appeal to a jury in the justice's court, the amount claimed being under $50.

(Syllabus by the Court.)

Error from superior court, Fulton county; MARSHALL J. CLARKE, Judge.

Petition for *certiorari* by C. J. Johnson. The *certiorari* was dismissed in the court below, and petitioner brings error. Affirmed.

One Cummings sued Johnson in a magistrate's court for $22.50, balance due for 10 quarter kegs of beer, the suit being brought by Cummings, "sole wholesale dealer in the Gerke Brewing Company's Cincinnati beer." The magistrate decided in favor of Cummings, and Johnson sued out a *certiorari* to the superior court, in which court the *certiorari* was dismissed, on the ground that the petition therefor and the magistrate's answer did not present questions of law alone, but questions of mixed law and fact, and that appeal to a jury in the magistrate's court, and not *certiorari*, was the proper remedy, to which ruling Johnson excepted.

Eugene M. Mitchell, for plaintiff in error. *J. C. Jenkins,* for defendant in error.

PER CURIAM. Judgment affirmed.

PHILLIPS v. O'NEAL.

(Supreme Court of Georgia. Oct. 19, 1891.)

VENDOR AND VENDEE — MISTAKE — BOUNDARIES— BEST AND SECONDARY EVIDENCE.

1. Where each of two coterminous proprietors recognizes the ownership of the other, and that the tract of each is bounded by that of the other, the ascertainment of the true line between them fixes the extent of their respective tracts.

2. If one by mistake purchases a strip of land from the other which really belongs to himself, though he acquire actual possession by reason of

his purchase, he is not bound to surrender the possession in order to avoid paying the purchase money, if the transaction was by mutual mistake, or if it was by mistake of the purchaser and fraud on the part of the vendor.

3. The rule that transactions in the sale and purchase of land which were evidenced by writing are not to be proved by parol, without first accounting for the absence of the writing, applies in this case.

4. The relevancy of possession, etc., of another tract by a third person is not apparent. There was no error in denying a new trial on any of the grounds set forth in the motion.

(Syllabus by the Court.)

Error from city court of Atlanta; HOWARD VAN EPPS, Judge.

Action by Mary S. Phillips against Hiram O'Neal, on notes given for the purchase price of land. Judgment for defendant. Plaintiff brings error. Affirmed.

Bruyles & Sons, for plaintiff in error. *Simmons & Corrigan,* for defendant in error.

BLECKLEY, C. J. This case has been here twice before. O'Neal v. Phillips, 83 Ga. 556, 10 S. E. Rep. 352; Phillips v. O'Neal, 85 Ga. 142, 11 S. E. Rep. 581. On the first occasion it was held that, if the pleas of O'Neal were found to be true, the verdict should be in his favor. At the trial which took place afterwards the verdict was in his favor, and this was a finding that the pleas were true. But the court having admitted some illegal evidence that may have influenced the jury in their opinion as to where the true boundary which originally divided the premises of the respective parties was located, a new trial was granted, not for the purpose of reopening the whole controversy, but for the purpose of ascertaining where the true boundary was. This court thought that the true issue remaining for trial was: "Where is the north boundary of the line of Phillips' land? Did Phillips' land, when she sold to O'Neal, extend north of Pine street? If it did, she is entitled to recover on the notes sued on; if it did not, she is not entitled to recover, for she only sold her interest in the land lying north of Pine street to O'Neal's land. If there was any of her land lying north of Pine street, then O'Neal purchased it, and would be bound to pay these notes; if not, he would not be bound to pay the notes." The court added: "We think the issue above stated should be submitted alone by the court to the jury, together with the question of interest, and nothing else." This course was pursued by the superior court at the last trial, and the jury again found in favor of O'Neal. Mrs. Phillips moved for a new trial, and the motion was overruled.

1. These parties were coterminous proprietors, and each acknowledged the ownership of the other, O'Neal by the deed from Love to him, which was dated August 20, 1883, and Mrs. Phillips by her bond for titles to O'Neal, which was dated September 21, 1885. O'Neal's tract, as described in the aforesaid deed, was bounded "south by Phillips' true line," and the description in the bond for titles from Mrs. Phillips to O'Neal was as follows: "A certain tract or parcel of land on the north side of Pine street, and east side of Fort,

adjoining the said Hiram O'Neal on the north and N. J. Hammond on the east, being all my interest north of Pine street;" and the obligation she assumed in the bond was "to make said O'Neal a title to all of her interest in and to all of her said lot north of Pine, warranting the same against her heirs and assigns." As the limit of O'Neal's tract was Mrs. Phillips' true line, and as Mrs. Phillips recognized that O'Neal's land extended to her line, the location of that line would show the true original boundary between their respective tracts. If that boundary was not north of Pine street, then Mrs. Phillips sold to O'Neal his own land, for she did not intend or undertake to sell anything south of that street, and she expressly declared that what she did sell was all her interest north of it. If she had no interest north of it, O'Neal acquired nothing by his purchase. There had been no dispute as to the boundary, and consequently no settlement of a dispute was involved in the transaction; there was nothing in the nature of a compromise or the adjustment of a controversy.

2. O'Neal sets up by his plea that he was ignorant of the location of the true line, and that both Mrs. Phillips and her husband, who represented her in the transaction, knew where it was, and did not inform him. He insists also that, if they did not know, this made a case of mutual mistake; and that, as they represented, in effect, that they did know, he is entitled to relief, inasmuch as he really received no consideration. To this it was answered, when the case was first here, that, as O'Neal acquired possession by reason of his purchase from Mrs. Phillips, he was bound to restore the possession or pay for the land. But that position was distinctly overruled, this court saying: "In a case like the present, it is not necessary that the contract should have been rescinded and the property restored to the vendor. Neither a court of law nor of equity could or would, under the facts alleged in these pleas, require a restoration of the property to the plaintiff. That would be to require one to restore to another property which belonged to himself. If A. purchase a horse from B., thinking at the time that the horse belongs to B., and give his note for the purchase price, B. knowing at the time that the horse belongs to A., the vendee, such note would be without consideration; and, inasmuch as the horse had got into the hands to which it belonged, it would be manifestly unjust to require it to be restored to a person to whom it did not belong. So, in this case, if the land belonged at the time of the purchase to the purchaser and not to the vendor, and the purchaser believed it belonged to the vendor, and the vendor knew that he had no title to it himself, there could be no sense or justice in requiring a restoration of possession of the property to the vendor. It would be taking the property that belonged to one man, and giving it to another, who had no claim to it." Nevertheless, at the last trial, the counsel for Mrs. Phillips requested the court to charge the jury thus: "If you believe from the evidence that O'Neal acquired posses-

sion of the land under and by virtue of his purchase from Mrs. Phillips, and that he still holds possession of the same, and has not been evicted and turned out of possession, you should find for the plaintiff, as it would be inequitable and unjust, under such a state of facts, for O'Neal to hold on to the property, and not pay for it." For three reasons the denial of this request was proper: (1) It was not law in its application to this case; (2) this court had so ruled in 83 Ga. 556, 10 S. E. Rep. 332; (3) it was wholly irrelevant upon the question whether the land of Mrs. Phillips extended north of Pine street, which was the issue on trial, if the decision of this court in 85 Ga. 142, 11 S. E. Rep. 581, was of any authority.

3. Another ground of the motion for a new trial complains that O'Neal, on cross-examination, was not required to answer as to certain transactions involving writings. It is enough to say that the writings, or some of them, were not produced or accounted for. Moreover, this testimony related to the fact of taking and retaining possession, which, as we have seen, was not material.

4. It is not clear to us that the court erred in excluding the evidence of Mulinax as to Crawford Munroe's occupation of a portion of the Brumby tract, and we think the court did not err in denying a new trial on any of the grounds set forth in the motion. Judgment affirmed.

RICHMOND & D. R. CO. v. WRIGHT.

(Supreme Court of Georgia. Oct. 19, 1891.)

MASTER AND SERVANT—NEGLIGENCE—ASSUMPTION OF RISK—EVIDENCE.

This case turned on the credibility of the witnesses, and there was no abuse of discretion by the court below in not granting a new trial.

(Syllabus by the Court.)

Error from city court of Atlanta; HOWARD VAN EPPS, Judge.

Action for personal injuries by Robert Wright against the Richmond & Danville Railroad Company. Judgment for plaintiff, and defendant appeals. Affirmed.

The following is the official report:

Wright sued the railroad company for damages for personal injuries, and obtained a verdict for $475. Defendant moved for a new trial, upon the grounds that the verdict was contrary to law, evidence, etc., and excessive. The motion was overruled, and it excepted. The evidence for plaintiff was, in brief, to the following effect: At the time he was hurt he was working for the Georgia Pacific Railway, which is controlled by defendant. He was hurt on the night of December 16, 1889, after he had been working a little over two weeks for that company. He was instructed by a conductor — one Guthrie—to couple an engine and cab to another cab, the latter being stationary. He gave the fireman of the engine, on whose side he was, a car-length signal to slack up; but he did not seem to slack up, and, just before he struck the standing cab, gave him a signal to stop. He did not stop, but struck the cab, and knocked it about two and a half or three feet. He theo signaled the fireman to stand still, and told him to stand still and let him go in and make the coupling. He went in to make the coupling, having a link and lamp in one hand and a stick in the other. He laid his lamp down on the end of the stationary car, and tried to get the pin out, but it was tight, and he could not shake it loose. He took the other link and commenced driving up the tight link, and all at once heard the engine exhaust, (when an engine is moving it will exhaust,) and he went to run out, and stumbled on something, and threw up his hand to catch. He threw up his hand on the dead-block, and just as he did so it was struck and caught. The fireman saw the signal he gave him to stand still, and the engine was standing completely still when he went in. It would have been plaintiff's duty to give him a signal to come forward; and plaintiff did not do so; he came forward without such signal. When plaintiff was driving the pin up he was stooping or squatting down. He had to do so. It was as much as he could do to drive it up with the link. It was very tight. When he went between the cars he was going to couple with his stick. It comes handier for him to couple with a stick than without one. Did not remember whether he laid it on the ground or the platform of the cab, but he knew he had to lay it down to drive out the pin. He could not get the pin out with the stick. He did not get up on the platform of the cab to get the pin out, because he could not get it out on the platform. Charles Simmons, another brakeman or switchman, saw the accident. He was there to give them the signals, but was not giving any signals that plaintiff knew of; and whether or not the engine was moved on Simmons' signal plaintiff did not know. Both of them gave the signal to stand still, which was the last signal made. Simmons was standing on one end of the cab and plaintiff on the other. Plaintiff did not make the coupling. No slack caught his hand. When he was hurt Guthrie told Simmons to cut the engine loose, and put plaintiff on it, and go up to the office, and he would telephone for the doctor, and have him come down to dress plaintiff's hand. The engine did not pull the cabs up to the office when plaintiff went with it. The cabs were left. He did not tell Guthrie he was hurt by the slack rolling out while he was pushing the pin. The engineer asked him how he got hurt, and whether he got hurt the second time he, the engineer, hit the cars, or the first time; and plaintiff told him he got hurt the second time. At that time he was between 28 and 29 years old, and was earning $1.25 a day; working during the week all the days and on Sunday night. He went to work again after the injury, the last of May. Worked for two or three days helping a man pile shingles and plank, and then drove a spring wagon. With the spring wagon he worked, until the weather commenced getting cold, for $4.50 a week. He is now working for defendant as a switchman, and has been working on this job since November or December, 1890. Has not

been working for them ever since. When he is able to go he is able to work. In February he lost nearly half. In December he did not know how much, but knew he drew $18 and something. Drew $16 and something in January, $20 in March. Did not remember what he drew in April. The last pay day, got about $20. He stopped off from work the second week before the trial, which occurred on May 18, 1891. Was not discharged,—just quit. He can now work tolerably well, but cannot do good work as he could before he got hurt. If he does two or three days' hard work, it will pain his hand so he can hardly stand it. Where the leaders are drawn he cannot bear for anything to touch his hand. It seems tender and sore all the time, unless he has a glove. His hand was "bursted" across, and then from two of his fingers out to his thumb. There was a hole that you could run your thumb in; and his first finger hasn't any feeling at all. It was the last of April when his hand healed up. He suffered about a month or six weeks. It seemed like pins or needles sticking all through his hand. He could not sleep day or night, and could not rest unless his hand was bound up tight. It pains him yet sometimes, etc. If he does any kind of heavy work, or any kind of lifting or straining, it pains him and hurts him for two or three days; or if he lifts as much as a 24-pound sack of flour it will pain him. In the fix his hand is now he cannot do near the work he could do before it was hurt. Before he could work all the time, and now can put in about three or four days a week, or not so many. Whether it was against the rules to go in between the cars he did not know. Supposed it was a rule of the company that couplings were to be made with sticks. No rules were read to him at all, and he could not read them himself. He did not know whether he made his mark or not to the agreement or rule hereafter to be mentioned. Guthrie asked him if he had ever signed the coupling list, and he told him, "No;" and Guthrie said, "Well, sign this here, and we will go home. It ain't no 'count nohow." Guthrie did not read it, and plaintiff did not hear it read. Plaintiff signed something. He did not know what it was. That was the second morning after Guthrie hired him. He was not made to sign the rule. Signed the next morning after they employed him. He had a stick that he coupled with, and used it all the time. The rules were never read to him, and never explained to him. There was a copy shown to him. He could not read them. If it was a rule to use a stick, it was not read to him, and he did not know it. No one explained any rules to him. What was required of a brakeman as to signals, switching, carrying keys, running an engine, and all, he learned when he first came to the railroad. The only caution Guthrie ever gave him was as he was going to make a coupling, and the end of a coal-car dropped out, and Guthrie came and looked at it, and told him he must be particular about going between those old coal-cars, because they were not safe.

Charles Simmons testified for plaintiff, among other things. He was present when plaintiff was hurt. Witness gave no signal; but while both the cabs were standing perfectly still plaintiff went between them, and got down to knock the pin out, so he could enter the link; and the engine moved the cab it was coupled to, without a signal, and plaintiff was hurt. Plaintiff did not finish the coupling, but witness went in and made the coupling; not right then, but a short time afterwards. The pin was a crooked one. It was not out when witness went in. When the engineer came ahead he came so quick plaintiff did not know it, and plaintiff raised his hands up, and the dead-block caught his hand. He had one hand on the top of the pin he was knocking under, and knocked that right straight up. He moved right quick, and that threw his hand up in the way of the draw-head. Witness was looking at him, and swears that was the way it happened. When he went on the engine with plaintiff after plaintiff was hurt the cabs were left. The pin was so crooked it was fastened. If it had been straight it would not have been hard to get out. It had to be knocked out. No sticks were ever furnished witness. He knew nothing about sticks. Never saw any rules; no instructions. Used sticks for putting on brakes. A physician testified for plaintiff that plaintiff's right hand was crushed, the injury being to the tendons of the flexor muscles, and also to the palmar surface, stiffening the hand. Witness found that plaintiff was unable either to open the hand or to close it or grasp anything, and that the injury was permanent. The tendons of the muscles were contracted permanently, and had lost elasticity, etc. The injury, as it appeared to him, would lessen plaintiff's capacity to earn a livelihood perhaps one-half, because there were certain kinds of labor he could not do. He would suffer more or less pain through life, witness thought, from looking at the back of his hand, the condition of the knuckles, etc.

The evidence for defendant, briefly stated, was: Charles Simmons was not close to plaintiff when plaintiff was hurt. The only signal that was given was to come ahead and couple. It was a car-length signal; and that was all that was done until plaintiff was brought to the engine and put on it after his hand was mashed. A car-length signal was given by a lamp held up, which was then lowered to a half car length, and then the engineer stopped. He found out plaintiff was hurt in a couple of minutes. Plaintiff told Guthrie they had mashed his hand. It was mashed the first time they approached it, (the cab.) The engine did not approach the cab when the coupling was made but the one time. It went back at a rate of speed reasonable to make a coupling. The engineer saw no signals except what were given him by the fireman. At the time of the trial the fireman was dead. When plaintiff was hurt he was put on the engine, and the engine moved off with the cabs. At that time the coupling was already made. Plaintiff did sign the rule or agree-

ment as to coupling, with his mark, and Guthrie witnessed the signature. When Guthrie hired plaintiff he asked plaintiff if he knew the rules of the road, and he said he did. Guthrie told him that there was a coupling form he must sign. Without that he was not allowed to work. Took him to the office, and gave him the paper. He (plaintiff) said he could not read or write, and for Guthrie to fill it out. Guthrie read it over to him, and filled it out, and plaintiff touched the pen to the mark, and used the stick afterwards. The other men used sticks furnished by the company. Guthrie had cautioned plaintiff about going between moving cars. Had seen him go in when he ought not to. The coupling to that car was made by plaintiff at that time. He told Guthrie, at the time, he entered the link, and went to push the pin down, and the slack rolled out ahead of the pin, and caught his hand. Defendant put in evidence the agreement or rule signed by plaintiff November 28, 1889, which was to the effect that plaintiff fully understood that the rules of defendant, lessee of the Georgia Pacific Railway, positively prohibited brakemen from coupling or uncoupling, except with a stick, and that brakemen or others must not go between cars under any circumstances for the purpose of coupling or uncoupling, or for adjusting pins, etc., when an engine was attached to such cars or train; and that, in consideration of being employed by such company, he agreed to be bound by said rule, and waived all or any liability of the company to him for any results of disobedience or infraction thereof. The agreement concluded with the statement, "I have read the above carefully, and fully understand it." It was attested by Guthrie, and accompanied by his certificate that plaintiff signed it, as appeared, by his "mark," and that he, Guthrie, read it over to plaintiff, and carefully explained it. Also by a note to the effect that, before any one was allowed to enter the service of the company as a brakeman, flagman, switchman, or fireman, he must sign one of these forms, and previous to signing it must insert, in his own handwriting, above his signature, the words, "I have read the above carefully, and fully understand it;" that, in cases where the would-be employe could not read or write, his signature must be made with his mark, and the witness must fill up the certificate, inserting the employe's name in the blank space left for that purpose, etc.

Jackson & Jackson, for plaintiff in error. *Bigby & Berry* and *John C. Reed,* for defendant in error.

PER CURIAM. Judgment affirmed.

GEORGIA RAILROAD & BANKING CO. *v* PENDLETON *et al.*

(*Supreme Court of Georgia.* Oct. 19, 1891.)

MORTGAGE — FORECLOSURE — WAIVER OF CONDITIONS—ACTION ON NOTE—JURY TRIAL.

1. If not in all cases whatsoever, certainly in any case admitting of doubt, the question of rendering a judgment by the superior court without a jury is one not involving jurisdiction, but the

proper exercise of jurisdiction, and the improper decision of it is mere error, and will not render the judgment void.

2. A joint action against the maker and indorsers of a promissory note is a civil case, founded on an unconditional contract in writing; and, where no issuable defense is filed under oath or affirmation, the court may render judgment thereon against all of the defendants without the verdict of a jury.

3. Where the maker of a promissory note executes a mortgage to secure the same, and in the mortgage stipulates for the payment of all expenses of collection, including 10 per cent. attorney's fees, and declares as a part of the mortgage deed that it may be foreclosed for such expenses and attorney's fees, together with the principal and interest of the note, and a judgment of foreclosure is afterwards rendered accordingly, and judgment upon the note against the maker and indorsers is also rendered in a proper action, and afterwards the indorsers waive in writing any objection to the stipulation in the mortgage as to attorney's fees, such waiver is a ratification by them of the maker's act in giving the mortgage, and they cannot afterwards insist that the judgment of foreclosure shall not operate against them as conclusive upon the question of the creditor's right to appropriate a sufficient amount of the proceeds of the mortgaged property to the payment of such fees.

4. One of the indorsers being the president of the corporation which executed the mortgage, and he signing the same as president, his assent to the stipulation as to attorney's fees was given thereby, and no further waiver as to him was necessary.

(Syllabus by the Court.)

Error from superior court, Fulton county; MARSHALL J. CLARKE, Judge.

Action by the Georgia Railroad & Banking Company against the Pendleton Guano Company, W. M. Pendleton, and others on a note. Judgment for plaintiff, and on levy of execution Pendleton and others, indorsers, filed affidavits of illegality. Judgment was rendered against plaintiff, who brings error. Reversed.

J. B. Cumming and *Hillyer & Bro.*, for plaintiff in error. *John L. Hopkins & Son, A. H. Cox,* and *Rosser & Carter,* for defendants in error.

LUMPKIN, J. The Pendleton Guano Company, a corporation, desiring to borrow money from the Georgia Railroad & Banking Company, executed, by its president, W. M. Pendleton, and its treasurer, E. A. Werner, a promissory note for $20,-000, payable to the order of Charles G. Goodrich, cashier, at the Gate City National Bank, Atlanta, Ga. The note was not indorsed by the payee, but was indorsed by M. Pendleton, C. K. Maddox, and others, all of whom were stockholders, and most of them directors, of the corporation, they simply signing their names across the back of the note. All this was done before the note was delivered to the banking company which advanced the money upon it, as above executed and indorsed. This note did not contain any stipulation for attorney's fees, but on the day of its execution the corporation, by its said president and treasurer, made a mortgage upon realty and personalty in favor of Goodrich, cashier, to secure said note; and the mortgage contained a stipulation that, in case said note was not paid at maturity, it might be foreclosed for principal, interest, and

the costs and expenses of collection, including 10 per cent. attorney's fees. Afterwards suit was brought on the note, judgment was rendered thereon by the court without the intervention of a jury, and the mortgage was foreclosed for principal, interest, costs, and 10 per cent. attorney's fees. The mortgage *fi. fa.* having been levied on the mortgaged property, the guano company was seeking, by equitable proceedings, to enjoin the sale under this levy, when an agreement was entered into between the plaintiff and the indorsers, who were interested in the corporation, and controlled its affairs, by the terms of which the sale was postponed until the following January, and the indorsers agreed to offer no further delay or obstacle to the sale, and also to make no resistance as to attorney's fees. This agreement was signed by all the indorsers except Pendleton, who, it will be remembered, was the president of the corporation. When the property of the corporation was sold under this *fi. fa.*, a portion of the proceeds was appropriated to the payment of the attorney's fees mentioned in the judgment of foreclosure. After all this was done, the *fi. fa.* issued from the common-law judgment was levied on property of the defendant indorsers, and they filed severally their affidavits of illegality.

1, 2. One of the grounds of the illegality was that the judgment was void as to these indorsers, for the reason, as alleged, that it was rendered by the court without the intervention of a jury, upon a contract which was not unconditional; the contention being that such indorsers were only liable on condition the note was duly presented to the principal at maturity, dishonored, and such fact duly notified to the indorsers. This contention assumes that the persons mentioned as indorsers were liable only as such, and not otherwise. Under the facts above recited, it would not, perhaps, be going too far to hold that these persons were not, in a strict sense, indorsers, but were really sureties, and liable as makers. It is unnecessary, however, to thus rule in this case. At best, the question whether or not the court should, without a jury, render judgment on this paper is not free from doubt; and, when a judgment upon such a paper is asked of the court, it may resolve the doubt by judicially determining whether it is a case requiring the verdict of a jury or not. As stated in the first head-note, we do not think the determination of this question is one involving the jurisdiction of the court, but rather how the court shall exercise the jurisdiction it undoubtedly has both of the persons and subject-matter before it, and the incorrect determination of the question would be simply an error which defendants should endeavor to prevent at the time of its commission, or, at least, seek to have the same corrected by a proper motion during the term when such error was made. We do not mean to hold that if suit was brought upon a written contract, which plainly and beyond all question was not unconditional, a judgment by the court without a jury would be valid; but we do mean to say that, in a case where it is doubtful whether there should be a verdict or a judgment without a verdict, and the court adjudicates that a jury is not necessary, and renders judgment accordingly, such judgment will not be absolutely void. If erroneously rendered, the error may be corrected as above indicated, but the judgment will not be open to attack by illegality after the expiration of the term at which it was rendered, especially when defendants have by their conduct acquiesced in its validity. The constitution provides that "the court shall render judgment without the verdict of a jury, in all civil cases founded on unconditional contracts in writing, where an issuable defense is not filed under oath or affirmation." So far as the maker is concerned, this note is undoubtedly an unconditional contract in writing; and, even if the persons described as indorsers are liable only as such, still they may be sued in the same action with the principal. When such a suit is brought, in determining whether or not the services of a jury are needed, the action must be classified, and the question must be settled whether it is or is not "founded on an unconditional contract in writing." Otherwise the curious result might follow that as to one of the defendants there should be a judgment of the court without a jury, and as to others there must be a verdict and judgment,—all in the same case. Our constitution and laws do not contemplate any such procedure as this, and therefore, in a case like the present, the same sort of judgment should be rendered against all of the defendants. In our opinion, there is no variance, either from truth or sound principle, in classifying this case as one founded upon an unconditional contract in writing, and the court properly rendered its judgment against all of the defendants without a jury.

3, 4. Other grounds of the affidavits of illegality made the point that if the money arising from the sale of the guano company's property under the mortgage fi. fa., which was appropriated to the payment of attorney's fees, had been applied to the common law fi. fa., such application, in connection with other credits thereon, would have satisfied the latter fi. fa., and therefore, so far as affiants are concerned, it has been paid. Granting all this to be true, a complete answer to it is that all these defendants, except W. M. Pendleton, expressly agreed in writing to make no resistance to the collection of these attorney's fees; and Mr. Pendleton, as president of the corporation, signed the mortgage agreeing to pay attorney's fees without objection to that stipulation therein, and without giving any notice to plaintiff that he would claim any exemption from liability in consequence of these fees being collected out of the proceeds of the mortgaged property. Hence we rule, in effect, in the third and fourth head-notes, that these indorsers waived all objections to the plaintiff, applying a sufficiency of the proceeds of the mortgaged property to the payment of these fees, and they are bound by such waivers. Judgment reversed.

SOUTHERN PAC. CO. v. STEWART.

(*Supreme Court of Georgia. Oct. 19, 1891.*)

REMOVAL OF CAUSES—ATTACHMENT.

1. Inasmuch as by the statute of the United States an application to remove a cause from a state court to the United States circuit court is in time if made "at the time, or at any time before, the defendant is required by the laws of the state, or the rule of the state court in which such suit is brought, to answer or plead to the declaration or complaint of the plaintiff;" and inasmuch as the law of Georgia entitles the defendant to plead at any time before final judgment, where the case is one commenced by attachment,—an application made to remove at any time before final judgment is not too late, where the defendant has filed no plea.

2. A stipulation between the parties, by which the plaintiff in attachment agrees to dispense with bond as a condition to dissolving the attachment, and the defendant agrees to be bound by any judgment rendered in the state court as if said company were within the jurisdiction of said court, and had been personally served, will not oust the right of removal or estop the defendant from exercising such right.

(*Syllabus by the Court.*)

Error from city court of Atlanta; HOWARD VAN EPPS, Judge.

Action aided by attachment by David O. Stewart against the Southern Pacific Company. Defendant brings error from an order refusing to remove the cause to the circuit court of the United States. Reversed.

Calhoun, King & Spalding and *J. T. Pendleton,* for plaintiff in error. *R. Arnold* and *R. R. Arnold,* for defendant in error.

BLECKLEY, C. J. This was an attachment for $10,000, sued out on the ground that the company was a non-resident of the state of Georgia, in favor of Stewart against the Southern Pacific Company. It was levied by the service of garnishment, and was returnable to the June term, 1890, of the city court. Before that term arrived, the parties entered into a written agreement, whereby it was stipulated that the company be relieved from the necessity of giving bond to dissolve the garnishment, and that it would enter a general appearance in lieu of giving bond and security. This clause was added: "The Southern Pacific Company fully consents to the jurisdiction of the city court of Atlanta, and agrees to be bound by any judgment rendered in said case as if said company was in the jurisdiction of said court, and had been personally served." By petition to the city court, presented on the 11th of May, 1891, the company applied to remove the case to the circuit court of the United States for the northern district of Georgia, alleging that the company was a citizen of Kentucky, and the plaintiff a citizen of Georgia. The court accepted the petition and the accompanying bond. Two days afterwards it ordered that the acceptance be revoked, holding that the case was not removable. The order of revocation is complained of as error.

1. One of the reasons assigned here in argument why the case is not removable is that the application came too late. It is contended that, under the stipulation

above recited, the case ceased to be an attachment proceeding, but was put upon the footing of an ordinary action, and that the time for filing a plea or answer was the appearance term, or certainly not later than the subsequent term. We think otherwise. The stipulation simply put the case where it would have stood if bond and security had been given to dissolve the garnishment, and we have no statute or rule of court which requires plea or answer earlier in an attachment case, where the attachment has been dissolved, than where it has not been dissolved. The only statute upon the subject is section 3310 of the Code, which says: "The defendant may appear by himself or attorney at law, and make his defense at any time before final judgment is rendered against him." This section was construed in Kimball v. Nicol, 58 Ga. 175, as holding the case open for appearance and defense down to the actual rendition of final judgment. So far as appears, the company in this case had not filed any plea or answer when the petition to remove was presented. Had a plea then been filed, it would have been in time; and, this being so, the right to remove had not been lost, the statute of the United States allowing the petition to be made and filed "at the time or any time before the defendant is required by the laws of the state or the rule of the state court in which such suit is brought to answer or plead to the declaration or complaint of the plaintiff." St. U. S. 1885-87, pp. 553, 554, § 3.

2. We can see no trace of any estoppel in the stipulation betweeen the parties. The company, by agreeing to be bound by any judgment rendered in the state court, did not expressly waive the right of removal. It does not now seek to controvert the jurisdiction of the city court, but simply to exercise a right consistent with that jurisdiction. It treats itself as upon the same footing as it would have occupied had the court obtained jurisdiction over its person by giving the notice provided for in section 3309 of the Code. The point raised in argument that the bond did not provide for entering special bail seems to have no merit. But, whether so or not, it was not passed upon by the court below, the court having revoked its acceptance of the petition and bond because the case was not removable, and not because of any defect in the bond tendered. Judgment reversed.

LASSITER v. CARROLL.

(Supreme Court of Georgia. Oct. 19, 1891.)

SERVICE OF PROCESS.

Where there was an original process attached to the declaration which was not copied and served on the defendant, the declaration alone being served, it was competent for the court, on motion of the plaintiff's counsel, to order the original process to be made returnable to the next term of the court, and that a copy be served on the defendant, notwithstanding the defendant had made a motion to dismiss the action.

(Syllabus by the Court.)

Error from city court of Atlanta; HOWARD VAN EPPS, Judge.

Action by Mattie Carroll against M. E. Lassiter. From an order overruling defendant's motion to dismiss the action, she brings error. Affirmed.

R. L. Rodgers, for plaintiff in error. *Simmons & Corrigan,* for defendant in error.

SIMMONS, J. The exceptions in this case were to an order of the court below overruling a motion to dismiss the case for lack of service, and granting time to perfect service. It appears that the defendant was served with a copy of the declaration, but no copy of the process was attached thereto, further than a printed form of process, with blanks not filled, and without the signature of the clerk. Regular process, however, was annexed to the declaration as filed, and upon this was an entry by the sheriff that the defendant had been served with a copy. At the appearance term the defendant traversed this return, and moved to dismiss as above stated. The court held that the defendant had not been properly served, but ordered that the original process be amended so as to be made returnable to the next term as the appearance term of the case, and that a copy of the declaration and of the process as amended be served on the defendant in terms of the law. We think the court had the right to do this. In the case of Peck v. La Roche, 86 Ga. 314, 12 S. E. Rep. 638, relied upon by counsel for the plaintiff in error, the question was not as to the power of the court to amend process, and extend the time for service; but as to the power of the clerk, without an order of court, to substitute for the original process a second returnable to another term. The other authorities relied upon, in which there was no original process, are inapplicable to this case. McGhee v. Mayor, etc., 78 Ga. 790, 3 S. E. Rep. 670; Ballard v. Bancroft, 31 Ga. 508; Reynolds v. Lyon, 20 Ga. 225; Brady v. Hardeman, 17 Ga. 67. It is clear that the entire absence of process cannot be supplied by amendment; but where there is original process, as in the present instance, it is in the power of the court to retain the case, allowing such amendment and granting such further time for service as may be required to give due notice to the defendant. It has been held that "the decisions made by this court as to the want of original process do not, in strictness, apply to a defect in the copy." Cochran v. Davis, 20 Ga. 581. In that case the copy was practically as ineffectual as in the present case, being without the signature of the clerk, but the court directed that the omission be supplied. This court has repeatedly recognized the right of the court below, in cases where there was no service of any kind, to pass an order amending the process, and extending the time for service. See Baker v. Thompson. 75 Ga. 166; Allen v. Banking Co., 86 Ga. 74, 12 S. E. Rep. 265 In the latter case it is said: If the court "was satisfied that the plaintiff had used due diligence to ascertain whether the declaration and process had been served, he then had a right to order the service perfected, as was done. The granting of such a motion is largely within the discretion of the court." In the present case there can be no question of the proper exercise of this discretion. The original process being regular, and the officer's return showing service, and it not appearing that the plaintiff knew of the omission complained of, no such lack of diligence is attributable to him as would call for the dismissal of his case; and, so far as the defendant was concerned, no harm could ensue from the action of the court, the notice provided for under the terms of the judge's order being quite as ample as he would have had if the case had been brought de novo. Judgment affirmed.

CLARK v. EMPIRE LUMBER CO.

(Supreme Court of Georgia. Oct. 19, 1891.)

TAXATION—HUSBAND AND WIFE—GIFT BETWEEN—LIS PENDENS—ATTACHMENT—EVIDENCE.

1. The books of tax returns in the office of the comptroller general are of equal rank as evidence with those in the proper offices of the respective counties, and the certificate of the comptroller general, touching the contents of such books, is no less admissible than the certificate of the proper county officer would be.

2. Objection to evidence which does not appear to have been presented in the court below will not be passed upon by the supreme court.

3. The evidence showing that land conveyed to a wife by a third person was paid for by her husband, and there being no evidence of any consideration advanced by her to the husband, the transaction is a gift from him to her.

4. After seizure of the land as his property by virtue of an attachment against him, a joint deed from the husband and wife to a purchaser from them is affected by the doctrine of *lis pendens*, and will not prevail over the lien of the attachment.

5. Where there is no evidence of any purchase by the wife from the husband, it is not error to omit or deny instructions on that subject in charging the jury.

6. Where the description in the levy of the attachment as returned by the officer is otherwise definite, the omission to set out the number of feet in the frontage of the premises on a certain street will not prevent the doctrine of *lis pendens* from applying to one who purchases the same pending the levy.

(Syllabus by the Court.)

Error from superior court, Fulton county; MARSHALL J. CLARKE, Judge.

Action aided by attachment by the Empire Lumber Company against one Montgomery. Plaintiff obtained judgment, and execution was levied on land as belonging to Montgomery. Frank Clark interposed a claim to the land, and from a judgment finding the property subject to the levy he brings error. Affirmed.

Mayson & Hill, for plaintiff in error. *P. L. Mynatt* and *Rosser & Carter*, for defendant in error.

SIMMONS, J. Montgomery gave to Willingham an order for 800,000 feet of lumber on the Empire Lumber Company. In payment for the lumber, Willingham, on March 29, 1888, conveyed to Mrs. Montgomery, at Montgomery's request, certain realty in the city of Atlanta. The lumber not having been paid for by Montgomery, the Empire Lumber Company commenced suit against Montgomery by attachment April 29, 1888, which attachment was on the same day levied on one

of the lots conveyed to Mrs. Montgomery. The attachment was filed in the clerk's office May 2, 1888; and on May 8, 1888, Montgomery and his wife conveyed the lot levied on by the attachment to Clark, the claimant in this case. The declaration in attachment was filed November 23, 1888, and on March 25, 1889, judgment was obtained thereon against Montgomery. In the description of the property levied on, made by the sheriff on the attachment, the number of feet in the frontage of the premises on a certain street was omitted. After the judgment was obtained, .the levy, declaration, and judgment were amended, under an order of court, so as to give the proper number of feet in the frontage of the lot. Execution was issued on this judgment, and levied upon the land, and Clark interposed a claim thereto. On the trial of the claim the jury found the property subject, and Clark made a motion for a new trial, which was overruled by the court.

1. The fourth ground of the motion for a new trial complains that the court erred in admitting the certificate of the comptroller general in evidence; such certificate, if admissible at all, not properly coming from his office, but from the county tax receiver. This ground of the motion does not state that the certificate of the comptroller general was objected to at the time it was offered in evidence, or, if any objection was made, what the objection was. The ground of the motion, when heard before the judge, was that the certificate should have been from the tax receiver of Dougherty county, instead of from the comptroller general. We have frequently decided that, where a motion for a new trial is made on the ground that the court admitted illegal evidence, the motion must state that the objection was made when the evidence was offered, and what the objection was; and, unless this is done, we will not consider such ground.

If, however, the reason assigned in this motion had been presented at the trial, there would have been no error in overruling the same. Under the law (Code, § 849) it is the duty of the tax receiver of each county in this state to make out three copies of the tax digest for his county. One of these copies it is his duty to transmit to the comptroller general, and it is filed in the latter's office; and section 3816 of the Code declares that that officer's certificate "shall give sufficient validity or authenticity to any copy or transcript of any record, document, paper, or file or other matter or thing" in that office, "or pertaining thereto, to admit the same in evidence in any court of this state." The comptroller general's certificate of the contents of the tax digest is therefore of equal rank as evidence with that of the ordinary or other proper officer of the county where the digest was made.

If the objection had been made to this certificate that it was not a certificate of the contents of the tax digest, but a certificate of the fact that the digest did not contain the name of Montgomery, it would have presented a very different question, and perhaps the court would

have sustained the objection, and ruled
out the certificate. Upon this question,
see Henderson v. Hackney, 16 Ga. 521;
Miller v. Reinhart, 18 Ga. 245; Dillon v.
Mattox, 21 Ga. 113; Martin v. Anderson,
Id. 308, Ferrell v Hurst, 68 Ga. 132.

2 The fifth ground complains, in substance, that the court erred in charging
that, if the jury should believe from the
evidence that the consideration for the
deed from Willingham to Mrs. Montgomery was furnished altogether by Mr. Montgomery, Mrs. Montgomery furnishing no
part of the consideration, this would be
a gift from Montgomery to her. The evidence discloses that Montgomery ordered
the lumber from the lumber company,
sold it to Willingham, and Willingham
paid Montgomery therefor by conveying
certain realty to the wife at the request
of the husband; and there is no evidence
that the wife paid or advanced any consideration whatever to the husband for
the land. Upon this state of facts this
would be clearly a gift by the husband to
the wife, and there was therefore no error
in the charge complained of.

3. The sixth ground complains of the
following charge: "If you should believe
from the evidence * * * that the deed
from Mr. Montgomery and Mrs. Montgomery to the claimant was executed
after the levy of the attachment in favor of
the plaintiff against the defendant, George
F. Montgomery, then it would be your
duty to find the property subject to the
execution." The objections to this charge
urged on the part of the plaintiff in error
were (1) that an attachment levied on the
property of Montgomery cannot affect
the purchaser for value and without fraud
who buys from Mrs. Montgomery; (2)
the doctrine of *lis pendens* only applies
where the parties to the record or liens
are the same with whom the purchaser
deals. The evidence shows that the attachment was levied upon the land as the
property of Montgomery, the husband,
April 29, 1888, and was filed in the clerk's
office May 2, 1888, and that on May 8, 1888,
Clark purchased the land from Montgomery and his wife, and the deed to him was
signed by the husband and wife. The
first objection was not sustained by the
evidence. Instead of purchasing from the
wife alone, the evidence shows that Clark
purchased from the husband and wife,
and the deed he took was signed by both;
and this purchase was made after the
land had been levied upon as the property
of the husband, and the levy had been filed
in the clerk's office. He was therefore
affected with notice of the pendency of the
suit, and of the seizure of the property as
the property of the husband. The doctrine of *lis pendens* clearly applies under
such a state of facts.

4. It was also objected to the charge of
the court that the doctrine of *lis pendens*
would not apply in this case because the
levy as entered on the attachment omitted to state the frontage of the lot, and,
as this error was not cured until after
judgment, when by order of court the levy
was amended by stating the proper frontage, *lis pendens* would only apply from
the time of the amendment. As to this

we hold that, where the description in the
levy of the attachment as returned by the
officer is otherwise definite, the omission
to set out the number of feet in the frontage of the premises on a certain street
will not prevent the doctrine of *lis pendens*
from applying to one who purchases the
same pending the levy. There was sufficient evidence to support the verdict, and
the charge of the court on the subject of
insolvency was legal and proper. Judgment affirmed.

COX v. RICHMOND & D. R. CO. MOSELEY v.
SAME. PERKINS v SAME.

(Supreme Court of Georgia. Oct. 19, 1891.)

CARRIERS OF PASSENGERS—EJECTION FROM TRAIN
—ACTION FOR DAMAGES—PLEADING.

1. A declaration sounding in tort, against a
railroad company for violation of its duty as a
common carrier, is not amendable by converting
it, in whole or in part, into an action upon contract to carry.

2. Where the declaration sets forth a cause
of action, and lays damages in general terms, it
is not vitiated by a clause which sets up that
"the entire injury is to her peace, happiness, and
feelings," although this theory of the injury be
incorrect. The action is maintainable for the
real injury embraced in the facts set out in the
declaration.

(Syllabus by the Court.)

Error from city court of Atlanta; How-
ARD VAN EPPS, Judge.

Separate actions by A. J. Cox, L. S.
Moseley, and C. I. Perkins against the
Richmond & Danville Railroad Com-
pany for wrongful ejection from a train.
Judgment for defendant in each case.
Plaintiffs bring error. Reversed.

Hoke & Burton Smith and *J. R. Whiteside,* for plaintiffs in error. *Jackson &
Jackson* and *W. S. Upshaw,* for defendant in error.

SIMMONS, J. These cases were argued
together. The petitions contained the
same allegations, and were dismissed by
the court for the same reasons, and the
decision in one case will control the others. They were actions for damages for a
tort committed upon the plaintiffs by the
servants of the railroad company, in causing them to leave the train at the wrong
station.

1. The allegations in the petitions were
sufficient to authorize a recovery by the
plaintiffs for the actual damages sustained,
and for the pain and suffering endured in
being left in the woods, and in traveling
to their homes on foot in the night-time.
The fact that they alleged "the entire injury" was to their "peace, happiness, and
feelings" did not destroy the force and
effect of their former allegation in regard
to their general damages. A court must
construe a declaration according to the
facts set out therein, and not according to
the conclusions of the pleader. If the allegations in the declaration set out facts
which make it an action on the case, and
the pleader erroneously styles it an action
of *assumpsit,* his calling it *assumpsit* does
not make it so if the facts pleaded show it
is case. We think, therefore, the court
erred in dismissing these cases because the
pleader alleged that the entire injury to

the plaintiffs was to their peace, happiness, and feelings. If the pleader had stated in the declarations that, upon the facts set out, no damages were claimed, except those arising from the injury to the peace, happiness, and feelings, possibly the court would have been right in dismissing the cases. But the pleader did not do this. He alleged sufficient facts to authorize the recovery of general damages, and, this being so, the fact that he undertook to classify the damages, and classified them wrong, would not authorize the court to dismiss the case when the declaration showed that she was entitled to recover general damages.

2. There was no error in disallowing the amendments offered by the plaintiffs in the court below. As we have already remarked, these were cases sounding in tort, and the amendments offered were counts sounding in contract; and we think, under our Code, an action sounding in tort cannot be amended by adding a count sounding in contract. Judgment reversed.

FULTON COUNTY ST. R. Co. *et al.* v. MC-
CONNELL.

(*Supreme Court of Georgia.* Oct. 19, 1891.)

STREET RAILWAYS—CONSTRUCTION OF ROAD—NEG-
LIGENCE OF CONTRACTOR.

1. Where a street-railway company, having authority under its charter to construct a railway in the public street, does the work by an independent contractor, and an injury to a person passing along the street is caused by the negligence of a servant of the contractor, which negligence consisted in unnecessarily and improperly laying down loose iron rails in advance of the workmen engaged in constructing the track, the contractor is liable for the consequences of such negligence, but the railway company is not, the latter company not having reserved any control over the conduct of the former in executing the work.

2. The evidence warranted the recovery against the contractor, and the judgment is affirmed to that extent, but reversed so far as the railway company is concerned.

(*Syllabus by the Court.*)

Error from city court of Atlanta; How-
ARD VAN EPPS, Judge.

Action for personal injuries by William McConnell against the Fulton County Street-Railroad Company and the Thomson-Houston Electric Company. Judgment for plaintiff against both defendants jointly. Defendants bring error. Affirmed as to the electric company, and reversed as to the railway company.

Candler & Thomson and *N. J. & T A. Hammond,* for plaintiffs in error. *J. L. McWhorter, R. Arnold,* and *R. R. Arnold,* for defendant in error.

SIMMONS, J. The Fulton County Street-Railroad Company obtained a charter from the legislature authorizing it to build a street railroad through certain streets of the city of Atlanta when it should obtain the consent of the municipal authorities. It seems this consent was obtained by the company, and it made a contract with the Thomson-Houston Electric Company, another corporation, whereby the latter undertook to furnish all the material and the entire construction of the road, with-

out any direction or control reserved to the street-railroad company. During the progress of the work upon West Peachtree street, the contractor laid the iron rails about eight feet apart on each side of the proposed road-bed, a considerable distance beyond and ahead of the place where its hands were taking up a pavement and preparing the road-bed for the cross-ties and iron. The rails thus laid furnished a continuous line on each side of where the road-bed was to be placed, for a considerable distance ahead of the hands. McConnell was riding on horseback upon that street, and, in attempting to cross the street where these iron rails were laid, the horse struck his foot against one of the rails, and fell, seriously injuring McConnell. He brought his action for damages against the street-railroad company and the Thomson-Houston Electric Company jointly. On the trial of the case, under the charge of the court, the jury returned a verdict against both defendants. A motion for a new trial was made, and overruled.

1. The first three grounds of the motion for a new trial are the usual ones, that the verdict was contrary to law, evidence, etc. The fourth ground complains that the verdict was contrary to law and evidence, in this: that there was no evidence showing that the injury to the plaintiff was occasioned by any act or acts of the defendants, or either of them, set forth in the declaration. There was sufficient evidence, in our opinion, to authorize the jury to find a verdict against the Thomson-Houston Electric Company. The evidence shows that the foreman of the squad of hands who were constructing the road upon this particular street had the iron rails taken from the gutters on each side of the street, and placed in the middle of the street for a considerable distance in advance of the place at which the hands were at work. The foreman testified, in substance, that it would have been safer to have let the rails remain in the gutters until they were actually needed; but to expedite the work, and to mark the lines to guide the hands in taking up the Belgian blocks and making the proper excavations, he had the rails taken from the gutters, and laid in the middle of the street in advance of the work, and that it was not necessary at that time to have placed the rails in the middle of the street; that the lines to guide the hands might have been made by other means, which would have been safe. His testimony shows that there were two ways to mark the lines to guide the hands,—one safe and the other unsafe. Where a person or corporation is authorized by law to obstruct the public streets of a city for any purpose, it is incumbent on him or it to exercise great care to prevent passengers along the streets from being injured; and if in the progress of the work it becomes necessary to do a certain thing, and there are two ways of doing it, one safe and the other unsafe and unnecessary, if the unsafe method is adopted, and a person is injured thereby, it is such negligence on the part of the person or corporation performing the work as would au-

thorize the party injured to recover damages. Although a person may have authority to obstruct the street for the purpose of constructing a railroad track therein, he has no right to obstruct more of that street than is necessary for the proper performance of his work at that time and place. He has no right to put obstructions far in advance of the work which is being performed, and which are unnecessary at that time to enable him to carry on his work. The people have a right to the use of the streets as well as the street-railroad companies or their contractors, and neither the companies nor their contractors have a right to prevent the free use of and access to the streets by the people, except at times and places where it is necessary for the companies or contractors to occupy them; and if they should place unnecessary obstructions in the street, and a passenger in the street should be injured thereby, they would be liable, unless the injury could have been avoided by the exercise of due care on the part of the passenger. We therefore think the court did not err in overruling the motion for a new trial as to the Thomson-Houston Electric Company

2. The case of the Fulton County Street-Railroad Company presents a different view. The evidence shows that it made a contract with the Thompson-Houston Electric Company to construct the road-bed of its line. The latter company was to furnish all the material, and was not to be subject to the direction or control of the former company This made it an independent contractor, and not the servant or agent of the Fulton County Street-Railroad Company. Our Code, § 2962, declares: "The employer is not responsible for torts committed by his employe when the latter exercises an independent business, and in it is not subject to the immediate direction and control of the employer." To this general principle we held in the case of Railroad Co. v. Kimberly, 13 S. E. Rep. 277, there are certain exceptions. The evidence does not show that this case falls within either or any of the exceptions stated in that case. The work in constructing the road was not wrongful in itself, the company having obtained authority from the legislature and the consent of the municipal authorities. Nor would the work result in a nuisance, for the same reason. Nor was it, according to previous knowledge and experience, in its nature dangerous to others, if carefully performed. It was not a violation of a duty imposed by express contract upon the employer. Nor was the duty of constructing the road imposed by statute upon the company obtaining the charter. The company did not retain the right, in its contract, to direct and control the time and manner of executing the work. Nor did it ratify the wrongful act of the contractor. So, as before remarked, the evidence does not bring the street-railroad company within any of the exceptions to the general rule laid down in the Kimberly Case. If the independent contractor is guilty of an act of negligence which causes injury to a third person, and the evidence shows that

the act does not fall within any of these exceptions, the employer is not liable. This is the rule in regard to all employers and independent contractors. It was argued, however, by counsel for the defendant in error, that this rule does not apply where the work is to be performed in a public thoroughfare; that the license to obstruct the street was given specially to the railroad company, and could not be delegated to the contractor; that where railroads are built in a public thoroughfare the rights of the public to the use of the thoroughfare are involved, and the rule should be stricter than where the rights of individuals merely are affected. We have been unable to find any case where this distinction is recognised; but, on the contrary, in Overton v. Freeman, 11 C. B 567, MAULE, J., in replying to this identical argument, says: "It is insisted that there is some greater degree of liability in respect of this being a public wrong than would ordinarily attach in the case of a mere private injury. I do not, however, perceive that there is any distinction between the two which is at all favorable to the plaintiff's argument. I rather think the liability for a public wrong is less extensive than the civil liability. A man is often civilly liable where no wrong was intended " The facts of that case are more like those of the case under consideration than are the facts of any other we have found. The parish officers of a certain district contracted with A. to pave a certain district, and A. entered into a subcontract with B., under which the latter was to lay down the paving of a street, the materials being supplied by A., and brought to the spot in his carts. Preparatory to the paving, the stones were laid, by laborers employed by B., on the pathway, and there left unguarded at night, in such a manner as to obstruct the same, and C. fell over them, and broke his leg. It was held that B. was responsible for this negligence, and not A. The rule announced in the Code,—which is simply declaratory of the common law,—is a broad one, and applies to all independent contractors, regardless of whether the work is to be performed in a thoroughfare, where public rights are involved, or in a place where private rights only are affected. The courts would have no right to apply it in the one class of cases and refuse to apply it in the other. The legislature alone can do this, if in its wisdom it sees proper. On the subject of employers and independent contractors, see Railroad Co. v. Kimberly, supra, and authorities cited; also Hackett v. Telegraph Co., (Wis.) 49 N. W. Rep. 822. We think, therefore, that the court erred in not granting a new trial to the Fulton County Street-Railroad Company. The judgment is affirmed as to the Thomson-Houston Electric Company, and reversed as to the Fulton County Street-Railroad Company.

POWELL v. STATE.

(Supreme Court of Georgia. Nov. 2, 1891.)

LARCENY—INDICTMENT—EVIDENCE—NEW TRIAL.

1. An indictment for larceny from the person which charges that the defendant "did wrong

fully and fraudulently and privately take from the person of one C. A. Dunwoody, Jr., and without the knowledge of the said Dunwoody, with intent to steal the same, one watch and chain of the value of seventy-five dollars, and the property of the said Dunwoody," is sufficiently specific in the description of the property stolen. Williams v State, 25 Ind. 150; 2 Bish. Crim. Proc. § 700; Sanders v. State, 86 Ga. 717, 13 S. E. Rep. 1058.

2. Where the indictment charges that the property stolen from the person was of the value of $75, and the jury return a general verdict of guilty, the conviction, under section 4411 of the Code, is one of felony, and not of misdemeanor; and, there being no evidence of the value of the property, the accused is entitled to a new trial.

(Syllabus by the Court.)

Error from superior court, Fulton county, RICHARD H. CLARK, Judge.

Indictment against Thomas Powell for larceny. Defendant was convicted, and brings error. Reversed.

The following is the official report·

Powell demurred to the indictment against him, upon the ground that the property charged to have been stolen was not sufficiently described in the indictment. The property was described as "one watch and chain of the value of $75." The demurrer was overruled, and to this he excepted. He was found guilty, and his motion for new trial was overruled, to which also he excepted. In addition to the usual grounds of the motion, that the verdict was contrary to law, evidence, etc., it was alleged therein that the court erred in charging: "Larceny is committed by privately, slyly, stealthily, committing the larceny upon the person, taking the property in question from the person." It was alleged that this was error, in that the most essential element of larceny from the person was left out, to-wit, "with intent to steal the same." In a note to this ground the court states that by reference to the general charge it would be found that, before charging as excepted to, he gave in full the definition of larceny as in the Code. It was also alleged that a new trial should be granted because the state failed to prove that the watch in question was of any value; that, while it was admitted in evidence without objection, the same was not turned over to the jury, nor did the jury handle it, nor did counsel for defendant know that it was not in the hands of the jury until they returned their verdict. In a note to this ground the court states. The bill of indictment charged the watch to be worth $75. There was no proof of the present value of the watch. It became a question after the rendition of the verdict whether the punishment should be as for a felony or misdemeanor. The solicitor general stated that he intended it as a misdemeanor, as he knew a second-hand watch that cost $75 was not worth as much as $50, and he so considered it during the trial. The solicitor general also contended that there was an agreement between him and defendant's counsel that the case should be judged a misdemeanor, but this defendant's counsel denied. Under the evidence and circumstances narrated, the court treated the conviction as for a misdemeanor, and made the penalty according-

ly. In an addition by the court to the brief of evidence, he states that the watch had the appearance of gold, was in full view of the jury, and in the progress of the case no question was made that it was not as it appeared, nor any question as to any defect in the watch.

R. J. Jordan, for plaintiff in error. C. D. Hill, Sol. Gen., for the State.

PER CURIAM. Judgment reversed.

BILLUPS v. STATE.

(Supreme Court of Georgia. Nov. 2, 1891.)

FORGERY—WHAT CONSTITUTES.

Under section 4451 of the Code, an indictment will lie for forging an instrument in the following terms: "Atlanta, Ga., May 9th, 1891. Mr. Williams: I will keep back two dollars a week from Bob's wages until the debt that he owes you is paid. I will be responsible for the two dollars as long as he works for me. Respectfully, HENRY AKINS;" the charge being that the act of forgery was done to defraud said Akins. This writing might have defrauded, or been used to defraud, Akins, and was therefore a subject-matter of forgery. Travis v. State, 83 Ga. 372, 9 S. E. Rep. 1063.

(Syllabus by the Court.)

Error from superior court, Fulton county; RICHARD H. CLARK, Judge.

Indictment against Bob Billups for forgery. Defendant was convicted, and brings error. Affirmed.

The following is the official report:

Billups was charged with forgery upon an indictment in the following terms: "For that the said Bob Billups, in the county aforesaid, on the 9th of May, in the year of our Lord eighteen hundred and ninety-one, with force and arms, did falsely and fraudulently make and forge the following writing, to-wit: 'Atlanta, Ga., May 9th, 1891. Mr Williams: I will keep back two dollars a week from Bob's wages until the debt that he owes you is paid. I will be responsible for the two dollars as long as he works for me. Respectfully, HENRY AKINS,'—with intent to defraud Henry Akins; and the said Bob Billups did utter and publish said writing as true upon James Williams, knowing the same to have been so falsely and fraudulently made and forged with intent to defraud him, the said Williams." The jury rendered a general verdict of guilty, and he moved in arrest of judgment, which motion was overruled, and to this he excepted. The motion was upon the following grounds: Because no legal judgment could be based upon the indictment; because the verdict was general, and did not specify upon which count in the indictment it was based; because no legal indictment, under section 4451 of the Code, had been found or returned; because the instrument alleged to have been forged was not such an instrument as to furnish the basis of a prosecution for forgery, in this: It was not an instrument calculated to deceive or defraud any one. It was not an unconditional promise to pay money or other thing of value. The labor or work by the defendant was of the essence of the order. The writing, if it showed anything, showed that Akins only agreed to pay the debt of another upon certain conditions, and nothing in the face of the writing or indictment showed that the conditions had been complied with, and nothing appeared on the face of the written instrument, showing that, if true and properly published and uttered, the party purporting to have executed the instrument would have been liable or bound, and no liability was created on the face of the paper.

J T. Spence, and *F. R. & J. G. Walker*, for plaintiff in error. *C. D. Hill*, Sol. Gen., for the State.

PER CURIAM. Judgment affirmed.

GEORGIA RAILROAD & BANKING CO. *v.* BAKER *et al.*

(*Supreme Court of Georgia.* Nov. 2, 1891.)

RAILROAD COMPANIES—CONSTRUCTION OF EMBANKMENT—ACTION FOR DAMAGES—INSTRUCTIONS.

1. The charge complained of in this case was that no express instruction to allow damage on account of depreciation of rental value as to the other property generally, and also for rent of the part of the alley occupied by the embankment; and, the amount of the verdict not appearing in the record, there is no presumption that the jury allowed such double damages.

2. The evidence warranted a recovery.

(*Syllabus by the Court.*)

Error from superior court, Fulton county; MARSHALL J. CLARKE, Judge.

Action by J. M. Baker and another against the Georgia Railroad & Banking Company. Judgment for plaintiffs. Defendant brings error. Affirmed.

The following is the official report:

· J. M. Baker, for himself and as next friend of his son, sued the railroad company for damages, which he alleged they sustained by the building of an embankment by the defendant, which projected 12 feet over their land, (a lot in the city of Atlanta, fronting for 100 feet the right of way of the railroad company, and running back 200 feet,) and by defendant's wrongfully causing water collected upon its premises to empty upon this lot. There was a verdict for the plaintiff, but what the amount of that verdict was does not appear, and the verdict was not specified in the bill of exceptions as a portion of the record which should be sent to this court. Defendant made a motion for a new trial, which was overruled, and to this it excepted. In addition to the general grounds of the motion that the verdict was contrary to law, evidence, etc., it was alleged therein that a new trial should be granted, because the damages found were excessive, and because the verdict was contrary to certain specified portions of the charge of the court. Also because the court erred in charging: "The plaintiff says that he has been damaged in two particulars: One is that he has been deprived by the embankment in question of the rental value of so much of the ground as it covers, the other is that, as the plaintiff says, the taking of this ground for the defendant's use, and the making of a ditch by the surface waters, has rendered the other part of his lot less valuable from the property. Now, you gentle-

men will look carefully into the evidence in regard to these matters, and make a verdict in accordance with the result which you reach." It was alleged that the error in this charge consisted in the submission of the case to the jury on the theory that plaintiffs could recover damages on the same piece of ground on account of being deprived of use of it by himself in both of two ways, each incompatible with the other, when, under the evidence, he could recover for only one of the uses of which he had been deprived. Also because the amount of the verdict was illegal and excessive, in this: Damages on the basis of what this strip of ground in question would rent for, if it had a valuable house on it, are too remote and hypothetical to support any recovery for the same.

J. B. Cumming, *Bryan Cumming*, and *Hillyer & Bro.*, for plaintiff in error. *E. W. Martin*, for defendants in error.

PER CURIAM. Judgment affirmed.

FOWLER *v* GATE CITY NAT. BANK.

(*Supreme Court of Georgia.* Nov. 2, 1891.)

BILLS OF EXCHANGE—ACCEPTANCE—INDORSEMENT—ACTION ON—PLEADING.

1. Where the drawee of a bill of exchange writes his name across the face of the bill, the statute requiring acceptance to be in writing is complied with, the legal significance of such an act being that the bill is thereby accepted.

2. The indorsee of a bill of exchange, in the absence of any notice on the subject, is entitled to treat the acceptor as the real debtor, and is under no duty to such acceptor to retain, or render available, collateral securities for the payment of the bill received from the payee and indorser thereof.

3. A plea of *non est factum* must be sworn to, and generally the affidavit must be made by the defendant, and not by an agent. The exception, if any, is stated in section 3449 of the Code.

4. A plea which neither admits nor denies that the plaintiff herself, or any one as her agent, accepted the bill sued on, but sets up merely that the acceptance is not binding on her for the reason that said act was not in her legitimate business or for her benefit, but for the benefit of a third party, and without authority, consent, or ratification on her part, is insufficient.

(*Syllabus by the Court.*)

Error from superior court, Fulton county, MARSHALL J. CLARKE, Judge.

Action by the Gate City National Bank against May E. Fowler and others. Judgment for plaintiff, and defendant Fowler brings error. Affirmed.

The following is the official report:

The Gate City National Bank sued the Tolleson Commission Company as drawer and indorser, May E. Fowler, doing business under the name and style of Fowler & Co., as acceptor, and E. L. Fowler as acceptor, of certain drafts or bills. Mrs. Fowler pleaded the general issue, and also a special plea denying that she composed the firm of Fowler & Co. On the trial of the case she offered the following plea: "If the jury should believe that the firm of Fowler & Co. was composed of this defendant, and that E. L. Fowler was her agent, then, in that event, she says that the writing of the name of Fowler & Co. on the face of said drafts or bills by said E. L. Fowler is not binding on her.

for the reason that said act was not in the legitimate business of this defendant, nor was it for her benefit, but for the benefit of a third party, and was without authority, consent, or ratification on her part. For further plea, this defendant says that the drafts or bills sued on were secured by bills of lading representing cars of grain, flour, and other stuff, turned over to plaintiff by J. R. Tolleson, representing the Tolleson Commission Company, as this defendant is informed; and if the plaintiff redelivered them to Tolleson, and he realized the money on the same, and it was not applied to these drafts, such conduct on the part of the plaintiff would discharge this defendant, she not consenting to the same; and, if the same is still in the possession of plaintiff, the railroad companies issuing the same are liable to plaintiff on said bills of lading; and, before this defendant could be held liable to plaintiff, said bills of lading should be brought into court, and tendered this defendant, as in law, if liable, she has a lien on the same." On motion of plaintiff, this plea was stricken by the court for insufficiency and as setting up no legal defense. To this ruling she excepted. After this plea was stricken she offered the following plea: "Now comes defendant, by her attorney, and withdraws the plea filed on the 15th day of June, 1888, to-wit, the special plea, and says the business being conducted at the time she was sued was a grocery business; that her husband was conducting the same, and the style of the firm was Fowler & Co.; that, acting as her agent, he wrote the name of Fowler & Co. on said drafts or bills, and the same was in no wise connected with the business of Fowler & Co., nor was any part of said money paid by plaintiffs on said drafts received by this defendant or her agent E. L. Fowler; that said act was without authority or consent on her part, nor did she know of it till long after said drafts were signed, nor has she in any way ratified said act; that, if anybody is liable to plaintiffs on said drafts, it is her agent, E. L. Fowler, and not this defendant." On motion of plaintiff, this plea was stricken by the court for insufficiency, and as not setting up any legal defense, and as not having been sworn to by her. (The plea was sworn to by E. L. Fowler, "agent for May E. Fowler.") To this ruling, also, she excepted. Upon the striking of this plea she offered the following plea: "Now comes defendant, May E. Fowler, and by leave of the court amends her plea, and says that if the name of Fowler & Co., written across the face of the drafts or bills sued on, is construed to be an acceptance, that it was an accommmodation acceptance; that she got no part of said money; and the same was applied by plaintiff to the credit of the Tolleson Commission Company, which was dealing with plaintiff. Defendant further says that the bills of lading attached to said drafts were turned over to plaintiff by defendant, the Tolleson Commission Company, and, if proper diligence had been used on part of plaintiff, the property represented by said bills of lading would have

more than canceled said drafts, and if plaintiff allowed the same to remain in the custody of the Tolleson Commission Company it was without her knowledge or consent; that said conduct increased her risk; and she is thereby discharged from any liability on said drafts or bills,"—which, on motion of plaintiff's counsel, was stricken, on the ground that it set up no legal defense. To this ruling, also, she excepted The drafts were then tendered in evidence, and objected to by her counsel, on the ground that she was sued as acceptor, and writing the name on the face of a draft, without more, did not constitute an acceptance under section 1950 of the Code. This objection was overruled, and the drafts admitted; to which ruling, also, she excepted. The drafts were drawn by the Tolleson Commission Company, payable to the order of that company, upon Fowler & Co., and written across their face was the name "Fowler & Co." The plea of the general issue was then withdrawn, and the plaintiff was allowed by the court to take judgment against her, plaintiff having dismissed as to the Tolleson Commission Company and as to E. L. Fowler; to which judgment, also, she excepted.

R. J. Jordan, for plaintiff in error. Calhoun, King & Spalding, for defendant in error.

Per Curiam. Judgment affirmed.

Livingston v. Wright et al.

(Supreme Court of Georgia. Nov. 2, 1891.)

Tax-Sale—Collusion—Rights of Mortgagee.

1. Where the claimant admits that he paid to the defendant a considerable amount on purchasing the land in question from a third person who had purchased at a tax-sale, it was not error for the court to charge the jury that if they believed from the evidence that the defendant, for the purpose of defrauding his creditors, suffered the property to go to sale for taxes, and that the purchaser at that sale at the time he received his deed either knew of this fraudulent purpose or had grounds for reasonable suspicion that it existed, and if they further believed that when the deed from such purchaser to the claimant was executed the claimant also knew of such fraudulent purpose on the part of the defendant or had grounds for reasonable suspicion, the jury ought to find that the tax-title is void as against the plaintiffs in fi. fa., (these plaintiffs being mortgagees of the property by a mortgage executed prior to the tax-sale, and the fi. fa. being founded on the judgment of foreclosure.)

2. The evidence warranted the verdict.

(Syllabus by the Court.)

Error from superior court, Fulton county; Marshall J. Clarke, Judge.

A mortgage fi. fa. in favor of Wright & Hilly against Charles Harper having been levied on the realty covered by the mortgage, Jackson Livingston filed a claim thereto. From a judgment against him claimant brings error. Affirmed.

The following is the official report:

A mortgage fi. fa. in favor of Wright & Hilly against Charles Harper was levied upon certain realty covered by the mortgage, and the same was claimed by Livingston under a tax-title, the sale for taxes having been made after the execution of the mortgage. The property was found subject, and Livingston's motion for a new trial was overruled, to which he excepted. In addition to the usual grounds of the motion that the verdict was contrary to law, evidence, etc., it was insisted therein that the verdict was contrary to a specified portion of the charge of the court, and also that the court erred in charging: "If you believe from the evidence that the defendant, Charles Harper, for the purpose of defrauding his creditors, suffered his property to go to sale for taxes; that at such sale John S. Owens became the purchaser; that a deed was executed to Owens in pursuance of such purchase; that Owens, at the time he received his deed, either knew of this fraudulent purpose on the part of Harper, or had ground for reasonable suspicion that it existed; and further believe that, when the deed was executed from Owens to Livingston, Livingston either knew of such fraudulent purpose on the part of Harper, or had grounds for reasonable suspicion that such purpose was entertained,—then you ought to find that the tax-title is void as against this mortgage fi. fa."

Blalock & Birney, for plaintiff in error.
Mayson & Hill, for defendant in error.

PER CURIAM. Judgment affirmed.

RICHMOND & D. R. Co. v. KERLER.

(Supreme Court of Georgia. Nov. 10, 1891.)

CARRIERS OF GOODS — NEGLIGENCE — ADMISSIONS.

1. The admissions contained in a letter are to be scanned with care if they are susceptible of more than one construction, and if, in order to discover their true meaning, attention should be directed to the precise terms employed by the writer.

2. The evidence warranted the verdict.

(Syllabus by the Court.)

Error from city court of Atlanta; HOWARD VAN EPPS, Judge.

Action by Charles Kerler, Jr., against the Richmond & Danville Railroad Company. Judgment for plaintiff. Defendant brings error. Affirmed.

Jackson & Jackson, for plaintiff in error.
Moyers & Skeen, for defendant in error.

SIMMONS, J. The plaintiff sued the railroad company for $500, on account of damages to certain furniture shipped over its line, and obtained a verdict for $225. On the trial, the defendant introduced in evidence, as an admission of the plaintiff as to the amount of damage, his letter to an agent of the defendant, setting forth his claim, in which he said, "$100 will not do more than cover the loss, and I hereby make claim for this amount." In regard to this testimony the court charged the jury as follows: "Admissions are to be scanned with care. If it appear to your satisfaction that the plaintiff made the statement or declaration which is contained in a letter introduced in evidence, you are to scan the same with care, giving to it such weight as you deem proper, taking into consideration the words and the circumstances under which they were

written, and all the facts and surrounding circumstances." This charge is excepted to as error. We find no error in the instruction complained of. The general rule was correctly stated by the court. The language of the Code is that "all admissions should be scanned with care." Section 3792. Where more than one construction of the statement is possible, this rule is especially applicable, and the jury should carefully consider the language used, and such facts and circumstances as may explain its true intent and meaning. Even if this were in terms a statement that $100 would cover the damage, it would not preclude the party making it from showing that he was mistaken, or anything else affecting its weight as an admission. The statement that "$100 will not do more than cover the loss, and I hereby make claim for this amount," is not necessarily an admission that $100 would cover the loss, even though such might be a reasonable construction. According to the testimony of the plaintiff, his damage was much greater than that amount; but his purpose in writing the letter was to fix upon that sum as an amount he would be willing to accept rather than to be put to the difficulty, expense, and delay of collecting his claim at law. The uncontradicted evidence, outside of this letter, was that the damage amounted to from $350 to $400. Under the evidence the charge of the court was proper, and the verdict should stand. See Stewart v. De Loach, 86 Ga. 729, 12 S. E. Rep. 1067. Judgment affirmed.

ATLANTA GLASS CO. v. NOIZET.

(Supreme Court of Georgia. Nov. 10, 1891.)

PLEADING — HARMLESS ERROR — HEARSAY EVIDENCE.

1. A plea which alleges no special damage is to be construed as one which claims general damages only; and where such a plea is improperly stricken, but the defendant is nevertheless allowed the benefit of it on the trial, the error of striking it is not cause for a new trial.

2. Unless it affirmatively appears that evidence is hearsay, it is not to be excluded as such where it is of a nature which admits of its resting on the personal knowledge of the witness.

(Syllabus by the Court.)

Error from superior court, Fulton county; MARSHALL J. CLARKE, Judge.

Action by L. Noizet against the Atlanta Glass Company. Judgment for plaintiff. Defendant brings error. Affirmed.

E. W. Martin, for plaintiff in error.
King & Anderson, for defendant in error.

SIMMONS, J. Noizet brought his action against the Atlanta Glass Company "for machinery furnished to it, and work and labor done in making said machinery, in attaching it to the premises of said company, and in repairing other machinery at the works of the company." The defendant filed the plea of the general issue, and several special pleas, denying in one of them that it had purchased the machinery sued for, or authorized any one else to purchase it, and alleging that the plaintiff and one Weyer colluded together for the purpose of defrauding in the matter; that he and Weyer were interested as partners in making the machinery; and that, for the purpose of defrauding the defendant, Weyer, who was the defendant's superintendent of the manufacture of glass, gave the orders for the machinery under the pretense that it was needed for the work of the defendant; and that the plaintiff was notified, before the machinery was furnished, not to furnish it, and that Weyer had no authority to order it. In another plea it was alleged that the machinery was furnished with the implied warranty that it was merchantable, and reasonably suited to the use intended, and that the plaintiff knew of no latent defects undisclosed; and the defendant averred that, on the contrary, it was useless. The fourth special plea was as follows: "The retorts and other things specified in the said account, by reason of defects both in the material and construction, had to be continually changed, which caused great detention in the work of manufacturing defendant's glass, owing to which defendant is damaged in the sum of five hundred dollars, which said sum defendant recoups for its damages for same against plaintiff." Another plea alleges that "the items in said account, which is the consideration of the demand sued on, were useless, and of no value for the purposes intended, and that the said consideration has totally failed." The fourth plea above set out was stricken on demurrer. The plaintiff had a verdict, and the defendant moved for a new trial. The motion was overruled, and it excepted. The main grounds relied on for reversal of the judgment of the court below were alleged error in striking the fourth plea of the defendant, and ruling out certain testimony of Pinson.

1. Treating the plea in question as a special plea of recoupment, the court would have been right in striking it if there had been a special demurrer thereto, and in refusing to allow the defendant to introduce any evidence thereunder tending to show special damages. A plea of recoupment is a cross-action by the defendant against the plaintiff, and should be as certain and definite in its allegations of damage as the allegations in a declaration should be. It should set out in detail how and when the damage was sustained. Simply saying that the machinery, "by reason of defects in material and construction, had to be continually changed, which caused great detention in the work of manufacturing defendant's glass, owing to which defendant was damaged in the sum of $500, which said sum defendant recoups for its damages for same against plaintiff," is not sufficient. "It states conclusions and not facts; it deals with generalities, and not in particulars." In the case of McKleroy v. Sewell, 73 Ga. 657, it is said: "To state in a plea of set-off that an overdose of ipecac damaged a man $200, without stating wherein and how, is too loose, and does not set out the defense plainly and distinctly." In the case of Kinard v. Sanford, 64 Ga. 630, it is said: "The plea of set-off being a cross-action brought by the defendant against the plaintiff, it

should set out his demand as fully and distinctly as though he were the plaintiff;" and it was further held that the plea of recoupment was not sufficient, the contract not being sufficiently set out, and the damages claimed appearing to be contingent and speculative. In Insurance Co. v. Carrugi, 41 Ga. 672, it is said: "Under our system of sending the whole case to the jury on the declaration and pleas, without a replication, we think it best that the pleas should go somewhat into detail."

Inasmuch as the plea contained no allegation of special damage, but only an allegation of general damages, and there being no special demurrer thereto, it should have been treated and considered by the court as a plea of general damages; and we are inclined to think the court erred in striking it. But, while the court may have erred in this, we do not think the error was a material one. The record shows that the defendant put in all the evidence he was entitled to introduce under this kind of plea. Where a plea is erroneously stricken by the court, and yet the defendant is allowed to introduce evidence to sustain the allegations therein, the striking of the plea is not reversible error. Insurance Co. v. Carrugi, supra. The jury must have considered it, because the verdict showed that they reduced the amount claimed by the plaintiff. The defendant was allowed to show all the damages it had well pleaded in the plea which had been stricken. That part of the testimony of Pinson set out in the eighth ground of the motion, which the court ruled out after the plea was stricken, and which related to profits and loss of the glass company, would not have been admissible, even if the demurrer to the plea had not been sustained. There was nothing in the plea to authorize that kind of testimony.

2. The plaintiff's testimony was taken by interrogatories, and in them he testified that he was employed by Weyer and Dr. Pinson; that Weyer received orders from Pinson, and transmitted them to Noiset, for all the articles mentioned between Nos. 2 and 3 in the interrogatories; that Weyer was the glass-maker of the company, and was the only man that knew anything about the glass factory, and the material it needed, but delivered orders, with Dr. Pinson's assent, for material and work mentioned in Exhibit A. This testimony was objected to because the answers were hearsay, as complained in the fourth and fifth grounds of the motion for a new trial. It is doubtful whether the witness was testifying from hearsay or from his own knowledge when he said Weyer received orders from Pinson, and delivered orders, with Pinson's assent, for material, etc. He may have been testifying from his own knowledge of the facts. He may have been present when Weyer received orders from Pinson, and may have heard Pinson assent to them. Taking the whole of the witness' testimony together, as it appears in this record it would seem that he was testifying of his own knowledge. However that may be, it does not appear to us affirm-

atively that he was testifying from hear-say; and, unless it should so appear, we could not hold that the court erred in allowing the testimony

3. There was no error in refusing to grant the motion upon the other grounds taken therein and not herein mentioned.

Judgment affirmed.

BRUNSWICK & W. R. Co. v. MAYOR, ETC., OF CITY OF WAYCROSS et al.

(*Supreme Court of Georgia.* Nov. 10, 1891.)

INJUNCTION—BUILDING RAILROAD TRACK.

There was no abuse of discretion in granting the injunction complained of.

(*Syllabus by the Court.*)

Error from superior court, Ware county; SPENCER R. ATKINSON, Judge.

Suit for an injunction by the Brunswick & Western Railroad Company against the mayor and council of Waycross and others. Defendants answered in the nature of a cross-bill, and prayed an injunction against the railroad company, which was granted. The railroad company brings error. Affirmed.

The following is the official report:

The Brunswick & Western Railroad Company commenced the construction of a side track or Y to make a connection with the track of another railroad. The line of this additional track crossed a street in the town of Waycross, which was already crossed by the main track of the Brunswick & Western Railroad. The city authorities interfered, and the railroad company made application for injunction. The city answered in the nature of a cross-bill, and prayed that the railroad company be enjoined from constructing the proposed track across the street. The judge below refused the injunction asked by the railroad company, and granted the injunction asked by the city. On the hearing for temporary injunction before the judge below, the following appeared: In September, 1860, the Brunswick & Florida Railroad Company, by purchase, acquired a strip of land 100 feet in width on each side, measured from the center of its track, through a lot of land in Ware county, and soon after constructed its road through the land, and has been, through its various successors, the last of which is the Brunswick & Western Railroad Company, in constant use and occupancy of its road-way to the present time, running and regularly operating it as a railroad. In 1872, long after the completion of the railroad, the town of Waycross was laid out, covering a portion of the lot of land mentioned. One of its streets, now known as "Plant Avenue," was laid out at right angles to and extending across the right of way and road-bed of the railroad company. There was no evidence of an express grant of the city authorities of this right so to lay off its streets, but the crossing so made has been in constant use by the city since it was first established, is now the principal thoroughfare of the city, and the crossing thus established has been maintained and kept up by the railroad company ever since. This street is the one along which most of the travel passes between the two sections of the town. Upon the strip of land 100 feet in width, lying to the northward of its track, the railroad company commenced the construction of the Y in question. It alleged in its petition that in the putting in of the Y it was its purpose to so construct it that it should be no obstruction to the passage of persons, vehicles, and property across Plant avenue; and that it was not its purpose to block up Plant avenue with cars, but solely to furnish a connection for the passage of cars and engines, and running the same from the main line of the Savannah, Florida & Western Railway to the railway yard of petitioner, and from its yard to the main line of the Savannah, Florida & Western Railway. No proceeding to condemn the way for Plant avenue across the railroad track was ever instituted, and no deed conveying to the town authorities the right to appropriate the land for the purpose of a street was shown. The judge below held that the city had acquired no right by prescription, for the reason that 20 years had not elapsed since the first appropriation by the city; but he further held that, under the facts above stated, the construction and use of the street across the railroad track, and through the strip of land, with the knowledge of the railroad company, its maintenance as a public way for so many years, until it became the principal thoroughfare in a now populous town, and the principal street leading to the public schools, and the railroad company having for many years kept up and maintained as public the crossing at this particular point, although it was under no obligation in law to maintain other than public crossings along the line of its tracks, a jury might find that the original entry by the public was with the consent of the railroad company, and that this permissive entry and subsequent recognition was sufficient evidence of an intention on its part to dedicate that portion of its right of way as a highway to the public; and that, by its constant use and maintenance as a street by the town authorities, a jury might find an acceptance upon the part of the public, which would make the dedication complete. He further held that, if the claim by the city of title by dedication were well founded, it would be as complete, and would as much entitle it to an uninterrupted use of the street, as though its claim were founded upon an express grant by the railroad company to the city; that if the dedication was made it was absolute, as it could not be said that a dedication once made, giving the public an absolute right, could afterwards be so modified by the grantor as to enable him to apply the fee to a use in conflict with the purposes of the dedication; and that the question was not then how great would be the inconvenience to the public, but should the public be subject to the inconvenience of the additional track or Y at all? the question of obstruction being one of principle, and not one of degree, etc.

Goodyear & Kay, S. W. Hitch, and *L. J.*

Brown, for plaintiff in error. *J. L. Sweat* and *L. A. Wilson*, for defendant in error.

PER CURIAM. Judgment affirmed.

WALLACE v. JOHNSON et al.

(Supreme Court of Georgia. Nov. 10, 1891.)

APPEAL—WHEN LIES.

Where three creditors petition under the traders' act of 1881 for injunction and the appointment of a receiver, and the petition is granted after making a fourth creditor a party to the petition, one of the creditors cannot bring to this court a writ of error, founded, not upon the judgment itself, but upon a reason given by the judge to the effect that, in granting the injunction and receiver, he did not consider this alleged creditor as having a valid debt, such reason being no adjudication of that question, and there being no order dismissing the petition as to any of the creditors. The statement of the judge as to his reason is no adjudication, final or otherwise, upon the rights of this particular creditor.

(Syllabus by the Court.)

Error from superior court, Fulton county; RICHARD H. CLARK, Judge.

Bill in the nature of a creditors' bill by F. M. Wallace and others against C. J. Johnson and another. The court granted the injunction, and appointed a receiver, but held that F. M. Wallace was not a creditor. F. M. Wallace brings error. Writ of error dismissed.

The following is the official report:

F. M. Wallace, G. W. Henderson, and the Atlanta City Brewing Company filed their equitable petition in the nature of a general creditors' bill against C. J. Johnson as their debtor, and Mrs. Emma Johnson, his sister-in-law, (to whom they alleged he had made a fraudulent sale of certain realty,) praying for injunction, receiver, etc. Upon the hearing the court granted the injunction, and appointed a receiver, but held that F. M. Wallace was not a creditor, and that Henderson was, which, leaving in the original petition but two creditors, the defect was allowed cured by an order making C. P. Johnson a party plaintiff. To the ruling that F. M. Wallace was not a creditor he excepted, and the case was brought to this court by "fast" bill of exceptions. The evidence produced in the court below, so far as relates to the question made in this court, was, on behalf of F. M. Wallace, as follows. On April 17, 1891, F. M. Wallace was in possession of and owned 2 barrels of whisky and 2,000 cigars. C. J. Johnson, through his agent, P. J. Wallace, told him, F. M. Wallace, to send down the goods in question to the store, and "they" would sell them, and account to F. M. for the value. He sent the goods to C. J. Johnson, and is informed that C. J. Johnson has disposed of them. Since that time Johnson has admitted that he owed F. M. Wallace the money for them. F. M. Wallace was engaged in the liquor, cigar, and tobacco business in the city of Atlanta prior to March 1, 1891. He had the goods mentioned above on hand at the time he quit business, and afterwards turned them over to C. J. Johnson, to be sold by him. He made no sale after these goods were turned over, and did not engage in the whisky and tobacco business after his city license expired. The goods were to be paid for by C. J. Johnson when sold. Wallace put in evidence a receipt from the tax collector of Fulton county, dated March 1, 1891, acknowledging the receipt of $50 from F. M. Wallace for special state tax on liquor for the year ending January 1, 1892. Also receipts showing that he had paid special taxes on his business as retail liquor dealer and as dealer in manufactured tobacco to the United States government. These were dated February 6, 1891. On behalf of the defendants evidence was introduced to the effect that the goods in question were not consigned by F. M. Wallace to C. J. Johnson, but were sold to Johnson & Henderson, a firm of which C. J. Johnson was then a partner; and the sale was made about the 10th or 11th of April, 1891, or between the 15th and 20th of April, 1891, or somewhere near the 10th of July, 1891. Defendants put in evidence the affidavit of one Bradly Slaughter, to the effect that the station-house docket showed that a case was made against F. M. Wallace for retailing spirituous and malt liquors without a license, March 11, 1891, and that on the hearing Wallace was adjudged guilty, and a fine was imposed upon him, which he paid; also, an affidavit from the clerk of the board of commissioners for Fulton county, to the effect that as such clerk he issues the county licenses to wholesale dealers in intoxicating liquors, and that no such license was issued to F. M. Wallace to cover any period during 1891. Defendant also put in evidence documents showing that P. J. Wallace had a license to sell whisky to June 30, 1891, and an application was made for the granting to F. M. Wallace of a license to sell whisky at the same place, which was refused by the city council of Atlanta. In his bill of exceptions F. M. Wallace alleged that the proof exclusively established the fact that C. J. Johnson was indebted to him, unless the debt was void on account of public policy, it being claimed that F. M. Wallace had no city license to sell whisky at wholesale, and that the debt was created by his selling a lot of whisky to C. J. Johnson; that F. M. Wallace claimed there was no evidence of any city ordinance of Atlanta prohibiting the sale of whisky at wholesale, no such ordinance having been introduced in evidence; and that, if such an ordinance had been introduced, the evidence did not show that Wallace had violated any such ordinance, because he had a right to sell out his stock of goods in bulk when he quit business as a retailer, without paying a special tax or license to either the city, state, and county, or to the United States, it being the policy of the law to tax a business, and not a single act, such as that in question. In a note by the court to the bill of exceptions it was stated: "It was in evidence that at the time Wallace sold liquors to Johnson he had a United States revenue license, but no license to sell at retail from the city, or license to sell at wholesale from the city or county, and upon that the court adjudged he could not legally collect his debt." As to the ordinances of the city on the subject there was no issue of fact, but it was treated by both sides as true and existing.

Simmons & Corrigan, for plaintiff in error. *R. J. Jordan*, for defendants in error.

PER CURIAM. Writ of error dismissed.

WILLIAMSBURG CITY FIRE INS. CO. v GWINN.

(*Supreme Court of Georgia.* Nov. 10, 1891.)

CONCURRENT INSURANCE — LIABILITY — CONTRIBUTION

Where one is insured concurrently in seven companies, and makes claim for his whole loss against six of the companies, and the whole loss is thus settled, conformably to the terms of the policies, and paid, the seventh company is discharged as to him, and its liability, if any, is to the other companies for contribution.

(*Syllabus by the Court.*)

Error from superior court, Fulton county; MARSHALL J. CLARKE, Judge.

Action by L. E. Gwinn against the Williamsburg Fire Insurance Company. Judgment for plaintiff. Defendant brings error. Reversed.

Calhoun, King & Spalding and *J. T. Pendleton*, for plaintiff in error. *Arnold & Arnold*, for defendant in error.

LUMPKIN, J. This case is controlled and disposed of by the principle announced in the head-note. It seems that Gwinn, the insured, had seven policies of insurance covering the property which was destroyed by fire. The sum total of all these policies amounted to considerably more than the loss sustained. It appears that at the time of the fire one of these policies, which was issued by the plaintiff in error, was not in Gwinn's possession, and that in making claim for his loss he made no demand upon this company. In the view we take of the case, it is immaterial whether he did this deliberately or by oversight. His contention was that this policy had been left with the agent of the Williamsburg City Company for the purpose of having permission for additional insurance indorsed thereon; that it was not returned to him, and at the time of the fire he overlooked the fact that he had such policy. The defense denied the existence of the policy altogether. Upon this question the testimony preponderates in favor of Gwinn's theory. Be this as it may, however, the great fact remains that he actually received from the other six companies the full amount of his loss. It is true, he testified in a general way that his settlement with those companies was the result of a compromise, and he did not receive the full amount to which he was entitled, and some of his witnesses swore that the settlement was not fair; but there were no facts or figures in proof bearing out these naked statements. The loss was arrived at and adjusted in the manner provided for by the policies themselves. It was fixed by competent appraisers, duly selected by the parties, after a careful examination into all the circumstances. The result was acceptable to Gwinn, and it nowhere appears that he made any objection to it at the time. The only just and fair conclusion from all the testimony on this subject is that Gwinn claimed and received from the six companies to whom he presented his demand full compensation for his loss. The verdict shows that the jury so believed. It is manifest they did not find that Gwinn's loss exceeded in amount the sum fixed by the appraisers. On the contrary, it appears that, taking this sum as a basis of calculation, they found one-sixth thereof against the Williamsburg City Company, with interest and attorney's fees added. It being quite plain that Gwinn has received the full amount of his loss, it seems too manifest for argument that he should not be allowed to receive or recover more than this from any source whatever. What then follows? If the Williamsburg City Company ought to have shared with the other companies in the payment of Gwinn's loss, and has not done so, and he has been paid in full, its liability ought to be to the other companies for contribution. This principle is clearly stated in 1 May, Ins. § 15. Having shown, we think, conclusively, that under the facts appearing in the record Gwinn can in no event recover of the Williamsburg City Company, the judgment below is reversed, with direction that the action be dismissed.

MOOMAUGH v. EVERETT et al.

EVERETT et al. v. MOOMAUGH.

(*Supreme Court of Georgia.* Nov. 10, 1891.)

PLEADING — REMITTITUR—APPEAL—NEW TRIAL.

1. Where the suit is in the short form of complaint for 210 bags of flour, of the value of $450, with no further allegation of damages, except that the defendants refuse to deliver the property or pay the profits thereof, there can be no recovery for more than $450, with interest thereon, there being no amendment of the declaration or offer to amend. Banking Co. v. Crawley, 87 Ga. 191, 13 S. E. Rep. 508.

2. Where the defendants in the court below move for a new trial, which is granted unless the plaintiff will write off a portion of his recovery, and thereupon the plaintiff, declining to write off, brings a writ of error upon the judgment granting a new trial, the defendants cannot by cross-bill of exceptions assign error, not as committed by the court in any of its ruling on the motion for a new trial, but as committed on the trial itself, and complained of in the motion.

(*Syllabus by the Court.*)

Cross-errors from city court of Atlanta; HOWARD VAN EPPS, Judge.

Action by Robert H. Moomaugh against George B. Everett & Co. Judgment for plaintiff, on condition that he would remit part of the verdict. Plaintiff brings error, and defendants file a cross-bill of exceptions. Judgment affirmed, with directions, and cross-bill of exceptions dismissed.

The following is the official report:

Moomaugh brought his action under section 3390 of the Code against G. B. Everett & Co. to recover 210 bags of flour, which he alleged to be of the value of $450. The action was brought on December 14, 1889, and on June 12, 1891, plaintiff obtained a verdict for $600. Defendants moved for a new trial, and the motion was granted, unless plaintiff would write off from the verdict all that was in excess of $450 as principal, with 7 per cent. interest on the same from the date of filing the declaration to the date of the verdict. To this ruling the plaintiff excepted. By cross-bill of exceptions, the defendants also excepted, alleging that the court below erred in certain charges and refusals to charge set out in the motion for a new trial, as follows: Because the court charged substantially: "This being an action to recover personal property, the plaintiff can make his election to have a verdict, either for the property, or for the highest proved value of the same between the conversion and the date of the trial. He has made this election on this trial, and if you find for him you should find such value." Because defendants' counsel claimed in his argument to the court that the rule mentioned in the last ground did not apply to such property and articles as are perishable in their nature, and likely to deteriorate rapidly in their value; and claimed, further, that the highest proved value to which the plaintiff was entitled would be that of the particular flour in question, and not that of other lots of flour of the same grade; and the court charged that, if the jury found for the plaintiff, they should find the highest proved value of flour of the same grade as that claimed in the declaration at any time since the conversion. And because the defendants' counsel made the following request to charge: "If plaintiff and Akers & Bros. agreed together to stop the flour in Atlanta, and allow Akers to substitute other goods for it, for the mutual benefit of the two parties, and against the rule and interests of the railroads, intending thereby to deprive the railroads of their proper freight charges, and such agreement was carried out without the knowledge and consent of the railroad officials, and Akers & Bros. thus got possession of plaintiff's flour, then both plaintiff and Akers & Bros. are in pari delicto, and plaintiff cannot recover possession from Akers & Bros., or from one who purchased from them bona fide;" which said request the court refused to charge, and charged instead that the only question for the jury was, who had the title to the flour at the time that the defendant acquired possession? and, even if Akers & Bros. got possession of plaintiff's flour in execution of the agreement set out in said request, the plaintiff could recover the same from them or from any one else holding under them. (The court said nothing in the rest of his charge which modified the passages recited above.) The other grounds of the motion were the general grounds that the verdict was contrary to law, evidence, etc., and that the verdict should be set aside because for an amount larger than was authorized by the declaration. In a note to the bill of exceptions the court states: "The court was of opinion it should have been left with the jury to say whether they would find the highest proved value, or the actual value, with interest. Having restricted them to the highest value alone, the excess was ordered written off."

Simmons & Corrigan, for plaintiff in error. *Cox & Reed,* for defendants in error.

PER CURIAM. Judgment affirmed, with direction. Cross-bill of exceptions dismissed.

SIBLEY v. MUTUAL RESERVE FUND LIFE ASS'N.

(Supreme Court of Georgia. Oct. 19, 1891.)

INSURANCE COMPANIES — CONTRACTS WITH AGENTS —APPEAL—RECORD.

1. Under the contract declared upon, the insurance company did not obligate itself unconditionally to open the states of Florida and Mississippi to the plaintiff for his operations as general agent of the company, nor was there any guaranty that such states were open to him at the time the contract was made. The plaintiff having failed to secure business to the amount of $50,000 per month in the state of Georgia, the company had a right to discontinue his services, and terminate the contract.

2. An amendment to the declaration which was offered at the time of hearing a demurrer to the declaration, and disallowed by the court, is no part of the record, and can only come to the supreme court by being set out in the bill of exceptions, or annexed to the same as an exhibit duly authenticated.

(Syllabus by the Court.)

Error from city court of Atlanta; HOWARD VAN EPPS, Judge.

Action by R. E. Sibley against the Mutual Reserve Fund Life Association. Judgment for defendant. Plaintiff brings error. Affirmed.

Fulton Colville, for plaintiff in error. *H. H. Gordon* and *J. H. Lumpkin,* for defendant in error.

BLECKLEY, C. J. These parties, in June, 1888, entered into a written contract, whereby the defendant appointed the plaintiff general agent of the association, with the title of "Manager of the Georgia Department," for the purpose of procuring and effecting applications for membership satisfactory to the association, and for collecting the admission fees on applications, and for securing agents, to be appointed by the association, for the purpose of procuring applications. One of the stipulations was as follows: "*Third.* The district in which said manager shall have the right to work and to appoint general agents, for the purpose of procuring applications as aforesaid, shall embrace the state of Georgia, and such healthy portions of Mississippi and Florida as may be acceptable to the association. Said right shall continue so long as the new business secured by said manager and his agents from said district shall, in each and every month, be not less than fifty thousand dollars, commencing from August 1st, 1888. This contract is made subject to the condition that the association is legally authorized to transact business in said district assigned; but should said association not now have such authority, or should said authority be at any time hereafter revoked, then this contract shall be null and void as to so much of said district as it may be prohibited from transacting business in, except upon business already done therein by said manager, or agents appointed by him, if any." Another stipulation was in these words: "Subject to all the provisions herein contained, this contract shall continue in force for the term of ten years." The plaintiff served seven months, and in that time the amount of business procured by him and his agents was $194,000. The company discontinued his services and terminated the contract. He brought his action for damages, and, the declaration being demurred to, the demurrer was sustained, and the action dismissed. The plaintiff contends that, notwithstanding he failed to obtain $50,000 new business in each and every month, he was wrongfully discharged, because his failure, as he contends, is to be attributed to his exclusion from the states of Mississippi and Florida. He contends that the language of the contract imports that the company represented and stipulated that it was entitled to transact business in all three of the states at the time the contract was made, or, if not, that it obligated itself unconditionally to open up the states of Florida and Mississippi, which it failed to do. We agree with the court below in the opinion that this is not a correct interpretation of the contract. The language, "This contract is made subject to the condition that the association is legally authorized to transact business in said district assigned," introduces a condition for the benefit of both parties, and not exclusively for the benefit of the plaintiff. It is immediately added: "But should said association not now have such authority, or should said authority be at any time hereafter revoked, then this contract shall be null and void as to so much of said district as it may be prohibited from transacting business in, except upon business already done therein by said manager, or agents appointed by him, if any." Here is no undertaking by the company to procure any authority which it did not already possess, and it did not guaranty or warrant that it possessed any whatever. It left that question open, and the contract was to be void or not void according as there might or might not be authority to transact business in the district. If there was authority for a part of the district only, the contract was to be good for that part, and void as to the rest. The effect was that the district would be narrowed down to fit the authority, and not that the authority would be widened to fit the district. Nor do we think that the plaintiff was relieved from raising the $50,000 per month in business because the district open to him proved to be the state of Georgia only. It appears from the declaration that the annual commissions which the company would realize on business was only $3 per thousand dollars, and at that rate it is fair to presume that nothing less than $50,000 in business per month would justify the company in maintaining a separate department, and employing a general agent or manager to attend to it. If the Georgia department failed to yield an income of $1,800 a year, there would seem to be no great inducement to keep the Georgia department on foot. Besides, the fruits to the extent of $50,000 per month in business were to be realized at once, commencing with the 1st of August, or else the right to go on was not to be absolute. Furthermore, as it was not the whole of Mississippi and Flori-

da, or either of them, but only such healthy portions thereof as might be acceptable to the company, that would belong to the district in any event, there is no way to apportion the $50,000 per month so as to ascertain how much of it should be discounted by reason of the district being confined to Georgia alone. Is it possible to tell how much the plaintiff was to realize per month in business, in order to entitle him to go on for 10 years, unless it was the $50,000 as a minimum? The parties having failed to stipulate expressly on this subject, or to furnish by their agreement any basis for reducing the $50,000 to any other sum, we can have no hesitation in holding that they did not contemplate any reduction of it whatever. The plaintiff, after trying seven months, failed by almost one-half to come up to the stipulated amount; and, so far from obtaining that amount in each and every month, it does not appear that he obtained it even for one month. It seems to us there can be no doubt that the company had the right to discontinue his services and terminate the contract.

2. The bill of exceptions states that an amendment to the declaration was offered at the time of the hearing of the demurrer, and disallowed by the court. That amendment did not become a part of the record so as to be authenticated by the clerk's certificate, and its contents are not set out in the bill of exceptions, nor is any copy of it annexed to the bill as an exhibit, or otherwise duly authenticated by the presiding judge. For this reason, although the record as sent up by the clerk is accompanied by what purports to be an amendment, without any mark of filing upon it, we do not consider it as properly before us. We have looked at it, however, and can see no reason to think that it was improperly disallowed. Judgment affirmed.

SMITH v. KRON et al., (two cases.)

(Supreme Court of North Carolina. Nov. 18 1891.)

AWARD — REVIEW ON APPEAL — CONCLUSIVENESS

1. Since arbitrators are not required to find a statement of facts and conclusions of law, unless the award contains erroneous views of the law as a basis of the award, their action, in the absence of fraud, will not be reviewed.

2. Where arbitrators, in making an award, gave the parties an opportunity of having the conclusions of law passed upon by the court, unless exceptions thereto are filed, the judgment is final

Appeal from superior court, Montgomery county; JESSE F. GRAVES, Judge.

Two actions pending in the superior court, one by Melissa A. Smith in her own right and one as administrator, against Adelaide and Elizabeth Kron, were submitted to arbitration, and an award was made in favor of defendants. No exceptions to the award being filed, final judgment was entered, from which plaintiff appeals. Affirmed.

STATEMENT BY THE COURT. On the 2d of April, 1890, the parties to each of these actions entered into an agreement to refer the matters in controversy involved in them to arbitrators. A portion of said agreement was in the following words: "Now, therefore, this agreement witnesseth that the said parties hereinbefore named have mutually agreed, and by these presents do mutually agree, to submit for arbitration, and do hereby submit for arbitration, to F. C. Robbins, M. S. Robbins, S. J. Pemberton, and H. B. Adams, all of the matters in litigation aforesaid, or about which there is any controversy, whether specially named herein or not, who shall hear and determine the said matters, and make their award in writing; and, in the event of the failure of any three of them to agree upon an award, they shall select a fifth man, who shall act as umpire, and the award of a majority of said arbitrators and umpire, when signed and delivered, shall be binding upon the said parties, and conclusive to all matters herein submitted to said arbitrators, and the said award so made shall be a rule of court in the cases now pending, and judgment according to said award shall be rendered in said actions, in so far as they shall be affected thereby." The arbitrators, having disagreed, chose Kerr Craige as umpire, and a majority made an award as to the issues involved in both actions. No exception having been filed to their report, judgment was rendered in each of the actions confirming the report, and making it a rule of court, and that defendants go without day, and recover costs. No exceptions were filed to the award. After judgment according to the record, "counsel for the plaintiff then stated that he did not think the findings of fact by the arbitrators justified the judgment or conclusions of law, and excepted and appealed to the supreme court."

Battle & Mordecai, for appellant.

AVERY, J. Arbitrators are not bound, like referees, under the statute, (Code, § 422,) to find the facts or state separately their conclusions of law and fact; but if they do attempt to state the law arising on the facts found by them, and "miss it," the error may be reviewed on exceptions, and the award set aside. Allison v. Bryson, 65 N. C. 44; Farmer v. Pickens, 83 N. C. 549. They are a law to themselves, are not bound to decide correctly, and unless they gratuitously incorporate in their award erroneous views of the law, as reasons for the conclusions reached, their action, in the absence of fraud, is not subject to review. Robbins v. Killebrew, 95 N. C. 19; Miller v. Bryan, 86 N. C. 167. But where they voluntarily extend to the parties litigant, as in our case, the opportunity to have their conclusions of law passed upon by the court, the practice is analogous to that adopted in references by consent. If objection is not taken by exception, pointing out the error complained of, before the rendition of judgment, an appellant has no more right to assign their mistakes of law as error in the court below or in this court, by virtue of the simple announcement when the judgment is filed that he appeals from it, than he would have had to except to a report of a referee after its confirmation. Keener v.

Goodson, 89 N. C. 276; Reisenstein v. Hahn, 107 N. C. 156, 12 S. E. Rep. 48. There is no error, and the judgment is affirmed.

MILLER et al. v. GROOME.

(Supreme Court of North Carolina. Nov. 18, 1891.)

REFERENCE—REVIEW BY COURT.

Under Code Civil Proc. N. C. § 423, giving plaintiff a right to except to a referee's report, it is the duty of the superior court to consider the exceptions, both as to findings of fact and conclusions of law, and pass judicially on the report.

Appeal from superior court, Guilford county; EDWIN T. BOYKIN, Judge.

Action by J. G. Miller & Co. against Z. Groome. From judgment for defendant on report of referee, plaintiff takes exceptions. Reversed.

STATEMENT BY THE COURT. The referee gave judgment for defendant, and plaintiff filed exceptions to his report. Upon the call of the case the pleadings, report, order of reference, and exceptions were read, when his honor asked if the law laid down by the referee was conceded to be correct on the facts found, and the plaintiff answered "Yes." His honor further asked if the testimony upon which the findings of fact were made was conflicting and contradictory, and, being answered by the plaintiff that it was, he declined to hear the testimony, overruled the exceptions, and the plaintiff appealed from the judgment rendered, assigning as error that his honor did not hear the testimony and pass upon the same, and that he overruled the exceptions.

J. T. Morehead, for appellant. *Dillard & King* and *Jas. E. Boyd,* for appellee.

DAVIS, J. This was a reference under the Code, and the referee, as was his duty, reported the facts found and his conclusions of law separately, and he also reported the evidence upon which he found the facts, and as a matter of right either party could file exceptions, appeal, and have the report reviewed by the judge of the superior court, whose duty it is to consider the exception, and set aside, modify, or confirm the report, according to his judgment; and his ruling upon the findings of fact is conclusive upon this court, but his rulings upon questions of law are subject to review here. Commissioners v. Magnin, 85 N. C. 114, and cases cited, McNeill v. Hodges, 105 N. C. 52, 11 S. E. Rep. 265. The plaintiff filed exceptions to the referee's report, both as to findings of fact and conclusions of law. One of the exceptions was to the competency of testimony, which, if overruled, would be the subject of review in this court. It was clearly the right of the appellant to have the report of the referee reviewed by the judge. Code, § 423. It was perfectly competent, upon review, if he so thought, to adopt the findings of fact and conclusions of law of the referee, and then they would become the findings and conclusions of the court; but it was error in his honor to summarily dispose of the exceptions by overruling them and confirming the report, without reviewing and passing upon them judicially. Error.

DICKENS et al. v. LONG et al.

(Supreme Court of North Carolina. Nov. 10, 1891.)

SALE OF DECEDENT'S LAND—ACTION TO SET ASIDE —PLEADING — HOMESTEAD EXEMPTIONS — JUDGMENT—COLLATERAL ATTACK.

1. In an action to set aside a sale of land under a decree in a special proceeding instituted before a clerk by the administrator of plaintiffs' deceased father for the purpose of selling land to pay debts of the estate, a complaint which, after stating that the sale was made under the decree in such proceeding, and that defendants claim thereunder, claims that plaintiffs were entitled to a homestead therein, and that the sale was therefore void under Const. N. C. art. 10, § 2, creating homestead exemptions, falls to state any cause of action, where it omits to state facts showing that the debt for which it was sold was not contracted before the adoption of the constitutional provision, and was not for taxes due the state or for the purchase money of the land, which are specially excepted from the provisions of said articles, the burden of proof to show the exemption being on plaintiffs.

2. In such action, those plaintiffs who were made defendants to the special proceeding cannot attack the judgment in that proceeding by claiming that it, together with the subsequent proceedings therein, did not constitute evidence that their right and title in the land derived from their father had not passed to the purchaser at the sale.

3. Under Code N. C. § 1468, providing that no order to sell real estate of a decedent shall be granted to the personal representative until the heirs of decedent shall have been made parties, one who claims to be an heir of decedent, and who was not made a party to the proceeding for a sale of his land, is not bound by the judgment and sale therein, and may therefore have a trial as to her interest, together with the preliminary question of whether she was an heir.

Appeal from superior court, Person county; EDWIN T. BOYKIN, Judge.

Action by Ellen Dickens and others against J. A. Long and others for possession of land, etc. From a judgment of nonsuit plaintiffs appeal. Reversed.

STATEMENT BY THE COURT. The defendants insisted that the complaint did not state facts sufficient to constitute a cause of action for reasons set out in their answer. to-wit: That the deed referred to in the complaint from Chambers, commissioner, to Sallie Barnett, could not be in this cause attacked, it being the deed under which defendants claimed the land in controversy. During the argument the court intimated an opinion that the deed could not be attacked in this suit, and also an opinion that the plaintiffs did not in their complaint affirmatively state that the defendants in the suit of Chambers v. Dickens (referred to in the complaint, said defendants being part of the plaintiffs herein) were entitled to a homestead in said land, and that it was not sold for debts good against the homestead. In deference thereto the plaintiffs submitted to a judgment of nonsuit, and appealed. The plaintiffs brought the action in the superior court, in term, to set aside a sale of the land in controversy, made by virtue of a decree rendered in March, 1883, in a special proceeding instituted before the clerk by the administrator of their deceased father for the purpose of selling land to pay debts, and also to recover the possession of the land from those

holding by mesne conveyances under the purchaser at the said administrator's sale. After setting forth that the sale was made, that one Sallie Barnett became the purchaser for the sum of $203, and that it was confirmed by the court, the cause of action is stated in the complaint, as follows: "(8) That the said order of sale was and is irregular, illegal, unjust, a fraud upon the plaintiffs' rights, and void, and the acts done thereunder are illegal and void, because— First. Isabella Edwards, a child and heir of said Mangum, and a plaintiff herein, and her husband, were not parties in and to said special proceeding. Second. The defendants in said special proceeding, who were then under the age of fourteen years, to-wit, said Lucy and Susan, were not summoned, as required by law, (Code, § 217,) which fact appears from the indorsement on the summons therein, it being as follows: 'Received Feb. 22d, 1883. Served on all the defendants, including J. S. Merritt, guardian ad litem, by reading the summons to each of them. This March 3d, 1883. Fee $7.30. C. G. MITCHELL, Sheriff Person County.' Third. The guardian ad litem for the infants in said special proceedings, said Vinie, Lucy, and Susan, whose answer was filed on March 12, 1883, as appears from same, was at the time of said filing, and at the time of said order and sale, representing interests adverse to his said wards, infants, which fact appears from the papers and accounts now filed in the clerk's office, in the administration of said Mangum's estate, one of which accounts, for the sum of $19.48, has upon its back the following indorsement: 'For value received I transfer this account to J. S. Merritt, this 1st March, 1883. JNO. C. PASS,'—the said Pass being then and ever since then the clerk of the superior court of Person county, and constituting the court herein mentioned, which said facts rendered, as plaintiffs are advised and believed, J. S. Merritt, who was appointed by the court, the said J. C. Pass, on February 22, 1883, guardian ad litem, as aforesaid, incompetent to act as such guardian; all of which facts were in the knowledge of the court. (9) That the said sale of said land was illegal, unjust, and void, because— First, the aforesaid order was void, and contained no authority to sell on account of the facts set forth in article 8 of this complaint; second, the homestead was not laid off and set apart before sale under said order; third, the homestead in said land was sold to pay debts, when it was exempt from the payment of such debts. (10) That the said minors Lucy and Susan are entitled to a homestead in said land. (11) That the plaintiffs are the owners, and entitled to the possession, of said land as heirs of Mangum Barnett, deceased, since, as they are informed and believed, the said sale was void, as aforesaid, as being contrary to the constitution and laws of North Carolina, and a great injustice upon their rights. (12) That the defendants J. A. Long, R. S. Baynes, R. C. Carver, J. C. Pass, W. T. Pass, R. A. Pass, Robt. Trotter, Sr., Ed. Chism, Taylor Stanfield, and Mary Farrar are in possession of said land, deriving their respective titles, claims, and interests, as plaintiffs are informed and believe, directly or indirectly through mesne conveyances from said Sallie Barnett, the purchaser, as aforesaid, at said illegal and void sale; and that said defendants do not claim as tenants in common, but each claims a separate, several lot or parcel of said tract of land, and all of them together, in that way and manner, claiming the whole of said tract of land. (13) That the defendants deny the title of the plaintiffs, who are the real owners of said land, and refuse to give possession of same to plaintiffs, who are justly entitled to it. (14) That by reason of the said facts complained of, and the occupation of said land by defendants, the plaintiffs have been greatly damaged, to-wit, in the sum of eight hundred dollars. (15) That the annual rents and profits of said land are worth a great sum, to-wit, two hundred dollars, the said land having increased greatly in value. Wherefore the plaintiffs demand judgment against the defendants J. A. Long, R. S. Baynes, R. C. Carver, J. C. Pass, R. A. Pass, W. T. Pass, Robt. Trotter, Sr., Ed. Chism, Taylor Stanfield, and Mary Farrar—*First*, for the recovery of the land above described; *second*, for the recovery of the sum of eight hundred dollars damages for the unlawful occupation of same, *third*, for six hundred dollars for the rents and profits of same for the last three years; *fourth*, that the said commissioner's deed to Sally Barnett be declared void; *fifth*, for their costs in this action sustained, and for any other just relief."

W. W. Kitchin, for appellants. John W. Graham, J. S. Merritt, and V. S. Bryant, for appellees.

Avery, J. Reversing the order in which the points were presented by counsel, and assuming for the present that the judgment in the special proceeding, by virtue of which Sallie Barnett bought the land in controversy, which she has since sold to several other defendants, cannot be attacked, on account of irregularities, in this action, brought in the superior court, it would only remain to determine whether, without impeaching that judgment, the plaintiffs, admitting the truth of every allegation contained in the complaint, have shown *prima facie* that they have title to the land in controversy. If the judgment be treated as valid, and the sale and confirmation unimpeachable for present purposes, then the deed executed to Sallie Barnett by the commissioner would, as against the parties to that record, claiming likewise through their father, (Mangum Barnett,) show title in her; and, unless it appeared from the complaint (if admitted to be true) that the sale was void because it was made in violation of article 10 of the constitution and the statutes enacted in pursuance of it in reference to homestead exemption, the plaintiffs cannot recover. Mobley v. Griffin, 104 N. C. 112, 10 S. E. Rep. 142. The burden was upon the plaintiffs, in view of such proof, to establish their right to have had a homestead allotted in

the land sold; and here the question to be determined, as on demurrer to the complaint, is whether, according to their own allegations, the sale may have been, in any phase of their statement, or under any state of facts that may be fairly inferred from it to have existed at that time, made without any infringement upon the right of the plaintiffs under the constitution and laws to claim and have assigned to them a homestead in a portion or all of the land sold. Mobley v. Griffin, supra; McCracken v. Adler, 98 N. C. 400, 4 S. E. Rep. 188; Wilson v. Taylor, 98 N. C. 275, 3 S. E. Rep. 492. If the debts of the intestate, to meet which the license was granted to the administrator to sell, were contracted before the homestead provision of the constitution became operative, or were taxes due the state, or were contracted for the purchase money of the land, the plaintiffs were not entitled to the homestead in the land sold under the decree against creditors holding such claims. Long v. Walker, 105 N. C. 90, 10 S. E. Rep. 858; Const. art 10, § 2. It has been expressly decided by this court that where a plaintiff offers in evidence, in an action involving the title and right to the possession of land, the record of the judgment, execution, levy, and sale of the land in controversy as the property of the defendant, or of one from whom the defendant is shown to derive title, the latter cannot rebut this *prima facie* proof of title by a simple denial, or by an allegation, without testimony tending to establish it, that he is entitled to the homestead in the land in dispute. Mobley v. Griffin, supra. Upon the same principle, if a plaintiff allege in his complaint facts which, if true, establish *prima facie* the title of the defendant as against him by a deed made in pursuance of a judgment of the court, the general allegation that such sale was void for failure to allot a homestead, without averring specifically the facts upon which the right to the homestead depends, so as to exclude the possibility of the validity of the sale, consistent with such statement, must be held insufficient to meet and rebut the apparent right of the plaintiff to recover. Upon a careful review of the complaint it appears that the plaintiffs have failed, if they could truthfully have done so, to negative the possibility that the land was sold to make assets to satisfy debts created before the right to such exemptions accrued. We concur with the judge below in the view that the facts alleged by the plaintiff are not sufficient to relieve them of the burden of showing their right to have a homestead assigned in said land. If we grant that the irregularities (if any appeared upon the face of the record of the special proceeding) would not be sufficient to destroy its efficacy as evidence of the validity of the sale under which Sallie Barnett, and the other defendants through her, claimed title.

But, recurring to the other question, which so frequently confronts us with slight variations in the facts, but no difference in the general principles applicable, we think it manifest that the judgment in the special proceeding can only be attacked directly by those who were parties to the proceeding, and that it would be a collateral impeachment of it to declare that, together with the subsequent orders of confirmation, etc., it did not constitute evidence that so much of the right and the title of Mangum Barnett as descended to those whose names appear as parties of record has passed to Sallie Barnett. England v. Garner, 90 N. C. 197; Fowler v. Poor, 93 N. C. 466; Ward v. Lowndes, 96 N. C. 367, 2 S. E. Rep. 591; Sumner v. Sessoms, 94 N. C. 371; Beard v. Hall, 63 N. C. 39; Simmons v. Hassell, 68 N. C. 213; Morris v. Gentry, 89 N. C. 248. But the plaintiffs allege that Isabella Edwards was a child and heir at law of Mangum Barnett, and that neither she nor her husband, Hal Edwards, were either real or nominal parties to the special proceedings, and that she is not concluded as to her rights in the land by the decree of sale. The defendants deny the allegations of fact that she is an heir at law of Mangum Barnett, and insist by way of argument that, if she is, she cannot now claim a homestead in the land, because she is more than 21 years of age. If Isabella Edwards is one of the heirs at law, and is not estopped by the judgment in the special proceeding from claiming title to the interest that descended to her in common with the other heirs of Mangum Barnett at his death, then she is entitled to recover possession of the land, and to be let in to the extent of her interest as tenant in common with the defendants who have acquired, so far as we can see in this action, the undivided interest of his other heirs at law. Gilchrist v. Middleton, 107 N. C. 663, 12 S. E. Rep. 85; Allen v. Salinger, 108 N. C. 14, 8 S. E. Rep. 913. If the sale under a judicial decree, purporting to authorize the administrator of Mangum Barnett to sell this particular piece of land for assets, gives to the purchaser who holds the deed of the personal representative for the land sold and those claiming under her a title good against an heir at law, who was not a party to the proceeding, then the plaintiff Isabella cannot demand that the question whether she is or is not an heir at law be passed upon by the jury. But if she is not concluded, and the jury find that she is an heir at law, it is obvious that she is entitled at least to be let into possession, and to have damages awarded in proportion to her interest. Gilchrist v. Middleton, supra. Section 1438 of the Code provides that no order to sell the real estate of a decedent shall be granted to the personal representative until the heirs or devisees of the decedent shall have been made parties, and the statute is now substantially the same that has been in force since 1846. Revised Code, c. 46, § 47; Thompson v. Cox, 8 Jones, (N. C.) 313. The law therefore obviously contemplates that those to whom any interest in the land has passed by descent or devise shall be made parties to any special proceeding instituted to subject such lands to pay the debts of the decedent. The general rule as to estoppels is that a decree of a court of competent jurisdiction is binding on the parties to the suit or proceeding in which it is entered, and on those who are in privity with them in all collateral actions or proceedings; but ordinarily it is not conclusive as to strangers. Bigelow, Estop. (4th Ed.) 24, 34; Edwards v. Baker, 99 N. C. 258, 6 S. E. Rep. 255; Coble v. Clapp, 1 Jones, Eq. 173; Falls v. Gamble, 66 N. C. 455; Tobacco Co. v. McElwee, 94 N. C. 425; Warden v. McKinnon, 99 N. C. 251, 5 S. E. Rep. 917. A judgment is not even binding on one who is not a party, at the time of its rendition, to the action or proceeding in which it is entered, though he had been a party previous to that time. Owens v. Alexander, 78 N. C. 1. The purchaser, Mrs. Barnett, might have successfully resisted the payment of the purchase money on the ground that Isabella Edwards, if indeed she was an heir at law of Mangum Barnett, had not been made a party, and concluded by the judgment. Edney v. Edney, 80 N. C. 81. But now that she has paid it in full, though she and those claiming under her may possibly resort to more than one remedy to make good their loss on account of the defective title, the doctrine of maintaining the integrity of judicial decrees cannot be pushed, as against strangers to the record, to the extremity of depriving them of their property without notice or a day in court. Isabella Edwards was not even a nominal party to the special proceeding, and the judgment did not purport to authorise the sale of any interest she might have. We think that there was error in the refusal to submit to the jury issues involving the title and right of possession of Isabella Edwards. The preliminary question whether she was an heir at law of Mangum Barnett could have been passed upon in considering the issue as to title. It was not alleged or contended that Isabella was an infant when the decree was made in the special proceeding. While we concur with the judge below in the general view which he seems to have taken of the law, we think that there was error in withdrawing from the jury the question whether Isabella Edwards was an heir at law of Mangum Barnett, and, as such, entitled to be let in as tenant in common with the defendants. Whether the action will be further prosecuted in her interest alone, or whether all will submit to nonsuit, and await the result of a direct proceeding, before moving for possession of the land, is a question addressed to the plaintiffs and their counsel. There is error, and a new trial is awarded.

STATE v. JOHNSON.

(*Supreme Court of North Carolina.* Nov. 10, 1891.)

APPEAL IN BASTARDY—SERVICE OF NOTICE.

1. Where the appeal from a judgment of acquittal in bastardy proceedings before a justice of the peace has not been taken at the trial, the burden is on plaintiff to show that the notice of appeal was served on defendant within 10 days thereafter, as required by Code N. C. § 876.

2. Where the acquittal was on March 4th, and Code N. C. § 876, required the notice of appeal to be served within 10 days thereafter, a finding of service "between March 4th and August term" was not sufficient to show compliance with the statute.

3. Service of the notice of appeal was made

by one not an officer. Code N. C. § 597, regulates the manner of service of notices, and subdivision 4 provides that a subpœna may be served by a person not an officer. *Held*, that service of the notice should have been made by an officer.

4. The fact that defendant's counsel had, soon after March 4th, a notice sent him by defendant, was too indefinite as to time, and was explained by evidence that the notice had been handed to defendant by one not an officer.

5. Service of the notice of appeal on the justice did not obviate the necessity of service on defendant. Green v. Hobgood, 74 N. C. 234, followed.

6. Where defendant's exception to the denial of his motion to dismiss was duly noted, his subsequent general appearance for trial was not a waiver of his rights under such exception.

Appeal from superior court, Duplin county; EDWIN T. BOYKIN, Judge.

Proceeding against P. P. Johnson to determine the paternity of the bastard child of Alice Wells. Defendant was acquitted before a justice of the peace, and the state appealed to the superior court. Defendant moved for a dismissal of the appeal, which was denied. Verdict of guilty, and judgment thereon. Motion for a new trial was denied. Defendant appealed. Appeal of state to superior court dismissed.

When the case was called for trial the defendant moved to dismiss the appeal for want of notice to him. Upon said motion his honor found the following facts: "That the proceeding was instituted before a justice of the peace of Duplin county, and was tried before him on the 4th day of March, 1891; that upon said trial the defendant was acquitted, and judgment rendered in his favor; that no notice of appeal was given at trial; that on the 10th day of March, 1891, the complainant, Alice Wells, served written notice of appeal on the justice who tried the case; that a notice of appeal signed by the complainant was handed to the defendant by a negro man, not a party, and not an officer, between the 4th day of March and the said August term, 1891, that shortly after the said 4th day of March, 1891, a notice corresponding with the said description was in possession of one of the defendant's attorneys, and said attorney admitted that said notice had been sent to him, by mail, by the defendant. The defendant was present in court with all his witnesses, who had been duly subpœnaed. Upon the above facts his honor held that the defendant had sufficient notice of the appeal, and overruled the motion, and the defendant excepted."

H. R. Kornegay and *Allen & Dortch*, for appellant. *O. H. Allen*, for the State. *A. D. Ward*, for Alice Wells.

CLARK, J. The court having refused the motion to dismiss, the defendant pursued the proper course in having his exception noted "to save his rights" and proceeding with the trial. Spaugh v. Boner, 85 N. C. 208. The final judgment being against him, the appeal now brings up the exception for review. The subsequent general appearance for the purposes of the trial did not waive his exception for the refusal to dismiss. Suiter v. Brittle, 90 N. C. 20.

On the facts found his honor erred in finding that there was sufficient service. The

statute requires (unless the appeal shall be taken at the trial) that notice of appeal shall be served in 10 days after judgment. As has been said, the burden is on appellant to show service within the prescribed time. Finlayson v. Accident Co., 13 S. E. Rep. 739, (at this term;) Spaugh v. Boner, 85 N. C. 208; Sparrow v. Davidson, 77 N. C. 35. The facts found do not show any service on defendant within that time, and the attempted service by one not an officer, "between March 4th and August term," was not only too late, but was not legal service of a notice required by the Code, § 597. A subpœna may be served by any person not a party to the action, and proven by his oath, (Code, § 597, subd. 4,) but the exception serves to prove the rule that service must be made by an officer, unless service is accepted. If the service of a notice is not legally made, service in any other mode is void. Allen v. Strickland, 100 N. C. 225, 6 S. E. Rep. 780.

The fact that defendant's counsel had, soon after March 4th, a notice sent him by the defendant, is not only indefinite as to time, but seems explained by the other evidence that such a paper had been handed defendant by one not an officer. The requirement of service by an officer is not only statutory, but reasonable, as it prevents disputes like this,—whether there has been service or not,—as is likewise the requirement that service must be within 10 days, for a party should not be indefinitely held in suspense, but should know when the matter is at an end. Any hardship which might, under any circumstances, be entailed on an appellant by failure to serve notice in a legal manner and within the statutory time is removed by the discretion reposed in the appellate court to permit notice to be given after that time. Marsh v. Cohen, 68 N. C. 283; Railroad Co. v. Richardson, 82 N. C. 343; West v. Reynolds, 94 N. C. 333. It seems there were not such circumstances in this case, as the court did not put an end to the controversy by permitting the notice to be given then and there, as it might have done.

It is, however, contended that, notice having been served on the justice, no notice to appellee was required. We have an express decision to the contrary, (Green v. Hobgood, 74 N. C. 234,) which is recognized in principle by Marsh v Cohen and Railroad Co. v. Richardson, supra, and Richardson v. Debnam, 75 N. C. 390. Besides, both the reason of the thing and a reasonable construction of the statute support this view. The notice to the justice is to send up the papers and transcript. The notice to the appellee is to have his witnesses, and be ready for trial, as the cause stands for trial at the first term of the superior court. Code, §§ 565, 880. Super. Ct. Rules, 24. The statute (Code, § 876) requires service of notice of appeal within 10 days, but nowhere provides directly on whom it may be served, except that inferentially it recognises in the next section (877) that it should be on both the justice and the appellant, as it provides that when the appeal is taken at the trial, and the adverse party is present, the appellant is not required to

give written notice, "either to the justice
or to the adverse party." It would be
unreasonable to fasten upon every party
who gains a cause in a magistrate's court
the duty of inquiring or watching out if
an appeal may not be sent up. When the
appellant does not crave an appeal at the
trial he should at least give the opposite
party notice, and must do so within 10
days. A party in court is fixed with notice of all orders and decrees taken at term,
for it is his duty to be there in person or
by attorney, (Clayton v. Jones, 68 N. C.
497;) but he is not held to have notice of
orders out of term, (Hemphill v. Moore,
104 N. C. 379, 10 S. E. Rep. 313; Branch v.
Walker, 92 N. C. 87, Code, § 546;) nor of
orders before the clerk, (Blue v. Blue, 79 N.
C. 69.) The same rule applies to appeals
from the superior court, as to which, if the
appeal is taken after the term is over, notice
must be served on the appellee, and within 10 days. Code, § 549, as amended by
Acts 1889, c. 161.
There having been no service of notice of
appeal, as required by statute, upon defendant within 10 days, and his honor not having exercised his discretionary power to relieve the appellant of the consequences,
and to permit notice to be given at the
trial, there was error in refusing the motion to dismiss. The power to relieve
from the failure to give due and proper
notice of appeal is vested in the wise discretion of the presiding judge, and should
only be exercised when there are facts and
circumstances which would make it a
hardship on the appellant not to permit
it to be done. The policy of legislation
and of the courts is to "require litigants
to be diligent in prosecuting appeals from
justices of the peace, and to prevent parties from using" such "as a means of causing useless delay." AVERY, J., in Ballard
v. Gay, 108 N. C. 544, 13 S. E. Rep. 207. Let
this be certified, that the appeal from the
justice may be dismissed in the superior
court. Error.

CITY COUNCIL OF CHARLESTON v. ASHLEY
PHOSPHATE CO., (two cases.)

(Supreme Court of South Carolina. Nov. 12,
1891.)

LICENSE FROM CITY — ACTION TO ENFORCE PAY-
MENT—PLEADING OF ORDINANCE—JUDICIAL NO-
TICE.

1. Act S. C. 1881 (17 St. 582) authorizes the
city council of Charleston to require the payment of certain licenses by persons engaged in
business in said city, and to pass such ordinances
as are necessary to carry the act into effect.
Held, that a complaint in an action to enforce
the payment of such licenses, alleging that the
city council, for the purpose of raising a revenue,
and in the exercise of the taxing power, passed
an ordinance entitled "An ordinance to regulate
licenses for the year 1889," whereby, inter alia,
it was provided that certain persons should obtain licenses, and should pay therefor a certain
sum, but not alleging that the said ordinance
contained any provision authorizing the enforcement of the payment of such licenses, was insufficient, for the reason that the courts do not
take judicial notice of city ordinances unless directed by charter or statute to do so, and such
ordinances, therefore, should be set out in the
pleadings, if not in hæc verba, at least in substance.

2. The city council of Charleston, having
passed an ordinance under said act of 1881 to reg-

ulate licenses, providing that, if any person
therein named should refuse to take out a license,
he should be liable to a penalty, but containing
no provision to the effect that he might also be
required to pay the license by an action for that
purpose, is confined to the mode therein prescribed for enforcing payment of such licenses,
and cannot resort to any other.

Appeal from common pleas circuit court
of Charleston county; JAMES ALDRICH,
Judge.
This comprises two actions, brought by
the city council of Charleston against the
Ashley Phosphate Company to recover the
amount of certain license taxes for the
years 1889 and 1890. The complaint in the
action for the license tax of 1889 is as follows: "Plaintiffs allege: (1) That they
are a corporation duly chartered under
and by the laws of the state of South Carolina, pursuant to an act of the general
assembly of the said state entitled 'An act
to incorporate Charleston,' and the acts
amendatory thereof. (2) That under and
by virtue of an act of the general assembly
of the said state entitled 'An act to authorize the city council of Charleston to
impose a license tax on all persons engaged
in any business, trade, or profession in the
city of Charleston,' approved the 17th December, 1881, the plaintiffs, on the 27th
day of December, 1888, for the purpose of
raising a revenue, and in exercise of the
taxing power, passed an ordinance entitled
'An ordinance to regulate licenses for the
year 1889,' whereby, inter alia, it is provided that phosphate rock mining or
manufacturing companies or agencies, engaged or intending to engage in business
in said city, shall, on or before the 20th
day of January, A. D. 1889, obtain each a
license therefor, and shall be required each
to pay for the same the sum of five hundred ($500) dollars. (3) That at the time
of the passage of the said ordinance the
defendant was, and now is, a corporation
duly created by and under the laws of
said state for the purpose of digging and
mining for phosphate rock, marl, lime, and
minerals, and of manufacturing the same,
and such other minerals or materials as
they may purchase or acquire, into chem-
icals, acids, and fertilizers, and of carrying
on trade therein. (4) That since the 1st
day of January, 1889, the defendant, being
a phosphate rock manufacturing company, as aforesaid, has carried on, and is
now carrying on, the business of selling
fertilizers in Charleston, aforesaid, having
an office on Brown's wharf in said city, for
a license to do which there was due and
payable to plaintiffs the sum of five hundred ($500) dollars, under the ordinance
aforesaid; but at no time during the said
year has the said company had, nor has
it now, a license to conduct the said business as required by law. (5) That no
part of the said five hundred ($500) dol-
lars due and payable by the defendant to
the plaintiffs as aforesaid has been paid.
Wherefore plaintiffs demand judgment
against the defendant for the sum of five
hundred dollars, and the costs and disbursements of this action." The complaint in the action for the license tax of
1890 is the same as the above, except that
the ordinance for that year is annexed

thereto. A demurrer was interposed to each complaint, and overruled. Defendants appeal. Reversed.

John F. Ficken and *Mitchell & Smith*, for appellant. *Charles Inglesby*, Corp. Counsel, for respondent.

McIVER, J. These two cases, though not involving all of the same questions, turning, as they do, in our judgment, upon the same question, may be considered together. Both were brought to recover the amount of certain license taxes, which plaintiff claimed defendant was liable for under an ordinance passed by the city council of Charleston, which will be more particularly referred to hereinafter. In each of the cases a demurrer was interposed upon the ground that the complaint did not state facts sufficient to constitute a cause of action, and in each case the demurrer was overruled, and the defendant appeals, raising the question common to both of the cases, though there are other questions raised in the last case which, under the view we take of the demurrer, cannot properly arise, and will not therefore be considered. We do not deem it necessary to set out in detail the several allegations contained in the complaints, though copies thereof should be inserted in the report of the case, for it is sufficient to say that in both of the cases the actions were brought to recover the sums which the ordinance, incorporated in the complaint in the second case, or, rather, made a part thereof as an exhibit, required persons or corporations engaging in the business in which it is claimed defendant was engaged to pay for a license to carry on such business within the city of Charleston. It is true that the ordinance imposing the license tax sued for in the first action is not set out in the "case," but the allegation of the complaint in that action shows that by such ordinance persons engaging in the business in which it is alleged defendant was engaged were required to take out a license, and pay therefor the sum of $500; and the further allegation is made that defendant has neither taken out such license nor paid the sum required for that purpose. But there is no allegation that plaintiff has been authorized, either by statute or ordinance, to enforce the payment of such sum by suit, and no such statute has been brought to our attention; nor is there any allegation in the complaint that no other mode has been provided, either by statute or ordinance, to enforce such payment. In the second case, however, brought to recover the amount of the license tax for the year 1890, the ordinance imposing that tax, which is made a part of the complaint, does show that another remedy has been provided, for the third section contains this provision: "If any person or persons shall exercise or carry on any trade, business, or profession, for the exercising, carrying on, or doing of which a license is required by this ordinance, without taking out such license as in that behalf required, he, she, or they shall for each and every offense be subject to a penalty not exceeding $100, as may be adjudged by the recorder or court trying the case,

and the same shall be entered up as a judgment of the court, and execution shall issue against the property of the defendants as for the collection of other taxes and penalties." This provision would seem to afford a most efficient remedy, for if a person should fail to take out a license as required, and continue business for any length of time, being liable to the penalty "for each and every offense," these penalties, under the decision in Jager's Case, 29 S. C. 446, 7 S. E. Rep. 605, might be swelled to a very large sum,—much larger than the sum required to be paid for the license. Whether the ordinance imposing the license tax for the year 1889—for the non-payment of which the first action was brought—contains a similar provision we are not informed; but from the fact that these two cases were submitted together, and our attention was not drawn to any difference between them in this respect, it would be reasonable to suppose that the two ordinances were substantially the same in this respect; but as we are, perhaps, not at liberty to assume this to be so, we have called attention above to the fact that there is no allegation in the complaint in the first case that no mode of enforcing the payment of the tax has been prescribed by any ordinance.

Confining our attention for the present to the first case, it seems to us that the practical question presented is whether a bare statement that a license tax has been imposed, that such license tax has not been paid, and that no license has been taken out, is sufficient to constitute a cause of action for the recovery of the amount required to be paid for such license. By the act of 1881 (17 St. 582) the city council of Charleston have been authorized "to require the payment of such sum or sums of money, not exceeding five hundred dollars, for license or licenses, as in their judgment be just and wise, by any person or persons engaged or intending to engage in any calling, business, or profession, in whole or in part, within the limits of the city of Charleston, except those engaged in the calling or profession of teachers and ministers of the gospel." And by the second section of that act the said city council are expressly authorized "to pass such ordinances as are necessary to carry the intent and purposes of this act into full effect." It is very manifest from the whole frame of the act that its main intent and purpose was to enable the city council, in addition to its other means of raising a revenue for the use of the corporation, to impose a license tax; and certainly, to carry such purpose into full effect, it was necessary to provide the means for enforcing the payment of such tax. Accordingly, by the second section, the city council were invested with power to pass such ordinances as might be necessary to enforce the payment of such tax. But there is no allegation in this complaint that any such ordinance has ever been passed. It is true that the complaint does contain an allegation that "the plaintiffs, on the 27th day of December, 1888, for the purpose of raising a revenue, and in exercise of the taxing power, passed an ordinance entitled 'An ordinance to regulate licenses for the year 1889,' whereby, *inter alia*, it is provided that phosphate rock mining or manufacturing companies or agencies engaged or intending to engage in business in said city shall, on or before the 20th day of January, A. D. 1889, obtain each a license therefor, and shall be required each to pay for the same the sum of five hundred ($500) dollars." But there is no allegation that such ordinance, thus referred to by date and title, contained any provision authorizing the enforcement of the payment of such license fee by suit or otherwise, (as the act above referred to authorized;) nor is there any allegation that such ordinance contained no provision at all for the enforcement of such payment. The reference to this ordinance by date and title is not sufficient, for, as is said in 1 Dill. Mun. Corp. (4th Ed) § 846: "The courts, unless it be the courts of the municipality, do not judicially notice the ordinances of a municipal corporation, unless directed by charter or statute to do so. Therefore such ordinances, when sought to be enforced by action, or when set up by the defendant as a protection, should be set out in the pleading. It is not sufficient that they be referred to generally by the title or section," though probably they need not be set out *in haec verba;* a statement of the substance with reference to the date, title, and section being sufficient. See, also, Information v. Oliver, 21 S. C. 323. Here, however, there is no allegation that the ordinance, in substance, provides for the enforcement of the payment of the license fee by action

It seems to us, therefore, that the allegations in this complaint are not sufficient to constitute the cause of action sought to be enforced therein; but that a further allegation was necessary for that purpose, either to the effect that provision had been made in the ordinance, as authorized by the act of 1881, supra, for the enforcement of the payment of such license tax by action, or that no provision whatever had been made for that purpose, which would have raised the question whether, in the absence of any provision at all, the court of common pleas, by virtue of its general jurisdiction, could enforce a right conferred by an ordinance of a municipal corporation by an ordinary action, where no other mode of doing so has been provided by the ordinance. Of course, these views are based upon the assumption that neither in the charter of the city nor in any other statute is there any provision authorizing the enforcement of the payment of taxes imposed by the city council by an ordinary action, for no such provision has been brought to our attention, and we are not aware of any. It is true that the counsel for respondent, in his argument in the second case, has cited us to certain sections in the Revised Ordinances of the City of Charleston, ratified 26th of September, 1882, containing such provisions; but, as we have seen, the court cannot take judicial notice of these ordinances, and they have not been set forth in the complaint, either *in haec verba* or in substance. The act of March 1,

1870, (14 St. 409,) also referred to by counsel in this connection, cannot affect the question for two reasons: (1) Because so much of that act as relates to license taxes has been declared unconstitutional in the case of City Council of Charleston v. Oliver, 16 S. C. 47, and therefore so much of the provisions of that act as relates to licenses must be regarded as if no such act had ever been passed. (2) Because even that act does not purport to give the city council authority to enforce the payment of taxes by action, but, in the section specially referred to, simply declares that the collection of taxes "shall be made by such officer or officers, and at such time or times, as the city council may direct;" and the last section of that act contains the same provision quoted above from the second section of the act of 1881. So that, while it is true that the legislature have, by statute, conferred upon the city council the power to provide the manner in which the payment of taxes may be enforced, the pleadings in this case do not show that such power has ever been exercised. Ordinarily, the payment of taxes, whether imposed by state or municipal authority, is not enforced by action, but some more summary and speedy remedy is usually resorted to. As is said in Cooley, Tax'n, 13, quoted with approval in Oliver's Case, supra: "Taxes are not debts in the ordinary sense of that term, and their collection will in general depend on the remedies which are given by statute for their enforcement." It seems to us, therefore, that when a municipal corporation resorts to the unusual remedy of an action, it must allege and prove its authority for so doing.

We come next to the consideration of the second of the cases above stated, in which the ordinance imposing the license tax sued for is made a part of the complaint. Here we find that the third section of the ordinance above set out does provide another remedy, and what seems to be, under the views announced in Jager's Case, supra, a most stringent one. It is there expressly provided that, if a person required to take out a license shall fail or refuse so to do, he is liable to a penalty; but there is no provision that he may also be required to pay the license fee by an action for that purpose. Practically he is offered the option either to take out the license by paying the amount specified or be subject to the penalty prescribed by the third section of the ordinance. There is no warrant in the ordinance for requiring both, for there is not only no provision in the ordinance that the payment of the license fee may be enforced by an action for the same, but there is an express provision that, if he fails to obtain the prescribed license, he is liable to a heavy penalty. In this respect the ordinance now under consideration differs widely from that which came under review in Oliver's Case, supra, for in that there was an express provision that, if any person shall pursue any of the occupations requiring a license without taking out one, he "shall, besides being liable to the payment for the license, be subject to a penalty of twenty per cent. of the amount of such license, to be sued for and collected in the city court, or any other court of competent jurisdiction, or to imprisonment not exceeding thirty days, as may be adjudged by the recorder." But in the present ordinance the only provision made is that the failure to take out a license when required subjects one to the penalties prescribed by the third section of the ordinance. It seems to us, therefore, that the city council of Charleston, having been invested with authority to require the payment of such sum as they may deem just for a license, and having been specially authorized by the same act (1881, supra) "to pass such ordinances as are necessary to carry the intent and purpose of this act (which, as we have seen, was to raise revenue by requiring the payment of license fees) into full effect," and the city council having passed no ordinance, so far as appears in this case, to carry such intent and purpose into full effect, except the ordinance providing that a failure to pay the amount required for a license will subject one to the penalties prescribed, they are confined to the mode which they have prescribed for enforcing the payment of license fees, and cannot resort to any other. We are therefore of opinion that the demurrers in both of these cases should have been sustained, upon the ground that the complainants in both of the cases fail to state facts sufficient to constitute a cause of action. The judgment of this court is that the judgment of the circuit court in each of the cases stated above be reversed.

McGOWAN, J., concurs.

C. AULTMAN & CO. v. UTSEY.[1]

(*Supreme Court of South Carolina.* Nov. 12, 1891.)

FRAUDULENT CONVEYANCES—BONA FIDE PURCHASERS—EVIDENCE.

1. In 1884, P., while indebted to plaintiffs, executed a mortgage on his house and lot to one C. to secure a debt due the latter. The mortgage was afterwards paid, but was never canceled of record. On December 7, 1886, P. conveyed the property to C. by a deed reciting a consideration of $5,000. In 1887, M., the brother of defendant, learning that she wished to buy the property, and being requested to see P., wrote him, asking the price. P. replied that the property belonged to C., whereupon M. agreed with the latter to purchase for $3,250. Defendant's husband afterwards, on October 26, 1887, went to see about the purchase, and met P. instead of C., who produced papers showing the chain of title, among which were the deed from him to C., and a deed of that date without warranty from C. to P.'s wife, reciting a consideration of $5,000, together with a deed of the same date from her to defendant, reciting a consideration of $3,250. The deeds were delivered to defendant's husband, and as her agent he paid the consideration. Previously plaintiffs had recovered judgment on their claim against P. In an action by plaintiffs to set aside the deeds, M. testified that he had actual notice of the mortgage. He also knew that after the deed from P. to C. the former remained in possession, and there was evidence tending to show that he regarded him as the owner of the property. He also knew, when negotiating for the property, that P. was financially embarrassed, and of the pendency of the suit in which plaintiffs obtained the judgment against him. The deed from P. was in fraud of his creditors. *Held,*

[1] Rehearing pending.

that the court was warranted in finding that defendant was not a *bona fide* purchaser, on the ground that her brother and husband, as her agents, had sufficient notice to put them on inquiry.

2. The question whether defendant had such notice was not affected by the fact that after the purchase she submitted the papers to an attorney for an examination of the title, and that he pronounced it good, since it was too late then to make inquiry.

3. Whether defendant's agents, in such case, had sufficient notice to put them on inquiry, was a question of fact, and not of law.

Appeal from common pleas circuit court of Abbeville county; JAMES F. IZLAR, Judge.

Action by C. Aultman & Co. against Mattie Utsey to set aside a mortgage as having been satisfied, and a deed as fraudulent against the grantor's creditors. Judgment for plaintiffs. Defendant appeals. Affirmed.

The decree of the lower court was as follows:

"The case was heard before me upon the pleadings and testimony taken by the master under an order of reference for that purpose. Full argument was made by the counsel on either side. In reference to the pleadings, I will say in the outset that, while the plea of purchaser for valuable consideration is not made specially and in the usual form, the issues raised are the same, and the answer is in effect a plea of purchaser for valuable consideration without notice, and in the consideration of the case I shall treat it as such. The evidence tends to sustain most of the material allegations of the complaint. There is no dispute that the defendant paid three thousand two hundred and fifty dollars for the house and lot; neither is there any dispute as to the fact that the deed from F. M. Pope to G. W. Connor, as also the deed from G. W. Connor to Mrs. Elizabeth M. Pope, the wife of F. M. Pope, was voluntary, and made without consideration; and the following facts, namely: That the deed from F. M. Pope to G. W. Connor was made at a time when F. M. Pope was largely indebted to the plaintiffs and others, and with intent to delay, hinder, and defraud the creditors of F. M. Pope, and that there was no change in the possession of said property after said conveyance; and that the judgment of the plaintiffs is still unpaid and unsatisfied,—are fully sustained by the testimony. The following facts, however, are seriously contested, and must therefore be considered and determined upon the testimony submitted, and the law applicable thereto, namely: Was the price paid by the defendant at the time of said purchase, for the premises, inadequate; and did the defendant at the time of said purchase have actual or constructive notice of the fraud in the conveyance by F. M. Pope to G. W. Connor in the first instance, and of the subsequent fraud in the conveyance by G. W. Connor to Elizabeth M. Pope, the immediate grantor of the defendant? I am satisfied from the evidence that the defendant had no actual notice of the fraud in either case. I am equally satisfied that the purchase price paid by the defendant for said property was not, under the circumstances, inadequate. So the issue is narrowed down to the single question, whether or not the defendant had constructive notice of the fraud in the transfers of F. M. Pope to G. W. Connor and of G. W. Connor to Elisabeth M. Pope. The answer to this question depends alone upon the fact whether the circumstances attending said transfers were sufficient to put the defendant or her agents upon the inquiry. The rule of law as to constructive notice is clearly and succinctly stated by our supreme court in the case of Black v. Childs, 14 S. C. 321. The court say: 'If there are circumstances sufficient to put a party upon the inquiry, he is held to have notice of everything which that inquiry, properly conducted, would certainly disclose; but constructive notice goes no further. It stands upon the principle that the party is bound to the exercise of due diligence, and is assumed to have the knowledge to which that diligence would lead him; but he is not held to have notice of matter which lies beyond the range of that inquiry, and which that diligence might not disclose. "There must appear to be, in the nature of the case, such a connection between the facts disclosed and the further facts to be discovered that the former could justly be viewed as furnishing a clue to the latter.'"

"Now, what are the facts here? The defendant was desirous of purchasing a house and lot in the town of Ninety-Six, where she formerly lived. She was residing at St. George's, in the county of Colleton, in this state, with her husband, W. B. Utsey. One L. M. Moore, a resident of Ninety-Six, wrote to her husband that the Pope house and lot were for sale, and could be bought for thirty-five hundred dollars, ($3,500.) W. B. Utsey, as the agent of his wife, the defendant herein, wrote to Moore that defendant would pay three thousand ($3,000) dollars for the property, and if it could be bought for that price to close the trade. Moore wrote to F. M. Pope at Greenville, where he had recently moved with his family, stating that Col. Utsey wanted to buy the property and wanted to know the least cash price, and to answer by return mail. F. M. Pope replied to Moore by return mail, saying he had referred his letter to G. W. Connor; that the property was Connor's; and that he would have to negotiate with him. Moore wrote at once to Connor, stating that Pope said the property was his, and asking the least price that would buy it, and that, if for sale, to come down at once. Connor came to Ninety-Six on the next train. Moore met him. Connor offered the property for $3,500. Moore told him that Utsey's figures were $3,000. Connor then proposed to split the difference, and take $3,250. Moore told him he was not authorized to give it, but would notify the party at once, and, if accepted, would wire him. Moore communicated with Utsey. Utsey wrote Moore that he would take the property at $3,250, and to notify Connor. Moore notified Connor by telegraph. On October 26, 1887, Moore telegraphed Utsey that Connor had accepted his offer, and would be at Ninety-Six on Thursday with the papers. Up to this point there was nothing to excite suspi-

cion or suggest any fraud between any of the parties to the transaction. Everything appeared to be open, fair, and bona fide; and, had the contract of purchase, as concluded between Connor and Utsey, been carried out in the regular way between Connor and Utsey, there would have been nothing in the circumstances to furnish knowledge of the fraud, or even a clue thereto,—nothing sufficient to put the defendant or her agents upon the inquiry. But let us examine the circumstances surrounding the execution of the contract made between Connor and the defendant. On the 27th day of October, 1887, W. B. Utsey, as the agent of his wife, the defendant, goes to Ninety-Six to meet Connor, who was to be there with the papers conveying said property to the defendant in pursuance of the previous contract entered into, as aforesaid, between them. In the place of Connor, Pope appears. Instead of a tender of Connor's deed, the deed of Connor to Elisabeth M. Pope, wife of F. M. Pope, without warranty of any description, and the deed of Elisabeth M. Pope to the defendant, were tendered. Pope consummates Connor's agreement to convey, in his absence, and receives the purchase money, exhibiting no other authority from Connor save the deed to his (Pope's) wife, without warranty. No reason or explanation was given or made for the conduct of Connor in conveying through Elizabeth M. Pope, and not directly. These deeds disclosed the fact Elisabeth M. Pope was disposing of property to the defendant at a price fixed by Connor, and which was $1,750 less than the price purported to have been paid by Elizabeth M. Pope for the identical property on the morning of the same day. Besides these facts, the mortgage upon said property executed by F. M. Pope to G. W. Connor for ten thousand dollars, and which had been duly recorded in the register's office for said county, was then open and unsatisfied. Of this mortgage the defendant and her agent had constructive notice at least. These facts, I am constrained to say, were, in my opinion, sufficient to put the defendant and her agents upon the inquiry. She and they were bound to the exercise of due diligence, and, with the facts and circumstances here disclosed, they certainly failed to exercise it. These facts and circumstances were more than enough to arouse suspicion. They demanded investigation and explanation, before complying with the agreement to purchase and paying over the purchase price. Had due diligence been exercised on this occasion, it would have led to the discovery of the fraud in the previous transaction between F. M. Pope and G. W. Connor. Connor testifies that Pope wanted him to make the transfer direct to Utsey, but that he declined; that he could not guaranty the title, and would not do it; that if it had been his father he would not have done it to protect him. Now, if inquiry had been made of Connor for an explanation of the peculiar and extraordinary circumstances attending the transfer of said property, it must have led up to the fact that the conveyance of F. M. Pope to G. W. Connor was purely voluntary, and made in fraud of the existing creditors of F. M. Pope, and to the further fact that the mortgage of F. M. Pope to G. W. Connor had been fully paid and satisfied by the conveyance of other property, and not by the house and lot in question. A diligent inquiry would, I am persuaded, have led to a discovery of the fraud; and have disclosed the secret which had theretofore been kept by G. W. Connor. The defendant must therefore be presumed to have had knowledge of all the facts which a diligent inquiry would have disclosed. In the very nature of the case, there was, in my opinion, such a connection between the facts disclosed and the further facts to be discovered that the former could justly be viewed as furnishing a clue to the latter. I am therefore of opinion that the defendant is not a *bona fide* purchaser for value without notice of the fraud affecting the title to the property described in the complaint herein. The question whether the defendant exercised due diligence cannot, in my opinion, be affected by the fact that counsel was employed to investigate the title after the agreement to convey had been executed by the delivery of the deeds, and the payment of the purchase price of the property. There is no testimony tending to show that the counsel was in possession of the facts and circumstances attending the making of the contract to purchase, and its execution; all counsel had was the chain of title, which appeared regular. It is a hard case, but the injury to the defendant, if any, arises, not from the application of the legal principles involved in this investigation, but from a want of due diligence on the part of those who acted in her behalf, and by whose acts she is bound. * * *"

Benet & Cason, for appellant. *Graydon & Graydon,* for respondents.

McIVER, J. On the 1st day of February, 1884, one F. M. Pope, being indebted at the time to plaintiffs and others to a large amount, executed a mortgage on a house and lot in the town of Ninety-Six to one G. W. Connor, to secure the sum of $10,-500, which Connor in his testimony says was intended to secure future advances as well as the amount then really due. The amount really due on this mortgage, ($5,045,) Connor says, was paid to him some time in the winter of 1884, though the mortgage was not canceled, and still remains of record, open and apparently unsatisfied. This payment was made by the sale to Connor of property other than that embraced in the mortgage. On the 7th of December, 1886, the house and lot above mentioned, which is the subject of this controversy, was conveyed by Pope to Connor by a deed, in which the consideration recited was the sum of $5,000, which deed seems to have been duly recorded, though the date of such record is not given. Some time in 1887, probably towards the latter part of that year, L. M. Moore, the brother-in-law of W. B. Utsey, who then resided in Ninety-Six, learning that Mrs. Utsey, the defendant herein, who then lived in Colleton county, desired to buy the house and lot in question, with a view to a return to Ninety-Six, where she had formerly resided, and being requested to see Pope, who was then supposed to be the owner of the property, and ascertain at what price the property could be bought, undertook the negotiation for the purchase. Accordingly Moore wrote to Pope, who had then recently removed to Greenville, asking the price of the property. Pope replied by the next mail, saying that the property belonged to Connor, and referring Moore to him. Thereupon Moore opened negotiations with Connor, which resulted in an agreement to sell for the sum of $3,250. W. B. Utsey, the husband of the defendant, being informed of this result, and being advised to go up on the following Thursday, which seems to have been the 26th of October, 1887, did so, and there met Pope instead of Connor, who produced the papers showing the chain of title, among which were the deed from Pope to Connor, above mentioned, and a deed without warranty from Connor to the wife of Pope, bearing date that day, in which the consideration recited was the sum of $5,000, together with a deed bearing the same date, signed by Mrs. Pope, to the defendant, in which the consideration recited was the price agreed upon, ($3,250;) and, upon the delivery of these deeds to W. B. Utsey, he, acting as the agent of his wife, settled with Pope by paying in cash $2,000 of the price, and the balance in an accepted draft at 60 days. After the trade was thus consummated, Utsey delivered the papers to his attorney for an examination of the title, who pronounced it good. In the mean time, however, to-wit, on the 25th of February, 1887, the plaintiffs had recovered a judgment on their claim against said Pope; and, under the execution issued to enforce that judgment, the said house and lot was levied on by the sheriff, and on the 2d of September, 1889, the same were sold and bid off by the plaintiffs, who, having complied with the terms of the sale, received titles from the sheriff. Very soon thereafter this action was commenced, in which plaintiffs, under the allegations that the deed from Pope to Connor was without consideration, and made with intent to hinder, delay, and defraud the creditors of Pope, and that the mortgage, if anything was ever due thereon, had been paid and satisfied, and that the deed from Connor to Mrs. Pope was also without consideration and made with like intent, demand judgment that the said deeds be declared fraudulent and void, and that the same, together with the mortgage, be canceled, and also for the possession of the premises. The defendant, in her answer, denies all the material allegations in the complaint, and sets up, in an informal manner, the defense that she is a purchaser for valuable consideration without notice. The case was heard by his honor, Judge IZLAR, upon the pleadings, the testimony taken by the master, and the argument of counsel; who having found, as matter of fact, that the deeds from Pope to Connor and from Connor to Mrs. Pope were not only without consideration, but made with intent to hinder, delay, and defraud the creditors of Pope, adjudged them fraudulent and void; and, having found that the mortgage had in fact been satisfied, directed that the same be so declared on the record by the clerk. He held that the only real question in the case was whether the defendant had such notice as would defeat her plea as purchaser for valuable consideration without notice. and upon that he found that, while she did not personally have such notice, yet she did have constructive notice, through her agents, sufficient to put them upon the inquiry, which, if followed up properly, would have led to the discovery of the defect in the title which she purchased; and he therefore overruled that plea, and rendered judgment that the deeds be delivered up, canceled, and the mortgage be marked satisfied, and directed that the issue of title and right of possession be referred to a jury for trial.

From this judgment defendant appeals upon the several grounds set out in the record, which raise, substantially, the single question whether there was error in holding that defendant had such notice as would defeat her plea of purchaser for valuable consideration without notice. The plaintiffs also, in accordance with the proper practice, give notice that they propose to sustain the judgment below upon other grounds than those stated in the decree, which are likewise set out in the record. But, as we are satisfied that the judgment must be sustained upon the grounds upon which it is based by the circuit judge, it will not be necessary for us to consider any of those additional grounds, some of which present important and very interesting questions, upon which we would prefer to have the aid of the circuit judge's views, as well as further argument of counsel, before undertaking to decide them, especially as it is not necessary to the decision of this case to do so now. We will, therefore, confine our attention to the question raised by counsel for the appellant, which is really more a question of fact than of law; and therefore, under the well-settled rule, the conclusion reached by the court below should not be disturbed here, unless it is either without any evidence to sustain it, or is manifestly against the weight of the evidence. But it is urged by appellant that, inasmuch as the appeal here does not impute error in the finding of any particular fact, but that such error lies in drawing an unwarranted inference from undisputed facts, a question of law, rather than of fact, is presented. If it could be shown that the law lays down any particular rule or rules by which to determine what facts are or are not sufficient to put a person upon inquiry, then there would be much force in the position. But, so far as we are informed, no specific rules have been laid down by which to determine whether the facts in a given case are or are not sufficient to put a party upon inquiry. Indeed, we do not see how it would be possible to formulate any specific rule of general applicability, as it is manifest that each case must depend largely upon its particular circumstances. The most that can be done is to lay down some general rules upon the subject; and that has been done by Mr. Justice Mc-

Gowan in Black v. Childs, 14 S. C. 312, probably as well as the nature of the subject permits, in the quotation from that case made by the circuit judge in his decree; for while it is undoubtedly true that "there must appear to be, in the nature of the case, such a connection between the facts disclosed and the further facts to be discovered that the former could justly be viewed as furnishing a clue to the latter," yet in every instance it will always be a question what is the nature of the case, and whether the facts disclosed can be re garded as furnishing a clue to the fact in question. This view may be illustrated by a case depending upon circumstantial evidence. While it is true that there are certain well-established general rules in regard to the consideration of that kind of testimony, yet, after all, it remains a question of fact whether, in a given case, the particular facts proved warrant the one or the other conclusion. For example, in the trial of a criminal case, where circumstantial evidence is relied upon to show the guilt of the accused, and where no error is imputed to the judge in laying down the general rules to be observed in considering that kind of testimony, it is always a question of fact, exclusively for the jury, whether the circumstances relied upon and established are sufficient to produce in the minds of the jury a conviction of the guilt of the accused. So in this case, where it does not appear that the circuit judge has violated or disregarded any of the general rules in respect to the subject under consideration, but, on the contrary, has expressly recognised and followed them, and the only error assigned is in applying them to the facts of the case, it seems to us that a question of fact only is presented. This view seems to have been adopted in Richardson v. Chappell, 6 S. C., at page 157, where it is said: "On the question of notice, the conclusions of the circuit judge appear to conform to the evidence. There was certainly evidence in the case from which a conclusion of fact could be drawn as to whether Simkins had, at the time of purchasing, knowledge of the existence of plaintiff's claim. * * * The question of notice was properly before the circuit judge as a question of fact to be determined from the testimony before him. There is no overbearing weight of evidence against his conclusions, such as would justify this court in setting them aside." And again: "We are not required to say what force these circumstances should have in the mind of the circuit judge, for the duty of drawing inferences rested primarily on him, and it is only where he acts in the face of and against the force of overbearing testimony that this court can properly disturb his conclusions." It seems to us, therefore, that the question of whether defendant had such notice as would defeat her plea of purchase for valuable consideration, without notice, was a question of fact, and that the conclusion reached by the circuit judge must, under the rule, be sustained, unless it is either without any evidence to sustain it, or is manifestly against the weight of the evidence, neither of which can be said in this case.

But in deference to the earnest and able efforts of counsel to relieve this unfortunate lady from a misfortune which has befallen her through no fault on her part, as it is entirely clear that there is not a shadow of reason for believing that she was guilty of any fraud herself, or connived at the fraud of others, or even had any personal knowledge that there had been any fraud committed, we are disposed to consider more fully the question than is usually done in cases where an appeal turns upon a question of fact, although it seems to us that the reasoning of the circuit judge in his decree, which we trust will be incorporated in the report of the case, is quite sufficient to vindicate the correctness of his conclusions. While, as we have said, it is clear that the defendant had no personal knowledge of any fraud, or of any circumstances calculated to excite inquiry, yet, under the well-settled doctrine that notice to the agent is notice to the principal, if her agents had notice she must be affected thereby The real question, therefore, is whether the agents of the defendant, one or both of them, had notice of such facts and circumstances as were calculated to excite inquiry, which, if followed up with due diligence, would have led to the discovery of the fraud; or, in other words, were the facts and circumstances, of which they unquestionably had notice, of such a character as would furnish a clue, which, if followed up with due diligence, would have led to the discovery of the fraud? In the first place, both of these agents certainly had constructive notice of the mortgage, which was spread upon the record, apparently unsatisfied, and one of them, (Moore,) who had conducted the negotiations up to the day when Utsey appeared for the purpose of consummating the trade, says he had actual knowledge of the mortgage; and when he learned that Pope had conveyed the property in question to Connor he assumed, without any inquiry whatever, that such conveyance had been made in satisfaction of the mortgage, which turns out not to have been the fact. Again, when Moore learned that the property had been conveyed to Connor some time before, he, at the same time, knew that Pope had retained possession, as long as he remained in Ninety-Six, up to a very short time before the sale to defendant, and this, of itself, was a circumstance well calculated to excite inquiry, especially in view of the fact that Moore still regarded Pope as the owner, as shown by his attempt to buy from him, as well as by his own direct testimony to that effect. Indeed, the remark made by Moore to Pope, after the sale had been consummated,—that he ought to pay him $100 for making the sale,—would seem to indicate that Moore still regarded Pope as the real owner, even after he had learned of the conveyance to Connor, and Pope's reply to that remark was not calculated to remove that impression, for he did not say that the property was not his, but said "the trouble of it was he did not get the money," but did not say who got it. Moore also knew that Pope was embarrassed at the time, to some extent

at least, and knew of the pendency of the action by plaintiffs against Pope, in which the judgment was recovered, under which the property was subsequently sold. Then, when Utsey appeared, as the agent of defendant, to consummate the trade which Moore had negotiated with Connor, he certainly had constructive notice of the mortgage. Common prudence required that he should examine the records of the county where the property which he proposed to purchase was located, and if he had done so he would have discovered, not only that there was a mortgage upon it, to secure the payment of a large sum of money, which was apparently open and unsatisfied, but that judgments to a large amount against the former owner (Pope) had been entered very soon after,—one of them only a few days. Pope had conveyed the property to Connor; yet it does not appear that he made any such examination, and made no inquiry, either as to the mortgage or anything else. Add to this the fact that, though Utsey had been informed only a day or two before that the agreement for the sale had been made with one person, (Connor,) he is met by another, (Pope,) and proceeds to consummate the trade with him, without any explanation whatever being given or asked for, as to why this sudden change in the vendor was made. But, more than this, when Pope presents the papers showing the chain of title, Utsey sees that one of them is a deed, dated that very day, from Connor to Mrs. Pope, the wife of F. M. Pope, a person whom he knew, or ought to have known, from the records, was heavily embarrassed, in which the consideration recited was $5,000, which deed contained no warranty whatever; and yet he takes a deed from Mrs. Pope, in which the consideration stated, and actually paid, was $1,750 less than the amount which her deed from Connor showed that she had, on the same day, paid for the very same property, without making any inquiry whatever, or receiving any explanation of these very singular circumstances. Here was not only a very sudden change in the vendor, but here was a married woman, whose husband had been the owner of the property within less than a year before, and who was then very much embarrassed, selling that property, which she held under a quitclaim deed, from a person who then held a mortgage, apparently unsatisfied, for a sum very much less than what the papers showed she had that very day given for it. Surely, these circumstances were well calculated to excite inquiry, and yet none was made. Indeed, some of the cases go so far as to hold that one who purchases from another holding under a quitclaim deed cannot, by reason of that fact, claim to be a purchaser without notice. See 2 Pom. Eq. Jur. § 753, where the cases, both *pro* and *con.*, are cited in a note. Among the cases cited in support of the proposition are two from the supreme court of the United States, (Oliver v. Platt, 3 How. 333, and May v. Le Claire, 11 Wall. 217.) The reason given is that such a purchaser buys no more than what his grantor can lawfully convey; to which we think might be added that the fact that the grantor is unwilling to warrant the title tends, at least, to show that there is some defect in the title, known to or apprehended by him, and therefore the purchaser is put upon inquiry. While we are not prepared, at present, to go to the full extent to which the doctrine has been carried by some of the cases, yet we are satisfied that the fact that the immediate grantor of the purchaser holds under a quitclaim deed is a circumstance well calculated to excite inquiry, which, if not pursued properly, will affect the purchaser with notice of every fact which such inquiry, pursued with due diligence, would disclose; and certainly when, as in this case, there are other circumstances of a very suspicious nature, connected with the fact that the immediate grantor of the purchaser held under a quitclaim deed, the conclusion reached by the circuit judge may well be sustained. It is urged, however, that if inquiry had been made, the defect in the title would not have been disclosed, as Connor would not have been likely to confess the fraud in which he had participated; for, to use the language of appellant's counsel: "Connor was anxious at that time to get out of the matter, as he had been a party in the fraud a good while before that time. We think it would be too much to ask any one to believe that he would have revealed the whole matter just at a time when he was about to get out of the difficulty." To say nothing of the fact that this would apply in every case of fraud, it is impossible for any one to say what Connor would have done if inquiry had been made of him before the sale, and the court is not at liberty to speculate about it. We do see, however, that the purchaser had notice, through her agents, of such facts and circumstances as demanded further inquiry, and that none was made. If inquiry had been made, and no information impugning the title had been obtained, that would have relieved the purchaser, but having failed to make inquiry, as the circumstances demanded, she cannot claim relief upon the ground of a mere speculation that the persons who could have furnished the desired information would have been unwilling to do so. That could only be tested by a trial, and none was made. But we are unable to see what difficulty, legally speaking, Connor was in, and wanted to get out of, though, morally considered, his conduct may well be viewed as reprehensible; and we do not see how his quitclaim deed to Mrs. Pope, for the purpose of enabling her to sell the property as her own, could relieve him from his moral delinquency. His debt secured by the mortgage had been extinguished by the conveyance of other property, and the fact that he held the property in question under a fraudulent deed, for which he had paid nothing could not involve him in any legal difficulty, as all he would have to do would be to surrender property, which had cost him nothing, to its rightful owner. But, more than this, the testimony shows that the first time Connor was called upon he stated fully, and no

doubt truthfully, all the circumstances. It seems to us that the fact that Utsey submitted the papers to an attorney for an examination of the title, who pronounced it good, after the sale had been made, titles executed, and the money paid, cannot affect this question. It was too late then to make the inquiry, which should have been made before. It seems to us, therefore, that there is much in the testimony to sustain the conclusion reached by the circuit judge; and certainly it cannot be said that it is either without any evidence to sustain it, or is against the manifest weight of the evidence. The judgment of this court is that the judgment of the circuit court be affirmed.

McGOWAN, J. I concur in the result. There was a complete chain of paper title, —deeds, purporting to be for valuable consideration, from Pope to Connor, and back again from Connor to Mrs. Pope. It is, however, perfectly clear ·that they were without consideration, fraudulent, and void. It is true that of this fraud Mrs. Utsey was entirely innocent. She had no connection whatever with it, or indeed knowledge of it. But, after some hesitation, I cannot resist the conclusion that there was, on the part of those who negotiated the purchase for Mrs. Utsey and paid her money, such a want of ordinary and proper care and inquiry as to prevent her from having the benefit of the plea of purchaser for valuable consideration without notice.

FISHER v. FAIR et al.

(Supreme Court of South Carolina. Nov. 27, 1891.)

REHEARING—WHEN GRANTED.

A motion for a rehearing will be denied where it appears that no material fact or principle of law was overlooked or misunderstood.

On rehearing. For former opinion, see 13 S. E. Rep. 470.

PER CURIAM. We have carefully examined this petition, and, finding that no material fact or important principle of law has been either overlooked or misunderstood, there is no ground for a rehearing. It is therefore ordered that the petition be dismissed.

COOLEY et al. (PIEDMONT MANUF'G CO., Interveners) v. PERRY et al.

(Supreme Court of South Carolina. Nov. 12, 1891.)

LANDLORD AND TENANT — DISTRESS — PRIORITY— RIGHTS OF OTHER CREDITORS—ASSIGNMENT.

1. Suit was commenced by the creditors of a firm to set aside an assignment, and subjecting the firm assets to its debts. A temporary order was granted restraining any one from interfering with the goods, and requiring defendants to show cause why the injunction should not be continued until the determination of the suit. Afterwards the landlord levied a distress upon the goods. An order was made setting aside the assignment, appointing a receiver, and requiring all creditors to prove their claims or be barred from participation in the fund. Held that, as the landlord was not a party until after the levy

of the distress, he was not bound by any order in the suit, but was entitled to priority over the other creditors, notwithstanding that the rent was not due when the assignment was made or when the suit was commenced.

2. As no order had been made authorizing any one to take possession of the goods, and hold the same subject to the direction of the court, they were not *in custodia legis*, and were therefore subject to levy under the distress.

Appeal from common pleas circuit court of Greenville county; JAMES F. IZLAR, Judge.

This was a suit by A. Cooley & Co. and others against Perry Bros. and others to set aside a deed of assignment, and to subject the assets of the defendants to the payment of the plaintiffs' debts. After commencement of suit, the Piedmont Manufacturing Company levied a distress for rent upon the stock of goods of the defendants, and applied for an order requiring the payment of the said rent. The order was granted, and plaintiffs appeal. Affirmed.

Perry & Heyward, for appellants. *T. Q. & A. H. Donaldson*, for respondents. *S. P. Dendy* and *M. F. Ansel*, for receiver.

McIVER, J. The defendants Perry Bros. occupied a store-house belonging to the petitioner, the Piedmont Manufacturing Company, under a contract for a lease thereof for the year 1889, at an annual rental of $500, payable in quarterly installments of $125 each, the last of which was due on the 1st of January, 1890. During the term the said Perry Bros. on the 19th of December, 1889, undertook to make an assignment to one J. Harper Donuald for the benefit of their creditors, and said assignee entered upon and used the said store-house until the end of the last quarter, and until the 8th of February, 1890, when the stock of goods in the store was sold under an order of the court, as will be hereinafter stated. On the 24th of December, 1889, this action was commenced for the benefit of all the creditors of Perry Bros., for the purpose, as we infer, of setting aside the deed of assignment above referred to, and subjecting the assets of the said Perry Bros. to the payment of their debts; and on that day an order was granted by his honor, Judge NORTON, at chambers, "enjoining and restraining the defendants and all other persons from interfering with or removing said goods, or seeking to carry out the terms of the assignment, and requiring the defendants to show cause before him, at Walhalla, on the 2d day of January, 1890, why said injunction should not be continued in force until the final determination of the action." In consequence of a failure to observe the provisions of subdivision 3 of rule 5 of the supreme court, requiring that the case shall set forth "the names of all the parties to the action," we are not informed as to who were made parties to the action; but we infer, from the manner in which the question which we are called upon to determine has been presented, that the Piedmont Manufacturing Company was not a party. On the 10th of January, 1890, the Piedmont Manufacturing Company, through its agent, "levied a distress warrant on the stock of goods in

said store-house, in the hands of J. H. Donuald, assignee," for the purpose of enforcing payment of the last quarter's rent, which fell due on the 1st of January, 1890. On the 18th of January, 1890, the temporary injunction previously granted, as above stated, was continued until the further order of the court; and on the 18th of January, 1890, it was agreed in writing "that the right of the Piedmont Manufacturing Company for rent be reserved, and transferred to the proceeds of sale of said stock of goods, the goods having been ordered to be sold by the court;" but when such order was granted does not appear, though the sale, as we have said, seems to have been made on the 8th of February, 1890. On the 28th of March, 1890, his honor, Judge ALDRICH, "made a consent order or decree, by which he set aside and declared void the assignment above-mentioned, and appointed the said J. Harper Donuald receiver of all and singular the property, both real and personal, of the said Perry Bros.," and required "all creditors to prove their claims before the receiver, or be barred from participating in the fund." At the ensuing term of the court an application was made to his honor, Judge IZLAR, for an order requiring the receiver to pay to the Piedmont Manufacturing Company the full amount of rent due for the quarter ending 1st January, 1890; which order, after hearing the facts as above stated, together with the argument of counsel, was granted. From this order plaintiffs appeal upon the grounds set out in the record.

Inasmuch as the so-called deed of assignment has been "declared void" by the judgment of a competent tribunal, the case must be considered as if no attempt had ever been made to execute an assignment. So considering it, there can be no doubt that the landlord had a perfect right to levy a distress warrant upon the goods of the lessee remaining on the leased premises, upon default in payment of the last quarter's rent, and this would give the landlord the first lien on such goods, which, by the agreement of the parties above stated, was transferred to the proceeds of the sale. Indeed, it would seem that, even if the deed of assignment had stood good, the landlord would still have the right to enforce payment of the rent due out of the goods in the hands of the assignee. Burrell, Assignm. § 374. It is contended, however, that the action in this case, being in the nature of a creditors' bill, having been commenced before the rent fell due, the distress warrant could not be legally levied on the goods, but that the landlord must come in under this action, and share alike with all the other creditors in the fund derived from the sale of the common debtor's goods. But it will be remembered that, so far as appears, the landlord was not a party to this action, and never was compelled to become so until the order calling in creditors was granted, and this was some time after the levy of the distress warrant.

Again, it is urged that the restraining order granted on the day of the commencement of the action—24th of December, 1889—was sufficient to prevent the execution of the distress warrant; but it will be observed that the landlord, not being a party to the action, could not be bound by any order therein; and, in addition to this, it would seem that the temporary restraining order was only operative to the 2d of January, 1890, and was not continued in force until the 13th of January, 1890, and that in the mean time, to-wit, on the 10th of January, 1890, the distress warrant was levied.

Finally, it is urged that the goods levied on under the distress warrant were *in custodia legis*, and therefore could not be the subject of such levy. While it is quite true that goods in the custody of the law cannot be the subject of levy, yet we are not prepared to admit that the goods in this case were in that condition when the distress warrant was levied. In Gilman v. Williams, 7 Wis. 329, which we find in a note to 4 Amer. & Eng. Enc. Law. 969, we see it was held that "property is in the custody of the law when it has been taken and is held by legal process in a lawful manner and for a lawful purpose." Looking to the reason of the rule, we think it may be said that property is in the custody of the law when it is found in the possession of some officer or agent of a court whose duty it is to hold and dispose of the same in accordance with the order or mandate of the court. Now, can this be said of the goods in this case when the distress warrant was levied? They were not in the possession of any officer or agent of any court; and, although the action when it was commenced did look to placing the property in that condition, yet it had not then been done, but the goods were actually in the possession and under the control of the debtor or his assignee, if the deed of assignment had not been declared void. No order had been passed requiring or authorizing any one to take possession and hold the same subject to the directions of the court, and we do not see how it can be said that the goods were *in custodia legis* at the time the distress warrant was levied. It seems to us, therefore, that, in any view of the case, the order appealed from must be sustained. The judgment of this court is that the order of the circuit court be affirmed.

McGOWAN, J.   I concur.

EAST TENNESSEE, V. & G. RY. CO. v. MARKENS.

(Supreme Court of Georgia.   Nov. 10, 1891.)

RAILROAD COMPANIES — ACCIDENT AT CROSSING — CARRIERS—IMPUTABLE NEGLIGENCE.

1. Where there is no evidence that a passenger in a public hack knew of danger from an approaching train on a public crossing, the judge may so state to the jury, and may say that there is no evidence of any failure in duty on the part of such passenger to avoid the injury.

2. In the case of a female passenger in a public hack, a charge to the jury as follows was correct: "I do charge you that the negligence of the driver, if he was negligent, is not imputable to her. A person who hires a public hack, and gives the driver directions as to the place where he wishes to be conveyed, but exercises no other control over the conduct of the driver, is not responsible for his acts of negligence, or

prevented from recovering against the railroad company for injuries suffered from a collision of its train with the hack, if the same was caused by the concurring negligence of both the manager of the train and the driver of the hack. The only negligence on the part of the driver which will defeat or otherwise affect the right of Mrs. Markens to recover is embodied in the following proposition: If the negligence of the driver was the sole cause and the real cause of the collision, she cannot recover. If the driver and the manager of the train were guilty of negligence, both concurring to bring the collision about, such negligence on the part of the driver cannot have the effect either to defeat or diminish the plaintiff's right to recover."

3. A female passenger in a public hack is under no duty to supervise the driver at a public crossing, nor to look or listen for approaching trains, unless she has some reason to distrust the diligence of the driver himself in respect to these matters.

4. The statute requiring the checking of trains and ringing of bells in approaching public crossings is applicable to this case, without reference to the distance from the crossing to the point at which the train started.

5. Though the court committed some slight errors in ruling upon the minor points of the case as set out in the motion for a new trial, there was no error in refusing a new trial upon any of the grounds stated in the motion.

(Syllabus by the Court.)

Error from city court of Atlanta; HOWARD VAN EPPS, Judge.

Action by one Markens against the East Tennessee, Virginia & Georgia Railway Company for personal injuries. Judgment for plaintiff. Defendant appeals. Affirmed.

Dorsey, Brewster & Howell, for plaintiff in error. *Mr. Hoke* and *Burton Smith,* for defendant in error.

LUMPKIN, J.   1. While a judge is forbidden to express or intimate his opinion concerning a question of fact about which there is any doubt whatever, he may with propriety say to the jury that there is no evidence to support an alleged fact, when such statement is unquestionably true. The object of section 3248 of the Code is to prevent judges from interfering with the functions of juries in determining contested issues of fact when there is proof on both sides; but when an alleged fact is entirely unsupported by evidence the judge may aid the jury by so informing them, thus relieving them of that much difficulty in reaching a correct conclusion in the case.

2 and 3. Whatever the law formerly may have been, it is now well settled that the propositions contained in the charge of the court below quoted in the second head-note are correct and sound. So well are we convinced of this, we deem an elaborate discussion of the questions involved unnecessary. In the American & English Encyclopedia of Law (volume 4, p. 83) we find the following: "It is now the rule in the United States courts, in England, and in most of the states of the United States, that the contributory negligence of a carrier is not attributable to a passenger." In volume 16, p. 447, of the same work, it is stated that "there can be no such thing as imputable negligence, except in cases where that privity which exists in law between master and servant and principal and agent is found."

In order for the negligence of one person to be properly imputable to another, the one to whom it is imputed must stand in such a relation of privity to the negligent person that the maxim *qui facit per alium facit per se* is directly applicable. It follows that all the cases in which the negligence of one person has been imputed to another in the absence of just this relation of privity are wrongly decided, and such is the effect of overwhelming recent cases." See, also, Flaherty v. Railway Co., (Minn.) 40 N. W. Rep. 160; Becke v. Railway Co., 102 Mo. 544, 13 S. W. Rep. 1053; Little v. Hackett, 116 U. S. 366, 6 Sup. Ct. Rep. 391, and authorities cited therein. And particularly see note by reporter (Irving Browne) to case of Borough of Carlisle v. Brisbane, 57 Amer. Rep. 488-511, inclusive, which treats of the subject in a most comprehensive manner. Also the following text-books: Deer. Neg. § 27; 1 Shear. & R. Neg. (4th Ed.) § 66; Whit. Smith, Neg. 405-407; Beach, Contrib. Neg. §§ 32-36; 1 Thomp. Neg. § 38; Thomp. Carr. 284 et seq.; Cooley, Torts, 684; Add. Torts, § 33; Whart. Neg. § 344a. These citations might be multiplied indefinitely, but even a casual examination of those above mentioned will suffice to establish the rule laid down by the court below. It will also appear from the foregoing authorities, and is entirely consistent with every-day experience, that a female passenger in a public hack may trust that the driver thereof will exercise proper caution and diligence in avoiding collisions with railroad trains or other things which would naturally result in injury to the vehicle or its occupants. If such driver were drunk, plainly incompetent to manage his team, or manifestly reckless, or if for any other reason it was apparent to the passenger that she could not safely rely upon him, probably the duty would be upon her to supervise his conduct, and compel him, if possible, to observe the requirements of ordinary care and prudence in the management of his vehicle, or else leave the same. No reason why the plaintiff should do either appeared in this case, and we therefore think she was under no obligation to overlook or undertake to control the driver's movements, or get out of the hack.

4. Section 708 of the Code, relating to the erection of blow-posts, the blowing of whistles, and the checking of trains in approaching public crossings, was by the act of 1875 (incorporated in section 710 of the Code) modified, so far as cities, towns, and villages are concerned, by dispensing with the posts, by substituting the tolling of bells for the blowing of whistles, and by requiring engineers to signal the approach of their trains to public crossings, no matter whether such trains were put in motion at a distance of 400 yards from such crossings or at a point less than that distance. We do not mean to say the act in precise terms makes these changes, but it seems unquestionable that they were intended to be made thereby. In the very nature of things, the legislature could not have intended that the approach of trains to public crossings in towns and cities ~ould be signaled only when the train be-

gan to move at a point 400 yards or more distant therefrom. The absolute absurdity of such intention in the legislative mind shows conclusively that it did not exist. The purpose of the act undoubtedly was to protect persons and property on street crossings in towns and cities, and this could not possibly be accomplished if warnings of the approach of trains and locomotives need be given only when they were set in motion nearly a quarter of a mile from any particular street crossing in question. The law meant that in towns and cities engineers and other persons in control of trains should always be cautious in approaching crossings, and have their powerful machines under such control as in every instance to be able to prevent collisions in such places. That this court has so regarded and construed the law is evident from its rulings in the following cases: Railroad v. Wyly, 65 Ga. 120; Railroad v. Carr, 73 Ga. 557; Railroad v. Russell, 75 Ga. 810; Railroad v. Young, 81 Ga. 417, 7 S. E. Rep. 912; Railroad v. Evans, (Ga.) 13 S. E. Rep. 580. Numerous other decisions of this court might be cited, but the above will suffice. The case of Morgan v. Railroad, 77 Ga. 788, even if correct in holding that section 708 of the Code does not apply to trains operating between points where blow-posts are or should be located, and public crossings, is not applicable here, because in that case the injury did not take place in a city, town, or village, and the case was not, therefore, within the act of 1875, above mentioned.

5. The motion for a new trial contains 35 grounds. We have carefully considered all of them, and find that the court did commit some slight errors in its rulings upon questions of minor importance, but none of them are sufficiently serious to authorize or require the granting of a new trial. The controlling questions in the case are those which we have already discussed. and, the court having ruled correctly upon these, we are of the opinion that the judgment below should be, and accordingly it is, affirmed.

UNDERWOOD v. STATE.

(*Supreme Court of Georgia.* Nov. 10, 1891.)

HOMICIDE—SELF-DEFENSE—INSTRUCTIONS—NEW TRIAL.

1. The prisoner's statement, if true, making a case from which the jury might conclude that the killing was necessary in self-defense; and his counsel having at the proper time requested the court in writing to instruct the jury that if they believed that at the time of the killing the deceased was making an unjustifiable assault upon the accused with a deadly weapon, with the purpose of taking his life, that the conduct of the accused was solely in defense against that assault, and was necessary in order to save his own life, and that under these circumstances he would not be guilty, and the jury should so find,—it was error, according to Hayden v. State, 69 Ga. 732, to deny such request. In Darby v. State, 79 Ga. 64, 3 S. E. Rep. 663, no request for any instruction based on the prisoner's statement appeared.

2. Taking into consideration all the rulings of the court so far as verified, and also the full charge given to the jury, it was not error to re-

fuse a new trial upon any of the grounds of the motion, save that which related to the above matter.

(*Syllabus by the Court.*)

Error from superior court, Fulton county; RICHARD H. CLARK, Judge.

Prosecution of E. A. Underwood for murder. From a judgment of conviction defendant appeals. Reversed.

Glenn & Maddox, for plaintiff in error. *C. D. Hill*, Sol. Gen., and *W. A. Little*, Asst. Sol. Gen., for the State.

BLECKLEY, C. J. 1. In a criminal case the accused is not a competent witness in his own behalf upon the trial, but by statute he has the right to make a statement to the court and jury. This right as to cases of felony was brought in by the act of 1868; by the act of 1874 it was extended so as to comprehend all criminal trials; and by amendment in 1879 it was enacted that the jury might believe the statement in preference to the sworn testimony in the case. The entire provision on the subject, as it stands now, appears in the Code of 1882, and reads as follows: "In all criminal trials in this state, the prisoner shall have the right to make to the court and jury such statement not to be under oath, and to have such force only as the jury may think right to give it; and the jury may believe such statement in preference to the sworn testimony in the case: provided, the prisoner shall not be compelled to answer any questions on cross-examination, should he or she think proper to decline to answer such questions." Code, § 4637. Exercising this statutory right, Underwood, on his trial for the killing of Sayer, made a statement consisting in part of the following: "Mr. Sayer was still talking in his room. I walked on back out there on the veranda near the cistern or well, going through the dining-room, and asked Mr. Sayer to be quiet; that Duggar was all right; there was nothing the matter with him. And I told him: 'Alexander, it is near time you were going to work. It is after three o'clock. Now go on to work. Everything is all right. Duggar seems to be quiet.' He remarked to me: 'You God damned son of a bitch, you are no friend to me either, and I will kill you.' He made at me with a knife or something in his hand, and I told him: 'Don't do nothing like that.' Mr. Sayer kept advancing, and then was when the work was done. I snatched my revolver just as quick as I could, and the firing was done in a second, and under the excitement, fearing my own life was in danger. I thought I would be murdered there. I didn't know I had fired two shots. I was under the impression it was one. He was advancing on me, and it was done in half a second. * * * It looked like a knife. * * * It looked like a knife to me." There was no sworn evidence to confirm this statement, but, on the contrary, the facts of the homicide, as testified to by the witnesses for the state, were wholly inconsistent with it. The court charged the jury upon murder and manslaughter, but gave no instruction whatever upon justi-

fiable homicide or the law of self-defense. Counsel for the accused, by a request made in writing at the proper time, called upon the court to charge the jury thus: "If you believe that, at that time of the killing, the deceased, Sayer, was making an unjustifiable assault upon the defendant with a deadly weapon with the purpose of taking defendant's life, that defendant's conduct was solely in defense against said assault thus made, and was necessary in order to save his own life, and that under these circumstances and for this purpose he shot and killed the deceased, he would not be guilty, and you should so find." The denial of this request is the subject-matter of the eleventh ground of the motion for a new trial. The court states, in a note to this ground, that it was his duty to charge the law of self-defense if warranted by the evidence, but he did not think it his duty to charge upon the statement of the defendant alone, unsupported by the evidence. It thus appears that the court was aware that counsel for the defendant desired to urge a substantive defense based on the statement of his client, and the sole reason assigned by the court for declining the request was that it rested on the statement alone. This reason was not legally sufficient, testing it by the only decision of this court of which we are aware that applies directly to the question. In the case of Hayden v. State, 69 Ga. 732, it was ruled by a full bench that "the statement of a prisoner is admissible by statute, to be weighed and passed upon by the jury, and they may believe it, notwithstanding it conflicts with the sworn testimony of witnesses. Therefore, when a legal and pertinent request to charge has been made in writing, based upon such statement, it should be given; otherwise the statement would be restricted in its effect." In the present case the request was in writing, and the matter of it was legal and pertinent; for, if the statement of the prisoner was true, the jury might have concluded from it that the homicide was committed in self-defense. By section 4330 of the Code, self-defense is a ground of justification, and the language of section 4333 is as follows: "If a person kill another in his defense, it must appear that the danger was so urgent and pressing at the time of the killing that, in order to save his own life, the killing of the other was absolutely necessary; and it must appear, also, that the person killed was the assailant, or that the slayer had really and in good faith endeavored to decline any further struggle before the mortal blow was given." Until reversed or modified in the manner prescribed by section 217 of the Code, the decision in Hayden v. State is binding, not only on the superior courts, but on this court. It was the legal right of the accused to have the rule there laid down administered on the trial of this case, and, however guilty he may be, we do not feel authorized to acquiesce in his conviction, and in the infliction of capital punishment upon him, until he has been legally tried. As the law has been hitherto expounded, it is only where a proper and pertinent request is presented in due time and manner that the accused is entitled to have instructions submitted to the jury upon the matters of defense raised by his statement. In Downing v. State, 66 Ga. 111, it was said: "If counsel representing the defendant in a criminal case desire special instructions in reference to the statement of the prisoner, in addition to the general charge as to the effect to be given it, they should make proper requests therefor." The contention in that case was that the court should have proceeded to inform the jury as to the legal effect of the statement, if true. In Darby v. State, 79 Ga. 63, 3 S. E. Rep. 663, no request for special instructions appeared, and it was held not to be the duty of the court to give in charge any theory of the case which arose, not from the evidence, but from the defendant's statement. In several cases where the charge of the court was entirely silent touching the statement, such silence, in the absence of a request, was held not to be cause for a new trial. Brassell v. State, 64 Ga. 318; Bray v. State, 69 Ga. 765; Seyden v. State, 78 Ga. 106. The statement stands upon a peculiar footing. It is often introduced for the mere purpose of explaining evidence, or as an attempt at mitigation. The accused and his counsel throw it in for what it may happen to be worth, and do not rely upon it as a substantive ground of acquittal. This may serve to explain why a request to charge upon it is frequently omitted. It is no injustice or hardship to treat the omission as a waiver. But where a stand is made upon the statement, and the court is formally requested to charge particularly touching the matter which it sets up, we can see no reason why it is not as much the right of the accused to have the charge given as it would be if the defense rested upon like matter brought out in the testimony. It is one thing to instruct the jury as to their right to credit the statement, and another thing to acquaint them with the legal effect of the contents of the statement in case they do give it credit. Upon each of these topics a proper request, when made, should be complied with. It is certainly in the power of the court to deal with them both without any request. In proper cases, the jury may be guarded by a charge from the court against giving the statement an undue effect in favor of the prisoner, as was done in Fry v. State, 81 Ga. 645, 8 S. E. Rep. 308. In that case the complaint was that the court, of its own motion, charged upon matter embraced in the prisoner's statement, and thus prevented him from getting the benefit before the jury of an excuse for the killing consisting of a mere provocation by words. It frequently happens in practice that the jury ought to be instructed upon the effect of the defense set up in the statement, in case the jury should believe the statement true. Otherwise the mistake might be made in the jury-box of treating as a good defense matter which is wholly insufficient in law. On the other hand, when the prisoner or his counsel requests it, a defense set up in the statement which is good should be so pronounced by the court, on condition that the jury consider it es-

tablished as matter of fact. In Ozburn v. State, (Ga.) 13 S. E. Rep. 247, there was a request in general terms to charge the sections of the Code relating to the law of voluntary manslaughter and of justifiable homicide. Such requests, when founded alone on the prisoner's statement, are altogether too comprehensive and indefinite, and for that reason their rejection would be warranted. The request, however, was complied with touching the law of voluntary manslaughter; and this court considered that the refusal in respect to the law of justifiable homicide was correct, inasmuch as no such defense was made out by the facts before the jury, in any view of the case. In writing out for the court the opinion in that case, Mr. Justice LUMPKIN said: "Indeed, the zealous and faithful counsel for the prisoner who argued the case before this court virtually conceded that the law of justifiable homicide had nothing to do with it." Had there been facts amounting to a justification, and also a specific request adjusted to them in their precise legal significance, as in the present case, a denial of such request would have been erroneous.

2. Many other grounds are contained in the motion for a new trial, but looking at the whole charge of the court and all of the rulings, so far as authenticated by the judge, we think the above matter is the only one upon which a new trial should have been granted. Some of the phraseology of the charge would need modification to adapt it to this matter as a part of the charge itself. On another trial, we doubt not that these modifications will be apparent to the presiding judge. Had not the error which we have discussed been committed, we should not have felt constrained to order another trial; for, testing the case by the evidence irrespective of the statement, the verdict of the jury was apparently correct. Judgment reversed.

NOTE. In addition to the cases cited in the opinion, the following are the rulings of the court heretofore made touching the prisoner's statement: (1) Practice: Prisoner's counsel cannot ask questions. Brown v. State, 58 Ga. 212. Court asking prisoner whether he meant to deny the testimony. Robinson v. State, 89 Ga. 535, 9 S. E. Rep. 528. (2) What it may embrace: Prisoner making long and rambling statement, or desiring to state matters grossly irrelevant, may be restrained by the court. Loyd v. State, 45 Ga. 58; Montross v. State, 72 Ga. 261; Howard v. State, 73 Ga. 68. But error to restrict to facts which would be admissible in evidence. Coxwell v. State, 66 Ga. 309. (3) Evidence: Admissible to rebut statement by testimony. Holsenbake v. State, 45 Ga. 44; Hanvey v. State, 68 Ga. 612. (witness not under rule;) Wilson v. State, 80 Ga. 357, 9 S. E. Rep. 1073; McKinne v. State, 81 Ga. 165, 9 S. E. Rep. 1091; Klug v. State, 77 Ga. 734; Bone v. State, 86 Ga. 108, 122, 12 S. E. Rep. 205, (witness heard statement;) Porter v. State, 86 Ga. 362, 12 S. E. Rep. 588, (proving abusive words not charged.) But bad character of prisoner, and that witness would not believe him on oath, not admissible. Doyle v. State, 77 Ga. 513. (4) Argument: Right of conclusion not lost by making statement. Farrow v. State, 48 Ga. 30; Seyden v. State, 78 Ga. 105. But evidence introduced in reply to rebuttal of statement loses conclusion. Downing v. State, 66 Ga. 110. Counsel for accused ought not to confound statement with testimony. Brown v. State, 60 Ga. 210. State's counsel ought not to argue on omission to make statement. Robinson v. State, 82 Ga. 535, 9 S. E. Rep. 528. (5) Failure to make statement and effect: Error to tell jury they might consider such failure. Bird v. State, 50 Ga. 585. Solicitor should not argue on such failure. Robinson v. State, supra. Failure by accident, ignorance, or neglect of counsel not ground for new trial. Dyson v. State, 72 Ga. 206; Hudson v. State, 76 Ga. 727. (6) Charge of the court: Not error, in connection with the general charge, to call attention to statements not being evidence, or not being under oath, or that defendant is under no penalty to speak the truth, and not subject to cross-examination without his consent. Ross v. State, 59 Ga. 248; Malone v. State, 66 Ga. 539; Wilson v. State, 69 Ga. 224; Poppell v. State, 71 Ga. 276; Hendricks v. State, 73 Ga. 577; Klug v. State, 77 Ga. 734; Ratteree v. State, Id. 774; Murray v. State, 85 Ga. 378, 11 S. E. Rep. 655. Jury may believe or disbelieve all or any part. Jones v. State, 65 Ga. 506; Stewart v. State, 68 Ga. 90; McConnell v. State, 67 Ga. 635. Restricting jury to testimony. Cox v. State, 64 Ga. 377; Hill v. State, Id. 453; Nixon v. State, 75 Ga. 362. Restricting effect of statement. Pease v. State, 68 Ga. 631; Lovejoy v. State, 82 Ga. 87, 8 S. E. Rep. 66; Harrison v. State, 83 Ga. 130, 9 S. E. Rep. 542. Court arguing on conflict with evidence, improper. Tucker v. State, 57 Ga. 508. Telling jury he charges them because the law obliges him to. McCord v. State, 83 Ga. 521, 10 S. E. Rep. 437. Referring to statement as "in contrast with" evidence, and as "defendant's version of it." Bone v. State, 86 Ga. 108, 113, 113, 12 S. E. Rep. 205. Language of statute recommended. Brown v. State, 60 Ga. 210; O'Connor v. State, 64 Ga. 125; Harrison v. State, 83 Ga. 130, 9 S. E. Rep. 542; Bone v. State, 86 Ga. 108, 12 S. E. Rep. 205. (7) Effect of statement before the act of 1879, Brown v. State, 60 Ga. 210; Day v. State, 63 Ga. 667; O'Connor v. State, 64 Ga. 125; after the act, Hayden v. State, 69 Ga. 731; Hendricks v. State, 73 Ga. 577. Admission proves fact admitted. Dumas v. State, 62 Ga. 58. Not impeaching testimony. Jones v. State, 48 Ga. 163.

SERLES v. CROMER.

(Supreme Court of Appeals of Virginia. Nov. 19, 1891.)

FINAL DECREE—SUSPENSION—REVIVAL.

1. A provision of a decree in favor of a receiver, that he shall execute a bond in a fixed penalty before receiving any money thereunder, does not prevent the decree being final, within the meaning of Code Va. 1873, c. 182, § 12, providing that an execution may be issued on a "final" decree within one year, or the same may be revived within ten years from its date.

2. Code Va. 1873, c. 182, § 13, provides that, in computing the time within which execution shall issue, or action be brought on a decree, the time during which such right "is suspended by the terms thereof, or by legal process, shall be omitted." *Held*, that there was no such suspension because of said provision, or by reason of an injunction whereby the sale of defendant's homestead was enjoined, as to permit its revival after 10 years had elapsed.

HINTON and FAUNTLEROY, JJ., dissenting.

Appeal from circuit court, Montgomery county. Affirmed.

Bill in equity by S. W. Cromer against Joseph Serles et al. to revive a decree against respondents in his favor. From a decree overruling a demurrer to the bill, defendant Serles appeals.

W. R. Staples and *G. W. Hansbrough,*

for appellant. *Mr. Tompkins, E. C. Burks,* and *Phlegar & Johnson,* for appellee.

LACY, J. This is an appeal from a decree of the circuit court of Montgomery county, rendered at its November term, 1888. The case, so far as it is necessary to be stated, is as follows: Cromer, the appellee, filed his bill, as the administrator of Stipes, in 1870, for the settlement of the executorial account of Stephen Childress, as the executor of the said Stipes, the said Childress having given as his securities as such executor Joseph Serles, William M. Childress, and Charles Howard, who were made defendants. At the May term, 1872, a decree was rendered against the said executor and his said securities for $1,312.- 14, with interest thereon from the 22d day of February, 1870, in favor of S. W. Cromer, receiver, the said receiver as such to execute a bond in the penalty of $3,000 before he received any money under the said decree. At the September term, 1874, this decree was amended, and the amount fixed at $1,385.25 and costs, and execution was directed to issue thereon, and the cause was continued for a report from the receiver. Upon this decree no execution issued within the year, and there was no proceeding to revive the decree until 1887, when a bill was filed for that purpose, to which the defendant Joseph Serles demurred and answered, and set up the defense of the statute of limitations. The court overruled the demurrer, and revived the decree; from which decree the appellant, Joseph Serles, applied for and obtained an appeal to this court.

The only error assigned is as to the action of the court in overruling the plea of the statute of limitations as a defense to the decree, the same being alleged to be barred at the institution of the said suit. Under our law, (section 12, c. 182, Code 1873,) an execution may be issued on a final decree within one year, or the same may be revived within ten years from its date. It is apparent from the record that no execution issued within the year, and there was no action brought to revive the same within ten years. But the claim is that the decree of 1874 was not a final decree, because the decree was in favor of a receiver, who was not authorized to collect any money under the decree until he executed a bond as such in a prescribed penalty, and that this bond was never executed, and that the decree was thus suspended by its own terms; whereas, section 13, c. 182, Code 1873, provides that "no execution shall issue, nor any *scire facias* or action be brought, on a judgment (or decree) in this state, other than for the commonwealth, after the time prescribed by the preceding section, except that, in computing the time, any time during which the right to sue out execution on the judgment (or decree) is suspended by the terms thereof, or by legal process, shall be omitted." It is provided by sections 1, 2, c. 182, supra, that a decree for money shall be embraced in the word "judgment" whenever used in this chapter, and chapters 183, 184, and 185. So that the questions whether this was a final decree, and, if so, whether it was suspended by the terms thereof, or by legal process, so as to save the running of the statute, are the only questions here involved.

Was the said decree a final decree? What is a final decree? This question has been so often answered by this court that the definition is familiar to the profession: "When a decree makes an end of a case, and decides the whole matter in contest, costs and all, leaving nothing further for the court to do, it is a final decree." Harvey v. Branson, 1 Leigh, 108; Vanmeter v. Vanmeters, 3 Grat. 148; Fleming v. Bolling, 8 Grat. 292; Ryan v. McLeod, 32 Grat. 376; Rawlings v. Rawlings, 75 Va. 76; Trust Co. v. Foster, 78 Va. 419; Yates' Adm'r v. Wilson, 86 Va. 627, 10 S. E. Rep. 976. But when the further action of the court in the cause is necessary to give completely the relief contemplated by the court it is not final; that is, the further action of the court in the cause, not that action of the court which is common to both final and interlocutory decrees, and is necessary for the execution of the decree, and is regarded not in, but beyond, the cause. Cocke v. Gilpin, 1 Rob. (Va.) 20;. Yates' Adm'r v. Wilson, supra. When no execution has issued on a final decree within the year, and no action has been brought to revive it within 10 years, the decree is barred. In the decree in question the amount of money due was ascertained, and a decree rendered for the amount, with costs, and execution was authorized to issue thereon. It is true, in the decree of 1872 the receiver was required to give a bond in the sum of $3,000, which was not given; but the court had fixed the amount and directed its execution. There was nothing more for the court judicially to do concerning it. The decree was as final as to this as any part of it. There was nothing more for the court to do. The receiver was to do this, and it was not to be done before nor in the court. The clerk takes this bond, and receives and passes upon the security, and, moreover, it cannot be regarded as a thing to be done in the cause, but beyond it.

But it is further insisted that an injunction suit was brought by the debtor, S. Childress, to enjoin the sale of his home place. But the decree of 1874 was not therein assailed, nor was the issuance of execution thereunder in any degree affected. Its pendency did not affect the question. There was no order nor other process asked for, nor made, restraining the issuance of any injunction. This proceeding did not bring the case within the saving of the thirteenth section, c. 182, supra. Straus v. Bodeker's Ex'x, 86 Va. 543, 10 S. E. Rep. 570; Dabney v. Shelton, 82 Va. 350. The defense of the statute of limitations was a complete bar to the action to revive the decree, and should have been allowed by the court, and the bill dismissed. The decree appealed from having decided otherwise, the same will be reversed and annulled, and such order entered here as the circuit ought to have rendered, and the bill dismissed.

FAUNTLEROY and HINTON, JJ., dissenting.

EVERITT v. WALKER et al.

(Supreme Court of North Carolina. Nov. 10, 1891.)

SUPPORT OF CHILD—LIABILITY OF FATHER.

1. In an action against a father to recover for the support of a child, the complaint alleged that the father became insane in 1880, and has continued so; that the mother died in October, 1880; that plaintiff was a sister of the deceased, who on her death-bed requested plaintiff to support the child, which plaintiff agreed to do; that plaintiff tried to obtain aid from other relatives of the child, which would have died or become a charge upon the county had not plaintiff supported it. The complaint failed to state that the father had abandoned or neglected the child, or that he knew of or promised to pay for the services of plaintiff. Held, that it did not state a cause of action.

2. Plaintiff could not support the child from motives of charity and love for her sister, without any intention of charging the father, and afterwards, when he became owner of property, compel him to pay for the support.

AVERY, J., dissenting.

Appeal from superior court, New Hanover county; EDWIN T. BOYKIN, Judge.

Action by Amanda Everett against C. C. Walker and others to recover for the support of a child. Defendants demurred to the complaint, which demurrer being overruled, they appeal. Reversed.

STATEMENT BY THE COURT. The following is a copy of the pleadings: "(1) That Mary C. Walker is the child of C. C. Walker and Mary C. Walker, his wife, and that said child was born July 29, 1879. (2) That C. C. Walker, the father, became insane in the summer of 1880, since which time he has been continuously insane and an inmate of the insane asylum at Raleigh, and that Mary C. Walker, the mother, died in October, 1880. (3) That the plaintiff is the sister of the child's mother, and that the mother on her death-bed requested the plaintiff to care for and support said child; that the plaintiff told her she would; and that she has supported her of her own labor since the mother's death, in 1880, the child being of too tender years to assist in her own support. (4) That the plaintiff tried to obtain aid from others of the child's relatives, but failed in her efforts, and that the child must have died or become a charge upon the county had not the plaintiff supported her. (5) That the plaintiff is dependent upon her own labor for her support. (6) That $100 per year for the first six years, and $200 per year for the remainder of the time, is a fair compensation for the expense of said child's maintenance, which, up to the institution of this action, will thus amount to $1,266, and for this amount the plaintiff claims that the defendant is justly indebted to her. (7) That the Wilmington Savings & Trust Company has been appointed by the clerk of the superior court of New Hanover county, guardian of C. C. Walker; that said company has qualified, and is now acting as such guardian. (8) That the said company has in its hands the sum of $1,900, more or less, personal property of C. C. Walker, and that there is a large undivided portion of the estate of John Walker, deceased, of which estate C. C. Walker is an heir and devisee. and that his portion of said undivided estate will be $4,000, more or less. Wherefore the plaintiff prays the judgment of the court for the sum of $1,266, the costs of this action, and for such other and further relief as the court shall think her entitled to." The defendants demur to the above complaint, upon the ground that it does not state facts sufficient to constitute a cause of action, in this: "(1) That it appears on the face of the complaint that there was no contract, either express or implied, upon the part of the defendants, or either of them, that the plaintiff should take upon herself the support of said child, or that they, or either of them, would pay for the support of said child. (2) That it appears upon the face of the complaint that the plaintiff took upon herself care and support of the said child out of pure benevolence, and solely at the request of its mother, and in fulfillment of a promise made to her by the plaintiff." The court overruled the demurrer, with leave to the defendants to answer, and they, having excepted, appealed to this court.

E. S. Martin and *Junius Davis*, for appellants. *P. B. Manning*, for appellee.

MERRIMON, C. J. We think the court should have sustained the demurrer upon the general ground that the complaint fails to state facts sufficient to constitute a cause of action. It is not alleged that the defendant Walker employed the plaintiff to do the service for his child for which she claims compensation, or that he promised, expressly or by implication, to pay her for the same; nor are facts alleged upon which the law implies his liability and obligation to pay therefor. It is not alleged that the father abandoned or neglected his child; that he would not or could not protect and provide for and support her; or that he knew of, recognized, approved of, and accepted the services of the plaintiff. That he was so in default, or promised to pay for the plaintiff's services, is left to mere inference and remote implication. If it be granted that a father is legally bound to provide for, protect, and support his child, it must be alleged, in a case like this, that he failed to do so, or that he promised expressly or by clear implication to pay for the services for which compensation is demanded. The facts stated in the fourth paragraph of the complaint are too indefinite, indirect, and inconclusive to constitute or be treated as a substitute for a material part of the allegation of a cause of action. Moreover, it appears from the complaint that at the time the services were rendered the father was insane and an inmate of the insane asylum, and, at least *prima facie*, incapable of promising to pay the plaintiff for her services.

Besides, it appears from the complaint that the plaintiff cared for and supported the child of her sister at the latter's request, made shortly before she died, as a work of benevolence and charity, for which she made no charge and expected no pecuniary compensation. She promised her sister not simply to care for, but to care for and support, her child. She said nothing of compensation at the time she made

the promise, or at any time afterwards, until she brought this action, so far as appears. She does not allege or intimate that she charged the father for her services, or that she expected compensation from him. It seems that at first the father was poor and insane; that afterwards, in some way, he came to have property; and the plaintiff then, and not until then, determined to ask for the compensation she seeks to recover by this action. This she cannot do. She could not support the child from motives of charity and love for her departed sister without any intention of charging the father for the same, and afterwards, when he came to be the owner of property, compel him to pay her for her good work of love and charity. She had, in such case, no valid claim at law or in equity. University v. McNair, 2 Ired. Eq. 605; Hedrick v. Wagoner, 8 Jones, (N. C.) 360; Miller v. Lash, 85 N. C. 54; Young v. Herman, 97 N. C. 280, 1 S. E. Rep. 792. There is error. The order overruling the demurrer must be reversed, and the case disposed of according to law. To that end let this opinion be certified to the superior court. It is so ordered.

AVERY, J., dissents.

STATE et al. v. GEORGIA CO.

(*Supreme Court of North Carolina.* Nov. 10, 1891.)

APPEAL — CERTIORARI — INTERLOCUTORY ORDER — PUBLICATION OF WRIT.

1. Appeal does not lie from an interlocutory ruling on objections to the jurisdiction of the court.

2. *Certiorari* does not lie as a substitute for an appeal from an interlocutory order of a superior court.

3. A daily publication of a summons in a newspaper from August 3d to August 31st, prior to the term of court beginning August 31st, was a sufficient publication, under Acts N. C. 1889, c. 106, which provides that, where service of summons by publication is required, the publication must be once a week for four weeks.

Application for *certiorari* to the superior court, Guilford county.

Action by the state of North Carolina and Guilford county against the Georgia Company was commenced by summons, and service was had by publication. The notice of summons was published from August 3d to August 31st, both inclusive, the last day being the day on which court opened. On September 5th the case was called in its order, when defendant appeared specially, and moved as follows: "(1) That this case go over to next term as return term of summons, because the notice of publication embraces only four weeks, and not four weeks and ten days. (2) The case is not properly constituted in this court, in that a copy of the summons and the proper title of action was not made in the publication. Both motions overruled. Defendant prayed an appeal to supreme court, which was refused. Plaintiff moved for judgment for want of an answer. Defendant, under protest, then entered a general appearance, and asked for 60 days to answer or demur as of this term. Plaintiff then withdraws its prayer for judgment, and

60 days granted by consent in which to file answer." Defendant having failed to give notice of appeal, to enter its appeal, and serve its case on appeal, now comes and asks for a writ of *certiorari* to bring up the case as on appeal. Denied.

L. M. Scott and *R. M. Douglas,* for plaintiff. *F. H. Busbee* and *P. B. Means,* for defendant.

CLARK, J. This application is for a *certiorari* as a substitute for an appeal claimed to have been denied by the judge. Skinner v. Maxwell, 67 N. C. 257. It is clear that an appeal did not lie from the interlocutory ruling of the court, and it was the duty of the judge not to suspend proceedings. Carleton v. Byers, 71 N. C. 331. If the defendant was not duly served with process properly returnable to such term, it could either have disregarded the further proceedings of the court,—which would have been a nullity as to it,—or it could have had its exception noted, and have proceeded with the trial, —the latter being the preferable and more commendable course. Plemmons v. Improvement Co., 108 N. C. 614, 13 S. E. Rep. 188. The manifest delays and inconveniences from entertaining premature and fragmentary appeals have, indeed, been often pointed out. Hines v. Hines, 84 N. C. 122; Commissioners v. Satchwell, 88 N. C. 1; White v. Utley, 94 N. C. 511; and in many other cases. As no appeal lay, a *certiorari,* as a substitute therefor, cannot be granted. Badger v. Daniel, 82 N. C. 468. Notwithstanding the petition must be denied, it may serve the end in view to pass upon the points presented, as has been sometimes, though rarely, done by the court, upon sufficient cause to justify it. McBryde v. Patterson, 78 N. C. 412; State v. Tyler, 85 N. C. 569; State v. Lockyear, 95 N. C. 633; State v. Nash, 97 N. C. 514, 2 S. E. Rep. 645; State v. Divine, 98 N. C. 778, 4 S. E. Rep. 477. The publication required by chapter 108, Acts 1889, is "once a week for four weeks." This, it appears from the petitioner's application, was made, for it avers the only publication in a newspaper from August 3 to August 31, 1891; and a publication on the four Mondays, August 3d, 10th, 17th, and 24th, was a publication "once a week for four weeks" prior to the term of court beginning Monday, August 31st. But if the requirement is construed to mean publication "for four weeks," still there was compliance under our statute, (Code, §§ 596, 602,) for, "excluding the first day, [August 3d,] and including the last day," August 31st, there was publication made for 28 days, or "four weeks." The same construction has always been given to the statute (Id. § 200) requiring personal service "ten days before the beginning of the term," for service before midnight of Friday, the tenth day before court, has always been held sufficient. Taylor v. Harris, 82 N. C. 25. We do not think that the defendant, when served by publication, is entitled to 10 days in addition to the four weeks. The publication "once a week for four weeks" is a substitute for and stands in lieu of the "ten days" which is allowed to a party on whom summons is personally served. This is not only consonant to the reason of the thing, but is in accordance with the express words of the statute. Code, § 227. "In the cases in which service by publication is allowed the summons shall be deemed served at the expiration of the time prescribed by the order of publication, and the party shall then be in court;" that is, exactly as a party who has had 10 days' personal notice of the summons would be in court. We are cited to the New York decisions, but the statute in that state (Code N. Y. § 441) differs essentially from ours, in the omission of the words, "and the party shall then be in court." Nor is there any force in the further objection that "a copy of the summons and the proper title of the action was not made in the publication." The publication, as set out in the petition, is a substantial publication of the summons, and a full compliance with the statute. It contains everything that is in the summons, and the additional matter in the publication, at the most, was mere surplusage. We cannot conceive how the defendant could have been prejudiced thereby. Motion denied.

CLEMENT v. COZART.

(Supreme Court of North Carolina. Nov. 12, 1891.)

FRAUDULENT CONVEYANCES—SECRET TRUST—SALE OF DECEDENT'S LAND.

1. Under Code N. C. § 1545, providing that fraudulent gifts, grants, etc., shall be void as to persons who "are, shall, or might be" thereby defrauded of their claims, a grant, made in contemplation of insolvency, without valuable consideration, and with the understanding that the land should be held for the benefit of the grantor, and shielded from such debts as he then owed or should incur, was void as to subsequent creditors.

2. It was immaterial that the conveyance was absolute on its face, and contained no clause of defeasance.

3. Decedent, with intent to defraud his creditors, conveyed land to his son, and the latter conveyed it to his brother, decedent's administrator, in trust for their father and his heirs. The administrator filed his final account, and left debts of decedent unpaid, without selling, or applying for license to sell, said land. *Held* that, under Code N. C. § 1436, providing that where a decedent's personalty is insufficient to pay his debts, his administrator shall, without undue delay, apply to the court for license to sell his real estate, and that the court may, at the instance of any creditor, compel him to perform his duty, there was no necessity that a creditor should demand of the administrator that he sell said land, before bringing an action to compel him to do so.

Appeal from superior court, Granville county: EDWIN T. BOYKIN, Judge.

Action by Thomas D. Clement, administrator of Amos Gooch, against W. W. Cozart, administrator of James C. Cozart, et al., to compel said defendant to render an account of his intestate's personal property, and to subject certain land, if necessary, to the payment of a debt due plaintiff's intestate.

STATEMENT BY THE COURT. The plaintiff, by leave of the court first had and obtained, files the following amended complaint, and alleges: "(1) That Amos Gooch, late of said county of Granville, died intestate in said county in the month of March, 1885. (2) That on the 16th of March, 1885, plaintiff was duly appointed and qualified as administrator upon said intestate's estate. (3) That on the 1st of September, 1877, the defendant Thomas I. Smith and James C. Cozart and John G. Harris, for a valuable consideration, executed and delivered to plaintiff's said intestate, Amos Gooch, their bond for the payment to him of the sum of one thousand dollars. (4) That at the September term, 1886, of the superior court of said county, plaintiff, as administrator as aforesaid, recovered judgment on said bond against the said Thomas I. Smith and the said James C. Cozart for $1,245, with interest on $1,000, the principal sum in said bond, at the rate of six per cent. per annum from the 6th day of February, 1886, until paid, and for his costs of action. (5) That on the 15th of February, 1888, said Smith, who was a son-in-law of the said James C., paid in part satisfaction of said judgment debt $468.32; that no other or further payments have been made towards the satisfaction of said debt, leaving a balance of $——, with interest as aforesaid from the —— day of ——, 18?—, still due and owing as aforesaid. (6) That by deed absolute on its face, dated 21st of November, 1871, the said James C. Cozart and his wife, Jane, for the recited consideration of $2,000, conveyed to their son-in-law the defendant David C. Lunsford, and to their son the defendant Thomas G. Cozart, three tracts of land, all lying near the waters of Tar river, in said county of Granville, to-wit: [The three tracts of land are set out by metes and bounds, aggregating 370 acres.] (7) That at the time of the execution of said deed the said James C. Cozart was greatly indebted, much beyond his ability to pay, and said deed was executed by him and his said wife with the intent to hinder, delay, and defraud the then and all subsequent creditors of said James C., and this covinous purpose of the said James C. and his said wife was well known to the said grantees and to the cestui que trusts in said deed at the time of the execution thereof as aforesaid. (8) That said deed was executed by said James C. and his said wife, as plaintiffs are informed and believe, upon some secret trust, for the use and benefit of the said grantors, in some way unknown to plaintiffs. (9) That no part of said recited consideration of $2,000 was ever paid by said grantees to said grantors, nor was it ever intended by either or any of the parties to said deed that said sum of $2,000, or any part thereof, ever should be paid, but said deed was in truth, and was intended by the parties to it to be, a voluntary conveyance. (10) That said James C. Cozart died intestate in said county of Granville in the year 1887. (11) That on the 23d of April, 1888, the defendant William W. Cozart, who was a son of the said James C. Cozart and his said wife, Jane, applied to the superior court of said county for letters of administration upon the estate of the said James C., and in his said application he swore that the personal estate of said James C. was worth about $5, and that

he, the said James C., owned no real property at the time of his death. (12) That on the 24th of April, 1888, the said William W. Cozart was duly and legally appointed administrator of the said James C. Cozart, and executed his bond as such administrator, with E. B. Cozart and A. S. Carrington as his sureties thereto in the penal sum of $10, conditioned according to law for the faithful performance of his duties as administrator of the estate of the said James C. (13) That on the 18th of September, 1889, the said William W., as administrator as aforesaid, filed in the office of the clerk of the superior court of said county an inventory of the personal estate of the said James C., of the value of about $350. (14) That on the 16th of April, 1890, the said William W., as administrator as aforesaid, filed on oath in the office of said clerk an account of the sales of the personal property belonging to the estate of the said James C., and of all receipts and disbursements on account of said estate, and that the receipts as returned by him into the office of said clerk aggregated $351.98, and the disbursements as returned by him as aforesaid aggregated $288.65, leaving a balance in his hands, as returned by him, of $63.33 only. (15) That said account of sales, as just above stated, and said disbursements, was intended by said William W. to be, and is, his final account with his said intestate's estate. (16) That the said James C., at the time of his death as aforesaid, left no money or effects or personal property of any kind whatsoever, beyond what is stated in said inventory and said account of sales of his said administrator, and that the same was insufficient to pay said James C. Cozart's debts, and the costs and charges of administering his estate, and it will be necessary to sell the real property, or some part thereof, to pay his debts, and the costs and charges of administering his estate. (17) That the said James C. Cozart died seized of the three (3) tracts of land, aggregating three hundred and seventy-two acres, set forth and described in article six of this complaint. (18) That on the 4th day of December, 1884, the defendants David C. Lunsford and his wife, Nancy J., and the defendants Thomas G. Cozart and his wife, Bettie F., for the recited consideration of $1, conveyed by deed said three (3) tracts of land to the defendant William W. Cozart and his heirs, in trust for the use and benefit of the said James C. and his said wife Jane, for their lives, and for the life of the survivor of them, and, at the death of the survivor of them two, to be sold by the said William W., and the proceeds of such sale to be by him, the said William W., divided among the children or heirs at law of the said James C. Cozart. (19) That the said Thomas I. Smith is insolvent. (20) That the said James C. Cozart left him surviving the following children, the defendants to this action, who are his only heirs at law, to-wit: William W. Cozart, Thomas G. Cozart, James H. Cozart, Frances Peed, Lucy Piper, Nancy I., wife of the defendant David C. Lunsford, Martha, wife of the defendant James Jones, Annetta, wife of the defendant

William C. Peed, Larcreasy, wife of the defendant Jesse V. Roberts, and Sally, wife of the defendant Thomas I. Smith. Wherefore the plaintiff demands judgment against the defendants—(1) That the defendant William W. Cozart, as administrator of James C. Cozart, render an account of the personal estate of his said intestate, which did come, or ought to have, to his hands to be administered by him as such administrator, and also of the debts and funeral expenses of the said James C., and also of the costs and charges of his said administrator. (2) That out of said personal property said administrator pay his intestate's debts, if there be a sufficiency thereof for that purpose. (3) That if, upon the taking and stating of such account, it shall appear that there is not in the hands of said administrator a sufficiency of personal assets to pay his intestate's debts, and the costs and charges of administering his estate, then, and in that event, said William W., as administrator as aforesaid, or as trustee as aforesaid, be ordered, adjudged, and decreed to sell said lands, or as much thereof as may be necessary to pay his intestate's debts, and out of the proceeds of said sale to pay said debts. (4) For their costs of action. (5) For such other and further relief," etc.

In this action the defendants demur to the amended complaint, that it does not state facts sufficient to constitute a cause of action—"(1) In that it appears that the conveyance of the tracts of land described in the complaint by James C. Cozart was made 21st November, 1871, and the debt on which judgment was taken by the plaintiff was not contracted until September 1, 1877; and, under section 1545 of the Code, plaintiff's intestate was not disturbed, hindered, delayed, or defrauded thereby. (2) That there is no allegation that any clause of defeasance was omitted by mistake from the said deed, which, being absolute on its face, even though voluntary, conveyed all interest which James C. Cozart had in the said tracts of land to his son and son-in-law upon good consideration; and no parol agreement in regard to any present or future interest therein, even if the same existed, as alleged in the complaint, (it not being stated that it was in writing, signed by David C. Lunsford and Thomas G. Cozart, as required by section 1554 of the Code,) could be enforced after the execution of said deed by James C. Cozart, nor by his subsequent creditors, who now ask to be subrogated to his rights. (3) In that it appears, from the allegations of said complaint, that after the debt on which this action is founded was contracted, James C. Cozart had no interest in said tracts of land except that acquired by the conveyance of David C. Lunsford and Thomas G. Cozart to W. W. Cozart as trustee, and such interest expired with the life of said James C. Cozart, and there was nothing left of which he was seised at his death which his administrators could sell. (4) That the allegations of said complaint, in regard to creditors of James C. Cozart in 1871, are vague and indefinite, and should be disregarded, as their claims are long since barred; and

besides, the plaintiff shows no connection of any creditors then existing, if there were such, as alleged, with this proceeding, nor is there any allegation that any rights of such creditors were assigned to the plaintiff's intestate. (5) That there is no allegation that the defendant W. W. Cozart, as administrator of James C. Cozart, has refused to bring suit to sell any land upon the request of the plaintiff, or in any way neglected to perform any duty in regard thereto. Wherefore the defendants demand judgment that the said plaintiff has no cause of action against them upon the facts alleged, and that the said James C. Cozart had no interest at his death in the said tracts of land, which could be sold by defendant W. W. Cozart, either as administrator or trustee, and that the plaintiff had made no request for such sale prior to this action, and for these reasons that this demurrer be sustained and said action be dismissed as to all the defendants; that as there appears from said complaint to be no necessity for an account of the administration of said estate, and it is alleged that there has been a final settlement thereof, this action be also dismissed as to the administrator."

Plaintiff appeals from a judgment sustaining a demurrer to his amended complaint. Reversed.

L. C. Edwards and *Batchelor & Devereux*, for appellant. *John W. Graham* and *A. W. Graham*, for appellee.

DAVIS, J. 1. The first ground of demurrer is based upon the fact, as appears in the complaint, that the debt of the plaintiff was not contracted until some time after the deed from James C. Cozart to his son-in-law was executed, and the deed could not, therefore, be embraced by the statute of frauds, (Code, § 1545,) which makes void fraudulent gifts, grants, etc., "only as against that person, his heirs, executors, and assigns, whose debts, accounts, damages, penalties, and forfeitures, by such fraudulent or covinous devices and practices aforesaid, are, shall, or might be in any wise disturbed, hindered, delayed, or defrauded," etc.; and it is insisted that a debt which had no existence when the deed was made could not be so disturbed, hindered, etc. We apprehend that if a deed be made, showing upon its face a full, valuable consideration, but upon the secret trust that the vendee shall not pay anything therefor, but shall hold the same in contemplation of insolvency for the benefit of the vendor, so as to protect and shield the property against any debts that he may owe at the time, or any liabilities that he may subsequently incur, such a deed would be void as to all persons whose claims "are, shall, or might be" defrauded thereby. As to pre-existing debts, such a deed would be *ipso facto* fraudulent and void. Morgan v. McLelland, 3 Dev. 82. "A voluntary conveyance is necessarily and in law fraudulent when opposed to the claim of a prior creditor;" as against subsequent creditors, whether fraudulent or not depends upon the *bona fides* of the transaction, and the question is one of intent, to be passed upon by the jury. O'Daniel v.

Crawford, 4 Dev. 197, in which the subject of fraudulent conveyances is elaborately discussed in concurring opinions by RUFFIN, C. J., and GASTON and DANIEL, JJ. The first ground of demurrer cannot be sustained.

2. The second ground of demurrer is that there is no allegation of any clause of defeasance, and, the deed being upon good consideration. the grantor had no interest in the land which could be enforced by him or his subsequent creditors. If the conveyance was made upon a fraudulent trust, of course the court would not aid the grantor in its enforcement, but the deed was void as to creditors, and no clause of defeasance was necessary as to them, and the second ground of demurrer cannot be sustained.

3. The third ground of demurrer cannot be sustained. The plaintiff's action rests upon the allegation that the deed of James C. Cosart to his son-in-law Lunsford was fraudulent and void as against creditors, and neither Lunsford nor W. W. Cosart, the trustee, acquired any title as against creditors.

4. The fourth ground of demurrer is based upon the assumption that the deed could only be fraudulent and void as against creditors existing at the time of the deed. As we have seen, this is a misapprehension, and the fourth ground of demurrer cannot be sustained.

5. It is alleged in the complaint, and the demurrer admits, that the personal property of the decedent was insufficient to pay his debts, and that a sale of his real estate was necessary for that purpose. The statute (Code, § 1436) makes it the duty of the administrator, without undue delay, to apply to the court for license to sell the real estate, etc., and the court, at the instance of the creditor, may compel him to perform this duty. Pelletier v. Saunders, 67 N. C. 261. For the purposes of demurrer, it is admitted that the deed of the decedent was made with the intent to hinder, delay, and defraud the then existing and subsequent creditors of the grantor. and that the defendant administrator was a party to this fraudulent transaction; that he had filed his final account, leaving debts of the decedent unpaid, without selling, or applying to the court for license to sell, the real estate of his intestate; and from the facts fully appearing in the complaint. and admitted by the demurrer, the administrator had designedly failed and neglected to perform his duty, and apply to the court for license to sell the land fraudulently conveyed by the deed of the intestate, under and through which he and the other defendants are beneficiaries, and from the facts appearing in the complaint no demand was necessary. Before the real estate of a decedent can be sold to pay debts, either upon the application of an administrator or at the instance of a creditor, under sections 1448 or 1474 of the Code, it must be made to appear that the personal estate has been exhausted or is insufficient to pay the debts of the decedent, and this may be, and usually is. ascertained by an account. This is well settled, as will appear by reference to the present

case, when before this court on a former appeal, (107 N. C. 695, 12 S. E. Rep. 254,) and cases there cited. And the fifth ground of demurrer cannot be sustained. There is error, and the demurrer must be overruled. Let this be certified, to the end that the defendants may answer or not, as they may be advised.

RICHMOND & D. R. CO. v. TOWN OF REIDSVILLE.

(Supreme Court of North Carolina. Dec. 1, 1891.)

RECOVERY OF INVALID TAX—DEMAND.

Act N. C. 1887, c. 137, § 84, provides that in every case where, for any reason, a tax paid is claimed to be invalid, the person paying the same may, within 30 days after payment, demand the same in writing from the treasurer of the town levying the tax; and, if the tax is not refunded within 90 days thereafter, a right of action therefor accrues against the town. Held, that a demand within 30 days after payment was a prerequisite to a right of action; and a complaint, in such case, which fails to allege such demand, is insufficient on demurrer.

Appeal from superior court, Rockingham county; JOHN G. BYNUM, Judge.

Action by the Richmond & Danville Railroad Company against the town of Reidsville to recover a tax claimed to be illegal, and paid under protest. From a judgment for defendant, plaintiff appeals. Affirmed.

STATEMENT BY THE COURT. The plaintiff brought this action to recover the sum of $200 which it alleges the defendant unlawfully collected from it as license tax. It alleges that it was a common carrier of freights and passengers into and out of this state into and from other states; that it was not subject to such tax; that such tax interfered with interstate commerce, and was imposed in violation of the constitution of the United States, etc. The defendant, among other defenses, pleaded "that plaintiff failed to make a demand for the taxes so paid within thirty days after payment thereof, as provided by law in such cases, and for this reason defendant says plaintiff company cannot maintain this action, and pleads the same in bar thereof." By consent of parties the court found the following facts: "(4) That in the years 1887 and 1888 the defendant levied a license tax of $50 for each of said years on the plaintiff company; the following being the town ordinance: 'For defraying the current expenses of the corporation for the year 1887, the following general (on real and personal estate) poll and license taxes shall be levied and collected, to-wit: On each railroad company a tax of fifty dollars.' That this tax was continued during the year 1888, but increased to one hundred dollars. (5) That on the 18th day of March, 1889, the taxes for the years 1887 and 1888 were demanded by the tax collector of the town of Reidsville of the plaintiff, and payment refused. That on the 19th of March, 1889, the tax collector levied on some of the cars of plaintiff for said tax, when plaintiff paid the same, under protest, to save its property from sale; the protest being as follows 'To the tax collector of Reidsville, North Carolina: Please take notice that the Richmond and Danville Railroad Company pays the one hundred dollars claimed by Reidsville against said company under protest, and that it will sue to recover the same in due time. D. SCHENCK, Counsel R. & D. R. R. Co. March 19th, 1889;' on the back of which is indorsed: 'I accept service of this protest. R. M. CLACK, Tax Collector.' That said Clack was tax collector at that time. That in June, 1889, the tax collector demanded the $100 tax levied for the year 1889, and payment was refused. That he levied, and the tax was paid, on the 22d of June, 1889, under like protest and proceedings as were had for the taxes of 1886 and 1887. (6) That on the 23d day of July, 1889, plaintiff demanded of defendant the refunding or repayment of the taxes paid or set out in finding of fact No. 5, which was refused." Thereupon the court gave judgment, whereof the following is a copy: "This cause coming on to be heard, a trial by jury having been waived, and the facts agreed to be admitted and found by the court, and being found and admitted, as set out in the case, it is ordered, adjudged, and decreed that the town of Reidsville is authorized to levy the tax imposed under the ordinance of said town against the plaintiff company, and that the same is not unconstitutional. The other questions are, therefore, not passed upon. And it is further considered by the court that the plaintiff take nothing by its writ; that the defendant go hence without day, and recover its costs of action, to be taxed by the clerk." The plaintiff excepted, and appealed to this court.

D. Schenck and Geo. F. Bason, for appellant.

MERRIMON, C. J. It is not questioned that the defendant, through its officers and agents, had power and authority, by the terms and purposes of the statute incorporating it, to impose and collect the license tax complained of by the plaintiff. The latter contends, however, that that statute and tax were unlawful and void, because, as it alleges, they were in contravention of the constitution of the United States, (article 1, § 8, par. 3,) which declares and provides "that congress shall have power * * * to regulate commerce with foreign nations, and among the several states, and with the Indian tribes." We are not called upon, nor would it be proper for us, to decide the grave question thus sought to be raised, because, apart from it, and upon another and different ground, the plaintiff is not entitled to recover. Whether the statute referred to is valid or not, it is very certain that the legislature deemed it valid, and intended further that such tax as that in question might be imposed and collected and treated as a tax. The statute so expressly declares. This being so, as soon as the defendant collected the tax complained of, the plaintiff, if it intended to insist that it was unlawfully imposed and collected, within 30 days next thereafter, ought to have demanded of the defendant that it refund the money so collected from it as a tax. The statute (Acts 1887, c. 137, § 84) provides and gives the remedy in such case. It forbids the grant of relief by injunction against the collection of any tax, and further provides that "in every case the person or persons claiming any tax, or any part thereof, to be for any reason invalid, or that the valuation of his property is excessive or unequal, who shall pay the same to the tax collector, or other proper authority, in all respects as though the same was legal and valid, such person may, at any time within thirty days after such payment, demand the same in writing from the treasurer of the state, or of the county, city, or town, for the benefit or under the authority or by the request of which the same was levied," etc. This statutory provision and regulation is significant and important in its purpose. It prescribes and establishes a method,—the method and procedure whereby, when an illegal or improper tax has been imposed and collected, the right of the party complaining may be settled, and the money improperly taken promptly refunded to him. The purpose is to require a prompt demand for the refunding of the money claimed, with a view to a settlement of the matter in dispute while the facts in respect thereto are fresh in the minds of those who know them, to expedite justice, prevent litigation if possible, and economize as to costs. To that end the proper authorities are required to examine and pass upon the merits of the claim, as they are required to do as to claims generally against the state, city, or town, as the case may be.

The demand within the time specified is made a prerequisite to an action to recover the money claimed. The section of the statute cited further provides that, if the money so demanded "shall not be refunded within ninety days thereafter, [the claimant] may sue such county, city, or town for the amount so demanded, including in his suit against the county both state and county tax; and if, upon the trial, it shall be determined that such tax, or any part thereof, was levied or assessed for an illegal or unauthorized purpose, or was for any reason invalid or excessive, judgment shall be rendered therefor, with interest," etc. Such prerequisite of demand is not confined to claims for refunding any particular class of taxes, or taxes illegal or invalid on any particular account or for any particular cause. The statute is broad and comprehensive in its terms and purposes, and applies to all taxes, on whatever account claimed to be illegally collected. The language employed is, "In every such case the person or persons claiming any tax, or any part thereof, to be for any reason invalid," etc. If it be granted that the statute under which the tax was imposed was void, this would not put the plaintiff's claim without the statute cited above. The defendant had at least colorable authority. The tax was imposed, collected, paid under protest as a tax, and so treated. We can see no reason why the plaintiff's claim is on a different footing from other taxes claimed to be unlawfully levied and collected. The statute embraces, by its broad terms and purposes, all such taxes. Nor is the prerequisite to bringing an action thus required unjust or unreasonable. The claimant has 30 days next after he pays the taxes alleged by him to be illegal, within which to make demand as required. The demand is simple, easily made, and the time allowed is ample for such purpose. If it shall not be complied with in 90 days after it is made, the claimant is allowed to bring his action. He is not deprived of his action, nor of just opportunity to assert his right. The preliminary requisite to bringing his action is for his benefit, as well as that of the state, county, city, or town. It is not unwarranted. The legislature clearly has power to prescribe and regulate by statute the method of preferring claims against the state and its agencies for taxes illegally levied and collected, as well as on other accounts, and how and when actions to establish and enforce such claims shall be brought and conducted. Railroad Co. v. Lewis, 99 N. C. 62, 5 S. E. Rep. 82; Mace v. Commissioners, 99 N. C. 65, 5 S. E. Rep. 740. The statutory provision under consideration is founded on justice, convenience, and sound policy. The class of claims to which it refers are against the state and its agencies. The latter are presumed to be honest and just, prepared and willing to allow and discharge all well-founded claims against them. They are not presumed to desire to litigate or withhold justice from any one; nor in their nature, business relations, and transactions can they know of the nature and merits of multitudes of claims and demands that may be made against them, in the absence of notice. It is therefore right, just, and expedient to require persons having such claims and demands to present them, and with reasonable promptness, before bringing actions to establish and enforce them. To so require imposes no unreasonable burden upon claimants; and the latter should not be allowed to delay making demand upon the public authorities that claims due them be recognized and paid, or denied and rejected. This is especially so as to claims for taxes improperly or unlawfully exacted. Such claims should be made and settled as soon as practicable.

It is insisted that the statute is only directory; that there are no negative words showing a purpose to prevent the recovery if the demand shall not be made within 30 days next after the collection of the illegal tax. The terms and purpose to require such demand, and within that time, are express; and, if there are no express words of negation, this appears by the strongest implication. If the demand may be made after the lapse of 30 days, within what time shall it be made? Will it be sufficient if made within 60 days, within 6 months, within 1 year, within 2 years, after the collection of the tax? The demand must be made within 30 days, else the statute has no reasonable or practical meaning. It must be alleged in the complaint that it was so made; otherwise, no sufficient cause of action is al-leged. It cannot be that the statute is meaningless,—a mere form. There are numerous statutes similar to the one under consideration, and they have been uniformly upheld and enforced. There is no reason why they should not be, where the regulations and prerequisites they prescribe are reasonable. Code, §§ 756, 757; Love v. Commissioners, 64 N. C. 706; Jones v. Commissioners, 73 N. C. 182; Hawley v. Fayetteville, 82 N. C. 22; Royster v. Commissioners, 98 N. C. 148, 3 S. E. Rep. 789.

The defendant expressly alleges in its answer, as a defense, that the plaintiff did not, within 30 days next after the payment of the alleged unlawful taxes, demand that it refund to the plaintiff the sum of money so collected; and the court so found the fact to be. As the demand was essential to the plaintiff's cause of action, and no such demand was alleged in the complaint, and it appears none was made within the time prescribed, the plaintiff cannot recover. The court, therefore, properly entered judgment, upon the facts found, for the defendant. It need not, however, have recited, as the reason for its judgment, that the statute alleged to be void was valid. Such recital was unnecessary, and, moreover, the proper ground upon which the judgment rests is that no demand was made as required by the statute, and the judgment upon that ground must be affirmed.

NATIONAL BANK OF CHAMBERSBURG V. GRIMM.

(Supreme Court of North Carolina. Nov. 17, 1891.)

SET-OFF—INDEPENDENT TRANSACTIONS.

Defendant gave his note to T. Mfg. Co., who, before maturity, sold it to plaintiff. After the transfer, and suit for its collection commenced, one M., who was attorney for plaintiff, and also treasurer of T. Mfg. Co., agreed that defendant should do certain work for T. Mfg. Co., and that his commissions, when collected, should be applied in payment of the note. T. Mfg. Co. became insolvent, and the commissions were not so applied or paid to defendant. *Held*, in the action on the note, that, as M.'s agreement to pay defendant commissions on work for T. Mfg. Co. had no connection with plaintiff, the commissions could not be set off against the note.

Appeal from superior court, Moore county; EDWIN T. BOYKIN, Judge.

Action on promissory note by National Bank of Chambersburg against Lewis Grimm. From a judgment for plaintiff defendant appeals. Affirmed.

STATEMENT BY THE COURT. The defendant made his promissory note to the Taylor Manufacturing Company for $401.-95, dated the 2d day of April, 1886, and due six months from date. Before the latter matured, this company indorsed the same for value to the plaintiff as collateral security for its indebtedness by notes to the plaintiff. This note was not paid at maturity on the 13th day of November, 1886, and the said company "took it up, along with several other past-due discounts, by giving to the bank (the plaintiff) a new note for an amount equal to the sum then due on the discount so taken up, and on the same day again deposited with the bank" the note now sued upon, as collateral security for the new note mentioned. There is due upon the latter note to the plaintiff from the company a sum of money largely in excess of the amount due upon the note sued upon. J. M. McDowell held the note sued upon as attorney for the plaintiff for collection, and he brought this action in April, 1888, and the defendant was then informed that the plaintiff owned it, and he knew that it had at first been indorsed to the plaintiff before maturity for value; but there was no evidence that he knew of subsequent dealings between the plaintiff and the company. There was no evidence that the said company owed the defendant any amount before the bringing of this action. The defendant testified, among other things, that the Taylor Manufacturing Company became indebted to him in the years 1889 and 1890 in an amount exceeding the note sued on, and that in June, 1890, the defendant called upon John M. McDowell, as attorney for plaintiff. That it was then and there agreed between them that, if the defendant would make sale of certain machinery for the Taylor Manufacturing Company, and send the notes for the same to the Taylor Manufacturing Company, which notes should include the defendant's commissions, the said commissions, when collected, should be applied to the defendant's note. That thereafter the defendant made such sales, and his commissions amounted to more than enough to pay the note, attorney's fee, and costs of suit; and that he sent the notes, which included his commissions, to the Taylor Manufacturing Company. A demand was made by plaintiff upon defendant before this action was commenced for the costs and attorney's fee, and defendant refused to pay the same. There was no evidence that the Taylor Manufacturing Company ever delivered such notes to the plaintiff. That it was agreed between the defendant and McDowell that upon receipt by the plaintiff of said notes plaintiff would, upon payment of attorney's fees and costs of the action, dismiss the same. That the defendant admitted that he had never paid the costs or attorney's fees, but testified that the notes which he forwarded to the Taylor Manufacturing Company included his commissions coming to him in excess of the amount sued upon and such costs and attorney's fees. There was evidence that the notes forwarded by him had been paid to the Taylor Manufacturing Company, but the date when paid was not stated. There was evidence that the Taylor Manufacturing Company failed and made an assignment for the benefit of creditors some time after said notes were forwarded, and before the trial of this action. There was no evidence that McDowell, as attorney of the bank, had any other authority than to collect the note sued upon. The following issues were submitted to the jury: "Did the Taylor Manufacturing Company transfer and assign to the plaintiff the note referred to in the complaint before maturity and for value? Answer. Yes. Has the defendant paid and satisfied the said note? A. No." It was in evidence by the defendant that he was informed of the first indorsement of the note sued upon, for value, before the maturity of the note. There is no evidence that he knew of the subsequent dealing of the bank and the Taylor Manufacturing Company until this suit was brought. The court then instructed the jury, if they believed the evidence, the plaintiff was entitled to recover the amount of its demands, and the jury should find the issues accordingly. The defendant excepted. Judgment for the plaintiff. Defendant appealed.

Douglass & Shaw, for appellant. *J. W. Hinsdale* and *Black & Adams*, for appellee.

MERRIMON, C. J. It appears that the defendant executed the note sued upon to the Taylor Manufacturing Company, and the latter company sold and indorsed it to the plaintiff. Whether it was negotiable or not, (and there was some question as to this,) it belonged to the plaintiff at and before the time this action began; and the defendant, the maker thereof, had knowledge of this fact then and ever thereafter. Moreover, so far as appears, he then had no debt, claim, or demand, legal or equitable, against the company to which he gave the note, that he could set off against it or avail himself of as a counter-claim or other defense, whereby to prevent the plaintiff from recovering from him the sum of money therein specified. He had no claim against that company until in the years 1889 and 1890. So that, at the time this action began, the plaintiff was plainly entitled to recover—the defendant then owed it—the amount of the note mentioned, which he was bound, and refused or failed, to pay. In June of the last-mentioned year the attorney of the plaintiff, who was also the treasurer of the manufacturing company named, and defendant agreed between themselves that, if the defendant would make sale of certain machinery of the company, take notes therefor, and deliver the same to the company, then, when the notes should be collected, the defendant's commissions for making such sales should be applied in payment of the note of the plaintiff sued upon. Thereafter the defendant made such sale, delivered the notes taken on account of the same to the company, and the latter collected the same. The defendant's commissions amounted to a sum of money more than sufficient to pay the note, the subject of this action. There was no evidence to show that the company ever delivered the notes taken for the machinery to the plaintiff, or that the defendant's commissions were ever applied to the payment of the note in question. Indeed, the jury found as a fact that it had never been paid. It appears that McDowell, as attorney for the plaintiff, only had authority to collect the note. He hence had no authority to go beyond that, and agree to take anything in discharge of the note but money. He had no authority to take the defendant's right to commissions for selling the machinery referred to in discharge of the note. It does not appear that he undertook to do so. Moye v. Cogdell, 69 N. C. 98; Herring v. Hottendorf,

74 N. C. 588; Williams v. Johnston, 92 N. C. 532; Ward v. Smith, 7 Wall. 447; 7 Wait, Act. & Def. 435. The fair and just interpretation of what he and the defendant agreed upon was that the commissions, when collected, should be applied to the payment of the plaintiff's note; that is, the treasurer of the company, as for it, agreed that when the notes should be collected, then the money received in payment of the defendant's commissions should be paid through its treasurer to the plaintiff. The plaintiff was not a party to that agreement, nor was it intended that it should be. The attorney intended no more than to say that he would take the commissions, when collected in cash, as payment. It was not intended, so far as appears from the evidence, that the arrangement should be accepted by the plaintiff in discharge of its note. The attorney had no authority to so agree, nor does it appear that he intended to do so. When, therefore, the manufacturing company collected the defendant's commissions for selling the machinery, and failed to pay the same to the plaintiff, and became insolvent, and made an assignment of its property, the loss of the commissions was not that of the plaintiff, but that of the defendant. It was his misfortune that he failed to follow up his right, and compel the appropriation of his commissions as contemplated by himself and McDowell. We are therefore of opinion that the court's instructions to the jury, complained of, were correct.

Judgment affirmed.

S. C. FORSAITH MACH. CO. *et al.* v HOPE MILLS LUMBER CO. *et al.*

(*Supreme Court of North Carolina.* Nov. 17, 1891.)

FINDINGS BY COURT—REDUCTION TO WRITING—APPOINTMENT OF RECEIVER — SALES—DISTRIBUTION OF PROCEEDS.

1. Where findings upon which a court appointed a receiver were not reduced to writing until three or four days after the order was made, the order will not be disturbed, where it does not appear that defendant suffered from such delay.

2. Where it is clear from the evidence and admissions of the parties that it is a case where a receiver should be appointed, and that defendant is insolvent, and all the property must be sold to pay the debts, an order appointing receivers, and directing them to sell all the property of defendant, is proper.

3. In disposing of the motion for a receiver, the court properly declined to pass on questions of fraud raised by the pleadings.

4. Where defendants did not consent that the court should direct the receivers to pay certain judgments, admitted to be just and valid, it was error to order their payment.

5. Where defendant did not demur on the ground that a proper party defendant was not joined, an objection by defendant on that ground will not be sustained.

6. Where the affidavits and exhibits offered by plaintiffs raised questions which should be submitted to a jury, the court properly refused to pass on such questions.

Appeal from superior court, Cumberland county; EDWIN T. BOYKIN, Judge.

Action by the S. C. Forsaith Machine Company and others against the Hope Mills Lumber Company, S. H. Cotton, H. C. Gadsby, R. M. Nimocks, and Z. B. Newton, to foreclose a real-estate mortgage, and set aside certain fraudulent mortgages and judgments. Plaintiffs moved for the appointment of receivers of defendant company's property, which motion was granted. From the order appointing the receivers, defendants appeal. Order modified.

STATEMENT BY THE COURT. The plaintiffs are creditors of the defendant corporation, having debts for very considerable sums of money. In the complaint they allege their debts; that they have a mortgage of the defendants' property, both real and personal, of large value, to secure the same; that the defendant company and its officers fraudulently prevented the registration of their mortgage until after it had confessed fraudulent judgments for divers large sums of money in favor of certain of its officers and stockholders, and had executed and registered a mortgage of all its property in their favor, and likewise a deed of trust conveying their property, to secure fraudulent debts, etc. They further allege that the defendant is insolvent, and that certain judgments in favor of parties named are valid and just, and executions upon them have been levied upon the defendant company's personal property. The purpose of this action is to foreclose the plaintiffs' mortgage, to have the judgments mentioned confessed, and the second mortgage and deed of trust executed by the defendant company declared fraudulent and void, etc. The defendants admit some of the material allegations of the complaint, confess and avoid others, and deny the alleged fraud, and aver that the judgments and mortgage and deed of trust complained of are honest, etc. In the course of the action the plaintiffs moved for a receiver to take charge and control of the defendant company's property, real and personal, and to collect debts due it, etc. The court heard the motion upon the complaint, answers, and affidavits used in support of and in opposition to it, and, upon finding the facts allowed the motion, and appointed receivers, charged to take all the property, both real and personal, of the defendant company into their possession and control, to sell the same, to collect all debts due it, to pay out of the fund collected certain judgments admitted to be just and valid, etc. The defendants appealed to this court, assigning error as follows: "(1) That his honor failed to find the facts upon which his judgment was based; (2) that by reason of his failure to find the facts the appellants could not specify their exceptions to the said judgment; (3) that the judgment directs the sale of real estate not levied on, and that the proceeds of same be applied to the payment of judgments in favor of Wallace McPherson and the Enterprise Lumber Company, which are prior to the judgments in favor of the Hope Mills Manufacturing Company, R. M. Nimocks, S. H. Cotton, and H. C. Gadsby, and R. M. Nimocks; (4) that there is a defect of parties defendant, in that J. T. Gardner, trustee in deed of May 6, 1891, has not been made party to the action; (5) that the plaintiffs' affidavits and exhibits offered raised issues of fact which should have been submitted to a jury."

Sutton & Cook, for appellee.

MERRIMON, C. J. The first exception is groundless. It appears from the record that the court did find the facts very fully from the evidence in favor of and against the motion for a receiver, and upon such findings based the order appealed from. It seems that the appellants objected that such findings were not reduced to writing at once before or after the entry of the order appointing the receivers. It was not essential that this should be done. It was sufficient that it was done within a reasonable time, though it would be better that it should be done as promptly as practicable. The case settled on appeal states that the facts were stated by the court "within three or four days after the entry of the order, and sent to counsel." It does not appear that the appellants suffered any prejudice by such brief delay. Moreover, this is a case in equity, and it becomes the duty of this court to review the evidence and findings of fact of the court below with a view to ascertain and determine that the order complained of was or was not a proper one. So that here the appellants have ample opportunity to make their objections to the order appealed from. This court has complete authority, in cases equitable in their nature, like this, to examine the whole matter of the motion in question, and to direct a reversal or modification of the order of the court below, if there be error.

We fully concur in the findings of fact by the court below. The evidence and admissions of the parties fully warrant them. It is clear that the facts present a case in which a receiver should be appointed to take charge of the property of the defendant corporation, and collect the debts due it, pending the litigation. The order appointing the receivers directs them to take immediate "possession of the property, real and personal, of said Hope Mills Lumber Company, and sell the same at public or private sale to the best advantage," and also to collect all the debts due it, and out of the proceeds of such sales or collections to pay certain specified judgments admitted to be just and valid, and hold the surplus subject to the further order of the court.

Ordinarily it is not proper to finally settle questions raised by the pleadings or the rights of the parties, in cases like this, in disposing of a motion for an injunction or a receiver pending the action. This should be done when the case is finally heard upon the whole merits of the matter in litigation, when the case, in every material aspect of it, is thoroughly scrutinized, and the rights of the parties settled and determined. Motions in the course of the action for an injunction, a receiver, and the like, are intended to serve some important incidental purpose pending the action, and the court looks into the case to see if there is reasonable ground for granting them. It generally and properly leaves the final decision of important questions as to the rights of the parties until the final hearing. Hence it was not necessary or proper at the present stage of the action to decide the questions raised as to the validity of the judgments confessed by the defendant corporation, and the mortgage and deed of trust executed by it in favor of certain of its officers and stockholders, and other important questions. These must be left to be determined at the final hearing.

Ordinarily, the receiver appointed pending the action, particularly as to real estate, should simply be directed by the court to take care of and let the property in proper cases, collect the rents, etc., and to collect debts, and hold funds coming into his hands, subject to the order of the court, from time to time, and when the action is determined. But there are cases in which it is expedient and very proper to direct a sale of the property, both real and personal. The court should always be careful to see, however, that a proper case is presented for the exercise of such power, and to see particularly that the owner of the property cannot be unduly prejudiced by a sale thereof. It should have in view the rights and advantage of all the parties, as nearly as may be. In this case it is very certain that the defendant corporation is insolvent, and all its property must be sold to satisfy the numerous debts of creditors, parties to the action. There appears no reason, therefore, why the property—all of it—shall not be sold at once, the fund arising from such sale to be held under the order of the court, to be distributed to the parties entitled to have it upon the final hearing and disposition of the case. No party on this account can suffer prejudice, and it is important that the property should be owned and used by some person for the practical purposes to which it is devoted. The court therefore properly directed a sale of the property, both real and personal; but the sale of the real property should be made with due care, and with the express sanction of the court. Sales of it should be reported to the court, and confirmed, and title made in pursuance of its order. This is important to the creditors, and as well to purchasers, for obvious reasons.

The defendants did not consent that the court should direct the receivers to pay the judgments specified in the order. Indeed, it seems that they objected upon the ground that some of them have judgments that should be first paid; and it may possibly so turn out,—it may not. We are therefore of opinion that the court should not have directed the receivers to pay the judgments referred to. It might do so by consent, but consent is not given. The property should, under the circumstances, be sold as above indicated, and the fund arising from all sources held under the direction of the court until the court shall upon the final hearing direct its application to be made.

The defendants did not demur upon the ground that a proper party defendant was not before the court. If need be, that party may yet be brought into the action for any proper purpose.

The fifth exception is unfounded. The court expressly declined to pass upon the questions of fraud raised. These, and other questions affecting the whole merits, will be disposed of upon the final hearing.

The order appealed from must be modified as indicated in this opinion, and, thus modified, affirmed. To that end, let this opinion be certified to the superior court. It is so ordered.

NATIONAL BANK OF WESTMINSTER V. BURNS et al.

(*Supreme Court of North Carolina.* Nov. 17, 1891.)

SUPPLEMENTARY PROCEEDINGS — SUFFICIENCY OF AFFIDAVIT—INJUNCTION.

1. An affidavit in supplementary proceedings alleged that defendants had not sufficient property subject to execution to satisfy the judgment, but that defendants had property not exempt from execution, which they refused to apply towards the satisfaction of the judgment, and that an execution had been issued, but not returned. *Held,* that the affidavit was sufficient, under Code N. C. § 488, par. 2, which provides that after issuing an execution, on proof by affidavit that debtors have property which they refuse to apply towards the satisfaction of a judgment, the court may by order require them to appear and answer concerning the same.

2. Where two of the defendants were judgment debtors, and the other three were not, the affidavit was sufficient when, from all its allegations, the words "not exempt" clearly related to property in the hands of the three, which was not part of the homestead or personal property exemption of such debtors. Hinsdale v. Sinclair, 83 N. C. 338, distinguished.

3. The restraining order, forbidding the other three defendants "to transfer or make any other disposition of any property belonging to said defendants not exempt by law from execution," was not intended to affect the three in their own property, but only such as belonged to the debtors. It was warranted by section 490, which provides that persons having property of the judgment debtor may be examined concerning the same.

4. If the three defendants claimed any interest in the property alleged to be in their possession, they could, by suggesting it, have the right litigated, as provided by Code N. C. § 497.

5. Where they claimed an interest in the property in their hands, the court had power to forbid a disposition of the same until a receiver could be appointed to litigate the matter.

6. The court could not restrain the transfer of property owned by one not a party to the action. Coates v. Wilkes, 94 N. C. 174, distinguished.

Appeal from superior court, Moore county; EDWIN T. BOYKIN, Judge.

Proceedings supplementary to execution instituted by the National Bank of Westminster against J. F. Burns, T. B. Burns, Robert L. Burns, and Ann R. Burns, to reach property belonging to J. F. Burns, the judgment debtor. Defendants moved to dismiss, and to modify the order, which motions were denied, and they appealed. Affirmed.

STATEMENT BY THE COURT. The plaintiff obtained its judgment against the defendants for $1,089.83, with interest, in the superior court of the county of Moore, on the 17th day of August, 1885, and the same was duly docketed in that county. No part of the same has been paid. It appears by the affidavit of the agent of the plaintiff that an execution upon the said judgment was, on June 26, 1890, issued to the sheriff of Moore county, in which both of the said defendants reside, said execution being against the property of both of said defendants, and that the said execution still remains in the hands of the

said sheriff, not having been returned by him; that affiant is informed and believes that the defendants have not sufficient property subject to execution in the state of North Carolina to satisfy the said judgment, but that the said defendants have property, money, and choses in action not exempt from execution, which they unjustly refuse to apply towards the satisfaction of the said judgment; that affiant is informed and believes T. B. Burns and Robert L. Burns and Ann R. Burns have property of J. F. Burns, one of the judgment debtors aforesaid, and are indebted to him in an amount exceeding $10. Thereupon, and on motion of the plaintiff, the court (the clerk) made its order on the 26th day of June, 1890, requiring the defendants to appear on the 8th day of July, 1890, "to be examined and make discovery on oaths concerning their property, joint and separate," and likewise requiring the said T. B. Burns, Robert L. Burns, and Ann R. Burns to appear also, "to be examined and answer on oath concerning the property of J. F. Burns," defendant, in their possession, and concerning their indebtedness to him, and an order was entered forbidding them "to transfer or make any other disposition of any property belonging to said defendants, not exempt by law from execution of said indebtedness, or in any manner to interfere therewith until further order in the premises." The defendants moved before the court (the clerk) to dismiss this proceeding supplementary to the execution, for insufficiency of the affidavit made by plaintiff, for the reason that said affidavit showed that execution had been issued, but not returned by the sheriff at the time of the commencement of the said proceedings, and that the defendants had property, money, and choses in action not exempt from execution; and in that said affidavit failed to show the existence of property, choses in action, and things of value unaffected by any lien, and incapable of levy. The defendants also moved, before said clerk, to modify the order issued by him, so as to dissolve the restraining order forbidding T. B. Burns and Robert L. Burns to dispose of any property in their hands, on the ground that no notice or any other process had been served on said T. B. Burns and Robert L. Burns, nor were they parties to said proceedings. The clerk refused to dismiss the proceedings for the alleged insufficiency of the affidavit, and also refused to modify said order; and from this ruling the defendants appealed. Upon the hearing the judge affirmed the ruling of the clerk, and refused to dismiss the proceedings, and to modify said order, and to this ruling the defendants excepted, and appealed to supreme court.

Douglass & Shaw, for appellants. *J. W. Hinsdale* and *Black & Adams,* for appellee.

MERRIMON, C. J. The statute (Code, § 488, par. 2) prescribes that, "after the issuing of an execution against property, and upon proof by affidavit of a party, his agent or attorney, to the satisfaction of the court or a judge thereof, that any judgment debtor residing in the judicial district where such judge or officer resides has property which he unjustly refuses to apply towards the satisfaction of the judgment, such court or judge may, by an order, require the judgment debtor to appear at a specified time and place to answer concerning the same," etc. The affidavit objected to substantially in all respects is a compliance with this statutory provision. It appears from it that an execution was in the hands of the sheriff; that the defendants therein had not property sufficient subject to execution to satisfy the judgment; that they "have property, money, and choses in action not exempt from execution, which they unjustly refuse to apply towards the satisfaction of the said judgment." Thus the foundation for the order complained of was laid almost in the very words of the statute, and the case was presented in which the judgment creditor became entitled to examine his judgment debtor. Although the execution was in the hands of the sheriff, it may be that the property so subject to execution could not be found; it may have been hidden. The debtors also may have had money, choses in action, etc. The statute intends that, when the debtor refuses to apply such property to the satisfaction of the judgment, he must, when duly required, answer concerning the same, to the end the court, in a proper way, may so apply the property to which the debtor may direct attention. It was said on the argument that, if the property is "not exempt from execution," as stated in the affidavit, why not levy upon and sell it? Why require the examination of the defendants? The explanation and reason are given above. Here, however, the words, "not exempt from execution," must be taken with the other parts of the affidavit, and it sufficiently appears that they were intended to imply that the defendants had such property not exempt from execution as part of the homestead or personal property exemption of the debtor. The affidavit states, in another part of the same paragraph of it, that the defendants "have not sufficient property subject to execution" to satisfy the judgment. Clearly, the affidavit was sufficient to warrant the order, under the clause of the statute cited above. Vegelahn v. Smith, 95 N. C. 254. The case of Hinsdale v. Sinclair, 83 N. C. 338, is not in point here, because the statute interpreted by it is not the same, in material respects, as the present pertinent statute. See Battle, Revisal, c. 17, § 264, par. 2. The present statute provides, as the former one did not, that the "creditor shall be entitled to the order of examination under this subdivision, and under subdivision 1 of this section, (that cited above,) although the judgment debtor may have an equitable estate in land subject to the lien of the judgment, or may have choses in action, or other things of value, unaffected by the lien of the judgment and incapable of levy."

The order forbidding T. B. Burns, Robert Burns, and Ann R. Burns "to transfer or make any other disposition of any property belonging to said defendants not exempt by law from execution" was not inappropriate or unwarranted. The purpose was not to restrain or affect these persons as to their own property, but expressly to prevent them from disposing of property of the judgment debtor in their hands, custody, and control. The statute (Code, § 490) expressly prescribes that persons having property of the judgment debtor may be examined in respect to the same, and mere notice is sufficient to bring them before the court, and make them subject to its jurisdiction, for the purpose of securing the debtor's property, not for the purpose of contesting any right of such persons having the same. If they claim an interest in the property, or that the same belongs to them, they may so properly suggest; in which case their rights may be litigated, as intended and provided by the statute. (Code, § 497. In such case the court has power to forbid the disposition of the property until a receiver can be appointed, and bring action to litigate the matter in dispute. But the court would not have authority in such proceedings to make a party subject to an injunction as to his own property, he not being a party to the action. The case of Coates v. Wilkes, 94 N. C. 174, cited by the defendants, has no application here. In that case, Wilkes, the wife, was not a party, nor did the order in question extend simply to the property of the judgment debtor. There is no error. To the end that further proceedings may be had in the proceeding supplementary to the execution, let this opinion be certified to the superior court. It is so ordered.

MOORE v. QUINCE et al.

(Supreme Court of North Carolina. Nov. 17, 1891.)

EQUITY—REFORMATION OF MARRIAGE SETTLEMENT.

By a deed of marriage settlement a wife gave all her property to a trustee, "his executors and administrators," to hold the same for her sole use, and provided that, if she should die during coverture, then he should hold it to the use of such child or children as she should leave surviving her, for them and their "legal representatives," unless she should otherwise direct by will; but if she should die intestate the property should become the property of the husband, and the trustee should reconvey to the wife or to the husband, or the survivor of them. *Held*, that there was sufficient evidence on the face of the deed to show that it was the intention of the parties to convey the property to the trustee and his heirs, instead of his personal representatives, and to insert words of inheritance, so that, in case of the husband's death, after the death of the wife without issue and intestate, the property should go to his heirs.

Appeal from superior court, New Hanover county; JAMES D. MCIVER, Judge.

Action by F. M. Moore against Mary E. Quince and others. Judgment for defendants. Plaintiff appeals. Reversed.

STATEMENT BY THE COURT. This was a civil action brought to restore a lost deed of marriage settlement, and to have it reformed by inserting words of inheritance. The defendants demurred to the evidence, and the only controverted question was whether there was sufficient evidence upon the face of the deed to show that it was the intention of the parties, by inserting the necessary words of inheritance, to provide for a reconveyance of the property in fee to the husband, James Moore, in case the wife should die intestate and without issue, and the husband should survive her. The marriage settlement was as follows: "Whereas, a marriage is shortly to be had and solemnized between James Moore, of the county of Chatham, state of North Carolina, and Sally J. Freeman, of the same county and state; and whereas, it has been agreed between the parties, with the consent of the said James Moore, which is evidenced by his signing this deed of conveyance, that the said Sally should settle for her sole use and benefit all her real and personal estate, so that the same shall in no wise be subject to the debts, liabilities, or contracts of her said intended husband, but that the said Sally may have and enjoy the same as if she was sole owner, notwithstanding the said marriage: Now, therefore, this deed witnesseth that the said Sally J. Freeman, for and in consideration of the premises and of one dollar to her in hand paid by Henry A. London, of said county and state, before the sealing and delivery of these presents, the receipt whereof is hereby acknowledged, hath given, granted, bargained, and sold, and by these presents doth give, grant, bargain, and sell, unto the said Henry A. London, his executors and administrators, all and singular, the following property, to-wit: All the lots and houses in the city of Columbia, South and Lower Carolina; all the houses and lots in the town of Wilmington, N. C., owned by the said Sally J. Freeman; together with all appurtenances thereunto belonging or in any wise appertaining; also all money, bonds, or evidence of debts due to her, the said Sally J. Freeman; also all furniture or other property of a personal nature. In special trust and confidence, nevertheless, that the said Henry A. London shall hold the said lots and houses, and money and bonds and furniture, to the sole and separate use of the said Sally J. Freeman until the celebration of the said contemplated marriage; and after the said contemplated marriage shall have been celebrated between the said parties the said Henry A. London, trustee aforesaid, shall hold the said lots and houses, money or bonds and furniture, and other property, in special trust for the sole and separate use of the said Sally J. Freeman, so that the same shall in no wise be responsible for the debts or contracts of the said James Moore; and it is further understood and agreed that the said trustee shall and will permit the said Sally J. Freeman to use any or all of the said property above described, in any way that she, in her own judgment, may deem proper; and if the said trustee shall rent out any or all of said lots and houses, or dispose of any of said property, at any time during the coverture of the said Sally J. Freeman, he shall pay over the said rents or other money derived from said property to the said Sally J. Freeman, and her receipt for the same shall be a sufficient discharge and acquittance for the same, notwithstanding her said coverture; and it is further understood and agreed that if the said Sally should die during the said coverture, that the said trustee shall hold the said property to the use and benefit of such child or children as the said Sally may leave surviving her, for them and their legal representatives, unless the said Sally by her last will and testament, duly executed, shall otherwise direct, which last will and testament it is agreed the said Sally may make, publish, and declare, notwithstanding her said coverture. But and if the said Sally shall die without making any last will and testament, then and in that case the said described property shall become the property of the said James Moore, and the said trustee shall reconvey to the said Sally, or to the said James, or the survivor of them, the said property above described, and the said trustee is in no wise responsible for any of the rents or profits of said property except such as may come actually into his hands. In testimony whereof the said James Moore, Sally J. Freeman, and Henry A. London, the trustee, have hereunto set their hands and seals this 19th day of April, 1867. JAMES MOORE. [Seal.] SALLY J. FREEMAN. [Seal.] HENRY A. LONDON. [Seal.] Signed, sealed, and delivered in presence of M. Q. WADDELL. [Jurat.] F. M. MOORE. L. P. WADDELL. [Jurat.]"

E. S. Martin and George Rountree, for appellant. Junius Davis, for appellees.

AVERY, J. It is settled law, not only that equity will not allow a trust to fall for want of a trustee, but that, when a trustee is named in a deed, and the nature of his fiduciary duties and the times at which they are to be performed, according to its terms, indicate clearly that the grantor contemplated either the certainty or possibility that the legal and equitable estates must be separated and the trust administered beyond the life-time of the trustee named, a court of equity will supply the words "and his heirs," after the name of the trustee, upon the ground that it was omitted by mistake of the draughtsman when the deed was drawn. Ryan v. McGehee, 83 N. C. 500; Perry, Trusts, § 320. Where the court is fully satisfied, from the expressed purpose of the grantor, the nature of the deed, and the context of that portion of it where the word "heirs" would naturally belong, that it was his intention to convey an estate in fee, and the omission of the prescribed technical words was an oversight, there is a plain equity to have the mistake corrected. Vickers v. Leigh, 104 N. C. 253, 10 S. E. Rep. 308; Rutledge v. Smith, Busb. Eq. 283. When, on the examination of an ordinary deed of conveyance to trustees on a marriage settlement, it appears manifest that a life-estate in the trustee is inadequate to the execution of the trust, and also that the obvious purpose of the grantor to dispose of the whole of the equitable estate will be defeated, unless the instrument can be construed to vest that estate in fee-simple in the beneficiaries, the concurrence of two reasons for supplying words of inheritance makes it more clearly the duty of the court to effectuate the intention of the grantor by correcting both mistakes or omissions.

The general purpose pervading the deed of settlement seems to have been to make a final disposition in any contingency of the real as well as the personal property of the wife, but the particular provisions of the deed, construed literally and according to technical rules, are strangely at war with what appears to have been the leading intent of the parties in entering into it. The deed provides for the disposition of the fund derived from the sale by the trustee of any of the property, without distinguishing between real and personal; but that clause is less indicative of the intent than some subsequent ones. The trustee, who, without enlargement beyond the words of the deed, takes but a life-estate, is, in case the wife dies during coverture, to hold "the said property to the use and benefit of such child or children as the said Sally may leave surviving her, for them and their legal representatives," unless the wife (Sally) should dispose of it by will, which she is empowered to make. The words "legal representatives" are often used (as we must gather from the context is their meaning here) in the sense of "heirs at law." Briggs v. Upton, L. R. 7 Ch. App. 376; Com. v. Bryan, 6 Serg. & R. 81; Delaunay v. Burnett, 4 Gilman, 454; Morehouse v. Phelps, 18 Ill. 472. It could not have been intended that the land in this case should go to any one who, by the proper authority, might be appointed a personal representative of a surviving child of the wife, and therefore the inevitable inference is that the words were used to mean the children and heirs at law of such children of Mrs. Moore as might die during her life, leaving issue who also should survive their grandmother. Bowman v. Long, 89 Ill. 19. If we construe the deed literally, supplying no ellipsis, the consequence would be that the trustee, who holds the legal estate in the land for life only, would be expected to discharge the trust for the wife, for the husband if she should die intestate during his life and without issue, and if she should die during coverture, leaving issue and also intestate, then for the benefit of the first and second generations of the issue, and, on failure of lineal descendants, for the heirs at law of such issue. The lands would not, without supplying words of inheritance, be finally disposed of by the deed except in the event that Mrs. Moore should devise in fee during coverture. We think it was the manifest purpose the marriage settlement to give Mrs. Moore the power to make a final disposition of the land and other property by will, but if she should fail to exercise that power during coverture, and there should also be a failure of issue of the marriage, then the intention was to clothe the trustee with power to convey the land in fee-simple to the survivor, whether James Moore or his wife. But, in the absence of words of inheritance appended to the names of both, any possible construction of the deed would lead to very absurd conclusions. If Mrs. Moore had outlived her husband, the trustee, London would have been required to reconvey to her, as survivor; yet if he took the legal estate under the settlement only

for his own life, he could convey to her an estate for the residue of his own life, and no longer. Now that James Moore was the survivor, and there was no issue of the marriage, it became the duty of the trustee to "reconvey" to him as survivor, and, as he has died since the death of his wife, to his only heir at law. Shall we hold that the trustee could have conveyed to him on the death of his wife only an estate *per outer vie*, and, in case of London's death during his life, that the remainder in fee would have passed to her heirs at law, leaving her husband then still living without any interest, and, for aught we know, without home or income? We are constrained to conclude that the word "reconvey" was used upon the assumption that the legal estate had previously passed in fee, and that the reconveyance was as necessary to revest the entire estate in the wife, if she should survive, as in the surviving husband, it being the purpose to give him, at her death without issue and intestate, just the same estate as would have been reconveyed to the wife. This view is strengthened by the consideration that the deed of settlement was executed in the year 1867, when, in the absence of any agreement, the husband would have become the owner of the whole of the personal property immediately upon the consummation of the marriage rites, and entitled to the contingent right to curtesy in the whole of her land; an estate for his own life being more advantageous than that for the life of London. It does not entirely destroy the force of this fact to admit, as we do, that the contemplated marriage was a consideration for some concessions on his part. But the fact that he surrendered such rights incident to the marriage adds some weight to the view that it was intended by the provision for reconveyance that, if she should die without issue and without availing herself of the power to provide by will for any favored one among her heirs at law, the reconveyance to her husband should pass the fee just as if made to herself. We conclude, therefore, that the judge erred in refusing to allow the deed to be reformed by inserting the words "and his heirs" after the name of James Moore, as proposed, on the ground that there was no sufficient evidence; and we think likewise that the manifest intention of the parties was to pass the legal estate in fee to the trustee London, and to use the words "and his heirs" in the *habendum* instead of "his executors and administrators." The deed must be reformed accordingly, and the trustee should be required then to reconvey in fee to the plaintiff, who is the only heir at law of the husband, James Moore. There is error, and the judgment must be reversed.

STATE v. NASH.

(*Supreme Court of North Carolina.* Nov. 10, 1891.)

ASSAULT WITH INTENT TO RAPE—EXAMINATION BY PHYSICIAN—INSTRUCTIONS—SENTENCE.

1. On a prosecution of a physician for assault with intent to rape on a girl 17 years of age, in that he took improper liberties with her person,

an instruction that if he acted in good faith as a physician, and did what he did as such, he is not guilty, "otherwise he is guilty," is erroneous, as, if she consented to the taking of the liberties, understanding that he was not acting in good faith as a physician, then he was not guilty.

2. Under Code N. C. § 987, providing that where no deadly weapon has been used, and no serious damage done, the punishment in cases of assault shall not exceed a fine of $50 or 30 days' imprisonment, provided that this shall not apply to cases of assault with intent to commit rape, on a conviction of a simple assault, where there is no evidence of bodily pain, there can be no greater punishment than therein prescribed, though the indictment was for assault with intent to commit rape.

Appeal from superior court, Granville county; ROBERT W. WINSTON, Judge.

H. A. Nash, indicted for assault with intent to commit rape, was convicted of a simple assault, and appeals. Reversed.

STATEMENT BY THE COURT. Defendant requested the court to charge the jury, in addition to other propositions, as follows: "(2) If defendant put his hand on the person of Susan with intent only to examine her as a physician, and with no intent to take indecent liberties with her, then defendant is not guilty of any assault, and the jury will return a verdict of not guilty. (3) If defendant put his hands on the person of Susan with her consent, and not against her will, the defendant is not guilty of any assault, and the jury will return a verdict of not guilty." The court gave the instruction embraced in the first proposition, but refused the other request, and told the jury that, "if Dr. Nash went to Susan's room, and to her bed, and with the desire to gratify any morbid curiosity, or to have to do with her, or for any other unlawful purpose, felt her breast or private parts, he is guilty, and it will be your duty to convict. If you find from the facts that defendant took advantage of his position as a physician, and as such, and with a bad purpose, felt the person of Susan, by pretending he would see if she had womb disease, you will find defendant guilty, even if she made no resistance, but consented to the same. But if defendant went in the room of Susan, and put his hands on her person, with no intent to take indecent liberties with her, but in good faith, at the request of Mrs. Goss, or because he thought she was sick, and needed his attention, and in good faith put his hands on her to examine her, he would not be guilty, and you will so find." At a later stage of the charge the judge added the following: "So that the question comes back again to what the court has already charged you: 'Did defendant do what he did to Susan in good faith, as her physician, or did he handle her person for a bad or unlawful purpose?' If he acted in good faith as a physician, and did what he did as such, he is not guilty; otherwise he is guilty." The question being only whether there was evidence to show consent obtained otherwise than fraudulently, it is unnecessary to set out all the evidence for the state.

L. C. Edwards and B. S. Royster, for appellant. J. W. Graham, Atty. Gen., and T. B. Womack, for the State.

AVERY, J. If it be conceded that where a physician induces a female to submit to an examination of her person by the false and fraudulent representation that he is putting his hands upon her in good faith, for the purpose of diagnosing and treating a disease, when in fact his object is only to gratify a licentious desire, he is equally guilty, in contemplation of law, with one who takes the same liberties against her consent, and with the avowed intention of gratifying his lusts, it is none the less a sound proposition of law that, whether the person charged with the assault be a physician or not, he may successfully meet such a charge by showing to the satisfaction of the jury that, without resorting to falsehood or deception, he had the consent of a girl, 17 years old, to put his hand upon her person as he did. Whether his intention was to desist after fondling her, or to have carnal intercourse with her, if she should continue to yield to him, he was not guilty if her consent was gained otherwise than by using his professional character to practice a fraud. There was serious conflict in the testimony of the prosecutrix and the defendant as to what the latter actually did and said at her bedside. The charge of the learned judge seems to have been founded upon the idea that the jury, in passing upon the facts, were so restricted that they must adopt either the theory of the state or that arising out of the defendant's testimony, and were not at liberty to take into consideration the whole of the evidence, and predicate their finding upon a hypothesis not entirely consistent with the theory advanced, or the testimony offered in support of it, by either the prosecution or the defense. Counsel may have contended before the jury that another witness corroborated the testimony of the plaintiff to the extent of showing that the mother of the prosecutrix had expressed apprehension as to the consequence to her daughter of overexertion on the previous afternoon. The jury may have concluded that, under the honest belief that the prosecutrix was suffering, and with the *bona fide* purpose of relieving her, the defendant first entered her room; but that subsequently, on discovering a willingness on her part to submit to liberties that, as she must have known, constituted no part of a legitimate medical or surgical examination, he determined to go further, and did so with her assent, plainly indicated. It appeared that two men, sleeping in the loft just above her, heard no outcry, nor loud remonstrance, and the prosecutrix did not say that she called for any one; yet, though she told the defendant that she was not sick, needed no attention, and pushed his hand away, she submitted without objection made in a tone sufficiently loud to be heard in the loft, to liberties, accompanied by expressions of endearment, and solicitations to go with him into the adjacent room, that counsel may have argued were inconsistent with the idea that she yielded only because he was conducting an examination as a physician authorised by her mother. The jury might have been influenced, too, by the fact that the father of the prosecutrix appeared, according to her testimony, at the door, and saw the defendant going out of her room twice; that he subsequently neither asked nor received a full explanation from his daughter for nearly two days after, though he ordered her to dress, and go to his son's house on that night. The rule laid down by Wharton (Crim. Law, § 1156) is that proof of the assent of the woman, given in ignorance of the fraud that was being practiced by the medical man, where the physician, under pretense of examination, has sexual intercourse, will not constitute a defense to the charge of assault. The principle was first established in the cases of Reg. v. Stanton, 1 Car. & K. 415, and Reg. v. Case, 4 Cox, Crim. Cas. 220. In the latter case, the instruction given by the recorder and approved by the court was "that the girl was of age to consent, and, if they thought she had consented to what the prisoner had done, they ought to acquit the prisoner; but if they were of opinion that she was ignorant of the nature of the prisoner's act, and made no resistance, solely from the belief that she was submitting to medical treatment, they ought to find him guilty." In that case the physician actually had carnal intercourse with a girl of 14, who had been placed under his care by her parents for medical treatment. We think that the questions whether the prosecutrix consented, after being kissed and told that she was a sweet girl, (even conceding the truth of her own statement,) to the still greater liberties with her person which she testifies that the defendant took, and whether, if she did consent, she was influenced to yield solely because she thought the defendant was making a medical examination of her person at the request of a parent, should have been fairly submitted to the jury; and, as in Reg. v. Case, the judge ought to have told the jury that in one view of the evidence the defendant was not guilty, as well as that in the other view he was guilty, of an assault. In Reg. v. Case it seemed to have been conceded, or not seriously disputed, that the girl of 14 was innocent, and did not understand what the physician was doing. In the case at bar there was evidence tending to show that the prosecutrix was not of good character, and it was admitted that she was in her eighteenth year. The defendant had a right to demand that the attention of the jury should be directed to the question whether she understood the manifest purpose of one who kissed and fondled her, and knew that his conduct was not that of a physician making a medical examination in good faith, but still submitted quietly until her father appeared upon the scene. But in response to the requests of the defendant the judge embodied his instruction upon this point in two or three propositions culminating in the sentence: "If he acted in good faith as a physician, and did what he did as such, he is not guilty; otherwise, he is guilty." So that the jury were not left at liberty to reach the belief from the evidence that, though the defendant was not in good faith examining the prosecutrix

as a physician, still that she understood and assented to what he did, or that she understood that he was putting his hands upon her with the purpose of gratifying his lusts, and made no objection because she was indifferent, or ready to submit to what he did, if not to still greater liberties.

Without adverting to the other exceptions, either to the admission of testimony or to the charge, and deciding questions that may not be raised upon another trial, it is perhaps best to advert to the exception to the judgment of the court. We think that there was error in imposing greater punishment than a fine of $50 or imprisonment for 30 days, when the defendant was found guilty of a simple assault only. In all of the cases cited by the attorney general in support of the judgment, this court laid stress upon the fact that the person assaulted suffered great bodily pain, though the physical injury did not prove permanent. In State v. Shelly, 98 N. C. 673, 4 S. E. Rep. 580, the opinion rested upon the ground that "the injury was not simply painful and humiliating, but disfigured the face seriously, bruised the eyes, closed one of them entirely, and probably permanently impaired the sight," and therefore that serious damage was done. The facts in State v. Roseman, 108 N. C. 765, 12 S. E. Rep. 1039, were that a female prisoner was whipped by a jailer with a buggy-whip, so as to cut the flesh on her back and arms. In State v. Huntley, 91 N. C. 621, though the court seem to have taken into consideration the mental anguish of the injured party, the reason for sustaining the jurisdiction of the superior court which is made most prominent was that the physical suffering of the injured party "must have been severe for a day or two, and more or less severe for several days." So that in every instance it has been declared essential, in order to give the superior court jurisdiction, that the bodily pain caused by the assault should be severe, if not permanent. The fact that in any given case the person injured must have endured mental anguish may aggravate the offense, but cannot, in the absence of physical injury giving rise to great bodily pain, constitute, within the meaning of the statute,[1] "serious injury." There was no evidence in our case tending to show that the prosecutrix suffered from bodily pain at all. The cases cited are distinguishable from that at bar in the fact that the jury found that the defendant was guilty of the offense charged in the indictment, which was within the jurisdiction of the superior court. In our case the defendant was found guilty of a simple assault only, and the jurisdiction of the

---

[1] Code N. C. § 987, provides that in all cases of an assault with or without intent to kill or injure, the person convicted shall be punished by fine or imprisonment, or both, at the discretion of the court: provided, that, where no deadly weapon has been used, and no serious damage done, the punishment in assaults, assaults and batteries, and affrays, shall not exceed a fine of $50 or imprisonment for 30 days; but that proviso shall not apply to cases of assault with intent to kill, or with intent to commit rape.

court is sustained on the ground that it is included in the higher offense with which he was charged. For the error pointed out the defendant is entitled to a new trial.

STATE v. MORRIS.

(Supreme Court of North Carolina. Nov. 17, 1891.)

APPEAL — REVIEW — DISCRETION — HEARSAY EVIDENCE.

1. On a trial for slandering an "innocent woman," after the examination of the prosecutrix, the court refused to allow defendant to ask her how many times she and her husband had separated, and the cause. *Held* that, since defendant had had fair opportunity for cross-examination, it was discretionary with the court to allow this question.

2. In such case the husband of the prosecutrix denied, on cross-examination, that he said he had sexual intercourse with the prosecutrix before he married her. Defendant offered to prove, by himself and another witness, that the husband said "that he would rather pay $2.50, and marry the woman, [the prosecutrix,] than have a bastard sworn to him." The trial court excluded the testimony. *Held,* that the testimony rejected was not competent to contradict the husband nor pertinent to prove the incontinency of the prosecutrix, and was simply hearsay.

3. The exercise of the discretion of the trial court in refusing to grant a new trial, on the ground of newly-discovered evidence, is not reviewable.

Appeal from superior court, Montgomery county; JESSE F. GRAVES, Judge.

Indictment of P. M. Morris for slander. Verdict and judgment of conviction. Defendant appeals. Affirmed.

The Attorney General and *Douglass & Shaw,* for the State.

MERRIMON, C. J. The defendant is indicted for slandering an "innocent woman" in violation of the statute. Code, § 1113. He pleaded not guilty. On the trial, the prosecutrix was examined as a witness for the state, and, after she was examined in chief, the defendant asked to be allowed to ask the witness one question. The solicitor, not knowing the nature of the question, did not at once object. The defendant then proposed this question: "How many times witness and her husband had separated," and asked the cause. The court said: "You may ask that question if its purpose is to impeach the witness." The counsel said: "We want to show the cause of the separation." The court said: "I cannot go into that investigation now;" and defendant excepted. The defendant had had fair opportunity, in the orderly course of the examination of the witness, to propound all proper questions, and it was discretionary with the court to allow or disallow the question propounded to be put to the witness. The defendant had no right to protract the examination indefinitely, particularly as to matters that the witness ought to have been examined about upon the cross-examination.

The husband of the prosecutrix was examined as a witness for the state, and on the cross-examination he was asked if he had not told a certain person named that

he had sexual intercourse with his wife (the prosecutrix) before he married her. The witness denied that he had said so. The defendant then offered to show, by himself and another witness, that the husband said to them "that he would rather pay two dollars and a half, and marry the woman, [the prosecutrix,] than have a bastard sworn to him." Upon objection, the court excluded the evidence, and the defendant excepted. The defendant was concluded by the answer of the husband when a witness to the question put to him, because it elicited matter wholly collateral to the purpose of the examination, and did not go to show bias. The evidence of the defendant rejected was hence not competent to contradict the husband, and it was not pertinent to prove the incontinency of the prosecutrix. It was simply hearsay. Kramer v. Light Co., 95 N. C. 277, and cases there cited; State v. Glisson, 93 N. C. 506.

The defendant moved for a new trial in the court below, assigning as ground for the motion that he had discovered since the trial important pertinent evidence that he could produce for his defense on another trial. The court, in the exercise of its discretion, denied the motion, and the defendant excepted. It is settled that such exercise of discretion is not reviewable. Carson v. Dellinger, 90 N. C. 226, and cases there cited. There is no error. Let this opinion be certified to the superior court according to law. It is so ordered.

STATE v. BLACK.

(Supreme Court of North Carolina. Nov. 17, 1891.)

ASSAULT AND BATTERY — CERTIORARI — CASE ON APPEAL.

1. The fact that defendant's hogs are impounded under an invalid ordinance will not justify a breach of the peace, and an assault on the officer in charge, in order to retake them.

2. Where a special instruction was asked in writing, and refused, and exception noted, but it does not appear that such exception was set out in the statement of the case on appeal, *certiorari* will not lie to have it incorporated in the "case settled."

Appeal from superior court, Moore county; EDWIN T. BOYKIN, Judge.

Indictment of W. E. Black for assault and battery, as follows: "The jurors for the state, upon their oath, present that W. E. Black, in Moore county, on the 24th day of July, 1891, did unlawfully and willfully assault and beat one J. M. Adams with deadly weapon, to-wit, a certain club, contrary to the statute in such case made and provided, and against the peace and dignity of the state." Verdict and judgment of conviction. Defendant appeals. Affirmed.

STATEMENT BY THE COURT. It appeared in evidence that defendant's hogs had been impounded by the town marshal of Carthage, and were in his custody. The marshal and two of the town commissioners, who were near the pound, saw the defendant going in the direction of the pound at night, and the defendant swore in their presence that, unless the marshal turned his hogs out, he would liberate them, and thereupon proceeded to the pound, and attempted to break the pound to turn the hogs out. The marshal and the two commissioners came up, and the marshal ordered the defendant to desist. He refused to desist. The marshal threatened to arrest him if he persisted in breaking the pound. There was also evidence that the marshal flourished a pistol when he threatened to arrest the defendant, who thereupon assaulted the marshal with a piece of scantling drawn in a striking attitude within striking distance. The marshal had no warrant. The defendant offered to introduce the ordinance under which his hogs had been impounded, for the purpose of showing that said ordinance was void. The court refused to admit the evidence. The exception for such refusal is the only exception presented for review. The case states that there was no exception to the charge. The defendant moved for a *certiorari*, as stated in the opinion.

Douglass & Shaw and *J. W. Hinsdale*, for appellant. *The Attorney General*, for the State.

CLARK, J. The affidavit in the petition for *certiorari* avers that a special prayer for instruction was asked in writing, and in proper time; that it was refused, and exception noted, but it is not alleged that such exception was set out in appellant's statement of case on appeal. As the appellant did not set it out as an exception in his case on appeal, he cannot complain that the judge did not incorporate it in the "case settled" by him. In Taylor v. Plummer, 105 N. C. 56, 11 S. E. Rep. 266, it is said: "Exceptions noted on the trial, and exceptions which, after the verdict, the losing party desires to assign to the charge, or to the refusal or granting of special instructions, must be set out by appellant in making out his statement of the case on appeal, (as required by Code, § 550,) or they are deemed waived." Had the exception for refusal of the special instruction (if asked in writing, and in apt time) been set out by appellant in making up his case on appeal, (Code, § 550, and Rule 27, Supreme Court, 12 S. E. Rep. vii.,) and the judge had omitted such prayer, and the exception for its refusal from the "case settled," a *certiorari* would lie to have them incorporated. Lowe v. Elliott, 107 N. C. 718, 12 S. E. Rep. 383. By not setting out such an exception in his statement of case on appeal, the appellant has waived the right to insist on it.

The only exception stated in the case on appeal is the refusal to admit the town ordinance in evidence, which was offered for the purpose of showing its invalidity. For the purpose of the exception, it must be taken that the hogs were impounded under an invalid ordinance; but they were in the custody of the officer, and the owner had no right to take the law in his own hands, and regain possession of his property by violence, and by tearing down the pound. The officer had a right to forbid him, and to prevent the property being taken out of his custody by force. This is not a case where the officer is on trial for using excessive force. Nor is it a case

where property is attempted to be taken under a void warrant, and the owner resists by force. For all that appears, the hogs were taken on process valid on its face, which the officer was compelled to execute, though issued, possibly, without sufficient legal ground; but that was not a matter for the officer to decide, nor the defendant. It was a matter to be settled by the court. Besides, the hogs had been taken previously, and were in the peaceable possession of the officer. The case presented is as to the right of the defendant to tear down the town pound to regain possession of his hogs, (taken under an illegal ordinance,) after being forbidden to do so, and his right to assault the officer who bade him desist, and who, when the defendant did not stop, with a flourish of his pistol had threatened to arrest him. That the defendant made an assault is uncontroverted. The defense set up by the exception, that the hogs had been taken under an invalid ordinance, is not sufficient. The defendant, after being forbidden by the officer, should have desisted, and have sought to get back his hogs by lawful process. He had no right to regain them by means of a breach of the peace. "Two wrongs will not make a right." In State v. Hedrick, 95 N. C. 624, an arrest was made by one who had been illegally deputed to serve a warrant in a civil action. On the party arrested attempting to escape, another party tripped up the acting officer, who was pursuing. It was held that such other party was guilty of an assault. In State v. Armistead, 106 N. C. 639, 10 S. E. Rep. 872, it is said that no one has a right to take a prisoner from the custody of an officer on the ground that such prisoner is unlawfully in arrest, since the lawfulness of the arrest must be inquired into without resort to force. The property being committed to the custody of the officer by process of law, he had the right to arrest any one attempting to take it from him, and without warrant. Braddy v. Hodges, 99 N. C. 319, 5 S. E. Rep. 17. The exigency would not permit him to get a warrant; for, while he was off looking up an officer to issue it, the property with whose safe-keeping he was charged would be taken. No error.

STATE v. FISHER.

(Supreme Court of North Carolina. Nov. 17, 1891.)

TRESPASS ON LAND—CRIMINAL LIABILITY.

A person who in good faith, believing that he has a right to do so, enters upon the lands of another after he had been forbidden, when he had no reasonable ground for such belief, is not excused from criminal liability under Code N. C. § 1120, which provides that, "if any person, after being forbidden to do so, shall go or enter upon the lands of another without a license therefor, he shall be guilty of a misdemeanor."

Appeal from superior court, Rowan county; JESSE F. GRAVES, Judge.

William Fisher was duly charged criminally in the court of a justice of the peace with having violated the statute, (Code, § 1120,) in that, after the prosecutor forbade him to go upon his land, he went up on the same, and hauled across the same cross-ties, without a license so to do. He was convicted in that court, and upon appeal he was afterwards likewise convicted in the superior court, upon the plea of not guilty. Thereupon he excepted, and appealed to this court. Affirmed.

The Attorney General, for the State.

MERRIMON, C. J., (*after stating the facts.*) The defendant insisted that he went upon the prosecutor's land in good faith, believing and claiming that he had the right to do so as the agent of a railroad company named, and therefore he was not guilty. The court held otherwise, and this is assigned as error. Unquestionably the railroad company had not the shadow of right to go upon the prosecutor's land and transport its cross-ties over the same, and no authority whatever to direct or authorize its agent or servant to do so. The statute (Code, § 1120) expressly provides that, "if any person, after being forbidden to do so, shall go or enter upon the lands of another without a license therefor, he shall be guilty of a misdemeanor," etc. The defendant is presumed to have knowledge of this statute, and the mere fact that he may have believed honestly that he had the right to go upon the prosecutor's land, after he was forbidden to do so, as agent of the railroad company, as the evidence went to prove he did, could not at all excuse him from criminal liability, unless he had reasonable ground for such belief; and there was no evidence from which the jury might so find. State v. Crawley, 103 N. C. 353, 9 S. E. Rep. 409. The court properly instructed the jury, in substance, that if they believed the evidence the defendant was guilty. State v. Bryson, 81 N. C. 595. There is no error. Let this be certified to the superior court according to law. It is so ordered.

BOYKIN *et al.* v. BUIE *et al.*

(*Supreme Court of North Carolina.* Nov. 17, 1891.)

COMPROMISE.

Under Code N. C. § 574, providing that, in all claims where an agreement is made and accepted for a less amount than that claimed, payment of such less amount shall be a complete discharge of the same, one of three joint judgment debtors, who proposes to pay a given sum provided the payment shall operate to relieve him from further liability, on acceptance of such offer and payment by check is entitled to have entry of satisfaction on the record as to the whole judgment as against him.

Appeal from superior court, Robeson county; JESSE F. GRAVES, Judge.

Action by Boykin, Carmer & Co. against D. B. Buie & Bros. Plaintiffs moved for leave to issue execution on a judgment. Motion denied. Plaintiffs appeal. Affirmed.

STATEMENT BY THE COURT. Judgment was rendered by a justice of the peace against the firm of D. B. Buie & Bros., composed of D. C. Buie, J. C. Buie, and the appellant M. C. Buie, in favor of the plaintiffs, which judgment was subsequently docketed in the superior court, and, at a subsequent term of the latter court, a judgment was rendered in favor of the plaintiffs against the defendants for the sum of ——. Both of these judgments were entered upon the judgment docket of the superior court. On the 5th of February, 1890, the defendant M. C. Buie wrote to the plaintiffs, proposing to pay 30 per cent. of both these judgments, provided that, upon payment of said sum, the said M. C. Buie should be released from any further obligation arising out of said judgments, and that the same should be satisfied so far as he is concerned. The plaintiffs replied as follows: "Replying to your favor of the 5th, just received, that you are prepared to pay 30 per cent. of the account against Buie, and that your brothers, you believe, will do the same: The claim now, with interest, amounts to $759.31, one-fifth of which will be $45.55, for which amount we will be pleased to give you a receipt against the claim, and trust your brothers will do the same." In answer to the letter of plaintiffs, the defendant M. C. Buie forwarded to the plaintiffs a check on the bank of Guilford, in Greensboro, N. C., for the sum of $45.55, setting forth in the check that it was in full of said judgments. The plaintiffs returned said check to said M. C. Buie, refusing to receive the same, except on condition that it should be entered as a credit *pro tanto* on the judgments. M. C. Buie sent the said check back a second and a third time, and each time it was returned in a letter giving the same reason for refusing to apply it. The defendant Buie has ever since kept funds in said bank to pay the amount of said check, and asks to be allowed to pay the amount into court, and have it entered as a payment in full of his indebtedness on said judgments. Upon the above facts, and from the affidavits, the court found that plaintiffs live in Baltimore, Md., and have their place of business there, and that defendant M. C. Buie lives at Red Springs, Robeson county, N. C., and that there was an acceptance by plaintiffs of the defendant M. C. Buie's offer of compromise, and that the tender of the check for $45.55 was a payment of the indebtedness of the defendant M. C. Buie, and he was entitled to have entry of satisfaction on the record as to the whole of the judgments as against him, and so ordered. The plaintiffs excepted, and appealed from the judgment rendered.

Strong & Stronach, for appellants.

AVERY, J. We concur with the judge who heard the motion in the court below, in the opinion that the plaintiffs accepted the proposal of the defendant M. C. Buie, and were bound, when he forwarded the check for $45.55, the sum mentioned in their letter, to apply the same in full discharge of his indebtedness by reason of said judgments. The defendant has the right to demand that the substance of the said agreement shall appear upon the judgment docket, so as to show that the plaintiffs can proceed no further by virtue of the judgments against him. Under the provisions of the statute, (Code, § 574,) where a creditor voluntarily accepts from the debtor a less sum than is actually due, by way of compromise and in lieu of the whole, the debt is discharged. Koonce v. Russell, 103 N. C. 179, 9 S. E. Rep. 316. When a proposal to pay a given sum, provided that the payment shall operate to relieve one of three joint judgment debtors, is accepted by the creditor, and the debtor within a reasonable time tenders the amount, he has the right to demand that it shall be received and applied in discharge of his obligation to make any further payment. There is no error, and the judgment is affirmed.

STATE v. WILLIAMS.

(Supreme Court of North Carolina. Nov. 3, 1891.)

CASE ON APPEAL—SUBSTITUTION—NOTICE OF TIME OF SETTLEMENT—BASTARDY—INSTRUCTIONS.

1. Appellant's statement of case on appeal will not be substituted for the "case" as settled by the judge after the expiration of the statutory time, since Code N. C. § 550, which imposes a penalty on the judge for failure to settle the "case" in time, does not deprive the appellee of his right to a settlement of the "case" by the judge on disagreement.

2. A judge need give notice of the time and place of settling the case on appeal only when "requested" to do so, under Code N. C. § 550. Walker v. Scott, 106 N. C. 56, 11 S. E. Rep. 364, followed.

3. Where a judge in charging the jury inadvertently spoke of a bastardy proceeding as an "indictment," the error, if any, was cured by his correcting the statement. State v. McNair, 93 N. C. 628, followed.

4. Under Code N. C. § 32, providing that in bastardy proceedings the examination of the woman before a justice of the peace, taken and returned, "shall be presumptive evidence against the person accused," but that it may be rebutted by other evidence, the jury were properly instructed that, if the oral evidence left them in doubt, then the presumption raised by the written examination would not be rebutted, and defendant would be guilty. State v. Rogers, 79 N. C. 609, followed.

Appeal from superior court, Alamance county; EDWIN T. BOYKIN, Judge.

Bastardy proceedings by the state of North Carolina against T. R. Williams on the complaint of Georgiana Hunter. Defendant was convicted, and appealed. Affirmed.

STATEMENT BY THE COURT. The prosecutrix, Georgiana Hunter, charged the defendant, T. R. Williams, with being the father of her bastard child. The state offered the affidavit of Georgiana Hunter, in which she stated that she had been delivered of a bastard child on the 21st of June, 1889; that she was a single woman; that the said bastard child was liable to become a charge to the county; and that the defendant, T. R. Williams, was the father of the child. The testimony being concluded, his honor charged the jury, and in conclusion said: "In an issue of paternity in a bastardy proceeding the written examination of the mother is presumptive evidence that defendant is the father of the child, and when such written examination is introduced by the state, as in this case, then it devolves on the defendant by a preponderance of evidence to show that he is not the father. Upon failure of the defendant to so show by a preponderance of evidence

that he is not the father, it is the duty of the jury to convict. If the defendant has satisfied the jury by a preponderance of evidence that he is not the father of the child, then the jury should acquit. If, however, the oral testimony, taken together, both for the prosecution and defense, left the minds of the jury in doubt, then the presumption raised by the written examination would not be rebutted, and the defendant would be guilty." Defendant excepted. In the opening of the charge to the jury, the judge inadvertently said that "this is an indictment against the defendant in bastardy," but afterwards, in the charge, this mistake was corrected, and the judge stated to the jury that it was a proceeding in bastardy, in which the defendant, T. R. Williams, was charged with the paternity of the bastard child of Georgiana Hunter, the prosecutrix, and that the issue was: "Is the defendant, T. R. Williams, the father of the bastard child in question?" Defendant excepted.

The Attorney General, for the State. *W. H. Carroll* and *L. M. Scott,* for defendant.

CLARK, J. The appellant's case on appeal, with the exceptions filed thereto, was handed to the judge, who failed to settle the case within 60 days after the courts of the district had closed. The appellant now asks that his statement of case on appeal should be taken instead of the "case" as since settled by the judge, on the ground that the judge, being liable to a penalty for the delay, cannot "settle the case." It is sufficient to say that though the Code, § 550, on the failure of the judge to settle the case in the prescribed time, permits an action against him for a penalty of $500, (if, indeed, he is liable in this case, as to which we express no opinion,) it does not subject the appellee to lose his right to have the case settled by the judge upon disagreement.

The appellant further insists that the judge should have given him notice of time and place of settling the case. But it does not appear that he requested this when sending the case to the judge, as required by the statute, (Code N. C. § 550,) nor afterwards. A case exactly in point is Walker v. Scott, 106 N. C. 56, 11 S. E. Rep. 364.

It is not seen how the inadvertence of the judge in referring to the action as an "indictment" prejudiced the defendant, but, if it could have had that effect, the error was cured by the judge correcting it in his charge. State v. McNair, 93 N. C. 628. The charge that, if the oral testimony offered by the prosecution and the defendant, taken together, "left the minds of the jury in doubt, then the presumption raised by the written examination [of the woman] would not be rebutted, and the defendant would be guilty," is correct. State v. Rogers, 79 N. C. 609; Code, § 32.[1] No error.

---

[1] Code N. C. § 32, provides that upon the trial of the issue of the paternity of a bastard the examination of the woman before a justice of the peace, taken and returned, "shall be presumptive evidence against the person accused," subject to be rebutted by other evidence.

STATE v. DUNN et ux.

(Supreme Court of North Carolina. Nov. 18, 1891.)

RESISTING OFFICER — INDICTMENT — ARREST OF JUDGMENT—TIME OF OFFENSE.

1. It is not necessary that an indictment, under Act N. C. 1889, c. 51, or at common law, for resisting an officer, should contain the warrant or name the party the officer was seeking to arrest when resisted.

2. Such an objection to an indictment could not be raised for the first time in arrest of judgment.

3. Where the date of the offense alleged is not traversable, a want of jurisdiction as to time must be shown by proof.

Appeal from superior court, Randolph county; JESSE F. GRAVES, Judge.

Indictment of George Dunn and wife for resisting an officer. From an order arresting judgment on conviction the state assigns error. Reversed.

The bill of indictment is, in substance, as follows: "The jurors present," etc., "that George Dunn and his wife, Mrs. George Dunn, * * * with force and arms, * * * in and upon one J. A. Brady, then being one of the constables in the township of Brower, in the county of Randolph, and in the due execution of his said office, did make an assault; and him, the said J. A. Brady, so being in the due execution of his said office, then and there willfully and unlawfully did resist, delay, obstruct, and hinder in discharging, and attempting to discharge, his duties as such constable, against the form of the statute," etc. "And the jurors," etc., "do further present * * * that the above-named defendants, with force and arms and with deadly weapons, to-wit, with a wagon tire of the weight of five pounds, did unlawfully make an assault upon one J. A. Brady, against the form of the statute," etc.

The Attorney General, for the State.

CLARK, J. There was error in granting the motion in arrest of judgment. It is not necessary, either under our statute (Act 1889, c. 51) or at common law, that the indictment for resisting an officer should "set out the warrant so as to show the title of the cause and name of the party named therein under which the officer attempted to make the arrest," when he was resisted, obstructed, etc., by the defendant. 1 Whart. Crim. Law, (9th Ed.) 650; Bowers v. People, 17 Ill. 373; McQuaid v. People, 3 Gilman, 76. Indeed, the indictment in this case seems to be a substantial copy of the form in 1 Archb. Crim. Pr. 941. It is sufficient to charge the assault as made upon the officer, etc., he being "in the due execution of his said office," and that thereby the defendant did willfully and unlawfully resist, hinder, and obstruct said officer in the discharge of his duties as such. Com. v. Kirby, 2 Cush. 577. If there had been any technical reason that the warrant should name the title of the writ, and the person to be arrested thereunder when the officer was assaulted and resisted by the defendant, this was cured by the verdict. It was too late to object on that ground after the merits had been passed on by a jury. But, as we

have seen, these details were matters of evidence, and need not be charged in the indictment. Had the defendant desired (as it seems he did not) this additional information to enable him to make a better defense, he should have moved the court before going into the trial for a bill of particulars. State v. Brady, 107 N. C. 822, 12 S. E. Rep. 325. Besides, the indictment was unquestionably good for the simple assault, (State v. Goldston, 103 N. C. 323, 9 S. E. Rep. 580;) and if any offense was charged, though not the one intended, it was error to quash or arrest the judgment, (State v. Evans, 27 N. C. 603.) If the indictment had been defective, except as to a charge of a simple assault, the jurisdiction of the court might have been ousted by showing that the offense took place within 12 months before indictment found, but the judgment could not be arrested on that ground, as the date alleged is not traversable, and the jurisdiction is in the superior court, unless it is shown in proof that the requisite time had not elapsed. State v. Taylor, 83 N. C. 601. The judgment in arrest must be set aside, and the case remanded, that judgment may be pronounced upon the verdict. Error.

JOHNSTON et al. v. DANVILLE, M. & S. W. R. CO.

(Supreme Court of North Carolina. Nov. 24, 1891.)

APPEAL — CERTIFICATE FROM SUPREME COURT— COST.

1. Laws N. C. 1887, c. 192, § 8, providing that "in civil cases, at the first term of the superior court after" the certificate of the supreme court "is received, if the judgment is affirmed the court below shall direct the execution thereof to proceed," is directory as to the mere forms to be observed; and it does not mean or intend that if, at the first term of the court below after it receives the certificate from the supreme court, it should fail for any cause to act upon the same, there could be no proper or sufficient action taken afterwards.

2. Judgment is entered in the supreme court for the costs of that court, and should not be entered in the court below.

Appeal from superior court, Rockingham county; JOHN GRAY BYNUM, Judge.

Johnston & Cheek sued Danville, Mocksville & Southwestern Railroad Company. Judgment for plaintiff. J. T. Morehead, receiver for defendant, appeals. Affirmed.

STATEMENT BY THE COURT. This case was before this court by a former appeal at the February term of 1890, (11 S. E. Rep. 535,) and the judgment appealed from was then affirmed. Thereupon the order and judgment of this court was certified to the superior court, and the following is a copy thereof: "This cause came on to be argued upon the transcript of the record from the superior court of Rockingham county; upon consideration whereof this court is of opinion that there is no error in the record and proceedings of the said superior court. It is therefore considered and adjudged by the court here that the opinion of the court as delivered by the Honorable A. S. MERRIMON, chief justice, be certified to the said superior court, to the intent that the judgment be affirmed. And it is considered and adjudged, further, that the appellant, J. Turner Morehead, do pay the costs of the appeal in this court incurred, to-wit, the sum of thirteen dollars, ($13,) and let execution issue therefor." In the superior court, at the January term, 1891, thereof, the court entered judgment in pursuance of the order here, as follows: "In this action J. Turner Morehead, receiver of the Danville, Mocksville & Southwestern Railroad Company, defendant, having taken an appeal from the judgment of MacRae, judge, entered on the 6th day of November, 1886, and the certificate having come down from the supreme court, and the same being now read and considered by the court, it is ordered and adjudged by this court now here, in obedience to said certificate from the supreme court, that the order of the said MacRae, judge, be, and the same is, affirmed and re-entered as the judgment and decree of this court, the costs in this court, together with the costs in the supreme court, to be paid as in said decree mentioned, and as directed by the judgment of the supreme court, by the said J. Turner Morehead, receiver." The appellant assigned error of this judgment as follows, and appealed to this court: "(1) That it does not comply with the mandatory statute of this state contained in chapter 192, § 3, Laws 1887: (a) In that it was not filed 'at the first term of the superior court after the certificate was received;' and (b) in that it fails to 'direct the execution thereof to proceed,' when said statute expressly commands that, 'if the judgment is affirmed, the court below shall direct the execution thereof to proceed.' (2) That there can be no legal process issued on the judgment until the 'order' is made therein to 'proceed.'" "(6) That this judgment is defective in form, and contrary to the course and practice of the court, in that it adjudges 'that the order of the said James C. MacRae, judge, be, and the same is, affirmed and re-entered as the judgment and decree of this court,' when the judgment should have been that the motion to vacate and set aside the judgment confessed in this action and court be denied and dismissed in accordance with the former judgment herein of Hon. James C. MacRae, judge, and the opinion of the supreme court in this cause. (7) That so much of this judgment as refers to cost is erroneous, in that it orders 'the cost * * * to be paid * * * as directed by the judgment of the supreme court by the said J. Turner Morehead, receiver,' when, according to the certificate from the supreme court, the judgment of the supreme court, as to cost, is against 'J. Turner Morehead.'"

Paul B. Means, for appellant. John W. Graham, for appellee.

Merrimon, C. J. The statute (Acts 1887, c. 192, § 3) among other things provides that, "in civil cases at the first term of the superior court after such certificate [that of the supreme court] is received, if the judgment is affirmed, the court below shall direct the execution thereof to proceed, and, if said judgment is modified, shall direct its modification and performance. If a new trial is ordered, the cause

shall stand in its regular order on the docket for trial at such first term after the receipt of the certificate from the supreme court." Obviously this statutory provision is directory as to the mere forms to be observed. It does not mean or intend that if, at the first term of the court below after it receives the certificate from this court, it should fail for any cause to act upon the same, there could be no proper or sufficient action taken afterwards. It directs the orderly course to be observed, but it will be sufficient if the substance of the purpose of the statute is pursued. In effectuating such purpose, the orderly course and forms prescribed are almost necessarily subject to well-known rules of practice that prevail in the courts. Regularly and orderly, the certificate from this court should be entered in the court below at the first term after it is received there, and the judgment there made to conform to it. If the judgment is affirmed, it would be sufficient to enter on the record, "And accordingly the judgment of this court is so affirmed; let execution issue," in proper cases. If the judgment is to be modified or amended, then it ought to be said, "Accordingly the judgment of this court is accordingly modified," (or "is accordingly amended,") "and it is considered and adjudged," etc.; or, if a new trial is directed, in that case it should be entered, if the certificate so directs, "Accordingly it is ordered and adjudged that the judgment of the court be reversed and a new trial awarded, and the case will stand for trial," etc. Such orders should be so framed as to meet the purpose of the directions of the court and the exigency of the case in the court below. Besides, in cases so requiring, the court below should enter appropriate judgments upon supersedeas undertakings, and for additional costs, when there are properly such. When the appropriate judgment is entered, it is better and more orderly to direct formally that execution issue; but, when judgment is entered by implication and the rules of practice, execution must issue in pursuance thereof, and according to the course of practice. The statute recited above so implies and intends. It is practical, and tends to promote and secure the ends of justice. In this case the judgment appealed from and complained of as to matters of form and order, though fuller than need be, and not so aptly expressed as it probably might be, is a substantial compliance with the order of this court, and with the statute above cited, except as to the costs of this court. Judgment is entered here for the costs of this court, and ought not to be entered in the court below, nor was it so intended in this case or directed. The certificate only embraced the judgment here for costs. It is so stated in the certificate, and this part of it might not inappropriately have been omitted. It was no more, however, than harmless, redundant matter, as was apparent. The judgment must be modified, in so far as it refers to and embraces the costs of this court, so as to omit such costs, and, thus modified, affirmed. To that end, let this opinion be certified to the superior court. It is so ordered.

STATE v. DAVIS et al.

(Supreme Court of North Carolina.   Nov. 24, 1891.)

FORCIBLE TRESPASS.

On an indictment for forcible entry, it appeared that the prosecutor had occupied a blacksmith-shop under a lease from defendant D. After the expiration of the lease, the prosecutor, without surrendering the premises, took a lease thereof from D.'s co tenant. While the prosecutor was standing about 100 yards from the shop, defendants, D. and four others, though forbidden to do so by the prosecutor, approached, and broke open the shop, and took possession. *Held*, that defendants were guilty of forcible entry. State v. Mills, 10 S. E. Rep. 676, 104 N. C. 905, distinguished.

Appeal from superior court, Iredell county; JESSE F. GRAVES, Judge.

J. A. Davis and others were indicted for forcible entry. Jury found a special verdict, upon which judgment was rendered for defendants. State appeals. Reversed.

STATEMENT BY THE COURT. Indictment for forcible entry. It is found by the special verdict that the prosecutor was in possession and daily use of a blacksmith-shop; that he had come from his home that morning, intending to work in the shop that day, and, while standing at a mill about 100 yards from the shop, the defendant Davis, with a crow-bar, and the other four defendants came down to a point half-way between the mill and the shop; that, leaving the other defendants there, Davis approached the prosecutor, and demanded the key of the shop, which was refused, and Davis then indicated his purpose to open it by force, and prosecutor forbade it. The defendants then went to the shop, prized the door open, threw down a part of the chimney, displaced the bellows, and took possession; the prosecutor had rented the shop for two years from defendant Davis, but, the term having expired, he had, without surrendering possession, leased the premises from one Morrison, who was a co-tenant of the premises with Davis; that, while defendants were at the shop, the prosecutor's son was present at the shop. The prosecutor himself went to the miller's house, within 75 yards of the shop. He testified that he was not afraid of the defendants, but did not go to the shop because he feared it might lead to a difficulty. The court adjudged the defendants not guilty on the special verdict.

The Attorney General, for the State. *Bingham & Caldwell,* for appellees.

CLARK, J. The question was discussed before us whether this was a case of forcible entry or forcible trespass. In State v. Jacobs, 94 N. C. 950, attention is called to the fact that forcible trespass applies to personal property, and forcible entry to land; but the distinction has not always been adverted to, and it is not very material what the offense is called in argument, if the indictment sufficiently charges a violation of the criminal law, and it is proven by evidence. State v. Evans, 27 N. C. 603. To constitute either offense, there must be either actual violence used, or such demonstration of force as was calculated to intimidate or tend to a breach of the peace. It is not necessary that the party be actually "put in fear." State v. Pearman, 61 N. C. 371. It is sufficient if there is such a demonstration of force as to create a reasonable apprehension that the party in possession must yield to avoid a breach of the peace. State v. Pollok, 26 N. C. 305; State v. Armfield, 27 N. C. 207. Such demonstration of force may be by a "multitude," or by weapons. State v. Ray, 32 N. C. 39, citing State v. Flowers, 6 N. C. 225; State v. Mills, 13 N. C. 420. The statute (Code, § 1028) provides: "No one shall make entry into any lands and tenements or term for years but in case where entry is given by law, and in such case not with strong hand, nor with a multitude of people, but only in a peaceable and easy manner; and if any man do the contrary he shall be guilty of a misdemeanor." The same, in effect, was the common-law rule: "Where the entry is lawful, it must not be made with a strong hand, or with a number of assailants; where it is not lawful, it must not be done at all." 2 Whart. Crim. Law, (9th Ed.) 1098. Following the analogy as to riots, three persons have been held enough to support the averment of a "multitude." State v. Simpson, 12 N. C. 504. If a breach of the peace did not actually take place, it was doubtless due to the defendant Davis' declaration of his purpose to enter, backed with a sufficient force to accomplish it in spite of the prohibition of the prosecutor. State v. Smith, 100 N. C. 466, 6 S. E. Rep. 84. The prosecutor need not have been on the exact spot. That he did not get closer than 75 yards was, he says, to avoid a breach of the peace. The defendants had shown themselves able by their numbers to render his closer approach of no avail. He forbade them, and in effect was present. In State v. Lawson, 98 N. C. 759, 4 S. E. Rep. 134, it was held that where the prosecutor was 50 or 75 yards distant when he forbade the entry, and the defendants persisted notwithstanding in making such entry, they were guilty; that it was not necessary for the party in possession to be on the very spot. Besides, in this case, the son of the prosecutor, after the prohibition to the defendants given by his father, was present at the shop when being forced open by them. The title to the premises could not be c .lled in question. The offense is the high-handed invasion of the possession of another, though such other need not be at all times personally present on the premises, if in actual exercise of authority and control over the same, (State v. Bryant, 103 N. C. 436, 9 S. E. Rep. 1,) and if present in person, or by some member of his family, at the time of the entry, and forbidding it. It is true that when the premises are withheld by one having a bare charge or custody, as a servant or a mere trespasser or intruder, the owner may break open doors, and forcibly enter, if unnecessary force is not used, (Whart. Crim. Law, 1087; 1 Russ. Crimes, 9th Ed., 420; 2 Bish. Crim. Law, 501;) but a landlord who violently dispossesses a tenant whose lease has expired is guilty of forcible entry, (Whart. Crim. Law, 9th Ed., 1087;) and a co-tenant may commit the offense of forcible entry, if the other co-tenant is in possession, and resists, (2

Bisl. Crim. Law, 501.) So, whether the prosecutor is treated as a tenant holding over, or as the lessee of the co-tenant, the taking the shop out of his possession by a multitude of persons in the manner stated, he being present, and forbidding, made the defendants guilty.

This case differs from State v. Mills, 104 N. C. 905, 10 S. E. Rep. 676, which is relied on by the defendants. In State v. Mills, the defendant, accompanied only by an old negro man, went to the house, and entered against remonstrance of the prosecutor, but without violence, or the display of weapons, of numbers, or other signs of force calculated to intimidate or create a breach of the peace; and the court held, citing State v. Covington, 70 N. C. 71, and State v. Lloyd, 85 N. C. 573, that "mere rudeness of language or slight demonstrations of force, against which ordinary firmness is a sufficient protection," was not indictable. Hence, though there the prosecutor left to avoid a breach of the peace, the demonstration of force was not sufficient ground for such apprehension. Here there were five men, one of them armed with a crow-bar. The language and conduct of the defendants indicated their purpose to take possession of the shop by force, though the prosecutor forbade them. This case differs also from State v. Laney, 87 N. C. 535, in that there, though the entry was made by numbers, there was no one present and forbidding the entry; hence no danger of a breach of the peace by such entry. Still the court intimated strongly that the defendants in that case were guilty of the forcible detainer. Upon the special verdict, the court should have rendered judgment against the defendants. Error.

HINKLE v. RICHMOND & D. R. Co.

(*Supreme Court of North Carolina.* Nov. 24, 1891.)

RAILROAD COMPANIES — ACCIDENTS AT CROSSINGS —NEGLIGENCE—EVIDENCE.

1. In the absence of statutes regulating the time and manner of giving signals, the failure of an engineer in charge of a locomotive to ring the bell or sound the whistle at the intersection of a mill-road, or a point where the public have been habitually permitted to cross, is evidence of negligence.

2. For a moving train to omit to give, in a reasonable time, some signal when approaching a highway from which the train is hidden by an embankment, cut, or curve, is negligence *per se.*

3. Where a railroad company has erected a whistle post at a proper distance from a crossing in order to notify engineers where to give warning, and the public are led to believe that a signal will be given at the post, it is negligence if the engineer, in passing with a freight or passenger train, fail to sound the whistle at such post.

4. Where the person injured would not have ventured upon the track at a crossing but for the negligence of the engineer in failing to give warning, the railroad company is liable, though plaintiff may have been careless in exposing himself.

5. In an action against a railroad company for damages resulting from personal injuries the court properly instructed the jury that it was the duty of plaintiff as well as the engineer to keep a proper lookout at a crossing, and that one time looking and listening at a distance from the track is not a proper lookout; that plaintiff should have used his senses of sight and hearing; and

that if, by failure to do so, he caused the injury, he could not recover.

6. Where the testimony in regard to contributory negligence was conflicting, the court rightly refused to charge that it was "the duty of plaintiff to see and hear," and that his failure to do so was equivalent to not looking or listening, since such a charge would decide the question of plaintiff's negligence.

7. Plaintiff testified that he and his father came along the highway in a covered wagon, and that plaintiff looked several times to see if a train was coming, and that when within about 90 yards of the crossing he stopped the wagon and listened, and then rode on the shaft, looking and listening, and did not see nor hear the train until the horse was on the track. *Held,* that testimony for the engineer, in which he was corroborated by another witness, that the track was visible for several hundred yards from the highway, did not warrant the court in instructing the jury that they must disregard plaintiff's statements and find against him, for in such a conflict the court could not instruct as to the weight of the evidence.

8. It was not the duty of plaintiff, if after listening at 90 yards' distance and riding on the shaft he neither heard nor saw an approaching train, to get down and look up and down the track, even though his view of the railroad line was obstructed.

9. If the engineer saw that the horse was attached to a covered wagon, and could see that the occupants were not on the outlook, but were inside the wagon, it was his duty to stop his engine.

10. If the engineer failed to give the usual signals, then it was his duty to keep a more vigilant watch along the track.

11. Plaintiff showed that soon after the accident defendant repaired the mill-road crossing where the accident took place. *Held,* that since such road may also have been a plantation road, which defendant was required to keep in repair under Code N. C. § 1975, it was not prejudicial to allow the testimony.

Appeal from superior court, Davidson county; R. F. ARMFIELD, Judge.

Action by David A. Hinkle, a minor without a guardian, by David Hinkle, his next friend, against the Richmond & Danville Railroad Company, to recover damages for personal injuries. Verdict and judgment for plaintiff. Defendant appeals. Affirmed.

D. Schenck and *George F. Bason,* for appellant. *Watson & Buxton,* for appellee.

AVERY, J. In the absence of statutes regulating the time and manner of giving signals, the failure of an engineer in charge of a locomotive to ring the bell or sound the whistle on approaching the crossing of a public highway or a point where the public have been habitually permitted to cross, as at the intersection of a mill-road or a farm road frequently used, is evidence of negligence to be submitted to the jury. 2 Shear. & R. Neg. §§ 463, 464; Warner v. Railroad Co., 44 N. Y. 465; Troy v. Railroad Co., 99 N. C. 298, 6 S. E. Rep. 77; 2 Woods, Ry. Law, p. 1292; Barry v. Railroad Co., 92 N. Y. 289. It is negligence *per se,* because of the peril both to passengers on trains and people using highways, to omit to give, in reasonable time, some signal from a train moving, whether at the rate of 20 or 40 miles an hour, when it is hidden from the view of travelers who may be approaching and in danger of coming in collision with it, by the cars of the company left standing on its track, or by an embankment, a cut, or a sharp curve in its line, or by any other obstruction allowed to be placed or placed in the way by the company. Randall v. Railroad Co., 104 N. C. 416, 10 S. E. Rep. 691; 2 Woods, Ry. Law, p. 1313, and note 3; Railroad Co. v. Goetz, 79 Ky. 442; Pennsylvania Co. v. Krick, 47 Ind. 368; Strong v. Railroad Co., 61 Cal. 326. Where a railroad company has erected a whistle post at a proper distance from a crossing in order to notify engineers where to give timely warning of the approach of a train to persons using the intersecting highway, and the purpose of the company is known to the public, so that persons generally are led to act on the supposition that a signal will be given at the post, it is also negligence on the part of the company, if the engineer fail to sound the whistle at the point so indicated, in passing with a freight or passenger train in his charge. 2 Woods, Ry. Law, p. 1313; Spencer v. Railroad Co., 29 Iowa, 55; Sweeny v. Railroad Co., 10 Allen, 368; Newson v. Railroad Co., 29 N. Y. 383. Where a jury find that the injured person would not have ventured upon the track at such a crossing, and would have incurred no risk of a collision with the train, but for the negligence of the engineer in failing to give timely warning of its approach, the corporation is liable to answer in damages, though the plaintiff may have been careless in exposing himself to danger. Deans v. Railroad Co., 107 N. C. 686, 12 S. E. Rep. 77, and cases cited.

In Randall v. Railroad Co., supra, the judge who tried the case below charged the jury, in effect, that if the engineer failed, in passing around a sharp curve, caused by a projecting cleft or mountain, to give the usual signal of approach to a crossing just beyond the curve, from which his train was not visible, the corporation was liable for injury to a team of oxen that were being driven along a parallel road beside the track and near said crossing, if, as the testimony tended to show, the owner would have driven them to a point more remote from the railroad, and where they would have been free from danger, had he heard the expected warning at the usual place. There was a conflict of testimony in that as in our case. The engineer testified that he blew at the usual point for the crossing, not far from the place where the animals were killed, while other witnesses contradicted this statement. Kinney, the engineer in the case at bar, testified that he blew at a post erected below Linwood station, which he located 342¼ yards south of that depot; that he passed the station, going north, without stopping, and blew again at the proper point to warn persons passing over the crossing of the Lexington road, which is 231 yards north of Linwood, but that he gave no other warning after passing that signal post till he struck the horse attached to the covered wagon in which the plaintiff and his father were riding, at the crossing of the mill-road, 652 yards north of the intersection with the Lexington road. It is admitted that there was a signal post erected on the west side of the track, or on the left of the engineer, going north, at a distance of 208 yards south of the mill-road crossing, and 444 yards north of the crossing of the Lexington road. Three witnesses for the plaintiff testified positively that the engineer blew the whistle at a bridge about a half mile south of Linwood, and far south of the first whistle post on his right, and did not blow again till the plaintiff was injured. Another witness, who lived within 60 or 70 yards of Linwood, stated that he did not hear any whistle after that given at the bridge. Conceding for the sake of the argument that the signal post on the left (208 yards from the mill-road crossing) was intended for trains moving north, and that the custom was to blow opposite to it to give notice of the approach of trains moving south to travelers on the Lexington road, we think that the judge below was not in error in telling the jury that a traveler had the right to rely on hearing the usual signal at posts known by the public to have been erected to indicate to engineers the point for blowing the whistle as a warning of the approach of a train. According to the testimony offered for the plaintiff the engineer failed to blow at the lower post (where he admits he ought to have given a signal, and says that he did) or below the Lexington road crossing, while the engineer testifies to the contrary. In Randall v. Railroad Co., supra, it was at the station below that the jury found the engineer had failed to give the signal, and he was near, not at, a crossing, and about 100 yards from the station, when his oxen jumped upon the track and were killed; yet, if he had heard the usual station blow at the point where he had a right to expect it, he would have removed his cattle out of danger, and thereby avoided the accident. But counsel pressed with much earnestness and ingenuity the more sweeping and general exception growing out of the tenth paragraph of his prayer for instructions,—that there was no evidence of negligence on the part of defendant company. Not only was the court justified, by the testimony tending to show the failure to sound the whistle at the lower post, in refusing to give this instruction, but the jury should have been left to determine (looking at every aspect of the testimony and the inferences to be drawn from it) whether the engineer blew the whistle before reaching the Lexington road, and whether his admitted failure, at the proper distance from the mill-road crossing, to repeat the warning, was the proximate cause of the injury; for if, by giving a signal at either place where plaintiff had a right to expect it, the accident would have been avoided, then such omission was the immediate cause of the injury, and the plaintiff was entitled to recover, though he may have shown a want of care in going upon the track. Lay v. Railroad Co., 106 N. C. 404, 11 S. E. Rep. 412; Deans v. Railroad Co., supra. In passing upon these questions the jury could have considered, and doubtless did, the contention, on the one hand, that the train was moving along a deep cut, up grade, and could not have been seen by the plaintiff, who had been stationed by his father on the shafts of the covered wagon, until the wagon was driven upon the track, and, on the other, that the train must have been distinctly visible to one looking out from the front of the wagon for 40 yards before they drove upon the crossing. The jury found, in response to the first issue, that the plaintiff was injured by the negligence of the defendant company, and, in answer to the second issue, that the plaintiff did not contribute to cause the injuries by his own negligence.

It was the duty of the plaintiff to look and listen before going upon the track, although it may not have been the hour when a regular train was expected. Randall v. Railroad Co., supra. "He is only bound to look, where to do so would aid him in determining whether a train is approaching. In all other respects he has a right to rely upon his ears. But when the proper signals are given, if a traveler ventures upon the track and miscalculates as to the chances of crossing, the risk is his unless some negligence can be imputed to the company which has directly caused the injury." 2 Wood Ry. Law, p. 1310, § 343, and note 2; Id. p. 1312, and note 1. The court instructed the jury upon this subject as follows: "It was the duty of the plaintiff to keep a proper lookout as well as the engineer, and one time looking and listening at a distance from the track is not a proper lookout. He ought to, have used his senses of sight and hearing all the time, and if he failed to do so, and thereby caused his injury, the answer to the second issue should be, 'Yes.'" If the court had, in compliance with the defendant's request, told the jury that it was "the duty of the plaintiff to see and hear," and his failure to do so was equivalent to not looking or listening at all, the instruction would unquestionably have been erroneous, and subject to well-grounded exception on the part of the plaintiff. It is manifest that the court had no right, where there was conflicting testimony, and more than one inference deducible from the evidence, to instruct the jury that they must find in any aspect of the case that the plaintiff by his own negligence contributed to bringing about the collision, much less that the negligence of the plaintiff was the direct cause of the injury. The plaintiff testified that he and his father (who is his next friend as plaintiff) started from the house of his brother, the witness A. A. Hinkle, near the Lexington road, in a covered wagon, and, as they traveled along the road, he looked out of the wagon two or three times to see if a train was coming, and that when they had gone down the hill, within about 20 yards of the crossing, he stopped the wagon and listened. The plaintiff then got out on the cross-piece of the shaft, and held the wagon with one hand while he rested the other on the horse's rump, and, as his father drove on, looked and listened, but neither heard nor saw an approaching train till the horse got upon the track, when he had but time to utter an exclamation, and fell back into the wagon with his father. They were carried and thrown about 75 feet and left in an insensible state by the train. It will

be observed that the boy, if he is to be believed, looked and listened, and neither saw nor heard anything. The judge had no right to tell the jury that because the engineer, however respectable or intelligent, testified to the height of the banks along the cut, and introduced a map to corroborate his opinion that a train on the track anywhere north of Linwood and south of the mill-road crossing was visible to a person passing along the road traveled by plaintiff from his brother's house to the crossing, they must disregard the plaintiff's statement, and answer the second issue "Yes." It was the province of the jury to determine whether the plaintiff did in fact, after stopping and listening at the foot of the hill, ride 60 feet, looking and listening still, but in vain, from the shaft, all the way for a train that could not be seen till the horse was upon the track, and to say whether it was possible for him to see the approaching train or hear the noise, in the absence of signals, as it moved up grade from the station. In such a conflict the court could not instruct the jury as to the weight of the testimony. Although the engineer may have failed to give the usual signals south of the depot or of either of the crossings, it was the duty of the plaintiff to look and listen before going upon the track, and he testified that he did. The jury were warranted by the testimony, therefore, in finding that he used ordinary care to guard against accident before attempting to cross. His father, according to the evidence, was deaf, and was compelled to rely upon the hearing of the plaintiff, a boy of 14. It was not the duty of the plaintiff, if after listening at 20 yards' distance and riding on the shaft he neither heard nor saw an approaching train, to get down and look up and down the track, even though his view of the railroad line was obstructed. Railroad Co. v. Ackerman, 74 Pa. St. 265.

It was not error in the court to give the jury the instruction as to the duty of the engineer to keep a vigilant outlook, which is the subject of exception. It was not contended that the proposition embodied in the instruction given was not a correct statement of the law, but that it was inapplicable to the facts and calculated to mislead the jury. There was some evidence that counsel had a right to comment upon, and to have submitted to the jury, as tending to show that after the engineer saw, or could by keeping a proper lookout have seen, the plaintiff's horse stepping upon the track, he might have stopped his train altogether before reaching the crossing, or have so lowered its speed as to strike with little force and diminish the chances of serious injury to the inmates of the wagon, who were thrown 75 feet by the violent concussion. The expert witness Rutherford, who was introduced for the defendant, testified that the engineer might have seen a man on his left within 9 or 10 feet of the track on the mill-road when the engine was 300 feet from the crossing, and that he could have seen a horse 6 feet from the track 1,000 feet from the crossing, and could have stopped his engine within 500 feet.

If the engineer could have seen or saw the horse, and was unable to tell whether he was harnessed, and he seemed to be approaching the track, it was his duty to slacken speed. Snowden v. Railroad Co., 95 N. C. 93; Carlton v. Railroad Co., 104 N. C. 365, 10 S. E. Rep. 516. If he saw that the horse was attached to a covered wagon, and could see that the inmates were not on the outlook, but were inside the wagon, it was his duty to stop his engine. If the jury believed that the engineer had failed to give the usual signals, then it was his duty to keep a more vigilant watch along the track. He had no right under such circumstances to keep his seat as he approached the crossing, and also to direct the fireman to put coal in the engine, so that neither could keep a proper outlook upon the crossing after he had neglected to whistle. We are assuming that the jury believed the whistle was not blown north of the bridge, in order to show that there were phases of the evidence that warranted the judge in giving, if they did not impose upon him the duty of giving, the instruction complained of. Counsel could not expect the court to find as a fact and tell the jury that the fireman could not look out on the left because his fire had gone down while the train was side-tracked at Holtsburg, and the engineer could not get out of his seat long enough to look first on one side and then on the other, while his subordinate replenished the supply of coal. Whether he could stand up and keep his hand upon the throttle of the engine under such circumstances, and whether it was necessary to do so in order to provide for the safety of all who might expose themselves to danger of being injured by his train, were questions, not for the court to pass upon, but for the jury to consider in their bearings upon the issues.

The court below permitted the plaintiff to show by a witness that soon after the accident the defendant company repaired the crossing at the mill-road so as to make it less difficult to get upon the track. The defendant objected then, and assigns as error now, the admission of the testimony. The court assigned as a reason for the ruling that it was competent to show in this way that the defendant knew of the existence of the crossing, and treated it as a public crossing, or one that the corporation was under obligations to keep in repair. Although the road may have been used as a mill-road, it may also, as a plantation road, have come within the requirement of section 1975 of the Code, which fact would have made it the duty of the company to keep it repaired. At that stage of the trial it is not difficult to see that it might become material for the jury to know whether such duty was imposed upon the defendant by law, especially if, in the further progress of the trial, it should appear that the engineer by keeping a proper outlook might have had reason to believe that the plaintiff's wagon was impeded by some defect in the crossing. Bullock v. Railroad Co., 105 N. C. 180, 10 S. E. Rep. 988. It is evident at any rate that the defendant was not prejudiced by the ruling, because it could not have materially influenced the jury in their findings.

The judge below had unquestionably the right, in the exercise of his discretion, to refuse the motion for a new trial on the ground of newly-discovered evidence in any case. Carson v. Dellinger, 90 N. C. 226. There is no error, and the motion for a new trial must be refused.

O'CONNOR v. O'CONNOR.

(Supreme Court of North Carolina. Nov. 24, 1891.)

DIVORCE—CRUELTY—CONDONATION.

1. Where a wife demands a divorce *a mensa et thoro* on the ground of personal violence, she must explicitly show in her complaint that the violence complained of was not due to any provocation on her part. White v. White, 84 N. C. 340, and Joyner v. Joyner, 6 Jones, Eq. 322, followed.

2. Under Code N. C. § 1286, subsec. 3, which provides for divorce from bed and board if either party "shall, by cruel or barbarous treatment, endanger the life of the other," to entitle plaintiff to divorce the jury must find that plaintiff's life was endangered; and defendant's dragging plaintiff off her chair and attempting to throw her out of the house is not sufficient.

3. A divorce on the ground of cruelty will not be granted where the parties lived together for 10 years after the alleged cruelty, and before the action was brought.

Appeal from superior court, Guilford county; ROBERT W. WINSTON, Judge.

Action by Mary O'Connor against Thomas O'Connor for divorce. Judgment for plaintiff. Defendant appeals. Reversed.

STATEMENT BY THE COURT. Twelve issues were submitted to the jury, being those tendered by defendant and adopted by the court. The issues and responses were as follows: "(1) Were the plaintiff and defendant lawfully married? Answer. Yes. (2) Have plaintiff and defendant resided in this state for two years next preceding this action? A. Yes. (3) Did the defendant, in 1878, violently choke, beat, and bruise the plaintiff, at the time she was pregnant? A. Yes. (4) Did the defendant, in September, 1884, strike the plaintiff with a gun? A. Yes. (5) Did the defendant, about the 15th day of October, 1889, violently throw the plaintiff against the door, hurting her head? A. Yes. (6) Did the defendant, on Thanksgiving day, 1890, drag plaintiff out of her chair, and attempt to throw her out of the house? A. Yes. (7) Did the defendant call plaintiff vile and opprobrious names, accusing her of a want of chastity, in the presence of her children and strangers? A. Yes. (8) If defendant did call plaintiff vile and opprobrious names, accusing her of a want of chastity, did he do so under provocation by plaintiff, and in a sudden fit of anger? A. Yes. (9) Was the notice in the newspaper made with intent to insult plaintiff, and bring her into humiliation and contempt? A. Yes. (10) Did defendant bring a strange woman in his house, and give her the management and control of his household affairs, to the exclusion of the plaintiff? A. No. (11) What amount of money, if any, has plaintiff let defendant have of her separate estate, and which is not repaid? A. $100. (12) Does the plaintiff now reside in her husband's dwelling because she has no means to support herself elsewhere, and no home to go to or friends to aid her? A. Yes." The plaintiff, in her own behalf, testified substantially to the several acts of cruelty, violence, and mistreatment on the part of the defendant, as set out in the complaint, and she further testified that each and every of the said acts and doings of the defendant were without cause or provocation on her part. Plaintiff also placed in evidence a copy of the Daily Workman containing the publication referred to in the complaint, which was identified and admitted as a newspaper published in and circulated at the time, as alleged. The defendant testified in his own behalf, and denied specifically each one of the several allegations of cruelty, violence, and mistreatment alleged in the complaint, and testified to by plaintiff, except he admitted that he did charge plaintiff with a want of chastity, but that he did this in the heat of passion, at a time when plaintiff had crossed and provoked him. He also admitted publishing the plaintiff in the Daily Workman, but said that he apprehended that plaintiff would make bills or get money, as she had declared her purpose (as witness stated) to do this, and leave, and go back north to her former home. Five of the children of plaintiff and defendant, three males and two females, all grown, and all residing with the defendant, were introduced by defendant as witnesses in his behalf, and each gave testimony tending to corroborate the defendant. After the verdict, the plaintiff, by leave of the court, amended the complaint by inserting in article 4, before each of the several allegations of cruelty, violence, and mistreatment the words, "without cause or provocation on her part." Defendant excepted to these amendments. Both parties then moved for judgment,—the plaintiff for a decree of separation and for alimony, the defendant for judgment in his favor on the complaint and findings of the jury. Judgment was entered for plaintiff. From the refusal of the court to grant his motion the defendant appealed.

Dillard & King and *Jas. T. Morehead,* for appellant. *Jas. E. Boyd* and *R. M. Douglas,* for appellee.

AVERY, J. It is true, as insisted by counsel in the brief, that a husband who brings his action for divorce from the bonds of matrimony is not required to "purge his conscience" by negativing, in his complaint, the possibility of unfaithfulness on his part, (Edwards v. Edwards, Phil. [N. C.] 534; Steele v. Steele, 104 N. C. 631, 10 S. E. Rep. 707;) but when the wife demands only a divorce *a mensa et thoro,* on the ground that the husband, by personal violence, has made her life intolerable and her condition burdensome, she must state specifically in her complaint what, if anything, was said or done by her just before or at the time when her husband struck her, or threatened her, or charged her with incontinency; or she must in some way negative, by explicitly setting forth what her conduct was, the

idea that any act or word on her part was calculated to arouse sudden passion on the part of the husband or put him on the defensive. White v. White, 84 N. C. 340; Joyner v. Joyner, 6 Jones, Eq. 322; Jackson v. Jackson, 105 N. C. 433, 11 S. E. Rep. 173; McQueen v. McQueen, 82 N. C. 471. In the case of White v. White, supra, the complainant alleged that an assault upon her by her husband, with a piece of iron about a foot and a half long, and another, with a stick about two and a half feet long, were committed on her person without any provocation; but, said the court, "she was entirely silent as to the antecedent and attending circumstances, and the causes which prompted the defendant thus to act. She makes no statement of her own conduct, nor of any facts in explanation of the three violent assaults described in the complaint, separated at long intervals from each other, so that the court can see whether there was any and what excuse or extenuation for such outbursts of temper in an old man, crippled, and verging upon 70 years of age." In that case the jury found, in response to an issue, that the defendant did "beat, abuse, and ill-treat the plaintiff, as alleged in the complaint." The fact that the jury find, in responding to four separate issues, that four assaults were committed at long intervals, instead of three, does not distinguish the case at bar, in principle, from White v. White, supra. The language of the amendment, "without cause or provocation on her part," made by the court after verdict, is substantially the same as that declared, in White v. White, insufficient to give the complainant a *status* in court. In Joyner v. Joyner, supra, the court held that, though the wife had been stricken by the husband with a horsewhip, and corrected with a switch, it was essential that she must set forth in her petition for divorce from bed and board the circumstances under which the blows were given, what her conduct was, and, especially, "what she had done or said to induce such violence on the part of the husband." The judge had the right to allow an amendment of the pleadings, so as to make an allegation conform to the proof, where both parties had offered testimony bearing upon the issue raised by such allegation and the defense to it; but, as the amendment itself was not sufficiently specific to show that the plaintiff's action was well grounded, it is not necessary to discuss the form of the issues. Where the pleadings raise an issue as to the conduct of the wife at the time of the assault, or when she was otherwise mistreated, the husband has the right to demand that the question so raised shall be passed upon by the jury through the medium of some issue submitted. White v. White, supra. It is intimated, rather than suggested, that the assault made in 1878, on account of the wife's condition, amounted to such cruel and barbarous treatment as to endanger her life, and that, therefore, the plaintiff may rightfully insist that she has brought the case within the meaning of subsection 3, § 1286. To this we answer: (1) That it is not found by the jury that her life was endangered, and the judgment cannot be predicated upon that view in the absence of such a finding; (2) that she had lived with her husband for 10 years after that assault, and before this action was brought. The court will not allow a separation for an offense so long ago condoned. The publication in the newspaper, and the assault on Thanksgiving day, were both causes of complaint that arose within six months before the issuing of the summons, which was the commencement of the action. Neither can be considered as grounds for granting the relief prayed for in this action. Jackson v. Jackson, supra. "The courts have held parties seeking divorce to strict proof, not only in conformity to a fair construction of the statutes relating to the subject, but in accordance with the dictates of public policy."

We think there was error in the refusal to grant the defendant's motion; but, as the amendment allowed by the court is not sufficient to give the plaintiff a *status* in court, a new trial will be awarded, and an opportunity extended to plaintiff to make the allegations more specific. Porter v. Railroad Co., 97 N. C. 66, 2 S. E. Rep. 581. New trial.

HOWELL et al. v. JONES et al.

(Supreme Court of North Carolina. Nov. 24, 1891.)

APPEAL—RECORD—DISMISSAL.

1. Where a case on appeal is signed only by appellant's counsel, and it does not appear that it was served on appellee, it must be treated as a nullity, but the appeal will not be dismissed on that ground, since there may be errors on the face of the record proper. Peebles v. Braswell, 107 N. C. 68, 12 S. E. Rep. 44, followed.

2. Where the record fails to show that an appeal was taken or notice of appeal given, the appeal must be dismissed. Manufacturing Co. v. Simmons, 1 S. E. Rep. 923, 97 N. C. 89, followed.

Appeal from superior court, Stanly county; JESSE F. GRAVES Judge.

Action by Howell and Hardister against W. C. Jones, P. S. Jones, and the Hearne Consolidated Mining Company Judgment for plaintiffs. Defendants appeal. Appeal dismissed.

Montgomery & Crowell, for appellants. *James A. Lockhart*, for appellees.

CLARK, J. There is no case on appeal settled by the judge nor signed by the parties, and nothing to show that any appeal was taken in open court, nor any service of notice, if appeal was taken out of court. There is a "case on appeal," signed only by appellants' counsel, but, as it does not appear that it was served on appellee within the required time, nor, indeed, at all, it must be treated as a nullity. Peebles v. Braswell, 107 N. C. 68, 12 S. E. Rep. 44. The appeal would not be dismissed on this ground, as it may be there are errors on the face of the record proper, as want of jurisdiction, or complaint not stating a cause of action, and the proper motion and order would be to affirm the judgment. It further fails to appear, however, that an appeal was taken or notice of appeal given. In such case the appeal must be dismissed. Manufacturing Co. v.

Simmons, 97 N. C. 89, 1 S. E. Rep. 923. In this last case it is said: "It does not appear [in the record] that an appeal was taken. It does not so appear in terms, nor is there any entry of record from which it may be inferred. It is not sufficient that the appellant intended to appeal, as perhaps he did, but it must appear of record that he did in fact appeal. This is essential to make the appeal effective, and put this court in relation with the superior court. Code, §§ 549, 550; Moore v. Vanderburg, 90 N. C. 10; Spence v. Tapscott, 93 N. C. 246; McCoy v. Lassiter, 94 N. C. 131; Brooks v. Austin, Id. 223." Appeal dismissed.

LONG v. FOUST.

(Supreme Court of North Carolina. Nov. 24, 1891.)

NUNCUPATIVE WILLS—WITNESSES.

Code N. C. § 2148, par. 3, relating to nuncupative wills, which provides that such wills must be proven "on the oath of at least two credible witnesses present at the making thereof, who state that they were specially required to bear witness thereto by the testator himself," is sufficiently complied with where a nuncupative will was declared in the presence of several persons competent to act as witnesses, and the testator, without naming them, called on all present to witness his will, and they heard and took notice.

Appeal from superior court, Randolph county; JOHN G. BYNUM, Judge.

Action by John W. Long against J. M. Foust, administrator, for the admission to probate of the nuncupative will of Henry C. Glosson, deceased. Judgment for propounder. Caveator appeals. Affirmed.

STATEMENT BY THE COURT. The following is so much of the case settled on appeal as need be reported: This was a proceeding begun before George S. Bradshaw, clerk of the superior court of Randolph county, by John W. Long, the propounder, who offered for probate the verbal or nuncupative will of Henry C. Glosson, who died in said county on the 23d day of December, 1888, which will was put in writing, and is in the following form, to-wit: "I give to Mrs. N. M. Patterson one hundred dollars out of my estate, and I appoint J. W. Long executor of my estate." A jury being duly sworn and impaneled to try the case, the court submitted the following issues, to-wit: "First issue: Did H. C. Glosson declare as his will in substance as follows: 'I give to Mrs. N. M. Patterson one hundred dollars out of my estate, and I appoint J. W. Long executor of my estate?' Second issue: At the time he made the declaration of what was his will, did H. C. Glosson have mind and intelligence sufficient to enable him to have a reasonable judgment of the kind and value of the property he proposed to will, and to whom he proposed to will it?" These issues were both found in the affirmative. The evidence produced on the trial, material here, was as follows: B. S. Williams, a witness called by the propounder, testified as follows: "I was there when Henry C. Glosson died. He died about nine o'clock at night. I had been there an hour, probably. Was in the room twice during that time. He was very low and weak. I heard him talk. Heard him say that he wanted Mrs. N. M. Patterson to have one hundred dollars for attending on him during his sickness, and wanted Dr. Long to settle or close out the estate. He called upon all in the room to witness his request. I may not have given his exact language, but have given the substance of what he said. He did not call upon any special person, but called all of us to come to his bed. I went to his bed, and so did Mr. Owen, Mr. Wrenn, and Mr. Johnson. I think there were other men there. Before he made the request, he called to us to come to him. When we came around his bed, he made the request. Then he asked Mrs. Patterson to read a psalm and have prayers, which she did. This was about fifteen minutes before he died. He talked after this, but I don't remember what he said. I think he had capacity and mind, at the time he made the request, to know what disposition he was making of his property. I heard no one called specially by name to hear the request, but all who were in the room were called, and all approached his bedside." W. B. Owen, another witness called by the propounder, testified that he was present at the time, and heard decedent say "that he wanted Dr. Long to be his guardian or administrator,"—witness is not certain which he said,—"and to settle his business." "He repeated this twice, and then asked Mrs. Patterson to read a chapter and have prayers, which she did. Immediately after prayers, he said he wanted Mrs. Patterson to have one hundred dollars for her trouble, and Dr. Long to settle his business, and called on all standing by to be witnesses, and repeated this the second time. When he called for witnesses, all approached a little nearer,—Johnson, Wrenn, Olive, Williams, Allred, Stroud, and myself. Mrs. Patterson and her three children were there. He called Mr. Johnson's name. Ain't positive of any other. I think he said, 'In presence of all these witnesses and Mr. Johnson, I make the bequest above;' and said, 'I want you all to take notice of it.' He was lying on his right side; turned his head, and looked to the crowd. From all appearance of his talk, his mind seemed clear. In my opinion, he knew what he was saying, and had capacity to dispose of his property." Millard Wrenn, a witness called for the propounder, testified that he was present about half an hour before his death. Decedent said he wanted Mrs. Patterson to reserve or have $100 out of his estate for her trouble, and he wanted his business settled up as quietly as possible, and he wanted Dr. Long to settle his estate. He called, and wanted to know if there were witnesses, or called witnesses. He called witnesses about the $100 to Mrs. Patterson, and also about Dr. Long settling the estate. Witness stated that, in his opinion, decedent had mind enough to know what he was doing. Witness had been there about half an hour when this conversation occurred. By permission of the court, the caveator was allowed to recall the witness Owen, who on his further cross-examination testified as follows: "I do not remember whether

I testified before the clerk that all of the bequests were made before he called the witnesses. I have stated it here as I remember it. Suppose I would have remembered better before the clerk, as it was nearer the time." The caveator then proposed to read in evidence the evidence of one Johnson and one Stroud, who were examined before the clerk when the will was propounded in common form, when the witnesses were subjected to a cross-examination. It was not shown that either of the witnesses were dead, or out of the jurisdiction of the court. The propounder objected. The objection was sustained. Defendant excepted. There was some evidence given by the caveator tending to disprove capacity in the decedent to make a will. Defendant asked for special instructions as follows: "(1) That the jury must be satisfied by the oath of at least two witnesses present at the making of the will, who stated that they were especially required to bear witness thereof by the testator himself. (2) That the jury must be satisfied by the weight of testimony that the alleged testator was in such a condition of mind as to understand what he was doing. (3) That the statute must be construed strictly, and all its provisions must be completely complied with; that, in calling upon persons to bear witness, the decedent must call specially upon each individual, or at least designate by either calling person by name, or in some other way selecting those whom he wished to be witnesses to the will; it is not sufficient to call up an indefinite group of persons standing by." The evidence being duly closed, his honor charged the jury that they must be satisfied by the oath of at least two credible witnesses present at the making of the will, who state that they were especially called on to bear witness thereto by the testator himself of the making of said nuncupative will; that they must also be satisfied from the evidence that said will was made in the testator's last sickness, in his own habitation, or where he had been previously resident for at least 10 days; and that the testator was at the time of sound and disposing mind, and knew the extent and effect of what he was doing, that he was disposing of his property, and how, and to whom. His honor called the attention of the jury to the language of the statute, and stated to them that all its provisions must be complied with, and its provisions strictly construed, and that they must be satisfied from the evidence that the witnesses were specially called upon by the testator to bear witness to what he was saying; that if they believed the evidence given in this case to be true, then he charged them that there was evidence before them from which they might find that the witnesses were specially called upon by the testator himself to bear witness to his will; that it was not necessary that the testator should call the names of the witnesses; that if he called upon them, or signified to them in any certain and distinct manner that he desired them to bear witness to what he was saying as his will, it was sufficient in law; that if they were satisfied from the evidence that Williams and Owen and others were in the room with the alleged testator at the time of his death, and he called all in the room to come to his bed and witness his request, although he did not call any by name, and Williams and Owen and others went to his bed in consequence of this request, and he declared his request in their presence, it would be a substantial compliance with the law. The court refused the second instruction of the caveator, and did not give the first and third, except in so far as stated in instructions as given. The caveator excepted to the charge as given, and to the refusal or omission to give the special instructions asked, and appealed.

J. A. Barringer, for appellant. *L. M. Scott*, for appellee.

MERRIMON, C. J. The statute (Code, § 2148, par. 3) in respect to nuncupative wills is strict in its terms and provisions. It must be strictly interpreted, and as strictly observed in all material respects; the purpose being to prevent and exclude mistake, misapprehension, imposition, and fraud, that might easily happen or be perpetrated when the alleged testator is in his last illness, and sometimes almost *in extremis.* Bundrick v. Haygood, 106 N. C. 468, 11 S. E. Rep. 423, and the cases there cited. While the evidence in this case was not very satisfactory, we think it was sufficient to go to the jury to prove the execution of the will as required by the statute, which provides that such a will must be proven "on the oath of at least two credible witnesses present at the making thereof, who state they were specially required to bear witness thereto by the testator himself." It is true, the testator did not specify by name the particular persons he required to witness his will as expressed by him; but the evidence of these witnesses went to prove that he was sensible, knew what he was doing, knew that several persons were present, saw them, and, without naming any of them but one, he expressly required all present to be witnesses. He called to them. They were present, near to him, heard and understood his request, and took notice of what he said. There were more than two persons eligible as witnesses for the purpose. The evidence tended to show the purpose and capacity of the testator to make a will, and that he did so in the presence of more than two credible witnesses who were present, and were specially required by the testator himself to bear witness thereto. It was sufficient that he saw the witnesses, and charged them to bear witness to his will, and they did so; and it is not a good objection that he failed to designate them particularly by name. That he required them each—all of them—to bear witness was what the statute required. The purpose is that the testator shall require two witnesses, at least, to take notice and bear witness that he makes his will. He must require—direct—a competent person, and that person must be able to testify that he was one of the persons—the witnesses—so required, and that he did take notice and bear witness. The witnesses here testified that they were called upon by the testator; that they

did take notice, and witnessed his will as expressed by him. This was sufficient. Haden v. Bradshaw, 1 Winst. 260; Smith v. Smith, 63 N. C. 637. We think the court gave the jury so much of the special instructions asked for as the caveator was entitled to have. The other exceptions are without merit. Judgment affirmed.

DRAKE v. WILHELM et al.

(*Supreme Court of North Carolina.* Nov. 24, 1891.)

LANDLORD AND TENANT—HOLDING OVER—WAIVER OF LANDLORD'S OPTION.

Shortly after the termination of a lease stipulating for a rent of $300 per year, payable monthly, the landlord visited the premises, which the tenants were still occupying, to collect the rent for the previous month. He offered to lease the place for $300, and then for $275, which the tenants rejected, but his proposal to let it for $250 was taken under consideration. *Held,* that by his conduct he had waived any right to treat them as tenants holding over for the following year.

Appeal from superior court, Iredell county; R. F. ARMFIELD, Judge.

Action by E. B. Drake against James Wilhelm and others, partners as Wilhelm & Allison, for rent. There was a nonsuit, and plaintiff appeals. Affirmed.

STATEMENT BY THE COURT. It appears that the plaintiff and T. M. Mills agreed with each other as follows: "This agreement between E. B. Drake and T. M. Mills witnesseth, that said Drake has rented to said Mills the store-room and building now occupied by him, west of the store of W. E. Anderson, Broad street, for the term of one year from January 1st, 1888, at the price of $250.00 per year, payable monthly, with the understanding that said Mills has the privilege to make such changes and alterations of interior part of the rooms, necessary to accommodate his business, as he shall deem proper, and at his own cost and expense, not to be thereafter removed. And it is further agreed that said Mills shall have an option to continue in and occupy said store and building for an additional year, from January 1st, 1889, for the sum of $300.00, payable monthly. E. B. DRAKE. T. M. MILLS. January 1, 1888." Mills occupied the store-house and premises from January, 1888, to April of the same year, when he sold and assigned the remainder of his term to the defendants, who at once took possession of and continued to occupy and pay rents for the same until February of 1890, the plaintiff suing for and recovering $25 as rents for the month of January of the latter year. That defendants then showed upon cross-examination of plaintiff that some time in January, 1890, and he thought about the 4th or 5th, he went into the store to collect the rent for December, 1889, when a conversation took place between him and defendants as to renting the store-house for the year 1890, when he asked them $300, but during the conversation he offered to take $275, and then $250, but defendants did not accept either of these offers, and asked a few days to consider, which he agreed to give, but returned the same day and said he wanted an answer sooner; and on the 24th day of January, 1890, he served on defendants the following written notice, having seen defendants' advertisement in the Landmark that defendants had rented another store, to-wit: "Statesville, January 24, 1890. Messrs. Wilhelm & Allison: Please take notice that the rent of the building and store you occupy for 1890 is $300.00 a year, payable monthly, and I withdraw all proposals for a change in terms. Respectfully, E. B. DRAKE." Plaintiff admitted that defendants did not actually occupy the store after January, 1890, and plaintiff closed his case, when his honor held that the conversation and transaction that took place between plaintiff and defendants in January, 1890, as to renting the house for that year, was a waiver of plaintiff's right to hold defendants as his tenants for the year 1890, and he should so instruct the jury; whereupon plaintiff submitted to a nonsuit, and appealed to the supreme court.

D. M. Furches, for appellant. Robbins & Long and R. Z. Linney, for appellees.

MERRIMON, C. J. It seems that the plaintiff accepted and treated the defendants as his tenants, and they intended to become such under the written lease above set forth. That lease terminated on the 1st day of January, 1890. If it be granted as contended that, as the defendants continued quietly to occupy the premises next after the written lease expired, the plaintiff might have treated them as his tenants for the year 1890 upon the same terms as to rent as those specified in the written lease referred to, the continued relation as landlord and tenant would arise only by implication. He was not bound to treat them as his tenants; he might have treated them as trespassers and ejected them; it was optional with him whether he would treat them as tenants or not, and he might waive his right of option by any act showing his purpose to do so. Taylor, Landl. & Ten. § 22. Then did the plaintiff waive such right or option in this case? We concur in the opinion of the court below that he did. The defendants were merchants doing business in the storehouse of the plaintiff. Their lease was just ended. Shortly after the 1st of January, and before the defendants had fixed upon their place of business for the year, the plaintiff called upon them to collect the rent then due for December of 1889. He and they then had a conversation looking to the lease of the premises for the year 1890. He did not then suggest that they were his tenants for that year,—that he so recognized them or intended to do so, as possibly he had the right to do. On the contrary, distinctly showing his purpose to make a new contract of lease on his part, he proposed that the rent should be $300. The defendants refused to agree to pay that sum. He then offered to take $275, and at last $250. The defendants did not accept his offers, but requested him to allow them a few days within which to consider his proposition to lease, and he allowed the request. The parties separated, but the plaintiff returned the same day, and said he wanted an earlier

answer. Now it seems to us obvious that the plaintiff did not treat or regard the defendants as his tenants, and that they did not so regard themselves. Why did the plaintiff offer to lease the premises, and at the reduced rent of $250? Did he not thereby give the defendants to understand and act upon the fact that he did not recognize or insist upon any implied lease for the year? Nor did he say aught to the contrary until he learned that the defendants had leased other premises. It was too late then for him to insist upon an advantage—if he ever had it—arising by implication that he might waive. From his conduct and what he said, the defendants might reasonably infer and believe that they were not his tenants or so recognized or treated by him, and that they might look elsewhere, as their interests might suggest, for a suitable store-house, as they did do, without peril as to any liability to him. He must justly be held to have waived any such right or option he may possibly have had. Judgment affirmed.

YOUNT v. MORRISON et ux.

(Supreme Court of North Carolina. Nov. 24, 1891.)

MORTGAGES—POWERS—EXECUTION BY EXECUTOR—EVIDENCE—COMPETENCY.

1. Under a mortgage authorizing the mortgagee or his executor to sell the land and execute a deed to the purchaser, a person appointed in the mortgagee's will as his executor may, on qualifying as such after the mortgagee's death, execute the power, the provision of the mortgage being a sufficiently certain designation of the person.

2. In an action for possession of land, where defendant, by her answer, alleges that she bid the land off at a mortgage sale, but never received a deed, and that it was thereafter paid for, and the mortgage discharged, evidence that S., who obtained a deed at such sale, and under whom plaintiff claimed, told witness a few days before the sale that arrangements had been made for defendant to purchase the land, and that he was going to pay for it for her, is incompetent.

Appeal from superior court, Iredell county; R. F. ARMFIELD, Judge.

Action by J. H. Yount against E. F. Morrison and Mary E. Morrison, his wife, for possession of land. E. F. Morrison put in no answer. Judgment for plaintiff, and defendant Mary E. Morrison appeals. Affirmed.

STATEMENT BY THE COURT. The complaint alleges that the plaintiff is the owner, and entitled to have possession of the land described therein; that the defendant is in possession thereof, and unlawfully withholds the same from him, etc. The answer denies such allegations, except as to the possession, which it is alleged is lawful, etc. It is further alleged therein that the husband of the feme defendant was the owner in fee of the land, and he and she, on or about the 14th of March, 1878, executed a deed of mortgage of the same to Franklin Gay, to secure a debt due from her husband to him for $600; that $96 of this debt was paid on the 14th of March, 1880; that, on the 22d of December, 1885, the said Gay having died, leaving a will, his executor, John B. Holman, sold the land by virtue of a power contained in said will, and the *feme* defendant bid the same off at the price of $900; that, since she so bought, the mortgage debt has been paid, and the mortgage discharged, but she never received a deed for the land; that the plaintiff, at the time he purchased any pretended interest in the land, had full knowledge of her rights as such purchaser, etc.; and the answer demands judgment that the said Holman and others make deed to her, etc. Among other appropriate issues which the court submitted to the jury is the following, to which they responded in the negative: "Did the defendant Mary E. Morrison purchase said land under the mortgage and at the mortgage sale, as she alleges in her answer?" On the trial the plaintiff put in evidence the mortgage deed referred to, which contained a power authorizing the mortgagee, Gay, and his executor to sell the land for the purpose of the mortgage. He then proved the death of the mortgagee, and the appointment and qualification of J. B. Holman as executor of his will. He further put in evidence a deed from the said executor to C. L. Summers, who purports to have been the purchaser of the land for him. This deed was objected to on the ground that the power of sale mentioned could only be executed by the heirs at law of said Gay, and not by the executor of his will. The court declined to sustain this objection, and this is assigned as error. The plaintiff then put in evidence a deed in trust for the land from said C. L. Summers to himself. "Defendant introduced at the trial one J. H. Stevenson, and proposed to prove by said witness that, a day or two before the mortgage sale by said Holman, at which sale defendant claimed to be purchaser, said C. L. Summers told him that the arrangement had been made for the defendant Mary E. Morrison to purchase the land as a home for herself and her children, and that he, Summers, was going to pay for it for her; said Holman having already testified for the plaintiff that no money was paid at said sale; that Mrs M. E. Morrison, the defendant, was the bidder; and that he took the note of said C. L. Summers for the purchase money, and returned the mortgage, marked 'Satisfied,' to E. F. Morrison, the mortgagor. Upon plaintiff objecting to this evidence the same was excluded, and the defendant excepted. The plaintiff, testifying in his own behalf, was asked what E. F. Morrison, husband of *feme* defendant, and who had put in no answer, said to witness, two or three years after the mortgage sale, about the wife's purchase of this land in controversy at the mortgage sale. The defendant objected to this evidence. Objection overruled. The evidence admitted as against E. F. Morrison only, he being, at the time of said declaration proposed to be proved, living upon the land with his wife, the *feme* defendant, and witness proceeded to state that E. F. Morrison told him that C. L. Summers had fixed things now to suit himself, and that said Summers might take what was his own, referring to defendant M. E. Morrison and her children, and he, E. F. Morrison, was going to Texas; that he would

give up the land without trouble; and that he had but recently heard of his wife's claim upon said land." The defendant appealed to this court.

Armfield & Turner, for appellant. *M. L. McCorkle,* for appellee.

MERRIMON, C. J. The appellant's principal contention is that the executor of Gay, the mortgagee, had not power under and in pursuance of the mortgage deed to sell the land in controversy, and execute to the purchaser a deed effectual to pass the title thereto to Summers. This objection is untenable. The deed of mortgage expressly empowered Gay, or his executor, to sell and convey the land, and there is no reason, in legal contemplation, why this might not be done. In and by the deed the mortgagor and mortgagee agreed that the latter might execute the power, and if, for any reason, he could or should not do so in his life-time, his executor after his death might. He made his will, and therein appointed an executor. He died, and the executor Holman qualified as such, sold and conveyed the land by deed, and thus the power was sufficiently executed. To provide that an executor shall execute a power designates with certainty the person to be charged for the purpose. If no executor had been appointed, then the appellant's objection might have had some force at the time the deed was executed. Demarest v. Wynkoop, 3 Johns. Ch. 145; 2 Jones, Mortg. § 1786. The statute, however, (Acts 1887, c. 147,) expressly confers upon the executor or administrator of a deceased mortgagee all the powers, rights, and duties he had to enforce the mortgage. This statute applies to cases where the executor is not mentioned in the power. In this case the executor was, in terms, authorized to execute it.

The evidence rejected offered by the appellant, so far as appears, was not pertinent for any proper purpose. She alleges in her answer that she bid the land off at the sale, and that it was thereafter paid for, and the mortgage discharged, but she does not at all allege that she paid for it, or that she gave her note or other obligation for the purchase money; nor does she allege that Summers gave his note for the purchase money and afterwards paid the same at her instance, and took the deed for the land for her benefit and that of her children, or that he agreed to do so. Much of this testimony was mere hearsay, and none of it was pertinent in any aspect of the pleadings. It was properly rejected.

The testimony of the plaintiff objected to, but admitted, on the trial, was, in view of the findings, scarcely pertinent, but it was harmless. In no view of the case, as it appears to us, was the appellant entitled to a verdict or judgment. Judgment affirmed.

<hr/>

LOVETT v. SLOCOMB.

(*Supreme Court of North Carolina.* Nov. 24, 1891.)

RECEIVERS—APPOINTMENT—POSSESSION OF LAND.

Where defendant, in an action to cancel a mortgage, sets up in his answer a release by plaintiff of all his interest in the mortgaged land,

and refers to the book and page of the record of the release; and plaintiff denies that he released or intended to release his interest in the land,— such denial raises no issue as to the execution of the release, but the record thereof is *prima facie* evidence that plaintiff's interest has been conveyed to defendant, and, plaintiff being in possession, defendant is entitled to the appointment of a receiver.

Appeal from superior court, Cumberland county; EDWIN T. BOYKIN, Judge.

Action by Richard Lovett against A. H. Slocomb to cancel a mortgage. Judgment for defendant. Plaintiff appeals. Affirmed.

STATEMENT BY THE COURT. The plaintiff, who is in possession of the land in controversy, brought his action for the surrender and cancellation of a mortgage deed executed by the plaintiff to his son Charles Lovett on the 14th of December, 1887, to secure the payment of a note of $200, due said Charles Lovett, and payable three years after December 14, 1887, or on December 14, 1890, and alleged that he had paid said note in full, and had it in his possession now, but that he was informed that the defendant Slocomb claimed an interest in the land by virtue of an alleged assignment of the mortgage deed by said Charles Lovett to him. The defendant Slocomb set up in his answer, for a first defense, substantially: (1) That he (Slocomb) was in possession as lessee of the land on December 14, 1887, when plaintiff executed the mortgage deed and note to Charles Lovett, and that on the 24th of January, 1889, the said Charles Lovett assigned the note secured by the mortgage before maturity to him, (Slocomb,) which still remained unpaid, and, if the plaintiff then held the note, he had gained possession of it by fraud. (2) That he (defendant Slocomb) was the owner in fee of an undivided third of the said land. (3) That he was the assignee also of a note for $180, executed by the plaintiff to Emily Lovett, (now Emily McPherson,) on said 14th of December, which note is secured by a prior mortgage to that executed to secure the note due Charles Lovett. (4) That plaintiff was in the wrongful possession of the land, and withholding it from the defendant, and, as defendant was informed, had dispossessed defendant's tenant by threats of violence. For a second defense, substantially: (1) That on the 5th day of December, 1887, the plaintiff leased to him (Slocomb) all of the plaintiff's interest in and to said land for a term of three years, (which lease was referred to as registered in a certain book,) and that on the 24th of December, 1888, (during said term,) the plaintiff, for value, released to said defendant all of plaintiff's right or interest in the said land, as will appear by the release, which is registered in Book No. 4, at page ——, of the register's office of said county. For a third defense, substantially: (1) That by virtue of the mortgages executed by plaintiff to secure the notes executed by him, respectively, to Emily Lovett and Charles Lovett, the defendant Slocomb (after due advertisement) sold the land in controversy on the 19th of March (after the action was brought) to satisfy said notes, at which sale the defendant Taylor

became the purchaser, and the defendant Slocomb has executed a deed to him for the land. The defendant Slocomb further avers that the plaintiff is in possession, and in reception of the rents and profits, and is totally insolvent; and demands judgment: (1) That a receiver be appointed to take possession of the rents; (2) for possession of the land, and damages for detention. The plaintiff, on return of an order to show cause, filed his own affidavit, and that of his daughter Emily McPherson, (formerly Emily Lovett.) The plaintiff swears that the note executed to Charles Lovett is paid in full, and both he and Emily McPherson make oath that the note executed to her, and secured by the prior mortgage, was deposited by her as collateral to secure a debt of $35 due the defendant Slocomb from her. The plaintiff averred his willingness and readiness to pay that sum and interest. The plaintiff does not deny the allegation that Slocomb is the owner of one undivided third interest in the land. To the allegation of Slocomb that the plaintiff released to him all of his title and interest in said land, the latter in his affidavit responds as follows: "The defendant denies that on the 24th day of December, 1888, or any other time, he released, or intended to release, his interest in the land to said A. H. Slocomb."

Geo. M. Rose, for appellant. *T. H. Sutton* and *James C. MacRae,* for appellee.

AVERY, J. Where a party to an action asks, for affirmative relief, the possession of land, and alleges that his adversary, who wrongfully withholds it, is insolvent, and the latter directly admits or fails to deny the allegation, it only remains for the action, in order to establish his right to demand the appointment of a receiver to take charge of the rents and profits, to show that he has set up in an affidavit filed under the sanction of the court, or in a verified pleading in the cause, used as an affidavit, an apparently good title, either not controverted at all, or not unequivocally and sufficiently denied by the affidavits of the claimant in possession. Code, § 379, subd. 1; McNair v. Pope, 96 N. C. 502, 2 S. E. Rep. 54; Levenson v. Elson, 88 N. C. 182; Twitty v. Logan, 80 N. C. 69; Bryan v. Moring, 94 N. C. 694; Oldham v. Bank, 84 N. C. 304. If we concede that no title passed to the defendant Taylor by the sale on the 19th of March, since this action was brought, it still appears that the defendant Slocomb claims title in himself to an undivided interest in the land in one paragraph of his answer, to-wit, one-third, and in another paragraph to the whole, by virtue of a deed of release executed by the plaintiff to him on December 24, 1888, whereby he surrendered to Slocomb all of his right, title, and interest. He refers, also, in his answer to the book and page of the register's records where the deed of release is recorded, in order to corroborate his statement, and to show that the deed is competent as evidence of title in him. The plaintiff fails to deny that Slocomb was, prior to the execution of any of the mortgage deeds mentioned, his tenant in common as to one-third. But, if he had controverted this claim, his denial of the allegation that he had released all of his right and title to Slocomb by a deed, which has been proved and recorded, is so equivocal that it must be regarded as an admission of the fact of executing it, with the qualification that he did not intend at the time to do so. The execution of the deed having been proved, there is a presumption that it is valid, and operates to pass the interest of the plaintiff in the land to Slocomb. If the plaintiff had sought to accomplish two objects,—first, to cancel that conveyance on the ground of fraud, and then the mortgage because the lien had been discharged by payment,—the burden would have rested on him to successfully impeach a deed which apparently passed a good title to the grantee. When he contents himself with the denial "that on the 24th of December, 1888, or any other time, he released, or intended to release, his interest in the land to said A. H. Slocomb," his statement is not a sufficiently explicit one to raise an issue as to its execution. The deed of release, having been proved and recorded, is of itself *prima facie* evidence that the interest of the plaintiff has been conveyed to Slocomb, and of his right as against the plaintiff to demand the appointment of a receiver. There is no error, and the judgment is affirmed.

STATE ex rel. RICE v. HEARN et al.

(*Supreme Court of North Carolina.* Nov. 24, 1891.)

SATISFACTION OF JUDGMENT—RIGHTS OF SURETIES.

Judgment was obtained against two of the sureties of a principal debtor, and they deposited the whole amount of the judgment, and procured an assignment thereof to a third person for their benefit, with the view of more easily compelling contribution from their co-sureties. The assignee then fraudulently sold the judgment to a purchaser with notice of the fraud. *Held*, that the sureties who paid the judgment had a right, on notice to the last assignee, to move that the satisfaction of the judgment be entered of record.

Appeal from superior court, Pitt county; SPIER WHITAKER, Judge.

Action by the state of North Carolina, on the relation of Laura M. Rice, against B. H. Hearn, administrator of H. Shepard, W. M. King, William Whitehead, and seven others, to recover on the official bond of Shepard, former clerk of court, Pitt county. Judgment for plaintiff, which defendants paid in full, and had transferred on the docket to S. A. Reddin, who fraudulently assigned it to Oscar Hooker. Motion was then made on behalf of William Whitehead to have the satisfaction of the judgment entered of record. Allowed. Hooker appeals. Affirmed.

STATEMENT BY THE COURT. It appears that the plaintiff obtained judgment against the appellees, and as sureties of the principal debtor defendant; that they deposited the whole amount of the judgment and costs, and, with a view the more conveniently to compel contribution by their co-sureties, had the plaintiff assign the same to S. A. Reddin, a nephew of one of the appellees, and insolvent, for their use and benefit; that afterwards Reddin fraudulently sold and assigned on the docket the said judgment, for same value, to the appellant, Oscar Hooker, who so purchased it with knowledge of facts and circumstances that put him on notice of such fraud. The appellees moved, upon notice to the appellant, that it be appropriately entered of record that the said judgment and costs had been satisfied and discharged, and the court allowed the motion. Thereupon the said Hooker excepted, and appealed to this court.

Jarvis & Blow and *C. M. Bernard*, for appellant. *T. F. Davidson*, for appellees.

MERRIMON, C. J. The assignment of the judgment to Reddin for the use and benefit of the appellees was a legitimate transaction, and the latter could compel him to a due observance of their equitable rights. It is very clear, as the authorities cited by the appellees' counsel abundantly show, that the appellant purchased the judgment subject to their rights and equities. Jordan v. Black, 2 Murph. 30; Moody v. Sitton, 2 Ired. Eq. 382; Bank v. Bynum, 84 N. C. 24; Havens v. Potts, 86 N. C. 31; Freem. Judgm. § 427; Black, Judgm. §§ 953, 956. See Sherwood v. Collier, 3 Dev. 380; Ferebee v. Doxey, 6 Ired. 446; Barringer v. Boyden, 7 Jones, (N. C.) 187. The appellees did not discharge the judgment by the deposit of money they made. It continued in force for their benefit. There was, however, no valid reason why they might not ask the court to declare and treat it as satisfied and discharged; and this might be done by motion, certainly in the absence of objection as to the course of procedure. Judgment affirmed.

KEERANS v. KEERANS et al.

(*Supreme Court of North Carolina.* Nov. 24, 1891.)

CERTIORARI—NOTICE TO ADVERSE PARTY.

Sup. Ct. Rule N. C. No. 43, (12 S. E. Rep. ix,) prescribing that a petitioner for *certiorari* shall not be heard unless he has given the adverse party 10 days' notice in writing, the application will be refused where there is nothing to show that such notice has been given.

Petition by R. N. Keerans against R. B. Keerans and others for a writ of *certiorari*. Denied.

Batchelor & Devereux, L. M. Scott, and *Douglass & Shaw*, for petitioner.

CLARK, J. This is an application for a writ of *certiorari*, filed April 25, 1890, and continued for the petitioner from time to time till the present term. Rule 43 prescribes that no petition for *certiorari* shall be heard "unless the petitioner shall have given the adverse party ten days' notice in writing." No counsel has at any time represented the adverse party in this court, and there is nothing to indicate that notice has been given as required by the rule. The application must therefore be refused. Motion denied.

HANES v. NORTH CAROLINA R. CO.

(*Supreme Court of North Carolina.* Nov. 24, 1891.)

CONDEMNATION PROCEEDINGS — EXCESSIVE DAMAGES — REPORT OF COMMISSIONERS — DIRECTORY STATUTE.

1. In special proceedings against a railroad company to assess damages for a right of way, defendant excepted to the commissioners' report on the ground that the damages were excessive. *Held,* that it was error for the court to refuse to hear affidavits on the ground that it had no legal power to pass on them, since Code N. C. § 1946, provides that "the court or judge on the hearing may direct a new appraisement, modify, or confirm the report, or make such order in the premises as to him shall seem right and proper."

2. The commissioners' report is not fatally defective because it does not contain a description of the land taken by defendant, since "that is certain which can be made certain."

3. The provision of Code N. C. § 1946, that the commissioners shall make their report under seal, is merely directory.

Appeal from superior court, Forsyth county; JOHN G. BYNUM, Judge.

Special proceedings by Mary C Hanes against North Carolina Railroad Company for damages for a right of way. Judgment for plaintiff. Defendant appeals. Reversed.

STATEMENT BY THE COURT. The report of the commissioners was as follows: "Obedient to a summons by the sheriff of Forsyth county, we, the undersigned commissioners, appointed by the clerk of Forsyth county superior court to assess the damages and benefits resulting to Mary C. Hanes by reason of the construction by the defendant company of a railroad through her lands, being duly sworn and having viewed the premises, do make the following report: Having taken into consideration the value of the plaintiff's land appropriated for the use of said railroad, and the disadvantages and inconveniences resulting to the plaintiff by reason of the construction of said railroad, we find that the plaintiff, Mary C. Hanes, is damaged to the amount of twelve hundred dollars, ($1,200.) We further find that the benefits arising to the plaintiff from the construction of said railroad are nothing. Respectfully submitted, this 24th day of February, 1890. J. A. NIFONG, C. T. POPE, THEO. KIMEL, Commissioners. The defendant excepted to the report of the commissioners: (1) Because the description of the condemned land was insufficient; (2) because the commissioners did not report under seal; (3) because "the damage was excessive, and out of all proportion to the value of the land condemned." The clerk made an order confirming the report, and from that order the defendant appealed. The judge entered the following judgment: "This cause coming on," etc., "all exceptions to said report are overruled, the court holding the report sufficiently definite; that the requirement that the report should be under seal is directory only. The court further held, in passing on exception 4, that he had no legal power to hear affidavits on the question of damages, nor to submit said question by issue to a jury, but that the act of the commissioners was conclusive as to the amount of damages,

there being no power in the court to review the amount assessed by them. It is adjudged that the report be confirmed, and that plaintiff recover $1,200 of defendant, and costs of action." The defendant appealed.

D. Schenck and *Glenn & Manly,* for appellant. *Eller & Starbuck,* for appellee.

AVERY, J. The statute (Code, § 1946,) provides that "the court or judge on the hearing may direct a new appraisement, modify or confirm the report, or make such order in the premises as to him shall seem right and proper." If, under the general statute regulating special proceedings, (Code, § 116,) the plaintiff had the right, before commissioners were appointed, to insist that the clerk should frame an issue involving the question of damages, and transmit the case to be tried in term-time by a jury, he could not, after acquiescing in the order appointing commissioners, and thereby assenting to that mode of trial, reassert and enforce that right after waiving it, and when he discovered that under the mode of trial agreed to, if not selected by him, the findings were not so favorable to him as he had expected. Railroad v. Parker, 105 N. C. 246, 11 S. E. Rep. 328. "The judge might have heard the affidavits, both of defendant and the plaintiff," as a help or guide in the exercise of the broad discretion given him by the statute. Skinner v. Carter, 108 N. C. 106, 12 S. E. Rep. 908. While his refusal to hear them, nothing more appearing, is not necessarily reviewable in this court, as it would have been presumed that he did so in the exercise of the power conferred by the statute, it was error to refuse to hear the affidavits on the ground that he had no legal power to pass upon them. He had authority unquestionably to set aside the report, and to direct a new appraisement by the same commissioners, or others appointed in their stead, on the ground that he thought the damage assessed was excessive, even though we should concede that, under the ruling of this court in Railroad Co. v. Ely, 101 N. C. 11, 7 S. E. Rep. 476, the judge could no more modify the findings of the commissioners in that respect by substituting a smaller sum than he could make the same change in the verdict of the jury. Skinner v. Carter, supra; Code, § 1946. He was clothed with the discretionary power to confirm the report, if such course seemed to him in all respects fair and proper, or "to make such order as seemed just," though he could no more annul the order appointing the commissioners and then direct an issue to be tried by a jury than he could have vacated a consent order of reference when one of the parties objected. But when the judge could not have called a jury, in aid of his conscience, to find the facts, how could he ascertain whether it was his duty to set aside the report, and direct a new assessment by the same or other commissioners, or to remand the case again for a new assessment, as he might have done, (Skinner v. Carter, supra,) unless he was at liberty to hear testimony in the form of affidavits, as on a motion to grant or dissolve an order of injunction, or in other cases where he was empowered to review the facts? We concur with his honor in the view that the description was not fatally defective, because the location of the right of way could be, and doubtless has been, made certain, so long as the road-bed shall be used, as a given number of feet from the known location of the track on either side. *Id certum est, quod certum reddi potest.* Beattie v. Railroad Co., 108 N. C. 425, 12 S. E. Rep. 913. The requirement of the statute, (Code, § 1946,) that the commissioners should attach a seal to their signatures, was unquestionably merely directory, not mandatory, as was declared by the court below. The clerk could not more readily vouch for the genuineness of a report, filed by persons selected by him because a seal was added to the signature, and the failure to append the seal does not in any way affect a substantial right of either of the parties. Code, § 289; Lineberger v. Tidwell, 104 N. C. 506, 10 S. E. Rep. 758; Matthews v. Joyce, 85 N. C. 258; Rollins v Henry, 78 N. C. 342. For the error in resting the refusal to hear affidavits upon the ground that he had no legal power to hear them in their bearing upon the question of setting aside the appraisement, the judgment is reversed, and the cause will stand for hearing upon the exceptions to the report of the commissioners filed before the clerk.

DAVIS v. POLLOCK.

(Supreme Court of South Carolina. Dec. 2, 1891.)

APPEAL—AGREED STATEMENT—RETURN—ILLNESS OF ATTORNEY.

1. The fact that the statement of the case for the supreme court agreed on by counsel for the respective parties does not specifically purport to be the return, will not deprive it of that character, as Code Civil Proc. S. C. § 345, subd. 5, provides that, where counsel for the respective parties agree on a statement of the case for the supreme court, "no return or other paper from the circuit court shall be required;" and rule 2 of the supreme court provides that such agreed statement, with the notice of appeal and exceptions, shall constitute the return. McNair v. Craig, (S. C.) 12 S. E. Rep. 664, followed.

2. Where the affidavits of appellant's attorneys allege that the failure to file the return within the time required by rule 1 of the supreme court was caused by the critical illness of the attorney having sole charge of the appeal, the court will reinstate the case on the calendar.

Appeal from common pleas circuit court of York county; KERSHAW, Judge.

Action by M. L. Davis against A. H. Pollock. Judgment for defendant. Plaintiff's appeal is dismissed under rule 1 of the supreme court. Motion to reinstate is granted.

Wilson & Wilson & McDow, for appellant. *Wm. B. McCaw,* for respondent.

PER CURIAM. This is a motion to reinstate the appeal of plaintiff, dismissed by the clerk under rule 1 of this court. Appellant's attorneys submitted the following affidavits in support of their motion: "South Carolina, York county. Personally appeared W. B. Wilson, Sr., of counsel for appellant in the case of M. L. Davis,

Appellant, against A. H. Pollock, Respondent, and makes oath that on 2d day of June, 1891, affiant and the counsel for respondent in said case agreed in writing upon a statement for the hearing of the appeal before the supreme court; that affiant was in sole charge of the appeal, and in sole possession of the papers therein, and soon after 2nd June, 1891, being in a critical state of ill health, left home for the Mineral Springs, and returned home in July; that he then sent the original papers in the case, not having full copy of the record, to the printer, and, as soon as he received the printed copies of the case, which was after the expiration of forty days from the 2d June, he filed the return with the clerk of the supreme court, and served three copies of same on the attorney for respondent. No notice was served upon appellant's attorneys in reference to service of printed copies of the case or as to filing the return. Said appeal was made in good faith, and, but for affiant's ill health and absence from home, would have received earlier attention. Printed copies of the case and points and authorities are on file with the clerk of this court. W. B. WILSON, Sr. Sworn to & subscribed before me, Oct. 22d, 1891. W. H. McCUKLE, Probate Judge & N. P."

"The State of South Carolina. In the supreme court, November term, 1891. M. L. Davis, Appellant, against A. H. Pollock, Respondent. Personally appears W. B. Wilson, Sr., and makes oath that in the appeal in above-stated case he omitted, by inadvertence, to have the return filed with the clerk of the supreme court within the time specified under rule 1 of said court; that, owing to an attack of grippe, he was then in a perilous condition. Affiant, in justice to himself, further says that in a practice of forty years at this bar this is the first instance in which his compliance with the rules of the court has been called in question. W. B. WILSON, Sr. Sworn to & subscribed before me, 20 Nov., 1891. W. H. McCUKLE, Probate Judge & N. P."

Counsel for respondent submitted the following affidavit:

"The State of South Carolina. In the supreme court, November term, 1891. M. L. Davis, Appellant, vs. A. H. Pollock, Respondent. Personally appeared Wm. B. McCaw, and made oath that when the counsel for appellant, Messrs. Wilson & Wilson & McDow and himself, as counsel for respondent, on the 2nd day of June, 1891, agreed upon a statement for the hearing of the foregoing appeal before the supreme court, the said counsel for appellant and respondent expressed in writing their consent at the foot of the said statement, as follows, to-wit: 'We consent that the foregoing shall constitute the "case" to be heard before the supreme court. [Signed] WILSON & WILSON & McDOW, Appellant's Attorneys. [Signed] WM. B. McCAW, Respondent's Attorney. June 2nd, 1891.' Deponent further makes oath that nothing was said in regard to what should constitute the return, and counsel for appellant did not request deponent to waive the requirements of rules 1 & 2 of the supreme court, and deponent did not agree to waive compliance with the said rules. Deponent swears further that at the trial of the case on circuit both W. B. Wilson, Sr., and W. B. Wilson, Jr., were engaged, and the latter was particularly active in the manipulation of the case. WM. B. McCAW. Sworn to and subscribed before me this 23d day of Nov., 1891. D. E. FINLEY, Notary Public."

After hearing argument *pro* and *con* the court decides as follows: The clerk was perfectly right in dismissing the appeal on the affidavit presented to him under rule 1. It will be observed that respondent's counsel object to the reinstatement of the appeal on two grounds: (1) Because the statement agreed upon was not intended for the return, but constituted the "case" for hearing; (2) because the return, assuming the agreed statement to be the return, was not filed in the time required by the rules of this court. The first objection is disposed of by the decision in the case of McNair v. Craig, (filed Jan. 19, 1891,) 12 S. E. Rep. 664, and the reasoning in the opinion then filed is adopted as the reasoning in this case. The fact that the statement of the case for the supreme court, agreed upon by counsel for the respective parties, does not specifically purport to be the return, will not deprive it of that character, as the Code of Civil Procedure, § 345, subd. 5, provides that, where counsel for the respective parties agree on a statement of the case for the supreme court, "no return or other paper from the circuit court shall be required;" and rule 2 of the supreme court provides that such agreed statement, with the notice of appeal and exceptions, shall constitute the return. This decision explains Nabors v. Latimer, 30 S. C. 607, 10 S. E. Rep. 390. The affidavits of appellant's attorneys concede that the return was not filed in the time required by the rule of court, but they allege that the critical illness of the attorney having sole charge of the appeal caused the delay. This is considered by the court a sufficient excuse for non-compliance with the rule of court.

STATE v. MERRIMAN.

(*Supreme Court of South Carolina.* Nov. 25, 1891.)

SUPREME COURT—MOTIONS—APPEALABLE ORDERS.

1. The provision of Sup. Ct. Rule S. C. No. 19, that a motion that "an appeal be dismissed or the cause stricken from the docket for any irregularity in the taking of the appeal or in the record filed in this court" must be made at the time assigned for the hearing of special motions, is imperative; but it does not apply to a motion to dismiss an appeal on the ground that the order from which the appeal was taken is not appealable.

2. An order of the court below, conforming to the directions contained in a judgment of the supreme court, previously rendered, is not appealable.

Mitchell v. Clayton, 11 S. E. Rep. 634, 33 S. C. 599, followed.

Appeal from general sessions circuit court of Chesterfield county; IZLAR, Judge. Appeal dismissed.

William D. Merriman was convicted of murder. The judgment was affirmed on appeal, and defendant now appeals from an order of the court below carrying out the judgment of the supreme court. For former reports, see 12 S. E. Rep. 619, 13 S. E. Rep. 328.

The following is the motion referred to in the opinion: "Take notice that the undersigned, attorney for plaintiff (respondent) in the above-stated case, will move before the supreme court on Tuesday, the 24th day of November, 1891, at 11 o'clock A. M., or as soon thereafter as counsel can be heard, for an order dismissing the appeal of defendant (appellant) from the order and sentence pronounced upon the defendant (appellant) by his honor Judge IZLAR at the fall term of the circuit court for Chesterfield county in copies of the 'case' as proposed by defendant, (appellant,) of the proposed amendments thereto by plaintiff, (respondent,) of the order of his honor Judge IZLAR settling the 'case,' of the notice of appeal of defendant, (appellant,) of the order and sentence from which the appeal is taken. and on the records and minutes of the supreme court in reference to the above-stated case from its original filing in the supreme court, upon the grounds that said appeal is taken from an order which merely carried out a previous judgment of the circuit court and the mandate of the supreme court, which order is therefore not appealable; and that, if the supreme court refuse to dismiss said appeal, a further motion will be made at the same time and place before the supreme court for an order requiring the above-stated case to be placed upon the docket of the supreme court, and set for a hearing on the first day assigned for the hearing of causes from the fourth circuit at the ensuing November, 1891, term of the supreme court. Take notice, further, that in moving for an order dismissing the appeal as hereinbefore noticed, the motion will be based on the additional ground that the facts and proceedings orally alleged as grounds for the motion submitted in arrest of judgment in the circuit court by defendant (appellant) were not before the circuit court in any competent form, so that the circuit court could take judicial cognizance thereof."

Hough & Kennedy and *Prince & Stevenson,* for appellant. *J. M. Johnson,* for the State.

McIVER, J. This is a motion by the state (respondent) to dismiss the appeal of the defendant, upon the ground that said appeal is taken from an order which merely carries out a previous judgment of the circuit court and the mandate of the supreme court, which order is therefore not appealable, which motion is hereunto attached. Before a consideration of this motion, it is necessary to dispose of a preliminary objection to its hearing at this time, made by appellant's attorney, to-wit, that under rule 19 of this court the motion cannot now be heard. Rule 19 is as follows: "(19) Motions, other than those that arise on the call of a cause, will be heard at the opening of the court on the morning of the day fixed for the call of causes from the circuit to which they appertain, and not afterwards, without the special leave of the court. When a party intends to move the court that an appeal be dismissed or the cause stricken from the docket, for any irregularity in the taking of the appeal, or in the record filed in this court, such motion must be made at the time assigned by this rule for the hearing of special motions. All motions, whether made before the court or a justice at chambers, as to all matters of fact involved, not appearing on the record filed in this court, and not appertaining to the class of which this court takes judicial notice, must be made on affidavits, copies of which must be served on the opposite party, with notice of the motion, in conformity with chapter 11, tit. 12, pt. 2, Code Proc., at least four days before the day on which such motion may be heard: provided, that upon a proper showing for that purpose the court or justice before whom the motion is made may prescribe a shorter time." It will be observed that this rule is not imperative, but permissive only. The second paragraph thereof is imperative; but this applies only to irregularities in the taking of the appeal, or in the record filed in this court, and is not applicable to this motion. A motion like the present motion can be heard at any time. In fact, such motions are often made and heard without reference to the time assigned for the call of cases from the circuit to which the case belongs. Is the motion well founded? There is no doubt in our minds that it is. In the case of Mitchell v. Clayton, 33 S. C. 599, 11 S. E. Rep. 634, the motion before this court was to dismiss the appeal from a judgment of the circuit court conforming to the directions contained in the judgment of this court previously rendered. This court granted the motion, saying: "This being an appeal from a judgment rendered by the circuit court in conformity to the instructions of this court at the hearing of the former appeal herein, the matter is clearly not appealable." There is no difference between this case and Clayton v. Mitchell, supra. The circuit judge was not required to resentence the defendant, but to assign a day for the execution of the sentence previously pronounced; and what he did in that respect was an act of supererogation. The circuit judge was bound to carry out the judgment of this court,—simply to fix a new day for the execution of the sentence. Such has been the practice for perhaps a century. See Miller's Compilation. There was nothing to appeal from. The circuit judge could not undertake to review the judgment of this court. This court may correct an error. If an error is supposed to have been made, there is a remedy, not by appeal, but by a motion in this court to recall the *remittitur* and have the matter reviewed by petition for a rehearing. But if the *remittitur* as not been recalled, the action of the circuit court thereupon is not appealable, because there is no judgment of the circuit court to appeal from. The court, therefore, made the following order: "[Caption.] It appearing to the satisfaction of the court that the appeal as above stated is made from the order of his honor Judge Izlar,

simply fixing and naming a new day for the execution of a previous judgment of the circuit court, which previous judgment had been appealed from and confirmed by this court, (any other matter in Judge Izlar's order being surplusage,) that said order of Judge Izlar is clearly not appealable, and therefore the motion is granted, and the appeal is dismissed."

STATE v. JAMES.

(*Supreme Court of South Carolina.* Nov. 25, 1891.)

DISMISSAL OF APPEAL.

A motion to dismiss an appeal to this court is premature when the notice of intention to appeal is the only record in the case, and the time for filing the return has not expired.

Appeal from general sessions circuit court of Darlington county; IZLAR, Judge. Denied.

Motion to dismiss the appeal from a conviction of Joseph W. James of murder.

E. Keith Dargan and *H. T. Thompson,* for appellant. *J. M. Johnson,* for the State.

PER CURIAM. The motion is not obnoxious to rule 19 of this court. Such motions can be heard at any time. State v. Merriman, 13 S. E. Rep. 898, (Nov. 25, 1891.) There is nothing before us of the record in this case but the notice of intention to appeal. No return has been filed, it appearing that the time in which the return is to be filed has not expired. We know nothing of the nature of the appeal. This motion is premature, and the motion cannot be considered for this reason alone. In the case of Pickens v. Quillian, 31 S. C. 602, 9 S. E. Rep. 743, the court held, on a motion in that case, that, the return not having been filed, it was without jurisdiction. For this reason alone the motion is refused.

HARRIS v. BRATTON *et al.* DE LOACH *et ux.* v. SAME. WILLIAMS v. SAME.

(*Supreme Court of South Carolina.* Nov. 27, 1891.)

A petition for rehearing will not be granted where no material fact or important principle of law has been overlooked or misunderstood.

On rehearing. For former report, see 13 S. E. Rep. 447.

PER CURIAM. We have carefully examined this petition, and, finding that no material fact or important principle of law has been overlooked or misunderstood, there is no ground for a rehearing. It is therefore ordered that this petition be dismissed.

AYRES *et al.* v. ALPHIN *et al.*

(*Supreme Court of Appeals of Virginia.* Nov. 19, 1891.)

REVIVAL OF CAUSES—PARTIES BY CONSENT.

Suit having been brought to enforce a vendor's lien, and a decree obtained, a judgment creditor of the vendee consented to a private sale upon condition that, after payment of the vendor, he should receive one-half the residue. Afterwards the purchaser defaulted, and a resale was ordered without the knowledge of the creditor. This second decree ignored the rights of the creditor, and directed the residue to be turned over to the vendee. *Held*, that the creditor by his consent to the first-named sale became in effect a party to the suit, and that it was erroneous to decree concerning his rights without reviving the cause against his administrator; the creditor and his counsel both having died before the second decree was entered.

W. E. Craig and *T. C. Elder*, for appellant. *S. H. Letcher*, for appellee.

LACY, J. This is an appeal from two decrees, rendered in this cause by the hustings court of Staunton city, respectively, on the 14th day of May, 1889, and on the 7th day of June, 1890. The case is as follows: On the 15th day of February, 1872, a bill was filed in the circuit court of Rockbridge county by D. C. E. Brady, executor of William Weaver, deceased, against the appellant William L. Ayres, to subject the land of the defendant (Ayres) in the bill mentioned, situated in the county of Rockbridge, to the lien reserved in the deed of the vendor to the said Ayres, to secure the purchase money for the said land,—a balance remaining unpaid by the said Ayres of $4,823.19. Ayres answered, admitting the correctness of the bill, except a failure to allow him credit for all of his payments, and admitting a balance to be still due and unpaid. The court referred the cause to a master to ascertain the true balance due. The commissioner reported the balance, which was not excepted to, and on the 10th day of December, 1872, a decree was rendered in the cause by consent, confirming the said report, and decreeing against that said defendant for a balance due of $4,991.19, and ordering a resale in default of payment by the defendant within 30 days, in whole or in parcels, of the said land, at public or private sale. The land was sold at private sale to one E. A. Quintard for the sum of $6,000, by the consent in writing both of the defendant William L. Ayres and of one William Alphin, the consent being both as to purchaser and the amount of the purchase money; the said William Alphin being a judgment creditor of William L. Ayres, by confession, in the sum of $3,138.28, with interest from the 1st day of January, 1871. This sale to Quintard at $6,000 was consented to by the said William Alphin, provided he (Alphin) should receive one-half of the residue after paying the balance due to Weaver's estate. which balance was about $1,000. Quintard paid a part of the purchase money, to-wit, $1,622.84, and defaulted as to the residue, and upon the petition of Weaver's executor, and proper proceedings thereon, on the 15th of May, 1875, a decree was rendered for a resale to satisfy the unpaid purchase money, which being executed, the said William L. Ayres became the purchaser at the price of $3,860, $336 being paid in cash, and bonds executed by Ayres, with M. E. Davidson as his security,—one bond, at four months, for $504, and three other annual bonds, each in the sum of $840,—which sale was confirmed by the court, and a commission-

er appointed and directed to collect these bonds and apply them to the payment of the Quintard bonds; and the commissioner, who was J. D. Davidson, was directed to convey the title when the same was fully paid. And subsequently, J. D. Davidson having died, C. A. Davidson was appointed a special receiver to collect the said bonds, and, he having partly collected the bonds and died, the general receiver of the court was ordered to collect the bonds, and to apply them as directed by former decree, and one J. G. Steele appointed to convey the title in lieu of the said J. D. Davidson, who had died. An account was ordered and taken, and report made of the balance due on the plaintiff's debt, and an account of the collection by the late special commissioner, C. A. Davidson, deceased. The commissioner reported that the last bond of Ayres was not necessary to pay the Weaver debt, and might be turned over to Ayres uncollected, which was decreed accordingly. It appeared from the said commissioner's report, further, that M. E. Davidson had paid for Ayres, as his security, $1,924.99, which had been repaid to the amount of $1,203.47, by her purchase of certain land of the said Ayres; and on March 15, 1884, the receiver was directed to turn over to Ayres his last bond of $840, and pay him the balance in his hands of $12.75; and, all matters being settled, as the decree recites, the cause was ordered to be stricken from the docket.

This decree having entirely ignored the rights of the said William Alphin, the judgment creditor, by whose consent the sale had been made to Quintard, upon the condition that he should receive from the said commissioner one-half of the last bond, which, as has been said, was turned over to the debtor (Ayres) in whole, on the 10th day of September, 1884, following the said March 15th, when the said decree was rendered, the administrator of Alphin, by leave of the court, filed his petition to review the said last-named decree for errors alleged to be apparent upon the record, wherein it was set forth that Alphin was the judgment creditor of Ayres in the sum of $3,138.28, with interest from January 1, 1871, and set forth the private sale to Quintard, made by the joint consent of Alphin and Ayres in writing, which was filed in the cause as the basis of the decree, as has been stated, and that the last decree was inadvertently and erroneously entered, to the prejudice of Alphin's rights, because at the time of the decree complained of Alphin was dead, and his counsel, J. D. Davidson, was dead, and the said petitioner, Alphin's administrator, was not aware of the entering of the decree in question until the time when the petition was filed, and asking that the said cause be reinstated upon the docket, and the petitioner, as administrator, be admitted a party to the cause, and the decree, so far as it directed the surrender of the last purchase-money bond, be set aside, and an account be taken between Ayres and petitioner, and petitioner be decreed his just rights under the agreement filed in the cause aforesaid. Ayres and M. E.

Davidson were summoned to answer this petition, which was returned executed on both Ayres and Davidson, and a decree of reference to a master to report on the matter involved in the petition. The said account was taken by the master, and report made that the decree of March 15, 1874, was erroneously and inadvertently entered, and that the said bond belonged to Alphin under his assignment aforesaid. Whereupon, it being suggested that the judge of the court should not sit in the cause, by reason of his relation to some of the parties by marriage, the cause was removed to the hustings court of Staunton on the 23d day of September, 1884. In the hustings court of Staunton, January 12, 1888, the said report of the master was confirmed, and the decree of March 15, 1884, was set aside and annulled, and the bond of $840 decreed to Alphin's administrator in accordance with the said commissioner's report, and decree rendered in his favor against Ayres and Davidson. In March following, Ayres and Davidson filed their bill of review to this decree, upon the facts as stated above, in which they allege that the decree setting aside the decree of March 15, 1884, was erroneous, because Alphin was not a party to the cause, and could not file the bill to set the decree aside, and that the same was done without notice to them, and the account was taken under the said decree without notice to them, and for other grounds. The appellee demurred to this bill, and it was dismissed, and from this decree Ayres and Davidson appealed. There is no error in this decree of which Ayres or Davidson can complain. The judgment of Alphin bound the interest of Ayres in the land held by him, and also the land sold to Davidson. It was erroneous to decree concerning the rights of Alphin's estate without reviving the case against his administrator. Alphin had been made a party, in effect, by consent in the decree confirming the sale to Quintard, and ascertaining his rights in the purchase money, and it was a fraud upon the rights of his estate to decree his interest in the fund to Ayres when he was not before the court, and was without counsel, his counsel having recently died. The order of revival was right and proper, and no injustice or injury has been done to the appellants by any of the decrees appealed from. The record shows that a large part of the money apparently paid by Ayres had been paid, in fact, for him by Alphin, who was his brother-in-law; and the device of depriving him of any interest in the fund was not thought of until after his death. The cause was not revived without notice to the appellants, but upon notice duly executed; and, being a party to the cause, the reference to the commissioner was a matter he was bound to take notice of, and, if notice was not given to him of the time of taking of the said account, he should have excepted upon that ground, which was not done. The report of the commissioner is not excepted to, and is in accordance with the just rights of the parties, and was properly confirmed by the court, and we are of opinion to affirm the decrees appealed from.

COMMONWEALTH v. LARKIN.

(Supreme Court of Appeals of Virginia. Nov. 19, 1891.)

PAYMENT OF ATTORNEY'S LICENSE — TENDER OF COUPONS—GENUINENESS—BURDEN OF PROOF.

1. On the trial of an indictment against an attorney at law for practicing without a revenue license it appeared that the defendant had tendered to the treasurer, in payment of his license, papers purporting to be coupons cut from the bonds of the state, tax-receivable and past due, and that the treasurer had refused to receive them, because the statutes prohibited him from doing so, and because he did not know whether they were genuine. Defendant, who was the only witness for the defense, testified that he had never seen the bonds from which said coupons were cut, but that he had handled many thousands of dollars worth of coupons, and that he believed himself an expert, competent to pass upon the genuineness of such coupons, and that he believed them to be genuine. He did not testify to any facts showing that he was an expert. Held, that an instruction that, if defendant showed "he believed" himself an expert, and that he believed the coupons tendered were genuine, the burden of proving their non-genuineness was shifted upon the commonwealth, was inapplicable and defective.

2. An instruction, without prelude or explanation, that it was "not necessary, independently of any collateral litigation, to establish the genuineness of coupons before or after tender, to entitle a tenderer to be free from molestation," only repeated the vice of the former instruction.

Indictment against W. W. Larkin, a licensed attorney, for practicing without a revenue license. There was a judgment of acquittal, and the commonwealth brings error. Reversed.

R. Taylor Scott, Atty. Gen., for the Commonwealth.

FAUNTLEROY, J. This is a writ of error by the commonwealth of Virginia to the judgment of the corporation court of the city of Lynchburg in the trial of an indictment therein pending against W. W. Larkin, had at the September term, 1890, for the violation of the revenue laws of the plaintiff in error. The accused pleaded "not guilty," but he filed no special plea, and he relied upon an alleged tender of coupons. Issue was joined, and, under instructions asked for by the defendant and given by the court, the jury found him "not guilty." Upon the trial the attorney for the commonwealth tendered and obtained his bill of exceptions, as follows: "The plaintiff, on the trial of this cause, to sustain the issue on its part, proves that the defendant, W. W. Larkin, was a duly-licensed attorney at law, and was practicing as such without having a revenue license, as required by law; that he tendered to the treasurer of Lynchburg, in payment of his license tax, papers purporting to be coupons cut from the bonds of this state, tax-receivable and past due; that the treasurer of the city of Lynchburg refused to receive them, because the statutes of Virginia prohibited him from receiving them; that he (the said treasurer) did not know whether they were genuine or not; that the bonds of this state, under the funding acts, required that said bonds should be signed by the state treasurer and auditor, and that the validity of the coupons depended on the proper and lawful issuance of the bond from which they were detached. The defendant, to sustain the issue on his part, proved that he tendered to the treasurer of the city of Lynchburg the amount of his license in coupons, which he believes to be genuine coupons, past due and tax-receivable, and cut from the bonds of this state; that he had never seen the bonds from which said coupons were cut, but that he had handled many thousand dollars' worth of coupons, and that he believed himself an expert, and believes the coupons tendered were genuine; that said coupons were still in his possession, and that he was ready to pay them over for his license; and thereupon he paid the same into court." Upon this testimony the court gave three instructions to the jury, the first of which was not objected to. The second instruction is: "After the defendant showed he believed himself to be an expert in reference to the genuineness of the coupons tendered, and that he believed those to be genuine he tendered in this case, the burden of proving non-genuineness is shifted to the commonwealth; and, if the commonwealth do not show non-genuineness, the jury must find the defendant not guilty." The plea of tender confessed the charge in the indictment that the license tax imposed by law upon the accused had not been paid, and it could only be a good defense when fully and properly proved. The *onus probandi* as to the genuineness of the coupons tendered was upon the tenderer. He must prove everything necessary to constitute a legal tender. In support of his plea, Mr. Larkin was the only witness for the defense, and he testified to no facts which showed him to be an expert, with knowledge, experience, or skill, which made him competent to testify as to the genuineness and tax-receivability of the coupons tendered by him in payment of his license tax. He had never seen the bonds, or any bonds, from which they had been cut, and, for aught that he knew or testified, *non constat* that they had ever been attached to any bond or legal obligation of the state of Virginia. They were mere printed or lithographed detached papers, which might have been printed or lithographed and put in circulation by irresponsible parties, either attached or unattached to simulated and unauthorized bonds. He merely expressed his belief that he was an expert; but he did not testify to any information, skill, or experience in printing, lithographing, or testing the genuineness of coupons, which could make him expert to detect and pronounce the spurious from the genuine coupon in circulation. Larkin's testimony was fatally defective, and it is clear from the record that he is not an expert as to the matters to which he undertook to testify, and that there was no expert witness before the jury. Yet the instruction of the court to the jury was that, if he showed he believed himself to be an expert, the burden of proving the genuineness of the coupons tendered by him was shifted from him to the commonwealth, who must prove the non-genuineness of the

coupons tendered by him. As formulated, there was no evidence which called for this instruction, and none to support it. It does not propound the law of the case as proven to the jury. It is defective and vicious, and the trial court erred in giving it. The third instruction told the jury, without prelude, explanation, or qualification: "Not necessary, independently of any collateral litigation, to establish the genuineness of coupons, before or after tender, to entitle a tenderer to be free from molestation." This repeats the vice of the second instruction, and gives a charter *ad libitum* to tender spurious coupons, and to be exempt, absolutely, from all obligation or requirement of proof of genuineness. The instructions were wholly erroneous, and misled the jury. The verdict must be set aside, the judgment reversed, and the case remanded to the corporation court of the city of Lynchburg for a new trial.

SIMMONS v. KRAMER.

(Supreme Court of Appeals of Virginia. Nov. 19, 1891.)

SPECIFIC PERFORMANCE—SALE OF LAND—AUTHORITY OF AGENT.

Suit was brought for the specific performance of a contract for the sale of lots. The person making the sale testified that he was the authorized agent of defendant, and that the following letter from defendant was received by him in answer to a letter asking for authority to sell: "Yours received. I cannot accept your offer, but my price is, at the present time, $10,000. * * * Will give you 2 per cent. commission. Awaiting a reply," etc. Defendant denied that he had ever received any letter from the agent, or that the latter had any authority to sell. The agent testified that it was agreed between defendant's attorney and himself that he should sell for $9,000, and that, if he had an offer for less, he should report it. The attorney testified that the understanding was that all offers should be communicated to defendant, and that, if defendant then determined to sell, he would advise the agent. The agent, having obtained an offer, wired defendant, "Can we sell" one lot for $3,000? to which the defendant replied: "I will take $3,000. * * * If you have sale for same, answer us soon as possible." *Held*, that the authority of the agent did not extend to making a sale, but only to finding a purchaser, and specific performance, therefore, would not be enforced. FAUNTLEROY, J., dissenting.

Suit by Simmons against F. C. Kramer for specific performance. There was a decree for defendant, and plaintiff appeals. Affirmed.

W. R. Staples and *Scott & Dupuy,* for appellant. *Phlegar & Johnson, Griffin & Watts,* and *Mr. Miller,* for appellee.

LEWIS, P. This was a suit in the hustings court of Roanoke city for the specific performance of an alleged contract for the sale of real estate. The bill which was filed by Simmons (the appellee here) alleges that on the 6th of October, 1888, the defendant, Kramer, through his authorized agents, R. H. Gray & Co., sold the three lots in question to the plaintiff for $10,000, on the terms of one-third cash, the balance on a credit of one and two years, payable in equal installments, as evidenced by a written contract of that date, signed by R. H. Gray & Co., a copy of which is exhibited with the bill. The defendant answered, denying that he had contracted to sell the property, or that he had authorized the firm of R. H. Gray & Co., or any one else, to do so for him. Depositions were taken, and when the cause came on to be heard the bill was dismissed by the decree complained of.

We are of opinion that there is no error in the decree. It is an established principle that, in cases like the present, to entitle the plaintiff to a decree for specific performance, the proof to establish the agency must be clear, certain, and specific. A bare preponderance of the evidence, it has been held, is not sufficient; but the proof must be so clear and distinct that a fair and candid person can see, without hesitation, that the alleged authority was given. This principle was recognized in the recent case of Blair v. Sheridan, 86 Va. 527, 10 S. E. Rep. 414, in which case Judge HINTON, speaking for the court, observed that, for the plaintiff to prevail in a case like the present, he must "show by evidence which is clear, competent, direct, and satisfactory, both the terms of the contract and the authority of the agent, or a ratification by the principal." And in the same case it was also said that, where an agent acts under a special or express authority, whether written or verbal, the party dealing with him is bound to know, at his peril, what the power of the agent is, and understand its legal effect, and that, if the agent exceeds the boundary of his power, the act, as it concerns the principal, is void. See, also, Davis v. Gordon, (Va.) 13 S. E. Rep. 35. In the present case the alleged authority of R. H. Gray & Co. was sought to be shown by the deposition of R. H. Gray and certain correspondence between the parties, which is filed with the record. In his deposition Gray testifies that his firm, who are real-estate agents at Roanoke, was authorized to sell the lots in question, a short while before the alleged sale, by W. A. Kramer, the son and accredited agent and attorney of the defendant, F. C. Kramer, (the latter being a resident of Carlisle, Pa.,) and that the authority thus given was afterwards ratified by the defendant. But this is distinctly denied by the Kramers in their depositions, and the documentary evidence relied on does not, in our opinion, when added to Gray's evidence, overcome the force of their denials. The writing relied on in the bill to establish the agency to sell is the following letter from the defendant to R. H. Gray & Co., viz.: "Carlisle, Pa., Oct. 3d, '88. R. H. Gray & Co., Roanoke, Va.—Gents: Yours received, and I cannot accept your offer, but my price is, at the present time, ten thousand dollars for my lots on Salem avenue; one-third cash, balance one and two years, 6 per cent., secured by deed of trust on the ground. Will give you 2 per cent. commission. Awaiting a reply, respectfully yours, F. C. KRAMER." Gray testifies that this letter was an answer to a letter previously addressed to the defendant by his firm, asking for authority to sell the lots in question; but the defendant denies having received any such letter. It is obviously, however, an answer to a communication of some sort, as it begins with the words, "Yours received." But, be that as it may, it cannot, by any fair interpretation, be construed as an authority to sell. At all events, rejecting a proposition, and mentioning the price at which the defendant held the property, is not the clear and satisfactory evidence of such an agency which the rule above mentioned requires. And the same may be said of the words, "I will pay you 2 per cent. commission," which may have been as appropriately addressed to a broker as to an agent to sell. Nor do we perceive that the words, "Awaiting a reply," have any special significance as tending to support the theory of the appellant. On the contrary, if they have any significance at all, they rather indicate that the letter was intended as a proposition, to which a reply was expected, than as conferring authority to sell. In Grant v. Ede, 85 Cal. 418, 24 Pac. Rep. 890, a letter to an agent, saying, "You stated you could get $30,000 for the place you occupy, and, if you can, we will sell at that price, and allow you 2¼ per cent. on said price," was held to authorize such agent to find a purchaser, but not to sell, and that a contract by such agent to sell conferred no rights on the purchaser as against the principal. "The expression, 'I will sell,' or its equivalent, accompanied by a specification of terms, does not confer any authority on an agent to make a contract of sale; neither does a correspondence between the owner and the agent, concerning the property, price, and terms of sale, confer any such authority." 1 Warv. Vend. 212; Bosseau v. O'Brien, 4 Biss. 395. Gray, in his deposition, says that it was agreed between young Kramer and himself that he (Gray) should sell for $9,000 cash, and that, if he had an offer for less, to report it. But Kramer testifies that the understanding was that any offer for the property should be telegraphed to his father by Gray, and that, if his father then determined to sell, he would telegraph him (Gray) to sell; and this version of the matter seems probable, for afterwards, to-wit, on the 21st of September, 1888, Gray & Co. telegraphed the defendant as follows: "Can we sell one lot, Salem avenue, to Campbell, three thousand dollars, third cash, balance one and two years? Answer." To which the defendant replied: "I will take $3,000, spot cash, for one lot on Salem avenue,—No. 91,—clear of all expenses. If you have sale for same, answer as soon as possible." It is contended that this conferred authority to sell. But it was, in fact, nothing more than giving the price at which the owner was willing to sell, and asking to be informed whether a purchaser could be found at that price. The question is, "Can we sell?" and the answer is, "I will take," etc., which is very different, as we have seen, from conferring an authority to make a contract of sale. In other words, it gave authority to R. H. Gray & Co. to act as agents in finding a purchaser, with a reservation of the power, on the part of the defendant, to make the contract of sale, in the event an acceptable offer should be reported. In short, we are of opinion, without going more fully into the case, that the appellant has not made out such a case as entitles him to the relief prayed for in the bill, and that the decree must be affirmed.

FAUNTLEROY, J., dissenting.

SMITH v. GEORGIA RAILROAD & BANKING CO.

(*Supreme Court of Georgia.* Nov. 28, 1891.)

NEGLIGENCE — INJURY TO EMPLOYE — PLEADING — AMENDMENT.

1. A declaration, filed by a track hand of a railroad company, alleging that plaintiff was injured by a fall of earth, caused by the negligence of the company, its agents and servants, is amendable by setting out the particulars constituting the alleged negligence, and also by averring that plaintiff himself was without fault. Ellison v. Railroad, etc., Co., 13 S. E. Rep. 809, 87 Ga. 691, (decided this term.)

2. The declaration, as amended, sets out a cause of action, although it does not distinctly allege that plaintiff was ignorant of the danger to which he was subjected.

(*Syllabus by the Court.*)

Error to superior court, Rockdale county; HINES, Judge. Reversed.

Action by one Smith against the Georgia Railroad & Banking Company for personal injuries. A demurrer to the complaint was sustained, and a proposed amendment was rejected. Plaintiff brings error.

In substance, the declaration alleged that plaintiff, employed by defendant as a section hand, was required, while loading a construction car with dirt from a grade excavated for a side track, to be near and face a high embankment; that he was under the orders and control of one Robinson, who was superintending the work for defendant; that the embankment, through defendant's negligence, had been excavated and undermined to a depth of several feet, and, becoming cracked on the upper surface from exposure to the weather, broke off, and fell on plaintiff, injuring him. The offered amendment alleged, in substance, that defendant was guilty of gross negligence in excavating the embankment, in that it was undermined 30 feet, and no supports were provided; that Robinson, under whose directions it was undermined, was agent of defendant; that the bank was not excavated in chambers or galleries,—the usual and proper method of doing such work,—but was undermined for a distance of 30 feet, and left exposed to the weather and the jarring of trains passing within a few feet, although defendant was bound to know the unsound condition of the embankment, that on the day after it had been so undermined plaintiff was ordered by Robinson to work near and under it, when it fell, and injured plaintiff; that these were acts of gross negligence on the part of defendant, through which plaintiff, wholly without fault or negligence on his part, was injured; that plaintiff was young and inexperienced, knowing nothing of the manner in which the work should be done, and that he was simply obeying the orders of his superior; and that Robinson, a skilled officer of defendant, was absent, and not attending to his

duties. This amendment was refused. on the ground that, no cause of action having been set forth in the declaration, there was nothing to amend by.

Calvin George and *G. W. Gleaton,* for plaintiff in error. *J. B. Cumming, A. C. McCalla,* and *Bryan Cumming,* for defendant in error.

PER CURIAM. Judgment reversed.

BARNETT v. EAST TENNESSEE, V. & G. RY. CO.

(*Supreme Court of Georgia.* Nov. 28, 1891.)

NEGLIGENCE—INJURY TO PASSENGER—AMENDMENT OF PLEADING—PRACTICE.

1. A declaration alleging that the conductor of a passenger train agreed with plaintiff to stop the train for him to get off at a point where there was no regular station, but at which defendant's road crossed another railroad at grade; that plaintiff paid his fare to this point; and that on reaching the same the train only slowed up, and did not stop, so that plaintiff, "in order to keep from being carried beyond his destination, was compelled to get from the moving train," and in so doing was seriously injured,— does not set forth a cause of action, it appearing from these allegations that plaintiff's injury was caused by his own voluntary act in taking a dangerous risk if the train was moving so rapidly as to make leaving it unsafe; or, if not, that the injury must have resulted from a mere accident, or from plaintiff's own carelessness in getting off.

2. Where an amendment to a declaration is offered, and disallowed by the court, it does not constitute a part of the record; and, in order to have this court review the ruling of the court below in rejecting such offered amendment, it should be set out in the bill of exceptions, or annexed to the same as an exhibit, properly authenticated. Sibley v. Association, 13 S. E. Rep. 838, 87 Ga. 732, (decided this term.)

(*Syllabus by the Court.*)

Error from superior court, Floyd county; MADDOX, Judge. Affirmed.

Action by one Barnett against the East Tennessee, Virginia & Georgia Railway Company for personal injuries. Judgment for defendant. Plaintiff brings error.

Dean & Smith, for plaintiff in error. *A. O. Bacon, Dorsey & Howell,* and *W. T. Turnbull,* for defendant in error.

PER CURIAM. Judgment affirmed.

MARKHAM v. WHITEHURST et al.

(*Supreme Court of North Carolina.* Nov. 24, 1891.)

FRAUDULENT CONVEYANCES—CONTRACT FOR LABOR — CONSIDERATION PAID TO WIFE.

1. Defendant was the inventor of a formula for the manufacture of medicated cigarettes. A company was formed to manufacture them, and, in consideration of his furnishing his services and formula in the business, a number of the shares of the stock were issued to his wife, for which she paid nothing. Defendant was insolvent at the time of the transaction. Held, that such stock was subject to the payment of his debts.

2. Though his creditors could have no lien on his skill in the manufacture of the cigarettes, and he could devote such skill to the support of his wife, yet he could not sell the formula, and agree to manufacture under it, and, by having the stock which he received in payment transferred to his wife, defeat the rights of his creditors. Osborne v. Wilkes, 13 S. E. Rep. 285, 108 N. C. 673, distinguished.

Appeal from superior court, Durham county; EDWIN T. BOYKIN, Judge.

Action by H. H. Markham, receiver, against R. F. Whitehurst and Sarah E. Whitehurst, his wife, to recover certain stock issued to the wife, to defraud creditors of the husband. Defendants' demurrer to the petition was overruled, and judgment entered for plaintiff. Defendants appeal. Affirmed.

Defendant R. F. Whitehurst was the inventor of a formula for the manufacture of medicated cigarettes. A company being formed to manufacture them, he contracted to furnish such formula and his services, in consideration of 98 shares of the company's stock, which were issued to his wife. He was insolvent at the time.

Boone & Parker, for appellants. *W. W. Fuller* and *J. S. Manning*, for appellee.

SHEPHERD, J. It is unquestionably true that the purely mental conception of a judgment debtor cannot be reached by his creditors, and subjected to the payment of his indebtedness. But says Lord ALVANLY, (referring to the proposition that an invention was an idea or scheme in a man's head, which could not be reached by process of law,) "if an inventor avail himself of his knowledge and skill, and thereby acquire a beneficial interest, which may be the subject of assignment, I cannot frame to myself an argument why that interest should not pass in the same manner as any other property acquired by his personal industry." Hesse v. Stevenson, 3 Bos. & P. 565; Walt, Fraud. Conv. § 38. Mr. Walt, in section 24, says "that the manifest tendency of the authorities is to reclaim every species of the debtor's property, prospective or contingent, for the creditor. As has been shown, [the further remarks,] transfers of intangible interests and rights in action, stocks, annuities, life insurance policies, book royalties, patent-rights, property of imprisoned felons, legacies, and choses in action generally, may be reached." See, also, Burton v. Farinholt, 86 N. C. 260, and Worthy v. Brady, 91 N. C. 265. If, therefore, as it appears in the present case, the judgment debtor acquired a right to the stock in controversy in consideration of the formula furnished by him for the manufacture of medicated cigarettes, such a right was a beneficial interest, which was subject to the demands of his creditors; and if he, being insolvent, and without reserving sufficient property to pay his existing indebtedness, caused the said stock to be issued in the name of his wife, (she not being a purchaser for value,) it would seem very clear that the plaintiff would be entitled to the relief prayed for.

It is insisted, however, that the creditor has no lien upon the labor, skill, or attainments of the debtor, and that he may gratuitously devote them to the support of his wife and family. Granting the principle as laid down and qualified in Osborne v. Wilkes, 108 N. C. 673, 13 S. E. Rep. 285, (and further than this we are not prepared to go,) we do not see how it applies to the case before us. The judgment debtor possesses a certain valuable formula, which he sells for so much stock, which stock he procures to be issued in the name of his wife. This, surely, is not merely devoting his personal services and skill for the wife's benefit, but it is the acquisition by him of a thing of value, which is subject to the claims of his creditors. Besides, it does not appear that he was to devote his services to the company except to the extent that he was to carry out the formula and make it valuable. Even if he had agreed to perform future personal services in consideration of the stock then issued, our case would not fall within the principle stated; for a debtor "is not permitted to treasure up a fund accruing from his labor or vocation, whatever it may be, and claim that it shall be protected for the benefit of himself or his family against the demands of creditors. Every agreement or contrivance entered into with such a view—to deprive his creditors of his future earnings, and enable him to retain and use them for his benefit and advantage, or to make a permanent provision for his family—is fraudulent and void." Bump, Fraud. Conv. 270, citing Hamilton v. Zimmerman, 5 Sneed, 39; Tripp v. Childs, 14 Barb. 85; Patterson v. Campbell, 9 Ala. 933; and other decisions. As it is not contended, upon the testimony, that the wife is a purchaser for value, we are of the opinion, for the foregoing reasons, that the plaintiff was entitled to recover, and that the judgment should be affirmed.

SOUTHERN FLOUR CO. v. McIVER *et al.*

(*Supreme Court of North Carolina.* Nov. 24, 1891.)

FRAUDULENT CONVEYANCES — EVIDENCE—CONSIDERATION.

In a creditor's action to set aside an assignment for fraud, a motion was made to have a preferred creditor refund to the assignee, on the ground of fraud, a payment to him as such creditor. Aside from the payment the only evidence in support of the motion was the sworn complaint, which alleged that the payment was fraudulent, that the preferred creditor was insolvent, and a son of one and a brother of the other member of the firm which made the assignment. The members of such firm, the assignee, and the preferred creditor all denied the alleged fraud. The preferred creditor gave evidence as to his solvency, and claimed that the payment was made for an honest debt. *Held,* that the motion was properly denied.

Appeal from superior court, Cumberland county; EDWIN T. BOYKIN, Judge.

Action by the Southern Flour Company against A. McIver & Son, H. L. Cook, and John S. McIver to set aside a payment made by Cook, as assignee, to John S. McIver, as preferred creditor of McIver & Son. Motion was made to have such money paid to the assignee pending a hearing on the merits. Motion denied, and plaintiff appeals. Affirmed.

STATEMENT BY THE COURT. This is a creditor's action. The complaint alleges that the defendants A. McIver & Son, merchants, became insolvent, and on the 20th of May, 1891, fraudulently conveyed their stock of goods and other property to the other defendants, H. L. Cook and John S. McIver, as assignees, ostensibly for the purpose of paying the debts of their numerous creditors; that they classified the latter, preferring some of them over others, and especially the said John S. as to a large debt, which it is alleged was without consideration and fraudulent. It alleges further that the conveyance so made is intended to hinder, delay, and defraud the creditors of said firm; that the said Cook and John S. McIver, assignees, are insolvent, etc. It demands judgment that a receiver be appointed; that the said assignees be restrained by injunction from disbursing any of the assets that have or shall come into their hands pending the action; that the deed of assignment be declared void for fraud; and that the proceeds of the property be distributed to the creditors according to their respective rights, etc. The defendants admit in their several answers the insolvency of the said firm and the execution of the deed, but positively deny, much in detail, all fraud, fraudulent purposes and practices; they deny that the said assignees are insolvent; and the said John S. and the said firm, especially, deny that his preferred debt is fraudulent and that he is insolvent, and he specifies much of his property, etc., and the consideration of his debt, etc. The court granted an injunction pending the action, but refused to appoint a receiver. It, however, directed that one of the said assignees, the said Cook, be charged with all the assets of all kinds conveyed to the said assignees; that he collect the assets and hold the same subject to the order of the court; and that he make report of assets that come into the hands of the said assignees and into his hands, and of disbursements made by them, etc. He made such report, from which, among other things, it appeared that he and the said John S. McIver, on the 27th of May, 1891, paid to the latter his said preferred debt. Thereupon a judge, in vacation, granted a rule upon the said John S. McIver to show cause why he should not refund to the said Cook the said sum of money so received by him. The court heard the motion in that respect at chambers. It found the facts and denied the motion, making record thereof as follows: "The deed of assignment was made on May 20th, 1891. The summons was issued May 28th, 1891, and on that day a restraining order was issued by WHITAKER, J., and served on defendant H. L. Cook on May 29th, 1891, and served on defendant John S. McIver on May 30th, 1891. On May 27th and 28th, 1891, the defendant John S. McIver received of H. L. Cook and John S. McIver, assignees, the sum of $103.31, and, upon a motion to show cause why he, the said John S. McIver, should not refund the said sum to H. L. Cook, who has charge of the fund under order of the court, the defendant comes in and filed the following answer, to-wit: 'John S. McIver, in answer to the order to show cause why he should not be required to pay over to H. L. Cook, assignee, the amount paid him on his debt, preferred in the deed of assignment, says that the amount of $103.31 was actually applied by said John S. McIver and H. L. Cook, assignees of A. McIver & Son, under the deed of assignment under which they

were acting, to the preferred debt of $1,000, before the service of the summons or restraining order herein, and before they had any notice of the same, or of an intention to bring suit; that said money was honestly and *bona fide* applied to said preferred debt in good faith, according to the direction and terms of said deed of assignment, and at the time before said suit or service of summons or restraining order the said money had been paid to said John S. McIver on his said debt; that he had no funds in his hands, as assignee, at the time of service of summons and restraining order, except what is accounted for in the report of H. L. Cook, assignee, and he has none now in his hands as assignee, nor since his removal. Affiant prays the court to grant an order dismissing the motion, and for such other and further relief as he may be entitled to.' Upon the hearing, the court denied the motion to require John S. McIver to refund the money to H. L. Cook, and the plaintiffs appealed from the judgment rendered."

Armistead Jones and *John W. Hinsdale,* for appellant. *Thos. H. Sutton* and *W. E. Murchison,* for appellees.

MERRIMON, C. J. If it be granted that the court had authority upon motion in the course of the action to grant relief in cases sufficiently proven, such as that invoked by the motion now under review, we think the court properly denied the motion. Apart fom the payment of the preferred debt of John S. McIver, one of the assignees, shortly before this action began, the only evidence to support the motion was the sworn complaint used as an affidavit. The allegation of fraud as to that debt was very general; the principal facts stated as evidence of it were that he was insolvent, and son of one and the brother of the other member of the firm which made the deed of assignment. But he and his co-defendants of the firm positively deny the alleged fraud, and aver the perfect honesty of the debt, stating the consideration thereof, and that a substantial part of it was money advanced to the firm to aid it in the prosecution of its business. He also denies that he was or is insolvent. He avers his solvency, and states facts much in detail as to his property, going to show that he is solvent. He further swears that the payment of the debt was made before this action began, in good faith, and that he had no notice of the action or a purpose to bring it; that such payment was made fairly, and with no fraudulent or dishonest intent. All the defendants positively deny all fraud and fraudulent intent, and give in evidence facts and circumstances tending more or less to sustain their denial as true. There is some evidence of bad faith and fraudulent purpose, but all this is strenuously denied by the defendants, and they give evidence of facts and circumstances that tend strongly to show good faith, and a purpose on the part of John S. McIver to avail himself of an advantage that he might not dishonestly take. The evidence preponderates, as we see it, in favor of the appellee. The plaintiffs are not entitled to the relief demanded by the motion, unless it appears with reasonable certainty that the transaction and acts complained of are fraudulent, and that they will suffer injustice and loss if relief shall not be granted pending the action until the hearing upon the merits. The evidence of the plaintiffs for the present purpose, in view of that of the defendants, is not satisfactory, or sufficient to entitle them to have their motion allowed. It appears strongly that John S. McIver is not insolvent, and they will have their remedy against him when the case shall be disposed of on the whole merits. If it turns out that he and others have perpetrated the alleged fraud, as he may have done, he will be amenable in this action. There is no error. Let this be certified to the superior court according to law. It is so ordered.

WALKER v. ADAMS.

(Supreme Court of North Carolina. Nov. 24, 1891.)

MARRIAGE LICENSE—EXAMINATION OF APPLICANT.

Where the register of deeds administers to the person applying for a marriage license an oath as to the legal capacity of the parties, in accordance with Acts N. C. 1887, c. 331, and the evidence is such as to render it probable there is no legal impediment, it is a sufficient compliance with Code N. C. § 1816, declaring it the duty of such officer to make reasonable inquiry as to whether there is any legal impediment to the proposed marriage, and the register is not liable for the statutory penalty.

Appeal from superior court, Wilkes county; JOHN G. BYNUM, Judge.

Action by J. F. Walker against J. M. Adams to recover a statutory penalty. Judgment for defendant. Plaintiff appeals. Affirmed.

STATEMENT BY THE COURT. This action was brought in the court of a justice of the peace to recover the penalty of $200, prescribed by Code, § 1816, which it is alleged the defendant incurred, in that, on the 9th of December, 1890, he, as register of deeds of the county of Wilkes, issued a license for the marriage of the male and female persons named in the pleadings, the female being a daughter of the plaintiff, residing with him, and at that time under the age of 15 years, without a written consent of the father, as required by Code, § 1814. In that court there was judgment for the defendant, and the plaintiff appealed to the superior court. In the latter court the parties agreed upon and submitted the material facts of the case to the court for its judgment. Thereupon there was judgment for the defendant, and the plaintiff excepted, and appealed to this court. It appeared that, when the said male person applied for the license, the defendant said to him: "Judging from your appearance, I take you to be of age; but I do not know the female whom you propose to marry." The latter said, "She is about 19 years old." The defendant said, "Will you make affidavit of that fact?" and he replied he would. The defendant administered an oath to the said person, and he testified by his affidavit that the persons for whom the license

was intended (he being the male) were of the lawful age to marry, and that he believed there was no legal cause or impediment in the way of their marriage. The affidavit was attached to the license. The defendant knew the male person so applying. He did not know his character, but had heard nothing against him.

A. E. Holton and *J. C. L. Harris,* for appellee.

MERRIMON, C. J. The statute (Code, § 1816) makes it the imperative duty of the register of deeds to make reasonable inquiry, before he issues a license for the marriage of any two persons, as to whether there is any legal impediment in the way of the proposed marriage, and whether either of the parties to be married is under the age of 18 years, and has not the consent in writing of the father or other person having the lawful care and control of such person, as prescribed by the statute, (Code, § 1814,) that such marriage may be had. If he issues license without such inquiry, and such impediment exists, he thereby incurs the penalty of $200 in favor of any person who shall sue for the same. This statute has been repeatedly interpreted by this court in varying aspects of it. Bowles v. Cochran, 93 N. C. 398; Williams v. Hodges, 101 N. C. 300, 7 S. E. Rep. 786; Maggett v. Roberts, 108 N. C. 174, 12 S. E. Rep. 890. In this case the male person proposing to be married applied to the defendant register of deeds for the marriage license. The defendant knew him, and, while he did not know his character, he knew nothing against him. He asked him as to the age of the female, and was assured that she was about 19 years of age. He was properly not content to accept the verbal statement of the person so applying, but he required him to make affidavit of the fact, and he did so, so far as the defendant could see, in good faith. He had no reason—none appears or is suggested—to believe the contrary. The statute (Acts 1887, c. 331) allows the register of deeds, when it shall appear to him that it is probable there is any legal impediment to the proposed marriage, to administer an oath to the person applying for the license as to the legal capacity of the parties to contract a marriage. The purpose of this statute is to facilitate and help the reasonable inquiry to be made by the register, and such inquiry is reasonable when the evidence before the register is such as renders it probable there is no legal impediment. Nothing to the contrary appearing, surely the affidavit of a party, known to the register, applying for a license, that there was no such impediment, and that the female to be married was above the age of 18 years, made it probable in the mind of the defendant that no legal objection to the marriage existed. If there had been other evidence and facts and circumstances tending to put the register on further inquiry, it might have been otherwise. But there was no such evidence, and, so far as appears, the defendant was cautious, and acted in good faith. The inquiry was reasonable, in contemplation of the statute, and the defendant, therefore, did not incur the penalty. See cases cited supra. Judgment affirmed.

PASS v. PASS et ux.

(Supreme Court of North Carolina. Nov. 24, 1891.)

COUNTER-CLAIM—INDEPENDENT TRANSACTION—NONSUIT.

In North Carolina where defendant, in an action to recover a debt and to foreclose a mortgage securing it, alleges, by way of counter-claim, that there is due him a sum of money placed in trust for him in plaintiff's hands, it is not a counter-claim growing out of and involving plaintiff's cause of action, and plaintiff may take a nonsuit.

Appeal from superior court, Surry county; JOHN G. BYNUM, Judge.

Action by E. H. Pass against John W. Pass and wife to foreclose a mortgage. At the proper time plaintiff asked to be allowed to take a nonsuit. Denied. Plaintiff appeals. Reversed.

STATEMENT BY THE COURT. The plaintiff brought this action to recover the debt and foreclose the mortgage of land to secure it, specified in the complaint. The answer denies the material allegations of the complaint, and among other things alleges "that said note and mortgage, referred to in the complaint, was a fraudulent arrangement entered into between plaintiff and defendant for the purpose and with the intent to hinder, delay, and defraud the creditors of this defendant at the request of plaintiff, and through the advice and counsel of plaintiff in this action, he being an older brother of defendant, and defendant relying upon his advice and counsel." It further alleges a counter-claim, which it is conceded may be litigated in this action, but it is not material here. The answer demands judgment that the said note be surrendered to the defendant, and that the mortgage be canceled, etc. The plaintiff asked at the proper time to be allowed to "take a nonsuit" as to his alleged cause of action, but the court denied his motion, and made an order, of which the following is a copy: "This cause coming on to be heard upon complaint, answer, and replication, and the plaintiff's motion for nonsuit, and it appearing that the defendants have set up an equitable defense to the plaintiff's cause of action, to-wit, that the bond and deed declared on by plaintiff were fraudulent, and insist upon the issue being tried by a jury, it is adjudged that plaintiff's motion be denied, and the cause stand for trial upon the issues raised by defendants' answer." Plaintiff excepted, and appealed to this court.

Watson & Buxton, for appellant. *T. C. Phillips* and *A. E. Holton,* for appellees.

MERRIMON, C. J. Very certainly the plaintiff had the right to dismiss as to his cause of action, and, in effect, become nonsuit under the present method of civil procedure, unless the defendant pleaded by his answer a counter-claim arising out of and involving the plaintiff's alleged cause of action. This is so whether the cause of action be legal or equitable, or both legal and equitable, and, for

---

the like reasons, that need not be here restated. Whedbee v. Leggett, 92 N. C. 469; Bank v. Stewart, 93 N. C. 402; McNeill v. Lawton, 97 N. C. 16, 1 S. E. Rep. 493; Bynum v. Powe, 97 N. C. 374, 2 S. E. Rep. 170; Gatewood v. Leak, 99 N. C. 363, 6 S. E. Rep. 706; Manufacturing Co. v. Buxton, 105 N. C. 74, 11 S. E. Rep. 264. Then did the defendant allege a counter-claim growing out of and involving the plaintiff's cause of action? We think not. He alleges, in general terms and effect, that the plaintiff's cause of action, the note and mortgage, was a fraudulent transaction suggested by the plaintiff, and participated in by the plaintiff and himself for the purpose of hindering, delaying, and defrauding the defendant's creditors. In such case the court will not help either of the parties. The cause of action is thoroughly tainted with fraud, and both parties are *particeps criminis.* The plaintiff alleges no honest cause of action, and the defendant has no counter-claim, in any aspect of the matter, that the court will take notice of and enforce. The parties are *in pari delicto.* Hence there is no reason why the plaintiff may not abandon his action, and go out of court. It seems that the defendant may have intended to allege the fraud of the plaintiff, and that he did not intentionally share therein; that the plaintiff was intelligent, and he was ignorant; that he hence confided in his brother, who misled, entrapped, deceived, and defrauded the defendant for his own gain and advantage; but clearly he did not so allege, in terms or effect. If he might have alleged a possible case in which the court could and would have granted relief to him, he might have asked leave to amend his answer, but he did not do so. Hence the plaintiff was entitled to have his motion allowed. There is error. The order appealed from must be reversed, and the motion of plaintiff allowed, unless the court shall, for cause satisfactory to it, allow the defendant to amend his answer. To that end let this opinion be certified to the superior court. It is so ordered.

JESTER et al. v. DAVIS et al.

(Supreme Court of North Carolina. Dec. 1, 1891.)

ADVERSE POSSESSION—TENANTS IN COMMON.

1. A tenant in common under a trustee cannot acquire title against his co-tenants by adverse possession for less than 20 years. Page v. Branch, 97 N. C. 97, 1 S. E. Rep. 625, followed.

2. A *cestui que trust* in possession under the trustee cannot, by adverse possession under a deed from the same grantor subsequent to the trust, acquire title against his trustee or his co-tenants.

Appeal from superior court, Yadkin county; W A. HOKE, Judge.

Special proceeding to try title by R. F. Jester against J. W. Davis and others. From a judgment for plaintiff, J. W. Davis appeals. Affirmed.

STATEMENT BY THE COURT. The defendant J. W. Davis answered and set up sole seisin. The plaintiffs introduced a deed from Josiah Davis to Stephen Davis, as trustee. Also deed marked "Exhibit B," for the sole purpose of estopping J. W. Davis. Defendant J. W. Davis introduced a deed from Josiah Davis to J. W. Davis. It was admitted that these deeds covered the *locus in quo*. Plaintiffs introduced A. J. McCollum, who testified that the plaintiffs and defendants are the children and grandchildren of Josiah Davis and Louisa Davis, and the children referred to in the first deed. That there were nine children, all of age, and living at the death of their mother,—four sons and five daughters. That three of the daughters were married before the death of their mother, and that T. J. McCollum lived on the lands about one year after the death of their mother, when they married and left. While they were there J. W. Davis supported them. That Josiah Davis died about two years ago, and his wife Louisa Davis died about twelve or thirteen years ago. That she lived with J. W. Davis on the lands after the deed from Josiah Davis to J. W. Davis was made, and up to the time of her death. That J. W. Davis supported her. On cross-examination witness stated that J. W. Davis had been in possession of the lands, cultivating them, since the death of Louisa Davis, "the mother." There was a dispute about it between him and the other children. They were claiming it, and he was holding it under his deed. That J. W. Davis has been on lands since the death of Louisa Davis, twelve or thirteen years ago; has cleared and fenced it. He has had exclusive possession since the date of the deed marked "Exhibit B." That J. F. Davis died about one year ago, and that his children are minors. Plaintiff rested. Defendant J. W. Davis claims under the deed marked "B," and contends that the claim of the plaintiffs and other defendants is barred by seven years' adverse possession. The court ruled that from the testimony the plaintiffs and defendants were tenants in common, and so instructed the jury. Judgment accordingly. Defendant J. W. Davis excepted and appealed.

A. E. Halton, for appellants. *T. C. Phillips*, for appellees.

SHEPHERD, J. We concur with his honor in his ruling that, taking the whole testimony, the defendant J. W. Davis had not sustained his plea of sole seisin of the land in controversy. In 1874 Josiah Davis conveyed the land to his brother Stephen in trust for the use and support of his wife and children, and after the death of the wife it was to be equally divided among them. The appellant, being one of the children, was an equitable tenant in common with his brothers and sisters, and although he was in possession, and took a deed to himself from the same grantor in 1877, charged with different trusts, and conceding that he was not estopped to claim under such deed, still his possession, being less than 20 years, would not have the effect of barring his co-tenants. However uncertain the decisions may have been upon this point, it may now be considered as settled. Page v. Branch, 97 N. C. 97, 1 S. E. Rep. 625; Gilchrist v. Middleton, 107 N. C. 663, 12 S. E. Rep. 85, and the cases cited. It is urged that the trustee is barred, and therefore the estate of the

plaintiffs must share the same fate. The defendant is presumed to have entered under the deed of 1874 as an equitable tenant in common. This being so, his possession was the possession of the trustee, and "there could be no adverse claim or possession during the continuance of the relation;" (2 Perry, Trusts, 863,) for a *cestui que trust* in actual possession is the tenant at will of the trustee, and the statute of limitation does not apply. (Wood, Lim. Act. 203; 2 Lewin, Trusts, 881; 2 Perry, Trusts, 863.) Holding as he does under the trustee, he cannot destroy that relation by setting up an adverse possession under a subsequent deed from the same grantor, and, even if he could do so, his disclaiming conduct must be of the same character as would create an adverse possession against a co-tenant in common. Busw. Lim. § 342. There is no error.

GORE v. LEWIS et ux.

(Supreme Court of North Carolina. Dec. 1, 1891.)

USURY AS A DEFENSE—CUSTOM.

1. Where plaintiff, in an action to foreclose a mortgage, seeks to recover usurious interest, and defendant alleges the usury as defense, he is entitled to the relief allowed by Code N. C. § 3836, which provides that the charging of usury shall be deemed a forfeiture of the whole interest, and the equitable rule that a mortgagor seeking relief should pay the sum owed, with legal interest, does not apply.

2. In North Carolina a local custom of merchants, warranting the taking of interest greater than that allowed by statute, cannot supersede or modify the statute.

Appeal from superior court, Columbus county; R. F. ARMFIELD, Judge. Reversed.

Action by D. L. Gore against R. B. Lewis and wife to foreclose a mortgage. From the judgment of the court below both parties appeal.

S. C. Weill, for plaintiff. *W. G. Burkehead* and *D. G. Lewis*, for defendants.

MERRIMON, C. J. The plaintiff brought this action to recover the money due upon two promissory notes executed by him by the defendants,—one for $250, due March 1, 1887; the other for $500, due March 1, 1888,—both bearing interest at the rate of 8 per centum per annum, and to foreclose a mortgage of the defendants' real and personal estate made to secure these notes. The defendants admit the execution of the notes and mortgage, but they allege that they are founded upon a usurious consideration, and hence the plaintiff has forfeited the entire interest which the notes carry with them. This is not a case where the debtor comes into the court asking equitable relief against the usurious debt or transaction of the defendants. The fact that the plaintiff asked the court for a decree of foreclosure did not deprive the defendants of their legal statutory defense. In such case, the plaintiff would be required to pay the honest debt and the lawful rate of interest, upon the just maxim that he who asks equity must do equity. Purnell v. Vaughan, 82 N. C. 134; Manning v. Elliott, 92 N. C. 48. But in cases like the present the strict rule of law applies. The creditor seeks to recover and enforce payment of his usurious debt, and the defendants, alleging the usury as matter of defense, are entitled to have the full measure of it as allowed by the statute, (Code, § 3836,) which provides that "the taking, receiving, reserving, or charging a rate of interest greater than is allowed by the preceding section, [that fixing the rate of interest,] when knowingly done, shall be deemed a forfeiture of the entire interest which the note or other evidence of debt carries with it, or which has been agreed to be paid thereon." And such defense may be alleged and proven in this and like actions to recover judgment upon the mortgage debt and foreclose the mortgage by a sale of the property. Arrington v. Jenkins, 95 N. C. 462; Grant v. Morris, 81 N. C. 150. The case, as it comes to us, is not very intelligible. The exceptions of the plaintiff and defendants to the report and amended report of the referee are confused. It seems that the facts found prove the alleged usury, but it likewise appears that the court allowed the plaintiff interest at the ordinary rate upon the principal of his debt, upon the ground, it seems, that the plaintiff was entitled to interest upon his debt purged of the usury. This is error. If usury is not proven, then the plaintiff is entitled to interest at the rate of 8 per centum per annum, as that rate is stipulated for in the notes. If the defense of usury shall be proven, then the plaintiff will forfeit the interest under the statute. It seems that the plaintiff insisted that a custom of merchants in the city of Wilmington, where he resides and does business as a merchant, warranted the taking of interest in a way that was greater than that allowed by the statute and stipulated for in the notes. This contention is without foundation. Such custom, whatever it may be, cannot supersede or modify the statute. It is possible that such custom might, in some possible view of the case, go to show that he did not in fact "knowingly" take, receive, or charge an unlawful rate of interest. As we see the reports of the referee and the exceptions thereto, they are not satisfactory; and we deem it proper, with a view to justice, to overrule and disregard the exceptions of the parties, and direct the court below to set the judgment aside, and recommit the report to the referee, with instructions to make inquiry and report as to the alleged usury, and restate the account in accordance with this opinion. Grant v. Bell, 90 N. C. 558; Burke v. Turner, 89 N. C. 246; McCampbell v. McClung, 75 N. C. 393. Both the plaintiff and defendants appealed, and what we have said applies to and disposes of both appeals. To the end that further action may be taken in the court below in accordance with this opinion, let the same be certified to that court. It is so ordered.

McLean v. Breece et al.

(Supreme Court of North Carolina. Dec. 1, 1891.)

Lunatic—Sale of Property for Debts.

1. In North Carolina, in an action to settle the account of the guardian of a lunatic, the facts as to each item must be shown, and it must appear that all expenditures were legal.

2. Under Code N. C. § 1401, providing that "vouchers are presumptive evidence of disbursement" by a guardian, such vouchers must state with reasonable particularity their purpose, on what account they were made, and the time when made, so that it may appear that the expenditure was proper.

3. Only so much of the property of a lunatic as exceeds the amount necessary for the support of his family will be sold by order of court.

Appeal from superior court, Cumberland county; James C. MacRae, Judge.

Action by John P. McLean, guardian, against Mrs. James Breece and others, to compel a settlement of plaintiff's accounts. Judgment for plaintiff. Defendants appeal. Reversed.

C. W. Broadfoot and John W. Hinsdale, for appellants. W. A. Guthrie, for appellee.

Merrimon, C. J. The late ward of the plaintiff was a lunatic many years next prior to his death in 1886, and this action is brought against his administrator and others, the widow and next of kin, to compel a settlement of the plaintiff's accounts as guardian. The record is imperfect and confused. It appears that a summons was issued and served, but neither the complaint nor answer appears, and the order of reference is scarcely discernible. The report of the referee is not satisfactory. The findings of fact in respect to several disbursements of money are imperfect, and it is impossible to see whether or not several items of the account should or should not have been allowed. The grounds of exception are that certain of the expenditures and disbursements were not for the benefit of the ward's wife and infant child, were not necessary for their support, and were not authorized by law. Evidence should have been required, and the facts found as to each item of the account questioned, and particularly, for the present purpose, as to the nature, purpose, and application of the expenditures and disbursements in question. The facts going to show that they were or were not proper ones should be found, and it should appear that all expenditures and disbursements were such as the law allowed. It was not sufficient, for example, that the plaintiff produced sundry vouchers for expenses incurred in going to and from the asylum to see the ward. It should have appeared, when these vouchers were questioned, that such visits were necessary, and the expenses reasonable. And so of other items of the account. It is true, as insisted for the plaintiff, that the statute (Code, § 1401[1]) makes vouchers presumptive evidence of disbursements, actually made, but not of their nature and purpose, and the necessity for them, when the same are not expressed in them. To make such vouchers presumptive evidence, they should state with reasonable particularity the purpose of them,—on what particular account they were made, the time made, etc.,—so as to make it appear by them that the expenditure or disbursement was a proper one. The property of the lunatic in the hands of the guardian

[1] Relating to executors, guardians, etc.

is *in custodia legis*, and all sales of such property to pay debts of the ward due or owing by him at the time he became a lunatic should he made by the guardian, with the sanction of the court, obtained as by the statute prescribed. Adams v. Thomas, 81 N. C. 296; Adams v. Thomas, 83 N. C. 521. The law intends that the debts of the lunatic shall be paid, if he has property sufficient for the purpose, after retaining a sufficient part thereof for the reasonable support of his wife and infant children. Property for the latter purpose ought not to be sold, and will not be, with the sanction of the court. But, where the lunatic has a surplus beyond that amount, property will be sold by order of the court, and assets so arising may be applied to the payment of the lunatic's debts by the guardian. And so, when the latter has money that came into his hands not so needed for the support of the lunatic and his family, he may in good faith pay debts of the ward; but he should be sure that the debts are justly due, and such as ought to be paid, otherwise he will not be allowed credit in his account for disbursements on such account. The guardian must be held to a strict and just account as to the property of his ward, and if, by his neglect or failure to observe the requirements of the statute in caring for and making sale of the same, the estate of the lunatic shall sustain damage, he will be required to account therefor in all proper ways and connections. When, however, he in good faith pays debts that ought to be paid, and by so doing the ward's estate suffers no prejudice, he will be allowed credit for disbursements of assets in his hands in such respect. The guardian always fails to observe statutory requirements affecting him, at his peril. It is his duty to observe statutory regulations, and in all things, in good faith, to have in view the good and just advantage of his ward. Several of the exceptions were properly abandoned in this court. We think that those must be sustained as to vouchers numbered, respectively, in the account stated by the referee as 2, 5, 6, 7, 10, 11, 12, 13, 14, 15, 16, 17, and as to the designated, "Sundry trips to Raleigh on account of ward." As to the vouchers thus designated, the referee must be required to inquire more particularly as to the nature and purpose of and the necessity for the expenditures and disbursements embraced by them, to the end the court may see and determine that they were substantially such as the law allowed to be made. To the end that such further inquiry may be made, and the judgment modified thereupon, if need be, let this opinion be certified to the superior court. It is so ordered.

BLACKBURN v. FAIR.

(Supreme Court of North Carolina. Dec. 1, 1891.)

APPEAL—OBJECTION NOT RAISED BELOW—INSTRUCTIONS.

Error cannot be predicated on the failure of the trial court to give instructions which were first suggested on a motion for a new trial.

Appeal from superior court, Stokes county; JESSE F. GRAVES, Judge. Affirmed.

Action by J. J. Blackburn against A. J. Fair for damages arising from the sale of an unsound horse. Judgment for plaintiff. Defendant appeals.

J. T. Morehead, for appellant. *Watson & Buxton*, for appellee.

MERRIMON, C. J. There was no exception to evidence received or to that excluded on the trial in this case; nor were there any objections to the instructions the court gave the jury. After verdict, on the motion for a new trial, the defendant, in support of his motion, contended that it should have given the jury certain instructions his counsel for the first time then suggested. The motion was denied. The court having given the jury appropriate instructions, as it appears it did without objection, if the defendant desired that it should give fuller or special instructions, he should have stated the same in apt time, and requested the court to give them. It was too late after verdict to complain that instructions that the court might have given were not given. Davis v. Council, 92 N. C. 725; Branton v. O'Briant, 93 N. C. 99; State v. Debnam, 98 N. C. 712, 3 S. E. Rep. 742; State v. Bailey, 100 N. C. 528, 6 S. E Rep. 872. Judgment affirmed.

ORRENDER v. CHAFFIN et al.

(Supreme Court of North Carolina. Dec. 1, 1891.)

TRIAL—DIRECTING VERDICT.

Where plaintiff, in an action for the possession of land, offers in evidence an administrator's deed of the land, which, on account of the inadequacy of consideration, is asserted by defendants to be fraudulent, it is error for the court to take the issue from the jury, and direct what their finding shall be, since inadequacy of price is but a badge of fraud, to be considered by the jury with other suspicious circumstances.

Appeals from superior court. Davie county; JOHN G. BYNUM, Judge. Reversed.

Action by W. C. Orrender against M. R. Chaffin and others to recover land. Judgment for defendants. Both parties appeal.

The other facts of the case appear in the following statement by AVERY, J.:

The plaintiff brought an action for possession of land, and offered the deed of an administrator *c. t. a.* to the land in controversy, made by virtue of a power contained in the will of David Call, executed in 1838, which power is construed in the case of Orrender v. Call, 101 N. C. 399, 7 S. E. Rep. 878, together with the will of David Call. The defendants claim through conveyances from the heirs at law of David Call, and set up, as a ground of affirmative relief, that there was a fraudulent combination or collusive arrangement between the plaintiff and the administrator to prevent a fair competition of bidders at the administrator's sale of the land, and that by reason of such collusive combination the plaintiff was enabled to buy at a grossly inadequate price. The defendants ask that the sale be declared fraudulent, and the deed executed in pursuance of it be declared void and canceled. There were many circumstances shown tending to prove such fraudulent combination, but, as the court directed a finding on the issues for the defendant, it is not necessary to give in full any testimony but that of the plaintiff. His wife was a daughter of Berry Call, and a devisee under his will. He testified as follows: "I was here on the day of sale. Chaffin put up the land for sale. Cornatzer stepped up and forbid the sale, and said he had a deed. Taylor did the same. They stopped the sale. Bailey said they were going to sell the land under the will of David Call, Sr., and if any others had any exceptions to come up. The lands were then put up. Several there. I bid ten dollars on the land. No bid against me. Bought the David Call land for five dollars. No other bids. It was knocked off to me. Chaffin did not know I was going to bid. I had no understanding with him." Cross-examined by defendant Cornatzer: "It was a fair sale. I had not been here in a month or two. I reckon I had some time before. I signed Chaffin's administration bond. Got him to administer. Did not talk with counsel about land before sale. I had counsel before sale. Mr. Bailey got him to examine will. He was also counsel for the administrator, Chaffin, and announced the terms of the sale. He said, 'We are going to sell under the will,' and asked, if others had objections, to state it. Chaffin did not say anything that I remember. I paid a low price. Did not pay the money that day. Gave a note at six months. Paid it, and got deed. There are 61 or 62 acres in the Dave Call place. There are 28 acres in the Cornatzer place. There are 225 or 230 acres in the John Taylor place. I did not know that Robertson had any of the land. If I have him sued, I don't know it. I brought suit against those in possession. Knew Taylor was claiming the land when I bought. Did not know Cornatzer was, before sale. Knew Dave Call was. The Dave Call land worth $300 or $400. I sold it for $500. Don't know how long before sale I employed counsel; five or six months. I got Chaffin to administer, and signed his bond. Don't know what commissions Chaffin got. I made no arrangements with him to get his pay." Cross-examined by defendant Chaffin: "Cornatzer never complained to me of the price I paid for the land. I gave bond for the purchase money to Chaffin on the day of sale. Don't know why land didn't bring more, only they forbid the sale, and the title was in dispute." Redirect examination: "I did not get any money for the Dave Call land I sold. I sold on credit. Have not been paid yet." The issues submitted, with the responses returned by direction of the court, were as follows: (1) Is the plaintiff the owner of the land in controversy? No. (2) What damage, if any, has the plaintiff sustained? (3) Was the sale of the administrator invalid, as alleged in the answer? Yes. The plaintiff and the defendant Chaffin both asked instructions. Among the requests by plaintiff was one that the burden was upon the defendant Cornatzer to prove the fraud al-

leged, and also a guilty participation in the fraud on the part of the plaintiff, Orrender. The court declined to give the instruction, and directed the jury to respond to the first issue "No," and to the third issue "Yes." To the refusal of the court to give the instructions asked, and to the ruling in directing the issues to be so found by the jury, the plaintiff excepted; as also did the defendant Chaffin.

Batchelor & Devereux, E. L. Gaither, and T. B. Bailey, for appellant. Watson & Buxton and A. E. Halton, for appellees.

AVERY, J., (*after stating the facts.*) The judge who tried the cause below erred in taking the issues away from the jury, and directing what their findings should be. There is a class of cases in which the court may declare that, in any aspect of the evidence, the party charged was guilty of fraud, and there is often an admitted state of facts which the court may tell the jury raises a presumption of fraud, and, in the absence of testimony tending to rebut the *prima facie* proof, the finding of the jury may be directed by the court. Berry v. Hall, 105 N. C. 163, 10 S. E. Rep. 903; Woodruff v. Bowles, 104 N. C. 197, 10 S. E. Rep. 482; State v. Mitchell, 102 N. C. 368, 9 S. E. Rep. 702; Hardy v. Simpson, 13 Ired. 132; Costen v. McDowell, 107 N. C. 546, 12 S. E. Rep. 432; McLeod v. Bullard, 84 N. C. 515; Lee v. Pearce, 68 N. C. 76. The case at bar does not fall within either of the classifications mentioned, but involves an issue the affirmative of which it is necessary to sustain by testimony satisfactory to the jury. Bobbitt v. Rodwell, 105 N. C. 236, 11 S. E. Rep. 245; Harding v. Long, 103 N. C. 1, 9 S. E. Rep. 445; Lee v. Pearce, supra. In Berry v. Hall, supra, the court say that "the fact that an inadequate price was paid is but a circumstance tending to show fraud, and, at most, is to be considered a badge of fraud that throws suspicion on the transaction, and calls for close scrutiny. * * * Proof of gross inadequacy of price, standing alone as a circumstance, in the absence of actual fraud or undue influence, is insufficient to warrant a decree declaring the conveyance void." See, also, Bump, Fraud. Conv. 76, 77, 87; Bigelow, Frauds, 136; Kerr, Fraud & M. 189; Potter v. Everitt, 7 Ired. Eq. 158; Moore v. Reed, 2 Ired. Eq. 540. In Osborne v. Wilker, 108 N. C. 671, 13 S. E. Rep. 285, this court said: "Inadequacy of price is not of itself in any case sufficient ground for setting aside a conveyance as fraudulent, but is a suspicious circumstance, to be considered in connection with other testimony tending to show fraud in procuring its execution. * * * If additional testimony were offered tending to show a fraudulent combination to prevent a fair competition of bidders on the part of her husband and others, in which she participated or of which she had notice before buying, then the jury would be justified in considering the inadequacy of the price paid for the Capps Mine, in connection with other badges of fraud, and with the fact that she was the wife of the debtor." In that case the sheriff sold under execution the Capps Mine, a tract of land that had once been sold for $13,000, and the wife of the judgment debtor bought it for $5. The judge below was asked to charge that there was a presumption of fraud in the purchase of the property, but, in lieu of the instruction asked, charged the jury that if the sale was *bona fide*, and not made in pursuance of an arrangement between the husband, acting for the wife, and the sheriff, to defraud creditors by getting property for a small price, it was valid, though $13,000 worth of property was bought for $5. If the testimony was not such as to show fraud in law, to be declared by the court, and did not raise a presumption that the land was sold by the administrator, and bought by the plaintiff, in pursuance of a collusive plan concocted by them, at a totally inadequate price, then the small sum paid by the purchaser was but a badge of fraud, to be considered by the jury in connection with other suspicious circumstances in passing upon an issue as to the alleged fraudulent combination between the administrator and the plaintiff to prevent a fair competition of bidders, and to enable the latter to buy the land at the sale at a grossly inadequate price, if such issue was fairly raised by the pleadings. In this case the plaintiff had the right, guarantied to him by the constitution, to demand that the jury should pass upon the issue involving the question of fraud, after appropriate instructions from the court, and to pass upon the weight of the testimony, and determine whether it was sufficient to satisfy them that there was such a fraudulent combination to prevent the property from bringing a higher price, and to enable the plaintiff to buy it far below its real value. Berry v. Hall, supra. If the administrator acted in good faith, or if Orrender did not participate in any wrongful purpose on the part of Chaffin, but bought the land upon his own judgment and upon advice as to title, despite the claim of Cornatzer and his openly forbidding the sale, then the right of Orrender as a *bona fide* purchaser is not impaired or vitiated because the defendant, by his own conduct at the sale, enabled him to get the land at but a nominal price.

Counsel for the plaintiff contended here, (stating that the case was presented in the same way to the court below,) not only that the judge was warranted in declaring that there was fraud and in taking the case out of the hands of the jury, on the ground that the price paid by the purchaser at execution sale was grossly inadequate, but that the testimony, in the aspect most favorable to the plaintiff, was sufficient to raise a presumption, at least, which was not rebutted by the other evidence, that there was a collusive combination between the administrator, Chaffin, and the plaintiff, Orrender, to cause the land to sell, and enable the latter to buy, at a price out of proportion to its true market value. In answer to this view of the subject, we need not look beyond the testimony of Orrender himself, to which counsel referred us. Orrender concluded his testimony with this statement: "Chaffin did not know I was going to bid; I had no understanding with him." If Orrender is

to be believed, there was no combination between the administrator and himself, and he had a right to demand that the jury pass upon his own statement, though the evidence of every other witness had been directly in conflict with it. It is true that there were many circumstances, mentioned by counsel, that could have been collated and presented to the jury, as tending to show that Orrender's statement was not true. The facts that he induced Chaffin to administer, signed his bond, and consulted with his counsel as to the title, and that the administrator advertised to sell in 30 days, refused to postpone the sale, and afterwards invited objections to selling, taken in connection with the very great inadequacy of the price and other circumstances, might have been presented by counsel in the argument as apparently inconsistent with and having a tendency to contradict the plaintiff's statement that he acted in good faith. If the answer distinctly charged a fraudulent combination, or was aided by the answer of Chaffin, so as to cure the defective pleading, an issue should have been submitted involving the question whether there was a fraudulent combination. It would seem now that, whatever defect there may be in the allegation of fraud, the answer is aided in this respect by the denial of collusion by the other party. The question whether Cornatzer forbade the sale, and thereby caused the land to bring a small price, would bear upon the main issue, but would not be decisive of the controversy. If Orrender acted in good faith, and the land sold for a song, simply because of the imprudent and unfortunate course pursued by the purchasers claiming under the heirs at law, the validity of the sale and of the sheriff's deed cannot be successfully assailed. His honor should have submitted an appropriate issue, involving and decisive of the questions whether the purchase was made in good faith, or whether there was a fraudulent combination which prevented the land from bringing a fair price. In his instruction to the jury it was his right, and might have been made by proper requests his duty, to recapitulate to the jury all of the testimony tending to establish or to disprove the allegation of fraud set up as a ground of affirmative relief.

Counsel did not insist, with apparent confidence, upon the view that the purchasers from the heirs at law took a good title despite the power of sale contained in the will. We will not, therefore, discuss that subject at any considerable length, as the will of David Call, Sr., was construed in the case of Orrender v. Call, 101 N. C. 399, 7 S. E. Rep. 878, and it was held that the administrator had power under the will to convey the land after the death of his widow. It was also held in that case that no alienation of a devisee operated to defeat the power of sale, and that the possession of the alienee under such deed was not adverse. It will be possible, if any mistake has been made as to the number of devisees under the will, to correct it when another judgment shall be entered. It was proper to make the administrator, Chaffin, a party defendant, as it was necessary to have him before the court before the demand for affirmative relief could be heard and granted. For the error of the court in directing the responses of the jury to the issues a new trial must be awarded to the plaintiff.

The defendant appeals from the ruling of the court directing the issues to be found in his favor, and for the refusal to give instructions prayed for. Under the circumstances, it is too plain for argument that there is no error in the ruling of the court of which the defendant Cornatzer could justly complain. There was no error assigned except that mentioned, which seems to have been the common ground of exception by both parties. There was no error.

KRAMER v. BLAIR et al.

(Supreme Court of Appeals of Virginia. Dec. 3, 1891.)

SALE OF LAND—AUTHORITY OF AGENT.

Real-estate agents wrote asking an owner of land for an opportunity to make a sale for him, and inquiring his terms. The owner replied, at different times, that his "price" for the property was $9,000; that he "would sell" for $10,000; and that he "had concluded to take" $10,000; but nowhere did he expressly authorize them to act as his agents. *Held*, that their authority did not extend to making a sale, but only to transmitting offers for the approval of the owner, and that it was incumbent upon a purchaser to look to their authority.

Bill by Blair and others against F. C. Kramer for the specific performance of a contract for the sale of land. There was a decree for complainants, and defendant appeals. Reversed.

Phlegar & Johnson, Griffin & Watts, and *Thos. W. Miller,* for appellant. *Hansbrough & Hansbrough* and *Penn & Cocke,* for appellees.

LACY, J. This is an appeal from a decree of the hustings court of Roanoke city, rendered at its May term, 1891. The bill was filed by the appellees to have specific performance of an alleged contract in writing for the sale of land against the appellant. The alleged contract set up in the bill was claimed to have been made with certain agents or brokers, doing business in the name and style of Hanckel, Kemp & Co. The said agents or brokers admit the contract, and seek to sustain it as against their alleged principal, (the appellant,) and insist upon their authority to bind their principal. The alleged principal denies the authority to bind him as his agents, and repudiates the contract altogether, and refuses to do any act to ratify the same. The evidence on both sides was taken in the form of depositions, and upon the hearing the said court decreed specific performance against the said appellant. From this decree the case is here on appeal. The questions arising for adjudication on this appeal are—*First,* whether any contract has been made binding upon the alleged principal, (the appellant;) and, in the *second* place, whether this contract, if so duly made, upon competent authority, should be specifically performed by the court. In the

first place, therefore, we will consider how far the said real-estate agents or brokers were clothed with authority to make a contract for the appellant, acting within the scope of their authority as his agents. "What authority had been conferred on the alleged agents by the appellant to make a complete sale of these lots?" is the first question argued by the learned counsel for the appellees. And it is said by the learned counsel for the appellant that "the first question that naturally arises in a case of this character is whether the alleged agents had the authority to make the sale that it is charged was made."

We will first consider this question upon the facts in the record. The whole matter rests in writing and in telegrams, so far as the principal and the agent are concerned. The first letter which passed between them is as follows: "Roanoke, Va., Sept. 19, 1888. F. C. Kramer, Esq., Carlisle, Pa.: Your son gave us your address, and said if we wrote you that we might get a chance to sell some of your property here. You have three lots between market-house and city hotel that we would like to get your figures on and terms,—if cash or part cash; also any other property you may give us. HANCKEL, KEMP & CO." The answer to this was as follows: Yours of Sept. 19th, 1888, to hand. My price is $9,000, cash, clear above commissions and expenses of any kind, for my three lots on Salem avenue, between Jefferson and Neeson streets. F. C. KRAMER." And the next letter is: "Yours to hand. I will sell lots on Salem avenue, running back to Campbell street, separately, $3,500 cash for lot 89; $3,250 cash for lot No. 90; $3,000 for lot No. 91. F. C. KRAMER." On September 26, 1888, Hanckel, Kemp & Co. wrote as follows to Kramer: "Your favor 1st to hand, and since wrote you, but have received no reply. We think if you would price these three lots at $10,000, one-third cash, balance one and two years, notes bearing interest at 6 per cent., one and two years, we can sell the lots, but find very much trouble in getting as much cash as you wish. Our commission on this would be $260. We would be glad if you would run down to our city, as I think it would be to your interest; also advise if you would sell one lot, giving price and terms." On the next day Kramer wrote to Hanckel, Kemp & Co.: "Your letter to hand. I will take for my lots on Salem ave. * * * $10,000, one-half cash," etc. "I have no objection to selling the lots separate." On October 3d he again wrote: "I have concluded to take $10,000 for my lots on Salem avenue; one-third cash, balance one and two years, 6 per cent., secured by deed of trust on the ground. Will give you 2 per cent. commission. Awaiting reply." On October 6th Hanckel, Kemp & Co. wrote: "We have just wired you that we closed sale of your Salem-Avenue lots, which we have done provided you will accept conditions which we think very liberal,"—setting out the terms proposed; and telegraphed. "Salem-Avenue lots sold if you will accept terms as per my letter of this morning;" and wrote same day: "We understand that some other agents have wired you that property was sold by them. We were the first to sell," etc., (this was the sale to Simmons, upon which Kramer was sued, disposed of at this term in suit of Simmons v. Kramer, (Va.) 13 S. E. Rep. 902¢) stated that they had wanted 60 days to raise the cash payment; but that they later in the day had heard from parties who would pay the $3,000 required in cash, (this being because other agents claimed to have sold to Simmons during the day;) adding: "In addition to this, if you will close sale with our parties, we will send you our check for $100, or you can deduct same from our commission;" and telegraphed on the same day: "Sold lots as per your letter. We claim first sale. Disregard my letter of this morning." On the same day other agents still telegraphed to Kramer, (Asbury, Greider & Co.:) "Will you take $11,000, third cash, on two years?" And on the same day Hanckel, Kemp & Co., later in the day, telegraphed: "Do not close for $11,000; might get you $12,000." On October 11th Hockaday & Co. wrote to this appellant that they had made sale of these same lots. The said firm, Hanckel, Kemp & Co., now claim to have made a sale, binding on Kramer, to the appellees; and this suit is brought by the appellees, as already stated, to compel Kramer to specifically perform the contract made for him by his said agents, Hanckel, Kemp & Co.

In the first place, it is clear that if Hanckel, Kemp & Co. have ever been appointed the agents of Kramer to make a sale for him, they have failed to produce any proof of their appointment as such. Kramer had said to them: "I will sell," etc.; "my price is," etc.; and "I have concluded to take." . But he has nowhere authorized them to act as his agents, and they themselves evidently did not claim any such authority at the time. In the letter announcing the alleged sale they say: "In addition to this, if you will close sale with our parties we will send you our check for one hundred dollars." Now, they say they had authority, and did at this date make a binding sale, on which the appellees, Blair, etc., brought their suit. And on the same day, after they had made a valid and binding sale, as they now claim, they telegraphed him: "Do not close for eleven thousand; might get you twelve thousand." How could they do this if they had already sold for $10,000? In addition, it is proved by the deposition of W. A. Kramer that the appellant declined to appoint them, or any other real-estate agents or brokers, his agents to make a binding sale for him. As has been said, Kramer had no dealings directly with the appellees. They claim only through their dealings with Hanckel, Kemp & Co., who were, as they themselves admit, agents with special and limited powers, to find a purchaser, subject to the ratification of Kramer. It was incumbent upon the buyers to look to the authority of the special agent, and they cannot derive any benefit from an unauthorized act of the agent. The record shows that pending the negotiations, and while they were trying to borrow the money to make the cash payment, and offering other terms, the appellees and the agents knew that other persons anxious

to become the purchasers had before that offered the price named.

As was said by Judge PENDLETON in Hooe v. Oxley, 1 Wash. (Va.) 23: "Agents may be clothed either with general or special powers. (1) A general agent may do everything which the principal may; powers of this sort are not usually granted, and none such appear in the present case. (2) Of the second sort are agents limited as to the objects or the business to be done, and left at large as to the mode of transacting it. If a particular mode is not prescribed by the original power, that which the agent may adopt the principal may, by approving, sanctify, and give to it equal validity as if it had made a part of the original authority, excluding the idea of collusion between the agent and the third party. To abuse the power conferred by the principal, such a circumstance would defeat the third party in his attempt to charge the principal. Special agents are limited as to the objects or business to be done, and must in all things pursue the power or authority which is given them, both as to the object and manner of effecting it, if that be also prescribed. They are the creatures of the power or authority, and therefore cannot in any manner exceed it or deviate from it, and, if they do, the principal is not bound." "If a person be appointed a general agent, as in the case of a factor for a merchant residing abroad, the principal is bound by his acts. But an agent constituted for a particular purpose, and under a limited and circumscribed power, cannot bind the principal by any act in which he exceeds his authority; for that would be to say that one man may bind another against his consent." Opinion of BULLER, J., in Fann v. Harrison, 3 Term R. 762; Bay v. Coddington, 5 Johns. Ch. 58. "A special agent, constituted for a particular purpose and under a limited power, cannot bind his principal beyond his authority. This is a very clear and settled rule." Chancellor KENT in Skinner v. Dayton, 5 Johns. Ch. 354; citing Nixon v. Hyserott, 5 Johns. 58; Gibson v. Colt, 7 Johns. 390. See, also, Denning v. Smith, 3 Johns. Ch. 345.

With respect to an agent constituted for a particular purpose, he who deals with him deals at his peril, if the agent passes the limit of his power; for it was his duty and his right to look to his instructions for the extent of his authority. It is said that a principal is liable to a third party for all contracts entered into by his broker or agent within the scope of his authority, as defined by direct instructions. The broker must obey his instructions in order to bind his principal. Siebold v. Davis, 67 Iowa, 560, 25 N. W. Rep. 778; Story, Ag. §§ 126, 127. Real-estate brokers or agents may be defined to be those who negotiate the sale or purchase of real property; but the power of a real-estate agent or broker does not generally extend to execute a sale, but merely to bring the parties together, or to negotiate for the contract. Pringle v. Spaulding, 53 Barb. 17; Haydock v. Stow, 40 N. Y. 363; Force v. Dutcher, 18 N. J. Eq. 401; Morris v. Ruddy, 20 N. J. Eq. 236. It is clear that there must be an appointment to constitute one an agent. It is a rule of law that no one can become an agent except by the will of the principal. Evans, Ag. 22; McGoldrick v. Willits, 52 N. Y. 612; Bank v. Bentley, 27 Minn. 87, 6 N. W. Rep. 422; Gifford v. Landrine, 37 N. J. Eq. 127. "In the absence of evidence of express appointment, of ratification, or of an estoppel, there is no sufficient evidence of agency." Alexander v. Rollins, 84 Mo. 657. It is said that an agency cannot be proved by general reputation, but is a fact to which a witness having knowledge of its existence may testify. Banking Co. v. Smith, 76 Ala. 572. When the principal, in a suit brought to enforce a contract entered into in his name by a supposed agent, denies the authority of the agent, the burden of proof to establish the agent's authority is on the party who seeks to enforce the contract. McCarty v. Straus, 21 La. Ann. 592. In the case of Grant v. Ede, 85 Cal. 418, 20 Amer. St. Rep. 237,[1] where the supposed authority to make a complete sale was as follows: "As you stated you could get $30,000 for the place you occupy on Market street, and if you can, we will sell at that price any time before Sept. 1st, 1887, and allow you 2½ per cent. on said price, and, if no sale is made, no expenses made to us;" and on this authority the agent, Martin, sold to Grant, (the appellant,) on the 23d of August, 1887, for $30,-000, $500 cash and residue on execution of deed by Ede, and signed himself as agent for Ede, and received $500 as part of purchase money,—it was held that "we will sell" does not mean that Martin is authorized to sell, the court saying: "A general authority to sell real estate includes merely the power to find a purchaser therefor, and the agent cannot conclude a contract which will be binding upon his principal." And Mr. Freeman appends a note to this case, citing Shults v. Griffin, (N. Y. App.) 18 Amer. St. Rep. 828,[2] saying: "Such letter does not constitute an agreement of the principal which such purchaser can enforce, as it merely fixes a price, and does not specify any form of deed, or time of payment or of delivery of possession, or authorize the agent to make such specifications."

In every letter written to these agents Kramer said, "I will take," or "I will sell," "I have concluded to sell," or "my price is," and nowhere appointed any agent to sell for him. He authorized them to find a purchaser, and agreed to pay them a commission for doing this. Their employment was to conduct negotiations for the sale of this real estate, and no one better understood this than these agents, who did not consider at the time that their employment was such as would authorize them to conclude any sale, except subject to the approval of their employer. And of these negotiations the evidence shows that the appellees were fully informed, the correspondence being conducted at their solicitation. See Fitch, Real-Estate Ag. pp. 7, 14. It is clear that Hanckel, Kemp & Co. had no authority to make a binding contract for their princi-

pal, and, having entered into one in his name, their act, so far as he is concerned, is null. There has been no sale made by Kramer, (the appellant,) nor by which he is in any degree bound. The hustings court of Roanoke city having decided otherwise, the decree so deciding and appealed from will be reversed and annulled, and such decree rendered here as the said court ought to have rendered. And this disposes of the case, so that it is unnecessary to consider the second branch of the case, as to the question whether the contract, if valid and binding on Kramer, is such that the court should, in the exercise of a judicial discretion, specifically perform. Decree reversed.

FAUNTLEROY, J., concurring in result.

JACKSON v. DU BOSE.

(Supreme Court of Georgia. Nov. 23, 1891.)

HOMESTEAD — EVIDENCE — DECLARATIONS — ABANDONMENT.

1. In an action of complaint for land, where both parties claim under the same person, any error of the court in admitting evidence to show title in such person is immaterial.

2. Where the question is whether a person has ceased to be a resident of Georgia and become a citizen of Alabama, his declarations, made in a certain city in Alabama, to the effect that he had made that place his home, and never expected to return to the county of his former residence in Georgia to live, are admissible in evidence in a controversy between his tenant and a third person respecting the cessation of his right of homestead in Georgia.

3. Where, after a levy upon land, an application is made for homestead, and, pending the application the land is sold by the sheriff under the levy, with notice to the purchaser of the pendency of the application, he acquires the whole interest of the defendant in execution, subject to the incumbrance of the homestead afterwards assigned, and on the expiration of that homestead interest is entitled to the possession of the premises. The case of Grace v. Kezar, 12 S. E. Rep. 1067, 86 Ga. 697, approved and adhered to. CLARK, J., dissenting.

4. The homestead interest is terminated by removal from the state. This is a sound proposition in itself, and is supported by the reasoning in Bank v. Smisson, 73 Ga. 429.

(Syllabus by the Court.)

Error from superior court, Hancock county; LUMPKIN, Judge. Affirmed.

Action by one Du Bose against one Jackson to recover land. Verdict and judgment for plaintiff. Defendant appeals.

The land in question was owned by one Lee. Defendant was his tenant, and plaintiff purchased the land at a sale under an execution against Lee. Plaintiff offered in evidence a deed executed to Lee and Forbes by one Turner, as guardian. This deed was objected to on the ground that, excepting recitals in the deed itself, there was nothing to show that Turner had ever been appointed guardian, or that he had authority from the court to sell the land. On a showing that it was a part of the chain of title under which both parties claimed, and that it was obtained from defendant under notice, it was admitted. A deed conveying Forbes' interest to Lee was introduced, and the sheriff's deed to plaintiff. Defendant, as a witness

---

for plaintiff, testified that he (defendant) rented the land from Lee, and had lived thereon for five years, but that Lee had lived during that time in Alabama. One Rogers testified that some months previously, in Birmingham, Ala., Lee told him that he had made that place his home, and never expected to return to Georgia to live. Defendant introduced evidence that in 1876 the land in question was set apart as a homestead on application of Lee's wife. Lee testified that at the time of his wife's death he and his wife and family lived on the land; that in 1880 he remarried; that, when he left it, it was his intention to return; that he had lived in Alabama and other states as a railroad contractor, but that it was still his intention to return to his home in Georgia. Defendant proved that an application for homestead was filed after the execution was levied, and the land was sold to plaintiff with public notice of the pending application

J. T. Jordan, for plaintiff in error.   *W. M. & M. P. Reese*, for defendant in error.

PER CURIAM.   Judgment affirmed.

STATE v. MATHIS.

(Supreme Court of North Carolina. Dec. 1, 1891.)

CRIMINAL LAW—DISMISSAL OF APPEAL—COMMUTATION OF SENTENCE.

An appeal from a judgment of death will be dismissed on defendant's motion when during the pendency of the appeal the governor commutes the sentence to life imprisonment, and the prisoner accepts the commutation.

Motion by defendant in the case of state of North Carolina against C. Mathis to dismiss defendant's appeal. Dismissed.

Glenn & Manly, for appellant.   *The Attorney General*, for the State.

MERRIMON, C. J.   The appellant prisoner was convicted of the crime of murder, and there was judgment of death against him, from which he appealed to this court. Pending the appeal, and before it was reached in its order to be heard and determined, the governor commuted his sentence of death to imprisonment for life in the penitentiary. The prisoner accepted such commutation, and, in pursuance of the same, he is now imprisoned in the penitentiary. When the appeal was called in its order to be heard the prisoner presented and exhibited before the court the order of commutation of his sentence, duly made and signed by the governor, and signified his acceptance of the same, and prayed the court that he be allowed freely to abandon his appeal, and that the court take no further notice of or action in and about the same. The attorney general admitted the commutation of the prisoner's sentence, and his acceptance of the same, and made no objection thereto, and prayed the court to make such disposition of the appeal as it might deem proper. After the prisoner was convicted, the governor had power and authority to commute the sentence of death against him to the lesser punishment of imprisonment for life in the penitentiary, (Const. art. 3, § 6; Code, § 1096.) The appeal did not, as formerly, vacate the judgment of death pending the appeal. It remained in full force to be executed, unless the court should adjudge there was error therein. The statute (Acts 1887, c. 191) so expressly provides, and hence no question such as that very seriously considered in State v. Alexander, 76 N. C. 231, arises here. It certainly appears to the court that the governor has granted such commutation of the prisoner's sentence; that the latter has accepted the same, and is now undergoing punishment in the penitentiary in pursuance of law in such cases. There is therefore no reason why he shall not be allowed to abandon his appeal. His application must be granted, and the appeal dismissed. Let a proper order for that purpose be entered.

Cox et al. v. PRUETT et al.

(Supreme Court of North Carolina. Dec. 1, 1891.)

CERTIORARI—LOST APPEAL.

A petition for a writ of *certiorari*, as a substitute for an appeal lost, alleged that within 10 days after notice of the order complained of notice of appeal was served on plaintiff, but it did not allege that defendants took an appeal within 10 days after notice, or within 10 days after the rendition of such order, nor that an appeal was entered in the judgment docket and notice given. It did not allege that the adverse party prevented defendants from taking an appeal, and it did not appear that an appeal was ever taken, and no reason was assigned for the neglect.   *Held*, that the writ would not issue.

Action by W. E. Cox and others against Martin Pruett and others. Defendants petition for a writ of *certiorari*. Petition dismissed.

R. A. Doughton, for plaintiffs.   *Q. F. Neal*, for defendants.

MERRIMON, C. J.   This is an application for the writ of *certiorari* as a substitute for an appeal lost. The petition alleges that, within 10 days next after the petitioners had notice of the order complained of, they placed a notice of an appeal in the hands of the sheriff to be served on the plaintiffs in the action, and that it was served. But it is not alleged, nor does it at all appear, that the petitioners took an appeal within 10 days after notice, or within 10 days after the rendition of such order; nor is it alleged, nor does it appear, that within that time the appellant caused his appeal to be entered by the clerk on the judgment docket, and notice thereof to be given to the adverse party, as required by the statute. Code, § 550. On the contrary, it appears by the affidavit of the clerk that no notice of appeal ever went to his office. It is not alleged, nor does it appear, that the adverse party in any way prevented the petitioners from taking an appeal within the time allowed by law. It does not appear that the petitioners ever took an appeal, nor is any proper reason assigned why they did not or could not. Clearly, the petitioners are not entitled to have their prayer granted. Let the petition be dismissed. It is so ordered.

FARTHING v. DARK.

(Supreme Court of North Carolina, Dec. 1, 1891.)

PROMISSORY NOTES—BONA FIDE PURCHASER—PROVINCE OF JURY.

1. A person unknown to plaintiff offered to sell him for $100 a note made by defendant, the face value of which was $125. Plaintiff, having learned on inquiry that defendant was solvent, purchased the note. In an action to recover its value the evidence introduced by plaintiff himself showed that the note was payable six months after date at a place which plaintiff was aware was not in existence, and that he knew that it was given "for some sort of a township right" on some contract not known to him. *Held,* that these facts were such as should have put plaintiff on further inquiry as to the validity of the note.

2. In an action on a promissory note, which defendant asserted to be fraudulent, it is error for the court to refuse to submit the question to the jury on all the evidence, and to tell the jury that, if they believed plaintiff's statement, they must answer the issue "Yes."

MERRIMON, C. J., and SHEPHERD, J., dissenting.

Appeal from superior court, Chatham county; ROBERT W. WINSTON, Judge. Reversed.

Action by C. C. Farthing against J. H. Dark on a promissory note. Judgment for plaintiff. Defendant appeals.

The other facts fully appear in the following statement by DAVIS, J.:

The plaintiff sued on a promissory note, of which the following is a copy: "$125.00. Durham, N. C., Feb'y 18th, 1891. Six months after date I promise to pay to the order of W. B. Pallett & Co. one hundred and twenty-five dollars, negotiable and payable at Durham Fence Factory, or office of Wortham, Warren & Co., Planing-Mills. Value received. J. H. DARK. No. ——. [Indorsed:] W. B. PALLETT & Co." The defendant admitted the execution, pleaded fraud in the *factum,* failure of consideration, and equities arising out of a contemporaneous contract, as set out in the answer, which is of record. The plaintiff introduced the note, and rested his case.

The execution of the note having been admitted, the burden was upon the defendant, and he offered in evidence an agreement between W. B. Pallett & Co. and himself, marked "A," which was, in substance, that whereas, W. B. Pallett & Co., of the town of Durham, had established a permanent industry in Durham for the purpose of manufacturing and selling the Champion combination slat and wire fence, upon the consideration named, they appointed the defendant agent to sell the manufactured fence in the township of Baldwin, Chatham county, and receive the compensation named. The said W. B. Pallett & Co. were at all times to furnish the defendant with the fence at the price of $45.50 per rod, according to the character of the fence, and the defendant was to pay Pallett & Co. 5 cents per rod of the commission after he had sold 1,000 rods of fence and received all the commission,—$250,—as he has this day secured to be paid $125 by execution of his note, being one-half of the commission on the first 1,000 rods of fence sold. And if 500 rods of fence are not sold at the end of six

months by the said second party, then said company, or their authorized representative, are fully empowered to cancel said agency, and appoint another agent in his stead. But if they decide to cancel said agency, which shall be at their option, they shall surrender said note, after first being paid one-half of the commission on the fence sold during the said six months. The defendant was then introduced in his own behalf, and testified: "One W. B. Pallett came to me and proposed to make me his agent for six months for my township in Chatham county, telling me he had established a permanent factory in the town of Durham for the manufacture of a wire fence described in circulars, which he read to me, and of which he gave me several copies. I executed my note, and we executed the contract in duplicate. He told me the note was simply to butt against the fence, and that at the end of six months it would be given up to me and canceled; and, if I sold no fence, I would have to pay nothing on it. In about two weeks after this I went to Durham, and went to see Wortham, Warren & Co. I found no fence, no factory, and that W. B. Pallett had left the country.' I went there to get the fence. I wanted some for my own farm, and some for my neighbors'. This is the only time I went or sent about buying the fence. I never wrote about it." The defendant rested his case.

G. C. Farthing, the plaintiff, testified in his own behalf as follows: "I bought the note sued on the 19th of February, 1891, and paid $100 for it. I did not know of the contract marked 'A.' I bought of W. B. Pallett & Co: I live in Durham, and have lived there for twenty-six years. I am a merchant, and am not a dealer in paper like this note. I had known Pallett but a few days. He was a stranger in Durham. Shortly after I purchased the note he left Durham. I heard of him in Danville. At the time I bought this note I purchased four others. He had previously sold nine others to J. F. Slaughter. Slaughter had spoken to me about them before I purchased. He had the pick, and paid $100 each for the ones he bought. I paid $100 each for three of those I bought; but for two, upon men I thought not good, I paid $62.50; making $425 in all for the five notes of $125 each. The notes Slaughter bought were for the same sums, and upon the same blanks, as the one sued on. I knew that the notes were given for some sort of a township right. Pallett told me. I didn't know what sort of a contract. I knew at that time that there was no factory in Durham called the 'Durham Fence Factory,' at which the notes were made payable. There is no such factory there now. I made inquiries of Make Jeans of the financial standing of the defendant, and of C. N. Justice, the obligor in another of the notes I bought, both of whom reside in Chatham county. He told me they were good for their debts. I did not tell him that I knew that there was any contract between Pallett and Dark by which Wortham, Warren & Co. were to furnish a fence. I saw C. N. Justice shortly after I purchased the notes, and offered to sell him his note for $110. I did not tell him that I gave that sum for it. I gave $100 for his note."

W. H. Wortham, a witness for the plaintiff, testified: "I am the Wortham of Wortham, Warren & Co., Planing-Mills. Pallett came to see me, and made a contract with me for the manufacture of wire fence. It is in writing. I am prepared to furnish the fence according to contract 'A,' and have been since about the 20th of February. We were the manufacturing agents of W. B. Pallett & Co. Pallett sent me machinery. I did not have room for it in my factory, and put it up outside. I did not tell Dark and Justice in the latter part of February, and after the purchase of the notes by plaintiff, that I had made no contract with Pallett, and that they could get no fence from there unless Pallett came back and made it. I did tell them that Pallett attempted to make me an agent for the sale of the fence, and that I refused to agree to become such agent for Durham township. I did not tell C. N. Justice, about the 10th of March last, near Farthing's store, at an auction sale of horses, that I had never given Pallett consent for the use of my name, and that I would not furnish any of the fence."

The plaintiff closed his case, and the defendant introduced Make Jeans as a witness, who testified: "I live in the town of Durham. The plaintiff came to my store, and said he was about to purchase the notes on the defendant, and on C. N. Justice, and asked their financial standing. I told him they were good; that Dark was my step-father. He said the notes had been given for the right to sell wire fence, which would be put up by Wortham, Warren & Co. Pallett had given me $25 for giving him the names of good farmers in Chatham county. I gave him the names of Dark and Justice."

C. N. Justice, a witness for the defendant, testified: "I am the obligor upon one of the notes mentioned. Shortly after the purchase of my note by the plaintiff, I went to see him in Durham. He proposed to sell me my note for $110, and said to me that was what he gave for it. About two weeks after the execution of my note I went with Mr. Dark to see Wortham, Warren & Co. Mr. Wortham told us that there was no fence there, and would not be unless Pallett came back and made it; that he would have nothing to do with it; that he would not let Pallett's machinery come into his house. About the 10th of March I saw him again, near Farthing's store, where there was an auction sale of horses, and he then told me that he had never authorized Pallett to use his name, and that he would furnish no fence. I never went to see about fence again."

J. H. Dark, recalled, testified: "I was with Mr. Justice when he went to see Mr. Wortham. He told us he was going to make no fence; that he would make none; that he would not even let Pallett's machinery come into his house. There was some machinery outside of the house setting on two scantlings about 4x4."

The defendant asked his honor to instruct the jury that, the defendant having pleaded fraud in the inception of the note,

and having introduced evidence tending to show fraud, the burden of proof was upon the plaintiff to show that he became the owner of the note before maturity, for value, and without notice of the fraud, and without notice of such facts and circumstances as would stimulate inquiry. His honor declined to give this instruction, and the defendant excepted. The defendant asked his honor to instruct the jury that, if they should believe that the plaintiff purchased the note sued on, together with four others of the same character, for the sum of $100 each for three notes, and $62.50 for each of two notes; that at the same time one J. F. Slaughter had purchased nine similar notes upon solvent men at the same discount, from the same person, paying $100 each for notes due in six months for $125 each; that plaintiff knew that the payee was then a stranger in the town in which plaintiff resided; that some of these notes were payable at the Durham Fence Factory; that plaintiff knew that there was no such factory in existence at Durham; that plaintiff made inquiries, and ascertained that defendant and others who gave said fourteen notes were all solvent men, except two, for which the plaintiff paid $62.50 each; that the plaintiff knew that all of these notes were given for some sort of a township right, and knew that they were given for the right to sell wire fence; that he knew that by such right the payees were to have wire fence made by Wortham, Warren & Co.; that plaintiff was not a dealer or trader in negotiable paper,—then the plaintiff had notice of the fraud and defenses of the defendant. This charge his honor declined to give, and the defendant excepted. The defendant asked the court to charge the jury that, if they believed the facts set forth in the preceding prayer, then the plaintiff had notice of such facts and circumstances as would stimulate an inquiry, and that he is presumed to have notice of all facts which such inquiry would have disclosed. This the court declined to give, and the defendant excepted. The defendant asked the court to instruct the jury that, if they found the facts as set forth in the preceding instruction but one, they could be considered by the jury in passing upon the question of notice. This the court declined to give, and the defendant excepted. His honor then charged the jury as follows: "The plaintiff having produced the note at the trial, and its execution being admitted, and being negotiable, the law presumes that the plaintiff is the owner. The only question for your consideration, the defendant having pleaded fraud, is, do you believe the statement made by the plaintiff that he paid value for the note before maturity, and had no notice of such fraud or equities? If so, you will answer the issue: 'Yes; $125, and interest from August 18, 1891.'" To which charge the defendant excepted. There was a verdict and judgment for the plaintiff, and appeal by the defendant.

Thos. B. Womack, for appellant. *J. S. Manning, W. W. Fuller,* and *F. L. Fuller,* for appellee.

DAVIS, J., (*after stating the facts.*) It is

insisted for the plaintiff that he purchased the note for value and without notice; that the note was negotiable, and there is a *prima facie* presumption of law, in favor of every holder of a negotiable note to the extent that he is the owner of it, and that he took it for value, and before dishonor, in the regular course of business; and, if there be fraud or illegality in the inception of it, the burden is upon the maker to show it. This proposition is supported by abundant authority, and will not be controverted; but the defendant says that there was evidence tending to rebut this presumption, and fix the plaintiff with notice, and that he was not a *bona fide* purchaser for value and without notice, and that the court erred in refusing to submit this evidence to the jury, and in instructing them that, if they believed the statement made by the plaintiff that he paid value for the note before maturity, without notice of any fraud or equities, they should answer the issue "Yes." Was there any evidence of facts and circumstances within the knowledge of the plaintiff calculated to attract attention and put him upon his guard and stimulate inquiry as to the character of the note which he purchased? "If so, it is well settled," says RUFFIN, C. J., in Bunting v. Ricks, 2 Dev. & B. Eq. 130, "that the person is affected with knowledge of all that the inquiry would disclose;" and this is reaffirmed in Hulbert v. Douglas, 94 N. C. 122. We think that the testimony of the plaintiff himself shows facts that should have put him on inquiry. He was careful to make inquiry as to the solvency of the maker of the note. This was prudent; but when he was offered a note by a perfect stranger, for $100, made by the defendant, whom he had, upon inquiry, ascertained to be perfectly solvent, for $125, payable six months after date, at a place named in his own town, which he knew to have no existence, and when he knew, as he says he did, that the note was given "for some sort of a township right," upon some sort of contract, he did not know what, would not ordinary prudence and a proper regard for the rights and interest of the debtor, whom he knew to be solvent, have suggested that he press his inquiry further, and ascertain something about the character of the payee in the note, and why it was made payable at a place which he knew had no existence, as well as to have inquired as to the solvency of the maker of the note? Conceding in favor of the purchaser of negotiable paper before maturity, that the simple fact that he purchased from a stranger, who sold for much less than its value, would not be sufficient, there was other conflicting testimony, and we think his honor erred in refusing to submit the question to the jury upon all the evidence. It was error to single out the testimony of the plaintiff, and tell the jury that, if they believed his statement, they must answer the issue "Yes." Long v. Hall, 97 N. C. 286, 2 S. E. Rep. 229; State v. Rogers, 93 N. C. 523, and cases cited. There was error.

MERRIMON, C. J., and SHEPHERD, J., dissented.

SNEEDEN v. HARRIS *et al.*

(*Supreme Court of North Carolina. Dec. 1, 1891.*)

MALICIOUS PROSECUTION — PLEADING — TERMINATION OF ACTION.

1. In an action for malicious prosecution, which alleges that plaintiff was arrested and imprisoned in an action for slander of title wrongfully instituted for the sole purpose of getting immediate possession of land claimed and occupied by him, it is not necessary that the complaint allege that such action had been finally determined.

2. Where the complaint alleged that W., one of the defendants, at the request of the others, signed the bond in the action for slander of title, but did not allege that he participated in the torts complained of, it failed to state a cause of action as to him.

Appeal from superior court, New Hanover county; JAMES D. McIVER, Judge. Modified.

Action by William H. Sneeden against George Harris, Julia Harris, D. L. Russell, and Henry P. West to recover damages for the malicious prosecution of an action for slander of title. Defendants demurred to the complaint, and from an order sustaining the demurrer plaintiff appeals.

The other facts fully appear in the following statement by DAVIS, J:

The complaint is as follows: "That during the summer and fall of 1887 plaintiff was in possession of a certain tract of land or island in New Hanover county, in Wrightsville sound, near the ocean, and known as 'Sneeden's Hammocks,' occupying same under a claim of title which he believed to be good and valid; that during that period there was a considerable discussion in the community about the probability of two railroads being constructed to the sound, and it was understood that both were desirous of securing possession of said property known as 'Sneeden's Hammocks,' the one the Wilmington Sea-Coast Railroad Company, intending it as their terminus, the other the Wilmington, Onslow & East Carolina Railroad Company, intending to make it the terminus of a branch road to the ocean, as plaintiff is informed and believes, and states for this reason the market value of his property became greatly enhanced. (3) That defendants George and Julia Harris also claim title to said island, and were negotiating with the railroad companies to make sale of it to one of them, and some time in October or November in that year entered into a contract with the Wilmington, Onslow & East Carolina Railroad Company, through defendant D. L. Russell, who was largely interested in said road, and its financial agent, projector, and manager, to sell one-half of said island to said railroad company, or to him and certain other divers persons interested with him, for $25,000, and, as the plaintiff has been informed by defendants Harris and Russell, the said contract would have been executed at that time but for the possession of the property by the plaintiff. (4) But, finding their bargain blocked by plaintiff's possession, the defendants George and Julia Harris (through her agent and husband George Harris) and D. L. Russell consulted together as to the best means to carry out their common object, and to obtain immediate possession of the property, so that they might make a sale thereof; and, well knowing there was no lawful means of accomplishing this, they determined upon and proceeded to execute the base, malicious, and illegal plan of suing out a writ of arrest and bail under the false and malicious pretense that plaintiff was slandering their title to the property by claiming it to be his own, and of having him arrested and removed from the property and imprisoned, so that they might take possession as soon as the plaintiff was removed; by which wrongful and malicious act the process of the court was abused and used for a purpose not set forth in the affidavit upon which the order of arrest was obtained. (5) In pursuance of this unlawful, base, and malicious design and purpose, they applied to Henry P. West, the other defendant, and induced him to sign a bond required by law, and then sued out before the clerk a writ of arrest and bail, and had the same placed in the sheriff's hands, who late in the afternoon, about the 1st day of November in said year, assaulted, arrested, and removed the plaintiff from the possession of the property which he was quietly enjoying, and believed to be his own; and, as soon as plaintiff was removed, the defendants took possession of and held the property until they sold it to the Wilmington Sea-Coast Railroad Company. (6) That defendants well knew at the time they made said affidavit that plaintiff was a very poor man, and that no damages could be obtained from him, and that the statements made in said affidavit that he was slandering their title were false, and that the purpose and object in bringing this suit was not to hold him to answer a claim for damages, but that it was, in truth and in fact, as above alleged, and as has been acknowledged by defendant George Harris, for the express and deliberate purpose of suing out a writ of arrest to obtain immediate possession of the property, which they could not otherwise secure, and in so doing they purposely and deliberately abused the process of the court. (7) That plaintiff was removed from possession as aforesaid, carried a distance of eight miles, to the common jail of the county, and then and there was incarcerated and restrained of his liberty for a period of ten days. (8) That plaintiff was an old man about 65 years of age, and at the time of his said imprisonment his wife was extremely ill of a sickness from which she shortly afterwards died, and at the time of his imprisonment he was daily expecting her death; and in order to avoid being separated from her, and to enable him to be present at her bedside to administer to her wants, and also to avoid the pain, suffering, and disgrace of going to jail, fearing the ill effects of close confinement upon one so old and infirm as himself, and well knowing his innocence of any unlawful act, and being too poor to give bond, he applied to several persons, through his friends, to give bail for him, but each of the persons applied to refused his petition. (9) That by reason of his imprisonment he was separated from

his wife, and unable to be with her in her last days, and was prevented from attending to his ordinary affairs, and greatly suffered in mind and body; by all of which he was damaged $5,000. (10) That as aforesaid, in pursuance of their illegal and evil purpose, immediately upon the removal of the plaintiff from the property, the defendants took possession, broke open his house, removed and scattered his effects, leveled his house with the ground, shot and destroyed his hogs and poultry, and committed other acts of violence, abuse, and spoliation, thereby showing their ill feelings, and the malice influencing the defendants towards the plaintiff; by all of which acts of violence the plaintiff was damaged five thousand dollars. Wherefore plaintiff demands judgment against defendants for $5,500 damages actually sustained by him from defendants' unlawful act; five thousand dollars punitory damages for suing out a writ contrary to law, and having plaintiff arrested and imprisoned upon a charge so false, and with a purpose so wrongful, illegal, and malicious; and for costs."

The defendants demurred to the complaint, and assigned several grounds of demurrer, but the only one relied upon in this court was "that the complaint does not allege or show upon its face that the civil action in which the warrant or writ of arrest was issued, whereunder the plaintiff was arrested and imprisoned, has been finally and legally determined and ended before the commencement of this action;" and, as to the defendant West, upon the additional ground that the complaint did not allege facts sufficient to constitute a cause of action as against him.

Thos. W. Strange, for appellant. *Junius Davis*, for appellees.

DAVIS, J., (*after stating the facts*.) The substance of the allegation, as to defendant West, is that, at the request of defendant Harris, he signed the usual undertaking required in arrest and bail, and it is not alleged that he participated in the torts alleged, nor does it appear that he was in any way liable for them except as surety on said undertaking, which would be *ex contractu*, and the demurrer as to him must be sustained.

As to the other defendants, the complaint clearly and distinctly alleges, in substance, that the plaintiff was in the quiet and peaceable possession of certain real property which he believed to be his own, but to which the defendants also claimed title; and that the defendants, desiring to get speedy possession of the said property without the risk and delay attending an action for the recovery of real property, conceived and executed a plan to have the plaintiff removed from the possession, by falsely and maliciously suing out a writ of arrest and bail for alleged slander of their title, and causing him to be arrested and imprisoned, and, while so removed from the possession and imprisoned, they entered upon the property, "broke open his house, removed and scattered his effects, leveled his house with the ground, shot and destroyed his hogs and poultry, and committed other acts of violence, abuse, and spoliation." The action of Harris v. Sneeden, in which the plaintiff in this action was taken under arrest and bail for "slander of title," was before this court at its September term, 1888, (101 N. C. 273, 7 S. E. Rep. 801;) and the court said it was questionable whether an action for slander of title was embraced by the statute on arrest and bail, (Code, § 290 et seq.;) but the court did not decide the question, and, for the reason presently to be stated, its decision is not necessary in this action.

It is proper to state that this court sustained the judgment of the court below in vacating the order of arrest, but the plaintiff in that action (defendants in this) had accomplished their purpose to get possession, while the defendant in that action (plaintiff in this) was in custody. The demurrer admits, for the purpose of this action, that Sneeden was in the quiet possession of the land, and that he believed it to be his; and whether an action for slander of title could be maintained, or whether the true title was in the plaintiff or defendants, is immaterial to the question now before whether the plaintiff can maintain this action without alleging the final legal determination of the action of the defendants against the plaintiff, in which the warrant or writ of arrest was issued and the plaintiff was imprisoned. This is not an action for malicious prosecution for an alleged crime, in which it would be necessary to allege and show a judicial determination of the prosecution in favor of the accused. Every good citizen is interested in the suppression of crime, and, if there be probable cause, may prosecute in the name of the state; and if the accused be adjudged guilty he will not be heard to complain of the prosecution, nor can he maintain an action against the prosecutor, whatever may have been his motive. This is an action for alleged malicious use and abuse of civil process.

But the council for the defendant says: "There is not the slightest proof [allegation] that the defendants gave the sheriff any instructions not enjoined by the exigency of the writ which he had in his hands." This action is not against the sheriff for abuse of the process in his hands, but against the defendants for having maliciously and fraudulently sued out a writ of arrest and bill for a purpose falsely alleged therein, when their real purpose, admitted by the demurrer, was not that named in the affidavit or process, but the ulterior object to get speedy possession of the land, and no instructions from them to the sheriff were necessary. They expected that he, in the discharge of his duty, would arrest Sneeden under the writ which they had sued out, and thereby enable them to get possession of the land, and level Sneeden's house with the ground, and destroy his property, so that he could not regain or reoccupy it.

Counsel for the defendants say: "Let us take it that Harris recovered judgment against the plaintiff in the original action of slander of title in which the writ was issued. Such a judgment would establish, as against the plaintiff, that the land in dispute belonged to Harris; that this plaintiff had no interest in it, and had taken possession of it, and set up title in himself, with the false and malicious intent to injure Harris. Then, if this action is sustained, we would have the singular spectacle of the plaintiff recovering damages from Harris because he basely and maliciously took possession of his own land after it had been left vacant in consequence of the lawful arrest and imprisonment of the plaintiff." It is true the sheriff did no wrong in discharging his duty, and arresting Sneeden in obedience to the command of the writ; but does it follow that, because it was the duty of the sheriff to arrest under the writ, the defendants could lawfully sue out the writ to enable them to procure the arrest of Sneeden, not for the purpose named in the writ, but for the admitted, ulterior, collateral purpose to get possession of the land, in dispute, as soon as it was made vacant by the arrest and imprisonment of the claimant in adverse possession, under the writ which they had falsely and fraudulently sued out for that purpose, instead of instituting an action to try the title to the land in dispute, and recover possession upon their title, if they had any? If, in their affidavit for arrest and bail, they had stated that their real, and, it appears, only, purpose was, as is admitted by the demurrer, to procure the arrest of Sneeden, to enable them to get possession of the land in dispute, instead of the recovery of damages for slander of title, no writ could have issued, and Sneeden could not have been lawfully arrested by the sheriff. Counsel for the defendants fail to note the marked distinction between a prosecution for the malicious use and abuse of process for ulterior purposes not named in the process and a prosecution for alleged crime. In the latter, there must be a final determination of the prosecution before an action for malicious prosecution can be maintained, and no citation of authority was needed for this; but in the former this is not necessary. In the one, the public have an interest; in the other, the individual only. And while it is true, as a general rule of law, that imprisonment under legal process is not duress, yet if one falsely, maliciously, and without probable cause procures the arrest and imprisonment of another on process legal and regular in form, and obtains thereby a deed from the party so arrested, such deed is void by reason of duress. Watkins v. Baird, 6 Mass. 506, and cases cited. When an action is for malicious abuse of legal process in order to compel a party to do a collateral thing or to accomplish an ulterior purpose, it is not necessary to allege that the process improperly employed is at an end. Prough v. Entriken, 11 Pa. St. 81, and the numerous cases there cited; Grainger v. Hill, 33 E. C. L. 675. Conceding that the defendants were the true owners of the property in dispute, the plaintiff was in possession claiming it as his own, and if, without any process, they had gone and taken forcible possession, and demolished the house claimed by him, and destroyed his property as alleged, it will not be denied that they would have subjected themselves to both civil and criminal actions. Did the fact that they got possession by the fraudulent use of legal process justify their acts, or were they not aggravated by making the strong arm of the law the instrument by which they were enabled to perpetrate them? "The law is just and good," and entitled to the obedience of all, the strong as well as the weak, and cannot sustain the perversion of its process to shield lawlessness and wrong, or permit it to be made the tool of trickery and cunning. The defendants admit that their purpose was not that named in their affidavit, but to get speedy possession of the land by having the plaintiff arrested and removed from it by the sheriff to enable them to enter upon it.

This case is distinguishable from that of Hewit v. Wooten, 7 Jones. (N. C.) 182. In that case it did not appear that the writ was sued out for the purpose of extorting money or any ulterior purpose. In this case the ulterior and wrongful purpose is alleged and admitted, which brings it clearly within the principle laid down in Grainger v. Hill, supra, and sanctioned in Hewit v. Wooten. Whether, under the old practice, the remedy of the plaintiff would have been trespass or case, is now immaterial, as the old technical distinctions in the form of actions (as between trespass and case) which so often perplex the profession have been abolished, (Code, § 133,) and the civil action, with its complaint stating clearly and concisely the facts constituting the cause of action, substituted, (Code, § 231 et seq.;) and, while the plaintiff's cause of action might have been more concisely stated, *utile per inutile non vitiatur*, and the demurrer must be overruled. Let this be certified, to the end that the defendants may answer if they shall be so advised, and the action proceeded with according to law.   Error.

DEWEY et al. v. SUGG.

(*Supreme Court of North Carolina.* Dec. 1, 1891.)

JUDGMENT LIEN—FAILURE TO RECORD AND INDEX.

Code N. C. §§ 83, 433-435, provide that a clerk of a superior court shall keep a judgment docket in which the substance of a judgment shall be recorded; that the entry of a judgment for money shall contain the names of the parties, the relief granted, the date of the judgment, and the date of its docketing, and that the clerk shall keep a cross-index, with the dates and numbers; that a judgment roll shall be made, and when filed such judgment shall become a lien on the debtor's real estate. *Held*, that in the entry of judgment against several, where the name of one is omitted from the caption and also from the cross-index, the judgment created no lien on his real estate as against judgments subsequently entered and indexed in accordance with the statutes.

Appeal from superior court, Pitt county; SPIER WHITAKER, Judge. Affirmed.

Petition of J. A. K. Tucker, sheriff, for instructions as to the payment of certain money in his hands.

The other facts in the case appear in the following statement by MERRIMON, C. J.:

It appears: (1) That previous to June term, 1887, of Pitt superior court, the plaintiffs brought their action in said court against B. F. Sugg for the recovery of certain personal property. (2) That B. F. Sugg gave bond for the return of the property seized by the sheriff, and I. A. Sugg and William Whitehead became his sureties upon said bond. (3) That at June term, 1887, the plaintiffs recovered a judgment against B. F. Sugg for the delivery of the property seized, and, in case a return thereof could not be had, then for five hundred and ten dollars, ($510,) the value thereof, both as against the said B F. Sugg and his sureties, I. A. Sugg and William Whitehead. (4) That this judgment was entitled, "Charles Dewey, George W. Dewey, and E. B. Dewey, trading as Dewey Brothers, against B. F. Sugg," and there was no reference in the caption to the said I. A. Sugg or the said William Whitehead, and nothing in said caption to indicate that either of them were parties to the said judgment. (5) That this judgment was shortly thereafter, and within 10 days after the said June term, copied upon the judgment docket, in book No. 9, exactly as it was originally written, and with no reference to the said I. A. Sugg or William Whitehead in the caption thereof, and with no minute of either of their names on the margin of the docket. (6) That the following is a copy of the judgment as it appears on the judgment docket No. 9, and as it was rendered, namely: "Charles Dewey, George W. Dewey, and E. B. Dewey, trading as Dewey Brothers, v. B. F. Sugg. Pitt county superior court.—June term, 1887. Before J. H. MERRIMON, Judge. Judgment was rendered in favor of the plaintiff, and against the defendants, for the possession of the property described in the complaint, and, if a return of the property cannot be had, that he recover of the defendant B. F. Sugg and William Whitehead and I. A. Sugg, the sureties on defendant's replevin bond, the sum of five hundred and ten dollars, with interest on same from 1st day of December, 1886, and the costs of this action." (7) That the docket upon which it is recorded, as set forth above, contains an index, but no cross-index, and upon said index there appears this entry, made at or about the time when said judgment was copied upon said docket, as follows: "Dewey Bros.—B. F. Sugg;" but there nowhere appears in said index the entry of said judgment as against the said I. A. Sugg and the said William Whitehead, nor was it ever indexed as to them. (8) That an index and a cross-index of judgments is kept in a separate book by the clerk of the superior court of Pitt county, and have been kept by him for more than five years, the names of the plaintiffs, followed by the names of the defendants, being written on the left-hand page, and the names of the defendants, followed by the names of the plaintiffs, being written on the opposite or right-hand page, under the appropriate letter of the alphabet. (9) That this judgment was, at or about the time of its being written on the docket, indexed on the said index under the letter "D," and on the left-hand page, and it is as follows: "Dewey Bros.—Sugg, B. F. & I. A.;" and the name of Whitehead did not appear as one of the defendants in said index. (10) That at the same time it was indexed on the cross-index under the letter "S," and on the right-hand page, as follows: "Sugg, B. F.—Dewey Bros;;" and the name of Whitehead did not appear in said index as one of the defendants in said judgment. (11) That the said judgment was not at that time cross-indexed either under the letter "W" or elsewhere, as to Whitehead. (12) That on the 15th day of December, 1890, the clerk of the superior court, under the letter "D," after the word "B. F. Sugg," added the words, "I. A. Sugg and William Whitehead," and on the cross-index on the right-hand page, under the letter "W," the said clerk, on the 15th day of December, 1890, made this entry: "Whitehead, William et al.—Dewey Bros." (18) That up to, and until the said 15th day of December, 1890, it did not appear, either from the index to docket No. 9, upon which the original judgment was recorded, or from the index or cross-index kept by the clerk of the superior court of Pitt county of all judgments filed in his office, that Charles Dewey, George W. Dewey, and E. B. Dewey, trading as Dewey Bros., had recovered any judgment against the said Whitehead for any amount, or that Dewey Bros. had recovered a judgment for any amount against said Whitehead. Upon this state of facts, the court held that the plaintiffs' judgment mentioned was not sufficiently docketed until the 15th of December, 1890; that it created and constituted no lien upon the lands of the said Whitehead in the county of Pitt prior to that time; and that the plaintiffs were not entitled to share in a fund the proceeds of his land sold by the sheriff under proper process, to satisfy divers judgments against him duly docketed before that time; and gave judgment accordingly. The plaintiffs excepted, and appealed to this court.

T. F. *Davidson* and *Jarvis & Blow,* for appellee.

MERRIMON, C. J., (*after stating the facts.*) The records of the courts are very important and essential in the administration of public justice. Appropriate statutes and general principles of law to some extent require the courts to make them, prescribe their purpose, where and by whom they shall be kept, and when and where they may be seen by every person interested to see them. While they are of great general utility, they import verity, and constitute the highest evidence of the rights and liabilities of all persons whom they directly concern and affect, and serve to give notice and information for the use and benefit of the public in many ways and for a variety of valuable purposes. It is hence essential that they should be made and kept substantially in all material respects as the law prescribes and requires. Otherwise they might fail of their purpose, and some person in some way interested must suffer detriment more or less serious. The statute (Code, § 83) requires the clerks of the several superior courts of this state to keep certain books specified, in which entries of the records of that court shall be made and preserved, and among them is "a judgment docket in which the substance of the judgment shall be recorded, and every proceeding subsequent thereto noted." This distinct judgment docket—its nature and purpose—is prescribed, and it is required to be kept for the purposes of the court. The law prescribes what shall be recorded on it, and everybody has notice that he may find there whatever ought to be there recorded, if, indeed, it exists. He is not required to look elsewhere for such matters. But he is required and bound to take notice, in proper connections, of what is there. The law charges him with such notice. The statute (Code § 433) further prescribes and requires that "every judgment of the superior court, affecting the right of real property, and any judgment requiring in whole or in part the payment of money, shall be entered by the clerk of said superior court on the judgment docket of said court. The entry shall contain the name of the parties, and the relief granted, date of judgment, and date of docketing; and the clerk shall keep a cross-index of the whole, with the dates and numbers thereof. All judgments rendered in any county by the superior court thereof, during a term of the court, and docketed during the same term, or within ten days thereafter, shall be held and deemed to have been rendered and docketed on the first day of said term." This section requires the classes of judgments specified to be docketed on the judgment docket, and directs how they shall be entered. It is not simply required that they shall be docketed, but it is further and of purpose required that they shall be docketed substantially in the way and manner prescribed. They are to be so entered, and in this way: "The entry shall contain the names of the parties, and the relief granted, date of judgment, and date of docketing; and the clerk shall keep a cross-index of the whole, with the dates and numbers thereof." The particularity thus required as to details is not merely directory and meaningless; it is intended to serve a substantial purpose,—that of giving information and notice, as to the particulars specified, to the public, everybody interested to have such information. It would be orderly, and much better, that such particulars should be set forth in the order directed by the statute. Still, if they appear in t' eir substance but disorderly, from the entry, this will be sufficient. The requirement that a cross-index shall be kept is not merely directory; it is important and necessary. It is intended to enable any person to learn that there is a docketed judgment in favor of a certain party or parties, and against certain other parties, and where to find it on the docket. The inquirer is not required to look through the whole docket to learn if there be a judgment against a particular person. He must be able to learn from such index that there is a judgment against him, and where he can find it on the docket, its nature, purpose, etc. When there are several judgment debtors in a docketed judgment, the index should and must specify the name of each one, because the index as to one would not point to all or any one of the others. The purpose is that the index shall point to a judgment against the particular person inquired about, if there be a judgment on the docket against him. A judgment not thus fully docketed does not serve the purpose of the statute, and is not docketed, in contemplation of law. The statute (Code, § 434) further prescribes and requires a judgment roll to be made up and filed as prescribed. It further prescribes, (section 435) that "upon filing a judgment roll upon a judgment affecting the title of real property, or directing in whole or in part the payment of money, it shall be docketed on the judgment docket of the superior court of the county where the judgment roll was filed, and may be docketed on the judgment docket of the superior court of any other county upon filing with the clerk thereof a transcript of the original docket, and shall be a lien on the real property in the county where the same is docketed, of every person against whom any such judgment shall be rendered, and which he may have at the time of the docketing thereof, in the county in which such real property is situated, or which he shall acquire at any time thereafter, for ten years from the date of the rendition of the judgment." A docketed judgment hence creates and secures a lien upon the judgment debtor's land. But a judgment, in order to create such lien, must be docketed in the way and manner above pointed out; otherwise, as we have seen, the judgment is not docketed, and no such or any lien arises. Holman v. Miller, 103 N. C. 118, 9 S. E. Rep. 429; 1 Black, Judgm. §§ 404, 406; Cummings v. Long, 16 Iowa, 41; Thomas v. Desney, 57 Iowa, 58, 10 N. W. Rep. 315; Nye v. Moody, 70 Tex. 434, 8 S. W. Rep. 606; Ridgway's Appeal, 15 Pa. St. 177; Hamilton's Appeal, 103 Pa. St. 368; Mets v. Bank, 7 Neb. 165. The important statutory provisions, above recited and referred to, prescribe and establish a method of creating judgment liens upon real property, and they must receive such reasonable interpretation as will give strength, certainty, and uniformity to that method, and effectuate its purposes. This can only be done by a strict observance of at least the substance of the requirements prescribed. Otherwise, uncertainty, confusion, and injustice must prevail to a greater or less extent in its administration. In the present case, we think the plaintiff's judgment was not sufficiently docketed to create a lien upon the real property of the defendant judgment debtor, William Whitehead. The judgment entered on the judgment docket is informal and disorderly; but granting that it is a judgment, and the entry contains sufficiently the names of the parties to it, the relief granted, the date of it, and the time of its docketing, still the index makes no mention whatever of this or any judgment against Whitehead. Any person looking on the index with a view to learn if there were a docketed judgment against him would have found nothing whatever leading him to examine or believe there was any such judgment. Thus such person would have been misled; such

a person may have been misled; numerous persons may have been misled. The law intends to prevent this, and that no such lien shall be created or exist to prejudice any person who cannot have the benefit of the means so provided to prevent prejudice thus arising. The judgment must be properly indexed as to each and all of the parties, in order to create the lien. The statute expressly makes it the duty of the clerk to make such entries, and he fails to do so at his peril. As the plaintiffs' judgment was not effectually docketed as to the defendant Whitehead, they could not share in the fund the proceeds of the sale of his lands under valid process issuing upon duly-docketed judgments, to the prejudice of the latter. Judgment affirmed.

BRISTOL v. PEARSON.

(Supreme Court of North Carolina. Dec. 9, 1891.)

CONTEMPT—DISOBEDIENCE OF ORDER—MOTION TO ATTACH—ABANDONMENT PENDING APPEAL.

1. Where an assignee for the benefit of creditors intentionally disobeys an order of court for the distribution of funds in his hands, and is attached for contempt upon the motion of a number of the creditors, from which he appeals, an application cannot be made in the lower court, pending the appeal, for leave to withdraw and abandon the motion, but the same must be disposed of in some appropriate way in the appellate court.

2. An application for such leave in the appellate court by the creditor who made the affidavit in support of the said motion must be allowed, but such allowance cannot affect the other creditors, where the motion was made at the instance of and for the benefit of the others as well as of himself.

3. Where an assignee for the benefit of creditors intentionally disobeys an order for the distribution of funds in his hands, the court may give judgment attaching him as for contempt.

Appeal from superior court, Burke county; WILLIAM A. HOKE, Judge. Affirmed.

The facts fully appear in the following statement by MERRIMON, C. J.:

The plaintiff, as assignee of certain property conveyed to him for the benefit of creditors named in the deed of trust, brought this action to have the property subject to the trust sold, and the proceeds of the sale thereof applied to the payment of debts of the creditors, according to their respective rights, etc., with the sanction and by the order of the court, etc. In the course of the action the court entered its decree directing a distribution of the fund in the hands of the plaintiff, trustee, to the parties therein specified. Thereafter, John A. Dickson, one of the defendant creditors, gave notice to the plaintiff of a motion to be made in the action to attach him for contempt of court, in that he had disobeyed the order of the court, etc. The motion was afterwards made, and the following is so much of the affidavit offered and considered by the court in support of the same as need be reported: "(8) That it was ordered by the court that the said L. A. Bristol, assignee, pay over one-half of the proceeds of sale of said specified property to J. H. and S. T. Pearson, and apply the remainder of said sum to the parties whose names are specified and mentioned in the report of G. P. Erwin, referee, filed in said cause; that, notwithstanding the order of the court, the said L. A. Bristol, assignee, in contempt of court, and in defiance of the advice of counsel, paid over to the said J. H. and S. T. Pearson the sum of twenty-one hundred and ninety-six dollars, when he should have paid him only the sum of seventeen hundred, (less their part of the cost,) and his so doing has prevented the other creditors, who should have received their *pro rata* share of said fund from being paid, as the order and decree of the court directed. Wherefore, the other creditors, whose names are specified in said report of said referee, pray the court that the said L. A. Bristol, assignee, be attached for contempt of court, and ordered and directed to distribute the fund received by him in accordance with the former decrees in this action." The court having found the facts of the matter, "being of opinion that the payment as made by the assignee (the plaintiff) was in willful disobedience of the decree of the superior court heretofore made, gave judgment attaching the assignee as for contempt," and the plaintiff, having excepted, appealed to this court. Pending the appeal in this court the said Dickson, who made the affidavit to support the motion to attach the plaintiff, moved in the court below to be allowed to withdraw and abandon the motion to attach, and his motion was there allowed, and a transcript of the record thereof was presented here at the time the appeal was called for argument; and also a motion was made here to allow him to withdraw and abandon his motion.

J. T. Perkins and Batchelor & Devereux, for appellant. S. J. Ervin, for appellee.

MERRIMON, C. J., (after stating the facts as above.) After the appeal was taken, bringing the whole matter of the motion into this court, it was irregular and improper to make the motion in the court below to withdraw and abandon the motion to attach, because the appeal brought the same here until it should be disposed of in some appropriate way. The court below did not have such control of the matter as to make an effectual disposition of it. The application of the defendant, (appellee,) John A. Dickson, to be allowed to abandon the motion to attach the plaintiff must be allowed, and an entry to that effect made in the court below. But this allowance cannot affect the motion as to other interested creditors, because the motion was applied for and allowed at the instance of and for the benefit of the others as well as himself. They were parties to the action, and the notice of the motion was signed by Dickson "for himself and other creditors," and the affidavit in support of the motion purported expressly to be for their benefit. Moreover, the counsel who made the motion represented all the interested creditors, and no one of them made any suggestion or opposition to it. Thus they, being before the court, and so represented by counsel, were at once

parties to and participating in the motion for their benefit; they were subject to the order of the court in that respect, and concluded by its order, and they were as well liable for costs. The motion was made at their instance, and for their benefit, as well as the same for Dickson. The affidavit made by the latter was sufficient to serve the common purpose of all the interested creditors. Who they were was shown by the record, and that was a sufficient designation of them, in connection with the motion; so that the appeal must be disposed of upon its merits, in the absence of a motion of the appellant to dismiss or withdraw it. It was found as a fact, and admitted, as appears from the case settled on appeal, that the plaintiff assignee had intentionally and willfully disbursed the funds in his hands wherewith he was charged otherwise than as by the decree and express order of the court. Obviously the court had authority to enforce its orders, decrees, and judgment by attachment, when the parties complained of were before it. It is a legitimate and approved method of enforcing its orders, as well as the order of and respect due the court. In re Daves, 81 N. C. 72; Bond v. Bond, 69 N. C. 97; Thompson v. Onley, 96 N. C. 9, 1 S. E. Rep. 620; In re Patterson, 99 N. C. 407, 6 S. E. Rep. 643.

Judgment affirmed.

WARD v. WILMINGTON & W. R. Co.

(*Supreme Court of North Carolina. Dec. 9, 1891.*)

RAILROAD COMPANIES — STOCK-KILLING CASES — OBSTRUCTIONS ON RIGHT OF WAY—DUTY TO REMOVE.

In an action against a railroad company for killing a horse, it appeared that the horse had been hidden from the sight of the engineer by high weeds and bushes growing within a few feet of the track, and that when the train was close upon him he had suddenly emerged. The court charged that it was negligence for the company to allow weeds and bushes to grow "near to" "or in close proximity" to the track, and that, if the injury resulted because the horse was so concealed that the engineer could not see him in time to stop, the company was liable. *Held* erroneous, in leaving uncertain the precise distance to which a railroad company must keep clear its right of way, and in fixing upon it the duty of taking possession of such parts of the right of way as are not actually needed for railroad purposes, and which custom has always allowed the abutting owners to cultivate. MERRIMON, C. J., dissenting.

Appeal from superior court, Pender county; R. F. ARMFIELD, Judge. Reversed.

This was an action by E. W. Ward against the Wilmington & Weldon Railroad Company to recover damages for the killing of plaintiff's horse. There was judgment for plaintiff, and defendant appeals.

The other facts fully appear in the following statement by AVERY, J.:

The issues submitted, with the responses by the jury, were as follows: "(1) Did defendant, by its negligence in moving its cars and engines, kill the horse of the plaintiff? Yes. (2) If yes, what damage has plaintiff sustained thereby? $88." There was testimony offered on the part of the plaintiff tending to show that within six months before the beginning of this action the defendant had killed the horse of the plaintiff by running against him, in the day-time, with a freight train running on defendant's road; and also testimony as to the value of the horse. Defendant introduced the engineer, fireman, and others who were on the train at the time of the killing of the horse. They testified that the train was a long and heavy freight train, running rapidly and with great momentum; that the engineer in charge of the train was on the vigilant lookout for stock in front of the train, but that weeds and bushes had grown up close to the track of defendant's road—at that point within two feet of the track—as high as plaintiff's horse; that the horse was concealed from the engineer by these weeds and bushes until the train was close upon him, when he suddenly emerged from the weeds and bushes onto the track; that the engineer, immediately on seeing the horse, he being on the lookout to the front, blew down brakes, blew the cattle alarm, and reversed his engine; that the brakes were applied, but that the horse was so close to the train that all these efforts were unavailing, and the train ran over the horse and killed him. Defendant asked his honor to instruct the jury: "If the jury believed that the engineer, as soon as he could, by looking out and being on the watch, discovered the horse, and then used all the efforts at his command to stop the train, and could not do so in time to keep from striking the horse, then the defendant was not guilty of negligence, and plaintiff could not recover." His honor told the jury that this would be true unless the defendant had negligently allowed bushes and weeds to grow on its right of way so close to its track that the horse was concealed thereby until it was too late to stop the train and prevent his destruction. Defendant further asked his honor to instruct that, "if the jury should believe that the engineer was prevented from seeing the horse, or would have been prevented from seeing the horse had he been on the careful lookout, by the weeds and bushes growing within two feet of the ends of the cross-ties on the side of the road on which the horse was killed, and the said bushes were three or four feet high, then the prima facie case in favor of the plaintiff would be rebutted, and jury should find first issue in favor of defendant." The substance of the instruction given is embodied in the opinion of the court There was a verdict for plaintiff. Defendant moved for a new trial on account of the refusal of the court to give the instructions asked for, and for alleged error in the instructions given.

Haywood & Haywood, for appellant.

AVERY, J., (*after stating the facts.*) It is settled law in this state that, if an engineer in charge of an engine sees, or can, by keeping a careful outlook, see, a cow or horse upon the track in his front, it is his duty to stop the train if he can do so without peril to the passengers and property under his charge by the use of all the

appliances for checking the speed at his command. Carlton v. Railroad Co., 104 N. C. 365, 10 S. E. Rep. 516; Wilson v. Railroad Co., 90 N. C. 69; Snowden v. Railroad Co., 95 N. C. 93; Bullock v. Railroad Co., 105 N. C. 180, 10 S. E. Rep. 988; Deans v. Railroad Co., 107 N. C. 686, 12 S. E. Rep. 77. If, by the exercise of ordinary care, the engineer can discover that an animal is greatly frightened, and is running apparently excitedly and wildly beside and near the track, or continues on and sometimes off it, it is the duty of the engineer to "slacken the speed, keep the engine under his control," and, if necessary, "stop it," until the animal is out of danger. Wilson v. Railroad Co., supra. "When the cattle are quietly grazing, resting, or moving near the track,—not on it,—manifesting no disposition to go on it, the speed of the train need not be checked." Wilson v. Railroad Co., supra. We have thus stated the general rules laid down by this court in reference to the negligence in injuring live-stock, in order the more intelligently to discuss the instruction given by the court in the case at bar, that, even though the engineer could not, by keeping the most vigilant outlook, discover that the plaintiff's horse was in the vicinity of the track in time to stop the engine, yet "it was the duty of the defendant to keep its right of way near its track reasonably clear of weeds and bushes, which might conceal stock approaching its road until it was too late to stop a train and prevent their destruction;" and that, "if they [the jury] believed that the horse was killed because he was so concealed by weeds and bushes, which the defendant had negligently permitted to grow up in close proximity to the track," that the engineer could not see in time to avert the injury, the defendant's negligence was the proximate cause of it. We take notice of the fact that, whatever may be the privilege of railroad companies to exercise dominion over their whole right of way, the universal custom has been to allow the abutting owner, whose land has been taken for the use of the public, to cultivate up to the side ditches that are kept open for the purposes of proper drainage by the company. While we concede that it is the duty of the corporation in constructing its road to cut down the large trees that might fall on or be thrown upon the track, we would be loth to give our sanction to any ruling that would make it incumbent upon them, in order to protect themselves from liability, to take actual possession of any portion of the right of way, not needed for corporate purposes proper, namely, to remove from it corn, grain, high grass, weeds, or bushes, that may spring up immediately outside of the ditches and grow upon cultivated land, high enough to conceal a horse or cow from the view of an engineer who is approaching with a moving train.

It is important that every principle of law, to which the conduct of the citizen is to be made to conform, should mark out the line of his duty with reasonable certainty. It is essential, in order to insure the transportation of passengers and freight with the dispatch and promptness that will meet the wants of a commercial people, that the managers of railroads should have a definite idea of the duties and liabilities of the companies, and should be able, by using proper precaution, to provide against them without subjecting the public to serious inconvenience or delay. If, therefore, the judge had told the jury that it was negligence to suffer weeds and bushes to grow in or upon the banks of the ditches of which the companies assume actual control and dominion to a sufficient height to obstruct the view of persons or animals from an approaching engine, he would have fixed a known and well-defined boundary line up to which the corporate authorities would be required to remove such obstructions, and would at the same time have held them bound to discharge a duty, which is but the exercise of ordinary diligence on their part. To burden these corporations with the further duty of removing such obstructions beyond the territory of which they assume actual control for corporate purposes is not only to license but to compel them, for their own security, to cut down corn or grain as well as weeds when it springs up so high as to hide cattle from view, and thus enable the engineer to see whether they are grazing quietly or moving about frantically as a train draws near to them. The court below laid down the indefinite rule that it was negligence to allow weeds or bushes to grow "near to" or "in close proximity" to the track. He left the precise distance to which the duty extended so vague and uncertain that railroad companies cannot provide against liability, however watchful their servants may be, except by assuming actual control and keeping clear of corn, grain, grass, weeds, and bushes the whole right of way, especially where there are curves so sharp that the line of vision of the engineer in looking to his front would cross the right of way at or near its outer boundary line. "Near," in common parlance, is understood and by lexicographers is defined to mean either "close" or "at no great distance;" while "in close proximity," or "in the immediate vicinity," are equivalent terms; and either of the expressions might have been understood by the jury as a declaration that it was negligence to leave weeds or bushes that would hide cattle from view anywhere on the right of way. One hundred feet from the center of the railroad (the ordinary limit of the right of way) would be considered by men of intelligence as at no great distance from or in the immediate vicinity of a track, and the instruction was therefore misleading, unless we intend to enjoin upon railroad companies the duty of ousting the owners of the abutting land and seeing that it is kept clear of corn-stalks or weeds, which, under good culture, would, after the crops are gathered, hide from view cattle on the right of way in the immediate vicinity of the track. In order to provide against liability under the rule laid down by his honor, railroad companies must either assume such control of the right of way, or the fast trains by which the companies have contracted for the expeditious transporta-

tion of the mails, persons, and property must stop and "beat the bushes" at every curve in the line where the soil is rich in order to ascertain whether a cow or horse can be made to emerge from them before proceeding on their important mission. Where bushes are allowed to grow in or inside of the ditches along the portion of the right of way of which the corporations assume actual control, so as to obstruct the view of an engineer on an approaching train, a greater degree of care does devolve upon the company, just as we have said in Hinkle v. Railroad Co., 13 S. E. Rep. 884, (decided at this term,) that where a company suffers cars or other obstructions to be placed on a side track, so as to shut off the view of a moving train from a traveler driving towards a crossing on the line, it is negligence in an engineer to fail to give notice of his approach. Loucks v. Railway Co., 19 Amer. & Eng. R. Cas. 312, notes and authorities cited; Railroad Co. v. Moody, 45 Amer. & Eng. R. Cas. 524, and notes, page 527 et seq. We think that the court below erred in fixing upon corporations the duty of re moving obstructions, such as weeds or corn-stalks, that are incident to the ordinary course of husbandry outside of the portions of the right of way, including side tracks under the actual control of the companies. It is, of course, the duty of the company to construct the road properly, and in such a manner as will not expose travelers to needless dangers. It is incumbent on them, as we have said, to remove all trees from the right of way, and also any structure that is liable to fall upon passing trains or upon the track so as to obstruct it. But in our case the question is as to their duty in reference to the right of way outside of the track and ditches, and after the completion of the road, in reference to weeds and bushes that may spring up while the land is being cultivated with ordinary care. There was error, for which the defendant is entitled to a new trial.

MERRIMON, C. J., dissented.

CLARK, J., (concurring.) It is the duty of a railroad company, as to its patrons, to keep the road-bed in good condition, and for that purpose to keep enough of its right of way clear to prevent accident from trees or limbs falling upon its track. It owes no duties as to the condition of its right of way or of its track as to others, except the statutory duty as to crossings. If a trestle is so defective that a foot-passenger, who chooses to walk thereon instead of in the highway, falls through and is hurt, would the company be liable? Or if a dead tree left standing on the right of way falls and kills stock pasturing there, must the company respond in damages? Or suppose stock frightened by the whistle or the noise of the train fall into a ditch on the right of way, must the corporation pay? I wot not. If accident from these causes occurs to those to whom the company owes duties, it would be liable; but it is no part of its duty to furnish a safe footpath for people or safe pasturage for cattle. If the man or the cattle are on the track, it is the duty of the company to avoid injury to them if, by the exercise of a proper lookout and care, it can do so. But the principle goes no further. There are in this state about 3,500 miles of railroad, and every year extends the mileage. If these companies are guilty of negligence, if they do not keep their right of way, 3,500 miles in length, and 200 feet wide, shrubbed, so that a piny-woods cow or a razor-back hog may not always be visible thereon, or in default of that are guilty of negligence if they do not slacken speed and "beat the bushes" whenever high enough and dense enough to conceal the recumbent forms of those interesting animals, who otherwise might be startled from their slumbers and rush upon the track, then the duty required of engineers, and the expense imposed upon the companies, will not be "trivial." The railroads own the right of way. It belongs to them for the purposes of their traffic. All that can be required of them, as to others than its passengers and freight, is the good old rule that it use its own in such manner as not to injure others. It is not required to put its track or right of way in good condition for the safe use of others, who pay nothing to them to enable them to do so. In those cases, where railroads have been held liable for fire originating on their right of way, the negligence was not in allowing the grass to grow there,—they are not expected to keep the right of way plowed up,—but in using defective spark-arresters, or negligently using them, so that fire is communicated to the inflammable grass or matter, and thence passes to the property of others, which is thereby destroyed. In the present case the prayer for instruction that if "the engineer did not, and by the exercise of a diligent lookout could not, have seen the stock on the track in time to avoid the injury, the issue should be answered in favor of the defendant," was warranted by Carlton's Case, 104 N. C. 365, 10 S. E. Rep. 516, and other precedents, and should have been given in the form asked, without the modification made by the court below.

MERRIMON, C. J., (dissenting.) In this state a railroad company is not required to inclose its railroad by fence or otherwise, and hence it is not regarded or treated in law as a trespass, if the live-stock of farmers and others at large in the forests or fields wander upon its road or graze upon its right of way. If such live-stock, so wandering, shall be negligently killed by its moving locomotives or trains, it will be answerable to the person whose property shall be so injured in damages. Indeed, the statute (Code, § 2326) prescribes that such killing of stock shall *prima facie* be negligently done, and the burden of proving the absence of negligence in such case is put upon the railroad company. Such company is bound to reasonable care and diligence in preventing such injuries. It is therefore its duty to keep its road-way in such reasonable condition as will prevent the killing of stock, and as well to prevent possible injury arising therefrom to passengers and

freight passing over its road, and injury to its own property. It is negligence on its part when it fails to do so. To prevent such injuries, it is bound to keep its road-way, as far as practicable, free from such things as will obstruct the view of the engine-man looking ahead of the moving train. He should be able to see stock of all kinds on the road or the road-way, in order that he may be able to sound the danger alarm as early as practicable, and frighten the stock away, and to put his engine in condition to stop the train promptly. If bushes, weeds, grass, and the like are permitted to grow upon the road-way, unrestrained, they not infrequently, particularly where the soil is rich, grow so high and thickly as to hide the animal grazing there, and prevent the engine-man from seeing it until the engine is almost upon it. He then sounds the alarm. This and the rushing train alarms the animal, and it at once springs upon the track, is killed, the train may be thrown off the track, passengers killed or wounded, or freight injured or ruined. All this may easily happen,—has happened. It may be easily prevented by keeping the road-way clear from bushes and high weeds that grow thickly. But for such growth, the stock would generally be seen in ample time to frighten them off, or stop the train, and thus sometimes prevent damage very serious in its extent and nature. The cost of keeping the road-way clear is trifling, compared with the loss occasioned by failing to do so. Indeed, one of the very purposes of the broad road-way allowed to railroad companies is to prevent injuries like those mentioned. It is expected and intended that it shall be kept reasonably clean and free from all such things as will give rise to injury and danger. Hence it has oftentimes been held that it is negligence to allow dry grass to remain on the road-way, or dry, decaying cross-ties and the like to remain there, because they easily take fire, and thus frequently spread devastation. In possible cases, no doubt, it may be that the road-way cannot be kept clear; but such cases are not general nor common. Nor is this any reason why it shall not be done when practicable. It is said that such a requirement will drive the railroad company to assert its right against farmers and others who are generally allowed as a matter of favor to cultivate the land freely and closely to the road track. This is an unfounded apprehension. Stock are not allowed to go at large in the fields where corn, wheat, rye, and tobacco and the like grow, and there is hence no danger arising from cattle straying in the cultivated fields. In the present case, if the bushes and grass had not been permitted to grow so high and stand in the road-way, the possibility, the strong probability, is that the animal would not have been killed, but in the bushes and grass the engine-man might—would have—seen the animal long before he did, and frightened it away, or he might readily have slackened the speed of the train, or, if need be, stopped it. It was fortunate that the train was not thrown from the track, and greater damage done. I cannot hesitate to say that, in my judgment, the defendant was justly chargeable with negligence, and that the charge of the court to the jury was reasonable and just.

DAVIS, J. I concur in the above dissenting opinion of the Chief Justice.

COWLES v. REAVIS.

(Supreme Court of North Carolina. Dec. 8, 1891.)

PROBATE OF WILL—EXECUTOR'S DEED—DESCRIPTION OF LAND.

1. A will admitted to probate prior to 1856 was governed by Rev. St. N. C. c. 122, § 6, which authorized the probate in common form by one subscribing witness, and not by Rev. Code N. C. c. 119, § 1.

2. Where a deed is executed by one of two executors under a provision of the will authorizing such executor to convey the land after the death of the co-executor, who was life-tenant of the land, the deed need not recite the death of the co executor, as that fact will be presumed.

3. If the beginning corner in the description of a tract of land has been destroyed, it is proper, in order to ascertain the true boundary, to survey the land by beginning at any known corner or point from which the boundaries may be located.

4. Where the last call in a grant of land is "125 poles, to the beginning," and the beginning point is established, the line must extend to or stop at it, regardless of distance.

Appeal from superior court, Wilkes county; JESSE F. GRAVES, Judge. Affirmed.

Action by C. J. Cowles against J. M. Reavis to determine the boundary of plaintiff's land. Judgment for plaintiff. Defendant appeals.

The other facts fully appear in the following statement by DAVIS, J.:

The plaintiff alleged that he was the owner of certain land described by metes and bounds in the complaint. The defendant by his answer denies the allegations of the complaint, and says that he is the owner of two tracts of land adjoining land of the plaintiff, set out by metes and bounds in the answer; and, if any portion of these tracts is covered by the boundaries alleged in the plaintiff's deed, then he is in possession of that portion of said land, and has been in possession for more than seven years under color of title, and is the owner thereof. At the trial the plaintiff offered in evidence a grant from the state to David Mickle, which he alleged covered the land in controversy. He then offered the will of David Mickle, dated August 13, 1840, attested by two subscribing witnesses, but only proved by one. The will is set out in the complaint, in which he gives certain property, including his "home tracts of land," to his wife, Lucy Mickle, for and during her life, and, among other things, he directs as follows: "I want my executor, hereinafter named, after the death of my beloved wife or widow, to sell the remainder of the estate, both real and personal," and divide the proceeds as directed by said will. He appoints his wife, Lucy Mickle, and his son Moses L. Mickle, "executors of this, my last

will and testament." The subscribing witnesses were Joshua Fletcher and W. Mastin, and the certificate of probate was as follows: "The execution of the within will was proved in open court by William Mastin, one of the subscribing witnesses thereto, and ordered to be recorded. [Signed] W. MASTIN, Clerk." The defendant objected to the introduction of this will, and insisted that there was no sufficient probate. Objection overruled, and defendant excepted. The plaintiff then offered in evidence a deed from Moses L Mickle, one of the executors named in the will of David Mickle, which recited that said land was sold under the authority of said will. The defendant objected to the introduction of this deed, because it was executed by only one executor, and because there was no evidence of the death of the life-tenant. Objection overruled, and defendant excepted. The call of the grant from the state and the deeds under which the plaintiff claims was as follows: "Beginning at a red oak, Adison Foster's south-east corner, runing south 76 poles, to a white oak; thence west with Hays' line 60 poles, to a stake; thence south 60 poles, to a stake; thence west 40 poles, to a stake; thence south 112 poles, to a stake; thence east 80 poles, to a stake; thence south 112 poles, with Joseph Law's, to a pine; thence east — poles, to a white oak, Brock's line; thence with his line 180 poles, to a poplar; thence west with Law's line 125 poles, to the beginning,— containing 200 acres, more or less." The red oak at the beginning corner could not be found, as all the land where it was had been cleared and cut down. There was much evidence tending to locate the white oak in Hays' line, the Hays' line west of the pine in Mickle and Lane's line, the white oak in Brooks' line, and the corner poplar of Mickle being his south-east corner.

The defendant asked the following instructions: "(1) What are the terms of a grant or deed is a matter of law for the court; where they are is for the jury. (2) In this case the beginning corner of plaintiff's grant must be located at the south-east corner of the Adison Foster tract, (and it cannot be at any other point on the line of said Foster's land.) (3) That if the jury failed to find the south-east corner of the Foster tract from the evidence, then the plaintiff must fail, the surveyor Somers and the plaintiff both being sworn; that if the beginning corner is the south-east corner of any tract located on the plat or shown in evidence, that then the plaintiff's grant would not cover any land in controversy. (4) That, in any aspect of this case, the last call of plaintiff's grant with John Law's line from the poplar must stop at the end of 125 poles, the distance in the grant. (5) That if the jury fail to locate the south-east corner of the Foster tract, but find from the evidence that the poplar in the last call of the plaintiff's grant is proven, then the beginning corner could not be nearer the defendant's land than where the distance gave out in running the calls of the line from the poplar. (6) If the defendant's grant and deed covers the land in controversy, and defendant, or those under whom he claims, have been in the actual adverse possession of any part of the land so conveyed by his grant and deed seven years next before the beginning of this action, the plaintiff cannot recover." His honor gave the first and sixth instructions asked for by plaintiff, modified the second by striking out the words in parentheses, and refused to give the third, fourth, and fifth. His honor further charged the jury on the question of the boundary as follows: "What are the boundaries is a question of law, to be settled by the court; but where the boundaries are, is a matter of fact for the jury. That the true and only beginning corner of plaintiff's deed is the south-east corner of the Adison Foster tract, and here the jury must begin, but it is for the jury to locate said corner, and say where it is. That, having located the south-east corner of Adison Foster's tract, they must begin there, and run the course and distance called for in the deed, stopping at the end of the course and distance, unless some natural object, line, etc., was called for, when they must run to the object called for, regardless of course and distance." He then charged the jury, with this rule to govern them, that they must run according to the calls of the deed; that in running the last call, thence west from the poplar with John Law's line 125 poles to the beginning, (which calls are set forth in the plat,) they must commence at the poplar, and run with Law's line to the beginning, (it having been established,) whether the number of poles gave out or not before reaching the beginning. There was much more of the charge not necessary for this case. Motion for a new trial by the defendant, assigning as error (1) the ruling of the court in admitting the will of David Mickle; (2) admitting the deed duly executed by one of the executors; (3) for failure of court to give instructions 2, 3, 4, and 5, asked by defendant; (4) because the court declined to tell jury in running last call from poplar that they must stop at the end of 125 poles. Rule discharged. Judgment for plaintiff. Appeal by defendant.

R. Z. Linney, for appellant. *Glenn & Manly*, for appellee.

DAVIS, J., (*after stating the facts.*) It appears upon the face of the will that there were two subscribing witnesses, and it was sufficient to pass the real estate of the testator. It is certified by the clerk that it was proved in open court by one of them, and this is sufficient evidence of probate. Harven v. Springs, 10 Ired. 180, and cases cited. The will was proved in common form, prior to 1856, and is governed by chapter 122, § 6, Rev. St., which authorized the probate in common form by one subscribing witness, and not by chapter 119, § 15, Rev. Code. Jenkins v. Jenkins, 96 N. C. 254, 2 S. E. Rep. 522. The case of Gerard's Will, 2 Hayw. (N. C.) 144, cited by counsel for defendant, has no application. That case only decides that the will must be proved in the court of the county in which the deceased resided. It was there proposed to prove the will of Gerard, who resided in Edgecombe county, in the superior court of Halifax county, and the court held that that could not be done. Nor is the case of Leatherwood v. Boyd, 1 Winst. 123, like this. PEARSON, C. J., says that, "had the certificate stopped after the words, 'the last will and testament of John Leatherwood was duly proved in common form by the oath of R. A. Edmundson, one of the subscribing witnesses thereto,' it would have been sufficient, for the presumption is that the court knew how to take the probate of a will, and saw that it was properly done. But, if there be anything on the face of the proceedings to show the contrary, that will rebut the presumption." In that case the certificate stated further facts that rebutted the maxim *omnia præsamuntur rite esse acta.* In this case nothing appears in the certificate to rebut the presumption. Marshall v. Fisher, 1 Jones, (N. C.) 111. The first exception was properly overruled.

The second exception is that the deed from Moses L. Mickle was improperly admitted, because executed by only one of the executors, and it does not appear in the face of the deed that the life-tenant was dead. It appears from the will itself that the deed could be only made by the executor Moses L. Mickle, for the executrix was the tenant for life, and the land was to be sold after her death. But chapter 46, § 40, was in force at the time, and expressly authorized the surviving executor to sell, and this exception cannot be sustained. Nor is there any force in the objection that it does not appear from the deed that Lucy Mickle, the devisee for life, was dead. This will be presumed. 1 Greenl. Ev. § 20; Hughes v. Hodges, 102 N. C. 202, 9 S. E. Rep. 437.

The third exception is to the refusal of the court to give instructions 2, 3, 4, and 5, asked by the defendant. It is too clear to need citation of authority that if the beginning corner has been destroyed, as in this case, it is competent, in order to ascertain the true boundary, to survey the land by beginning at any known corner or point from which the boundaries may be located, and the second instruction asked for was given as far as the defendant was entitled to it. The 3d, 4th, and 5th instructions were properly refused, and the charge of his honor upon the question of boundary covered all that the defendant was entitled to. The last call was 125 poles, to the beginning, and, the beginning point having been established, the line must extend to or stop at it, regardless of distance. No error.

STATE v. AVERY.

(*Supreme Court of North Carolina.* Dec. 8, 1891.)

BURNING COTTON IN CARS.

Code, § 985, par. 5, as amended by Acts 1885, c. 42, which makes it a misdemeanor to "willfully burn or destroy any other person's corn. cotton, * * * shucks, or other provender, in a stack, hill, or pen, or secured in any other way, out of doors, grass or sedge on the land," does not embrace cotton stored in a car standing on a railroad track. CLARK, J., dissenting.

Appeal from superior court, Burke county; JOHN GRAY BYNUM, Judge. Reversed.

Joe Avery was convicted of burning cotton in a car, and appeals.

The other facts fully appear in the following statement by MERRIMON, C. J.:

The indictment charges that "the defendant, at," etc., "willfully and unlawfully did burn and destroy twenty bales of cotton, the property of the Dunevant Cotton Manufacturing Company, which said cotton being then and there secured on a car, the property of the Richmond & Danville Railroad Company, against the form of the statute," etc. The defendant pleaded not guilty. On the trial it was in evidence that the defendant and two other small boys were playing in a box-car loaded with cotton, standing on the railroad at the depot at Morganton; that the defendant lighted a candle, and fastened it in the floor, and near the cotton, when one of the boys was about to put it out, and he prevented him, saying he would watch it. The cotton was soon on fire, and it and the car were burned and destroyed. There was also evidence of threats made by the defendant that he would get even with the railroad company, if he had to burn the depot, for cutting off his leg, etc. The defendant requested the court to instruct the jury "that, unless the cotton was out of doors, the defendant cannot be convicted, and, the cotton not being out of doors, he cannot be convicted." There was a verdict of guilty, and the defendant moved in arrest of judgment upon the ground that it appears by the indictment that the cotton charged to have been burned was cotton in bales secured in a car, and the statute alleged to have been violated has no application; that it applies only to cases where cotton and other things therein specified, burned or destroyed, are "out of doors;" that is, in the field, etc. The court denied the motion, and entered judgment against the defendant, and he excepted, and appealed to this court.

Batchelor & Devereux, for appellant. *The Attorney General,* for the State.

MERRIMON, C. J., *(after stating the facts.)* The statute, (Code, § 985, par. 5,) as amended by the subsequent statute, (Act 1885, c. 42,) provides that "any person who shall willfully burn or destroy any other person's corn, cotton, wheat, barley, rye, oats, buckwheat, rice, tobacco, hay, straw, fodder, shucks, or other provender, in a stack, hill, or pen, or secured in any other way, out of doors, grass or sedge standing on the land, shall be guilty of a misdemeanor," etc. In our judgment, this statute plainly refers to and embraces only cotton and the other things specified therein, not within doors,—not housed and thus secured, as in a barn, gin-house, or the like. It refers to cotton and the other things secured in any other way,— "out of doors;" in the field; "on the land;"

the farm where they were produced, or some other land, so as to be in some way secured without doors: without the barn, ginhouse, or other like inclosure. The words, "in a stack, hill, or pen," "out of doors," "the grass or sedge standing on the land," applied to the several things specified in their connection, are apt and appropriate to refer to and imply such things so situate and secured "out of doors." The purpose is to protect such things so exposed and imperfectly secured "out of doors," in the fields, on the farm, "the land" of the person who owns or has control of them. In any reasonable view of their meaning, application, and connections, they cannot refer to and embrace cotton stored in a railroad car standing on a railroad track at a depot, whether to be thus and there secured temporarily or shipped to some other place. Cotton and the other things specified, secured in a car on the railroad, are not secured in some other way out of doors on the land, in the sense of the statute. When thus secured on the car, they have been taken from the place,—the land where they were secured "out of doors." —and are on the way to market, to be used, or on the way to be again housed, or secured in a stack, hill, or pen, or in some other way, "out of doors." The burning or destruction of such things on a car does not come within the mischief to be remedied by the statute,—the burning or destruction of them when they are ordinarily secured out of doors. The indictment should appropriately, in the proper connections, charge that the cotton or other thing burned or destroyed was in a stack, or as otherwise, in a way described, secured "out of doors." In this case it fails, as to matter of substance, to charge the offense defined by the statute. It does not charge, in substance or effect, that the cotton in some way described was secured "out of doors;" it simply charges the burning on the railroad in a railroad car. For the reasons stated, this is not sufficient. It seems that the legislature supposed and intended that the statute (Code, § 985, pars. 6, 7) in respect to burning barns, gin-houses, and other buildings would be sufficient to protect grain, cotton, and the like stored in them,—in doors on the land. This appears to be a case in which the defendant might appropriately have been indicted for malicious injury to personal property, as defined by the statute, (Code, § 1082,) but in no view of the present indictment will it suffice to charge that offense. There is error. The judgment must be reversed, and judgment arrested. To that end let this opinion be certified to the superior court. It is so ordered.

CLARK, J., *(dissenting.)* The statute (Code, § 985, par. 5) makes it indictable to willfully burn or destroy any of the articles therein named, when "in a stack, hill, or pen, or secured in any other way, out of doors." The expression "out of doors" means simply "not in a house." If in a house, then these articles are protected by paragraphs 6 and 7 of this section in regard to burning barns, gin-houses, and other buildings. This subsection 5 was intended to protect them when not so housed, but "in a stack, hill, or pen, or otherwise secured." The article here (cotton) is one of those enumerated. It was "out of doors;" that is, not in a house. Though not in a hill, stack, or pen, it was "otherwise secured," and is properly charged in the indictment as " then and there secured in a car, the property of the Richmond & Danville Railroad Company." It seems conceded in the opinion of the court that property of the description named is not protected against burning when off the premises where grown, except in those cases where an indictment would lie for injury to personal property. Code, § 1082. If this is so, the defendant, who has been found guilty of the "willful and unlawful" burning of 20 bales of cotton secured out of doors, has been guilty of no offense, because the cotton was in transit and off the farm where grown, and he and others would be at full liberty to "willfully and unlawfully burn or destroy" the vast amount of farm produce daily in transit on railroads and other conveyances, or camped out at night in the country wagons, covered and uncovered, which bring such a large part of the farm produce mentioned in this subsection to market. I do not think so broad a "casus omissus" was left by the law-making power. There are no words in the statute restricting its application to the burning and destruction if done on the farm, and the courts are not called on by a fair and reasonable interpretation of the statute to leave farm produce "secured out of doors" unprotected, if it is being moved from the place of its production, for section 1082, supra, does not make any burning or destruction indictable if done merely "willfully and unlawfully." The words "on the land" are not in the original act, and the amendment refers only to "grass or sedge standing on the land."

STATON v. NORFOLK & C. R. CO.

(Supreme Court of North Carolina. Dec. 8, 1891.)

CONSTRUCTION OF RAILROAD — FLOWING LANDS— NATURAL DRAINS—SURFACE WATER.

1. In an action against a railroad company, the complaint alleged that the company, by means of a ditch along its right of way, had diverted water, and emptied it on plaintiff's land. The company owned the right of way, and its evidence tended to prove that it was not on plaintiff's land; that the ditch was on its right of way beside the track, and was necessary to the construction of the road; that it was to convey surface water along its road to a natural outlet; that the ditch was sufficient to carry the water into such outlet without flooding it. *Held,* that it was error not to instruct that if the ditch was necessary in the construction of the road, and the water was additional surface water, the company had a right to drain the road as it did.

2. It was error to refuse to instruct that the company had a right to drain its road-bed, and that if the ditch was cut through to a natural drain, and it could not have been drained in any other direction without overflowing the lands of other persons, then the company had a right to drain into such natural drain. SHEPHERD, J., dissenting.

3. The company had no right to collect surface water in its right of way and divert it into a channel where it would not naturally flow, and which was inadequate to receive it.

Appeal from superior court, Halifax county; SPIER WHITAKER, Judge. Reversed.

Action by Thomas M Staton against the Norfolk & Carolina Railroad Company to recover damages for flooding his land. Verdict and judgment for plaintiff. Defendant appeals.

The other facts fully appear in the following statement by MERRIMON, C. J.:

The following is a copy of the material parts of the complaint: (2) That the plaintiff is the owner of a farm in said county, containing about 160 acres, and the defendant, some time during the year 1889, located and constructed its road near said farm. (3) That he planted a large portion of said farm in corn and other crops the said year. (4) That the defendant, some time during said year, negligently, wrongfully, and unlawfully cut a ditch, through which great quantities of water from a large pocoson were diverted from their natural course, and from the way in which it had been accustomed to flow, and emptied upon his said farm. (5) That on account of the negligent, wrongful, and unlawful cutting of said ditch, the negligent and unlawful diversion of the course of said water, the plaintiff's farm was constantly kept overflowed during said year, and the crops therein planted were entirely drowned and destroyed. (6) That on account of the negligent, unlawful, and wrongful cutting of said ditch, and the unlawful and negligent diversion of the course of said water, the plaintiff's farm has been sobbed, soured, and its fertility destroyed, and rendered unfit for agricultural purposes. (7) That, on account of said negligent, unlawful, and wrongful acts of the defendant, the plaintiff has been damaged to the amount of $1,000. The defendant denied these allegations. The parties agreed upon and the court submitted the following issues to the jury, and they responded as follows: "(1) Is the plaintiff the owner of the farm described in the complaint? Yes. (2) Did the defendant locate its road near the farm? Yes. (3) Was the ditch cut by defendant negligently, wrongfully, and unlawfully cut? Yes. (4) Did the cutting of said ditch cause the water from the pocoson to overflow the land of the plaintiff in 1889? Yes. (5) Was the overflow, if any, caused by surface water? Yes. (6) Did the defendant negligently damage the plaintiff's land for agricultural purposes? Yes. (7) What damage, if any, has the plaintiff sustained? $220." The plaintiff produced evidence on the trial tending to prove the allegations of the complaint. It was admitted that the defendant owned the right of way for the proper purposes of its railroad. It likewise produced evidence going to prove that its road-way was not situate upon any part of the plaintiff's land; that the ditch mentioned and complained of was cut along-side of the railroad track; that it was necessary to the construction and uses of the road; that its purpose was to convey surface water from a pocoson, and along the road, to Indian branch. One witness testified for the defendant that "in March, 1889, I had charge of railroad grading and ditching in this pocoson ditch cut along railroad down to Indian branch, to relieve the road-bed of the surface water. We began down at Indian branch, and worked up towards pocoson; cut the ditch from a branch up through a field to pocoson. We stopped from the 26th of March to the 1st of April, 1889. About one-half foot of water in pocoson. If ditch had not been cut, we could not have made a solid road-bed. We could not have gotten dirt to make the road-bed unless water in pocoson gets very high. Ditch through Mark Bell's field does not carry off any water. This ditch in poor condition. Logs in it. The water drained off by railroad. Surface water. Ditch cut in pretty fair shape." Another witness testified: "Civil engineer eleven years. Have examined the locality. Measured ditch and taken measurements of that country. (Exhibits and explains a map of that locality, made by him.) Condition of Deep creek, May 14, 1890, 700 feet wide. Opposite plaintiff's lands water rises three or four feet, and five or six feet at dam. The ditch cut by R. R. necessary to build road. Ditch through pocoson 2x2; through field, 5x6. Difference in capacity between Indian branch and R. R. ditch, 1 to 50. For rains ordinarily expected, ditch sufficient to carry off the water without overflow on plaintiff's land. Ditch skillfully constructed." Another testified: "I had contract for building this part of road. I cut the ditch under direction of civil engineer of defendant company. The work was skillfully done. The R. R. embankment acts as a dam against upper part of pocoson. Work began on pocoson in March, 1889. In 1888 little or no water in pocoson. In 1889, except after rain, little or no water. '89 very wet year. Capacity of ditch sufficient to relieve road of surface water in 1889. Ditch could not carry water enough to flood Indian branch. Ditch sufficient to carry the water which came down ditch along R. R., unless in case of extra heavy rain. Ditch we dug would carry all water which came from the pocoson and Indian branch. Mark Bell's ditch was filled up." The defendant requested the court to give the jury sundry special instructions, which it gave, and to give the following, which it refused to give, and thereupon the defendant excepted: "(3) If the ditch was necessary in the construction of the road, the right of way being condemned and paid for, and the water additional surface water, then the defendant had a right to cut a ditch and drain the road as it did." "(8) The defendant had a right to drain its road-bed, and if the ditch was cut through to a natural drain, and it could not have been drained in any other direction without overflowing the lands of other persons, then they had a right to drain the surface water into a natural drain, and the plaintiff cannot recover." There was a verdict and judgment for the plaintiff, and the defendant appealed.

T. N. Hill and *W. H. Day*, for appellant. *W. A. Dunn*, for appellee.

MERRIMON, C. J., (*after stating the facts.*) Unquestionably the defendant had the right to cut through and along its right of way, and keep in repair, such appropriate ditches and culverts as were necessary to carry off the surface water coming upon the right of way to a natural drain or outlet adequate to receive it. There was evidence of the defendant tending to prove that the ditch complained of was wholly situate upon its right of way: that the ditch was necessary, skillfully constructed, and that it was adequate in its capacity to carry the surface water into a natural drain, without flooding the latter, unless in case of an extraordinary rain-fall. In view of the contention of the parties, the evidence and conflict of the same, we think the court should have given the jury the third instruction asked for by the defendant, which was denied. It may be that the jury believed that the defendant had no right to divert the surface water on its right of way to a natural outlet, even though this were done altogether upon its own land. The instruction might have prevented such possible misapprehension.

And for the like reason the court should have given the eighth instruction denied, except so much thereof as implied that the plaintiff could not recover.

The defendant had no right to collect surface water in its right of way, and divert it, by cutting a ditch for the purpose, into a channel where it would not naturally flow, and which was not adequate to receive it, and thus flood and injure the land of another. A party must submit to the natural disadvantages and inconveniences incident to his land, unless he can in some lawful way avoid or remove and rid himself of them. But he has no right, as a general rule, to rid himself of them by shifting them by artificial means to the land of another, when naturally and in the order of things they would not go upon such land or affect it adversely. Porter v. Durham, 74 N. C. 767; Washb. Easem. 353 et seq. Nor is a railroad company or other corporation ordinarily on any footing in such respect other than a natural person. There is error. The judgment must be reversed, and a new trial granted. To that end let this opinion be certified to the superior court. It is so ordered

SHEPHERD, J., (*dissenting.*) Conceding that the defendant has a right to cut the ditch and conduct the surface water into a natural stream passing through its right of way, the privilege must necessarily be attended with the qualification that the ditch should not be so constructed as to divert the surface water from the direction in which, by the general inclination of the land, it naturally flows, and discharge it, to the injury of others, into a stream which is inadequate to receive it. I think that from the testimony of the plaintiff (who was examined in his own behalf) there was some evidence of this latter view, and, although it may have been slight, it warranted his honor in refusing instructions which entirely ignored the very important qualification I have mentioned.

MILLER v. BUMGARDNER et al.

(Supreme Court of North Carolina. Dec. 8, 1891.)

ADVERSE POSSESSION—TACKING—BURDEN OF PROOF—INFANCY—COVERTURE.

1. Plaintiff took possession of land under a deed from a married woman, who was not privily examined, and held the same until it was sold under execution to defendant's grantor. Upon the second marriage of plaintiff's grantor, subsequent to said sale under execution, she joined her husband in another conveyance to plaintiff. Held, that plaintiff's possession had been under color of title, and, as defendant was in privity with her, he could set up the same against her by connecting it with the possession of himself and his grantor.

2. Plaintiff sought to prove that her grantor was an infant during her widowhood, and that consequently, being under the disability of either marriage or infancy all the time, said adverse possession was not a defense. Held, that the burden of such proof was upon plaintiff, and any doubt should have been resolved in defendant's favor.

3. If plaintiff's grantor became of age during her widowhood the statute thereupon began to run, and it was not interrupted by her marriage.

Appeal from superior court, Ashe county; W. A. HOKE, Judge. Affirmed.

Action by Betsy Jane Miller against David Bumgardner et al. to recover possession of land. From a judgment for defendants, plaintiff appeals.

Geo. W. Bower, for appellees.

AVERY, J. It was admitted that prior to the year 1876 one Mollie Cox was the owner of the land in dispute, and that she married one Denton Williams, and during coverture, in September, 1876, a deed, signed by her husband, Denton Williams, and herself, was delivered to the plaintiff, Betsy Jane Miller, but the feme covert was not privily examined as to its execution. The defendant, relying on this deed or paper, delivered to the plaintiff as color of title, offered evidence tending to show that Betsey Jane Miller, the plaintiff, took possession under it at the date of its execution in September, 1876, and remained in possession continuously till January 3, 1883, when Williams Miller, under whom the defendant Bumgardner holds, was placed in possession by the sheriff by virtue of a writ of possession issued in an action brought by him, claiming title and possession of said land against the plaintiff. It was in evidence also that the said Williams Miller prior to the institution of said suit had purchased a note, given by plaintiff to said Mollie Williams for the purchase money, recovered judgment on the same against plaintiff, bought at sale under execution issued on said judgment, and recovered in said action on the sheriff's deed. Avoiding the estoppel growing out of that action, the plaintiff, Betsy Jane Miller, offered as evidence of title a deed executed by Mollie Robertson, (who was first Mollie Cox, then married Denton Williams,

and after his death married Robertson,) in which her husband joined, dated July 28, 1888, which was duly proven. As both parties to the action acknowledged in the pleadings that the title was in Mollie Robertson, (née Mollie Cox,) this deed offered by the plaintiff was prima facie proof that the title had passed from Mollie Robertson, and was in the plaintiff at the time when the action was brought, and, nothing more appearing, the plaintiff was entitled to recover upon it, the possession by defendants being admitted. To meet this apparently sufficient title the defendants offered testimony tending to show the continuous possession by Betsy Jane Miller, the plaintiff in this action, for over six years, between dates already given, under the paper purporting to be a deed from Denton Williams and his wife, Mollie, to her, and to connect with that occupancy by her that of Williams Miller, under whom defendants claim, and who took possession in 1883 as the purchaser of her interest at execution sale. Williams Miller and those claiming under him were clearly in privity with her as to her claim of title by virtue of the occupancy under the paper purporting to have been executed by Williams and wife; and, while the plaintiff was not estopped from setting up the subsequent deed as evidence of title, she was a stranger and adverse to, while the defendants were in privity with, her former claim of title under that paper as color. There was no error in the charge of the court that the paper was sufficient to show color of title in Betsy Miller during her occupancy under it. Avent v. Arrington, 105 N. C. 377, 10 S. E. Rep. 991. There is as little doubt that the defendants, being in privity with her former claim as claimants under the purchaser at execution sale, might avail themselves of her possession from September, 1876, to January 3, 1883. Wood, Lim. § 271. But it was admitted on the trial that Mollie Williams was a feme covert, as she purported to be on the face of the paper, which was offered and is relied on by defendant as color of title. The plaintiff having shown an apparently good title from the common source, the defendants had the right to set up adverse possession under the general denial. (Freeman v. Sprague, 82 N. C. 366;) but the burden was upon them, nevertheless, to prove continuous possession under the paper offered as color for such period as was necessary to vest the title in Williams Miller, under whom they claimed. This they did by connecting his possession in his own proper person with that of plaintiff, and proving that it continued from January 3, 1883, when the sheriff put him in, till this action was brought, on the 6th of August, 1888. The plaintiff then offered testimony tending to show that Mollie Cox was laboring under the disability of infancy when she married Denton Williams, and did not arrive at the age of 21 years until after he had died, in 1877, and until she had, on November 3, 1880, married her present husband. The plaintiff thus took the burden again upon herself in attempting to destroy the force of the proof of continuous possession for the statutory period. Bailey, Onus Probandi,

p. 258. On the other hand, the defendants offered testimony tending to show · that Mollie Robertson became 21 years old in 1878, prior to her second marriage, and that the statute began to run before the second disability supervened. There was no error in the instruction given that, if the statute began to run during her discoverture, it continued to run after her second marriage, and that consequently the possession of defendants and those under whom they claimed was adverse from 1878 till the action was brought, in 1888; and, if she was 21 years old in 1878, the plaintiff could not recover. The jury came in, after having retired for some time, to request further instruction from the court, "saying their minds were agreed on all but one point, and that was as to when Mollie Robertson became 21,—whether before or after her second marriage,—and as to that their minds were about balanced, and asked what they must do." The court charged them that the burden of establishing the affirmative of the issue of title was upon the plaintiff, and "if the evidence left their minds in doubt on this question" they would answer that issue, "No." The plaintiff had offered the evidence as to the disability of the *feme covert* to meet the testimony as to possession, and the burden was on her to show the supervening disability, which prevented the statute from running. It was not incumbent on the defendants to negative the possibility of her infancy and of its continuance until another disability supervened. Proof of possession under color for seven years extending from the period of her widowhood in 1878 till the action began, the title being admitted to be out of the state, was presumptive evidence that it vested in Williams Miller to the boundaries described in the paper under which he claimed. McLean v. Smith, 106 N. C. 172, 11 S. E. Rep. 184; Ruffin v. Overby, 105 N. C. 78, 11 S. E. Rep. 251. The burden was upon the plaintiff, therefore, to show by a preponderance of evidence that the disability of infancy continued till the second marriage, and if she failed to satisfy the jury by the greater weight of testimony, so as to leave the scales (figuratively speaking) no longer evenly balanced as to this question, it was their duty to find for the defendants, and it was not error in the court to so instruct them. State v. Rogers, 79 N. C. 609. The presumption is in favor of the title of one who is in possession, and a plaintiff cannot overcome that presumption except by satisfying the jury by the greater weight of evidence of the truth of such facts as it is incumbent on him to prove. For the reasons given we think that there was no error in the instruction of the court to the jury to which the plaintiff excepted. No error.

TILLEY et al. v. KING et al.

(Supreme Court of North Carolina. Dec. 8, 1891.)

CONSTRUCTION OF WILLS—RIGHTS OF DEVISEES—CONDITIONAL BEQUEST.

1. A will provided that if T. would stay with the testator and his wife until after their deaths, and take care of them, "then" the testator gave and bequeathed to T. certain land. The testator and his wife had no children living with them. T. was their grandchild, and with his father was otherwise provided for in the will. *Held,* that T.'s living with the testator and wife during their lives was a condition precedent.

2. The testator's meaning being clear, it was immaterial that there was no limitation over in case of T.'s failure to perform the condition.

Appeal from superior court, Stokes county; JESSE F. GRAVES, Judge. Reversed.

Action by Amer Tilley and others against Lucy King and others to assert an interest in certain lands. Judgment of nonsuit. Plaintiffs appeal.

Glenn & Manly, for appellants. *Watson & Buxton, R. F. Haymore,* and *J. T. Morehead,* for appellees.

SHEPHERD, J. The only question material to be considered is whether his honor was correct in ruling that in the will of A. B. Tilley there was no condition precedent to the vesting of an estate in his grandson P. H. Tilley, and that the latter took a vested remainder expectant upon the determination of the life-estate of his grandmother. The words to be construed are as follows: "And if Powell H. Tilley stays with us until after our deaths, and takes care of us, then I give and bequeath this tract of land to him forever." The testator provided for his wife and children, among whom was the father of P. H. Tilley, and there is no mention of the latter in any other part of the will; nor is there anything in that instrument which in any way explains or controls the ordinary meaning of the above words. The language is, to our minds, entirely explicit, and must be construed to mean precisely what it declares, unless some rule of interpretation is met which imperatively requires us to do otherwise. Now, it is well settled "that there are no precise technical words in wills, nor even in deeds, to make a stipulation a condition precedent or subsequent, * * * [and] that it is to be construed according to the intention as gathered from the whole instrument." 2 Minor, Inst. 260; 4 Kent, Comm. 125. Even according to technical rules, the words used by the testator are words of strict condition; but, regardless of such rules, it is clear to us that it was not the intention of the testator that any estate should vest in his grandson until after the death of his wife, and then only in the event of his having fully performed the conditions imposed. How could this intention have been more clearly emphasized than by the use of the word "then?" And what, we ask, is there in the will that authorizes us to give a different meaning to the language employed? The cases cited by counsel for the defendants are where the devising clause is followed by or coupled with a proviso that the devisee shall pay to another a specific sum, (Woods v. Woods, Busb. 290; Whitehead, v. Thompson, 79 N. C. 450,) or to support or maintain a certain person, (Misenheimer v. Sifford, 94 N. C. 592.) In these and other similar cases to be found in the text-books, the courts have been astute in holding such provisions to be either conditions subsequent or trusts or vesting of the estate is clearly postponed until the performance of the conditions. Even if we could ignore the plain meaning of the language, it would be difficult to put the case within the principle of the decisions mentioned, because from the very nature of a part of the condition (that is, to live with the grandparents and give them the comfort of his society) it could not be enforced by way of trust or charge. The testator and his wife had no children living with them, and it was natural that they should desire the society of their grandchild in their declining years. The father of this child had already been provided for, and, under the circumstances, we cannot hesitate in holding that the testator intended to create a condition precedent. It is insisted that, where the condition requires something to be done which will take time, it should be construed as a condition subsequent. But, says a writer of high authority, if there be "a condition which involves anything in the nature of a consideration, it is in general a condition precedent." Theob. Wills, 400. As we have seen that the living with these old people was a material inducement to the making of the devise, the principle referred to has no application.

Again, it is urged that there is no limitation over to a third person upon a failure to perform the conditions. This undoubtedly has great weight where the intention is left in doubt, but it can have no influence where the meaning is clearly expressed; for it is an elementary principle that a condition precedent may be created without an ulterior limitation. For the reasons given we think that there should be a new trial.

BLACKBURN v. BLACKBURN.

(*Supreme Court of North Carolina.* Dec. 8, 1891.)

DECLARATION OF TRUST-DEED—INDORSEMENT.

Where a deed is executed in fee-simple, and the grantor makes before delivery the following indorsement, signed and sealed in the presence of witnesses: "Accordance deed. I, the said Eli Blackburn, Sr., do hereby certify that Sarah Blackburn, a daughter of said Blackburn, doth hold a life-time possession in the said Eli deed," —the grantee takes the land in trust for Sarah during her natural life.

Appeal from superior court, Wilkes county; M. L. McCORKLE, Judge. Affirmed.

Special proceedings by Sarah Ann Blackburn against Sarah Blackburn and others. Judgment for defendants. Plaintiff appeals.

The other facts fully appear in the following statement by SHEPHERD, J.:

The only point presented for review is whether the indorsement on the deed vested an estate, either in law or equity, in Sarah Blackburn. The following is the case agreed: Eli Blackburn, Sr., executed on the 11th day of May, 1872, a deed in fee-simple to Eli Blackburn, Jr., for the following described land, situate in Wilkes county, (description given.) On the back

to Eli Blackburn, Jr., to-wit: "Accordance deed. I, the said Eli Blackburn, Sr., do hereby certify that Sarah Blackburn, a daughter of said Blackburn, doth hold a life-time possession in the said Eli deed." (Signed and sealed in the presence of witnesses.) It is agreed that the said indorsement has reference to the said deed executed May 11, 1872, by Eli Blackburn, Sr., to Eli Blackburn, Jr.

Glenn & Manly, for appellee.

SHEPHERD, J. It is very clear that the indorsement on the deed did not operate as an exception or reservation so as to vest an estate for life in Sarah Blackburn. Exceptions and reservations inure only to the benefit of the grantor, and those claiming under him, and have no effect by way of passing an estate to a third party. Tied. Real Prop. 843; 2 Devl. Deeds, 979. We think, however, (without passing upon the question whether the language used can be construed into a covenant to stand seised to uses,) that the judgment of his honor may be sustained on the ground that the indorsement, made before or at the time of the delivery, amounted to a declaration of trust, to-wit, that the grantee should hold the land for the use of the said Sarah for life. Even without consideration, an oral declaration of trust in favor of a third person, made contemporaneously with the transmission of the legal title, will, when established by competent testimony, be recognized and enforced in a court of equity. Pittman v. Pittman, 107 N. C. 159, 12 S. E. Rep. 61. If this be so, *a fortiori* will the court give effect to such a contemporaneous declaration when made in writing under seal and for a good consideration. No particular form of words is necessary to establish such a trust. "The intent is what the courts look to." 2 Fonbl. Eq. 36, note; 3 Ves. 9; Bisp. Eq. 98. The language in our case is very similar to that used in Fisher v. Fields, 10 Johns. 494, which was held to be sufficient; and indeed, upon looking over the many cases in the reports, there can be no doubt upon the question. The grantee, then, taking the title accompanied with this contemporaneous declaration, must be declared seised of the land in trust for Sarah Blackburn for the term of her natural life. Affirmed.

WHITEHURST et al. v. MERCHANTS' & FARMERS' TRANSP. CO.

(*Supreme Court of North Carolina.* Dec. 8, 1891.)

SETTING ASIDE JUDGMENT — DOCKETING JUSTICE COURT JUDGMENT.

The docketing of a justice court judgment in a superior court, as allowed by Code N. C. § 839, does not give the superior court jurisdiction of an action to set aside such judgment for want of service of summons, but a motion for that purpose must be made in the justice's court.

Appeal from superior court, Beaufort county; HENRY R. BRYAN, Judge. Affirmed.

Action by J. B. Whitehurst, S. Whitehurst, and C. W. Whitehurst against the

Merchants' & Farmers' Transportation Company to set aside a judgment. On defendant's motion the action was dismissed, and plaintiffs appeal.

The other facts fully appear in the statement by MERRIMON, C. J.:

The present defendant brought its action in the court of a justice of the peace against the present plaintiffs to recover the sum of $75, and obtained judgment on the 18th of November, 1886, and afterwards filed and docketed a transcript of its judgment in the office of the superior court clerk of the county where the judgment was rendered, as allowed by the statute. Code, § 839 The present plaintiffs allege that the summons in the action just mentioned was served on J. B. Whitehurst, one of the defendants therein named, (who is one of the present plaintiffs;) that it was never served on S. Whitehurst or C. W. Whitehurst, therein named, who are two of the present plaintiffs; that nevertheless the said summons purports to have been served upon all the persons named as defendants therein. This action is brought by the plaintiffs for the purpose of having the judgment above mentioned set aside and declared to be void, and to obtain relief by injunction, etc., upon the ground that no summons was ever served upon them. Counsel for the defendant moved that the action be dismissed, "because a motion in the original cause was the proper remedy," etc. The court gave judgment dismissing the action, and the plaintiffs, having excepted, appealed to this court.

John H. Small, for appellants. Chas. F. Warren, for appellee.

MERRIMON, C. J., (after stating the facts.) A judgment against a party who has not submitted himself to the jurisdiction of the court granting it for that purpose, and who has not in fact been served with original leading process, though the same purports to have been served, is irregular, and may be avoided; the remedy being a motion in the cause to set the judgment aside for irregularity. Such judgment is not void, it is only voidable, because it appears by the record (the return) that the original summons was served upon the party against whom it is entered. It, however, so appears in such case by inadvertence, mistake, or the false return of the summons by the sheriff. The court is careful to see that it has jurisdiction, and that its course of action in the progress of the action is orderly and duly observed. When there is irregularity in any material respect appearing upon the face of the record, to the prejudice of a party, it will ex mero motu correct the same; or within a reasonable period, on the mere motion of the party prejudiced, it will correct, set aside, or modify, if need be, the order, judgment, or other matter or thing complained of. And as to the jurisdiction of the party, and perhaps in some other possible cases, it will, there being no laches, on motion in the cause, supported by affidavits, inquire whether it has such jurisdiction, although upon the face of the record it appears to have the same. Thus, if the original summons

in the action be returned by the sheriff "served" upon the defendant therein named, it will so inquire whether in fact such service was made, or whether the return is made untruly by inadvertence, mistake, or falsely on purpose. This is important and necessary, because the service of the summons is essential to the jurisdiction, unless the party submits himself to the court. and besides to give the party his day in court, as the law contemplates he shall have the same. Keaton v. Banks, 10 Ired. 381; Mason v. Miles, 63 N. C. 564; Cowles v. Hayes, 69 N. C. 406; Doyle v. Brown, 72 N. C. 393; Koonce v. Butler, 84 N. C. 221; Brickhouse v. Sutton, 99 N. C. 103, 5 S. E. Rep. 380; and there are numerous other cases. Although the court of a justice of the peace is not a court of record, its proceedings are authoritative and judicial in their nature, and its judgments are conclusive and binding until they shall in an orderly way be set aside, reversed, or modified. Such judgments cannot be attacked when it appears from the proceedings that the court had jurisdiction for irregularity or other cause. The remedy for irregularity is by a motion in the action before the justice of the peace who granted the judgment, or before his successor in office. The office of justice of the peace is continuous in its nature, and filled by the incumbent, and to be filled after him by his successors. He is required to keep dockets, enter minutes of proceedings before him, keep and preserve his official papers, and transfer the same to his successors. Code, §§ 828, 831. So that it is orderly, convenient, necessary, and appropriate to make pertinent motions of all kinds in an action in such court, just as like motions may be made in actions in the superior courts. If a motion should be made to set aside a judgment in the court of a justice of the peace, and it should be allowed or denied improperly, the complaining party might appeal to the superior court. Hooks v. Moses, 8 Ired. 88; McKee v. Angel, 90 N. C. 60; Moore v. Edwards, 92 N. C. 43. That a judgment of a justice of the peace has been docketed in the office of the superior court clerk, as allowed by the statute, (Code, § 839,) does not give the superior court jurisdiction of the action in which such judgment was rendered. The docketing makes the judgment that of the superior court in all respects only for the purpose of creating a lien upon the real estate of the judgment debtor, and enforcing the same by execution and otherwise. Hence the latter court has no authority to set the judgment aside for irregularity, or upon the ground that the summons in the action in which it was rendered had not in fact been served upon the defendant therein named, while the return of the same showed that it had been. Ledbetter v. Osborne, 66 N. C. 379; Birdsey v. Harris, 68 N. C. 92; Morton v. Rippy, 84 N. C. 611. If a judgment of a justice of the peace shall have been docketed, and afterwards set aside in the way above indicated, the defendant in the action should apply by motion to the superior court to set the judgment there aside, and the court should grant the motion, basing its action upon that of the court of the justice of the peace. Thus complete and effectual relief would be granted. So that the plaintiffs in the present action should have sought the relief they demand by a motion in the action mentioned in the court of the justice of the peace. This action was improvidently brought, and the court properly dismissed it. Judgment affirmed.

STATE v. PARKS.

(Supreme Court of North Carolina. Dec. 8, 1891.)

CRIMINAL LAW—EVIDENCE—CHARACTER.

1. Where defendant, in a trial for burning a barn, put his character in issue, and a witness testifies that, prior to the burning, defendant, in reference to a robbery lately perpetrated, said, "Damn them, [the robbers,] * * * there is going to be a battle in this neighborhood before three weeks, and I be d——d if I care how quick it comes," such evidence, though but slightly relevant, is competent as bearing on defendant's character.

2. In such case it is proper to admit, as bearing on defendant's character, evidence that, shortly before daylight on the morning when defendant was arrested, there were with him, at his mother-in-law's house, several persons, two or three of whom had guns.

Appeal from superior court, Randolph county; JESSE F. GRAVES, Judge. Affirmed.

Riley Parks was convicted of burning a barn and appeals.

The Attorney General, for the State.

MERRIMON, C. J. The defendant is indicted for setting fire to and burning a barn, the property of the prosecutor, in violation of the statute. Code, § 985, par. 6. He pleaded not guilty. On the trial, much evidence was produced, both by the state and the defendant. The latter produced evidence of his good character, and thus put the same in question. A witness for the state testified that he had a conversation with defendant some time —how long did not appear—before the barn was burned, in which reference was made to the robbing of a house which had been lately perpetrated, and the defendant said in that connection: "God damn them [referring to the robbers] to hell; there's going to be a battle in this neighborhood before three weeks, and I be damned if I care how quick it comes." No objection to this evidence was made until after it came out. Then the defendant requested the court to withdraw and exclude it. The court declined to do so, and the defendant excepted. This evidence was slight. It tended not strongly to show a threatening purpose, and as well the character and disposition of the defendant in a light adverse to him. In its instruction to the jury the court cautioned them as to such evidence, saying: "Evidence of threats, while admissible, is regarded as unreliable, and ought to have little weight, unless clearly directed against" the party whose barn was burned. In view of the whole evidence, including that as to his character produced by the defendant, that which the court refused to withdraw from the jury had slight relevancy and pertinency. It bore upon the character of the defendant, and in reply was competent. The defendant was examined as a witness in his own behalf, and on cross-examination he was asked who were present with him at his mother-in-law's on the morning shortly before daylight, when the officer arrested him for the alleged burning of the barn? He objected to the question, on the ground of incompetency, in that its purpose was to elicit immaterial evidence. The court declined to sustain the objection. The defendant then testified that there were several persons named, and two or three of them had guns, coming in the house. This evidence was also slight. Still, in view of all the evidence, it had some bearing, standing along with other evidence, to show the character of the defendant, he having put it in issue. But if this were not so, and the evidence was irrelevant, the mere fact that it appeared that the persons named were present, and two of them simply had their guns, did not tend of itself to prejudice the defendant. In that case, he ought to have shown at the proper time that it probably did prejudice him before the jury. The admission of merely irrelevant evidence is not ground for a new trial, unless it of itself tends to prejudice the complaining party, or it appears in some way that it probably did prejudice him. There is no error, and the judgment must be affirmed.

HARRISON et al. v. HARGROVE et al.

(Supreme Court of North Carolina. Dec. 9, 1891.)

RES JUDICATA.

Defendants purchased land sold by an administrator under a decree reciting the personal service of summons upon plaintiffs, who were decedent's devisees. Nineteen years thereafter plaintiffs moved to set aside the decree and sale on the ground that they had not been, in fact, so summoned. The motion was granted, and the proceedings were declared irregular and void; but it was ordered that all the papers in the cause should remain on file for the use of the purchaser when his rights should be questioned. Held, in an action of ejectment brought 17 years after the decree and sale, that as plaintiffs were guilty of laches by reason of both their long acquiescence in defendant's possession, and their delay in seeking to set aside decree and sale, in the absence of an explanation thereof, said proceedings would not be deemed to have been declared void as to defendants.

Appeal from superior court, Vance county; THOMAS B. WOMACK, Judge. Reversed.

Action of ejectment by Judith L. Harrison et al. against Mary L. Hargrove et al. From a judgment for plaintiffs, defendants appeal.

E. C. Smith, M. V. Lanier, and A. W. Graham, for appellants. Batchelor & Devereux, for appellees.

SHEPHERD, J. This was an action of ejectment prosecuted by Judith and Rebecca Harrison, as the devisees of their father, Robert Harrison. The defendants purchased the land in controversy at a sale made by the administrator c. t. a. of said Robert, pursuant to a decree of the superior court of Granville county. The decree recited that personal service of the summons had been made on the plaintiffs and other devisees; and, being unable to attack it collaterally, the plaintiffs, in 1889, moved in the original cause (that is, in the special proceeding just mentioned) to set aside the said sale and decree, on the ground that no service was in fact ever made upon them, and that there had been no appearance by any one in their behalf. The motion was allowed, the court declaring the proceedings irregular and void, but at the same time requiring that all of the papers in the cause should remain on file for the use of the purchaser when his rights should be questioned. This order of the judge was affirmed by this court, (Harrison v. Harrison, 106 N. C. 282, 11 S. E. Rep. 356;) but, owing to its peculiar terms, the rights of the defendants, *bona fide* purchasers, were left undetermined, and, so far as they are concerned, the question here presented is whether, as against them, the decree in a direct proceeding should have been set aside. We must, of course, treat it in this way, for, if the decree be considered now as absolutely set aside for want of jurisdiction of the parties, it is very clear that it can afford the defendants no protection, and it must also follow that the provisions of the order apparently saving the rights of the purchasers, and looking to their future litigation, would be ignored. After very great consideration, we have concluded that the important questions so ably argued by counsel (involving, as they do, the conclusiveness of judicial records, and especially their recitals of jurisdictional facts) need not be passed upon in this appeal. It is generally stated that courts will correct their records, and set aside irregular judgments at any time; but where there has been long delay, and especially when the rights of third persons can be affected, they will require satisfactory explanation of such laches, as well as meritorious grounds for such relief. Whatever may be the effect of setting aside a decree like this for want of service of process, it is well settled by our decisions and other authorities that, the vice being a secret one, and the record reciting the necessary jurisdictional facts, such a decree is voidable only, and comes within the principle we have just stated. Doyle v. Brown, 72 N. C. 898; 1 Womack, Dig. 2336; Freem. Judgm. 116. This principle requires the party making the application to act in good faith and with ordinary diligence, "and relief will not be granted if he has knowingly acquiesced in the judgment complained of, or has been guilty of laches or unreasonable delay in seeking his remedy." 1 Black, Judgm. 313.

Under the circumstances of this case, it seems very plain that we should not—as against these defendants—give any relief until the want of notice is negatived and the long delay explained. The decree and sale were made in 1870, and this action was brought in 1887. The motion to set aside the decree was made in 1889, and thus we have 17 years or more of inaction on the part of the plaintiffs, who during all this time were under no disabilities whatever. In addition to this, the purchaser was in the possession of the property, and there is evidence showing that these plaintiffs, with their mother, lived about 300 yards distant, on an adjoining tract. It is true that the mother, under the will, had a life-estate in the land, and that she did not die until 1887; but the land was, says the will, "to be used by her for the support of herself, and all my children who may choose to live with her," etc. These plaintiffs, having a right to be supported from said land during the life of their mother, and also entitled in remainder, could have moved to set aside the decree at any time after it was rendered; but, for some cause, they failed to do so until 1889. Taking these circumstances, together with the fact that they must have known of the long and adverse possession by the defendants of the adjoining land, and we are entirely clear that we should not exercise this "*quasi* equitable" (Black, Judgm. supra) power of the court, and grant the plaintiffs relief as upon setting aside the decree. Indeed, if there is anything in the rule which requires long delay to be explained, and knowledge of a decree to be negatived, we can conceive of no stronger case for its application than the present one. With the exception of the finding, on the motion to set aside, that the plaintiffs were not served with process, and had no notice, (and this must, of course, refer to the time of the decree,) there is nothing in the record to negative any subsequent knowledge of the proceedings, nor is there any explanation of their acquiescence in the long possession of the defendants. These circumstances, while insufficient to estop the plaintiffs, if there were no decree in their way, do, in our opinion, (in view of the peculiar terms of the order mentioned,) warrant the court in refusing to treat the decree as having been set aside as to these defendants. New trial.

STATE v. BROWN.

(Supreme Court of North Carolina. Dec. 8, 1891.)

VIOLATION OF ORDINANCE—DRIVING ON SIDEWALK.

The violation of a city ordinance against driving on a sidewalk cannot be justified on the ground of necessity arising from the muddy condition of a street, where such condition was known to defendant before he started to drive along it, and where, to avoid unloading his wagon, he drove on the sidewalk, though such street was the only passage to his place of business.

Appeal from superior court, Forsyth county; JOHN G. BYNUM, Judge. Affirmed.

Indictment against R. D. Brown for a violation of a city ordinance. Defendant was convicted, and, his motion for a new trial being denied, he appeals.

The other facts fully appear in the following statement by AVERY, J.:

This was an indictment for a violation of a city ordinance. The ordinance imposed a penalty for driving or leading horses on a sidewalk, and it was admitted that the defendant's driver, under his order, drove his wagon partly on a sidewalk for a distance of 90 feet along the street. The defendant relied upon necessity, growing out of the impassable condition of the streets on account of the mud for a number of yards, as a defense. The defendant excepted to the refusal of the court to permit him to prove that he could not drive a loaded wagon along the street without going on the sidewalk, with safety to the load or his wagon. The court permitted defendant's counsel to ask him "if the condition of the street at that place was not of such dangerous character that the traveler's person or property would have been endangered unless he used the sidewalk, or partially used the sidewalk." The defendant admitted that he knew the condition of the street before he started his loaded wagon along it, and in answer to the last question said only "that the boxes of tobacco would have to have been unloaded, as the team could not pull it." There was evidence tending to show that there was no other possible way from defendant's building to haul out his tobacco except by the south street, over which he hauled it, the street north of it being wholly impassable. The sidewalk, where the defendant drove upon it, was not paved. The defendant excepted to the refusal of the judge to charge that 'he was not guilty in driving upon the sidewalk to avert danger to his person or property, and to the refusal of the court to admit testimony offered. Motion for new trial. Appeal.

Glenn & Manly, for appellant. *The Attorney General*, for the State.

AVERY, J., (*after stating the facts*.) It is admitted to have been the well-settled law in England that where a highway became obstructed and impassable from temporary causes, a traveler might go extra viam upon the adjacent land, without subjecting himself to liability in an action of trespass, brought by the owner. 2 Bl. Comm. 86; Bullard v. Harrison, 4 Maule & S. 387, 393; Taylor v. Whitehead, 2 Doug. 744–748. This extraordinary rule was subsequently recognized by the courts of this country, and the right to do with impunity what would ordinarily subject a person to liability in an action for damages was generally held to rest upon the doctrine of necessity. Campbell v. Race, 7 Cush. 408. The right on the part of the traveler is, according to the definition of BIGELOW, C. J., "confined to those cases of inevitable necessity or unavoidable accident arising from sudden and recent causes, which have occasioned temporary and impassable obstructions in the highway." Campbell v. Race, supra. When a traveler has notice of the existence of the obstruction, and can reach his destination with his vehicle by another route, which is more circuitous, but not unreasonably long, he will not be permitted, merely for the sake of convenience, to pass, without incurring liability in a civil action, by the more direct way over the land of an abutting proprietor. Farrelly v. City of Cincinnati, 2 Disn. 516. The objection that the rule licenses the taking of private property for public use without compensation is met by the argument that the grant of the easement in the highway carried with it the right in a case of supreme necessity to pass over adjacent land. The principle has been heretofore invoked, so far as our investigations have extended, only for the

purpose of avoiding responsibility for damages in civil actions. The rule is said to have originated in England at a time when there were no public officials who were liable to indictment or to respond in damages for permitting the highways to become impassable. Where there is a town ordinance forbidding persons to lead or drive horses along the sidewalk, which is the portion of the street intended for the use of pedestrians, and a violation of the ordinance is an indictable offense, and where at the same time the commissioners of the city are liable criminally for failure to keep the streets proper in passable condition for vehicles of all kinds, an individual who, deliberately and with full notice of the state of the street, loads his wagon, and drives along it to the dangerous point, will not be allowed to evade punishment for violating the letter of the law on the ground that it was absolutely necessary to do so in order to escape danger to his property, which he has willfully put in peril. Especially will this principle hold good in a case like that at bar, where, in order to avert danger, the traveler insists that he may drive upon the sidewalk, and make it impassable for foot passengers, to whose exclusive use it is by law devoted, and escape liability under an indictment on the plea of necessity, when he could have unloaded his tobacco even after his team was in the mud, and have moved the wagon back or forward. Pedestrians have rights that are intended to be protected by such ordinances, and among them that of carrying their wares, as well as passing safely, by the public footway. The man who transports his goods on wheels must, when the street proper becomes impassable, join the caravan of footmen till such time as those charged with the duty can be induced or driven to repair it, rather than rush his team over the sidewalk, and render it also perilous or disagreeable for the larger number of persons for whose comfort and convenience the protective ordinance was passed, merely in order to ship his goods more rapidly. The fact that the foot-way had not been paved made it only more susceptible to injury from hauling heavily loaded wagons over it, and rendered it more important to pedestrians that the ordinance should be rigidly enforced. In our geographical location, where the climate is milder, carriages are not often subject to delay by immense blocks of snow and ice, suddenly deposited in highways, as in the colder regions of the northern and northwestern states of this country, or in the higher latitude of England, and, while our public roads are often rendered temporarily and for short distances impassable on account of sudden washes, no case involving the claim of right on the part of a traveler to go *extra viam* has hitherto arisen in this state. Mud, rather than ice or snow, is the common enemy of those who travel our highways on foot or in carriages; but it must be only in exceptional instances that mud or anything except a sudden wash renders highways absolutely impassable. It is usually held to be the duty of the traveler to remove brush or other slight obstructions to his passage along a public road, when he can do so with little trouble or delay, rather than go upon the premises of the adjacent owner. The law provides generally, as far as it is practicable, for the uninterrupted use by wagons and carriages of that portion of the highway intended as a pass-way for them; but it is the duty of the owner of such vehicles to beware, in the exercise of their own rights, not to infringe upon those of other citizens, just as the same limit is fixed by the law to the enjoyment of their own exclusive property. *Sic utere tuo, ut non alienum lædas.*

But the particular question presented by this appeal is whether there were such circumstances shown, looking at any and every phase of the evidence, as would, if believed, have justified the violation of the criminal law on the ground of necessity. It is admitted that the defendant's conduct brought him within its letter; but it is contended that the evidence offered takes the case out of its spirit. Whether the authorities of a town are guilty of nuisance in placing an actual obstruction upon the streets, or by reason of their failure to repair, they are indictable at common law, and usually under some statute also. Elliott, Roads & S. 493; State v. Wilson, 107 N. C. 869, 12 S. E. Rep. 320; Code, § 3803. Evidence that the defendant's teamster drove his team upon the sidewalk, if believed, made a *prima facie* case of guilt, and it was incumbent on the defendant, if he relied upon the defense that it was necessary, "to show that it was done under circumstances that rendered it lawful" or excusable. State v. Wray, N. C. 253; Wharton, (Crim. Law, § 90c,) in treating of homicide through necessity, says: "But it must be remembered that necessity of this class must be strictly limited. It exists only when the act in question is necessary for the preservation of life, or the preservation of the life of relatives in the first degree." The same author (section 90d) takes issue with writers who have maintained that the accused could not set up as a defense a necessity that was the result of his own culpable act. He limits the right of such wrong-doers to avail themselves of that defense when accused of homicide in extreme cases, such as that of one who carelessly sets fire to a house, and runs over and crushes another in the attempt to escape the flames; or that of a thief, who falls overboard while engaged in stealing fish from a boat, and in the struggle for life upsets the boat, and causes another to be drowned. The violation of the letter of the law has been excused in criminal cases generally on no other ground except that a human being was thereby saved from death or peril, or relieved from severe suffering. State v. Mc-Brayer, 98 N. C. 619, 2 S. E. Rep. 755; Randall v. Railroad Co., 107 N. C. 753, 12 S. E. Rep. 605. In State v. Wray, supra, it was found as a fact that it was absolutely necessary for the safety of a patient that the druggist should furnish her brandy on the physician's certificate. The facts found were a special verdict established the necessity for administering it as a medicine, yet this court, in State v. McBrayer,

supra, declared that the extreme limit to which necessity could be made available as a defense was marked in State v. Wray. Wharton (section 2441,) maintains that in such cases nothing short of an exception in the statute would excuse a sale even to a sick person in violation of the letter of the law. But, accepting the doctrine laid down in State v. Wray as the true interpretation of the law, the defendant has failed to offer any testimony tending to show that he or his driver was in danger of death or bodily harm or injury to health which could not be averted except by driving the team over the sidewalk. The admitted violation of the letter of the ordinance, therefore, could not have been declared excusable on the ground that the wagon or horses were in a position of peril, in which the defendant had knowingly and purposely placed them, and from which he could, according to his own statement, have relieved them by unloading the wagon, and turning it and the team back or moving them forward. In answer to the direct question the defendant would not say that the person of himself or driver was in peril, from which either could escape only by driving on the sidewalk. On the contrary, he said the wagon and horses could not pass without unloading. It was the duty of the city authorities to repair the portion of the streets intended for the passage of wagons; but their failure to do so did not justify the defendant, though it may have been his only route for transporting his tobacco to a warehouse or shipping point, in defying the law making it indictable to violate a city ordinance, and in disregarding the rights of pedestrians, protected by the penalty imposed under such by-law. If the law were as contended for the defendant it might, indeed, be possible to drive a wagon, if not a coach, through many criminal laws and statutes made to protect the premises of land-owners from unnecessary invasion. We must not be understood as holding that, where a person incurs no liability to indictment by going *extra viam*, there may not be instances where the highways are temporarily rendered impassable by the mud, and where all of the circumstances may be such that the abutting proprietor cannot recover in an action brought against one who passes out of the public road, and over his premises, far enough to avoid the dangerous point. In the case at bar, if the judge below erred, it was in stating the law more favorably to the defendant than the testimony in any aspect justified him in doing. There was no testimony that the person of the defendant was put in peril, and no necessity for submitting that question to the jury. The motion for a new trial is refused, and the judgment affirmed.

PEARSON v. BARRINGER.

(*Supreme Court of North Carolina.* Dec. 8, 1891.)

ESTABLISHMENT OF BOUNDARIES—AWARD OF ARBITRATORS—SETTING ASIDE.

1. Arbitrators, chosen to declare and establish the true boundary line between litigants, de

not exceed their authority when they award that the line shall be five feet from the fence, and shall "come off" defendant's land, and be "added to" plaintiff's land, since these expressions simply describe the line as established, and do not show an unwarranted taking of land.

2. Where an affidavit alleges that one of the arbitrators was surety on plaintiff's prosecution bond in the action, and prejudiced in his favor, and that defendant was ignorant of this at the time he was chosen, but the affidavit does not deny that defendant had such knowledge in time to object to the making of the award, the court will not interfere.

Appeal from superior court, Burke county; JOHN G. BYNUM, Judge. Affirmed.

Action by D. C. Pearson against Rufus Barringer to determine a boundary line. Judgment for plaintiff. Defendant appeals.

Batchelor & Devereux, for appellant. *S. J. Ervin,* for appellee.

SHEPHERD, J. Only two reasons for setting aside the award were insisted upon on the argument before us:

1. The first is that the arbitrators exceeded their authority, in that they undertook to take five feet from the defendant's land, and "add" it to that of the plaintiff; whereas, they were only authorised "to declare and establish the line in dispute between the plaintiff and the defendant," etc. We do not think that the award is susceptible of the construction that the arbitrators assumed to try the title, or to divest the estate of one party and put it in the other. Very clearly the authority to declare and establish the line necessarily implied the right to so fix the line that one of the parties would get less land than he claimed. The award upon this point is as follows: "We find that the line between Pearson and Barringer shall be five feet from the present fence as it now stands, clear through from King to College streets, to come off Barringer's lots Nos. 42 and 51, and added to Nos. 41 and 52, Pearson lots." The court is entirely satisfied that the use of the words "come off" and "added to" was simply for the purpose of describing the line as established by the arbitrators, and that in no sense can it be understood as an assumption of authority on their part to arbitrarily take land from one party and give it to the other.

2. It is earnestly insisted that the award should be set aside because Bristol, the arbitrator chosen by the plaintiff, was a surety on the prosecution bond, and therefore an interested party. It is well settled that parties "knowing the facts may submit their differences to any person, whether he is interested in the matters involved, (Navigation Co. v. Fenlon, 4 Watts & S. 205,) or is related to one of the parties, and the award will be binding upon them," (6 Wait. Act. & Def. 519; Morse, Arb. 105;) but, if the submission be made in ignorance of such incompetency, the award may be avoided. No relief, however, will be granted unless objection is made as soon as the aggrieved party becomes aware of the facts; and if, after the submission, he acquires such knowledge and permits the award to be made without objection, it is treated as a waiv-

er, and the award will not be disturbed. Davis v. Forshee, 34 Ala. 107. A party, says Morse on Arbitration, supra, "will not be allowed to lie by after he has attained the knowledge and proceed with the hearing without objection, thereby accumulating expense and taking his chance of a decision in his favor, and then, at a later stage, or after a decision has been or seems likely to be rendered against him, for the first time produce and urge his objection." From these and other authorities it would seem clear that when one seeks to impeach an award he must show that he made objection as soon as he discovered the disqualifying facts. The affidavit of the defendant in this case does not show this. It simply states that such facts were unknown to him "at the time said Bristol was appointed as arbitrator," but it does not negative the existence of such knowledge in time to object before the making of the award. We think this was necessary, and, in its absence, we must decline to interfere. The other points made by defendants are without merit. Affirmed.

STATE v. RHYNE.

(Supreme Court of North Carolina. Dec. 8, 1891.)

LARCENY—CROSS-EXAMINATION—RULINGS ON EVIDENCE.

1. On a prosecution for larceny, a witness for the state testified that on one occasion there was a two-dollar bill in the cash drawer when he went to dinner; that defendant was the only clerk left in the store; and that when witness returned the bill was gone. It was not shown that defendant was charged with taking the bill. *Held,* that a question, on cross-examination, as to whether, on witness' return to the store, he asked defendant what had become of the bill, and what his reply was, was properly ruled out.

2. Where it was not stated what defendant expected to show by the question, and it therefore does not appear that he was injured, it was not error to exclude the question.

Appeal from superior court, Gaston county; JESSE F. GRAVES, Judge. Affirmed.

Prosecution against Rhyne for larceny. Defendant was convicted, and appeals.

Geo. F. Bason, for appellant. *The Attorney General,* for the State.

CLARK, J. The state offered as a witness a clerk in the store of the prosecutors, who testified that on one occasion when he went to dinner there was a two-dollar bill in the cash-drawer; that when he left the store the defendant was the only clerk left there; and that when witness returned from dinner the two-dollar bill was gone. On cross-examination, this witness was asked if he inquired of defendant upon his return to the store what had become of the two-dollar bill, and if defendant gave any explanation. The evidence on objection was ruled out, and defendant excepted. There was much other evidence not objected to.

If the state had brought out that the defendant was accused of the crime, it would have been competent for the defendant to have rebutted the implied admission of guilt which might have been argued from his silence by giving his reply. State v. Patterson, 63 N. C. 520; State v. Worthington, 64 N. C. 594. But it was certainly not competent for the defendant to give in evidence the fact that he was so charged for the purpose of giving his unsworn declarations, when they were no part of the *res gestæ.* State v Scott, 8 N. C. 24; State v. Hildreth, 31 N. C. 440; State v. Brandon, 53 N. C. 463; State v. McNair, 93 N. C. 628. He could not thus make testimony for himself. Had the defendant testified that the charge was untrue, he could have shown, as corroborative evidence, either by himself or by this witness, that he made a similar statement when first charged. State v. Whitfield, 92 N. C. 831. But this evidence is neither asked to rebut an implied admission from his silence nor as corroborative evidence.

The objection is further to be sustained on the ground that it is not stated what the defendant expected to show by the inquiry, and it does not therefore appear that he was injured by its exclusion. Knight v. Killebrew, 86 N. C. 400, and cases there cited. The other exception was abandoned on the argument. No error.

McQUAY v. RICHMOND & D. R. Co.

(Supreme Court of North Carolina. Dec. 9, 1891.)

TRIAL—INSTRUCTIONS—ASSUMPTION OF FACT.

In an action for injury by a railroad engine, defendant's request to charge that, "if the jury believe the evidence, the plaintiff could have extricated himself from any danger after he saw the engine," was properly refused, since the proposition was an inference to be made by the jury from all the circumstances in evidence.

Appeal from superior court, Mecklenburg county; JAMES H. MERRIMON, Judge. Affirmed.

Action by R. E. McQuay against the Richmond & Danville Railroad Company for damage from being struck by an engine while crossing defendant's tracks. On the trial the following issues were submitted to the jury: (1) Was the plaintiff's injury caused by the negligence of the defendant as alleged in the complaint? (2) Did the plaintiff, by his own negligence, contribute to his injury? (3) What damages did plaintiff sustain? Among other instructions asked by defendant was the following: "(8) If the jury believe the evidence, the plaintiff could have extricated himself from any danger after he saw the engine, and if he could have done so, and failed to do it, and took the risk of the engine's frightening his horse, he cannot recover unless the engine made unusual and unnecessary noises; and if they believe no such unusual and unnecessary noise was made, the answer to the second issue should be, 'Yes.'" The court declined to instruct the jury that "if they believed the evidence the plaintiff could have extricated himself from any danger after he saw the engine," but told them that it was for them to say, upon the evidence, whether "the plaintiff could have extricated himself from any danger after he saw the engine."

The other part of defendant's eighth special instruction was given, and defendant excepted to the modification made by the court. The jury answered the first issue, "Yes," the second issue, "No," and the third issue "$400," and there was judgment accordingly. Defendant moved the court for a new trial, for the refusal of the court to instruct the jury as requested in the eighth prayer of defendant, and for that the damages assessed were excessive.l Motion overruled. Defendant appeals.

D. Schenck and *Geo. F. Bason,* for appellant. *Burwell & Walker,* for appellee.

SHEPHERD, J. The defendant conceded that it was guilty of negligence, but alleged that the plaintiff, by his own negligent conduct, had contributed to the injury of which he complained. The only exception insisted upon is the refusal of the court to charge the jury that, "if they believed the evidence, the plaintiff could have extricated himself from any danger after he saw the engine." "When the evidence is direct, so as to leave nothing to inference, and the evidence, if believed, is the same thing as the fact sought to be proved, the judge is at liberty to instruct the jury that if they believe the witness they should find for the plaintiff or for the defendant." Gaither v. Ferebee, 1 Winst. 310. Applying this principle to the testimony before us, we are of the opinion that the ruling of his honor was correct, and that the proposition embodied in the instruction prayed for was an inference to be made by the jury from all of the circumstances in evidence. We think that "two reasonable and fairminded men" (Deans v. Railroad Co., 107 N. C. 686, 12 S. E. Rep. 77) might have reached different conclusions, or at least have been left in serious doubt, as to whether the plaintiff could have extricated himself as alleged. No error.

CURTIS v. PIEDMONT LUMBER, RANCH & MIN. Co.

(Supreme Court of North Carolina. Dec. 14, 1891.)

CONTRACTS OF CORPORATION—ABATEMENT—ANOTHER ACTION PENDING.

1. In an action against a corporation on a contract alleged to have been entered into by it, it is error for the court to refuse to instruct, when the evidence warranted, that "the contract not being in writing, and a liability in excess of one hundred dollars being imposed on defendant under said contract, plaintiff cannot recover;" Code, § 683, providing that contracts of a corporation by which a liability of more than $100 is imposed on the corporation "shall be in writing, and either under the common seal of the corporation or signed by some officer of the company authorized thereto."

2. The pendency of an action is a bar to another action in the same court, between the same parties, founded on the same cause of action, even if plaintiff submitted to a nonsuit in the first action.

Appeal from superior court, McDowell county; JOHN GRAY BYNUM, Judge. Reversed.

Action by A. T. Curtis against the Piedmont Lumber, Ranch & Mining Company to recover money. Judgment for plaintiff. Defendant appeals.

The other facts fully appear in the following statement by MERRIMON, C. J.:

The plaintiff alleges in his complaint that he contracted with the defendant at a time specified to deliver to it, at a place designated, a certain number of poplar logs, containing and aggregating 90,000 feet, at the price of $12 per thousand feet, making the sum of $1,530; that he delivered the logs at the place specified, and notified the defendant that he had done so; that the latter refused to receive the same without lawful excuse; that the logs became injured by exposure to the weather; that at the last he sold the same for the largest price he could get for them; that in all things he complied with and performed his part of said contract, and the defendant, without excuse, refused and neglected to do so on its part, etc.; and demands judgment for the balance due upon said contract, $455, and costs. The defendant denies that it contracted with the plaintiff as alleged, and alleges a materially different contract it made with the plaintiff which he failed to keep and perform, etc. It further alleges and pleads as a bar that, at and before this action began, another action, brought by the plaintiff against the defendant, founded upon the same alleged cause of action, was pending and undetermined in the superior court of the county of McDowell. It alleges and pleads, as a further defense, that the contract alleged by the plaintiff involved and imposed on the defendant a liability in favor of the plaintiff for a sum of money greater than $100; that such contract was not reduced to writing and under the seal of the defendant corporation, nor was any such contract signed by any officer of the defendant authorised to sign the same, and that such alleged contract was void under the statute. Code, § 683. Upon the trial of the issues of fact submitted to the jury, "it was admitted that, when the summons was issued in this case, another suit was pending in McDowell county, another suit (the present plaintiff) was plaintiff and the same defendant, for the same cause of action; that the summons issued April 9, 1890, and a nonsuit was entered at fall term, 1890." This action began July 17, 1890. The defendant asked the court to instruct the jury: "(1) The contract not being in writing, and a liability in excess of one hundred dollars being imposed upon the defendant under said contract, the plaintiff was not entitled to recover." The court refused to grant this instruction, but said to the jury: "If you find that the contract was verbal; that the plaintiff went to work under it; that Martin, as agent of the company, recognized it in letters introduced, and made the plaintiff payments under the contract,—then the contract would be good in law, and plaintiff can recover for a breach of it." The defendant excepted. There was a verdict for the plaintiff. The "defendant moved for judgment against plaintiff for costs, on the ground that the action pending when this suit was brought was a bar to this action. Motion denied, and defendant excepted." Judgment was entered for plaintiff, and defendant appealed to this court.

S. J. Ervin, for appellant.

MERRIMON, C. J., (after stating the facts.) The statute (Code, § 683; Acts 1871-72, c. 199, § 28) prescribes that "every contract of every corporation, by which a liability may be incurred by the company exceeding one hundred dollars, shall be in writing, and either under the common seal of the corporation, or signed by some officer of the company authorised thereto." The provision is important, and not merely directory. Its purpose is to protect corporations against the hasty or fraudulent acts and practices of their incautious or faithless officers and agents, and as well those persons who deal with them, in respect to contracts involving pecuniary liability of importance. They must necessarily act and contract by and through their officers and agents, and it is wise and salutary to protect them and those who deal with them in the way thus provided. Such contracts must be in writing, and under the common seal of the corporation, or signed by some one of its officers authorised thereto. It is not sufficient to simply recognise, by such officer or agent, a merely verbal contract to give it efficiency. It must be done in writing, and in such way as to give evidence of the nature, purpose, and substance of the contract. Otherwise the statute would be practically nugatory. In this case the defendant is a corporation of this state, and clearly comes within the purpose of the statute above recited. The plaintiff alleges specifically a merely verbal contract with it, whereby a liability of it to the plaintiff might be incurred for a sum much greater than $100. The defendant, in order to avail itself of the defense of the statute, must plead it specifically. It must appear from the pleadings that it intends to rely upon the same. Here the defendant does plead it specifically, and relies upon it as a particular ground of defense. The plaintiff relies upon divers letters written by the defendant's treasurer to him to show that he, for the defendant, recognised the alleged contract in writing. These letters are set forth in the case stated on appeal, and we have examined them carefully. They do not, in any reasonable interpretation of them, refer to or at all purport to recognise the contract alleged. They do not refer to this or any particular contract. They simply refer to logs that the plaintiff sent and was expected to send to the defendant; but when or to what point they were to be sent, what number, what kind, and at what price does not appear by terms or the remotest implication. There was no evidence to go to the jury to prove the contract in writing signed by the defendant's officer, and hence the plea should have been sustained. Kenner v. Manufacturing Co., 91 N. C. 421; Rumbough v. Improvement Co., 106 N. C. 461, 11 S. E. Rep. 528. The statute refers to executory contracts which create liabilities and obligations of the corporation, not to cases where they have received and availed themselves of property sold and actually delivered to them. No doubt the defendant might be compelled to pay the fair value of any logs it received and accepted from the plaintiff, but no question in that respect is presented here.

The defendant also pleaded specifically the pending of another action in the same court, between the same parties, founded on the same cause of action as in this case. It could not avail itself of such defense, except by demurrer in proper cases, or by pleading the same specifically in the answer, and it may be pleaded with other defenses. Code, § 239, par. 3; Blackwell v. Dibbrell, 103 N. C. 270, 9 S. E. Rep. 192; Montague v. Brown, 104 N. C. 161, 10 S. E. Rep. 186. Such defense is a good one, when well pleaded, and should be sustained. Woody v. Jordan, 69 N. C. 189; Smith v. Moore, 79 N. C. 82; Tuttle v. Harrill, 85 N. C. 456; Sloan v. McDowell, 75 N. C. 29; Long v. Jarratt, 94 N. C. 443; 1 Chit. Pl. 454. Here it is admitted that there was an action pending in the same court, between the same parties, founded upon and involving the same cause of action, as in the present action, when the latter began. That the plaintiff in the former action submitted to a judgment of nonsuit after the present one began could not alter the case. He should have done so before this action began, if for any cause he could not proceed in the former one. Upon the admission of the pending of the former action, the court should at once have sustained the defendant's plea, and dismissed the action. There is error. The defendant is entitled to a new trial, and we so adjudge. To that end let this opinion be certified to the superior court.

It is so ordered.

GRESHAM v. TURNER.

(Supreme Court of Georgia. Dec. 7, 1891.)

RECORD ON APPEAL—INSUFFICIENCY—AMENDMENT OF CERTIFICATE—DISMISSAL.

1. Where neither the certificate of the judge nor that of the clerk is such as is prescribed by the act of November, 1889, for bringing cases to this court, and where some of the record which the judge certifies to be necessary does not appear in the transcript sent up by the clerk, the writ of error will be dismissed.

2. The act prescribes the terms of the certificate which the judge is required to sign, and directs that, if needful, he shall change the bill of exceptions so as to make it conform to the truth and contain all the evidence, and refer to all the record, necessary to a clear understanding of the errors complained of. The needful changes are to be made in the bill of exceptions, but no change in the certificate is allowable.

(Syllabus by the Court.)

Error from superior court, Douglas county; R. H. CLARK, Judge.

Action by Samuel Turner against A. S. Gresham. From a judgment for plaintiff, defendant brings error. Dismissed.

The following is the official report:

The bill of exceptions in this case makes certain assignments of error based upon the overruling of a motion for new trial, and sets forth that certain portions of the evidence were material to a clear understanding of the errors complained of, and that it was contained in exhibits to the bill of exceptions, with the exception of part of a certain bill in equity. The judge's certificate to the bill of exceptions states

that the bill of exceptions is true, and specifies all of the evidence, and specifies all of the record material to a clear understanding of the errors complained of, except the motion for new trial and the brief of evidence, "all of which must also be sent up, including the whole charge of the court," and the clerk of the superior court was ordered to make out a complete copy of "such record, and parts of the record," as were in the bill of exceptions specified "and directed by the court," certify the same as such, etc. The record, as transmitted by the clerk of the superior court, does not contain the brief of evidence nor the charge of the court. Hence no further report is made.

J. S. James, for plaintiff in error. *W. A. James*, for defendant in error.

PER CURIAM. Writ of error dismissed.

GREEN v. ALEXANDER.

(Supreme Court of Georgia. Dec. 7, 1891.)

JUDGMENT BY JUSTICE OF THE PEACE—AFFIDAVIT OF ILLEGALITY.

A judgment of the superior court rendered on appeal from a justice's court is not void so as to be attacked by affidavit of illegality on the ground that the justice's court was not held "at a court-house established according to law," both parties having had their day in the superior court. Code, § 3671.

(Syllabus by the Court.)

Error from superior court, Clayton county; R. H. CLARK, Judge.

Action by Simon Alexander against R. W. Green. Judgment for plaintiff. Defendant brings error. Affirmed.

The following is the official report:

Green, defendant in *fi. fa.*, filed separate affidavits of illegality to three *fi. fas.* issued against him in favor of Alexander. When the cases thus made were called in the superior court, the plaintiff in *fi. fa.* demurred orally to the illegalities, and they were dismissed upon the grounds of insufficiency of the statements therein, lack of clearness, and because they were not issuable, to which decisions Green excepted. Two of the affidavits of illegality were alike, and were upon the following grounds: "(1) Because the court rendered a judgment upon the intervention of a jury, the cause of action being an unconditional contract in writing, the same having been appealed by defendant from a justice court, there being no plea in the justice court, nor none filed under oath nor otherwise to said appeal, nor said defendant having no counsel, nor appearing at time of said judgment. (2) Because said *fi. fa.* issued from a judgment of the superior court of said county, based upon an appeal from the judgment of the justice court of the 1088th dist., G. M., said county. which said justice court judgment is null and void. because not rendered at a court-house established according to law in said 1088th dist., G. M." The other affidavit was upon the following grounds: "(1) Because the court rendered a judgment upon the verdict of a jury, the cause of action being an unconditional contract in writing, the same having been appealed by defendant from a justice court, there being no plea in the justice court, nor never filed under oath nor otherwise to the appeal, nor having counsel, nor appearing at the time of the same." (2) Similar to the second ground in the affidavit above stated. "(8) Because the minutes of the court failed to show the signature of the judge to the judgment who presided when said judgment was rendered. In each of the three bills of exceptions the same judgment upon demurrer is set out, to-wit, that "plaintiff in fi. fa., by his counsel, demurred to said illegality for insufficiency and clearness and distinctness of the allegations therein contained, and because the same were not issuable on its face; the said superior court sustained said demurrer," etc. In each the judgment sustaining the demurrer is specified as a portion of the record material to be transmitted to this court, but in only one of the records is the judgment similar to that set out in the bills of exceptions. In one of the other records it is stated in the judgment that the demurrer was for insufficiency of statement, and because the affidavit did not present any issuable fact; and in the remaining record that it was because the allegations therein (in the affidavit) were not something the reporter could not read, "and issuable as they stood."

Hutcheson & Key, for plaintiff in error.
Roan & Golightly, for defendant in error.

PER CURIAM. Judgment affirmed.

IVEY v. EAST TENNESSEE, V. & G. RY. CO.

(*Supreme Court of Georgia.* Nov. 28, 1891.)

ACCIDENT TO PERSON ON RAILROAD TRACK—CONTRIBUTORY NEGLIGENCE.

The testimony of the plaintiff himself being confused and contradictory, it is not apparent to this court that there was any error in granting a nonsuit. Considered all together, the testimony, construed fairly and naturally, shows that, notwithstanding the train by which the plaintiff was injured was running too fast and that the bell was not rung in approaching the crossing, the injury did not take place at the crossing, but some distance beyond it, and did not result directly from the company's negligence, but from the sudden and unnecessary conduct of the plaintiff himself in stepping upon the track immediately in front of the train, and so near to the locomotive that it was impossible to avoid striking him after he thus put himself in a position of danger.

(*Syllabus by the Court.*)

Error from city court of Atlanta; HOWARD VAN EPPS, Judge.

Action by Ivey against East Tennessee, Virginia & Georgia Railway Company for damages for personal injuries. Judgment of nonsuit for defendant. Plaintiff brings error.

The following is the official report:

Ivey sued the East Tennessee, Virginia & Georgia Railway Company for damages for personal injuries. At the trial of the case after the introduction of the testimony for the plaintiff, defendant moved for a nonsuit, which motion was granted, and to this the plaintiff excepted.

The plaintiff testified: He went at night between 9 and 10 o'clock to where Victoria street, in the city of Atlanta, crosses a number of railroad tracks, approaching the crossing from the north side. He did not see any train at all while coming across the track, except a switch-engine, which was on the south side, making switches. He looked both ways. He stood there about 20 minutes waiting for the train, which was across the main crossing, and a very long train, to pull up. It did not seem to get across the crossing. It made two or three switches as it pulled on up towards the freight depot. He went on, starting towards the switchman, coming from near the end of the train, west of the crossing. The switchman hallooed, "Look out!" and there was at that time a train coming in front of witness, the switch-engine being right by side of him, and he was watching the train in front. The switchman hallooed again, and the third time, and by that time witness looked back and saw a train was very nearly on him, and jumped, and before his feet could hit the ground the train threw him. This was on the main line,—the Georgia Pacific track,—which was used both by that road and by defendant. It was about 50 or 60 feet from the crossing. Witness does not know what engine hit him. He did not hear anything but the noise of the train, and heard that all the time, because the other train was pulling up towards the depot, and the train that was going that way he did not pay any attention to, because he knew it had passed him. The train that struck him was not ringing the bell, and he does not know how fast it was running. There was no bell ringing at all. He could not detect the train was on him until he jumped, and when he jumped it was so close to him it hit him before he knew anything. The switchman said, "Look out!" that train was coming there, or some way. Witness did not exactly understand him, but knows he threw up his lantern and told witness to "look out." Witness was watching the train coming in front of him, but does not know what train that was. He crossed the railroad because he could not get across "there," and because they were making up their freight there, and they retained the track so long he had either to go back the other way, or go where the switchman was. At the place where he attempted to cross, people crossed very often, and they crossed there because the crossing was blocked with trains. He supposes that he was on the identical track where the engine hit him about a minute and a half. He saw the train was on it when he stepped on the track. Supposes he was on there more than two minutes, and as soon as he stepped on the track he glanced his eye, and saw the train coming, and about that minute, before he hit the ground, the train hit him. He understood the switchman to be alluding to the train that was coming in front of him when the switchman was calling to him. There are five or six tracks at this place, and of these the Western & Atlantic Railroad had two. The cars that were blockading the street were on the track that ran by the freight depot, which was the track of the Georgia Pacific, and not of defendant. The Georgia Pacific is at the crossing on the south side of these tracks, but the East Tennessee depot is about a mile away. There was no train on the tracks next to Marietta street,—the side from which he approached,—and the blockading train was on the far side of the five tracks. He stopped next to the track that this train was on, right between two tracks, having crossed over four tracks, and was waiting to get over that last track; and the train not moving, after he had waited a while, he walked down the track, in order to get to the end of the train, and go around it. He did not get up on the track, but went between the last two tracks. He did not go to where he wanted to cross because the train had stopped, and there was a train coming on the same track, which threw him between the two trains. The switchman hallooed, "Look out!" and witness could not go that way, but had to come back, so he turned to his right to get on the other side, stepped back, and crossed the other track to between the second and third tracks. When the switchman still hallooed, "Look out!" he turned himself "that way," and found the train was on him. It was while he was walking to get around the blockading train that the cry "Look out!" was given, and he did not get to the end of the blockading train, which train was facing towards the city. The two tracks were about three feet—the regular distance—apart. People can walk between them, and when trains are on them a man could stand, but he did not know that it would be safe to walk unless one walked "mighty straight;" if he stood still, the train might pass him without his being hit. The switchman was at the switch below him west of the crossing; the city side being east of the crossing. At the time the switchman spoke to him he was walking between the tracks, and the train he saw moving then was coming right towards him on the right on his right, from towards the river,—the west side. The blockading train was "puffing about; kind of shifting." He does not know what it was doing. It was not coming fast, and the engine or train that was coming towards him was not coming very fast. The head-light was shining in his face. When he heard the switchman halloo, "Look out!" he thought he meant the engine was coming towards him, and did not look back to see whether there was one on the other side coming. After the switchman hallooed, and witness turned to his right and stepped across the track, this put him between the third and fourth tracks; and just as he stepped there he looked back, and saw the train was right on him, and that he could not risk himself there between those two tracks, where he first caught sight of this train. He got upon the third track; tried to jump over it. He did not get on it, he "dont reckon." He does not know how he did, but knows he jumped. When the warning to "look out" was given he was between the third and fourth tracks, having crossed over one track, and the third track was the main line. Does

not know how he got on that track. He jumped right there. Just as he crossed the track on the right, and got in between the others, he looked back, and saw this train was right on him. Supposed he must have been on the track when he saw the train was on him. He could not tell the position he was in right then, because he got a little "sorter" excited, and knew it was dangerous, and made a jump. He "aimed" to jump clean out of the way. When he got the first notice to "look out" he was between the fourth and fifth tracks, and saw an engine coming down the fourth, and he crossed over the fourth, and then the switchman hallooed again to "look out," and he looked in the rear. He got another notice after he was between the third and fourth tracks, and he looked out about the third time the switchman hallooed. He never looked for the engine coming from towards the city, but looked right in front of him, taking it for granted that was the train the switchman was talking about. Never looked the other way until after he got on that track. He was crossing back towards Marietta street when he got hit. That was the only way to get out of danger. He was quite familiar with that place, and had been crossing there about five years, twice a day. Had a bottle of whisky in his pocket at the time he was hurt, but had not drank a drop of it. Had taken two glasses of beer that night,—the last about 20 or 25 minutes before he left Marietta street. He heard the switchman when he first called out; and, as they have a usual way of hallooing at each other on the switch, he had no idea the switchman was talking to him, but left the place where he was because the switchman kept hallooing and throwing the lantern, and that attracted his attention. The main line where he got hurt is straight, and perfectly open. He could have heard a bell if they were ringing it, but there was no bell rung. If he had been paying attention and listening to see whether trains were coming or not, he could have heard the noise of the train that hit him, in spite of what was going on around him. He was not paying attention in the direction in which the train was coming that struck him, but all his attention was on the train that was coming from the west. The train that hit him had a head-light on it, and, if he had been looking that way, he could have seen it approaching for several hundred yards.

The switchman testified for plaintiff: It was the pilot of one of defendant's engines which struck plaintiff. Witness saw plaintiff about three minutes before, and he (plaintiff) was going between the No. 1 side track and the main line, walking on the end of the ties, right by the side of the track. Witness' train (Georgia Pacific) was in motion at the same time, coming back on No. 1 side track. Both of the trains were in motion. Plaintiff "aimed" to go around by witness, and witness hallooed to him to "look out." If he had come around where witness was, witness' train would have caught him. There was a Western & Atlantic switch-engine right across the track, blowing off steam, and defendant's passenger train coming, and witness supposes plaintiff did not know which one hallooed at him. The train which struck him was running fast enough for a man to get off and on,—witness supposes about 10 miles an hour. It was about three car-lengths from the street crossing, and when the train was coming towards the crossing witness did not hear it ringing a bell. Does not know whether the Western & Atlantic train was ringing a bell. If it was, he did not hear it. Could not have heard it if it had been, because of the noise of witness' own train that he was working with. Plaintiff touched the track, and started across, and before he got across the engine struck him. It was about three seconds or a minute; something like that. If a man were crossing at Victoria street he would have to cross three of the Georgia Pacific tracks, counting the main line, and three of the Western & Atlantic. The Western & Atlantic engine was coming from the river towards the city, and was on the track next to the main line. Plaintiff was coming down the main line on the side of the track and next to the track witness' train was on, and was about three car-lengths from witness when witness hallooed at him, looking right at the engine. The reflection of the light of the Western & Atlantic shone right in his face. Witness saw the engine coming behind him. Could have seen the engine three or four hundred yards. The main line was between the track witness' engine was on and the track Western & Atlantic engine was coming on, and when witness hallooed at plaintiff he did not cross the track the Western & Atlantic engine was on, but started across the main line, and before he got across was struck. If he had looked back he could have seen the train coming. He was watching witness. The Western & Atlantic engine was ringing a bell. It was letting off steam; and witness' engine was backing and making a noise, and the steam was escaping from it. Does not remember whether it was ringing a bell or not. Because of the noise the Western & Atlantic was making, witness could not tell whether the train that was coming out was making a noise or not. Thinks it was running about 10 or 12 miles an hour. Saw nothing of any whisky when he picked up plaintiff. Saw the bottle where it was broken, and smelt some whisky when he picked him up, but paid no attention to his breath, and does not know whether he had drank any or not. He did not see plaintiff when plaintiff was standing at the crossing; there were so many standing there. The tracks were about six feet, he supposes, from one rail to the other, which is the regular distance. When he first saw plaintiff, plaintiff was walking straight.

Plaintiff also put in evidence as to the extent of his injuries, earnings, age, etc., and also an ordinance of the city to the effect that any engineer or other person in charge of an engine, with or without cars attached, who should run the same through any part of the city at a greater rate of speed than six miles an hour,

should, on conviction, be punished in a manner prescribed in the ordinance.

Cox & Reed, for plaintiff in error. *Dorsey, Brewster & Howell*, for defendant in error.

PER CURIAM. Judgment affirmed.

SIMMONS, J., not presiding.

LUKENS v. FORD.

(Supreme Court of Georgia. July 13, 1891.)

INSTRUCTIONS—TRESPASS.

1. Construing all the charge together, there was no material error committed by the judge in the trial of this case.

2. The verdict was warranted by the evidence.

(Syllabus by the Court.)

Error from superior court, Whitfield county; THOMAS W. MILNER, Judge.

Action by Olive A. Lukens against Timothy Ford. Verdict and judgment for defendant. Plaintiff brings error. Affirmed.

The following is the official report:

In September, 1887, Mrs. Lukens sued Ford for damages alleged to have been caused by his backing water in and upon her spring, and otherwise injuring it, by erecting an embankment across the mouth of the spring, and erecting and maintaining a fish-pond immediately below the spring. She obtained a verdict against the defendant for $20, in April, 1888, and, a new trial being denied Ford, he brought the case to this court, where the judgment of the court below was affirmed at the October term, 1888. 81 Ga. 633, 8 S. E. Rep. 813. In March, 1889, she again sued Ford for the continuation of the trespass, which was the cause of action in the former suit. Ford, by way of defense, set up that she had injured him by turning her hogs into his dams, in cutting his dams and letting in surface water, causing his fish to escape, by filling up his drain and protection ditches, by driving stock over the dams and riding over them, and by shutting up and locking her gates, forcing him to go around a longer and worse road. The jury gave Ford a verdict for $25, and plaintiff's motion for a new trial was overruled, which she alleges was error. In addition to the usual grounds of the motion for new trial, that the verdict was contrary to law, evidence, etc., it was alleged that the court erred in charging: "This case is to be tried by the evidence before you, and not upon evidence or conclusions drawn from evidence in another case." Plaintiff insists that the last clause of the charge was misleading, because it excluded, or might have been understood as excluding, from the consideration of the jury, the force and effect of a former judgment (admitted to have been rendered) in favor of plaintiff against the defendant; the evidence showing that the conditions of the spring, dam, and pond remained for a portion of the time covered by the present case just as they were during the period covered by the former suit; plaintiff insisting, also, that the evidence showed that the items for which defendant claimed damages in this case were passed upon by the jury in the former suit. It was also alleged that the court erred in charging "that under the contract Ford would have no right to dig down and lower the spring without consent of plaintiff. She had a right to keep it as it then stood, if it was not below the natural height." Plaintiff insists that this charge was misleading, and may have misled the jury, plaintiff not having insisted that defendant had lowered the spring, but that the water was dammed in the spring higher than its natural height, by *debris*, etc., when Ford erected the dam and pond complained of, and that plaintiff had the right to reduce the spring to its natural depth and flow. Plaintiff further insists that the statement by the court that Ford had no right to dig down and lower the spring may have led the jury to infer that he had a right to seize and keep the water at the height he found it when he constructed the dam and pond, and the evidence showing that the depth of the spring was then greater than the natural depth; and plaintiff further insists that the second clause of the charge quoted might have misled the jury to believe that she, too, was entitled to hold the water at that height, and not lower. It was also alleged that the court erred in charging: "Under this contract defendant could construct one or more ponds until he completed his system or exhausted the grant, and this he could do without any further consent on the part of the owner of the land." Plaintiff insists that this charge was erroneous because it did not, nor did the court elsewhere, submit to the jury, under proper instructions, whether Ford had exhausted his right to construct dams or ponds, the evidence showing that Ford had constructed and finished a series of dams and ponds in 1885, and did not commence the pond complained of until the fall of 1886. Plaintiff further insists that the charge complained of also excluded from the consideration of the jury the question whether Ford had commenced and prosecuted the work in good faith for the purpose contemplated by the contract, to-wit, raising fish and making profit thereby for himself and plaintiff, or for the purpose of selling the ponds and speculating upon them, the latter being his purpose, as insisted by plaintiff. It was further alleged that a new trial should have been granted, because the case was submitted to and tried by the jury on the assumed theory that Ford had not exhausted his grant under the contract when he completed a series of ponds in 1885, and suspended his work of construction until the fall of 1886, and a new trial should have been granted, that the question whether or not Ford had exhausted the grant before the erection of the nuisance complained of might be properly submitted and tried. It was further alleged that the court erred in charging: "The defendant would be entitled to recover damages caused by the cutting down of the dams by the plaintiff or her agent, causing an escape of his fish, if you find from the evidence she or her agents so cut the dam." Plaintiff alleges that this charge was erroneous, because it excluded from the jury the question whether such cutting by plaintiff's agent was not necessary for the protection of plaintiff's rights, and also because it holds by implication that plaintiff had no right to abate a nuisance created by defendant in the prosecution of the business, she insisting that defendant had created such nuisance, as shown by the evidence, and further, that the only cutting of the dam was considered by the jury in the former suit, and that this fact was shown by the evidence. It was also alleged that the court erred in refusing to charge "that defendant, Ford, had no right, under his contract, to open the gate of the dwelling inclosure of plaintiff, and to drive his wagons through the house-yard of plaintiff, provided there was any other reasonable and practicable way over plaintiff's land; that, while the plaintiff was bound by the contract to allow Ford a right of way over his land, that would not mean that he could make a wagon way through the house inclosure and yard of plaintiff, against his will, unless there was no other practicable way for the wagon to go on plaintiff's land;" plaintiff insisting that the evidence showed there was another way equally as good and practicable, which had been selected and used by Ford for some time before he sought to go through the inclosure and yard, and Ford insisting upon plaintiff's refusal to permit him to drive his wagon through the inclosure and yard as an item upon which he was entitled to damages. It was also alleged that the court erred in charging: "Under the law, as given in charge, you will find what damages, if any, the plaintiff is entitled to recover from the defendant; and likewise what damages, if any, the defendant is entitled to recover from the plaintiff, and then take the one sum from the other, and, if the balance is in favor of the plaintiff, then your verdict should be in her favor against the defendant for that amount; but, if the balance is in favor of the defendant, then your verdict should be in his favor for that amount against the plaintiff." Plaintiff insists that the jury should have found specifically whether or not Ford had exceeded his rights under the contract in the erection of the dams and ponds complained of, and the court should have so directed, but no such direction was given, and no other form of verdict was submitted or given to the jury, and the charge complained of inhibited the jury from saying in their verdict whether defendant had exceeded his rights under the contract.

Plaintiff insists that the court erred in refusing a new trial, for the reason that defendant proposed to admit that plaintiff had a right of action when she sued, and in ordering the admission to be entered of record, and that a new trial should have been awarded, notwithstanding such admission was made and entered of record. The admission referred to was that plaintiff had a right of action against defendant in the suit tried, and that the foundation of the verdict was solely on the defendant's set-off. It was expressly stated that this admission was made to end the present litigation, and, if not accepted, and a new trial should be granted by the superior court or supreme court, then this admission to be of no force. The court ordered this admission to be made a part of the record, and in his order overruling the motion for new trial recited that the respondent, having made and filed an admission that he would not insist upon the verdict and judgment as a bar to movant's rights, and that plaintiff had a right of action when she sued, it was ordered that a new trial be refused. The contract in question was made between Ford and one Rowley, under whom plaintiff derives title to the premises upon which the alleged trespass was committed. By this contract Rowley conveyed to Ford the right to enter upon Rowley's lands "lying along and contiguous to the spring branch," and to construct and keep upon the land one or more or a series of fish-ponds; and for this purpose it was agreed that Ford might enter upon the land, and cut ditches, drains, etc., and build dams, make embankments, and stop and dam up the water, and change and divert the course thereof as far as necessary for the purpose indicated, but should not have the right to dam up the water so as in any wise to overflow or injure the main spring. It was further stipulated that Ford should have the right of passage over any lands for all purposes necessary to the building and managing said ponds; and that Ford was in good faith to commence work by September, 1883, and prosecute it with reasonable diligence; Ford agreeing that one-third of the fish taken from the ponds by him should belong to Rowley, and that Rowley, his heirs and assigns, should have and own one-third of the ponds and all advantages derived therefrom, Ford to have the management and control of taking the fish therefrom, and to build, keep up, and stock the pond or ponds at his own charges. Upon the hearing of the motion for new trial it was insisted by plaintiff that the verdict was contrary to law and evidence, for the reason that the clause of the contract giving Ford the right to enter upon the land and construct and maintain the pond or ponds, properly construed, authorised Ford to construct ponds upon the land adjacent to the branch, but not to cover the branch by and embrace it in a pond or ponds, the evidence showing that the pond complained of had entirely covered and absorbed the branch, and that Ford had thus exceeded his rights under the contract; and plaintiff alleges that the court, by refusing a new trial, dissented from the construction of the clause insisted upon, and which plaintiff insists is the proper construction.

McCutchen & Shumate, for plaintiff in error. *W. K. Moore* and *R. J. & J. Mc-Camy*, for defendant in error.

BLECKLEY, C. J. In the ornithology of litigation this case is a tomtit furnished with a garb of feathers ample enough for a turkey. Measured by the verdict, its tiny body has only the bulk of $25, but it struts with a display of record expanded into 83 pages of manuscript. It seems to us that a more contracted plumage might serve for so small a bird, but perhaps we are mistaken. In every forensic season, we have a considerable flock of such cases, to be stripped and dissected for the cabinets of jurisprudence. We endeavor to pick our overfledged poultry with judicial assiduity and patience.

1. The motion for a new trial contains eight grounds, five of them alleging error in the charge of the court. The full charge is set out in the record, and we have examined it minutely. Reading it altogether, and construing it as a whole, it is free from material error. We see nothing misleading in the statement that "this case is to be tried by the evidence before you, and not upon the evidence or the conclusions drawn from evidence in another case." It appears to us that it was not prejudicial to the plaintiff to instruct the jury, at the request of defendant's counsel, that, under the contract governing the relation of the parties to each other, "Ford would have no right to dig down and lower plaintiff's stream without her consent. She had a right to keep it at the height it then stood, if it was not below the natural height." This looks like it was true, as far as it went; and, if it did not fit onto the grounds of the suit, or square with the contention of plaintiff's counsel at the trial, it had only the vice of irrelevancy. The charge in full contained ample matter that did apply to the real issues, and which expounded the law of them clearly and correctly. By some casualty the charge is blank as to one of them, but this is not complained of. Why the defendant should have requested the court to instruct that he, the defendant, had no right to dig down and lower the spring, and that the plaintiff had a right to keep the water in it as it stood at the date of the contract, if it was not below the natural height, we are at some loss to conjecture; but we cannot order a new trial because the defendant requested instructions apparently favorable to his adversary, and the court gave them in compliance with the request. Perhaps the object of the defendant was to curry favor with the jury by showing them that he was willing to make concessions, and was not disposed to controvert what was of no consequence to the merits of the dispute. But we do not know this to be so; and, if we did, we hardly think that such a light touch in currying favor would vitiate the trial. We agree with the court in thinking that under the contract the defendant "could construct one or more ponds, from time to time, till he completed his system or exhausted the grant; and this he could do without any further consent on the part of the owner of the land." Regarded in the light of the evidence and of the whole charge, we indorse the instruction that "the defendant would be entitled to recover damages caused by the cutting down of the dams by the plaintiff or her agent, causing an escape of his fish, if you find from the evidence that she or her agent so cut the dams." The pleadings of the defendant brought before the court and jury his claim for the damages here referred to. The instructions given to the jury as to the form of their verdict were undoubtedly correct,

and they were broad enough to guide the jury in finding for either party. It was not incumbent upon the court to give more specific or extensive instructions unless they had been requested. So far as appears, there was not even any suggestion from counsel when the verdict was returned that it should settle anything but what it expressed. Had there been at that time a request to send the jury out again to find a more comprehensive verdict, the court might have complied with it. There is a strong flavor of afterthought in what the motion for a new trial has to say touching the form of the verdict. The observations we have made dispose of objections to the charge of the court. One of the grounds of the motion complains of a refusal to charge as requested, but the request was not presented in writing, and the language of it was not so perspicuous as to make clear to the mind at once that it lays down sound law. Indeed, after reading its terms over and over, we are not quite certain that the request is sound as it stands in the record. We rather think it should have been qualified by some reference to the way, if any, actually used under the contract before any dispute about the means of ingress and egress arose. But what we decide is that the accuracy of the request is not so apparent as to make it error to decline giving it in charge on the report of the ear alone, with no aid from the aye. We might add that we deem the matter to which the request relates rather too inconsiderable to warrant the grant of a new trial on account of it alone. To reopen this fierce but petty litigation because of a slight error would not be wholesome practice. This is the second of the spring and fish-pond cases. The first is reported in 81 Ga. 633, 8 S. E. Rep. 818.

2. The remaining two grounds of the motion are the general ones attacking the verdict as contrary to law and evidence. In so far as our duty requires us to verify the correctness of the verdict, we regard it as sound enough to be upheld by the presiding judge in the exercise of his discretion. Judgment affirmed.

EAST TENNESSEE, V. & G. RY. CO. v. PERKINS.

(*Supreme Court of Georgia.* Oct. 19, 1891.)

INJURY TO EMPLOYE—DEFECTIVE APPLIANCES—EVIDENCE.

1. There was no error in failing to give any of the requests for instruction; the court having covered the same by the general charge, in so far as they were legal and appropriate.

2. The charge as a whole was correct, and covered all substantial questions involved in the case.

3. The verdict was not warranted by the evidence, under the law; there being no sufficient ground for imputing to the defendant any negligence whatever in the matter of furnishing to the plaintiff an unfit instrument for the work in hand, but the evidence showing, on the contrary, that the plaintiff did not wait to have furnished to him such an instrument as the superintendent considered suitable, and promised to furnish.

(*Syllabus by the Court.*)

Error from superior court, Fulton county; MARSHALL J. CLARKE, Judge.

The following is the official report: Perkins sued for damages, alleging as follows: He was employed by the defendant railway company in its shops as a machinist, and in the discharge of his duty endeavored to insert a set-screw in an eccentric. The hole was not properly tapped out, and as a consequence the screw would not go in correctly. It was impossible for him to detect this defect in the hole until he inserted the screw, as it was very small. As soon as he found that the screw would not go in, he notified the foreman, who endeavored to put it in, but could only put it partly in. It had now got fastened in the hole, and the foreman directed him to cut the screw out with a chisel, which he endeavored to do, and had cut out the greater part of it, when the tapering form of the hole made it necessary for him to take another chisel. At the first blow he struck with the other chisel, the chisel blurred; and by reason of this a chip of steel from the screw flew into his eye, destroying the sight. He was without fault or negligence. He had nothing to do with the tempering or preparation of the chisel. He could not have known of its defective tempering. It was the duty of a blacksmith, another employe of defendant, to temper the chisel; and any competent blacksmith, in tempering a tool, can put on it the proper temper. It was one of the tools furnished by defendant for his use; and the agent of defendant, the blacksmith, failed to temper it properly. The chisel blurred, and broke off the chip of steel, instead of cutting it off. Defendant was negligent in furnishing an improper chisel, and one improperly tempered, and not satisfactorily hard, and in not properly supervising the tempering and preparation of tools for petitioner, and in other respects. Petitioner could not have avoided the injury by the use of ordinary care. At the close of the testimony for plaintiff the defendant moved for a nonsuit, which motion was overruled, and to this it excepted. Plaintiff obtained a verdict for $1,111, and defendant's motion for a new trial was overruled, to which it excepted. In addition to the general grounds of the motion, that the verdict was contrary to law, evidence, etc., it was alleged therein that the court erred in refusing to give in charge the following written requests: "Although the chisel may have been tempered too soft, and although you may believe the company knew it, or ought to have known it, by the exercise of ordinary care and diligence, still the plaintiff would not be entitled to recover if the injury did not occur on that account, as, for instance, if the plaintiff was hurt because of the chisel being too large to do the work in hand, he could not recover, and you should find for the defendant." "If the company in this case exercised due care in selecting the blacksmith to do the work of repairing the chisel used by the plaintiff, and if there is no reason shown by the evidence why he should not be trusted as an expert blacksmith, you should find for the defendant, although the chisel may have proved by use to have been defective." "If the defendant company exercised ordinary care in repairing the chisel used by the plaintiff, it would not be liable for an injury to the plaintiff, although it should turn out that it was not properly tempered. The defendant company is not an insurer of the safety of tools furnished to employes. It is only bound to the exercise of ordinary care and diligence in purchasing and repairing the tools so furnished its employes." "Before he can recover, he must not only show that the chisel he used was defective, but that the defendant knew it, or could have known it by the exercise of ordinary care and diligence. The mere fact that the chisel may have been defective is not sufficient to authorize the jury to infer negligence on the part of the company. If the chisel was defective, and that defect was not known to the company, or could not have been known by the use of ordinary care on its part, you should find for the defendant. If the defect in the chisel, if there was a defect, was latent,—that is, hidden from view,—there could be no recovery by the plaintiff. It would be an accident, in law, for which no one could be held responsible." Also, because the court erred in failing to charge upon the duty of the employe to exercise care in discerning defects; the law being that any defect which may become apparent in their use it is the duty of the employe to observe and report to his employer, if the servant have the means of discovering any such defect which the master does not possess. Also, error in failing to charge upon the question of what would be ordinary risks of employment, although the court charged, "the defendant would not be liable for the ordinary risks of employment,"—the law being that it is not negligence in the employer if the tools break, whether from internal, original fault not apparent when the tools were at first provided or furnished, or from an external, apparent one, produced by time and use, not brought to the master's knowledge. These are the ordinary risks of employment which the servant takes upon himself. Also, because the court erred in confusing the jury in determining the question of the plaintiff's negligence to two things,—"whether he disobeyed the instructions of his superior," and "whether he selected an improper tool."—when the evidence would have authorized the jury to have imputed negligence to plaintiff as to other parts of the transaction in which he got hurt, as, for instance, in the method of holding his head over the hole in which he was using the chisel, and in various other things. Because the court erred in failing to charge the jury, as the evidence required, that if the defect in the chisel was such a defect as to deceive human judgment the plaintiff, as well as the defendant, stands excused for using it in its defective condition. If it appeared safe to him, and no reason is shown why the defendant could have known or suspected it to be defective, then, it being demonstrated to be defective only in its use, the plaintiff could not recover. In such a case, it would be only a risk assumed by the plaintiff when he went into the defendant's employment.

A. O. Bacon and Dorsey, Brewster & Howell, for plaintiff in error. Hode & Burton Smith and J. R. Whiteside, for defendant in error.

LUMPKIN, J. 1, 2. Plaintiff in error made to the court below several written requests to charge the jury, many of which were legal, and some of which were not. The general charge was a correct presentation of the law applicable, and covered not only the above-mentioned requests, in so far as they were legal, but also all substantial questions involved in the case. This is all a charge should be required to do.

3. The facts adduced upon the trial appear in the reporter's statement, and show, we think, that the verdict should have been in favor of the defendant. It was not foreseen that any instrument specially adapted to the work in which plaintiff was engaged at the time he was injured would be needed, because this particular work was itself made necessary by an accident. As soon as the emergency arose, the superintendent not only offered to supply plaintiff with a proper instrument with which to do this work, but promptly went off to secure one, and was actually bringing it to plaintiff when the injury occurred. Plaintiff, however, chose to rely upon his own experience and judgment, selected a tool from a large number which had been put in his charge, and began work before the superintendent could possibly supply one which would be proper. The instruments from which plaintiff made his selection were not specially designed to do the particular work made necessary by the emergency which had arisen; the evidence showing that such work required a more perfect tool. It is probably true that the tool with which plaintiff attempted to do this work was not a proper one for the purpose, but the company did not hold it out as such, as plaintiff must have known; and, to say the least, he might have waited until the return of the superintendent with what the latter considered a proper instrument for this occasion. Such an accident as this is likely to happen at any time, and may have occurred, no matter what sort of chisel the plaintiff had used. It was one of those unfortunate occurrences incident to the employment in which he was engaged,—an accident which, in all probability, no amount of diligence on the part of either plaintiff or defendant could have prevented. It is a well established rule of law that every man, when he enters upon a particular employment, must assume the risks and hazards usually pertaining thereto; and, accordingly, the plaintiff, under the facts disclosed by the record, was not entitled to any recovery against the defendant. Judgment reversed.

HOUSTON v. CULVER et al.

(Supreme Court of Georgia. Nov. 10, 1891.)

MASTER AND SERVANT — NEGLIGENCE — RISKS OF EMPLOYMENT.

The action being for employing an incompetent superintendent, and for negligence on the part of the superintendent in directing a hole to be drilled for blasting where a charge blast was already in, and there being no evidence either of the incompetency of the superintendent, or that, if competent, he could by the use of proper diligence have known that the previous charge had not been exploded, the judgment of nonsuit was correct.

(Syllabus by the Court.)

Error from city court of Atlanta; Howard Van Epps, Judge.

Action by O. A. Houston against Culver, Reynolds & Co. for personal injuries. Judgment for defendants. Plaintiff brings error. Affirmed.

The following is the official report:

Houston sued Culver, Reynolds & Co. for damages for personal injuries which he alleged he received while working at a rock quarry conducted by them. At the close of the testimony for plaintiff the court granted a nonsuit, upon the ground that Peter Hill (whose connection with the matter will hereafter appear) and plaintiff were fellow-servants, and defendants were not liable for the negligence of Peter Hill; to which decision plaintiff excepted. The testimony for plaintiff, so far as material, was to the following effect: He had been working at a rock quarry for about 10 days. Peter Hill was in charge of the quarry, and employed and discharged the hands. Some of the hands were drilling holes, some blasting and some hauling rocks. Peter Hill had control of all these men, and directed when and where and how they should work. He fixed the pay of the men who worked there. On the day when plaintiff was injured, Hill directed him and the men who worked with him to drill a hole at a certain point, indicating the place. Plaintiff cleared away the rubbish, consisting of dirt and loose rock, and found a hole very near the place where Hill had directed him to drill the hole. Plaintiff had heard that a hole ought not to be drilled near an old hole, and told Hill about the hole, and he directed plaintiff to drill in the old hole. They commenced drilling, plaintiff holding the drill and another man striking. Plaintiff was on his knees holding the drill close to the mouth of the hole, which was about 2½ feet deep when they commenced to drill. When they had got down to about 3½ feet from the top there was an explosion, which hurt plaintiff very badly. Culver, one of the firm, used to come to the quarry two or three times a week and talk with Hill and give directions about the work, and another of the defendant firm used to pay off the hands Saturday evenings at the house of the third member of the firm. Plaintiff had worked in the quarry before, but not where dynamite was used; he knew nothing about dynamite, and relied upon the knowledge of Hill in working with it; did not know there was any dynamite in the hole. Three holes had been drilled and charged with power and dynamite, and the fuse lit to fire them off, but only two explosions were heard by a witness, who testified as to this point, and Hill was told that it was thought all three had not fired. Hill said the dynamite had gone out at the bottom through the crevices in the rock. The witness did not think so, because he heard only two explosions, and could see no sign of the powder having blackened the rock at the bottom of the ledge, which he thought would have been there if the powder had gone out that way, but the witness yielded his opinion, as he thought Hill knew more about it than he did. Hill then ordered that hole, which was full at the top, rimmed about three feet, and a second bottom put in above the point where the crevices would be. He then charged this hole again and fired it, and it did not break up the rock from the bottom, but simply around the top, which was the condition of the hole when plaintiff commenced to drill in it. The explosion which injured plaintiff was of the dynamite below the second bottom, which had never exploded. Culver discharged Hill when plaintiff was injured, and he has never worked there since, until about a week before the trial.

Calhoun, King & Spalding and J. T. Pendleton, for plaintiff in error. N. J. & T. A. Hammond, for defendants in error.

Lumpkin, J. The declaration charges the defendants and their foreman with being negligent. The alleged negligence of Hill, the foreman or boss, consisted in removing the cap from the dynamite cartridge, thereby rendering it less liable to explode; "in recharging said hole and putting the charge below the said recharge, and thus endeavoring to fire off said dynamite;" in not knowing that the charge of dynamite in the old hole had not been exploded; and in ordering the plaintiff to drill in said hole. The alleged negligence of the defendants consisted in knowingly employing an unskilled and incompetent foreman, and holding him out to the plaintiff as competent to direct the work of blasting. From an examination of the evidence, the substance of which appears in the report, it will be seen that there is no proof that the cap was removed from the dynamite cartridge, or that this was an unusual or improper act in the operation of blasting. Nor is it shown that the method adopted on the second attempt to fire the unexploded dynamite, by putting in a "second bottom," charging the hole with powder and firing it, was not proper, or would not ordinarily accomplish the desired result. Nor does it appear that Hill neglected any precautionary measure to ascertain whether the second effort to explode the dynamite had succeeded, or how, by the use of proper diligence, he could have known that fact. Consequently, to order the plaintiff to drill in the old hole was not shown to be an act of negligence. As to the alleged negligence of the defendants in knowingly employing an incompetent foreman, there is not a particle of proof of Hill's incompetency, or of knowledge thereof on the part of the defendants. Such incompetency could not be inferred from his conduct in this transaction, because, as shown above, it was not proved to be in any respect negligent. The evidence only shows that the plaintiff suffered a misfortune incident to the dangerous class of work in which he engaged. No one seems to have suspected that the dynamite was still unexploded at the time when the plaintiff was ordered to drill. Hill and Holden differed in opinion as to whether the first firing had sent off the dynamite; but, after the explosion of the second charge of powder in the same hole, there appears no reason why either should think that the dynamite still lay there unexploded, not having "gone out at the bottom through the crevices or fissures in the rock," as Hill believed it had done on the first explosion. The plaintiff, as he alleges in his declaration, objected to drilling near the old hole, not because of any possible danger there, but because he "had been informed that a hole drilled too near to another hole that had been previously blasted was liable to be defective for the purpose of the blasting, by reason of fissures liable to be made by the prior blasting in the rock." There being no evidence of negligence on the part either of the foreman or of the defendants the judgment of nonsuit was proper. The court below rested its judgment on the ground that the plaintiff and Hill were fellow-servants, and the defendants were not liable for the negligence of Hill. The plaintiff contends that Hill was the defendants' "general superintendent," standing in their place and representing them. The declaration calls him by the less pretentious designations of "foreman" and "boss," and it is not clear from the evidence that he was anything more at the time of the injury. It may be that the court rightly granted the nonsuit for the reason above stated. Whether this is true or not, on the evidence adduced by the plaintiff there could be no recovery. Judgment affirmed.

AUSTIN et al. v. APPLING.

(Supreme Court of Georgia. Nov. 10, 1891.)

INSTRUCTIONS — INJURY TO EMPLOYE — ASSUMPTION OF RISK — ACTION AGAINST PARTNERSHIP — LIABILITIES OF RETIRING PARTNER.

1. It was not error for the court to address the jury in this case in the same terms as were used in Parker v. Railway Co., 83 Ga. 540, 10 S. E. Rep. 233.

2. It was not error to decline to charge that, if the plaintiff had the same means of knowing the defect in the fastening of the rope as the defendant had, he cannot recover; it appearing that the duty of inspection did not rest upon him. Nor was it error to decline to charge that if the plaintiff commenced to use the door knowing its condition, and continued in defendant's service, the door remaining in the same condition, his continuance in the service would be a waiver of any claim upon the defendants to furnish greater safeguards; the evidence being that the door did not continue in the same condition.

3. Where three persons are sued as a partnership, and two of them file pleas of non-partnership, and the whole case is tried together, a verdict against all three by name, construed in the light of the pleadings, is a finding that they are all liable as partners, and is equivalent to a verdict against the partnership.

4. Where three persons compose a partnership under a name, such as the Fulton Lumber & Manufacturing Company, which does not disclose the individual name of any partner, and two of them withdraw, and the third continues business at the same place, and under the same partnership name, a person dealing with him cannot hold the retired members of the firm responsible, if he had never dealt with the firm before dissolution,

and had no knowledge of the persons constituting the same, either before the dissolution or at the time of the dealing in question. This is true although no notice of the dissolution had ever been given in any manner.

5. Where three persons are sued as partners, and no partnership is established, the verdict may be against one only.

6. The recovery being correct as to one of the defendants, and obviously incorrect as to the other two, the judgment is affirmed as to the former, but reversed as to the latter, with direction that the action be dismissed as to them.

(Syllabus by the Court.)

Error from city court of Atlanta; HOWARD VAN EPPS, Judge.

Action by H. B. Appling against T. H. Austin and others. Verdict and judgment for plaintiff. Defendants bring error. Modified.

Candler & Thomson and W. A. Haygood, for plaintiffs in error. P. L. Mynatt & Son, for defendant in error.

LUMPKIN, J. 1. Juries ought to agree upon verdicts whenever they can conscientiously do so, and it is not improper for the court to aid them in reconciling their differences of opinion by such language as the following: "If you disagreed about a matter of law, I could aid you; but, as it is a matter of evidence, I cannot aid you, as you are judges of the evidence, except by some rules of law for your guidance. I can, however, give you this rule: In civil cases, where the jury cannot reconcile the testimony of witnesses conflicting, they can find a verdict according to the preponderance of the testimony. This jury is, in the eyes of the law, as capable of deciding this case, and reaching a verdict, as any other that may be impaneled hereafter; and I am disposed to give you some further opportunity to consider your verdict. Go to your room, and make an honest effort to agree on a verdict, and follow the rules I have given you, and I do not think it will trouble you in agreeing." Parker v. Railway Co., 83 Ga. 540, 10 S. E. Rep. 233.

2. Appling was employed as a common laborer, and it was proved that it was no part of his duty to inspect the machinery and appliances used in the prosecution of the business. If such a duty had devolved upon him, he might have been chargeable with knowledge of any defect which existed in the fastening of the rope. Otherwise, he had a right to rely upon the judgment of the superintendent; it not appearing that the defect, if it existed, could be readily detected. It appears that the door did not remain in the same condition in which it was when Appling commenced to use it, and that the change in its condition, or in the fastening of the rope attached to it, caused it to fall. Under these circumstances, the court did right in declining to give the charges set forth in the second head-note.

3. Verdicts must have a reasonable construction in the light of the pleadings upon which they are based. Hence, where three persons are sued as a partnership, and two of them file pleas denying the partnership, and the question whether these two were in fact partners is one of the most seriously contested issues

the jury intended to make them all liable as partners. This, certainly, is a common-sense view of such a verdict, under these circumstances; and we are not aware of any rule of construction which should prevent giving it the effect it was manifestly intended to have.

4 The evidence shows beyond controversy that Appling had no dealings with either Austin or Boylston, and that he did not even know they had been members of the firm composing the Fulton Lumber & Manufacturing Company until after he was injured. He was not even acquainted with them, and in no way acted on the faith of their being members of such firm. In point of fact, they were not members of it when he began work at the lumber-yard as a laborer. Before this time they had been members of this firm, but had retired from it. It is true that, after their retirement, Dobbs, the remaining member, retained the same firm name, kept its sign over the door, and used some of the letter-heads and bill-heads of the old concern. These letter-heads and bill-heads, however, did not disclose who composed the old firm. On them it appeared that T. H. Austin was president; W. E. Dobbs, general manager; A. D. Boylston, secretary and treasurer; and John M. La Fontaine, superintendent.—of the Fulton Lumber & Manufacturing Company. The natural impression would be that this company was a corporation having these persons for its officers. La Fontaine, in point of fact, was never a member of the firm, but any inference that either of the others was such member would be equally applicable to him; yet there is no pretense that he could be made liable to the plaintiff in this case. Section 1895 of the Code provides as follows: "The dissolution of a partnership by the retiring of an ostensible partner must be made known to creditors and to the world. By the retiring of a dormant partner, it must be made known to all who had knowledge of his connection with the firm." In a case like this, where the style of the firm does not disclose the individual name of any partner, although the members of the firm may not, strictly speaking, be dormant partners, yet it would seem that the law as to the kind of notice which should be given where a dormant partner retires would justly be applicable. In such cases, as appears by the section quoted, the notice need be given to those only who had knowledge of such partner's connection with the firm. This application of the law can surely work no hardship, certainly not in a case of this kind. Appling did not engage in the service of Dobbs upon the idea that Austin and Boylston were his partners, and his injury was in no wise occasioned by reason of an erroneous supposition upon his part that they belonged to the firm, or had ever belonged to it. He treated with Dobbs alone, not knowing, and doubtless not caring, whether he had partners or not, or, if so, who they were. It would therefore seem entirely contrary to justice to make Austin and Boylston liable to

Partn. p. *43; Richards v. Hunt, 65 Ga. 342; Richards v. Butler, Id. 593.

5 and 6. Where a suit is brought against three persons as partners, charging them with the perpetration of a tort whereby the plaintiff was injured, and he fails to establish the existence of the partnership, but does show by the testimony that one of these three persons, and that one only, is liable to him for the injury sustained, a verdict against the latter would be proper. The ruling here made is in harmony with the principle laid down in many authorities, that for torts partners are jointly and severally liable; and this court has settled the doctrine that in this state, even in a suit against a partnership founded on contract, a verdict against only one of the alleged partners, if warranted by the evidence, is sustainable. Wooten v. Nall, 18 Ga. 609; Francis v. Dickel, 68 Ga. 255; Maynard v. Ponder, 75 Ga. 664; Ledbetter v. Dean, 82 Ga. 790, 9 S. E. Rep. 720; Scofield v. Jones, 85 Ga. 816, 823, 11 S. E. Rep. 1032. The evidence, we think, is sufficient to sustain the verdict as to the defendant Dobbs. We have already shown it cannot be sustained as to the other two defendants. Inasmuch, therefore, as the verdict might have been found against Dobbs alone, the same result may, we think, be properly accomplished by confining it to him. Accordingly, as to Dobbs the judgment is affirmed, and as to Austin and Boylston it is reversed, and we direct that as to them the action be dismissed. Judgment affirmed in part and reversed in part, with direction.

PALMER et al. v. SMITH.

(Supreme Court of Georgia. Nov. 23, 1891.)

DEED BY MARRIED WOMAN—VALIDITY—CONVEYANCE OF HOMESTEAD.

1. A conveyance of land, executed by a married woman in payment of her husband's debt, though declared by the statute absolutely void, is only so as against her, and upon her election to treat it as void; coverture being a personal privilege, which is not available in behalf of a stranger to her title.

2. That a deed by a husband and wife, made in 1869, recites on its face that the property had been set apart as a homestead, without specifying to whom or as whose property it had been so set apart, will not defeat the deed as a conveyance of the wife's prior title to the premises, the deed being executed in the state of Alabama, and no actual occupation of the property as a homestead then or previously being shown, and it not appearing that the makers of the deed then or afterwards resided in Georgia.

(Syllabus by the Court.)

Error from superior court, Fulton county; MARSHALL J. CLARKE, Judge.

Suit by Palmer, Stewart & Co. against J. M. Smith to recover land. Verdict and judgment for defendant. Plaintiffs bring error. Reversed.

The following is the official report:

Palmer, Stewart & Co. brought complaint against Smith for a certain tract of land in Fulton county. The evidence showed that in 1860 one James Jett was in possession of the land, and had been for several years previously. He conveyed it to Thrasher, who conveyed it to one Sells in 1865 or 1866, and Sells went into possession, and conveyed to one Boyd in 1866. Boyd, in March, 1869, conveyed to Mrs. Walls, the wife of W. W. Walls. Walls was indebted to the plaintiffs on three notes, and plaintiffs took a deed to the property from Mrs. Walls and W. W. Walls in October, 1869, in settlement of the notes. This last deed contained the following clause: "The said premises described having been recently set apart as a homestead by the ordinary of Fulton county. Ga., to-wit, in the month of April, 1869." Walls testified, among other things, that he bought the land from Boyd, and the deed was made to his (Walls') wife, and he and his wife afterwards sold to plaintiffs. Defendant is now in possession of the premises, but the nature of his possession or of his claim to the property does not appear. Plaintiffs have, through their agent, been paying taxes on the property since the deed was made them, but have not been in possession of the lot. The jury, under direction of the court, returned a verdict for defendant, and plaintiffs moved for a new trial, which motion was overruled, and they excepted. The grounds of the motion were that the verdict was contrary to law, evidence, etc.; that the court erred in charging the jury to find for the defendant; and for newly-discovered evidence. In support of the last-mentioned ground the plaintiffs produced the affidavit of their attorney, to the following effect: He had received letters from W. W. Walls, attached as exhibits to his affidavits, since the verdict was rendered, in which Walls states that his wife is dead, leaving only one child; that this knowledge has come to deponent since the verdict, and he did not know of it until he received the letter; that the evidence is material under the ruling of the court that the deed from Mrs. Walls to plaintiffs was void; that deponent, as attorney for plaintiffs, who reside in Virginia, has had the sole management and care of the case in its preparation and trial, and the facts thereof connected with this motion are only known to him; that he has not obtained the affidavit of Walls to the facts, because Walls is inimical to the interest and recovery of plaintiffs; and from other letters received from Walls, who lives in Alabama, he knew it was useless to ask him to give his affidavit to the truth of the facts; and that deponent had used due diligence in discovering and preparing the evidence in the case. The first of the two letters attached as exhibits stated that the writer had noticed in a paper the decision in this case; that his son, who was just of age, was going to commence suit for the property; and the writer saw nothing to keep this son, the only child of Mrs. Walls, from recovering the property. The other letter stated that the writer did not know that he could claim any of his deceased wife's estate, as the money that paid for the land belonged to her and not him, and as he had deeded his rights away, if he ever had any, though that did not affect the claim of his son, who could recover, etc.

Fulton Colville, fo *John L. Hopkins &* error.

SIMMONS, J. 1. Un the judge directed th dict in favor of Sml the ground that the from Walls and his art & Co. was made ment of her husban therefore void under Smith, the defendant The record does not privy in blood or e Where a married wol rate estate, conveys third person in paym debts, and afterward property, or to cance will be declared voi against all persons w it was made for such she has conveyed he payment of her hus party, and another of the property, wh with her in blood c therefor by the vende fendant cannot set u the deed is void becau of the husband's del wife is a personal p her or her privies; ar not set it up, no stran do so. The property der such circumstanc and, if she honestly w the hands of her vend husband's just debts, to claim it for herse stranger, who does no set up this defense, an to his pocket? The personal privilege, and fant can avail himsel usury is also a person one but the party pro privies, can take adv in cases of insolvency. of coverture is also a the wife, and can ava self and her privies. that under the facts as ord the deed from Wal er, Stewart & Co. wi tween these parties. Ga. 746, 11 S. E. Rep. 4 62 Ga. 741; 1 Wait, Act v. Johnson, (Ind. S 413; Bennett v. Matti N. E. Rep. 290, and 11 surance Co. v. Baker, 7

2. The deed above re the following clause: described having been as a homestead by the county, Georgia, to-wi April, 1869." Counsel error contended that stead property, and e be maintained upon th are seeking to recover h on that deed, and the denied to the court the or enforcing such a jud facts reported, the prii

does not apply. The evidence does not show to whom or out of whose property the homestead was set apart. It does not show that Walls and his wife ever occupied the land as a homestead, nor does it show that they ever resided in the state of Georgia; but we can infer that, if they ever did reside in Georgia, they had removed to the state of Alabama, because the deed in controversy was executed in that state, and the two letters from Walls, the husband, attached to the motion for a new trial, show that he still resides in Alabama. If they had never resided in this state, no homestead could have been set apart to them under its laws. If they had had a homestead set apart to them, and removed from this state to another, under the reasoning of the decision in the case of Bank v. Smisson, 73 Ga. 422, they lost their homestead rights in the property. If this property was the wife's, its homestead could not have been set apart to them out of it. We think, therefore, that the facts as disclosed by the record could not defeat the deed as a conveyance of the wife's prior title to the premises. Judgment reversed.

MARTIN v. BURGWYN et al.

(Supreme Court of Georgia. Nov. 28, 1891.)

PETITION FOR INJUNCTION—VERIFICATION—RESCISSION OF SALE — APPOINTMENT OF RECEIVER—CONTEMPT.

1. Although the act of 1887 requires a petition for injunction and receiver to be verified, yet, where the verification is imperfect, the deficiency may be supplied by affidavits at the hearing in case the presiding judge shall think proper, in the exercise of his discretion, to proceed on the defective verification. It is best, however, to require proper verification before any action is taken on the petition.

2. A petition by the vendors of goods against an insolvent purchaser, alleging fraud in the purchase and repudiating the contract of sale on that account, has equity on which to proceed to reclaim the goods or their proceeds in the hands of such purchaser. This equity holds equally whether the term of credit has expired or not. In such case a receiver may be appointed to take charge of money and books of account.

3. An order appointing a receiver is sufficiently specific in its description as to notes and books of account which specifies them thus: "The books, notes, and accounts of all kinds of the said defendant in the business of selling cigars, snuff, tobacco, and other goods."

4. Where, in his sworn answer to a rule for contempt in not surrendering up to a receiver his money, books, notes, and accounts, the defendant alleges that he cannot make the surrender because, at the filing of the petition, he paid the money and transferred the other assets to his sister in discharge of a bona fide indebtedness to her; that she now has possession of the money, books, notes, and accounts, and they are not now in his power, possession, or control,—and where this answer is supported by the affidavit of the sister, whose credibility as a witness is unimpeached, she admitting on oath that she has the assets, and it further appearing that she is solvent and able to respond to the plaintiffs or the receiver for the same, and that she is a resident of the county where the suit is pending, the answer thus supported is sufficient to relieve the defendant from the imputation of willful contempt, and the rule against him should be discharged; more especially as the plaintiffs, under the facts, are not dependent upon this harsh proceeding to realize the assets in question, but may reach the same, if the testimony above recited

be false, either by making the sister a party defendant in the cause, or by a regular action against her at the suit of the receiver.

5. Irregularities in proceedings for contempt are immaterial where the result is a sufficient purging of the contempt, and a consequent discharge of the rule. Judgment affirmed as to the injunction and receiver, but reversed as to the attachment for contempt.

(Syllabus by the Court.)

Error from superior court, Fulton county; R. H. CLARK, Judge.

Petition of W. H. S. Burgwyn and others against J. W. Martin. Judgment for plaintiffs for an injunction and receiver, and attachment against defendant for contempt in failure to turn over certain property to the receiver. Defendant brings error. Modified.

Mayson & Hill and Hopkins & Son, for plaintiff in error. Glenn & Maddox, Benj. Phillips, and Well & Goodwin, for defendants in error.

SIMMONS, J. The original petition of the plaintiffs was sworn to by Haralson, their agent, who made affidavit "that the facts stated in the foregoing petition, so far as they were stated on his own knowledge, were true, and, so far as stated upon the knowledge of others, he believed them to be true." At the hearing the defendant moved to dismiss the petition on the ground that it was not sufficiently verified. The motion was overruled, and the hearing was had, when an amendment was filed, and the affidavit to which stated positively that the facts contained therein were true. Affidavits from other persons were also filed, sustaining the allegations in the bill and amendments. While the act of 1887 (Acts 1887, p. 64) declares that a petition which seeks an extraordinary equitable relief or remedy must be verified, and while we think it is the better practice for a judge to require petitions seeking extraordinary equitable relief or remedies to be positively verified before he grants any order thereon, still, if the petition should be imperfectly verified, the deficiency may be supplied at the hearing by a new affidavit to the petition, or by the affidavits of other persons, if, in the exercise of his discretion, he should think proper to proceed on the defective verification. If the judge should refuse to proceed on account of the insufficiency of the verification, we would not hold the ruling to be erroneous. Boykin v. Epstein, 87 Ga. 26, 13 S. E. Rep. 15. If, however, the judge sees proper, in the exercise of his discretion, to allow the petition to be properly verified, either by a new affidavit of the plaintiff, or by affidavits of others who know the facts, we will not control his discretion in so doing. Shannon v. Fechheimer, 76 Ga. 86; Alspaugh v. Adams, 80 Ga. 345, 5 S. E. Rep. 496.

2. The defendant also moved to dismiss the petition on the ground "that the petition and amendments did not make out a case for the relief sought; that the evidence did not authorize the appointment of a receiver; that no receiver could be had for money in the hands of defendant; that the appointment of a receiver for books, notes, and accounts was unauthor-

ized, as the remedy at law was complete; and that the debts of the petitioners were not due." The petition charges, in substance, that the defendant was insolvent; that, at the time he made the purchase of goods from the plaintiffs, he had no intention or purpose to pay for the same, but his intention was to dispose of them, and put the money in his own pocket; that he did sell a large part of them to Gregg & Co. with intent to get the stock of goods so sold beyond the reach of his creditors; that his plan was to acquire goods from the plaintiffs and other creditors fraudulently, sell and dispose of them in like maner, and appropriate the proceeds to himself; that he refused to make any payments on his debts, and had evaded all his creditors, and declined to make settlements with them; that Gregg & Co. claim they are bona fide purchasers without notice; that the defendant sold to them with the intent and purpose to delay, defraud, and hinder the petitioners in the collection of their debts, and to put the said assets, which in justice and equity belonged to the petitioners and other creditors, in the shape of money, and thus perfect his scheme to defraud them of their goods; that, if petitioners failed to reach the money which Gregg & Co. paid the defendant, they would lose their entire indebtedness; that this money ought to be appropriated to the payment of all the creditors, and the only method of reaching it was through the action of the court; that they had sold the defendant goods on the faith of certain representations as to his solvency made by him to Dun & Co., and that said representations were false; that he was insolvent at the time the statements were made; that, the goods being sold on the faith of the statements, and they being false, the contract for the sale thereof was void, and they repudiated it; and, the defendant having sold the goods to a bona fide purchaser, the courts would follow the proceeds of the sale, because the defendant, not having acquired title to the goods, had no title to the proceeds thereof, but held the same for the use of the parties from whom he obtained the goods. It may be fairly inferred from these and other allegations that the notes, accounts, and money were the proceeds of the goods sold defendant by the plaintiffs; and we think the facts alleged were sufficient to authorise the plaintiffs to proceed to reclaim their goods in the hands of the purchaser, or reclaim the proceeds thereof, in case they had been disposed of to innocent purchasers. According to these allegations, the defendant was insolvent at the time of the purchase of the goods, and did not intend at that time to pay for the same. If that be true, the sale was void, at the election of the vendors. The purchaser obtained no title to the goods, and the vendors could reclaim them wherever found, unless they had been sold to innocent purchasers; and in that event they would have a right to the proceeds of the goods if such proceeds were found in the defendant's possession, custody, or control. Under this state of facts, it was immaterial whether the debt was due or not. Where a debtor by fraudulent means has obtained a credit in the purchase of goods, the vendor, upon ascertaining the fraud, can rescind the sale, and institute proceedings to claim the goods or the proceeds thereof, whether the time of credit given the purchaser has expired or not. The contract to give time to pay for the goods is, at the instance of the seller, as void as the contract of sale. And if, in such case, it is necessary for the protection of the rights and interests of the plaintiffs, the court may appoint a receiver, and require the debtor to turn over to such receiver his books of account, and notes, and the money arising from the sale of the goods. Benj. Sales, § 451, (Bennett's Amer. Notes, Ed. 1888, p. 443;) Cohen v. Meyers, 42 Ga. 46; Johnson v. O'Donnell, 75 Ga. 453.

3. The order appointing the receiver provided, among other things, that he should turn over "the books, notes, and accounts of all kinds of the said defendant in the business of selling cigars, snuff, tobacco, and other goods." Objection was made by the defendant in the court below to this part of the order because it did not specify what books, notes, and accounts he must turn over to the receiver, and it was impossible to comply with it as it stood. We think the order was sufficiently specific to put the defendant on notice of what books, notes, and accounts he must turn over. In fact the order specifies that they were the books, notes, and accounts "in the business of selling cigars, snuff, tobacco," etc. The defendant was a cigar and tobacco dealer. Plaintiffs had sold him cigars and tobacco, and they had instituted this suit to recover the articles sold, or the proceeds thereof. The litigation was entirely about these matters. So far as the record discloses, the defendant had no other business than that of dealing in cigars and tobacco; and, if he had, the order did not call for the books, notes, etc., in any other business. It seems to us that the order was sufficiently specific to put a man of the weakest mind on notice of what books, notes, and accounts were required of him.

4, 5. The fourth head-note fully covers the question decided, and needs no further elaboration. The fifth head-note likewise covers some minor points of irregularity made in the bill of exceptions; and it is needless to comment upon them, as we hold that the defendant had sufficiently purged himself of contempt. Judgment affirmed as to injunction and receiver, but reversed as to the attachment for contempt.

HATHCOCK v. STATE.

(Supreme Court of Georgia.　Nov. 23, 1891.)

SWINDLING — REPRESENTATIONS AS TO WEALTH— INDICTMENT — VERDICT — SENTENCE — SEVERAL COUNTS—EVIDENCE—CHARACTER.

1. Representations, by a party applying for credit, that he was perfectly solvent, and responsible for his debts, and was good for his obligations, are representations of his respectability and wealth, and, if false, are within section 4587 of the Code, which declares that, "if any person, by false representation of his own respectability, wealth, or mercantile correspond-

a cheat and swindler."

2. Where the trial is had at the same time on two counts in an accusation, a verdict of guilty on one count alone is an acquittal on the other; but such acquittal does not vitiate the conviction, although both counts may relate to the same transaction.

3. Where goods are obtained by false representations mixed with true ones, if the false are separable from the true, and are material, and had a material influence in effecting the fraud, they alone may be alleged in the indictment or accusation, and the conviction will be upheld although other representations, not false, constituted a material part of the inducement on which the prosecutor gave the credit, and parted with his goods.

4. Where the fruits of a criminal fraud amounted to more than $900, a fine of $1,000 is not an excessive or unusual punishment.

5. The sentence, being that the accused "pay a fine of one thousand dollars, and costs of this prosecution, or be confined in the common jail for twelve months," is in the alternative. When in the alternative, the imprisonment is a part of the punishment, and cannot exceed the limit of six months. Direction given to modify sentence as to imprisonment in jail in accordance with section 4705 of the Code.

6. An affidavit on which an accusation is founded in the city court may charge two misdemeanors of the same class as committed by the same person, and the accusation founded thereon may consist of two counts, each charging one of the offenses set forth in the affidavit; and the prosecutor will not be compelled to elect between these counts at the trial, where it appears from the evidence that both of them relate to the same transaction.

7. Where the affidavit sets out one of the offenses, and adds the facts concerning the other, introducing these facts with the phrase, "the deponent further charges and accuses the said W. M. Hathcock with misdemeanor in this," the verification of the affidavit is not confined to these terms of accusation, but extends also to the facts as set out in the subjoined statement as to the mode of committing the misdemeanor.

8. That the accused had unlimited credit with another house was not relevant upon the question of whether he had misrepresented his solvency to the prosecutor, and thereby defrauded him.

9. Promissory notes of the accused, executed after the misrepresentation complained of, in renewal of debts existing before, were admissible in evidence to show the amount of his liabilities at the time he represented himself as solvent.

10. Objection to evidence generally, with no statement of the grounds on which the objection was based at the time it was made, will not be considered.

11. Proof of good character will not hinder conviction if the guilt of the defendant is plainly proved to the satisfaction of the jury, and so to instruct the jury is not "gratuitous, unnecessary, argumentative, and hurtful to the defendant."

12. The verdict was warranted by the evidence.

(Syllabus by the Court.)

Error from city court of Atlanta; Howard Van Epps, Judge.

Prosecution against W. M. Hathcock for making fraudulent representations as to his financial responsibility. Verdict of guilty, and judgment thereon. Defendant brings error. Affirmed.

J. W. Longino, W. Y. Atkinson, Arnold & Arnold, and T. W. Latham, for plaintiff in error. F. M. O'Bryan, City Sol., and Rosser & Carter, for the State.

Hathcock, in Fulton county, on or about May 28, 1889, did, by false and fraudulent representations as to his own respectability, wealth, and commercial standing, cheat and defraud A. P. Morgan out of certain merchandise to the value of $921.35, to-wit: The said W. M. Hathcock represented to said Morgan that he (Hathcock) was the owner of a certain tract of land in Campbell county, Georgia, containing six hundred acres, and also was the sole owner of two certain mills, in his own right and title, and upon these representations induced Morgan to extend to him credit for a lot of corn, bran, oats, and hay to the said amount of $921.35, when in truth and in fact one of these mills did not belong to Hathcock, and he had no title to it, as he represented. Said Hathcock, by said false and fraudulent representations, induced said Morgan to part with his property as aforesaid, and thereby cheated and defrauded him out of the amount of $921.35; said Hathcock knowing at the time he made said representations that they were false, and were made for the purpose of cheating and defrauding said Morgan, as aforesaid, and did thereby cheat and defraud him." The second count (omitting the formal part) charged that Hathcock represented to Morgan that he was "perfectly solvent and responsible for his debts, and was good for his obligations, and thereby induced the said Morgan to part with certain merchandise to the value of nine hundred and twenty-one and 35-100 dollars, * * * when in truth and fact the said Hathcock was then and there deeply insolvent, and he knew the same when he made the aforesaid false and fraudulent representations; and said false representations were made for the purpose of cheating and defrauding the said A. P. Morgan, and did thereby cheat and defraud him, as aforesaid. The said A. P. Morgan was induced to extend credit to the said Hathcock upon his false and fraudulent statements, believing at the time that they were true; but the said Hathcock, knowing that they were false and fraudulent, made the same for the purpose of cheating and defrauding, and thereby did cheat and defraud, as aforesaid, contrary to law," etc. The defendant demurred to the second count of the accusation on the ground that it set forth no offense under the laws of Georgia. The demurrer was overruled, and he excepted. A trial was had, and the defendant was convicted on the second count; and he moved in arrest of judgment on the ground taken in the demurrer, and also upon the ground that "he had been acquitted on the first count, and, having been so acquitted, it was not lawful that he should be convicted on the second count, because the charges therein made were covered by the charge in the first count. If the representations stated in the second count were made, they were made at the time of the representations charged in the first count; and the charge in the second relates to and is covered by the transactions which relate to and are covered by the first count." This motion was also overruled. The defendant then made a motion for a new trial on the several grounds set out in the report, which was overruled, and he excepted.

1. Counsel for the plaintiff in error contended that the court erred in overruling his demurrer to the second count of the accusation, and in refusing to arrest the judgment entered thereon. He contended that the allegations in the second count were not sufficient in law to authorize a conviction. Our Code, § 4587, provides that "if any person, by false representation of his own respectability, wealth, or mercantile correspondence and connections, shall obtain a credit, and thereby defraud any person or persons of any money, goods, chattels," etc., such person, on conviction, shall be punished, etc. We think that where one person falsely represents to another that he is perfectly solvent and responsible for his debts, and is good for his obligations, and by means of such false representations obtains a credit, and defrauds another of goods, such false representations are within the statute. A representation of solvency and ability to pay debts is a representation, to a certain extent, of his wealth. It is not necessary that he should represent that he is wealthy before he can be indicted under this section. A representation of solvency is a declaration that he has property sufficient to pay all his debts, and the one about to be incurred; and when he adds thereto that he is responsible for his debts, and good for his obligations, it emphasizes the representation, and is more likely to deceive the creditor. If the representations thus made are fraudulent, and the creditor is thereby defrauded, the person making them is guilty, under this section of the Code. This is certainly in accordance with good morals, sound principle, and right dealing between man and man. A man who has defrauded his neighbor by such false representations, and has obtained his goods, and refused to pay for them, has no right to complain if he is adjudged guilty, and punished for the fraudulent act. Clifford v. State, 56 Ind. 245; Com. v. Wallace, 114 Pa. St. 405, 6 Atl. Rep. 685.

2. Counsel for the plaintiff in error claimed that the court erred in not arresting the judgment, because the jury acquitted the defendant on the first count; and, it being the same transaction, he was necessarily acquitted on the second. He cites on this point Roberts v. State, 14 Ga. 8, and Blair v. State, 81 Ga. 631, 7 S. E. Rep. 855; but it will be seen by reference to these cases that they refer to separate and independent trials on different indictments. Neither of the cases holds, where a person is tried at one time upon two counts of an indictment, an acquittal on one amounts to an acquittal on the other. On the contrary, the law is that, where a trial is had at the same time on two counts of an indictment or accusation, a verdict of guilty on one count alone is an acquittal on the other; but such acquittal does not vitiate the conviction, although both counts may relate to the same transaction.

3. It is also conten[ded] showed that the rep[...] made at the same ti[...] defendant said that [...] land and two mills, a[...] ent and responsible [...] good for his obliga[...] prosecutor testified t[...] it on the faith of all [...] and not one alone, ar[...] the jury had found [...] tions concerning the [...] were true, he could no[...] only one of the repres[...] We think that, where [...] resentations to anot[...] of obtaining credit, a[...] resentations are true, [...] false, and he knows [...] time, and the false o[...] from those that are t[...] ly influenced the min[...] in giving credit, the [...] may be alleged alone [...] the indictment or ac[...] viction thereon will [...] the other representa[...] stituted a material pa[...] on which the prosecu[...] and parted with his go[...] this statute, it is not [...] to sustain a convictio[...] the representations w[...] so, a conviction unde[...] rarely be had, becaus[...] tended to defraud and [...] sentations could alwa[...] with the false to prev[...] Bish. Crim. Law, § 4[...] Law, § 776; People v.[...] 314; Beasley v. State,[...]

4 and 5. The bill of e[...] after the motion in [...] was overruled the cou[...] fendant to pay a fine [...] confined in the commo[...] for a period of 12 mor[...] was excepted to on t[...] punishment was exce[...] In the fourth head-n[...] that where the fruits [...] amounted to more th[...] 000 is not an excessive [...] ment. But while that [...] the fine imposed, the b[...] tified to by the judge [...] tence was in the alt[...] pay a fine of $1,000, o[...] months in jail. The ju[...] tence upon a crimina[...] misdemeanor, can, if h[...] sentence in the alterna[...] does so, his discretion [...] is limited by section [...] which prescribes that [...] common jail shall not [...] If, however, he simply [...] criminal, it seems tha[...] payment of that fine i[...] prisonment in jail; an [...] imprisonment does no [...] although the judge c[...] authority may afterwa[...] oner from jail. Brock[...] McMeekin v. State, 48[...] Hab. Corp. § 308; Fisc[...] Rep. 71. But, inasmuc[...]

ternative sentence, and the imprisonment inflicted was not to enforce the payment of a fine, but as a punishment, the court exceeded its powers in respect to imprisonment in jail. Where the imprisonment is a part of the punishment, and not to enforce a fine, six months in the common jail is the limit. We therefore direct that the judge modify the imprisonment part of the sentence so as not to exceed the limits authorized by the statute.

6. There were other grounds taken in the bill of exceptions and in the motion for a new trial which are fully covered by the 6th, 7th, 8th, 9th, 10th, 11th, and 12th headnotes; and we deem it unnecessary to elaborate them further. Judgment affirmed, with direction.

ROGERS et al. v. ROBERTS, Judge.

(*Supreme Court of Georgia.* Nov. 23, 1891.)

MANDAMUS TO JUDGE — CORRECTIONS IN BILL OF EXCEPTIONS.

After a judge has corrected, signed, and certified a bill of exceptions, having interlined in the certificate a reference to the corrections made by him, and the plaintiff in error has served and filed the bill of exceptions thus certified, and caused it, together with the record, to be transmitted to this court, thereby recognizing and adopting such bill of exceptions as sufficient, it is too late to apply to this court for a *mandamus* to compel the judge to omit the corrections he had made in the bill of exceptions as originally presented to him, and sign another certificate, free from such interlineation.

(*Syllabus by the Court.*)

Application of J. S. Rogers and others for a writ of *mandamus* to D. M. Roberts, judge, to compel him to omit certain corrections in a bill of exceptions. Writ denied.

A. C. Pate and *J. H. Martin*, for movants.

Mandamus denied.

RODGERS v. MOORE.

(*Supreme Court of Georgia.* Nov. 23, 1891.)

COMPETENCY OF WITNESS — TRANSACTIONS WITH DECEDENT—DEED A MORTGAGE—EVIDENCE.

1. Where an attorney was employed to procure a bond for one charged with a criminal offense, and did so, taking from the person so charged a deed to indemnify him against loss on account of said bond, and afterwards the defendant in such criminal case borrowed money from another to settle the same, and the attorney, at the request of the defendant, quitclaimed the property to the lender as a security for such money, *held*, that in a controversy as to the title of the land between the estate of the lender and that of the defendant in the criminal case, both being dead, such attorney was a competent witness to prove the above-recited facts, and also an admission by the lender that the money he advanced upon such quitclaim deed had all been repaid.

2. When the question at issue is whether a deed was made as an absolute conveyance of property or simply as a security for money advanced to the maker, evidence of the value of the property at the time the deed was made is pertinent and material.

3. None of the questions made in the bill of exceptions furnish any cause for reversing the judgment.

(*Syllabus by the Court.*)

Error from superior court, Fulton county; MARSHALL J. CLARKE, Judge.

Suit by Robert L. Rodgers, administrator, against Sarah Moore to recover land. Judgment for defendant. Plaintiff brings error. Affirmed.

Robt. L. Rodgers, for plaintiff in error. *Spears & Roan* and *Rosser & Carter*, for defendant in error.

SIMMONS, J. Rodgers, as administrator of Beck, brought complaint for land against Sarah Moore. The title he relied on was a deed from Giles and Sarah Moore to Daniel, and a deed from Daniel to Beck. It seems that Giles Moore was charged with some criminal offense, and placed in jail, and that he sent for Daniel, an attorney, and procured him to have a bond made for his (Moore's) appearance at court, so that he might be discharged from jail until his trial. Daniel got up the bond, and Moore, to secure Daniel, made him a deed to the land in dispute. Moore subsequently settled the criminal case by paying $110. He borrowed this money from Beck, and requested Daniel to make a deed to the land to Beck, to secure him in the payment of the money borrowed. Daniel was not Moore's attorney except in procuring his appearance bond. He was not his attorney in the settlement of the case, nor when Moore borrowed the money from Beck, nor when the deed was made to Beck at Moore's request. Beck afterwards told Daniel that Moore had paid him the money borrowed. Moore and Beck both died before the commencement of this action. When Daniel was placed upon the stand by the defendant, and asked about the deed he had made to Beck, the plaintiff objected on the ground that Beck was dead, and that the witness was attorney for Giles Moore. The court overruled the objection, and allowed the witness to testify, and to this the plaintiff excepted.

1. We know of no reason which rendered Daniel incompetent to testify as to the matters inquired about. The plaintiff relied upon the deed from Moore to Daniel and the deed from Daniel to Beck to recover the land. The defendant set up that the deed from Daniel to Beck was given to secure a loan which Beck had made to Moore, and that the loan had been repaid by Moore. Daniel was never the attorney of Beck, nor was he attorney for Moore, except to procure a bond. After the bond was procured, his relationship to Moore as attorney ceased. After it ceased, Moore borrowed the money from Beck, and requested Daniel to make Beck a quitclaim deed to the land to secure Beck for the money borrowed. The bond procured by Daniel for Moore had served its purpose, and he was discharged from jail. Moore had settled the criminal case, and had borrowed the money from Beck to make the settlement, and in these transactions Daniel was not his attorney or agent in any manner. There was no reason why Daniel should be incompetent to testify as to the transaction between Moore and Beck. He had no interest in the matter, and was not at that time the agent or attorney of either of them. Nor

was there any reason why he should not
testify to the admissions of Beck that
Moore had paid him the money. He
would not have been incompetent under
the evidence act of 1866, nor was he under
the amendatory act of 1889.

2. Sarah Moore, the defendant, had filed
a plea that the deed was made to secure
a loan from Beck to Moore, and that the
loan had been paid off. The consideration expressed in the deed was $110.
When the plaintiff was testifying as a witness, the defendant's counsel asked him
the value of the land, to which he objected. The court overruled the objection, and compelled the plaintiff to testify
as to its value. He testified that it was
worth between $400 and $500, or may be
$500 or $600. The question at issue being
whether the deed was an absolute conveyance or simply a security for money
advanced to the maker, evidence of the
value of the property at the time the deed
was made was pertinent and material.
Evidence that at the time the deed was
made the property was worth $500 or
$600, the consideration of the deed being
only $110, was strong proof to sustain
the defendant's plea, and the court was
right in overruling the objection.

3. There are other questions made in
the bill of exceptions, but none of them
furnish any cause for reversing the judgment. Judgment affirmed.

STILLWELL et al. v. SAVANNAH GROCERY
Co. et al.

(Supreme Court of Georgia. Nov. 28, 1891.)

FRAUDULENT CONVEYANCES—APPOINTMENT OF RE-
CEIVER—INTERLOCUTORY INJUNCTION.

1. In so far as the petition in this case rests
on the insolvent traders' act or on the assignment
act, it is unsupported by the facts in evidence.
Granting that the evidence makes a *prima facie*
case of fraudulent conveyance by an insolvent
firm of all of its property to a single creditor, to
the injury of the other creditors, the purchasing
creditor being solvent and able to respond, and
the complaining creditors being without judgments or other liens, and having no claim to the
property by reason of fraud in the creation of
their demands or otherwise, no sufficient cause
for an interlocutory injunction and receiver as to
this property appears. It was certainly error to
appoint a receiver unconditionally, without
offering the purchaser the alternative of giving
bond and security in lieu of surrendering the
property to a receiver.

2. The case of De Lacy v. Hurst, 83 Ga. 223, 9
S. E. Rep. 1052, rules nothing as to interlocutory
injunctions or receivers. The uniformity procedure act of 1887 does not make extraordinary remedies applicable or available where they were not
so before.

(Syllabus by the Court.)

Error from superior court, Montgomery
county; D. M. ROBERTS, Judge. Reversed.

Creditors' bill by Savannah Grocery
Company and others against Stillwell,
Millen & Co. Order granting an injunction and appointing a receiver. Defendants bring error.

The following is the official report:

The Savannah Grocery Company et al.,
creditors of Peacock, Peterson & Co., filed
their petition in the nature of a general
creditors' bill, alleging they are creditors of
the firm named, which is composed of G. W.

Peacock and of W. M. and C. R. Peterson.
Peacock, Peterson & Co. are merchants of
Montgomery county, and are also engaged in the saw-mill business, and as
such traders and lumber manufacturers
bought from petitioners, from time to
time, goods to be used by them in the
course of their business, in their store as
well as in carrying on their saw-mill; and
are indebted as set out in an exhibit. Petitioners have demanded payment of such
of their debts as have matured, which has
been refused. Peacock, Peterson & Co.
own a large amount of real and personal
property located principally in Montgomery county, and have enjoyed good credit
with petitioners and others, based upon
the knowledge of creditors of the large
amount of assets of the firm, as well as
upon the good standing of its members.
They did business in Savannah with Stillwell, Millen & Co. as factors, who claim
to be creditors of Peacock, Peterson &
Co. for some $10,000, and they have upheld
the credit of Peacock, Peterson & Co. in
Savannah to petitioners, whenever inquiry was made of them, asserting that
Peacock, Peterson & Co. were good and
solvent, and that, while they held a mortgage to secure their debt, the property
upon which it was given was worth four
times their debt; and in this way aided
greatly Peacock, Peterson & Co. in obtaining credit from petitioners. On January 16, 1891, Stillwell, Millen & Co. obtained a mortgage from Peacock, Peterson & Co. to secure a debt of $7,000 princi-
pal, with interest, due in 90 days; on March
6, 1891, another mortgage, further securing the $7,000; and upon March 16, 1891,
another, securing payment of a note of
$5,000, payable four months after date,
and dated March 6, 1891; all of which
mortgages are of record. These mortgages covered all the partnership property, embracing property described in the
petition, and were given subject to a
mortgage for $6,000, dated November 8,
1890, to the Hawkinsville Bank & Trust
Company, upon which last-named debt
only $2,000 principal remained due. On May
1, 1891, the three members of the firm of Peacock, Peterson & Co., who were in Savannah at the special instance of Stillwell, Millen & Co., made a conveyance to the latter
in consideration of thirteen thousand one or
two hundred dollars, of which $400 was to
be paid W. M. and $200 C. R. Peterson,
conveying all the partnership property
and assets of Peacock, Peterson & Co. in
payment of the balance due Stillwell, Millen & Co., of between $9,000 and $10,000,
and the balance of the debt due the bank
and trust company, of about $2,000, and
about $1,800 alleged to be due for labor
claims at the mills of Peacock, Peterson
& Co.; Stillwell, Millen & Co. agreeing
then and there with Peacock, Peterson &
Co. that they would pay all the claims
against Peacock, Peterson & Co. which
were liens or were for supplies or goods
furnished them in their saw-mill and mercantile business, and would assist them in
arranging their other indebtedness; and
also agreeing that Peacock, Peterson &
Co. should have the privilege of paying
the money named in the conveyance to

Stillwell, Millen & Co. within a reasonable time, whereupon they would convey back the property, if that course were desired by Peacock, Peterson & Co.; Stillwell, Millen & Co. expressly stating that they did not desire the property, but only payment of their debt, and asserting that it would be in every way better for Peacock, Peterson & Co. to put the title in them of all the assets than to have a foreclosure of the mortgage, as the expense of the foreclosure would be very great, and would amount to a breaking up in business. At the time of and immediately after the signing of said conveyance Stillwell advised Peacock to go home and sell out all his private property as soon as possible. On May 2d, W. M. Peterson went to Stillwell, Millen & Co., and requested, in conformity with the promise made by them, that they pay the debt due by Peacock, Peterson & Co. to a lumber company, which request Stillwell refused, alleging he would pay nothing, and claiming title and ownership to all the property conveyed in the deed of May 1st. Peterson then, finding that they would not conform to the agreement made with them, informed some of the Savannah creditors of the state of affairs, among them the Savannah Grocery Company, whereupon Deitsch, vice-president of that company, on Saturday, May 2d, went to the office of Stillwell, Millen & Co., accompanied by both the Petersons, and in the name of the Savannah Grocery Company, a corporation of large means, expressly stating that the offer was on behalf of Peacock, Peterson & Co. and their creditors at large, tendered Stillwell, Millen & Co. the full amount of the consideration of said debt, to be paid then and there; whereupon Stillwell refused to receive the money for his firm, alleging that the property belonged to it, and they would not give it up. Then W. M. Peterson increased the offer, offering to pay $1,000 more than the amount of the indebtedness, which Stillwell, Millen & Co. refused to accept, claiming the property was theirs, and they would not dispose of it. The deed referred to was a quitclaim conveyance, with no inventory attached to it, and no schedule of assets made out and sworn to by Peacock, Peterson & Co., so that it was not executed according to law, if intended as an assignment of all the property of Peacock, Peterson & Co.; and it was made to hinder and delay their creditors, such intention being known to Stillwell, Millen & Co. The property mentioned in it was worth largely more than the consideration thereof, and at the lowest valuation worth double the same. The sale was not bona fide in payment of a debt, but there was a gross undervaluation of the property, and an element of trust therein, by reason of the agreement that Stillwell, Millen & Co. would pay out of the proceeds of the property certain other creditors of Peacock, Peterson & Co., and assist Peacock, Peterson & Co. in making a compromise of their other debts; the understanding between the parties being that, while the title was put in Stillwell, Millen & Co., the transaction was also to benefit Peacock, Peterson & Co., so as to give them a surplus out of the property, either by compromise or by the transfer of Stillwell, Millen & Co. of all the property upon the payment of the indebtedness named as consideration by some outside party, the result being a secret trust, though the deed, upon its face, showed a transfer for value. Upon the ascertainment by Peacock, Peterson & Co. that Stillwell, Millen & Co. would not carry out the scheme agreed on, Peacock, Peterson & Co. have refused to give them possession of the property, have remained in possession of it, and are now in possession. Peacock, Peterson & Co. are insolvent. Their property is of such peculiar character—machinery, saw-mills, and other adjuncts of a saw-mill business—that, while there might be assets more than enough to pay off all debts, (and the total indebtedness will amount to nearly, if not over, $30,000,) yet, by shutting down the business, which has now occurred, there will be a large depreciation in values, and, much of the property being not yet fully paid for, the sums paid upon the same will, in all likelihood, be lost, and may be accounted as no assets by reason of the stoppage of the business, (an example being given.) During the last days of April, at the suggestion of Stillwell, Millen & Co., Peacock, Peterson & Co. sold out their merchandise stock for $2,000 to a Dr. Terrell for part cash, part being still due; so that, at the special instance and request of Stillwell, Millen & Co. during the week before the presentation of this petition, Peacock, Peterson & Co. disposed of to them and Terrell all the assets of Peacock, Peterson & Co. which were charged with the payments of their debts; the whole scheme tending, with the full knowledge of Stillwell, Millen & Co., to hinder, delay, and defraud the creditors of Peacock, Peterson & Co. Peacock, Peterson & Co. were threatened by Stillwell, Millen & Co. with the foreclosure of the mortgage immediately, unless they signed the deed. They were loath to sign it, and stated to Stillwell, Millen & Co. that they desired to have a meeting of their creditors, which Stillwell urged them not to do, and, by pressure and threats, induced them to convey the title as above mentioned. While Stillwell, Millen & Co. may have had a valid claim for money due under their mortgages, by their conduct in colluding with Peacock, Peterson & Co. they are liable in law to petitioners for the full amount of their debts against Peacock, Peterson & Co., because they aided Peacock, Peterson & Co. in the disposition and concealment of their assets, as stated above, and because of this conduct have no right to any claim of lien or preference, and should not participate in any of the assets of Peacock, Peterson & Co. until after the claims of petitioners and the other creditors have been fully satisfied. Peacock owns valuable real estate, besides personal property, and W. M. Peterson owns a house and lot, and the members of the firm own other property, all of which private property is chargeable with the payment of the debts of the creditors.

Petitioners prayed for the appointment

of a receiver of all the property of the firm, including that mentioned in the conveyance to Stillwell, Millen & Co., and all of the private property of each of the copartners; that Peacock, Peterson & Co. and the members of the firm be enjoined from disposing of any of their property, and ordered to turn it over to the receiver; that they be made to account for all money paid over to them, and concerning their alleged debt; that the deed to Stillwell, Millen & Co. be decreed void and canceled; that petitioners might have judgment for their several claims against Peacock, Peterson & Co., and also against Stillwell, Millen & Co., for process, etc., and for temporary restraining order. An affidavit to this petition was made by Deitsch, alleging immediate necessity for a retraining order, injunction, and receiver, etc. A temporary restraining order was granted, and a temporary receiver appointed, on May 9, 1891, and a rule granted requiring defendants to show cause why a permanent receiver should not be appointed. Stillwell, Millen & Co. answered: They and their predecessors in business have had dealings with Peacock & Peterson and the predecessors of that firm for about 10 years, making them large advances, the advances being secured by mortgages executed from time to time, and always duly and promptly recorded. Attached is a statement showing the indebtedness at various times, covering the period from April 16, 1887, to May 1, 1891. On October 7, 1890, this indebtedness was $4,175, and on that day Peacock & Peterson represented to these defendants that their total indebtedness, including what they owed these defendants, amounted to but $11,500, and that, if these defendants would make additional advances up to that amount, they would be enabled to pay off their entire indebtedness, leaving these defendants their only creditor. Defendants agreed to do this, and the mortgage and notes for $11,500 were duly executed by W. M. Peterson, for himself and for the firm, and were taken by him for the purpose of having Peacock execute them. Afterwards, however, Peacock & Peterson stated that they had concluded not to borrow the additional amounts needed from these defendants, and were about to negotiate a loan with the bank and trust company. During November, 1890, this indebtedness was reduced to about $2,500, and remained about that figure until January 16, 1891, when Peacock & Peterson applied for an additional advance of about $4,500, at that time assuring defendants that outside of their indebtedness to them and the bank and trust company they owed only $6,000; and that, if the additional credit of $4,500 was given them, it would enable them to pay off all this outside indebtedness, except a few minor and unimportant matters, which were not pressing, and that these, as well as the bank and trust company notes, they could and would provide for out of the regular and current earnings of their business. Relying upon these statements, these defendants agreed to make the additional advances, and Peacock, Peterson & Co. (C. R. Peterson hav-

ing in the mean time been admitted to the firm) executed to these defendants a mortgage to secure the sum of $7,000. About March 6, 1891, Peacock, Peterson & Co. informed them that they would not be able to meet the notes held by the bank and trust company as they had anticipated, and if these defendants would give them further credit of $5,000 they would be enabled, with these additional advances, to take up said notes as they fell due, and then assured defendants that, outside of the indebtedness to them and the bank and trust company, they owed only a few thousand dollars, none of which was pressing, and they could readily pay off all of it from their regular earnings. Relying upon these statements, defendants agreed to make this additional advance, and Peacock, Peterson & Co. executed another mortgage to secure it, including in it all the property embraced in the mortgage for $7,000, and other property, and at the same time executed a new mortgage as additional security for the indebtedness of $7,000, covering the additional property not embraced in the prior mortgage for that amount; it being then and always previously distinctly understood and agreed that the mortgages given by the firm to secure their indebtedness to defendants should cover all of their property. These defendants at that time believed that the property embraced in the mortgages much exceeded in value the indebtedness to them, else they would not have agreed to make any additional advances. It was distinctly agreed that the indebtedness of Peacock, Peterson & Co. to them should not exceed $12,000, and that this should include the amount due the bank and trust company, whose mortgage was prior to those held by defendants, and whose notes were to be paid with the advances thus to be made by them. It was distinctly agreed that Peacock, Peterson & Co. would pay their labor account, and meet the notes of the bank and trust company, and that no further advances beyond the $12,000 so secured would be required by them or would be made by these defendants; and that Peacock, Peterson & Co. would pay off their small outside indebtedness out of their regular earnings. On April 10, 1891, Peacock, Peterson & Co. obtained from defendants $500 to pay laborers, representing that that was all they owed for labor. Later in the month they presented a statement showing they owed a further amount of about $1,000 for labor, which statement was sworn to by them as correct, and as being all they then owed for labor. These defendants sent a representative for the purpose of paying off this labor account, but Peacock, Peterson & Co. declined to allow this to be done. Defendants then ascertained that this statement was incomplete, and that there was more due for labor than appeared thereon, and sent for Peacock, Peterson & Co., who, in response to their request, came to Savannah, and defendants then ascertained that they really owed for labor about $2,000, and that the amounts thus due for labor, with the notes held by the bank and trust company, for which Peacock, Peterson & Co. were not providing, as they had agreed to do, would make their indebtedness to defendant considerably exceed $12,000, if said labor account and notes were paid by defendants. During the month of April they ascertained that the indebtedness of Peacock, Peterson & Co. was very much greater than they had represented it to be, and that they owed a great deal more on their timber leases than they had represented, and that, therefore, the property covered by the mortgage of these defendants was not nearly so valuable as Peacock, Peterson & Co. stated it to be. They also learned that said firm had been purchasing costly machinery and other things, not warranted by their business, and for which they could not reasonably expect to pay. Accordingly, when Peacock, Peterson & Co. came to Savannah, about May 1st, defendants informed them they could not make any further advances, and, one of the mortgages being overdue, that they would be compelled to foreclose it. The matter was discussed, and finally it was agreed that Peacock, Peterson & Co. should make an absolute deed to Stillwell, Millen & Co. of all their property in satisfaction of their indebtedness to Stillwell, Millen & Co.; and these defendants did at the time state to Peacock, Peterson & Co. that they did not desire the property, but would much prefer the money, and would take $1,000 off their account in order to get a money settlement, but Peacock, Peterson & Co. stated that they were unable to do this, and had reached the point where they could not go on with their business, and agreed to execute the deed as the best and only settlement they could make. There were no conditions, reservations, or understanding with reference to the deed, but it was understood that it was, as it purports to be, absolute and unconditional. The consideration named in it, $13,265, was thus arrived at: The indebtedness of Peacock, Peterson & Co. was estimated and fixed at $10,500. At that time they were entitled to credit for lumber sold for their account, of which measurements had not been received, so that it was impossible then to state with certainty what this credit should be. There were also freight-bills, which had not then been received, for shipments of lumber embraced in previous accountings. Defendants knew the indebtedness would reach at least $10,500, but have since ascertained that it was really about $100 more. The labor account was agreed to be $2,000, and this had to be estimated, because, in addition to the itemized statement presented by Peacock, Peterson & Co., there were amounts on loose memoranda, which they stated had to be added, and the statement and memoranda showed the labor account to be about $2,000.

There was also a mortgage upon the house and lot of W. M. Peterson, upon which there was due, as defendants were then informed, $400, which had been given, as they were informed, by him to secure a loan with which to pay the amount due on account of an engine bought by the firm. There was also $165 due for an

engine, and $200 due for timber. These sums made the consideration mentioned in the deed. After this amount was fixed, and the purchase agreed on, defendants also promised to pay a bill for food for mules, amounting to $100. There was no agreement or understanding of any kind that defendants were to pay or would assume any of the debts of Peacock, Peterson & Co., except those which made up the consideration of the deed and the debt of $100 last mentioned. They knew that the deed was subject to the mortgage of the bank and trust company, and that it was subject to the claims for labor, of which they then had actual notice, those labor claims, however, being included in said consideration; and also knew that, if they desired to take any of the timber mentioned in the timber leases, which had then not been furnished and paid for, they would be compelled to provide for its payment where title remained in the vendor or lessor. There were also a few liens which are specifically mentioned in the mortgages held by these defendants, and they understood their deed was subject to these, and they would have to satisfy these if they desired to hold the property covered by them, but were under no obligation to take any property which was subject to specific and prior liens, unless they saw fit; and this was thoroughly understood. The deed was executed May 1st, and on the evening of May 2d Deitsch came to their office with both of the Petersons, and stated that they had informed him that Stillwell had promised he would cancel the deed whenever the indebtedness of Peacock, Peterson & Co. to these defendants was paid; and he inquired of Stillwell whether this were true, and Stillwell replied that the statement was not true; that the deed was an absolute deed, and, if proposals to purchase the property were made, he would consult the other partners who were interested. At this point W. M. Peterson asked whether, if $500 were added to the amount, these defendants would cancel the deed, to which Stillwell replied: "The deed is absolute, and we will not talk about canceling it." Deitsch then rejoined that that was all right; that he only came to verify the statement of the Petersons; that he understood it now; that the deed was an absolute one to these defendants, and that settled it. As they were going off, Stillwell called back the Petersons, and stated that, while he could not admit the right of any one to have the deed canceled, it being absolute, he did not desire to keep the property, but wished to sell it, and, if Peacock, Peterson & Co., or Deitsch, or the creditors, or any one, offered the money, he would quickly close with the offer, and was willing to sell to any one who would pay these defendants the consideration of the deed. He also called to the attention of the Petersons that Deitsch had made no offer of any kind, and that he did not believe Deitsch was authorized to do so, being under the impression that the president of the grocery company was absent; and he did not think Deitsch had then conferred with the creditors, or that he had authority to make any offer. Stillwell then and there distinctly stated that any one who desired the property could get it for what these defendants gave for it. On the evening of Saturday, May 2d, these defendants sent a representative of their firm to receive possession of the property under their deed, and they are informed that the possession was actually and duly delivered to him. On Monday they received a telegram from him that during the day, and after the possession had been delivered to him, Deitsch arrived, and at once busied himself with efforts to impede and embarrass their control and management of the property. They learned that Deitsch had advised the laborers not to work for them, nor to receive any money from them, and had prevented their representative from getting the pay-roll and paying off the laborers. They had forwarded by express the requisite money—over $1,800—to pay off the laborers, having paid at Savannah the balance of the labor account, and their representative was unable to use the money for this purpose because of Deitsch's interference, and finally it was returned to them. They are informed that by various contrivances Deitsch managed to add seriously to the demoralization that already existed among the laborers, and obstructed and embarrassed, in every way his craft and cunning could suggest, the agents and employes of these defendants in their control and operation of the property. All this was done by Deitsch without the slightest warrant or authority or intimation on his part that would lead them to suspect he contemplated any such proceedings. On the contrary, his observations, tone, and bearing at his interview with Stillwell, above mentioned, were such as to lead them to believe he was entirely satisfied they had made an absolute purchase of the property, and that he had no intention of questioning the transaction. On Wednesday, May 6th, Myers, the president of the grocery company, asked Stillwell if he would be willing to sell the property conveyed for the consideration mentioned in the deed, and Stillwell replied he would, to any one who would pay these defendants the amount they gave for the property. Myers then stated he had been informed that the indebtedness of Peacock, Peterson & Co. was not as much as the amount named as the consideration of the deed; and Stillwell replied that that was true: that the consideration not only included the actual indebtedness of Peacock, Peterson & Co., which then amounted to about $10,500, but also included certain amounts for labor, etc., which these defendants had agreed to pay; and that, if the amount which represented the indebtedness of Peacock, Peterson & Co. on May 1st were paid, he would be willing to make a quitclaim deed to the property, provided the purchaser would assume these additional amounts, which were included in the consideration. To this Myers replied that that was all right; that the creditors were then endeavoring to arrange the matter, and he thought they would purchase the property from these defendants upon these terms. On Thursday Myers again called, and stated to Stillwell

that the matter was progressing favorably, and that the creditors expected to purchase the property from these defendants upon the terms stated, and he thought the matter would soon be adjusted upon this basis. Later during the day, one who was representing Peacock, Peterson & Co., and was advising with their creditors, called at the office of these defendants, and stated that he was sent by the creditors and by their attorneys to advise these defendants that the arrangements were progressing very favorably, and that they expected on the following Saturday to close the matter and purchase the property by paying these defendants the consideration of their deed; and he stated further that W. M. Peterson had been sent to Montgomery county to get certain papers, and that on Saturday morning the creditors expected to finally adjust the matter. On Saturday morning, instead of the adjustment promised, and which these defendants, in entire reliance upon the good faith of the creditors, were awaiting, they were served by the attorney of the creditors with a telegram from Judge Roberts, which stated that a restraining order on tne creditors' petition had been granted by him at 8 o'clock A. M. that day, and a temporary receiver appointed, etc. These defendants at once endeavored to get further information than that conveyed by the telegram, with reference to the character and effect of the proceeding, and sought to procure a copy of the petition, but were unable to obtain the information or procure a copy until the following Monday, and then read with amazement its allegations, and observed that it had been sworn to by Deitsch on May 8th, at a time when the negotiations for a friendly adjustment were still pending.

It is not true, as stated in the petition, that Peacock, Peterson & Co. were, when the petition was filed, merchants or traders, but they had entirely ceased to do business, are not now traders, and have not been since May 1st, and on May 1st the firm was actually dissolved by written agreement. On several occasions inquiries have been made of Stillwell with reference to Peacock, Peterson & Co. The particular circumstances attending each inquiry, or the persons making them, these defendants cannot state, but they have on each occasion answered them fairly and frankly, giving the facts as they understood them. They have informed the inquirers of their mortgages upon all the property of Peacock, Peterson & Co., and, with reference to the value of the property or any other matter, have given the information they had received from Peacock, Peterson & Co., stating expressly that their statements were based upon the information thus received from Peacock, Peterson & Co. They could have no possible motive to uphold the credit of Peacock, Peterson & Co. They were always, as they thought, fully secured by promptly recorded mortgages; and they have no recollection of ever having stated that the property covered by their mortgages was worth four times the indebtedness to them, but there are times when this statement might have been made, because there are times when it was true. It is not true that $700 of the consideration named in the deed was to be paid to W. M. Peterson. In the statement of the account for labor there was included $200, due C. R. Peterson for labor by the old firm before C. R. was admitted into the firm. It is not true that they agreed with Peacock, Peterson & Co. to pay all the claims against that firm which were liens, or were for supplies or goods furnished them in the saw-mill or mercantile business; nor that they agreed to assist them in arranging their other indebtedness; nor that they agreed with Peacock, Peterson & Co. that they were to have the privilege of paying the sum named in the conveyance to these defendants within a reasonable time after the signing of the deed, and that they would convey back the property if that course were desired by Peacock, Peterson & Co. It is true, these defendants stated, before the settlement was made, that they did not desire the property, but only the payment of their debt. It is untrue that Stillwell advised Peacock to go home and sell out all his private property as soon as possible. It is untrue that W. M. Peterson requested them to pay the debt mentioned in the petition, and if the request had been made it would have been refused, for they had not assumed the payment of this debt; but it was distinctly understood they would not assume the payment of any of the debts except those included in the consideration of the deed, and the small bill of $100 mentioned. It is not true that on Saturday, May 2d, Deitsch tendered these defendants the full amount of the consideration of the debt, stating that the offer was made on behalf of Peacock, Peterson & Co. and the creditors at large, or that Stillwell refused to receive the money, or stated that they would not dispose of the property. No tender has ever been made them, but, on the contrary, Deitsch, Myers, and the other petitioners know that they could now get and could at any time have gotten a quitclaim deed to the property from these defendants by paying the consideration of the deed to them, or by paying the actual indebtedness of Peacock, Peterson & Co. to them on May 1st, and assuming the other amounts assumed by defendants and included in the consideration. The deed was not made to hinder and delay the creditors, nor was such intention known to these defendants. The property was not worth largely more than the consideration named in the deed. The sale was bona fide in payment of a debt, and there was not a gross undervaluation of the property. The statement that there was an element of trust in the deed, etc., was false, as was the statement that there was an understanding between the parties that, while the title was put in these defendants, the transaction was also to benefit Peacock, Peterson & Co. so as to give them a surplus out of the property, etc. All the statements and suggestions of the petition which in any way impeach the bona fides of the deed, or charged these defendants with fraud, or with participation in fraud, are infamous falsehoods. It

is not true that Peacock, Peterson & Co. refused to give possession of the property to these defendants, or were in possession of it at the time the petition was filed, but possession was duly delivered by them to the representative of these defendants on Monday, May 4th. These defendants, after their purchase and the execution of the deed, agreed to employ the Petersons at Verbena at salaries of $75 per month,—W. M. until January 1st, and C. R. as long as it was mutually satisfactory,—these defendants intending to operate the Verbena mill, and the Petersons being familiar with the property and business at that point, and being then without other employment. At once, upon turning over the property to defendants' representative, the Petersons went regularly to work under him, faithfully performing their duties as directed by him. They and the other employes were proceeding harmoniously under the supervision of the representative until the advent of Deitsch, who succeeded, by inducements and chicanery of various kinds, in dissatisfying W. M. Peterson, and in alienating him from the employment he had undertaken with these defendants. The possession of the property, however, remained with these defendants until they turned it over to the receiver, under the order of Judge Roberts, on May 11th, the receiver giving their representative his receipt for the property. Up to that time they were in the full possession and control of the property. It is true that by the shutting down of the business, which has now occurred, there will be a large depreciation in value, and, as the result of the granting of the injunction and receivership, these defendants have already incurred large damages, which are being daily augmented. It is untrue that Peacock, Peterson & Co. sold out their merchandise stock to Terrell at the suggestion or special instance and request of these defendants, for these defendants did not know of the sale until after it was effected. It is true these defendants have advised Peacock, Peterson & Co. it was not good business policy to run a merchandise store in connection with their saw-mill business, and that this had been their experience, and that in consequence, in their own business, they had for some time discontinued such a practice. They have no recollection of having any conversation with Peacock, Peterson & Co. at all upon the subject within a month or so prior to May 1st, and their advice, as given previously, was only with reference to the inexpediency generally of attempting to run a store and saw-mill at the same time. It is untrue that Peacock, Peterson & Co. were loath to sign the deed, or that they stated they desired to have a meeting of their creditors, or that Stillwell urged them not to do so, and by pressure and threats prevailed upon and induced them to execute the deed. The matter was fully and carefully considered by Peacock, Peterson & Co., and fully discussed by them with Stillwell, representing his firm; and the deed was executed by them freely and voluntarily, and no improper influences of any kind were attempted or thought of. These defendants accepted the deed in entire good faith in satisfaction of the indebtedness to them, which, as well as the mortgages securing it, was unquestioned. Far from any desire to take advantage of their debtors or the other creditors in receiving the deed, these defendants preferred to have a settlement at a loss to them of $1,000, rather than take the property in satisfaction of their debt. It is difficult to say what the market value of the property is, the prices of lumber having greatly fallen since January 1st, and all kinds of saw-mill property having greatly depreciated in value. It is untrue that they colluded with Peacock, Peterson & Co. to hinder and delay the creditors, or aided and assisted them in the disposition and concealment of their assets in fraud of the rights of creditors. These defendants have been engaged in business in Savannah for many years, are possessed of large capital, and are amply able to respond to all claims against them. The actual expenses now accruing, and which will continue to accrue while this injunction and receivership are continued, on account of the care and preservation of the large amount of property which remains idle and employed, are very great, and probably $50 a day would be a moderate estimate of the actual daily expenses. The property is just of that character that depreciates rapidly by reason of non-use. The machinery deteriorates. The logs, if there be any in the woods, will be destroyed by the worms, and the property generally will necessarily suffer great injury from remaining unused and idle. Besides all this, the labor will become demoralized and scattered. There have been employed about 75 laborers about the mill at Verbena, who are in a state of demoralization, threatening serious trouble. These have not been paid off for some time, despite the willingness of these defendants to pay them off. Many of them are skilled and familiar with the work, and especially familiar with this mill, and it will be exceedingly difficult and expensive to supply their places. A large element in the value of property of this kind is dependent upon its continuous use and employment. While it is impossible now to calculate exactly what the damages will be that will result from a continuance of the injunction and receivership, they will be very large, and such continuance must result most disastrously. Wherefore they prayed that the order granted without notice to them on May 4th be set aside, and that the prayers of petitioners be denied, and the property embraced in the deed to them be restored to them.

Upon the hearing much evidence was introduced upon both sides, most of it being in the shape of affidavits, which are set out in full in the bill of exceptions. On June 1st the judge below granted the injunction prayed for, appointed J. H. Sapp permanent receiver, in accordance with the prayers of the petition, of the estate of Peacock, Peterson & Co. and of each of the members of that firm, and ordered the receiver at his earliest convenience to reduce the property to money by sale of the same at either public or private sale, as might seem to him to the best interest of

all parties concerned, etc. To the order granting the injunction and receiver, and to the order requiring the receiver to sell the property, Stillwell, Millen & Co. excepted on the following grounds: Because each of the orders was contrary to law; because the judge had no jurisdiction to grant either of them; because, under the averments of the petition, the grant of each of them was contrary to law; because the evidence submitted did not authorize the grant of either of them; because petitioners were not lien or judgment creditors, and were not asserting any claim to title, and therefore were not entitled to an injunction or receiver; because Peacock, Peterson & Co. were not traders when the petition was filed, and therefore petitioners had no right to an injunction or receiver; because petitioners had an adequate remedy by attachment; because it was not alleged or claimed that Stillwell, Millen & Co. were insolvent, but it was shown that they were solvent; because no necessity for the injunction or receiver, or for sale of the property as ordered, was shown or appeared; because each of the orders was contrary to law and evidence; and because the original restraining order and appointment of a receiver was granted without notice to Stillwell, Millen & Co.

Denmark, Adams & Adams, A. C. Wright, and Pate & Warren, for plaintiffs in error. Smith & Clements, Garrard & Meldrim, W. L. Clarke, and R. R. Norman, for defendants in error.

BLECKLEY, C. J. The facts are stated in the official report. The judgment below was acquiesced in by the debtors. Peacock, Peterson & Co., the excepting parties being Stillwell, Millen & Co. alone. In so far, therefore, as the granting of an injunction and the appointment of a receiver concern any property not conveyed by the former of these firms to the latter, the decision of the presiding judge, whether correct or incorrect, should not and could not be disturbed on this writ of error. What we shall rule will have relation only to the property embraced in the conveyance to which we have referred, leaving the individual property of the several persons composing the firm of Peacock, Peterson & Co. to be dealt with by the receiver as though it alone had been the subject-matter of the receivership.

1. The petitioning creditors attack this conveyance as fraudulent. Giving the petition the widest possible range, it has three aspects. It rests—First, upon the insolvent traders' act, (Code, § 3149a et seq.;) secondly, upon the assignment act of 1881, (Acts 1880–81, p. 174;) Code, Addenda, § 1953d, p. X. as amended by the act of 1885, (Acts 1884–85, p. 100;) and, thirdly, upon the general law making void all conveyances intended to hinder, delay, or defraud creditors. If the evidence supports any one of these aspects of the petition, it is the last one. It does not support the first, because the partnership of Peacock, Peterson & Co. had been dissolved and had ceased to carry on the firm business before the petition was filed. In this

respect the case is within the ruling on that subject in Kimbrell v. Walters, 86 Ga. 99, 12 S. E. Rep. 305, and previous cases therein cited. The evidence does not support the second aspect of the petition, because it shows, not an assignment, but an absolute conveyance, made in payment of a pre-existing debt, together with an undertaking by the purchasers, Stillwell, Millen & Co., to pay certain other debts, not out of the proceeds of the property, but absolutely, as a part of the agreed price. Touching this element, the case is ruled by Powell v. Kelly, 82 Ga. 1, 9 S. E. Rep. 278 By a very decided preponderance of the evidence the conveyance was made free from any trust, open or secret, in favor of the debtors or any creditor or any other person. It was an absolute and unconditional sale, and the only element of suspicion attaching to it results from apparent inadequacy of price. There is no doubt that the property covered by the conveyance, estimated at its normal value, was very much in excess of the purchasing creditors' debt, and of the whole consideration expressed in the conveyance. Various facts are set up by Stillwell, Millen & Co. to account for and vindicate the transaction, notwithstanding this excess, the principal fact being that much of the property embraced in the deed had not been paid for by Peacock, Peterson & Co., and was still subject to claims for its own purchase money. Conceding all the consequences that could be drawn from the excess of value over the price paid, the case is that of a conveyance by an insolvent partnership to one of the firm creditors at an undervaluation, made to hinder, delay, or defeat the other firm creditors. What, then, is the rule of law governing the grant of an injunction and the appointment of a receiver as against such purchasing creditor, the attacking creditors being without judgments or other liens, and claiming no title to the property, either by reason of fraud in procuring credit therefor in the creation of their demands or otherwise? There can be no doubt that, generally, creditors complaining of a fraudulent conveyance of his property by their debtor are not entitled to an interlocutory injunction and receiver. The present case falls within this general rule, inasmuch as there is no allegation of the insolvency of the alleged fraudulent purchasers, Stillwell, Millen & Co. The case of Mayer v. Wood, 56 Ga. 427, is a direct authority upon the subject, so far as an injunction is concerned; and the principle of that case, fairly carried out, will extend also to the element of appointing a receiver. Where injunction to restrain a solvent purchaser from disposing of the property embraced in his fraudulent purchase would not be granted, we can see no reason why a receiver should be appointed. That the solvency of the purchaser would be security against ultimate loss by the attacking creditors in case they should establish their debts and prove the fraud, would stand as well for a reason against appointing an *ad interim* receiver as against granting an injunction. It is obvious that merely to enjoin a man temporarily from disposing of property to which he claims title is a milder interference with his dominion over it than to take it from him and put it in the hands of a receiver. Indeed, before the order granting an injunction in Mayer v. Wood was brought to this court for review, it had been so far modified, with the consent of the parties, as to allow the fraudulent purchasers to sell the goods and hold up the proceeds, thus virtually converting them into receivers for that purpose. Nevertheless, the order itself, after this modification, was held erroneous. Tested by the case cited and by the main current of the authorities, we are of opinion that no receiver for the property purchased by Stillwell, Millen & Co. should have been appointed. And we are clear that the discretion of the judge was not well exercised in appointing such receiver absolutely and unconditionally, without offering Stillwell, Millen & Co. the alternative of giving bond and security either for the forthcoming of the property or for the eventual condemnation money in this cause. The property consisted partly of real estate, which could not disappear; partly of a saw-mill and fixtures; and partly of a large number of animals used in connection therewith. These animals would be expensive to keep in the hands of a receiver. They would have to be sold speedily, or else the receiver would have to operate the saw-mill at a heavy daily expense, and under many hazards of loss. In the exercise of a wise judicial discretion, it could not be otherwise than desirable, in behalf of the interest of all parties concerned, to keep such property out of the hands of a receiver; and, if that could be done by exacting bond and security, this exaction ought to have been made, and opportunity afforded to comply with it. In Cohen v. Meyers, 42 Ga. 46, the receiver was appointed *ex parte*, but on hearing the matter after answer the chancellor recognized as a basis for discharging the receiver the alternative of giving bond and security for the payment of any recovery which might be had in the case. It may be asserted as a general proposition that a bond with good security is always a better form of protecting creditors likely to be injured by fraud than the appointment of a receiver for property perishable in its nature or expensive to keep. And in most cases the liability of a solvent party without bond and security would itself be preferable to an expensive receivership. The answer of Stillwell, Millen & Co. alleged that they were solvent, and fully able to respond. This was not contradicted by any evidence or by any allegation in the petition. By no disposition or misappropriation of the property pending suit against them to set the conveyance aside could they evade their responsibility to the plaintiffs for any fraud complained of in the petition, should that fraud be established at the final trial of the cause. Being solvent, they are virtually sureties to the petitioning creditors for the forthcoming of the property should the conveyance be set aside, or for its value in excess of their own debt and the residue of the price at which they purchased it.

2. It developed in argument at the bar that the case of De Lacy v. Hurst, 83 Ga. 223, 9 S. E. Rep. 1052, was susceptible of being misunderstood by learned counsel. That case holds that in one and the same suit creditors may proceed for judgment on their debts, and to set aside fraudulent conveyances; but it nowhere suggests that an *ad interim* injunction or receiver can be had in any case in which the like extraordinary remedy could not be invoked prior to the passage of the uniformity procedure act of 1887. On the contrary, in the statement of facts with which the opinion in that case opens it is said: "The trial judge refused to grant the injunction or to appoint a receiver." This refusal was acquiesced in, and consequently the element of injunction and receiver had been eliminated from the case before it reached this court. We adhere to the decision in De Lacy v. Hurst, but cannot apply it to this case at its present stage further than to hold that the creditors attacking this conveyance are *recti in curia* as to the ultimate purposes of their action; these purposes being to establish their claims against Peacock, Peterson & Co. and set aside an alleged fraudulent conveyance made by them to their codefendants, Stillwell, Millen & Co. The judge erred in granting an injunction as to Stillwell, Millen & Co., in appointing a receiver for the property embraced in the conveyance to them, and in ordering a sale of that property by the receiver.

Judgment reversed.

DOTTERER *et al.* v. HARDEN, Judge.

(Supreme Court of Georgia. Nov. 28, 1891.)

RECORD ON APPEAL—MANDAMUS TO JUDGE — REFUSAL TO SIGN BILL OF EXCEPTIONS—JUDGMENT LIEN—VALIDITY OF ASSIGNMENT.

1. Where the only error assigned is upon the rendition of a decree founded on the verdict of a jury, none of the evidence adduced on the trial is requisite in reviewing the decree; nor is anything the judge may have stated orally at the time of rendering the decree, or previously, material.

2. The supreme court will not grant a *mandamus nisi*, to the end that a bill of exceptions may be signed and certified, where it affirmatively appears on the face of the application that the decision complained of, and sought to be excepted to, was correct, inasmuch as in such case the *mandamus* would be of no practical benefit to the applicant.

3. In a contest between a judgment creditor and the assignees of a money demand against a county, the lien of the judgment not having attached upon the fund before it was brought into court, such judgment will not take precedence of the assignments, though they were made after the judgment was rendered.

4. Though the assignments are not set forth in the pleadings fully and specifically, yet, if they be alleged substantially, and the jury have found them to be valid, they ought to be so treated in rendering the decree; no motion for a new trial or other attack upon the verdict having been made by any of the parties in due time.

(Syllabus by the Court.)

Application of Dotterer, trustee, and others, for a writ of *mandamus* to William D. Harden, acting as judge of the superior court of Chatham county, to compel him to certify a bill of exceptions. Writ denied.

F. H. Miller, R. G. Erwin, W. S. Chisholm, and *Harrison & Peeples,* for petitioners.

LUMPKIN, J. Dotterer, trustee, et al., applied to this court for a writ of *mandamus nisi* requiring the Honorable WILLIAM D. HARDEN (judge of the city court of Savannah, who presided in the superior court of Chatham county in the place of Hon. ROBERT FALLIGANT, disqualified) to show cause why the former should not certify a bill of exceptions duly tendered to him in the case of Bowe v. County of Chatham et al.; his honor, Judge HARDEN, having refused to certify the same as presented. It appears that Judge HARDEN declined to certify the bill of exceptions unless counsel for the plaintiff in error would set forth therein the evidence adduced on the trial, and also certain reasons given orally by the judge at the time of rendering the decree for the conclusions he had reached. This the counsel refused to do. As ruled in the first head-note, we do not think the proposed corrections were material or necessary. Even if they had been, still if the bill of exceptions as tendered set forth no erroneous ruling by the court below, the writ of *mandamus* ought to be denied. It was conceded by the learned and able counsel who presented this application that if it appeared from the bill of exceptions sought to be certified that there was no error in the rulings of the court below, the writ of *mandamus* should be denied; and so it was held by this court in Pitts v. Hall, 60 Ga. 389. It only remains, therefore, to be shown that the bill of exceptions tendered to Judge HARDEN set forth no error requiring correction by this court; and this will appear from a brief discussion of the merits of the case.

Bowe filed in Chatham superior court an equitable petition alleging, among other things, that he had contracted to build a jail for said county for $47,780, of which sum a large amount was still due him; that he had found it impossible to complete the work without becoming indebted in large sums to various persons for work done and materials furnished in carrying out his work; for said work and materials suits had been instituted and judgments obtained against him by the Fred Myers Manufacturing Company, Andrew Hanley, Charles A. Robbe, Frank Smyth, and W. P. Bailey & Co., upon which judgments summonses of garnishment had been issued, directed to the county of Chatham, and were still due him; that, in the progress of the work of building said jail, petitioner had been compelled to assign to one John O. Smith certain amounts due to petitioner under his contract with the county, and that the said Smith had filed said assignment with the commissioners of the county; that because of said garnishments and assignment the county commissioners refused to pay to petitioner the alleged balance due him on the contract; and that petitioner was willing to pay the amount due him by the county to such persons as were lawfully entitled to receive the same. The petition prayed that the county of

Chatham be required to pay into the registry of the court the amount due petitioner, and that the above-named parties be required to appear and interplead, and have determined their respective rights and priorities to so much of said money as might be due to them, or to either of them, and that process be issued and directed accordingly. The county filed an answer denying many of the allegations of the petition, but admitting an indebtedness to petitioner in the sum of $4,735.95, which it averred its willingness to pay into court, to be disposed of as the court might order and decree. The Fred Myers Manufacturing Company, Andrew Hanley, Charles A. Robbe, and Frank Smyth filed separate answers setting forth the amounts, respectively, due them by Bowe for work done and materials furnished in the construction of the jail; that they had obtained judgments against Bowe for the same: that Bowe had given them written orders upon the county commissioners for these amounts, which orders were assignments of said funds by Bowe to them; that these orders had been duly filed with the county commissioners, and that upon them there were still due to these defendants the several amounts of their respective judgments. The answer of W. P. Bailey & Co. alleged that Bowe was indebted to them in the amount therein named on a judgment obtained against him, based on an indebtedness for bricks furnished in the construction of the jail, but their answer did not claim that Bowe had made to them an assignment of any part of the amount due to him by the county. The answer of John O. Smith alleged an indebtedness to him by Bowe of a large sum of money for work and materials in the building of the jail, and that Bowe had assigned to him a sufficiency of the amount due Bowe by the county to pay such indebtedness, and that Bowe had given him a power of attorney to collect the same. After these answers had been filed, and before Dotterer became a party to the case, a consent order was passed, adjudging that the county of Chatham pay into the registry of the court $6,436.73, and, after said payment, be released and absolved from all further liability either to Bowe or to any of his creditors in the petition mentioned. This order was passed March 4, 1891. Thereafter, on the same day, Dotterer, trustee, was made a party defendant to the case, and filed an answer alleging that Bowe was indebted to him, in an amount therein named, upon a judgment he had obtained on the 10th day of June, 1887, and praying that said judgment be satisfied out of the fund paid into court by the commissioners of Chatham county. During the same term of the court certain issues of fact were submitted to the jury, and they found substantially as follows: First, that the claims of all the respondents, as set forth in their respective answers, were valid and just, and that all of them were in judgment except that of John O. Smith; second, that the assignments given by Bowe to Robbe, Smyth, and John O. Smith were valid; third, that the claims of all these respondents, except Dotterer, were founded on amounts due by Bowe for labor, materials, etc., furnished in connection with the building of the jail, and that Dotterer's judgment was based upon a matter foreign to the construction of said jail. There was no finding by the jury that Hanley or W. P. Bailey & Co. had assignments from Bowe of any part of the funds due him by the county. There was no motion for a new trial, or any effort made by any of the respondents to set aside the verdict. At the next term of the court, upon the petition, answers, and verdict as they stood, a final decree was entered, which after allowing Bowe's solicitors $600 for bringing the fund into court, and providing for the payment of costs, divided the balance of the fund among Robbe, Smyth, and John O. Smith, the three latter receiving the amounts awarded them pro rata upon their respective claims: the fund being insufficient to pay them in full. As will be seen, the claims of Hanley, W. P. Bailey & Co., and Dotterer were excluded from any participation in the fund. The judge evidently was of the opinion that only those creditors of Bowe who had assignments from him were entitled to share in the money paid into court by the county. Dotterer's judgment being older than any of the orders on the county, or assignments given by Bowe, he claims that his judgment was entitled to priority, and that the judge erred in holding otherwise. We think the judge's ruling was correct. Dotterer's judgment gave him no lien on this fund in the hands of the county. Indeed, it was expressly ruled in Dotterer v. Bowe that he could not reach this money by a garnishment. 84 Ga. 769, 11 S. E. Rep. 896. If he had no lien on the fund while it remained in the county treasury, and could not reach it there by process of garnishment, we see no reason why the lien of his judgment should attach to the money after it was, at the instance of Bowe, brought into court for distribution. Moreover, the finding of the jury, of which Dotterer did not complain, established that this money had been lawfully assigned by Bowe to Robbe, Smyth, and John O. Smith, and consequently it belonged to them. It is true that in none of the answers above referred to were the assignments alleged to have been made by Bowe as clearly and distinctly set forth as they might have been; and probably, on special demurrer, an objection to this effect would have been sustained. In the absence of such demurrer the allegations concerning the assignments were sufficient, and should be so treated, especially after the jury have found them to be valid. Whether this finding was right in fact, or sound in law, is immaterial. Until set aside, it is binding and conclusive upon all of these parties; and, this being true, the judge could not do otherwise than decree, as he did, that the money be awarded to those to whom, under the verdict, it belonged. It appears, therefore, that, if the bill of exceptions had been certified by the judge precisely as it was presented to him, it would have resulted in no practical service to the plaintiff in error, and nothing beneficial would be accomplished by ordering the writ of *mandamus* to issue. Assuming, for argument's sake, that the bill of exceptions ought to have been signed as tendered, and supposing the same was now being considered upon its own merits, the judgment of the court below would be affirmed. For this reason, the propriety of refusing the writ is manifest. *Mandamus* denied.

VIRGINIA FIRE & MARINE INS. CO. v. BUCK et al.

(*Supreme Court of Appeals of Virginia.* Dec. 14, 1891.)

ACTIONS ON INSURANCE POLICIES—EVIDENCE—APPLICATIONS—RIGHT TO FILE SPECIAL PLEAS.

1. The statute which allows the defendant to plead as many matters of defense as he may elect, does not confer upon him an absolute right to file special pleas setting up defenses which are already covered by other pleas; and, although such a plea has been received, and issue joined upon it, it is still competent for the court to strike it out.

2. In an action on an insurance policy the refusal to allow the defendant on cross-examination to ask a witness, who has previously testified that he had been employed as watchman, how much he was paid for his services, is not error, as the jury cannot measure the watchman's diligence by the amount of his pay, and the only inquiry is whether he was in fact so employed.

3. An insurance company has no right, in an action on a policy, to inquire whether a certain person had obtained "other insurance" for the plaintiff in violation of a provision of the policy, without having first established that the said person was the plaintiff's agent, or at least satisfied the court that it would subsequently do so.

4. One of the questions in an application for insurance was as to the length of time that the plaintiff had been merchandising, and who slept in the store. The answer was, "Four years; watchman on premises at night." *Held*, that the answer amounted only to a warranty that the plaintiff had a watchman on the premises at the time of the application, not that he would continue to keep one there; and hence the absence of the watchman without the plaintiff's knowledge on the night of the fire was no defense.

Error to circuit court, Montgomery county.

This was an action by Buck & Newsom against the Virginia Fire & Marine Insurance Company on a policy of insurance. There was judgment for plaintiffs and defendant brings error. Affirmed.

W. W. & B. T. Crump, for plaintiff in error. *Burks & Campbell*, for defendants in error.

HINTON, J. This was an action of case in *assumpsit* on a policy of insurance. Issue was joined on the plea of *non assumpsit*, and the defendant company, in accordance with a practice common in the circuit courts of this state, obtained leave to file special pleas within 60 days. The effect of granting leave to file these pleas in the clerk's office is twofold: It gives the defendant additional time within which to plead, and it gives the plaintiff timely notice of the defense to be set up, and thus prevents surprise and delay at the succeeding term. In these respects the practice is convenient. It seems, however, to have no other advantage, since the clerk can only receive and file the pleas, and the plaintiff cannot reply or demur to the pleas,

and make up an issue. Three special pleas were filed in the clerk's office. To the first of these no objection was made; but the plaintiffs, treating the other two as tendered by the filing in the clerk's office, moved the court to reject them, which was accordingly done. The defendant then tendered a fifth plea, which, on the plaintiffs' motion, was also rejected. The rejection of these three pleas constitutes the first assignment of error. Upon this point we shall spend but little time, because, in the opinion of this court, every fact might have been proved under the general issue in the case which could have been proved under either of these pleas. Their rejection, therefore, could not have prejudiced the defendant. "The fact is undeniable," says Mr. Minor, in his Institutes, "that for more than a century past there has been admitted, under the plea of *non assumpsit*, in all actions of *assumpsit*, whether founded on an implied or express promise, any matter of defense whatever (the same as in the case of *nil debit*) which tends to deny his liability to the plaintiff's demands." 4 Minor Inst. p. 645. And at page 641 of the same volume the author says: "Under the plea of *nil debit* the defendant may prove at the trial coverture when the promise was made, lunacy, duress, infancy, release, arbitrament, award and satisfaction, payment, a want of consideration for the promise, failure or fraud in the consideration, and, in short, anything which shows there is no existing debt due. The statute of limitations, bankruptcy, and tender are believed to be the only defenses which may not be proved under this plea, and they are excepted because they do not contest that the debt is owing, but insist only that no action can be maintained for it." And to the same effect seem to be all the authorities. 1 Chit. Pl. (4th Amer. Ed.) § 18; Steph. Pl. (4th Amer. Ed.) p. 162, note 20; 1 Rob. Pr. 210; 5 Rob. Pr. 259. Nor can this court assent to the proposition that the statute which allows the defendant to plead as many matters of defense as he may elect confers upon him the "absolute right" to file special pleas setting up defenses covered by a plea already received. Such a construction of the statute would be inconsistent with the authorities already cited, and, so far as we can see, could serve no good purpose. This same suggestion seems to have been made in Fant v. Miller, 17 Grat. 47; but said JOYNES, J.: "I think the object of the [special] plea was to set up the defense that the plaintiffs were not *bona fide* holders of the note on which the action was founded. That defense, however, might have been made, as, in point of fact, it was made, under the plea of *nil debit*, upon which issue had already been joined in 1853. The plea was therefore wholly unnecessary, and this would have been good ground for rejecting it when offered, if it had been objected to, (Reed v. Hanna's Ex'r, 3 Rand. (Va.) 56; and it was competent for the court to strike it out after it was received, even though issue had been joined upon it. Kemp v. Mundell, 9 Leigh, 12. The plaintiffs in error, not having been deprived of any de-

and ought not to be encouraged, 'except in cases where, by law, the defense would otherwise be excluded or rendered unavailing.'" It is suggested, however, if we correctly apprehend the brief of the plaintiff in error, that the plaintiffs below ought to have demurred to those pleas "if insufficient in law," and should not have moved the court to reject them. But this, as the defendants in error point out in their brief, is generally an unsafe practice; the better way undoubtedly being to move the court, when it has not been received, to reject it. In Reed v. Hanna's Ex'r, 3 Rand. (Va.) 62, the court said: "Where the objection to a second plea * * * is that the matter of that plea is already put in issue, the party ought not to be put to the hazard of a demurrer in order to avail himself of that objection, the proper and safe practice being to try that question on a motion to reject the plea, or strike it out, if it has been entered on the record."

The next assignment of error is that the court declined to permit the defendant to ask, on cross-examination, the witness, Wilkes, who had previously testified that he had been employed as night watchman, and paid for his services as such, how much he was paid. But we perceive no error in this action of the court. The jury could not measure the watchman's diligence by the amount of his pay. The real inquiry was whether he was employed by the plaintiffs, and acted under such employment, and that question was submitted to the jury.

The next objection seems equally groundless. The defendant clearly had no right to go into the inquiry whether or no the firm of Johnson & Co. had obtained "other insurance" for the plaintiffs, in violation of a provision of the policy sued on, without having first established that they were the plaintiffs' agents, or, at least, had satisfied the court that they would subsequently do so.

Passing over several minor exceptions, which seem to be fully answered by the facts of the case, we come now to what may be regarded as the most formidable objection to the action of the circuit court, viz., that it erred in giving the following instruction: "That if they believe from the evidence that the policy in suit was based on a written application, authorized by the plaintiffs, or either of them, said application thereby became a part of said policy, and the answer to the eighteenth question in said application is a warranty on the part of said plaintiffs that a watchman was kept on the premises at night. But what constitutes a 'watchman,' within the meaning of said application, is a matter of fact to be determined by the jury, and, if they believe from the evidence that at the time of said application the plaintiffs had such watchman on the premises at night, and continued to keep one in their employment on said premises at night continuously from that date until the destruction of the man was, without the knowledge or consent of the plaintiffs, or either of them, absent from the premises." The great fact relied on by the defendant as its ground of defense being that the watchman who usually slept on the premises was absent on the night of the fire, it is insisted that the instruction tells the jury, in effect, that, after they shall have found that there was a warranty of a watchman on the premises at night, and have determined the meaning of the word "watchman" as used in the application, and that such watchman was kept on the premises, yet the law dispensed with his presence on the night of the fire, unless his absence was known to the plaintiffs. We do not think the instruction fairly susceptible of this construction. That instruction, it is true, left it to the jury to determine what constituted a "watchman" within the meaning of the application, and then declared that, if the plaintiffs had such watchman on the premises at the time of the application, and continued to keep him in their employment on the premises from that date until the destruction of the property by fire, then there was no breach of the warranty. And this was going further than the plaintiffs need have gone. It certainly, however, could not have hurt the defendant, and did not intimate that the defendant would be excused if the warranty was found to be promissory and continuing. And, moreover, it was just and proper in the circumstances of this case, where, as we shall proceed to show, the warranty was merely affirmative. "Warranties," says Mr. May, "are distinguished into two kinds,—affirmative, or those which allege the existence at the time of a particular fact, and avoid the contract if the allegation be untrue; and promissory, or those which require that something shall be done or omitted after the insurance takes effect and during its continuance, and avoid the contract if the thing to be done or omitted be not done or omitted according to the terms of the warranty." May, Ins. § 157; O'Neil v. Insurance Co., 3 N. Y. 122. And the rule is that the courts will never construe a warranty as promissory and continuing if any other reasonable construction can be given. Blood v. Insurance Co., 12 Cush. 472; Schmidt v. Insurance Co. 41 Ill., 295; Hosford v. Insurance Co., 127 U. S. 399, 8 Sup. Ct. Rep. 1199; Insurance Co. v. Eddy, 55 Ill. 213; Gates v. Insurance Co., 5 N. Y. 469; May v. Insurance Co., 25 Wis. 291; Stout v. Insurance Co., 12 Iowa. 371; Insurance Co. v. Kimberly, 34 Md. 224; Frisbie v. Insurance Co., 27 Pa. St. 325; and other cases too numerous to mention. Without reference to this last-mentioned rule, however, we think it perfectly plain that the answer to the eighteenth question in the application amounted only to a statement that the plaintiffs had in their employ a watchman, whose usual place for sleeping was on the premises. Now, this statement is merely affirmative of the usual and existing state of things, and has nothing promissory as to the future. That such is the case seems to us clear from the circumstances under which the answer was made. The question was: "How long have you been merchandising, and who sleeps in the store, and what clerks are employed?" To which the answer in the application, written admittedly by the defendant's agent, and not signed by the plaintiffs, or either of them, is: "Four years; watchman on premises at night." The question, as the plaintiffs say in their brief, manifestly relates to the present, and not to the future. It was intended to get information as to the present state of things, and not to exact a promise that such state should continue. It is only necessary to add that the court did not err in refusing to set aside the verdict and grant a new trial. The case being before us as upon a demurrer to evidence, we must exclude the evidence of Kelsey, the agent of the defendant, to the effect that the answer to the question just mentioned was authorized by the plaintiffs; and we must therefore take the fact to be as Mr. Buck says it was,—that no such statement or reply was authorized. We see no error in the judgment of the circuit court, and the same must be affirmed.

TYLER v. CHESAPEAKE & O. R. CO.

(Supreme Court of Appeals of Virginia. Nov.
12, 1891.)

ACTIONS AGAINST RAILROAD COMPANIES—INSTRUCTIONS — PROVINCE OF JURY — PERSONAL INJURIES.

Plaintiff and two other boys obtained permission from a section-master, who was going with the sectionmen on a hand-car to load some scrap-iron, to go with him if they would assist in loading the iron. On their return the hand-car collided with a rapidly moving train. Plaintiff was injured, and sued the railroad company. He asked the court to charge that, if the section-master was in the habit of employing and discharging the men under him, and was in control of the said car, and plaintiff was on the car by his permission, and without knowing that it was contrary to the rules of the company, and the injuries sustained by him resulted from the gross negligence of defendant, he was entitled to recover, and that the relation between a section master and the men under him was that of superior and subordinates; and that, if one employed by the section-master was injured by the section-master's negligence, the company could not escape liability on the ground that the injured party was a co-employe. The court rejected the instructions of plaintiff as calculated to mislead the jury, and as inapplicable to the evidence. It then charged that, although plaintiff was permitted to ride on the hand-car, upon condition that he would assist in loading the said iron, this did not make him an employe, so as to obligate the company to protect him from injury; and that, unless defendant authorized the section-master to permit him so to ride, the jury must find for the defendant. *Held,* that the said rulings were an invasion of the province of the jury, in assuming to decide for them questions of fact, and in directing their verdict. FAUNTLEROY, J., dissenting.

This was an action by Tyler, an infant, by his next friend, against the Chesapeake & Ohio Railroad Company, to recover for personal injuries. There was judgment for defendant, and plaintiff brings error. Reversed.

T. C. Elder and *G. M. Cochran,* for plaintiff in error. *R. L. Parrish* and *W. J. Robertson,* for defendant in error.

LACY, J. This is a writ of error to a judgment of the circuit court of Augusta county, rendered on the 22d of November, 1890. The action was by an infant, by his next friend, in trespass on the case, for injuries, against the defendant company. Upon the trial the demurrer was sustained by the court to the fifth count of the plaintiff's declaration, and the same overruled. As to the other four counts of the declaration evidence was taken on both sides, and the court gave certain instructions, and the jury, by their verdict, found for the defendant under the instructions of the court, and judgment was rendered on the verdict for the defendant, and, he having excepted to the several rulings of the court refusing instructions asked for by him, and giving others for the defendant, the plaintiff moved the court to set aside the verdict and grant him a new trial, upon the ground that the court had misinstructed the jury as to the law, which motion the court overruled, and the plaintiff applied for and obtained a writ of error to this court. The case, briefly stated, is as follows: The plaintiff, a boy less than 17 years of age, in company with another boy, whose age is not stated, was joined by another boy, 14 years of age, and encountered a section-master of the defendant company, who had a hand-car and some hands going a few miles out on the railway, west of the city of Staunton, to do some work in gathering up scraps of iron and some heavy frogs which had been left out in recent track repairs. It was agreed between the plaintiff and the other boys on the one hand and the section-master on the other that these boys could ride on the hand-car to the point indicated if they would work like other hands in gathering up the iron in question. This was agreed to, and, the iron having been collected and loaded on the hand-car, except heavy frogs, which were loaded on a freight train, the hand-car started back in command of the section-master, and, by putting forward a flagman, and stopping a freight train they encountered on the way, and unloading the hand-car and taking the same off the track, it escaped collision. But, loading up again, and starting towards Staunton, the grade descending, and the hand-car heavy with the iron, the speed became greater than is usual on hand-cars,—25 miles an hour,—and, no flagman being out, and no brakes on the hand-car, except a stick held by the section-master, they encountered a train running rapidly out of Staunton, flat-car in front, and, the shock occurring almost without warning, the other parties jumped off, but the plaintiff was struck and injured, as were others who jumped, and three men were killed on the flat-car on the train, and nothing was found of the hand-car but one wheel. The plaintiff was seriously injured, and the evidence tends to show that these were permanent injuries. He has, according to that, lost the use of his right arm, which might freeze or mortify without his knowing it; and his head has been so injured by the hurts he received that they are worse than those in his limbs. He is unfitted for any business requiring a strong mind or strong body. He is blighted every way in body and mind. The accident happened at a critical period of his life, and seriously interfered with his development, and he never can be the man he would have been if he had not sustained the injuries proven in the case.

The plaintiff asked the court to instruct the jury: "(1) If the jury shall believe from the evidence that at the time of the collision which resulted in the injuries to the plaintiff of which he complains in this action, G. C. Ellis, as section-master of the defendant company on that part of said company's road on which the collision occurred, was on the hand-car involved in said collision, and in the control and management of the same, and that the plaintiff was then and there on said hand-car by permission of said Ellis, and without knowing that it was contrary to the rules of the defendant company to be on said hand-car, and that the injuries sustained by the plaintiff in said collision resulted from the gross negligence of the defendant company, or of its agents, or any of them, while the plaintiff was on said hand-car, then the court instructs the jury that the defendant company is liable to the plaintiff in this action for said injuries. (2) If the jury believe from the evidence that when the collision occurred between the hand-car and train, which resulted in the injuries to the plaintiff for which he seeks to recover in the action, G. C. Ellis was the section-master of the defendant company on that part of said company's road upon which said collision took place, and that, as such section-master, he was then on the aforesaid hand-car, and in the actual control and management of the same and of the laborers thereon, and was in the habit of employing and discharging and controlling the laborers under him, and did, on the day upon which the collision occurred, and but an hour or two before its occurrence, agree with the plaintiff that he would take him on said hand-car with his force from West End, a suburb of Staunton, to La Grange, a point on defendant's road, three or four miles west of said starting-point, and bring him back on said hand-car in a short time on the same day, upon the condition and understanding that the plaintiff would aid in loading scrap-iron along the track at and near La Grange on said hand car, to be brought to Staunton, and that the plaintiff, in ignorance of any regulation of the company which forbade his being on the hand-car so under the control of said Ellis, did go thereon to La Grange, and did, according to his undertaking, aid in loading scrap-iron on said hand-car, and that, in returning from La Grange on said hand-car, the plaintiff, by reason of the gross negligence of the defendant company, or of its agents and representatives, in permitting the aforesaid collision to take place, was seriously and permanently injured, then the court instructs the jury

that the plaintiff is entitled to recover of the defendant for such injuries. (3) The court instructs the jury that a section-master of a railroad company, in charge of a particular section of the company's road, with a force of hands under him, to take care of and preserve said section, is not merely a co-employe with said hands, on an equal footing with them, but that the relations between the section-master and those working under him are those which exist between a superior and a subordinate, and that, in all matters pertaining to the particular department in which the section-master is engaged, he is the representative of the company, and, therefore, if one who is employed by the section-master to work under him on his section is injured by the negligence of the section-master while engaged in and about said employment, the company cannot escape liability for said injury upon the ground that the injured party was the co-employe of the section-master; but the jury are further instructed that this will not prevent the company from showing, if it can, that on other grounds or for other reasons it is not liable to the injured party for the injuries he has sustained." Which instructions the court refused to give; but, at the instance of the defendant, instructed the jury, among other things, that "(3) although the jury may believe from the evidence that the plaintiff requested Section-Master Ellis to permit him to ride on the hand-car to La Grange, and that said Ellis replied that said plaintiff might go on the car if he would help to pick up scrap-iron, they are instructed that said request and reply did not make the plaintiff an employe of the railroad company, and did not give the plaintiff any right to ride on said hand-car, and did not obligate the company to protect the plaintiff from hurt and injury while riding on the same; and that, therefore, they must find a verdict for the defendant, unless the plaintiff has proven by a preponderance of evidence that the defendant company had authorized said Ellis to allow the plaintiff to ride on said hand-car." And the court, being of opinion that it could not fairly be inferred from the testimony that the plaintiff was either a passenger or an employe of the company, and that, from the familiarity of the plaintiff with its (defendant's) railroad and its employes, it was fairly to be inferred that he was aware of the rules and regulations of the company prohibiting persons from riding on the hand-cars, rejected plaintiff's first and second instructions, supra, as calculated to mislead the jury; and, being also of opinion that the third (supra) instruction of the plaintiff was not applicable to the testimony in the case, rejected that also, but gave the fourth instruction; to which action of the court the plaintiff excepted.

It is elementary, and is firmly settled in Virginia, that the court responds to questions of law and the jury to questions of fact. The court must decide on the admissibility of evidence, that being a question of law; but not as to its weight after it is admitted, that being a question of fact. McDowell v. Crawford, 11 Grat. 377. The decided cases evince a jealous care to watch over and protect the legitimate powers of a jury. They show that the court must be very careful not to overstep the line which separates law from fact. They establish the fact that when evidence is parol, any opinion as to the weight, effect, or sufficiency of the evidence submitted to the jury, any assumption of a fact as proved, will be an invasion of the province of the jury. Bart. L. Pr. 214, and cited cases; Baring v. Reeder, 1 Hen. & M. 174; Moore v. Chapman, 3 Hen. & M. 266; Fisher's Ex'r v. Duncan, 1 Hen. & M. 576; Whitacre v. McIlhaney, 4 Munf. 310; McRae v. Scott, 4 Rand. (Va.) 463; Cornett v. Rhudy, 80 Va. 710. For making observations or instructions to the jury as to the weight to be given by them to any part of the testimony or the whole evidence, the cause may be reversed, and a new trial awarded. Bart. L. Pr., supra; Davis v. Miller, 14 Grat. 1; Hopkins v. Richardson, 9 Grat. 486. In this case, the court, after duly impaneling a jury, undertook to decide for them every question of fact involved, and instructed them as to the weight of the testimony, and, in effect, directed their verdict; and the jury, recognizing that this had been done, in effect rendered a special verdict, divesting themselves of all responsibilities whatever for the result, announced their verdict as directed by the court's instructions, and the court, against the exception of the plaintiff, rendered judgment thereon. There has, in fact, been no trial by the jury in this case, as that term is properly understood and defined, and the verdict and judgment must be set aside, reversed, and annulled, because of the misdirection of the court, which erred in rejecting the plaintiff's instructions and in giving the instructions given on the motion of the defendant; and, as the cause must go back for a new trial, we will say that the fifth count of the plaintiff's declaration stated a good cause of action, and the demurrer thereto should have been overruled by the court, and the action of the court in sustaining said demurrer to the said fifth count is erroneous. For the foregoing reasons we are of opinion to reverse the judgment of the circuit court of Augusta herein, and to remand the case for a new trial to be had therein in the said circuit court. Judgment reversed.

FAUNTLEROY, J., dissenting.

Rehearing refused.

McCLANAHAN v. WESTERN LUNATIC ASYLUM.
(Supreme Court of Appeals of Virginia. Dec. 3, 1891.)

LIMITATIONS—APPLICABILITY TO PUBLIC CORPORATIONS.

Public corporations, such as lunatic asylums, when clothed with capacity to sue and be sued, are amenable, in actions instituted by such corporations, to the defense of the statute of limitations, as well as to all other defenses, the same as natural persons are amenable.

This was an action by the Western Lunatic Asylum against S. R. McClanahan, administrator of R. S. McClanahan, a patient in the said asylum, to recover for the

board and attendance of the said patient. There was judgment for plaintiff, and defendant appeals. Reversed.

J. C. Gibson and *Rixey & Barbour,* for plaintiff in error. *Thos. C. Elder* and *J. N. Opie,* for defendant in error.

FAUNTLEROY, J. The plaintiff in error complains of a judgment of the hustings court of the city of Staunton, entered therein on the 11th day of July, 1890, against him as administrator of R. S. McClanahan, deceased. On the 20th of March, 1878, Robert S. McClanahan, a son of the plaintiff in error, was admitted into the Western Lunatic Asylum at Staunton, as a patient thereof, at the age of 15 years, and he died therein September 7, 1882, at the age of 19 years. As a condition precedent to the admission of the said infant patient a writing obligatory was executed on the 20th of March, 1878, by the said S. R. McClanahan and Robert Stringfellow, binding them on demand to pay to the Western Lunatic Asylum, for the board, fuel, lights, washing, and medical attendance of the said patient, the sum of $25 per month, or such sum as the directors may from time to time assess. On the 20th of June, 1878, the said obligor S. R. McClanahan paid to the said asylum the sum of $75 in full for three months' board, etc., of the said patient. On the '6th of September, 1878, a resolution was adopted and entered of record by the board of directors of the said asylum "that the said Dr. S. R. McClanahan be released from his obligation for the support of his son, R. S. McClanahan, in the asylum from the 20th of June, 1878, forward." On the 10th day of June, 1890, the said Western Lunatic Asylum exhibited to the said hustings court of the city of Staunton its account against the plaintiff in error as administrator of the said R. S. McClanahan, deceased, in the sum of $1,504.35 as of October 1, 1890, together with a notice of a motion to be made on the same day for a judgment for the same. Thereupon the defendant (plaintiff in error) filed—*First,* a general plea of the statute of limitations; *second,* a plea of *non assumpsit;* and, *third,* a special plea of release of the debt claimed, by virtue of the aforesaid order of release made by the board of directors of the said asylum as of September 6, 1878. The plaintiff demurred to the defendant's plea of the statute of limitations, and issue was joined upon the said demurrer, and, both sides waiving a jury, the whole case was submitted to the court, whereupon the court sustained the demurrer to the defendant's plea of the statute of limitations, and, having considered the evidence submitted, gave and entered judgment against the defendant, as administrator aforesaid, in the sum of $1,504.35, with interest on $998.88, part thereof, from October 1, 1890, till paid, and the costs. The court overruled a motion to set the said judgment aside as being contrary to the law and the evidence, and certified the facts proved upon the hearing.

The first assignment of error is that the hustings court erred in sustaining the plaintiff's demurrer to the defendant's plea of the statute of limitations, and this is the only real or material question presented by the record for the decision of this court. The last item in the account or bill of particulars moved on is dated September 7, 1882, and this action was instituted on the 10th of July, 1890. The contention is that the Western Lunatic Asylum, plaintiff, asserting this demand against a patient or his estate for support and maintenance in the said asylum, stands *quoad hoc* in the shoes of the state, and that the maxim "*nullum tempus occurrit regi*" is applicable and obtains in the case. We are of opinion that this contention is not sound, and that the error assigned is well taken. The Western Lunatic Asylum is a corporation, an organized legal entity, a personality in law, with power to sue and be sued, to plead and to be impleaded, and, being endowed with this capacity, it is thereby entitled to and amenable to all legal defenses which pertain to private persons. In the case of Bank of U. S. v. Planters' Bank of Georgia, 9 Wheat. 904, Chief Justice MARSHALL says: "The state does not, by becoming a corporation, identify itself with the corporation. The Planters' Bank of Georgia is not the state of Georgia, although the state holds an interest in it. * * * The state of Georgia, by giving to the bank the capacity to sue and be sued, voluntarily strips itself of its sovereign character, so far as respects the transactions of the bank, and waives all the privileges of that character. As a member of a corporation, a government never exercises its sovereignty. It acts merely as a corporator, and exercises no other power in the management of the affairs of the corporation than are expressly given by the incorporating act." "So with respect to the present Bank of the United States. Suits brought by or against it are not understood to be brought by or against the United States." See, also, Osborn v. Bank, 9 Wheat. 738; McCulloch v. State of Maryland, 4 Wheat. 816. In the case of Asylum v. Miller, 29 W. Va. 326, 1 S. E. Rep. 740, the court of appeals of that state in an able and convincing opinion entered into a full discussion of the powers, responsibilities, and capabilities of corporations to sue and be sued, and decided that the plea of the statute of limitations was a good, proper, and legal defense to an action instituted by this same Western Lunatic Asylum. The judgment complained of is wholly erroneous, and it is reversed and annulled; and this court, proceeding to enter such judgment as the hustings court of the city of Staunton ought to have entered, will overrule the demurrer to the plea of the statute of limitations, and dismiss the plaintiff's motion, with costs. Reversed.

LACY, J., concurring in result, but not in the views expressed in opinion.

TYLER v. SITES' ADM'R.

(*Supreme Court of Appeals of Virginia.* Dec. 3, 1891.)

RAILROAD COMPANIES — ACCIDENTS ON TRACK— CONTRIBUTORY NEGLIGENCE—INSTRUCTIONS.

1. Plaintiff's intestate was killed while walking on a railroad track. The deceased, who was a deaf-mute, had once before received an injury in a similar manner, and had been repeatedly warned about walking upon the railroad. Only a few minutes before he was killed, he had been so warned. The accident occurred in an open plain, where the view was unobstructed for nearly a mile. Deceased, although a deaf-mute, was possessed of all his other faculties, including that of sight, and was a strong, active man, about 32 years of age. He was walking directly towards the train, on the ends of the ties, on the side opposite the engineer. The latter saw him until he came within 25 or 30 yards, when the projecting front of the locomotive intervened. He supposed, however, the deceased would step off. *Held,* that the deceased's own negligence was the proximate cause of the injury, and plaintiff was not entitled to recover.

2. The defendant requested the court to charge that the company was bound to keep a reasonable lookout for trespassers on its track, and to exercise such care as the circumstances might require to prevent injury to them; if a trespasser was an adult, and apparently possessed of his faculties, the company had a right to presume that he would remove himself from his dangerous position, and if he failed to do so the fault was his own, "and there is, in the absence of willful negligence on its part, no remedy against it for the results of an injury brought upon him by his own recklessness." If the company or its employes used reasonable care after discovering the perilous position of the deceased to avoid injuring him, plaintiff was not entitled to recover. The court modified the said instructions by striking out the words quoted. *Held* erroneous, as the said words were necessary to the correct statement of the rule. Railroad Co. v. Harman's Adm'r, 8 S. E. Rep. 851, 83 Va. 553, followed.

3. The defendant requested the court to charge—*First,* that certain acts and conduct of the deceased, if proven, constituted gross negligence on his part; and, *second,* that if guilty of such negligence the plaintiff could not recover unless the injury was willfully committed. The court modified the said instruction by adding: Unless the injury could have been prevented by the exercise of reasonable care on the part of the trainmen after they discovered the peril of the deceased. *Held,* that the modification was unwarranted, as there was no evidence to show that the peril of the deceased was discovered, or that the injury could have been prevented by the exercise of reasonable care.

This was an action by V. H. Tain, administrator of Thomas H. Sites, against S. F. Tyler, receiver of the Shenandoah Valley Railroad Company, to recover for the killing of plaintiff's intestate. There was judgment for plaintiff, and defendant brings error. Reversed.

W. H. Travers and *Sipe & Harris,* for appellant. *J. E. Roller* and *C. D. Harris,* for appellee.

RICHARDSON, J. This is a writ of error to a judgment of the circuit court of Rockingham county, rendered on the 21st day of October, 1890, in a certain action of trespass on the case, wherein V. H. Tain, sheriff of Rockingham county, and as such, administrator of the estate of Thomas H. Sites, deceased, was plaintiff, and S. F. Tyler, receiver of the Shenandoah Valley Railroad Company, was defendant. The trial court certifies, not the facts proved, but the evidence adduced at the trial. From an inspection of the evidence thus certified, it is impossible to perceive why the court below did not abbreviate the matter by certifying the facts proved, as there certainly is no conflict of evidence as to any material question arising in the case. But, be this as it may, the material facts as established by the plaintiff's testimony alone are these:

Thomas H. Sites, the plaintiff's intestate, who was a deaf-mute, was on the 24th day of May, 1887, while walking on or very near the railroad track of the Shenandoah Valley Railroad Company, about two miles north of Elkton, a station on said road, struck and killed by an engine attached to and drawing a train of freight-cars on said road, which engine and train were then in the control and management of the employes, agents, and servants of said company. From Elkton the Shenandoah Valley Railroad extends northward for nearly three miles through a "level, cleared plain, comprising the rich cultivated river bottoms lying along the east side of the Shenandoah river in that locality. In the midst of this plain, and about two miles from Elkton, the accident occurred, at a point where the track is elevated upon a slight fill, estimated at three feet, with nothing to obstruct the view of the track for a distance of nearly a mile to the north, and an equal distance to the south." About 600 yards north of the point where the accident occurred, a public road crosses the railway, and a short distance beyond, on the left or west side of the railroad, and some 75 yards distant therefrom, is the residence of Mr. Thomas Naylor, at or near whose residence the plaintiff's intestate started to go to the house of Decatur Bear, and seems to have walked along near, but not on, the railroad track, for some distance, and then on the track, or on the ends of the ties on the side of the track, and was so walking when he met the train, by the engine of which he was struck and killed. The accident occurred in the midst of the open plain above described, where there was no obstruction to the view of the track for the distance of near one mile north or south, and at the time of the accident the train was running north, and the plaintiff's intestate walking south, meeting it.

Thomas Naylor, above referred to, was introduced as a witness for the plaintiff, and testified that he lives in Rockingham, six or seven hundred yards from Bear Lithia Springs; that the most direct foot route from his house to the springs is the railway, up to the crossing; that people are in the habit of using this route, and that witness himself used it; that witness knew the plaintiff's intestate, and that he was at the house of the witness on the morning of the accident; that he (Sites) said he was going to Decatur Bear's, which is further south; that the direct route to Decatur Bear's is by the railroad; that he came on the railroad about 75 yards from witness' house, about 2 miles from Elkton; that it was about 500 yards from the house of witness to where he could see the road straight; that he (plaintiff's intestate) could not be seen all the way from Elkton,—trees would be in the way at the curve; that witness was at home that day, and knew of the accident; that he had heard the whistle for "down brakes;" heard the trainmen say to the section boss that they had struck a

man. They went back. running. When witness got there, he saw Sites. He was then dead. He remained there some time. And that witness heard no whistle before the one for "down brakes." Such is the testimony in chief of Thomas Naylor, and it signifies but little. However, his evidence on cross-examination was more to the point. He says he had heard the whistle of the train at Elkton; that Sites said, "I believe I will go up to Decatur Bear's;" that witness told him not to go until after the train came down; that Sites said he would not walk on the railroad; that witness wrote on a little tablet, that Sites carried with him, that the train was in Elkton; that Sites kept next to the fence until he came to the crossing; that he went upon the track at the crossing, and that at about 150 yards, or perhaps 200 yards, from the crossing, he was killed, only 2 miles from Elkton; that the train stopped 500 yards from where it struck Sites; that they were trying to stop. They stopped and backed back. It was a heavy train. Was still down grade from Elkton to where Sites was killed. The grade rises towards the north at crossing. He was walking towards the train when struck. He walked from place to place. Was a good workman. Wrote a good hand, and spelled well.

George W. Murray, another witness introduced by the plaintiff, testified that he is a plasterer, and was on the day of the accident working on Bear's Hotel, in East Rockingham; that he was working on the north end of the hotel, about 100 yards from the Shenandoah Valley Railroad, 2 miles from Elkton; that Whitlock, witness' son, and a colored man were with him; that the colored man is now dead; that witness saw the accident; that at the time they were working on the hotel, overlooking railroad; that witness' son was looking through a fieldglass. "We came up to the window. We saw a man walking pretty fast on the track, with his head down. He was on the far side from us, on the outside of the rails. While looking, we saw a train approaching. Had heard no warning or signal. Was surprised to see it. Were not expecting it. They came right together. It knocked him off. Ran fifty yards, blew 'down brakes,' and stopped. The train had knocked Sites down the bank. The men came back and looked at him. A material train from Elkton came down, and picked him up, and carried him to Elkton. Was familiar with footpath. A man going from Naylor's would have taken that route. People were in the habit of taking this course. Have not noticed particular, but have seen several people passing from that route. Was well acquainted with Sites. He was deaf and mute. On one occasion, he called my attention to the fact that he could hear a little. I do not remember his ever having shown that he ever heard a train whistle. He was in a bending position when I saw him, and recognised him as Sites. It was down grade to near the point where he was killed, but grade on a rise where it struck him. He was walking on the outside of the rail, on the end of the ties, when he was struck." That there was a slight ascending grade north of the point where the accident occurred, but witness could not state the distance from the crossing or the grade, and that there were about 18 cars in the train, but witness did not know whether they were loaded or not. On cross-examination this witness testified that it was up grade, going north from the point of the accident; that the accident occurred 200 yards south of the crossing, and 500 or 600 yards of Bear's house; that witness paid no attention to the distance; that the train was an ordinary freight train composed of 18 or 19 cars; that, for a portion of the way from Elkton, it was down grade; that Sites was working at Bear's as a farm hand, but witness did not know what wages he got, but supposed he could earn $15 or $20 per month; that witness had had no experience with deaf-mutes; thought Sites had heard knocking in the building; that he had on one occasion called witness' attention, by putting his hands to his ears, that he heard the sound of the hammer. And the witness further said: "He [Sites] was a mute, and you know how much a deaf-mute can hear. Sites made the impression upon my mind that he heard better than Decatur Bear. Bear could hear trains whistle at Elkton, and Sites could hear better." On redirect examination, this witness (Murray) stated that there was no obstruction in the way of seeing the train, looking south to Elkton, for a mile or more; that the train was nearly 100 yards from Sites when witness and those with him first saw it; that the train was moving slowly,—was creeping upon him,—and that there was no trouble about getting out of the way, if he saw it.

A. J. Whitlock, another witness introduced by the plaintiff, testified that he is a plasterer; was working for Murray at Bear's Spring at the time of the accident; was on the third story of the building; that Murray and Murray's son were there; no one else than he saw the accident; that he was fixing to go to work; that Murray said, "There is a train coming," and handed him the glasses; that by the time he caught the focus the train was nearly opposite the hotel; that he saw a man on the track whom he took to be Sites, who was walking with his head hanging down; that witness saw him throw up his hands just as the engine struck him; that, when the train passed, some one said, "Where is the man who was on the track?" The train stopped, and train hands came back, and some one joined him, and went back. That after a while a train came from Elkton, and took him (Sites) to Elkton; that the train came for that purpose. It was an hour after the accident. That there was a rain and thunder storm, and it had not quit raining when the train came down; that witness had known Sites all his life; that Sites could not talk any, and could hear but very little; that he was a stout man, and, as witness supposed, was 24 or 25 years old. On cross-examination this witness testifies that Sites was several hundred yards ahead of the train when witness first saw him; that witness cannot tell whether he was on the track or not. He was on opposite side from witness, and witness could not tell whether he was on the track or on the side. That his hands went up just as the train got there; that witness was not certain whether the train struck him or not. And on re-examination this witness says that he heard no whistle or noise before the man was struck; that he heard the noise of the train when it came opposite Bear's house, and that the train whistled several times after it ran past, and stopped. On recross-examination the same witness testifies that Sites could not hear any one talk to him; that witness had seen him point up when it thundered; that he could not communicate except by writing; and that, if one could walk up behind him and halloo, he could hear.

Such is the testimony of the three witnesses, Thomas Naylor, George Murray, and A. J. Whitlock; and they testified to the only really material facts in the case. They, except the witness Naylor, were at work on Bear's hotel, 500 yards distant from the place of the accident, and at that distance witnessed what they testified to. The witness Naylor was at the time of the accident at his house, the point from which the plaintiff's intestate took his departure for Decatur Bear's, just a short time before the accident. One of these witnesses, George W. Murray, as before stated, testified that the plaintiff's intestate, Thomas H. Sites, made the impression on his mind that he could hear better than Decatur Bear, who could from his house hear a train whistle at Elkton, a distance of 500 yards.

Other witnesses introduced by the plaintiff testify as to Sites' capacity for hearing. For instance, George Clatterbuck testifies that he lives about 3½ miles from Harrisonburg. Knew Sites tolerably well, and had worked with him on farm and sawmill. That Sites could not talk, but he could make a noise; that, when the engine would pop off, he would look around and grin, and that witness noticed that he could hear;" that, when fencing plank were carried out, he would look up, and when they were thrown down would motion to his ear as if he felt the jar; that when he was about the mill the engineman, when he wanted him to do anything, would blow the whistle, and Sites would look up, and then they would motion to him what they wanted him to do. And on cross-examination this witness stated that "Sites would be 30 or 40 yards off when the whistle would blow, and that it was in the winter of 1882 that he saw him hear the whistle." Abraham Billhimer testifies that he knew Sites all his life. Lived near him until 1870, and then moved off four miles. That Sites was a deaf-mute, and could not hear anything except something loud and terrific, like thunder, which seemed to scare him very much; that witness was with him a good deal; that, after witness moved to the mountains, Sites came to pick cherries; that the whistle blew at a mile, one-fourth to one-half of a mile, off, and Sites motioned to witness that it was dinner-time, and that he knew because the whistle had blown. On cross-examination this witness stated that Sites had motioned to him that he knew it was dinner-time because he had heard the whistle, and that this occurred eight years before. This witness also undertook to repeat the signs by which he communicated with Sites on the occasion referred to. The plaintiff also introduced Mrs. Mary Sites, who testifies that she lives near Keezletown; that Tom Sites was her son; that she does not know where her husband is; that he is an old man, 75 years old, and did not contribute to her support in 1887; that Tom was all her support in 1887, and that he was in his thirty-second or thirty-third year when he was killed; that he was a good hand, quiet and industrious, but was high-tempered when provoked. On cross-examination, Mrs. Sites testified that her son Tom was away from home a great deal; that he was hurt by a train at Linville on the Baltimore & Ohio Railroad; that he knew the train time, but the train was late at the time he was hurt at Linville; that witness had often cautioned him about going on the railroads; that she had so cautioned him in the last 12 months before he was killed; that she could not estimate what he had furnished her, but that he would bring her flour, sugar, and coffee, meat, etc., just when she needed it, and that he had no family. The plaintiff also introduced the tables of life expectancy in Matthew's Guide. And V. H. Tain, the plaintiff in the cause, was introduced on his own behalf, and testified that Tom Sites' father was an old man, and was in the almshouse. This is all the testimony on behalf of the plaintiff.

The defendant then introduced C. W. S. Turner, who testified that he knew Tom Sites very well; that witness used the sign language, was born of deaf and mute parents, and had taught at the Deaf, Dumb, and Blind Institution in Staunton; had known Sites 20 years; that Sites was at the Deaf, Dumb, and Blind Institution in Staunton six years; that witness had at his own house frequently conversed with Sites about the danger of being on railroads; that, just after the accident at Linville, witness, having seen him on the railroad track, again cautioned him that all pupils at the Deaf, Dumb, and Blind Institution are first instructed to keep off the railroad track; saw him on the track at Elkton, and told him he had no business on the track, and that Sites said he knew it; that Sites was a total deaf-mute, and was placed at the Deaf, Dumb, and Blind Institution. He spoke no intelligible words. Deaf-mutes are sensible to jars and concussions, but the difficulty is to distinguish what they are, or from what source they come. They cannot analyse the sound. That witness saw signs made by Billhimer in his testimony, and by which he professed to have communicated with Sites in manner stated by him, and the signs which he repeated simply mean, in deaf-mute language, the word "two," and nothing more; that, as to Sites' habits, he would do a little work around; people treated him charitably and kindly; that witness regarded him as an object

of charity, and that he often asked witness for money with which to buy tobacco. On cross-examination this witness stated that Sites was a totally deaf mute; that he feels sounds, but does not hear them; "he feels the noise of a plank when it falls, but does not hear it." And on re-examination this witness stated, in substance, that the difficulty with deaf-mutes is to locate the sound and concussions felt by them, that Sites' mathematics were limited; that he could probably keep his accounts of his daily work; that witness had known his father, who is a deaf-mute, when there was cannonading at Richmond, to recognise the fact by putting his hands against the window; that it was sensation without the power of location; that he was totally deaf, notwithstanding these sensations. And witness, as an expert, states that, when a man reproduces sound, he hears, and not otherwise. As an evidence that deaf-mutes do not hear sounds, they look round, up, and try to locate the cause. C. C. Diehl, another witness introduced by defendant, said that he was the conductor on the train in question; that he was in his cabin at the time of the accident, but knew nothing of the accident until he was told by one of his brakemen that a man had been struck; that witness' position on a train is first one place, and then another; that witness got off as soon as he could, and found a man lying down the bank, head foremost; that the body was left in charge of Brakeman Sandridge, as his train had to go on; that he did not know how many cars were in his train, but thought there were from 15 to 20 loads; that the grade was a descending grade; and that between 700 to 900 yards would be required to stop a train at that point, running 20 miles an hour, if it were running on schedule time,—sometimes more, sometimes less. Did not remember any signal for "down brakes." Ran 200 or 300 yards beyond dead body, owing to rising grade. Stopped in that distance. That Mr. Cranch was engineman; that he is a steady, sober, cautious engine-driver and man; that deceased was killed 200 yards north of curve, which is sharp; that trains could be seen a half-mile from where Sites was killed, looking south; was killed between two curves,—one north, the other south. "We could have seen him. Nothing to obstruct the view except some trees, and we could have seen through or by them." William Mills, another witness introduced by the defendant, testified that he was working on the road-bed of the Shenandoah Valley Railroad, north of the place of the accident about 2,300 feet, at the time of the accident. First heard the train blow "down brakes." By the time it came near witness, it stopped. Sandridge said a man was struck. Witness ran back with train hands to where he was, and the train followed. He was lying with his head down the bank. The ballast train came down, and took him to Elkton. The track hands were working opposite Naylor's house. Grade is down where Sites was struck. "It rises just after you reach the crossing. It is 1,890 feet from public road crossing to where Sites was struck. There was no fog or anything to obscure the view from point of accident. Could see one mile or three-quarters any way. Could see the mill south of the place of the accident. There were some trees, but they did not intercept the view of the train. Could see engine clear back to Elkton. The track is on a fill of about three feet at the point of the accident."

The defendant also introduced I. B. Cranch, the engineman in charge of the engine in question, who testified that he saw a man walking in front of the train, and coming towards the engine, on the left side of the track. The engine was a Baldwin engine, with an extension boiler, and on this engine, for 25 or 30 yards ahead, the engineman cannot see a man on the left side of the track. Witness did not see the man when he was struck. When witness last saw him, he was walking right towards the train, on the left side of the track, and did not pay much attention to him. As he was walking towards the train, going towards the left, witness supposed he would step off. Witness saw the man about the time the injector flew off. This means that the water stopped flowing into the boiler. Witness shut off the steam to correct this, which did not require a minute. Witness did not take much notice of the man, because at the time there were other objects on the track beyond that attracted his attention, which proved to be workmen at work on the track in a cut some distance beyond. Witness never gives signals when persons are coming towards the train, and never stops train for persons on the track, because he supposes they will get off. That witness had never made a run without meeting people on the track, and they always got off. It is down grade from Elkton to place of accident. The train was equal to 18 loaded cars; 1½ empty cars being counted as a loaded car. Could not have stopped train under 200 or 300 yards by blowing down brakes and reversing engine. The fireman said, "You have knocked a man off the track." "Stopped train as soon as I could. Backed train two train-lengths; got off, and went back. There was a bruise on the face, which was the only part hurt. The end of pilot seemed to have struck him. If standing on the ground beyond the track, a man would be struck in that way at this point. Left a brakeman in charge with him. Did not know the man. Had no knowledge of his condition. He could have seen the train for some distance. If we had to stop every time we see a person on the track we would have no schedule at all for running trains. I saw Sites some distance down the track. View not obstructed when injector flies off. You must shut off steam, and then engine can run some minutes in that way." P. P. Shiflett, another witness introduced by the defendant, testified that, as justice of the peace, he presided at the inquest upon the body of Thomas H. Sites. Saw that his face was bruised, but did not remember which side of the face. That the body was lying at the station for some hours, and no steps taken to bury it; that

a subscription was proposed, and a few did the necessary work to get the body ready for burial; and that Mr. Shipp read the finding of the jury. W. J. Runkle, another witness for the defendant, testified that he was one of the coroner's jury: that the face of the deceased was bruised on the left cheek; was cut and bleeding; that the body was brought there several hours after the accident; that there was no injury back of the head; only injury was on the face. On cross-examination, witness stated that the body was placed in the depot several hours after the accident, and remained there until 12 o'clock next day; no coffin; that it was sent for by Mr. Sites' friends from 10 to 2 o'clock on the day after he was killed; that the citizens had taken some steps to have the body buried; and that the coroner's inquest was at night. And then the plaintiff introduced R. A. Thurmond, who testified that he knew Tom Sites; that Sites lived near Taylor Springs, and had worked for witness; that he was not a lazy man, by any means; was a good hand in harvest field; took most of his wages in bacon, etc., which he took home to his mother; and that witness paid him 50 cents a day in harvest. On cross-examination the witness stated that Sites helped him to harvest in 1886; that he worked for witness whenever witness called on him; and that witness employed him two or three days at a time.

This, as certified by the trial court, was all the evidence adduced at the trial; and it is the subject of the defendant's bill of exceptions No. 1, when, in the nature of things, it should have been the last bill of exceptions taken by the defendant. Taken all together, it cannot in reason be said that there is any real conflict between the evidence of the plaintiff and that of the defendant. It is true that four of the witnesses introduced for the plaintiff, to-wit, George W. Murray, A. J. Whitlock, George Clatterbuck, and Abraham Billhimer, testify to circumstances from which they seem to draw the inference that the deceased was not entirely bereft of the sense of hearing, or, in other words, that he was not a totally deaf mute, but could hear some. For instance the witness Murray, a plasterer, who says that he had had no experience with deaf-mutes, yet testifies that he thought Sites had heard knocking in the building, as he had called witness' attention on one occasion, by putting his hands to his ears, that he heard the sound of the hammer, and he adds: "He was a mute, and you know how much a deaf-mute can hear. Sites made the impression on my mind that he could hear better than Decatur Bear. Bear could hear trains whistle at Elkton, and Sites could hear better." Now, we are not informed whether or not Decatur Bear was a deaf-mute; but he certainly was not if, as stated by Murray, he could hear the sound of the whistle from Elkton to his house, a distance of not less than 500 yards; and if the plaintiff's intestate, Sites, could hear better than Decatur Bear, then he was not totally deaf,—a circumstance which, if true, could by no means enhance the plaintiff's claim to a right of recovery against the defendant. But it was indisputably established that the deceased was a totally deaf mute. It is therefore obvious that Murray's statement, though not corruptly so, was false. He ignorantly failed to distinguish between concussion or violent agitation of the air, which is felt by a deaf-mute, and not heard, and the sound produced by the same concussion, which is heard by one who is possessed of the sense of hearing. This is fully explained by the witness C. W. S. Turner, introduced by the defendant, who knew the deceased well, and had known him for 20 years; that witness was born of deaf-mute parents, used the sign language, and had taught at the Deaf, Dumb, and Blind Institution in Staunton, and that Sites was at said institution six or seven years; that Sites was a totally deaf mute, and was placed at the Deaf, Dumb, and Blind institution among the totally deaf mutes; that he spoke no intelligible words; that deaf-mutes are sensible to jars and concussions, but that the difficulty is to distinguish what they are, or from what source they come. This witness, who evidently understood the subject about which he testified, effectually disposes of the false or mistaken testimony of the four witnesses who testified to the effect that in their opinion Sites was not a totally deaf mute, and he specially explodes the simulated testimony of the witness Billhimer, who says that Sites came to his house to get cherries, and that while there the whistle blew at a mill from a quarter to one-half mile distant; that Sites motioned to him (Billhimer) that it was dinner-time, and that he (Sites) knew because the whistle had blown. And on cross-examination this witness (Billhimer) stated that Sites had motioned to him that he (Sites) knew it was dinner-time because he had heard the whistle, and the witness Billhimer undertook to repeat the signs by which he communicated with Sites on the occasion referred to. The witness C. W. S. Turner, who was present when Billhimer testified, and witnessed the signs repeated by him, says that the signs repeated by Billhimer, and by which he professed to have communicated with Sites, simply mean, in deaf-mute language, the word "two," and nothing more. And the witness Turner, an expert in the treatment of deaf-mutes, and who knew Sites well, says that he was a totally deaf mute; that he felt sounds, but did not hear them; that the concussion or shock felt by deaf-mutes was sensation without the power of location; and as an expert the witness states that, when a man reproduces sound, he hears, and not otherwise, and, as evidence that the deaf-mutes do not hear sounds, they look up and around, and try to locate the cause. This witness knew the facts which he testified, and, under all the circumstances, his testimony should have been received and treated as absolutely conclusive of the fact that the plaintiff's testate was a deaf-mute, and could not hear sounds. And on the other hand the testimony of Murray, Whitlock, Clatterick, and Billhimer should have been disgarded, because neither of them was informed as to the fact about which he testified, and because their evidence went to the establishment of a fact, the existence of which was, in the nature of things, impossible. It is therefore clear that in no just sense can it be said that there was any real conflict of evidence on the point under consideration. Hence the facts, which are few and simple, and not the evidence, should have been certified.

Then, whether viewed in the light of all the evidence adduced on both sides, or in the light of the evidence of the plaintiff (defendant in error) alone, the simple case presented is this: On the 24th day of May, 1887, Thomas H. Sites, a deaf-mute, who had once before received an injury by being in or near the railroad track, and who had been repeatedly warned by friends and acquaintances to keep off the railroad track, and who had been so warned on the day of his death, and only a very short time before he was killed, while walking on or near the track of the Shenandoah Valley Railroad in the county of Rockingham, and meeting a train on said road approaching him from the direction opposite to that in which he was going, was struck and killed by the engine attached to and drawing said train, the accident occurring on an open plain, where the view of the approaching train was unobstructed for a distance of near one mile. The deceased, though a deaf-mute, was possessed of his other faculties unimpaired, including that of sight, and was an active, strong man, some 32 or 33 years of age. At the time of the accident the train was going north, and Sites was coming, meeting it, and walking on the left side of the track, on the outside of the rail, viewed from the position of the engineman and the direction the train was moving. And the undisputed testimony is that the blow received by the deceased was on the left side of the face, there being no sign of a blow elsewhere on his body; that the deceased was walking rapidly, meeting the train, with his head down; that the engineman saw deceased approaching the train on left side of the track, and supposed he would get off; that the engine was a Baldwin engine, with an extension boiler, on which, for 25 or 30 yards ahead, the engineman cannot see a man on the left side of the track; that the engineman did not see deceased when he was struck, but was told of it by the fireman, whose position was on the left side of the boiler; that when the train was stopped, as soon as could be, and was backed two train-lengths, and was stopped, the trainmen alighted, walked back to the point of collision, and found deceased lying with his head down the bank, dead; and that signals are never given when persons are coming towards a train, and trains are never stopped for persons on the track, because it is supposed they will get off.

Such being the facts, we may safely venture the remark that not only was there no ground upon which the plaintiff (the defendant in error here) could possibly be entitled to a recovery from the defendant, (the plaintiff in error here,) but that, if there was ever a case more clearly than all others a case of contributory negligence on the part of the party complaining, this is that case. In the light of the simple and undisputed facts of this case, there can be no difficulty in ascertaining and applying the principles of law appropriate thereto. Though there is in no just sense any conflict of evidence as to any material fact, yet, excluding all the evidence of the defendant, (the plaintiff in error here,) there can be no doubt that the facts established by the evidence of the plaintiff (the defendant in error here) present in the most unquestionable form a plain case of gross negligence on the part of the plaintiff's intestate,—a case so plain and clear as to preclude the idea of any just claim to a legal recovery against the railroad company. That evidence fails to disclose any fact or circumstance upon which to base any just claim to a recovery, nor can any just inference be drawn therefrom to warrant such a recovery. In other words, when all the evidence of the plaintiff below (the defendant in error here) is carefully scrutinized and weighed, not even one fact or circumstance is disclosed which reasonably tends to show any carelessness or neglect of duty on the part of the railroad company or its agents, servants, or employes. The substance of the charge in the declaration is that the deceased came to his death by reason of the carelessness and negligence of the agents, servants, and employes of the railroad company in running the engine and train in question. Such being the complaint, it must be established by proof, or there can be no recovery.

In the present case, just before the accident the plaintiff's intestate was at the house of Thomas Naylor, a witness for the plaintiff, who lived within 75 yards of the railroad track, and some 2 miles north of Elkton station. The plaintiff's intestate expressed his intention to go to Decatur Bear's, in the direction from which the train was to come, and Naylor, who had heard the train whistle at Elkton, informed the deceased that the train was then at Elkton, and that he had better not start until the train passed; but deceased persisted in his purpose, saying he would not walk on the track, and started, walking in a pathway near the track until he reached the road crossing, some 200 yards distant, where he got on the track, and kept it until he was knocked down and killed, and at a point where the view of the approaching train was unobstructed for the distance of near one mile.

Now, what is the law of the case? This court, in Railroad Co. v. Harman's Adm'r, 83 Va. 553, 8 S. E Rep. 251, approving the rule as laid down in 2 Wood, Ry. Law, 1267, said: "The rule may be said to be that a railroad company is bound to keep a reasonable lookout for trespassers upon its track, and is bound to exercise such care as the circumstances require to prevent injury to them. If the person seen upon the track is an adult person, and apparently in the possession of his or her faculties, the company has a right to presume that he will exercise his senses, and remove himself from his dangerous position, and if he fails to do so, and is injured, the fault is his own, and there is, in

the absence of willful negligence on its part, no remedy against the company for the results of an injury brought upon him by his own recklessness." The plaintiff's intestate was a trespasser upon the company's track, with fresh warning of the early approach of the train. Naylor said to him, by writing on the little tablet he carried with him: "The train is at Elkton. Now, don't go up to Bear's until the train comes down." He replied, by the same medium of communication: "I won't walk on the track." But he was heedless of the warning, and of his promise not to walk on the track, and in a very few minutes got on the track, and met a horrible death. Though a deaf-mute, his vision was perfect, and it was all the more incumbent upon him to look and see the approaching train, the full view of which was in no way obstructed, and to leave the track, but this he did not do. To all appearances, he was in possession of all his faculties, and the company had the right to presume that he would exercise his sense, and get off the track. That his own careless and reckless act was the sole, proximate cause of his death is a proposition too clear for argument. The case is in every essential particular ruled by the case of Railroad Co. v. Harman's Adm'r, supra. It follows, therefore, that the court below erred in overruling the defendant's motion to set aside the verdict of the jury and grant a new trial.

At the trial below the defendant asked for five several instructions to the jury, the 5th and last of which the court gave, but refused to give the 1st, 2d, 3d, and 4th of the series as asked, and modified each of them, and as modified gave them. To which action of the court, modifying said instructions 1, 2, 3, and 4, the defendant excepted; and this is the subject of the defendant's second bill of exceptions. The first instruction is in these words: "The court instructs the jury that a railroad company is bound to keep a reasonable lookout for trespassers on its track, and to exercise such care as the circumstances require to prevent injury to them. If trespasser is adult, and apparently possesses his faculties, the company has a right to presume that he will exercise his senses, and remove himself from his dangerous position, and if he fails to do so, and is injured, the fault is his own, and there is, in the absence of willful negligence on its part, no remedy against it for the results of an injury brought upon him by his own recklessness, and he is not entitled to recover if the defendant or his employes used reasonable care, after the discovery of the plaintiff's perilous position, to avoid injury to him." The court modified this instruction by striking out, in the latter part thereof, the words, "and there is, in the absence of willful negligence on its part, no remedy against it for the results of an injury brought upon him by his own recklessness." That the court erred in thus emasculating this instruction is too plain for argument. The words stricken out are essential features of the rule laid down in Railroad Co. v. Harman's Adm'r, and the precise words were employed by this court in laying down the rule in that case, and they are essential to the correct statement of the rule itself. In thus striking out these words in the presence of the jury, the court not only deprived the defendant of the benefit of a well-settled principle, peculiarly applicable to its case, but in effect said to the jury that the language stricken out was no part of the rule, and that there was, in the absence of willful negligence on the part of the defendant, a remedy against it for the results of an injury brought upon the deceased by his own recklessness. It is useless to pursue the subject further. The error of the court is palpable.

The 2d, 3d, and 4th instructions, in the main, simply assert two propositions: *First*, that certain acts and conduct of the deceased, put in issue in the cause, if proven, constitute gross negligence on his part; and, *second*, that if guilty of such contributory negligence the plaintiff could not recover, unless the injury was willfully committed. Each of these instructions was modified by the addition of the words, "unless they shall further believe from the evidence that the injury could have been prevented by the exercise of reasonable care by the servants of the defendant in charge of the train, after they discovered the plaintiff's intestate in a perilous position." Not only did the court err in making this addition, or additions of similar import, to each of these instructions, but there was not a *scintilla* of evidence in the cause upon which to predicate the modification. By this modification the court, without warrant, assumed that the deceased was discovered by the agents and servants of the company in charge of the train in a perilous position, and the jury were left to infer that by the exercise of reasonable care the injury could have been prevented. There is not only no evidence that the peril of the deceased was observed, or that, in the exercise of reasonable care, it could have been discovered in time to prevent the mischief, but, on the contrary, the proof is positive and conclusive that while the engine man saw the deceased, an adult, and apparently in the possession of all his faculties, on the track, and coming, meeting the train, and inclining to the left side of the track in the direction the train was going, by reason of the extension boiler the engineman's view of the deceased was obstructed for the distance of 25 or 30 yards ahead, and that the engineman, from the direction the deceased when last seen by him was taking, supposed he would step off and out of danger. The law is that he had a right to presume that the deceased, an adult and apparently in the possession of his senses, would use them, and remove himself from his position of danger. Having the right, under the well-settled law, to so presume, that is the end of the matter. It is not pretended that the engineman knew the deceased, or knew that he was a deaf-mute. In fact the deafness of the deceased in no way palliated his gross negligence, which was the sole, proximate cause of his death. For these reasons the judgment of the court below must be reversed and annulled, and the verdict of the jury set aside, and the cause remanded for a new trial to be had therein in accordance with the views expressed in this opinion.

FOWLER v. HESS.

(Supreme Court of Appeals of Virginia. Dec. 3, 1891.)

Appeal from circuit court, Amherst county.

Suit by Fowler against Hess for an accounting. Judgment dismissing the bill. Complainant appeals. Reversed.

C. L. Scott, for appellant.

LEWIS, P. Without going into the voluminous details of the accounts between the parties, which fully appear from the commissioner's report and the depositions returned therewith, we will say that we see no reason to distrust the result reached by the commissioner, except as to the following items, viz.: $258.33 charged against the defendant for 15¼ months' services, $155 for board for the same time, and $179.21 for use and occupation of the farm; the last item being charged against the plaintiff. We are of opinion that these three items ought to be stricken out of the report. The evidence does not show that the plaintiff was entitled to anything as compensation for his services in looking after the farm and other interests of the defendant, or that, over and above the use and occupation of the farm, and the products thereof which were received by the plaintiff, anything ought to be paid him. There was no definite contract between the parties on the subject, and the proof does not show that his services were reasonably worth more. With these items stricken out of the account, there would be a balance due the plaintiff of $143.31, for which sum he is entitled to a decree. The decree dismissing the bill will therefore be reversed, and a decree entered here in favor of the appellant for the last-mentioned sum, and costs.

HUMPHREYS v. RICHMOND & M. R. Co.

(Supreme Court of Appeals of Virginia. Dec. 3, 1891.)

RIGHT OF WAY — CONTRACT — DELIVERY — PAROL EVIDENCE.

1. An agreement to deed a right of way through certain land, in consideration of the construction of the road, may be shown by parol evidence to have been delivered to the president of the road, on condition that it should not be used unless the withholding of it would defeat the building of the road, or the board of directors of the road should make compensation for the right of way.

2. After the completion of the road, although there had been no necessity for using the contract, and although no compensation had been made by the directory, and none asked of them, the president turned the contract over to the right-of-way agent of the road, who had knowledge of the conditions on which it was delivered to the president. *Held*, that the contract was void, and the owner might recover the damages to his land.

Suit by T. F. Humphreys against the Richmond & Mecklenburg Railroad Company for the enjoining of an action at law, to have a contract declared void, and for other relief. From a decree for defendant, complainant appeals. Reversed.

W. W. Henry and *Finch & Atkins*, for appellant. *T. N. Williams* and *B. B. Munford*, for appellee.

RICHARDSON, J. This is an appeal from a decree of the circuit court of Mecklenburg county, rendered on the 15th day of April, 1889, in the suit in chancery therein pending, wherein T. F. Humphreys was plaintiff, and the Richmond & Mecklenburg Railroad Company was defendant. The case, briefly outlined, is as follows: In the year 1863, T. F. Humphreys purchased a tract of land in the county of Mecklenburg, on Roanoke river, near the town of Clarksville, of one Joseph G. Snead. Subsequent to this purchase, in a suit brought to enforce a prior lien, the same land was sold on the 5th day of July, 1870, under a decree of court, and was bought in by said Humphreys, and he thereby became the owner in fee of said land. Prior to the purchase by Humphreys, to-wit, in the year 1860, the Roanoke Valley Railroad Company had entered upon said land without taking the steps required by law for the purpose, and, without any title to same, had erected thereon earth-works and masonry for the purposes of its railway, and in the construction of said earth-works and masonry took or occupied and seriously damaged several acres of valuable river bottom land belonging to said tract. The Roanoke Valley Railroad Company became insolvent, and did not complete any part of its proposed line of railway, and some time in the year 1880 the Richmond & Mecklenburg Railroad Company became the owner of the property, rights, and franchises of said Roanoke Valley Railroad Company. Thereupon the Richmond & Mecklenburg Railroad Company entered into an agreement with the Richmond & West Point Railway & Warehouse Company, through the Richmond & Danville Railroad Company, which controlled said Richmond & West Point Railway & Warehouse Company, to build the proposed Richmond & Mecklenburg Railroad from Charlottesville to Keysville, in the county of Charlotte, and a point on the Richmond & Danville Railroad, for a certain amount of the first mortgage bonds of the Richmond & Mecklenburg Railroad Company; but upon the following conditions: (1) That the Richmond & Mecklenburg Railroad Company should acquire a perfect title to all the franchises, property, rights of way, and road-bed of the old Roanoke Valley Railroad Company, the same having been mortgaged and in the hands of trustees; the same to be purchased from said trustees for $300,000, payable in the paid-up capital stock of the Richmond & Mecklenburg Railroad Company. (2) That the said trustees should transfer and assign to the said terminal and warehouse company the said $300,000 of paid-up stock of the Richmond & Mecklenburg Railroad Company. This arrangement having been effected, and the conditions aforesaid complied with, thereupon P. F. Howard was employed by the Richmond & Mecklenburg Railroad Company to acquire for it the rights of way along the line of the proposed road. In furtherance of that object, he and John B. McPhail, the president of the Richmond & Mecklenburg Railroad Company, approached T. F. Humphreys, and requested him to donate the right of way through his said land; but Humphreys declined to do so, saying he had already subscribed $1,000 to the capital stock of said company, which was as much as he was able to give it. It seems, however, to have been thought by McPhail that the refusal of Humphreys to donate the right of way through his land, if known, would be injurious to the scheme for securing the donation of the right of way from others along the line. He therefore called on Humphreys again, and proposed a special arrangement. Land-owners along the line having been asked to sign a general paper binding them, respectively, to donate the right of way through their lands, Humphreys was asked to sign a separate paper, of similar import, which was to be held by McPhail, and not to be delivered to the railroad company unless compensation was allowed him or the construction of the road would be prevented by withholding such paper; and, McPhail insisting that the demand for compensation might endanger the building of the road, Humphreys signed and delivered to McPhail the paper, to be held by him subject to the conditions aforesaid. But, after securing said paper, under such circumstances, without securing compensation to Humphreys, or making any effort to do so, although the company had ample assets out of which to make the compensation, McPhail, long after the building of said road was assured, delivered the paper so executed by Humphreys to said P. F. Howard, the regularly employed agent of said Richmond & Mecklenburg Railroad Company, to acquire for it the rights of way along the line of its road, and who was present when said paper was executed and delivered by Humphreys to McPhail, and was fully cognizant of the condition aforesaid upon which it was executed and delivered. Subsequently, and prior to the institution of the present suit, the Richmond & Mecklenburg Railroad Company brought an action at law in the circuit court of Mecklenburg county against said T. F. Humphreys, the object of which was to collect from him $700, the balance claimed to be due on his said subscription of $1,000; and at the October term, 1885, of said court, with the leave of court, said Humphreys filed his bill against said Richmond & Mecklenburg Railroad Company, setting forth substantially the facts above stated, and praying for an injunction to restrain said railroad company from proceeding in said action at law until the further order of the court; that said paper of October 3, 1881, be declared null and void; that the damages to the plaintiff's land be set off against said subscription; and that the defendant company be required to answer, but waiving answer under oath; and for general relief. A temporary injunction was accordingly awarded the plaintiff, but on condition of his confessing judgment in said action at law for the said balance due on said subscription, which was done. The Richmond & Mecklenburg Railroad Company answered the plaintiff's bill, and claimed that while it may be true, as alleged, that the Roanoke Valley Railroad Company entered upon the land in question about the year 1860, without any authority, and while it may be true that said corporation had no title to said right of way, yet insists that the plaintiff is estopped from raising a question of title as to that corporation, for the reason that about October, 1881, by a certain paper, he gave the unconditional right of way through his low grounds to Maj. John B. McPhail, then and now president of the Richmond & Mecklenburg Railroad Company, and with its answer exhibited said paper, or a copy thereof, marked "A." And the said company in its answer denies that it ever entered upon the lands of the plaintiff without permission and in disregard of his rights, but says "that the authority under the paper writing referred to was complete, and which authority was never questioned by the plaintiff, although it was a long time after the paper was executed by him and delivered to Maj. John B. McPhail before respondent began to work on that part of the right of way given by said paper, which intervening time afforded every opportunity for the plaintiff to make any demand he thought proper for compensation, or to object to a continuance of work, and yet said complainant never in any way objected to the work, or said one thing about pay, which, respondent submits, is very strange upon his part, if, under said paper, he was entitled to it." The defendant company denies having ever injured the lands of complainant, but say that said land, if injured, was injured long before by the same embankment placed there by another railroad company, and that, even if the lands have been injured, it is by no fault of respondent, etc. Such is the answer, omitting its merely argumentative features, except that it concludes with a prayer that the injunction awarded the plaintiff be dissolved, and that he be required to specifically perform his agreement to convey said right of way to respondent, etc. Depositions were taken by both parties, and on the 15th day of April, 1889, the cause came on to be heard, when a decree was rendered dissolving the injunction theretofore awarded in the cause, and dismissing the plaintiff's bill, and from that decree the case is here on appeal.

The case presented for our determination turns upon the legal effect of Paper A, executed on the 3d of October, 1881, by the appellant, T. F. Humphreys, and delivered to John B. McPhail, to be delivered by him to the Richmond & Mecklenburg Railroad Company upon certain conditions; which paper is as follows: "In consideration of the advantage to be derived from the construction of the Richmond & Mecklenburg Railroad, I promise and bind myself that I will, when thereto requested by the president of the Richmond & Mecklenburg Railroad Company, or such person as may be

authorized by him to make the request, grant and convey to the said company so much of my land as will be sufficient for the construction and convenient use of said railroad through my tract of land, not exceeding the width limited by the law of Virginia in case of condemnation of lands for railroads; such grant to be with condition that, in using such land for the railroad, cattle-guards shall be provided where fences cross, if there be any such places, and also the necessary road crossings over the railroad. Given under my hand and seal this 3d day of October, 1881. The words 'so much of my land,' at the beginning of the seventh line above, interlined before signing. [Signed] T. F. HUMPHREYS. [Seal.] Signed, sealed, and delivered in presence of [Signed] J. R. MOPHAIL, Jr. [Signed] P. F. HOWARD."

On the part of the appellant, Humphreys, it is contended that this paper was signed by him and delivered to McPhail upon the express condition, orally agreed upon and understood between them before said paper was signed, that it should be held by McPhail, and not delivered or used, until the directory of the Richmond & Mecklenburg Railroad Company should allow Humphreys compensation for the right of way through his land, unless the withholding of said paper would defeat or imperil the building of the proposed railroad, McPhail agreeing and undertaking, as the agent of Humphreys, to present his claim for compensation to said directory, and to endeavor to secure its allowance, the amount of which was left to the discretion of McPhail. On the other hand, the appellee, the Richmond & Mecklenburg Railroad Company, insists that the paper, on its face, expresses all that was agreed upon and understood between Humphreys and McPhail; that its terms are absolute and unconditional; and that the paper was not signed by Humphreys and delivered to McPhail upon the condition alleged, or upon any condition other than what is expressed on the face of the paper itself; and that the appellant (Humphreys) is bound thereby.

The parties being thus at issue, we must first find whether the fact is as alleged by the appellant; and, second, if so, whether or not such fact may be established by parol evidence, notwithstanding the unconditional character of the paper on its face. The question of fact must be determined by the evidence. Aside from Paper A, relied on by the appellee, the only material evidence introduced on behalf of the railroad company is found in the deposition of John B. McPhail, who was then and is yet the president of the Richmond & Mecklenburg Railroad Company. Contrary to the usual order of procedure, McPhail was the first witness whose deposition was taken in the cause. The only material evidence introduced on behalf of the appellant (Humphreys) is found in the deposition of McPhail himself, and in the deposition of W. W. Wood, who was, at the time of the execution of Paper A, the general counsel of the Richmond & Mecklenburg Railroad Company, and in the depositions of F. J. Lupfort, and the appellant, T. F. Humphreys. These depositions will be referred to in the order named; but it is not necessary to enter into a critical analysis of all that is said in them, much of which is either useless repetition or is matter wholly immaterial.

Omitting all useless repetition, and all irrelevant and immaterial matter, John B. McPhail deposes substantially as follows: That he was president of the Richmond & Mecklenburg Railroad Company in October, 1881, when Paper A was signed by Humphreys and delivered to him, by which Humphreys obligated himself to convey to said railroad company the right of way through his land when requested to do so by said company; that P. F. Howard was at the time accompanying him along the line of road, for the purpose of writing agreements securing to the company rights of way, and that said Howard was, he thinks, present when Paper A was signed by Humphreys and delivered to witness; that the Richmond & Mecklenburg Railroad was built by contract with the Richmond & West Point Terminal Company, and that, by the arrangement between the Richmond & Mecklenburg Company and the Richmond & West Point Terminal Company, one of the conditions imposed by the latter upon the former was that, before it would enter into any contract to build the road, the former should acquire title to the right of way, and turn the same over to the Richmond & West Point Terminal Company, and that this condition was embodied in a proposition submitted by the president (McPhail) of the Richmond & Mecklenburg Railroad Company to the trustees holding the franchises, right of way, and property of the old Roanoke Valley Railroad Company for the county of Mecklenburg, and to such private individuals through whose lands the line of road was located, and who had not conveyed the right of way to the Richmond & Mecklenburg Company. And, in answer to a question, the witness further says: "I have a memorandum which I read to the trustees in submitting the proposition referred to, which is marked '1, 2, 3,' and filed by the witness as part of his deposition." The last question asked McPhail in his examination-in-chief was this: "Did you or did you not agree, as an officer or agent of the Richmond & Mecklenburg Railroad, to pay Mr. T. F. Humphreys for the right of way through his low grounds above referred to?" He answers: "I did not." It may here be observed that this question and answer are not responsive to, but evades, the issue joined between the parties. The allegation in the appellant's bill is not that McPhail, as an officer or agent of the Richmond & Mecklenburg Railroad Company, agreed to pay the appellant (Humphreys) for the right of way in question; but that he, as the agent of Humphreys, agreed and undertook to present his claim to compensation for the right of way to the board of directors of said company, and to urge its allowance, but that he failed to perform his agreement and undertaking, and, in violation of the conditions upon which Paper A was signed by the appellant and delivered ͡ him, he, when neither of the conditions

had happened, and long after the building of the road was assured, delivered said paper to the railroad company, when he should have returned it to the appellant, Humphreys. McPhail was subjected to a very long and searching cross-examination; then to long re-examination and re-cross-examination; and finally was subjected, in effect, to a cross-examination by the counsel of the railroad company, in behalf of which he was introduced as a witness. The substance of this cross-examination, so far as relevant and material, is substantially as follows: In answer to the first question propounded to him, "When you first approached T. F. Humphreys to secure the right of way through his low grounds for the Richmond & Mecklenburg Railroad, did he not decline very promptly to give the same?" McPhail answered, "My recollection is that Mr. Humphreys hesitated, and urged that he should have some compensation for the right of way through his lands." He was then asked whether he secured Paper A at the first interview he had with Humphreys, and he answered that he did not remember. Being asked, "Did you not, in securing the right of way for the Richmond & Mecklenburg Railroad, use a paper with the heading obligating the signers to said paper to give the right of way to said road, and which paper was generally used for that purpose?" McPhail answered: "The papers relating to the right of way were drawn by P. F. Howard, who was employed by the company for that purpose. Some years having elapsed, I do not remember the exact form used. I do not remember whether there was a paper for general signature. I know that single papers were used in many cases." Being then asked to state as many instances where single papers were used as he could remember, he answered that he could not remember any particular number; and, being asked to name a single instance, he failed to recall even one, but said he was unable to give names without refreshing his memory by the record. He was then asked how, not being able to remember a single instance, he was able to swear that in many instances single papers were used, and he answered that he had stated to the best of his knowledge and belief that many single papers were used, and that he could remember transactions without being able to remember the names of parties; but he added: "I am entirely confident that the right-of-way papers will sustain my recollection that single papers were used in numbers of cases." Now, however true all this may be, still the fact stands boldly out that McPhail did not resort to the records to verify the correctness of his statement; nor does he satisfactorily explain why he so confidently remembered that in many cases single papers were used, when he could only recall one single instance, and could not remember the person with whom the transaction was had, and yet failed to remember that when he first approached the appellant, Humphreys, he presented to him the paper for general signature, which he refused to sign, and refused to give the right of way through his land without just compensation. These matters, under other circumstances, would amount to little or nothing; but they become important in view of the fact that the appellant, Humphreys, whose deposition is in the record, among other things testifies positively that McPhail first approached him with the paper for general signature, and solicited his signature thereto, but that he positively refused to sign it or to donate the right of way, giving as a reason for his refusal that he had already subscribed $1,000 to the capital stock of the company, which was as much, if not more, than he was able to give, and that, if the company needed any more of his property, he was entitled to and demanded just compensation therefor. The appellant, Humphreys, made substantially the same statement to W. W. Wood and F. J. Lupfort, as appears from their depositions. In the course of his cross-examination, McPhail was asked this question: "Have you no recollection of any reason assigned by Mr. Humphreys, on your first interview with him, why he declined to give Paper A? Answer. I do not remember that Mr. Humphreys, at any time, positively declined to give the right of way; but I do remember that he hesitated, and urged that he should have some compensation."

Now, this is a singular statement, especially in view of the facts disclosed in the depositions of W. W. Wood, the then general counsel of the Richmond & Mecklenburg Railroad Company, and who had repeated conferences with McPhail, the president of said company, with respect to the refusal of Humphreys to give the right of way through his land, and of F. J. Lupfort, both of whom testify positively that McPhail told them that Humphreys had refused to give the right of way, and urged and induced them, as friends of Humphreys, to see him and use their influence to induce him to recede from the position he had taken, and at the same time urged them to be quiet, and to say nothing about it, as it might influence others who had promised to give the right of way through their lands. They both did call on the same day, though not at the same time, Wood calling once and Lupfort twice; and to each of them Humphreys gave his reasons for refusing to give the right of way when solicited to do so by McPhail, and to each of them he positively refused to recede from his position, and earnestly insisted upon just compensation for the right of way through his land. Lupfort's first visit to Humphreys was in the forenoon; his second, in the afternoon of the same day, when he, in company with McPhail himself, went into the back room of Humphreys' store, where they found P. F. Howard and Humphreys engaged in discussing the matter of the right of way. On this second visit of Lupfort he took no part in the discussion, but stood by and listened to the discussion between Humphreys on the one hand, and McPhail and Howard on the other; and Lupfort says that Humphreys still firmly refused to donate the right of way, and demanded compensation therefor. In the light of the direct

and positive testimony of these two witnesses, it is passing strange that McPhail should say, as he did, that he did not remember that Mr. Humphreys, at any time, positively declined to give the right of way. Moreover, as to what transpired from the time McPhail first approached Humphreys and urged him to donate the right of way until the execution of Paper A, Humphreys himself testifies as follows: "As the work progressed upon the road, before the completion to Clarksville, when sitting at my place of business, two gentlemen entered, one of whom was Maj. McPhail, the other a stranger to me, who was introduced by Maj. McPhail as Mr. Howard, agent of the Richmond & Mecklenburg Railroad to secure the right of way to lands through which it passed, and requesting me to give the right of way through my land. Knowing that it would require some time to explain to Maj. McPhail my position with regard to the matter, I invited him into the rear of my store, to be seated, that I might set forth the facts. I then stated to him that I declined to give the right of way; that I had already subscribed my full share, and all that I felt able to subscribe; and that I thought, if the railroad company required any other property that I had, they ought to pay me its value. In the same conversation I stated to him that I had taken a similar position a few years before, when applied to by the Southern Security Company for right of way. The major seemed much surprised and disappointed, and earnestly urged that I should recede from my position. I was firm, and stated to him that, when taking a similar position with the Southern Security Company, I had stated the facts to a mutual friend, whose name I gave, who fully approved of the position I took. I also think I stated that I would derive neither profit, honor, nor thanks from making a donation to the corporation. Maj. McPhail urged that the effect would be bad, expressed his regrets, and left with Mr. Howard, evidently discomfited. The next day parties came to me and expressed surprise at what they had heard about my declining to give the right of way, and repeating some fabulous stories as to charges that I had proposed to make for the right of way. Later in the day Maj. McPhail again came in, and wished to know if I had reconsidered the matter. I told him I had thought over it, but saw no reason to change my position, and again repeated the arguments used on the previous day. The major then suggested that he had devised a plan which he thought would meet the case. He then suggested that, as I refused to sign the general paper for relinquishment of lands, he would prepare a special paper for my case, and put it in his pocket, and present it to the board, and he thought he might be able to get me compensation, at the same time alleging that the not granting the right of way might imperil the building of the road, and alluded to my being especially friendly to the road, and so looked upon by the community. I promptly met that by stating that nothing that I should ever do should ever imperil the building of the road, and at once acquiesced in the proposition to give a separate right of way, with the proviso that it was not to be used unless the non-use of it obstructed the building of the road, or a directory made me an allowance for the right of way. That seemed to be satisfactory to the major. He then left, stating that he would prepare, or have prepared, the paper. A few days after, he came in with Mr. Howard, and produced the prepared paper for signature, which I promptly signed, without any further conversation as to the conditions. Many months elapsed, and I heard nothing further from it. Finally the major, meeting me on the street, remarked to me that he had not yet presented the paper. After several months more we met again, and he then stated to me that he had presented that paper, and that the board refused to make any allowance. I promptly remarked: 'Well, you know, major, the conditions upon which that paper was given.' He did not seem fully to comprehend my meaning, and I repeated what I understood to be the understanding,—that that paper was not to be used unless the non-use of it obstructed the building of the road or the board made me an allowance for the right of way. I also stated: 'If you will say, major, that the non-use of that paper would have stopped the building of the road, I have nothing more to say.' He promptly stated: 'I will say that if you and others had withheld the right of way it would have obstructed the building of the road.' I stated that that was not what I said."

Having made this full and clear circumstantial statement, which is natural and consistent in all its parts, and is fully corroborated, in its most important features, by the testimony of W. W. Wood and F. J. Lupfort, Humphreys is asked this question: "Is your memory clear and distinct upon the conditions on which you signed this Paper A? Answer. Perfectly so; as much so as any event in my past life, having thought of it hundreds of times, and feeling at the same time that all I risked in acceding to the major's proposition was that the directory might have made me a pitifully small allowance for the right of way." The appellant, Humphreys, was further examined in chief, as follows: "Question. Was it your understanding that you would be bound by the paper given by you to Maj. McPhail if the directory did not allow you a satisfactory compensation? Answer. It was my understanding that Maj. McPhail had the right to exercise his discretion in turning the paper over, however small the compensation, provided he believed that the non-use of that paper would have prevented the building of the road. At the time the paper was given the building of the road had progressed so far that I felt that I incurred no risk with that proviso attached, except in the smallness of the allowance that might be made for the right of way, feeling that, if they made no allowance, the proviso came in and nullified it. Q. In your previous answer you have stated that when Maj. 'cPhail informed you, you promptly re-

marked, 'Well, you know, major, the conditions upon which that paper was given;' and that you repeated to him what you understood to be the understanding with which that paper was executed, to-wit, that that paper was not to be used unless the non-use of it obstructed the building of the road, or the board would make you an allowance for the right of way. When you told him this, did he deny that these were the conditions upon which the paper was executed? A. He did not, but asserted that he would say that, if others had done the same thing, it would have obstructed the building of the road. I regarded that as an evasion, and we had no further conversation on the subject." Now, recurring briefly to the deposition of McPhail, we find in his cross-examination the following: "Question. Have you no recollection of saying to Mr. Humphreys that if he would sign Paper A you would go before your board of directors and get them to allow him compensation for the right of way through his low grounds, or something to that amount? Answer. No, sir; I never, at any time, gave Mr. Humphreys the least encouragement that I could get him compensation. The Richmond & Mecklenburg Railroad Company had agreed to acquire title to right of way, and was incompetent to make any such concession without the consent of the terminal company, to which it was under obligations to acquire the right of way. On the contrary, Mr. Humphreys gave the right of way, with the request that I would use my best endeavor to get him some compensation, but named no particular amount. An agreement requiring compensation would have been of no conceivable value, such terms being already provided by law, referring to condemnation of lands for such purposes. I would not have held the paper upon condition that I was to get compensation. It was distinctly understood that I should pass the paper to the company if I could not get compensation, and that the matter of compensation should not be pressed to the hazard of building the road."

Now, observe that McPhail, after returning a plain negative answer to a very simple question, goes on to say that he never at any time gave Humphreys any encouragement as to securing compensation for him. Then enters upon the absurd statement that, inasmuch as the Richmond & Mecklenburg Company, by its arrangement with the terminal company, had bound itself to secure the right of way, it was therefore not competent for that company to do what it had bound itself to the terminal company to do. But in the last sentence of the answer above McPhail practically admits all that is claimed by Humphreys, when he says: "It was distinctly understood that I should pass the paper to the company if I could not get compensation, and that the matter of compensation should not be pressed to the hazard of building the road." And again: "Question. Did this question of compensation by your board arise at the first interview with Mr. Humphreys? Answer. Yes, sir; Mr.

Humphreys' withholding right of way for compensation was the first suggestion that crossed my mind in regard to compensation in his case. Q. In answer to question 28, you say that Mr. Humphreys stated to you that he would sign the paper with the understanding that you would try to get him compensation. Now, was this said to you at the first or at a subsequent interview with him? A. As that seems to be the end of the transaction, it must have been at the last interview or conclusion of the negotiation. Q. Did you ever try to get compensation for Mr. Humphreys; and, if so, when and from whom, and what was the result of your effort? A. Yes, sir; our only appeal in the matter was to the terminal company, the Richmond & Mecklenburg Railroad Company being utterly destitute of means, except such as had already been contracted to be expended in the construction of the road. I repeatedly made efforts to get money to purchase right of way. Matters were then very shaky. The terminal company showed no eagerness to complete the work, and any faltering on our part as to the condition imposed on us, I feared, would be fatal. I dared not press them harder than I did to do that which we had agreed to do ourselves. I did all that could have been expected or desired by Mr. Humphreys, or that I would have desired or expected from Mr. Humphreys, had our positions been changed." Now, in his answers to the last three questions, as above set forth, McPhail, notwithstanding his previous statements to the contrary, makes two things certain: (1) That Humphreys did withhold the right of way through his land for compensation; or, in other words, that he did refuse to give the right of way without compensation. (2) That, notwithstanding his admission that the distinct agreement was that he was to try to get Humphreys compensation, he admits that he never made any effort to do so. He was to make application for the allowance of compensation to his board,—the board of directors of the Richmond & Mecklenburg Railroad Company,—of which he was the president; but he admits that the only application ever made was to the terminal company, a company that was confessedly under no obligation, either to the Richmond & Mecklenburg Company or to Humphreys, to pay for rights of way either to Humphreys or any one else, and a company with which Humphreys had no concern whatever. And as to the statement of McPhail that the Richmond & Mecklenburg Company was utterly without means, except such as had already been pledged to the construction of its road, it is not only not borne out by the record, but the contrary clearly appears. As already stated, the terminal company agreed with the Richmond & Mecklenburg Company to construct the road of the latter company upon two conditions: (1) That the Richmond & Mecklenburg Company should acquire a perfect title to all the franchises, property, rights of way, and road-bed of the old Roanoke Valley Railroad Company, then held by trustees for the county of Mecklenburg, by pur-

chasing the same from them for $300,000, payable in the paid-up capital stock of the Richmond & Mecklenburg Railroad Company. (2) That said trustees should transfer and assign the said $300,000 of stock to the construction company. Both of these conditions were performed; but it will be seen that they did not involve the acquisition, by gift, of the right of way and road-bed through the land of Humphreys or any one else. On the contrary, inasmuch as the old Roanoke Valley Company had never acquired the right of way through the land of Humphreys, the Richmond & Mecklenburg Railroad Company was not only left free to purchase, out of their assets, such rights of way and road-bed, but actually bound itself to the terminal company to do so. And, having performed the conditions aforesaid, the Richmond & Mecklenburg Company, on the 27th day of October, 1881, consummated its agreement with said terminal company, whereby the said terminal or construction company agreed to build the Richmond & Mecklenburg railroad for the sum of $400,000 of first mortgage bonds of said railroad company, to be secured by a deed of trust "on all the works, property, rights, assets, and franchises of the said Richmond & Mecklenburg Railroad Company, as well those which it now owns as those which it may hereafter acquire." This contract and deed of trust were both made long prior to the delivery of Paper A by McPhail to the Richmond & Mecklenburg Railroad Company. This contract imposed no prohibition upon the purchase or condemnation by the Richmond & Mecklenburg Railroad Company of rights of way or road-bed, and, in fact, it had to condemn and pay for some of the lands along the line of its road. Nor did the said deed of trust convey the debts due to the Richmond & Mecklenburg Railroad Company. But, as the deed of trust purported to be upon all the assets of the Richmond & Mecklenburg Company, some of the directors thereof declined to execute it until provision was distinctly made for the debts due by the Richmond & Mecklenburg Railroad Company. This was effected by leaving with the said company $10,000 of the said first mortgage bonds, for the purpose of discharging said indebtedness, which consisted of some $7,000 for commissions due to subscription agents along the line of the road, and other obligations due by the company to parties who could not give the right of way.

Thus it will be seen that there were not only ample assets of the Richmond & Mecklenburg Company to pay for the right of way through the land of Humphreys out of this $10,000 of its first mortgage bonds, which, so far as shown by the record, would have been ample; but, in addition, the company held and controlled its subscription list to its stock, amounting to $87,167, of which $55,744 was to be paid in land, $3,800 in materials, $6,400 in labor, and $21,223 in money. Moreover, the company retained and held the subscription of Humphreys for $1,000, for the balance of which the company sued in its own name and right. This balance on subscription the company could, with convenience and justice, have applied, so far as it might go, in compensating Humphreys for the right of way through his land. It is therefore obvious that there is nothing in McPhail's statement as to the then impecunious condition of the Richmond & Mecklenburg Railroad Company. But it is immaterial what was the then condition of the company. If it took his land and property, and has used and enjoyed it, without rightful authority, it is liable therefor.

Recurring again to McPhail's cross-examination, it is important to call attention to the last question propounded to him by counsel for the plaintiff (the appellant here) on his recross-examination, and to his answer thereto, as follows: "Question. Are you not now, and have you not continuously been, the president of the Richmond & Mecklenburg Railroad Company since its organization in 1880? Answer. I have. I desire to state, further, in acting for Mr. Humphreys, so far as relates to holding the paper, I acted in my individual capacity, and held the paper, so to speak, in escrow." Here is a purely voluntary statement, not called for by the question put to him, in which McPhail plainly and unequivocally admits all that is claimed by Humphreys. But the witness is taken in hand by counsel for the railroad company, on whose behalf the witness was introduced, and is examined as follows: First question: "In legal definition, 'escrow' means a paper held under condition, not to be delivered until the conditions therein specified had been complied with. Was this such a paper? Answer. The conditions specified in the paper have been complied with by the railroad company, and all other conditions relating to the matter imposed upon me, by writing or otherwise." Second question: "Was there any understanding between you and Mr. Humphreys that the railroad company had to do anything as a condition precedent to you passing the paper to the company? Answer. None." Third question: "In answer to a question by plaintiff's counsel you state that, in acting for Mr. Humphreys, as relating to holding the paper, you acted in your individual capacity, and held the paper, so to speak, as an escrow. What did you mean by holding it in escrow? Answer. In using the words, so to speak, I meant something like, and used them only in reference to the conditions referring to compensation, which conditions are not stated in the paper, and which were complied with before the paper passed out of my hands." Here ends the deposition of Maj. McPhail. While it contains many inconsistent and irreconcilable statements,—due, doubtless, not to any deliberate purpose to misrepresent the facts, but to the want of a retentive memory,—yet the deposition, taken altogether, is more in favor of than opposed to the claim asserted by Humphreys, as to the conditions upon which Paper A was signed by him and delivered to McPhail. But, independently of the testimony of McPhail, the evidence clearly sustains the contention of Humphreys, which is that the paper was not to be used unless the

withholding of it would defeat the building of the road, or the board of directors of the Richmond & Mecklenburg Railroad Company should make him compensation. Soon after the execution of Paper A the arrangement for building the Richmond & Mecklenburg road by the terminal company was consummated. Henceforth the building of the road was assured, and the only remaining duty imposed upon McPhail was to secure compensation to Humphreys or to return the paper to him. But he admits that he never presented the claim to the board of directors of the Richmond & Mecklenburg Railroad Company, of which he was the president, and that he never even made known the existence of the paper; yet, long after the building of the road was assured, he delivered the paper to Howard, the company's agent, who was fully cognizant of the conditions upon which the paper was signed by Humphreys, and delivered to him. Howard's knowledge was the company's knowledge, and the delivery to him was unauthorized, null, and void.

These being the facts, it only remains to show that they may unquestionably be established by parol. It is undeniably true that, to have made the delivery in question a valid delivery to the railroad company, it must have been delivered to McPhail, as the agent of the company, "for the use and benefit of the company, and with intent to pass an absolute property or interest in the deed delivered." Insurance, etc., Co. v. Cole, 4 Fla. 359. In Devlin on Deeds, § 316, it is said: "A delivery of a deed, with the intention of passing the title, made to an officer of a corporation, is a delivery to the corporation itself, if it be done for the use and benefit of the corporation. But a deed may be delivered to an officer of a corporation, to take effect as an escrow, upon the performance of a condition, as there is no such personal identity between a corporation and its officers as will prevent a delivery to the latter as an escrow." For this position the author quotes abundant authority. See the case just cited, and Bank v. Bailhache, 65 Cal. 326, 4 Pac. Rep. 106; Bowker v. Burdekin, 11 Mees. & W. 145; Flagg v. Mason, 2 Sum. 510; Millership v. Brookes, 5 Hurl. & N. 797. In the same section Devlin says: "It is not an inevitable conclusion that the mere delivery of manual possession is a valid delivery of the deed. If the acceptance of an agency from both parties will involve no violation of duty to either, the releasor may make the agent of the releasee his own agent, for the purpose of holding the deed as an escrow, and returning it to him in case a stipulated condition is not performed. The rule that a delivery to an agent of the grantee is equivalent to a delivery to the grantee himself would not apply in such a case, because there is not that personal identity between the releasee and his agent upon which the reason of the rule depends." Railroad Co. v. Iliff, 13 Ohio St. 235; Railroad Co. v. Hall, 1 Ill. App. 612. Howard was the agent of the company, charged with the preparation of deeds to rights of way and the obtaining of their execution. When Howard received the paper, for the purpose of getting a deed, he was fully aware of the conditions on which it had been delivered to McPhail, he having been present when they were agreed upon, and he and McPhail being the attesting witnesses to the paper. This knowledge on the part of Howard must be attributed to the company, of which he was agent. Newlin v. Beard, 6 W. Va. 110. See, also, Ward v. Churn, 18 Grat. 813, where it is said: "If the delivery is upon a condition made known to the obligee, his assent to it will be presumed from the acceptance of the instrument; and he will not be allowed to repudiate the condition thus assented to, and to treat the delivery as absolute and unconditional." So, too, in Nash v. Fugate, 32 Grat. 595, which turned upon an instruction "that a bond, perfect on its face, is invalid in the hands of the obligee if he had notice of the conditions on which it was signed by the defendant." In that case the instruction was sustained, and Judge STAPLES, delivering the unanimous opinion of the court, cites with approval. among others, the case of Millett v. Parker. 2 Metc. (Ky.) 608. See, also, Harris v. Harris, 23 Grat. 778, and Newlin v. Beard, supra. When a deed is delivered to a person to be held until certain conditions are performed, and then to be delivered to the grantee or obligee, it is an escrow; but the person to whom the deed is delivered in the first instance must be the judge as to when the condition is performed, in order to act. His judgment, however. is always subject to review by a court. Devl. Deeds, § 327. And so, if it is delivered before the condition is performed, equity will declare such delivery void. Id. §§ 321. 322; Hicks v. Goode, 12 Leigh, 490, 491. The depositary of an escrow is, in fact, the agent of both parties. As the agent of the grantor, it is his business to withhold the deed until the condition is performed; as the agent of the grantee, it is his business to hold it for him, and to deliver it to him after the condition is performed. Devl. Deeds, § 327. The duty imposed upon McPhail in the present case was to ascertain whether the withholding of Paper A would prevent the construction of the road. By his own admission he ascertained that it would not. His only remaining duty, then, was to get compensation for Humphreys, and, failing this, to return the paper to Humphreys. But he utterly ignored the obligations thus resting upon him; hence his delivery of the paper was without authority, null, and void. Id. § 322; Hicks v. Goode, supra; Nash v. Fugate, 24 Grat. 208. 209. We are therefore of opinion that, on the facts and the law applicable thereto, the case is clearly with the appellant, Humphreys, and that the court below erred in dissolving the injunction and dismissing the bill.

There is much evidence in the record as to the damage done to the appellant by the railroad company in occupying his land, earth-works, and masonry, and also as to damages to the residue of his tract of land by reason of said earth-works or embankment. But this court will not invade the legitimate province of a jury by undertaking to ascertain such damages upon the varient estimates of

v.18s.E.no.37—68

witnesses, when the object can be better and more safely accomplished by a jury of the vicinage; but will enter a decree reversing and annulling the decree appealed from, and remanding the cause to said circuit court, with instructions to restore the case to its place on the docket, to be proceeded in to a final decree, and with a further instruction that, when the case is matured for hearing, an issue *quantum damnificatus* be directed to be tried at the bar of said court, on the law side thereof. to ascertain the damages aforesaid, and that the same, when so ascertained and duly certified to the chancery side of said court, be set off against said judgment at law confessed by the apppellant in favor of the said Richmond & Mecklenburg Railroad Company, and that the excess of said damages, if any, over and above said judgment, be decreed against said railroad company in favor of the appellant, Humphreys.

Decree reversed.

GRIGG *et al.* v. DALSHEIMER *et al.*

(*Supreme Court of Appeals of Virginia.* Dec. 10, 1891.)

WRIT OF PROHIBITION — WHEN LIES — VALIDITY OF JUDGMENT.

Code Va. § 3286, provides that when, in an action of *assumpsit*, an affidavit is filed with the declaration, no plea in bar shall be received unless supported by the affidavit; and, if such plea and affidavit are not filed, there shall be no inquiry of damages, but judgment shall be for plaintiff for the amount claimed in the affidavit filed with the declaration. *Held*, that where a plea of *non assumpsit* unaccompanied by affidavit was stricken out, and the subsequent tender of a plea accompanied by affidavit refused, a final judgment given by the court for plaintiffs was not void, as the court had jurisdiction, though it would have been the duty of the clerk to enter judgment at rules, and therefore its enforcement would not be restrained. FAUNTLEROY, J., dissenting.

Application of Griggs & Cross for writ of prohibition to restrain proceedings for collection of a judgment entered by the court for respondents, S. Dalsheimer & Bro., in an action of *assumpsit* by respondents against petitioners, the court having in such case stricken out petitioners' plea of *non assumpsit* for the reason that it was not accompanied by affidavit, and refused to receive another plea of *non assumpsit* supported by a proper affidavit. Writ denied.

Geo. P. Haw, for petitioners. Jo. Lane Stern, for respondents.

LEWIS, P. Section 3286 of the Code provides that when, in an action of *assumpsit* for money, (except where the process is served by publication,) an affidavit is filed with the declaration, stating that the amount claimed is justly due, and the time from which interest is claimed, no plea in bar shall be received, either at rules or in court, unless accompanied by an affidavit in support thereof; and then it is further enacted that, "if such plea and affidavit be not filed by the defendant, there shall be no inquiry of damages, but judgment shall be for the plaintiff for the amount claimed in the affidavit filed with the declaration." These provisions relative to the action of *assumpsit* were for the first time incorporated into the statute law of the state upon the adoption of the new Code. Their obvious purpose is to prevent delay, and, with that object in view, to simplify and shorten the proceedings. It will be observed that the provision is express that no plea in bar shall be received unless accompanied by an affidavit; so that, without the requisite affidavit, such a plea is, in legal effect, a nullity. There can be no doubt, therefore, that the motion to strike out the plea in the present case was rightly granted, nor that the case stood, before the motion was granted, in contemplation of the statute, as though no plea had been tendered at rules. The question, then, is not whether the circuit court erred in refusing to remand the case to rules, or to allow a plea and affidavit to be filed in court, but whether, in giving final judgment as it did, it exceeded its jurisdiction. In other words, is the judgment void? for, unless it is. the case is not a proper one for a prohibition. The office of the writ of prohibition, we need hardly say, is not the correction of errors. The writ lies only to restrain an inferior court from acting in a matter of which it has no jurisdiction, or from exceeding the bounds of its jurisdiction. Hence, if the inferior court has jurisdiction of the subject-matter of the controversy, and the parties are before it, or have had notice and an opportunity to be heard, a mistaken exercise of that jurisdiction does not render its judgment void, or justify a resort to the extraordinary remedy by prohibition; or, as it has been tersely expressed, the writ of prohibition does not lie to prevent a subordinate court from deciding erroneously, or from enforcing an erroneous judgment, in a case in which it has a right to adjudicate. High, Extr. Rem. § 772; Hogan v. Guigon, 29 Grat. 705; Nelms v. Vaughan, 84 Va. 696, 5 S. E. Rep. 704. In the present case the circuit court had jurisdiction both of the subject-matter and of the parties. The defendants appeared to the action and pleaded, though their plea, as we have seen, was, in effect, a nullity. They, however, had their day in court, and they were not arbitrarily put out of court, and denied an opportunity to make defense, as was the defendant in the celebrated McVeigh Cases, cited and relied on by counsel, viz., McVeigh v. U. S., 11 Wall. 259; Windsor v. McVeigh, 93 U. S. 274; Underwood v. McVeigh, 23 Grat. 409. Nor had they an absolute right under the statute to plead a second time. Their first plea, moreover, being a nullity, the effect was the same as if they had not pleaded at all, in which case it would have been the duty of the clerk to enter a judgment at rules for the plaintiff, since the statute is imperative that in such a case there shall be no inquiry of damages, but judgment shall be for the plaintiff. In short, whatever may be said as to the correctness of the judgment,—and we do not mean to intimate that it is erroneous,—it is not void, and that is decisive of the case. If the defendants have lost a good defense by neglecting to seasonably assert it in the manner prescribed by the statute, they cannot now obtain the benefit of it, or be relieved from the consequences of their own neglect by a writ of prohibition.

FAUNTLEROY, J., dissenting.

BONSACK MACH. CO. v. WOODRUM.

(Supreme Court of Appeals of Virginia. Dec. 10, 1891.)

PAROL EVIDENCE—RELEASE OF CONTRACT.

An agreement that "all matters and things embraced by the within contract have been fully adjusted and settled, and this contract is, for value received, declared ended and settled," cannot, in the absence of fraud or mutual mistake, be shown by parol testimony to have referred only to money accounts between the parties to the contract, and not to have included a covenant therein, on the part of the party paying the consideration for the release, not to engage in a certain business with any one else for a certain time.

Appeal from circuit court of city of Roanoke.

Suit by the Bonsack Machine Company against R. F. Woodrum for specific performance, injunction, and damages. The bill was dismissed, and complainant appeals. Affirmed.

Hansbrough & Hansbrough and *A. H. Burroughs,* for appellant. *Phlegar & Johnson, Penn & Cocke,* and *W. R. Staples,* for appellee.

FAUNTLEROY, J. The petition of the Bonsack Machine Company complains of a decree pronounced by the circuit court for the city of Roanoke, Va., in vacation, on the 30th day of April, 1890, in the suit of the said Bonsack Machine Company against R. H. Woodrum. The bill is for specific performance of the covenant contained in the clause of an agreement, under seal, entered into on the 10th day of July, 1888, between the Bonsack Machine Company, of Salem, Va., of the first part, and R. H. Woodrum, of Roanoke, Va., of the second part, as follows: "And it is expressly agreed by the said Woodrum that he shall, in no event, either directly or indirectly, have anything to do with any other cigarette-machine than those of the said company, unless by the full consent in writing of the said company, and under such contract and arrangements as the said company may provide; and this last provision shall continue for twenty years from this date. The object of latter clause, as to other machines, being to prevent the said Woodrum, after establishing to any extent a business for the said company in South America, from forming any combination, directly or indirectly, or in any manner whatsoever, by purchase or otherwise, with the owner or controller of any other cigarette-machine, the said Woodrum being the agent of the said company, and the latter not being in a position to protect itself against any arrangement which he might make to the injury of the said company; and on this account it is distinctly agreed that said Woodrum shall not abandon this agency, or cause the said company to revoke it, and, after connection with this company has ceased from any cause whatever, in any manner whatever, directly or indirectly, become interested in any other cigarette-machine in South America, or in any country to which a machine of the said party of the first part had been sent, for twenty years from the date hereof." And the further object of the bill is to enjoin the said R. H. Woodrum from acting with or for another company, and to recover damages for his having been connected or interested in and with and for another company, to-wit, the Ludington Cigarette-Machine Company, thereby supplanting and breaking down the interest and business of his principal, the Bonsack Cigarette-Machine Company. As a defense to this suit, Woodrum pleaded that after the contract sued on and exhibited with the bill, dated July 10, 1888, was made and delivered, to-wit, on the 6th day of August, 1889. the plaintiff, the Bonsack Cigarette-Machine Company, for a valuable consideration, to-wit, $20,000, paid to it by the defendant, Woodrum, by a writing dated August 6, 1889, signed by it, by D. B. Strouse, its president, and by the said Woodrum, which was indorsed on the said contract of July 10, 1888, contracted and agreed that all matters and things embraced by said contract of July 10, 1888, were fully adjusted and settled, and the said contract itself was ended and settled, and did thereby agree to release and absolve the defendant from all the liability, obligations, and restrictions imposed by the said contract, and the said Woodrum did thereby release the said plaintiff from all liability, obligations, and restrictions imposed by the said contract. And that afterwards, to-wit, on the 7th day of September, 1889, the plaintiff, the Bonsack Cigarette-Machine Company, did, by its board of directors, who were thereunto duly authorized, by a resolution duly adopted and authenticated by the corporate seal of the said plaintiff and the signature of and certificate of P. A. Krise, its secretary, confirm and ratify the settlement and contract made between the plaintiff, by D. B. Strouse, president, and the said Woodrum, on the 6th day of August, 1889, as aforesaid. A motion was made by the complainant to strike out and reject this plea; which motion was overruled. A special replication was then tendered, which alleges that the matter set up in the bill was not intended to be embraced by the contract of August 6, 1889. This special replication was rejected; but an agreement was made that the cause might be heard and determined upon a general replication as it would be on a good special replication; and the cause was so heard, and the bill dismissed.

We are of opinion that the written agreement of August 6, 1889, did embrace and abrogate the provision in the contract of July 10, 1888, which prohibited Woodrum from becoming interested in, or connected with, the cigarette-machines of other companies. There is no pretense, nor can there be, that there is any patent ambiguity; and the words are too plain, positive, and pointed to admit the possibility of any occult or latent meaning. "All matters and things embraced by the within contract have been fully adjusted and settled, and this contract is, for value received, declared ended and settled." It is contended by the appellant, that the "settlement," "receipt," and "release," expressed and embodied in the explicit and all-embracing terms of the contract of August 6, 1889, embraced and referred to the settlement, adjustment, and satisfaction of only the money accounts in controversy between the parties to the contract of July 10, 1888, and do not affect or embrace the covenant contained in the said contract, which restrained Woodrum, for 20 years from its date, from any connection with, or interest in, the cigarette-machines of any other competing company. But, if it be possible to hold that the terms, "all matters and things embraced by the within contract have been fully adjusted and settled," relate only to money accounts between Woodrum, agent, and the Bonsack Machine Company, principal, yet there are the express words added, "and this contract is, for value received, declared ended and settled." The contract itself is abrogated,—"ended." What does "ended" mean? It means final, definitive, complete, conclusive. It imports what will be when the apocalyptic angel, with one foot on the sea and the other upon the earth, shall lift his hand to heaven, and swear, by Him that liveth forever and ever, that there shall be "time no longer!" It will not then be admissible to offer parol testimony to alter, vary, and contradict the explicit terms of the awful declaration, and to prove that, non obstante the unambiguous words themselves, "time [still] rolls his ceaseless course" for some of the provisions of man's tenure upon earth. There is no intimation of fraud or of mutual mistake; and, though in a court of law a covenant cannot be released by parol agreement alone, yet this is an executed written agreement for valuable consideration, accepted and retained by the complainant, who, offering to return none of it, asks a court of equity to say it is not bound, because it did not put its seal to the writing indorsed upon the contract under seal, and which was adopted, ratified, and approved by its own resolution August 24, 1889, certified under its seal, and delivered to the defendant, who then and thereupon paid to the said company the additional sum of $500, which, with the $20,000 already paid by him to the said company, was the consideration moving from him for his release from the contract itself, of July 10, 1888. See the following authorities: 7 Wait, Act. & Def. 454, 455; Pom. Eq. Jur. §§ 70, 378, 383; Towner v. Lucas, 13 Grat. 705; Colhoun v. Wilson, 27 Grat. 639; Barnett v. Barnett, 83 Va. 504, 2 S. E. Rep. 733; 2 Starkie, Ev. p. 547; Woodward v. Foster, 18 Grat. 200, 207, and cases there referred to; Knick v. Knick, 75 Va. 12; French v. Williams, 82 Va. 462; Yates v. Town of Warrenton, 84 Va. 337, 4 S. E. Rep. 818; Redd v. Com., 85 Va. 648, 8 S. E. Rep. 490; 2 Phil. Ev. 559, 531, 958, 961, 754, and 3 Phil. Ev. 292, and note; Crawford v. Jarrett, 2 Leigh, 630. We find no error in the record, and our judgment is to affirm the decree appealed from.

Judgment affirmed.

MORGANTOWN BANK v. FOSTER.

(Supreme Court of Appeals of West Virginia. Dec. 7, 1891.)

ASSUMPSIT — PLEADING — OVERRULING DEMURRER —JUDGMENT.

1. Issue was joined on the plea of *non assumpsit.* Defendant then filed two special pleas, to which plaintiff demurred. The court overruled the demurrers, and gave final judgment for the defendant. *Held,* this was error, as there should have been no final judgment without the issue on the plea of *non assumpsit* having been tried, withdrawn, or otherwise disposed of.

2. If there be one or more pleas, and the demurrer thereto be sustained, the party may plead further if he has any other defense, but, if not, judgment may be rendered, if it is such a case as that judgment by default or without a jury might have been rendered on it; otherwise, a writ of inquiry, or its equivalent, must be executed.

(Syllabus by the Court.)

Error to circuit court, Tyler county.

Action of *assumpsit* by the Morgantown Bank against Cyrus A. Foster. Judgment for defendant, and plaintiff brings error. Reversed.

Thos. J. Stealey, B. Engle, and *Daniel D. Johnson,* for plaintiff in error. *J. V. Blair,* for defendant in error.

HOLT, J. This was an action of *assumpsit,* brought by the Morgantown Bank on the 21st day of July, 1881, in the circuit court of Tyler county, against C. A. Foster. The declaration avers, in substance, that on 27th November, 1874, one James Wells executed to C. A. Foster his writing obligatory of that date, whereby he promised and bound himself to pay to Foster on or before the 1st day of April, 1878, the sum of $250; that afterwards, for value received, Foster indorsed and assigned the same to one C. Shriver; that afterwards, to-wit, on 5th September, 1878, Shriver, for value received, indorsed and assigned the same, it being then due and unpaid, to plaintiff, without any recourse on him; that the said Wells was, at the time said bond became due, totally and notoriously insolvent, and unable to pay the same, and has so remained insolvent ever since, and has never paid said bond, of all which premises Foster had notice; by reason whereof Foster became liable to pay plaintiff the said sum of $250, with interest from the 1st day of April, 1878, until paid, and, being so liable, and in consideration thereof, on the day aforesaid undertook and promised the plaintiff to pay it said sum of $250, with interest as aforesaid, when defendant should be thereunto afterwards requested, but, although requested, has neglected and refused, and still doth neglect and refuse, to pay the same, to plaintiff's damage $500, and therefore it brings suit, etc. On the 17th of April, 1882, defendant, C. A. Foster, appeared, and pleaded *non assumpsit,* to which plaintiff replied by adding the *similiter.* Issue was joined, and the cause was continued. On 22d August, 1883, a jury was impaneled and sworn to try the cause, but, being unable to agree, was discharged, and the cause continued. On 11th April, 1889, defendant asked leave to withdraw his plea of *non assumpsit,* which motion the court overruled, and defendant there-

upon demurred to plaintiff's declaration, which demurrer the court also overruled. Thereupon defendant tendered two special pleas in writing, marked, respectively, "No. 1" and "No. 2," and asked leave to file the same, to which plaintiff objected, but the court overruled the objection, and permitted the pleas to be filed, which was done, and plaintiff excepted, and prayed that its exception be made a part of the record, which was done. Plaintiff then replied generally to each of the pleas, issues were joined thereon, and the cause continued. On August 20, 1889, the plaintiff asked the court to set aside the issues joined on these two special pleas, and for leave to withdraw its replications to the pleas, to which defendant objected, but the court overruled the objection, set aside said issues joined on the two special pleas, gave leave to plaintiff to withdraw its replications to said pleas, which was done, and thereupon plaintiff demurred generally to each of said special pleas in writing, in which demurrer defendant joined. The court overruled the demurrer to each plea, and gave final judgment for defendant. These special pleas are as follows:

"First special plea· The Morgantown Bank, which sues, etc., plaintiff, vs. C. A. Foster, defendant. And the said defendant, by his attorney, comes, and for a further plea in this behalf says that on the 27th day of November, 1874, he sold and conveyed to one James Wells, of Monongalia county, of this state, certain real estate situated therein, for the price and consideration of $2,250, of which $500 was then and there paid in land, and $500 in money, and for the balance two bonds for $500 each and one bond for $250 were given by said Wells to this defendant; and in the deed of conveyance made by him to said Wells he expressly reserved a vendor's lien on said real estate to secure the payment of said bonds. That subsequently this defendant assigned the said bond for $250 to one Cannon Shriver, and the other two for $500 each to the plaintiff in this action, the assignment of the $250 bond to Shriver being made first in time. That on the —— day of March, 1877, said plaintiff brought a suit in chancery in the circuit court of said Monongalia county to enforce said vendor's lien against said Wells, to which said Shriver was a defendant. That in said suit a decree was rendered by which said real estate was ordered to be sold, and the same was afterwards sold for the sum of $774.17. That an answer was filed for said Shriver in said suit, but it failed to set up the right of said Shriver to have the said bond for $250 assigned to him as aforesaid first paid, and no provision was made in the decree rendered by said court therein for such payment to said Shriver. That said plaintiff had knowledge and notice before said decree for sale was made, and before said sale was made, that the bond for $250 was assigned to said Shriver before the other two bonds for $500 each were assigned to it. That the price for which said land was sold was not sufficient to pay off all three of said bonds, and the proceeds of said sale were applied to the payment of the balance due on said bonds for $500 each, and of the costs of said suit; and said proceeds were only sufficient for that purpose. And this defendant further says that by reason of said Shriver's failure to assert the priority of his said lien in his said answer, and by reason of his having been made a party to said suit and having elected his remedy on the lien, he lost and waived his right of recourse against this defendant; and defendant further says that by said Shriver's assignment of said bond for $250 to the said plaintiff there was no right of recourse against this defendant assigned to the said plaintiff, and this the said defendant is ready to verify. C. A. FOSTER. By his Attorneys.

"Second special plea: The Morgantown Bank, which sues, etc., plaintiff, vs. C. A. Foster, defendant. And the said defendant, by his attorneys, comes, and for a further plea in this behalf says that on the 27th day of November, 1874, he sold and conveyed to one James Wells, of Monongalia county, of this state, certain real estate therein situated for the consideration and price of $2,250, of which $500 was then and there paid in land and $500 in cash, and for the balance the said Wells then and there executed and delivered to this defendant two bonds for $500 each, and one bond for $250; and in the deed of conveyance made by him to said Wells he expressly reserved a vendor's lien on said real estate to secure the payment of said bonds. That afterwards this defendant assigned said bond for $250 to one Cannon Shriver, and the two bonds for $500 to the plaintiff, the assignment to Shriver being made first. That on the —— day of March, 1877, said plaintiff commenced a suit in chancery in the circuit court of said Monongalia county to enforce the said vendor's lien and sell said real estate. That neither this defendant nor said Shriver was made a party to said suit by service of summons or by voluntary appearance or by attorney authorized by them, or either of them, or in person. That said plaintiff had notice, before any proceedings were had in said suit, and before said two bonds for $500 each were assigned to it as aforesaid, that said bond for $250 had been assigned to said Shriver. That, if this defendant had been made party to this suit, and if he had received notice of the proceedings in said suit, he could have made said real estate sell for enough to pay off in full all three of said bonds and the costs of said suit. That a decree was rendered in said suit to sell said real estate, and in pursuance thereof it was afterwards sold for the sum of $774.17, and said sale was, by a further decree of said court, confirmed. And this defendant further says that the jurisdiction of said circuit court of said Monongalia county in said chancery suit over the person of this defendant and said Shriver was obtained and the decrees made therein were rendered by and through the fraud and covin of said plaintiff; that is to say, by the said plaintiff falsely and fraudulently, through its attorneys, Keck and Hough, entering the appearance of this defendant and said Shriver in said suit, and by filing separate answers for them therein without their authority and consent, and by concealing and suppressing from said court in its said bill and in said answer filed in said suit the fact that the said bond for $250 was assigned to said Shriver before the two bonds for $500 each were assigned to said plaintiff. And said defendant further says that by reason of the said fraud and covin of the plaintiff, as is hereinbefore set forth, the said court ordered said $774.17, after the payment of costs, to be applied to the payment of balance due on the bonds assigned to and held by said plaintiff, and there was nothing left of the proceeds of said sale, after such application was made, to pay on the bond for $250; whereas, said proceeds should have been first applied to the payment of said last-named bond; and that the said real estate at the time it was so sold was reasonably worth $1,500, of which said plaintiff then and there had notice, and this the said defendant is ready to verify. C. A. FOSTER. By his attorneys."

It was error to give final judgment against the plaintiff, with the issue on the plea of *non assumpsit* left standing and undetermined. There could properly be no final judgment until the issue joined upon the plea of *non assumpsit* was tried. Wilson v. Davisson, 5 Munf. 178. For this error the judgment of the court below must be reversed, and the cause remanded for a new trial. But, in order to avoid delay, it is proper to pass now upon the declaration and the two special pleas.

The declaration seems to be in the usual form, and I am unable to discover any substantial defect.

Special plea No. 1. The plaintiff, in the declaration, avers the various matters constituting the premises, and of which defendant had notice. It then avers that by reason thereof defendant became liable to pay the $250, etc., and defendant, being so liable in consideration thereof, undertook and promised the plaintiff that he would pay it the said sum of $250, etc. An action of *assumpsit* lies upon a promise expressly made or upon a promise implied by law as a legal inference from a given state of facts. But there is no such thing as an implied promise in pleading. That fact comes out only in the evidence, so that the promise, whether express or implied as matter of law, must, as matter of pleading, be alleged as an express promise; and, except in the cases of bills of exchange, promissory notes, and checks, the declaration must also disclose the consideration upon which the contract or promise is founded. Each party tacitly admits all such traversable allegations made on the opposite side as he does not traverse. Therefore each party must be allowed to deny in some form, either by the general traverse of the general issue or precise traverse, all material facts alleged against him. This promise, alleged in the declaration as an express one, constitutes its essential part, and must be denied or avoided. The general issue *non assumpsit* is a denial, for that covers the whole declaration, and puts the plaintiff to the proof of every material fact. But *assumpsit* is only a species of the more general class of actions of trespass on the case, and is treated, like all its class, with liberality as to the pleadings by relaxing some of the common rules. Hence in trespass on the case, whether growing out of tort or contract, many defenses strictly in avoidance may be given in evidence under the general issue, and therefore need not be specially pleaded. Hence it is commonly said that anything may be given in evidence under the plea of *non assumpsit* except the statute of limitations and tender. Set-off, with us, need not be specially pleaded, but, when specified in an account filed, may be proved without any plea except *non assumpsit*. But discharge in bankruptcy must be specially pleaded. It follows from this that the defense, if good in law, attempted to be set up in these two special pleas, could have been proved under the general issue. But it does not follow that they amount to the general issue, for, if they may be taken as confessing the truth of the declaration, and as setting up a bar by way of confession and avoidance, then such matters may be specially pleaded. But these pleas are not good as special pleas in bar by way of confession and avoidance because they do not attempt to confess and avoid the promise laid in the declaration as expressly made; and if the object was to deny such express promise, and no more, they could not do it in better form or more effectually than they had done by the pleas of *non assumpsit* already in, and still standing on the record undecided. Therefore both special pleas should have been rejected in answer to plaintiff's motion to reject when they were tendered.

Special plea No. 2. This is so obscure and confused, rambling, and inconclusive that nothing further need be said about it than to say that I suppose it was intended to present with some variations the defense intended by plea No. 1, with a few other half-way pleas thrown in for good measure.

Special plea No. 1. From this plea it is easy to gather that defendant meant to say, and in substance does say, that Shriver, the intermediate assignee from defendant and plaintiff's immediate assignor, was a party to a chancery suit in which the fund out of which his bond of $250 was first entitled to be paid, had willfully waived his right of priority, or had lost such plain and easy mode of receiving payment by his own negligence, not being willing even to put out his hand, and take the money in court, ready for him, or ready to be set apart for him, in a chancery suit to which he was a party. Such willful waiver of his right to be paid first out of the fund in court, or his negligence in permitting such an opportunity to be paid to pass away, would have constituted, unexplained or unavoided, a good defense under the plea of *non assumpsit;* for section 14, c. 99, of the Code, (1869 and 1891,) provides that "the assignee of any bond, note, account, or writing not negotiable may maintain thereupon any action in his own name, without the addition of 'assignee,' which the original obligee or payee might have brought; but shall allow all just discounts, not only

against himself but against the assignor, before the defendant had notice of the assignment;" and the term "discount," as here used, embraces any right which Foster has to an abatement of the demands against him, as against his assignee, Shriver, for there is no privity of contract by assignment between defendant, Foster, and the plaintiff, the remote assignee. It is only by virtue of this statute that plaintiff can sue the defendant, Foster, at all; and Shriver cannot put his assignee on any higher ground than he occupies himself without some act of Foster. And it is no answer to say that it is just as broad as it is long,—that, if the $250 had been taken out of the proceeds of sale of the land, it would have left a deficiency of that amount on the two $500 bonds that Foster himself directly assigned to the bank. That is a wholly disconnected matter. No one in this suit knows what the grounds of defense may be in that one. Defendant may be able to show that he assigned to the bank the two $500 bonds without recourse, or that he only received $750 for them, and therefore nothing more would be due on recourse. It is enough to say at this time and according to this record that that case has nothing to do with this case. The $250 bond, as the first assigned, gave to Shriver, the assignee, the right to have it first paid out of the proceeds of the sale of the land, to enforce the vendor's lien, in which the $250 was included. The assignment of the $250 bond by defendant, Foster, to Shriver carried with it, as an incident thereto, the vendor's lien expressly reserved on the face of the conveyance, and entitled Shriver, as assignee of such bond, as the one first assigned, to be first paid out of the proceeds of the sale of the land. Jenkins v. Hawkins, 34 W. Va. 799, 12 S. E. Rep. 1090; Tingle v. Fisher, 20 W. Va. 497. It is true, Shriver was not bound as a condition precedent to his right of recourse to follow up this incident of the assignment. He could show debtor's insolvency when the bond was due, so that suit would be known in advance as sure to turn out to be unavailing; or he could bring suit at law, and prosecute it diligently to *nulla bona.* None of these he saw fit to do, but, when in a court of equity as party to a suit in which the proceeds of the sale of the land to enforce the vendor's lien were in court ready to be given to him for the asking, he, according to the substance of this plea, waived his right, or negligently failed to put out his hand and take the money there ready for him. Therefore, by reason of such waiver or negligence on the part of Shriver, there was no implied promise raised by implication of law out of the facts stated as inducement to show a consideration in plaintiff's declaration with these new facts put in with them, and that was already sufficiently said by the plea of *non assumpsit,* which puts in issue the implied promise as well as the express one; whereas this special plea, if it puts in issue anything, does not expressly traverse either the implied or express promise alleged in the declaration. In saying that such defense is admissible under the plea of *non assumpsit,*

I do not mean to say that it could not be well pleaded specially, and in such a way as to separate the law from the facts, so that the sufficiency of such defense could be settled on demurrer, but only that defendant has not done so in this plea. For the error, already mentioned, of giving final judgment on demurrer to these two special pleas, leaving the issue joined on the plea of *non assumpsit* still standing wholly undetermined, the judgment must be reversed, and the cause remanded.

SMITH v. LOWTHER et al.

(Supreme Court of Appeals of West Virginia.
Nov. 14, 1891.)

MORTGAGES—SALE UNDER TRUST—PLEADING—
PRACTICE.

1. A trustee in a deed of trust executed to him upon a tract of land to secure the payment of money, when required to sell under said trust-deed, must be personally present at the time and place of sale, and supervise the same, and cannot delegate his powers to a stranger, authorizing such stranger to make the sale in his absence, unless authorized so to do by the deed of trust.

2. Matters not charged in the bill or averred in the answer, and not put in issue in any manner by the pleadings in the cause, are not proper to be considered at the hearing, and should have no weight in determining the cause.

(Syllabus by the Court.)

Appeal from circuit court, Doddridge county.

Bill by Stephen J. Smith against A. J. Lowther and others to set aside a sale under a deed of trust. Decree for defendants. Plaintiff appeals. Reversed.

Geo. W. Farr, for appellant. *Laird & Turner,* for appellees.

ENGLISH, J. On the 11th day of April, 1887, Stephen J. Smith filed his bill in the circuit court of Doddridge county, in which he alleged, in substance, that being the owner of a tract of land situated in said county containing 167 acres, and being indebted to his brother Vincent Smith in the sum of $281, he executed a deed of trust upon said tract of land to C. C. Cole, trustee, to secure the payment of said note; that on the 11th day of November, 1872, said trustee was proceeding to sell said land to satisfy said debt, and said S. J. Smith employed A. J. Lowther to attend at the time and place of sale to buy in and redeem said land by paying the amount of said note, amounting to $287.37, including principal and interest and costs of sale, $15.68, which several amounts of money were furnished to said A. J. Lowther by said Stephen J. Smith, who paid said Lowther for his services in the premises; that said Lowther, in pursuance of his agreement with said Stephen J. Smith, attended said sale, and became the *quasi* purchaser of said land for the sum of $299, the same being the amount of said note, interest, and costs; that it was agreed between said Stephen J. Smith and said Lowther that said land was to be bought in by said Lowther for said S. J. Smith, and said Lowther was not to take possession of said land, or require a deed therefor under said sale, which fact was known to the said trustee, and was

recognized by said trustee as being a payment of said debt, and a redemption of said land by said Smith, who paid said purchase money and took up the note which evidenced said indebtedness; that said S. J. Smith remained in possession of said land up to some time in 1883, when said Lowther took possession of the same under a deed made by said C. C. Cole, trustee, to him on the 16th day of September, 1882, which was recorded on the 9th day of January, 1883; that on the 5th day of February, 1877, said Stephen J. Smith conveyed 50 acres of said tract of land to one Thomas Brown, upon which portion said Brown paid the taxes, and he (Smith) paid the taxes upon the residue of the same up to the time said Lowther took possession thereof under the deed from said trustee in 1883. He also alleged that the deed procured by the said A. J. Lowther from said trustee was procured by and through misrepresentation and fraud, and without the knowledge and consent of complainant, and in direct violation of the agreement above stated; and that said Lowther well knew that said tract of land was the property of the plaintiff before and from the time of said pretended sale up to and at the time that he procured said fraudulent conveyance, except the 50 acres sold to Brown as aforesaid. To this bill A. J. Lowther, Mary A. Lowther, Martha J. Taylor, and Zachariah Taylor, her husband, C. C. Cole, trustee, Thomas Brown, Vincent Smith, C. J. Stuart, and J. V. Blair were made defendants. And the complainant further alleged that the said A. J. Lowther, by himself, his agents and attorneys, falsely and fraudulently, after the lapse of about 10 years from the date of said *quasi* sale, without the knowledge of complainant, represented to the said C. C. Cole, trustee, that he, the said Lowther, had been the *bona fide* purchaser of said land at said sale, and was entitled to a deed from said trustee therefor, and demanded the same; and said trustee, relying upon said false and fraudulent representations as being true, and through and by his request and mistake, and without the knowledge or consent of complainant, executed said deed to him, although he was not entitled to the same. The complainant further alleged that, in furtherance of said fraud and deception, the said A. J. Lowther, on the 21st day of December, 1882, conveyed said tract of land to his two daughters, Martha J. Taylor and Mary A. Lowther, who were not innocent purchasers of said land, and that the same was conveyed without valuable consideration; that said land, except the 50 acres conveyed by him to Thomas Brown, was assessed on the land books of said county to complainant, and had been ever since he acquired his title; and that he (complainant) paid the taxes on said land up to and including the year 1882; and that he made great improvements on said land by clearing and fencing a large portion of the same, and erecting buildings thereon, thus greatly increasing the value thereof; and said Brown had greatly improved the portion thereof that had been sold to him; and that the amount said land was sold for by said trustee was not more than one-third of its real value. Said Stephen J. Smith also alleged in his bill that said land was not sold by said trustee at public auction, or advertised as required by law; and for that reason the proceedings under said trust were null and void, and no title could pass from said trustee to said Lowther; and that the deed made by said trustee Cole to said Lowther on the 16th day of September, 1882, is null and void; and he prayed that said deed from said trustee to said A. J. Lowther, and from said A. J. Lowther to his said two daughters, might be set aside and declared null and void, and that said trustee, C. C. Cole, be required to convey said land to complainant.

This bill was answered by C. C. Cole, who in his answer alleged that said trust sale was made in all respects as required by law; that the said sale was made at the instance and suggestion of the plaintiff; that for some reason the plaintiff wanted said land sold under said trust-deed, and on the 11th of November, 1872, it was offered for sale in front of the court-house, and he received only one bid therefor, which was made by the defendant A. J. Lowther, in the presence of the complainant, who became the purchaser for the sum of $299, the same being the amount due on the note secured by said deed of trust, including interest to the day of sale and the expenses of sale; that he was informed by the said complainant and the said Lowther, on the day of sale, that said Lowther would purchase said land at said sale for a sum just sufficient to pay the said debt, interest, and costs of sale, unless there was a higher bid for the same; and he was informed by one or both of them at that time that the said Lowther did not then have sufficient money to pay the entire amount, and the respondent consented, at the request of one or both of said persons, to accept from the said Lowther, in case he became the purchaser of said land, a part of the money then due on said debt, and take the note on said Lowther, with the complainant as surety, for the residue; that after said Lowther purchased said land he paid to respondent on the same day $120, and executed to respondent his note, due one day after date, for $179, for the residue, which note was signed by complainant as surety for said Lowther; that the greater part of said note was soon after paid by said Lowther, but a portion thereof remained until about the 16th day of September, 1882, at which time the said Lowther paid respondent the balance remaining due on said note, and he executed a deed to him for the land, as he is advised and believes it was his duty to do, and he disclaims any knowledge of any arrangement between the plaintiff and said Lowther as is set forth in the plaintiff's bill.

The defendant Thomas Brown also filed an answer to complainant's bill, in which, after stating the facts with reference to his purchase of said 50 acres, part of said 167-acre tract, from said Stephen J. Smith, he alleges that said S. J. Smith and A. J. Lowther each told to him, and said in his presence, that the said Stephen J. Smith furnished, out of his own means, property and money, and placed the same in the hands of said A. J. Lowther, to pay off and satisfy said deed of trust, and that said Lowther had taken the same and paid off and satisfied said debt of $281, together with the proper charges due thereon, and that the note was then delivered to the said Stephen J. Smith by the holder thereof, and that said tract of land was thereby released from any liability on account of said debt, and that said Lowther was at that time only acting as agent for said S. J. Smith in the matter; and that, relying upon these representations so made to him by the said Smith and Lowther, he was induced to and did purchase a part of said 167-acre tract of land, and at once took possession thereof, and so remained until quite recently, and made valuable improvements thereon, and that, after being in possession of said land for nearly 10 years, he was approached by the said Lowther, who represented that he had a deed from C. C. Cole, trustee, for the 167 acres of land, and that the 50 acres bought and paid for by him was a part of said 167-acre tract; and further represented that he had bought said land at the trustee's sale made on the 11th of November, 1872, and had furnished the money to pay off said deed of trust, and demanded payment for said 50 acres, or that he should surrender possession thereof, and the said S. J. Smith having removed to the West, and the said Cole, trustee, having left the county, and moved to some place unknown to respondent, and respondent being ignorant on matters of law, and having no time or opportunity to investigate the matter, he was induced by the representations of said Lowther, on the 9th of January, 1883, to execute his obligations to Mary A. Lowther for the sum of $300, payable as set forth in a bill which had been filed against him by her, said Lowther agreeing to convey to respondent such title as was vested in him by the deed of said C. C. Cole, trustee. Respondent Brown also alleged that the said C. C. Cole, trustee, could not make, and did not make, any title to said land so attempted by him to be conveyed to the said A. J. Lowther on the 16th day of September, 1882; that said pretended deed was a nullity, and did not operate to pass any title for said land, because the land was not advertised and sold as provided for on the face of the deed, or as required by law. He alleges that he purchased said 50 acres of land on the representations, both of Stephen J. Smith and A. J. Lowther, that the land belonged to said Smith, and expended large sums of money in improving it, and only executed the $300 note to said Mary A. Lowther by reason of the false and fraudulent representations of said A. J. Lowther. He reiterates the allegations of the bill as to the fraudulent acts of said A. J. Lowther, and he prayed, by way of affirmative relief, that the written obligations given by him to Mary A. Lowther on January 9, 1883, on which suit was then pending in the name of Mary A. Lowther against him and others, in said circuit court, might be by the court canceled and declared null and void, and that the deed from C. C. Cole, trustee, to A. J. Lowther, dated September 16, 1882, might be set aside and annulled, so far, at least, as respondent was interested, and that the deed made by A. J. Lowther to Mary A. Lowther for said land might also be set aside, and if the court might be of opinion that the title to said real estate was yet in said C. C. Cole, trustee, that he might be required to convey said 50 acres of land to respondent, and that he be relieved from paying said $300 to said Mary A. Lowther.

The defendant A. J. Lowther also answered the complainant's bill, admitting that said trust sale was made by W. L. Cole as agent for C. C. Cole, trustee, and avers that said sale was made by said W. L. Cole with and by the consent and at the request of said C. C. Cole, Vincent Smith, and Stephen J. Smith; and also avers that said Stephen J. Smith, being present at said sale, and consenting thereto, and acquiescing therein, cannot now complain; and by said answer he puts in issue all of the other material allegations of complainant's bill.

Numerous depositions were taken in the cause, and, by agreement, the depositions taken in the case of Mary A. Lowther v. Thomas Brown, pending in said circuit court, were read in this cause; and on the 25th day of November, 1889, this cause was heard upon the bill, and the answers of A. J. Lowther, Mary A. Lowther, and Martha J. Taylor, and C. C. Cole, with replications thereto, and upon the exhibits filed, the depositions taken in the cause, and the depositions read therein by agreement, on consideration whereof the court held that the allegations of the bill were not sustained by the evidence; that the cause made by the bill was not the same made out by the proofs; and that the plaintiff, Stephen J. Smith, joined in and colluded with the principal defendant, A. J. Lowther, for the purpose of defrauding and did defraud A. J. Furby; and that the two parties, Smith and Lowther, are in pari delicto; and for other reasons the court was of opinion that the plaintiff, Stephen J. Smith, was not entitled to the relief prayed for by him; and proceeded to dismiss the plaintiff's bill, with costs; and from this decree said Stephen J. Smith appealed.

The first error assigned by the appellant presents the question as to the validity of the title claimed by A. J. Lowther, the same having been acquired by reason of his purchase at said trust sale. The bill, as we have seen, alleges that said sale was not made by C. C. Cole, trustee, as required by law. This question is raised both by the complainant's bill and the answer of Thomas Brown. Let us then look at the facts in reference to said sale, and we find that W. L. Cole, in answer to the third question asked him, says, among other things: "No payment was made on this note to 11th of November, 1872. On that day land was sold under the deed of trust after proper advertisement. The trustee himself not being present, I acted for him in making the sale, by consent, and at the request of said Smith. At that sale A. J. Lowther became the purchaser for the

sum of $299, that being the exact amount of the debt, interest, and expenses of sale." He had just been speaking of both Vincent Smith and Stephen J. Smith, so it is difficult to determine which one was referred to when he spoke of "making the sale by consent, and at the request of said Smith." The receipt for the cash payment for said land on the day of sale was signed, "C. C. Cole, by W. L. Cole," showing that W. L. Cole was acting for C. C. Cole in making the sale. Can a trustee in a deed of trust delegate his powers? This question must be met and answered in determining upon the validity of this trust sale under which A. J. Lowther claims to have derived his title to said tract of land. It has been frequently held that the trustee in a deed of trust is the agent of both the grantor and the cestui que trust, and his duty requires him to act impartially between them. A confidence is reposed in him by both parties, and he is to use discretion in making the sale. It is his duty to offer the property at public auction, but he must exercise discretion as to the length of time the biddings shall continue, consistent with obtaining the best price for the property; and for this reason the parties interested have the right to select a trustee with such qualities of character and judgment as will enable him to make a judicious and honest disposition of the same, and when the selection is made the law provides that they shall have the benefit of their selection. It is true that it is also said that no trust shall fail for want of a trustee, but when a trustee is wanting, by reason of death or removal, etc., the mode is pointed out for substituting one in his stead by action of the court. Neither the grantor in said deed of trust, nor the cestui que trust, could by their several verbal consent authorize a stranger to make sale thereunder. Neither could they, by their joint verbal consent, legalize a sale made by a person other than the trustee named in the deed of trust. The act which was in force at the time said sale was made, was passed February 28, 1870, and it provided that "the trustee in any such deed, except so far as may be therein otherwise provided, shall, whenever required by any creditor secured, or any surety indemnified, by the deed, * * * sell the property conveyed by the deed," etc., and if it was intended that the grantor in such deed and the cestui que trust could, by agreement, nominate and appoint a stranger, and confer upon him the power to execute such trust-deed, why the necessity of resorting to the courts, as the statute says you must do, when the office of a trustee is vacated by death, removal, or refusal to act? Prof. Minor, in his Institutes, (volume 2, p. 286,) in speaking of the mode of sale by a trustee, says: "He must conform to the terms of the deed in respect to the time and manner of giving notice, and the time and manner of sale, as well as in all other particulars; and in all points where the deed is silent he must govern himself by the general rule to sell to the best advantage, and with an impartial regard to the rights and interests of both parties. It is a principle, also, of such transactions that the trustee is charged with a personal confidence, and must therefore act in person, and not by agent. In the American & English Encyclopedia of Law, under the head of "Agency," p. 368, we find it said: "An agent who has a bare power or authority must execute it himself, and cannot delegate his authority to another." See note 4, where the authorities are fully collated. In Lomax, Dig. p. 427, the author says: "If the trustee dies, the legal title descends to his heirs. But the trust was in some measure personal to the trustee, and the confidence which was reposed in his capacity cannot descend to his heirs, who by their number, their infancy, and their dispersed situation, or other circumstances, may not have the same facilities to sell as the trustee himself had. In the case of the death of the trustee, therefore, a new trustee to sell must be supplied by the court of chancery, and the sale must be made under the authority of the court." Our statute, however, (Code, c. 132, § 5,) provides that, in case of death or removal of the trustee beyond the limits of the state, or, the trustee named shall decline to accept the trust or refuse to act, any person interested in the execution of the deed may apply, by motion, to the circuit court, after 10 days' notice to the persons therein mentioned, and have a trustee appointed, who shall be substituted to all of the powers, rights, duties, and responsibilities of the trustee named in said deed; and the next section provides that "the personal representative of a sole or surviving trustee shall execute the trust, or so much as remained unexecuted at the death of such trustee, (whether the trust subject be real or personal estate,) unless the instrument creating the trust otherwise direct, or some other trustee be appointed for the purpose by a court of chancery having jurisdiction of the case." There would surely be no necessity for these provisions if the grantor in a deed of trust, or the *cestui que trust*, could consent that a stranger could carry the trust into execution, and confer title on a purchaser, to the same extent as if the trustee himself was present and acting in the premises. We must therefore conclude that W. L. Cole, in the absence of C. C. Cole, trustee, had no power or authority to make sale of the 167 acres of land mentioned in said deed of trust.

Again, it appears in the evidence adduced in the cause that in 1872, about the month of March, the appellant, Stephen J. Smith, sold the tract of land in controversy to one A. J. Furby for six dollars per acre; and before the first payment was due he refused to make the payment, because he claimed there was something wrong with the title, and said he was going to hold the land until the last note was due, and in the mean time would take off the timber, and appellant could not help himself, and that the sale was made under said trust-deed in order to dispossess said Furby; and the circuit court, on the face of its decree, recites that, "it appearing that the allegations of the bill are not sustained by the evidence in this case; that the cause made in the bill is

not the same made out by the proofs; and that the plaintiff, Stephen J. Smith, joined in and colluded with the principal defendant, A. J. Lowther, for the purpose of defrauding, and did defraud, A. J. Furby; and that the two said parties, Smith and Lowther, are *in pari delicto;* and for other reasons,—the court is of opinion that the plaintiff, Stephen J. Smith, is not entitled to the relief prayed for by him." In this case, however, the said A. J. Furby is no party, by petition or otherwise, and he is not complaining of the action of either Smith or Lowther in the premises. No allegation of fraudulent conduct towards said Furby is presented by any of the pleadings in the cause, and no question as to the effect of the sale under said trust, upon the rights and interests of said Furby, is in any manner put in issue or brought before the court by the pleadings, and it is difficult to conceive how a decree could be predicated upon any evidence in relation to said collusion or fraud against the rights of said Furby. This court has held in the case of Burley v. Weller, 14 W. Va. 264, (section 1 of syllabus,) that "matters not charged in the bill or averred in the answer, and not in issue in the cause, are not proper to be considered in the hearing." See, also, Hunter's Ex'rs y. Hunter, 10 W. Va. 321, where the same principle is decided. And as the decree in this case appears to have been based to some extent, at least, upon a matter which was not presented to the court for consideration, we must regard it as error.

Having arrived at these conclusions, it would appear unnecessary to enter into any analysis or discussion of the evidence which has been taken in the cause, for the reason that it bears mainly upon the question as to who was the real purchaser of the tract of land in controversy at the attempted sale made by W. L. Cole on the 11th day of November, 1872, and who paid said purchase money, what amount was paid, and how it was applied. It does appear, however, that on the 11th day of November, 1872, a receipt signed. "C. C. Cole, by W. L. Cole," was executed on the 11th day of November, 1872, to A. J. Lowther for $120, part payment for said tract of land; and on the same day, a single bill, which was joint and several, was executed to C. C. Cole, trustee, by A. J. Lowther and S. Smith, which single bill is indorsed with several credits, reducing the balance due on the 7th of October, 1873, to $71. The deposition of W. L. Cole discloses the fact that the entire amount of the balance of the purchase money was paid on the 20th of October, 1873, in a chancery suit which had been instituted by C. C. Cole, trustee, against A. J. Lowther, Stephen J. Smith, and Vincent Smith. Subsequent to this time, something near 10 years, and after Stephen J. Smith had gone west to live, it appears that W. L. Cole, by mistake, collected from A. J. Lowther a sum of money, (the exact amount of which does not appear,) but which he claimed to be still due upon said purchase money, and procured a deed to be made to said A. J. Lowther for said 167 acres of land by said C. C. Cole, trustee, dated on the 10th day of September, 1882. From what has been said, it follows that A. J. Lowther derived no title by reason of said deed from C. C. Cole, trustee; and, of course, he could confer none upon Martha J. Taylor and Mary J., Lowther, his daughters, and both of said deeds must be set aside and held for naught; but as it does not clearly and definitely appear who paid the debt due to Vincent Smith, and an account may be necessary to adjust and settle the differences between Stephen J. Smith and A. J. Lowther as to the payment of said indebtedness, the decree complained of is reversed, and the cause is remanded to the circuit court of Doddridge county, with leave to the parties to amend their pleadings if they think proper in order to settle and adjust said matters of account, and the appellant, Stephen J. Smith, must be paid the costs of this appeal by the appellee A. J. Lowther.

McCLAIN v. LOWTHER.

(*Supreme Court of Appeals of West Virginia. Nov. 14, 1891.*)

ACTION ON CHECK — PLEADING — DELAY IN PRESENTING—BURDEN OF PROOF.

1. The drawing and delivery of a check implies the indebtedness of the drawer to the payee to the amount of the check, and in an action upon the check it is unnecessary to aver in the declaration any further consideration.

2. Where a check is not presented in time, and notice of non payment is not given, injury to the drawer will be presumed; but a check is always presumed to be drawn on actual funds; and while if the holder has been guilty of laches in not presenting it in due time, or in failing to give notice of non-payment, it becomes incumbent upon him to show that the drawer has not been injured by the dereliction, yet, on the other hand, if he shows that the drawer had no funds in the bank against which he drew, the burden of proving actual damage is shifted upon the drawer, and, in the absence of such proof, the plaintiff is entitled to recover.

(*Syllabus by the Court.*)

Error to circuit court, Doddridge county.

Action of *assumpsit* by U. D. McClain, administrator, etc., against Oliver Lowther, on a check drawn by defendant. Judgment for plaintiff, and defendant brings error. Affirmed.

R. S. Blair, for plaintiff in error. *Laird & Turner*, for defendant in error.

LUCAS, P. This was an action of *assumpsit* in the circuit court of Doddridge county upon a check for $500, drawn by Oliver Lowther on the Second National Bank of Parkersburg, payable to the order of A. J. Lowther. After the plaintiff had closed his case, the defendant demurred to the evidence, and, the plaintiff having joined in the demurrer, the jury found a conditional verdict on the issue of *non assumpsit*, and the court gave judgment for the full amount of the check, with interest and costs against the defendant. From that judgment this writ of error is prosecuted.

The testimony, in substance, proved the execution and delivery of the check; also that the payee, A. J. Lowther, indorsed the check to one Maurice Prager, who presented it to the bank, and payment

was refused. This was done several times, and the cashier informed Mr. Prager that there were no funds in the bank to meet the check. The cashier of the bank testified that the check was presented, but it was not paid, the drawer, Oliver Lowther, not having money there sufficient to meet the check; nor did he (Oliver Lowther) have sufficient money there to meet the check during the month of December, on the 7th of which month the check bore date. And this was all the evidence. Upon this evidence we are required to decide whether judgment was properly rendered in favor of the plaintiff. There was a general demurrer to the declaration, but not to each and every count, and, as the declaration contained the common counts in *assumpsit*, the demurrer was, of course, properly overruled. The special count on the check seems liable to no valid exception. It is true that it avers no consideration for the giving of the check, nor was any proved, but that was plainly unnecessary, as the drawing and delivery of the check implied the indebtedness of the drawer to the payee to the amount of the check, as was held in Ford v McClung, 5 W. Va. 156. See, also, Peasley v. Boatwright, 2 Leigh, 195, and Terry v. Ragsdale, 33 Grat. 342. In the case of Ford, 5 W. Va. 165, the law upon the subject of checks and orders is thus correctly defined: "The drawer of a bill of exchange or order is not directly liable to the payee or his indorsee, but his implied obligation or contract is to pay in the event the amount is not paid by the drawee. And the general rule is well established that the drawers and indorsers are entitled to prompt notice of the non-acceptance or non-payment, in order that the former may look after his funds, and withdraw or secure the same, and that the latter may take the necessary steps to secure himself, and that, upon the failure to receive such notice, they are discharged from liability; and the bill or order, as between the drawer and payee or indorsee, will be considered paid. 1 Tuck. Comm. Laws, and note; Bank v. Vanmeter, 4 Rand. (Va.) 553. But there are well-defined exceptions to this rule, and numerous cases may be found in which, under the peculiar circumstances of the case, the holder has been excused from presenting the bill or order to the drawee or giving notice of the non-acceptance or non-payment thereof." And where a check is not presented in time, and notice of non-acceptance given, injury to the drawer will be presumed. But a check is always presumed to be drawn on actual funds; and while if the holder has been guilty of laches in not presenting it in due time, or in failing to give notice of non-payment, it becomes incumbent upon him to show that the drawer has not been injured by the delay, yet, on the other hand, if he shows that the drawer had no funds in the bank against which he drew, the burden of proving actual damage is shifted upon the drawer. Edw. Bills & N. § 552. In the present case the check was dated the 6th of December, and there is no proof that it was ever presented for payment until about the middle of that month, and no notice of non-acceptance was proved to have been given to the drawer. But, on the other hand, the cashier of the bank proves that the drawer had no sufficient funds to meet the check during the entire month of December. The drawer, it is true, had presented a note for discount about the time that he drew the check, but the discount was refused, and the note returned to him. Under these circumstances, we think the plaintiff has fully met the burden and responsibility of proving that the defendant had no funds to draw against, and that he had knowledge of this fact, and consequently no notice of non-payment was necessary; nor was he injured, so far as the evidence discloses, by the failure to give him notice. We think the judgment of the circuit court was proper, and the same must be affirmed.

SPENCE v. ROBINSON et al.

(Supreme Court of Appeals of West Virginia. Nov. 21, 1891.)

NEGOTIABLE INSTRUMENTS — INDORSEMENT AND TRANSFER—ACTIONS—PLEADING—REVIEW.

1. Where there is error in the declaration, pleadings, or judgment, committed against the protest, or over the demurrer or other objection, of a party as shown by the record, the same may be reviewed and corrected in this court, although no motion has been made for a new trial in the court below, and no exception was reserved by bill of exceptions or otherwise.

2. If a negotiable instrument, not payable to bearer, be indorsed specially to a particular person, while such person remains the holder and legal owner the right of action is in him alone, and none but he, or his personal representative, can sue.

3. If a special replication has been permitted to be filed over the objection of the defendant, and his demurrer thereto overruled to his manifest injury, the error will be corrected in this court by setting aside the judgment, and directing the trial court to award a new trial.

(Syllabus by the Court.)

Error to circuit court, Taylor county.

Action by L. Spence, for the use, etc., against Joshua G. Robinson and another, on a note. The action was commenced before a justice, where plaintiff had judgment. Defendants appealed to the circuit court, where judgment was again rendered for plaintiff. Defendants bring error. Reversed.

B. F. Martin, for plaintiffs in error. John Bassel, for defendant in error.

LUCAS, P. This was an action instituted before GEORGE W. BROWN, justice of the peace for Taylor county, in which the defendants, Robinson and Dunham, were summoned to answer the complaint "of L. Spence, use of Noah Beck, in a civil action for the recovery of money due on contract." The defendants failed to appear, and the plaintiff had judgment for the sum of $154.40, with interest and costs. Thereupon the defendants took an appeal to the circuit court. The cause was there docketed, and the defendants filed two pleas to the complaint of the plaintiff. The first amounted to a plea of nil debit, and the second set up a failure of consideration. It averred that on the 14th day of August, 1887, the defendants bought from said L. Spence a portable steam-engine for

$500, and executed and delivered to said L. Spence "the note in controversy for $150, and two other notes, of $175 each, of same date, for the price of said engine." The plea then alleges a specific warranty of the engine by Spence, and its utter failure to come up to the warranty, and that by reason of the breach they are damaged to the extent of $500, against which they offer to allow the amount of the note sued on, with interest from said 14th day of August, 1887, as an offset. These pleas were at first replied to generally, but subsequently the plaintiff withdrew his general replication to the second plea, and tendered a "replication in writing to the said plea, to the filing of which the defendants objected, and moved the court to reject the same." At a subsequent day the court overruled the motion to reject the special replication, and allowed the same to be filed. The special replication is as follows: "L. Spence, for use of Noah Beck, v. J. G. Robinson et als. Appeal. The plaintiff says he ought not to be barred of having and maintaining his action against the defendants by reason of the matters contained in the plea in writing by them secondly above pleaded, because he says that the promissory note mentioned and described in the summons in this action, and filed therewith, was upon the face thereof made by the defendants payable to the plaintiff at Martin's Ferry, in the state of Ohio, and by the laws of said state said promissory note is negotiable; and the plaintiff, for a valuable consideration, before the maturity of said promissory note, indorsed the same to the person for whose use this action is brought, said indorsement being made at said Martin's Ferry, in the said state of Ohio, and said indorsee having no notice of the matters alleged in the said plea at the time said indorsement was so made to him. And this the plaintiff is ready to verify, etc. J. BASSEL, Atty." And on a subsequent day the defendants demurred to this replication, but the court overruled the demurrer, and gave judgment, after trial and verdict, in favor of the plaintiff against the defendants and their sureties on the appeal-bond. No bill of exceptions was taken, nor was there any motion for a new trial in the court below. Neither does the record disclose that any exception was taken by the defendant to the action of the court in overruling his objection to filing the special replication, or in overruling his demurrer to the same.

Is that replication a part of the record, and can we review the action of the circuit court, as above described? Code, c. 131, § 9, provides that "any party may avail himself of any error appearing on the record, by which he is prejudiced, without excepting thereto." In the leading case of Danks v. Rhodehaver, 26 W. Va. 274, 287, Judge GREEN suggests that this sentence should read as if it were written, "without taking a formal bill of exceptions," this court having previously in several other cases made a similar suggestion. Perry v. Horn, 22 W. Va. 381. I doubt, however, whether we are at liberty to curtail the remedial efficacy of the act by interpolating any other language than that employed in the act itself, which is perfectly free from all ambiguity. The state of our law upon this subject will be found more accurately stated by Judge SNYDER in Bank v. Showacre, 26 W. Va. 50: "A party may take advantage in the appellate court of an error committed by the trial court in permitting a plea to be filed, where the record shows that such party objected to the filing of such plea in the trial court, and that he need not in such case take a bill of exceptions, or except to the action of the court overruling his objection. This rule is equally applicable to the filing of a replication." It is true, as a general rule, that if errors, or supposed errors, are committed by a court in its rulings during the trial of a case by a jury, the appellate court cannot review those rulings, unless they were objected to at the time, and a bill of exceptions filed during the term, and a new trial asked of the court below, and refused. See leading case of Danks v. Rhodeheaver, 26 W. Va. 274. But in this leading case reference is made, and approvingly, to what was said in State v. Phares, 24 W. Va. 657, as follows: "Of course, it is different if the error is in the pleadings, as in such case there was a mistrial." And in the latest case on this subject (Brown v. Brown, 29 W. Va. 778, 2 S. E. Rep. 808) it is said, in substance, that, if a demurrer to the declaration has been improperly overruled, the appellate court will reverse, though no bill of exceptions was taken, and although there was no motion for a new trial. The reasons for this distinction are not very satisfactory. Nevertheless, we may regard it as firmly established in this state that where there is error in the declaration, pleadings, or judgment, committed against the protest, or over the demurrer or other objection, of a party, the same may be reviewed and corrected in this court, although no motion has been made for a new trial in the court below, and no exception was reserved by bills of exceptions or otherwise.

Let us apply these principles to the case in hand. No exception was taken, nor was there any motion for a new trial. The special replication marked "No. 2" was filed over the objection of the defendants, and their demurrer thereto was overruled, and this, as we have seen, was all that was necessary for the purposes of review by this court. Was the demurrer to the said replication properly overruled? For the purpose of demurrer, the facts stated in the replication must be taken as true. Therefore, without looking at the note itself, we must regard it as a negotiable instrument, indorsed for value to a special indorsee, suit upon which has been brought by the payee for the use of the special indorsee and holder. If the note were not negotiable, this could be done under our statute, which declares that the assignee of any bond, note, account, or writing not negotiable may maintain thereupon any action, in his own name, without the addition of "assignee," which the original obligee or payee might have brought, but shall allow all just discounts, not only against himself, but against the assignor, before the defendant had notice of the assignment. According

to the practice under the Code of Virginia, the assignee could institute the suit, where the instrument was not negotiable, either in his own name, or in the name of his assignor for his use. But this was in express derogation of the rule of the common law that only he who had the strict legal title and interest had the right of action. In cases not provided for by the statute, the principle of the common law must be held still to prevail. If, therefore, by the indorsement of a negotiable instrument to a specific indorsee by the law-merchant, the legal title becomes vested in said indorsee, in the absence of any statutory provision he alone can sue upon the instrument. It is very true he may transfer his right to another, but so long as the legal title remains in him, together with the possession of the note or other instrument, the right of action is vested in him alone. Upon principle, this would seem to be a correct conclusion, and, although cases may be found tending in an opposite direction, this position is sustained by a large majority of the better authorities. The text-writers agree with considerable unanimity in stating the law to be as I have construed it. Thus, Mr. Edwards says: "The plaintiff, in an action upon a bill, check, or note, must show in his declaration his right to sue thereon in the same manner as every other plaintiff must show a sufficient title to enable him to maintain his suit. If he sues as the indorsee or bearer of a bill, he must show that it was drawn in a transferable form, and that the transfer to him was made in the manner permitted by its terms; in short, he must allege all that is necessary to show the legal title vested in himself." Edw. Bills & N. §§ 928, 962. So, also, Mr. Daniel: "In the first place, an indorsement in full is one which mentions the name of the person in whose favor it is made, and to whom or to whose order the sum is to be paid. For instance, 'Pay to B. or order,' signed 'A.,' is an indorsement in full by A., the payee or holder of the paper, to B. An indorsement in full prevents the bill or note from being indorsed by any one but the indorsee, and none but the special indorsee or his representative can sue upon it." 1 Daniel, Neg. Inst. § 692. Likewise Mr. Parsons: "But if the plaintiff has neither the possession of the paper, nor any right to it by reason of any interest in it, he cannot recover upon it. The legal interest, however, is sufficient to support the action, although the entire beneficial interest has been transferred. And an agent who holds a bill or note payable to bearer or indorsed in blank, or to whom it has been indorsed for the purpose of collection, may sue on it in his own name." 2 Pars. Notes & B. 443. It will be observed that the author is here speaking of notes payable to bearer, or indorsed in blank, and Mr. Robinson in his second volume of Practice, (page 229,) to which we are cited by counsel for defendant in error, holds the same language. He says: "The beneficial owner of a bill of exchange or negotiable note, which is payable to bearer or is indorsed in blank, may, says Chancellor WALWORTH, institute a suit thereon in a court of law in the name of any one who is willing to allow his name to be used for that purpose; and, where the defendant has no legal or equitable defense to the bill or note as against the real owner thereof, he cannot be permitted to show that the nominal plaintiff, in whose name the suit is so brought, is not the real party in interest." On the same page, however, Mr. Robinson draws the proper distinction, and says: "As a person who has no interest in, or possession of, a bill cannot maintain an action upon it, it is a valid defense that the bill was not indorsed to the plaintiff, and that he is not the holder of it." See, also, pages 227, 228. The distinction between a note indorsed in blank and one indorsed to a special indorsee is a natural and proper one, because, in a suit by a holder upon the former, a recovery is a perfect defense to the maker against any future action, and he is deprived of no defense which he might legitimately make. On the other hand, if there is a special indorsee, the defendant has a right to inquire in what manner the title to the note has passed away from such indorsee, and a recovery by a person not entitled to the note would be no defense in a subsequent action by the party entitled. In the case of Ritchie v. Moore, 5 Munf. 388, it was held that the holder of a bill of exchange, with several indorsements in blank, could maintain a suit upon it, because he had the right to write such assignment as he though proper over the blank indorsements. On the other hand, in the case of Myers v. Friend, 1 Rand. (Va.) 14, in speaking of an instrument transferable by delivery or indorsement only, the court says: "In the case before us the appellee should have deduced his title from the note under that cashier to whom it was confided and indorsed. He could acquire no property in it from another,—from a man who only had the possession of it." It seems quite clear, therefore, if a negotiable instrument not payable to bearer be indorsed specially to a particular person, while such person remains the holder and legal owner, the right of action is in him alone, and none but he, or his personal representative, can sue. If this conclusion be, then, correct, it follows that the demurrer to the special replication should have been sustained, because, if the matter therein contained were true, the plaintiff had no case and no right of recovery. It is hardly necessary to add that the defendants were manifestly injured by the filing of this improper replication, and the judgment of the circuit court must be reversed, with directions to that court to award a new trial, to be conducted upon the principles herein announced, and otherwise according to law.

STATE v. PEARIS.

(Supreme Court of Appeals of West Virginia. Nov. 21, 1891.)

OFFENSES AGAINST ELECTION LAWS—GIVING LIQUOR TO VOTER — INDICTMENT — JURY — CHALLENGES.

1. The latter clause of section 10, c. 5, Code, reads: "And if any person, whether a candidate or not, offer, give, or distribute any intoxicating drink to any voter on the day of an election, he shall forfeit not less than ten, nor more than fifty, dollars." *Held* that, in an indictment based on this section of the statute, it being charged that the person to whom the intoxicating drink was given was a legally qualified voter, it is not necessary to state the facts constituting such person a qualified voter.

2. In such indictment it is not necessary to allege any special criminal intent, but the *scienter*, or general criminal intent, that is, that the accused knowingly and willfully did the unlawful act, is sufficient.

3. The offense here charged, being a misdemeanor, is not within the meaning of the term "civil case," as used in section 31, c. 116, Code, and therefore the accused was not entitled to a special jury.

4. But under section 17, c. 116, the accused was entitled to challenge four jurors peremptorily, and, this having been refused, the judgment and verdict are set aside, and a new trial is awarded.

(Syllabus by the Court.)

Error to circuit court, Mercer county; A. C. SNYDER, Judge.

Indictment of George W. Pearis for giving intoxicating drinks to a voter on the day of an election. Defendant was convicted, and brings error. Reversed.

David E. Johnston, for plaintiff in error. *Alfred Caldwell*, Atty. Gen., for the State.

HOLT, J. On the 12th of March, 1889, the grand jury of the circuit court of Mercer county found an indictment against George W. Pearis, founded on the latter clause of section 10, c. 5, Code (2d Ed.) 1891, p. 95. The whole section is as follows: "If any person who is a candidate for any office under the constitution and laws of this state shall, himself or by another, offer to give or distribute among the voters any intoxicating drink on the day of the election, he shall, if elected, forfeit his office, and on proof of the fact be removed therefrom; and if any person, whether a candidate or not, offer, give, or distribute any intoxicating drink to any voter on the day of an election, he shall forfeit not less than ten, nor more than fifty, dollars." The indictment was demurred to, and the demurrer was overruled. This is one of the errors complained of, and I give the indictment in full: "State of West Virginia, Mercer county, to-wit: The grand jurors of the state of West Virginia, in and for the body of the county of Mercer, upon their oaths present that on the 6th day of November, 1888, in the said county of Mercer and state of West Virginia, at an election then and there held in said county for the election of state, county, and district officers, under the laws of the state of West Virginia, George W. Pearis did then and there, to-wit, in the said county of Mercer, on the 6th day of November, 1888, willfully, wrongfully, knowingly, and unlawfully give to one Joseph R. Johnston an intoxicating drink, the said Joseph R. Johnston being then and there a legally qualified voter, against the peace and dignity of the state. J. W. HALE, Pros. Atty. Found upon the evidence of Joseph R. Johnston." It is alleged on the part of defendant that this indictment is bad, because, in averring that Joseph R. Johnston is a qualified voter, it charges only the legal result of certain facts, whereas it should charge the facts out of which the legal result arises, that is, the facts showing that Johnston was a qualified voter; and that it fails to charge the wrongful or criminal intent, without which the offense does not exist.

In this offense no special criminal intent is necessary. All that is needed is the averment of the *scienter*,—the general criminal intent,—and that this indictment contains,"—willfully" and "knowingly" did the act which the statute forbids; and, being conclusively presumed to know the law, the only criminal intent needed is both alleged and proved. As to the other objection, this indictment follows the language of the statute in describing the offense, and, in alleging that it was committed, fully, directly, and expressly alleges, without any uncertainty or ambiguity, all the essential facts of time, place, person, and other circumstances, so as to fix the instance given as a definite and particular violation of the statute. It alleges that Johnston, to whom the intoxicating drink was given, was a legally qualified voter, and that, for this purpose, is a matter of fact, although his right to vote is made by law to depend on the existence of quite a number of facts. Any other rule would require the allegation that he was a male citizen of the state, etc., (section 1, art. 4, Const. W. Va.,) and here we would be where we started; for citizen or not a citizen is, in the same sense, also a question of law and fact. All facts with which the law deals are more or less complex, involving matters of law, and such a mode of separation of law from fact would involve us in an endless maze of averments, confusing and perplexing the accused, rather than giving him notice of the accusation. If it had been an indictment against Johnston for illegal voting, then it might be necessary to state the precise facts which disqualified him. Pearce v. State, 1 Sneed, 63. We think the indictment good, and the demurrer properly overruled. The defendant was not entitled to a special jury, for section 21, c. 116, Code, p. 778, (Ed. 1891,) allows a special jury in civil cases only; but by the seventeenth section of chapter 116 he did have the right to challenge four jurors peremptorily. State v. Railroad Co., 15 W. Va. 364. This the circuit court denied him, and for this cause the judgment and verdict must be set aside, and a new trial awarded, and the cause is remanded.

WATT et al. v. BROOKOVER et al.

(Supreme Court of Appeals of West Virginia. Nov. 21, 1891.)

DEATH OF PLAINTIFF BEFORE JUDGMENT—ATTORNEY—POWER TO COMPROMISE.

1. The fact that a sole plaintiff, or one of several plaintiffs, is dead at the time of the institution of an action, such death not appearing on the record, does not render a judgment therein void, but only erroneous, and such judgment is a lien on real estate.

2. An attorney at law, employed to collect a debt merely as such, has no power to compromise after judgment, and accept a sum of money less than the full amount of the judgment as satisfaction.

(Syllabus by the Court.)

Appeal from circuit court, Monongalia county.

Suit by Watt, Lang & Co., for use of Stephen A. Shepherd, against Joseph S. Brookover, to enforce a judgment. The bill was dismissed, and plaintiffs appeal. Reversed.

Keck & Son, for appellants. *Berkshire & Sturgiss,* for appellees.

BRANNON, J. A judgment was rendered in the circuit court of Monongalia county in favor of plaintiffs for $307.22, with interest and costs, in an action by Watt, Lang & Co., for the use of Stephen A. Shepherd, against Joseph S. Brookover; and a chancery suit was brought by Watt, Lang & Co. and Shepherd against Brookover to enforce the judgment against a tract of 45 acres of land, and, the bill having been dismissed, the plaintiffs appeal to this court. It is assigned as error that an amended answer was allowed to be filed by Brookover. He filed an answer, setting up that he had compromised and settled the judgment, and the cause was then referred to a commissioner to ascertain the lands of the judgment debtor and the liens upon it. Depositions were taken by both sides. The commissioner filed a report allowing the plaintiffs their debt in full, and Brookover excepted to it. Then the decree of dismissal was entered. In this decree it is stated that an answer and amended answer of Brookover were read, though I see no prior order filing such amended answer. This amended answer sets up that defendant Brookover had learned since the filing of his original answer that John W. Watt, of the firm of Watt, Lang & Co., and a plaintiff in the chancery suit, and also in the action in which the judgment had been rendered, had died before the action at law was brought, and that the said judgment was a nullity and void, and no lien on his land. The plaintiff objected, and excepted to said amended answer as irrelevant and immaterial and as offered too late. The decree does not pass on the exception, but reads the amended answer on the hearing, and impliedly overruled the exception. It is sufficient to say of this answer, though taken to be true, in the absence of a replication, that the fact which it presents as a defense—that is, the death of Watt—was immaterial, and presented no defense to the bill. As regards a judgment against a party dead at its rendition, this court, in King v. Burdett, 28 W. Va. 601, held such judgment not void for the fact of death not appearing on the record, and that it was a lien enforceable in chancery, and such death could not be set up in defense of a bill to enforce it. In Evans v. Spurgin, 6 Grat. 107, it was held that, the death of a defendant not having been suggested, a decree cannot be impeached in a collateral action by evidence of his death. I think these decisions are binding authority on us, and in principle decide this point in the case. I shall not advert to the many decisions upholding them, as Pres. JOHNSON fully discussed them in King v. Burdett. In Neale v. Utz, 75 Va. 480, a judgment against a convict was held unimpeachable in a collateral proceeding, though the party was *civiliter mortuus.* True, these cases were cases of judgment against persons, while here it is the case of one of the partners plaintiff dead at the institution of the action; but I concur in the opinion expressed in 1 Black, Judgm. § 204, that such a case" cannot be distinguished in principle from that of a defendant dying while the action is pending, where, as already shown, (section 200,) the great preponderance of authority sustains the rule that the judgment is at least impervious to collateral attack, and must be vacated or reversed by proper proceedings. Both cases are equally governed by the principle that, when once the jurisdiction has attached, no subsequent error or irregularity in the exercise of that jurisdiction can make its judgment void." Here the party was dead at the institution of the action in which judgment was rendered. Mr. Black, supra, states the law to be that, if an action is commenced in the name of a person already dead, (as, where the decedent is the nominal plaintiff, and the one for whose benefit the suit is prosecuted is the real party in interest,) or if one of several joint claimants is dead before action brought, it is held that the defendant must take advantage of the fact by plea in abatement, at the peril of being estopped by his silence, and the judgment for plaintiff will not be disturbed." (The fact that defendant did not know of his death can make no difference as to this point.) In Powell v. Washington, 15 Ala. 803, it was held that where one, having the beneficial interest in a note, sued in the name of a dead payee, and there was judgment by default, the judgment was valid, and could not even be vacated by a proper proceeding to vacate it. In Milam Co. v. Robertson, 47 Tex. 222, and Case v. Ritelin, 1 J. J. Marsh, 29, it was held that a judgment for or against a party dead at the time, his death not appearing, is not void. Freeman on Judgments, § 153, states it as law that judgments for or against deceased parties are not void, and that, even where the fact of the death appears in the record, they are not void, but only voidable, and are to be affected only by appeal. I am of opinion that, where the fact of death is apparent in the record of the judgment, its rendition would be error of law, to be corrected by appellate process; and, where it does not appear in the record, but is to be shown *aliunde,* it is called error in fact, to be corrected at common law by writ of error *coram vobis,* and now, under our Code, (1889,) c. 135, § 1, by motion in lieu of that writ. 2 Tuck Com. Laws, 328; 4 Minor, Inst. 848. I do not intimate whether this judgment could have been affected in any way; whether the naming as a plaintiff a dead partner, when the cause of action survived to the other, who was also a party, would render the judgment erroneous. Some cases cited by authors as holding that judgments against dead persons are null do not do so. The word "void" may be used in them, but in the sense of "erroneous." They were cases where, by proper proceedings, they were sought to be re-

versed, not attacked collaterally. Such are the cases of Colson v. Wade, 1 Murph. 43; Burke v. Stokely, 65 N. C. 569; Moore v. Easley, 18 Ala. 619. There is a wide difference between a judgment null and void and one erroneous and voidable; the one is no lien, the other is until reversed. This judgment is not a nullity, but a valid lien on the land sought to be subjected.

Now, as to the defense of payment. The defendant, Brookover, gives evidence to show that he compromised the judgment with Hough, one of the firm of Kreck & Hough, attorneys, who recovered the judgment, and paid Hough $100 in satisfaction of it. In Wiley v. Mahood, 10 W. Va. 206, and Harper v. Harvey, 4 W. Va. 539, it was held that an attorney employed to collect a debt can only receive money for payment, and cannot, without authority, accept other things in satisfaction of it. Here money was received, but much less than the debt. Is this compromise valid? Has an attorney to collect a debt authority simply as such to compromise and accept only part of a debt as full satisfaction? Chief Justice MARSHALL, in Holker v. Parker, 7 Cranch, 496, said that he had not. I do not here refer to the question of the power of an attorney to compromise pending litigation to obtain judgment. In England it seems to be settled in such case that he has authority to compromise, but in America there is great conflict of decision on the subject, the preponderance of authority seeming to be against such power, though, as that point is not involved here, I have not fully examined the authorities. See note to section 24, Story, Ag. (9th Ed.;) Preston v. Hill, 50 Cal. 43, 19 Amer. Rep. 647, note in 41 Amer. Rep. 847; De Louis v. Meek, 50 Amer. Dec. 491; Huston v. Mitchell, 16 Amer. Dec. 506; 1 Lawson, Rights, Rem. & Pr. § 171, and notes. This is a case where there was no appearance of contention as to the right to the debt, and its amount has been fixed by final judgment, but there was some considerable doubt whether the judgment could be realized. It is clear that no express authority to compromise the debt was given. We are of opinion that under these circumstances the attorney had no implied authority to receive part of the judgment in full. In Granger v. Batchelder, 54 Vt. 248, 41 Amer. Rep. 846, an attorney received part of a judgment in money, and the execution which had been levied on property claimed by others was returned satisfied. The court held that the attorney had no power to receive less than the full amount. So in Robinson v. Murphy the supreme court of Alabama said that the judgment terminated the litigation and its uncertainties, and conclusively ascertained that the plaintiff was to have from the defendant a fixed amount; that the powers of the attorney are not co-equal and co-extensive with those of the client, and he could accept nothing less than the full amount of the judgment. See note to Granger v. Batchelder, 41 Amer. Rep. 847. So it was held in Beers v. Hendrickson, 45 N. Y. 665; Lewis v. Woodruff, 15 How. Pr. 539; Wilson v. Wadleigh, 36 Me. 496; Harrow v. Farrow, 7 B. Mon. 126; Chambers v. Miller,

7 Watts, 63; Town of Whitehall v. Keller, 100 Pa. St. 105; 1 Lawson, Rights, Rem. & Pr. 171; 2 Black, Judgm. § 989. I see no authority to the reverse. But, though this compromise will not discharge the judgment, we think the judgment should be credited with $100 paid under said compromise as of 15th day of April, 1884. Here it is useless to detail evidence further than to say that Brookover swears positively to the payment, and Gallagher that he saw the receipt, since lost, which had been given by Hough. The evidence is not entirely convincing, but we conclude that it should be allowed. The decree is reversed, and the cause remanded, with direction to enter a decree for the judgment, subject to such credit, and to enforce it as a lien against the land in the record described.

TAYLOR v. OHIO RIVER R. CO.

(Supreme Court of Appeals of West Virginia. Nov. 21, 1891.)

ACTION AGAINST DOMESTIC RAILROAD COMPANY—SERVICE OF SUMMONS.

Service of a summons in an action before a justice against a domestic railroad corporation upon its president must be in the county in which he resides, and the return must show that fact, else it is invalid. A judgment based on a return of service not showing that fact, there being no appearance, is void.

(Syllabus by the Court.)

Error to circuit court, Mason county.

Action by Adam Taylor against the Ohio River Railroad Company. Judgment for plaintiff, and defendant brings error. Reversed.

V. B. Archer, for plaintiff in error. Simpson & Howard and James B. Menager, for defendant in error.

BRANNON, J. Adam Taylor recovered judgment before a justice of Mason county against the Ohio River Railroad Company upon the verdict of a jury, and the case went to the circuit court by certiorari; and, the judgment having been there affirmed, the company brought the case to this court. The point of error assigned against the judgment is that the return of service of the summons to answer the action, upon the president, while it shows such service to have been made in Mason county, does not show that it is the county of his residence. The Code, (Ed. 1887,) c. 50, § 34, reads as follows: "(34) Unless otherwise specially provided, such process or order, and any notice against a corporation, may be served upon the president, cashier, treasurer, or chief officer thereof, or if there be no such officer, or if he be absent, on any officer, director, trustee, or agent of the corporation, at its principal office or place of business, or in any county in which a director or other officer or any agent of said corporation may reside. But service at any time may be made upon any corporation in the manner prescribed for similar proceedings in the circuit court." Sections 35-37 provide for service on foreign corporations, foreign insurance and express companies and banks, and need not be further mentioned. Then section 38 provides as follows: "(38)

v.13s.e.no.37—64

Service on any person under either of the last four sections shall be in the county in which he resides, and the return must show this, and state on whom and when the service was; otherwise the service shall not be valid." Leaving out the closing clause of section 34, authorizing for process in justices' courts similar service to that for process in suits in circuit courts, it would seem to be very plain that a return of service on a president of a domestic corporation, not showing that the service was made in the county of his residence, would be bad. But it is contended that said closing clause adds to its preceding provisions, and gives an additional mode of service, provided by another section of the Code, namely, section 7, c. 124, and that this service and return will be sustained by that section. That section is as follows: "(7) It shall be sufficient to serve any process against or notice to a corporation on its mayor, president, or other chief officer, or any person appointed pursuant to law to accept service of process for it, or in his absence from the county or municipal corporation, to the officer of which the process is directed, it shall be sufficient to serve the notice or process, if the corporation to be served he a city, town, or village, on two members of the council, and if it be not a city, town, or village, on the secretary, cashier, or treasurer, and if there be none such, or he be absent, on a member of the board of trustees, directors, or visitors. If there be not within the state any other person on whom there can be service as aforesaid, service on a director, agent, (including, in the case of a railroad company, a depot or station agent in actual employment of the company,) or other officer of the corporation against which the case is, shall be sufficient."

To justify the omission of the return to show that this service was in the county in which the president of the company resided, it is urged that while, if the service were tested only by section 34 of chapter 50 without its closing clause, the return would be bad, yet as under such closing clause the service may be under section 7 of chapter 124, and as this section does not require the return to show that the service was in the county in which the president resided, the return is good. If this be so, then this unreasonable result would follow, namely: Service on the corporation president is authorized under both sections. You serve on such president. One section requires the return to show that it was in the county of his residence; the other does not. In one breath the law says that fact must be shown; in the same, that it need not: an enactment and repeal in the same act; a command and a retraction in the same instant. If there were any persons named in section 34 for service of process not named in section 7, it might be said with some force that where service was on one named in section 34, but not in section 7, the return must show service in his county, but, if on one named in both, it need not; but there are none named in section 34 not named in section 7, and there are some named in section 7 not named in section 34. Until chapter 59, Acts 1887, was adopted, section 34 did not contain said closing clause; but in 1887 the section was amended by adding, "or in any county in which a director or other officer or any agent of said corporation may reside. But service at any time may be made upon any corporation in the manner prescribed for similar proceedings in the circuit court." Here, as pertinent to the legislative intent, it is to be noted that at the date of this amendment the legislature still held to the policy of having the service in justices' courts in the county where the person served resided; for, while intending no longer to limit the place of service on any officer, director, trustee, or agent of the corporation to the principal office or place of business, but extending it to the extent of the county, yet it limited it to the county of residence; a circumstance tending to show that, in making the closing clause, it did not intend to dispense with the provision of section 38 requiring service in the county of residence. What does this closing clause mean? It had been found that the law did not afford sufficient facility of service of process issued by justices, and it was thought proper to give the right to serve such process on the same persons on whom process in other courts might be served. There were some persons specified in section 7 on whom circuit court process could be served, but on whom justices' process could not be served; for instance, a person appointed under section 37, c 54, to accept service of process, and especially railroad station agents, included in section 7, but not in section 34, and perhaps others, such as mayor, councilmen, and trustees, so as to expressly name them, to avoid question as to whether they would be included under section 34. It was simply to make the right to serve justices' process co-extensive with process of other courts, so far as regards the persons on whom service should be made, and not to dispense with the requirements of section 38 of the justices' chapter, touching only the place of service and the return, requiring the service to be in the county of residence of the person served, and that the return should show that fact, and the person and date of service. If the legislature intended that those requirements should cease, why did it leave section 38 intact? Did it amend section 34 by adding the closing clause with the very purpose of no longer requiring service in the county wherein the person served resided, and yet forget section 38, and leave it standing? We cannot say this; and, if its continuance was in fact by inadvertence, that does not alter it, for there it stands, and this court cannot repeal it. All these provisions are in the Code, and are in pari materia, and, under the familiar rule, all these sections must be held up before our eyes, and each given a force and meaning, and assigned a function, if not in utter and irreconcilable conflict. Thus we give section 38 the plain meaning spoken by its letter, requiring process against corporations, emanating from justices' courts, no matter on what person served, whether one named in sec-

tion 34 of chapter 50 or section 7 of chapter 124, to be served in the county in which the person served resides, and the return to show that fact. Suppose the legislature, in amending section 34, instead of amending by adding the closing clause, had incorporated in the section every one of the persons specified in section 7 for service of process. Who would doubt that section 38, requiring service to be in the county of residence, would apply? Has it not in effect done the same thing by the closing clause? For the purposes of this question, every person specified in section 7 is to be regarded as if specified expressly in section 34, and then comes section 38, broadly declaring that service on any person under either of the last four sections—34 being one of them—shall be in the county in which the person resides, and that the return must show that fact or be invalid. The case of Railway Co. v. Ryan, 31 W. Va. 364, 6 S. E. Rep. 924, is pointed authority to overthrow the return of service in this case, as it holds that a return of service of a summons from a justice against a corporation, showing a service on an attorney in fact appointed to accept service of process, was bad, because it failed to show that it was served in the county of his residence; and the judgment was held void. Now note that such attorney to accept service is one not named in section 34, c. 50, but named in section 7, c. 124; yet it was necessary, that case held, to serve in the county of his residence. But it is said that the court in that case overlooked entirely the closing clause of section 34. True, it is not mentioned in the opinion, but we must not assume that it was overlooked; and, moreover, it could not have altered the decision. But for the suggestion that said clause was overlooked, we should not have reconsidered the question.

Therefore we reach the conclusion that the judgment of the justice was erroneous, —indeed void,—as being rendered without appearance upon a return of service branded by law as invalid; a judgment without service of process, and therefore without jurisdiction of the person. Railway Co. v. Ryan, supra; Freem. Judgm. §§ 495, 521; 1 Black, Judgm. § 220; Capehart v. Cunningham, 12 W. Va. 750. For these reasons the judgment of the circuit court is reversed and annulled; and, this court rendering such judgment as that court should have rendered, the judgment of the justice is reversed and annulled, the verdict of the jury set aside, and the case remanded to the circuit court.

LONG v. OHIO RIVER R. CO.

(Supreme Court of Appeals of West Virginia.
Nov. 28, 1891.)

CERTIORARI TO JUSTICE—FILING PETITION—
LACHES.

1. In applying to the circuit court for a writ of *certiorari* to the judgment of a justice, under chapter 110 of the Code, the general rule is that the petitioner must present his petition within 10 days after the judgment complained of is rendered, according to the analogy of appeals in section 164, chapter 50, of the Code.

2. But it may, and in a proper case should,

be granted after the expiration of 10 days, and within 90 days after the date of the judgment, when the party otherwise entitled to the writ shall show, by his own oath or otherwise, good cause for his not having applied for such writ within the 10 days.

3. A case in which the above rule against laches is laid down and applied.

(Syllabus by the Court.)

Appeal from circuit court, Mason county.

Petition of the Ohio River Railroad Company for a writ of *certiorari* to review the judgment of a justice of the peace. The court quashed and dismissed the writ, and petitioner appeals. Affirmed.

V. B. Archer, for appellant. *Simpson & Howard*, for appellee.

Holt, J. On the 28th of December, 1889, J. M. Long, plaintiff below and appellee, brought suit before a justice of Mason county against the Ohio River Railroad Company, the appellant, for the recovery of $200, the value of one mare, the property of the plaintiff, killed by defendant on its railroad. The defendant appeared, and the case was fixed for trial to be had on January 31, 1890. Plaintiff demanded a jury, and a jury of six, having been duly selected and sworn, and having heard the evidence and received the instructions given by the justice at the instance of the defendant, and without objection by plaintiff, rendered a verdict for plaintiff, assessing his damages at $200. Defendant at once moved the justice to set aside the verdict, and grant a new trial. The justice overruled the motion, and defendant excepted, and prayed that bill of exceptions No. 1 be signed, sealed, and made part of the record, "which bill of exceptions [quoting from the docket of the magistrate] has not been taken as yet." On the verdict, judgment was rendered. Under chapter 110, § 4, of the Code, the judge of the circuit court of Mason county awarded defendant a writ of *certiorari* on 28th April, 1890, the day of defendant's application. On 15th May, 1890, plaintiff, Long, by his attorneys, moved the circuit court of Mason county to quash and dismiss the writ of *certiorari* upon the ground, as appears by the argument, that neither bill of exceptions nor writ of *certiorari* were applied for and obtained in due time; and the cause is here for review on writ of error obtained by defendant.

The counsel have argued the case mainly upon the merits. The principal use of this writ with us before 1868 was to bring up records, in whole or in part, in aid of some other proceeding; but the statute of 1882, as now found in the Code, p. 742, c. 110, has very much enlarged its scope, giving power to rehear after judgment on the evidence certified, as well as correct errors in law, and in a proper case to retain for trial *de novo*, being thus in effect an appeal from the judgment of a justice in a certain class of cases. In obedience to the writ, the record should be certified and returned "in the condition in which it was when the writ came to the court below." "In all such cases removed as aforesaid from before a justice to the circuit court, wherein the amount in controversy is more than fifteen dollars, and in which the judgment of the justice is set aside, [the case] shall be retained in said court, and disposed of as if originally brought therein." Section 3, c. 110, Code. It lay at common law in all civil actions before judgment, where the courts of king's bench and common pleas had jurisdiction, and could administer the same justice to the parties as the court below, and was there retained and tried. Under our statute, it lies after judgment, and the circuit court, after reversing the judgment complained of, retains it for final disposition if the amount in controversy is more than $15. The petition for the writ should disclose a proper case upon its face, and when issued it may be dismissed without a hearing, when improvidently awarded. But it is now under our statute a remedy of great importance, and constant use, and should be upheld and applied, within its proper scope, to the end of meting out substantial justice. In a proper case the writ may on motion be superseded before its return, as that it was improvidently awarded; and by motion to quash it may be quashed on any proper ground after the return. But the language of the motion is not material, so that it give notice of the thing asked to be done; nor the language of the order of the court, if it properly directs that it be done. "It should not be granted where the party seeking it has been guilty of laches, and generally, and in analogy to the writ of error" (or appeal,) not where the time within which these latter could be brought has expired. See 3 Amer. & Eng. Enc. Law, p. 64, and authorities cited; Poe v. Machine-Works, 24 W. Va. 517, 521, where the general doctrine of the writ as at common law, and as modified by our recent statute, is stated and discussed. See, also, 1 Tidd, Pr. 399. And, in cases where the party has permitted the time for appeal to expire, *certiorari* will not issue for relief unless upon a special showing unmixed with any blame on the part of such party. Poe v. Machine-Works, 24 W. Va. 517.

Following the analogy here pointed out to appeals from justices under sections 164-174 of chapter 50 of the Code, as applied to like cases, the petition for the writ should be presented within 10 days after the judgment is rendered by the justice; or, if not within that time, then it must be presented within 90 days after the date of the judgment complained of, and in addition the petitioner must show, by his own oath or otherwise, good cause for his not having applied for the writ within the 10 days. As to what constitutes good cause, see Lowther v. Davis, 33 W. Va. 132, 10 S. E. Rep. 20; Hubbard v. Yocum, 30 W. Va. 740, 5 S. E. Rep. 867; Machine Co. v. Floding, 27 W. Va. 540; Ruffner v. Love, 24 W. Va. 181. It appears by the petition for the writ of *certiorari*, and from the transcript returned, that the judgment was rendered on the 31st day of January, 1890, and, by the vacation order allowing the writ, that it was presented to the judge on the 28th April, 1890, being within the 90 days; but the petitioner, the Ohio River Railroad Company, does not state or show in the petition, or in any other mode, any cause in excuse or justification of its not having presented such petition for the writ within the 10 days. "In all cases the party praying for this remedy must have merit on his side, and pursue it in proper time. Time has always been considered an important circumstance in the application for the writ, and redress by this means should be sought as soon as possible after the happening of the event which rendered it necessary to resort to it." See Poe v. Machine-Works, 24 W. Va. 517, and cases cited. Some limit of time must be adopted, and the one stated above as to appeals seems to furnish a peculiarly fit and appropriate analogy. Whether it is to be adhered to with the same inflexibility as if it were prescribed by statute, need not be considered in advance of the occasion. Whether in a proper case, upon a special showing, it may be granted after the 90 days, no opinion is now given. The railroad company in this case has been guilty of laches in applying for the writ, for which no excuse or justification has been alleged or shown, so that the judgment of the circuit court of Mason county of 15th May, 1890, quashing and dismissing the writ of *certiorari*, must be affirmed.

BURDETT v. ALLEN.

*(Supreme Court of Appeals of West Virginia.
Dec. 7, 1891.)*

ANIMALS RUNNING AT LARGE—IMPOUNDING—CONSTITUTIONAL LAW.

The charter of a city or town located in this state, and the ordinances ordained by its council in pursuance of the provisions of sections 28 and 29 of chapter 47 of the Code, may, as an act of police regulation and power, provide for the taking up and impounding cattle, hogs, horses, sheep, and other animals found running at large in the public streets during the night, and for selling them to pay charges for impounding, etc., without judicial inquiry or determination, upon notice being given to the owner; and such provisions will not be unconstitutional, as authorizing the forfeiture or confiscation of property without due process of law, or without compensation.

(Syllabus by the Court.)

Error to circuit court, Kanawha county.

Action of detinue by S. C. Burdett against Dover Allen. Judgment for plaintiff. Defendant brings error. Reversed.

W. S. Laidley, for plaintiff in error. *S. C. Burdett*, in pro. per.

ENGLISH, J. On the 7th day of August, 1889, S. C. Burdett instituted an action of detinue against Dover Allen before C. W. Hall, a justice of the peace of Kanawha county, in which the plaintiff complained that the defendant unlawfully withheld from him one brindle cow of the value of $50. The plaintiff filed affidavit and gave bond for the immediate possession of the property. On the 28th day of August the case was heard, and judgment was rendered for the plaintiff that he retain possession of the property, and that he recover from the defendant his costs in said suit. From this judgment the defendant took an appeal to the circuit court of said county, and on the 10th day of April, 1890, said appeal was submitted to the circuit court of Kanawha county upon an agreed statement of the facts, upon consideration whereof, and after hearing the

argument of counsel thereon, the said court was of opinion that the ordinance of the city of Charleston in relation to the impounding and sale of animals is unconstitutional, and rendered judgment for the plaintiff for said property claimed in said action, and for costs, and from this judgment the defendant applied for and obtained this writ of error.

It was agreed between the plaintiff and the defendant that the following are the facts to be taken as proven by the respective parties: By the plaintiff: That he lives in Charleston, and that he is the owner of the cow which the suit is about; that on the evening of the 7th day of August, 1889, the plaintiff found his said cow in charge of Dover Allen, the city pound-master, and that he demanded the release of his cow, which was refused until the charges thereon were paid, and to pay the same or any sum the plaintiff declined, and thereupon he brought said action, and the said cow was delivered to him by the constable on the order of the justice aforesaid, and that on the trial of said action before the said justice judgment was given for the plaintiff, the said court holding that said ordinance under which the said cow was held was unconstitutional and void. Also the charter and ordinances of the city were put in evidence. By the defendant: That he was on the 6th day of August, 1889, and has since been, and is yet, pound-master of the city of Charleston; that he was then, and is yet, exercising the duties of said office under and by virtue of the ordinances of said city; that on the night of the 6th day of August, 1889, between 10 and 12 o'clock, the said Allen, with two boys he had to assist him in hunting for and driving in stray cows, were out on the street, and found said cow of plaintiff in the public street, and that they drove her to the city pound, and fastened her therein that night, and kept her in said pound until taken away by the constable the next day; that on the evening of the 7th of August the plaintiff came and demanded his cow, claiming her, and defendant demanded his fees, etc., allowed him by the city ordinance, which at that time amounted to two dollars, and the plaintiff refused to pay the same, and thereupon the defendant refused to give up the cow, and the plaintiff brought said action before Justice HALL, and upon his order the constable took the cow from the defendant; that the said charges of two dollars are still unpaid; that upon the trial before the said justice his decision was that the said city ordinance was unconstitutional and void, and he gave judgment for the plaintiff, from which judgment the said defendant appealed; that the said lot in which said cow was impounded was the city pound, made so under and by virtue of an ordinance adopted June 30, 1887; and this was all the evidence adduced.

The counsel for the defendant in error contends that the ordinance of the city of Charleston under which the property of said defendant in error was seized and impounded is void because (1) there is no express authority conferred by the charter, either in chapter 47 of the Code or the special charter of the city of Charleston; that the power to impound and sell animals must be expressly conferred, and a general authority given to prevent animals from running at large is not sufficient. The first section of chapter 47 of the Code provides that "a city, town, or village heretofore established, (other than the city of Wheeling,) may exercise all the powers conferred by this chapter, although the same may not be conferred by their charter, and that, so far as said chapter confers powers on the municipal authorities of a city, town, or village, (other than said ci'y of Wheeling,) not conferred by the charter of any such city, town, or village, the same shall be deemed an amendment to said charter;" and section 28, which prescribes the powers and duties of the council, provides, among other things, that such council shall have power therein "to prevent hogs, cattle, horses, sheep, and other animals and fowls of all kinds from going at large in such city, town, or village;" and section 29 of said chapter provides that, "to carry into effect these enumerated powers and all others conferred upon such city, town, or village, or its council, by this chapter, or by any future act of the legislature of this state, the council shall have the power to make and pass all needful orders, by-laws, ordinances, resolutions, rules, and regulations not contrary to the constitution and laws of the state, and to prescribe, impose, and enact reasonable fines, penalties, and imprisonments in the county jail. * * * Such fines, penalties, and imprisonments shall be recovered and enforced under the judgment of the mayor of such city, town, or village or the person lawfully exercising his functions." The ordinance of the city of Charleston in reference to the public pound was put in evidence in this case, and the first section thereof provides that the inclosure attached to the city hall be, until otherwise ordained by the council, constituted the public pound for the impounding of animals therein subject to be impounded. It also provides in section 2 that "it shall be unlawful for any person being the owner or having charge of any cow, calf, or ox to allow the same to run at large between sunset and sunrise in any of the streets, lanes, alleys, or commons of said city below the Elk and Piedmont roads;" and section 4 provides: "It shall be the duty of the pound-master, on view or information, forthwith to take up all or any such animals running at large as aforesaid, and shut up the same in the public pound," there to be retained and fed until disposed of as thereinafter provided. Section 5 provides that the owner shall be notified forthwith; and section 6 provides that, in case the owner shall not within 48 hours after giving said notice appear and prove his right to such animal, the pound-master shall make his return to the mayor, setting forth the number and kind of animals taken up, time when taken, owner of the animal, if known, the fact of giving the notice, and that 48 hours have passed since such notice was given or posted, and that the animal or animals still remain in the pound unclaimed. Section 7 provides that

the mayor shall then direct the sergeant to advertise and sell said animals, and prescribes the mode of advertisement; and further directs that the sergeant shall make return to the mayor of his proceedings, and shall pay all surplus money arising from said sales to the treasurer; and section 9 provides that "any person being the owner * * * of such animal," who shall within one year show to the mayor that he was such owner, shall have any surplus in the hands of the treasurer arising from the sale of such animal paid over to him, said surplus to be paid on the order of the council. These ordinances, enacted under the power so to do conferred by section 29 of chapter 47 of the Code, appear to me to confer express authority upon the pound-master, acting in connection with, and under the supervision of, the mayor, to impound cattle found running at large in the city, and hold them until the fees and costs are paid, or to sell the same after notice to the owner, and, after deducting said costs and fees, to pay the residue to the owner when he asserts his claim thereto. It is true that Dillon on Municipal Corporations (volume 1, § 150) states that "power to impound and forfeit domestic animals must be expressly granted to the corporation, and that laws or ordinances authorizing the officers of the corporation to impound, and, upon taking specified proceedings, to sell, the property, are penal in their nature, and, where doubtful in their meaning, will not be construed to produce a forfeiture of the property, but rather the reverse;" and then proceeds to state that the powers conferred must be strictly followed in order to constitute a valid sale of such animal. In the case under consideration, however, no sale took place; the animal was only taken up and impounded, and, under section 28 of chapter 47, providing that the council of such city, etc., shall have power therein to prevent cattle from going at large therein, taken in connection with section 29 of the same chapter, authorizing the council to make and pass all needful orders, by-laws, ordinances, and resolutions, etc., not contrary to the constitution and laws of the state, to carry into effect said power, the impounding officer, under the provisions of the ordinances above mentioned, would surely have the authority to take up and impound such animal found running at large at night in the streets of the city.

There were no steps taken in this case, so far as the evidence discloses, to sell the cow that had been impounded, and the question raised by the action of detinue was simply whether the animal was unlawfully detained by the pound-master at the time said action of detinue was instituted. The evidence shows that the cow was impounded on the night of the 6th of August; that the plaintiff demanded her on the 7th, and, said demand being refused unless the charges were paid, said plaintiff at once brought his action of detinue; so that the only question really presented for our consideration is whether the cow was lawfully detained at the time said action was brought. As is suggested by counsel for the plaintiff, however, our

Code, c. 61, provides for taking up estrays found upon the land of a person, and, after giving the notice therein prescribed, if the owner does not appear in four weeks, the person taking up such estray may have the same appraised, as therein provided, by three freeholders, who shall return their certificate with the warrant to the clerk of the county court, who shall record it, and post a copy at the front door of the court-house on the next court-day; and, if the owner of such property shall not appear in 30 days after said copy has been so posted, and the valuation thereof be under $15, or if such value be as much as $15, and the owner does not appear after the said certificate has been published as aforesaid, and also three times in a newspaper published nearest to the place where such property was taken up, it shall belong to the owner of the land on which it was taken, and the former owner may at any time recover the valuation money after deducting the fees and charges. This has been the law of Virginia and of this state for many years, and, so far as we know, no question has been raised in regard to the constitutionality or validity of the law. Again, it is an every-day occurrence in the cities of our state that men are arrested for disorderly conduct and violation of the city ordinances, and, if found guilty, they are not only locked up, but are compelled to work on the streets to pay their fines, and thus their labor, which is their property as much as anything else they have, is taken from them to discharge the penalty. Under the common law the right of distress damage feasant existed, and the cattle found trespassing were liable to distress, and it was held in the case of Anscomb v. Shore, 1 Taunt. 261, that no action lies against one who distrains cattle damage feasant for impounding them, instead of accepting compensation for the damages tendered before the cattle were impounded. See 6 Wait, Act. & Def. c. 17, p. 639, where the authorities are collated upon this subject, so that this matter of impounding cattle is not a mere creature of the statute, but existed at common law.

Counsel for the defendant in error contends that the property taken, as the cow in this case was, was so taken without due process of law, and refers to Cooley, Const. Lim. pp. 363, 364, but we find the author says: "A statute which authorizes a party to seize the property of another without process or warrant, and to sell without notification to the owner for the punishment of a private trespass, and in order to enforce a penalty against the owner, can find no justification in the constitution." Cattle running at large at night in a public street of a city or town cannot, however, be regarded as committing a private trespass. Section 5 of the ordinance proven in this case provides that the pound-master shall forthwith notify the owner, etc., and section 7 of the same ordinance provides that the mayor shall direct the sergeant to advertise and sell, etc. Thus it appears that the pound-master's duty is to take up the animal, notify the owner, and report the facts to the mayor; and when a sale is to be made

it is made by the sergeant under the direction of the mayor, who, by section 39 of chapter 47 of the Code, is ex officio a justice and conservator of the peace within the limits of the city. In the case of Davidson v. New Orleans, 96 U. S. 97, the court holds in the second point of the syllabus as follows: "The court suggests the difficulty and danger of attempting an authoritative definition of what it is for a state to deprive a person of life, liberty, or property without due process of law, within the meaning of the fourteenth amendment, and holds that the enunciation of the principles which govern each case as it arises is the better mode of arriving at a sound definition;" and in point 3 the court says: "This court has heretofore decided that due process of law does not in all cases require a resort to a court of justice to assert the rights of the parties against the individual, or to impose burdens upon his property for the public use;" citing Murray v. Improvement Co., 18 How. 272, and McMillen v. Anderson, 95 U. S. 37. In 1 Dill. Mun. Corp. 481, note 2, we find "an ordinance directing the impounding and sale of animals for costs and expenses," but not imposing a penalty, held valid under a charter authorizing the impounding and sale "for any penalty imposed by any ordinance or regulation and all costs;" citing Ft. Smith v. Dodson, 46 Ark. 296; that "such an ordinance is valid and takes effect whether the owner resides in the town or not;" citing Rose v. Hardie, 98 N. C. 44, 4 S. E. Rep. 41. We also find that Tiedeman, in his valuable work on Limitations of Police Power, says on page 506: "The clash of interest between stock-raising and farming calls for the interference of the state by the institution of police regulations; and whether the regulations shall subordinate the stock-raising interest to that of farming, or vice versa, in the case of an irreconcilable difference, as is the case with respect to the going at large of cattle, is a matter for the legislative discretion, and is not a judicial question. In the exercise of this general power of control over the keeping of live-stock the state or municipal corporation may prohibit altogether the running at large of such animals, and compel the owners to keep them within their own inclosures, and provide as a remedy for enforcing the law that the animals found astray shall be sold, after proper notice to the owner, and time allowed for redemption, paying over to the owner the proceeds of sale, after deducting what is due to the state in the shape of penalty." The power granted by the legislature to the cities and towns of our state to prevent cattle and other animals from running at large in their streets is a police power, intended for the protection of the citizens, and to enable them to enjoy the streets and public thoroughfares, and to prevent depredations on yards and gardens by breachy stock during the night, when the same are unwatched and unprotected. There is necessity for immediate action when cattle are found upon the public street at night. As is frequently the case, the officer may be ignorant as to the ownership of the cattle thus found on the street, and, in order that the object of the ordinance may be made effective, he must proceed at once, and arrest the animal, without waiting for any judicial investigation as to whether the seizure may be lawful. If it were otherwise, and the officer waited until a judicial investigation should take place, the animal would be gone, and the ordinance would prove abortive and inoperative. In order, then, to enforce the ordinance, such cattle must be impounded; they must also be cared for and fed, and, if no owner comes for them, they must be sold, to use a common expression, "to prevent them from eating their heads off."

This question has been before the courts in the state of New York, and in the case of Cook v. Gregg, 46 N. Y. 439, the court held that the provisions of the acts authorizing the seizure of animals trespassing upon private premises are constitutional; that "the act does not impose a penalty for the trespass, but simply prescribes and fixes a remedy therefor; and remedies are clearly within the peculiar province of legislation. The temporary seizure and detention of property as authorized by the statute, awaiting judicial action, is not violative of the provision of article 1, section 6, of the constitution, directing that no person shall be deprived of property without due process of law." See, also. Hard v. Nearing, 44 Barb. 472. Also, in the case of Campau v. Langley, 39 Mich. 451, it was held that "a statute allowing animals running at large in a public highway to be taken by any person and publicly sold by a public officer, and providing that, after the expenses of the proceedings and of keeping the animals were paid, the remainder should be paid over to the owner, who should be allowed a certain time within which to redeem them, is to remedy a public grievance, and is not unconstitutional, as divesting property rights without due process of law." Also, in the case of Wilcox v. Hemming, 58 Wis. 144, 15 N. W. Rep. 435, it was held that "a city charter and ordinances may, as an exercise of police power, provide for the taking up and impounding of animals found running at large in the public streets, and for selling them to pay the expenses of impounding, etc., without judicial inquiry or determination; and such provisions will not be unconstitutional, as authorizing the forfeiture, condemnation, or confiscation of property without due process of law or without compensation." Judge Cooley, in his work on Constitutional Limitations, p. 588, says: "So beasts may be prohibited from running at large under the penalty of being seized or sold;" citing numerous authorities in support of the proposition. And Sedgwick on the Construction of Statutory and Constitutional Law, p. 435, under the head of "Police Powers," says: "The clause prohibiting the taking of private property without compensation is not intended as a limitation of the exercise of those police powers which are necessary to the tranquility of every well-ordered community, nor of that general power over private property which is necessary for the orderly

existence of all governments;" and in a note we find that "summary statutory proceedings for the seizure, detention, and sale of stray animals running at large have been sustained;" citing numerous authorities. Numerous other authorities might be cited in support of the validity of such laws and ordinances, but, as we think, enough have been mentioned to show how said statutes and ordinances are regarded, and how the question is considered by the elementary authors upon the subject and by the highest courts of the different states, at least to indicate the weight of authority so far as I have had an opportunity of examining them upon the subject. There can be no question that the city of Charleston, under its charter as amended by chapter 47 of the Code, and the ordinances which were in evidence, had the right to take up and impound the cow of the defendant in error, which was all that had been done at the time the owner took possession of her by giving the required bond in his action of detinue; but, if the defendant in error had not seen proper to bring said action, and had allowed said cow to be sold after the requirements of said ordinance had been complied with, in my opinion a sale of said animal under the provisions of said ordinance, and a disposition of the proceeds of said sale as therein directed, would have violated no provision of the constitution. For these reasons the judgment complained of must be reversed, and the defendant in error must pay the costs, and the cause is remanded to the circuit court of Kanawha county.

THOMPSON et al. *v.* DOUGLASS et al.

(Supreme Court of Appeals of West Virginia. Dec. 7, 1891.)

WHAT CONSTITUTES SALE — LIABILITY OF PERSON RECEIVING GOODS—EXCLUSION OF JUROR.

1. The mere exclusion of a juror upon a challenge for cause upon insufficient ground will not be cause for reversal.

2. Where one sends goods to another as under a sale, and at the same time sends a bill of the goods, and the goods and bill reach the one to whom they are sent, whether he ordered them or not, in law, he will be regarded as a purchaser, unless within reasonable time he either returns the goods, or notifies the sender that he will not accept them.

3. What is reasonable time, is a question of fact for the jury.

4. Where such goods reach the person to whom they are so sent, though not ordered by him, he will be regarded as purchaser, if he exercises acts of ownership over them, or treats them in a way inconsistent with a recognition of another's ownership.

5. Where one so sends goods to another, and he disclaims to have purchased them, but permits a third person to take them, and convert them to his own use, this will make him liable as purchaser.

(Syllabus by the Court.)

Error to circuit court, Barbour county.

Action of *assumpsit* by G. W. Thompson and H. C. Jackson, partners trading as Thompson & Jackson, against S. C. Douglass and others, partners trading as S. C. Douglass & Co. Judgment for plaintiffs, and defendants bring error. Reversed.

Melville Peck, for plaintiffs in error.

Sam V. Woods and *William T. Ice,* for defendants in error.

BRANNON, J. Thompson & Jackson brought an action of *assumpsit* against S. C. Douglass & Co. in the circuit court of Barbour county, and recovered judgment; and the defendants brought the case to this court. The first point of error made against the judgment is that the court excluded five persons from the jury because they were indebted to one of the defendant firm. Challenges of jurors, called challenges to the polls, are of two kinds,—peremptory and for cause. Lord Coke said, as we can say, to-day, that peremptory challenges were allowed the party "upon his own dislike, without showing any cause." Our law allows each party in civil cases four such challenges; and in felony cases, to the state, two, and the accused, six. Challenges for cause are divided by the common law into challenges for principal cause and challenges to the favor,—the former being where the cause assigned positively disqualified; the latter being causes which, though not conclusively disqualifying, yet threw suspicion of bias on the juror. Principal challenges were tried by the court, challenges to the favor by three triers; and, while these different modes of trial of challenge existed, it was very important to preserve this distinction, to determine in which class the challenge would fall, in view of the different methods of trial of each. But our statute law requires challenges to be tried by the court, and thus the distinction between principal cause of challenge and challenge to the favor has become unimportant, and we commonly call all challenges for cause, challenges for cause. As Lord COKE said centuries ago may be said now: "The causes of favor are infinite." No enumeration was ever attempted of what causes might be alleged as grounds of challenges to the favor. It would be impossible to specify all that should be allowed in advance by a statute, for they depend upon each particular case, and the circumstances and parties to it. All concede that statutory disqualifications are not the only ones. Thomp. & M. Jur. § 175; Dilworth's Case, 12 Grat. 689; Amer. & Eng. Enc. Law, 360. See, also, Thomp. & M. Jur. §§ 152, 170, 171; 1 Thomp. Trials, § 331.

The cause assigned for the challenge of these jurors would fall under the head of challenge to the favor. But is the fact that a man is indebted to another good cause of challenge to exclude the indebted party from sitting as a juror in a case wherein the creditor is a party? Would a feeling of favor or fear move him, in the eye of the law, to render a false verdict? Practically, there is some force to say that where a party is greatly favored by a creditor, by indulgence, he would feel a favor towards his friend; and, with perhaps more force, that one largely indebted to another, so much indebted as to be at his mercy for his solvency, and even his home, might from fear fail to render a just verdict adverse to his creditor. On the other hand, it would be going quite far to say that simply the fact that one man is in-

debted to another would disqualify; that if he owes only a small sum, which he is able to pay at any time, or is a man of large means, or has more means than has his creditor, he should be rejected. I do not say that no case of indebtedness—one showing the debtor to be at the mercy and in the power of his creditor—might not exclude. I have, however, met with no case excluding, or of attempt to exclude, a juror for such cause, except one cited by counsel, (Bank v. Smith, 19 Johns. 115,) where, because the juror was an indorser on a note held by a bank, he was held disqualified by the triers, not by the court,—the court having allowed that fact to go before the triers as an item of evidence to show bias; and, as the court above said, it was a decision on the admissibility, not on the sufficiency, of the evidence to show bias; and the judge in the opinion pointedly says that he would not undertake to say that the single circumstance that one was indorser on a note to the bank would of itself support a challenge to the favor, yet it was easy to imagine that an indorser might have bias, as in case the maker was insolvent, and the indorser in great danger at the hands of the bank. No other case is cited. In this present case simply the fact of indebtedness is shown, without any appearance of amounts or the relative pecuniary standing of the parties. We therefore think the jurors were improperly excluded.

What then? Is it reversible error, or harmless error? Where a disqualified juror is put on a jury, it is of course error; but, where a qualified juror is improperly rejected, it is a wholly different thing. In such case the man taking his place is qualified and unexceptionable. Is he not as good a juror as the excluded one? Has not the party had what the law designs, —a trial by an impartial jury? If you set aside the verdict, upon a new trial he cannot get that rejected man. Is that man better than all the balance of the citizens of the state qualified for jury service? Shall a long, costly trial be upturned for such a cause only to give the party what he has already had,—a fair jury? Is the administration of justice to bear the odium of such technicality? In Montague's Case, 10 Grat. 767, point 4 of the syllabus is: "The decision of a court allowing a challenge on the part of the commonwealth, or disallowing a challenge on the part of the accused, whether such challenge be a principal challenge, or a challenge to the favor, is matter of exception on the part of the accused, which it is his right to have reviewed in an appellate court." I am of opinion that this decision is erroneous, and hurtful to the practice of the courts and the administration of justice, and ought not longer to prevail. The doctrine that harmless error shall not reverse and render fair trials abortive has made great progress since the date of the decision cited. Judge LEE gave no reasons in the opinion, except that in criminal cases the law would intend harm to an accused where he is deprived of a right. He did not even refer to the *quære* in Clore's Case, 8 Grat. 606, and the strong argument of Judge LOMAX, probably overlooking them.

That argument is, in my judgment, unanswerable. He said: " When, upon the commonwealth's challenge, one of the *venire* is erroneously excluded from the panel, the effect is materially different from that produced by erroneously overruling the prisoner's challenge to a venire-man. In the former case the exclusion of a particular man from the jury does not throw any obstacle in the way of impaneling an impartial jury of qualified jurors. The effect is only to set aside one alleged to be disqualified, and put in his place one that is qualified. This exclusion and substitution can in no wise affect the fairness and impartiality of the trial, because the trial is still had before a jury, all the members of which are free from exception. Not so in the other case. Then a disqualified juror is imposed upon the accused. He has not been tried by 12 qualified jurors, as the law entitled him; and the disqualification of the juror thus imposed upon him vitiates the verdict. Overruling his challenge, therefore, is just ground of exception on his part; and he is allowed to complain of the error, because he has been aggrieved. He has not been tried, as he was entitled to be, by 12 duly-qualified jurors. But in the other case, notwithstanding the exclusion complained of, of one of the *venire*, he has had all that any prisoner can be entitled to demand,—a fair and impartial trial before 12 jurors free from all exception. And again, if the exclusion of the venire-man upon the commonwealth's challenge be a matter of exception and ground of error on the part of the accused, how can the supposed wrong that the error has inflicted upon him be repaired? It is only upon the reversal of the judgment to award a new *venire facias;* not that he may have the excluded venire-man impaneled on his jury, but that he may again be tried by 12 qualified jurors; in other words, that he may have another trial,—such precisely, in all respects, as that fair and impartial trial before a jury free from exception that he has already had." As the juror's exclusion in that case was justified on its merits, the point was not decided, but put as a *quære.* Henry's Case, 4 Humph. 270, and Arthur's Case, 2 Dev. 217, are cited by Judge LOMAX as sustaining his position. I will add some others. Snow v. Weeks, 75 Me. 105, holds that the exclusion of a qualified juror is not reviewable; that the judge "may put a legal juror off, but cannot allow an illegal juror to go on." In Sutton v. Fox, 55 Wis. 531, 13 N. W. Rep. 477, is a *quære* whether the rejection of a competent juror would be error; but the opinion strongly maintains that it is not. In Tatum v. Young, 1 Port. (Ala.) 298, it was held that " when a cause has been tried by a legally impartial jury, though the judge, on the application of the plaintiff, against the consent of the defendant, may have rejected a juror for a cause somewhat questionable as to its sufficiency, such rejection of the juror is not available in error " The opinion draws the line between the erroneous rejection and admission of a juror, and says, where the trial has been by a fair jury, there can be no prejudice, and quotes with approval what Judge STORY said in U. S.

v. Cornell, 2 Mason, 91: " Even if a juror has been set aside for insufficient cause, I do not know that it is matter of error, if the trial has been by a jury duly sworn and impaneled, and above all exception. Neither the prisoner nor the government in such case can have suffered any injury." In O'Brien v. Iron Works, 7 Mo. App. 257, it was held that "the improper exclusion of a juror upon a challenge is not sufficient ground for reversal, where it does not appear that the party was prejudiced thereby." In Maner v. State, 8 Tex. App. 361, held, that excusing juror for insufficient cause was no material error, when it is not shown that the defendant was prejudiced. See Dodge v. People, 4 Neb. 220; John D. C. v. State, 16 Fla. 554; Railroad Co. v. Franklin, 23 Kan. 74; State v. Ward, 39 Vt. 225; Watson v. State, 63 Ind. 548. There are some authorities to the opposite. I notice that a very limited number cited to sustain the contrary by prisoner's counsel in Montague's Case do so; perhaps only two of the American cases. An abuse of discretion by a court, or where it appears that prejudice in the particular case resulted from the exclusion, would be subject to review. Nothing of this kind appears here, and we are of opinion that the exclusion of these jurors, though on insufficient ground, is not reversible error.

The appellants assign error in the refusal of instructions asked by them, and in giving those asked by the plaintiffs. The plaintiffs' claim was for a car-load of flour which, upon the order of their traveling agent, they shipped to S. C. Douglass & Co., the defendants, but which the defendants deny having purchased. They claim that the order for the flour given by J. E. Heatherly to the plaintiffs' agent was for another firm, J. E. Heatherly & Co., and not for S. E. Douglass & Co. (J. E. Heatherly was a member of both firms.) The defendants claim that at once on receipt of the bill for the flour, as for a sale to them, they wrote to the plaintiffs that the flour had arrived, that they did not order it, and refused to take it. The plaintiffs claim that as soon as they received this notification they ordered their agent to go to Phillippi, where Douglass & Co. did business, and the point to which the flour was consigned, and take charge of the flour, and that he did go there within three or four days from the date of the notification from Douglass & Co., and, when he reached Phillippi, did not find the flour there, but found that J. E. Heatherly had, under an arrangement with S. C. Douglass, one of the defendants, and with his consent, removed the car of flour to Belington for the use of J. E. Heatherly & Co., and that even if in fact the sale had not been made to S. C. Douglass & Co., yet by reason of such removal from the place of consignment, and its conversion to the use of J. E. Heatherly & Co., with the knowledge and consent of Douglass, the law made the defendants liable as if the sale had been made to them. These facts so alleged by plaintiffs were denied by the defendants.

Three instructions asked by the defense were refused.

Defendants' instruction No. 2: "If the jury find that S. C. Douglass, one of the defendants, notified the plaintiffs by letter, on the day said car and goods were removed by said Heatherly, that the firm of S. C. Douglass & Co. had not purchased said goods, and that said J. E. Heatherly had taken the same into his possession, claiming to have bought the same from the plaintiffs, and had removed the same to Belington, and that plaintiffs had time to follow said goods to Belington and reclaim the same, and failed to do so, then the plaintiffs would be in default for such negligence, and the jury should find for the defendants." So far as this instruction goes, it is good; but what if the removal was with the consent of S. C. Douglass? What if the sale was in fact to S. C. Douglass & Co.? It was claimed by plaintiffs, and they gave evidence tending to show, that the sale was to S. C. Douglass & Co., not to Heatherly or Heatherly & Co.; but this instruction omits this contention. Suppose everything in this instruction true, and yet that the sale was in fact to Douglass & Co.; there ought not to have been a verdict for defendants. It was claimed by plaintiffs that, even if the flour had not been ordered by S. C. Douglass & Co., yet it was consigned to them, and reached Phillippi in their name, which they knew, and that they received a bill of it as sold to them, and then S. C. Douglass, under an understanding with J. E. Heatherly, allowed him to take the flour to Belington for the use of J. E. Heatherly & Co. Suppose this to be so, then the verdict could not go for the defense, for these principles of law are laid down in Bartholomae v. Paull, 18 W. Va. 771, namely: "Where one merchant sends goods to another, and at the same time sends invoices of such goods, and the goods and invoices are received, and he, disclaiming to have purchased them, permits another to take them, and use them, this is an act of ownership, making him liable as purchaser. Though he did not order them, he will in law be regarded as purchaser if he exercises acts of ownership over them, or treats them in a way inconsistent with another ownership." An instruction cannot take only a portion of the facts involved in a case under the evidence, and erect an hypothesis upon them only, disregarding others, and tell the jury, if that hypothesis be true, to find accordingly, because such hypothesis is not as broad as the scope of the evidence, and the contention before the jury. True, an instruction may present a partial hypothesis, but it must not make that partial hypothesis all-controlling in the case. Storrs v. Feick, 24 W. Va. 606.

I do not see why defendants' instruction No. 3 is not good, under Bartholomae v. Paull. It presented the whole theory of their defense,—the scope of their case; and they were entitled to a declaration of the law upon the facts stated in it, if found to exist by the jury. I do not see that any other instruction performed its office. Other instructions given at defendants' instance are not in the record. No criticism upon this instruction is given

by counsel, or upon any of those offered by the defense. I have perceived no objection to this instruction.

Defendants' instruction No. 3: "The jury are instructed that if they believe from the evidence that the sale of the flour in controversy was made by Robt. Felty to J. E. Heatherly for the firm of J. E. Heatherly & Co., at Belington, and the said Felty caused the said flour to be shipped by plaintiffs to S. C. Douglass & Co. without instructions from S. C. Douglass & Co., or from J. E. Heatherly, one of said firm of S. C. Douglass & Co., and that S. C. Douglass & Co. notified the plaintiffs within a reasonable time after the arrival of the flour at Phillippi of their mistake in the shipping the flour, and that S. E. Douglass & Co. exercised no act of ownership over said flour after they ascertained the contents of the car by opening it, then the jury should find for the defendant."

Defendants' instruction No. 5: "If the jury believe from the evidence that after the arrival of the flour in controversy at Phillippi the defendant S. C. Douglass, for S. C. Douglass & Co., refused to accept or receive the flour, for the reason that said firm had not bought or ordered the same from the plaintiffs, and that S. C. Douglass, by mistake, permitted or consented to the defendant J. E. Heatherly's removing the same to Belington, believing that he had bought the goods, and notified the plaintiffs by mail of such fact, and such notice was given to the plaintiffs in time for them to have reclaimed the goods at Belington, but that the plaintiffs declined and failed to do so, then the plaintiffs are not entitled to recover in this action." This instruction is bad. If S. C. Douglass consented to Heatherly's taking the flour away from the point to which plaintiffs consigned it, and where it should have remained, so that they could find it there when they should come to reclaim it, though Douglass acted through mistake, it was his own mistake, for which plaintiffs were not responsible. If he trusted Heatherly's statement that he had bought the flour, it was his own act. He knew the flour had been consigned to S. C. Douglass & Co., and had received the bill as for a sale to them; and he must, at his peril, know the true facts as to a sale to Heatherly, and could not actively and knowingly participate by consent in the removal of the flour, and its conversion to the use of J. E. Heatherly & Co. Plaintiffs did not have to go to any other persons or place than those of consignment to exercise the right of reclamation.

I do not discover any error in the five instructions given at plaintiffs' instance. They seem supported by the principles announced in Bartholomae v. Paull, supra. Criticism is made upon the word "received," used in the instructions, because it might be construed as "accepted;" but I do not think it is to be so construed, but as meaning that the flour came to hand, or reached its destination.

It is argued that the purchase, if made for S. C. Douglass & Co., was not within the scope of the partnership. The nature of that partnership is not fully developed in the record, but from what appears we could not say that it was not within such scope: nor can we say that Douglass' participation in the removal of the flour would not bind the partnership, if he did participate. As Justice MATTHEWS said in Irwin v. Williar, 110 U. S. 506, 4 Sup. Ct. Rep. 160, what is the nature of the business of a partnership, what is necessary and proper in its prosecution, what is involved in the usual and ordinary course of its management by those engaged in it, at the place and time where and when carried on, are all questions of fact to be decided by a jury from a consideration of all the circumstances which, singly or in combination, affect its character or determine its peculiarities, and from them all its province is to ascertain and say whether the transaction in question is one which those dealing with the firm had reason to believe was authorized. And under the motion for a new trial we shall express no opinion upon that or other questions of fact, but leave them to the decision of a jury, where they, in the first instance, belong. Because of the refusal of defendants' instruction No. 3, we must reverse and set aside the judgment, and remand it for a new trial.

GILLIS v. WILMINGTON, O. & E. C. R. Co.

(Supreme Court of North Carolina. April 7, 1891.)

For majority opinion, see 13 S. E. Rep. 11.

CLARK, J., *(concurring.)* Agreeing in the conclusion reached, I cannot concur with so much of the opinion as holds that such sufficient search had been made for the missing documents as would admit of parol evidence of their contents. The judge in this case having set out the facts, his conclusion thereon was one of law, and subject to review. There were two depositories, in both of which the papers were sometimes kept, and I think it was error to admit parol proof of their contents, unless it had been shown that, after search in both the trunks, the papers could not be found.

STATE v. EASTMAN.

(Supreme Court of North Carolina. Dec. 8, 1891.)

OBSTRUCTION OF HIGHWAY—INDICTMENT.

1. An indictment charging an obstruction of "a certain public square and common public highway," and stating facts descriptive of its location, bounds, the uses to which it is put, and how and where it was obstructed, clearly charges but a single offense.

2. The public square of a county around and about the court-house is a highway, and to obstruct it is indictable under Code, § 2065, inflicting a penalty for the obstruction of highways.

Appeal from superior court, Burke county; W. A. HOKE, Judge. Affirmed.

J. S. Eastman was convicted of obstructing a public highway, and appeals.

The other facts fully appear in the following statement by MERRIMON, C. J.:

The indictment charged that the defendant at, etc., "unlawfully and willfully did obstruct a certain public square and common public highway there situate next and adjoining the court-house in the said county-seat of Morganton, and leading to and away from, as well as around one side of, the said court-house, from Sterling street, in said town, on the south-west side of said court-house, into Green street, on the south-east side of said court-house, by then and there digging holes in, and erecting a line of posts in, upon, and across, said public square and common public highway, over, upon, and across which said public square and common public highway the citizens of the state were and long have been accustomed to pass and repass, so that the citizens of the state were prevented from going in, upon, and over said public square and common public highway for a long space of time, to-wit, for the space of a day, and could not go, return, pass, and travel as they ought and were accustomed to do, and had a right to do, to the great damage and annoyance and to the common nuisance of the citizens and people of the state, and contrary to the peace and dignity of the state." Defendant pleaded not guilty. Upon the trial there was a verdict of guilty, whereupon the "defendant moved to set aside the verdict on the ground that there was not sufficient evidence to justify and sustain it. Motion overruled. The defendant then moved in arrest of judgment (1) for redundancy, in that the bill attempted to charge the defendant with two distinct and separate offenses in one count, to-wit, a nuisance in obstructing a public common, and an obstruction to a public highway; (2) for that the court had no jurisdiction of the offense of obstructing a public highway. Motion denied." Thereupon the court entered judgment against the defendant, who, having excepted, appealed to this court.

Batchelor & Devereux and *Isaac T. Avery,* for appellant. *The Attorney General* and *John T. Perkins,* for the State.

MERRIMON, C. J., *(after stating the facts.)* It would be better if the indictment were fuller and more precise in describing the "public square and common highway" as part of the public square of the county of Burke on which is situate the court-house of that county. Still it appears sufficiently to be seen and understood that the highway charged to have been obstructed by the defendant was part and parcel of that square. The objection that the indictment is bad because it charges two distinct offenses is unfounded. It charges, and its clear purpose is to charge, that the defendant did obstruct "a certain public square and common public highway there situate," and charges facts descriptive of it,—its location, bounds, the uses to which it is devoted, and how and where it was obstructed. It charges also the obstruction of the highway described, and, though there may be some redundancy of facts charged, and it might have been framed with greater technical precision and formality, it charges but a single offense, with sufficient clearness to enable the court to see what it is, and the defendant to make any defense he may have.

It does not charge, as suggested, the obstruction of the public square as "a public common," and the obstruction of a separate and distinct highway; it charges the obstruction of the public square as constituting a highway,—as such square and highway. The redundancy of statement complained of does not confuse or obscure the charge in any substantial respect. The indictment is certainly sufficient in substance. So much of such public square as is around and about the court-house and devoted to the purpose of a highway becomes such not simply by the use of it for such purpose, but as well by virtue of the statute, which empowers the proper county authorities to purchase real property for proper public buildings, and to designate and direct the use of the same. Parts of it may be, and not infrequently are, devoted to the use of pedestrians, while other parts are used for and devoted to the purpose of passing and repassing, going to and from, with carriages, wagons, carts, horses, etc. The purpose is to enable all persons—the people—going to and from the court-house to have ample and convenient public way and means to do so. This is a material part of the purpose of what is commonly and not inaptly called the "public square" of the county. It belongs to the county. The court-house is erected upon it, and so much of it as is used for the moving about of the people constitutes and is a highway recognized, allowed, and protected by the law. It belongs to the public, and they use it of right until public authority shall abolish it. Ordinarily, an overseer and laborers are not formally assigned to "work it" and keep it in order, as in the case of a public road; but the board of commissioners of the county have charge and supervision of it, and it is their duty to keep it in repair and order to that end, and as well to protect it against invasion and injury that might be done by unwarranted intruders. An overseer is not essential to the existence of a highway; and, though there be none, still no one has the right or privilege to obstruct it. The statute (Code, § 2065) expressly makes it indictable to obstruct it, and the superior court has jurisdiction of such offense. The public square of a county around and about the court-house being a highway, it is indictable to obstruct the same. State v. Long, 94 N. C. 896; State v. Smith, 100 N. C. 550, 6 S. E. Rep. 251; Elliott, Roads & S. 2 et seq.

The defendant insisted that "there was not sufficient evidence to justify and sustain" the verdict of guilty. If there was any evidence to go to the jury, it was their province to determine its weight and sufficiency to warrant a verdict of guilty. The court below might, in its sound discretion, set the verdict aside, and grant a new trial, if it deemed the verdict against the weight of evidence; but the exercise of that discretion is not reviewable here. If the defendant meant to insist that there was not evidence to go to the jury, then his contention is certainly groundless. There was abundant evidence of witnesses, to which there was no objection, certainly so far as appears, tending to prove the charge as laid in the indictment. It may be that a material part of this evidence was not the best evidence, and that it might have been excluded if objection had been made in apt time; but no objection was made, and, in the absence of objection, it might properly go to the jury. The learned counsel of the defendant brought to our attention the statute (Private Acts 1885, c. 120, § 62) which confers upon the mayor of the town of Morganton, in which the public square referred to is situate, to sell the part thereof to which the indictment has reference, and he insisted that it ought to be interpreted as abolishing so much of the public square as it refers to and embraces. Such defense, so far as appears, was not made or relied upon in the court below. The statute, if we could properly take notice of it, did not of itself abolish or purport to abolish the public square; it simply conferred upon the mayor power to sell it for the purpose and in the way prescribed, and it does not appear that he ever exercised the power, or at all disturbed the use of it as a highway. In no aspect of it, as it appears to us, can it be treated as serving the purpose for which it is invoked here. There is no error, and the judgment must be affirmed. Let this opinion be certified to the superior court according to law. It is so ordered.

HART v. HART.

(Supreme Court of North Carolina. Dec. 11, 1891.)

HUSBAND AND WIFE—ACTIONS BETWEEN—FRAUDULENT CONVEYANCE—EVIDENCE.

Where a wife sues to recover from her husband the price of her land sold by him, which money he had retained, and, to establish her title to the land, produces a deed from her husband to herself, and the husband in his answer alleges that the deed was made in fraud of creditors, it is error for the court to reject evidence tending to prove the husband's allegation. SHEPHERD, J., dissenting.

Appeal from superior court, New Hanover county; J. F. GRAVES, Judge. Reversed.

Action by Julia M. Hart against God frey Hart to recover property. Judgment for plaintiff. Defendant appeals.

The other facts fully appear in the following statement by MERRIMON, C. J.:

The plaintiff alleges in her complaint that the defendant, her husband, on the 23d day of October, 1873, conveyed to her, in consideration of love and affection and five dollars, the real and personal property specified in the deed; that thereafter, on the 2d day of January, 1875, her husband induced her to unite with him in conveying said land to one Lomax for the sum of $1,000, all of which was paid to the defendant, and she received no part thereof; that the defendant received for the land $1,375, which was and is the property of plaintiff; that before bringing this action she demanded of the defendant that he pay the said sum and interest, etc. She demands judgment for the same, etc. The defendant denies that any title to the said land ever passed to the plaintiff by virtue o' said deed. "On the contrary, the defendant alleges that any deed which he may have made to plaintiff was with the un-

derstanding that it should not be registered unless defendant should so direct,
and that it never has been registered, as
defendant is informed and believes, and
that the same had not been registered as
late as the month of April, 1888; and the
defendant further alleges that any deed
which he may have made to plaintiff was
a deed of gift, without any valuable consideration whatever, and that it was his
purpose, well known to the plaintiff, to
register said deed only in the event that
judgments by creditors should be recovered
or threatened. (2) That the conveyance
of the defendant to the plaintiff was for
the purpose of hindering and delaying
creditors, as was well known to the plaintiff, and was with the distinct understanding that plaintiff would convey to the defendant or any other person, as the defendant might direct; and so the defendant alleges that the plaintiff was in equal
wrong with the defendant." "(4) That
at the time of the conveyance by the defendant to the plaintiff in October, 1873,
the defendant was largely indebted to various persons, besides the debt above mentioned, and was insolvent; and all this
was explained to the plaintiff, and well
understood by her; and the deed to her
was made for the purpose of securing
compromises and settlement of his debts,
as the plaintiff was fully advised; and
with the understanding between the plaintiff and the defendant that she would at
any and all times convey the land according as the defendant should direct."

The following issues were submitted to
the jury, and their responses thereto:
"*First*. What amount was received, if
any, from the sale of the land in controversy? Answer. $1,300.00. *Second*. Did
the plaintiff agree to allow the defendant
to take the proceeds for his own use? A.
No. *Third*. How much did defendant pay
out to remove incumbrances, clear the
title, and protect and keep up the premises? A. $150.00. *Fourth*. What amount,
if any, was received from the sale of personal effects? A. $150.00. *Fifth*. Is the
defendant indebted to the plaintiff on the
first cause of action? If so, how much?
A. $1,150.00. *Sixth*. Is the defendant in-
debted to the plaintiff on the second cause
of action? If so, how much? A. None."
The defendant asked that an issue be
submitted to the jury as to whether the
causes of action set out in the complaint
were barred by the statute of limitations.
His honor refused to submit this issue,
and held, as a matter of law, that the statute of limitations could not apply as between husband and wife. It was admitted by the plaintiff that her husband had
abandoned her prior to the commencement
of this action, and that actions of divorce
were mutually depending between them.
The defendant excepted.

The deed from the defendant to the
plaintiff was not duly registered. "The
defendant objected to the introduction
of said deed in evidence on the ground
that its registration was unauthorized
and void, and no title has passed. His
honor held that said deed was not void
between the parties, and permitted the
deed to be introduced. Defendant except-

ed. The defendant was introduced as a
witness in his own behalf: 'Was married
to plaintiff in 1873. I made deed to her
when in financial difficulty.' The defendant proposes to show that no money
was paid by plaintiff to defendant as a
consideration for the deed, and that he
was in financial trouble when he made
deed, and that deed was made to defraud
creditors. Plaintiff objects. Objections
sustained. Defendant excepts. The defendant proposes to show by this witness
a parol agreement, made at the time of the
deed between himself and plaintiff, that
he was to have the proceeds of the land.
Plaintiff objects. Objection sustained.
Defendant excepts. The defendant proposes to show by this witness that, subsequently to the making of the deed to
plaintiff, plaintiff agreed that the proceeds
of the land should be his. The plaintiff
objects. Objection sustained. Defendant
excepts. The defendant proposes to show
that at the time of the sale to Lomax
the plaintiff agreed for him to take
the proceeds for his own use and benefit.
The plaintiff objects. Objection sustained, and defendant excepts. Witness
testified that plaintiff never said one word
about the money after the sale to Lomax. 'I paid out $50 to Lawyer French
to foreclose mortgage given me by Lomax, and paid taxes and insurance and
other expenses for keeping up property,
amounting to $100.' Witness further testi-
fied that at the time of making deed to
plaintiff there was a mortgage on said
property to one W. G. Curtis, and that
after date of deed to wife he paid off balance due on said mortgage, amounting to
about $600. On cross-examination plain-
tiff asked defendant what he was worth
to-day. Defendant objects. Objection
overruled. Defendant excepts. 'Answer.
I am worth $5,000.'" His honor charged
the jury as follows: "That the effect of
the deed from defendant to plaintiff was
to convey to her the property, real and
personal, therein described. On the sale
of the property, the proceeds were due
to the plaintiff, and she will be entitled
to recover it, unless she gave the same to
the defendant." The defendant asked the
court to charge the jury as to the effect
of the recital of the deed to Lomax from
plaintiff as bearing upon second issue;
and, further, that the recital in said deed
is admission by plaintiff that she claimed
the land, not as the owner, but only
claimed her marital right of dower. This
instruction was refused, and no instruction was given as to the effects of said recital in deed as bearing upon second issue,
and appealed to this court. Defendant
assigns error—*First*, the admission of the
evidence to which objection was made
by defendant; *second*, the refusal to admit the evidence offered by defendant;
third, the ruling of court that the deed
from defendant to plaintiff passed the title
to the property therein described.

S. C. Weill, for appellant.   *T. W. Strange*,
for appellee.

MERRIMON, C. J., (*after stating the facts.*)
Passing by any question as to the sufficiency of the deed from the defendant hus-

band to the plaintiff, his wife, as an unregistered deed, we think the defendant is entitled to a new trial upon another and different ground. The defendant alleges in his answer that at the time he executed the deed in question he was largely indebted to divers persons; that he was then insolvent and financially embarrassed, and that this deed was executed in fraud of and to defraud his creditors; that it was executed for that express purpose, and the plaintiff so well understood; that she was so "fully advised, and with the understanding between the plaintiff [and defendant] that she would at any and all times convey the land according as the defendant should direct;" and that it was understood by the parties that the deed was to be registered "only in the event that judgments by creditors should be recovered or threatened." It appeared on the trial that the deed was not offered for registration until August, 1889, being after the execution of a deed to Lomax, in which the plaintiff joined in order to conclude her as to her right of dower. The defendant was a witness in his own behalf, and offered to testify that he was pecuniarily embarrassed, and that the deed was made for the fraudulent purpose as alleged by him; but, the plaintiff objecting, the proposed evidence was rejected. In this there is error. The evidence should have been received. The plaintiff's right is founded upon this deed. If it is fraudulent, as alleged, and therefore void, she is not entitled to the money she seeks to recover. Her claim springs out of and is founded in a fraudulent transaction, and the defendant, a party to it, having the money, the fruit of it, the court will not help her to recover it from him. That the plaintiff is a married woman, and the wife of the defendant, cannot help her or alter the case. A married woman can acquire, hold, and dispose of property in a large sense as a feme sole. She has capacity to perpetrate and participate in a fraud,—the fraudulent purposes and transactions of her husband. She has no right or privilege or disability that excuses her as to such fraudulent transactions in which she participates, nor that protects her against their consequences,—not even as against her husband,—when she must invoke the aid of the courts to assert her claim. She has privileges and immunities in some respects, but not such as will help her to share in a fraud with impunity when she must go into a court of justice to enforce her claims growing out of it. The law abhors fraud, and will not help any person to take advantage of and have benefit of it. It would be singular and monstrous —a great reproach to the courts of justice —if a husband and his wife could perpetrate a fraud upon his creditors, and the courts would afterwards help her to assert a claim against her husband growing out of that fraud. In such case, the wife must be on the same footing as a feme sole, and treated as such. Burns v. McGregor, 90 N. C. 222; Walker v. Brooks, 99 N. C. 207, 6 S. E. Rep. 63; Loftin v. Crossland, 94 N. C. 76; Boyd v. Turpin, Id. 137. The evidence rejected was relevant and pertinent, —it tended directly to prove the fraud as alleged. If it be said that it did not go to prove that the plaintiff had knowledge of and participated in the same, the answer is, it was relevant and competent, and ought to have been received. It may be that the defendant would have testified that the plaintiff had such knowledge, or it might be that he would have proven such knowledge by some other witness or in some other way. But why should he do so after the court had excluded the proposed evidence of fraud? Besides, there was some evidence of the plaintiff's knowledge of it. The deed was executed in 1873. She did not offer it for registration until 1889, more than 15 years having elapsed; and in the mean time, in 1875, she joined her husband in executing a deed conveying the land, in which it was recited that she did so in order to relinquish her right of dower. This recital, perhaps, did not conclude her as to any other right she might have; but it was some evidence that she did not at that time regard the deed in question as having been made as a bona fide conveyance of the land to her. There is error. The defendant is entitled to a new trial, and we so adjudge. To that end let this opinion be certified to the superior court. It is so ordered.

SHEPHERD, J., dissents.

COWEN v. WITHROW et al.

(Supreme Court of North Carolina. Dec. 15, 1891.)

JUDICIAL SALES—RECORD OF PRIOR DEED—NOTICE.

1. Act 1885, c. 147, providing that no conveyance or lease of land for more than three years shall be valid, as against creditors or purchasers for a valuable consideration from the bargainor or lessor, but from the registration thereof, applies to a purchaser at sheriff's sale founded upon judgments docketed against the bargainor or lessor prior to the registration of the said deed, and allows him to recover the land as against the person claiming thereunder.

2. Act 1885, c. 147, providing that no purchase from any such bargainor or lessor shall avail to pass title as against any unregistered deed executed prior to December 1, 1885, when the person claiming under such deed shall be in the actual possession and enjoyment of such land, does not apply to purchasers at sheriff's sale, but only to purchasers from the bargainor or lessor.

Appeal from superior court, Rutherford county; JAMES H. MERRIMON, Judge.

Action by J. C. Cowen against T. J. Withrow and P. J. Withrow to recover the possession of land. There was judgment for defendant, and plaintiff appeals. Reversed.

The other facts fully appear in the following statement by MERRIMON, J.:

This action is brought to recover possession of the land described in the complaint. The pleadings raised issues of fact that put in question the sufficiency of the plaintiff's title. On the trial he put in evidence a deed from the sheriff of Rutherford county to him, purporting to convey the interest and title of the husband, defendant, in the land. This deed was dated the 3d of December, 1888, and registered on the 11th day of the same month. The plaintiff further put in evidence executions authorizing a sale of the land by the sheriff founded upon judgments docketed in that county before the registration of the deed under which the defendant wife claims title. The defendant wife put in evidence a deed from her said husband, dated August 5, 1882, purporting to convey the same land to her, which deed was registered on the 25th of November, 1889. She also produced evidence tending to show that she was in possession of the land, living with her husband. The plaintiff's counsel asked the court to charge the jury that under the act of 1885, c. 147, p. 233, providing that "no conveyance of land nor contract to convey, or lease of land for more than three years, shall be valid to pass any property, as against creditors or purchasers for a valuable consideration from the donor, bargainor, or lessor, but from the registration thereof within the county where the land lieth," the plaintiff was entitled to recover the land mentioned in the pleadings. The court refused to charge the jury as prayed, and the plaintiff excepted. The plaintiff's counsel asked the court to charge the jury that the second saving clause of the act of 1885, c. 147, providing "that no purchase from any such donor, bargainor, or lessor shall avail to pass title as against any unregistered deed executed prior to the 1st day of December, 1885, when the person or persons holding or claiming under such unregistered deed shall be in the actual possession and enjoyment of such land, either in person, or by his, her, or their tenants, at the time of the execution of such second deed," etc., did not apply to judgment creditors, and those claiming under the sheriff's deed, but only to purchasers from the bargainor, grantor, or lessor. His honor refused to give the instruction, and the plaintiff excepted. The plaintiff asked the court to charge the jury that if they believed P. J. Withrow was in possession of the land in December, 1888, and was living with her husband, and had been living with him prior to and at the time of the execution of the deed, in 1882, this was not the kind of possession contemplated in the second saving clause of § 1, c. 147, Acts 1885; and, further, that the possession of the wife was the possession of the husband, and as the defendant P. J. Withrow claims title by deed from defendant T. J. Withrow, registered on November 27, 1880, and the plaintiff claims title by sheriff's deed for the interest of T. J. Withrow in said land, registered on the 11th day of December, 1888, the plaintiff is entitled to recover. The court refused to give this instruction. The plaintiff excepted. There was evidence tending to show the actual possession of the land by the feme defendant, but there was no exception to the instructions of the court as to her possession. After verdict and judgment for the defendant, the plaintiff appealed to this court.

Justice & Justice, for appellant. *J. A. Forney,* for appellees.

MERRIMON, C. J., *(after stating the facts.)* We are of opinion that the court erred in refusing to give the jury the special instructions above set forth, as requested by the plaintiff, or the substance of them.

The purpose of the statute (Acts 1885, c. 147) is to require all conveyances of land to be registered as therein prescribed, and to render the same ineffectual without registration. The first clause thereof material here provides: "No conveyance of land nor contract to convey, or lease of land for more than three years, shall be valid to pass any property, as against creditors or purchasers for a valuable consideration from the donor, bargainor, or lessor, but from the registration thereof in the county were the land lieth." It seems to us clear that this case comes directly within the letter and purpose of this provision, unless it comes within the meaning of the proviso presently to be considered. The plaintiff was a purchaser of the land for a valuable consideration, and his deed was registered long before that under which the defendant claims. The title of the defendant husband had passed to the plaintiff before the *feme* defendant's deed became operative and effectual as against creditors or purchasers for value. The statute cited, however, contains a proviso as to the clause above recited, which provides as follows: "Provided, further, that no purchase from any such donor, bargainor, or lessor shall avail to pass title as against any unregistered deed executed prior to December 1, 1885, when the person or persons claiming or holding under such unregistered deed shall be in the actual possession and enjoyment of such land," etc. It is insisted that the *feme* defendant's deed comes within the saving purpose of this proviso. We do not think so. The saving extends only to cases where the purchase is "from any donor, bargainor, or lessor." The plaintiff did not purchase from a donor, bargainor, or lessor, in the sense of this proviso. He purchased at the sheriff's sale made under and in pursuance of executions to enforce and satisfy docketed judgments against the husband defendant, which were liens upon the land. The sheriff was not a donor or bargainor or lessor. He was the agent of the law to sell the property, and pass the title of the defendant in the executions to the purchaser. There is a substantial reason why the saving does not extend to purchasers at sheriff's sale. It is founded upon the "actual possession and enjoyment of such land" by the person claiming under the unregistered deed, "either in person or by his, her, or their tenants, at the time of the execution of such second deed, or when the person or persons claiming under or taking such second deed had at the time of taking or purchasing under such deed actual or constructive notice of such unregistered deed, or the claim of the person or persons holding or claiming thereunder." Such actual possession and enjoyment of the land is treated as notice to a donee, bargainee, or lessee. It is supposed that such persons will take notice of the land, and have opportunity and be interested and disposed to see and make inquiries of those in possession as to the nature of their possession, their claim and title. But at the sheriff's sale, made not on the land, but at the court-house,—a place perhaps distant from it,—the purchaser has not opportunity on the day of sale to see it, and learn who is in possession, and the nature of his claim and title. Here the plaintiff purchased the land at the sheriff's sale. He may have purchased without notice. He may have purchased suddenly, and without opportunity to see who was in possession thereof. It would tend to discourage such sales if purchasers at them were charged by the statute with such notice. Uninformed persons would not buy, or they would bid only nominal prices. The purpose of the law is not to discourage, but to encourage, bidding at such sales. The saving clause in question does not contain this and like cases in terms; nor, for the reasons stated, does it do so by implication. Moreover, persons so claiming under an unregistered deed are charged with notice of docketed judgments against the donor, bargainor, or lessor under whom they claim. They have constructive notice of the sheriff's sale of land, and it is their own laches if they fail to give notice at the sale of their claim and unregistered deed. They could not—might not ordinarily—have such opportunity or information as would enable them to give notice of their deed to subsequent donees, bargainees, and lessees of the same land. It is not probable that a bargainor would give notice to the holder of the unregistered deed that he had sold the land a second time to another person. The defendant's deed does not, therefore, come within the saving provision of the proviso, but does come within the clause of the statute first above recited.

There is error. The plaintiff is entitled to a new trial, and we so adjudge. To that end let this opinion be certified to the superior court.

END OF VOLUME 13.

INDEX.

ABATEMENT AND REVIVAL.

Plea in abatement, see *Criminal Law,* 7, 8.

When action survives.

1. Acts Ga. 1889, p. 73, amending Code Ga. § 2967, and providing that "no action for homicide, injury to person, or injury to property shall abate by death," applies to actions against a railroad company for personal injuries, as actions for "injury to person."—Pritchard v. Savannah St. & R. R. R. Co., (Ga.) 13 S. E. 493.

2. Acts Ga. 1889, p. 73, amending Code Ga. § 2967, and providing that "no action for homicide, injury to person, or injury to property shall abate by death," applies to actions pending at the time of its passage, its language being sufficiently comprehensive to include them.—Johnson v. Bradstreet Co., (Ga.) 13 S. E. 250; Pritchard v. Savannah St. & R. R. R. Co., Id. 493.

3. Acts Ga. 1889, p. 73, amending Code Ga. § 2967, and providing that "no action for homicide, injury to person, or injury to property shall abate by death," applies to actions for libel, as actions for "injury to person."—Johnson v. Bradstreet Co., (Ga.) 13 S. E. 250.

Objections to jurisdiction—Waiver.

4. Where one files a plea to the merits he thereby waives the question of jurisdiction of the person.—Perseverance Min. Co. v. Bisaner, (Ga.) 13 S. E. 461.

Pendency of another action.

5. The pendency of an action is a bar to another action in the same court, between the same parties, founded on the same cause of action, even if plaintiff submitted to a nonsuit in the first action.—Curtis v. Piedmont Lumber, Ranch & Min. Co., (N. C.) 13 S. E. 944.

6. Pendency of a prior suit in one state cannot be pleaded in abatement of a suit between the same parties, for the same cause, in a court of another state.—Chattanooga, R. & C. R. Co. v. Jackson, (Ga.) 13 S. E. 109.

Death of party—Substitution of representative.

7. Suit having been brought to enforce a vendor's lien, and a decree obtained, a judgment creditor of the vendee consented to a private sale upon condition that, after payment of the vendor, he should receive one-half the residue. Afterwards the purchaser defaulted, and a resale was ordered without the knowledge of the creditor. This second decree ignored the rights of the creditor, and directed the residue to be turned over to the vendee. *Held,* that the creditor by his consent to the first-named sale became in effect a party to the suit, and that it was erroneous to decree concerning his rights without reviving the cause against his administrator; the creditor and his counsel both having died before the second decree was entered.—Ayres v. Alphin, (Va.) 13 S. E. 899.

ABDUCTION.

Civil action.

1. In an action by a father for damages for the abduction of his daughter for immoral pur-

poses, it is no answer that she, as well as plaintiff's whole family, was of a loose and immoral character.—Dobson v. Cothran, (S. C.) 13 S. E. 679.

2. In an action by a father for damages for abducting his daughter for immoral purposes, although defendants did not entice the daughter from home, if they persuaded her, after she came to their house, to lead a life of shame, and when plaintiff came for her hid her from him, he was entitled to recover.—Dobson v. Cothran, (S. C.) 13 S. E. 679.

3. In an action by a father for damages for abducting his daughter for immoral purposes, where the daughter was intoxicated and much excited when taken by plaintiff out of a wardrobe at defendants' house, and had no recollection of seeing plaintiff on that occasion, it was not error to rule out a question put to her as to whether she did not tell him that she would not go home until she got the money she made at defendants' house.—Dobson v. Cothran, (S. C.) 13 S. E. 679.

Acceptance.

Of draft, see *Negotiable Instruments,* 6.
order, see *Orders.*

Accident.

At railroad crossing, see *Railroad Companies,* 20–48.
To railroad train, see *Railroad Companies,* 18, 19.
Insurance against, see *Insurance,* 18.

Accord and Satisfaction.

See *Compromise; Payment.*

Accounting.

By guardian, see *Guardian and Ward,* 1, 2; *Insanity,* 1–3.
In equity, see *Equity,* 6.

Acknowledgment.

Of debt, see *Limitation of Actions,* 19–21.
deed, see *Deed,* 3–5.

ACTION.

By and against executors and administrators, see *Executors and Administrators,* 27–31.
—— husband and wife, see *Husband and Wife,* 24–29.
—— partnership, see *Partnership,* 10.
For abduction, see *Abduction.*
assault, see *Assault and Battery,* 2.
breach of covenant, see *Covenants,* 2, 3.
enticing away servant, see *Master and Servant,* 1–4.
nuisance, see *Nuisance,* 2.
price of goods, see *Sale,* 18, 19.
On contract, see *Contracts,* 4.
insurance policy, see *Insurance,* 12–17.
negotiable instruments, see *Negotiable Instruments,* 9–13.

Survival of, see *Abatement and Revival*, 1–8.
To set aside conveyances, see *Fraudulent Conveyances*, 16–19.

Who may sue.

1. Where a railroad company and its employe are both injured by the same negligence of another railroad company, the former has no right, in an action for its own damages against the latter, to sue also, though it may be for the use of its employe, to recover the damages sustained by him in excess of those already paid to him by it in compromise.—Central Railroad & Banking Co. v. Brunswick & W. R. Co., (Ga.) 13 S. E. 520.

Joinder.

2. Under Code Ga. § 3261, allowing all causes of action of a like kind between the same parties to be joined in one action, two bonds for the forthcoming of personal property levied upon by the sheriff by virtue of two executions in favor of the same plaintiff against the same defendant, one of them being also against another defendant, may, after breach thereof, be sued upon by the sheriff in one action, the makers of both bonds being the same persons, and the sheriff being the obligee in both.—Aycock v. Austin, (Ga.) 13 S. E. 582.

Election.

3. Where a declaration against a common carrier is susceptible of being construed equally as an action upon contract or an action of tort based upon an alleged violation of a public duty by the carrier, and the same is not demurred to, the plaintiff at the trial may, at his option, elect to treat it as either species of action.—Central Railroad & Banking Co. v. Pickett, (Ga.) 13 S. E. 750.

Adjournment.

See *Continuance.*

Administration.

See *Executors and Administrators.*

Admissions.

See *Criminal Law*, 83–86; *Evidence*, 20–29.

ADULTERY.

As ground for divorce, see *Divorce*, 1.

Indictment.

1. An indictment charging that defendants "unlawfully did associate, bed, and cohabit together, and then and there did commit fornication and adultery, contrary to the form of the statute," etc., and that they "were not united together in marriage," implies that they did "lewdly and lasciviously associate," as forbidden by Code N. C. § 1041, and sufficiently charges the offense.—State v. Stubbs, (N. C.) 13 S. E. 90.

Evidence—Admissibility.

2. On an indictment for adultery, evidence of a declaration of the *feme* defendant, made after the offense charged, but not as part of the *res gestæ*, that her brother had driven her from home, and her father had paid the male defendant to take her on his farm as a work-hand, was inadmissible.—State v. Stubbs, (N. C.) 13 S. E. 90.

3. Evidence that the defendants had been seen driving together since the prosecution began was admissible when received with other evidence tending to show their adulterous association.—State v. Stubbs, (N. C.) 13 S. E. 90.

—— Sufficiency.

4. Where, on the trial of a man for fornication and adultery with a woman who lived at his house, it does not appear that the woman was single, or that she was not defendant's wife, or that her child, born while she lived at defend-

ant's house, was a bastard, there is insufficient evidence to go to the jury.—State v. Pope, (N. C.) 13 S. E. 700.

ADVERSE POSSESSION.

Against co-tenant, see *Tenancy in Common and Joint Tenancy*, 2.

What constitutes.

1. Land was conveyed to W., his heirs and assigns, in trust for the sole use and enjoyment of K. during her life, and not liable for the debts of her husband; and at her death to be divided among any children she might leave surviving her. Thereafter the husband of K. executed a deed of the land, and she signed it, but her name nowhere else appeared in the deed except in the attestation clause, and the deed did not refer in any way to the trust-estate. *Held*, in an action by the children of K. after her death against a party claiming by mesne conveyances from the grantee in the deed of K. and her husband, and who had been in possession, claiming adversely for the statutory period, that, as said deed was not in fact executed by K., and her husband had no interest to convey, the trustee could have maintained an action against defendant at any time, and therefore the trustee's estate was barred.—King v. Rhew, (N. C.) 13 S. E. 174.

2. Where a husband brought suit against his divorced wife to recover an undivided half interest in certain land, alleging in his declaration that she had been in the exclusive and adverse possession of this land, without interruption, for more than 15 years, holding under a deed fraudulently made to her and her children, which should have been to herself and him, and it further appears from the declaration that he had actual knowledge of the alleged fraud from the time her adverse possession began, but failed sooner to bring his suit because of ignorance of his legal rights, and the testimony substantially sustains the allegations of the declaration, a nonsuit was properly awarded.—Alford v. Hays, (Ga.) 13 S. E. 315.

3. In an action against one formerly plaintiff's guardian, and administrator of his father, for alleged fraudulent misappropriation of money received in such capacities, plaintiff can recover lands not administered, but fraudulently merged into the administrator's estate, and mesne profits thereon, since no prescriptive title can ripen from a possession originating in fraud.—Lane v. Lane, (Ga.) 13 S. E. 335.

4. Plaintiff took possession of land under a deed from a married woman, who was not privily examined, and held the same until it was sold under execution to defendant's grantor. Upon the second marriage of plaintiff's grantor, subsequent to said sale under execution, she joined her husband in another conveyance to plaintiff. *Held*, that plaintiff's possession had been under color of title, and, as defendant was in privity with her, he could set up the same against her by connecting it with the possession of himself and his grantor.—Miller v. Bumgardner, (N. C.) 13 S. E. 93.

Evidence.

5. The direct testimony of a witness that a certain person was in possession of land is the statement of a simple fact, and, as such, evidence of actual possession and occupation, for the purpose of establishing adverse possession.—Bryan v. Spivey, (N. C.) 13 S. E. 766.

6. Testimony that a certain person, and those claiming under him, had certain land in possession during a certain period, immediately followed by testimony of the same witness giving the names of the heirs and devisees of such person, and the successive descents and devises down to the date of the conveyance of the property to plaintiff, warranted a finding that these were the persons claiming under such person, and that they were in possession as stated by witness.—Bryan v. Spivey, (N. C.) 13 S. E. 766.

Effect on remainder-men.

7. Where certain children had but a contingent remainder in a trust-estate, the legal title to the fee of which vested in the trustee, and his estate was barred, that of the remainder-men was also barred.—King v. Rhew, (N. C.) 13 S. E. 174.

Interruption.

8. Title to land acquired by prescription is not lost by ceasing to hold actual possession for 12 months or more, if the *animus revertendi* existed.—Milliken v. Kennedy, (Ga.) 13 S. E. 685.

9. Plaintiff took possession of land under a deed from a married woman, who was not privily examined, and held the same until it was sold under execution to defendant's grantor. Upon the second marriage of plaintiff's grantor, subsequent to said sale under execution, she joined her husband in another conveyance to plaintiff. Plaintiff sought to prove that her grantor was an infant during her widowhood, and that consequently, being under the disability of either marriage or infancy during the possession of defendant and his grantor, such adverse possession was not a defense. *Held*, that the burden of such proof was upon plaintiff, and any doubt should have been resolved in defendant's favor.—Miller v. Bumgardner, (N. C.) 13 S. E. 935.

By cestui que trust.

10. A *cestui que trust* in possession as a tenant in common under a trustee cannot, by adverse possession under a deed from the same grantor subsequent to the trust, acquire title against his trustee or his co-tenants.—Jester v. Davis, (N. C.) 13 S. E. 908.

Color of title.

11. Where, in an action of trespass for cutting timber from certain land, plaintiff's title is brought in issue, but it is proved that he or his grantors have been in continuous possession for more than seven years, a deed to land lying in two counties, including the *locus in quo* and constituting a link in plaintiff's title, though properly proved and registered only in one county, is admissible to show color of title, under Code N. C. § 1245, which provides that, where real estate is situate in two or more counties, probate of the deed conveying same, made before the clerk of the superior court of either county, is sufficient.—Lewis v. Roper Lumber Co., (N. C.) 13 S. E. 701.

12. Plaintiff's admission that defendants were for a certain time in adverse possession of certain land, claiming in the same manner as a certain witness, is not an admission that they were claiming under color of title,—the testimony of said witness being, first, that he claimed under a deed to one S. in trust for the people of J.; and, next, that he claimed his lot in severalty, though under such deed the beneficiaries would take as tenants in common; and, next, that he claimed in the same way he did when he first went on the land, though the deed was executed several years thereafter.—Bryan v. Spivey, (N. C.) 13 S. E. 766.

Affidavit.

In attachment, see *Attachment*, 1.
   bastardy proceeding, see *Bastardy*, 1.
   criminal cases, see *Criminal Law*, 8.
   supplementary proceedings, see *Execution*, 24, 25.
Of claim, see *Replevin*, 3.
   illegality of execution, see *Execution*, 9–11.

Agency.

See *Principal and Agent*.

Aider by Verdict.

See *Indictment and Information*, 4; *Pleading*, 22.

Alcoholic Liquors.

See *Intoxicating Liquors*.

Alibi.

Burden of proof, see *Criminal Law*, 43.

Amendment.

Of answer in *certiorari* proceedings, see *Certiorari*, 10.
   pleading, see *Pleading*, 8–17.
   record, see *Records*, 1.
   return, see *Writs*, 7, 8.
   statute, see *Statutes*, 2, 3.

ANIMALS.

Killing of stock on railroad track, see *Railroad Companies*, 55–56.
Live-stock shipments, see *Carriers*, 3–4.
Power of municipalities to impound, see *Municipal Corporations*, 2.

Vicious dogs—Liability of owner.

Under Code Ga. § 2964, declaring that where a person keeps a vicious or dangerous animal, and by the careless management of the same, or by allowing the same to go at liberty, another, "without fault on his part," is injured thereby, such owner or keeper shall be liable in damages for such injury, one who keeps a ferocious dog, knowing that it is accustomed to bite, loose in his back yard, with the gate open, is liable for injuries to a person who enters the yard in search of work, though such person may be a trespasser.—Conway v. Grant, (Ga.) 13 S. E. 803.

APPEAL.

I. JURISDICTION.
II. PRACTICE.
III. REVIEW.
IV. EFFECT OF APPEAL.
V. DECISION.
VI. LIABILITIES ON APPEAL-BONDS.

See, also, *Certiorari; Exceptions, Bill of; New Trial*.

Certiorari as a substitute, see *Certiorari*, 3–7.
Change of venue, review of order, see *Venue in Civil Cases*, 2.
Costs on, see *Costs*, 4–6.
From judgment on referee's report, see *Reference*, 10.
   order granting injunction, see *Injunction*, 19.
In condemnation proceedings, see *Eminent Domain*, 8.
   criminal cases, see *Criminal Law*, 67–84.

I. JURISDICTION.

Appealable judgments and orders.

1. An order of the court below, conforming to the directions contained in a judgment of the supreme court, previously rendered, is not appealable. Mitchell v. Clayton, 11 S. E. 684, 82 S. C. 599, followed.—State v. Merriman, (S. C.) 13 S. E. 898.

2. Appeal does not lie from an interlocutory ruling on objections to the jurisdiction of the court.—State v. Georgia Co., (N. C.) 13 S. E. 861.

3. A judgment allowing a garnishee to file an answer after default is not final, and an appeal will not lie therefrom under Code Ga. § 4250, which provides that no cause shall be carried to the supreme court upon any bill of exceptions so long as the same is pending in the court below.—Moore v. Hill, (Ga.) 13 S. E. 259.

4. Where three creditors petition for an injunction and the appointment of a receiver, under the traders' act of Georgia, (1881,) requiring that number of creditors to institute such a suit, and the petition is granted after making a fourth creditor a party to the petition, one of the cred-

pires will be dismissed on motion.—**Logan v. Western & A. R. Co.,** (Ga.) 13 S. E. 516.

86. Where the record fails to show that an appeal was taken or notice of appeal given, the appeal must be dismissed. **Manufacturing Co. v. Simmons,** 1 S. E. 923, 97 N. C. 89 followed.—**Howell v. Jones,** (N. C.) 13 S. E. 889.

87. Where an appeal is not docketed in the supreme court at the term succeeding the trial of the case in the court below, and no excuse is shown for the delay, the appeal will be dismissed.—**State v. James,** (N. C.) 13 S. E. 112.

Dismissal—Notice of motion.

88. Notice of motion to dismiss an appeal is not required.—**Johnston v. Whitehead,** (N. C.) 13 S. E. 731.

—— Time of making motion.

89. The provision of Sup. Ct. Rule S. C. No. 19, that a motion that "an appeal be dismissed or the cause stricken from the docket for any irregularity in the taking of the appeal or in the record filed in this court" must be made at the time assigned for the hearing of special motions, is imperative; but it does not apply to a motion to dismiss an appeal on the ground that the order from which the appeal was taken is not appealable. **Mitchell v. Clayton,** 11 S. E. 634, 88 S. C. 599, followed.—**State v. Merriman,** (S. C.) 13 S. E. 898.

—— Reinstatement.

90. Under Sup. Ct. N. C. rule 17, providing that, if an appeal be not docketed before the call of the district to which it belongs, the appellee may have it dismissed, and that if improperly dismissed the motion to reinstate should be made "during the term," an agreement of counsel to give until January 31, 1891, to perfect an appeal, while ground to resist a motion to dismiss if made at the fall term of 1890, when the appeal should in due course have been docketed, was no excuse for the appeal not being docketed or a *certiorari* applied for at the spring term of 1891, and a motion to reinstate at the next term thereafter was too late.—**Johnston v. Whitehead,** (N. C.) 13 S. E. 731.

91. Though Act S. C. Dec. 24, 1889, § 2, (20 St. 356,) requires appellant to serve his case with exceptions on the opposite party or his attorney within 30 days after service of the notice of appeal, the trial judge may extend his time; and when he has done so, and the clerk, without knowledge of the extension, has dismissed the appeal, under supreme court rule No. 1, the appeal will be reinstated.—**Cunningham v. Cauthen,** (S. C.) 13 S. E. 829.

Modification of judgment.

92. Where, on appeal in an action against three persons as partners for a tort, the judgment is correct as to one of them, and obviously incorrect as to the other two, no partnership being established, the judgment will be affirmed as to the former, but reversed as to the latter.—**Austin v. Appling,** (Ga.) 13 S. E. 955.

Remandment.

93. Where, on appeal from a writ of *habeas corpus,* granted by the superior court, awarding to a mother the possession of her minor children, it appears that she has since become insane and has been committed to the insane asylum, the case will be remanded, under Code N. C. § 905, providing that a case may be remanded for further proceedings, "whenever it shall appear necessary for the purposes of justice."—**Jones v. Cotten,** (N. C.) 13 S. E. 161.

94. On appeal, a cause may be remanded for a special finding as to the right to costs.—**Smith v. Smith,** (N. C.) 13 S. E. 113.

—— Proceedings below.

95. Laws N. C. 1887, c. 192, § 3, providing that "in civil cases, at the first term of the superior court after" the certificate of the supreme court "is received, if the judgment is affirmed the court below shall direct the execution thereof to pro-

ceed," is directory as to the mere forms to be observed; and it does not mean or intend that if, at the first term of the court below after it receives the certificate from the supreme court, it should fail for any cause to act upon the same, there could be no proper or sufficient action taken afterwards.—**Johnston v. Danville, M. & S. W. R. Co.,** (N. C.) 13 S. E. 881.

96. On application by a mother for the apprenticeship of her minor child, the superior court affirmed the action of the clerk in apprenticing the child to defendant, against the mother's wishes. *Held,* that a reversal of this decision by the supreme court on appeal, which did not render a final judgment in the matter, but simply remanded the cause for a new trial to the court below, did not warrant the mother in instituting *habeas corpus* proceedings to regain the custody of the child from defendant, as the order of the superior court apprenticing the child to him still remained in force.—**Ashby v. Page,** (N. C.) 13 S. E. 90.

97. The reversal by the supreme court of the judgment of the superior court, refusing to apprentice a minor child to his step-father, on the ground that the facts found did not warrant the judgment that the mother was not entitled to the custody of her child, does not preclude the superior court, on a new trial, from hearing additional testimony, nor from finding the facts in accordance therewith.—**Ashby v. Page,** (N. C.) 13 S. E. 90.

98. After remand for a new trial, the refusal to allow further pleadings is within the discretion of the trial court, and not reviewable, unless the refusal is based on want of power.—**Beville v. Cox,** (N. C.) 13 S. E. 800.

VI. LIABILITIES ON APPEAL-BONDS.

Release of sureties.

99. A judgment against defendant having been affirmed, he obtained, without the consent of L., the surety on the *supersedeas* bond, an injunction against further proceedings, giving an injunction bond, with R. as surety. An action against the heirs of R. was compromised, and in a subsequent suit on the *supersedeas* bond against the heirs of L. the court held that defendants were released to the extent of the value of the property of R. which had been released by the compromise, and directed that defendants be credited such amount. It appeared that at the administrator's sale of R.'s property the entire property had been purchased by R.'s heirs at very much less than its value. *Held,* that the actual value of R.'s property, and not the price for which it sold, should determine the amount to be credited defendants.—**Lewis v. Hill,** (Ga.) 13 S. E. 588.

Application.

For insurance, see *Insurance,* 1–5.
Of payments, see *Payment,* 3.
To remove cause to federal court, see *Removal of Causes.*

APPRENTICE.

Apprenticing fatherless child.

A finding by the court that a mother is a woman of bad character, and not a fit person to have the custody of her child, whose father is dead, brings the case within Acts N. C. 1889, c. 169, § 2, subd. 4, and authorizes the apprenticeship of the child to a stranger.—**Ashby v. Page,** (N. C.) 13 S. E. 90.

ARBITRATION AND AWARD.

Scope of submission.

1. Arbitrators, chosen to declare and establish the true boundary line between litigants, do not exceed their authority when they award that the line shall be five feet from the fence, and shall "come off" defendant's land, and be "added

to" plaintiff's land, since these expressions simply describe the line as established, and do not show an unwarranted taking of land.—Pearson v. Barringer, (N. C.) 13 S. E. 942.

Award—Conclusiveness.

2. Since arbitrators are not required to find a statement of facts and conclusions of law, unless the award contains erroneous views of the law as a basis of the award, their action, in the absence of fraud, will not be reviewed.—Smith v. Kron, (N. C.) 13 S. E. 839.

3. Where arbitrators, in making an award, gave the parties an opportunity of having the conclusions of law passed upon by the court, unless exceptions thereto are filed, the judgment is final. —Smith v. Kron, (N. C.) 13 S. E. 839.

Setting aside award.

4. Where an affidavit alleges that one of the arbitrators was surety on plaintiff's prosecution bond in the action, and prejudiced in his favor, and that defendant was ignorant of this at the time he was chosen, but the affidavit does not deny that defendant had such knowledge in time to object to the making of the award, the court will not interfere.—Pearson v. Barringer, (N. C.) 13 S. E. 942.

5. By the terms of a submission of a controversy relating to party lines, the arbitrators were to settle the lines between plaintiff and defendant, and all matters of difference in relation thereto. Plaintiff offered in evidence certain deeds and plats for the purpose of showing his lines. Held, that the award should be set aside for the refusal of the arbitrators to consider such evidence.—Hurdle v. Stallings, (N. C.) 13 S. E. 720.

Argument of Counsel.

See Criminal Law, 25–28; Trial, 9–11.

Arrest of Judgment.

See Criminal Law, 56, 57.

ARSON.

Evidence.

1. In a prosecution for setting fire to an unoccupied dwelling-house, which was only partially completed when burned, the evidence showed that when the fire was discovered the flames were bursting out at every opening, and that the fire appeared to have been set in several places. It was also shown that defendant entertained hostile feelings towards the owner of the building; that he had repeatedly threatened to burn it; that, after the fire, he was seen to stand on the site of the house, and hold up his hands, and yell as if in delight; and that he had admitted to several witnesses that he had burned the house. Held, that the evidence so clearly established defendant's guilt that an erroneous ruling by the court, excluding evidence offered to impeach one of the commonwealth's witnesses, was no ground for reversal, since such exclusion could not have harmed defendant.—Sawyers v. Commonwealth, (Va.) 13 S. E. 708.

Instructions.

2. When on the trial of a defendant for setting fire to a guard-house the issue was whether he attempted to burn a hole in the door solely for the purpose of effecting his escape, or set fire to the house maliciously and with intent to burn it, and the court, in its charge, after stating in detail a number of alleged acts of defendant, instructed the jury they should look to the circumstances and to the conduct of defendant in determining what his intention was, the court should also instruct the jury they might look to defendant's statement, and decide whether or not the statement successfully rebutted any inferences of guilty intention, provided there were such, which might be drawn from the testimony.—Washington v. State, (Ga.) 13 S. E. 131.

3. On a trial for arson involving an issue as to whether defendant set fire to a guard-house for the sole purpose of effecting his escape, it is error to charge as follows: "A man has the same right to burn a hole in the house to get into it as to burn a hole into it to get out of it. He has exactly the same right to burn a hole into a dwelling-house for the purpose of getting inside of it that he would have to burn a hole into the guard-house to get out of it."—Washington v. State, (Ga.) 13 S. E. 131.

ASSAULT AND BATTERY.

With intent to kill, see Homicide, 22, 23.
—— to rape, see Rape, 2–6.

Criminal prosecution—Justification.

1. The fact that defendant's hogs are impounded under an invalid ordinance will not justify a breach of the peace, and an assault on the officer in charge, in order to retake them.—State v. Black, (N. C.) 13 S. E. 877.

Civil action—Defense.

2. In an action to recover damages for an alleged assault and battery, an affirmative answer which alleges that plaintiff first assaulted defendant, who committed the acts complained of in self defense, is sufficient on demurrer, under Code S. C. § 170, which provides that the defendant may set up any matter which will constitute a defense to the action.—Hughey v. Kellar, (S. C.) 13 S. E. 475.

ASSIGNMENT.

See, also, Assignment for Benefit of Creditors.
Of errors, see Appeal, 18.

What constitutes.

1. A creditor drew on his debtor through a bank for the amount of the debt, payable in 15 days, "as advised," and at the same time wrote the debtor either to pay the draft when due, or remit to the bank; saying that the drawer had gotten money from the bank, and wanted to transfer to it the balance due from the drawee. The bank, and not the drawer, was afterwards regarded by all the parties as the owner of the debt, and the party to whom the debtor was to pay it. Held, that the debt was assigned to the bank, and that it was entitled to it as against a subsequent garnishing creditor of the drawer.— First Nat. Bank v. Hartman Steel Co., (Ga.) 13 S. E. 586.

What is assignable.

2. In Georgia a right of action for a tort is not assignable.—Central Railroad & Banking Co. v. Brunswick & W. R. Co., (Ga.) 13 S. E. 520.

ASSIGNMENT FOR BENEFIT OF CREDITORS.

See, also, Insolvency.

What constitutes.

1. A conveyance by a debtor of all his property to a single creditor, the grantee agreeing absolutely out of the proceeds of the property to pay certain of the other debts, is not an assignment, and will not support a petition by the other creditors to set it aside as fraudulent under the assignment act of 1881, (Acts 1880–81, p. 174.)—Stillwell v. Savannah Grocery Co., (Ga.) 13 S. E. 963.

Rights of creditors.

2. After a debtor had made an assignment for benefit of creditors, one of them filed a petition to have the assignment set aside, alleging that it was void because it preferred persons who were not creditors of the assignor, and because the schedule of liabilities was not full and complete. The petition also alleged that his debt was secured by a real-estate mortgage not yet due, and valid as between the parties there-

to, but void as against innocent purchasers, because attested by only one witness, and that the assignee was threatening to sell the property, as empowered by the assignment. Defendants alleged that the assignment was valid, and at the trial each party offered evidence in support of its allegations. *Held*, that the appointment of a receiver of the property of the assignor, and the granting of an injunction against the sale of the property by the assignee, was not an abuse of the discretion vested in the trial court.—Buena Vista Manuf'g Co. v. Chattanooga Door & Sash Co., (Ga.) 13 S. E. 684.

Associations.

See *Building and Loan Associations; Corporations; Religious Societies.*

ASSUMPSIT.

Money had and received.

1. Where one who has bought a water-wheel on trial sells both it and the mill with which it is connected for a gross sum, and there is nothing to show the amount obtained for the wheel, the seller is not entitled to recover from the second purchaser upon an implied contract as for money had and received.—Glascock v. Hazell, (N. C.) 13 S. E. 789.

Money paid to another's use.

2. Plaintiff was the clerk of an agent for an express company. He received a money package, and delivered it to the consignee, but neglected to take a receipt. The latter having denied receiving the package, the agent was required by the express company to make good the loss. Plaintiff paid the money to the agent, who sent it to the consignor, and the latter credited it on his account against the consignee. *Held*, in a suit to which the agent, the consignor, and the consignee were made parties, that the consignee was liable to the plaintiff for the money paid by him.—Houser v. McGinnis, (N. C.) 13 S. E. 139.

Practice.

3. After issue was joined on the plea of *non assumpsit*, defendant filed two special pleas, to which plaintiff demurred. The court overruled the demurrers, and gave final judgment for defendant. *Held*, this was error, as there could be no final judgment unless the issue on the plea of *non assumpsit* had been tried, withdrawn, or otherwise disposed of.—Morgantown Bank v. Foster, (W. Va.) 13 S. E. 996.

ATTACHMENT.

See, also, *Execution; Garnishment; Writs.*

Affidavit.

1. Where the affidavit supporting the petition for an attachment issued on the ground of fraud is not positive, but only "to the best of affiant's knowledge and belief," the burden of proof on the hearing of an application to dissolve the attachment is on plaintiff.—Kenny v. Wallace, (Ga.) 13 S. E. 744.

Bond.

2. Under Code Va. § 2968, providing that, in attachments, if the plaintiff shall file a bond, etc., the sheriff shall take the property attached into his possession, a bond is not required unless the sheriff is directed to take the property into his possession.—Kenefick v. Caulfield, (Va.) 13 S. E. 848.

Attestation.

Of deed, see *Deed*, 6–8.
will, see *Wills*, 1.

ATTORNEY AND CLIENT.

Absence of attorney, continuance, see *Criminal Law*, 11.

Argument of counsel, see *Criminal Law*, 23–26; *Trial*, 9–11.
Privileged communications between, see *Witness*, 3, 4.

Authority of attorney.

1. An attorney employed to prosecute a suit, in the absence of direction from his client, cannot delegate his authority as such to another attorney.—Crotty v. Eagle's Adm'r, (W. Va.) 13 S. E. 59.

2. An attorney at law cannot by an agreement *in pais* commute the debt of his client, or compromise his suit, without express authority so to do.—Crotty v. Eagle's Adm'r, (W. Va.) 13 S. E. 59.

3. Where infants, interested as distributees in the estate of a decedent, sue in equity by a *prochein ami* to compel the administrator to settle his accounts, and such *prochein ami* employs an attorney to represent their interests, such attorney cannot bind said infants by an agreement to waive proof of the vouchers and accounts presented by the administrator, or to allow commissions to such administrator which are not allowed by statute.—Crotty v. Eagle's Adm'r, (W. Va.) 13 S. E. 59.

—— Satisfaction of judgment.

4. Although there was no direct evidence that an attorney was authorized to satisfy a judgment obtained in a suit by him, yet, as his client claimed through the act of that attorney in procuring the judgment, it will be presumed, so far as a third person relying on such satisfaction is concerned, that the attorney was authorized to satisfy the judgment.—Wheeler v. Alderman, (S. C.) 13 S. E. 673.

5. An attorney only employed to collect a debt has no power after judgment to accept a sum of money less than the full amount of the judgment as satisfaction.—Watt v. Brookover, (W. Va.) 13 S. E. 1007.

Purchase at judicial sale.

6. An attorney who brings an equitable petition to marshal and administer the assets of a corporation, and who, by a consent decree, is to be paid for his services out of the proceeds of a receiver's sale of the property, so far represents the corporation that he cannot purchase the property for himself at the sale at a grossly inadequate price.—Crayton v. Spullock, (Ga.) 13 S. E. 561.

License—Payment in state coupons.

7. On the trial of an indictment against an attorney at law for practicing without a revenue license, it appeared that the defendant had tendered to the treasurer, in payment of his license, papers purporting to be coupons cut from the bonds of the state, tax-receivable and past due, and that the treasurer had refused to receive them, because the statutes prohibited him from doing so, and because he did not know whether they were genuine. Defendant, who was the only witness for the defense, testified that he had never seen the bonds from which said coupons were cut, but that he had handled many thousands of dollars' worth of coupons, and that he believed himself an expert, competent to pass upon the genuineness of such coupons, and that he believed them to be genuine. He did not testify to any facts showing that he was an expert. *Held*, that an instruction that, if defendant showed "he believed" himself an expert, and that he believed the coupons tendered were genuine, the burden of proving their non-genuineness was shifted upon the commonwealth, was inapplicable and defective.—Commonwealth v. Larkin, (Va.) 13 S. E. 901.

8. An instruction, without prelude or explanation, that it was "not necessary, independently of any collateral litigation, to establish the genuineness of coupons before or after tender, to entitle a tenderer to be free from molestation," is erroneous.—Commonwealth v. Larkin, (Va.) 13 S. E. 901.

Award.

See *Arbitration and Award.*

the tract of each is bounded by that of the other, the ascertainment of the true line between them fixes the extent of their respective tracts.—Phillips v. O'Neal, (Ga.) 18 S. E. 819.

Evidence.

5. It is competent to establish the lines and courses of a tract of land by showing where the surveyor actually ran when making the boundaries at the instance of the parties to the conveyance, and with a view to its execution.—Euliss v. McAdams, (N. C.) 18 S. E. 162.

6. A junior deed is not admissible as evidence to locate the corner of land conveyed by an older deed.—Euliss v. McAdams, (N. C.) 18 S. E. 162.

Purchase with reference to boundary.

7. S. and G., owning a lot in common, divided it between them, and their portions, by mesne conveyances, became vested in plaintiff and defendant, respectively, through an intermediate grantee of both portions. The deeds of S.'s portion down to defendant described the tract as containing 98 acres, more or less, and the deeds from G. down to defendant described his portion as containing 100 acres, more or less. The land in dispute was a tract midway of the lot which each claimed to be included in his portion. *Held*, that if plaintiff first purchased from such grantee with reference to a boundary established by S. and G., he would be entitled to take up to that boundary only, whether the tract so determined contained the number of acres called for by his deed or not; but, if he purchased by an imaginary boundary, he would be entitled to 98 acres, though it might leave defendant, who purchased after him, less than the number of acres called for by his deed.—Adams v. Powell, (Ga.) 13 S. E. 280.

8. S. and G., owning a lot in common, divided it between them, and their portions, by mesne conveyances, became vested in plaintiff and defendant, respectively, through an intermediate grantee of both portions. The deeds of S.'s portion down to defendant described the tract as containing 98 acres, more or less, and the deeds from G. down to defendant described his portion as containing 100 acres, more or less. The land in dispute was a tract midway of the lot which each claimed to be included in his portion. The evidence tended to show that a boundary line had been established between S. and G., which was recognized by subsequent purchasers. *Held*, that it was error to charge that, if defendant had 100 acres without taking in the tract in dispute, and plaintiff did not have 98 acres without including it, plaintiff should recover the tract; since if S. and G. had established a boundary line, and defendant had purchased his tract with reference to it, he would be entitled to hold it, though it contained more than 100 acres.—Adams v. Powell, (Ga.) 13 S. E. 280.

BRIDGES.

Construction—Approval of justices.

Defendants, county commissioners, contracted in writing to pay plaintiff the actual cost of constructing a bridge upon a highway in the county. A majority of the justices of the county, not then in session, executed a writing ratifying the contract, and afterwards, at a regular joint meeting of the commissioners and justices, a quorum of the latter voted in ratification of said contract. *Held*, that under Code N. C. § 707, subsec. 10, providing that where the cost of a bridge exceeds $500 the commissioners can order its construction only with the concurrence of a majority of the justices of the peace, the approval of the contract by a majority of the justices sitting as an organized body is a sufficient compliance therewith. MERRIMON, C. J., and CLARK, J., dissenting.—Cleveland Cotton-Mills v. Commissioners of Cleveland County, (N. C.) 18 S. E. 271.

Brokers.

See *Factors and Brokers.*

BUILDING AND LOAN ASSOCIATIONS.

Dissolution.

Where a building and loan association sells out, and assigns in writing all its claims for unpaid loans, thereby realizing a fund sufficient to raise the value of its stock to the maximum fixed by the constitution or the by-laws, and with this fund, in connection with other assets, pays off and satisfies all its stockholders, and entirely ceases to transact business, it is virtually dissolved, and is incapable of further prosecuting a pending action founded upon a bond so transferred and assigned after the action was brought.—Van Pelt v. Home Building & Loan Ass'n, (Ga.) 18 S. E. 574.

BURGLARY.

Indictment.

1. An indictment for burglary which does not allege that the breaking and entering was "feloniously and burglariously" done is bad, and the defect is not cured by verdict.—State v. McClung, (W. Va.) 18 S. E. 654.

2. A count of an indictment alleging a breaking and entering into a dwelling with intent to steal goods therein, and actual larceny therein, is not bad as a count for burglary, because that part charging larceny is not drawn with sufficient precision to support a conviction of larceny, where the breaking and entering are charged to have been done with intent to commit larceny, since the charge of actual larceny may be rejected as surplusage.—State v. McClung, (W. Va.) 18 S. E. 654.

Evidence.

3. Recent possession, not satisfactorily explained, of goods stolen from the house at the time the alleged burglary was committed, may be sufficient as a basis of conviction of burglary, where the burglary has been established, and the jury believe from all the evidence beyond a reasonable doubt that defendant is guilty.—Mangum v. State, (Ga.) 18 S. E. 558.

4. Where a burglary is fully established, and the whole contest, in a prosecution therefor, is as to the identity of the burglar, the positive testimony of one witness that she recognized the accused as the burglar, and the less confident testimony of another that she also recognized him, both of them being on the premises when the offense was committed, and the moon giving considerable light, warrants a verdict of guilty.—Matthews v. State, (Ga.) 18 S. E. 16.

5. On an indictment for burglary it was shown that a dwelling had been broken open and some bacon and meal stolen. The articles were found in defendant's possession, and at first she denied taking them, but afterwards, being told that she had better confess it if she took them, she confessed in the presence of three men that one P. helped her to burst in the door, and they got the meat and meal, and carried them off and divided them. *Held*, that a verdict of guilty was warranted.—Matthews v. State, (Ga.) 13 S. E. 16.

CARRIERS.

See, also, *Railroad Companies.*

Of goods—Liability for loss.

1. Though goods saved by a carrier from the perils of a freshet were damaged by passing through the freshet without its fault, yet if some not saved are unaccounted for, and it is not shown that the freshet caused their loss, or what their condition was when they disappeared, a recovery for their full value may be had.—Charlotte, C. & A. R. Co. v. Wooten, (Ga.) 18 S. E. 509.

—— Live-stock shipments.

2. The shipper of live-stock by railway, under a special contract in which he agrees that, "in case of accidents to or delays of train from

any cause whatever," he "is to feed, water, and take proper care of the stock at his own expense," cannot recover damages resulting from his own failure to perform his part of the contract, although the company may have consumed more time than necessary in effecting the transportation. — Boaz v. Central Railroad & Banking Co., (Ga.) 13 S. E. 711.

3. Where a railroad company transporting live-stock has actual knowledge that they suffered injury from the beginning of the journey, and has consented to their removal from the car before reaching destination, the shipper may recover for the injuries, though he has not given the company notice thereof, as required by the contract of shipment.—Central Railroad & Banking Co. v. Pickett, (Ga.) 13 S. E. 750.

4. In an action against a carrier for injuries sustained by cattle and hogs during transportation, it is not a material variance that they are described in the written contract of shipment as one car-load of cattle; the action being treated as one of tort, and not as founded on the contract.—Central Railroad & Banking Co. v. Pickett, (Ga.) 13 S. E. 750.

—— Limitation of liability.

5. Where there is a special contract varying the common-law liability of the carrier, the action is properly brought on the special contract, and not on the common-law liability.—Boaz v. Central Railroad & Banking Co., (Ga.) 13 S. E. 711.

—— Connecting lines.

6. Under Code N. C. § 1963, providing that common carriers may require prepayment of freight in all cases, a railroad company may lawfully refuse to receive freight offered by a connecting railway company without prepayment, though it does not demand prepayment of others, if the connecting railroad has notice that prepayment is required.—Randall v. Richmond & D. R. Co., (N. C.) 13 S. E. 137.

7. In an action for damages for refusal to receive from a connecting line without prepayment freight billed to a certain flag station, defendant may show that it had a fixed regulation requiring prepayment on all freight consigned to that station, and that both plaintiff and the connecting line knew of that fact.—Randall v. Richmond & D. R. Co., (N. C.) 13 S. E. 137.

Injuries to passengers.

8. A freight train, with caboose for passengers, stopped at a certain station, and the conductor, though he saw several persons approaching with baggage, ordered the engineer to back the train. Without warning, the train was violently backed while the passengers were boarding it, fatally injuring a boy between five and six years old, standing on the ends of the ties, and about to get on. Held, that the railroad was negligent. — Norfolk & W. R. Co. v. Groseclose's Adm'r, (Va.) 13 S. E. 454.

9. A declaration alleging that the conductor on a passenger train agreed with plaintiff, who was a passenger, to stop the train for him to get off at a point where there was no regular station, but at which defendant's road crossed another railroad at grade; that plaintiff paid his fare to this point; and that on reaching the same the train only slowed up, and did not stop, so that plaintiff, "in order to keep from being carried beyond his destination, was compelled to get from the moving train," and in so doing was seriously injured,—does not set forth a cause of action, it appearing from these allegations that plaintiff's injury was caused by his own voluntary act in taking a dangerous risk, if the train was moving so rapidly as to make leaving it unsafe; or, if not, that the injury must have resulted from a mere accident, or from plaintiff's own carelessness in getting off.—Barnett v. East Tennessee, V. & G. Ry. Co., (Ga.) 13 S. E. 904.

10. Although a railroad required fare for all children over five years old, the fact that a father purchased no ticket for his child, six years old, will not bar recovery for injuries causing his death; and whether or not he knew that a ticket was required is immaterial.—Norfolk & W. R. Co. v. Groseclose's Adm'r, (Va.) 13 S. E. 454.

11. Though the accident was occasioned by the train leaving the main track at the switch, and then running into freight-cars standing on the side track, leaving such freight-cars standing on the side track is not negligence where they do not interfere with travel when the tracks are in order.—Grant v. Raleigh & G. R. Co., (N. C.) 13 S. E. 209.

—— Evidence.

12. In an action for injuries to plaintiff, a mail agent on defendant's train, received in an accident at a switch, the exclusion of a question whether there was not a subsequent accident at the same switch is harmless error where another witness testifies as to such accident.—Grant v. Raleigh & G. R. Co., (N. C.) 13 S. E. 209.

13. It is not error to exclude a question whether, if a switch be worn, the flanges of the engine wheels might not throw it open, when the witness is not an expert, and there is no evidence that the switch was worn.—Grant v. Raleigh & G. R. Co., (N. C.) 13 S. E. 209.

14. Evidence of the condition of defendant's track at other places and of other switches in the vicinity is inadmissible.—Grant v. Raleigh & G. R. Co., (N. C.) 13 S. E. 209.

Cemeteries.

Regulation of, police power, see *Constitutional Law*, 13.

Certificate.

To record on appeal, see *Appeal*, 36–38.

CERTIORARI.

When lies.

1. The statute providing for elections respecting fences and stock law in and for a single militia district makes no provision for a counter-petition, or for any contest or hearing before the ordinary; and the ordinary's action upon such a petition is ministerial, and *certiorari* will not lie to correct any error or mistake in his conduct. Affirming 10 S. E. 904.—Meadows v. Taylor, (Ga.) 13 S. E. 155.

2. Where the facts are not disputed, *certiorari* is the proper remedy to review the judgment of a justice of the peace on questions of law.—Greenwood v. Boyd & Baxter Furniture Factory, (Ga.) 13 S. E. 123.

—— Substitute for appeal.

3. Where there are issues of fact, and the amount involved is less than $50, *certiorari* will not lie to a judgment of a justice of the peace. Appeal is the proper remedy.—Bernstein v. Clark, (Ga.) 13 S. E. 336.

4. Since under the Code the writ of *certiorari* to a judgment of a justice has the scope of an appeal, it should be applied for within the time in which an appeal can be taken, and as Code, c. 50, §§ 164–174, provide that such an appeal must be taken within 10 days after judgment, or may be granted after the expiration of 10 days and within 90 days, if appellant show good cause for not having taken the appeal within the 10 days, a writ of *certiorari* will be denied where the petition therefor is not filed until nearly 90 days after the judgment, and no excuse is given for the delay.—Long v. Ohio River R. Co., (W. Va.) 13 S. E. 1010.

5. A petition for a writ of *certiorari*, as a substitute for an appeal lost, alleged that within 10 days after notice of the order complained of notice of appeal was served on plaintiff, but it did not allege that defendants took an appeal within 10 days after notice, or within 10 days after the rendition of such order, nor that an appeal was entered in the judgment docket and notice given. It did not allege that the adverse party prevented defendants from taking an appeal, and it did not appear that an appeal was

ever taken, and no reason was assigned for the neglect. *Held*, that the writ would not issue.—Cox v. Pruett, (N. C.) 13 S. E. 917.

6. *Certiorari* does not lie as a substitute for an appeal from an interlocutory order of a superior court.—State v. Georgia Co., (N. C.) 13 S. E. 861.

7. Where a judgment has been rendered by a justice in an action on account, in which a question of fact was involved, the remedy is by appeal, and not by *certiorari*.—Johnson v. Cummings, (Ga.) 13 S. E. 819.

Notice of hearing.

8. Under Sup. Ct. Rule N. C. No. 43, (12 S. E. ix.,) prescribing that a petitioner for *certiorari* shall not be heard unless he has given the adverse party 10 days' notice in writing, the application will be refused where there is nothing to show that such notice has been given.—Keerans v. Keerans, (N. C.) 13 S. E. 895.

Bond.

9. Where a petition for *certiorari* is sanctioned by the judge and filed with the clerk of the superior court, but no bond as required by law is filed, and no writ is issued, it is too late, after the expiration of the time allowed by law for obtaining the writ, to file such bond; and it is not error to dismiss the case in the absence of plaintiff's attorney, to whom the judge has granted leave of absence for the balance of the term, this being the only legal disposition that could have been made of the case, even if the attorney had been present.—Baker v. McDaniel, (Ga.) 13 S. E. 130.

Amendment of answer.

10. On a writ of *certiorari* to review a conviction, in a municipal court, for violation of a city ordinance, the answer of the judge of the court was defective, in omitting to set out the ordinance on which the proceeding was founded. *Held*, that it might be amended by the judge in this respect, after he had retired from office, and had become assistant city attorney of the city prosecuting the proceeding, it not appearing that he had taken any part in or been connected with the *certiorari* proceeding, and his amended answer being supported by his affidavit, as required by Code Ga. § 4063, in case of such an answer "made after the party making the same has retired from office."—Phillips v. City of Atlanta, (Ga.) 13 S. E. 201.

Decision.

11. Upon the hearing of a *certiorari* in the superior court, in which no issues of fact are involved, and the determination of the case depends entirely upon legal questions, it is the duty of that court to render a final judgment.—Greenwood v. Boyd & Baxter Furniture Factory, (Ga.) 13 S. E. 123.

Challenge.

Of jurors, see *Jury*, 12-14.

Change of Venue.

See *Venue in Civil Cases*, 2.

Character.

Evidence as to, see *Criminal Law*, 37-39.

Charter.

See *Corporations*, 1.

CHATTEL MORTGAGES.

Description.

1. A chattel mortgage on "all my entire crop, now growing or to be grown the present year on my own land," describes with sufficient certainty the property intended to be mortgaged; but a further description, covering the crop which the mortgagor might raise on "any other land," is too indefinite, because it points to no

particular land.—Weil v. Flowers, (N. C.) 13 S. E. 761.

2. In January, 1889, a mortgage was given on "the entire crop of cotton to be raised by me or my tenants on all my lands during the year 1889." The mortgagor had for 15 years been in possession of a tract of land known as his. There was then pending a suit for the recovery of the land, in which judgment was entered against him 10 days after the mortgage was given. He then leased the land, and planted it in cotton. *Held*, that the mortgage covered the crop raised, subject to the landlord's lien for rent. Following Rawlings v. Hunt, 90 N. C. 270.—Brown v. Miller, (N. C.) 13 S. E. 167.

Liens—Priorities.

3. Under a mortgage on a crop of cotton "for supplies," where it does not appear how, or on what account, or for what purpose, the supplies were furnished, the mortgagee acquires no preference over a prior mortgage under Code N. C. § 1799, providing for such a preference for advances for supplies. Following Rawlings v. Hunt, 90 N. C. 270.—Brown v. Miller, (N. C.) 13 S. E. 167.

Record.

4. Plaintiffs held a chattel mortgage on certain horses and other personal property, which were in the possession of the mortgagor, in North Carolina. The mortgage was duly recorded in the county where the property was situated, and also in the county where the mortgagor resided. While the mortgage debt was unpaid, the mortgagor took the property into Virginia, where it was seized and sold on attachment by defendants, who were creditors of the mortgagor, and the proceeds were applied in part payment of their judgments against him. Plaintiffs brought an action against defendants to recover the debt secured by such mortgage. *Held*, that they were entitled to recover, though the mortgage was not recorded in Virginia.—Hornthall v. Burwell, (N. C.) 13 S. E. 721.

Claim and Delivery.

See *Replevin*.

Collateral Attack.

On judgment, see *Judgment*, 26-28.

Color of Title.

See *Adverse Possession*, 11, 12.

Commerce.

Regulation by state, see *Constitutional Law*, 10.

Common Carrier.

See *Carriers*.

Comparative Negligence.

See *Negligence*, 4; *Railroad Companies*, 42.

Compensation.

In condemnation proceedings, see *Eminent Domain*, 9, 10.
Of child for services to parent, see *Parent and Child*, 4.

Complaint.

See *Pleading*, 1.

COMPROMISE.

See, also, *Payment*.
Authority of attorney to compromise suit, see *Attorney and Client*, 2.

Effect.

1. An agreement in compromise of an action brought by the next friend of a lunatic against

his committee for an accounting of the trust-estate, which was not submitted to and approved by the court, is not a bar to an action by the administrator of the lunatic against the administrator of the committee involving the same matter.—Clark v. Crout, (S. C.) 13 S. E. 602.

2. In compromise of a litigation instituted by the administrator c. t. a. contesting the validity of a will, the devisees, on the payment of a spec ified sum to them, executed a deed conveying to the administrator all their "right, title, interest, and claim which they have" in and to the property devised. *Held*, that this deed conveyed to the administrator all rents which had theretofore accrued on the devised property, and which had never been paid over to the devisees, as the title to the rents was dependent on that to the property devised, and the title thereto had never vested in the devisees because the devise had not been assented to by the administrator c. t. a., as required by Code Ga. § 2451. SIMMONS, J., dissenting.—Chisholm v. Spullock, (Ga.) 13 S. E. 571.

Condition.

Conditional acceptance of order, see *Orders*.
—— sale, see *Sale*, 22, 23.
In insurance policy, see *Insurance*, 6–9.

Confession.

See *Criminal Law*, 33–35.

CONFLICT OF LAWS.

Contracts.

1. Where a note made in Georgia bears a rate of interest allowed by the state laws, and is secured by mortgage on land in this state which provides that "the contract * * * shall in all respects be construed according to the laws of Georgia," the note is not usurious, though it is payable in a state in which the highest rate of interest allowed is less than that agreed to be paid.—New England Mortgage Security Co. v. McLaughlin, (Ga.) 13 S. E. 81.

2. Where a married woman enters into a contract in a state by the laws of which she may contract as if unmarried, and suit is brought in a state in which she is subjected to the common-law disability of coverture, and it appears that she was at the commencement of the suit and has since been a resident of the latter state, it will be presumed that at the time of the contract she was domiciled in the state in which it was made, and the contract will be enforced against her.—Taylor v. Sharp, (N. C.) 13 S. E. 133.

Consideration.

Of contract, see *Contracts*, 1.
Parol evidence of, see *Evidence*, 40, 41.

Constable.

See *Sheriffs and Constables*.

CONSTITUTIONAL LAW.

Public schools, exaction of fees from pupils, see *Schools and School-Districts*, 3–4.
Title of acts, see *Statutes*, 1.

Local or special law.

1. Act Ga. 1881, (Code, § 3149a et seq.,) for putting the assets of insolvent traders into the hands of a receiver, is a general law, and is constitutional.—Allen v. Nussbaum, (Ga.) 13 S. E. 635.

2. Act Ga. 1872, providing for the establishment of county courts, and Act 1879, amending the same, inasmuch as they except certain counties from their operation, are not general laws, within the meaning of Const. Ga. art. 1, § 4, par. 1, (Code, § 5027,) declaring that laws of a general nature shall have uniform operation through

out the state, and no special law shall be enacted in any case for which provision has been made by an existing general law, and did not prevent the passage of the special act of 1887, organizing the county court of Early county.—Lorentz v. Alexander, (Ga.) 13 S. E. 632.

3. Act Ga. 1879, (Code, § 279 et seq.,) is a general law in so far as it establishes uniformity as to jurisdiction, powers, proceedings, and practice of all county courts, and, in so far as the special law of 1887, establishing the county court of Early county, conflicts with the same, the special law is unconstitutional; but this does not vitiate such act in so far as it establishes the county court of Early county, and ordains jurisdiction, powers, proceedings, and practice in conformity to the general law.—Lorentz v. Alexander, (Ga.) 13 S. E. 632.

4. Sp. Acts Ga. of September 5, 1885, and October 1, 1887, empowering the mayor and aldermen of Savannah to improve the streets and levy local assessments therefor, do not violate Const. Ga. art. 1, § 4, par. 1, (Code, § 5027,) prohibiting any special law in any case for which provision has been made by an existing general law, since there is no general law as to how cities shall make public improvements and collect the cost thereof; nor do they violate the provision that no general law affecting private rights shall be varied in any particular case by special legislation, etc., since there is no general statute exempting citizens of cities in the state from assessments for public improvements.—Weed v. City of Savannah, (Ga.) 13 S. E. 529.

5. Since by the general law (Code Ga. § 1684) every corporation is dissolved by expiration of its charter, and as the constitution declares that laws general in their nature shall have uniform operation throughout the state, the legislature cannot by a special law extend the charter of a corporation existing under the general laws, after it has expired, for the purpose of terminating suits pending against it.—Logan v. Western & A. R. Co., (Ga.) 13 S. E. 516.

6. Since the general laws of Georgia provide for enforcing the rights of creditors against corporations after dissolution, and the constitution inhibits the enactment of any special law in a case provided for by an existing general law, a special act extending the charter of a corporation existing under the general law, for the purpose of terminating suits pending against it, is unconstitutional.—Logan v. Western & A. R. Co., (Ga.) 13 S. E. 516.

Retrospective laws.

7. Gen. St. S. C. 1882, § 1831, passed in 1879, providing that no mortgage, judgment, decree, or other lien on real estate shall constitute a lien on any real estate after the lapse of 20 years from the date of the creation of the same, unless the holder shall record or file a note of some payment or acknowledgment, in which case the 20 years shall date from the time of acknowledgment or payment, does not apply to mortgages executed prior to its passage. Henry v. Henry, 31 S. C. 1, 9 S. E. 726, distinguished.—Curtis v. Renneker, (S. C.) 13 S. E. 664.

8. Acts Ga. 1889, p. 73, amending Code Ga. § 2967, and providing that no action for homicide, injury to the person or property, shall abate by death, is not unconstitutional, in that it applies to actions pending at the time of its passage.—Pritchard v. Savannah St. & R. R. R. Co., (Ga.) 13 S. E. 493.

Obligation of contracts.

9. Const. N. C. 1868, art. 4, § 9, provides that the supreme court shall have original jurisdiction of claims against the state, but that its decisions shall be merely recommendatory, and shall be reported to the legislature for action. *Held*, that Const. 1880, art. 1, § 6, amendatory thereto, which provides that the legislature shall not pay, "either directly or indirectly," any debt or bond incurred or issued by the convention of 1868, or by the legislature of that year, with certain exceptions unless the proposition therefor

be submitted to the voters of the state, is not obnoxious to Const. U. S. art. 1, § 10, in impairing the obligation of contracts, since no one has any right of action against the state except as given by its constitution and laws. Baltzer v. State, 104 N. C. 265, 10 S. E. 153, followed.—Baltzer v. State, (N. C.) 13 S. E. 734.

Regulation of commerce.

10. Code Va. § 3801, forbidding the running of trains on Sunday between sunrise and sunset, except wrecking, passenger, stock, and United States mail trains, conflicts with Const. U. S. art. 1, § 8, providing that congress shall have power to regulate commerce among the several states, and is void as to trains running between points in different states. LACY, J., dissenting.—Norfolk & W. R. Co. v. Commonwealth, (Va.) 13 S. E. 340.

Trial by jury.

11. Under Bill of Rights W. Va. § 14, declaring that trials of crimes and misdemeanors shall be by a jury of 12 men, where the record shows that the prisoner was tried by a jury of 18 jurymen, instead of 12, the verdict should be set aside and a new trial awarded.—State v. Hudkins, (W. Va.) 13 S. E. 367.

Due process of law.

12. An ordinance providing for the impounding of cattle found running at large in the public streets, and for selling them to pay charges, on notice to the owner, without judicial inquiry or determination, is not unconstitutional as authorizing the taking of property without due process of law, or without compensation.—Burdett v. Allen, (W. Va.) 13 S. E. 1012.

Police power.

13. The ownership of a lot in a cemetery, or license to inter therein, is subject to the police power of the state, and interments may be forbidden, and bodies already interred removed, by ordinance of the city, if authorized by act of the legislature.—Humphrey v. Board of Trustees of M. E. Church, (N. C.) 13 S. E. 798.

Taxation.

14. Const. Ga. 1877, (Code, § 5181,) declaring that all taxation shall be uniform upon the same class of subjects, and ad valorem on all property "subject to be taxed" within the territorial limits of the authority levying the tax, does not prohibit taxing one railroad company ad valorem on its property, and taxing another railroad company only up to a certain per cent., where such limitation is prescribed by the latter company's charter, granted before the constitution of 1877 took effect.—Atlanta & F. R. Co. v. Wright, (Ga.) 13 S. E. 578.

15. Since Const. Ga. 1877, (Code, § 5181,) requires taxes to be levied and collected under general laws, the legislature has no power to impose a pecuniary penalty for non-payment upon one class of tax-payers exclusively, leaving all other classes exempt from any penalty whatever.—Atlanta & F. R. Co. v. Wright, (Ga.) 13 S. E. 578.

16. Since Const. Ga. 1877, (Code, § 5181,) requires taxes to be levied and collected under general laws, the legislature cannot subject one class of tax-payers to execution for taxes on the 1st of October, when the great mass of the tax-payers are exempt until the 20th of December.—Atlanta & F. R. Co. v. Wright, (Ga.) 13 S. E. 578.

CONTEMPT.

What constitutes.

1. Where, in his sworn answer to a rule for contempt in not surrendering up to a receiver his money, books, notes, and accounts, as ordered, defendant alleges that he cannot make the surrender because, before the filing of the petition, he paid the money and transferred the other assets to his sister in discharge of a bona fide indebtedness to her; that she now has possession of such assets, and they are not in defendant's control, and where this answer is supported by the affidavit of the sister, whose credibility as a witness is unimpeached, she admitting on oath that she has the assets, and it further appearing that she is solvent and able to respond to plaintiffs or the receiver for the same, and that she is a resident of the county where the suit is pending,—the answer thus supported is sufficient to relieve defendant from the imputation of willful contempt, and the rule against him should be discharged.—Martin v. Burgwyn, (Ga.) 13 S. E. 958.

2. Where an assignee for the benefit of creditors intentionally disobeys an order for the distribution of funds in his hands, the court may give judgment attaching him as for contempt.—Bristol v. Pearson, (N. C.) 13 S. E. 925.

Procedure.

3. Irregularities in proceedings for contempt are immaterial where the result is a sufficient purging of the contempt, and a consequent discharge of the rule.—Martin v. Burgwyn, (Ga.) 13 S. E. 958.

CONTINUANCE.

In criminal cases, see Criminal Law, 10, 11.
On appeal, see Appeal, 40; Criminal Law, 76.

Newly-discovered evidence.

1. After the evidence in a case has been closed, and the opening argument of plaintiff's counsel has been made, there is no abuse of discretion in denying a continuance on account of newly-discovered evidence, where it does not appear, otherwise than by hearsay, that the newly-discovered witness could or would testify to any material fact whatever, the party or his counsel not having had any personal communication with him.—Central Railroad & Banking Co. v. Curtis, (Ga.) 13 S. E. 757; Curtis v. Central Railroad & Banking Co., Id.

Amendment of pleading.

2. The court may refuse defendant a continuance on the ground of surprise by an amendment, where a copy of the amendment was served on it in December, and the trial was not had until the following October, though the original was not filed in the clerk's office until three days before trial.—Southern Bell Tel., etc., Co. v. Jordan, (Ga.) 13 S. E. 202.

3. Service on a corporation having been acknowledged in defendant's proper name, an amendment of the petition substituting the correct name was no ground for continuance.—Chattanooga, R. & C. R. Co. v. Jackson, (Ga.) 13 S. E. 109.

CONTRACTS.

See, also, Arbitration and Award; Assignment; Assignment for Benefit of Creditors; Attorney and Client; Bonds; Carriers; Chattel Mortgages; Compromise; Covenants; Deed; Factors and Brokers; Frauds, Statute of; Fraudulent Conveyances; Insurance; Interest; Master and Servant; Mortgages; Negotiable Instruments; Partnership; Principal and Agent; Principal and Surety; Sale; Specific Performance; Usury; Vendor and Vendee.

Damages for breach of, see Damages, 1, 2.
Enforcement in equity, see Specific Performance, 1–4.
For sale of land, see Vendor and Vendee, 1, 2.
Impairing obligation of, see Constitutional Law, 9.
Of corporation, see Corporations, 3.
 married woman, see Husband and Wife, 14–17.
Reformation, see Equity, 3, 4.
Rescission, see Equity, 5.
Sunday contract, see Sunday.
To make will, see Wills, 14, 15.
What law governs, see Conflict of Laws.

Illegal considerations.

1. Under Code Ga. § 2745, declaring that, if the consideration of a contract be illegal in

whole or in part, the whole promise fails, a note and mortgage given in part upon an agreement, express or implied, to settle or prevent a criminal prosecution, and in part to repay money due the mortgagee, are void, unless the case falls within some express statute authorizing settlement.—Small v. Williams, (Ga.) 13 S. E. 589.

Construction — Province of court and jury.

2. In an action for the price of goods sold by parol, which defendant had refused to receive, the latter swore that the goods were to be delivered in two weeks, which was denied by plaintiffs. Held, that it was error to charge the jury that, if they found that such agreement was made, then they must determine whether the parties understood that the plaintiffs were to insure the delivery within that time, or merely whether they were to use all due diligence in forwarding the goods by the common carrier; the interpretation of the contract was a question of law for the court. MERRIMON, C. J., dissenting. — Spragins v. White, (N. C.) 13 S. E. 171.

Modification.

3. Where one contracted with a person since deceased to build a church, the fact that, before proceeding, the contractor secured the guaranty of the church trustees that he should be paid the contract price, and as much in excess of it as the work should cost, and that he then sublet the work to another, did not bar a recovery against the estate on the original contract.—Ferguson's Adm'r v. Wills, (Va.) 13 S. E. 392.

Actions on—Burden of proof.

4. Where a contract with a railroad company for furnishing ties provided that they should be accepted or rejected by the company's inspector, the burden of proof is on the company to show that ties, used by it without such inspection, were defective.—Draffin v. Charleston, C. & C. R. Co., (S. C.) 13 S. E. 427.

Contribution.

Between insurance companies, see *Insurance*, 10.
—— sureties, see *Principal and Surety*, 3.

Contributory Negligence.

See *Master and Servant*, 19-28; *Railroad Companies*, 34-42.

Conversion.

See *Trover and Conversion*.

Conveyances.

See *Chattel Mortgages; Deed; Fraudulent Conveyances; Mortgages; Sale; Vendor and Vendee*.

CORPORATIONS.

See, also, *Building and Loan Associations; Carriers; Insurance; Municipal Corporations; Railroad Companies; Religious Societies; Telegraph Companies*.
Dissolution, effect on appeal, see *Appeal*, 35.
Public corporations, running of statute of limitations, see *Limitation of Actions*, 1.
Service of process on, see *Writs*, 3.
—— by publication, see *Writs*, 6.
Special legislation concerning, see *Constitutional Law*, 6.

Charter—Alteration by special law.

1. Since Code Ga. § 1679, declares that all corporations have the right to sue and be sued, to have and use a common seal, to make by-laws, to receive donations, to purchase and hold property necessary for the purposes of their organization, and to do all acts necessary for the legitimate execution of this purpose, the legislature cannot hinder the charter of a business corporation from expiring, and the corporation from being dis-

v.13s.E.—66

solved, by enacting a special law declaring that the charter be continued in force only for the purpose of terminating suits and litigation pending against it. Provisions applicable alike to all corporations under the general law must remain applicable to each until changed by the general law.—Logan v. Western & A. R. Co., (Ga.) 13 S. E. 516.

Corporate existence—Evidence.

2. Certified copies of letters of incorporation are *prima facie* evidence of such incorporation, under Code N. C. §§ 677-682, providing that letters of incorporation, certified by the clerk of the supreme court, shall be admissible in judicial proceedings, and be deemed *prima facie* evidence of the organization of a company purporting thereby to be established.—Marshall v. Macon County Sav. Bank, (N. C.) 13 S. E. 182.

Contracts.

3. In an action against a corporation on a contract alleged to have been entered into by it, it is error for the court to refuse to instruct, when the evidence warranted, that "the contract not being in writing, and a liability in excess of one hundred dollars being imposed on defendant under said contract, plaintiff cannot recover;" Code, § 683, providing that contracts of a corporation by which a liability of more than $100 is imposed on the corporation "shall be in writing, and either under the common seal of the corporation or signed by some officer of the company authorized thereto."—Curtis v. Piedmont Lumber, Ranch & Min. Co., (N. C.) 13 S. E. 944.

Subscription—Liability on.

4. Where a person's name is on the subscription list of a corporation with his consent, he is *prima facie* bound to pay for his stock, and his liability is not discharged by a private agreement with a third person that the latter should pay for it.—Williams v. Benet, (S. C.) 13 S. E. 97.

Foreign corporations.

5. Under Act Ga. Feb. 28, 1877, prohibiting foreign corporations from owning more than 5,000 acres of land in the state, the state alone can question a foreign corporation's title to land in excess of that amount.—American Mortg. Co. of Scotland v. Tennille, (Ga.) 13 S. E. 153.

6. Under Acts Ga. 1853-54, p. 464, authorizing a foreign corporation to build a railroad in Georgia, and declaring that it shall be subject to suit by citizens of the state in the county in which it is located, a foreign corporation, which acquires the franchises of the said corporation, is subject to whatever suits could have been maintained against that company.—Alabama G. S. R. Co. v. Fulgham, (Ga.) 13 S. E. 649.

COSTS.

On creditors' bill, see *Creditors' Bill*, 3.

Who liable.

1. Under Code N. C. § 525, plaintiff is entitled to costs of course upon recovery in an action for the possession of personal property; and where other defendants intervene in such a case, and file a joint answer with the original defendant, and make a joint defense, the costs which occur after the intervention should be taxed, not merely against the interveners, but against all the defendants.—Spruill v. Arrington, (N. C.) 13 S. E. 779.

2. In an action to set aside a power of attorney on account of the maker's want of mental capacity, next friends, appointed by the clerk to conduct the action, may, on a verdict finding the maker sane, be taxed with costs, if they officiously and unnecessarily caused themselves to be appointed, but there must be a special finding of such fact by the court. Modifying 13 S. E. 1045.—Smith v. Smith, (N. C.) 13 S. E. 113.

Security for costs.

3. After the jury is impaneled, a motion to nonsuit plaintiffs, on the ground that the prose-

cution bond is improperly executed, will be denied where plaintiffs offer to perfect the bond.—Albertson v. Terry, (N. C.) 13 S. E. 713.

Costs on appeal.

4. Judgment is entered in the supreme court for the costs of that court, and should not be entered in the court below.—Johnston v. Danville, M. & S. W. R. Co., (N. C.) 13 S. E. 881.

5. Where the successful party on appeal could have condensed his brief to 10 pages, for which number of pages he is permitted to tax costs by Sup. Ct. Rule N. C. 87, no costs will be allowed him for the excess.—Town of Durham v. Richmond & D. R. Co., (N. C.) 13 S. E. 1.

6. Sup. Ct. Rule N. C. 31, limits the costs for printing the record to 20 pages, unless otherwise specially ordered by the court. *Held*, that where the "case on appeal," as settled by the judge, exceeds 20 printed pages, the supreme court will permit the costs of the excess to be taxed in favor of the unsuccessful party, as such "case" is required to be printed as part of the record by rule 29, but no costs will be taxed for printing other parts of the record, not embraced in the "case on appeal," and presenting no question to be reviewed.—Town of Durham v. Richmond & D. R. Co., (N. C.) 13 S. E. L.

Co-Tenancy.

See *Tenancy in Common and Joint Tenancy.*

Counter-Claim.

See *Set-Off and Counter-Claim.*

COUNTIES.

See, also, *Bridges; Highways; Schools and School-Districts.*

County commissioners—Liabilities.

1. Under Code N. C. § 711, making a county commissioner liable to a penalty of $200 if he neglect to perform any duty required of him by law as a member of the board, where a sheriff fails both to make an annual renewal of his bonds and to produce receipts, failure to do either of which creates a vacancy in the office by the provisions of section 2070, but one penalty can be recovered against a commissioner for failure to declare the office vacant, and to fill the same by appointment, though section 720 provides that, whenever a vacancy shall occur in the office of sheriff, the board of county commissioners shall fill it by appointment; and section 1875 provides that, on failure of any such officer to make an annual renewal of his bond, it shall be the duty of the board of commissioners to declare his office vacant, and to appoint a successor; the duties of the commissioners prescribed by the several sections being substantially the same.—Bray v. Barnard, (N. C.) 13 S. E. 729.

2. Under Code N. C. § 775, providing that, for failure of the sheriff to perform certain duty, the board of county commissioners "may forthwith" bring suit on his official bond, in an action against a commissioner to recover the penalty prescribed by section 711 for failure to perform any duty required of him by law, it is not enough that the complaint allege that the sheriff failed to perform the duty, and the commissioners failed to sue on his bond, as the statute leaves it to their sound discretion whether they will sue or not, and therefore the complaint should at least allege facts showing negligent failure or willful refusal of the commissioners to exercise their authority.—Bray v. Barnard, (N. C.) 13 S. E. 729.

COURTS.

See, also, *Judge; Justices of the Peace; Removal of Causes.*

County courts, special legislation concerning, see *Constitutional Law*, 2, 3.

Mandamus to, see *Mandamus*, 1, 2.
Trial by, see *Trial*, 54–57.

Jurisdiction—Of supreme court of appeals.

1. Code Va. § 3086, giving the supreme court of appeals original jurisdiction to issue writs of *mandamus* in all cases in which it may be "necessary to prevent a failure of justice," in which a *mandamus* may issue according to the principles of the common law, does not take a case of which the circuit court also has jurisdiction out of the original jurisdiction of said court on the ground that, since the circuit court has jurisdiction, the interposition of the court of appeals is not necessary to prevent a failure of justice. LACY, J., dissenting.—Clay v. Ballard, (Va.) 13 S. E. 262.

2. Code Va. § 3438, provides that when a circuit or corporation court or judge thereof shall refuse to award an injunction, a copy of the proceedings in court, and the original papers presented to the judge in vacation, with his order of refusal, may be presented to a judge of the court of appeals, who may thereupon award an injunction. In an action to set aside a deed of trust an order was granted restraining the trustee from selling the goods therein conveyed. Upon the trial the order was dissolved, and the prayer for the appointment of a receiver denied. Upon the following day a judge of this court, upon the original bill, and without notice to defendants, granted the injunction and appointment of a receiver. After the entry of this order, and in the absence of counsel for defendants, a judgment of the lower court granted an order directing the sheriff to put the receiver in possession of the property. *Held*, that the statute confers no authority upon a judge of the court of appeals to reinstate an injunction order that has been dissolved on the merits in the lower court, and both orders are void. LACY and RICHARDSON, JJ., dissenting.—Fredenheim v. Rohr, (Va.) 13 S. E. 193.

—— Of court of common pleas.

3. Since the court of equity in South Carolina, as a separate tribunal, has been abolished, and its jurisdiction vested in the court of common pleas, the common pleas may take jurisdiction of an action to recover possession of land, for the purpose of partition among plaintiffs.—Westlake v. Farrow, (S. C.) 13 S. E. 469.

—— Of actions arising in another state.

4. Acts Ga. 1853-54, p. 464, authorizing a foreign corporation to build a railroad in Georgia, and declaring that it shall be subject to suit by citizens of the state, in the county in which it is located, allows service of process to be made as upon a domestic corporation; and a brakeman who is a citizen and runs upon one train, partly in Georgia and partly in Alabama, is entitled to maintain an action in Georgia for an injury sustained in Alabama.—Alabama G. S. R. Co. v. Fulgham, (Ga.) 13 S. E. 649.

COVENANTS.

Warranty.

1. A general warranty in a deed conveying the "entire interest" of the grantor in land is limited and restricted to the interest conveyed, and does not warrant the land.—Hull's Adm'r v. Hull's Heirs, (W. Va.) 13 S. E. 49; Dudley v. Same, Id.

Action for breach.

2. An action for breach of covenant can be maintained upon the mere claim of title paramount by another, where no disturbance of possession is shown.—Jones v. Richmond, (Va.) 13 S. E. 414.

3. An action for breach of covenant cannot be maintained by one who has parted with the title conveyed by the deed, the covenants of which are alleged to have been broken.—Jones v. Richmond, (Va.) 13 S. E. 414.

decree has, upon disaffirmance of the sale, been substituted to the right of the creditor, he may maintain a bill to enforce such right, and as incident to his relief make his bill a creditors' bill.—Hull's Adm'r v. Hull's Heirs, (W. Va.) 13 S. E. 49, Dudley v. Same, Id.

2. A court of equity has jurisdiction to pass upon the validity and regularity of the record of a deed in the office of the clerk of the county court in a suit by creditors' bill which alleges that by reason of defects in the acknowledgment such deed must be postponed to the liens sought to be enforced by the bill.—Janesville Hay Tool Co. v. Boyd, (W. Va.) 13 S. E. 381.

Costs.

3. Where a petition in equity in the nature of a creditors' bill is filed, alleging the insolvency of a partnership, and praying an injunction and appointment of a receiver, creditors who on their own application are made plaintiffs after the receiver is appointed become chargeable with their proportion of counsel fees for filing the petition, as provided by Code Ga. § 3149c, though the appointment of the receiver was unnecessary, because such creditors have mortgages which will absorb the entire assets.—Lowry Banking Co. v. Abbott, (Ga.) 13 S. E. 204.

CRIMINAL LAW.

See, also, *Bail; Grand Jury; Indictment and Information; Witness.*
Criminal trespass, see *Trespass.*
Illegal sale of liquor, see *Intoxicating Liquors,* 4–10.
Non-payment of license tax by attorney, see *Attorney and Client,* 7, 8.
Offenses against election laws, see *Elections and Voters,* 3, 4.
Particular crimes, see *Adultery; Arson; Assault and Battery,* 1; *Bastardy; Burglary; Disturbance of Public Worship; False Pretenses; Forgery; Fornication; Homicide; Larceny; Malicious Mischief; Obstructing Justice; Perjury; Poison; Rape; Robbery.*
Slandering innocent woman, see *Libel and Slander,* 6, 7.
Unlawful seizure of crop by landlord, see *Landlord and Tenant,* 15.

Jurisdiction.

1. Code N. C. § 892, restricting the jurisdiction of the superior courts for assault, where no deadly weapon is used, and no serious damage done, to cases where justices of the peace neglect for six months to take official cognizance of the offense, does not oust the jurisdiction of the court where the indictment charges an assault with a deadly weapon, although the evidence shows only a simple assault, committed within six months of the finding of the indictment.—State v. Fesperman, (N. C.) 13 S. E. 14.

2. Const. N. C. art. 4, § 27, restricts the jurisdiction of magistrates to cases where the punishment cannot exceed $50 fine or 30 days' imprisonment. Code, § 987, prescribes that an assault with a deadly weapon may be punished by fine and imprisonment, in the discretion of the court. *Held,* that section 892, as amended by chapter 152, Acts 1891, giving magistrates jurisdiction of all assaults in which no serious damage is done, where the punishment shall not exceed $50 fine or 30 days' imprisonment, does not confer jurisdiction in cases where, although no serious damage is inflicted, the use of a deadly weapon is charged.—State v. Fesperman, (N. C.) 13 S. E. 14.

Affidavit—Verification.

3. Where the affidavit on which an accusation of a crime is founded, charging two misdemeanors of the same class, sets out one of the offenses, and adds the facts concerning the other, introducing such facts with the phrase, "the

in the subjoined statement as to the mode of committing the misdemeanor.—Hathcock v. State, (Ga.) 13 S. E. 959.

Indictment—Demurrer.

4. A demurrer to an indictment containing several counts is properly overruled if either count is good.—State v. McClung, (W. Va.) 13 S. E. 654.

—— Motion to quash.

5. An indictment for perjury under Acts N. C. 1889, c. 83, which fails to allege that defendant knew the false statement alleged to have been made by him to be false, or that he was ignorant whether or not the statement was true, is defective, since the act specially requires such allegations; but such defect is not ground for quashing the indictment, the proper action being for the court to hold the prisoner, and permit the solicitor to send a new bill curing the defect.—State v. Flowers, (N. C.) 13 S. E. 718.

Motion to dismiss—Waiver of objections.

6. Where defendant's exception to the denial of his motion to dismiss was duly noted, his subsequent general appearance for trial was not a waiver of his rights under such exception.—State v. Johnson, (N. C.) 13 S. E. 843.

Pleas in abatement.

7. Objection that no *venire facias* was issued must be made before plea to the merits. FAUNTLEROY and HINTON, JJ., dissenting.—Watson v. Commonwealth, (Va.) 13 S. E. 22.

8. Setting aside a verdict and granting a new trial in a criminal case does not expunge the plea of not guilty previously entered, and it is too late for defendant, on the new trial, while the plea is standing, to plead in abatement · that the record does not show that a *venire facias* was issued to summon the grand jury by which the indictment was found.—Custis v. Commonwealth, (Va.) 13 S. E. 73.

Change of venue—Record.

9. Code Va. § 4016, providing that, where one indicted in the county court for a felony elects to be tried in the circuit court, the clerk shall transmit to the clerk of the latter court "a transcript of the record of the proceedings in said county court in relation to the prosecution, and copies of the indictment and recognizances and other papers connected with the case," does not require the record to show affirmatively that a *venire facias* was issued in summoning the grand jury. FAUNTLEROY and HINTON, JJ., dissenting.—Watson v Commonwealth, (Va.) 13 S. E. 23.

Continuance.

10. Having subpoenaed a witness who did not appear, defendant, on the court's suggestion, obtained a rule against him, but the officer returned that the witness was sick. Defendant's motion to adjourn was overruled, on the ground, as stated by the judge, that when the case was balled in the morning no motion for continuance was made because of the absence of such witness. Defendant made no objection to this statement, nor did he show that the evidence of such witness would not be merely cumulative. *Held,* the court was justified in proceeding with the trial.—Thompson v. Commonwealth, (Va.) 13 S. E. 304.

11. A showing for a continuance on the ground of the absence and illness of leading counsel is not complete without a statement on oath that the application is not made for delay only, as required by Code Ga. § 3525; and where the showing is thus deficient, and the presiding judge has given notice to both the leading and associate counsel a month before the trial that the case would not again be continued for illness of the former, it having been previously continued on the same ground, there is no abuse of discretion

and connected by a chain with the buggy in which he was riding, in company with an officer who had in his pocket the warrant under which he had been committed on a charge of larceny, do not of themselves constitute duress, so as to exclude any material declaration made to the officer in reference to the crime; and, unless it appears that the defendant was induced to make the declaration by some advantageous offer, or by threats, or actual force, arousing hope or exciting fear in his mind, it is not error to admit the officer's testimony.—State v. Whitfield, (N. C.) 13 S. E. 726.

34. Where an exclamation made by a person at night, while in bed, not addressed to any one, is offered against her in evidence on trial for murder, and objected to, because made in sleep, and it does not appear whether the person was asleep or awake, it was properly allowed to go to the jury.—State v. Morgan, (W. Va.) 13 S. E. 385.

35. Under Code Ga. § 3792, providing that "a confession alone uncorroborated by other evidence will not justify a conviction," a doubtful or contradictory confession by a man of good moral character will not warrant a conviction of larceny where the *corpus delicti* is uncertain.—Johnson v. State, (Ga.) 13 S. E. 282.

36. What a witness voluntarily testified at a former trial of another party for the homicide is not privileged on a trial of the witness himself for the same homicide. It may be given in evidence against him as an admission.—Burnett v. State, (Ga.) 13 S. E. 552.

—— Character.

37. Where defendant, in a trial for burning a barn, put his character in issue, and a witness testifies that, prior to the burning, defendant, in reference to a robbery lately perpetrated, said, "Damn them, [the robbers,] * * * there is going to be a battle in this neighborhood before three weeks, and I be d——d if I care how quick it comes," such evidence, though but slightly relevant, is competent as bearing on defendant's character.—State v. Parks, (N. C.) 13 S. E. 939.

38. In such case it is proper to admit, as bearing on defendant's character, evidence that, shortly before daylight on the morning when defendant was arrested, there were with him, at his mother-in-law's house, several persons, two or three of whom had guns.—State v. Parks, (N. C.) 13 S. E. 939.

39. It is not competent, on the issue of defendant's character, to ask a witness how it was rumored that a "hung jury" stood on a former trial of an indictment against him, the witness having testified that he did not know how they stood.—State v. Austin, (N. C.) 13 S. E. 219.

Instructions.

40. Upon the trial of a felony, it is not error for the court to charge the jury that they should not be controlled in making up their verdict by any fear as to what the punishment may be, but that they were sworn to find according to the evidence.—Brantley v. State, (Ga.) 13 S. E. 257.

41. A statement by the court that defendant had offered no evidence to contradict the testimony of the state's witnesses, which is true, is relieved of any possible prejudicial effect by the further statement that it is a question for the jury whether there is any contradiction between the state's witnesses.—State v. Brabham, (N. C.) 13 S. E. 217.

42. Where defendant is indicted as a principal, an instruction as to the law applying to an accessory is irrelevant.—State v. Morgan, (W. Va.) 13 S. E. 385.

—— Reasonable doubt.

43. Where the jury were instructed to find for defendant, unless the state proved everything essential to the establishment of the charge to the exclusion of a reasonable doubt, it was not error to charge, immediately afterwards, that "the burden rests upon the commonwealth to make out its case, * * * to the exclusion of a reasonable doubt, but, where the accused * * * attempts to prove an *alibi*, * * * the

burden of proving the *alibi* rests upon him."—Thompson v. Commonwealth, (Va.) 13 S. E. 304.

44. An instruction that if the jury find that no motive on the part of the prisoner existed for the commission of the crime, that itself is sufficient to raise a reasonable doubt of guilt, is bad.—State v. Morgan, (W. Va.) 13 S. E. 385.

Separation of jurors.

45. Of persons summoned on a *venire* in a felony case, six, who were found free from exception, were allowed to separate during an adjournment to a future day of the term, being cautioned not to converse about the case, and were subsequently sworn as jurors without being again examined on their *voir dire*. *Held* no error.—Custis v. Commonwealth, (Va.) 13 S. E. 73.

Verdict.

46. Where the record shows that Jeremiah S. Peirpoint is one of the jury sworn in the case, the verdict is not invalid because signed by J. S. Peirpoint.—State v. Morgan, (W. Va.) 13 S. E. 385.

47. Defendants cannot complain of the reception of the verdict by the clerk during the judge's absence from the court-room, where they failed to object at the time to its being so received, though they had opportunity to do so.—State v. Austin, (N. C.) 13 S. E. 219.

48. On a trial for burglary it is not error to refuse to receive a verdict of "guilty of receiving stolen goods," and to direct the jury that they would have to find a verdict of guilty or not guilty.—Mangum v. State, (Ga.) 13 S. E. 558.

49. On the trial of a felony, it is not error for the court to allow the solicitor general, at the request of the jury, to reduce their verdict of conviction to proper form, they having stated that the verdict as formulated was their real finding.—Brantley v. State, (Ga.) 13 S. E. 257.

50. Where four defendants, jointly indicted for riot, have been put upon trial, and the state announces that it will claim no conviction as to two of them, and then examines these two as witnesses against the other two, a verdict of guilty as to all is not void, and may be set aside as to the two examined as witnesses, and left to stand as to the other two.—Sims v. State, (Ga.) 13 S. E. 551.

—— Different counts.

51. Upon a count properly alleging both burglary and larceny, there may be a conviction of either, but not of both.—State v. McClung, (W. Va.) 13 S. E. 654.

52. Though, where trial is had at the same time on two counts in an accusation, a verdict of guilty on one count alone is an acquittal on the other, such acquittal does not vitiate the conviction, though both counts may relate to the same transaction.—Hathcock v. State, (Ga.) 13 S. E. 959.

Judgment and sentence.

53. Under an indictment consisting of two counts, where there was no instruction refused or exception taken to the charge as to one of them, and there was a general verdict of guilty on both counts, and but one sentence imposed, the law will apply it to the verdict upon the count to which no exception was assigned.—State v. Hall, (N. C.) 13 S. E. 189.

54. A sentence that accused "pay a fine of one thousand dollars and costs of this prosecution, or be confined in the common jail for twelve months," being in the alternative, the imprisonment is a part of the punishment, and is error, since, under Code, § 4705, the discretion of the judge, when he makes such a sentence, is limited, as to imprisonment, to six months.—Hathcock v. State, (Ga.) 13 S. E. 959.

55. Upon a general verdict of guilty on a count in an indictment charging both burglary and larceny, the sentence would be for burglary, not for both larceny and burglary or for larceny.—State v. McClung, (W. Va.) 13 S. E. 654.

the record of a deed executed out of the state it must be "attested * * * by a commissioner of deeds for the state of Georgia, or * * * [the certificate of these officers, under their seals, being evidence of the fact] by a judge of a court of record in the state where executed, with a certificate of the clerk, under the seal of such court, as to the genuineness of the signature of such judge." *Held*, that the attestation of a commissioner of deeds for Georgia, under his seal, is sufficient without a formal certificate verifying his identity and official character.—Hadden v. Larned, (Ga.) 13 S. E. 806.

7. In attesting a deed executed in another state, a commissioner of deeds for Georgia erased the printed words describing him, which by mistake were opposite the name of another attesting witness, and interlined such words in their proper place, without explanation of the erasure, and attached his seal as commissioner. *Held*, that the erasure explained itself, and did not vitiate the attestation.—Hadden v. Larned, (Ga.) 13 S. E. 806.

8. A deed saying nothing of delivery in the attestation clause is nevertheless prepared for record if attested by two witnesses, one of whom was the clerk of the superior court, who signed the attestation in his official character.—Blalock v. Miland, (Ga.) 13 S. E. 551.

Description—Parol evidence to explain.

9. Where a deed describes land as "all their land lying between Haw river and Stony creek, up to the line of" H., and refers to the title papers, evidence *aliunde* is admissible to identify the land.—Euliss v. McAdams, (N. C.) 13 S. E. 162.

10. A description of land in a deed as "the Sellars Tract" is not too vague to admit of evidence *aliunde* of its location, for the purpose of establishing a corner.—Euliss v. McAdams, (N. C.) 13 S. E. 162.

Record.

11. An unrecorded deed to a husband and wife passes only an equitable title, to be perfected by registration.—Phillips v. Hodges, (N. C.) 13 S. E. 769.

12. Under Act N. C. 1885, c. 147, which provided that no deed of conveyance then executed should be valid as against an innocent purchaser for value unless recorded prior to January 1, 1886, no claim can be asserted against such purchaser under a deed given in 1852, which was not recorded until January 11, 1886.—Phillips v. Hodges, (N. C.) 13 S. E. 769.

13. The fact that the official seal of a commissioner of deeds for Georgia, attached to his attestation of a deed executed in another state, is not copied or referred to in the record of the deed, though an imperfection, will not affect the sufficiency of the recording.—Hadden v. Larned, (Ga.) 13 S. E. 806.

14. In an action to recover land, the issue was as to whether a certain deed was filed for registration before December 30, 1889, and the deed contained an indorsement by the register that it was "filed for registration at 12 o'clock M., July 27, 1889, subject to the annexed facts;" that, no fees having been paid, it was left open to the inspection of the public until December 30, 1889, when the fees were paid, and it was duly filed and recorded. The register and others testified that he expressly refused to receive the deed till the fees were paid. *Held* that, under Code N. C. § 3654, which requires the register to "indorse on each deed in trust and mortgage the day on which it is presented to him for registration," and section 3758, which provides that he shall not be compelled to perform any service, unless his fee be paid or tendered, except in criminal actions, it was error to refuse to charge that, if the jury believed the evidence, they should find that the deed had not been "filed for registration" prior to December 30, 1889.—Cunninggim v. Peterson, (N. C.) 13 S. E. 714.

refused record by the clerk, whereupon the maker acknowledged it before him, and he signed his name officially as a witness, though he had not seen the deed executed, instead of certifying to the acknowledgment.' The deed was then recorded. Code Ga. § 2705, requires a deed to be either attested by one of certain officials, the clerk among them, or, subsequent to its execution, to be acknowledged before one of them, and the acknowledgment to be certified on the deed. *Held*, that the deed was not legally recorded, and was not notice to a creditor of the grantor, who, between its execution and record, gave credit on the faith of the property conveyed, under Code Ga. § 1778, declaring that the record of a deed legally recorded within three months of its execution shall be constructive notice, taking effect from the date of the deed itself.—White v. Magarahan, (Ga.) 13 S. E. 509.

16. Act 1885, c. 147, providing that no conveyance or lease of land for more than three years shall be valid, as against creditors or purchasers for a valuable consideration from the bargainor or lessor, but from the registration thereof, applies to a purchaser at sheriff's sale founded upon judgments docketed against the bargainor or lessor prior to the registration of the said deed, and allows him to recover the land as against the person claiming thereunder.—Cowen v. Withrow, (N. C.) 13 S. E. 1022.

Nature of estate conveyed.

17. A conveyance to a trustee by a husband forever in fee-simple for the use of his wife and her children then, born and to be born, with a condition in the *habendum* that, if he should survive her, the whole property should revert to him free from the trust, creates a fee in the trustee, defeasible on the contingency specified; and, on the happening of that contingency, the title revests in the husband, and thenceforth the property is his absolutely.—Woods v. Woods, (Ga.) 13 S. E. 692.

18. A deed providing that "in consideration that he, the said J., is to live with me, the said M., and take care of me, the said M., and my wife, Sally, so long as we both live, and that I, the said M., doth give to the said J. all of the tract of land whereon I now live, at my death, containing * * *, and that I, the said M., do hereby warrant and defend the right and title of said land to J. and his heirs, forever, against the claims of all persons whatsoever," will be so construed that the words, "his heirs, forever," in the warranty, will be held to operate both to pass a remainder in fee and define the extent of the warranty.—Mitchell v. Mitchell, (N. C.) 13 S. E. 187.

Default.

Judgment by, see *Judgment*, 1, 2.

Delivery.

Of goods sold, see *Sale*, 10, 11.

Demand.

To give right of action for recovery of taxes, see *Taxation*, 18.

Demonstrative Legacies.

See *Wills*, 18.

Demurrer.

To evidence, review on appeal, see *Appeal*, 71, 72.
indictment, see *Indictment and Information*, 4.

DESCENT AND DISTRIBUTION.

See, also, *Executors and Administrators; Wills*.

Illegitimate children.

The rights given by Code N. C. § 1281, rules 9, 10, permitting illegitimate children born

Dying Declarations.

See *Homicide*, 38.

EASEMENTS.

By prescription.

1. Though a lane established by two coterminous proprietors, and embracing an equal strip from the land of each, was originally intended only as a way for cattle, yet, if used for more than seven years as a general way by both proprietors and their grantees, the successors of neither can close it up as against the successors of the other, since Code Ga. § 731, declares that when a person has laid out a private way, and has been in the use and enjoyment of it for seven years, of which the owners have had six months' knowledge, without moving for damages, his right to use becomes complete, and the owners are barred of damages.—Thompson v. Easley, (Ga.) 13 S. E. 511.

Conveyance.

2. Where the owner of a lot grants the use of a private alley-way, entirely upon his lot, to an adjoining property owner, his heirs and assigns, and provides that the grantee shall have the right to convey the privilege granted to certain persons named, the grant is one in gross, and does not become appurtenant to the land of the grantee, and he cannot convey the easement thereby obtained to persons other than those named in the grant, and he cannot invest others with the powers conferred upon him by deed of indenture. —Fisher v. Fair, (S. C.) 13 S. E. 470.

EJECTMENT.

See, also, *Adverse Possession.*

Title to support.

1. Where a city granted land to a railroad company upon conditions as to the use of the land which were not complied with, and afterwards another railroad company took possession of the same, the city, which had a clear legal title to the land except as affected by such grant, could maintain an action against the latter company for such land without a previous demand. — Georgia Railroad & Banking Co. v. City of Macon, (Ga.) 13 S. E. 21.

2. Proof by an heir or devisee, suing in ejectment, that his ancestor died in possession of the land under a *bona fide* claim of right thereto, establishes a *prima facie* case in favor of plaintiff, and he is entitled to recover unless defendant shows a better adverse title.—Wolfe v. Baxter, (Ga.) 13 S. E. 18.

3. A grant of land by the commonwealth as waste and unappropriated gives the grantee *prima facie* title, which cannot be resisted in ejectment by a defendant who has taken possession without color of title, and relies on the fact that the land had been conveyed by an old colonial grant to a third person before the grant by the commonwealth. LACY and HINTON, JJ., dissenting.—Holloran v. Meisel, (Va.) 13 S. E. 38.

—— Common source.

4. In ejectment it appeared that S. and G. divided a lot which they owned in common, and that by mesne conveyances the title to the share of S. vested in defendant. The source of plaintiff's title to G.'s portion was a deed from one A., made after the partition, but his title was not shown to be connected with G.'s. The property in dispute was a small tract claimed by each to be included in his portion of the lot. *Held* that, as plaintiff's title was not connected with S. or G., it was error to charge the jury that, if they believed that plaintiff's and defendant's titles originated in S. or G., and from them came down to plaintiff and defendant, there was a common owner under whom both claimed, and that there was no dispute as to the title being in S. or G., and those who claimed under them.—Adams v. Powell, (Ga.) 13 S. E. 280.

Evidence.

5. In ejectment, since the plaintiff must recover on the strength of his own title, defendant may show that the title to the land passed from plaintiff by a sheriff's deed to a third person, without connecting himself with the title of such person.—Thomas v. Hunsucker, (N. C.) 13 S. E. 221.

6. In an ejectment suit by heirs, a patent to the land in controversy, issued to their ancestor by the state, lacking the state seal, was excluded until the plaintiffs introduced evidence that the seal was upon it when issued. The court then allowed it to go to the jury, but required a finding as to whether or not the seal had been attached. *Held* error, since the patent should have gone to the jury with an instruction that its validity depended upon its legal execution. LEWIS, P., dissenting. — Carter's Heirs v. Edwards, (Va.) 13 S. E. 352.

7. The exclusion of a copy of a patent, from the state, duly signed, sealed, and verified, was error. LEWIS, P., dissenting.—Carter's Heirs v. Edwards, (Va.) 13 S. E. 352.

Practice—Repeal of statute.

8. Act Va. March 9, 1880, providing that "in all cases of ejectment * * * in the counties of Buchanan, Dickenson, and Wise the plaintiff shall file with his declaration, 30 days before trial, the written and record evidence on which he relies, and unless he does so the defendant may have a continuation," etc., is a "general" law, within Code Va. 1887, § 4202, which provides that upon the adoption of the Code all acts of a "general" nature shall be repealed. LEWIS, P., dissenting.—Carter's Heirs v. Edwards, (Va.) 13 S. E. 352.

Improvements.

9. Code N. C. § 473, provides that any defendant against whom a judgment shall be rendered for land may present a petition stating that, "while holding the premises under a color of title believed by him * * * to be good," he has made valuable improvements thereon; and the court may, if satisfied of the probable truth of the allegation, impanel a jury to assess the allowance to defendant for such improvements. Section 481 provides that nothing herein shall apply to any suit brought by a mortgagee, or his heirs or assigns, against a mortgagor, or his heirs or assigns, for the recovery of the mortgaged premises. The grantees of land as part of the transaction conveyed the land in trust to secure the grantors, but afterwards, without authority from the grantors, conveyed a portion to a stranger, who had notice that the trust had not been received. *Held*, that though the purchaser of said portion did not hold the premises "under a color of title believed by him * * * to be good," and was therefore not entitled to betterments, yet the suit was within the spirit of section 481, and, in assessing the grantor's damages for the use and detention of the land, it was proper to make allowance to said purchaser for permanent improvements thereon.—Browne v. Davis, (N. C.) 13 S. E. 703.

Election.

Between causes of action, see *Action*, 3.
—— counts, see *Criminal Law*, 18.

ELECTIONS AND VOTERS.

Mandamus to election officers, see *Mandamus*, 4, 5.

School-district election, see *Schools and School-Districts*, 1.

Election officers—Resignation.

1. A registrar of voters cannot legally resign by merely sending his resignation to the clerk of the electoral board, and receiving from him an acknowledgment of its receipt, without an express or implied acceptance thereof by the board. LACY and RICHARDSON, JJ., dissenting.—Coleman v. Sands, (Va.) 13 S. E. 148.

on condition that it should not be used unless withholding it would defeat the building of the road. After the completion of the road, although there had been no necessity for using the contract, and although no compensation had been made by the directory, and none asked of them, the president turned the contract over to the right-of-way agent of the road, who had knowledge of the conditions on which it was delivered to the president. *Held*, that the contract was void, and the owner might recover the damages to his land.—Humphreys v. Richmond & M. R. Co., (Va.) 13 S. E. 985.

—— Of mortgages.

15. Where the mortgagor of land grants a right of way to a railroad company without the consent of the mortgagee, and without any proceeding against the mortgagee to condemn the land, the mortgagee's interest is not affected, and the purchaser at a foreclosure sale under the mortgage, or his grantee, may sue the company for compensation, though he cannot recover damages incident to the entry before he acquired title.—Livermon v. Roanoke & T. R. R. Co., (N. C.) 13 S. E. 784.

—— Limitation.

16. Since Code N. C. § 701, provides that the general railroad act (Code, c. 49) shall apply to railroad corporations created by special act of assembly, and shall govern and control, anything in the special act to the contrary notwithstanding, unless in such special act the sections of the general act intended to be repealed shall be specially referred to, and as such specially repealed, the provision in the charter of the Roanoke & Tar River Railroad Company, by which it is granted "the powers and incidents of the North Carolina Railroad Company, and other corporations of like nature created by the laws of the state," does not make applicable the provision in the charter of the North Carolina Railroad Company, that two years shall bar the claim for damages or compensation by the owner of land over which it has constructed its road, nor prevent the application of the general railroad act, under which a railroad company can only acquire title to a right of way by purchase or condemnation, and under which, so long as the company occupies the land without title, the owner is not barred unless its possession has been adverse for a length of time sufficient to mature title.—Livermon v. Roanoke & T. R. R. Co., (N. C.) 13 S. E. 784.

Entirety, Estate by.

Liability for husband's debts, see *Husband and Wife*, 1.

EQUITY.

See, also, *Creditors' Bill; Fraudulent Conveyances; Injunction; Mortgages; Partition; Receivers; Reference; Specific Performance; Trusts.*

Abatement of liquor nuisance, see *Intoxicating Liquors*, 11.

Forfeiture of interest for usury, see *Usury*, 2.

Relief against judgment, see *Judgment*, 40–44.

Jurisdiction.

1. A court of equity will not settle the title and boundaries of land when the plaintiff has no equity against the party who is holding the land.—Bright v. Knight, (W. Va.) 13 S. E. 63.

2. Where several executions in favor of different plaintiffs have been levied on the same property, and the owner has filed in resistance to each levy a separate claim, and the claim cases thus made are pending in court, all involving the same question, upon the decision of which the subjection or non-subjection of the property to all the executions depends, a petition in equity will lie in favor of the claimant against all the plaintiffs jointly, to bring to trial all of the claims together, and dispose of them by one verdict and judgment.—Smith v. Dobbins, (Ga.) 13 S. E. 496.

Jurisdiction—Reformation.

3. In an action to reform a deed plaintiff testified that his written contract with defendant provided for the mutual exchange of all their lands, but that by mistake defendant's deed omitted one 50-acre tract. Defendant denied that the contract included his tract, and that there was any mistake in the deed. It appeared that the contract was written by plaintiff, and had been lost. The deed was drawn under plaintiff's directions, and in his presence, defendant being absent, and was, after execution, accepted and placed on record by plaintiff. Plaintiff's witnesses testified merely that, in conversations with defendant, he had said nothing about reserving this tract. When defendant moved, he left his mother in possession of it, and at his instance she forbade defendant to remove a house therefrom. *Held*, that the burden of proof was on plaintiff, and that the mistake was not clearly established by the evidence.—French v. Chapman, (Va.) 13 S. E. 479.

4. Where a grantor intended to make an actual conveyance, and the seal was omitted by mistake, a court of equity will regard the instrument as a deed, and supply a seal.—Trustees of Wadsworthville Poor School v. Bryson, (S. C.) 13 S. E. 619.

—— Rescission.

5. In an action by an executrix to recover on three bonds of $917, $1,250, and $2,492.81, respectively, executed to testator by his daughter and her husband, the only competent witness of a settlement had between them, on the day when the last bond was signed, was the daughter's attorney, who testified that testator presented a claim for several thousand dollars paid for the daughter's husband; that the latter and testator had small memorandum books, and pieces of paper with memoranda on them; that the "$1,250 note" was not executed at this time; that, as to the bond for $917, "there was no dispute over this debt;" that the bond of a third person for $2,900, which he thought, from the testimony of another witness, may have been erroneously charged against the daughter, "entered into the result which was arrived at;" that testator contended that the daughter's husband owed the bond under some agreement they had made; and that he had no recollection of the various items, which amounted to a considerable sum. Testator's will gave none of his estate to the daughter, reciting that he had already given considerable property to her and her husband. *Held* insufficient to prove that the bonds were executed under a mistake of fact.—Chapman v. Persinger's Ex'x, (Va.) 13 S. E. 549.

—— Accounting.

6. Where one is employed at a certain amount per cord to purchase wood to be delivered by the vendors to the purchasing agent's employers, and the single question in dispute between such employee and his employers is the quantity of wood purchased and delivered, there is no ground for equity jurisdiction, though the account is a long one, and the delivery of a large number of lots is disputed.—Goddin v. Bland, (Va.) 13 S. E. 145.

—— Usury.

7. Plaintiffs sued to enjoin a foreclosure and compel an accounting between them and defendant. The mortgage was collateral to a bond executed by plaintiffs to secure defendant for such money as it might thereafter advance to a firm composed of two of the obligors, in an amount not exceeding $5,000, such advances to be discounted after three days, with interest, and the balance existing one year after date of the bond to become payable at 8 per cent. interest. The account embraced dealings prior to the execution of the bond, and also showed that defendant had charged the firm daily on balances at the rate of 12 per cent. interest, which it had paid monthly by checks. *Held*, that the defendant is entitled to judgment against the firm for the balance upon the whole dealings, without regard to the usury, as plain-

tiffs' remedy for such illegal payments was by action to recover the same within two years, under Code N. C. § 3886, and equity could not relieve plaintiffs, as such payments of usury were transactions distinct from the indebtedness to defendant.—Rogers v. Bank of Oxford, (N. C.) 18 S. E. 245.

8. The surety on the bond is liable only for the balance of the money so advanced by defendant, with interest at 8 per cent. after one year, said balance to be ascertained by allowing defendant interest at 6 per cent. on the advances, it not being within the meaning of the bond that the surety should be liable for usurious interest. —Rogers v. Bank of Oxford, (N. C.) 18 S. E. 245.

Laches.

9. Laches will not be attributed to the heirs of a lunatic for failure to bring an action to prevent waste during his life, where his administrator sued for an accounting against the committee shortly after the lunatic's death.—Clark v. Crout, (N. C.) 18 S. E. 602.

Pleading—Multifariousness.

10. A bill which alleges that one of the defendants, a judgment debtor, has made various fraudulent transfers to the other defendants, and which seeks to have them set aside, and asks for an injunction and receiver, is not multifarious, having for its single object the subjection of the property of the judgment debtor to the lien of plaintiff's judgment and execution.—Thomas v. Sellman, (Va.) 18 S. E. 146.

Parties.

11. Where a creditor files a bill to set aside a voluntary conveyance by his debtor, and pending the suit the debt is paid by the indorser of the notes representing it, and the notes delivered to him, such indorser cannot prosecute the suit in the name of the original plaintiff. RICHARDSON, J., dissenting.—Campbell v. Shipman, (Va.) 18 S. E. 114.

Master's report.

12. When exceptions to a master's report have not been filed within the time allowed by the court for that purpose, it is within the discretion of the court to allow them to be filed thereafter upon proper cause shown. — Stewart v. Crane, (Ga.) 18 S. E. 552.

13. Code Ga. § 4208, which provides that a master's report, when returned to "court," shall be subject to exceptions for such time as the "court" may allow, does not confer on a judge at chambers any authority to pass an ex parte order extending the time for filing such exceptions beyond the time originally fixed by the court for that purpose.—Stewart v. Crane, (Ga.) 18 S. E. 552.

14. The finding of a master that there was no fraud or collusion in setting aside the satisfaction of a judgment is not conclusive, even though the trial court did not disturb such finding.— Wheeler v. Alderman, (S. C.) 18 S. E. 673.

Decree — Adjudicating rights of stranger.

15. In a suit to set aside a sale under a deed of trust, brought by the grantor therein against the purchaser and others, a decree dismissing the bill, and reciting as one of the reasons for such dismissal that plaintiff and the purchaser colluded at the sale to defraud one F., to whom plaintiff had previously sold the land, and were therefore in pari delicto, is error, where F. was not a party to the suit, and is not complaining, and no issues as to his rights are raised by the pleadings.—Smith v. Lowther, (W. Va.) 18 S. E. 999.

Bill of review.

16. Where a sale was made of "one-half" of a certain tract of land in gross, and a deed executed, based upon a subsequent survey which so defined the boundaries as to inclose 102 acres less than the parties supposed the one-half contained, a bill of review of a judgment for the balance of the purchase money recovered by the grantor's executor should be granted, where it was dis-

covered after judgment that the surveyor acted fraudulently as to both parties in so defining the boundaries, and that upon discovering that fact the grantor avowed his purpose to correct the injustice thus done, although in the main action the mistake had been alleged by the grantee as ground for an equitable abatement of the purchase money, and the judgment had been affirmed on appeal. LACY, J., dissenting. — Reynolds v. Reynolds' Ex'r, (Va.) 18 S. E. 895; Id. 596.

17. One of the essential qualifications of a bill in chancery is that it should, either in the caption or in the body of the bill, name some person or persons as parties defendant, and describe them as having some interest in the subject-matter of the suit, and these requisites are as essential to a bill of review as to an original bill, and without them a paper purporting to be a bill of review should be dismissed on demurrer, or stricken from the files on motion.—Kanawha Valley Bank v. Wilson, (W. Va.) 18 S. E. 58.

Error, Writ of.

See Appeal; Certiorari; Exceptions, Bill of; New Trial.

Estates.

See Dower; Easements; Homestead; Tenancy in Common and Joint Tenancy.

By entirety, see Husband and Wife, 1.
Nature of estate created by deed, see Deed, 18.
—— estate devised, see Wills, 6-11.

ESTOPPEL.

By compromise, see Compromise.
—— judgment, see Judgment, 4-18.
To attack validity of execution, see Execution, 4.
—— claim dower, see Dower, 1, 2.

By deed.

1. The signers of a bond are estopped, after the death of the obligee, to aver that they were induced to sign it by his promise to give it to them.—Chapman v. Persinger's Ex'x, (Va.) 18 S. E. 549.

By record.

2. A debtor conveyed certain land to a person who, in consideration thereof, agreed to pay certain of the former's debts, and subsequently conveyed a portion to the debtor's mother in satisfaction of a judgment. P. and another, creditors of the debtor, filed a petition in bankruptcy, seeking to set aside the original conveyances as made to defraud creditors. A compromise was effected, wherein the bankruptcy proceedings were abandoned, and the mother gave her notes to P. and the other creditor, and placed the land in trust as security. Another creditor sued, and the trust property was sold, under decree of court, to satisfy his claim, and P. became one of the purchasers. Held, in an action by another creditor of the debtor to set aside all these conveyances as in fraud of creditors, that the allegations of fraud in the bankruptcy proceedings instituted by P. did not estop him to maintain that he was an innocent purchaser.—Penn's Ex'r v. Penn, (Va.) 18 S. E. 707.

In pais.

3. In an action on contract for furnishing ties, the court charged that the defendant had set up admissions of plaintiff that a very large amount of ties had been paid for, which was a question for the jury to determine. He then charged that such admissions must be received and weighed with great care, and would not estop plaintiff, "unless defendant has done something or in some way acted upon them." Held not erroneous, as invading the province of the jury, nor as inapplicable to the case.—Draffin v. Charleston, C. & C. R. Co., (S. C.) 18 S. E. 427.

4. The fact that a bond given by a married woman to secure the payment of money borrowed by the husband for his own use was given in 1884, and thereafter assigned to defendant, who sought

to foreclose in 1889, and that plaintiff had not claimed that the money was not borrowed for her use, will not operate as an estoppel, especially when she did nothing to induce the defendant to take the assignment.—Griffin v. Earle, (S. C.) 13 S. E. 478.

5. Code Ga. § 2966, provides that "one who silently stands by and permits another to purchase his property without disclosing his title is guilty of such fraud as estops him from subsequently setting up such title against the purchaser." A. executed a mortgage to B. to secure her on a note, and thereafter died. At maturity of the note, plaintiffs, as the deceased mortgagor's executors, tried to borrow money to pay the note, and failed, whereupon B. paid the note, advertised the property under the power of the sale in the mortgage, and sold it. Two of plaintiffs were present at the sale, and made no objections. The purchaser, as the agent of the mortgagee, drew the notice of sale, and was a brother of deceased mortgagor in possession of the facts of title. *Held*, that the plaintiffs were not estopped from contesting the validity of the sale.—Wilkins v. McGehee, (Ga.) 13 S. E. 84.

6. In 1875 defendant conveyed property to a bank to secure his notes to a third person, but the deed was not properly acknowledged. In 1878 he gave a deed of trust to secure to the bank any debt for which he should be liable jointly with M. as one of the sureties on the bond of the cashier who had defaulted. M. sought to enforce the deed of 1878 for contribution, claiming that it was paramount to the defectively acknowledged deed of 1875. *Held* that, since the bank had knowledge of the deed of 1875, and could not set up the deed of 1878 against it, M. could not do so, since he could only claim through the bank.—Barton's Ex'r v. Brent, (Va.) 13 S. E. 29.

—— To assert title.

7. Ratification by the wife of a deed of gift by her to her husband may operate as an estoppel, and not merely as an admission, after it has been acted upon as affording security for money advanced upon the faith of it.—Hadden v. Larned, (Ga.) 13 S. E. 806.

8. Admissions of a father that he had donated certain land to his son, of which the latter was in possession, will not estop the father from asserting his title as against the son's creditor, to whom the admissions were not made, and who merely heard of them, where it does not appear that such admissions were made with any design or intention that they should be acted on.—Harvey v. West, (Ga.) 13 S. E. 693.

9. A husband and wife took a deed of land on April 2, 1852, but did not record it until January 11, 1886. April 28, 1852, the husband alone deeded back to their grantor, S., who reconveyed the same, and his grantee died in 1880, and the land was sold to defendant at administrator's sale. S. publicly stated at the sale, in presence of the husband and wife, that the title was perfect, and they made no objection. The husband acted as auctioneer. Defendant had no notice of the deed to the husband and wife, and went into possession, and in 1884 recorded his deed. *Held*, that the wife's conduct at the sale did not estop her from asserting her right of survivorship to the land.—Phillips v. Hodges, (N. C.) 13 S. E. 769.

EVIDENCE.

Judicial notice.

1. Act S. C. 1881 (17 St. 582) authorizes the city council of Charleston to require the payment of certain licenses by persons engaged in business in said city, and to pass such ordinances as are necessary to carry the act into effect. *Held*, that a complaint in an action to enforce the payment of such licenses, alleging that the city council, for the purpose of raising a revenue, and in the exercise of the taxing power, passed an ordinance entitled "An ordinance to regulate licenses for the year 1889," whereby, *inter alia*, it was provided that certain persons should obtain licenses, and should pay therefor a certain sum, but not alleging that the said ordinance contained any provision authorizing the enforcement of the payment of such licenses, was insufficient, for the reason that the courts do not take judicial notice of city ordinances unless directed by charter or statute to do so, and such ordinances, therefore, should be set out in the pleadings, if not *in hæc verba*, at least in substance.—City Council of Charleston v. Ashley Phosphate Co., (S. C.) 13 S. E. 845.

2. Courts of a municipal corporation will take judicial notice of its ordinances without allegation or proof of their existence.—Town of Moundsville v. Velton, (W. Va.) 13 S. E. 373.

3. Where, upon conviction of a violation of an ordinance of a municipal corporation before its mayor, an appeal is taken to the circuit court, under Code W. Va. c. 50, § 220, and chapter 47, § 89, providing for a trial *de novo* in such cases, on the trial of such appeal the circuit court will take judicial notice of such ordinance.—Town of Moundsville v. Velton, (W. Va.) 13 S. E. 373.

Presumption—Non-production of witness.

4. In an action against a railroad company for injuries sustained by falling over a stool on the car platform, defendant contended that the stool was at the bottom of the car-steps at the time of the accident, in accordance with its custom to keep it there until the train started, to assist lady passengers in getting on. *Held* that, where defendant failed to produce the employe whose duty it was to place the stool in position, and did not show that he was inaccessible or that defendant was ready to produce him, it was *not* error for the court, in charging the jury, to call their attention to his absence or non-production as a fact to be considered by them in connection with the evidence in the case.—Atlanta & W. P. R. Co. v. Holcombe, (Ga.) 13 S. E. 751.

Best and secondary.

5. A memorandum of the names of customers, as shown by the books of a firm, is not admissible, where the books themselves are not tendered nor accounted for.—Phillips v. Trowbridge Furniture Co., (Ga.) 13 S. E. 19.

6. The entry in a "fiduciary book," in which Code Va. 1849, c. 132, § 1, and Code 1860, c. 132, § 1, required the clerk of the court to keep a record of personal representatives and their sureties, is, in the absence of the bond and other records, which were lost during the war, sufficient to show the fact of the suretyship of the persons named therein. HINTON and RICHARDSON, JJ., dissenting.—Timberlake's Adm'r v. Jennings, (Va.) 13 S. E. 98.

in which the land was situated, are admissible to show that he has ceased to be a resident of the latter state, for the purpose of showing that he no longer has a homestead interest in the land.—Jackson v. Du Bose, (Ga.) 13 S. E. 916.

27. In an action against a carrier of goods for $500 damages for injury to goods shipped, plaintiff recovered a verdict of $225. At the trial defendant introduced in evidence, as an admission, a letter from plaintiff reciting, "$100 will not do more than cover the loss, and I hereby make claim for this amount." The uncontradicted evidence outside of the letter was that the damage was from $350 to $400. *Held*, that the court did not err in charging the jury that admissions should be scanned with care; that, if it should appear to their satisfaction that plaintiff made the statement contained in the letter, they should scan the same with care, giving it such weight as they might deem proper, taking into consideration the words, and the circumstances under which they were written.—Richmond & D. R. Co. v. Kerler, (Ga.) 13 S. E. 833.

28. On an issue as to whether defendant was a partner of one N., it is error to admit a statement made by N. to another person, not in defendant's presence or with her knowledge, that defendant was going into partnership with him.—Phillips v Trowbridge Furniture Co., (Ga.) 13 S. E. 19.

—— Res gestæ.

29. Pertinent declarations, made by a person while on his way to procure the execution of a mortgage to secure an antecedent debt or liability, the expedition having resulted in its procurement, are admissible in evidence, as part of the *res gestæ*, against the mortgagee on the question whether the mortgage was procured by fraud or duress, irrespective of the relation of agency between the mortgagee and the person making the declaration.—Small v. Williams, (Ga.) 13 S. E. 589.

Opinions.

30. In an action for injuries sustained by an employe of a railroad company in coupling cars, plaintiff cannot testify that he acted cautiously, as he thereby states a conclusion, and not facts.—Mayfield v. Savannah, G. & N. A. R. Co., (Ga.) 13 S. E. 459

—— Expert testimony.

31. Expert testimony is not admissible to aid in the interpretation of an indorsement on a note having a definite legal import, and being expressed in terms free from ambiguity.—Freeman v. Exchange Bank, (Ga.) 13 S. E. 160.

32. In the examination of an expert as to plaintiff's condition, it is proper to put hypothetical questions based on plaintiff's testimony.—Southern Bell Tel., etc., Co. v. Jordan, (Ga.) 13 S. E. 202.

Public records—Certified copies.

33. Code Ga. § 849, requires the tax receiver of each county to make out three copies of the tax digest of his county, and transmit one to the comptroller general, to be filed in his office, and section 3816 declares that the certificate of any public officer of the state, or any county thereof, shall give sufficient validity or authenticity to any copy or transcript of any record, document, paper, or file, or other matter or thing in their respective offices, or pertaining thereto, to admit the same in evidence in any court of the state. *Held*, that the books of tax returns in the office of the comptroller general are of equal rank as evidence with those in the proper offices of the respective counties, and the certificate of the comptroller general, touching the contents of such books, is no less admissible than the certificate of the proper county officer would be.—Clark v. Empire Lumber Co., (Ga.) 13 S. E. 826.

—— Statutes of foreign state.

34. Notwithstanding Code Ga. § 3824, provides that the public laws of the several states, as published by authority, shall be judicially recognized without proof, there is no error in receiving the

testimony of skilled attorneys to aid in coming to a correct conclusion as to the laws, and especially as to the practice of the courts of their state.—Chattanooga, R. & C. R. Co. v. Jackson. (Ga.) 13 S. E. 109.

Parol evidence.

35. Oral testimony is inadmissible to show the grounds on which a preceding judge overruled a written demurrer.—Baker v Garris, (N. C.) 13 S. E. 2.

36. Evidence of negotiations between the parties which culminated in a written agreement was incompetent.—Fishburne v. Smith, (S. C.) 13 S. E. 525.

37. An agreement that "all matters and things embraced by the within contract have been fully adjusted and settled, and this contract is, for value received, declared ended and settled," cannot, in the absence of fraud or mutual mistake, be shown by parol testimony to have referred only to money accounts between the parties to the contract, and not to have included a covenant therein, on the part of the party paying the consideration for the release, not to engage in a certain business with any one else for a certain time.—Bonsack Mach. Co. v. Woodrum, (Va.) 13 S. E. 994.

38. An agreement to deed a right of way through certain land, in consideration of the construction of the road, may be shown by parol evidence to have been delivered to the president of the road, on condition that it should not be used unless the withholding of it would defeat the building of the road, or the board of directors of the road should make compensation for the right of way.—Humphreys v. Richmond & M. R. Co., (Va.) 13 S. E. 985.

39. Where defendant obtained a license from a land company to cut timber from its land, knowing at the time the superior rights of plaintiff lumber company, plaintiff, being a stranger to the contract between defendant and the land company, may by parol evidence show the true meaning and scope thereof.—Bruce v. John L. Roper Lumber Co., (Va.) 13 S. E. 153.

—— Consideration.

40. Where defendant's father, in his life-time, conveyed to defendant land worth $1,900, reciting in the deed as the consideration $400, which was paid, it may be shown by parol evidence, after the father's death, that the excess was intended as an advancement from his estate. 13 S. E. 215, affirmed.—Barbee v. Barbee, (N. C.) 13 S. E. 792.

41. The recital in a deed of the receipt of the purchase money, not being contractual in its nature, is only *prima facie* evidence of payment, and hence, though deeds from a father to his children recite the receipt of a consideration, parol evidence is admissible to show that the conveyances were intended as advancements.—Barbee v. Barbee, (N. C.) 13 S. E. 215.

—— To explain ambiguities.

42. A written contract, silent or ambiguous as to certain matters, may, as to them, be explained by parol evidence, not conflicting with anything plainly expressed in such contract.—Johnston v. Patterson, (Ga.) 13 S. E. 17.

43. If a partner, after dissolution of the partnership, on receiving notice from a bank that a note of the firm has been protested, which note was indorsed in the firm name by another partner, for his own accommodation, with the knowledge of the bank, writes the bank that he has bought out his copartner's interest, and will pay the notes of the firm, as he has assumed the firm's liabilities, the *prima facie* effect of the writing is to ratify the indorsement; but the writing, being ambiguous, is open to explanation by extrinsic evidence as to whether there was an intention to ratify the indorsement or not.—American Exch. Nat. Bank v. Georgia Const. & Inv. Co., (Ga.) 13 S. E. 505.

Evidence at former trial.

44. The deposition of a draughtsman, admitted to have been regularly taken, and allowed in a

previous action between the same parties, and in relation to the same subject-matter, is competent, though no proceedings have been taken to make it competent in the present action.—Stewart v. Register, (N. C.) 13 S. E. 234.

45. A synopsis of the evidence of a deceased witness, agreed upon by both parties, and approved by the court, together with the stenographer's report in full of said evidence, is admissible on a second trial of the cause.—Lathrop v. Adkinson, (Ga.) 13 S. E. 517.

46. A record of a suit by an administrator and widow of a decedent, brought in Virginia against his heirs, to sell lands there to pay debts and satisfy the widow's dower, wherein debts are decreed against the decedent's estate and subjecting its assets, is not evidence, in a suit in this state against such heirs to subject lands of such decedent to pay such debts, to establish such debts or their amounts.—Hull's Adm'r v. Hull's Heirs, (W. Va.) 13 S. E. 49; Dudley v. Same, Id.

Examination.

Of witness, see *Witness*, 14–16.

EXCEPTIONS, BILL OF.

See, also, *Appeal; Certiorari; New Trial.*
Mandamus to compel signing, see *Mandamus*, 1.

Settlement and signing.

1. After a judge has corrected, signed, and certified a bill of exceptions, having interlined in the certificate a reference to the corrections made by him, and the plaintiff in error has served and filed the bill of exceptions thus certified, and caused it, together with the record, to be transmitted to this court, thereby recognizing and adopting such bill of exceptions as sufficient, it is too late to apply to this court for a *mandamus* to compel the judge to omit the corrections he had made in the bill of exceptions as originally presented to him, and sign another certificate, free from such interlineation.— Rogers v. Roberts, (Ga.) 13 S. E. 962.

2. The constitution of Georgia confers jurisdiction upon the supreme court for the trial and determination of writs of error from the superior and city courts. The writ of error provided for by statute prior to the act of 1889 was abolished by that act, and the one prescribed must have a clause in the judge's certificate showing that the bill of exceptions specifies all of the errors complained of, or else that none of the record is material.—Pendly v. State, (Ga.) 13 S. E. 443.

3. In Georgia it is not the duty of the judges of the superior or city courts to prepare or correct certificates to bills of exceptions, but only to sign such as are presented to them when they are in the form prescribed by statute.—Pendly v. State, (Ga.) 13 S. E. 443.

Service.

4. Where plaintiff in error fails to serve his bill of exceptions on the opposing party within the time limited by the statute after the signing thereof by the judge, a subsequent certificate of the judge, to the effect that such failure of service arose through his delay, cannot be considered to relieve the party in default.—Greer v. Holdridge, (Ga.) 13 S. E. 106.

Necessary contents.

5. It is not the office of the bill of exceptions to verify and bring up a transcript of the record. The transcript is to be certified and sent up by the clerk, and the bill of exceptions should deal with the record no further than to specify such parts thereof as are material.—Lewis v. Clegg, (Ga.) 13 S. E. 608.

Excessive Damages.

See *Damages*, 4.

EXECUTION.

See, also, *Attachment; Exemptions; Garnishment; Judicial Sales.*
Equitable jurisdiction over claim case, see *Equity*, 2.
To collect taxes, see *Taxation*, 3–5.

Issue and validity.

1. Code Va. 1873, c. 182, § 13, provides that, in computing the time within which execution shall issue, or action be brought on a decree, the time during which such right "is suspended by the terms thereof, or by legal process, shall be omitted." *Held*, that there was no such suspension because of said provision, or by reason of an injunction whereby the sale of defendant's homestead was enjoined, as to permit its revival after 10 years had elapsed.—Serles v. Cromer, (Va.) 13 S. E. 859.

2. Code Proc. S. C. 306, (the original Code,) provided that "the party in whose favor judgment has been heretofore or shall hereafter be given * * * may, at any time within five years after the entry of judgment, proceed to enforce the same, as prescribed by this title." Section 307 provided that, "after the lapse of five years from the entry of judgment, an execution can only be issued by leave of court. * * * But the leave shall not be necessary when execution has been issued on the judgment within five years, and returned unsatisfied, in whole or in part." Section 315 provided that, "if the first execution is returned unsatisfied, in whole or in part, another execution, as of course, may be issued at any time within the period limited by this act for issuing executions." *Held*, that the issuance of a second execution at any time within five years from the return, unsatisfied, of the first execution was not authorized by the statute, but a second execution, as of course, must be issued within five years from the entry of the judgment.—Garvin v. Garvin, (S. C.) 13 S. E. 625.

3. Though a *fi. fa.* appear on its face to carry interest upon interest accrued up to the time prior to the judgment, the fact will not render it inadmissible in evidence, since the presumption is that the *fi. fa.* followed the judgment, and it was legally possible for the judgment to be correct, though requiring interest to be computed on interest, as it could have been stipulated for by contract.—Hadden v. Larned, (Ga.) 13 S. E. 806.

—— Estoppel to attack.

4. Defendant in a *fi. fa.* issued upon a revived judgment, after litigating the legality of a levy, and after final judgment that the levy proceed, cannot raise the question, by a subsequent affidavit of illegality, of proper service upon him in the proceedings to revive the judgment before the *fi. fa.* issued, both because the question is *res judicata*, and because of rule 31 of the superior courts in Georgia, declaring that a second affidavit of illegality cannot be filed "for causes which existed and were known, or in the exercise of a reasonable diligence might have been known, at the time of filing the first."—Fuller v. Vining, (Ga.) 13 S. E. 635.

Property subject to.

5. Under Code N. C. § 1840, which provides that no land belonging to the wife shall be disposed of by the husband for his own life or any less term without her assent, and that no interest of the husband shall be subject to sale to satisfy any execution obtained against him, the husband's curtesy initiate in his wife's land is not such an interest as can be subjected to sale to satisfy a judgment against the husband.—Bruce v. Sugg, (N. C.) 13 S. E. 790.

6. Code W. Va. c. 100, § 13, provides that "if any person shall transact business as a trader with the addition of the words 'factor,' 'agent,' 'and company,' or 'and Co.,' and fail to disclose the name of his principal or partner by a sign in letters easy to be read, placed conspicuously at the house wherein such business is transacted, and also by a notice published for two weeks in a

newspaper (if any) printed in the town or county wherein the same is transacted, or if any person transact such business in his own name without any such addition, all the property, stock, choses in action acquired or used in such business shall, as to the creditors of such person, be liable for the debts of such person." *Held*, that a party whose entire business consists in selling agricultural implements, as agent for the manufacturer thereof, receiving a commission for his services, cannot be regarded either as a trader or commission merchant; and although his name, with the addition of the words "Mfrs'. Agent," be on a sign nailed on the outside of the building in which he does business, in a conspicuous place, farming implements which he has on sale as an agent for the manufacturer are not liable to execution and sale as his property under this section.— Brown Manuf'g Co. v. William Deering & Co., (W. Va.) 13 S. E. 883.

7. Under Code Ga. § 2664, which raises a conclusive presumption of a gift from the fact that a child has been in possession of his father's land for seven years, land held by a son for less than seven years under a parol gift from his father is not subject to execution in favor of the son's creditor against the claim of the father, though the son may have erected valuable improvements on the faith of the gift. The legal title remaining in the father, and the son's remedy being by a suit for specific performance of the voluntary agreement, his creditor must resort to a like remedy.—Harvey v. West, (Ga.) 13 S. E. 693.

Levy—By what officer.

8. Since an execution on a justice's judgment is directed to any constable of the county, an entry thereon by a constable is legal, though he is not an officer of the militia district in which the execution issued, and will keep the judgment alive.—Neal v. Brookhan, (Ga.) 13 S. E. 288.

—— Trial of illegality.

9. Code Ga. § 3666, provides that where an execution is levied and an affidavit of illegality is filed thereto, the officer shall return the execution, affidavit, and bond to "the court from which the execution issued," and the issue of illegality shall be tried in that court. *Held*, that an execution issued from a justice court should be returned to such court, and not to the superior court, for trial of the issue of exemption of the land as a homestead.—Moore v. O'Barr, (Ga.) 13 S. E. 464.

10. A judgment of the superior court rendered on appeal from a justice's court is not void so as to be attacked by affidavit of illegality of execution issued thereon, on the ground that the justice's court was not held "at a court-house established according to law," both parties having had their day in the superior court, since Code, § 3671, provides that if defendant in execution has had his day in court, he cannot go behind the judgment by affidavit of illegality.— Green v. Alexander, (Ga.) 13 S. E. 946.

11. A motion to dismiss an affidavit of illegality is rightly denied when one of the grounds thereof presents a legal defense against the further progress of the execution.—American Mortg. Co. of Scotland v. Tennille, (Ga.) 13 S. E. 158.

Forthcoming bond—Breach.

12. Where the defendant in *fi. fa.* gives to the sheriff a forthcoming bond for the production of the property at the time and place of sale, and afterwards the levy is duly advertised and the property not produced, the bond is broken, notwithstanding a third person may, on the day of sale, interpose a claim thereto, and the sheriff accepts a claim affidavit and bond; and a recovery may be had on the forthcoming bond pending such claim.—Aycock v. Austin, (Ga.) 13 S. E. 582.

Claims of third persons.

13. Although it may be irregular to dismiss, for want of evidence to support it, the claim of a third person to property levied on under a *fi. fa.*, yet if the claimant, after admitting posses-

sion in the defendant in *fi. fa.* at the time of the levy, thus making a *prima facie* case for the plaintiff, closes his evidence without showing anything to overcome the effect of his admission, the error is immaterial, and the judgment will not be reversed.—Jordan v. Grogan, (Ga.) 13 S. E. 552.

14. When, on trial of a claim case, there was no evidence at all showing that the property levied on either belonged to, or was in possession of, the defendant in *fi. fa.*, the court rightly ordered the levy to be dismissed. — Freeman v. Sturgis Nat. Bank, (Ga.) 13 S. E. 29.

15. Where all the pertinent facts on behalf of the claimant of property levied on under execution are admissible in evidence in a claim case, and actually admitted, the refusal of the court to allow an amendment to the claim affidavit, setting out these facts in detail, is of no consequence.—Hadden v. Larned, (Ga.) 13 S. E. 806.

16. When, in a claim case, the execution levy has been improperly dismissed, the court may correct the error at the same term by reinstating the case on motion.—Wilson v. Herrington, (Ga.) 13 S. E. 129.

Sale—Title of purchaser.

17. Under Gen. St. S. C. § 685, providing that "the sheriff shall pay over the proceeds of sale of any real estate sold by him to any judgment having prior lien thereon," the title of a purchaser at a sale under an execution, junior to a conveyance made by the debtor, may be referred to and supported by a judgment senior to the conveyance, though no valid execution thereon had been issued.—Garvin v. Garvin, (S. C.) 13 S. E. 695.

Relief against execution.

18. In an action to enjoin the sale of land on execution the complaint alleged fraud and collusion. It appeared that the owner of certain land confessed judgment in favor of his brother, the defendant; that he and the attorney who acted in taking the judgment represented to one who was about to advance money upon a mortgage on the land that the judgment had been paid, and the attorney then entered a satisfaction of record as attorney of defendant; that, relying upon such representations and satisfaction, the money was loaned on the mortgage; that plaintiff afterwards purchased the land at a sale under a foreclosure of the mortgage, and had no notice of defendant's claim; that defendant afterwards, without notice to plaintiff, had the satisfaction of his judgment set aside, and sought to sell the land on execution. *Held*, that the facts entitled plaintiff to equitable relief.—Wheeler v. Alderman, (S. C.) 13 S. E. 673.

Supplementary proceedings.

19. In supplementary proceedings instituted against the judgment debtors and three co-defendants, to whom it was alleged the debtors had transferred property, an order forbidding the co-defendants "to transfer or make any other disposition of any property belonging to said defendants, not exempt by law from execution," was not intended to affect the co-defendants in their own property, but only such as belonged to the debtors. It was warranted by Code N. C. § 490, which provides that persons having property of the judgment debtor may be examined concerning the same.—National Bank v. Burns, (N. C.) 13 S. E. 871.

20. Where the co-defendants claimed an interest in the property in their hands, the court had power to forbid a disposition of the same until a receiver could be appointed to litigate the matter. —National Bank v. Burns, (N. C.) 13 S. E. 871.

21. If the co-defendants claimed any interest in the property alleged to be in their possession, they could, by suggesting it, have the right litigated, as provided by Code N. C. § 497.—National Bank v. Burns, (N. C.) 13 S. E. 871.

22. In supplementary proceedings, the court cannot restrain the transfer of property owned by one not a party to the action. Coates v.

Wilkes, 94 N. C. 174, distinguished.—National Bank v. Burns, (N. C.) 13 S. E. 871.

23. While creditors may subject, in a supplementary proceeding, the debtor's choses in action, including a claim for compensation due for service rendered under an express or implied contract, they have no lien on his skill or attainments, and cannot compel him to exact compensation for managing his wife's property, or for service rendered to any person with the understanding that it was gratuitous.—Osborne v. Wilkes, (N. C.) 13 S. E. 285.

Supplementary proceedings—Affidavit.

24. An affidavit in supplementary proceedings alleged that defendants had not sufficient property subject to execution to satisfy the judgment, but that defendants had property not exempt from execution, which they refused to apply towards the satisfaction of the judgment, and that an execution had been issued, but not returned. Held, that the affidavit was sufficient, under Code N. C. § 488, par. 2, which provides that after issuing an execution, on proof by affidavit that debtors have property which they refuse to apply towards the satisfaction of a judgment, the court may by order require them to appear and answer concerning the same.—National Bank v. Burns, (N. C.) 13 S. E. 871.

25. An affidavit in supplementary proceedings alleged that the judgment debtors had not sufficient property subject to execution to satisfy the judgment, but that they had property "not exempt" from execution, which they had placed in the hands of their co-defendants, and which they refused to apply to the satisfaction of the judgment. Held, that the affidavit was sufficient when, from all its allegations, the words "not exempt" clearly related to property in the hands of the co-defendants, which was not part of the homestead or personal property exemption of the judgment debtors. Hinsdale v. Sinclair, 83 N. C. 338, distinguished.—National Bank v. Burns, (N. C.) 13 S. E. 871.

Service of order.

26. Leaving a copy of an order on a judgment debtor to appear and answer in supplemental proceedings with the debtor's wife was a sufficient service.—Turner v. Holden, (N. C.) 13 S. E. 731.

EXECUTORS AND ADMINISTRATORS.

See, also, Descent and Distribution; Wills.
Acknowledgment of debt by, see Limitation of Actions, 20, 21.
Subrogation of administrator to rights of creditors, see Subrogation, 2.

Appointment.

1. Where a person having a right to administer within the time allowed, has renounced her right in favor of her nominee, it is error to refuse to appoint him.—Williams v. Neville, (N. C.) 13 S. E. 240.

2. Where a person having a right to administer has not renounced or otherwise lost it, it is error to refuse her application to remove an administrator already appointed.—Williams v. Neville, (N. C.) 13 S. E. 240.

3. The fact that, pending an appeal from an order refusing to appoint a nominee of the person entitled to administer, the latter has not applied for appointment within the statutory period therefor, will not bar his appointment. — Williams v. Neville, (N. C.) 13 S. E. 240.

4. Code N. C. § 1373, provides that when any person applies for administration, and any other person has a prior right thereto, a written renunciation of such right must be filed with the clerk of the superior court. Held, that a verbal statement made by a person having such right, to one who desires to be appointed, that she will not administer upon an estate, does not constitute a renunciation.—Williams v. Neville, (N. C.) 13 S. E. 240.

5. A letter, by one having such right to administer, to the clerk of the superior court having jurisdiction, stating that she intends to renounce in favor of her nominee before the clerk of another county, does not constitute a renunciation.—Williams v. Neville, (N. C.) 13 S. E. 240.

Bonds—Release of sureties.

6. The fact that the heirs of an intestate and the administrator entered into an agreement by which the administrator delayed the creditors in collecting their debts will not discharge the sureties on the administrator's bond for waste committed by the administrator pending litigation with the creditors, since the heirs had a right to co-operate with the administrator in resisting the claims of creditors by all lawful means.—McMahon v. Paris, (Ga.) 13 S. E. 573.

Presentation and allowance of claims.

7. Under Code N. C. § 164, providing that, if claims against a decedent's estate are filed within a year after appointment of the administrator, and allowed, it shall not be necessary to bring suit thereon to prevent a bar, claims filed within the year will not be barred by subsequent lapse of time pending the administration, and the statute of limitations cannot be pleaded against them.—Turner v. Shuffler, (N. C.) 13 S. E. 243.

8. Code N. C. provides that, where an action is brought on a claim which was not presented within 12 months from the first publication of a notice to creditors, the administrator shall not be chargeable for assets he may have distributed before such action was commenced. An administrator published a notice to all persons having claims against the estate to exhibit them within 12 months thereafter. After the expiration of the year he paid part of the assets to the next of kin on account of their distributive shares. Plaintiff sued on a claim that had not been presented within 12 months from the first publication of the notice. Held, that defendant is not chargeable with the amount of money he paid to the distributees.—Mallard v. Patterson, (N. C.) 13 S. E. 93.

9. Where one contracted with a person since deceased to build a church, the fact that the administrator, shortly after the work was commenced, gave notice not to proceed therewith, and that the estate would not be responsible therefor, was no bar to a recovery for work afterwards done, when the church was completed according to the contract.—Ferguson's Adm'r v. Wills, (Va.) 13 S. E. 392.

10. It is the duty of an administrator to protect the estate of his decedent by interposing every legal defense, and he cannot by an agreement in pais, where infants are concerned and are made parties, either obtain commissions as administrator, to which he is not entitled by statute, or provide for the allowance of claims against said estate without proof of their correctness and validity.—Crotty v. Eagle's Adm'r, (W. Va.) 13 S. E. 59.

Powers of commissioner.

11. A commissioner appointed to ascertain the debts of a decedent, and their order of priority, has no authority to go behind a judgment rendered against the decedent in his life-time; and since Acts Va. 1865-66, c. 171, §§ 1, 2, provide for setting up the fact of a Confederate transaction only as a defense to a suit while pending, so as to reduce the judgment to be rendered, the action of the commissioner in scaling the judgment as a Confederate transaction will not affect the judgment creditor, who was no party to and had no notice of the proceedings. RICHARDSON and HINTON, JJ., dissenting.—Marshall's Adm'r v. Cheatham, (Va.) 13 S. E. 308.

12. Code Va. 1873, c. 177, which provides for corrections of mistakes, errors in calculation, and misrecitals in judgments, within five years after their rendition, does not apply to the scaling of a judgment as a Confederate transaction, since this fact might have been interposed as a defense to the suit; and hence the action of the commissioner in scaling such a judgment seven years after its rendition cannot be justified under this

chapter. RICHARDSON and HINTON, JJ., dissenting.—Marshall's Adm'r v. Cheatham, (Va.) 13 S.
E. 308.

Duties.

13. An executor, in dividing the property in
which he had an equal share, should set apart a
share for himself equal with the shares of the
others; should execute a writing that in such division his share had been allotted to him, which
should be proven and recorded; and he should
also take and file his own receipt for his share.
—Johnston v. Johnston, (N. C.) 13 S. E. 183.

14. Where a will provided for a division of the
estate or a sale and division of the proceeds, in
case of an actual division, the devisee or legatee
would take under the will, and it would be sufficient for the executor to execute a paper under
his hand and seal specifying the division made
and the allotment, making appropriate reference
to the will and his power thereunder, such writing to be proved and registered as in the case of
deeds.—Johnston v. Johnston, (N. C.) 13 S. E. 183.

Liabilities.

15. The mere fact that an executor made no
attempt to collect the unsecured note of a solvent
person will not render him liable to the remainder-men for loss occasioned by the unforeseen
failure of such person, especially when the executor was deterred from suing by the express objections of the life-tenant.—OTT v. ORR, (S. C.)
13 S. E. 467.

16. The testimony of an executor that his
mother, the life-tenant, objected to his suing
upon a note, the maker of which became insolvent, was competent as bearing upon his bona
fides.—Orr v. Orr, (S. C.) 13 S. E. 467.

17. In an action by an heir against the administrator of the estate and others, the petition alleged that, though the administrators had ample
personalty to pay decedent's debts, they mismanaged the estate so as to procure an order for the
sale of the larger part of the realty, in pursuance of a conspiracy between themselves and
their co-defendants to convert the estate to their
own use; that petitioner was then a minor; that
the other heirs were women, unused to business,
that the co-defendants, who were the persons on
whom petitioner's mother chiefly relied, represented to her that the administrators had so mismanaged the estate as to prevent bidding at the
sale; that, relying on such representations, the
heirs sold their interest in the land to the co-defendants for $5,400; that petitioner was repre-
sented in this transaction by his mother as guardian; that his share of the price was only $1,800,
though his interest in the land was well worth
$20,000; and that the lands or their proceeds
were divided between the administrators and
their co-defendants. The petition also alleged
that the administrators had permitted another
tract of land to be recovered from the estate on a
fraudulent title set up thereto; that they had
sold the balance of the lands to their co-defendants for a grossly inadequate price; that they
had turned over all the personalty of the estate,
worth $10,000, to their co-defendants; and that
they had then procured themselves to be discharged. The petition prayed that all the various sales be set aside; that petitioner be permitted to recover a one-fourth interest in the
lands or their proceeds; and that the administrators be compelled to account for the rents and
profits of the lands, and also for the personal
estate. Held, that the petition set forth a
cause of action, and that it was error to dismiss
the case on demurrer.—Dees v. Freeman, (Ga.)
13 S. E. 747.

—— Release from.

18. Under the provision of a will that in case
any of testator's children shall have issue which
shall reach majority then the gift to them shall
vest in such children absolutely, "released and
discharged from all terms, limitations, and provisions herein imposed," the receipt given to the
executor from a devisee or legatee having issue
of age need not specify the terms, conditions

and limitations otherwise required, but should
recite the arrival of such issue at majority.—
Johnston v. Johnston, (N. C.) 13 S. E. 183.

Sales under order of court.

19. Under Code N. C. § 1438, providing that
no order to sell real estate of a decedent shall be
granted to the personal representative until the
heirs of decedent shall have been made parties,
one who claims to be an heir of decedent, and
who was not made a party to the proceeding for
a sale of his land, is not bound by the judgment
and sale therein, and may therefore have a trial
as to her interest, together with the preliminary
question of whether she was an heir.—Dickens v.
Long, (N. C.) 13 S. E. 841.

20. Decedent, with intent to defraud his
creditors, conveyed land to his son, and the latter conveyed it to his brother, decedent's administrator, in trust for their father and his heirs.
The administrator filed his final account, and
left debts of decedent unpaid, without selling, or
applying for license to sell, said land. Held,
that, under Code N. C. § 1436, providing that
where a decedent's personalty is insufficient to
pay his debts, his administrator shall, without
undue delay, apply to the court for license to
sell his real estate, and that the court may, at
the instance of any creditor, compel him to perform his duty, there was no necessity that a
creditor should demand of the administrator that
he sell said land, before bringing an action to
compel him to do so.—Clement v. Cozart, (N. C.)
13 S. E. 862.

21. In a proceeding to sell land to pay decedent's debts the realty is liable for the costs of
an action against the executor as well as for the
debt, unless the judgment taxed the costs against
the executor personally, or against the plaintiff.
—Long v. Oxford, (N. C.) 13 S. E. 112.

22. In a proceeding to sell land to pay decedent's debts a judgment against the executor is
conclusive against the heirs and devisees unless
fraud or collusion is shown, and they cannot
plead the statute of limitations or other defenses
which might have been set up in the original action.—Long v. Oxford, (N. C.) 13 S. E. 112.

—— Setting aside.

23. Where, in proceedings to set aside an administrator's sale because made indirectly to the
administrator, the referee finds that the sale was
not in fact so made, but that it was bona fide,
and that the purchaser, after paying a fair price,
and taking a proper deed, then conveyed the
property to the administrator, such finding will
not be reviewed on appeal if there was any evidence to warrant it, and if the sale was approved.
—Turner v. Shuffler, (N. C.) 13 S. E. 243.

24. In an action to set aside a sale of land under a decree in a special proceeding by the administrator of plaintiffs' deceased father for the
purpose of selling land to pay debts of the estate,
a complaint which, after stating that the sale was
made under the decree in such proceeding, and
that defendants claim thereunder, claims that
plaintiffs were entitled to a homestead therein,
and that the sale was therefore void under Const.
N. C. art. 10, § 2, creating homestead exemptions,
fails to state any cause of action, where it omits
to state facts showing that the debt for which it
was sold was not contracted before the adoption
of the constitutional provision, and was not for
taxes due the state or for the purchase money of
the land, which are specially excepted from the
provisions of said articles, the burden of proof to
show the exemption being on plaintiffs.—Dickens
v. Long, (N. C.) 13 S. E. 841.

25. In an action to set aside a sale of land under a decree in a special proceeding by the administrator of plaintiffs' deceased father for the
purpose of selling land to pay debts of the estate, those plaintiffs who were made defendants
to the special proceeding cannot attack the judgment in that proceeding by claiming that it, together with the subsequent proceedings therein,
did not constitute evidence that their right and
title in the land derived from their father had not

passed to the purchaser at the sale.—Dickens v. Long, (N. C.) 18 S. E. 841.

Allowance to widow and children.

26. Under Act Ga. Oct. 9, 1885, authorizing the allowance of a year's support for the widow and minors out of the estate of a deceased husband and father, which provides that on application for such relief citation shall issue, and notice be published, as required in the appointment of permanent administrators, objections to granting such application may be filed at or before the term of court referred to in the citation. Parks v. Johnson, 79 Ga. 567, 5 S. E. 245, followed.—Laslie v. Laslie, (Ga.) 18 S. E. 596.

Actions by.

27. It is error to disregard a plea of *plene administravit præter* in an action against an administrator, since any recovery would be subject to such plea, if sustained.—Clark v. Crout, (S. C.) 18 S. E. 602.

28. An executor cannot recover in ejectment without producing the will. Sorrell v. Ham, 9 Ga. 55, and Mays v. Killen, 56 Ga. 527, followed.—Horne v. Johnson, (Ga.) 18 S. E. 683.

Actions against.

29. Where a plaintiff has a suit pending against defendant as executor, all proceedings in other courts intended to create evidence to be used in such suit should be against him in the same character, and not in the character of administrator, since an executor represents primarily the devisees and legatees, and the administrator represents the heirs at law.—Fulgham v. Carruthers, (Ga.) 18 S. E. 597.

30. Under the law as it existed prior to July, 1869, (Code N. C. §§ 1476, 1477,) a judgment against an administrator by default fixes him with assets with which to satisfy it, and he cannot set up in defense to a suit on such judgment that he had no assets when it was rendered.—Brown v. Walker (N. C.) 18 S. E. 3.

31. An executor may plead the coverture of his testatrix in actions to charge her separate estate with debt.—Baker v. Garris, (N. C.) 18 S. E. 2.

EXEMPTIONS.

See, also, *Homestead.*

Goods in custodia legis.

Suit was commenced by the creditors of a firm to set aside an assignment, and subject the firm assets to its debts. *Held*, that a temporary order restraining any one from interfering with the goods of the firm, and requiring defendants to show cause why the injunction should not be continued, but not authorizing any one to take possession of the goods, and hold them subject to the direction of the court, did not operate to place the goods *in custodia legis*, so as to invalidate a subsequent levy of a distress on the goods by the landlord for his rent.—Cooley v. Perry, (S. C.) 18 S. E. 853.

Expert Evidence.

See *Evidence*, 31, 32.

Express Trusts.

See *Trusts*, 1, 2.

FACTORS AND BROKERS.

Real-estate agents—Authority.

1. Real-estate agents wrote asking an owner of land for an opportunity to make a sale for him, and inquiring his terms. The owner replied, at different times, that his "price" for the property was $9,000; that he "would sell" for $10,000; and that he "had concluded to take" $10,-000; but nowhere did he expressly authorize them to act as his agents. *Held*, that their authority did not extend to making a sale, but only to transmitting offers for the approval of the owner, and that it was incumbent upon a purchaser to look to their authority.—Kramer v. Blair, (Va.) 18 S. E. 914.

2. An owner of land employed real-estate agents to sell it, without fixing a definite price. These agents had previously sold other land for the owner; but in each case, before closing the contract, the offer was submitted to the owner for his approval or rejection. Not being able to sell the land, it was platted into lots, with a view of selling at auction. On consultation with the owner, he fixed the minimum price, and advised the agents to sell the property as a whole, or to first put up the lots furthest from the corner. The auction sale was abandoned. For seven months thereafter, no sale was effected, and no definite price for the lots was agreed on; but the owner on several occasions conferred with the agents about the market, asked if they had any offer to submit on the lots, and required the property to be sold as a whole, or the lots furthest from the corner first. *Held*, that the agents, being employed to effect the sale of only the one parcel of land in a specified manner, were special agents, and not general agents; that the owner was not bound by a sale of the corner lots made by them in his absence, and without his consent, at a price below the minimum fixed for the auction sale, and at a time when the demand for the lots had greatly increased on account of public improvements to be made in the vicinity; and that the purchasers from the agent could not specifically enforce the contract as against the owner.—Davis v. Gordon, (Va.) 18 S. E. 35.

3. The fact that the proposed auction sale was advertised in several newspapers by the real-estate agents, and that the bill for such advertising was paid by the owner, did not convert the special agency into a general agency, with authority in the agents, seven months later, to effect a private sale of the lots in a manner and at a price wholly different from what was arranged for the contemplated auction sale.—Davis v. Gordon, (Va.) 18 S. E. 35.

4. The fact that the real-estate agents erected a sign on the property, showing that it was for sale by them, without mentioning the owner's name, does not constitute a holding out of the agents, by the owner, to the public, as having a general authority to bind him by a sale of the property.—Davis v. Gordon, (Va.) 18 S. E. 35.

FALSE PRETENSES.

See, also, *Deceit; Fraudulent Conveyances.*

What constitutes.

1. One who applies for and obtains credit by falsely representing that he is perfectly solvent, and responsible for his debts, and is good for his obligations, is guilty, under Code, § 4587, declaring any person a cheat and swindler who "by false representation of his own respectability, wealth, or mercantile correspondence and connections," shall obtain credit, and thereby defraud any person of money, etc.—Hathcock v. State, (Ga.) 18 S. E. 959.

2. Where goods are obtained by false representations mixed with true ones, if the false are separable from the true, and are material, and had a material influence in effecting the fraud, they alone may be alleged in the indictment or accusation, and the conviction will be upheld though the true representations constituted a material part of the inducement on which the prosecutor gave the credit and parted with his goods.—Hathcock v. State, (Ga.) 18 S. E. 959.

Evidence.

3. On a prosecution for obtaining goods on credit, and thereby defrauding the seller, by falsely representing solvency, evidence that defendant had unlimited credit with another house is irrelevant.—Hathcock v. State, (Ga.) 18 S. E. 959.

4. On a prosecution for obtaining goods on credit, and thereby defrauding the seller by falsely representing solvency, promissory notes of defendant, executed after the misrepresenta-

FRAUDS, STATUTE OF.

Enforcement of parol contract, see *Specific Performance*, 4.

Promise to answer for another's debt.

1. Where one has a statutory lien for supplies upon personal property belonging to a firm, which is sold to another firm, composed in part of the same members, and the purchasing firm, to prevent a foreclosure and sale under the lien, agrees with the creditor to pay the debt if he will grant certain indulgence, and furnish other like supplies to them for their use, and the creditor complies with his undertaking, the case is not within the statute of frauds, and he may recover of the second firm upon their contract to pay the debt of the first firm.—Wooten v. Wilcox, (Ga.) 13 S. E. 595.

Agreement relating to land.

2. Plaintiff's father conveyed land to defendant upon a parol trust to pay certain judgments, which were afterwards discharged with the proceeds of other land, which the father had intended to convey to plaintiff, with the understanding with defendant that he should convey the land held in trust by him to plaintiff. *Held*, that the agreement to convey to plaintiff, not being in writing, was void under the statute of frauds.—Dover v. Rhea, (N. C.) 13 S. E. 164.

FRAUDULENT CONVEYANCES.

See, also, *Creditors' Bill*.
Action to set aside, limitation, see *Limitation of Actions*, 5.

What constitutes.

1. An agreement between an insolvent debtor, whose land has been sold at sheriff's sale under execution, and the purchaser thereat, by which the latter gives the former a year's time to refund the purchase money with interest, and agrees on his doing so to convey to him the land, the plaintiff in *fi. fa.* not participating in the agreement, is not *per se* fraudulent as against the debtor's creditors. Nor is it rendered fraudulent by a stipulation that the debtor shall have the crop then upon the land without paying for it, nor by a stipulation that the succeeding year's crop shall be the property of the purchaser in case the debtor fails to take the land, and pay for it within the time agreed upon. Nor is it rendered fraudulent by the fact that the purchaser afterwards pays the debtor or his assigns for a release from the agreement.—Smith v. Dobbins, (Ga.) 13 S. E. 406.

2. When a course of dealings covering a period of only a few months begins between a seller and purchaser, and credit is extended by the seller on the faith of land, set forth in a statement by the purchaser to a mercantile agency, the presumption is that the land is relied on for all credit given while the dealings continued, until there is some notice or agreement to the contrary; and where the seller sells goods on the credit of such land, after conveyance thereof by the purchaser to his wife without notice to the seller, the deed is void as to the seller.—White v. Magarahan, (Ga.) 13 S. E. 509.

Consideration.

3. In the absence of a statute prohibiting preferences by an insolvent debtor, a deed by an insolvent to his wife, in consideration of the release of *bona fide* debts due from him to third persons, is valid.—Barton's Ex'r v. Brent, (Va.) 13 S. E. 29.

Knowledge of grantee.

4. In an action to set aside a deed as in fraud of the grantor's creditor, the question whether defendant had sufficient notice to put her on inquiry is not affected by the fact that after the purchase she submitted the papers to an attorney for an examination of the title, and that he pronounced it good, since it was too late then to make inquiry.—C. Aultman & Co. v. Utsey, (S. C.) 13 S. E. 848.

5. In an action to set a deed as in fraud of the grantor's creditor, whether defendant's agents had sufficient notice to put them on inquiry was a question of fact, and not of law.—C. Aultman & Co. v. Utsey, (S. C.) 13 S. E. 848.

6. Land was levied on under execution on a judgment of foreclosure, and a claim was made by one who had purchased from one O., the latter having purchased the land at a tax-sale subsequent to execution of the mortgage. Claimant admitted that he had paid defendant a considerable amount on purchasing from O. *Held*, that it was not error to charge the jury that if they believed from the evidence that defendant, for the purpose of defrauding his creditors, suffered the property to go to sale for taxes, and that O., when he received his deed, knew of such purpose, or had grounds for reasonable suspicion that it existed, and if they further believed that when the deed from O. to the claimant was executed the claimant also knew, or had grounds for reasonable suspicion, of such purpose on the part of defendant, they ought to find that the tax title was void as against the plaintiffs in *fi. fa.*—Livingston v. Wright, (Ga.) 13 S. E. 833.

Wife as grantee.

7. The fact that a husband retained possession of land conveyed by him to his wife until his death, being consistent with the nature of the marriage relation, is not a badge of fraud.—Trustees of Wadsworthville Poor School v. Bryson, (S. C.) 13 S. E. 619.

8. Defendant was the inventor of a formula for the manufacture of medicated cigarettes. A company was formed to manufacture them, and, in consideration of his furnishing his services and formula in the business, a number of the shares of the stock were issued to his wife, for which she paid nothing. Defendant was insolvent at the time of the transaction. *Held*, that such stock was subject to the payment of his debts.—Markham v. Whitehurst, (N. C.) 13 S. E. 904.

9. Though his creditors could have no lien on his skill in the manufacture of the cigarettes, and he could devote such skill to the support of his wife, yet he could not sell the formula, and agree to manufacture under it, and, by having the stock which he received in payment transferred to his wife, defeat the rights of his creditors. Osborne v. Wilkes, 13 S. E. 285, 108 N. C. 673, distinguished.—Markham v. Whitehurst, (N. C.) 13 S. E. 904.

10. M., a creditor of W., bought at execution sale a lot belonging to the latter for $7,000. In consideration of $3,000, advanced for the benefit of W.'s wife by S., her brother, and four notes for $3,000 each, signed by W. and his wife, secured by reconveyance in trust, M., in pursuance of a previous agreement with the attorney of S., conveyed the land to W.'s wife. W. and his wife conveyed the equity of redemption to S. by deed absolute upon its face to secure the payment of the $3,000 advanced. *Held*, that the transaction was not fraudulent in law, nor did the admitted facts raise a presumption of fraud; but it was proper for the court to leave the jury to determine whether the purchase was made for the husband in the wife's name in order to evade the payment of his debts, and whether she participated in the fraud, or she or her agent had notice of a fraudulent purpose to defraud the husband's creditors.—Osborne v. Wilkes, (N. C.) 13 S. E. 285.

Secret trusts.

11. Under Code N. C. § 1545, providing that fraudulent gifts, grants, etc., shall be void as to persons who "are, shall, or might be" thereby defrauded of their claims, a grant, made in contemplation of insolvency, without valuable consideration, and with the understanding that the land should be held for the benefit of the grantor, and shielded from such debts as he then owed or should incur, was void as to subsequent creditors.—Clement v. Cozart, (N. C.) 13 S. E. 862.

12. It was immaterial that the conveyance was absolute on its face, and contained no clause of defeasance.—Clement v. Cozart, (N. C.) 13 S. E. 862.

Rights of creditors.

13. Where a fraudulent grantee of property has sold such property to a *bona fide* purchaser, and realized money therefrom, the defrauded creditor may have a money recovery against the purchaser.— Ringold v. Suiter, (W. Va.) 13 S. E. 46.

14. A creditor cannot have a judgment for the recovery of money against a grantee of the debtor on mere proof that the conveyance was fraudulent.—Ringold v. Suiter, (W. Va.) 13 S. E. 46.

Right of grantor to set up illegality of conveyance.

15. Where a wife sues to recover from her husband the price of her land sold by him, which money he had retained, and, to establish her title to the land, produces a deed from her husband to herself, and the husband in his answer alleges that the deed was made in fraud of creditors, it is error for the court to reject evidence tending to prove the husband's allegation. SHEPHERD, J., dissenting.—Hart v. Hart, (N. C.) 13 S. E. 1020.

Actions to set aside.

16. The purchaser at execution sale of land of which there has been a voluntary conveyance by the judgment debtor since the debt was contracted may sue to set aside such conveyance, though he had actual notice thereof when he purchased, where the judgment creditor in whose behalf the land was sold had no notice thereof.—McGee v. Jones, (S. C.) 13 S. E. 326.

17. Where many circumstances are shown tending to prove that conveyances were made to the wife to evade the payment of a certain debt due from the husband, it is competent for him to show in rebuttal that he voluntarily allowed the judgment in favor of that creditor to be renewed after it was barred by the statute of limitation. — Osborne v. Wilkes, (N. C.) 13 S. E. 285.

18. Where, in an action by creditors to set aside as fraudulent an assignment of a life insurance policy to decedent's brothers, the defense was that the latter had theretofore paid a number of decedent's debts; that one of them, as co-executor with him of their father's estate, was obliged to pay large sums on account of his default; and that the sums so paid were a just and fair price for the assignment,—evidence as to such payments was material to prove the consideration for the assignment, and the *bona fide* character of the transaction.—Watts v. Warren, (N. C.) 13 S. E. 232.

19. In a creditor's action to set aside an assignment for fraud, a motion was made to have a preferred creditor refund to the assignee, on the ground of fraud, a payment to him as such creditor. Aside from the payment, the only evidence in support of the motion was the sworn complaint, which alleged that the payment was fraudulent, that the preferred creditor was insolvent, and a son of one and a brother of the other member of the firm which made the assignment. The members of such firm, the assignee, and the preferred creditor all denied the alleged fraud. The preferred creditor gave evidence as to his solvency, and claimed that the payment was made for an honest debt. *Held,* that the motion was properly denied.—Southern Flour Co. v. McIver, (N. C.) 13 S. E. 905.

Evidence.

20. In an action to set aside a mortgage of a stock of goods purporting to secure $1,200 as in fraud of the mortgagor's creditors, the mortgagee testified that, before and at the time of the execution of the mortgage, he loaned the mortgagee $1,000, and agreed to advance the remaining $200 afterwards, and that he estimated the value of the stock of goods at $1,200. There was other evidence that the goods were worth only $800. The mortgagee did not show where he obtained the money alleged to have been loaned, and the tax-books did not show that he owned any property during the year before or the year after the execution of the mortgage. The mortgage was not recorded for more than two months, and after the bill to set it aside had been filed. The note secured was payable 9 months after date, and there was no stipulation that it should bear interest before maturity. *Held,* that the evidence was sufficient to sustain a finding of actual fraud, which should vitiate the mortgage *in toto,* though part of the debt secured was *bona fide.*—Kea v. Epstein, (Ga.) 13 S. E. 312.

21. A debtor in Texas gave a bill of sale to a creditor in that state of his interest in his father's estate in Georgia. Before an attorney in Georgia could collect the same, the administrator was garnished by another creditor. The debtor then gave his first creditor 24 notes, aggregating the amount of his indebtedness, dated in 1887, due in 30 days, but in fact executed in February, 1888. The debtor went to Georgia ostensibly on other business, but returned without attending to it, after summonses were served upon him in a justice court on each of the 24 notes. *Held* sufficient to sustain a finding that the judgments were obtained by collusion, to defeat the rights of the garnishing creditor.—Beach v. Atkinson, (Ga.) 13 S. E. 591.

GARNISHMENT.

See, also, *Attachment; Writs.*

Property subject to.

1. Where one person takes out a policy of insurance on the goods of another, the policy is the property of him to whom it is issued, and cannot be subjected to garnishment as a liability on the part of the company, in case of loss, to the owner of the goods.—Tim v. Franklin, (Ga.) 13 S. E. 259; Levi v. Same, Id.

2. A power of attorney authorizing one to collect a fire insurance policy, payable to the assured, accompanied by oral instructions to apply the proceeds, when collected, to a debt due by the assured to the attorney in fact, does not operate as a transfer of such policy to the latter, or prevent the money due on such policy, and still in the company's hands, from being reached by a garnishment sued out in favor of another creditor of the assured.—Greenwood v. Boyd & Baxter Furniture Factory, (Ga.) 13 S. E. 128.

3. When the payee of a bill of exchange indorses it, "For deposit to the credit" of himself, the proceeds belong to him, and are subject to garnishment for his debt in the hands of a third indorsee, to whom the bill was indorsed by the second indorsee "For collection" to his own account, as the third indorsee is the mere agent for collection for the payee.—Freeman v. Exchange Bank, (Ga.) 13 S. E. 160.

Lien.

4. Code W. Va. c. 106, § 9, provides that the lien of an attachment served on a garnishee begins with the service of the attachment. Section 14 provides that if it appears on examination of the garnishee that at or after the service of the writ he was indebted to the defendant, or had in his control any goods, etc., belonging to defendant, the court may order him to pay, etc. *Held,* that an attachment served on a garnishee binds debts existing or effects in the garnishee's hands at the date of service of the attachment, as also debts arising or effects coming to the hands of the garnishee until the answer of such garnishee, but not later than such answer.—Ringold v. Suiter, (W. Va.) 13 S. E. 46.

Parties.

5. Where one person takes out a policy of insurance on the goods of another, the policy cannot be held to be the property of the owner of the goods in a garnishment proceeding without making the holder of the policy a party thereto.—Tim v. Franklin, (Ga.) 13 S. E. 259; Levi v. Same, Id.

GIFTS.

Evidence.

In order for the heir of a deceased donee to set up a deed of gift made to her by her father, it is not necessary that it should appear that the donee or her heir ever had possession of the premises, or that either of them ever had actual custody of the deed.—Blalock v. Miland, (Ga.) 18 S. E. 551.

GRAND JURY.

Powers of special jury.

Under Acts Va. 1889-90, p. 91, providing that at least seven of a regular grand jury must concur in finding an indictment in any case, while in the case of a special grand jury only five of its members need concur, there is no ground for holding that an indictment for a capital felony can be found only by a regular grand jury.—Lyles v. Commonwealth, (Va.) 18 S. E. 802.

GUARDIAN AND WARD.

Accounting.

1. Under Code N. C. § 1401, providing that "vouchers are presumptive evidence of disbursement" by a guardian, such vouchers must state with reasonable particularity their purpose, on what account they were made, and the time when made, so that it may appear that the expenditure was proper.—McLean v. Breece, (N. C.) 18 S. E. 910.

2. A decree approving the accounts of a guardian, but failing to direct how certain moneys in bank are to be disposed of, and how costs thereafter accruing are to be provided for, is not final, but interlocutory.—Whitehead v. Bradley, (Va.) 18 S. E. 195.

Sale of ward's realty.

3. A purchaser at a void guardian's sale cannot recover the land from one holding the legal title, and he cannot complain of a decree directing a sale of the property, and a return to him of the purchase money, with interest.—Dooley v. Bell, (Ga.) 18 S. E. 284.

4. Where land is sold by one professing to act as guardian, who in fact is not, for the reason that his appointment was void, the sale is likewise void, and passes no title to the purchaser, although he buys in good faith, and without actual notice of any defect in the guardian's appointment or his authority to sell.—Dooley v. Bell, (Ga.) 18 S. E. 284.

5. Code Va. § 2609, provides that the circuit court may, on the application of a guardian, order the sale of an infant's real estate, when it shall be necessary for his proper maintenance and education, and may also, from time to time, make such decrees as are proper to secure the due expenditure of the proceeds. *Held*, that such authority must be given before, and not after, such expenditures are made; and therefore, when a guardian, without first obtaining an order for that purpose, makes such expenditures, the court has no authority afterwards to ratify the same.—Whitehead v. Bradley, (Va.) 18 S. E. 195.

6. Where the purchase money, under an order directing the sale of an infant's real estate, is paid to an unbonded commissioner, who, without previous sanction of the court, pays the same to the infant's guardian, and a petition is then filed against the purchasers to show cause why the property should not be resold, and alleging the guardian's insolvency, an objection that the remedy against the guardian and his sureties was not first exhausted comes too late when made for the first time in the appellate court.—Whitehead v. Bradley, (Va.) 18 S. E. 195.

Harmless Error.

Hearsay Evidence.

HIGHWAYS.

Dedication.

1. A railroad company owned a right of way of 100 feet on each side of its track. Afterwards a city was laid out, the principal street of which crossed the track. The city had not acquired the right to use the property of the railroad company for the street either by deed or by prescription, but the company acquiesced for a number of years in its use, and maintained a crossing of the track for the use of the city. The court below held that the conduct of the company amounted to a dedication of the street to the city, and enjoined the company from constructing switching tracks across the street, on the ground that it would inconvenience the public. *Held*, that the court did not abuse its discretion in granting the injunction.—Brunswick & W. R. Co. v. City of Waycross, (Ga.) 18 S. E. 835.

Establishment—Appeal.

2. An appeal from an order of the county commissioners establishing a public road, and directing a jury to be summoned to lay it out and assess damages, may be taken as well after the confirmation of the report of the jury as before.—Lambe v. Love, (N. C.) 18 S. E. 773.

Levy of road-tax.

3. Under the general law of Virginia, the board of supervisors of Pulaski county were given authority to assess and levy a road tax on property in the county, including the town of Pulaski, not only on the fourth Monday of July, but, if not done then, as soon thereafter as practicable during the tax year. Act of February 22, 1890, which took effect from its passage, made the town a separate and distinct road-district of the county, and provided that no road-tax should be levied on the property within the limits of the town, except by the town council, which tax should be expended on streets and roads within the limits of the town, under the direction and supervision of the council. *Held*, that the act of February, 1890, repealed the general law in so far as the latter authorized the board of supervisors to levy a road-tax on property in the town, and after its passage they had no authority to levy such tax for the tax year beginning on the first Monday of July, 1889, and ending the first Monday of July, 1890.—Bertha Zinc Co. v. Board Sup'rs Pulaski County, (Va.) 18 S. E. 740.

Failure to work on road.

4. A warrant simply charged that defendant willfully refused to attend and work on the public road after being lawfully warned, contrary to the statute, etc., but did not negative the payment of one dollar in discharge of his liability to perform the labor. *Held*, that a motion in arrest of judgment should have been allowed.—State v. Neal, (N. C.) 18 S. E. 784.

5. In proceedings before a justice of the peace, a warrant that charges that defendant was liable and duly assigned to work on a public road specified; that he was within the ages of 18 and 45 years; that he was duly summoned to work on that road at the time specified; and that he willfully and unlawfully failed and omitted to work as he was bound to do, etc.,—sufficiently discloses an offense, under Act N. C. 1885, c. 134.—State v. Baker, (N. C.) 18 S. E. 214.

6. Where, under a road law (Acts N. C. 1885, c. 134, § 8) requiring the township trustees to "divide their respective townships into suitable road-districts," and to "furnish each supervisor with a plat of his district," it appears that no new division was made, but that the trustees "adopted the districts of the old board" of supervisors, created under Code, § 2014, "making such alterations as they thought advisable, allot-

ting certain farms to a section," and that no map or plat was furnished to the supervisors, such division into sections, and assignment of the hands liable to road service, is sufficiently definite to fix the duty and liability of the defendant for a refusal to work it.—State v. Baker, (N. C.) 13 S. E. 214.

7. It appeared from the evidence of the supervisor that he personally notified defendant to work on the road; that he told him to meet him "at Hunter's branch to work the road" on the mornings specified, but without mentioning any road; that defendant had previously received a like notice to work the same road, and had worked as directed. Held, that the notice, though informal, was sufficient.—State v. Baker, (N. C.) 13 S. E. 214.

Obstruction.

8. An indictment charging an obstruction of "a certain public square and common public highway," and stating facts descriptive of its location, bounds, the uses to which it is put, and how and where it was obstructed, clearly charges but a single offense.—State v. Eastman, (N. C.) 13 S. E. 1019.

9. The public square of a county around and about the court-house is a highway, and to obstruct it is indictable under Code, § 2065, inflicting a penalty for the obstruction of highways.—State v. Eastman, (N. C.) 13 S. E. 1019.

10. An indictment against a railroad company charged it with obstructing a public highway by placing in and across the highway certain plank. The evidence showed that the company's road where it crossed the highway was about 10 inches above the highway, and that one of the planks used to raise the highway to a level with the railroad had slid down, leaving a hole about eight inches deep. Held, that the variance was fatal.—State v. Roanoke Railroad & Lumber Co., (N. C.) 13 S. E. 719.

Defective highways.

11. Where one receives injuries from defects in a road which is a deviation from the regular highway laid out by the overseer of the roadhands at the suggestion of the neighbors, and without the authority of the county commissioners, who alone are empowered by law to alter highways, he cannot recover against the county under Gen. St. S. C. § 1087, which provides that "any person who shall receive bodily injury * * * through a defect in the repair of a high way * * * may recover in an action against the county," etc.—Hill v. Laurens County, (S. C.) 13 S. E. 318.

HOMESTEAD.

Rights of divorced wife in, see Divorce, 7.

In general.

1. Possession by the husband with the wife, he being the head of the family, is presumptively his possession; and, if the premises occupied be homestead property, the creditor of the wife is chargeable with constructive notice of its homestead character, though the formal paper title be in the wife.—Broome v. Davis, (Ga.) 13 S. E. 749.

2. Homestead property cannot be charged with claims against it by attachment, and a sale of it under attachment for such claims is void.—Burns v. Lewis, (Ga.) 13 S. E. 123.

In partnership property.

3. A homestead may lawfully be assigned to a partner out of partnership property; and, where all the partners gave their assent at the time of the allotment, a creditor of the partnership cannot attack the validity of the proceedings, and subject the land assigned to a judgment in his favor.—McMillan v. Parker, (N. C.) 13 S. E. 764.

Rights of wife and children.

4. Where a homestead is set apart to a mother and her children, on the ground that they are minors, the fact that thereafter, and before he came of age, one of the children became imbecile and dependent, will not keep the homestead alive after the mother's death, and the attainment of their majority by all the children.—Neal v. Brookhan, (Ga.) 13 S. E. 283.

5. Const. N. C. art. 10, § 2, provides that "every homestead, * * * not exceeding in value one thousand dollars, to be selected" by the owner, or, in lieu thereof, any town lot, with the buildings thereon of like value, owned and occupied by him, shall be exempt from debt; and section 3 provides that the homestead, after the death of the owner, shall be so exempt during the minority of any of his children. Held, that when a man dies without having had a homestead allotted, and dower is assigned to the widow, the minor children are not entitled to homestead in lands covered by the dower. Following Watts v. Leggett, 66 N. C. 197.—Graves v. Hines, (N. C.) 13 S. E. 15.

6. A homestead was set apart to a widow, as the head of a family consisting of herself and a minor child, out of her deceased husband's estate. The homestead was subsequently sold by order of court, and one claiming under the adult heirs of the husband brought an action against the purchaser to contest his title as to the share of such heirs which would accrue to them after the widow's death. Held that, as the widow did not take the homestead as her own individual share of the realty belonging to her husband's estate, evidence was not admissible to show that the homestead was not more than her own interest in the estate would have amounted to.—Fleetwood v. Lord, (Ga.) 13 S. E. 574.

Conveyance.

7. Land paid for with homestead land is homestead property, though the deed be taken in the name of the wife, when it should have been taken in the name of the husband; and the homestead right can be asserted against the wife's mortgagee, with notice of the homestead character of the land.—Broome v. Davis, (Ga.) 13 S. E. 749.

8. The fact that a deed by a husband and wife recites on its face that the property had been set apart as a homestead will not defeat the deed as a conveyance of the wife's prior title to the premises, if it does not appear to whom or as whose property it had been so set apart, and if it was executed in another state, and no actual occupation of the property as a homestead then or previously is shown, and if it does not appear that the grantors then or afterwards resided in Georgia.—Palmer v. Smith, (Ga.) 13 S. E. 956.

9. Code Ga. § 2025, declares that the sale of a homestead under an order of court "shall operate to pass to the purchaser the entire interest and title of the beneficiaries in the exempted property, and also the entire interest and title owned before the exemption was made by the party out of whose estate the property was so exempted." Held that, where a homestead has been set apart to a widow, as the head of a family consisting of herself and minor child, out of her deceased husband's estate, and the adult heirs have acquiesced in the same, a subsequent sale of the homestead, under said section 2025, transfers to the purchaser not only the title of the widow and minor child, but that of the estate, so as to bar the rights of the adult heirs, and all persons claiming under them; their rights being transferred to the property in which the proceeds of the sale were invested.—Fleetwood v. Lord, (Ga.) 13 S. E. 574.

10. Where a debtor, after judgment has been rendered against him, conveyed by voluntary deed land in which he is entitled to a homestead, (Code Ga. § 2040,) but has never parted with possession, he is still entitled to the exemption as against a sale of the land by virtue of the judgment; no present interest or estate in land beyond that implied in the fact of possession being requisite to sustain the claim of exemption, as against a debt or lien inferior to the exemption right.—Pendleton v. Hooper, (Ga.) 13 S. E. 318.

11. Suicide is an unlawful act, and when one, in attempting to commit suicide, takes the life of another, it is murder.—State v. Levelle, (S. C.) 13 S. E. 319.

12. On a murder trial it appeared that defendant was engaged in building a fence on his land, which he had removed from the line between him and deceased, contrary to the prohibition of the latter, although the fence was owned by defendant. Deceased's son testified for the state that deceased came up to the draw-bars, and an altercation occurred, in which the lie was given and returned, and that thereupon defendant drew his pistol, and shot deceased, who was unarmed and standing still. The defense proved that, as soon as the lie was passed, deceased assaulted defendant, inflicting injuries upon him with a knife, and that he retreated, when thus attacked, about nine steps from the draw-bars to a fence, and, while warding blows from the knife, drew his pistol, and fired the fatal shot. Held error to instruct that defendant was guilty of murder if deceased was going from the draw-bars towards his home, and defendant, advancing towards him, drew a pistol, which he had concealed about his person, and shot him, he neither making nor attempting to make an assault, since there was no evidence that defendant either pursued the deceased, or had concealed the pistol.—Hash v. Commonwealth, (Va.) 13 S. E. 398.

Manslaughter.

13. No words, however opprobrious, furnish sufficient provocation to reduce a killing with a deadly weapon from murder to manslaughter.—State v. Levelle, (S. C.) 13 S. E. 319.

14. On trial for homicide, the evidence for the state made out a case of murder. The evidence for defendant showed that defendant, on being run over by two men at a dance, told them to watch out or he would cripple somebody; that a woman thereupon hit at him several times with a torch, and, on defendant's making a motion as if to strike her, deceased came up with a pistol, and said he would take her part; that deceased snapped the pistol at defendant, and shot at him twice after he got into the yard; that defendant came back into the house, and, when deceased advanced on him with pistol in hand, dropped on his knees and shot deceased. Held, that the evidence warranted a verdict of voluntary manslaughter.—Jones v. State, (Ga.) 13 S. E. 591.

15. Defendant and deceased met after work hours to fight in accordance with an agreement made earlier in the day, when deceased had dunned defendant for money and cursed him. The wound from which deceased died was a cut in the bowels. Besides this, he received a cut in the right shoulder, and one in the left arm, all made with a knife. Defendant received some bruises, and had the skin on his head torn somewhat, but was not severely injured. There was no witness at the commencement of the fight, which started behind a shed. The evidence for the state was that when first seen deceased was running with nothing in his hands, and defendant was running after him with a knife in his hand; that when defendant overtook deceased the latter picked up a stone, and threw it at defendant; that deceased slipped and fell, and defendant jumped on him and cut him. Defendant testified that when they met for the fight deceased hit him on the head with a plow-point, and he fell, and deceased got on him, and he then cut deceased; that he then ran, and deceased threatened to knock his brains out if he made another move; that deceased hit him on the shoulder with a rock, knocking him down; and that he then cut deceased in the bowels, as the latter reached for some other implement; and that he then got up and ran, with deceased after him. Held, that the evidence was sufficient to sustain a verdict of voluntary manslaughter.—Robertson v. State, (Ga.) 13 S. E. 696.

Self-defense.

16. On a murder trial it appeared that defendant was engaged in building a fence on his land, which he had removed from the line between him and deceased, contrary to the prohibition of the latter, although the fence was owned by defendant. Held, that the removal of the fence, notwithstanding the prohibition of deceased, was not an unlawful act; and it was error to charge that if defendant built it upon the line, so that it rested partly on the land of each, and it had been used as a line fence for a number of years, and deceased had notified defendant not to remove it, and that defendant, arming himself with a pistol, went to the fence to remove it by force, if necessary, and did remove it, he was guilty of an unlawful act, and if, while removing it, a conflict arose on account thereof, in which defendant killed deceased, then defendant cannot avail himself of the plea of necessary self-defense.—Hash v. Commonwealth, (Va.) 13 S. E. 398.

17. It is error to charge that "a man cannot in any case justify the killing of another upon the pretense of self-defense unless he be without fault in bringing the necessity of so doing upon himself," since the instruction does not distinguish between controversies provoked in order to furnish a pretext for killing and those provoked without such felonious intent.—Hash v. Commonwealth, (Va.) 13 S. E. 398.

18. It was error to refuse to charge that the accused must have been without fault in bringing on the combat, and must not have provoked it, or produced the occasion for the killing of deceased; but if he was so at fault, or provoked the combat or produced the occasion in order to have a pretext for the killing, yet, if he fairly declined the combat by retreating as far as he could, and then killed deceased in self-defense, he is not guilty.—Hash v. Commonwealth, (Va.) 13 S. E. 398.

19. Where an instruction, asked by defendant, that if deceased had threatened to kill him, and the threats were made known to him, and if, before the fatal shot was fired, deceased did some overt act from which defendant could reasonably infer that he intended to execute the threats, the killing would be excusable homicide, is modified by the insertion of the clause, "and that defendant killed deceased to prevent him from killing him, or doing him great bodily harm," defendant cannot complain, since the modification could not injure him. FAUNTLEROY and HINTON, JJ., dissenting.—Watson v. Commonwealth, (Va.) 13 S. E. 29.

20. An instruction, asked by defendant, that if he went to the house where the killing occurred to stop a quarrel between deceased and deceased's wife, and to demand an apology for slanderous words previously spoken by deceased, and if, when he attempted to do so, deceased attacked him with a deadly weapon, the killing of deceased is not murder, is properly modified by requiring that defendant shall have gone to the house for the purpose of "peaceably" stopping the quarrel, and demanding an apology. FAUNTLEROY and HINTON, JJ., dissenting.—Watson v. Commonwealth, (Va.) 13 S. E. 29.

21. Code Ga. § 4637, provides that, in a criminal case, the prisoner shall have a right to make a statement, not under oath, in his defense, to have such force as the jury may see fit to give it, and that the jury may believe such statement in preference to the sworn testimony in the case. Held, that on a prosecution for murder, where the prisoner's statement, if true, makes a case from which the jury may conclude that the killing was in self-defense, though the sworn testimony is inconsistent therewith, it is error to refuse an instruction on self-defense, requested in writing at the proper time by defendant's counsel. Hayden v. State, 69 Ga. 782, followed. Darby v. State, 79 Ga. 64, 3 S. E. 663, distinguished.—Underwood v. State, (Ga.) 13 S. E. 856.

Assault with intent to kill.

22. Where the testimony of defendant and that of the other witnesses upon a trial for assault with intent to kill failed to show that defendant shot at a person under the fear that such person was about to commit a felonious assault upon him,

it was unnecessary for the court to charge that defendant was not justified in shooting unless he had reasonable grounds to apprehend that such an assault was about to be committed.—Brantley v. State, (Ga.) 13 S. E. 957.

23. In a prosecution for a secret assault, the prosecutor testified that he was fired on in the evening by some one standing behind a fence six feet distant, whose size, height, complexion, and appearance were those of defendant; that at the time of the shooting it was possible for witness to see a man plainly 50 yards distant; and that the shirt worn by his assailant was the same as that worn by defendant at the preliminary hearing, two days afterwards. It was also shown that the tracks made by the assailant corresponded with the shoes worn by defendant. *Held*, that the evidence identifying defendant was sufficient to warrant its submission to the jury, and that a verdict of guilty would not be disturbed.—State v. Telfair, (N. C.) 13 S. E. 726.

Indictment.

24. A joint indictment for murder is sufficiently definite as to the persons charged with the crime, where a comma is inserted between the names of defendants, although the word "and" is omitted.—Hash v. Commonwealth, (Va.) 13 S. E. 398.

Evidence.

25. Upon an indictment in the form prescribed by Code W. Va. 1887, c. 144, § 1, for murder, which does not prescribe any mode of killing, the state may prove any manner of killing or different manners of killing.—State v. Morgan, (W. Va.) 13 S. E. 385.

26. At the trial of an indictment for murder, a witness testified to the good character of defendant for peaceableness, and that he had never heard of defendant having a difficulty before. *Held*, that he might be asked on cross-examination if he had never heard of defendant's shooting any one before, and if he had never heard of his shooting a man in another state.—Ozburn v. State, (Ga.) 13 S. E. 247.

27. On indictment for murder, where defendant testifies that he killed deceased because he had spoken insultingly of his wife, he may be asked on cross-examination whether the woman was lawfully married to him. FAUNTLEROY and HINTON, JJ., dissenting.— Watson v. Commonwealth, (Va.) 13 S. E. 22.

28. Proof that deceased died from wounds on the left side of his head is not a material variance from an allegation that the wounds were on the right side.—Custis v. Commonwealth, (Va.) 13 S. E. 73.

29. On a trial for murder, verbal directions given by deceased to his brother to follow accused, and see that he did not leave the road in which the homicide shortly afterwards occurred, and over which deceased and his brother were about to pass, being in evidence, the state, in order to show that this request was meant as a precaution for defense, and not as a measure of attack, may prove that it followed and was connected with a suggestion made by a third person that the accused would "waylay the boys tonight," though the accused was not present, and did not hear the conversation.—Ponder v. State, (Ga.) 13 S. E. 464.

30. A question put to a physician examined as an expert, whether it was possible for deceased to have inflicted on himself, in a scuffle with defendant, the knife wound of which he died, is properly excluded, as it calls for the opinion of a witness in a matter requiring no special skill or knowledge.—State v. Bradley, (S. C.) 13 S. E. 315.

31. On an indictment for murder, where the evidence for the state is entirely circumstantial, evidence is admissible as to the unnatural behavior of defendant shortly after the homicide took place.—State v. Brabham, (N. C.) 13 S. E. 217.

32. Where it is shown that deceased was killed with an iron coupling-pin, and a witness has testified that he saw a man who looked like defendant drop the pin near the place of the homicide, and shortly after its occurrence, evidence is admissible that such a pin was seen near defendant's house the day before the homicide, which shortly disappeared therefrom.—State v. Brabham, (N. C.) 13 S. E. 217.

—— Dying declarations.

33. Dying declarations are admissible, on an indictment for murder, where they indicate that deceased fully expected to die, and where he in fact did die a few hours after making them.— State v. Bradley, (S. C.) 13 S. E 315.

Instructions.

34. On a murder trial, when the court fails to charge fully, to the satisfaction of counsel for the accused, on the prisoner's statement, attention should be called to the omission.—Pool v. State, (Ga.) 13 S. E. 556.

35. On a murder trial, a request to charge with reference to doubt, with no qualification as to the doubt being reasonable, was properly refused.—Pool v. State, (Ga.) 13 S. E. 556.

36. On a murder trial, it was not error to decline to charge the abstract proposition that, when the conduct of the accused is equally susceptible of two constructions, the one in favor of the hypothesis of innocence is the one that ought to be adopted, there being no conduct in evidence specially requiring the application of this principle.—Pool v. State, (Ga.) 13 S. E. 556.

37. On a murder trial, the court is not bound to instruct the jury that, when the proof in favor of defendant is stronger and more direct than the evidence against him, there is room for doubt, and he ought not to be convicted.—Pool v. State, (Ga.) 13 S. E. 556.

38. A charge which is based upon and recites the evidence for the state is erroneous in failing to recite that of the defense also, and to give an hypothetical alternative instruction based thereon.—Hash v. Commonwealth, (Va.) 13 S. E. 398.

39. At the trial of an indictment for murder, defendant requested the court to give in charge to the jury the sections of the Code relating to the law of voluntary manslaughter and of justifiable homicide, and the court complied with the request as made, except as to justifiable homicide; it plainly appearing that in no view of the case was the law of justifiable homicide applicable. *Held*, that the omission was not error.— Ozburn v. State, (Ga.) 13 S. E. 247.

40. On a trial for murder, where the judge recharges the jury without verifying for himself the prisoner's presence, and it afterwards appears that the prisoner was in an adjoining room, in the custody of an officer, and did not know that the jury was being recharged, and knowledge did not come to him until after such recharge was concluded, a new trial should be granted.—Wilson v. State, (Ga.) 13 S. E. 566.

Arguments of counsel.

41. The jury in a case of murder having the right to avert the death penalty by recommending imprisonment for life as a punishment, it is not improper for the prosecuting counsel to argue before them the propriety of their making such recommendation.—Ozburn v. State, (Ga.) 13 S. E. 247.

Recommendation to mercy.

42. The jury having found a verdict for the offense of murder, and desiring to recommend imprisonment in the penitentiary for life, it was proper for the court, in the presence of the jury, and at their request, to allow this recommendation to be put in proper form by the solicitor general, and thus prepare the verdict for signature by the foreman.—Pool v. State, (Ga.) 13 S. E. 556.

New trial.

43. A statement in the motion for a new trial that the court allowed evidence to go to the jury, over objection of defendant's counsel, relating to a subsequent difficulty with another party, without specifying what the evidence was, is not sufficiently full and certain as a basis for assigning error; more especially where, according to

the testimony of one of the state's witnesses as set forth in the brief of evidence, the difficulty with the third person was apparently a part of the *res gestæ* of the homicide, and material in determining whether the shooting was willful or accidental.—Pool v. State, (Ga.) 13 S. E. 556.

HUSBAND AND WIFE.

See, also, *Divorce; Dower; Homestead; Marriage.*
Allowance to widow out of husband's estate, see *Executors and Administrators,* 26.
Competency as witnesses, see *Witness,* 2.
Conveyances to, survivorship, see *Tenancy in Common and Joint Tenancy,* 1.

Estate by entireties—Liability for husband's debts.

1. Under Code N. C. § 1840, which provides that no land belonging to the wife shall be disposed of by the husband for his own life or any less term without her assent, and that no interest of the husband shall be subject to sale to satisfy any execution obtained against him, a tract of land held by the husband and wife by entireties cannot be sold on execution against the husband so as to pass any title during their joint lives, or as against the wife if she survives.—Bruce v. Sugg, (N. C.) 13 S. E. 790.

Liability of wife—Contract before marriage.

2. Where a *feme sole* employed plaintiff, and after her marriage died, plaintiff has an action against her estate before a justice of the peace for services rendered before the marriage.—Beville v. Cox, (N. C.) 13 S. E. 800.

Wife's choses in action.

3. Under Laws N. Y. 1884, c. 381, providing that a married woman may contract as if she were a *feme sole* except where the contract is made with her husband, she is bound by the indorsement of a note executed by her husband to her order, and by her indorsed for his accommodation. Following Bank v. Sniffen, 7 N. Y. S. 520.—Taylor v. Sharp, (N. C.) 13 S. E. 138.

4. Where in a state in which the common law obtains, the husband permits his wife to relinquish her right to her choses in action, and unites with her in a disposition of them, he constitutes himself a trustee for her benefit in respect to the property, and cannot recover it back from the person to whom he and she have paid it over on the ground that it was his by right of marriage.—Taylor v. Sikes, (N. C.) 13 S. E. 136.

Wife's separate estate.

5. Where a wife's earnings were allowed to accumulate with her employer for the express purpose of providing a fund for the purchase of a home for her, and the husband, both before and after the purchase, always spoke of the money as hers, and never on any occasion as his own, the inference is irresistible that he had given it to her, though, under the law as it then stood, it could not have become hers in any other way; and the fact that the property purchased with such earnings was taken in the husband's name is not sufficient to overcome the undisputed evidence of his declarations that it was paid for with his wife's money.—Grantham v. Grantham, (S. C.) 13 S. E. 675.

6. A sealed instrument, executed in 1862 by a husband to an administrator acknowledging the receipt of money as his wife's share of her parents' estate, which he bound himself to return to her to dispose of as she saw fit, sufficiently shows an intent to create a separate estate in the money in his wife, and his marital rights do not attach thereto.—Trustees of Wadsworthville Poor School v. Bryson, (S. C.) 13 S. E. 619.

7. A husband who paid for land with his own money, and took a conveyance in 1881, describing himself in the deed as trustee for his wife, acquired the property for her, and it became her sep-

arate estate, both legally and equitably.—Payton v. Payton, (Ga.) 13 S. E. 127.

—— Charges on.

8. A bond given by a married woman to secure the payment of money borowed by the husband for his own use is void, and cannot be enforced as against her separate estate.—Griffin v. Earle, (S. C.) 13 S. E. 473.

9. A husband, representing himself as agent of his wife, made an application in the name of the wife for a loan to be secured by a bond and mortgage upon her property, which were accordingly delivered to the lender by the husband, who received the money. The wife admitted the execution of the bond and mortgage. *Held,* that the husband was acting as agent for his wife, and the lender was justified in presuming that the loan was for the benefit of her separate estate.—Hibernia Sav. Inst. v. Luhn, (S. C.) 13 S. E. 357.

10. Where a married woman, either directly or through her agent, borrows money, the money so borrowed becomes at once a part of her separate estate, and her contract to repay the same is a contract with reference to her separate estate, which may be enforced, unless it is shown that the lender had notice that the money was not for her use.—Hibernia Sav. Inst. v. Luhn, (S. C.) 13 S. E. 357.

11. Under Code N. C. § 1826, providing that no woman during her coverture shall, without her husband's written consent, make any contract to affect her real estate, except for her necessary personal expenses, etc., unless she be a free trader, a married woman is not liable for labor and material furnished for her real estate under her husband's contract, although the evidence tends to show that she was aware of said contract, and ratified and approved it. Farthing v. Shields, 106 N. C. 289, 10 S. E. 998, followed.—Weir v. Page, (N. C.) 13 S. E. 773.

—— Conveyance.

12. A conveyance of land, executed by a married woman in payment of her husband's debt, though declared by the statute absolutely void, is only so as against her, or her privies, and upon her or their election to treat it as void; coverture being a personal privilege, which is not available in behalf of a stranger to her title.—Palmer v. Smith, (Ga.) 13 S. E. 956.

13. Act Va. April 4, 1876, provides that a married woman shall have power to make a contract for the disposition of her separate estate, provided her husband shall join therein. The law in force March 1, 1880, provided that if the wife, "on being examined privily and apart from her husband, and having the writing fully explained to her, acknowledged the same to be her act, and declared that she had willingly executed it, and does not retract it, such privy examination, acknowledgment, and declaration shall thereupon be recorded," etc. *Held,* that a certificate reciting that a husband and wife, who executed a deed, "personally appeared before the undersigned, * * * and acknowledged the same to be their act and deed, the said" wife "being examined separate and apart from her husband, to the effect that she signed the said deed willingly, and that she does not wish to retract from it," though insufficient to render the deed a valid instrument of conveyance, still renders it a valid executory contract of sale.—Virginia Coal & Iron Co. v. Roberson, (Va.) 13 S. E. 350.

Contracts of wife.

14. Where a married woman, not being a free trader, carries on the business of manufacturing on her own property, she may employ the husband as her agent to manage the business, and the fact that she employs him raises no presumption of a purpose to defraud his creditors, but it is competent, in trying an issue of fraud, to show his manner of conducting the business. — Osborne v. Wilkes, (N. C.) 13 S. E. 285.

15. A married woman cannot make any valid contract of suretyship, but she can enter into an

occupying her property, of which he was in possession when she separated from him.—Payton v. Payton, (Ga.) 13 S. E. 127.

7. A majority of the complainants having voted in favor of the approval of a local school law, and all of them having acquiesced in the result of the election until after a school was established and put into operation, an interlocutory injunction restraining the collection of a tax authorized by the local law, and levied for supporting the public school system provided for by said law, is properly denied.—Irvin v. Gregory, (Ga.) 13 S. E. 120.

8. A temporary injunction restraining the construction of a side track for a steam railway in the streets of a city may be granted at the instance of a citizen alleging special damage to his land in the vicinity of the nuisance, and, though the evidence be conflicting as to whether he will sustain special damage or not, the discretion of the judge in granting the injunction will not be controlled unless abused.—Savannah & W. R. Co. v. Woodruff, (Ga.) 13 S. E. 156.

9. It is no legal bar to an injunction restraining the construction of side-tracks in the streets that plaintiff may have acquired his title to adjacent property from collateral motives, and very recently before the work complained of began.—Savannah & W. R. Co. v. Woodruff, (Ga.) 13 S. E. 156.

Pleading.

10. Where a petition by the manufacturer of a certain medicine to enjoin a person who owned a large quantity thereof, which had been in a burned building, alleged that the medicine had a large sale; that it was composed of vegetable substances, and that, by reason of the great heat to which it had been subjected, its medicinal properties were dissipated, and that the sale thereof under petitioner's trade-mark would cause great damage to petitioner's business; but failed to allege that defendant was insolvent, or to show wherein petitioner would suffer irreparable injury, or wherein the medicine had lost its virtue,—there was no abuse of discretion in denying the injunction.—Swift Specific Co. v. Jacobs, (Ga.) 13 S. E. 643.

11. One against whom an injunction is prayed may in his answer set up that he did the acts complained of as agent for another, and this is no cause for striking his answer.—Cobb v. Hogue, (Ga.) 13 S. E. 633.

—— Verification.

12. The refusal by a judge of the superior court to hear and determine a petition for injunction, and the appointment of a receiver, before the same has been verified as required by law, was not error.—Boykin v. Epstein, (Ga.) 13 S. E. 15.

13. Though Acts 1887, p. 64, requires a petition for an injunction and a receiver to be verified, yet, where the verification is imperfect, as where it is only on information and belief, the deficiency may be supplied by affidavits at the hearing in case the presiding judge shall think proper, in the exercise of his discretion, to proceed on the defective verification. — Martin v. Burgwyn, (Ga.) 13 S. E. 958.

Practice.

14. After a full hearing on an application for temporary injunction, and after the judge has announced his purpose to deny the injunction, plaintiff still has the right to dismiss his bill.—Bryant v. Jones, (Ga.) 13 S. E. 636.

15. It is discretionary with the judge sitting at chambers, upon an application for injunction, to reopen the case for more testimony, upon discovery of additional witnesses by one of the parties after argument, and while holding up the matter for decision.—Electric Ry. Co. v. Savannah, F. & W. Ry. Co., (Ga.) 13 S. E. 512.

16. The fact that some of the defendants in a suit for an injunction failed to answer does not make it an abuse of the court's discretion to refuse the injunction as to all.—Cobb v. Hogue, (Ga.) 13 S. E. 633.

17. Error cannot be predicated on an order in chambers refusing an injunction which does not decide the merits of the main case, though the reason for the refusal was that, according to the court's view of the merits, there was no ground for the injunction.—Sease v. Dobson, (S. C.) 13 S. E. 530.

—— Dissolution.

18. Where a creditor files a bill attacking the validity of an assignment for the benefit of creditors on the ground that a preferred claim to the debtor's mother is fictitious, and that the mother was in fact a secret partner, and obtains an injunction against the payment of that claim, but fails for more than a year to adduce any evidence to substantiate the charges of the bill, which are specifically denied by the answer setting out how the debt was contracted, the injunction is properly dissolved upon the motion of the preferred creditor.—Motley v. Frank, (Va.) 13 S. E. 26.

—— Appeal.

19. An appeal from the granting of a petition for an injunction against the sale of goods by a trustee and the appointment of a receiver, by a judge of the court of appeals, will not lie, especially where the property is in the hands of the receiver, and no motion was made below to dissolve the injunction, and no proofs taken. Per LACY and RICHARDSON, JJ., dissenting.—Fredenheim v. Rohr, (Va.) 13 S. E. 266.

In Pais.

See Estoppel, 8–9.

INSANITY.

Accounting by guardian.

1. Where a committee of an insane person received a trust fund in gold or its equivalent in 1857, and retained it in his possession, he thereby became a debtor of the estate, and could not allege, in defense to an action for accounting, that a portion of it was lost by an investment in Confederate bonds in 1864, although at that time such bonds were current in the community.—Clark v. Crout, (S. C.) 13 S. E. 602.

2. Where a trust fund in the hands of a committee was not exhausted, a counter-claim for the lunatic's support was properly disallowed on an accounting.—Clark v. Crout, (S. C.) 13 S. E. 602.

3. In North Carolina, in an action to settle the account of the guardian of a lunatic, the facts as to each item must be shown, and it must appear that all expenditures were legal.—McLean v. Breece, (N. C.) 13 S. E. 910.

Sale of lunatic's property.

4. Only so much of the property of a lunatic as exceeds the amount necessary for the support of his family will be sold by order of court.—McLean v. Breece, (N. C.) 13 S. E. 910.

INSOLVENCY.

See, also, Assignment for Benefit of Creditors.

Who entitled to benefits of act.

1. The insolvent trader's act, (Code, § 3149a et seq.,) providing for closing up an insolvent firm of traders, and the appointment of a receiver, does not apply where the firm has been dissolved, and has ceased to carry on business, before the petition is filed.—Stillwell v. Savannah Grocery Co., (Ga.) 13 S. E. 963.

2. A merchant, whose store has been closed and whose stock has been seized by the sheriff in proceedings to foreclose a chattel mortgage, is not a trader, within the meaning of the Georgia traders' act of 1881, which authorizes the appointment of a receiver of traders unable to pay their debts on demand, and the closing up of their business, at the suit of their creditors.—Hobbs v. Sheffield, (Ga.) 13 S. E. 686.

Action on policy—Limitation.

12. A condition in a policy, that no suit against the insurer shall be sustained unless commenced "within 12 months" next after the loss, is not in contravention of Code N. C. § 3076, which forbids the insurer to limit the term within which suit shall be brought "to a period less than one year."—Muse v. London Assur. Corp., (N. C.) 13 S. E. 94.

—— Evidence.

13. In an action on a policy of fire insurance covering a stock of tobacco, a question propounded by defendant to a witness as to what commission he was to receive if he sold plaintiff's tobacco is properly excluded as irrelevant. RICHARDSON, J., dissenting.—Wytheville Ins. & Bkg. Co. v. Stultz, (Va.) 13 S. E. 77.

14. In an action on an insurance policy the refusal to allow the defendant on cross-examination to ask a witness, who has previously testified that he had been employed as watchman, how much he was paid for his services, is not error, as the jury cannot measure the watchman's diligence by the amount of his pay, and the only inquiry is whether he was in fact so employed.—Virginia Fire & Marine Ins. Co. v. Buck, (Va.) 13 S. E. 973.

15. An insurance company has no right, in an action on a policy, to inquire whether a certain person had obtained "other insurance" for the plaintiff in violation of a provision of the policy, without having first established that the said person was the plaintiff's agent, or at least satisfied the court that it would subsequently do so.—Virginia Fire & Marine Ins. Co. v. Buck, (Va.) 13 S. E. 973.

—— Submission of special issue.

16. There was no error in refusing to submit a special issue as to whether the fact that additional insurance was taken was made known to the company before the loss, as such inquiry was immaterial where the defense was that the condition in the policy forbidding such insurance was waived.—Grubbs v. North Carolina Home Ins. Co., (N. C.) 13 S. E. 236.

—— Damages.

17. There is no error in an instruction that the measure of damages is the fair cash value of goods at the time and place of the fire.—Grubbs v. North Carolina Home Ins. Co., (N. C.) 13 S. E. 236.

Accident insurance.

18. If both parties engage willingly in a personal rencounter, it is a mutual combat or fight, and death resulting therefrom is not included in a policy of accident insurance which excepts from the risk death or injury which may have been caused by fighting; and it makes no difference, in such case, whether the slayer was sane or insane.—Grosham v. Equitable Life & Acc. Ins. Co., (Ga.) 13 S. E. 752.

Mutual benefit insurance—Forfeiture of membership.

19. In an action on a certificate of membership binding the insured to pay such assessment as should be levied and required by the supreme commandery, the declaration alleged that an unpaid assessment was one of which the insured had no notice whatever, and also that under the charter and by-laws of the association 30 days after the assessment is due were allowed holders of certificates and beneficiaries thereof to pay such assessment, and that he should have died within the 30 days, and that before the 30 days had expired the beneficiaries tendered the unpaid assessment, and the association refused to receive it. *Held*, on demurrer, that the declaration was sufficient to show that no forfeiture of the policy resulted from the non-payment of the assessment, more especially as the declaration also alleged that the association continued to treat the assured as a member in good standing, by making a subsequent assessment against him. — Wright v. Supreme Commandery of Golden Rule, (Ga.) 13 S. E. 564.

INTEREST.

See, also, *Usury.*

Rate, custom as to, see *Custom and Usage,* 1.

Right to interest.

1. In an action of debt on a decree for the payment of a certain amount of interest, interest on the amount of the decree can be recovered in the shape of damages for its detention.—Stuart v. Hurt, (Va.) 13 S. E. 488.

2. A bond reciting, "in consideration of professional services rendered to me by H., I owe, and hereby promise to pay to him, $10,000," is a promise of payment *in præsenti,* and bears interest from date.—McVeigh's Ex'r v. Howard, (Va.) 13 S. E. 81.

3. Defendants executed certain bonds to secure plaintiff, a banking corporation, for advancements to be made to a firm, not to exceed $5,000, and to "include and to secure all amounts drawn by them for any purpose whatsoever," to terminate October 31, 1886, and the obligors to be held for whatever balance thereafter appeared, at 8 per cent. per annum. In an action on the bonds the referee found that plaintiff charged on the daily balances of advancements 1 per cent. per month, and compounded same from month to month, and that on October 31st there was due plaintiff $5,031.82, which was reduced by credits, leaving due $4,043.72, September 1, 1887. Judgment was entered for the latter amount without interest. *Held,* that the bonds covered any balance found due October 31st, with 8 per cent. interest therefrom, and plaintiff was entitled to interest on the amount due from September 1, 1887, at 8 per cent. MERRIMON, C. J., and CLARK, J., dissenting.—Bank of Oxford v. Bobbitt, (N. C.) 13 S. E. 177.

Rate.

4. Where a note stipulates for interest at 12 per cent. per annum, it is proper to allow interest at the same rate on the judgment thereon, since by the law of Georgia judgments bear interest at the contract rate.—Neal v. Brockhan, (Ga.) 13 S. E. 283.

5. In an action for breach of a contract to accept grain which plaintiffs sold defendants, plaintiffs are entitled to interest on the amount fixed as the measure of damages, and it may be incorporated in the aggregate sum of damages found.—Woods v. Cramer, (S. C.) 13 S. E. 660.

Interstate Commerce.

See *Constitutional Law,* 10.

Intervention.

See *Parties,* 5.

INTOXICATING LIQUORS.

Gift to voter on election day, see *Elections and Voters,* 3, 4.

License—Revocation.

1. Under the charter of the city of Atlanta, (Acts Ga. 1874, p. 122, § 27,) conferring on the mayor and council "full power and authority to regulate the retail of ardent spirits," and, "at their discretion, to issue license to retail or to withhold the same," they have authority to pass an ordinance that conviction of violation of the state statute prohibiting the sale of liquor to a minor shall work an immediate revocation of the license.—Sprayberry v. City of Atlanta, (Ga.) 13 S. E. 197.

2. A license to sell liquors is a mere privilege to carry on the business subject to the will of the grantor, and not a contract, and is not property, and a forfeiture thereof does not deprive the licensee of his property without due process of law.—Sprayberry v. City of Atlanta, (Ga.) 13 S. E. 197.

3. Where a license itself contains the conditions of forfeiture as prescribed by the ordinance

under which it was granted, the licensee, who has been convicted of selling liquor to a minor, is not entitled to any notice of the forfeiture of his license.—Sprayberry v. City of Atlanta, (Ga.) 13 S. E. 197.

Illegal sales.

4. On indictment for retailing spirituous liquors without a license it appeared that defendant, the steward of a club, was given a jug of liquor by the individual members thereof, who owned the liquor in common, and that he gave one of such members a drink from the jug, taking 10 cents in exchange. The amount received was just about the value of the liquor furnished, and with other money so received was used in replenishing the jug. *Held*, that there was a sale. Following State v. Lockyear, 95 N. C. 633.—State v. Neis, (N. C.) 13 S. E. 225.*

5. In a prohibition county, one who receives money from another with a request to procure whisky, and who shortly afterwards delivers the whisky, may be treated as the seller if no other person filling that character appears, and if it is not shown where, how, or from whom the whisky was obtained. Paschal v. State, 84 Ga. 326, 10 S. E. 821, followed.—Grant v. State, (Ga.) 13 S. E. 554.

6. A writing by which a father authorizes a saloon-keeper to sell liquor to his son, without limit as to time or quantity, will not justify a sale under Code Ga. § 4540a, making it an offense to sell intoxicating liquors to any minor "without first obtaining written authority from the parent or guardian."—Gill v. State, 13 S. E. 86, 86 Ga. 751; Dixon v. State, 13 S. E. 87, 86 Ga. 754.

—— Indictment.

7. An indictment under Act Ga. Feb. 22, 1877, making it unlawful to sell "spirituous" liquors, which charges in general terms the sale of intoxicating liquors, without alleging that they were spirituous, does not set forth the offense with requisite certainty.—McDuffie v. State, (Ga.) 13 S. E. 596.

—— Variance.

8. An indictment charging a sale of whisky as made to a person named will be supported by evidence that it was made to him through his servant or messenger, and the latter need not be mentioned by name or otherwise in the indictment.—Hall v. State, (Ga.) 13 S. E. 634.

9. On an indictment charging the sale of whisky to two named persons, proof of a sale to either of them will warrant a conviction.—Hall v. State, (Ga.) 13 S. E. 634.

—— Evidence.

10. On a prosecution for the illegal sale of intoxicating liquor, evidence that defendant refused to sell liquor to another is not admissible to show that he did not sell to the prosecuting witness on a different occasion.—Corley v. State, (Ga.) 13 S. E. 556.

Injunction against liquor nuisance.

11. Code W. Va. c. 32, § 18, provides that "all houses, buildings, and places of every description where intoxicating liquors are sold or vended contrary to law shall be held, taken, and deemed to be common and public nuisances, and may be abated as such upon the conviction of the owner or keeper thereof, as hereinafter provided; and courts of equity shall have jurisdiction by injunction to restrain and abate any such nuisance upon bill filed by any citizen." *Held*, that a court of equity cannot restrain by injunction a party charged with selling intoxicating liquors contrary to law, or abate the house, building, or place where such intoxicating liquors are alleged to be sold contrary to law, until the owner or keeper of such house or place has been convicted of such unlawful selling at the place named in the bill. HOLT and BRANNON, JJ., dissenting.—Hartley v. Henretta, (W. Va.) 13 S. E. 375; Lutes v. Riley, Id.; Stidger v. Kelley, Id.; Dick v. Kull, Id.

Joinder.

Of actions, see *Action*, 2; *Pleading*, 1.

JUDGE.

See, also, *Justices of the Peace*.

Powers.

Under Gen. St. S. C. §§ 2116, 2117, relative to the functions of circuit judges, which provide that a circuit judge shall have jurisdiction to discharge all the duties of his office within the circuit where he resides, except the holding of circuit courts therein, when some other circuit judge shall be engaged in holding said courts, a judge has no jurisdiction to grant a writ of *certiorari* in a case tried in another circuit, while the judge thereof is holding court therein.—State v. Black, (S. C.) 13 S. E. 361.

JUDGMENT.

Action on, limitation, see *Limitation of Actions*, 8.
Appealable judgments, see *Appeal*, 1-11.
Arrest of, in criminal cases, see *Criminal Law*, 56, 57.
Attack on, by affidavit of illegality, see *Execution*, 10.
Bill to review, see *Equity*, 16, 17.
Decree in equity, see *Equity*, 15.
In action to enforce mechanic's lien, see *Mechanics' Liens*, 4, 5.
    criminal cases, see *Criminal Law*, 53-58.
    trover, see *Trover and Conversion*, 2-4.
Modification of, on appeal, see *Appeal*, 92.
Satisfaction by attorney, see *Attorney and Client*, 4, 5.
Scaling judgment as Confederate transaction, see *Executors and Administrators*, 11, 12.
Subrogation to rights of judgment creditor, see *Subrogation*, 3, 4.

By default.

1. The fact that defendant's counsel failed to enter an appearance in a case wherein judgment was had against defendant by default is not ground to set aside the judgment, though such counsel is insolvent, and unable to respond in damages for the injury to his client.—Phillips v. Collier, (Ga.) 13 S. E. 260.

2. Where, in an action on an unconditional contract in writing, no plea on the part of the defense is filed, and counsel's name is not marked upon the docket, a request by one of defendants to the clerk to mark the name of counsel on the docket, and the fact that such counsel was a member of the legislature in session when the case was called, are not sufficient grounds for setting aside the judgment, under the rule requiring counsel to file his pleas at the first term of court, and to mark or have marked his name on the docket.—Bentley v. Finch, (Ga.) 13 S. E. 155.

Rendition.

3. A joint action against the maker and indorsers of a promissory note is a civil case, founded on an unconditional contract in writing; and, where no issuable defense is filed under oath or affirmation, the court may render judgment thereon against all of the defendants without the verdict of a jury, under Const. Ga. art. 6, § 14, par. 7, authorizing such rendition of judgment.—Georgia Railroad & Banking Co. v. Pendleton, (Ga.) 13 S. E. 822.

Res judicata—Parties.

4. A creditor, in whose favor a judgment has been passed that land belonged to the deceased husband, is estopped from afterwards claiming that it was not the property of the husband, and that therefore the widow is not entitled to dower therein.—Jefferies v. Allen, (S. C.) 13 S. E. 365.

5. In an action to recover amount realized from sale of property placed in the hands of a judgment creditor to be sold and applied on the judgment, which plaintiff claimed was not so applied, it appeared that prior to this action plain-

tiff was cited to show cause why execution should not issue on said judgment, and in that proceeding alleged that the execution was paid by the proceeds of the property, which question was then adjudicated. *Held*, that plaintiff was estopped from again trying the issue.—Moore v. Garner, (N. C.) 18 S. E. 768.

6. Where the administrator of a surety on an administrator's bond is sued together with the other sureties and the principal, and fails to appear, though served with process, the judgment for plaintiffs is conclusive against him, and he cannot, in a suit to enforce that judgment, set up defenses which he might have pleaded in the original action.—Brown v. Walker, (N. C.) 18 S. E. 3.

7. Defendants purchased land sold by an administrator under a decree reciting the personal service of summons upon plaintiffs, who were decedent's devisees. Nineteen years thereafter plaintiffs moved to set aside the decree and sale on the ground that they had not been, in fact, so summoned. The motion was granted, and the proceedings were declared irregular and void; but it was ordered that all the papers in the cause should remain on file for the use of the purchaser when his rights should be questioned. *Held*, in an action of ejectment brought 17 years after the decree and sale, that as plaintiffs were guilty of laches by reason of both their long acquiescence in defendant's possession, and their delay in seeking to set aside said decree and sale, in the absence of an explanation thereof, said proceedings would not be deemed to have been declared void as to defendants.—Harrison v. Hargrove, (N. C.) 18 S. E. 989.

8. Plaintiff obtained judgment against defendant in a Tennessee justice court. Defendant, after appealing to the circuit court, dismissed his appeal, and the court confirmed the justice's judgment. Plaintiff then dismissed his case. In Tennessee an appeal from a justice court vacates the judgment. The amount of the judgment was paid by defendant to the circuit court clerk. But it does not appear that the clerk was the proper party to receive it, or that it was ever paid to plaintiff. *Held*, in an action in Georgia, that a plea in abatement of prior judgment which had been satisfied was properly overruled.—Chattanooga, R. & C. R. Co. v. Jackson, (Ga.) 18 S. E. 109.

9. Where both husband and wife were defendants in *fi. fa.*, the fact that the husband made an affidavit of illegality, claiming the property levied upon as a homestead, which was determined in a court which had no jurisdiction, does not bind the wife, and she may thereafter make an affidavit claiming the land upon the same ground, and have it determined by a court of competent jurisdiction. — Moore v. O'Barr, (Ga.) 18 S. E. 464.

Res judicata—Questions determined.

10. The fact that plaintiff recovered only nominal damages in an action for a continuing tort is not conclusive against his right to maintain another action for the same tort seven or eight years later.—Stafford v. Maddox, (Ga.) 18 S. E. 559.

11. In an action on a bond, evidence is admissible as to whether the merits were inquired into upon rendering a judgment in a justice court in another action on the same bond.—Davie v. Davis, (N. C.) 18 S. E. 240.

12. In a suit to enjoin a sale of land under a decree, a contention that there is a defect in the title will not be considered, where the original case was fully investigated by a referee, and his report confirmed by the circuit court, and an appeal to the supreme court dismissed.—Hudson v. Yost, (Va.) 18 S. E. 436.

13. A judgment for the rent only, in what was essentially a special proceeding to establish an agricultural lien on crops for rent and advances, but which in form was an action by summons and complaint, in which an agreement for a lien was held invalid as an agricultural lien, because not signed by both parties, is not a bar to an action in equity to declare the agreement an equitable chattel mortgage on the crop, and for an accounting of the amount due thereon for the advances.—Sease v. Dobson, (S. C.) 18 S. E. 590.

14. In an action to reform a deed by inserting the words "and their heirs," omitted by mistake from the proper place to pass the fee, it appeared that a special proceeding was previously brought against plaintiffs, who set this up as an equitable counter-claim, and that the question was decided in their favor, but was reversed in the supreme court. The reversal, however, was never entered below, the action and the counter-claim being withdrawn by common consent. *Held*, that such proceeding did not constitute an estoppel. —Stewart v. Register, (N. C.) 18 S. E. 234.

15. Five notes were given under a contract in payment of personal property of the value of $2,500, to be paid at a specified time by delivering a certain number of brick to the payee. The first two payments were not made as agreed, and, before maturity of the last three, suit was brought to recover the value of the brick which should have been delivered on the first two notes, alleging that the notes were two of the five given, and laying the damages at $3,055. The maker filed a counter-claim. Judgment was rendered for $1,186.07. Afterwards suit was brought on the last three of the five notes, and the maker filed a plea of *res judicata*. *Held* proper, in the second suit, to admit parol evidence to prove the issues presented to the jury in the first suit.—McMakin v. Fowler, (S. C.) 18 S. E. 584.

16. Where, in an action on a bond in a justice's court, it is adjudged, after hearing the evidence, that the suit be dismissed as to one of the defendants on the ground that no obligee was named in the bond at the time such defendant signed it, and plaintiff did not present on the trial any equitable claim he might have had against defendant on account of his having executed said bond, the judgment is one upon the merits, that concludes the parties to all matters that were and could have been pleaded.—Davie v. Davis, (N. C.) 18 S. E. 240.

17. Where wages are garnished, and after the garnishee, in discharge of a judgment against him rendered by a justice's court, has paid the money to the constable, the laborer claims the fund as exempt, and such claim is adjudicated against him in the justice's court, he cannot maintain a rule against the constable in the superior court for the money, founded on his exemption right, since the matter is *res adjudicata*. —La Motte v. Harper, (Ga.) 18 S. E. 804.

18. Where an application for removal to the federal court has been denied on the ground that the allegations therein as to the citizenship of the parties were insufficient, the court below might in its discretion have allowed an amendment at the proper time, but after an appeal from the order of denial, and an affirmance by the supreme court, the matter has become *res adjudicata*, although it was an interlocutory or incidental order, and an amendment cannot be allowed.—Herndon v. Ætna Ins. Co., (N. C.) 18 S. E. 188.

Lien.

19. In a contest between a judgment creditor and the assignees of a money demand against a county, the lien of the judgment not having attached upon the fund before it was brought into court, such judgment will not take precedence of the assignments, though they were made after the judgment was rendered. — Dotterer v. Harden, (Ga.) 18 S. E. 971.

20. Under Code Ga. § 3460, which declares that parties by consent cannot give jurisdiction to the court as to the person or subject-matter of a suit, so as to prejudice third parties, the maker of certain notes, by not objecting to action thereon before the notes were due, could not waive jurisdiction to the prejudice of another garnishing creditor.—Beach v. Atkinson, (Ga.) 18 S. E. 591.

21. Where lands are bought under a parol agreement, and the price is paid, and visible

possession taken before notice of the rendition of a judgment, the subsequent docketing of a judgment against the vendor before the deed to the land is recorded creates no lien.—Brown v. Butler, (Va.) 13 S. E. 71.

22. Code N. C. § 435, providing that a judgment shall be a lien on the real property of every person against whom it shall be rendered, and which the said person may then have or shall thereafter acquire at any time during 10 years, does not vest in the judgment creditor any estate or interest in the land, but only secures his right to have the judgment satisfied out of the proceeds of a sale made under an ordinary process of execution; and the lien in such a case embraces only such estate, legal or equitable, as may be sold at the time it attaches.—Bruce v. Sugg, (N. C.) 13 S. E. 790.

23. Code N. C. §§ 83, 433-435, provide that a clerk of a superior court shall keep a judgment docket in which the substance of a judgment shall be recorded; that the entry of a judgment for money shall contain the names of the parties, the relief granted, the date of the judgment, and the date of its docketing, and that the clerk shall keep a cross-index, with the dates and numbers; that a judgment roll shall be made, and when filed such judgment shall become a lien on the debtor's real estate. Held, that in the entry of judgment against several, where the name of one is omitted from the caption and also from the cross-index, the judgment created no lien on his real estate as against judgments subsequently entered and indexed in accordance with the statutes.—Dewey v. Sugg, (N. C.) 13 S. E. 928.

24. A judgment rendered in 1868 against a debtor in L. county became, by the law then in force, a lien on the debtor's land in that county, and an execution was issued and returned unsatisfied. In 1871, A. county was created (14 St. S. C. 695) out of a portion of L. county, including the land which was subject to the judgment rendered in 1868. The act creating A. county contained no provision affecting the lien on lands within such county of judgments theretofore rendered. In 1874 the judgment debtor sold the land (then in A. county) to defendant. In 1875 the judgment creditor filed in A. county a transcript of his judgment, as authorized by Act S. C. 1873, § 14, (15 St. 499,) which provides that "from the date of the filing of such transcript it shall have the same force and effect as if the judgment had been originally entered in the county in which said transcript is filed." Held, under Code Proc. S. C. 306, (the original Code,) which provides that "the party in whose favor judgment has been heretofore or shall hereafter be given * * * may, at any time within five years after the entry of judgment, proceed to enforce the same, as prescribed by this title," that an execution issued on the judgment in question, immediately on filing the transcript thereof in A. county, was valid as against the land in defendant's hands, and authorized the sheriff to sell such land under a judgment rendered in A. county against the same judgment debtor after the conveyance by the debtor to defendant; and the purchaser at such sale acquired a title superior to that of defendant.—Garvin v. Garvin, (S. C.) 13 S. E. 625.

25. Where a new county is created out of a portion of an existing county, the lien of judgments theretofore rendered is not affected as to lands included within the new county, where the act creating it contains no retroactive provisions relating to such judgments.—Garvin v. Garvin, (S. C.) 13 S. E. 625.

Collateral attack.

26. The fact that a sole plaintiff, or one of several plaintiffs, was dead at the time of the institution of an action, such death not appearing on the record, does not render a judgment therein void, but only erroneous.—Watt v. Brookover, (W. Va.) 13 S. E. 1007.

27. A judgment rendered by a court of competent jurisdiction, and a sale under execution thereon, are not void on the ground that when the judgment was rendered and sale made defendant was insane; and cannot be collaterally attacked in ejectment by defendant, where the sheriff's deed is introduced to show that plaintiff in ejectment has no title.—Thomas v. Hunsucker, (N. C.) 13 S. E. 231.

28. Const. Ga. provides that "the court shall render judgment without the verdict of a jury in all civil cases founded on unconditional contracts in writing, where an issuable defense is not filed under oath or affirmation." Held that, if not in all cases whatsoever, certainly in any case admitting of doubt as to whether a contract sued on is unconditional, the question of rendering a judgment without a jury is one not involving jurisdiction, but the proper exercise of jurisdiction, and the improper decision of it is mere error, and will not render the judgment void.—Georgia Railroad & Banking Co. v. Pendleton, (Ga.) 13 S. E. 823.

Satisfaction.

29. Judgment was obtained against two of the sureties of a principal debtor, and they deposited the whole amount of the judgment, and procured an assignment thereof to a third person for their benefit, with the view of more easily compelling contribution from their co-sureties. The assignee then fraudulently sold the judgment to a purchaser with notice of the fraud. Held, that the sureties who paid the judgment had a right, on notice to the last assignee, to move that the satisfaction of the judgment be entered of record.—State v. Hearn, (N. C.) 13 S. E. 995.

30. Under Code N. C. § 574, providing that, in all claims where an agreement is made and accepted for a less amount than that claimed, payment of such less amount shall be a complete discharge of the same, one of three joint judgment debtors, who proposes to pay a given sum provided the payment shall operate to relieve him from further liability, on acceptance of such offer and payment by check is entitled to have entry of satisfaction on the record as to the whole judgment as against him.—Boykin v. Buie, (N. C.) 13 S. E. 879.

Revivor.

31. A provision of a decree in favor of a receiver, that he shall execute a bond in a fixed penalty before receiving any money thereunder, does not prevent the decree being final, within the meaning of Code Va. 1873, c. 182, § 12, providing that an execution may be issued on a "final" decree within one year, or the same may be revived within ten years from its date.—Serles v. Cromer, (Va.) 13 S. E. 859.

Vacating.

32. The docketing of a justice court judgment in a superior court, as allowed by Code N. C. § 839, does not give the superior court jurisdiction of an action to set aside such judgment for want of service of summons, but a motion for that purpose must be made in the justice's court.—Whitehurst v. Merchants' & Farmers' Transp. Co., (N. C.) 13 S. E. 937.

33. A verdict and judgment for costs alone against plaintiff will not be set aside on the ground that the court in which his action was brought had no jurisdiction of the subject-matter of the suit.—Parker v. Belcher, (Ga.) 13 S. E. 314.

34. A joint verdict and judgment against several defendants, some of whom were never served, and had not waived service by appearance, should be set aside on motion made at the same term.—Haralson v. McArthur, (Ga.) 13 S. E. 594.

35. An independent action is not the proper remedy for setting aside a judgment, entered in a special proceeding, on the ground that a summons, necessary to give the court jurisdiction, was not served; but relief can be obtained only by a motion in the cause.—Grant v. Harrell, (N. C.) 13 S. E. 718.

36. Plaintiff, in a pending action in which he had employed two counsel to represent him, absented himself without leave of court, and against the advice of one of his counsel. Plaintiff's lead-

ing counsel was absent at the same time, with leave of court. The cause was regularly called for trial during such absence, and the counsel present allowed judgment to be taken against plaintiff, without moving for a continuance on the ground of the absence of the leading counsel with leave of court, or on any other ground. *Held*, that the judgment would not be set aside.— Parker v. Belcher, (Ga.) 13 S. E. 814.

37. The fact that a letter to counsel to appear in a case reached him a half-hour after the case was set for trial furnished no ground for opening the judgment, there having been plenty of time to secure counsel by telegraphing, and it being negligence not to do so.—Finlayson v. American Acc. Co., (N. C.) 13 S. E. 739.

38. Where defendant's attorney is absent with leave of court on account of sickness, and his relationship to the case is known to counsel for plaintiff, though his name is not marked on the docket, his leave of absence applied to the case, and, if his client is also absent on account of a public announcement made by the judge in open court (she being then present and hearing it) that no case would be taken up in which the absent counsel was concerned, a judgment against such defendant ought to be set aside upon application made at the same term, supported by an affidavit of a meritorious defense.—Haralson v. McArthur, (Ga.) 13 S. E. 594.

39. Where an attorney is engaged simply to employ counsel to appear at another place, he is a mere agent, and his negligence to employ the counsel is the negligence of his principal.—Finlayson v. American Acc. Co., (N. C.) 13 S. E. 739.

Equitable relief.

40. Judgment was rendered in favor of the payee of a promissory note given "for a patent-right to the Shellnut water-engine" for a designated county. *Held*, that the collection of this judgment would not be enjoined at the suit of the maker, because no assignment of the patent had ever been made to him, where he himself introduced in evidence an instrument executed by the patentee's agent, authorizing him "to use and sell the said patent" within the designated county.—Moore v. Garland, (Ga.) 13 S. E. 576.

41. A court of equity will not restrain the enforcement of a judgment on the ground that defendant was never served with process, where the record shows no flaw or defect in the service, and where defendant does not state any facts imparting to the case some feature of equitable cognizance, such as fraud, accident, or mistake; defendant having a plain, speedy, and adequate remedy by a motion to vacate the judgment in the court and in the action wherein it was rendered. —Crocker v. Allen, (S. C.) 13 S. E. 650.

42. The mere fact that the judgment was recovered on the equity side of the court will not authorize the maintenance of the separate equitable action to set the judgment aside.—Crocker v. Allen, (S. C.) 13 S. E. 650.

43. The fact that an injunction may be necessary to make the relief on the motion for the vacation of the judgment effectual is not sufficient to give a court of equity jurisdiction, since that relief was always obtainable by a motion to stay the execution, even before the enactment of Gen. St. S. C. § 2115, expressly conferring such power on a circuit judge in chambers.—Crocker v. Allen, (S. C.) 13 S. E. 650.

44. Code Va. § 3286, provides that when, in an action of *assumpsit*, an affidavit is filed with the declaration, no plea in bar shall be received unless supported by the affidavit; and, if such plea and affidavit are not filed, there shall be no inquiry of damages, but judgment shall be for plaintiff for the amount claimed in the affidavit filed with the declaration. *Held*, that where a plea of *non assumpsit* unaccompanied by affidavit was stricken out, and the subsequent tender of a plea accompanied by affidavit refused, a final judgment given by the court for plaintiffs was not void, as the court had jurisdiction, though it would have been the duty of the clerk to enter judgment at rules, and therefore its enforcement

would not be restrained. FAUNTLEROY, J., dissenting.—Grigg v. Dalsheimer, (Va.) 13 S. E. 993.

Judicial Notice.

See *Evidence*, 1–3.

JUDICIAL SALES.

By executors and administrators, see *Executors and Administrators*, 19–25.
Foreclosure sale, see *Mortgages*, 11–14.
For non-payment of taxes, see *Taxation*, 9.
Of lunatic's property, see *Insanity*, 4.
Under execution, see *Execution*, 17.

Order of sale.

1. A decree which simply confirms a commissioner's report of debts, and directs a sale of lands therefor in default of payment, though that report specifies the debts and priorities, is erroneous, because the decree does not itself adjudicate and declare what debts are to be paid, and fix their order and priority as to the lands to be sold therefor.—Hull's Adm'r v. Hull's Heirs, (W. Va.) 13 S. E. 49; Dudley v. Same, Id.

2. An agreement was made between a mortgagor and mortgagee that proceedings to foreclose the mortgage, which were then pending, should be withdrawn, and the land conveyed to trustees, who were authorized to sell the land, if the mortgage debt should not be paid on a certain day. A sale by the trustees was set aside in an action brought by the mortgagor, and a resale was ordered to be made by the master. *Held*, that it was error to order the sale without a formal discontinuance of the foreclosure suit, as the pendency of such suit was a cloud on the title, and deterred bidding at the sale. — Fishburne v. Smith, (S. C.) 13 S. E. 525.

—— Setting aside.

3. After the termination of a special proceeding, wherein a sale of a testator's lands was ordered for the payment of his debts, a motion in the cause is not the proper remedy for setting aside for fraud the orders directing the sale, but this can be done only by an independent action. —Carter v. Rountree, (N. C.) 13 S. E. 716.

4. But such motion, if made within a reasonable time, is the proper remedy for setting the orders aside for irregularities; and the fact that the motion alleges fraud in addition to the irregularities is immaterial, since such allegations will be treated as surplusage.—Carter v. Rountree, (N. C.) 13 S. E. 716.

Confirmation.

5. The confirmation of a judicial sale for about $4,000 will not be vacated on the ground that the price was grossly inadequate, when, on two prior sales within two years preceding such sale the land, after wide advertisements, brought $1,550 and $2,650, respectively; and the purchaser at the last sale agreed to sell the land to a third person for $5,000.—Allison v. Allison, (Va.) 13 S. E. 549.

6. The fact that the attorney of the owner of land sold at a judicial sale died about two weeks before the confirmation of the sale, and that the owner had notice of motion for confirmation only from Saturday until Monday, are not sufficient grounds for vacating such confirmation, when the owner had several days' notice of the death of his attorney, and lived only three or four hours' ride from the place where the motion was made.—Allison v. Allison, (Va.) 13 S. E. 549.

Payment of price.

7. A purchaser of land under a void decree, whose money has been applied upon liens on the land valid against the owner, will be entitled to charge such money upon the land by substitution to the right of the creditor, upon disaffirmance of the sale.—Hull's Adm'r v. Hull's Heirs, (W. Va.) 13 S. E. 49; Dudley v. Same, Id.

8. Where the purchase money at a judicial sale is paid to a commissioner, who has failed to give bond, as required by the decree, and also

by Code Va. § 3397, such payment is invalid, and does not discharge the purchaser.—Whitehead v. Bradley, (Va.) 13 S. E. 195.

9. Where payments of purchase money at a judicial sale are void, because made to an unbonded commissioner, proceedings against the purchasers to show cause why the property should not be resold are not within Code Va. § 3425, which declares that the purchaser's title at a sale made under a decree six months after the date thereof, and confirmed, shall not be affected by a subsequent reversal; since the object of such proceedings is not to set aside the sale, but to compel the purchasers to comply with their respective contracts.—Whitehead v. Bradley, (Va.) 13 S. E. 195.

Record of deed.

10. Act 1885, c. 147, providing that no purchase from a bargainor or lessor whose deed or lease is unregistered shall avail to pass title as against any unregistered deed executed prior to December 1, 1885, when the person claiming under such deed shall be in the actual possession and enjoyment of such land, does not apply to purchasers at sheriff's sale, but only to purchasers from the bargainor or lessor.—Cowen v. Withrow, (N. C.) 13 S. E. 1022.

Jurisdiction.

See *Courts.*
In criminal cases, see *Criminal Law,* 1, 2.
   equity, see *Equity,* 1–8.
Objections to, see *Abatement and Revival,* 4.
Of justice, see *Justices of the Peace,* 1–7.
On appeal, see *Appeal,* 1–15.

JURY.

Disqualification, waiver of objection, see *Criminal Law,* 59.
Misconduct of, see *New Trial,* 6, 7.
Province of, invasion by instructions, see *Trial,* 31–37.
Right to trial by, see *Constitutional Law,* 11.
Separation of, in criminal case, see *Criminal Law,* 45.
Taking papers to jury-room, see *Trial,* 3.

Competency.

1. The persons filling the offices of treasurer and councilman of a city are not disqualified to serve in the hustings court thereof, in a criminal case.—Thompson v. Commonwealth, (Va.) 13 S. E. 304.

2. A juror should not be excluded in a civil case merely because he is indebted to defendant, in the absence of any showing that he is by reason thereof at the mercy of defendant, or that he has been treated with such indulgence as to make him favor him.—Thompson v. Douglass, (W. Va.) 13 S. E. 1015.

3. A juror in a capital case, who swears on his *voir dire* that he is opposed to capital punishment, is properly rejected. Affirming 12 S. E. 657.—State v. James, (S. C.) 13 S. E. 325.

4. The impressions of a juror as to defendant's guilt, based on what he "had heard," do not disqualify him, where he states on his *voir dire* that he can render a fair and impartial judgment according to the law and the evidence. Affirming 12 S. E. 657.—State v. James, (S. C.) 13 S. E. 325.

5. Objection to the competency of a juror is properly overruled where he states that he is impartial, and can give the prisoner a fair trial, and that he has no opinion about the case, though he had previously stated that at the time of its commission he heard some talk about it, and might then have had some opinion about it, but did not remember whether he had or not.—Lyles v. Commonwealth, (Va.) 13 S. E. 802.

Summoning and impaneling.

6. The irregularity in a *venire facias* ordered in vacation, that it commands the summoning of 40 persons for the trial of two persons

and others charged with felony, but not jointly indicted with the two, not being prejudicial, cannot, by the provisions of Acts Va. 1887–88, p. 18, for the first time be objected to after verdict.—Lyles v. Commonwealth. (Va.) 13 S. E. 802.

7. The appearance of 16 of the 20 persons ordered to be summoned from the list furnished by the judge to serve as jurors is sufficient, under Code Va. § 4019, providing that in cases of felony, "where a sufficient number of jurors to constitute a panel of sixteen persons free from exception cannot be had from those summoned," additional persons may be summoned from the bystanders; and it is not error for the court to refuse to cause the appearance of the four persons originally summoned.—Custis v. Commonwealth, (Va.) 13 S. E. 73.

8. When Acts N. C. 1885, c. 180, was passed, prescribing that certain terms of the superior court of the county of Wake should continue for three weeks for the trial of civil business alone, (there having previously been no longer terms than two weeks,) Code N. C. c. 39, in respect to jurors, providing in terms for the drawing of them by the county commissioners for each week of the terms of the courts lasting two weeks, was by necessary implication extended to authorize the commissioners to draw jurors for the third week of the newly-established terms.—Leach v. Linde, (N. C.) 13 S. E. 213.

9. Where the county commissioners fail to draw jurors for the third week of a term, the court may direct a jury to be drawn and summoned, as prescribed by Code N. C. § 1732, providing for drawing a jury in case the commissioners fail to do so.—Leach v. Linde, (N. C.) 13 S. E. 213.

10. Where, on the trial of a felony, after several of the jury have been selected, but not sworn in chief, one of them becomes sick, it is not error to excuse him, and then proceed regularly to complete the panel to the number of twelve; and this the court may do without summoning a physician to determine that the juror is sick.—Ozburn v. State, (Ga.) 13 S. E. 247.

11. The offense of giving intoxicating drink to a voter at an election, in violation of Code, c. 5, § 10, providing as a penalty therefor a fine of not less than $10 nor more than $50, being a misdemeanor, defendant, on an indictment therefor, is not entitled to a special jury, under Code, c. 116, § 21, authorizing the court to allow a special jury in any civil case.—State v. Pearis, (W. Va.) 13 S. E. 1006.

Challenges.

12. The mere exclusion of a juror upon a challenge for cause upon insufficient ground will not be cause for reversal.—Thompson v. Douglass, (W. Va.) 13 S. E. 1015.

13. Since under Code, c. 116, § 17, "in every case, the plaintiff and defendant may each challenge four jurors peremptorily," the refusal by the court, on the trial of an indictment for a misdemeanor, to allow defendant such challenges, is reversible error.—State v. Pearis, (W. Va.) 13 S. E. 1006.

14. After a jury has been stricken, it is not error to refuse to allow a restriking because counsel for one of the parties simply states in his place that he had by oversight left on the jury a man who, for reasons alleged, would, in his opinion, be partial and prejudiced against his client; it not appearing that, even if these things were true, any diligence was shown to ascertain the same, or that they might not easily have been known by proper and timely inquiry.—Central Railroad & Banking Co. v. Kent, (Ga.) 13 S. E. 502.

JUSTICES OF THE PEACE.

Appeal from, see *Appeal,* 43–47.
Jurisdiction of action against married woman, see *Husband and Wife,* 24.

Jurisdiction.

1. An issue as to whether land is exempt from levy and sale under an execution as a home-

stead does not bring the title of the land in question.—Moore v. O'Barr, (Ga.) 13 S. E. 464.

2. Under Code N. C. § 871, forbidding a justice of the peace to issue process to any county other than his own where there is only one defendant, and section 191, (applicable to proceedings in superior courts,) providing that an action for the recovery of a penalty must be brought in the county where the cause arose, a justice has jurisdiction of an action against a resident of his county for a penalty incurred in another county, in the absence of any provision extending the provision of section 191 to justices' courts.—Fisher v. Bullard, (N. C.) 13 S. E. 799.

3. Where plaintiffs' contract provided for furnishing defendant with certain lumber, and on a performance of their contract the amount due them exceeded the jurisdiction of a justice of the peace, they could not split the amount so as to bring three actions within such jurisdiction, though the lumber had been delivered by installments.—McPhail v. Johnson, (N. C.) 13 S. E. 799.

4. Where the face of a note, with the attorney's fee provided therein, is in excess of the amount of the jurisdiction of a justice of the peace, the judgment rendered therein by him is void.—Beach v. Atkinson, (Ga.) 13 S. E. 591.

5. Under Code Va. § 2939, providing, among other things, that a justice of the peace shall have jurisdiction of any claim to any fine if the amount thereof does not exceed $20, and of other claims where the amount does not exceed $100, a justice has no jurisdiction of an action for the $100 penalty imposed by section 1292 upon telegraph companies for failure to deliver a dispatch, since such penalty is a fine within the meaning of the statute.—Western Union Tel Co. v. Pettyjohn, (Va.) 13 S. E. 431.

6. Under Code N. C. § 834, which provides that justices of the peace shall have exclusive original jurisdiction of all civil actions founded on contracts, except where the demand exceeds $200, or the title to real estate is in controversy, a justice has no jurisdiction in ejectment, where the issue is whether a contract to purchase the land was abandoned by defendant, and a suit for specific performance of the contract, instituted by defendant, is pending in the superior court.—Boone v. Drake, (N. C.) 13 S. E. 724.

7. Code N. C. § 1159, authorizing two justices of the peace to sit together in criminal proceedings, and giving them the same powers and duties as are given to any justice sitting alone, was authorized by Const. N. C. art. 4, § 12, empowering the general assembly to allot and distribute the judicial power and jurisdiction which does not pertain to the supreme court in such manner as they may deem best.—State v. Flowers, (N. C.) 13 S. E. 718.

Procedure.

8. A justice of the peace cannot instruct the jury.—Freeman v. Exchange Bank, (Ga.) 13 S. E. 160.

9. On a trial in a justice's court it is not error in the magistrate to allow a note, the foundation of the action, to be read in evidence pending the argument to the jury, and the opposite party, if desirous of doing so, would be permitted to introduce evidence also.—Davis v. Mobley, (Ga.) 13 S. E. 596.

10. A conviction for a violation of an ordinance of a municipal corporation will not be reversed for want of a plea by the defendant, since under the laws of West Virginia formal pleadings are not necessary before a justice.—Town of Moundsville v. Velton, (W. Va.) 13 S. E. 373.

Justification.

For assault, see *Assault and Battery*, 1.

Killing Stock.

See *Railroad Companies*, 53–56.

Laches.

See *Equity*, 9.

LANDLORD AND TENANT.

Action by tenant on covenants.

1. Where a lessor prevents the lessee from enjoying the leased property by a preliminary injunction, which is afterwards dissolved, the fact that the lessee has a right of action on the injunction bond will not bar his action of covenant.—Hubble v. Cole, (Va.) 13 S. E. 441.

Tenancy at will—Termination.

2. Where one gives a tenant, after the end of his term, permission to occupy a house until a tenant is obtained for the year, the occupant is entitled to reasonable notice that a tenant has been obtained.—Sloat v. Rountree, (Ga.) 13 S. E. 637.

Holding over.

3. In an action against a tenant for holding over after expiration of a definite term, it is a sufficient defense that the landlord consented for defendant to hold over; and, if the real cause of action be damages resulting from the violation of the terms of this consent, that cause should be alleged in the declaration.—Sloat v. Rountree, (Ga.) 13 S. E. 637.

4. Shortly after the termination of a lease stipulating for a rent of $300 per year, payable monthly, the landlord visited the premises, which the tenants were still occupying, to collect the rent for the previous month. He offered to lease the place for $300, and then for $275, which the tenants rejected, but his proposal to let it for $250 was taken under consideration. Held, that by his conduct he had waived any right to treat them as tenants holding over for the following year.—Drake v. Wilhelm, (N. C.) 13 S. E. 891.

Rent—Apportionment.

5. Code N. C. § 1748, provides that, when rents are payable to successive owners, and the right of any owner is terminable by death or other uncertain event, the payment following shall be apportioned among the said owners. Section 1749 provides that when a farm lease determines by the happening of an uncertain event, determining the estate of the lessor, the tenant shall continue to the end of the year, and shall pay to the succeeding owner a proportionate part of the rent. Held, that a foreclosure is not such an uncertain event as to entitle one to the apportionment of a crop which is planted after the sale, and on which he has made advances with knowledge of the foreclosure decree.—Spruill v. Arrington, (N. C.) 13 S. E. 779.

—— Action on rent note.

6. Under Code Ga. § 2288, providing that "judgments upon suits for rent may be rendered at the first term," an action by the payee of a note, which states on its face that it was given for rent, and which is attached to the declaration, is in order for judgment at the first term. The declaration need not allege the relation of landlord and tenant.—Simpson v. Earle, (Ga.) 13 S. E. 446.

7. Where judgment has been entered by default on a joint note, which recites on its face that it was given for rent, one of the makers cannot, eight years afterwards, in resisting execution on the ground that the judgment was illegal, show by parol evidence that he was merely surety on the note, and that the relation of landlord and tenant did not exist between him and the payee.—Simpson v. Earle, (Ga.) 13 S. E. 446.

Landlord's lien.

8. Code N. C. § 1754, provides that the landlord shall have a lien on crops which shall "be preferred to all other liens," and that the crops shall be "vested in possession of the lessor" until

the rents are paid. Section 1800 provides that the lien in favor of those making advances on crops "shall not affect the rights of the landlords to their proper share of rents." *Held*, that a purchaser at foreclosure sale who enters upon the land before the crop is planted, and rents it to the mortgagor in possession, is entitled to the rights of a landlord, notwithstanding that at the time of the sale considerable advances have been made upon the crop. Killebrew v. Hines, 104 N. C. 182, 10 S. E. 159, 251, distinguished.—Spruill v. Arrington, (N. C.) 13 S. E. 779.

9. Code N. C. § 1754, provides that crops raised on leased land shall, unless otherwise agreed, be deemed vested in possession of the lessor until the rent is paid, and the lessor reimbursed for all "advancements" in making and saving said crops. *Held*, that where the lessor furnishes table board to the lessee and his family, in order that the latter may make and save his crops, such board at once becomes an advancement, and the lessor is not required to prove an express agreement showing that it was to be so considered between the parties.—Brown v. Brown, (N. C.) 13 S. E. 797.

10. Under Code N. C. § 1754, giving a landlord a lien on the whole of the tenant's crop for the rent, and providing that the crop is "held to be vested in possession of the lessor" until the rent is paid, and giving the landlord an action of claim and delivery if the crop, or any part thereof, shall be removed from the land without the consent of the lessor, the landlord may maintain the action for a certain part only of the crop, though all of it has been delivered to a third person.—Boone v. Darden, (N. C.) 13 S. E. 728.

11. Plaintiffs, the owners of a fish-scrap and oil factory, contracted to furnish W. & Co. the factory, a seine, and some boats, while W. & Co. agreed to deliver to them one-fourth of the gross product of oil and scraps, and to pay all running expenses of factory. W. & Co., instead of delivering the one-fourth of the product to plaintiffs, sold it all to defendant. *Held*, in an action to recover said one-fourth or the value thereof, that said agreement constituted a lease, rent to be paid in kind; and that as the only statutory provision giving the landlord a lien, until a division had been made and his share set apart to him in severalty, was in the case of leases for agricultural purposes, (Code N. C. § 1754,) plaintiffs' only remedy was against their lessees.—Howland v. Forlaw, (N. C.) 13 S. E. 173.

12. Suit was commenced by the creditors of a firm to set aside an assignment, and subject the firm assets to its debts. A temporary order was granted restraining any one from interfering with the goods, and requiring defendants to show cause why the injunction should not be continued until the determination of the suit. Afterwards the landlord levied a distress upon the goods. An order was made setting aside the assignment, appointing a receiver, and requiring all creditors to prove their claims or be barred from participation in the fund. *Held* that, as the landlord was not a party until after the levy of the distress, he was not bound by any order in the suit, but was entitled to priority over the other creditors, notwithstanding that the rent was not due when the assignment was made or when the suit was commenced.—Cooley v. Perry, (S. C.) 13 S. E. 553.

13. A landlord having, as surety with his tenant and another person, signed a note for supplies purchased by the tenant, but not having purchased or ordered them himself, cannot have a lien therefor on the tenant's crop, though he is obliged to pay the note at its maturity.—Brimberry v. Mansfield, (Ga.) 13 S. E. 189.

—— Distress.

14. Where the entry of a levy upon a distress warrant included among other things "one crop cotton growing," allowing such levy to be read to the jury on the trial of an issue made by a counter-affidavit to the distress warrant was no ground for a new trial.—Johnston v. Patterson, (Ga.) 13 S. E. 17.

Landlord's lien — Unlawful seizure of crop by landlord.

15. Code N. C. § 1754, provides that crops on land leased for agricultural purposes shall be deemed in possession of the lessor until all rents are paid. Section 1755 gives the lessee a civil remedy, if the lessor obtains actual possession otherwise than as mentioned in the preceding section. Section 1759 makes it a misdemeanor for the lessor to unlawfully and knowingly seize the crop when there is nothing due him. Section 1762 extends these provisions to leases of turpentine trees. *Held*, that a lessor, who, after receiving all rent due, forbade the lessee to gather part of his crop, and leased the trees to others, before the first lease terminated, and allowed them to take the balance of the crop, was guilty of a misdemeanor under section 1759.—State v. Ewing, (N. C.) 13 S. E. 10.

LARCENY.

Jurisdiction.

1. Where defendant, who had found a pocket-book with a check therein, which was only of the value of $10.79, converted it with intent to steal, the offense is only petit larceny; and, where the conversion occurred in a county different from the one in which the pocket-book was lost, the county court of the latter county has no jurisdiction of the matter. RICHARDSON, J., dissenting.—Perrin v. Commonwealth, (Va.) 13 S. E. 76.

What constitutes.

2. On an indictment for privily stealing from the person, where the jury has been instructed that the taking must have been secret in order to make out the offense, it is not error to add that it is not necessary for the state to prove that no force was used.—State v. Chavis, (S. C.) 13 S. E. 817.

Indictment.

3. An indictment for larceny from the person which charges that the defendant did take from the person of one C. "one watch and chain of the value of $75, and the property of the said C.," is sufficiently specific in the description of the property stolen.—Powell v. State, (Ga.) 13 S. E. 829.

4. An indictment charging burglary with intent to commit larceny, which alleges that one pair of pants "and other goods," of the value of $24, without specifying the other goods, were stolen, is not a good indictment for grand larceny.—State v. McClung, (W. Va.) 13 S. E. 654.

5. To support a conviction of larceny under a count of an indictment charging both burglary and larceny, the charge of larceny must be well laid, as in an indictment for larceny.—State v. McClung, (W. Va.) 13 S. E. 654.

6. Code Ga. § 4394, provides that horse-stealing shall be denominated "simple larceny," and the term "horse" shall include "mule" and "ass," and each animal of both sexes, and without regard to the alterations which may be made by artificial means. Section 4395 provides that the indictment for such an offense shall designate the nature, character, and sex of the animal, and give some other description by which its identity may be established. *Held*, that an indictment charging the theft of "one dark bay horse, with one spot on the end of his nose," etc., did not sufficiently indicate the character and sex of the animal, notwithstanding the use of the pronoun "his."—Brown v. State, (Ga.) 13 S. E. 20.

Evidence.

7. The theft of a lot of canned goods from a wholesale store is not established by finding a lot of such goods in the possession of accused when it is not shown that the goods were missed from the stock, nor that the stock was short, as it will be presumed that the goods in question were sold to retail dealers, and by them sold to accused.—Johnson v. State, (Ga.) 13 S. E. 282.

8. On trial for the larceny of a pocket-book containing $100 in money and a check for $10.79,

the evidence showed that the pocket-book had been lost in a public road. The next day, defendant, a colored man, unable to either read or write, in passing along the road, saw some papers along the wayside, and picked up two of them, one of which was the check in question, which was made payable to a third person, and did not have the owner's name thereon. On the same day defendant showed the check to a neighbor, who was unable to tell him what it was. Some weeks after this defendant accidentally disclosed his possession of the check, and reluctantly parted with it in payment of a bill, stating that the check had been given him in payment for work done. *Held,* that the evidence was not sufficient to show that defendant ever had possession of the pocket-book or its contents, except the check; and that, as there was nothing to show that he knew the owner at the time of the finding, and as the owner's name did not appear on the check, a conviction would be set aside as without evidence in its support. RICHARDSON, J., dissenting.—Perrin v. Commonwealth, (Va.) 13 S. E. 76.

9. Where an indictment for larceny from the person charges that the property stolen was of the value of $75, and the jury return a general verdict of guilty, the conviction is one of felony, and not of misdemeanor, under Code Ga. § 4411, making larceny from the person of an article of a greater value than $50 punishable by imprisonment in the penitentiary, and, if there is no evidence of the value of the property, the accused is entitled to a new trial.—Powell v. State, (Ga.) 13 S. E. 839.

Legacy.

See *Wills.*

Levy.

Of execution, see *Execution,* 8–11.

LIBEL AND SLANDER.

Death of plaintiff, survival of action, see *Abatement and Revival,* 8.

What is actionable.

1. Where perjury is punishable by confinement in the penitentiary, a false charge that a person swore lies at a certain trial is actionable *per se.*—Gudger v. Penland, (N. C.) 13 S. E. 168.

Privileged communications.

2. An alleged libel consisted in a letter written by the defendant to the superintendent of the United States census, wherein it was stated that the defendant thought himself entitled to recommend some of his political friends in the district in which he lived, and have them appointed as enumerators; that the supervisor, however, had paid no attention to his recommendations, but had appointed the plaintiff, a man who had since the war murdered two Union soldiers, and been instrumental also in defrauding the defendant out of his election to the legislature. There was evidence that the charges were untrue, and that the character of the plaintiff was good. There was no evidence in reply, and the answer admitted that the object of the defendant was to secure plaintiff's removal from office. *Held,* that the communication was one only of qualified privilege, and that, as there was evidence tending to show malice, the case should have been submitted to the jury.—Ramsey v. Cheek, (N. C.) 13 S. E. 775; Bradsher v. Same, Id. 777.

3. Where the complaint in an action for slander in making a false charge that a person swore lies at a certain trial does not show whether the charge was made at or after the trial, or that defendant sustained such relation to the trial as would exempt him from liability for his utterance, the complaint is not demurrable on the ground that the charge was made pending a judicial investigation.—Gudger v. Penland, (N. C.) 13 S. E. 168.

Action for—Pleading.

4. In an action of slander, in that defendant accused plaintiff of false swearing at a trial, plaintiff need not set forth the language or substance of the testimony referred to by defendant, unless defendant, in uttering the slanderous words, specified what plaintiff swore, or in what particulars his testimony was false.—Gudger v. Penland, (N. C.) 13 S. E. 168.

5. Though an action could be maintained and damages recovered by proving the utterance of slanderous words set forth in more than one paragraph of the complaint, where the language used in each instance amounts to a charge of perjury in the same judicial proceeding, and at the same time, it is not necessary that a separate demand for damages be appended to each paragraph.—Gudger v. Penland, (N. C.) 13 S. E. 168.

Criminal prosecution—Indictment.

6. An indictment which, in the language of Code N. C. § 1113, creating the offense, charges that defendant, attempting wantonly and maliciously to injure and destroy the reputation of L. B., an innocent and virtuous woman, did, by words spoken, declare, in substance, that she was an incontinent woman, is sufficient, without setting forth the words by which the attempt was made.—State v. Haddock, (N. C.) 13 S. E. 714.

—— Evidence.

7. On a trial for slandering an "innocent woman," the husband of the prosecutrix denied, on cross-examination, that he said he had sexual intercourse with the prosecutrix before he married her. Defendant offered to prove, by himself and another witness, that the husband said "that he would rather pay $2.50, and marry the woman, [the prosecutrix,] than have a bastard sworn to him." The trial court excluded the testimony. *Held,* that the testimony rejected was not competent to contradict the husband nor pertinent to prove the incontinency of the prosecutrix, and was simply hearsay.—State v. Morris, (N. C.) 13 S. E. 877.

LICENSE.

Of attorney, payment in state coupons, see *Attorney and Client,* 7, 8.
sale of liquor, see *Intoxicating Liquors,* 1–3.
To marry, see *Marriage.*

Business tax.

1. Under an ordinance providing "that all persons coming into the town of Rock Hill to engage therein in the business of a merchant for a shorter period than one year shall pay a license tax of $50," a tax is invalid which is assessed upon a merchant who, having conducted a dry goods store for 75 days, changes his business to that of selling produce, where the evidence shows that he had leased his store building for one year, with the privilege of two years.—White v. Town Council of Rock Hill, (S. C.) 13 S. E. 416.

Revocation.

2. Where, without express statutory authority, a city authorizes a licensed fish dealer to place a fish-box in a street, it may at any time require its removal, though by so doing it breaks up his business as a fish dealer before his license expires.—Laing v. City of Americus, (Ga.) 13 S. E. 107.

Liens.

See *Mechanics' Liens.*
chattel mortgage, see *Chattel Mortgages,* 3.
judgment, see *Judgment,* 19–25.
landlord, see *Landlord and Tenant,* 8–15.
mortgage, see *Mortgages,* 5, 6.
tax execution, see *Taxation,* 8.
Vendor's lien, see *Vendor and Vendee,* 7.

Life Insurance.

See *Insurance.*

LIMITATION OF ACTIONS.

See, also, *Adverse Possession.*
Against railroad company, see *Eminent Domain,*
16.
On insurance policy, see *Insurance,* 12–17.

Public corporations.

1. Public corporations, such as lunatic asylums, when clothed with capacity to sue and be sued, are amenable, in actions instituted by such corporations, to the defense of the statute of limitations, as well as to all other defenses, the same as natural persons are amenable.—McClanahan v. Western Lunatic Asylum, (Va.) 13 S. E. 977.

Action against guardian and administrator.

2. An action against one formerly plaintiff's guardian, and administrator of his father, for alleged fraudulent misappropriation of money received in such capacities, is barred by limitations where the administration was closed 26 years, and plaintiff reached his majority 13 years, prior to the commencement thereof.—Lane v. Lane, (Ga.) 13 S. E. 385.

Action on judgment.

3. Code Va. § 3573, prohibits the enforcement of a judgment lien upon which the right to issue execution or bring *scire facias* or action is barred by sections 3577 and 3578. Section 3577 provides that execution may issue within a year, and a *scire facias* or action may be brought within 10 years after judgment, and, where execution issues within the year, other executions may be issued, or a *scire facias* or action may be brought within 10 years from the return-day of an execution on which there is no return, or within 20 years from the return-day of an execution on which there is such return. Judgment in a justice court was obtained February 28, 1866, duly docketed, but upon which no execution was issued, and a judgment of the circuit court of November 2, 1866, also was duly docketed, on which no execution was issued. Suit was brought to enforce the liens of the judgments, April 30, 1887. *Held,* that the right was barred by limitation.—Brown v. Butler, (Va.) 13 S. E. 71.

Vendor's lien.

4. The statute of limitation does not apply to a lien for purchase money reserved in a conveyance of land.—Hull's Adm'r v. Hull's Heirs, (W. Va.) 13 S. E. 49; Dudley v. Same, Id.

Fraudulent conveyances.

5. Under Code N. C. § 155, subsecs. 4, 9, and section 158, limiting the bringing of actions based on fraud to 3 years after the discovery of the fraud, and placing a general limitation of 10 years on all actions, an action by a creditor to set aside his debtor's conveyances to his wife, brought 16 years after knowledge of such conveyances, is barred. Shepherd, J., dissenting.—Osborne v. Wilkes, (N. C.) 13 S. E. 285.

Running of statute.

6. Though an amendment of a summons and complaint was not made within a year, yet being merely as to the name of a party, and not the insertion of a new cause of action, it did not come within the statute of limitations, which required the action to be commenced within a year.—Bray v. Creekmore, (N. C.) 13 S. E. 723.

7. Though a third person has actual notice of the fraud infecting a conveyance, his right of action to set it aside only accrues upon his purchase of the land, and the statute does not begin to run against his action until then.—McGee v. Jones, (S. C.) 13 S. E. 826.

8. In a suit by an administrator and widow of a decedent, brought in Virginia against his heirs, to sell lands there to pay debts and satisfy the widow's dower, a decree adjudicating against existing against the decedent's estate, and subjecting its assets, will not save such debts from the statute of limitations for the purposes of a suit prosecuted in this state against lands here.—Hull's Adm'r v. Hull's Heirs, (W. Va.) 13 S. E. 49; Dudley v. Same, Id.

Trusts.

9. Where defendant agreed orally to hold the lands in trust, and that on a sale certain advances made by the parties, respectively, should be repaid out of the proceeds, and the balance equally divided between them, the statute of limitations does not run until the lands are sold by defendant.—Sprague v. Bond, (N. C.) 13 S. E. 143.

10. The rendition of a judgment against an administratrix, trustee of a continuing trust, and her failure to appeal therefrom, do not evidence a purpose on her part to throw off the trust; and the statute of limitations does not then begin to run against an action by the probate court against her sureties.—Burnside v. Donnon, (S. C.) 13 S. E. 465.

11. Where a ward writes her guardian demanding what is due her, and the guardian replies denying that anything is due, there is an express repudiation of his trust by the guardian, and an action against him and his sureties is barred within three years, under Code N. C. § 155, subd. 6, providing that actions against sureties on guardians' bonds shall be barred within three years after the breach complained of. Merrimon, C. J., dissenting.—Kennedy v. Cromwell, (N. C.) 13 S. E. 135.

Disabilities and exceptions.

12. An order enjoining creditors from prosecuting actions at law against an estate, and fixing a time for proving their claims in the action in which the injunction was granted, will not suspend the running of the statute of limitations against a creditor who brings suit on a simple contract claim more than six years after the time so fixed.—McLure v. Melton, (S. C.) 13 S. E. 615; In re Hardin, Id.

13. An action on a note against which the statute of limitations has run is not taken out of the statute because plaintiff also attempts to found the action on a mortgage securing the note, which mortgage contains a covenant binding the mortgagor to pay all reasonable attorneys' fees of collecting the note, if not paid at maturity, since the covenant in the mortgage is to be construed as applying to attorneys' fees incurred in proceedings to collect the note, commenced while it was collectible by law, and not after the bar of the statute had attached.—Allen v. Glenn, (Ga.) 13 S. E. 565.

14. In an action against the sureties on an administratrix's bond, the presumption that the administratrix has discharged her liability, if it arises from the fact that more than 20 years have elapsed since the execution of the administration bond, is rebutted by the collection, subsequent to the commencement of the action, of a judgment in favor of the estate against one of the sureties.—Burnside v. Donnon, (S. C.) 13 S. E. 465.

Coverture.

15. When the statute of limitations begins to run, the subsequent marriage of the *feme* plaintiff will not stop it.—Kennedy v. Cromwell, (N. C.) 13 S. E. 135.

16. Code Va. § 2933, provides that where a right accrues against a person who had before resided in the state, and who departs therefrom, or by any other indirect means obstructs the prosecution of such right, the time such obstruction continues shall not be computed as part of the time within which the right should have been prosecuted. A judgment debtor at the date of the judgment resided in the state, and was a carpenter by trade, and for several years after judgment he went from place to place in different states, working at his trade, leaving his family all the time in the place where the judgment was obtained. His wife testified that only three months before her deposition he wrote "he was coming home," and that his family were expecting him home, had he not died. *Held,* that there was no such obstruction as contemplated by the statute, as the judgment debtor had not

MANDAMUS.

To courts.

1. The supreme court will not grant a *mandamus nisi*, to the end that a bill of exceptions may be signed and certified, where it affirmatively appears on the face of the application that the decision complained of, and sought to be excepted to, was correct. — Dotterer v. Harden, (Ga.) 13 S. E. 971.

2. Code Va. § 3438, provides that, where a circuit judge refuses to award an injunction, a copy of the proceedings may be presented to a judge of the court of appeals, who may award the injunction. *Held*, that where a circuit judge has denied a petition for an injunction, and the appointment of a receiver, and a judge of the court of appeals has granted same, the circuit judge has no right to refuse to enforce his order; and the fact that the petition was a second and supplemental one is immaterial, and *mandamus* will lie to compel him to carry out the order of the appellate judge. LEWIS, P., and FAUNTLEROY, J., dissenting.—Wilder v. Kelley, (Va.) 13 S. E. 488.

To sheriff.

3. Gen. St. S. C. § 1817, provides that, on the determination of a lease of lands, when the lessee shall hold over, any two justices in the county may, on proof by the lessor, summon a jury to try the case, and, if they shall find that the lessor is entitled to the possession of the premises, the justices shall thereupon issue their warrant, commanding the sheriff to deliver to such lessor full possession of the premises. *Held*, that where, on verdict against the lessee and one holding under him, the justices have issued the proper warrant to the sheriff, *mandamus* will lie to compel him to execute same; and the fact that *certiorari* proceedings are pending before a judge of another circuit is immaterial, when such proceedings are void for lack of jurisdiction.—State v. Black, (S. C.) 13 S. E. 361.

To registrar of election.

4. Under Code Va. § 88, providing that if any person shall offer to be registered, and shall be rejected by the registrar, he may take an appeal to the court of his county or corporation, or to the judge thereof in vacation, and that on application of such appellant the registrar shall transmit to the court or judge a written statement of the ground relied on by appellant, and the reasons of the registrar that appellant did not offer to qualify as to his right to vote, and that he is not entitled to register, is no defense to an application for *mandamus* to compel him to transmit such statement to the county judge. LACY and RICHARDSON, JJ., dissenting.—Coleman v. Sands, (Va.) 13 S. E. 148.

5. Any qualified voter has such interest as entitles him to petition for *mandamus* to compel the registrar of voters to allow him to inspect or take copies of the registration books. LACY, J., dissenting.—Clay v. Ballard, (Va.) 13 S. E 262.

Manslaughter.

See *Homicide*, 13-15.

MARRIAGE.

See, also, *Divorce; Dower; Homestead; Husband and Wife.*

Effect on statute of limitations, see *Limitation of Actions*, 15, 16.

Marriage settlements, see *Husband and Wife*, 18-20.

License—Duty of officer.

Where the register of deeds administers to the person applying for a marriage license an oath as to the legal capacity of the parties, in accordance with Acts N. C. 1887, c. 331, and the evidence is such as to render it probable there is no legal impediment, it is a sufficient compliance with Code N. C. § 1816, declaring it the duty of such officer to make reasonable inquiry as to whether there is any legal impediment to the proposed marriage, and the register is not liable for the statutory penalty.—Walker v. Adams, (N. C.) 13 S. E. 907.

MASTER AND SERVANT.

Enticing away servant.

1. In an action for enticing a servant from his employer, an instruction, asked by defendant, that to constitute the relation of master and servant the terms of the employment must bind the servant to give his exclusive personal service to the master for the whole time agreed, was properly modified to the effect that the relation existed if the servant was bound to render services for such time as was usual and necessary in the work for which he was engaged.—Duckett v. Pool, (S. C.) 13 S. E. 542.

2. One who entices away a servant being liable to the master in damages by the common law, it was harmless error to charge that such entice ment was a "violation of our statute for which damages could be recovered," though no such statute existed.—Duckett v. Pool, (S. C.) 13 S. E. 542.

3. An instruction that if defendant, knowing that the servant was under contract with plaintiff, induced him to leave plaintiff's employ before the contract was terminated, defendant would be liable unless the servant voluntarily left before the inducement was offered, is not objectionable as not stating the time when the inducement was made, and when it contemplated the servant's abandoning his employment.— Duckett v. Pool, (S. C.) 13 S. E. 542.

Exemplary damages.

4. Where the testimony showed that defendant acted maliciously or in wanton disregard of plaintiff's rights in enticing away his servant, the court properly charged that exemplary damages could be awarded.—Duckett v. Pool, (S. C.) 13 S. E. 542.

Liability of master to third persons.

5. The owner of a horse, having rented a warehouse to a certain firm, left the horse with them, and used the horse in common with the firm. A clerk of the firm obtained the horse from the firm, without the knowledge of the owner, to drive to a picnic, the firm telling him to send the horse back if he had opportunity, which he did by a minor not in the employ of the firm or of the owner. The minor left the horse standing in the street, and it ran away, and killed plaintiff's horse. *Held*, that the firm were not liable, because the minor was not in their employ, and the clerk, as to the use of the horse, was not acting in the scope of his employment.—Thorp v. Minor, (N. C.) 13 S. E. 702.

Independent contractor.

6. Where a street-railway company, having authority to construct a railway in a street, does the work by an independent contractor, and an injury to a person passing along the street is caused by the negligence of a servant of the contractor, in unnecessarily laying loose rails in advance of the work, the contractor is liable for the injury, but the railway company is not, if it has not reserved any control over the conduct of the contractor in executing the work.—Fulton County St. R. Co. v. McConnell, (Ga.) 13 S. E. 828.

7. A railroad company which has employed an independent contractor to construct its road is not liable for the damages resulting from a nuisance created by such contractor, consisting of a pond on plaintiff's land, the result of failure to drain through an embankment, and the accumulation therein of filth from the camp of the contractor's workmen; the nuisance not being one necessarily incident to the construction of the road, and the railroad company having retained

no control over the manner of constructing it.—Atlanta & F. R. Co. v. Kimberly, (Ga.) 13 S. E. 277.

8. Where possession of the road was not yet delivered to the railroad company at the time of the injuries complained of, there is no such ratification of the contractor's acts as will render it liable therefor.—Atlanta & F. R. Co. v. Kimberly, (Ga.) 13 S. E. 277.

Negligence of master.

9. In an action against a railroad company for personal injuries the contention was that plaintiff had sued the defendant, when he should have sued the company which operated the road. Plaintiff testified that he kept the books at one of defendant's stations for a short time; that he made his remittances to the operating company, and may possibly have been paid by it, but that he did not know it was operating the road; that he afterwards became a brakeman on the train of a conductor who had been for a long time in defendant's employ; that the cars were marked with the name of that company, and that the superintendent to whom he applied for the position was the superintendent of both companies. The time schedules published in a newspaper were headed by the name of the defendant, and were separate from those of the operating company. The proprietor of the newspaper received separate passes for their publication. The name of the operating company appeared on the books of the station. Held, that the testimony as to which company was the employer was sufficient to go to the jury, and that it was error to grant a nonsuit.—Barnett v. Northeastern R. Co., (Ga.) 13 S. E. 646.

10. In an action to recover for personal injuries it appeared that plaintiff was employed to operate a machine in defendant's oil-mill; that while so doing he was required to do very rapid work, and that he was supplied with bags, which were placed on top of the machine by other employes; that it was necessary, for the safety of the machine operator, that these bags should be free from holes; that, if the operator discovered any hole in a bag, he would throw it out; and that the injury resulted from the use of a bag with a hole in it. Held error to nonsuit plaintiff upon the ground that no negligence was shown. Distinguishing Davis v. Railroad Co., 21 S. C. 93.—Carter v. Oliver Oil Co., (S. C.) 13 S. E. 419.

11. Plaintiff, who was employed by defendants in their quarry, was injured by the explosion of dynamite in a hole which he was drilling, and in which he had no knowledge that there was dynamite. It appeared that the hole had previously been charged with dynamite, and, with three others, sought to be exploded. The foreman thought that the charge had gone out through fissures at the bottom. He afterwards recharged the hole with powder, and exploded it. Afterwards he ordered plaintiff to drill into the hole, supposing that the explosion of the powder would have exploded the dynamite had it been there. The complaint alleged that defendant was negligent in employing an incompetent foreman, and in recharging the hole. There was no evidence that the foreman was incompetent, or that, if competent, he could by the use of due diligence have known that the previous charge had not exploded. Held, that a nonsuit was properly granted.—Houston v. Culver, (Ga.) 13 S. E. 953.

12. In an action against a railroad company for personal injuries, plaintiff, a brakeman, testified that he went behind the engine to uncouple it; that it was standing still at the time, but afterwards, without any signal from him, backed up, and caused him to catch his hand between the bumpers; and that he would not have been hurt but for its unexpected movement. He knew it was an ordinary coupling, and that the drag-bar, which they generally used, had been broken a day or two before; and did not think the engine and car could have come together if the drag-bar had been in position. He further testified, on cross-examination, that to the best of his recollection he had uncoupled the link before

he was hurt, and that in that case the cars would have come together even if the drag-bar had been there. Held, that the evidence of the company's negligence was sufficient to go to the jury, and that it was error to grant a nonsuit.—Barnett v. Northeastern R. Co., (Ga.) 13 S. E. 646.

13. In an action against a railroad company by its engineer for personal injuries sustained in running his train into a washout, it appeared that the culvert at which the washout occurred had withstood storms for 30 years, and that there was no reason for suspecting it of weakness; that shortly before the washout, which was from 30 minutes to two hours and a half before the accident, the sectionman examined the culvert, and, it appearing perfectly safe, went four miles up the track, where he apprehended danger, and watched. While there a severe and unprecedented water-spout, which he had no reason to apprehend, and of which he knew nothing until after the accident, occurred at the culvert, causing the washout. Held, that an instruction basing defendant's liability on the question whether there was sufficient time between the washout and the accident for defendant to learn of the washout, without calling the jury's attention to the other facts, was error.—Central Railroad & Banking Co. v. Kent, (Ga.) 13 S. E. 502.

14. Where an employe of a railroad company engages another to work in his place, and the latter is injured, evidence of private instructions, given by the former to the latter, as to how the work should be done, is not admissible in an action against the company for such injuries.—Mayfield v. Savannah, G. & N. A. R. Co., (Ga.) 13 S. E. 459.

—— Defective appliances.

15. In an action for personal injuries by a brakeman against a railroad company, it appeared that plaintiff, on a car on the front end of the train, attempted to descend to uncouple the engine. The bottom rung of the car ladder was missing, and, while feeling for it with his foot, the engineer, without the customary signal, suddenly backed the engine against plaintiff and injured him. The night was dark, and the bumper on the end of the car was broken off, so that the tender came up close to it. Plaintiff did not know the bumper had been broken off, and it was shown that the train was made up under the supervision of the regular car inspector, who was not called as a witness by the company. Held, the defective condition of the car was the proximate cause of the injury, and defendant was liable, although the negligence of a fellow-servant, the engineer, contributed to the injury.—Richmond & D. R. Co. v. George, (Va.) 13 S. E. 429.

16. In an action to recover damages for wrongful death, the evidence showed that a train of six cars was being run along a coal wharf, upon a wooden structure 25 feet high, and about 300 feet long. The only obstruction on the end of the structure was a log chained to the wharf. The chain gave way, and let the cars pass over the end thereof, killing plaintiff's intestate, who was a brakeman. It further appeared that the company had ordered timbers four years before, intending to build a dead-block, but the same was not built. Held sufficient to show negligence on the part of the company.—Norfolk & W. R. Co. v. Gilman's Adm'x, (Va.) 13 S. E. 475.

17. In an action by an employe for injuries sustained by reason of the falling of a door because of a defect in the rope suspending it, an instruction that, if plaintiff had the same means of knowing the defect in the fastening of the rope as defendant had, he cannot recover is properly refused if the duty of inspection did not rest upon him.—Austin v. Appling, (Ga.) 13 S. E. 955.

Negligence of fellow-servant.

18. A laborer employed by a railroad company in transferring freight was directed by his superior to assist a line repairer in putting up some wires. He did so, and was injured by falling to the ground with the ladder on which he was at

work, owing to the negligence of the line repairer, who was also in the railroad company's employment. *Held*, in an action for the injuries, that the question whether or not the laborer was injured by the negligence of a fellow-servant was for the jury, and it was error to grant a nonsuit.—Reedy v. East Tennessee, V. & G. Ry. Co., (Ga.) 13 S. E. 555.

Contributory negligence.

19. In an action for personal injuries it appeared that plaintiff, a machinist in defendant's employ, was told by the foreman to cut out with a chisel a screw which had become fastened, and in doing so the chisel blurred, causing a chip of steel to fly into his eye; that the foreman had gone to get a tool for plaintiff to do the work with, but that plaintiff, instead of awaiting his return, used a chisel which had been furnished him by defendant for other work, and which was not well tempered. *Held*, that a verdict for plaintiff was not warranted.—East Tennessee, V. & G. Ry. Co. v. Perkins, (Ga.) 13 S. E. 952.

20. A laborer employed by a railroad company in transferring freight was directed by his superior to assist a line repairer in putting up some wires. He did so, and carried some wire part way up a ladder, but refused to go to the top. The line repairer, who had been holding the ladder, then ran up it, passed the laborer, taking the wire with him, and sprang onto the roof of the depot, against which the ladder had been placed, causing the ladder to fall to the ground. *Held*, in an action against the company for the injuries sustained by the laborer in the fall, that the questions whether or not his own negligence contributed to the injury, and whether he could have prevented it by the exercise of ordinary care, were questions for the jury, and that it was error to grant a nonsuit.—Reedy v. East Tennessee, V. & G. Ry. Co., (Ga.) 13 S. E. 555.

21. Though attempting to couple cars when the engine is running at a speed of 15 miles an hour is apparently not only dangerous, but reckless, yet if it be true in the experience of engineers and railroad men that it is safe, provided the engine is properly managed, and if the failure in question resulted solely from the fault of the engineer in manipulating the engine, the high speed will be no obstacle to a recovery by the car-coupler for a personal injury sustained by him in making the attempt. Though to non-experts its truth would seem in a high degree improbable, if not impossible, yet, there being direct and positive evidence tending to support the theory of safety, the court erred in granting a nonsuit.—Rebb v. East Tennessee, V. & G. R. Co., (Ga.) 13 S. E. 566.

22. In an action by an engineer against a railroad company for personal injuries sustained by running his train into a washout, evidence that he was an experienced and reliable engineer is not pertinent on the question whether he was to blame for not seeing the washout in time to avoid the accident.—Central Railroad & Banking Co. v. Kent, (Ga.) 13 S. E. 502.

23. At the trial of an action against a railway company for damage for the death of a flagman on a freight train, killed by the running of the engine of a passenger train into the cab at the rear of the freight train where he was asleep, it appeared that the freight train was, at the time, on the main track, because of the derailment of its engine, and that deceased had been directed by the conductor to go into the cab and go to sleep, as he had worked hard and needed rest; and that, although the employes in charge of the freight train knew that the passenger train was approaching, and was due in about an hour and a half, deceased had reason to believe, from the assurance of the conductor that he would have deceased awaked in time to flag the passenger train, and from the placing of signals, and other circumstances, that that train would be stopped in time to avoid a collision. *Held*, that, in the absence of evidence showing how the duties of deceased were defined or regulated, otherwise

v. 13s. E.—69

than by the orders of the conductor, the question whether deceased was guilty of negligence in obeying the conductor's directions was one of fact for the jury, and it was error to grant a nonsuit on that ground.—Mills v. East Tennessee, V. & G. Ry. Co., (Ga.) 13 S. E. 205.

24. An employe of a railroad company, who, to couple cars, attempts, while an engine is running at the rate of four miles an hour, to jump upon a rim around the pilot which is only one and one-half inches wide, is guilty of contributory negligence, and cannot recover if injured.—Mayfield v. Savannah, G. & N. A. R. Co., (Ga.) 13 S. E. 459.

25. A railroad brakeman who, in coupling cars, with knowledge that the couplings are mismatched, places the pin in the moving car, and remains between the two cars to shake the pin into position, when he might have safely made the coupling by placing the pin in the standing car and permitting it to be shaken into position by the concussion of the two cars, is guilty of negligence, and no recovery can be had for his death resulting from being crushed between the two cars.—Norfolk & W. R. Co. v. McDonald's Adm'r, (Va.) 13 S. E. 706.

26. Plaintiff, an experienced railroad laborer on defendant's road, who knew that it was rough and crooked, was riding on a material train running very rapidly. He was in a closed car, having a large opening in one of its sides, and moved from the rear of the car, where he was protected, towards the stove, located in the center; and as he passed by the opening the train made a swift curve, which threw him out of the car. *Held*, that plaintiff was guilty of contributory negligence in passing by the opening without supporting himself, when he might have reached the place he intended to occupy by passing along the side of the car opposite to the opening.—Taylor v. Richmond & D. R. Co., (N. C.) 13 S. E. 736.

27. The fact that plaintiff left his position of safety in the rear of the car through fear of an accident, and to be near the opening, so that he might jump off the car in case of an emergency, does not relieve him from negligence in passing unsupported by the opening, when he might have safely reached the position he intended to occupy by passing along the opposite side of the car.—Taylor v. Richmond & D. R. Co., (N. C.) 13 S. E. 736.

28. In an action against a railroad company for personal injuries sustained by plaintiff while employed by defendant in coupling cars, the testimony for plaintiff showed that, being directed by a conductor to couple an engine and cab to another cab which was stationary, he gave the fireman a car-length signal to slack up, but the fireman did not do so; that he struck the cab, after which, on a signal, he stood still; that plaintiff then went between the cars to make the coupling; that after he had stooped down, and was hammering up the link, which was tight, he suddenly heard the engine exhaust, which it always did when moving; that in running out he stumbled, and, throwing up his hand, struck the dead block, and was caught, his hand being mashed. Plaintiff testified that no rules of the company requiring him to make a coupling in any other way had ever been read or explained to him; that he made his mark to some paper, but could not read, and did not know what it was. There was testimony for defendant contradicting plaintiff's evidence as to the cause of the accident, and the rules of the company were put in evidence, signed by plaintiff, requiring him to proceed otherwise than he did in coupling cars. The rules recited that they had been explained and were understood by the signers, and there was evidence that they had been read to plaintiff when he signed them. There was a verdict for plaintiff. *Held*, that the court did not abuse its discretion in refusing a new trial.—Richmond & D. R. Co. v. Wright, (Ga.) 13 S. E. 820.

Risks of employment.

29. A brakeman who enters into the employ of a railroad company owning cars, the couplings

of which are mismatched, and who continues to use such couplings for over a year without any promise by the company to change them, assumes the extra hazard incident to the use of the mismatched couplings; and no recovery can be had from the company for his death resulting from their use.—Norfolk & W. R. Co. v. McDonald's Adm'r, (Va.) 18 S. E. 706.

30. In an action by an employe for injuries sustained by reason of the falling of a door because of a defect in the rope suspending it, an instruction that if plaintiff commenced to use the door knowing its condition, and continued in defendants' service, the door remaining in the same condition, his continuance in the service would be a waiver of any claim upon defendants to furnish greater safeguards, is properly refused where the evidence shows that the door did not continue in the same condition.—Austin v. Appling, (Ga.) 18 S. E. 955.

31. In an action against a railroad company for injuries received by a section hand by reason of the falling of an embankment on defendant's right of way, where plaintiff was at work, the declaration alleged the particulars of defendant's negligence in undermining the embankment, and further alleged that plaintiff was young and inexperienced, knowing nothing of the manner in which the work should be done, and that in working near the embankment he was simply obeying the orders of the superintendent. *Held*, that the declaration was sufficient, though it did not distinctly allege that plaintiff was ignorant of the danger to which he was subjected.—Smith v. Georgia Railroad & Banking Co., (Ga.) 18 S. E. 904.

Master in Chancery.

See *Equity*, 12–14.

Measure of Damages.

See *Damages*.

MECHANICS' LIENS.

For construction of railroad.

1. Code Ga. § 1979, which gives railroad contractors a lien on the railroad for their work, contemplates a lien on the whole railroad; and a contractor cannot set up and enforce a lien on a part of the road, though such part may be all of the road which he constructed or added to construct.—Farmers' Loan & Trust Co. v. Candler, (Ga.) 18 S. E. 560.

Part performance of contract.

2. Plaintiffs contracted to furnish an apparatus at a fixed price sufficient to heat part of defendant's hotel. It was verbally agreed that the hotel halls should be kept closed, and not be included in this contract. Plaintiffs agreed to do extra work, and furnish materials, for which no price was agreed upon. Plaintiffs sued for a lien covering the whole amount. A portion of the claim had been paid, and plaintiff quit before completing the extra work for fear he would not get his pay. There was a dispute as to the price of the extra work. The court charged: "If the plaintiffs quit the extra work for fear they would not get their pay, they had the right to do so, and a failure to complete the extra work for that reason would not defeat their lien." *Held*, that under Code Ga. § 1980, which requires that there shall be "a compliance with his contract by the person claiming a lien," the plaintiffs, having failed to do the work, are not entitled to a lien for so much of the extra work as they have done, but as to such work are entitled to a general judgment upon a *quantum meruit*.—Rome Hotel Co. v. Warlick, (Ga.) 18 S. E. 116.

Enforcement.

3. A proceeding to foreclose a subcontractor's lien is a suit in equity.—Bailey Const. Co. v. Purcell, (Va.) 18 S. E. 456.

Enforcement—Verdict and judgment.

4. A verdict describing the lien intended to be allowed thereby in these terms: "That the plaintiff have a lien as a contractor to build railroads upon that part of the Gainesville & Dahlonega Railroad from its terminus, in the city of Gainesville, to the Chattahoochee river, in Hall county, including its right of way, road-bed, depot grounds, and all other property belonging to said railroad company, for the sum aforesaid," etc.,—does not set up a lien upon the whole railroad referred to, but only attempts to do so upon the part extending from Gainesville to the Chattahoochee river.—Farmers' Loan & Trust Co. v. Candler, (Ga.) 18 S. E. 560.

5. Since Code Ga. § 1990, declares that, in an action to enforce a mechanic's lien, the verdict must set forth the lien allowed, and the judgment and execution must be awarded accordingly, a verdict and judgment which attempt to set up and enforce, in favor of a contractor, a lien on a specified portion of a railroad, instead of on the whole road, are void on their face.—Farmers' Loan & Trust Co. v. Candler, (Ga.) 18 S. E. 560.

Memorandum.

To refresh memory of witness, see *Witness*, 14.

Minor.

See *Apprentice; Guardian and Ward; Infancy; Parent and Child*.

Mistake.

As ground for equitable relief, see *Equity*, 3–5. In purchase of land, see *Vendor and Vendee*, 5.

Money.

Had and received, see *Assumpsit*, 1. Paid to another's use, see *Assumpsit*, 2.

MORTGAGES.

See, also, *Chattel Mortgages*. Right of mortgagee on condemnation of land, see *Eminent Domain*, 15.

Absolute deed.

1. When the question at issue is whether a deed was made as an absolute conveyance of property or simply as a security for money advanced to the maker, evidence of the value of the property at the time the deed was made is pertinent and material.—Rodgers v. Moore, (Ga.) 18 S. E. 963.

Indorsement of mortgage note—Adoption of mortgage.

2. Where one, who, as president of a corporation, has executed a note and mortgage, subsequently indorses the note individually, he is bound by all the stipulations in the mortgage.—Georgia Railroad & Banking Co. v. Pendleton, (Ga.) 18 S. E. 823.

Description.

3. The W. turnpike ran in a northerly and southerly direction through plaintiff's plantation. West of this turnpike, also running north and south, was the A. canal. A road, known as the "Old Military Road," running nearly easterly and westerly, intersected the canal. A trust-deed executed by plaintiff on part of his plantation described the mortgaged land as being west of the W. turnpike, and then specifically bounded it, but by mistake the A. canal was given as the southern boundary instead of the eastern, and the old military road as the eastern, instead of the southern. *Held* that, as the parties could not reasonably have intended to locate the canal on the south when it was actually on the east, the true eastern boundary of the mortgaged land should be regarded as the canal, and that the land lying between it and the W. turnpike did

20. Where the mortgagee bid a certain sum at the trustee's sale, but withdrew the bid at the suggestion of the trustee, and afterwards bid in the property for a much smaller sum, the sale was void.—Fishburne v. Smith, (S. C.) 13 S. E. 525.

Motion.

To quash indictment, see *Indictment*, 1.

Multifariousness.

In pleading, see *Equity*, 10.

MUNICIPAL CORPORATIONS.

See, also, *Bridges; Counties; Highways; Schools and School-Districts; Towns.*

Appeals from Charleston city court, see *Appeal*, 13-15.

Grant of license by city, see *License.*

License of sale of liquor by, revocation, see *Intoxicating Liquors*, 1-3.

Ordinances, judicial notice of, see *Evidence*, 1-3.
—— regulation of speed of railroad trains, see *Railroad Companies*, 13, 14.

Special legislation concerning, see *Constitutional Law*, 4.

Streets, use by railroad, see *Railroad Companies*, 7, 8.

Ordinances—Driving on sidewalk.

1. The violation of a city ordinance against driving on a sidewalk cannot be justified on the ground of necessity arising from the muddy condition of a street, where such condition was known to defendant before he started to drive along it, and where, to avoid unloading his wagon, he drove on the sidewalk, though such street was the only passage to his place of business.—State v. Brown, (N. C.) 13 S. E. 940.

—— Impounding cattle.

2. Code, c. 47, § 28, provides that the council of a city shall have power to prevent cattle from going at large in the city, and section 29 declares that to carry into effect the powers conferred on a city the council shall have the power to pass all needful ordinances not contrary to the constitution and laws of the state, and to prescribe reasonable fines and penalties. *Held*, that the council could provide for the taking up and impounding of cattle found running at large in the public streets, and for selling them to pay charges. —Burdett v. Allen, (W. Va.) 13 S. E. 1012.

—— Punishment for violation.

3. A city ordinance prescribed, as a punishment for carrying on, without registration, a business required to be registered, a fine not exceeding a certain sum for each day the business was so carried on. *Held* that, on a summons expressly limited to one day's business, it was error to impose a fine of the maximum amount for three days' business; but that a violation of the ordinance being established by the evidence, the court on appeal could correct the error by reducing the fine to the maximum amount for so carrying on business for one day.—Phillips v. City of Atlanta, (Ga.) 13 S. E. 201.

4. The city council of Charleston, having passed an ordinance to regulate licenses, providing that, if any person therein named should refuse to take out a license, he should be liable to a penalty, but containing no provision to the effect that he might also be required to pay the license by an action for that purpose, is confined to the mode therein prescribed for enforcing payment of such licenses, and cannot resort to any other. —City Council of Charleston v. Ashley Phosphate Co., (S. C.) 13 S. E. 845.

Streets—Use by railroads.

5. The power to authorize the public streets of the city of Macon to be longitudinally occupied and used by a steam railroad resides exclusively in the legislature, and the municipal government is without authority to grant such a privilege to a railway company. Daly v. Railroad Co., 80 Ga. 793, 7 S. E. 146, followed.—Davis v. East Tennessee, V. & G. Ry. Co., (Ga.) 13 S. E. 567.

—— Removal of obstruction.

6. Under the charter of the city of Americus, (section 20,) declaring that the mayor and council shall have power to remove any building or other obstruction from the streets of the city, this power may, after notice to remove, be exercised summarily, and without a preliminary hearing. —Laing v. City of Americus, (Ga.) 13 S. E. 107.

7. The municipal authorities of a city cannot, on complaint of a citizen, cause an obstruction to be removed from a street which exists only in the plan of such city, and which has not been actually opened or worked by the municipal authorities, and used by the public, but, on the contrary, has been in private occupation for 30 or 40 years.—Bryans v. Almand, (Ga.) 13 S. E. 554.

—— Liability for defects.

8. In an action against a city for personal injuries caused by a defective sidewalk, there was evidence that the walk was in a bad condition, being of dirt, only about two feet wide, and sloping towards a ditch between it and the street, and that plaintiff, in walking along it at night, by reason of the edge crumbling away, fell into the ditch, and was injured. The city had been notified of the defect before the injury, and some time before had made some repairs, but the weather previous to the accident had made the walk crumble and wash. There was evidence that plaintiff and her husband, who walked part of the way with her on the night of the accident, and then let her go on alone, were familiar with the walk, and knew there was a better one on the other side of the street. Plaintiff testified that she was careful, and did not know the walk was so narrow. *Held*, that a verdict for plaintiff was warranted.—City of Atlanta v. Martin, (Ga.) 13 S. E. 805.

9. In an action against a city for personal injuries sustained by falling into an open sewer, it appeared that the city had left it open for years, and that it was on a principal street, and in a neighborhood that was badly lighted. Plaintiff, a woman of 24, was familiar with the locality, and knew the sewer was there, but thought it extended above the ground, and expected to strike it with her feet as she felt her way along. She had been away from the city for two years, during which the sewer was changed, so as to be level with the ground. The jury viewed the ground, and brought in a verdict for $500 damages. *Held*, that the verdict should not be disturbed.—City of Milledgeville v. Brown, (Ga.) 13 S. E. 688.

Public improvements—Property subject to assessment.

10. A local statute (Acts Ga. 1880-81, p. 356) which confers upon the municipal government power and authority to assess one-third of the cost of grading, paving, macadamizing, and otherwise improving the road-way or street proper on real estate abutting on each side of the street improved, subjects alike all real estate owned by individuals or private corporations, without respect to the purpose or use for which the property is held or to which it is devoted. Churches are not exempt; and, after paying such assessment, the religious corporation to which a church belongs cannot recover back the money so paid into the city treasury. Overruling Trustees, etc., v. City of Atlanta, 76 Ga. 181.—City of Atlanta v. First Presbyterian Church, (Ga.) 13 S. E. 252.

Bonds—Assent of voters.

11. Under Const. N. C. art. 7, § 7, prohibiting a municipal corporation from contracting any debt unless authorized by a majority of its qualified voters, the issuance of township bonds will not be compelled when plaintiff alleges that it was authorized by "a majority of the votes cast."

—Lynchburg & D. R. Co. v. Board Com'rs Person County, (N. C.) 13 S. E. 783.

12. Acts N. C. 1891, c. 206, authorized the school trustees to issue bonds, secured by a mortgage, and sell them; to take up other bonds previously issued for the purpose of paying for and repairing graded schools in a certain township; and, to raise a fund to pay the interest, and provide a sinking fund to pay the principal, allowed said trustees to appropriate annually a sufficient amount of the school fund going into their hands; and then provided that if they failed to do so the county commissioners should levy a tax on the taxable property and polls of the township for such purpose. *Held*, that the purpose of the act, in directing the county commissioners to levy a tax on the township property to pay the bonds in case the trustees should not do so, was to make the township assume and pay a debt other than for its necessary expenses, and, not having been sanctioned by a majority of the voters of the township, was to that extent in violation of Const. N. C. art. 7, § 7, which provides that no municipal corporation shall contract any debt, nor shall any tax be levied or collected by any officers of the same, except for the necessary expenses thereof, unless by a vote of a majority of the qualified voters therein.—Trustees of Goldsborough Graded School v. Broadhurst, (N. C.) 13 S. E. 781.

Murder.

See *Homicide*, 1-12.

Mutual Benefit Insurance.

See *Insurance*, 19.

Navigable Waters.

See *Riparian Rights; Water and Water-Courses.*

Necessary Parties.

See *Parties*, 1-3.

NEGLIGENCE.

Defective highways, see *Highways*, 11.
—— streets, see *Municipal Corporations*, 8, 9.
Liability of bailee, see *Bailment*, 2.
—— of carrier, see *Carriers*.
—— of infant, see *Infancy*, 2.
—— of railroad companies, see *Railroad Companies*, 15-17.
Of fellow-servant, see *Master and Servant*, 18.
master, see *Master and Servant*, 9-17.

Runaway horses.

1. The owner of a horse, having rented a warehouse to a certain firm, left the horse with them, and used the horse in common with the firm. A clerk of the firm obtained the horse from the firm, without the knowledge of the owner, to drive to a picnic, the firm telling him to send the horse back if he had opportunity, which he did by a minor not in the employ of the firm or of the owner. The minor left the horse standing in the street, and it ran away, and killed plaintiff's horse. *Held*, that the facts fail to show any negligence on the part of the owner.—Thorp v. Minor, (N C.) 13 S. E. 702.

Dangerous premises.

2. A person having authority from a city to construct a railway in a street caused loose rails to be taken from the gutter and placed in the street far in advance of the work, to expedite the work, and guide the workmen in making the proper excavations. The street was safe with the rails in the gutter, but unsafe with them on the street, and there was a safe way of marking the lines in advance of the work without using the rails. *Held*, that it was negligence to place the rails in the street.—Fulton County St. R. Co. v. McConnell, (Ga.) 13 S. E. 896.

Contributory negligence—Of child.

3. In an action against a railroad company by a child under 14 years of age for personal injuries, where there is no demurrer, and the case is submitted to the jury, there is no presumption, on account of the child's age, that it did not have sufficient capacity to be sensible of danger, and power to avoid it, but the jury are to determine the child's capacity according to the facts of each case.—Central Railroad & Banking Co. v. Ryles, (Ga.) 13 S. E. 584.

Comparative negligence.

4. Code Ga. § 2972, provides that in suits for personal injuries, if by ordinary care the plaintiff could have avoided the consequences of the defendant's negligence, he cannot recover. Section 3084 provides that, if the plaintiff and the defendant are both in fault, the former may recover, but the jury shall diminish the damage in proportion to his fault. *Held*, that it was error to charge in the language of the two sections, without telling the jury that the last section applies only to cases in which the plaintiff could not have avoided the consequences of the defendant's negligence.—Americus, P. & L. R. R. v. Luckie, (Ga.) 13 S. E. 105.

Imputed negligence.

5. Two railway companies, each under its own franchise, used the track of one of them in common. *Held* that, in an action against the owner of the track for the death of an employe of the other company caused by defendant's neglect to render harmless a low bridge over the track, though it be not alleged that the company not owning the track was ignorant of the danger or of the conditions which caused it, it will not be assumed, in deciding upon a demurrer to the declaration, that it was negligent in running the train to which the employe was attached when injured, so that the question whether any negligence of that company could be imputed to the employe is immaterial.—Ellison v. Georgia Railroad & Banking Co., (Ga.) 13 S. E. 809; Georgia Railroad & Banking Co. v. Ellison, Id.

6. In a suit by the administrator of an infant for injuries causing his death, the contributory negligence of the parents cannot be imputed to him, and is therefore immaterial.—Norfolk & W. R. Co. v. Groseclose's Adm'r, (Va.) 13 S. E. 454.

7. In an action against a railroad company for injuries sustained by plaintiff at a crossing, while being driven in a public hack, the court charged the jury that negligence of the driver was not imputable in law to her; that a person who hired a public hack and directed the driver where she wished to be conveyed, but exercised no other control over his conduct, was not responsible for his negligence, or prevented from recovering against the railroad company for injuries suffered from a collision of its train with the hack caused by the concurring negligence of both the manager of the train and the driver of the hack; that the only negligence of the driver which would defeat her right to recover was where his negligence was the sole and real cause of the collision. *Held*, that the charge was correct.—East Tennessee, V. & G. Ry. Co. v. Markens, (Ga.) 13 S. E. 855.

8. A passenger in a public hack is under no duty to supervise the driver at a railroad crossing, nor to look or listen for approaching trains, unless she has some reason to distrust the diligence of the driver.—East Tennessee, V. & G. Ry. Co. v. Markens, (Ga.) 13 S. E. 855.

Pleading.

9. The owner of a horse, having rented a warehouse to a certain firm, left the horse with them, and used the horse in common with the firm. A clerk of the firm obtained the horse from the firm, without the knowledge of the owner, to drive to a picnic, the firm telling him to send the horse back if he had opportunity, which he did by a minor not in the employ of the firm or of the owner. The minor left the horse standing in the street, and it ran away, and killed plaintiff's

horse. *Held*, that the clerk was not liable, because there were no allegations against him in the complaint.—Thorp v. Minor, (N. C.) 13 S. E. 702.

10. Where the declaration charges that the damages were occasioned by the negligence of the defendant, it is sufficient on demurrer, although there is no denial of contributory negligence.—Norfolk & W. R. Co. v. Gilman's Adm'x. (Va.) 13 S. E. 475.

NEGOTIABLE INSTRUMENTS.

Indorsement of mortgage note, adoption of mortgage, see *Mortgages*, 2.

Date of maturity.

1. Notes being executed in February, 1888, payable in 30 days, were not due until 30 days thereafter, notwithstanding that they bore date in 1887. Raefle v. Moore, 58 Ga. 94, followed.—Beach v. Atkinson, (Ga.) 13 S. E. 591.

Indorsement and transfer.

2. Where, in order to have a note discounted at bank, a partner indorsed it in his own name, and also in the partnership name, and the undisputed evidence shows that the bank would not make the discount and advance the money without the latter indorsement, there is no ground in the evidence for charging the jury as to the effect of the transaction, if based on the credit of the one partner only; and this is so, although the bank knew that, before the partnership indorsement would be binding on the firm, ratification by the other partner would be necessary.—American Exch. Nat. Bank v. Georgia Const. & Inv. Co., (Ga.) 13 S. E. 505.

3. The indorsee of a bill of exchange, in the absence of any notice on the subject, is entitled to treat the acceptor as the real debtor, and is under no duty to such acceptor to retain or render available collateral securities for the payment of the bill received from the payee and indorser.—Fowler v. Gate City Nat. Bank, (Ga.) 13 S. E. 831.

4. Where the maker of a note executes a mortgage to secure the same, and stipulates therein for the payment of attorney's fees in case of collection, declaring as a part of the mortgage deed that it may be foreclosed for such fees, together with the principal and interest of the note, and a judgment of foreclosure is afterwards rendered accordingly, and judgment on the note against the maker and indorsers is also rendered in a proper action, a subsequent waiver by the indorsers in writing of any objection to the stipulation in the mortgage as to attorney's fees is a ratification by them of the maker's act in giving the mortgage, which will estop them from afterwards insisting that the judgment of foreclosure shall not operate against them as conclusive upon the question of the creditor's right to appropriate a sufficient amount of the proceeds of the mortgaged property to the payment of such fees.—Georgia Railroad & Banking Co. v. Pendleton, (Ga.) 13 S. E. 823.

—— Bona fide purchaser.

5. A person unknown to plaintiff offered to sell him for $100 a note made by defendant, the face value of which was $125. Plaintiff, having learned on inquiry that defendant was solvent, purchased the note. In an action to recover its value the evidence introduced by plaintiff himself showed that the note was payable six months after date at a place which plaintiff was aware was not in existence, and that he knew that it was given "for some sort of a township right" on some contract not known to him. *Held*, that these facts were such as should have put plaintiff on further inquiry as to the validity of the note.—Farthing v. Dark, (N. C.) 13 S. E. 918.

Acceptance.

6. Where the drawee of a bill of exchange writes his name across the face thereof, Code Ga. § 1950, requiring acceptance to be in writing, is complied with, the legal significance of such an

act being that the bill is thereby accepted.—Fowler v. Gate City Nat. Bank, (Ga.) 13 S. E. 831.

Protest and notice of dishonor.

7. The certificate of protest of a note payable in New York, by a notary there, is no evidence of dishonor, in a suit on it in Virginia, since there is no statute in Virginia making such protest evidence.—Corbin v. Planters' Nat. Bank (Va.) 13 S. E. 98.

8. Where a note was due on the 14th of the month in New York, and on the 17th the holder received notice of its dishonor in Richmond, Va., which on the same day he forwarded to the indorser. there is no proof of due notice of dishonor, as it does not appear when the notice was mailed in New York.—Corbin v. Planters' Nat. Bank, (Va.) 13 S. E. 98.

Actions on—Parties.

9. The payee of a negotiable instrument, not payable to bearer, after indorsing the same specially to another person, cannot sue thereon for the use of the indorsee, but the indorsee alone can sue, so long as he is the legal holder of the instrument.—Spence v. Robinson, (W. Va.) 13 S. E. 1004.

10. The maker and indorsers of a promissory note, executed in another state, under the laws of which it is negotiable, are not jointly liable to a holder who discounts it in Virginia, and such holder cannot, therefore, sue the maker and indorsers jointly.—Corbin v. Planters' Nat. Bank, (Va.) 13 S. E. 98.

—— Pleading.

11. The giving of a check implies indebtedness to the amount thereof, and in an action upon the check it is unnecessary to plead consideration.—McClain v. Lowther, (W. Va.) 13 S. E. 1008.

—— Burden of proof.

12. In an action on a check, where plaintiff shows that there were no funds in the bank to pay it, the burden as to proof of injury or no injury, because of laches in presenting the check, or failure to notify the drawer of its non-payment, is shifted from plaintiff to defendant.—McClain v. Lowther, (W. Va.) 13 S. E. 1008.

Newly-Discovered Evidence.

See *Criminal Law*, 61–66; *New Trial*, 12, 13. As ground for continuance, see *Continuance*, 1.

NEW TRIAL.

In criminal cases, see *Criminal Law*, 59–66; *Homicide*, 43.

Application.

1. A motion for a new trial on the ground that the court admitted illegal evidence must state that objection was made when the evidence was offered, and what the objection was, or the objection will not be considered on appeal.—Clark v. Empire Lumber Co., (Ga.) 13 S. E. 836.

—— Verification.

2. The recital of facts in a motion for a new trial is verified where the bill of exceptions sets forth in detail all the grounds, and adds: "The recitals of fact contained in the motion for new trial, and in each of the foregoing six grounds thereof, are true and correct."—Starling v. Thorne, (Ga.) 13 S. E. 552.

—— Brief of evidence.

3. Superior court rule 49 (Code Ga. p. 1352) provides that, "in every application for a new trial, a brief of the testimony in the cause shall be filed by the party applying for such new trial, under the revision and approval of the court." *Held*, that the court has power to pass an order during term allowing until the hearing of the motion to file the brief of evidence; and if the hearing by subsequent order be regularly continued from one time in vacation to another, the

case having in term been set down for hearing in vacation, the judge may approve and allow the brief of evidence to be filed at or before the hearing, though he may not be absolutely bound to do so.—Central Railroad & Banking Co. v. Curtis, (Ga.) 13 S. E. 757; Curtis v. Central Railroad & Banking Co., Id.

—— Exception to rulings.

4. Where a motion was made at one term of the court to dismiss a motion for a new trial, and was overruled, it was too late at the next term to assign error thereon in a bill of exceptions to the final judgment of the court granting a new trial in the case, no exceptions *pendente lite* having been taken and filed at the term when the rulings complained of were made.—Hyfield v. Sims, (Ga.) 13 S. E. 554.

—— Hearing.

5. An allowance of seven days for preparing to argue a motion for a new trial, and bringing the same for a hearing, is no abuse of discretion by the trial court, though one of such days is a Sunday, and another day falls in a term of court in which all the counsel were practitioners.—Greer v. State, (Ga.) 13 S. E. 552.

Misconduct of jury.

6. The verdict of a jury in a justice's court is not vitiated because the jury, after deliberating for some hours, came into court, announced that they could not agree unless they could have before them a certain cash-book, and, upon being informed by the presiding justice that the book was not legal evidence, returned to their room, under the direction of the justice, to resume their deliberations, and in a few minutes brought in a verdict. Though it was irregular for the jury to call for more evidence, it was not such misconduct as to render their subsequent finding illegal.—Nolen v. Heard, (Ga.) 13 S. E. 554.

—— Strangers in jury-room.

7. The losing party is entitled to a new trial where it appears that a man who was not a member of the jury, and whose name was not on the list, did, without the knowledge or consent of such party or his counsel, accompany the jury to their room, remain there with them, and participate in the formation and rendition of the verdict.—Starling v. Thorne, (Ga.) 13 S. E. 552.

Conflicting evidence.

8. Where the evidence on the second trial of an action is irreconcilable, and the verdict results in favor of the same party as at the first trial, the supreme court will not interfere with the refusal of the trial judge to grant a new trial on condition that a part of the recovery be remitted, which condition has been complied with.—Jones v. Farmer, (Ga.) 13 S. E. 554.

9. The evidence having been conflicting, and the court having been satisfied with the verdict, there is no error in refusing a new trial on the grounds that the verdict was contrary to the law and evidence.—Hooks v. Hayes, (Ga.) 13 S. E. 134.

10. Where a cause of action is set forth in the declaration, and the evidence adduced at the trial is sufficient to support it, it is not error to refuse to grant a new trial.—Georgia Railroad & Banking Co. v. Rhodes, (Ga.) 13 S. E. 637.

11. There is no abuse of discretion in refusing a new trial where the evidence upon the main issue was conflicting.—Miller v. Miller, (Ga.) 13 S. E. 635.

Newly-discovered evidence.

12. Newly-discovered evidence which is cumulative, or which only tends to discredit a witness, is not cause for a new trial.—Johnson v. Palmour, (Ga.) 13 S. E. 637.

13. It was proper to refuse to grant a new trial upon the ground of newly-discovered evidence when the affidavit in support thereof does not give the date or details of a conversation between affiant and defendant, which is made the basis of the motion, as in such case the relevancy of the testimony does not appear.—Grayson v. Buchanan, (Va.) 13 R. E. 457.

Non Compos Mentis.

See *Insanity.*

Nonsuit.

See *Practice in Civil Cases,* 2, 3.

Notice.

Of appeal, in criminal cases, see *Criminal Law,* 68–73.
application for certiorari, see *Certiorari,* 3.
dishonor of note, see *Negotiable Instruments,* 7, 8.
motion to dismiss appeal, see *Appeal,* 38.

NOVATION.

What constitutes.

The fact that a construction company agreed with a railway company to pay the salaries of its officers does not relieve the latter from liability in the absence of an agreement to that effect.—Bowen v. Carolina, C. G. & C. R. Co., (S. C.) 13 S. E. 421.

NUISANCE.

Liquor nuisance, abatement in equity, see *Intoxicating Liquors,* 11.

Indictment.

1. An indictment against a railroad company charged it with obstructing a public highway by placing in and across the highway certain plank. *Held* that, where the indictment did not show in what way the plank was misused or misapplied at the crossing, or that defendant allowed the plank to become out of repair, and in such improper condition as to obstruct the highway, it failed to appropriately charge a nuisance.—State v. Roanoke Railroad & Lumber Co., (N. C.) 13 S. E. 719.

Action for damages—Evidence.

2. Plaintiff, in an action for damages from a nuisance, testified that the malaria of which he complained resulted from four causes, viz.: An embankment of loose earth, a dam, a horse lot, and a hog lot,—all maintained by the contractor near his house. There being no allegation in the petition as to the horse and hog lots, they were stricken from his testimony. *Held,* that it was error to admit the testimony as changed, since it made the injury dependent upon two causes only, while plaintiff assigned four.—Atlanta & F. R. Co. v. Kimberly, (Ga.) 13 S. E. 277.

Nuncupative Will.

See *Wills,* 2.

Obligation of Contracts.

See *Constitutional Law,* 9.

OBSTRUCTING JUSTICE.

Resisting officer—Indictment.

It is not necessary that an indictment, under Act N. C. 1889, c. 51, or at common law, for resisting an officer, should contain the warrant or name the party the officer was seeking to arrest when resisted.—State v. Dunn, (N. C.) 13 S. E. 881.

Office and Officer.

See *Judge; Justices of the Peace; Receivers· Sheriffs and Constables.*
Election officer, resignation, see *Elections and Voters,* 1.

Opinion Evidence.

See *Evidence*, 30-32.

ORDERS.

Appealable orders, see *Appeal*, 1-11.

Conditional acceptance.

An order was drawn by contractors for a specific sum, with direction to "charge the same to firm on account of work done and to be done on your building now in process of erection," and was accepted in these terms, "I agree to pay the within order when the building is finished and received by B. & M." *Held*, that the acceptance was conditional on completion of the building by the drawer; and since, without fault of the acceptor, he failed to complete it, and the acceptor had it completed by others at his own expense, there can be no recovery on the acceptance.—Baker v. Dobbins, (Ga.) 13 S. E. 594.

Ordinance.

See *Municipal Corporations*, 1-4.

PARENT AND CHILD.

Abduction of child, action by father, see *Abduction*.
Allowance to children out of father's estate, see *Executors and Administrators*, 26.
Apprenticing child, see *Apprentice*.
Damages for killing child, see *Death by Wrongful Act*, 3, 4.

Support of children.

1. A widow, who has not sufficient property of her own to support minor children, may resort to the children's property for that purpose; and therefore, where she arranges with her father to furnish the support, agreeing to allow him as consideration the use of the children's land, from which he derives an income less in value than the support, neither she nor they have any claim against his estate.—Rhode v. Tuten, (S. C.) 13 S. E. 676.

2. In an action against a father to recover for the support of a child, the complaint alleged that the father became insane in 1880, and has continued so; that plaintiff was a sister of the deceased, who on her death-bed requested plaintiff to support the child, which plaintiff agreed to do; that plaintiff tried to obtain aid from other relatives of the child which would have died or become a charge upon the county had not plaintiff supported it. The complaint failed to state that the father had abandoned or neglected the child, or that he knew of or promised to pay for the services of plaintiff. *Held*, that it did not state a cause of action.—Everitt v. Walker, (N. C.) 13 S. E. 860.

3. Plaintiff could not support the child from motives of charity and love for her sister, without any intention of charging the father, and afterwards, when he became owner of property, compel him to pay for the support.—Everitt v. Walker, (N. C.) 13 S. E. 860.

Services of child for father — Compensation.

4. On a trial to recover for services rendered for defendant's decedent by his daughter, two witnesses testified that they had heard the father say the daughter ought to be paid for her services. Another testified that she had heard him say that she ought to have "extra pay for her services to him." *Held* insufficient to create a legal obligation, as in such cases the presumption is that the services were gratuitous, which must be overcome by proof of an express agreement to pay.—In re Kirkpatrick's Estate, (S. C.) 13 S. E. 450.

Parol Evidence.

See *Evidence*, 35-43.

PARTIES.

Action on note, see *Negotiable Instruments*, 9, 10.
Amendment of pleadings as to, see *Pleading*, 14, 15.
In condemnation proceedings, see *Eminent Domain*, 4.
equity, see *Equity*, 11.
Joinder of husband and wife, see *Husband and Wife*, 25, 26.

Necessary parties.

1. The next friend, being one of the heirs of a lunatic, is a necessary party to an action by the administrator of the lunatic against the administrator of the committee for an accounting, where the amount of the recovery would be affected by the construction of an agreement by the next friend with the committee for a settlement of the account.—Clark v. Crout, (S. C.) 13 S. E. 602.

2. Land was devised to a married woman for the life of her husband, with a charge thereon for the support and maintenance of her husband during his life; after his death, his minor children to take the fee. *Held*, that such a minor had not, during the lives of his parents, such an interest in the land as rendered him a necessary party to an action resulting in a verdict and judgment by consent that the claim be a special lien on the crops, to be enforced in three annual installments.—Watson v. Goolsby, (Ga.) 13 S. E. 106.

3. Under Code N. C. § 186, providing that persons severally liable upon the same obligation or instrument, including the parties to bills of exchange and promissory notes, may all or any of them be included in the same action, at the option of the plaintiff, the administrator and other sureties on his bond are not necessary parties to a suit by the distributees against one of the sureties to enforce a judgment recovered against the administrator and all of his sureties.—Brown v. Walker, (N. C.) 13 S. E. 8.

Defect of parties.

4. Where defendant did not demur on the ground that a proper party defendant was not joined, an objection by defendant on that ground will not be sustained.—S. C. Forsaith Mach. Co. v. Hope Mills Lumber Co., (N. C.) 13 S. E. 869.

Intervention.

5. Judgment creditors are not entitled to be made party defendants in foreclosure proceedings for the purpose of proving collusion between the mortgagor and mortgagee to the prejudice of themselves and other creditors, and to contest the validity of the mortgage, but the proper remedy is by an independent action for that purpose.—Bruce v. Sugg, (N. C.) 13 S. E. 790.

PARTITION.

Owelty—How enforced.

A decree of partition having charged the dividend of superior value with a sum of money to make equality, payment must be enforced by the writ of *venditioni exponas* granted on motion or petition in the partition proceedings, and not by independent action. Following Herman v. Watts, 13 S. E. 437.—Pardue v. Givens, (N. C.) 13 S. E. 112.

PARTNERSHIP.

Appointment of receiver, see *Receivers*, 7, 8.

Power of partner to bind firm.

1. A partner has the right to give a mortgage on personal property to secure a partnership debt, and also to agree to its cancellation, and the other partner is not injured thereby.—Phillips v Trowbridge Furniture Co., (Ga.) 13 S. E. 19.

—— Ratification.

2. An indorsement in the partnership name to raise funds for the indorsing partner or for a third person will not bind the partnership with-

out ratification, where the bank discounting the paper knows such ratification to be necessary, though the funds be entered in the bank-books to the credit of the partnership, and afterwards drawn out on checks of the partnership signed by the partner not privy to the transaction; but if the proceeds of such checks, or some of them, be used for the benefit of the partnership, and any of them be retained after notice of the material facts has been acquired, it will be a ratification.—American Exch. Nat. Bank v. Georgia Const. & Inv. Co., (Ga.) 13 S. E. 505.

Firm and private creditors.

3. Where the business is carried on by one visible partner, who is known to the creditor to be advertised as the sole proprietor of the firm, such partner has power to assign the firm assets to pay his individual debts in preference over partnership creditors.—Motley v. Frank, (Va.) 13 S. E. 36.

4. If two members of a partnership unite in selling the firm assets to pay individual debts, and the share of one of them in the assets exceeds the amount of his debts settled by the sale, it amounts in law to a donation by him to his partner of such excess, which will be held void as against firm creditors.—Ellison v. Lucas, (Ga.) 13 S. E. 445.

5. The members of a partnership, though it be insolvent, may unite in selling the entire assets in payment of their individual debts, and such a sale, if made in good faith, is valid as against the firm creditors, if not obnoxious to the statutes against voluntary conveyances by insolvent debtors.—Ellison v. Lucas, (Ga.) 13 S. E. 445.

Retiring partners — Liability for firm debts.

6. Where three persons compose a partnership under a name which does not disclose the individual name of any partner, and two of them withdraw, and the third continues business at the same place, and under the same partnership name, a person dealing with him, even though no notice of the dissolution had ever been given in any manner, cannot hold the retired members of the firm responsible, if he had never dealt with the firm before dissolution, and had no knowledge of the persons constituting the same, either before the dissolution or at the time of the dealing in question.—Austin v. Appling, (Ga.) 13 S. E. 955.

7. In an action against a retiring partner for goods alleged to have been sold to the partnership without notice of the dissolution, it is proper to refuse an instruction that the retiring partner is not liable if the goods were purchased by his copartner before the dissolution, to be delivered to the latter after the dissolution, with knowledge by plaintiff of this fact, where the only evidence relating to the dissolution shows that it had taken place before the sale in question.—McGee v. Potts, (Ga.) 13 S. E. 746.

8. In an action for goods alleged to have been sold to a partnership, plaintiff's evidence showed that they were sold without information of the dissolution of the partnership, though with notice of an intention to dissolve in the future. Plaintiff also showed that the retiring partner had subsequently paid for a portion of the goods. Held, that the evidence was sufficient to warrant a finding by the jury that the sale was to the partnership, and that the retiring partner was liable, though defendant's evidence showed that plaintiff was informed of the dissolution of the partnership before he sold the goods, and that the portion paid for by the retiring partner had been used by him in his individual business.—McGee v. Potts, (Ga.) 13 S. E. 746.

Liability of partners for tort.

9. Where three persons are sued as partners for a tort, and no partnership is established, the verdict may be against one only, if the tort is established as against him.—Austin v. Appling, (Ga.) 13 S. E. 955.

Actions.

10. That the name of a partnership was inverted in making a written contract for the shipment of live-stock will not defeat an action brought in tort against the carrier by the partnership in its proper name for injuries to the property during transportation.—Central Railroad & Banking Co. v. Pickett, (Ga.) 13 S. E. 750.

11. Where three persons are sued as partners, and two of them file pleas of non-partnership, and the whole case is tried together, a verdict against all three by name, construed in the light of the pleadings, is a finding that they are all liable as partners, and is equivalent to a verdict against the partnership. — Austin v. Appling, (Ga.) 13 S. E. 955.

Part Performance.

See *Specific Performance*, 4.

Passengers.

See *Carriers*, 8–14.

PAYMENT.

See, also, *Compromise*.
Of loss by insurance company, see *Insurance*, 10.
taxes, see *Taxation*, 6, 7.

Evidence.

1. Where the state makes a grant of land to a city, to be absolute upon the payment of $10,-000 by the city to the state, within a given time, the original receipt of the comptroller general for said sum of money was properly admitted as evidence of such payment.—Georgia Railroad & Banking Co. v. City of Macon, (Ga.) 13 S. E. 21.

—— Province of jury.

2. In an action against defendant for $254 due plaintiff's intestate, where there was evidence tending to show that defendant had nearly paid the whole claim during the life-time of deceased, the jury were the judges as to the amount paid, and it was error for the court to instruct them that they could not find that defendant had paid more than $96.—Benton v. Toler, (N. C.) 13 S. E. 768.

Application.

3. A chattel mortgage on a growing crop and other property, given to secure a note executed by the mortgagor and future advances to be made on the crop, empowered the mortgagees to sell the crop, and apply the proceeds in payment of the advances and the note. Held, that the acceptance by the mortgagees of a second mortgage covering property already embraced in the first mortgage, as security for another debt, did not modify the provision in the first mortgage as to the application of payments; and a direction of the mortgagor that the mortgagees apply the proceeds of the crop to the payment of the debt secured by the second mortgage was not binding on them.—Weil v. Flowers, (N. C.) 13 S. E. 761.

Penalty.

For failure to deliver message, see *Telegraph Companies*.

PERJURY.

Indictment.

Under Acts N. C. 1889, c. 83, prescribing a form for indictments for perjury, and requiring them to state the court in which the perjury was committed, it is not error, in an indictment for perjury committed at a trial in a justice's court, to give, in addition to the name of the court, the names of the justices who sat at the trial.—State v. Flowers, (N. C.) 13 S. E. 718.

PLEADING.

Alleging damages, see *Damages*, 5–7.
—— negligence, see *Negligence*, 9, 10.

Complaint—Joinder of causes.

1. A complaint which alleges ownership of certain lands, and that defendant is in possession, claiming to have some interest, and wrongfully withholds the same from plaintiffs, and that they own no other land in common with defendant, contains but one cause of action, namely, to recover land, though the prayer of judgment is for an accounting and partition, as the prayer is no part of the cause of action.—Westlake v. Farrow, (S. C.) 13 S. E. 469.

Plea.

2. The statute which allows the defendant to plead as many matters of defense as he may elect, does not confer upon him an absolute right to file special pleas setting up defenses which are already covered by other pleas; and, although such a plea has been received, and issue joined upon it, it is still competent for the court to strike it out.—Virginia Fire & Marine Ins. Co. v. Buck, (Va.) 13 S. E. 973.

3. In an action for the price of land, a plea of set-off, showing that there was a partial failure of consideration, in that a spring was represented to be on the land, when in fact it was not, and that there was a deficiency of 14 acres in the tract, is not double.—Grayson v. Buchanan, (Va.) 13 S. E. 457.

Striking out allegations—Harmless error.

4. Where a plea is improperly stricken, but defendant is nevertheless allowed the benefit of it on the trial, the error of striking it is not cause for a new trial.—Atlanta Glass Co. v. Noizet, (Ga.) 13 S. E. 833.

5. In an action by a father for damages for abducting his daughter for immoral purposes, where on demurrer allegations of the immoral character of the daughter and of plaintiff's whole family were stricken out of the answer, but all the evidence offered to prove the same was received, defendants were not prejudiced, even though the allegations were material.—Dobson v. Cothran, (S. C.) 13 S. E. 679.

Verification.

6. A plea of *non est factum* must be sworn to, and generally the affidavit must be made by the defendant, and not by an agent, except, it may be, under Code Ga. § 3449, where, in civil cases, on unconditional contracts in writing, there is an issuable defense, and defendant does not reside in the county wherein the writ is pending.—Fowler v. Gate City Nat. Bank, (Ga.) 13 S. E. 831.

7. A note for a stated sum, with interest from maturity, provided that, if placed in the hands of an attorney for collection, the maker would pay 10 per cent. of the attorney's fees, and that it might be assigned without notice. The recited consideration was the price of certain machinery which the vendors had sold on condition that the title should remain in them till the purchase price was paid. On default, the vendor could take possession of the machinery, the maker to pay all damage for such default, and waive all equities. *Held*, that where, in an action on this note, no pleas on oath or affirmation were filed, judgment was properly rendered for the payee, under Code Ga. 1882, § 5145, which provides that "the court shall render judgment without the verdict of a jury, in all civil cases founded on unconditional contracts in writing, where an issuable defense is not filed under oath or affirmation."—Brewster v. Hamilton, (Ga.) 13 S. E. 660.

Amendment.

8. In Georgia a declaration sounding in tort against a railroad company for violation of its duty as a common carrier, is not amendable by converting it, in whole or in part, into an action upon contract to carry.—Cox v. Richmond & D. R. Co., (Ga.) 13 S. E. 627; Moseley v. Same, Id.; Perkins v. Same, Id.

9. In order for a declaration to be amendable in form, a substantial cause of action must appear; otherwise there is not "enough to amend by."—Ellison v. Georgia Railroad & Banking Co., (Ga.) 13 S. E. 809; Georgia Railroad & Banking Co. v. Ellison, Id.

10. Code Ga. §§ 3479, 3480, provide that all parties, whether at law or in equity, may, at any stage of the cause, "as matter of right," amend their pleadings in all respects, whether in matter of form or of substance, "provided there is enough in the pleadings to amend by," and that no amendment "adding a new and distinct cause of action" shall be allowed unless expressly provided for by law. *Held*, that a plaintiff has a right to amend his declaration in matter of substance, though, as it stands, it does not set forth in substance a full and complete cause of action, provided it does show a plaintiff and defendant, jurisdiction of the court, and facts enough to indicate and identify some particular cause of action as the one intended to be declared upon, so as to enable the court to determine whether the facts proposed to be introduced by the amendment are part and parcel of that same cause. Martin v. Railroad, 78 Ga. 307, overruled.—Ellison v. Georgia Railroad & Banking Co., (Ga.) 13 S. E. 809; Georgia Railroad & Banking Co. v. Ellison, Id.

11. Any amendment of substance in a pleading, which, if allowed, would leave the cause of action incomplete, should be rejected.—Ellison v. Georgia Railroad & Banking Co., (Ga.) 13 S. E. 809; Georgia Railroad & Banking Co. v. Ellison, Id.

12. A declaration, filed by a track hand of a railroad company, alleging that plaintiff was injured by a fall of earth, caused by the negligence of the company, its agents and servants, is amendable by setting out the particulars constituting the alleged negligence, and also by averring that plaintiff himself was without fault, under Code, § 3479, allowing parties as a matter of right to amend their pleadings either in matter of form or of substance, provided there is enough in the pleadings to amend by. Ellison v. Railroad, etc. Co., 13 S. E. 809, 97 Ga. 691, followed.—Smith v. Georgia Railroad & Banking Co., (Ga.) 13 S. E. 904.

—— New cause of action.

13. Petitioner, as guardian for A., brought suit against defendants to recover land, alleging that A.'s father, as trustee, purchased the land with the proceeds of a trust-estate which he held for the use of his wife during her life, and at her death for her children; that, as trustee, he went into possession, and so remained until 1871, when he left the state, leaving tenants in possession, who so remained until after his death, in 1872, leaving A. sole heir, his wife having died before him. Defendants claimed that they had acquired the land absolutely, petitioner claiming that they had taken possession only until the rents should pay a debt due them from her father. A., having reached her majority, and her guardian having died pending the suit, she filed an amended petition, asking that the cause continue in her own name. The amendment alleged that her father had been indebted to defendants, and had moved out of the state and

died; that her guardian made an arrangement with defendants that the rents of the land should go to them until the debt should be paid; that the debt had been more than paid; and that petitioner was entitled to recover the land and the rents for four years. *Held*, that the amendment did not introduce a new cause of action.—Lathrop v. Adkinson, (Ga.) 13 S. E. 517.

—— Parties.

14. There is no error in permitting the amendment of a petition by the substitution of a word so as to give the defendant its proper corporate name, as this is simply correcting a misnomer, and not an introduction of a new party.—Chattanooga, R. & C. R. Co. v. Jackson, (Ga.) 13 S. E. 109.

15. Where the real defendant has been made a party to the suit, so as to give the court jurisdiction of her person, the fact that she does not live in the county where the suit is pending cannot be urged against plaintiff's right to amend.—Lathrop v. Adkinson, (Ga.) 13 S. E. 517.

—— Time of making.

16. After a general demurrer to a declaration has been sustained, and the cause dismissed, by the superior court, and that judgment affirmed in the supreme court without condition or direction, the declaration is not amendable. King v. King, 45 Ga. 195, overruled.—Central Railroad & Banking Co. v. Patterson, (Ga.) 13 S. E. 525.

17. Under Code Ga. § 3479, providing that plaintiff or defendant, in any court except the supreme court, whether at law or in equity, may, at any stage of the case, amend the pleadings in all respects, it is reversible error to refuse an amendment to defendant's plea of the general issue, by filing a plea of the statute of limitations after the cause has been submitted, and the jury have retired, and been out all night.—Savannah, F. & W. R. Co. v. Watson, (Ga.) 13 S. E. 156.

Pleading and proof.

18. A complaint alleged defendant's indebtedness for services rendered from March 1, 1881, to November 15, 1889, in the sum of $15 per month. The answer denied the allegations, pleaded the statute of limitations, and set up a counter-claim for board. Plaintiff's reply alleged that defendant agreed in consideration of the services named to board plaintiff, and leave him all his property at his decease; but that on November 15, 1889, defendant dismissed him from service. On the trial plaintiff testified that he hired to defendant in 1881, and was to be paid whatever was right, and worked a year; that in 1883 he made a contract with defendant to stay with him as long as defendant lived, he to make plaintiff heir to all his property; and that plaintiff lived with him for five years, when defendant discharged him. Plaintiff testified his services were worth from $20 to $35 per month. *Held*, that the allegations of the complaint were broad enough to cover evidence given of the special contract set up in the replication.—Fulps v. Mock, (N. C.) 13 S. E. 99.

Waiver of defects.

19. Where defendant's demurrer, on the ground of no cause of action, is overruled, the fact that he answers over, and goes to trial on the merits, does not waive the insufficiency of the complaint.—Baker v. Garris, (N. C.) 13 S. E. 2.

20. Where defendant's demurrer, on the ground of no cause of action, is erroneously overruled, and he answers over and goes to trial, he may take advantage of the defect in the appellate court by a motion to dismiss the case. Merrimon, C. J., dissenting.—Baker v. Garris, (N. C.) 13 S. E. 2.

21. It is too late on a motion for a new trial to, for the first time, complain of the allowance of amendments to a petition for foreclosure, the one adding a prayer for counsel fees, the other making the administrator of plaintiff's assignor a party plaintiff suing for the use of plaintiff.—Hooks v. Hayes, (Ga.) 13 S. E. 134.

Aider by verdict.

22. In a suit to set aside assignments of a money demand, and subject the same to the satisfaction of judgments against the assignor, though the assignments are not set forth in the pleadings fully and specifically, yet, if they be alleged substantially, and the jury have found them to be valid, they ought to be so treated in rendering the decree; no motion for a new trial or other attack upon the verdict having been made by any of the parties in due time.—Dotterer v. Harden, (Ga.) 13 S. E. 971.

PLEDGE.

Liability of pledgee—Change of security.

When a pledgee of a note as collateral changes the character of collateral to land without the consent of the pledgor, he holds the new collateral on the same terms as he held the old, and if rents or profits are made by him he must account therefor to the pledgeor; and if the rents or profits are sufficient to pay the debt it becomes canceled, and the pledgeor is entitled to recover the lands.—Lathrop v. Adkinson, (Ga.) 13 S. E. 517.

POISON.

Attempt to murder—Evidence.

On the trial of a husband, a day-laborer, for attempting to poison his wife, it appeared that he had at one time abandoned his family, but was then living with them; that he and his wife had been at enmity for a long time, and he was enamored of another woman. On the day of the alleged poisoning the daughter had prepared dinner. While he and the children were eating, the wife came in and went into the sitting-room. The children soon after followed her, leaving the husband alone at the table. When the wife came to dinner he brought her some bread. Presently she called out that the gravy was "awful bitter," and spit out what she had taken. The children said there was nothing the matter with it; that they had all eaten of it; but when they came to taste it again they too pronounced it bitter. The son gave it to the dog, and, the mother feeling sick, they gave her some milk as an antidote. The husband said, if milk was good for her to give some to the dog, which was in great suffering, and died shortly after. The doctor found her suffering with some of the symptoms of strychnine poison. No analysis was made of the gravy or of the stomach of the dog; and the husband gave no explanation as to where the poison came from, or who put it in the gravy. Many witnesses testified to his steady habits and previous good character. *Held*, that a conviction would not be disturbed.—Bell v. Commonwealth, (Va.) 13 S. E. 742.

Police Power.

See *Constitutional Law*, 18.

POWERS.

Of sale in mortgage, see *Mortgages*, 15–20.

Revocation—Death of donor.

1. A mortgage given as collateral security to a note containing a power of sale does not convey such an interest in the estate as to render the power irrevocable by the death of the mortgagor, under Code Ga. § 2133, providing that the death of a person creating a power of agency revokes it, unless the power is coupled with an interest in the agent himself.—Wilkins v. McGehee, (Ga.) 13 S. E. 84.

Execution.

2. On a sale of property under a power in a will the executor should execute a deed to the purchaser, with reference to the will, and his power thereunder.—Johnston v. Johnston, (N. C.) 13 S. E. 183.

3. In case any of the devisees purchased, the executor should in like manner execute a deed to him.—Johnston v. Johnston, (N. C.) 13 S. E. 188.

Testamentary powers.

4. Where a deed is executed by one of two executors under a provision of the will authorizing such executor to convey the land after the death of the co-executor, who was life-tenant of the land, the deed need not recite the death of the co-executor, as that fact will be presumed.—Cowles v. Reavis, (N. C.) 13 S. E. 930.

PRACTICE IN CIVIL CASES.

See, also, *Appeal; Assumpsit,* 3; *Certiorari; Costs; Ejectment,* 8; *Equity; Evidence; Exceptions, Bill of; Judgment; Jury; Mandamus; New Trial; Parties; Pleading; Reference; Removal of Causes; Trial; Venus in Civil Cases; Writs.*

Dismissal, appeal from order refusing, see *Appeal,* 6–11.

In equity, see *Equity,* 12–17.

On appeal, see *Appeal,* 16–47.

Withdrawal from jury — Discretion of court.

1. After a demurrer has been overruled, the court may, in its discretion, withdraw the case from the jury, and suspend the trial, for the purpose of allowing defendant an opportunity of taking the case to the supreme court in advance of a trial by jury on the issue of fact; but there is no duty requiring it to do so.—Augusta Factory v. Davis, (Ga.) 13 S. E. 577.

Nonsuit.

2. In South Carolina the question of contributory negligence cannot be considered on motion for nonsuit.—Carter v. Oliver Oil Co., (S. C.) 13 S. E. 419.

3. In North Carolina, where defendant, in an action to recover a debt and to foreclose a mortgage securing it, alleges, by way of counter-claim, that there is due him a sum of money placed in trust for him in plaintiff's hands, it is not a counter-claim growing out of and involving plaintiff's cause of action, and plaintiff may take a nonsuit.—Pass v. Pass, (N. C.) 13 S. E. 906.

Leave to file verified answer.

4. In an action against an administrator, defendant made default in answering the verified complaint, and after time was granted him to file his pleading an unverified answer appeared among the papers. After the lapse of five years defendant was allowed to file a verified answer, setting up meritorious pleas, exclusive of a plea of the running of the statute of limitations. *Held,* that leave to file the verified answer, with the limitation, was discretionary with the court below, and is not reviewable on appeal.—Mallard v. Patterson, (N. C.) 13 S. E. 93.

Prescription.

See *Adverse Possession; Limitation of Actions.*

Creation of easement by, see *Easements,* 1.

Presumption.

See *Evidence,* 4.

On appeal, see *Appeal,* 62, 63.

PRINCIPAL AND AGENT.

See, also, *Attorney and Client; Factors and Brokers.*

Insurance agents, see *Insurance,* 11.

Powers of agent.

1. Suit was brought for the specific performance of a contract for the sale of lots. The person making the sale testified that he was the authorized agent of defendant, and that the following letter from defendant was received by him in answer to a letter asking for authority to sell: "Yours received. I cannot accept your offer, but my price is, at the present time, $10.000. * * * Will give you 2 per cent. commission. Awaiting a reply," etc. Defendant denied that he had ever received any letter from the agent, or that the latter had any authority to sell. The agent testified that it was agreed between defendant's attorney and himself that he should sell for $9,000, and that, if he had an offer for less, he should report it. The attorney testified that the understanding was that all offers should be communicated to defendant, and that, if defendant then determined to sell, he would advise the agent. The agent, having obtained an offer, wired defendant, "Can we sell" one lot for $3,000?—to which the defendant replied: "I will take $3,000. * * * If you have sale for same, answer as soon as possible." *Held,* that the authority of the agent did not extend to making a sale, but only to finding a purchaser, and specific performance, therefore, would not be enforced. FAUNTLEROY, J., dissenting. — Simmons v. Kramer, (Va.) 13 S. E. 902.

2. The sayings of an alleged agent *dum fervet opus,* while not evidence to prove his agency, may be looked to on the question whether he was acting as agent, there being other sufficient evidence to establish the agency. —Small v. Williams, (Ga.) 13 S. E. 589.

3. Code Ga. § 2207, provides that any act authorized or required to be done under the Code, by any person in the prosecution of his legal remedies, may be done by his agents; and for this purpose he is authorized to make an affidavit and execute any bond required, though his agency be created by parol. Plaintiff foreclosed a chattel mortgage in justice's court, and levied on the mortgaged property. A., as defendants' special agent appointed by parol, filed an affidavit of illegality. *Held,* that the verbal appointment of the agent sufficiently authorized his filing the affidavit in behalf of his principal.—Cook v. Buchanan, (Ga.) 13 S. E. 83.

Ratification.

4. Appealing a case after judgment, giving an appeal-bond, and offering to subscribe the affidavit in the superior court, is a ratification by a principal of his agent's acts, authorizing the lower court to hear and determine a claim of illegality on its merits.—Cook v. Buchanan, (Ga.) 13 S. E. 83.

Liability of agent to principal.

5. Where notes held by a creditor as collateral security are in the hands of the principal debtor for collection, with the understanding that the proceeds are to be and remain the property of the creditor until the principal debt is paid, cotton received in payment of the collateral notes, and sent to an agent of the creditor for sale, must be accounted for by such agent to the creditor as property belonging to the latter.—Sibley v. Ober & Sons Co., 13 S. E. 711, 87 Ga. 55.

PRINCIPAL AND SURETY.

See, also, *Bonds.*

Release of surety on receiver's bond, see *Receivers,* 18.

Sureties on administrator's bond, see *Executors and Administrators,* 6.

—— on appeal-bond, release, see *Appeal,* 99.

Remedies against sureties.

1. In an action at law on a joint note, all the makers except one appearing on its face as sureties, a verdict cannot be rendered against some of the sureties for the whole amount of the note, and against one of them for half that amount, on the ground that he notified the payee that he would only be surety for half the amount of the note; but, in case of such verdict, plaintiff may enter judgment against all the sureties for the lesser sum.—Jones v. Lewis, (Ga.) 13 S. E. 578.

roborated by another witness, that the track was visible for several hundred yards from the highway, did not warrant the court in instructing the jury that they must disregard plaintiff's statements, and find against him, for in such a conflict the court could not instruct as to the weight of the evidence.—Hinkle v. Richmond & D. R. Co., (N. C.) 13 S. E. 884.

39. Where a boy of 13 years, familiar with a railroad crossing at which, on account of a deep cut, a train could not be seen until one was on the track, drives upon it with his ears covered up on account of the cold, though he had just been told at the post office that the train was late, and would probably reach the crossing at about the same time he did, he is guilty of contributory negligence which will prevent recovery for his death, though the train was running at a high rate of speed, and the whistle was not blown.—Norfolk & W. R. Co. v. Stone's Adm'r, (Va.) 13 S. E. 432.

40. A person who, after standing near a railroad crossing, towards which a train has commenced to back in obedience to the signal of a brakeman in full view from where she stood, attempts to cross the track when the train is but seven feet from, and moving towards, her, is guilty of contributory negligence, and cannot recover for the injuries she receives, though the railroad company is guilty of negligence in backing the train.—Marks' Adm'r v. Petersburg R. Co., (Va.) 13 S. E. 299.

41. The fact that a person who is injured by her own negligence at a railroad crossing is blind in one eye will not excuse her, but only imposes the duty of a higher degree of care to avoid danger.—Marks' Adm'r v. Petersburg R. Co., (Va.) 13 S. E. 299.

42. In an action by a father against a railroad company for the negligent killing of his son at a public crossing, where deceased was not killed while jumping on or off cars, his previous habit of doing so at the crossing is irrelevant.—Georgia Midland & G. R. Co. v. Evans, (Ga.) 13 S. E. 580.

Accidents at crossings — Comparative negligence.

43. Where the person injured would not have ventured upon the track at a crossing but for the negligence of the engineer in failing to give warning, the railroad company is liable, though plaintiff may have been careless in exposing himself.—Hinkle v. Richmond & D. R. Co., (N. C.) 13 S. E. 884.

Injuries to persons on track.

44. In an action against a railroad company to recover damages for the negligent killing of plaintiff's decedent, it appeared that deceased was a jeweler, and often went to defendant's office to obtain the correct time; that it was not necessary for him to cross the track, but that on the day of the accident he went to see an engine which was being repaired on the side track, and while standing between the tracks (there being a space of about 10 to 15 feet between them) he was struck by the steps of a passing coach, and thrown under the wheels. The accident occurred in the yard while the switch-engine was shifting cars, and running at the rate of about 10 miles per hour. The yard was surrounded by public streets. No signals were given of the approaching train. Held, that the company was not liable.—Hale v. Columbia & G. R. Co., (S. C.) 13 S. E. 537.

45. Gen. St. S. C. § 1483, required railway corporations to ring a bell or sound a whistle at a distance of 500 yards from all public crossings. Section 1529 makes a railway corporation liable for injuries to persons resulting from collisions at such crossings for failure to give the signals, unless the person injured was guilty of gross negligence. Held, that one injured while standing in the switch-yard of the railroad company, and not passing over a crossing, could not recover under the above statutes, though the yard was surrounded by streets, and the required signals were not given by the company. Neely v

Railroad Co., 11 S. E. 686, followed.—Hale v. Columbia & G. R. Co., (S. C.) 13 S. E. 537.

46. Actual or implied license by a railroad company to use as a foot-way its tracks, laid on what was previously a highway, does not relieve a pedestrian of the duty of exercising care.—Meredith v. Richmond & D. R. Co., (N. C.) 13 S. E. 137.

—— Deaf persons.

47. Plaintiff's intestate was killed while walking on a railroad track. The deceased, who was a deaf-mute, had once before received an injury in a similar manner, and had been repeatedly warned about walking upon the railroad. Only a few minutes before he was killed, he had been so warned. The accident occurred in an open plain, where the view was unobstructed for nearly a mile. Deceased, although a deaf-mute, was possessed of all his other faculties, including that of sight, and was a strong, active man, about 32 years of age. He was walking directly towards the train, on the ends of the ties, on the side opposite the engineer. The latter saw him until he came within 25 or 30 yards, when the projecting front of the locomotive intervened. He supposed, however, the deceased would step off. Held, that the deceased's own negligence was the proximate cause of the injury, and plaintiff was not entitled to recover.—Tyler v. Sites' Adm'r, (Va.) 13 S. E. 978.

48. The defendant requested the court to charge that the company was bound to keep a reasonable lookout for trespassers on its track, and to exercise such care as the circumstances might require to prevent injury to them; if a trespasser was an adult, and apparently possessed of his faculties, the company had a right to presume that he would remove himself from his dangerous position, and if he failed to do so the fault was his own, "and there is, in the absence of willful negligence on its part, no remedy against it for the results of an injury brought upon him by his own recklessness." If the company or its employes used reasonable care after discovering the perilous position of the deceased to avoid injuring him, plaintiff was not entitled to recover. The court modified the said instructions by striking out the words quoted. Held erroneous, as the said words were necessary to the correct statement of the rule. Railroad Co. v. Harman's Adm'r, 8 S. E. 251, 83 Va. 553, followed.—Tyler v. Sites' Adm'r, (Va.) 13 S. E. 978.

49. The defendant requested the court to charge—First, that certain acts and conduct of the deceased, if proven, constituted gross negligence on his part; and, second, that if guilty of such negligence the plaintiff could not recover unless the injury was wilfully committed. The court modified the said instruction by adding: "Unless the injury could have been prevented by the exercise of reasonable care on the part of the trainmen after they discovered the peril of the deceased." Held, that the modification was unwarranted, as there was no evidence to show that the peril of the deceased was discovered, or that the injury could have been prevented by the exercise of reasonable care.—Tyler v. Sites' Adm'r, (Va.) 13 S. E. 978.

—— Children.

50. In an action against a railroad company for personal injuries, plaintiff, a bright boy of 13, showed that what had previously been a highway had been filled for a considerable distance by defendant's tracks; that while walking thereon he passed a train going in the opposite direction, and, seeing another coming along the track on which he was walking, he stepped off, and was struck and injured by the backing of the first train, which he did not see. Held contributory negligence, and plaintiff was properly nonsuited.—Meredith v. Richmond & D. R. Co., (N. C.) 13 S. E. 137.

51. Where a boy 13 years old, and "apparently capable of appreciating the peril of his situation," is walking on the track in front of a locomotive, and there is an opportunity for him to avert the danger by stepping off, the engineer is justified

in assuming that he will step off.—Meredith v. Richmond & D. R. Co., (N. C.) 13 S. E. 137.

—— **Contributory negligence.**

52. Deceased was killed by a train at the north end of a trestle 150 yards long and from 12 to 15 feet high. She and another woman had been to a water-tank at the other end of the trestle, and were on their way back. They did not commence to run until the train had passed the water-tank, where they thought it would stop. Deceased fell, and her companion tried to help her up, but before she could do so she was hit by the train, and thrown from the track, and deceased was run over and killed. The train stopped with the front driving-wheels on her. *Held,* that a nonsuit was properly granted, as it was gross negligence for them to go on the trestle about the time when a train was due, and where all that was possible was done to stop the train after they were discovered.—Phillips v. East Tennessee, V. & G. Ry. Co., (Ga.) 13 S. E. 644.

Stock-killing cases.

53. In an action against a railroad company for killing a horse, it appeared that the horse had been hidden from the sight of the engineer by high weeds and bushes g. owing within a few feet of the track, and that when the train was close upon him he had suddenly emerged. The court charged that it was negligence for the company to allow weeds and bushes to grow "near to" "or in close proximity" to the track, and that, if the injury resulted because the same so concealed that the engineer could not see him in time to stop, the company was liable. *Held* erroneous, in leaving uncertain the precise distance to which a railroad company must keep clear its right of way, and in fixing upon it the duty of taking possession of such parts of the right of way as are not actually needed for railroad purposes, and which custom has always allowed the abutting owners to cultivate. MERRIMON, C. J., dissenting.—Ward v. Wilmington & W. R. Co., (N. C.) 13 S. E. 926.

54. In an action against a railroad company for killing stock, an instruction in general terms that a less degree of diligence in looking out for stock is required in a county where the stock law prevails than in a county in which it does not, or while running through inclosed lands than while running through uninclosed lands, is properly refused, since Code Ga. § 3033, requires "ordinary and reasonable" care in all cases.—Central Railroad & Banking Co. v. Summerford, (Ga.) 13 S. E. 588.

55. In an action against a railroad company for the negligent killing of a cow, the fact that the people of a certain section held a mass-meeting and agreed to disregard the "stock law," does not repeal the law, and evidence of such fact is inadmissible.—Georgia Railroad & Banking Co. v. Walker, (Ga.) 13 S. E. 511.

56. In an action against a railroad company for the negligent killing of a cow, evidence that the company at different times paid other persons for cattle killed by its trains at the same place is inadmissible.—Georgia Railroad & Banking Co. v. Walker, (Ga.) 13 S. E. 511.

RAPE.

Instructions.

1. Where the evidence shows the consummation of the offense of rape, it is not incumbent on the court to charge the jury on the minor offense of an assault with intent to rape.—Berry v. State, (Ga.) 13 S. E. 690.

Assault with intent to rape.

2. On a prosecution of a physician for assault with intent to rape on a girl 17 years of age, in that he took improper liberties with her person, an instruction that if he acted in good faith as a physician, and did what he did as such, he is not guilty, "otherwise he is guilty," is erroneous, as, if she consented to the taking of the lib-

v. 13 s. e.—70

erties, understanding that he was not acting in good faith as a physician, then he was not guilty.—State v. Nash, (N. C.) 13 S. E. 874.

3. Under Code N. C. § 987, providing that where no deadly weapon has been used, and no serious damage done, the punishment in cases of assault shall not exceed a fine of $50 or 30 days' imprisonment, provided that this shall not apply to cases of assault with intent to commit rape, on a conviction of a simple assault, where there is no evidence of bodily pain, there can be no greater punishment than therein prescribed, though the indictment was for assault with intent to commit rape.—State v. Nash, (N. C.) 13 S. E. 874.

4. The commonwealth's evidence showed that the prosecutrix and defendant were employed as cooks at the same hotel. Defendant made an indecent proposal to her, which she rejected. A few nights thereafter she was awakened by a man in her room, who put his hand on her person, and who said he was going to do what he came to do. The prosecutrix recognized defendant, and began to scream, when defendant choked her. Her screams aroused another servant in the same room, who lit a lamp, when defendant escaped. *Held,* that the evidence was sufficient to support a verdict of guilty, though defendant and several of his witnesses testified to an *alibi.*—Cunningham v. Commonwealth, (Va.) 13 S. E. 309.

—— **Indictment.**

5. Under Code Va. § 3888, which provides that every person who attempts to commit an offense, "and in such attempt does any act towards its commission," shall be punished, etc., an indictment for an attempt to commit a rape must aver the act or acts done by defendant towards the commission of the crime.—Cunningham v. Commonwealth, (Va.) 13 S. E. 309.

6. An indictment for an assault with intent to rape, which alleges that defendant violently and feloniously made an assault on a female, and feloniously did attempt to ravish her and carnally know her, against her will and by force, sufficiently charges an act done towards the commission of the offense.—Cunningham v. Commonwealth, (Va.) 13 S. E. 309.

Ratification.

Of agent's acts, see *Principal and Agent,* 4.
Sunday contract, see *Sunday,* 2.

Real-Estate Agents.

See *Factors and Brokers.*

Reasonable Doubt.

See *Criminal Law,* 43, 44.

RECEIVERS.

Appointment.

1. Where the court appointed two receivers, the mere fact that one of them was attorney for complainant will not be deemed an abuse of discretion, where the other was attorney for defendant.—Shannon v. Hanks, (Va.) 13 S. E. 437.

2. After a decree in an action to subject property fraudulently conveyed, a receiver may be appointed, though not prayed in the bill, where the circumstances justify it.—Shannon v. Hanks, (Va.) 13 S. E. 437.

3. Where it is clear from the evidence and admissions of the parties that it is a case where a receiver should be appointed, and that defendant is insolvent, and all the property must be sold to pay the debts, an order appointing receivers, and directing them to sell all the property of defendant, is proper.—S. C. Forsaith Mach. Co. v. Hope Mills Lumber Co., (N. C.) 13 S. E. 869.

4. A petition by the vendors of goods against an insolvent purchaser, alleging fraud in the purchase, and repudiating the contract of sale

on that account, has equity on which to proceed to reclaim the goods or their proceeds in the hands of such purchaser, whether the term of credit has expired or not, and in such case a receiver may be appointed to take charge of money and books of account.—Martin v. Burgwyn, (Ga.) 13 S. E. 958.

5. In a suit by creditors of an insolvent firm for a receiver and an injunction, and to set aside a conveyance by the firm of all its property to one creditor, though such conveyance is fraudulent as to the other creditors, yet if the purchasing creditor is solvent, and the complaining creditors are without judgments or other liens, and have no claim to the property by reason of fraud in the creation of their demands or otherwise, an injunction should not be granted nor a receiver appointed.—Stillwell v. Savannah Grocery Co., (Ga.) 13 S. E. 963.

6. In a suit by creditors of an insolvent firm for a receiver and an injunction, and to set aside, as fraudulent as against them, a conveyance by the firm of all its property to a single creditor, who is solvent, where the property is perishable and hard to keep, it is error to appoint a receiver unconditionally, without offering such creditor the alternative of giving bond or security, either for the forthcoming of the property, or for the proceeds.—Stillwell v. Savannah Grocery Co., (Ga.) 13 S. E. 963.

Appointment—Of partnership.

7. Where a receiver of the assets of a partnership was appointed, and the failure of the judge to appoint a member of the firm such receiver is assigned as error, and it appears that no request was made to him that such member should be so appointed, his action is not subject to review.—Bliley v. Taylor, (Ga.) 13 S. E. 288.

8. Where a judge appointed as receiver of an insolvent firm a proper person, who was the choice of a large majority, in amount and number, of the creditors, and no good reason appeared why he should have appointed another person at the instance of a single creditor, whose claim against the firm was comparatively small, such action will not be disturbed on appeal.—Jacoby v. Kiesling, (Ga.) 13 S. E. 161.

—— Of real property.

9. Where defendant, in an action to cancel a mortgage, sets up in his answer a release by plaintiff of all his interest in the mortgaged land, and refers to the book and page of the record of the release; and plaintiff denies that he released or intended to release his interest in the land,— such denial raises no issue as to the execution of the release, but the record thereof is *prima facie* evidence that plaintiff's interest has been conveyed to defendant, and, plaintiff being in possession, defendant is entitled to the appointment of a receiver.—Lovett v. Slocomb, (N. C.) 13 S. E. 896.

10. W. conveyed land to H., and took a deed of trust to secure notes for the purchase money. After some of the notes were paid, a second deed of trust was given on the same property, to secure the notes remaining unpaid. Default was made in the payment of one of these notes, and the trustee was requested to sell under the last-named deed of trust. During the pendency of the advertisement, H. confessed a judgment to his father for over $8,000, which was docketed. On the day of sale the father was present, and publicly announced, through his attorney, that his judgment was a lien upon said property, and entitled to priority; and the land was bid off by the father for $4,900, but he failed to pay the purchase money, claiming that he was entitled to it by virtue of his judgment. The trustee filed a bill, supported by affidavits, setting forth these facts, and alleging that H. was insolvent, and had been allowing the land to run down, and was cultivating it in a wasteful and destructive manner. *Held*, that a receiver was properly appointed to take charge of the land, and to rent and preserve the same, until the conflicting claims asserted could be adjusted.—Dunlap v. Hedges, (W. Va.) 13 S. E. 656.

11. The fact appearing from the commissioner's report that, independent of the land sought to be subjected, the annual value of defendant's real estate is only about $300, and the liens thereon amount to about $20,000, justifies the appointment of a receiver.—Shannon v. Hanks, (Va.) 13 S. E. 487.

—— Questions considered.

12. In disposing of the motion for a receiver, the court properly declined to pass on questions of fraud raised by the pleadings.—S. C. Forsaith Mach. Co. v. Hope Mills Lumber Co., (N. C.) 13 S. E. 869.

Bonds—Release of surety.

13. Where the court, at the instance of a party to the case, requires a receiver to execute a new bond in the same penalty and conditioned as the old bond, the new bond will not operate to discharge the surety on the old bond from liability for future defaults of the receiver, in the absence of circumstances to show that the second bond was intended as a substitute for rather than as supplemental to the first.—Stewart v. Johnston, (Ga.) 13 S. E. 258.

Orders of court.

14. Where defendants did not consent that the court should direct the receivers to pay certain judgments, admitted to be just and valid, it was error to order their payment.—S. C. Forsaith Mach. Co. v. Hope Mills Lumber Co., (N. C.) 13 S. E. 869.

15. In an action, against a cigar and tobacco dealer by a creditor who has sold him tobacco and cigars, to recover the articles sold, or the proceeds thereof, and for a receiver, an order appointing the receiver is sufficiently specific in its description as to notes and books of account to be turned over to him which specifies them as "the books, notes, and accounts of all kinds of the said defendant in the business of selling cigars, snuff, tobacco, and other goods."—Martin v. Burgwyn, (Ga.) 13 S. E. 958.

Reconvention.

See *Set-Off* and *Counter-Claim.*

RECORDS.

Estoppel by, see *Estoppel*, 2.
Of chattel mortgage, see *Chattel Mortgages*, 4.
    deed, see *Deed*, 11-16.
    sheriff's deed, see *Judicial Sales*, 10.
On appeal, see *Appeal*, 19-39, 73, 74.
    change of venue, see *Criminal Law*, 9.
Public records, certified copies as evidence, see *Evidence*, 33, 34.
Registration of voters, right to make copies, see *Elections and Voters*, 2.

Amendment.

1. Under Code Ga. § 203, which empowers every court to amend its own records so as to make them conform to the truth, the records of the board of county commissioners, when they fail to speak the truth, may be corrected by an order *nunc pro tunc.*—Foster v. Foster, (Ga.) 13 S. E. 558.

Establishment of lost records.

2. Under Act Ga. Oct. 22, 1887, which provides the procedure by which lost records may be established, and which empowers the auditor appointed to hear the evidence to summon witnesses, and compel the production of books and papers, under such rules and regulations as are now practiced in courts of law in this state, " a witness cannot be compelled, by a *subpœna duces tecum*, to make discovery of the contents of lost public records in a proceeding to establish a copy of such records, where the pleadings for the purpose do not allege or set out anything whatever as the specific contents to be proved.—Ex parte Calhoun, (Ga.) 13 S. E. 694.

3. In proceedings to establish lost county records, the secretary and treasurer of a private abstract company is not bound to obey a *subpœna duces tecum* calling on him to produce "all the abstract books of the company, in which appear the abstracts of Deed Books B, F, and H, and Mortgage Book E," since such information is valuable, and its disclosure is not sought as testimony for the proof of any alleged fact, but as a substitute in the first instance for the allegation of facts unknown, or not known sufficiently to enable the plaintiff to set them forth conformably to general laws applicable to pleading.—Ex parte Calhoun, (Ga.) 13 S. E. 694.

Redemption.

From tax-sale, see *Taxation*, 12.

REFERENCE.

To master in chancery, see *Equity*, 12–14.

When granted.

1. Code Civil Proc. S. C. § 298, provides that the court may, upon application, or of its own motion, except where the investigation will require the decision of difficult questions of law, direct a reference, "where the trial of an issue of fact shall require the examination of a long account on either side." *Held* that, in an action to set aside a deed and mortgage upon the grounds of fraud, where the court heard statements of counsel upon the nature of the case, which statements are not in the record, and made an order of reference, it will be presumed, upon appeal, that the statements showed that there was a long account involved.—Ferguson v. Harrison, (S. C.) 13 S. E. 332.

—— Objections to reference.

2. Where one appears before an auditor at the time and place fixed for a hearing, and moves to continue the same, which is granted, he cannot thereafter at the hearing object for the first time to the auditor taking the testimony upon the ground that the place fixed was outside of the county where the suit was pending.—Perseverance Min. Co. v. Bisaner, (Ga.) 13 S. E. 461.

Powers of referee.

3. Where an action against the sureties of an administrator has been referred to an auditor to find who were the heirs of the intestate, the auditor has no authority to investigate the question of the administrator's solvency or insolvency, or of the time when he became insolvent.—McMahon v. Paris, (Ga.) 13 S. E. 572.

4. It was proper for an auditor to refuse to suspend a hearing until the evidence of plaintiff was transcribed, so that defendant might make a motion of nonsuit, as an auditor cannot grant a nonsuit.—Perseverance Min. Co. v. Bisaner, (Ga.) 13 S. E. 461.

5. An auditor cannot hear and determine a demurrer to the declaration. Such pleading can only be filed in the court where the cause is pending.—Perseverance Min. Co. v. Bisaner, (Ga.) 13 S. E. 461.

Report and findings.

6. An auditor's finding that the court had jurisdiction is immaterial when no such issue is raised by the pleadings in the superior court.—Perseverance Min. Co. v. Bisaner, (Ga.) 13 S. E. 461.

—— Exceptions and objections.

7. Under Code Civil Proc. N. C. § 422, giving plaintiff a right to except to a referee's report, it is the duty of the superior court to consider the exceptions, both as to findings of fact and conclusions of law, and pass judicially on the report.—Miller v. Groome, (N. C.) 13 S. E. 840.

8. Where an auditor's report has been recommitted for further findings on the joint exception of both defendants, and the supplemental report has been excepted to by only one of them, the court at the trial may permit the other defendant to join in the exceptions, under Code Ga. § 4208, which provides that an auditor's report shall be subject to exceptions for such time as the court may allow, and that the time may be extended in the discretion of the court.—McMahon v. Paris, (Ga.) 13 S. E. 572.

9. Where plaintiffs omitted to file exceptions to the referee's report, but, at a term when a final amended report under a re-reference was filed, filed a motion in writing embracing specified objections to such report, having all the effect of exceptions thereto, and no objection is made by defendant, the hearing and overruling of such motion cures any irregularity as to the time of filing same.—Rogers v. Bank of Oxford, (N. C.) 13 S. E. 245.

Judgment on report—Appeal.

10. A judgment overruling exceptions to an auditor's report, and not excepted to *pendente lite*, as required by Code Ga. § 4254, nor within 60 days after its rendition, as required by section 4952, is not open to review and reversal by the supreme court.—Van Pelt v. Home Building & Loan Ass'n, (Ga.) 13 S. E. 574.

Reformation.

Of contracts, see *Equity*, 3, 4.

Refreshing Memory.

Of witness, see *Witness*, 14.

Rehearing.

On appeal, see *Appeal*, 41, 42.

Release and Discharge.

See *Compromise; Payment*.
Of mortgage, see *Mortgages*, 7.
   surety on appeal-bond, see *Appeal*, 99.

RELIGIOUS SOCIETIES.

Assessment of property for public improvements, see *Municipal Corporations*, 10.
Condemnation of church property by railroad, see *Eminent Domain*, 1.

Power of members to bind church.

A deed from certain members of a church, who had no authority to make the same, purporting to convey to a railway company a right of way over land belonging to the church, does not authorize the company to take such land for the purpose designated in said deed, where the transaction is afterwards repudiated by the church, and the consideration paid by the railway company is returned to it.—Macon & A. Ry. Co. v. Riggs, (Ga.) 13 S. E. 812.

Remandment.

Of case to trial court, see *Appeal*, 98–96.

REMOVAL OF CAUSES.

Time of application.

1. Under St. U. S. 1885–87, pp. 553, 554, § 3, allowing an application to remove a cause from a state court to the United States circuit court to be made at the time, or at any time before, defendant is required by the laws of the state, or the rule of the state court, to answer or plead to the declaration or complaint; and Code Ga. § 3310, allowing defendant to plead at any time before final judgment, where the case is one commenced by attachment,—an application made to remove a case commenced by attachment at any time before final judgment is not too late where defendant has filed no plea.—Southern Pac. Co. v. Stewart, (Ga.) 13 S. E. 824.

2. A stipulation by which plaintiff in attachment agrees to dispense with bond as a condition

4. On indictment for robbery, although the prosecutor was intoxicated when robbed, it is not competent evidence for accused that three nights previous thereto he was in a certain saloon intoxicated, and complained that two men were trying to rob him, but that he was prepared for them, and only carried two or three dollars with him, either to discredit the prosecutor, where he has testified that he did not go to the saloon, and did not make the statements attributed to him, nor as tending to show that he was in a state of drunkenness for several days prior to the alleged robbery, and while in that state was under the delusion that he was being robbed.—Lampkin v. State, (Ga.) 13 S. E. 523.

SALE.

See, also, *Judicial Sales; Vendor and Vendee.*
By executors and administrators, see *Executors and Administrators,* 19–25.
Foreclosure sale, see *Mortgages,* 11–14.
For non-payment of taxes, see *Taxation,* 9.
Of ward's realty, see *Guardian and Ward,* 3–6.
Under execution, see *Execution,* 17.

What constitutes.

1. Where one sends goods to another as under a sale, and at the same time sends a bill therefor, and the goods and bill reach him, whether he ordered the goods or not, he will be regarded as a purchaser, unless within reasonable time he either returns the goods, or notifies the sender that he will not accept them.—Thompson v. Douglass, (W. Va.) 13 S. E. 1015.

2. Where one sends goods to another, as on a sale, and the latter disclaims to have purchased them, but permits a third person to take them, and convert them to his own use, he will be liable as purchaser; and this, notwithstanding he may have allowed them to be taken by mistake.—Thompson v. Douglass, (W. Va.) 13 S. E. 1015.

The contract.

3. A written offer to sell defendant 100 tons of fertilizer, "with the privilege of 200 tons more at the same price if in stock unsold, or when wanted" by defendant, was made by plaintiff's salesman, subject to approval by plaintiff's general agent, and was returned, indorsed "Approved" by the general agent, with a letter, written by his direction, stating that the contract for 100 tons was approved, but that plaintiff could not now promise to supply more than that. *Held,* that the court properly charged, in an action for the price of the 100 tons, that, if the offer was approved by the general agent, and the letter written by his direction, and the two were sent together to defendant, the original offer and the letter constituted the contract between the parties.—Atlantic Phosphate Co. v. Sullivan, (S. C.) 13 S. E. 539.

4. Where a person writes, "Please send me the following" goods promptly, on his letter-head paper, the printed part of which reads, "General Merchandise Broker" "Consignments solicited." and, after receiving the goods, assigns them, the letter, together with the printed letter-head, is competent evidence to go to the jury on the question whether the goods were sold or consigned to the person ordering them.—Simpson v. Pegram, (N. C.) 13 S. E. 7.

—— Damages for breach.

5. Plaintiffs having sold defendants bacon, to be paid for on delivery, shipped it, and drew on them a draft payable on demand, which was presented for payment before arrival of the bacon. Payment was refused by defendants, and on arrival of the bacon they refused to accept it on the ground that plaintiffs had violated their contract in demanding payment before the money was due. Plaintiffs' agent thereupon sold the bacon for the best price that could be obtained. *Held,* that defendants were liable to plaintiffs for the difference between the contract price and the net proceeds of the bacon.—McCord v. Laidley, (Ga.) 13 S. E. 509.

6. In an action for the price of a "ledger, index, check-books, and other stationery," it appeared that plaintiffs prepared the articles at defendant's request. They were only useful for it, and it, without cause, refused to accept and pay for them. The court charged that if defendant ordered the goods, and plaintiffs thereby prepared the same, and the order was countermanded thereafter, plaintiffs are entitled to damages, which would be the difference between the contract price and present value; and, if the goods were of no value except to defendant, the measure of damages would be the contract price. Judgment was entered for plaintiffs. *Held,* that there was evidence warranting the instructions.—Marshall v. Macon County Sav. Bank, (N. C.) 13 S. E. 182.

7. In an action for breach of a contract to accept grain which plaintiffs sold defendants, and which defendants refused to accept because not up to sample, but which they did afterwards accept, an exception that the court charged that the measure of damages was the difference between the contract price and the net proceeds realized by plaintiffs at an auction sale, whereas it should have been the difference between such net proceeds and the price at the time of such acceptance, could not be sustained, even if well taken, if defendants offered no proof of the price of such grain at the time of acceptance.—Woods v. Cramer, (S. C.) 13 S. E. 660.

8. Where the purchaser of grain by sample, after refusing to accept on the ground that it was not up to sample, agrees to accept it without any new arrangement as to price, he becomes liable for the contract price, and, if he afterwards fails to accept, and the seller has to sell the grain at auction, he is liable to the seller for the difference between the contract price and the price realized at such sale, together with costs of storage and other expenses necessitated by his failure to accept.—Woods v. Cramer, (S. C.) 13 S. E. 660.

9. Defendant claimed damages for non-compliance by plaintiff with an offer to sell defendant 100 tons of fertilizer, "with the privilege of 200 tons more at the same price if in stock unsold, or when wanted." *Held,* that the court properly refused to charge at defendant's request that, if plaintiff had on hand or could have shipped when demanded the 200 tons, and failed to do so, plaintiff was responsible for damages sustained by defendant because of such failure.—Atlantic Phosphate Co. v. Sullivan, (S. C.) 13 S. E. 539.

Delivery.

10. A charge that if a merchant in Atlanta ordered goods to be shipped to him by a railroad company from Virginia, delivery to the railroad company by the seller would be delivery to the purchaser, in contemplation of law, is correct, in the absence of a contract to deliver the goods in Atlanta.—Falvey v. Richmond, (Ga.) 13 S. E. 261.

11. A contract for the sale of oats, f. o. b. cars at a given point, does not contemplate that delivery to the carrier at that point shall be a delivery to the purchaser, where the seller takes the bill of lading to his own order, and attaches it to a draft on the buyer, which he transmits to a banker of the city of the buyer's residence; but under such circumstances the fair inference is that both parties contemplated delivery at such city, and payment of the price on delivery.—Erwin v. Harris, (Ga.) 13 S. E. 513.

Rescission.

12. In an action by a husband and wife and W. to recover certain horses, the property of the wife and W., it appeared that W. sold them to defendant, to be paid for in cash on delivery; that by exhibiting a check, which he claimed he would get cashed as soon as a bank was open, and would pay for the property, defendant got possession of the horses, and when W. demanded payment therefor defendant tendered a note which he held against W., who refused to accept it. *Held,* that this rendered the contract voidable at the instance of the owners.—Blake v. Blackley, (N. C.) 13 S. E. 786.

13. In an action to recover certain horses, it appeared that plaintiff sold them to defendant, to be paid for in cash on delivery; that by exhibiting a check, which he claimed he would get cashed as soon as a bank was open, and would pay for the property, defendant got possession of the horses, and when plaintiff demanded payment therefor defendant tendered a note which he held against plaintiff, who refused to accept it. *Held*, that the *gravamen* of the fraud was in impressing plaintiff with the idea that defendant would procure the money by means of the check, and pay for the horses, when in fact he intended to acquire possession of them and credit their value on the note; and it is immaterial whether his language was such as to convey the idea that his money was on deposit in a bank in R. or elsewhere.—Blake v. Blackley, (N. C.) 13 S. E. 786.

14. Defendant's representation that he wished to start the horses early in the morning, his transferring them from the road ordinarily traveled to his home to another road not so well known, and his declaration before he acquired possession that he intended to play a trick on plaintiff, were sufficient to warrant a verdict for plaintiffs.—Blake v. Blackley, (N. C.) 13 S. E. 786.

Rights of purchaser.

15. Although machinery purchased for $600 is, in its present condition, inefficient and worthless, yet where, by undisputed testimony, it appears that, by the expenditure of $50, it can be repaired and made to perform good work, it is not worthless so as to entitle the purchaser to keep it without paying for it.—Trippe v. McLain, (Ga.) 13 S. E. 522.

Failure to deliver goods.

16. On a sale of five car-loads of oats by sample, the buyer is entitled to inspect the oats before paying a draft drawn for the price; and where the shipment embraces two car-loads only, and the buyer refuses to pay the draft covering the price of these, upon the ground that the cars have not arrived, and he has had no opportunity to inspect, and thereupon the banker causes the draft to be protested for non-payment, this does not justify the seller in not sending forward the other three cars.—Erwin v. Harris, (Ga.) 13 S. E. 513.

17. A subsequent purchase of the same car-loads of oats from the broker of the seller by the purchaser after having for good reason refused to accept them under his original contract to purchase, and after the seller has declined to forward other car-loads, as called for by his contract, is no waiver of the right of action for the breach of contract by the seller in refusing to furnish the other car-loads.—Erwin v. Harris, (Ga.) 13 S. E. 513.

Action for price.

18. In an action for the balance due on goods, though defendant testifies that they were only worth one cent a pound, which amount he paid, a verdict for plaintiff is warranted, where defendant admits on his examination that the contract price was a cent and a half per pound.—Falvey v. Richmond, (Ga.) 13 S. E. 261.

19. In an action for the price of machinery, defendants filed a counter-claim for plaintiffs' failure to deliver the machinery promptly, according to their contract. Plaintiffs replied that they were merely defendants' agents to purchase the machinery specified, and were in no wise responsible for the delay. The evidence was conflicting as to whether plaintiffs were such agents, or whether the machinery was purchased directly from them. *Held*, that it was error to instruct the jury to find that plaintiffs had not failed to comply with their contract.—Powers v. Erwin, (N. C.) 13 S. E. 208.

Bona fide purchaser.

20. A deed of trust, given to secure creditors of the grantor, who act in good faith, and without notice either to them or the trustee that the goods conveyed by the deed were obtained by the grantor by fraud, will not be set aside at the suit of the creditors from whom the goods were so obtained.—Oberdorfer v. Meyer, (Va.) 13 S. E. 756.

21. Although notes embracing a contract of conditional sale may not have been legally recorded, yet, if defendants, before they purchased from one who bought from plaintiff, had actual notice of the retention of title by plaintiff and that some of the notes were unpaid, the defective recording is of no consequence as to them; Code Ga., § 1955a, providing that the existing statutes and laws relating to the recording of chattel mortgages shall apply to conditional sales of personal property.—Morton v. Frick Co., (Ga.) 13 S. E. 463.

Conditional sale.

22. Code N. C. § 1275, requiring conditional sales of personal property to be reduced to writing and registered, does not render such sales invalid as between the parties, nor affect the remedies of the parties against each other, unless it is complied with; and, in an action by the seller against the buyer, a note for the purchase money may be put in evidence, although it has not been registered.—Kornegay v. Kornegay, (N. C.) 13 S. E. 770.

—— Sale on approval.

23. Where property is not sold absolutely, but only delivered on approval, and the buyer fails to signify his approval, or make the payments required by the contract, the title still remains in the seller.—Glascock v. Hazell, (N. C.) 13 S. E. 789.

Satisfaction.

Of judgment, see *Judgment*, 29, 30.

SCHOOLS AND SCHOOL-DISTRICTS.

Election—Notice.

1. Where the advertisement prescribed by Act Ga. 1889, pp. 1305, 1306, providing for a local election to determine whether a local school should be established, was published once a week for four weeks, and the last publication was inadvertently omitted, but the other three were duly made, the omission may be treated as a mere irregularity if more than two-thirds of the qualified voters actually voted, and if the result has been acquiesced in until after action has been taken on the faith thereof by which substantial rights have arisen.—Irvin v. Gregory, (Ga.) 13 S. E. 120.

Exaction of fees from pupils.

2. Under Const. Ga., (Code, § 5304,) providing that public schools shall be free to all children, a municipal public school established under a local act (Acts 1889, pp. 1305, 1306) cannot exact incidental fees from resident scholars.—Irvin v. Gregory, (Ga.) 13 S. E. 120.

3. The main purpose of Acts Ga. 1889, pp. 1305, 1306, passed by the general assembly, and approved by two-thirds of the qualified voters of a given town, being to establish and maintain a system of public schools in the town, an unconstitutional requirement therein, which exacts an incidental fee annually of all pupils, thereby including resident as well as non-resident pupils, will not vitiate the whole statute. If, as matter of fact, the means otherwise provided for establishing and maintaining the schools are sufficient, the law can have effect, notwithstanding the unconstitutional requirement.—Irvin v. Gregory, (Ga.) 13 S. E. 120.

4. In a local statute (Acts Ga. 1889, pp. 1305, 1306) authorising the establishment of public schools in a town, a provision that the local board may admit pupils not residents of the town on such terms as the board may prescribe does not allow the board to prescribe terms which would cast upon the town or its inhabitants any part of the expense of educating non-resident pupils. Such pupils cannot be received at a less rate per scholar than the inhabitants of the town pay by taxation

for their children, nor can they be received at all to the exclusion of resident children who would otherwise attend.—Irvin v. Gregory, (Ga.) 13 S. E. 190.

Taxation.

5. Acts N. C. 1881, c. 189, and Acts 1887, c. 382, authorizing the levy of taxes on the taxable property and polls of Goldsborough township for the purpose of establishing and for the annual support of graded schools in that township, do not, either in terms or by implication, authorize the board of county commissioners to levy taxes to pay the interest or principal of any debt created for that purpose.—Trustees of Goldsborough Graded School v. Broadhurst, (N. C.) 13 S. E. 781.

Secondary Evidence.

See *Evidence*, 5–15.

Sentence.

See *Criminal Law*, 53–58.

Service of Process.

See *Writs*, 1–4.

SET-OFF AND COUNTER-CLAIM.

Counter-claim as affecting plaintiff's right to non-suit, see *Practice in Civil Cases*, 8.

When allowable.

1. Where an association sues its former treasurer and her attorney for money due it, the treasurer cannot set off against the plaintiff's demand damages and expenses resulting from a malicious prosecution for embezzling the funds in her hands; nor can such attorney set off his claim for fees for services rendered in defending the treasurer, either in the prosecution or the action for the money; there being no allegation that the association was insolvent.—Houston v. Ladies' Union Branch Ass'n, (Ga.) 13 S. E. 684.

2. The defendant in a distress warrant, after arresting the levy thereof by filing the affidavit prescribed by the statute, may, on the trial of the issue thus formed, prove, by way of recoupment against the plaintiff's demand, damages resulting from a breach by the plaintiff of his own stipulations in the rent contract, and in order to do this it is not necessary to amend his counter-affidavit to set out the grounds of such recoupment.—Johnston v. Patterson, (Ga.) 13 S. E. 17.

3. Code Va. § 3999, provides that, "in any action on a contract, the defendant may file a plea, alleging any such failure in the consideration of the contract * * * as would entitle him to recover damages at law, * * * or to relief in equity, * * * alleging any such matter arising under the contract, existing before its execution, as would entitle him to relief in equity." *Held* that, in an action to recover the purchase price of land, the vendee may plead, by way of set-off, and prove by parol, that the vendor falsely represented that a certain spring was upon the land, although such spring was not mentioned in the contract of sale.—Grayson v. Buchanan, (Va.) 13 S. E. 457.

4. Defendant gave his note to T. Mfg. Co., who, before maturity, sold it to plaintiff. After the transfer, and suit for its collection commenced, one M., who was attorney for plaintiff, and also treasurer of T. Mfg. Co., agreed that defendant should do certain work for T. Mfg. Co., and that his commissions, when collected, should be applied in payment of the note. T. Mfg. Co. became insolvent, and the commissions were not so applied or paid to defendant. *Held*, in the action on the note, that, as M.'s agreement to pay defendant commissions on work for T. Mfg. Co. had no connection with plaintiff, the commissions could not be set off against the note.—National Bank v. Grimm, (N. C.) 13 S. E. 867.

5. A plea of set-off alleging against the plaintiff in a distress warrant items of indebtedness entirely independent of and disconnected with the rent contract is not allowable.—Johnston v. Patterson, (Ga.) 13 S. E. 17.

6. Code N. C. § 244, provides that in an action arising on contract any other cause of action arising on contract, and existing at the commencement of the action, may be set up as a counter-claim. Plaintiff sold to defendants cotton, and received from their agent a ticket on defendants for the cash, which ticket was presented for payment, but defendants refused to pay the cash, and against plaintiff's consent they applied the amount on a balance due them from plaintiff on notes given about two years previous. Plaintiff sued them for conversion, and defendants set up the old debt as a counter-claim. *Held* that, as the action was one for tort, the counter claim did not come within the statute.—Smith v. Young, (N. C.) 13 S. E. 735.

Pleading.

7. Where a plea in recoupment contains no allegation of special damage, but only an allegation of general damages, and there is only a general demurrer thereto, it should not be stricken out, but should be treated as a plea of general damages.—Atlanta Glass Co. v. Noizet, (Ga.) 13 S. E. 833.

8. In an action for machinery furnished defendant, a plea which merely alleges that the machinery, "by reason of defects in material and construction, had to be continually changed, which caused great detention in the work of manufacturing defendant's glass, owing to which defendant was damaged in the sum of $500, which said sum defendant recoups for its damages for same against plaintiff," is not sufficient, since a plea in recoupment, being a cross-action, must state the particulars of defendant's demand.—Atlanta Glass Co. v. Noizet, (Ga.) 13 S. E. 833.

—— **Reply.**

9. The allegations of a counter-claim are sufficiently put in issue by a reply stating that plaintiff, "replying to the counter-claim, denies the same."—Atlantic Phosphate Co. v. Sullivan, (S. C.) 13 S. E. 539.

Settlement.

See *Compromise*.

Of bill of exceptions, see *Exceptions, Bill of*, 1–3.

SHERIFFS AND CONSTABLES.

Mandamus to compel execution of warrant, see *Mandamus*, 3.

Appointment of deputy—Minor.

In the absence of any statute making a deputy-sheriff an officer, or making provisions as to his age, a minor may be appointed deputy, though Const. N. C. art. 6, §§ 4, 5, provide that an officer shall be 21 years old.—Jamesville & W. R. Co. v. Fisher, (N. C.) 13 S. E. 696.

Signals.

At railroad crossings, see *Railroad Companies*, 28–33.

Slander.

See *Libel and Slander*.

Societies.

See *Building and Loan Associations; Corporations; Religious Societies*.

Special Laws.

See *Constitutional Law*, 1–6.

STATUTES CITED AND CONSTRUED.

Stock.

Killed by railroad, see *Railroad Companies,* 53-56.

Live-stock shipments, see *Carriers,* 2-7.

Street.

See *Municipal Corporations,* 5-9.

SUBROGATION.

When allowed.

1. The grantees of land, as part of the transaction, conveyed the land in trust to secure the grantors, but afterwards, without authority from the grantors, conveyed a portion thereof to a stranger, who had notice that the trust had not been satisfied. The register recorded in the margin of the record of the trust-deed a memorandum, not under seal, reciting that the trustee, for value received, thereby released from the trust said portion of land, and this entry was signed by the trustee. *Held,* in a decree awarding to the grantors the portion of land attempted to be sold by the trustee, that it was proper to charge the land with the amount paid therefor to the grantors through the trustee, since a person cannot repudiate a transaction made in his behalf, and retain the fruits thereof.—Browne v. Davis, (N. C.) 13 S. E. 703.

2. Where an administrator, being in doubt as to what is properly assets in his hands, inadvertently pays some of the debts of his intestate out of his own funds, he does not thereby become an intermeddler, but is entitled to subrogation to the rights of those creditors whose claims he has paid.—Turner v. Shuffler, (N. C.) 13 S. E. 243.

To rights of judgment creditor.

3. A. sold real estate to B., with general warranty, receiving therefor four sealed notes, secured by mortgage. At maturity A. surrendered the notes and mortgage in consideration of B.'s unsealed agreement to pay a judgment against A., which was a lien on the land when sold. B. did not pay the judgment, and afterwards made a voluntary conveyance, with warranty, to trustees for the benefit of his wife and children. The trustees conveyed without warranty to plaintiff, who in turn sold the premises with warranty, and afterwards paid the judgment in exoneration of his covenants. *Held,* that plaintiff was not entitled to be subrogated to the rights of the judgment creditor against B.'s estate, nor to the rights of A.'s estate against it, since he did not pay the judgment for the benefit of A.'s estate, but in performance of his own covenants.—McLure v. Melton, (S. C.) 13 S. E. 615; In re Hardin, Id.

4. Plaintiff's father conveyed land to defendant upon a parol trust to pay certain judgments, which were afterwards discharged with the proceeds of other land, which the father had intended to convey to plaintiff, with the understanding with defendant that he should convey the land held in trust by him to plaintiff. *Held,* that plaintiff is not entitled to the land by way of subrogation, since she had no interest in the land intended for her.—Dover v. Rhea, (N. C.) 13 S. E. 164.

Subscription.

To corporate stock, see *Corporations,* 4.

Summons.

See *Writs.*

SUNDAY.

Running of trains, interstate commerce, see *Constitutional Law,* 10.

Execution of contract.

1. Since in Georgia a contract made on Sunday is void, and, if not executed, cannot be enforced, a sale made on Sunday without delivery of the property is void, though the parties may have intended to waive delivery, since no valid agreement to waive delivery can be made on Sunday.—Calhoun v. Phillips, (Ga.) 13 S. E. 598.

—— Ratification on week-day.

2. Ratification on a week-day by the vendee alone of a sale made on Sunday, by allowing the vendor a credit on his account, does not validate the sale, where it does not appear that the vendor ever took or claimed the benefit of the credit.—Calhoun v. Phillips, (Ga.) 13 S. E. 598.

Supplementary Proceedings.

See *Execution,* 19-26.

SURFACE WATER.

Obstruction of flow by railroad embankment, see *Railroad Companies,* 9-11.

Diversion by railroad company.

A railroad company has no right to collect surface water in its right of way, and divert it into a channel where it would not naturally flow, and which is inadequate to receive it.—Staton v. Norfolk & C. R. Co., (N. C.) 13 S. E. 958.

TAXATION.

Assessments for public improvements, property subject to, see *Municipal Corporations,* 10.

Constitutionality of laws, see *Constitutional Law,* 14, 15.

For school purposes, see *Schools and School-Districts,* 5.

Road tax, see *Highways,* 3.

Property subject to.

1. Under Acts Va. 1883-84, § 17, p. 568, providing for a state tax on the assessed market value of the shares of banks located in the state, regardless of the residence of the stockholders, and Code Va. § 833, cl. 2, providing that the board of supervisors of each county shall order a levy on all property assessed with a state tax within the county, the board has power to levy a tax for county purposes on the shares of stock of a bank located in the county, although some of its stockholders are non-residents of the state. HINTON and LACY, JJ., dissenting.—Stockholders of Bank of Abingdon v. Board of Sup'rs Washington County, (Va.) 13 S. E. 407.

To whom taxable.

2. Real estate in Savannah, Ga., held by purchase from the city, the terms of purchase being the payment of an annual ground-rent forever, or, at the election of the purchaser, his heirs, executors, administrators, or assigns, the payment in full of the stipulated purchase money at any time, is taxable by the municipal government as the property of the purchaser or his successor in the title.—Wells v. City of Savannah, (Ga.) 13 S. E. 442.

Collection—By execution.

3. The omission of the tax collector to attach an unsigned receipt to the tax execution, as required by Act Ga. 1885, does not render the execution void, but only irregular.—Wilson v. Herrington, (Ga.) 13 S. E. 129.

4. Code Ga. § 3641, providing that, when a defendant in *fi. fa.* shall point out any property on which to levy, which is in the hands of a person not a party to the judgment, the officer shall not levy thereon, applies only to executions on judgments, and not to *fi. fas.* issued by a tax collector under section 891, which provides that defendant "shall have the privilege of pointing out property," but that the execution may be levied upon any property when the collector deems it necessary; and in the latter case the officer may levy on lands in the possession of another claiming title, although defendant possesses other property subject to levy. Affirming Wilson v. Boyd, 10 S. E. 499.—Boyd v. Wilson, (Ga.) 13 S. E. 426.

Title.

Color of, see *Adverse Possession*, 11, 12.
Derived from state, see *Public Lands*.
Estoppel to assert, see *Estoppel*, 7-9.
Of statute, see *Statutes*, 1.
Tax-titles, see *Taxation*, 10, 11.
To support ejectment, see *Ejectment*, 1-4.

Torts.

See *Abduction; Assault and Battery*, 2; *Death by Wrongful Act; Deceit; Libel and Slander; Malicious Prosecution; Negligence; Nuisance; Trespass; Trover and Conversion*.
Assignment of right of action for, see *Assignment*, 2.
Measure of damages for, see *Damages*, 3.
Of infant, see *Infancy*, 2.

TOWNS.

Liability and indebtedness.

Under Const. N. C. art. 7, § 7, prohibiting a municipal corporation from contracting any debt unless authorized by a majority of its qualified voters, in the absence of such authority, a township is not bound by the appointment of agents by the county commissioners and township justices to subscribe for railroad stock on behalf of the township, and to represent it and vote at meetings of stockholders, and by the exercise of such authority by said agents. Jones v. Commissioners, 107 N. C. 248, 12 S. E. 69, distinguished.—Lynchburg & D. R. Co. v. Board Com'rs Person County, (N. C.) 13 S. E. 788.

Transactions with Decedents.

See *Witness*, 5-9.

TRESPASS.

Criminal trespass.

1. A person who in good faith, believing that he has a right to do so, enters upon the lands of another after he had been forbidden, when he had no reasonable ground for such belief, is not excused from criminal liability under Code N. C. § 1120, which provides that, "if any person, after being forbidden to do so, shall go or enter upon the lands of another without a license therefor, he shall be guilty of a misdemeanor."—State v. Fisher, (N. C.) 13 S. E. 878.

2. On an indictment for forcible entry, it appeared that the prosecutor had occupied a blacksmith-shop under a lease from defendant D. After the expiration of the lease, the prosecutor, without surrendering the premises, took a lease thereof from D.'s co tenant. While the prosecutor was standing about 100 yards from the shop, defendants, D. and four others, though forbidden to do so by the prosecutor, approached, and broke open the shop, and took possession. *Held*, that defendants were guilty of forcible entry. State v. Mills, 10 S. E. 676, 104 N. C. 905, distinguished.—State v. Davis, (N. C.) 13 S. E. 888.

TRIAL.

See, also, *Appeal; Certiorari; Evidence; Exceptions, Bill of; Judgment; Jury; New Trial; Pleading; Practice in Civil Cases; Witness*.
Conduct of, in criminal cases, see *Criminal Law*, 12-28.

Remarks of judge.

1. A verdict which is manifestly right, and the only one that could have resulted from the pleadings and evidence, will not be set aside because the court, when the jury were about to consider of their verdict, said, "You can retire, if you wish to do so," and sent an officer to them a few minutes after they had retired, with instructions to inquire "what was the difficulty."—

Houston v. Ladies' Union Branch Ass'n, (Ga.) 12 S. E. 634.

2. Where the jury came into court on Saturday of the first week of the term, and announced that they could not agree as to the facts, it was not error for the judge to say that there were two more weeks of the term, and he would give them plenty of time to consider, and then to direct the sheriff to provide comfortable accommodations for them.—Osborne v. Wilkes, (N. C.) 13 S. E. 285.

Taking papers to jury-room.

3. The fact that the plaintiff's counsel handed the interrogatories of plaintiff to the jury when they retired, and that they kept them until the verdict was announced, is not ground for a new trial, where counsel make affidavit that they did so inadvertently, and the foreman of the jury makes affidavit that they did not examine the interrogatories, and did not know that they had them.—Falvey v. Richmond, (Ga.) 13 S. E. 261.

Reception of evidence.

4. In an action by a father for damages for abducting his daughter for immoral purposes, where the daughter was examined as to declarations made to her father while he was carrying her home, and witnesses were afterwards examined to contradict her testimony, defendants were not prejudiced by not allowing them to examine plaintiff as to such declarations.—Dobson v. Cothran, (S. C.) 13 S. E. 679.

5. It was no abuse of discretion for the court to not allow a Bible to be exhibited in evidence after the testimony was closed, and argument by counsel commenced.—Dobson v. Cothran, (S. C.) 13 S. E. 679.

6. Though evidence be improperly rejected, if the verdict is correct, and the excluded evidence could not properly have changed it, the error is immaterial.—Harvey v. West, (Ga.) 13 S. E. 693.

—— Reopening case.

7. It is discretionary with the court to reopen a case for the re-examination of a witness.—Central Railroad & Banking Co. v. Curtis, (Ga.) 13 S. E. 757; Curtis v. Central Railroad & Banking Co., Id.

Objections to evidence.

8. An exception to the sufficiency of evidence to identify land described in a deed cannot be raised for the first time on appeal.—Euliss v. McAdams, (N. C.) 13 S. E. 162.

Arguments of counsel.

9. The fact that a witness for defendant, in an action on an insurance policy, who was present and aiding its counsel in the conduct of the case, was not examined to contradict the plaintiff as to what occurred when he and another came to adjust the loss, was a matter which counsel was properly allowed to use as an argument that plaintiff's testimony should be believed.—Grubbs v. North Carolina Home Ins. Co., (N. C.) 13 S. E. 236.

10. Though it is improper for counsel, on a motion to reopen the case for more evidence, made while the argument by opposing counsel is in progress, to give the names of witnesses, and state what their evidence would be, without first requesting the court to cause the jury to retire, the impropriety will not necessarily work a new trial, if it does not appear that he acted in bad faith, or with any purpose to get facts before the jury by artful practice.—Georgia Midland & G. R. Co. v. Evans, (Ga.) 13 S. E. 580.

—— Right to open and close.

11. On the trial of a claim case, claimant demanded the right to assume the burden of proof, and to open and conclude the argument, but made no offer to admit any particular fact or facts. It appeared that claimant was in possession of a portion of the property levied on, and defendant in fi. fa. was in possession of the remaining portion. *Held*, there was no error in refusing to allow claimant's demand.—Johnson v. Palmour, (Ga.) 13 S. E. 657.

Instructions.

12. Where, in an action to recover salary by a railroad president, it is claimed that his services were gratuitous, and that he did not intend to charge therefor at the time they were rendered, it is not error to charge that "the position of the defense is that the president did not intend to charge, * * * and that he never thought about charging till he got out of office."—Bowen v. Carolina, C. G. & C. R. Co., (S. C.) 13 S. E. 421.

13. One who, against objection, introduces testimony upon a point not raised by the pleadings, cannot object to the giving of a charge based upon such testimony.—Bowen v. Carolina, C. G. & C. R. Co., (S. C.) 13 S. E. 421.

14. In an action to recover for a heating apparatus furnished an hotel, where the defense is a failure to heat properly, it is not error to charge: "If it was the contract that the hotel company was to close up the halls by storm-doors, and if the hotel company failed to close up the halls, and if there was a failure to produce the proper degree of heat by reason of such neglect to put in storm doors, then the plaintiffs would not be responsible for the failure," though the main contract was a written one, and the contract as to the doors was in parol, where the testimony as to the closing of the halls was first brought out by defendant on cross-examination of plaintiffs' witness, and an issue was made thereon without objection.—Rome Hotel Co. v. Warlick, (Ga.) 13 S. E. 116.

15. Where plaintiff and defendant are the principal witnesses, and the former testifies distinctly to one contract and its breach by defendant, who testifies as distinctly to another and a different contract, it is not error to charge that, if the jury find that plaintiff has stated the contract correctly, they will find for him, but, if defendant stated it correctly, then the verdict should be for him.—Barringer v. Burns, (N. C.) 13 S. E. 142.

16. The judge invited argument, in the presence of the jury, when plaintiff rested, as to whether he had made a *prima facie* case, and then he directed defendants to proceed in the development of their case, and told the jury then, and subsequently charged them, that they must not be influenced in favor of defendants by his inviting argument, nor against them by his order to proceed with the introduction of their testimony. *Held* not to be error.—Osborne v. Wilkes, (N. C.) 13 S. E. 285.

17. Where, if defendants had pleaded separately, the charge correctly laid down the law as to what facts would implicate one or more of them, and left it to the jury to say whether such facts were established, the charge was not erroneous.—Dobson v. Cothran, (S. C.) 13 S. E. 679.

—— Misleading instructions.

18. It is not misleading to refer inadvertently to the "claim for injuries made by defendant" instead of by plaintiff.—Southern Bell Tel., etc., Co. v. Jordan, (Ga.) 13 S. E. 202.

—— Requests to charge.

19. It is not error to refuse to consider written requests for instructions, unless presented to the court at or before the close of the testimony.—Grubbs v. North Carolina Home Ins. Co., (N. C.) 13 S. E. 236.

20. Where an instruction covering the law of the case has been given, it is not error to refuse to give another, though it state the law correctly in a different manner.—Ferguson's Adm'r v. Wills, (Va.) 13 S. E. 392.

21. A request to charge in terms not applicable to the facts in evidence, or which in laying down a proposition omits some of the material elements to be considered, is properly refused.—Georgia Midland & G. R. Co. v. Evans, (Ga.) 13 S. E. 580.

22. Where no request is made to charge as to the burden of proof or the preponderance of evidence, mere failure to charge on such topics will not require a new trial.—Small v. Williams, (Ga.) 13 S. E. 589.

Instructions—Evidence to support.

23. Where the evidence shows that the deed in question was executed freely and voluntarily, and there is no testimony from which the jury could rightly infer that it was the result of duress or fraud, the court is not warranted in charging on these subjects.—Campbell v. Higginbotham, (Ga.) 13 S. E. 556.

24. Instructions should be refused unless there is evidence to which they are pertinent, and which warrante them.—Leach v. Linde, (N. C.) 13 S. E. 212.

25. An instruction which takes only a portion of the facts involved in a case under the evidence, and erects an hypothesis on them only, disregarding others, and tells the jury that if the hypothesis be true they shall find accordingly, is properly refused, though it may be good as far as it goes.—Thompson v. Douglass, (W. Va.) 13 S. E. 1015.

26. Where there is no evidence in support of requests to charge, they are properly refused.—Humphrey v. Board of Trustees of M. E. Church, (N. C.) 13 S. E. 793.

—— Construction as a whole.

27. Though an instruction embraces only the aspects of the case favorable to one party, it is not erroneous if the entire charge fairly presents the case to the jury.—Barringer v. Burns, (N. C.) 13 S. E. 142.

28. The alternative of a legal proposition favorable to one party, if fairly given in charge, need not be in immediate connection with the alternative in favor of the other party.—Small v. Williams, (Ga.) 13 S. E. 589.

—— Harmless error.

29. Though the charge of the court was in part not strictly accurate, yet where, in view of the substantial merits of the case, the inaccuracy did no harm, it is not cause for a new trial.—Hadden v. Larned, (Ga.) 13 S. E. 806.

—— Return of jury for further instructions.

30. Where the jury in a negligence case come into court without having agreed on a verdict, it is not error for the court, in telling them to return to their room, and try to find a verdict, to say to them that they are as capable as any jury will ever be to reach a verdict, and that, if they will follow the rules he has given them, he does not think they will have trouble in agreeing. Parker v. Railway Co., 83 Ga. 540, 10 S. E. 233, followed.—Austin v. Appling, (Ga.) 13 S. E. 955.

—— Province of jury.

31. In an action to recover for services as railway president upon a *quantum meruit*, a charge that "the salaries of railway presidents are very high, and much higher than of state officials, and are made so because of the great responsibility attached to the office, and the high order of ability required," is not erroneous as violating the constitutional provision prohibiting a charge upon the facts.—Bowen v. Carolina, C. G. & C. R. Co., (S. C.) 13 S. E. 421.

32. Where plaintiff, in an action for the possession of land, offers in evidence an administrator's deed of the land, which, on account of the inadequacy of consideration, is asserted by defendants to be fraudulent, it is error for the court to take the issue from the jury, and direct what their finding shall be, since inadequacy of price is but a badge of fraud, to be considered by the jury with other suspicious circumstances.—Orrender v. Chaffin, (N. C.) 13 S. E. 911.

33. Since, under the procedure in North Carolina, issues are submitted to the jury, and on their findings the court adjudges the recovery, it was not error in the court to refuse defendant's request to instruct the jury that upon the evidence plaintiff could not recover.—Bottoms v. Seaboard & R. R. Co., (N. C.) 13 S. E. 738.

34. Plaintiff and two other boys obtained permission from a section-master, who was going with the sectionmen on a hand-car to load some

scrap-iron, to go with him if they would assist in loading the iron. On their return the hand-car collided with a rapidly moving train. Plaintiff was injured, and sued the railroad company. He asked the court to charge that, if the section-master was in the habit of employing and discharging the men under him, and was in control of the said car, and plaintiff was on the car by his permission, and without knowing that it was contrary to the rules of the company, and the injuries sustained by him resulted from the gross negligence of defendant, he was entitled to recover, and that the relation between a section-master and the men under him was that of superior and subordinates; and that, if one employed by the section-master was injured by the section-master's negligence, the company could not escape liability on the ground that the injured party was a co-employe. The court rejected the instructions of plaintiff as calculated to mislead the jury, and as inapplicable to the evidence. It then charged that, although plaintiff was permitted to ride on the hand-car, upon condition that he would assist in loading the said iron, this did not make him an employe, so as to obligate the company to protect him from injury; and that, unless defendant authorized the section-master to permit him so to ride, the jury must find for the defendant. *Held*, that the said rulings were an invasion of the province of the jury, in assuming to decide for them questions of fact, and in directing their verdict. FAUNTLEROY, J., dissenting.—Tyler v. Chesapeake & O. R. Co., (Va.) 13 S. E. 975.

35. Under Code, § 413, which provides that no judge, in giving an instruction to the petit jury, shall give an opinion whether a fact is fully or sufficiently proven, an instruction that no charge in the bill of particulars appears against one of the defendants which is not paid, as shown by copies of receipts filed, was properly refused, as invading the province of the jury.—Albertson v. Terry, (N. C.) 13 S. E. 713.

36. In an action for injury by a railroad engine, defendant's request to charge that, "if the jury believe the evidence, the plaintiff could have extricated himself from any danger after he saw the engine," was properly refused, since the proposition was an inference to be made by the jury from all the circumstances in evidence.—McQuay v. Richmond & D. R. Co., (N. C.) 13 S. E. 944.

37. Code Ga. § 3248, prohibiting a judge in his charge to the jury, or during the progress of a trial, to express or intimate his opinion as to what has or has not been proved, does not prohibit a judge from stating to the jury that there is no evidence to support an alleged fact, when such statement is unquestionably true.—East Tennessee, V., & G. Ry. Co. v. Markens, (Ga.) 13 S. E. 855.

Instructions — Objections and exceptions.

38. If the matter of a lengthy extract from the charge of the court is sound in part, any unsound part must be specifically pointed out in the motion for a new trial.—Small v. Williams, (Ga.) 13 S. E. 589.

39. An exception "to the charge as given" is too vague and indefinite to be considered on appeal.—Bottoms v. Seaboard & R. R. Co., (N. C.) 13 S. E. 738.

40. Where an exception to the charge was based upon the assumption that defendants pleaded separate defenses, when the record shows that they did not, the exception will not be sustained.—Dobson v. Cothran, (S. C.) 13 S. E. 679.

41. Where an exception charges error in giving an instruction, but contains no specifications as to what the error was, the exception will not be sustained.—Dobson v. Cothran, (S. C.) 13 S. E. 679.

42. A misstatement of the testimony in the charge to the jury is a cause for a new trial, and cannot be presented for the first time in the supreme court.—Bowen v. Carolina, C. G. & C. R. Co., (S. C.) 13 S. E. 421.

43. Error cannot be predicated on the failure of the trial court to give instructions which were first suggested on a motion for a new trial.—Blackburn v. Fair, (N. C.) 13 S. E. 911.

—— Directing verdict.

44. When a case turns on a question of law which is decisive of its merits, and the court directs a verdict for defendant, though irregular, the error is harmless.—Laing v. City of Americus, (Ga.) 13 S. E. 107.

Verdict.

45. In an action against two defendants sued jointly, a general verdict for plaintiff is a finding against both, and is sufficiently certain.—Houston v. Ladies' Union Branch Ass'n, (Ga.) 13 S. E. 684.

46. Where the verdict is for a larger sum than is sued for, and no amendment covering the excess is offered, the court should set it aside or require a *remittitur*, though interest added to the damages proved would equal the verdict.—Georgia Railroad & Banking Co. v. Crawley, (Ga.) 13 S. E. 508.

47. When the vendor represented that the tract contained 140 acres, and included within its boundaries one-half of a certain spring, when in fact it only contained 126 acres, and did not include the spring, a verdict assessing defendant's damages at $600 for loss of one-half of the spring, and $540 for the loss of 14 acres of land, and directing the manner in which this sum shall be applied towards the purchase price, is not vague and uncertain.—Grayson v. Buchanan, (Va.) 13 S. E. 457.

48. The findings, in an action on a note, where defendant filed a counter-claim, that defendant owed plaintiff $45, and that he was entitled to $22.50 damages, were not intelligible, for the reason that it could not be determined whether the jury meant that defendant owed plaintiff $45 and that his damages should be deducted from that sum, or whether the damages should be recovered by defendant and plaintiff should recover nothing, or that defendant was damaged $45, and in addition $22.50.—Kornegay v. Kornegay, (N. C.) 13 S. E. 770.

49. Evidence certified cannot be read to find facts essential to judgment, which should have been, but were not, found by verdict.—Ringold v. Suiter, (W. Va.) 13 S. E. 46.

—— Exceptions.

50. An exception based upon the allegation that the damages found by the jury are excessive cannot be considered by this court. Steele v. Railroad Co., 11 S. C. 589; Petrie v. Railroad Co., 29 S. C. 303, 7 S. E. 515,—followed.—Dobson v. Cothran, (S. C.) 13 S. E. 679.

51. An exception, "because the finding of the jury was contrary to the clear preponderance of the testimony," is insufficient.—Dobson v. Cothran, (S. C.) 13 S. E. 679.

—— Special findings.

52. In an action by plaintiff against a railroad company for injury to his child the following issues were submitted to the jury: "(2) Was the defendant guilty of negligence in respect to the injury of plaintiff's child? Answer. Yes. (3) Was the plaintiff guilty of contributory negligence in respect to the injury of his child? A. Yes. (4) Was the plaintiff's child injured by defendant's negligence? A. Yes." *Held* that, as the material facts found are confused, a new trial will be ordered.—Bottoms v. Seaboard & R. R. Co., (N. C.) 13 S. E. 738.

53. Plaintiff sued on a note given in part payment for a horse, which he claimed was to remain his until the note was paid. Defendant alleged that he bought the horse, paying part cash, and giving his note for $45 for the balance; that plaintiff warranted the horse to be sound, whereas in fact it was unsound; and claimed damages for breach of warranty. The jury found that plaintiff was not the owner of the horse; that defendant owed him for the same $45; that his representations in regard to its soundness were

false; and that the defendant was entitled to $22.50 damages. *Held*, that the finding in regard to ownership was material, and not inconsistent with the other findings or with the general verdict, and that the court erred in adjudging that it was mere surplusage and that the plaintiff was the owner.—Kornegay v. Kornegay, (N. C.) 13 S. E. 770.

Trial by court.

54. Where the judge, acting as a jury, decides the case long after hearing the evidence and argument, he may act upon his recollection of the written evidence without having it in his possession at the time of deciding, provided he is satisfied that he remembers it, and especially if he remains of the same opinion as to the effect of it after reviewing it upon a motion for a new trial, in deciding which motion the evidence was all put before him again and re-examined. —Sibley v. Ober & Sons Co., 13 S. E. 711, 87 Ga 55.

55. When a case is submitted to the judge on the law and the facts, to be tried by him without the intervention of a jury, and he finds on the facts and decides the questions of law, the losing party may either move for a new trial or file his bill of exceptions, as he may see proper; but when, by agreement of the parties, a verdict is actually taken in accordance with the judge's finding, a motion for a new trial is indispensable to review the finding.—Hyfield v. Sims, (Ga.) 13 S. E. 554.

—— Findings.

56. Where findings upon which a court appointed a receiver were not reduced to writing until three or four days after the order was made, the order will not be disturbed, where it does not appear that defendant suffered from such delay. —S. C. Forsaith Mach. Co. v. Hope Mills Lumber Co., (N. C.) 13 S. E. 869.

57. The failure of the record to show that the court made specific findings of fact will not invalidate its judgment, where it does not appear that findings were requested.—Carter v. Rountree, (N. C.) 13 S. E. 716.

TROVER AND CONVERSION.

Conversion by mortgagee.

1. In January, 1889, a mortgage was given on "the entire crop of cotton to be raised by me or my tenants on all my lands during the year 1889." The mortgagor planted some leased land in cotton, and gave a second mortgage to the defendants, and was directed to deliver to them a bale of cotton due his landlord for rent. The mortgagor delivered a bale to the defendants for his landlord, but they insisted on applying it on account of their mortgage. The mortgagor said he was willing if his landlord was, and the next week he delivered to the landlord another bale in payment of the rent. *Held*, that the defendants were liable to the first mortgagee for the conversion of the bale delivered to them.—Following Rawlings v. Hunt, 90 N. C. 270.—Brown v. Miller, (N. C.) 13 S. E. 167.

Verdict and judgment.

2. In trover by the seller of goods, the title to which he retained as security for the price, where plaintiff elects, under Code Ga. § 3564, to take a verdict for the property and its hire, and where no plea has been filed except the general issue, and there is no evidence as to the value of the goods, defendant is entitled to no deduction from the amount of hire on account of partial payments made to plaintiff on the price.—Morton v. Frick Co., (Ga.) 13 S. E. 463.

3. Where, in an action under Code Ga. § 3890, prescribing a short form of complaint for the recovery of personal property, and declaring that the verdict and judgment under such form may be the same as in actions of trover, the complaint is for 210 bags of flour, of the value of $450, with no further allegation of damages, except that the defendants refuse to deliver the property or pay the profits thereof, there can be no recovery for more than $450, with interest thereon, there being no amendment of the declaration, or offer to amend.—Moomaugh v. Everett, (Ga.) 13 S. E. 337; Everett v. Moomaugh, Id.

—— Remittitur.

4. In Georgia, when personal property has been sold for $375, and $250 thereof has been paid to the seller, who, having retained the title to the property to secure the purchase money, recovers in an action of trover the property itself and $100 for hire, the supreme court will direct that the judgment in favor of plaintiff may be discharged by defendants' paying the balance of the purchase money and interest thereon, and costs of the action, within 10 days from the time the *remittitur* is made the judgment of the court below: and, if not so paid, then the original judgment in favor of plaintiff to stand of full force.—Morton v. Frick Co., (Ga.) 13 S. E. 463.

Trustee Process.

See *Garnishment.*

TRUSTS.

Action against trustee, limitation, see *Limitation of Actions*, 9-11.
Adverse possession by *cestui que trust*, see *Adverse Possession*, 10.

Express trust.

1. Where a deed is executed in fee-simple, and the grantor makes before delivery the following indorsement, signed and sealed in the presence of witnesses: "Accordance deed. I, the said Eli Blackburn, Sr., do hereby certify that Sarah Blackburn, a daughter of said Blackburn, doth hold a life-time possession in the said Eli deed," —the grantee takes the land in trust for Sarah during her natural life.—Blackburn v. Blackburn, (N. C.) 13 S. E. 987.

—— Establishment by parol.

2. In an action to establish a parol trust in personal property it appeared that 28 years prior to the suit, plaintiffs' mother, desiring to divide a sum of money among her children, delivered certain portions of it to some of them in person, and directed defendant to take the shares of plaintiffs, invest it for them, and pay them only the interest. No demand was made by plaintiffs upon defendant for the principal or interest of their shares for a series of years, although two of them were in needy circumstances, and had frequently requested pecuniary assistance from defendant. The testimony of the plaintiffs was vague and uncertain, and the details of the original transaction were stated in three different ways. *Held*, that the evidence was insufficient to establish the trust.—Harris v. Bratt., (S. C.) 13 S. E. 447; De Loach v. Same, Id.; Williams v. Same, Id.

Resulting trust.

3. A deed from a father-in-law, made in consideration of $500, "less $300 for the love and affection the said W. [grantor] bears to his daughter, [the grantee's wife,] donated out of the $500 at and before the sealing and delivery of these presents," and conveying the premises to the son-in-law, with warranty title, vests the title in him for his own use, and no trust results in favor of the daughter.—Hawks v. Sailors, (Ga.) 13 S. E. 638.

4. Plaintiff's father conveyed land to defendant upon a parol trust to pay certain judgments, which were afterwards discharged with the proceeds of other land, which the father had intended to convey to plaintiff, with the understanding with defendant that he should convey the land held in trust by him to plaintiff. *Held*, that a trust in the land conveyed to defendant resulted to plaintiff's father, and went to his heirs. There being no transfer of the legal title contemporaneous with the parol understanding that defendant should convey to plaintiff, no trust

proceeds thus arising to be paid to the widow, and the remainder to be divided among the six heirs. At the death or marriage of the widow, the executor was to elect to take the homestead at $40 per acre, or to sell it at auction, and divide the proceeds equally among the six heirs. At the death of the widow, the homestead was sold at auction. The proceeds of the personalty and of the land were insufficient to pay the debts and the legacy of $700, without resorting to the proceeds of the sale of the homestead. *Held*, that the devise to the six heirs was a demonstrative legacy, while the $700 bequest was a general legacy, and hence the latter must abate to pay debts before the former could be touched.—Meyers v. Meyers' Ex'r, (Va.) 13 S. E. 346.

Contract to make will.

14. Where a father has agreed to will his son property on consideration of the son's moving to the father's house and taking care of him during his life, no change in the contract can result from an agreement made by the children after the father has become insane, and unable to make the will.—Hudson v. Hudson, (Ga.) 13 S. E. 583.

15. Where a son removes himself and family to the residence of his father, on an express promise by the latter to will him his home place if he will attend to and take care of him for life, and performs his part of the contract, but the father fails to make the agreed will, because of his becoming and dying insane, the son should recover of the father's administrator, upon a *quantum meruit*, the actual value of his services, not to exceed the value of the home place; but he should account for and have deducted from the full amount he is entitled to all he has received from the property over what was necessary for the father's support during his lifetime.—Hudson v. Hudson, (Ga.) 13 S. E. 583.

WITNESS.

See, also, *Evidence*.
Absence of, continuance, see *Criminal Law*, 10, 11.
Failure to produce, presumption, see *Evidence*, 4.
Separation of, during trial, see *Criminal Law*, 19.

Competency—Interest.

1. A trustee is a "person interested in the result of a suit," instituted by the beneficiaries of the trust against the surviving members of a firm to charge them with trust funds invested by the trustee in land which he subsequently sold to the firm, within the meaning of the Georgia witness act of 1889, cl. d, which forbids "a person interested in the result of a suit" from testifying therein, if, as a party, he would for any cause be incompetent.—Morgan v. Harrold, (Ga.) 13 S. E. 710.

—— Husband and wife.

2. Where a wife and her husband are both parties to an action, but she alone is interested in the result, she is competent as a witness.— Thomas v. Sellman, (Va.) 13 S. E. 146.

—— Privileged communications.

3. An attorney was employed only to procure a bond for one charged with a criminal offense, and did so, taking from him a deed to indemnify him against loss on account of said bond, and afterwards the defendant in such criminal case borrowed money from another to settle the same, and the attorney, at the request of said defendant, quitclaimed the property to the lender as a security for such money. *Held*, that in a controversy as to the title of the land between the estate of the lender and that of said defendant, both being dead, the attorney was a competent witness to prove the above-recited facts, and also an admission by the lender that the money he advanced upon such quitclaim deed had all been repaid.—Rodgers v. Moore, (Ga.) 13 S. E. 962.

tion, has deuied that he had ever told his attorney that a confession of the crime had been procured from him by the threats of the sheriff, does not thereby waive the privileged character of his communications to the attorney, and the latter cannot be compelled to disclose them for the purpose of impeaching the witness. Affirming 12 S. E. 657.—State v. James, (S. C.) 13 S. E. 225.

—— Transactions with decedents.

5. In partition between heirs at law evidence by some of the parties that in a division of lands by their father among them it was agreed that some of them should pay certain sums to others for owelty of partition is incompetent under Code N. C. § 590, where one of the heirs, a party to such agreement, is dead.—Barbee v. Barbee, (N. C.) 13 S. E. 215.

6. A wife was competent to testify that she had no conversations with a deceased mortgagee who held a mortgage upon the separate property of the wife, in an action to enjoin the sale of the premises upon the ground that the husband received the benefits of the mortgage, in regard to the transaction.—Griffin v. Earle, (S. C.) 13 S. E. 473.

7. Code N. C. § 590, provides that no one interested in an action adversely to a deceased person shall be examined as a witness in his own behalf, "concerning a personal transaction or communication between the witness and the deceased person." *Held*, in an action to set aside an assignment to decedent's brothers of a life insurance policy, that defendants, although incompetent under said section to prove the contract of assignment, or the consideration agreed upon therefor with decedent, could testify to their transactions with third persons in that regard, and show what money they had paid in settlement of decedent's debts, and also what sums they had been compelled to pay on account of decedent's default as co-executor of their father's estate.—Watts v. Warren, (N. C.) 13 S. E. 232.

8. In an action against a railroad company for injuries sustained by an employe, alleged to have resulted from the negligent act of defendant's engineer in managing his engine, plaintiff is incompetent to testify as to the alleged negligence of the engineer if the latter is dead, and no other officer or agent of defendant was present, under Act Ga. Oct. 29, 1889, (Pamphlet, p. 85,) which provides that where suit is defended by a corporation the opposite party shall not be admitted to testify in his own behalf to transactions solely with a deceased officer or agent of the corporation, and not also with surviving persons, officers, or agents.—Mayfield v. Savannah, G. & N. A. R. Co., (Ga.) 13 S. E. 459.

9. In an action by a son against his brother, as administrator of his father, to recover for services rendered the father in his life-time, plaintiff may testify, in answer to the testimony of the administrator, as to occurrences between him and plaintiff before their father's death, not in the presence of the father, and not participated in by him.—Hudson v. Hudson, (Ga.) 13 S. E. 583.

—— Interest of witness.

10. In an action by the beneficiaries of a trust fund against the surviving members of a firm which was alleged to have purchased land from the trustee with knowledge of its trust character, the trustee is *prima facie* incompetent as a witness for the plaintiffs to affect the partnership with notice of the trust, by means of a transaction or communication between himself and a member of the partnership now deceased, since the Georgia witness act of 1889, cl. b, renders a party to an action against partners incompetent to testify in his own favor as to a transaction with a deceased partner, and clause d renders a "person interested in the result of the suit" incompetent to testify if he would be incompetent party.—Morgan v. Harrold, (Ga.) 13 S. E.

11. The defendant purchased land, taking bond for a deed. After he had paid the purchase money, the vendor executed to a daughter of the defendant a warranty deed. In a suit by her heirs to recover the land, the defendant contended that at the request of his wife, and to satisfy her, his vendor executed the deed and delivered it to the defendant, telling him to keep it, and not deliver it to the daughter, and at the proper time the vendor would make a deed to him. With this understanding the defendant surrendered his bond, and took the deed, which was never delivered to his daughter, but was, without his knowledge, abstracted from his house and put on record. Code Ga. § 3854, par. 1, provides that, "where one of the original parties to the contract or cause of action is dead, * * * the other party shall not be admitted to testify in his own favor." *Held*, that the defendant was not, but that his vendor was, a competent witness to establish the defense.—Harrison v. Perry, (Ga.) 13 S. E. 88.

12. Under Code S. C. § 400, which provides "that no * * * person who has a legal or equitable interest which may be affected by the event of the action * * * shall be examined in regard to any transaction * * * between such witness and a person at the time of such examination deceased," a husband may testify as to conversations had with a deceased mortgagee who held a mortgage upon the separate property of the wife, when she seeks to enjoin the sale of the premises upon the ground that the husband received the benefits of the mortgage.—Griffin v. Earle, (S. C.) 13 S. E. 473.

13. A witness not a party or interested in the issue can testify to a contract made in his hearing whereby defendant's mortgagee, since deceased, sold the mortgage to plaintiff.—Hooks v. Hayes, (Ga.) 13 S. E. 134.

Examination—Refreshing memory.

14. A witness may refresh his memory by a memorandum taken from his books if, after so refreshing it, he can and does testify to the facts from his own recollection.—Finch v. Barclay, (Ga.) 13 S. E. 566.

—— Cross-examination.

15. On a prosecution for larceny, a witness for the state testified that on one occasion there was a two-dollar bill in the cash drawer when he went to dinner; that defendant was the only clerk left in the store; and that when witness returned the bill was gone. It was not shown that defendant was charged with taking the bill. *Held*, that a question, on cross-examination, as to whether, on witness' return to the store, he asked defendant what had become of the bill, and what his reply was, was properly ruled out.—State v. Rhyne, (N. C.) 13 S. E. 943.

16. On a trial for slandering an "innocent woman," after the examination of the prosecutrix, the court refused to allow defendant to ask her how many times she and her husband had separated, and the cause. *Held* that, since defendant had fair opportunity for cross-examination, it was discretionary with the court to allow this question.—State v. Morris, (N. C.) 13 S. E. 877.

Credibility.

17. The evidence being in direct conflict, and the jury having credited a single witness in opposition to two others, the verdict was not without evidence to support it.—Nolen v. Heard, (Ga.) 13 S. E. 554.

18. The credibility of a witness, on whose testimony a conviction for murder rests, and who admitted having made different statements; is a matter for the determination of the jury.—Lyles v. Commonwealth, (Va.) 13 S. E. 802.

19. Where, in a murder trial, deceased's son testifies that he knew the hour at which the assault occurred, because he looked at a clock in the house, and his sisters testify that there was no clock, the value of his evidence is for the jury, and an instruction is properly refused declaring that, if the witness swore falsely in this respect,

his whole testimony is destroyed, and should be disregarded.—Hash v. Commonwealth, (Va.) 13 S. E. 398.

—— Impeachment.

20. On a trial for slandering an "innocent woman" the husband of the prosecutrix denied, on cross-examination, that he said he had sexual intercourse with the prosecutrix before he married her. *Held* that, the answer of the husband involving merely collateral matters, he could not be contradicted by evidence that he had said that he would rather pay $250 and marry the woman (the prosecutrix) than have a bastard sworn to him.—State v. Morris, (N. C.) 13 S. E. 877.

21. It is competent, on cross-examination, for the purpose of attacking the witness' credibility, to ask him whether he has ever been convicted of larceny. Affirming 12 S. E. 619.—State v. Merriman, (S. C.) 13 S. E. 328.

22. The fact that a person was induced by others to prosecute for a criminal offense should not discredit his testimony before the jury, nor should the trial judge allow the fact to be proven for that purpose.—Allgood v. State, (Ga.) 13 S. E. 569.

23. An accused person who becomes a witness in his own behalf assumes the position of an ordinary witness; and where he has put his character for peaceableness in issue he may be cross-examined as to particular acts of violence which he is alleged to have committed. Affirming 12 S. E. 619.—State v. Merriman, (S. C.) 13 S. E. 328.

24. A witness for the defense, who testifies that defendant is of a peaceable character, may be asked, on cross-examination, if he knows of certain particular acts of violence committed by defendant, for the purpose of showing that he gives defendant a character inconsistent with that inferable from facts known to him. Affirming 12 S. E. 619.—State v. Merriman, (S. C.) 13 S. E. 328.

25. He may also be asked whether he ever told persons named of an act of violence which he at one time purposed, but was prevented from consummating, with a view to contradicting him by the evidence of the persons named. Affirming 12 S. E. 619.—State v. Merriman, (S. C.) 13 S. E. 328.

26. In a criminal prosecution the state cannot impeach its own witness by evidence of previous declarations by him at variance with his testimony, unless it has been deceived or entrapped by the witness.—Dixon v. State, (Ga.) 13 S. E. 87.

27. Where defendant, in an action for enticing a servant from his employer, offers the servant to prove there was no contract of employment, plaintiff, having laid the foundation on cross-examination, may prove in reply that the servant had admitted the contract to others, for the purpose of discrediting the testimony of the servant.—Duckett v. Pool, (S. C.) 13 S. E. 542.

Words and Phrases.

"Heirs," see *Wills*, 5.
"Injury to person," see *Abatement and Revival*, 1.
"Lend," see *Wills*, 8.
"Person interested in result of suit," see *Witness*, 1.
"Traders," see *Insolvency*, 2.
"Traveled place," see *Railroad Companies*, 31.

WRITS.

See, also, *Attachment; Certiorari; Execution; Garnishment; Injunction; Mandamus; Replevin.*
Service of order in supplementary proceedings, see *Execution*, 26.
—— of process on minors, see *Infancy*, 1.

Service of process.

1. Under Code W. Va. c. 124, providing that any process may be executed on or before the return-day thereof, process to commence a civil action returnable to the first Monday in a month as

a rule day may be dated, issued, and executed on the return-day. The provisions of the statute that any process shall be returnable within 90 days from its date, and that the time within which any act is to be done shall be computed by excluding the first day and including the last, do not preclude the execution of the writ on the day of its issuance.—Spragins v. West Virginia, C. & P. Ry. Co., (W. Va.) 13 S. E. 45.

2. Where an amendment of a summons and complaint was formal, and defendant could derive no benefit from a service of the summons and complaint as amended, such service is unnecessary.—Bray v. Creekmore, (N. C.) 13 S. E. 723.

3. Code, c. 50, § 34, provides that process against a corporation, in an action before a justice, may be served on the president, and other specified officers or agents, at its place of business, or in any county in which such officer or agent resides, and further provides: "But service at any time may be made upon any corporation in the manner prescribed for similar proceedings in the circuit court." Section 36 declares that service on any person under section 34 shall be in the county in which he resides, and that the service will be invalid unless the return shows such fact. Chapter 124, § 7, which applies to circuit courts, declares that it shall be sufficient to serve process against a corporation on certain officers, which include the president, and does not require such service to be in the county in which the officer resides. No persons were named in chapter 50, § 34, not named in chapter 124, § 7, while some are named in section 7 not named in section 34. *Held,* that service of summons in an action before a justice against a domestic railroad corporation upon its president must be in the county in which he resides, and the return is invalid unless it shows that fact. —Taylor v. Ohio River R. Co., (W. Va.) 13 S. E. 1009.

—— Remedy for defective service.

4. Where there was attached to the declaration an original process which was not copied and served on the defendant, the declaration alone being served, it is competent for the court, on motion of plaintiff, to order the original process to be made returnable to the next term of the court, and that a copy be served on defendant, notwithstanding defendant had made a motion to dismiss.—Lassiter v. Carroll, (Ga.) 13 S. E. 895.

Publication.

5. A daily publication of a summons in a newspaper from August 3d to August 31st, prior to the term of court beginning August 31st, was a sufficient publication, under Acts N. C. 1889, c. 108, which provides that, where service of summons by publication is required, the publication must be once a week for four weeks.—State v. Georgia Co., (N. C.) 13 S. E. 861.

6. The fact that an insurance company also does a banking business does not, in an action on a policy, necessitate the service of process on it in the mode prescribed for service of process on banks; and where the action is brought in the county in which the property was situated, and there is no agent of the company resident in that county, the process may be served by publication, as provided by Code Va. § 3225, for service against corporations generally with the exception of banks. RICHARDSON, J., dissenting.—Wytheville Ins. & Bkg. Co. v. Stults, (Va.) 13 S. E. 77.

Return—Amendment.

7. Where the sheriff's return on a notice to a judgment debtor to appear and answer in supplemental proceedings did not show that the person with whom it was left was defendant's wife, and a person of suitable age and discretion, it was proper to allow an amendment so as to show such facts.—Turner v. Holden, (N. C.) 13 S. E. 781.

8. The power of amendment of pleadings, process, and proceedings, given to the trial court by Code N. C. § 273, will not enable it to bring in a new party defendant without its consent, except by the issue and service of an amended summons, and where the summons commands the sheriff to summon "B., president of the Southern Improvement Co.," and it was so served, the added words are merely *descriptio personæ,* and B. alone is summoned; and an amendment striking out the words "B., president of," will not have the effect to make the improvement company a defendant.—Flemmons v. Southern Imp. Co., (N. C.) 13 S. E. 188.

TABLES OF SOUTHEASTERN CASES

IN

STATE REPORTS.

VOL. 86, GEORGIA REPORTS.

VOL. 87, GEORGIA REPORTS.

VOL. 107, NORTH CAROLINA REPORTS.

VOL. 108, NORTH CAROLINA REPORTS.

VOL. 32, SOUTH CAROLINA REPORTS.

VOL. 33, SOUTH CAROLINA REPORTS.

VOL. 87, VIRGINIA REPORTS.

VOL. 34, WEST VIRGINIA REPORTS.